ST/ESA/SER.A/245

Department of Economic and Social Affairs
Population Division

World Population Prospects
The 2004 Revision

Volume II
Sex and Age Distribution of the World Population

Ipas Resource Center

United Nations
New York, 2005

DESA

The Department of Economic and Social Affairs of the United Nations Secretariat is a vital interface between global policies in the economic, social and environmental spheres and national action. The Department works in three main interlinked areas: (i) it compiles, generates and analyses a wide range of economic, social and environmental data and information on which States Members of the United Nations draw to review common problems and take stock of policy options; (ii) it facilitates the negotiations of Member States in many intergovernmental bodies on joint courses of action to address ongoing or emerging global challenges; and (iii) it advises interested Governments on the ways and means of translating policy frameworks developed in United Nations conferences and summits into programmes at the country level and, through technical assistance, helps build national capacities.

Note

ST/ESA/SER.A/245
ISBN 92-1-151408-8

PREFACE

The *2004 Revision* of *World Population Prospects* represents the latest global demographic estimates and projections prepared by the Population Division of the Department of Economic and Social Affairs of the United Nations Secretariat. This volume of the *2004 Revision* shows the age and sex distribution of populations of these official United Nations world population estimates and projections. Covering the 1950-2050 time period, age and sex distributions are provided for each development group, major area, region and country with more than 100,000 inhabitants in 2000. In all data tables, figures for 1950-2005 are estimates and those thereafter are projections, presented as medium, high and low-fertility variants. The tables are accompanied by an executive summary of the results and the assumptions underlying the *2004 Revision*. The executive summary and the assumptions have been translated into the six official United Nations languages.

The full results of the *2004 Revision* are presented in a series of three volumes. In addition to the present volume, the first volume[1] provides the comprehensive tables displaying demographic profiles and major demographic indicators for each development group, major area, region and country for 1950-2050; and the third volume[2] is devoted to an analysis of the results obtained. Summary findings of the *2004 Revision* are also shown in a wall chart[3].

In addition, data are distributed in digital form. Interested users can purchase one of three different CD-ROMs[4] containing the major results of the 2004 Revision in different amount of details. A description of the data provided on the CD-ROMs and an order form are presented on pages 3-12 of this publication and are also posted on the Population Division's web site (*www.unpopulation.org*).

Responsibility for the *2004 Revision* rests with the Population Division. Preparation of the *2004 Revision* was facilitated by the collaboration of the Regional Commissions, the specialized agencies and other relevant bodies of the United Nations with the Population Division. The Population Division is also grateful to the Statistics Division of the Department of Economic and Social Affairs for its continuing cooperation.

Selected output from the *2004 Revision* as well as other population information may be accessed on the website of the Population Division at *www.unpopulation.org*. For further information about the *2004 Revision*, please contact, the Director, Population Division, Department of Economic and Social Affairs, United Nations, New York, NY 10017, USA (fax: 1-212-963-2147).

---

[1] *World Population Prospects: The 2004 Revision*, vol. I, *Comprehensive Tables* (United Nations publication, Sales No. E.05.XIII.5).

[2] *World Population Prospects: The 2004 Revision*, vol. III, *Analytical Report* (United Nations publication, forthcoming).

[3] *World Population Prospects: The 2004 Revision*, *Wall Chart* (United Nations publication, Sales No. E.05.XIII.4).

[4] *World Population Prospects: The 2004 Revision*, *CD-ROM Edition* (United Nations publication, Basic Dataset, Sales No. E.05.XIII.10; Comprehensive Dataset, Sales No. E.05.XIII.11; Extended Dataset, Sales No. E.05.XIII.12).

CONTENTS

Explanatory notes

The following symbols have been used in the tables throughout this report:

Two dots (..) indicate that data are not available or are not separately reported.
A hyphen (-) indicates that the item is not applicable.
A minus sign (-) before a figure indicates a decrease.
A full stop (.) is used to indicate decimals.
Years given start on 1 July.
Use of a hyphen (-) between years, for example, 1995-2000, signifies the full period involved, from 1 July of the first year to 1 July of the second year.

References to countries, territories and areas

The designations employed and the material in this publication do not imply the expression of any opinion whatsoever on the part of the Secretariat of the United Nations concerning the legal status of any country, territory or area or its authorities, or concerning the delimitation of its frontiers or boundaries.

The designation "more developed" and "less developed" regions are intended for statistical convenience and do not necessarily express a judgment about the stage reached by a particular country or area in the development process. The term "country" as used in this publication also refers, as appropriate, to territories or areas.

More developed regions comprise all regions of Europe plus Northern America, Australia/New Zealand and Japan.

Less developed regions comprise all regions of Africa, Asia (excluding Japan) and Latin America and the Caribbean, as well as Melanesia, Micronesia and Polynesia.

The group of least developed countries, as defined by the United Nations General Assembly in 2003, comprises 50 countries, of which 34 are in Africa, 10 in Asia, 1 in Latin America and the Caribbean, and 5 in Oceania.

Names and compositions of geographical areas follow those of "Standard country or area codes for statistical use" (ST/ESA/STAT/SER.M/49/Rev.3), available at http://unstats.un.org/unsd/methods/m49/m49.htm.

The following abbreviations have been used

AIDS	Acquired Immunodeficiency Syndrome.
DESA	Department of Economic and Social Affairs.
HIV	Human Immunodeficiency Virus.
SAR	Special administrative region.
UNAIDS	Joint United Nations Programme on HIV/AIDS.
UNHCR	Office of the United Nations High Commissioner for Refugees.

For analytical purposes, the following country groupings have been used:

CLASSIFICATION OF COUNTRIES BY MAJOR AREA AND REGION OF THE WORLD

Africa

Eastern Africa	*Middle Africa*	*Northern Africa*	*Western Africa*
Burundi	Angola	Algeria	Benin
Comoros[5]	Cameroon	Egypt	Burkina Faso
Djibouti	Central African Republic	Libyan Arab Jamahiriya	Cape Verde
Eritrea	Chad	Morocco	Côte d'Ivoire
Ethiopia	Congo	Sudan	Gambia
Kenya	Democratic Republic of the	Tunisia	Ghana
Madagascar	Congo	Western Sahara	Guinea
Malawi	Equatorial Guinea		Guinea-Bissau
Mauritius[6]	Gabon	*Southern Africa*	Liberia
Mozambique	Sao Tome and Principe		Mali
Réunion		Botswana	Mauritania
Rwanda		Lesotho	Niger
Seychelles*		Namibia	Nigeria
Somalia		South Africa	Saint Helena[7] *
Uganda		Swaziland	Senegal
United Republic of Tanzania			Sierra Leone
Zambia			Togo
Zimbabwe			

Asia

Eastern Asia	*South-central Asia*[8]	*South-eastern Asia*	*Western Asia*
China	Afghanistan	Brunei Darussalam	Armenia
China, Hong Kong SAR	Bangladesh	Cambodia	Azerbaijan
China, Macao SAR	Bhutan	Democratic Republic of	Bahrain
Democratic People's	India	Timor-Leste	Cyprus
Republic of Korea	Iran (Islamic Republic of)	Indonesia	Georgia
Japan	Kazakhstan	Lao People's Democratic	Iraq
Mongolia	Kyrgyzstan	Republic	Israel
Republic of Korea	Maldives	Malaysia	Jordan
	Nepal	Myanmar	Kuwait
	Pakistan	Philippines	Lebanon
	Sri Lanka	Singapore	Occupied Palestinian
	Tajikistan	Thailand	Territory
	Turkmenistan	Viet Nam	Oman
	Uzbekistan		Qatar
			Saudi Arabia
			Syrian Arab Republic
			Turkey
			United Arab Emirates
			Yemen

---

[5] Including the island of Mayotte.
[6] Including the islands of Agalega, Rodrigues, and Saint Brandon.
[7] Including the islands of Ascension and Tristan da Cunha.
[8] The regions Southern Asia and Central Asia are combined into South-central Asia.

CLASSIFICATION OF COUNTRIES (*continued*)

Europe

Eastern Europe

Belarus
Bulgaria
Czech Republic
Hungary
Poland
Republic of Moldova
Romania
Russian Federation
Slovakia
Ukraine

Northern Europe

Channel Islands[9]
Denmark
Estonia
Faeroe Islands*
Finland[10]
Iceland
Ireland
Isle of Man*
Latvia
Lithuania
Norway[11]
Sweden
United Kingdom of Great
   Britain and Northern
   Ireland[12]

Southern Europe

Albania
Andorra*
Bosnia and Herzegovina
Croatia
Gibraltar*
Greece
Holy See*
Italy
Malta
Portugal
San Marino*
Serbia and Montenegro
Slovenia
Spain
The former Yugoslav
   Republic of Macedonia[13]

Western Europe

Austria
Belgium
France
Germany
Liechtenstein*
Luxembourg
Monaco*
Netherlands
Switzerland

Latin America and the Caribbean

Caribbean

Anguilla*
Antigua and Barbuda*
Aruba*
Bahamas
Barbados
British Virgin Islands*
Cayman Islands*
Cuba
Dominica*
Dominican Republic
Grenada*
Guadeloupe
Haiti
Jamaica
Martinique
Montserrat*
Netherlands Antilles
Puerto Rico
Saint Kitts and Nevis*
Saint Lucia
Saint Vincent and the
   Grenadines
Trinidad and Tobago
Turks and Caicos Islands*
United States Virgin Islands

Central America

Belize
Costa Rica
El Salvador
Guatemala
Honduras
Mexico
Nicaragua
Panama

South America

Argentina
Bolivia
Brazil
Chile
Colombia
Ecuador
Falkland Islands (Malvinas)*
French Guiana
Guyana
Paraguay
Peru
Suriname
Uruguay
Venezuela

---

[9] Including the islands of Guernsey and Jersey.
[10] Including Åland Islands.
[11] Including Svalbard and Jan Mayen Islands.
[12] Also referred to as United Kingdom.
[13] Also referred to as TFYR Macedonia.

CLASSIFICATION OF COUNTRIES (*continued*)

Northern America

Bermuda*
Canada
Greenland*
Saint Pierre et Miquelon*
United States of America

Oceania

Australia/New Zealand	*Melanesia*	*Micronesia*	*Polynesia*
Australia[14]	Fiji	Guam	American Samoa*
New Zealand	New Caledonia	Kiribati*	Cook Islands*
	Papua New Guinea	Marshall Islands*	French Polynesia
	Solomon Islands	Micronesia	Niue*
	Vanuatu	(Federated States of)	Pitcairn*
		Nauru*	Samoa
		Northern Mariana Islands*	Tokelau*
		Palau*	Tonga
			Tuvalu*
			Wallis and Futuna Islands*

Sub-Saharan Africa

Angola	Côte d'Ivoire	Kenya	Nigeria	Swaziland
Benin	Democratic Republic	Lesotho	Réunion	Togo
Botswana	of the Congo	Liberia	Rwanda	Uganda
Burkina Faso	Djibouti	Madagascar	Saint Helena	United Republic
Burundi	Equatorial Guinea	Malawi	Sao Tome and Principe	of Tanzania
Cameroon	Eritrea	Mali	Senegal	Zambia
Cape Verde	Ethiopia	Mauritania	Seychelles	Zimbabwe
Central African	Gabon	Mauritius	Sierra Leone	
Chad	Gambia	Mozambique	Somalia	
Comoros	Ghana	Namibia	South Africa	
Congo	Guinea	Niger	Sudan	
	Guinea-Bissau			

---

[14] Including Christmas Island, Cocos (Keeling) Islands, and Norfolk Island.

CLASSIFICATION OF COUNTRIES (*continued*)

Least developed countries

Afghanistan	Ethiopia	Niger
Angola	Gambia	Rwanda
Bangladesh	Guinea	Samoa
Benin	Guinea-Bissau	Sao Tome and Principe
Bhutan	Haiti	Senegal
Burkina Faso	Kiribati	Sierra Leone
Burundi	Lao People's Democratic Republic	Solomon Islands
Cambodia	Lesotho	Somalia
Cape Verde	Liberia	Sudan
Central African Republic	Madagascar	Togo
Chad	Malawi	Tuvalu
Comoros	Maldives	Uganda
Democratic Republic of the Congo	Mali	United Republic of Tanzania
Democratic Republic of Timor-Leste	Mauritania	Vanuatu
Djibouti	Mozambique	Yemen
Equatorial Guinea	Myanmar	Zambia
Eritrea	Nepal	

Note: Countries with a population of less than 100,000 in 2000 are indicated by an asterisk (*).

EXECUTIVE SUMMARY

The *2004 Revision* is the nineteenth round of official United Nations population estimates and projections prepared by the Population Division of the Department of Economic and Social Affairs of the United Nations Secretariat. These are used throughout the United Nations system as the basis for activities requiring population information. The *2004 Revision* is the first to incorporate the full results of the 2000 round of national population censuses. It also takes into account the results of recent specialized surveys carried out in developing countries to provide both demographic and other information to assess the progress made in achieving the internationally agreed development goals, including the Millennium Development Goals (MDGs). The comprehensive review of past worldwide demographic trends and future prospects presented in the *2004 Revision* provides the population basis for the assessment of those goals.

The *2004 Revision* confirms the variety of demographic dynamics of our times. While the population at the global level continues to increase, that of the more developed regions as a whole is hardly changing and virtually all population growth is occurring in the less developed regions. Especially rapid population growth characterizes the group of 50 least developed countries.

Underlying these varied patterns of growth are distinct trends in fertility and mortality. Below-replacement fertility prevails in the more developed regions and is expected to continue to 2050. Fertility is still high in most least developed countries and, although it is expected to decline, it will remain higher than in the rest of the world. In the rest of the developing countries, fertility has declined markedly since the late 1960s and is expected to reach below-replacement levels by 2050 in most of these developing countries.

Mortality in the established market economies of the developed world is low and continues to decline, but it has been stagnant or even increasing in a number of countries with economies in transition, largely as a result of deteriorating social and economic conditions and, in some cases, because of the spread of HIV. Mortality is also decreasing in the majority of developing countries, but in those highly affected by the HIV/AIDS epidemic, mortality has been increasing. Given the ongoing efforts to provide antiretroviral treatment to 3 million AIDS patients by 2005 and the expectation of further expansion of that treatment thereafter, the *2004 Revision* assumes a longer average survivorship for people living with HIV than the *2002 Revision* did and therefore projects somewhat lower future mortality levels in HIV-affected countries than the previous *Revision*.

The HIV/AIDS epidemic continues to spread. The number of countries with a significant number of infected people in the *2004 Revision* is 60, up from 53 in the *2002 Revision*. Although HIV prevalence levels in some countries have been revised downward as better statistics become available. Nevertheless, the toll of the disease continues to be high and is expected to remain so, despite projected reductions in the prevalence of HIV/AIDS. Lower projected levels of HIV prevalence depend on the realization of the commitments made by Governments in the 2000 Millennium Declaration[1] and the 2001 United Nations Declaration of Commitment on HIV/AIDS[2].

---

[1] See General Assembly Resolution A/Res/55/2.
[2] See General Assembly Resolution A/Res/S-26/2.

The key findings from the *2004 Revision* can be summarized as follows:

1. By July 2005, the world will have 6.5 billion inhabitants, 380 million more than in 2000 or a gain of 76 million annually. Despite the declining fertility levels projected over 2005-2050 the world population is expected to reach 9.1 billion according to the medium variant and will still be adding 34 million persons annually by mid-century.

2. Today, 95 per cent of all population growth is absorbed by the developing world and 5 per cent by the developed world. By 2050, according to the medium variant, the population of the more developed countries as a whole would be declining slowly by about 1 million persons a year and that of the developing world would be adding 35 million annually, 22 million of whom would be absorbed by the least developed countries.

3. Future population growth is highly dependent on the path that future fertility takes. In the medium variant, fertility is projected to decline from 2.6 children per woman today to slightly over 2 children per woman in 2050. If fertility were to remain about half a child above the levels projected in the medium variant, world population would reach 10.6 billion by 2050. A fertility path half a child below the medium would lead to a population of 7.6 billion by mid-century. That is, at the world level, continued population growth until 2050 is inevitable even if the decline of fertility accelerates.

TABLE 1. POPULATION OF THE WORLD, MAJOR DEVELOPMENT GROUPS AND MAJOR AREAS, 1950, 1975, 2005 AND 2050, BY PROJECTION VARIANTS

Major area	Population (millions)			Population in 2050 (millions)			
	1950	1975	2005	Low	Medium	High	Constant
World...	2 519	4 074	6 465	7 680	9 076	10 646	11 658
More developed regions	813	1 047	1 211	1 057	1 236	1 440	1 195
Less developed regions....................	1 707	3 027	5 253	6 622	7 840	9 206	10 463
Least developed countries.............	201	356	759	1 497	1 735	1 994	2 744
Other less developed countries	1 506	2 671	4 494	5 126	6 104	7 213	7 719
Africa...	224	416	906	1 666	1 937	2 228	3 100
Asia...	1 396	2 395	3 905	4 388	5 217	6 161	6 487
Europe	547	676	728	557	653	764	606
Latin America and the Caribbean	167	322	561	653	783	930	957
Northern America............................	172	243	331	375	438	509	454
Oceania...	13	21	33	41	48	55	55

Source: Population Division of the Department of Economic and Social Affairs of the United Nations Secretariat (2005). *World Population Prospects: The 2004 Revision. Highlights.* New York: United Nations.

Figure 1. Population of the world, 1950-2050, by projection variants

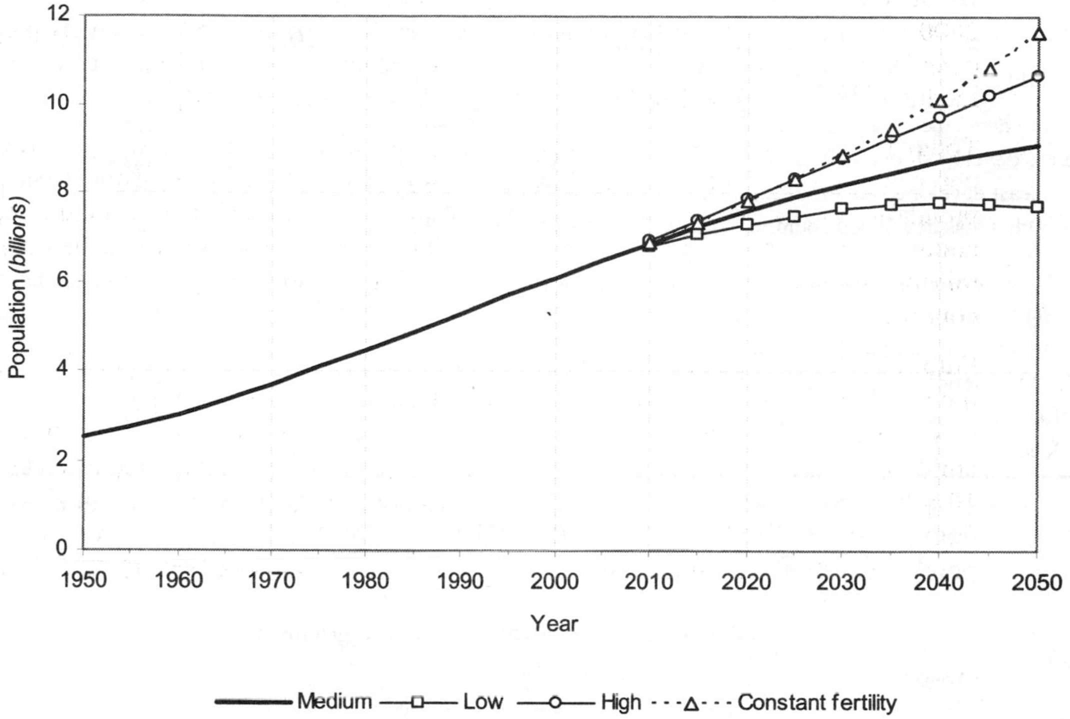

Source: Population Division of the Department of Economic and Social Affairs of the United Nations Secretariat (2005). *World Population Prospects: The 2004 Revision. Highlights.* New York: United Nations.

4. Because of its low and declining rate of growth, the population of developed countries as a whole is expected to remain virtually unchanged between 2005 and 2050, at about 1.2 billion. In contrast, the population of the 50 least developed countries is projected to more than double, passing from 0.8 billion in 2005 to 1.7 billion in 2050. Growth in the rest of the developing world is also projected to be robust, though less rapid, with its population rising from 4.5 billion to 6.1 billion between 2005 and 2050.

5. Very rapid population growth is expected to prevail in a number of developing countries, the majority of which are least developed. Between 2005 and 2050, the population is projected to at least triple in Afghanistan, Burkina Faso, Burundi, Chad, Congo, the Democratic Republic of Congo, the Democratic Republic of Timor-Leste, Guinea-Bissau, Liberia, Mali, Niger and Uganda.

6. The population of 51 countries or areas, including Germany, Italy, Japan, the Baltic States and most of the successor states of the former Soviet Union, is expected to be lower in 2050 than in 2005.

7. During 2005-2050, nine countries are expected to account for half of the world's projected population increase: India, Pakistan, Nigeria, the Democratic Republic of Congo, Bangladesh, Uganda, the United States of America, Ethiopia and China, listed according to the size of their contribution to population growth during that period.

TABLE 2. AVERAGE ANNUAL RATE OF CHANGE OF THE TOTAL POPULATION AND THE POPULATION IN BROAD AGE GROUPS, BY MAJOR AREA, 2005-2050 (MEDIUM VARIANT)

Major area	0-14	15-59	60+	80+	Total population
World	0.01	0.63	2.39	3.37	0.75
More developed regions	-0.14	-0.38	1.10	2.13	0.05
Less developed regions	0.03	0.82	2.88	4.19	0.89
Least developed countries	1.02	2.15	3.32	4.03	1.84
Other less developed countries	-0.29	0.54	2.84	4.21	0.68
Africa	0.87	2.00	3.12	3.86	1.69
Asia	-0.29	0.47	2.70	4.04	0.64
Europe	-0.36	-0.75	0.90	1.98	-0.24
Latin America and the Caribbean	-0.38	0.61	2.98	3.99	0.74
Northern America	0.23	0.37	1.67	2.30	0.62
Oceania	0.09	0.65	2.11	2.89	0.81

Source: Population Division of the Department of Economic and Social Affairs of the United Nations Secretariat (2005). *World Population Prospects: The 2004 Revision. Highlights.* New York: United Nations.

Figure 2. Population dynamics by development groups, 1950-2050

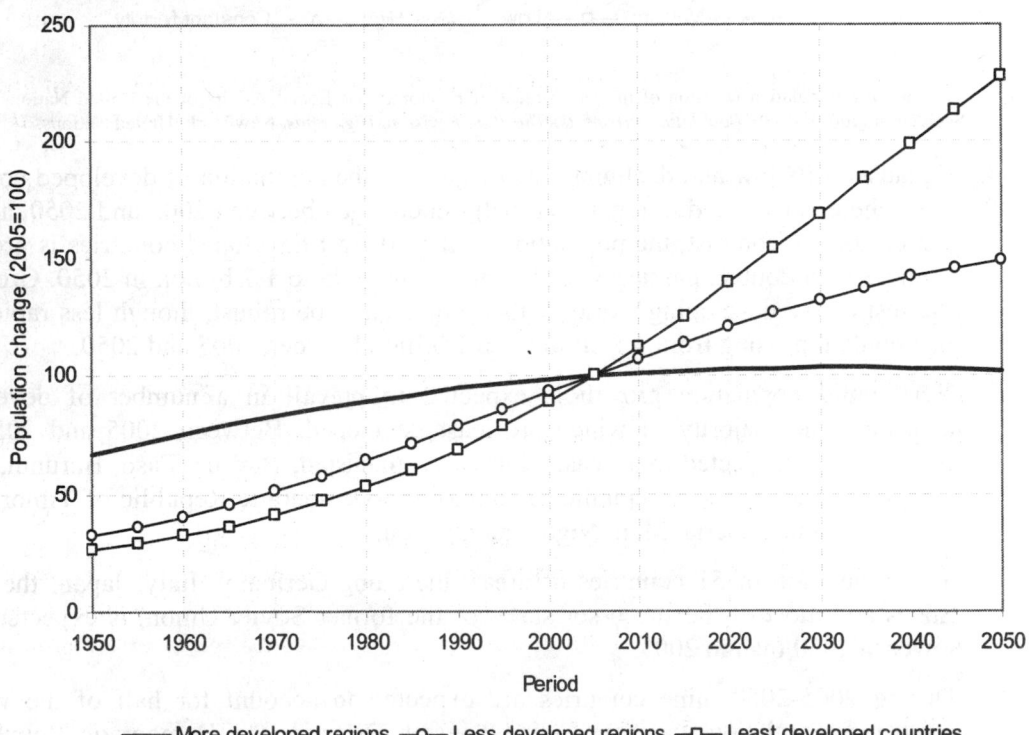

Source: Population Division of the Department of Economic and Social Affairs of the United Nations Secretariat (2005). *World Population Prospects: The 2004 Revision. Highlights.* New York: United Nations.

TABLE 3. TOTAL FERTILITY FOR THE WORLD, MAJOR DEVELOPMENT GROUPS AND MAJOR AREAS, 1970-1975, 2000-2005 AND 2045-2050, BY PROJECTION VARIANTS

| Major area | Total fertility (children per woman) | | | | | |
| | 1970-1975 | 2000-2005 | 2045-2050 | | | |
			Low	Medium	High	Constant
World..............................	4.49	2.65	1.56	2.05	2.53	3.50
More developed regions	2.12	1.56	1.34	1.84	2.34	1.67
Less developed regions.....................	5.44	2.90	1.59	2.07	2.56	3.69
Least developed countries	6.61	5.02	2.08	2.57	3.05	5.56
Other less developed countries	5.28	2.58	1.42	1.92	2.41	3.06
Africa.................................	6.72	4.97	2.03	2.52	3.00	5.50
Asia	5.08	2.47	1.42	1.91	2.41	2.98
Europe	2.16	1.40	1.33	1.83	2.33	1.45
Latin America and the Caribbean	5.05	2.55	1.36	1.86	2.36	2.69
Northern America..........................	2.01	1.99	1.35	1.85	2.35	1.99
Oceania	3.23	2.32	1.42	1.92	2.42	2.72

Source: Population Division of the Department of Economic and Social Affairs of the United Nations Secretariat (2005). *World Population Prospects: The 2004 Revision. Highlights.* New York: United Nations.

8. In 2000-2005, fertility at the world level stood at 2.65 children per woman, about half the level it had in 1950-1955 (5 children per women). In the medium variant, global fertility is projected to decline further to 2.05 children per woman by 2045-2050. Average world levels result from quite different trends by major development group. In developed countries as a whole fertility is currently 1.56 children per woman and is projected to increase slowly to 1.84 children per woman in 2045-2050. In the least developed countries, fertility is 5 children per woman and is expected to drop by about half, to 2.57 children per woman by 2045-2050. In the rest of the developing world, fertility is already moderately low at 2.58 children per woman and is expected to decline further to 1.92 children per woman by mid century, thus nearly converging to the fertility levels by then typical of the developed world. Realization of the fertility declines projected is contingent on access to family planning, especially in the least developed countries.

9. In 2000-2005, fertility remains above 5 children per woman in 35 of the 148 developing countries, 30 of which are least developed countries, while the pace of decline in several countries of sub-Saharan Africa and South-central Asia has been slower than anticipated. Overall, the countries with high fertility account for 10 per cent of the world population. In contrast, fertility has reached below-replacement levels in 23 developing countries accounting for 25 per cent of the world population. This group includes China whose fertility during 2000-2005 is estimated at 1.7 children per woman.

10. Fertility levels in the 44 developed countries, which account for 19 per cent of the world population, are currently very low. All except Albania have fertility below replacement level and 15, mostly located in Southern and Eastern Europe, have reached levels of fertility unprecedented in human history (below 1.3 children per woman). Since 1990-1995, fertility decline has been the rule among most developed countries. The few increases recorded, such as those in Belgium, France, Germany, the Netherlands and the United States, have been small.

TABLE 4. LIFE EXPECTANCY AT BIRTH FOR THE WORLD, MAJOR DEVELOPMENT
GROUPS AND MAJOR AREAS, 2000-2005 AND 2045-2050

Major area	2000-2005	2045-2050
World	65.4	75.1
More developed regions............................	75.6	82.1
Less developed regions.............................	63.4	74.0
Least developed countries	51.0	66.5
Other less developed countries...............	66.1	76.3
Africa...	49.1	65.4
Asia...	67.3	77.2
Europe...	73.7	80.6
Latin America and Caribbean	71.5	79.5
Northern America	77.6	82.7
Oceania	74.0	81.2

Source: Population Division of the Department of Economic and Social Affairs
of the United Nations Secretariat (2005). *World Population Prospects: The 2004
Revision. Highlights.* New York: United Nations.

11. Global life expectancy at birth, which is estimated to have risen from 47 years in 1950-1955 to 65 years in 2000-2005, is expected to keep on rising to reach 75 years in 2045-2050. In the more developed regions, the projected increase is from 76 years today to 82 years by mid-century. Among the least developed countries, where life expectancy today is 51 years, it is expected to be 67 years in 2045-2050. Because many of these countries are highly affected by the HIV/AIDS epidemic, the projected increase in life expectancy is dependent on the implementation of effective programmes to prevent and treat HIV infection. In the rest of the developing world, under similar conditionalities, life expectancy is projected to rise from 66 years today to 76 years by mid-century.

12. Mortality in Eastern Europe has been increasing since the late 1980s. In 2000-2005 life expectancy in the region, at 67.9 years, was lower than it had been in 1960-1965 (68.6 years). The Russian Federation and the Ukraine are particularly affected by rises in mortality resulting partly from the spread of HIV.

13. Twenty-five years into the HIV/AIDS epidemic, the impact of the disease is evident in terms of increased morbidity and mortality and slower population growth. In Southern Africa, the region with the highest HIV/AIDS prevalence of the disease, life expectancy has fallen from 62 years in 1990-1995 to 48 years in 2000-2005, and is projected to decrease further to 43 years over the next decade before a slow recovery starts. As a consequence, population growth in the region is expected to stall between 2005 and 2020. In Botswana, Lesotho and Swaziland, the population is projected to decrease as deaths outnumber births. In most of the other developing countries affected by the epidemic, population growth will continue to be positive because their moderate or high fertility more than counterbalances the rise in mortality.

14. The primary consequence of fertility decline, especially if combined with increases in life expectancy, is population ageing, whereby the share of older persons in a population grows relative to that of younger persons. Globally, the number of persons aged 60 years or over is expected almost to triple, increasing from 672 million in 2005 to nearly 1.9 billion by 2050. Whereas 6 out of every 10 of those older persons live today in developing countries, by 2050, 8 out of every 10 will do so. An even more

marked increase is expected in the number of the oldest-old (persons aged 80 years or over): from 86 million in 2005 to 394 million in 2050. In developing countries, the rise will be from 42 million to 278 million, implying that by 2050 most oldest-old will live in the developing world.

15. In developed countries, 20 per cent of today's population is aged 60 years or over and by 2050 that proportion is projected to be 32 per cent. The elderly population in developed countries has already surpassed the number of children (persons aged 0-14) and by 2050 there will be 2 elderly persons for every child. In the developing world, the proportion of the population aged 60 or over is expected to rise from 8 per cent in 2005 to close to 20 per cent by 2050.

16. Increases in the median age, the age at which 50 per cent of the population is older and 50 per cent younger than that age, are indicative of population ageing. Today, just 11 developed countries have a median age above 40 years. By 2050, there will be 89 countries in that group, 45 in the developing world. Population aging, which is becoming a pervasive reality in developed countries, is also inevitable in the developing world and will occur faster in developing countries.

17. Countries where fertility remains high and has declined only moderately will experience the slowest population ageing. By 2050, about one in five countries is still projected to have a median age equal or less than 30 years. The youngest populations will be found in least developed countries, 11 of which are projected to have median ages equal to or less than 23 years in 2050, including Afghanistan, Angola, Burundi, Chad, the Democratic Republic of Congo, Equatorial Guinea, Guinea-Bissau, Liberia, Mali, Niger and Uganda.

18. During 2005-2050, the net number of international migrants to more developed regions is projected to be 98 million or an average of 2.2 million annually. The same number will leave the less developed regions. For the developed world, such a level of net migration will largely offset the expected excess of deaths over births during 2005-2050, which amounts to a loss of 73 million people. For the developing world, the 98 million emigrants represent scarcely less than 4 per cent of expected population growth.

19. Over the period 2000-2005, 74 countries were net receivers of migrants. In 64 of these countries, the net migration projected reinforces population growth and in 7 countries, it reverses the trend of population decline (Austria, Croatia, Germany, Greece, Italy, Slovakia and Slovenia) In three countries, the migration slows down population decline but does not reverse it (Czech Republic, Hungary and the Russian Federation).

20. In terms of annual averages for the period 2005-2050, the major net receivers of international migrants are projected to be the United States (1.1 million annually), Germany (202,000), Canada (200,000), the United Kingdom (130,000), Italy (120,000) and Australia (100,000). The major countries of net emigration are projected to be China (-327,000 annually), Mexico (-293,000), India (-241,000), the Philippines (-180,000), Indonesia (-164,000), Pakistan (-154,000) and the Ukraine (-100,000).

ASSUMPTIONS UNDERLYING THE *2004 REVISION*

To project population until 2050, the United Nations Population Division applies assumptions regarding future trends in fertility, mortality, and migration. Because future trends cannot be known with certainty, a number of projection variants are produced. The Highlights focus on the medium variant of the *2004 Revision*. The assumptions of the medium variant are outlined in detail in section A of this chapter.

The *2004 Revision* includes five additional variants: the high, low, constant-fertility, constant-mortality, and zero-migration variants. The assumptions that differentiate these variants from the medium variant are described in section B. Detailed results of these variants will be made available in forthcoming publications.

The future population of each country is projected from an estimated population for 1 July 2005. Because actual population data for 2005 are not yet available, the 2005 estimate is based upon the most recent population data available for each country, derived usually from a census or population register, updated to 2005 using all available data on fertility, mortality and international migration. In cases where very recent data are not available, estimated demographic trends are short term projections from the most recent available data. Population data from all sources are evaluated for completeness, accuracy and consistency, and adjusted where necessary.[3]

A. ASSUMPTIONS OF THE MEDIUM VARIANT

1. Fertility assumptions: Convergence toward total fertility below replacement

Total fertility in all countries is assumed to converge eventually toward a level of 1.85 children per woman. However, not all countries reach this level during the projection period, that is, by 2050. The basic principle of fertility projection is the same for all countries, but projection procedures are slightly different depending on whether countries had a total fertility above or below 1.85 children per woman in 2000-2005.

For those countries with total fertility above 1.85 children per woman, fertility is assumed to follow a path derived from models of fertility decline established by the United Nations Population Division on the basis of the past experience of all countries with declining fertility during 1950-2000. The models relate the level of total fertility during a period to the average expected decline in total fertility during the next period. If the total fertility projected by a model for a country falls to 1.85 children per woman before 2050, total fertility is held constant at that level for the remainder of the projection period (that is, until 2050).

In all cases, the projected fertility paths yielded by the models are checked against recent trends in fertility for each country. When a country's recent fertility trends deviate considerably from those consistent with the models, fertility is projected over an initial period of 5 or 10 years in such a way that it follows recent experience. The model projection takes over after that transition period. For instance, in countries where fertility has stalled or where there is no evidence of fertility decline, fertility is projected to remain constant for several more years before a declining path sets in.

---

[3] For a general description of the procedures used in revising estimates of population dynamics, see *World Population Prospects: The 2002 Revision, Volume III: Analytical Report*, pp. 180-182.

For countries where total fertility was below 1.85 children per woman in 2000-2005, it is assumed that over the first 5 or 10 years of the projection period fertility will follow the recently observed trends in each country. After that transition period, fertility is assumed to increase linearly at a rate of 0.07 children per woman per quinquennium. Thus, countries whose fertility is currently very low need not reach a level of 1.85 children per woman by 2050.

2. Mortality assumptions: Increasing life expectancy except when affected by HIV/AIDS

a. Normal mortality assumptions

Mortality is projected on the basis of models of change of life expectancy produced by the United Nations Population Division. These models produce smaller gains the higher the life expectancy already reached. The selection of a model for each country is based on recent trends in life expectancy by sex. For countries highly affected by the HIV/AIDS epidemic, the model incorporating a slow pace of mortality decline has generally been used to project the reduction of general mortality risks not related to HIV/AIDS.

b. The impact of HIV/AIDS on mortality

For the 60 countries highly affected by the HIV/AIDS epidemic (listed in table VIII.21), estimates of the impact of HIV/AIDS are made by explicitly modelling the course of the epidemic and by projecting the yearly incidence of HIV infection. The model developed by the UNAIDS Reference Group on Estimates, Modelling and Projections[4] is used to fit past estimates of HIV prevalence provided by UNAIDS so as to derive the parameters determining the past dynamics of the epidemic. For most countries, the model is fitted assuming that the relevant parameters have remained constant in the past. Beginning in 2005, the parameter PHI, which reflects the rate of recruitment of new individuals into the high-risk or susceptible group, is projected to decline by half every thirty years. The parameter R, which represents the force of infection, is projected to decline in the same manner. The reduction in R reflects the assumption that changes in behaviour among those subject to the risk of infection, along with increases in access to treatment for those infected, will reduce the chances of transmitting the virus. The rate of mother-to-child transmission is projected to decline at varying rates, depending on each country's progress in increasing access to treatment. In addition, the component of the Reference Group model relative to the survivorship of infected children has been updated: in the *2004 Revision* it is assumed that 50 per cent of children infected through mother-to-child transmission will survive to age two.

The *2004 Revision* incorporates for the first time a longer survival for persons receiving treatment with highly active antiretroviral therapy (ART). The proportion of the HIV-positive population receiving treatment in each country is consistent with estimates prepared by the World Health Organization for the end of 2004[5]. Coverage is projected to reach between 40 percent and 85 per cent by 2015, depending on the current level of coverage. It is assumed that, on average, annual survival probabilities increase to at least 80 per cent for individuals receiving ART. Under this assumption, mean survival from the initiation of therapy is 3.1 years (median 4.5 years). In contrast, in the absence of treatment mean survival after progression to AIDS is assumed to be just one year.

---

[4] Improved methods and assumptions for estimation of the HIV/AIDS epidemic and its impact: Recommendations of the UNAIDS Reference Group on Estimates, Modelling and Projections. AIDS, vol. 16, pp. W1-W14 (UNAIDS Reference Group on Estimates, Modelling and Projections, 2002).
[5] World Health Organization. "3 by 5" Progress Report, December 2004/WHO and UNAIDS.

3. International migration assumptions

The future path of international migration is set on the basis of past international migration estimates and an assessment of the policy stance of countries with regard to future international migration flows.

B. PROJECTION VARIANTS

The *2004 Revision* includes five projection variants in addition to the medium variant. Three variants—high, low and constant-fertility—differ from the medium variant only in the projected level of total fertility. In the high variant, total fertility is projected to remain 0.5 children above the total fertility in the medium variant over most of the projection period. For example, countries reaching a total fertility of 1.85 in the medium variant reach a total fertility of 2.35 in the high variant. In the low variant, total fertility is projected to remain 0.5 children below the total fertility in the medium variant. In the constant-fertility variant, total fertility remains constant at the level estimated for 2000-2005.

A constant-mortality variant and a zero-migration variant have also been prepared. They both have the same fertility assumption as the medium variant. Furthermore, the constant-mortality variant has the same international migration assumption as the medium variant. Consequently, the results of the constant-mortality variant can be compared with those of the medium variant to assess the effect that changing mortality has on other demographic parameters. Similarly, the zero-migration variant differs from the medium variant only with respect to the underlying assumption regarding international migration. Therefore, the zero-migration variant allows an assessment of the effect that non-zero migration has on other demographic parameters.

C. METHODOLOGICAL CHANGES MADE FOR THE *2004 REVISION*

- In the medium variant, the fertility of countries with a total fertility below 1.85 children per woman in 2000-2005 is projected first by continuing recent trends and then by increasing fertility linearly at a rate of 0.07 children per woman per quinquennium. These countries do not necessarily reach a level of 1.85 children per woman by 2050.

- In the *2004 Revision*, additional models of mortality change have been used to capture the diversity of historical experience in the rise of life expectancy. Specifically, very slow and very fast models of change have been developed and added to the previously existing slow, medium and fast models.

- The impact of HIV/AIDS on mortality is modelled explicitly for all countries that had adult HIV prevalence of one per cent or greater in 2003.

- Treatment with antiretroviral therapy is explicitly incorporated into the projection of HIV/AIDS for affected countries. In addition, the rate of mother-to-child transmission of HIV is projected to decline at a rate consistent with projected progress in expanding access to treatment.

تصدير

يقدم هذا التقرير موجزا للنتائج التي توصل إليها *تنقيح عام ٢٠٠٤* بشأن التقديرات والتوقعات السكانية الرسمية في العالم التي أعدتها شعبة السكان التابعة لإدارة الشؤون الاقتصادية والاجتماعية بالأمانة العامة للأمم المتحدة. وبالإضافة إلى ذلك، يورد هذا التقرير استعراضا عاما للافتراضات المتعلقة بالخصوبة ومعدل الوفيات والهجرة، التي تستند إليها التوقعات، فضلا عن تقديم موجز للتغيرات والتعديلات التي أدخلت على *تنقيح عام ٢٠٠٤*، فيما يخص الإجراءات المتبعة في *تنقيح عام ٢٠٠٢*. ويمثّل *تنقيح عام ٢٠٠٤* الجولة التاسعة عشرة للتقديرات والتوقعات الديموغرافية العالمية التي دأبت شعبة السكان على إعدادها منذ عام ١٩٥٠.

وسترد النتائج الكاملة *للتنقيح لعام ٢٠٠٤* في سلسلة من ثلاثة مجلدات. فيحتوي المجلد الأول[(١)] جداول شاملة تتضمن المؤشرات الديموغرافية الرئيسية لكل بلد خلال الفترة ١٩٥٠-٢٠٥٠. ويحتوي المجلد الثاني[(٢)] على التوزيع السكاني لكل بلد حسب العمر ونوع الجنس خلال الفترة ١٩٥٠-٢٠٥٠. أما المجلد الثالث[(٣)] فسيخصص لتحليل النتائج التي يتم التوصل إليها.

وستوزع البيانات أيضا في شكل رقمي. ويمكن للمستعملين المهتمين شراء قرص حاسوبي مدمج CD-ROM يتضمن النتائج الرئيسية *لتنقيح عام ٢٠٠٤*. ويتوافر بموقع شعبة السكان على الشبكة www.unpopulation.org وصف، للبيانات التي يحتوي عليها القرص الحاسوبي المدمج واستمارة طلب شراء.

وشعبة السكان هي المسؤولة عن *تنقيح عام ٢٠٠٤*. ولقد سهّل من عملية إعداد *تنقيح عام ٢٠٠٤* تعاون اللجان الإقليمية والوكالات المتخصصة، وغيرها من هيئات الأمم المتحدة المعنية، مع شعبة السكان.

وعلى وجه الخصوص، فقد شكلت الحولية الديموغرافية للأمم المتحدة مع قواعد بياناتها التي تعدها وتستكملها شعبة الأمم المتحدة للإحصاءات التابعة لإدارة الشؤون

---

(١) ''التوقعات السكانية في العالم: تنقيح عام ٢٠٠٤''، المجلد الأول، ''جداول شاملة'' (منشورات الأمم المتحدة، No Sales.E .٠٥.XIII.٥).

(٢) ''التوقعات السكانية في العالم: تنقيح عام ٢٠٠٤''، المجلد الثاني، ''توزيع سكان العالم حسب نوع الجنس والسن'' (منشورات الأمم المتحدة، No Sales.E .٠٥.XIII.٦).

(٣) ''التوقعات السكانية في العالم: تنقيح عام ٢٠٠٤''، المجلد الثالث، ''تقرير تحليلي'' (منشورات الأمم المتحدة، سيصدر عما قريب).

الاقتصادية والاجتماعية، أحد المصادر الرئيسية للإحصاءات السكانية الوطنية الرسمية الـتي استخدمت في إعداد هذه التقديرات والتوقعات. وتُعرب شعبة السكان عن امتنانِها لـشعبة الإحصاءات لتعاونِها المستمر.

ويمكـــن الوصـــول إلى نواتـــج منتقـــاة مـــن تنقـــيح عـــام ٢٠٠٤، فضلا عن معلومات أخرى تتعلق بالسكان، على موقع شعبة السكان على الـشبكة العالميــة www.unpopulation.org. وللحصول على مزيد من المعلومات عن تنقيح عام ٢٠٠٤ يرجى الاتصال على العنوان التــالي: Ms. Hania Zlotnik, Director, Population Division, United Nations, New York, NY 10017, USA (fax: 1 212 963 2147).

موجز

يمثل *تنقيح عام ٢٠٠٤* الجولة التاسعة عشرة للتقديرات والتوقعات السكانية الرسمية للأمم المتحدة التي أعدتها شعبة السكان التابعة لإدارة الشؤون الاقتصادية والاجتماعية بالأمانة العامة للأمم المتحدة. وتُستخدم هذه التقديرات والتوقعات في كامل منظومة الأمم المتحدة أساسا للأنشطة التي تتطلب معلومات سكانية. وتنقيح عام ٢٠٠٤ هو أول تنقيح يضم كل نتائج جولة الإحصاءات السكانية الوطنية لعام ٢٠٠٠. ويضم بالمثل نتائج الدراسات الاستقصائية المتخصصة التي أجريت مؤخرا في البلدان النامية لتوفير المعلومات الديمغرافية وغيرها من المعلومات لتقييم التقدم المحرز في تحقيق الأهداف الإنمائية المتفق عليها دوليا، بما في ذلك الأهداف الإنمائية للألفية. ويوفر الاستعراض الشامل للاتجاهات الديمغرافية على نطاق العالم في الماضي، وكذلك التوقعات في المستقبل المعروضة في تنقيح عام ٢٠٠٤، الأساس السكاني لتقييم هذه الأهداف.

ويؤكد *تنقيح عام ٢٠٠٤* تباين الديناميات الديمغرافية السائدة في عصرنا هذا. ففي الوقت الذي يستمر فيه حاليا تزايد السكان على مستوى العالم، فإن التزايد في المناطق الأكثر تقدما ككل لا يكاد يطرأ عليه تغيير، فيما يحدث كل النمو السكاني تقريبا في المناطق الأقل تقدما. وبوجه خاص، فإن مجموعة أقل البلدان نموا وعددها ٥٠ بلدا يغلب عليها النمو السكاني السريع.

وتستند هذه الأنماط المتباينة في النمو إلى اتجاهات مختلفة في معدلات الخصوبة والوفيات. فتسود في المناطق الأكثر تقدما معدلات خصوبة دون مستوى الإحلال، ويتوقع أن تستمر هذه المعدلات حتى عام ٢٠٥٠. وما زالت معدلات الخصوبة عالية في معظم أقل البلدان نموا؛ وبالرغم من توقع انخفاض هذه المعدلات، فستظل أعلى من معدلات بقية العالم. وفي بقية البلدان النامية، انخفضت معدلات الخصوبة انخفاضا ملحوظا منذ أواخر الستينيات، ومن المتوقع أن تصل إلى ما دون مستوى الإحلال مع مقدم عام ٢٠٥٠ في معظم هذه البلدان النامية.

ويلاحظ انخفاض معدلات الوفيات في اقتصادات السوق الراسخة في البلدان المتقدمة النمو ولا تزال آخذة في الانخفاض، لكنها ظلت ثابتة بل وفي ازدياد في عدد من البلدان التي تمر اقتصاداتها بمرحلة انتقالية، وذلك إلى حد كبير نتيجة لتدهور الأوضاع الاجتماعية والاقتصادية وفي بعض الحالات بسبب انتشار فيروس نقص المناعة البشرية. كما تتناقص معدلات الوفيات في أكثرية البلدان النامية، غير أن معدلات الوفيات لا تزال في ازدياد في البلدان المتأثرة بوباء فيروس نقص المناعة البشرية/متلازمة نقص المناعة المكتسب (الإيدز).

ونظرا للجهود المبذولة حاليا لتوفير علاجات مضادة للفيروسات الرجعية لثلاثة ملايين مـن مرضى الإيدز بحلول عام ٢٠٠٥ ، وتوقع زيادة توسيع نطاق هذا العلاج فيما بعد، يفترض تنقيح ٢٠٠٤ متوسط بقاء على قيد الحياة للمصابين بالفيروس يزيد عمـا افترضه تنقيح ٢٠٠٢، وبالتالي فهو يفترض انخفاض معدلات الوفيات في المستقبل إلى حد ما في البلدان المتضررة بالفيروس مقارنة بنظيرتها في التنقيح السابق.

ويستمر وباء الفيروس/الإيدز في الانتشار. فقد ارتفع عدد البلدان التي بها عدد كبير من المصابين في تنقيح عام ٢٠٠٤ إلى ٦٠ بلدا من ٥٣ بلدا في تنقيح عام ٢٠٠٢، بـالرغم من تنقيح معدلات انتشار الفيروس وتخفيضها في بعض البلدان مع توافر إحصاءات أفـضل. ومع ذلك، فإن نسبة الإصابة بالمرض لا تزال عالية ومن المتوقع أن تظل كذلك، بالرغم مـن توقع حدوث انخفاض في انتشار الفيروس/الإيدز. ويتوقف انخفاض المعدلات المتوقعة لانتشار الفيروس على تحقيق الالتزامات التي قطعتها الحكومات في إعلان الألفيـة لعـام ٢٠٠٠[٤] وإعلان الأمم المتحدة بشأن الفيروس/الإيدز[٥].

ويمكن إيجاز النتائج الرئيسية المستخلصة من تنقيح عام ٢٠٠٤ على النحو التالي:

١ -   مع حلول تموز/يوليه ٢٠٠٥، سيبلغ عدد سكان العالم ٦,٥ بلايين نـسمة، أي بزيادة قدرها ٣٨٠ مليون نسمة مقارنة بعام ٢٠٠٠ أو بزيادة ٧٦ مليون نسمة كل عـام. وعلى الرغم من الانخفاض المتوقع في معدلات الخصوبة للفترة ٢٠٠٥-٢٠٥٠، يتوقع أن يبلغ عدد سكان العالم ٩,١ بلايين نسمة حسب متغير الخصوبة المتوسط، وأن ينضاف رغم ذلك ٣٤ مليون نسمة كل عام مع حلول منتصف القرن.

٢ -   واليوم، يستوعب العالم النامي ٩٥ في المائة من مجموع النمو السكاني فيما يمثل العالم المتقدم ٥ في المائة في المجموع. وبحلول ٢٠٥٠، يشير متغير الخصوبة المتوسط إلى أن عـدد سكان البلدان الأكثر تقدما ككل سيتناقص تدريجيا بحوالي مليون نـسمة في العـام، فيمـا سيضيف العالم النامي ٣٥ مليون نسمة في العام، منها ٢٢ مليون نسمة تضيفها أقل البلدان نموا.

٣ -   ويتوقف النمو السكاني في المستقبل بدرجة كبيرة على المنحى الذي سيتخذه معـدل الخصوبة في المستقبل. وبحسب متغير الخصوبة المتوسط، يتوقع أن ينخفض معدل الخصوبة من ٢,٦ طفل لكل امرأة اليوم إلى ما يربو بقليل على طفلين لكل امرأة في عام ٢٠٥٠. وإذا

---

(٤) انظر قرار الجمعية العامة ٢/٥٥.

(٥) انظر قرار الجمعية العامة د إ ٢٦/٢.

استقر معدل الخصوبة عند نحو ٠,٥ طفل فوق المعدلات المتوقعة بحسب المتغير المتوسط، فقد يبلغ عدد سكان العالم ١٠,٦ بلايين نسمة بحلول عام ٢٠٥٠ . وسوف يـؤدي اتجـاه الخصوبة إذا تحدد بـ ٠,٥ طفل دون المتوسط إلى بلوغ عدد السكان ٧,٦ بلايـين نـسمة بحلول منتصف القرن. وهذا يعني على مستوى العالم أن اطراد النمو السكاني إلى غاية عـام ٢٠٥٠ أمر حتمي حتى وإن تسارع انخفاض معدل الخصوبة.

الجدول ١

عدد سكان العالم وسكان المجموعات الإنمائية الرئيسية والمناطق الرئيـسية في الأعـوام ١٩٥٠ و ١٩٧٥ و ٢٠٠٥ و٢٠٥٠ حسب متغيرات الإسقاط

الخصوبة الثابتة	متغير الخصوبة العالي	متغير الخصوبة المتوسط	متغير الخصوبة المنخفض	٢٠٠٥	١٩٧٥	١٩٥٠	المنطقة الرئيسية
عدد السكان في سنة ٢٠٥٠ (بالملايين)				عدد السكان (بالملايين)			
١١ ٦٥٨	١٠ ٦٤٦	٩ ٠٧٦	٧ ٦٨٠	٦ ٤٦٥	٤ ٠٧٤	٢ ٥١٩	العالم
١ ١٩٥	١ ٤٤٠	١ ٢٣٦	١ ٠٥٧	١ ٢١١	١ ٠٤٧	٨١٣	المناطق الأكثر تقدما
١٠ ٤٦٣	٩ ٢٠٦	٧ ٨٤٠	٦ ٦٢٢	٥ ٢٥٣	٣ ٠٢٧	١ ٧٠٧	المناطق الأقل تقدما
٢ ٧٤٤	١ ٩٩٤	١ ٧٣٥	١ ٤٩٧	٧٥٩	٣٥٦	٢٠١	أقل البلدان نموا
٧ ٧١٩	٧ ٢١٣	٦ ١٠٤	٥ ١٢٦	٤ ٤٩٤	٢ ٦٧١	١ ٥٠٦	البلدان الأخرى الأقل تقدما
٣ ١٠٠	٢ ٢٢٨	١ ٩٣٧	١ ٦٦٦	٩٠٦	٤١٦	٢٢٤	أفريقيا
٦ ٤٨٧	٦ ١٦١	٥ ٢١٧	٤ ٣٨٨	٣ ٩٠٥	٢ ٣٩٥	١ ٣٩٦	آسيا
٦٠٦	٧٦٤	٦٥٣	٥٥٧	٧٢٨	٦٧٦	٥٤٧	أوروبا
٩٥٧	٩٣٠	٧٨٣	٦٥٣	٥٦١	٣٢٢	١٦٧	أمريكا اللاتينية ومنطقة البحر الكاريبي
٤٥٤	٥٠٩	٤٣٨	٣٧٥	٣٣١	٢٤٣	١٧٢	أمريكا الشمالية
٥٥	٥٥	٤٨	٤١	٣٣	٢١	١٣	أوقيانوسيا

المصدر: شعبة السكان التابعة لإدارة الشؤون الاقتصادية والاجتماعية بالأمانة العامة للأمم المتحدة (٢٠٠٥). التوقعـات السكانية في العالم: تنقيح عام ٢٠٠٤ . الملامح الرئيسية. نيويورك، الأمم المتحدة.

الشكل الأول

سكان العالم ، ١٩٥٠-٢٠٥٠ ، حسب متغيرات الإسقاط

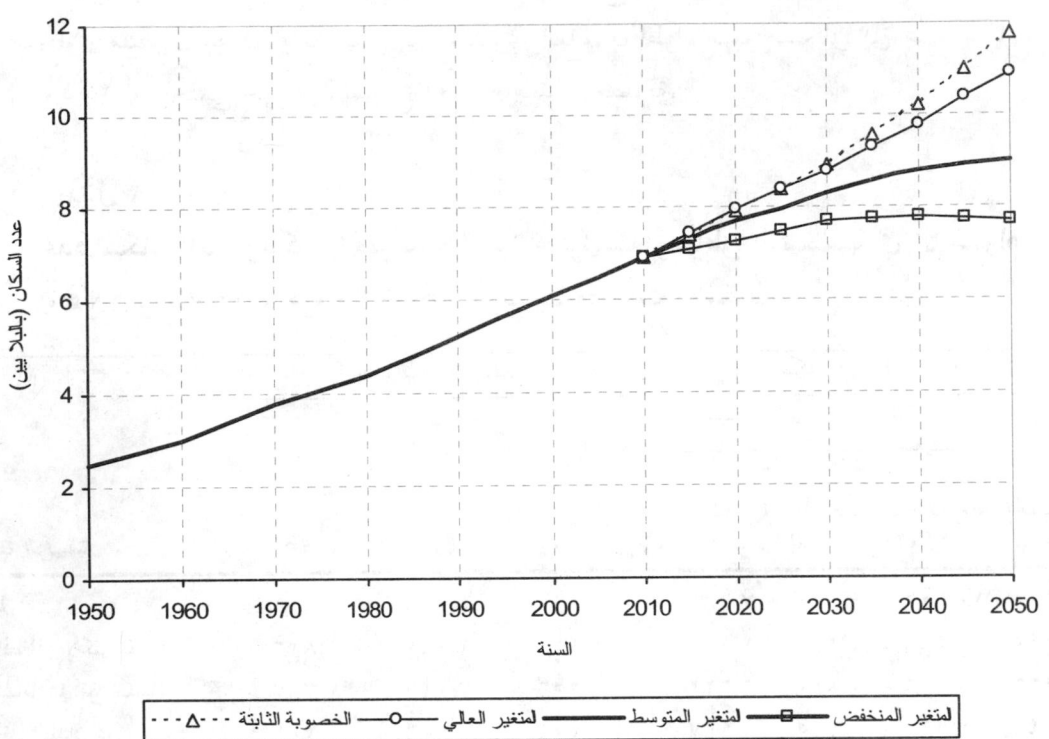

السنة

| لمتغير المنخفض ━□━ | لمتغير المتوسط ━━━ | لمتغير العالي ━○━ | الخصوبة الثابتة △--- |

المصدر: شعبة السكان التابعة لإدارة الشؤون الاقتصادية والاجتماعية بالأمانة العامة للأمم المتحدة (٢٠٠٥). التوقعات السكانية في العالم: تنقيح عام ٢٠٠٤. الملامح الرئيسية. نيويورك، الأمم المتحدة.

٤ - ومن المتوقع أن يظل عدد سكان البلدان المتقدمة ككل دون تغيير يذكر في الفترة بين ٢٠٠٥ و ٢٠٥٠ عند حوالي ١,٢ بليون نسمة، وذلك بسبب معدل النمو المتدني المستمر في الانخفاض. وفي المقابل، يُتوقع أن يرتفع عدد سكان أقل البلدان نموا، وعددها ٥٠ بلدا، إلى أكثر من الضعف، من ٠,٨ بليون نسمة في عام ٢٠٠٥ إلى ١,٧ بليون نسمة في عام ٢٠٥٠. ويتوقع أيضا أن يكون النمو قويا في باقي بلدان العالم النامي وإن كان أقل سرعة، بحيث يرتفع عدد سكانها من ٤,٥ بلايين نسمة إلى ٦,١ بلايين نسمة بين عامي ٢٠٠٥ و ٢٠٥٠.

٥ - ويُتوقع أن يزيد النمو السكاني بوتيرة سريعة جدا في عدد من البلدان النامية، معظمها من أقل البلدان نموا. وفي الفترة بين عامي ٢٠٠٥ و٢٠٥٠، يُتوقع أن يتضاعف

عدد السكان ثلاث مرات على الأقل في أفغانستان وأوغندا وبوركينــا فاســو وبورونــدي وتشاد وجمهورية تيمور – ليشتي الديمقراطية وجمهورية الكونغو الديمقراطية وغينيا – بيـساو والكونغو وليبريا ومالي والنيجر.

٦ – ومن المتوقع أن ينخفض عدد السكان في عام ٢٠٥٠ مقارنة بعام ٢٠٠٥، في ٥١ بلدا أو منطقة، بما في ذلك ألمانيا وإيطاليا واليابان ودول البلطيق ومعظم الدول التي خلفــت الاتحاد السوفياتي السابق.

٧ – وخلال الفترة ٢٠٠٥ – ٢٠٥٠، يُتوقع أن تكون تسعة بلدان مسؤولة عن نــصف الزيادة المتوقعة في عدد سكان العالم، وهي: الهند وباكستان ونيجيريا وجمهوريــة الكونغــو الديمقراطية وبنغلاديش وأوغندا والولايات المتحدة الأمريكية وإثيوبيا والصين؛ وهي مرتبة هنا حسب حجم مساهمتها في النمو السكاني خلال الفترة المذكورة.

الجدول ٢

متوسط معدل النمو السنوي لمجموع السكان والفئات العمرية العريضة للسكان، حسب المناطق الرئيسية، ٢٠٠٥–٢٠٥٠ (متغير الخصوبة المتوسط)

(نسبة مئوية)

مجموع السكان	+٨٠	+٦٠	١٥-٥٩	صفر-١٤	المنطقة الرئيسية
٠,٧٥	٣,٣٧	٢,٣٩	٠,٦٣	٠,٠١	العالم
٠,٠٥	٢,١٣	١,١٠	٠,٣٨-	٠,١٤-	المناطق الأكثر تقدما
٠,٨٩	٤,١٩	٢,٨٨	٠,٨٢	٠,٠٣	المناطق الأقل تقدما
١,٨٤	٤,٠٣	٣,٣٢	٢,١٥	١,٠٢	أقل البلدان نموا
٠,٦٨	٤,٢١	٢,٨٤	٠,٥٤	٠,٢٩-	البلدان الأخرى الأقل تقدما
١,٦٩	٣,٨٦	٣,١٢	٢,٠٠	٠,٨٧	أفريقيا
٠,٦٤	٤,٠٤	٢,٧٠	٠,٤٧	٠,٢٩-	آسيا
٠,٢٤-	١,٩٨	٠,٩٠	٠,٧٥-	٠,٣٦-	أوروبا
٠,٧٤	٣,٩٩	٢,٩٨	٠,٦١	٠,٣٨-	أمريكا اللاتينية ومنطقة البحر الكاريبي
٠,٦٢	٢,٣٠	١,٦٧	٠,٣٧	٠,٢٣	أمريكا الشمالية
٠,٨١	٢,٨٩	٢,١١	٠,٦٥	٠,٠٩	أوقيانوسيا

المصدر: شعبة السكان التابعة لإدارة الشؤون الاقتصادية والاجتماعية بالأمانة العامة للأمم المتحــدة (٢٠٠٥). التوقعات السكانية في العالم: تنقيح عام ٢٠٠٤. الملامح الرئيسية. نيويورك، الأمم المتحدة.

الشكل الثاني

ديناميات السكان حسب المجموعات الإنمائية، ١٩٥٠–٢٠٥٠

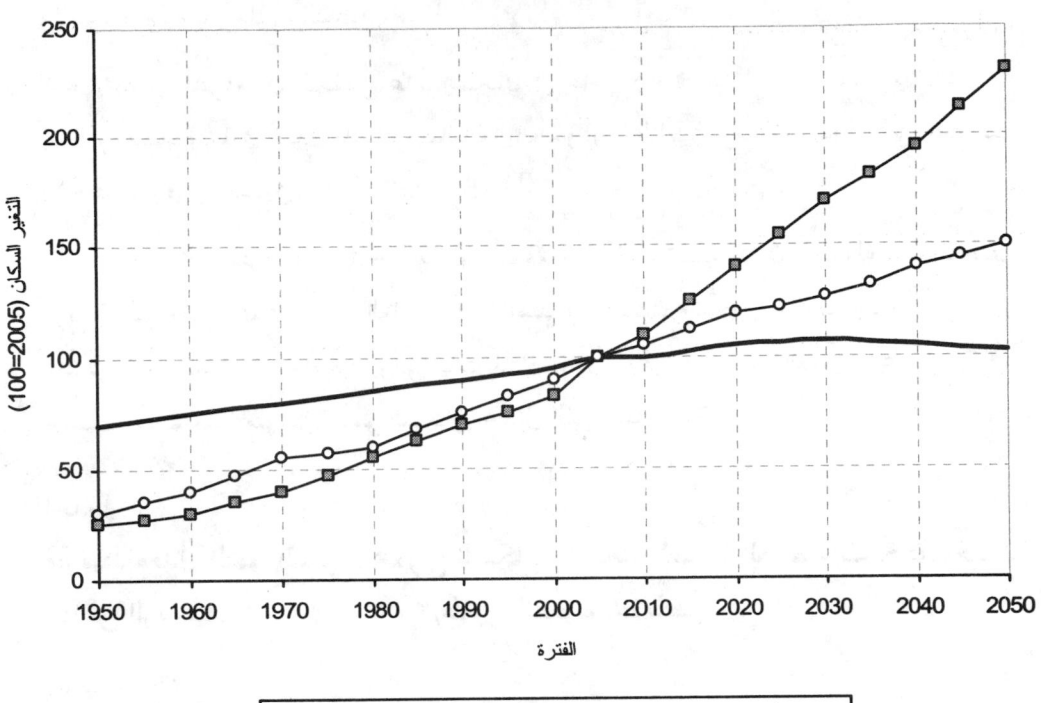

المصدر: شعبة السكان التابعة لإدارة الشؤون الاقتصادية والاجتماعية بالأمانة العامة للأمم المتحدة
(٢٠٠٥). التوقعات السكانية في العالم: تنقيح عام ٢٠٠٤. الملامح الرئيسية. نيويـــورك، الأمـــم
المتحدة.

الخصوبة الكلية في العالم وفي المجموعات الإنمائية الرئيسية وللمناطق الرئيسية في الفترات ١٩٧٠-١٩٧٥ و ٢٠٠٠-٢٠٠٥ و٢٠٤٥-٢٠٥٠ حــسب متغيِّــرات الإسقاطات

	الخصوبة الكلية (متوسط عدد الأطفال لكل امرأة)					
	٢٠٤٥-٢٠٥٠					
المنطقة الرئيسية	١٩٧٠-١٩٧٥	٢٠٠٠-٢٠٠٥	متغير الخصوبة المنخفض	متغير الخصوبة المتوسط	متغير الخصوبة العالي	الخصوبة الثابتة
العالم	٤,٤٩	٢,٦٥	١,٥٦	٢,٠٥	٢,٥٣	٣,٥٠
المناطق الأكثر تقدما	٢,١٢	١,٥٦	١,٣٤	١,٨٤	٢,٣٤	١,٦٧
المناطق الأقل تقدما	٥,٤٤	٢,٩٠	١,٥٩	٢,٠٧	٢,٥٦	٣,٦٩
أقل البلدان نموا	٦,٦١	٥,٠٢	٢,٠٨	٢,٥٧	٣,٠٥	٥,٥٦
البلدان الأخرى الأقل تقدما	٥,٢٨	٢,٥٨	١,٤٢	١,٩٢	٢,٤١	٣,٠٦
أفريقيا	٦,٧٢	٤,٩٧	٢,٠٣	٢,٥٢	٣,٠٠	٥,٥٠
آســـيا	٥,٠٨	٢,٤٧	١,٤٢	١,٩١	٢,٤١	٢,٩٨
أوروبا	٢,١٦	١,٤٠	١,٣٣	١,٨٣	٢,٣٣	١,٤٥
أمريكا اللاتينية ومنطقة البحر الكاريبي	٥,٠٥	٢,٥٥	١,٣٦	١,٨٦	٢,٣٦	٢,٦٩
أمريكا الشمالية	٢,٠١	١,٩٩	١,٣٥	١,٨٥	٢,٣٥	١,٩٩
أوقيانوسيا	٣,٢٣	٢,٣٢	١,٤٢	١,٩٢	٢,٤٢	٢,٧٢

المصدر: شعبة السكان التابعة لإدارة الشؤون الاقتصادية والاجتماعية بالأمانة العامة للأمم المتحدة (٢٠٠٥). التوقعات السكانية في العالم: تنقيح عام ٢٠٠٤. المجلد الأول، الملامح الرئيسية. نيويورك، الأمم المتحدة.

٨ - في الفترة ٢٠٠٠-٢٠٠٥، بلغ معدل الخصوبة على مستوى العالم ٢,٦٥ طفل لكل امرأة، أي حوالي نصف معدلها المسجل للفترة ١٩٥٠-١٩٥٥ (٥ أطفال لكل امرأة). وبحسب متغير الخصوبة المتوسط، يتوقع أن يستمر انخفاض معدل الخصوبة الكلي في العالم إلى ٢,٠٥ طفل لكل امرأة بحلول ٢٠٤٥ - ٢٠٥٠. وتأتي متوسطات المعدلات العالميــة نتيجة اتجاهات متباينة تماما فيما بين المجموعات الإنمائية الرئيسية. ففي البلدان المتقدمة ككل، يبلغ معدل الخصوبة حاليا ١,٥٦ طفل لكل امرأة، ويتوقع أن يشهد ارتفاعا بطيئــا ليبلــغ ١,٨٤ طفل لكل امرأة في الفترة ٢٠٤٥-٢٠٥٠. وفي أقل البلدان نموا، يبلغ معدل الخصوبة ٥ أطفال لكل امرأة، ويتوقع أن ينخفض بحوالي النصف إلى ٢,٥٧ طفل لكل امرأة بحلول الفترة ٢٠٤٥-٢٠٥٠. وفي باقي بلدان العالم النامي، انخفض معدل الخصوبة فعلا بصــورة معقولة، إذ يبلغ ٢,٥٨ طفل لكل امرأة، ومن المتوقع أن يــستمر في الانخفاض إلى ١,٩٢ طفل لكل امرأة بحلول منتصف القرن، بحيث يناهز معدلات الخصوبة التي ستغلب على العالم المتقدم في تلك الفترة. ويبقى تحقق توقعات الانخفاض في معدل الخصوبة رهنا بانتشار تنظيم الأسرة، لا سيما في أقل البلدان نموا.

٩ - وفي الفترة ٢٠٠٠-٢٠٠٥، يظل معدل الخصوبة فوق ٥ أطفال لكل امرأة في ٣٥ من بين ١٤٨ بلدا ناميا، منها ٣٠ بلدا من أقل البلدان نموا، فيما كانت وتيرة الانخفاض في العديد من بلدان أفريقيا جنوب الصحراء الكبرى وجنوب آسيا الوسطى أكثر بطئا مـن المتوقع. وإجمالا، تمثل البلدان التي تتسم بخصوبة عالية ١٠ في المائة من سكان العالـم. وفي المقابل، فقد انخفض معدل الخصوبة دون مستويات الإحلال في ٢٣ من البلدان النامية تمثـل ٢٥ في المائة من سكان العالم. وتشمل هذه المجموعة الصين التي يقدر معدل الخصوبة فيهـا خلال الفترة ٢٠٠٠-٢٠٠٥ بما نسبته ١,٧ طفل لكل امرأة.

١٠ - أما مستويات الخصوبة الحالية في البلدان المتقدمة، وعددها ٤٤ بلدا تمثل ١٩ في المائة من سكان العالم، فإنها تتسم بالانخفاض الشديد، ومعدل الخصوبة فيها جميعهـا، باستثناء ألبانيا، دون مستوى الإحلال و ١٥ منها، معظمها يقع في جنوب وشرق أوروبـا، بلغـت معدلات خصوبة لم يسبق لها مثيل في تاريخ البشرية (أقل من ١,٣ طفل لكل امرأة). ومنـذ ١٩٩٠-١٩٩٥، أصبح انخفاض معدل الخصوبة هو القاعدة في معظم البلـدان المتقدمـة. والارتفاعات القليلة التي سُجلت، كما هو الحال في ألمانيـا وبلجيكـا وفرنسا وهولنـدا والولايات المتحدة الأمريكية، ارتفاعات ضئيلة.

الجدول ٤

متوسط العمر المتوقع عند الولادة في العالم والمجموعات الإنمائيـة الرئيسية والمنـاطق الرئيسية، ٢٠٠٠-٢٠٠٥ و ٢٠٤٥-٢٠٥٠

المنطقة الرئيسية	٢٠٠٠-٢٠٠٥	٢٠٤٥-٢٠٥٠
العالم	٦٥,٤	٧٥,١
المناطق الأكثر تقدما	٧٥,٦	٨٢,١
المناطق الأقل تقدما	٦٣,٤	٧٤,٠
أقل البلدان نموا	٥١,٠	٦٦,٥
البلدان الأقل تقدما الأخرى	٦٦,١	٧٦,٣
أفريقيا	٤٩,١	٦٥,٤
آسيــــا	٦٧,٣	٧٧,٢
أوروبا	٧٣,٧	٨٠,٦
أمريكا اللاتينية ومنطقة البحر الكاريبي	٧١,٥	٧٩,٥
أمريكا الشمالية	٧٧,٦	٨٢,٧
أوقيانوسيا	٧٤,٠	٨١,٢

المصدر: شعبة السكان التابعة لإدارة الشؤون الاقتصادية والاجتماعية بالأمانة العامة للأمـم المتحدة (٢٠٠٥). التوقعات السكانية العالمية: تنقيح عام ٢٠٠٤، الملامح الرئيسية. نيويورك: الأمم المتحدة.

١١ - يتوقع أن يستمر ارتفاع متوسط العمر المتوقع عند الولادة، الذي يُقدر أنه ارتفع على الصعيد العالمي من ٤٧ سنة في الفترة ١٩٥٠-١٩٥٥ إلى ٦٥ سنة في الفترة ٢٠٠٠-٢٠٠٥، فيصل إلى ٧٥ سنة في الفترة ٢٠٤٥-٢٠٥٠. وفي المناطق الأكثر تقدما، يتوقع ارتفاع متوسط العمر من ٧٦ سنة حاليا إلى ٨٢ سنة بحلول منتصف القرن. ويتوقع في البلدان الأقل نموا، حيث يبلغ متوسط العمر المتوقع حاليا ٥١ سنة، أن يرتفع المتوسط إلى ٦٧ سنة في الفترة ٢٠٤٥-٢٠٥٠. وبما أن العديد من هذه البلدان يتأثر كثيرا بوباء الفيروس/الإيدز، فإن الارتفاع المتوقع في متوسط العمر يتوقف على تنفيذ البرامج الفعالة للوقاية من الإصابة بفيروس نقص المناعة البشرية والعلاج منه. أما في باقي بلدان العالم النامي ذات الظروف المشابهة، فمن المنتظر أن يرتفع متوسط العمر المتوقع من ٦٦ سنة حاليا إلى ٧٦ سنة في منتصف القرن.

١٢ - وقد أخذت تزداد الوفيات في أوروبا الشرقية منذ أواخر الثمانينات. وأصبح متوسط العمر المتوقع في الفترة ٢٠٠٠-٢٠٠٥ في المنطقة، ٦٧,٩ سنة، أقل مما كان عليه في الفترة ١٩٦٠-١٩٦٥ عندما بلغ ٦٨,٦ سنة. وتأثر الاتحاد الروسي وأوكرانيا على نحو خاص بالارتفاع في الوفيات الناجم جزئيا عن انتشار فيروس نقص المناعة البشرية.

١٣ - وبعد خمس وعشرين سنة من بدء انتشار وباء الفيروس/الإيدز، يبدو تأثير المرض جليا من حيث زيادة الاعتلال والوفيات وتباطؤ النمو السكاني. ففي الجنوب الأفريقي، وهو المنطقة التي تعرف أعلى معدل لانتشار وباء الفيروس/الإيدز، انخفض متوسط العمر المتوقع من ٦٢ سنة في الفترة ١٩٩٠-١٩٩٥ إلى ٤٨ سنة في الفترة ٢٠٠٠-٢٠٠٥، ويتوقع أن ينخفض أكثر إلى ٤٣ سنة خلال العقد المقبل قبل أن يبدأ تحسن بطيء. ونتيجة لذلك، يتوقع أن يتوقف النمو السكاني في المنطقة بين عامي ٢٠٠٠ و ٢٠٢٠. وفي بوتسوانا وليسوتو وسوازيلند، يتوقع أن ينخفض عدد السكان نظرا لزيادة عدد الوفيات على عدد المواليد. وفي أغلب البلدان النامية الأخرى المتأثرة بالوباء، سيواصل النمو السكاني اتجاهه الإيجابي ذلك أن معدل الخصوبة بها، معتدلا كان أم عاليا، يتجاوز الزيادة في الوفيات.

١٤ - وأولى نتائج تراجع الخصوبة، وخاصة مع زيادة متوسط العمر المتوقع، هي شيوخة السكان، حيث يزداد عدد كبار السن من السكان مقارنا بعدد الشباب. وعلى الصعيد العالمي، يتوقع أن يبلغ عدد الأشخاص ٦٠ سنة أو أكثر ثلاثة أضعافه تقريبا، فيزداد عددهم من ٦٧٢ مليون نسمة سنة ٢٠٠٥ إلى قرابة ١,٩ بليون نسمة مع حلول سنة ٢٠٥٠. وفي حين أن ٦ من كل ١٠ من هؤلاء المسنين يعيشون حاليا في البلدان النامية، فإن عددهم في تلك المناطق سيكون ٨ من كل ١٠ مع حلول سنة ٢٠٥٠. بل يتوقع حدوث زيادة

ملحوظة بصورة أكبر في عدد أكبر المسنين سنا (٨٠ سنة فأكثر)، من ٨٦ مليون نسمة عام ٢٠٠٥ إلى ٣٩٤ مليون نسمة عام ٢٠٠٥. وفي البلدان النامية، سيزداد العدد من ٤٢ مليون نسمة إلى ٢٧٨ مليون نسمة، مما يعني أن العالم النامي سيكون به معظم أكبر المسنين سنا مع حلول عام ٢٠٥٠.

١٥ – وفي البلدان المتقدمة، يبلغ عمر ٢٠ في المائة من السكان حاليا ٦٠ سنة أو أكثر ويتوقع أن تصل هذه النسبة مع حلول ٢٠٥٠ إلى ٣٢ في المائة. وبالفعل فقد تجاوز عدد المسنين في البلدان المتقدمة عدد الأطفال (ممن تتراوح أعمارهم بين صفر و ١٤ سنة)، ومـع حلول عام ٢٠٥٠ سيكون هناك مسنان لكل طفل واحد. وفي العالم النامي، يتوقع أن ترتفع نسبة السكان البالغة أعمارهم ٦٠ سنة أو أكثر من ٨ في المائة سنة ٢٠٠٥ إلى قرابة ٢٠ في المائة مع حلول ٢٠٥٠.

١٦ – وتعد الزيادات في العمر المتوسط، أي العمر الذي يزيد عنه ٥٠ في المائة من السكان ويقل عنده الـ ٥٠ في المائة الآخرون، مؤشرا على شيوخة السكان. واليوم لا يزيـد عـن ١١ بلدا عدد البلدان المتقدمة التي يربو فيها العمر المتوسط على ٤٠ سنة. ومع حلول عـام ٢٠٥٠، سيبلغ عدد بلدان هذه المجموعة ٨٩ بلدا، ٤٥ منها في العالم النامي. فشيوخة السكان التي اتسعت وازدادت في البلدان المتقدمة أمر لا مفر منه في العالم النامـي أيضا. وستحل هذه الشيوخة بوتيرة أسرع في البلدان النامية.

١٧ – وستشهد البلدان، التي تبقى الخصوبة عالية فيها و لم تتراجع إلا بشكل معتدل، أبطـأ معدل لشيوخة السكان. وما زال يتوقع بحلول عام ٢٠٥٠ أن هناك بلد من كل خمسة بلدان يبلغ فيه العمر المتوسط ٣٠ سنة أو يقل عن ٣٠ سنة. وسنجد أقل السـكان سـنا يعيشون في أقل البلدان نموا، حيث يتوقع أن يبلغ العمر المتوسط في ١١ بلدا منها ٢٣ سنة أو أقل عام ٢٠٥٠، ومن بين هذه البلدان أفغانستان وأنغولا وأوغندا وبورونـدي وتـشاد وجمهورية الكونغو الديمقراطية وغينيا الاستوائية وغينيا – بيساو وليبيريا ومالي والنيجر.

١٨ – ويتوقع، خلال الفترة ٢٠٠٥-٢٠٥٠، أن يبلغ صافي عدد المهاجرين على الـصعيد الدولي إلى المناطق الأكثر تقدما ٩٨ مليون مهاجر أو ما متوسطه ٢,٢ مليـون مهـاجر في السنة. وسيغادر هذا العدد نفسه المناطق الأقل تقدما. وفيما يتعلق بالعالم المتقدم، فـإن مـن شأن هذا المعدل الصافي للهجرة أن يعوض الزيادة المتوقعة في الوفيات على المواليـد خـلال الفترة ٢٠٠٥-٢٠٥٠، وهي تعادل فقدان ٧٣ مليون نسمة. وبالنسبة للعالم النامي، يمثل ٩٨ مليون مهاجر بالكاد أقل من ٤ في المائة من النمو المتوقع للسكان.

١٩ - وخلال الفترة ٢٠٠٠-٢٠٠٥، بلغ عدد البلدان المستقبلة الصافية للمهاجرين ٧٤ بلدا. وفي ٦٤ بلدا من هذه البلدان، يضيف صافي الهجرة المتوقع إلى النمو السكاني ويؤدي في ٧ بلدان إلى عكس اتجاه الانخفاض السكان (ألمانيا وإيطاليا وكرواتيا والنمسا وسلوفاكيا وسلوفينيا واليونان). وفي ثلاثة بلدان، تبطئ الهجرة معدل الانخفاض السكاني لكنها لا تعكس اتجاهه (الاتحاد الروسي والجمهورية التشيكية وهنغاريا).

٢٠ - وفيما يتعلق بالمتوسطات السنوية للفترة ٢٠٠٥-٢٠٥٠، يتوقع أن يكون أكبر البلدان المتلقية الصافية للمهاجرين الدوليين هي الولايات المتحدة (١,١ مليون مهاجر سنويا) وألمانيا (٢٠٢ ٠٠٠) وكندا (٢٠٠ ٠٠٠) والمملكة المتحدة (١٣٠ ٠٠٠) وإيطاليا (١٢٠ ٠٠٠) وأستراليا (١٠٠ ٠٠٠). ويتوقع أن تكون البلدان الرئيسية الموفدة الصافية للمهاجرين هي الصين (- ٣٢٧ ٠٠٠ مهاجر سنويا) والمكسيك (- ٢٩٣ ٠٠٠) والهند (- ٢٤١ ٠٠٠) والفلبين (- ١٨٠ ٠٠٠) وإندونيسيا (- ١٦٤ ٠٠٠) وباكستان (- ١٥٤ ٠٠٠) وأوكرانيا (- ١٠٠ ٠٠٠).

الافتراضات التي يرتكز عليها تنقيح ٢٠٠٤

لإعداد التوقعات السكانية لغاية ٢٠٥٠، تطبق شعبة السكان بالأمم المتحدة افتراضات تتعلق بالاتجاهات المستقبلية للخصوبة والوفيات والهجرة. وبما أنه لا يمكن معرفة الاتجاهات المستقبلية على وجه اليقين، يوضع عدد من متغيرات الإسقاطات. وتركز الملامح الرئيسية لتنقيح ٢٠٠٤ على متغير الخصوبة المتوسط للتنقيح. وترد الافتراضات المتعلقة بالمتغير المتوسط موضحة بتفصيل في القسم ألف من هذا الفصل.

ويتضمن تنقيح ٢٠٠٤ خمسة متغيرات إضافية: متغيرات الخصوبة العالية والمنخفضة والثابتة والوفيات الثابتة والهجرة الصفرية. وترد الافتراضات التي تميز هذه المتغيرات عن المتغير المتوسط موضحة في القسم باء. وستقدم النتائج المفصلة لهذه المتغيرات في المنشورات المقبلة.

وقد أعدت الإسقاطات السكانية المستقبلية لكل بلد انطلاقا من تقديرات عدد السكان في ١ تموز/يوليه ٢٠٠٥. وبما أن البيانات السكانية الفعلية لسنة ٢٠٠٥ ليست متاحة بعد، فإن تقديرات ٢٠٠٥ تقوم على أحدث البيانات السكانية المتاحة عن كل بلد والتي تشتق عادة من تعداد سكاني أو سجل سكاني تم استكماله لسنة ٢٠٠٥ باستخدام كل البيانات المتاحة عن الخصوبة والوفيات والهجرة الدولية. وفي الحالات التي لا تتوافر فيها بيانات حديثة جدا، تكون الاتجاهات الديمغرافية المقدرة عبارة عن إسقاطات قصيرة الأجل

لأحدث البيانات المتاحة. وتُقيَّم البيانات السكانية من كل المصادر من حيث التمام والدقــة والاتساق وتعدل حيثما تدعو الضرورة[6].

ألف – افتراضات المتغير المتوسط

١ – افتراضات الخصوبة: الاقتراب نحو خصوبة كلية أقل من مستوى الإحلال

يُفترض في النهاية أن تقترب الخصوبة الكلية في البلدان كافة من معدل ١,٨٥ طفل لكل امرأة. ومع ذلك، لا تبلغ كل البلدان هذا المعدل خلال فترة الإسقاط، أي، مع حلــول ٢٠٥٠. فالمبدأ الأساسي لإسقاط الخصوبة لا يتغير بالنسبة لكل البلدان، لكـن إجــراءات الإسقاط تختلف بعض الشيء بحسب المعدل الكلي للخصوبة في البلدان وما إذا كـان هـذا المعدل أعلى أو أقل من ١,٨٥ طفل لكل امرأة في الفترة ٢٠٠٠–٢٠٠٥.

فبالنسبة للبلدان التي يزيد فيها معدل الخصوبة الكلية على ١,٨٥ طفل لكل امــرأة، يُقدر أن تتبع الخصوبة مسارا من مسارات نماذج انخفاض الخصوبة الـتي وضعتها شعبة السكان بالأمم المتحدة على أساس المشهد الماضي لكل البلدان التي انخفضت فيها الخصوبة خلال الفترة ١٩٥٠–٢٠٠٠. وتربط هذه النماذج معدل الخصوبة الكلية خلال كل فتـرة بمتوسط الانخفاض المتوقع في الخصوبة الكلية خلال الفترة التالية. فإذا انخفضت الخصوبة الكلية المسقطة بحسب نموذج البلد إلى ١,٨٥ طفل لكل امرأة قبل ٢٠٥٠، فإنــه يُحتفظ بالخصوبة الكلية ثابتة عند هذا المعدل خلال ما تبقى من فتـرة الإسقاط (أي، إلى غايـة ٢٠٥٠).

وفي كل الحالات، يُتحقق من مسارات الخصوبة المسقطة المستقاة مـن النمـاذج بمقارنتها مع الاتجاهات الحديثة للخصوبة في كل بلد. وعندما تحيد اتجاهات الخصوبة الحديثة بدرجة كبيرة في بلد ما عن الاتجاهات التي تتفق وهذه النماذج، تُعد إسقاطات الخصوبة على مدى فترة أولية من ٥ سنوات أو ١٠ سنوات بحيث تراعي ما استجد حديثا. ويحذو نموذج الإسقاط حذو تلك الفترة الانتقالية. فعلى سبيل المثال، يتوقع أن تبقى الخصوبة، في البلـدان التي توقفت فيها الخصوبة أو التي لا توجد فيها دلائل على انخفاض الخصوبة، ثابتـة لعـدة سنوات أخرى قبل أن تبدأ في التناقص.

وفيما يتعلق بالبلدان التي تبلغ فيها الخصوبة الكلية أقل من ١,٨٥ طفل لكل امرأة في الفترة ٢٠٠٠–٢٠٥٠، يُفترض أن يتبع إسقاط الخصوبة خلال فترة الإسقاط الأولى من

---

(٦) للإطلاع على وصف عام للإجراءات المتبعة في تنقيح تقديرات الدينامية السكانية، انظر توقعات سكان العالم: تنقيح سنة ٢٠٠٢، المجلد الثالث، التقرير التحليلي، الصفحات ١٨٠–١٨٢ (من النص الانكليزي).

٥ أو ١٠ سنوات الاتجاهات الملاحظة حديثا في كل بلد. وبعد تلك الفترة الانتقالية، يفترض أن ترتفع الخصوبة خطيا بمعدل ٠٫٠٧ طفل لكل امرأة كل خمس سنوات.

٢ – *افتراضات الوفيات: زيادة العمر المتوقع باستثناء أثر الإصابة بفيروس نقص المناعة البشرية/الإيدز*

أ – *افتراضات الوفيات العادية*

تقوم إسقاطات الوفيات على أساس نماذج تغير متوسط الزيادة في العمر المتوقع عند الولادة التي صاغتها شعبة السكان بالأمم المتحدة. وتكشف هذه النماذج عن تناقص معدل الزيادة من هذه الناحية كلما كان متوسط العمر المتوقع عاليا بالفعل من قبل. ويقوم اختيار النموذج لكل بلد على الاتجاهات الحديثة للعمر المتوقع حسب نوع الجنس. فبالنسبة للبلدان المتأثرة كثيرا بالفيروس/الإيدز، يستخدم عموما نموذج الانخفاض البطيء في الوفيات لإعداد إسقاطات الوفيات العامة غير المرتبطة بالفيروس/الإيدز، وهذه تكون مائلة إلى الانخفاض.

ب – *تأثير الفيروس/الإيدز*

فيما يتعلق بالـ ٦٠ بلدا المتضررة بصورة كبيرة من وباء الفيروس/الإيدز (ترد قائمة بأسمائها في الجدول الثامن – ٢١)، تُعد تقديرات أثر هذا الوباء من خلال وضع نماذج واضحة لمسار الوباء وحساب المعدل السنوي المتوقع للإصابة بالفيروس. ويستخدم النموذج الذي وضعه فريق الإحالة المعني بالتقديرات ووضع النماذج والإسقاطات التابع لبرنامج الأمم المتحدة المشترك المعني بفيروس نقص المناعة البشرية/الإيدز[7] بما يتمشى والتقديرات الماضية لانتشار الفيروس التي قدمها برنامج الأمم المتحدة المشترك المعني بالإيدز بغية استقاء المحددات التي تظهر من خلالها دينامية الوباء في السابق. وفيما يتعلق بمعظم البلدان، يكيف النموذج على افتراض أن المحددات ذات الصلة ظلت ثابتة في الماضي. وانطلاقا من ٢٠٠٥، يتوقع أن ينخفض المحدد المتعلق بنسبة الانتشار المرتفعة للوباء PHI، الذي يبين معدل دخول أفراد جدد إلى المجموعات المعرضة لخطر كبير أو السريعة التأثر، بواقع النصف كل ثلاثين سنة. كما يتوقع أن ينخفض المحدد R، الذي يمثل شدة خطر الإصابة، بالطريقة نفسها. ويعكس الانخفاض في المحدد المتعلق بشدة خطر الإصابة R افتراضا مؤداه أن التغيرات التي تطرأ على سلوك الأشخاص المعرضين لخطر الإصابة، إضافة إلى زيادة توفير العلاج للمصابين، ستقلل

---

(٧) أساليب وافتراضات محسنة للتقديرات المتعلقة بوباء فيروس نقص المناعة البشرية/الإيدز وآثاره: توصيات فريق الإحالة المعني بالتقديرات ووضع النماذج والإسقاطات التابع لبرنامج الأمم المتحدة المعني بالإيدز. الإيدز، المجلد ١٦، الصفحات W1-W14 من النص الانكليزي (فريق الإحالة المعني بالتقديرات ووضع النماذج والإسقاطات التابع لبرنامج الأمم المتحدة المعني بالإيدز، ٢٠٠٢).

من فرص انتقال الفيروس. كما يتوقع أن تنخفض نسبة انتقال المرض مـن الأم إلى الطفـل بمعدلات مختلفة حسب تقدم كل بلد في مجال توفير العلاج. وإضافة إلى ذلـك، اسـتُكمل مكون نموذج فريق الإحالة المتعلق ببقاء الأطفال المصابين: ففي تنقيـح ٢٠٠٤ يُفترض أن ٥٠ في المائة من الأطفال المصابين نتيجة انتقال المرض من الأم إلى الطفل سيعيـشون حـتى السنة الثانية من العمر.

ويشير تنقيح ٢٠٠٤ لأول مرة إلى زيادة أعمار الأشخاص الذين يتلقون علاجـا مضادا للفيروسات الرجعية شديد الفعالية. وتتوافق نسبة السكان المصابين بالفيروس الـذين يتلقون علاجا في كل بلد مع التقديرات التي أعدتها منظمة الـصحة العالميـة لنهايـة سـنة ٢٠٠٤[(٨)]. ويتوقع أن يصل معدل التغطية بالعلاج إلى ما بين ٤٠ و ٨٥ في المائة مع حلـول سنة ٢٠١٥، استنادا إلى المعدل الحالي للتغطية. ومن المفترض أن تزداد احتمالات البقاء على قيد الحياة سنويا، في المتوسط، إلى ما لا يقل عن ٨٠ في المائة بالنـسبة للأشخاص الـذين يتلقون العلاج المضاد للفيروسات الرجعية. وحسب هذا الافتراض، فإن متوسط البقاء بعـد الشروع في العلاج هو ٣,١ سنوات (العمر المتوسط هو ٤,٥ سنوات). وبالمقابل يُفترض أن متوسط البقاء في غياب العلاج بعد تقدم الإصابة نحو الإيدز يكون سنة واحدة فحسب.

٣ - الافتراضات المتعلقة بالهجرة الدولية

يحدد المسار المستقبلي للهجرة الدولية استنادا إلى تقديرات الهجرة الدولية الـسابقة وإلى تقييم الموقف السياسي للبلدان تجاه التدفقات المستقبلية للهجرة الدولية.

باء - متغيرات الإسقاط

يتضمن تنقيح ٢٠٠٤ خمسة متغيرات إسقاط إضافة إلى المتغير المتوسط. ولا تختلـف ثلاثة متغيرات - الخصوبة المرتفعة والمنخفضة والثابتة - عن المتغير المتوسط إلا فيما يتعلـق بالمعدل المسقط للخصوبة الكلية. ففي إطار المتغير المرتفع، يتوقع أن تظل الخصوبة الكليـة أعلى بمعدل ٥,٠ طفل عن الخصوبة الكلية في المتغير المتوسط خلال معظم فترة الإسـقاط. وعلى سبيل المثال، فإن البلدان التي تبلغ فيها الخصوبة الكلية ١,٨٥ طفل لكل امرأة في إطار المتغير المتوسط تبلغ معدل خصوبة كليا قدره ٢,٣٥ طفل في إطار المتغير المرتفع. وفي إطـار المتغير المنخفض، يتوقع أن تظل الخصوبة الكلية أدنى بنسبة ٥,٠ طفل من الخصوبة الكلية في

(٨) منظمة الصحة العالمية. التقرير المرحلي "معالجة ٣ ملايـين شخص بحلول عـام ٢٠٠٥"، كـانون الأول/ديسمبر ٢٠٠٤/منظمة الصحة العالمية وبرنامج الأمم المتحدة المشترك المعني بفيروس نقـص المناعـة البشرية/الإيدز.

إطار المتغير المتوسط. وفي إطار متغير الخصوبة الثابت، تظل الخصوبة الكلية ثابتة عند المعدل المقدر للفترة ٢٠٠٠-٢٠٥٠.

كما تم إعداد متغير وفيات ثابت ومتغير هجرة صغرى. وكلاهما له ذات الافتراض المتعلق بالخصوبة الذي يقوم عليه متغير الخصوبة المتوسط. وعلاوة على ذلك، فلمتغير الوفيات الثابت ذات الافتراض المتعلق بالهجرة الدولية الذي يقوم عليه متغير الخصوبة المتوسط. ونتيجة لذلك، يمكن مقارنة نتائج متغير الوفيات الثابت مع نتائج متغير الخصوبة المتوسط لتقييم الأثر الذي يحدثه تغير الوفيات على المحددات الديمغرافية الأخرى. وعلى هذا النحو، لا يختلف متغير الهجرة الصفري عن متغير الخصوبة المتوسط إلا فيما يتعلق بالافتراض الأساسي بخصوص الهجرة الدولية. وبالتالي، يتيح متغير الهجرة الصفري تقييما للأثر الـذي يحدثه متغير الهجرة غير الصفري على المحددات الديمغرافية الأخرى.

جيم – التغييرات المنهجية التي أُدخلت من أجل تنقيح ٢٠٠٤

• في إطار متغير الخصوبة المتوسط، يتوقع أن تستمر خصوبة البلدان ذات الخصوبة الكلية الأقل من ١,٨٥ طفل لكل امرأة في الفترة ٢٠٠٠-٢٠٠٥، وذلك في البداية بتواصل الاتجاهات الحديثة، ثم بتزايد الخصوبة خطيا بمعدل ٠,٠٧ طفل لكل امرأة كل خمس سنوات. ولا تصل هذه البلدان بالضرورة إلى معدل ١,٨٥ طفـل لكـل امرأة مع حلول ٢٠٥٠.

• وفي تنقيح ٢٠٠٤، استُخدمت نماذج إضافية لتغير الوفيات لبيـان تنـوع الواقـع التاريخي من حيث زيادة العمر المتوقع. وعلى وجه التحديد، وضعت نمـاذج تغييـر بطيئة جدا وسريعة جدا أُضيفت إلى النماذج البطيئة والمتوسطة السـرعة والسـريعة الموجودة بالفعل.

• ووضعت نماذج واضحة لتأثير الفيروس/الإيدز على الوفيات لكل البلدان التي كـان معدل انتشار الفيروس لديها بين البالغين ١ في المائة أو أكثر سنة ٢٠٠٣.

• وأُدمج العلاج المضاد للفيروسات الرجعية صراحة في الإسقاطات المتعلقة بالبلدان المتأثرة بالفيروس/الإيدز. وإضافة إلى ذلك، يتوقع أن يتراجع معدل انتقال الإصابة من الأم إلى الطفل بمعدل يتناسب والتقدم المتوقع في زيادة توفير العلاج.

———————

前言

本报告是联合国秘书处经济和社会事务部人口司编制的世界人口正式估算和预测《2004 年修订本》的结果执行摘要。此外，本报告概述了据以作出人口预测的生育力、死亡率和移徙的各种假设和《2004 年修订本》对《2002 年修订本》采用的程序作出的改动和调整。《2004 年修订本》是人口司自 1950 年以来进行的第十九回合的全球人口估算和预测。

《2004 年修订本》的全部结果将分三卷印发。第一卷[1]为综合表，列出了 1950-2050 年每个国家的主要人口指标；第二卷[2]是按年龄和性别分列的 1950-2050 年期间每个国家的人口分布情况；第三卷[3]对得到的有关结果进行了分析。

还将用数字形式分发有关数据。感兴趣的用户可购买内有《2004 年修订本》主要结果的光盘。人口司的网址（www.unpopulation.org）上会有光盘数据的说明和订购单。

人口司对《2004 年修订本》负责。人口司同联合国各区域委员会、专门机构和其他有关机构的合作有助于《2004 年修订本》的编写工作。

尤其是用于编制这些估算和预测的正式国家人口统计主要来源为联合国经济和社会事务部统计司编制和保有的《联合国人口统计年鉴》及其有关数据库。人口司感谢统计司继续给予合作。

可从人口司的网址（www.unpopulation.org）查阅《2004 年修订本》的一些内容和其他人口信息。如需《2004 年修订本》的进一步资料，请接洽 Ms. Hania Zlotnik, Director, Population Division, United Nations, New York, NY 10017, USA（传真：1 212 963 2147）。

---

[1] 《世界人口前景：2004 年修订本》第一卷，《综合表》（联合国出版物，Sales No. E. 05. XIII. 5）。

[2] 《世界人口前景：2004 年修订本》第二卷，《世界人口的性别和年龄分布情况》（联合国出版物，Sales No. E. 05. XIII. 6）。

[3] 《世界人口前景：2004 年修订本》第三卷，《分析报告》（联合国出版物，即将发行）。

执行摘要

《2004 年修订本》是联合国秘书处经济和社会事务部人口司编制的第十九次联合国正式人口估算和预测。整个联合国系统根据这些估算和预测来开展那些利用人口资料的活动。《2004 年修订本》首度将 2000 年回合的国家人口普查全部结果纳入。其中也考虑到了最近在发展中国家进行的专门调查的结果，提供人口统计资料和其他资料，以供评估在实现国际商定的发展目标，包括实现《千年发展目标》方面所取得的进展。《2004 年修订本》中对过去的世界人口趋势和未来前景所作的全面审查为评估这些目标提供了人口基础。

《2004 年修订本》确认了我们当代的各种人口动态。虽然全球一级的人口继续增加，但较发达区域整体几乎没有改变，实际上所有人口增长都是出现在较不发达区域。50 个最不发达国家的群组呈现了人口尤其快速增长的特点。

在这些不同类型的增长之下是不同的生育力和死亡率趋势。较发达区域存在生育力未达更替生育率的情况，这种情况预期将持续到 2050 年。多数最不发达国家的生育力仍然偏高，虽预期会下降，但仍预期高出世界其他国家。从 1960 年代末期以来，其余发展中国家的生育力显著下降，预期到 2050 年，这些国家的多数的生育力将达到低于更替生育率的水平。

拥有市场经济的发达世界死亡率偏低，并持续下降，但若干转型经济国家的死亡率出现停滞甚至上升的情况，这主要是由于社会和经济状况日益恶化，有时是由于艾滋病毒蔓延。多数发展中国家的死亡率也日益下降，但是在深受艾滋病毒/艾滋病流行病困扰的国家，死亡率则在上升。由于不断努力在 2005 年之前向 300 万名艾滋病人提供抗逆转录病毒疗法和在 2005 年之后进一步扩大这种治疗，《2004 年修订本》对带有艾滋病毒者的平均存活率的假设较《2002 年修订本》为高，因此对受到艾滋病毒之害国家的未来死亡率的预测比前一个修订本的预测要低一些。

艾滋病毒/艾滋病流行病继续扩散。《2004 年修订本》中有相当人数受到感染的国家有 60 个，多于《2002 年修订本》中的 53 个。不过有些国家艾滋病毒流行率因采用了更好的统计方法而有所下降。然而，尽管预测艾滋病毒/艾滋病流行率会下降，染病人数仍然且将继续很高。艾滋病毒流行率的下降取决于各国政府是否履行《2000 年千年宣言》[4] 和《2001 年联合国关于艾滋病毒/艾滋病问题的承诺宣言》[5] 的承诺。

---

[4] 见大会第 A/RES/55/2 号决议。

[5] 见大会第 A/RES/S-26/2 号决议。

以下摘述《2004 年修订本》的主要结论：

1. 到 2005 年 7 月，世界居民将达 65 亿人，比 2000 年多出 3.8 亿人，每年增加 7 600 万人。尽管 2005-2050 年生育力预测继续下降，但按中变式计算，至本世纪中期，世界人口预期达到 91 亿人，每年增加 3 400 万人。

2. 今天有 95% 人口增长出现在发展中世界，5% 出现在发达世界。按中变式计算，到 2050 年，较发达世界整体每年将缓慢减少人口约 100 万人，发展中世界每年增加 3 500 万人，其中 2 200 万人出现在最不发达国家。

3. 进一步的人口增长高度取决于未来生育力的走向。按中变式计算，预测生育力将由今天的每一妇女生 2.6 个子女降至 2050 年每一妇女生育略多于 2 个子女。如果生育力停留在比按中变式计算的预测人数多出约半个子女，到 2050 年世界人口将达 106 亿人。如生育力走向为比中变数低半个子女，到本世纪中期人口将达 76 亿人。也就是说，即使生育力的下降速度加快，到 2050 年世界人口将持续增长的趋势仍不可避免。

表 1
1950、1975、2005 和 2050 年按预测变式计算的世界、主要发展群组和主要地区人口

主要地区	人口（百万）			人口 2050（百万）			
	1950	1975	2005	低	中	高	不变
世界.................	2 519	4 074	6 465	7 680	9 076	10 646	11 658
较发达区域.............	813	1 047	1 211	1 057	1 236	1 440	1 195
较不发达区域...........	1 707	3 027	5 253	6 622	7 840	9 206	10 403
最不发达国家.......	201	356	759	1 497	1 735	1 994	2 744
其他较不发达国家...	1 506	2 671	4 494	5 126	6 104	7 213	7 719
非洲.................	224	416	906	1 666	1 937	2 228	3 100
亚洲.................	1 396	2 395	3 905	4 388	5 217	6 161	6 487
欧洲.................	547	676	728	557	653	764	606
拉丁美洲和加勒比.......	167	322	561	653	783	930	957
北美洲...............	172	243	331	375	438	509	454
大洋洲...............	13	21	33	41	48	55	55

资料来源：联合国秘书处经济和社会事务部人口司（2005 年）。《世界人口前景：2004 年修订本》概要，纽约：联合国。

图 1

1950-2050 年按预测变式计算的世界人口

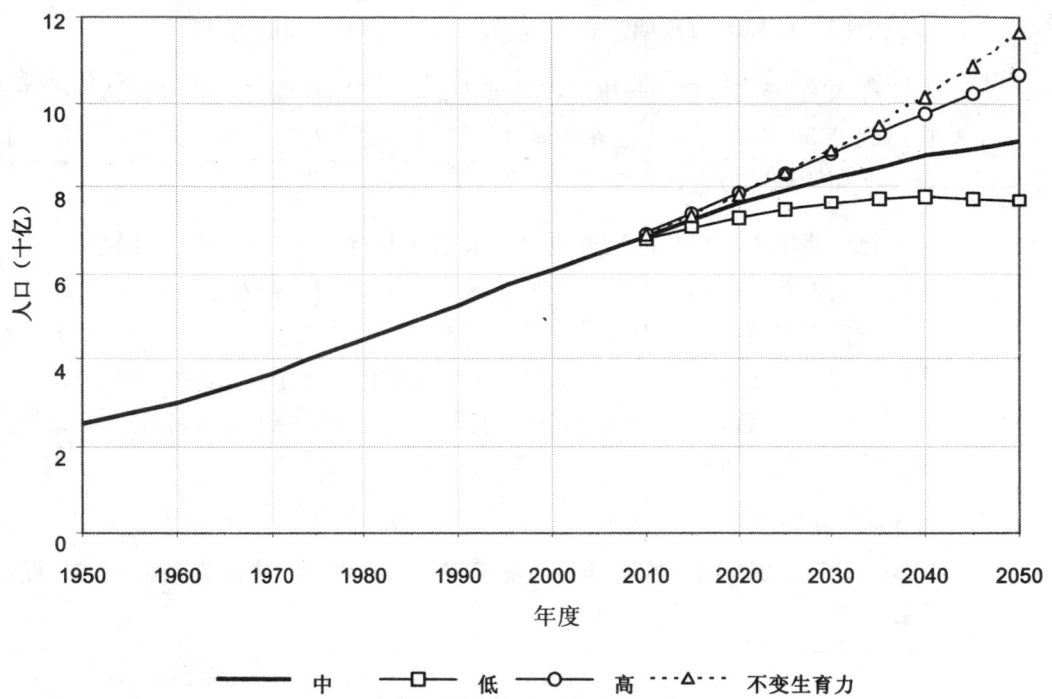

资料来源：联合国秘书处经济和社会事务部人口司（2005 年）。《世界人口前景：2004 年修订本》概要，纽约：联合国。

4.　发达国家整体的人口由于增长率低且不断下降，预期 2005 至 2050 年期间实际上将保持不变，约为 12 亿人。相对的，50 个最不发达国家的人口预测将增加一倍以上，由 2005 年的超出 8 亿人增加到 2050 年的 17 亿人。发展中世界其余国家的增长虽预测不那么快，仍增加很多，从 2005 年的 45 亿人增加到 2050 年的 61 亿人。

5.　若干发展中国家的人口预期增长非常快速，主要是在最不发达国家。2005 年至 2050 年期间，阿富汗、布基纳法索、布隆迪、乍得、刚果、刚果民主共和国、东帝汶民主共和国、几内亚比绍、利比里亚、马里、尼日尔和乌干达的人口预测增长两倍。

6.　有 51 个国家或地区，包括德国、意大利、日本、波罗的海国家和前苏联的多数继承国家 2050 年的人口预期将低于 2005 年。

7. 2005 年至 2050 年期间，世界人口的增加预测有一半出现在九个国家，按其这一期间人口增长的多少排列，这些国家为：印度、巴基斯坦、尼日利亚、刚果民主共和国、孟加拉国、乌干达、美利坚合众国、埃塞俄比亚和中国。

表 2

2005-2050 年按主要地区计算的总人口和广泛年龄群体年平均变动率（按中变式）

主要地区	0-14	15-59	60+	80+	人口总数
世界....................	0.01	0.63	2.39	3.37	0.75
较发达区域.............	-0.14	-0.38	1.10	2.13	0.05
较不发达区域.............	0.03	0.82	2.88	4.19	0.89
最不发达国家.......	1.02	2.15	3.32	4.03	1.84
其他较不发达国家...	-0.29	0.54	2.84	4.21	0.68
非洲....................	0.87	2.00	3.12	3.86	1.69
亚洲....................	-0.29	0.47	2.70	4.04	0.64
欧洲....................	-0.36	-0.75	0.90	1.98	-0.24
拉丁美洲和加勒比.......	-0.38	0.61	2.98	3.99	0.74
北美洲................	0.23	0.37	1.67	2.30	0.62
大洋洲................	0.09	0.65	2.11	2.89	0.81

资料来源：联合国秘书处经济和社会事务部人口司（2005 年）。《世界人口前景：2004 年修订本》概要，纽约：联合国。

图 2

1950-2050 年按发展群组计算的世界人口动态

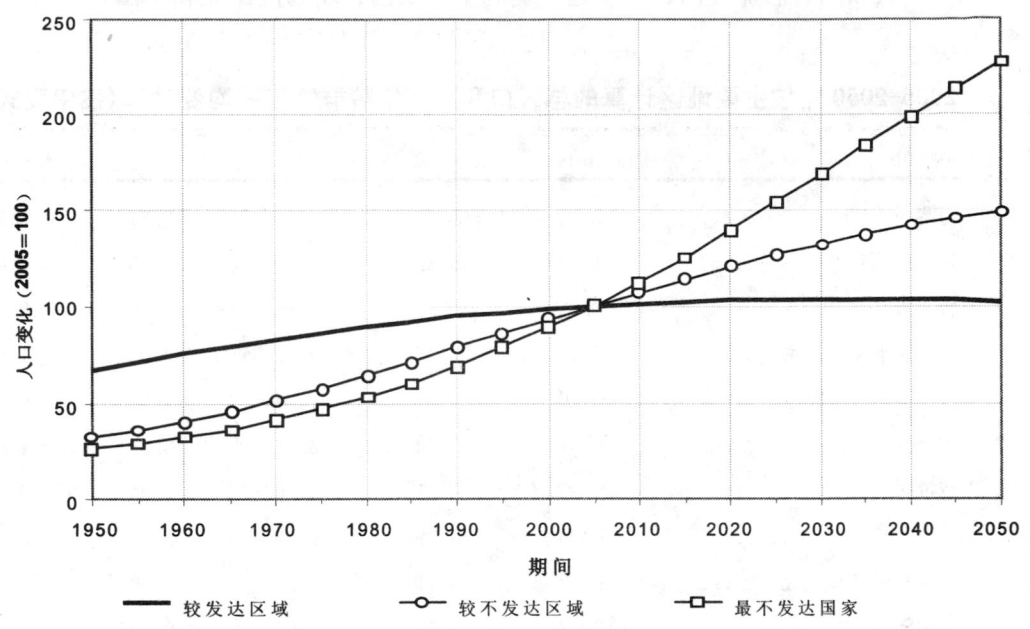

资料来源：联合国秘书处经济和社会事务部人口司（2005 年）。《世界人口前景：2004 年修订本》概要，纽约：联合国。

表 3

1970-1975、2000-2005 和 2045-2050 年按预测变式计算的世界、主要发展群组和主要地区的总生育力

| 主要地区 | 总生育力（每一妇女所生子女数） | | | | | |
| | 1970-1975 | 2000-2005 | 2045-2050 | | | |
			低	中	高	不变
世界................	4.49	2.65	1.56	2.05	2.53	3.50
较发达区域............	2.12	1.56	1.34	1.84	2.34	1.67
较不发达区域..........	5.44	2.90	1.59	2.07	2.56	3.69
最不发达国家.......	6.61	5.02	2.08	2.57	3.05	5.56
其他较不发达国家...	5.28	2.58	1.42	1.92	2.41	3.06
非洲.................	6.72	4.97	2.03	2.52	3.00	5.50
亚洲.................	5.08	2.47	1.42	1.91	2.41	2.98
欧洲.................	2.16	1.40	1.33	1.83	2.33	1.45
拉丁美洲和加勒比......	5.05	2.55	1.36	1.86	2.36	2.69
北美洲...............	2.01	1.99	1.35	1.85	2.35	1.99
大洋洲...............	3.23	2.32	1.42	1.92	2.42	2.72

资料来源：联合国秘书处经济和社会事务部人口司（2005 年）。《世界人口前景：2004 年修订本》概要，纽约：联合国。

8.   在 2000-2005 年期间，世界生育力水平为每一妇女生 2.65 个子女，约为 1950-1955 年的半数（每一妇女生 5 个子女）。按中变式计算，到 2045-2050 年全球生育力预测将进一步下降到每一妇女生 2.05 个子女。按主要发展群组计算，世界平均生育力水平呈现极为不同的趋势。在发达国家整体，目前的生育力为每一妇女生 1.56 个子女，到 2045-2050 年期间预测将缓慢增加到每一妇女生 1.84 个子女。在最不发达国家，生育力为每一妇女生 5 个子女，到 2045-2050 年预测将下降一半，为每一妇女生 2.57 个子女。在发展中世界其余国家，生育力已经较低，为每一妇女生 2.58 个子女，预期到本世纪中期将进一步降到每一妇女生 1.92 个子女，因此几乎与发达世界到时的典型生育力水平趋同。要实现所预测的生育力下降取决于是否能获得计划生育，尤其是在最不发达国家。

9.   在 2000-2005 年期间，148 个发展中国家中有 35 个国家的生育力仍为每一妇女生 5 个子女以上，其中 30 个国家为最不发达国家，而撒哈拉以南非洲国家和南-中亚国家中有数个国家的下降速度比预期的低。总体来说，生育力高的国家占世界人口的 10%。相对来说，有 23 个发展中国家的生育力低于更替生育水平，

它们的人口占世界人口的 25%。这一群组包括中国，2000-2005 年期间其生育力估计为每一妇女生 1.7 个子女。

10. 占世界人口 19% 的 44 个发达国家目前的生育力水平很低。除阿尔巴尼亚外，这所有国家的生育力都低于更替生育水平，其中主要是在南欧和东欧的 15 个国家已达到了人类史上前所未有的生育力水平（每一妇女生 1.3 个子女）。从 1990-1995 年以来，多数发达国家的生育力都在下降。少数国家象比利时、法国、德国、荷兰和美国的生育力有增加，但增加不多。

表 4

2000-2005 和 2045-2050 年世界、主要发展群组和主要地区的预期寿命

主要地区	2000-2005	2045-2050
世界.................................	65.4	75.1
较发达区域........................	75.6	82.1
较不发达区域......................	63.4	74.0
最不发达国家....................	51.0	66.5
其他较不发达国家...............	66.1	76.3
非洲...............................	49.1	65.4
亚洲...............................	67.3	77.2
欧洲...............................	73.7	80.6
拉丁美洲和加勒比.................	71.5	79.5
北美洲.............................	77.6	82.7
大洋洲.............................	74.0	81.2

资料来源：联合国秘书处经济和社会事务部人口司（2005 年）。《世界人口前景：2004 年修订本》概要，纽约：联合国。

11. 全球出生时预期寿命估计从 1950-1955 年的 47 岁上升到 2000-2005 年的 65 岁，预期将升到 2045-2050 年的 75 岁。在较发达区域，预期从今天的 76 岁上升到本世纪中期的 82 岁。最不发达国家今天的预期寿命为 51 岁，预计将升到 2045-2050 年的 67 岁。由于这许多国家高度受到艾滋病毒/艾滋病流行病之害，预期寿命的预计增长取决于能否执行有效的艾滋病毒感染预防和治疗方案。在具有类似条件的其余发展中世界，预计预期寿命将从今天的 66 岁增加到本世纪中期的 76 岁。

12. 从 1980 年代末期以来东欧的死亡率一直在上升。2000-2005 年该区域的预期寿命为 67.9 岁，比 1960-1965 年（68.6 岁为低）。俄罗斯联邦和乌克兰特别受到部分由于艾滋病毒扩散所造成的死亡率上升的影响。

13. 艾滋病毒/艾滋病流行病已经存在了二十五年，在增加发病率和死亡率并减缓人口增长方面，这一疾病的影响非常明显。南部非洲是艾滋病毒/艾滋病最猖獗的区域，预期寿命从 1990-1995 年的 62 岁减到了 2000-2005 年的 48 岁，预期在缓慢回升之前，下一个十年还会进一步减到 43 岁。因此，在 2005 至 2020 年之间，该区域的人口增长预期会停滞。在博茨瓦纳、莱索托和斯威士兰，因死亡人数超过出生人数，人口预计会减少。在受到上述流行病影响的其他发展中国家，因其略高或很高的生育力足以抵销死亡率的上升，人口将继续呈现正数增长。

14. 生育力下降，尤其是预期寿命也同时增加时，就会造成人口老化的主要结果，人口当中的老人比例随着年轻人增长。全球 60 岁以上的人数预期会增加两倍，从 2005 年的 6.27 亿人增加到 2050 年的将近 19 亿人。今天每 10 个老人当中有 6 个人是住在发展中国家，到 2050 年时则每 10 个有 8 人是住在发展中国家。预期更明显增加的是最老的老人（80 岁以上）：从 2005 年的 8 600 万人增加到 2050 年的 3.94 亿人。在发展中国家，将从 4 200 万人增加到 2.78 亿人，意味着到 2050 年时，多数最老的老人将住在发展中国家。

15. 在发达国家，今天有 20% 的人口是在 60 岁以上，到 2050 年这一部分的人口预测达到 32%。发达国家的老年人口已经超过了儿童人数（0-14 岁的人口），到 2050 年时每两个老人对 1 个儿童。在发展中世界，60 岁以上人口的比例预期从 2005 年的 8% 增加到 2050 年的 20%。

16. 中位年龄（即有 50% 的人口已经高出和有 50% 的人口尚未达到的年龄）的增加是人口老化的迹象。今天只有 11 个发达国家的中位年龄为 40 岁以上。到 2050 年时将有 89 个国家属于这一群组，其中有 45 个在发展中世界。人口老化已日益成为发达国家的当前现实，发展中世界也不可避免，而且在发展中国家会出现得更快。

17. 生育力仍旧很高而且只略有下跌的国家将经历最缓慢的人口老化。到 2050 年，每五个国家中约有一个仍预测保有等于或少于 30 岁的中位年龄。最不发达国家将拥有最年轻的人口，预测其中 11 个国家到 2050 年时将保有等于或少于 23 岁的中位年龄，其中包括以下国家：阿富汗、安哥拉、布隆迪、乍得、刚果民主共和国、赤道几内亚、几内亚比绍、利比里亚、马里、尼日尔和乌干达。

18. 在 2005-2050 年期间，预测移往发达区域的国际移民净人数达 9 800 万人，平均每年 220 万人。同等人数将离开较不发达区域。对发达世界而言，这一数目的净移徙将因 2005-2050 年预期死亡人数超过出生人数所造成的 7 300 万人损失而大部分得到抵销。对发展中世界而言，9 800 万的外移人数只占预期人口增长的 4% 不到。

19. 在 2005-2050 年期间，有 74 个国家为净移入国。预测其中 64 个国家的净移入加强了人口的增长，另 7 个国家有助于扭转人口下降的趋势（奥地利、克罗地亚、德国、希腊、意大利、斯洛伐克和斯洛文尼亚）。有三个国家的人口移入减缓了人口的下降，但未扭转其下降趋势（捷克共和国、匈牙利和俄罗斯联邦）。

20. 就 2005-2050 年的年平均数而言，预测净接收国际移民的主要国家为：美国（每年 110 万人）、德国（202 000 人）、加拿大（200 000 人）、联合王国（130 000 人）、意大利（120 000 人）和澳大利亚（100 000 人）。预测主要净移出国为中国（每年减 327 000 人）、墨西哥（减 293 000 人）、印度（减 241 000 人）、菲律宾（减 180 000 人）、印度尼西亚（减 164 000 人）、巴基斯坦（减 154 000 人）和乌克兰（减 100 000 人）。

《2004 年修订本》的基本假设

为预测到 2050 年的人口，联合国人口司运用了关于未来生育力、死亡率和人口移徙趋势的一些假设。由于未来的趋势无法确知，因此采用了若干预测变式。本摘要着重于《2004 年修订本》的中变式。本章 A 节细述了中变式的各种假设。

《2004 年修订本》列有五种另外的变式：高、低、不变生育力、不变死亡率和零移徙变式。B 节说明了区分这些变式与中变式的各种不同假设。将要出版的出版物中将提供这些变式的详细结果。

每个国家的未来人口是从 2005 年 7 月 1 日的估算人口去预测。由于 2005 年的实际人口数据尚未出来，2005 年的人口估算是依据通常取自人口普查或人口登记并利用关于生育力、死亡率和国际移徙的所有现有数据修订到 2005 年的最新各国现有最近人口数据计算得出。如无法取得最新的数据，估算的人口数据则采用利用可取得的最近数据作出的短期预测。所有来源的人口数据都要评价其完整性、正确性和一致性，必要时加以调整。[6]

A. 中变式的假设

1. 生育力假设：共同走向总生育力低于更替生育水平

所有国家的总生育力是假设最后会共同走向每一妇女生 1.85 个子女的水平。但是，并非所有国家在这一预测期间，即到 2050 年会达到这个水平。生育力预测的基本原则同样适用于所有国家，但预测程序视各国在 2000-2005 年期间的总生育力是否高于或低于每个妇女生 1.85 个子女而略有不同。

对于总生育力高于每个妇女生 1.85 个子女的国家来说，其生育力是假设遵循联合国人口司依据 1950-2000 年生育力下降的所有国家的过去经验建立的生育力下降模式得出的走向而加以计算。这些模式将某一期间的总生育力水平联系到下一期间总生育力的预期平均下降值。如果某一模式预测某一国家 2050 年之前的总生育力下降到每一妇女生 1.85 个子女，则剩余预测期间（即到 2050 年为止）的总生育力维持在这一不变的水平上。

---

[6] 关于人口动态订正估算所用程序的一般说明，见《世界人口前景：2002 年修订本》，第三卷：分析报告，英文本第 180-182 页。

在所有情况中，这些模式得出的预测生育力走向将与每个国家最近的趋势核对。当一国最近的趋势偏离符合这些模式的趋势甚多时，头 5 或 10 年的生育力预测是按最近的经验进行。过了这一过渡期间后，则采用模式预测方式。举例来说，在生育力停滞或无生育力下降证据的国家，在定出下降走向之前多年，生育力预测是按保持不变进行。

对于 2000-2005 年总生育力低于每一妇女生 1.85 个子女的国家，是假设预测期头 5 或 10 年的生育力将遵循每一国家最近呈现的趋势。过了过渡期间后，生育力是假设按每五年每一妇女生 0.07 个子女的线性增长增加。因此，目前生育力极低的国家无需在 2050 年之前达到每一妇女生 1.85 个子女的水平。

2. 死亡率假设：除受到艾滋病毒/艾滋病影响外预期寿命会增加

a. 正常死亡率假设

死亡率假设是根据联合国人口司建立的预期寿命变化模式来预测的。预期寿命越高，这些模式建立的增长越小。一国模式的选择是根据按性别区分的最近预期寿命趋势。对于高度受到艾滋病毒/艾滋病流行病影响的国家，通常是采用采纳了较缓慢死亡率下降速度的模式来预测与艾滋病毒/艾滋病无关的一般死亡率风险的减少情况。

b. 艾滋病毒/艾滋病对死亡率的影响

对于受到艾滋病毒/艾滋病流行病高度影响的 60 个国家（在表八.21 列出），艾滋病毒/艾滋病影响估算是以明确定出流行病过程模式和预测每年发生艾滋病毒感染人数的方式进行。联合国艾滋病毒/艾滋病联合规划署(艾滋病规划署)估计、模式和预测咨商小组制作的模式[7]是用于切入艾滋病规划署过去提供的艾滋病毒流行估算，以得出确定这一流行病的过去动态的参数。对大部分国家来说，切入的模式是假设有关的参数在过去保持不变。从 2005 年起，反映将新人纳入高危险群体或易感染群体的比例的 PHI 参数是按每三十年下降一半预测。代表感染力量的 R 参数也按同样方式预测。R 的减少反映了会受感染者的行为变化和受感染者治疗途径的增加会减少病毒传染机会的假设。视每一国家治疗途径增加的进展情况而定，按不同比率预测，母婴传播比率会降低。此外，咨商小组关于受感染儿童的成活率的部分已经更新：《2004 年修订本》假设母婴传播的受感染儿童有 50％可活到两岁。

《2004 年修订本》首度指出接受积极抗逆转录病毒疗法的病人可成活较久。每一国家接受抗逆转录病毒疗法的艾滋病毒抗体阳性人口比例，符合世界卫生组

---

[7] 评估艾滋病毒/艾滋病流行病及其影响的改良方法和假设：艾滋病规划署估计、模式和预测咨商小组的建议。艾滋病，第 16 卷，英文本第 W1-W14 页（艾滋病规划署估计、模式和预测咨商小组，2002 年）。

织 2004 年年底的估算。[8] 视目前的治疗人数而定，到 2015 年治疗面预测将达
40-85％之间。接受抗逆转录病毒疗法的病人每年的成活机率假设为至少 80％。
根据这一假设，从开始接受治疗算起的平均成活期为 3.1 年。相对的，艾滋病开
始出现后不接受治疗的成活期仅假设为一年。

3. 国际移徙假设

在估算以往国际移徙人数和评估各国对今后国际移民流动的政策立场的基
础上，设定了今后的国际移徙走向。

B. 预测变式

《2004 年修订本》除中变式外，还列有五种预测变式。生育力高、低和不变
三种变式仅在预测的总生育力上与中变式有别。按高变式，预计在预测期间的大
部分时间，总生育力保持在比中变式的总生育力多出 0.5 个子女的水平上。举例
来说，按中变式总生育力达到 1.85 个子女的国家，按高变式则为 2.35 个子女。
低变式的总生育力预测比中变式的总生育力少 0.5 个子女。不变生育力变式的总
生育力与 2000-2005 年的估算水平保持不变。

也计算了不变死亡率变式和零移徙变式。两者都采用与中变式相同的假设。
另外，不变死亡率变式与中变式有相同的国际移徙假设。因此，不变死亡率变式
的结果可与中变式的结果对比，以评估不断改变的死亡率对其他人口统计参数的
影响。同样的，零移徙变式与中变式的差别仅在于对国际移徙的根本假设。因此，
零移徙变式可供评估非零移徙对其他人口统计参数的影响。

C. 就《2004 年修订本》所作方法改变

- 在中变式中，2000-2005 年总生育力低于每一妇女生 1.85 个子女的国家
  的生育力首先是按持续最近的趋势预测，而后按每五年每一妇女增生
  0.07 个子女的比例线性增加生育力。这些国家不一定会在 2050 年之前
  达到每一妇女生 1.85 个子女的水平。

- 在《2004 年修订本》中使用了另外的死亡率变化模式以了解预期寿命上
  升的历史经验的多样性。具体来说，制作了极缓慢和极快速的变化模式，
  加入先前存在的缓慢、中等和快速变化模式。

- 对 2003 年成人艾滋病毒流行率为 1％以上的所有国家明确采用艾滋病
  毒/艾滋病对死亡率的影响模式。

---

[8] 世界卫生组织，"三五"进度报告，2004 年 12 月/卫生组织和艾滋病规划署。

- 抗逆转录病毒疗法明确纳入对受到影响国家的艾滋病毒/艾滋病预测。此外，预测母婴传播艾滋病毒的比率将按照符合扩大该治疗途径的预测进展度而降低。

———————

Préface

On trouvera dans le présent rapport le résumé des résultats de la *Révision de 2004* des estimations et projections officielles concernant la population mondiale établies par la Division de la population du Département des affaires économiques et sociales du Secrétariat de l'ONU. En outre, le rapport donne un aperçu des hypothèses concernant la fécondité, la mortalité et les migrations utilisées pour l'établissement des projections ainsi qu'un résumé des modifications et ajustements introduits dans la *Révision de 2004* par rapport aux procédures suivies dans la *Révision de 2002*. La *Révision de 2004* est fondée sur les résultats de la dix-neuvième série d'estimations et projections démographiques mondiales entreprises par la Division de la population depuis 1950.

Les résultats complets de la *Révision de 2004* seront publiés dans une série de trois volumes. Le premier volume[1] contiendra les tableaux détaillés relatifs aux principaux indicateurs démographiques pour chaque pays, de 1950 à 2050; le deuxième volume[2] présentera la répartition par âge et par sexe de la population de chaque pays au cours de la période 1950-2050; et le troisième volume[3] sera consacré à une analyse des résultats obtenus.

Les données seront également disponibles sous forme numérique. Les utilisateurs intéressés peuvent acheter un CD-ROM contenant les principaux résultats de la *Révision de 2004*. Une description des données contenues dans le CD-ROM et un formulaire de commande seront affichés sur le site Web de la Division de la population à l'adresse <www.unpopulation.org>.

La responsabilité de la *Révision de 2004* incombe à la Division de la population. L'élaboration de la *Révision de 2004* a été facilitée par la collaboration offerte à la Division de la population par les commissions régionales, les institutions spécialisées et d'autres organes pertinents des Nations Unies.

En particulier, il a été fait appel pour l'établissement de ces estimations et projections à une source essentielle de statistiques officielles nationales sur la population, l'*Annuaire démographique des Nations Unies* et ses bases de données, élaborées et tenues à jour par la Division de statistique du Département des affaires économiques et sociales de l'ONU. La Division de la population remercie la Division de statistique de la coopération qu'elle ne cesse de lui apporter.

On trouvera certains résultats de la *Révision de 2004* ainsi que d'autres informations démographiques sur le site Web de la Division de la population à l'adresse <www.unpopulation.org>. Pour tout complément d'information au sujet de la *Révision de 2004*, veuillez entrer en contact avec Mme Hania Zlotnik, Directrice de la Division de la population, Nations Unies, New York, NY 10017, États-Unis (télécopie : 1 (212) 963-2147).

---

[1] *World Population Prospects: The 2004 Revision*, vol. I, *Comprehensive Tables* (publication des Nations Unies, Sales No. E.05.XIII.5).

[2] *World Population Prospects: The 2004 Revision*, vol. II, *Sex and Age Distribution of the World Population* (publication des Nations Unies, Sales No. E.05.XIII.6).

[3] *World Population Prospects: The 2004 Revision*, vol. III, *Analytical Report* (publication des Nations Unies, à paraître).

Résumé

La *Révision de 2004* est fondée sur les résultats de la dix-neuvième série d'estimations et projections démographiques officielles de l'ONU établis par la Division de la population du Département des affaires économiques et sociales du Secrétariat de l'Organisation. Ces estimations et projections sont utilisées dans l'ensemble du système des Nations Unies où elles servent de base aux activités pour lesquelles des informations démographiques sont nécessaires. La *Révision de 2004* est la première qui intègre les résultats complets de la série des recensements nationaux de la population de 2000. Elle tient également compte des résultats d'enquêtes spécialisées effectuées récemment dans des pays moins développés pour recueillir des données démographiques et autres permettant d'évaluer les progrès réalisés en vue des objectifs de développement convenus sur le plan international, y compris les objectifs du Millénaire pour le développement (OMD). L'inventaire détaillé des tendances passées et futures de la population mondiale présenté dans la *Révision de 2004* constitue la base de données démographiques indispensable pour une évaluation des progrès accomplis dans cette voie.

La *Révision de 2004* confirme la diversité de la dynamique démographique de notre époque. S'il est vrai que la population mondiale continue d'augmenter, il n'y a guère de changements dans la population des régions développées du monde, et la croissance de la population a lieu en quasi-totalité dans les régions moins développées. Le groupe des 50 pays les moins avancés connaît une croissance démographique particulièrement rapide.

Ces différents schémas de croissance s'expliquent par les tendances différentes de la fécondité et de la mortalité. Des niveaux de fécondité inférieurs au seuil de remplacement s'observent dans les régions développées et cette tendance devrait se poursuivre jusqu'en 2050. La fécondité est encore élevée dans la plupart des pays les moins avancés et, même s'il faut s'attendre à une baisse, elle restera plus élevée dans ces pays que dans le reste du monde. Dans les autres pays moins développés, la fécondité a nettement diminué depuis la fin des années 60 et, pour la plupart des pays inclus dans ce groupe, la fécondité devrait tomber en dessous du seuil de remplacement d'ici à 2050.

Dans les économies de marché traditionnelles du monde développé, la mortalité est faible et continue à baisser, mais elle a été stationnaire ou a même augmenté dans bon nombre de pays à économie en transition, en grande partie sous l'effet de la dégradation des conditions sociales et économiques et, dans certains cas, en raison de la propagation du VIH. La mortalité diminue également dans la plupart des pays moins développés, mais elle a augmenté dans ceux qui sont gravement touchés par l'épidémie de VIH/sida. Étant donné les efforts entrepris actuellement pour dispenser d'ici à 2005 un traitement antirétroviral à trois millions de patients atteints du sida et compte tenu de l'expansion de ce traitement attendue par la suite, la *Révision de 2004* part de l'hypothèse d'une période de survie plus longue pour les personnes vivant avec le VIH que ce n'était le cas dans la *Révision de 2002* et indique en conséquence pour les pays touchés par le VIH des niveaux de mortalité futurs qui sont inférieurs aux niveaux prévus dans la *Révision* précédente.

L'épidémie de VIH/sida continue de s'étendre. Le nombre de pays comptant un effectif important de personnes atteintes est de 60 dans la *Révision de 2004*, alors qu'il était de 53 dans la *Révision de 2002*. Bien que les taux de prévalence du VIH dans quelques pays aient été révisés en baisse à mesure que les statistiques améliorées devenaient disponibles, le tribut payé à la maladie est encore très lourd et le restera probablement, malgré les réductions prévues de la prévalence du VIH/sida. La baisse attendue des taux de prévalence du VIH dépend de l'exécution par les gouvernements des engagements qu'ils ont pris dans la Déclaration du Millénaire[4] et dans la Déclaration d'engagement des Nations Unies de 2001 sur le VIH/sida[5].

Les principales conclusions de la *Révision de 2004* peuvent se résumer comme suit :

1.   En juillet 2005, le monde comptera 6,5 milliards d'habitants, 380 millions de plus qu'en 2000, ce qui représente un accroissement annuel de 76 millions d'êtres humains. Malgré la baisse de fécondité prévue pour la période 2005-2050, la population mondiale devrait atteindre 9,1 milliards de personnes d'après la variante moyenne et s'accroîtra encore de 34 millions de personnes par an au milieu du siècle.

2.   Aujourd'hui, 95 % de toute la croissance démographique mondiale est absorbée par les régions moins développées et 5 % par les régions développées. D'ici à 2050, d'après la variante moyenne, la population de l'ensemble des pays développés devrait diminuer lentement, d'environ 1 million de personnes par an, et les régions moins développées devraient augmenter chaque année de 35 millions d'habitants, dont 22 millions seraient absorbés par les pays les moins avancés.

3.   La croissance future de la population est largement liée aux tendances futures de la fécondité. La variante moyenne anticipe une baisse de fécondité, allant de 2,6 enfants par femme aujourd'hui à un peu plus de 2 enfants par femme en 2050. Si la fécondité demeurait à un niveau supérieur d'environ 0,5 enfant par femme aux niveaux prévus dans la variante moyenne, le monde compterait 10,6 milliards d'habitants en 2050. Une évolution de la fécondité se traduisant par un niveau inférieur de 0,5 enfant par femme aux niveaux de la variante moyenne se traduirait par une population mondiale de 7,7 milliards au milieu du siècle. Cela veut dire qu'au niveau mondial la poursuite de la croissance démographique est inévitable jusqu'en 2050 même si la baisse de la fécondité s'accélère.

---

[4] Voir la résolution A/Res/55/2 de l'Assemblée générale.
[5] Voir la résolution A/Res/S-26/2 de l'Assemblée générale.

Tableau 1
**Population mondiale selon les différentes variantes de la projection,
par grande région, 1950, 1975, 2005 et 2050**

	Population (millions)			Population en 2050 (millions)			
Grande région	1950	1975	2005	Variante faible	Variante moyenne	Variante élevée	Variante constante
Ensemble du monde	2 519	4 074	6 465	7 680	9 076	10 646	11 658
Régions développées	813	1 047	1 211	1 057	1 236	1 440	1 195
Régions moins développées	1 707	3 027	5 253	6 622	7 840	9 206	10 463
Pays les moins avancés	201	356	759	1 497	1 735	1 994	2 744
Autres pays moins développés	1 506	2 671	4 494	5 126	6 104	7 213	7 719
Afrique	224	416	906	1 666	1 937	2 228	3 100
Asie	1 396	2 395	3 905	4 388	5 217	6 161	6 487
Europe	547	676	728	557	653	764	606
Amérique latine et Caraïbes	167	322	561	653	783	930	957
Amérique du Nord	172	243	331	375	438	509	454
Océanie	13	21	33	41	48	55	55

Source : Division de la population du Département des affaires économiques et sociales du
Secrétariat de l'ONU (2005). *World Population Prospects: The 2004 Revision Highlights*.
New York: Nations Unies.

Figure 1
Population mondiale selon les différentes variantes de la projection, 1950-2050

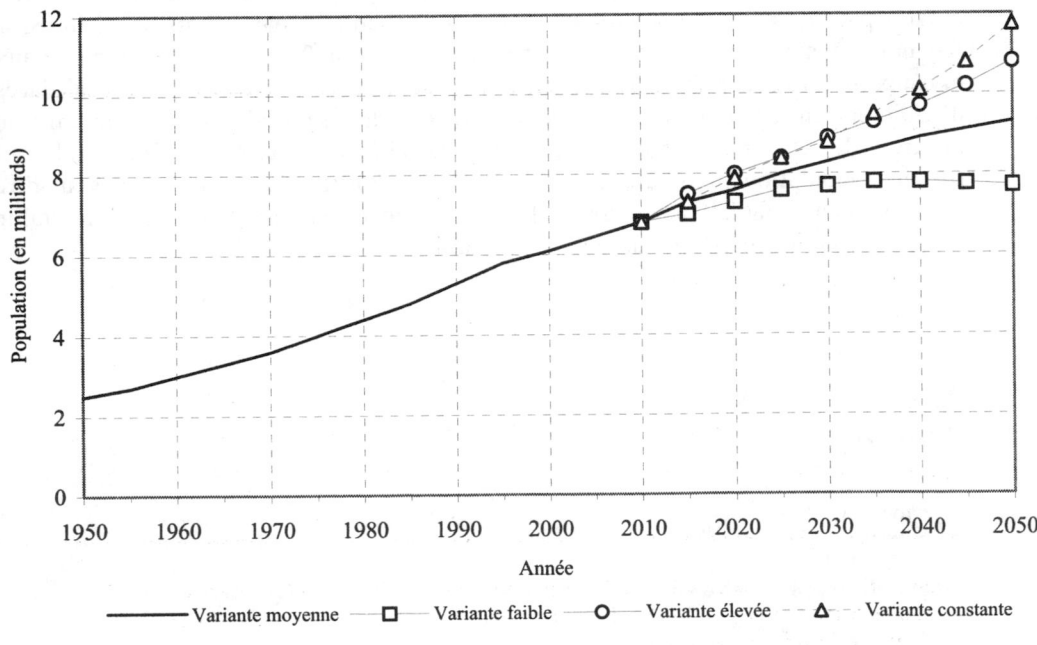

Source : Division de la population du Département des affaires économiques et sociales du
Secrétariat de l'ONU (2005). *World Population Prospects: The 2004 Revision Highlights*.
New York: Nations Unies.

4.   En raison de son taux de croissance relativement faible et en déclin, la population de l'ensemble des pays développés devrait rester pratiquement inchangée entre 2005 et 2050, avec environ 1,2 milliard d'habitants. En revanche, la population des 50 pays les moins avancés devrait plus que doubler, d'après les projections, passant de 0,8 milliard en 2005 à 1,7 milliard en 2050. Les prévisions font également apparaître une croissance vigoureuse, mais moins rapide, pour les autres pays moins développés, dont la population devrait passer de 4,5 milliards à 6,1 milliards entre 2005 et 2050.

5.   Une très forte croissance démographique est anticipée dans un certain nombre de pays moins développés, dont la plupart sont parmi les pays les moins avancés. Entre 2005 et 2050, la population devrait au moins tripler en Afghanistan, au Burkina Faso, au Burundi, au Congo, en Guinée-Bissau, au Libéria, au Mali, au Niger, en Ouganda, en République démocratique du Congo, en République démocratique du Timor-Leste et au Tchad.

6.   La population de 51 pays ou régions, y compris l'Allemagne, l'Italie, le Japon, les États baltes et la plupart des États successeurs de l'ex-Union soviétique, sera probablement moins nombreuse en 2050 qu'en 2005.

7.   En 2005-2050, neuf pays devraient être à l'origine de la moitié de l'augmentation prévue de la population mondiale : l'Inde, le Pakistan, le Nigeria, la République démocratique du Congo, le Bangladesh, l'Ouganda, les États-Unis d'Amérique, l'Éthiopie et la Chine, énumérés dans l'ordre selon l'ampleur de leur contribution à la croissance de la population au cours de cette période.

Tableau 2
Taux annuel de variation de la population selon les grands groupes d'âge, par grande région, 2005-2050 (variante moyenne)

Grande région	0-14	15-59	60+	80+	Population totale
Ensemble du monde	- 0,01	0,63	2,39	3,37	0,75
Régions développées	- 0,14	- 0,38	1,10	2,13	0,05
Régions moins développées	0,03	0,82	2,88	4,19	0,89
Pays les moins avancés	1,02	2,15	3,32	4,03	1,84
Autres pays moins développés	- 0,29	0,54	2,84	4,21	0,68
Afrique	0,87	2,00	3,12	3,86	1,69
Asie	- 0,29	0,47	2,70	4,04	0,64
Europe	- 0,36	- 0,75	0,90	1,98	- 0,24
Amérique latine et Caraïbes	- 0,38	0,61	2,98	3,99	0,74
Amérique du Nord	0,23	0,37	1,67	2,30	0,62
Océanie	0,09	0,65	2,11	2,89	0,81

Source : Division de la population du Département des affaires économiques et sociales du Secrétariat de l'ONU (2005). *World Population Prospects: The 2004 Revision Highlights*. New York: Nations Unies.

Figure 2
Dynamique de la population, par grande région, 1950-2050 (variante moyenne)

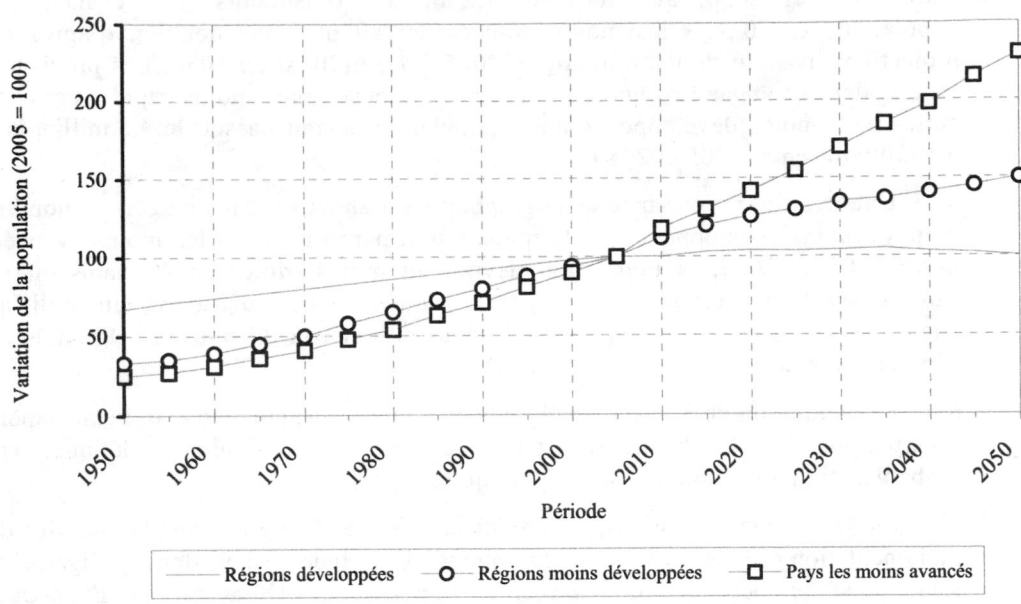

Régions développées — O — Régions moins développées — □ — Pays les moins avancés

Source : Division de la population du Département des affaires économiques et sociales du
Secrétariat de l'ONU (2005). *World Population Prospects: The 2004 Revision Highlights.*
New York: Nations Unies.

Tableau 3
**Indice synthétique de fécondité selon les différentes variantes de la projection,
par grande région, 1970-1975, 2000-2005 et 2045-2050**

Grande région	Indice synthétique de fécondité (nombre d'enfants par femme)		2045-2050			
	1970-1975	2000-2005	Variante faible	Variante moyenne	Variante élevée	Variante constante
Ensemble du monde	4,49	2,65	1,56	2,05	2,53	3,50
Régions développées	2,12	1,56	1,34	1,84	2,34	1,67
Régions moins développées	5,44	2,90	1,59	2,07	2,56	3,69
Pays les moins avancés	6,61	5,02	2,08	2,57	3,05	5,56
Autres pays moins développés	5,28	2,58	1,42	1,92	2,41	3,06
Afrique	6,72	4,97	2,03	2,52	3,00	5,50
Asie	5,08	2,47	1,42	1,91	2,41	2,98
Europe	2,16	1,40	1,33	1,83	2,33	1,45
Amérique latine et Caraïbes	5,05	2,55	1,36	1,86	2,36	2,69
Amérique du Nord	2,01	1,99	1,35	1,85	2,35	1,99
Océanie	3,23	2,32	1,42	1,92	2,42	2,72

Source : Division de la population du Département des affaires économiques et sociales du
Secrétariat de l'ONU (2005). *World Population Prospects: The 2004 Revision Highlights.*
New York: Nations Unies.

8.   En 2000-2005, la fécondité à l'échelle mondiale était de 2,65 enfants par femme, soit environ la moitié du niveau des années 1950-1955 (5 enfants par femme). Dans la variante moyenne, les projections indiquent que la fécondité mondiale atteindra 2,05 enfants par femme en 2045-2050. Les niveaux de fécondité à l'échelle mondiale résultent d'évolutions très différentes parmi les pays développés et les pays moins développés. Dans l'ensemble des pays développés, la fécondité est aujourd'hui de 1,56 enfant par femme et devrait progresser lentement pour atteindre 1,84 enfant par femme en 2045-2050. Dans les pays les moins avancés, la fécondité est de 5 enfants par femme et devrait diminuer environ de moitié, pour tomber à 2,57 enfants par femme en 2045-2050. Pour les autres pays moins développés, la fécondité est déjà relativement faible, avec 2,58 enfants par femme, et devrait diminuer davantage pour atteindre 1,92 enfant par femme d'ici le milieu du siècle, ce qui la ferait pratiquement converger avec les niveaux de fécondité typiques observés à cette date dans les régions développées. Cette baisse anticipée de la fécondité présuppose un accès continu aux services de planification familiale, d'autant plus dans les pays les moins avancés.

9.   En 2000-2005, la fécondité est encore supérieure à 5 enfants par femme dans 35 des 148 pays moins développés, dont 30 font partie des pays les moins avancés, et la baisse observée dans plusieurs pays d'Afrique subsaharienne et d'Asie méridionale et centrale a été plus lente que prévue. Dans l'ensemble, les pays à forte fécondité représentent 10 % de la population mondiale. En revanche, la fécondité a atteint des taux inférieurs au seuil de remplacement dans 23 pays moins développés où vit 25 % de la population mondiale. Ce groupe comprend la Chine, où la fécondité pour la période 2000-2005 est estimée à 1,7 enfant par femme.

10.   Les niveaux de fécondité dans les 44 pays développés, où vit 19 % de la population mondiale, sont aujourd'hui très bas. Tous, à l'exception de l'Albanie, ont des niveaux de fécondité inférieurs au seuil de remplacement et 15, situés pour la plupart en Europe méridionale et orientale, ont atteint un niveau de fécondité sans précédent dans l'histoire humaine (moins de 1,3 enfant par femme). Depuis 1990-1995, la baisse de la fécondité a été la règle dans la plupart des pays développés. Les quelques augmentations enregistrées, par exemple en Allemagne, en Belgique, aux États-Unis, en France et aux Pays-Bas, ont été minimes.

11.   Pour l'ensemble du monde, l'espérance de vie à la naissance a augmenté de 47 ans en 1950-1955 à 65 ans en 2000-2005, et devrait continuer de progresser pour atteindre 75 ans en 2045-2050. Dans les régions développées, l'accroissement prévu amènerait l'espérance de vie de 76 ans aujourd'hui à 82 ans au milieu du siècle. Dans les pays les moins avancés, l'espérance de vie est aujourd'hui de 51 ans; elle devrait atteindre 67 ans en 2045-2050. Étant donné que bon nombre de ces pays sont gravement touchés par l'épidémie du VIH/sida, l'accroissement de l'espérance de vie indiquée par les projections dépend de la mise en œuvre de programmes efficaces de prévention et de traitement de l'infection à VIH. Pour les autres pays moins développés, et compte tenu des mêmes réserves, l'espérance de vie devrait passer de 66 ans aujourd'hui à 76 ans au milieu du siècle.

Tableau 4
Espérance de vie à la naissance, par grande région, 2000-2005 et 2045-2050

Grande région	2000-2005	2045-2050
Ensemble du monde	65,4	75,1
Régions développées	75,6	82,1
Régions moins développées	63,4	74,0
Pays les moins avancés	51,0	66,5
Autres pays moins développés	66,1	76,3
Afrique	49,1	65,4
Asie	67,3	77,2
Europe	73,7	80,6
Amérique latine et Caraïbes	71,5	79,5
Amérique du Nord	77,6	82,7
Océanie	74,0	81,2

Source : Division de la population du Département des affaires économiques et sociales du Secrétariat de l'ONU (2005). *World Population Prospects: The 2004 Revision. Highlights.* New York: Nations Unies.

12. La mortalité a augmenté en Europe orientale depuis la fin des années 80. En 2000-2005, l'espérance de vie, qui est de 67,9 ans dans la région, avait diminué par rapport au niveau de la période 1960-1965 (68,6 ans). La Fédération de Russie et l'Ukraine sont particulièrement touchées par l'augmentation de la mortalité qui résulte en partie de la propagation du VIH.

13. Vingt-cinq ans après le déclenchement de l'épidémie du VIH/sida, l'impact de la maladie ressort clairement de l'accroissement de la morbidité et de la mortalité et du ralentissement de la croissance démographique. En Afrique australe, région qui connaît le niveau le plus élevé de prévalence du VIH/sida, l'espérance de vie a diminué, tombant de 62 ans en 1990-1995 à 48 ans en 2000-2005, et devrait encore se réduire pour tomber à 43 ans au cours de la prochaine décennie avant d'amorcer une lente reprise. En conséquence, la croissance démographique de la région sera probablement nulle entre 2005 et 2020. Pour le Botswana, le Lesotho et le Swaziland, les projections indiquent une diminution de la population, avec des décès plus nombreux que les naissances. Dans la plupart des autres pays moins développés touchés par l'épidémie, la population devrait continuer à croître car les taux de natalité modérés ou dynamiques compensent pour l'augmentation de la mortalité.

14. La principale conséquence d'une baisse de la fécondité, surtout lorsqu'elle s'accompagne d'un accroissement de l'espérance de vie, est le vieillissement de la population, selon lequel la proportion de personnes âgées dans une population augmente par rapport à la proportion de jeunes. À l'échelle mondiale, l'effectif de personnes âgées de 60 ans ou plus devrait pratiquement tripler, passant de 672 millions de personnes en 2005 à près de 1,9 milliard en 2050. Alors que 6 sur 10 de ces personnes âgées vivent aujourd'hui dans les régions moins développées, en 2050, on en comptera 8 sur 10. Les prévisions indiquent une augmentation plus forte encore du nombre des personnes très âgées (80 ans ou plus) : de 86 millions en 2005 à 394 millions en 2050. Dans les pays moins développés, leur nombre passera

de 42 millions à 278 millions, ce qui signifie qu'en 2050 la plupart des personnes très âgées vivront dans les régions moins développées.

15.   Dans les pays développés, 20 % de la population d'aujourd'hui est âgée de 60 ans ou davantage et en 2050 cette proportion devrait être de 32 % d'après les projections. La population âgée des pays développés est déjà plus nombreuse que les enfants (personnes âgées de 0 à 14 ans), et en 2050 il y aura 2 personnes âgées pour 1 enfant. Dans les régions moins développées, la proportion de la population âgée de 60 ans ou plus devrait augmenter, passant de 8 % en 2005 à près de 20 % en 2050.

16.   L'augmentation de l'âge médian, c'est-à-dire l'âge qui constitue la limite entre les 50 % de la population qui ont plus que cet âge et les 50 % qui ont moins que cet âge, est un signe de vieillissement de la population. Aujourd'hui, l'âge médian est supérieur à 40 ans dans seulement 11 pays développés. En 2050, il est prévu que 89 pays auront un âge médian de cet ordre, dont 45 pays moins développés. Le vieillissement de la population, phénomène qui prend actuellement beaucoup d'ampleur dans les pays développés, est également inévitable dans les pays moins développés, où, dans l'ensemble, il se manifestera à un rythme plus accéléré.

17.   Les pays où la fécondité demeure élevée et n'a diminué que modérément sont ceux où le vieillissement de la population se produira le plus lentement. En 2050, d'après les projections, il devrait y avoir encore un pays sur cinq où l'âge médian sera égal ou inférieur à 30 ans. Les populations les plus jeunes se trouveront dans les pays les moins avancés, dont 11 devraient enregistrer, d'après les prévisions, un âge médian égal ou inférieur à 23 ans en 2050, notamment l'Afghanistan, l'Angola, le Burundi, la Guinée-Bissau, la Guinée équatoriale, le Libéria, le Mali, le Niger, l'Ouganda, la République démocratique du Congo et le Tchad.

18.   Pendant la période 2005-2050, le solde migratoire des régions développées devrait être de 98 millions, soit en moyenne 2,2 millions par an. Un nombre égal de personnes quittera les régions moins développées. Pour le monde développé, un tel niveau de migrations nettes compensera largement l'excédent des décès par rapport aux naissances prévisibles pour la période 2005-2050, qui représente une perte de 73 millions de personnes. Pour les régions moins développées, les 98 millions d'émigrants représentent moins de 4 % de l'accroissement anticipé de la population.

19.   Au cours de la période 2000-2005, 74 pays ont été, en termes de migration nette, des pays d'accueil de migrants. Dans 64 de ces pays, la migration nette renforce la croissance de la population, et dans 7 autres, elle inverse la tendance au déclin démographique (Allemagne, Autriche, Croatie, Grèce, Italie, Slovaquie et Slovénie). Dans trois pays, les migrations ralentissent le déclin de la population mais ne l'inversent pas (Fédération de Russie, Hongrie et République tchèque).

20.   Sur la base des moyennes annuelles pour la période 2005-2050, les principaux pays d'accueil de migrants internationaux devraient être, en chiffres nets, les États-Unis (1,1 million par an), l'Allemagne (202 000), le Canada (200 000), le Royaume-Uni (130 000), l'Italie (120 000) et l'Australie (100 000). Les principaux pays d'émigration nette seront, d'après les projections, la Chine (- 327 000 par an), le Mexique (- 293 000), l'Inde (- 241 000), les Philippines (- 180 000), l'Indonésie (- 164 000), le Pakistan (- 154 000) et l'Ukraine (- 100 000).

Hypothèses sur lesquelles la *Révision de 2004* est fondée

Pour établir ces projections de la population jusqu'en 2050, la Division de la population de l'Organisation des Nations Unies applique des hypothèses concernant les tendances futures de la fécondité, de la mortalité et des migrations. Parce que les tendances futures ne peuvent pas être connues avec certitude, les projections comportent plusieurs variantes. Le document met l'accent sur la variante moyenne de la *Révision de 2004*. Les hypothèses sur lesquelles la variante moyenne repose sont décrites en détail à la section A du présent chapitre.

La *Révision de 2004* comporte cinq variantes supplémentaires : les variantes fondées sur l'hypothèse d'une fécondité élevée, faible ou constante, d'une mortalité constante et de migrations nulles. Les hypothèses qui font que ces variantes diffèrent de la variante moyenne sont décrites à la section B. Les résultats détaillés de ces variantes feront l'objet de publications futures.

Les projections concernant la population future de chaque pays sont établies à partir du chiffre de la population estimée à la date du 1er juillet 2005. Étant donné que les données relatives à la population réelle pour 2005 ne sont pas encore disponibles, l'estimation de la population repose sur les données démographiques les plus récentes disponibles pour chaque pays, tirées généralement d'un recensement ou d'un registre de la population, mis à jour jusqu'en 2005 en utilisant toutes les données disponibles concernant la fécondité, la mortalité et les migrations internationales. Lorsqu'il n'y a pas de données vraiment récentes disponibles, les données démographiques estimées sont des projections à court terme établies sur la base des données disponibles les plus récentes. Les données démographiques de toutes sources sont évaluées du point de vue de leur exhaustivité, de leur exactitude et de leur cohérence, et ajustées si nécessaire[6].

A.   Hypothèses sur lesquelles la variante moyenne repose

1.   Hypothèses concernant la fécondité : convergence vers un niveau de fécondité inférieur au seuil de remplacement

L'hypothèse retenue pour tous les pays est que l'indice synthétique de fécondité converge finalement vers un niveau de 1,85 enfant par femme. Cependant, tous les pays n'atteignent pas ce niveau au cours de la période de la projection, c'est-à-dire d'ici à 2050. Le principe de base de la projection concernant la fécondité est le même pour tous les pays, mais les méthodes de projection sont légèrement différentes lorsque les pays ont un indice synthétique de fécondité soit supérieur ou inférieur à 1,85 enfant par femme dans la période 2000-2005.

Pour les pays dont l'indice synthétique de fécondité est supérieur à 1,85 enfant par femme, on suppose que la fécondité baissera en suivant une trajectoire tirée des modèles de la baisse de la fécondité mis au point par la Division de la population des Nations Unies, sur la base de l'expérience passée de tous les pays où la fécondité a diminué de 1950 à 2000. Les modèles établissent un lien entre le niveau de fécondité au cours d'une période et la baisse moyenne prévue de la fécondité au cours de la période suivante. Lorsque la fécondité projetée par un modèle pour un

---

[6] Pour une description générale des procédures utilisées pour réviser les estimations de la dynamique de la population, voir *World Population Prospects: The 2002 Revision, Volume III: Analytical Report*, p. 180 à 182.

pays atteint 1,85 enfant par femme avant 2050, la fécondité est présumée constante à ce niveau pour le reste de la période couverte par la projection (c'est-à-dire jusqu'en 2050). Dans tous les cas, l'évolution prévue de la fécondité indiquée par les modèles est comparée aux tendances récentes de la fécondité dans chaque pays. Lorsque les tendances récentes de la fécondité dans un pays donné s'écartent considérablement des tendances compatibles avec les modèles, il est établi pour une période initiale de cinq à 10 ans une projection de la fécondité qui reflète l'expérience de la période récente. La projection du modèle prend ensuite le relais après cette période de transition. Par exemple, dans les pays où la fécondité a été stationnaire ou dans les pays pour lesquels il n'y a pas d'indications d'une baisse de la fécondité, on présume que la fécondité demeure constante pendant quelques années avant d'amorcer un déclin.

Pour les pays dont l'indice synthétique de fécondité était inférieur à 1,85 enfant par femme dans la période 2000-2005, on suppose qu'au cours des cinq ou 10 dernières années de la période de la projection, la fécondité suivra l'évolution récemment observée dans chaque pays. Après cette période de transition, on suppose que la fécondité suivra une progression linéaire au rythme de 0,07 enfant par femme tous les cinq ans. Ainsi, les pays où la fécondité est actuellement très faible n'atteindront pas nécessairement un niveau de 1,85 enfant par femme en 2050.

2. **Hypothèses concernant la mortalité : l'espérance de vie progresse, sauf dans les pays touchés par le VIH/sida**

a) *Hypothèses fondées sur un taux de mortalité normal*

Les projections concernant la mortalité sont fondées sur des modèles de l'évolution de l'espérance de vie élaborés par la Division de la population du Secrétariat de l'ONU. Ces modèles indiquent des progrès d'autant plus modestes que l'espérance de vie déjà atteinte est plus élevée. Le choix d'un modèle pour un pays quelconque est réalisé en fonction des tendances récentes de l'espérance de vie à la naissance pour chaque sexe. Dans le cas des pays fortement touchés par l'épidémie de VIH/sida, le modèle qui invoque un rythme lent de la baisse de la mortalité a généralement été utilisé pour les projections concernant la réduction des risques généraux de mortalité qui ne sont pas liés au VIH/sida.

b) *L'impact du VIH/sida sur la mortalité*

Pour les 60 pays fortement touchés par l'épidémie de VIH/sida (dont la liste figure au tableau VIII.21), les estimations de l'impact du VIH/sida sont effectuées explicitement sur la base d'hypothèses concernant l'évolution de l'épidémie – c'est-à-dire en établissant des projections concernant le nombre annuel de nouveaux cas d'infection à VIH. Le modèle élaboré par le Groupe de référence d'ONUSIDA sur les estimations, les modèles et les projections[7] a été utilisé pour ajuster les estimations d'ONUSIDA sur la prévalence du VIH afin de dégager les paramètres déterminants de la dynamique passée de l'épidémie. Pour la plupart des pays, le modèle est ajusté en partant de l'hypothèse que les paramètres pertinents sont restés constants dans le passé. À partir de 2005, le paramètre PHI, qui rend compte du taux de recrutement de nouveaux individus dans le groupe à haut risque ou vulnérable,

---

[7] Improved methods and assumptions for estimation of the HIV/AIDS epidemic and its impact: Recommendations of the UNAIDS Reference Group on Estimates, Modelling and Projections. AIDS, vol. 16, p. W1 à W14 (Groupe de référence d'ONUSIDA sur les estimations, les modèles et les projections, 2002).

devrait diminuer de moitié tous les 30 ans. Le paramètre R, qui représente la force de l'infection, devrait diminuer dans la même proportion. La réduction du paramètre R se fonde sur l'hypothèse que les changements de comportement parmi les sujets exposés aux risques d'infection, parallèlement à l'amélioration de l'accès au traitement pour les personnes infectées, réduiront les risques de transmission du virus. Le taux de transmission de la mère à l'enfant devrait diminuer dans des proportions variables, selon les progrès réalisés dans chaque pays en ce qui concerne l'amélioration de l'accès au traitement. De plus, l'élément du modèle de référence qui a trait à la survie des enfants infectés a été mis à jour : la *Révision de 2004* se fonde sur l'hypothèse que 50 % des enfants infectés à la suite d'une transmission de la mère à l'enfant survivront jusqu'à l'âge de 2 ans.

La *Révision de 2004* considère pour la première fois une période de survie plus longue pour les personnes recevant un traitement de trithérapie antirétrovirale (ART). La proportion de la population séropositive bénéficiant d'un traitement dans chaque pays est compatible avec les estimations établies par l'Organisation mondiale de la santé pour la fin de 2004[8]. Il est prévu que les taux de couverture atteindront des niveaux allant de 40 % à 85 % en 2015 selon le taux de couverture actuel. Les projections partent de l'hypothèse que les probabilités annuelles de survie augmentent en moyenne d'au moins 80 % pour les sujets recevant un traitement de trithérapie antirétrovirale. Sur la base de cette hypothèse, la survie moyenne à partir du début du traitement est de 3,1 ans (avec une survie médiane de 4,5 ans). En revanche, la projection se fonde sur l'hypothèse d'une survie moyenne d'un an seulement après le passage au sida en l'absence de traitement.

3. Hypothèses concernant les migrations internationales

L'évolution future des migrations internationales est déterminée sur la base des estimations passées des migrations internationales et d'une évaluation de la politique des pays en ce qui concerne les flux migratoires internationaux futurs.

B. Variantes de la projection

La *Révision 2004* comporte, en plus de la variante moyenne, cinq variantes de la projection. Trois variantes – fécondité élevée, faible et constante – ne diffèrent de la variante moyenne que par l'indice synthétique de fécondité retenu. Dans le cadre de la variante élevée, le niveau de fécondité demeure supérieur de 0,5 enfant au niveau utilisé dans la variante moyenne, pour pratiquement toute la période de la projection. Par exemple, les pays qui atteignent un indice synthétique de fécondité de 1,85 dans la variante moyenne ont également un niveau de fécondité de 2,35 dans la variante élevée. Dans le cas de la variante faible, la fécondité reste inférieure de 0,5 enfant à la fécondité retenue dans la variante moyenne. Dans la variante à fécondité constante, la fécondité demeure constante tout au long de la période de projection au niveau estimé pour la période 2000-2005.

Une variante avec mortalité constante et une variante avec migrations nulles ont également été élaborées. Dans ces deux variantes, l'hypothèse retenue en ce qui concerne la fécondité est la même que dans la variante moyenne. En outre, dans la variante à mortalité constante, l'hypothèse retenue en ce qui concerne les migrations

---

[8] Organisation mondiale de la santé. "3 by 5" Progress Report, December 2004/WHO and UNAIDS.

internationales est la même que dans la variante moyenne. Ainsi, les résultats de la variante avec mortalité constante peuvent être comparés avec ceux de la variante moyenne pour évaluer l'effet d'une variation du taux de mortalité sur les autres paramètres démographiques. De même, la variante avec migrations nulles ne diffère de la variante moyenne que par l'hypothèse retenue en ce qui concerne les migrations internationales. En conséquence, la variante avec migrations nulles permet d'évaluer l'effet de migrations nulles sur les autres paramètres démographiques.

C. Modifications méthodologiques introduites dans la *Révision 2004*

- Dans la variante moyenne, la fécondité des pays dont la fécondité est inférieure à 1,85 enfant par femme en 2000-2005 est projetée, dans un premier temps, en fonction des tendances récentes et amorce ensuite une progression linéaire au taux de 0,07 enfant par femme tous les cinq ans. Ces pays n'atteignent pas nécessairement un niveau de 1,85 enfant par femme en 2050.

- Dans la *Révision 2004*, des modèles supplémentaires de l'évolution de la mortalité ont été utilisés pour tenir compte de la diversité de l'expérience historique en ce qui concerne l'accroissement de l'espérance de vie. Plus précisément, des modèles à taux de variation très lent et très rapide ont été élaborés et ajoutés aux modèles à taux lent, moyen et rapide existant précédemment.

- L'impact du VIH/sida sur la mortalité a été expressément incorporé aux modèles pour tous les pays où la prévalence du VIH dans la population adulte était égale ou supérieure à 1 % en 2003.

- Le traitement par trithérapie antirétrovirale est expressément pris en compte dans la projection du VIH/sida pour les pays touchés. De plus, les projections se fondent sur l'hypothèse que le taux de transmission du VIH de la mère à l'enfant diminue à un rythme compatible avec les progrès prévus en ce qui concerne l'accès au traitement.

———————

Резюме

Обзор 2004 года основан на результатах девятнадцатого раунда официальных демографических оценок и прогнозов Организации Объединенных Наций, которые были подготовлены Отделом народонаселения Департамента по экономическим и социальным вопросам Секретариата Организации Объединенных Наций. Эти данные используются в рамках всей системы Организации Объединенных Наций в качестве основы для проведения мероприятий, которые требуют демографической информации. В *Обзор 2004 года* впервые включена полная информация о результатах цикла национальных переписей населения 2000 года. В нем также учтены результаты специализированных обследований, недавно проведенных в развивающихся странах в целях сбора как демографических, так и других данных для оценки прогресса, достигнутого в деле достижения согласованных на международном уровне целей в области развития, включая цели, сформулированные в Декларации тысячелетия. Всеобъемлющий обзор мировых демографических тенденций прошлых лет и перспектив на будущее, представленный в *Обзоре 2004 года*, обеспечивает демографическую основу для проведения оценки этих целей.

Обзор 2004 года подтверждает разнообразие современных демографических процессов. Хотя численность населения мира продолжает расти, в более развитых регионах в целом она почти не меняется, а весь прирост населения мира происходит за счет менее развитых регионов. Особенно быстрый прирост населения характерен для группы 50 наименее развитых стран.

В основе таких разнообразных моделей роста лежат различные тенденции в области рождаемости и смертности. В более развитых регионах показатели рождаемости ниже уровня воспроизводства населения, и ожидается, что эта тенденция сохранится до 2050 года. По-прежнему высокие показатели рождаемости наблюдаются в наименее развитых странах, и, хотя ожидается их снижение, рождаемость в этих странах сохранится на более высоком уровне, чем в других странах мира. В остальных развивающихся странах, начиная с конца 60-х годов, наблюдалось заметное снижение показателей рождаемости, и ожидается, что к 2050 году уровень рождаемости в этих странах будет ниже уровня воспроизводства населения.

Показатели смертности в развитых странах с рыночной экономикой остаются на низком уровне и продолжают снижаться, однако в некоторых странах с переходной экономикой они оставались на том же уровне или даже росли, главным образом в результате ухудшения социально-экономических условий и в некоторых случаях из-за распространения ВИЧ. В большинстве развивающихся стран также наблюдается снижение показателей смертности, однако в странах, наиболее пострадавших от эпидемии ВИЧ/СПИДа, показатели смертности повышаются. Учитывая предпринимаемые в настоящее время усилия по охвату к 2005 году антиретровирусной терапией 3 млн. больных СПИДом и ожидания, связанные с дальнейшим расширением сферы охвата, в *Обзоре 2004 года*, предполагается рост среднего показателя доживаемости для людей, живущих с ВИЧ-инфекцией, по сравнению с оценкой, содержащейся в *Обзоре 2002 года*, и в этой связи в затронутых ВИЧ-инфекцией странах прогнозируются несколько более низкие показатели смертности в будущем, чем в предыдущем *Обзоре*.

Эпидемия ВИЧ/СПИДа продолжает распространяться. Количество стран, в которых отмечается значительное число инфицированных людей, выросло с 53 согласно данным *Обзора 2002 года* до 60 согласно *Обзору 2004 года*. И это происходит несмотря на то, что благодаря повышению качества статистических данных показатели распространенности ВИЧ в некоторых странах были пересмотрены в сторону понижения. Тем не менее потери в результате этого заболевания остаются высокими, и ожидается, что такое положение сохранится, несмотря на прогнозируемое сокращение распространенности ВИЧ/ СПИДа. Более низкие прогнозируемые показатели распространенности ВИЧ зависят от выполнения обязательств, взятых на себя правительствами в Декларации тысячелетия 2000 года[1] и в Декларации о приверженности делу борьбы с ВИЧ/СПИДом 2001 года[2].

Ключевые выводы *Обзора 2004 года* можно суммировать следующим образом:

1.   К июлю 2005 года население мира составит 6,5 миллиарда человек, т.е. на 380 миллионов человек больше, чем в 2000 году, что означает прирост населения в количестве 76 миллионов человек в год. Несмотря на снижение показателей рождаемости, прогнозируемых на период 2005–2050 годов, мировая численность населения при варианте со средним уровнем рождаемости достигнет, как ожидается, 9,1 миллиарда человек, и до середины века ежегодный прирост населения будет составлять 34 миллиона человек.

2.   В настоящее время на развивающиеся страны приходится 95 процентов всего прироста населения, на развитые страны — 5 процентов. Согласно варианту со средним уровнем рождаемости к 2050 году население более развитых стран в целом будет медленно сокращаться приблизительно на 1 миллион человек в год, а прирост населения развивающихся стран будет ежегодно составлять 35 миллионов человек, из которых 22 миллиона человек будет приходиться на наименее развитые страны.

3.   Рост численности населения в будущем в значительной степени зависит от тенденций в области рождаемости. Согласно варианту со средним уровнем рождаемости прогнозируется снижение показателей рождаемости с 2,6 ребенка на женщину сегодня до чуть больше двух детей на женщину в 2050 году. Если бы показатель рождаемости оставался хотя бы на половину пункта выше показателя, прогнозируемого в среднем варианте, то к 2050 году численность населения мира увеличилась бы до 10,6 миллиарда человек. При снижении этого показателя на половину пункта ниже среднего варианта численность населения к середине века составила бы 7,6 миллиарда человек. Это означает, что в мировом масштабе численность населения до 2050 года будет неизбежно увеличиваться, даже если падение рождаемости ускорится.

---

[1] См. резолюцию 55/2 Генеральной Ассамблеи.
[2] См. резолюцию S-26/2 Генеральной Ассамблеи.

Таблица 1

**Численность населения мира, основных групп стран и основных регионов
в 1950, 1975, 2005 и 2050 годах при разных вариантах прогнозирования**

Основной регион	Население (в млн. человек)			Численность населения в 2050 году (в млн. человек)			
	1950 год	1975 год	2005 год	Низкий уровень рождаемости	Средний уровень рождаемости	Высокий уровень рождаемости	Неизменный уровень рождаемости
Весь мир	2 519	4 074	6 465	7 680	9 076	10 646	11 658
Более развитые регионы	813	1 047	1 211	1 057	1 236	1 440	1 195
Менее развитые регионы	1 707	3 027	5 253	6 622	7 840	9 206	10 463
Наименее развитые страны	201	356	759	1 497	1 735	1 994	2 744
Другие менее развитые страны	1 506	2 671	4 494	5 126	6 104	7 213	7 719
Африка	224	416	906	1 666	1 937	2 228	3 100
Азия	1 396	2 395	3 905	4 388	5 217	6 161	6 487
Европа	547	676	728	557	653	764	606
Латинская Америка и Карибский бассейн	167	322	561	653	783	930	957
Северная Америка	172	243	331	375	438	509	454
Океания	13	21	33	41	48	55	55

Источник: Отдел народонаселения Департамента по экономическим и социальным вопросам Секретариата Организации Объединенных Наций (2005 год). *Мировые демографические перспективы: Обзор 2004 года. Основные выводы.* Нью-Йорк: Организация Объединенных Наций.

Рисунок 1

**Численность населения в мире при разных вариантах прогнозирования
(1950–2050 годы)**

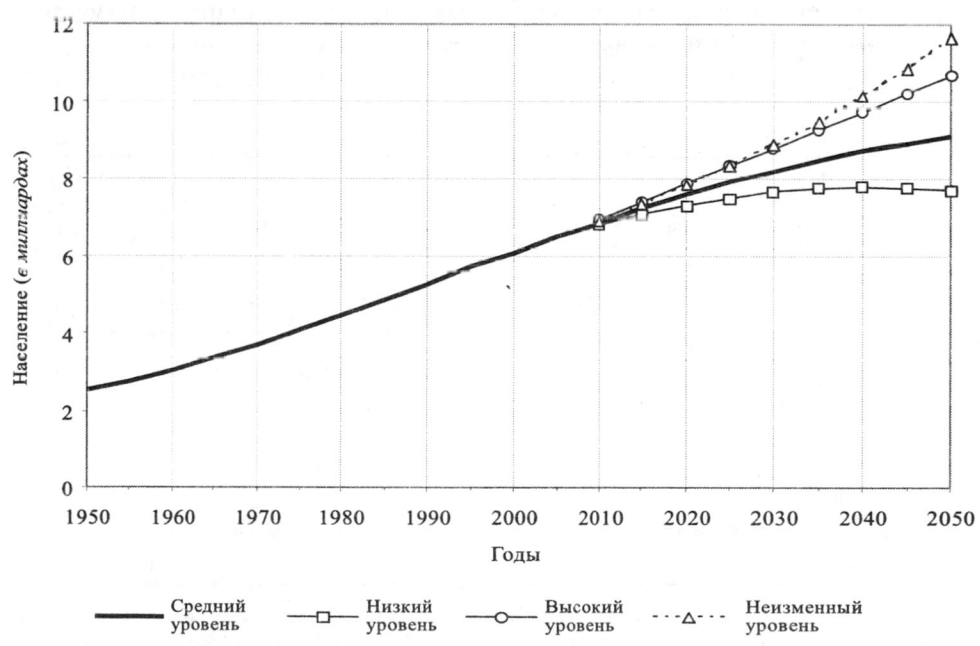

Источник: Отдел народонаселения Департамента по экономическим и социальным вопросам Секретариата Организации Объединенных Наций (2005 год). *Мировые демографические перспективы: Обзор 2004 года. Основные выводы.* Нью-Йорк: Организация Объединенных Наций.

4.   Численность населения развитых стран в целом в результате низких и сокращающихся темпов прироста в период 2005–2050 годов останется, как ожидается, фактически неизменной и будет составлять 1,2 миллиарда человек, тогда как численность населения 50 наименее развитых стран, напротив, согласно прогнозу, увеличится более чем в два раза — с 0,8 миллиарда человек в 2005 году до 1,7 миллиарда человек в 2050 году. В остальных развивающихся странах также прогнозируется рост численности населения, хотя и более медленными темпами, и в период 2005–2050 годов она увеличится с 4,5 миллиарда человек до 6,1 миллиарда человек.

5.   Весьма быстрый рост численности населения ожидается в ряде развивающихся стран, большинство из которых составляют наименее развитые страны. Прогнозируется, что в период 2005–2050 годов численность населения увеличится по меньшей мере втрое в Афганистане, Буркина-Фасо, Бурунди, Гвинее-Бисау, Демократической Республике Конго, Демократической Республике Тимор-Лешти, Конго, Либерии, Мали, Нигере, Уганде и Чаде.

6.   Ожидается, что численность населения 51 страны или районов, в том числе Германии, Италии, Японии, стран Балтии и большинства государств-преемников бывшего Советского Союза, будет в 2050 году ниже, чем в 2005 году.

7.   В период 2005–2050 годов на девять стран, как ожидается, будет приходиться половина прогнозируемого увеличения численности населения: Индия, Пакистан, Нигерия, Демократическая Республика Конго, Бангладеш, Уганда, Соединенные Штаты Америки, Эфиопия и Китай, которые перечислены в порядке их вклада в рост населения в течение этого периода.

Таблица 2
Среднегодовые темпы изменения общей численности населения и численности населения в крупных возрастных группах в разбивке по основным регионам, 2005–2050 годы (средний вариант)

Основной район	0–14	15–59	60+	80+	Общая численность населения
Весь мир	0,01	0,63	2,39	3,37	0,75
Более развитые регионы	-0,14	-0,38	1,10	2,13	0,05
Менее развитые регионы	0,03	0,82	2,88	4,19	0,89
Наименее развитые страны	1,02	2,15	3,32	4,03	1,84
Другие менее развитые страны	-0,29	0,54	2,84	4,21	0,68
Африка	0,87	2,00	3,12	3,86	1,69
Азия	-0,29	0,47	2,70	4,04	0,64
Европа	-0,36	-0,75	0,90	1,98	-0,24
Латинская Америка и Карибский бассейн	-0,38	0,61	2,98	3,99	0,74
Северная Америка	0,23	0,37	1,67	2,30	0,62
Океания	0,09	0,65	2,11	2,89	0,81

Источник: Отдел народонаселения Департамента по экономическим и социальным вопросам Секретариата Организации Объединенных Наций (2005 год). *Мировые демографические перспективы: Обзор 2004 года. Основные выводы*. Нью-Йорк: Организация Объединенных Наций.

Рисунок 2

Динамика роста численности населения по группам развития, 1950–2050 годы

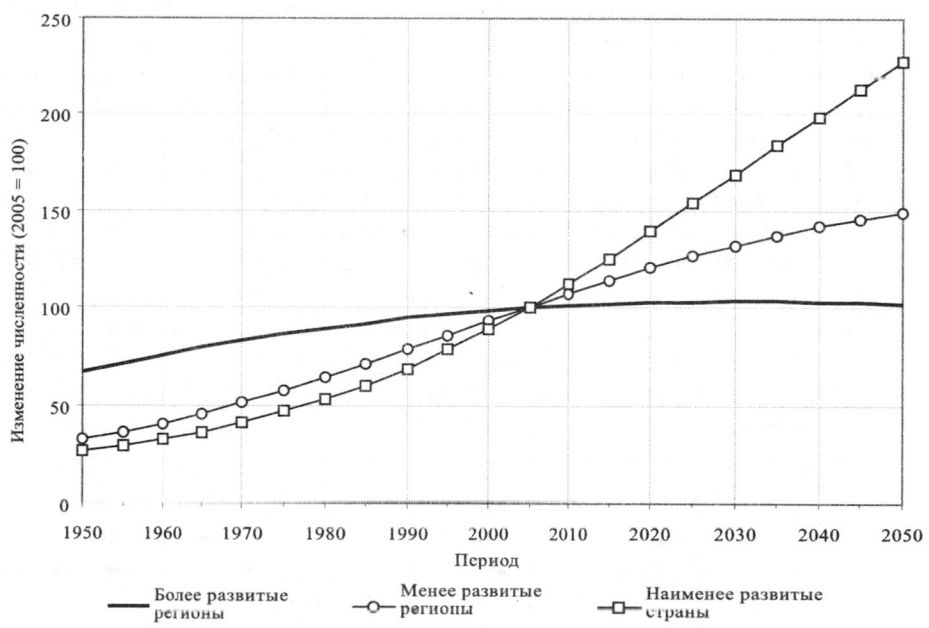

Источник: Отдел народонаселения Департамента по экономическим и социальным вопросам Секретариата Организации Объединенных Наций (2005 год). *Мировые демографические перспективы: Обзор 2004 года. Основные выводы.* Нью-Йорк: Организация Объединенных Наций.

Таблица 3

Суммарный коэффициент рождаемости во всем мире, по основным группам развития и основным районам в 1970–1975, 2000–2005 и 2045–2050 годах при различных вариантах прогноза

| Основной район | Общий показатель рождаемости (число детей в расчете на одну женщину) | | | | | |
| | 1970–1975 годы | 2000–2005 годы | 2045–2050 годы | | | |
			Низкий уровень	Средний уровень	Высокий уровень	Неизменный уровень
Весь мир	4,49	2,65	1,56	2,05	2,53	3,50
Более развитые регионы	2,12	1,56	1,34	1,84	2,34	1,67
Менее развитые регионы	5,44	2,90	1,59	2,07	2,56	3,69
Наименее развитые страны	6,61	5,02	2,08	2,57	3,05	5,56
Другие менее развитые страны	5,28	2,58	1,42	1,92	2,41	3,06
Африка	6,72	4,97	2,03	2,52	3,00	5,50
Азия	5,08	2,47	1,42	1,91	2,41	2,98
Европа	2,16	1,40	1,33	1,83	2,33	1,45
Латинская Америка и Карибский бассейн	5,05	2,55	1,36	1,86	2,36	2,69
Северная Америка	2,01	1,99	1,35	1,85	2,35	1,99
Океания	3,23	2,32	1,42	1,92	2,42	2,72

Источник: Отдел народонаселения Департамента по экономическим и социальным вопросам Секретариата Организации Объединенных Наций (2005 год). *Мировые демографические перспективы: Обзор 2004 года. Основные выводы.* Нью-Йорк: Организация Объединенных Наций.

8.   В 2000–2005 годах среднемировой уровень рождаемости составлял 2,65 ребенка на женщину, что почти наполовину меньше уровня, зафиксированного в 1950–1955 годах (5 детей на женщину). По среднему варианту прогноза среднемировой уровень рождаемости к 2045–2050 годам сократится до 2,05 ребенка на женщину. Среднемировые показатели формируются в результате действия весьма различных тенденций в группах стран. В развитых странах в целом суммарный коэффициент рождаемости в настоящее время составляет 1,56 ребенка на женщину, а к 2045–2050 годам прогнозируется его медленное увеличение до 1,84 ребенка на женщину. В группе наименее развитых стран этот показатель составляет 5 детей на женщину, а к 2045–2050 годам снизится наполовину — т.е. до 2,57 ребенка на женщину. В группе остальных развивающихся стран этот показатель уже находится на довольно низком уровне и составляет 2,58 ребенка на женщину; ожидается его дальнейшее снижение до 1,92 ребенка на женщину к середине века — таким образом, он вплотную приблизится к уровню, прогнозируемому для того периода в развитых странах. Реализация этих прогнозов снижения рождаемости зависит от доступа к услугам по планированию семьи, особенно в наименее развитых странах.

9.   В 2000–2005 годах уровень рождаемости превышал 5 детей на женщину в 35 из 148 развивающихся стран, 30 из которых являются наименее развитыми странами. Кроме того, в некоторых странах Африки к югу от Сахары и южной части Центральной Азии эти показатели снижались более медленными темпами, чем предполагалось. В итоге на страны с высокой рождаемостью приходится 10 процентов мирового населения. И наоборот, в 23 развивающихся странах, на долю которых приходится 25 процентов мирового населения, рождаемость упала ниже уровня, обеспечивающего воспроизводство населения. В эту группу стран входит Китай, где уровень рождаемости в 2000–2005 годах составляет, по оценкам, 1,7 ребенка на женщину.

10.   Рождаемость в 44 развитых странах, на долю которых приходится 19 процентов мирового населения, в настоящее время очень низка. Во всех странах, за исключением Албании, рождаемость не обеспечивает воспроизводство населения, а в 15 странах, главным образом расположенных в Южной и Восточной Европе, уровни рождаемости достигли беспрецедентных за всю историю значений (ниже 1,3 ребенка на женщину). С периода 1990–1995 годов снижение рождаемости характерно для большинства развитых стран. Лишь в немногих странах, таких, как Бельгия, Германия, Нидерланды, Соединенные Штаты Америки и Франция, был зафиксирован их незначительный рост.

Таблица 4

Показатели ожидаемой продолжительности жизни при рождении во всем мире, основных группах развития и основных регионах в 2000–2005 годах и в 2045–2050 годах

Основной район	2000–2005 годы	2045–2050 годы
Весь мир	65,4	75,1
Более развитые регионы	75,6	82,1
Менее развитые регионы	63,4	74,0
Наименее развитые страны	51,0	66,5
Другие менее развитые страны	66,1	76,3
Африка	49,1	65,4
Азия	67,3	77,2
Европа	73,7	80,6
Латинская Америка и Карибский бассейн	71,5	79,5
Северная Америка	77,6	82,7
Океания	74,0	81,2

Источник: Отдел народонаселения Департамента по экономическим и социальным вопросам Секретариата Организации Объединенных Наций (2005 год). *Мировые демографические перспективы: Обзор 2004 года. Основные выводы*. Нью-Йорк: Организация Объединенных Наций.

11. Ожидается, что среднемировой показатель ожидаемой продолжительности жизни при рождении, который вырос с 47 лет в период 1950–1955 годов до 65 лет в период 2000–2005 годов, будет продолжать повышаться и в 2045–2050 годах достигнет 75 лет. В более развитых регионах прогнозируется рост продолжительности жизни с 76 лет в настоящее время до 82 лет в середине века. Среди наименее развитых стран продолжительность жизни составляет 51 год и, как ожидается, повысится в 2045–2050 годах до 67 лет. Поскольку во многих этих странах распространена эпидемия ВИЧ/СПИДа, прогнозируемый рост продолжительности жизни зависит от осуществления эффективных программ профилактики и лечения ВИЧ-инфекции. В остальных развивающихся странах, находящихся в подобных условиях, прогнозируется повышение этого показателя с 66 лет в настоящее время до 76 лет к середине века.

12. В Восточной Европе смертность росла начиная с конца 80-х годов. В 2000–2005 годах продолжительность жизни в этом регионе (67,9 года) была ниже, чем в 1960–1965 годах (68,6 года). Наиболее заметно смертность выросла в Российской Федерации и Украине, в том числе и в результате распространения ВИЧ.

13. Спустя 25 лет после начала эпидемии ВИЧ/СПИДа воздействие этой болезни наглядно проявляется в повышении уровней заболеваемости, смертности и в замедлении роста численности населения. В регионе южной части Африки, где наблюдается самый высокий показатель распространенности ВИЧ/СПИДа, продолжительность жизни сократилась с 62 лет в период 1990–1995 годов до 48 лет в период 2000–2005 годов; в течение следующего десятилетия ожидается ее дальнейшее сокращение до 43 лет и лишь затем начнется медленное восстановление. Поэтому предполагается, что

в период 2005–2020 годов роста численности населения в регионе не будет. В Ботсване, Лесото и Свазиленде прогнозируется сокращение численности населения, поскольку число умерших превысит число родившихся. В большинстве других развивающихся стран, затронутых эпидемией, население будет расти вследствие того, что фиксируемые в них умеренные или высокие показатели рождаемости более чем компенсируют рост смертности.

14.   Главным следствием падения рождаемости, особенно в сочетании с ростом продолжительности жизни, является старение населения, при котором доля пожилых людей в общей численности населения возрастает по сравнению с долей более молодых людей. Ожидается, что на глобальном уровне число пожилых людей в возрасте 60 лет или старше почти утроится, увеличившись с 672 млн. в 2005 году почти до 1,9 млрд. в 2050 году. В настоящее время 6 из каждых 10 пожилых людей живут в развивающихся странах, а к 2050 году 8 из 10 пожилых будут жить в развивающихся странах. Число людей в возрасте 80 лет или старше будет расти еще быстрее: с 86 млн. в 2005 году до 394 млн. в 2050 году. В развивающихся странах их численность увеличится с 42 млн. до 278 млн., что означает, что к 2050 году в развивающихся странах будет сосредоточено большинство самых пожилых людей.

15.   В развитых странах доля населения в возрасте 60 лет или старше составляет в настоящее время 20 процентов, а к 2050 году прогнозируется ее увеличение до 32 процентов. Численность пожилого населения в развитых странах уже превысила численность детей (лиц в возрасте от 0 до 14 лет), а к 2050 году на каждого ребенка будет приходиться по два пожилых человека. В развивающихся странах прогнозируется увеличение доли населения в возрасте 60 лет или старше с 8 процентов в 2005 году до примерно 20 процентов в 2050 году.

16.   Увеличение медианного возраста, т.е. такого возраста, при котором 50 процентов населения его старше и 50 процентов моложе, означает старение населения. Сегодня лишь в 11 развитых странах медианный возраст превышает 40 лет. К 2050 году в эту группу войдут 89 стран, в том числе 45 развивающихся стран. Старение населения, которое становится в развитых странах повсеместно распространенным явлением, также неизбежно и в развивающихся странах, где оно будет происходить более высокими темпами.

17.   В странах, где рождаемость снизилась лишь незначительно и сохраняется на высоком уровне, старение населения будет происходить самыми медленными темпами. Согласно прогнозам, к 2050 году примерно в каждой пятой стране медианный возраст не будет превышать 30 лет. В наименее развитых странах будет самое молодое население. В 2050 году медианный возраст не будет превышать 23 лет в 11 наименее развитых странах — Афганистане, Анголе, Бурунди, Гвинее-Бисау, Демократической Республике Конго, Либерии, Мали, Нигере, Чаде, Экваториальной Гвинее и Уганде.

18.   В период 2005–2050 годов международная нетто-миграция в более развитые регионы прогнозируется на уровне 98 млн. человек, т.е. в среднем 2,2 млн. человек в год. Такое же количество людей покинет менее развитые регионы. В развитых странах мира такой показатель чистой миграции более чем компенсирует ожидаемое превышение числа смертей над числом рождений, которое составит 73 млн. в период 2005–2050 годов. Что касается развивающегося мира, то 98 млн. эмигрантов представляют собой чуть меньше 4 процентов ожидаемого прироста населения.

19.   В период 2000–2005 годов нетто-миграция в 74 странах была положительной. В 64 из них нетто-миграция содействовала росту населения, а

в 7 странах изменила тенденцию к снижению численности населения на противоположную (Австрия, Германия, Греция, Италия, Словакия, Словения и Хорватия). В трех странах миграция замедлила, но не компенсировала, сокращение численности населения (Венгрия, Российская Федерация и Чешская Республика).

20.   Что касается среднегодовых объемов нетто-миграции в 2005–2050 годах, то, согласно прогнозам, основными принимающими странами будут Соединенные Штаты Америки (1,1 млн. мигрантов в год), Германия (202 000), Канада (200 000), Соединенное Королевство (130 000), Италия (120 000) и Австралия (100 000), а основными поставщиками мигрантов будут Китай (-327 000 мигрантов в год), Мексика (-293 000), Индия (-241 000), Филиппины (-180 000), Индонезия (-164 000), Пакистан (-154 000) и Украина (-100 000).

Гипотезы, заложенные в *Обзор 2004 года*

Для прогнозирования численности населения до 2050 года Отдел народонаселения Организации Объединенных Наций применяет гипотезы в отношении будущих тенденций рождаемости, смертности и миграции. Поскольку достоверно определить будущие тенденции невозможно, подготавливается несколько вариантов прогноза. В Резюме рассматривается средний вариант прогноза. Гипотезы, заложенные в средний вариант прогноза, подробно рассматриваются в разделе А настоящей главы.

Обзор 2004 года включает пять дополнительных вариантов: вариант с высоким уровнем рождаемости, вариант с низким уровнем рождаемости, вариант с неизменным уровнем рождаемости, вариант с неизменным уровнем смертности и вариант с нулевой миграцией. Отличия соответствующих гипотез от среднего варианта изложены в разделе В. Подробная информация о результатах их применения будет опубликована в следующих изданиях.

Будущая численность населения каждой страны прогнозируется на основе оценок численности населения по состоянию на 1 июля 2005 года. Поскольку фактических данных по народонаселению за 2005 год пока еще нет, оценки за этот год основываются на самой последней демографической информации о каждой стране, источником которой является, как правило, перепись населения или регистр населения, скорректированные на 2005 год на основе всех имеющихся данных о рождаемости, смертности и международной миграции. В тех случаях, когда свежая информация отсутствует, используются краткосрочные прогнозы, составленные на основе самых последних имеющихся данных. Данные по народонаселению из всех источников оцениваются с точки зрения их полноты, точности и взаимосогласованности и при необходимости корректируются[3].

---

[3] Общее описание методик, применяемых при пересмотре оценок динамики народонаселения, см. *Мировые демографические перспективы: Обзор 2002 года, том III: Аналитический доклад,* стр. 180–182.

A. Гипотезы среднего варианта прогноза

1. Гипотезы в отношении рождаемости: сближение суммарных коэффициентов на уровне ниже воспроизводства населения

Предполагается, что коэффициенты суммарной рождаемости повсеместно достигнут 1,85 ребенка на женщину. Вместе с тем не все страны достигнут этого уровня в течение прогнозируемого периода, т.е. к 2050 году. Основной принцип прогнозирования рождаемости одинаков для всех стран, однако методики прогнозирования несколько различаются в зависимости от того, был ли суммарный коэффициент рождаемости выше или ниже 1,85 ребенка на женщину в 2000–2025 годах.

Предполагается, что в странах, где этот показатель в настоящее время выше 1,85 ребенка на женщину, будущая динамика рождаемости определяется моделями, разработанными Отделом народонаселения Организации Объединенных Наций на основе предыдущего опыта всех стран, где рождаемость снижалась в период 1950–2000 годов. Эти модели устанавливают зависимость между уровнем рождаемости в течение каждого периода времени и средней величиной ожидаемого снижения рождаемости в следующем периоде. Если прогнозируемый таким образом суммарный коэффициент рождаемости снижается до 1,85 ребенка на женщину до 2050 года, предполагается, что он останется на этом уровне вплоть до конца периода прогнозирования (то есть до 2050 года).

Для каждой страны прогнозируемые на основе моделей траектории рождаемости сопоставляются с последними тенденциями рождаемости. В тех случаях, когда последние тенденции рождаемости в стране значительно отклоняются от модельных траекторий, для первых 5 или 10 лет периода прогнозирования траектория рождаемости выбирается в соответствии с последними тенденциями. После такого переходного периода применяется прогнозная модель. Например, для стран, где снижение рождаемости прекратилось, или отсутствует информация, подтверждающая снижение рождаемости, прогнозируется ее сохранение на неизменном уровне в течение еще нескольких лет, прежде чем начнется снижение.

Для стран, в которых в 2000–2005 годах суммарный коэффициент рождаемости был рассчитан ниже 1,85 ребенка на женщину, допускается, что в течение первых 5 или 10 лет прогнозируемого периода этот показатель будет следовать наблюдаемым в последнее время тенденциям. Предполагается, что после этого переходного периода суммарный коэффициент рождаемости будет линейно расти на 0,07 ребенка на женщину за пятилетний период. Таким образом, страны с нынешним очень низким уровнем рождаемости не обязательно достигнут к 2050 году уровня 1,85 ребенка на одну женщину.

2. Гипотезы в отношении смертности: повышение средней продолжительности жизни, за исключением стран, пострадавших от эпидемии ВИЧ/СПИДа

a) Нормальная гипотеза в отношении смертности

Показатели смертности прогнозируются на основе моделей изменения продолжительности жизни, разработанных Отделом народонаселения Организации Объединенных Наций. В соответствии с этими моделями, прирост продолжительности жизни тем меньше, чем выше ее уже достигнутый уровень. Отбор моделей для каждой страны производится на основе последних тенденций в динамике продолжительности жизни по полу. Для стран, сильно пострадавших от эпидемии ВИЧ/СПИДа, прогнозы общих рисков умереть от не связанных с ВИЧ/СПИДом причин обычно основываются на моделях медленного снижения смертности.

b)   Воздействие ВИЧ/СПИДа на смертность

Для 60 стран, которые серьезно пострадали от эпидемии ВИЧ/СПИДа (они перечислены в таблице VIII.21), оценка воздействия ВИЧ/СПИДа проводится с использованием модели динамики эпидемии, а также путем прогнозирования годового числа новых случаев инфицирования ВИЧ-инфекцией в отношении к численности населения. Модель, разработанная методической группой по вопросам оценки, моделирования и прогнозирования[4] Объединенной программы Организации Объединенных Наций по ВИЧ/СПИДу (ЮНЭЙДС), применялась для расчета параметров динамики эпидемии в прошлом на основе осуществленных ЮНЭЙДС оценок распространенности ВИЧ. Для большинства стран эта модель пригодна при допущении, что полученные ранее соответствующие параметры оставались в прошлом неизменными. В соответствии с прогнозом параметр PHI, отражающий темп вовлечения новых лиц в группу высокого риска или восприимчивых к этой инфекции, будет, начиная с 2005 года, снижаться наполовину каждые 30 лет. Предполагается, что параметр R, который отражает интенсивность инфекции, будет снижаться по такой же схеме. Снижение показателя R основывается на том допущении, что изменения в поведении лиц, подверженных риску инфекции, наряду с расширением доступа инфицированных к лечению, приведут к снижению шансов передачи этого вируса. Предполагается также, что частота передачи вируса от матери к ребенку будет сокращаться различными темпами в зависимости от прогресса, достигнутого каждой страной в деле расширения доступа к лечению. Кроме того, был обновлен компонент разработанной методической группой модели, отражающий показатель дожития инфицированных детей: в *Обзоре 2004 года* предполагается, что 50 процентов детей, инфицированных в результате передачи вируса от матери к ребенку, доживут до двухлетнего возраста.

Впервые в *Обзор 2004 года* закладываются более высокие коэффициенты дожития лиц, получающих лечение с применением высокоактивной антиретровирусной терапии. Для каждой страны доля проходящего лечение ВИЧ-инфицированного населения соответствует оценкам, подготовленным Всемирной организацией здравоохранения по состоянию на конец 2004 года[5] Предполагается, что к 2015 году охват ВИЧ-инфицированного населения лечением составит от 40 до 85 процентов, в зависимости от сегодняшнего уровня. Предполагается, что вероятность прожить по меньшей мере еще год для лиц, проходящих курс высокоактивного антиретровирусного терапевтического лечения, в среднем повышается по меньшей мере до 80 процентов. Согласно этому допущению, продолжительность жизни с момента начала терапевтического лечения составляет в среднем 3,1 года (медианное значение 4,5 года). И наоборот, в том случае, если курс терапевтического лечения не проводится, средняя продолжительность жизни с

---

[4] Усовершенствованные методы и допущения для оценки распространения эпидемии ВИЧ/СПИДа и ее последствий: рекомендации методической группы ЮНЭЙДС по вопросам оценки, моделирования и прогнозирования (AIDS, vol. 16, pp. W1-W14, UNAIDS Reference Group on Estimates, Modeling and Projections, 2002).

[5] World Health Organization. "3 by 5" Progress Report, December 2004/WHO and UNAIDS.

момента перехода инфицированности ВИЧ в стадию СПИДа, составляет, согласно допущениям, один год.

3. **Гипотеза в отношении международной миграции**

Будущая траектория международной миграции установлена на основе оценок международной миграции в прошлом и оценок позиций государств в отношении будущих миграционных потоков.

B. Варианты прогнозов

Помимо среднего варианта *Обзор 2004 года* включает пять вариантов прогноза. Три варианта — с высокой, низкой и неизменной рождаемостью — отличаются от среднего варианта лишь прогнозируемыми уровнями суммарного коэффициента рождаемости. Вариант с высоким уровнем рождаемости предполагает, что в течение большей части периода прогнозирования суммарный коэффициент рождаемости будет превышать рождаемость среднего варианта на 0,5 ребенка на одну женщину. Например, страны, достигающие рождаемости на уровне 1,85 ребенка на женщину в варианте со средним уровнем рождаемости, достигают уровня 2,35 ребенка на одну женщину. В варианте с низким уровнем рождаемости ее суммарный коэффициент будет на 0,5 ребенка на одну женщину меньше, чем в среднем варианте. превышать рождаемость среднего варианта на 0,5 ребенка на одну женщину. В варианте с неизменным уровнем рождаемости суммарный коэффициент остается постоянным на уровне 2000–2005 годов.

Подготовлены также варианты с неизменной смертностью и вариант с нулевой миграцией. В отношении рождаемости в них была заложена та же гипотеза, что и в среднем варианте. Помимо этого, вариант с неизменной смертностью использует ту же гипотезу в отношении миграции, что и средний вариант. Следовательно, результаты варианта с неизменной смертностью можно сравнивать с результатами среднего варианта для оценки воздействия меняющейся смертности на другие демографические параметры. Аналогичным образом, вариант с нулевой миграцией отличается от среднего варианта только гипотезой в отношении миграции. Поэтому этот вариант позволяет оценить воздействие миграции на другие демографические параметры.

C. Методологические изменения, сделанные в *Обзоре 2004 года*

- В среднем варианте траектория рождаемости в странах, где ее уровень в 2000–2005 годах ниже 1,85 ребенка на женщину, прогнозируется первоначально как продолжение последних тенденций, переходящих в линейный рост с добавлением 0,07 ребенка на женщину за каждый пятилетний период. Эти страны необязательно достигнут уровня 1,85 ребенка на женщину к 2050 году.

- В *Обзоре 2004 года* дополнительные модели изменения смертности использованы для того, чтобы отразить все разнообразие исторического опыта в деле увеличения продолжительности жизни. В частности, в дополнение к ранее созданным моделям медленных, средних и быстрых изменений были разработаны и внедрены модели очень медленных и очень быстрых темпов изменений.

- Воздействие эпидемии ВИЧ/СПИДа на смертность смоделировано для всех стран, где в 2003 году доля ВИЧ-инфицированных составляла не менее 1 процента взрослого населения.

- Лечение с использованием антиретровирусной терапии специально включено в прогноз распространения ВИЧ/СПИДа для этих стран. Кроме того, снижение частоты передачи ВИЧ-инфекции от матери к ребенку прогнозируется темпами, соответствующими предполагаемому прогрессу в деле расширения доступа к лечению.

Prefacio

El presente informe contiene el resumen ejecutivo de los resultados de la *Revisión de 2004* de las estimaciones y proyecciones oficiales de población en el mundo que prepara la División de Población del Departamento de Asuntos Económicos y Sociales de la Secretaría de las Naciones Unidas. En el informe se presenta, además, una perspectiva general de las hipótesis de fecundidad, mortalidad y migración en que se basan las proyecciones y un resumen de los cambios y ajustes introducidos en la *Revisión de 2004* en relación con los procedimientos seguidos en la *Revisión de 2002*. La *Revisión de 2004* es la 19ª serie de estimaciones y proyecciones demográficas mundiales que prepara la División de Población desde 1950.

Los resultados completos de la *Revisión de 2004* se publicarán en una serie de tres volúmenes. En el primer volumen[1] figurarán los cuadros completos en que se recogen los principales indicadores demográficos correspondientes a cada país respecto del período 1950-2050; en el segundo volumen[2] se presentará la distribución por edad y sexo de la población de cada país respecto del período 1950-2050, y en el tercero[3] se hará un análisis de los resultados obtenidos.

Los datos estarán también disponibles en formato digital. Los usuarios interesados podrán adquirir un CD-ROM con los principales resultados de la *Revisión de 2004*. En el sitio de la División de Población en la Web (*www.unpopulation.org*) se publicará una descripción de los datos que contiene el CD-ROM y un formulario para encargarlo.

La *Revisión de 2004* es responsabilidad de la División de Población. Las comisiones regionales, los organismos especializados y otros órganos pertinentes de las Naciones Unidas que colaboraron con la División de Población facilitaron su preparación.

Entre las fuentes más importantes de estadísticas de población nacionales oficiales consultadas para la preparación de las estimaciones y proyecciones destacan el *Demographic Yearbook* de las Naciones Unidas y sus bases de datos complementarias, preparadas y mantenidas por la División de Estadística del Departamento de Asuntos Económicos y Sociales de las Naciones Unidas. La División de Población agradece también a la División de Estadística del Departamento de Asuntos Económicos y Sociales su permanente cooperación.

En el sitio de la División de Población en la Web (*www.unpopulation.org*) se pueden consultar algunos resultados de la *Revisión de 2004*, así como información

---

[1] *World Population Prospects: The 2004 Revision,* vol. I, *Comprehensive Tables* (publicación de las Naciones Unidas, Sales No. E.05.XIII.5).

[2] *World Population Prospects: The 2004 Revision,* vol. II, *Sex and Age Distribution of the World Population* (publicación de las Naciones Unidas, Sales No. E.05.XIII.6).

[3] *World Population Prospects: The 2004 Revision,* vol. III, *Analytical Report* (publicación de las Naciones Unidas, de próxima aparición).

demográfica de diversa índole. Para más información acerca de la *Revisión de 2004*, se ruega dirigirse a la Sra. Hania Zlotnik, Directora de la División de Población, Naciones Unidas, Nueva York, NY 10017 (Estados Unidos de América) (fax: 1 212 963 2147).

Resumen ejecutivo

La *Revisión de 2004* es la 19ª serie de estimaciones y proyecciones demográficas oficiales de las Naciones Unidas que prepara la División de Población del Departamento de Asuntos Económicos y Sociales de la Secretaría de las Naciones Unidas. Esas estimaciones y proyecciones se utilizan en todo el sistema de las Naciones Unidas como base para actividades en que se precisa información demográfica. La *Revisión de 2004* es la primera en que se incorporan los resultados completos de la serie de censos de población nacionales de 2000. Además, en ella se tienen en cuenta los resultados de estudios especializados realizados recientemente en países en desarrollo, a fin de proporcionar información demográfica y de otra índole para determinar los avances realizados en el cumplimiento de los objetivos de desarrollo convenidos internacionalmente, incluidos los objetivos de desarrollo del Milenio. El examen exhaustivo de las tendencias demográficas mundiales hasta la fecha y las proyecciones para el futuro que se presentan en la *Revisión de 2004* ofrecen la información sobre población que se necesita para evaluar el cumplimiento de esos objetivos.

La *Revisión de 2004* confirma la variedad de dinámicas demográficas que existen en nuestros tiempos. Aunque la población mundial continúa aumentando, la del conjunto de las regiones más desarrolladas apenas varía y prácticamente todo el crecimiento demográfico se está produciendo en las regiones menos desarrolladas. El grupo de los 50 países menos adelantados se caracteriza por un crecimiento demográfico especialmente rápido.

Detrás de las distintas pautas de crecimiento hay tendencias diferenciadas de fecundidad y mortalidad. En las regiones más desarrolladas, predominan las tasas de fecundidad por debajo del nivel de reemplazo y se prevé que esa tendencia persista hasta 2050. La fecundidad sigue siendo alta en la mayoría de los países menos adelantados y, aunque está previsto que descienda, seguirá siendo mayor que en el resto del mundo. En los demás países en desarrollo, la fecundidad ha descendido notablemente desde finales de los años sesenta y se prevé que en 2050 la mayoría de esos países tendrán tasas de fecundidad por debajo del nivel de reemplazo.

La mortalidad en los países del mundo desarrollado con economías de mercado establecidas es baja y continúa descendiendo, pero se ha estancado e incluso está aumentando en algunos países con economías en transición, en buena parte como consecuencia del deterioro de las condiciones sociales y económicas y, en algunos casos, a causa de la propagación del virus de la inmunodeficiencia humana (VIH). La mortalidad está disminuyendo también en la mayoría de los países en desarrollo, pero ha aumentado en los países muy afectados por la epidemia del VIH y el síndrome de inmunodeficiencia adquirida (SIDA). Habida cuenta de los esfuerzos que se están realizando para suministrar tratamiento antirretroviral a 3 millones de enfermos de SIDA antes de que concluya 2005 y de la expectativa de que posteriormente el acceso al tratamiento se amplíe aún más, en la *Revisión de 2004* se presupone una supervivencia media de las personas que viven con el VIH mayor que en la *Revisión de 2002*; de ahí que en los países afectados por el VIH se prevean unos niveles de mortalidad futuros algo más bajos que en la *Revisión* anterior.

La epidemia del VIH/SIDA continúa propagándose. En la *Revisión de 2004* aparecen 60 países con un número considerable de personas infectadas, frente a 53 en la *Revisión de 2002*, aun cuando la prevalencia del VIH en algunos países se revisó a la baja después de que se reunieran mejores estadísticas. De todos modos, la enfermedad sigue cobrándose muchas víctimas y parece que continuará siendo así, a pesar de la disminución prevista de la prevalencia del VIH/SIDA. Esa disminución dependerá del cumplimiento de los compromisos contraídos por los gobiernos en la Declaración del Milenio[4], aprobada en 2000, y la Declaración de las Naciones Unidas de compromiso en la lucha contra el VIH/SIDA[5], aprobada en 2001.

A continuación se resumen las principales conclusiones de la *Revisión de 2004*:

1. En julio de 2005, el mundo tendrá 6.500 millones de habitantes, 380 millones más que en 2000, lo que supone un incremento de 76 millones al año. Pese a que, con arreglo a las proyecciones, los niveles de fecundidad descenderán entre 2005 y 2050, según la variante media, a mediados de siglo la población mundial alcanzará los 9.100 millones de personas y seguirá aumentando 34 millones al año.

2. Actualmente, el 95% del crecimiento demográfico mundial corresponde al mundo en desarrollo y el otro 5% al mundo desarrollado. Según la variante media, en 2050 la población del conjunto de los países más desarrollados estará descendiendo lentamente, esto es, disminuirá en 1 millón de personas al año, aproximadamente, y la del mundo en desarrollo se estará incrementando en 35 millones de personas al año, de los cuales 22 millones corresponderán a los países menos adelantados.

3. El crecimiento demográfico futuro dependerá en gran medida de la evolución de la fecundidad. En la variante media, se prevé que las tasas de fecundidad descenderán del nivel actual de 2,6 hijos por mujer a poco más de 2 hijos por mujer en 2050. Si la fecundidad se mantuviera aproximadamente medio hijo por encima de los niveles previstos en la variante media, la población mundial alcanzaría los 10.600 millones de personas en 2050. Si, en cambio, evolucionara medio hijo por debajo de los niveles de la variante media, la población mundial a mediados de siglo sería de 7.600 millones de personas. En otras palabras, aunque el descenso de la fecundidad se acelere, el crecimiento constante de la población mundial hasta 2050 es inevitable.

---

[4] Véase la resolución 55/2 de la Asamblea General.
T[5] Véase la resolución S-26/2 de la Asamblea General.

Cuadro 1
Población mundial, desglosada por principales grupos de desarrollo y zonas (1950, 1975 y 2005) y por variante de proyección (2050)

Zonas principales	Población (en millones de habitantes)			Población en 2050 (en millones de habitantes)			
	1950	1975	2005	Baja	Media	Alta	Constante
Mundo	2 519	4 074	6 465	7 680	9 076	10 646	11 658
Regiones más desarrolladas	813	1 047	1 211	1 057	1 236	1 440	1 195
Regiones menos desarrolladas	1 707	3 027	5 253	6 622	7 840	9 206	10 463
Países menos adelantados	201	356	759	1 497	1 735	1 994	2 744
Otros países menos adelantados	1 506	2 671	4 494	5 126	6 104	7 213	7 719
África	224	416	906	1 666	1 937	2 228	3 100
Asia	1 396	2 395	3 905	4 388	5 217	6 161	6 487
Europa	547	676	728	557	653	764	606
América Latina y el Caribe	167	322	561	653	783	930	957
América del Norte	172	243	331	375	438	509	454
Oceanía	13	21	33	41	48	55	55

Fuente: División de Población del Departamento de Asuntos Económicos y Sociales de la Secretaría de las Naciones Unidas (2005). *World Population Prospects: The 2004 Revision. Highlights*. Nueva York, Naciones Unidas.

Gráfico 1
Población mundial, de 1950 a 2050, por variante de proyección

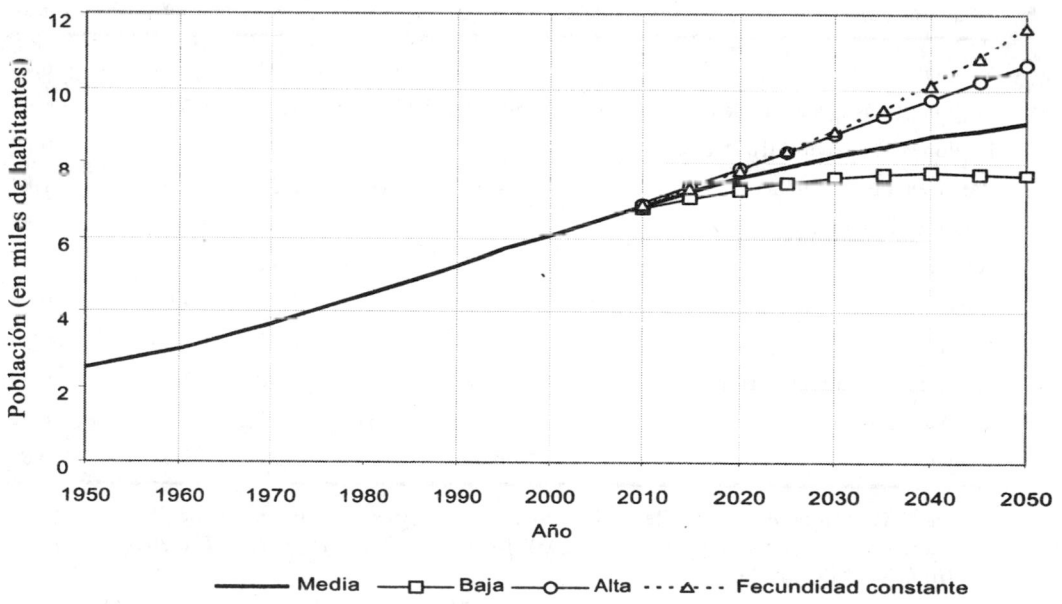

Fuente: División de Población del Departamento de Asuntos Económicos y Sociales de la Secretaría de las Naciones Unidas (2005). *World Population Prospects: The 2004 Revision. Highlights*. Nueva York, Naciones Unidas.

4.	La tasa de crecimiento de la población del conjunto de los países desarrollados es baja y está en disminución, por lo que se prevé que el número de habitantes de esos países apenas variará entre 2005 y 2050, y se mantendrá en unos 1.200 millones de personas. En cambio, según las proyecciones, la población de los 50 países menos adelantados aumentará más del doble, y pasará de 800 millones de personas en 2005 a 1.700 en 2050. En el resto del mundo en desarrollo también se prevé un crecimiento considerable, aunque menos rápido, ya que la población aumentará de 4.500 a 6.100 millones de habitantes entre 2005 y 2050.

5.	Según las previsiones, se producirá un crecimiento demográfico muy rápido en algunos países en desarrollo, la mayoría de ellos del grupo de países menos adelantados. Se prevé que entre 2005 y 2050 la población del Afganistán, Burkina Faso, Burundi, el Chad, el Congo, Guinea-Bissau, Liberia, Malí, el Níger, la República Democrática del Congo, la República Democrática de Timor-Leste y Uganda como mínimo se triplicará.

6.	Por otra parte, se prevé que en 2050 la población de 51 países o zonas, entre ellos Alemania, Italia, el Japón, los países bálticos y la mayoría de los Estados sucesores de la antigua Unión Soviética, habrá disminuido con respecto a 2005.

7.	De acuerdo con las previsiones, entre 2005 y 2050, la mitad del aumento proyectado de la población mundial corresponderá a nueve países: la India, el Pakistán, Nigeria, la República Democrática del Congo, Bangladesh, Uganda, los Estados Unidos de América, Etiopía y China, por orden de contribución al crecimiento demográfico en ese período.

Cuadro 2

Tasa media anual de variación de la población total y de la población desglosada por grupos de edad y zonas principales, 2005-2050 (variante media)

Zonas principales	0-14	15-59	60+	80+	Población total
Mundo	0,01	0,63	2,39	3,37	0,75
Regiones más desarrolladas	-0,14	-0,38	1,10	2,13	0,05
Regiones menos desarrolladas	0,03	0,82	2,88	4,19	0,89
Países menos adelantados	1,02	2,15	3,32	4,03	1,84
Otros países menos desarrollados	-0,29	0,54	2,84	4,21	0,68
África	0,87	2,00	3,12	3,86	1,69
Asia	-0,29	0,47	2,70	4,04	0,64
Europa	-0,36	-0,75	0,90	1,98	-0,24
América Latina y el Caribe	-0,38	0,61	2,98	3,99	0,74
América del Norte	0,23	0,37	1,67	2,30	0,62
Oceanía	0,09	0,65	2,11	2,89	0,81

Fuente: División de Población del Departamento de Asuntos Económicos y Sociales de la Secretaría de las Naciones Unidas (2005). *World Population Prospects: The 2004 Revision. Highlights.* Nueva York, Naciones Unidas.

Gráfico 2

Dinámica demográfica por grupo de desarrollo, 1950-2050

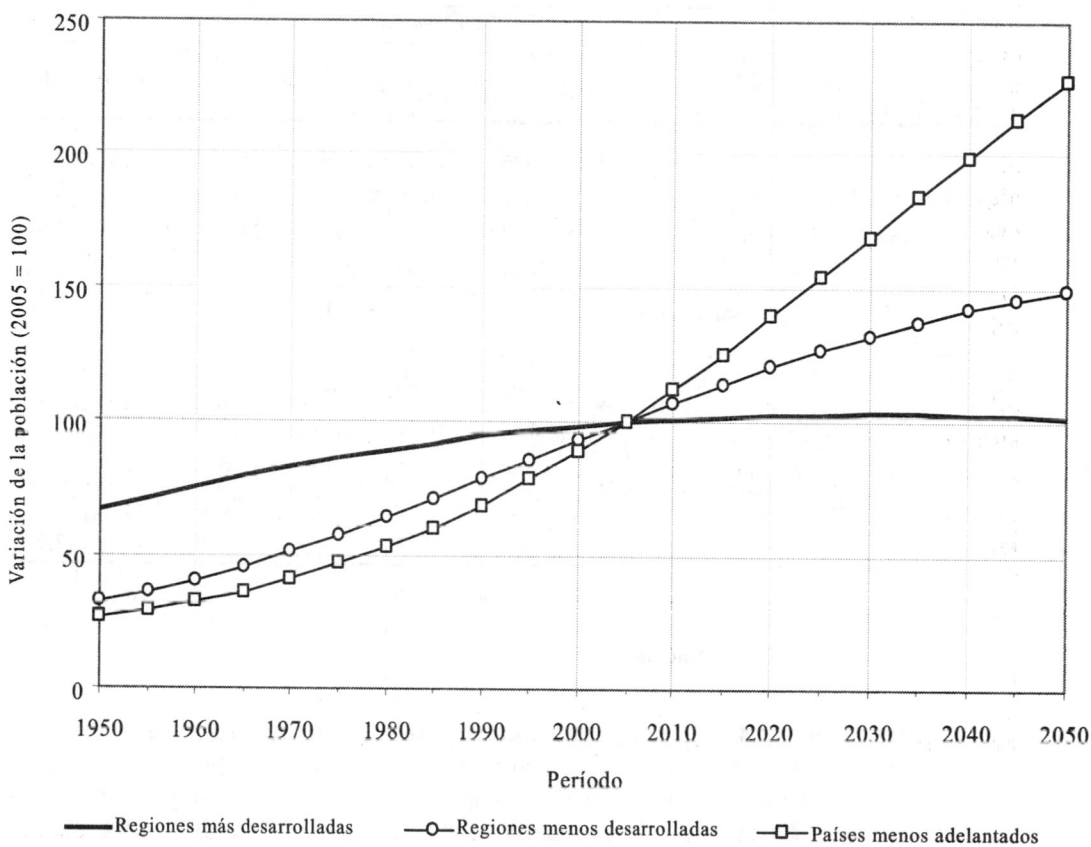

Fuente: División de Población del Departamento de Asuntos Económicos y Sociales de la
Secretaría de las Naciones Unidas (2005). *World Population Prospects: The 2004 Revision.*
Highlights. Nueva York, Naciones Unidas.

Cuadro 3

Fecundidad mundial total, desglosada por principales grupos de desarrollo y zonas (1970-1975 y 2000-2005) y por variante de proyección (2045-2050)

Zonas principales	Fecundidad total (número de hijos por mujer)					
			2045-2050			
	1970-1975	2000-2005	Baja	Media	Alta	Constante
Mundo	4,49	2,65	1,56	2,05	2,53	3,50
Regiones más desarrolladas	2,12	1,56	1,34	1,84	2,34	1,67
Regiones menos desarrolladas	5,44	2,90	1,59	2,07	2,56	3,69
Países menos adelantados	6,61	5,02	2,08	2,57	3,05	5,56
Otros países menos desarrollados	5,28	2,58	1,42	1,92	2,41	3,06
África	6,72	4,97	2,03	2,52	3,00	5,50
Asia	5,08	2,47	1,42	1,91	2,41	2,98
Europa	2,16	1,40	1,33	1,83	2,33	1,45
América Latina y el Caribe	5,05	2,55	1,36	1,86	2,36	2,69
América del Norte	2,01	1,99	1,35	1,85	2,35	1,99
Oceanía	3,23	2,32	1,42	1,92	2,42	2,72

Fuente: División de Población del Departamento de Asuntos Económicos y Sociales de la Secretaría de las Naciones Unidas (2005). *World Population Prospects: The 2004 Revision. Highlights*. Nueva York, Naciones Unidas.

8.   Entre 2000 y 2005, la tasa de fecundidad mundial fue de 2,65 hijos por mujer, prácticamente la mitad de la registrada entre 1950 y 1955 (5 hijos por mujer). Según las proyecciones de la variante media, la tasa de fecundidad mundial continuará disminuyendo y será de 2,05 hijos por mujer en el período 2045-2050. Los niveles mundiales medios son resultado de tendencias muy diferentes en los distintos grupos de desarrollo principales. En el conjunto de los países desarrollados, la tasa de fecundidad actual es de 1,56 hijos por mujer y se prevé que aumentará lentamente a 1,84 hijos por mujer en el período 2045-2050. En los países menos adelantados, la tasa de fecundidad es de 5 hijos por mujer y está previsto que, en el período 2045-2050, se habrá reducido a casi la mitad, es decir, a 2,57 hijos por mujer. En el resto del mundo en desarrollo, la tasa de fecundidad es ya moderadamente baja, de 2,58 hijos por mujer, y se estima que seguirá descendiendo hasta situarse en 1,92 hijos por mujer a mediados de siglo, con lo cual prácticamente coincidirá con los niveles de fecundidad que se registrarán en ese momento en el mundo desarrollado. El descenso proyectado de la fecundidad dependerá de las posibilidades de acceso a la planificación familiar, en especial en los países menos adelantados.

9.   En el período 2000-2005, la tasa de fecundidad ha seguido siendo superior a 5 hijos por mujer en 35 de los 148 países en desarrollo, de los cuales 30 se consideran países menos adelantados, mientras que en varios países del África subsahariana y el Asia centromeridional esa tasa ha disminuido a un ritmo más lento de lo previsto. En conjunto, los países con tasas de fecundidad altas reúnen el 10% de la población mundial. Por el contrario, la fecundidad se ha situado por debajo del nivel de reemplazo en 23 países en desarrollo en los que vive el 25% de la población

mundial. En este grupo está China, con una tasa de fecundidad estimada de 1,7 hijos por mujer durante el período 2000-2005.

10. Los 44 países desarrollados, a los que corresponde el 19% de la población mundial, tienen actualmente unos niveles de fecundidad muy bajos. Todos, excepto Albania, presentan tasas de fecundidad por debajo del nivel de reemplazo y en 15 de ellos, casi todos del sur y el este de Europa, se han registrado niveles de fecundidad sin precedentes en la historia de la humanidad (menos de 1,3 hijos por mujer). Desde el período 1990-1995, el descenso de la fecundidad ha sido generalizado en los países más desarrollados. Los contados aumentos que se han producido, por ejemplo, en Alemania, Bélgica, los Estados Unidos, Francia y los Países Bajos, han sido leves.

Cuadro 4

Esperanza de vida al nacer a nivel mundial, por principales grupos de desarrollo y zonas 2000-2005 y 2045-2050

Zonas principales	2000-2005	2045-2050
Mundo	65,4	75,1
Regiones más desarrolladas	75,6	82,1
Regiones menos desarrolladas	63,4	74,0
Países menos adelantados	51,0	66,5
Otros países menos desarrollados	66,1	76,3
África	49,1	65,4
Asia	67,3	77,2
Europa	73,7	80,6
América Latina y el Caribe	71,5	79,5
América del Norte	77,6	82,7
Oceanía	74,0	81,2

Fuente: División de Población del Departamento de Asuntos Económicos y Sociales de la Secretaría de las Naciones Unidas (2005). *World Population Prospects: The 2004 Revision. Highlights*. Nueva York, Naciones Unidas.

11. Según las previsiones, la esperanza de vida al nacer a nivel mundial, que se estima que ha pasado de 47 años en el período 1950-1955 a 65 años en el período 2000-2005, seguirá aumentando y se situará en 75 años en el período 2045-2050. En las regiones más desarrolladas se prevé que pase de los 76 años en que se sitúa ahora a 82 años a mediados de siglo. En los países menos adelantados, la esperanza de vida, que es actualmente de 51 años, será de 67 años en el período 2045-2050. Dado que muchos de esos países se ven gravemente afectados por la epidemia del VIH/SIDA, el incremento proyectado de la esperanza de vida dependerá de que se apliquen programas eficaces de prevención y tratamiento de la infección por VIH. En el resto del mundo en desarrollo, se prevé que la esperanza de vida aumente del nivel actual, que es de 66 años, a 76 a mediados de siglo, aunque ese incremento estará supeditado a condiciones similares.

12. La mortalidad en Europa oriental ha aumentado sin parar desde finales de los años ochenta. En el período 2000-2005, la esperanza de vida en la región era de 67,9 años, esto es, inferior a la del período 1960-1965 (68,6 años). La mortalidad ha aumentado especialmente en la Federación de Rusia y Ucrania, como consecuencia, en parte, de la propagación del VIH.

13. Tras 25 años de epidemia del VIH/SIDA, las repercusiones de la enfermedad se sienten en el aumento de la morbilidad y la mortalidad y la ralentización del crecimiento de la población. En el África meridional, la región con mayor prevalencia del VIH/SIDA, la esperanza de vida ha caído de 62 años en el período 1990-1995 a 48 años en el período 2000-2005 y, según las previsiones, seguirá descendiendo hasta situarse en 43 años en el próximo decenio, antes de empezar a repuntar lentamente. Como consecuencia, se prevé que el crecimiento demográfico en la región se estanque entre 2005 y 2020. En Botswana, Lesotho y Swazilandia está previsto que disminuya la población, debido a que el número de defunciones supera el de nacimientos. En la mayoría de los demás países en desarrollo afectados por la epidemia, el crecimiento demográfico seguirá siendo positivo, ya que las tasas de fecundidad son moderadas o altas y compensan sobradamente el aumento de la mortalidad.

14. La consecuencia principal del descenso de la fecundidad, especialmente si va unido a un incremento de la esperanza de vida, es el envejecimiento de la población, que hace que aumente el peso relativo de las personas de edad en el conjunto de la población. Se prevé que, a nivel mundial, el número de personas de 60 años o más casi se triplique y pase de 672 millones en 2005 a cerca de 1.900 millones en 2050. Si bien actualmente 6 de cada 10 personas de ese grupo de edad viven en países en desarrollo, en 2050 la proporción será de 8 de cada 10. Se prevé que el aumento del número de personas de edad muy avanzada (personas de 80 años o más) será aún más pronunciado: de 86 millones en 2005 a 394 millones en 2050. En los países en desarrollo, el número de personas de edad muy avanzada pasará de 42 a 278 millones, de manera que en 2050 la mayoría de esas personas vivirá en el mundo en desarrollo.

15. En los países desarrollados, la población de 60 años o más constituye actualmente el 20% de la población y se prevé que en 2050 constituirá el 32%. En los países desarrollados, la población anciana ha superado ya a la infantil (personas de 0 a 14 años) y en 2050 habrá dos personas ancianas por cada niño. Según las previsiones, en el mundo en desarrollo, la proporción de personas de 60 años o más aumentará de un 8% en 2005 a cerca de un 20% en 2050.

16. El aumento de la edad mediana, es decir, la edad con respecto a la cual la mitad de la población es mayor y la otra mitad menor, es sintomático del envejecimiento de la población. Actualmente, sólo en 11 países desarrollados la edad mediana es superior a los 40 años. En 2050 pertenecerán a ese grupo 89 países, 45 de ellos del mundo en desarrollo. El envejecimiento de la población, fenómeno cada vez más generalizado en los países desarrollados, es también inexorable en el mundo en desarrollo, donde se producirá con mayor rapidez.

17. En los países en que la fecundidad sigue siendo elevada y sólo ha bajado moderadamente, el envejecimiento de la población será más lento. Según las proyecciones, en 2050, la edad mediana será todavía igual o inferior a 30 años en aproximadamente uno de cada cinco países. Las poblaciones más jóvenes se encontrarán en los países menos adelantados; en 11 de esos países, a saber, el Afganistán, Angola, Burundi, el Chad, Guinea-Bissau, Guinea Ecuatorial, Liberia, Malí, el Níger, la

República Democrática del Congo y Uganda, se prevé que la edad mediana será igual o inferior a 23 años en 2050.

18.   Según las proyecciones, en el período comprendido entre 2005 y 2050, el número neto de migrantes internacionales a las regiones más desarrolladas ascenderá a 98 millones, lo que representa un promedio de 2,2 millones al año. El mismo número de personas abandonará las regiones menos desarrolladas. En lo que respecta al mundo desarrollado, ese nivel de migración neta compensará sobradamente el crecimiento demográfico negativo previsto para el período 2005-2050, que es de -73 millones de personas. En lo que respecta al mundo en desarrollo, los 98 millones de emigrantes representarán algo menos del 4% del crecimiento demográfico previsto.

19.   En el período 2000-2005, 74 países fueron receptores netos de migrantes. En 64 de ellos, la migración neta prevista reforzará el crecimiento de la población y en 7 países, invertirá la tendencia a la disminución de la población (Alemania, Austria, Croacia, Eslovaquia, Eslovenia, Grecia e Italia). En tres países, la migración ralentizará el descenso de la población, pero no llegará a invertir esa tendencia (Federación de Rusia, Hungría y República Checa).

20.   Teniendo en cuenta las medias anuales previstas para el período 2005-2050, los principales receptores netos de migrantes internacionales serán los Estados Unidos (1,1 millones de personas por año), Alemania (202.000), el Canadá (200.000), el Reino Unido (130.000), Italia (120.000) y Australia (100.000). Se prevé que los países de los que saldrá el mayor número neto de emigrantes serán China (327.000 por año), México (293.000), la India (241.000), Filipinas (180.000), Indonesia (164.000), el Pakistán (154.000) y Ucrania (100.000).

Hipótesis en que se basa la *Revisión de 2004*

Para elaborar las proyecciones demográficas hasta 2050, la División de Población de las Naciones Unidas parte de la hipótesis sobre las tendencias futuras con respecto a la fecundidad, la mortalidad y la migración. Dado que las tendencias futuras no se pueden conocer con certeza, se preparan diversas variantes de proyección. Las proyecciones presentadas en *Highlights* se basan en la variante media de la *Revisión de 2004*. Las hipótesis de la variante media se exponen en detalle en la sección A de este capítulo.

La *Revisión de 2004* incluye otras cinco variantes: las variantes alta, baja, de fecundidad constante, de mortalidad constante y de migración cero. Las hipótesis que diferencian a estas variantes de la variante media se describen en la sección B. Los resultados pormenorizados de estas variantes se podrán consultar en publicaciones de próxima aparición.

Las proyecciones de la población de cada país se realizan a partir de la población estimada al 1º de julio de 2005. Como aún no se dispone de datos reales de la población en 2005, la estimación correspondiente a 2005 se basa en los últimos datos de población que se conocen de cada país, los cuales se obtienen normalmente de los censos o registros de población y se ajustan a 2005 aplicando todos los datos conocidos sobre fertilidad, mortalidad y migración internacional. Cuando no se dispone de datos muy recientes, las estimaciones de las tendencias demográficas son proyecciones a corto plazo realizadas a partir de los últimos datos conocidos. Los datos sobre población de todas las fuentes se analizan para determinar si son exhaustivos, exactos y coherentes, y se ajustan en caso necesario[6].

A. Hipótesis de la variante media

1. Hipótesis de fecundidad: convergencia hacia una fecundidad total inferior al nivel de reemplazo

Se parte del supuesto de que la fecundidad total en todos los países acabará por converger en una tasa de 1,85 hijos por mujer. No obstante, no todos los países alcanzarán ese nivel en el período de la proyección, es decir, de aquí a 2050. El principio en que se basan las proyecciones en materia de fecundidad es el mismo para todos los países, pero los procedimientos para hacer esas proyecciones son ligeramente diferentes, dependiendo de si los países han tenido una tasa de fecundidad total superior o inferior a 1,85 hijos por mujer en el período 2000-2005.

En lo que respecta a los países con una tasa de fecundidad total superior a 1,85 hijos por mujer, se supone que la fecundidad seguirá una trayectoria deducida de los modelos de disminución de la fecundidad establecidos por la División de Población de las Naciones Unidas sobre la base de lo ocurrido en todos los países en que la fecundidad se redujo entre 1950 y 2000. Los modelos relacionan el nivel de fecundidad total durante un período determinado con la disminución media prevista de la fecundidad total en el período siguiente. Si la fecundidad total prevista en un modelo para un país desciende por debajo de 1,85 hijos por mujer antes de 2050, la tasa

---

[6] Para una descripción general de los procedimientos empleados para examinar las estimaciones de la dinámica demográfica, véase *World Population Prospects: The 2002 Revision, Volume III: Analytical Report*, págs. 180 a 182.

de fecundidad total se mantiene constante a ese nivel en el resto del período de la proyección (es decir, hasta 2050).

En todos los casos, la evolución prevista de la fecundidad de acuerdo con los modelos se coteja con las tendencias recientes de la fecundidad en cada país. Cuando las tendencias recientes de la fecundidad de un país se desvían considerablemente de las definidas a partir de los modelos, se hace una proyección de la fecundidad para un período inicial de cinco o diez años de manera que se ajuste a lo observado recientemente. Las proyecciones a partir de los modelos vuelven a aplicarse después de ese período de transición. Por ejemplo, en los países en que la fecundidad se ha estancado o no hay indicios de un descenso de la fecundidad, se prevé que la fecundidad se mantenga constante unos años antes de empezar a disminuir.

En lo que respecta a los países con una tasa de fecundidad total inferior a 1,85 hijos por mujer en el período 2000-2005, se supone que en los primeros cinco o diez años del período de la proyección la fecundidad seguirá las tendencias más recientes observadas en cada país. Después de ese período de transición, se supone que la fecundidad aumentará de forma lineal a un ritmo de 0,07 hijos por mujer y quinquenio. Así pues, los países que actualmente tienen una fecundidad muy baja quizá no hayan alcanzado el nivel de 1,85 hijos por mujer en 2050.

2. Hipótesis de mortalidad: aumento de la esperanza de vida, excepto en los países afectados por el VIH/SIDA

a. Hipótesis de mortalidad normal

La proyección de la mortalidad se realiza partiendo de los modelos de evolución de la esperanza de vida preparados por la División de Población de las Naciones Unidas. Según esos modelos, cuanto más alta sea la esperanza de vida ya alcanzada, menor será el incremento. La elección del modelo adecuado para cada país se basa en las tendencias más recientes de la esperanza de vida por sexo. En el caso de los países muy afectados por la epidemia del VIH/SIDA, por lo general se ha utilizado el modelo que prevé un ritmo lento de disminución de la mortalidad para tener en cuenta la reducción de los riesgos de mortalidad general no relacionados con el VIH/SIDA.

b. Influencia del VIH/SIDA en la mortalidad

En lo que respecta a los 60 países muy afectados por la epidemia del VIH/SIDA (enumerados en el cuadro VIII.21), para estimar la influencia del VIH/SIDA se preparan modelos explícitos de la evolución futura de la epidemia y proyecciones de la incidencia anual de la infección por el VIH. El modelo desarrollado por el Grupo de Referencia del ONUSIDA sobre estimaciones, modelos y proyecciones[7] se utiliza para ajustar las estimaciones previas de la prevalencia del VIH obtenidas del ONUSIDA y deducir los parámetros que han determinado la dinámica de la epidemia hasta el momento. En el caso de la mayoría de los países, el modelo se ajusta partiendo del supuesto de que los parámetros pertinentes se han mantenido constantes en el pasado. A partir de 2005, las proyecciones indican que el parámetro

---

[7] Improved methods and assumptions for estimation of the HIV/AIDS epidemic and its impact: Recommendations of the UNAIDS Reference Group on Estimates, Modelling and Projections. AIDS, vol. 16, págs. W1 a W14 (Grupo de Referencia del ONUSIDA sobre estimaciones, modelización y proyecciones, 2002).

FI[Φ], que representa la tasa de ingreso de nuevos individuos en el grupo de alto riesgo o vulnerable, se reducirá a la mitad cada 30 años. Según las proyecciones, el parámetro R, que representa la intensidad de la infección, registrará la misma disminución. La reducción del parámetro R se basa en la hipótesis de que los cambios de comportamiento entre quienes están expuestos al riesgo de infección, unidos a un mayor acceso de las personas infectadas al tratamiento, reducirán las posibilidades de transmisión del virus. Se prevé que la tasa de transmisión de la madre al niño se reducirá a distintos ritmos, en función de lo que avance cada país en la ampliación del acceso al tratamiento. Además, se ha actualizado el componente del modelo del Grupo de Referencia relativo a la supervivencia de los niños infectados: en la *Revisión de 2004* se presupone que el 50% de los niños infectados como consecuencia de la transmisión del VIH de la madre a hijo cumplirá los 2 años de edad.

En la *Revisión de 2004* se prevé por primera vez una supervivencia más larga para las personas que reciben terapia antirretroviral de gran actividad. La proporción de personas seropositivas que reciben tratamiento en cada país coincide con las estimaciones de la Organización Mundial de la Salud para finales de 2004[8]. Según las proyecciones, la proporción de personas con acceso a tratamiento oscilará entre un 40% y un 85% en 2015, dependiendo del actual nivel de acceso. Se supone que, por término medio, la probabilidad de supervivencia anual aumenta hasta al menos el 80% en el caso de los pacientes que reciben terapia antirretroviral. Con arreglo a esta hipótesis, la supervivencia media desde que se inicia la terapia es de 3,1 años (la supervivencia mediana es de 4,5 años). En cambio, se presupone que, sin tratamiento, la supervivencia media una vez que se manifiesta el SIDA es de solamente un año.

3. Hipótesis de migración internacional

La evolución futura de la migración internacional se determina sobre la base de las estimaciones pasadas de la migración internacional y de una evaluación de la orientación de las políticas de los países con respecto a las corrientes futuras de migración internacional.

B. Variantes de la proyección

La *Revisión de 2004* incluye cinco variantes de proyección, además de la variante media. Tres de ellas (alta, baja y de fecundidad constante) difieren de la variante media únicamente en lo que respecta a la tasa de fecundidad total prevista. De acuerdo con la variante alta, se prevé que la fecundidad total se mantendrá 0,5 hijos por encima de la fecundidad total de la variante media durante la mayor parte del período que abarca la proyección. Por ejemplo, que los países con una fecundidad total de 1,85 hijos por mujer en la variante media tienen en la variante alta una fecundidad total de 2,35 hijos por mujer. En la variante baja se prevé que la fecundidad total se mantendrá 0,5 hijos por debajo de la fecundidad total de la variante media. De acuerdo con la variante de fecundidad constante, la fecundidad total se mantiene constante en el nivel estimado para el período 2000-2005.

---

[8] Organización Mundial de la Salud. Informe sobre los progresos realizados en la aplicación de la iniciativa "3 por 5", diciembre de 2004, OMS y ONUSIDA

También se han preparado una variante de mortalidad constante y una variante de migración cero. Ambas parten de la misma hipótesis de fecundidad que la variante media. La variante de mortalidad constante parte además de la misma hipótesis de migración internacional que la variante media. En consecuencia, los resultados de la variante de mortalidad constante se pueden comparar con los de la variante media para determinar la influencia que tienen los cambios de la mortalidad en otros parámetros demográficos. De igual manera, la variante de migración cero difiere de la variante media únicamente en la hipótesis de base relativa a la migración internacional. Por tanto, la variante de migración cero permite evaluar la influencia que una migración por encima o por debajo de cero tiene en otros parámetros demográficos.

C. Cambios metodológicos introducidos en la *Revisión de 2004*

- En la variante media, las proyecciones de la fecundidad de los países con una fecundidad total inferior a 1,85 hijos por mujer en el período 2000-2005 se han hecho partiendo del supuesto de que las tendencias más recientes se mantendrán en un primer momento e incrementando después la fecundidad de forma lineal a un ritmo de 0,07 hijos por mujer y quinquenio. En esos países no se habrá alcanzado necesariamente el nivel de 1,85 hijos por mujer en 2050.

- En la *Revisión de 2004*, se han utilizado nuevos modelos de variación de la mortalidad, a fin de tener en cuenta las distintas tendencias históricas en el aumento de la esperanza de vida. En concreto, se han preparado modelos de variaciones muy lentas y variaciones muy rápidas, como complemento de los modelos de variación lenta, media y rápida ya existentes.

- La influencia del VIH/SIDA en la mortalidad se determina mediante modelos explícitos en el caso de todos los países en que la prevalencia del VIH entre adultos era de un 1% o más en 2003.

- La terapia antirretroviral se ha incorporado explícitamente en las proyecciones relativas al VIH/SIDA en los países afectados. Además, se prevé que la tasa de transmisión del VIH de la madre al niño disminuya a un ritmo paralelo a los avances previstos en la ampliación del acceso al tratamiento.

I. INTRODUCTION

Timely and accurate information about population trends is in high demand. Knowledge about the current size and structure of a country's population is needed for the formulation and implementation of policies and programmes in almost all areas of public life. Because policies are aimed at achieving goals in the future, knowledge about future population trends is required. What is true for individual countries also holds for the international community. United Nations activities in areas as diverse as health and environment, poverty reduction and promoting social progress and economic growth, rely on comprehensive and consistent demographic information. The population estimates and projections prepared by the Population Division of the United Nations Department of Economic and Social Affairs (DESA) provide that information.

The Population Division has been preparing the official United Nations estimates and projections of the world's population since 1951. The *2004 Revision* of *World Population Prospects* is the nineteenth set of global estimates and projections completed by the Population Division since that date. Until 1978, revisions of the global set of population projections were published every five years, but since that date the Population Division has issued revisions of the estimates and projections for all countries and areas of the world every two years.

The data produced for each revision of *World Population Prospects* represent a unique set of comprehensive, consistent and internationally comparable estimates and projections of population by age and sex as well as estimates and projections of mortality and fertility schedules by age and sex, and estimates of net international migration for each country. Such data serve as a basis for the calculation of sectoral estimates and projections produced by the various agencies and bodies of the United Nations system. Given the numerous uses of the Population Division's estimates and projections as well as the fact that future world population trends are inherently uncertain, it is important to ensure that the official set of population estimates and projections of the United Nations system are kept as up-to-date as possible. This goal is met by revising the official set of projections every two years and, in the process, incorporating the most recent demographic information available for each country of the world.

The results of the *2004 Revision* are published in three volumes. Volume I presents all major demographic indicators, for all countries and their aggregates, in the form of demographic profiles and indicator-specific data tables. Volume II presents detailed information about the composition of populations by age and sex. Volume III is devoted to an analysis of the results, the methodological underpinnings and the documentation of the data sources of the *2004 Revision*. In addition, the results of the *2004 Revision* are available in digital form on three CD-ROMs, as well as on the Population Division's website at *http://www.unpopulation.org*. A wall chart showing population estimates and projections for 2005, 2025, and 2050 for all countries of the world and corresponding demographic indicators has also been issued.

The *2004 Revision* provides estimates and projections for 228 countries. For 192 countries of the world that had an estimated population of 100,000 inhabitants or more in the year 2000, the projections are carried out using the cohort-component method, which requires explicit assumptions on future fertility, mortality and migration trends for each country. For 36 countries that in 2000 had less than 100,000 inhabitants, projections of the total population are made on the basis of assumptions about the future rate of population growth. Such methodology does not require or produce information on future fertility, mortality and migration levels.

Estimates and projections are made and presented for each country separately. The estimates cover the period 1950-2005 and the projections cover the period 2005-2050. Results are also presented for the world as a whole, its 21 regions and six major areas. In addition, countries are organized by level of development. The sets of countries that constitute each region, major area and development group are shown in the explanatory notes.

The *2004 Revision* includes seven projection variants and three AIDS scenarios. The seven variants are: low, medium, high, constant-fertility, instant-replacement-fertility, constant-mortality, and zero-migration. The first five variants, namely, low, medium, high, constant-fertility and instant-replacement-fertility, differ among themselves exclusively in the assumptions made regarding the future path of fertility. The sixth variant, named constant-mortality, differs from the medium variant with regard to the path followed by future mortality. The seventh variant, named zero-migration, differs from the medium variant only with regard to the path followed by future international migrations. Projection variants differ from each other only for the period 2005-2050. The low, medium and high variants constitute the core of the official projections. They encompass the likely future path of population growth for each country of the world. The low and high variants provide lower and upper bounds for that growth. The medium variant is a useful central reference for trends over the longer term. The constant-fertility, instant-replacement-fertility, constant-mortality, and zero-migration variants have been produced for illustrative purposes, to permit an assessment of the effects that future assumptions on fertility, mortality and international migration in the medium variant have in relation to these scenarios.

In addition, the *2004 Revision* includes three AIDS scenarios named No-AIDS, high-AIDS and AIDS-vaccine. These scenarios are variations of the medium variant and differ from each other and from that variant on the path of mortality because they are based on different assumptions regarding the course of the HIV/AIDS epidemic. Note that only 60 countries are considered to be significantly affected by the epidemic. Consequently, the AIDS scenarios produce different projections only for those countries.

The No-AIDS scenario applies the mortality likely to be exhibited by the non-infected population to the whole population, thus excluding the direct impacts of the epidemic. The high-AIDS scenario assumes that the AIDS modeling parameters determining the path of the HIV/AIDS epidemic remain constant at their 2005 level. The AIDS-vaccine scenario assumes that there are no new HIV infections starting in 2006. The estimates associated with the No-AIDS scenario (that is, the figures for 1980-2005) differ from the estimates of the other variants because AIDS started affecting the populations in the majority of the highly-affected countries around 1980. By comparing these results with those of the estimates and medium variant that include explicitly the effects of the HIV/AIDS epidemic, the user can infer the impact of the epidemic. The two other AIDS scenarios (high-AIDS and AIDS-Vaccine) provide alternative bounds on the possible course of the epidemic.

Volumes I, II and III present results for the three main variants, medium, high and low. Additionally, projection results from the constant-fertility variant are shown in volume I. The results of the three additional variants, instant-replacement, constant-mortality and zero-migration, and the three special HIV/AIDS scenarios are not included in the volumes. However, the results of these additional variants and scenarios are contained in the CD-ROMs entitled "Comprehensive" and "Extended" (see order form, chapter II).

Data in volume II are presented for the world and its development groups, followed by alphabetically sorted major areas, their regions and the countries in alphabetical order. The population data are tabulated by five-year age groups and sex for the period 1950 to 2050 and for three projection variants. Data on the aggregates are followed by population figures for 192 countries which had a population of 100,000 people or more in 2000.

In addition to the data tables, this report includes an executive summary of the main results and a summary of the assumptions of the *2004 Revision* in all six official languages of the United Nations. A more detailed description of the assumptions is provided in volume III.

II. ORDERING THE WORLD POPULATION PROSPECTS DATA ON CD-ROM

The *2004 Revision* of the *World Population Prospects,* prepared by the United Nations Population Division, provides a comprehensive and consistent set of population data for the world's countries and their aggregates.

The results of this Revision are available on three CD-ROM editions that differ with regard to the data included and their prices (table 1). All three CDs contain estimates and projections of national populations by five-year age groups and sex for 1950-2050 and demographic indicators for the same period. Data for 1950-2005 are estimates and those thereafter are projections.

The Basic CD-ROM contains all essential data from the medium variant (total births, total deaths, total net number of migrants, the respective crude rates, life expectancy at birth by sex, infant and child mortality, total fertility, net reproduction rate and population growth rates for 1950-2050 by five-year periods). It also includes population figures by five-year age groups and sex for every fifth year, beginning in 1950, as well as interpolated annual total population. The data are tabulated in Excel worksheets and correspond to the first three datasets listed in table 1.

The Comprehensive CD-ROM includes all the data from the Basic CD, plus the same data for the low, high and constant-fertility projection variants, births and deaths by five-year age groups, the corresponding age-specific fertility and mortality rates and abridged life tables (survivors and life expectancies at specific ages). It also comprises a standard set of demographic indicators and population by age groups and sex for the instant-replacement-fertility, constant-mortality and zero-migration variants as well as for different AIDS scenarios. All data on this CD are presented in Excel worksheets and correspond to the datasets 1 to 3 and 5 to 13 listed in table 1.

The Extended CD-ROM contains all the data from the Comprehensive CD, plus population figures by single calendar year and single age groups for 1950-2050. This CD also provides interpolated demographic indicators for single calendar years (total births and deaths, their respective crude rates, life expectancy at birth by sex, infant and child mortality, survivors to age 1, total fertility), urban population, population density and interpolated total population by main age groups and sex, and their respective percentage distributions and sex ratios. The data are presented in Excel and database formats (ASCII comma delimited format for all datasets and Microsoft Access for interpolated population by age and sex) and correspond to all datasets listed in table 1.

All CDs show data for 228 countries and areas, 33 country aggregates, including the world as a whole, the more and the less developed regions, and the major areas. For the AIDS scenarios (datasets 10-13), special aggregations by region and HIV prevalence level in 2003 are provided for 60 countries affected by the HIV/AIDS epidemic. The Microsoft Excel files correspond to version 5.0/95 and later of this software. For a detailed listing of the contents of each CD, see table 2. Data files in database formats are shown in table 3. All CDs include the images of volumes I and II of *World Population Prospects: The 2004 Revision* in Adobe Acrobat PDF format.

For information on how to order this CD-ROM please see the order form at the end.

Table 1. Summary contents of each CD-ROM

Description: Datasets included on CD-ROM	Basic CD (Medium variant only)	Comprehensive CD	Extended CD
1. Period indicators, five-year periods	X	X	X
2. Stock indicators, five-year periods (and annual population)	X	X	X
3. Population by five-year age groups and sex, five-year periods	X	X	X
4. Population by five year age groups and sex, annual			X
5. Mortality indicators by age and sex, five-year periods		X	X
6. Fertility indicators by age, five-year periods		X	X
7. Zero-migration variant		X	X
8. Constant-mortality variant		X	X
9. Instant-replacement-fertility variant		X	X
10. No-AIDS mortality scenario		X	X
11. AIDS mortality scenario (medium/default)		X	X
12. High-AIDS mortality scenario		X	X
13. AIDS-Vaccine mortality scenario		X	X
14. Interpolated demographic and population indicators, annual			X
15. Population (by sex and both sexes combined) interpolated by single years of age and single calendar years			X
Price ($US)	$50	$250	$800

United Nations Department of Economic and Social Affairs/Population Division
World Population Prospects: The 2004 Revision, Volume II: Sex and Age Distribution of the World Population

3

TABLE 2. CONTENTS OF DATASETS IN DIGITAL FORM

Dataset and File	Indicators	CD-ROM Edition[1]	Number of countries or areas	Projection variants or scenarios (starting in 2005) Note: Basic dataset includes only the medium variant	Periods covered	Age groups
Dataset 1. Period indicators, five-year periods						
F1.	Total fertility	B/C/E	192	Low, medium, high, constant-fertility	1950-1955,....2045-2050	---
F2.	Net reproduction rate	B/C/E	192	Low, medium, high, constant-fertility	1950-1955,....2045-2050	---
F3.	Crude birth rate	B/C/E	192	Low, medium, high, constant-fertility	1950-1955,....2045-2050	---
F4.	Births	B/C/E	192	Low, medium, high, constant-fertility	1950-1955,....2045-2050	---
F5.	Life expectancy at birth by sex	B/C/E	192	Medium	1950-1955,....2045-2050	---
F6.	Infant mortality, q(1)	B/C/E	192	Medium	1950-1955,....2045-2050	---
	Under-five mortality, q(5)	B/C/E	192	Medium	1995-2000,....2045-2050	---
F7.	Crude death rate	B/C/E	192	Low, medium, high, constant-fertility	1950-1955,....2045-2050	---
F8.	Total number of deaths (both sexes)	B/C/E	192	Low, medium, high, constant-fertility	1950-1955,....2045-2050	---
F8.	Total number of male deaths	B/C/E	192	Low, medium, high, constant-fertility	1950-1955,....2045-2050	---
F8.	Total number of female deaths	B/C/E	192	Low, medium, high, constant-fertility	1950-1955,....2045-2050	---
F9.	Net migration rate	B/C/E	192	Low, medium, high, constant-fertility	1950-1955,....2045-2050	---
F10.	Net number of migrants (both sexes)	B/C/E	192	Medium	1950-1955,....2045-2050	---
F11.	Average annual rate of population change	B/C/E	228	Low, medium, high, constant-fertility	1950-1955,....2045-2050	---
F12.	Rate of natural increase	B/C/E	192	Low, medium, high, constant-fertility	1950-1955,....2045-2050	---
F13.	Sex ratio at birth	B/C/E	192	Medium	2000-2005,....2045-2050	---
Dataset 2. Stock indicators						
F1.	Total population (both sexes), annual	B/C/E	228	Low, medium, high, constant-fertility	1950, 1951,....2049, 2050	---
F2.	Male population, annual	B/C/E	192	Low, medium, high, constant-fertility	1950, 1951,....2049, 2050	---
F3.	Female population, annual	B/C/E	192	Low, medium, high, constant-fertility	1950, 1951,....2049, 2050	---
F4.	Sex ratio of the population	B/C/E	192	Low, medium, high, constant-fertility	1950, 1955,....2045, 2050	---
F5.	Dependency ratio (0-14 and 65+ by 15-64)	B/C/E	192	Low, medium, high, constant-fertility	1950, 1955,....2045, 2050	---
F6.	Median age of the population	B/C/E	192	Low, medium, high, constant-fertility	1950, 1955,....2045, 2050	---
F7.	Total population by main age groups	B/C/E	192	Low, medium, high, constant-fertility	1950, 1955,....2045, 2050	0-4, 5-14, 0-14, 15-24, 15-59, 15-64, 60+, 65+, 80+, 90+
F8.	Percentage total population by main age groups	B/C/E	192	Low, medium, high, constant-fertility	1950, 1955,....2045, 2050	0-4, 5-14, 0-14, 15-24, 15-59, 15-64, 60+, 65+, 80+, 90+
F9.	Sex ratio and feminity ratio by main age groups	B/C/E	192	Low, medium, high, constant-fertility	1950, 1955,....2045, 2050	0-4, 5-14, 0-14, 15-24, 15-59, 15-64, 60+, 65+, 80+, 90+
F10.	Population density	B/C/E	228	Low, medium, high, constant-fertility	1950, 1955,....2045, 2050	---
Dataset 3. Population by age and sex, five-year periods						
F1.	Population by five-year age groups (both sexes)	B/C/E	192	Low, medium, high, constant-fertility	1950, 1955,....1985, 1990	0-4, 5-9,...75-79, 80+
					1995, 2000,....2045, 2050	0-4, 5-9, ...95-99, 100+

TABLE 2. CONTENTS OF DATASETS IN DIGITAL FORM

Dataset and File	Indicators	CD-ROM Edition[1]	Number of countries or areas	Projection variants or scenarios (starting in 2005) Note: Basic dataset includes only the medium variant	Periods covered	Age groups
F2.	Male population by five-year age groups	B/C/E	192	Low, medium, high, constant-fertility	1950, 1955,...1985, 1990	0-4, 5-9,...75-79, 80+
					1995, 2000,...2045, 2050	0-4, 5-9,...95-99, 100+
F3.	Female population by five-year age groups	B/C/E	192	Low, medium, high, constant-fertility	1950, 1955,...1985, 1990	0-4, 5-9,...75-79, 80+
					1995, 2000,...2045, 2050	0-4, 5-9,...95-99, 100+
Dataset 4. Population by age and sex, annual						
F1.	Population by five-year age groups (both sexes)	E	192	Medium	1950, 1951,...1994	0-4, 5-9,...75-79, 80+
					1995, 1996,...2050	0-4, 5-9,...95-99, 100+
F2.	Population by five-year age groups (male)	E	192	Medium	1950, 1951,...1994	0-4, 5-9,...75-79, 80+
					1995, 1996,...2050	0-4, 5-9,...95-99, 100+
F3.	Population by five-year age groups (female)	E	192	Medium	1950, 1951,...1994	0-4, 5-9,...75-79, 80+
					1995, 1996,...2050	0-4, 5-9,...95-99, 100+
Dataset 5. Mortality indicators by age and sex, five-year periods						
F1.	Deaths by five-year age groups (both sexes)	C/E	192	Low, medium, high, constant-fertility	1995-2000,...2045-2050	0-4, 5-9,...90-94, 95+
F2.	Deaths by five-year age groups (male)	C/E	192	Low, medium, high, constant-fertility	1995-2000,...2045-2050	0-4, 5-9,...90-94, 95+
F3.	Deaths by five-year age groups (female)	C/E	192	Low, medium, high, constant-fertility	1995-2000,...2045-2050	0-4, 5-9,...90-94, 95+
F4.	Life table l(x) values by sex	C/E	192	Medium	1995-2000,...2045-2050	0, 1, 5, 10,...80, 85
F5.	Life expectancy at age (x) by sex	C/E	192	Medium	1995-2000,...2045-2050	0, 1, 5, 10,...95, 100
Dataset 6. Fertility indicators by age, five-year periods						
F1.	Births by five-year age groups of mother	C/E	192	Medium	1995-2000,...2045-2050	15-19, 20-24,...45-49
F2.	Age-specific fertility rates	C/E	192	Medium	1995-2000,...2045-2050	15-19, 20-24,...45-49
Dataset 7. Zero-migration variant						
F1.	Population by five-year age groups and sex	C/E	192	Zero-migration	2010, 2015,... 2045, 2050	0-4, 5-9,...95-99, 100+
F2.	Total population (both sexes)	C/E	192	Zero-migration	1950, 1955,...2045, 2050	---
F3.	Median age of the population	C/E	192	Zero-migration	1950, 1955,...2045, 2050	---
F4.	Dependency ratio (0-14 and 65+ by 15-64)	C/E	192	Zero-migration	1950, 1955,...2045, 2050	---
F5.	Crude birth rate	C/E	192	Zero-migration	1950-1955,...2045-2050	---
F6.	Crude death rate	C/E	192	Zero-migration	1950-1955,...2045-2050	---
F7.	Average annual rate of population change	C/E	192	Zero-migration	1950-1955,...2045-2050	---
Dataset 8. Constant-mortality variant						
F1.	Population by five-year age groups and sex	C/E	192	Constant-mortality	2010, 2015,...2045, 2050	0-4, 5-9,...95-99, 100+
F2.	Total population (both sexes)	C/E	192	Constant-mortality	1950, 1955,...2045, 2050	---
F3.	Median age of the population	C/E	192	Constant-mortality	1950, 1955,...2045, 2050	---
F4.	Dependency ratio (0-14 and 65+ by 15-64)	C/E	192	Constant-mortality	1950, 1955,...2045, 2050	---

TABLE 2. CONTENTS OF DATASETS IN DIGITAL FORM

Dataset and File	Indicators	CD-ROM Edition[1]	Number of countries or areas	Projection variants or scenarios (starting in 2005) Note: Basic dataset includes only the medium variant	Periods covered	Age groups
F5.	Deaths by five-year age groups and sex	C/E	192	Constant-mortality	2005-2010, ... 2045-2050	0-4, 5-9, ...95+
F6.	Life expectancy at birth by sex	C/E	192	Constant-mortality	1950-1955,...2045-2050	---
F7.	Crude birth rate	C/E	192	Constant-mortality	1950-1955,...2045-2050	---
F8.	Crude death rate	C/E	192	Constant-mortality	1950-1955,...2045-2050	---
F9.	Average annual rate of population change	C/E	192	Constant-mortality	1950-1955,...2045-2050	---
Dataset 9. Instant-replacement-fertility variant						
F1.	Population by five-year age groups and sex	C/E	192	Instant-replacement-fertility	2010, 2015,... 2045, 2050	0-4, 5-9, ...95-99, 100+
F2.	Total population (both sexes)	C/E	192	Instant-replacement-fertility	1950, 1955,...2045, 2050	---
F3.	Median age of the population	C/E	192	Instant-replacement-fertility	1950, 1955,...2045, 2050	---
F4.	Dependency ratio (0-14 and 65+ by 15-64)	C/E	192	Instant-replacement-fertility	1950, 1955,...2045, 2050	---
F5.	Total fertility	C/E	192	Instant-replacement-fertility	1950-1955,...2045-2050	---
F6.	Crude birth rate	C/E	192	Instant-replacement-fertility	1950-1955,...2045-2050	---
F7.	Crude death rate	C/E	192	Instant-replacement-fertility	1950-1955,...2045-2050	---
F8.	Average annual rate of population change	C/E	192	Instant-replacement-fertility	1950-1955,...2045-2050	---

AIDS Scenarios for 60 countries affected by the HIV/AIDS epidemic and 13 special aggregations (by region and HIV prevalence level in 2003)

Dataset and File	Indicators	CD-ROM Edition[1]	Number of countries or areas	Projection variants or scenarios	Periods covered	Age groups
Dataset 10. No-AIDS scenario						
10.1 Period indicators						
F2.	Net reproduction rate	C/E	60	No-AIDS	1980-1985,...2045-2050	---
F3.	Crude birth rate	C/E	60	No-AIDS	1980-1985,...2045-2050	---
F4.	Births	C/E	60	No-AIDS	1980-1985,...2045-2050	---
F5.	Life expectancy at birth by sex	C/E	60	No-AIDS	1980-1985,...2045-2050	---
F6.	Infant mortality, q(1)	C/E	60	No-AIDS	1980-1985,...2045-2050	---
	Under-five mortality, q(5)	C/E	60	No-AIDS	1995-2000,...2045-2050	---
F7.	Crude death rate	C/E	60	No-AIDS	1980-1985,...2045-2050	---
F8.	Total number of deaths (both sexes)	C/E	60	No-AIDS	1980-1985,...2045-2050	---
F8.	Total number of male deaths	C/E	60	No-AIDS	1980-1985,...2045-2050	---
F8.	Total number of female deaths	C/E	60	No-AIDS	1980-1985,...2045-2050	---
F11.	Average annual rate of population change	C/E	60	No-AIDS	1980-1985,...2045-2050	---
F12.	Rate of natural increase	C/E	60	No-AIDS	1980-1985,...2045-2050	---
10.2 Stock indicators						
F1.	Total population (both sexes), annual	C/E	60	No-AIDS	1980, 1981,...2049, 2050	---
F2.	Male population, annual	C/E	60	No-AIDS	1980, 1981,...2049, 2050	---
F3.	Female population, annual	C/E	60	No-AIDS	1980, 1981,...2049, 2050	---
F4.	Sex ratio of the population	C/E	60	No-AIDS	1980, 1985,...2045, 2050	---

TABLE 2. CONTENTS OF DATASETS IN DIGITAL FORM

Dataset and File	Indicators	CD-ROM Edition[1]	Number of countries or areas	Projection variants or scenarios (starting in 2005) Note: Basic dataset includes only the medium variant	Periods covered	Age groups
F5.	Dependency ratio (0-14 and 65+ by 15-64)	C/E	60	No-AIDS	1980, 1985,....2045, 2050	--
F6.	Median age of the population	C/E	60	No-AIDS	1980, 1985,....2045, 2050	--
10.3	**Population by age and sex, five-year periods**					
F1.	Population by five-year age groups (both sexes)	C/E	60	No-AIDS	1980, 1985,....1985, 1990 / 1995, 2000,....2045, 2050	0-4, 5-9,...75-79, 80+ / 0-4, 5-9,....95-99, 100+
F2.	Male population by five-year age groups	C/E	60	No-AIDS	1980, 1985,....1985, 1990 / 1995, 2000,....2045, 2050	0-4, 5-9,...75-79, 80+ / 0-4, 5-9,....95-99, 100+
F3.	Female population by five-year age groups	C/E	60	No-AIDS	1980, 1985,....1985, 1990 / 1995, 2000,....2045, 2050	0-4, 5-9,...75-79, 80+ / 0-4, 5-9,....95-99, 100+
10.4	**Population by age and sex, annual**					
F1.	Population by five-year age groups (both sexes)	C/E	60	No-AIDS	1980, 1981,....1994 / 1995, 1996,....2050	0-4, 5-9,...75-79, 80+ / 0-4, 5-9,....95-99, 100+
F2.	Population by five-year age groups (male)	C/E	60	No-AIDS	1980, 1981,....1994 / 1995, 1996,....2050	0-4, 5-9,...75-79, 80+ / 0-4, 5-9,....95-99, 100+
F3.	Population by five-year age groups (female)	C/E	60	No-AIDS	1980, 1981,....1994 / 1995, 1996,....2050	0-4, 5-9,...75-79, 80+ / 0-4, 5-9,....95-99, 100+
10.5	**Mortality indicators by age and sex, five-year periods**					
F1.	Deaths by five-year age groups (both sexes)	C/E	60	No-AIDS	1980-1985,....2045-2050	0-4, 5-9,...90-94, 95+
F2.	Deaths by five-year age groups (male)	C/E	60	No-AIDS	1980-1985,....2045-2050	0-4, 5-9,...90-94, 95+
F3.	Deaths by five-year age groups (female)	C/E	60	No-AIDS	1980-1985,....2045-2050	0-4, 5-9,...90-94, 95+
F4.	Life table l(x) values by sex	C/E	60	No-AIDS	1995-2000,....2045-2050	0, 1, 5, 10,....80, 85
F5.	Life expectancy at age (x) by sex	C/E	60	No-AIDS	1995-2000,....2045-2050	0, 1, 5, 10,....95, 100
10.6	**Fertility indicators by age, five-year periods**					
F1.	Births by five-year age groups of mother	C/E	60	No-AIDS	1995-2000,....2045-2050	15-19, 20-24,...45-49
F2.	Age-specific fertility rates	C/E	60	No-AIDS	1995-2000,....2045-2050	15-19, 20-24,...45-49
Dataset 11. AIDS scenario (medium/default)						
F1.	Population by five-year age groups and sex	C/E	60	AIDS (medium)	1980, 1985,....1985, 1990 / 1995, 2000,....2045, 2050	0-4, 5-9,...75-79, 80+ / 0-4, 5-9,....95-99, 100+
F2.	Total population (both sexes)	C/E	60	AIDS (medium)	1980, 1985,....2045, 2050	--
F3.	Median age of the population	C/E	60	AIDS (medium)	1980, 1985,....2045, 2050	--
F4.	Dependency ratio (0-14 and 65+ by 15-64)	C/E	60	AIDS (medium)	1980, 1985,....2045, 2050	--
F5.	Deaths by five-year age groups and sex	C/E	60	AIDS (medium)	1980, 1985,....2045, 2050	0-4, 5-9,...95+
F6.	Life expectancy at birth by sex	C/E	60	AIDS (medium)	1980-1985,....2045-2050	--
F7.	Crude birth rate	C/E	60	AIDS (medium)	1980-1985,....2045-2050	--
F8.	Crude death rate	C/E	60	AIDS (medium)	1980-1985,....2045-2050	--

TABLE 2. CONTENTS OF DATASETS IN DIGITAL FORM

Dataset and File	Indicators	CD-ROM Edition[1]	Number of countries or areas	Projection variants or scenarios (starting in 2005) Note: Basic dataset includes only the medium variant	Periods covered	Age groups
F9.	Average annual rate of population change	C/E	60	AIDS (medium)	1980-1985,...2045-2050	---
Dataset 12. High-AIDS scenario (2005 situation constant until 2050)						
F1.	Population by five-year age groups and sex	C/E	60	High-AIDS	2010, 2015,... 2045, 2050	0-4, 5-9, ...95-99, 100+
F2.	Total population (both sexes)	C/E	60	High-AIDS	1980, 1985,...2045, 2050	---
F3.	Median age of the population	C/E	60	High-AIDS	1980, 1985,...2045, 2050	---
F4.	Dependency ratio (0-14 and 65+ by 15-64)	C/E	60	High-AIDS	1980, 1985,...2045, 2050	---
F5.	Deaths by five-year age groups and sex	C/E	60	High-AIDS	1980, 1985,...2045, 2050	0-4, 5-9, ...95+
F6.	Life expectancy at birth by sex	C/E	60	High-AIDS	1980-1985,...2045-2050	---
F7.	Crude birth rate	C/E	60	High-AIDS	1980-1985,...2045-2050	---
F8.	Crude death rate	C/E	60	High-AIDS	1980-1985,...2045-2050	---
F9.	Average annual rate of population change	C/E	60	High-AIDS	1980-1985,...2045-2050	---
Dataset 13. AIDS-Vaccine scenario (no new HIV infection starting in 2006)						
F1.	Population by five-year age groups and sex	C/E	60	AIDS-Vaccine	2010, 2015,...2045, 2050	0-4, 5-9, ...95-99, 100+
F2.	Total population (both sexes)	C/E	60	AIDS-Vaccine	1980, 1985,...2045, 2050	---
F3.	Median age of the population	C/E	60	AIDS-Vaccine	1980, 1985,...2045, 2050	---
F4.	Dependency ratio (0-14 and 65+ by 15-64)	C/E	60	AIDS-Vaccine	1980, 1985,...2045, 2050	---
F5.	Deaths by five-year age groups and sex	C/E	60	AIDS-Vaccine	1980, 1985,...2045, 2050	0-4, 5-9, ...95+
F6.	Life expectancy at birth by sex	C/E	60	AIDS-Vaccine	1980-1985,...2045-2050	---
F7.	Crude birth rate	C/E	60	AIDS-Vaccine	1980-1985,...2045-2050	---
F8.	Crude death rate	C/E	60	AIDS-Vaccine	1980-1985,...2045-2050	---
F9.	Average annual rate of population change	C/E	60	AIDS-Vaccine	1980-1985,...2045-2050	---
Dataset 14. Interpolated annual Indicators (SUPPLEMENT)						
F1.	Total number of deaths (both sexes)	E	192	Medium	1950, 1951,...2029, 2030	---
F1.	Crude death rate	E	192	Medium	1950, 1951,...2029, 2030	---
F1.	Life expectancy at birth by sex	E	192	Medium	1950, 1951,...2029, 2030	---
F1.	Infant deaths (under age 1)	E	192	Medium	1950, 1951,...2029, 2030	---
F1.	Infant mortality, q(1)	E	192	Medium	1950, 1951,...2029, 2030	---
F1.	Survivors to age 1	E	192	Medium	1950, 1951,...2029, 2030	---
F1.	Under-five mortality, q(5)	E	192	Medium	1950, 1951,...2029, 2030	---
F1.	Births	E	192	Medium	1950, 1951,...2029, 2030	---
F1.	Crude birth rate	E	192	Medium	1950, 1951,...2029, 2030	---
F1.	Total fertility	E	192	Medium	1950, 1951,...2029, 2030	---
F1.	Rate of natural increase	E	192	Medium	1950, 1951,...2029, 2030	---

TABLE 2. CONTENTS OF DATASETS IN DIGITAL FORM

Dataset and File	Indicators	CD-ROM Edition[1]	Number of countries or areas	Projection variants or scenarios (starting in 2005) Note: Basic dataset includes only the medium variant	Periods covered	Age groups
F2.	Interpolated population by main age groups	E	192	Medium	1950, 1951,... 2029, 2030	<1, <5, <15, <18, 5-14, 6-11, 12-14, 15-17, 15-24, 18-23, 15-59, 15-64, 60+, 65+, 80+, 90+
F2.	Interpolated female population in reproductive ages	E	192	Medium	1950, 1951,... 2029, 2030	15-49
F2.	Interpolated total population	E	192	Medium	1950, 1951,... 2029, 2030	---
F2.	Interpolated urban population	E	192	Medium	1950, 1951,... 2029, 2030	---
F3.	Percentage of total population by main age groups	E	192	Medium	1950, 1951,... 2029, 2030	<1, <5, <15, <18, 5-14, 6-11, 12-14, 15-17, 15-24, 18-23, 15-59, 15-64, 60+, 65+, 80+, 90+
F3.	Percentage of female population in reproductive ages in total population	E	192	Medium	1950, 1951,... 2029, 2030	15-49
F3.	Interpolated percentage urban population	E	192	Medium	1950, 1951,... 2029, 2030	---
F3.	Interpolated population density	E	192	Medium	1950, 1951,... 2029, 2030	---
Dataset 15. Interpolated annual populations by single age (INTERPOLATED)						
F1.	Population by single age (both sexes)	E	192	Medium	1950, 1951,....1994	0, 1, 2,... 79, 80+
					1995, 1996,....2050	0, 1, 2,... 98, 99, 100+
F2.	Population by single age (male)	E	192	Medium	1950, 1951,....1994	0, 1, 2,... 79, 80+
					1995, 1996,....2050	0, 1, 2,... 98, 99, 100+
F3.	Population by single age (female)	E	192	Medium	1950, 1951,....1994	0, 1, 2,... 79, 80+
					1995, 1996,....2050	0, 1, 2,... 98, 99, 100+

Note: (1) CD-ROM editions are: B = Basic, C = Comprehensive, E = Extended

Datasets 10 to 13 present, in addition to the default AIDS mortality scenario (medium), three other AIDS scenarios for 60 countries affected by the HIV/AIDS epidemic: (1) the No-AIDS scenario assumes that there is no AIDS or, more specifically, reflects the mortality levels of that segment of the population of each country that is not infected with HIV; (2) the High-AIDS scenario assumes that the AIDS modelling parameters determining the path of the HIV/AIDS epidemic remain constant at their 2005 level; and (3) the AIDS-Vaccine scenario assumes that there are no new HIV infections starting in 2006. The estimates associated with the No-AIDS scenario (that is, the figures for 1980-2005) differ from the estimates of the other variants because AIDS started affecting the populations in the majority of the highly-affected countries around 1980. By comparing these results with those of the estimates and medium variant that include explicitly the effects of the HIV/AIDS epidemic, the user can infer the impact of the epidemic. The two other AIDS scenarios (High-AIDS mortality and AIDS-Vaccine mortality) provide alternative bounds on the possible course of the epidemic.

9

TABLE 3. DATA FILES IN DATABASE FORMAT INCLUDED IN THE EXTENDED CD-ROM EDITION

Topic / Data file	Description	Data file format[1]	Number of indicators[2]	Number of records
DB01. Period indicators				
DB01_Period_Indicators.csv	All period indicators (total fertility, net reproduction rate, crude birth rate, births, life expectancy at birth, infant mortality, under-five mortality, crude death rate, number of deaths (by sex), net migration rate, net number of migrants, average annual rate of population change, rate of natural increase, sex ratio at birth) by major area, region and country, for estimates and all 10 projection variants or scenarios, 1950-2050. Data only for 1980-2050 for AIDS scenarios.	CSV	18	25,067
DB02. Stock indicators				
DB02_Populations_Annual.csv	Total population (by sex and both sexes combined) and average annual rate of population change, by major area, region and country, for estimates and all 10 projection variants or scenarios, annually for 1950-2050. Data only for 1980-2050 for AIDS scenarios.	CSV	4	125,744
DB02_Populations_Main_Age_Groups.csv	Total population by main age groups (by sex and both sexes combined) by major area, region and country, for estimates and all 10 projection variants or scenarios, 1950-2050. Data only for 1980-2050 for AIDS scenarios.	CSV	54	22,452
DB02_Stock_Indicators.csv	All stock indicators (total population by sex, dependency ratio, sex ratio, median age, population density, percentage by main age groups, sex ratio (M/F) and feminity ratio (F/M) by main age groups), by major area, region and country, for estimates and all 10 projection variants or scenarios, 1950-2050. Data only for 1980-2050 for AIDS scenarios.	CSV	92	22,452
DB03. Population by age and sex, five-year periods	Population by age group and sex, by major area, region and country, for estimates and all 10 projection variants or scenarios, 1950-2050. Data only for 1980-2050 for AIDS scenarios.			
DB03_Population_Quinquennial.csv	Database format with sex and age in rows.	CSV	1	1,430,136
DB03_Population_By_Sex_Quinquennial.csv	Database format with sex in column and age in row.	CSV	3	476,712
DB03_Population_By_Age_Quinquennial.csv	Database format with sex in row and age from 0 to 100+ in column.	CSV	21	70,020
DB04. Population by age and sex, annual	Population by age group and sex, by major area, region and country, annually for 1950-2050 (estimates and 6 projection variants or scenarios: Medium, Instant-replacement-fertility, and 4 AIDS mortality scenarios). Data only for 1980-2050 for AIDS scenarios.			
DB04_Population_Annual.csv	Database format with sex and age in rows.	CSV	1	3,229,434
DB04_Population_By_Sex_Annual.csv	Database format with sex in column and age in row.	CSV	3	1,076,478
DB04_Population_By_Age_Annual.csv	Database format with sex in row and age from 0 to 100+ in column.	CSV	21	163,374
DB05. Mortality indicators by age and sex	Total deaths by age group and sex, by major area, region and country, for estimates and all 10 projection variants or scenarios,1995-2050. Data only for 1980-2050 for AIDS scenarios.			
DB05_Deaths.csv	Database format with sex and age in rows.	CSV	1	1,203,240
DB05_Deaths_By_Sex.csv	Database format with sex in column and age in row.	CSV	3	401,080
DB05_Deaths_By_Age.csv	Database format with sex in row and age from 0 to 100+ in column.	CSV	21	60,162

TABLE 3. DATA FILES IN DATABASE FORMAT INCLUDED IN THE EXTENDED CD-ROM EDITION

Topic / Data file	Description	Data file format[1]	Number of indicators[2]	Number of records
DB05_Life_Table.csv	Life Table (by sex and both sexes combined) by major area, region and country,1995-2050 (estimates, medium variant and No-AIDS scenario).	CSV	2	217,074
DB05_Life_Table_lx_By_Age.csv	Life table survivors, (l(x)), and life expectancy at exact age, e(x) (by sex and both sexes combined). Database format with sex and age in rows. Life table survivors, (l(x)), at exact age (x) (by sex and both sexes combined). Database format with sex in row and age from 0 to 85 in column.	CSV	18	9,867
DB05_Life_Table_ex_By_Age.csv	Life expectancy at exact age, e(x) (by sex and both sexes combined). Database format with sex in row and age from 0 to 100 in column.	CSV	21	9,867
DB06. Fertility indicators by age	Births by age group of mother and age-specific fertility rates, by major area, region and country, for estimates and all 10 projection variants or scenarios, 1995-2050. Data only for 1980-2050 for AIDS scenarios.			
DB06_Fertility_Indicators.csv	Database format with indicators in column and age groups in row.	CSV	2	140,378
DB06_Fertility_Indicators_By_Age.csv	Database format with indicators by age groups in column.	CSV	14	20,054
DB14. Interpolated annual indicators				
WPP2004_SUP_F1_Annual_Demographic_Indicators.csv	Interpolated demographic indicators by major area, region and country, annually for 1950-2050 (estimates and medium variant).	CSV	15	22,725
WPP2004_SUP_F2_Annual_Population_Indicators.csv	Interpolated total population by main age groups and urban population, by major area, region and country, annually for 1950-2050 (estimates and medium variant).	CSV	21	22,725
WPP2004_SUP_F3_Annual_Population_Indicators_Percentage.csv	Percentage of total population by main age groups, percentage urban and population density, by major area, region and country, annually for 1950-2050 (estimates and medium variant).	CSV	19	22,725
DB15. Interpolated annual populations by single age	Population (by sex and both sexes combined) interpolated by single years of age and single calendar years, by major area, region and country, annual y for 1950-2050 (estimates and medium variant).			
WPP2004_AnnualAgeSex.mdb	Microsoft Access 2000 database tables, with simple user interface for querying and downloading data for population interpolated by single years of age and single calendar years, by major area, region and country, annually for 1950-2050 (estimates and medium variant).	MDB	101	241MB
WPP2004_INT_Population_Annual_Single.csv	Database format with sex and age in rows.	CSV	1	6,278,175
WPP2004_INT_Population_By_Sex_Annual_Single.csv	Database format with sex in column and age in row.	CSV	3	2,092,725
WPP2004_INT_Population_By_Age_Annual_Single.csv	Database format with sex in row and age from 0 to 100+ in column.	CSV	101	68,175

(1) File format is: CSV for ASCII comma delimited data files (.csv) with field names in header, or MDB for Microsoft Access 2000 compatible database files.

(2) Number of indicators does not include descriptive fields like codes and names for location, projection variant/scenario, calendar year or period, age group and/or sex.

UNITED NATIONS  NATIONS UNIES

POPULATION DIVISION
Department of Economic and Social Affairs

World Population Prospects: The 2004 Revision - CD-ROM Edition

Date: _____

Order Form

CD-ROM requested

CD	Description	Price in US$	Quantity	Total Price in US$
[ ]	Basic dataset (Excel and PDF files)	$50	...	...
[ ]	Comprehensive dataset (Excel and PDF files)	$250	...	...
[ ]	Extended dataset (Excel and PDF files, and data in database format)	$800	...	...
		Total	...	...

SHIP TO:

Name: ....

Institution: ....

Address: ....

....

Telephone: .... Fax No: ....

e-mail address ....

For overnight or express mail delivery, please provide a billing account number: ....

Notes

1. Data contained in the above datasets are copyrighted by the United Nations. No portion of the data files contained on diskettes or CD-ROMs can be reproduced, distributed or used to prepare derivative works or for any other purpose without the express permission of the United Nations, to be obtained from the Secretary of the United Nations Publications Board. For further information, please contact the Director, Population Division/DESA, United Nations, New York, NY 10017, U.S.A., telephone no. 1-212-963-3179; fax no. 1-212-963-2147.

2. The order form should be accompanied by a cheque or an international money order in **US dollars drawn on a United States Bank** for the correct amount, payable to the UNITED NATIONS POPULATION DIVISION and mailed to: The Director, Population Division/DESA, United Nations, DC2-1950, New York, NY 10017, U.S.A. **Credit cards are not accepted**.

III. BIBLIOGRAPHY

United Nations (2000). *United Nations Millennium Declaration*. General Assembly Resolution A/Res/55/2 on its Fifty-fifth Session, Agenda item 60 (b), 18 September 2000.

United Nations (2001). *United Nations Declaration of Commitment on HIV/AIDS*. General Assembly Resolution A/Res/S-26/2 on its Twenty-sixth Special Session, Agenda item 8 on 2 August 2001.

United Nations (2005). World Population Prospects: The 2004 Revision, Highlights. ESA/P/WP.193.

United Nations (2003). *World Population Prospects: The 2002 Revision*, vol. 3, *Analytical Report* (United Nations publication, Sales No. E.03.XII.10).

UNAIDS (2002). Improved methods and assumptions for estimation of the HIV/AIDS epidemic and its impact: Recommendations of the UNAIDS Reference Group on Estimates, Modelling and Projections. *AIDS* (Geneva, Switzerland), vol. 16, pp. W1-W14.

World Health Organization (2005). *"3 by 5" Progress Report, December 2004*. World Health Organization and Joint United Nations Programme on HIV/AIDS.

United Nations Department of Economic and Social Affairs/Population Division
World Population Prospects: The 2004 Revision, Volume II: Sex and Age Distribution of the World Population

13

IV. LIST OF PREVIOUS REVISIONS OF THE WORLD POPULATION PROSPECTS

"The past and future growth of world population—a long-range view", *Population Bulletin of the United Nations*, No. 1—December 1951 (United Nations publication, Sales No. 52.XIII.2), pp. 1-12.

"The past and future population of the world and its continents" and "Framework for the future population estimates, 1950-1980, by world regions", *Proceedings of the World Population Conference, 1954*, vol. III (United Nations publication, Sales No. 55.XIII.8), pp. 265-282 and 283-328.

The Future Growth of World Population (United Nations publication, Sales No. 66.XIII.2).

World Population Prospects as Assessed in 1973 (United Nations publication, Sales No. E.76.XIII.4 and corrigenda).

World Population Trends and Prospects by Country, 1950-2000: Summary Report of the 1978 Assessment (ST/ESA/SER.R/33).

Selected Demographic Indicators by Country, 1950-2000: Demographic Estimates and Projections as Assessed in 1978 (ST/ESA/SER.R/38).

World Population Prospects as Assessed in 1980 (United Nations publication, Sales No. E.81.XIII.8).

Demographic Indicators of Countries: Estimates and Projections as Assessed in 1980 (United Nations publication, Sales No. E.82.XIII.5 and corrigendum).

World Population Prospects: Estimates and Projections as Assessed in 1982 (United Nations publication, Sales No. E.83.XIII.5).

World Population Prospects: Estimates and Projections as Assessed in 1984 (United Nations publication, Sales No. E.86.XIII.3).

World Population Prospects 1988 (United Nations publication, Sales No. E.88.XIII.7).

The Sex and Age Distributions of Population: The 1990 Revision (United Nations publication, Sales No. E.90.XIII.33).

World Population Prospects: The 1990 Revision (United Nations publication, Sales No. E.91.XIII.4).

The Sex and Age Distribution of the World Populations: The 1992 Revision (United Nations publication, Sales No. E.93.XIII.3).

World Population Prospects: The 1992 Revision (United Nations publication, Sales No. E.93.XIII.7).

The Sex and Age Distribution of the World Populations: The 1994 Revision (United Nations publication, Sales No. E.95.XIII.2).

World Population Prospects: The 1994 Revision (United Nations publication, Sales No. E.95.XIII.16).

The Sex and Age Distribution of the World Populations: The 1996 Revision (United Nations publication, Sales No. E.98.XIII.2).

World Population Prospects: The 1996 Revision (United Nations publication, Sales No. E.98.XIII.5).

World Population Prospects: The 1998 Revision, vol. I, Comprehensive Tables (United Nations publication, Sales No. E.99.XIII.9).

World Population Prospects: The 1998 Revision, vol. II, Sex and Age Distribution of the World Population (United Nations publication, Sales No. E.99.XIII.8).

World Population Prospects: The 1998 Revision, vol. III, Analytical Report (United Nations publication, Sales No. E.99.XIII.10).

World Population Prospects: The 2000 Revision, vol. I, Comprehensive Tables (United Nations publication, Sales No. E.01.XIII.8 and corrigendum).

World Population Prospects: The 2000 Revision, vol. II, Sex and Age Distribution of the World Population (United Nations publication, Sales No. E.01.XIII.9 and corrigendum).

World Population Prospects: The 2000 Revision, vol. III, Analytical Report (United Nations publication, Sales No. E.01.XIII.20).

World Population Prospects: The 2002 Revision, vol. I, Comprehensive Tables (United Nations publication, Sales No. E.03.XIII.6).

World Population Prospects: The 2002 Revision, vol. II, Sex and Age Distribution of the World Population (United Nations publication, Sales No. E.03.XIII.7).

World Population Prospects: The 2002 Revision, vol. III, *Analytical Report* (United Nations publication, Sales No. E.03.XIII.10).

ANNEX TABLES

A.1. POPULATION BY SEX AND AGE FOR THE WORLD, MAJOR AREAS, REGIONS AND SPECIAL GROUPS: ESTIMATES AND MEDIUM, HIGH AND LOW VARIANTS, 1950-2050

POPULATION BY AGE AND SEX (in thousands)

Age group	1950 Both sexes	Males	Females	1955 Both sexes	Males	Females	1960 Both sexes	Males	Females	1965 Both sexes	Males	Females
All ages	2 519 470	1 257 101	1 262 368	2 757 399	1 376 939	1 380 461	3 023 812	1 511 816	1 511 995	3 337 974	1 671 790	1 666 184
0-4	337 882	172 803	165 079	399 397	203 719	195 678	428 986	218 975	210 011	478 129	244 414	233 715
5-9	269 483	137 049	132 435	314 555	161 119	153 436	375 475	191 907	183 567	407 029	208 313	198 716
10-14	256 774	131 248	125 526	264 593	134 751	129 842	309 548	158 624	150 924	369 936	189 303	180 633
15-19	238 745	122 153	116 591	252 441	128 948	123 493	260 006	132 401	127 605	304 997	156 200	148 797
20-24	220 642	111 901	108 742	232 731	118 724	114 006	247 216	125 974	121 242	254 718	129 450	125 269
25-29	193 784	96 681	97 103	214 643	108 621	106 021	226 897	115 647	111 249	241 986	123 184	118 802
30-34	164 819	82 380	82 439	187 967	93 627	94 340	209 084	105 759	103 325	221 372	112 812	108 559
35-39	161 448	80 037	81 411	158 325	78 935	79 390	182 025	90 449	91 576	203 679	102 897	100 783
40-44	146 434	72 730	73 704	154 625	76 209	78 416	152 057	75 434	76 623	176 133	87 186	88 947
45-49	126 889	62 933	63 956	137 962	67 871	70 091	147 364	72 018	75 346	145 265	71 579	73 686
50-54	107 109	52 425	54 684	118 771	57 839	60 932	130 088	63 160	66 928	139 156	67 263	71 893
55-59	90 098	43 500	46 598	96 225	45 909	50 316	108 714	51 812	56 903	120 431	57 431	63 000
60-64	74 488	34 993	39 495	79 572	37 524	42 048	84 759	39 300	45 459	96 793	44 983	51 810
65-69	56 548	25 177	31 371	61 580	28 131	33 449	66 614	30 545	36 069	71 315	31 865	39 451
70-74	38 290	16 648	21 642	42 777	18 402	24 375	47 429	20 860	26 570	52 241	23 008	29 233
75-79	22 257	9 208	13 049	25 154	10 484	14 671	28 724	11 805	16 920	32 546	13 594	18 952
80 +	13 780	5 237	8 543	16 080	6 124	9 956	18 826	7 148	11 678	22 247	8 309	13 937

Age group	1970 Both sexes	Males	Females	1975 Both sexes	Males	Females	1980 Both sexes	Males	Females	1985 Both sexes	Males	Females
All ages	3 696 588	1 853 966	1 842 622	4 073 740	2 046 860	2 026 880	4 442 295	2 233 880	2 208 415	4 843 947	2 436 945	2 407 002
0-4	520 132	265 967	254 165	542 093	277 212	264 881	540 080	276 177	263 903	581 955	297 826	284 129
5-9	458 395	234 783	223 612	502 136	257 405	244 731	523 700	268 228	255 472	522 552	267 466	255 085
10-14	402 204	206 102	196 102	453 336	232 496	220 839	497 193	254 867	242 326	519 582	266 112	253 471
15-19	365 417	186 890	178 527	397 339	203 739	193 601	448 228	229 673	218 554	493 914	253 080	240 834
20-24	299 401	152 751	146 650	359 817	183 697	176 120	391 969	200 817	191 153	443 760	227 004	216 757
25-29	249 646	126 834	122 811	295 290	150 600	144 690	354 936	181 112	173 824	387 652	198 204	189 448
30-34	237 125	120 522	116 603	245 145	124 529	120 616	291 820	148 522	143 298	350 608	178 650	171 958
35-39	216 093	109 986	106 107	232 725	118 094	114 632	239 790	121 703	118 087	287 422	146 013	141 409
40-44	198 181	99 842	98 339	210 860	107 143	103 717	228 377	115 577	112 800	234 913	118 814	116 099
45-49	169 992	83 704	86 288	192 424	96 558	95 866	204 357	103 362	100 996	221 498	111 371	110 127
50-54	138 186	67 456	70 730	163 201	79 617	83 584	185 196	92 249	92 947	196 228	98 294	97 934
55-59	129 919	61 871	68 047	129 637	62 400	67 238	154 294	74 286	80 008	174 832	85 877	88 955
60-64	108 783	50 690	58 092	118 078	55 113	62 965	118 407	55 924	62 483	141 467	66 733	74 734
65-69	83 367	37 388	45 979	94 333	42 505	51 829	102 404	46 374	56 030	103 500	47 390	56 110
70-74	56 337	23 953	32 384	66 302	28 408	37 893	77 015	33 109	43 906	84 257	36 390	47 868
75-79	36 665	15 280	21 384	39 574	15 792	23 781	48 580	19 450	29 130	56 116	22 571	33 545
80 +	26 746	9 945	16 801	31 451	11 552	19 899	35 948	12 450	23 498	43 691	15 151	28 540

Age group	1990 Both sexes	Males	Females	1995 Both sexes	Males	Females	2000 Both sexes	Males	Females	2005 Both sexes	Males	Females
All ages	5 279 519	2 658 290	2 621 229	5 692 353	2 865 516	2 826 837	6 085 572	3 060 338	3 025 234	6 464 750	3 248 919	3 215 831
0-4	625 813	321 294	304 520	621 141	318 870	302 270	613 840	314 912	298 928	617 149	316 403	300 746
5-9	566 910	290 505	276 404	610 563	313 665	296 897	607 066	311 719	295 348	600 596	308 175	292 421
10-14	519 906	266 137	253 769	563 200	288 519	274 681	606 996	311 731	295 265	603 299	309 720	293 579
15-19	514 729	263 314	251 415	516 082	263 963	252 119	560 166	286 788	273 378	603 908	309 941	293 967
20-24	487 227	248 511	238 716	507 854	259 205	248 649	510 560	260 545	250 015	554 967	283 559	271 407
25-29	438 148	223 299	214 849	480 571	244 462	236 109	501 166	255 040	246 126	503 445	256 343	247 101
30-34	383 536	195 934	187 602	432 532	219 769	212 762	473 435	240 045	233 389	492 699	250 214	242 485
35-39	346 068	176 119	169 950	377 555	192 193	185 363	425 102	215 140	209 962	464 766	235 005	229 761
40-44	282 145	143 058	139 087	339 557	172 124	167 433	369 864	187 377	182 486	416 318	209 863	206 455
45-49	229 188	115 450	113 738	275 447	138 894	136 553	331 077	166 713	164 364	360 710	181 700	179 010
50-54	213 541	106 641	106 900	221 633	110 679	110 954	266 200	132 957	133 243	320 515	160 070	160 445
55-59	185 796	92 038	93 758	202 734	99 853	102 881	210 859	103 886	106 973	253 992	125 352	128 641
60-64	161 105	77 594	83 511	171 720	83 373	88 348	187 891	90 656	97 235	196 667	95 224	101 443
65-69	124 648	57 133	67 515	142 753	66 688	76 065	152 784	72 085	80 699	168 235	79 019	89 215
70-74	85 385	37 498	47 887	103 672	45 448	58 224	119 287	53 411	65 876	128 935	58 559	70 376
75-79	62 330	25 272	37 057	63 768	26 331	37 437	79 026	32 576	46 450	91 901	38 969	52 932
80 +	53 044	18 493	34 551	61 571	21 479	40 091	70 254	24 758	45 495	86 648	30 804	55 844

United Nations Department of Economic and Social Affairs/Population Division
World Population Prospects: The 2004 Revision, Volume II: Sex and Age Distribution of the World Population

20

POPULATION BY AGE AND SEX (in thousands)

Age group	2005 Both sexes	Males	Females	2010 Both sexes	Males	Females	2015 Both sexes	Males	Females	2020 Both sexes	Males	Females
All ages	6 464 750	3 248 919	3 215 831	6 842 923	3 436 848	3 406 075	7 219 431	3 623 546	3 595 885	7 577 889	3 800 469	3 777 420
0-4	617 149	316 403	300 746	632 987	324 453	308 534	647 844	332 039	315 805	647 342	331 693	315 649
5-9	600 596	308 175	292 421	604 673	310 015	294 658	621 557	318 538	303 019	637 732	326 749	310 983
10-14	603 299	309 720	293 579	596 751	306 139	290 612	600 892	308 007	292 885	618 076	316 675	301 401
15-19	603 908	309 941	293 967	600 530	308 098	292 432	594 213	304 640	289 573	598 530	306 601	291 929
20-24	554 967	283 559	271 407	599 042	306 893	292 149	596 093	305 304	290 789	590 193	302 101	288 092
25-29	503 445	256 343	247 101	547 701	279 307	268 394	591 880	302 710	289 170	589 439	301 466	287 972
30-34	492 699	250 214	242 485	494 597	251 422	243 175	538 477	274 237	264 240	582 537	297 630	284 907
35-39	464 766	235 005	229 761	483 327	244 875	238 451	485 107	246 105	239 002	528 408	268 671	259 737
40-44	416 318	209 863	206 455	455 447	229 493	225 954	473 846	239 300	234 546	475 599	240 576	235 023
45-49	360 710	181 700	179 010	406 679	203 967	202 712	445 668	223 555	222 113	464 042	233 340	230 701
50-54	320 515	160 070	160 445	349 729	174 821	174 908	395 306	196 891	198 415	434 141	216 395	217 746
55-59	253 992	125 352	128 641	306 723	151 458	155 265	335 515	165 933	169 582	380 487	187 646	192 841
60-64	196 667	95 224	101 443	238 058	115 546	122 512	288 478	140 169	148 308	316 577	154 173	162 404
65-69	168 235	79 019	89 215	177 555	83 920	93 635	216 374	102 585	113 790	263 400	125 080	138 321
70-74	128 935	58 559	70 376	143 154	64 828	78 326	152 724	69 795	82 930	187 745	86 126	101 619
75-79	91 901	38 969	52 932	100 557	43 393	57 164	112 863	48 624	64 239	122 106	53 235	68 872
80-84	53 212	20 226	32 986	62 669	24 624	38 045	69 610	27 908	41 702	79 266	31 789	47 478
85-89	22 751	7 718	15 033	29 930	10 130	19 800	35 857	12 594	23 263	40 625	14 568	26 057
90-94	8 491	2 375	6 116	9 826	2 814	7 012	13 398	3 802	9 596	16 421	4 849	11 572
95-99	1 929	436	1 493	2 596	580	2 017	3 165	711	2 454	4 489	985	3 505
100 +	265	50	216	392	71	321	560	97	463	733	122	611

Age group	2025 Both sexes	Males	Females	2030 Both sexes	Males	Females	2035 Both sexes	Males	Females	2040 Both sexes	Males	Females
All ages	7 905 239	3 960 700	3 944 539	8 199 104	4 103 073	4 096 032	8 463 265	4 230 138	4 233 127	8 701 319	4 344 282	4 357 037
0-4	635 905	325 722	310 183	624 428	319 583	304 845	619 965	317 265	302 700	621 236	317 918	303 319
5-9	638 575	327 067	311 509	628 376	321 715	306 662	618 018	316 147	301 871	614 493	314 303	300 190
10-14	631 769	325 144	309 626	636 103	325 705	310 398	626 354	320 583	305 771	616 373	315 210	301 163
15-19	615 903	315 364	300 539	632 798	323 933	308 865	634 364	324 615	309 749	624 845	319 616	305 229
20-24	594 745	304 191	290 554	612 293	313 041	299 252	629 387	321 722	307 665	631 209	322 553	308 656
25-29	583 984	298 527	285 457	588 852	300 790	288 062	606 699	309 806	296 893	624 130	318 679	305 451
30-34	580 547	296 688	283 859	575 645	294 072	281 573	580 988	296 607	284 381	599 266	305 864	293 402
35-39	572 223	291 965	280 258	570 701	291 300	279 391	566 507	289 160	277 347	572 385	292 016	280 369
40-44	518 415	262 912	255 503	562 119	286 170	275 950	561 244	285 990	275 255	557 601	284 164	273 437
45-49	465 986	234 768	231 218	508 516	256 958	251 558	552 110	280 176	271 934	551 823	280 402	271 421
50-54	452 598	226 210	226 388	454 953	227 899	227 054	497 140	249 882	247 259	540 524	272 982	267 542
55-59	418 986	206 930	212 055	437 590	216 797	220 793	440 437	218 782	221 656	482 091	240 418	241 673
60-64	360 452	175 198	185 254	398 253	194 019	204 234	416 921	203 862	213 059	420 372	206 194	214 178
65-69	290 323	138 301	152 022	332 305	158 169	174 135	368 720	176 083	192 637	387 233	185 746	201 487
70-74	229 798	105 630	124 168	254 828	117 664	137 164	293 646	135 645	158 001	327 576	151 973	175 602
75-79	151 811	66 460	85 351	187 086	82 109	104 977	209 175	92 344	116 830	243 082	107 478	135 604
80-84	87 294	35 499	51 795	110 173	45 013	65 160	136 829	56 060	80 769	154 660	63 833	90 827
85-89	47 127	16 928	30 199	53 152	19 406	33 746	68 394	25 099	43 295	85 634	31 500	54 134
90-94	19 073	5 737	13 336	22 646	6 846	15 800	26 312	8 101	18 211	34 616	10 721	23 895
95-99	5 666	1 291	4 375	6 798	1 569	5 230	8 278	1 928	6 349	9 942	2 358	7 584
100 +	1 058	168	890	1 408	225	1 183	1 775	280	1 495	2 226	352	1 874

Age group	2045 Both sexes	Males	Females	2050 Both sexes	Males	Females
All ages	8 907 417	4 442 962	4 464 455	9 075 903	4 523 474	4 552 428
0-4	616 551	315 509	301 041	604 373	309 246	295 127
5-9	616 597	315 374	301 223	612 670	313 347	299 322
10-14	613 160	313 525	299 635	615 530	314 727	300 803
15-19	615 074	314 355	300 719	612 046	312 766	299 280
20-24	621 962	317 712	304 250	612 458	312 603	299 855
25-29	626 389	319 751	306 638	617 635	315 178	302 457
30-34	617 189	314 998	302 191	620 090	316 401	303 690
35-39	591 138	301 541	289 597	609 597	310 960	298 637
40-44	563 981	287 333	276 648	583 156	297 109	286 048
45-49	548 801	278 980	269 821	555 630	282 438	273 193
50-54	540 858	273 625	267 233	538 484	272 626	265 858
55-59	525 036	263 234	261 802	526 080	264 345	261 736
60-64	461 124	227 224	233 900	503 215	249 467	253 748
65-69	391 383	188 451	202 932	430 578	208 450	222 128
70-74	345 518	161 154	184 364	350 409	164 204	186 205
75-79	273 061	121 376	151 685	289 727	129 607	160 120
80-84	181 681	75 173	106 508	205 929	85 742	120 187
85-89	98 200	36 476	61 724	116 980	43 611	73 368
90-94	43 568	13 531	30 037	50 770	15 995	34 775
95-99	13 377	3 200	10 178	16 806	4 049	12 757
100 +	2 768	441	2 327	3 739	604	3 135

POPULATION BY AGE AND SEX (in thousands)

Age group	2005 Both sexes	2005 Males	2005 Females	2010 Both sexes	2010 Males	2010 Females	2015 Both sexes	2015 Males	2015 Females	2020 Both sexes	2020 Males	2020 Females
All ages	6 464 750	3 248 919	3 215 831	6 903 276	3 467 899	3 435 377	7 382 434	3 707 364	3 675 070	7 873 172	3 952 211	3 920 961
0-4	617 149	316 403	300 746	693 340	355 503	337 837	751 161	385 152	366 009	780 905	400 294	380 611
5-9	600 596	308 175	292 421	604 673	310 016	294 657	681 243	349 242	332 001	739 990	379 307	360 683
10-14	603 299	309 720	293 579	596 751	306 140	290 611	600 892	308 008	292 884	677 538	347 257	330 281
15-19	603 908	309 941	293 967	600 530	308 098	292 432	594 213	304 641	289 572	598 530	306 602	291 928
20-24	554 967	283 559	271 407	599 042	306 893	292 149	596 093	305 304	290 789	590 193	302 102	288 091
25-29	503 445	256 343	247 101	547 701	279 307	268 394	591 880	302 710	289 170	589 439	301 466	287 972
30-34	492 699	250 214	242 485	494 597	251 422	243 175	538 477	274 237	264 240	582 537	297 630	284 907
35-39	464 766	235 005	229 761	483 327	244 875	238 451	485 107	246 105	239 002	528 408	268 671	259 737
40-44	416 318	209 863	206 455	455 447	229 493	225 954	473 846	239 300	234 546	475 599	240 576	235 023
45-49	360 710	181 700	179 010	406 679	203 967	202 712	445 668	223 555	222 113	464 042	233 340	230 702
50-54	320 515	160 070	160 445	349 729	174 821	174 908	395 306	196 891	198 415	434 141	216 395	217 746
55-59	253 992	125 352	128 641	306 723	151 458	155 265	335 515	165 933	169 582	380 488	187 646	192 841
60-64	196 667	95 224	101 443	238 058	115 546	122 512	288 478	140 169	148 308	316 577	154 173	162 404
65-69	168 235	79 019	89 215	177 555	83 920	93 635	216 375	102 585	113 790	263 400	125 080	138 321
70-74	128 935	58 559	70 376	143 154	64 828	78 326	152 724	69 795	82 930	187 745	86 126	101 619
75-79	91 901	38 969	52 932	100 557	43 393	57 164	112 863	48 624	64 239	122 106	53 235	68 872
80-84	53 212	20 226	32 986	62 669	24 624	38 045	69 610	27 908	41 702	79 266	31 789	47 478
85-89	22 751	7 718	15 033	29 930	10 130	19 800	35 857	12 594	23 263	40 625	14 568	26 057
90-94	8 491	2 375	6 116	9 826	2 814	7 012	13 398	3 802	9 596	16 421	4 849	11 572
95-99	1 929	436	1 493	2 596	580	2 017	3 165	711	2 454	4 489	985	3 505
100 +	265	50	216	392	71	321	560	97	463	733	122	611

Age group	2025 Both sexes	2025 Males	2025 Females	2030 Both sexes	2030 Males	2030 Females	2035 Both sexes	2035 Males	2035 Females	2040 Both sexes	2040 Males	2040 Females
All ages	8 336 867	4 182 374	4 154 493	8 784 155	4 403 317	4 380 838	9 237 907	4 627 451	4 610 457	9 709 446	4 861 127	4 848 319
0-4	773 986	396 592	377 394	779 897	399 294	380 603	812 134	415 799	396 335	858 172	439 409	418 764
5-9	770 911	395 016	375 895	765 312	391 972	373 340	772 346	395 244	377 103	805 444	412 175	393 269
10-14	736 677	377 510	359 168	768 029	393 427	374 602	762 914	390 630	372 284	770 333	394 099	376 234
15-19	675 205	345 850	329 354	734 445	376 143	358 302	765 975	392 148	373 827	761 100	389 480	371 621
20-24	594 745	304 192	290 553	671 364	343 382	327 982	730 657	373 696	356 961	762 357	389 797	372 561
25-29	583 984	298 528	285 456	588 852	300 791	288 062	665 402	339 932	325 470	724 802	370 309	354 494
30-34	580 548	296 688	283 859	575 645	294 072	281 573	580 988	296 608	284 380	657 468	335 719	321 749
35-39	572 223	291 965	280 258	570 782	291 390	279 391	566 508	289 161	277 346	572 385	292 017	280 368
40-44	518 415	262 912	255 503	562 120	286 170	275 950	561 245	285 990	275 255	557 601	284 165	273 436
45-49	465 986	234 768	231 218	508 516	256 958	251 558	552 110	280 176	271 934	551 824	280 402	271 421
50-54	452 598	226 210	226 388	454 953	227 899	227 054	497 141	249 882	247 259	540 525	272 982	267 542
55-59	418 986	206 930	212 055	437 590	216 797	220 793	440 438	218 782	221 656	482 092	240 418	241 674
60-64	360 452	175 198	185 254	398 253	194 019	204 234	416 921	203 862	213 059	420 372	206 194	214 178
65-69	290 323	138 301	152 022	332 305	158 169	174 135	368 721	176 083	192 638	387 233	185 746	201 488
70-74	229 798	105 630	124 168	254 828	117 664	137 164	293 646	135 645	158 001	327 576	151 974	175 602
75-79	151 811	66 460	85 351	187 087	82 109	104 977	209 175	92 344	116 830	243 082	107 478	135 604
80-84	87 294	35 499	51 795	110 173	45 013	65 160	136 829	56 060	80 769	154 660	63 833	90 827
85-89	47 127	16 928	30 199	53 152	19 406	33 746	68 394	25 099	43 295	85 634	31 501	54 134
90-94	19 073	5 737	13 336	22 646	6 846	15 800	26 312	8 101	18 211	34 616	10 721	23 895
95-99	5 666	1 291	4 375	6 798	1 569	5 230	8 278	1 928	6 349	9 942	2 358	7 584
100 +	1 058	168	890	1 408	225	1 183	1 775	280	1 495	2 226	352	1 874

Age group	2045 Both sexes	2045 Males	2045 Females	2050 Both sexes	2050 Males	2050 Females
All ages	10 184 739	5 097 576	5 087 163	10 646 311	5 328 002	5 318 309
0-4	890 269	455 828	434 441	903 065	462 318	440 747
5-9	852 245	436 155	416 090	885 105	452 950	432 155
10-14	803 721	411 173	392 547	850 767	435 268	415 499
15-19	768 717	393 052	375 666	802 256	410 200	392 056
20-24	757 766	387 293	370 473	765 630	391 004	374 626
25-29	756 806	386 577	370 230	752 737	384 359	368 378
30-34	717 057	366 198	350 859	749 532	382 711	366 821
35-39	648 798	331 100	317 698	708 598	361 694	346 904
40-44	563 982	287 334	276 647	640 271	326 357	313 913
45-49	548 802	278 981	269 821	555 630	282 439	273 192
50-54	540 858	273 625	267 233	538 484	272 626	265 858
55-59	525 037	263 235	261 802	526 081	264 345	261 736
60-64	461 124	227 224	233 900	503 216	249 468	253 748
65-69	391 383	188 451	202 932	430 578	208 450	222 128
70-74	345 518	161 154	184 364	350 410	164 204	186 205
75-79	273 061	121 376	151 685	289 727	129 607	160 120
80-84	181 682	75 173	106 508	205 930	85 742	120 188
85-89	98 200	36 476	61 724	116 980	43 611	73 368
90-94	43 568	13 531	30 037	50 770	15 995	34 775
95-99	13 377	3 200	10 178	16 806	4 049	12 757
100 +	2 768	441	2 327	3 739	604	3 135

United Nations Department of Economic and Social Affairs/Population Division
World Population Prospects: The 2004 Revision, Volume II: Sex and Age Distribution of the World Population

POPULATION BY AGE AND SEX (in thousands)

Age group	2005			2010			2015			2020		
	Both sexes	Males	Females	Both sexes	Males	Females	Both sexes	Males	Females	Both sexes	Males	Females
All ages	6 464 750	3 248 919	3 215 831	6 781 431	3 405 228	3 376 203	7 054 584	3 538 811	3 515 773	7 280 148	3 647 499	3 632 649
0-4	617 149	316 403	300 746	571 495	292 832	278 663	543 773	278 551	265 222	513 136	262 764	250 372
5-9	600 596	308 175	292 421	604 673	310 016	294 657	560 782	287 289	273 492	534 729	273 824	260 906
10-14	603 299	309 720	293 579	596 751	306 140	290 611	600 892	308 008	292 884	557 545	285 559	271 986
15-19	603 908	309 941	293 967	600 530	308 098	292 432	594 213	304 641	289 572	598 530	306 602	291 928
20-24	554 967	283 559	271 407	599 042	306 893	292 149	596 093	305 304	290 789	590 193	302 102	288 091
25-29	503 445	256 343	247 101	547 701	279 307	268 394	591 880	302 710	289 170	589 438	301 466	287 972
30-34	492 699	250 214	242 485	494 597	251 422	243 175	538 477	274 237	264 240	582 537	297 630	284 907
35-39	464 766	235 005	229 761	483 327	244 875	238 451	485 107	246 105	239 002	528 408	268 670	259 737
40-44	416 318	209 863	206 455	455 447	229 493	225 953	473 846	239 300	234 546	475 599	240 576	235 023
45-49	360 710	181 700	179 010	406 679	203 967	202 712	445 668	223 555	222 113	464 042	233 340	230 701
50-54	320 515	160 070	160 445	349 729	174 821	174 908	395 306	196 891	198 415	434 141	216 395	217 746
55-59	253 992	125 352	128 641	306 723	151 458	155 265	335 515	165 933	169 582	380 487	187 646	192 841
60-64	196 667	95 224	101 443	238 058	115 546	122 512	288 478	140 169	148 308	316 577	154 173	162 404
65-69	168 235	79 019	89 215	177 555	83 920	93 635	216 374	102 585	113 790	263 400	125 080	138 320
70-74	128 935	58 559	70 376	143 154	64 828	78 326	152 724	69 795	82 930	187 745	86 126	101 619
75-79	91 901	38 969	52 932	100 557	43 393	57 164	112 863	48 624	64 239	122 106	53 235	68 872
80-84	53 212	20 226	32 986	62 669	24 624	38 045	69 610	27 908	41 702	79 266	31 789	47 478
85-89	22 751	7 718	15 033	29 930	10 130	19 800	35 857	12 594	23 263	40 625	14 568	26 057
90-94	8 491	2 375	6 116	9 826	2 814	7 012	13 398	3 802	9 596	16 421	4 849	11 572
95-99	1 929	436	1 493	2 596	580	2 017	3 165	711	2 454	4 489	985	3 505
100 +	265	50	216	392	71	321	560	97	463	733	122	611

Age group	2025			2030			2035			2040		
	Both sexes	Males	Females	Both sexes	Males	Females	Both sexes	Males	Females	Both sexes	Males	Females
All ages	7 471 426	3 737 040	3 733 485	7 618 083	3 804 943	3 813 140	7 712 423	3 845 110	3 867 313	7 753 745	3 858 606	3 895 139
0-4	498 069	254 979	243 090	475 152	243 059	232 093	447 560	228 896	218 664	421 090	215 334	205 756
5-9	505 600	258 791	246 809	491 686	251 585	240 101	469 856	240 224	229 633	443 224	226 553	216 671
10-14	532 126	272 415	250 711	503 539	257 807	245 802	490 040	250 664	239 376	468 573	239 490	229 083
15-19	555 544	284 350	271 194	530 422	271 364	259 058	502 117	256 758	245 359	498 835	249 880	248 955
20-24	594 745	304 192	290 553	552 179	282 181	269 998	527 395	269 394	258 001	499 425	254 985	244 440
25-29	583 984	298 527	285 456	588 852	300 791	288 062	546 979	279 174	267 805	522 753	266 705	256 048
30-34	580 547	296 688	283 859	575 645	294 072	281 573	580 988	296 608	284 380	540 081	275 520	264 561
35-39	572 223	291 965	280 258	570 701	291 390	279 391	566 507	289 161	277 346	572 385	292 017	280 368
40-44	518 415	262 912	255 503	562 119	286 170	275 049	561 244	285 989	275 255	557 600	284 165	273 436
45-49	465 986	234 768	231 218	508 516	256 958	251 558	552 110	280 176	271 934	551 823	280 402	271 421
50-54	452 598	226 210	226 388	454 953	227 900	227 054	497 140	249 802	247 268	540 524	272 982	267 542
55-59	418 985	206 930	212 055	437 590	216 797	220 792	440 437	218 781	221 656	482 091	240 418	241 670
60-64	360 452	175 198	185 254	398 253	194 019	204 234	416 921	203 862	213 059	420 372	206 194	214 178
65-69	290 323	138 301	152 022	332 305	158 169	174 135	368 720	176 083	192 637	387 233	185 746	201 487
70-74	229 708	105 639	124 168	254 828	117 664	137 164	293 646	135 645	158 001	327 576	151 973	175 602
75-79	151 811	66 460	85 351	187 086	82 109	104 977	209 173	92 344	116 830	243 082	107 478	135 604
80-84	87 294	35 499	51 795	110 173	45 013	65 160	136 829	56 060	80 769	154 660	63 833	90 827
85-89	47 127	16 928	30 199	53 152	19 406	33 746	68 394	25 099	43 295	85 634	31 500	54 134
90-94	19 073	5 737	13 336	22 646	6 846	15 800	26 312	8 101	18 211	34 616	10 721	23 895
95-99	5 666	1 291	4 375	6 798	1 569	5 230	8 278	1 928	6 349	9 942	2 358	7 584
100 +	1 058	168	890	1 409	225	1 183	1 775	280	1 495	2 226	352	1 874

Age group	2045			2050		
	Both sexes	Males	Females	Both sexes	Males	Females
All ages	7 741 810	3 845 776	3 896 034	7 679 714	3 808 429	3 871 285
0-4	394 108	201 519	192 590	368 384	188 347	180 036
5-9	417 594	213 420	204 174	391 326	199 970	191 356
10-14	442 256	225 983	216 273	416 892	212 985	203 907
15-19	467 581	238 821	228 760	441 469	225 423	216 045
20-24	486 403	248 258	238 146	465 426	237 357	228 069
25-29	495 341	252 604	242 737	482 780	246 124	236 656
30-34	516 640	263 465	253 176	490 023	249 772	240 251
35-39	532 532	271 510	261 022	509 942	259 906	250 036
40-44	563 981	287 334	276 647	525 129	267 406	257 723
45-49	548 801	278 981	269 820	555 630	282 438	273 192
50-54	540 858	273 625	267 233	538 483	272 626	265 857
55-59	525 036	263 234	261 802	526 080	264 345	261 735
60-64	461 124	227 224	233 900	503 215	249 467	253 748
65-69	391 382	188 450	202 932	430 577	208 450	222 127
70-74	345 518	161 154	184 364	350 409	164 204	186 205
75-79	273 061	121 376	151 685	289 727	129 607	160 120
80-84	181 681	75 173	106 508	205 929	85 742	120 187
85-89	98 200	36 476	61 724	116 980	43 611	73 368
90-94	43 568	13 531	30 037	50 770	15 995	34 775
95-99	13 377	3 200	10 178	16 806	4 049	12 757
100 +	2 768	441	2 327	3 739	604	3 135

POPULATION BY AGE AND SEX (in thousands)

Age group	1950 Both sexes	Males	Females	1955 Both sexes	Males	Females	1960 Both sexes	Males	Females	1965 Both sexes	Males	Females
All ages	812 772	387 257	425 515	863 220	412 835	450 385	915 300	439 115	476 185	966 633	465 232	501 402
0-4	81 556	41 663	39 893	86 811	44 429	42 382	89 769	45 852	43 916	89 338	45 693	43 645
5-9	68 224	34 626	33 598	80 993	41 344	39 649	86 499	44 217	42 283	89 592	45 733	43 859
10-14	72 534	36 620	35 914	68 366	34 670	33 695	80 924	41 251	39 673	86 548	44 228	42 320
15-19	67 671	34 043	33 627	72 022	36 218	35 805	67 773	34 213	33 559	80 884	41 115	39 769
20-24	70 708	34 708	35 999	66 888	33 373	33 515	71 417	35 729	35 688	67 665	33 916	33 749
25-29	63 193	29 432	33 762	70 117	34 334	35 783	66 583	33 287	33 295	71 519	35 811	35 708
30-34	50 496	23 498	26 999	62 825	29 202	33 622	69 590	34 018	35 572	66 596	33 331	33 265
35-39	58 881	27 094	31 787	49 779	23 105	26 674	62 142	28 786	33 356	69 317	33 839	35 477
40-44	56 119	26 256	29 863	58 117	26 668	31 449	49 111	22 716	26 395	61 574	28 438	33 135
45-49	49 359	23 056	26 303	54 161	25 226	28 935	56 893	25 941	30 952	48 111	22 120	25 991
50-54	42 887	19 690	23 197	48 413	22 350	26 063	52 900	24 386	28 514	55 072	24 874	30 198
55-59	35 797	16 106	19 690	40 361	18 176	22 185	46 051	20 850	25 201	50 507	22 847	27 659
60-64	31 314	13 877	17 436	33 166	14 548	18 618	37 394	16 378	21 016	42 458	18 718	23 739
65-69	25 243	10 921	14 322	27 534	11 771	15 763	29 267	12 351	16 917	33 044	13 872	19 172
70-74	18 563	7 823	10 740	20 374	8 442	11 933	22 452	9 133	13 319	24 275	9 685	14 590
75-79	11 709	4 734	6 976	13 297	5 324	7 973	14 836	5 801	9 034	16 580	6 297	10 283
80 +	8 518	3 110	5 408	9 995	3 654	6 341	11 699	4 206	7 493	13 556	4 714	8 842

Age group	1970 Both sexes	Males	Females	1975 Both sexes	Males	Females	1980 Both sexes	Males	Females	1985 Both sexes	Males	Females
All ages	1 007 673	485 738	521 935	1 047 196	505 725	541 471	1 082 539	523 379	559 161	1 114 785	539 588	575 197
0-4	82 711	42 312	40 399	81 129	41 527	39 603	78 444	40 162	38 283	78 462	40 159	38 303
5-9	89 351	45 659	43 692	83 086	42 460	40 626	81 242	41 559	39 683	78 331	40 066	38 265
10-14	89 914	45 904	44 010	89 441	45 736	43 705	83 452	42 648	40 803	81 933	41 920	40 013
15-19	86 382	43 971	42 411	89 665	45 682	43 983	89 486	45 699	43 786	84 524	43 199	41 326
20-24	80 109	40 317	39 792	86 643	43 834	42 809	90 119	45 820	44 299	90 271	45 902	44 369
25-29	67 537	33 932	33 605	81 094	41 023	40 071	87 017	43 955	43 062	90 411	45 696	44 715
30-34	71 225	35 623	35 602	67 644	33 977	33 668	81 734	41 148	40 586	86 971	43 727	43 245
35-39	66 013	32 969	33 043	70 900	35 305	35 595	66 433	33 222	33 211	81 220	40 694	40 525
40-44	68 416	33 274	35 142	65 408	32 512	32 895	70 525	34 930	35 595	65 993	32 794	33 199
45-49	60 375	27 755	32 620	67 115	32 401	34 714	63 991	31 526	32 464	68 921	33 833	35 088
50-54	46 657	21 247	25 410	58 881	26 674	32 207	65 337	31 229	34 109	62 230	30 269	31 961
55-59	52 493	23 291	29 201	44 689	19 956	24 733	56 882	25 314	31 568	62 649	29 385	33 264
60-64	46 848	20 607	26 241	48 996	21 176	27 819	41 925	18 248	23 676	53 466	23 194	30 272
65-69	38 006	16 017	21 989	42 066	17 665	24 401	43 486	18 006	25 480	38 118	15 972	22 146
70-74	27 573	10 853	16 720	31 514	12 484	19 030	35 843	14 163	21 680	37 948	14 848	23 099
75-79	18 121	6 684	11 437	20 548	7 455	13 093	24 673	8 977	15 696	27 684	10 081	17 603
80 +	15 943	5 322	10 621	18 378	5 858	12 520	21 951	6 773	15 178	25 654	7 850	17 804

Age group	1990 Both sexes	Males	Females	1995 Both sexes	Males	Females	2000 Both sexes	Males	Females	2005 Both sexes	Males	Females
All ages	1 148 572	556 821	591 752	1 173 983	569 773	604 210	1 193 354	578 859	614 495	1 211 265	587 635	623 630
0-4	78 036	39 965	38 071	71 303	36 554	34 748	66 126	33 918	32 208	66 119	33 932	32 187
5-9	78 804	40 255	38 549	78 781	40 333	38 448	72 088	36 931	35 157	66 739	34 223	32 515
10-14	79 181	40 448	38 733	79 997	40 845	39 152	80 153	41 008	39 145	73 014	37 401	35 612
15-19	82 830	42 301	40 529	80 629	41 176	39 453	81 941	41 860	40 081	81 687	41 778	39 909
20-24	84 728	43 041	41 688	83 909	42 734	41 174	82 086	41 735	40 351	83 673	42 612	41 061
25-29	90 651	45 790	44 861	85 939	43 475	42 463	85 322	43 140	42 182	83 598	42 324	41 274
30-34	91 196	45 810	45 386	91 520	46 038	45 482	86 984	43 759	43 225	86 387	43 500	42 887
35-39	87 211	43 606	43 606	91 131	45 533	45 598	91 596	45 797	45 799	87 325	43 727	43 599
40-44	80 599	40 217	40 382	86 490	42 973	43 517	90 296	44 772	45 525	91 111	45 286	45 825
45-49	65 277	32 295	32 981	79 561	39 403	40 158	85 035	41 845	43 190	89 176	43 869	45 307
50-54	67 363	32 783	34 580	64 056	31 330	32 726	77 749	38 032	39 717	83 293	40 542	42 751
55-59	59 976	28 746	31 230	64 704	30 914	33 790	61 859	29 767	32 092	75 062	36 193	38 869
60-64	59 314	27 131	32 182	56 641	26 457	30 184	61 108	28 432	32 677	59 037	27 853	31 184
65-69	48 892	20 529	28 363	54 156	23 867	30 289	51 874	23 426	28 448	56 124	25 284	30 840
70-74	33 619	13 447	20 172	42 773	17 111	25 662	47 252	19 855	27 397	45 757	19 789	25 968
75-79	30 118	10 971	19 147	27 038	10 124	16 915	34 966	13 094	21 872	38 695	15 320	23 376
80 +	30 779	9 488	21 292	35 356	10 905	24 451	36 918	11 489	25 429	44 469	14 002	30 467

(*) More developed regions comprise Europe, Northern America, Australia/New Zealand and Japan.

United Nations Department of Economic and Social Affairs/Population Division
World Population Prospects: The 2004 Revision, Volume II: Sex and Age Distribution of the World Population

24

POPULATION BY AGE AND SEX (in thousands)

Age group	2005 Both sexes	2005 Males	2005 Females	2010 Both sexes	2010 Males	2010 Females	2015 Both sexes	2015 Males	2015 Females	2020 Both sexes	2020 Males	2020 Females
All ages	1 211 265	587 635	623 630	1 225 678	594 532	631 145	1 236 561	599 731	636 829	1 244 413	603 443	640 970
0-4	66 119	33 932	32 187	66 676	34 220	32 455	65 936	33 841	32 095	64 729	33 222	31 508
5-9	66 739	34 223	32 515	66 680	34 205	32 474	67 207	34 479	32 728	66 474	34 104	32 370
10-14	73 014	37 401	35 612	67 621	34 672	32 948	67 525	34 636	32 888	68 049	34 908	33 141
15-19	81 687	41 778	39 909	74 448	38 114	36 334	69 016	35 370	33 646	68 922	35 336	33 586
20-24	83 673	42 612	41 061	83 201	42 415	40 786	75 960	38 776	37 185	70 573	36 067	34 506
25-29	83 598	42 324	41 274	84 864	43 035	41 829	84 366	42 849	41 517	77 262	39 312	37 950
30-34	86 387	43 500	42 887	84 334	42 515	41 819	85 499	43 191	42 308	85 085	43 073	42 012
35-39	87 325	43 727	43 599	86 483	43 342	43 141	84 367	42 348	42 019	85 547	43 050	42 496
40-44	91 111	45 286	45 825	86 840	43 254	43 587	85 979	42 877	43 102	83 918	41 937	41 981
45-49	89 176	43 869	45 307	90 038	44 437	45 601	85 964	42 564	43 400	85 182	42 250	42 932
50-54	83 293	40 542	42 751	87 406	42 555	44 851	88 437	43 258	45 180	84 673	41 606	43 067
55-59	75 062	36 193	38 869	80 472	38 608	41 864	84 628	40 658	43 970	85 911	41 537	44 374
60-64	59 037	27 853	31 184	71 688	33 907	37 781	76 899	36 203	40 697	81 089	38 279	42 810
65-69	56 124	25 284	30 840	54 866	25 204	29 661	66 795	30 790	36 005	71 765	32 944	38 821
70-74	45 757	19 789	25 968	49 669	21 460	28 209	49 299	21 846	27 453	60 239	26 820	33 418
75-79	38 695	15 320	23 376	38 032	15 550	22 482	41 501	16 988	24 514	41 989	17 715	24 274
80-84	25 653	8 782	16 871	28 603	10 392	18 211	28 699	10 798	17 901	31 602	11 945	19 657
85-89	11 816	3 582	8 234	15 975	4 827	11 148	18 101	5 829	12 272	18 704	6 242	12 462
90-94	5 459	1 345	4 113	5 715	1 439	4 275	7 954	1 993	5 961	9 265	2 482	6 783
95-99	1 353	264	1 089	1 792	341	1 451	2 031	386	1 645	2 936	552	2 383
100 +	188	28	160	277	39	238	396	52	344	501	63	438

Age group	2025 Both sexes	2025 Males	2025 Females	2030 Both sexes	2030 Males	2030 Females	2035 Both sexes	2035 Males	2035 Females	2040 Both sexes	2040 Males	2040 Females
All ages	1 248 954	605 461	643 493	1 250 658	606 038	644 620	1 249 903	605 533	644 370	1 247 071	604 307	642 765
0-4	63 288	32 481	30 806	62 734	32 198	30 536	63 030	32 351	30 679	63 741	32 717	31 024
5-9	65 277	33 489	31 787	63 844	32 754	31 089	63 297	32 475	30 822	63 597	32 630	30 967
10-14	67 322	34 307	32 706	66 130	33 926	32 204	64 703	33 194	31 509	64 160	32 917	31 243
15-19	69 450	35 612	33 838	68 730	35 246	33 485	67 546	34 640	32 906	66 127	33 911	32 213
20-24	70 493	36 045	34 448	71 034	36 331	34 703	70 329	35 976	34 352	69 161	35 383	33 778
25-29	71 942	36 654	35 288	71 877	36 647	35 230	72 430	36 944	35 486	71 748	36 607	35 141
30-34	78 154	39 657	38 497	72 916	37 059	35 857	72 867	37 067	35 800	73 436	37 379	36 057
35-39	85 210	42 999	42 220	78 469	39 700	38 761	73 331	37 179	36 152	73 305	37 208	36 098
40-44	85 130	42 671	42 459	84 877	42 678	42 199	78 317	39 518	38 700	73 297	37 069	36 228
45-49	83 208	41 378	41 830	84 457	42 145	42 312	84 279	42 209	42 070	77 935	39 196	38 739
50-54	84 664	41 070	43 625	82 136	40 576	41 560	83 422	41 373	42 049	83 334	41 501	41 833
55-59	82 517	40 137	42 380	81 987	39 992	41 995	80 241	39 283	40 957	81 575	40 114	41 461
60-64	82 653	39 342	43 311	79 706	38 233	41 473	79 348	38 193	41 154	77 756	37 587	40 169
65-69	75 939	35 009	40 930	77 800	36 248	41 552	75 401	35 471	39 930	75 257	35 555	39 702
70-74	64 849	28 772	36 077	68 920	30 762	38 159	71 076	32 143	38 933	69 325	31 721	37 604
75-79	51 574	21 893	29 681	55 677	23 570	32 107	59 514	25 396	34 118	61 903	26 838	35 066
80-84	32 760	12 808	19 953	40 575	16 002	24 573	44 000	17 337	26 662	47 413	18 883	28 530
85-89	20 908	7 037	13 871	22 395	7 809	14 587	28 115	9 926	18 189	30 690	10 857	19 832
90-94	9 968	2 762	7 205	11 391	3 199	8 192	12 719	3 702	9 017	16 283	4 826	11 457
95-99	3 563	717	2 846	4 036	835	3 201	4 752	1 002	3 750	5 568	1 215	4 352
100 +	737	91	646	966	123	843	1 187	152	1 035	1 462	191	1 272

Age group	2045 Both sexes	2045 Males	2045 Females	2050 Both sexes	2050 Males	2050 Females
All ages	1 242 398	602 562	639 836	1 236 200	600 391	635 810
0-4	64 054	32 878	31 176	63 613	32 651	30 962
5-9	64 311	32 998	31 313	64 627	33 161	31 467
10-14	64 463	33 074	31 389	65 180	33 443	31 737
15-19	65 591	33 641	31 950	65 899	33 801	32 098
20-24	67 757	34 668	33 089	67 234	34 404	32 830
25-29	70 608	36 032	34 576	69 232	35 334	33 897
30-34	72 789	37 065	35 724	71 690	36 514	35 176
35-39	73 898	37 537	36 361	73 294	37 249	36 045
40-44	73 304	37 121	36 184	73 927	37 470	36 457
45-49	73 053	36 839	36 215	73 104	36 918	36 185
50-54	77 249	38 664	38 585	72 538	36 420	36 118
55-59	81 594	40 314	41 280	75 834	37 699	38 135
60-64	79 146	38 450	40 695	79 291	38 734	40 557
65-69	73 866	35 074	38 792	75 316	35 970	39 347
70-74	69 445	31 946	37 499	68 313	31 618	36 696
75-79	60 883	26 765	34 118	61 311	27 135	34 176
80-84	49 903	20 256	29 647	49 655	20 486	29 169
85-89	33 453	12 007	21 447	35 825	13 157	22 668
90-94	17 918	5 353	12 565	19 812	6 041	13 772
95-99	7 307	1 639	5 668	8 099	1 852	6 247
100 +	1 807	242	1 565	2 406	336	2 070

United Nations Department of Economic and Social Affairs/Population Division
World Population Prospects: The 2004 Revision, Volume II: Sex and Age Distribution of the World Population

25

POPULATION BY AGE AND SEX (in thousands)

Age group	2005 Both sexes	Males	Females	2010 Both sexes	Males	Females	2015 Both sexes	Males	Females	2020 Both sexes	Males	Females
All ages	1 211 265	587 635	623 630	1 236 012	599 841	636 171	1 262 834	613 222	649 612	1 289 550	626 617	662 933
0-4	66 119	33 932	32 187	77 010	39 527	37 483	81 891	42 033	39 857	83 622	42 921	40 701
5-9	66 739	34 223	32 515	66 680	34 206	32 474	77 526	39 776	37 749	82 408	42 284	40 124
10-14	73 014	37 401	35 612	67 621	34 673	32 948	67 525	34 637	32 888	78 359	40 201	38 158
15-19	81 687	41 778	39 909	74 448	38 114	36 334	69 016	35 371	33 645	68 922	35 337	33 585
20-24	83 673	42 612	41 061	83 201	42 415	40 786	75 960	38 776	37 185	70 573	36 068	34 505
25-29	83 598	42 324	41 274	84 864	43 035	41 829	84 366	42 849	41 517	77 262	39 312	37 950
30-34	86 387	43 500	42 887	84 334	42 515	41 819	85 499	43 191	42 308	85 085	43 073	42 012
35-39	87 325	43 727	43 599	86 483	43 342	43 141	84 367	42 348	42 019	85 547	43 050	42 496
40-44	91 111	45 286	45 825	86 840	43 254	43 587	85 979	42 877	43 102	83 918	41 937	41 981
45-49	89 176	43 869	45 307	90 038	44 437	45 601	85 964	42 564	43 400	85 182	42 250	42 932
50-54	83 293	40 542	42 751	87 406	42 555	44 851	88 437	43 258	45 180	84 673	41 606	43 067
55-59	75 062	36 193	38 869	80 472	38 608	41 864	84 628	40 658	43 970	85 911	41 537	44 374
60-64	59 037	27 853	31 184	71 688	33 907	37 781	76 899	36 203	40 697	81 089	38 279	42 810
65-69	56 124	25 284	30 840	54 866	25 204	29 661	66 795	30 790	36 005	71 765	32 944	38 821
70-74	45 757	19 789	25 968	49 669	21 460	28 209	49 299	21 846	27 453	60 239	26 820	33 418
75-79	38 695	15 320	23 376	38 032	15 550	22 482	41 501	16 988	24 514	41 989	17 715	24 274
80-84	25 653	8 782	16 871	28 603	10 392	18 211	28 699	10 798	17 901	31 602	11 945	19 657
85-89	11 816	3 582	8 234	15 975	4 827	11 148	18 101	5 829	12 272	18 704	6 242	12 462
90-94	5 459	1 345	4 113	5 715	1 439	4 275	7 954	1 993	5 961	9 265	2 482	6 783
95-99	1 353	264	1 089	1 792	341	1 451	2 031	386	1 645	2 936	552	2 383
100 +	188	28	160	277	39	238	396	52	344	501	63	438

Age group	2025 Both sexes	Males	Females	2030 Both sexes	Males	Females	2035 Both sexes	Males	Females	2040 Both sexes	Males	Females
All ages	1 312 272	637 965	674 307	1 333 175	648 389	684 786	1 355 347	659 640	695 706	1 381 006	673 021	707 985
0-4	81 513	41 838	39 675	82 000	42 089	39 911	86 068	44 180	41 888	92 409	47 437	44 972
5-9	84 148	43 177	40 971	82 051	42 101	39 950	82 545	42 356	40 189	86 614	44 447	42 168
10-14	83 244	42 710	40 534	84 991	43 607	41 384	82 901	42 535	40 366	83 399	42 792	40 607
15-19	79 749	40 897	38 852	84 637	43 408	41 229	86 391	44 311	42 080	84 311	43 245	41 066
20-24	70 493	36 046	34 447	81 310	41 599	39 710	86 204	44 117	42 087	87 973	45 031	42 942
25-29	71 942	36 655	35 287	71 877	36 647	35 230	82 669	42 189	40 480	87 573	44 715	42 858
30-34	78 154	39 657	38 497	72 916	37 060	35 857	72 867	37 068	35 799	83 624	42 593	41 031
35-39	85 219	42 999	42 220	78 469	39 708	38 761	73 331	37 180	36 151	73 305	37 208	36 097
40-44	85 130	42 671	42 459	84 877	42 678	42 199	78 317	39 518	38 799	73 297	37 070	36 227
45-49	83 208	41 378	41 830	84 457	42 145	42 312	84 279	42 209	42 070	77 935	39 196	38 739
50-54	84 004	41 370	42 635	82 136	40 576	41 560	83 422	41 373	42 049	83 334	41 501	41 833
55-59	82 517	40 137	42 380	81 987	39 992	41 995	80 241	39 283	40 957	81 575	40 114	41 461
60-64	82 653	39 342	43 311	79 706	38 233	41 473	79 348	38 193	41 154	77 756	37 587	40 169
65-69	75 939	35 009	40 930	77 800	36 248	41 552	75 401	35 471	39 930	75 257	35 555	39 702
70-74	64 849	28 772	36 077	68 920	30 762	38 159	71 076	32 143	38 933	69 325	31 721	37 604
75-79	51 574	21 893	29 681	55 677	23 570	32 107	59 514	25 396	34 118	61 903	26 838	35 066
80-84	32 760	12 808	19 953	40 575	16 002	24 573	44 000	17 337	26 662	47 413	18 883	28 530
85-89	20 908	7 037	13 871	22 395	7 809	14 587	28 115	9 926	18 189	30 690	10 857	19 832
90-94	9 968	2 762	7 205	11 391	3 199	8 192	12 719	3 702	9 017	16 283	4 826	11 457
95-99	3 563	717	2 846	4 036	835	3 201	4 752	1 002	3 750	5 568	1 215	4 352
100 +	737	91	646	966	123	843	1 187	152	1 035	1 462	191	1 272

Age group	2045 Both sexes	Males	Females	2050 Both sexes	Males	Females
All ages	1 409 776	688 421	721 355	1 439 850	704 835	735 015
0-4	97 752	50 180	47 572	100 220	51 446	48 775
5-9	92 956	47 704	45 252	98 301	50 448	47 852
10-14	87 471	44 884	42 586	93 814	48 143	45 671
15-19	84 817	43 507	41 309	88 892	45 602	43 290
20-24	85 915	43 981	41 934	86 434	44 252	42 182
25-29	89 370	45 647	43 722	87 347	44 620	42 727
30-34	88 543	45 131	43 413	90 383	46 088	44 295
35-39	84 025	42 714	41 311	88 967	45 266	43 701
40-44	73 304	37 121	36 183	83 988	42 605	41 383
45-49	73 053	36 839	36 214	73 104	36 919	36 185
50-54	77 249	38 664	38 585	72 538	36 421	36 117
55-59	81 594	40 314	41 280	75 834	37 699	38 135
60-64	79 146	38 450	40 695	79 291	38 734	40 557
65-69	73 866	35 074	38 792	75 316	35 970	39 347
70-74	69 445	31 946	37 499	68 313	31 618	36 696
75-79	60 883	26 765	34 118	61 311	27 135	34 176
80-84	49 903	20 256	29 647	49 655	20 486	29 169
85-89	33 453	12 007	21 447	35 825	13 157	22 668
90-94	17 918	5 353	12 565	19 812	6 041	13 772
95-99	7 307	1 639	5 668	8 099	1 852	6 247
100 +	1 807	242	1 565	2 406	336	2 070

United Nations Department of Economic and Social Affairs/Population Division
World Population Prospects: The 2004 Revision, Volume II: Sex and Age Distribution of the World Population

26

POPULATION BY AGE AND SEX (in thousands)

Age group	2005 Both sexes	Males	Females	2010 Both sexes	Males	Females	2015 Both sexes	Males	Females	2020 Both sexes	Males	Females
All ages	1 211 265	587 635	623 630	1 215 277	589 195	626 082	1 210 085	586 143	623 943	1 198 800	580 032	618 768
0-4	66 119	33 932	32 187	56 275	28 881	27 394	49 846	25 581	24 265	45 562	23 382	22 180
5-9	66 739	34 223	32 515	66 680	34 206	32 474	56 822	29 149	27 673	50 405	25 856	24 549
10-14	73 014	37 401	35 612	67 621	34 673	32 948	67 525	34 637	32 888	57 673	29 584	28 089
15-19	81 687	41 778	39 909	74 448	38 114	36 334	69 016	35 371	33 645	68 922	35 337	33 585
20-24	83 673	42 612	41 061	83 201	42 415	40 786	75 960	38 776	37 185	70 573	36 068	34 505
25-29	83 598	42 324	41 274	84 864	43 035	41 829	84 366	42 849	41 517	77 262	39 312	37 950
30-34	86 387	43 500	42 887	84 334	42 515	41 819	85 499	43 191	42 308	85 085	43 073	42 012
35-39	87 325	43 727	43 599	86 483	43 342	43 141	84 367	42 348	42 019	85 547	43 050	42 496
40-44	91 111	45 286	45 825	86 840	43 254	43 587	85 979	42 877	43 102	83 918	41 937	41 981
45-49	89 176	43 869	45 307	90 038	44 437	45 601	85 964	42 564	43 400	85 182	42 250	42 932
50-54	83 293	40 542	42 751	87 406	42 555	44 851	88 437	43 258	45 180	84 673	41 606	43 067
55-59	75 062	36 193	38 869	80 472	38 608	41 864	84 628	40 658	43 970	85 911	41 537	44 374
60-64	59 037	27 853	31 184	71 688	33 907	37 781	76 899	36 203	40 697	81 089	38 279	42 810
65-69	56 124	25 284	30 840	54 866	25 204	29 661	66 795	30 790	36 005	71 765	32 944	38 821
70-74	45 757	19 789	25 968	49 669	21 460	28 209	49 299	21 846	27 453	60 239	26 820	33 418
75-79	38 695	15 320	23 376	38 032	15 550	22 482	41 501	16 988	24 514	41 989	17 715	24 274
80-84	25 653	8 782	16 871	28 603	10 392	18 211	28 699	10 798	17 901	31 602	11 945	19 657
85-89	11 816	3 582	8 234	15 975	4 827	11 148	18 101	5 829	12 272	18 704	6 242	12 462
90-94	5 459	1 345	4 113	5 715	1 439	4 275	7 954	1 993	5 961	9 265	2 482	6 783
95-99	1 353	264	1 089	1 792	341	1 451	2 031	386	1 645	2 936	552	2 383
100 +	188	28	160	277	39	238	396	52	344	501	63	438

Age group	2025 Both sexes	Males	Females	2030 Both sexes	Males	Females	2035 Both sexes	Males	Females	2040 Both sexes	Males	Females
All ages	1 185 003	572 641	612 361	1 168 279	563 768	604 511	1 147 542	553 022	594 520	1 121 890	540 101	581 788
0-4	44 905	23 045	21 860	44 238	22 704	21 534	42 937	22 037	20 900	40 745	20 912	19 833
5-9	46 131	23 662	22 468	45 479	23 329	22 150	44 818	22 990	21 827	43 521	22 326	21 195
10-14	51 264	26 295	24 968	46 996	24 106	22 890	46 347	23 774	22 573	45 689	23 437	22 252
15-19	59 086	30 295	28 791	52 688	27 015	25 673	48 420	24 824	23 597	47 785	24 503	23 282
20-24	70 493	36 046	34 447	60 692	31 030	29 662	54 318	27 768	26 550	50 075	25 597	24 479
25-29	71 942	36 655	35 287	71 877	36 647	35 230	62 125	31 668	30 458	55 789	28 432	27 357
30-34	78 154	39 657	38 497	72 916	37 060	35 857	72 867	37 068	35 799	63 182	32 134	31 049
35-39	85 219	42 000	43 220	78 469	39 708	38 761	73 331	37 180	36 151	73 305	37 208	36 097
40-44	85 130	42 671	42 459	84 877	42 670	42 100	78 317	39 518	38 799	73 297	37 070	36 227
45-49	83 208	41 378	41 830	84 457	42 145	42 312	84 279	42 209	42 070	77 935	39 196	38 739
50-54	84 004	41 370	42 635	82 136	40 576	41 560	83 422	41 373	42 049	83 334	41 501	41 833
55-59	82 517	40 137	42 380	81 987	39 992	41 995	80 041	39 293	40 957	81 575	40 114	41 461
60-64	82 653	39 342	43 311	79 706	38 233	41 473	79 348	38 193	41 154	77 756	37 587	40 169
65-69	75 939	35 009	40 930	77 800	36 248	41 552	75 401	35 471	39 930	75 257	35 555	39 702
70-74	64 849	28 772	36 077	68 920	30 762	38 159	71 076	32 143	38 933	69 325	31 721	37 604
75-79	51 574	21 893	29 681	55 677	23 570	32 107	59 514	25 396	34 118	61 903	26 838	35 066
80-84	32 760	12 808	19 953	40 575	16 002	24 573	44 000	17 337	26 662	47 410	18 883	28 530
85-89	20 908	7 037	13 871	22 395	7 809	14 587	28 115	9 926	18 189	30 690	10 857	19 832
90-94	9 968	2 762	7 205	11 391	3 199	8 192	12 719	3 702	9 017	16 283	4 826	11 457
95-99	3 563	717	2 846	4 036	835	3 201	4 752	1 002	3 750	5 568	1 215	4 352
100 +	737	91	646	966	123	843	1 187	152	1 035	1 462	191	1 272

Age group	2045 Both sexes	Males	Females	2050 Both sexes	Males	Females
All ages	1 091 378	525 119	566 259	1 057 486	508 767	548 718
0-4	37 966	19 486	18 481	35 591	18 265	17 325
5-9	41 334	21 204	20 130	38 559	19 779	18 780
10-14	44 395	22 774	21 621	42 212	21 654	20 557
15-19	47 133	24 170	22 963	45 844	23 510	22 334
20-24	49 443	25 276	24 167	48 800	24 950	23 851
25-29	51 575	26 280	25 295	50 960	25 970	24 990
30-34	56 900	28 931	27 968	52 728	26 804	25 923
35-39	63 704	32 328	31 377	57 487	29 165	28 322
40-44	73 304	37 121	36 183	63 800	32 302	31 497
45-49	73 053	36 839	36 214	73 104	36 919	36 185
50-54	77 249	38 664	38 585	72 538	36 421	36 117
55-59	81 594	40 314	41 280	75 834	37 699	38 135
60-64	79 146	38 450	40 695	79 291	38 734	40 557
65-69	73 866	35 074	38 792	75 316	35 970	39 347
70-74	69 445	31 946	37 499	68 313	31 618	36 696
75-79	60 883	26 765	34 118	61 311	27 135	34 176
80-84	49 903	20 256	29 647	49 655	20 486	29 169
85-89	33 453	12 007	21 447	35 825	13 157	22 668
90-94	17 918	5 353	12 565	19 812	6 041	13 772
95-99	7 307	1 639	5 668	8 099	1 852	6 247
100 +	1 807	242	1 565	2 406	336	2 070

United Nations Department of Economic and Social Affairs/Population Division
World Population Prospects: The 2004 Revision, Volume II: Sex and Age Distribution of the World Population

27

POPULATION BY AGE AND SEX (in thousands)

Age group	1950 Both sexes	Males	Females	1955 Both sexes	Males	Females	1960 Both sexes	Males	Females	1965 Both sexes	Males	Females
All ages	1 706 698	869 844	836 854	1 894 179	964 103	930 076	2 108 512	1 072 701	1 035 810	2 371 340	1 206 558	1 164 782
0-4	256 326	131 140	125 186	312 586	159 290	153 296	339 217	173 123	166 095	388 792	198 722	190 070
5-9	201 259	102 423	98 837	233 562	119 775	113 787	288 976	147 691	141 285	317 437	162 581	154 857
10-14	184 240	94 628	89 612	196 228	100 081	96 147	228 624	117 373	111 251	283 388	145 075	138 312
15-19	171 074	88 110	82 964	180 419	92 730	87 688	192 233	98 188	94 045	224 113	115 085	109 029
20-24	149 935	77 193	72 742	165 842	85 351	80 491	175 799	90 245	85 554	187 053	95 534	91 519
25-29	130 591	67 250	63 341	144 525	74 287	70 238	160 314	82 360	77 954	170 467	87 373	83 094
30-34	114 323	58 882	55 441	125 143	64 425	60 718	139 494	71 741	67 753	154 775	79 481	75 294
35-39	102 567	52 943	49 624	108 545	55 829	52 716	119 883	61 663	58 220	134 363	69 057	65 305
40-44	90 315	46 474	43 841	96 508	49 541	46 967	102 946	52 718	50 227	114 559	58 747	55 812
45-49	77 530	39 877	37 653	83 801	42 645	41 156	90 471	46 077	44 394	97 154	49 458	47 696
50-54	64 222	32 735	31 487	70 358	35 489	34 869	77 188	38 774	38 414	84 084	42 389	41 695
55-59	54 302	27 394	26 908	55 864	27 733	28 131	62 663	30 962	31 701	69 924	34 584	35 340
60-64	43 174	21 116	22 059	46 406	22 976	23 430	47 365	22 922	24 443	54 335	26 265	28 071
65-69	31 304	14 255	17 049	34 046	16 360	17 686	37 347	18 194	19 153	38 272	17 992	20 279
70-74	19 727	8 825	10 903	22 403	9 960	12 442	24 977	11 727	13 251	27 966	13 323	14 643
75-79	10 547	4 474	6 073	11 858	5 160	6 697	13 889	6 003	7 885	15 966	7 297	8 669
80 +	5 262	2 127	3 135	6 085	2 469	3 616	7 127	2 942	4 185	8 691	3 595	5 096

Age group	1970 Both sexes	Males	Females	1975 Both sexes	Males	Females	1980 Both sexes	Males	Females	1985 Both sexes	Males	Females
All ages	2 688 915	1 368 228	1 320 687	3 026 543	1 541 134	1 485 409	3 359 755	1 710 501	1 649 254	3 729 162	1 897 357	1 831 805
0-4	437 421	223 656	213 766	460 963	235 685	225 278	461 636	236 015	225 620	503 493	257 667	245 826
5-9	369 044	189 124	179 920	419 049	214 945	204 104	442 457	226 669	215 788	444 221	227 401	216 820
10-14	312 290	160 198	152 092	363 894	186 760	177 134	413 742	212 219	201 523	437 649	224 191	213 458
15-19	279 036	142 919	136 117	307 675	158 057	149 618	358 742	183 974	174 768	409 390	209 881	199 509
20-24	219 291	112 434	106 858	273 174	139 863	133 311	301 850	154 997	146 853	353 490	181 102	172 388
25-29	182 109	92 903	89 206	214 197	109 577	104 619	267 919	137 157	130 762	297 241	152 508	144 733
30-34	165 900	84 899	81 001	177 500	90 552	86 948	210 086	107 375	102 712	263 636	134 923	128 713
35-39	150 080	77 016	73 064	161 826	82 789	79 037	173 357	88 481	84 876	206 202	105 318	100 884
40-44	129 765	66 568	63 197	145 452	74 631	70 822	157 852	80 647	77 205	168 920	86 020	82 900
45-49	109 617	55 950	53 668	125 309	64 157	61 152	140 367	71 836	68 531	152 577	77 538	75 039
50-54	91 529	46 209	45 320	104 320	52 942	51 377	119 859	61 020	58 838	133 998	68 026	65 972
55-59	77 426	38 580	38 846	84 948	42 444	42 504	97 412	48 973	48 439	112 183	56 492	55 691
60-64	61 935	30 083	31 851	69 082	33 937	35 145	76 483	37 676	38 807	88 000	43 539	44 462
65-69	45 361	21 371	23 990	52 267	24 840	27 428	58 918	28 368	30 550	65 382	31 418	33 964
70-74	28 764	13 100	15 664	34 788	15 924	18 864	41 172	18 945	22 227	46 310	21 541	24 768
75-79	18 544	8 597	9 947	19 026	8 338	10 688	23 907	10 473	13 433	28 432	12 490	15 942
80 +	10 803	4 622	6 180	13 073	5 694	7 379	13 997	5 677	8 320	18 037	7 301	10 736

Age group	1990 Both sexes	Males	Females	1995 Both sexes	Males	Females	2000 Both sexes	Males	Females	2005 Both sexes	Males	Females
All ages	4 130 947	2 101 469	2 029 478	4 518 369	2 295 742	2 222 627	4 892 218	2 481 479	2 410 740	5 253 484	2 661 284	2 592 200
0-4	547 777	281 328	266 449	549 838	282 316	267 522	547 714	280 994	266 720	551 030	282 471	268 559
5-9	488 106	250 251	237 855	531 782	273 333	258 449	534 979	274 788	260 191	533 858	273 952	259 906
10-14	440 725	225 690	215 036	483 202	247 674	235 529	526 843	270 723	256 121	530 286	272 318	257 967
15-19	431 899	221 013	210 886	435 453	222 787	212 666	478 225	244 928	233 297	522 221	268 163	254 058
20-24	402 499	205 470	197 028	423 945	216 470	207 475	428 474	218 810	209 664	471 294	240 948	230 346
25-29	347 497	177 509	169 988	394 632	200 986	193 646	415 844	211 900	203 944	419 847	214 019	205 828
30-34	292 340	150 124	142 216	341 011	173 731	167 280	386 450	196 286	190 164	406 312	206 714	199 599
35-39	258 857	132 513	126 344	286 425	146 660	139 765	333 506	169 342	164 163	377 440	191 278	186 163
40-44	201 546	102 841	98 705	253 067	129 151	123 916	279 567	142 606	136 961	325 207	164 577	160 630
45-49	163 911	83 155	80 756	195 886	99 491	96 396	246 042	124 868	121 175	271 534	137 831	133 704
50-54	146 179	73 858	72 320	157 577	79 349	78 228	188 451	94 925	93 526	237 222	119 528	117 694
55-59	125 820	63 292	62 528	138 030	68 939	69 092	148 999	74 118	74 881	178 930	89 158	89 772
60-64	101 791	50 462	51 329	115 079	56 915	58 164	126 783	62 224	64 559	137 630	67 371	70 260
65-69	75 756	36 605	39 152	88 597	42 821	45 776	100 910	48 659	52 251	112 111	53 736	58 375
70-74	51 767	24 052	27 715	60 899	28 337	32 563	72 035	33 557	38 479	83 178	38 771	44 408
75-79	32 211	14 301	17 910	36 729	16 208	20 522	44 060	19 482	24 578	53 206	23 649	29 557
80 +	22 265	9 005	13 259	26 215	10 574	15 641	33 336	13 270	20 066	42 179	16 802	25 377

(*) Less developed regions comprise all regions of Africa, Asia (except Japan), Latin America and the Caribbean plus Melanesia, Micronesia and Polynesia.

United Nations Department of Economic and Social Affairs/Population Division
World Population Prospects: The 2004 Revision, Volume II: Sex and Age Distribution of the World Population

POPULATION BY AGE AND SEX (in thousands)

Age group	2005 Both sexes	Males	Females	2010 Both sexes	Males	Females	2015 Both sexes	Males	Females	2020 Both sexes	Males	Females
All ages	5 253 484	2 661 284	2 592 200	5 617 246	2 842 315	2 774 930	5 982 871	3 023 815	2 959 056	6 333 475	3 197 026	3 136 450
0-4	551 030	282 471	268 559	566 311	290 233	276 078	581 908	298 198	283 711	582 613	298 471	284 141
5-9	533 858	273 952	259 906	537 993	275 810	262 183	554 350	284 059	270 291	571 258	292 646	278 612
10-14	530 286	272 318	257 967	529 130	271 466	257 663	533 367	273 371	259 997	550 027	281 767	268 260
15-19	522 221	268 163	254 058	526 082	269 984	256 099	525 198	269 270	255 927	529 608	271 265	258 344
20-24	471 294	240 948	230 346	515 841	264 478	251 363	520 133	266 528	253 605	519 620	266 034	253 586
25-29	419 847	214 019	205 828	462 837	236 272	226 565	507 514	259 861	247 653	512 176	262 154	250 022
30-34	406 312	206 714	199 599	410 263	208 908	201 356	452 978	231 046	221 932	497 452	254 557	242 895
35-39	377 440	191 278	186 163	396 844	201 533	195 311	400 740	203 757	196 983	442 861	225 620	217 241
40-44	325 207	164 577	160 630	368 606	186 239	182 367	387 867	196 423	191 445	391 681	198 639	193 042
45-49	271 534	137 831	133 704	316 641	159 530	157 111	359 704	180 991	178 713	378 860	191 091	187 769
50-54	237 222	119 528	117 694	262 324	132 266	130 057	306 869	153 634	153 235	349 468	174 789	174 679
55-59	178 930	89 158	89 772	226 251	112 849	113 402	250 888	125 275	125 612	294 577	146 109	148 468
60-64	137 630	67 371	70 260	166 370	81 640	84 730	211 578	103 967	107 612	235 488	115 894	119 594
65-69	112 111	53 736	58 375	122 690	58 716	63 974	149 579	71 795	77 785	191 635	92 136	99 500
70-74	83 178	38 771	44 408	93 485	43 368	50 118	103 425	47 949	55 476	127 506	59 305	68 200
75-79	53 206	23 649	29 557	62 525	27 842	34 683	71 362	31 637	39 725	80 117	35 520	44 598
80-84	27 559	11 444	16 115	34 066	14 232	19 834	40 911	17 110	23 801	47 664	19 844	27 820
85-89	10 934	4 135	6 799	13 955	5 303	8 652	17 756	6 765	10 991	21 921	8 327	13 595
90-94	3 033	1 030	2 003	4 112	1 375	2 736	5 444	1 809	3 635	7 156	2 367	4 789
95-99	576	172	404	805	239	566	1 135	325	810	1 554	432	1 121
100 +	78	21	56	115	32	83	164	44	119	232	60	173

Age group	2025 Both sexes	Males	Females	2030 Both sexes	Males	Females	2035 Both sexes	Males	Females	2040 Both sexes	Males	Females
All ages	6 656 285	3 355 239	3 301 047	6 948 446	3 497 035	3 451 412	7 213 362	3 624 604	3 588 757	7 454 248	3 739 975	3 714 272
0-4	572 617	293 240	279 377	561 694	287 385	274 309	556 935	284 914	272 021	557 496	285 201	272 295
5-9	573 298	293 577	279 721	564 533	288 960	275 572	554 721	283 673	271 049	550 896	281 673	269 223
10-14	567 448	290 607	276 841	569 973	291 779	278 194	561 652	287 389	274 262	552 214	282 294	269 920
15-19	546 453	279 752	266 701	564 068	288 687	275 381	566 818	289 975	276 843	558 718	285 702	273 016
20-24	524 252	268 146	256 105	541 259	276 710	264 549	559 058	285 745	273 313	562 048	287 170	274 878
25-29	512 042	261 873	250 169	516 975	264 143	252 832	534 269	272 862	261 408	552 382	282 072	270 310
30-34	502 394	257 031	245 362	502 729	257 013	245 716	508 121	259 540	248 581	525 830	268 485	257 345
35-39	487 004	248 966	238 038	492 313	251 683	240 630	493 176	251 981	241 195	499 080	254 808	244 272
40-44	433 285	220 241	213 044	477 242	243 492	233 751	482 927	246 471	236 456	484 304	247 096	237 209
45-49	382 778	193 390	189 388	424 059	214 813	209 246	467 831	237 967	229 864	473 888	241 206	232 683
50-54	368 594	184 840	183 754	372 817	187 323	185 494	413 718	208 509	205 209	457 191	231 482	225 709
55-59	336 469	166 793	169 676	355 603	176 805	178 797	360 197	179 498	180 698	400 516	200 304	200 212
60-64	277 799	135 856	141 943	318 547	155 786	162 761	337 574	165 669	171 905	342 616	168 607	174 009
65-69	214 384	103 292	111 092	254 505	121 922	132 583	293 320	140 612	152 707	311 976	150 190	161 786
70-74	164 949	76 858	88 091	185 908	86 903	99 005	222 570	103 502	119 068	258 251	120 252	137 999
75-79	100 237	44 567	55 670	131 410	58 540	72 870	149 660	56 948	92 712	181 179	80 641	100 538
80-84	54 533	22 691	31 843	69 598	29 011	40 586	92 829	38 722	54 107	107 247	44 950	62 297
85-89	26 219	9 891	16 328	30 757	11 597	19 160	40 279	15 173	25 106	54 945	20 643	34 302
90-94	9 105	2 975	6 130	11 255	3 647	7 608	13 593	4 400	9 193	18 333	5 895	12 438
95-99	2 103	574	1 529	2 762	734	2 028	3 525	926	2 599	4 375	1 143	3 232
100 +	321	78	244	442	102	340	588	128	460	763	162	602

Age group	2045 Both sexes	Males	Females	2050 Both sexes	Males	Females
All ages	7 665 019	3 840 400	3 824 619	7 839 702	3 923 083	3 916 619
0-4	552 497	282 631	269 866	540 760	276 595	264 164
5-9	552 286	282 376	269 910	548 042	280 187	267 855
10-14	548 697	280 451	268 246	550 350	281 284	269 066
15-19	549 483	280 714	268 769	546 147	278 965	267 182
20-24	554 205	283 044	271 161	545 224	278 199	267 025
25-29	555 781	283 718	272 063	548 404	279 843	268 560
30-34	544 401	277 933	266 467	548 400	279 886	268 514
35-39	517 240	264 004	253 236	536 303	273 711	262 592
40-44	490 677	250 213	240 464	509 230	259 639	249 591
45-49	475 748	242 141	233 607	482 526	245 519	237 007
50-54	463 609	234 961	228 648	465 946	236 205	229 740
55-59	443 443	222 920	220 522	450 246	226 646	223 600
60-64	381 979	188 774	193 205	423 924	210 733	213 191
65-69	317 516	153 376	164 140	355 261	172 480	182 781
70-74	276 073	129 209	146 865	282 096	132 586	149 510
75-79	212 178	94 611	117 567	228 416	102 472	125 944
80-84	131 779	54 917	76 862	156 275	65 256	91 018
85-89	64 747	24 469	40 278	81 155	30 454	50 700
90-94	25 650	8 178	17 472	30 958	9 955	21 003
95-99	6 070	1 560	4 510	8 707	2 197	6 510
100 +	961	199	762	1 333	268	1 065

United Nations Department of Economic and Social Affairs/Population Division
World Population Prospects: The 2004 Revision, Volume II: Sex and Age Distribution of the World Population

29

POPULATION BY AGE AND SEX (in thousands)

Age group	2005 Both sexes	Males	Females	2010 Both sexes	Males	Females	2015 Both sexes	Males	Females	2020 Both sexes	Males	Females
All ages	5 253 484	2 661 284	2 592 200	5 667 265	2 868 058	2 799 206	6 119 600	3 094 142	3 025 458	6 583 622	3 325 594	3 258 028
0-4	551 030	282 471	268 559	616 330	315 976	300 354	669 270	343 118	326 152	697 283	357 373	339 910
5-9	533 858	273 952	259 906	537 993	275 810	262 183	603 717	309 466	294 252	657 582	337 023	320 559
10-14	530 286	272 318	257 967	529 130	271 466	257 663	533 367	273 371	259 997	599 179	307 056	292 123
15-19	522 221	268 163	254 058	526 082	269 984	256 099	525 198	269 270	255 927	529 608	271 265	258 344
20-24	471 294	240 948	230 346	515 841	264 478	251 363	520 133	266 528	253 605	519 620	266 034	253 586
25-29	419 847	214 019	205 828	462 837	236 272	226 565	507 514	259 861	247 653	512 177	262 154	250 022
30-34	406 312	206 714	199 599	410 263	208 908	201 356	452 978	231 046	221 932	497 452	254 557	242 895
35-39	377 440	191 278	186 163	396 844	201 533	195 311	400 740	203 757	196 983	442 861	225 620	217 241
40-44	325 207	164 577	160 630	368 606	186 239	182 367	387 867	196 423	191 445	391 681	198 639	193 042
45-49	271 534	137 831	133 704	316 641	159 530	157 111	359 704	180 991	178 713	378 860	191 091	187 769
50-54	237 222	119 528	117 694	262 324	132 266	130 057	306 869	153 634	153 235	349 468	174 789	174 679
55-59	178 930	89 158	89 772	226 251	112 849	113 402	250 888	125 275	125 612	294 577	146 109	148 468
60-64	137 630	67 371	70 260	166 370	81 640	84 730	211 578	103 967	107 612	235 488	115 894	119 594
65-69	112 111	53 736	58 375	122 690	58 716	63 974	149 579	71 795	77 785	191 635	92 136	99 500
70-74	83 178	38 771	44 408	93 485	43 368	50 118	103 425	47 949	55 476	127 506	59 305	68 200
75-79	53 206	23 649	29 557	62 525	27 842	34 683	71 362	31 637	39 725	80 117	35 520	44 598
80-84	27 559	11 444	16 115	34 066	14 232	19 834	40 911	17 110	23 801	47 664	19 844	27 820
85-89	10 934	4 135	6 799	13 955	5 303	8 652	17 756	6 765	10 991	21 921	8 327	13 595
90-94	3 033	1 030	2 003	4 112	1 375	2 736	5 444	1 809	3 635	7 156	2 367	4 789
95-99	576	172	404	805	239	566	1 135	325	810	1 554	432	1 121
100 +	78	21	56	115	32	83	164	44	119	232	60	173

Age group	2025 Both sexes	Males	Females	2030 Both sexes	Males	Females	2035 Both sexes	Males	Females	2040 Both sexes	Males	Females
All ages	7 024 595	3 544 409	3 480 185	7 450 980	3 754 927	3 696 052	7 882 561	3 967 810	3 914 751	8 328 440	4 188 105	4 140 334
0-4	692 473	354 754	337 719	697 896	357 205	340 692	726 066	371 619	354 447	765 763	391 971	373 792
5-9	686 763	351 839	334 924	683 261	349 871	333 390	689 801	352 888	336 913	718 830	367 728	351 102
10-14	653 433	334 800	318 633	683 039	349 820	333 218	680 013	348 095	331 918	686 933	351 306	335 627
15-19	595 456	304 954	290 502	649 808	332 735	317 073	679 584	347 837	331 746	676 789	346 234	330 555
20-24	524 252	268 146	256 105	590 054	301 783	288 272	644 453	329 579	314 874	674 384	344 766	329 618
25-29	512 042	261 873	250 169	516 975	264 143	252 832	582 733	297 743	284 990	637 230	325 594	311 636
30-34	502 394	257 031	245 363	502 729	257 013	245 716	508 121	259 540	248 581	573 845	293 126	280 718
35-39	487 005	248 966	238 038	492 313	251 683	240 630	493 177	251 981	241 196	499 080	254 808	244 272
40-44	433 285	220 241	213 044	477 242	243 492	233 751	482 928	246 471	236 456	484 304	247 095	237 209
45-49	382 778	193 390	189 388	424 059	214 813	209 246	467 831	237 967	229 864	473 889	241 206	232 683
50-54	368 594	184 840	183 754	372 817	187 323	185 494	413 718	208 509	205 209	457 191	231 482	225 709
55-59	336 469	166 793	169 676	355 603	176 806	178 797	360 197	179 498	180 699	400 516	200 304	200 212
60-64	277 799	135 856	141 943	318 547	155 786	162 761	337 574	165 669	171 905	342 616	168 608	174 009
65-69	214 384	103 292	111 092	254 505	121 922	132 583	293 320	140 612	152 707	311 977	150 191	161 786
70-74	164 949	76 858	88 091	185 908	86 903	99 005	222 570	103 502	119 068	258 251	120 252	137 999
75-79	100 237	44 567	55 670	131 410	58 540	72 870	149 661	66 948	82 712	181 179	80 641	100 538
80-84	54 533	22 691	31 843	69 598	29 011	40 586	92 829	38 722	54 107	107 247	44 950	62 297
85-89	26 219	9 891	16 328	30 757	11 597	19 160	40 279	15 173	25 106	54 945	20 643	34 302
90-94	9 105	2 975	6 130	11 255	3 647	7 608	13 593	4 400	9 193	18 333	5 895	12 438
95-99	2 103	574	1 529	2 762	734	2 028	3 525	926	2 599	4 375	1 143	3 232
100 +	321	78	244	442	102	340	588	128	460	763	162	602

Age group	2045 Both sexes	Males	Females	2050 Both sexes	Males	Females
All ages	8 774 963	4 409 155	4 365 808	9 206 461	4 623 167	4 583 294
0-4	792 517	405 648	386 869	802 844	410 872	391 972
5-9	759 289	388 451	370 839	786 804	402 501	384 303
10-14	716 250	366 289	349 961	756 954	387 126	369 828
15-19	683 901	349 544	334 357	713 364	364 598	348 766
20-24	671 852	343 312	328 539	679 196	346 752	332 444
25-29	667 437	340 929	326 508	665 390	339 739	325 651
30-34	628 514	321 067	307 447	659 150	336 624	322 526
35-39	564 772	288 386	276 386	619 630	316 428	303 203
40-44	490 677	250 213	240 464	556 283	283 753	272 531
45-49	475 748	242 142	233 607	482 527	245 519	237 007
50-54	463 610	234 961	228 649	465 946	236 205	229 741
55-59	443 443	222 921	220 523	450 247	226 646	223 601
60-64	381 979	188 774	193 205	423 925	210 734	213 191
65-69	317 517	153 376	164 140	355 262	172 481	182 781
70-74	276 074	129 209	146 865	282 096	132 586	149 510
75-79	212 178	94 611	117 567	228 416	102 472	125 944
80-84	131 779	54 917	76 862	156 275	65 256	91 019
85-89	64 747	24 469	40 278	81 155	30 454	50 700
90-94	25 650	8 178	17 472	30 958	9 955	21 003
95-99	6 070	1 560	4 510	8 707	2 197	6 510
100 +	961	199	762	1 333	268	1 065

United Nations Department of Economic and Social Affairs/Population Division
World Population Prospects: The 2004 Revision, Volume II: Sex and Age Distribution of the World Population

30

POPULATION BY AGE AND SEX (in thousands)

Age group	2005 Both sexes	2005 Males	2005 Females	2010 Both sexes	2010 Males	2010 Females	2015 Both sexes	2015 Males	2015 Females	2020 Both sexes	2020 Males	2020 Females
All ages	5 253 484	2 661 284	2 592 200	5 566 154	2 816 033	2 750 121	5 844 499	2 952 668	2 891 830	6 081 348	3 067 467	3 013 881
0-4	551 030	282 471	268 559	515 220	263 951	251 269	493 927	252 970	240 957	467 574	239 382	228 192
5-9	533 858	273 952	259 906	537 993	275 810	262 183	503 960	258 141	245 819	484 325	247 968	236 357
10-14	530 286	272 318	257 967	529 130	271 466	257 663	533 367	273 371	259 997	499 872	255 975	243 896
15-19	522 221	268 163	254 058	526 082	269 984	256 099	525 198	269 270	255 927	529 608	271 265	258 344
20-24	471 294	240 948	230 346	515 841	264 478	251 363	520 133	266 528	253 605	519 620	266 034	253 586
25-29	419 847	214 019	205 828	462 837	236 272	226 565	507 514	259 861	247 653	512 176	262 154	250 022
30-34	406 312	206 714	199 599	410 263	208 908	201 356	452 978	231 046	221 932	497 452	254 557	242 895
35-39	377 440	191 278	186 163	396 844	201 533	195 311	400 740	203 757	196 983	442 861	225 620	217 241
40-44	325 207	164 577	160 630	368 606	186 239	182 367	387 867	196 423	191 445	391 681	198 639	193 042
45-49	271 534	137 831	133 704	316 641	159 530	157 111	359 704	180 991	178 713	378 860	191 091	187 769
50-54	237 222	119 528	117 694	262 324	132 266	130 057	306 869	153 634	153 235	349 468	174 789	174 679
55-59	178 930	89 158	89 772	226 251	112 849	113 402	250 888	125 275	125 612	294 577	146 109	148 468
60-64	137 630	67 371	70 260	166 370	81 640	84 730	211 578	103 967	107 612	235 488	115 894	119 594
65-69	112 111	53 736	58 375	122 690	58 716	63 974	149 579	71 795	77 785	191 635	92 136	99 500
70-74	83 178	38 771	44 408	93 485	43 368	50 118	103 425	47 949	55 476	127 506	59 305	68 200
75-79	53 206	23 649	29 557	62 525	27 842	34 683	71 362	31 637	39 725	80 117	35 520	44 598
80-84	27 559	11 444	16 115	34 066	14 232	19 834	40 911	17 110	23 801	47 664	19 844	27 820
85-89	10 934	4 135	6 799	13 955	5 303	8 652	17 756	6 765	10 991	21 921	8 327	13 595
90-94	3 033	1 030	2 003	4 112	1 375	2 736	5 444	1 809	3 635	7 156	2 367	4 789
95-99	576	172	404	805	239	566	1 135	325	810	1 554	432	1 121
100 +	78	21	56	115	32	83	164	44	119	232	60	173

Age group	2025 Both sexes	2025 Males	2025 Females	2030 Both sexes	2030 Males	2030 Females	2035 Both sexes	2035 Males	2035 Females	2040 Both sexes	2040 Males	2040 Females
All ages	6 286 423	3 165 299	3 121 124	6 449 804	3 241 175	3 208 629	6 564 881	3 292 088	3 272 793	6 631 856	3 318 505	3 313 351
0-4	453 164	231 934	221 230	430 914	220 355	210 559	404 623	206 859	197 764	380 344	194 421	185 923
5-9	459 469	235 128	224 341	446 207	228 257	217 950	425 039	217 233	207 805	399 703	204 227	195 476
10-14	480 863	246 120	234 740	455 549	232 551	222 992	443 692	226 890	216 802	422 884	216 053	206 831
15-19	496 458	254 055	242 403	477 734	244 348	233 385	453 689	231 927	221 762	441 050	225 377	215 672
20-24	524 252	268 146	256 105	491 487	251 151	240 336	473 077	241 626	231 451	449 350	229 389	219 961
25-29	512 042	261 873	250 169	516 975	264 143	252 832	484 854	247 507	237 348	466 964	238 273	228 691
30-34	502 394	257 031	245 362	502 729	257 012	245 716	508 121	259 540	248 581	476 899	243 387	233 512
35-39	487 004	248 966	238 038	492 313	251 682	240 630	493 176	251 981	241 195	499 080	254 808	244 272
40-44	433 285	220 241	213 044	477 242	243 491	233 750	482 927	246 471	236 456	404 304	247 095	237 209
45-49	382 778	193 390	189 388	424 058	214 813	209 246	467 830	237 966	229 864	473 888	241 206	232 682
50-54	355 594	184 840	170 754	372 817	187 323	185 494	413 718	208 509	205 209	457 190	231 481	225 709
55-59	336 469	166 793	169 676	355 602	176 805	178 797	360 197	179 498	180 698	400 816	200 004	200 812
60-64	277 799	135 856	141 943	318 547	155 786	162 761	337 574	165 669	171 904	342 616	168 607	174 009
65-69	214 384	103 292	111 092	254 505	121 922	132 583	293 320	140 612	152 707	311 976	150 190	161 786
70-74	164 949	76 858	88 091	185 908	86 903	99 005	222 570	103 502	119 067	258 250	120 252	137 998
75-79	100 237	44 567	55 670	131 410	58 540	72 070	149 660	66 948	82 712	181 179	80 641	100 538
80-84	54 533	22 691	31 843	69 598	29 011	40 586	92 829	38 722	54 107	107 247	44 950	62 297
85-89	26 219	9 891	16 328	30 757	11 597	19 160	40 279	15 173	25 106	54 945	20 643	34 302
90-94	9 105	2 975	6 130	11 255	3 647	7 608	13 593	4 400	9 193	18 333	5 895	12 438
95-99	2 103	574	1 529	2 762	734	2 028	3 525	926	2 599	4 375	1 143	3 232
100 +	321	78	244	442	102	340	588	128	460	763	162	602

Age group	2045 Both sexes	2045 Males	2045 Females	2050 Both sexes	2050 Males	2050 Females
All ages	6 650 432	3 320 657	3 329 775	6 622 229	3 299 662	3 322 567
0-4	356 142	182 033	174 109	332 793	170 082	162 711
5-9	376 259	192 216	184 044	352 767	180 191	172 576
10-14	397 861	203 208	194 652	374 680	191 331	183 349
15-19	420 449	214 651	205 798	395 625	201 913	193 712
20-24	436 960	222 982	213 978	416 626	212 407	204 218
25-29	443 766	226 324	217 441	431 820	220 154	211 666
30-34	459 741	234 533	225 207	437 295	222 968	214 327
35-39	468 828	239 182	229 645	452 455	230 741	221 714
40-44	490 677	250 213	240 464	461 329	235 103	226 226
45-49	475 748	242 141	233 606	482 526	245 519	237 007
50-54	463 609	234 961	228 648	465 945	236 205	229 740
55-59	443 442	222 920	220 522	450 246	226 646	223 600
60-64	381 978	188 773	193 205	423 924	210 733	213 191
65-69	317 516	153 376	164 140	355 261	172 480	182 781
70-74	276 073	129 208	146 865	282 096	132 586	149 509
75-79	212 178	94 611	117 567	228 415	102 472	125 944
80-84	131 779	54 917	76 862	156 274	65 256	91 018
85-89	64 747	24 469	40 278	81 155	30 454	50 700
90-94	25 650	8 178	17 472	30 958	9 955	21 003
95-99	6 070	1 560	4 510	8 707	2 197	6 510
100 +	961	199	762	1 333	268	1 065

POPULATION BY AGE AND SEX (in thousands)

Age group	1950 Both sexes	Males	Females	1955 Both sexes	Males	Females	1960 Both sexes	Males	Females	1965 Both sexes	Males	Females
All ages	200 789	100 980	99 809	221 538	111 364	110 174	246 910	124 028	122 882	277 308	139 195	138 113
0-4	33 540	16 828	16 712	38 377	19 355	19 022	43 383	21 897	21 486	49 363	24 931	24 432
5-9	26 332	13 187	13 145	29 397	14 768	14 629	34 108	17 226	16 882	38 950	19 682	19 268
10-14	22 614	11 338	11 276	25 289	12 682	12 607	28 336	14 251	14 085	32 963	16 666	16 297
15-19	19 925	10 061	9 864	21 830	10 959	10 871	24 485	12 290	12 195	27 483	13 830	13 653
20-24	17 486	8 849	8 636	19 022	9 592	9 430	20 912	10 478	10 434	23 487	11 762	11 724
25-29	15 070	7 637	7 433	16 519	8 334	8 184	18 043	9 064	8 979	19 861	9 911	9 950
30-34	13 054	6 639	6 415	14 168	7 169	7 000	15 600	7 853	7 748	17 070	8 552	8 518
35-39	11 472	5 936	5 536	12 195	6 195	6 000	13 301	6 717	6 584	14 685	7 374	7 311
40-44	10 074	5 186	4 888	10 630	5 481	5 149	11 362	5 748	5 614	12 438	6 254	6 184
45-49	8 079	4 086	3 993	9 240	4 720	4 521	9 813	5 019	4 794	10 532	5 285	5 247
50-54	6 763	3 406	3 357	7 294	3 646	3 648	8 400	4 243	4 158	8 961	4 533	4 428
55-59	5 467	2 714	2 753	5 931	2 946	2 985	6 451	3 181	3 270	7 470	3 723	3 746
60-64	4 271	2 083	2 187	4 568	2 234	2 334	5 008	2 451	2 557	5 493	2 668	2 825
65-69	3 069	1 449	1 621	3 292	1 581	1 711	3 572	1 719	1 853	3 962	1 907	2 055
70-74	1 966	890	1 075	2 094	970	1 123	2 290	1 079	1 211	2 526	1 192	1 334
75-79	1 063	459	604	1 108	489	619	1 213	548	665	1 359	624	735
80 +	547	233	313	584	242	342	632	264	368	705	300	406

Age group	1970 Both sexes	Males	Females	1975 Both sexes	Males	Females	1980 Both sexes	Males	Females	1985 Both sexes	Males	Females
All ages	314 107	157 518	156 588	355 870	178 371	177 499	402 902	201 624	201 278	457 958	229 113	228 845
0-4	56 220	28 386	27 834	63 531	32 119	31 412	71 271	36 049	35 222	81 549	41 273	40 276
5-9	44 834	22 658	22 176	51 319	25 927	25 392	58 282	29 484	28 797	65 645	33 216	32 429
10-14	37 831	19 132	18 699	43 494	21 991	21 503	49 690	25 102	24 588	56 524	28 605	27 919
15-19	32 100	16 236	15 864	36 733	18 577	18 156	42 212	21 316	20 896	48 250	24 364	23 886
20-24	26 468	13 285	13 183	30 830	15 550	15 280	35 330	17 783	17 547	40 581	20 426	20 155
25-29	22 414	11 173	11 241	25 225	12 591	12 634	29 419	14 742	14 677	33 706	16 881	16 825
30-34	18 888	9 392	9 495	21 283	10 564	10 719	23 976	11 893	12 083	27 960	13 953	14 007
35-39	16 166	8 076	8 090	17 848	8 845	9 004	20 142	9 938	10 204	22 718	11 224	11 494
40-44	13 818	6 908	6 910	15 194	7 556	7 638	16 741	8 233	8 508	18 963	9 306	9 658
45-49	11 605	5 788	5 816	12 893	6 399	6 494	14 158	6 962	7 196	15 679	7 650	8 030
50-54	9 690	4 809	4 881	10 680	5 277	5 404	11 869	5 810	6 058	13 071	6 362	6 709
55-59	8 040	4 014	4 026	8 717	4 277	4 440	9 607	4 674	4 934	10 760	5 199	5 560
60-64	6 422	3 153	3 269	6 948	3 425	3 523	7 570	3 661	3 908	8 374	4 013	4 361
65-69	4 409	2 105	2 304	5 199	2 516	2 683	5 665	2 746	2 919	6 228	2 960	3 267
70-74	2 854	1 346	1 508	3 223	1 512	1 711	3 826	1 814	2 012	4 206	1 993	2 213
75-79	1 537	706	831	1 789	824	965	2 022	924	1 098	2 423	1 115	1 309
80 +	811	350	460	966	423	543	1 123	493	630	1 322	573	748

Age group	1990 Both sexes	Males	Females	1995 Both sexes	Males	Females	2000 Both sexes	Males	Females	2005 Both sexes	Males	Females
All ages	521 816	260 942	260 874	596 962	298 400	298 562	673 524	336 756	336 768	759 389	380 048	379 341
0-4	90 779	45 964	44 815	101 447	51 353	50 094	109 289	55 346	53 944	119 353	60 451	58 902
5-9	76 074	38 507	37 567	85 572	43 317	42 256	95 656	48 400	47 256	103 834	52 555	51 279
10-14	64 153	32 469	31 685	74 659	37 803	36 856	83 967	42 504	41 463	94 103	47 615	46 488
15-19	55 202	27 924	27 277	63 029	31 855	31 174	73 423	37 159	36 263	82 912	41 950	40 963
20-24	46 608	23 445	23 163	53 729	27 008	26 721	61 330	30 906	30 423	71 932	36 312	35 620
25-29	38 852	19 436	19 416	44 804	22 363	22 441	51 377	25 745	25 632	59 140	29 744	29 396
30-34	32 161	16 018	16 143	37 264	18 539	18 726	42 296	21 075	21 221	48 796	24 482	24 314
35-39	26 611	13 213	13 398	30 848	15 305	15 543	35 102	17 416	17 686	39 944	19 919	20 025
40-44	21 523	10 569	10 954	25 485	12 610	12 876	29 072	14 357	14 714	33 159	16 420	16 739
45-49	17 855	8 691	9 164	20 522	10 025	10 498	23 994	11 786	12 208	27 457	13 489	13 968
50-54	14 603	7 051	7 552	16 876	8 157	8 719	19 176	9 270	9 906	22 537	10 976	11 561
55-59	11 936	5 738	6 198	13 553	6 485	7 068	15 520	7 405	8 116	17 750	8 478	9 272
60-64	9 495	4 519	4 977	10 719	5 093	5 626	12 096	5 697	6 399	13 969	6 562	7 407
65-69	6 970	3 280	3 691	8 069	3 782	4 287	9 069	4 229	4 840	10 345	4 782	5 564
70-74	4 697	2 183	2 514	5 390	2 484	2 906	6 235	2 857	3 378	7 109	3 240	3 869
75-79	2 716	1 248	1 468	3 122	1 408	1 714	3 605	1 613	1 992	4 252	1 891	2 361
80 +	1 581	688	893	1 873	816	1 057	2 319	991	1 327	2 797	1 182	1 615

(*) The least developed countries, as defined by the United Nations General Assembly in 2003, included 50 countries, of which 34 are in Africa, 10 in Asia, 1 in Latin America and the Caribbean, and 5 in Oceania.

United Nations Department of Economic and Social Affairs/Population Division
World Population Prospects: The 2004 Revision, Volume II: Sex and Age Distribution of the World Population

POPULATION BY AGE AND SEX (in thousands)

Age group	2005 Both sexes	Males	Females	2010 Both sexes	Males	Females	2015 Both sexes	Males	Females	2020 Both sexes	Males	Females
All ages	759 389	380 048	379 341	852 025	426 835	425 190	951 610	477 138	474 472	1 057 086	530 392	526 694
0-4	119 353	60 451	58 902	129 959	65 825	64 134	140 185	71 015	69 171	148 568	75 274	73 295
5-9	103 834	52 555	51 279	113 675	57 532	56 143	124 327	62 912	61 416	134 916	68 272	66 644
10-14	94 103	47 615	46 488	102 024	51 634	50 390	111 734	56 537	55 197	122 404	61 919	60 485
15-19	82 912	41 950	40 963	92 876	46 969	45 907	100 712	50 937	49 775	110 393	55 817	54 577
20-24	71 932	36 312	35 620	81 241	41 010	40 232	91 090	45 961	45 129	98 925	49 916	49 009
25-29	59 140	29 744	29 396	69 446	35 007	34 439	78 553	39 605	38 948	88 380	44 533	43 847
30-34	48 796	24 482	24 314	56 239	28 339	27 900	66 202	33 442	32 759	75 150	37 970	37 180
35-39	39 944	19 919	20 025	46 129	23 189	22 940	53 260	26 900	26 360	62 929	31 867	31 062
40-44	33 159	16 420	16 739	37 779	18 823	18 955	43 722	21 972	21 750	50 609	25 564	25 045
45-49	27 457	13 489	13 968	31 366	15 466	15 900	35 839	17 790	18 049	41 597	20 837	20 760
50-54	22 537	10 976	11 561	25 837	12 596	13 241	29 614	14 499	15 115	33 960	16 746	17 213
55-59	17 750	8 478	9 272	20 922	10 077	10 846	24 080	11 615	12 465	27 722	13 435	14 287
60-64	13 969	6 562	7 407	16 038	7 544	8 494	19 008	9 021	9 987	22 001	10 461	11 541
65-69	10 345	4 782	5 564	12 021	5 541	6 480	13 905	6 417	7 488	16 610	7 737	8 873
70-74	7 109	3 240	3 869	8 184	3 695	4 489	9 614	4 328	5 287	11 246	5 068	6 178
75-79	4 252	1 891	2 361	4 910	2 171	2 739	5 738	2 512	3 226	6 850	2 988	3 862
80-84	1 972	849	1 123	2 365	1 012	1 353	2 781	1 182	1 599	3 315	1 394	1 921
85-89	665	273	392	802	327	476	984	398	586	1 182	475	707
90-94	140	54	86	182	68	114	225	84	142	283	105	178
95-99	18	6	12	24	8	16	32	11	22	41	13	28
100 +	1	0	1	2	1	1	3	1	2	4	1	3

Age group	2025 Both sexes	Males	Females	2030 Both sexes	Males	Females	2035 Both sexes	Males	Females	2040 Both sexes	Males	Females
All ages	1 167 461	586 040	581 421	1 281 335	643 318	638 017	1 397 057	701 391	695 666	1 512 643	759 220	753 422
0-4	155 569	78 844	76 725	161 320	81 779	79 541	165 866	84 103	81 763	168 770	85 598	83 173
5-9	143 792	72 772	71 020	151 298	76 594	74 704	157 561	79 787	77 774	162 591	82 356	80 235
10-14	133 180	67 367	65 813	142 260	71 960	70 298	149 965	75 883	74 082	156 400	79 159	77 241
15-19	121 088	61 203	59 884	131 916	66 671	65 245	141 078	71 304	69 774	148 898	75 255	73 902
20-24	108 610	54 787	53 823	119 306	60 164	59 142	130 156	65 634	64 522	139 375	70 291	69 084
25-29	96 223	48 481	47 742	105 889	53 331	52 558	116 576	58 693	57 883	127 452	64 170	63 282
30-34	84 919	42 859	42 060	92 738	46 784	45 955	102 362	51 602	50 760	113 028	56 947	56 081
35-39	71 719	36 317	35 402	81 402	41 153	40 249	89 173	45 046	44 127	98 747	49 834	48 914
40-44	60 052	30 412	29 639	68 712	34 790	33 922	78 276	39 560	38 710	85 095	43 425	42 570
45-49	48 309	24 330	23 979	57 574	29 072	28 502	66 086	33 366	32 720	75 523	38 067	37 456
50-54	39 565	19 697	19 868	46 122	23 090	23 032	55 174	27 702	27 473	63 512	31 893	31 620
55-59	31 941	15 598	16 344	37 378	18 434	18 945	43 736	21 696	22 040	52 520	26 137	26 383
60-64	25 485	12 178	13 307	29 536	14 224	15 312	34 737	16 901	17 836	40 820	19 983	20 836
65-69	19 383	9 045	10 338	22 628	10 611	12 016	26 412	12 485	13 927	31 257	14 930	16 327
70-74	13 590	6 182	7 409	16 031	7 302	8 728	18 903	8 652	10 251	22 276	10 272	12 004
75-79	8 143	3 555	4 589	9 994	4 401	5 593	11 954	5 269	6 685	14 291	6 319	7 971
80-84	4 045	1 694	2 351	4 910	2 055	2 856	6 142	2 592	3 550	7 492	3 152	4 339
85-89	1 443	573	870	1 807	714	1 093	2 248	887	1 361	2 890	1 140	1 750
90-94	347	128	220	435	158	277	560	202	358	722	256	466
95-99	53	17	36	66	21	45	85	26	58	114	35	79
100 +	5	1	4	6	2	5	8	2	6	11	2	8

Age group	2045 Both sexes	Males	Females	2050 Both sexes	Males	Females
All ages	1 626 025	815 748	810 277	1 735 368	870 016	865 352
0-4	169 910	86 199	83 711	169 623	86 068	83 554
5-9	165 973	84 091	81 882	167 560	84 916	82 643
10-14	161 586	81 804	79 782	165 112	83 608	81 504
15-19	155 376	78 568	76 807	160 648	81 252	79 396
20-24	147 230	74 276	72 954	153 839	77 633	76 206
25-29	136 764	68 868	67 896	144 749	72 913	71 836
30-34	123 943	62 436	61 508	133 383	67 186	66 196
35-39	109 397	55 166	54 231	120 352	60 665	59 686
40-44	95 524	48 189	47 336	106 149	53 506	52 643
45-49	83 189	41 904	41 285	92 663	46 637	46 026
50-54	72 798	36 505	36 293	80 384	40 294	40 089
55-59	60 639	30 193	30 447	69 717	34 677	35 040
60-64	49 237	24 189	25 048	57 052	28 054	28 998
65-69	36 927	17 750	19 177	44 797	21 615	23 182
70-74	26 586	12 385	14 201	31 635	14 830	16 805
75-79	17 062	7 591	9 471	20 596	9 250	11 345
80-84	9 131	3 837	5 294	11 103	4 676	6 427
85-89	3 621	1 412	2 209	4 530	1 746	2 784
90-94	962	336	626	1 245	423	823
95-99	153	45	108	213	60	153
100 +	15	3	11	21	4	16

POPULATION BY AGE AND SEX (in thousands)

Age group	2005 Both sexes	Males	Females	2010 Both sexes	Males	Females	2015 Both sexes	Males	Females	2020 Both sexes	Males	Females
All ages	759 389	380 048	379 341	858 183	429 964	428 219	970 119	486 538	483 582	1 093 369	548 801	544 568
0-4	119 353	60 451	58 902	136 117	68 954	67 163	152 746	77 393	75 353	166 804	84 522	82 282
5-9	103 834	52 555	51 279	113 675	57 532	56 143	130 276	65 933	64 343	147 083	74 446	72 637
10-14	94 103	47 615	46 488	102 024	51 634	50 390	111 734	56 537	55 197	128 285	64 905	63 380
15-19	82 912	41 950	40 963	92 876	46 969	45 907	100 712	50 937	49 775	110 393	55 817	54 577
20-24	71 932	36 312	35 620	81 241	41 010	40 232	91 090	45 961	45 129	98 925	49 916	49 009
25-29	59 140	29 744	29 396	69 446	35 007	34 439	78 553	39 605	38 948	88 380	44 533	43 847
30-34	48 796	24 482	24 314	56 239	28 339	27 900	66 202	33 442	32 759	75 150	37 970	37 180
35-39	39 944	19 919	20 025	46 129	23 189	22 940	53 260	26 900	26 360	62 929	31 867	31 062
40-44	33 159	16 420	16 739	37 779	18 823	18 955	43 722	21 972	21 750	50 609	25 564	25 045
45-49	27 457	13 489	13 968	31 366	15 466	15 900	35 839	17 790	18 049	41 597	20 837	20 760
50-54	22 537	10 976	11 561	25 837	12 596	13 241	29 614	14 499	15 115	33 960	16 746	17 213
55-59	17 750	8 478	9 272	20 922	10 077	10 846	24 080	11 615	12 465	27 722	13 435	14 287
60-64	13 969	6 562	7 407	16 038	7 544	8 494	19 008	9 021	9 987	22 001	10 461	11 541
65-69	10 345	4 782	5 564	12 021	5 541	6 480	13 905	6 417	7 488	16 610	7 737	8 873
70-74	7 109	3 240	3 869	8 184	3 695	4 489	9 614	4 328	5 287	11 246	5 068	6 178
75-79	4 252	1 891	2 361	4 910	2 171	2 739	5 738	2 512	3 226	6 850	2 988	3 862
80-84	1 972	849	1 123	2 365	1 012	1 353	2 781	1 182	1 599	3 315	1 394	1 921
85-89	665	273	392	802	327	476	984	398	586	1 182	475	707
90-94	140	54	86	182	68	114	225	84	142	283	105	178
95-99	18	6	12	24	8	16	32	11	22	41	13	28
100 +	1	0	1	2	1	1	3	1	2	4	1	3

Age group	2025 Both sexes	Males	Females	2030 Both sexes	Males	Females	2035 Both sexes	Males	Females	2040 Both sexes	Males	Females
All ages	1 224 160	614 791	609 369	1 362 935	684 680	678 255	1 510 525	758 889	751 635	1 666 501	837 175	829 326
0-4	176 640	89 532	87 108	186 999	94 807	92 191	198 702	100 766	97 936	210 442	106 748	103 694
5-9	161 542	81 765	79 777	171 892	87 029	84 863	182 747	92 552	90 195	194 886	98 728	96 158
10-14	145 223	73 477	71 746	159 861	80 878	78 983	170 410	86 237	84 173	181 433	91 840	89 593
15-19	126 923	64 164	62 759	143 873	72 733	71 140	158 559	80 150	78 409	169 186	85 542	83 644
20-24	108 610	54 787	53 823	125 082	63 091	61 991	141 995	71 628	70 367	156 696	79 042	77 654
25-29	96 223	48 481	47 742	105 889	53 331	52 558	122 258	61 570	60 687	139 106	70 066	69 040
30-34	84 919	42 859	42 060	92 738	46 784	45 955	102 362	51 602	50 760	118 583	59 763	58 820
35-39	71 719	36 317	35 402	81 402	41 153	40 249	89 173	45 046	44 127	98 747	49 834	48 914
40-44	60 052	30 412	29 639	68 712	34 790	33 922	78 276	39 560	38 716	85 995	43 425	42 570
45-49	48 309	24 330	23 979	57 574	29 072	28 502	66 086	33 366	32 720	75 523	38 067	37 456
50-54	39 565	19 697	19 868	46 122	23 090	23 032	55 174	27 702	27 473	63 512	31 893	31 620
55-59	31 941	15 598	16 344	37 378	18 434	18 945	43 736	21 696	22 040	52 520	26 137	26 383
60-64	25 485	12 178	13 307	29 536	14 224	15 312	34 737	16 901	17 836	40 820	19 983	20 836
65-69	19 383	9 045	10 338	22 628	10 611	12 016	26 412	12 485	13 927	31 257	14 930	16 327
70-74	13 590	6 182	7 409	16 031	7 302	8 728	18 903	8 652	10 251	22 276	10 272	12 004
75-79	8 143	3 555	4 589	9 994	4 401	5 593	11 954	5 269	6 685	14 291	6 319	7 971
80-84	4 045	1 694	2 351	4 910	2 055	2 856	6 142	2 592	3 550	7 492	3 152	4 339
85-89	1 443	573	870	1 807	714	1 093	2 248	887	1 361	2 890	1 140	1 750
90-94	347	128	220	435	158	277	560	202	358	722	256	466
95-99	53	17	36	66	21	45	85	26	58	114	35	79
100 +	5	1	4	6	2	5	8	2	6	11	2	8

Age group	2045 Both sexes	Males	Females	2050 Both sexes	Males	Females
All ages	1 828 505	918 334	910 171	1 993 676	1 000 885	992 791
0-4	220 209	111 732	108 477	227 542	115 473	112 069
5-9	207 062	104 926	102 136	217 269	110 124	107 144
10-14	193 718	98 086	95 633	206 025	104 343	101 683
15-19	180 283	91 176	89 107	192 637	97 449	95 188
20-24	167 389	84 463	82 926	178 560	90 129	88 431
25-29	153 827	77 482	76 345	164 638	82 956	81 682
30-34	135 351	68 212	67 138	150 097	75 632	74 465
35-39	114 820	57 918	56 902	131 501	66 317	65 184
40-44	95 524	48 189	47 336	111 451	56 196	55 256
45-49	83 189	41 904	41 285	92 663	46 637	46 026
50-54	72 798	36 505	36 293	80 384	40 294	40 089
55-59	60 639	30 193	30 447	69 717	34 677	35 040
60-64	49 237	24 189	25 048	57 052	28 054	28 998
65-69	36 927	17 750	19 177	44 797	21 615	23 182
70-74	26 586	12 385	14 201	31 635	14 830	16 805
75-79	17 062	7 591	9 471	20 596	9 250	11 345
80-84	9 131	3 837	5 294	11 103	4 676	6 427
85-89	3 621	1 412	2 209	4 530	1 746	2 784
90-94	962	336	626	1 245	423	823
95-99	153	45	108	213	60	153
100 +	15	3	11	21	4	16

United Nations Department of Economic and Social Affairs/Population Division
World Population Prospects: The 2004 Revision, Volume II: Sex and Age Distribution of the World Population

34

POPULATION BY AGE AND SEX (in thousands)

Age group	2005 Both sexes	Males	Females	2010 Both sexes	Males	Females	2015 Both sexes	Males	Females	2020 Both sexes	Males	Females
All ages	759 389	380 048	379 341	844 949	423 247	421 703	931 868	467 128	464 740	1 019 517	511 348	500 100
0-4	119 353	60 451	58 902	122 884	62 237	60 647	127 261	64 459	62 802	130 252	65 984	64 268
5-9	103 834	52 555	51 279	113 675	57 532	56 143	117 510	59 457	58 053	122 394	61 927	60 467
10-14	94 103	47 615	46 488	102 024	51 634	50 390	111 734	56 537	55 197	115 673	58 509	57 164
15-19	82 912	41 950	40 963	92 876	46 969	45 907	100 712	50 937	49 775	110 393	55 817	54 577
20-24	71 932	36 312	35 620	81 241	41 010	40 232	91 090	45 961	45 129	98 925	49 916	49 009
25-29	59 140	29 744	29 396	69 446	35 007	34 439	78 553	39 605	38 948	88 380	44 533	43 847
30-34	48 796	24 482	24 314	56 239	28 339	27 900	66 202	33 442	32 759	75 150	37 970	37 180
35-39	39 944	19 919	20 025	46 129	23 189	22 940	53 260	26 900	26 360	62 929	31 867	31 062
40-44	33 159	16 420	16 739	37 779	18 823	18 955	43 722	21 972	21 750	50 609	25 564	25 045
45-49	27 457	13 489	13 968	31 366	15 466	15 900	35 839	17 790	18 049	41 597	20 837	20 760
50-54	22 537	10 976	11 561	25 837	12 596	13 241	29 614	14 499	15 115	33 960	16 746	17 213
55-59	17 750	8 478	9 272	20 922	10 077	10 846	24 080	11 615	12 465	27 722	13 435	14 287
60-64	13 969	6 562	7 407	16 038	7 544	8 494	19 008	9 021	9 987	22 001	10 461	11 541
65-69	10 345	4 782	5 564	12 021	5 541	6 480	13 905	6 417	7 488	16 610	7 737	8 873
70-74	7 109	3 240	3 869	8 184	3 695	4 489	9 614	4 328	5 287	11 246	5 068	6 178
75-79	4 252	1 891	2 361	4 910	2 171	2 739	5 738	2 512	3 226	6 850	2 988	3 862
80-84	1 972	849	1 123	2 365	1 012	1 353	2 781	1 182	1 599	3 315	1 394	1 921
85-89	665	273	392	802	327	476	984	398	586	1 182	475	707
90-94	140	54	86	182	68	114	225	84	142	283	105	178
95-99	18	6	12	24	8	16	32	11	22	41	13	28
100 +	1	0	1	2	1	1	3	1	2	4	1	3

Age group	2025 Both sexes	Males	Females	2030 Both sexes	Males	Females	2035 Both sexes	Males	Females	2040 Both sexes	Males	Females
All ages	1 109 526	556 681	552 845	1 198 987	601 601	597 386	1 284 532	644 404	640 129	1 363 517	683 707	679 810
0-4	134 529	68 172	66 356	136 106	68 990	67 116	134 691	68 289	66 401	130 859	66 363	64 496
5-9	125 962	63 739	62 223	130 737	66 177	64 560	132 840	67 262	65 578	131 938	66 824	65 114
10-14	120 791	61 092	59 698	124 582	63 010	61 574	129 554	65 547	64 007	131 830	66 717	65 113
15-19	114 413	57 824	56 589	119 618	60 446	59 172	123 518	62 418	61 100	126 304	61 996	63 578
20-24	108 610	54 787	53 823	112 706	56 828	55 878	117 982	59 482	58 500	121 976	61 500	60 476
25-29	96 223	48 481	47 742	105 889	53 331	52 558	110 094	55 419	54 674	115 476	58 123	57 353
30-34	84 919	42 859	42 060	92 738	46 784	45 955	102 362	51 602	50 760	106 705	53 750	52 955
35-39	71 719	36 317	35 402	81 402	41 153	40 249	89 173	45 046	44 127	98 747	49 834	48 914
40-44	60 052	30 412	29 639	68 712	34 790	33 922	78 276	39 560	38 716	85 995	43 425	42 570
45-49	48 309	24 330	23 979	57 574	29 072	28 502	66 086	33 366	32 720	75 523	38 067	37 456
50-54	39 565	19 697	19 868	48 122	23 090	23 032	55 174	27 702	27 473	63 512	31 893	31 620
55-59	31 941	15 598	16 344	37 378	18 434	18 945	43 736	21 696	22 040	50 520	25 137	26 383
60-64	25 485	12 178	13 307	29 536	14 224	15 312	34 737	16 901	17 836	40 820	19 983	20 836
65-69	19 383	9 045	10 338	22 628	10 611	12 016	26 412	12 485	13 927	31 257	14 930	16 327
70-74	13 500	6 182	7 409	16 031	7 302	8 728	18 903	8 652	10 251	22 276	10 272	12 004
75-79	8 143	3 555	4 589	9 994	4 401	5 593	11 954	5 269	6 685	14 291	6 319	7 971
80-84	4 045	1 694	2 351	4 910	2 055	2 856	6 142	2 592	3 550	7 492	3 152	4 339
85-89	1 443	573	870	1 807	714	1 093	2 248	887	1 361	2 890	1 140	1 750
90-94	347	128	220	435	158	277	560	202	358	722	256	466
95-99	53	17	36	66	21	45	85	26	58	114	35	79
100 +	5	1	4	6	2	5	8	2	6	11	2	8

Age group	2045 Both sexes	Males	Females	2050 Both sexes	Males	Females
All ages	1 434 476	718 753	715 723	1 496 542	749 080	747 461
0-4	125 798	63 813	61 985	120 272	61 019	59 253
5-9	128 601	65 150	63 451	123 976	62 821	61 155
10-14	131 092	66 361	64 732	127 904	64 760	63 144
15-19	130 933	66 200	64 733	130 294	65 892	64 403
20-24	127 105	64 108	62 998	129 582	65 376	64 206
25-29	119 623	60 214	59 409	124 896	62 890	62 006
30-34	112 236	56 518	55 718	116 592	58 702	57 890
35-39	103 241	52 050	51 191	108 926	54 885	54 041
40-44	95 524	48 189	47 336	100 145	50 467	49 678
45-49	83 189	41 904	41 285	92 663	46 637	46 026
50-54	72 798	36 505	36 293	80 384	40 294	40 089
55-59	60 639	30 193	30 447	69 717	34 677	35 040
60-64	49 237	24 189	25 048	57 052	28 054	28 998
65-69	36 927	17 750	19 177	44 797	21 615	23 182
70-74	26 586	12 385	14 201	31 635	14 830	16 805
75-79	17 062	7 591	9 471	20 596	9 250	11 345
80-84	9 131	3 837	5 294	11 103	4 676	6 427
85-89	3 621	1 412	2 209	4 530	1 746	2 784
90-94	962	336	626	1 245	423	823
95-99	153	45	108	213	60	153
100 +	15	3	11	21	4	16

POPULATION BY AGE AND SEX (in thousands)

Age group	1950 Both sexes	1950 Males	1950 Females	1955 Both sexes	1955 Males	1955 Females	1960 Both sexes	1960 Males	1960 Females	1965 Both sexes	1965 Males	1965 Females
All ages	1 505 909	768 864	737 045	1 672 641	852 740	819 902	1 861 602	948 674	912 928	2 094 033	1 067 364	1 026 669
0-4	222 786	114 312	108 474	274 209	139 935	134 274	295 834	151 226	144 608	339 428	173 791	165 638
5-9	174 928	89 236	85 692	204 165	105 007	99 157	254 868	130 465	124 403	278 487	142 899	135 589
10-14	161 625	83 290	78 336	170 939	87 399	83 540	200 287	103 122	97 166	250 425	128 410	122 016
15-19	151 148	78 049	73 100	158 589	81 771	76 817	167 748	85 897	81 851	196 631	101 255	95 376
20-24	132 449	68 343	64 106	146 821	75 759	71 061	154 887	79 767	75 120	163 567	83 772	79 795
25-29	115 522	59 613	55 909	128 007	65 953	62 054	142 271	73 296	68 975	150 606	77 462	73 144
30-34	101 269	52 243	49 026	110 974	57 256	53 718	123 894	63 888	60 006	137 705	70 929	66 776
35-39	91 095	47 007	44 088	96 351	49 635	46 716	106 582	54 946	51 636	119 677	61 683	57 994
40-44	80 241	41 288	38 954	85 878	44 060	41 818	91 583	46 970	44 613	102 121	52 494	49 627
45-49	69 451	35 791	33 660	74 561	37 926	36 635	80 658	41 058	39 600	86 622	44 173	42 449
50-54	57 460	29 330	28 130	63 064	31 843	31 221	68 788	34 531	34 257	75 123	37 855	37 268
55-59	48 835	24 680	24 155	49 933	24 787	25 146	56 212	27 781	28 431	62 455	30 861	31 594
60-64	38 904	19 032	19 871	41 839	20 742	21 097	42 357	20 471	21 886	48 843	23 597	25 246
65-69	28 235	12 807	15 428	30 754	14 778	15 976	33 775	16 475	17 300	34 309	16 085	18 224
70-74	17 762	7 935	9 827	20 309	8 990	11 319	22 687	10 647	12 040	25 441	12 131	13 310
75-79	9 484	4 015	5 469	10 750	4 671	6 078	12 675	5 455	7 220	14 607	6 673	7 934
80 +	4 715	1 894	2 821	5 501	2 227	3 274	6 495	2 679	3 816	7 986	3 296	4 690

Age group	1970 Both sexes	1970 Males	1970 Females	1975 Both sexes	1975 Males	1975 Females	1980 Both sexes	1980 Males	1980 Females	1985 Both sexes	1985 Males	1985 Females
All ages	2 374 809	1 210 710	1 164 099	2 670 674	1 362 764	1 307 910	2 956 853	1 508 877	1 447 976	3 271 204	1 668 244	1 602 959
0-4	381 201	195 269	185 932	397 432	203 567	193 866	390 365	199 967	190 398	421 944	216 394	205 550
5-9	324 210	166 467	157 744	367 730	189 018	178 713	384 176	197 185	186 991	378 576	194 185	184 391
10-14	274 460	141 066	133 394	320 400	164 769	155 631	364 051	187 117	176 934	381 125	195 587	185 539
15-19	246 935	126 683	120 253	270 942	139 480	131 462	316 530	162 658	153 872	361 140	185 517	175 623
20-24	192 824	99 149	93 675	242 344	124 313	118 031	266 520	137 214	129 306	312 909	160 676	152 233
25-29	159 695	81 730	77 965	188 972	96 986	91 986	238 500	122 415	116 086	263 535	135 628	127 908
30-34	147 012	75 506	71 506	156 217	79 988	76 230	186 110	95 481	90 629	235 677	120 970	114 706
35-39	133 914	68 941	64 974	143 978	73 944	70 033	153 215	78 542	74 672	183 484	94 094	89 390
40-44	115 947	59 660	56 287	130 258	67 075	63 183	141 111	72 414	68 697	149 956	76 714	73 242
45-49	98 013	50 161	47 852	112 416	57 758	54 658	126 208	64 874	61 335	136 898	69 888	67 010
50-54	81 839	41 400	40 439	93 639	47 666	45 973	107 990	55 210	52 780	120 927	61 664	59 263
55-59	69 386	34 565	34 820	76 231	38 167	38 065	87 805	44 299	43 506	101 423	51 292	50 131
60-64	55 512	26 930	28 582	62 135	30 512	31 622	68 913	34 014	34 898	79 627	39 526	40 101
65-69	40 952	19 266	21 686	47 068	22 324	24 744	53 253	25 622	27 631	59 155	28 458	30 697
70-74	25 910	11 754	14 156	31 564	14 412	17 152	37 346	17 131	20 215	42 104	19 549	22 555
75-79	17 007	7 891	9 116	17 237	7 514	9 723	21 885	9 549	12 336	26 009	11 376	14 633
80 +	9 992	4 272	5 720	12 107	5 271	6 836	12 874	5 185	7 690	16 715	6 728	9 987

Age group	1990 Both sexes	1990 Males	1990 Females	1995 Both sexes	1995 Males	1995 Females	2000 Both sexes	2000 Males	2000 Females	2005 Both sexes	2005 Males	2005 Females
All ages	3 609 131	1 840 527	1 768 604	3 921 407	1 997 342	1 924 065	4 218 694	2 144 723	2 073 972	4 494 095	2 281 237	2 212 859
0-4	456 998	235 364	221 634	448 391	230 963	217 428	438 425	225 648	212 776	431 677	222 020	209 657
5-9	412 032	211 744	200 289	446 209	230 016	216 193	439 323	226 388	212 935	430 024	221 397	208 627
10-14	376 572	193 221	183 351	408 543	209 871	198 672	442 876	228 218	214 658	436 183	224 704	211 479
15-19	376 698	193 089	183 609	372 424	190 932	181 491	404 802	207 769	197 033	439 308	226 213	213 095
20-24	355 891	182 025	173 865	370 217	189 463	180 754	367 144	187 904	179 240	399 362	204 636	194 726
25-29	308 645	158 073	150 572	349 829	178 623	171 205	364 467	186 155	178 312	360 707	184 275	176 432
30-34	260 179	134 106	126 073	303 747	155 193	148 555	344 154	175 211	168 943	357 517	182 232	175 285
35-39	232 247	119 301	112 946	255 576	131 355	124 221	298 404	151 926	146 477	337 496	171 359	166 137
40-44	180 023	92 271	87 751	227 582	116 541	111 040	250 496	128 248	122 247	292 048	148 157	143 891
45-49	146 056	74 463	71 593	175 364	89 466	85 898	222 049	113 082	108 967	244 077	124 342	119 735
50-54	131 576	66 807	64 769	140 701	71 192	69 509	169 275	85 655	83 621	214 684	108 551	106 133
55-59	113 884	57 554	56 330	124 477	62 453	62 024	133 479	66 713	66 766	161 180	80 681	80 499
60-64	92 295	45 944	46 352	104 361	51 823	52 538	114 687	56 527	58 160	123 661	60 808	62 853
65-69	68 786	33 325	35 461	80 528	39 039	41 489	91 841	44 430	47 411	101 765	48 954	52 811
70-74	47 070	21 869	25 201	55 509	25 853	29 657	65 801	30 700	35 101	76 070	35 531	40 539
75-79	29 496	13 053	16 442	33 607	14 800	18 807	40 455	17 869	22 585	48 954	21 758	27 196
80 +	20 684	8 318	12 366	24 342	9 758	14 583	31 017	12 279	18 739	39 382	15 620	23 762

United Nations Department of Economic and Social Affairs/Population Division
World Population Prospects: The 2004 Revision, Volume II: Sex and Age Distribution of the World Population

LESS DEVELOPED REGIONS, EXCLUDING LEAST DEVELOPED COUNTRIES

POPULATION BY AGE AND SEX (in thousands)

Age group	2005 Both sexes	Males	Females	2010 Both sexes	Males	Females	2015 Both sexes	Males	Females	2020 Both sexes	Males	Females
All ages	4 494 095	2 281 237	2 212 859	4 765 221	2 415 480	2 349 741	5 031 261	2 546 677	2 484 584	5 276 399	2 666 633	2 609 756
0-4	431 677	222 020	209 657	436 352	224 408	211 944	441 723	227 183	214 540	434 044	223 198	210 847
5-9	430 024	221 397	208 627	424 319	218 278	206 041	430 023	221 148	208 875	436 342	224 374	211 968
10-14	436 183	224 704	211 479	427 106	219 832	207 273	421 633	216 833	204 799	427 623	219 848	207 775
15-19	439 308	226 213	213 095	433 206	223 015	210 191	424 486	218 333	206 152	419 215	215 448	203 767
20-24	399 362	204 636	194 726	434 600	223 468	211 132	429 043	220 567	208 475	420 695	216 118	204 577
25-29	360 707	184 275	176 432	393 391	201 265	192 126	428 962	220 256	208 705	423 796	217 621	206 175
30-34	357 517	182 232	175 285	354 024	180 568	173 456	386 776	197 604	189 173	422 302	216 587	205 715
35-39	337 496	171 359	166 137	350 714	178 344	172 371	347 480	176 857	170 623	379 932	193 753	186 179
40-44	292 048	148 157	143 891	330 828	167 416	163 411	344 145	174 450	169 695	341 073	173 075	167 997
45-49	244 077	124 342	119 735	285 275	144 064	141 210	323 865	163 201	160 664	337 263	170 253	167 010
50-54	214 684	108 551	106 133	236 486	119 670	116 816	277 255	139 135	138 120	315 508	158 042	157 466
55-59	161 180	80 681	80 499	205 328	102 773	102 556	226 808	113 661	113 147	266 855	132 674	134 180
60-64	123 661	60 808	62 853	150 332	74 096	76 236	192 570	94 946	97 624	213 486	105 433	108 053
65-69	101 765	48 954	52 811	110 668	53 175	57 494	135 675	65 378	70 297	175 025	84 399	90 626
70-74	76 070	35 531	40 539	85 301	39 672	45 629	93 811	43 621	50 190	116 260	54 237	62 023
75-79	48 954	21 758	27 196	57 615	25 671	31 944	65 623	29 125	36 498	73 267	32 531	40 736
80-84	25 587	10 595	14 992	31 700	13 220	18 481	38 130	15 928	22 202	44 349	18 450	25 899
85-89	10 269	3 863	6 406	13 153	4 977	8 176	16 772	6 367	10 405	20 740	7 852	12 888
90-94	2 892	976	1 917	3 929	1 307	2 622	5 219	1 725	3 494	6 873	2 262	4 611
95-99	557	165	392	781	231	550	1 102	314	788	1 512	419	1 093
100 +	76	21	55	113	31	82	161	44	117	229	59	170

Age group	2025 Both sexes	Males	Females	2030 Both sexes	Males	Females	2035 Both sexes	Males	Females	2040 Both sexes	Males	Females
All ages	5 488 825	2 769 199	2 719 626	5 667 111	2 853 717	2 813 395	5 816 304	2 923 213	2 893 091	5 941 605	2 980 755	2 960 850
0-4	417 048	214 397	202 652	400 374	205 606	194 768	391 069	200 810	190 258	388 725	199 603	189 122
5-9	429 507	220 805	208 702	413 235	212 366	200 868	397 160	203 886	193 275	388 305	199 317	188 988
10-14	434 267	223 240	211 028	427 707	219 810	207 896	411 686	211 506	200 180	395 814	203 135	192 679
15-19	425 365	218 549	206 816	432 151	222 016	210 135	425 740	218 670	207 069	409 861	210 448	199 413
20-24	415 642	213 359	202 283	421 952	216 546	205 406	428 902	220 112	208 790	422 673	216 870	205 794
25-29	415 818	213 392	202 427	411 087	210 813	200 274	417 693	214 168	203 525	424 931	217 902	207 028
30-34	417 475	214 172	203 302	409 990	210 229	199 762	405 760	207 938	197 822	412 802	211 538	201 265
35-39	415 285	212 649	202 637	410 011	210 529	200 382	404 004	206 935	197 068	400 333	204 975	195 358
40-44	373 204	189 829	183 405	408 530	208 701	199 829	404 651	206 911	197 740	398 300	203 671	194 639
45-49	334 469	169 060	165 409	366 485	185 741	180 744	401 745	204 601	197 144	398 365	203 139	195 226
50-54	329 000	165 143	163 886	326 696	164 233	162 462	358 544	180 807	177 736	393 678	199 589	194 089
55-59	304 527	151 195	153 332	318 224	158 372	159 853	310 401	157 902	158 659	347 996	174 168	173 829
60-64	252 315	123 678	128 636	289 011	141 562	147 449	302 837	148 768	154 068	301 797	148 624	153 172
65-69	195 002	94 247	100 754	231 877	111 310	120 567	266 907	128 127	138 780	280 719	135 260	145 459
70-74	151 358	70 676	80 682	169 877	79 601	90 277	203 667	94 850	108 816	235 975	109 980	125 995
75-79	92 094	41 013	51 081	121 416	54 139	67 277	137 707	61 679	76 028	166 888	74 322	92 566
80-84	50 489	20 997	29 492	64 687	26 957	37 731	86 687	36 131	50 556	99 755	41 797	57 958
85-89	24 776	9 318	15 458	28 949	10 883	18 066	38 031	14 287	23 745	52 055	19 503	32 552
90-94	8 758	2 847	5 911	10 820	3 490	7 331	13 033	4 198	8 835	17 611	5 639	11 972
95-99	2 050	557	1 493	2 696	713	1 983	3 441	900	2 541	4 261	1 108	3 152
100 +	316	76	240	435	100	335	580	126	454	753	159	594

Age group	2045 Both sexes	Males	Females	2050 Both sexes	Males	Females
All ages	6 038 994	3 024 652	3 014 342	6 104 334	3 053 068	3 051 267
0-4	382 587	196 432	186 155	371 137	190 527	180 610
5-9	386 313	198 284	188 028	380 483	195 270	185 212
10-14	387 111	198 647	188 464	385 238	197 676	187 563
15-19	394 108	202 146	191 962	385 499	197 713	187 786
20-24	406 975	208 768	198 207	391 385	200 566	190 819
25-29	419 017	214 850	204 167	403 655	206 930	196 724
30-34	420 457	215 498	204 960	415 017	212 700	202 317
35-39	407 843	208 838	199 005	415 951	213 046	202 906
40-44	395 153	202 024	193 129	403 081	206 133	196 947
45-49	392 559	200 238	192 321	389 864	198 882	190 982
50-54	390 812	198 456	192 356	385 562	195 911	189 651
55-59	382 803	192 728	190 076	380 529	191 969	188 560
60-64	332 742	164 585	168 157	366 873	182 680	184 193
65-69	280 589	135 626	144 963	310 465	150 865	159 599
70-74	249 487	116 823	132 664	250 461	117 756	132 705
75-79	195 115	87 020	108 095	207 820	93 221	114 598
80-84	122 647	51 080	71 567	145 171	60 580	84 591
85-89	61 126	23 057	38 068	76 625	28 708	47 917
90-94	24 688	7 842	16 846	29 713	9 532	20 181
95-99	5 917	1 515	4 402	8 494	2 137	6 357
100 +	946	196	750	1 312	264	1 048

United Nations Department of Economic and Social Affairs/Population Division
World Population Prospects: The 2004 Revision, Volume II: Sex and Age Distribution of the World Population

37

POPULATION BY AGE AND SEX (in thousands)

Age group	2005 Both sexes	2005 Males	2005 Females	2010 Both sexes	2010 Males	2010 Females	2015 Both sexes	2015 Males	2015 Females	2020 Both sexes	2020 Males	2020 Females
All ages	4 494 095	2 281 237	2 212 859	4 809 081	2 438 094	2 370 987	5 149 481	2 607 604	2 541 876	5 490 253	2 776 794	2 713 460
0-4	431 677	222 020	209 657	480 213	247 022	233 191	516 524	265 725	250 799	530 480	272 851	257 629
5-9	430 024	221 397	208 627	424 318	218 278	206 041	473 441	243 533	229 908	510 499	262 577	247 922
10-14	436 183	224 704	211 479	427 106	219 832	207 273	421 633	216 833	204 799	470 894	242 151	228 743
15-19	439 308	226 213	213 095	433 206	223 015	210 192	424 486	218 333	206 152	419 215	215 448	203 767
20-24	399 362	204 636	194 726	434 600	223 468	211 132	429 043	220 567	208 475	420 695	216 118	204 577
25-29	360 707	184 275	176 432	393 391	201 265	192 126	428 962	220 256	208 705	423 796	217 621	206 175
30-34	357 517	182 232	175 285	354 024	180 568	173 456	386 776	197 604	189 173	422 302	216 587	205 715
35-39	337 496	171 359	166 137	350 714	178 344	172 371	347 480	176 857	170 623	379 932	193 753	186 179
40-44	292 048	148 157	143 891	330 828	167 416	163 411	344 145	174 450	169 695	341 073	173 075	167 997
45-49	244 077	124 342	119 735	285 275	144 064	141 210	323 865	163 201	160 664	337 263	170 254	167 010
50-54	214 684	108 551	106 133	236 486	119 670	116 816	277 255	139 135	138 120	315 508	158 042	157 466
55-59	161 180	80 681	80 499	205 328	102 773	102 556	226 808	113 661	113 147	266 855	132 674	134 180
60-64	123 661	60 808	62 853	150 332	74 096	76 236	192 570	94 946	97 624	213 486	105 433	108 053
65-69	101 765	48 954	52 811	110 668	53 175	57 494	135 675	65 378	70 297	175 025	84 399	90 626
70-74	76 070	35 531	40 539	85 301	39 672	45 629	93 811	43 621	50 190	116 260	54 237	62 023
75-79	48 954	21 758	27 196	57 615	25 671	31 944	65 623	29 125	36 498	73 267	32 531	40 736
80-84	25 587	10 595	14 992	31 700	13 220	18 481	38 130	15 928	22 202	44 349	18 450	25 899
85-89	10 269	3 863	6 406	13 153	4 977	8 176	16 772	6 367	10 405	20 740	7 852	12 888
90-94	2 892	976	1 917	3 929	1 307	2 622	5 219	1 725	3 494	6 873	2 262	4 611
95-99	557	165	392	781	231	550	1 102	314	788	1 512	419	1 093
100 +	76	21	55	113	31	82	161	44	117	229	59	170

Age group	2025 Both sexes	2025 Males	2025 Females	2030 Both sexes	2030 Males	2030 Females	2035 Both sexes	2035 Males	2035 Females	2040 Both sexes	2040 Males	2040 Females
All ages	5 800 434	2 929 618	2 870 816	6 088 044	3 070 248	3 017 797	6 372 036	3 208 921	3 163 115	6 661 939	3 350 930	3 311 009
0-4	515 833	265 222	250 611	510 897	262 397	248 500	527 364	270 853	256 511	555 321	285 223	270 098
5-9	525 221	270 075	255 146	511 369	262 842	248 526	507 055	260 337	246 718	523 944	269 000	254 944
10-14	508 210	261 323	246 887	523 177	268 942	254 235	509 603	261 858	247 745	505 500	259 466	246 034
15-19	468 533	240 789	227 743	505 935	260 002	245 934	521 025	267 688	253 338	507 604	260 692	246 911
20-24	415 642	213 359	202 283	464 972	238 692	226 280	502 458	257 951	244 507	517 688	265 724	251 965
25-29	415 819	213 392	202 427	411 087	210 813	200 274	460 475	236 173	224 302	498 124	255 528	242 596
30-34	417 475	214 172	203 303	409 990	210 229	199 762	405 760	207 938	197 822	455 262	233 363	221 899
35-39	415 286	212 649	202 637	410 911	210 529	200 382	404 004	206 935	197 068	400 333	204 975	195 358
40-44	373 234	189 829	183 405	408 530	208 701	199 829	404 652	206 911	197 740	398 310	203 671	194 639
45-49	334 469	169 060	165 409	366 485	185 741	180 744	401 745	204 601	197 144	398 366	203 139	195 227
50-54	329 029	165 143	163 886	326 696	164 233	162 462	358 544	180 807	177 737	393 679	199 589	194 089
55-59	304 527	151 195	153 332	318 224	158 372	159 853	316 461	157 802	158 659	347 996	174 168	173 829
60-64	252 315	123 678	128 636	289 011	141 562	147 449	302 837	148 768	154 069	301 797	148 624	153 172
65-69	195 002	94 247	100 754	231 877	111 310	120 567	266 908	128 127	138 780	280 719	135 261	145 459
70-74	151 358	70 676	80 682	169 877	79 601	90 277	203 667	94 851	108 816	235 975	109 980	125 995
75-79	92 094	41 013	51 081	121 416	54 139	67 277	137 707	61 679	76 028	166 888	74 322	92 566
80-84	50 489	20 997	29 492	64 687	26 957	37 731	86 687	36 131	50 556	99 755	41 797	57 958
85-89	24 776	9 318	15 458	28 949	10 883	18 066	38 031	14 287	23 745	52 055	19 503	32 552
90-94	8 758	2 847	5 911	10 820	3 490	7 331	13 033	4 198	8 835	17 611	5 639	11 972
95-99	2 050	557	1 493	2 696	713	1 983	3 441	900	2 541	4 261	1 108	3 152
100 +	316	76	240	435	100	335	580	126	454	753	159	594

Age group	2045 Both sexes	2045 Males	2045 Females	2050 Both sexes	2050 Males	2050 Females
All ages	6 946 458	3 490 821	3 455 637	7 212 786	3 622 282	3 590 504
0-4	572 308	293 915	278 392	575 302	295 399	279 903
5-9	552 227	283 525	268 702	569 536	292 377	277 158
10-14	522 531	268 203	254 328	550 928	282 783	268 145
15-19	503 618	258 368	245 250	520 727	267 149	253 578
20-24	504 462	258 849	245 613	500 635	256 623	244 012
25-29	513 610	263 447	250 163	500 752	256 784	243 969
30-34	493 163	252 855	240 309	509 052	260 992	248 061
35-39	449 952	230 468	219 484	488 129	250 111	238 018
40-44	395 153	202 024	193 129	444 832	227 557	217 275
45-49	392 559	200 238	192 321	389 864	198 882	190 982
50-54	390 812	198 456	192 356	385 563	195 911	189 652
55-59	382 804	192 728	190 076	380 530	191 970	188 560
60-64	332 742	164 585	168 157	366 873	182 680	184 193
65-69	280 590	135 626	144 964	310 465	150 866	159 600
70-74	249 487	116 823	132 664	250 461	117 756	132 705
75-79	195 116	87 020	108 095	207 820	93 222	114 599
80-84	122 647	51 080	71 567	145 171	60 580	84 591
85-89	61 126	23 057	38 068	76 625	28 708	47 917
90-94	24 688	7 842	16 846	29 713	9 532	20 181
95-99	5 917	1 515	4 402	8 494	2 137	6 357
100 +	946	196	750	1 312	264	1 048

United Nations Department of Economic and Social Affairs/Population Division
World Population Prospects: The 2004 Revision, Volume II: Sex and Age Distribution of the World Population

LOW VARIANT

LESS DEVELOPED REGIONS, EXCLUDING LEAST DEVELOPED COUNTRIES

POPULATION BY AGE AND SEX (in thousands)

Age group	2005 Both sexes	2005 Males	2005 Females	2010 Both sexes	2010 Males	2010 Females	2015 Both sexes	2015 Males	2015 Females	2020 Both sexes	2020 Males	2020 Females
All ages	4 494 095	2 281 237	2 212 859	4 721 204	2 392 787	2 326 418	4 912 631	2 485 540	2 427 091	5 061 831	2 556 118	2 505 712
0-4	431 677	222 020	209 657	392 336	201 714	190 622	366 666	188 511	178 155	337 322	173 398	163 924
5-9	430 024	221 397	208 627	424 319	218 278	206 041	386 450	198 684	187 766	361 931	186 041	175 890
10-14	436 183	224 704	211 479	427 106	219 832	207 273	421 633	216 834	204 799	384 198	197 466	186 732
15-19	439 308	226 213	213 095	433 206	223 015	210 191	424 486	218 333	206 152	419 215	215 448	203 767
20-24	399 362	204 636	194 726	434 600	223 468	211 132	429 042	220 567	208 475	420 695	216 118	204 577
25-29	360 707	184 275	176 432	393 391	201 265	192 126	428 962	220 256	208 705	423 796	217 621	206 175
30-34	357 517	182 232	175 285	354 024	180 568	173 456	386 776	197 604	189 172	422 302	216 587	205 715
35-39	337 496	171 359	166 137	350 714	178 344	172 371	347 480	176 857	170 623	379 932	193 753	186 179
40-44	292 048	148 157	143 891	330 828	167 416	163 411	344 145	174 450	169 695	341 072	173 075	167 997
45-49	244 077	124 342	119 735	285 275	144 064	141 210	323 865	163 201	160 664	337 263	170 253	167 010
50-54	214 684	108 551	106 133	236 486	119 670	116 816	277 254	139 135	138 120	315 508	158 042	157 466
55-59	161 180	80 681	80 499	205 328	102 773	102 556	226 808	113 661	113 147	266 855	132 674	134 180
60-64	123 661	60 808	62 853	150 332	74 096	76 236	192 570	94 946	97 624	213 486	105 433	108 053
65-69	101 765	48 954	52 811	110 668	53 175	57 494	135 675	65 378	70 297	175 025	84 399	90 626
70-74	76 070	35 531	40 539	85 301	39 672	45 629	93 811	43 621	50 190	116 260	54 237	62 023
75-79	48 954	21 758	27 196	57 615	25 671	31 944	65 623	29 125	36 498	73 267	32 531	40 736
80-84	25 587	10 595	14 992	31 700	13 220	18 481	38 130	15 928	22 202	44 349	18 450	25 899
85-89	10 269	3 863	6 406	13 153	4 977	8 176	16 772	6 367	10 405	20 740	7 852	12 888
90-94	2 892	976	1 917	3 929	1 307	2 622	5 219	1 725	3 494	6 873	2 262	4 611
95-99	557	165	392	781	231	550	1 102	314	788	1 512	419	1 093
100 +	76	21	55	113	31	82	161	44	117	229	59	170

Age group	2025 Both sexes	2025 Males	2025 Females	2030 Both sexes	2030 Males	2030 Females	2035 Both sexes	2035 Males	2035 Females	2040 Both sexes	2040 Males	2040 Females
All ages	5 176 896	2 608 618	2 568 279	5 250 817	2 639 574	2 611 243	5 280 349	2 647 684	2 632 665	5 268 338	2 634 798	2 633 541
0-4	318 636	163 761	154 874	294 808	151 364	143 443	269 933	138 570	131 363	249 485	128 058	121 427
5-9	333 507	171 389	162 118	315 470	162 080	153 390	292 199	149 971	142 227	267 765	137 403	130 362
10-14	360 072	185 027	175 045	331 951	170 533	161 418	314 138	161 343	152 795	291 053	149 336	141 718
15-19	382 045	196 231	185 814	358 116	183 902	174 214	330 171	169 508	160 662	312 486	160 392	152 094
20-24	415 642	213 359	202 283	378 781	194 323	184 458	355 096	182 144	172 951	327 374	167 889	159 485
25-29	415 818	213 392	202 427	411 087	210 813	200 274	374 760	192 087	182 673	351 488	180 150	171 338
30-34	417 475	214 172	203 302	409 990	210 229	199 761	405 760	207 938	197 822	370 194	189 637	180 558
35-39	415 285	212 649	202 637	410 911	210 629	200 382	404 003	206 935	197 068	400 333	204 975	195 358
40-44	373 234	189 829	183 405	408 530	208 701	199 828	404 651	206 911	197 740	398 309	203 671	194 638
45-49	334 469	169 060	165 409	366 485	185 741	180 744	401 745	204 601	197 144	398 365	203 139	195 226
50-54	329 028	165 140	163 886	326 695	164 233	162 462	358 543	180 807	177 736	393 678	199 589	194 089
55-59	304 527	151 195	153 332	318 224	158 372	159 853	316 461	157 803	158 658	347 996	174 167	173 828
60-64	252 315	123 678	128 636	289 011	141 562	147 449	302 836	148 768	154 068	301 796	148 624	153 172
65-69	195 002	94 247	100 754	231 877	111 310	120 567	266 907	128 127	138 780	280 719	135 260	145 459
70-74	151 358	70 676	80 682	169 877	79 601	90 277	203 667	94 850	108 816	235 974	109 980	125 995
75-79	92 094	41 013	51 081	121 410	54 139	67 277	137 707	61 679	76 028	166 888	74 322	92 566
80-84	50 489	20 997	29 492	64 687	26 957	37 731	86 687	36 131	50 556	99 755	41 797	57 958
85-89	24 776	9 318	15 458	28 949	10 883	18 066	38 031	14 287	23 745	52 055	19 503	32 552
90-94	8 758	2 847	5 911	10 820	3 490	7 331	13 033	4 198	8 835	17 611	5 639	11 972
95-99	2 050	557	1 493	2 696	713	1 983	3 441	900	2 541	4 261	1 108	3 152
100 +	316	76	240	435	100	335	580	126	454	753	159	594

Age group	2045 Both sexes	2045 Males	2045 Females	2050 Both sexes	2050 Males	2050 Females
All ages	5 215 956	2 601 904	2 614 052	5 125 687	2 550 502	2 575 106
0-4	230 344	118 220	112 124	212 521	109 063	103 458
5-9	247 658	127 065	120 593	228 791	117 369	111 422
10-14	266 768	136 847	129 921	246 776	126 571	120 206
15-19	289 516	148 452	141 064	265 330	136 021	129 309
20-24	309 855	158 874	150 981	287 044	147 031	140 013
25-29	324 142	166 110	158 032	306 923	157 264	149 659
30-34	347 504	178 015	169 489	320 703	164 265	156 437
35-39	365 587	187 133	178 454	343 529	175 856	167 673
40-44	395 152	202 024	193 129	361 185	184 636	176 548
45-49	392 559	200 237	192 321	389 863	198 882	190 982
50-54	390 811	198 456	192 355	385 562	195 910	189 651
55-59	382 803	192 728	190 075	380 529	191 969	188 560
60-64	332 741	164 584	168 157	366 872	182 679	184 193
65-69	280 589	135 626	144 963	310 464	150 865	159 599
70-74	249 487	116 823	132 664	250 460	117 756	132 704
75-79	195 115	87 020	108 095	207 820	93 221	114 598
80-84	122 647	51 080	71 567	145 171	60 580	84 591
85-89	61 126	23 057	38 068	76 625	28 708	47 917
90-94	24 688	7 842	16 846	29 713	9 532	20 181
95-99	5 917	1 515	4 402	8 494	2 137	6 357
100 +	946	196	750	1 312	264	1 048

United Nations Department of Economic and Social Affairs/Population Division
World Population Prospects: The 2004 Revision, Volume II: Sex and Age Distribution of the World Population

39

POPULATION BY AGE AND SEX (in thousands)

Age group	1950 Both sexes	Males	Females	1955 Both sexes	Males	Females	1960 Both sexes	Males	Females	1965 Both sexes	Males	Females
All ages	1 149 774	580 530	569 244	1 282 503	648 005	634 498	1 447 772	732 544	715 228	1 638 248	829 456	808 793
0-4	180 068	90 827	89 241	211 698	107 798	103 900	245 329	125 152	120 177	275 960	140 727	135 233
5-9	144 367	72 520	71 847	163 182	82 595	80 587	194 827	99 532	95 295	228 256	116 748	111 509
10-14	130 689	65 787	64 902	140 590	70 760	69 829	159 534	80 916	78 618	190 824	97 583	93 241
15-19	116 492	59 028	57 464	127 836	64 425	63 411	137 624	69 346	68 278	155 992	79 174	76 817
20-24	102 690	52 172	50 517	113 080	57 243	55 837	124 378	62 618	61 760	133 556	67 237	66 318
25-29	87 045	44 353	42 692	98 937	50 144	48 792	109 389	55 267	54 122	120 160	60 398	59 762
30-34	74 550	38 042	36 508	83 551	42 584	40 967	95 440	48 421	47 019	105 475	53 269	52 206
35-39	66 670	34 266	32 404	71 132	36 310	34 822	80 123	40 841	39 282	91 670	46 471	45 199
40-44	57 707	29 689	28 018	63 209	32 362	30 847	67 748	34 487	33 261	76 468	38 875	37 593
45-49	48 096	24 718	23 377	54 158	27 678	26 480	59 620	30 353	29 266	64 025	32 448	31 578
50-54	40 288	20 325	19 963	44 507	22 615	21 892	50 436	25 568	24 868	55 637	28 077	27 560
55-59	32 753	16 549	16 204	36 135	17 982	18 154	40 298	20 232	20 067	46 077	23 088	22 989
60-64	26 426	13 023	13 403	28 275	14 012	14 262	31 551	15 509	16 041	35 441	17 553	17 888
65-69	18 713	8 556	10 158	20 925	10 160	10 765	22 839	11 184	11 655	26 111	12 615	13 496
70-74	12 589	5 864	6 725	13 518	6 051	7 468	15 472	7 364	8 109	17 165	8 237	8 928
75-79	6 936	3 157	3 779	7 585	3 449	4 137	8 390	3 670	4 720	9 866	4 587	5 279
80 +	3 697	1 654	2 043	4 184	1 836	2 348	4 774	2 084	2 691	5 567	2 369	3 198

Age group	1970 Both sexes	Males	Females	1975 Both sexes	Males	Females	1980 Both sexes	Males	Females	1985 Both sexes	Males	Females
All ages	1 854 045	938 746	915 299	2 094 087	1 060 905	1 033 182	2 355 588	1 193 037	1 162 550	2 653 225	1 343 084	1 310 140
0-4	304 507	155 290	149 217	334 112	170 420	163 691	361 374	184 268	177 106	401 596	204 796	196 800
5-9	258 763	132 216	126 547	287 697	147 019	140 678	317 455	162 192	155 263	345 132	176 242	168 890
10-14	223 891	114 594	109 297	254 312	130 039	124 273	283 026	144 691	138 335	313 003	159 947	153 056
15-19	187 366	95 790	91 576	219 830	112 558	107 272	249 939	127 735	122 204	278 984	142 559	136 425
20-24	151 917	77 001	74 917	182 466	93 166	89 301	214 404	109 495	104 909	245 129	125 133	119 996
25-29	129 325	64 954	64 371	147 459	74 557	72 902	177 922	90 700	87 222	210 248	107 267	102 981
30-34	116 131	58 262	57 869	125 265	62 849	62 416	143 545	72 504	71 041	174 227	88 814	85 413
35-39	101 775	51 354	50 422	112 507	56 440	56 067	121 372	60 901	60 472	140 228	70 789	69 439
40-44	87 917	44 447	43 470	98 111	49 511	48 600	108 696	54 409	54 287	117 602	58 854	58 748
45-49	72 758	36 797	35 961	84 364	42 553	41 811	94 003	47 237	46 766	104 465	52 002	52 463
50-54	60 159	30 240	29 919	68 869	34 624	34 244	79 998	40 028	39 970	89 078	44 355	44 723
55-59	51 188	25 559	25 629	55 604	27 674	27 930	63 778	31 724	32 054	74 227	36 656	37 572
60-64	40 850	20 180	20 670	45 420	22 400	23 020	49 853	24 458	25 395	57 050	27 907	29 143
65-69	29 731	14 477	15 254	34 330	16 674	17 656	38 647	18 713	19 934	42 132	20 193	21 939
70-74	19 808	9 389	10 419	22 691	10 853	11 837	26 602	12 639	13 963	30 039	14 097	15 943
75-79	11 168	5 229	5 939	13 115	6 060	7 054	15 351	7 137	8 213	18 221	8 319	9 902
80 +	6 790	2 969	3 821	7 937	3 508	4 429	9 624	4 207	5 417	11 863	5 155	6 707

Age group	1990 Both sexes	Males	Females	1995 Both sexes	Males	Females	2000 Both sexes	Males	Females	2005 Both sexes	Males	Females
All ages	2 969 565	1 502 432	1 467 133	3 292 439	1 664 159	1 628 279	3 611 159	1 822 847	1 788 312	3 930 140	1 981 897	1 948 242
0-4	428 364	218 583	209 782	446 186	227 636	218 550	451 856	230 489	221 367	466 236	237 783	228 453
5-9	386 129	197 129	189 000	413 387	211 104	202 283	432 034	220 505	211 529	438 511	223 726	214 785
10-14	340 919	174 056	166 862	381 546	194 758	186 788	408 776	208 706	200 070	427 567	218 176	209 391
15-19	308 647	157 629	151 018	336 063	171 420	164 643	376 968	192 271	184 696	404 526	206 384	198 142
20-24	273 487	139 432	134 056	301 481	153 587	147 894	329 774	167 893	161 881	370 646	188 688	181 959
25-29	240 295	122 378	117 917	266 583	135 558	131 025	294 344	149 646	144 698	321 918	163 609	158 309
30-34	205 969	105 025	100 944	234 674	119 157	115 517	259 423	131 524	127 899	285 729	145 064	140 665
35-39	170 079	86 588	83 492	200 873	102 093	98 780	228 130	115 393	112 737	251 426	127 174	124 252
40-44	136 023	68 474	67 549	165 358	83 908	81 449	195 000	98 678	96 322	220 879	111 296	109 582
45-49	113 490	56 531	56 959	131 518	65 864	65 653	159 749	80 526	79 223	188 175	94 666	93 509
50-54	99 286	49 016	50 270	108 548	53 617	54 931	125 704	62 337	63 366	152 825	76 366	76 459
55-59	82 920	40 778	42 143	93 234	45 459	47 775	101 986	49 700	52 287	118 438	58 005	60 433
60-64	66 822	32 430	34 392	75 352	36 453	38 899	85 064	40 750	44 314	93 490	44 794	48 695
65-69	48 655	23 280	25 375	57 801	27 446	30 355	65 611	31 036	34 575	74 596	34 924	39 672
70-74	33 182	15 440	17 742	38 964	18 118	20 846	46 762	21 569	25 193	53 644	24 636	29 009
75-79	20 945	9 458	11 487	23 577	10 572	13 004	28 161	12 622	15 539	34 329	15 236	19 093
80 +	14 352	6 207	8 145	17 293	7 407	9 887	21 816	9 201	12 615	27 206	11 372	15 834

United Nations Department of Economic and Social Affairs/Population Division
World Population Prospects: The 2004 Revision, Volume II: Sex and Age Distribution of the World Population

40

POPULATION BY AGE AND SEX (in thousands)

Age group	2005 Both sexes	Males	Females	2010 Both sexes	Males	Females	2015 Both sexes	Males	Females	2020 Both sexes	Males	Females
All ages	3 930 140	1 981 897	1 948 242	4 254 820	2 143 963	2 110 857	4 581 633	2 307 035	2 274 590	4 900 947	2 466 079	2 434 868
0-4	466 236	237 783	228 453	481 033	245 327	235 706	491 774	250 782	240 992	494 067	251 932	242 135
5-9	438 511	223 726	214 785	453 564	231 322	222 241	469 401	239 340	230 061	481 429	245 410	236 019
10-14	427 567	218 176	209 391	433 953	221 346	212 607	449 076	228 968	220 108	465 212	237 128	228 084
15-19	404 526	206 384	198 142	423 652	216 022	207 630	430 271	219 306	210 965	445 522	226 989	218 533
20-24	370 646	188 688	181 959	398 749	203 083	195 666	418 239	212 907	205 331	425 161	216 365	208 796
25-29	321 918	163 609	158 309	362 935	184 496	178 439	391 308	199 049	192 259	411 098	209 066	202 032
30-34	285 729	145 064	140 665	313 124	159 019	154 106	353 991	179 881	174 110	382 409	194 519	187 890
35-39	251 426	127 174	124 252	277 237	140 526	136 711	304 535	154 492	150 043	344 969	175 187	169 782
40-44	220 879	111 296	109 582	243 786	122 904	120 882	269 491	136 223	133 268	296 606	150 121	146 485
45-49	188 175	94 666	93 509	213 674	107 105	106 570	236 508	118 686	117 822	262 099	131 929	130 170
50-54	152 825	76 366	76 459	180 654	90 163	90 491	205 873	102 441	103 432	228 590	113 938	114 652
55-59	118 438	58 005	60 433	144 636	71 443	73 193	171 761	84 794	86 967	196 545	96 791	99 753
60-64	93 490	44 794	48 695	109 247	52 637	56 610	134 242	65 276	68 966	160 293	77 932	82 361
65-69	74 596	34 924	39 672	82 653	38 730	43 923	97 428	45 924	51 503	120 643	57 416	63 227
70-74	53 644	24 636	29 009	61 708	28 043	33 666	69 125	31 457	37 669	82 395	37 716	44 679
75-79	34 329	15 236	19 093	40 020	17 679	22 341	46 760	20 422	26 337	53 141	23 235	29 905
80-84	17 570	7 520	10 050	21 880	9 256	12 623	26 018	10 938	15 080	31 031	12 864	18 167
85-89	7 110	2 888	4 222	8 946	3 608	5 338	11 413	4 535	6 878	13 910	5 464	8 446
90-94	2 069	797	1 272	2 720	1 025	1 695	3 531	1 310	2 221	4 635	1 680	2 955
95-99	402	147	254	566	201	366	770	264	506	1 029	342	688
100 +	56	20	36	83	29	54	119	40	79	163	53	110

Age group	2025 Both sexes	Males	Females	2030 Both sexes	Males	Females	2035 Both sexes	Males	Females	2040 Both sexes	Males	Females
All ages	5 205 974	2 617 406	2 588 568	5 492 853	2 758 943	2 733 910	5 761 032	2 890 386	2 870 646	6 011 289	3 012 343	2 998 946
0-4	491 032	250 386	240 646	485 967	247 797	238 170	482 835	246 190	236 645	482 515	246 027	236 488
5-9	485 024	247 201	237 823	483 173	246 243	236 930	479 181	244 198	234 983	476 960	243 049	233 911
10-14	477 765	243 458	234 307	481 844	245 487	236 356	480 418	244 745	235 673	476 779	242 880	233 899
15-19	461 831	235 233	226 598	474 576	241 655	232 921	476 000	242 702	235 076	477 649	243 158	234 491
20-24	440 577	224 127	216 450	457 022	232 429	224 593	469 942	238 944	230 998	474 455	241 206	233 248
25-29	418 324	212 679	205 646	433 926	220 518	213 408	450 601	228 935	221 666	463 803	235 604	228 199
30-34	402 390	204 644	197 747	409 935	208 407	201 528	425 810	216 377	209 433	442 810	224 961	217 849
35-39	373 322	180 826	183 496	393 448	200 030	193 418	401 318	203 968	197 350	417 499	212 103	205 396
40-44	336 625	170 619	166 006	364 929	185 243	179 687	385 143	195 512	189 632	393 327	199 640	193 687
45-49	289 059	145 746	143 313	328 716	166 035	162 681	356 918	180 609	176 308	377 208	190 944	186 264
50-54	254 012	127 063	126 960	280 788	140 743	140 045	319 950	160 720	159 230	347 968	175 187	172 781
55-59	219 003	108 094	110 909	244 115	120 968	123 140	270 521	134 400	136 121	308 942	153 897	155 045
60-64	184 336	89 437	94 898	206 285	100 371	105 913	230 780	112 792	117 988	256 526	125 769	130 757
65-69	145 047	69 033	76 014	167 867	79 765	88 102	188 839	90 031	98 809	212 244	101 701	110 544
70-74	103 033	47 622	55 411	125 001	57 788	67 212	145 848	67 322	78 525	165 178	76 531	88 647
75-79	64 209	28 211	36 029	81 421	36 125	45 297	99 958	44 325	55 633	117 900	52 183	65 717
80-84	35 915	14 880	21 035	44 293	18 414	25 879	57 031	23 889	33 142	71 116	29 711	41 406
85-89	17 009	6 558	10 452	20 156	7 750	12 406	25 474	9 779	15 695	33 473	12 876	20 597
90-94	5 799	2 060	3 739	7 317	2 537	4 780	8 903	3 061	5 842	11 562	3 939	7 623
95-99	1 383	443	940	1 780	552	1 228	2 311	692	1 619	2 877	848	2 029
100 +	218	67	151	295	86	209	383	106	277	499	132	368

Age group	2045 Both sexes	Males	Females	2050 Both sexes	Males	Females
All ages	6 238 434	3 122 367	3 116 067	6 437 641	3 218 119	3 219 522
0-4	478 304	243 874	234 430	469 957	239 611	230 346
5-9	477 452	243 289	234 163	473 979	241 506	232 473
10-14	474 849	241 878	232 971	475 589	242 242	233 346
15-19	474 199	241 391	232 808	472 442	240 478	231 964
20-24	473 467	240 701	232 765	470 251	239 065	231 186
25-29	468 680	238 059	230 621	468 109	237 775	230 335
30-34	456 413	231 831	224 582	461 821	234 551	227 270
35-39	434 853	220 873	213 980	448 890	227 966	220 924
40-44	409 788	207 942	201 847	427 452	216 889	210 563
45-49	385 692	195 263	190 428	402 379	203 711	198 668
50-54	368 293	185 555	182 739	377 061	190 059	187 001
55-59	336 626	168 147	168 479	356 911	178 493	178 418
60-64	293 772	144 495	149 278	320 849	158 337	162 512
65-69	236 862	113 920	122 941	272 226	131 430	140 796
70-74	186 797	87 030	99 767	209 559	98 050	111 509
75-79	134 710	59 857	74 854	153 578	68 643	84 935
80-84	85 098	35 451	49 646	98 361	41 112	57 249
85-89	42 605	16 277	26 328	51 936	19 734	32 202
90-94	15 523	5 264	10 259	20 226	6 764	13 462
95-99	3 827	1 109	2 717	5 236	1 495	3 741
100 +	626	160	466	830	207	623

POPULATION BY AGE AND SEX (in thousands)

Age group	2005 Both sexes	2005 Males	2005 Females	2010 Both sexes	2010 Males	2010 Females	2015 Both sexes	2015 Males	2015 Females	2020 Both sexes	2020 Males	2020 Females
All ages	3 930 140	1 981 897	1 948 242	4 292 547	2 163 234	2 129 313	4 686 135	2 360 405	2 325 730	5 094 950	2 565 127	2 529 824
0-4	466 236	237 783	228 453	518 760	264 598	254 162	559 158	285 194	273 964	584 743	298 222	286 520
5-9	438 511	223 726	214 785	453 563	231 322	222 241	506 518	258 298	248 221	547 837	279 316	268 521
10-14	427 567	218 176	209 391	433 953	221 346	212 607	449 076	228 967	220 108	502 131	255 980	246 151
15-19	404 526	206 384	198 142	423 652	216 022	207 630	430 271	219 306	210 965	445 522	226 989	218 533
20-24	370 646	188 688	181 959	398 749	203 083	195 666	418 239	212 907	205 331	425 161	216 365	208 796
25-29	321 918	163 609	158 309	362 935	184 496	178 439	391 308	199 049	192 259	411 098	209 066	202 033
30-34	285 729	145 064	140 665	313 124	159 019	154 106	353 991	179 881	174 110	382 409	194 519	187 890
35-39	251 426	127 174	124 252	277 237	140 526	136 711	304 535	154 492	150 043	344 969	175 187	169 782
40-44	220 879	111 296	109 582	243 786	122 904	120 882	269 491	136 223	133 268	296 606	150 121	146 485
45-49	188 175	94 666	93 509	213 674	107 105	106 570	236 508	118 686	117 822	262 099	131 929	130 170
50-54	152 825	76 366	76 459	180 654	90 163	90 491	205 873	102 441	103 432	228 590	113 938	114 652
55-59	118 438	58 005	60 433	144 636	71 443	73 193	171 761	84 794	86 967	196 545	96 791	99 753
60-64	93 490	44 794	48 695	109 247	52 637	56 610	134 242	65 276	68 966	160 293	77 932	82 361
65-69	74 596	34 924	39 672	82 653	38 730	43 923	97 428	45 924	51 503	120 643	57 416	63 227
70-74	53 644	24 636	29 009	61 708	28 043	33 666	69 125	31 457	37 669	82 395	37 716	44 679
75-79	34 329	15 236	19 093	40 020	17 679	22 341	46 760	20 422	26 337	53 141	23 235	29 905
80-84	17 570	7 520	10 050	21 880	9 256	12 623	26 018	10 938	15 080	31 031	12 864	18 167
85-89	7 110	2 888	4 222	8 946	3 608	5 338	11 413	4 535	6 878	13 910	5 464	8 446
90-94	2 069	797	1 272	2 720	1 025	1 695	3 531	1 310	2 221	4 635	1 680	2 955
95-99	402	147	254	566	201	366	770	264	506	1 029	342	688
100 +	56	20	36	83	29	54	119	40	79	163	53	110

Age group	2025 Both sexes	2025 Males	2025 Females	2030 Both sexes	2030 Males	2030 Females	2035 Both sexes	2035 Males	2035 Females	2040 Both sexes	2040 Males	2040 Females
All ages	5 496 051	2 765 462	2 730 589	5 893 663	2 963 453	2 930 210	6 298 166	3 164 372	3 133 794	6 715 087	3 371 253	3 343 834
0-4	588 690	300 240	288 450	598 541	305 264	293 277	621 439	316 942	304 496	652 186	332 633	319 553
5-9	574 558	292 892	281 666	579 756	295 527	284 229	590 683	301 092	289 591	614 420	313 184	301 237
10-14	543 864	277 196	266 668	571 015	290 978	280 037	576 664	293 841	282 823	587 947	299 587	288 360
15-19	498 617	254 006	244 610	540 453	275 262	265 191	567 766	289 121	278 645	573 627	292 094	281 533
20-24	440 577	224 127	216 450	493 626	251 090	242 536	535 509	272 360	263 149	562 961	286 292	276 669
25-29	418 325	212 679	205 646	433 926	220 518	213 408	486 918	247 433	239 485	528 884	268 746	260 137
30-34	402 390	204 644	197 747	409 935	208 407	201 528	425 810	216 377	209 433	478 740	243 257	235 483
35-39	373 322	189 826	183 496	393 448	200 030	193 418	401 318	203 968	197 350	417 499	212 103	205 396
40-44	336 625	170 619	166 006	364 930	185 243	179 687	385 144	195 512	189 632	393 328	199 640	193 688
45-49	289 059	145 746	143 313	328 716	166 035	162 681	356 918	180 609	176 309	377 208	190 944	186 264
50-54	254 013	127 053	126 960	280 788	140 743	140 045	319 950	160 720	159 230	347 968	175 187	172 781
55-59	219 003	108 094	110 909	244 115	120 969	123 146	270 521	134 400	136 121	308 943	153 898	155 045
60-64	184 336	89 437	94 898	206 285	100 371	105 913	230 780	112 792	117 988	256 526	125 769	130 757
65-69	145 047	69 033	76 014	167 867	79 765	88 102	188 839	90 031	98 809	212 245	101 701	110 544
70-74	103 033	47 622	55 411	125 001	57 789	67 212	145 848	67 322	78 525	165 178	76 531	88 647
75-79	64 269	28 241	36 029	81 421	36 125	45 297	99 958	44 325	55 633	117 900	52 183	65 717
80-84	35 915	14 880	21 035	44 293	18 414	25 879	57 031	23 889	33 142	71 116	29 711	41 406
85-89	17 009	6 558	10 452	20 156	7 750	12 406	25 474	9 779	15 695	33 473	12 876	20 597
90-94	5 799	2 060	3 739	7 317	2 537	4 780	8 903	3 061	5 842	11 562	3 939	7 623
95-99	1 383	443	940	1 780	552	1 228	2 311	692	1 619	2 877	848	2 029
100 +	218	67	151	295	86	209	383	106	277	499	132	368

Age group	2045 Both sexes	2045 Males	2045 Females	2050 Both sexes	2050 Males	2050 Females
All ages	7 135 374	3 579 677	3 555 697	7 548 087	3 784 177	3 763 910
0-4	675 352	344 442	330 909	688 289	351 033	337 255
5-9	645 919	329 236	316 683	669 827	341 407	328 420
10-14	611 959	311 814	300 146	643 685	327 975	315 710
15-19	585 086	297 929	287 158	609 240	310 224	299 017
20-24	569 052	289 394	279 658	580 724	295 345	285 379
25-29	556 569	282 800	273 770	563 085	286 126	276 959
30-34	520 845	264 639	256 206	548 889	278 869	270 019
35-39	470 371	238 954	231 417	512 630	260 413	252 217
40-44	409 788	207 942	201 847	462 564	234 746	227 818
45-49	385 692	195 263	190 429	402 379	203 711	198 668
50-54	368 294	185 555	182 739	377 061	190 059	187 002
55-59	336 627	168 147	168 479	356 911	178 493	178 418
60-64	293 773	144 495	149 278	320 850	158 337	162 512
65-69	236 862	113 920	122 942	272 226	131 430	140 796
70-74	186 797	87 030	99 767	209 559	98 050	111 509
75-79	134 711	59 857	74 854	153 578	68 643	84 935
80-84	85 098	35 451	49 646	98 361	41 112	57 249
85-89	42 605	16 277	26 328	51 936	19 734	32 202
90-94	15 523	5 264	10 259	20 226	6 764	13 462
95-99	3 827	1 109	2 717	5 236	1 495	3 741
100 +	626	160	466	830	207	623

United Nations Department of Economic and Social Affairs/Population Division
World Population Prospects: The 2004 Revision, Volume II: Sex and Age Distribution of the World Population

42

POPULATION BY AGE AND SEX (in thousands)

Age group	2005 Both sexes	Males	Females	2010 Both sexes	Males	Females	2015 Both sexes	Males	Females	2020 Both sexes	Males	Females
All ages	3 930 140	1 981 897	1 948 242	4 216 021	2 124 154	2 091 867	4 475 488	2 252 845	2 222 643	4 704 963	2 366 042	2 338 922
0-4	466 236	237 783	228 453	442 234	225 517	216 716	423 770	216 063	207 707	403 024	205 454	197 570
5-9	438 511	223 726	214 785	453 564	231 322	222 241	431 260	219 869	211 391	414 412	211 205	203 207
10-14	427 567	218 176	209 391	433 953	221 346	212 607	449 076	228 968	220 109	427 290	217 775	209 515
15-19	404 526	206 384	198 142	423 652	216 022	207 630	430 271	219 306	210 965	445 522	226 989	218 533
20-24	370 646	188 688	181 959	398 749	203 083	195 666	418 239	212 907	205 331	425 161	216 365	208 796
25-29	321 918	163 609	158 309	362 935	184 496	178 439	391 308	199 049	192 259	411 098	209 066	202 032
30-34	285 729	145 064	140 665	313 124	159 019	154 106	353 991	179 881	174 110	382 409	194 519	187 890
35-39	251 426	127 174	124 252	277 237	140 526	136 711	304 535	154 492	150 043	344 969	175 187	169 782
40-44	220 879	111 296	109 582	243 786	122 904	120 882	269 491	136 223	133 268	296 606	150 121	146 485
45-49	188 175	94 666	93 509	213 674	107 105	106 570	236 508	118 686	117 822	262 099	131 929	130 170
50-54	152 825	76 366	76 459	180 654	90 163	90 491	205 873	102 441	103 432	228 590	113 938	114 652
55-59	118 438	58 005	60 433	144 636	71 443	73 193	171 761	84 794	86 967	196 545	96 791	99 753
60-64	93 490	44 794	48 695	109 247	52 637	56 610	134 242	65 276	68 966	160 293	77 932	82 361
65-69	74 596	34 924	39 672	82 653	38 730	43 923	97 428	45 924	51 503	120 643	57 416	63 227
70-74	53 644	24 636	29 009	61 708	28 043	33 666	69 125	31 457	37 669	82 395	37 716	44 679
75-79	34 329	15 236	19 093	40 020	17 679	22 341	46 760	20 422	26 337	53 141	23 235	29 905
80-84	17 570	7 520	10 050	21 880	9 256	12 623	26 018	10 938	15 080	31 031	12 864	18 167
85-89	7 110	2 888	4 222	8 946	3 608	5 338	11 413	4 535	6 878	13 910	5 464	8 446
90-94	2 069	797	1 272	2 720	1 025	1 695	3 531	1 310	2 221	4 635	1 680	2 955
95-99	402	147	254	566	201	366	770	264	506	1 029	342	688
100 +	56	20	36	83	29	54	119	40	79	163	53	110

Age group	2025 Both sexes	Males	Females	2030 Both sexes	Males	Females	2035 Both sexes	Males	Females	2040 Both sexes	Males	Females
All ages	4 914 304	2 468 559	2 445 745	5 094 568	2 555 751	2 538 817	5 238 800	2 624 050	2 614 750	5 345 691	2 672 986	2 672 705
0-4	393 738	200 718	193 020	377 488	192 425	185 063	356 597	181 762	174 836	336 168	171 342	164 827
5-9	395 124	201 324	193 800	386 953	197 145	189 807	371 754	189 389	182 366	351 793	179 199	172 594
10-14	411 068	209 426	201 642	392 309	199 811	192 498	384 534	195 834	188 700	369 678	188 254	181 424
15-19	424 053	215 963	208 090	408 106	207 756	200 349	389 608	198 280	191 329	382 034	194 408	187 626
20-24	440 577	224 127	216 450	419 443	213 282	206 161	403 788	205 242	198 546	385 587	195 936	189 651
25-29	418 324	212 679	205 645	433 926	220 518	213 408	413 334	209 964	203 370	398 151	202 183	195 967
30-34	402 390	204 643	197 747	409 935	208 407	201 528	425 810	216 377	209 433	405 963	206 207	199 756
35-39	373 322	189 826	183 496	393 448	200 030	193 418	401 317	203 967	197 350	417 499	212 103	205 396
40-44	336 625	170 619	166 006	364 929	185 242	179 687	385 143	195 512	189 632	393 327	199 640	193 687
45-49	289 059	145 746	143 313	328 716	166 035	162 681	356 917	180 609	176 308	377 207	190 944	186 264
50-54	254 012	127 053	126 960	280 787	140 743	140 045	319 949	160 720	159 229	347 967	175 187	172 781
55-59	219 003	108 094	110 909	244 115	120 969	123 146	270 521	134 466	136 121	000 040	153 997	155 045
60-64	184 335	89 437	94 898	206 284	100 371	105 913	230 779	112 792	117 988	256 525	125 769	130 757
65-69	145 047	69 032	76 014	167 867	79 765	88 102	188 839	90 031	98 809	212 244	101 701	110 543
70-74	103 033	47 622	55 411	125 001	57 788	67 212	145 848	67 322	78 525	165 178	76 531	88 647
75-79	64 209	28 241	36 020	81 421	36 125	45 297	99 958	44 325	55 633	117 900	52 183	65 717
80-84	35 915	14 880	21 035	44 293	18 414	25 879	57 031	23 889	33 142	71 116	29 711	41 406
85-89	17 009	6 558	10 452	20 156	7 750	12 406	25 474	9 779	15 695	33 473	12 876	20 597
90-94	5 799	2 060	3 739	7 317	2 537	4 780	8 903	3 061	5 842	11 562	3 939	7 623
95-99	1 383	443	940	1 780	552	1 228	2 311	692	1 619	2 877	848	2 029
100 +	218	67	151	295	86	209	383	106	277	499	132	368

Age group	2045 Both sexes	Males	Females	2050 Both sexes	Males	Females
All ages	5 413 510	2 701 877	2 711 634	5 442 474	2 710 962	2 731 512
0-4	315 161	160 625	154 536	295 054	150 369	144 685
5-9	332 181	169 193	162 988	311 871	158 832	153 039
10-14	350 014	178 216	171 797	330 651	168 339	162 312
15-19	367 374	186 931	180 443	347 900	176 995	170 905
20-24	378 244	192 194	186 049	363 834	184 858	178 975
25-29	380 432	193 136	187 296	373 497	189 609	183 888
30-34	391 435	198 758	192 676	374 398	190 051	184 347
35-39	398 455	202 353	196 101	384 629	195 265	189 365
40-44	409 788	207 941	201 847	391 492	198 609	192 883
45-49	385 691	195 263	190 428	402 379	203 711	198 668
50-54	368 293	185 555	182 738	377 060	190 059	187 001
55-59	336 626	168 147	168 479	356 910	178 493	178 417
60-64	293 772	144 494	149 277	320 849	158 337	162 512
65-69	236 861	113 920	122 941	272 226	131 430	140 796
70-74	186 797	87 029	99 767	209 559	98 050	111 509
75-79	134 710	59 857	74 854	153 577	68 643	84 935
80-84	85 097	35 451	49 646	98 361	41 112	57 249
85-89	42 605	16 277	26 328	51 936	19 734	32 202
90-94	15 523	5 264	10 259	20 226	6 764	13 462
95-99	3 827	1 109	2 717	5 236	1 495	3 741
100 +	626	160	466	830	207	623

POPULATION BY AGE AND SEX (in thousands)

Age group	1950 Both sexes	Males	Females	1955 Both sexes	Males	Females	1960 Both sexes	Males	Females	1965 Both sexes	Males	Females
All ages	179 956	88 745	91 210	200 707	99 106	101 601	225 790	111 632	114 158	255 825	126 567	129 258
0-4	31 041	15 584	15 457	35 630	17 895	17 735	40 539	20 373	20 166	46 440	23 348	23 092
5-9	24 241	12 115	12 125	27 209	13 637	13 572	31 606	15 849	15 758	36 387	18 234	18 153
10-14	20 772	10 357	10 415	23 256	11 626	11 631	26 188	13 127	13 061	30 507	15 270	15 236
15-19	18 184	9 084	9 101	20 098	10 021	10 077	22 559	11 277	11 283	25 428	12 743	12 685
20-24	15 740	7 851	7 889	17 455	8 690	8 764	19 349	9 616	9 733	21 728	10 824	10 905
25-29	13 510	6 701	6 810	14 971	7 428	7 542	16 661	8 253	8 408	18 484	9 140	9 345
30-34	11 624	5 749	5 874	12 792	6 324	6 468	14 228	7 037	7 191	15 857	7 828	8 029
35-39	9 825	4 855	4 971	10 937	5 398	5 540	12 083	5 959	6 124	13 468	6 643	6 825
40-44	8 283	4 062	4 221	9 165	4 509	4 656	10 250	5 037	5 214	11 358	5 577	5 781
45-49	6 935	3 357	3 577	7 647	3 716	3 931	8 510	4 151	4 359	9 548	4 653	4 895
50-54	5 771	2 737	3 034	6 310	3 015	3 295	7 004	3 362	3 642	7 816	3 767	4 048
55-59	4 685	2 171	2 515	5 111	2 386	2 726	5 630	2 650	2 981	6 290	2 976	3 315
60-64	3 637	1 652	1 985	3 966	1 803	2 163	4 368	2 003	2 365	4 854	2 245	2 609
65-69	2 628	1 166	1 461	2 849	1 267	1 582	3 149	1 403	1 746	3 513	1 578	1 934
70-74	1 694	735	959	1 822	788	1 035	2 016	873	1 142	2 268	984	1 284
75-79	910	379	531	975	405	570	1 080	448	632	1 226	510	716
80 +	477	191	285	514	199	315	571	217	353	652	246	406

Age group	1970 Both sexes	Males	Females	1975 Both sexes	Males	Females	1980 Both sexes	Males	Females	1985 Both sexes	Males	Females
All ages	292 004	144 662	147 343	335 017	166 141	168 875	386 979	192 172	194 807	448 051	222 669	225 383
0-4	53 417	26 863	26 553	61 731	31 079	30 652	71 303	35 937	35 366	82 753	41 737	41 017
5-9	42 114	21 130	20 984	48 830	24 505	24 325	56 928	28 610	28 319	66 156	33 285	32 871
10-14	35 234	17 653	17 580	40 844	20 481	20 362	47 494	23 828	23 666	55 532	27 901	27 632
15-19	29 715	14 873	14 842	34 301	17 175	17 126	39 929	20 022	19 907	46 499	23 313	23 186
20-24	24 590	12 292	12 298	28 725	14 328	14 398	33 396	16 676	16 721	38 804	19 391	19 413
25-29	20 867	10 354	10 513	23 648	11 758	11 890	27 832	13 828	14 005	32 244	16 023	16 221
30-34	17 691	8 728	8 963	19 995	9 888	10 107	22 854	11 344	11 510	26 786	13 258	13 529
35-39	15 101	7 443	7 658	16 856	8 294	8 562	19 214	9 489	9 725	21 914	10 844	11 071
40-44	12 736	6 261	6 475	14 301	7 021	7 280	16 058	7 877	8 181	18 332	9 021	9 312
45-49	10 636	5 185	5 451	11 957	5 838	6 118	13 512	6 592	6 920	15 211	7 412	7 798
50-54	8 819	4 250	4 569	9 854	4 756	5 097	11 156	5 394	5 763	12 634	6 102	6 532
55-59	7 047	3 349	3 697	7 986	3 801	4 185	8 989	4 283	4 706	10 226	4 881	5 345
60-64	5 442	2 530	2 912	6 141	2 875	3 265	7 020	3 287	3 732	7 951	3 729	4 223
65-69	3 921	1 775	2 145	4 450	2 032	2 418	5 073	2 329	2 745	5 847	2 684	3 163
70-74	2 546	1 113	1 433	2 895	1 281	1 614	3 326	1 480	1 846	3 816	1 705	2 112
75-79	1 391	580	811	1 619	685	934	1 855	791	1 064	2 136	912	1 224
80 +	740	281	459	885	343	542	1 036	404	632	1 211	475	735

Age group	1990 Both sexes	Males	Females	1995 Both sexes	Males	Females	2000 Both sexes	Males	Females	2005 Both sexes	Males	Females
All ages	517 253	257 066	260 187	592 126	294 348	297 778	670 317	333 624	336 693	751 273	374 877	376 397
0-4	93 663	47 282	46 381	103 978	52 539	51 439	113 932	57 608	56 324	124 959	63 211	61 748
5-9	77 262	38 904	38 358	87 351	44 040	43 311	97 383	49 149	48 234	106 761	53 922	52 839
10-14	64 731	32 559	32 173	75 190	37 854	37 336	85 507	43 104	42 403	94 995	47 938	47 057
15-19	54 400	27 308	27 093	63 253	31 756	31 496	73 926	37 202	36 723	83 970	42 313	41 657
20-24	45 138	22 528	22 610	52 825	26 346	26 479	61 443	30 778	30 664	71 797	36 068	35 730
25-29	37 366	18 543	18 823	43 225	21 422	21 803	49 889	24 854	25 035	57 843	29 027	28 816
30-34	30 942	15 284	15 659	35 618	17 597	18 021	40 029	19 842	20 186	45 477	22 836	22 642
35-39	25 627	12 615	13 012	29 487	14 510	14 977	32 942	16 235	16 707	36 165	18 033	18 132
40-44	20 858	10 258	10 600	24 393	11 957	12 436	27 389	13 399	13 990	29 949	14 758	15 191
45-49	17 331	8 458	8 872	19 758	9 653	10 104	22 732	11 039	11 693	25 117	12 210	12 907
50-54	14 228	6 858	7 370	16 248	7 852	8 396	18 350	8 854	9 496	20 901	10 035	10 866
55-59	11 597	5 528	6 069	13 104	6 239	6 864	14 891	7 090	7 801	16 743	7 961	8 782
60-64	9 084	4 265	4 819	10 334	4 851	5 483	11 677	5 463	6 214	13 262	6 202	7 060
65-69	6 671	3 065	3 606	7 649	3 524	4 126	8 738	4 018	4 720	9 902	4 534	5 368
70-74	4 445	1 985	2 460	5 108	2 287	2 821	5 910	2 654	3 256	6 799	3 045	3 753
75-79	2 491	1 067	1 423	2 929	1 257	1 672	3 422	1 479	1 943	4 004	1 736	2 268
80 +	1 419	559	860	1 676	664	1 013	2 157	856	1 301	2 626	1 047	1 579

United Nations Department of Economic and Social Affairs/Population Division
World Population Prospects: The 2004 Revision, Volume II: Sex and Age Distribution of the World Population

44

POPULATION BY AGE AND SEX (in thousands)

Age group	2005 Both sexes	2005 Males	2005 Females	2010 Both sexes	2010 Males	2010 Females	2015 Both sexes	2015 Males	2015 Females	2020 Both sexes	2020 Males	2020 Females
All ages	751 273	374 877	376 397	839 012	419 849	419 163	904 260	468 641	465 619	1 034 722	520 043	514 680
0-4	124 959	63 211	61 748	135 909	68 753	67 156	145 584	73 662	71 922	152 723	77 295	75 428
5-9	106 761	53 922	52 839	117 574	59 399	58 175	128 829	65 075	63 754	139 122	70 286	68 836
10-14	94 995	47 938	47 057	104 049	52 542	51 507	114 773	57 966	56 807	126 139	63 692	62 447
15-19	83 970	42 313	41 657	93 394	47 109	46 284	102 443	51 703	50 740	113 116	57 095	56 022
20-24	71 797	36 068	35 730	81 818	41 159	40 659	91 258	45 951	45 306	100 305	50 531	49 773
25-29	57 843	29 027	28 816	68 039	34 250	33 789	77 994	39 301	38 692	87 446	44 082	43 364
30-34	45 477	22 836	22 642	53 021	26 868	26 153	62 928	31 966	30 962	72 698	36 932	35 766
35-39	36 165	18 033	18 132	41 075	20 840	20 235	48 331	24 740	23 592	57 805	29 644	28 161
40-44	29 949	14 758	15 191	32 770	16 417	16 353	37 498	19 129	18 369	44 458	22 869	21 589
45-49	25 117	12 210	12 907	27 376	13 456	13 921	30 118	15 074	15 044	34 701	17 688	17 013
50-54	20 901	10 035	10 866	23 053	11 107	11 946	25 232	12 313	12 919	27 912	13 883	14 028
55-59	16 743	7 961	8 782	19 074	9 035	10 038	21 126	10 057	11 069	23 235	11 216	12 019
60-64	13 262	6 202	7 060	14 958	6 991	7 967	17 128	7 981	9 147	19 073	8 940	10 134
65-69	9 902	4 534	5 368	11 306	5 176	6 130	12 851	5 881	6 970	14 817	6 764	8 053
70-74	6 799	3 045	3 753	7 771	3 466	4 305	8 966	3 999	4 967	10 301	4 594	5 707
75-79	4 004	1 736	2 268	4 666	2 018	2 649	5 413	2 330	3 083	6 336	2 728	3 608
80-84	1 861	766	1 095	2 215	915	1 300	2 633	1 085	1 549	3 114	1 277	1 837
85-89	622	235	387	752	287	465	917	352	565	1 118	428	690
90-94	126	41	84	169	56	113	210	70	139	263	89	174
95-99	16	4	12	21	6	16	29	8	22	38	10	27
100 +	1	0	1	2	0	1	2	0	2	3	1	3

Age group	2025 Both sexes	2025 Males	2025 Females	2030 Both sexes	2030 Males	2030 Females	2035 Both sexes	2035 Males	2035 Females	2040 Both sexes	2040 Males	2040 Females
All ages	1 139 564	573 540	566 024	1 248 262	628 802	619 460	1 359 719	685 262	674 457	1 472 119	741 972	730 147
0-4	158 576	80 286	78 290	163 843	82 980	80 863	168 285	85 254	83 031	171 059	86 676	84 383
5-9	147 001	74 288	72 714	153 566	77 636	75 930	159 497	80 667	78 830	164 538	83 240	81 298
10-14	136 795	69 080	67 715	145 022	73 251	71 771	151 885	76 746	75 139	158 063	79 896	78 167
15-19	124 526	62 834	61 692	135 270	68 259	67 012	143 614	72 481	71 133	150 596	76 030	74 566
20-24	110 962	55 901	55 061	122 375	61 628	60 747	133 161	67 064	66 097	141 600	71 328	70 273
25-29	96 533	48 654	47 878	107 193	54 003	53 190	118 652	59 732	58 919	129 542	65 206	64 336
30-34	82 110	41 666	40 445	91 243	46 225	45 018	101 938	51 561	50 377	113 491	57 314	56 178
35-39	67 338	34 487	32 851	76 661	39 149	37 512	85 809	43 691	42 118	96 548	49 027	47 521
40-44	53 542	27 576	25 966	62 865	32 298	30 567	72 036	36 872	35 164	81 176	41 400	39 776
45-49	41 412	21 279	20 134	50 202	25 818	24 384	59 289	30 408	28 882	68 305	34 897	33 408
50-54	32 356	16 396	15 960	38 849	19 844	19 004	47 331	24 201	23 130	56 167	28 645	27 522
55-59	25 847	12 728	10 110	30 140	15 129	15 011	36 373	18 410	17 962	44 521	22 564	21 957
60-64	21 104	10 040	11 064	23 624	11 477	12 147	27 707	13 731	13 976	33 613	16 804	16 809
65-69	16 622	7 639	8 983	18 530	8 652	9 877	20 887	9 970	10 917	24 661	12 019	12 642
70-74	12 001	5 341	6 659	13 599	6 099	7 500	15 302	6 981	8 321	17 400	8 125	9 275
75-79	7 389	3 182	4 207	8 732	3 754	4 977	10 022	4 347	5 676	11 411	5 042	6 369
80-84	3 715	1 524	2 191	4 417	1 814	2 603	5 310	2 181	3 129	6 197	2 568	3 629
85-89	1 353	516	838	1 654	631	1 023	2 013	769	1 244	2 477	946	1 530
90-94	329	111	218	410	138	272	514	173	341	641	216	424
95-99	48	13	35	63	17	46	80	22	59	104	28	76
100 +	4	1	3	6	1	5	7	1	6	10	2	8

Age group	2045 Both sexes	2045 Males	2045 Females	2050 Both sexes	2050 Males	2050 Females
All ages	1 583 371	797 839	785 532	1 691 763	851 930	839 834
0-4	171 881	87 106	84 775	171 330	86 832	84 498
5-9	167 882	84 948	82 933	169 230	85 642	83 589
10-14	163 317	82 573	80 744	166 849	84 371	82 478
15-19	156 889	79 232	77 657	162 254	81 958	80 296
20-24	148 703	74 931	73 772	155 128	78 194	76 934
25-29	138 184	69 557	68 627	145 540	73 274	72 266
30-34	124 564	62 854	61 710	133 520	67 334	66 185
35-39	108 210	54 816	53 394	119 476	60 430	59 045
40-44	91 938	46 741	45 197	103 668	52 555	51 114
45-49	77 410	39 404	38 006	88 146	44 729	43 418
50-54	65 004	33 032	31 972	74 013	37 483	36 530
55-59	53 065	26 832	26 233	61 673	31 081	30 592
60-64	41 351	20 706	20 645	49 514	24 743	24 771
65-69	30 099	14 803	15 296	37 251	18 353	18 898
70-74	20 716	9 887	10 829	25 479	12 275	13 203
75-79	13 113	5 941	7 172	15 770	7 314	8 456
80-84	7 153	3 026	4 127	8 319	3 616	4 702
85-89	2 938	1 136	1 802	3 443	1 363	2 080
90-94	808	273	535	975	334	641
95-99	132	36	96	171	46	125
100 +	13	2	11	17	3	14

POPULATION BY AGE AND SEX (in thousands)

Age group	2005 Both sexes	Males	Females	2010 Both sexes	Males	Females	2015 Both sexes	Males	Females	2020 Both sexes	Males	Females
All ages	751 273	374 877	376 397	844 681	422 721	421 960	951 170	477 205	473 965	1 068 632	537 205	531 428
0-4	124 959	63 211	61 748	141 578	71 625	69 953	157 095	79 493	77 602	170 311	86 200	84 111
5-9	106 761	53 922	52 839	117 574	59 399	58 175	134 225	67 805	66 419	150 157	75 868	74 289
10-14	94 995	47 938	47 057	104 049	52 542	51 507	114 773	57 966	56 807	131 426	66 366	65 059
15-19	83 970	42 313	41 657	93 394	47 109	46 284	102 443	51 703	50 740	113 116	57 095	56 022
20-24	71 797	36 068	35 730	81 818	41 159	40 659	91 258	45 951	45 306	100 305	50 531	49 773
25-29	57 843	29 027	28 816	68 039	34 250	33 789	77 994	39 301	38 692	87 446	44 082	43 364
30-34	45 477	22 836	22 642	53 021	26 868	26 153	62 928	31 966	30 962	72 698	36 932	35 766
35-39	36 165	18 033	18 132	41 075	20 840	20 235	48 331	24 740	23 592	57 805	29 644	28 161
40-44	29 949	14 758	15 191	32 770	16 417	16 353	37 498	19 129	18 369	44 458	22 869	21 589
45-49	25 117	12 210	12 907	27 376	13 456	13 921	30 118	15 074	15 044	34 701	17 688	17 013
50-54	20 901	10 035	10 866	23 053	11 107	11 946	25 232	12 313	12 919	27 912	13 883	14 028
55-59	16 743	7 961	8 782	19 074	9 035	10 038	21 126	10 057	11 069	23 235	11 216	12 019
60-64	13 262	6 202	7 060	14 958	6 991	7 967	17 128	7 981	9 147	19 073	8 940	10 134
65-69	9 902	4 534	5 368	11 306	5 176	6 130	12 851	5 881	6 970	14 817	6 764	8 053
70-74	6 799	3 045	3 753	7 771	3 466	4 305	8 966	3 999	4 967	10 301	4 594	5 707
75-79	4 004	1 736	2 268	4 666	2 018	2 649	5 413	2 330	3 083	6 336	2 728	3 608
80-84	1 861	766	1 095	2 215	915	1 300	2 633	1 085	1 549	3 114	1 277	1 837
85-89	622	235	387	752	287	465	917	352	565	1 118	428	690
90-94	126	41	84	169	56	113	210	70	139	263	89	174
95-99	16	4	12	21	6	16	29	8	22	38	10	27
100 +	1	0	1	2	0	1	2	0	2	3	1	3

Age group	2025 Both sexes	Males	Females	2030 Both sexes	Males	Females	2035 Both sexes	Males	Females	2040 Both sexes	Males	Females
All ages	1 193 073	600 613	592 460	1 325 680	667 963	657 717	1 467 672	739 862	727 810	1 618 814	816 168	802 646
0-4	179 024	90 643	88 380	188 758	95 604	93 154	200 093	101 375	98 719	211 538	107 194	104 344
5-9	163 976	82 868	81 107	173 414	87 675	85 739	183 800	92 964	90 835	195 691	99 008	96 684
10-14	147 654	74 571	73 083	161 779	81 719	80 061	171 529	86 677	84 852	182 163	92 085	90 079
15-19	129 753	65 476	64 277	146 021	73 691	72 330	160 223	80 868	79 356	170 089	85 876	84 213
20-24	110 962	55 901	55 061	127 522	64 226	63 296	143 758	72 409	71 349	157 995	79 590	78 405
25-29	96 533	48 654	47 878	107 193	54 003	53 190	123 642	62 251	61 390	139 854	70 406	69 448
30-34	82 110	41 666	40 445	91 243	46 225	45 018	101 938	51 561	50 377	118 252	59 727	58 525
35-39	67 338	34 487	32 851	76 661	39 149	37 512	85 809	43 691	42 118	96 548	49 027	47 521
40-44	53 542	27 576	25 966	62 865	32 298	30 567	72 036	36 872	35 164	81 176	41 400	39 776
45-49	41 412	21 279	20 134	50 202	25 818	24 384	59 289	30 408	28 882	68 305	34 897	33 408
50-54	32 356	16 396	15 960	38 849	19 844	19 004	47 331	24 201	23 130	56 167	28 645	27 522
55-59	25 847	12 728	13 119	30 140	15 129	15 011	36 373	18 410	17 962	44 521	22 564	21 957
60-64	21 104	10 040	11 064	23 624	11 477	12 147	27 707	13 731	13 976	33 613	16 804	16 809
65-69	16 622	7 639	8 983	18 530	8 652	9 877	20 887	9 970	10 917	24 661	12 019	12 642
70-74	12 001	5 341	6 659	13 599	6 099	7 500	15 302	6 981	8 321	17 400	8 125	9 275
75-79	7 389	3 182	4 207	8 732	3 754	4 977	10 022	4 347	5 676	11 411	5 042	6 369
80-84	3 715	1 524	2 191	4 417	1 814	2 603	5 316	2 181	3 135	6 197	2 568	3 629
85-89	1 353	516	838	1 654	631	1 023	2 013	769	1 244	2 477	946	1 530
90-94	329	111	218	410	138	272	514	173	341	641	216	424
95-99	48	13	35	63	17	46	80	22	59	104	28	76
100 +	4	1	3	6	1	5	7	1	6	10	2	8

Age group	2045 Both sexes	Males	Females	2050 Both sexes	Males	Females
All ages	1 776 855	895 711	881 144	1 939 041	977 019	962 021
0-4	221 000	112 005	108 995	228 050	115 585	112 465
5-9	207 666	105 086	102 580	217 648	110 151	107 497
10-14	194 258	98 223	96 035	206 409	104 383	102 027
15-19	180 827	91 328	89 500	193 013	97 502	95 511
20-24	167 971	84 645	83 326	178 821	90 143	88 678
25-29	154 189	77 619	76 570	164 407	82 780	81 627
30-34	134 468	67 865	66 603	148 970	75 136	73 835
35-39	112 735	57 119	55 616	128 958	65 242	63 717
40-44	91 938	46 741	45 197	107 995	54 759	53 236
45-49	77 410	39 404	38 006	88 146	44 729	43 418
50-54	65 004	33 032	31 972	74 013	37 483	36 530
55-59	53 065	26 832	26 233	61 673	31 081	30 592
60-64	41 351	20 706	20 645	49 514	24 743	24 771
65-69	30 099	14 803	15 296	37 251	18 353	18 898
70-74	20 716	9 887	10 829	25 479	12 275	13 203
75-79	13 113	5 941	7 172	15 770	7 314	8 456
80-84	7 153	3 026	4 127	8 319	3 616	4 702
85-89	2 938	1 136	1 802	3 443	1 363	2 080
90-94	808	273	535	975	334	641
95-99	132	36	96	171	46	125
100 +	13	2	11	17	3	14

United Nations Department of Economic and Social Affairs/Population Division
World Population Prospects: The 2004 Revision, Volume II: Sex and Age Distribution of the World Population

46

POPULATION BY AGE AND SEX (in thousands)

Age group	2005 Both sexes	Males	Females	2010 Both sexes	Males	Females	2015 Both sexes	Males	Females	2020 Both sexes	Males	Females
All ages	751 273	374 877	376 397	832 395	416 501	415 894	915 714	459 261	456 453	999 198	502 075	497 123
0-4	124 959	63 211	61 748	129 291	65 404	63 887	133 326	67 458	65 868	135 108	68 376	66 732
5-9	106 761	53 922	52 839	117 574	59 399	58 175	122 539	61 897	60 642	127 374	64 349	63 025
10-14	94 995	47 938	47 057	104 049	52 542	51 507	114 773	57 966	56 807	119 978	60 580	59 398
15-19	83 970	42 313	41 657	93 394	47 109	46 284	102 443	51 703	50 740	113 116	57 095	56 022
20-24	71 797	36 068	35 730	81 818	41 159	40 659	91 258	45 951	45 306	100 305	50 531	49 773
25-29	57 843	29 027	28 816	68 039	34 250	33 789	77 994	39 301	38 692	87 446	44 082	43 364
30-34	45 477	22 836	22 642	53 021	26 868	26 153	62 928	31 966	30 962	72 698	36 932	35 766
35-39	36 165	18 033	18 132	41 075	20 840	20 235	48 331	24 740	23 592	57 805	29 644	28 161
40-44	29 949	14 758	15 191	32 770	16 417	16 353	37 498	19 129	18 369	44 458	22 869	21 589
45-49	25 117	12 210	12 907	27 376	13 456	13 921	30 118	15 074	15 044	34 701	17 688	17 013
50-54	20 901	10 035	10 866	23 053	11 107	11 946	25 232	12 313	12 919	27 912	13 883	14 028
55-59	16 743	7 961	8 782	19 074	9 035	10 038	21 126	10 057	11 069	23 235	11 216	12 019
60-64	13 262	6 202	7 060	14 958	6 991	7 967	17 128	7 981	9 147	19 073	8 940	10 134
65-69	9 902	4 534	5 368	11 306	5 176	6 130	12 851	5 881	6 970	14 817	6 764	8 053
70-74	6 799	3 045	3 753	7 771	3 466	4 305	8 966	3 999	4 967	10 301	4 594	5 707
75-79	4 004	1 736	2 268	4 666	2 018	2 649	5 413	2 330	3 083	6 336	2 728	3 608
80-84	1 861	766	1 095	2 215	915	1 300	2 633	1 085	1 549	3 114	1 277	1 837
85-89	622	235	387	752	287	465	917	352	565	1 118	428	690
90-94	126	41	84	169	56	113	210	70	139	263	89	174
95-99	16	4	12	21	6	16	29	8	22	38	10	27
100 +	1	0	1	2	0	1	2	0	2	3	1	3

Age group	2025 Both sexes	Males	Females	2030 Both sexes	Males	Females	2035 Both sexes	Males	Females	2040 Both sexes	Males	Females
All ages	1 084 421	545 653	538 769	1 169 376	588 914	580 462	1 251 383	630 490	620 892	1 328 074	669 145	658 929
0-4	138 082	69 906	68 176	139 065	70 427	68 638	137 524	69 667	67 857	133 576	67 680	65 895
5-9	130 000	65 691	64 309	133 673	67 575	66 098	135 330	68 441	66 890	134 414	67 998	66 416
10-14	124 336	62 341	61 995	128 238	64 770	63 469	132 197	66 794	65 403	134 099	67 780	66 320
15-19	118 437	59 761	58 677	123 829	62 483	61 046	126 979	64 082	62 897	131 001	66 100	64 907
20-24	110 962	55 901	55 061	116 384	58 611	57 773	121 884	61 382	60 502	125 180	63 053	62 128
25-29	96 533	48 654	47 878	107 193	54 003	53 190	112 842	56 806	56 036	118 569	59 679	58 890
30-34	82 110	41 666	40 445	91 243	46 225	45 018	101 938	51 561	50 377	107 944	54 509	53 435
35-39	67 338	34 487	32 851	76 661	39 149	37 512	85 809	43 691	42 118	96 548	49 027	47 521
40-44	53 542	27 576	25 966	62 865	32 298	30 567	72 036	36 872	35 164	81 176	41 400	39 776
45-49	41 412	21 279	20 134	50 202	25 818	24 384	59 289	30 408	28 882	68 305	34 897	33 408
50-54	32 356	16 396	15 960	38 849	19 844	19 004	47 331	24 201	23 130	56 167	28 645	27 522
55-59	25 847	12 728	13 119	30 140	15 129	15 011	36 373	18 410	17 962	44 601	22 644	21 957
60-64	21 104	10 040	11 064	23 624	11 477	12 147	27 707	13 731	13 976	33 613	16 804	16 809
65-69	16 622	7 639	8 983	18 530	8 652	9 877	20 887	9 970	10 917	24 661	12 019	12 642
70-74	12 001	5 341	6 659	13 599	6 099	7 500	15 302	6 981	8 321	17 400	8 125	9 275
75-79	7 389	3 182	4 207	8 700	3 764	4 977	10 022	4 347	5 676	11 411	5 042	6 369
80-84	3 715	1 524	2 191	4 417	1 814	2 603	5 316	2 181	3 135	6 197	2 568	3 629
85-89	1 353	516	838	1 654	631	1 023	2 013	769	1 244	2 477	946	1 530
90-94	329	111	218	410	138	272	514	173	341	641	216	424
95-99	48	13	35	63	17	46	80	22	59	104	28	76
100 +	4	1	3	6	1	5	7	1	6	10	2	8

Age group	2045 Both sexes	Males	Females	2050 Both sexes	Males	Females
All ages	1 397 994	704 101	693 894	1 460 338	734 896	725 443
0-4	128 206	64 970	63 236	122 382	62 022	60 360
5-9	131 048	66 308	64 740	126 184	63 855	62 330
10-14	133 401	67 444	65 957	130 225	65 848	64 376
15-19	133 087	67 208	65 879	132 515	66 933	65 582
20-24	129 394	65 197	64 197	131 572	66 317	65 255
25-29	122 155	61 483	60 672	126 633	63 749	62 884
30-34	114 028	57 532	56 497	118 047	59 522	58 525
35-39	102 934	52 138	50 795	109 389	55 320	54 070
40-44	91 938	46 741	45 197	98 622	49 991	48 631
45-49	77 410	39 404	38 006	88 146	44 729	43 418
50-54	65 004	33 032	31 972	74 013	37 483	36 530
55-59	53 065	26 832	26 233	61 673	31 081	30 592
60-64	41 351	20 706	20 645	49 514	24 743	24 771
65-69	30 099	14 803	15 296	37 251	18 353	18 898
70-74	20 716	9 887	10 829	25 479	12 275	13 203
75-79	13 113	5 941	7 172	15 770	7 314	8 456
80-84	7 153	3 026	4 127	8 319	3 616	4 702
85-89	2 938	1 136	1 802	3 443	1 363	2 080
90-94	808	273	535	975	334	641
95-99	132	36	96	171	46	125
100 +	13	2	11	17	3	14

POPULATION BY AGE AND SEX (in thousands)

Age group	1950 Both sexes	Males	Females	1955 Both sexes	Males	Females	1960 Both sexes	Males	Females	1965 Both sexes	Males	Females
All ages	224 068	110 844	113 224	250 253	123 948	126 305	281 659	139 724	141 935	318 937	158 357	160 580
0-4	38 312	19 257	19 055	44 145	22 215	21 930	50 362	25 388	24 975	57 644	29 065	28 579
5-9	29 910	14 964	14 947	33 864	16 998	16 866	39 447	19 835	19 612	45 707	23 024	22 684
10-14	25 792	12 877	12 914	28 786	14 410	14 376	32 707	16 429	16 278	38 258	19 215	19 042
15-19	22 664	11 334	11 330	25 001	12 486	12 515	27 872	13 955	13 918	31 456	15 777	15 679
20-24	19 654	9 820	9 834	21 771	10 856	10 915	24 023	11 958	12 065	26 517	13 199	13 318
25-29	16 863	8 386	8 477	18 713	9 307	9 406	20 759	10 303	10 456	22 776	11 262	11 514
30-34	14 496	7 198	7 299	15 988	7 927	8 061	17 794	8 826	8 968	19 698	9 739	9 959
35-39	12 292	6 103	6 189	13 669	6 771	6 897	15 101	7 470	7 631	16 800	8 313	8 488
40-44	10 384	5 129	5 255	11 497	5 684	5 813	12 815	6 322	6 493	14 150	6 979	7 171
45-49	8 712	4 253	4 459	9 616	4 707	4 908	10 682	5 240	5 442	11 887	5 831	6 056
50-54	7 256	3 476	3 780	7 949	3 831	4 118	8 812	4 266	4 546	9 782	4 759	5 023
55-59	5 900	2 759	3 142	6 443	3 039	3 405	7 093	3 370	3 723	7 994	3 825	4 168
60-64	4 586	2 106	2 480	5 005	2 297	2 708	5 514	2 557	2 957	6 223	2 918	3 305
65-69	3 327	1 499	1 828	3 601	1 620	1 980	3 991	1 798	2 193	4 555	2 083	2 473
70-74	2 157	949	1 208	2 334	1 024	1 310	2 591	1 141	1 451	2 967	1 313	1 654
75-79	1 165	491	674	1 230	521	708	1 385	587	798	1 635	704	931
80 +	597	242	354	641	253	388	709	279	430	888	353	535

Age group	1970 Both sexes	Males	Females	1975 Both sexes	Males	Females	1980 Both sexes	Males	Females	1985 Both sexes	Males	Females
All ages	363 535	180 530	183 005	415 824	206 717	209 107	478 824	238 358	240 466	553 255	275 604	277 651
0-4	65 534	33 070	32 464	75 620	38 140	37 479	86 544	43 707	42 837	99 757	50 407	49 350
5-9	52 629	26 524	26 105	60 266	30 362	29 904	69 922	35 214	34 708	80 964	40 832	40 132
10-14	44 425	22 384	22 041	51 026	25 712	25 315	58 593	29 518	29 075	68 411	34 443	33 968
15-19	37 257	18 704	18 553	43 084	21 695	21 390	49 639	24 953	24 686	57 480	28 928	28 552
20-24	30 224	15 084	15 140	35 793	17 872	17 921	41 724	20 859	20 865	48 273	24 179	24 094
25-29	25 261	12 468	12 793	28 905	14 312	14 593	34 605	17 179	17 426	40 252	20 050	20 203
30-34	21 705	10 664	11 042	24 147	11 889	12 259	27 941	13 839	14 102	33 465	16 596	16 869
35-39	18 820	9 260	9 560	20 822	10 229	10 594	23 270	11 508	11 762	27 024	13 372	13 652
40-44	15 906	7 828	8 078	17 928	8 807	9 121	20 084	9 864	10 219	22 320	10 999	11 321
45-49	13 241	6 486	6 755	15 050	7 373	7 677	17 109	8 403	8 706	19 106	9 306	9 800
50-54	11 022	5 349	5 673	12 360	6 006	6 355	14 238	6 916	7 322	16 046	7 785	8 262
55-59	8 883	4 257	4 626	10 020	4 809	5 212	11 320	5 443	5 877	13 101	6 280	6 822
60-64	7 050	3 304	3 747	7 757	3 673	4 085	8 916	4 222	4 695	10 064	4 766	5 298
65-69	5 143	2 359	2 784	5 783	2 667	3 116	6 544	3 048	3 497	7 478	3 474	4 004
70-74	3 426	1 524	1 902	3 816	1 717	2 099	4 386	1 985	2 401	4 972	2 258	2 713
75-79	1 875	802	1 073	2 182	942	1 240	2 517	1 100	1 417	2 851	1 242	1 609
80 +	1 134	462	672	1 263	515	748	1 471	600	871	1 689	686	1 003

Age group	1990 Both sexes	Males	Females	1995 Both sexes	Males	Females	2000 Both sexes	Males	Females	2005 Both sexes	Males	Females
All ages	635 685	316 691	318 993	722 669	360 039	362 630	812 466	405 067	407 399	905 936	452 505	453 431
0-4	110 951	56 115	54 836	120 332	60 892	59 440	129 819	65 719	64 101	141 914	71 867	70 046
5-9	93 923	47 399	46 523	104 383	52 739	51 644	113 582	57 418	56 164	122 531	61 968	60 563
10-14	79 427	40 047	39 380	91 750	46 295	45 456	102 464	51 761	50 703	111 134	56 173	54 961
15-19	66 943	33 675	33 268	77 693	39 140	38 553	90 302	45 528	44 774	100 762	50 865	49 897
20-24	55 585	27 830	27 755	64 834	32 438	32 396	75 505	37 934	37 571	87 835	44 171	43 664
25-29	46 510	23 120	23 390	53 225	26 417	26 808	61 519	30 718	30 801	71 552	35 952	35 600
30-34	38 856	19 272	19 584	44 602	22 048	22 553	49 808	24 710	25 098	56 883	28 569	28 315
35-39	32 256	15 953	16 303	37 346	18 479	18 867	41 807	20 629	21 178	45 831	22 845	22 986
40-44	25 920	12 774	13 146	30 973	15 278	15 695	35 156	17 317	17 839	38 723	19 103	19 620
45-49	21 276	10 421	10 855	24 766	12 143	12 623	29 207	14 298	14 909	32 772	16 062	16 710
50-54	17 999	8 683	9 316	20 079	9 748	10 332	23 209	11 254	11 955	27 204	13 189	14 015
55-59	14 808	7 093	7 715	16 667	7 944	8 723	18 528	8 867	9 661	21 379	10 224	11 155
60-64	11 715	5 525	6 190	13 294	6 274	7 020	14 978	7 013	7 964	16 649	7 827	8 821
65-69	8 510	3 951	4 560	9 970	4 611	5 358	11 363	5 250	6 113	12 856	5 888	6 968
70-74	5 751	2 602	3 149	6 601	2 984	3 617	7 814	3 519	4 296	8 981	4 038	4 943
75-79	3 293	1 439	1 854	3 853	1 677	2 176	4 494	1 959	2 535	5 399	2 343	3 056
80 +	1 963	793	1 170	2 300	931	1 369	2 909	1 172	1 737	3 532	1 421	2 111

United Nations Department of Economic and Social Affairs/Population Division
World Population Prospects: The 2004 Revision, Volume II: Sex and Age Distribution of the World Population

48

POPULATION BY AGE AND SEX (in thousands)

Age group	2005 Both sexes	2005 Males	2005 Females	2010 Both sexes	2010 Males	2010 Females	2015 Both sexes	2015 Males	2015 Females	2020 Both sexes	2020 Males	2020 Females
All ages	905 936	452 505	453 431	1 006 905	504 029	502 875	1 115 358	559 357	556 002	1 228 276	616 892	611 384
0-4	141 914	71 867	70 046	153 783	77 879	75 904	163 771	82 950	80 821	170 550	86 405	84 146
5-9	122 531	61 968	60 563	134 432	68 002	66 431	146 623	74 155	72 467	157 241	79 535	77 706
10-14	111 134	56 173	54 961	119 771	60 560	59 211	131 588	66 543	65 045	143 894	72 749	71 144
15-19	100 762	50 865	49 897	109 386	55 250	54 136	118 027	59 633	58 395	129 800	65 586	64 214
20-24	87 835	44 171	43 664	98 302	49 506	48 796	106 960	53 898	53 062	115 612	58 274	57 338
25-29	71 552	35 952	35 600	83 754	42 140	41 614	94 170	47 443	46 727	102 857	51 833	51 023
30-34	56 883	28 569	28 315	66 520	33 667	32 853	78 441	39 734	38 707	88 685	44 959	43 726
35-39	45 831	22 845	22 986	52 369	26 514	25 855	61 722	31 480	30 242	73 212	37 355	35 857
40-44	38 723	19 103	19 620	42 353	21 184	21 169	48 711	24 758	23 953	57 766	29 564	28 202
45-49	32 772	16 062	16 710	36 045	17 742	18 303	39 601	19 786	19 815	45 809	23 258	22 551
50-54	27 204	13 189	14 015	30 529	14 851	15 678	33 720	16 491	17 229	37 217	18 488	18 730
55-59	21 379	10 224	11 155	25 119	12 028	13 091	28 323	13 624	14 699	31 434	15 212	16 222
60-64	16 649	7 827	8 821	19 302	9 074	10 228	22 821	10 752	12 069	25 881	12 259	13 621
65-69	12 856	5 888	6 968	14 357	6 604	7 753	16 793	7 725	9 068	20 016	9 235	10 781
70-74	8 981	4 038	4 943	10 254	4 566	5 688	11 554	5 169	6 384	13 678	6 120	7 558
75-79	5 399	2 343	3 056	6 292	2 724	3 567	7 289	3 123	4 167	8 321	3 582	4 739
80-84	2 492	1 034	1 458	3 054	1 260	1 795	3 632	1 494	2 138	4 300	1 744	2 556
85-89	844	323	521	1 023	393	630	1 286	492	795	1 578	597	980
90-94	173	58	115	229	77	152	284	96	189	371	124	248
95-99	22	6	16	29	8	21	39	10	29	51	14	37
100 +	2	0	1	2	0	2	3	1	2	4	1	3

Age group	2025 Both sexes	2025 Males	2025 Females	2030 Both sexes	2030 Males	2030 Females	2035 Both sexes	2035 Males	2035 Females	2040 Both sexes	2040 Males	2040 Females
All ages	1 344 491	675 951	668 540	1 463 493	736 208	727 285	1 584 258	797 136	787 121	1 704 870	857 749	847 121
0-4	175 832	89 111	86 721	180 697	91 605	89 092	184 959	93 792	91 167	187 563	95 131	92 432
5-9	164 769	83 363	81 406	170 770	86 433	84 337	176 304	89 268	87 036	181 169	91 756	89 412
10-14	154 878	78 308	76 570	162 758	82 309	80 449	169 060	85 527	83 533	174 843	88 482	86 361
15-19	142 156	71 810	70 347	153 232	77 407	75 825	161 232	81 463	79 769	167 657	84 737	82 920
20-24	127 375	64 210	63 165	139 700	70 420	69 313	150 859	76 037	74 822	158 960	80 137	78 823
25-29	111 556	56 208	55 348	123 325	62 126	61 199	135 736	68 345	67 391	146 965	73 997	72 968
30-34	97 339	49 308	48 031	106 091	53 674	52 417	117 897	59 581	58 317	130 405	65 825	64 580
35-39	83 225	42 462	40 763	91 801	46 747	45 054	100 575	51 100	49 476	112 428	57 009	55 418
40-44	68 864	35 242	33 623	78 675	40 232	38 443	87 111	44 437	42 674	95 087	47 982	47 105
45-49	54 608	27 910	26 697	65 406	33 418	31 988	74 989	38 281	36 708	83 287	42 412	40 876
50-54	43 273	21 849	21 424	51 835	26 348	25 487	62 314	31 667	30 647	71 654	36 390	35 264
55-59	34 859	17 146	17 713	40 736	20 377	20 359	49 004	24 685	24 318	59 123	29 785	29 337
60-64	28 889	13 775	15 114	32 209	15 624	16 586	37 831	18 675	19 156	45 714	22 737	22 977
65-69	22 872	10 615	12 257	25 718	12 022	13 696	28 850	13 732	15 118	34 088	16 526	17 561
70-74	16 495	7 403	9 092	19 046	8 602	10 444	21 618	9 838	11 780	24 445	11 341	13 104
75-79	10 019	4 308	5 711	12 279	5 295	6 984	14 376	6 239	8 137	16 523	7 227	9 296
80-84	5 005	2 035	2 969	6 167	2 499	3 668	7 737	3 133	4 604	9 010	3 553	5 457
85-89	1 928	713	1 214	2 304	853	1 452	2 929	1 072	1 857	3 779	1 377	2 402
90-94	475	154	321	605	190	416	750	234	516	990	302	689
95-99	69	18	51	93	23	70	125	29	95	161	37	124
100 +	6	1	5	8	1	7	11	2	9	16	2	13

Age group	2045 Both sexes	2045 Males	2045 Females	2050 Both sexes	2050 Males	2050 Females
All ages	1 823 062	916 880	906 182	1 936 952	973 525	963 426
0-4	188 069	95 406	92 663	187 004	94 864	92 141
5-9	184 346	93 384	90 962	185 370	93 912	91 458
10-14	179 923	91 075	88 848	183 289	92 793	90 496
15-19	173 557	87 745	85 812	178 749	90 389	88 360
20-24	165 509	83 468	82 041	171 544	86 540	85 004
25-29	155 273	78 187	77 085	162 078	81 634	80 445
30-34	141 820	71 546	70 273	150 443	75 867	74 576
35-39	125 046	63 290	61 755	136 655	69 086	67 569
40-44	107 763	54 696	53 066	120 449	61 002	59 447
45-49	92 039	46 742	45 296	103 887	52 638	51 248
50-54	79 798	40 433	39 365	88 467	44 715	43 753
55-59	68 182	34 340	33 843	76 133	38 268	37 865
60-64	55 377	27 557	27 820	64 069	31 888	32 181
65-69	41 410	20 240	21 171	50 415	24 665	25 751
70-74	29 108	13 771	15 337	35 615	17 001	18 614
75-79	18 881	8 433	10 448	22 716	10 367	12 348
80-84	10 773	4 429	6 344	12 489	5 261	7 228
85-89	4 623	1 693	2 930	5 545	2 053	3 491
90-94	1 330	401	929	1 687	511	1 176
95-99	223	50	174	317	69	248
100 +	22	3	18	32	4	27

POPULATION BY AGE AND SEX (in thousands)

Age group	2005 Both sexes	2005 Males	2005 Females	2010 Both sexes	2010 Males	2010 Females	2015 Both sexes	2015 Males	2015 Females	2020 Both sexes	2020 Males	2020 Females
All ages	905 936	452 505	453 431	1 014 194	507 729	506 465	1 136 732	570 199	566 533	1 270 382	638 240	632 142
0-4	141 914	71 867	70 046	161 073	81 579	79 493	178 132	90 236	87 896	191 878	97 221	94 657
5-9	122 531	61 968	60 563	134 432	68 002	66 431	153 634	77 711	75 923	171 119	86 569	84 550
10-14	111 134	56 173	54 961	119 771	60 560	59 211	131 588	66 543	65 045	150 794	76 247	74 547
15-19	100 762	50 865	49 897	109 386	55 250	54 136	118 027	59 633	58 395	129 800	65 586	64 214
20-24	87 835	44 171	43 664	98 302	49 506	48 796	106 960	53 898	53 062	115 612	58 274	57 338
25-29	71 552	35 952	35 600	83 754	42 140	41 614	94 170	47 443	46 727	102 857	51 833	51 023
30-34	56 883	28 569	28 315	66 520	33 667	32 853	78 441	39 734	38 707	88 685	44 959	43 726
35-39	45 831	22 845	22 986	52 369	26 514	25 855	61 722	31 480	30 242	73 212	37 355	35 857
40-44	38 723	19 103	19 620	42 353	21 184	21 169	48 711	24 758	23 953	57 766	29 564	28 202
45-49	32 772	16 062	16 710	36 045	17 742	18 303	39 601	19 786	19 815	45 809	23 258	22 551
50-54	27 204	13 189	14 015	30 529	14 851	15 678	33 720	16 491	17 229	37 217	18 488	18 730
55-59	21 379	10 224	11 155	25 119	12 028	13 091	28 323	13 624	14 699	31 434	15 212	16 222
60-64	16 649	7 827	8 821	19 302	9 074	10 228	22 821	10 752	12 069	25 881	12 259	13 621
65-69	12 856	5 888	6 968	14 357	6 604	7 753	16 793	7 725	9 068	20 016	9 235	10 781
70-74	8 981	4 038	4 943	10 254	4 566	5 688	11 554	5 169	6 384	13 678	6 120	7 558
75-79	5 399	2 343	3 056	6 292	2 724	3 567	7 289	3 123	4 167	8 321	3 582	4 739
80-84	2 492	1 034	1 458	3 054	1 260	1 795	3 632	1 494	2 138	4 300	1 744	2 556
85-89	844	323	521	1 023	393	630	1 286	492	795	1 578	597	980
90-94	173	58	115	229	77	152	284	96	189	371	124	248
95-99	22	6	16	29	8	21	39	10	29	51	14	37
100 +	2	0	1	2	0	2	3	1	2	4	1	3

Age group	2025 Both sexes	2025 Males	2025 Females	2030 Both sexes	2030 Males	2030 Females	2035 Both sexes	2035 Males	2035 Females	2040 Both sexes	2040 Males	2040 Females
All ages	1 410 045	709 177	700 868	1 557 193	783 689	773 504	1 713 638	862 688	850 950	1 879 362	946 157	933 205
0-4	200 141	101 443	98 698	209 866	106 407	103 459	221 935	112 559	109 376	234 440	118 927	115 513
5-9	185 475	93 852	91 623	194 474	98 444	96 030	204 855	103 739	101 116	217 485	110 168	107 317
10-14	168 578	85 249	83 329	183 244	92 681	90 562	192 556	97 427	95 129	203 189	102 843	100 346
15-19	148 995	75 274	73 721	166 819	84 287	82 533	181 566	91 751	89 815	190 998	96 550	94 448
20-24	127 375	64 210	63 165	146 493	73 842	72 650	164 288	82 825	81 462	179 072	90 296	88 776
25-29	111 556	56 208	55 348	123 325	62 126	61 199	142 330	71 681	70 649	160 103	80 637	79 466
30-34	97 339	49 308	48 031	106 091	53 674	52 417	117 897	59 581	58 317	136 766	69 053	67 713
35-39	83 225	42 462	40 763	91 801	46 747	45 054	100 575	51 100	49 476	112 428	57 009	55 418
40-44	68 864	35 242	33 623	78 675	40 232	38 443	87 111	44 437	42 674	95 887	48 782	47 105
45-49	54 608	27 910	26 697	65 406	33 418	31 988	74 989	38 281	36 708	83 287	42 412	40 876
50-54	43 273	21 849	21 424	51 835	26 348	25 487	62 314	31 667	30 647	71 654	36 390	35 264
55-59	34 859	17 146	17 713	40 736	20 377	20 359	49 004	24 685	24 318	59 123	29 785	29 337
60-64	28 889	13 775	15 114	32 209	15 624	16 586	37 831	18 675	19 156	45 714	22 737	22 977
65-69	22 872	10 615	12 257	25 718	12 022	13 696	28 850	13 732	15 118	34 088	16 526	17 561
70-74	16 495	7 403	9 092	19 046	8 602	10 444	21 618	9 838	11 780	24 445	11 341	13 104
75-79	10 019	4 308	5 711	12 279	5 295	6 984	14 376	6 239	8 137	16 523	7 227	9 296
80-84	5 005	2 035	2 969	6 167	2 498	3 669	7 727	3 133	4 594	9 213	3 756	5 457
85-89	1 928	713	1 214	2 304	853	1 452	2 929	1 072	1 857	3 779	1 377	2 402
90-94	475	154	321	605	190	416	750	234	516	990	302	689
95-99	69	18	51	93	23	70	125	29	95	161	37	124
100 +	6	1	5	8	1	7	11	2	9	16	2	13

Age group	2045 Both sexes	2045 Males	2045 Females	2050 Both sexes	2050 Males	2050 Females
All ages	2 051 804	1 032 785	1 019 019	2 227 675	1 120 840	1 106 835
0-4	244 676	124 137	120 539	251 958	127 835	124 123
5-9	230 521	116 796	113 725	241 279	122 260	119 019
10-14	216 023	109 367	106 656	229 237	116 077	113 160
15-19	201 737	102 011	99 727	214 664	108 572	106 092
20-24	188 619	95 145	93 474	199 473	100 655	98 818
25-29	174 988	88 142	86 846	184 781	93 098	91 683
30-34	154 542	77 993	76 550	169 597	85 557	84 040
35-39	131 167	66 406	64 761	148 950	75 330	73 620
40-44	107 763	54 696	53 066	126 365	64 015	62 350
45-49	92 039	46 742	45 296	103 887	52 638	51 248
50-54	79 798	40 433	39 365	88 467	44 715	43 753
55-59	68 182	34 340	33 843	76 133	38 268	37 865
60-64	55 377	27 557	27 820	64 069	31 888	32 181
65-69	41 410	20 240	21 171	50 415	24 665	25 751
70-74	29 108	13 771	15 337	35 615	17 001	18 614
75-79	18 881	8 433	10 448	22 716	10 367	12 348
80-84	10 773	4 429	6 344	12 489	5 261	7 228
85-89	4 623	1 693	2 930	5 545	2 053	3 491
90-94	1 330	401	929	1 687	511	1 176
95-99	223	50	174	317	69	248
100 +	22	3	18	32	4	27

United Nations Department of Economic and Social Affairs/Population Division
World Population Prospects: The 2004 Revision, Volume II: Sex and Age Distribution of the World Population

50

POPULATION BY AGE AND SEX (in thousands)

Age group	2005 Both sexes	Males	Females	2010 Both sexes	Males	Females	2015 Both sexes	Males	Females	2020 Both sexes	Males	Females
All ages	905 936	452 505	453 431	998 659	499 849	498 809	1 092 313	547 678	544 635	1 184 495	594 707	589 788
0-4	141 914	71 867	70 046	145 537	73 699	71 838	148 638	75 277	73 361	149 167	75 560	73 607
5-9	122 531	61 968	60 563	134 432	68 002	66 431	138 709	70 149	68 561	142 626	72 134	70 492
10-14	111 134	56 173	54 961	119 771	60 560	59 211	131 588	66 543	65 045	136 111	68 810	67 301
15-19	100 762	50 865	49 897	109 386	55 250	54 136	118 027	59 633	58 395	129 800	65 586	64 214
20-24	87 835	44 171	43 664	98 302	49 506	48 796	106 960	53 898	53 062	115 612	58 274	57 338
25-29	71 552	35 952	35 600	83 754	42 140	41 614	94 170	47 443	46 727	102 857	51 833	51 023
30-34	56 883	28 569	28 315	66 520	33 667	32 853	78 441	39 734	38 707	88 685	44 959	43 726
35-39	45 831	22 845	22 986	52 369	26 514	25 855	61 722	31 480	30 242	73 212	37 355	35 857
40-44	38 723	19 103	19 620	42 353	21 184	21 169	48 711	24 758	23 953	57 766	29 564	28 202
45-49	32 772	16 062	16 710	36 045	17 742	18 303	39 601	19 786	19 815	45 809	23 258	22 551
50-54	27 204	13 189	14 015	30 529	14 851	15 678	33 720	16 491	17 229	37 217	18 488	18 730
55-59	21 379	10 224	11 155	25 119	12 028	13 091	28 323	13 624	14 699	31 434	15 212	16 222
60-64	16 649	7 827	8 821	19 302	9 074	10 228	22 821	10 752	12 069	25 881	12 259	13 621
65-69	12 856	5 888	6 968	14 357	6 604	7 753	16 793	7 725	9 068	20 016	9 235	10 781
70-74	8 981	4 038	4 943	10 254	4 566	5 688	11 554	5 169	6 384	13 678	6 120	7 558
75-79	5 399	2 343	3 056	6 292	2 724	3 567	7 289	3 123	4 167	8 321	3 582	4 739
80-84	2 492	1 034	1 458	3 054	1 260	1 795	3 632	1 494	2 138	4 300	1 744	2 556
85-89	844	323	521	1 023	393	630	1 286	492	795	1 578	597	980
90-94	173	58	115	229	77	152	284	96	189	371	124	248
95-99	22	6	16	29	8	21	39	10	29	51	14	37
100 +	2	0	1	2	0	2	3	1	2	4	1	3

Age group	2025 Both sexes	Males	Females	2030 Both sexes	Males	Females	2035 Both sexes	Males	Females	2040 Both sexes	Males	Females
All ages	1 277 247	641 881	635 366	1 368 390	688 033	680 356	1 454 977	731 659	723 317	1 534 382	771 402	762 980
0-4	151 480	76 758	74 722	151 786	76 937	74 849	149 449	75 773	73 676	144 554	73 305	71 249
5-9	144 007	72 847	71 161	147 025	74 402	72 623	148 010	74 929	73 081	146 302	74 085	72 217
10-14	140 455	71 007	69 448	142 217	71 909	70 308	145 523	73 606	71 917	146 755	74 255	72 500
15-19	134 449	67 912	66 538	138 931	70 173	68 758	140 844	71 148	69 697	144 276	72 904	71 372
20-24	127 375	64 210	63 165	132 132	66 585	65 547	136 728	68 900	67 828	138 794	69 950	68 844
25-29	111 556	56 208	55 348	123 325	62 126	61 199	128 315	64 598	63 717	133 144	67 018	66 126
30-34	97 339	49 308	48 031	106 091	53 674	52 417	117 897	59 581	58 317	123 250	62 202	61 049
35-39	83 225	42 462	40 763	91 801	46 747	45 054	100 575	51 100	49 476	112 428	57 009	55 418
40-44	68 864	35 242	33 623	78 675	40 232	38 443	87 111	44 437	42 674	95 887	48 782	47 105
45-49	54 600	27 910	26 697	65 406	33 418	31 988	74 989	38 281	36 708	83 287	42 412	40 876
50-54	43 273	21 849	21 424	51 835	26 348	25 487	62 314	31 667	30 647	71 654	36 390	35 264
55-59	34 859	17 146	17 713	40 736	20 377	20 359	49 004	24 685	24 318	59 123	29 785	29 337
60-64	28 889	13 775	15 114	32 209	15 624	16 585	37 831	18 675	19 156	45 714	22 737	22 977
65-69	22 872	10 615	12 257	25 718	12 022	13 696	28 850	13 732	15 118	34 088	16 526	17 561
70-74	16 495	7 403	9 092	19 046	8 602	10 444	21 618	9 838	11 780	24 445	11 341	13 104
75-79	10 019	4 308	5 711	12 279	5 295	6 984	14 376	6 239	8 137	16 523	7 227	9 296
80-84	5 005	2 035	2 969	6 167	2 498	3 669	7 727	3 133	4 594	9 213	3 756	5 457
85-89	1 928	713	1 214	2 304	853	1 452	2 929	1 072	1 857	3 779	1 377	2 402
90-94	475	154	321	605	190	416	750	234	516	990	302	689
95-99	69	18	51	93	23	70	125	29	95	161	37	124
100 +	6	1	5	8	1	7	11	2	9	16	2	13

Age group	2045 Both sexes	Males	Females	2050 Both sexes	Males	Females
All ages	1 605 112	806 485	798 628	1 666 475	836 519	829 957
0-4	138 220	70 101	68 119	131 532	66 710	64 822
5-9	141 991	71 914	70 076	136 164	68 969	67 195
10-14	145 266	73 519	71 747	141 147	71 443	69 703
15-19	145 634	73 613	72 021	144 273	72 939	71 334
20-24	142 360	71 772	70 588	143 872	72 558	71 315
25-29	135 504	68 206	67 299	139 338	70 151	69 187
30-34	128 441	64 775	63 666	131 238	66 151	65 087
35-39	118 166	59 796	58 370	123 733	62 531	61 203
40-44	107 763	54 696	53 066	113 805	57 625	56 180
45-49	92 039	46 742	45 296	103 887	52 638	51 248
50-54	79 798	40 433	39 365	88 467	44 715	43 753
55-59	68 182	34 340	33 843	76 133	38 268	37 865
60-64	55 377	27 557	27 820	64 069	31 888	32 181
65-69	41 410	20 240	21 171	50 415	24 665	25 751
70-74	29 108	13 771	15 337	35 615	17 001	18 614
75-79	18 881	8 433	10 448	22 716	10 367	12 348
80-84	10 773	4 429	6 344	12 489	5 261	7 228
85-89	4 623	1 693	2 930	5 545	2 053	3 491
90-94	1 330	401	929	1 687	511	1 176
95-99	223	50	174	317	69	248
100 +	22	3	18	32	4	27

POPULATION BY AGE AND SEX (in thousands)

Age group	1950 Both sexes	1950 Males	1950 Females	1955 Both sexes	1955 Males	1955 Females	1960 Both sexes	1960 Males	1960 Females	1965 Both sexes	1965 Males	1965 Females
All ages	64 986	32 072	32 914	72 872	35 965	36 907	82 487	40 722	41 764	94 360	46 606	47 753
0-4	11 707	5 855	5 852	13 440	6 701	6 739	15 339	7 657	7 681	17 752	8 875	8 877
5-9	8 940	4 455	4 485	10 215	5 097	5 118	11 901	5 921	5 980	13 806	6 877	6 929
10-14	7 573	3 768	3 804	8 523	4 248	4 275	9 784	4 883	4 902	11 460	5 702	5 758
15-19	6 641	3 315	3 326	7 299	3 632	3 666	8 240	4 107	4 133	9 492	4 735	4 757
20-24	5 697	2 838	2 859	6 352	3 160	3 192	7 005	3 474	3 530	7 930	3 939	3 991
25-29	4 842	2 405	2 437	5 401	2 676	2 725	6 047	2 992	3 055	6 691	3 303	3 388
30-34	4 140	2 058	2 082	4 566	2 261	2 305	5 118	2 528	2 590	5 755	2 839	2 916
35-39	3 476	1 732	1 744	3 880	1 925	1 955	4 301	2 125	2 175	4 845	2 388	2 457
40-44	2 908	1 445	1 463	3 229	1 602	1 626	3 626	1 792	1 833	4 042	1 990	2 052
45-49	2 440	1 191	1 249	2 675	1 318	1 358	2 990	1 473	1 517	3 379	1 658	1 721
50-54	1 940	915	1 025	2 212	1 066	1 146	2 442	1 189	1 254	2 749	1 339	1 410
55-59	1 559	722	837	1 713	795	918	1 969	934	1 034	2 194	1 053	1 141
60-64	1 219	553	666	1 314	598	717	1 462	667	795	1 700	794	906
65-69	890	393	497	953	424	529	1 045	466	578	1 182	529	653
70-74	568	246	322	614	265	350	674	293	381	757	330	427
75-79	302	125	178	325	135	189	364	151	213	413	173	240
80 +	144	56	88	161	61	99	182	69	112	212	81	131

Age group	1970 Both sexes	1970 Males	1970 Females	1975 Both sexes	1975 Males	1975 Females	1980 Both sexes	1980 Males	1980 Females	1985 Both sexes	1985 Males	1985 Females
All ages	108 818	53 769	55 049	125 811	62 189	63 622	145 906	72 139	73 767	169 622	83 924	85 698
0-4	20 594	10 303	10 291	23 922	11 982	11 940	27 650	13 874	13 776	31 887	16 007	15 880
5-9	16 163	8 062	8 100	18 873	9 422	9 451	22 054	11 026	11 028	25 653	12 848	12 805
10-14	13 369	6 659	6 711	15 661	7 810	7 851	18 271	9 119	9 152	21 452	10 722	10 730
15-19	11 152	5 547	5 605	12 999	6 472	6 528	15 209	7 577	7 632	17 845	8 901	8 944
20-24	9 164	4 556	4 608	10 751	5 326	5 425	12 567	6 222	6 345	14 763	7 330	7 433
25-29	7 608	3 761	3 847	8 774	4 340	4 434	10 345	5 090	5 255	12 139	5 983	6 156
30-34	6 396	3 147	3 249	7 258	3 575	3 683	8 423	4 145	4 279	9 966	4 887	5 079
35-39	5 475	2 694	2 781	6 080	2 982	3 098	6 934	3 400	3 534	8 072	3 959	4 113
40-44	4 583	2 250	2 333	5 178	2 537	2 641	5 763	2 814	2 949	6 602	3 225	3 378
45-49	3 791	1 853	1 938	4 302	2 097	2 205	4 876	2 373	2 503	5 452	2 646	2 807
50-54	3 130	1 520	1 610	3 518	1 702	1 816	4 010	1 937	2 073	4 557	2 197	2 360
55-59	2 490	1 197	1 293	2 842	1 362	1 480	3 218	1 539	1 679	3 679	1 755	1 924
60-64	1 913	904	1 009	2 182	1 032	1 149	2 516	1 189	1 327	2 851	1 343	1 508
65-69	1 391	638	753	1 578	732	846	1 824	849	975	2 104	977	1 127
70-74	873	382	491	1 039	465	573	1 200	545	654	1 381	628	753
75-79	476	201	276	559	236	322	682	297	386	777	341	436
80 +	250	97	154	297	115	181	365	144	221	441	177	264

Age group	1990 Both sexes	1990 Males	1990 Females	1995 Both sexes	1995 Males	1995 Females	2000 Both sexes	2000 Males	2000 Females	2005 Both sexes	2005 Males	2005 Females
All ages	197 630	97 700	99 931	224 430	110 893	113 537	255 681	126 506	129 175	287 707	142 825	144 883
0-4	36 623	18 397	18 226	40 155	20 185	19 970	44 430	22 353	22 076	48 807	24 568	24 240
5-9	29 992	15 025	14 966	33 924	17 007	16 917	37 962	19 046	18 916	41 858	21 019	20 839
10-14	25 230	12 632	12 598	28 808	14 425	14 383	33 412	16 743	16 669	37 006	18 559	18 447
15-19	21 063	10 514	10 549	24 336	12 136	12 201	28 495	14 258	14 237	32 872	16 460	16 412
20-24	17 344	8 600	8 744	20 176	9 954	10 222	23 719	11 795	11 924	27 753	13 855	13 897
25-29	14 226	6 997	7 228	16 290	7 990	8 300	18 918	9 330	9 588	22 339	11 137	11 201
30-34	11 634	5 683	5 951	13 292	6 507	6 785	14 836	7 290	7 546	17 060	8 516	8 543
35-39	9 521	4 632	4 889	10 883	5 304	5 579	12 091	5 908	6 183	13 187	6 548	6 639
40-44	7 679	3 736	3 942	8 921	4 334	4 587	9 986	4 837	5 149	10 839	5 311	5 527
45-49	6 242	3 021	3 221	7 162	3 470	3 692	8 259	3 972	4 287	9 070	4 373	4 697
50-54	5 109	2 451	2 658	5 771	2 770	3 001	6 641	3 176	3 466	7 557	3 596	3 960
55-59	4 199	1 999	2 200	4 668	2 213	2 445	5 304	2 507	2 797	6 054	2 854	3 200
60-64	3 292	1 547	1 745	3 724	1 751	1 973	4 181	1 952	2 229	4 738	2 202	2 536
65-69	2 416	1 117	1 299	2 774	1 282	1 491	3 185	1 468	1 717	3 570	1 634	1 936
70-74	1 621	734	887	1 859	840	1 019	2 178	983	1 195	2 506	1 128	1 378
75-79	917	402	515	1 076	470	606	1 270	556	714	1 498	656	842
80 +	522	212	311	622	254	368	812	332	480	994	407	588

United Nations Department of Economic and Social Affairs/Population Division
World Population Prospects: The 2004 Revision, Volume II: Sex and Age Distribution of the World Population

52

POPULATION BY AGE AND SEX (in thousands)

Age group	2005 Both sexes	2005 Males	2005 Females	2010 Both sexes	2010 Males	2010 Females	2015 Both sexes	2015 Males	2015 Females	2020 Both sexes	2020 Males	2020 Females
All ages	287 707	142 825	144 883	323 485	161 104	162 381	362 790	181 151	181 639	404 347	202 328	202 019
0-4	48 807	24 568	24 240	53 659	27 018	26 641	57 852	29 144	28 708	60 763	30 621	30 142
5-9	41 858	21 019	20 839	46 179	23 198	22 980	51 215	25 736	25 479	55 690	28 003	27 687
10-14	37 006	18 559	18 447	40 740	20 448	20 292	45 099	22 643	22 456	50 203	25 213	24 990
15-19	32 872	16 460	16 412	36 396	18 239	18 157	40 145	20 133	20 012	44 500	22 323	22 177
20-24	27 753	13 855	13 897	32 082	16 032	16 051	35 609	17 808	17 801	39 368	19 701	19 667
25-29	22 339	11 137	11 201	26 341	13 178	13 163	30 590	15 314	15 277	34 155	17 099	17 056
30-34	17 060	8 516	8 543	20 469	10 321	10 148	24 328	12 293	12 035	28 496	14 390	14 106
35-39	13 187	6 548	6 639	15 347	7 762	7 585	18 623	9 497	9 126	22 313	11 393	10 920
40-44	10 839	5 311	5 527	11 903	5 952	5 952	13 999	7 126	6 874	17 113	8 779	8 334
45-49	9 070	4 373	4 697	9 885	4 840	5 045	10 950	5 473	5 477	12 964	6 599	6 365
50-54	7 557	3 596	3 960	8 320	3 982	4 338	9 129	4 442	4 687	10 170	5 056	5 115
55-59	6 054	2 854	3 200	6 906	3 247	3 658	7 648	3 620	4 028	8 434	4 063	4 372
60-64	4 738	2 202	2 536	5 427	2 519	2 909	6 231	2 887	3 345	6 938	3 238	3 700
65-69	3 570	1 634	1 936	4 064	1 853	2 211	4 693	2 137	2 556	5 428	2 468	2 959
70-74	2 506	1 128	1 378	2 828	1 265	1 563	3 253	1 449	1 804	3 795	1 689	2 106
75-79	1 498	656	842	1 740	760	980	1 990	864	1 127	2 322	1 004	1 318
80-84	702	295	407	839	353	487	993	417	576	1 155	482	673
85-89	238	93	144	287	113	174	351	139	212	424	168	257
90-94	48	17	31	64	23	42	80	28	52	100	36	64
95-99	6	2	4	8	2	6	11	3	8	14	4	10
100 +	0	0	0	1	0	0	1	0	1	1	0	1

Age group	2025 Both sexes	2025 Males	2025 Females	2030 Both sexes	2030 Males	2030 Females	2035 Both sexes	2035 Males	2035 Females	2040 Both sexes	2040 Males	2040 Females
All ages	447 683	224 341	223 342	492 698	247 103	245 596	539 141	270 486	268 655	586 272	294 117	292 155
0-4	63 077	31 802	31 275	65 320	32 944	32 376	67 511	34 057	33 453	69 093	34 863	34 231
5-9	58 901	29 629	29 273	61 495	30 948	30 547	63 991	32 217	31 774	66 391	33 434	32 957
10-14	54 847	27 562	27 285	58 208	29 260	28 948	60 925	30 640	30 285	63 517	31 954	31 563
15-19	49 625	24 899	24 726	54 308	27 264	27 044	57 717	28 983	28 734	60 482	30 385	30 098
20-24	43 722	21 884	21 838	48 842	24 450	24 392	53 536	26 815	26 720	56 982	28 550	28 432
25-29	37 929	18 987	18 943	42 279	21 157	21 122	47 394	23 711	23 683	52 111	26 082	26 030
30-34	32 063	16 161	15 903	35 843	18 033	17 810	40 184	20 186	19 998	45 296	22 730	22 566
35-39	26 377	13 433	12 943	29 914	15 174	14 740	33 673	17 024	16 649	38 001	19 163	18 838
40-44	20 659	10 600	10 059	24 625	12 582	12 043	28 094	14 282	13 812	31 820	16 112	15 709
45-49	15 947	8 177	7 769	19 386	9 935	9 450	23 239	11 853	11 385	26 637	13 515	13 122
50-54	12 108	6 131	5 977	14 983	7 641	7 342	18 305	9 329	8 976	22 039	11 179	10 860
55-59	9 445	4 652	4 793	11 709	5 676	5 677	14 063	7 109	6 954	17 267	8 719	8 548
60-64	7 695	3 657	4 038	8 669	4 216	4 453	10 438	5 175	5 263	13 044	6 515	6 529
65-69	6 086	2 790	3 296	6 797	3 175	3 622	7 709	3 687	4 022	9 340	4 556	4 783
70-74	4 436	1 973	2 463	5 021	2 252	2 769	5 658	2 587	3 071	6 470	3 031	3 439
75-79	2 747	1 186	1 561	3 257	1 406	1 851	3 734	1 626	2 108	4 256	1 891	2 365
80-84	1 372	570	802	1 653	687	967	1 999	830	1 169	2 327	975	1 351
85-89	505	199	306	613	241	372	754	296	458	933	367	566
90-94	124	44	79	150	54	97	187	67	120	235	84	151
95-99	18	5	13	22	7	16	28	8	19	35	11	25
100 +	2	0	1	2	0	2	3	1	2	3	1	2

Age group	2045 Both sexes	2045 Males	2045 Females	2050 Both sexes	2050 Males	2050 Females
All ages	633 087	317 490	315 597	678 716	340 141	338 574
0-4	69 743	35 199	34 544	69 683	35 174	34 509
5-9	68 165	34 336	33 829	68 982	34 757	34 225
10-14	65 995	33 209	32 786	67 833	34 141	33 691
15-19	63 117	31 718	31 399	65 632	32 989	32 643
20-24	59 792	29 972	29 819	62 475	31 329	31 146
25-29	55 628	27 846	27 781	58 532	29 312	29 220
30-34	50 057	25 114	24 943	53 676	26 922	26 755
35-39	43 117	21 703	21 414	47 917	24 099	23 818
40-44	36 137	18 242	17 894	41 243	20 774	20 469
45-49	30 330	15 327	15 003	34 622	17 444	17 178
50-54	25 365	12 800	12 565	29 007	14 583	14 424
55-59	20 860	10 492	10 369	24 100	12 061	12 038
60-64	16 082	8 030	8 052	19 521	9 704	9 817
65-69	11 739	5 770	5 969	14 553	7 150	7 402
70-74	7 901	3 778	4 123	10 003	4 818	5 185
75-79	4 917	2 241	2 676	6 066	2 823	3 243
80-84	2 690	1 151	1 539	3 148	1 383	1 765
85-89	1 105	439	666	1 300	527	773
90-94	298	107	191	360	131	229
95-99	45	14	31	59	18	41
100 +	4	1	3	5	1	4

United Nations Department of Economic and Social Affairs/Population Division
World Population Prospects: The 2004 Revision, Volume II: Sex and Age Distribution of the World Population

53

POPULATION BY AGE AND SEX (in thousands)

Age group	2005 Both sexes	2005 Males	2005 Females	2010 Both sexes	2010 Males	2010 Females	2015 Both sexes	2015 Males	2015 Females	2020 Both sexes	2020 Males	2020 Females
All ages	287 707	142 825	144 883	325 684	162 211	163 473	369 284	184 420	184 864	417 499	208 947	208 552
0-4	48 807	24 568	24 240	55 859	28 125	27 733	62 248	31 358	30 889	67 627	34 080	33 547
5-9	41 858	21 019	20 839	46 179	23 198	22 980	53 314	26 790	26 523	59 922	30 131	29 791
10-14	37 006	18 559	18 447	40 740	20 448	20 292	45 099	22 643	22 456	52 259	26 245	26 014
15-19	32 872	16 460	16 412	36 396	18 239	18 157	40 145	20 133	20 012	44 500	22 323	22 177
20-24	27 753	13 855	13 897	32 082	16 032	16 051	35 609	17 808	17 801	39 368	19 701	19 667
25-29	22 339	11 137	11 201	26 341	13 178	13 163	30 590	15 314	15 277	34 155	17 099	17 056
30-34	17 060	8 516	8 543	20 469	10 321	10 148	24 328	12 293	12 035	28 496	14 390	14 106
35-39	13 187	6 548	6 639	15 347	7 762	7 585	18 623	9 497	9 126	22 313	11 393	10 920
40-44	10 839	5 311	5 527	11 903	5 952	5 952	13 999	7 126	6 874	17 113	8 779	8 334
45-49	9 070	4 373	4 697	9 885	4 840	5 045	10 950	5 473	5 477	12 964	6 599	6 365
50-54	7 557	3 596	3 960	8 320	3 982	4 338	9 129	4 442	4 687	10 170	5 056	5 115
55-59	6 054	2 854	3 200	6 906	3 247	3 658	7 648	3 620	4 028	8 434	4 063	4 372
60-64	4 738	2 202	2 536	5 427	2 519	2 909	6 231	2 887	3 345	6 938	3 238	3 700
65-69	3 570	1 634	1 936	4 064	1 853	2 211	4 693	2 137	2 556	5 428	2 468	2 959
70-74	2 506	1 128	1 378	2 828	1 265	1 563	3 253	1 449	1 804	3 795	1 689	2 106
75-79	1 498	656	842	1 740	760	980	1 990	864	1 127	2 322	1 004	1 318
80-84	702	295	407	839	353	487	993	417	576	1 155	482	673
85-89	238	93	144	287	113	174	351	139	212	424	168	257
90-94	48	17	31	64	23	42	80	28	52	100	36	64
95-99	6	2	4	8	2	6	11	3	8	14	4	10
100 +	0	0	0	1	0	0	1	0	1	1	0	1

Age group	2025 Both sexes	2025 Males	2025 Females	2030 Both sexes	2030 Males	2030 Females	2035 Both sexes	2035 Males	2035 Females	2040 Both sexes	2040 Males	2040 Females
All ages	468 593	234 863	233 731	523 178	262 437	260 741	581 923	292 006	289 917	644 701	323 509	321 192
0-4	71 128	35 861	35 268	75 235	37 944	37 292	80 255	40 485	39 770	85 357	43 068	42 289
5-9	65 558	32 977	32 581	69 347	34 900	34 448	73 707	37 107	36 600	78 927	39 745	39 182
10-14	59 016	29 657	29 359	64 788	32 567	32 220	68 707	34 553	34 154	73 164	36 807	36 358
15-19	51 659	25 919	25 740	58 437	29 337	29 100	64 244	32 261	31 984	68 210	34 266	33 944
20-24	43 722	21 884	21 838	50 845	25 453	25 392	57 608	28 856	28 753	63 429	31 780	31 648
25-29	37 929	18 987	18 943	42 279	21 157	21 122	49 334	24 682	24 652	56 073	28 065	28 007
30-34	32 063	16 161	15 903	35 843	18 033	17 810	40 184	20 186	19 998	47 143	23 659	23 485
35-39	26 377	13 433	12 943	29 914	15 174	14 740	33 673	17 024	16 649	38 001	19 163	18 838
40-44	20 659	10 600	10 059	24 625	12 582	12 043	28 094	14 282	13 812	31 820	16 112	15 709
45-49	15 947	8 177	7 769	19 386	9 935	9 450	23 239	11 853	11 385	26 637	13 515	13 122
50-54	12 108	6 131	5 977	14 983	7 641	7 342	18 305	9 329	8 976	22 039	11 179	10 860
55-59	9 445	4 652	4 793	11 309	5 676	5 633	14 063	7 109	6 954	17 257	8 719	8 538
60-64	7 695	3 657	4 038	8 669	4 216	4 453	10 438	5 175	5 263	13 044	6 515	6 529
65-69	6 086	2 790	3 296	6 797	3 175	3 622	7 709	3 687	4 022	9 340	4 556	4 783
70-74	4 436	1 973	2 463	5 021	2 252	2 769	5 658	2 587	3 071	6 470	3 031	3 439
75-79	2 747	1 186	1 561	3 257	1 406	1 851	3 734	1 626	2 108	4 256	1 891	2 365
80-84	1 372	570	802	1 653	687	967	1 999	830	1 169	2 327	975	1 351
85-89	505	199	306	613	241	372	754	296	458	933	367	566
90-94	124	44	79	150	54	97	187	67	120	235	84	151
95-99	18	5	13	22	7	16	28	8	19	35	11	25
100 +	2	0	1	2	0	2	3	1	2	3	1	2

Age group	2045 Both sexes	2045 Males	2045 Females	2050 Both sexes	2050 Males	2050 Females
All ages	710 473	356 424	354 049	777 989	390 096	387 894
0-4	89 545	45 191	44 354	92 660	46 771	45 890
5-9	84 214	42 418	41 796	88 572	44 626	43 946
10-14	78 459	39 479	38 980	83 806	42 179	41 627
15-19	72 706	36 536	36 170	78 032	39 221	38 811
20-24	67 434	33 803	33 631	71 970	36 090	35 881
25-29	61 920	30 997	30 923	66 012	33 058	32 954
30-34	53 853	27 021	26 832	59 742	29 966	29 775
35-39	44 867	22 586	22 281	51 541	25 924	25 616
40-44	36 137	18 242	17 894	42 911	21 617	21 294
45-49	30 330	15 327	15 003	34 622	17 444	17 178
50-54	25 365	12 800	12 565	29 007	14 583	14 424
55-59	20 860	10 492	10 369	24 100	12 061	12 038
60-64	16 082	8 030	8 052	19 521	9 704	9 817
65-69	11 739	5 770	5 969	14 553	7 150	7 402
70-74	7 901	3 778	4 123	10 003	4 818	5 185
75-79	4 917	2 241	2 676	6 066	2 823	3 243
80-84	2 690	1 151	1 539	3 148	1 383	1 765
85-89	1 105	439	666	1 300	527	773
90-94	298	107	191	360	131	229
95-99	45	14	31	59	18	41
100 +	4	1	3	5	1	4

United Nations Department of Economic and Social Affairs/Population Division
World Population Prospects: The 2004 Revision, Volume II: Sex and Age Distribution of the World Population

54

POPULATION BY AGE AND SEX (in thousands)

Age group	2005 Both sexes	Males	Females	2010 Both sexes	Males	Females	2015 Both sexes	Males	Females	2020 Both sexes	Males	Females
All ages	287 707	142 825	144 883	320 959	159 832	161 127	355 633	177 549	178 084	390 522	195 371	195 151
0-4	48 807	24 568	24 240	51 134	25 747	25 388	53 107	26 754	26 353	53 873	27 149	26 724
5-9	41 858	21 019	20 839	46 179	23 198	22 980	48 804	24 524	24 279	51 119	25 705	25 414
10-14	37 006	18 559	18 447	40 740	20 448	20 292	45 099	22 643	22 456	47 839	24 025	23 813
15-19	32 872	16 460	16 412	36 396	18 239	18 157	40 145	20 133	20 012	44 500	22 323	22 177
20-24	27 753	13 855	13 897	32 082	16 032	16 051	35 609	17 808	17 801	39 368	19 701	19 667
25-29	22 339	11 137	11 201	26 341	13 178	13 163	30 590	15 314	15 277	34 155	17 099	17 056
30-34	17 060	8 516	8 543	20 469	10 321	10 148	24 328	12 293	12 035	28 496	14 390	14 106
35-39	13 187	6 548	6 639	15 347	7 762	7 585	18 623	9 497	9 126	22 313	11 393	10 920
40-44	10 839	5 311	5 527	11 903	5 952	5 952	13 999	7 126	6 874	17 113	8 779	8 334
45-49	9 070	4 373	4 697	9 885	4 840	5 045	10 950	5 473	5 477	12 964	6 599	6 365
50-54	7 557	3 596	3 960	8 320	3 982	4 338	9 129	4 442	4 687	10 170	5 056	5 115
55-59	6 054	2 854	3 200	6 906	3 247	3 658	7 648	3 620	4 028	8 434	4 063	4 372
60-64	4 738	2 202	2 536	5 427	2 519	2 909	6 231	2 887	3 345	6 938	3 238	3 700
65-69	3 570	1 634	1 936	4 064	1 853	2 211	4 693	2 137	2 556	5 428	2 468	2 959
70-74	2 506	1 128	1 378	2 828	1 265	1 563	3 253	1 449	1 804	3 795	1 689	2 106
75-79	1 498	656	842	1 740	760	980	1 990	864	1 127	2 322	1 004	1 318
80-84	702	295	407	839	353	487	993	417	576	1 155	482	673
85-89	238	93	144	287	113	174	351	139	212	424	168	257
90-94	48	17	31	64	23	42	80	28	52	100	36	64
95-99	6	2	4	8	2	6	11	3	8	14	4	10
100 +	0	0	0	1	0	0	1	0	1	1	0	1

Age group	2025 Both sexes	Males	Females	2030 Both sexes	Males	Females	2035 Both sexes	Males	Females	2040 Both sexes	Males	Females
All ages	426 080	213 471	212 609	461 574	231 445	230 128	496 091	248 832	247 258	528 684	265 151	263 533
0-4	54 997	27 729	27 268	55 445	27 964	27 481	55 134	27 815	27 319	53 932	27 214	26 718
5-9	52 219	26 268	25 951	53 614	26 982	26 631	54 313	27 345	26 968	54 216	27 303	26 912
10-14	50 345	25 300	25 045	51 603	25 940	25 663	53 115	26 713	26 403	53 909	27 121	26 788
15-19	47 287	23 726	23 561	49 847	25 025	24 822	51 105	26 008	25 472	52 720	26 488	26 248
20-24	43 722	21 884	21 838	46 539	23 298	23 242	49 136	24 612	24 524	50 510	25 307	25 203
25-29	37 929	18 987	18 943	42 279	21 157	21 122	45 159	22 593	22 567	47 830	23 938	23 892
30-34	32 063	16 161	15 903	35 843	18 033	17 810	40 184	20 186	19 998	43 163	21 659	21 504
35-39	26 377	13 433	12 943	29 914	15 174	14 740	33 673	17 024	16 649	38 001	19 163	18 838
40-44	20 650	10 600	10 059	24 625	12 582	12 043	28 094	14 282	13 812	31 820	16 112	15 709
45-49	15 947	8 177	7 769	19 386	9 935	9 450	23 239	11 863	11 385	26 637	13 515	13 122
50-54	12 108	6 131	5 977	14 983	7 641	7 342	18 305	9 329	8 976	22 039	11 179	10 860
55-59	9 445	4 652	4 793	11 309	5 676	5 633	14 062	7 100	6 961	17 257	8 719	8 538
60-64	7 695	3 657	4 038	8 669	4 216	4 453	10 438	5 175	5 263	13 044	6 515	6 529
65-69	6 086	2 790	3 296	6 797	3 175	3 622	7 709	3 687	4 022	9 340	4 556	4 783
70-74	4 436	1 973	2 463	5 021	2 252	2 769	5 658	2 587	3 071	6 470	3 031	3 439
75-79	2 747	1 186	1 561	3 257	1 406	1 851	3 734	1 626	2 108	4 256	1 891	2 365
80-84	1 372	570	802	1 653	687	967	1 999	830	1 169	2 327	975	1 351
85-89	505	199	306	613	241	372	754	296	458	933	367	566
90-94	124	44	79	150	54	97	187	67	120	235	84	151
95-99	18	5	13	22	7	16	28	8	19	35	11	25
100 +	2	0	1	2	0	2	3	1	2	3	1	2

Age group	2045 Both sexes	Males	Females	2050 Both sexes	Males	Females
All ages	558 627	280 032	278 596	585 423	293 202	292 220
0-4	52 023	26 258	25 765	49 769	25 124	24 646
5-9	53 203	26 801	26 402	51 452	25 926	25 526
10-14	53 890	27 119	26 771	52 941	26 647	26 293
15-19	53 566	26 919	26 646	53 589	26 937	26 652
20-24	52 121	26 127	25 994	53 017	26 586	26 431
25-29	49 311	24 684	24 628	51 024	25 551	25 473
30-34	45 950	23 052	22 898	47 589	23 867	23 723
35-39	41 089	20 681	20 408	43 992	22 122	21 870
40-44	36 137	18 242	17 894	39 306	19 797	19 509
45-49	30 330	15 327	15 003	34 622	17 444	17 178
50-54	25 365	12 800	12 565	29 007	14 583	14 424
55-59	20 860	10 492	10 369	24 100	12 061	12 038
60-64	16 082	8 030	8 052	19 521	9 704	9 817
65-69	11 739	5 770	5 969	14 553	7 150	7 402
70-74	7 901	3 778	4 123	10 003	4 818	5 185
75-79	4 917	2 241	2 676	6 066	2 823	3 243
80-84	2 690	1 151	1 539	3 148	1 383	1 765
85-89	1 105	439	666	1 300	527	773
90-94	298	107	191	360	131	229
95-99	45	14	31	59	18	41
100 +	4	1	3	5	1	4

POPULATION BY AGE AND SEX (in thousands)

Age group	1950 Both sexes	1950 Males	1950 Females	1955 Both sexes	1955 Males	1955 Females	1960 Both sexes	1960 Males	1960 Females	1965 Both sexes	1965 Males	1965 Females
All ages	26 332	12 631	13 701	28 902	13 919	14 983	32 184	15 561	16 623	36 102	17 522	18 581
0-4	4 383	2 171	2 212	4 947	2 464	2 483	5 631	2 808	2 823	6 457	3 225	3 233
5-9	3 462	1 701	1 761	3 802	1 877	1 926	4 348	2 158	2 190	4 984	2 478	2 506
10-14	2 985	1 459	1 525	3 301	1 621	1 679	3 647	1 800	1 847	4 168	2 068	2 100
15-19	2 619	1 276	1 343	2 878	1 407	1 471	3 198	1 571	1 627	3 531	1 742	1 789
20-24	2 291	1 108	1 183	2 514	1 221	1 293	2 776	1 354	1 422	3 082	1 509	1 573
25-29	1 983	949	1 034	2 177	1 047	1 130	2 403	1 161	1 242	2 652	1 286	1 365
30-34	1 713	816	898	1 873	894	979	2 069	992	1 077	2 282	1 099	1 183
35-39	1 467	694	773	1 606	762	843	1 767	841	926	1 952	933	1 019
40-44	1 246	585	661	1 362	641	721	1 502	710	792	1 655	784	871
45-49	1 049	486	563	1 145	533	613	1 262	589	673	1 393	653	740
50-54	877	401	476	949	433	516	1 046	479	566	1 154	531	623
55-59	711	320	391	772	346	426	844	378	465	933	421	512
60-64	549	241	308	599	264	335	658	290	369	722	318	404
65-69	410	178	232	424	182	242	470	203	268	522	225	297
70-74	284	121	163	280	118	162	296	124	173	334	140	194
75-79	173	72	101	160	65	95	162	65	97	176	70	106
80 +	130	54	76	113	44	69	105	40	65	103	38	65

Age group	1970 Both sexes	1970 Males	1970 Females	1975 Both sexes	1975 Males	1975 Females	1980 Both sexes	1980 Males	1980 Females	1985 Both sexes	1985 Males	1985 Females
All ages	41 104	20 023	21 082	46 987	22 971	24 016	54 357	26 661	27 696	62 926	30 946	31 980
0-4	7 472	3 737	3 735	8 686	4 350	4 336	10 208	5 117	5 091	11 863	5 948	5 914
5-9	5 812	2 894	2 918	6 766	3 375	3 391	7 971	3 982	3 989	9 376	4 688	4 688
10-14	4 821	2 397	2 425	5 614	2 795	2 819	6 574	3 278	3 296	7 731	3 860	3 871
15-19	4 066	2 018	2 049	4 690	2 330	2 360	5 488	2 730	2 758	6 415	3 196	3 218
20-24	3 427	1 685	1 741	3 933	1 946	1 987	4 560	2 259	2 301	5 330	2 643	2 687
25-29	2 968	1 446	1 522	3 295	1 613	1 681	3 803	1 874	1 930	4 407	2 173	2 234
30-34	2 542	1 229	1 313	2 840	1 381	1 459	3 174	1 551	1 623	3 662	1 799	1 863
35-39	2 175	1 045	1 130	2 416	1 166	1 250	2 720	1 320	1 399	3 038	1 482	1 556
40-44	1 847	880	968	2 053	982	1 071	2 298	1 105	1 193	2 586	1 251	1 335
45-49	1 551	729	822	1 730	818	912	1 938	921	1 017	2 169	1 036	1 132
50-54	1 289	597	692	1 434	667	767	1 613	755	858	1 807	851	957
55-59	1 042	473	570	1 165	532	633	1 309	601	708	1 473	681	792
60-64	809	358	450	907	405	503	1 026	461	565	1 154	522	632
65-69	585	252	333	661	287	374	752	329	423	853	377	476
70-74	381	160	221	431	181	250	495	210	285	565	241	324
75-79	205	83	123	238	96	142	277	112	165	319	129	189
80 +	111	41	70	128	47	81	151	56	95	179	67	112

Age group	1990 Both sexes	1990 Males	1990 Females	1995 Both sexes	1995 Males	1995 Females	2000 Both sexes	2000 Males	2000 Females	2005 Both sexes	2005 Males	2005 Females
All ages	72 913	35 924	36 989	85 589	42 229	43 360	96 040	47 466	48 575	109 641	54 313	55 329
0-4	13 701	6 873	6 828	15 989	8 021	7 968	17 553	8 801	8 752	20 197	10 133	10 064
5-9	10 957	5 481	5 476	12 890	6 450	6 440	14 448	7 229	7 220	16 194	8 099	8 096
10-14	9 127	4 562	4 566	10 852	5 427	5 425	12 311	6 158	6 152	14 015	7 010	7 005
15-19	7 563	3 774	3 788	9 091	4 541	4 550	10 440	5 218	5 222	12 046	6 024	6 022
20-24	6 226	3 093	3 134	7 469	3 716	3 752	8 674	4 321	4 353	10 119	5 045	5 074
25-29	5 127	2 529	2 598	6 038	2 987	3 051	6 959	3 457	3 502	8 202	4 083	4 119
30-34	4 221	2 073	2 148	4 924	2 421	2 503	5 498	2 725	2 773	6 405	3 198	3 207
35-39	3 493	1 710	1 783	4 040	1 976	2 065	4 456	2 191	2 265	5 002	2 491	2 511
40-44	2 884	1 400	1 484	3 338	1 623	1 714	3 663	1 783	1 880	4 061	1 997	2 064
45-49	2 440	1 172	1 269	2 750	1 322	1 427	3 034	1 463	1 571	3 355	1 624	1 731
50-54	2 026	958	1 068	2 308	1 095	1 213	2 491	1 183	1 307	2 779	1 325	1 454
55-59	1 655	769	886	1 882	878	1 004	2 061	964	1 097	2 256	1 057	1 199
60-64	1 304	594	710	1 489	681	808	1 632	749	883	1 817	836	981
65-69	965	429	536	1 109	496	613	1 220	549	672	1 364	615	749
70-74	645	278	367	744	323	421	825	361	464	931	409	522
75-79	367	150	217	428	177	251	477	200	277	545	231	314
80 +	210	79	131	249	94	155	299	114	184	353	137	216

United Nations Department of Economic and Social Affairs/Population Division
World Population Prospects: The 2004 Revision, Volume II: Sex and Age Distribution of the World Population

56

POPULATION BY AGE AND SEX (in thousands)

Age group	2005 Both sexes	Males	Females	2010 Both sexes	Males	Females	2015 Both sexes	Males	Females	2020 Both sexes	Males	Females
All ages	109 641	54 313	55 329	125 472	62 282	63 190	143 346	71 262	72 084	162 070	81 111	81 002
0-4	20 197	10 133	10 064	23 099	11 591	11 508	25 832	12 964	12 869	28 100	14 108	13 992
5-9	16 194	8 099	8 096	18 733	9 372	9 361	21 542	10 773	10 768	24 301	12 152	12 149
10-14	14 015	7 010	7 005	15 711	7 853	7 858	18 181	9 090	9 091	20 974	10 481	10 493
15-19	12 046	6 024	6 022	13 721	6 859	6 862	15 383	7 684	7 699	17 832	8 908	8 925
20-24	10 119	5 045	5 074	11 694	5 833	5 862	13 338	6 649	6 689	14 988	7 465	7 523
25-29	8 202	4 083	4 119	9 601	4 783	4 818	11 133	5 548	5 585	12 750	6 349	6 401
30-34	6 405	3 198	3 207	7 584	3 797	3 787	8 920	4 467	4 453	10 395	5 205	5 190
35-39	5 002	2 491	2 511	5 845	2 938	2 908	6 954	3 504	3 450	8 217	4 141	4 076
40-44	4 061	1 997	2 064	4 563	2 277	2 286	5 356	2 698	2 658	6 396	3 232	3 165
45-49	3 355	1 624	1 731	3 722	1 823	1 900	4 197	2 087	2 110	4 943	2 483	2 460
50-54	2 779	1 325	1 454	3 075	1 474	1 601	3 422	1 661	1 761	3 870	1 909	1 961
55-59	2 256	1 057	1 199	2 521	1 186	1 335	2 798	1 325	1 474	3 125	1 499	1 626
60-64	1 817	836	981	1 995	920	1 075	2 238	1 037	1 201	2 496	1 164	1 332
65-69	1 364	615	749	1 526	689	837	1 684	762	922	1 902	865	1 037
70-74	931	409	522	1 048	462	586	1 181	522	659	1 316	583	734
75-79	545	231	314	621	264	357	707	302	405	807	346	461
80-84	251	101	151	290	117	173	336	137	199	389	159	230
85-89	83	30	52	97	36	61	114	43	71	135	51	84
90-94	16	5	11	21	7	14	25	8	17	30	10	20
95-99	2	0	1	2	1	2	3	1	2	4	1	3
100 +	0	0	0	0	0	0	0	0	0	0	0	0

Age group	2025 Both sexes	Males	Females	2030 Both sexes	Males	Females	2035 Both sexes	Males	Females	2040 Both sexes	Males	Females
All ages	184 332	91 821	92 511	207 223	103 287	103 936	231 125	115 251	115 874	255 411	127 393	128 018
0-4	30 299	15 221	15 078	32 273	16 223	16 051	33 761	16 982	16 779	34 649	17 438	17 210
5-9	26 659	13 338	13 321	28 958	14 499	14 459	31 052	15 561	15 491	32 668	16 386	16 283
10-14	23 750	11 866	11 884	26 150	13 071	13 079	28 491	14 252	14 239	30 628	15 334	15 294
15-19	20 609	10 289	10 320	23 382	11 670	11 712	25 790	12 877	12 913	28 144	14 062	14 082
20-24	17 408	8 671	8 737	20 158	10 035	10 123	22 913	11 404	11 509	25 320	12 607	12 713
25-29	14 374	7 150	7 224	16 743	8 328	8 415	19 449	9 668	9 781	22 175	11 020	11 155
30-34	11 964	5 982	5 982	13 546	6 762	6 784	15 849	7 909	7 940	18 495	9 219	9 276
35-39	9 624	4 846	4 777	11 141	5 598	5 543	12 678	6 357	6 321	14 913	7 470	7 443
40-44	7 591	3 836	3 755	8 942	4 513	4 429	10 406	5 208	5 100	11 905	5 978	5 927
45-49	5 925	2 986	2 939	7 070	3 564	3 506	8 369	4 214	4 155	9 788	4 916	4 872
50-54	4 575	2 281	2 294	5 510	2 758	2 753	6 605	3 308	3 297	7 856	3 931	3 925
55-59	3 549	1 731	1 818	4 216	2 080	2 136	5 103	2 528	2 575	6 147	3 049	3 098
60-64	2 802	1 325	1 477	3 200	1 540	1 660	3 824	1 862	1 962	4 654	2 277	2 377
65-69	2 136	978	1 158	2 415	1 122	1 293	2 778	1 315	1 463	3 343	1 602	1 742
70-74	1 501	668	833	1 703	763	939	1 944	885	1 059	2 259	1 048	1 211
75-79	912	392	520	1 055	456	599	1 213	528	684	1 403	621	782
80-84	452	186	267	521	215	306	611	255	356	718	301	417
85-89	159	61	99	190	73	117	224	87	137	270	106	164
90-94	36	12	24	44	15	29	54	19	35	65	23	42
95-99	5	1	4	6	2	4	7	2	5	9	3	7
100 +	0	0	0	0	0	0	1	0	0	1	0	1

Age group	2045 Both sexes	Males	Females	2050 Both sexes	Males	Females
All ages	279 587	139 456	140 131	303 349	151 280	152 070
0-4	35 067	17 656	17 411	35 228	17 743	17 485
5-9	33 696	16 912	16 784	34 255	17 201	17 054
10-14	32 291	16 181	16 110	33 368	16 732	16 637
15-19	30 299	15 151	15 148	31 985	16 008	15 978
20-24	27 679	13 792	13 886	29 844	14 884	14 960
25-29	24 576	12 219	12 358	26 939	13 403	13 536
30-34	21 180	10 551	10 630	23 572	11 742	11 830
35-39	17 497	8 750	8 747	20 139	10 059	10 080
40-44	14 081	7 062	7 019	16 606	8 312	8 294
45-49	11 254	5 639	5 615	13 375	6 694	6 681
50-54	9 230	4 608	4 622	10 660	5 311	5 349
55-59	7 345	3 642	3 703	8 670	4 291	4 379
60-64	5 638	2 763	2 875	6 773	3 318	3 454
65-69	4 098	1 973	2 125	4 998	2 411	2 588
70-74	2 744	1 289	1 455	3 394	1 602	1 792
75-79	1 652	746	906	2 031	930	1 102
80-84	845	361	484	1 010	441	569
85-89	322	128	194	387	157	230
90-94	81	29	52	99	36	63
95-99	12	4	8	15	5	10
100 +	1	0	1	1	0	1

United Nations Department of Economic and Social Affairs/Population Division
World Population Prospects: The 2004 Revision, Volume II: Sex and Age Distribution of the World Population

57

POPULATION BY AGE AND SEX (in thousands)

Age group	2005 Both sexes	Males	Females	2010 Both sexes	Males	Females	2015 Both sexes	Males	Females	2020 Both sexes	Males	Females
All ages	109 641	54 313	55 329	125 806	62 449	63 357	144 879	72 031	72 849	167 029	83 145	83 884
0-4	20 197	10 133	10 064	23 434	11 759	11 675	27 053	13 576	13 476	30 700	15 413	15 287
5-9	16 194	8 099	8 096	18 733	9 372	9 361	21 855	10 930	10 925	25 452	12 728	12 724
10-14	14 015	7 010	7 005	15 711	7 853	7 858	18 181	9 090	9 091	21 279	10 634	10 645
15-19	12 046	6 024	6 022	13 721	6 859	6 862	15 383	7 684	7 699	17 832	8 908	8 925
20-24	10 119	5 045	5 074	11 694	5 833	5 862	13 338	6 649	6 689	14 988	7 465	7 523
25-29	8 202	4 083	4 119	9 601	4 783	4 818	11 133	5 548	5 585	12 750	6 349	6 401
30-34	6 405	3 198	3 207	7 584	3 797	3 787	8 920	4 467	4 453	10 395	5 205	5 190
35-39	5 002	2 491	2 511	5 845	2 938	2 908	6 954	3 504	3 450	8 217	4 141	4 076
40-44	4 061	1 997	2 064	4 563	2 277	2 286	5 356	2 698	2 658	6 396	3 232	3 165
45-49	3 355	1 624	1 731	3 722	1 823	1 900	4 197	2 087	2 110	4 943	2 483	2 460
50-54	2 779	1 325	1 454	3 075	1 474	1 601	3 422	1 661	1 761	3 870	1 909	1 961
55-59	2 256	1 057	1 199	2 521	1 186	1 335	2 798	1 325	1 474	3 125	1 499	1 626
60-64	1 817	836	981	1 995	920	1 075	2 238	1 037	1 201	2 496	1 164	1 332
65-69	1 364	615	749	1 526	689	837	1 684	762	922	1 902	865	1 037
70-74	931	409	522	1 048	462	586	1 181	522	659	1 316	583	734
75-79	545	231	314	621	264	357	707	302	405	807	346	461
80-84	251	101	151	290	117	173	336	137	199	389	159	230
85-89	83	30	52	97	36	61	114	43	71	135	51	84
90-94	16	5	11	21	7	14	25	8	17	30	10	20
95-99	2	0	1	2	1	2	3	1	2	4	1	3
100 +	0	0	0	0	0	0	0	0	0	0	0	0

Age group	2025 Both sexes	Males	Females	2030 Both sexes	Males	Females	2035 Both sexes	Males	Females	2040 Both sexes	Males	Females
All ages	191 301	95 314	95 988	217 786	108 579	109 206	246 405	122 906	123 499	276 963	138 192	138 771
0-4	33 370	16 764	16 606	36 065	18 129	17 936	38 726	19 480	19 247	41 251	20 761	20 490
5-9	29 130	14 574	14 556	31 899	15 972	15 927	34 705	17 392	17 313	37 478	18 798	18 680
10-14	24 877	12 429	12 447	28 576	14 284	14 292	31 386	15 701	15 686	34 234	17 139	17 094
15-19	20 909	10 439	10 471	24 492	12 224	12 268	28 185	14 073	14 112	31 006	15 492	15 514
20-24	17 408	8 671	8 737	20 452	10 181	10 270	24 002	11 946	12 056	27 673	13 779	13 894
25-29	14 374	7 150	7 224	16 743	8 328	8 415	19 733	9 809	9 923	23 228	11 544	11 684
30-34	11 964	5 982	5 982	13 546	6 762	6 784	15 849	7 909	7 940	18 763	9 353	9 410
35-39	9 624	4 846	4 777	11 141	5 598	5 543	12 678	6 357	6 321	14 913	7 470	7 443
40-44	7 591	3 836	3 755	8 942	4 513	4 429	10 406	5 238	5 168	11 905	5 978	5 927
45-49	5 925	2 986	2 939	7 070	3 564	3 506	8 369	4 214	4 155	9 788	4 916	4 872
50-54	4 575	2 281	2 294	5 510	2 758	2 753	6 605	3 308	3 297	7 856	3 931	3 925
55-59	3 549	1 731	1 818	4 216	2 080	2 136	5 103	2 528	2 575	6 147	3 049	3 098
60-64	2 802	1 325	1 477	3 200	1 540	1 660	3 824	1 862	1 962	4 654	2 277	2 377
65-69	2 136	978	1 158	2 415	1 122	1 293	2 778	1 315	1 463	3 343	1 602	1 742
70-74	1 501	668	833	1 703	763	939	1 944	885	1 059	2 259	1 048	1 211
75-79	912	392	520	1 055	456	599	1 213	528	684	1 403	621	782
80-84	452	186	267	521	215	306	614	255	359	718	301	417
85-89	159	61	99	190	73	117	224	87	137	270	106	164
90-94	36	12	24	44	15	29	54	19	35	65	23	42
95-99	5	1	4	6	2	4	7	2	5	9	3	7
100 +	0	0	0	0	0	0	1	0	0	1	0	1

Age group	2045 Both sexes	Males	Females	2050 Both sexes	Males	Females
All ages	309 045	154 220	154 825	342 148	170 730	171 418
0-4	43 418	21 861	21 557	45 144	22 738	22 406
5-9	40 122	20 138	19 984	42 418	21 300	21 118
10-14	37 048	18 565	18 483	39 735	19 924	19 811
15-19	33 868	16 936	16 932	36 699	18 367	18 332
20-24	30 495	15 196	15 299	33 360	16 638	16 723
25-29	26 860	13 355	13 506	29 680	14 767	14 913
30-34	22 185	11 051	11 133	25 762	12 834	12 928
35-39	17 749	8 876	8 873	21 093	10 536	10 557
40-44	14 081	7 062	7 019	16 844	8 431	8 413
45-49	11 254	5 639	5 615	13 375	6 694	6 681
50-54	9 230	4 608	4 622	10 660	5 311	5 349
55-59	7 345	3 642	3 703	8 670	4 291	4 379
60-64	5 638	2 763	2 875	6 773	3 318	3 454
65-69	4 098	1 973	2 125	4 998	2 411	2 588
70-74	2 744	1 289	1 455	3 394	1 602	1 792
75-79	1 652	746	906	2 031	930	1 102
80-84	845	361	484	1 010	441	569
85-89	322	128	194	387	157	230
90-94	81	29	52	99	36	63
95-99	12	4	8	15	5	10
100 +	1	0	1	1	0	1

United Nations Department of Economic and Social Affairs/Population Division
World Population Prospects: The 2004 Revision, Volume II: Sex and Age Distribution of the World Population

58

POPULATION BY AGE AND SEX (in thousands)

Age group	2005 Both sexes	Males	Females	2010 Both sexes	Males	Females	2015 Both sexes	Males	Females	2020 Both sexes	Males	Females
All ages	109 641	54 313	55 329	124 523	61 806	62 718	140 681	69 925	70 755	157 833	78 535	79 297
0-4	20 197	10 133	10 064	22 151	11 115	11 036	24 054	12 071	11 983	25 501	12 802	12 698
5-9	16 194	8 099	8 096	18 733	9 372	9 361	20 655	10 330	10 325	22 624	11 313	11 311
10-14	14 015	7 010	7 005	15 711	7 853	7 858	18 181	9 090	9 091	20 110	10 049	10 061
15-19	12 046	6 024	6 022	13 721	6 859	6 862	15 383	7 684	7 699	17 832	8 908	8 925
20-24	10 119	5 045	5 074	11 694	5 833	5 862	13 338	6 649	6 689	14 988	7 465	7 523
25-29	8 202	4 083	4 119	9 601	4 783	4 818	11 133	5 548	5 585	12 750	6 349	6 401
30-34	6 405	3 198	3 207	7 584	3 797	3 787	8 920	4 467	4 453	10 395	5 205	5 190
35-39	5 002	2 491	2 511	5 845	2 938	2 908	6 954	3 504	3 450	8 217	4 141	4 076
40-44	4 061	1 997	2 064	4 563	2 277	2 286	5 356	2 698	2 658	6 396	3 232	3 165
45-49	3 355	1 624	1 731	3 722	1 823	1 900	4 197	2 087	2 110	4 943	2 483	2 460
50-54	2 779	1 325	1 454	3 075	1 474	1 601	3 422	1 661	1 761	3 870	1 909	1 961
55-59	2 256	1 057	1 199	2 521	1 186	1 335	2 798	1 325	1 474	3 125	1 499	1 626
60-64	1 817	836	981	1 995	920	1 075	2 238	1 037	1 201	2 496	1 164	1 332
65-69	1 364	615	749	1 526	689	837	1 684	762	922	1 902	865	1 037
70-74	931	409	522	1 048	462	586	1 181	522	659	1 316	583	734
75-79	545	231	314	621	264	357	707	302	405	807	346	461
80-84	251	101	151	290	117	173	336	137	199	389	159	230
85-89	83	30	52	97	36	61	114	43	71	135	51	84
90-94	16	5	11	21	7	14	25	8	17	30	10	20
95-99	2	0	1	2	1	2	3	1	2	4	1	3
100 +	0	0	0	0	0	0	0	0	0	0	0	0

Age group	2025 Both sexes	Males	Females	2030 Both sexes	Males	Females	2035 Both sexes	Males	Females	2040 Both sexes	Males	Females
All ages	176 228	87 761	88 467	195 325	97 327	97 997	214 283	106 815	107 468	232 390	115 861	116 530
0-4	27 156	13 642	13 514	28 257	14 204	14 054	28 532	14 352	14 180	28 089	14 137	13 952
5-9	24 187	12 101	12 086	25 950	12 993	12 957	27 183	13 622	13 561	27 603	13 845	13 758
10-14	22 110	11 046	11 063	23 724	11 858	11 866	25 529	12 770	12 759	26 810	13 422	13 387
15-19	19 760	9 865	9 895	21 765	10 863	10 903	23 396	11 681	11 715	25 217	12 599	12 617
20-24	17 408	8 671	8 707	19 326	9 621	9 705	21 328	10 615	10 713	22 968	11 436	11 532
25-29	14 374	7 150	7 224	16 743	8 328	8 415	18 647	9 269	9 378	20 641	10 258	10 383
30-34	11 964	5 982	5 982	13 546	6 762	6 784	15 849	7 909	7 940	17 732	8 839	8 893
35-39	9 624	4 846	4 777	11 141	5 598	5 543	12 678	6 357	6 321	14 913	7 470	7 443
40-44	7 591	3 836	3 755	8 942	4 513	4 429	10 406	5 238	5 168	11 905	5 978	5 927
45-49	5 925	2 986	2 939	7 070	3 564	3 506	8 369	4 214	4 155	9 788	4 916	4 872
50-54	4 575	2 281	2 294	5 510	2 758	2 753	6 605	3 308	3 297	7 856	3 931	3 925
55-59	3 549	1 731	1 818	4 216	2 080	2 136	5 103	2 528	2 575	6 147	3 049	3 098
60-64	2 802	1 325	1 477	3 200	1 540	1 660	3 824	1 862	1 962	4 654	2 277	2 377
65-69	2 136	978	1 158	2 415	1 122	1 293	2 778	1 315	1 463	3 343	1 602	1 742
70-74	1 501	668	833	1 703	763	939	1 944	885	1 059	2 259	1 048	1 211
75-79	912	392	520	1 055	456	599	1 213	528	684	1 403	621	782
80-84	452	186	267	521	215	306	614	255	359	718	301	417
85-89	159	61	99	190	73	117	224	87	137	270	106	164
90-94	36	12	24	44	15	29	54	19	35	65	23	42
95-99	5	1	4	6	2	4	7	2	5	9	3	7
100 +	0	0	0	0	0	0	1	0	0	1	0	1

Age group	2045 Both sexes	Males	Females	2050 Both sexes	Males	Females
All ages	249 264	124 261	125 003	264 703	131 910	132 793
0-4	27 268	13 730	13 539	26 289	13 241	13 048
5-9	27 312	13 708	13 604	26 632	13 373	13 259
10-14	27 282	13 671	13 611	27 043	13 560	13 483
15-19	26 519	13 261	13 258	27 021	13 523	13 498
20-24	24 798	12 356	12 441	26 119	13 026	13 093
25-29	22 293	11 083	11 210	24 134	12 007	12 127
30-34	19 715	9 820	9 895	21 382	10 651	10 731
35-39	16 775	8 389	8 387	18 747	9 363	9 384
40-44	14 081	7 062	7 019	15 922	7 969	7 953
45-49	11 254	5 639	5 615	13 375	6 694	6 681
50-54	9 230	4 608	4 622	10 660	5 311	5 349
55-59	7 345	3 642	3 703	8 670	4 291	4 379
60-64	5 638	2 763	2 875	6 773	3 318	3 454
65-69	4 098	1 973	2 125	4 998	2 411	2 588
70-74	2 744	1 289	1 455	3 394	1 602	1 792
75-79	1 652	746	906	2 031	930	1 102
80-84	845	361	484	1 010	441	569
85-89	322	128	194	387	157	230
90-94	81	29	52	99	36	63
95-99	12	4	8	15	5	10
100 +	1	0	1	1	0	1

United Nations Department of Economic and Social Affairs/Population Division
World Population Prospects: The 2004 Revision, Volume II: Sex and Age Distribution of the World Population

59

POPULATION BY AGE AND SEX (in thousands)

Age group	1950 Both sexes	Males	Females	1955 Both sexes	Males	Females	1960 Both sexes	Males	Females	1965 Both sexes	Males	Females
All ages	53 302	26 681	26 621	59 797	29 954	29 843	67 381	33 835	33 546	76 075	38 261	37 814
0-4	8 925	4 506	4 419	10 318	5 232	5 086	11 875	6 053	5 822	13 542	6 901	6 641
5-9	6 954	3 493	3 461	8 112	4 094	4 019	9 437	4 792	4 645	11 142	5 710	5 432
10-14	6 105	3 066	3 040	6 761	3 402	3 358	7 917	4 004	3 913	9 280	4 717	4 563
15-19	5 410	2 717	2 693	5 954	2 992	2 961	6 506	3 277	3 229	7 379	3 713	3 666
20-24	4 709	2 367	2 342	5 212	2 614	2 598	5 686	2 849	2 837	5 934	2 949	2 985
25-29	4 028	2 021	2 007	4 501	2 256	2 245	4 954	2 477	2 477	5 257	2 603	2 654
30-34	3 442	1 731	1 710	3 839	1 922	1 917	4 288	2 148	2 140	4 653	2 314	2 339
35-39	2 947	1 488	1 460	3 268	1 640	1 628	3 626	1 812	1 814	4 014	2 007	2 006
40-44	2 502	1 266	1 236	2 781	1 398	1 384	3 068	1 534	1 533	3 361	1 683	1 679
45-49	2 104	1 057	1 047	2 339	1 174	1 166	2 589	1 294	1 295	2 807	1 408	1 399
50-54	1 753	871	882	1 937	962	975	2 148	1 070	1 079	2 349	1 178	1 171
55-59	1 444	698	746	1 570	768	802	1 729	848	881	2 007	996	1 011
60-64	1 135	545	590	1 235	587	648	1 349	652	698	1 597	781	816
65-69	838	399	439	899	424	475	997	468	530	1 206	581	625
70-74	556	258	298	608	282	326	680	317	364	810	379	431
75-79	305	136	169	309	141	168	363	166	197	471	222	249
80 +	145	62	82	155	67	88	169	74	94	269	120	149

Age group	1970 Both sexes	Males	Females	1975 Both sexes	Males	Females	1980 Both sexes	Males	Females	1985 Both sexes	Males	Females
All ages	86 229	43 214	43 015	97 863	49 111	48 752	111 816	56 194	55 621	128 585	64 669	63 916
0-4	14 797	7 566	7 231	17 013	8 648	8 365	18 834	9 597	9 238	21 084	10 748	10 336
5-9	12 609	6 453	6 156	13 903	7 106	6 797	15 927	8 092	7 835	18 227	9 284	8 943
10-14	10 940	5 614	5 326	12 234	6 267	5 967	13 541	6 927	6 614	15 797	8 023	7 774
15-19	9 021	4 577	4 443	10 507	5 390	5 117	11 751	5 963	5 788	13 421	6 850	6 571
20-24	6 934	3 443	3 491	8 518	4 275	4 244	10 033	5 043	4 991	11 497	5 811	5 686
25-29	5 488	2 660	2 828	6 524	3 186	3 338	8 200	4 068	4 132	9 695	4 874	4 822
30-34	4 933	2 392	2 541	5 215	2 530	2 686	6 330	3 114	3 215	8 086	4 044	4 043
35-39	4 489	2 199	2 290	4 854	2 375	2 479	5 094	2 535	2 559	6 330	3 135	3 195
40-44	3 811	1 884	1 927	4 365	2 151	2 214	4 887	2 414	2 473	5 002	2 481	2 520
45-49	3 135	1 561	1 574	3 703	1 834	1 868	4 309	2 161	2 148	4 730	2 306	2 425
50-54	2 633	1 309	1 324	3 005	1 491	1 514	3 662	1 805	1 857	4 094	2 016	2 078
55-59	2 179	1 073	1 106	2 429	1 197	1 232	2 796	1 383	1 413	3 421	1 662	1 759
60-64	1 871	898	973	1 921	942	979	2 253	1 103	1 149	2 536	1 238	1 298
65-69	1 407	670	737	1 552	738	814	1 730	840	890	1 937	934	1 004
70-74	998	466	532	1 059	499	560	1 228	582	646	1 357	646	711
75-79	552	253	299	639	291	348	754	350	404	829	381	448
80 +	431	197	235	422	191	232	486	218	268	540	237	304

Age group	1990 Both sexes	Males	Females	1995 Both sexes	Males	Females	2000 Both sexes	Males	Females	2005 Both sexes	Males	Females
All ages	144 498	72 719	71 779	159 895	80 446	79 449	175 051	87 992	87 059	190 895	95 863	95 032
0-4	21 546	11 002	10 543	20 982	10 712	10 270	20 888	10 661	10 227	22 171	11 317	10 854
5-9	20 422	10 408	10 014	21 041	10 739	10 302	20 593	10 506	10 087	20 507	10 458	10 049
10-14	17 976	9 154	8 822	20 227	10 305	9 922	20 872	10 648	10 224	20 403	10 405	9 999
15-19	15 351	7 791	7 560	17 646	9 011	8 635	19 965	10 150	9 816	20 598	10 486	10 112
20-24	12 783	6 481	6 302	14 740	7 473	7 267	17 181	8 735	8 446	19 503	9 860	9 643
25-29	11 076	5 548	5 528	12 258	6 131	6 127	14 266	7 193	7 073	16 688	8 430	8 257
30-34	9 516	4 791	4 725	10 846	5 385	5 462	11 952	5 958	5 994	13 909	6 994	6 915
35-39	7 961	4 004	3 958	9 400	4 739	4 661	10 652	5 287	5 365	11 722	5 843	5 880
40-44	6 210	3 085	3 125	7 855	3 956	3 899	9 240	4 651	4 589	10 463	5 187	5 276
45-49	4 893	2 430	2 463	6 099	3 028	3 071	7 687	3 860	3 827	9 043	4 541	4 502
50-54	4 542	2 202	2 340	4 722	2 331	2 390	5 887	2 904	2 983	7 436	3 712	3 724
55-59	3 829	1 864	1 965	4 275	2 050	2 226	4 462	2 177	2 284	5 584	2 724	2 860
60-64	3 110	1 488	1 622	3 513	1 687	1 826	3 942	1 858	2 084	4 128	1 981	2 147
65-69	2 191	1 050	1 141	2 728	1 279	1 449	3 100	1 456	1 644	3 504	1 613	1 891
70-74	1 538	723	815	1 767	823	943	2 226	1 014	1 212	2 559	1 167	1 392
75-79	935	430	505	1 081	490	591	1 263	566	697	1 620	708	912
80 +	619	266	353	715	306	409	874	367	507	1 059	439	620

United Nations Department of Economic and Social Affairs/Population Division
World Population Prospects: The 2004 Revision, Volume II: Sex and Age Distribution of the World Population

60

POPULATION BY AGE AND SEX (in thousands)

Age group	2005 Both sexes	Males	Females	2010 Both sexes	Males	Females	2015 Both sexes	Males	Females	2020 Both sexes	Males	Females
All ages	190 895	95 863	95 032	208 146	104 456	103 690	225 131	112 914	112 217	241 089	120 834	120 255
0-4	22 171	11 317	10 854	23 241	11 864	11 377	23 602	12 050	11 551	23 273	11 888	11 385
5-9	20 507	10 458	10 049	21 932	11 186	10 746	23 020	11 742	11 278	23 395	11 936	11 459
10-14	20 403	10 405	9 999	20 427	10 412	10 014	21 838	11 132	10 705	22 909	11 680	11 229
15-19	20 598	10 486	10 112	20 236	10 298	9 938	20 257	10 304	9 952	21 651	11 016	10 635
20-24	19 503	9 860	9 643	20 248	10 255	9 993	19 892	10 071	9 821	19 906	10 075	9 831
25-29	16 688	8 430	8 257	19 096	9 602	9 494	19 844	10 000	9 844	19 490	9 818	9 672
30-34	13 909	6 994	6 915	16 372	8 253	8 120	18 760	9 416	9 344	19 506	9 814	9 692
35-39	11 722	5 843	5 880	13 699	6 887	6 813	16 133	8 132	8 000	18 498	9 287	9 212
40-44	10 463	5 187	5 276	11 560	5 757	5 803	13 509	6 788	6 722	15 916	8 020	7 895
45-49	9 043	4 541	4 502	10 291	5 093	5 198	11 373	5 656	5 717	13 295	6 672	6 623
50-54	7 436	3 712	3 724	8 802	4 398	4 405	10 033	4 942	5 092	11 099	5 496	5 603
55-59	5 584	2 724	2 860	7 115	3 515	3 600	8 447	4 178	4 269	9 652	4 708	4 943
60-64	4 128	1 981	2 147	5 218	2 503	2 715	6 680	3 248	3 432	7 960	3 877	4 083
65-69	3 504	1 613	1 891	3 706	1 738	1 968	4 716	2 210	2 505	6 074	2 887	3 187
70-74	2 559	1 167	1 392	2 934	1 309	1 625	3 127	1 421	1 706	4 017	1 823	2 193
75-79	1 620	708	912	1 898	830	1 068	2 207	943	1 264	2 384	1 035	1 348
80-84	739	314	424	973	403	570	1 163	481	682	1 388	555	832
85-89	259	103	156	318	125	193	429	164	264	535	201	334
90-94	54	19	35	71	25	46	89	31	58	127	42	85
95-99	7	2	5	9	2	6	11	3	8	15	4	11
100 +	0	0	0	1	0	0	1	0	1	1	0	1

Age group	2025 Both sexes	Males	Females	2030 Both sexes	Males	Females	2035 Both sexes	Males	Females	2040 Both sexes	Males	Females
All ages	255 959	128 172	127 787	269 743	134 928	134 814	282 428	141 098	141 330	293 827	146 596	147 231
0-4	22 771	11 639	11 132	22 427	11 469	10 958	22 238	11 378	10 861	21 992	11 256	10 736
5-9	23 101	11 793	11 308	22 627	11 559	11 068	22 305	11 401	10 904	22 136	11 319	10 816
10-14	23 301	11 883	11 418	23 022	11 748	11 274	22 560	11 521	11 039	22 247	11 367	10 880
15-19	22 735	11 570	11 164	23 135	11 778	11 357	22 865	11 648	11 217	22 411	11 426	10 985
20-24	21 310	10 792	10 518	22 402	11 352	11 050	22 812	11 566	11 246	22 552	11 442	11 110
25-29	19 513	9 827	9 685	20 925	10 550	10 376	22 030	11 116	10 914	22 452	11 336	11 116
30-34	19 164	9 639	9 525	19 199	9 655	9 544	20 623	10 382	10 240	21 742	10 956	10 787
35-39	19 256	9 691	9 565	18 929	9 524	9 405	18 977	9 547	9 430	20 412	10 279	10 133
40-44	18 276	9 173	9 103	19 048	9 584	9 463	18 735	9 426	9 309	18 795	9 455	9 340
45-49	15 688	7 897	7 791	18 042	9 046	8 996	18 824	9 464	9 360	18 528	9 315	9 213
50-54	12 999	6 498	6 502	15 370	7 708	7 662	17 706	8 847	8 859	18 498	9 271	9 227
55-59	10 704	5 253	5 451	12 570	6 231	6 339	14 899	7 414	7 485	17 202	8 532	8 670
60-64	9 132	4 388	4 744	10 161	4 917	5 245	11 969	5 854	6 115	14 228	6 990	7 238
65-69	7 278	3 466	3 812	8 396	3 947	4 449	9 384	4 446	4 937	11 097	5 320	5 777
70-74	5 224	2 403	2 821	6 311	2 908	3 403	7 339	3 338	4 001	8 255	3 789	4 466
75-79	3 108	1 344	1 765	4 099	1 793	2 306	5 013	2 194	2 819	5 899	2 546	3 353
80-84	1 536	620	916	2 051	817	1 234	2 761	1 107	1 654	3 441	1 377	2 064
85-89	668	237	431	767	271	496	1 060	364	696	1 473	504	969
90-94	169	52	117	225	64	161	273	75	197	396	104	292
95-99	24	6	18	35	8	27	50	10	40	65	12	53
100 +	2	0	1	3	0	2	4	1	4	7	1	6

Age group	2045 Both sexes	Males	Females	2050 Both sexes	Males	Females
All ages	303 710	151 324	152 386	311 893	155 201	156 693
0-4	21 558	11 036	10 522	20 950	10 725	10 225
5-9	21 904	11 206	10 698	21 480	10 992	10 488
10-14	22 085	11 290	10 795	21 859	11 179	10 679
15-19	22 104	11 276	10 829	21 947	11 201	10 746
20-24	22 106	11 224	10 882	21 808	11 079	10 729
25-29	22 206	11 220	10 986	21 772	11 008	10 764
30-34	22 180	11 184	10 996	21 952	11 075	10 876
35-39	21 547	10 859	10 687	22 002	11 095	10 907
40-44	20 238	10 191	10 047	21 384	10 776	10 608
45-49	18 598	9 349	9 249	20 044	10 085	9 959
50-54	18 220	9 133	9 087	18 302	9 173	9 129
55-59	17 999	8 958	9 041	17 750	8 839	8 911
60-64	16 473	8 073	8 400	17 277	8 502	8 775
65-69	13 245	6 384	6 861	15 398	7 411	7 987
70-74	9 824	4 568	5 256	11 803	5 528	6 275
75-79	6 707	2 926	3 780	8 066	3 576	4 490
80-84	4 132	1 632	2 501	4 788	1 922	2 866
85-89	1 895	647	1 249	2 358	800	1 558
90-94	579	150	428	783	205	578
95-99	100	17	83	157	27	130
100 +	9	1	8	15	2	14

United Nations Department of Economic and Social Affairs/Population Division
World Population Prospects: The 2004 Revision, Volume II: Sex and Age Distribution of the World Population

61

POPULATION BY AGE AND SEX (in thousands)

Age group	2005 Both sexes	Males	Females	2010 Both sexes	Males	Females	2015 Both sexes	Males	Females	2020 Both sexes	Males	Females
All ages	190 895	95 863	95 032	210 105	105 456	104 649	230 541	115 676	114 865	251 071	125 931	125 141
0-4	22 171	11 317	10 854	25 201	12 865	12 336	27 067	13 820	13 247	27 874	14 239	13 635
5-9	20 507	10 458	10 049	21 932	11 186	10 746	24 964	12 734	12 230	26 839	13 693	13 145
10-14	20 403	10 405	9 999	20 427	10 412	10 014	21 838	11 132	10 705	24 847	12 669	12 179
15-19	20 598	10 486	10 112	20 236	10 298	9 938	20 257	10 304	9 952	21 651	11 016	10 635
20-24	19 503	9 860	9 643	20 248	10 255	9 993	19 892	10 071	9 821	19 906	10 075	9 831
25-29	16 688	8 430	8 257	19 096	9 602	9 494	19 844	10 000	9 844	19 490	9 818	9 672
30-34	13 909	6 994	6 915	16 372	8 253	8 120	18 760	9 416	9 344	19 506	9 814	9 692
35-39	11 722	5 843	5 880	13 699	6 887	6 813	16 133	8 132	8 000	18 498	9 287	9 212
40-44	10 463	5 187	5 276	11 560	5 757	5 803	13 509	6 788	6 722	15 916	8 020	7 895
45-49	9 043	4 541	4 502	10 291	5 093	5 198	11 373	5 656	5 717	13 295	6 672	6 623
50-54	7 436	3 712	3 724	8 802	4 398	4 405	10 033	4 942	5 092	11 099	5 496	5 603
55-59	5 584	2 724	2 860	7 115	3 515	3 600	8 447	4 178	4 269	9 652	4 708	4 943
60-64	4 128	1 981	2 147	5 218	2 503	2 715	6 680	3 248	3 432	7 960	3 877	4 083
65-69	3 504	1 613	1 891	3 706	1 738	1 968	4 716	2 210	2 505	6 074	2 887	3 187
70-74	2 559	1 167	1 392	2 934	1 309	1 625	3 127	1 421	1 706	4 017	1 823	2 193
75-79	1 620	708	912	1 898	830	1 068	2 207	943	1 264	2 384	1 035	1 348
80-84	739	314	424	973	403	570	1 163	481	682	1 388	555	832
85-89	259	103	156	318	125	193	429	164	264	535	201	334
90-94	54	19	35	71	25	46	89	31	58	127	42	85
95-99	7	2	5	9	2	6	11	3	8	15	4	11
100 +	0	0	0	1	0	0	1	0	1	1	0	1

Age group	2025 Both sexes	Males	Females	2030 Both sexes	Males	Females	2035 Both sexes	Males	Females	2040 Both sexes	Males	Females
All ages	270 732	135 716	135 017	289 854	145 198	144 656	309 029	154 683	154 346	328 444	164 278	164 167
0-4	27 601	14 109	13 492	27 812	14 223	13 588	28 787	14 729	14 058	30 085	15 399	14 686
5-9	27 677	14 130	13 548	27 436	14 016	13 420	27 671	14 144	13 527	28 666	14 659	14 006
10-14	26 735	13 635	13 100	27 588	14 079	13 509	27 359	13 972	13 387	27 604	14 105	13 499
15-19	24 668	12 556	12 112	26 562	13 525	13 036	27 422	13 973	13 448	27 201	13 871	13 330
20-24	21 310	10 792	10 518	24 328	12 333	11 995	26 227	13 305	12 922	27 094	13 757	13 337
25-29	19 513	9 827	9 685	20 925	10 550	10 376	23 946	12 091	11 855	25 851	13 067	12 784
30-34	19 164	9 639	9 525	19 199	9 655	9 544	20 623	10 382	10 240	23 647	11 925	11 723
35-39	19 256	9 691	9 565	18 929	9 524	9 405	18 977	9 547	9 430	20 412	10 279	10 133
40-44	18 276	9 173	9 103	19 048	9 584	9 463	18 735	9 426	9 309	18 795	9 455	9 340
45-49	15 688	7 897	7 791	18 042	9 046	8 996	18 824	9 464	9 360	18 528	9 315	9 213
50-54	12 999	6 498	6 502	15 370	7 708	7 662	17 706	8 847	8 859	18 498	9 271	9 227
55-59	10 704	5 253	5 451	12 570	6 231	6 339	14 899	7 414	7 485	17 202	8 532	8 670
60-64	9 132	4 388	4 744	10 161	4 917	5 245	11 969	5 854	6 115	14 228	6 990	7 238
65-69	7 278	3 466	3 812	8 396	3 947	4 449	9 384	4 446	4 937	11 097	5 320	5 777
70-74	5 224	2 403	2 821	6 311	2 908	3 403	7 339	3 338	4 001	8 255	3 789	4 466
75-79	3 108	1 344	1 765	4 099	1 793	2 306	5 013	2 194	2 819	5 899	2 546	3 353
80-84	1 536	620	916	2 051	817	1 234	2 761	1 107	1 654	3 441	1 377	2 064
85-89	668	237	431	767	271	496	1 060	364	696	1 473	504	969
90-94	169	52	117	225	64	161	273	75	197	396	104	292
95-99	24	6	18	35	8	27	50	10	40	65	12	53
100 +	2	0	1	3	0	2	4	1	4	7	1	6

Age group	2045 Both sexes	Males	Females	2050 Both sexes	Males	Females
All ages	347 732	173 813	173 918	366 287	182 991	183 295
0-4	31 060	15 901	15 159	31 444	16 098	15 346
5-9	29 978	15 337	14 641	30 963	15 846	15 117
10-14	28 606	14 625	13 982	29 923	15 305	14 618
15-19	27 452	14 008	13 445	28 458	14 529	13 929
20-24	26 883	13 661	13 222	27 141	13 801	13 340
25-29	26 730	13 525	13 205	26 531	13 434	13 097
30-34	25 563	12 905	12 657	26 455	13 368	13 086
35-39	23 440	11 823	11 618	25 365	12 806	12 559
40-44	20 238	10 191	10 047	23 265	11 732	11 533
45-49	18 598	9 349	9 249	20 044	10 085	9 959
50-54	18 220	9 133	9 087	18 302	9 173	9 129
55-59	17 999	8 958	9 041	17 750	8 839	8 911
60-64	16 473	8 073	8 400	17 277	8 502	8 775
65-69	13 245	6 384	6 861	15 398	7 411	7 987
70-74	9 824	4 568	5 256	11 803	5 528	6 275
75-79	6 707	2 926	3 780	8 066	3 576	4 490
80-84	4 132	1 632	2 501	4 788	1 922	2 866
85-89	1 895	647	1 249	2 358	800	1 558
90-94	579	150	428	783	205	578
95-99	100	17	83	157	27	130
100 +	9	1	8	15	2	14

United Nations Department of Economic and Social Affairs/Population Division
World Population Prospects: The 2004 Revision, Volume II: Sex and Age Distribution of the World Population

62

POPULATION BY AGE AND SEX (in thousands)

Age group	2005 Both sexes	Males	Females	2010 Both sexes	Males	Females	2015 Both sexes	Males	Females	2020 Both sexes	Males	Females
All ages	190 895	95 863	95 032	206 179	103 451	102 728	219 690	110 136	109 554	231 047	115 707	115 340
0-4	22 171	11 317	10 854	21 274	10 860	10 414	20 113	10 268	9 844	18 644	9 523	9 121
5-9	20 507	10 458	10 049	21 932	11 186	10 746	21 068	10 746	10 322	19 928	10 166	9 762
10-14	20 403	10 405	9 999	20 427	10 412	10 014	21 838	11 132	10 705	20 964	10 688	10 276
15-19	20 598	10 486	10 112	20 236	10 298	9 938	20 257	10 304	9 952	21 651	11 016	10 635
20-24	19 503	9 860	9 643	20 248	10 255	9 993	19 892	10 071	9 821	19 906	10 075	9 831
25-29	16 688	8 430	8 257	19 096	9 602	9 494	19 844	10 000	9 844	19 490	9 818	9 672
30-34	13 909	6 994	6 915	16 372	8 253	8 120	18 760	9 416	9 344	19 506	9 814	9 692
35-39	11 722	5 843	5 880	13 699	6 887	6 813	16 133	8 132	8 000	18 498	9 287	9 212
40-44	10 463	5 187	5 276	11 560	5 757	5 803	13 509	6 788	6 722	15 916	8 020	7 895
45-49	9 043	4 541	4 502	10 291	5 093	5 198	11 373	5 656	5 717	13 295	6 672	6 623
50-54	7 436	3 712	3 724	8 802	4 398	4 405	10 033	4 942	5 092	11 099	5 496	5 603
55-59	5 584	2 724	2 860	7 115	3 515	3 600	8 447	4 178	4 269	9 652	4 708	4 943
60-64	4 128	1 981	2 147	5 218	2 503	2 715	6 680	3 248	3 432	7 960	3 877	4 083
65-69	3 504	1 613	1 891	3 706	1 738	1 968	4 716	2 210	2 505	6 074	2 887	3 187
70-74	2 559	1 167	1 392	2 934	1 309	1 625	3 127	1 421	1 706	4 017	1 823	2 193
75-79	1 620	708	912	1 898	830	1 068	2 207	943	1 264	2 384	1 035	1 348
80-84	739	314	424	973	403	570	1 163	481	682	1 388	555	832
85-89	259	103	156	318	125	193	429	164	264	535	201	334
90-94	54	19	35	71	25	46	89	31	58	127	42	85
95-99	7	2	5	9	2	6	11	3	8	15	4	11
100 +	0	0	0	1	0	0	1	0	1	1	0	1

Age group	2025 Both sexes	Males	Females	2030 Both sexes	Males	Females	2035 Both sexes	Males	Females	2040 Both sexes	Males	Females
All ages	241 133	120 602	120 531	249 728	124 708	125 020	256 432	127 823	128 609	260 872	129 765	131 107
0-4	17 948	9 174	8 775	17 191	8 791	8 400	16 198	8 287	7 911	14 957	7 655	7 302
5-9	18 496	9 441	9 055	17 826	9 106	8 720	17 088	8 734	8 355	16 114	8 239	7 874
10-14	19 843	10 119	9 724	18 427	9 402	9 024	17 767	9 073	8 695	17 038	8 705	8 333
15-19	20 795	10 581	10 213	19 686	10 020	9 666	18 280	9 309	8 971	17 627	8 983	8 644
20-24	21 310	10 792	10 518	20 470	10 368	10 102	19 374	9 814	9 560	17 981	9 112	8 869
25-29	19 513	9 827	9 685	20 925	10 550	10 376	20 107	10 137	9 969	19 029	9 594	9 435
30-34	19 164	9 639	9 525	19 199	9 655	9 544	20 623	10 382	10 240	19 830	9 983	9 847
35-39	19 256	9 691	9 565	18 929	9 524	9 405	18 977	9 547	9 430	20 412	10 279	10 133
40-44	18 276	9 173	9 103	19 048	9 584	9 463	18 735	9 426	9 309	18 795	9 455	9 340
45-49	15 688	7 897	7 791	18 042	9 046	8 996	18 824	9 464	9 360	18 528	9 315	9 213
50-54	12 999	6 498	6 502	15 370	7 708	7 662	17 706	8 847	8 859	18 498	9 271	9 227
55-59	10 704	5 253	5 451	12 570	6 231	6 339	14 899	7 414	7 485	17 200	8 530	8 670
60-64	9 132	4 388	4 744	10 161	4 917	5 245	11 969	5 854	6 115	14 228	6 990	7 238
65-69	7 278	3 466	3 812	8 396	3 947	4 449	9 384	4 446	4 937	11 097	5 320	5 777
70-74	5 224	2 403	2 821	6 311	2 908	3 403	7 339	3 338	4 001	8 255	3 789	4 466
75-79	3 109	1 344	1 765	4 099	1 793	2 306	5 013	2 194	2 819	5 899	2 546	3 353
80-84	1 536	620	916	2 051	817	1 234	2 761	1 107	1 654	3 441	1 377	2 064
85-89	668	237	431	767	271	496	1 060	364	696	1 473	504	969
90-94	169	52	117	225	64	161	273	75	197	396	104	292
95-99	24	6	18	35	8	27	50	10	40	65	12	53
100 +	2	0	1	3	0	2	4	1	4	7	1	6

Age group	2045 Both sexes	Males	Females	2050 Both sexes	Males	Females
All ages	262 976	130 518	132 458	262 887	130 168	132 719
0-4	13 684	7 005	6 679	12 561	6 430	6 131
5-9	14 886	7 615	7 271	13 623	6 970	6 652
10-14	16 071	8 215	7 856	14 848	7 593	7 255
15-19	16 904	8 619	8 285	15 942	8 132	7 810
20-24	17 337	8 791	8 546	16 621	8 431	8 190
25-29	17 653	8 901	8 753	17 020	8 585	8 435
30-34	18 775	9 451	9 324	17 420	8 767	8 653
35-39	19 646	9 892	9 753	18 615	9 372	9 243
40-44	20 238	10 191	10 047	19 496	9 816	9 680
45-49	18 598	9 349	9 249	20 044	10 085	9 959
50-54	18 220	9 133	9 087	18 302	9 173	9 129
55-59	17 999	8 958	9 041	17 750	8 839	8 911
60-64	16 473	8 073	8 400	17 277	8 502	8 775
65-69	13 245	6 384	6 861	15 398	7 411	7 987
70-74	9 824	4 568	5 256	11 803	5 528	6 275
75-79	6 707	2 926	3 780	8 066	3 576	4 490
80-84	4 132	1 632	2 501	4 788	1 922	2 866
85-89	1 895	647	1 249	2 358	800	1 558
90-94	579	150	428	783	205	578
95-99	100	17	83	157	27	130
100 +	9	1	8	15	2	14

United Nations Department of Economic and Social Affairs/Population Division
World Population Prospects: The 2004 Revision, Volume II: Sex and Age Distribution of the World Population

63

POPULATION BY AGE AND SEX (in thousands)

Age group	1950 Both sexes	Males	Females	1955 Both sexes	Males	Females	1960 Both sexes	Males	Females	1965 Both sexes	Males	Females
All ages	15 624	7 747	7 877	17 529	8 712	8 817	19 773	9 837	9 936	22 572	11 168	11 405
0-4	2 410	1 207	1 203	2 864	1 472	1 393	3 258	1 665	1 593	3 752	1 901	1 851
5-9	1 963	982	981	2 244	1 130	1 114	2 695	1 390	1 306	3 148	1 589	1 559
10-14	1 710	854	855	1 941	969	972	2 221	1 117	1 104	2 693	1 358	1 335
15-19	1 534	781	752	1 684	838	846	1 913	952	961	2 186	1 095	1 090
20-24	1 351	702	649	1 494	756	738	1 641	811	830	1 866	920	945
25-29	1 188	604	584	1 307	674	633	1 446	726	720	1 596	782	814
30-34	1 082	544	538	1 143	577	566	1 259	644	614	1 404	700	704
35-39	937	471	466	1 035	517	518	1 095	549	547	1 214	617	597
40-44	812	396	416	886	442	444	982	486	496	1 046	519	527
45-49	665	318	346	757	365	392	829	409	421	924	452	472
50-54	564	265	298	607	286	320	695	330	365	761	369	392
55-59	470	215	255	500	231	269	543	252	291	636	296	339
60-64	370	165	205	400	178	221	431	194	236	479	216	262
65-69	263	115	148	296	128	169	325	140	185	358	156	202
70-74	172	73	99	194	81	113	222	91	131	250	102	148
75-79	90	36	53	112	45	68	129	50	79	153	58	94
80 +	44	17	28	64	23	41	86	30	57	109	36	72

Age group	1970 Both sexes	Males	Females	1975 Both sexes	Males	Females	1980 Both sexes	Males	Females	1985 Both sexes	Males	Females
All ages	25 668	12 719	12 949	29 302	14 537	14 765	33 182	16 432	16 751	37 720	18 672	19 047
0-4	4 253	2 139	2 114	4 775	2 402	2 373	5 238	2 634	2 604	5 752	2 896	2 856
5-9	3 632	1 835	1 797	4 135	2 074	2 061	4 657	2 336	2 322	5 136	2 576	2 560
10-14	3 112	1 568	1 544	3 595	1 813	1 782	4 097	2 051	2 046	4 626	2 316	2 310
15-19	2 662	1 341	1 321	3 082	1 551	1 531	3 554	1 787	1 766	4 066	2 030	2 035
20-24	2 153	1 078	1 075	2 631	1 324	1 307	3 020	1 512	1 508	3 510	1 757	1 753
25-29	1 834	906	928	2 128	1 066	1 062	2 562	1 282	1 281	2 976	1 483	1 493
30-34	1 567	771	796	1 809	897	912	2 066	1 030	1 036	2 522	1 259	1 263
35-39	1 369	685	684	1 535	759	776	1 750	864	886	2 027	1 012	1 015
40-44	1 166	592	574	1 323	662	661	1 473	725	749	1 705	842	863
45-49	986	486	500	1 106	558	549	1 252	620	632	1 415	692	724
50-54	848	409	439	912	443	469	1 023	507	516	1 174	574	601
55-59	672	319	353	756	356	399	816	387	429	930	451	479
60-64	532	240	293	568	260	308	643	292	351	708	324	384
65-69	371	158	212	417	177	240	449	193	256	519	222	297
70-74	250	100	149	262	104	159	299	116	182	331	131	200
75-79	151	56	95	154	56	98	165	58	107	194	68	126
80 +	111	36	74	113	36	77	118	37	81	128	39	89

Age group	1990 Both sexes	Males	Females	1995 Both sexes	Males	Females	2000 Both sexes	Males	Females	2005 Both sexes	Males	Females
All ages	42 161	20 799	21 362	47 806	23 503	24 304	52 069	25 528	26 542	54 055	26 498	27 557
0-4	5 870	2 959	2 911	6 122	3 089	3 033	6 169	3 115	3 053	6 075	3 070	3 006
5-9	5 658	2 843	2 816	5 789	2 913	2 876	6 040	3 043	2 997	6 009	3 031	2 978
10-14	5 101	2 555	2 546	5 627	2 824	2 804	5 769	2 900	2 869	6 003	3 022	2 981
15-19	4 581	2 285	2 296	5 102	2 546	2 555	5 618	2 817	2 801	5 753	2 891	2 861
20-24	3 990	1 974	2 017	4 644	2 295	2 349	5 021	2 503	2 517	5 462	2 746	2 716
25-29	3 434	1 701	1 733	4 087	1 997	2 090	4 451	2 190	2 260	4 481	2 255	2 225
30-34	2 920	1 444	1 476	3 533	1 733	1 800	3 900	1 889	2 011	3 795	1 880	1 915
35-39	2 465	1 222	1 243	3 011	1 475	1 536	3 392	1 644	1 748	3 359	1 620	1 739
40-44	1 959	969	991	2 522	1 238	1 284	2 898	1 399	1 499	2 991	1 429	1 562
45-49	1 625	792	833	1 980	968	1 011	2 421	1 168	1 253	2 611	1 234	1 377
50-54	1 324	635	689	1 602	768	834	1 880	900	979	2 206	1 037	1 169
55-59	1 071	510	561	1 261	590	671	1 491	696	795	1 709	793	915
60-64	815	381	434	962	442	520	1 131	510	621	1 327	595	732
65-69	583	252	331	678	300	378	813	353	460	961	409	552
70-74	392	155	238	446	178	268	530	218	312	644	259	384
75-79	222	79	143	268	94	173	314	113	200	378	141	238
80 +	149	44	105	174	51	122	233	68	164	292	87	205

United Nations Department of Economic and Social Affairs/Population Division
World Population Prospects: The 2004 Revision, Volume II: Sex and Age Distribution of the World Population

64

POPULATION BY AGE AND SEX (in thousands)

Age group	2005 Both sexes	Males	Females	2010 Both sexes	Males	Females	2015 Both sexes	Males	Females	2020 Both sexes	Males	Females
All ages	54 055	26 408	27 557	54 150	26 868	27 591	54 578	27 150	27 428	54 857	27 492	27 365
0-4	6 075	3 070	3 006	5 778	2 922	2 857	5 584	2 825	2 759	5 487	2 777	2 710
5-9	6 009	3 031	2 978	5 851	2 953	2 898	5 594	2 826	2 768	5 466	2 763	2 703
10-14	6 003	3 022	2 981	5 890	2 968	2 922	5 667	2 858	2 809	5 444	2 749	2 696
15-19	5 753	2 891	2 861	5 985	3 013	2 972	5 857	2 952	2 905	5 629	2 840	2 789
20-24	5 462	2 746	2 716	5 629	2 837	2 792	5 874	2 965	2 909	5 760	2 911	2 849
25-29	4 481	2 255	2 225	4 919	2 517	2 402	5 163	2 644	2 519	5 433	2 783	2 650
30-34	3 795	1 880	1 915	3 620	1 890	1 729	4 100	2 182	1 918	4 392	2 331	2 061
35-39	3 359	1 620	1 739	3 000	1 530	1 470	2 849	1 558	1 291	3 328	1 848	1 480
40-44	2 991	1 429	1 562	2 743	1 335	1 408	2 397	1 257	1 140	2 321	1 306	1 015
45-49	2 611	1 234	1 377	2 547	1 207	1 340	2 288	1 121	1 168	2 021	1 070	951
50-54	2 206	1 037	1 169	2 295	1 063	1 232	2 209	1 035	1 174	1 998	971	1 027
55-59	1 709	793	915	1 967	898	1 069	2 034	920	1 114	1 968	904	1 065
60-64	1 327	595	732	1 509	673	836	1 736	764	973	1 807	789	1 018
65-69	961	409	552	1 129	478	651	1 291	545	745	1 497	625	872
70-74	644	259	384	768	303	465	910	358	552	1 052	414	637
75-79	378	141	238	467	170	297	565	202	364	680	242	438
80-84	192	61	131	236	78	158	297	95	202	367	115	251
85-89	77	20	56	94	26	68	118	33	85	152	42	110
90-94	19	4	15	28	6	22	35	8	27	45	10	35
95-99	3	1	3	5	1	4	7	1	6	9	1	7
100 +	0	0	0	0	0	0	1	0	1	1	0	1

Age group	2025 Both sexes	Males	Females	2030 Both sexes	Males	Females	2035 Both sexes	Males	Females	2040 Both sexes	Males	Females
All ages	55 136	27 805	27 331	55 323	28 024	27 299	55 425	28 156	27 269	55 531	28 262	27 269
0-4	5 339	2 703	2 635	5 113	2 591	2 523	4 878	2 472	2 405	4 684	2 374	2 309
5-9	5 409	2 737	2 673	5 287	2 676	2 611	5 080	2 573	2 507	4 855	2 460	2 395
10-14	5 373	2 715	2 658	5 351	2 705	2 645	5 251	2 657	2 594	5 058	2 561	2 497
15-19	5 418	2 736	2 681	5 358	2 708	2 649	5 342	2 702	2 639	5 246	2 656	2 590
20-24	5 543	2 803	2 740	5 342	2 704	2 638	5 290	2 680	2 610	5 281	2 678	2 603
25-29	5 358	2 739	2 619	5 183	2 644	2 539	5 025	2 560	2 465	5 003	2 549	2 454
30-34	4 682	2 473	2 209	4 671	2 445	2 225	4 570	2 374	2 196	4 484	2 317	2 167
35-39	3 624	1 998	1 626	3 927	2 138	1 789	3 974	2 129	1 846	3 949	2 086	1 863
40-44	2 759	1 573	1 186	3 052	1 718	1 334	3 055	1 552	1 502	3 445	1 862	1 583
45-49	1 983	1 125	857	2 387	1 369	1 018	2 671	1 506	1 164	2 971	1 639	1 332
50-54	1 781	937	844	1 762	994	768	2 139	1 218	921	2 416	1 350	1 065
55-59	1 794	856	938	1 610	833	777	1 602	890	712	1 958	1 098	860
60-64	1 761	783	978	1 616	749	867	1 457	734	723	1 457	790	668
65-69	1 571	653	918	1 544	655	889	1 425	632	793	1 291	625	666
70-74	1 232	481	752	1 307	508	798	1 294	515	779	1 203	503	700
75-79	796	285	511	945	335	610	1 013	359	654	1 013	369	644
80-84	448	141	307	500	100	065	640	202	411	699	219	479
85-89	192	51	141	241	64	177	294	78	215	362	95	266
90-94	59	13	46	77	16	61	100	21	79	125	26	99
95-99	12	2	10	16	3	13	22	3	18	29	4	25
100 +	1	0	1	2	0	2	3	0	2	4	0	3

Age group	2045 Both sexes	Males	Females	2050 Both sexes	Males	Females
All ages	55 710	28 387	27 323	56 004	28 548	27 456
0-4	4 527	2 296	2 231	4 390	2 227	2 163
5-9	4 668	2 366	2 302	4 517	2 290	2 227
10-14	4 842	2 453	2 390	4 661	2 362	2 299
15-19	5 057	2 562	2 495	4 844	2 456	2 388
20-24	5 193	2 635	2 558	5 013	2 546	2 466
25-29	5 027	2 562	2 465	4 974	2 536	2 438
30-34	4 519	2 331	2 188	4 600	2 369	2 231
35-39	3 934	2 061	1 873	4 029	2 103	1 926
40-44	3 474	1 847	1 627	3 513	1 850	1 663
45-49	3 088	1 665	1 423	3 153	1 671	1 482
50-54	2 713	1 482	1 230	2 848	1 521	1 327
55-59	2 227	1 226	1 001	2 520	1 357	1 163
60-64	1 791	981	810	2 050	1 104	946
65-69	1 297	679	618	1 603	850	753
70-74	1 095	503	592	1 105	552	553
75-79	949	365	584	867	369	498
80-84	707	229	478	669	229	439
85-89	401	106	295	413	112	301
90-94	158	32	126	180	36	144
95-99	37	5	32	49	7	42
100 +	5	0	5	7	1	6

POPULATION BY AGE AND SEX (in thousands)

Age group	2005 Both sexes	Males	Females	2010 Both sexes	Males	Females	2015 Both sexes	Males	Females	2020 Both sexes	Males	Females
All ages	54 055	26 498	27 557	54 991	27 137	27 854	55 973	27 855	28 118	57 364	28 760	28 604
0-4	6 075	3 070	3 006	6 311	3 191	3 120	6 463	3 270	3 193	6 632	3 357	3 275
5-9	6 009	3 031	2 978	5 851	2 953	2 898	6 110	3 087	3 023	6 327	3 199	3 128
10-14	6 003	3 022	2 981	5 890	2 968	2 922	5 667	2 858	2 809	5 946	3 002	2 944
15-19	5 753	2 891	2 861	5 985	3 013	2 972	5 857	2 952	2 905	5 629	2 840	2 789
20-24	5 462	2 746	2 716	5 629	2 837	2 792	5 874	2 965	2 909	5 760	2 911	2 849
25-29	4 481	2 255	2 225	4 919	2 517	2 402	5 163	2 644	2 519	5 433	2 783	2 650
30-34	3 795	1 880	1 915	3 620	1 890	1 729	4 100	2 182	1 918	4 392	2 331	2 061
35-39	3 359	1 620	1 739	3 000	1 530	1 470	2 849	1 558	1 291	3 328	1 848	1 480
40-44	2 991	1 429	1 562	2 743	1 335	1 408	2 397	1 257	1 140	2 321	1 306	1 015
45-49	2 611	1 234	1 377	2 547	1 207	1 340	2 288	1 121	1 168	2 021	1 070	951
50-54	2 206	1 037	1 169	2 295	1 063	1 232	2 209	1 035	1 174	1 998	971	1 027
55-59	1 709	793	915	1 967	898	1 069	2 034	920	1 114	1 968	904	1 065
60-64	1 327	595	732	1 509	673	836	1 736	764	973	1 807	789	1 018
65-69	961	409	552	1 129	478	651	1 291	545	745	1 497	625	872
70-74	644	259	384	768	303	465	910	358	552	1 052	414	637
75-79	378	141	238	467	170	297	565	202	364	680	242	438
80-84	192	61	131	236	78	158	297	95	202	367	115	251
85-89	77	20	56	94	26	68	118	33	85	152	42	110
90-94	19	4	15	28	6	22	35	8	27	45	10	35
95-99	3	1	3	5	1	4	7	1	6	9	1	7
100 +	0	0	0	0	0	0	1	0	1	1	0	1

Age group	2025 Both sexes	Males	Females	2030 Both sexes	Males	Females	2035 Both sexes	Males	Females	2040 Both sexes	Males	Females
All ages	58 809	29 663	29 146	60 294	30 539	29 755	61 929	31 448	30 481	63 825	32 465	31 360
0-4	6 539	3 312	3 228	6 447	3 266	3 181	6 471	3 280	3 191	6 596	3 344	3 252
5-9	6 537	3 307	3 230	6 476	3 278	3 198	6 404	3 243	3 161	6 441	3 263	3 177
10-14	6 219	3 142	3 077	6 466	3 269	3 196	6 430	3 253	3 177	6 375	3 228	3 148
15-19	5 916	2 988	2 928	6 199	3 133	3 066	6 453	3 264	3 189	6 422	3 251	3 171
20-24	5 543	2 803	2 740	5 834	2 952	2 882	6 121	3 099	3 022	6 380	3 233	3 147
25-29	5 358	2 739	2 619	5 183	2 644	2 539	5 489	2 795	2 694	5 792	2 949	2 843
30-34	4 682	2 473	2 209	4 671	2 445	2 225	4 570	2 374	2 196	4 898	2 530	2 368
35-39	3 624	1 998	1 626	3 927	2 138	1 789	3 974	2 129	1 846	3 949	2 086	1 863
40-44	2 759	1 573	1 186	3 052	1 718	1 334	3 355	1 852	1 502	3 445	1 862	1 583
45-49	1 983	1 125	857	2 387	1 369	1 018	2 671	1 506	1 164	2 971	1 639	1 332
50-54	1 781	937	844	1 762	994	768	2 139	1 218	921	2 416	1 350	1 065
55-59	1 794	856	938	1 610	833	777	1 602	890	712	1 958	1 098	860
60-64	1 761	783	978	1 616	749	867	1 457	734	723	1 457	790	668
65-69	1 571	653	918	1 544	655	889	1 425	632	793	1 291	625	666
70-74	1 232	481	752	1 307	508	798	1 294	515	779	1 203	503	700
75-79	796	285	511	945	335	610	1 013	359	654	1 013	369	644
80-84	448	141	307	533	169	365	643	202	441	699	219	479
85-89	192	51	141	241	64	177	294	78	215	362	95	266
90-94	59	13	46	77	16	61	100	21	79	125	26	99
95-99	12	2	10	16	3	13	22	3	18	29	4	25
100 +	1	0	1	2	0	2	3	0	2	4	0	3

Age group	2045 Both sexes	Males	Females	2050 Both sexes	Males	Females
All ages	65 985	33 603	32 383	68 378	34 839	33 539
0-4	6 712	3 404	3 308	6 763	3 431	3 332
5-9	6 574	3 332	3 242	6 695	3 395	3 300
10-14	6 422	3 253	3 169	6 562	3 325	3 237
15-19	6 372	3 228	3 144	6 421	3 254	3 166
20-24	6 359	3 225	3 134	6 317	3 206	3 111
25-29	6 076	3 094	2 982	6 093	3 104	2 990
30-34	5 232	2 697	2 535	5 561	2 861	2 700
35-39	4 297	2 251	2 047	4 664	2 433	2 231
40-44	3 474	1 847	1 627	3 838	2 020	1 818
45-49	3 088	1 665	1 423	3 153	1 671	1 482
50-54	2 713	1 482	1 230	2 848	1 521	1 327
55-59	2 227	1 226	1 001	2 520	1 357	1 163
60-64	1 791	981	810	2 050	1 104	946
65-69	1 297	679	618	1 603	850	753
70-74	1 095	503	592	1 105	552	553
75-79	949	365	584	867	369	498
80-84	707	229	478	669	229	439
85-89	401	106	295	413	112	301
90-94	158	32	126	180	36	144
95-99	37	5	32	49	7	42
100 +	5	0	5	7	1	6

United Nations Department of Economic and Social Affairs/Population Division
World Population Prospects: The 2004 Revision, Volume II: Sex and Age Distribution of the World Population

66

POPULATION BY AGE AND SEX (in thousands)

Age group	2005			2010			2015			2020		
	Both sexes	Males	Females	Both sexes	Males	Females	Both sexes	Males	Females	Both sexes	Males	Females
All ages	54 055	26 498	27 557	53 926	26 598	27 328	53 183	26 444	26 738	52 350	26 224	26 126
0-4	6 075	3 070	3 006	5 245	2 652	2 593	4 704	2 380	2 324	4 342	2 198	2 144
5-9	6 009	3 031	2 978	5 851	2 953	2 898	5 079	2 566	2 513	4 606	2 328	2 277
10-14	6 003	3 022	2 981	5 890	2 968	2 922	5 667	2 858	2 809	4 943	2 495	2 447
15-19	5 753	2 891	2 861	5 985	3 013	2 972	5 857	2 952	2 905	5 629	2 840	2 789
20-24	5 462	2 746	2 716	5 629	2 837	2 792	5 874	2 965	2 909	5 760	2 911	2 849
25-29	4 481	2 255	2 225	4 919	2 517	2 402	5 163	2 644	2 519	5 433	2 783	2 650
30-34	3 795	1 880	1 915	3 620	1 890	1 729	4 100	2 182	1 918	4 392	2 331	2 061
35-39	3 359	1 620	1 739	3 000	1 530	1 470	2 849	1 558	1 291	3 328	1 848	1 480
40-44	2 991	1 429	1 562	2 743	1 335	1 408	2 397	1 257	1 140	2 321	1 306	1 015
45-49	2 611	1 234	1 377	2 547	1 207	1 340	2 288	1 121	1 168	2 021	1 070	951
50-54	2 206	1 037	1 169	2 295	1 063	1 232	2 209	1 035	1 174	1 998	971	1 027
55-59	1 709	793	915	1 967	898	1 069	2 034	920	1 114	1 968	904	1 065
60-64	1 327	595	732	1 509	673	836	1 736	764	973	1 807	789	1 018
65-69	961	409	552	1 129	478	651	1 291	545	745	1 497	625	872
70-74	644	259	384	768	303	465	910	358	552	1 052	414	637
75-79	378	141	238	467	170	297	565	202	364	680	242	438
80-84	192	61	131	236	78	158	297	95	202	367	115	251
85-89	77	20	56	94	26	68	118	33	85	152	42	110
90-94	19	4	15	28	6	22	35	8	27	45	10	35
95-99	3	1	3	5	1	4	7	1	6	9	1	7
100 +	0	0	0	0	0	0	1	0	1	1	0	1

Age group	2025			2030			2035			2040		
	Both sexes	Males	Females	Both sexes	Males	Females	Both sexes	Males	Females	Both sexes	Males	Females
All ages	51 474	25 953	25 521	50 421	25 545	24 877	49 154	24 982	24 171	47 765	24 327	23 438
0-4	4 148	2 100	2 047	3 838	1 945	1 894	3 448	1 747	1 700	3 069	1 556	1 513
5-9	4 281	2 166	2 116	4 108	2 079	2 029	3 814	1 931	1 882	3 433	1 739	1 694
10-14	4 528	2 288	2 240	4 236	2 142	2 094	4 081	2 065	2 016	3 798	1 923	1 875
15-19	4 920	2 485	2 435	4 516	2 283	2 233	4 231	2 141	2 090	4 079	2 066	2 013
20-24	5 543	2 803	2 740	4 851	2 456	2 395	4 458	2 260	2 198	4 182	2 123	2 059
25-29	5 358	2 739	2 619	5 183	2 644	2 539	4 561	2 325	2 236	4 215	2 150	2 065
30-34	4 682	2 473	2 209	4 671	2 445	2 225	4 570	2 374	2 196	4 070	2 104	1 965
35-39	3 024	1 990	1 020	3 927	2 130	1 709	3 974	2 129	1 846	3 940	2 086	1 863
40-44	2 759	1 573	1 186	3 052	1 718	1 334	3 355	1 852	1 502	3 445	1 862	1 583
45-49	1 983	1 125	857	2 387	1 369	1 018	2 671	1 506	1 164	2 971	1 639	1 332
50-54	1 781	937	844	1 762	994	768	2 139	1 218	921	2 416	1 350	1 065
55-59	1 794	856	938	1 610	833	777	1 602	890	712	1 958	1 098	860
60-64	1 761	783	978	1 616	749	867	1 457	734	723	1 457	790	668
65-69	1 571	653	918	1 544	655	889	1 425	632	793	1 291	625	666
70-74	1 232	481	752	1 307	508	798	1 294	515	779	1 203	503	700
75-79	796	285	511	945	335	610	1 013	360	654	1 013	360	611
80-84	448	141	307	533	169	365	643	202	441	699	219	479
85-89	192	51	141	241	64	177	294	78	215	362	95	266
90-94	59	13	46	77	16	61	100	21	79	125	26	99
95-99	12	2	10	16	3	13	22	3	18	29	4	25
100 +	1	0	1	2	0	2	3	0	2	4	0	3

Age group	2045			2050		
	Both sexes	Males	Females	Both sexes	Males	Females
All ages	46 381	23 651	22 730	45 092	22 998	22 094
0-4	2 762	1 401	1 362	2 535	1 286	1 249
5-9	3 060	1 551	1 509	2 757	1 398	1 359
10-14	3 425	1 735	1 690	3 057	1 549	1 508
15-19	3 800	1 926	1 874	3 429	1 739	1 690
20-24	4 038	2 051	1 986	3 766	1 915	1 850
25-29	3 977	2 030	1 947	3 864	1 973	1 891
30-34	3 806	1 965	1 841	3 639	1 876	1 762
35-39	3 571	1 872	1 699	3 394	1 773	1 621
40-44	3 474	1 847	1 627	3 189	1 679	1 509
45-49	3 088	1 665	1 423	3 153	1 671	1 482
50-54	2 713	1 482	1 230	2 848	1 521	1 327
55-59	2 227	1 226	1 001	2 520	1 357	1 163
60-64	1 791	981	810	2 050	1 104	946
65-69	1 297	679	618	1 603	850	753
70-74	1 095	503	592	1 105	552	553
75-79	949	365	584	867	369	498
80-84	707	229	478	669	229	439
85-89	401	106	295	413	112	301
90-94	158	32	126	180	36	144
95-99	37	5	32	49	7	42
100 +	5	0	5	7	1	6

POPULATION BY AGE AND SEX (in thousands)

Age group	1950 Both sexes	Males	Females	1955 Both sexes	Males	Females	1960 Both sexes	Males	Females	1965 Both sexes	Males	Females
All ages	63 823	31 712	32 111	71 153	35 398	35 756	79 834	39 769	40 065	89 827	44 800	45 027
0-4	10 887	5 518	5 369	12 576	6 347	6 229	14 259	7 204	7 055	16 141	8 164	7 977
5-9	8 591	4 333	4 258	9 491	4 801	4 690	11 066	5 574	5 492	12 627	6 369	6 258
10-14	7 419	3 730	3 689	8 261	4 169	4 092	9 138	4 625	4 513	10 656	5 370	5 287
15-19	6 461	3 245	3 215	7 187	3 616	3 571	8 015	4 048	3 968	8 869	4 491	4 378
20-24	5 606	2 805	2 801	6 200	3 107	3 094	6 915	3 470	3 445	7 705	3 881	3 824
25-29	4 821	2 407	2 415	5 328	2 654	2 674	5 909	2 948	2 962	6 580	3 287	3 293
30-34	4 119	2 048	2 071	4 568	2 274	2 293	5 060	2 514	2 546	5 604	2 787	2 816
35-39	3 466	1 719	1 747	3 880	1 926	1 954	4 313	2 143	2 169	4 776	2 368	2 408
40-44	2 916	1 438	1 479	3 239	1 600	1 639	3 638	1 799	1 839	4 046	2 002	2 044
45-49	2 454	1 201	1 254	2 698	1 318	1 380	3 012	1 476	1 536	3 384	1 660	1 724
50-54	2 122	1 023	1 098	2 244	1 084	1 160	2 481	1 198	1 282	2 769	1 342	1 427
55-59	1 717	804	913	1 888	897	991	2 008	957	1 051	2 225	1 060	1 165
60-64	1 313	601	712	1 458	671	787	1 614	754	859	1 725	809	916
65-69	927	414	512	1 028	462	566	1 153	521	632	1 287	592	695
70-74	577	250	326	637	279	359	718	316	402	817	361	455
75-79	294	122	172	324	136	188	367	155	212	422	180	242
80 +	134	53	81	148	58	90	168	65	102	194	76	118

Age group	1970 Both sexes	Males	Females	1975 Both sexes	Males	Females	1980 Both sexes	Males	Females	1985 Both sexes	Males	Females
All ages	101 716	50 805	50 910	115 861	57 909	57 952	133 564	66 932	66 631	154 402	77 393	77 009
0-4	18 418	9 326	9 092	21 223	10 758	10 465	24 614	12 485	12 129	29 171	14 807	14 364
5-9	14 413	7 279	7 133	16 589	8 384	8 205	19 312	9 778	9 534	22 571	11 435	11 136
10-14	12 183	6 147	6 036	13 922	7 026	6 896	16 110	8 144	7 966	18 806	9 522	9 283
15-19	10 356	5 221	5 135	11 807	5 952	5 855	13 638	6 895	6 743	15 733	7 950	7 783
20-24	8 546	4 321	4 225	9 960	5 002	4 958	11 543	5 823	5 720	13 172	6 637	6 535
25-29	7 362	3 695	3 667	8 185	4 106	4 079	9 693	4 866	4 827	11 035	5 537	5 498
30-34	6 267	3 124	3 143	7 025	3 507	3 518	7 949	3 999	3 950	9 229	4 607	4 621
35-39	5 312	2 638	2 675	5 937	2 947	2 990	6 772	3 388	3 384	7 557	3 784	3 773
40-44	4 499	2 223	2 276	5 008	2 475	2 533	5 662	2 806	2 856	6 425	3 201	3 224
45-49	3 778	1 857	1 921	4 209	2 066	2 143	4 735	2 328	2 407	5 339	2 627	2 712
50-54	3 123	1 516	1 607	3 492	1 702	1 789	3 930	1 912	2 017	4 414	2 148	2 266
55-59	2 498	1 195	1 303	2 828	1 361	1 468	3 182	1 534	1 648	3 599	1 731	1 868
60-64	1 926	904	1 022	2 180	1 034	1 146	2 480	1 177	1 303	2 816	1 339	1 477
65-69	1 389	641	748	1 576	733	842	1 790	836	954	2 064	965	1 099
70-74	923	416	508	1 025	468	557	1 163	531	632	1 338	612	726
75-79	491	210	280	592	263	329	639	283	356	733	324	409
80 +	230	91	139	303	126	178	351	146	205	401	167	234

Age group	1990 Both sexes	Males	Females	1995 Both sexes	Males	Females	2000 Both sexes	Males	Females	2005 Both sexes	Males	Females
All ages	178 483	89 551	88 933	204 949	102 969	101 980	233 624	117 575	116 049	263 636	133 005	130 631
0-4	33 211	16 883	16 327	37 085	18 886	18 199	40 781	20 788	19 992	44 663	22 780	21 884
5-9	26 893	13 642	13 251	30 739	15 631	15 108	34 539	17 594	16 944	37 961	19 361	18 600
10-14	21 994	11 144	10 849	26 236	13 314	12 922	30 100	15 312	14 788	33 706	17 178	16 528
15-19	18 385	9 310	9 075	21 518	10 906	10 612	25 783	13 085	12 698	29 495	15 004	14 490
20-24	15 242	7 683	7 559	17 806	9 000	8 807	20 911	10 580	10 331	24 997	12 664	12 333
25-29	12 647	6 344	6 303	14 552	7 312	7 240	16 924	8 547	8 378	19 843	10 046	9 797
30-34	10 565	5 281	5 284	12 006	6 003	6 004	13 621	6 848	6 773	15 715	7 981	7 735
35-39	8 814	4 385	4 430	10 013	4 986	5 028	11 215	5 599	5 616	12 561	6 344	6 217
40-44	7 188	3 584	3 604	8 338	4 127	4 211	9 369	4 646	4 723	10 370	5 179	5 190
45-49	6 075	3 007	3 069	6 775	3 353	3 421	7 807	3 836	3 971	8 693	4 290	4 403
50-54	4 998	2 437	2 561	5 677	2 783	2 894	6 311	3 091	3 219	7 227	3 519	3 708
55-59	4 054	1 951	2 103	4 590	2 213	2 377	5 210	2 522	2 688	5 776	2 796	2 980
60-64	3 193	1 514	1 679	3 606	1 713	1 893	4 092	1 945	2 147	4 639	2 214	2 425
65-69	2 355	1 103	1 253	2 682	1 254	1 428	3 045	1 424	1 621	3 457	1 616	1 840
70-74	1 554	712	842	1 785	820	965	2 055	943	1 112	2 342	1 074	1 267
75-79	852	377	475	1 000	445	555	1 171	524	647	1 358	607	750
80 +	463	193	271	542	226	316	691	290	401	834	352	482

United Nations Department of Economic and Social Affairs/Population Division
World Population Prospects: The 2004 Revision, Volume II: Sex and Age Distribution of the World Population

68

POPULATION BY AGE AND SEX (in thousands)

Age group	2005 Both sexes	Males	Females	2010 Both sexes	Males	Females	2015 Both sexes	Males	Females	2020 Both sexes	Males	Females
All ages	263 636	133 006	130 631	286 311	140 321	146 020	320 514	166 000	102 004	365 010	185 120	179 000
0-4	44 663	22 780	21 884	48 005	24 484	23 521	50 900	25 967	24 934	52 926	27 009	25 917
5-9	37 961	19 361	18 600	41 738	21 293	20 445	45 252	23 078	22 174	48 389	24 681	23 708
10-14	33 706	17 178	16 528	37 003	18 879	18 124	40 804	20 820	19 984	44 363	22 627	21 737
15-19	29 495	15 004	14 490	33 048	16 842	16 206	36 386	18 560	17 826	40 188	20 499	19 688
20-24	24 997	12 664	12 333	28 649	14 550	14 099	32 246	16 404	15 842	35 589	18 122	17 467
25-29	19 843	10 046	9 797	23 798	12 059	11 739	27 439	13 938	13 501	31 030	15 785	15 245
30-34	15 715	7 981	7 735	18 476	9 406	9 070	22 333	11 375	10 957	25 896	13 219	12 678
35-39	12 561	6 344	6 217	14 477	7 398	7 080	17 162	8 789	8 373	20 856	10 686	10 169
40-44	10 370	5 179	5 190	11 584	5 863	5 720	13 449	6 889	6 559	16 019	8 226	7 792
45-49	8 693	4 290	4 403	9 599	4 779	4 820	10 793	5 449	5 344	12 585	6 434	6 151
50-54	7 227	3 519	3 708	8 036	3 935	4 102	8 927	4 413	4 515	10 081	5 056	5 024
55-59	5 776	2 796	2 980	6 611	3 182	3 429	7 396	3 582	3 814	8 254	4 039	4 216
60-64	4 639	2 214	2 425	5 153	2 459	2 694	5 936	2 817	3 119	6 679	3 191	3 488
65-69	3 457	1 616	1 840	3 933	1 846	2 086	4 409	2 070	2 339	5 116	2 389	2 727
70-74	2 342	1 074	1 267	2 677	1 228	1 449	3 083	1 419	1 663	3 498	1 611	1 887
75-79	1 358	607	750	1 565	700	865	1 820	813	1 007	2 129	955	1 174
80-84	607	262	345	716	309	407	843	364	479	1 001	432	569
85-89	188	76	112	227	93	134	274	112	162	332	136	196
90-94	34	12	22	45	17	29	56	21	35	70	26	44
95-99	4	1	3	5	1	3	7	2	5	8	3	6
100 +	0	0	0	0	0	0	0	0	0	1	0	0

Age group	2025 Both sexes	Males	Females	2030 Both sexes	Males	Females	2035 Both sexes	Males	Females	2040 Both sexes	Males	Females
All ages	401 381	203 812	197 569	438 506	222 866	215 640	476 139	242 146	233 993	513 830	261 381	252 449
0-4	54 346	27 745	26 601	55 563	28 379	27 184	56 572	28 903	27 669	57 145	29 199	27 945
5-9	50 699	25 868	24 831	52 403	26 751	25 652	53 876	27 517	26 359	55 119	28 158	26 961
10-14	47 607	24 281	23 325	50 027	25 524	24 503	51 833	26 457	25 376	53 393	27 266	26 127
15-19	43 769	22 315	21 454	47 050	23 987	23 063	49 518	25 252	24 266	51 374	26 208	25 165
20-24	39 392	20 060	19 333	42 993	21 884	21 110	46 308	23 572	22 736	48 825	24 860	23 965
25-29	34 382	17 505	16 876	38 194	19 447	18 748	41 838	21 290	20 548	45 223	23 009	22 215
30-34	29 466	15 053	14 413	32 832	16 778	16 055	36 672	18 729	17 942	40 387	20 602	19 785
35-39	24 344	12 493	11 852	27 890	14 313	13 577	31 273	16 044	15 230	35 151	18 010	17 141
40-44	19 579	10 060	9 519	23 008	11 835	11 173	26 521	13 638	12 883	29 922	15 375	14 546
45-49	15 065	7 724	7 341	18 522	9 504	9 018	21 887	11 244	10 643	25 364	13 027	12 337
50-54	11 809	6 002	5 807	14 209	7 247	6 963	17 558	8 965	8 593	20 846	10 659	10 187
55-59	9 366	4 653	4 713	11 031	5 557	5 474	13 337	6 745	6 592	16 560	8 388	8 172
60-64	7 499	3 622	3 877	8 562	4 202	4 360	10 144	5 051	5 093	12 330	6 165	6 165
65-69	5 801	2 728	3 073	6 567	3 123	3 443	7 554	3 652	3 902	9 017	4 423	4 594
70-74	4 102	1 878	2 223	4 704	2 170	2 534	5 383	2 513	2 870	6 258	2 970	3 288
75-79	2 456	1 102	1 354	2 924	1 305	1 618	3 404	1 531	1 872	3 953	1 800	2 153
80-84	1 106	518	677	1 409	611	790	1 710	738	971	2 029	883	1 146
85-89	404	166	238	494	204	290	597	247	350	741	305	436
90-94	87	33	54	108	41	67	136	52	84	168	64	104
95-99	11	3	7	14	4	9	18	6	12	23	8	15
100 +	1	0	1	1	0	1	1	0	1	2	0	1

Age group	2045 Both sexes	Males	Females	2050 Both sexes	Males	Females
All ages	550 968	280 224	270 744	586 989	298 356	288 634
0-4	57 164	29 209	27 955	56 754	28 995	27 760
5-9	55 912	28 563	27 349	56 135	28 671	27 464
10-14	54 710	27 943	26 767	55 568	28 379	27 189
15-19	52 980	27 038	25 942	54 341	27 735	26 606
20-24	50 739	25 844	24 895	52 406	26 703	25 703
25-29	47 836	24 340	23 496	49 862	25 375	24 487
30-34	43 882	22 366	21 516	46 643	23 758	22 885
35-39	38 951	19 917	19 034	42 567	21 730	20 838
40-44	33 833	17 354	16 479	37 702	19 290	18 412
45-49	28 768	14 762	14 006	32 693	16 744	15 949
50-54	24 270	12 409	11 861	27 651	14 127	13 524
55-59	19 751	10 022	9 729	23 094	11 720	11 374
60-64	15 393	7 711	7 682	18 448	9 259	9 189
65-69	11 032	5 434	5 598	13 863	6 843	7 021
70-74	7 545	3 633	3 912	9 310	4 501	4 809
75-79	4 657	2 155	2 502	5 686	2 669	3 016
80-84	2 399	1 056	1 343	2 873	1 285	1 588
85-89	899	374	526	1 086	456	630
90-94	214	82	132	266	103	163
95-99	29	10	19	37	13	25
100 +	2	1	2	3	1	2

United Nations Department of Economic and Social Affairs/Population Division
World Population Prospects: The 2004 Revision, Volume II: Sex and Age Distribution of the World Population

69

POPULATION BY AGE AND SEX (in thousands)

Age group	2005 Both sexes	Males	Females	2010 Both sexes	Males	Females	2015 Both sexes	Males	Females	2020 Both sexes	Males	Females
All ages	263 636	133 005	130 631	297 608	150 476	147 132	336 055	170 217	165 837	377 418	191 457	185 961
0-4	44 663	22 780	21 884	50 269	25 640	24 629	55 301	28 212	27 090	59 046	30 132	28 914
5-9	37 961	19 361	18 600	41 738	21 293	20 445	47 392	24 170	23 222	52 579	26 818	25 761
10-14	33 706	17 178	16 528	37 003	18 879	18 124	40 804	20 820	19 984	46 463	23 698	22 765
15-19	29 495	15 004	14 490	33 048	16 842	16 206	36 386	18 560	17 826	40 188	20 499	19 688
20-24	24 997	12 664	12 333	28 649	14 550	14 099	32 246	16 404	15 842	35 589	18 122	17 467
25-29	19 843	10 046	9 797	23 798	12 059	11 739	27 439	13 938	13 501	31 030	15 785	15 245
30-34	15 715	7 981	7 735	18 476	9 406	9 070	22 333	11 375	10 957	25 896	13 219	12 678
35-39	12 561	6 344	6 217	14 477	7 398	7 080	17 162	8 789	8 373	20 856	10 686	10 169
40-44	10 370	5 179	5 190	11 584	5 863	5 720	13 449	6 889	6 559	16 019	8 226	7 792
45-49	8 693	4 290	4 403	9 599	4 779	4 820	10 793	5 449	5 344	12 585	6 434	6 151
50-54	7 227	3 519	3 708	8 036	3 935	4 102	8 927	4 413	4 515	10 081	5 056	5 024
55-59	5 776	2 796	2 980	6 611	3 182	3 429	7 396	3 582	3 814	8 254	4 039	4 216
60-64	4 639	2 214	2 425	5 153	2 459	2 694	5 936	2 817	3 119	6 679	3 191	3 488
65-69	3 457	1 616	1 840	3 933	1 846	2 086	4 409	2 070	2 339	5 116	2 389	2 727
70-74	2 342	1 074	1 267	2 677	1 228	1 449	3 083	1 419	1 663	3 498	1 611	1 887
75-79	1 358	607	750	1 565	700	865	1 820	813	1 007	2 129	955	1 174
80-84	607	262	345	716	309	407	843	364	479	1 001	432	569
85-89	188	76	112	227	93	134	274	112	162	332	136	196
90-94	34	12	22	45	17	29	56	21	35	70	26	44
95-99	4	1	3	5	1	3	7	2	5	8	3	6
100 +	0	0	0	0	0	0	0	0	0	1	0	0

Age group	2025 Both sexes	Males	Females	2030 Both sexes	Males	Females	2035 Both sexes	Males	Females	2040 Both sexes	Males	Females
All ages	420 609	213 622	206 987	466 081	236 936	229 145	514 352	261 645	252 707	565 428	287 713	277 715
0-4	61 502	31 398	30 104	64 306	32 844	31 462	67 696	34 586	33 110	71 150	36 355	34 796
5-9	56 573	28 864	27 709	59 316	30 279	29 037	62 368	31 853	30 515	65 974	33 702	32 272
10-14	51 731	26 385	25 346	55 826	28 482	27 345	58 674	29 948	28 726	61 812	31 564	30 248
15-19	45 843	23 373	22 470	51 130	26 068	25 062	55 262	28 180	27 082	58 158	29 668	28 490
20-24	39 392	20 060	19 333	45 034	22 923	22 111	50 330	25 619	24 710	54 497	27 747	26 750
25-29	34 382	17 505	16 876	38 194	19 447	18 748	43 829	22 304	21 525	49 159	25 012	24 147
30-34	29 466	15 053	14 413	32 832	16 778	16 055	36 672	18 729	17 942	42 314	21 586	20 728
35-39	24 344	12 493	11 852	27 890	14 313	13 577	31 273	16 044	15 230	35 151	18 010	17 141
40-44	19 579	10 060	9 519	23 008	11 835	11 173	26 521	13 638	12 883	29 922	15 375	14 546
45-49	15 065	7 724	7 341	18 522	9 504	9 018	21 887	11 244	10 643	25 364	13 027	12 337
50-54	11 809	6 002	5 807	14 209	7 247	6 963	17 558	8 965	8 593	20 846	10 659	10 187
55-59	9 366	4 653	4 713	11 031	5 557	5 474	13 337	6 745	6 592	16 560	8 388	8 172
60-64	7 499	3 622	3 877	8 562	4 202	4 360	10 144	5 051	5 093	12 330	6 165	6 165
65-69	5 801	2 728	3 073	6 567	3 123	3 443	7 554	3 652	3 902	9 017	4 423	4 594
70-74	4 102	1 878	2 223	4 704	2 170	2 534	5 383	2 513	2 870	6 258	2 970	3 288
75-79	2 456	1 102	1 354	2 924	1 305	1 618	3 404	1 531	1 872	3 953	1 800	2 153
80-84	1 196	518	677	1 409	611	798	1 710	738	971	2 029	883	1 146
85-89	404	166	238	494	204	290	597	247	350	741	305	436
90-94	87	33	54	108	41	67	136	52	84	168	64	104
95-99	11	3	7	14	4	9	18	6	12	23	8	15
100 +	1	0	1	1	0	1	1	0	1	2	0	1

Age group	2045 Both sexes	Males	Females	2050 Both sexes	Males	Females
All ages	618 570	314 725	303 844	672 873	342 184	330 689
0-4	73 942	37 780	36 161	75 947	38 798	37 149
5-9	69 634	35 571	34 063	72 630	37 094	35 537
10-14	65 488	33 446	32 042	69 211	35 344	33 867
15-19	61 340	31 303	30 036	65 053	33 201	31 852
20-24	57 449	29 261	28 188	60 684	30 920	29 764
25-29	53 402	27 172	26 230	56 465	28 735	27 730
30-34	47 710	24 318	23 392	52 078	26 527	25 551
35-39	40 813	20 870	19 943	46 287	23 630	22 657
40-44	33 833	17 354	16 479	39 507	20 215	19 293
45-49	28 768	14 762	14 006	32 693	16 744	15 949
50-54	24 270	12 409	11 861	27 651	14 127	13 524
55-59	19 751	10 022	9 729	23 094	11 720	11 374
60-64	15 393	7 711	7 682	18 448	9 259	9 189
65-69	11 032	5 434	5 598	13 863	6 843	7 021
70-74	7 545	3 633	3 912	9 310	4 501	4 809
75-79	4 657	2 155	2 502	5 686	2 669	3 016
80-84	2 399	1 056	1 343	2 873	1 285	1 588
85-89	899	374	526	1 086	456	630
90-94	214	82	132	266	103	163
95-99	29	10	19	37	13	25
100 +	2	1	2	3	1	2

United Nations Department of Economic and Social Affairs/Population Division
World Population Prospects: The 2004 Revision, Volume II: Sex and Age Distribution of the World Population

70

POPULATION BY AGE AND SEX (in thousands)

Age group	2005 Both sexes	2005 Males	2005 Females	2010 Both sexes	2010 Males	2010 Females	2015 Both sexes	2015 Males	2015 Females	2020 Both sexes	2020 Males	2020 Females
All ages	263 636	133 005	130 631	293 071	148 162	144 909	323 127	163 623	159 504	352 744	178 870	173 874
0-4	44 663	22 780	21 884	45 732	23 325	22 407	46 661	23 804	22 857	46 807	23 887	22 920
5-9	37 961	19 361	18 600	41 738	21 293	20 445	43 104	21 983	21 121	44 349	22 621	21 728
10-14	33 706	17 178	16 528	37 003	18 879	18 124	40 804	20 820	19 984	42 256	21 552	20 704
15-19	29 495	15 004	14 490	33 048	16 842	16 206	36 386	18 560	17 826	40 188	20 499	19 688
20-24	24 997	12 664	12 333	28 649	14 550	14 099	32 246	16 404	15 842	35 589	18 122	17 467
25-29	19 843	10 046	9 797	23 798	12 059	11 739	27 439	13 938	13 501	31 030	15 785	15 245
30-34	15 715	7 981	7 735	18 476	9 406	9 070	22 333	11 375	10 957	25 896	13 219	12 678
35-39	12 561	6 344	6 217	14 477	7 398	7 080	17 162	8 789	8 373	20 856	10 686	10 169
40-44	10 370	5 179	5 190	11 584	5 863	5 720	13 449	6 889	6 559	16 019	8 226	7 792
45-49	8 693	4 290	4 403	9 599	4 779	4 820	10 793	5 449	5 344	12 585	6 434	6 151
50-54	7 227	3 519	3 708	8 036	3 935	4 102	8 927	4 413	4 515	10 081	5 056	5 024
55-59	5 776	2 796	2 980	6 611	3 182	3 429	7 396	3 582	3 814	8 254	4 039	4 216
60-64	4 639	2 214	2 425	5 153	2 459	2 694	5 936	2 817	3 119	6 679	3 191	3 488
65-69	3 457	1 616	1 840	3 933	1 846	2 086	4 409	2 070	2 339	5 116	2 389	2 727
70-74	2 342	1 074	1 267	2 677	1 228	1 449	3 083	1 419	1 663	3 498	1 611	1 887
75-79	1 358	607	750	1 565	700	865	1 820	813	1 007	2 129	955	1 174
80-84	607	262	345	716	309	407	843	364	479	1 001	432	569
85-89	188	76	112	227	93	134	274	112	162	332	136	196
90-94	34	12	22	45	17	29	56	21	35	70	26	44
95-99	4	1	3	5	1	3	7	2	5	8	3	6
100 +	0	0	0	0	0	0	0	0	0	1	0	0

Age group	2025 Both sexes	2025 Males	2025 Females	2030 Both sexes	2030 Males	2030 Females	2035 Both sexes	2035 Males	2035 Females	2040 Both sexes	2040 Males	2040 Females
All ages	382 333	194 095	188 238	411 342	209 008	202 334	439 018	223 207	215 811	464 671	236 299	228 373
0-4	47 230	24 113	23 117	47 055	24 034	23 021	46 137	23 573	22 564	44 506	22 743	21 764
5-9	44 824	22 871	21 953	45 527	23 242	22 286	45 611	23 297	22 314	44 936	22 958	21 978
10-14	43 630	22 254	21 376	44 228	22 566	21 662	45 030	22 986	22 044	45 200	23 083	22 116
15-19	41 689	21 255	20 434	43 117	21 983	21 134	43 773	22 324	21 450	44 627	22 767	21 859
20-24	39 392	20 060	19 333	40 946	20 842	20 104	42 431	21 599	20 832	43 153	21 973	21 181
25-29	34 382	17 505	16 876	38 194	19 447	18 748	39 841	20 274	19 567	41 430	21 079	20 351
30-34	29 466	15 053	14 413	32 832	16 778	16 055	36 672	18 729	17 942	38 456	19 617	18 839
35-39	24 344	12 493	11 852	27 890	14 313	13 577	31 273	16 044	15 230	35 151	18 010	17 141
40-44	19 579	10 060	9 519	23 008	11 835	11 173	26 521	13 638	12 883	29 922	15 375	14 546
45-49	15 065	7 724	7 341	18 522	9 504	9 018	21 887	11 244	10 643	25 364	13 027	12 337
50-54	11 809	6 002	5 807	14 209	7 247	6 963	17 558	8 965	8 593	20 846	10 659	10 187
55-59	9 366	4 653	4 712	11 021	5 657	5 474	13 237	6 745	6 592	16 560	8 388	8 172
60-64	7 499	3 622	3 877	8 562	4 202	4 360	10 144	5 051	5 093	12 330	6 165	6 165
65-69	5 801	2 728	3 073	6 567	3 123	3 443	7 554	3 652	3 902	9 017	4 423	4 594
70-74	4 102	1 878	2 223	4 704	2 170	2 534	5 383	2 513	2 870	6 258	2 970	3 288
75-79	2 456	1 102	1 354	2 924	1 305	1 618	3 404	1 531	1 872	3 953	1 800	2 153
80-84	1 196	518	677	1 409	611	798	1 710	738	971	2 029	883	1 146
85-89	404	166	238	494	204	290	597	247	350	741	305	436
90-94	87	33	54	108	41	67	136	52	84	168	64	104
95-99	11	3	7	14	4	9	18	6	12	23	8	15
100 +	1	0	1	1	0	1	1	0	1	2	0	1

Age group	2045 Both sexes	2045 Males	2045 Females	2050 Both sexes	2050 Males	2050 Females
All ages	487 865	248 023	239 841	508 371	258 240	250 130
0-4	42 481	21 708	20 774	40 378	20 630	19 748
5-9	43 530	22 240	21 290	41 700	21 301	20 399
10-14	44 599	22 781	21 818	43 258	22 094	21 163
15-19	44 845	22 888	21 957	44 292	22 608	21 684
20-24	44 067	22 447	21 621	44 349	22 599	21 751
25-29	42 269	21 508	20 761	43 295	22 034	21 262
30-34	40 195	20 486	19 708	41 208	20 990	20 218
35-39	37 085	18 962	18 122	38 985	19 901	19 085
40-44	33 833	17 354	16 479	35 894	18 364	17 529
45-49	28 768	14 762	14 006	32 693	16 744	15 949
50-54	24 270	12 409	11 861	27 651	14 127	13 524
55-59	19 751	10 022	9 729	23 094	11 720	11 374
60-64	15 393	7 711	7 682	18 448	9 259	9 189
65-69	11 032	5 434	5 598	13 863	6 843	7 021
70-74	7 545	3 633	3 912	9 310	4 501	4 809
75-79	4 657	2 155	2 502	5 686	2 669	3 016
80-84	2 399	1 056	1 343	2 873	1 285	1 588
85-89	899	374	526	1 086	456	630
90-94	214	82	132	266	103	163
95-99	29	10	19	37	13	25
100 +	2	1	2	3	1	2

United Nations Department of Economic and Social Affairs/Population Division
World Population Prospects: The 2004 Revision, Volume II: Sex and Age Distribution of the World Population

71

POPULATION BY AGE AND SEX (in thousands)

Age group	1950 Both sexes	Males	Females	1955 Both sexes	Males	Females	1960 Both sexes	Males	Females	1965 Both sexes	Males	Females
All ages	1 396 254	714 860	681 394	1 539 784	787 135	752 650	1 699 137	868 148	830 989	1 896 875	969 503	927 372
0-4	201 941	103 799	98 142	245 542	125 531	120 011	259 572	132 937	126 636	296 407	152 093	144 314
5-9	159 325	81 409	77 916	184 853	95 338	89 515	228 058	117 053	111 004	243 974	125 572	118 402
10-14	148 162	76 561	71 601	155 699	79 764	75 935	181 351	93 633	87 718	224 082	115 283	108 800
15-19	140 394	72 730	67 664	145 314	75 139	70 175	152 725	78 385	74 340	178 378	92 131	86 248
20-24	123 016	63 659	59 357	136 235	70 525	65 710	141 800	73 207	68 593	149 189	76 578	72 611
25-29	107 127	55 244	51 882	118 817	61 424	57 393	132 022	68 266	63 756	138 294	71 380	66 914
30-34	94 234	48 635	45 599	102 839	53 043	49 796	115 040	59 588	55 452	128 021	66 253	61 768
35-39	85 585	44 335	41 250	89 498	46 129	43 369	98 779	50 920	47 859	111 326	57 642	53 684
40-44	75 908	39 280	36 627	80 600	41 505	39 095	85 098	43 664	41 433	94 766	48 703	46 063
45-49	65 608	34 023	31 585	70 419	36 018	34 402	75 659	38 634	37 025	80 547	41 069	39 478
50-54	54 204	27 943	26 261	59 471	30 205	29 266	64 939	32 779	32 160	70 522	35 635	34 887
55-59	46 236	23 610	22 626	46 977	23 541	23 436	52 988	26 308	26 680	58 844	29 214	29 629
60-64	37 085	18 290	18 795	39 518	19 790	19 728	39 746	19 378	20 368	45 830	22 235	23 595
65-69	27 018	12 260	14 758	29 202	14 143	15 059	31 794	15 660	16 135	31 935	15 074	16 861
70-74	17 040	7 579	9 461	19 344	8 550	10 794	21 438	10 120	11 318	23 750	11 411	12 338
75-79	8 996	3 771	5 225	10 276	4 430	5 846	11 984	5 128	6 856	13 612	6 230	7 382
80 +	4 376	1 732	2 644	5 179	2 060	3 119	6 145	2 489	3 656	7 397	3 000	4 397

Age group	1970 Both sexes	Males	Females	1975 Both sexes	Males	Females	1980 Both sexes	Males	Females	1985 Both sexes	Males	Females
All ages	2 140 425	1 094 279	1 046 146	2 395 218	1 225 954	1 169 264	2 630 386	1 346 409	1 283 977	2 887 969	1 477 665	1 410 303
0-4	334 682	171 775	162 908	345 735	177 545	168 190	330 471	169 734	160 736	355 282	182 627	172 655
5-9	283 269	145 901	137 369	322 948	166 530	156 417	334 139	172 123	162 017	319 526	164 474	155 052
10-14	240 485	124 046	116 439	280 230	144 638	135 592	319 800	164 918	154 882	331 323	170 692	160 631
15-19	220 888	113 713	107 175	237 795	122 922	114 873	277 103	142 988	134 115	317 329	163 655	153 674
20-24	175 321	90 420	84 901	217 200	111 901	105 299	234 176	121 224	112 952	274 248	141 528	132 720
25-29	146 036	74 985	71 051	172 161	88 738	83 423	213 873	110 352	103 521	231 819	120 041	111 778
30-34	135 304	69 794	65 509	143 114	73 564	69 549	169 581	87 365	82 216	211 322	109 078	102 244
35-39	124 617	64 491	60 126	132 559	68 378	64 181	140 286	72 128	68 158	167 238	86 142	81 095
40-44	107 952	55 824	52 127	121 272	62 773	58 499	129 737	66 837	62 899	137 295	70 466	66 830
45-49	91 171	46 645	44 526	104 761	54 073	50 688	117 393	60 589	56 804	125 893	64 550	61 342
50-54	76 198	38 521	37 677	87 127	44 331	42 796	100 534	51 607	48 927	112 577	57 677	54 900
55-59	65 110	32 519	32 591	71 048	35 533	35 515	81 732	41 181	40 552	94 593	48 059	46 534
60-64	52 205	25 438	26 767	58 412	28 730	29 682	64 198	31 631	32 567	74 249	36 804	37 444
65-69	38 319	18 077	20 242	44 302	21 076	23 226	49 984	24 061	25 924	55 189	26 484	28 705
70-74	23 970	10 918	13 052	29 529	13 484	16 045	35 146	16 124	19 022	39 681	18 400	21 280
75-79	15 769	7 352	8 417	15 873	6 915	8 958	20 407	8 858	11 549	24 609	10 733	13 876
80 +	9 129	3 861	5 269	11 154	4 824	6 330	11 827	4 690	7 137	15 795	6 255	9 541

Age group	1990 Both sexes	Males	Females	1995 Both sexes	Males	Females	2000 Both sexes	Males	Females	2005 Both sexes	Males	Females
All ages	3 168 616	1 621 724	1 546 892	3 430 323	1 753 835	1 676 488	3 675 799	1 875 830	1 799 969	3 905 415	1 989 639	1 915 776
0-4	386 350	199 537	186 813	378 012	195 216	182 795	366 079	188 895	177 184	356 879	183 988	172 891
5-9	346 737	178 760	167 977	377 732	195 367	182 364	370 675	191 591	179 084	360 222	185 996	174 227
10-14	318 151	163 882	154 269	344 401	177 516	166 885	375 167	193 991	181 175	368 884	190 620	178 264
15-19	327 748	168 725	159 023	315 337	162 336	153 001	341 722	176 054	165 668	373 045	192 812	180 233
20-24	313 404	161 016	152 388	323 086	166 184	156 903	311 983	160 491	151 492	338 588	174 290	164 298
25-29	270 906	139 561	131 345	309 007	158 659	150 348	319 522	164 113	155 408	308 492	158 431	150 061
30-34	229 174	118 967	110 207	267 294	137 482	129 812	305 215	156 288	148 927	315 613	161 697	153 916
35-39	208 520	107 766	100 753	225 470	116 752	108 718	263 414	135 039	128 376	301 024	153 672	147 351
40-44	164 183	84 567	79 615	204 608	105 462	99 146	221 553	114 323	107 229	259 002	132 298	126 705
45-49	133 827	68 475	65 352	160 351	82 257	78 094	200 039	102 574	97 465	216 668	111 266	105 402
50-54	121 160	61 821	59 339	129 304	65 709	63 594	155 097	78 948	76 149	193 983	98 796	95 186
55-59	106 201	53 950	52 251	115 004	58 027	56 977	122 921	61 727	61 194	148 153	74 638	73 514
60-64	86 195	43 104	43 091	97 659	48 764	48 895	106 161	52 628	53 533	114 217	56 447	57 770
65-69	64 220	31 051	33 169	75 547	36 801	38 745	86 139	41 897	44 242	94 470	45 714	48 756
70-74	44 052	20 384	23 668	52 125	24 185	27 940	61 942	29 011	32 931	71 660	33 638	38 021
75-79	27 931	12 306	15 624	31 659	13 828	17 831	38 195	16 736	21 458	46 410	20 671	25 739
80 +	19 857	7 850	12 007	23 727	9 289	14 438	29 974	11 522	18 453	38 104	14 663	23 441

United Nations Department of Economic and Social Affairs/Population Division
World Population Prospects: The 2004 Revision, Volume II: Sex and Age Distribution of the World Population

72

POPULATION BY AGE AND SEX (in thousands)

Age group	2005 Both sexes	2005 Males	2005 Females	2010 Both sexes	2010 Males	2010 Females	2015 Both sexes	2015 Males	2015 Females	2020 Both sexes	2020 Males	2020 Females
All ages	3 905 415	1 989 639	1 915 776	4 130 383	2 100 604	2 029 779	4 351 001	2 208 851	2 142 151	4 553 791	2 307 407	2 246 384
0-4	356 879	183 988	172 891	360 579	185 853	174 727	366 684	188 990	177 694	361 301	186 152	175 149
5-9	360 222	185 996	174 227	351 948	181 529	170 419	356 341	183 706	172 636	363 064	187 121	175 943
10-14	368 884	190 620	178 264	358 641	185 133	173 508	350 523	180 745	169 777	355 073	183 000	172 073
15-19	373 045	192 812	180 233	367 107	189 623	177 483	357 073	184 244	172 829	349 123	179 944	169 178
20-24	338 588	174 290	164 298	370 281	191 227	179 054	364 638	188 195	176 443	354 882	182 984	171 898
25-29	308 492	158 431	150 061	335 275	172 309	162 965	367 067	189 285	177 782	361 684	186 443	175 240
30-34	315 613	161 697	153 916	304 853	156 173	148 681	331 614	170 041	161 573	363 307	186 973	176 334
35-39	301 024	153 672	147 351	311 436	159 049	152 387	300 919	153 695	147 224	327 499	167 469	160 030
40-44	259 002	132 298	126 705	296 416	150 756	145 660	306 875	156 160	150 715	296 588	150 968	145 620
45-49	216 668	111 266	105 402	253 906	129 089	124 817	291 066	147 389	143 677	301 577	152 815	148 762
50-54	193 983	98 796	95 186	210 528	107 405	103 123	247 367	124 987	122 381	284 132	143 034	141 098
55-59	148 153	74 638	73 514	185 991	93 797	92 194	202 314	102 237	100 077	238 481	119 403	119 077
60-64	114 217	56 447	57 770	138 557	68 755	69 802	174 721	86 815	87 906	190 628	94 952	95 675
65-69	94 470	45 714	48 756	102 494	49 506	52 988	125 352	60 834	64 518	158 961	77 267	81 694
70-74	71 660	33 638	38 021	79 450	37 167	42 284	87 144	40 740	46 404	107 701	50 623	57 078
75-79	46 410	20 671	25 739	54 621	24 434	30 187	61 407	27 398	34 008	68 336	30 504	37 832
80-84	24 448	9 958	14 491	30 423	12 650	17 772	36 563	15 276	21 287	41 856	17 459	24 397
85-89	9 981	3 610	6 370	12 872	4 695	8 177	16 510	6 159	10 351	20 377	7 626	12 751
90-94	2 996	928	2 068	4 003	1 219	2 783	5 395	1 636	3 759	7 175	2 231	4 945
95-99	603	151	452	880	212	667	1 235	285	950	1 758	395	1 363
100 +	76	16	60	123	23	100	193	32	161	290	44	245

Age group	2025 Both sexes	2025 Males	2025 Females	2030 Both sexes	2030 Males	2030 Females	2035 Both sexes	2035 Males	2035 Females	2040 Both sexes	2040 Males	2040 Females
All ages	4 728 131	2 390 814	2 337 317	4 872 472	2 458 372	2 414 101	4 991 992	2 513 197	2 478 795	5 091 829	2 558 300	2 533 529
0-4	347 167	178 791	168 376	332 969	171 247	161 721	325 749	167 505	158 243	325 162	167 193	157 969
5-9	358 232	184 548	173 685	344 588	177 427	167 161	330 804	170 095	160 709	323 891	166 509	157 381
10-14	361 927	186 481	175 446	357 217	183 970	173 248	343 705	176 921	166 783	330 034	169 655	160 379
15-19	353 788	182 259	171 529	360 735	185 791	174 944	356 115	183 330	172 785	342 687	176 333	166 354
20-24	347 136	178 800	168 336	351 947	181 195	170 752	359 008	184 795	174 213	354 501	182 408	172 094
25-29	352 229	181 425	170 804	344 772	177 416	167 356	349 791	179 938	169 852	357 024	183 649	173 375
30-34	358 190	184 324	173 867	349 144	179 573	169 571	342 080	175 812	166 269	347 384	178 513	168 870
35-39	359 053	184 329	174 724	354 357	181 974	172 383	345 789	177 535	168 254	339 162	174 053	165 109
40-44	323 042	164 680	158 362	354 594	181 552	173 042	350 378	179 517	170 861	342 290	175 395	166 898
45-49	291 677	147 880	143 707	318 129	161 601	156 528	349 701	178 491	171 210	345 959	176 771	169 188
50-54	294 782	148 536	146 246	285 475	143 976	141 499	311 896	157 675	154 222	343 392	174 518	168 875
55-59	274 625	137 060	137 574	285 606	142 070	142 000	270 941	135 576	135 366	303 187	152 156	151 030
60-64	225 672	111 418	114 254	260 830	128 433	132 397	271 910	134 143	137 767	264 291	130 623	133 668
65-69	174 151	84 915	89 237	207 378	100 282	107 097	240 876	116 255	124 621	252 063	121 988	130 075
70-74	137 529	64 757	72 772	151 562	71 667	79 896	181 921	85 371	96 550	212 724	99 704	113 020
75-79	85 622	38 437	47 185	110 286	49 603	60 683	122 554	55 425	67 129	148 632	66 733	81 899
80-84	47 449	19 806	27 643	60 518	25 398	35 120	78 731	33 092	45 639	88 460	37 433	51 027
85-89	23 850	8 910	14 940	27 681	10 363	17 319	36 145	13 600	22 545	47 480	17 875	29 605
90-94	9 126	2 835	6 290	10 951	3 406	7 545	13 088	4 089	8 999	17 530	5 506	12 024
95-99	2 435	560	1 875	3 195	733	2 462	3 931	908	3 023	4 844	1 128	3 716
100 +	437	62	375	637	91	546	879	123	756	1 129	158	971

Age group	2045 Both sexes	2045 Males	2045 Females	2050 Both sexes	2050 Males	2050 Females
All ages	5 168 280	2 592 141	2 576 139	5 217 202	2 612 844	2 604 358
0-4	320 981	165 026	155 955	311 407	160 087	151 321
5-9	323 538	166 312	157 226	319 566	164 252	155 314
10-14	323 204	166 116	157 088	322 918	165 954	156 963
15-19	329 089	169 111	159 977	322 315	165 607	156 707
20-24	341 182	175 482	165 700	327 682	168 326	159 356
25-29	352 688	181 371	171 317	339 547	174 560	164 988
30-34	354 853	182 368	172 485	350 764	180 242	170 523
35-39	344 771	176 945	167 826	352 498	180 959	171 539
40-44	336 082	172 181	163 902	341 978	175 256	166 722
45-49	338 352	172 958	165 394	332 544	170 005	162 538
50-54	340 132	173 108	167 023	333 054	169 639	163 415
55-59	334 406	168 814	165 592	331 693	167 754	163 939
60-64	290 110	143 910	146 200	320 722	160 152	160 570
65-69	245 674	119 195	126 478	270 656	131 919	138 738
70-74	223 797	105 284	118 514	218 970	103 361	115 609
75-79	175 427	78 717	96 710	185 971	83 846	102 124
80-84	108 756	45 669	63 087	130 026	54 586	75 440
85-89	54 109	20 561	33 548	67 719	25 515	42 204
90-94	23 064	7 253	15 811	26 644	8 509	18 135
95-99	6 629	1 558	5 071	8 567	2 034	6 532
100 +	1 437	202	1 235	1 963	282	1 681

POPULATION BY AGE AND SEX (in thousands)

Age group	2005 Both sexes	2005 Males	2005 Females	2010 Both sexes	2010 Males	2010 Females	2015 Both sexes	2015 Males	2015 Females	2020 Both sexes	2020 Males	2020 Females
All ages	3 905 415	1 989 639	1 915 776	4 168 227	2 120 156	2 048 071	4 453 009	2 261 527	2 191 482	4 737 350	2 402 138	2 335 212
0-4	356 879	183 988	172 891	398 423	205 404	193 018	431 193	222 291	208 902	443 456	228 526	214 931
5-9	360 222	185 996	174 227	351 948	181 529	170 419	393 840	203 081	190 759	427 062	220 156	206 906
10-14	368 884	190 620	178 264	358 641	185 133	173 508	350 522	180 745	169 777	392 477	202 321	190 156
15-19	373 045	192 812	180 233	367 107	189 623	177 483	357 073	184 244	172 829	349 123	179 944	169 178
20-24	338 588	174 290	164 298	370 281	191 227	179 054	364 638	188 195	176 443	354 882	182 984	171 898
25-29	308 492	158 431	150 061	335 275	172 309	162 965	367 067	189 285	177 782	361 684	186 443	175 240
30-34	315 613	161 697	153 916	304 853	156 173	148 681	331 614	170 041	161 573	363 307	186 973	176 334
35-39	301 024	153 672	147 351	311 436	159 049	152 387	300 919	153 695	147 224	327 499	167 470	160 030
40-44	259 002	132 298	126 705	296 416	150 756	145 660	306 875	156 160	150 715	296 588	150 968	145 620
45-49	216 668	111 266	105 402	253 906	129 089	124 817	291 066	147 389	143 677	301 577	152 815	148 762
50-54	193 983	98 796	95 186	210 528	107 405	103 123	247 367	124 987	122 381	284 132	143 034	141 098
55-59	148 153	74 638	73 514	185 991	93 797	92 194	202 314	102 237	100 077	238 481	119 403	119 077
60-64	114 217	56 447	57 770	138 557	68 755	69 802	174 721	86 815	87 906	190 628	94 952	95 675
65-69	94 470	45 714	48 756	102 494	49 506	52 988	125 352	60 834	64 518	158 961	77 267	81 694
70-74	71 660	33 638	38 021	79 450	37 167	42 284	87 144	40 740	46 404	107 701	50 623	57 078
75-79	46 410	20 671	25 739	54 621	24 434	30 187	61 407	27 398	34 008	68 336	30 504	37 832
80-84	24 448	9 958	14 491	30 423	12 650	17 772	36 563	15 276	21 287	41 856	17 459	24 397
85-89	9 981	3 610	6 370	12 872	4 695	8 177	16 510	6 159	10 351	20 377	7 626	12 751
90-94	2 996	928	2 068	4 003	1 219	2 783	5 395	1 636	3 759	7 175	2 231	4 945
95-99	603	151	452	880	212	667	1 235	285	950	1 758	395	1 363
100 +	76	16	60	123	23	100	193	32	161	290	44	245

Age group	2025 Both sexes	2025 Males	2025 Females	2030 Both sexes	2030 Males	2030 Females	2035 Both sexes	2035 Males	2035 Females	2040 Both sexes	2040 Males	2040 Females
All ages	4 994 396	2 528 142	2 466 254	5 230 880	2 643 061	2 587 819	5 464 680	2 756 616	2 708 064	5 704 887	2 873 851	2 831 036
0-4	430 622	221 797	208 825	425 948	219 086	206 862	441 032	226 823	214 208	466 811	240 080	226 731
5-9	439 853	226 638	213 215	427 571	220 179	207 392	423 331	217 688	205 643	438 691	225 563	213 129
10-14	425 782	219 434	206 348	438 681	225 967	212 714	426 549	219 592	206 958	422 427	217 169	205 259
15-19	391 121	201 537	189 584	424 481	218 676	205 805	437 459	225 252	212 207	425 423	218 935	206 488
20-24	347 136	178 800	168 336	389 181	200 409	188 772	422 604	217 584	205 020	435 680	224 223	211 457
25-29	352 229	181 425	170 805	344 772	177 416	167 356	386 883	199 064	187 819	420 411	216 309	204 102
30-34	358 190	184 324	173 867	349 144	179 573	169 571	342 080	175 812	166 269	384 296	197 531	186 764
35-39	359 053	184 329	174 724	354 358	181 974	172 384	345 789	177 535	168 254	339 162	174 053	165 109
40-44	323 042	164 680	158 362	354 594	181 552	173 043	350 378	179 518	170 861	342 293	175 395	166 898
45-49	291 677	147 880	143 797	318 129	161 601	156 528	349 701	178 491	171 210	345 959	176 771	169 188
50-54	294 782	148 536	146 246	285 476	143 976	141 499	311 896	157 675	154 222	343 393	174 518	168 875
55-59	274 635	137 060	137 574	285 506	142 676	142 830	276 942	138 576	138 366	303 187	152 156	151 031
60-64	225 672	111 418	114 254	260 830	128 433	132 397	271 910	134 143	137 767	264 291	130 624	133 668
65-69	174 151	84 915	89 237	207 378	100 282	107 097	240 876	116 255	124 621	252 063	121 988	130 075
70-74	137 529	64 757	72 772	151 562	71 667	79 896	181 922	85 371	96 550	212 724	99 704	113 020
75-79	85 622	38 437	47 185	110 286	49 603	60 683	122 554	55 425	67 129	148 632	66 733	81 899
80-84	47 449	19 806	27 643	60 518	25 398	35 120	78 731	33 092	45 639	88 460	37 433	51 027
85-89	23 850	8 910	14 940	27 681	10 363	17 319	36 145	13 600	22 545	47 480	17 875	29 605
90-94	9 126	2 835	6 290	10 951	3 406	7 545	13 088	4 089	8 999	17 530	5 506	12 024
95-99	2 435	560	1 875	3 195	733	2 462	3 931	908	3 023	4 844	1 128	3 716
100 +	437	62	375	637	91	546	879	123	756	1 129	158	971

Age group	2045 Both sexes	2045 Males	2045 Females	2050 Both sexes	2050 Males	2050 Females
All ages	5 940 910	2 989 657	2 951 253	6 160 528	3 097 998	3 062 530
0-4	482 150	247 937	234 213	484 007	248 852	235 155
5-9	464 683	238 919	225 764	480 245	246 888	233 357
10-14	437 863	225 085	212 778	463 915	238 471	225 445
15-19	421 373	216 557	204 816	436 854	224 501	212 353
20-24	423 767	217 988	205 779	419 816	215 676	204 140
25-29	433 639	223 046	210 593	421 933	216 944	204 989
30-34	417 976	214 871	203 104	431 436	221 753	209 683
35-39	381 482	195 844	185 638	415 328	213 291	202 037
40-44	336 083	172 181	163 902	378 464	194 020	184 444
45-49	338 352	172 958	165 394	332 544	170 006	162 538
50-54	340 132	173 109	167 023	333 054	169 639	163 415
55-59	334 407	168 814	165 593	331 693	167 754	163 940
60-64	290 110	143 910	146 200	320 722	160 152	160 570
65-69	245 674	119 196	126 478	270 657	131 919	138 738
70-74	223 797	105 284	118 514	218 970	103 361	115 609
75-79	175 428	78 717	96 710	185 971	83 846	102 124
80-84	108 756	45 669	63 087	130 026	54 586	75 440
85-89	54 109	20 561	33 548	67 720	25 515	42 205
90-94	23 064	7 253	15 811	26 644	8 509	18 135
95-99	6 629	1 558	5 071	8 567	2 034	6 532
100 +	1 437	202	1 235	1 963	282	1 681

United Nations Department of Economic and Social Affairs/Population Division
World Population Prospects: The 2004 Revision, Volume II: Sex and Age Distribution of the World Population

74

POPULATION BY AGE AND SEX (in thousands)

Age group	2005 Both sexes	Males	Females	2010 Both sexes	Males	Females	2015 Both sexes	Males	Females	2020 Both sexes	Males	Females
All ages	3 905 415	1 989 639	1 915 776	4 092 422	2 080 993	2 011 429	4 249 014	2 156 187	2 092 828	4 369 930	2 212 524	2 157 406
0-4	356 879	183 988	172 891	322 619	166 242	156 377	302 317	155 762	146 555	278 846	143 625	135 222
5-9	360 222	185 996	174 227	351 948	181 529	170 419	318 721	164 269	154 452	299 186	154 149	145 036
10-14	368 884	190 620	178 264	358 641	185 133	173 508	350 523	180 745	169 777	317 545	163 616	153 929
15-19	373 045	192 812	180 233	367 107	189 623	177 483	357 073	184 244	172 829	349 123	179 944	169 179
20-24	338 588	174 290	164 298	370 281	191 227	179 054	364 638	188 195	176 443	354 882	182 984	171 898
25-29	308 492	158 431	150 061	335 275	172 309	162 965	367 067	189 285	177 782	361 684	186 443	175 240
30-34	315 613	161 697	153 916	304 853	156 173	148 681	331 614	170 041	161 573	363 307	186 973	176 334
35-39	301 024	153 672	147 351	311 436	159 049	152 387	300 919	153 695	147 224	327 499	167 469	160 030
40-44	259 002	132 298	126 705	296 416	150 756	145 660	306 875	156 160	150 715	296 588	150 968	145 620
45-49	216 668	111 266	105 402	253 906	129 089	124 817	291 066	147 389	143 677	301 577	152 815	148 762
50-54	193 983	98 796	95 186	210 528	107 405	103 123	247 367	124 987	122 381	284 132	143 034	141 097
55-59	148 153	74 638	73 514	185 991	93 797	92 194	202 314	102 237	100 077	238 481	119 403	119 077
60-64	114 217	56 447	57 770	138 557	68 755	69 802	174 721	86 815	87 906	190 628	94 952	95 675
65-69	94 470	45 714	48 756	102 494	49 506	52 988	125 352	60 834	64 518	158 961	77 267	81 694
70-74	71 660	33 638	38 021	79 450	37 167	42 284	87 144	40 740	46 404	107 701	50 623	57 078
75-79	46 410	20 671	25 739	54 621	24 434	30 187	61 407	27 398	34 008	68 336	30 504	37 832
80-84	24 448	9 958	14 491	30 423	12 650	17 772	36 563	15 276	21 287	41 856	17 459	24 397
85-89	9 981	3 610	6 370	12 872	4 695	8 177	16 510	6 159	10 351	20 377	7 626	12 751
90-94	2 996	928	2 068	4 003	1 219	2 783	5 395	1 636	3 759	7 175	2 231	4 945
95-99	603	151	452	880	212	667	1 235	285	950	1 758	395	1 363
100 +	76	16	60	123	23	100	193	32	161	290	44	245

Age group	2025 Both sexes	Males	Females	2030 Both sexes	Males	Females	2035 Both sexes	Males	Females	2040 Both sexes	Males	Females
All ages	4 461 882	2 253 498	2 208 384	4 518 542	2 275 991	2 242 551	4 537 392	2 279 098	2 258 294	4 521 131	2 264 571	2 256 561
0-4	264 031	135 948	128 084	244 456	125 708	118 748	224 104	115 214	108 890	207 853	106 843	101 010
5-9	276 315	142 306	134 009	261 922	134 836	127 085	242 723	124 790	117 933	222 670	114 451	108 220
10-14	298 187	153 590	144 597	275 458	141 821	133 638	261 177	134 413	126 764	242 080	124 425	117 655
15-19	310 332	162 920	153 412	297 101	152 965	144 136	274 476	141 256	133 219	260 267	133 893	126 374
20-24	347 136	178 800	168 336	314 589	161 919	152 670	295 520	152 064	143 457	273 029	140 441	132 587
25-29	352 229	181 425	170 804	344 772	177 416	167 356	312 573	160 750	151 823	293 742	151 045	142 696
30-34	358 190	184 324	173 867	349 143	179 572	169 571	342 080	175 812	166 269	310 348	159 433	150 914
35-39	359 053	184 329	174 724	354 357	181 974	172 383	346 790	177 536	169 254	339 162	174 063	165 100
40-44	323 042	164 680	158 362	354 594	181 552	173 042	350 378	179 517	170 861	342 292	175 395	166 898
45-49	291 677	147 880	143 797	318 129	161 601	156 528	349 701	178 491	171 210	345 959	176 771	169 188
50-54	294 782	148 536	146 246	285 475	143 976	141 499	311 896	157 674	154 222	343 392	174 518	168 874
55-59	274 635	137 060	137 574	285 506	142 676	142 830	276 941	138 576	138 366	303 186	152 156	151 030
60-64	225 672	111 418	114 254	260 830	128 433	132 397	271 910	134 143	137 767	264 291	130 623	133 668
65-69	174 151	84 915	89 237	207 378	100 281	107 097	240 876	116 255	124 621	252 063	121 988	130 075
70-74	137 529	64 757	72 772	151 562	71 667	79 896	181 921	85 371	96 550	212 724	99 704	113 020
75-79	85 622	38 437	47 185	110 296	49 603	60 693	122 554	55 424	67 129	148 621	66 733	81 889
80-84	47 449	19 806	27 643	60 518	25 398	35 120	78 731	33 092	45 639	88 460	37 433	51 027
85-89	23 850	8 910	14 940	27 681	10 363	17 319	36 145	13 600	22 545	47 480	17 875	29 605
90-94	9 126	2 835	6 290	10 951	3 406	7 545	13 088	4 089	8 999	17 530	5 506	12 024
95-99	2 435	560	1 875	3 195	733	2 462	3 931	908	3 023	4 844	1 128	3 716
100 +	437	62	375	637	91	546	879	123	756	1 129	158	971

Age group	2045 Both sexes	Males	Females	2050 Both sexes	Males	Females
All ages	4 470 610	2 233 221	2 237 389	4 387 784	2 186 314	2 201 409
0-4	192 520	98 952	93 569	177 896	91 431	86 465
5-9	206 648	106 196	100 452	191 501	98 401	93 100
10-14	222 109	114 133	107 977	206 150	105 912	100 238
15-19	241 237	123 946	117 291	221 325	113 690	107 635
20-24	258 913	133 138	125 774	239 974	123 251	116 723
25-29	271 444	139 546	131 899	257 477	132 337	125 140
30-34	291 830	149 918	141 912	269 801	138 581	131 220
35-39	307 937	157 985	149 952	289 765	148 680	141 085
40-44	336 082	172 180	163 902	305 371	156 432	148 939
45-49	338 352	172 958	165 394	332 543	170 005	162 538
50-54	340 131	173 108	167 023	333 053	169 639	163 415
55-59	334 406	168 814	165 592	331 692	167 753	163 939
60-64	290 109	143 910	146 200	320 721	160 152	160 570
65-69	245 673	119 195	126 478	270 656	131 919	138 737
70-74	223 797	105 283	118 513	218 969	103 360	115 609
75-79	175 427	78 717	96 710	185 970	83 846	102 124
80-84	108 756	45 669	63 087	130 026	54 586	75 440
85-89	54 109	20 561	33 548	67 719	25 515	42 204
90-94	23 064	7 253	15 811	26 644	8 509	18 135
95-99	6 629	1 558	5 071	8 567	2 034	6 532
100 +	1 437	202	1 235	1 963	282	1 681

POPULATION BY AGE AND SEX (in thousands)

Age group	1950 Both sexes	1950 Males	1950 Females	1955 Both sexes	1955 Males	1955 Females	1960 Both sexes	1960 Males	1960 Females	1965 Both sexes	1965 Males	1965 Females
All ages	670 985	345 682	325 303	734 105	376 351	357 754	792 228	404 993	387 235	874 284	446 877	427 407
0-4	92 075	48 399	43 676	114 935	58 666	56 269	108 344	55 381	52 964	127 730	65 641	62 090
5-9	70 683	36 876	33 807	85 618	44 973	40 645	107 995	55 218	52 778	103 410	53 120	50 289
10-14	66 167	35 237	30 930	69 231	36 210	33 022	84 195	44 159	40 036	106 297	54 481	51 816
15-19	66 296	34 997	31 298	65 041	34 596	30 445	67 892	35 560	32 332	83 024	43 471	39 553
20-24	57 621	30 178	27 443	64 259	33 852	30 407	63 456	33 627	29 829	66 482	34 778	31 705
25-29	52 012	26 863	25 149	55 636	29 095	26 540	62 163	32 698	29 465	62 312	32 981	29 331
30-34	46 902	24 201	22 701	49 853	25 695	24 158	53 926	28 223	25 703	60 476	31 820	28 656
35-39	42 705	21 965	20 740	44 329	22 759	21 570	47 865	24 602	23 264	52 473	27 433	25 041
40-44	38 538	19 731	18 807	39 870	20 317	19 553	41 956	21 397	20 559	46 032	23 574	22 458
45-49	34 643	17 792	16 851	35 351	17 755	17 596	37 198	18 732	18 466	39 681	20 062	19 619
50-54	28 349	14 639	13 710	30 733	15 284	15 449	32 199	15 860	16 339	34 536	17 189	17 347
55-59	25 234	12 671	12 563	23 807	11 742	12 064	26 964	12 956	14 007	28 975	13 961	15 014
60-64	19 783	9 554	10 229	21 317	10 474	10 843	19 514	9 183	10 331	23 051	10 700	12 351
65-69	14 873	6 715	8 158	15 610	7 325	8 284	17 228	8 261	8 967	15 338	6 850	8 488
70-74	8 660	3 598	5 062	10 636	4 638	5 999	11 476	5 213	6 264	12 960	6 030	6 930
75-79	4 433	1 639	2 795	5 345	2 123	3 222	6 694	2 796	3 899	7 449	3 250	4 198
80 +	2 009	625	1 385	2 533	845	1 688	3 160	1 128	2 032	4 056	1 536	2 520

Age group	1970 Both sexes	1970 Males	1970 Females	1975 Both sexes	1975 Males	1975 Females	1980 Both sexes	1980 Males	1980 Females	1985 Both sexes	1985 Males	1985 Females
All ages	986 777	504 673	482 103	1 096 726	561 731	534 995	1 177 958	603 729	574 229	1 257 927	644 518	613 408
0-4	148 646	76 450	72 196	143 639	73 852	69 787	115 060	59 336	55 725	115 159	59 700	55 459
5-9	125 067	64 501	60 565	146 980	75 958	71 022	141 605	73 006	68 599	113 478	58 557	54 921
10-14	102 543	52 852	49 690	124 342	64 302	60 040	146 475	75 633	70 842	141 549	72 940	68 609
15-19	105 064	53 906	51 158	101 991	52 734	49 256	123 661	63 866	59 796	146 137	75 423	70 714
20-24	82 143	42 857	39 285	104 067	53 442	50 625	101 171	52 491	48 680	122 728	63 322	59 406
25-29	65 658	34 384	31 274	81 466	42 466	39 000	103 353	53 209	50 143	100 600	52 096	48 503
30-34	61 699	32 624	29 076	65 133	34 179	30 954	81 159	42 248	38 911	102 698	52 838	49 859
35-39	59 367	31 212	28 156	61 179	32 306	28 873	64 817	34 014	30 802	80 755	42 009	38 747
40-44	51 428	26 869	24 559	58 266	30 591	27 675	60 867	32 114	28 753	64 066	33 540	30 526
45-49	44 678	22 791	21 887	50 367	26 239	24 128	57 049	29 910	27 139	59 678	31 316	28 362
50-54	37 738	18 905	18 833	43 007	21 808	21 199	49 032	25 469	23 563	55 404	28 845	26 559
55-59	31 980	15 700	16 280	35 438	17 548	17 890	40 848	20 524	20 324	46 849	24 123	22 726
60-64	25 826	12 129	13 698	29 085	14 018	15 067	32 330	15 754	16 576	37 862	18 700	19 161
65-69	19 294	8 586	10 709	22 211	10 109	12 102	25 173	11 831	13 343	28 511	13 477	15 035
70-74	11 573	4 863	6 710	15 171	6 425	8 746	18 216	7 886	10 330	20 586	9 254	11 332
75-79	8 928	4 001	4 927	7 857	3 078	4 779	10 925	4 310	6 615	13 163	5 351	7 812
80 +	5 144	2 043	3 101	6 529	2 677	3 851	6 216	2 128	4 088	8 705	3 028	5 677

Age group	1990 Both sexes	1990 Males	1990 Females	1995 Both sexes	1995 Males	1995 Females	2000 Both sexes	2000 Males	2000 Females	2005 Both sexes	2005 Males	2005 Females
All ages	1 349 695	692 302	657 392	1 419 717	727 502	692 215	1 479 233	756 549	722 683	1 524 380	778 496	745 884
0-4	131 505	68 993	62 512	115 425	60 771	54 653	107 175	56 344	50 831	95 070	49 968	45 103
5-9	115 431	60 030	55 401	130 415	68 434	61 982	114 665	60 344	54 321	106 624	56 042	50 582
10-14	114 290	59 070	55 220	115 015	59 770	55 244	130 057	68 203	61 853	114 414	60 190	54 225
15-19	140 043	71 994	68 050	113 758	58 739	55 019	114 586	59 489	55 097	129 663	67 948	61 715
20-24	144 511	73 948	70 563	139 064	71 360	67 704	113 017	58 249	54 768	113 936	59 059	54 877
25-29	121 493	62 385	59 108	143 426	73 250	70 176	138 005	70 666	67 338	112 171	57 691	54 481
30-34	100 031	52 020	48 011	120 588	61 803	58 785	142 301	72 518	69 783	136 995	70 003	66 993
35-39	101 970	52 602	49 368	99 083	51 414	47 669	119 532	61 116	58 416	141 197	71 801	69 396
40-44	80 047	41 700	38 347	100 720	51 815	48 905	97 973	50 691	47 282	118 369	60 370	57 999
45-49	62 976	32 897	30 079	78 795	40 891	37 904	99 142	50 804	48 339	96 600	49 816	46 784
50-54	58 187	30 451	27 736	61 383	31 870	29 513	76 902	39 667	37 235	97 038	49 480	47 559
55-59	53 007	27 436	25 571	55 790	28 885	26 905	59 020	30 317	28 702	74 300	37 991	36 309
60-64	43 376	21 998	21 379	49 424	25 103	24 320	52 249	26 559	25 690	55 692	28 160	27 532
65-69	33 491	16 078	17 413	38 721	19 028	19 694	44 386	21 858	22 528	47 418	23 476	23 942
70-74	23 278	10 532	12 746	27 730	12 611	15 119	32 436	15 159	17 277	37 814	17 852	19 962
75-79	14 817	6 232	8 584	17 094	7 141	9 953	20 827	8 764	12 063	25 064	11 000	14 064
80 +	11 242	3 938	7 303	13 286	4 617	8 668	16 959	5 800	11 159	22 013	7 650	14 363

United Nations Department of Economic and Social Affairs/Population Division
World Population Prospects: The 2004 Revision, Volume II: Sex and Age Distribution of the World Population

76

POPULATION BY AGE AND SEX (in thousands)

Age group	2005 Both sexes	Males	Females	2010 Both sexes	Males	Females	2015 Both sexes	Males	Females	2020 Both sexes	Males	Females
All ages	1 524 390	778 406	746 984	1 566 168	709 043	767 126	1 604 611	816 484	788 126	1 635 403	830 122	805 361
0-4	95 070	49 968	45 103	95 053	49 918	45 136	99 576	52 257	47 319	97 699	51 233	46 466
5-9	106 624	56 042	50 582	94 682	49 754	44 929	94 709	49 722	44 987	99 259	52 069	47 189
10-14	114 414	60 190	54 225	106 443	55 929	50 514	94 538	49 665	44 874	94 571	49 638	44 934
15-19	129 663	67 948	61 715	114 132	60 008	54 124	106 206	55 776	50 430	94 349	49 542	44 807
20-24	113 936	59 059	54 877	129 073	67 564	61 510	113 616	59 670	53 945	105 764	55 487	50 276
25-29	112 171	57 691	54 481	113 188	58 566	54 622	128 196	66 978	61 217	112 812	59 137	53 675
30-34	136 995	70 003	66 993	111 359	57 149	54 210	112 260	57 941	54 319	127 027	66 194	60 833
35-39	141 197	71 801	69 396	135 955	69 315	66 640	110 385	56 496	53 889	111 133	57 184	53 949
40-44	118 369	60 370	57 999	139 899	70 962	68 936	134 633	68 445	66 189	109 191	55 701	53 490
45-49	96 600	49 816	46 784	116 856	59 411	57 444	138 127	69 831	68 297	132 883	67 312	65 571
50-54	97 038	49 480	47 559	94 685	48 600	46 085	114 673	58 031	56 641	135 596	68 228	67 368
55-59	74 300	37 991	36 309	93 955	47 515	46 439	91 830	46 762	45 068	111 407	55 947	55 460
60-64	55 692	28 160	27 532	70 419	35 489	34 930	89 264	44 513	44 751	87 463	43 943	43 520
65-69	47 418	23 476	23 942	50 921	25 126	25 795	64 753	31 888	32 865	82 350	40 154	42 195
70-74	37 814	17 852	19 962	40 807	19 426	21 381	44 287	21 052	23 236	56 759	26 980	29 779
75-79	25 064	11 000	14 064	29 700	13 219	16 481	32 484	14 607	17 877	35 773	16 101	19 672
80-84	13 866	5 284	8 583	17 126	6 866	10 260	20 706	8 435	12 271	23 060	9 520	13 539
85-89	5 850	1 848	4 003	7 704	2 505	5 199	9 861	3 394	6 466	12 239	4 289	7 950
90-94	1 847	449	1 399	2 526	614	1 912	3 499	870	2 629	4 665	1 246	3 420
95-99	398	65	333	599	99	500	863	139	724	1 268	207	1 060
100 +	51	5	46	88	8	79	145	14	132	225	20	205

Age group	2025 Both sexes	Males	Females	2030 Both sexes	Males	Females	2035 Both sexes	Males	Females	2040 Both sexes	Males	Females
All ages	1 651 971	836 063	815 908	1 655 077	834 957	820 120	1 648 856	829 367	819 489	1 635 952	820 839	815 113
0-4	90 557	47 454	43 102	84 495	44 084	40 411	82 681	43 125	39 557	83 481	43 533	39 948
5-9	97 420	51 064	46 356	90 325	47 313	43 011	84 303	43 967	40 336	82 516	43 024	39 492
10-14	99 109	51 980	47 129	97 273	50 978	46 295	90 198	47 239	42 959	84 199	43 906	40 293
15-19	94 397	49 526	44 871	98 938	51 871	47 067	97 113	50 876	46 237	90 055	47 148	42 907
20-24	93 968	49 296	44 672	94 045	49 300	44 745	98 599	51 654	46 945	96 794	50 672	46 122
25-29	105 040	55 015	50 025	93 366	48 908	44 457	93 503	48 954	44 549	98 091	51 331	46 760
30-34	111 736	58 430	53 306	104 120	54 423	49 697	92 637	48 445	44 192	92 868	48 553	44 315
35-39	125 643	65 276	60 367	110 579	57 678	52 901	103 171	53 817	49 354	91 900	47 979	43 921
40-44	109 047	56 033	53 014	124 228	64 051	59 077	109 457	56 950	52 504	102 256	53 200	49 020
45-49	107 734	54 755	52 979	108 441	55 424	53 017	122 752	63 404	59 348	108 284	56 205	52 079
50-54	130 503	65 796	64 707	105 891	53 581	52 310	106 728	54 336	52 392	120 941	62 255	58 685
55-59	131 878	65 863	66 014	127 116	63 639	63 477	103 306	51 935	51 370	104 323	52 805	51 517
60-64	106 411	52 753	53 658	126 232	62 275	63 958	121 990	60 380	61 611	99 374	49 433	49 940
65-69	81 003	39 834	41 169	98 979	48 080	50 899	117 815	57 012	60 803	114 295	55 561	58 734
70-74	72 472	34 139	38 333	71 728	34 133	37 595	88 205	41 538	46 667	105 504	49 556	55 948
75-79	46 326	20 896	25 430	59 436	26 603	32 832	59 360	26 899	32 461	73 572	33 053	40 519
80-84	26 885	10 718	16 168	33 070	14 106	18 897	40 766	10 100	25 658	44 255	18 577	25 670
85-89	13 957	4 965	8 992	16 068	5 758	10 310	21 441	7 775	13 666	27 636	10 000	17 637
90-94	5 965	1 623	4 341	6 993	1 943	5 049	8 295	2 345	5 950	11 246	3 249	7 997
95-99	1 768	316	1 452	2 332	428	1 905	2 812	532	2 280	3 442	671	2 771
100 +	351	31	320	519	50	469	722	72	650	921	94	827

Age group	2045 Both sexes	Males	Females	2050 Both sexes	Males	Females
All ages	1 615 599	809 164	806 435	1 586 704	793 912	792 792
0-4	82 640	43 090	39 551	79 111	41 245	37 866
5-9	83 333	43 445	39 888	82 510	43 012	39 498
10-14	82 428	42 972	39 456	83 262	43 399	39 862
15-19	84 070	43 824	40 246	82 308	42 896	39 413
20-24	89 763	46 962	42 801	83 798	43 651	40 146
25-29	96 332	50 379	45 953	89 350	46 700	42 650
30-34	97 513	50 967	46 546	95 826	50 060	45 766
35-39	92 231	48 152	44 079	96 938	50 606	46 332
40-44	91 182	47 524	43 658	91 602	47 755	43 847
45-49	101 276	52 612	48 664	90 392	47 025	43 367
50-54	106 806	55 269	51 537	100 004	51 808	48 196
55-59	118 347	60 602	57 745	104 648	53 891	50 757
60-64	100 635	50 455	50 180	114 318	58 026	56 292
65-69	93 422	45 698	47 725	94 986	46 900	48 086
70-74	102 926	48 642	54 284	84 551	40 272	44 279
75-79	88 649	39 784	48 864	87 202	39 453	47 748
80-84	55 398	23 087	32 310	67 434	28 143	39 291
85-89	28 417	10 471	17 945	36 015	13 231	22 785
90-94	14 341	4 151	10 189	15 019	4 462	10 557
95-99	4 723	955	3 768	5 840	1 197	4 642
100 +	1 169	124	1 045	1 591	180	1 411

United Nations Department of Economic and Social Affairs/Population Division
World Population Prospects: The 2004 Revision, Volume II: Sex and Age Distribution of the World Population

77

POPULATION BY AGE AND SEX (in thousands)

Age group	2005			2010			2015			2020		
	Both sexes	Males	Females	Both sexes	Males	Females	Both sexes	Males	Females	Both sexes	Males	Females
All ages	1 524 380	778 496	745 884	1 579 159	805 386	773 773	1 641 023	835 587	805 436	1 698 715	863 283	835 432
0-4	95 070	49 968	45 103	109 044	57 261	51 783	122 043	64 042	58 001	124 592	65 330	59 262
5-9	106 624	56 042	50 582	94 682	49 754	44 929	108 654	57 040	51 615	121 661	63 816	57 845
10-14	114 414	60 190	54 225	106 443	55 929	50 514	94 538	49 665	44 874	108 498	56 944	51 554
15-19	129 663	67 948	61 715	114 132	60 008	54 124	106 206	55 776	50 430	94 349	49 542	44 807
20-24	113 936	59 059	54 877	129 073	67 564	61 510	113 616	59 670	53 945	105 764	55 487	50 276
25-29	112 171	57 691	54 481	113 188	58 566	54 622	128 196	66 978	61 217	112 812	59 137	53 675
30-34	136 995	70 003	66 993	111 359	57 149	54 210	112 260	57 941	54 319	127 027	66 194	60 833
35-39	141 197	71 801	69 396	135 955	69 315	66 640	110 385	56 496	53 889	111 133	57 184	53 949
40-44	118 369	60 370	57 999	139 899	70 962	68 936	134 633	68 445	66 189	109 191	55 701	53 490
45-49	96 600	49 816	46 784	116 856	59 411	57 444	138 127	69 831	68 297	132 883	67 312	65 571
50-54	97 038	49 480	47 559	94 685	48 600	46 085	114 673	58 031	56 641	135 596	68 228	67 368
55-59	74 300	37 991	36 309	93 955	47 515	46 439	91 830	46 762	45 068	111 407	55 947	55 460
60-64	55 692	28 160	27 532	70 419	35 489	34 930	89 264	44 513	44 751	87 463	43 943	43 520
65-69	47 418	23 476	23 942	50 921	25 126	25 795	64 753	31 888	32 865	82 350	40 154	42 195
70-74	37 814	17 852	19 962	40 807	19 426	21 381	44 287	21 052	23 236	56 759	26 980	29 779
75-79	25 064	11 000	14 064	29 700	13 219	16 481	32 484	14 607	17 877	35 773	16 101	19 672
80-84	13 866	5 284	8 583	17 126	6 866	10 260	20 706	8 435	12 272	23 060	9 520	13 539
85-89	5 850	1 848	4 003	7 704	2 505	5 199	9 861	3 394	6 466	12 239	4 289	7 950
90-94	1 847	449	1 399	2 526	614	1 912	3 499	870	2 629	4 665	1 246	3 420
95-99	398	65	333	599	99	500	863	139	724	1 268	207	1 060
100 +	51	5	46	88	8	79	145	14	132	225	20	205

Age group	2025			2030			2035			2040		
	Both sexes	Males	Females	Both sexes	Males	Females	Both sexes	Males	Females	Both sexes	Males	Females
All ages	1 740 039	882 219	857 820	1 769 409	894 802	874 608	1 796 748	906 699	890 050	1 826 229	920 247	905 982
0-4	115 520	60 532	54 988	110 906	57 863	53 042	116 439	60 734	55 705	126 150	65 787	60 363
5-9	124 243	65 118	59 124	115 231	60 356	54 875	110 661	57 714	52 947	116 215	60 597	55 618
10-14	121 481	63 708	57 772	124 059	65 011	59 048	115 073	60 263	54 810	110 528	57 636	52 892
15-19	108 307	56 821	51 486	121 284	63 583	57 701	123 871	64 891	58 980	114 906	60 157	54 749
20-24	93 968	49 296	44 672	107 927	56 577	51 350	120 906	63 342	57 565	123 511	64 661	58 850
25-29	105 040	55 015	50 025	93 366	48 908	44 457	107 338	56 201	51 137	120 333	62 977	57 355
30-34	111 736	58 430	53 307	104 120	54 423	49 697	92 637	48 445	44 192	106 637	55 759	50 877
35-39	125 643	65 276	60 367	110 579	57 678	52 901	103 172	53 817	49 355	91 900	47 979	43 921
40-44	109 847	56 333	53 514	124 228	64 351	59 877	109 457	56 953	52 504	102 256	53 233	49 023
45-49	107 734	54 755	52 979	108 441	55 424	53 017	122 752	63 404	59 348	108 284	56 205	52 079
50-54	130 504	65 796	64 707	105 891	53 582	52 310	106 728	54 336	52 392	120 941	62 256	58 685
55-59	131 878	65 863	66 014	127 116	63 639	63 477	103 306	51 936	51 370	104 323	52 806	51 517
60-64	106 411	52 753	53 658	126 233	62 275	63 958	121 990	60 380	61 611	99 374	49 433	49 940
65-69	81 003	39 834	41 169	98 979	48 080	50 899	117 815	57 012	60 803	114 295	55 561	58 734
70-74	72 472	34 139	38 333	71 728	34 133	37 595	88 205	41 538	46 667	105 505	49 556	55 948
75-79	46 326	20 896	25 430	59 436	26 603	32 832	59 360	26 899	32 461	73 572	33 053	40 520
80-84	25 885	10 718	15 168	33 973	14 136	19 837	43 766	18 108	25 658	44 255	18 577	25 679
85-89	13 957	4 965	8 992	16 068	5 758	10 310	21 441	7 775	13 666	27 636	10 000	17 637
90-94	5 965	1 623	4 341	6 993	1 943	5 049	8 295	2 345	5 950	11 246	3 249	7 997
95-99	1 768	316	1 452	2 332	428	1 905	2 812	532	2 280	3 442	671	2 771
100 +	351	31	320	519	50	469	722	72	650	921	94	827

Age group	2045			2050		
	Both sexes	Males	Females	Both sexes	Males	Females
All ages	1 853 309	933 267	920 041	1 872 926	943 259	929 666
0-4	130 455	68 021	62 434	128 095	66 782	61 313
5-9	125 938	65 659	60 279	130 263	67 906	62 356
10-14	116 096	60 527	55 568	125 835	65 594	60 241
15-19	110 377	57 540	52 837	115 950	60 435	55 515
20-24	114 579	59 949	54 630	110 071	57 346	52 725
25-29	122 981	64 325	58 656	114 112	59 653	54 459
30-34	119 666	62 558	57 107	122 386	63 951	58 435
35-39	105 927	55 313	50 614	118 991	62 136	56 855
40-44	91 182	47 524	43 658	105 219	54 866	50 352
45-49	101 276	52 612	48 664	90 392	47 025	43 367
50-54	106 806	55 269	51 537	100 005	51 809	48 196
55-59	118 347	60 602	57 745	104 649	53 891	50 757
60-64	100 635	50 455	50 180	114 319	58 026	56 292
65-69	93 423	45 698	47 725	94 986	46 900	48 086
70-74	102 926	48 642	54 284	84 551	40 272	44 279
75-79	88 649	39 784	48 864	87 202	39 453	47 749
80-84	55 398	23 087	32 310	67 434	28 143	39 291
85-89	28 417	10 471	17 945	36 015	13 231	22 785
90-94	14 341	4 151	10 189	15 019	4 462	10 557
95-99	4 723	955	3 768	5 840	1 197	4 642
100 +	1 169	124	1 045	1 591	180	1 411

United Nations Department of Economic and Social Affairs/Population Division
World Population Prospects: The 2004 Revision, Volume II: Sex and Age Distribution of the World Population

POPULATION BY AGE AND SEX (in thousands)

Age group	2005 Both sexes	Males	Females	2010 Both sexes	Males	Females	2015 Both sexes	Males	Females	2020 Both sexes	Males	Females
All ages	1 524 380	778 406	745 004	1 551 102	790 631	760 471	1 568 145	797 354	770 791	1 572 172	796 931	775 241
0-4	95 070	49 968	45 103	81 047	42 566	38 481	77 071	40 452	36 619	70 761	37 112	33 649
5-9	106 624	56 042	50 582	94 683	49 754	44 929	80 748	42 397	38 352	76 819	40 303	36 516
10-14	114 414	60 190	54 225	106 443	55 929	50 514	94 538	49 665	44 874	80 629	42 323	38 305
15-19	129 663	67 948	61 715	114 132	60 008	54 124	106 206	55 776	50 430	94 349	49 542	44 807
20-24	113 936	59 059	54 877	129 073	67 564	61 510	113 616	59 670	53 945	105 764	55 487	50 276
25-29	112 171	57 691	54 481	113 188	58 566	54 622	128 196	66 978	61 217	112 812	59 137	53 675
30-34	136 995	70 003	66 993	111 359	57 149	54 210	112 260	57 941	54 319	127 026	66 194	60 833
35-39	141 197	71 801	69 396	135 955	69 315	66 640	110 385	56 496	53 889	111 133	57 184	53 949
40-44	118 369	60 370	57 999	139 899	70 962	68 936	134 633	68 445	66 189	109 191	55 701	53 490
45-49	96 600	49 816	46 784	116 856	59 411	57 444	138 127	69 831	68 296	132 883	67 312	65 571
50-54	97 038	49 480	47 559	94 685	48 600	46 085	114 673	58 031	56 641	135 596	68 228	67 368
55-59	74 300	37 991	36 309	93 955	47 515	46 439	91 830	46 762	45 068	111 407	55 947	55 460
60-64	55 692	28 160	27 532	70 419	35 489	34 930	89 264	44 513	44 751	87 463	43 943	43 520
65-69	47 418	23 476	23 942	50 921	25 126	25 795	64 753	31 888	32 865	82 350	40 154	42 195
70-74	37 814	17 852	19 962	40 807	19 426	21 381	44 287	21 052	23 236	56 759	26 980	29 779
75-79	25 064	11 000	14 064	29 700	13 219	16 481	32 484	14 607	17 877	35 773	16 101	19 672
80-84	13 866	5 284	8 583	17 126	6 866	10 260	20 706	8 435	12 271	23 060	9 520	13 539
85-89	5 850	1 848	4 003	7 704	2 505	5 199	9 861	3 394	6 466	12 239	4 289	7 950
90-94	1 847	449	1 399	2 526	614	1 912	3 499	870	2 629	4 665	1 246	3 420
95-99	398	65	333	599	99	500	863	139	724	1 268	207	1 060
100 +	51	5	46	88	8	79	145	14	132	225	20	205

Age group	2025 Both sexes	Males	Females	2030 Both sexes	Males	Females	2035 Both sexes	Males	Females	2040 Both sexes	Males	Females
All ages	1 563 822	789 865	773 956	1 542 070	775 805	766 265	1 507 142	755 260	751 881	1 460 492	729 160	731 332
0-4	65 611	34 387	31 225	59 492	31 040	28 451	53 779	28 048	25 731	49 461	25 790	23 671
5-9	70 551	36 986	33 565	65 436	34 280	31 156	59 350	30 954	28 396	53 664	27 978	25 685
10-14	76 701	40 232	36 468	70 441	36 921	33 520	65 341	34 225	31 117	59 273	30 909	28 364
15-19	80 471	42 222	38 249	76 555	40 190	36 116	70 060	35 587	34 472	65 222	34 148	31 074
20-24	93 968	49 296	44 672	80 146	42 013	38 133	76 255	39 947	36 307	70 033	36 660	33 372
25-29	105 039	55 015	50 025	93 366	48 908	44 457	79 651	41 698	37 954	75 812	39 666	36 146
30-34	111 736	58 430	53 306	104 120	54 423	49 697	92 636	48 445	44 191	79 082	41 338	37 744
35-39	125 643	65 276	60 367	110 579	57 677	52 901	103 171	53 817	49 354	91 900	47 979	43 921
40-44	109 047	55 533	53 514	124 227	64 351	59 877	109 457	56 953	52 504	102 256	53 233	49 023
45-49	107 734	54 755	52 979	108 440	55 424	53 016	122 752	63 404	59 348	108 284	56 205	52 079
50-54	130 503	65 796	64 707	105 891	53 581	52 309	106 728	54 336	52 392	120 940	62 255	58 685
55-59	131 878	65 863	66 014	127 116	63 639	63 477	102 206	51 035	51 070	104 022	52 005	51 517
60-64	106 411	52 753	53 658	126 232	62 275	63 958	121 990	60 379	61 610	99 373	49 433	49 940
65-69	81 003	39 834	41 169	98 979	48 080	50 899	117 815	57 012	60 803	114 295	55 561	58 734
70-74	72 472	34 139	38 333	71 728	34 133	37 595	88 205	41 538	46 667	105 504	49 556	55 948
75-79	46 326	20 896	25 430	59 436	26 603	32 832	59 360	26 899	32 461	73 572	33 053	40 519
80-84	25 885	10 718	15 168	33 973	14 136	19 837	43 766	18 108	25 658	44 255	18 577	25 679
85-89	13 957	4 965	8 992	16 068	5 758	10 310	21 441	7 775	13 666	27 636	10 000	17 637
90-94	5 965	1 623	4 341	6 993	1 943	5 049	8 295	2 345	5 950	11 246	3 249	7 997
95-99	1 768	316	1 452	2 332	428	1 905	2 812	532	2 280	3 442	671	2 771
100 +	351	31	320	519	50	469	722	72	650	921	94	827

Age group	2045 Both sexes	Males	Females	2050 Both sexes	Males	Females
All ages	1 403 628	698 483	705 145	1 338 194	664 226	673 967
0-4	45 766	23 862	21 904	42 124	21 962	20 162
5-9	49 364	25 733	23 631	45 684	23 813	21 870
10-14	53 603	27 942	25 660	49 318	25 703	23 614
15-19	59 166	30 840	28 325	53 506	27 880	25 626
20-24	64 964	33 984	30 980	58 925	30 687	28 237
25-29	69 637	36 409	33 228	64 605	33 756	30 849
30-34	75 323	39 357	35 966	69 220	36 145	33 075
35-39	78 520	40 984	37 536	74 847	39 057	35 790
40-44	91 182	47 524	43 658	77 969	40 636	37 333
45-49	101 275	52 611	48 664	90 391	47 024	43 367
50-54	106 805	55 268	51 537	100 004	51 808	48 196
55-59	118 346	60 602	57 744	104 648	53 891	50 757
60-64	100 635	50 455	50 180	114 318	58 026	56 292
65-69	93 422	45 697	47 725	94 985	46 899	48 086
70-74	102 926	48 642	54 284	84 550	40 272	44 279
75-79	88 648	39 784	48 864	87 202	39 453	47 748
80-84	55 397	23 087	32 310	67 434	28 143	39 291
85-89	28 416	10 471	17 945	36 015	13 231	22 785
90-94	14 341	4 151	10 189	15 019	4 462	10 557
95-99	4 723	955	3 768	5 840	1 197	4 642
100 +	1 169	124	1 045	1 591	180	1 411

United Nations Department of Economic and Social Affairs/Population Division
World Population Prospects: The 2004 Revision, Volume II: Sex and Age Distribution of the World Population

79

POPULATION BY AGE AND SEX (in thousands)

Age group	1950 Both sexes	Males	Females	1955 Both sexes	Males	Females	1960 Both sexes	Males	Females	1965 Both sexes	Males	Females
All ages	496 092	254 995	241 097	549 611	282 995	266 616	616 999	318 136	298 863	693 602	357 800	335 802
0-4	75 500	38 167	37 333	88 036	45 296	42 740	101 279	52 215	49 064	112 978	58 189	54 790
5-9	60 382	30 430	29 952	67 546	34 460	33 086	80 346	41 711	38 635	93 467	48 554	44 914
10-14	55 586	28 121	27 465	58 912	29 788	29 124	66 206	33 878	32 328	78 818	41 015	37 804
15-19	50 233	25 724	24 509	54 548	27 661	26 887	57 978	29 381	28 597	65 052	33 360	31 692
20-24	44 774	23 085	21 690	48 906	25 071	23 835	53 343	27 082	26 262	56 506	28 678	27 828
25-29	37 994	19 764	18 230	43 280	22 341	20 938	47 514	24 395	23 120	51 740	26 296	25 445
30-34	32 793	17 155	15 638	36 576	19 076	17 500	41 906	21 683	20 223	45 991	23 647	22 344
35-39	29 260	15 466	13 794	31 402	16 461	14 941	35 238	18 409	16 829	40 432	20 935	19 497
40-44	25 539	13 612	11 927	27 839	14 702	13 137	30 057	15 747	14 310	33 801	17 638	16 163
45-49	21 093	11 269	9 825	24 066	12 765	11 301	26 411	13 884	12 527	28 591	14 914	13 678
50-54	17 872	9 376	8 497	19 570	10 377	9 193	22 482	11 839	10 643	24 759	12 918	11 841
55-59	14 699	7 894	6 805	16 108	8 365	7 743	17 815	9 353	8 462	20 558	10 717	9 842
60-64	11 913	6 232	5 680	12 612	6 708	5 903	14 014	7 199	6 815	15 629	8 112	7 518
65-69	8 235	3 737	4 498	9 453	4 903	4 550	10 195	5 371	4 824	11 475	5 826	5 649
70-74	5 667	2 746	2 921	5 787	2 609	3 178	6 815	3 502	3 313	7 470	3 894	3 576
75-79	3 029	1 460	1 569	3 279	1 586	1 693	3 479	1 557	1 922	4 186	2 126	2 061
80 +	1 522	757	765	1 692	826	866	1 920	929	991	2 147	984	1 162

Age group	1970 Both sexes	Males	Females	1975 Both sexes	Males	Females	1980 Both sexes	Males	Females	1985 Both sexes	Males	Females
All ages	780 020	402 355	377 665	876 102	452 240	423 862	978 034	504 609	473 425	1 096 754	565 132	531 623
0-4	124 077	63 875	60 202	135 464	69 870	65 595	143 928	74 043	69 885	163 574	83 999	79 574
5-9	105 337	54 616	50 721	116 683	60 494	56 189	128 238	66 490	61 748	136 601	70 641	65 960
10-14	91 888	47 829	44 059	103 658	53 858	49 800	114 949	59 685	55 265	126 097	65 444	60 653
15-19	77 586	40 443	37 143	90 508	47 183	43 324	102 108	53 115	48 993	113 476	58 975	54 502
20-24	63 573	32 639	30 934	75 965	39 578	36 387	88 733	46 276	42 457	100 819	52 518	48 301
25-29	54 962	27 919	27 044	61 771	31 675	30 096	74 221	38 694	35 527	87 446	45 671	41 775
30-34	50 245	25 564	24 682	53 249	27 056	26 193	60 337	30 975	29 363	72 857	38 024	34 833
35-39	44 518	22 904	21 613	48 698	24 814	23 883	51 614	26 245	25 369	58 973	30 267	28 706
40-44	38 935	20 136	18 799	43 112	22 230	20 882	47 115	23 980	23 135	50 131	25 448	24 682
45-49	32 285	16 779	15 506	37 547	19 430	18 117	41 389	21 270	20 118	45 316	22 954	22 361
50-54	26 925	13 949	12 976	30 793	15 944	14 849	35 638	18 331	17 307	39 217	19 987	19 230
55-59	22 771	11 764	11 008	25 000	12 856	12 144	28 639	14 699	13 940	32 978	16 764	16 214
60-64	18 161	9 357	8 804	20 252	10 359	9 892	22 422	11 394	11 028	25 341	12 819	12 522
65-69	12 954	6 640	6 314	15 159	7 726	7 433	17 099	8 632	8 467	18 574	9 248	9 326
70-74	8 552	4 286	4 265	9 775	4 963	4 813	11 606	5 835	5 771	12 962	6 365	6 596
75-79	4 681	2 408	2 273	5 449	2 704	2 745	6 394	3 190	3 204	7 734	3 766	3 968
80 +	2 571	1 247	1 323	3 019	1 499	1 520	3 604	1 756	1 848	4 660	2 241	2 419

Age group	1990 Both sexes	Males	Females	1995 Both sexes	Males	Females	2000 Both sexes	Males	Females	2005 Both sexes	Males	Females
All ages	1 225 578	630 821	594 756	1 356 969	697 154	659 815	1 484 624	761 138	723 486	1 610 896	823 953	786 943
0-4	176 119	90 454	85 665	182 445	93 602	88 843	180 153	92 394	87 759	181 481	93 049	88 432
5-9	156 577	80 775	75 802	170 094	87 653	82 442	176 955	91 000	85 956	175 717	90 279	85 438
10-14	134 833	69 774	65 059	155 303	80 143	75 159	168 444	86 809	81 635	175 698	90 349	85 349
15-19	124 666	64 758	59 908	133 554	69 125	64 429	153 902	79 420	74 482	167 156	86 137	81 018
20-24	111 826	58 156	53 669	122 292	63 483	58 809	131 752	68 154	63 598	151 921	78 347	73 574
25-29	99 260	51 702	47 558	109 292	56 735	52 557	120 244	62 299	57 945	129 458	66 810	62 648
30-34	85 944	44 903	41 041	97 089	50 476	46 613	107 289	55 552	51 737	117 923	60 871	57 052
35-39	71 422	37 252	34 170	84 003	43 797	40 206	95 124	49 303	45 821	105 094	54 180	50 914
40-44	57 391	29 396	27 994	69 599	36 201	33 398	81 986	42 583	39 403	92 954	47 947	45 006
45-49	48 520	24 518	24 002	55 516	28 304	27 212	67 490	34 915	32 576	79 690	41 149	38 541
50-54	43 113	21 672	21 441	46 306	23 218	23 089	53 134	26 875	26 259	64 855	33 284	31 570
55-59	36 414	18 349	18 065	40 267	20 000	20 267	43 430	21 519	21 911	50 124	25 061	25 063
60-64	29 406	14 714	14 692	32 708	16 226	16 482	36 366	17 769	18 597	39 585	19 300	20 286
65-69	21 201	10 516	10 685	24 981	12 245	12 737	27 971	13 586	14 385	31 489	15 050	16 439
70-74	14 297	6 935	7 363	16 601	8 023	8 578	19 766	9 433	10 333	22 480	10 624	11 856
75-79	8 810	4 194	4 616	9 902	4 655	5 247	11 693	5 478	6 215	14 207	6 556	7 651
80 +	5 778	2 752	3 026	7 017	3 269	3 748	8 925	4 051	4 873	11 065	4 958	6 107

United Nations Department of Economic and Social Affairs/Population Division
World Population Prospects: The 2004 Revision, Volume II: Sex and Age Distribution of the World Population

80

POPULATION BY AGE AND SEX (in thousands)

Age group	2005 Both sexes	Males	Females	2010 Both sexes	Males	Females	2015 Both sexes	Males	Females	2020 Both sexes	Males	Females
All ages	1 610 896	823 953	786 943	1 738 693	887 356	851 337	1 865 884	950 322	915 562	1 987 494	1 010 265	977 228
0-4	181 481	93 049	88 432	184 895	94 771	90 124	187 031	95 828	91 203	184 990	94 755	90 236
5-9	175 717	90 279	85 438	177 688	91 216	86 472	181 610	93 156	88 454	184 239	94 432	89 808
10-14	175 698	90 349	85 349	174 612	89 698	84 915	176 675	90 676	85 999	180 722	92 674	88 049
15-19	167 156	86 137	81 018	174 635	89 783	84 852	173 674	89 188	84 487	175 826	90 206	85 621
20-24	151 921	78 347	73 574	165 545	85 250	80 295	173 207	88 984	84 223	172 381	88 453	83 929
25-29	129 458	66 810	62 648	149 898	77 159	72 739	163 707	84 168	79 539	171 494	87 972	83 522
30-34	117 923	60 871	57 052	127 292	65 480	61 811	147 810	75 894	71 917	161 707	82 965	78 742
35-39	105 094	54 180	50 914	115 701	59 471	56 230	125 197	64 179	61 018	145 695	74 598	71 097
40-44	92 954	47 947	45 006	102 876	52 776	50 100	113 509	58 092	55 417	123 094	62 872	60 223
45-49	79 690	41 149	38 541	90 573	46 444	44 129	100 499	51 277	49 221	111 147	56 608	54 540
50-54	64 855	33 284	31 570	76 858	39 375	37 483	87 653	44 610	43 043	97 566	49 435	48 131
55-59	50 124	25 061	25 063	61 476	31 199	30 277	73 192	37 094	36 099	83 824	42 221	41 603
60-64	39 585	19 300	20 286	46 039	22 655	23 384	56 841	28 400	28 441	68 089	33 982	34 107
65-69	31 489	15 050	16 439	34 643	16 528	18 115	40 692	19 597	21 094	50 669	24 783	25 886
70-74	22 480	10 624	11 856	25 665	11 927	13 738	28 607	13 274	15 333	34 016	15 934	18 082
75-79	14 207	6 556	7 651	16 460	7 520	8 940	19 129	8 578	10 551	21 678	9 704	11 974
80-84	7 157	3 237	3 920	8 904	3 960	4 945	10 552	4 641	5 911	12 536	5 395	7 141
85-89	2 889	1 274	1 616	3 588	1 569	2 019	4 576	1 961	2 615	5 566	2 353	3 212
90-94	836	366	470	1 092	467	625	1 387	586	801	1 816	748	1 069
95-99	162	72	90	222	95	127	295	123	172	383	156	227
100 +	21	10	12	30	13	17	41	17	24	55	22	33

Age group	2025 Both sexes	Males	Females	2030 Both sexes	Males	Females	2035 Both sexes	Males	Females	2040 Both sexes	Males	Females
All ages	2 098 694	1 064 703	1 033 991	2 197 640	1 112 670	1 084 971	2 286 126	1 155 084	1 131 042	2 367 026	1 193 500	1 173 527
0-4	179 074	91 704	87 370	172 243	88 188	84 055	168 279	86 127	82 151	168 079	85 998	82 081
5-9	182 623	93 554	89 069	177 077	90 677	86 400	170 569	87 319	83 250	166 845	85 375	81 470
10-14	183 464	94 003	89 461	181 939	93 169	88 770	176 484	90 341	86 144	170 050	87 024	83 026
15-19	179 044	91 837	87 707	182 746	93 597	89 150	181 276	92 791	88 485	175 860	90 991	85 870
20-24	174 639	89 522	85 117	178 838	91 593	87 245	181 708	92 990	88 718	180 298	92 222	88 076
25-29	170 821	87 531	83 291	173 212	88 672	84 539	177 520	90 805	86 716	180 495	92 266	88 228
30-34	169 614	86 854	82 760	169 124	86 524	82 599	171 681	87 762	83 919	176 145	89 988	86 157
35-39	159 652	81 725	77 928	167 695	85 708	81 987	167 405	85 502	81 904	170 151	86 855	83 297
40-44	143 541	73 274	70 267	157 563	80 450	77 110	165 739	84 521	81 218	165 653	84 446	81 207
45-49	120 805	61 443	59 362	141 178	71 805	69 374	155 237	79 007	76 230	163 530	83 160	80 370
50-54	108 204	54 756	53 449	117 912	59 621	58 291	138 124	69 878	68 246	152 155	77 066	75 090
55-59	83 891	46 001	40 070	104 223	52 245	51 978	113 905	57 086	56 818	133 788	67 130	66 658
60-64	78 407	38 899	39 508	88 052	43 527	44 526	98 385	48 613	49 772	107 909	53 339	54 569
65-69	61 169	29 887	31 282	70 933	34 453	36 480	80 160	38 807	41 353	90 044	43 590	46 454
70-74	42 799	20 359	22 440	52 172	24 787	27 385	61 023	28 816	32 207	69 519	32 722	36 797
75-79	26 172	11 817	14 355	33 361	15 288	18 073	41 172	18 830	22 342	48 709	22 123	26 586
80-84	14 481	6 212	8 269	17 804	7 692	10 112	23 041	10 085	12 956	28 901	12 596	16 305
85-89	6 770	2 789	3 981	7 991	3 276	4 715	10 037	4 124	5 913	13 269	5 483	7 786
90-94	2 267	916	1 350	2 828	1 108	1 720	3 420	1 325	2 095	4 415	1 696	2 719
95-99	511	202	309	653	252	401	835	309	527	1 040	374	665
100 +	72	28	44	96	36	60	125	46	79	163	56	107

Age group	2045 Both sexes	Males	Females	2050 Both sexes	Males	Females
All ages	2 437 637	1 226 667	1 210 969	2 495 028	1 253 110	1 241 919
0-4	165 893	84 856	81 037	161 130	82 406	78 724
5-9	166 831	85 332	81 500	164 814	84 271	80 543
10-14	166 380	85 109	81 271	166 405	85 088	81 318
15-19	169 476	86 698	82 778	165 840	84 804	81 036
20-24	174 949	89 459	85 489	168 612	86 203	82 409
25-29	179 176	91 556	87 619	173 927	88 857	85 070
30-34	179 262	91 535	87 727	178 085	90 911	87 174
35-39	174 783	89 183	85 600	178 061	90 829	87 233
40-44	168 582	85 915	82 666	173 373	88 345	85 027
45-49	163 650	83 220	80 430	166 749	84 802	81 946
50-54	160 540	81 286	79 254	160 884	81 495	79 389
55-59	147 691	74 236	73 455	156 130	78 497	77 633
60-64	127 195	62 993	64 202	140 804	69 899	70 905
65-69	99 234	48 087	51 147	117 531	57 099	60 431
70-74	78 646	37 025	41 621	87 227	41 115	46 112
75-79	56 081	25 384	30 697	64 052	28 984	35 068
80-84	34 699	14 994	19 705	40 524	17 414	23 110
85-89	17 010	6 959	10 051	20 830	8 398	12 432
90-94	5 974	2 286	3 688	7 859	2 945	4 914
95-99	1 378	485	893	1 914	659	1 254
100 +	207	68	139	278	88	190

POPULATION BY AGE AND SEX (in thousands)

Age group	2005 Both sexes	2005 Males	2005 Females	2010 Both sexes	2010 Males	2010 Females	2015 Both sexes	2015 Males	2015 Females	2020 Both sexes	2020 Males	2020 Females
All ages	1 610 896	823 953	786 943	1 754 761	895 590	859 172	1 910 305	973 085	937 220	2 069 126	1 052 085	1 017 041
0-4	181 481	93 049	88 432	200 964	103 005	97 959	215 636	110 481	105 155	222 640	114 033	108 607
5-9	175 717	90 279	85 438	177 688	91 216	86 472	197 425	101 266	96 160	212 464	108 894	103 570
10-14	175 698	90 349	85 349	174 612	89 698	84 915	176 675	90 676	85 999	196 479	100 751	95 728
15-19	167 156	86 137	81 018	174 635	89 783	84 852	173 674	89 188	84 487	175 826	90 206	85 621
20-24	151 921	78 347	73 574	165 545	85 250	80 295	173 207	88 984	84 223	172 381	88 453	83 929
25-29	129 458	66 810	62 648	149 898	77 159	72 739	163 707	84 168	79 539	171 494	87 972	83 522
30-34	117 923	60 871	57 052	127 292	65 480	61 811	147 810	75 894	71 917	161 707	82 965	78 742
35-39	105 094	54 180	50 914	115 701	59 471	56 230	125 197	64 179	61 018	145 695	74 598	71 097
40-44	92 954	47 947	45 006	102 876	52 776	50 100	113 509	58 092	55 417	123 094	62 872	60 223
45-49	79 690	41 149	38 541	90 573	46 444	44 129	100 499	51 277	49 221	111 147	56 608	54 540
50-54	64 855	33 284	31 570	76 858	39 375	37 483	87 653	44 610	43 043	97 566	49 435	48 131
55-59	50 124	25 061	25 063	61 476	31 199	30 277	73 192	37 094	36 099	83 824	42 221	41 603
60-64	39 585	19 300	20 286	46 039	22 655	23 384	56 841	28 400	28 441	68 089	33 982	34 107
65-69	31 489	15 050	16 439	34 643	16 528	18 115	40 692	19 597	21 094	50 669	24 783	25 886
70-74	22 480	10 624	11 856	25 665	11 927	13 738	28 607	13 274	15 333	34 016	15 934	18 082
75-79	14 207	6 556	7 651	16 460	7 520	8 940	19 129	8 578	10 551	21 678	9 704	11 974
80-84	7 157	3 237	3 920	8 904	3 960	4 945	10 552	4 641	5 911	12 536	5 395	7 141
85-89	2 889	1 274	1 616	3 588	1 569	2 019	4 576	1 961	2 615	5 566	2 353	3 212
90-94	836	366	470	1 092	467	625	1 387	586	801	1 816	748	1 069
95-99	162	72	90	222	95	127	295	123	172	383	156	227
100 +	21	10	12	30	13	17	41	17	24	55	22	33

Age group	2025 Both sexes	2025 Males	2025 Females	2030 Both sexes	2030 Males	2030 Females	2035 Both sexes	2035 Males	2035 Females	2040 Both sexes	2040 Males	2040 Females
All ages	2 219 849	1 126 750	1 093 099	2 364 246	1 197 961	1 166 285	2 508 914	1 269 089	1 239 825	2 658 045	1 342 359	1 315 686
0-4	219 117	112 203	106 913	218 250	111 736	106 514	225 095	115 197	109 898	237 089	121 295	115 794
5-9	219 878	112 632	107 246	216 765	110 993	105 772	216 229	110 685	105 545	223 292	114 248	109 044
10-14	211 601	108 417	103 184	219 101	112 193	106 909	216 089	110 607	105 482	215 628	110 341	105 287
15-19	195 663	100 293	95 371	210 825	107 976	102 849	218 374	111 776	106 599	215 414	110 220	105 194
20-24	174 639	89 522	85 117	194 509	99 620	94 889	209 711	107 323	102 388	217 315	111 157	106 159
25-29	170 821	87 531	83 291	173 212	88 672	84 539	193 125	98 791	94 334	208 396	106 538	101 858
30-34	169 614	86 854	82 760	169 124	86 524	82 599	171 681	87 762	83 919	191 665	97 925	93 740
35-39	159 652	81 725	77 928	167 695	85 708	81 987	167 405	85 502	81 904	170 151	86 855	83 297
40-44	143 541	73 274	70 267	157 563	80 450	77 113	165 739	84 521	81 218	165 653	84 446	81 207
45-49	120 805	61 443	59 362	141 178	71 805	69 374	155 237	79 007	76 230	163 530	83 160	80 370
50-54	108 204	54 756	53 449	117 912	59 621	58 291	138 124	69 878	68 246	152 155	77 066	75 090
55-59	93 664	46 991	46 673	104 223	52 245	51 978	113 905	57 086	56 818	133 788	67 130	66 658
60-64	78 407	38 899	39 508	88 052	43 527	44 526	98 385	48 613	49 772	107 909	53 339	54 569
65-69	61 169	29 887	31 282	70 933	34 453	36 480	80 160	38 807	41 353	90 044	43 590	46 454
70-74	42 799	20 359	22 440	52 172	24 787	27 385	61 023	28 816	32 207	69 519	32 722	36 797
75-79	26 172	11 817	14 355	33 361	15 288	18 073	41 172	18 830	22 342	48 709	22 123	26 586
80-84	14 481	6 212	8 269	17 804	7 692	10 112	23 041	10 085	12 956	28 901	12 596	16 305
85-89	6 770	2 789	3 981	7 991	3 276	4 715	10 037	4 124	5 913	13 269	5 483	7 786
90-94	2 267	916	1 350	2 828	1 108	1 720	3 420	1 325	2 095	4 415	1 696	2 719
95-99	511	202	309	653	252	401	835	309	527	1 040	374	665
100 +	72	28	44	96	36	60	125	46	79	163	56	107

Age group	2045 Both sexes	2045 Males	2045 Females	2050 Both sexes	2050 Males	2050 Females
All ages	2 806 355	1 415 200	1 391 156	2 948 052	1 484 673	1 463 379
0-4	244 535	125 068	119 467	246 528	126 066	120 462
5-9	235 457	120 419	115 037	243 083	124 276	118 807
10-14	222 739	113 930	108 809	234 939	120 120	114 818
15-19	214 994	109 978	105 015	222 132	113 583	108 549
20-24	214 416	109 641	104 775	214 050	109 435	104 615
25-29	216 082	110 424	105 658	213 296	108 980	104 315
30-34	207 036	105 734	101 302	214 856	109 702	105 154
35-39	190 209	97 066	93 143	205 694	104 947	100 747
40-44	168 582	85 915	82 666	188 693	96 166	92 527
45-49	163 650	83 220	80 430	166 749	84 802	81 946
50-54	160 540	81 286	79 254	160 884	81 495	79 389
55-59	147 691	74 236	73 455	156 130	78 497	77 633
60-64	127 195	62 993	64 202	140 804	69 899	70 905
65-69	99 234	48 087	51 147	117 531	57 099	60 431
70-74	78 646	37 025	41 621	87 227	41 115	46 112
75-79	56 081	25 384	30 697	64 052	28 984	35 068
80-84	34 699	14 994	19 705	40 524	17 414	23 110
85-89	17 010	6 959	10 051	20 830	8 398	12 432
90-94	5 974	2 286	3 688	7 859	2 945	4 914
95-99	1 378	485	893	1 914	659	1 254
100 +	207	68	139	278	88	190

United Nations Department of Economic and Social Affairs/Population Division
World Population Prospects: The 2004 Revision, Volume II: Sex and Age Distribution of the World Population

82

POPULATION BY AGE AND SEX (in thousands)

Age group	2005 Both sexes	Males	Females	2010 Both sexes	Males	Females	2015 Both sexes	Males	Females	2020 Both sexes	Males	Females
All ages	1 610 896	823 953	786 943	1 722 753	879 188	843 565	1 821 980	927 826	894 154	1 906 259	968 652	937 608
0-4	181 481	93 049	88 432	168 955	86 603	82 352	158 822	81 380	77 443	147 249	75 429	71 820
5-9	175 717	90 279	85 438	177 688	91 216	86 472	165 914	85 108	80 806	156 385	80 160	76 224
10-14	175 698	90 349	85 349	174 612	89 698	84 915	176 675	90 676	85 999	165 083	84 657	80 427
15-19	167 156	86 137	81 018	174 635	89 783	84 852	173 674	89 188	84 487	175 826	90 206	85 621
20-24	151 921	78 347	73 574	165 545	85 250	80 295	173 207	88 984	84 223	172 381	88 453	83 929
25-29	129 458	66 810	62 648	149 898	77 159	72 739	163 707	84 168	79 539	171 494	87 972	83 522
30-34	117 923	60 871	57 052	127 292	65 480	61 811	147 810	75 894	71 917	161 707	82 965	78 742
35-39	105 094	54 180	50 914	115 701	59 471	56 230	125 197	64 179	61 018	145 695	74 598	71 097
40-44	92 954	47 947	45 006	102 876	52 776	50 100	113 509	58 092	55 417	123 094	62 872	60 223
45-49	79 690	41 149	38 541	90 573	46 444	44 129	100 499	51 277	49 221	111 147	56 608	54 540
50-54	64 855	33 284	31 570	76 858	39 375	37 483	87 653	44 610	43 043	97 566	49 435	48 131
55-59	50 124	25 061	25 063	61 476	31 199	30 277	73 192	37 094	36 099	83 824	42 221	41 603
60-64	39 585	19 300	20 286	46 039	22 655	23 384	56 841	28 400	28 441	68 089	33 982	34 107
65-69	31 489	15 050	16 439	34 643	16 528	18 115	40 692	19 597	21 094	50 669	24 783	25 886
70-74	22 480	10 624	11 856	25 665	11 927	13 738	28 607	13 274	15 333	34 016	15 934	18 082
75-79	14 207	6 556	7 651	16 460	7 520	8 940	19 129	8 578	10 551	21 678	9 704	11 974
80-84	7 157	3 237	3 920	8 904	3 960	4 945	10 552	4 641	5 911	12 536	5 395	7 141
85-89	2 889	1 274	1 616	3 588	1 569	2 019	4 576	1 961	2 615	5 566	2 353	3 212
90-94	836	366	470	1 092	467	625	1 387	586	801	1 816	748	1 069
95-99	162	72	90	222	95	127	295	123	172	383	156	227
100 +	21	10	12	30	13	17	41	17	24	55	22	33

Age group	2025 Both sexes	Males	Females	2030 Both sexes	Males	Females	2035 Both sexes	Males	Females	2040 Both sexes	Males	Females
All ages	1 978 214	1 003 003	975 211	2 033 994	1 028 894	1 005 100	2 072 686	1 045 863	1 026 823	2 096 468	1 055 107	1 041 362
0-4	139 313	71 349	67 964	128 529	65 814	62 715	117 876	60 339	57 537	110 239	56 413	53 825
5-9	145 277	74 430	70 848	137 670	70 505	67 164	127 184	65 117	62 067	116 767	59 760	57 007
10-14	155 692	79 778	75 914	144 688	74 099	70 589	137 160	70 217	66 943	126 742	64 868	61 874
15-19	164 342	84 242	80 101	155 030	79 405	75 625	144 087	73 760	70 328	136 603	69 903	66 700
20-24	174 639	89 522	85 117	163 282	83 626	79 655	154 061	78 842	75 219	143 192	73 242	69 950
25-29	170 821	87 531	83 291	173 212	88 672	84 539	162 028	82 877	79 151	152 943	78 176	74 767
30-34	169 614	86 854	82 760	169 124	86 524	82 599	171 681	87 762	83 919	160 735	82 108	78 628
35-39	159 652	81 725	77 928	167 695	85 708	81 987	167 405	85 502	81 904	170 151	86 855	83 297
40-44	143 541	73 274	70 267	157 563	80 450	77 113	165 739	84 521	81 218	165 653	84 446	81 207
45-49	120 805	61 443	59 362	141 178	71 805	69 374	155 237	79 007	76 230	163 530	83 160	80 370
50-54	108 204	54 756	53 449	117 912	59 621	58 291	138 124	69 878	68 246	152 155	77 066	75 090
55-59	93 664	46 991	46 673	104 223	52 245	51 978	113 905	57 086	56 818	133 788	67 130	66 658
60-64	78 407	38 899	39 508	89 053	43 527	44 526	98 806	49 010	49 772	107 903	53 335	54 569
65-69	61 169	29 887	31 282	70 933	34 453	36 480	80 160	38 807	41 353	90 044	43 590	46 454
70-74	42 799	20 359	22 440	52 172	24 787	27 385	61 023	28 816	32 207	69 519	32 722	36 797
75-79	26 172	11 817	14 355	33 361	15 288	18 073	41 172	18 830	22 342	48 709	22 123	26 586
80-84	14 481	6 212	8 269	17 804	7 692	10 112	23 041	10 085	12 956	28 901	12 596	16 305
85-89	6 770	2 789	3 981	7 991	3 276	4 715	10 037	4 124	5 913	13 269	5 483	7 786
90-94	2 267	916	1 350	2 828	1 108	1 720	3 420	1 325	2 095	4 415	1 696	2 719
95-99	511	202	309	653	252	401	835	309	527	1 040	374	665
100 +	72	28	44	96	36	60	125	46	79	163	56	107

Age group	2045 Both sexes	Males	Females	2050 Both sexes	Males	Females
All ages	2 104 490	1 056 324	1 048 166	2 096 268	1 049 284	1 046 984
0-4	102 446	52 412	50 034	94 530	48 355	46 175
5-9	109 312	55 922	53 390	101 670	51 996	49 675
10-14	116 380	59 540	56 839	108 963	55 724	53 239
15-19	126 226	64 578	61 648	115 899	59 271	56 628
20-24	135 760	69 420	66 340	125 437	64 128	61 309
25-29	142 180	72 643	69 538	134 836	68 875	65 962
30-34	151 833	77 515	74 318	141 225	72 074	69 151
35-39	159 466	81 356	78 110	150 768	76 886	73 882
40-44	168 582	85 915	82 666	158 159	80 579	77 580
45-49	163 650	83 220	80 430	166 749	84 802	81 946
50-54	160 540	81 286	79 254	160 884	81 495	79 389
55-59	147 691	74 236	73 455	156 130	78 497	77 633
60-64	127 195	62 993	64 202	140 804	69 899	70 905
65-69	99 234	48 087	51 147	117 531	57 099	60 431
70-74	78 646	37 025	41 621	87 227	41 115	46 112
75-79	56 081	25 384	30 697	64 052	28 984	35 068
80-84	34 699	14 994	19 705	40 524	17 414	23 110
85-89	17 010	6 959	10 051	20 830	8 398	12 432
90-94	5 974	2 286	3 688	7 859	2 945	4 914
95-99	1 378	485	893	1 914	659	1 254
100 +	207	68	139	278	88	190

United Nations Department of Economic and Social Affairs/Population Division
World Population Prospects: The 2004 Revision, Volume II: Sex and Age Distribution of the World Population

83

POPULATION BY AGE AND SEX (in thousands)

Age group	1950			1955			1960			1965		
	Both sexes	Males	Females	Both sexes	Males	Females	Both sexes	Males	Females	Both sexes	Males	Females
All ages	178 073	88 731	89 342	197 592	98 588	99 003	222 799	111 304	111 495	252 018	126 002	126 016
0-4	26 631	13 295	13 336	32 742	16 544	16 198	38 466	19 471	18 995	42 826	21 695	21 132
5-9	22 146	11 003	11 143	24 301	12 140	12 161	30 276	15 294	14 982	35 930	18 176	17 754
10-14	20 467	10 178	10 289	21 555	10 721	10 834	23 740	11 868	11 872	29 661	14 988	14 673
15-19	18 484	9 231	9 254	19 930	9 928	10 002	21 059	10 487	10 572	23 273	11 642	11 632
20-24	15 933	8 026	7 907	17 829	8 908	8 921	19 307	9 618	9 689	20 449	10 177	10 272
25-29	13 543	6 855	6 687	15 243	7 675	7 568	17 148	8 560	8 588	18 629	9 267	9 363
30-34	11 709	5 917	5 792	12 886	6 522	6 364	14 587	7 341	7 246	16 472	8 214	8 257
35-39	10 632	5 403	5 229	11 060	5 584	5 477	12 252	6 193	6 060	13 932	6 999	6 933
40-44	9 192	4 658	4 533	9 954	5 038	4 916	10 431	5 244	5 186	11 611	5 843	5 768
45-49	7 619	3 827	3 792	8 517	4 280	4 236	9 292	4 667	4 626	9 790	4 884	4 905
50-54	6 047	3 002	3 044	6 937	3 443	3 493	7 818	3 885	3 933	8 589	4 266	4 323
55-59	4 935	2 376	2 559	5 354	2 619	2 735	6 202	3 035	3 167	7 046	3 451	3 594
60-64	3 984	1 889	2 095	4 171	1 973	2 198	4 587	2 205	2 382	5 369	2 583	2 787
65-69	2 986	1 381	1 605	3 122	1 447	1 675	3 336	1 544	1 792	3 725	1 753	1 973
70-74	1 997	917	1 079	2 114	955	1 160	2 246	1 016	1 230	2 451	1 104	1 348
75-79	1 143	506	636	1 188	526	662	1 298	565	734	1 419	618	800
80 +	626	265	362	688	286	402	753	311	442	847	344	502

Age group	1970			1975			1980			1985		
	Both sexes	Males	Females	Both sexes	Males	Females	Both sexes	Males	Females	Both sexes	Males	Females
All ages	285 793	142 965	142 828	321 293	160 742	160 551	357 948	178 927	179 021	398 420	199 153	199 268
0-4	47 738	24 191	23 546	50 412	25 547	24 865	52 998	26 912	26 086	56 001	28 448	27 553
5-9	40 375	20 419	19 956	45 294	22 920	22 374	48 335	24 466	23 869	51 331	26 023	25 308
10-14	35 239	17 813	17 425	39 630	20 027	19 603	44 518	22 505	22 013	47 784	24 175	23 609
15-19	29 103	14 709	14 395	34 577	17 462	17 115	38 897	19 621	19 276	43 874	22 155	21 719
20-24	22 688	11 344	11 344	28 365	14 316	14 050	33 690	16 959	16 731	38 002	19 123	18 880
25-29	19 794	9 841	9 954	22 025	10 997	11 027	27 460	13 806	13 655	32 768	16 446	16 321
30-34	17 967	8 929	9 037	19 151	9 513	9 638	21 221	10 550	10 671	26 664	13 373	13 291
35-39	15 802	7 867	7 935	17 302	8 585	8 717	18 365	9 079	9 286	20 553	10 190	10 362
40-44	13 281	6 647	6 634	15 111	7 495	7 616	16 472	8 121	8 351	17 684	8 705	8 979
45-49	10 965	5 480	5 485	12 595	6 261	6 334	14 303	7 025	7 278	15 794	7 740	8 055
50-54	9 110	4 497	4 612	10 238	5 067	5 171	11 767	5 777	5 990	13 526	6 588	6 938
55-59	7 797	3 819	3 978	8 316	4 050	4 266	9 354	4 558	4 796	10 932	5 301	5 631
60-64	6 158	2 965	3 193	6 856	3 298	3 557	7 366	3 528	3 838	8 394	4 022	4 372
65-69	4 421	2 081	2 340	5 110	2 405	2 705	5 750	2 706	3 044	6 286	2 946	3 340
70-74	2 802	1 283	1 519	3 349	1 532	1 817	3 922	1 795	2 126	4 508	2 060	2 447
75-79	1 586	688	898	1 848	815	1 033	2 231	987	1 244	2 695	1 189	1 506
80 +	967	392	575	1 114	451	663	1 299	533	767	1 625	670	955

Age group	1990			1995			2000			2005		
	Both sexes	Males	Females	Both sexes	Males	Females	Both sexes	Males	Females	Both sexes	Males	Females
All ages	439 846	219 945	219 901	481 081	240 501	240 580	518 867	259 107	259 760	555 815	277 230	278 585
0-4	56 575	28 789	27 786	57 041	29 052	27 989	54 291	27 666	26 625	54 970	28 021	26 949
5-9	54 503	27 648	26 855	55 503	28 207	27 296	56 187	28 581	27 606	53 625	27 293	26 332
10-14	51 008	25 839	25 169	54 074	27 407	26 667	55 127	27 998	27 129	55 909	28 422	27 487
15-19	47 191	23 839	23 353	50 337	25 470	24 866	53 484	27 085	26 399	54 731	27 765	26 966
20-24	43 071	21 680	21 391	46 042	23 207	22 835	49 260	24 856	24 403	52 759	26 628	26 131
25-29	37 212	18 679	18 532	41 883	20 998	20 884	44 809	22 452	22 357	48 370	24 277	24 094
30-34	32 126	16 113	16 012	36 391	18 181	18 210	40 976	20 408	20 568	43 930	21 891	22 039
35-39	26 083	13 068	13 015	31 507	15 746	15 761	35 734	17 764	17 969	40 170	19 912	20 258
40-44	19 994	9 887	10 107	25 613	12 807	12 807	30 992	15 442	15 550	34 976	17 310	17 667
45-49	17 051	8 357	8 694	19 582	9 652	9 931	25 122	12 514	12 608	30 189	14 966	15 223
50-54	15 052	7 321	7 730	16 483	8 017	8 466	18 988	9 292	9 697	24 240	11 991	12 249
55-59	12 659	6 100	6 559	14 292	6 866	7 426	15 713	7 553	8 160	18 033	8 730	9 302
60-64	9 925	4 732	5 193	11 693	5 539	6 154	13 269	6 267	7 002	14 540	6 876	7 664
65-69	7 230	3 390	3 840	8 733	4 074	4 660	10 373	4 807	5 566	11 758	5 429	6 329
70-74	5 007	2 281	2 726	5 880	2 684	3 196	7 174	3 256	3 919	8 553	3 850	4 703
75-79	3 153	1 391	1 762	3 584	1 578	2 006	4 281	1 888	2 392	5 259	2 300	2 959
80 +	2 006	830	1 176	2 444	1 015	1 429	3 088	1 279	1 809	3 803	1 570	2 233

United Nations Department of Economic and Social Affairs/Population Division
World Population Prospects: The 2004 Revision, Volume II: Sex and Age Distribution of the World Population

POPULATION BY AGE AND SEX (in thousands)

Age group	2005 Both sexes	Males	Females	2010 Both sexes	Males	Females	2015 Both sexes	Males	Females	2020 Both sexes	Males	Females
All ages	555 815	277 230	278 585	591 021	294 590	296 411	623 101	310 546	312 555	652 400	324 809	327 594
0-4	54 970	28 021	26 949	54 151	27 635	26 516	52 762	26 945	25 817	50 911	26 011	24 900
5-9	53 625	27 293	26 332	54 432	27 722	26 710	53 703	27 386	26 317	52 386	26 736	25 650
10-14	55 909	28 422	27 487	53 399	27 164	26 235	54 226	27 604	26 622	53 523	27 283	26 240
15-19	54 731	27 765	26 966	55 559	28 215	27 345	53 083	26 976	26 106	53 945	27 436	26 509
20-24	52 759	26 628	26 131	54 075	27 351	26 724	54 937	27 821	27 116	52 550	26 654	25 897
25-29	48 370	24 277	24 094	51 925	26 089	25 836	53 289	26 842	26 446	54 246	27 407	26 839
30-34	43 930	21 891	22 039	47 568	23 772	23 796	51 140	25 599	25 542	52 589	26 430	26 159
35-39	40 170	19 912	20 258	43 183	21 438	21 745	46 855	23 346	23 509	50 435	25 186	25 249
40-44	34 976	17 310	17 667	39 432	19 477	19 955	42 470	21 023	21 447	46 153	22 938	23 214
45-49	30 189	14 966	15 223	34 182	16 845	17 338	38 622	19 008	19 614	41 676	20 559	21 116
50-54	24 240	11 991	12 249	29 245	14 411	14 835	33 210	16 276	16 934	37 610	18 413	19 197
55-59	18 033	8 730	9 302	23 141	11 338	11 803	28 024	13 685	14 339	31 925	15 509	16 416
60-64	14 540	6 876	7 664	16 799	8 009	8 789	21 676	10 468	11 208	26 361	12 692	13 669
65-69	11 758	5 429	6 329	12 990	6 011	6 979	15 122	7 060	8 063	19 643	9 289	10 353
70-74	8 553	3 850	4 703	9 798	4 394	5 404	10 926	4 913	6 013	12 848	5 823	7 025
75-79	5 259	2 300	2 959	6 371	2 762	3 609	7 389	3 189	4 200	8 346	3 604	4 743
80-84	2 583	1 090	1 493	3 236	1 351	1 885	3 996	1 650	2 346	4 720	1 926	2 794
85-89	959	383	575	1 190	473	717	1 526	597	930	1 940	740	1 201
90-94	228	85	143	298	109	188	381	138	243	509	176	333
95-99	31	10	21	43	14	29	59	19	40	79	24	55
100 +	2	1	2	3	1	2	5	1	3	7	2	5

Age group	2025 Both sexes	Males	Females	2030 Both sexes	Males	Females	2035 Both sexes	Males	Females	2040 Both sexes	Males	Females
All ages	678 347	337 557	340 791	700 930	348 503	352 427	719 810	357 486	362 324	734 755	364 478	370 277
0-4	49 780	25 447	24 334	48 611	24 853	23 757	47 395	24 244	23 151	46 392	23 742	22 651
5-9	50 598	25 838	24 761	49 519	25 301	24 219	48 389	24 730	23 659	47 203	24 138	23 065
10-14	52 229	26 646	25 583	50 463	25 760	24 704	49 400	25 232	24 168	48 282	24 670	23 613
15-19	53 264	27 128	26 136	51 992	26 504	25 489	50 245	25 630	24 616	49 197	25 112	24 085
20-24	53 439	27 130	26 309	52 788	26 839	25 949	51 544	26 233	25 311	49 822	25 376	24 446
25-29	51 918	26 276	25 641	52 838	26 770	26 067	52 218	26 500	25 718	51 002	25 913	25 089
30-34	53 592	27 023	26 570	51 328	25 930	25 398	52 277	26 442	25 834	51 688	26 192	25 495
35-39	51 935	26 049	25 886	52 990	26 670	26 319	50 787	25 616	25 171	51 765	26 148	25 617
40-44	49 747	24 787	24 960	51 302	25 680	25 621	52 400	26 330	26 073	50 267	25 316	24 950
45-49	45 377	22 487	22 890	48 989	24 344	24 645	50 595	25 266	25 329	51 745	25 945	25 800
50-54	40 670	19 967	20 703	44 385	21 899	22 486	48 004	23 756	24 248	49 665	24 710	24 955
55-59	36 251	17 600	18 651	39 310	19 147	20 162	43 014	21 065	21 948	46 627	22 915	23 712
60-64	30 155	14 450	15 705	34 363	16 463	17 900	37 392	17 982	19 411	41 048	19 862	21 186
65-69	24 022	11 330	12 692	27 643	12 980	14 664	31 656	14 864	16 792	34 608	16 324	18 284
70-74	16 843	7 734	9 110	20 767	9 510	11 257	24 113	10 986	13 127	27 802	12 668	15 133
75-79	9 957	4 327	5 630	13 234	5 821	7 413	16 536	7 242	9 294	19 441	8 463	10 978
80-84	5 428	2 209	3 220	6 625	2 701	3 924	9 020	3 704	5 324	11 497	4 682	6 816
85-89	2 348	875	1 473	2 771	1 021	1 750	3 536	1 288	2 248	4 983	1 811	3 172
90-94	671	222	449	842	267	575	1 049	322	727	1 414	423	991
95-99	112	31	80	155	40	115	208	50	158	274	63	211
100 +	10	2	8	15	3	12	22	4	18	32	5	27

Age group	2045 Both sexes	Males	Females	2050 Both sexes	Males	Females
All ages	745 564	369 397	376 167	752 254	372 327	379 927
0-4	45 014	23 195	22 118	44 209	22 636	21 573
5-9	46 222	23 649	22 574	45 161	23 113	22 048
10-14	47 106	24 083	23 023	46 133	23 599	22 534
15-19	48 090	24 557	23 534	46 923	23 977	22 947
20-24	48 792	24 871	23 921	47 701	24 327	23 374
25-29	49 307	25 074	24 233	48 299	24 583	23 716
30-34	50 502	25 623	24 878	48 836	24 802	24 035
35-39	51 208	25 917	25 292	50 055	25 367	24 688
40-44	51 274	25 866	25 408	50 753	25 656	25 097
45-49	49 683	24 974	24 709	50 724	25 545	25 180
50-54	50 867	25 416	25 450	48 898	24 503	24 396
55-59	48 341	23 895	24 446	49 602	24 635	24 967
60-64	44 627	21 680	22 946	46 395	22 687	23 708
65-69	38 157	18 121	20 036	41 652	19 877	21 775
70-74	30 600	14 012	16 588	33 941	15 660	18 281
75-79	22 636	9 847	12 790	25 148	10 997	14 151
80-84	13 780	5 562	8 218	16 271	6 553	9 718
85-89	6 530	2 343	4 187	8 037	2 847	5 190
90-94	2 086	617	1 469	2 832	822	2 010
95-99	397	88	309	615	133	481
100 +	45	7	38	70	11	59

United Nations Department of Economic and Social Affairs/Population Division
World Population Prospects: The 2004 Revision, Volume II: Sex and Age Distribution of the World Population

85

POPULATION BY AGE AND SEX (in thousands)

Age group	2005 Both sexes	Males	Females	2010 Both sexes	Males	Females	2015 Both sexes	Males	Females	2020 Both sexes	Males	Females
All ages	555 815	277 230	278 585	596 673	297 463	299 209	638 686	318 345	320 341	680 127	338 988	341 139
0-4	54 970	28 021	26 949	59 803	30 518	29 285	62 431	31 882	30 549	63 416	32 399	31 017
5-9	53 625	27 293	26 332	54 432	27 722	26 710	59 318	30 248	29 070	62 003	31 642	30 361
10-14	55 909	28 422	27 487	53 399	27 164	26 235	54 226	27 604	26 622	59 125	30 137	28 988
15-19	54 731	27 765	26 966	55 559	28 215	27 345	53 083	26 976	26 106	53 945	27 436	26 509
20-24	52 759	26 628	26 131	54 075	27 351	26 724	54 937	27 821	27 116	52 550	26 654	25 897
25-29	48 370	24 277	24 094	51 925	26 089	25 836	53 289	26 842	26 446	54 246	27 407	26 839
30-34	43 930	21 891	22 039	47 568	23 772	23 796	51 140	25 599	25 542	52 589	26 430	26 159
35-39	40 170	19 912	20 258	43 183	21 438	21 745	46 855	23 346	23 509	50 435	25 186	25 249
40-44	34 976	17 310	17 667	39 432	19 477	19 955	42 470	21 023	21 447	46 153	22 938	23 214
45-49	30 189	14 966	15 223	34 182	16 845	17 338	38 622	19 008	19 614	41 676	20 559	21 116
50-54	24 240	11 991	12 249	29 245	14 411	14 835	33 210	16 276	16 934	37 610	18 413	19 197
55-59	18 033	8 730	9 302	23 141	11 338	11 803	28 024	13 685	14 339	31 925	15 509	16 416
60-64	14 540	6 876	7 664	16 799	8 009	8 789	21 676	10 468	11 208	26 361	12 692	13 669
65-69	11 758	5 429	6 329	12 990	6 011	6 979	15 122	7 060	8 063	19 643	9 289	10 353
70-74	8 553	3 850	4 703	9 798	4 394	5 404	10 926	4 913	6 013	12 848	5 823	7 025
75-79	5 259	2 300	2 959	6 371	2 762	3 609	7 389	3 189	4 200	8 346	3 604	4 743
80-84	2 583	1 090	1 493	3 236	1 351	1 885	3 996	1 650	2 346	4 720	1 926	2 794
85-89	959	383	575	1 190	473	717	1 526	597	930	1 940	740	1 201
90-94	228	85	143	298	109	188	381	138	243	509	176	333
95-99	31	10	21	43	14	29	59	19	40	79	24	55
100 +	2	1	2	3	1	2	5	1	3	7	2	5

Age group	2025 Both sexes	Males	Females	2030 Both sexes	Males	Females	2035 Both sexes	Males	Females	2040 Both sexes	Males	Females
All ages	718 901	358 255	360 646	755 610	376 411	379 199	791 290	393 970	397 320	826 439	411 281	415 158
0-4	62 698	32 049	30 649	62 843	32 129	30 714	64 326	32 904	31 423	66 762	34 165	32 597
5-9	63 048	32 193	30 855	62 390	31 875	30 515	62 579	31 982	30 598	64 093	32 774	31 319
10-14	61 827	31 541	30 286	62 891	32 102	30 789	62 252	31 795	30 457	62 456	31 910	30 545
15-19	58 853	29 974	28 879	61 571	31 386	30 185	62 652	31 958	30 694	62 030	31 662	30 368
20-24	53 439	27 130	26 309	58 359	29 673	28 686	61 094	31 096	29 998	62 197	31 683	30 514
25-29	51 918	26 276	25 641	52 838	26 770	26 067	57 767	29 320	28 447	60 520	30 755	29 765
30-34	53 592	27 023	26 570	51 328	25 930	25 398	52 277	26 442	25 834	57 213	28 998	28 215
35-39	51 935	26 049	25 886	52 990	26 670	26 319	50 787	25 616	25 171	51 765	26 148	25 617
40-44	49 747	24 787	24 960	51 302	25 680	25 621	52 403	26 330	26 073	50 267	25 316	24 950
45-49	45 377	22 487	22 890	48 989	24 344	24 645	50 595	25 266	25 329	51 745	25 945	25 800
50-54	40 670	19 967	20 703	44 385	21 899	22 486	48 004	23 756	24 248	49 665	24 710	24 955
55-59	36 251	17 600	18 651	39 310	19 147	20 162	43 014	21 065	21 948	46 627	22 915	23 712
60-64	30 155	14 450	15 705	34 363	16 463	17 900	37 392	17 982	19 411	41 048	19 862	21 186
65-69	24 022	11 330	12 692	27 643	12 980	14 664	31 656	14 864	16 792	34 608	16 324	18 284
70-74	16 843	7 734	9 110	20 767	9 510	11 257	24 113	10 986	13 127	27 802	12 668	15 133
75-79	9 957	4 327	5 630	13 234	5 821	7 413	16 536	7 242	9 294	19 441	8 463	10 978
80-84	5 428	2 208	3 220	6 625	2 701	3 924	9 028	3 704	5 324	11 497	4 682	6 816
85-89	2 348	875	1 473	2 771	1 021	1 750	3 536	1 288	2 248	4 983	1 811	3 172
90-94	671	222	449	842	267	575	1 049	322	727	1 414	423	991
95-99	112	31	80	155	40	115	208	50	158	274	63	211
100 +	10	2	8	15	3	12	22	4	18	32	5	27

Age group	2045 Both sexes	Males	Females	2050 Both sexes	Males	Females
All ages	860 462	428 060	432 401	892 526	443 959	448 567
0-4	68 734	35 183	33 551	69 839	35 759	34 080
5-9	66 550	34 047	32 503	68 541	35 077	33 464
10-14	63 979	32 708	31 270	66 442	33 986	32 456
15-19	62 245	31 785	30 460	63 777	32 589	31 188
20-24	61 596	31 402	30 194	61 829	31 537	30 292
25-29	61 645	31 356	30 288	61 069	31 092	29 976
30-34	59 983	30 444	29 539	61 131	31 059	30 072
35-39	56 708	28 707	28 000	59 495	30 164	29 331
40-44	51 274	25 866	25 408	56 221	28 429	27 792
45-49	49 683	24 974	24 709	50 724	25 545	25 180
50-54	50 867	25 416	25 450	48 898	24 503	24 396
55-59	48 341	23 895	24 446	49 602	24 635	24 967
60-64	44 627	21 680	22 946	46 395	22 687	23 708
65-69	38 157	18 121	20 036	41 652	19 877	21 775
70-74	30 600	14 012	16 588	33 941	15 660	18 281
75-79	22 636	9 847	12 790	25 148	10 997	14 151
80-84	13 780	5 562	8 218	16 271	6 553	9 718
85-89	6 530	2 343	4 187	8 037	2 847	5 190
90-94	2 086	617	1 469	2 832	822	2 010
95-99	397	88	309	615	133	481
100 +	45	7	38	70	11	59

United Nations Department of Economic and Social Affairs/Population Division
World Population Prospects: The 2004 Revision, Volume II: Sex and Age Distribution of the World Population

86

POPULATION BY AGE AND SEX (in thousands)

Age group	2005 Both sexes	Males	Females	2010 Both sexes	Males	Females	2015 Both sexes	Males	Females	2020 Both sexes	Males	Females
All ages	555 815	277 230	278 585	585 141	291 580	293 561	607 600	302 525	305 158	624 097	310 394	313 704
0-4	54 970	28 021	26 949	48 271	24 635	23 636	42 883	21 901	20 982	38 255	19 546	18 709
5-9	53 625	27 293	26 332	54 432	27 722	26 710	47 863	24 409	23 454	42 562	21 723	20 839
10-14	55 909	28 422	27 487	53 399	27 164	26 235	54 226	27 604	26 622	47 697	24 314	23 383
15-19	54 731	27 765	26 966	55 559	28 215	27 345	53 083	26 976	26 106	53 945	27 436	26 509
20-24	52 759	26 628	26 131	54 075	27 351	26 724	54 937	27 821	27 116	52 550	26 654	25 897
25-29	48 370	24 277	24 094	51 925	26 089	25 836	53 289	26 842	26 446	54 246	27 407	26 839
30-34	43 930	21 891	22 039	47 568	23 772	23 796	51 140	25 599	25 542	52 589	26 430	26 159
35-39	40 170	19 912	20 258	43 183	21 438	21 745	46 855	23 346	23 509	50 435	25 186	25 249
40-44	34 976	17 310	17 667	39 432	19 477	19 955	42 470	21 023	21 447	46 153	22 938	23 214
45-49	30 189	14 966	15 223	34 182	16 845	17 338	38 622	19 008	19 614	41 676	20 559	21 116
50-54	24 240	11 991	12 249	29 245	14 411	14 835	33 210	16 276	16 934	37 610	18 413	19 197
55-59	18 033	8 730	9 302	23 141	11 338	11 803	28 024	13 685	14 339	31 925	15 509	16 416
60-64	14 540	6 876	7 664	16 799	8 009	8 789	21 676	10 468	11 208	26 361	12 692	13 669
65-69	11 758	5 429	6 329	12 990	6 011	6 979	15 122	7 060	8 063	19 643	9 289	10 353
70-74	8 553	3 850	4 703	9 798	4 394	5 404	10 926	4 913	6 013	12 848	5 823	7 025
75-79	5 259	2 300	2 959	6 371	2 762	3 609	7 389	3 189	4 200	8 346	3 604	4 743
80-84	2 583	1 090	1 493	3 236	1 351	1 885	3 996	1 650	2 346	4 720	1 926	2 794
85-89	959	383	575	1 190	473	717	1 526	597	930	1 940	740	1 201
90-94	228	85	143	298	109	188	381	138	243	509	176	333
95-99	31	10	21	43	14	29	59	19	40	79	24	55
100 +	2	1	2	3	1	2	5	1	3	7	2	5

Age group	2025 Both sexes	Males	Females	2030 Both sexes	Males	Females	2035 Both sexes	Males	Females	2040 Both sexes	Males	Females
All ages	637 223	316 567	320 656	646 252	320 597	325 655	650 047	321 880	328 167	648 013	320 203	327 810
0-4	36 870	18 848	18 022	34 949	17 869	17 080	32 176	16 460	15 717	29 248	14 969	14 279
5-9	38 000	19 406	18 594	36 656	18 730	17 927	34 769	17 770	16 998	32 022	16 376	15 646
10-14	42 425	21 645	20 780	37 886	19 341	18 545	36 555	18 673	17 883	34 678	17 720	16 959
15-19	47 452	24 169	23 284	42 208	21 517	20 691	37 690	19 226	18 464	36 371	18 565	17 806
20-24	53 439	27 130	26 309	46 996	23 893	23 103	41 788	21 265	20 522	37 298	18 994	18 304
25-29	51 918	26 276	25 641	52 838	26 770	26 067	46 449	23 569	22 880	41 281	20 968	20 313
30-34	53 592	27 023	26 570	51 328	25 930	25 398	52 277	26 442	25 834	45 945	23 277	22 669
35-39	51 935	26 049	25 886	52 990	26 670	26 319	50 787	25 616	25 171	51 765	26 148	25 617
40-44	49 747	24 787	24 960	51 302	25 680	25 621	52 403	26 330	26 073	50 267	25 316	24 950
45-49	45 377	22 487	22 890	48 989	24 344	24 645	50 595	25 266	25 329	51 745	26 045	25 800
50-54	40 670	19 967	20 703	44 385	21 899	22 486	48 004	23 756	24 248	49 665	24 710	24 955
55-59	36 251	17 600	18 651	39 310	19 147	20 162	43 014	21 065	21 948	46 627	22 915	23 712
60-64	30 155	14 450	15 705	34 363	16 463	17 900	37 392	17 982	19 411	41 048	19 862	21 186
65-69	24 022	11 330	12 692	27 643	12 980	14 664	31 656	14 864	16 792	34 608	16 324	18 284
70-74	16 843	7 734	9 110	20 767	9 510	11 257	24 113	10 986	13 127	27 802	12 668	15 133
75-79	9 957	4 327	5 630	13 234	5 821	7 413	16 536	7 242	9 294	19 441	8 463	10 978
80-84	5 428	2 208	3 220	6 625	2 701	3 924	9 028	3 704	5 324	11 497	4 682	6 816
85-89	2 348	875	1 473	2 771	1 021	1 750	3 536	1 288	2 248	4 983	1 811	3 172
90-94	671	222	449	842	267	575	1 049	322	727	1 414	423	991
95-99	112	31	80	155	40	115	208	50	158	274	63	211
100 +	10	2	8	15	3	12	22	4	18	32	5	27

Age group	2045 Both sexes	Males	Females	2050 Both sexes	Males	Females
All ages	640 268	315 647	324 621	627 439	308 606	318 833
0-4	26 555	13 594	12 961	24 441	12 515	11 926
5-9	29 114	14 897	14 217	26 436	13 531	12 905
10-14	31 941	16 331	15 610	29 040	14 856	14 184
15-19	34 504	17 618	16 885	31 775	16 236	15 539
20-24	35 995	18 344	17 651	34 141	17 407	16 734
25-29	36 823	18 716	18 106	35 537	18 078	17 459
30-34	40 819	20 700	20 119	36 395	18 469	17 925
35-39	45 495	23 018	22 477	40 415	20 469	19 947
40-44	51 274	25 866	25 408	45 075	22 777	22 298
45-49	49 683	24 974	24 709	50 724	25 545	25 180
50-54	50 867	25 416	25 450	48 898	24 503	24 396
55-59	48 341	23 895	24 446	49 602	24 635	24 967
60-64	44 627	21 680	22 946	46 395	22 687	23 708
65-69	38 157	18 121	20 036	41 652	19 877	21 775
70-74	30 600	14 012	16 588	33 941	15 660	18 281
75-79	22 636	9 847	12 790	25 148	10 997	14 151
80-84	13 780	5 562	8 218	16 271	6 553	9 718
85-89	6 530	2 343	4 187	8 037	2 847	5 190
90-94	2 086	617	1 469	2 832	822	2 010
95-99	397	88	309	615	133	481
100 +	45	7	38	70	11	59

POPULATION BY AGE AND SEX (in thousands)

Age group	1950 Both sexes	1950 Males	1950 Females	1955 Both sexes	1955 Males	1955 Females	1960 Both sexes	1960 Males	1960 Females	1965 Both sexes	1965 Males	1965 Females
All ages	51 104	25 453	25 652	58 477	29 200	29 276	67 111	33 715	33 396	76 970	38 823	38 147
0-4	7 735	3 939	3 796	9 829	5 025	4 804	11 483	5 870	5 613	12 873	6 569	6 303
5-9	6 114	3 100	3 015	7 388	3 765	3 623	9 440	4 831	4 610	11 167	5 722	5 445
10-14	5 943	3 026	2 917	6 001	3 045	2 956	7 210	3 728	3 482	9 306	4 799	4 507
15-19	5 381	2 778	2 603	5 795	2 954	2 841	5 796	2 958	2 839	7 028	3 658	3 370
20-24	4 687	2 370	2 317	5 241	2 694	2 547	5 694	2 881	2 813	5 752	2 945	2 806
25-29	3 577	1 762	1 816	4 659	2 313	2 346	5 196	2 613	2 584	5 612	2 837	2 776
30-34	2 830	1 362	1 468	3 523	1 750	1 773	4 621	2 341	2 280	5 083	2 572	2 511
35-39	2 988	1 501	1 487	2 707	1 325	1 382	3 423	1 717	1 707	4 489	2 276	2 214
40-44	2 639	1 279	1 360	2 938	1 448	1 490	2 654	1 275	1 378	3 323	1 648	1 674
45-49	2 252	1 135	1 117	2 485	1 217	1 269	2 757	1 351	1 407	2 485	1 209	1 276
50-54	1 936	925	1 010	2 231	1 100	1 131	2 438	1 194	1 244	2 638	1 262	1 376
55-59	1 368	668	700	1 708	815	893	2 007	963	1 044	2 265	1 085	1 180
60-64	1 405	614	791	1 418	634	783	1 631	791	841	1 780	841	940
65-69	924	426	498	1 018	468	550	1 035	483	552	1 396	645	751
70-74	716	317	399	807	349	458	900	390	511	868	384	484
75-79	390	166	225	463	195	268	513	211	301	558	235	322
80 +	218	86	132	265	103	162	311	120	191	348	136	212

Age group	1970 Both sexes	1970 Males	1970 Females	1975 Both sexes	1975 Males	1975 Females	1980 Both sexes	1980 Males	1980 Females	1985 Both sexes	1985 Males	1985 Females
All ages	87 835	44 286	43 549	101 097	51 241	49 856	116 446	59 143	57 303	134 867	68 863	66 004
0-4	14 222	7 259	6 963	16 220	8 276	7 944	18 484	9 443	9 041	20 549	10 480	10 069
5-9	12 492	6 365	6 126	13 991	7 158	6 833	15 961	8 160	7 801	18 115	9 252	8 863
10-14	10 816	5 552	5 264	12 599	6 450	6 149	13 857	7 095	6 762	15 894	8 133	7 760
15-19	9 135	4 655	4 480	10 720	5 542	5 178	12 437	6 386	6 051	13 842	7 102	6 740
20-24	6 917	3 580	3 337	8 803	4 566	4 237	10 582	5 498	5 084	12 700	6 567	6 133
25-29	5 621	2 841	2 779	6 899	3 599	3 300	8 838	4 643	4 196	11 006	5 828	5 178
30-34	5 392	2 678	2 715	5 580	2 816	2 764	6 864	3 592	3 271	9 103	4 843	4 260
35-39	4 930	2 508	2 422	5 381	2 673	2 707	5 490	2 789	2 701	6 957	3 677	3 280
40-44	4 308	2 173	2 135	4 783	2 457	2 326	5 283	2 623	2 660	5 415	2 773	2 642
45-49	3 243	1 595	1 648	4 252	2 142	2 110	4 651	2 383	2 268	5 105	2 541	2 564
50-54	2 426	1 170	1 256	3 088	1 512	1 576	4 098	2 030	2 068	4 430	2 257	2 174
55-59	2 561	1 236	1 325	2 294	1 080	1 214	2 891	1 400	1 492	3 835	1 872	1 963
60-64	2 059	987	1 072	2 220	1 055	1 165	2 079	955	1 124	2 651	1 262	1 389
65-69	1 651	770	880	1 822	835	986	1 962	892	1 070	1 818	813	1 004
70-74	1 043	486	557	1 234	565	670	1 402	608	794	1 625	720	905
75-79	574	254	320	719	318	401	857	371	486	1 017	427	590
80 +	447	178	269	492	196	296	707	273	434	806	316	490

Age group	1990 Both sexes	1990 Males	1990 Females	1995 Both sexes	1995 Males	1995 Females	2000 Both sexes	2000 Males	2000 Females	2005 Both sexes	2005 Males	2005 Females
All ages	153 498	78 655	74 843	172 556	88 679	83 877	193 075	99 035	94 040	214 323	109 959	104 364
0-4	22 152	11 302	10 850	23 101	11 791	11 310	24 460	12 492	11 968	25 358	12 951	12 407
5-9	20 226	10 307	9 919	21 719	11 074	10 645	22 868	11 666	11 202	24 256	12 381	11 874
10-14	18 019	9 199	8 820	20 010	10 195	9 815	21 538	10 980	10 558	22 862	11 659	11 204
15-19	15 847	8 134	7 713	17 688	9 002	8 686	19 750	10 061	9 689	21 495	10 962	10 533
20-24	13 996	7 231	6 765	15 689	8 134	7 555	17 953	9 231	8 722	19 972	10 256	9 716
25-29	12 942	6 795	6 146	14 407	7 676	6 731	16 464	8 696	7 768	18 493	9 654	8 839
30-34	11 073	5 931	5 142	13 226	7 022	6 204	14 649	7 810	6 839	16 765	8 932	7 833
35-39	9 045	4 844	4 201	10 877	5 795	5 082	13 024	6 855	6 169	14 562	7 779	6 783
40-44	6 751	3 584	3 167	8 676	4 640	4 036	10 603	5 608	4 995	12 703	6 670	6 033
45-49	5 281	2 703	2 577	6 457	3 410	3 047	8 285	4 342	3 943	10 189	5 335	4 854
50-54	4 808	2 377	2 431	5 132	2 604	2 527	6 073	3 114	2 959	7 850	4 041	3 809
55-59	4 121	2 065	2 055	4 655	2 275	2 379	4 759	2 338	2 421	5 696	2 856	2 841
60-64	3 487	1 661	1 826	3 835	1 895	1 939	4 278	2 034	2 244	4 400	2 111	2 288
65-69	2 297	1 067	1 231	3 111	1 455	1 655	3 409	1 647	1 762	3 805	1 758	2 046
70-74	1 470	637	833	1 914	867	1 047	2 566	1 163	1 403	2 813	1 313	1 501
75-79	1 151	489	662	1 079	454	625	1 394	606	787	1 880	815	1 065
80 +	832	330	502	981	388	592	1 002	391	611	1 223	485	737

United Nations Department of Economic and Social Affairs/Population Division
World Population Prospects: The 2004 Revision, Volume II: Sex and Age Distribution of the World Population

88

POPULATION BY AGE AND SEX (in thousands)

Age group	2005			2010			2015			2020		
	Both sexes	Males	Females	Both sexes	Males	Females	Both sexes	Males	Females	Both sexes	Males	Females
All ages	214 323	109 959	104 364	235 501	120 626	114 875	257 105	131 498	125 607	278 401	142 170	136 231
0-4	25 358	12 951	12 407	26 480	13 530	12 950	27 316	13 960	13 356	27 700	14 154	13 547
5-9	24 256	12 381	11 874	25 145	12 837	12 308	26 320	13 442	12 878	27 180	13 885	13 296
10-14	22 862	11 659	11 204	24 187	12 342	11 844	25 083	12 801	12 282	26 256	13 406	12 851
15-19	21 495	10 962	10 533	22 780	11 618	11 162	24 111	12 304	11 806	25 002	12 760	12 242
20-24	19 972	10 256	9 716	21 588	11 063	10 526	22 878	11 720	11 158	24 187	12 390	11 797
25-29	18 493	9 654	8 839	20 264	10 496	9 768	21 876	11 297	10 579	23 132	11 927	11 204
30-34	16 765	8 932	7 833	18 634	9 771	8 864	20 403	10 607	9 796	21 985	11 384	10 600
35-39	14 562	7 779	6 783	16 596	8 825	7 772	18 482	9 674	8 808	20 236	10 501	9 735
40-44	12 703	6 670	6 033	14 208	7 540	6 668	16 263	8 601	7 662	18 150	9 457	8 693
45-49	10 189	5 335	4 854	12 295	6 389	5 906	13 818	7 272	6 546	15 871	8 336	7 535
50-54	7 850	4 041	3 809	9 740	5 020	4 719	11 832	6 069	5 763	13 360	6 958	6 402
55-59	5 696	2 856	2 841	7 420	3 745	3 675	9 268	4 697	4 571	11 325	5 726	5 599
60-64	4 400	2 111	2 288	5 301	2 602	2 699	6 941	3 434	3 507	8 714	4 335	4 379
65-69	3 805	1 758	2 046	3 940	1 841	2 099	4 785	2 289	2 496	6 299	3 040	3 260
70-74	2 813	1 313	1 501	3 181	1 419	1 762	3 324	1 501	1 823	4 078	1 886	2 192
75-79	1 880	815	1 065	2 090	933	1 157	2 404	1 024	1 380	2 539	1 095	1 444
80-84	842	347	495	1 156	473	683	1 308	551	757	1 540	617	923
85-89	283	106	177	390	148	241	547	206	341	632	244	388
90-94	85	29	56	87	29	58	127	42	85	185	61	124
95-99	12	4	8	17	5	12	18	5	13	29	7	21
100 +	1	0	1	1	0	1	2	0	2	2	0	2

Age group	2025			2030			2035			2040		
	Both sexes	Males	Females	Both sexes	Males	Females	Both sexes	Males	Females	Both sexes	Males	Females
All ages	299 119	152 492	146 627	318 826	162 243	156 583	337 200	171 261	165 940	354 096	179 484	174 612
0-4	27 756	14 186	13 571	27 620	14 121	13 499	27 393	14 010	13 384	27 210	13 920	13 290
5-9	27 592	14 092	13 499	27 666	14 135	13 531	27 543	14 078	13 465	27 327	13 972	13 354
10-14	27 125	13 852	13 272	27 542	14 064	13 479	27 622	14 109	13 513	27 503	14 055	13 448
15-19	26 183	13 369	12 814	27 058	13 819	13 239	27 481	14 034	13 447	27 566	14 083	13 483
20-24	25 090	12 852	12 238	26 276	13 463	12 813	27 157	13 918	13 240	27 587	14 137	13 451
25-29	24 450	12 603	11 848	25 357	13 065	12 292	26 550	13 680	12 870	27 437	14 138	13 299
30-34	23 248	12 018	11 230	24 572	12 695	11 877	25 486	13 162	12 324	26 684	13 780	12 903
35-39	21 823	11 280	10 543	23 094	11 918	11 176	24 425	12 600	11 825	25 346	13 072	12 274
40-44	19 908	10 286	9 622	21 502	11 070	10 431	22 780	11 713	11 066	24 117	12 400	11 717
45-49	17 760	9 195	8 566	19 522	10 029	9 493	21 117	10 814	10 302	22 400	11 461	10 939
50-54	15 404	8 017	7 387	17 288	8 875	8 413	19 041	9 704	9 336	20 632	10 487	10 144
55-59	12 842	6 606	6 236	14 857	7 644	7 213	16 717	8 489	8 229	18 449	9 306	9 144
60-64	10 099	5 017	5 082	12 102	6 108	6 014	14 143	7 168	6 974	15 960	7 988	7 972
65-69	7 957	3 863	4 093	9 824	4 769	5 055	11 245	5 572	5 673	13 116	6 513	6 603
70-74	5 414	2 525	2 889	6 895	3 237	3 658	8 580	4 031	4 549	9 899	4 758	5 141
75-79	3 167	1 397	1 770	4 255	1 891	2 364	5 486	2 454	3 032	6 909	3 094	3 815
80-84	1 654	668	986	2 115	869	1 246	2 895	1 194	1 701	3 806	1 579	2 228
85-89	776	281	495	851	308	543	1 130	413	717	1 592	581	1 011
90-94	223	73	150	288	88	201	324	97	227	454	137	318
95-99	44	11	33	56	14	42	76	17	59	88	20	68
100 +	4	1	3	7	1	6	9	1	8	13	2	11

Age group	2045			2050		
	Both sexes	Males	Females	Both sexes	Males	Females
All ages	369 481	186 912	182 568	383 216	193 495	189 721
0-4	27 134	13 885	13 249	26 957	13 799	13 158
5-9	27 151	13 887	13 264	27 081	13 856	13 225
10-14	27 290	13 952	13 339	27 117	13 868	13 249
15-19	27 452	14 032	13 420	27 243	13 931	13 312
20-24	27 679	14 191	13 489	27 571	14 144	13 427
25-29	27 873	14 362	13 511	27 972	14 420	13 551
30-34	27 576	14 242	13 334	28 018	14 470	13 548
35-39	26 548	13 693	12 855	27 444	14 157	13 287
40-44	25 045	12 876	12 169	26 250	13 500	12 751
45-49	23 744	12 153	11 591	24 679	12 634	12 045
50-54	21 919	11 137	10 781	23 267	11 833	11 434
55-59	20 028	10 081	9 946	21 314	10 731	10 583
60-64	17 653	8 781	8 872	19 205	9 541	9 665
65-69	14 860	7 290	7 571	16 488	8 043	8 445
70-74	11 625	5 605	6 020	13 251	6 313	6 938
75-79	8 061	3 702	4 359	9 569	4 412	5 157
80-84	4 880	2 026	2 854	5 797	2 476	3 321
85-89	2 153	788	1 365	2 837	1 040	1 798
90-94	663	198	465	934	280	653
95-99	131	30	101	199	45	154
100 +	16	2	14	24	4	20

United Nations Department of Economic and Social Affairs/Population Division
World Population Prospects: The 2004 Revision, Volume II: Sex and Age Distribution of the World Population

89

POPULATION BY AGE AND SEX (in thousands)

Age group	2005 Both sexes	2005 Males	2005 Females	2010 Both sexes	2010 Males	2010 Females	2015 Both sexes	2015 Males	2015 Females	2020 Both sexes	2020 Males	2020 Females
All ages	214 323	109 959	104 364	237 634	121 717	115 917	262 996	134 510	128 486	289 382	147 782	141 600
0-4	25 358	12 951	12 407	28 613	14 621	13 992	31 083	15 886	15 197	32 808	16 764	16 044
5-9	24 256	12 381	11 874	25 145	12 837	12 308	28 442	14 527	13 915	30 934	15 804	15 131
10-14	22 862	11 659	11 204	24 187	12 342	11 844	25 083	12 801	12 282	28 375	14 489	13 887
15-19	21 495	10 962	10 533	22 780	11 618	11 162	24 111	12 304	11 806	25 002	12 760	12 242
20-24	19 972	10 256	9 716	21 588	11 063	10 526	22 878	11 720	11 158	24 187	12 390	11 797
25-29	18 493	9 654	8 839	20 264	10 496	9 768	21 876	11 297	10 579	23 132	11 927	11 204
30-34	16 765	8 932	7 833	18 634	9 771	8 864	20 403	10 607	9 796	21 985	11 384	10 600
35-39	14 562	7 779	6 783	16 596	8 825	7 772	18 482	9 674	8 808	20 236	10 501	9 735
40-44	12 703	6 670	6 033	14 208	7 540	6 668	16 263	8 601	7 662	18 150	9 457	8 693
45-49	10 189	5 335	4 854	12 295	6 389	5 906	13 818	7 272	6 546	15 871	8 336	7 535
50-54	7 850	4 041	3 809	9 740	5 020	4 719	11 832	6 069	5 763	13 360	6 958	6 402
55-59	5 696	2 856	2 841	7 420	3 745	3 675	9 268	4 697	4 571	11 325	5 726	5 599
60-64	4 400	2 111	2 288	5 301	2 602	2 699	6 941	3 434	3 507	8 714	4 335	4 379
65-69	3 805	1 758	2 046	3 940	1 841	2 099	4 785	2 289	2 496	6 299	3 040	3 260
70-74	2 813	1 313	1 501	3 181	1 419	1 762	3 324	1 501	1 823	4 078	1 886	2 192
75-79	1 880	815	1 065	2 090	933	1 157	2 404	1 024	1 380	2 539	1 095	1 444
80-84	842	347	495	1 156	473	683	1 308	551	757	1 540	617	923
85-89	283	106	177	390	148	241	547	206	341	632	244	388
90-94	85	29	56	87	29	58	127	42	85	185	61	124
95-99	12	4	8	17	5	12	18	5	13	29	7	21
100 +	1	0	1	1	0	1	2	0	2	2	0	2

Age group	2025 Both sexes	2025 Males	2025 Females	2030 Both sexes	2030 Males	2030 Females	2035 Both sexes	2035 Males	2035 Females	2040 Both sexes	2040 Males	2040 Females
All ages	315 608	160 918	154 690	341 614	173 887	167 728	367 727	186 858	180 869	394 173	199 963	194 210
0-4	33 288	17 013	16 274	33 950	17 358	16 591	35 171	17 988	17 183	36 811	18 833	17 978
5-9	32 685	16 694	15 990	33 185	16 955	16 230	33 861	17 308	16 553	35 091	17 944	17 148
10-14	30 874	15 768	15 106	32 630	16 662	15 968	33 136	16 926	16 209	33 816	17 282	16 534
15-19	28 298	14 449	13 849	30 801	15 731	15 070	32 561	16 628	15 934	33 073	16 895	16 177
20-24	25 090	12 852	12 238	28 385	14 539	13 846	30 892	15 823	15 069	32 657	16 723	15 934
25-29	24 450	12 603	11 848	25 357	13 065	12 292	28 653	14 752	13 901	31 162	16 038	15 124
30-34	23 248	12 018	11 230	24 572	12 695	11 877	25 486	13 162	12 324	28 781	14 849	13 932
35-39	21 823	11 280	10 543	23 094	11 918	11 176	24 425	12 600	11 825	25 346	13 072	12 274
40-44	19 908	10 286	9 622	21 502	11 070	10 431	22 780	11 713	11 066	24 117	12 400	11 717
45-49	17 760	9 195	8 566	19 522	10 029	9 493	21 117	10 814	10 302	22 400	11 461	10 939
50-54	15 404	8 017	7 387	17 288	8 875	8 413	19 041	9 704	9 336	20 632	10 487	10 144
55-59	12 842	6 606	6 236	14 857	7 644	7 213	16 717	8 489	8 229	18 449	9 306	9 144
60-64	10 699	5 317	5 382	12 182	6 168	6 014	14 143	7 169	6 974	15 960	7 988	7 972
65-69	7 957	3 863	4 093	9 824	4 769	5 055	11 245	5 572	5 673	13 116	6 513	6 603
70-74	5 414	2 525	2 889	6 895	3 237	3 658	8 580	4 031	4 549	9 899	4 758	5 141
75-79	3 167	1 397	1 770	4 255	1 891	2 364	5 486	2 454	3 032	6 909	3 094	3 815
80-84	1 654	668	986	2 115	869	1 246	2 895	1 194	1 701	3 806	1 579	2 228
85-89	776	281	495	851	308	543	1 130	413	717	1 592	581	1 011
90-94	223	73	150	288	88	201	324	97	227	454	137	318
95-99	44	11	33	56	14	42	76	17	59	88	20	68
100 +	4	1	3	7	1	6	9	1	8	13	2	11

Age group	2045 Both sexes	2045 Males	2045 Females	2050 Both sexes	2050 Males	2050 Females
All ages	420 784	213 130	207 654	447 025	226 107	220 917
0-4	38 425	19 665	18 760	39 545	20 245	19 301
5-9	36 739	18 793	17 946	38 358	19 628	18 730
10-14	35 050	17 920	17 130	36 699	18 770	17 929
15-19	33 758	17 254	16 504	34 995	17 894	17 101
20-24	33 176	16 996	16 180	33 866	17 359	16 507
25-29	32 931	16 941	15 991	33 456	17 218	16 238
30-34	31 291	16 135	15 156	33 063	17 041	16 023
35-39	28 638	14 757	13 881	31 148	16 044	15 104
40-44	25 045	12 876	12 169	28 331	14 558	13 773
45-49	23 744	12 153	11 591	24 679	12 634	12 045
50-54	21 919	11 137	10 781	23 267	11 833	11 434
55-59	20 028	10 081	9 946	21 314	10 731	10 583
60-64	17 653	8 781	8 872	19 205	9 541	9 665
65-69	14 860	7 290	7 571	16 488	8 043	8 445
70-74	11 625	5 605	6 020	13 251	6 313	6 938
75-79	8 061	3 702	4 359	9 569	4 412	5 157
80-84	4 880	2 026	2 854	5 797	2 476	3 321
85-89	2 153	788	1 365	2 837	1 040	1 798
90-94	663	198	465	934	280	653
95-99	131	30	101	199	45	154
100 +	16	2	14	24	4	20

United Nations Department of Economic and Social Affairs/Population Division
World Population Prospects: The 2004 Revision, Volume II: Sex and Age Distribution of the World Population

90

POPULATION BY AGE AND SEX (in thousands)

Age group	2005 Both sexes	Males	Females	2010 Both sexes	Males	Females	2015 Both sexes	Males	Females	2020 Both sexes	Males	Females
All ages	214 323	109 959	104 364	233 366	119 534	113 832	251 208	128 482	122 725	267 401	136 548	130 854
0-4	25 358	12 951	12 407	24 345	12 438	11 907	23 542	12 030	11 512	22 581	11 537	11 044
5-9	24 256	12 381	11 874	25 145	12 837	12 308	24 196	12 356	11 840	23 420	11 963	11 457
10-14	22 862	11 659	11 204	24 187	12 342	11 844	25 083	12 801	12 282	24 136	12 322	11 814
15-19	21 495	10 962	10 533	22 780	11 618	11 162	24 111	12 304	11 806	25 002	12 760	12 242
20-24	19 972	10 256	9 716	21 588	11 063	10 526	22 878	11 720	11 158	24 187	12 390	11 797
25-29	18 493	9 654	8 839	20 264	10 496	9 768	21 876	11 297	10 579	23 132	11 927	11 204
30-34	16 765	8 932	7 833	18 634	9 771	8 864	20 403	10 607	9 796	21 985	11 384	10 600
35-39	14 562	7 779	6 783	16 596	8 825	7 772	18 482	9 674	8 808	20 236	10 501	9 735
40-44	12 703	6 670	6 033	14 208	7 540	6 668	16 263	8 601	7 662	18 150	9 457	8 693
45-49	10 189	5 335	4 854	12 295	6 389	5 906	13 818	7 272	6 546	15 871	8 336	7 535
50-54	7 850	4 041	3 809	9 740	5 020	4 719	11 832	6 069	5 763	13 360	6 958	6 402
55-59	5 696	2 856	2 841	7 420	3 745	3 675	9 268	4 697	4 571	11 325	5 726	5 599
60-64	4 400	2 111	2 288	5 301	2 602	2 699	6 941	3 434	3 507	8 714	4 335	4 379
65-69	3 805	1 758	2 046	3 940	1 841	2 099	4 785	2 289	2 496	6 299	3 040	3 260
70-74	2 813	1 313	1 501	3 181	1 419	1 762	3 324	1 501	1 823	4 078	1 886	2 192
75-79	1 880	815	1 065	2 090	933	1 157	2 404	1 024	1 380	2 539	1 095	1 444
80-84	842	347	495	1 156	473	683	1 308	551	757	1 540	617	923
85-89	283	106	177	390	148	241	547	206	341	632	244	388
90-94	85	29	56	87	29	58	127	42	85	185	61	124
95-99	12	4	8	17	5	12	18	5	13	29	7	21
100 +	1	0	1	1	0	1	2	0	2	2	0	2

Age group	2025 Both sexes	Males	Females	2030 Both sexes	Males	Females	2035 Both sexes	Males	Females	2040 Both sexes	Males	Females
All ages	282 623	144 063	138 560	296 225	150 695	145 531	307 517	156 095	151 423	316 158	160 100	156 057
0-4	22 237	11 364	10 873	21 486	10 984	10 501	20 272	10 367	9 905	18 905	9 670	9 235
5-9	22 487	11 484	11 003	22 159	11 321	10 839	21 421	10 948	10 473	20 217	10 336	9 881
10-14	23 370	11 934	11 436	22 443	11 459	10 984	22 121	11 298	10 822	21 386	10 928	10 458
15-19	24 068	12 288	11 779	23 309	11 904	11 404	22 389	11 434	10 955	22 071	11 277	10 795
20-24	25 090	12 852	12 238	24 165	12 385	11 779	23 417	12 009	11 408	22 506	11 544	10 962
25-29	24 450	12 603	11 848	25 357	13 065	12 292	24 444	12 606	11 838	23 706	12 236	11 470
30-34	23 248	12 018	11 230	24 572	12 695	11 877	25 486	13 162	12 324	24 585	12 711	11 874
35-39	21 823	11 280	10 543	23 094	11 918	11 176	24 425	12 600	11 825	25 346	13 072	12 274
40-44	19 908	10 286	9 622	21 502	11 070	10 431	22 780	11 713	11 066	24 117	12 400	11 717
45-49	17 760	9 195	8 566	19 522	10 029	9 493	21 117	10 814	10 302	22 400	11 461	10 939
50-54	15 404	8 017	7 387	17 288	8 875	8 413	19 041	9 704	9 336	20 632	10 487	10 144
55-59	12 842	6 606	6 236	14 857	7 644	7 213	16 717	8 409	8 309	18 440	9 306	9 144
60-64	10 699	5 317	5 382	12 182	6 168	6 014	14 143	7 169	6 974	15 960	7 988	7 972
65-69	7 957	3 863	4 093	9 824	4 769	5 055	11 245	5 572	5 673	13 116	6 513	6 603
70-74	5 414	2 525	2 889	6 895	3 237	3 658	8 580	4 031	4 549	9 899	4 758	5 141
75-79	3 167	1 397	1 770	4 255	1 891	2 364	5 486	2 454	3 032	6 909	3 094	3 815
80-84	1 654	668	986	2 115	869	1 246	2 895	1 194	1 701	3 806	1 579	2 228
85-89	776	281	495	851	308	543	1 130	413	717	1 592	581	1 011
90-94	223	73	150	288	88	201	324	97	227	454	137	318
95-99	44	11	33	56	14	42	76	17	59	88	20	68
100 +	4	1	3	7	1	6	9	1	8	13	2	11

Age group	2045 Both sexes	Males	Females	2050 Both sexes	Males	Females
All ages	322 224	162 766	159 457	325 883	164 198	161 684
0-4	17 753	9 083	8 670	16 801	8 599	8 202
5-9	18 858	9 644	9 213	17 711	9 061	8 650
10-14	20 186	10 319	9 867	18 830	9 629	9 201
15-19	21 341	10 909	10 432	20 145	10 303	9 843
20-24	22 195	11 391	10 803	21 471	11 028	10 442
25-29	22 804	11 777	11 027	22 499	11 629	10 870
30-34	23 855	12 346	11 509	22 961	11 892	11 068
35-39	24 456	12 627	11 828	23 735	12 268	11 467
40-44	25 045	12 876	12 169	24 168	12 440	11 728
45-49	23 744	12 153	11 591	24 679	12 634	12 045
50-54	21 919	11 137	10 781	23 267	11 833	11 434
55-59	20 028	10 081	9 946	21 314	10 731	10 583
60-64	17 653	8 781	8 872	19 205	9 541	9 665
65-69	14 860	7 290	7 571	16 488	8 043	8 445
70-74	11 625	5 605	6 020	13 251	6 313	6 938
75-79	8 061	3 702	4 359	9 569	4 412	5 157
80-84	4 880	2 026	2 854	5 797	2 476	3 321
85-89	2 153	788	1 365	2 837	1 040	1 798
90-94	663	198	465	934	280	653
95-99	131	30	101	199	45	154
100 +	16	2	14	24	4	20

POPULATION BY AGE AND SEX (in thousands)

Age group	1950 Both sexes	1950 Males	1950 Females	1955 Both sexes	1955 Males	1955 Females	1960 Both sexes	1960 Males	1960 Females	1965 Both sexes	1965 Males	1965 Females
All ages	547 405	255 320	292 085	575 186	270 068	305 118	604 406	285 304	319 102	634 032	301 090	332 942
0-4	50 382	25 740	24 642	54 837	28 092	26 746	57 283	29 269	28 014	56 924	29 135	27 789
5-9	42 559	21 556	21 004	49 876	25 450	24 426	54 425	27 851	26 574	56 920	29 071	27 849
10-14	50 300	25 331	24 968	42 420	21 467	20 954	49 748	25 355	24 392	54 309	27 789	26 520
15-19	46 042	23 122	22 920	50 011	25 152	24 860	42 247	21 301	20 947	49 720	25 329	24 391
20-24	48 798	23 801	24 998	45 653	22 874	22 779	49 494	24 835	24 659	42 106	21 214	20 892
25-29	42 192	19 246	22 946	48 170	23 386	24 784	44 916	22 431	22 485	49 250	24 700	24 550
30-34	31 349	14 189	17 160	41 739	18 970	22 770	47 486	22 953	24 533	44 718	22 328	22 390
35-39	40 505	18 072	22 433	30 645	13 796	16 849	41 080	18 564	22 516	47 207	22 800	24 407
40-44	39 416	17 936	21 480	39 939	17 740	22 199	30 151	13 503	16 648	40 660	18 312	22 348
45-49	35 505	16 009	19 496	38 317	17 315	21 001	39 007	17 208	21 799	29 530	13 146	16 385
50-54	29 667	13 080	16 587	34 115	15 223	18 893	37 016	16 554	20 462	37 785	16 479	21 306
55-59	24 342	10 409	13 933	27 944	12 071	15 873	32 389	14 195	18 194	35 245	15 473	19 771
60-64	21 388	8 989	12 399	22 330	9 306	13 024	25 829	10 857	14 973	30 032	12 794	17 238
65-69	17 218	7 123	10 095	18 720	7 600	11 120	19 760	7 917	11 843	22 839	9 187	13 652
70-74	13 194	5 342	7 852	14 153	5 609	8 544	15 363	5 936	9 427	16 384	6 224	10 160
75-79	8 471	3 284	5 187	9 367	3 599	5 768	10 198	3 811	6 387	11 246	4 058	7 187
80 +	6 077	2 091	3 986	6 948	2 418	4 530	8 015	2 764	5 250	9 158	3 053	6 106

Age group	1970 Both sexes	1970 Males	1970 Females	1975 Both sexes	1975 Males	1975 Females	1980 Both sexes	1980 Males	1980 Females	1985 Both sexes	1985 Males	1985 Females
All ages	655 862	312 637	343 225	675 548	322 694	352 854	692 435	331 619	360 816	706 017	338 703	367 314
0-4	52 649	26 935	25 713	51 267	26 230	25 037	49 893	25 538	24 355	49 365	25 266	24 099
5-9	56 616	28 942	27 675	52 680	26 913	25 766	51 033	26 087	24 946	49 588	25 350	24 238
10-14	56 939	29 080	27 858	56 403	28 856	27 547	52 657	26 901	25 756	51 155	26 164	24 992
15-19	54 219	27 676	26 543	56 414	28 770	27 644	56 062	28 655	27 407	52 971	27 069	25 903
20-24	49 129	24 988	24 142	54 143	27 433	26 710	56 402	28 766	27 636	56 243	28 610	27 633
25-29	41 590	20 941	20 649	49 238	24 959	24 279	53 946	27 296	26 651	56 188	28 462	27 726
30-34	48 603	24 291	24 312	41 181	20 685	20 496	49 541	24 974	24 567	53 521	26 933	26 588
35-39	44 107	21 992	22 115	48 250	23 980	24 270	40 061	20 027	20 033	48 874	24 506	24 367
40-44	46 431	22 303	24 129	43 516	21 525	21 990	47 793	23 574	24 219	39 697	19 700	19 996
45-49	39 651	17 745	21 906	45 436	21 648	23 788	42 378	20 772	21 606	46 447	22 674	23 773
50-54	28 552	12 574	15 978	38 795	17 062	21 732	44 134	20 808	23 327	40 991	19 789	21 202
55-59	35 975	15 418	20 557	27 373	11 796	15 577	37 493	16 172	21 321	42 028	19 368	22 660
60-64	32 818	14 003	18 815	33 585	14 005	19 580	25 547	10 698	14 848	35 006	14 661	20 344
65-69	26 806	10 915	15 891	29 261	11 904	17 357	29 327	11 683	17 643	23 031	9 232	13 798
70-74	19 037	7 185	11 852	22 203	8 480	13 723	24 918	9 502	15 415	25 482	9 534	15 948
75-79	12 149	4 265	7 884	13 931	4 839	9 092	17 100	5 980	11 119	18 768	6 529	12 239
80 +	10 590	3 385	7 206	11 873	3 608	8 264	14 151	4 184	9 967	16 663	4 857	11 806

Age group	1990 Both sexes	1990 Males	1990 Females	1995 Both sexes	1995 Males	1995 Females	2000 Both sexes	2000 Males	2000 Females	2005 Both sexes	2005 Males	2005 Females
All ages	721 390	346 863	374 527	727 885	350 623	377 262	728 463	350 497	377 966	728 389	350 386	378 003
0-4	48 308	24 741	23 566	41 263	21 166	20 097	36 896	18 934	17 962	36 605	18 801	17 804
5-9	49 336	25 174	24 162	48 662	24 911	23 751	41 588	21 307	20 281	37 098	19 030	18 068
10-14	49 807	25 406	24 401	49 869	25 428	24 441	49 227	25 172	24 054	41 769	21 394	20 375
15-19	51 338	26 179	25 159	50 327	25 657	24 670	50 723	25 879	24 844	49 682	25 383	24 299
20-24	52 751	26 776	25 975	51 724	26 338	25 386	50 776	25 745	25 031	51 347	26 100	25 247
25-29	56 132	28 357	27 775	53 157	26 916	26 241	52 121	26 318	25 803	51 184	25 843	25 341
30-34	56 435	28 381	28 054	56 392	28 392	28 001	53 362	26 850	26 512	52 319	26 295	26 024
35-39	53 524	26 765	26 758	56 219	28 125	28 094	56 131	28 055	28 076	53 310	26 672	26 638
40-44	48 350	24 138	24 211	52 930	26 278	26 651	55 390	27 440	27 950	55 600	27 580	28 020
45-49	39 249	19 391	19 858	47 494	23 491	24 003	51 691	25 326	26 365	54 459	26 691	27 768
50-54	45 227	21 859	23 368	38 346	18 665	19 681	46 091	22 406	23 685	50 343	24 296	26 047
55-59	39 331	18 668	20 663	43 056	20 336	22 720	36 734	17 499	19 234	44 081	21 023	23 058
60-64	39 677	17 758	21 919	36 804	16 923	19 881	40 316	18 413	21 903	34 829	16 183	18 645
65-69	31 775	12 825	18 950	35 786	15 303	20 483	33 300	14 697	18 603	36 555	16 049	20 507
70-74	20 232	7 699	12 533	27 428	10 468	16 960	30 720	12 411	18 310	28 903	12 122	16 781
75-79	19 809	6 832	12 977	15 826	5 590	10 236	21 999	7 777	14 223	24 578	9 276	15 303
80 +	20 110	5 914	14 196	22 602	6 635	15 967	21 398	6 268	15 130	25 726	7 647	18 078

United Nations Department of Economic and Social Affairs/Population Division
World Population Prospects: The 2004 Revision, Volume II: Sex and Age Distribution of the World Population

92

POPULATION BY AGE AND SEX (in thousands)

Age group	2005 Both sexes	2005 Males	2005 Females	2010 Both sexes	2010 Males	2010 Females	2015 Both sexes	2015 Males	2015 Females	2020 Both sexes	2020 Males	2020 Females
All ages	728 389	350 386	378 003	725 786	348 904	376 882	721 111	346 491	374 620	714 959	343 434	371 524
0-4	36 605	18 801	17 804	36 593	18 797	17 796	35 736	18 359	17 377	34 615	17 784	16 832
5-9	37 098	19 030	18 068	36 763	18 869	17 894	36 730	18 855	17 875	35 881	18 421	17 460
10-14	41 769	21 394	20 375	37 246	19 102	18 144	36 894	18 933	17 961	36 864	18 920	17 943
15-19	49 682	25 383	24 299	42 140	21 555	20 585	37 604	19 261	18 343	37 259	19 097	18 162
20-24	51 347	26 100	25 247	50 102	25 495	24 607	42 583	21 702	20 881	38 090	19 441	18 649
25-29	51 184	25 843	25 341	51 450	26 038	25 412	50 206	25 455	24 751	42 825	21 764	21 061
30-34	52 319	26 295	26 024	51 060	25 651	25 409	51 252	25 825	25 427	50 094	25 311	24 783
35-39	53 310	26 672	26 638	52 017	25 985	26 032	50 700	25 333	25 367	50 906	25 533	25 372
40-44	55 600	27 580	28 020	52 749	26 213	26 536	51 425	25 526	25 899	50 148	24 919	25 229
45-49	54 459	26 691	27 768	54 703	26 876	27 827	52 007	25 643	26 364	50 737	25 004	25 734
50-54	50 343	24 296	26 047	53 079	25 648	27 431	53 472	25 958	27 514	51 023	24 909	26 114
55-59	44 081	21 023	23 058	48 196	22 816	25 381	50 974	24 203	26 772	51 584	24 672	26 912
60-64	34 829	16 183	18 645	41 789	19 441	22 348	45 714	21 116	24 599	48 527	22 528	26 000
65-69	36 555	16 049	20 507	32 015	14 403	17 612	38 499	17 348	21 151	42 203	18 887	23 316
70-74	28 903	12 122	16 781	31 819	13 292	18 527	28 367	12 233	16 134	34 221	14 790	19 431
75-79	24 578	9 276	15 303	23 501	9 251	14 250	25 998	10 209	15 789	23 701	9 670	14 031
80-84	15 655	5 010	10 645	17 568	6 025	11 544	17 172	6 166	11 006	19 169	6 890	12 279
85-89	6 252	1 772	4 480	9 272	2 609	6 662	10 534	3 187	7 348	10 622	3 368	7 254
90-94	3 054	716	2 338	2 746	655	2 091	4 253	999	3 253	4 951	1 253	3 698
95-99	690	136	554	867	164	702	837	158	679	1 376	252	1 125
100 +	74	13	61	111	18	93	151	23	129	164	23	141

Age group	2025 Both sexes	2025 Males	2025 Females	2030 Both sexes	2030 Males	2030 Females	2035 Both sexes	2035 Males	2035 Females	2040 Both sexes	2040 Males	2040 Females
All ages	707 235	339 616	367 619	698 140	335 121	363 019	688 041	330 230	357 811	677 191	325 150	352 041
0-4	33 338	17 128	16 210	32 503	16 701	15 802	32 405	16 653	15 753	32 679	16 795	15 884
5-9	34 768	17 850	16 918	33 498	17 199	16 298	32 668	16 775	15 893	32 574	16 729	15 845
10-14	36 018	18 489	17 530	34 910	17 921	16 989	33 644	17 273	16 371	32 818	16 850	15 967
15-19	37 229	19 086	18 144	36 389	18 658	17 731	35 285	18 094	17 191	34 025	17 440	16 575
20-24	37 754	19 285	18 469	37 733	19 282	18 451	36 902	18 862	18 040	35 810	18 307	17 503
25-29	38 389	19 547	18 841	38 061	19 402	18 659	38 047	19 406	18 641	37 234	19 001	18 234
30-34	42 875	21 734	21 141	38 509	19 569	18 940	38 188	19 434	18 754	38 183	19 448	18 735
35-39	49 826	25 081	24 744	42 777	21 623	21 154	38 403	19 516	18 976	38 185	19 394	18 791
40-44	50 379	25 147	25 232	49 365	24 749	24 616	42 491	21 412	21 079	38 304	19 371	18 933
45-49	49 524	24 451	25 073	49 784	24 708	25 076	48 833	24 359	24 473	42 159	21 159	21 000
50-54	49 832	24 328	25 504	48 691	23 833	24 858	48 978	24 113	24 865	48 102	23 819	24 283
55-59	49 416	23 821	25 595	48 317	23 305	25 012	47 252	22 866	24 387	47 575	23 171	24 404
60-64	49 367	23 153	26 214	47 523	22 518	25 005	46 533	22 073	24 460	45 559	21 695	23 864
65-69	45 010	20 289	24 721	46 088	21 057	25 031	44 626	20 656	23 970	43 772	20 293	23 479
70-74	37 613	16 149	21 465	40 352	17 490	22 862	41 664	18 371	23 293	40 644	18 210	22 434
75-79	28 722	11 751	16 972	31 095	12 002	19 010	34 277	14 101	20 176	35 782	15 035	20 747
80-84	17 971	6 741	11 230	21 946	8 270	13 677	24 382	9 137	15 245	26 684	10 159	16 525
85-89	12 054	3 840	8 215	11 729	3 907	7 822	14 522	4 873	9 650	16 318	5 450	10 868
90-94	5 212	1 381	3 831	6 063	1 621	4 442	6 187	1 731	4 456	7 833	2 216	5 617
95-99	1 666	328	1 338	1 852	379	1 473	2 232	464	1 768	2 411	522	1 889
100 +	271	36	235	358	50	308	431	61	370	543	78	464

Age group	2045 Both sexes	2045 Males	2045 Females	2050 Both sexes	2050 Males	2050 Females
All ages	665 637	319 921	345 716	653 323	314 470	338 854
0-4	32 723	16 818	15 905	32 211	16 555	15 656
5-9	32 850	16 873	15 978	32 896	16 897	15 999
10-14	32 726	16 806	15 921	33 004	16 950	16 054
15-19	33 204	17 030	16 173	33 115	16 988	16 128
20-24	34 561	17 671	16 890	33 749	17 259	16 491
25-29	36 164	18 460	17 704	34 937	17 838	17 099
30-34	37 397	19 060	18 337	36 360	18 538	17 821
35-39	38 193	19 419	18 774	37 439	19 050	18 389
40-44	38 016	19 263	18 753	38 041	19 300	18 741
45-49	38 083	19 193	18 891	37 822	19 103	18 719
50-54	41 665	20 781	20 884	37 727	18 907	18 819
55-59	46 788	22 938	23 850	40 648	20 103	20 545
60-64	45 921	22 023	23 899	45 239	21 858	23 382
65-69	42 913	19 987	22 927	43 322	20 334	22 988
70-74	39 966	17 945	22 021	39 258	17 725	21 533
75-79	35 244	15 093	20 151	34 790	14 943	19 847
80-84	28 286	11 051	17 235	28 234	11 278	16 957
85-89	18 188	6 197	11 991	19 722	6 936	12 787
90-94	8 960	2 528	6 433	10 255	2 967	7 288
95-99	3 151	694	2 458	3 703	814	2 889
100 +	636	94	542	850	128	722

POPULATION BY AGE AND SEX (in thousands)

Age group	2005 Both sexes	Males	Females	2010 Both sexes	Males	Females	2015 Both sexes	Males	Females	2020 Both sexes	Males	Females
All ages	728 389	350 386	378 003	732 049	352 124	379 925	736 773	354 541	382 232	741 277	356 960	384 317
0-4	36 605	18 801	17 804	42 856	22 016	20 840	45 147	23 195	21 951	45 292	23 271	22 021
5-9	37 098	19 030	18 068	36 763	18 870	17 893	42 983	22 068	20 915	45 277	23 249	22 028
10-14	41 769	21 394	20 375	37 246	19 103	18 143	36 894	18 934	17 960	43 109	22 129	20 980
15-19	49 682	25 383	24 299	42 140	21 555	20 585	37 604	19 262	18 342	37 259	19 098	18 161
20-24	51 347	26 100	25 247	50 102	25 495	24 607	42 583	21 702	20 881	38 090	19 442	18 648
25-29	51 184	25 843	25 341	51 450	26 038	25 412	50 206	25 455	24 751	42 825	21 764	21 061
30-34	52 319	26 295	26 024	51 060	25 651	25 409	51 252	25 825	25 427	50 094	25 311	24 783
35-39	53 310	26 672	26 638	52 017	25 985	26 032	50 700	25 333	25 367	50 906	25 533	25 372
40-44	55 600	27 580	28 020	52 749	26 213	26 536	51 425	25 526	25 899	50 148	24 919	25 229
45-49	54 459	26 691	27 768	54 703	26 876	27 827	52 007	25 643	26 364	50 737	25 004	25 734
50-54	50 343	24 296	26 047	53 079	25 648	27 431	53 472	25 958	27 514	51 023	24 909	26 114
55-59	44 081	21 023	23 058	48 196	22 816	25 381	50 974	24 203	26 772	51 584	24 672	26 912
60-64	34 829	16 183	18 645	41 789	19 441	22 348	45 714	21 116	24 599	48 527	22 528	26 000
65-69	36 555	16 049	20 507	32 015	14 403	17 612	38 499	17 348	21 151	42 203	18 887	23 316
70-74	28 903	12 122	16 781	31 819	13 292	18 527	28 367	12 233	16 134	34 221	14 790	19 431
75-79	24 578	9 276	15 303	23 501	9 251	14 250	25 998	10 209	15 789	23 701	9 670	14 031
80-84	15 655	5 010	10 645	17 568	6 025	11 544	17 172	6 166	11 006	19 169	6 890	12 279
85-89	6 252	1 772	4 480	9 272	2 609	6 662	10 534	3 187	7 348	10 622	3 368	7 254
90-94	3 054	716	2 338	2 746	655	2 091	4 253	999	3 253	4 951	1 253	3 698
95-99	690	136	554	867	164	702	837	158	679	1 376	252	1 125
100 +	74	13	61	111	18	93	151	23	129	164	23	141

Age group	2025 Both sexes	Males	Females	2030 Both sexes	Males	Females	2035 Both sexes	Males	Females	2040 Both sexes	Males	Females
All ages	743 369	358 183	385 186	744 424	358 899	385 525	746 559	360 287	386 271	751 058	363 086	387 972
0-4	43 184	22 189	20 995	42 698	21 942	20 756	44 716	22 982	21 734	48 156	24 753	23 403
5-9	45 431	23 329	22 102	43 333	22 254	21 079	42 852	22 009	20 843	44 872	23 050	21 821
10-14	45 406	23 311	22 095	45 565	23 396	22 170	43 473	22 323	21 150	42 996	22 081	20 915
15-19	43 467	22 289	21 178	45 766	23 474	22 292	45 931	23 562	22 369	43 846	22 495	21 351
20-24	37 754	19 286	18 468	43 954	22 473	21 481	46 258	23 663	22 595	46 435	23 761	22 674
25-29	38 388	19 548	18 841	38 061	19 403	18 658	44 239	22 579	21 660	46 551	23 777	22 774
30-34	42 875	21 734	21 141	38 509	19 570	18 939	38 188	19 435	18 754	44 334	22 597	21 737
35-39	49 826	25 081	24 744	42 777	21 623	21 154	38 493	19 517	18 976	38 185	19 395	18 790
40-44	50 379	25 147	25 232	49 365	24 749	24 616	42 491	21 412	21 079	38 304	19 371	18 932
45-49	49 524	24 451	25 073	49 784	24 708	25 076	48 833	24 359	24 473	42 159	21 159	21 000
50-54	49 832	24 328	25 504	48 691	23 833	24 858	48 978	24 113	24 865	48 102	23 819	24 283
55-59	49 416	23 821	25 595	48 317	23 305	25 012	47 252	22 866	24 387	47 575	23 171	24 404
60-64	49 367	23 153	26 214	47 523	22 518	25 005	46 533	22 073	24 460	45 559	21 695	23 864
65-69	45 010	20 289	24 721	46 088	21 057	25 031	44 626	20 656	23 970	43 772	20 293	23 479
70-74	37 613	16 149	21 465	40 352	17 490	22 862	41 664	18 371	23 293	40 644	18 210	22 434
75-79	28 722	11 751	16 972	31 695	12 882	18 813	34 277	14 101	20 176	35 782	15 035	20 747
80-84	17 971	6 741	11 230	21 946	8 270	13 677	24 382	9 137	15 245	26 684	10 159	16 525
85-89	12 054	3 840	8 215	11 729	3 907	7 822	14 522	4 873	9 650	16 318	5 450	10 868
90-94	5 212	1 381	3 831	6 063	1 621	4 442	6 187	1 731	4 456	7 833	2 216	5 617
95-99	1 666	328	1 338	1 852	379	1 473	2 232	464	1 768	2 411	522	1 889
100 +	271	36	235	358	50	308	431	61	370	543	78	464

Age group	2045 Both sexes	Males	Females	2050 Both sexes	Males	Females
All ages	757 434	367 059	390 375	764 242	371 419	392 824
0-4	50 837	26 132	24 705	51 573	26 510	25 063
5-9	48 312	24 822	23 491	50 995	26 202	24 793
10-14	45 018	23 124	21 895	48 460	24 895	23 564
15-19	43 374	22 256	21 118	45 399	23 300	22 099
20-24	44 366	22 705	21 661	43 905	22 474	21 431
25-29	46 752	23 891	22 861	44 713	22 854	21 859
30-34	46 658	23 804	22 854	46 896	23 939	22 957
35-39	44 297	22 540	21 756	46 638	23 758	22 880
40-44	38 016	19 264	18 752	44 094	22 390	21 704
45-49	38 083	19 193	18 890	37 822	19 104	18 719
50-54	41 665	20 781	20 884	37 727	18 908	18 819
55-59	46 788	22 938	23 850	40 648	20 103	20 545
60-64	45 921	22 023	23 899	45 239	21 858	23 382
65-69	42 913	19 987	22 927	43 322	20 334	22 988
70-74	39 966	17 945	22 021	39 258	17 725	21 533
75-79	35 244	15 093	20 151	34 790	14 943	19 847
80-84	28 286	11 051	17 235	28 234	11 278	16 957
85-89	18 188	6 197	11 991	19 722	6 936	12 787
90-94	8 960	2 528	6 433	10 255	2 967	7 288
95-99	3 151	694	2 458	3 703	814	2 889
100 +	636	94	542	850	128	722

POPULATION BY AGE AND SEX (in thousands)

Age group	2005 Both sexes	Males	Females	2010 Both sexes	Males	Females	2015 Both sexes	Males	Females	2020 Both sexes	Males	Females
All ages	728 389	350 386	378 003	719 473	345 662	373 810	705 302	338 371	366 930	688 271	329 727	358 544
0-4	36 605	18 801	17 804	30 280	15 554	14 725	26 229	13 474	12 755	23 715	12 183	11 532
5-9	37 098	19 030	18 068	36 763	18 870	17 893	30 429	15 619	14 810	26 388	13 545	12 843
10-14	41 769	21 394	20 375	37 246	19 103	18 143	36 894	18 934	17 960	30 569	15 688	14 880
15-19	49 682	25 383	24 299	42 140	21 555	20 585	37 604	19 262	18 342	37 259	19 098	18 161
20-24	51 347	26 100	25 247	50 102	25 495	24 607	42 583	21 702	20 881	38 090	19 442	18 648
25-29	51 184	25 843	25 341	51 450	26 038	25 412	50 206	25 455	24 751	42 825	21 764	21 061
30-34	52 319	26 295	26 024	51 060	25 651	25 409	51 252	25 825	25 427	50 094	25 311	24 783
35-39	53 310	26 672	26 638	52 017	25 985	26 032	50 700	25 333	25 367	50 906	25 533	25 372
40-44	55 600	27 580	28 020	52 749	26 213	26 536	51 425	25 526	25 899	50 148	24 919	25 229
45-49	54 459	26 691	27 768	54 703	26 876	27 827	52 007	25 643	26 364	50 737	25 004	25 734
50-54	50 343	24 296	26 047	53 079	25 648	27 431	53 472	25 958	27 514	51 023	24 909	26 114
55-59	44 081	21 023	23 058	48 196	22 816	25 381	50 974	24 203	26 772	51 584	24 672	26 912
60-64	34 829	16 183	18 645	41 789	19 441	22 348	45 714	21 116	24 599	48 527	22 528	26 000
65-69	36 555	16 049	20 507	32 015	14 403	17 612	38 499	17 348	21 151	42 203	18 887	23 316
70-74	28 903	12 122	16 781	31 819	13 292	18 527	28 367	12 233	16 134	34 221	14 790	19 431
75-79	24 578	9 276	15 303	23 501	9 251	14 250	25 998	10 209	15 789	23 701	9 670	14 031
80-84	15 655	5 010	10 645	17 568	6 025	11 544	17 172	6 166	11 006	19 169	6 890	12 279
85-89	6 252	1 772	4 480	9 272	2 609	6 662	10 534	3 187	7 348	10 622	3 368	7 254
90-94	3 054	716	2 338	2 746	655	2 091	4 253	999	3 253	4 951	1 253	3 698
95-99	690	136	554	867	164	702	837	158	679	1 376	252	1 125
100 +	74	13	61	111	18	93	151	23	129	164	23	141

Age group	2025 Both sexes	Males	Females	2030 Both sexes	Males	Females	2035 Both sexes	Males	Females	2040 Both sexes	Males	Females
All ages	670 554	320 777	349 777	651 734	311 292	340 443	631 212	301 054	330 158	608 439	289 859	318 579
0-4	23 314	11 978	11 337	22 732	11 680	11 052	21 905	11 256	10 649	20 631	10 602	10 029
5-9	23 882	12 258	11 624	23 486	12 056	11 430	22 907	11 760	11 147	22 084	11 338	10 746
10-14	26 534	13 618	12 916	24 031	12 334	11 698	23 638	12 133	11 505	23 062	11 838	11 224
15-19	30 943	15 859	15 083	26 915	13 794	13 121	24 417	12 514	11 904	24 027	12 315	11 712
20-24	37 754	19 286	18 468	31 462	16 067	15 396	27 450	14 014	13 436	24 963	12 742	12 222
25-29	38 388	19 548	18 841	38 061	19 403	18 658	31 805	16 210	15 595	27 821	14 176	13 644
30-34	42 875	21 734	21 141	38 509	19 570	18 939	38 188	19 435	18 754	31 983	16 276	15 707
35-39	40 826	26 081	21 744	42 777	21 623	21 154	38 493	19 517	18 976	38 185	19 395	18 790
40-44	50 379	25 147	25 232	49 365	24 749	24 616	42 491	21 412	21 079	38 304	19 371	18 932
45-49	49 524	24 451	25 073	49 784	24 708	25 076	48 833	24 359	24 473	42 159	21 159	21 000
50-54	49 832	24 328	25 504	48 691	23 833	24 858	48 978	24 113	24 865	48 102	23 819	24 283
55-59	49 416	23 821	25 595	48 317	23 305	25 012	47 252	22 866	24 387	47 575	23 171	24 404
60-64	49 367	23 153	26 214	47 523	22 518	25 005	46 533	22 073	24 460	45 559	21 695	23 864
65-69	45 010	20 289	24 721	46 088	21 057	25 031	44 626	20 656	23 970	43 772	20 293	23 479
70-74	37 613	16 149	21 465	40 352	17 490	22 862	41 664	18 371	23 293	40 644	18 210	22 434
75-79	28 700	11 761	16 972	31 695	12 882	18 813	34 277	14 101	20 176	35 782	15 035	20 747
80-84	17 971	6 741	11 230	21 946	8 270	13 677	24 382	9 137	15 245	26 684	10 159	16 525
85-89	12 054	3 840	8 215	11 729	3 907	7 822	14 522	4 873	9 650	16 318	5 450	10 868
90-94	5 212	1 381	3 831	6 063	1 621	4 442	6 187	1 731	4 456	7 833	2 216	5 617
95-99	1 666	328	1 338	1 852	379	1 473	2 232	464	1 768	2 411	522	1 889
100 +	271	36	235	358	50	308	431	61	370	543	78	464

Age group	2045 Both sexes	Males	Females	2050 Both sexes	Males	Females
All ages	583 337	277 682	305 656	556 608	264 841	291 767
0-4	18 995	9 762	9 233	17 559	9 024	8 536
5-9	20 813	10 686	10 127	19 179	9 847	9 332
10-14	22 241	11 418	10 823	20 972	10 767	10 205
15-19	23 455	12 023	11 432	22 637	11 605	11 032
20-24	24 580	12 548	12 032	24 015	12 261	11 754
25-29	25 355	12 918	12 437	24 985	12 733	12 252
30-34	28 039	14 267	13 772	25 605	13 027	12 578
35-39	32 040	16 274	15 766	28 145	14 294	13 851
40-44	38 016	19 264	18 752	31 940	16 187	15 753
45-49	38 083	19 193	18 890	37 822	19 104	18 719
50-54	41 665	20 781	20 884	37 727	18 908	18 819
55-59	46 788	22 938	23 850	40 648	20 103	20 545
60-64	45 921	22 023	23 899	45 239	21 858	23 382
65-69	42 913	19 987	22 927	43 322	20 334	22 988
70-74	39 966	17 945	22 021	39 258	17 725	21 533
75-79	35 244	15 093	20 151	34 790	14 943	19 847
80-84	28 286	11 051	17 235	28 234	11 278	16 957
85-89	18 188	6 197	11 991	19 722	6 936	12 787
90-94	8 960	2 528	6 433	10 255	2 967	7 288
95-99	3 151	694	2 458	3 703	814	2 889
100 +	636	94	542	850	128	722

POPULATION BY AGE AND SEX (in thousands)

Age group	1950 Both sexes	1950 Males	1950 Females	1955 Both sexes	1955 Males	1955 Females	1960 Both sexes	1960 Males	1960 Females	1965 Both sexes	1965 Males	1965 Females
All ages	220 199	98 437	121 762	237 123	107 532	129 591	253 475	116 279	137 196	266 945	123 545	143 400
0-4	21 294	10 866	10 427	25 949	13 302	12 647	27 001	13 778	13 223	24 197	12 370	11 826
5-9	16 866	8 472	8 394	21 171	10 799	10 372	25 747	13 182	12 566	26 777	13 658	13 118
10-14	23 755	11 865	11 891	16 844	8 461	8 384	21 076	10 743	10 333	25 620	13 109	12 511
15-19	20 413	10 208	10 205	23 702	11 827	11 875	16 713	8 374	8 339	20 953	10 663	10 290
20-24	23 081	11 022	12 059	20 295	10 130	10 165	23 397	11 636	11 761	16 564	8 282	8 282
25-29	16 963	7 246	9 717	22 877	10 867	12 010	20 016	9 943	10 074	23 173	11 468	11 705
30-34	12 185	5 105	7 079	16 806	7 143	9 663	22 594	10 677	11 917	19 787	9 779	10 008
35-39	17 138	7 032	10 105	12 039	5 010	7 029	16 519	6 958	9 560	22 286	10 464	11 822
40-44	15 481	6 486	8 995	16 813	6 832	9 981	11 800	4 875	6 924	16 226	6 779	9 447
45-49	13 245	5 288	7 958	15 036	6 216	8 820	16 320	6 566	9 754	11 499	4 696	6 803
50-54	10 190	4 073	6 117	12 682	4 968	7 713	14 401	5 858	8 543	15 680	6 199	9 481
55-59	8 118	3 256	4 862	9 565	3 728	5 837	11 930	4 562	7 368	13 625	5 416	8 208
60-64	7 121	2 721	4 401	7 384	2 861	4 523	8 741	3 289	5 452	10 976	4 057	6 919
65-69	5 510	2 003	3 507	6 192	2 255	3 937	6 443	2 378	4 064	7 697	2 766	4 931
70-74	4 095	1 396	2 699	4 549	1 570	2 979	4 999	1 720	3 279	5 328	1 866	3 462
75-79	2 690	841	1 848	2 925	934	1 991	3 233	1 032	2 201	3 661	1 170	2 491
80 +	2 054	557	1 497	2 293	628	1 665	2 546	707	1 839	2 898	803	2 095

Age group	1970 Both sexes	1970 Males	1970 Females	1975 Both sexes	1975 Males	1975 Females	1980 Both sexes	1980 Males	1980 Females	1985 Both sexes	1985 Males	1985 Females
All ages	276 419	128 648	147 771	285 700	133 414	152 287	294 976	138 458	156 518	303 395	143 029	160 366
0-4	20 934	10 686	10 247	22 471	11 456	11 014	23 544	12 004	11 541	24 202	12 345	11 857
5-9	24 062	12 287	11 775	20 888	10 631	10 256	22 321	11 370	10 951	23 509	11 972	11 537
10-14	26 700	13 609	13 091	23 760	12 151	11 608	20 719	10 548	10 171	22 312	11 376	10 936
15-19	25 501	13 030	12 471	26 098	13 291	12 807	23 250	11 870	11 380	20 722	10 556	10 166
20-24	20 764	10 536	10 227	25 161	12 733	12 428	25 952	13 244	12 707	23 191	11 785	11 407
25-29	16 378	8 141	8 238	20 613	10 385	10 228	25 026	12 618	12 408	25 848	13 095	12 753
30-34	22 969	11 316	11 654	16 282	8 042	8 240	21 159	10 595	10 564	24 853	12 458	12 395
35-39	19 495	9 587	9 909	22 659	11 063	11 596	15 290	7 498	7 792	20 832	10 348	10 483
40-44	21 855	10 181	11 673	19 050	9 261	9 789	22 247	10 738	11 509	14 998	7 283	7 715
45-49	15 847	6 547	9 300	21 269	9 804	11 465	18 239	8 749	9 489	21 528	10 242	11 286
50-54	11 064	4 439	6 625	15 560	6 246	9 313	20 564	9 370	11 194	17 476	8 194	9 283
55-59	14 825	5 710	9 115	10 621	4 126	6 495	15 175	5 949	9 227	19 378	8 538	10 840
60-64	12 585	4 819	7 766	13 756	5 140	8 617	9 745	3 628	6 117	13 932	5 231	8 700
65-69	9 744	3 411	6 333	11 135	4 019	7 116	11 906	4 188	7 718	8 574	3 000	5 574
70-74	6 382	2 145	4 237	7 952	2 614	5 338	9 397	3 148	6 249	9 927	3 231	6 696
75-79	3 977	1 272	2 705	4 608	1 422	3 186	6 001	1 778	4 223	6 790	2 050	4 740
80 +	3 337	932	2 405	3 818	1 029	2 789	4 442	1 162	3 280	5 323	1 324	3 999

Age group	1990 Both sexes	1990 Males	1990 Females	1995 Both sexes	1995 Males	1995 Females	2000 Both sexes	2000 Males	2000 Females	2005 Both sexes	2005 Males	2005 Females
All ages	310 854	147 250	163 604	309 904	146 944	162 960	304 636	143 713	160 923	297 328	139 737	157 592
0-4	23 468	11 988	11 480	17 459	8 955	8 505	14 093	7 228	6 866	14 192	7 286	6 906
5-9	24 197	12 321	11 876	23 591	12 047	11 544	17 582	9 001	8 581	14 027	7 190	6 837
10-14	23 560	11 987	11 573	24 272	12 357	11 915	23 873	12 176	11 697	17 519	8 963	8 556
15-19	22 372	11 397	10 975	23 579	11 985	11 594	24 688	12 558	12 129	23 775	12 104	11 670
20-24	20 617	10 506	10 111	22 236	11 366	10 870	23 572	11 918	11 654	24 444	12 370	12 074
25-29	23 094	11 685	11 408	20 392	10 370	10 022	22 048	11 123	10 924	23 155	11 603	11 552
30-34	25 688	12 907	12 781	22 956	11 527	11 429	20 184	10 102	10 082	21 597	10 782	10 815
35-39	24 604	12 253	12 351	25 302	12 576	12 727	22 542	11 136	11 406	19 713	9 746	9 967
40-44	20 340	10 017	10 322	24 108	11 841	12 267	24 596	11 992	12 605	21 883	10 638	11 245
45-49	14 621	7 015	7 606	19 529	9 444	10 085	23 137	11 080	12 057	23 682	11 308	12 374
50-54	20 657	9 652	11 004	14 083	6 575	7 508	18 566	8 699	9 867	21 993	10 243	11 750
55-59	16 529	7 531	8 998	19 283	8 677	10 607	13 045	5 833	7 211	17 325	7 819	9 505
60-64	17 884	7 537	10 347	15 034	6 507	8 528	17 485	7 412	10 074	11 835	5 028	6 808
65-69	12 353	4 379	7 974	15 584	6 118	9 466	12 977	5 235	7 742	15 157	5 982	9 175
70-74	7 113	2 303	4 810	10 100	3 286	6 814	12 604	4 529	8 075	10 573	3 914	6 659
75-79	7 411	2 174	5 237	5 248	1 534	3 715	7 443	2 179	5 263	9 270	2 994	6 277
80 +	6 348	1 598	4 750	7 146	1 781	5 365	6 202	1 510	4 691	7 188	1 766	5 422

United Nations Department of Economic and Social Affairs/Population Division
World Population Prospects: The 2004 Revision, Volume II: Sex and Age Distribution of the World Population

POPULATION BY AGE AND SEX (in thousands)

Age group	2005 Both sexes	2005 Males	2005 Females	2010 Both sexes	2010 Males	2010 Females	2015 Both sexes	2015 Males	2015 Females	2020 Both sexes	2020 Males	2020 Females
All ages	297 328	139 737	157 592	290 411	135 985	154 426	283 267	132 260	151 007	275 581	128 401	147 181
0-4	14 192	7 286	6 906	14 701	7 549	7 153	14 215	7 300	6 915	13 149	6 754	6 394
5-9	14 027	7 190	6 837	14 127	7 248	6 879	14 640	7 513	7 127	14 162	7 270	6 893
10-14	17 519	8 963	8 556	13 980	7 162	6 818	14 079	7 220	6 858	14 594	7 486	7 107
15-19	23 775	12 104	11 670	17 452	8 914	8 537	13 935	7 128	6 807	14 037	7 189	6 848
20-24	24 444	12 370	12 074	23 554	11 937	11 617	17 321	8 812	8 509	13 840	7 052	6 787
25-29	23 155	11 603	11 552	23 996	12 043	11 953	23 177	11 665	11 512	17 073	8 635	8 438
30-34	21 597	10 782	10 815	22 634	11 228	11 405	23 456	11 672	11 784	22 716	11 357	11 359
35-39	19 713	9 746	9 967	21 050	10 383	10 667	22 060	10 832	11 228	22 890	11 297	11 594
40-44	21 883	10 638	11 245	19 132	9 318	9 814	20 441	9 951	10 490	21 473	10 432	11 041
45-49	23 682	11 308	12 374	21 064	10 032	11 031	18 470	8 842	9 628	19 794	9 498	10 296
50-54	21 993	10 243	11 750	22 544	10 478	12 066	20 100	9 339	10 761	17 713	8 306	9 407
55-59	17 325	7 819	9 505	20 594	9 252	11 342	21 185	9 521	11 664	18 961	8 543	10 418
60-64	11 835	5 028	6 808	15 807	6 794	9 013	18 888	8 103	10 784	19 519	8 401	11 118
65-69	15 157	5 982	9 175	10 389	4 139	6 251	13 975	5 650	8 325	16 802	6 800	10 002
70-74	10 573	3 914	6 659	12 430	4 497	7 934	8 664	3 189	5 475	11 761	4 407	7 354
75-79	9 270	2 994	6 277	7 905	2 640	5 265	9 394	3 057	6 337	6 682	2 227	4 455
80-84	4 721	1 225	3 496	5 943	1 697	4 246	5 186	1 529	3 657	6 259	1 789	4 469
85-89	1 598	364	1 234	2 379	534	1 846	3 065	751	2 314	2 762	689	2 073
90-94	731	149	582	558	109	449	869	161	708	1 167	233	934
95-99	127	25	102	156	29	128	127	21	106	209	31	178
100 +	12	3	9	16	3	12	21	4	17	19	3	16

Age group	2025 Both sexes	2025 Males	2025 Females	2030 Both sexes	2030 Males	2030 Females	2035 Both sexes	2035 Males	2035 Females	2040 Both sexes	2040 Males	2040 Females
All ages	267 149	124 256	142 893	258 264	119 973	138 291	249 401	115 843	133 559	240 753	111 989	128 764
0-4	11 886	6 107	5 779	11 162	5 736	5 426	11 141	5 727	5 414	11 378	5 849	5 529
5-9	13 104	6 728	6 375	11 847	6 085	5 763	11 127	5 716	5 411	11 108	5 708	5 400
10-14	14 121	7 246	6 875	13 068	6 708	6 360	11 816	6 067	5 749	11 098	5 700	5 398
15-19	14 555	7 457	7 098	14 088	7 220	6 867	13 039	6 685	6 354	11 701	6 047	5 744
20-24	13 948	7 119	6 829	14 470	7 391	7 079	14 011	7 162	6 849	12 973	6 634	6 339
25-29	13 642	6 915	6 727	13 754	6 988	6 766	14 280	7 266	7 014	13 837	7 048	6 789
30-34	16 767	8 435	8 332	13 399	6 762	6 637	13 513	6 842	6 671	14 044	7 127	6 917
35-39	22 223	11 039	11 184	16 433	8 228	8 205	13 139	6 607	6 532	13 260	6 696	6 563
40-44	22 324	10 920	11 403	21 712	10 708	11 003	16 084	8 010	8 074	12 875	6 447	6 427
45-49	20 865	10 017	10 848	21 731	10 523	11 208	21 167	10 351	10 816	15 719	7 775	7 943
50-54	19 063	8 987	10 076	20 165	9 535	10 629	21 038	10 051	10 987	20 529	9 918	10 611
55-59	16 808	7 678	9 130	18 171	8 371	9 800	19 289	8 936	10 353	20 167	9 455	10 712
60-64	17 548	7 595	9 954	15 658	6 904	8 754	17 013	7 591	9 422	18 131	8 157	9 974
65-69	17 455	7 107	10 348	15 773	6 477	9 296	14 183	5 967	8 216	15 501	6 623	8 878
70-74	14 251	5 358	8 893	14 898	5 649	9 249	13 548	5 198	8 350	12 296	4 863	7 433
75-79	9 181	3 122	6 060	11 242	3 841	7 400	11 855	4 098	7 757	10 868	3 814	7 054
80-84	4 561	1 338	3 222	6 370	1 905	4 465	7 919	2 387	5 533	8 454	2 585	5 869
85-89	3 420	820	2 600	2 572	626	1 946	3 687	917	2 770	4 683	1 176	3 507
90-94	1 098	217	881	1 409	264	1 145	1 105	206	899	1 647	315	1 332
95-99	298	47	251	296	43	253	398	55	343	327	43	285
100 +	30	4	26	45	6	39	49	6	44	68	7	61

Age group	2045 Both sexes	2045 Males	2045 Females	2050 Both sexes	2050 Males	2050 Females
All ages	232 194	108 313	123 882	223 539	104 639	118 900
0-4	11 316	5 818	5 498	10 811	5 559	5 252
5-9	11 346	5 831	5 515	11 286	5 801	5 484
10-14	11 079	5 692	5 388	11 318	5 816	5 503
15-19	11 076	5 682	5 394	11 059	5 675	5 384
20-24	11 735	6 003	5 731	11 025	5 642	5 383
25-29	12 819	6 534	6 285	11 600	5 914	5 686
30-34	13 625	6 924	6 701	12 639	6 427	6 212
35-39	13 799	6 988	6 810	13 410	6 803	6 607
40-44	13 006	6 546	6 460	13 556	6 845	6 711
45-49	12 605	6 278	6 328	12 752	6 386	6 365
50-54	15 288	7 485	7 803	12 287	6 064	6 223
55-59	19 719	9 363	10 356	14 731	7 103	7 628
60-64	19 007	8 670	10 338	18 623	8 617	10 006
65-69	16 599	7 173	9 426	17 458	7 662	9 795
70-74	13 541	5 461	8 081	14 590	5 972	8 618
75-79	9 976	3 632	6 344	11 098	4 141	6 958
80-84	7 835	2 441	5 394	7 300	2 375	4 925
85-89	5 090	1 301	3 790	4 798	1 256	3 542
90-94	2 154	416	1 738	2 402	475	1 928
95-99	515	69	445	699	95	604
100 +	63	6	57	96	9	87

POPULATION BY AGE AND SEX (in thousands)

Age group	2005			2010			2015			2020		
	Both sexes	Males	Females	Both sexes	Males	Females	Both sexes	Males	Females	Both sexes	Males	Females
All ages	297 328	139 737	157 592	293 241	137 438	155 803	290 269	135 855	154 414	286 987	134 257	152 730
0-4	14 192	7 286	6 906	17 531	9 002	8 530	18 395	9 448	8 948	17 569	9 025	8 544
5-9	14 027	7 190	6 837	14 127	7 248	6 879	17 462	8 961	8 501	18 332	9 410	8 922
10-14	17 519	8 963	8 556	13 980	7 162	6 818	14 079	7 220	6 858	17 410	8 931	8 479
15-19	23 775	12 104	11 670	17 452	8 914	8 537	13 935	7 128	6 807	14 037	7 189	6 848
20-24	24 444	12 370	12 074	23 554	11 937	11 617	17 321	8 812	8 509	13 840	7 052	6 787
25-29	23 155	11 603	11 552	23 996	12 043	11 953	23 177	11 665	11 512	17 073	8 635	8 438
30-34	21 597	10 782	10 815	22 634	11 228	11 405	23 456	11 672	11 784	22 716	11 357	11 359
35-39	19 713	9 746	9 967	21 050	10 383	10 667	22 060	10 832	11 228	22 890	11 297	11 594
40-44	21 883	10 638	11 245	19 132	9 318	9 814	20 441	9 951	10 490	21 473	10 432	11 041
45-49	23 682	11 308	12 374	21 064	10 032	11 031	18 470	8 842	9 628	19 794	9 498	10 296
50-54	21 993	10 243	11 750	22 544	10 478	12 066	20 100	9 339	10 761	17 713	8 306	9 407
55-59	17 325	7 819	9 505	20 594	9 252	11 342	21 185	9 521	11 664	18 961	8 543	10 418
60-64	11 835	5 028	6 808	15 807	6 794	9 013	18 888	8 103	10 784	19 519	8 401	11 118
65-69	15 157	5 982	9 175	10 389	4 139	6 251	13 975	5 650	8 325	16 802	6 800	10 002
70-74	10 573	3 914	6 659	12 430	4 497	7 934	8 664	3 189	5 475	11 761	4 407	7 354
75-79	9 270	2 994	6 277	7 905	2 640	5 265	9 394	3 057	6 337	6 682	2 227	4 455
80-84	4 721	1 225	3 496	5 943	1 697	4 246	5 186	1 529	3 657	6 259	1 789	4 469
85-89	1 598	364	1 234	2 379	534	1 846	3 065	751	2 314	2 762	689	2 073
90-94	731	149	582	558	109	449	869	161	708	1 167	233	934
95-99	127	25	102	156	29	128	127	21	106	209	31	178
100 +	12	3	9	16	3	12	21	4	17	19	3	16

Age group	2025			2030			2035			2040		
	Both sexes	Males	Females	Both sexes	Males	Females	Both sexes	Males	Females	Both sexes	Males	Females
All ages	282 333	132 051	150 282	277 485	129 838	147 648	273 796	128 359	145 437	271 591	127 809	143 782
0-4	15 686	8 060	7 626	15 231	7 828	7 403	16 371	8 415	7 956	17 918	9 212	8 706
5-9	17 514	8 993	8 521	15 640	8 033	7 607	15 188	7 803	7 385	16 329	8 391	7 938
10-14	18 285	9 383	8 902	17 473	8 969	8 504	15 605	8 012	7 592	15 156	7 784	7 372
15-19	17 366	8 898	8 468	18 244	9 352	8 892	17 438	8 942	8 495	15 575	7 990	7 586
20-24	13 948	7 119	6 829	17 269	8 824	8 445	18 152	9 283	8 869	17 357	8 881	8 476
25-29	13 642	6 915	6 727	13 754	6 988	6 766	17 055	8 684	8 371	17 946	9 150	8 796
30-34	16 767	8 435	8 332	13 399	6 762	6 637	13 513	6 842	6 671	16 784	8 526	8 259
35-39	22 223	11 039	11 184	16 433	8 228	8 205	13 139	6 607	6 532	13 260	6 696	6 563
40-44	22 324	10 920	11 403	21 712	10 708	11 003	16 084	8 010	8 074	12 875	6 447	6 427
45-49	20 865	10 017	10 848	21 731	10 523	11 208	21 167	10 351	10 816	15 719	7 775	7 943
50-54	19 063	8 987	10 076	20 165	9 535	10 629	21 038	10 051	10 987	20 529	9 918	10 611
55-59	16 808	7 678	9 130	18 171	8 371	9 800	19 289	8 936	10 353	20 167	9 455	10 712
60-64	17 548	7 595	9 954	15 658	6 904	8 754	17 013	7 591	9 422	18 131	8 157	9 974
65-69	17 455	7 107	10 348	15 773	6 477	9 296	14 183	5 967	8 216	15 501	6 623	8 878
70-74	14 251	5 358	8 893	14 898	5 649	9 249	13 548	5 198	8 350	12 296	4 863	7 433
75-79	9 181	3 122	6 060	11 242	3 841	7 400	11 855	4 098	7 757	10 868	3 814	7 054
80-84	4 561	1 338	3 222	6 370	1 905	4 465	7 919	2 387	5 533	8 454	2 585	5 869
85-89	3 420	820	2 600	2 572	626	1 946	3 687	917	2 770	4 683	1 176	3 507
90-94	1 098	217	881	1 409	264	1 145	1 105	206	899	1 647	315	1 332
95-99	298	47	251	296	43	253	398	55	343	327	43	285
100 +	30	4	26	45	6	39	49	6	44	68	7	61

Age group	2045			2050		
	Both sexes	Males	Females	Both sexes	Males	Females
All ages	270 126	127 771	142 355	268 578	127 740	140 838
0-4	18 555	9 540	9 014	18 106	9 310	8 795
5-9	17 876	9 188	8 688	18 514	9 517	8 997
10-14	16 297	8 372	7 925	17 844	9 169	8 675
15-19	15 129	7 763	7 366	16 271	8 352	7 919
20-24	15 507	7 938	7 570	15 068	7 717	7 352
25-29	17 175	8 764	8 411	15 351	7 836	7 515
30-34	17 688	9 001	8 687	16 952	8 634	8 318
35-39	16 500	8 365	8 135	17 421	8 851	8 570
40-44	13 006	6 546	6 460	16 216	8 198	8 019
45-49	12 605	6 278	6 328	12 752	6 386	6 365
50-54	15 288	7 485	7 803	12 287	6 064	6 223
55-59	19 719	9 363	10 356	14 731	7 103	7 628
60-64	19 007	8 670	10 338	18 623	8 617	10 006
65-69	16 599	7 173	9 426	17 458	7 662	9 795
70-74	13 541	5 461	8 081	14 590	5 972	8 618
75-79	9 976	3 632	6 344	11 098	4 141	6 958
80-84	7 835	2 441	5 394	7 300	2 375	4 925
85-89	5 090	1 301	3 790	4 798	1 256	3 542
90-94	2 154	416	1 738	2 402	475	1 928
95-99	515	69	445	699	95	604
100 +	63	6	57	96	9	87

United Nations Department of Economic and Social Affairs/Population Division
World Population Prospects: The 2004 Revision, Volume II: Sex and Age Distribution of the World Population

98

POPULATION BY AGE AND SEX (in thousands)

Age group	2005 Both sexes	Males	Females	2010 Both sexes	Males	Females	2015 Both sexes	Males	Females	2020 Both sexes	Males	Females
All ages	297 328	139 737	157 592	287 584	134 533	153 051	276 231	128 647	147 583	264 006	122 458	141 548
0-4	14 192	7 286	6 906	11 874	6 097	5 777	9 998	5 134	4 863	8 593	4 414	4 179
5-9	14 027	7 190	6 837	14 127	7 248	6 879	11 822	6 067	5 755	9 956	5 110	4 846
10-14	17 519	8 963	8 556	13 980	7 162	6 818	14 079	7 220	6 858	11 780	6 043	5 737
15-19	23 775	12 104	11 670	17 452	8 914	8 537	13 935	7 128	6 807	14 037	7 189	6 848
20-24	24 444	12 370	12 074	23 554	11 937	11 617	17 321	8 812	8 509	13 840	7 052	6 787
25-29	23 155	11 603	11 552	23 996	12 043	11 953	23 177	11 665	11 512	17 073	8 635	8 438
30-34	21 597	10 782	10 815	22 634	11 228	11 405	23 456	11 672	11 784	22 716	11 357	11 359
35-39	19 713	9 746	9 967	21 050	10 383	10 667	22 060	10 832	11 228	22 890	11 297	11 594
40-44	21 883	10 638	11 245	19 132	9 318	9 814	20 441	9 951	10 490	21 473	10 432	11 041
45-49	23 682	11 308	12 374	21 064	10 032	11 031	18 470	8 842	9 628	19 794	9 498	10 296
50-54	21 993	10 243	11 750	22 544	10 478	12 066	20 100	9 339	10 761	17 713	8 306	9 407
55-59	17 325	7 819	9 505	20 594	9 252	11 342	21 185	9 521	11 664	18 961	8 543	10 418
60-64	11 835	5 028	6 808	15 807	6 794	9 013	18 888	8 103	10 784	19 519	8 401	11 118
65-69	15 157	5 982	9 175	10 389	4 139	6 251	13 975	5 650	8 325	16 802	6 800	10 002
70-74	10 573	3 914	6 659	12 430	4 497	7 934	8 664	3 189	5 475	11 761	4 407	7 354
75-79	9 270	2 994	6 277	7 905	2 640	5 265	9 394	3 057	6 337	6 682	2 227	4 455
80-84	4 721	1 225	3 496	5 943	1 697	4 246	5 186	1 529	3 657	6 259	1 789	4 469
85-89	1 598	364	1 234	2 379	534	1 846	3 065	751	2 314	2 762	689	2 073
90-94	731	149	582	558	109	449	869	161	708	1 167	233	934
95-99	127	25	102	156	29	128	127	21	106	209	31	178
100 +	12	3	9	16	3	12	21	4	17	19	3	16

Age group	2025 Both sexes	Males	Females	2030 Both sexes	Males	Females	2035 Both sexes	Males	Females	2040 Both sexes	Males	Females
All ages	251 706	116 329	135 378	239 122	110 149	128 973	226 176	103 927	122 248	212 825	97 665	115 160
0-4	7 997	4 109	3 888	7 431	3 819	3 612	7 001	3 598	3 402	6 579	3 382	3 197
5-9	8 558	4 394	4 164	7 966	4 091	3 875	7 403	3 803	3 600	6 975	3 584	3 391
10-14	9 921	5 090	4 831	8 528	4 377	4 151	7 938	4 076	3 863	7 377	3 788	3 589
15-19	11 747	6 017	5 730	9 895	5 070	4 825	8 506	4 359	4 147	7 919	4 060	3 859
20-24	13 948	7 119	6 829	11 674	5 960	5 714	9 834	5 022	4 812	8 455	4 318	4 136
25-29	13 642	6 915	6 727	13 754	6 988	6 766	11 507	5 849	5 658	9 690	4 927	4 763
30-34	16 767	8 435	8 332	13 399	6 762	6 637	13 513	6 842	6 671	11 305	5 730	5 576
35-39	22 223	11 039	11 184	16 433	8 228	8 205	13 139	6 607	6 532	13 260	6 696	6 563
40-44	22 324	10 920	11 403	21 712	10 708	11 003	16 084	8 010	8 074	12 875	6 447	6 427
45-49	20 865	10 017	10 848	21 731	10 523	11 208	21 167	10 351	10 816	15 719	7 775	7 943
50-54	19 063	8 987	10 076	20 165	9 535	10 629	21 038	10 051	10 987	20 529	9 918	10 611
55-59	16 808	7 678	9 130	18 171	8 371	9 800	19 253	8 900	10 353	20 167	9 455	10 712
60-64	17 548	7 595	9 954	15 658	6 904	8 754	17 013	7 591	9 422	18 131	8 157	9 974
65-69	17 455	7 107	10 348	15 773	6 477	9 296	14 183	5 967	8 216	15 501	6 623	8 878
70-74	14 251	5 358	8 893	14 898	5 649	9 249	13 548	5 198	8 350	12 296	4 863	7 433
75-79	9 181	3 122	6 060	11 242	3 841	7 400	11 855	4 098	7 757	10 868	3 814	7 054
80-84	4 561	1 338	3 222	6 370	1 905	4 465	7 919	2 387	5 533	8 454	2 585	5 009
85-89	3 420	820	2 600	2 572	626	1 946	3 687	917	2 770	4 683	1 176	3 507
90-94	1 098	217	881	1 409	264	1 145	1 105	206	899	1 647	315	1 332
95-99	298	47	251	296	43	253	398	55	343	327	43	285
100 +	30	4	26	45	6	39	49	6	44	68	7	61

Age group	2045 Both sexes	Males	Females	2050 Both sexes	Males	Females
All ages	199 090	91 336	107 754	185 224	84 994	100 230
0-4	5 998	3 084	2 914	5 418	2 786	2 632
5-9	6 554	3 369	3 186	5 975	3 071	2 904
10-14	6 950	3 570	3 380	6 530	3 355	3 175
15-19	7 360	3 774	3 586	6 934	3 556	3 378
20-24	7 873	4 023	3 850	7 318	3 740	3 578
25-29	8 330	4 235	4 095	7 760	3 947	3 813
30-34	9 525	4 829	4 697	8 194	4 153	4 041
35-39	11 100	5 613	5 487	9 363	4 736	4 626
40-44	13 006	6 546	6 460	10 898	5 494	5 404
45-49	12 605	6 278	6 328	12 752	6 386	6 365
50-54	15 288	7 485	7 803	12 287	6 064	6 223
55-59	19 719	9 363	10 356	14 731	7 103	7 628
60-64	19 007	8 670	10 338	18 623	8 617	10 006
65-69	16 599	7 173	9 426	17 458	7 662	9 795
70-74	13 541	5 461	8 081	14 590	5 972	8 618
75-79	9 976	3 632	6 344	11 098	4 141	6 958
80-84	7 835	2 441	5 394	7 300	2 375	4 925
85-89	5 090	1 301	3 790	4 798	1 256	3 542
90-94	2 154	416	1 738	2 402	475	1 928
95-99	515	69	445	699	95	604
100 +	63	6	57	96	9	87

POPULATION BY AGE AND SEX (in thousands)

Age group	1950 Both sexes	Males	Females	1955 Both sexes	Males	Females	1960 Both sexes	Males	Females	1965 Both sexes	Males	Females
All ages	77 293	37 475	39 819	78 835	38 132	40 703	80 962	39 152	41 810	84 128	40 880	43 248
0-4	6 933	3 550	3 383	6 299	3 224	3 075	6 544	3 348	3 195	7 229	3 699	3 530
5-9	5 966	3 043	2 924	6 858	3 509	3 349	6 204	3 169	3 036	6 537	3 342	3 195
10-14	5 418	2 746	2 671	5 872	2 994	2 879	6 799	3 468	3 331	6 206	3 169	3 037
15-19	5 260	2 653	2 607	5 341	2 695	2 646	5 872	2 979	2 893	6 813	3 477	3 336
20-24	5 546	2 776	2 769	5 182	2 598	2 584	5 332	2 683	2 649	5 900	2 993	2 908
25-29	5 853	2 902	2 950	5 412	2 684	2 727	5 149	2 581	2 568	5 369	2 718	2 650
30-34	5 307	2 632	2 674	5 776	2 834	2 941	5 331	2 623	2 708	5 173	2 622	2 552
35-39	5 808	2 859	2 949	5 159	2 523	2 635	5 669	2 770	2 900	5 336	2 654	2 682
40-44	5 757	2 836	2 921	5 674	2 766	2 908	5 116	2 489	2 627	5 680	2 786	2 894
45-49	5 272	2 545	2 727	5 594	2 740	2 854	5 564	2 700	2 864	5 019	2 447	2 572
50-54	4 651	2 162	2 489	5 111	2 452	2 659	5 420	2 635	2 785	5 407	2 597	2 810
55-59	4 020	1 829	2 191	4 384	2 002	2 382	4 855	2 290	2 565	5 165	2 467	2 698
60-64	3 542	1 580	1 962	3 696	1 634	2 062	4 063	1 807	2 256	4 511	2 078	2 433
65-69	2 983	1 304	1 679	3 103	1 328	1 775	3 278	1 385	1 893	3 580	1 516	2 063
70-74	2 330	1 002	1 329	2 436	1 009	1 427	2 542	1 024	1 518	2 708	1 077	1 631
75-79	1 523	636	887	1 665	668	997	1 760	678	1 083	1 868	691	1 176
80 +	1 126	419	707	1 274	471	803	1 465	523	942	1 627	546	1 080

Age group	1970 Both sexes	Males	Females	1975 Both sexes	Males	Females	1980 Both sexes	Males	Females	1985 Both sexes	Males	Females
All ages	86 526	42 160	44 366	88 211	43 019	45 192	89 093	43 412	45 681	90 201	43 935	46 266
0-4	6 975	3 575	3 400	6 383	3 277	3 107	5 646	2 895	2 751	5 816	2 980	2 836
5-9	7 225	3 700	3 525	6 999	3 589	3 410	6 344	3 255	3 090	5 682	2 913	2 770
10-14	6 701	3 435	3 265	7 160	3 670	3 490	6 975	3 575	3 400	6 330	3 246	3 084
15-19	6 286	3 225	3 061	6 617	3 394	3 223	7 138	3 650	3 489	7 073	3 629	3 444
20-24	6 793	3 456	3 337	6 318	3 233	3 085	6 592	3 367	3 225	7 310	3 719	3 591
25-29	5 921	3 012	2 910	6 740	3 429	3 311	6 265	3 188	3 077	6 593	3 339	3 253
30-34	5 220	2 645	2 575	5 703	2 900	2 803	6 715	3 387	3 329	6 214	3 140	3 074
35-39	5 019	2 523	2 496	5 218	2 639	2 579	5 667	2 865	2 802	6 675	3 359	3 316
40-44	5 233	2 588	2 645	5 007	2 509	2 498	5 181	2 612	2 569	5 643	2 842	2 801
45-49	5 424	2 644	2 780	5 190	2 554	2 636	4 938	2 466	2 472	5 087	2 539	2 548
50-54	4 963	2 402	2 561	5 420	2 618	2 802	5 060	2 472	2 588	4 810	2 375	2 435
55-59	5 094	2 427	2 667	4 665	2 223	2 441	5 226	2 492	2 734	4 845	2 337	2 508
60-64	4 816	2 248	2 568	4 836	2 246	2 590	4 383	2 045	2 339	4 841	2 260	2 581
65-69	4 037	1 780	2 256	4 320	1 927	2 393	4 309	1 923	2 387	3 970	1 781	2 188
70-74	3 016	1 194	1 821	3 371	1 384	1 988	3 671	1 543	2 128	3 696	1 557	2 140
75-79	1 968	719	1 249	2 232	800	1 432	2 596	972	1 624	2 829	1 082	1 747
80 +	1 835	584	1 251	2 032	626	1 405	2 385	707	1 679	2 784	836	1 948

Age group	1990 Both sexes	Males	Females	1995 Both sexes	Males	Females	2000 Both sexes	Males	Females	2005 Both sexes	Males	Females
All ages	91 712	44 359	47 353	92 901	45 067	47 834	94 157	45 818	48 338	95 792	46 804	48 988
0-4	6 215	3 195	3 020	6 055	3 100	2 955	5 585	2 863	2 722	5 397	2 768	2 629
5-9	5 833	2 948	2 885	6 169	3 172	2 997	6 106	3 126	2 979	5 618	2 879	2 739
10-14	5 782	2 925	2 857	5 847	2 951	2 896	6 262	3 209	3 052	6 162	3 157	3 005
15-19	6 211	3 142	3 069	5 801	2 946	2 855	5 906	3 011	2 895	6 439	3 307	3 132
20-24	6 822	3 375	3 448	6 191	3 111	3 080	5 832	2 925	2 907	6 123	3 122	3 001
25-29	7 040	3 468	3 572	6 897	3 381	3 517	6 366	3 158	3 209	6 015	3 032	2 983
30-34	6 600	3 259	3 341	7 167	3 531	3 636	7 135	3 528	3 607	6 502	3 234	3 267
35-39	6 294	3 110	3 184	6 657	3 300	3 357	7 224	3 588	3 636	7 226	3 573	3 653
40-44	6 667	3 354	3 313	6 245	3 094	3 151	6 573	3 271	3 302	7 247	3 593	3 654
45-49	5 706	2 869	2 837	6 560	3 303	3 257	6 090	3 023	3 067	6 514	3 234	3 280
50-54	5 030	2 504	2 526	5 618	2 801	2 816	6 559	3 263	3 296	6 000	2 962	3 038
55-59	4 731	2 321	2 410	4 813	2 365	2 448	5 306	2 616	2 690	6 377	3 148	3 229
60-64	4 676	2 210	2 466	4 444	2 139	2 305	4 565	2 209	2 356	5 080	2 473	2 607
65-69	4 421	2 017	2 404	4 270	1 965	2 305	4 091	1 919	2 171	4 244	2 014	2 231
70-74	3 519	1 516	2 003	3 837	1 673	2 163	3 727	1 646	2 081	3 632	1 647	1 985
75-79	2 915	1 136	1 780	2 812	1 122	1 689	3 115	1 263	1 852	3 081	1 285	1 796
80 +	3 250	1 011	2 239	3 518	1 112	2 407	3 716	1 201	2 515	4 135	1 377	2 758

100

United Nations Department of Economic and Social Affairs/Population Division
World Population Prospects: The 2004 Revision, Volume II: Sex and Age Distribution of the World Population

POPULATION BY AGE AND SEX (in thousands)

Age group	2005 Both sexes	2005 Males	2005 Females	2010 Both sexes	2010 Males	2010 Females	2015 Both sexes	2015 Males	2015 Females	2020 Both sexes	2020 Males	2020 Females
All ages	95 792	46 804	48 988	97 145	47 551	49 594	98 538	40 299	50 238	100 095	49 111	50 983
0-4	5 397	2 768	2 629	5 312	2 723	2 589	5 411	2 774	2 637	5 673	2 909	2 764
5-9	5 618	2 879	2 739	5 442	2 783	2 659	5 358	2 739	2 619	5 457	2 790	2 667
10-14	6 162	3 157	3 005	5 660	2 902	2 758	5 485	2 806	2 678	5 401	2 763	2 638
15-19	6 439	3 307	3 132	6 313	3 225	3 088	5 812	2 971	2 842	5 638	2 875	2 762
20-24	6 123	3 122	3 001	6 637	3 385	3 252	6 514	3 306	3 208	6 016	3 053	2 963
25-29	6 015	3 032	2 983	6 294	3 207	3 087	6 809	3 471	3 338	6 688	3 393	3 295
30-34	6 502	3 234	3 267	6 113	3 080	3 032	6 393	3 256	3 137	6 909	3 522	3 388
35-39	7 226	3 573	3 653	6 561	3 262	3 300	6 177	3 111	3 066	6 458	3 287	3 171
40-44	7 247	3 593	3 654	7 228	3 568	3 661	6 571	3 262	3 309	6 192	3 115	3 078
45-49	6 514	3 234	3 280	7 188	3 556	3 631	7 177	3 537	3 640	6 530	3 237	3 293
50-54	6 000	2 962	3 038	6 423	3 173	3 249	7 096	3 497	3 600	7 095	3 484	3 611
55-59	6 377	3 148	3 229	5 859	2 871	2 989	6 283	3 083	3 200	6 954	3 405	3 549
60-64	5 080	2 473	2 607	6 123	2 990	3 133	5 639	2 734	2 905	6 060	2 944	3 116
65-69	4 244	2 014	2 231	4 750	2 272	2 478	5 751	2 762	2 989	5 315	2 536	2 778
70-74	3 632	1 647	1 985	3 792	1 742	2 051	4 275	1 984	2 291	5 209	2 433	2 776
75-79	3 081	1 285	1 796	3 025	1 300	1 726	3 189	1 392	1 797	3 630	1 607	2 023
80-84	2 276	843	1 433	2 286	875	1 411	2 276	902	1 374	2 432	983	1 448
85-89	1 203	380	823	1 401	457	944	1 438	487	951	1 462	516	945
90-94	509	127	382	557	147	410	673	184	488	712	204	508
95-99	130	25	105	157	30	126	180	37	143	227	49	179
100 +	17	2	15	24	3	20	30	4	26	37	5	31

Age group	2025 Both sexes	2025 Males	2025 Females	2030 Both sexes	2030 Males	2030 Females	2035 Both sexes	2035 Males	2035 Females	2040 Both sexes	2040 Males	2040 Females
All ages	101 674	49 912	51 762	102 977	50 559	52 418	103 892	51 013	52 879	104 527	51 344	53 183
0-4	5 842	2 995	2 846	5 773	2 960	2 812	5 624	2 884	2 740	5 563	2 853	2 710
5-9	5 719	2 925	2 794	5 888	3 012	2 876	5 819	2 977	2 843	5 671	2 901	2 770
10-14	5 500	2 814	2 686	5 762	2 949	2 814	5 931	3 036	2 896	5 863	3 001	2 862
15-19	5 554	2 832	2 722	5 654	2 883	2 770	5 916	3 018	2 898	6 086	3 105	2 980
20-24	5 842	2 959	2 884	5 760	2 916	2 843	5 861	2 969	2 892	6 123	3 104	3 020
25-29	6 193	3 143	3 050	6 021	3 050	2 971	5 940	3 008	2 931	6 041	3 061	2 980
30-34	6 790	3 445	3 345	6 298	3 197	3 101	6 127	3 105	3 022	6 047	3 064	2 983
35-39	6 975	3 554	3 421	6 859	3 480	3 379	6 369	3 233	3 136	6 201	3 142	3 058
40-44	6 475	3 292	3 183	6 993	3 559	3 434	6 880	3 488	3 393	6 395	3 244	3 151
45-49	6 158	3 094	3 064	6 443	3 273	3 170	6 961	3 540	3 421	6 853	3 472	3 381
50-54	6 462	3 192	3 270	6 100	3 055	3 045	6 387	3 235	3 152	6 905	3 502	3 402
55-59	6 964	3 400	3 564	6 351	3 100	3 231	6 003	2 991	3 012	6 291	3 171	3 120
60-64	6 723	3 262	3 461	6 748	3 267	3 482	6 164	3 004	3 160	5 835	2 886	2 949
65-69	5 730	2 743	2 987	6 376	3 051	3 326	6 421	3 068	3 353	5 879	2 831	3 049
70-74	4 838	2 247	2 591	5 239	2 444	2 795	5 857	2 735	3 122	5 926	2 767	3 158
75-79	4 461	1 992	2 469	4 174	1 856	2 318	4 549	2 036	2 513	5 120	2 298	2 821
80-84	2 808	1 157	1 651	3 493	1 457	2 036	3 304	1 370	1 020	3 639	1 529	2 109
85-89	1 594	577	1 016	1 878	697	1 181	2 381	898	1 482	2 291	865	1 426
90-94	746	224	522	837	259	578	1 015	323	691	1 322	432	891
95-99	251	57	194	273	65	208	318	78	240	400	102	298
100 +	48	7	41	57	9	48	65	11	54	79	14	65

Age group	2045 Both sexes	2045 Males	2045 Females	2050 Both sexes	2050 Males	2050 Females
All ages	105 051	51 643	53 408	105 602	51 976	53 626
0-4	5 618	2 881	2 736	5 748	2 948	2 800
5-9	5 610	2 870	2 740	5 665	2 898	2 767
10-14	5 715	2 925	2 790	5 654	2 894	2 760
15-19	6 018	3 071	2 947	5 870	2 995	2 875
20-24	6 293	3 191	3 102	6 226	3 157	3 069
25-29	6 304	3 197	3 108	6 475	3 284	3 190
30-34	6 149	3 117	3 032	6 413	3 253	3 159
35-39	6 122	3 102	3 019	6 224	3 156	3 068
40-44	6 228	3 154	3 074	6 151	3 115	3 036
45-49	6 374	3 232	3 142	6 211	3 145	3 066
50-54	6 804	3 439	3 365	6 333	3 204	3 128
55-59	6 808	3 438	3 370	6 716	3 381	3 335
60-64	6 124	3 066	3 058	6 638	3 331	3 307
65-69	5 579	2 729	2 850	5 868	2 907	2 961
70-74	5 447	2 566	2 881	5 188	2 487	2 702
75-79	5 216	2 347	2 869	4 824	2 193	2 631
80-84	4 135	1 748	2 387	4 257	1 809	2 448
85-89	2 561	980	1 581	2 957	1 144	1 814
90-94	1 304	428	876	1 492	498	993
95-99	540	143	397	551	147	404
100 +	102	19	83	142	27	115

United Nations Department of Economic and Social Affairs/Population Division
World Population Prospects: The 2004 Revision, Volume II: Sex and Age Distribution of the World Population

101

POPULATION BY AGE AND SEX (in thousands)

Age group	2005 Both sexes	Males	Females	2010 Both sexes	Males	Females	2015 Both sexes	Males	Females	2020 Both sexes	Males	Females
All ages	95 792	46 804	48 988	97 924	47 950	49 974	100 577	49 345	51 232	103 738	50 980	52 758
0-4	5 397	2 768	2 629	6 091	3 123	2 968	6 674	3 422	3 252	7 277	3 732	3 545
5-9	5 618	2 879	2 739	5 442	2 783	2 659	6 136	3 138	2 998	6 719	3 437	3 281
10-14	6 162	3 157	3 005	5 660	2 902	2 758	5 485	2 806	2 678	6 178	3 162	3 017
15-19	6 439	3 307	3 132	6 313	3 225	3 088	5 812	2 971	2 842	5 638	2 875	2 762
20-24	6 123	3 122	3 001	6 637	3 385	3 252	6 514	3 306	3 208	6 016	3 053	2 963
25-29	6 015	3 032	2 983	6 294	3 207	3 087	6 809	3 471	3 338	6 688	3 393	3 295
30-34	6 502	3 234	3 267	6 113	3 080	3 032	6 393	3 256	3 137	6 909	3 522	3 388
35-39	7 226	3 573	3 653	6 561	3 262	3 300	6 177	3 111	3 066	6 458	3 287	3 171
40-44	7 247	3 593	3 654	7 228	3 568	3 661	6 571	3 262	3 309	6 192	3 115	3 078
45-49	6 514	3 234	3 280	7 188	3 556	3 631	7 177	3 537	3 640	6 530	3 237	3 293
50-54	6 000	2 962	3 038	6 423	3 173	3 249	7 096	3 497	3 600	7 095	3 484	3 611
55-59	6 377	3 148	3 229	5 859	2 871	2 989	6 283	3 083	3 200	6 954	3 405	3 549
60-64	5 080	2 473	2 607	6 123	2 990	3 133	5 639	2 734	2 905	6 060	2 944	3 116
65-69	4 244	2 014	2 231	4 750	2 272	2 478	5 751	2 762	2 989	5 315	2 536	2 778
70-74	3 632	1 647	1 985	3 792	1 742	2 051	4 275	1 984	2 291	5 209	2 433	2 776
75-79	3 081	1 285	1 796	3 025	1 300	1 726	3 189	1 392	1 797	3 630	1 607	2 023
80-84	2 276	843	1 433	2 286	875	1 411	2 276	902	1 374	2 432	983	1 448
85-89	1 203	380	823	1 401	457	944	1 438	487	951	1 462	516	945
90-94	509	127	382	557	147	410	673	184	488	712	204	508
95-99	130	25	105	157	30	126	180	37	143	227	49	179
100 +	17	2	15	24	3	20	30	4	26	37	5	31

Age group	2025 Both sexes	Males	Females	2030 Both sexes	Males	Females	2035 Both sexes	Males	Females	2040 Both sexes	Males	Females
All ages	106 897	52 592	54 306	109 774	54 046	55 729	112 481	55 419	57 063	115 387	56 915	58 472
0-4	7 423	3 807	3 616	7 350	3 770	3 580	7 420	3 806	3 614	7 839	4 021	3 818
5-9	7 322	3 747	3 575	7 469	3 823	3 646	7 396	3 786	3 610	7 466	3 822	3 644
10-14	6 761	3 461	3 300	7 364	3 770	3 594	7 512	3 846	3 665	7 439	3 809	3 630
15-19	6 331	3 231	3 101	6 914	3 530	3 384	7 518	3 840	3 678	7 665	3 916	3 750
20-24	5 842	2 959	2 884	6 536	3 315	3 222	7 120	3 614	3 506	7 724	3 924	3 799
25-29	6 193	3 143	3 050	6 021	3 050	2 971	6 715	3 406	3 309	7 299	3 706	3 593
30-34	6 790	3 445	3 345	6 298	3 197	3 101	6 127	3 105	3 022	6 821	3 461	3 360
35-39	6 975	3 554	3 421	6 859	3 480	3 379	6 369	3 233	3 136	6 201	3 142	3 058
40-44	6 475	3 292	3 183	6 993	3 559	3 434	6 880	3 488	3 393	6 395	3 244	3 151
45-49	6 158	3 094	3 064	6 443	3 273	3 170	6 961	3 540	3 421	6 853	3 472	3 381
50-54	6 462	3 192	3 270	6 100	3 055	3 045	6 387	3 235	3 152	6 905	3 502	3 402
55-59	6 964	3 400	3 564	6 351	3 120	3 231	6 002	2 991	3 012	6 291	3 171	3 120
60-64	6 723	3 262	3 461	6 748	3 267	3 482	6 164	3 004	3 160	5 835	2 886	2 949
65-69	5 730	2 743	2 987	6 376	3 051	3 326	6 421	3 068	3 353	5 879	2 831	3 049
70-74	4 838	2 247	2 591	5 239	2 444	2 795	5 857	2 735	3 122	5 926	2 767	3 158
75-79	4 461	1 992	2 469	4 174	1 856	2 318	4 549	2 036	2 513	5 120	2 298	2 821
80-84	2 808	1 157	1 651	3 493	1 457	2 036	3 304	1 376	1 929	3 638	1 529	2 109
85-89	1 594	577	1 016	1 878	697	1 181	2 381	898	1 482	2 291	865	1 426
90-94	746	224	522	837	259	578	1 015	323	691	1 322	432	891
95-99	251	57	194	273	65	208	318	78	240	400	102	298
100 +	48	7	41	57	9	48	65	11	54	79	14	65

Age group	2045 Both sexes	Males	Females	2050 Both sexes	Males	Females
All ages	118 719	58 654	60 065	122 451	60 619	61 832
0-4	8 434	4 327	4 107	8 940	4 586	4 353
5-9	7 885	4 037	3 848	8 480	4 343	4 137
10-14	7 510	3 846	3 664	7 929	4 061	3 867
15-19	7 593	3 879	3 714	7 664	3 916	3 748
20-24	7 872	4 001	3 871	7 800	3 965	3 836
25-29	7 903	4 016	3 887	8 052	4 093	3 959
30-34	7 405	3 761	3 644	8 009	4 072	3 938
35-39	6 894	3 498	3 396	7 478	3 799	3 680
40-44	6 228	3 154	3 074	6 922	3 510	3 412
45-49	6 374	3 232	3 142	6 211	3 145	3 066
50-54	6 804	3 439	3 365	6 333	3 204	3 128
55-59	6 808	3 438	3 370	6 716	3 381	3 335
60-64	6 124	3 066	3 058	6 638	3 331	3 307
65-69	5 579	2 729	2 850	5 868	2 907	2 961
70-74	5 447	2 566	2 881	5 188	2 487	2 702
75-79	5 216	2 347	2 869	4 824	2 193	2 631
80-84	4 135	1 748	2 387	4 257	1 809	2 448
85-89	2 561	980	1 581	2 957	1 144	1 814
90-94	1 304	428	876	1 492	498	993
95-99	540	143	397	551	147	404
100 +	102	19	83	142	27	115

United Nations Department of Economic and Social Affairs/Population Division
World Population Prospects: The 2004 Revision, Volume II: Sex and Age Distribution of the World Population

102

POPULATION BY AGE AND SEX (in thousands)

Age group	2005 Both sexes	Males	Females	2010 Both sexes	Males	Females	2015 Both sexes	Males	Females	2020 Both sexes	Males	Females
All ages	95 792	46 804	48 988	90 305	47 151	40 015	06 497	47 253	49 245	96 455	47 245	49 211
0-4	5 397	2 768	2 629	4 532	2 323	2 209	4 151	2 128	2 023	4 072	2 087	1 984
5-9	5 618	2 879	2 739	5 442	2 783	2 659	4 578	2 339	2 239	4 198	2 145	2 054
10-14	6 162	3 157	3 005	5 660	2 902	2 758	5 485	2 806	2 678	4 621	2 363	2 258
15-19	6 439	3 307	3 132	6 313	3 225	3 088	5 812	2 971	2 842	5 638	2 875	2 762
20-24	6 123	3 122	3 001	6 637	3 385	3 252	6 514	3 306	3 208	6 016	3 053	2 963
25-29	6 015	3 032	2 983	6 294	3 207	3 087	6 809	3 471	3 338	6 688	3 393	3 295
30-34	6 502	3 234	3 267	6 113	3 080	3 032	6 393	3 256	3 137	6 909	3 522	3 388
35-39	7 226	3 573	3 653	6 561	3 262	3 300	6 177	3 111	3 066	6 458	3 287	3 171
40-44	7 247	3 593	3 654	7 228	3 568	3 661	6 571	3 262	3 309	6 192	3 115	3 078
45-49	6 514	3 234	3 280	7 188	3 556	3 631	7 177	3 537	3 640	6 530	3 237	3 293
50-54	6 000	2 962	3 038	6 423	3 173	3 249	7 096	3 497	3 600	7 095	3 484	3 611
55-59	6 377	3 148	3 229	5 859	2 871	2 989	6 283	3 083	3 200	6 954	3 405	3 549
60-64	5 080	2 473	2 607	6 123	2 990	3 133	5 639	2 734	2 905	6 060	2 944	3 116
65-69	4 244	2 014	2 231	4 750	2 272	2 478	5 751	2 762	2 989	5 315	2 536	2 778
70-74	3 632	1 647	1 985	3 792	1 742	2 051	4 275	1 984	2 291	5 209	2 433	2 776
75-79	3 081	1 285	1 796	3 025	1 300	1 726	3 189	1 392	1 797	3 630	1 607	2 023
80-84	2 276	843	1 433	2 286	875	1 411	2 276	902	1 374	2 432	983	1 448
85-89	1 203	380	823	1 401	457	944	1 438	487	951	1 462	516	945
90-94	509	127	382	557	147	410	673	184	488	712	204	508
95-99	130	25	105	157	30	126	180	37	143	227	49	179
100 +	17	2	15	24	3	20	30	4	26	37	5	31

Age group	2025 Both sexes	Males	Females	2030 Both sexes	Males	Females	2035 Both sexes	Males	Females	2040 Both sexes	Males	Females
All ages	96 446	47 230	49 216	96 198	47 082	49 116	95 509	46 713	48 796	94 317	46 107	48 210
0-4	4 251	2 179	2 071	4 219	2 163	2 056	4 015	2 059	1 957	3 729	1 912	1 817
5-9	4 119	2 104	2 015	4 298	2 196	2 102	4 267	2 180	2 087	4 063	2 076	1 987
10-14	4 242	2 169	2 073	4 162	2 128	2 034	4 342	2 220	2 122	4 311	2 204	2 106
15-19	4 775	2 433	2 343	4 396	2 238	2 158	4 317	2 198	2 119	4 497	2 290	2 206
20-24	5 842	2 959	2 884	4 982	2 518	2 464	4 604	2 324	2 280	4 526	2 284	2 241
25-29	6 193	3 143	3 050	6 021	3 050	2 971	5 163	2 610	2 553	4 786	2 418	2 368
30-34	6 790	3 445	3 345	6 298	3 197	3 101	6 127	3 105	3 022	5 271	2 667	2 605
35-39	6 975	3 554	3 421	6 859	3 480	3 379	6 369	3 233	3 136	6 201	3 142	3 058
40-44	6 475	3 292	3 183	6 993	3 559	3 434	6 000	6 488	3 393	6 395	3 244	3 151
45-49	6 158	3 094	3 064	6 443	3 273	3 170	6 961	3 540	3 421	6 853	3 472	3 381
50-54	6 462	3 192	3 270	6 100	3 055	3 045	6 387	3 235	3 152	6 905	3 502	3 402
55-59	6 094	2 400	3 564	6 351	3 120	3 231	6 002	2 991	3 012	6 291	3 171	3 120
60-64	6 723	3 262	3 461	6 748	3 267	3 482	6 164	3 004	3 160	5 835	2 886	2 949
65-69	5 730	2 743	2 987	6 376	3 051	3 326	6 421	3 068	3 353	5 879	2 831	3 049
70-74	4 838	2 247	2 591	5 239	2 444	2 795	5 857	2 735	3 122	5 926	2 767	3 158
75-79	4 461	1 992	2 469	4 174	1 856	2 318	4 549	2 036	2 513	5 120	2 298	2 821
80-84	2 808	1 157	1 651	3 493	1 457	2 000	3 004	1 376	1 929	3 638	1 529	2 109
85-89	1 594	577	1 016	1 878	697	1 181	2 381	898	1 482	2 291	865	1 426
90-94	746	224	522	837	259	578	1 015	323	691	1 322	432	891
95-99	251	57	194	273	65	208	318	78	240	400	102	298
100 +	48	7	41	57	9	48	65	11	54	79	14	65

Age group	2045 Both sexes	Males	Females	2050 Both sexes	Males	Females
All ages	92 691	45 303	47 388	90 822	44 394	46 428
0-4	3 461	1 775	1 686	3 317	1 701	1 616
5-9	3 777	1 929	1 848	3 509	1 792	1 717
10-14	4 107	2 100	2 007	3 822	1 954	1 868
15-19	4 466	2 275	2 191	4 263	2 171	2 092
20-24	4 706	2 377	2 329	4 675	2 362	2 314
25-29	4 708	2 378	2 330	4 888	2 471	2 418
30-34	4 896	2 475	2 421	4 819	2 436	2 383
35-39	5 348	2 706	2 642	4 973	2 515	2 458
40-44	6 228	3 154	3 074	5 379	2 720	2 659
45-49	6 374	3 232	3 142	6 211	3 145	3 066
50-54	6 804	3 439	3 365	6 333	3 204	3 128
55-59	6 808	3 438	3 370	6 716	3 381	3 335
60-64	6 124	3 066	3 058	6 638	3 331	3 307
65-69	5 579	2 729	2 850	5 868	2 907	2 961
70-74	5 447	2 566	2 881	5 188	2 487	2 702
75-79	5 216	2 347	2 869	4 824	2 193	2 631
80-84	4 135	1 748	2 387	4 257	1 809	2 448
85-89	2 561	980	1 581	2 957	1 144	1 814
90-94	1 304	428	876	1 492	498	993
95-99	540	143	397	551	147	404
100 +	102	19	83	142	27	115

United Nations Department of Economic and Social Affairs/Population Division
World Population Prospects: The 2004 Revision, Volume II: Sex and Age Distribution of the World Population

103

POPULATION BY AGE AND SEX (in thousands)

Age group	1950 Both sexes	1950 Males	1950 Females	1955 Both sexes	1955 Males	1955 Females	1960 Both sexes	1960 Males	1960 Females	1965 Both sexes	1965 Males	1965 Females
All ages	108 996	52 874	56 122	113 588	55 339	58 250	118 067	57 552	60 516	122 979	59 947	63 032
0-4	10 819	5 527	5 292	10 763	5 512	5 251	11 093	5 671	5 422	11 642	5 974	5 668
5-9	9 431	4 793	4 638	10 584	5 392	5 191	10 477	5 370	5 106	10 837	5 538	5 300
10-14	9 886	5 017	4 869	9 297	4 709	4 587	10 478	5 329	5 149	10 336	5 302	5 034
15-19	10 056	5 032	5 024	9 730	4 926	4 804	9 107	4 568	4 539	10 304	5 225	5 079
20-24	9 757	4 855	4 902	9 876	4 924	4 952	9 416	4 720	4 696	8 817	4 383	4 434
25-29	8 922	4 304	4 619	9 517	4 726	4 792	9 463	4 675	4 788	9 124	4 525	4 599
30-34	6 680	3 183	3 497	8 741	4 216	4 525	9 191	4 540	4 651	9 186	4 494	4 692
35-39	7 409	3 557	3 852	6 333	3 022	3 311	8 473	4 065	4 408	8 964	4 398	4 566
40-44	7 311	3 555	3 756	7 397	3 560	3 837	6 140	2 915	3 224	8 265	3 939	4 326
45-49	6 385	3 093	3 292	7 011	3 401	3 610	7 160	3 431	3 730	5 962	2 810	3 151
50-54	5 546	2 604	2 943	6 056	2 917	3 139	6 737	3 248	3 489	6 929	3 293	3 635
55-59	4 509	2 029	2 480	5 187	2 382	2 805	5 737	2 730	3 007	6 420	3 051	3 369
60-64	3 983	1 773	2 210	4 118	1 825	2 293	4 786	2 161	2 625	5 340	2 485	2 855
65-69	3 141	1 393	1 748	3 456	1 510	1 946	3 647	1 576	2 072	4 188	1 827	2 362
70-74	2 434	1 055	1 380	2 594	1 118	1 476	2 871	1 208	1 662	2 989	1 243	1 745
75-79	1 577	661	916	1 672	706	966	1 878	787	1 091	2 050	830	1 221
80 +	1 150	444	706	1 258	494	764	1 413	557	856	1 626	630	996

Age group	1970 Both sexes	1970 Males	1970 Females	1975 Both sexes	1975 Males	1975 Females	1980 Both sexes	1980 Males	1980 Females	1985 Both sexes	1985 Males	1985 Females
All ages	127 244	62 140	65 104	132 472	64 660	67 812	137 905	67 497	70 408	140 566	68 756	71 809
0-4	11 503	5 900	5 603	11 297	5 805	5 491	10 684	5 511	5 173	9 087	4 686	4 401
5-9	11 452	5 859	5 593	11 508	5 895	5 614	11 257	5 785	5 472	10 421	5 360	5 061
10-14	10 690	5 467	5 223	11 449	5 858	5 591	11 612	5 951	5 661	11 309	5 808	5 501
15-19	10 080	5 114	4 966	10 594	5 388	5 206	11 488	5 877	5 611	11 672	5 968	5 705
20-24	9 838	4 992	4 846	9 979	5 033	4 947	10 564	5 365	5 199	11 441	5 822	5 619
25-29	8 212	4 074	4 138	9 665	4 849	4 816	9 900	4 999	4 901	10 428	5 252	5 176
30-34	8 672	4 262	4 409	8 082	3 987	4 095	9 541	4 765	4 776	9 724	4 884	4 840
35-39	8 954	4 420	4 534	8 688	4 258	4 430	8 120	4 017	4 103	9 368	4 680	4 687
40-44	8 777	4 299	4 477	8 923	4 383	4 541	8 868	4 354	4 515	8 230	4 069	4 161
45-49	8 018	3 835	4 183	8 594	4 185	4 409	8 894	4 354	4 540	8 542	4 186	4 357
50-54	5 732	2 689	3 043	7 768	3 675	4 093	8 419	4 068	4 351	8 685	4 222	4 463
55-59	6 624	3 117	3 507	5 501	2 539	2 962	7 445	3 472	3 972	8 120	3 874	4 246
60-64	6 063	2 830	3 233	6 216	2 856	3 360	5 199	2 358	2 841	7 127	3 261	3 866
65-69	4 831	2 180	2 651	5 406	2 438	2 969	5 663	2 514	3 149	4 806	2 115	2 691
70-74	3 545	1 476	2 069	4 031	1 721	2 311	4 619	1 989	2 630	4 960	2 099	2 860
75-79	2 231	883	1 348	2 564	1 007	1 557	3 114	1 246	1 867	3 552	1 414	2 138
80 +	2 022	742	1 281	2 204	784	1 421	2 517	871	1 646	3 093	1 058	2 036

Age group	1990 Both sexes	1990 Males	1990 Females	1995 Both sexes	1995 Males	1995 Females	2000 Both sexes	2000 Males	2000 Females	2005 Both sexes	2005 Males	2005 Females
All ages	142 737	69 767	72 970	144 103	70 421	73 682	146 081	71 359	74 722	149 389	73 012	76 377
0-4	8 009	4 121	3 888	7 541	3 882	3 658	7 266	3 741	3 525	7 439	3 837	3 602
5-9	8 845	4 546	4 299	7 980	4 095	3 884	7 561	3 884	3 677	7 377	3 796	3 581
10-14	10 170	5 216	4 954	8 977	4 602	4 375	8 056	4 134	3 922	7 644	3 924	3 719
15-19	11 348	5 802	5 547	10 400	5 322	5 077	9 124	4 675	4 449	8 232	4 219	4 013
20-24	11 414	5 806	5 608	11 438	5 834	5 604	10 605	5 417	5 188	9 473	4 844	4 628
25-29	11 329	5 719	5 610	11 505	5 828	5 676	11 611	5 909	5 702	11 019	5 619	5 400
30-34	10 518	5 282	5 235	11 209	5 637	5 572	11 512	5 816	5 696	11 956	6 078	5 879
35-39	9 769	4 894	4 875	10 394	5 202	5 193	11 241	5 634	5 607	11 771	5 941	5 830
40-44	9 362	4 668	4 695	9 654	4 824	4 830	10 437	5 204	5 233	11 412	5 714	5 699
45-49	8 160	4 035	4 126	9 306	4 619	4 687	9 587	4 772	4 815	10 510	5 230	5 280
50-54	8 392	4 096	4 297	8 010	3 927	4 083	9 220	4 548	4 672	9 567	4 740	4 827
55-59	8 354	4 030	4 324	8 147	3 926	4 221	7 920	3 842	4 078	9 103	4 452	4 650
60-64	7 885	3 701	4 183	8 070	3 820	4 251	7 861	3 725	4 136	7 707	3 684	4 023
65-69	6 742	3 014	3 728	7 348	3 348	4 001	7 667	3 534	4 133	7 445	3 443	4 002
70-74	4 412	1 857	2 555	5 963	2 547	3 416	6 673	2 916	3 757	6 954	3 081	3 873
75-79	3 957	1 573	2 384	3 486	1 379	2 107	4 929	1 979	2 951	5 646	2 325	3 321
80 +	4 069	1 407	2 662	4 676	1 628	3 048	4 811	1 629	3 182	6 135	2 084	4 050

104

United Nations Department of Economic and Social Affairs/Population Division
World Population Prospects: The 2004 Revision, Volume II: Sex and Age Distribution of the World Population

POPULATION BY AGE AND SEX (in thousands)

Age group	2005			2010			2015			2020		
	Both sexes	Males	Females	Both sexes	Males	Females	Both sexes	Males	Females	Both sexes	Males	Females
All ages	149 389	73 012	76 377	150 789	73 707	77 082	150 881	73 770	77 110	150 145	73 442	76 703
0-4	7 439	3 837	3 602	7 390	3 813	3 577	6 954	3 589	3 365	6 490	3 350	3 141
5-9	7 377	3 796	3 581	7 492	3 863	3 629	7 427	3 831	3 595	6 989	3 606	3 383
10-14	7 644	3 924	3 719	7 429	3 822	3 607	7 532	3 883	3 649	7 467	3 851	3 616
15-19	8 232	4 219	4 013	7 731	3 966	3 765	7 493	3 852	3 641	7 597	3 915	3 683
20-24	9 473	4 844	4 628	8 371	4 284	4 087	7 821	4 008	3 813	7 585	3 895	3 689
25-29	11 019	5 619	5 400	9 623	4 914	4 709	8 464	4 326	4 138	7 917	4 052	3 865
30-34	11 956	6 078	5 879	11 140	5 673	5 467	9 697	4 946	4 751	8 541	4 361	4 180
35-39	11 771	5 941	5 830	12 054	6 117	5 936	11 200	5 695	5 505	9 760	4 972	4 789
40-44	11 412	5 714	5 699	11 839	5 965	5 874	12 092	6 127	5 965	11 241	5 707	5 534
45-49	10 510	5 230	5 280	11 420	5 703	5 717	11 829	5 945	5 884	12 085	6 109	5 976
50-54	9 567	4 740	4 827	10 448	5 174	5 274	11 342	5 639	5 703	11 759	5 886	5 873
55-59	9 103	4 452	4 650	9 425	4 630	4 795	10 286	5 054	5 233	11 184	5 520	5 664
60-64	7 707	3 684	4 023	8 845	4 266	4 579	9 151	4 435	4 716	10 011	4 858	5 153
65-69	7 445	3 443	4 002	7 321	3 420	3 901	8 402	3 965	4 438	8 711	4 136	4 575
70-74	6 954	3 081	3 873	6 780	3 020	3 760	6 700	3 022	3 679	7 717	3 523	4 194
75-79	5 646	2 325	3 321	5 919	2 476	3 443	5 809	2 449	3 359	5 795	2 481	3 314
80-84	3 700	1 359	2 341	4 282	1 617	2 665	4 541	1 746	2 796	4 512	1 754	2 758
85-89	1 548	490	1 058	2 320	746	1 575	2 740	908	1 832	2 969	1 004	1 965
90-94	721	197	524	725	189	536	1 135	300	835	1 386	379	1 007
95-99	153	36	118	215	46	169	230	46	185	386	77	309
100 +	12	2	10	22	4	18	35	5	30	42	5	37

Age group	2025			2030			2035			2040		
	Both sexes	Males	Females	Both sexes	Males	Females	Both sexes	Males	Females	Both sexes	Males	Females
All ages	148 866	72 840	76 025	147 342	72 093	75 248	145 681	71 253	74 428	143 796	70 288	73 508
0-4	6 233	3 217	3 016	6 222	3 211	3 011	6 376	3 291	3 085	6 503	3 356	3 147
5-9	6 526	3 367	3 159	6 270	3 235	3 034	6 259	3 230	3 029	6 414	3 310	3 104
10-14	7 027	3 625	3 402	6 563	3 386	3 177	6 307	3 254	3 053	6 298	3 249	3 049
15-19	7 529	3 881	3 648	7 089	3 655	3 434	6 625	3 416	3 209	6 369	3 285	3 085
20-24	7 689	3 958	3 731	7 622	3 926	3 696	7 181	3 700	3 482	6 717	3 461	3 256
25-29	7 683	3 942	3 741	7 788	4 005	3 783	7 721	3 974	3 748	7 281	3 748	3 533
30-34	7 997	4 090	3 908	7 765	3 981	3 784	7 872	4 045	3 827	7 806	4 014	3 792
35-39	8 608	4 390	4 217	8 068	4 122	3 946	7 838	4 014	3 823	7 946	4 080	3 866
40-44	9 804	4 987	4 817	8 658	4 411	4 246	8 123	4 146	3 977	7 896	4 041	3 855
45-49	11 237	5 693	5 544	9 810	4 981	4 829	8 674	4 412	4 262	8 146	4 152	3 994
50-54	12 017	6 051	5 966	11 180	5 643	5 536	9 768	4 943	4 825	8 647	4 385	4 262
55-59	11 608	5 771	5 837	11 871	5 940	5 931	11 052	5 545	5 506	9 666	4 864	4 802
60-64	10 006	5 022	5 504	11 040	5 579	5 701	11 611	5 752	5 859	10 820	5 378	5 441
65-69	9 560	4 550	5 010	10 447	5 008	5 439	10 892	5 271	5 621	11 173	5 450	5 723
70-74	8 022	3 691	4 332	8 850	4 090	4 760	9 717	4 531	5 186	10 171	4 797	5 374
75-79	6 711	2 916	3 795	7 009	3 076	3 934	7 792	3 442	4 349	8 618	3 852	4 766
80-84	4 570	1 809	2 761	5 343	2 153	3 190	5 626	2 295	3 331	6 332	2 608	3 723
85-89	3 012	1 034	1 978	3 124	1 094	2 030	3 715	1 330	2 385	3 966	1 442	2 524
90-94	1 554	433	1 120	1 629	462	1 167	1 748	507	1 241	2 133	636	1 497
95-99	497	102	395	587	122	465	646	137	510	726	157	569
100 +	75	9	65	107	13	94	139	17	122	168	21	146

Age group	2045			2050		
	Both sexes	Males	Females	Both sexes	Males	Females
All ages	141 514	69 129	72 386	138 716	67 728	70 988
0-4	6 471	3 340	3 132	6 271	3 237	3 035
5-9	6 542	3 376	3 166	6 511	3 360	3 151
10-14	6 454	3 330	3 124	6 583	3 396	3 187
15-19	6 361	3 281	3 081	6 519	3 362	3 157
20-24	6 463	3 330	3 133	6 457	3 327	3 129
25-29	6 818	3 510	3 307	6 565	3 381	3 184
30-34	7 367	3 790	3 577	6 903	3 552	3 351
35-39	7 881	4 050	3 832	7 443	3 826	3 617
40-44	8 006	4 107	3 899	7 943	4 078	3 865
45-49	7 924	4 049	3 874	8 036	4 117	3 919
50-54	8 130	4 132	3 998	7 915	4 034	3 880
55-59	8 568	4 323	4 245	8 066	4 080	3 986
60-64	9 474	4 725	4 748	8 411	4 209	4 202
65-69	10 427	5 107	5 319	9 144	4 498	4 646
70-74	10 466	4 983	5 482	9 789	4 686	5 103
75-79	9 075	4 113	4 962	9 384	4 303	5 082
80-84	7 086	2 964	4 122	7 534	3 206	4 327
85-89	4 552	1 678	2 874	5 190	1 952	3 238
90-94	2 327	708	1 620	2 747	850	1 897
95-99	921	206	715	1 038	238	801
100 +	202	26	176	266	36	231

POPULATION BY AGE AND SEX (in thousands)

Age group	2005			2010			2015			2020		
	Both sexes	Males	Females	Both sexes	Males	Females	Both sexes	Males	Females	Both sexes	Males	Females
All ages	149 389	73 012	76 377	152 081	74 376	77 705	154 013	75 390	78 623	155 323	76 118	79 205
0-4	7 439	3 837	3 602	8 681	4 480	4 201	8 796	4 540	4 256	8 538	4 407	4 131
5-9	7 377	3 796	3 581	7 492	3 864	3 628	8 717	4 498	4 219	8 830	4 557	4 273
10-14	7 644	3 924	3 719	7 429	3 822	3 607	7 532	3 884	3 648	8 756	4 517	4 239
15-19	8 232	4 219	4 013	7 731	3 966	3 765	7 493	3 853	3 640	7 597	3 915	3 682
20-24	9 473	4 844	4 628	8 371	4 284	4 087	7 821	4 008	3 813	7 585	3 896	3 689
25-29	11 019	5 619	5 400	9 623	4 914	4 709	8 464	4 326	4 138	7 917	4 052	3 865
30-34	11 956	6 078	5 879	11 140	5 673	5 467	9 697	4 946	4 751	8 541	4 361	4 180
35-39	11 771	5 941	5 830	12 054	6 117	5 936	11 200	5 695	5 505	9 760	4 972	4 789
40-44	11 412	5 714	5 699	11 839	5 965	5 874	12 092	6 127	5 965	11 241	5 707	5 534
45-49	10 510	5 230	5 280	11 420	5 703	5 717	11 829	5 945	5 884	12 085	6 109	5 976
50-54	9 567	4 740	4 827	10 448	5 174	5 274	11 342	5 639	5 703	11 759	5 886	5 873
55-59	9 103	4 452	4 650	9 425	4 630	4 795	10 286	5 054	5 233	11 184	5 520	5 664
60-64	7 707	3 684	4 023	8 845	4 266	4 579	9 151	4 435	4 716	10 011	4 858	5 153
65-69	7 445	3 443	4 002	7 321	3 420	3 901	8 402	3 965	4 438	8 711	4 136	4 575
70-74	6 954	3 081	3 873	6 780	3 020	3 760	6 700	3 022	3 679	7 717	3 523	4 194
75-79	5 646	2 325	3 321	5 919	2 476	3 443	5 809	2 449	3 359	5 795	2 481	3 314
80-84	3 700	1 359	2 341	4 282	1 617	2 665	4 541	1 746	2 796	4 512	1 754	2 758
85-89	1 548	490	1 058	2 320	746	1 575	2 740	908	1 832	2 969	1 004	1 965
90-94	721	197	524	725	189	536	1 135	300	835	1 386	379	1 007
95-99	153	36	118	215	46	169	230	46	185	386	77	309
100 +	12	2	10	22	4	18	35	5	30	42	5	37

Age group	2025			2030			2035			2040		
	Both sexes	Males	Females	Both sexes	Males	Females	Both sexes	Males	Females	Both sexes	Males	Females
All ages	155 949	76 500	79 448	156 404	76 775	79 629	157 124	77 163	79 961	158 238	77 745	80 493
0-4	8 142	4 203	3 939	8 207	4 237	3 970	8 764	4 524	4 240	9 513	4 911	4 602
5-9	8 572	4 424	4 148	8 177	4 221	3 957	8 243	4 254	3 988	8 801	4 543	4 258
10-14	8 867	4 575	4 292	8 608	4 442	4 166	8 214	4 239	3 975	8 281	4 273	4 007
15-19	8 818	4 547	4 271	8 928	4 605	4 323	8 668	4 471	4 197	8 275	4 269	4 006
20-24	7 689	3 959	3 730	8 908	4 590	4 318	9 018	4 648	4 370	8 759	4 515	4 244
25-29	7 683	3 942	3 740	7 788	4 006	3 782	9 006	4 636	4 370	9 115	4 694	4 421
30-34	7 997	4 090	3 908	7 765	3 981	3 784	7 872	4 046	3 826	9 088	4 675	4 413
35-39	8 608	4 390	4 217	8 068	4 122	3 946	7 838	4 015	3 823	7 946	4 081	3 865
40-44	9 804	4 987	4 817	8 658	4 411	4 246	8 123	4 146	3 977	7 896	4 042	3 855
45-49	11 237	5 693	5 544	9 810	4 981	4 829	8 674	4 412	4 262	8 146	4 152	3 994
50-54	12 017	6 051	5 966	11 180	5 643	5 536	9 768	4 943	4 825	8 647	4 385	4 262
55-59	11 608	5 771	5 837	11 871	5 940	5 931	11 052	5 545	5 506	9 666	4 864	4 802
60-64	10 906	5 322	5 584	11 340	5 579	5 761	11 611	5 752	5 859	10 820	5 378	5 441
65-69	9 560	4 550	5 010	10 447	5 008	5 439	10 892	5 271	5 621	11 173	5 450	5 723
70-74	8 022	3 691	4 332	8 850	4 090	4 760	9 717	4 531	5 186	10 171	4 797	5 374
75-79	6 711	2 916	3 795	7 009	3 076	3 934	7 792	3 442	4 349	8 618	3 852	4 766
80-84	4 570	1 809	2 761	5 343	2 153	3 190	5 626	2 295	3 331	6 332	2 608	3 723
85-89	3 012	1 034	1 978	3 124	1 094	2 030	3 715	1 330	2 385	3 966	1 442	2 524
90-94	1 554	433	1 120	1 629	462	1 167	1 748	507	1 241	2 133	636	1 497
95-99	497	102	395	587	122	465	646	137	510	726	157	569
100 +	75	9	65	107	13	94	139	17	122	168	21	146

Age group	2045			2050		
	Both sexes	Males	Females	Both sexes	Males	Females
All ages	159 461	78 393	81 068	160 382	78 909	81 472
0-4	9 991	5 158	4 833	10 011	5 168	4 843
5-9	9 551	4 930	4 621	10 029	5 177	4 853
10-14	8 840	4 562	4 278	9 590	4 950	4 641
15-19	8 343	4 304	4 039	8 903	4 593	4 310
20-24	8 367	4 313	4 054	8 437	4 350	4 087
25-29	8 856	4 562	4 294	8 466	4 361	4 105
30-34	9 197	4 733	4 464	8 938	4 601	4 337
35-39	9 160	4 708	4 452	9 268	4 766	4 502
40-44	8 006	4 108	3 898	9 217	4 733	4 484
45-49	7 924	4 050	3 874	8 036	4 118	3 918
50-54	8 130	4 132	3 998	7 915	4 035	3 880
55-59	8 568	4 323	4 245	8 066	4 080	3 986
60-64	9 474	4 725	4 748	8 411	4 209	4 202
65-69	10 427	5 107	5 319	9 144	4 498	4 646
70-74	10 466	4 983	5 482	9 789	4 686	5 103
75-79	9 075	4 113	4 962	9 384	4 303	5 082
80-84	7 086	2 964	4 122	7 534	3 206	4 327
85-89	4 552	1 678	2 874	5 190	1 952	3 238
90-94	2 327	708	1 620	2 747	850	1 897
95-99	921	206	715	1 038	238	801
100 +	202	26	176	266	36	231

United Nations Department of Economic and Social Affairs/Population Division
World Population Prospects: The 2004 Revision, Volume II: Sex and Age Distribution of the World Population

106

POPULATION BY AGE AND SEX (in thousands)

Age group	2005 Both sexes	Males	Females	2010 Both sexes	Males	Females	2015 Both sexes	Males	Females	2020 Both sexes	Males	Females
All ages	149 389	73 012	76 377	149 487	73 037	76 450	147 699	72 131	75 568	144 863	70 720	74 143
0-4	7 439	3 837	3 602	6 088	3 142	2 946	5 073	2 619	2 454	4 388	2 265	2 123
5-9	7 377	3 796	3 581	7 492	3 864	3 628	6 126	3 161	2 965	5 110	2 637	2 473
10-14	7 644	3 924	3 719	7 429	3 822	3 607	7 532	3 884	3 648	6 166	3 181	2 986
15-19	8 232	4 219	4 013	7 731	3 966	3 765	7 493	3 853	3 640	7 597	3 915	3 682
20-24	9 473	4 844	4 628	8 371	4 284	4 087	7 821	4 008	3 813	7 585	3 896	3 689
25-29	11 019	5 619	5 400	9 623	4 914	4 709	8 464	4 326	4 138	7 917	4 052	3 865
30-34	11 956	6 078	5 879	11 140	5 673	5 467	9 697	4 946	4 751	8 541	4 361	4 180
35-39	11 771	5 941	5 830	12 054	6 117	5 936	11 200	5 695	5 505	9 760	4 972	4 789
40-44	11 412	5 714	5 699	11 839	5 965	5 874	12 092	6 127	5 965	11 241	5 707	5 534
45-49	10 510	5 230	5 280	11 420	5 703	5 717	11 829	5 945	5 884	12 085	6 109	5 976
50-54	9 567	4 740	4 827	10 448	5 174	5 274	11 342	5 639	5 703	11 759	5 886	5 873
55-59	9 103	4 452	4 650	9 425	4 630	4 795	10 286	5 054	5 233	11 184	5 520	5 664
60-64	7 707	3 684	4 023	8 845	4 266	4 579	9 151	4 435	4 716	10 011	4 858	5 153
65-69	7 445	3 443	4 002	7 321	3 420	3 901	8 402	3 965	4 438	8 711	4 136	4 575
70-74	6 954	3 081	3 873	6 780	3 020	3 760	6 700	3 022	3 679	7 717	3 523	4 194
75-79	5 646	2 325	3 321	5 919	2 476	3 443	5 809	2 449	3 359	5 795	2 481	3 314
80-84	3 700	1 359	2 341	4 282	1 617	2 665	4 541	1 746	2 796	4 512	1 754	2 758
85-89	1 548	490	1 058	2 320	746	1 575	2 740	908	1 832	2 969	1 004	1 965
90-94	721	197	524	725	189	536	1 135	300	835	1 386	379	1 007
95-99	153	36	118	215	46	169	230	46	185	386	77	309
100 +	12	2	10	22	4	18	35	5	30	42	5	37

Age group	2025 Both sexes	Males	Females	2030 Both sexes	Males	Females	2035 Both sexes	Males	Females	2040 Both sexes	Males	Females
All ages	141 647	69 119	72 528	138 213	67 388	70 825	134 499	65 490	69 009	130 272	63 318	66 954
0-4	4 293	2 216	2 077	4 306	2 223	2 083	4 315	2 227	2 087	4 151	2 143	2 008
5-9	4 425	2 284	2 141	4 331	2 235	2 096	4 345	2 242	2 102	4 354	2 247	2 107
10-14	5 149	2 656	2 492	4 463	2 303	2 160	4 369	2 254	2 115	4 384	2 262	2 122
15-19	6 230	3 212	3 018	5 212	2 688	2 524	4 526	2 334	2 192	4 433	2 286	2 147
20-24	7 689	3 959	3 730	6 324	3 258	3 067	5 307	2 734	2 573	4 621	2 381	2 240
25-29	7 683	3 942	3 740	7 788	4 006	3 782	6 426	3 307	3 119	5 410	2 785	2 625
30-34	7 997	4 090	3 908	7 765	3 981	3 784	7 872	4 046	3 826	6 514	3 350	3 164
35-39	8 608	4 390	4 217	8 068	4 122	3 946	7 838	4 015	3 823	7 946	4 081	3 865
40-44	9 804	4 987	4 817	8 658	4 411	4 246	8 123	4 146	3 977	7 896	4 042	3 855
45-49	11 237	5 693	5 544	9 810	4 981	4 829	8 674	4 412	4 202	8 146	4 152	3 994
50-54	12 017	6 051	5 966	11 180	5 643	5 536	9 768	4 943	4 825	8 647	4 385	4 262
55-59	11 608	5 771	5 837	11 871	5 940	5 931	11 052	5 545	5 506	9 668	4 864	4 802
60-64	10 906	5 322	5 584	11 340	5 579	5 761	11 611	5 752	5 859	10 820	5 378	5 441
65-69	9 560	4 550	5 010	10 447	5 008	5 439	10 892	5 271	5 621	11 173	5 450	5 723
70-74	8 022	3 691	4 332	8 850	4 090	4 760	9 717	4 531	5 186	10 171	4 797	5 374
75-79	6 711	2 916	3 795	7 009	3 076	3 934	7 792	3 442	4 349	8 618	3 852	4 766
80-84	4 570	1 809	2 761	5 343	2 153	3 190	5 626	2 295	3 331	6 332	2 608	3 723
85-89	3 012	1 034	1 978	3 124	1 094	2 030	3 715	1 330	2 385	3 966	1 442	2 524
90-94	1 554	433	1 120	1 629	462	1 167	1 748	507	1 241	2 133	636	1 497
95-99	497	102	395	587	122	465	646	137	510	726	157	569
100 +	75	9	65	107	13	94	139	17	122	168	21	146

Age group	2045 Both sexes	Males	Females	2050 Both sexes	Males	Females
All ages	125 341	60 795	64 546	119 726	57 945	61 781
0-4	3 806	1 965	1 842	3 436	1 773	1 662
5-9	4 191	2 163	2 028	3 847	1 985	1 862
10-14	4 395	2 267	2 127	4 232	2 184	2 049
15-19	4 448	2 294	2 154	4 461	2 300	2 160
20-24	4 528	2 333	2 195	4 545	2 342	2 203
25-29	4 724	2 432	2 292	4 633	2 385	2 247
30-34	5 499	2 829	2 670	4 814	2 477	2 337
35-39	6 592	3 388	3 205	5 579	2 868	2 711
40-44	8 006	4 108	3 898	6 658	3 419	3 239
45-49	7 924	4 050	3 874	8 036	4 118	3 918
50-54	8 130	4 132	3 998	7 915	4 035	3 880
55-59	8 568	4 323	4 245	8 066	4 080	3 986
60-64	9 474	4 725	4 748	8 411	4 209	4 202
65-69	10 427	5 107	5 319	9 144	4 498	4 646
70-74	10 466	4 983	5 482	9 789	4 686	5 103
75-79	9 075	4 113	4 962	9 384	4 303	5 082
80-84	7 086	2 964	4 122	7 534	3 206	4 327
85-89	4 552	1 678	2 874	5 190	1 952	3 238
90-94	2 327	708	1 620	2 747	850	1 897
95-99	921	206	715	1 038	238	801
100 +	202	26	176	266	36	231

POPULATION BY AGE AND SEX (in thousands)

Age group	1950			1955			1960			1965		
	Both sexes	Males	Females	Both sexes	Males	Females	Both sexes	Males	Females	Both sexes	Males	Females
All ages	140 916	66 534	74 383	145 640	69 065	76 575	151 902	72 321	79 581	159 981	76 719	83 262
0-4	11 336	5 797	5 540	11 826	6 053	5 773	12 646	6 471	6 175	13 856	7 091	6 764
5-9	10 296	5 248	5 048	11 263	5 749	5 513	11 996	6 130	5 866	12 769	6 533	6 236
10-14	11 240	5 703	5 537	10 407	5 303	5 104	11 395	5 815	5 580	12 147	6 208	5 938
15-19	10 313	5 228	5 084	11 238	5 704	5 534	10 555	5 380	5 176	11 650	5 964	5 687
20-24	10 414	5 148	5 267	10 300	5 222	5 078	11 349	5 795	5 554	10 825	5 557	5 268
25-29	10 454	4 794	5 660	10 364	5 110	5 254	10 287	5 231	5 055	11 584	5 988	5 596
30-34	7 178	3 268	3 910	10 417	4 776	5 641	10 370	5 113	5 257	10 572	5 433	5 138
35-39	10 151	4 624	5 527	7 114	3 241	3 873	10 419	4 772	5 648	10 620	5 283	5 337
40-44	10 868	5 060	5 808	10 055	4 582	5 472	7 096	3 224	3 872	10 489	4 808	5 681
45-49	10 602	5 084	5 519	10 677	4 959	5 717	9 963	4 512	5 451	7 051	3 193	3 859
50-54	9 279	4 241	5 038	10 267	4 885	5 381	10 457	4 813	5 645	9 770	4 390	5 380
55-59	7 695	3 295	4 400	8 807	3 958	4 849	9 867	4 613	5 254	10 035	4 539	5 496
60-64	6 741	2 915	3 827	7 132	2 986	4 146	8 240	3 599	4 640	9 205	4 175	5 031
65-69	5 583	2 423	3 160	5 969	2 507	3 462	6 392	2 578	3 815	7 373	3 077	4 296
70-74	4 335	1 890	2 445	4 575	1 913	2 662	4 952	1 984	2 968	5 360	2 038	3 322
75-79	2 682	1 146	1 536	3 106	1 291	1 815	3 326	1 314	2 012	3 667	1 368	2 299
80 +	1 748	671	1 076	2 123	825	1 298	2 591	977	1 614	3 009	1 074	1 935

Age group	1970			1975			1980			1985		
	Both sexes	Males	Females	Both sexes	Males	Females	Both sexes	Males	Females	Both sexes	Males	Females
All ages	165 674	79 689	85 984	169 165	81 601	87 563	170 462	82 252	88 210	171 855	82 983	88 873
0-4	13 238	6 775	6 463	11 116	5 692	5 425	10 019	5 129	4 890	10 260	5 254	5 006
5-9	13 878	7 095	6 783	13 284	6 799	6 486	11 110	5 677	5 433	9 975	5 105	4 870
10-14	12 847	6 568	6 279	14 035	7 178	6 857	13 351	6 827	6 523	11 204	5 734	5 470
15-19	12 351	6 306	6 045	13 106	6 698	6 408	14 186	7 258	6 928	13 504	6 916	6 588
20-24	11 735	6 004	5 731	12 684	6 435	6 249	13 293	6 789	6 504	14 302	7 285	7 017
25-29	11 079	5 715	5 364	12 220	6 295	5 925	12 756	6 490	6 266	13 318	6 775	6 543
30-34	11 742	6 068	5 674	11 114	5 755	5 358	12 125	6 227	5 898	12 730	6 451	6 279
35-39	10 638	5 461	5 177	11 684	6 019	5 665	10 984	5 647	5 337	11 999	6 119	5 880
40-44	10 566	5 234	5 332	10 535	5 373	5 163	11 497	5 870	5 627	10 825	5 506	5 319
45-49	10 362	4 719	5 644	10 383	5 105	5 278	10 307	5 203	5 104	11 289	5 707	5 582
50-54	6 793	3 044	3 749	10 047	4 523	5 524	10 091	4 897	5 194	10 019	4 998	5 021
55-59	9 432	4 164	5 268	6 587	2 908	3 679	9 647	4 259	5 388	9 684	4 619	5 065
60-64	9 354	4 104	5 249	8 777	3 763	5 013	6 220	2 668	3 552	9 106	3 909	5 197
65-69	8 194	3 544	4 650	8 400	3 520	4 880	7 449	3 059	4 390	5 681	2 336	3 345
70-74	6 095	2 370	3 725	6 848	2 762	4 086	7 231	2 823	4 409	6 900	2 648	4 252
75-79	3 973	1 390	2 583	4 527	1 609	2 917	5 389	1 984	3 406	5 597	1 982	3 614
80 +	3 396	1 126	2 270	3 818	1 169	2 649	4 806	1 444	3 361	5 463	1 640	3 823

Age group	1990			1995			2000			2005		
	Both sexes	Males	Females	Both sexes	Males	Females	Both sexes	Males	Females	Both sexes	Males	Females
All ages	176 087	85 487	90 600	180 977	88 191	92 786	183 589	89 607	93 982	185 879	90 833	95 047
0-4	10 616	5 438	5 178	10 208	5 229	4 979	9 952	5 102	4 850	9 578	4 911	4 666
5-9	10 461	5 359	5 102	10 922	5 597	5 326	10 339	5 296	5 043	10 075	5 165	4 910
10-14	10 295	5 278	5 017	10 772	5 518	5 255	11 036	5 653	5 383	10 444	5 349	5 096
15-19	11 406	5 838	5 568	10 548	5 404	5 144	11 005	5 634	5 370	11 237	5 753	5 484
20-24	13 897	7 090	6 808	11 858	6 027	5 832	10 767	5 485	5 282	11 308	5 764	5 543
25-29	14 669	7 484	7 185	14 363	7 336	7 027	12 096	6 128	5 968	10 994	5 588	5 406
30-34	13 630	6 933	6 697	15 061	7 697	7 364	14 530	7 403	7 127	12 263	6 200	6 063
35-39	12 857	6 509	6 348	13 866	7 048	6 817	15 124	7 697	7 428	14 600	7 412	7 187
40-44	11 980	6 100	5 881	12 922	6 519	6 403	13 783	6 973	6 810	15 058	7 636	7 422
45-49	10 762	5 472	5 290	12 099	6 125	5 974	12 878	6 451	6 426	13 753	6 919	6 834
50-54	11 148	5 606	5 541	10 635	5 362	5 273	11 746	5 896	5 850	12 783	6 351	6 432
55-59	9 718	4 786	4 932	10 813	5 369	5 444	10 463	5 208	5 255	11 277	5 604	5 673
60-64	9 233	4 310	4 923	9 256	4 458	4 798	10 405	5 067	5 338	10 207	4 998	5 209
65-69	8 259	3 415	4 844	8 584	3 872	4 712	8 565	4 008	4 557	9 709	4 610	5 099
70-74	5 188	2 023	3 165	7 528	2 961	4 567	7 717	3 320	4 397	7 745	3 480	4 265
75-79	5 525	1 949	3 576	4 280	1 555	2 725	6 513	2 356	4 157	6 581	2 672	3 909
80 +	6 442	1 898	4 545	7 262	2 115	5 147	6 669	1 928	4 741	8 268	2 420	5 848

United Nations Department of Economic and Social Affairs/Population Division
World Population Prospects: The 2004 Revision, Volume II: Sex and Age Distribution of the World Population

POPULATION BY AGE AND SEX (in thousands)

Age group	2005			2010			2015			2020		
	Both sexes	Males	Females	Both sexes	Males	Females	Both sexes	Males	Females	Both sexes	Males	Females
All ages	185 070	90 023	95 047	187 110	91 661	95 770	188 127	92 162	96 266	189 129	92 490	96 657
0-4	9 578	4 911	4 666	9 189	4 712	4 477	9 157	4 696	4 461	9 303	4 771	4 532
5-9	10 075	5 165	4 910	9 702	4 975	4 727	9 306	4 771	4 534	9 273	4 755	4 518
10-14	10 444	5 349	5 096	10 177	5 217	4 961	9 799	5 023	4 775	9 403	4 820	4 582
15-19	11 237	5 753	5 484	10 644	5 449	5 195	10 364	5 310	5 053	9 987	5 118	4 868
20-24	11 308	5 764	5 543	11 540	5 889	5 651	10 928	5 577	5 350	10 650	5 440	5 210
25-29	10 994	5 588	5 406	11 537	5 874	5 663	11 756	5 993	5 764	11 147	5 683	5 463
30-34	12 263	6 200	6 063	11 174	5 669	5 505	11 706	5 951	5 755	11 927	6 071	5 856
35-39	14 600	7 412	7 187	12 352	6 223	6 129	11 264	5 695	5 568	11 797	5 978	5 819
40-44	15 058	7 636	7 422	14 550	7 363	7 187	12 321	6 186	6 135	11 242	5 664	5 577
45-49	13 753	6 919	6 834	15 032	7 584	7 447	14 531	7 319	7 213	12 328	6 159	6 169
50-54	12 783	6 351	6 432	13 665	6 823	6 842	14 934	7 484	7 450	14 455	7 233	7 223
55-59	11 277	5 604	5 673	12 318	6 063	6 255	13 221	6 546	6 675	14 485	7 204	7 281
60-64	10 207	4 998	5 209	11 014	5 392	5 623	12 037	5 843	6 193	12 937	6 325	6 612
65-69	9 709	4 610	5 099	9 555	4 573	4 982	10 370	4 971	5 399	11 376	5 415	5 961
70-74	7 745	3 480	4 265	8 817	4 034	4 783	8 728	4 038	4 690	9 534	4 428	5 106
75-79	6 581	2 672	3 909	6 652	2 836	3 816	7 606	3 311	4 295	7 593	3 354	4 239
80-84	4 958	1 583	3 375	5 057	1 836	3 221	5 169	1 989	3 179	5 966	2 363	3 603
85-89	1 903	538	1 366	3 171	873	2 298	3 291	1 041	2 251	3 430	1 159	2 272
90-94	1 093	242	850	906	209	696	1 576	353	1 223	1 686	437	1 249
95-99	280	51	229	339	59	280	299	54	246	554	95	459
100 +	34	6	27	50	8	42	66	10	56	66	9	57

Age group	2025			2030			2035			2040		
	Both sexes	Males	Females	Both sexes	Males	Females	Both sexes	Males	Females	Both sexes	Males	Females
All ages	189 546	92 607	96 939	189 558	92 496	97 062	189 067	92 122	96 945	188 115	91 530	96 586
0-4	9 377	4 809	4 568	9 346	4 793	4 553	9 264	4 751	4 513	9 236	4 736	4 499
5-9	9 419	4 830	4 589	9 493	4 868	4 625	9 463	4 852	4 610	9 381	4 810	4 571
10-14	9 370	4 804	4 566	9 516	4 879	4 637	9 590	4 917	4 673	9 559	4 901	4 658
15-19	9 591	4 915	4 676	9 558	4 899	4 659	9 705	4 974	4 731	9 778	5 012	4 766
20-24	10 275	5 249	5 026	9 881	5 048	4 833	9 849	5 032	4 817	9 996	5 108	4 888
25-29	10 871	5 548	5 323	10 498	5 358	5 140	10 106	5 158	4 948	10 075	5 143	4 932
30-34	11 320	5 763	5 557	11 047	5 629	5 418	10 677	5 442	5 235	10 286	5 243	5 044
35-39	12 020	6 098	5 921	11 417	5 793	5 623	11 146	5 661	5 485	10 779	5 475	5 303
40-44	11 778	5 948	5 829	12 002	6 070	5 932	11 405	5 768	5 636	11 138	5 630	5 400
45-49	11 264	5 647	5 617	11 801	5 931	5 869	12 030	6 056	5 975	11 441	5 760	5 681
50-54	12 290	6 098	6 192	11 246	5 599	5 647	11 786	5 885	5 901	12 021	6 013	6 008
55-59	14 035	6 971	7 064	11 924	5 874	6 050	10 909	5 394	5 516	11 451	5 681	5 770
60-64	14 189	6 974	7 214	13 777	6 768	7 008	11 745	5 725	6 020	10 773	5 273	5 499
65-69	12 265	5 889	6 376	13 491	6 521	6 970	13 130	6 351	6 780	11 218	5 389	5 830
70-74	10 503	4 853	5 650	11 366	5 308	6 058	12 542	5 907	6 635	12 251	5 783	6 468
75-79	8 368	3 720	4 648	9 270	4 108	5 162	10 081	4 526	5 556	11 176	5 070	6 106
80-84	6 002	2 407	3 595	6 740	2 754	3 986	7 530	3 080	4 450	8 260	3 436	4 824
85-89	4 028	1 408	2 620	4 154	1 490	2 664	4 740	1 727	3 012	5 379	1 967	3 411
90-94	1 814	506	1 308	2 188	636	1 552	2 320	695	1 625	2 730	833	1 898
95-99	620	123	497	695	149	547	869	194	675	957	220	737
100 +	119	16	103	149	22	127	177	27	150	228	36	192

Age group	2045			2050		
	Both sexes	Males	Females	Both sexes	Males	Females
All ages	186 877	90 837	96 041	185 467	90 128	95 339
0-4	9 318	4 779	4 539	9 380	4 811	4 569
5-9	9 352	4 796	4 557	9 434	4 838	4 596
10-14	9 478	4 859	4 619	9 449	4 845	4 605
15-19	9 748	4 997	4 752	9 667	4 955	4 712
20-24	10 070	5 146	4 924	10 041	5 132	4 910
25-29	10 223	5 220	5 003	10 298	5 259	5 039
30-34	10 256	5 229	5 028	10 405	5 305	5 099
35-39	10 391	5 278	5 113	10 363	5 265	5 098
40-44	10 775	5 456	5 319	10 391	5 261	5 130
45-49	11 181	5 634	5 547	10 824	5 455	5 369
50-54	11 444	5 725	5 719	11 192	5 604	5 588
55-59	11 694	5 814	5 880	11 135	5 538	5 596
60-64	11 316	5 562	5 754	11 568	5 701	5 867
65-69	10 308	4 978	5 330	10 852	5 266	5 585
70-74	10 512	4 935	5 577	9 691	4 580	5 111
75-79	10 976	5 001	5 976	9 484	4 307	5 177
80-84	9 230	3 897	5 333	9 144	3 887	5 256
85-89	5 984	2 238	3 746	6 777	2 584	4 193
90-94	3 175	976	2 199	3 613	1 143	2 470
95-99	1 176	276	901	1 415	335	1 080
100 +	270	43	227	346	56	289

POPULATION BY AGE AND SEX (in thousands)

Age group	2005 Both sexes	Males	Females	2010 Both sexes	Males	Females	2015 Both sexes	Males	Females	2020 Both sexes	Males	Females
All ages	185 879	90 833	95 047	188 803	92 360	96 443	191 914	93 950	97 964	195 229	95 604	99 625
0-4	9 578	4 911	4 666	10 553	5 411	5 141	11 281	5 785	5 496	11 909	6 107	5 802
5-9	10 075	5 165	4 910	9 702	4 975	4 727	10 668	5 470	5 198	11 396	5 844	5 553
10-14	10 444	5 349	5 096	10 177	5 217	4 961	9 799	5 023	4 775	10 765	5 519	5 246
15-19	11 237	5 753	5 484	10 644	5 449	5 195	10 364	5 310	5 053	9 987	5 118	4 868
20-24	11 308	5 764	5 543	11 540	5 889	5 651	10 928	5 577	5 350	10 650	5 440	5 210
25-29	10 994	5 588	5 406	11 537	5 874	5 663	11 756	5 993	5 764	11 147	5 683	5 463
30-34	12 263	6 200	6 063	11 174	5 669	5 505	11 706	5 951	5 755	11 927	6 071	5 856
35-39	14 600	7 412	7 187	12 352	6 223	6 129	11 264	5 695	5 568	11 797	5 978	5 819
40-44	15 058	7 636	7 422	14 550	7 363	7 187	12 321	6 186	6 135	11 242	5 664	5 577
45-49	13 753	6 919	6 834	15 032	7 584	7 447	14 531	7 319	7 213	12 328	6 159	6 169
50-54	12 783	6 351	6 432	13 665	6 823	6 842	14 934	7 484	7 450	14 455	7 233	7 223
55-59	11 277	5 604	5 673	12 318	6 063	6 255	13 221	6 546	6 675	14 485	7 204	7 281
60-64	10 207	4 998	5 209	11 014	5 392	5 623	12 037	5 843	6 193	12 937	6 325	6 612
65-69	9 709	4 610	5 099	9 555	4 573	4 982	10 370	4 971	5 399	11 376	5 415	5 961
70-74	7 745	3 480	4 265	8 817	4 034	4 783	8 728	4 038	4 690	9 534	4 428	5 106
75-79	6 581	2 672	3 909	6 652	2 836	3 816	7 606	3 311	4 295	7 593	3 354	4 239
80-84	4 958	1 583	3 375	5 057	1 836	3 221	5 169	1 989	3 179	5 966	2 363	3 603
85-89	1 903	538	1 366	3 171	873	2 298	3 291	1 041	2 251	3 430	1 159	2 272
90-94	1 093	242	850	906	209	696	1 576	353	1 223	1 686	437	1 249
95-99	280	51	229	339	59	280	299	54	246	554	95	459
100 +	34	6	27	50	8	42	66	10	56	66	9	57

Age group	2025 Both sexes	Males	Females	2030 Both sexes	Males	Females	2035 Both sexes	Males	Females	2040 Both sexes	Males	Females
All ages	198 189	97 040	101 150	200 760	98 240	102 520	203 157	99 346	103 811	205 843	100 617	105 226
0-4	11 932	6 119	5 813	11 910	6 108	5 802	12 161	6 236	5 924	12 885	6 608	6 277
5-9	12 024	6 166	5 858	12 047	6 178	5 869	12 025	6 166	5 859	12 276	6 295	5 981
10-14	11 492	5 892	5 600	12 120	6 214	5 906	12 143	6 226	5 917	12 121	6 215	5 906
15-19	10 952	5 613	5 339	11 680	5 987	5 693	12 307	6 308	5 998	12 330	6 320	6 010
20-24	10 275	5 249	5 026	11 240	5 745	5 496	11 968	6 118	5 850	12 596	6 440	6 155
25-29	10 871	5 548	5 323	10 498	5 358	5 140	11 463	5 853	5 610	12 191	6 227	5 964
30-34	11 320	5 763	5 557	11 047	5 629	5 418	10 677	5 442	5 235	11 641	5 936	5 705
35-39	12 020	6 098	5 921	11 417	5 793	5 623	11 146	5 661	5 485	10 779	5 475	5 303
40-44	11 776	5 948	5 829	12 002	6 070	5 932	11 405	5 768	5 636	11 138	5 639	5 499
45-49	11 264	5 647	5 617	11 801	5 931	5 869	12 030	6 056	5 975	11 441	5 760	5 681
50-54	12 290	6 098	6 192	11 246	5 599	5 647	11 786	5 885	5 901	12 021	6 013	6 008
55-59	14 035	6 971	7 064	11 924	5 874	6 050	10 909	5 394	5 516	11 451	5 681	5 770
60-64	14 189	6 974	7 214	13 777	6 768	7 008	11 745	5 725	6 020	10 773	5 273	5 499
65-69	12 265	5 889	6 376	13 491	6 521	6 970	13 130	6 351	6 780	11 218	5 389	5 830
70-74	10 503	4 853	5 650	11 366	5 308	6 058	12 542	5 907	6 635	12 251	5 783	6 468
75-79	8 368	3 720	4 648	9 270	4 108	5 162	10 081	4 526	5 556	11 176	5 070	6 106
80-84	6 032	2 437	3 595	6 740	2 754	3 986	7 533	3 080	4 453	8 260	3 436	4 824
85-89	4 028	1 408	2 620	4 154	1 490	2 664	4 740	1 727	3 012	5 379	1 967	3 411
90-94	1 814	506	1 308	2 188	636	1 552	2 320	695	1 625	2 730	833	1 898
95-99	620	123	497	695	149	547	869	194	675	957	220	737
100 +	119	16	103	149	22	127	177	27	150	228	36	192

Age group	2045 Both sexes	Males	Females	2050 Both sexes	Males	Females
All ages	209 128	102 241	106 888	212 832	104 151	108 681
0-4	13 857	7 107	6 750	14 517	7 445	7 072
5-9	13 000	6 667	6 334	13 972	7 165	6 807
10-14	12 372	6 343	6 029	13 097	6 715	6 382
15-19	12 309	6 310	5 999	12 560	6 439	6 122
20-24	12 620	6 453	6 167	12 600	6 443	6 157
25-29	12 819	6 549	6 269	12 844	6 563	6 281
30-34	12 368	6 310	6 059	12 996	6 632	6 364
35-39	11 743	5 969	5 773	12 470	6 343	6 127
40-44	10 775	5 456	5 319	11 738	5 949	5 789
45-49	11 181	5 634	5 547	10 824	5 455	5 369
50-54	11 444	5 725	5 719	11 192	5 604	5 588
55-59	11 694	5 814	5 880	11 135	5 538	5 596
60-64	11 316	5 562	5 754	11 568	5 701	5 867
65-69	10 308	4 978	5 330	10 852	5 266	5 585
70-74	10 512	4 935	5 577	9 691	4 580	5 111
75-79	10 976	5 001	5 976	9 484	4 307	5 177
80-84	9 230	3 897	5 333	9 144	3 887	5 256
85-89	5 984	2 238	3 746	6 777	2 584	4 193
90-94	3 175	976	2 199	3 613	1 143	2 470
95-99	1 176	276	901	1 415	335	1 080
100 +	270	43	227	346	56	289

United Nations Department of Economic and Social Affairs/Population Division
World Population Prospects: The 2004 Revision, Volume II: Sex and Age Distribution of the World Population

110

POPULATION BY AGE AND SEX (in thousands)

Age group	2005 Both sexes	Males	Females	2010 Both sexes	Males	Females	2015 Both sexes	Males	Females	2020 Both sexes	Males	Females
All ages	185 879	90 833	95 047	186 036	90 941	95 095	184 874	90 340	94 535	182 947	89 305	93 641
0-4	9 578	4 911	4 666	7 786	3 992	3 793	7 007	3 593	3 414	6 663	3 417	3 246
5-9	10 075	5 165	4 910	9 702	4 975	4 727	7 903	4 052	3 851	7 124	3 653	3 471
10-14	10 444	5 349	5 096	10 177	5 217	4 961	9 799	5 023	4 775	8 001	4 102	3 899
15-19	11 237	5 753	5 484	10 644	5 449	5 195	10 364	5 310	5 053	9 987	5 118	4 868
20-24	11 308	5 764	5 543	11 540	5 889	5 651	10 928	5 577	5 350	10 650	5 440	5 210
25-29	10 994	5 588	5 406	11 537	5 874	5 663	11 756	5 993	5 764	11 147	5 683	5 463
30-34	12 263	6 200	6 063	11 174	5 669	5 505	11 706	5 951	5 755	11 927	6 071	5 856
35-39	14 600	7 412	7 187	12 352	6 223	6 129	11 264	5 695	5 568	11 797	5 978	5 819
40-44	15 058	7 636	7 422	14 550	7 363	7 187	12 321	6 186	6 135	11 242	5 664	5 577
45-49	13 753	6 919	6 834	15 032	7 584	7 447	14 531	7 319	7 213	12 328	6 159	6 169
50-54	12 783	6 351	6 432	13 665	6 823	6 842	14 934	7 484	7 450	14 455	7 233	7 223
55-59	11 277	5 604	5 673	12 318	6 063	6 255	13 221	6 546	6 675	14 485	7 204	7 281
60-64	10 207	4 998	5 209	11 014	5 392	5 623	12 037	5 843	6 193	12 937	6 325	6 612
65-69	9 709	4 610	5 099	9 555	4 573	4 982	10 370	4 971	5 399	11 376	5 415	5 961
70-74	7 745	3 480	4 265	8 817	4 034	4 783	8 728	4 038	4 690	9 534	4 428	5 106
75-79	6 581	2 672	3 909	6 652	2 836	3 816	7 606	3 311	4 295	7 593	3 354	4 239
80-84	4 958	1 583	3 375	5 057	1 836	3 221	5 169	1 989	3 179	5 966	2 363	3 603
85-89	1 903	538	1 366	3 171	873	2 298	3 291	1 041	2 251	3 430	1 159	2 272
90-94	1 093	242	850	906	209	696	1 576	353	1 223	1 686	437	1 249
95-99	280	51	229	339	59	280	299	54	246	554	95	459
100 +	34	6	27	50	8	42	66	10	56	66	9	57

Age group	2025 Both sexes	Males	Females	2030 Both sexes	Males	Females	2035 Both sexes	Males	Females	2040 Both sexes	Males	Females
All ages	180 755	88 099	92 656	178 202	86 673	91 528	175 028	84 925	90 103	171 025	82 769	88 255
0-4	6 773	3 473	3 300	6 775	3 475	3 301	6 574	3 371	3 203	6 172	3 165	3 007
5-9	6 781	3 477	3 304	6 891	3 533	3 357	6 893	3 535	3 358	6 692	3 432	3 260
10-14	7 222	3 702	3 520	6 878	3 526	3 352	6 988	3 583	3 406	6 991	3 584	3 407
15-19	8 190	4 197	3 993	7 412	3 798	3 613	7 068	3 622	3 446	7 178	3 679	3 499
20-24	10 275	5 249	5 026	8 482	4 331	4 151	7 705	3 933	3 772	7 362	3 758	3 604
25-29	10 871	5 548	5 323	10 498	5 358	5 140	8 709	4 443	4 266	7 934	4 047	3 887
30-34	11 320	5 763	5 557	11 047	5 629	5 418	10 677	5 442	5 235	8 892	4 529	4 363
35-39	12 020	6 098	5 921	11 417	5 793	5 623	11 146	5 661	5 485	10 779	5 475	5 303
40-44	11 776	5 948	5 829	12 002	6 070	5 932	11 405	5 768	5 636	11 138	5 639	5 499
45-49	11 264	5 647	5 617	11 801	5 931	5 869	12 030	6 056	5 975	11 441	5 760	5 681
50-54	12 290	6 098	6 192	11 246	5 599	5 647	11 786	5 885	5 901	12 021	6 013	6 008
55-59	14 033	6 971	7 004	11 924	5 874	6 050	10 909	5 099	5 810	11 451	5 681	5 770
60-64	14 189	6 974	7 214	13 777	6 768	7 008	11 745	5 725	6 020	10 773	5 273	5 499
65-69	12 265	5 889	6 376	13 491	6 521	6 970	13 130	6 351	6 780	11 218	5 389	5 830
70-74	10 503	4 853	5 650	11 366	5 308	6 058	12 542	5 907	6 635	12 251	5 783	6 468
75-79	8 368	3 720	4 648	9 270	4 108	5 162	10 081	4 526	5 556	11 176	5 070	6 106
80-84	6 032	2 437	3 595	6 740	2 754	3 986	7 533	3 080	4 453	8 260	3 436	4 824
85-89	4 028	1 408	2 620	4 154	1 490	2 664	4 740	1 727	3 012	5 379	1 967	3 411
90-94	1 814	506	1 308	2 188	636	1 552	2 320	695	1 625	2 730	833	1 898
95-99	620	123	497	695	149	547	869	194	675	957	220	737
100 +	119	16	103	149	22	127	177	27	150	228	36	192

Age group	2045 Both sexes	Males	Females	2050 Both sexes	Males	Females
All ages	166 215	80 247	85 968	160 836	77 508	83 329
0-4	5 729	2 938	2 791	5 389	2 764	2 625
5-9	6 290	3 226	3 065	5 848	2 999	2 849
10-14	6 790	3 481	3 309	6 388	3 275	3 113
15-19	7 181	3 680	3 500	6 980	3 578	3 403
20-24	7 473	3 815	3 658	7 476	3 817	3 659
25-29	7 592	3 872	3 720	7 704	3 930	3 774
30-34	8 119	4 135	3 985	7 779	3 961	3 818
35-39	9 000	4 567	4 433	8 230	4 174	4 056
40-44	10 775	5 456	5 319	9 005	4 553	4 451
45-49	11 181	5 634	5 547	10 824	5 455	5 369
50-54	11 444	5 725	5 719	11 192	5 604	5 588
55-59	11 694	5 814	5 880	11 135	5 538	5 596
60-64	11 316	5 562	5 754	11 568	5 701	5 867
65-69	10 308	4 978	5 330	10 852	5 266	5 585
70-74	10 512	4 935	5 577	9 691	4 580	5 111
75-79	10 976	5 001	5 976	9 484	4 307	5 177
80-84	9 230	3 897	5 333	9 144	3 887	5 256
85-89	5 984	2 238	3 746	6 777	2 584	4 193
90-94	3 175	976	2 199	3 613	1 143	2 470
95-99	1 176	276	901	1 415	335	1 080
100 +	270	43	227	346	56	289

POPULATION BY AGE AND SEX (in thousands)

Age group	1950 Both sexes	1950 Males	1950 Females	1955 Both sexes	1955 Males	1955 Females	1960 Both sexes	1960 Males	1960 Females	1965 Both sexes	1965 Males	1965 Females
All ages	167 321	83 727	83 594	191 034	95 607	95 427	218 577	109 328	109 249	250 774	125 360	125 414
0-4	26 819	13 562	13 257	31 914	16 152	15 762	36 727	18 591	18 136	42 247	21 393	20 854
5-9	21 343	10 769	10 574	25 443	12 844	12 598	30 498	15 406	15 093	35 231	17 790	17 441
10-14	18 773	9 480	9 293	21 043	10 615	10 428	25 104	12 664	12 440	30 046	15 153	14 893
15-19	16 377	8 254	8 123	18 506	9 331	9 176	20 698	10 420	10 278	24 677	12 423	12 254
20-24	14 779	7 425	7 354	16 026	8 050	7 975	18 052	9 064	8 989	20 205	10 142	10 063
25-29	12 577	6 314	6 263	14 392	7 212	7 180	15 565	7 785	7 781	17 558	8 782	8 776
30-34	10 626	5 323	5 302	12 229	6 128	6 101	13 970	6 975	6 995	15 126	7 537	7 590
35-39	9 617	4 816	4 801	10 334	5 168	5 166	11 851	5 918	5 933	13 553	6 745	6 808
40-44	8 388	4 201	4 187	9 244	4 619	4 625	9 924	4 948	4 976	11 428	5 688	5 740
45-49	7 135	3 576	3 559	8 023	3 999	4 024	8 840	4 396	4 444	9 509	4 718	4 791
50-54	6 067	2 990	3 077	6 713	3 343	3 370	7 545	3 736	3 809	8 351	4 124	4 227
55-59	4 863	2 374	2 488	5 578	2 723	2 855	6 188	3 052	3 136	7 005	3 434	3 571
60-64	3 756	1 801	1 956	4 338	2 091	2 247	4 993	2 405	2 588	5 581	2 713	2 868
65-69	2 696	1 273	1 423	3 171	1 494	1 677	3 696	1 750	1 946	4 300	2 033	2 267
70-74	1 790	824	966	2 093	967	1 126	2 510	1 158	1 352	2 971	1 375	1 597
75-79	1 060	471	588	1 216	545	671	1 473	663	810	1 805	809	996
80 +	656	274	382	771	324	447	942	398	543	1 178	500	677

Age group	1970 Both sexes	1970 Males	1970 Females	1975 Both sexes	1975 Males	1975 Females	1980 Both sexes	1980 Males	1980 Females	1985 Both sexes	1985 Males	1985 Females
All ages	285 196	142 522	142 674	322 449	160 996	161 453	362 210	180 569	181 641	402 992	200 521	202 471
0-4	45 406	23 014	22 392	48 804	24 716	24 088	52 380	26 553	25 827	54 992	27 979	27 012
5-9	40 791	20 609	20 182	44 086	22 286	21 800	47 656	24 080	23 576	51 439	26 046	25 394
10-14	34 809	17 555	17 254	40 320	20 342	19 979	43 639	22 036	21 603	47 233	23 833	23 400
15-19	29 581	14 884	14 697	34 297	17 253	17 044	39 703	19 967	19 736	42 925	21 575	21 350
20-24	24 080	12 073	12 007	28 908	14 477	14 431	33 377	16 665	16 713	38 611	19 278	19 333
25-29	19 630	9 824	9 806	23 504	11 737	11 767	28 165	14 012	14 153	32 515	16 124	16 391
30-34	17 047	8 507	8 541	19 160	9 556	9 604	22 940	11 388	11 552	27 499	13 602	13 897
35-39	14 671	7 290	7 381	16 616	8 263	8 353	18 702	9 283	9 418	22 354	11 035	11 319
40-44	13 095	6 497	6 598	14 234	7 047	7 187	16 145	7 987	8 157	18 170	8 967	9 204
45-49	10 955	5 426	5 529	12 621	6 232	6 389	13 739	6 764	6 976	15 591	7 656	7 935
50-54	9 014	4 441	4 572	10 433	5 131	5 302	12 065	5 917	6 148	13 128	6 397	6 731
55-59	7 781	3 805	3 976	8 438	4 120	4 318	9 810	4 779	5 030	11 346	5 490	5 856
60-64	6 353	3 070	3 284	7 094	3 424	3 671	7 743	3 728	4 016	8 989	4 297	4 692
65-69	4 850	2 316	2 534	5 558	2 635	2 923	6 272	2 968	3 304	6 835	3 205	3 629
70-74	3 485	1 610	1 875	3 967	1 849	2 118	4 607	2 130	2 477	5 174	2 365	2 809
75-79	2 164	972	1 192	2 576	1 153	1 423	2 979	1 347	1 632	3 438	1 520	1 918
80 +	1 484	629	856	1 832	776	1 056	2 288	963	1 324	2 754	1 152	1 602

Age group	1990 Both sexes	1990 Males	1990 Females	1995 Both sexes	1995 Males	1995 Females	2000 Both sexes	2000 Males	2000 Females	2005 Both sexes	2005 Males	2005 Females
All ages	443 747	220 364	223 383	483 615	239 654	243 960	522 929	258 610	264 319	561 346	277 161	284 185
0-4	56 065	28 527	27 538	56 377	28 705	27 671	56 690	28 881	27 809	56 936	29 025	27 911
5-9	54 122	27 501	26 621	55 264	28 079	27 185	55 642	28 294	27 348	56 009	28 502	27 507
10-14	51 012	25 798	25 214	53 672	27 243	26 429	54 825	27 831	26 995	55 202	28 048	27 153
15-19	46 484	23 375	23 109	50 241	25 322	24 919	52 864	26 745	26 119	54 067	27 366	26 702
20-24	41 687	20 784	20 903	45 235	22 550	22 684	48 865	24 423	24 442	51 598	25 914	25 684
25-29	37 619	18 641	18 978	40 586	20 061	20 525	44 063	21 791	22 272	47 735	23 696	24 039
30-34	31 743	15 632	16 111	36 713	18 050	18 664	39 642	19 450	20 192	43 105	21 180	21 925
35-39	26 840	13 192	13 648	31 006	15 159	15 847	35 893	17 524	18 369	38 812	18 923	19 889
40-44	21 771	10 678	11 093	26 150	12 762	13 389	30 247	14 686	15 561	35 085	17 017	18 068
45-49	17 590	8 617	8 973	21 120	10 280	10 840	25 411	12 310	13 100	29 452	14 198	15 254
50-54	14 933	7 259	7 674	16 912	8 206	8 706	20 366	9 824	10 542	24 565	11 796	12 768
55-59	12 377	5 947	6 430	14 142	6 784	7 358	16 091	7 716	8 375	19 440	9 270	10 170
60-64	10 461	4 970	5 491	11 478	5 423	6 055	13 185	6 229	6 955	15 074	7 124	7 950
65-69	8 014	3 736	4 278	9 390	4 360	5 029	10 394	4 806	5 588	11 999	5 554	6 446
70-74	5 726	2 597	3 129	6 812	3 078	3 734	8 085	3 645	4 440	9 030	4 056	4 974
75-79	3 954	1 730	2 224	4 472	1 945	2 527	5 428	2 358	3 070	6 536	2 832	3 704
80 +	3 347	1 378	1 970	4 047	1 647	2 400	5 238	2 098	3 140	6 700	2 660	4 041

United Nations Department of Economic and Social Affairs/Population Division
World Population Prospects: The 2004 Revision, Volume II: Sex and Age Distribution of the World Population

112

POPULATION BY AGE AND SEX (in thousands)

Age group	2005 Both sexes	Males	Females	2010 Both sexes	Males	Females	2015 Both sexes	Males	Females	2020 Both sexes	Males	Females
All ages	561 346	277 161	284 185	598 771	295 354	303 417	634 104	312 497	321 607	666 955	328 408	338 547
0-4	56 936	29 025	27 911	56 529	28 850	27 680	55 744	28 458	27 286	54 716	27 942	26 774
5-9	56 009	28 502	27 507	56 341	28 703	27 638	55 992	28 559	27 433	55 267	28 200	27 067
10-14	55 202	28 048	27 153	55 638	28 296	27 342	55 998	28 512	27 486	55 680	28 385	27 295
15-19	54 067	27 366	26 702	54 566	27 653	26 913	55 058	27 935	27 123	55 469	28 185	27 284
20-24	51 598	25 914	25 684	52 977	26 654	26 322	53 579	27 010	26 569	54 156	27 350	26 806
25-29	47 735	23 696	24 039	50 592	25 276	25 317	52 058	26 071	25 986	52 744	26 481	26 263
30-34	43 105	21 180	21 925	46 858	23 142	23 716	49 748	24 742	25 007	51 284	25 582	25 701
35-39	38 812	18 923	19 889	42 341	20 702	21 639	46 085	22 659	23 426	48 997	24 272	24 725
40-44	35 085	17 017	18 068	38 061	18 453	19 608	41 579	20 226	21 353	45 318	22 180	23 138
45-49	29 452	14 198	15 254	34 271	16 518	17 753	37 239	17 948	19 291	40 751	19 716	21 035
50-54	24 565	11 796	12 768	28 567	13 661	14 906	33 315	15 935	17 380	36 277	17 360	18 917
55-59	19 440	9 270	10 170	23 545	11 186	12 359	27 465	12 998	14 467	32 119	15 211	16 908
60-64	15 074	7 124	7 950	18 306	8 607	9 699	22 260	10 428	11 831	26 061	12 166	13 895
65-69	11 999	5 554	6 446	13 815	6 400	7 415	16 867	7 774	9 093	20 610	9 467	11 143
70-74	9 030	4 056	4 974	10 522	4 733	5 789	12 215	5 500	6 715	15 017	6 726	8 290
75-79	6 536	2 832	3 704	7 403	3 196	4 207	8 724	3 770	4 954	10 234	4 426	5 809
80-84	3 917	1 617	2 300	4 806	1 977	2 829	5 533	2 264	3 268	6 612	2 707	3 905
85-89	1 906	736	1 170	2 432	935	1 496	3 049	1 166	1 883	3 576	1 358	2 218
90-94	685	244	440	920	322	597	1 203	418	785	1 542	532	1 010
95-99	164	53	111	239	76	162	329	103	226	436	134	302
100 +	28	9	19	44	14	30	65	20	44	88	27	61

Age group	2025 Both sexes	Males	Females	2030 Both sexes	Males	Females	2035 Both sexes	Males	Females	2040 Both sexes	Males	Females
All ages	696 541	342 649	353 892	722 377	354 999	367 378	743 926	365 177	378 749	761 268	373 251	388 018
0-4	53 389	27 271	26 118	51 818	26 474	25 344	50 131	25 617	24 514	48 768	24 925	23 843
5-9	54 272	27 702	26 570	52 965	27 042	25 923	51 421	26 260	25 161	49 758	25 416	24 342
10-14	54 969	28 034	26 935	53 985	27 542	26 442	52 689	26 888	25 801	51 155	26 113	25 042
15-19	55 167	28 069	27 098	54 466	27 724	26 742	53 497	27 243	26 255	52 216	26 599	25 617
20-24	54 590	27 617	26 973	54 298	27 507	26 791	53 623	27 181	26 442	52 678	26 718	25 960
25-29	53 349	26 843	26 506	53 790	27 113	26 678	53 529	27 025	26 504	52 885	26 722	26 163
30-34	52 016	26 023	25 993	52 630	26 389	26 241	53 099	26 678	26 421	52 870	26 613	26 257
35-39	50 575	25 141	25 434	51 335	25 596	25 739	51 975	25 980	25 996	52 473	26 287	26 185
40-44	48 236	23 706	24 440	49 836	24 677	25 159	50 636	25 156	25 480	51 306	25 557	25 749
45-49	44 473	21 657	22 816	47 380	23 262	24 118	40 000	24 160	24 849	49 851	24 663	25 188
50-54	39 771	19 113	20 658	43 457	21 028	22 430	46 348	22 616	23 732	48 007	23 528	24 479
55-59	35 080	16 818	18 442	38 516	18 346	20 170	42 148	20 217	21 931	45 013	21 779	23 234
60-64	30 574	14 287	16 288	33 474	15 669	17 805	36 863	17 345	19 518	40 415	19 152	21 263
65-69	24 234	11 093	13 142	28 551	13 098	15 454	31 365	14 418	16 947	34 649	16 014	18 635
70-74	18 459	8 238	10 221	21 846	9 731	12 115	25 861	11 546	14 314	28 536	12 769	15 768
75-79	12 688	5 453	7 235	15 752	6 758	8 994	18 773	8 035	10 739	22 364	9 591	12 773
80-84	7 850	3 211	4 639	9 872	4 018	5 854	12 373	5 021	7 352	14 875	6 016	8 860
85-89	4 346	1 648	2 698	5 263	1 994	3 269	6 704	2 522	4 182	8 499	3 184	5 315
90-94	1 841	628	1 213	2 301	784	1 517	2 824	958	1 866	3 647	1 226	2 421
95-99	566	172	395	693	206	486	878	260	618	1 083	319	765
100 +	114	34	80	149	43	106	179	50	129	221	61	160

Age group	2045 Both sexes	Males	Females	2050 Both sexes	Males	Females
All ages	774 255	379 176	395 079	782 903	382 994	399 909
0-4	47 421	24 241	23 180	46 151	23 594	22 557
5-9	48 415	24 736	23 679	47 086	24 061	23 025
10-14	49 502	25 274	24 228	48 167	24 598	23 569
15-19	50 695	25 832	24 863	49 054	25 002	24 053
20-24	51 420	26 090	25 329	49 920	25 339	24 581
25-29	51 972	26 282	25 690	50 744	25 677	25 068
30-34	52 263	26 335	25 928	51 387	25 920	25 467
35-39	52 279	26 245	26 034	51 712	25 994	25 718
40-44	51 833	25 883	25 950	51 676	25 864	25 812
45-49	50 551	25 081	25 470	51 108	25 424	25 684
50-54	48 891	24 053	24 838	49 622	24 487	25 135
55-59	46 697	22 699	23 998	47 624	23 244	24 380
60-64	43 235	20 670	22 565	44 935	21 589	23 347
65-69	38 077	17 723	20 353	40 817	19 169	21 648
70-74	31 651	14 241	17 410	34 886	15 806	19 080
75-79	24 819	10 665	14 154	27 665	11 954	15 711
80-84	17 857	7 231	10 626	19 948	8 090	11 858
85-89	10 324	3 847	6 477	12 501	4 660	7 840
90-94	4 678	1 563	3 115	5 741	1 904	3 837
95-99	1 412	411	1 001	1 824	526	1 298
100 +	265	73	192	335	92	242

POPULATION BY AGE AND SEX (in thousands)

Age group	2005 Both sexes	Males	Females	2010 Both sexes	Males	Females	2015 Both sexes	Males	Females	2020 Both sexes	Males	Females
All ages	561 346	277 161	284 185	604 577	298 318	306 259	649 643	320 429	329 213	695 013	342 732	352 281
0-4	56 936	29 025	27 911	62 335	31 813	30 522	65 505	33 442	32 063	67 288	34 363	32 925
5-9	56 009	28 502	27 507	56 341	28 703	27 638	61 770	31 507	30 263	64 986	33 161	31 825
10-14	55 202	28 048	27 153	55 638	28 296	27 342	55 998	28 512	27 486	61 447	31 327	30 120
15-19	54 067	27 366	26 702	54 566	27 653	26 913	55 058	27 935	27 123	55 469	28 185	27 284
20-24	51 598	25 914	25 684	52 977	26 654	26 322	53 579	27 010	26 569	54 156	27 350	26 806
25-29	47 735	23 696	24 039	50 592	25 276	25 317	52 058	26 071	25 986	52 744	26 481	26 263
30-34	43 105	21 180	21 925	46 858	23 142	23 716	49 748	24 742	25 007	51 284	25 582	25 701
35-39	38 812	18 923	19 889	42 341	20 702	21 639	46 085	22 659	23 426	48 997	24 272	24 725
40-44	35 085	17 017	18 068	38 061	18 453	19 608	41 579	20 226	21 353	45 318	22 180	23 138
45-49	29 452	14 198	15 254	34 271	16 518	17 753	37 239	17 948	19 291	40 751	19 716	21 035
50-54	24 565	11 796	12 768	28 567	13 661	14 906	33 315	15 935	17 380	36 277	17 360	18 917
55-59	19 440	9 270	10 170	23 545	11 186	12 359	27 465	12 998	14 467	32 119	15 211	16 908
60-64	15 074	7 124	7 950	18 306	8 607	9 699	22 260	10 428	11 831	26 061	12 166	13 895
65-69	11 999	5 554	6 446	13 815	6 400	7 415	16 867	7 774	9 093	20 610	9 467	11 143
70-74	9 030	4 056	4 974	10 522	4 733	5 789	12 215	5 500	6 715	15 017	6 726	8 290
75-79	6 536	2 832	3 704	7 403	3 196	4 207	8 724	3 770	4 954	10 234	4 426	5 809
80-84	3 917	1 617	2 300	4 806	1 977	2 829	5 533	2 264	3 268	6 612	2 707	3 905
85-89	1 906	736	1 170	2 432	935	1 496	3 049	1 166	1 883	3 576	1 358	2 218
90-94	685	244	440	920	322	597	1 203	418	785	1 542	532	1 010
95-99	164	53	111	239	76	162	329	103	226	436	134	302
100 +	28	9	19	44	14	30	65	20	44	88	27	61

Age group	2025 Both sexes	Males	Females	2030 Both sexes	Males	Females	2035 Both sexes	Males	Females	2040 Both sexes	Males	Females
All ages	737 878	363 751	374 126	778 928	383 862	395 065	818 679	403 319	415 359	857 442	422 307	435 134
0-4	66 748	34 096	32 652	67 149	34 309	32 841	68 500	35 005	33 495	70 419	35 993	34 426
5-9	66 796	34 097	32 699	66 275	33 839	32 435	66 701	34 066	32 635	68 072	34 774	33 298
10-14	64 671	32 985	31 686	66 487	33 925	32 563	65 978	33 674	32 304	66 414	33 906	32 508
15-19	60 919	31 001	29 919	64 145	32 659	31 486	65 972	33 606	32 366	65 479	33 366	32 113
20-24	54 590	27 617	26 973	60 026	30 421	29 606	63 264	32 088	31 176	65 110	33 049	32 061
25-29	53 349	26 843	26 506	53 790	27 113	26 678	59 226	29 916	29 310	62 479	31 595	30 884
30-34	52 016	26 023	25 993	52 630	26 389	26 241	53 099	26 678	26 421	58 531	29 479	29 052
35-39	50 575	25 141	25 434	51 335	25 596	25 739	51 975	25 980	25 996	52 473	26 287	26 185
40-44	48 236	23 796	24 440	49 836	24 677	25 159	50 636	25 156	25 480	51 306	25 557	25 749
45-49	44 473	21 657	22 816	47 380	23 262	24 118	49 009	24 160	24 849	49 851	24 663	25 188
50-54	39 771	19 113	20 658	43 457	21 028	22 430	46 348	22 616	23 732	48 007	23 528	24 479
55-59	35 060	16 618	18 442	38 516	18 346	20 170	42 148	20 217	21 931	45 013	21 779	23 234
60-64	30 574	14 287	16 288	33 474	15 669	17 805	36 863	17 345	19 518	40 415	19 152	21 263
65-69	24 234	11 093	13 142	28 551	13 098	15 454	31 365	14 418	16 947	34 649	16 014	18 635
70-74	18 459	8 238	10 221	21 846	9 731	12 115	25 861	11 546	14 314	28 536	12 769	15 768
75-79	12 688	5 453	7 235	15 752	6 758	8 994	18 773	8 035	10 739	22 364	9 591	12 773
80-84	7 850	3 211	4 639	9 872	4 018	5 854	12 373	5 021	7 352	14 875	6 016	8 860
85-89	4 346	1 648	2 698	5 263	1 994	3 269	6 704	2 522	4 182	8 499	3 184	5 315
90-94	1 841	628	1 213	2 301	784	1 517	2 824	958	1 866	3 647	1 226	2 421
95-99	566	172	395	693	206	486	878	260	618	1 083	319	765
100 +	114	34	80	149	43	106	179	50	129	221	61	160

Age group	2045 Both sexes	Males	Females	2050 Both sexes	Males	Females
All ages	894 637	440 563	454 074	929 846	457 902	471 945
0-4	71 935	36 774	35 161	73 107	37 377	35 729
5-9	70 007	35 771	34 237	71 540	36 562	34 978
10-14	67 793	34 618	33 174	69 735	35 619	34 116
15-19	65 927	33 606	32 320	67 315	34 325	32 990
20-24	64 641	32 827	31 814	65 108	33 082	32 026
25-29	64 348	32 573	31 775	63 911	32 374	31 537
30-34	61 800	31 169	30 631	63 697	32 165	31 532
35-39	57 897	29 083	28 814	61 184	30 784	30 400
40-44	51 833	25 883	25 950	57 244	28 669	28 575
45-49	50 551	25 081	25 470	51 108	25 424	25 684
50-54	48 891	24 053	24 838	49 622	24 487	25 135
55-59	46 697	22 699	23 998	47 624	23 244	24 380
60-64	43 235	20 670	22 565	44 935	21 589	23 347
65-69	38 077	17 723	20 353	40 817	19 169	21 648
70-74	31 651	14 241	17 410	34 886	15 806	19 080
75-79	24 819	10 665	14 154	27 665	11 954	15 711
80-84	17 857	7 231	10 626	19 948	8 090	11 858
85-89	10 324	3 847	6 477	12 501	4 660	7 840
90-94	4 678	1 563	3 115	5 741	1 904	3 837
95-99	1 412	411	1 001	1 824	526	1 298
100 +	265	73	192	335	92	242

United Nations Department of Economic and Social Affairs/Population Division
World Population Prospects: The 2004 Revision, Volume II: Sex and Age Distribution of the World Population

114

POPULATION BY AGE AND SEX (in thousands)

Age group	2005			2010			2015			2020		
	Both sexes	Males	Females	Both sexes	Males	Females	Both sexes	Males	Females	Both sexes	Males	Females
All ages	561 346	277 161	284 185	592 949	292 382	300 567	618 519	304 541	313 978	638 791	314 029	324 761
0-4	56 936	29 025	27 911	50 707	25 878	24 830	45 953	23 458	22 495	42 084	21 490	20 594
5-9	56 009	28 502	27 507	56 341	28 703	27 638	50 198	25 602	24 596	45 518	23 224	22 294
10-14	55 202	28 048	27 153	55 638	28 296	27 342	55 998	28 512	27 486	49 897	25 435	24 462
15-19	54 067	27 366	26 702	54 566	27 653	26 913	55 058	27 935	27 123	55 469	28 185	27 284
20-24	51 598	25 914	25 684	52 977	26 654	26 322	53 579	27 010	26 569	54 156	27 350	26 806
25-29	47 735	23 696	24 039	50 592	25 276	25 317	52 058	26 071	25 986	52 744	26 481	26 263
30-34	43 105	21 180	21 925	46 858	23 142	23 716	49 748	24 742	25 007	51 284	25 582	25 701
35-39	38 812	18 923	19 889	42 341	20 702	21 639	46 085	22 659	23 426	48 997	24 272	24 725
40-44	35 085	17 017	18 068	38 061	18 453	19 608	41 579	20 226	21 353	45 318	22 180	23 138
45-49	29 452	14 198	15 254	34 271	16 518	17 753	37 239	17 948	19 291	40 751	19 716	21 035
50-54	24 565	11 796	12 768	28 567	13 661	14 906	33 315	15 935	17 380	36 277	17 360	18 917
55-59	19 440	9 270	10 170	23 545	11 186	12 359	27 465	12 998	14 467	32 119	15 211	16 908
60-64	15 074	7 124	7 950	18 306	8 607	9 699	22 260	10 428	11 831	26 061	12 166	13 895
65-69	11 999	5 554	6 446	13 815	6 400	7 415	16 867	7 774	9 093	20 610	9 467	11 143
70-74	9 030	4 056	4 974	10 522	4 733	5 789	12 215	5 500	6 715	15 017	6 726	8 290
75-79	6 536	2 832	3 704	7 403	3 196	4 207	8 724	3 770	4 954	10 234	4 426	5 809
80-84	3 917	1 617	2 300	4 806	1 977	2 829	5 533	2 264	3 268	6 612	2 707	3 905
85-89	1 906	736	1 170	2 432	935	1 496	3 049	1 166	1 883	3 576	1 358	2 218
90-94	685	244	440	920	322	597	1 203	418	785	1 542	532	1 010
95-99	164	53	111	239	76	162	329	103	226	436	134	302
100 +	28	9	19	44	14	30	65	20	44	88	27	61

Age group	2025			2030			2035			2040		
	Both sexes	Males	Females	Both sexes	Males	Females	Both sexes	Males	Females	Both sexes	Males	Females
All ages	655 199	321 544	333 655	666 549	326 506	340 044	671 815	328 385	343 430	671 086	327 256	343 830
0-4	40 129	20 496	19 632	37 216	19 013	18 203	33 683	17 211	16 473	30 471	15 572	14 899
5-9	41 689	21 277	20 412	39 754	20 295	19 459	36 868	18 826	18 042	33 360	17 038	16 322
10-14	45 237	23 068	22 169	41 422	21 130	20 293	39 498	20 153	19 345	36 622	18 690	17 932
15-19	49 399	25 129	24 270	44 758	22 774	21 984	40 963	20 849	20 114	39 051	19 881	19 170
20-24	54 590	27 617	26 973	48 554	24 585	23 970	43 951	22 258	21 693	40 187	20 356	19 831
25-29	53 349	26 843	26 506	53 790	27 113	26 678	47 816	24 126	23 690	43 262	21 835	21 427
30-34	52 016	26 023	25 993	52 630	26 389	26 241	53 099	26 678	26 421	47 194	23 739	23 455
35-39	50 575	25 141	25 434	51 005	25 506	25 739	51 975	25 980	25 996	52 473	26 287	26 185
40-44	48 236	23 796	24 440	49 836	24 677	25 159	50 636	25 156	25 480	51 306	25 557	25 749
45-49	44 473	21 657	22 816	47 380	23 262	24 118	49 009	24 160	24 849	49 851	24 663	25 188
50-54	39 771	19 113	20 658	43 457	21 028	22 430	46 348	22 616	23 732	48 007	23 528	24 479
55-59	35 060	16 618	18 442	38 516	18 346	20 170	42 148	20 217	21 931	45 013	21 779	23 234
60-64	30 574	14 287	16 288	33 474	15 669	17 805	36 863	17 345	19 518	40 415	19 152	21 263
65-69	24 234	11 093	13 142	28 551	13 098	15 454	31 365	14 418	16 947	34 649	16 014	18 635
70-74	18 459	8 238	10 221	21 846	9 731	12 115	25 861	11 546	14 314	28 536	12 769	15 768
75-79	12 688	5 453	7 235	15 752	6 768	8 994	18 773	8 035	10 739	22 364	9 591	12 773
80-84	7 850	3 211	4 639	9 872	4 018	5 854	12 373	5 021	7 352	14 875	6 016	8 860
85-89	4 346	1 648	2 698	5 263	1 994	3 269	6 704	2 522	4 182	8 499	3 184	5 315
90-94	1 841	628	1 213	2 301	784	1 517	2 824	958	1 866	3 647	1 226	2 421
95-99	566	172	395	693	206	486	878	260	618	1 083	319	765
100 +	114	34	80	149	43	106	179	50	129	221	61	160

Age group	2045			2050		
	Both sexes	Males	Females	Both sexes	Males	Females
All ages	664 628	323 286	341 342	652 858	316 723	336 135
0-4	27 682	14 149	13 533	25 359	12 963	12 396
5-9	30 169	15 411	14 758	27 395	13 996	13 399
10-14	33 124	16 908	16 216	29 941	15 285	14 656
15-19	36 189	18 427	17 761	32 704	16 654	16 050
20-24	38 297	19 404	18 893	35 456	17 966	17 490
25-29	39 538	19 961	19 576	37 675	19 029	18 646
30-34	42 696	21 486	21 210	39 019	19 645	19 374
35-39	46 645	23 400	23 245	42 211	21 189	21 022
40-44	51 833	25 883	25 950	46 092	23 052	23 040
45-49	50 551	25 081	25 470	51 108	25 424	25 684
50-54	48 891	24 053	24 838	49 622	24 487	25 135
55-59	46 697	22 699	23 998	47 624	23 244	24 380
60-64	43 235	20 670	22 565	44 935	21 589	23 347
65-69	38 077	17 723	20 353	40 817	19 169	21 648
70-74	31 651	14 241	17 410	34 886	15 806	19 080
75-79	24 819	10 665	14 154	27 665	11 954	15 711
80-84	17 857	7 231	10 626	19 948	8 090	11 858
85-89	10 324	3 847	6 477	12 501	4 660	7 840
90-94	4 678	1 563	3 115	5 741	1 904	3 837
95-99	1 412	411	1 001	1 824	526	1 298
100 +	265	73	192	335	92	242

United Nations Department of Economic and Social Affairs/Population Division
World Population Prospects: The 2004 Revision, Volume II: Sex and Age Distribution of the World Population

115

POPULATION BY AGE AND SEX (in thousands)

Age group	1950 Both sexes	Males	Females	1955 Both sexes	Males	Females	1960 Both sexes	Males	Females	1965 Both sexes	Males	Females
All ages	17 027	8 574	8 454	18 604	9 338	9 266	20 423	10 210	10 212	22 655	11 296	11 359
0-4	2 566	1 288	1 278	2 822	1 428	1 394	3 099	1 570	1 529	3 695	1 870	1 825
5-9	2 143	1 075	1 068	2 389	1 197	1 192	2 678	1 352	1 326	2 915	1 468	1 447
10-14	1 866	938	927	2 075	1 040	1 035	2 346	1 173	1 173	2 568	1 284	1 283
15-19	1 586	790	796	1 783	890	893	1 977	981	996	2 199	1 085	1 114
20-24	1 429	706	724	1 493	736	757	1 663	816	848	1 842	906	936
25-29	1 215	605	611	1 333	657	676	1 385	672	713	1 572	768	804
30-34	1 144	573	571	1 140	566	574	1 261	616	645	1 329	644	684
35-39	1 064	537	526	1 105	550	555	1 101	544	557	1 213	594	619
40-44	905	463	441	978	493	485	1 029	515	514	1 039	517	522
45-49	804	423	380	866	441	425	940	474	465	974	488	486
50-54	636	333	303	748	393	355	800	408	392	868	439	429
55-59	501	261	240	576	299	277	680	356	324	735	373	362
60-64	409	209	200	455	233	221	516	266	251	614	317	296
65-69	312	158	154	346	174	172	387	195	192	445	227	218
70-74	223	110	113	244	122	122	273	135	138	315	156	159
75-79	141	67	74	145	71	74	168	82	86	193	94	99
80 +	85	37	48	106	47	58	119	54	65	140	65	76

Age group	1970 Both sexes	Males	Females	1975 Both sexes	Males	Females	1980 Both sexes	Males	Females	1985 Both sexes	Males	Females
All ages	24 832	12 404	12 428	27 121	13 530	13 591	29 215	14 565	14 651	31 564	15 729	15 834
0-4	3 754	1 906	1 848	3 715	1 886	1 829	3 518	1 788	1 730	3 785	1 925	1 860
5-9	3 546	1 791	1 755	3 650	1 850	1 800	3 618	1 836	1 782	3 434	1 746	1 688
10-14	2 853	1 435	1 418	3 467	1 748	1 720	3 585	1 819	1 767	3 591	1 821	1 770
15-19	2 454	1 222	1 231	2 754	1 381	1 373	3 349	1 684	1 665	3 520	1 779	1 741
20-24	2 062	1 011	1 050	2 326	1 153	1 173	2 542	1 261	1 281	3 174	1 584	1 590
25-29	1 703	838	865	1 960	956	1 004	2 182	1 073	1 110	2 430	1 198	1 232
30-34	1 462	720	742	1 628	797	830	1 891	923	968	2 122	1 039	1 083
35-39	1 244	607	637	1 409	692	717	1 598	783	815	1 820	887	933
40-44	1 137	561	576	1 193	581	612	1 379	677	702	1 548	759	789
45-49	964	481	483	1 088	535	552	1 152	561	590	1 334	654	679
50-54	899	451	449	906	450	456	1 038	510	528	1 101	537	564
55-59	795	402	394	830	414	416	852	422	430	979	480	499
60-64	667	335	331	722	362	360	769	380	389	780	384	396
65-69	540	278	262	580	288	292	654	322	331	685	335	350
70-74	360	182	178	438	222	216	489	239	250	543	264	280
75-79	221	107	113	262	127	134	333	167	166	382	182	200
80 +	173	78	95	193	87	105	267	120	147	336	155	181

Age group	1990 Both sexes	Males	Females	1995 Both sexes	Males	Females	2000 Both sexes	Males	Females	2005 Both sexes	Males	Females
All ages	33 823	16 821	17 002	35 707	17 745	17 963	37 456	18 588	18 868	39 129	19 405	19 724
0-4	3 989	2 030	1 959	3 776	1 926	1 850	3 655	1 863	1 792	3 657	1 867	1 790
5-9	3 695	1 877	1 818	3 897	1 980	1 917	3 685	1 875	1 810	3 575	1 821	1 754
10-14	3 391	1 719	1 671	3 638	1 846	1 792	3 849	1 954	1 895	3 637	1 850	1 787
15-19	3 486	1 764	1 723	3 294	1 668	1 627	3 559	1 804	1 755	3 784	1 920	1 865
20-24	3 302	1 658	1 645	3 331	1 675	1 655	3 120	1 570	1 549	3 445	1 743	1 702
25-29	3 023	1 498	1 525	3 139	1 564	1 574	3 172	1 584	1 588	2 978	1 495	1 483
30-34	2 328	1 137	1 190	2 887	1 422	1 465	3 020	1 498	1 521	3 026	1 506	1 520
35-39	2 035	991	1 043	2 223	1 082	1 140	2 769	1 359	1 411	2 887	1 426	1 460
40-44	1 766	858	908	1 941	942	999	2 117	1 028	1 089	2 652	1 294	1 358
45-49	1 489	728	761	1 690	817	873	1 852	895	956	2 020	975	1 045
50-54	1 265	618	647	1 421	692	730	1 615	777	838	1 765	848	917
55-59	1 030	498	531	1 194	579	614	1 347	651	696	1 526	727	798
60-64	904	439	465	952	457	495	1 108	532	576	1 251	598	653
65-69	708	343	365	811	390	420	869	410	459	1 004	474	530
70-74	577	277	300	599	286	313	701	330	370	750	345	404
75-79	427	202	225	449	210	240	473	220	253	561	255	305
80 +	408	184	224	467	208	259	547	238	310	613	261	351

United Nations Department of Economic and Social Affairs/Population Division
World Population Prospects: The 2004 Revision, Volume II: Sex and Age Distribution of the World Population

116

POPULATION BY AGE AND SEX (in thousands)

Age group	2005			2010			2015			2020		
	Both sexes	Males	Females	Both sexes	Males	Females	Both sexes	Males	Females	Both sexes	Males	Females
All ages	39 129	19 405	19 724	40 748	20 206	20 543	42 249	20 952	21 297	43 568	21 609	21 959
0-4	3 657	1 867	1 790	3 637	1 857	1 780	3 584	1 831	1 753	3 493	1 785	1 708
5-9	3 575	1 821	1 754	3 582	1 827	1 755	3 567	1 820	1 747	3 522	1 798	1 724
10-14	3 637	1 850	1 787	3 529	1 797	1 732	3 536	1 804	1 732	3 523	1 798	1 725
15-19	3 784	1 920	1 865	3 577	1 819	1 758	3 471	1 767	1 704	3 479	1 774	1 705
20-24	3 445	1 743	1 702	3 675	1 861	1 814	3 473	1 764	1 710	3 370	1 713	1 656
25-29	2 978	1 495	1 483	3 306	1 669	1 636	3 541	1 791	1 750	3 350	1 699	1 651
30-34	3 026	1 506	1 520	2 833	1 420	1 413	3 162	1 596	1 566	3 402	1 720	1 682
35-39	2 887	1 426	1 460	2 895	1 437	1 458	2 703	1 353	1 349	3 028	1 528	1 500
40-44	2 652	1 294	1 358	2 772	1 365	1 407	2 781	1 377	1 404	2 589	1 294	1 295
45-49	2 020	975	1 045	2 552	1 239	1 313	2 672	1 310	1 362	2 683	1 323	1 359
50-54	1 765	848	917	1 934	927	1 007	2 459	1 188	1 271	2 579	1 258	1 321
55-59	1 526	727	798	1 676	798	878	1 843	877	966	2 357	1 130	1 227
60-64	1 251	598	653	1 428	672	755	1 576	742	834	1 739	817	921
65-69	1 004	474	530	1 143	538	606	1 314	609	705	1 456	674	782
70-74	750	345	404	877	405	473	1 009	463	546	1 167	527	640
75-79	561	255	305	610	271	339	724	322	402	841	372	469
80-84	335	149	187	407	176	231	450	190	260	543	229	314
85-89	185	77	108	204	84	120	254	102	151	286	112	174
90-94	72	28	44	86	33	54	98	37	61	124	45	79
95-99	18	6	11	23	8	15	29	9	19	33	11	23
100 +	3	1	2	4	1	3	5	1	3	6	2	4

Age group	2025			2030			2035			2040		
	Both sexes	Males	Females	Both sexes	Males	Females	Both sexes	Males	Females	Both sexes	Males	Females
All ages	44 663	22 154	22 509	45 524	22 585	22 939	46 126	22 887	23 238	46 475	23 065	23 410
0-4	3 377	1 726	1 651	3 254	1 664	1 590	3 132	1 602	1 530	3 020	1 545	1 475
5-9	3 436	1 755	1 681	3 325	1 699	1 626	3 206	1 639	1 567	3 088	1 579	1 509
10-14	3 480	1 777	1 703	3 397	1 735	1 662	3 288	1 680	1 608	3 171	1 621	1 550
15-19	3 467	1 769	1 698	3 426	1 749	1 677	3 045	1 700	1 636	3 237	1 654	1 582
20-24	3 380	1 722	1 658	3 369	1 717	1 652	3 330	1 699	1 631	3 251	1 659	1 592
25-29	3 249	1 650	1 599	3 260	1 660	1 601	3 253	1 657	1 596	3 218	1 640	1 577
30-34	3 221	1 633	1 588	3 123	1 586	1 537	3 137	1 597	1 540	3 134	1 597	1 537
35-39	3 269	1 652	1 616	3 098	1 571	1 527	3 004	1 527	1 478	3 022	1 540	1 482
40-44	2 908	1 466	1 443	3 149	1 590	1 558	2 988	1 514	1 474	2 899	1 473	1 426
45-49	2 492	1 242	1 250	2 805	1 410	1 395	3 044	1 534	1 510	2 893	1 463	1 430
50-54	2 591	1 272	1 319	2 403	1 192	1 211	2 710	1 357	1 353	2 947	1 480	1 468
55-59	2 477	1 200	1 277	2 492	1 215	1 276	2 308	1 138	1 170	2 606	1 295	1 311
60-64	2 236	1 061	1 176	2 357	1 130	1 226	2 374	1 146	1 227	2 197	1 072	1 125
65-69	1 613	746	867	2 088	975	1 113	2 206	1 042	1 164	2 226	1 059	1 167
70-74	1 301	587	714	1 449	654	795	1 890	862	1 028	2 004	925	1 079
75-79	982	426	555	1 105	480	625	1 238	538	700	1 630	717	912
80-84	639	267	372	758	312	447	861	354	507	971	399	572
85-89	351	137	214	423	164	260	510	193	316	585	222	363
90-94	143	50	93	182	64	119	224	77	147	274	92	181
95-99	43	14	30	52	16	36	67	20	47	84	25	59
100 +	7	2	5	10	3	7	12	3	9	15	4	11

Age group	2045			2050		
	Both sexes	Males	Females	Both sexes	Males	Females
All ages	46 575	23 119	23 456	46 438	23 054	23 384
0-4	2 909	1 488	1 421	2 806	1 436	1 370
5-9	2 980	1 524	1 456	2 871	1 469	1 402
10-14	3 055	1 563	1 493	2 948	1 508	1 440
15-19	3 121	1 596	1 525	3 006	1 538	1 469
20-24	3 145	1 606	1 539	3 032	1 549	1 483
25-29	3 143	1 603	1 539	3 041	1 552	1 489
30-34	3 104	1 583	1 521	3 036	1 550	1 487
35-39	3 024	1 542	1 481	3 001	1 532	1 469
40-44	2 921	1 488	1 433	2 927	1 492	1 434
45-49	2 809	1 424	1 385	2 835	1 441	1 393
50-54	2 806	1 413	1 392	2 727	1 378	1 349
55-59	2 843	1 419	1 424	2 711	1 358	1 353
60-64	2 488	1 226	1 262	2 719	1 344	1 375
65-69	2 061	990	1 070	2 339	1 135	1 204
70-74	2 028	943	1 085	1 877	881	996
75-79	1 737	774	962	1 763	791	972
80-84	1 294	541	753	1 387	587	800
85-89	666	252	414	898	347	551
90-94	318	107	211	366	123	243
95-99	104	30	74	123	35	88
100 +	20	5	14	25	6	18

United Nations Department of Economic and Social Affairs/Population Division
World Population Prospects: The 2004 Revision, Volume II: Sex and Age Distribution of the World Population

117

POPULATION BY AGE AND SEX (in thousands)

Age group	2005 Both sexes	Males	Females	2010 Both sexes	Males	Females	2015 Both sexes	Males	Females	2020 Both sexes	Males	Females
All ages	39 129	19 405	19 724	41 124	20 398	20 726	43 239	21 458	21 781	45 334	22 512	22 823
0-4	3 657	1 867	1 790	4 013	2 050	1 963	4 201	2 146	2 055	4 276	2 185	2 091
5-9	3 575	1 821	1 754	3 582	1 827	1 755	3 940	2 011	1 929	4 133	2 111	2 023
10-14	3 637	1 850	1 787	3 529	1 797	1 732	3 536	1 804	1 732	3 893	1 987	1 906
15-19	3 784	1 920	1 865	3 577	1 819	1 758	3 471	1 767	1 704	3 479	1 774	1 705
20-24	3 445	1 743	1 702	3 675	1 861	1 814	3 473	1 764	1 710	3 370	1 713	1 656
25-29	2 978	1 495	1 483	3 306	1 669	1 636	3 541	1 791	1 750	3 350	1 699	1 651
30-34	3 026	1 506	1 520	2 833	1 420	1 413	3 162	1 596	1 566	3 402	1 720	1 682
35-39	2 887	1 426	1 460	2 895	1 437	1 458	2 703	1 353	1 349	3 028	1 528	1 500
40-44	2 652	1 294	1 358	2 772	1 365	1 407	2 781	1 377	1 404	2 589	1 294	1 295
45-49	2 020	975	1 045	2 552	1 239	1 313	2 672	1 310	1 362	2 683	1 323	1 359
50-54	1 765	848	917	1 934	927	1 007	2 459	1 188	1 271	2 579	1 258	1 321
55-59	1 526	727	798	1 676	798	878	1 843	877	966	2 357	1 130	1 227
60-64	1 251	598	653	1 428	672	755	1 576	742	834	1 739	817	921
65-69	1 004	474	530	1 143	538	606	1 314	609	705	1 456	674	782
70-74	750	345	404	877	405	473	1 009	463	546	1 167	527	640
75-79	561	255	305	610	271	339	724	322	402	841	372	469
80-84	335	149	187	407	176	231	450	190	260	543	229	314
85-89	185	77	108	204	84	120	254	102	151	286	112	174
90-94	72	28	44	86	33	54	98	37	61	124	45	79
95-99	18	6	11	23	8	15	29	9	19	33	11	23
100 +	3	1	2	4	1	3	5	1	3	6	2	4

Age group	2025 Both sexes	Males	Females	2030 Both sexes	Males	Females	2035 Both sexes	Males	Females	2040 Both sexes	Males	Females
All ages	47 230	23 466	23 764	48 983	24 352	24 631	50 649	25 198	25 450	52 262	26 022	26 240
0-4	4 187	2 140	2 047	4 158	2 126	2 032	4 213	2 155	2 058	4 308	2 204	2 104
5-9	4 214	2 152	2 061	4 129	2 110	2 019	4 104	2 098	2 006	4 163	2 128	2 034
10-14	4 090	2 088	2 001	4 172	2 131	2 041	4 089	2 090	1 999	4 067	2 079	1 988
15-19	3 837	1 958	1 879	4 034	2 060	1 974	4 117	2 103	2 014	4 036	2 062	1 974
20-24	3 380	1 722	1 658	3 737	1 905	1 832	3 935	2 007	1 928	4 020	2 052	1 968
25-29	3 249	1 650	1 599	3 260	1 660	1 601	3 618	1 843	1 775	3 818	1 947	1 871
30-34	3 221	1 633	1 588	3 123	1 586	1 537	3 137	1 597	1 540	3 494	1 781	1 713
35-39	3 269	1 652	1 616	3 098	1 571	1 527	3 004	1 527	1 478	3 022	1 540	1 482
40-44	2 908	1 466	1 443	3 149	1 590	1 558	2 988	1 514	1 474	2 899	1 473	1 426
45-49	2 492	1 242	1 250	2 805	1 410	1 395	3 044	1 534	1 510	2 893	1 463	1 430
50-54	2 591	1 272	1 319	2 403	1 192	1 211	2 710	1 357	1 353	2 947	1 480	1 468
55-59	2 477	1 200	1 277	2 492	1 215	1 276	2 308	1 138	1 170	2 608	1 298	1 311
60-64	2 236	1 061	1 176	2 357	1 130	1 226	2 374	1 146	1 227	2 197	1 072	1 125
65-69	1 613	746	867	2 088	975	1 113	2 206	1 042	1 164	2 226	1 059	1 167
70-74	1 301	587	714	1 449	654	795	1 890	862	1 028	2 004	925	1 079
75-79	982	426	555	1 105	480	625	1 238	538	700	1 630	717	912
80-84	639	267	372	758	312	447	861	354	507	971	399	572
85-89	351	137	214	423	164	260	510	193	316	585	222	363
90-94	143	50	93	182	64	119	224	77	147	274	92	181
95-99	43	14	30	52	16	36	67	20	47	84	25	59
100 +	7	2	5	10	3	7	12	3	9	15	4	11

Age group	2045 Both sexes	Males	Females	2050 Both sexes	Males	Females
All ages	53 797	26 809	26 988	55 223	27 544	27 679
0-4	4 374	2 238	2 136	4 408	2 256	2 152
5-9	4 261	2 180	2 081	4 330	2 216	2 115
10-14	4 127	2 110	2 016	4 227	2 162	2 064
15-19	4 015	2 053	1 962	4 076	2 085	1 991
20-24	3 942	2 013	1 929	3 923	2 004	1 919
25-29	3 907	1 993	1 914	3 833	1 956	1 877
30-34	3 698	1 886	1 812	3 792	1 935	1 857
35-39	3 379	1 723	1 656	3 587	1 831	1 756
40-44	2 921	1 488	1 433	3 277	1 671	1 606
45-49	2 809	1 424	1 385	2 835	1 441	1 393
50-54	2 806	1 413	1 392	2 727	1 378	1 349
55-59	2 843	1 419	1 424	2 711	1 358	1 353
60-64	2 488	1 226	1 262	2 719	1 344	1 375
65-69	2 061	990	1 070	2 339	1 135	1 204
70-74	2 028	943	1 085	1 877	881	996
75-79	1 737	774	962	1 763	791	972
80-84	1 294	541	753	1 387	587	800
85-89	666	252	414	898	347	551
90-94	318	107	211	366	123	243
95-99	104	30	74	123	35	88
100 +	20	5	14	25	6	18

United Nations Department of Economic and Social Affairs/Population Division
World Population Prospects: The 2004 Revision, Volume II: Sex and Age Distribution of the World Population

118

POPULATION BY AGE AND SEX (in thousands)

Age group	2005 Both sexes	Males	Females	2010 Both sexes	Males	Females	2015 Both sexes	Males	Females	2020 Both sexes	Males	Females
All ages	39 129	19 405	19 724	40 372	20 013	20 358	41 255	20 444	20 811	41 795	20 703	21 092
0-4	3 657	1 867	1 790	3 260	1 665	1 596	2 963	1 514	1 450	2 706	1 383	1 323
5-9	3 575	1 821	1 754	3 582	1 827	1 755	3 194	1 630	1 564	2 906	1 484	1 423
10-14	3 637	1 850	1 787	3 529	1 797	1 732	3 536	1 804	1 732	3 151	1 608	1 543
15-19	3 784	1 920	1 865	3 577	1 819	1 758	3 471	1 767	1 704	3 479	1 774	1 705
20-24	3 445	1 743	1 702	3 675	1 861	1 814	3 473	1 764	1 710	3 370	1 713	1 656
25-29	2 978	1 495	1 483	3 306	1 669	1 636	3 541	1 791	1 750	3 350	1 699	1 651
30-34	3 026	1 506	1 520	2 833	1 420	1 413	3 162	1 596	1 566	3 402	1 720	1 682
35-39	2 887	1 426	1 460	2 895	1 437	1 458	2 703	1 353	1 349	3 028	1 528	1 500
40-44	2 652	1 294	1 358	2 772	1 365	1 407	2 781	1 377	1 404	2 589	1 294	1 295
45-49	2 020	975	1 045	2 552	1 239	1 313	2 672	1 310	1 362	2 683	1 323	1 359
50-54	1 765	848	917	1 934	927	1 007	2 459	1 188	1 271	2 579	1 258	1 321
55-59	1 526	727	798	1 676	798	878	1 843	877	966	2 357	1 130	1 227
60-64	1 251	598	653	1 428	672	755	1 576	742	834	1 739	817	921
65-69	1 004	474	530	1 143	538	606	1 314	609	705	1 456	674	782
70-74	750	345	404	877	405	473	1 009	463	546	1 167	527	640
75-79	561	255	305	610	271	339	724	322	402	841	372	469
80-84	335	149	187	407	176	231	450	190	260	543	229	314
85-89	185	77	108	204	84	120	254	102	151	286	112	174
90-94	72	28	44	86	33	54	98	37	61	124	45	79
95-99	18	6	11	23	8	15	29	9	19	33	11	23
100 +	3	1	2	4	1	3	5	1	3	6	2	4

Age group	2025 Both sexes	Males	Females	2030 Both sexes	Males	Females	2035 Both sexes	Males	Females	2040 Both sexes	Males	Females
All ages	42 096	20 843	21 253	42 110	20 840	21 269	41 767	20 660	21 106	41 063	20 300	20 763
0-4	2 574	1 315	1 258	2 394	1 224	1 170	2 172	1 110	1 061	1 945	995	950
5-9	2 656	1 356	1 299	2 527	1 291	1 236	2 352	1 202	1 150	2 133	1 091	1 043
10-14	2 867	1 464	1 403	2 620	1 338	1 281	2 493	1 274	1 219	2 320	1 186	1 134
15-19	3 097	1 580	1 517	2 815	1 407	1 377	2 660	1 313	1 257	2 444	1 249	1 195
20-24	3 380	1 722	1 658	3 000	1 529	1 471	2 721	1 388	1 333	2 478	1 265	1 214
25-29	3 249	1 650	1 599	3 260	1 660	1 601	2 887	1 471	1 416	2 614	1 332	1 281
30-34	3 221	1 633	1 588	3 123	1 586	1 537	3 137	1 597	1 540	2 773	1 413	1 360
35-39	3 269	1 652	1 616	3 098	1 571	1 527	3 004	1 527	1 478	3 022	1 540	1 482
40-44	2 908	1 466	1 443	3 149	1 590	1 558	2 988	1 514	1 474	2 899	1 473	1 426
45-49	2 492	1 242	1 250	2 805	1 410	1 395	3 044	1 534	1 510	2 893	1 463	1 430
50-54	2 591	1 272	1 319	2 403	1 192	1 211	2 710	1 357	1 353	2 947	1 480	1 468
55-59	2 477	1 200	1 277	2 492	1 215	1 276	2 308	1 138	1 170	2 608	1 290	1 011
60-64	2 236	1 061	1 176	2 357	1 130	1 226	2 374	1 146	1 227	2 197	1 072	1 125
65-69	1 613	746	867	2 088	975	1 113	2 206	1 042	1 164	2 226	1 059	1 167
70-74	1 301	587	714	1 449	654	795	1 890	862	1 028	2 004	925	1 079
75-79	981	426	555	1 105	480	625	1 238	538	700	1 630	717	912
80-84	639	267	372	758	312	447	861	354	507	971	399	572
85-89	351	137	214	423	164	260	510	193	316	585	222	363
90-94	143	50	93	182	64	119	224	77	147	274	92	181
95-99	43	14	30	52	16	36	67	20	47	84	25	59
100 +	7	2	5	10	3	7	12	3	9	15	4	11

Age group	2045 Both sexes	Males	Females	2050 Both sexes	Males	Females
All ages	40 025	19 772	20 253	39 697	19 098	20 598
0-4	1 741	891	850	1 576	807	770
5-9	1 910	977	933	1 709	874	835
10-14	2 103	1 076	1 027	1 881	963	919
15-19	2 271	1 162	1 110	2 056	1 052	1 004
20-24	2 355	1 203	1 152	2 185	1 116	1 068
25-29	2 376	1 212	1 164	2 256	1 152	1 105
30-34	2 507	1 279	1 229	2 277	1 162	1 115
35-39	2 667	1 360	1 307	2 411	1 231	1 180
40-44	2 921	1 488	1 433	2 576	1 313	1 262
45-49	2 809	1 424	1 385	2 835	1 441	1 393
50-54	2 806	1 413	1 392	2 727	1 378	1 349
55-59	2 843	1 419	1 424	2 711	1 358	1 353
60-64	2 488	1 226	1 262	2 719	1 344	1 375
65-69	2 061	990	1 070	2 339	1 135	1 204
70-74	2 028	943	1 085	1 877	881	996
75-79	1 737	774	962	1 763	791	972
80-84	1 294	541	753	1 387	587	800
85-89	666	252	414	898	347	551
90-94	318	107	211	366	123	243
95-99	104	30	74	123	35	88
100 +	20	5	14	25	6	18

United Nations Department of Economic and Social Affairs/Population Division
World Population Prospects: The 2004 Revision, Volume II: Sex and Age Distribution of the World Population

119

POPULATION BY AGE AND SEX (in thousands)

Age group	1950 Both sexes	1950 Males	1950 Females	1955 Both sexes	1955 Males	1955 Females	1960 Both sexes	1960 Males	1960 Females	1965 Both sexes	1965 Males	1965 Females
All ages	37 299	18 677	18 622	42 759	21 400	21 359	49 722	24 881	24 841	58 023	29 030	28 992
0-4	6 440	3 264	3 176	7 776	3 939	3 837	9 224	4 671	4 553	10 714	5 425	5 289
5-9	5 073	2 573	2 500	6 009	3 048	2 961	7 358	3 728	3 630	8 794	4 448	4 347
10-14	4 268	2 178	2 090	4 965	2 517	2 447	5 905	2 994	2 910	7 236	3 661	3 575
15-19	3 714	1 893	1 821	4 168	2 120	2 048	4 869	2 461	2 408	5 801	2 935	2 867
20-24	3 139	1 588	1 551	3 581	1 812	1 769	4 044	2 043	2 001	4 744	2 390	2 354
25-29	2 687	1 351	1 336	3 014	1 515	1 498	3 461	1 742	1 719	3 911	1 966	1 945
30-34	2 078	1 042	1 036	2 575	1 288	1 287	2 907	1 454	1 453	3 342	1 673	1 669
35-39	1 850	922	927	1 983	990	994	2 476	1 232	1 244	2 803	1 394	1 409
40-44	1 670	824	846	1 756	871	886	1 897	941	956	2 376	1 174	1 201
45-49	1 494	732	763	1 576	772	804	1 669	822	847	1 812	893	919
50-54	1 324	640	684	1 391	674	717	1 480	719	761	1 574	769	806
55-59	1 131	542	589	1 207	577	630	1 281	615	666	1 371	660	711
60-64	911	432	480	997	471	526	1 079	510	569	1 154	548	606
65-69	659	307	352	762	356	406	851	398	454	929	433	496
70-74	433	199	234	510	234	277	608	280	329	690	318	372
75-79	266	120	146	300	135	166	370	166	204	452	204	247
80 +	161	70	91	190	82	108	243	106	137	320	140	180

Age group	1970 Both sexes	1970 Males	1970 Females	1975 Both sexes	1975 Males	1975 Females	1980 Both sexes	1980 Males	1980 Females	1985 Both sexes	1985 Males	1985 Females
All ages	67 897	33 961	33 936	79 155	39 537	39 617	90 719	45 217	45 502	101 559	50 434	51 124
0-4	12 556	6 369	6 188	14 495	7 357	7 138	15 130	7 688	7 442	15 226	7 751	7 475
5-9	10 284	5 199	5 085	12 109	6 131	5 978	14 092	7 140	6 953	14 742	7 476	7 266
10-14	8 657	4 371	4 286	10 104	5 098	5 006	11 914	6 021	5 894	13 842	6 994	6 848
15-19	7 097	3 577	3 520	8 430	4 234	4 196	9 822	4 925	4 897	11 464	5 725	5 739
20-24	5 625	2 827	2 798	6 796	3 389	3 407	8 039	3 984	4 055	9 220	4 538	4 682
25-29	4 587	2 298	2 289	5 389	2 682	2 706	6 504	3 209	3 295	7 635	3 732	3 903
30-34	3 781	1 891	1 891	4 410	2 192	2 217	5 185	2 556	2 629	6 236	3 048	3 188
35-39	3 232	1 610	1 623	3 645	1 811	1 834	4 257	2 102	2 155	4 992	2 441	2 551
40-44	2 702	1 338	1 365	3 114	1 542	1 572	3 516	1 735	1 782	4 102	2 010	2 092
45-49	2 272	1 116	1 156	2 590	1 275	1 315	2 991	1 471	1 520	3 377	1 654	1 723
50-54	1 714	839	875	2 156	1 050	1 106	2 470	1 206	1 264	2 850	1 387	1 463
55-59	1 464	707	756	1 602	777	824	2 022	975	1 048	2 323	1 123	1 200
60-64	1 239	589	650	1 331	636	695	1 468	702	766	1 859	885	974
65-69	1 001	469	532	1 085	507	578	1 175	551	624	1 306	613	693
70-74	758	348	410	826	379	446	906	414	492	991	454	537
75-79	517	234	283	575	258	317	636	284	352	708	314	394
80 +	409	179	230	499	218	282	590	254	336	684	291	393

Age group	1990 Both sexes	1990 Males	1990 Females	1995 Both sexes	1995 Males	1995 Females	2000 Both sexes	2000 Males	2000 Females	2005 Both sexes	2005 Males	2005 Females
All ages	112 798	55 852	56 946	124 623	61 506	63 118	136 039	66 942	69 096	147 029	72 168	74 861
0-4	15 901	8 089	7 812	16 550	8 423	8 127	16 367	8 328	8 040	16 161	8 225	7 936
5-9	14 853	7 544	7 309	15 561	7 894	7 667	16 222	8 235	7 987	16 060	8 151	7 909
10-14	14 497	7 340	7 156	14 621	7 411	7 211	15 324	7 757	7 567	15 992	8 102	7 890
15-19	13 406	6 727	6 678	14 073	7 074	6 998	14 180	7 133	7 047	14 892	7 485	7 407
20-24	10 792	5 289	5 503	12 735	6 274	6 461	13 365	6 595	6 770	13 494	6 669	6 826
25-29	8 771	4 257	4 514	10 345	4 998	5 347	12 261	5 966	6 295	12 906	6 297	6 610
30-34	7 339	3 551	3 788	8 479	4 069	4 410	10 035	4 799	5 236	11 949	5 765	6 183
35-39	6 031	2 926	3 105	7 143	3 429	3 714	8 273	3 941	4 332	9 822	4 666	5 156
40-44	4 828	2 344	2 484	5 865	2 825	3 041	6 968	3 323	3 645	8 091	3 830	4 261
45-49	3 957	1 926	2 030	4 682	2 258	2 424	5 708	2 733	2 975	6 802	3 225	3 577
50-54	3 232	1 568	1 664	3 808	1 837	1 971	4 526	2 165	2 360	5 538	2 632	2 907
55-59	2 686	1 291	1 395	3 066	1 470	1 596	3 636	1 737	1 899	4 340	2 058	2 282
60-64	2 150	1 028	1 122	2 505	1 192	1 313	2 882	1 372	1 510	3 437	1 630	1 807
65-69	1 668	780	889	1 948	916	1 032	2 295	1 078	1 217	2 659	1 251	1 408
70-74	1 114	511	603	1 443	660	783	1 709	791	918	2 031	939	1 092
75-79	785	349	436	897	399	497	1 185	530	655	1 420	643	776
80 +	789	332	457	904	377	526	1 102	459	643	1 434	599	835

United Nations Department of Economic and Social Affairs/Population Division
World Population Prospects: The 2004 Revision, Volume II: Sex and Age Distribution of the World Population

120

POPULATION BY AGE AND SEX (in thousands)

Age group	2005 Both sexes	Males	Females	2010 Both sexes	Males	Females	2015 Both sexes	Males	Females	2020 Both sexes	Males	Females
All ages	147 029	72 168	74 861	157 478	77 193	80 285	167 528	82 031	85 497	177 089	86 638	90 451
0-4	16 161	8 225	7 936	15 625	7 975	7 650	15 428	7 877	7 551	15 208	7 768	7 440
5-9	16 060	8 151	7 909	15 881	8 074	7 807	15 375	7 840	7 535	15 205	7 757	7 448
10-14	15 992	8 102	7 890	15 862	8 037	7 825	15 701	7 970	7 731	15 213	7 747	7 466
15-19	14 892	7 485	7 407	15 624	7 865	7 760	15 530	7 823	7 707	15 404	7 779	7 625
20-24	13 494	6 669	6 826	14 290	7 084	7 206	15 078	7 501	7 577	15 041	7 499	7 543
25-29	12 906	6 297	6 610	13 082	6 412	6 670	13 912	6 849	7 063	14 733	7 286	7 447
30-34	11 949	5 765	6 183	12 624	6 120	6 505	12 820	6 248	6 572	13 669	6 696	6 973
35-39	9 822	4 666	5 156	11 739	5 636	6 104	12 422	5 995	6 427	12 630	6 131	6 499
40-44	8 091	3 830	4 261	9 646	4 556	5 090	11 554	5 519	6 035	12 240	5 881	6 359
45-49	6 802	3 225	3 577	7 922	3 731	4 191	9 465	4 449	5 016	11 357	5 401	5 956
50-54	5 538	2 632	2 907	6 622	3 118	3 504	7 732	3 619	4 113	9 256	4 325	4 931
55-59	4 340	2 058	2 282	5 335	2 514	2 821	6 401	2 990	3 411	7 493	3 480	4 013
60-64	3 437	1 630	1 807	4 122	1 940	2 183	5 086	2 377	2 709	6 122	2 836	3 287
65-69	2 659	1 251	1 408	3 190	1 495	1 695	3 844	1 786	2 058	4 762	2 196	2 565
70-74	2 031	939	1 092	2 373	1 098	1 276	2 867	1 319	1 547	3 474	1 584	1 890
75-79	1 420	643	776	1 707	771	936	2 014	908	1 106	2 453	1 099	1 354
80-84	875	380	495	1 068	468	600	1 304	568	736	1 558	676	882
85-89	393	161	232	544	223	321	681	281	400	849	347	501
90-94	135	49	85	178	65	113	257	94	162	332	123	209
95-99	28	8	20	38	11	26	53	16	37	80	25	56
100 +	3	1	2	4	1	3	6	1	4	8	2	6

Age group	2025 Both sexes	Males	Females	2030 Both sexes	Males	Females	2035 Both sexes	Males	Females	2040 Both sexes	Males	Females
All ages	185 678	90 752	94 927	193 104	94 277	98 827	199 297	97 183	102 114	204 147	99 420	104 727
0-4	14 759	7 540	7 219	14 209	7 261	6 948	13 700	7 002	6 698	13 187	6 741	6 446
5-9	14 993	7 652	7 341	14 550	7 428	7 122	14 006	7 152	6 854	13 503	6 896	6 607
10-14	15 047	7 666	7 381	14 838	7 563	7 275	14 398	7 341	7 057	13 856	7 066	6 790
15-19	14 920	7 559	7 362	14 758	7 480	7 277	14 551	7 379	7 172	14 115	7 159	6 956
20-24	14 920	7 458	7 462	14 442	7 242	7 201	14 284	7 167	7 117	14 083	7 069	7 014
25-29	14 703	7 288	7 414	14 588	7 253	7 335	14 117	7 041	7 076	13 965	6 971	6 994
30-34	14 492	7 135	7 357	14 469	7 143	7 326	14 362	7 112	7 250	13 899	6 907	6 993
35-39	13 482	6 581	6 901	14 307	7 021	7 285	14 291	7 034	7 257	14 191	7 008	7 182
40-44	12 453	6 020	6 433	13 306	6 471	6 835	14 131	6 911	7 220	14 122	6 928	7 194
45-49	12 043	5 763	6 280	12 261	5 905	6 056	13 112	6 354	6 758	13 935	6 793	7 142
50-54	11 124	5 261	5 862	11 806	5 620	6 186	12 029	5 764	6 265	12 876	6 210	6 666
55-59	9 099	4 160	4 810	10 010	5 000	5 700	11 405	5 404	6 001	11 720	5 580	6 143
60-64	7 185	3 308	3 877	8 637	3 971	4 666	10 413	4 848	5 566	11 078	5 191	5 887
65-69	5 752	2 629	3 123	6 770	3 075	3 695	8 157	3 699	4 458	9 853	4 524	5 328
70-74	4 325	1 957	2 369	5 248	2 350	2 897	6 198	2 758	3 440	7 490	3 326	4 164
75-79	2 994	1 326	1 668	3 750	1 646	2 104	4 574	1 986	2 588	5 426	2 338	3 088
80-84	1 919	825	1 094	2 364	1 003	1 361	2 985	1 253	1 732	3 666	1 520	2 146
85-89	1 033	420	613	1 292	520	772	1 610	639	972	2 055	805	1 250
90-94	425	157	269	530	194	336	675	245	430	854	305	550
95-99	108	34	74	143	44	98	182	57	125	237	74	163
100 +	13	3	10	18	5	13	25	7	18	32	9	23

Age group	2045 Both sexes	Males	Females	2050 Both sexes	Males	Females
All ages	207 594	100 967	106 628	209 557	101 789	107 768
0-4	12 711	6 499	6 213	12 236	6 256	5 979
5-9	12 994	6 638	6 357	12 522	6 397	6 125
10-14	13 356	6 812	6 544	12 849	6 555	6 294
15-19	13 577	6 887	6 690	13 078	6 635	6 444
20-24	13 651	6 853	6 798	13 117	6 583	6 534
25-29	13 769	6 877	6 892	13 343	6 665	6 679
30-34	13 754	6 841	6 913	13 565	6 752	6 813
35-39	13 737	6 809	6 928	13 598	6 747	6 851
40-44	14 030	6 907	7 123	13 585	6 713	6 872
45-49	13 934	6 814	7 119	13 848	6 797	7 051
50-54	13 694	6 644	7 050	13 699	6 669	7 030
55-59	12 561	6 018	6 543	13 368	6 444	6 924
60-64	11 310	5 336	5 974	12 130	5 761	6 369
65-69	10 497	4 851	5 646	10 729	4 992	5 737
70-74	9 067	4 077	4 990	9 676	4 378	5 299
75-79	6 581	2 828	3 752	7 986	3 475	4 511
80-84	4 373	1 797	2 576	5 326	2 181	3 145
85-89	2 547	984	1 563	3 059	1 171	1 888
90-94	1 105	390	715	1 384	481	903
95-99	305	94	211	401	122	279
100 +	43	12	31	57	16	41

POPULATION BY AGE AND SEX (in thousands)

Age group	2005 Both sexes	Males	Females	2010 Both sexes	Males	Females	2015 Both sexes	Males	Females	2020 Both sexes	Males	Females
All ages	147 029	72 168	74 861	159 073	78 008	81 065	171 810	84 219	87 591	184 851	90 604	94 247
0-4	16 161	8 225	7 936	17 221	8 790	8 430	18 121	9 254	8 867	18 700	9 553	9 147
5-9	16 060	8 151	7 909	15 881	8 074	7 807	16 964	8 651	8 313	17 889	9 128	8 761
10-14	15 992	8 102	7 890	15 862	8 037	7 825	15 701	7 970	7 731	16 799	8 557	8 243
15-19	14 892	7 485	7 407	15 624	7 865	7 760	15 530	7 823	7 707	15 404	7 779	7 625
20-24	13 494	6 669	6 826	14 290	7 084	7 206	15 078	7 501	7 577	15 041	7 499	7 543
25-29	12 906	6 297	6 610	13 082	6 412	6 670	13 912	6 849	7 063	14 733	7 286	7 447
30-34	11 949	5 765	6 183	12 624	6 120	6 505	12 820	6 248	6 572	13 669	6 696	6 973
35-39	9 822	4 666	5 156	11 739	5 636	6 104	12 422	5 995	6 427	12 630	6 131	6 499
40-44	8 091	3 830	4 261	9 646	4 556	5 090	11 554	5 519	6 035	12 240	5 881	6 359
45-49	6 802	3 225	3 577	7 922	3 731	4 191	9 465	4 449	5 016	11 357	5 401	5 956
50-54	5 538	2 632	2 907	6 622	3 118	3 504	7 732	3 619	4 113	9 256	4 325	4 931
55-59	4 340	2 058	2 282	5 335	2 514	2 821	6 401	2 990	3 411	7 493	3 480	4 013
60-64	3 437	1 630	1 807	4 122	1 940	2 183	5 086	2 377	2 709	6 122	2 836	3 287
65-69	2 659	1 251	1 408	3 190	1 495	1 695	3 844	1 786	2 058	4 762	2 196	2 565
70-74	2 031	939	1 092	2 373	1 098	1 276	2 867	1 319	1 547	3 474	1 584	1 890
75-79	1 420	643	776	1 707	771	936	2 014	908	1 106	2 453	1 099	1 354
80-84	875	380	495	1 068	468	600	1 304	568	736	1 558	676	882
85-89	393	161	232	544	223	321	681	281	400	849	347	501
90-94	135	49	85	178	65	113	257	94	162	332	123	209
95-99	28	8	20	38	11	26	53	16	37	80	25	56
100 +	3	1	2	4	1	3	6	1	4	8	2	6

Age group	2025 Both sexes	Males	Females	2030 Both sexes	Males	Females	2035 Both sexes	Males	Females	2040 Both sexes	Males	Females
All ages	197 129	96 603	100 527	208 758	102 275	106 483	219 945	107 732	112 214	230 665	112 965	117 700
0-4	18 467	9 436	9 031	18 437	9 423	9 014	18 731	9 575	9 155	19 107	9 769	9 338
5-9	18 473	9 430	9 043	18 247	9 318	8 930	18 223	9 308	8 915	18 521	9 462	9 058
10-14	17 726	9 035	8 692	18 313	9 338	8 975	18 090	9 228	8 862	18 068	9 219	8 849
15-19	16 503	8 367	8 137	17 432	8 846	8 586	18 021	9 151	8 870	17 801	9 043	8 759
20-24	14 920	7 458	7 462	16 021	8 046	7 974	16 951	8 527	8 424	17 543	8 835	8 708
25-29	14 703	7 288	7 414	14 588	7 253	7 335	15 689	7 841	7 848	16 622	8 324	8 298
30-34	14 492	7 135	7 357	14 469	7 143	7 326	14 362	7 112	7 250	15 464	7 702	7 762
35-39	13 482	6 581	6 901	14 307	7 021	7 285	14 291	7 034	7 257	14 191	7 008	7 182
40-44	12 453	6 020	6 433	13 306	6 471	6 835	14 131	6 911	7 220	14 122	6 928	7 194
45-49	12 043	5 763	6 280	12 261	5 905	6 356	13 112	6 354	6 758	13 935	6 793	7 142
50-54	11 124	5 261	5 862	11 806	5 620	6 186	12 029	5 764	6 265	12 876	6 210	6 666
55-59	8 988	4 169	4 819	10 819	5 082	5 738	11 495	5 434	6 061	11 723	5 580	6 143
60-64	7 185	3 308	3 877	8 637	3 971	4 666	10 413	4 848	5 566	11 078	5 191	5 887
65-69	5 752	2 629	3 123	6 770	3 075	3 695	8 157	3 699	4 458	9 853	4 524	5 328
70-74	4 325	1 957	2 369	5 248	2 350	2 897	6 198	2 758	3 440	7 490	3 326	4 164
75-79	2 994	1 326	1 668	3 750	1 646	2 104	4 574	1 986	2 588	5 426	2 338	3 088
80-84	1 919	825	1 094	2 364	1 003	1 361	2 985	1 253	1 732	3 666	1 520	2 146
85-89	1 033	420	613	1 292	520	772	1 610	639	972	2 055	805	1 250
90-94	425	157	269	530	194	336	675	245	430	854	305	550
95-99	108	34	74	143	44	98	182	57	125	237	74	163
100 +	13	3	10	18	5	13	25	7	18	32	9	23

Age group	2045 Both sexes	Males	Females	2050 Both sexes	Males	Females
All ages	240 749	117 898	122 851	249 965	122 420	127 545
0-4	19 414	9 928	9 486	19 579	10 014	9 565
5-9	18 901	9 659	9 242	19 212	9 820	9 392
10-14	18 368	9 375	8 993	18 750	9 573	9 177
15-19	17 782	9 036	8 746	18 084	9 193	8 891
20-24	17 328	8 730	8 599	17 313	8 726	8 587
25-29	17 218	8 634	8 583	17 009	8 534	8 475
30-34	16 399	8 186	8 213	16 998	8 499	8 500
35-39	15 292	7 597	7 695	16 228	8 082	8 146
40-44	14 030	6 907	7 123	15 128	7 494	7 634
45-49	13 934	6 814	7 119	13 848	6 797	7 051
50-54	13 694	6 644	7 050	13 699	6 669	7 030
55-59	12 561	6 018	6 543	13 368	6 444	6 924
60-64	11 310	5 336	5 974	12 130	5 761	6 369
65-69	10 497	4 851	5 646	10 729	4 992	5 737
70-74	9 067	4 077	4 990	9 676	4 378	5 299
75-79	6 581	2 828	3 752	7 986	3 475	4 511
80-84	4 373	1 797	2 576	5 326	2 181	3 145
85-89	2 547	984	1 563	3 059	1 171	1 888
90-94	1 105	390	715	1 384	481	903
95-99	305	94	211	401	122	279
100 +	43	12	31	57	16	41

United Nations Department of Economic and Social Affairs/Population Division
World Population Prospects: The 2004 Revision, Volume II: Sex and Age Distribution of the World Population

POPULATION BY AGE AND SEX (in thousands)

Age group	2005 Both sexes	Males	Females	2010 Both sexes	Males	Females	2015 Both sexes	Males	Females	2020 Both sexes	Males	Females
All ages	147 020	72 160	74 861	155 000	76 077	70 504	160 004	70 807	80 007	160 206	80 656	86 640
0-4	16 161	8 225	7 936	14 029	7 160	6 869	12 725	6 496	6 229	11 696	5 973	5 724
5-9	16 060	8 151	7 909	15 881	8 074	7 807	13 784	7 027	6 757	12 512	6 381	6 131
10-14	15 992	8 102	7 890	15 862	8 037	7 825	15 701	7 970	7 731	13 626	6 936	6 689
15-19	14 892	7 485	7 407	15 624	7 865	7 760	15 530	7 823	7 707	15 404	7 779	7 625
20-24	13 494	6 669	6 826	14 290	7 084	7 206	15 078	7 501	7 577	15 041	7 499	7 543
25-29	12 906	6 297	6 610	13 082	6 412	6 670	13 912	6 849	7 063	14 733	7 286	7 447
30-34	11 949	5 765	6 183	12 624	6 120	6 505	12 820	6 248	6 572	13 669	6 696	6 973
35-39	9 822	4 666	5 156	11 739	5 636	6 104	12 422	5 995	6 427	12 630	6 131	6 499
40-44	8 091	3 830	4 261	9 646	4 556	5 090	11 554	5 519	6 035	12 240	5 881	6 359
45-49	6 802	3 225	3 577	7 922	3 731	4 191	9 465	4 449	5 016	11 357	5 401	5 956
50-54	5 538	2 632	2 907	6 622	3 118	3 504	7 732	3 619	4 113	9 256	4 325	4 931
55-59	4 340	2 058	2 282	5 335	2 514	2 821	6 401	2 990	3 411	7 493	3 480	4 013
60-64	3 437	1 630	1 807	4 122	1 940	2 183	5 086	2 377	2 709	6 122	2 836	3 287
65-69	2 659	1 251	1 408	3 190	1 495	1 695	3 844	1 786	2 058	4 762	2 196	2 565
70-74	2 031	939	1 092	2 373	1 098	1 276	2 867	1 319	1 547	3 474	1 584	1 890
75-79	1 420	643	776	1 707	771	936	2 014	908	1 106	2 453	1 099	1 354
80-84	875	380	495	1 068	468	600	1 304	568	736	1 558	676	882
85-89	393	161	232	544	223	321	681	281	400	849	347	501
90-94	135	49	85	178	65	113	257	94	162	332	123	209
95-99	28	8	20	38	11	26	53	16	37	80	25	56
100 +	3	1	2	4	1	3	6	1	4	8	2	6

Age group	2025 Both sexes	Males	Females	2030 Both sexes	Males	Females	2035 Both sexes	Males	Females	2040 Both sexes	Males	Females
All ages	174 229	84 901	89 327	177 691	86 403	91 289	179 451	87 045	92 406	179 376	86 769	92 607
0-4	11 084	5 661	5 422	10 220	5 221	4 999	9 231	4 716	4 515	8 215	4 197	4 017
5-9	11 492	5 862	5 629	10 885	5 554	5 331	10 028	5 118	4 910	9 044	4 616	4 428
10-14	12 358	6 293	6 065	11 342	5 777	5 565	10 738	5 470	5 268	9 884	5 035	4 848
15-19	13 336	6 751	6 586	12 074	6 110	5 963	11 062	5 597	5 465	10 461	5 293	5 168
20-24	14 920	7 458	7 462	12 863	6 437	6 426	11 607	5 802	5 806	10 602	5 293	5 309
25-29	14 703	7 288	7 414	14 588	7 253	7 335	12 544	6 241	6 303	11 298	5 612	5 685
30-34	14 492	7 135	7 357	14 469	7 143	7 326	14 362	7 112	7 250	12 334	6 112	6 222
35-39	13 482	6 581	6 901	14 307	7 021	7 285	14 291	7 034	7 257	14 191	7 008	7 182
40-44	12 453	6 020	6 433	13 300	6 471	6 835	14 131	6 911	7 220	14 122	6 928	7 194
45-49	12 043	5 763	6 280	12 261	5 905	6 356	13 112	6 354	6 758	13 935	6 793	7 142
50-54	11 124	5 261	5 862	11 806	5 620	6 186	12 029	5 764	6 265	12 876	6 210	6 666
55-59	8 900	4 169	4 819	10 019	5 082	5 730	11 495	5 434	6 061	11 720	5 580	6 143
60-64	7 185	3 308	3 877	8 637	3 971	4 666	10 413	4 848	5 566	11 078	5 191	5 887
65-69	5 752	2 629	3 123	6 770	3 075	3 695	8 157	3 699	4 458	9 853	4 524	5 328
70-74	4 325	1 957	2 369	5 248	2 350	2 897	6 198	2 758	3 440	7 490	3 326	4 164
75-79	2 994	1 326	1 668	3 750	1 646	2 104	4 574	1 986	2 588	5 426	2 338	3 088
80-84	1 919	825	1 094	2 304	1 003	1 301	2 985	1 253	1 732	3 660	1 520	2 140
85-89	1 033	420	613	1 292	520	772	1 610	639	972	2 055	805	1 250
90-94	425	157	269	530	194	336	675	245	430	854	305	550
95-99	108	34	74	143	44	98	182	57	125	237	74	163
100 +	13	3	10	18	5	13	25	7	18	32	9	23

Age group	2045 Both sexes	Males	Females	2050 Both sexes	Males	Females
All ages	177 525	85 614	91 911	173 956	83 617	90 339
0-4	7 348	3 754	3 593	6 620	3 382	3 237
5-9	8 033	4 100	3 933	7 169	3 659	3 510
10-14	8 903	4 535	4 368	7 893	4 020	3 873
15-19	9 610	4 860	4 750	8 632	4 362	4 270
20-24	10 006	4 992	5 014	9 159	4 562	4 597
25-29	10 300	5 109	5 191	9 710	4 812	4 898
30-34	11 099	5 491	5 608	10 111	4 994	5 117
35-39	12 181	6 020	6 161	10 959	5 408	5 551
40-44	14 030	6 907	7 123	12 040	5 932	6 109
45-49	13 934	6 814	7 119	13 848	6 797	7 051
50-54	13 694	6 644	7 050	13 699	6 669	7 030
55-59	12 561	6 018	6 543	13 368	6 444	6 924
60-64	11 310	5 336	5 974	12 130	5 761	6 369
65-69	10 497	4 851	5 646	10 729	4 992	5 737
70-74	9 067	4 077	4 990	9 676	4 378	5 299
75-79	6 581	2 828	3 752	7 986	3 475	4 511
80-84	4 373	1 797	2 576	5 326	2 181	3 145
85-89	2 547	984	1 563	3 059	1 171	1 888
90-94	1 105	390	715	1 384	481	903
95-99	305	94	211	401	122	279
100 +	43	12	31	57	16	41

United Nations Department of Economic and Social Affairs/Population Division
World Population Prospects: The 2004 Revision, Volume II: Sex and Age Distribution of the World Population

123

POPULATION BY AGE AND SEX (in thousands)

Age group	1950			1955			1960			1965		
	Both sexes	Males	Females	Both sexes	Males	Females	Both sexes	Males	Females	Both sexes	Males	Females
All ages	112 995	56 476	56 519	129 671	64 869	64 802	148 432	74 237	74 196	170 096	85 033	85 063
0-4	17 812	9 009	8 803	21 316	10 785	10 531	24 404	12 350	12 054	27 839	14 099	13 740
5-9	14 127	7 121	7 007	17 045	8 600	8 445	20 462	10 326	10 136	23 523	11 875	11 648
10-14	12 639	6 364	6 276	14 003	7 057	6 946	16 853	8 496	8 356	20 242	10 208	10 035
15-19	11 077	5 571	5 506	12 555	6 321	6 235	13 852	6 978	6 874	16 677	8 404	8 273
20-24	10 210	5 131	5 080	10 952	5 502	5 450	12 345	6 205	6 141	13 619	6 846	6 773
25-29	8 674	4 358	4 317	10 045	5 041	5 005	10 719	5 371	5 348	12 075	6 048	6 027
30-34	7 404	3 709	3 695	8 514	4 275	4 240	9 802	4 905	4 897	10 455	5 219	5 236
35-39	6 704	3 357	3 347	7 246	3 628	3 618	8 274	4 142	4 132	9 537	4 756	4 780
40-44	5 813	2 913	2 900	6 509	3 256	3 254	6 999	3 492	3 507	8 014	3 997	4 017
45-49	4 837	2 421	2 416	5 581	2 787	2 795	6 231	3 100	3 131	6 724	3 337	3 387
50-54	4 108	2 017	2 091	4 574	2 276	2 298	5 265	2 609	2 656	5 909	2 917	2 992
55-59	3 231	1 572	1 659	3 795	1 847	1 948	4 227	2 080	2 146	4 899	2 401	2 498
60-64	2 436	1 160	1 276	2 887	1 387	1 500	3 398	1 629	1 769	3 813	1 848	1 965
65-69	1 724	808	917	2 063	964	1 099	2 457	1 157	1 300	2 925	1 373	1 553
70-74	1 134	515	619	1 339	612	727	1 629	743	886	1 966	901	1 066
75-79	653	285	368	770	339	431	936	414	521	1 161	511	650
80 +	410	167	243	475	194	281	580	239	341	718	296	422

Age group	1970			1975			1980			1985		
	Both sexes	Males	Females	Both sexes	Males	Females	Both sexes	Males	Females	Both sexes	Males	Females
All ages	192 467	96 157	96 310	216 173	107 929	108 245	242 276	120 787	121 488	269 870	134 357	135 512
0-4	29 097	14 740	14 356	30 594	15 473	15 121	33 732	17 077	16 655	35 980	18 304	17 677
5-9	26 960	13 619	13 341	28 327	14 305	14 022	29 946	15 105	14 841	33 263	16 824	16 440
10-14	23 299	11 748	11 551	26 749	13 496	13 253	28 139	14 197	13 943	29 800	15 018	14 781
15-19	20 030	10 084	9 946	23 113	11 638	11 476	26 533	13 358	13 175	27 941	14 072	13 869
20-24	16 393	8 235	8 158	19 786	9 936	9 850	22 796	11 420	11 376	26 217	13 156	13 061
25-29	13 340	6 689	6 652	16 155	8 098	8 057	19 479	9 730	9 749	22 449	11 194	11 256
30-34	11 804	5 896	5 908	13 123	6 567	6 556	15 864	7 909	7 955	19 141	9 515	9 626
35-39	10 195	5 073	5 121	11 561	5 760	5 801	12 846	6 398	6 448	15 542	7 707	7 835
40-44	9 255	4 599	4 657	9 927	4 924	5 003	11 250	5 576	5 674	12 520	6 197	6 322
45-49	7 719	3 829	3 890	8 943	4 422	4 521	9 597	4 732	4 865	10 881	5 348	5 532
50-54	6 400	3 152	3 248	7 371	3 631	3 740	8 557	4 201	4 355	9 178	4 474	4 704
55-59	5 522	2 696	2 826	6 006	2 929	3 078	6 936	3 383	3 553	8 043	3 887	4 157
60-64	4 447	2 145	2 302	5 042	2 426	2 616	5 507	2 645	2 861	6 350	3 028	3 322
65-69	3 310	1 569	1 741	3 893	1 840	2 053	4 443	2 094	2 349	4 844	2 257	2 586
70-74	2 367	1 080	1 287	2 703	1 247	1 456	3 212	1 477	1 735	3 640	1 647	1 992
75-79	1 426	631	795	1 740	768	972	2 010	896	1 114	2 348	1 024	1 324
80 +	903	372	531	1 139	471	668	1 431	590	841	1 734	706	1 028

Age group	1990			1995			2000			2005		
	Both sexes	Males	Females	Both sexes	Males	Females	Both sexes	Males	Females	Both sexes	Males	Females
All ages	297 126	147 691	149 435	323 284	160 404	162 880	349 434	173 079	176 355	375 187	185 588	189 599
0-4	36 175	18 409	17 766	36 051	18 357	17 694	36 667	18 689	17 978	37 118	18 933	18 185
5-9	35 574	18 079	17 495	35 807	18 205	17 602	35 735	18 184	17 551	36 373	18 530	17 843
10-14	33 124	16 738	16 386	35 413	17 986	17 426	35 652	18 120	17 532	35 573	18 096	17 477
15-19	29 592	14 884	14 708	32 874	16 580	16 294	35 124	17 807	17 317	35 391	17 960	17 431
20-24	27 593	13 838	13 755	29 169	14 601	14 568	32 381	16 258	16 123	34 659	17 502	17 156
25-29	25 825	12 886	12 939	27 102	13 498	13 603	28 630	14 241	14 389	31 851	15 905	15 946
30-34	22 077	10 944	11 133	25 348	12 559	12 788	26 588	13 153	13 435	28 130	13 910	14 221
35-39	18 774	9 275	9 499	21 641	10 648	10 993	24 851	12 225	12 626	26 103	12 830	13 273
40-44	15 177	7 476	7 701	18 344	8 995	9 349	21 162	10 335	10 827	24 342	11 893	12 449
45-49	12 144	5 963	6 181	14 749	7 205	7 543	17 851	8 682	9 169	20 630	9 998	10 632
50-54	10 436	5 074	5 362	11 682	5 677	6 005	14 225	6 881	7 343	17 261	8 317	8 944
55-59	8 662	4 158	4 504	9 882	4 735	5 147	11 108	5 327	5 781	13 574	6 485	7 089
60-64	7 407	3 504	3 904	8 021	3 774	4 247	9 195	4 326	4 869	10 387	4 896	5 490
65-69	5 638	2 613	3 025	6 630	3 053	3 577	7 230	3 318	3 912	8 336	3 829	4 508
70-74	4 035	1 810	2 226	4 770	2 132	2 638	5 675	2 524	3 152	6 249	2 771	3 477
75-79	2 742	1 179	1 563	3 126	1 336	1 790	3 771	1 608	2 163	4 555	1 933	2 622
80 +	2 151	863	1 288	2 677	1 062	1 615	3 588	1 401	2 188	4 654	1 799	2 854

United Nations Department of Economic and Social Affairs/Population Division
World Population Prospects: The 2004 Revision, Volume II: Sex and Age Distribution of the World Population

124

POPULATION BY AGE AND SEX (in thousands)

Age group	2005 Both sexes	Males	Females	2010 Both sexes	Males	Females	2015 Both sexes	Males	Females	2020 Both sexes	Males	Females
All ages	375 187	185 588	189 599	400 544	197 955	202 590	424 327	209 514	214 813	446 297	220 161	226 136
0-4	37 118	18 933	18 185	37 267	19 017	18 250	36 732	18 750	17 983	36 015	18 389	17 626
5-9	36 373	18 530	17 843	36 877	18 802	18 076	37 050	18 898	18 151	36 540	18 645	17 895
10-14	35 573	18 096	17 477	36 246	18 461	17 786	36 761	18 738	18 023	36 944	18 840	18 104
15-19	35 391	17 960	17 431	35 365	17 969	17 396	36 057	18 345	17 713	36 586	18 631	17 955
20-24	34 659	17 502	17 156	35 012	17 709	17 303	35 028	17 745	17 283	35 745	18 138	17 607
25-29	31 851	15 905	15 946	34 205	17 194	17 011	34 605	17 432	17 173	34 662	17 497	17 165
30-34	28 130	13 910	14 221	31 401	15 603	15 798	33 766	16 898	16 869	34 212	17 166	17 046
35-39	26 103	12 830	13 273	27 707	13 629	14 078	30 960	15 311	15 650	33 339	16 613	16 726
40-44	24 342	11 893	12 449	25 643	12 532	13 111	27 245	13 330	13 914	30 490	15 006	15 484
45-49	20 630	9 998	10 632	23 797	11 547	12 249	25 101	12 188	12 913	26 712	12 992	13 720
50-54	17 261	8 317	8 944	20 011	9 615	10 396	23 125	11 129	11 996	24 442	11 776	12 666
55-59	13 574	6 485	7 089	16 534	7 873	8 661	19 221	9 130	10 090	22 270	10 601	11 669
60-64	10 387	4 896	5 490	12 756	5 995	6 761	15 598	7 310	8 288	18 200	8 513	9 688
65-69	8 336	3 829	4 508	9 482	4 368	5 114	11 710	5 380	6 330	14 392	6 597	7 796
70-74	6 249	2 771	3 477	7 271	3 231	4 040	8 339	3 718	4 621	10 375	4 615	5 760
75-79	4 555	1 933	2 622	5 086	2 154	2 932	5 986	2 540	3 446	6 940	2 955	3 985
80-84	2 706	1 088	1 618	3 332	1 333	1 998	3 779	1 507	2 272	4 511	1 802	2 708
85-89	1 328	498	830	1 683	628	1 055	2 115	783	1 332	2 441	899	1 542
90-94	478	167	311	656	225	431	848	288	561	1 086	364	722
95-99	118	39	79	178	57	121	247	78	170	322	99	224
100 +	23	7	15	37	12	25	54	18	37	74	23	51

Age group	2025 Both sexes	Males	Females	2030 Both sexes	Males	Females	2035 Both sexes	Males	Females	2040 Both sexes	Males	Females
All ages	466 200	229 743	236 457	483 749	238 137	245 611	498 503	245 106	253 396	510 647	250 766	259 881
0-4	35 252	18 004	17 248	34 355	17 550	16 806	33 299	17 013	16 286	32 560	16 639	15 921
5-9	35 843	18 295	17 548	35 090	17 915	17 175	34 209	17 470	16 739	33 167	16 941	16 226
10-14	36 442	18 591	17 851	35 750	18 244	17 506	35 003	17 868	17 136	34 127	17 425	16 702
15-19	36 780	18 741	18 030	36 283	18 404	17 788	35 601	18 155	17 446	34 864	17 785	17 079
20-24	36 290	18 437	17 853	36 487	18 548	17 939	36 008	18 315	17 693	35 344	17 989	17 355
25-29	35 398	17 904	17 493	35 942	18 201	17 742	36 159	18 326	17 832	35 703	18 111	17 591
30-34	34 303	17 255	17 048	35 038	17 660	17 378	35 600	17 968	17 632	35 837	18 109	17 728
35-39	33 824	16 907	16 917	33 930	17 004	16 926	34 681	17 419	17 262	35 260	17 739	17 521
40-44	32 875	16 310	16 565	33 382	16 616	16 766	33 517	16 732	16 786	34 285	17 157	17 128
45-49	29 939	14 653	15 286	32 313	15 947	16 367	32 853	16 271	16 581	33 022	16 407	16 615
50-54	26 056	12 580	13 477	29 248	14 216	15 033	31 609	15 495	16 114	32 183	15 838	16 345
55-59	23 594	11 249	12 346	25 205	12 049	13 156	28 344	13 645	14 699	30 682	14 902	15 780
60-64	21 153	9 918	11 235	22 480	10 568	11 912	24 076	11 351	12 725	27 139	12 889	14 250
65-69	16 870	7 718	9 151	19 694	9 048	10 646	21 002	9 677	11 326	22 570	10 431	12 139
70-74	12 833	5 695	7 138	15 149	6 727	8 422	17 772	7 926	9 846	19 042	8 517	10 525
75-79	8 713	3 701	5 012	10 897	4 631	6 265	12 961	5 511	7 450	15 308	6 535	8 773
80-84	5 292	2 119	3 173	6 750	2 703	4 047	8 527	3 414	5 113	10 238	4 097	6 141
85-89	2 961	1 091	1 871	3 548	1 311	2 238	4 584	1 691	2 894	5 859	2 157	3 702
90-94	1 272	422	851	1 589	526	1 063	1 926	637	1 289	2 519	829	1 690
95-99	415	124	291	498	146	352	629	183	446	763	220	542
100 +	94	29	65	121	35	85	143	40	102	173	48	125

Age group	2045 Both sexes	Males	Females	2050 Both sexes	Males	Females
All ages	520 086	255 091	264 995	526 907	258 151	268 756
0-4	31 801	16 254	15 547	31 109	15 902	15 207
5-9	32 441	16 574	15 867	31 693	16 195	15 498
10-14	33 091	16 900	16 191	32 369	16 535	15 834
15-19	33 997	17 349	16 649	32 969	16 829	16 140
20-24	34 624	17 632	16 992	33 772	17 207	16 565
25-29	35 060	17 802	17 259	34 360	17 460	16 900
30-34	35 405	17 911	17 494	34 786	17 619	17 167
35-39	35 518	17 895	17 624	35 113	17 715	17 398
40-44	34 882	17 488	17 394	35 164	17 659	17 506
45-49	33 808	16 842	16 966	34 425	17 185	17 240
50-54	32 391	15 996	16 395	33 196	16 440	16 756
55-59	31 293	15 262	16 031	31 545	15 442	16 102
60-64	29 437	14 108	15 329	30 087	14 484	15 602
65-69	25 519	11 882	13 637	27 749	13 042	14 707
70-74	20 556	9 222	11 334	23 333	10 547	12 786
75-79	16 502	7 063	9 439	17 916	7 688	10 228
80-84	12 190	4 893	7 297	13 234	5 322	7 913
85-89	7 111	2 611	4 500	8 544	3 142	5 402
90-94	3 255	1 066	2 189	3 991	1 300	2 691
95-99	1 003	287	716	1 300	369	931
100 +	203	56	147	254	70	183

United Nations Department of Economic and Social Affairs/Population Division
World Population Prospects: The 2004 Revision, Volume II: Sex and Age Distribution of the World Population

125

POPULATION BY AGE AND SEX (in thousands)

Age group	2005 Both sexes	Males	Females	2010 Both sexes	Males	Females	2015 Both sexes	Males	Females	2020 Both sexes	Males	Females
All ages	375 187	185 588	189 599	404 379	199 911	204 468	434 594	214 753	219 841	464 828	229 617	235 211
0-4	37 118	18 933	18 185	41 101	20 974	20 128	43 183	22 042	21 141	44 312	22 625	21 687
5-9	36 373	18 530	17 843	36 877	18 802	18 076	40 866	20 845	20 021	42 964	21 922	21 041
10-14	35 573	18 096	17 477	36 246	18 461	17 786	36 761	18 738	18 023	40 754	20 783	19 971
15-19	35 391	17 960	17 431	35 365	17 969	17 396	36 057	18 345	17 713	36 586	18 631	17 955
20-24	34 659	17 502	17 156	35 012	17 709	17 303	35 028	17 745	17 283	35 745	18 138	17 607
25-29	31 851	15 905	15 946	34 205	17 194	17 011	34 605	17 432	17 173	34 662	17 497	17 165
30-34	28 130	13 910	14 221	31 401	15 603	15 798	33 766	16 898	16 869	34 212	17 166	17 046
35-39	26 103	12 830	13 273	27 707	13 629	14 078	30 960	15 311	15 650	33 339	16 613	16 726
40-44	24 342	11 893	12 449	25 643	12 532	13 111	27 245	13 330	13 914	30 490	15 006	15 484
45-49	20 630	9 998	10 632	23 797	11 547	12 249	25 101	12 188	12 913	26 712	12 992	13 720
50-54	17 261	8 317	8 944	20 011	9 615	10 396	23 125	11 129	11 996	24 442	11 776	12 666
55-59	13 574	6 485	7 089	16 534	7 873	8 661	19 221	9 130	10 090	22 270	10 601	11 669
60-64	10 387	4 896	5 490	12 756	5 995	6 761	15 598	7 310	8 288	18 200	8 513	9 688
65-69	8 336	3 829	4 508	9 482	4 368	5 114	11 710	5 380	6 330	14 392	6 597	7 796
70-74	6 249	2 771	3 477	7 271	3 231	4 040	8 339	3 718	4 621	10 375	4 615	5 760
75-79	4 555	1 933	2 622	5 086	2 154	2 932	5 986	2 540	3 446	6 940	2 955	3 985
80-84	2 706	1 088	1 618	3 332	1 333	1 998	3 779	1 507	2 272	4 511	1 802	2 708
85-89	1 328	498	830	1 683	628	1 055	2 115	783	1 332	2 441	899	1 542
90-94	478	167	311	656	225	431	848	288	561	1 086	364	722
95-99	118	39	79	178	57	121	247	78	170	322	99	224
100 +	23	7	15	37	12	25	54	18	37	74	23	51

Age group	2025 Both sexes	Males	Females	2030 Both sexes	Males	Females	2035 Both sexes	Males	Females	2040 Both sexes	Males	Females
All ages	493 519	243 683	249 836	521 187	257 236	263 952	548 085	270 390	277 695	574 515	283 321	291 194
0-4	44 093	22 519	21 574	44 554	22 759	21 795	45 557	23 276	22 281	47 003	24 019	22 984
5-9	44 109	22 514	21 595	43 899	22 412	21 487	44 374	22 660	21 714	45 389	23 183	22 205
10-14	42 855	21 862	20 993	44 003	22 455	21 548	43 799	22 357	21 442	44 279	22 608	21 672
15-19	40 579	20 676	19 903	42 679	21 754	20 925	43 835	22 352	21 483	43 642	22 261	21 381
20-24	36 290	18 437	17 853	40 269	20 469	19 799	42 377	21 554	20 824	43 546	22 163	21 384
25-29	35 398	17 904	17 493	35 942	18 201	17 742	39 919	20 232	19 687	42 039	21 325	20 714
30-34	34 303	17 255	17 048	35 038	17 660	17 378	35 600	17 968	17 632	39 573	19 997	19 576
35-39	33 824	16 907	16 917	33 930	17 004	16 926	34 681	17 419	17 262	35 260	17 739	17 521
40-44	32 875	16 310	16 565	33 382	16 616	16 766	33 517	16 732	16 786	34 285	17 157	17 128
45-49	29 939	14 653	15 286	32 313	15 947	16 367	32 853	16 271	16 581	33 022	16 407	16 615
50-54	26 056	12 580	13 477	29 248	14 216	15 033	31 609	15 495	16 114	32 183	15 838	16 345
55-59	23 594	11 249	12 346	25 205	12 049	13 156	28 344	13 645	14 699	30 682	14 902	15 780
60-64	21 153	9 918	11 235	22 480	10 568	11 912	24 076	11 351	12 725	27 139	12 889	14 250
65-69	16 870	7 718	9 151	19 694	9 048	10 646	21 002	9 677	11 326	22 570	10 431	12 139
70-74	12 833	5 695	7 138	15 149	6 727	8 422	17 772	7 926	9 846	19 042	8 517	10 525
75-79	8 713	3 701	5 012	10 897	4 631	6 265	12 961	5 511	7 450	15 308	6 535	8 773
80-84	5 292	2 119	3 173	6 750	2 703	4 047	8 527	3 414	5 113	10 238	4 097	6 141
85-89	2 961	1 091	1 871	3 548	1 311	2 238	4 584	1 691	2 894	5 859	2 157	3 702
90-94	1 272	422	851	1 589	526	1 063	1 926	637	1 289	2 519	829	1 690
95-99	415	124	291	498	146	352	629	183	446	763	220	542
100 +	94	29	65	121	35	85	143	40	102	173	48	125

Age group	2045 Both sexes	Males	Females	2050 Both sexes	Males	Females
All ages	600 091	295 855	304 236	624 658	307 938	316 720
0-4	48 146	24 608	23 538	49 120	25 108	24 012
5-9	46 845	23 932	22 913	47 998	24 526	23 472
10-14	45 298	23 133	22 165	46 758	23 884	22 874
15-19	44 130	22 517	21 612	45 155	23 047	22 108
20-24	43 370	22 085	21 286	43 872	22 352	21 521
25-29	43 223	21 945	21 278	43 069	21 884	21 185
30-34	41 703	21 097	20 606	42 906	21 731	21 175
35-39	39 226	19 763	19 464	41 368	20 871	20 497
40-44	34 882	17 488	17 394	38 839	19 504	19 335
45-49	33 808	16 842	16 966	34 425	17 185	17 240
50-54	32 391	15 996	16 395	33 196	16 440	16 756
55-59	31 293	15 262	16 031	31 545	15 442	16 102
60-64	29 437	14 108	15 329	30 087	14 484	15 602
65-69	25 519	11 882	13 637	27 749	13 042	14 707
70-74	20 556	9 222	11 334	23 333	10 547	12 786
75-79	16 502	7 063	9 439	17 916	7 688	10 228
80-84	12 190	4 893	7 297	13 234	5 322	7 913
85-89	7 111	2 611	4 500	8 544	3 142	5 402
90-94	3 255	1 066	2 189	3 991	1 300	2 691
95-99	1 003	287	716	1 300	369	931
100 +	203	56	147	254	70	183

United Nations Department of Economic and Social Affairs/Population Division
World Population Prospects: The 2004 Revision, Volume II: Sex and Age Distribution of the World Population

126

POPULATION BY AGE AND SEX (in thousands)

Age group	2005 Both sexes	Males	Females	2010 Both sexes	Males	Females	2015 Both sexes	Males	Females	2020 Both sexes	Males	Females
All ages	375 187	185 588	189 599	396 696	195 991	200 705	414 029	204 259	209 770	427 700	210 670	217 029
0-4	37 118	18 933	18 185	33 418	17 053	16 365	30 265	15 449	14 816	27 681	14 134	13 547
5-9	36 373	18 530	17 843	36 877	18 802	18 076	33 219	16 945	16 274	30 100	15 359	14 741
10-14	35 573	18 096	17 477	36 246	18 461	17 786	36 761	18 738	18 023	33 120	16 891	16 230
15-19	35 391	17 960	17 431	35 365	17 969	17 396	36 057	18 345	17 713	36 586	18 631	17 955
20-24	34 659	17 502	17 156	35 012	17 709	17 303	35 028	17 745	17 283	35 745	18 138	17 607
25-29	31 851	15 905	15 946	34 205	17 194	17 011	34 605	17 432	17 173	34 662	17 497	17 165
30-34	28 130	13 910	14 221	31 401	15 603	15 798	33 766	16 898	16 869	34 212	17 166	17 046
35-39	26 103	12 830	13 273	27 707	13 629	14 078	30 960	15 311	15 650	33 339	16 613	16 726
40-44	24 342	11 893	12 449	25 643	12 532	13 111	27 245	13 330	13 914	30 490	15 006	15 484
45-49	20 630	9 998	10 632	23 797	11 547	12 249	25 101	12 188	12 913	26 712	12 992	13 720
50-54	17 261	8 317	8 944	20 011	9 615	10 396	23 125	11 129	11 996	24 442	11 776	12 666
55-59	13 574	6 485	7 089	16 534	7 873	8 661	19 221	9 130	10 090	22 270	10 601	11 669
60-64	10 387	4 896	5 490	12 756	5 995	6 761	15 598	7 310	8 288	18 200	8 513	9 688
65-69	8 336	3 829	4 508	9 482	4 368	5 114	11 710	5 380	6 330	14 392	6 597	7 796
70-74	6 249	2 771	3 477	7 271	3 231	4 040	8 339	3 718	4 621	10 375	4 615	5 760
75-79	4 555	1 933	2 622	5 086	2 154	2 932	5 986	2 540	3 446	6 940	2 955	3 985
80-84	2 706	1 088	1 618	3 332	1 333	1 998	3 779	1 507	2 272	4 511	1 802	2 708
85-89	1 328	498	830	1 683	628	1 055	2 115	783	1 332	2 441	899	1 542
90-94	478	167	311	656	225	431	848	288	561	1 086	364	722
95-99	118	39	79	178	57	121	247	78	170	322	99	224
100 +	23	7	15	37	12	25	54	18	37	74	23	51

Age group	2025 Both sexes	Males	Females	2030 Both sexes	Males	Females	2035 Both sexes	Males	Females	2040 Both sexes	Males	Females
All ages	438 874	215 799	223 074	446 748	219 263	227 486	450 598	220 680	229 918	450 647	220 187	230 461
0-4	26 471	13 520	12 952	24 602	12 567	12 034	22 280	11 384	10 897	20 312	10 380	9 932
5-9	27 541	14 058	13 483	26 341	13 449	12 892	24 488	12 506	11 982	22 182	11 331	10 851
10-14	30 012	15 311	14 701	27 461	14 015	13 446	26 267	13 409	12 856	24 419	12 469	11 950
15-19	32 966	16 798	16 168	29 870	15 227	14 643	27 332	13 939	13 393	26 146	13 339	12 807
20-24	36 290	18 437	17 853	32 691	16 619	16 072	29 623	15 068	14 554	27 107	13 798	13 309
25-29	35 398	17 904	17 493	35 942	18 201	17 742	32 385	16 414	15 971	29 350	14 890	14 461
30-34	34 303	17 255	17 048	35 038	17 660	17 378	35 600	17 968	17 632	32 087	16 214	15 873
35-39	33 024	16 007	16 017	33 930	17 004	16 926	34 681	17 419	17 262	35 260	17 739	17 521
40-44	32 875	16 310	16 565	33 382	16 616	16 766	33 517	16 732	16 786	34 285	17 157	17 128
45-49	29 939	14 653	15 286	32 313	15 947	16 367	32 853	16 271	16 581	33 022	16 407	16 615
50-54	26 056	12 580	13 477	29 248	14 216	15 033	31 609	15 495	16 114	32 183	15 838	16 345
55-59	23 594	11 249	12 346	25 205	12 049	13 156	28 344	13 645	14 699	30 602	14 902	15 700
60-64	21 153	9 918	11 235	22 480	10 568	11 912	24 076	11 351	12 725	27 139	12 889	14 250
65-69	16 870	7 718	9 151	19 694	9 048	10 646	21 002	9 677	11 326	22 570	10 431	12 139
70-74	12 833	5 695	7 138	15 149	6 727	8 422	17 772	7 926	9 846	19 042	8 517	10 525
75-79	9 710	3 701	5 012	10 897	4 631	6 265	12 961	5 511	7 450	15 308	6 535	8 773
80-84	5 292	2 119	3 173	6 750	2 703	4 047	8 527	3 414	5 113	10 238	4 097	6 141
85-89	2 961	1 091	1 871	3 548	1 311	2 238	4 584	1 691	2 894	5 859	2 157	3 702
90-94	1 272	422	851	1 589	526	1 063	1 926	637	1 289	2 519	829	1 690
95-99	415	124	291	498	146	352	629	183	446	763	220	542
100 +	94	29	65	121	35	85	143	40	102	173	48	125

Age group	2045 Both sexes	Males	Females	2050 Both sexes	Males	Females
All ages	447 078	217 901	229 177	440 205	214 008	226 197
0-4	18 593	9 503	9 090	17 163	8 773	8 390
5-9	20 226	10 334	9 892	18 517	9 463	9 054
10-14	22 118	11 297	10 822	20 167	10 303	9 864
15-19	24 308	12 406	11 902	22 016	11 240	10 776
20-24	25 936	13 209	12 727	24 113	12 288	11 825
25-29	26 862	13 640	13 222	25 709	13 065	12 644
30-34	29 090	14 717	14 373	26 631	13 489	13 142
35-39	31 797	16 020	15 777	28 840	14 550	14 290
40-44	34 882	17 488	17 394	31 476	15 807	15 670
45-49	33 808	16 842	16 966	34 425	17 185	17 240
50-54	32 391	15 996	16 395	33 196	16 440	16 756
55-59	31 293	15 262	16 031	31 545	15 442	16 102
60-64	29 437	14 108	15 329	30 087	14 484	15 602
65-69	25 519	11 882	13 637	27 749	13 042	14 707
70-74	20 556	9 222	11 334	23 333	10 547	12 786
75-79	16 502	7 063	9 439	17 916	7 688	10 228
80-84	12 190	4 893	7 297	13 234	5 322	7 913
85-89	7 111	2 611	4 500	8 544	3 142	5 402
90-94	3 255	1 066	2 189	3 991	1 300	2 691
95-99	1 003	287	716	1 300	369	931
100 +	203	56	147	254	70	183

POPULATION BY AGE AND SEX (in thousands)

Age group	1950 Both sexes	1950 Males	1950 Females	1955 Both sexes	1955 Males	1955 Females	1960 Both sexes	1960 Males	1960 Females	1965 Both sexes	1965 Males	1965 Females
All ages	171 615	85 831	85 784	186 882	92 924	93 958	204 149	101 249	102 901	219 567	108 486	111 081
0-4	18 882	9 652	9 230	21 217	10 840	10 376	23 097	11 796	11 301	22 723	11 611	11 113
5-9	15 109	7 719	7 390	18 951	9 686	9 265	21 300	10 873	10 428	23 230	11 851	11 379
10-14	12 706	6 464	6 242	15 382	7 850	7 532	19 039	9 725	9 315	21 451	10 950	10 501
15-19	12 301	6 215	6 086	12 546	6 292	6 253	15 181	7 682	7 499	19 113	9 696	9 417
20-24	13 365	6 660	6 706	12 053	5 900	6 153	12 739	6 337	6 403	15 371	7 634	7 737
25-29	13 991	6 960	7 032	13 468	6 722	6 746	12 592	6 318	6 274	12 952	6 465	6 488
30-34	13 182	6 560	6 622	14 097	7 002	7 095	13 680	6 829	6 850	12 737	6 398	6 339
35-39	12 533	6 241	6 292	13 228	6 585	6 643	14 125	7 014	7 111	13 666	6 809	6 857
40-44	11 529	5 762	5 767	12 420	6 187	6 234	13 115	6 511	6 604	14 028	6 940	7 089
45-49	9 225	4 705	4 521	10 787	5 415	5 372	12 263	6 072	6 191	12 853	6 340	6 513
50-54	9 295	4 626	4 669	9 846	4 887	4 959	11 002	5 425	5 577	11 829	5 816	6 012
55-59	8 209	4 079	4 130	8 707	4 251	4 455	9 419	4 563	4 856	10 613	5 112	5 501
60-64	7 189	3 567	3 621	7 884	3 803	4 081	8 148	3 850	4 298	8 543	4 035	4 508
65-69	5 905	2 835	3 070	6 466	3 075	3 391	6 941	3 225	3 716	7 216	3 274	3 942
70-74	3 845	1 829	2 015	4 554	2 115	2 440	5 185	2 351	2 834	5 816	2 536	3 280
75-79	2 401	1 115	1 285	2 876	1 305	1 571	3 471	1 525	1 946	4 001	1 691	2 309
80 +	1 950	844	1 106	2 398	1 008	1 390	2 850	1 153	1 697	3 424	1 330	2 095

Age group	1970 Both sexes	1970 Males	1970 Females	1975 Both sexes	1975 Males	1975 Females	1980 Both sexes	1980 Males	1980 Females	1985 Both sexes	1985 Males	1985 Females
All ages	231 931	114 073	117 859	243 417	119 776	123 641	255 545	125 433	130 112	269 015	132 067	136 948
0-4	19 678	10 056	9 622	18 362	9 402	8 960	18 577	9 510	9 067	20 174	10 323	9 851
5-9	22 936	11 707	11 230	19 961	10 191	9 770	18 673	9 559	9 114	18 802	9 621	9 180
10-14	23 520	12 000	11 520	23 192	11 841	11 351	20 258	10 346	9 912	19 158	9 802	9 356
15-19	21 635	10 977	10 659	23 720	12 064	11 656	23 573	12 013	11 561	20 945	10 699	10 247
20-24	18 961	9 319	9 641	21 942	11 083	10 859	24 272	12 278	11 994	24 222	12 307	11 916
25-29	15 744	7 900	7 844	19 771	9 983	9 787	22 497	11 343	11 154	24 830	12 493	12 337
30-34	13 256	6 640	6 616	16 136	8 110	8 026	20 097	10 084	10 013	22 918	11 494	11 424
35-39	12 775	6 380	6 395	13 263	6 618	6 645	16 055	8 030	8 025	20 204	10 082	10 121
40-44	13 658	6 796	6 862	12 808	6 419	6 389	13 410	6 690	6 720	16 013	7 956	8 057
45-49	13 884	6 845	7 039	13 445	6 658	6 787	12 659	6 278	6 381	13 268	6 571	6 697
50-54	12 490	6 113	6 377	13 447	6 560	6 887	13 147	6 449	6 698	12 434	6 109	6 325
55-59	11 327	5 452	5 875	11 902	5 718	6 184	12 957	6 219	6 738	12 728	6 157	6 571
60-64	9 681	4 542	5 139	10 468	4 913	5 555	11 186	5 252	5 934	12 239	5 754	6 485
65-69	7 735	3 479	4 256	8 838	3 946	4 892	9 587	4 294	5 293	10 228	4 651	5 577
70-74	6 030	2 550	3 480	6 358	2 689	3 669	7 450	3 144	4 306	8 358	3 573	4 786
75-79	4 446	1 790	2 656	4 733	1 836	2 897	5 248	2 031	3 217	6 050	2 385	3 665
80 +	4 176	1 527	2 649	5 069	1 744	3 325	5 899	1 913	3 986	6 444	2 089	4 355

Age group	1990 Both sexes	1990 Males	1990 Females	1995 Both sexes	1995 Males	1995 Females	2000 Both sexes	2000 Males	2000 Females	2005 Both sexes	2005 Males	2005 Females
All ages	283 361	139 192	144 169	299 028	146 954	152 074	314 968	154 903	160 065	330 608	162 738	167 870
0-4	21 652	11 084	10 568	22 459	11 503	10 956	21 601	11 067	10 533	22 115	11 333	10 783
5-9	20 426	10 449	9 977	21 968	11 245	10 722	22 831	11 693	11 138	21 983	11 263	10 720
10-14	19 268	9 859	9 410	21 068	10 777	10 291	22 708	11 626	11 082	23 555	12 067	11 488
15-19	19 824	10 146	9 678	20 180	10 334	9 846	22 111	11 322	10 790	23 722	12 156	11 566
20-24	21 555	10 968	10 588	20 650	10 531	10 120	21 187	10 819	10 368	23 096	11 797	11 300
25-29	24 756	12 500	12 256	22 320	11 279	11 040	21 639	10 966	10 673	22 163	11 253	10 910
30-34	25 230	12 625	12 605	25 273	12 680	12 593	23 076	11 603	11 473	22 413	11 309	11 103
35-39	23 026	11 484	11 543	25 372	12 614	12 757	25 554	12 758	12 796	23 418	11 729	11 689
40-44	20 147	9 991	10 156	22 958	11 375	11 583	25 366	12 548	12 818	25 590	12 724	12 866
45-49	15 859	7 830	8 030	19 971	9 840	10 131	22 796	11 241	11 555	25 210	12 423	12 788
50-54	13 054	6 417	6 638	15 627	7 654	7 974	19 706	9 653	10 053	22 510	11 043	11 467
55-59	12 075	5 864	6 211	12 735	6 187	6 549	15 255	7 401	7 853	19 249	9 349	9 899
60-64	12 075	5 739	6 336	11 525	5 506	6 019	12 178	5 832	6 346	14 623	7 000	7 622
65-69	11 261	5 151	6 110	11 168	5 175	5 993	10 699	4 998	5 701	11 355	5 322	6 033
70-74	8 990	3 926	5 063	9 966	4 391	5 575	9 924	4 447	5 477	9 564	4 325	5 239
75-79	6 859	2 761	4 098	7 442	3 074	4 368	8 281	3 471	4 810	8 303	3 544	4 759
80 +	7 302	2 399	4 903	8 346	2 789	5 557	10 056	3 457	6 599	11 740	4 101	7 639

United Nations Department of Economic and Social Affairs/Population Division
World Population Prospects: The 2004 Revision, Volume II: Sex and Age Distribution of the World Population

128

POPULATION BY AGE AND SEX (in thousands)

Age group	2005 Both sexes	Males	Females	2010 Both sexes	Males	Females	2015 Both sexes	Males	Females	2020 Both sexes	Males	Females
All ages	330 608	162 738	167 870	346 062	170 480	175 582	360 905	177 901	183 003	375 000	184 898	190 101
0-4	22 115	11 333	10 783	22 810	11 689	11 120	23 150	11 863	11 286	23 277	11 928	11 348
5-9	21 983	11 263	10 720	22 493	11 526	10 967	23 177	11 878	11 300	23 515	12 051	11 465
10-14	23 555	12 067	11 488	22 701	11 633	11 068	23 189	11 885	11 304	23 869	12 234	11 635
15-19	23 722	12 156	11 566	24 558	12 591	11 967	23 677	12 144	11 534	24 160	12 393	11 767
20-24	23 096	11 797	11 300	24 696	12 627	12 069	25 505	13 049	12 456	24 624	12 603	12 021
25-29	22 163	11 253	10 910	24 057	12 225	11 833	25 625	13 039	12 586	26 432	13 461	12 971
30-34	22 413	11 309	11 103	22 928	11 594	11 334	24 791	12 549	12 242	26 354	13 361	12 994
35-39	23 418	11 729	11 689	22 763	11 444	11 319	23 265	11 723	11 543	25 124	12 674	12 450
40-44	25 590	12 724	12 866	23 485	11 718	11 767	22 840	11 442	11 398	23 349	11 724	11 625
45-49	25 210	12 423	12 788	25 446	12 606	12 840	23 378	11 625	11 754	22 758	11 363	11 395
50-54	22 510	11 043	11 467	24 903	12 212	12 691	25 151	12 400	12 750	23 143	11 455	11 687
55-59	19 249	9 349	9 899	22 006	10 710	11 297	24 366	11 856	12 510	24 641	12 059	12 582
60-64	14 623	7 000	7 622	18 480	8 863	9 616	21 166	10 178	10 987	23 482	11 298	12 185
65-69	11 355	5 322	6 033	13 680	6 416	7 264	17 338	8 158	9 180	19 919	9 408	10 511
70-74	9 564	4 325	5 239	10 209	4 639	5 571	12 363	5 632	6 731	15 738	7 204	8 534
75-79	8 303	3 544	4 759	8 065	3 480	4 585	8 678	3 771	4 907	10 582	4 621	5 961
80-84	6 222	2 414	3 808	6 298	2 494	3 804	6 187	2 485	3 702	6 730	2 730	4 000
85-89	3 519	1 190	2 329	4 022	1 385	2 637	4 133	1 460	2 673	4 119	1 482	2 637
90-94	1 489	402	1 087	1 807	505	1 302	2 105	602	1 503	2 200	650	1 550
95-99	427	84	343	549	111	439	680	143	537	808	175	633
100 +	83	11	72	107	14	93	140	19	121	176	25	151

Age group	2025 Both sexes	Males	Females	2030 Both sexes	Males	Females	2035 Both sexes	Males	Females	2040 Both sexes	Males	Females
All ages	388 032	191 295	196 737	400 079	197 142	202 937	410 996	202 425	208 571	420 805	207 218	213 587
0-4	23 239	11 909	11 330	23 524	12 055	11 470	23 864	12 229	11 636	24 244	12 423	11 821
5-9	23 644	12 116	11 528	23 607	12 097	11 510	23 894	12 243	11 650	24 234	12 418	11 817
10-14	24 208	12 407	11 800	24 337	12 473	11 864	24 302	12 454	11 847	24 588	12 601	11 987
15-19	24 841	12 743	12 099	25 183	12 918	12 265	25 314	12 985	12 329	25 281	12 967	12 313
20-24	25 111	12 855	12 256	25 796	13 207	12 589	26 141	13 384	12 757	26 276	13 454	12 822
25-29	25 559	13 020	12 539	26 050	13 275	12 775	26 739	13 630	13 109	27 089	13 810	13 279
30-34	27 167	13 787	13 381	26 307	13 354	12 953	26 804	13 612	13 192	27 500	13 971	13 529
35-39	26 691	13 487	13 204	27 513	13 918	13 594	26 668	13 496	13 172	27 175	13 760	13 415
40-44	25 207	12 674	12 533	26 779	13 480	13 290	27 612	13 927	13 685	26 786	13 517	13 270
45-49	23 278	11 651	11 627	25 137	12 600	12 538	26 713	13 418	13 295	27 557	13 862	13 695
50-54	22 558	11 215	11 343	23 093	11 512	11 581	24 950	12 459	12 491	26 530	13 278	13 253
55-59	22 719	11 166	11 553	22 183	10 855	11 328	22 739	11 200	11 470	24 393	12 007	12 386
60-64	23 801	11 525	12 276	22 000	10 705	11 295	21 534	10 535	10 998	22 119	10 861	11 259
65-69	22 170	10 487	11 683	22 542	10 744	11 798	20 909	10 024	10 884	20 533	9 907	10 626
70-74	18 158	8 356	9 803	20 297	9 368	10 929	20 725	9 652	11 073	19 306	9 055	10 250
75-79	13 556	5 960	7 596	15 733	6 964	8 769	17 690	7 868	9 822	18 158	8 163	9 995
80-84	8 283	3 384	4 899	10 707	4 414	6 293	12 536	5 215	7 322	14 210	5 952	8 259
85-89	4 540	1 655	2 884	5 664	2 086	3 578	7 418	2 764	4 654	8 790	3 314	5 476
90-94	2 229	674	1 555	2 500	768	1 732	3 174	989	2 186	4 226	1 337	2 889
95-99	859	193	666	889	205	684	1 019	240	779	1 320	317	1 003
100 +	214	31	183	237	35	202	253	39	214	290	46	244

Age group	2045 Both sexes	Males	Females	2050 Both sexes	Males	Females
All ages	429 669	211 653	218 016	437 950	215 915	222 035
0-4	24 534	12 571	11 963	24 734	12 673	12 061
5-9	24 615	12 612	12 003	24 906	12 761	12 145
10-14	24 930	12 775	12 154	25 311	12 970	12 340
15-19	25 569	13 115	12 454	25 912	13 290	12 622
20-24	26 246	13 439	12 808	26 538	13 588	12 950
25-29	27 229	13 883	13 346	27 205	13 871	13 333
30-34	27 857	14 156	13 701	28 004	14 234	13 771
35-39	27 879	14 125	13 754	28 246	14 316	13 930
40-44	27 305	13 789	13 516	28 020	14 160	13 860
45-49	26 756	13 467	13 289	27 288	13 747	13 540
50-54	27 389	13 731	13 658	26 619	13 355	13 264
55-59	26 176	13 027	13 150	27 054	13 491	13 563
60-64	23 964	11 798	12 167	25 551	12 618	12 933
65-69	21 155	10 253	10 902	22 980	11 178	11 803
70-74	19 041	9 000	10 041	19 699	9 364	10 335
75-79	17 005	7 712	9 294	16 869	7 722	9 147
80-84	14 690	6 232	8 458	13 858	5 943	7 915
85-89	10 081	3 837	6 244	10 537	4 074	6 463
90-94	5 084	1 633	3 451	5 918	1 926	3 993
95-99	1 791	438	1 352	2 192	547	1 645
100 +	372	61	312	508	85	423

United Nations Department of Economic and Social Affairs/Population Division
World Population Prospects: The 2004 Revision, Volume II: Sex and Age Distribution of the World Population

129

POPULATION BY AGE AND SEX (in thousands)

Age group	2005 Both sexes	Males	Females	2010 Both sexes	Males	Females	2015 Both sexes	Males	Females	2020 Both sexes	Males	Females
All ages	330 608	162 738	167 870	348 916	171 943	176 974	368 525	181 807	186 718	388 779	191 960	196 818
0-4	22 115	11 333	10 783	25 664	13 152	12 512	27 919	14 308	13 611	29 442	15 088	14 354
5-9	21 983	11 263	10 720	22 493	11 526	10 967	26 028	13 339	12 689	28 280	14 493	13 787
10-14	23 555	12 067	11 488	22 701	11 633	11 068	23 189	11 885	11 304	26 718	13 694	13 024
15-19	23 722	12 156	11 566	24 558	12 591	11 967	23 677	12 144	11 534	24 160	12 393	11 767
20-24	23 096	11 797	11 300	24 696	12 627	12 069	25 505	13 049	12 456	24 624	12 603	12 021
25-29	22 163	11 253	10 910	24 057	12 225	11 833	25 625	13 039	12 586	26 432	13 461	12 971
30-34	22 413	11 309	11 103	22 928	11 594	11 334	24 791	12 549	12 242	26 354	13 361	12 994
35-39	23 418	11 729	11 689	22 763	11 444	11 319	23 265	11 723	11 543	25 124	12 674	12 450
40-44	25 590	12 724	12 866	23 485	11 718	11 767	22 840	11 442	11 398	23 349	11 724	11 625
45-49	25 210	12 423	12 788	25 446	12 606	12 840	23 378	11 625	11 754	22 758	11 363	11 395
50-54	22 510	11 043	11 467	24 903	12 212	12 691	25 151	12 400	12 750	23 143	11 455	11 687
55-59	19 249	9 349	9 899	22 006	10 710	11 297	24 366	11 856	12 510	24 641	12 059	12 582
60-64	14 623	7 000	7 622	18 480	8 863	9 616	21 166	10 178	10 987	23 482	11 298	12 185
65-69	11 355	5 322	6 033	13 680	6 416	7 264	17 338	8 158	9 180	19 919	9 408	10 511
70-74	9 564	4 325	5 239	10 209	4 639	5 571	12 363	5 632	6 731	15 738	7 204	8 534
75-79	8 303	3 544	4 759	8 065	3 480	4 585	8 678	3 771	4 907	10 582	4 621	5 961
80-84	6 222	2 414	3 808	6 298	2 494	3 804	6 187	2 485	3 702	6 730	2 730	4 000
85-89	3 519	1 190	2 329	4 022	1 385	2 637	4 133	1 460	2 673	4 119	1 482	2 637
90-94	1 489	402	1 087	1 807	505	1 302	2 105	602	1 503	2 200	650	1 550
95-99	427	84	343	549	111	439	680	143	537	808	175	633
100 +	83	11	72	107	14	93	140	19	121	176	25	151

Age group	2025 Both sexes	Males	Females	2030 Both sexes	Males	Females	2035 Both sexes	Males	Females	2040 Both sexes	Males	Females
All ages	408 225	201 643	206 582	427 327	211 104	216 224	446 607	220 669	225 938	466 602	230 675	235 927
0-4	29 664	15 201	14 463	30 599	15 680	14 919	32 257	16 529	15 728	34 474	17 665	16 809
5-9	29 803	15 273	14 530	30 027	15 387	14 640	30 962	15 865	15 096	32 620	16 714	15 905
10-14	28 970	14 848	14 122	30 493	15 628	14 865	30 718	15 743	14 976	31 654	16 221	15 432
15-19	27 688	14 201	13 487	29 940	15 355	14 585	31 465	16 136	15 329	31 692	16 252	15 440
20-24	25 111	12 855	12 256	28 637	14 661	13 975	30 890	15 816	15 074	32 417	16 598	15 819
25-29	25 559	13 020	12 539	26 050	13 275	12 775	29 573	15 080	14 494	31 828	16 235	15 593
30-34	27 167	13 787	13 381	26 307	13 354	12 953	26 804	13 612	13 192	30 325	15 415	14 910
35-39	26 691	13 487	13 204	27 513	13 918	13 594	26 668	13 496	13 172	27 175	13 760	13 415
40-44	25 207	12 674	12 533	26 779	13 489	13 290	27 612	13 927	13 685	26 786	13 517	13 270
45-49	23 278	11 651	11 627	25 137	12 600	12 536	26 713	13 418	13 295	27 557	13 862	13 695
50-54	22 558	11 215	11 343	23 093	11 512	11 581	24 950	12 459	12 491	26 530	13 278	13 253
55-59	22 719	11 166	11 553	22 183	10 955	11 228	22 739	11 263	11 475	24 592	12 207	12 385
60-64	23 801	11 525	12 276	22 000	10 705	11 295	21 534	10 535	10 998	22 119	10 861	11 259
65-69	22 170	10 487	11 683	22 542	10 744	11 798	20 909	10 024	10 884	20 533	9 907	10 626
70-74	18 158	8 356	9 803	20 297	9 368	10 929	20 725	9 652	11 073	19 306	9 055	10 250
75-79	13 556	5 960	7 596	15 733	6 964	8 769	17 690	7 868	9 822	18 158	8 163	9 995
80-84	8 283	3 384	4 899	10 707	4 414	6 293	12 536	5 215	7 322	14 210	5 952	8 259
85-89	4 540	1 655	2 884	5 664	2 086	3 578	7 418	2 764	4 654	8 790	3 314	5 476
90-94	2 229	674	1 555	2 500	768	1 732	3 174	989	2 186	4 226	1 337	2 889
95-99	859	193	666	889	205	684	1 019	240	779	1 320	317	1 003
100 +	214	31	183	237	35	202	253	39	214	290	46	244

Age group	2045 Both sexes	Males	Females	2050 Both sexes	Males	Females
All ages	487 424	241 228	246 196	508 991	252 284	256 706
0-4	36 554	18 730	17 824	38 102	19 523	18 579
5-9	34 836	17 850	16 987	36 917	18 915	18 002
10-14	33 312	17 070	16 241	35 529	18 206	17 323
15-19	32 629	16 732	15 898	34 289	17 582	16 707
20-24	32 648	16 717	15 932	33 589	17 199	16 390
25-29	33 358	17 019	16 339	33 595	17 141	16 454
30-34	32 582	16 572	16 011	34 118	17 359	16 759
35-39	30 694	15 562	15 133	32 956	16 721	16 235
40-44	27 305	13 789	13 516	30 822	15 588	15 234
45-49	26 756	13 467	13 289	27 288	13 747	13 540
50-54	27 389	13 731	13 658	26 619	13 355	13 264
55-59	26 176	13 027	13 150	27 054	13 491	13 563
60-64	23 964	11 798	12 167	25 551	12 618	12 933
65-69	21 155	10 253	10 902	22 980	11 178	11 803
70-74	19 041	9 000	10 041	19 699	9 364	10 335
75-79	17 005	7 712	9 294	16 869	7 722	9 147
80-84	14 690	6 232	8 458	13 858	5 943	7 915
85-89	10 081	3 837	6 244	10 537	4 074	6 463
90-94	5 084	1 633	3 451	5 918	1 926	3 993
95-99	1 791	438	1 352	2 192	547	1 645
100 +	372	61	312	508	85	423

United Nations Department of Economic and Social Affairs/Population Division
World Population Prospects: The 2004 Revision, Volume II: Sex and Age Distribution of the World Population

130

POPULATION BY AGE AND SEX (in thousands)

Age group	2005 Both sexes	Males	Females	2010 Both sexes	Males	Females	2015 Both sexes	Males	Females	2020 Both sexes	Males	Females
All ages	330 608	162 738	167 870	343 208	169 017	174 191	353 283	173 995	179 288	361 215	177 834	183 302
0-4	22 115	11 333	10 783	19 955	10 226	9 729	18 379	9 419	8 961	17 107	8 766	8 341
5-9	21 983	11 263	10 720	22 493	11 526	10 967	20 326	10 416	9 910	18 750	9 608	9 142
10-14	23 555	12 067	11 488	22 701	11 633	11 068	23 189	11 885	11 304	21 019	10 773	10 246
15-19	23 722	12 156	11 566	24 558	12 591	11 967	23 677	12 144	11 534	24 160	12 393	11 767
20-24	23 096	11 797	11 300	24 696	12 627	12 069	25 505	13 049	12 456	24 624	12 603	12 021
25-29	22 163	11 253	10 910	24 057	12 225	11 833	25 625	13 039	12 586	26 432	13 461	12 971
30-34	22 413	11 309	11 103	22 928	11 594	11 334	24 791	12 549	12 242	26 354	13 361	12 994
35-39	23 418	11 729	11 689	22 763	11 444	11 319	23 265	11 723	11 543	25 124	12 674	12 450
40-44	25 590	12 724	12 866	23 485	11 718	11 767	22 840	11 442	11 398	23 349	11 724	11 625
45-49	25 210	12 423	12 788	25 446	12 606	12 840	23 378	11 625	11 754	22 758	11 363	11 395
50-54	22 510	11 043	11 467	24 903	12 212	12 691	25 151	12 400	12 750	23 143	11 455	11 687
55-59	19 249	9 349	9 899	22 006	10 710	11 297	24 366	11 856	12 510	24 641	12 059	12 582
60-64	14 623	7 000	7 622	18 480	8 863	9 616	21 166	10 178	10 987	23 482	11 298	12 185
65-69	11 355	5 322	6 033	13 680	6 416	7 264	17 338	8 158	9 180	19 919	9 408	10 511
70-74	9 564	4 325	5 239	10 209	4 639	5 571	12 363	5 632	6 731	15 738	7 204	8 534
75-79	8 303	3 544	4 759	8 065	3 480	4 585	8 678	3 771	4 907	10 582	4 621	5 961
80-84	6 222	2 414	3 808	6 298	2 494	3 804	6 187	2 485	3 702	6 730	2 730	4 000
85-89	3 519	1 190	2 329	4 022	1 385	2 637	4 133	1 460	2 673	4 119	1 482	2 637
90-94	1 489	402	1 087	1 807	505	1 302	2 105	602	1 503	2 200	650	1 550
95-99	427	84	343	549	111	439	680	143	537	808	175	633
100 +	83	11	72	107	14	93	140	19	121	176	25	151

Age group	2025 Both sexes	Males	Females	2030 Both sexes	Males	Females	2035 Both sexes	Males	Females	2040 Both sexes	Males	Females
All ages	367 887	180 971	186 916	373 182	183 360	189 822	376 593	184 800	191 793	377 841	185 213	192 628
0-4	16 866	8 643	8 223	16 754	8 585	8 169	16 329	8 367	7 962	15 640	8 014	7 626
5-9	17 480	8 957	8 523	17 240	8 834	8 406	17 129	8 777	8 352	16 705	8 559	8 146
10-14	19 445	9 966	9 478	18 177	9 316	8 861	17 937	9 193	8 744	17 827	9 136	8 691
15-19	21 995	11 284	10 711	20 425	10 480	9 945	19 159	9 831	9 328	18 922	9 709	9 212
20-24	25 111	12 855	12 256	22 955	11 752	11 203	21 391	10 952	10 439	20 131	10 307	9 824
25-29	25 559	13 020	12 539	26 050	13 275	12 775	23 905	12 180	11 725	22 350	11 385	10 964
30-34	27 167	13 787	13 381	26 307	13 354	12 953	26 804	13 612	13 192	24 674	12 527	12 147
35-39	26 691	13 487	13 204	27 513	13 918	13 594	26 668	13 496	13 172	27 175	13 760	13 415
40-44	26 207	12 674	12 533	26 779	13 489	13 290	27 812	10 927	13 685	26 786	13 517	13 270
45-49	23 278	11 651	11 627	25 137	12 600	12 536	26 713	13 418	13 295	27 557	13 862	13 695
50-54	22 559	11 216	11 343	23 093	11 512	11 581	24 950	12 459	12 491	26 530	13 278	13 253
55-59	22 719	11 166	11 553	22 183	10 955	11 228	22 739	11 263	11 475	24 503	12 207	12 385
60-64	23 801	11 525	12 276	22 000	10 705	11 295	21 534	10 535	10 998	22 119	10 861	11 259
65-69	22 170	10 487	11 683	22 542	10 744	11 798	20 909	10 024	10 884	20 533	9 907	10 626
70-74	18 158	8 356	9 803	20 297	9 368	10 929	20 725	9 652	11 073	19 306	9 055	10 250
75-79	13 556	5 960	7 596	16 700	6 931	8 769	17 690	7 868	9 822	18 158	8 163	9 995
80-84	8 283	3 384	4 899	10 707	4 414	6 293	12 536	5 215	7 322	14 210	5 952	8 258
85-89	4 540	1 655	2 884	5 664	2 086	3 578	7 418	2 764	4 654	8 790	3 314	5 476
90-94	2 229	674	1 555	2 500	768	1 732	3 174	989	2 186	4 226	1 337	2 889
95-99	859	193	666	889	205	684	1 019	240	779	1 320	317	1 003
100 +	214	31	183	237	35	202	253	39	214	290	46	244

Age group	2045 Both sexes	Males	Females	2050 Both sexes	Males	Females
All ages	377 111	184 741	192 370	375 046	183 714	191 332
0-4	14 881	7 625	7 256	14 309	7 331	6 978
5-9	16 017	8 207	7 811	15 260	7 818	7 442
10-14	17 403	8 919	8 484	16 716	8 567	8 150
15-19	18 813	9 654	9 159	18 391	9 437	8 954
20-24	19 897	10 187	9 709	19 791	10 133	9 657
25-29	21 097	10 745	10 351	20 867	10 628	10 238
30-34	23 130	11 740	11 390	21 887	11 106	10 780
35-39	25 064	12 688	12 376	23 535	11 910	11 624
40-44	27 305	13 789	13 516	25 217	12 731	12 486
45-49	26 756	13 467	13 289	27 288	13 747	13 540
50-54	27 389	13 731	13 658	26 619	13 355	13 264
55-59	26 176	13 027	13 150	27 054	13 491	13 563
60-64	23 964	11 798	12 167	25 551	12 618	12 933
65-69	21 155	10 253	10 902	22 980	11 178	11 803
70-74	19 041	9 000	10 041	19 699	9 364	10 335
75-79	17 005	7 712	9 294	16 869	7 722	9 147
80-84	14 690	6 232	8 458	13 858	5 943	7 915
85-89	10 081	3 837	6 244	10 537	4 074	6 463
90-94	5 084	1 633	3 451	5 918	1 926	3 993
95-99	1 791	438	1 352	2 192	547	1 645
100 +	372	61	312	508	85	423

United Nations Department of Economic and Social Affairs/Population Division
World Population Prospects: The 2004 Revision, Volume II: Sex and Age Distribution of the World Population

131

POPULATION BY AGE AND SEX (in thousands)

Age group	1950 Both sexes	1950 Males	1950 Females	1955 Both sexes	1955 Males	1955 Females	1960 Both sexes	1960 Males	1960 Females	1965 Both sexes	1965 Males	1965 Females
All ages	12 807	6 519	6 288	14 260	7 257	7 003	15 884	8 064	7 820	17 788	8 994	8 794
0-4	1 546	792	754	1 741	888	853	1 943	994	949	2 183	1 117	1 066
5-9	1 237	633	604	1 568	802	766	1 747	890	857	1 966	1 005	961
10-14	1 042	534	508	1 262	646	616	1 599	818	781	1 790	913	877
15-19	966	498	468	1 062	548	514	1 281	658	624	1 652	845	808
20-24	1 030	536	494	993	519	473	1 107	573	533	1 330	683	646
25-29	1 036	532	504	1 082	569	513	1 042	545	497	1 155	595	560
30-34	931	474	457	1 075	556	518	1 115	587	528	1 072	558	514
35-39	915	469	446	951	485	466	1 089	562	527	1 127	588	539
40-44	809	421	387	925	475	450	953	486	468	1 101	565	536
45-49	704	367	338	800	417	383	914	468	446	939	476	463
50-54	620	310	310	677	351	326	774	400	374	886	449	437
55-59	549	270	279	576	285	292	637	324	313	731	373	359
60-64	484	240	244	497	236	261	528	254	275	584	288	296
65-69	385	187	198	419	199	220	433	196	237	471	215	256
70-74	264	124	140	298	136	162	342	153	189	353	149	204
75-79	165	75	90	190	84	106	213	90	123	247	101	146
80 +	125	54	70	143	60	83	166	66	100	201	74	127

Age group	1970 Both sexes	1970 Males	1970 Females	1975 Both sexes	1975 Males	1975 Females	1980 Both sexes	1980 Males	1980 Females	1985 Both sexes	1985 Males	1985 Females
All ages	19 639	9 926	9 713	21 284	10 723	10 561	22 893	11 491	11 402	24 700	12 385	12 315
0-4	2 183	1 116	1 066	2 305	1 179	1 126	2 215	1 134	1 081	2 386	1 225	1 161
5-9	2 154	1 101	1 052	2 195	1 122	1 073	2 275	1 164	1 111	2 233	1 145	1 089
10-14	2 027	1 037	990	2 163	1 107	1 056	2 246	1 148	1 098	2 302	1 178	1 124
15-19	1 837	937	900	2 029	1 036	993	2 147	1 097	1 049	2 264	1 155	1 109
20-24	1 687	868	818	1 831	931	900	2 019	1 025	993	2 163	1 102	1 061
25-29	1 385	716	669	1 712	872	840	1 850	931	920	2 048	1 034	1 014
30-34	1 210	626	584	1 406	725	681	1 720	871	849	1 882	946	936
35-39	1 103	573	530	1 215	626	589	1 417	726	691	1 729	875	854
40-44	1 139	594	545	1 102	571	531	1 209	624	585	1 418	726	692
45-49	1 090	557	533	1 111	575	536	1 079	556	522	1 193	612	581
50-54	910	457	453	1 038	527	512	1 078	552	525	1 052	538	514
55-59	843	420	423	856	423	432	981	492	489	1 036	524	512
60-64	675	334	341	761	369	392	817	393	424	920	451	469
65-69	514	242	272	591	277	314	690	321	369	740	342	397
70-74	388	165	223	429	189	239	509	223	286	590	259	331
75-79	261	100	162	279	108	171	329	133	196	400	161	239
80 +	232	82	151	261	85	175	312	99	213	345	112	233

Age group	1990 Both sexes	1990 Males	1990 Females	1995 Both sexes	1995 Males	1995 Females	2000 Both sexes	2000 Males	2000 Females	2005 Both sexes	2005 Males	2005 Females
All ages	26 721	13 457	13 264	28 834	14 411	14 422	30 949	15 431	15 518	33 056	16 490	16 566
0-4	2 487	1 288	1 199	2 698	1 387	1 310	2 754	1 416	1 339	2 699	1 388	1 311
5-9	2 366	1 223	1 143	2 554	1 323	1 230	2 748	1 415	1 333	2 753	1 415	1 338
10-14	2 242	1 146	1 095	2 440	1 260	1 180	2 605	1 349	1 256	2 756	1 418	1 338
15-19	2 392	1 214	1 178	2 305	1 174	1 131	2 444	1 261	1 183	2 630	1 360	1 270
20-24	2 245	1 138	1 107	2 325	1 163	1 161	2 244	1 133	1 111	2 503	1 287	1 215
25-29	2 225	1 119	1 105	2 276	1 129	1 147	2 303	1 134	1 169	2 318	1 167	1 151
30-34	2 097	1 056	1 041	2 257	1 118	1 139	2 331	1 144	1 186	2 366	1 164	1 202
35-39	1 903	958	944	2 142	1 063	1 080	2 302	1 135	1 167	2 372	1 164	1 207
40-44	1 775	908	867	1 938	970	968	2 152	1 064	1 089	2 318	1 142	1 176
45-49	1 386	716	670	1 746	883	863	1 933	963	970	2 148	1 060	1 088
50-54	1 168	602	565	1 365	698	667	1 731	871	860	1 910	949	961
55-59	1 004	516	488	1 131	575	556	1 330	675	654	1 690	846	844
60-64	982	498	484	961	482	478	1 074	540	534	1 275	641	634
65-69	867	420	447	894	437	456	889	437	452	1 000	494	506
70-74	635	290	346	741	342	399	801	379	422	797	380	417
75-79	484	204	280	517	218	298	628	275	354	676	304	372
80 +	464	158	306	548	189	360	679	241	438	847	312	535

132

United Nations Department of Economic and Social Affairs/Population Division
World Population Prospects: The 2004 Revision, Volume II: Sex and Age Distribution of the World Population

POPULATION BY AGE AND SEX (in thousands)

Age group	2005 Both sexes	Males	Females	2010 Both sexes	Males	Females	2015 Both sexes	Males	Females	2020 Both sexes	Males	Females
All ages	33 056	16 490	16 566	35 017	17 477	17 540	38 952	18 450	18 502	38 909	19 430	19 479
0-4	2 699	1 388	1 311	2 693	1 385	1 308	2 760	1 420	1 340	2 884	1 483	1 400
5-9	2 753	1 415	1 338	2 697	1 387	1 310	2 694	1 386	1 308	2 763	1 422	1 342
10-14	2 756	1 418	1 338	2 755	1 415	1 339	2 700	1 388	1 312	2 698	1 387	1 311
15-19	2 630	1 360	1 270	2 774	1 426	1 348	2 773	1 424	1 350	2 720	1 397	1 323
20-24	2 503	1 287	1 215	2 683	1 384	1 300	2 828	1 450	1 377	2 829	1 449	1 380
25-29	2 318	1 167	1 151	2 572	1 319	1 253	2 753	1 416	1 337	2 898	1 483	1 415
30-34	2 366	1 164	1 202	2 377	1 196	1 182	2 631	1 347	1 284	2 814	1 445	1 369
35-39	2 372	1 164	1 207	2 402	1 182	1 221	2 416	1 214	1 201	2 670	1 366	1 304
40-44	2 318	1 142	1 176	2 384	1 170	1 214	2 416	1 188	1 228	2 431	1 222	1 209
45-49	2 148	1 060	1 088	2 309	1 136	1 173	2 376	1 165	1 211	2 409	1 184	1 225
50-54	1 910	949	961	2 122	1 044	1 078	2 281	1 119	1 162	2 349	1 149	1 200
55-59	1 690	846	844	1 866	922	944	2 074	1 016	1 058	2 230	1 089	1 140
60-64	1 275	641	634	1 624	806	818	1 795	879	916	1 998	970	1 028
65-69	1 000	494	506	1 194	591	603	1 527	746	781	1 691	816	875
70-74	797	380	417	899	432	468	1 082	522	560	1 391	663	728
75-79	676	304	372	676	308	368	767	353	414	931	431	500
80-84	478	193	285	520	218	302	525	224	301	601	260	341
85-89	248	86	162	310	113	198	344	131	214	353	137	216
90-94	95	27	68	122	37	86	159	50	109	181	60	121
95-99	22	5	17	33	8	25	45	11	33	60	16	44
100 +	3	1	3	5	1	4	8	2	6	11	2	9

Age group	2025 Both sexes	Males	Females	2030 Both sexes	Males	Females	2035 Both sexes	Males	Females	2040 Both sexes	Males	Females
All ages	40 809	20 375	20 434	42 543	21 231	21 312	44 052	21 972	22 080	45 356	22 614	22 742
0-4	2 940	1 512	1 427	2 917	1 501	1 416	2 855	1 469	1 387	2 820	1 451	1 370
5-9	2 890	1 487	1 403	2 948	1 517	1 431	2 927	1 506	1 421	2 867	1 475	1 392
10-14	2 769	1 424	1 345	2 897	1 490	1 407	2 955	1 520	1 435	2 935	1 509	1 426
15-19	2 720	1 397	1 323	2 792	1 435	1 358	2 921	1 501	1 420	2 980	1 531	1 449
20-24	2 779	1 424	1 355	2 781	1 425	1 355	2 854	1 463	1 391	2 983	1 530	1 454
25-29	2 902	1 483	1 419	2 854	1 459	1 395	2 858	1 462	1 396	2 933	1 500	1 433
30-34	2 959	1 513	1 447	2 965	1 514	1 452	2 919	1 490	1 429	2 925	1 494	1 431
35-39	2 854	1 464	1 390	3 000	1 532	1 467	3 007	1 534	1 473	2 963	1 512	1 451
40-44	2 005	1 073	1 312	2 870	1 471	1 399	3 016	1 540	1 476	3 025	1 543	1 482
45-49	2 426	1 218	1 208	2 680	1 369	1 311	2 865	1 467	1 398	3 010	1 536	1 475
50-54	2 383	1 168	1 214	2 402	1 203	1 198	2 654	1 352	1 302	2 839	1 451	1 388
55-59	2 298	1 119	1 179	2 332	1 139	1 193	2 354	1 175	1 179	2 603	1 320	1 282
60-64	2 148	1 041	1 108	2 217	1 070	1 146	2 251	1 090	1 160	2 275	1 126	1 149
65-69	1 885	902	983	2 028	968	1 059	2 095	998	1 097	2 129	1 017	1 111
70-74	1 544	727	817	1 725	806	918	1 857	866	991	1 921	894	1 027
75-79	1 204	552	652	1 342	608	734	1 504	677	827	1 623	730	893
80-84	737	321	416	962	416	546	1 080	462	618	1 217	518	700
85-89	409	161	248	510	203	307	676	268	409	768	300	468
90-94	190	64	126	225	78	148	288	100	188	391	135	256
95-99	70	20	51	76	22	55	93	27	66	123	36	87
100 +	15	3	12	19	4	15	22	5	17	27	6	21

Age group	2045 Both sexes	Males	Females	2050 Both sexes	Males	Females
All ages	46 514	23 191	23 323	47 572	23 726	23 847
0-4	2 832	1 457	1 376	2 866	1 474	1 392
5-9	2 833	1 457	1 376	2 846	1 464	1 383
10-14	2 875	1 479	1 397	2 842	1 461	1 381
15-19	2 960	1 521	1 439	2 901	1 490	1 411
20-24	3 043	1 561	1 483	3 024	1 551	1 473
25-29	3 063	1 567	1 496	3 124	1 599	1 525
30-34	3 001	1 533	1 468	3 132	1 600	1 531
35-39	2 971	1 516	1 454	3 048	1 556	1 491
40-44	2 983	1 522	1 461	2 993	1 527	1 465
45-49	3 021	1 539	1 482	2 982	1 520	1 462
50-54	2 983	1 519	1 464	2 995	1 523	1 472
55-59	2 787	1 418	1 369	2 928	1 485	1 443
60-64	2 517	1 267	1 250	2 699	1 362	1 336
65-69	2 154	1 052	1 102	2 387	1 186	1 202
70-74	1 954	914	1 041	1 981	947	1 034
75-79	1 684	756	928	1 716	774	941
80-84	1 319	561	758	1 374	584	790
85-89	875	341	534	956	373	582
90-94	452	154	298	525	179	346
95-99	171	49	122	203	57	146
100 +	36	8	28	51	12	39

POPULATION BY AGE AND SEX (in thousands)

Age group	2005 Both sexes	Males	Females	2010 Both sexes	Males	Females	2015 Both sexes	Males	Females	2020 Both sexes	Males	Females
All ages	33 056	16 490	16 566	35 313	17 629	17 684	37 751	18 861	18 891	40 371	20 181	20 190
0-4	2 699	1 388	1 311	2 989	1 537	1 452	3 264	1 679	1 585	3 549	1 825	1 723
5-9	2 753	1 415	1 338	2 697	1 387	1 310	2 989	1 537	1 452	3 266	1 680	1 586
10-14	2 756	1 418	1 338	2 755	1 415	1 339	2 700	1 388	1 312	2 993	1 539	1 454
15-19	2 630	1 360	1 270	2 774	1 426	1 348	2 773	1 424	1 350	2 720	1 397	1 323
20-24	2 503	1 287	1 215	2 683	1 384	1 300	2 828	1 450	1 377	2 829	1 449	1 380
25-29	2 318	1 167	1 151	2 572	1 319	1 253	2 753	1 416	1 337	2 898	1 483	1 415
30-34	2 366	1 164	1 202	2 377	1 196	1 182	2 631	1 347	1 284	2 814	1 445	1 369
35-39	2 372	1 164	1 207	2 402	1 182	1 221	2 416	1 214	1 201	2 670	1 366	1 304
40-44	2 318	1 142	1 176	2 384	1 170	1 214	2 416	1 188	1 228	2 431	1 222	1 209
45-49	2 148	1 060	1 088	2 309	1 136	1 173	2 376	1 165	1 211	2 409	1 184	1 225
50-54	1 910	949	961	2 122	1 044	1 078	2 281	1 119	1 162	2 349	1 149	1 200
55-59	1 690	846	844	1 866	922	944	2 074	1 016	1 058	2 230	1 089	1 140
60-64	1 275	641	634	1 624	806	818	1 795	879	916	1 998	970	1 028
65-69	1 000	494	506	1 194	591	603	1 527	746	781	1 691	816	875
70-74	797	380	417	899	432	468	1 082	522	560	1 391	663	728
75-79	676	304	372	676	308	368	767	353	414	931	431	500
80-84	478	193	285	520	218	302	525	224	301	601	260	341
85-89	248	86	162	310	113	198	344	131	214	353	137	216
90-94	95	27	68	122	37	86	159	50	109	181	60	121
95-99	22	5	17	33	8	25	45	11	33	60	16	44
100 +	3	1	3	5	1	4	8	2	6	11	2	9

Age group	2025 Both sexes	Males	Females	2030 Both sexes	Males	Females	2035 Both sexes	Males	Females	2040 Both sexes	Males	Females
All ages	42 954	21 478	21 476	45 403	22 702	22 701	47 745	23 871	23 874	50 095	25 051	25 044
0-4	3 626	1 865	1 761	3 637	1 871	1 766	3 694	1 900	1 794	3 873	1 992	1 881
5-9	3 553	1 828	1 725	3 632	1 869	1 764	3 645	1 875	1 770	3 704	1 905	1 799
10-14	3 271	1 682	1 589	3 559	1 830	1 729	3 639	1 871	1 767	3 652	1 878	1 774
15-19	3 015	1 549	1 466	3 293	1 692	1 601	3 582	1 841	1 741	3 662	1 882	1 780
20-24	2 779	1 424	1 355	3 074	1 576	1 498	3 354	1 720	1 634	3 643	1 869	1 774
25-29	2 902	1 483	1 419	2 854	1 459	1 395	3 151	1 612	1 539	3 431	1 756	1 675
30-34	2 959	1 513	1 447	2 965	1 514	1 452	2 919	1 490	1 429	3 217	1 644	1 573
35-39	2 854	1 464	1 390	3 000	1 532	1 467	3 007	1 534	1 473	2 963	1 512	1 451
40-44	2 685	1 373	1 312	2 870	1 471	1 399	3 016	1 540	1 476	3 025	1 543	1 482
45-49	2 426	1 218	1 208	2 680	1 369	1 311	2 865	1 467	1 398	3 010	1 536	1 475
50-54	2 383	1 168	1 214	2 402	1 203	1 198	2 654	1 352	1 302	2 839	1 451	1 388
55-59	2 298	1 119	1 179	2 332	1 139	1 193	2 354	1 175	1 179	2 603	1 320	1 282
60-64	2 148	1 041	1 108	2 217	1 070	1 146	2 251	1 090	1 160	2 275	1 126	1 149
65-69	1 885	902	983	2 028	968	1 059	2 095	998	1 097	2 129	1 017	1 111
70-74	1 544	727	817	1 725	806	918	1 857	866	991	1 921	894	1 027
75-79	1 204	552	652	1 342	608	734	1 504	677	827	1 623	730	893
80-84	737	321	416	962	416	546	1 080	462	618	1 217	518	700
85-89	409	161	248	510	203	307	676	268	409	768	300	468
90-94	190	64	126	225	78	148	288	100	188	391	135	256
95-99	70	20	51	76	22	55	93	27	66	123	36	87
100 +	15	3	12	19	4	15	22	5	17	27	6	21

Age group	2045 Both sexes	Males	Females	2050 Both sexes	Males	Females
All ages	52 530	26 284	26 246	55 029	27 559	27 470
0-4	4 117	2 117	2 000	4 317	2 220	2 097
5-9	3 885	1 998	1 887	4 129	2 124	2 006
10-14	3 711	1 909	1 803	3 892	2 001	1 891
15-19	3 676	1 889	1 787	3 736	1 920	1 816
20-24	3 725	1 911	1 814	3 739	1 919	1 821
25-29	3 721	1 905	1 816	3 804	1 948	1 856
30-34	3 498	1 788	1 710	3 789	1 938	1 851
35-39	3 261	1 666	1 596	3 543	1 811	1 733
40-44	2 983	1 522	1 461	3 282	1 676	1 606
45-49	3 021	1 539	1 482	2 982	1 520	1 462
50-54	2 983	1 519	1 464	2 995	1 523	1 472
55-59	2 787	1 418	1 369	2 928	1 485	1 443
60-64	2 517	1 267	1 250	2 699	1 362	1 336
65-69	2 154	1 052	1 102	2 387	1 186	1 202
70-74	1 954	914	1 041	1 981	947	1 034
75-79	1 684	756	928	1 716	774	941
80-84	1 319	561	758	1 374	584	790
85-89	875	341	534	956	373	582
90-94	452	154	298	525	179	346
95-99	171	49	122	203	57	146
100 +	36	8	28	51	12	39

United Nations Department of Economic and Social Affairs/Population Division
World Population Prospects: The 2004 Revision, Volume II: Sex and Age Distribution of the World Population

134

POPULATION BY AGE AND SEX (in thousands)

Age group	2005 Both sexes	Males	Females	2010 Both sexes	Males	Females	2015 Both sexes	Males	Females	2020 Both sexes	Males	Females
All ages	33 056	16 490	16 566	34 720	17 325	17 396	36 153	18 039	18 114	37 446	18 677	18 768
0-4	2 699	1 388	1 311	2 396	1 232	1 164	2 256	1 161	1 095	2 217	1 141	1 076
5-9	2 753	1 415	1 338	2 697	1 387	1 310	2 398	1 234	1 165	2 261	1 164	1 098
10-14	2 756	1 418	1 338	2 755	1 415	1 339	2 700	1 388	1 312	2 403	1 236	1 167
15-19	2 630	1 360	1 270	2 774	1 426	1 348	2 773	1 424	1 350	2 720	1 397	1 323
20-24	2 503	1 287	1 215	2 683	1 384	1 300	2 828	1 450	1 377	2 829	1 449	1 380
25-29	2 318	1 167	1 151	2 572	1 319	1 253	2 753	1 416	1 337	2 898	1 483	1 415
30-34	2 366	1 164	1 202	2 377	1 196	1 182	2 631	1 347	1 284	2 814	1 445	1 369
35-39	2 372	1 164	1 207	2 402	1 182	1 221	2 416	1 214	1 201	2 670	1 366	1 304
40-44	2 318	1 142	1 176	2 384	1 170	1 214	2 416	1 188	1 228	2 431	1 222	1 209
45-49	2 148	1 060	1 088	2 309	1 136	1 173	2 376	1 165	1 211	2 409	1 184	1 225
50-54	1 910	949	961	2 122	1 044	1 078	2 281	1 119	1 162	2 349	1 149	1 200
55-59	1 690	846	844	1 866	922	944	2 074	1 016	1 058	2 230	1 089	1 140
60-64	1 275	641	634	1 624	806	818	1 795	879	916	1 998	970	1 028
65-69	1 000	494	506	1 194	591	603	1 527	746	781	1 691	816	875
70-74	797	380	417	899	432	468	1 082	522	560	1 391	663	728
75-79	676	304	372	676	308	368	767	353	414	931	431	500
80-84	478	193	285	520	218	302	525	224	301	601	260	341
85-89	248	86	162	310	113	198	344	131	214	353	137	216
90-94	95	27	68	122	37	86	159	50	109	181	60	121
95-99	22	5	17	33	8	25	45	11	33	60	16	44
100 +	3	1	3	5	1	4	8	2	6	11	2	9

Age group	2025 Both sexes	Males	Females	2030 Both sexes	Males	Females	2035 Both sexes	Males	Females	2040 Both sexes	Males	Females
All ages	38 657	19 269	19 389	39 686	19 762	19 924	40 434	20 112	20 322	40 866	20 306	20 560
0-4	2 249	1 157	1 092	2 207	1 136	1 072	2 090	1 075	1 015	1 941	998	943
5-9	2 226	1 145	1 080	2 259	1 162	1 097	2 219	1 142	1 077	2 103	1 082	1 021
10-14	2 268	1 166	1 102	2 233	1 148	1 084	2 267	1 166	1 101	2 227	1 145	1 082
15-19	2 426	1 246	1 180	2 292	1 177	1 115	2 258	1 160	1 098	2 292	1 178	1 115
20-24	2 779	1 424	1 355	2 487	1 275	1 213	2 355	1 207	1 148	2 322	1 190	1 132
25-29	2 902	1 483	1 419	2 854	1 459	1 395	2 565	1 311	1 254	2 435	1 244	1 190
30-34	2 959	1 513	1 447	2 965	1 514	1 452	2 919	1 490	1 429	2 633	1 344	1 289
35-39	2 854	1 464	1 390	3 000	1 532	1 467	3 007	1 534	1 473	2 963	1 512	1 451
40-44	2 685	1 373	1 312	2 870	1 471	1 399	3 016	1 540	1 476	3 025	1 543	1 482
45-49	2 426	1 218	1 208	2 680	1 369	1 311	2 865	1 467	1 398	3 010	1 536	1 475
50-54	2 383	1 168	1 214	2 402	1 203	1 198	2 654	1 352	1 302	2 839	1 451	1 388
55-59	2 298	1 119	1 179	2 332	1 139	1 193	2 354	1 175	1 179	2 603	1 320	1 282
60-64	2 148	1 041	1 108	2 217	1 070	1 146	2 251	1 090	1 160	2 275	1 126	1 149
65-69	1 885	902	983	2 028	968	1 059	2 095	998	1 097	2 129	1 017	1 111
70-74	1 544	727	817	1 725	806	918	1 857	866	991	1 921	894	1 027
75-79	1 204	552	652	1 342	608	734	1 504	677	827	1 623	730	893
80-84	737	321	416	962	416	546	1 080	462	618	1 217	519	700
85-89	409	161	248	510	203	307	676	268	409	768	300	468
90-94	190	64	126	225	78	148	288	100	188	391	135	256
95-99	70	20	51	76	22	55	93	27	66	123	36	87
100 +	15	3	12	19	4	15	22	5	17	27	6	21

Age group	2045 Both sexes	Males	Females	2050 Both sexes	Males	Females
All ages	41 012	20 362	20 650	40 942	20 317	20 625
0-4	1 811	931	880	1 728	888	839
5-9	1 956	1 006	950	1 827	939	887
10-14	2 112	1 086	1 026	1 965	1 010	955
15-19	2 253	1 157	1 096	2 138	1 098	1 040
20-24	2 357	1 208	1 149	2 319	1 188	1 131
25-29	2 403	1 228	1 175	2 439	1 247	1 192
30-34	2 504	1 278	1 226	2 473	1 262	1 211
35-39	2 680	1 367	1 313	2 553	1 302	1 250
40-44	2 983	1 522	1 461	2 703	1 379	1 324
45-49	3 021	1 539	1 482	2 982	1 520	1 462
50-54	2 983	1 519	1 464	2 995	1 523	1 472
55-59	2 787	1 418	1 369	2 928	1 485	1 443
60-64	2 517	1 267	1 250	2 699	1 362	1 336
65-69	2 154	1 052	1 102	2 387	1 186	1 202
70-74	1 954	914	1 041	1 981	947	1 034
75-79	1 684	756	928	1 716	774	941
80-84	1 319	561	758	1 374	584	790
85-89	875	341	534	956	373	582
90-94	452	154	298	525	179	346
95-99	171	49	122	203	57	146
100 +	36	8	28	51	12	39

POPULATION BY AGE AND SEX (in thousands)

Age group	1950 Both sexes	Males	Females	1955 Both sexes	Males	Females	1960 Both sexes	Males	Females	1965 Both sexes	Males	Females
All ages	10 127	5 103	5 024	11 337	5 732	5 605	12 648	6 387	6 262	14 153	7 125	7 029
0-4	1 117	572	545	1 238	633	605	1 381	708	673	1 487	762	725
5-9	884	450	434	1 173	600	573	1 275	651	624	1 444	739	705
10-14	733	373	360	922	470	451	1 217	623	594	1 343	687	656
15-19	691	353	338	762	391	372	954	489	466	1 274	653	621
20-24	785	404	381	731	380	352	822	424	399	1 019	523	496
25-29	824	419	405	858	450	408	801	417	384	896	460	436
30-34	750	377	373	880	452	428	905	475	431	848	439	409
35-39	762	387	375	786	397	390	909	466	444	939	488	451
40-44	682	353	329	787	402	386	804	406	398	941	480	462
45-49	600	311	289	689	358	331	791	403	388	808	406	402
50-54	534	264	270	588	304	284	678	350	328	782	395	387
55-59	491	239	252	507	248	259	563	286	277	652	332	320
60-64	435	214	221	452	213	239	474	225	248	527	260	268
65-69	342	164	178	386	181	204	401	179	221	432	196	236
70-74	234	108	126	271	123	149	320	143	177	330	138	192
75-79	148	66	82	173	76	98	198	83	116	236	96	140
80 +	115	49	66	133	55	78	156	61	95	193	71	122

Age group	1970 Both sexes	Males	Females	1975 Both sexes	Males	Females	1980 Both sexes	Males	Females	1985 Both sexes	Males	Females
All ages	15 548	7 823	7 725	16 708	8 376	8 332	17 751	8 858	8 893	18 916	9 425	9 491
0-4	1 505	770	735	1 557	796	761	1 381	706	674	1 475	756	718
5-9	1 558	798	760	1 543	790	754	1 551	792	758	1 421	727	694
10-14	1 503	770	733	1 583	811	771	1 603	819	783	1 592	814	778
15-19	1 389	710	679	1 523	779	744	1 586	812	774	1 640	837	803
20-24	1 327	683	644	1 403	714	689	1 539	782	756	1 616	824	791
25-29	1 083	559	524	1 372	698	674	1 442	724	718	1 581	797	784
30-34	952	490	462	1 121	576	545	1 395	704	691	1 490	747	743
35-39	885	457	428	972	497	475	1 147	584	563	1 419	715	705
40-44	957	497	460	901	464	437	981	503	478	1 162	592	570
45-49	939	477	461	944	486	457	893	458	435	981	501	481
50-54	789	394	396	904	457	447	928	474	454	883	449	434
55-59	749	372	377	751	370	381	864	432	432	904	456	448
60-64	609	301	308	684	330	354	732	350	382	823	402	421
65-69	469	220	249	541	253	288	631	292	339	672	309	362
70-74	361	152	208	398	175	223	473	207	267	548	239	309
75-79	248	94	155	262	100	162	309	124	184	376	151	225
80 +	223	78	146	250	80	170	300	94	206	332	107	225

Age group	1990 Both sexes	Males	Females	1995 Both sexes	Males	Females	2000 Both sexes	Males	Females	2005 Both sexes	Males	Females
All ages	20 284	10 108	10 176	21 598	10 671	10 928	22 890	11 281	11 608	24 184	11 932	12 251
0-4	1 515	776	739	1 583	813	770	1 574	807	767	1 527	783	744
5-9	1 499	768	731	1 608	824	784	1 670	858	812	1 600	820	780
10-14	1 479	758	721	1 581	810	771	1 673	857	817	1 689	868	821
15-19	1 680	859	821	1 562	796	766	1 604	821	783	1 715	877	838
20-24	1 623	825	798	1 637	821	816	1 527	769	758	1 687	860	827
25-29	1 677	844	833	1 671	825	846	1 638	803	835	1 623	815	809
30-34	1 657	832	825	1 726	850	876	1 743	849	893	1 720	842	878
35-39	1 546	772	774	1 716	845	871	1 788	875	913	1 800	877	923
40-44	1 489	757	732	1 594	790	804	1 744	855	889	1 823	892	931
45-49	1 160	594	566	1 475	740	734	1 608	794	814	1 760	862	897
50-54	973	496	477	1 158	586	572	1 480	741	740	1 608	793	815
55-59	856	434	423	957	482	475	1 144	577	567	1 464	730	734
60-64	869	433	436	835	414	421	925	462	463	1 115	558	557
65-69	785	371	414	805	388	417	790	385	405	880	433	447
70-74	580	258	323	682	309	373	737	346	392	724	343	380
75-79	451	185	266	481	199	282	591	255	336	634	283	350
80 +	445	148	297	527	177	350	652	228	424	817	298	519

United Nations Department of Economic and Social Affairs/Population Division
World Population Prospects: The 2004 Revision, Volume II: Sex and Age Distribution of the World Population

POPULATION BY AGE AND SEX (in thousands)

Age group	2005 Both sexes	Males	Females	2010 Both sexes	Males	Females	2015 Both sexes	Males	Females	2020 Both sexes	Males	Females
All ages	24 184	11 932	12 251	25 070	12 630	12 843	26 552	13 121	13 431	27 742	13 712	14 030
0-4	1 527	783	744	1 547	793	754	1 610	826	784	1 701	873	828
5-9	1 600	820	780	1 550	794	755	1 570	805	765	1 633	837	796
10-14	1 689	868	821	1 613	827	787	1 563	801	762	1 584	812	772
15-19	1 715	877	838	1 723	884	839	1 648	843	805	1 599	818	781
20-24	1 687	860	827	1 791	913	878	1 800	921	879	1 726	880	845
25-29	1 623	815	809	1 779	904	875	1 884	957	927	1 893	965	928
30-34	1 720	842	878	1 701	852	849	1 856	941	915	1 962	995	967
35-39	1 800	877	923	1 773	868	905	1 755	878	876	1 911	968	943
40-44	1 823	892	931	1 831	892	939	1 805	884	922	1 788	895	893
45-49	1 760	862	897	1 836	898	938	1 846	899	947	1 821	892	930
50-54	1 608	793	815	1 758	860	898	1 835	896	939	1 846	898	948
55-59	1 464	730	734	1 590	781	809	1 739	848	891	1 817	885	932
60-64	1 115	558	557	1 426	706	720	1 552	757	794	1 700	824	876
65-69	880	433	447	1 063	524	538	1 362	666	697	1 486	716	770
70-74	724	343	380	809	388	421	982	473	508	1 263	603	659
75-79	634	283	350	627	285	342	706	325	381	861	399	461
80-84	457	183	274	496	207	289	496	212	285	564	245	320
85-89	240	82	158	302	109	193	334	126	207	340	132	208
90-94	93	26	67	120	36	84	156	49	107	177	59	119
95-99	22	5	17	33	8	25	44	11	33	59	16	44
100 +	3	1	3	5	1	4	8	2	6	11	2	9

Age group	2025 Both sexes	Males	Females	2030 Both sexes	Males	Females	2035 Both sexes	Males	Females	2040 Both sexes	Males	Females
All ages	28 868	14 266	14 602	29 873	14 755	15 118	30 726	15 167	15 559	31 455	15 523	15 932
0-4	1 731	888	843	1 720	883	838	1 697	870	826	1 701	873	828
5-9	1 724	884	840	1 754	900	855	1 743	894	849	1 720	882	838
10-14	1 647	844	803	1 738	891	847	1 768	907	862	1 757	901	856
15-19	1 619	829	790	1 682	861	821	1 773	908	865	1 804	924	880
20-24	1 676	855	821	1 697	866	831	1 761	899	862	1 852	946	906
25-29	1 820	925	894	1 771	901	870	1 792	912	880	1 855	945	911
30-34	1 972	1 004	968	1 899	964	935	1 850	940	911	1 871	951	921
35-39	2 016	1 022	995	2 027	1 031	996	1 954	991	963	1 906	967	939
40-44	1 944	984	960	2 050	1 038	1 012	2 061	1 048	1 014	1 989	1 009	980
45-49	1 805	903	902	1 961	992	969	2 067	1 046	1 021	2 079	1 056	1 023
50-54	1 823	891	932	1 808	903	904	1 963	992	971	2 070	1 046	1 023
55-59	1 830	888	942	1 809	882	926	1 795	895	900	1 950	983	967
60-64	1 778	861	917	1 793	865	928	1 774	861	914	1 762	874	889
65-69	1 631	781	850	1 710	818	892	1 727	824	903	1 712	822	890
70-74	1 382	652	730	1 521	714	808	1 599	750	849	1 620	758	862
75-79	1 113	512	601	1 225	557	668	1 355	613	741	1 430	648	782
80-84	694	303	391	900	390	510	1 005	432	574	1 120	480	641
85-89	392	155	237	489	196	294	648	257	390	729	287	442
90-94	185	63	123	219	76	143	280	98	182	379	132	248
95-99	70	19	50	75	21	54	92	26	65	121	35	85
100 +	15	3	12	19	4	15	22	5	17	27	6	21

Age group	2045 Both sexes	Males	Females	2050 Both sexes	Males	Females
All ages	32 109	15 852	16 258	32 729	16 173	16 556
0-4	1 739	892	847	1 790	918	871
5-9	1 724	884	840	1 762	904	858
10-14	1 734	889	845	1 738	891	847
15-19	1 793	918	875	1 770	906	863
20-24	1 882	961	921	1 872	956	916
25-29	1 947	992	955	1 978	1 008	970
30-34	1 935	984	952	2 027	1 031	996
35-39	1 928	979	949	1 992	1 012	980
40-44	1 942	985	957	1 964	997	967
45-49	2 008	1 018	990	1 961	995	967
50-54	2 082	1 057	1 025	2 012	1 019	993
55-59	2 056	1 037	1 019	2 070	1 048	1 022
60-64	1 916	961	955	2 022	1 015	1 007
65-69	1 704	836	867	1 854	921	933
70-74	1 610	759	852	1 606	775	831
75-79	1 456	659	797	1 453	663	790
80-84	1 191	511	680	1 221	524	697
85-89	823	323	500	886	349	537
90-94	436	150	287	503	172	330
95-99	168	48	120	199	56	142
100 +	36	8	27	51	12	39

POPULATION BY AGE AND SEX (in thousands)

Age group	2005 Both sexes	Males	Females	2010 Both sexes	Males	Females	2015 Both sexes	Males	Females	2020 Both sexes	Males	Females
All ages	24 184	11 932	12 251	25 584	12 638	12 946	27 116	13 410	13 706	28 760	14 235	14 526
0-4	1 527	783	744	1 758	902	857	1 963	1 007	956	2 155	1 106	1 049
5-9	1 600	820	780	1 550	794	755	1 781	913	868	1 986	1 018	968
10-14	1 689	868	821	1 613	827	787	1 563	801	762	1 795	920	875
15-19	1 715	877	838	1 723	884	839	1 648	843	805	1 599	818	781
20-24	1 687	860	827	1 791	913	878	1 800	921	879	1 726	880	845
25-29	1 623	815	809	1 779	904	875	1 884	957	927	1 893	965	928
30-34	1 720	842	878	1 701	852	849	1 856	941	915	1 962	995	967
35-39	1 800	877	923	1 773	868	905	1 755	878	876	1 911	968	943
40-44	1 823	892	931	1 831	892	939	1 805	884	922	1 788	895	893
45-49	1 760	862	897	1 836	898	938	1 846	899	947	1 821	892	930
50-54	1 608	793	815	1 758	860	898	1 835	896	939	1 846	898	948
55-59	1 464	730	734	1 590	781	809	1 739	848	891	1 817	885	932
60-64	1 115	558	557	1 426	706	720	1 552	757	794	1 700	824	876
65-69	880	433	447	1 063	524	538	1 362	666	697	1 486	716	770
70-74	724	343	380	809	388	421	982	473	508	1 263	603	659
75-79	634	283	350	627	285	342	706	325	381	861	399	461
80-84	457	183	274	496	207	289	496	212	285	564	245	320
85-89	240	82	158	302	109	193	334	126	207	340	132	208
90-94	93	26	67	120	36	84	156	49	107	177	59	119
95-99	22	5	17	33	8	25	44	11	33	59	16	44
100 +	3	1	3	5	1	4	8	2	6	11	2	9

Age group	2025 Both sexes	Males	Females	2030 Both sexes	Males	Females	2035 Both sexes	Males	Females	2040 Both sexes	Males	Females
All ages	30 337	15 020	15 317	31 796	15 741	16 054	33 171	16 421	16 750	34 566	17 119	17 447
0-4	2 183	1 120	1 063	2 175	1 116	1 059	2 220	1 139	1 081	2 369	1 215	1 153
5-9	2 178	1 117	1 061	2 205	1 131	1 074	2 198	1 127	1 070	2 243	1 150	1 092
10-14	2 000	1 025	975	2 191	1 124	1 068	2 219	1 138	1 081	2 212	1 134	1 077
15-19	1 830	937	893	2 035	1 042	993	2 227	1 141	1 086	2 255	1 155	1 100
20-24	1 676	855	821	1 908	974	934	2 113	1 079	1 034	2 305	1 178	1 127
25-29	1 820	925	894	1 771	901	870	2 002	1 020	983	2 207	1 125	1 082
30-34	1 972	1 004	968	1 899	964	935	1 850	940	911	2 082	1 058	1 023
35-39	2 016	1 022	995	2 027	1 031	996	1 954	991	963	1 906	967	939
40-44	1 944	984	960	2 050	1 038	1 012	2 061	1 048	1 014	1 989	1 009	980
45-49	1 805	903	902	1 961	992	969	2 067	1 046	1 021	2 079	1 056	1 023
50-54	1 823	891	932	1 808	903	904	1 963	992	971	2 070	1 046	1 023
55-59	1 830	888	942	1 809	882	926	1 795	895	900	1 950	983	967
60-64	1 778	861	917	1 793	865	928	1 774	861	914	1 762	874	889
65-69	1 631	781	850	1 710	818	892	1 727	824	903	1 712	822	890
70-74	1 382	652	730	1 521	714	808	1 599	750	849	1 620	758	862
75-79	1 113	512	601	1 225	557	668	1 355	613	741	1 430	648	782
80-84	694	303	391	906	393	512	1 005	432	574	1 120	480	641
85-89	392	155	237	489	196	294	648	257	390	729	287	442
90-94	185	63	123	219	76	143	280	98	182	379	132	248
95-99	70	19	50	75	21	54	92	26	65	121	35	85
100 +	15	3	12	19	4	15	22	5	17	27	6	21

Age group	2045 Both sexes	Males	Females	2050 Both sexes	Males	Females
All ages	36 048	17 872	18 176	37 604	18 674	18 930
0-4	2 568	1 318	1 250	2 729	1 401	1 329
5-9	2 392	1 227	1 165	2 591	1 329	1 262
10-14	2 257	1 157	1 099	2 406	1 234	1 172
15-19	2 247	1 151	1 096	2 292	1 174	1 118
20-24	2 333	1 193	1 140	2 326	1 189	1 137
25-29	2 399	1 224	1 176	2 428	1 238	1 189
30-34	2 287	1 164	1 123	2 479	1 263	1 216
35-39	2 138	1 086	1 051	2 343	1 192	1 151
40-44	1 942	985	957	2 173	1 104	1 069
45-49	2 008	1 018	990	1 961	995	967
50-54	2 082	1 057	1 025	2 012	1 019	993
55-59	2 056	1 037	1 019	2 070	1 048	1 022
60-64	1 916	961	955	2 022	1 015	1 007
65-69	1 704	836	867	1 854	921	933
70-74	1 610	759	852	1 606	775	831
75-79	1 456	659	797	1 453	663	790
80-84	1 191	511	680	1 221	524	697
85-89	823	323	500	886	349	537
90-94	436	150	287	503	172	330
95-99	168	48	120	199	56	142
100 +	36	8	27	51	12	39

United Nations Department of Economic and Social Affairs/Population Division
World Population Prospects: The 2004 Revision, Volume II: Sex and Age Distribution of the World Population

138

POPULATION BY AGE AND SEX (in thousands)

Age group	2005 Both sexes	Males	Females	2010 Both sexes	Males	Females	2015 Both sexes	Males	Females	2020 Both sexes	Males	Females
All ages	24 184	11 932	12 251	25 161	12 421	12 740	25 987	12 831	13 156	26 721	13 189	13 533
0-4	1 527	783	744	1 335	685	650	1 257	645	612	1 245	639	606
5-9	1 600	820	780	1 550	794	755	1 358	696	662	1 280	656	624
10-14	1 689	868	821	1 613	827	787	1 563	801	762	1 372	703	669
15-19	1 715	877	838	1 723	884	839	1 648	843	805	1 599	818	781
20-24	1 687	860	827	1 791	913	878	1 800	921	879	1 726	880	845
25-29	1 623	815	809	1 779	904	875	1 884	957	927	1 893	965	928
30-34	1 720	842	878	1 701	852	849	1 856	941	915	1 962	995	967
35-39	1 800	877	923	1 773	868	905	1 755	878	876	1 911	968	943
40-44	1 823	892	931	1 831	892	939	1 805	884	922	1 788	895	893
45-49	1 760	862	897	1 836	898	938	1 846	899	947	1 821	892	930
50-54	1 608	793	815	1 758	860	898	1 835	896	939	1 846	898	948
55-59	1 464	730	734	1 590	781	809	1 739	848	891	1 817	885	932
60-64	1 115	558	557	1 426	706	720	1 552	757	794	1 700	824	876
65-69	880	433	447	1 063	524	538	1 362	666	697	1 486	716	770
70-74	724	343	380	809	388	421	982	473	508	1 263	603	659
75-79	634	283	350	627	285	342	706	325	381	861	399	461
80-84	457	183	274	496	207	289	496	212	285	564	245	320
85-89	240	82	158	302	109	193	334	126	207	340	132	208
90-94	93	26	67	120	36	84	156	49	107	177	59	119
95-99	22	5	17	33	8	25	44	11	33	59	16	44
100 +	3	1	3	5	1	4	8	2	6	11	2	9

Age group	2025 Both sexes	Males	Females	2030 Both sexes	Males	Females	2035 Both sexes	Males	Females	2040 Both sexes	Males	Females
All ages	27 390	13 508	13 882	27 942	13 764	14 178	28 322	13 934	14 389	28 509	14 011	14 497
0-4	1 273	653	620	1 267	650	617	1 222	627	595	1 157	594	563
5-9	1 268	650	618	1 297	665	632	1 290	662	629	1 245	639	607
10-14	1 294	663	631	1 282	657	625	1 311	672	639	1 305	669	636
15-19	1 407	720	687	1 330	680	649	1 318	674	644	1 347	689	658
20-24	1 676	855	821	1 486	758	728	1 408	718	690	1 397	712	684
25-29	1 820	925	894	1 771	901	870	1 581	803	777	1 504	764	739
30-34	1 972	1 004	968	1 899	964	935	1 850	940	911	1 661	843	818
35-39	2 016	1 022	995	2 027	1 031	996	1 954	991	963	1 906	967	939
40-44	1 944	984	960	2 050	1 038	1 012	2 001	1 040	1 014	1 989	1 009	980
45-49	1 805	903	902	1 961	992	969	2 067	1 046	1 021	2 079	1 056	1 023
50-54	1 823	891	932	1 808	903	904	1 963	992	971	2 070	1 046	1 023
55-59	1 830	888	942	1 809	882	926	1 795	895	900	1 950	983	967
60-64	1 778	861	917	1 793	865	928	1 774	861	914	1 762	874	889
65-69	1 631	781	850	1 710	818	892	1 727	824	903	1 712	822	890
70-74	1 382	652	730	1 521	714	808	1 599	750	849	1 620	758	862
75-79	1 110	512	601	1 225	557	668	1 355	613	741	1 430	648	782
80-84	694	303	391	906	393	512	1 005	432	574	1 120	480	641
85-89	392	155	237	489	196	294	648	257	390	729	287	442
90-94	185	63	123	219	76	143	280	98	182	379	132	248
95-99	70	19	50	75	21	54	92	26	65	121	35	85
100 +	15	3	12	19	4	15	22	5	17	27	6	21

Age group	2045 Both sexes	Males	Females	2050 Both sexes	Males	Females
All ages	28 523	14 012	14 511	28 420	13 963	14 457
0-4	1 097	563	534	1 064	546	518
5-9	1 180	605	575	1 120	574	546
10-14	1 259	646	614	1 195	612	582
15-19	1 340	686	655	1 295	663	633
20-24	1 425	727	698	1 419	724	695
25-29	1 492	758	734	1 521	773	748
30-34	1 584	804	780	1 573	798	775
35-39	1 717	871	846	1 641	832	809
40-44	1 942	985	957	1 754	889	865
45-49	2 008	1 018	990	1 961	995	967
50-54	2 082	1 057	1 025	2 012	1 019	993
55-59	2 056	1 037	1 019	2 070	1 048	1 022
60-64	1 916	961	955	2 022	1 015	1 007
65-69	1 704	836	867	1 854	921	933
70-74	1 610	759	852	1 606	775	831
75-79	1 456	659	797	1 453	663	790
80-84	1 191	511	680	1 221	524	697
85-89	823	323	500	886	349	537
90-94	436	150	287	503	172	330
95-99	168	48	120	199	56	142
100 +	36	8	27	51	12	39

United Nations Department of Economic and Social Affairs/Population Division
World Population Prospects: The 2004 Revision, Volume II: Sex and Age Distribution of the World Population

139

POPULATION BY AGE AND SEX (in thousands)

Age group	1950 Both sexes	1950 Males	1950 Females	1955 Both sexes	1955 Males	1955 Females	1960 Both sexes	1960 Males	1960 Females	1965 Both sexes	1965 Males	1965 Females
All ages	2 289	1 207	1 082	2 483	1 293	1 190	2 735	1 418	1 317	3 056	1 571	1 485
0-4	363	186	176	424	215	209	470	239	230	590	301	289
5-9	299	155	144	333	170	163	394	199	195	432	220	212
10-14	264	138	126	289	149	140	322	164	157	372	188	183
15-19	235	123	112	255	133	122	278	144	135	320	161	159
20-24	205	109	97	221	117	104	241	126	115	262	134	128
25-29	179	95	84	191	101	90	206	110	96	219	114	105
30-34	155	83	72	165	88	77	178	95	82	188	100	88
35-39	132	71	61	140	75	65	152	81	70	158	85	73
40-44	110	60	51	119	63	56	129	69	60	134	71	62
45-49	91	48	42	96	51	46	105	56	49	111	59	52
50-54	75	41	35	76	40	36	83	43	39	89	46	42
55-59	50	27	23	60	32	28	63	33	31	67	34	33
60-64	42	23	19	38	20	18	47	25	23	48	24	24
65-69	38	21	18	28	15	14	27	14	13	33	16	17
70-74	27	15	12	24	12	12	19	9	9	19	9	10
75-79	15	8	7	14	7	7	13	6	7	9	4	5
80 +	8	5	3	9	5	5	9	4	5	7	3	4

Age group	1970 Both sexes	1970 Males	1970 Females	1975 Both sexes	1975 Males	1975 Females	1980 Both sexes	1980 Males	1980 Females	1985 Both sexes	1985 Males	1985 Females
All ages	3 426	1 761	1 665	3 865	1 981	1 884	4 363	2 234	2 130	4 923	2 517	2 406
0-4	564	288	276	640	327	312	720	369	350	783	403	381
5-9	493	251	242	545	278	267	620	317	302	704	362	342
10-14	435	222	214	485	247	238	541	276	265	609	311	297
15-19	376	190	185	425	216	209	472	240	232	525	267	258
20-24	302	155	147	360	181	179	405	204	200	461	233	228
25-29	256	133	123	291	149	142	346	175	171	394	199	194
30-34	217	115	102	243	127	116	277	143	135	331	168	164
35-39	185	99	86	207	110	98	232	121	110	264	137	128
40-44	154	82	71	171	91	80	193	102	91	218	114	104
45-49	128	68	60	142	76	67	159	84	75	180	95	85
50-54	102	53	49	113	59	54	127	66	60	143	75	68
55-59	79	40	39	89	45	43	99	51	48	111	58	54
60-64	56	28	28	64	32	32	71	36	35	80	41	40
65-69	38	18	19	42	20	22	48	23	25	56	27	29
70-74	23	11	12	26	12	14	29	14	16	34	16	18
75-79	11	5	6	14	6	8	16	7	9	19	8	11
80 +	7	3	4	8	4	4	9	4	5	10	4	6

Age group	1990 Both sexes	1990 Males	1990 Females	1995 Both sexes	1995 Males	1995 Females	2000 Both sexes	2000 Males	2000 Females	2005 Both sexes	2005 Males	2005 Females
All ages	5 475	2 852	2 623	6 184	3 201	2 983	6 935	3 576	3 359	7 661	3 941	3 719
0-4	838	444	394	977	504	473	1 041	537	504	1 031	532	499
5-9	747	393	354	813	431	382	950	490	460	1 015	524	491
10-14	654	332	322	739	389	351	803	425	378	940	485	455
15-19	609	301	308	641	325	316	727	382	345	790	418	372
20-24	528	263	265	596	295	301	626	317	308	711	374	337
25-29	467	234	233	514	257	257	579	287	292	610	310	300
30-34	370	188	181	449	226	223	499	250	249	564	280	284
35-39	300	158	142	358	183	175	434	219	215	483	243	240
40-44	240	128	113	286	150	136	342	175	168	417	210	207
45-49	190	104	86	228	120	108	270	141	129	324	165	160
50-54	164	90	74	173	94	79	210	110	100	250	129	120
55-59	123	69	53	146	79	67	154	82	71	188	97	91
60-64	92	54	38	102	56	46	123	65	58	131	69	62
65-69	67	41	26	72	40	31	80	43	37	97	50	47
70-74	45	28	17	46	27	19	50	27	23	57	29	28
75-79	26	16	10	28	16	12	28	15	13	32	16	16
80 +	15	9	6	16	10	7	20	11	9	21	11	11

United Nations Department of Economic and Social Affairs/Population Division
World Population Prospects: The 2004 Revision, Volume II: Sex and Age Distribution of the World Population

140

POPULATION BY AGE AND SEX (in thousands)

Age group	2005 Both sexes	Males	Females	2010 Both sexes	Males	Females	2015 Both sexes	Males	Females	2020 Both sexes	Males	Females
All ages	7 661	3 941	3 719	8 355	4 293	4 062	9 041	4 641	4 400	9 744	4 999	4 746
0-4	1 031	532	499	1 009	521	488	1 016	525	491	1 052	544	508
5-9	1 015	524	491	1 008	521	487	990	512	478	999	517	482
10-14	940	485	455	1 005	519	486	999	516	483	982	508	475
15-19	790	418	372	927	478	449	993	512	480	988	510	478
20-24	711	374	337	775	410	364	911	470	441	978	505	473
25-29	610	310	300	695	366	329	760	403	357	897	463	434
30-34	564	280	284	596	303	293	681	359	322	747	396	350
35-39	483	243	240	548	273	275	581	297	285	667	352	315
40-44	417	210	207	466	234	232	531	264	266	565	288	277
45-49	324	165	160	397	200	197	446	223	223	510	254	257
50-54	250	129	120	302	152	150	372	186	186	420	209	211
55-59	188	97	91	225	115	110	275	137	138	342	169	173
60-64	131	69	62	162	82	80	196	99	98	243	119	124
65-69	97	50	47	105	53	52	132	65	68	162	79	83
70-74	57	29	28	71	35	37	79	38	41	101	47	54
75-79	32	16	16	37	18	19	47	21	26	53	24	29
80-84	14	7	7	17	8	9	20	9	11	27	11	15
85-89	6	3	3	6	3	3	7	3	4	9	4	5
90-94	1	1	1	2	1	1	2	1	1	2	1	1
95-99	0	0	0	0	0	0	0	0	0	0	0	0
100 +	0	0	0	0	0	0	0	0	0	0	0	0

Age group	2025 Both sexes	Males	Females	2030 Both sexes	Males	Females	2035 Both sexes	Males	Females	2040 Both sexes	Males	Females
All ages	10 461	5 363	5 098	11 142	5 708	5 434	11 758	6 019	5 739	12 307	6 294	6 013
0-4	1 080	558	522	1 071	554	518	1 038	536	501	1 004	519	485
5-9	1 038	537	501	1 068	552	515	1 061	548	512	1 028	532	497
10-14	993	514	480	1 032	534	498	1 062	549	513	1 056	546	510
15-19	973	503	470	985	509	476	1 024	529	495	1 055	545	510
20-24	976	504	472	963	497	465	975	504	471	1 015	525	491
25-29	965	498	467	965	498	467	953	492	461	967	499	467
30-34	883	456	427	953	492	461	955	493	461	944	488	456
35-39	734	390	344	870	450	420	941	486	454	944	488	456
40-44	651	344	307	718	382	336	854	441	412	925	478	447
45-49	546	278	268	631	333	298	698	370	328	833	430	403
50-54	484	239	245	521	264	257	605	317	287	672	355	317
55-59	389	192	197	451	221	230	488	245	243	569	296	273
60-64	304	147	157	349	169	180	408	196	212	445	219	225
65-69	203	96	107	257	121	137	299	140	159	353	165	188
70-74	125	58	67	159	72	87	204	92	113	240	108	133
75-79	69	30	39	88	38	50	114	48	66	149	62	87
80-84	31	13	18	42	17	25	54	21	32	72	28	44
85-89	12	5	8	15	5	9	20	7	13	27	10	17
90-94	3	1	2	4	1	3	5	2	4	8	2	5
95-99	0	0	0	1	0	0	1	0	1	1	0	1
100 +	0	0	0	0	0	0	0	0	0	0	0	0

Age group	2045 Both sexes	Males	Females	2050 Both sexes	Males	Females
All ages	12 706	6 537	6 260	13 231	6 750	6 482
0-4	985	509	476	973	503	471
5-9	996	515	481	977	505	473
10-14	1 024	529	495	992	513	480
15-19	1 049	542	507	1 018	526	492
20-24	1 047	541	506	1 042	538	504
25-29	1 008	520	487	1 040	537	503
30-34	959	495	463	1 000	517	484
35-39	935	483	451	950	491	459
40-44	930	481	449	922	477	446
45-49	905	467	438	912	470	441
50-54	804	413	391	876	450	426
55-59	635	333	303	764	389	374
60-64	522	267	255	586	302	284
65-69	388	186	202	459	228	230
70-74	287	128	159	320	147	173
75-79	178	75	103	216	90	125
80-84	95	37	59	116	45	71
85-89	37	13	24	50	17	33
90-94	10	3	7	15	4	10
95-99	2	0	2	3	1	2
100 +	0	0	0	0	0	0

United Nations Department of Economic and Social Affairs/Population Division
World Population Prospects: The 2004 Revision, Volume II: Sex and Age Distribution of the World Population

141

POPULATION BY AGE AND SEX (in thousands)

Age group	2005 Both sexes	Males	Females	2010 Both sexes	Males	Females	2015 Both sexes	Males	Females	2020 Both sexes	Males	Females
All ages	7 661	3 941	3 719	8 428	4 330	4 097	9 244	4 746	4 498	10 130	5 198	4 932
0-4	1 031	532	499	1 083	559	523	1 147	593	554	1 236	639	597
5-9	1 015	524	491	1 008	521	487	1 062	549	513	1 129	584	545
10-14	940	485	455	1 005	519	486	999	516	483	1 054	545	509
15-19	790	418	372	927	478	449	993	512	480	988	510	478
20-24	711	374	337	775	410	364	911	470	441	978	505	473
25-29	610	310	300	695	366	329	760	403	357	897	463	434
30-34	564	280	284	596	303	293	681	359	322	747	396	350
35-39	483	243	240	548	273	275	581	297	285	667	352	315
40-44	417	210	207	466	234	232	531	264	266	565	288	277
45-49	324	165	160	397	200	197	446	223	223	510	254	257
50-54	250	129	120	302	152	150	372	186	186	420	209	211
55-59	188	97	91	225	115	110	275	137	138	342	169	173
60-64	131	69	62	162	82	80	196	99	98	243	119	124
65-69	97	50	47	105	53	52	132	65	68	162	79	83
70-74	57	29	28	71	35	37	79	38	41	101	47	54
75-79	32	16	16	37	18	19	47	21	26	53	24	29
80-84	14	7	7	17	8	9	20	9	11	27	11	15
85-89	6	3	3	6	3	3	7	3	4	9	4	5
90-94	1	1	1	2	1	1	2	1	1	2	1	1
95-99	0	0	0	0	0	0	0	0	0	0	0	0
100 +	0	0	0	0	0	0	0	0	0	0	0	0

Age group	2025 Both sexes	Males	Females	2030 Both sexes	Males	Females	2035 Both sexes	Males	Females	2040 Both sexes	Males	Females
All ages	11 050	5 667	5 383	11 961	6 132	5 830	12 853	6 585	6 268	13 739	7 034	6 705
0-4	1 286	665	621	1 305	674	631	1 317	680	637	1 346	695	651
5-9	1 221	631	589	1 272	658	614	1 293	668	624	1 306	675	631
10-14	1 122	580	542	1 214	628	586	1 267	655	612	1 288	666	622
15-19	1 045	540	505	1 113	575	538	1 206	623	582	1 259	651	608
20-24	976	504	472	1 034	534	500	1 103	570	533	1 196	618	578
25-29	965	498	467	965	498	467	1 023	529	495	1 093	565	529
30-34	883	456	427	953	492	461	955	493	461	1 014	524	490
35-39	734	390	344	870	450	420	941	486	454	944	488	456
40-44	651	344	307	718	382	336	854	441	412	925	478	447
45-49	546	278	268	631	333	298	698	370	328	833	430	403
50-54	484	239	245	521	264	257	605	317	287	672	355	317
55-59	389	192	197	451	221	230	488	245	243	569	296	273
60-64	304	147	157	349	169	180	408	196	212	445	219	225
65-69	203	96	107	257	121	137	299	140	159	353	165	188
70-74	125	58	67	159	72	87	204	92	113	240	108	133
75-79	69	30	39	88	38	50	114	48	66	149	62	87
80-84	31	13	18	42	17	25	54	21	32	72	28	44
85-89	12	5	8	15	5	9	20	7	13	27	10	17
90-94	3	1	2	4	1	3	5	2	4	8	2	5
95-99	0	0	0	1	0	0	1	0	1	1	0	1
100 +	0	0	0	0	0	0	0	0	0	0	0	0

Age group	2045 Both sexes	Males	Females	2050 Both sexes	Males	Females
All ages	14 627	7 482	7 145	15 510	7 927	7 584
0-4	1 390	718	672	1 429	738	691
5-9	1 336	691	646	1 381	713	668
10-14	1 302	673	629	1 332	688	644
15-19	1 280	661	619	1 295	669	626
20-24	1 249	645	604	1 272	657	615
25-29	1 187	613	574	1 241	641	600
30-34	1 085	560	524	1 179	609	570
35-39	1 004	519	485	1 075	556	519
40-44	930	481	449	991	512	479
45-49	905	467	438	912	470	441
50-54	804	413	391	876	450	426
55-59	635	333	303	764	389	374
60-64	522	267	255	586	302	284
65-69	388	186	202	459	228	230
70-74	287	128	159	320	147	173
75-79	178	75	103	216	90	125
80-84	95	37	59	116	45	71
85-89	37	13	24	50	17	33
90-94	10	3	7	15	4	10
95-99	2	0	2	3	1	2
100 +	0	0	0	0	0	0

United Nations Department of Economic and Social Affairs/Population Division
World Population Prospects: The 2004 Revision, Volume II: Sex and Age Distribution of the World Population

142

POPULATION BY AGE AND SEX (in thousands)

Age group	2005 Both sexes	Males	Females	2010 Both sexes	Males	Females	2015 Both sexes	Males	Females	2020 Both sexes	Males	Females
All ages	7 661	3 941	3 719	8 282	4 255	4 027	8 839	4 536	4 302	9 359	4 799	4 559
0-4	1 031	532	499	936	484	453	886	458	428	867	448	419
5-9	1 015	524	491	1 008	521	487	918	475	443	870	450	420
10-14	940	485	455	1 005	519	486	999	516	483	911	471	440
15-19	790	418	372	927	478	449	993	512	480	988	510	478
20-24	711	374	337	775	410	364	911	470	441	978	505	473
25-29	610	310	300	695	366	329	760	403	357	897	463	434
30-34	564	280	284	596	303	293	681	359	322	747	396	350
35-39	483	243	240	548	273	275	581	297	285	667	352	315
40-44	417	210	207	466	234	232	531	264	266	565	288	277
45-49	324	165	160	397	200	197	446	223	223	510	254	257
50-54	250	129	120	302	152	150	372	186	186	420	209	211
55-59	188	97	91	225	115	110	275	137	138	342	169	173
60-64	131	69	62	162	82	80	196	99	98	243	119	124
65-69	97	50	47	105	53	52	132	65	68	162	79	83
70-74	57	29	28	71	35	37	79	38	41	101	47	54
75-79	32	16	16	37	18	19	47	21	26	53	24	29
80-84	14	7	7	17	8	9	20	9	11	27	11	15
85-89	6	3	3	6	3	3	7	3	4	9	4	5
90-94	1	1	1	2	1	1	2	1	1	2	1	1
95-99	0	0	0	0	0	0	0	0	0	0	0	0
100 +	0	0	0	0	0	0	0	0	0	0	0	0

Age group	2025 Both sexes	Males	Females	2030 Both sexes	Males	Females	2035 Both sexes	Males	Females	2040 Both sexes	Males	Females
All ages	9 872	5 058	4 814	10 328	5 288	5 041	10 690	5 467	5 223	10 944	5 590	5 354
0-4	874	452	422	844	436	408	778	402	376	705	364	341
5-9	855	442	413	863	447	417	834	432	403	771	398	372
10-14	864	447	417	850	439	410	859	444	415	830	429	401
15-19	902	466	436	857	443	414	843	436	407	852	440	412
20-24	976	504	472	892	461	431	848	438	410	835	431	403
25-29	965	498	467	965	498	467	883	456	427	840	434	406
30-34	883	456	427	953	492	461	955	493	461	874	452	423
35-39	734	390	344	870	450	420	941	486	454	944	488	456
40-44	651	344	307	718	382	336	854	441	412	925	478	447
45-49	546	278	268	631	333	298	608	370	328	833	430	403
50-54	484	239	245	521	264	257	605	317	287	672	355	317
55-59	389	192	197	451	221	230	488	245	243	569	296	273
60-64	304	147	157	349	169	180	408	196	212	445	219	225
65-69	203	96	107	257	121	137	299	140	159	353	165	188
70-74	125	58	67	159	72	87	204	92	113	240	108	133
75-79	69	30	39	88	38	50	114	48	66	149	62	87
80-84	31	13	18	42	17	25	54	21	32	72	28	44
85-89	12	5	8	15	5	9	20	7	13	27	10	17
90-94	3	1	2	4	1	3	5	2	4	8	2	5
95-99	0	0	0	1	0	0	1	0	1	1	0	1
100 +	0	0	0	0	0	0	0	0	0	0	0	0

Age group	2045 Both sexes	Males	Females	2050 Both sexes	Males	Females
All ages	11 100	5 660	5 440	11 173	5 686	5 486
0-4	646	333	312	604	312	292
5-9	698	361	337	640	331	309
10-14	767	396	371	695	359	336
15-19	824	426	398	761	393	368
20-24	845	436	408	817	422	395
25-29	828	427	400	839	433	406
30-34	833	430	403	822	424	397
35-39	866	448	418	825	427	399
40-44	930	481	449	854	441	413
45-49	905	467	438	912	470	441
50-54	804	413	391	876	450	426
55-59	635	333	303	764	389	374
60-64	522	267	255	586	302	284
65-69	388	186	202	459	228	230
70-74	287	128	159	320	147	173
75-79	178	75	103	216	90	125
80-84	95	37	59	116	45	71
85-89	37	13	24	50	17	33
90-94	10	3	7	15	4	10
95-99	2	0	2	3	1	2
100 +	0	0	0	0	0	0

POPULATION BY AGE AND SEX (in thousands)

Age group	1950 Both sexes	Males	Females	1955 Both sexes	Males	Females	1960 Both sexes	Males	Females	1965 Both sexes	Males	Females
All ages	148	85	63	164	91	73	184	98	86	211	111	99
0-4	22	11	11	27	14	13	32	16	16	35	18	17
5-9	16	8	8	20	10	10	27	13	13	31	16	15
10-14	14	7	7	17	9	8	21	11	10	26	13	13
15-19	15	10	6	16	9	6	16	9	7	19	10	9
20-24	18	13	5	17	11	6	16	9	7	19	11	8
25-29	14	8	5	13	8	6	13	7	6	15	8	7
30-34	11	7	4	12	7	5	14	8	6	14	8	6
35-39	9	5	4	10	6	4	11	7	5	12	7	5
40-44	7	4	3	8	4	3	9	5	4	10	6	4
45-49	6	3	2	6	3	3	7	4	3	8	4	4
50-54	4	2	2	5	3	2	5	3	2	6	3	3
55-59	3	2	2	4	2	2	4	2	2	5	2	2
60-64	3	1	1	3	1	1	3	2	2	4	2	2
65-69	2	1	1	2	1	1	2	1	1	3	1	1
70-74	2	1	1	1	1	1	2	1	1	2	1	1
75-79	1	0	1	1	0	1	1	0	1	1	0	1
80 +	1	0	0	1	0	0	1	0	0	1	0	0

Age group	1970 Both sexes	Males	Females	1975 Both sexes	Males	Females	1980 Both sexes	Males	Females	1985 Both sexes	Males	Females
All ages	242	127	115	267	138	129	301	154	147	353	181	172
0-4	39	20	19	41	21	20	45	23	22	53	27	26
5-9	35	18	17	39	20	19	41	21	20	45	23	22
10-14	31	16	15	33	17	16	38	19	18	40	20	19
15-19	25	13	12	29	15	14	32	17	16	38	19	18
20-24	23	13	10	26	14	12	29	15	14	34	18	16
25-29	16	9	8	19	10	9	25	13	13	31	16	15
30-34	15	8	7	16	9	8	21	11	10	27	14	13
35-39	13	7	6	13	7	6	15	8	7	20	11	9
40-44	11	6	5	12	6	5	12	6	6	15	8	7
45-49	9	5	4	10	5	5	10	5	5	12	6	6
50-54	7	4	3	8	4	4	9	5	4	11	6	5
55-59	6	3	3	7	4	3	8	4	4	9	4	4
60-64	4	2	2	5	3	3	6	3	3	7	4	4
65-69	3	1	2	4	2	2	4	2	2	5	3	3
70-74	2	1	1	2	1	1	3	1	1	3	2	2
75-79	1	1	1	1	1	1	2	1	1	2	1	1
80 +	1	0	1	1	0	1	1	1	1	2	1	1

Age group	1990 Both sexes	Males	Females	1995 Both sexes	Males	Females	2000 Both sexes	Males	Females	2005 Both sexes	Males	Females
All ages	418	216	203	469	240	230	505	256	250	556	280	275
0-4	59	30	29	63	32	31	62	32	30	67	34	33
5-9	53	27	26	58	30	28	56	29	27	61	32	30
10-14	44	23	22	52	27	26	56	28	27	56	28	27
15-19	40	21	20	44	22	21	50	25	25	55	28	27
20-24	41	22	19	39	20	19	40	20	20	49	25	24
25-29	37	19	18	40	21	20	39	19	19	39	19	19
30-34	33	17	16	38	19	19	41	21	21	38	19	19
35-39	28	15	13	33	17	16	38	19	19	41	21	21
40-44	21	11	10	28	14	13	32	16	16	37	19	19
45-49	15	8	7	21	11	10	26	14	13	32	16	16
50-54	12	6	6	14	7	7	20	10	10	26	13	13
55-59	10	5	5	12	6	6	13	7	7	19	10	9
60-64	9	4	4	10	5	5	11	5	6	12	6	6
65-69	6	3	3	7	4	4	9	4	4	10	5	5
70-74	4	2	2	5	3	3	6	3	3	7	3	4
75-79	3	1	1	3	1	2	4	2	2	4	2	2
80 +	2	1	1	2	1	1	3	1	2	3	1	2

United Nations Department of Economic and Social Affairs/Population Division
World Population Prospects: The 2004 Revision, Volume II: Sex and Age Distribution of the World Population

144

POPULATION BY AGE AND SEX (in thousands)

Age group	2005 Both sexes	2005 Males	2005 Females	2010 Both sexes	2010 Males	2010 Females	2015 Both sexes	2015 Males	2015 Females	2020 Both sexes	2020 Males	2020 Females
All ages	556	280	275	603	303	300	646	324	322	687	344	343
0-4	67	34	33	66	34	32	66	34	32	66	34	32
5-9	61	32	30	66	34	32	66	34	32	66	34	32
10-14	56	28	27	61	31	29	65	33	32	65	33	32
15-19	55	28	27	55	28	27	60	31	29	64	33	31
20-24	49	25	24	53	27	26	53	27	26	58	29	28
25-29	39	19	19	47	23	24	51	26	25	51	25	25
30-34	38	19	19	38	19	19	46	23	23	50	25	25
35-39	41	21	21	38	19	19	38	19	19	45	22	23
40-44	37	19	19	41	20	20	37	18	19	37	18	19
45-49	32	16	16	37	18	18	40	20	20	36	18	18
50-54	26	13	13	31	15	15	35	18	18	39	19	20
55-59	19	10	9	24	12	12	29	15	15	34	17	17
60-64	12	6	6	18	9	9	23	11	12	28	14	14
65-69	10	5	5	11	5	6	16	8	8	21	10	11
70-74	7	3	4	8	4	4	9	4	5	14	7	7
75-79	4	2	2	6	2	3	6	3	4	7	3	4
80-84	2	1	1	3	1	2	4	1	2	4	2	3
85-89	1	0	1	1	0	1	1	1	1	2	1	1
90-94	0	0	0	0	0	0	0	0	0	0	0	0
95-99	0	0	0	0	0	0	0	0	0	0	0	0
100 +	0	0	0	0	0	0	0	0	0	0	0	0

Age group	2025 Both sexes	2025 Males	2025 Females	2030 Both sexes	2030 Males	2030 Females	2035 Both sexes	2035 Males	2035 Females	2040 Both sexes	2040 Males	2040 Females
All ages	724	361	363	757	377	380	787	391	396	813	403	410
0-4	65	33	32	64	33	31	63	32	31	62	32	30
5-9	65	33	32	64	33	31	63	32	31	63	32	30
10-14	65	33	32	64	33	31	63	32	31	62	32	30
15-19	64	33	31	64	33	31	63	32	31	62	32	30
20-24	62	32	31	62	31	30	62	31	30	61	31	30
25-29	56	28	27	60	30	30	60	30	30	60	30	30
30-34	50	25	25	55	27	27	59	30	29	59	30	29
35-39	49	25	25	49	24	25	54	27	27	59	29	29
40-44	45	22	23	49	24	25	49	24	24	53	27	27
45-49	36	18	18	44	22	22	48	24	24	48	24	24
50-54	36	17	18	35	17	18	43	21	22	47	23	24
55-59	37	18	19	34	17	18	34	17	18	42	20	21
60-64	32	16	17	36	17	18	33	16	17	33	16	17
65-69	25	12	13	30	14	16	33	16	17	30	14	16
70-74	18	8	10	22	10	12	26	12	14	29	13	16
75-79	11	5	6	14	6	8	18	8	10	22	9	12
80-84	5	2	3	8	3	4	10	4	6	13	5	8
85-89	2	1	1	3	1	2	4	1	3	6	2	4
90-94	1	0	0	1	0	1	1	0	1	2	0	1
95-99	0	0	0	0	0	0	0	0	0	0	0	0
100 +	0	0	0	0	0	0	0	0	0	0	0	0

Age group	2045 Both sexes	2045 Males	2045 Females	2050 Both sexes	2050 Males	2050 Females
All ages	834	412	421	849	419	430
0-4	60	31	29	57	29	28
5-9	61	32	30	59	30	29
10-14	62	32	30	61	31	30
15-19	61	31	30	61	31	30
20-24	60	31	30	60	30	29
25-29	59	30	29	58	30	29
30-34	59	30	29	58	29	29
35-39	58	29	29	58	29	29
40-44	58	29	29	58	29	29
45-49	53	26	26	58	29	29
50-54	47	23	24	52	26	26
55-59	46	23	23	46	22	23
60-64	40	19	21	44	21	23
65-69	31	14	16	37	18	20
70-74	27	12	15	27	12	15
75-79	24	11	14	23	10	13
80-84	16	6	9	18	7	11
85-89	8	3	5	9	3	6
90-94	3	1	2	3	1	2
95-99	1	0	0	1	0	1
100 +	0	0	0	0	0	0

POPULATION BY AGE AND SEX (in thousands)

Age group	2005 Both sexes	2005 Males	2005 Females	2010 Both sexes	2010 Males	2010 Females	2015 Both sexes	2015 Males	2015 Females	2020 Both sexes	2020 Males	2020 Females
All ages	556	280	275	609	306	302	661	332	329	714	358	357
0-4	67	34	33	72	37	35	76	39	37	78	40	38
5-9	61	32	30	66	34	32	71	36	35	75	38	37
10-14	56	28	27	61	31	29	65	33	32	70	36	34
15-19	55	28	27	55	28	27	60	31	29	64	33	31
20-24	49	25	24	53	27	26	53	27	26	58	29	28
25-29	39	19	19	47	23	24	51	26	25	51	25	25
30-34	38	19	19	38	19	19	46	23	23	50	25	25
35-39	41	21	21	38	19	19	38	19	19	45	22	23
40-44	37	19	19	41	20	20	37	18	19	37	18	19
45-49	32	16	16	37	18	18	40	20	20	36	18	18
50-54	26	13	13	31	15	15	35	18	18	39	19	20
55-59	19	10	9	24	12	12	29	15	15	34	17	17
60-64	12	6	6	18	9	9	23	11	12	28	14	14
65-69	10	5	5	11	5	6	16	8	8	21	10	11
70-74	7	3	4	8	4	4	9	4	5	14	7	7
75-79	4	2	2	6	2	3	6	3	4	7	3	4
80-84	2	1	1	3	1	2	4	1	2	4	2	3
85-89	1	0	1	1	0	1	1	1	1	2	1	1
90-94	0	0	0	0	0	0	0	0	0	0	0	0
95-99	0	0	0	0	0	0	0	0	0	0	0	0
100 +	0	0	0	0	0	0	0	0	0	0	0	0

Age group	2025 Both sexes	2025 Males	2025 Females	2030 Both sexes	2030 Males	2030 Females	2035 Both sexes	2035 Males	2035 Females	2040 Both sexes	2040 Males	2040 Females
All ages	765	382	383	814	406	408	862	429	433	910	453	458
0-4	78	40	38	79	41	39	82	42	40	85	43	41
5-9	77	40	38	77	40	38	78	40	38	81	42	40
10-14	74	38	36	77	39	37	77	39	37	78	40	38
15-19	70	36	34	73	37	36	76	39	37	76	39	37
20-24	62	32	31	68	34	33	71	36	35	74	38	36
25-29	56	28	27	60	30	30	66	33	32	69	35	34
30-34	50	25	25	55	27	27	59	30	29	64	32	32
35-39	49	25	25	49	24	25	54	27	27	59	29	29
40-44	45	22	23	49	24	25	49	24	24	53	27	27
45-49	36	18	18	44	22	22	48	24	24	48	24	24
50-54	36	17	18	35	17	18	43	21	22	47	23	24
55-59	37	18	19	34	17	18	34	17	18	42	20	21
60-64	32	16	17	36	17	18	33	16	17	33	16	17
65-69	25	12	13	30	14	16	33	16	17	30	14	16
70-74	18	8	10	22	10	12	26	12	14	29	13	16
75-79	11	5	6	14	6	8	18	8	10	22	9	12
80-84	5	2	3	8	3	4	10	4	6	13	5	8
85-89	2	1	1	3	1	2	4	1	3	6	2	4
90-94	1	0	0	1	0	1	1	0	1	2	0	1
95-99	0	0	0	0	0	0	0	0	0	0	0	0
100 +	0	0	0	0	0	0	0	0	0	0	0	0

Age group	2045 Both sexes	2045 Males	2045 Females	2050 Both sexes	2050 Males	2050 Females
All ages	957	476	481	1 001	497	504
0-4	86	44	42	86	44	42
5-9	84	43	41	85	44	42
10-14	80	41	39	83	43	41
15-19	77	39	38	80	41	39
20-24	74	38	36	75	38	37
25-29	72	36	35	72	36	35
30-34	68	34	34	71	36	35
35-39	64	32	32	68	34	34
40-44	58	29	29	63	32	32
45-49	53	26	26	58	29	29
50-54	47	23	24	52	26	26
55-59	46	23	23	46	22	23
60-64	40	19	21	44	21	23
65-69	31	14	16	37	18	20
70-74	27	12	15	27	12	15
75-79	24	11	14	23	10	13
80-84	16	6	9	18	7	11
85-89	8	3	5	9	3	6
90-94	3	1	2	3	1	2
95-99	1	0	0	1	0	1
100 +	0	0	0	0	0	0

POPULATION BY AGE AND SEX (in thousands)

Age group	2005 Both sexes	Males	Females	2010 Both sexes	Males	Females	2015 Both sexes	Males	Females	2020 Both sexes	Males	Females
All ages	556	280	275	598	301	297	632	017	015	000	330	330
0-4	67	34	33	61	31	30	57	29	28	53	27	26
5-9	61	32	30	66	34	32	60	31	29	56	29	27
10-14	56	28	27	61	31	29	65	33	32	60	30	29
15-19	55	28	27	55	28	27	60	31	29	64	33	31
20-24	49	25	24	53	27	26	53	27	26	58	29	28
25-29	39	19	19	47	23	24	51	26	25	51	25	25
30-34	38	19	19	38	19	19	46	23	23	50	25	25
35-39	41	21	21	38	19	19	38	19	19	45	22	23
40-44	37	19	19	41	20	20	37	18	19	37	18	19
45-49	32	16	16	37	18	18	40	20	20	36	18	18
50-54	26	13	13	31	15	15	35	18	18	39	19	20
55-59	19	10	9	24	12	12	29	15	15	34	17	17
60-64	12	6	6	18	9	9	23	11	12	28	14	14
65-69	10	5	5	11	5	6	16	8	8	21	10	11
70-74	7	3	4	8	4	4	9	4	5	14	7	7
75-79	4	2	2	6	2	3	6	3	4	7	3	4
80-84	2	1	1	3	1	2	4	1	2	4	2	3
85-89	1	0	1	1	0	1	1	1	1	2	1	1
90-94	0	0	0	0	0	0	0	0	0	0	0	0
95-99	0	0	0	0	0	0	0	0	0	0	0	0
100 +	0	0	0	0	0	0	0	0	0	0	0	0

Age group	2025 Both sexes	Males	Females	2030 Both sexes	Males	Females	2035 Both sexes	Males	Females	2040 Both sexes	Males	Females
All ages	684	341	343	703	349	354	717	355	362	724	357	367
0-4	52	26	25	49	25	24	47	24	23	43	22	21
5-9	53	27	26	51	26	25	49	25	24	46	24	22
10-14	55	28	27	52	27	25	50	26	24	48	24	23
15-19	59	30	29	55	28	27	51	26	25	49	25	24
20-24	62	32	01	57	29	28	53	27	26	49	25	24
25-29	56	28	27	60	30	30	55	28	27	51	26	25
30-34	50	25	25	55	27	27	59	30	29	54	27	27
35-39	49	25	25	49	24	25	54	27	27	59	29	29
40-44	45	22	23	49	24	25	49	24	24	53	27	27
45-49	36	18	18	44	22	22	48	24	24	48	24	24
50-54	36	17	18	35	17	18	43	21	22	47	23	24
55-59	37	18	19	34	17	18	34	17	18	42	20	21
60-64	32	16	17	36	17	18	33	16	17	33	16	17
65-69	25	12	13	30	14	16	33	16	17	30	14	16
70-74	18	8	10	22	10	12	26	12	14	29	13	16
75-79	11	5	6	14	6	8	18	8	10	22	9	12
80-84	5	2	3	9	3	4	10	4	6	13	5	8
85-89	2	1	1	3	1	2	4	1	3	6	2	4
90-94	1	0	0	1	0	1	1	0	1	2	0	1
95-99	0	0	0	0	0	0	0	0	0	0	0	0
100 +	0	0	0	0	0	0	0	0	0	0	0	0

Age group	2045 Both sexes	Males	Females	2050 Both sexes	Males	Females
All ages	723	356	367	716	351	365
0-4	39	20	19	35	18	17
5-9	43	22	21	38	20	19
10-14	45	23	22	42	21	20
15-19	47	24	23	44	23	22
20-24	47	24	23	45	23	22
25-29	47	24	23	46	23	23
30-34	50	25	25	46	23	23
35-39	53	27	27	49	25	25
40-44	58	29	29	53	26	26
45-49	53	26	26	58	29	29
50-54	47	23	24	52	26	26
55-59	46	23	23	46	22	23
60-64	40	19	21	44	21	23
65-69	31	14	16	37	18	20
70-74	27	12	15	27	12	15
75-79	24	11	14	23	10	13
80-84	16	6	9	18	7	11
85-89	8	3	5	9	3	6
90-94	3	1	2	3	1	2
95-99	1	0	0	1	0	1
100 +	0	0	0	0	0	0

POPULATION BY AGE AND SEX (in thousands)

Age group	1950 Both sexes	Males	Females	1955 Both sexes	Males	Females	1960 Both sexes	Males	Females	1965 Both sexes	Males	Females
All ages	242	124	118	276	141	135	317	162	156	368	187	181
0-4	44	23	21	53	27	26	61	31	30	70	36	34
5-9	37	19	18	42	22	20	51	26	25	58	30	29
10-14	31	16	15	35	18	17	39	20	19	49	25	24
15-19	25	12	12	29	15	14	33	17	16	38	20	19
20-24	21	10	11	23	12	11	27	14	13	30	15	15
25-29	18	9	9	20	10	10	22	11	11	26	13	12
30-34	15	8	7	17	9	9	19	9	9	21	11	10
35-39	13	6	6	14	7	7	17	8	8	18	9	9
40-44	10	5	5	11	6	5	13	6	6	16	8	8
45-49	8	4	4	9	5	4	11	6	5	12	6	6
50-54	7	3	3	7	4	4	8	4	4	10	5	5
55-59	5	2	2	6	3	3	6	3	3	7	4	4
60-64	4	2	2	4	2	2	5	2	2	5	3	3
65-69	3	1	1	3	1	2	3	1	1	4	2	2
70-74	2	1	1	2	1	1	2	1	1	2	1	1
75-79	1	1	0	1	0	1	1	1	1	1	1	1
80 +	1	0	0	1	0	0	1	0	0	1	0	0

Age group	1970 Both sexes	Males	Females	1975 Both sexes	Males	Females	1980 Both sexes	Males	Females	1985 Both sexes	Males	Females
All ages	423	215	208	445	228	217	477	246	232	507	261	246
0-4	74	38	36	68	35	33	70	36	34	74	38	36
5-9	67	34	33	68	35	33	65	34	31	63	32	30
10-14	58	29	28	62	32	30	65	33	32	62	32	30
15-19	47	24	23	52	27	25	57	30	27	61	32	29
20-24	35	18	17	42	22	20	47	24	23	51	27	25
25-29	29	15	14	30	15	15	37	19	18	43	22	21
30-34	25	13	12	26	14	13	28	14	13	34	17	17
35-39	21	11	10	23	12	11	24	13	12	25	13	12
40-44	17	9	9	19	10	9	22	12	10	22	12	10
45-49	14	7	7	16	8	8	17	9	8	19	10	9
50-54	11	5	5	13	6	6	14	7	7	15	8	7
55-59	9	5	4	9	5	4	11	6	6	12	6	6
60-64	6	3	3	8	4	4	8	4	4	10	5	5
65-69	4	2	2	5	2	2	6	3	3	7	3	3
70-74	2	1	1	3	1	2	4	2	2	5	2	2
75-79	1	1	1	2	1	1	2	1	1	3	1	1
80 +	1	0	1	1	1	1	2	1	1	2	1	1

Age group	1990 Both sexes	Males	Females	1995 Both sexes	Males	Females	2000 Both sexes	Males	Females	2005 Both sexes	Males	Females
All ages	543	281	262	581	300	282	619	318	301	656	336	320
0-4	74	39	36	74	38	36	78	40	38	74	38	36
5-9	68	35	33	75	39	36	72	37	34	77	40	37
10-14	64	33	31	67	34	32	73	38	35	71	37	34
15-19	62	33	29	58	30	28	63	33	30	69	36	33
20-24	53	28	25	53	28	25	52	27	25	56	29	27
25-29	44	23	21	50	26	24	47	24	23	46	23	22
30-34	38	19	18	43	22	21	48	24	23	45	22	22
35-39	29	15	14	35	18	17	42	21	21	47	24	23
40-44	24	12	12	30	15	15	34	18	16	41	21	20
45-49	21	11	10	22	11	11	28	15	14	32	17	16
50-54	18	9	9	20	10	9	21	11	10	27	14	13
55-59	15	8	7	17	9	8	19	10	9	20	10	10
60-64	12	6	6	13	7	7	15	8	7	17	9	8
65-69	9	4	4	10	5	5	11	6	5	13	7	6
70-74	6	3	3	7	3	4	8	4	4	9	4	5
75-79	4	2	2	5	2	2	5	2	3	6	3	3
80 +	3	1	2	3	1	2	4	2	2	5	2	3

United Nations Department of Economic and Social Affairs/Population Division
World Population Prospects: The 2004 Revision, Volume II: Sex and Age Distribution of the World Population

148

POPULATION BY AGE AND SEX (in thousands)

Age group	2005 Both sexes	Males	Females	2010 Both sexes	Males	Females	2015 Both sexes	Males	Females	2020 Both sexes	Males	Females
All ages	656	336	320	690	351	338	713	364	349	736	375	361
0-4	74	38	36	70	36	34	67	34	33	65	34	32
5-9	77	40	37	73	37	35	68	35	33	65	34	32
10-14	71	37	34	76	39	37	71	37	35	67	35	33
15-19	69	36	33	68	36	33	73	38	35	68	35	33
20-24	56	29	27	64	33	30	63	33	30	68	35	33
25-29	46	23	22	51	26	25	58	30	28	57	30	28
30-34	45	22	22	43	21	21	48	24	24	55	28	27
35-39	47	24	23	44	22	22	42	21	21	47	24	23
40-44	41	21	20	46	24	22	42	21	21	40	21	20
45-49	32	17	16	39	20	19	44	23	22	41	21	20
50-54	27	14	13	31	16	15	38	20	19	43	22	21
55-59	20	10	10	26	13	13	30	15	15	37	19	18
60-64	17	9	8	18	9	9	24	12	12	28	14	14
65-69	13	7	6	15	7	7	16	8	8	21	11	11
70-74	9	4	5	11	5	5	12	6	6	14	6	7
75-79	6	3	3	7	3	4	8	4	4	10	4	5
80-84	3	1	2	4	2	2	5	2	3	6	2	3
85-89	1	1	1	2	1	1	2	1	1	3	1	2
90-94	0	0	0	1	0	0	1	0	1	1	0	1
95-99	0	0	0	0	0	0	0	0	0	0	0	0
100 +	0	0	0	0	0	0	0	0	0	0	0	0

Age group	2025 Both sexes	Males	Females	2030 Both sexes	Males	Females	2035 Both sexes	Males	Females	2040 Both sexes	Males	Females
All ages	756	384	371	771	391	380	780	395	385	781	395	386
0-4	64	33	31	62	32	30	58	30	28	53	27	26
5-9	64	33	31	63	32	30	61	31	29	57	29	27
10-14	64	33	31	63	32	30	61	32	30	59	31	29
15-19	64	33	31	61	32	30	60	31	29	58	30	28
20-24	63	33	31	59	31	29	56	29	27	55	28	26
25-29	62	32	30	58	30	28	53	27	26	51	26	25
30-34	55	28	27	59	30	29	55	28	27	50	26	25
35-39	54	28	26	54	27	26	58	29	29	54	27	27
40-44	46	23	23	53	27	26	52	27	26	57	29	28
45-49	39	20	19	44	22	22	52	27	25	51	26	25
50-54	40	20	20	38	19	19	43	22	21	51	26	24
55-59	42	21	20	38	19	19	37	19	18	40	21	21
60-64	34	17	17	39	20	19	36	18	18	35	18	17
65-69	25	13	12	31	15	16	36	18	18	33	16	17
70-74	18	9	10	22	10	11	27	13	14	31	15	16
75-79	11	5	6	15	7	8	17	8	10	22	10	12
80-84	7	0	4	8	3	4	10	4	6	13	5	7
85-89	3	1	2	4	1	2	4	2	3	6	2	4
90-94	1	0	1	1	0	1	2	0	1	2	1	2
95-99	0	0	0	0	0	0	0	0	0	1	0	0
100 +	0	0	0	0	0	0	0	0	0	0	0	0

Age group	2045 Both sexes	Males	Females	2050 Both sexes	Males	Females
All ages	775	391	384	763	384	379
0-4	49	25	24	45	23	22
5-9	52	27	25	47	24	23
10-14	56	29	27	51	26	25
15-19	56	29	27	53	27	25
20-24	54	28	26	52	27	25
25-29	49	25	24	48	25	23
30-34	48	24	24	46	23	23
35-39	50	25	25	47	24	23
40-44	53	27	26	49	25	24
45-49	55	28	27	51	26	25
50-54	50	26	24	54	28	27
55-59	49	25	24	49	25	24
60-64	40	20	20	47	24	23
65-69	32	16	16	37	18	18
70-74	29	14	15	29	14	15
75-79	26	12	14	25	11	13
80-84	16	7	10	19	8	11
85-89	8	3	5	10	4	7
90-94	3	1	2	4	1	3
95-99	1	0	1	1	0	1
100 +	0	0	0	0	0	0

United Nations Department of Economic and Social Affairs/Population Division
World Population Prospects: The 2004 Revision, Volume II: Sex and Age Distribution of the World Population

149

POPULATION BY AGE AND SEX (in thousands)

Age group	2005 Both sexes	Males	Females	2010 Both sexes	Males	Females	2015 Both sexes	Males	Females	2020 Both sexes	Males	Females
All ages	656	336	320	692	354	338	729	373	357	767	391	376
0-4	74	38	36	76	39	37	77	40	38	79	41	39
5-9	77	40	37	73	37	35	74	38	36	76	39	37
10-14	71	37	34	76	39	37	71	37	35	73	38	36
15-19	69	36	33	68	36	33	73	38	35	68	35	33
20-24	56	29	27	64	33	30	63	33	30	68	35	33
25-29	46	23	22	51	26	25	58	30	28	57	30	28
30-34	45	22	22	43	21	21	48	24	24	55	28	27
35-39	47	24	23	44	22	22	42	21	21	47	24	23
40-44	41	21	20	46	24	22	42	21	21	40	21	20
45-49	32	17	16	39	20	19	44	23	22	41	21	20
50-54	27	14	13	31	16	15	38	20	19	43	22	21
55-59	20	10	10	26	13	13	30	15	15	37	19	18
60-64	17	9	8	18	9	9	24	12	12	28	14	14
65-69	13	7	6	15	7	7	16	8	8	21	11	11
70-74	9	4	5	11	5	5	12	6	6	14	6	7
75-79	6	3	3	7	3	4	8	4	4	10	4	5
80-84	3	1	2	4	2	2	5	2	3	6	2	3
85-89	1	1	1	2	1	1	2	1	1	3	1	2
90-94	0	0	0	1	0	0	1	0	1	1	0	1
95-99	0	0	0	0	0	0	0	0	0	0	0	0
100 +	0	0	0	0	0	0	0	0	0	0	0	0

Age group	2025 Both sexes	Males	Females	2030 Both sexes	Males	Females	2035 Both sexes	Males	Females	2040 Both sexes	Males	Females
All ages	801	408	393	832	423	409	858	435	423	880	445	434
0-4	79	41	38	78	40	38	75	39	37	74	38	36
5-9	78	40	38	77	40	37	76	39	37	74	38	36
10-14	75	39	36	77	40	37	76	39	37	75	39	36
15-19	70	36	34	72	37	35	74	38	36	73	38	35
20-24	63	33	31	65	34	32	67	35	32	69	36	33
25-29	62	32	30	58	30	28	60	31	29	61	31	30
30-34	55	28	27	59	30	29	55	28	27	57	29	28
35-39	54	28	26	54	27	26	58	29	29	54	27	27
40-44	46	23	23	53	27	26	52	27	26	57	29	28
45-49	39	20	19	44	22	22	52	27	25	51	26	25
50-54	40	20	20	38	19	19	43	22	21	51	26	24
55-59	42	21	20	38	19	19	37	19	18	42	21	21
60-64	34	17	17	39	20	19	36	18	18	35	18	17
65-69	25	13	12	31	15	16	36	18	18	33	16	17
70-74	18	9	10	22	10	11	27	13	14	31	15	16
75-79	11	5	6	15	7	8	17	8	10	22	10	12
80-84	7	3	4	8	3	4	10	4	6	13	5	7
85-89	3	1	2	4	1	2	4	2	3	6	2	4
90-94	1	0	1	1	0	1	2	0	1	2	1	2
95-99	0	0	0	0	0	0	0	0	0	1	0	0
100 +	0	0	0	0	0	0	0	0	0	0	0	0

Age group	2045 Both sexes	Males	Females	2050 Both sexes	Males	Females
All ages	898	454	444	913	461	452
0-4	73	38	36	73	37	35
5-9	72	37	35	72	37	35
10-14	73	37	35	71	37	35
15-19	72	37	35	70	36	34
20-24	68	35	33	67	35	32
25-29	63	32	31	63	32	30
30-34	58	30	29	60	31	30
35-39	56	28	28	57	29	28
40-44	53	27	26	55	28	27
45-49	55	28	27	51	26	25
50-54	50	26	24	54	28	27
55-59	49	25	24	49	25	24
60-64	40	20	20	47	24	23
65-69	32	16	16	37	18	18
70-74	29	14	15	29	14	15
75-79	26	12	14	25	11	13
80-84	16	7	10	19	8	11
85-89	8	3	5	10	4	7
90-94	3	1	2	4	1	3
95-99	1	0	1	1	0	1
100 +	0	0	0	0	0	0

United Nations Department of Economic and Social Affairs/Population Division
World Population Prospects: The 2004 Revision, Volume II: Sex and Age Distribution of the World Population

150

POPULATION BY AGE AND SEX (in thousands)

Age group	2005 Both sexes	Males	Females	2010 Both sexes	Males	Females	2015 Both sexes	Males	Females	2020 Both sexes	Males	Females
All ages	666	336	330	680	348	332	696	356	341	706	360	346
0-4	74	38	36	64	33	31	57	29	27	52	27	25
5-9	77	40	37	73	37	35	62	32	30	55	28	27
10-14	71	37	34	76	39	37	71	37	35	61	31	30
15-19	69	36	33	68	36	33	73	38	35	68	35	33
20-24	56	29	27	64	33	30	63	33	30	68	35	33
25-29	46	23	22	51	26	25	58	30	28	57	30	28
30-34	45	22	22	43	21	21	48	24	24	55	28	27
35-39	47	24	23	44	22	22	42	21	21	47	24	23
40-44	41	21	20	46	24	22	42	21	21	40	21	20
45-49	32	17	16	39	20	19	44	23	22	41	21	20
50-54	27	14	13	31	16	15	38	20	19	43	22	21
55-59	20	10	10	26	13	13	30	15	15	37	19	18
60-64	17	9	8	18	9	9	24	12	12	28	14	14
65-69	13	7	6	15	7	7	16	8	8	21	11	11
70-74	9	4	5	11	5	5	12	6	6	14	6	7
75-79	6	3	3	7	3	4	8	4	4	10	4	5
80-84	3	1	2	4	2	2	5	2	3	6	2	3
85-89	1	1	1	2	1	1	2	1	1	3	1	2
90-94	0	0	0	1	0	0	1	0	1	1	0	1
95-99	0	0	0	0	0	0	0	0	0	0	0	0
100 +	0	0	0	0	0	0	0	0	0	0	0	0

Age group	2025 Both sexes	Males	Females	2030 Both sexes	Males	Females	2035 Both sexes	Males	Females	2040 Both sexes	Males	Females
All ages	711	362	350	712	361	351	705	357	349	690	348	342
0-4	50	26	24	47	24	23	43	22	21	36	19	18
5-9	50	26	24	48	25	23	46	24	22	41	21	20
10-14	54	28	26	49	25	24	47	24	23	45	23	22
15-19	58	30	28	51	26	25	46	24	22	44	23	21
20-24	63	33	31	53	27	26	46	24	22	41	21	20
25-29	62	32	30	58	30	28	47	24	23	40	21	20
30-34	55	28	27	59	30	29	55	28	27	44	22	22
35-39	54	28	26	54	27	26	58	29	29	54	27	27
40-44	46	23	23	53	27	26	52	27	26	57	29	28
45-49	39	20	19	44	22	22	52	27	25	51	26	25
50-54	40	20	20	38	19	19	43	22	21	51	26	24
55-59	42	21	20	38	19	19	37	19	18	42	21	21
60-64	34	17	17	39	20	19	36	18	18	35	18	17
65-69	25	13	12	31	15	16	36	18	18	33	16	17
70-74	18	9	10	22	10	11	27	13	14	31	15	16
75-79	11	5	6	15	7	8	17	8	10	22	10	12
80-84	7	3	4	8	3	4	10	4	6	13	5	7
85-89	3	1	2	4	1	2	4	2	3	6	2	4
90-94	1	0	1	1	0	1	2	0	1	2	1	2
95-99	0	0	0	0	0	0	0	0	0	1	0	0
100 +	0	0	0	0	0	0	0	0	0	0	0	0

Age group	2045 Both sexes	Males	Females	2050 Both sexes	Males	Females
All ages	665	334	331	633	317	316
0-4	30	15	15	25	13	12
5-9	35	18	17	29	15	14
10-14	40	21	19	34	17	16
15-19	42	22	20	37	19	18
20-24	39	20	19	37	19	18
25-29	35	18	17	33	17	16
30-34	37	19	19	33	16	16
35-39	44	22	22	37	19	18
40-44	53	27	26	43	22	21
45-49	55	28	27	51	26	25
50-54	50	26	24	54	28	27
55-59	49	25	24	49	25	24
60-64	40	20	20	47	24	23
65-69	32	16	16	37	18	18
70-74	29	14	15	29	14	15
75-79	26	12	14	25	11	13
80-84	16	7	10	19	8	11
85-89	8	3	5	10	4	7
90-94	3	1	2	4	1	3
95-99	1	0	1	1	0	1
100 +	0	0	0	0	0	0

United Nations Department of Economic and Social Affairs/Population Division
World Population Prospects: The 2004 Revision, Volume II: Sex and Age Distribution of the World Population

152

A.2. POPULATION BY SEX AND AGE FOR COUNTRIES AND AREAS: ESTIMATES AND MEDIUM, HIGH AND LOW VARIANTS, 1950-2050

POPULATION BY AGE AND SEX (in thousands)

Age group	1950 Both sexes	1950 Males	1950 Females	1955 Both sexes	1955 Males	1955 Females	1960 Both sexes	1960 Males	1960 Females	1965 Both sexes	1965 Males	1965 Females
All ages	8 151	4 220	3 932	8 971	4 646	4 325	9 966	5 162	4 805	11 158	5 778	5 380
0-4	1 433	736	698	1 551	797	754	1 753	900	852	1 988	1 021	966
5-9	1 091	565	527	1 206	624	582	1 321	684	637	1 513	783	730
10-14	951	494	458	1 051	545	505	1 164	604	560	1 279	664	615
15-19	833	434	399	920	479	441	1 019	530	488	1 131	589	542
20-24	719	375	344	794	414	380	880	459	421	977	509	468
25-29	615	320	294	679	354	325	753	392	360	837	436	401
30-34	525	274	251	580	303	277	643	336	307	716	374	342
35-39	447	234	213	494	259	236	548	287	261	609	319	291
40-44	378	198	181	418	218	200	464	242	221	516	270	246
45-49	318	165	153	351	182	169	389	202	187	433	225	208
50-54	262	135	127	289	149	141	321	165	156	358	184	174
55-59	210	107	103	231	118	114	257	131	126	287	146	141
60-64	158	80	79	175	88	87	195	98	97	218	110	108
65-69	108	54	54	119	60	60	134	67	67	151	75	76
70-74	63	32	32	70	35	35	78	39	39	90	45	45
75-79	28	14	14	31	16	16	36	18	18	42	21	21
80 +	10	5	5	11	6	5	13	6	6	15	8	7

Age group	1970 Both sexes	1970 Males	1970 Females	1975 Both sexes	1975 Males	1975 Females	1980 Both sexes	1980 Males	1980 Females	1985 Both sexes	1985 Males	1985 Females
All ages	12 596	6 520	6 076	14 319	7 409	6 910	15 209	7 866	7 344	13 912	7 191	6 721
0-4	2 267	1 165	1 102	2 593	1 334	1 260	2 778	1 429	1 349	2 592	1 334	1 259
5-9	1 741	900	841	2 013	1 040	972	2 165	1 119	1 046	1 996	1 032	964
10-14	1 469	762	707	1 695	879	816	1 822	944	878	1 678	869	809
15-19	1 246	648	597	1 434	745	688	1 537	799	739	1 414	734	680
20-24	1 088	567	521	1 203	627	576	1 288	670	618	1 182	614	568
25-29	933	486	447	1 044	544	500	1 073	559	514	985	512	472
30-34	799	417	382	894	467	428	931	486	445	818	426	391
35-39	681	356	325	763	399	365	795	415	380	710	371	340
40-44	577	301	275	647	338	309	675	352	323	603	314	289
45-49	484	252	233	544	283	261	568	295	273	508	264	244
50-54	400	206	194	450	232	218	471	243	228	422	217	204
55-59	322	164	158	363	185	178	381	194	187	342	174	167
60-64	246	124	122	278	140	138	294	148	146	265	133	131
65-69	172	86	86	196	98	99	209	104	105	190	94	96
70-74	104	51	52	120	59	61	130	64	66	120	59	61
75-79	49	24	25	58	29	30	65	32	33	61	30	31
80 +	18	9	9	23	11	12	26	13	14	26	12	13

Age group	1990 Both sexes	1990 Males	1990 Females	1995 Both sexes	1995 Males	1995 Females	2000 Both sexes	2000 Males	2000 Females	2005 Both sexes	2005 Males	2005 Females
All ages	14 606	7 547	7 059	20 669	10 670	9 999	23 735	12 245	11 489	29 863	15 404	14 459
0-4	2 766	1 423	1 343	3 977	2 044	1 933	4 561	2 344	2 217	5 535	2 847	2 688
5-9	2 139	1 105	1 033	3 072	1 587	1 485	3 584	1 849	1 735	4 540	2 343	2 196
10-14	1 766	915	852	2 539	1 314	1 225	2 959	1 531	1 428	3 811	1 969	1 841
15-19	1 487	772	716	2 101	1 090	1 011	2 449	1 269	1 179	3 151	1 632	1 518
20-24	1 243	645	597	1 753	910	843	2 009	1 042	967	2 586	1 341	1 245
25-29	1 033	537	496	1 457	756	700	1 668	865	802	2 112	1 095	1 016
30-34	860	448	412	1 210	629	581	1 384	719	665	1 750	909	841
35-39	711	371	340	1 004	523	481	1 146	596	550	1 449	753	696
40-44	615	321	295	828	431	397	946	492	454	1 194	620	574
45-49	519	269	250	709	367	341	774	401	373	978	506	472
50-54	431	222	209	590	304	286	655	337	318	791	406	384
55-59	350	178	171	480	244	235	533	271	262	653	332	321
60-64	272	137	135	374	188	186	416	209	207	511	256	254
65-69	196	97	99	271	134	136	302	150	152	372	185	188
70-74	125	61	64	174	85	89	195	96	100	241	118	123
75-79	65	31	33	91	44	47	103	50	54	128	62	67
80 +	28	14	15	41	20	22	49	23	26	63	29	33

United Nations Department of Economic and Social Affairs/Population Division
World Population Prospects: The 2004 Revision, Volume II: Sex and Age Distribution of the World Population

154

POPULATION BY AGE AND SEX (in thousands)

Age group	2005 Both sexes	2005 Males	2005 Females	2010 Both sexes	2010 Males	2010 Females	2015 Both sexes	2015 Males	2015 Females	2020 Both sexes	2020 Males	2020 Females
All ages	29 863	15 404	14 459	35 642	18 382	17 260	41 401	21 348	20 053	48 000	24 704	23 296
0-4	5 535	2 847	2 688	6 488	3 338	3 150	7 426	3 823	3 604	8 417	4 335	4 083
5-9	4 540	2 343	2 196	5 269	2 721	2 548	6 055	3 127	2 928	6 984	3 608	3 376
10-14	3 811	1 969	1 841	4 585	2 370	2 215	5 186	2 681	2 505	5 970	3 086	2 883
15-19	3 151	1 632	1 518	3 853	1 994	1 859	4 515	2 336	2 179	5 115	2 647	2 468
20-24	2 586	1 341	1 245	3 162	1 639	1 523	3 768	1 950	1 818	4 426	2 291	2 136
25-29	2 112	1 095	1 016	2 583	1 339	1 244	3 079	1 596	1 484	3 680	1 904	1 775
30-34	1 750	909	841	2 107	1 093	1 013	2 512	1 303	1 209	3 003	1 557	1 446
35-39	1 449	753	696	1 741	904	837	2 043	1 060	983	2 443	1 267	1 176
40-44	1 194	620	574	1 434	744	690	1 680	871	809	1 978	1 025	953
45-49	978	506	472	1 173	606	567	1 374	710	665	1 615	834	781
50-54	791	406	384	949	487	462	1 111	570	541	1 306	670	636
55-59	653	332	321	751	382	369	880	447	433	1 034	525	509
60-64	511	256	254	596	300	297	671	337	334	791	397	394
65-69	372	185	188	437	216	220	501	248	253	568	281	287
70-74	241	118	123	285	139	146	329	161	169	382	186	196
75-79	128	62	67	153	74	79	179	86	93	211	101	110
80-84	49	23	26	59	28	31	71	33	37	85	40	45
85-89	12	5	6	14	7	8	18	8	10	21	10	12
90-94	2	1	1	2	1	1	2	1	1	3	1	2
95-99	0	0	0	0	0	0	0	0	0	0	0	0
100 +	0	0	0	0	0	0	0	0	0	0	0	0

Age group	2025 Both sexes	2025 Males	2025 Females	2030 Both sexes	2030 Males	2030 Females	2035 Both sexes	2035 Males	2035 Females	2040 Both sexes	2040 Males	2040 Females
All ages	55 443	28 581	26 862	63 424	32 693	30 732	71 759	36 985	34 773	80 267	41 362	38 905
0-4	9 318	4 801	4 517	10 009	5 159	4 850	10 479	5 404	5 075	10 783	5 561	5 222
5-9	7 975	4 121	3 854	8 890	4 595	4 295	9 612	4 970	4 642	10 120	5 235	4 885
10-14	6 898	3 567	3 332	7 890	4 080	3 810	8 809	4 556	4 253	9 538	4 935	4 604
15-19	5 897	3 051	2 846	6 825	3 531	3 294	7 817	4 044	3 772	8 739	4 522	4 217
20-24	5 025	2 601	2 424	5 806	3 004	2 802	6 732	3 484	3 249	7 725	3 997	3 728
25-29	4 333	2 243	2 091	4 932	2 553	2 379	5 711	2 956	2 755	6 637	3 435	3 202
30-34	3 597	1 862	1 735	4 247	2 198	2 048	4 845	2 508	2 336	5 623	2 911	2 712
35-39	2 928	1 517	1 411	3 517	1 820	1 697	4 162	2 154	2 008	4 759	2 463	2 296
40-44	2 372	1 228	1 143	2 850	1 475	1 375	3 432	1 774	1 650	4 072	2 105	1 967
45-49	1 907	984	923	2 293	1 184	1 110	2 764	1 426	1 338	3 337	1 720	1 617
50-54	1 540	790	750	1 824	935	888	2 200	1 129	1 071	2 659	1 364	1 295
55-59	1 220	620	601	1 445	734	711	1 719	873	845	2 081	1 058	1 023
60-64	905	439	466	1 110	556	554	1 322	663	659	1 580	793	787
65-69	675	334	342	805	398	408	964	476	488	1 157	572	586
70-74	440	214	226	529	257	272	639	310	329	774	375	398
75-79	249	119	130	291	139	153	357	169	187	438	208	230
80-84	102	48	55	124	57	66	148	68	80	190	85	100
85-89	27	12	15	33	15	18	41	18	23	50	22	28
90-94	4	2	2	5	2	3	6	3	4	8	3	5
95-99	0	0	0	0	0	0	0	0	0	1	0	0
100 +	0	0	0	0	0	0	0	0	0	0	0	0

Age group	2045 Both sexes	2045 Males	2045 Females	2050 Both sexes	2050 Males	2050 Females
All ages	88 831	45 757	43 074	97 324	50 101	47 223
0-4	10 986	5 666	5 320	11 082	5 714	5 368
5-9	10 471	5 414	5 057	10 719	5 540	5 179
10-14	10 056	5 204	4 852	10 415	5 386	5 029
15-19	9 473	4 902	4 571	9 997	5 173	4 823
20-24	8 651	4 476	4 175	9 393	4 860	4 533
25-29	7 631	3 949	3 682	8 561	4 430	4 131
30-34	6 547	3 389	3 159	7 542	3 903	3 639
35-39	5 535	2 864	2 671	6 458	3 341	3 117
40-44	4 666	2 412	2 254	5 440	2 811	2 628
45-49	3 968	2 045	1 923	4 559	2 350	2 209
50-54	3 220	1 650	1 570	3 840	1 969	1 871
55-59	2 524	1 283	1 241	3 067	1 558	1 509
60-64	1 923	965	958	2 344	1 176	1 167
65-69	1 394	689	706	1 709	845	865
70-74	939	455	484	1 144	555	589
75-79	539	255	284	665	314	351
80-84	233	107	126	293	134	159
85-89	65	28	36	84	37	47
90-94	10	4	6	13	5	8
95-99	1	0	1	1	0	1
100 +	0	0	0	0	0	0

POPULATION BY AGE AND SEX (in thousands)

Age group	2005 Both sexes	Males	Females	2010 Both sexes	Males	Females	2015 Both sexes	Males	Females	2020 Both sexes	Males	Females
All ages	29 863	15 404	14 459	36 015	18 574	17 441	42 645	21 989	20 656	49 893	25 724	24 169
0-4	5 535	2 847	2 688	6 860	3 530	3 330	8 322	4 284	4 038	9 092	4 682	4 410
5-9	4 540	2 343	2 196	5 269	2 721	2 548	6 403	3 307	3 096	7 827	4 043	3 784
10-14	3 811	1 969	1 841	4 585	2 370	2 215	5 186	2 681	2 505	6 313	3 264	3 049
15-19	3 151	1 632	1 518	3 853	1 994	1 859	4 515	2 336	2 179	5 115	2 647	2 468
20-24	2 586	1 341	1 245	3 162	1 639	1 523	3 768	1 950	1 818	4 426	2 291	2 136
25-29	2 112	1 095	1 016	2 583	1 339	1 244	3 079	1 596	1 484	3 680	1 904	1 775
30-34	1 750	909	841	2 107	1 093	1 013	2 512	1 303	1 209	3 003	1 557	1 446
35-39	1 449	753	696	1 741	904	837	2 043	1 060	983	2 443	1 267	1 176
40-44	1 194	620	574	1 434	744	690	1 680	871	809	1 978	1 025	953
45-49	978	506	472	1 173	606	567	1 374	710	665	1 615	834	781
50-54	791	406	384	949	487	462	1 111	570	541	1 306	670	636
55-59	653	332	321	751	382	369	880	447	433	1 034	525	509
60-64	511	256	254	596	300	297	671	337	334	791	397	394
65-69	372	185	188	437	216	220	501	248	253	568	281	287
70-74	241	118	123	285	139	146	329	161	169	382	186	196
75-79	128	62	67	153	74	79	179	86	93	211	101	110
80-84	49	23	26	59	28	31	71	33	37	85	40	45
85-89	12	5	6	14	7	8	18	8	10	21	10	12
90-94	2	1	1	2	1	1	2	1	1	3	1	2
95-99	0	0	0	0	0	0	0	0	0	0	0	0
100 +	0	0	0	0	0	0	0	0	0	0	0	0

Age group	2025 Both sexes	Males	Females	2030 Both sexes	Males	Females	2035 Both sexes	Males	Females	2040 Both sexes	Males	Females
All ages	58 089	29 948	28 141	67 167	34 626	32 540	77 148	39 770	37 377	87 845	45 279	42 566
0-4	10 153	5 231	4 922	11 163	5 754	5 409	12 200	6 291	5 908	13 069	6 740	6 329
5-9	8 614	4 451	4 163	9 687	5 007	4 680	10 720	5 543	5 177	11 783	6 095	5 687
10-14	7 731	3 997	3 734	8 523	4 407	4 116	9 600	4 965	4 635	10 639	5 504	5 135
15-19	6 236	3 227	3 010	7 649	3 958	3 692	8 444	4 369	4 075	9 523	4 928	4 595
20-24	5 025	2 601	2 424	6 140	3 177	2 963	7 546	3 905	3 641	8 345	4 318	4 027
25-29	4 333	2 243	2 091	4 932	2 553	2 379	6 040	3 126	2 914	7 439	3 850	3 589
30-34	3 597	1 862	1 735	4 247	2 198	2 048	4 845	2 508	2 336	5 946	3 078	2 868
35-39	2 928	1 517	1 411	3 517	1 820	1 697	4 162	2 154	2 008	4 759	2 463	2 296
40-44	2 372	1 228	1 143	2 850	1 475	1 375	3 432	1 774	1 658	4 072	2 105	1 967
45-49	1 907	984	923	2 293	1 184	1 110	2 764	1 426	1 338	3 337	1 720	1 617
50-54	1 540	790	750	1 824	935	888	2 200	1 129	1 071	2 659	1 364	1 295
55-59	1 220	620	601	1 445	734	711	1 719	873	845	2 081	1 058	1 023
60-64	935	469	466	1 110	556	554	1 322	663	659	1 580	793	787
65-69	675	334	342	805	398	408	964	476	488	1 157	572	586
70-74	440	214	226	529	257	272	639	310	329	774	375	398
75-79	249	119	130	291	139	153	357	169	187	438	208	230
80-84	102	48	55	124	57	66	148	68	80	186	85	100
85-89	27	12	15	33	15	18	41	18	23	50	22	28
90-94	4	2	2	5	2	3	6	3	4	8	3	5
95-99	0	0	0	0	0	0	0	0	0	1	0	0
100 +	0	0	0	0	0	0	0	0	0	0	0	0

Age group	2045 Both sexes	Males	Females	2050 Both sexes	Males	Females
All ages	98 952	50 989	47 963	110 322	56 818	53 504
0-4	13 642	7 036	6 606	14 084	7 262	6 823
5-9	12 691	6 562	6 129	13 311	6 880	6 432
10-14	11 708	6 059	5 649	12 623	6 528	6 095
15-19	10 566	5 467	5 098	11 640	6 024	5 616
20-24	9 428	4 878	4 549	10 477	5 421	5 056
25-29	8 243	4 266	3 977	9 330	4 828	4 502
30-34	7 339	3 798	3 541	8 147	4 216	3 931
35-39	5 853	3 028	2 825	7 239	3 745	3 494
40-44	4 666	2 412	2 254	5 753	2 973	2 780
45-49	3 968	2 045	1 923	4 559	2 350	2 209
50-54	3 220	1 650	1 570	3 840	1 969	1 871
55-59	2 524	1 283	1 241	3 067	1 558	1 509
60-64	1 923	965	958	2 344	1 176	1 167
65-69	1 394	689	706	1 709	845	865
70-74	939	455	484	1 144	555	589
75-79	539	255	284	665	314	351
80-84	233	107	126	293	134	159
85-89	65	28	36	84	37	47
90-94	10	4	6	13	5	8
95-99	1	0	1	1	0	1
100 +	0	0	0	0	0	0

United Nations Department of Economic and Social Affairs/Population Division
World Population Prospects: The 2004 Revision, Volume II: Sex and Age Distribution of the World Population

156

POPULATION BY AGE AND SEX (in thousands)

Age group	2005 Both sexes	Males	Females	2010 Both sexes	Males	Females	2015 Both sexes	Males	Females	2020 Both sexes	Males	Females
All ages	29 863	15 404	14 459	35 416	18 265	17 150	40 744	21 010	19 735	46 730	24 092	22 638
0-4	5 535	2 847	2 688	6 261	3 222	3 040	6 981	3 593	3 388	7 743	3 987	3 756
5-9	4 540	2 343	2 196	5 269	2 721	2 548	5 843	3 018	2 825	6 565	3 392	3 174
10-14	3 811	1 969	1 841	4 585	2 370	2 215	5 186	2 681	2 505	5 761	2 978	2 783
15-19	3 151	1 632	1 518	3 853	1 994	1 859	4 515	2 336	2 179	5 115	2 647	2 468
20-24	2 586	1 341	1 245	3 162	1 639	1 523	3 768	1 950	1 818	4 426	2 291	2 136
25-29	2 112	1 095	1 016	2 583	1 339	1 244	3 079	1 596	1 484	3 680	1 904	1 775
30-34	1 750	909	841	2 107	1 093	1 013	2 512	1 303	1 209	3 003	1 557	1 446
35-39	1 449	753	696	1 741	904	837	2 043	1 060	983	2 443	1 267	1 176
40-44	1 194	620	574	1 434	744	690	1 680	871	809	1 978	1 025	953
45-49	978	506	472	1 173	606	567	1 374	710	665	1 615	834	781
50-54	791	406	384	949	487	462	1 111	570	541	1 306	670	636
55-59	653	332	321	751	382	369	880	447	433	1 034	525	509
60-64	511	256	254	596	300	297	671	337	334	791	397	394
65-69	372	185	188	437	216	220	501	248	253	568	281	287
70-74	241	118	123	285	139	146	329	161	169	382	186	196
75-79	128	62	67	153	74	79	179	86	93	211	101	110
80-84	49	23	26	59	28	31	71	33	37	85	40	45
85-89	12	5	6	14	7	8	18	8	10	21	10	12
90-94	2	1	1	2	1	1	2	1	1	3	1	2
95-99	0	0	0	0	0	0	0	0	0	0	0	0
100 +	0	0	0	0	0	0	0	0	0	0	0	0

Age group	2025 Both sexes	Males	Females	2030 Both sexes	Males	Females	2035 Both sexes	Males	Females	2040 Both sexes	Males	Females
All ages	53 360	27 506	25 854	60 340	31 100	29 240	67 334	34 699	32 635	74 103	38 176	35 927
0-4	8 495	4 377	4 118	8 955	4 616	4 339	9 076	4 680	4 395	8 967	4 625	4 343
5-9	7 336	3 791	3 545	8 104	4 189	3 915	8 600	4 447	4 153	8 765	4 534	4 231
10-14	6 484	3 353	3 132	7 257	3 753	3 504	8 031	4 154	3 877	8 534	4 415	4 119
15-19	5 691	3 045	2 710	6 415	3 313	3 050	7 190	3 720	3 470	7 966	4 122	3 844
20-24	5 025	2 601	2 424	5 603	2 899	2 704	6 328	3 274	3 054	7 105	3 677	3 429
25-29	4 333	2 243	2 091	4 932	2 553	2 379	5 511	2 852	2 659	6 238	3 228	3 010
30-34	3 597	1 862	1 735	4 247	2 198	2 048	4 845	2 508	2 336	5 426	2 809	2 617
35-39	2 928	1 517	1 411	3 517	1 820	1 697	4 162	2 154	2 008	4 759	2 463	2 296
40-44	2 372	1 228	1 143	2 850	1 475	1 375	3 432	1 774	1 658	4 072	2 105	1 967
45-49	1 907	984	923	2 293	1 184	1 110	2 764	1 426	1 338	3 337	1 720	1 617
50-54	1 540	790	750	1 824	935	888	2 200	1 129	1 071	2 659	1 364	1 295
55-59	1 220	620	601	1 445	734	711	1 718	873	845	2 081	1 058	1 023
60-64	935	469	466	1 110	556	554	1 322	663	659	1 580	793	787
65-69	675	334	342	805	398	408	964	476	488	1 157	572	586
70-74	440	214	226	529	257	272	639	310	329	774	375	398
75-79	249	119	130	291	139	153	357	169	187	438	208	230
80-84	102	48	55	124	57	66	148	68	80	186	85	100
85-89	27	12	15	33	15	18	41	18	23	50	22	28
90-94	4	2	2	5	2	3	6	3	4	8	3	5
95-99	0	0	0	0	0	0	0	0	0	1	0	0
100 +	0	0	0	0	0	0	0	0	0	0	0	0

Age group	2045 Both sexes	Males	Females	2050 Both sexes	Males	Females
All ages	80 545	41 474	39 071	86 571	44 543	42 027
0-4	8 772	4 524	4 248	8 514	4 389	4 124
5-9	8 708	4 502	4 205	8 558	4 423	4 135
10-14	8 709	4 507	4 202	8 660	4 479	4 182
15-19	8 475	4 386	4 090	8 657	4 480	4 177
20-24	7 886	4 081	3 806	8 403	4 348	4 055
25-29	7 018	3 632	3 386	7 804	4 038	3 766
30-34	6 154	3 185	2 969	6 936	3 589	3 347
35-39	5 341	2 763	2 578	6 070	3 140	2 930
40-44	4 666	2 412	2 254	5 249	2 713	2 536
45-49	3 968	2 045	1 923	4 559	2 350	2 209
50-54	3 220	1 650	1 570	3 840	1 969	1 871
55-59	2 524	1 283	1 241	3 067	1 558	1 509
60-64	1 923	965	958	2 344	1 176	1 167
65-69	1 394	689	706	1 709	845	865
70-74	939	455	484	1 144	555	589
75-79	539	255	284	665	314	351
80-84	233	107	126	293	134	159
85-89	65	28	36	84	37	47
90-94	10	4	6	13	5	8
95-99	1	0	1	1	0	1
100 +	0	0	0	0	0	0

United Nations Department of Economic and Social Affairs/Population Division
World Population Prospects: The 2004 Revision, Volume II: Sex and Age Distribution of the World Population

157

POPULATION BY AGE AND SEX (in thousands)

Age group	1950			1955			1960			1965		
	Both sexes	Males	Females	Both sexes	Males	Females	Both sexes	Males	Females	Both sexes	Males	Females
All ages	1 215	612	603	1 379	694	685	1 611	811	799	1 870	943	927
0-4	173	88	86	219	110	108	280	143	138	316	162	154
5-9	154	78	75	168	85	83	214	108	106	274	140	134
10-14	146	74	72	153	78	75	168	85	83	213	107	105
15-19	121	61	60	145	74	71	153	78	75	167	85	82
20-24	107	53	53	120	61	59	145	73	71	152	78	74
25-29	76	38	38	105	53	53	119	60	59	143	73	71
30-34	72	37	35	75	38	37	105	52	52	118	60	59
35-39	68	34	34	71	37	35	75	37	37	103	52	52
40-44	55	28	27	67	34	33	70	36	34	73	37	37
45-49	45	23	22	54	27	27	66	33	33	69	35	34
50-54	42	21	21	44	22	22	53	26	26	64	32	32
55-59	32	15	17	40	20	21	42	21	21	50	25	25
60-64	37	18	19	30	14	16	37	18	19	39	19	20
65-69	32	16	17	33	16	17	26	12	14	33	16	18
70-74	25	12	12	26	13	13	27	13	14	22	10	12
75-79	17	8	8	17	8	9	18	9	10	19	9	10
80 +	11	6	6	12	6	6	13	6	7	14	7	8

Age group	1970			1975			1980			1985		
	Both sexes	Males	Females	Both sexes	Males	Females	Both sexes	Males	Females	Both sexes	Males	Females
All ages	2 136	1 079	1 057	2 401	1 214	1 187	2 671	1 379	1 293	2 957	1 525	1 432
0-4	322	165	157	336	173	164	344	178	166	361	187	174
5-9	311	159	152	315	161	154	316	164	152	343	178	165
10-14	273	139	134	307	157	150	298	154	144	317	165	152
15-19	212	107	105	270	137	132	306	162	143	308	162	146
20-24	166	84	82	209	105	104	268	142	126	300	158	142
25-29	151	77	74	163	83	81	208	109	99	263	138	125
30-34	142	72	70	149	76	73	162	85	77	203	106	98
35-39	117	59	58	139	71	69	147	78	69	159	83	76
40-44	102	51	51	115	58	57	137	72	66	144	75	68
45-49	72	36	36	99	50	50	113	58	54	134	69	65
50-54	67	34	33	70	35	35	97	50	47	109	56	53
55-59	61	30	31	64	32	32	72	34	38	97	47	50
60-64	47	23	24	57	28	29	65	31	34	66	32	34
65-69	35	17	18	42	20	22	57	26	31	58	28	30
70-74	28	13	15	29	14	15	39	17	21	47	22	26
75-79	16	7	9	21	9	11	24	10	13	28	13	16
80 +	16	7	9	16	7	9	20	8	12	22	9	13

Age group	1990			1995			2000			2005		
	Both sexes	Males	Females	Both sexes	Males	Females	Both sexes	Males	Females	Both sexes	Males	Females
All ages	3 289	1 687	1 602	3 133	1 579	1 554	3 062	1 523	1 539	3 130	1 552	1 578
0-4	389	202	187	329	170	159	282	145	137	253	131	123
5-9	352	184	168	349	180	169	315	162	152	278	143	135
10-14	337	174	163	315	159	156	324	165	158	312	161	151
15-19	326	168	158	273	135	137	291	143	148	312	159	153
20-24	316	163	153	257	128	129	230	110	120	270	132	138
25-29	311	160	151	256	128	128	212	101	110	211	99	111
30-34	264	136	128	256	129	127	219	106	113	197	93	104
35-39	199	103	96	231	118	113	221	110	111	209	100	109
40-44	152	80	72	178	92	86	213	108	105	213	106	107
45-49	152	79	73	144	75	69	164	84	80	207	104	103
50-54	129	69	60	134	70	65	138	71	67	159	81	78
55-59	106	55	51	120	63	57	121	62	59	133	68	65
60-64	82	39	43	96	50	46	111	57	54	115	58	57
65-69	69	32	37	75	35	40	85	44	41	102	51	51
70-74	43	20	24	58	26	33	65	29	36	73	36	37
75-79	36	14	21	32	13	19	44	17	26	49	19	29
80 +	28	10	18	29	9	20	29	8	21	37	10	26

United Nations Department of Economic and Social Affairs/Population Division
World Population Prospects: The 2004 Revision, Volume II: Sex and Age Distribution of the World Population

158

POPULATION BY AGE AND SEX (in thousands)

Age group	2005 Both sexes	Males	Females	2010 Both sexes	Males	Females	2015 Both sexes	Males	Females	2020 Both sexes	Males	Females
All ages	3 130	1 552	1 578	3 216	1 601	1 625	3 325	1 642	1 683	3 420	1 685	1 735
0-4	253	131	123	257	133	124	265	137	128	260	135	126
5-9	278	143	135	250	129	121	255	132	123	263	136	127
10-14	312	161	151	276	142	134	249	128	121	254	131	123
15-19	312	159	153	303	156	147	270	139	131	243	125	118
20-24	270	132	138	296	151	146	293	151	142	260	133	127
25-29	211	99	111	255	124	132	286	145	141	283	145	138
30-34	197	93	104	200	93	106	248	120	128	279	141	138
35-39	209	100	109	189	89	100	194	90	104	242	116	126
40-44	213	106	107	203	97	106	185	87	99	191	88	102
45-49	207	104	103	209	103	105	200	95	105	182	85	97
50-54	159	81	78	203	101	101	205	101	104	196	93	103
55-59	133	68	65	154	78	77	197	98	99	200	98	102
60-64	115	58	57	127	64	63	148	74	74	190	93	97
65-69	102	51	51	106	52	53	117	58	60	138	67	71
70-74	73	36	37	87	42	46	92	43	49	103	48	54
75-79	49	19	29	55	24	31	67	29	38	72	31	41
80-84	26	8	18	30	10	21	35	13	22	43	15	28
85-89	8	2	6	12	2	9	14	3	11	17	4	12
90-94	2	0	2	2	0	2	4	0	3	5	0	4
95-99	0	0	0	0	0	0	0	0	0	1	0	1
100 +	0	0	0	0	0	0	0	0	0	0	0	0

Age group	2025 Both sexes	Males	Females	2030 Both sexes	Males	Females	2035 Both sexes	Males	Females	2040 Both sexes	Males	Females
All ages	3 484	1 713	1 771	3 512	1 723	1 790	3 520	1 723	1 796	3 513	1 718	1 795
0-4	240	124	116	216	112	104	205	106	99	204	105	98
5-9	258	134	125	238	123	115	215	111	104	204	105	98
10-14	262	135	127	257	133	124	237	123	114	214	111	103
15-19	248	128	120	256	132	124	251	130	121	231	120	112
20-24	233	120	113	238	122	115	246	127	119	241	125	117
25-29	250	128	122	223	114	109	228	117	111	236	122	115
30-34	275	141	134	243	124	119	216	110	105	221	113	107
35-39	273	138	135	270	138	132	237	121	116	211	108	103
40-44	238	114	124	269	136	133	266	136	130	234	119	115
45-49	187	86	101	235	112	123	266	134	132	262	134	129
50-54	179	83	96	184	85	100	231	110	121	262	131	130
55-59	192	90	101	175	81	94	180	82	98	227	107	119
60-64	193	93	99	185	86	99	169	77	92	174	79	96
65-69	177	85	92	181	85	95	174	79	95	160	71	88
70-74	121	56	65	157	72	85	161	73	88	157	68	88
75-79	81	35	46	97	41	56	128	54	74	133	56	77
80-84	47	17	31	55	19	35	67	24	43	91	33	58
85-89	22	5	17	25	6	19	30	7	22	38	10	28
90-94	6	1	5	8	1	7	10	1	9	12	2	11
95-99	1	0	1	1	0	1	2	0	2	3	0	3
100 +	0	0	0	0	0	0	0	0	0	0	0	0

Age group	2045 Both sexes	Males	Females	2050 Both sexes	Males	Females
All ages	3 494	1 709	1 785	3 458	1 694	1 764
0-4	201	104	97	191	99	92
5-9	202	105	98	199	103	96
10-14	202	105	98	201	104	97
15-19	208	108	100	197	102	95
20-24	221	114	107	198	102	96
25-29	232	119	112	212	109	103
30-34	229	118	111	224	115	109
35-39	215	110	105	224	115	109
40-44	207	105	101	212	108	104
45-49	230	117	113	204	104	100
50-54	259	132	127	227	115	112
55-59	257	128	129	254	129	125
60-64	220	103	117	249	124	126
65-69	165	73	92	209	96	112
70-74	144	62	82	150	64	86
75-79	131	53	78	122	49	73
80-84	96	35	61	97	34	62
85-89	53	14	39	58	16	42
90-94	17	3	14	24	4	20
95-99	4	0	3	5	0	5
100 +	0	0	0	1	0	1

United Nations Department of Economic and Social Affairs/Population Division
World Population Prospects: The 2004 Revision, Volume II: Sex and Age Distribution of the World Population

159

POPULATION BY AGE AND SEX (in thousands)

Age group	2005 Both sexes	2005 Males	2005 Females	2010 Both sexes	2010 Males	2010 Females	2015 Both sexes	2015 Males	2015 Females	2020 Both sexes	2020 Males	2020 Females
All ages	3 130	1 552	1 578	3 248	1 607	1 641	3 410	1 686	1 725	3 570	1 763	1 808
0-4	253	131	123	289	149	140	319	165	154	326	169	158
5-9	278	143	135	250	129	121	287	148	139	316	163	153
10-14	312	161	151	276	142	134	249	128	121	285	147	138
15-19	312	159	153	303	156	147	270	139	131	243	125	118
20-24	270	132	138	296	151	146	293	151	142	260	133	127
25-29	211	99	111	255	124	132	286	145	141	283	145	138
30-34	197	93	104	200	93	106	248	120	128	279	141	138
35-39	209	100	109	189	89	100	194	90	104	242	116	126
40-44	213	106	107	203	97	106	185	87	99	191	88	102
45-49	207	104	103	209	103	105	200	95	105	182	85	97
50-54	159	81	78	203	101	101	205	101	104	196	93	103
55-59	133	68	65	154	78	77	197	98	99	200	98	102
60-64	115	58	57	127	64	63	148	74	74	190	93	97
65-69	102	51	51	106	52	53	117	58	60	138	67	71
70-74	73	36	37	87	42	46	92	43	49	103	48	54
75-79	49	19	29	55	24	31	67	29	38	72	31	41
80-84	26	8	18	30	10	21	35	13	22	43	15	28
85-89	8	2	6	12	2	9	14	3	11	17	4	12
90-94	2	0	2	2	0	2	4	0	3	5	0	4
95-99	0	0	0	0	0	0	0	0	0	1	0	1
100 +	0	0	0	0	0	0	0	0	0	0	0	0

Age group	2025 Both sexes	2025 Males	2025 Females	2030 Both sexes	2030 Males	2030 Females	2035 Both sexes	2035 Males	2035 Females	2040 Both sexes	2040 Males	2040 Females
All ages	3 696	1 823	1 874	3 791	1 867	1 924	3 882	1 911	1 972	3 984	1 961	2 022
0-4	302	156	146	283	146	136	290	150	140	312	161	150
5-9	324	168	157	300	155	145	281	145	135	288	149	139
10-14	315	163	152	323	167	156	299	155	144	280	145	135
15-19	279	144	135	309	160	150	317	164	153	293	152	142
20-24	233	120	113	269	139	131	299	154	145	307	158	148
25-29	250	128	122	223	114	109	259	133	126	289	149	140
30-34	275	141	134	243	124	119	216	110	105	252	129	123
35-39	273	138	135	270	138	132	237	121	116	211	108	103
40-44	238	114	124	269	136	133	266	136	130	234	119	115
45-49	187	86	101	235	112	123	266	134	132	262	134	129
50-54	179	83	96	184	85	100	231	110	121	262	131	130
55-59	192	90	101	175	81	94	180	82	98	227	107	119
60-64	193	93	99	185	86	99	169	77	92	174	79	96
65-69	177	85	92	181	85	95	174	79	95	160	71	88
70-74	121	56	65	157	72	85	161	73	88	157	68	88
75-79	81	35	46	97	41	56	128	54	74	133	56	77
80-84	47	17	31	55	19	35	67	24	43	91	33	58
85-89	22	5	17	25	6	19	30	7	22	38	10	28
90-94	6	1	5	8	1	7	10	1	9	12	2	11
95-99	1	0	1	1	0	1	2	0	2	3	0	3
100 +	0	0	0	0	0	0	0	0	0	0	0	0

Age group	2045 Both sexes	2045 Males	2045 Females	2050 Both sexes	2050 Males	2050 Females
All ages	4 084	2 014	2 070	4 169	2 061	2 108
0-4	321	166	155	312	162	151
5-9	310	160	150	319	165	154
10-14	287	149	138	309	160	149
15-19	274	142	132	281	146	136
20-24	283	146	137	264	136	127
25-29	297	153	144	273	141	132
30-34	282	145	137	290	149	141
35-39	247	126	120	277	142	135
40-44	207	105	101	243	124	119
45-49	230	117	113	204	104	100
50-54	259	132	127	227	115	112
55-59	257	128	129	254	129	125
60-64	220	103	117	249	124	126
65-69	165	73	92	209	96	112
70-74	144	62	82	150	64	86
75-79	131	53	78	122	49	73
80-84	96	35	61	97	34	62
85-89	53	14	39	58	16	42
90-94	17	3	14	24	4	20
95-99	4	0	3	5	0	5
100 +	0	0	0	1	0	1

United Nations Department of Economic and Social Affairs/Population Division
World Population Prospects: The 2004 Revision, Volume II: Sex and Age Distribution of the World Population

160

POPULATION BY AGE AND SEX (in thousands)

Age group	2005			2010			2015			2020		
	Both sexes	Males	Females	Both sexes	Males	Females	Both sexes	Males	Females	Both sexes	Males	Females
All ages	3 130	1 552	1 578	3 186	1 576	1 610	3 241	1 598	1 643	3 270	1 608	1 662
0-4	253	131	123	226	117	109	213	110	103	194	100	94
5-9	278	143	135	250	129	121	224	115	108	211	109	102
10-14	312	161	151	276	142	134	249	128	121	222	115	108
15-19	312	159	153	303	156	147	270	139	131	243	125	118
20-24	270	132	138	296	151	146	293	151	142	260	133	127
25-29	211	99	111	255	124	132	286	145	141	283	145	138
30-34	197	93	104	200	93	106	248	120	128	279	141	138
35-39	209	100	109	189	89	100	194	90	104	242	116	126
40-44	213	106	107	203	97	106	185	87	99	191	88	102
45-49	207	104	103	209	103	105	200	95	105	182	85	97
50-54	159	81	78	203	101	101	205	101	104	196	93	103
55-59	133	68	65	154	78	77	197	98	99	200	98	102
60-64	115	58	57	127	64	63	148	74	74	190	93	97
65-69	102	51	51	106	52	53	117	58	60	138	67	71
70-74	73	36	37	87	42	46	92	43	49	103	48	54
75-79	49	19	29	55	24	31	67	29	38	72	31	41
80-84	26	8	18	30	10	21	35	13	22	43	15	28
85-89	8	2	6	12	2	9	14	3	11	17	4	12
90-94	2	0	2	2	0	2	4	0	3	5	0	4
95-99	0	0	0	0	0	0	0	0	0	1	0	1
100 +	0	0	0	0	0	0	0	0	0	0	0	0

Age group	2025			2030			2035			2040		
	Both sexes	Males	Females	Both sexes	Males	Females	Both sexes	Males	Females	Both sexes	Males	Females
All ages	3 272	1 603	1 668	3 240	1 582	1 658	3 179	1 547	1 632	3 093	1 501	1 592
0-4	178	92	86	155	80	75	137	71	66	123	64	59
5-9	193	100	93	176	91	85	154	80	74	136	70	65
10-14	209	108	101	191	99	92	175	91	84	153	79	74
15-19	217	112	105	204	105	98	186	96	90	169	88	82
20-24	233	120	113	207	106	100	194	100	94	176	91	85
25-29	250	128	122	223	114	109	197	101	96	184	95	89
30-34	275	141	134	243	124	119	216	110	105	190	97	92
35-39	273	138	135	270	138	132	237	121	116	211	108	103
40-44	238	114	124	260	130	133	266	136	130	234	119	115
45-49	187	86	101	235	112	123	266	134	132	262	134	129
50-54	179	83	96	184	85	100	231	110	121	262	131	130
55-59	192	90	101	175	81	94	180	82	98	227	107	110
60-64	193	93	99	185	86	99	169	77	92	174	79	96
65-69	177	85	92	181	85	95	174	79	95	160	71	88
70-74	121	56	65	157	72	85	161	73	88	157	68	88
75-79	81	35	46	97	41	56	128	54	74	133	56	77
80-84	47	17	31	55	19	35	67	24	43	91	33	58
85-89	22	5	17	25	6	19	30	7	22	38	10	28
90-94	6	1	5	8	1	7	10	1	9	12	2	11
95-99	1	0	1	1	0	1	2	0	2	3	0	3
100 +	0	0	0	0	0	0	0	0	0	0	0	0

Age group	2045			2050		
	Both sexes	Males	Females	Both sexes	Males	Females
All ages	2 985	1 446	1 539	2 859	1 384	1 475
0-4	112	58	54	100	52	48
5-9	122	63	59	110	57	53
10-14	134	70	65	121	63	58
15-19	147	76	71	129	67	62
20-24	159	82	77	137	71	66
25-29	166	86	81	150	77	73
30-34	177	91	86	159	82	77
35-39	185	94	90	172	88	84
40-44	207	105	101	181	92	89
45-49	230	117	113	204	104	100
50-54	259	132	127	227	115	112
55-59	257	128	129	254	129	125
60-64	220	103	117	249	124	126
65-69	165	73	92	209	96	112
70-74	144	62	82	150	64	86
75-79	131	53	78	122	49	73
80-84	96	35	61	97	34	62
85-89	53	14	39	58	16	42
90-94	17	3	14	24	4	20
95-99	4	0	3	5	0	5
100 +	0	0	0	1	0	1

United Nations Department of Economic and Social Affairs/Population Division
World Population Prospects: The 2004 Revision, Volume II: Sex and Age Distribution of the World Population

161

POPULATION BY AGE AND SEX (in thousands)

Age group	1950 Both sexes	Males	Females	1955 Both sexes	Males	Females	1960 Both sexes	Males	Females	1965 Both sexes	Males	Females
All ages	8 753	4 465	4 288	9 715	4 927	4 788	10 800	5 436	5 364	11 923	5 990	5 933
0-4	1 390	699	691	1 627	829	798	1 960	1 011	949	2 326	1 181	1 145
5-9	1 122	558	564	1 289	646	642	1 510	768	742	1 789	922	867
10-14	1 001	499	502	1 099	547	552	1 256	630	626	1 434	730	704
15-19	876	441	435	978	487	491	1 063	527	536	1 184	594	590
20-24	756	385	371	839	420	419	913	447	466	975	480	495
25-29	649	333	315	717	363	354	775	380	395	827	401	426
30-34	555	291	265	613	313	300	658	327	331	694	337	357
35-39	479	257	222	522	271	251	559	279	280	585	288	297
40-44	410	224	185	447	237	210	472	239	233	489	241	248
45-49	353	192	160	377	204	173	398	206	192	406	203	203
50-54	299	159	139	319	171	147	331	174	157	336	172	164
55-59	268	133	135	263	138	126	272	142	130	271	142	129
60-64	213	106	108	227	110	117	217	110	107	215	111	104
65-69	166	84	83	169	82	88	181	86	95	161	81	80
70-74	122	58	63	129	62	67	134	63	71	134	63	71
75-79	64	30	34	67	32	35	69	32	37	67	31	36
80 +	31	14	17	32	15	17	32	14	17	30	13	16

Age group	1970 Both sexes	Males	Females	1975 Both sexes	Males	Females	1980 Both sexes	Males	Females	1985 Both sexes	Males	Females
All ages	13 746	6 721	7 025	16 018	7 901	8 117	18 811	9 440	9 371	22 097	11 112	10 985
0-4	2 674	1 364	1 310	3 005	1 533	1 472	3 359	1 712	1 647	3 841	1 961	1 880
5-9	2 195	1 118	1 078	2 517	1 281	1 236	2 826	1 439	1 387	3 284	1 675	1 609
10-14	1 779	907	872	2 104	1 071	1 033	2 437	1 241	1 196	2 800	1 426	1 374
15-19	1 395	711	684	1 642	837	805	2 050	1 045	1 005	2 426	1 235	1 191
20-24	1 021	484	537	1 326	662	664	1 589	810	778	2 043	1 041	1 003
25-29	790	348	442	1 011	478	533	1 350	686	664	1 580	805	775
30-34	711	319	392	742	338	404	953	458	496	1 338	679	659
35-39	678	308	370	724	331	393	748	363	385	940	451	490
40-44	524	243	281	644	299	345	746	358	388	734	356	378
45-49	408	193	215	523	245	277	690	343	347	730	350	381
50-54	374	176	198	429	202	226	530	256	274	667	331	337
55-59	337	158	179	377	177	200	422	205	217	503	242	261
60-64	293	138	155	305	143	162	354	171	183	389	187	202
65-69	219	102	116	265	124	141	277	133	144	312	149	164
70-74	153	70	83	183	84	99	228	108	121	226	106	120
75-79	98	43	55	119	52	67	132	61	72	164	73	91
80 +	99	40	59	102	43	59	119	51	67	120	48	72

Age group	1990 Both sexes	Males	Females	1995 Both sexes	Males	Females	2000 Both sexes	Males	Females	2005 Both sexes	Males	Females
All ages	25 291	12 739	12 552	28 271	14 255	14 016	30 463	15 360	15 103	32 854	16 577	16 277
0-4	3 841	1 963	1 878	3 639	1 858	1 780	3 012	1 540	1 472	3 160	1 616	1 544
5-9	3 786	1 934	1 852	3 800	1 941	1 858	3 604	1 841	1 764	2 991	1 529	1 462
10-14	3 258	1 661	1 597	3 763	1 922	1 841	3 778	1 929	1 848	3 589	1 832	1 757
15-19	2 769	1 409	1 360	3 230	1 646	1 584	3 716	1 895	1 821	3 748	1 912	1 835
20-24	2 390	1 214	1 175	2 737	1 391	1 346	3 170	1 611	1 559	3 676	1 872	1 804
25-29	2 013	1 024	989	2 362	1 199	1 163	2 688	1 362	1 326	3 136	1 591	1 545
30-34	1 556	792	764	1 989	1 011	979	2 324	1 176	1 147	2 661	1 346	1 314
35-39	1 313	665	648	1 533	779	754	1 954	990	964	2 296	1 161	1 135
40-44	921	440	480	1 291	653	638	1 502	762	740	1 926	975	951
45-49	718	347	370	903	431	471	1 263	638	625	1 477	748	729
50-54	708	338	370	698	337	361	876	417	459	1 232	621	611
55-59	637	314	322	678	323	355	667	320	346	842	399	442
60-64	468	224	244	594	292	303	633	299	334	626	299	327
65-69	348	165	182	420	198	222	534	259	275	573	267	306
70-74	259	120	139	291	135	156	352	162	190	452	214	238
75-79	166	74	93	192	85	108	216	95	121	265	117	149
80 +	139	53	86	151	56	95	176	65	111	203	76	128

162

United Nations Department of Economic and Social Affairs/Population Division
World Population Prospects: The 2004 Revision, Volume II: Sex and Age Distribution of the World Population

POPULATION BY AGE AND SEX (in thousands)

Age group	2005 Both sexes	Males	Females	2010 Both sexes	Males	Females	2015 Both sexes	Males	Females	2020 Both sexes	Males	Females
All ages	32 854	16 577	16 277	35 420	17 874	17 546	38 088	19 217	18 868	40 624	20 491	20 133
0-4	3 160	1 616	1 544	3 442	1 760	1 683	3 616	1 848	1 769	3 579	1 829	1 750
5-9	2 991	1 529	1 462	3 142	1 607	1 535	3 427	1 751	1 676	3 603	1 840	1 763
10-14	3 589	1 832	1 757	2 979	1 522	1 457	3 132	1 601	1 531	3 417	1 745	1 672
15-19	3 748	1 912	1 835	3 555	1 813	1 742	2 949	1 505	1 444	3 102	1 584	1 518
20-24	3 676	1 872	1 804	3 699	1 884	1 816	3 510	1 786	1 724	2 907	1 480	1 427
25-29	3 136	1 591	1 545	3 635	1 847	1 788	3 661	1 860	1 801	3 474	1 763	1 711
30-34	2 661	1 346	1 314	3 103	1 572	1 532	3 603	1 828	1 775	3 631	1 842	1 789
35-39	2 296	1 161	1 135	2 629	1 328	1 301	3 073	1 554	1 519	3 572	1 810	1 763
40-44	1 926	975	951	2 265	1 144	1 121	2 600	1 311	1 288	3 043	1 537	1 506
45-49	1 477	748	729	1 896	959	937	2 234	1 127	1 107	2 567	1 294	1 274
50-54	1 232	621	611	1 443	730	713	1 857	937	920	2 192	1 103	1 089
55-59	842	399	442	1 187	596	591	1 394	702	692	1 799	904	895
60-64	626	299	327	794	374	420	1 124	560	564	1 325	662	663
65-69	573	267	306	570	268	301	726	337	389	1 032	507	525
70-74	452	214	238	488	222	266	488	224	264	627	283	343
75-79	265	117	149	343	156	188	375	163	212	379	166	213
80-84	134	54	80	166	67	99	217	91	126	242	97	145
85-89	54	18	36	62	21	41	78	27	51	104	37	66
90-94	13	3	10	16	4	12	19	5	14	24	6	18
95-99	2	0	2	2	0	2	3	0	3	4	1	3
100 +	0	0	0	0	0	0	0	0	0	0	0	0

Age group	2025 Both sexes	Males	Females	2030 Both sexes	Males	Females	2035 Both sexes	Males	Females	2040 Both sexes	Males	Females
All ages	42 871	21 613	21 258	44 706	22 515	22 191	46 217	23 240	22 978	47 508	23 843	23 665
0-4	3 347	1 711	1 635	3 082	1 577	1 505	2 950	1 511	1 440	2 957	1 514	1 442
5-9	3 569	1 823	1 746	3 338	1 707	1 631	3 075	1 573	1 502	2 944	1 508	1 437
10-14	3 595	1 836	1 760	3 562	1 820	1 743	3 332	1 704	1 629	3 070	1 571	1 499
15-19	3 396	1 733	1 663	3 574	1 824	1 751	3 542	1 808	1 734	3 313	1 693	1 621
20-24	3 072	1 566	1 507	3 366	1 715	1 651	3 545	1 806	1 739	3 514	1 791	1 723
25-29	2 883	1 465	1 418	3 048	1 551	1 497	3 343	1 701	1 642	3 522	1 792	1 730
30-34	3 452	1 750	1 702	2 863	1 453	1 410	3 029	1 540	1 490	3 324	1 689	1 635
35-39	3 607	1 828	1 779	3 430	1 738	1 693	2 846	1 443	1 403	3 012	1 530	1 482
40-44	3 544	1 794	1 750	3 581	1 814	1 767	3 408	1 725	1 683	2 827	1 433	1 394
45-49	3 011	1 519	1 491	3 511	1 776	1 735	3 550	1 797	1 753	3 380	1 710	1 669
50-54	2 525	1 270	1 255	2 965	1 494	1 471	3 462	1 748	1 713	3 503	1 771	1 733
55-59	2 130	1 068	1 062	2 458	1 231	1 227	2 892	1 451	1 441	3 382	1 702	1 680
60-64	1 716	855	860	2 037	1 013	1 024	2 357	1 171	1 186	2 780	1 384	1 396
65-69	1 223	602	621	1 591	782	810	1 897	929	968	2 203	1 079	1 124
70-74	898	430	468	1 072	513	558	1 403	670	733	1 684	803	881
75-79	494	212	281	714	325	388	861	392	469	1 140	518	622
80-84	250	101	150	333	130	203	409	202	207	601	249	352
85-89	121	41	80	129	43	86	177	56	121	267	91	176
90-94	34	9	25	42	10	33	48	11	37	70	15	54
95-99	5	1	4	7	1	6	10	1	9	12	1	11
100 +	0	0	0	1	0	1	1	0	1	1	0	1

Age group	2045 Both sexes	Males	Females	2050 Both sexes	Males	Females
All ages	48 635	24 361	24 274	49 500	24 745	24 755
0-4	3 034	1 554	1 480	3 026	1 550	1 476
5-9	2 951	1 511	1 440	3 029	1 551	1 478
10-14	2 940	1 505	1 435	2 947	1 509	1 438
15-19	3 052	1 560	1 491	2 922	1 495	1 427
20-24	3 286	1 676	1 610	3 025	1 544	1 481
25-29	3 492	1 777	1 714	3 264	1 663	1 602
30-34	3 504	1 781	1 723	3 473	1 766	1 707
35-39	3 306	1 679	1 627	3 486	1 771	1 715
40-44	2 994	1 520	1 474	3 288	1 669	1 619
45-49	2 804	1 420	1 384	2 971	1 507	1 464
50-54	3 338	1 687	1 651	2 771	1 401	1 370
55-59	3 428	1 726	1 702	3 270	1 647	1 623
60-64	3 259	1 628	1 631	3 310	1 655	1 655
65-69	2 609	1 281	1 328	3 069	1 514	1 556
70-74	1 970	940	1 030	2 347	1 125	1 222
75-79	1 385	630	755	1 638	748	890
80-84	814	338	476	1 007	421	586
85-89	340	118	222	476	168	308
90-94	109	26	83	146	37	109
95-99	19	2	17	31	4	27
100 +	2	0	2	3	0	3

POPULATION BY AGE AND SEX (in thousands)

Age group	2005 Both sexes	2005 Males	2005 Females	2010 Both sexes	2010 Males	2010 Females	2015 Both sexes	2015 Males	2015 Females	2020 Both sexes	2020 Males	2020 Females
All ages	32 854	16 577	16 277	35 781	18 058	17 723	39 083	19 727	19 356	42 449	21 423	21 026
0-4	3 160	1 616	1 544	3 804	1 944	1 859	4 255	2 174	2 081	4 408	2 252	2 155
5-9	2 991	1 529	1 462	3 142	1 607	1 535	3 787	1 935	1 852	4 240	2 166	2 074
10-14	3 589	1 832	1 757	2 979	1 522	1 457	3 132	1 601	1 531	3 777	1 929	1 848
15-19	3 748	1 912	1 835	3 555	1 813	1 742	2 949	1 505	1 444	3 102	1 584	1 518
20-24	3 676	1 872	1 804	3 699	1 884	1 816	3 510	1 786	1 724	2 907	1 480	1 427
25-29	3 136	1 591	1 545	3 635	1 847	1 788	3 661	1 860	1 801	3 474	1 763	1 711
30-34	2 661	1 346	1 314	3 103	1 572	1 532	3 603	1 828	1 775	3 631	1 842	1 789
35-39	2 296	1 161	1 135	2 629	1 328	1 301	3 073	1 554	1 519	3 572	1 810	1 763
40-44	1 926	975	951	2 265	1 144	1 121	2 600	1 311	1 288	3 043	1 537	1 506
45-49	1 477	748	729	1 896	959	937	2 234	1 127	1 107	2 567	1 294	1 274
50-54	1 232	621	611	1 443	730	713	1 857	937	920	2 192	1 103	1 089
55-59	842	399	442	1 187	596	591	1 394	702	692	1 799	904	895
60-64	626	299	327	794	374	420	1 124	560	564	1 325	662	663
65-69	573	267	306	570	268	301	726	337	389	1 032	507	525
70-74	452	214	238	488	222	266	488	224	264	627	283	343
75-79	265	117	149	343	156	188	375	163	212	379	166	213
80-84	134	54	80	166	67	99	217	91	126	242	97	145
85-89	54	18	36	62	21	41	78	27	51	104	37	66
90-94	13	3	10	16	4	12	19	5	14	24	6	18
95-99	2	0	2	2	0	2	3	0	3	4	1	3
100 +	0	0	0	0	0	0	0	0	0	0	0	0

Age group	2025 Both sexes	2025 Males	2025 Females	2030 Both sexes	2030 Males	2030 Females	2035 Both sexes	2035 Males	2035 Females	2040 Both sexes	2040 Males	2040 Females
All ages	45 502	22 957	22 545	48 145	24 272	23 873	50 580	25 469	25 111	53 037	26 670	26 368
0-4	4 156	2 125	2 031	3 894	1 992	1 901	3 880	1 986	1 893	4 130	2 115	2 015
5-9	4 395	2 246	2 150	4 146	2 120	2 026	3 886	1 988	1 898	3 872	1 983	1 890
10-14	4 231	2 160	2 071	4 388	2 241	2 147	4 140	2 116	2 024	3 880	1 985	1 895
15-19	3 754	1 916	1 838	4 210	2 148	2 062	4 366	2 229	2 138	4 120	2 105	2 015
20-24	3 072	1 566	1 507	3 724	1 898	1 827	4 179	2 130	2 050	4 337	2 211	2 126
25-29	2 883	1 465	1 418	3 048	1 551	1 497	3 700	1 883	1 817	4 155	2 115	2 040
30-34	3 452	1 750	1 702	2 863	1 453	1 410	3 029	1 540	1 490	3 680	1 871	1 809
35-39	3 607	1 828	1 779	3 430	1 738	1 693	2 846	1 443	1 403	3 012	1 530	1 482
40-44	3 544	1 794	1 750	3 581	1 814	1 767	3 408	1 725	1 682	2 827	1 433	1 394
45-49	3 011	1 519	1 491	3 511	1 776	1 735	3 550	1 797	1 753	3 380	1 710	1 669
50-54	2 525	1 270	1 255	2 965	1 494	1 471	3 462	1 748	1 713	3 503	1 771	1 733
55-59	2 130	1 068	1 062	2 458	1 231	1 227	2 892	1 451	1 441	3 382	1 702	1 680
60-64	1 716	855	860	2 037	1 013	1 024	2 357	1 171	1 186	2 780	1 384	1 396
65-69	1 223	602	621	1 591	782	810	1 897	929	968	2 203	1 079	1 124
70-74	898	430	468	1 072	513	558	1 403	670	733	1 684	803	881
75-79	494	212	281	714	325	388	861	392	469	1 140	518	622
80-84	250	101	150	333	130	203	489	202	287	601	249	352
85-89	121	41	80	129	43	86	177	56	121	267	91	176
90-94	34	9	25	42	10	33	48	11	37	70	15	54
95-99	5	1	4	7	1	6	10	1	9	12	1	11
100 +	0	0	0	1	0	1	1	0	1	1	0	1

Age group	2045 Both sexes	2045 Males	2045 Females	2050 Both sexes	2050 Males	2050 Females
All ages	55 604	27 925	27 680	58 087	29 136	28 950
0-4	4 482	2 295	2 186	4 654	2 384	2 271
5-9	4 123	2 111	2 011	4 475	2 292	2 183
10-14	3 867	1 980	1 887	4 118	2 108	2 009
15-19	3 861	1 974	1 887	3 848	1 969	1 879
20-24	4 091	2 088	2 004	3 833	1 957	1 876
25-29	4 313	2 196	2 117	4 068	2 073	1 995
30-34	4 135	2 103	2 032	4 293	2 184	2 109
35-39	3 662	1 860	1 801	4 116	2 092	2 024
40-44	2 994	1 520	1 474	3 641	1 849	1 792
45-49	2 804	1 420	1 384	2 971	1 507	1 464
50-54	3 338	1 687	1 651	2 771	1 401	1 370
55-59	3 428	1 726	1 702	3 270	1 647	1 623
60-64	3 259	1 628	1 631	3 310	1 655	1 655
65-69	2 609	1 281	1 328	3 069	1 514	1 556
70-74	1 970	940	1 030	2 347	1 125	1 222
75-79	1 385	630	755	1 638	748	890
80-84	814	338	476	1 007	421	586
85-89	340	118	222	476	168	308
90-94	109	26	83	146	37	109
95-99	19	2	17	31	4	27
100 +	2	0	2	3	0	3

United Nations Department of Economic and Social Affairs/Population Division
World Population Prospects: The 2004 Revision, Volume II: Sex and Age Distribution of the World Population

164

POPULATION BY AGE AND SEX (in thousands)

Age group	2005 Both sexes	Males	Females	2010 Both sexes	Males	Females	2015 Both sexes	Males	Females	2020 Both sexes	Males	Females
All ages	32 854	16 577	16 277	35 058	17 689	17 370	37 086	18 706	18 379	38 800	19 559	19 241
0-4	3 160	1 616	1 544	3 081	1 575	1 506	2 977	1 521	1 456	2 751	1 406	1 345
5-9	2 991	1 529	1 462	3 142	1 607	1 535	3 067	1 567	1 500	2 966	1 515	1 451
10-14	3 589	1 832	1 757	2 979	1 522	1 457	3 132	1 601	1 531	3 058	1 562	1 496
15-19	3 748	1 912	1 835	3 555	1 813	1 742	2 949	1 505	1 444	3 102	1 584	1 518
20-24	3 676	1 872	1 804	3 699	1 884	1 816	3 510	1 786	1 724	2 907	1 480	1 427
25-29	3 136	1 591	1 545	3 635	1 847	1 788	3 661	1 860	1 801	3 474	1 763	1 711
30-34	2 661	1 346	1 314	3 103	1 572	1 532	3 603	1 828	1 775	3 631	1 842	1 789
35-39	2 296	1 161	1 135	2 629	1 328	1 301	3 073	1 554	1 519	3 572	1 810	1 763
40-44	1 926	975	951	2 265	1 144	1 121	2 600	1 311	1 288	3 043	1 537	1 506
45-49	1 477	748	729	1 896	959	937	2 234	1 127	1 107	2 567	1 294	1 274
50-54	1 232	621	611	1 443	730	713	1 857	937	920	2 192	1 103	1 089
55-59	842	399	442	1 187	596	591	1 394	702	692	1 799	904	895
60-64	626	299	327	794	374	420	1 124	560	564	1 325	662	663
65-69	573	267	306	570	268	301	726	337	389	1 032	507	525
70-74	452	214	238	488	222	266	488	224	264	627	283	343
75-79	265	117	149	343	156	188	375	163	212	379	166	213
80-84	134	54	80	166	67	99	217	91	126	242	97	145
85-89	54	18	36	62	21	41	78	27	51	104	37	66
90-94	13	3	10	16	4	12	19	5	14	24	6	18
95-99	2	0	2	2	0	2	3	0	3	4	1	3
100 +	0	0	0	0	0	0	0	0	0	0	0	0

Age group	2025 Both sexes	Males	Females	2030 Both sexes	Males	Females	2035 Both sexes	Males	Females	2040 Both sexes	Males	Females
All ages	40 241	20 269	19 972	41 285	20 767	20 518	41 939	21 053	20 886	42 223	21 141	21 082
0-4	2 538	1 298	1 240	2 286	1 170	1 116	2 088	1 069	1 019	1 944	996	948
5-9	2 743	1 401	1 342	2 531	1 294	1 237	2 280	1 167	1 113	2 083	1 067	1 017
10-14	2 959	1 511	1 448	2 737	1 398	1 339	2 526	1 291	1 235	2 276	1 164	1 112
15-19	3 037	1 550	1 487	2 939	1 499	1 440	2 718	1 387	1 331	2 508	1 281	1 227
20-24	3 072	1 566	1 507	3 008	1 533	1 476	2 911	1 483	1 429	2 692	1 371	1 320
25-29	2 883	1 465	1 418	3 048	1 551	1 497	2 986	1 518	1 467	2 889	1 469	1 420
30-34	3 452	1 750	1 702	2 863	1 453	1 410	3 029	1 540	1 490	2 968	1 508	1 460
35-39	3 607	1 828	1 779	3 430	1 738	1 693	2 846	1 443	1 403	3 012	1 530	1 482
40-44	3 544	1 794	1 750	3 581	1 814	1 767	3 408	1 725	1 682	2 827	1 433	1 394
45-49	3 011	1 519	1 491	3 511	1 776	1 735	3 550	1 707	1 753	3 000	1 710	1 009
50-54	2 525	1 270	1 255	2 965	1 494	1 471	3 462	1 748	1 713	3 503	1 771	1 733
55-59	2 130	1 068	1 062	2 458	1 231	1 227	2 892	1 451	1 441	3 382	1 702	1 680
60-64	1 716	855	860	2 037	1 013	1 024	2 057	1 171	1 186	2 780	1 384	1 396
65-69	1 223	602	621	1 591	782	810	1 897	929	968	2 203	1 079	1 124
70-74	898	430	468	1 072	513	558	1 403	670	733	1 684	803	881
75-79	494	212	281	714	325	388	861	392	469	1 140	518	622
80-84	250	101	150	333	130	203	489	202	287	601	249	352
85-89	121	41	80	129	43	86	177	56	121	267	91	176
90-94	34	9	25	42	10	33	48	11	37	70	15	54
95-99	5	1	4	7	1	6	10	1	9	12	1	11
100 +	0	0	0	1	0	1	1	0	1	1	0	1

Age group	2045 Both sexes	Males	Females	2050 Both sexes	Males	Females
All ages	42 177	21 059	21 118	41 769	20 792	20 977
0-4	1 853	949	904	1 744	893	851
5-9	1 939	993	946	1 849	947	902
10-14	2 079	1 064	1 015	1 936	991	944
15-19	2 258	1 154	1 104	2 062	1 055	1 007
20-24	2 482	1 266	1 217	2 233	1 139	1 094
25-29	2 670	1 358	1 312	2 462	1 253	1 209
30-34	2 872	1 459	1 413	2 654	1 348	1 306
35-39	2 951	1 498	1 453	2 856	1 450	1 407
40-44	2 994	1 520	1 474	2 934	1 488	1 445
45-49	2 804	1 420	1 384	2 971	1 507	1 464
50-54	3 338	1 687	1 651	2 771	1 401	1 370
55-59	3 428	1 726	1 702	3 270	1 647	1 623
60-64	3 259	1 628	1 631	3 310	1 655	1 655
65-69	2 609	1 281	1 328	3 069	1 514	1 556
70-74	1 970	940	1 030	2 347	1 125	1 222
75-79	1 385	630	755	1 638	748	890
80-84	814	338	476	1 007	421	586
85-89	340	118	222	476	168	308
90-94	109	26	83	146	37	109
95-99	19	2	17	31	4	27
100 +	2	0	2	3	0	3

POPULATION BY AGE AND SEX (in thousands)

Age group	1950 Both sexes	Males	Females	1955 Both sexes	Males	Females	1960 Both sexes	Males	Females	1965 Both sexes	Males	Females
All ages	4 148	2 034	2 113	4 531	2 221	2 310	5 011	2 456	2 556	5 505	2 699	2 806
0-4	703	351	352	833	413	420	945	469	476	1 057	526	531
5-9	538	267	271	582	289	293	699	345	354	791	391	400
10-14	467	232	235	505	251	254	548	272	276	650	321	329
15-19	415	206	209	445	221	224	483	240	243	515	256	259
20-24	366	181	185	393	195	198	422	209	213	451	223	228
25-29	319	157	162	343	169	174	369	182	187	391	193	198
30-34	277	136	141	297	146	151	320	157	163	340	167	173
35-39	238	116	121	255	125	130	275	135	140	292	143	149
40-44	201	98	103	217	106	111	234	114	120	249	121	127
45-49	168	81	87	181	87	94	196	95	101	209	101	108
50-54	138	65	73	149	71	78	161	77	85	173	82	90
55-59	111	51	59	118	55	64	128	60	69	138	64	74
60-64	78	36	43	90	41	49	97	44	53	104	48	57
65-69	58	26	32	58	26	32	67	30	37	73	32	40
70-74	38	17	22	37	16	21	37	16	21	44	19	25
75-79	20	8	11	19	8	11	19	8	11	20	8	12
80 +	11	5	7	10	4	6	9	4	6	9	4	6

Age group	1970 Both sexes	Males	Females	1975 Both sexes	Males	Females	1980 Both sexes	Males	Females	1985 Both sexes	Males	Females
All ages	6 083	2 985	3 098	6 813	3 347	3 466	7 835	3 853	3 982	9 276	4 565	4 711
0-4	1 166	581	585	1 296	647	649	1 523	760	763	1 820	909	911
5-9	895	444	451	1 009	501	508	1 150	572	578	1 390	692	698
10-14	737	364	372	845	419	426	971	482	489	1 136	565	571
15-19	612	302	310	702	347	355	820	407	414	967	480	487
20-24	482	239	243	580	286	295	678	334	344	813	402	411
25-29	419	206	213	453	223	230	556	272	284	667	327	340
30-34	361	177	184	392	192	199	432	212	220	544	266	279
35-39	312	153	159	336	165	171	371	182	189	421	207	214
40-44	266	130	136	287	140	147	316	154	161	359	175	183
45-49	224	108	116	242	117	125	267	130	138	302	146	155
50-54	185	88	97	201	96	105	222	106	116	252	121	131
55-59	149	70	79	162	76	86	180	85	95	205	96	108
60-64	113	52	62	124	57	67	139	64	75	159	73	85
65-69	79	35	44	88	40	49	99	45	55	114	52	63
70-74	48	21	28	55	24	31	63	27	35	72	32	41
75-79	24	10	14	28	11	16	32	14	19	38	16	22
80 +	10	4	6	12	5	8	15	6	9	18	7	11

Age group	1990 Both sexes	Males	Females	1995 Both sexes	Males	Females	2000 Both sexes	Males	Females	2005 Both sexes	Males	Females
All ages	10 532	5 186	5 346	12 280	6 047	6 233	13 841	6 818	7 022	15 941	7 861	8 081
0-4	2 075	1 036	1 039	2 406	1 202	1 204	2 573	1 286	1 286	2 974	1 487	1 487
5-9	1 592	792	799	1 875	933	942	2 142	1 067	1 075	2 348	1 170	1 178
10-14	1 315	654	661	1 551	772	779	1 791	891	900	2 085	1 038	1 047
15-19	1 084	539	545	1 292	643	649	1 494	743	751	1 760	876	885
20-24	917	454	463	1 056	523	532	1 235	612	622	1 456	722	734
25-29	765	376	389	880	433	448	989	488	501	1 181	584	597
30-34	625	306	319	730	357	373	811	398	413	928	459	470
35-39	507	247	260	594	289	305	669	326	343	752	369	383
40-44	389	190	199	480	232	248	544	263	281	620	301	319
45-49	328	159	169	365	177	189	438	210	228	504	242	262
50-54	273	131	142	305	146	159	331	158	173	404	191	213
55-59	222	105	117	247	117	131	271	127	143	300	141	159
60-64	173	80	93	194	90	104	212	98	114	237	110	128
65-69	125	57	68	141	64	77	156	71	85	175	79	95
70-74	80	35	45	90	40	51	101	45	57	116	51	64
75-79	42	18	24	48	20	28	55	23	32	64	27	37
80 +	21	8	13	24	9	15	30	12	18	37	14	22

166

United Nations Department of Economic and Social Affairs/Population Division
World Population Prospects: The 2004 Revision, Volume II: Sex and Age Distribution of the World Population

POPULATION BY AGE AND SEX (in thousands)

Age group	2005 Both sexes	Males	Females	2010 Both sexes	Males	Females	2015 Both sexes	Males	Females	2020 Both sexes	Males	Females
All ages	15 941	7 861	8 081	18 327	9 045	9 282	20 947	10 347	10 600	23 777	11 752	12 025
0-4	2 974	1 487	1 487	3 379	1 689	1 690	3 775	1 887	1 888	4 125	2 063	2 062
5-9	2 348	1 170	1 178	2 726	1 358	1 368	3 110	1 548	1 562	3 500	1 741	1 759
10-14	2 085	1 038	1 047	2 285	1 138	1 147	2 643	1 315	1 328	3 016	1 499	1 517
15-19	1 760	876	885	2 048	1 019	1 029	2 237	1 114	1 124	2 583	1 284	1 299
20-24	1 456	722	734	1 716	851	865	1 992	988	1 004	2 173	1 078	1 095
25-29	1 181	584	597	1 391	688	703	1 640	811	829	1 905	942	963
30-34	928	459	470	1 106	548	558	1 303	647	656	1 541	764	777
35-39	752	369	383	862	427	435	1 024	509	514	1 208	602	606
40-44	620	301	319	697	341	355	796	394	401	945	471	475
45-49	504	242	262	575	277	298	644	314	330	735	362	372
50-54	404	191	213	465	220	245	529	252	277	592	286	306
55-59	300	141	159	367	171	196	422	197	225	480	226	255
60-64	237	110	128	264	122	142	324	148	175	373	171	202
65-69	175	79	95	197	89	108	220	100	121	271	122	149
70-74	116	51	64	131	58	73	149	66	83	168	74	94
75-79	64	27	37	74	32	43	86	36	49	99	42	57
80-84	27	11	16	33	13	19	38	16	23	45	18	27
85-89	8	3	5	10	4	6	12	4	8	14	5	9
90-94	1	0	1	2	1	1	2	1	2	3	1	2
95-99	0	0	0	0	0	0	0	0	0	0	0	0
100 +	0	0	0	0	0	0	0	0	0	0	0	0

Age group	2025 Both sexes	Males	Females	2030 Both sexes	Males	Females	2035 Both sexes	Males	Females	2040 Both sexes	Males	Females
All ages	26 829	13 267	13 563	30 050	14 863	15 186	33 376	16 512	16 864	36 751	18 184	18 566
0-4	4 422	2 214	2 209	4 666	2 338	2 328	4 851	2 432	2 418	4 979	2 498	2 480
5-9	3 860	1 922	1 938	4 171	2 078	2 093	4 433	2 211	2 222	4 641	2 317	2 324
10-14	3 410	1 695	1 716	3 775	1 877	1 898	4 091	2 036	2 055	4 360	2 172	2 188
15-19	2 954	1 467	1 487	3 348	1 661	1 686	3 712	1 843	1 869	4 031	2 003	2 028
20-24	2 514	1 246	1 268	2 880	1 426	1 455	3 271	1 618	1 653	3 635	1 799	1 836
25-29	2 084	1 031	1 053	2 418	1 195	1 223	2 778	1 371	1 407	3 164	1 561	1 603
30-34	1 798	890	907	1 973	977	996	2 297	1 136	1 161	2 650	1 309	1 341
35-39	1 436	714	722	1 684	836	848	1 856	921	935	2 170	1 075	1 095
40-44	1 120	558	562	1 339	666	673	1 578	783	795	1 747	867	880
45-49	876	434	442	1 043	518	526	1 253	621	633	1 484	734	750
50-54	678	331	347	812	399	413	972	479	493	1 173	576	596
55-59	540	257	283	621	300	321	747	363	384	899	438	461
60-64	426	107	229	482	226	256	558	265	292	675	323	352
65-69	314	141	173	362	164	198	412	190	222	481	225	256
70-74	209	92	118	245	108	137	285	126	159	328	148	181
75-79	113	48	65	142	60	82	169	72	97	200	86	114
80-84	53	21	31	62	25	37	79	32	47	96	39	57
85-89	17	6	11	21	8	13	25	9	16	33	12	21
90-94	4	1	2	5	1	3	6	2	4	7	2	5
95-99	0	0	0	1	0	0	1	0	1	1	0	1
100 +	0	0	0	0	0	0	0	0	0	0	0	0

Age group	2045 Both sexes	Males	Females	2050 Both sexes	Males	Females
All ages	40 137	19 862	20 275	43 501	21 526	21 976
0-4	5 066	2 545	2 522	5 124	2 575	2 549
5-9	4 793	2 396	2 397	4 905	2 454	2 451
10-14	4 574	2 281	2 293	4 733	2 363	2 370
15-19	4 302	2 140	2 162	4 520	2 251	2 269
20-24	3 954	1 959	1 995	4 228	2 096	2 131
25-29	3 526	1 741	1 785	3 846	1 900	1 946
30-34	3 029	1 495	1 534	3 389	1 674	1 716
35-39	2 514	1 244	1 271	2 888	1 427	1 461
40-44	2 052	1 017	1 035	2 389	1 182	1 208
45-49	1 650	816	834	1 947	962	985
50-54	1 394	685	710	1 558	765	793
55-59	1 090	530	560	1 302	633	669
60-64	817	392	424	996	478	518
65-69	586	276	310	715	338	377
70-74	387	177	210	477	220	257
75-79	233	102	132	279	124	155
80-84	116	48	68	138	58	80
85-89	41	16	26	51	20	31
90-94	9	3	6	12	4	8
95-99	1	0	1	2	0	1
100 +	0	0	0	0	0	0

POPULATION BY AGE AND SEX (in thousands)

Age group	2005			2010			2015			2020		
	Both sexes	Males	Females	Both sexes	Males	Females	Both sexes	Males	Females	Both sexes	Males	Females
All ages	15 941	7 861	8 081	18 458	9 111	9 347	21 316	10 531	10 785	24 493	12 109	12 384
0-4	2 974	1 487	1 487	3 509	1 754	1 755	4 025	2 012	2 013	4 493	2 247	2 245
5-9	2 348	1 170	1 178	2 726	1 358	1 368	3 230	1 607	1 623	3 732	1 857	1 875
10-14	2 085	1 038	1 047	2 285	1 138	1 147	2 643	1 315	1 328	3 132	1 557	1 575
15-19	1 760	876	885	2 048	1 019	1 029	2 237	1 114	1 124	2 583	1 284	1 299
20-24	1 456	722	734	1 716	851	865	1 992	988	1 004	2 173	1 078	1 095
25-29	1 181	584	597	1 391	688	703	1 640	811	829	1 905	942	963
30-34	928	459	470	1 106	548	558	1 303	647	656	1 541	764	777
35-39	752	369	383	862	427	435	1 024	509	514	1 208	602	606
40-44	620	301	319	697	341	355	796	394	401	945	471	475
45-49	504	242	262	575	277	298	644	314	330	735	362	372
50-54	404	191	213	465	220	245	529	252	277	592	286	306
55-59	300	141	159	367	171	196	422	197	225	480	226	255
60-64	237	110	128	264	122	142	324	148	175	373	171	202
65-69	175	79	95	197	89	108	220	100	121	271	122	149
70-74	116	51	64	131	58	73	149	66	83	168	74	94
75-79	64	27	37	74	32	43	86	36	49	99	42	57
80-84	27	11	16	33	13	19	38	16	23	45	18	27
85-89	8	3	5	10	4	6	12	4	8	14	5	9
90-94	1	0	1	2	1	1	2	1	2	3	1	2
95-99	0	0	0	0	0	0	0	0	0	0	0	0
100 +	0	0	0	0	0	0	0	0	0	0	0	0

Age group	2025			2030			2035			2040		
	Both sexes	Males	Females	Both sexes	Males	Females	Both sexes	Males	Females	Both sexes	Males	Females
All ages	27 960	13 830	14 130	31 720	15 696	16 024	35 773	17 707	18 066	40 092	19 851	20 242
0-4	4 869	2 437	2 431	5 246	2 628	2 618	5 629	2 822	2 806	5 990	3 006	2 984
5-9	4 204	2 093	2 111	4 592	2 288	2 304	4 985	2 486	2 499	5 385	2 689	2 696
10-14	3 636	1 807	1 829	4 112	2 044	2 067	4 505	2 242	2 263	4 902	2 442	2 460
15-19	3 068	1 523	1 544	3 569	1 771	1 798	4 043	2 008	2 035	4 438	2 205	2 232
20-24	2 514	1 246	1 268	2 992	1 481	1 511	3 487	1 725	1 762	3 959	1 960	1 999
25-29	2 084	1 031	1 053	2 418	1 195	1 223	2 886	1 424	1 461	3 373	1 664	1 709
30-34	1 798	890	907	1 973	977	996	2 297	1 136	1 161	2 752	1 359	1 393
35-39	1 436	714	722	1 684	836	848	1 856	921	935	2 170	1 075	1 095
40-44	1 120	558	562	1 339	666	673	1 578	783	795	1 747	867	880
45-49	876	434	442	1 043	518	526	1 253	621	633	1 484	734	750
50-54	678	331	347	812	399	413	972	479	493	1 173	576	596
55-59	540	257	283	621	300	321	747	363	384	899	438	461
60-64	426	197	229	482	226	256	558	265	292	675	323	352
65-69	314	141	173	362	164	198	412	190	222	481	225	256
70-74	209	92	118	245	108	137	285	126	159	328	148	181
75-79	113	48	65	142	60	82	169	72	97	200	86	114
80-84	53	21	31	62	25	37	79	32	47	96	39	57
85-89	17	6	11	21	8	13	25	9	16	33	12	21
90-94	4	1	2	5	1	3	6	2	4	7	2	5
95-99	0	0	0	1	0	0	1	0	1	1	0	1
100 +	0	0	0	0	0	0	0	0	0	0	0	0

Age group	2045			2050		
	Both sexes	Males	Females	Both sexes	Males	Females
All ages	44 636	22 106	22 530	49 365	24 452	24 913
0-4	6 311	3 169	3 141	6 594	3 314	3 280
5-9	5 767	2 883	2 884	6 110	3 057	3 053
10-14	5 308	2 647	2 661	5 695	2 843	2 852
15-19	4 837	2 406	2 431	5 246	2 612	2 634
20-24	4 353	2 157	2 197	4 754	2 357	2 396
25-29	3 841	1 896	1 945	4 235	2 093	2 142
30-34	3 230	1 594	1 635	3 692	1 823	1 869
35-39	2 612	1 292	1 320	3 080	1 522	1 558
40-44	2 052	1 017	1 035	2 482	1 227	1 254
45-49	1 650	816	834	1 947	962	985
50-54	1 394	685	710	1 558	765	793
55-59	1 090	530	560	1 302	633	669
60-64	817	392	424	996	478	518
65-69	586	276	310	715	338	377
70-74	387	177	210	477	220	257
75-79	233	102	132	279	124	155
80-84	116	48	68	138	58	80
85-89	41	16	26	51	20	31
90-94	9	3	6	12	4	8
95-99	1	0	1	2	0	1
100 +	0	0	0	0	0	0

POPULATION BY AGE AND SEX (in thousands)

Age group	2005			2010			2015			2020		
	Both sexes	Males	Females	Both sexes	Males	Females	Both sexes	Males	Females	Both sexes	Males	Females
All ages	15 941	7 861	8 081	18 196	8 980	9 216	20 577	10 162	10 415	23 062	11 395	11 667
0-4	2 974	1 487	1 487	3 248	1 623	1 624	3 526	1 762	1 763	3 757	1 879	1 878
5-9	2 348	1 170	1 178	2 726	1 358	1 368	2 990	1 488	1 502	3 269	1 626	1 643
10-14	2 085	1 038	1 047	2 285	1 138	1 147	2 643	1 315	1 328	2 899	1 441	1 458
15-19	1 760	876	885	2 048	1 019	1 029	2 237	1 114	1 124	2 583	1 284	1 299
20-24	1 456	722	734	1 716	851	865	1 992	988	1 004	2 173	1 078	1 095
25-29	1 181	584	597	1 391	688	703	1 640	811	829	1 905	942	963
30-34	928	459	470	1 106	548	558	1 303	647	656	1 541	764	777
35-39	752	369	383	862	427	435	1 024	509	514	1 208	602	606
40-44	620	301	319	697	341	355	796	394	401	945	471	475
45-49	504	242	262	575	277	298	644	314	330	735	362	372
50-54	404	191	213	465	220	245	529	252	277	592	286	306
55-59	300	141	159	367	171	196	422	197	225	480	226	255
60-64	237	110	128	264	122	142	324	148	175	373	171	202
65-69	175	79	95	197	89	108	220	100	121	271	122	149
70-74	116	51	64	131	58	73	149	66	83	168	74	94
75-79	64	27	37	74	32	43	86	36	49	99	42	57
80-84	27	11	16	33	13	19	38	16	23	45	18	27
85-89	8	3	5	10	4	6	12	4	8	14	5	9
90-94	1	0	1	2	1	1	2	1	2	3	1	2
95-99	0	0	0	0	0	0	0	0	0	0	0	0
100 +	0	0	0	0	0	0	0	0	0	0	0	0

Age group	2025			2030			2035			2040		
	Both sexes	Males	Females	Both sexes	Males	Females	Both sexes	Males	Females	Both sexes	Males	Females
All ages	25 702	12 704	12 998	28 397	14 039	14 357	31 036	15 345	15 690	33 544	16 586	16 959
0-4	3 979	1 992	1 987	4 101	2 055	2 046	4 114	2 063	2 051	4 047	2 031	2 016
5-9	3 516	1 750	1 766	3 753	1 870	1 883	3 896	1 943	1 953	3 935	1 965	1 970
10-14	3 185	1 583	1 602	3 438	1 710	1 729	3 681	1 832	1 849	3 831	1 908	1 923
15-19	2 840	1 410	1 429	3 126	1 551	1 575	3 381	1 679	1 702	3 626	1 802	1 824
20-24	2 514	1 246	1 268	2 769	1 370	1 399	3 054	1 511	1 544	3 310	1 638	1 672
25-29	2 084	1 031	1 053	2 418	1 195	1 223	2 671	1 318	1 353	2 954	1 457	1 497
30-34	1 798	890	907	1 973	977	996	2 297	1 136	1 161	2 547	1 258	1 289
35-39	1 436	714	722	1 684	836	848	1 856	921	935	2 170	1 075	1 095
40-44	1 120	558	562	1 339	666	673	1 578	783	795	1 747	867	880
45-49	876	434	442	1 043	518	526	1 253	621	633	1 484	734	750
50-54	678	331	347	812	399	413	972	479	493	1 173	576	596
55-59	540	257	283	621	300	321	747	363	384	899	438	461
60-64	420	197	229	482	226	256	558	265	292	675	323	352
65-69	314	141	173	362	164	198	412	190	222	481	225	256
70-74	209	92	118	245	108	137	285	126	159	328	148	181
75-79	113	48	65	142	60	82	169	72	97	200	86	114
80-84	53	21	31	62	25	37	79	32	47	86	30	57
85-89	17	6	11	21	8	13	25	9	16	33	12	21
90-94	4	1	2	5	1	3	6	2	4	7	2	5
95-99	0	0	0	1	0	0	1	0	1	1	0	1
100 +	0	0	0	0	0	0	0	0	0	0	0	0

Age group	2045			2050		
	Both sexes	Males	Females	Both sexes	Males	Females
All ages	35 895	17 746	18 149	38 072	18 817	19 255
0-4	3 949	1 983	1 966	3 836	1 928	1 908
5-9	3 896	1 947	1 949	3 823	1 913	1 910
10-14	3 878	1 934	1 944	3 847	1 921	1 927
15-19	3 780	1 881	1 900	3 833	1 909	1 924
20-24	3 557	1 762	1 795	3 715	1 842	1 873
25-29	3 211	1 585	1 626	3 460	1 710	1 750
30-34	2 829	1 396	1 432	3 087	1 524	1 562
35-39	2 417	1 196	1 221	2 697	1 333	1 364
40-44	2 052	1 017	1 035	2 297	1 136	1 161
45-49	1 650	816	834	1 947	962	985
50-54	1 394	685	710	1 558	765	793
55-59	1 090	530	560	1 302	633	669
60-64	817	392	424	996	478	518
65-69	586	276	310	715	338	377
70-74	387	177	210	477	220	257
75-79	233	102	132	279	124	155
80-84	116	48	68	138	58	80
85-89	41	16	26	51	20	31
90-94	9	3	6	12	4	8
95-99	1	0	1	2	0	1
100 +	0	0	0	0	0	0

POPULATION BY AGE AND SEX (in thousands)

Age group	1950 Both sexes	Males	Females	1955 Both sexes	Males	Females	1960 Both sexes	Males	Females	1965 Both sexes	Males	Females
All ages	17 150	8 827	8 323	18 928	9 666	9 261	20 616	10 470	10 146	22 283	11 244	11 039
0-4	1 947	992	955	2 158	1 096	1 062	2 261	1 148	1 113	2 343	1 189	1 154
5-9	1 710	867	843	1 941	988	952	2 140	1 086	1 054	2 245	1 140	1 105
10-14	1 579	801	778	1 725	874	850	1 943	989	954	2 142	1 087	1 055
15-19	1 568	796	772	1 619	818	801	1 738	882	857	1 955	995	960
20-24	1 579	802	777	1 612	815	797	1 632	825	807	1 750	887	863
25-29	1 469	749	720	1 599	810	790	1 614	816	798	1 634	825	809
30-34	1 320	673	647	1 473	749	724	1 592	806	786	1 607	811	796
35-39	1 241	639	602	1 315	668	646	1 460	741	719	1 578	797	781
40-44	1 127	594	534	1 225	628	597	1 295	656	639	1 440	728	711
45-49	974	526	448	1 098	574	524	1 194	608	586	1 265	637	629
50-54	797	431	366	932	497	435	1 053	544	510	1 149	578	571
55-59	632	345	288	744	395	349	874	458	416	992	502	490
60-64	486	260	226	570	303	267	676	350	326	796	405	391
65-69	329	170	159	417	216	201	494	255	240	589	292	297
70-74	201	99	102	263	130	132	338	168	170	401	196	206
75-79	110	51	59	144	67	77	191	90	102	248	116	132
80 +	82	33	49	94	38	56	120	49	71	149	61	88

Age group	1970 Both sexes	Males	Females	1975 Both sexes	Males	Females	1980 Both sexes	Males	Females	1985 Both sexes	Males	Females
All ages	23 962	12 019	11 943	26 049	13 004	13 046	28 094	13 860	14 233	30 305	14 913	15 392
0-4	2 461	1 249	1 212	2 804	1 424	1 381	3 330	1 691	1 639	3 274	1 663	1 611
5-9	2 328	1 181	1 147	2 463	1 249	1 214	2 787	1 414	1 373	3 325	1 688	1 637
10-14	2 248	1 140	1 107	2 344	1 188	1 156	2 456	1 245	1 211	2 796	1 416	1 380
15-19	2 153	1 092	1 061	2 286	1 160	1 126	2 316	1 164	1 152	2 464	1 246	1 218
20-24	1 966	1 000	967	2 197	1 113	1 084	2 214	1 092	1 122	2 325	1 166	1 158
25-29	1 752	887	865	1 989	1 010	979	2 132	1 054	1 078	2 211	1 089	1 122
30-34	1 628	821	807	1 759	889	870	1 928	955	973	2 117	1 045	1 072
35-39	1 592	801	791	1 623	816	807	1 720	857	863	1 909	944	965
40-44	1 554	781	773	1 576	790	786	1 582	785	797	1 695	842	853
45-49	1 406	705	700	1 523	759	763	1 528	755	773	1 547	762	785
50-54	1 219	605	614	1 358	673	686	1 468	723	745	1 477	721	756
55-59	1 083	533	550	1 155	562	593	1 287	624	662	1 396	674	722
60-64	906	444	462	997	475	522	1 065	502	563	1 193	562	631
65-69	695	338	357	799	374	425	884	403	481	953	430	523
70-74	482	227	255	575	265	310	665	294	371	744	320	425
75-79	297	136	161	361	159	202	433	185	247	508	208	300
80 +	191	78	113	239	96	143	298	116	182	372	140	232

Age group	1990 Both sexes	Males	Females	1995 Both sexes	Males	Females	2000 Both sexes	Males	Females	2005 Both sexes	Males	Females
All ages	32 581	15 997	16 584	34 835	17 086	17 749	36 896	18 059	18 836	38 747	18 949	19 799
0-4	3 395	1 726	1 670	3 496	1 778	1 719	3 457	1 758	1 699	3 340	1 699	1 641
5-9	3 280	1 666	1 615	3 392	1 723	1 669	3 487	1 772	1 715	3 430	1 744	1 687
10-14	3 338	1 689	1 649	3 283	1 665	1 619	3 387	1 720	1 667	3 466	1 761	1 705
15-19	2 803	1 415	1 387	3 336	1 685	1 650	3 257	1 647	1 610	3 370	1 710	1 660
20-24	2 467	1 243	1 224	2 797	1 409	1 388	3 301	1 661	1 640	3 234	1 632	1 602
25-29	2 336	1 167	1 169	2 464	1 238	1 226	2 764	1 387	1 378	3 274	1 644	1 630
30-34	2 210	1 084	1 126	2 327	1 159	1 168	2 434	1 217	1 217	2 739	1 370	1 369
35-39	2 097	1 033	1 065	2 192	1 072	1 119	2 298	1 139	1 159	2 409	1 200	1 209
40-44	1 883	927	956	2 071	1 016	1 055	2 158	1 050	1 109	2 267	1 119	1 148
45-49	1 659	818	841	1 847	904	943	2 029	989	1 041	2 119	1 024	1 095
50-54	1 497	729	768	1 609	785	824	1 794	869	925	1 976	954	1 022
55-59	1 406	673	733	1 430	683	746	1 542	741	801	1 722	823	900
60-64	1 297	608	689	1 313	611	702	1 341	625	715	1 449	680	769
65-69	1 071	483	588	1 172	527	645	1 192	534	658	1 221	549	672
70-74	807	343	464	917	390	527	1 012	430	582	1 035	439	597
75-79	574	227	347	633	247	385	731	286	445	814	319	495
80 +	460	166	293	558	194	364	711	234	478	880	281	599

United Nations Department of Economic and Social Affairs/Population Division
World Population Prospects: The 2004 Revision, Volume II: Sex and Age Distribution of the World Population

170

POPULATION BY AGE AND SEX (in thousands)

Age group	2005 Both sexes	2005 Males	2005 Females	2010 Both sexes	2010 Males	2010 Females	2015 Both sexes	2015 Males	2015 Females	2020 Both sexes	2020 Males	2020 Females
All ages	38 747	18 949	19 799	40 738	19 923	20 815	42 677	20 877	21 800	44 486	21 767	22 719
0-4	3 340	1 699	1 641	3 436	1 749	1 687	3 454	1 758	1 696	3 398	1 730	1 668
5-9	3 430	1 744	1 687	3 335	1 696	1 639	3 431	1 746	1 685	3 450	1 756	1 694
10-14	3 466	1 761	1 705	3 428	1 742	1 686	3 334	1 695	1 639	3 430	1 745	1 685
15-19	3 370	1 710	1 660	3 464	1 759	1 706	3 427	1 740	1 687	3 333	1 693	1 640
20-24	3 234	1 632	1 602	3 364	1 704	1 659	3 459	1 754	1 706	3 423	1 736	1 687
25-29	3 274	1 644	1 630	3 222	1 623	1 599	3 353	1 696	1 657	3 450	1 745	1 704
30-34	2 739	1 370	1 369	3 257	1 631	1 626	3 207	1 611	1 596	3 339	1 685	1 654
35-39	2 409	1 200	1 209	2 720	1 356	1 363	3 236	1 616	1 620	3 187	1 598	1 590
40-44	2 267	1 119	1 148	2 385	1 184	1 201	2 694	1 339	1 355	3 207	1 597	1 611
45-49	2 119	1 024	1 095	2 233	1 096	1 136	2 351	1 161	1 190	2 658	1 315	1 343
50-54	1 976	954	1 022	2 069	992	1 077	2 184	1 064	1 120	2 302	1 128	1 174
55-59	1 722	823	900	1 904	907	997	1 999	946	1 053	2 114	1 017	1 097
60-64	1 449	680	769	1 627	760	867	1 806	842	964	1 903	882	1 021
65-69	1 221	549	672	1 329	603	726	1 501	678	823	1 674	756	918
70-74	1 035	439	597	1 071	457	614	1 176	507	668	1 338	576	762
75-79	814	319	495	845	331	514	886	351	535	983	395	588
80-84	518	181	337	590	207	383	625	220	405	666	238	428
85-89	257	76	181	313	93	220	366	110	256	398	121	277
90-94	87	21	66	116	27	89	147	35	112	178	44	134
95-99	17	3	13	26	5	21	36	6	30	48	9	39
100 +	1	0	1	3	0	2	4	1	4	6	1	5

Age group	2025 Both sexes	2025 Males	2025 Females	2030 Both sexes	2030 Males	2030 Females	2035 Both sexes	2035 Males	2035 Females	2040 Both sexes	2040 Males	2040 Females
All ages	46 115	22 563	23 552	47 534	23 250	24 284	48 727	23 819	24 908	49 786	24 319	25 467
0-4	3 298	1 679	1 618	3 185	1 622	1 563	3 075	1 566	1 509	3 073	1 565	1 508
5-9	3 395	1 728	1 667	3 295	1 677	1 617	3 183	1 621	1 562	3 073	1 565	1 509
10-14	3 449	1 755	1 694	3 394	1 727	1 667	3 295	1 677	1 618	3 183	1 620	1 563
15-19	3 430	1 744	1 686	3 449	1 754	1 695	3 395	1 727	1 668	3 296	1 677	1 619
20-24	3 331	1 690	1 641	3 428	1 740	1 687	3 448	1 751	1 696	3 394	1 725	1 670
25-29	3 415	1 729	1 686	3 324	1 684	1 640	3 421	1 735	1 686	3 442	1 746	1 696
30-34	3 436	1 735	1 701	3 403	1 720	1 683	3 313	1 675	1 637	3 411	1 727	1 684
35-39	3 320	1 671	1 649	3 418	1 722	1 696	3 386	1 708	1 679	3 298	1 665	1 633
40-44	3 161	1 580	1 582	3 094	1 554	1 541	3 394	1 705	1 688	3 363	1 692	1 672
45-49	3 167	1 570	1 598	3 124	1 554	1 570	3 258	1 628	1 630	3 358	1 680	1 678
50-54	2 607	1 280	1 327	3 109	1 530	1 579	3 070	1 517	1 553	3 205	1 591	1 613
55-59	2 233	1 082	1 151	2 533	1 230	1 303	3 027	1 473	1 553	2 993	1 462	1 530
60-64	2 018	952	1 065	2 137	1 016	1 121	2 430	1 159	1 271	2 909	1 392	1 517
65-69	1 773	797	976	1 886	865	1 021	2 005	928	1 077	2 286	1 062	1 224
70-74	1 502	648	854	1 601	688	912	1 711	752	959	1 826	811	1 015
75-79	1 130	454	676	1 281	517	764	1 376	554	822	1 480	611	869
80-84	750	273	477	875	319	555	1 003	368	635	1 089	400	688
85-89	433	134	299	496	157	339	588	188	401	684	220	464
90-94	199	49	149	222	57	165	259	68	191	313	83	230
95-99	60	11	48	68	13	55	78	16	62	93	20	74
100 +	9	1	7	11	2	9	13	2	11	15	3	12

Age group	2045 Both sexes	2045 Males	2045 Females	2050 Both sexes	2050 Males	2050 Females
All ages	50 683	24 736	25 947	51 382	25 052	26 331
0-4	3 053	1 555	1 498	3 005	1 530	1 475
5-9	3 072	1 564	1 508	3 052	1 554	1 498
10-14	3 074	1 564	1 509	3 073	1 564	1 509
15-19	3 185	1 620	1 564	3 076	1 565	1 511
20-24	3 296	1 675	1 621	3 185	1 619	1 566
25-29	3 390	1 720	1 669	3 292	1 671	1 621
30-34	3 433	1 739	1 694	3 381	1 714	1 668
35-39	3 397	1 716	1 681	3 419	1 729	1 690
40-44	3 277	1 650	1 627	3 376	1 702	1 675
45-49	3 330	1 668	1 662	3 246	1 628	1 618
50-54	3 306	1 644	1 662	3 281	1 634	1 647
55-59	3 127	1 537	1 590	3 230	1 590	1 639
60-64	2 882	1 386	1 495	3 016	1 460	1 557
65-69	2 745	1 281	1 464	2 726	1 279	1 447
70-74	2 092	934	1 158	2 520	1 132	1 389
75-79	1 589	665	925	1 830	771	1 059
80-84	1 180	446	734	1 277	490	787
85-89	753	243	510	824	275	549
90-94	370	100	271	413	112	302
95-99	115	24	90	138	30	108
100 +	18	3	15	22	4	18

United Nations Department of Economic and Social Affairs/Population Division
World Population Prospects: The 2004 Revision, Volume II: Sex and Age Distribution of the World Population

171

POPULATION BY AGE AND SEX (in thousands)

Age group	2005 Both sexes	2005 Males	2005 Females	2010 Both sexes	2010 Males	2010 Females	2015 Both sexes	2015 Males	2015 Females	2020 Both sexes	2020 Males	2020 Females
All ages	38 747	18 949	19 799	41 118	20 116	21 002	43 692	21 394	22 298	46 316	22 698	23 618
0-4	3 340	1 699	1 641	3 815	1 942	1 874	4 090	2 082	2 008	4 214	2 146	2 068
5-9	3 430	1 744	1 687	3 335	1 696	1 639	3 810	1 939	1 872	4 085	2 079	2 006
10-14	3 466	1 761	1 705	3 428	1 742	1 686	3 334	1 695	1 639	3 808	1 937	1 871
15-19	3 370	1 710	1 660	3 464	1 759	1 706	3 427	1 740	1 687	3 333	1 693	1 640
20-24	3 234	1 632	1 602	3 364	1 704	1 659	3 459	1 754	1 706	3 423	1 736	1 687
25-29	3 274	1 644	1 630	3 222	1 623	1 599	3 353	1 696	1 657	3 450	1 745	1 704
30-34	2 739	1 370	1 369	3 257	1 631	1 626	3 207	1 611	1 596	3 339	1 685	1 654
35-39	2 409	1 200	1 209	2 720	1 356	1 363	3 236	1 616	1 620	3 187	1 598	1 590
40-44	2 267	1 119	1 148	2 385	1 184	1 201	2 694	1 339	1 355	3 207	1 597	1 611
45-49	2 119	1 024	1 095	2 233	1 096	1 136	2 351	1 161	1 190	2 658	1 315	1 343
50-54	1 976	954	1 022	2 069	992	1 077	2 184	1 064	1 120	2 302	1 128	1 174
55-59	1 722	823	900	1 904	907	997	1 999	946	1 053	2 114	1 017	1 097
60-64	1 449	680	769	1 627	760	867	1 806	842	964	1 903	882	1 021
65-69	1 221	549	672	1 329	603	726	1 501	678	823	1 674	756	918
70-74	1 035	439	597	1 071	457	614	1 176	507	668	1 338	576	762
75-79	814	319	495	845	331	514	886	351	535	983	395	588
80-84	518	181	337	590	207	383	625	220	405	666	238	428
85-89	257	76	181	313	93	220	366	110	256	398	121	277
90-94	87	21	66	116	27	89	147	35	112	178	44	134
95-99	17	3	13	26	5	21	36	6	30	48	9	39
100 +	1	0	1	3	0	2	4	1	4	6	1	5

Age group	2025 Both sexes	2025 Males	2025 Females	2030 Both sexes	2030 Males	2030 Females	2035 Both sexes	2035 Males	2035 Females	2040 Both sexes	2040 Males	2040 Females
All ages	48 795	23 927	24 868	51 171	25 101	26 070	53 490	26 242	27 248	55 885	27 421	28 464
0-4	4 150	2 113	2 037	4 145	2 111	2 034	4 206	2 142	2 064	4 417	2 250	2 168
5-9	4 210	2 143	2 067	4 146	2 111	2 035	4 142	2 109	2 033	4 204	2 140	2 063
10-14	4 084	2 078	2 006	4 208	2 142	2 067	4 145	2 110	2 035	4 141	2 108	2 033
15-19	3 808	1 936	1 872	4 083	2 076	2 007	4 208	2 141	2 068	4 146	2 109	2 037
20-24	3 331	1 690	1 641	3 805	1 932	1 873	4 080	2 073	2 008	4 206	2 137	2 069
25-29	3 415	1 729	1 686	3 324	1 684	1 640	3 797	1 925	1 872	4 073	2 066	2 007
30-34	3 436	1 735	1 701	3 403	1 720	1 683	3 313	1 675	1 637	3 786	1 916	1 869
35-39	3 320	1 671	1 649	3 418	1 722	1 696	3 386	1 708	1 679	3 298	1 665	1 633
40-44	3 161	1 580	1 582	3 294	1 654	1 641	3 394	1 705	1 688	3 363	1 692	1 672
45-49	3 167	1 570	1 598	3 124	1 554	1 570	3 258	1 628	1 630	3 358	1 680	1 678
50-54	2 607	1 280	1 327	3 109	1 530	1 579	3 070	1 517	1 553	3 205	1 591	1 613
55-59	2 233	1 082	1 151	2 533	1 230	1 303	3 027	1 473	1 553	2 993	1 463	1 529
60-64	2 018	952	1 065	2 137	1 016	1 121	2 430	1 159	1 271	2 909	1 392	1 517
65-69	1 773	797	976	1 886	865	1 021	2 005	928	1 077	2 286	1 062	1 224
70-74	1 502	648	854	1 601	688	912	1 711	752	959	1 826	811	1 015
75-79	1 130	454	676	1 281	517	764	1 376	554	822	1 480	611	869
80-84	750	273	477	875	319	555	1 003	368	635	1 089	400	688
85-89	433	134	299	496	157	339	588	188	401	684	220	464
90-94	199	49	149	222	57	165	259	68	191	313	83	230
95-99	60	11	48	68	13	55	78	16	62	93	20	74
100 +	9	1	7	11	2	9	13	2	11	15	3	12

Age group	2045 Both sexes	2045 Males	2045 Females	2050 Both sexes	2050 Males	2050 Females
All ages	58 315	28 618	29 698	60 709	29 793	30 916
0-4	4 598	2 342	2 256	4 714	2 400	2 313
5-9	4 415	2 248	2 167	4 595	2 340	2 256
10-14	4 203	2 139	2 063	4 414	2 247	2 167
15-19	4 142	2 107	2 034	4 204	2 139	2 065
20-24	4 144	2 106	2 038	4 141	2 105	2 036
25-29	4 199	2 131	2 068	4 138	2 101	2 037
30-34	4 061	2 057	2 004	4 188	2 123	2 065
35-39	3 770	1 905	1 865	4 045	2 045	2 000
40-44	3 277	1 650	1 627	3 747	1 888	1 858
45-49	3 330	1 668	1 662	3 246	1 628	1 618
50-54	3 306	1 644	1 662	3 281	1 634	1 647
55-59	3 127	1 537	1 590	3 230	1 590	1 639
60-64	2 882	1 386	1 495	3 016	1 460	1 557
65-69	2 745	1 281	1 464	2 726	1 279	1 447
70-74	2 092	934	1 158	2 520	1 132	1 389
75-79	1 589	665	925	1 830	771	1 059
80-84	1 180	446	734	1 277	490	787
85-89	753	243	510	824	275	549
90-94	370	100	271	413	112	302
95-99	115	24	90	138	30	108
100 +	18	3	15	22	4	18

United Nations Department of Economic and Social Affairs/Population Division
World Population Prospects: The 2004 Revision, Volume II: Sex and Age Distribution of the World Population

POPULATION BY AGE AND SEX (in thousands)

Age group	2005 Both sexes	Males	Females	2010 Both sexes	Males	Females	2015 Both sexes	Males	Females	2020 Both sexes	Males	Females
All ages	38 747	18 949	19 799	40 359	19 730	20 629	41 661	20 000	21 301	42 659	20 836	21 822
0-4	3 340	1 699	1 641	3 056	1 555	1 501	2 817	1 434	1 383	2 584	1 316	1 268
5-9	3 430	1 744	1 687	3 335	1 696	1 639	3 053	1 553	1 499	2 815	1 432	1 382
10-14	3 466	1 761	1 705	3 428	1 742	1 686	3 334	1 695	1 639	3 052	1 552	1 500
15-19	3 370	1 710	1 660	3 464	1 759	1 706	3 427	1 740	1 687	3 333	1 693	1 640
20-24	3 234	1 632	1 602	3 364	1 704	1 659	3 459	1 754	1 706	3 423	1 736	1 687
25-29	3 274	1 644	1 630	3 222	1 623	1 599	3 353	1 696	1 657	3 450	1 745	1 704
30-34	2 739	1 370	1 369	3 257	1 631	1 626	3 207	1 611	1 596	3 339	1 685	1 654
35-39	2 409	1 200	1 209	2 720	1 356	1 363	3 236	1 616	1 620	3 187	1 598	1 590
40-44	2 267	1 119	1 148	2 385	1 184	1 201	2 694	1 339	1 355	3 207	1 597	1 611
45-49	2 119	1 024	1 095	2 233	1 096	1 136	2 351	1 161	1 190	2 658	1 315	1 343
50-54	1 976	954	1 022	2 069	992	1 077	2 184	1 064	1 120	2 302	1 128	1 174
55-59	1 722	823	900	1 904	907	997	1 999	946	1 053	2 114	1 017	1 097
60-64	1 449	680	769	1 627	760	867	1 806	842	964	1 903	882	1 021
65-69	1 221	549	672	1 329	603	726	1 501	678	823	1 674	756	918
70-74	1 035	439	597	1 071	457	614	1 176	507	668	1 338	576	762
75-79	814	319	495	845	331	514	886	351	535	983	395	588
80-84	518	181	337	590	207	383	625	220	405	666	238	428
85-89	257	76	181	313	93	220	366	110	256	398	121	277
90-94	87	21	66	116	27	89	147	35	112	178	44	134
95-99	17	3	13	26	5	21	36	6	30	48	9	39
100 +	1	0	1	3	0	2	4	1	4	6	1	5

Age group	2025 Both sexes	Males	Females	2030 Both sexes	Males	Females	2035 Both sexes	Males	Females	2040 Both sexes	Males	Females
All ages	43 451	21 207	22 244	43 977	21 440	22 538	44 181	21 506	22 676	44 127	21 440	22 687
0-4	2 459	1 252	1 207	2 289	1 166	1 123	2 080	1 059	1 021	1 953	995	958
5-9	2 582	1 314	1 268	2 457	1 251	1 206	2 288	1 165	1 123	2 080	1 059	1 021
10-14	2 814	1 432	1 382	2 582	1 314	1 268	2 458	1 251	1 207	2 289	1 165	1 124
15-19	3 052	1 551	1 501	2 815	1 432	1 384	2 584	1 314	1 270	2 460	1 251	1 209
20-24	3 331	1 690	1 641	3 051	1 549	1 502	2 815	1 430	1 385	2 585	1 313	1 272
25-29	3 415	1 729	1 686	3 324	1 684	1 640	3 046	1 544	1 501	2 811	1 426	1 385
30-34	3 436	1 735	1 701	3 403	1 720	1 683	3 313	1 675	1 637	3 037	1 537	1 500
35-39	3 320	1 671	1 649	3 418	1 722	1 696	3 386	1 708	1 679	3 298	1 665	1 633
40-44	3 161	1 580	1 582	3 294	1 654	1 641	3 394	1 705	1 688	3 363	1 692	1 672
45-49	3 167	1 570	1 598	3 124	1 554	1 570	3 258	1 628	1 630	3 358	1 680	1 678
50-54	2 607	1 280	1 327	3 109	1 530	1 579	3 070	1 517	1 553	3 205	1 591	1 613
55-59	2 233	1 082	1 151	2 533	1 230	1 303	3 027	1 473	1 553	2 993	1 463	1 529
60-64	2 018	952	1 065	2 137	1 016	1 121	2 430	1 159	1 271	2 909	1 392	1 517
65-69	1 773	797	976	1 886	865	1 021	2 005	928	1 077	2 286	1 062	1 224
70-74	1 502	648	854	1 601	688	912	1 711	752	959	1 826	811	1 015
75-79	1 130	454	676	1 281	517	764	1 376	554	822	1 480	611	869
80-84	750	273	477	875	319	555	1 003	368	635	1 099	400	688
85-89	433	134	299	496	157	339	588	188	401	684	220	464
90-94	199	49	149	222	57	165	259	68	191	313	83	230
95-99	60	11	48	68	13	55	78	16	62	93	20	74
100 +	9	1	7	11	2	9	13	2	11	15	3	12

Age group	2045 Both sexes	Males	Females	2050 Both sexes	Males	Females
All ages	43 800	21 236	22 564	43 202	20 894	22 308
0-4	1 819	926	893	1 693	862	831
5-9	1 953	994	959	1 819	926	893
10-14	2 081	1 059	1 022	1 954	995	959
15-19	2 291	1 166	1 126	2 084	1 060	1 024
20-24	2 461	1 251	1 211	2 293	1 166	1 128
25-29	2 582	1 310	1 272	2 459	1 248	1 211
30-34	2 804	1 420	1 384	2 576	1 306	1 271
35-39	3 024	1 528	1 496	2 794	1 412	1 381
40-44	3 277	1 650	1 627	3 006	1 515	1 491
45-49	3 330	1 668	1 662	3 246	1 628	1 618
50-54	3 306	1 644	1 662	3 281	1 634	1 647
55-59	3 127	1 537	1 590	3 230	1 590	1 639
60-64	2 882	1 386	1 495	3 016	1 460	1 557
65-69	2 745	1 281	1 464	2 726	1 279	1 447
70-74	2 092	934	1 158	2 520	1 132	1 389
75-79	1 589	665	925	1 830	771	1 059
80-84	1 180	446	734	1 277	490	787
85-89	753	243	510	824	275	549
90-94	370	100	271	413	112	302
95-99	115	24	90	138	30	108
100 +	18	3	15	22	4	18

United Nations Department of Economic and Social Affairs/Population Division
World Population Prospects: The 2004 Revision, Volume II: Sex and Age Distribution of the World Population

173

POPULATION BY AGE AND SEX (in thousands)

Age group	1950			1955			1960			1965		
	Both sexes	Males	Females	Both sexes	Males	Females	Both sexes	Males	Females	Both sexes	Males	Females
All ages	1 354	642	711	1 564	747	816	1 867	901	966	2 205	1 072	1 133
0-4	150	73	77	235	121	114	317	163	153	346	178	168
5-9	109	51	57	154	75	79	242	124	118	324	167	157
10-14	191	94	98	113	53	59	159	77	82	249	127	121
15-19	150	76	74	196	96	100	117	55	62	164	80	85
20-24	159	80	78	154	78	76	201	98	103	122	57	64
25-29	80	36	44	161	81	80	158	80	78	204	100	105
30-34	48	20	28	82	37	45	165	83	82	163	82	81
35-39	75	31	44	49	20	29	84	38	46	167	84	84
40-44	74	33	41	76	31	44	50	21	30	86	38	47
45-49	66	29	37	74	32	42	76	31	45	51	21	30
50-54	46	23	23	65	28	37	74	32	42	76	30	45
55-59	39	21	18	44	21	23	64	27	37	72	30	42
60-64	53	26	28	37	19	18	42	20	22	60	25	36
65-69	42	20	23	47	22	25	33	16	17	38	17	21
70-74	33	14	19	35	15	19	39	17	22	28	13	15
75-79	21	9	13	24	10	14	26	10	15	30	12	17
80 +	16	6	10	18	7	11	21	8	13	24	9	15

Age group	1970			1975			1980			1985		
	Both sexes	Males	Females	Both sexes	Males	Females	Both sexes	Males	Females	Both sexes	Males	Females
All ages	2 518	1 230	1 288	2 826	1 379	1 447	3 096	1 509	1 587	3 339	1 633	1 706
0-4	292	150	142	301	154	148	331	169	162	378	193	184
5-9	358	184	174	306	156	149	304	155	149	324	166	158
10-14	337	174	163	364	187	177	307	157	150	305	155	149
15-19	259	132	126	342	173	169	362	184	178	301	154	147
20-24	171	83	88	269	133	136	354	175	179	346	172	174
25-29	127	60	67	178	87	91	262	127	135	336	165	171
30-34	210	102	108	132	63	69	181	88	93	257	124	132
35-39	168	84	84	213	104	109	120	58	62	175	85	90
40-44	171	85	86	169	85	84	207	100	107	117	56	61
45-49	88	39	49	171	84	87	165	82	83	202	98	104
50-54	52	21	31	92	39	53	172	84	88	162	80	83
55-59	75	30	45	54	21	33	95	40	55	166	80	86
60-64	70	29	41	72	28	43	53	20	33	89	37	52
65-69	56	22	34	63	25	38	64	24	39	47	17	30
70-74	33	14	19	46	18	28	53	21	32	54	20	34
75-79	22	10	12	25	11	15	37	14	23	41	15	25
80 +	29	11	18	30	11	18	31	12	19	39	14	24

Age group	1990			1995			2000			2005		
	Both sexes	Males	Females	Both sexes	Males	Females	Both sexes	Males	Females	Both sexes	Males	Females
All ages	3 545	1 719	1 825	3 227	1 532	1 695	3 082	1 450	1 632	3 016	1 406	1 610
0-4	389	198	191	290	150	140	198	106	92	162	87	75
5-9	369	187	182	344	174	170	273	141	132	194	104	90
10-14	318	161	157	317	158	159	327	165	162	271	140	131
15-19	278	144	134	261	127	135	298	147	150	320	161	159
20-24	283	141	142	217	106	110	240	113	127	282	137	145
25-29	336	162	174	218	103	115	193	91	102	219	100	120
30-34	328	159	169	276	127	149	189	86	103	175	79	96
35-39	251	120	131	277	130	147	249	112	138	176	77	99
40-44	170	81	89	212	98	114	251	114	137	238	104	134
45-49	114	54	60	140	65	75	193	87	106	241	108	134
50-54	196	93	103	93	43	51	123	56	67	184	81	103
55-59	157	75	82	176	81	95	81	36	46	115	50	65
60-64	156	72	84	135	63	72	158	70	88	74	31	43
65-69	79	32	48	134	60	75	113	51	62	140	59	81
70-74	39	13	26	64	24	40	109	46	63	93	40	53
75-79	40	14	26	29	9	20	48	17	31	83	33	50
80 +	40	14	26	43	14	29	38	11	27	49	15	34

United Nations Department of Economic and Social Affairs/Population Division
World Population Prospects: The 2004 Revision, Volume II: Sex and Age Distribution of the World Population

174

POPULATION BY AGE AND SEX (in thousands)

Age group	2005 Both sexes	Males	Females	2010 Both sexes	Males	Females	2015 Both sexes	Males	Females	2020 Both sexes	Males	Females
All ages	3 016	1 406	1 610	2 981	1 382	1 599	2 970	1 374	1 596	2 952	1 363	1 589
0-4	162	87	75	176	94	82	184	96	88	172	88	84
5-9	194	104	90	159	86	73	174	93	81	182	95	87
10-14	271	140	131	193	103	90	158	85	73	174	93	81
15-19	320	161	159	266	137	129	189	101	88	155	83	72
20-24	282	137	145	307	152	155	258	131	126	183	96	86
25-29	219	100	120	266	127	140	297	145	151	249	126	123
30-34	175	79	96	206	91	115	256	120	136	289	140	148
35-39	176	77	99	165	72	93	198	86	113	250	116	134
40-44	238	104	134	168	72	96	159	68	91	193	82	111
45-49	241	108	134	230	99	131	162	68	94	155	65	89
50-54	184	81	103	233	102	131	223	94	129	157	65	93
55-59	115	50	65	174	75	100	222	95	127	214	88	125
60-64	74	31	43	106	45	61	162	67	95	207	86	121
65-69	140	59	81	65	26	39	94	38	56	146	58	88
70-74	93	40	53	116	46	70	54	20	34	80	30	49
75-79	83	33	50	72	29	43	91	34	56	43	15	28
80-84	32	10	22	56	21	35	49	19	31	63	22	41
85-89	10	3	7	17	5	12	31	10	20	27	9	18
90-94	5	1	4	4	1	3	7	2	5	13	4	9
95-99	1	0	1	1	0	1	1	0	1	2	0	2
100 +	0	0	0	0	0	0	0	0	0	0	0	0

Age group	2025 Both sexes	Males	Females	2030 Both sexes	Males	Females	2035 Both sexes	Males	Females	2040 Both sexes	Males	Females
All ages	2 908	1 340	1 568	2 843	1 308	1 535	2 768	1 272	1 496	2 690	1 237	1 453
0-4	148	76	72	130	67	63	126	65	61	131	67	64
5-9	170	87	83	147	75	71	129	66	63	124	64	61
10-14	181	95	86	169	87	82	146	75	71	128	66	62
15-19	171	91	80	178	93	85	167	85	82	143	73	70
20-24	149	79	70	164	87	78	172	89	83	160	81	79
25-29	174	91	83	140	74	67	156	81	75	164	83	80
30-34	242	121	121	167	86	81	133	69	64	149	77	72
35-39	282	100	146	235	116	119	161	82	79	128	65	63
40-44	244	112	132	276	132	144	230	113	117	157	70	78
45-49	188	79	109	239	108	131	271	128	143	225	110	116
50-54	150	62	87	183	76	107	233	105	129	264	124	141
55-59	151	61	90	144	59	85	177	72	105	225	105	120
60-64	200	80	120	142	55	86	136	54	82	167	66	101
65-69	187	75	113	182	70	112	130	49	81	124	48	77
70-74	124	47	78	161	61	100	158	58	100	113	41	73
75-79	64	23	41	100	36	65	131	47	84	130	45	85
80-84	30	10	20	46	15	30	73	24	49	96	32	64
85-89	36	11	25	18	5	13	27	8	19	44	13	31
90-94	12	3	8	16	4	12	8	2	6	13	3	9
95-99	4	1	3	3	1	3	5	1	4	3	0	2
100 +	0	0	0	1	0	1	1	0	1	1	0	1

Age group	2045 Both sexes	Males	Females	2050 Both sexes	Males	Females
All ages	2 605	1 200	1 405	2 500	1 157	1 340
0-4	134	69	65	125	64	61
5-9	130	67	63	133	68	64
10-14	124	63	60	129	66	63
15-19	125	64	61	121	62	59
20-24	137	69	68	119	60	59
25-29	152	76	76	129	64	65
30-34	157	79	78	145	71	74
35-39	143	73	71	151	75	76
40-44	124	62	61	139	70	69
45-49	153	77	76	120	60	60
50-54	220	106	114	149	74	75
55-59	256	118	138	213	101	112
60-64	213	92	121	243	110	133
65-69	154	59	95	197	82	114
70-74	109	40	69	136	50	86
75-79	94	32	62	91	31	59
80-84	96	31	65	70	22	48
85-89	59	17	42	60	17	43
90-94	21	5	16	28	7	21
95-99	4	1	3	7	1	6
100 +	1	0	1	1	0	1

United Nations Department of Economic and Social Affairs/Population Division
World Population Prospects: The 2004 Revision, Volume II: Sex and Age Distribution of the World Population

175

POPULATION BY AGE AND SEX (in thousands)

Age group	2005 Both sexes	Males	Females	2010 Both sexes	Males	Females	2015 Both sexes	Males	Females	2020 Both sexes	Males	Females
All ages	3 016	1 406	1 610	3 014	1 400	1 614	3 056	1 419	1 637	3 094	1 437	1 657
0-4	162	87	75	210	112	98	237	124	113	228	117	111
5-9	194	104	90	159	86	73	208	111	97	235	123	112
10-14	271	140	131	193	103	90	158	85	73	207	111	96
15-19	320	161	159	266	137	129	189	101	88	155	83	72
20-24	282	137	145	307	152	155	258	131	126	183	96	86
25-29	219	100	120	266	127	140	297	145	151	249	126	123
30-34	175	79	96	206	91	115	256	120	136	289	140	148
35-39	176	77	99	165	72	93	198	86	113	250	116	134
40-44	238	104	134	168	72	96	159	68	91	193	82	111
45-49	241	108	134	230	99	131	162	68	94	155	65	89
50-54	184	81	103	233	102	131	223	94	129	157	65	93
55-59	115	50	65	174	75	100	222	95	127	214	88	125
60-64	74	31	43	106	45	61	162	67	95	207	86	121
65-69	140	59	81	65	26	39	94	38	56	146	58	88
70-74	93	40	53	116	46	70	54	20	34	80	30	49
75-79	83	33	50	72	29	43	91	34	56	43	15	28
80-84	32	10	22	56	21	35	49	19	31	63	22	41
85-89	10	3	7	17	5	12	31	10	20	27	9	18
90-94	5	1	4	4	1	3	7	2	5	13	4	9
95-99	1	0	1	1	0	1	1	0	1	2	0	2
100 +	0	0	0	0	0	0	0	0	0	0	0	0

Age group	2025 Both sexes	Males	Females	2030 Both sexes	Males	Females	2035 Both sexes	Males	Females	2040 Both sexes	Males	Females
All ages	3 094	1 437	1 657	3 076	1 428	1 647	3 065	1 426	1 639	3 070	1 433	1 637
0-4	193	99	94	177	91	86	190	98	93	215	110	105
5-9	226	116	110	191	98	93	175	90	85	189	97	92
10-14	234	122	112	225	116	110	190	98	93	174	90	85
15-19	204	109	95	231	120	111	222	114	109	188	96	92
20-24	149	79	70	198	104	93	224	116	108	216	109	106
25-29	174	91	83	140	74	67	189	99	90	216	111	105
30-34	242	121	121	167	86	81	133	69	64	182	94	88
35-39	282	136	146	235	116	119	161	82	79	128	65	63
40-44	244	112	132	276	132	144	230	113	117	157	79	78
45-49	188	79	109	239	108	131	271	128	143	225	110	116
50-54	150	62	87	183	76	107	233	105	129	264	124	141
55-59	151	61	90	144	59	85	177	72	105	225	99	126
60-64	200	80	120	142	55	86	136	54	82	167	66	101
65-69	187	75	113	182	70	112	130	49	81	124	48	77
70-74	124	47	78	161	61	100	158	58	100	113	41	73
75-79	64	23	41	100	36	65	131	47	84	130	45	85
80-84	30	10	20	46	15	30	73	24	49	96	32	64
85-89	36	11	25	18	5	13	27	8	19	44	13	31
90-94	12	3	8	16	4	12	8	2	6	13	3	9
95-99	4	1	3	3	1	3	5	1	4	3	0	2
100 +	0	0	0	1	0	1	1	0	1	1	0	1

Age group	2045 Both sexes	Males	Females	2050 Both sexes	Males	Females
All ages	3 075	1 442	1 633	3 062	1 443	1 619
0-4	225	115	109	212	109	103
5-9	213	110	104	223	115	109
10-14	188	97	92	213	109	103
15-19	172	88	84	185	95	91
20-24	181	92	89	165	84	82
25-29	208	104	103	173	86	87
30-34	209	106	103	200	99	101
35-39	177	90	86	203	102	101
40-44	124	62	61	172	87	85
45-49	153	77	76	120	60	60
50-54	220	106	114	149	74	75
55-59	256	118	138	213	101	112
60-64	213	92	121	243	110	133
65-69	154	59	95	197	82	114
70-74	109	40	69	136	50	86
75-79	94	32	62	91	31	59
80-84	96	31	65	70	22	48
85-89	59	17	42	60	17	43
90-94	21	5	16	28	7	21
95-99	4	1	3	7	1	6
100 +	1	0	1	1	0	1

United Nations Department of Economic and Social Affairs/Population Division
World Population Prospects: The 2004 Revision, Volume II: Sex and Age Distribution of the World Population

176

POPULATION BY AGE AND SEX (in thousands)

Age group	2005 Both sexes	Males	Females	2010 Both sexes	Males	Females	2015 Both sexes	Males	Females	2020 Both sexes	Males	Females
All ages	3 018	1 408	1 610	2 947	1 364	1 583	2 884	1 329	1 555	2 809	1 288	1 520
0-4	162	87	75	143	76	67	131	68	63	115	59	56
5-9	194	104	90	159	86	73	141	75	66	129	68	62
10-14	271	140	131	193	103	90	158	85	73	140	75	65
15-19	320	161	159	266	137	129	189	101	88	155	83	72
20-24	282	137	145	307	152	155	258	131	126	183	96	86
25-29	219	100	120	266	127	140	297	145	151	249	126	123
30-34	175	79	96	206	91	115	256	120	136	289	140	148
35-39	176	77	99	165	72	93	198	86	113	250	116	134
40-44	238	104	134	168	72	96	159	68	91	193	82	111
45-49	241	108	134	230	99	131	162	68	94	155	65	89
50-54	184	81	103	233	102	131	223	94	129	157	65	93
55-59	115	50	65	174	75	100	222	95	127	214	88	125
60-64	74	31	43	106	45	61	162	67	95	207	86	121
65-69	140	59	81	65	26	39	94	38	56	146	58	88
70-74	93	40	53	116	46	70	54	20	34	80	30	49
75-79	83	33	50	72	29	43	91	34	56	43	15	28
80-84	32	10	22	56	21	35	49	19	31	63	22	41
85-89	10	3	7	17	5	12	31	10	20	27	9	18
90-94	5	1	4	4	1	3	7	2	5	13	4	9
95-99	1	0	1	1	0	1	1	0	1	2	0	2
100 +	0	0	0	0	0	0	0	0	0	0	0	0

Age group	2025 Both sexes	Males	Females	2030 Both sexes	Males	Females	2035 Both sexes	Males	Females	2040 Both sexes	Males	Females
All ages	2 719	1 242	1 477	2 612	1 188	1 424	2 489	1 128	1 361	2 352	1 062	1 290
0-4	102	53	50	88	45	43	77	40	38	72	37	35
5-9	113	58	55	101	52	49	87	45	42	76	39	37
10-14	129	67	61	112	58	55	100	51	49	86	44	42
15-19	138	73	64	126	65	60	110	56	54	97	50	48
20-24	149	79	70	131	69	62	119	61	58	103	52	51
25-29	174	91	83	140	74	67	123	64	59	111	56	55
30-34	242	121	121	167	86	81	133	69	64	116	59	57
35-39	282	136	146	235	116	119	161	82	79	128	65	63
40-44	244	112	132	276	132	144	230	113	117	157	79	78
45-49	188	79	109	239	108	131	271	128	143	225	110	116
50-54	150	62	87	183	76	107	233	105	129	264	124	141
55-59	151	61	90	144	59	85	177	72	105	225	99	126
60-64	200	80	120	142	55	86	136	54	82	167	66	101
65-69	187	75	113	182	70	112	130	49	81	124	48	77
70-74	124	47	78	161	61	100	158	58	100	113	41	73
75-79	64	23	41	100	36	65	131	47	84	130	45	85
80-84	30	10	20	46	15	30	73	24	49	96	32	64
85-89	36	11	25	18	5	13	27	8	19	44	13	31
90-94	12	3	8	16	4	12	8	2	6	13	3	9
95-99	4	1	3	3	1	3	5	1	4	3	0	2
100 +	0	0	0	1	0	1	1	0	1	1	0	1

Age group	2045 Both sexes	Males	Females	2050 Both sexes	Males	Females
All ages	2 201	991	1 210	2 038	916	1 123
0-4	67	35	33	60	31	29
5-9	70	36	34	66	34	32
10-14	75	39	37	70	36	34
15-19	83	42	41	73	37	36
20-24	91	46	46	77	38	39
25-29	95	47	49	83	40	43
30-34	104	51	53	88	42	46
35-39	111	55	55	99	48	51
40-44	124	62	61	107	53	54
45-49	153	77	76	120	60	60
50-54	220	106	114	149	74	75
55-59	256	118	138	213	101	112
60-64	213	92	121	243	110	133
65-69	154	59	95	197	82	114
70-74	109	40	69	136	50	86
75-79	94	32	62	91	31	59
80-84	96	31	65	70	22	48
85-89	59	17	42	60	17	43
90-94	21	5	16	28	7	21
95-99	4	1	3	7	1	6
100 +	1	0	1	1	0	1

United Nations Department of Economic and Social Affairs/Population Division
World Population Prospects: The 2004 Revision, Volume II: Sex and Age Distribution of the World Population

177

POPULATION BY AGE AND SEX (in thousands)

Age group	1950 Both sexes	Males	Females	1955 Both sexes	Males	Females	1960 Both sexes	Males	Females	1965 Both sexes	Males	Females
All ages	8 219	4 144	4 075	9 201	4 657	4 544	10 276	5 195	5 082	11 525	5 807	5 719
0-4	885	453	432	985	503	482	1 092	560	532	1 184	607	577
5-9	707	360	347	941	482	459	1 021	522	499	1 151	590	561
10-14	587	299	288	740	377	362	980	502	478	1 082	553	529
15-19	558	285	273	613	315	299	771	395	377	1 031	529	502
20-24	645	332	313	593	309	285	670	347	324	832	427	405
25-29	681	348	333	705	370	335	655	342	313	732	377	355
30-34	614	310	304	727	374	353	747	393	355	700	363	337
35-39	625	318	307	646	328	319	755	388	368	777	404	373
40-44	555	288	267	647	332	316	661	335	326	783	400	384
45-49	491	255	236	563	294	269	652	333	319	665	335	330
50-54	439	217	222	478	248	230	554	287	267	646	327	319
55-59	408	199	209	417	204	213	460	234	226	533	272	261
60-64	356	175	181	374	176	198	389	184	204	430	212	219
65-69	273	130	143	316	148	167	332	148	183	354	160	194
70-74	182	83	99	214	97	118	262	117	145	273	115	158
75-79	119	52	67	135	58	78	155	64	92	195	80	115
80 +	94	40	54	106	43	63	121	46	75	155	56	99

Age group	1970 Both sexes	Males	Females	1975 Both sexes	Males	Females	1980 Both sexes	Males	Females	1985 Both sexes	Males	Females
All ages	12 728	6 414	6 315	13 625	6 838	6 787	14 638	7 310	7 329	15 669	7 816	7 853
0-4	1 208	619	589	1 254	642	613	1 133	580	553	1 227	629	598
5-9	1 255	643	611	1 240	635	605	1 266	647	619	1 169	598	570
10-14	1 208	619	589	1 264	649	615	1 303	666	637	1 301	666	636
15-19	1 127	576	551	1 225	627	598	1 284	657	626	1 342	685	657
20-24	1 096	565	532	1 146	583	564	1 271	646	625	1 334	682	652
25-29	900	467	433	1 129	576	554	1 205	606	599	1 315	665	650
30-34	789	408	381	922	476	446	1 159	586	574	1 246	626	620
35-39	737	381	355	805	413	392	957	489	468	1 180	595	585
40-44	797	414	383	744	384	361	814	419	395	971	496	475
45-49	783	399	384	785	405	380	747	384	363	816	418	398
50-54	650	325	325	748	378	369	774	395	379	740	376	363
55-59	619	308	311	619	306	313	717	359	359	756	380	375
60-64	497	246	250	560	270	289	605	290	315	685	334	350
65-69	381	179	203	440	205	234	518	240	278	558	257	301
70-74	295	124	171	322	142	180	386	168	218	453	198	255
75-79	205	77	128	215	82	133	252	101	151	309	124	186
80 +	181	62	118	206	66	140	247	78	170	267	86	182

Age group	1990 Both sexes	Males	Females	1995 Both sexes	Males	Females	2000 Both sexes	Males	Females	2005 Both sexes	Males	Females
All ages	16 873	8 426	8 448	17 941	8 868	9 072	19 071	9 410	9 662	20 155	9 953	10 202
0-4	1 237	634	603	1 301	667	634	1 292	662	630	1 253	642	611
5-9	1 244	637	607	1 317	674	643	1 378	708	671	1 313	673	641
10-14	1 214	623	591	1 314	673	641	1 373	703	670	1 390	713	676
15-19	1 388	711	677	1 296	661	635	1 337	684	653	1 405	718	687
20-24	1 345	686	660	1 362	684	678	1 282	648	634	1 410	718	692
25-29	1 401	708	692	1 395	691	704	1 380	680	699	1 372	691	682
30-34	1 384	698	686	1 430	706	724	1 452	710	742	1 454	717	738
35-39	1 296	648	648	1 428	704	724	1 479	725	754	1 503	735	768
40-44	1 255	640	615	1 336	663	673	1 457	715	742	1 510	740	769
45-49	973	500	473	1 231	619	613	1 353	669	685	1 471	722	749
50-54	813	416	397	969	492	478	1 240	621	619	1 354	668	686
55-59	715	362	352	796	402	395	960	485	475	1 226	612	615
60-64	726	362	364	698	346	353	771	386	385	936	469	467
65-69	658	311	347	671	322	348	663	322	340	735	362	373
70-74	480	214	267	567	256	311	617	288	329	608	288	320
75-79	375	154	221	398	165	233	495	213	282	532	237	295
80 +	368	122	246	432	145	287	541	190	352	684	250	434

(*) Including Christmas Island, Cocos (Keeling) Islands, and Norfolk Island.

United Nations Department of Economic and Social Affairs/Population Division
World Population Prospects: The 2004 Revision, Volume II: Sex and Age Distribution of the World Population

POPULATION BY AGE AND SEX (in thousands)

Age group	2005 Both sexes	2005 Males	2005 Females	2010 Both sexes	2010 Males	2010 Females	2015 Both sexes	2015 Males	2015 Females	2020 Both sexes	2020 Males	2020 Females
All ages	20 155	9 953	10 202	21 201	10 476	10 725	22 250	11 000	11 250	23 317	11 529	11 788
0-4	1 253	642	611	1 278	655	623	1 345	689	655	1 433	735	698
5-9	1 313	673	641	1 274	653	621	1 299	666	634	1 366	700	666
10-14	1 390	713	676	1 325	678	646	1 285	658	627	1 311	671	639
15-19	1 405	718	687	1 421	728	693	1 356	693	663	1 317	673	644
20-24	1 410	718	692	1 478	752	726	1 495	763	732	1 431	729	702
25-29	1 372	691	682	1 500	761	739	1 569	796	773	1 586	807	779
30-34	1 454	717	738	1 448	727	721	1 576	798	778	1 645	833	812
35-39	1 503	735	768	1 506	742	764	1 500	753	747	1 629	824	805
40-44	1 510	740	769	1 535	750	784	1 538	758	781	1 533	769	764
45-49	1 471	722	749	1 524	747	777	1 550	758	792	1 555	766	789
50-54	1 354	668	686	1 471	721	750	1 526	747	779	1 552	758	794
55-59	1 226	612	615	1 340	659	681	1 458	712	746	1 513	738	774
60-64	936	469	467	1 197	593	604	1 310	640	670	1 426	692	734
65-69	735	362	373	894	442	452	1 146	560	586	1 257	606	651
70-74	608	288	320	677	325	352	827	399	428	1 063	508	556
75-79	532	237	295	528	239	289	592	273	319	727	337	389
80-84	384	154	230	418	174	244	420	178	241	475	206	269
85-89	201	69	132	254	92	162	282	106	176	288	111	177
90-94	77	22	56	101	30	71	132	41	91	150	49	101
95-99	18	4	14	27	7	21	37	9	28	51	13	37
100 +	3	1	2	4	1	3	7	1	5	10	2	7

Age group	2025 Both sexes	2025 Males	2025 Females	2030 Both sexes	2030 Males	2030 Females	2035 Both sexes	2035 Males	2035 Females	2040 Both sexes	2040 Males	2040 Females
All ages	24 329	12 025	12 304	25 238	12 466	12 772	26 022	12 843	13 179	26 706	13 175	13 531
0-4	1 459	748	711	1 451	744	707	1 435	736	699	1 445	741	704
5-9	1 454	745	709	1 481	759	722	1 473	755	718	1 456	746	710
10-14	1 378	706	672	1 466	751	715	1 492	765	728	1 485	761	724
15-19	1 343	686	656	1 410	721	689	1 498	766	732	1 525	780	745
20-24	1 392	709	683	1 418	722	695	1 485	757	728	1 573	802	771
25-29	1 523	773	750	1 484	754	731	1 510	767	743	1 577	802	776
30-34	1 663	844	819	1 600	811	789	1 562	792	770	1 588	805	783
35-39	1 698	860	839	1 717	871	846	1 654	838	816	1 616	819	798
40-44	1 662	840	821	1 731	876	856	1 750	887	862	1 688	855	833
45-49	1 550	777	773	1 679	848	830	1 748	884	865	1 767	896	871
50-54	1 558	766	791	1 554	779	775	1 682	849	833	1 752	885	867
55-59	1 540	750	790	1 547	759	788	1 544	772	772	1 672	842	830
60-64	1 482	719	763	1 511	732	779	1 519	741	778	1 517	754	763
65-69	1 371	657	713	1 427	684	742	1 457	698	759	1 467	708	759
70-74	1 170	552	618	1 280	601	679	1 336	627	708	1 368	642	726
75-79	999	432	567	1 038	472	566	1 141	517	624	1 196	543	653
80-84	587	257	330	765	332	433	854	366	487	945	405	541
85-89	330	131	200	415	166	249	548	217	331	620	243	377
90-94	157	53	104	185	64	121	238	83	155	322	111	211
95-99	59	16	43	64	18	46	78	22	56	103	30	73
100 +	13	3	10	17	4	13	19	4	15	23	5	18

Age group	2045 Both sexes	2045 Males	2045 Females	2050 Both sexes	2050 Males	2050 Females
All ages	27 335	13 488	13 847	27 940	13 707	14 142
0-4	1 486	762	724	1 536	788	748
5-9	1 466	752	715	1 507	773	735
10-14	1 468	752	716	1 478	757	721
15-19	1 517	776	741	1 500	768	733
20-24	1 600	816	784	1 592	812	780
25-29	1 666	847	819	1 693	861	832
30-34	1 655	840	815	1 744	886	858
35-39	1 643	832	810	1 710	867	843
40-44	1 651	836	815	1 677	850	827
45-49	1 706	864	843	1 670	845	824
50-54	1 772	898	875	1 712	866	846
55-59	1 742	878	864	1 763	891	872
60-64	1 644	824	820	1 715	860	855
65-69	1 468	723	745	1 593	791	802
70-74	1 381	654	726	1 385	669	715
75-79	1 230	559	671	1 246	572	674
80-84	998	429	569	1 033	445	589
85-89	696	272	423	743	293	451
90-94	372	127	245	426	145	281
95-99	143	41	103	171	48	123
100 +	31	7	24	44	10	34

United Nations Department of Economic and Social Affairs/Population Division
World Population Prospects: The 2004 Revision, Volume II: Sex and Age Distribution of the World Population

179

POPULATION BY AGE AND SEX (in thousands)

Age group	2005 Both sexes	Males	Females	2010 Both sexes	Males	Females	2015 Both sexes	Males	Females	2020 Both sexes	Males	Females
All ages	20 155	9 953	10 202	21 379	10 567	10 811	22 724	11 243	11 481	24 171	11 967	12 204
0-4	1 253	642	611	1 456	746	709	1 641	841	800	1 813	930	884
5-9	1 313	673	641	1 274	653	621	1 477	757	720	1 662	852	810
10-14	1 390	713	676	1 325	678	646	1 285	658	627	1 488	762	726
15-19	1 405	718	687	1 421	728	693	1 356	693	663	1 317	673	644
20-24	1 410	718	692	1 478	752	726	1 495	763	732	1 431	729	702
25-29	1 372	691	682	1 500	761	739	1 569	796	773	1 586	807	779
30-34	1 454	717	738	1 448	727	721	1 576	798	778	1 645	833	812
35-39	1 503	735	768	1 506	742	764	1 500	753	747	1 629	824	805
40-44	1 510	740	769	1 535	750	784	1 538	758	781	1 533	769	764
45-49	1 471	722	749	1 524	747	777	1 550	758	792	1 555	766	789
50-54	1 354	668	686	1 471	721	750	1 526	747	779	1 552	758	794
55-59	1 226	612	615	1 340	659	681	1 458	712	746	1 513	738	774
60-64	936	469	467	1 197	593	604	1 310	640	670	1 426	692	734
65-69	735	362	373	894	442	452	1 146	560	586	1 257	606	651
70-74	608	288	320	677	325	352	827	399	428	1 063	508	556
75-79	532	237	295	528	239	289	592	273	319	727	337	389
80-84	384	154	230	418	174	244	420	178	241	475	206	269
85-89	201	69	132	254	92	162	282	106	176	288	111	177
90-94	77	22	56	101	30	71	132	41	91	150	49	101
95-99	18	4	14	27	7	21	37	9	28	51	13	37
100 +	3	1	2	4	1	3	7	1	5	10	2	7

Age group	2025 Both sexes	Males	Females	2030 Both sexes	Males	Females	2035 Both sexes	Males	Females	2040 Both sexes	Males	Females
All ages	25 561	12 657	12 904	26 850	13 292	13 558	28 074	13 895	14 179	29 322	14 516	14 806
0-4	1 837	942	895	1 833	940	893	1 875	962	914	2 009	1 030	979
5-9	1 834	940	894	1 859	953	906	1 854	951	904	1 897	972	924
10-14	1 674	857	816	1 846	946	900	1 870	958	912	1 866	956	910
15-19	1 520	777	743	1 706	873	833	1 878	961	917	1 902	974	929
20-24	1 392	709	683	1 595	813	782	1 780	908	872	1 953	997	956
25-29	1 523	773	750	1 484	754	731	1 687	858	830	1 873	953	920
30-34	1 663	844	819	1 600	811	789	1 562	792	770	1 765	896	869
35-39	1 698	859	839	1 717	871	846	1 654	838	816	1 616	819	798
40-44	1 662	840	821	1 731	876	856	1 750	887	862	1 688	855	833
45-49	1 550	777	773	1 679	848	830	1 748	884	865	1 767	896	871
50-54	1 558	766	791	1 554	779	775	1 682	849	833	1 752	885	867
55-59	1 540	750	790	1 547	759	788	1 544	772	772	1 672	842	830
60-64	1 482	719	763	1 511	732	779	1 519	741	778	1 517	754	763
65-69	1 371	657	713	1 427	684	742	1 457	698	759	1 467	708	759
70-74	1 170	552	618	1 280	601	679	1 336	627	708	1 368	642	726
75-79	939	432	507	1 038	472	566	1 141	517	624	1 196	543	653
80-84	587	257	330	765	332	433	854	366	487	945	405	541
85-89	330	131	200	415	166	249	548	217	331	620	243	377
90-94	157	53	104	185	64	121	238	83	155	322	111	211
95-99	59	16	43	64	18	46	78	22	56	103	30	73
100 +	13	3	10	17	4	13	19	4	15	23	5	18

Age group	2045 Both sexes	Males	Females	2050 Both sexes	Males	Females
All ages	30 651	15 188	15 463	32 050	15 905	16 145
0-4	2 188	1 122	1 066	2 333	1 197	1 136
5-9	2 031	1 041	990	2 209	1 133	1 077
10-14	1 908	978	930	2 042	1 047	995
15-19	1 898	971	927	1 941	993	947
20-24	1 977	1 009	968	1 973	1 007	966
25-29	2 045	1 042	1 004	2 070	1 054	1 016
30-34	1 950	991	959	2 123	1 080	1 043
35-39	1 819	923	896	2 005	1 018	986
40-44	1 651	836	815	1 853	940	913
45-49	1 706	864	843	1 670	845	824
50-54	1 772	898	875	1 712	866	846
55-59	1 742	878	864	1 763	891	872
60-64	1 644	824	820	1 715	860	855
65-69	1 468	723	745	1 593	791	802
70-74	1 381	654	726	1 385	669	715
75-79	1 230	559	671	1 246	572	674
80-84	998	429	569	1 033	445	589
85-89	696	272	423	743	293	451
90-94	372	127	245	426	145	281
95-99	143	41	103	171	48	123
100 +	31	7	24	44	10	34

United Nations Department of Economic and Social Affairs/Population Division
World Population Prospects: The 2004 Revision, Volume II: Sex and Age Distribution of the World Population

180

POPULATION BY AGE AND SEX (in thousands)

Age group	2005 Both sexes	Males	Females	2010 Both sexes	Males	Females	2015 Both sexes	Males	Females	2020 Both sexes	Males	Females
All ages	20 155	9 953	10 202	21 023	10 385	10 638	21 775	10 756	11 019	22 460	11 089	11 370
0-4	1 253	642	611	1 100	564	536	1 048	537	511	1 050	538	512
5-9	1 313	673	641	1 274	653	621	1 121	574	547	1 069	548	521
10-14	1 390	713	676	1 325	678	646	1 285	658	627	1 133	580	553
15-19	1 405	718	687	1 421	728	693	1 356	693	663	1 317	673	644
20-24	1 410	718	692	1 478	752	726	1 495	763	732	1 431	729	702
25-29	1 372	691	682	1 500	761	739	1 569	796	773	1 586	807	779
30-34	1 454	717	738	1 448	727	721	1 576	798	778	1 645	833	812
35-39	1 503	735	768	1 506	742	764	1 500	753	747	1 629	824	805
40-44	1 510	740	769	1 535	750	784	1 538	758	781	1 533	769	764
45-49	1 471	722	749	1 524	747	777	1 550	758	792	1 555	766	789
50-54	1 354	668	686	1 471	721	750	1 526	747	779	1 552	758	794
55-59	1 226	612	615	1 340	659	681	1 458	712	746	1 513	738	774
60-64	936	469	467	1 197	593	604	1 310	640	670	1 426	692	734
65-69	735	362	373	894	442	452	1 146	560	586	1 257	606	651
70-74	608	288	320	677	325	352	827	399	428	1 063	508	556
75-79	532	237	295	528	239	289	592	273	319	727	337	389
80-84	384	154	230	418	174	244	420	178	241	475	206	269
85-89	201	69	132	254	92	162	282	106	176	288	111	177
90-94	77	22	56	101	30	71	132	41	91	150	49	101
95-99	18	4	14	27	7	21	37	9	28	51	13	37
100 +	3	1	2	4	1	3	7	1	5	10	2	7

Age group	2025 Both sexes	Males	Females	2030 Both sexes	Males	Females	2035 Both sexes	Males	Females	2040 Both sexes	Males	Females
All ages	23 087	11 388	11 699	23 616	11 634	11 982	24 001	11 807	12 195	24 226	11 903	12 323
0-4	1 075	551	524	1 071	549	522	1 035	531	504	984	505	479
5-9	1 072	549	523	1 097	562	535	1 092	560	533	1 056	541	515
10-14	1 081	554	527	1 083	555	528	1 108	568	541	1 104	566	539
15-19	1 165	595	570	1 113	569	544	1 116	570	545	1 141	583	558
20-24	1 392	709	683	1 240	631	609	1 188	605	584	1 191	606	585
25-29	1 523	773	750	1 484	754	731	1 333	676	657	1 282	650	632
30-34	1 663	844	819	1 600	811	789	1 562	792	770	1 411	715	696
35-39	1 698	859	839	1 717	871	846	1 654	838	816	1 616	819	798
40-44	1 662	840	821	1 731	876	856	1 750	887	862	1 688	855	833
45-49	1 550	777	773	1 679	848	830	1 748	884	865	1 767	896	871
50-54	1 558	766	791	1 554	779	775	1 682	849	833	1 752	885	867
55-59	1 540	750	790	1 547	759	788	1 544	772	772	1 672	842	830
60-64	1 482	719	763	1 511	732	779	1 519	741	778	1 517	754	763
65-69	1 371	657	713	1 427	684	742	1 457	698	759	1 467	708	759
70-74	1 170	552	618	1 280	601	679	1 336	627	708	1 368	642	726
75-79	939	432	507	1 038	472	566	1 141	517	624	1 196	543	653
80-84	587	257	330	765	332	433	854	366	487	945	405	541
85-89	330	131	200	415	166	249	548	217	331	620	243	377
90-94	157	53	104	185	64	121	238	83	155	322	111	211
95-99	59	16	43	64	18	46	78	22	56	103	30	73
100 +	13	3	10	17	4	13	19	4	15	23	5	18

Age group	2045 Both sexes	Males	Females	2050 Both sexes	Males	Females
All ages	24 310	11 937	12 373	24 300	11 931	12 369
0-4	940	482	458	918	471	447
5-9	1 006	515	490	961	493	469
10-14	1 068	547	521	1 018	521	496
15-19	1 137	581	556	1 101	563	538
20-24	1 216	619	597	1 212	617	595
25-29	1 284	652	633	1 310	665	645
30-34	1 360	689	671	1 363	690	673
35-39	1 466	742	724	1 415	716	699
40-44	1 651	836	815	1 501	760	741
45-49	1 706	864	843	1 670	845	824
50-54	1 772	898	875	1 712	866	846
55-59	1 742	878	864	1 763	891	872
60-64	1 644	824	820	1 715	860	855
65-69	1 468	723	745	1 593	791	802
70-74	1 381	654	726	1 385	669	715
75-79	1 230	559	671	1 246	572	674
80-84	998	429	569	1 033	445	589
85-89	696	272	423	743	293	451
90-94	372	127	245	426	145	281
95-99	143	41	103	171	48	123
100 +	31	7	24	44	10	34

United Nations Department of Economic and Social Affairs/Population Division
World Population Prospects: The 2004 Revision, Volume II: Sex and Age Distribution of the World Population

181

POPULATION BY AGE AND SEX (in thousands)

Age group	1950 Both sexes	Males	Females	1955 Both sexes	Males	Females	1960 Both sexes	Males	Females	1965 Both sexes	Males	Females
All ages	6 935	3 216	3 719	6 947	3 231	3 716	7 048	3 282	3 766	7 271	3 404	3 867
0-4	514	263	251	487	249	238	573	293	280	641	327	314
5-9	565	287	278	505	258	247	483	246	237	568	290	278
10-14	502	255	247	556	283	273	503	257	246	489	249	240
15-19	457	233	224	494	251	243	556	283	273	501	256	245
20-24	491	240	251	446	227	219	481	247	234	541	275	266
25-29	523	223	300	481	235	246	422	214	208	475	243	232
30-34	334	143	191	511	218	293	466	227	239	422	214	208
35-39	511	225	286	332	142	190	496	210	286	464	227	237
40-44	541	246	295	490	215	275	324	138	186	491	208	283
45-49	543	256	287	526	238	288	475	207	268	319	135	184
50-54	484	220	264	518	242	276	508	227	281	462	200	262
55-59	400	173	227	454	203	251	493	226	267	484	213	271
60-64	351	150	201	365	153	212	419	180	239	455	202	253
65-69	288	123	165	302	125	177	322	128	194	369	152	218
70-74	218	92	126	229	93	136	243	94	149	266	99	167
75-79	132	55	77	151	60	91	162	61	101	179	64	116
80 +	81	32	49	100	39	61	122	44	78	143	49	94

Age group	1970 Both sexes	Males	Females	1975 Both sexes	Males	Females	1980 Both sexes	Males	Females	1985 Both sexes	Males	Females
All ages	7 467	3 518	3 949	7 579	3 581	3 998	7 549	3 567	3 982	7 578	3 599	3 979
0-4	608	311	297	498	255	243	430	220	210	455	232	223
5-9	641	328	314	612	313	299	497	254	243	429	220	209
10-14	569	291	278	650	331	319	615	314	301	501	256	245
15-19	502	255	247	583	296	287	657	333	325	626	319	307
20-24	509	260	249	516	260	256	590	296	294	664	336	328
25-29	532	272	261	520	266	254	509	255	254	590	297	293
30-34	473	242	231	534	272	262	509	258	251	506	253	252
35-39	426	218	208	473	241	231	526	265	260	503	254	249
40-44	464	227	237	422	214	208	465	235	230	519	261	259
45-49	485	205	280	455	221	235	412	207	206	456	229	227
50-54	312	131	181	473	197	276	441	211	230	401	198	203
55-59	444	189	255	300	124	176	453	185	268	423	198	225
60-64	449	191	258	415	172	243	282	113	169	427	169	258
65-69	401	169	232	402	163	239	375	148	227	257	99	158
70-74	300	114	186	331	129	202	337	127	210	322	119	203
75-79	192	65	127	219	75	144	247	87	160	258	88	170
80 +	158	50	109	175	51	124	204	59	144	239	69	170

Age group	1990 Both sexes	Males	Females	1995 Both sexes	Males	Females	2000 Both sexes	Males	Females	2005 Both sexes	Males	Females
All ages	7 729	3 711	4 018	8 047	3 902	4 144	8 096	3 946	4 151	8 189	4 003	4 186
0-4	447	230	218	469	241	229	407	209	198	384	197	187
5-9	462	237	226	464	238	226	470	241	229	410	210	200
10-14	437	225	212	479	245	234	466	239	227	476	244	232
15-19	519	265	254	459	236	223	482	247	235	474	243	231
20-24	653	334	320	560	282	278	465	238	227	498	252	246
25-29	685	350	334	703	360	343	567	284	283	482	243	239
30-34	600	305	295	718	371	348	705	360	344	575	288	287
35-39	514	259	255	621	318	302	717	369	348	706	361	346
40-44	505	255	250	528	268	260	617	316	301	715	367	348
45-49	515	258	258	510	258	252	523	264	258	613	313	300
50-54	448	223	225	509	253	256	500	251	249	515	259	256
55-59	388	188	199	438	215	223	493	243	251	486	242	244
60-64	400	182	218	371	176	195	424	205	219	487	236	251
65-69	394	150	244	371	163	208	351	162	190	412	195	217
70-74	226	82	144	350	126	224	331	139	193	317	140	177
75-79	258	88	170	187	63	124	293	98	195	281	111	170
80 +	276	79	197	310	89	222	284	81	203	359	103	256

United Nations Department of Economic and Social Affairs/Population Division
World Population Prospects: The 2004 Revision, Volume II: Sex and Age Distribution of the World Population

182

POPULATION BY AGE AND SEX (in thousands)

Age group	2005 Both sexes	2005 Males	2005 Females	2010 Both sexes	2010 Males	2010 Females	2015 Both sexes	2015 Males	2015 Females	2020 Both sexes	2020 Males	2020 Females
All ages	8 199	4 003	4 196	8 240	4 082	4 187	8 288	4 107	4 181	8 320	4 144	4 176
0-4	384	197	187	362	186	176	359	184	175	369	189	179
5-9	410	210	200	387	198	188	365	187	178	362	186	176
10-14	476	244	232	412	211	201	388	199	189	366	188	178
15-19	474	243	231	482	247	234	418	215	203	394	203	191
20-24	498	252	246	489	252	236	496	257	239	433	224	208
25-29	482	243	239	516	263	253	507	264	243	515	269	246
30-34	575	288	287	498	253	244	532	274	258	522	274	248
35-39	706	361	346	585	294	290	508	260	248	542	280	261
40-44	715	367	348	711	364	347	590	298	292	514	264	249
45-49	613	313	300	714	367	347	710	363	347	591	299	292
50-54	515	259	256	607	309	298	707	362	345	705	360	345
55-59	486	242	244	505	252	252	596	302	295	696	355	341
60-64	487	236	251	470	232	238	490	243	247	580	291	289
65-69	412	195	217	461	219	242	446	216	230	467	228	239
70-74	317	140	177	375	171	204	422	194	227	411	193	217
75-79	281	111	170	271	114	158	323	141	183	367	162	205
80-84	222	68	154	215	79	136	211	83	128	255	104	150
85-89	83	23	60	140	39	102	139	46	93	140	50	90
90-94	45	10	34	38	9	29	67	16	51	69	20	50
95-99	9	2	7	12	2	10	11	2	9	22	4	18
100 +	1	0	1	1	0	1	2	0	2	2	0	2

Age group	2025 Both sexes	2025 Males	2025 Females	2030 Both sexes	2030 Males	2030 Females	2035 Both sexes	2035 Males	2035 Females	2040 Both sexes	2040 Males	2040 Females
All ages	8 339	4 171	4 168	8 333	4 182	4 151	8 296	4 176	4 120	8 237	4 158	4 079
0-4	372	191	181	367	188	179	358	184	174	357	183	174
5-9	371	191	181	375	192	183	370	190	180	361	185	176
10-14	364	187	177	373	191	182	377	193	183	372	191	181
15-19	373	192	181	370	191	179	379	195	184	383	197	186
20-24	409	213	197	388	202	186	385	200	185	394	205	189
25-29	451	237	215	428	225	203	407	214	193	404	213	191
30-34	530	279	251	467	247	220	444	236	209	423	225	198
35-39	533	281	251	541	286	255	478	254	224	455	243	212
40-44	548	285	263	539	285	253	547	290	257	484	259	226
45-49	516	266	250	550	286	264	541	287	254	549	292	257
50-54	588	297	291	514	264	249	548	285	263	540	286	254
55-59	694	353	341	580	292	288	509	261	247	542	281	261
60-64	678	343	335	678	342	335	568	284	284	498	254	244
65-69	554	274	280	650	324	325	651	325	326	547	271	276
70-74	432	205	227	514	249	266	606	296	309	610	299	311
75-79	360	163	197	381	175	206	457	214	243	542	257	284
80-84	293	122	171	291	125	166	312	136	176	378	169	209
85-89	173	65	108	203	78	125	206	82	124	225	91	134
90-94	72	23	50	93	30	62	113	38	75	119	42	77
95-99	24	5	18	26	7	20	36	9	26	46	13	33
100 +	4	1	4	5	1	4	6	1	5	9	2	7

Age group	2045 Both sexes	2045 Males	2045 Females	2050 Both sexes	2050 Males	2050 Females
All ages	8 164	4 132	4 032	8 073	4 097	3 976
0-4	364	187	177	365	188	178
5-9	360	185	175	367	188	179
10-14	363	186	177	362	186	176
15-19	378	195	183	369	190	179
20-24	398	207	191	393	204	189
25-29	413	218	196	417	219	198
30-34	420	223	197	429	228	201
35-39	434	232	202	431	231	200
40-44	462	247	214	440	237	204
45-49	487	261	227	465	250	215
50-54	548	291	257	487	261	226
55-59	535	283	252	544	288	255
60-64	532	275	258	526	277	249
65-69	481	243	238	515	264	252
70-74	514	250	264	454	226	228
75-79	549	262	287	466	221	245
80-84	452	206	246	462	212	251
85-89	277	116	162	337	144	193
90-94	134	48	85	169	63	106
95-99	50	15	36	59	18	41
100 +	12	2	10	14	3	11

POPULATION BY AGE AND SEX (in thousands)

Age group	2005 Both sexes	2005 Males	2005 Females	2010 Both sexes	2010 Males	2010 Females	2015 Both sexes	2015 Males	2015 Females	2020 Both sexes	2020 Males	2020 Females
All ages	8 189	4 003	4 186	8 310	4 093	4 217	8 447	4 188	4 259	8 597	4 286	4 311
0-4	384	197	187	424	217	206	456	234	222	487	250	237
5-9	410	210	200	387	198	188	426	219	208	459	236	224
10-14	476	244	232	412	211	201	388	199	189	428	220	208
15-19	474	243	231	482	247	234	418	215	203	394	203	191
20-24	498	252	246	489	252	236	496	257	239	433	224	208
25-29	482	243	239	516	263	253	507	264	243	515	269	246
30-34	575	288	287	498	253	244	532	274	258	522	274	248
35-39	706	361	346	585	294	290	508	260	248	542	280	261
40-44	715	367	348	711	364	347	590	298	292	514	264	249
45-49	613	313	300	714	367	347	710	363	347	591	299	292
50-54	515	259	256	607	309	298	707	362	345	705	360	345
55-59	486	242	244	505	252	252	596	302	295	696	355	341
60-64	487	236	251	470	232	238	490	243	247	580	291	289
65-69	412	195	217	461	219	242	446	216	230	467	228	239
70-74	317	140	177	375	171	204	422	194	227	411	193	217
75-79	281	111	170	271	114	158	323	141	183	367	162	205
80-84	222	68	154	215	79	136	211	83	128	255	104	150
85-89	83	23	60	140	39	102	139	46	93	140	50	90
90-94	45	10	34	38	9	29	67	16	51	69	20	50
95-99	9	2	7	12	2	10	11	2	9	22	4	18
100 +	1	0	1	1	0	1	2	0	2	2	0	2

Age group	2025 Both sexes	2025 Males	2025 Females	2030 Both sexes	2030 Males	2030 Females	2035 Both sexes	2035 Males	2035 Females	2040 Both sexes	2040 Males	2040 Females
All ages	8 727	4 370	4 357	8 829	4 437	4 392	8 918	4 495	4 423	9 022	4 561	4 462
0-4	484	248	235	475	244	231	484	248	236	520	267	253
5-9	490	251	238	486	250	237	478	245	233	487	250	237
10-14	461	236	224	491	252	239	488	251	238	480	246	234
15-19	434	224	211	467	240	227	498	256	242	494	254	240
20-24	409	213	197	449	233	216	482	250	232	513	266	247
25-29	451	237	215	428	225	203	468	245	222	501	262	238
30-34	530	279	251	467	247	220	444	236	209	484	256	228
35-39	533	281	251	541	286	255	478	254	224	455	243	212
40-44	548	284	263	539	285	253	547	290	257	484	259	226
45-49	516	266	250	550	286	264	541	287	254	549	292	257
50-54	588	297	291	514	264	249	548	285	263	540	286	254
55-59	694	353	341	580	292	288	508	261	247	542	281	261
60-64	678	343	335	678	342	335	568	284	284	498	254	244
65-69	554	274	280	650	324	325	651	325	326	547	271	276
70-74	432	205	227	514	249	266	606	296	309	610	299	311
75-79	360	163	197	381	175	206	457	214	243	542	257	284
80-84	293	122	171	291	125	166	312	136	176	378	169	209
85-89	173	65	108	203	78	125	206	82	124	225	91	134
90-94	72	23	50	93	30	62	113	38	75	119	42	77
95-99	24	5	18	26	7	20	36	9	26	46	13	33
100 +	4	1	4	5	1	4	6	1	5	9	2	7

Age group	2045 Both sexes	2045 Males	2045 Females	2050 Both sexes	2050 Males	2050 Females
All ages	9 149	4 637	4 512	9 277	4 715	4 562
0-4	565	290	275	585	300	285
5-9	523	269	255	568	291	276
10-14	489	251	238	525	269	256
15-19	486	250	236	495	255	240
20-24	509	264	245	501	260	241
25-29	532	278	253	528	277	252
30-34	517	273	244	547	289	259
35-39	495	263	231	528	280	247
40-44	462	247	214	501	268	234
45-49	487	261	227	465	250	215
50-54	548	291	257	487	261	226
55-59	535	283	252	544	288	255
60-64	532	275	258	526	277	249
65-69	481	243	238	515	264	252
70-74	514	250	264	454	226	228
75-79	549	262	287	466	221	245
80-84	452	206	246	462	212	251
85-89	277	116	162	337	144	193
90-94	134	48	85	169	63	106
95-99	50	15	36	59	18	41
100 +	12	2	10	14	3	11

United Nations Department of Economic and Social Affairs/Population Division
World Population Prospects: The 2004 Revision, Volume II: Sex and Age Distribution of the World Population

184

LOW VARIANT   **AUSTRIA**

POPULATION BY AGE AND SEX (in thousands)

Age group	2005 Both sexes	Males	Females	2010 Both sexes	Males	Females	2015 Both sexes	Males	Females	2020 Both sexes	Males	Females
All ages	8 189	4 003	4 186	8 186	4 030	4 157	8 128	4 025	4 103	8 040	4 000	4 040
0-4	384	197	187	300	154	146	261	134	127	248	128	121
5-9	410	210	200	387	198	188	303	155	147	264	136	129
10-14	476	244	232	412	211	201	388	199	189	304	156	148
15-19	474	243	231	482	247	234	418	215	203	394	203	191
20-24	498	252	246	489	252	236	496	257	239	433	224	208
25-29	482	243	239	516	263	253	507	264	243	515	269	246
30-34	575	288	287	498	253	244	532	274	258	522	274	248
35-39	706	361	346	585	294	290	508	260	248	542	280	261
40-44	715	367	348	711	364	347	590	298	292	514	264	249
45-49	613	313	300	714	367	347	710	363	347	591	299	292
50-54	515	259	256	607	309	298	707	362	345	705	360	345
55-59	486	242	244	505	252	252	596	302	295	696	355	341
60-64	487	236	251	470	232	238	490	243	247	580	291	289
65-69	412	195	217	461	219	242	446	216	230	467	228	239
70-74	317	140	177	375	171	204	422	194	227	411	193	217
75-79	281	111	170	271	114	158	323	141	183	367	162	205
80-84	222	68	154	215	79	136	211	83	128	255	104	150
85-89	83	23	60	140	39	102	139	46	93	140	50	90
90-94	45	10	34	38	9	29	67	16	51	69	20	50
95-99	9	2	7	12	2	10	11	2	9	22	4	18
100 +	1	0	1	1	0	1	2	0	2	2	0	2

Age group	2025 Both sexes	Males	Females	2030 Both sexes	Males	Females	2035 Both sexes	Males	Females	2040 Both sexes	Males	Females
All ages	7 944	3 969	3 976	7 831	3 924	3 906	7 684	3 862	3 822	7 499	3 779	3 720
0-4	258	132	125	259	133	126	248	127	121	231	119	112
5-9	251	129	122	260	134	127	262	134	128	251	129	122
10-14	266	136	129	253	130	123	262	135	128	264	135	128
15-19	311	160	150	272	140	132	259	134	126	269	139	130
20-24	409	213	197	326	170	156	287	150	137	275	144	131
25-29	451	237	215	428	225	203	345	182	162	306	163	144
30-34	530	279	251	467	247	220	444	236	209	361	193	168
35-39	533	281	251	541	286	255	478	254	224	455	243	212
40-44	548	284	263	539	285	253	517	260	257	484	259	226
45-49	516	266	250	550	286	264	541	287	254	549	292	257
50-54	588	297	291	514	264	249	548	285	263	540	286	254
55-59	694	353	341	580	292	288	508	261	247	542	281	261
60-64	678	343	335	678	342	335	568	284	284	498	254	244
65-69	554	274	280	650	324	325	651	325	326	547	271	276
70-74	432	205	227	514	249	266	606	296	309	610	299	311
75-79	360	163	197	381	175	206	457	214	243	542	257	284
80-84	293	122	171	291	125	166	312	136	170	378	168	209
85-89	173	65	108	203	78	125	206	82	124	225	91	134
90-94	72	23	50	93	30	62	113	38	75	119	42	77
95-99	24	5	18	26	7	20	36	9	26	46	13	33
100 +	4	1	4	5	1	4	6	1	5	9	2	7

Age group	2045 Both sexes	Males	Females	2050 Both sexes	Males	Females
All ages	7 277	3 677	3 600	7 022	3 558	3 464
0-4	214	110	104	200	103	97
5-9	234	120	114	217	111	106
10-14	253	130	123	236	121	115
15-19	270	139	131	259	134	125
20-24	284	148	135	285	149	136
25-29	294	156	138	303	161	142
30-34	323	173	149	310	167	143
35-39	372	200	172	334	181	153
40-44	462	247	214	379	205	174
45-49	487	261	227	465	250	215
50-54	548	291	257	487	261	226
55-59	535	283	252	544	288	255
60-64	532	275	258	526	277	249
65-69	481	243	238	515	264	252
70-74	514	250	264	454	226	228
75-79	549	262	287	466	221	245
80-84	452	206	246	462	212	251
85-89	277	116	162	337	144	193
90-94	134	48	85	169	63	106
95-99	50	15	36	59	18	41
100 +	12	2	10	14	3	11

POPULATION BY AGE AND SEX (in thousands)

Age group	1950 Both sexes	1950 Males	1950 Females	1955 Both sexes	1955 Males	1955 Females	1960 Both sexes	1960 Males	1960 Females	1965 Both sexes	1965 Males	1965 Females
All ages	2 896	1 363	1 533	3 326	1 575	1 751	3 894	1 864	2 031	4 574	2 209	2 366
0-4	300	148	151	485	251	234	724	372	352	836	427	408
5-9	232	111	121	299	148	151	472	244	228	709	364	345
10-14	405	197	208	239	114	125	298	147	151	471	243	228
15-19	341	175	165	416	202	214	238	113	124	297	147	151
20-24	301	155	146	348	179	170	413	200	213	237	113	124
25-29	173	77	96	307	158	150	345	176	168	409	198	211
30-34	124	51	73	176	78	98	303	155	148	341	174	167
35-39	178	73	106	125	51	74	173	76	97	298	152	147
40-44	166	71	96	179	72	107	122	49	73	170	74	96
45-49	148	61	87	165	68	97	173	68	105	119	47	72
50-54	115	54	61	144	58	86	157	64	93	165	64	101
55-59	91	46	45	109	50	59	134	52	81	147	58	89
60-64	123	57	65	83	40	43	97	43	55	121	46	76
65-69	88	39	49	107	48	59	71	33	38	84	35	49
70-74	57	25	32	72	30	42	85	36	49	57	25	32
75-79	31	14	18	41	17	24	51	20	31	62	25	38
80 +	23	9	14	30	12	18	39	15	24	50	18	33

Age group	1970 Both sexes	1970 Males	1970 Females	1975 Both sexes	1975 Males	1975 Females	1980 Both sexes	1980 Males	1980 Females	1985 Both sexes	1985 Males	1985 Females
All ages	5 172	2 511	2 661	5 689	2 774	2 915	6 161	3 000	3 161	6 670	3 248	3 422
0-4	753	383	370	699	356	343	706	360	346	808	415	393
5-9	822	420	402	759	385	374	677	344	333	700	358	342
10-14	707	363	344	820	422	398	745	378	367	679	347	333
15-19	470	242	228	686	351	336	803	410	393	723	367	356
20-24	296	146	150	462	234	228	680	340	339	754	371	383
25-29	235	112	124	296	145	152	449	218	230	635	309	326
30-34	406	196	210	234	113	121	306	148	157	441	215	226
35-39	337	171	166	400	194	206	211	102	109	299	145	154
40-44	293	148	145	324	165	159	385	185	200	208	101	107
45-49	165	71	94	283	140	143	316	159	157	374	179	195
50-54	114	44	70	167	67	99	280	136	144	307	151	156
55-59	156	59	97	111	41	70	165	66	98	264	126	139
60-64	134	51	83	132	50	82	104	36	68	150	59	91
65-69	107	38	69	114	41	73	110	40	70	91	31	61
70-74	70	28	42	82	29	53	92	32	60	91	31	60
75-79	43	18	25	53	19	34	60	20	40	68	22	46
80 +	64	22	42	67	24	43	74	24	50	78	23	55

Age group	1990 Both sexes	1990 Males	1990 Females	1995 Both sexes	1995 Males	1995 Females	2000 Both sexes	2000 Males	2000 Females	2005 Both sexes	2005 Males	2005 Females
All ages	7 212	3 529	3 683	7 791	3 815	3 976	8 143	3 974	4 169	8 411	4 083	4 328
0-4	942	486	456	899	462	437	690	360	330	602	314	288
5-9	819	421	399	933	480	453	891	457	434	679	354	325
10-14	710	363	346	814	416	398	939	482	457	888	455	433
15-19	702	367	335	691	348	343	807	409	398	930	476	455
20-24	681	328	353	676	345	332	659	321	339	788	395	393
25-29	695	330	365	666	314	352	628	302	326	636	304	332
30-34	577	278	299	700	332	369	645	294	351	607	286	321
35-39	424	206	218	585	282	302	720	345	375	627	281	346
40-44	262	127	136	418	203	215	601	294	307	702	332	370
45-49	268	129	139	243	117	126	409	199	210	582	280	302
50-54	327	156	171	238	113	125	215	104	112	391	186	205
55-59	274	131	143	301	140	160	196	92	104	202	94	107
60-64	225	101	124	248	116	133	264	119	145	179	80	99
65-69	118	45	73	191	83	107	216	97	119	234	100	133
70-74	82	27	54	88	33	55	152	65	87	181	77	104
75-79	68	23	45	52	17	35	61	22	38	117	47	70
80 +	38	11	26	48	14	34	50	14	36	66	19	46

United Nations Department of Economic and Social Affairs/Population Division
World Population Prospects: The 2004 Revision, Volume II: Sex and Age Distribution of the World Population

186

POPULATION BY AGE AND SEX (in thousands)

Age group	2005			2010			2015			2020		
	Both sexes	Males	Females	Both sexes	Males	Females	Both sexes	Males	Females	Both sexes	Males	Females
All ages	8 411	4 082	4 329	8 741	4 236	4 506	9 083	4 390	4 692	9 004	4 522	4 862
0-4	602	314	288	650	339	311	694	359	335	685	352	334
5-9	679	354	325	593	309	284	642	335	307	686	354	332
10-14	888	455	433	676	353	324	591	308	283	640	334	307
15-19	930	476	455	883	452	431	672	349	322	587	305	282
20-24	788	395	393	919	468	452	872	444	428	662	342	320
25-29	636	304	332	774	385	389	905	457	448	859	434	425
30-34	607	286	321	623	294	329	761	375	385	891	447	444
35-39	627	281	346	595	278	318	612	286	326	749	367	382
40-44	702	332	370	615	273	342	584	270	314	601	278	323
45-49	582	280	302	685	320	365	601	263	338	571	260	311
50-54	391	186	205	562	266	296	663	304	358	582	251	332
55-59	202	94	107	370	172	198	533	247	286	632	284	348
60-64	179	80	99	185	84	102	343	154	188	496	222	273
65-69	234	100	133	159	68	91	165	71	94	307	132	175
70-74	181	77	104	198	81	117	135	55	80	141	58	84
75-79	117	47	70	140	56	84	154	59	95	106	41	66
80-84	41	13	27	79	29	50	96	35	61	107	37	70
85-89	16	4	12	23	7	17	45	15	31	56	18	38
90-94	7	2	6	7	1	6	10	2	8	20	5	15
95-99	1	0	1	2	0	2	2	0	2	3	1	3
100 +	0	0	0	0	0	0	1	0	0	1	0	0

Age group	2025			2030			2035			2040		
	Both sexes	Males	Females	Both sexes	Males	Females	Both sexes	Males	Females	Both sexes	Males	Females
All ages	9 596	4 609	4 988	9 713	4 648	5 065	9 759	4 657	5 103	9 763	4 649	5 114
0-4	627	322	305	564	289	274	535	275	260	542	279	264
5-9	679	348	331	621	318	303	559	287	272	531	273	258
10-14	684	353	331	677	347	330	620	317	302	557	286	272
15-19	636	331	305	680	350	330	673	344	329	616	315	301
20-24	578	298	279	627	324	303	671	343	327	664	337	326
25-29	650	333	317	566	289	276	615	315	300	659	334	324
30-34	845	424	421	638	324	314	555	281	273	604	307	297
35-39	879	438	441	834	416	418	628	317	311	545	274	271
40-44	737	358	379	866	429	438	822	407	415	618	310	309
45-49	588	269	319	722	347	375	850	417	433	808	397	411
50-54	554	249	305	572	258	314	703	334	369	829	402	427
55-59	557	234	323	530	233	297	549	243	306	676	316	360
60-64	589	256	333	522	212	310	498	213	286	517	222	294
65-69	447	192	255	534	223	311	476	186	290	455	187	268
70-74	264	108	156	386	158	228	465	185	280	416	155	261
75-79	112	43	69	211	81	130	311	120	191	377	141	236
80-84	76	36	40	80	28	52	151	50	90	225	79	145
85-89	63	19	44	44	13	31	48	15	33	92	28	64
90-94	25	7	19	29	7	22	21	5	16	23	6	17
95-99	7	1	5	8	2	7	10	2	8	7	1	6
100 +	1	0	1	1	0	1	2	0	2	2	0	2

Age group	2045			2050		
	Both sexes	Males	Females	Both sexes	Males	Females
All ages	9 725	4 628	5 097	9 631	4 587	5 044
0-4	553	285	269	540	278	262
5-9	538	277	262	550	283	267
10-14	530	272	258	537	276	261
15-19	554	283	271	526	269	257
20-24	607	308	299	545	277	268
25-29	652	328	323	595	300	296
30-34	648	326	321	641	320	321
35-39	594	300	294	638	319	319
40-44	537	268	269	586	294	292
45-49	607	302	305	527	262	266
50-54	789	384	405	593	292	301
55-59	799	382	417	761	365	396
60-64	638	291	347	755	353	402
65-69	474	197	277	585	258	327
70-74	399	157	242	417	166	251
75-79	341	120	221	328	122	206
80-84	275	94	180	251	81	170
85-89	138	43	95	171	52	119
90-94	44	11	33	67	17	50
95-99	8	1	6	15	3	12
100 +	2	0	2	2	0	2

United Nations Department of Economic and Social Affairs/Population Division
World Population Prospects: The 2004 Revision, Volume II: Sex and Age Distribution of the World Population

187

POPULATION BY AGE AND SEX (in thousands)

Age group	2005 Both sexes	Males	Females	2010 Both sexes	Males	Females	2015 Both sexes	Males	Females	2020 Both sexes	Males	Females
All ages	8 411	4 083	4 328	8 833	4 283	4 550	9 328	4 518	4 811	9 811	4 742	5 069
0-4	602	314	288	742	387	355	849	439	410	869	446	423
5-9	679	354	325	593	309	284	733	382	351	840	433	406
10-14	888	455	433	676	353	324	591	308	283	731	381	350
15-19	930	476	455	883	452	431	672	349	322	587	305	282
20-24	788	395	393	919	468	452	872	444	428	662	342	320
25-29	636	304	332	774	385	389	905	457	448	859	434	425
30-34	607	286	321	623	294	329	761	375	385	891	447	444
35-39	627	281	346	595	278	318	612	286	326	749	367	382
40-44	702	332	370	615	273	342	584	270	314	601	278	323
45-49	582	280	302	685	320	365	601	263	338	571	260	311
50-54	391	186	205	562	266	296	663	304	358	582	251	332
55-59	202	94	107	370	172	198	533	247	286	632	284	348
60-64	179	80	99	185	84	102	343	154	188	496	222	273
65-69	234	100	133	159	68	91	165	71	94	307	132	175
70-74	181	77	104	198	81	117	135	55	80	141	58	84
75-79	117	47	70	140	56	84	154	59	95	106	41	66
80-84	41	13	27	79	29	50	96	35	61	107	37	70
85-89	16	4	12	23	7	17	45	15	31	56	18	38
90-94	7	2	6	7	1	6	10	2	8	20	5	15
95-99	1	0	1	2	0	2	2	0	2	3	1	3
100 +	0	0	0	0	0	0	1	0	0	1	0	0

Age group	2025 Both sexes	Males	Females	2030 Both sexes	Males	Females	2035 Both sexes	Males	Females	2040 Both sexes	Males	Females
All ages	10 183	4 910	5 272	10 461	5 033	5 428	10 718	5 149	5 569	10 997	5 283	5 714
0-4	788	404	384	727	373	354	748	384	364	820	422	399
5-9	861	441	420	781	400	381	722	370	352	742	381	361
10-14	838	432	405	859	440	419	779	399	380	720	369	351
15-19	726	378	349	833	429	404	854	437	418	775	396	379
20-24	578	298	279	717	371	346	823	422	401	845	430	415
25-29	650	333	317	566	289	276	704	361	343	811	413	398
30-34	845	424	421	638	324	314	555	281	273	693	353	340
35-39	879	438	441	834	416	418	628	317	311	545	274	271
40-44	737	358	379	866	428	438	822	407	415	618	310	309
45-49	588	269	319	722	347	375	850	417	433	808	397	411
50-54	554	249	305	572	258	314	703	334	369	829	402	427
55-59	557	234	323	530	233	297	549	243	306	676	316	360
60-64	589	256	333	522	212	310	498	213	286	517	222	294
65-69	447	192	255	534	223	311	476	186	290	455	187	268
70-74	264	108	156	386	158	228	465	185	280	416	155	261
75-79	112	43	69	211	81	130	311	120	191	377	141	236
80-84	75	26	49	80	28	52	151	53	98	225	79	145
85-89	63	19	44	44	13	31	48	15	33	92	28	64
90-94	25	7	19	29	7	22	21	5	16	23	6	17
95-99	7	1	5	8	2	7	10	2	8	7	1	6
100 +	1	0	1	1	0	1	2	0	2	2	0	2

Age group	2045 Both sexes	Males	Females	2050 Both sexes	Males	Females
All ages	11 273	5 423	5 850	11 496	5 544	5 952
0-4	871	448	423	862	443	418
5-9	815	419	396	866	445	421
10-14	741	380	361	814	418	396
15-19	716	366	350	737	377	359
20-24	766	389	376	707	360	347
25-29	832	421	412	754	381	373
30-34	799	404	395	821	412	409
35-39	683	346	337	789	397	392
40-44	537	268	269	674	339	335
45-49	607	302	305	527	262	266
50-54	789	384	405	593	292	301
55-59	799	382	417	761	365	396
60-64	638	291	347	755	353	402
65-69	474	197	277	585	258	327
70-74	399	157	242	417	166	251
75-79	341	120	221	328	122	206
80-84	275	94	180	251	81	170
85-89	138	43	95	171	52	119
90-94	44	11	33	67	17	50
95-99	8	1	6	15	3	12
100 +	2	0	2	2	0	2

United Nations Department of Economic and Social Affairs/Population Division
World Population Prospects: The 2004 Revision, Volume II: Sex and Age Distribution of the World Population

188

POPULATION BY AGE AND SEX (in thousands)

Age group	2005			2010			2015			2020		
	Both sexes	Males	Females	Both sexes	Males	Females	Both sexes	Males	Females	Both sexes	Males	Females
All ages	8 411	4 083	4 328	8 651	4 188	4 463	8 840	4 264	4 575	8 957	4 302	4 655
0-4	602	314	288	560	292	268	540	279	261	500	257	243
5-9	679	354	325	593	309	284	553	288	265	534	276	258
10-14	888	455	433	676	353	324	591	308	283	551	287	264
15-19	930	476	455	883	452	431	672	349	322	587	305	282
20-24	788	395	393	919	468	452	872	444	428	662	342	320
25-29	636	304	332	774	385	389	905	457	448	859	434	425
30-34	607	286	321	623	294	329	761	375	385	891	447	444
35-39	627	281	346	595	278	318	612	286	326	749	367	382
40-44	702	332	370	615	273	342	584	270	314	601	278	323
45-49	582	280	302	685	320	365	601	263	338	571	260	311
50-54	391	186	205	562	266	296	663	304	358	582	251	332
55-59	202	94	107	370	172	198	533	247	286	632	284	348
60-64	179	80	99	185	84	102	343	154	188	496	222	273
65-69	234	100	133	159	68	91	165	71	94	307	132	175
70-74	181	77	104	198	81	117	135	55	80	141	58	84
75-79	117	47	70	140	56	84	154	59	95	106	41	66
80-84	41	13	27	79	29	50	96	35	61	107	37	70
85-89	16	4	12	23	7	17	45	15	31	56	18	38
90-94	7	2	6	7	1	6	10	2	8	20	5	15
95-99	1	0	1	2	0	2	2	0	2	3	1	3
100 +	0	0	0	0	0	0	1	0	0	1	0	0

Age group	2025			2030			2035			2040		
	Both sexes	Males	Females	Both sexes	Males	Females	Both sexes	Males	Females	Both sexes	Males	Females
All ages	9 007	4 305	4 702	8 970	4 266	4 704	8 847	4 188	4 659	8 645	4 075	4 570
0-4	462	237	225	409	210	199	363	186	176	334	172	162
5-9	495	253	241	458	235	223	405	208	197	360	185	175
10-14	532	275	258	493	253	241	456	234	223	404	207	197
15-19	547	284	263	528	272	256	489	250	239	453	231	222
20-24	578	298	279	538	278	260	519	265	254	480	243	237
25-29	650	333	317	566	289	276	526	269	257	508	257	251
30-34	845	424	421	638	324	314	555	281	273	515	261	254
35-39	879	438	441	834	416	418	628	317	311	545	274	271
40-44	737	358	379	866	428	438	822	407	415	618	310	309
45-49	588	269	319	722	347	375	817	417	400	808	397	411
50-54	554	249	305	572	258	314	703	334	369	829	402	427
55-59	557	237	320	500	233	267	540	234	306	676	316	360
60-64	589	256	333	522	212	310	498	213	286	517	222	294
65-69	447	192	255	534	223	311	476	186	290	455	187	268
70-74	264	108	156	386	158	228	465	185	280	416	155	261
75-79	112	43	69	211	81	130	311	120	191	377	141	236
80-84	75	26	49	80	28	52	151	53	98	225	79	145
85-89	63	19	44	44	13	31	48	15	33	92	28	64
90-94	25	7	19	29	7	22	21	5	16	23	6	17
95-99	7	1	5	8	2	7	10	2	8	7	1	6
100 +	1	0	1	1	0	1	2	0	2	2	0	2

Age group	2045			2050		
	Both sexes	Males	Females	Both sexes	Males	Females
All ages	8 372	3 934	4 438	8 037	3 769	4 268
0-4	315	162	153	295	152	143
5-9	331	170	161	312	161	152
10-14	359	184	175	330	170	161
15-19	400	204	196	355	181	174
20-24	444	225	219	392	198	194
25-29	469	235	234	433	217	216
30-34	497	249	248	459	228	231
35-39	507	255	252	489	243	246
40-44	537	268	269	499	249	250
45-49	607	302	305	527	262	266
50-54	789	384	405	593	292	301
55-59	799	382	417	761	365	396
60-64	638	291	347	755	353	402
65-69	474	197	277	585	258	327
70-74	399	157	242	417	166	251
75-79	341	120	221	328	122	206
80-84	275	94	180	251	81	170
85-89	138	43	95	171	52	119
90-94	44	11	33	67	17	50
95-99	8	1	6	15	3	12
100 +	2	0	2	2	0	2

POPULATION BY AGE AND SEX (in thousands)

Age group	1950 Both sexes	Males	Females	1955 Both sexes	Males	Females	1960 Both sexes	Males	Females	1965 Both sexes	Males	Females
All ages	79	37	42	89	41	47	110	52	57	140	69	72
0-4	12	6	6	14	7	7	19	10	10	26	13	13
5-9	10	5	5	11	6	6	15	8	8	21	11	11
10-14	9	5	4	10	5	5	12	6	6	15	8	8
15-19	8	3	4	8	4	4	9	5	5	12	6	6
20-24	7	3	4	7	3	4	9	4	5	12	6	6
25-29	6	3	3	6	3	4	8	4	4	11	5	5
30-34	5	2	3	6	2	3	7	3	4	9	4	4
35-39	5	2	3	6	3	3	6	3	3	8	4	4
40-44	4	2	2	5	2	3	5	2	3	6	3	3
45-49	3	1	2	4	2	2	5	2	2	6	3	3
50-54	3	1	2	3	1	2	4	2	2	5	2	3
55-59	2	1	1	2	1	1	3	1	1	3	2	2
60-64	2	1	1	2	1	1	2	1	1	3	1	2
65-69	1	1	1	2	1	1	2	1	1	2	1	1
70-74	1	0	1	1	0	1	1	0	1	1	0	1
75-79	1	0	0	1	0	0	1	0	0	1	0	0
80 +	0	0	0	1	0	0	1	0	0	1	0	1

Age group	1970 Both sexes	Males	Females	1975 Both sexes	Males	Females	1980 Both sexes	Males	Females	1985 Both sexes	Males	Females
All ages	170	84	86	189	93	96	210	104	106	233	116	118
0-4	27	14	13	27	14	13	26	13	13	29	15	14
5-9	26	13	13	27	14	14	28	14	14	26	13	13
10-14	21	10	10	24	12	12	27	14	13	28	14	14
15-19	15	7	8	19	10	10	26	13	13	27	13	13
20-24	13	6	6	16	8	8	21	10	11	26	13	13
25-29	14	7	7	15	7	8	16	8	8	21	10	11
30-34	12	6	6	12	6	6	13	6	7	16	8	8
35-39	9	5	5	11	5	5	12	6	6	13	6	7
40-44	8	4	4	9	4	4	10	5	5	11	6	6
45-49	6	3	3	7	3	4	8	4	4	9	5	5
50-54	6	3	3	6	3	3	6	3	3	7	4	4
55-59	5	2	2	5	2	2	5	2	3	6	3	3
60-64	3	2	2	4	2	2	4	2	2	4	2	2
65-69	3	1	1	3	1	2	4	2	2	4	2	2
70-74	1	1	1	2	1	1	2	1	1	3	1	2
75-79	1	0	1	1	0	1	1	1	1	2	1	1
80 +	1	0	1	1	0	1	1	0	1	1	1	1

Age group	1990 Both sexes	Males	Females	1995 Both sexes	Males	Females	2000 Both sexes	Males	Females	2005 Both sexes	Males	Females
All ages	255	126	129	279	137	142	301	147	154	323	157	166
0-4	28	14	14	31	16	15	30	16	15	30	15	15
5-9	29	15	14	28	14	14	31	16	15	30	15	15
10-14	26	13	13	29	15	14	28	14	14	31	16	15
15-19	28	14	14	26	13	13	29	14	15	28	14	14
20-24	26	13	13	28	14	14	26	13	13	29	14	15
25-29	26	13	13	26	13	13	27	13	14	25	12	13
30-34	20	10	10	25	12	13	25	12	13	26	13	14
35-39	15	7	8	20	10	10	24	12	12	24	11	13
40-44	12	6	6	15	7	8	19	9	10	23	11	12
45-49	11	5	6	12	6	6	15	7	8	19	9	10
50-54	9	4	5	11	5	6	12	6	6	15	7	8
55-59	7	3	4	9	4	5	11	5	6	12	5	6
60-64	5	3	3	7	3	3	8	4	4	10	5	5
65-69	4	2	2	5	2	3	6	3	3	8	4	4
70-74	3	1	2	3	1	2	4	2	2	5	2	3
75-79	2	1	1	3	1	2	3	1	2	4	1	2
80 +	2	1	1	2	1	1	3	1	2	4	1	2

United Nations Department of Economic and Social Affairs/Population Division
World Population Prospects: The 2004 Revision, Volume II: Sex and Age Distribution of the World Population

190

POPULATION BY AGE AND SEX (in thousands)

Age group	2005 Both sexes	2005 Males	2005 Females	2010 Both sexes	2010 Males	2010 Females	2015 Both sexes	2015 Males	2015 Females	2020 Both sexes	2020 Males	2020 Females
All ages	323	157	166	344	167	177	365	177	180	005	100	199
0-4	30	15	15	30	15	15	30	15	15	30	15	15
5-9	30	15	15	30	15	15	30	15	15	30	15	15
10-14	31	16	15	30	15	15	30	15	15	30	15	15
15-19	28	14	14	31	15	15	30	15	15	30	15	15
20-24	29	14	15	28	14	14	31	15	15	30	15	15
25-29	25	12	13	29	14	15	28	13	14	30	15	16
30-34	26	13	14	25	12	13	28	13	15	27	13	14
35-39	24	11	13	26	12	13	25	12	13	28	13	15
40-44	23	11	12	24	11	12	26	12	13	24	12	13
45-49	19	9	10	23	11	12	23	11	12	25	12	13
50-54	15	7	8	19	9	10	23	11	12	23	11	12
55-59	12	5	6	14	7	8	18	8	10	22	10	12
60-64	10	5	5	11	5	6	14	6	7	17	8	9
65-69	8	4	4	9	4	5	10	5	6	13	6	7
70-74	5	2	3	7	3	4	8	4	5	9	4	5
75-79	4	1	2	4	2	3	6	2	3	7	3	4
80-84	2	1	1	3	1	2	3	1	2	4	2	3
85-89	1	0	1	1	0	1	2	1	1	2	1	1
90-94	0	0	0	1	0	0	1	0	0	1	0	1
95-99	0	0	0	0	0	0	0	0	0	0	0	0
100 +	0	0	0	0	0	0	0	0	0	0	0	0

Age group	2025 Both sexes	2025 Males	2025 Females	2030 Both sexes	2030 Males	2030 Females	2035 Both sexes	2035 Males	2035 Females	2040 Both sexes	2040 Males	2040 Females
All ages	403	194	210	420	201	219	434	208	226	446	213	233
0-4	29	15	14	29	15	14	28	14	14	28	14	14
5-9	30	15	15	29	15	14	28	15	14	28	14	14
10-14	30	15	15	30	15	15	29	15	14	29	15	14
15-19	30	15	15	30	15	15	30	15	15	29	15	15
20-24	30	15	15	30	15	15	30	15	15	30	15	15
25-29	30	15	15	30	15	15	30	15	15	30	15	15
30-34	30	14	16	30	14	15	30	15	15	30	14	15
35-39	27	13	14	30	14	16	30	14	15	30	14	15
40-44	28	13	15	27	13	14	00	14	15	30	14	15
45-49	24	12	13	28	13	14	27	13	14	30	14	15
50-54	25	12	13	24	12	13	27	13	14	27	13	14
55-59	23	11	12	25	12	13	24	11	12	27	13	14
60-64	21	10	11	22	10	12	24	11	13	23	11	12
65-69	16	7	9	20	9	11	21	9	11	22	10	12
70-74	11	5	7	15	6	9	18	8	10	19	8	11
75-79	8	3	5	10	4	6	13	5	8	16	7	9
80-84	5	2	3	6	2	4	0	0	5	11	4	7
85-89	3	1	2	4	1	3	4	1	3	6	2	4
90-94	1	0	1	2	0	1	2	1	2	3	1	2
95-99	0	0	0	0	0	0	1	0	1	1	0	1
100 +	0	0	0	0	0	0	0	0	0	0	0	0

Age group	2045 Both sexes	2045 Males	2045 Females	2050 Both sexes	2050 Males	2050 Females
All ages	457	218	239	466	221	244
0-4	28	14	14	27	14	13
5-9	28	14	14	28	14	14
10-14	28	14	14	28	14	14
15-19	29	14	14	28	14	14
20-24	29	15	15	29	14	14
25-29	30	15	15	29	14	15
30-34	30	14	15	30	14	15
35-39	30	14	15	30	14	15
40-44	30	14	16	30	14	15
45-49	30	14	15	30	15	16
50-54	29	14	15	30	14	15
55-59	26	12	14	29	14	15
60-64	26	12	14	25	12	13
65-69	22	10	12	25	11	13
70-74	21	9	11	20	9	11
75-79	17	7	10	18	8	11
80-84	13	5	8	14	5	8
85-89	8	2	5	10	3	6
90-94	3	1	3	5	1	3
95-99	1	0	1	2	0	1
100 +	0	0	0	0	0	0

POPULATION BY AGE AND SEX (in thousands)

Age group	2005 Both sexes	2005 Males	2005 Females	2010 Both sexes	2010 Males	2010 Females	2015 Both sexes	2015 Males	2015 Females	2020 Both sexes	2020 Males	2020 Females
All ages	323	157	166	348	169	179	374	181	193	402	194	208
0-4	30	15	15	33	17	16	36	18	17	37	19	18
5-9	30	15	15	30	15	15	33	17	16	36	18	17
10-14	31	16	15	30	15	15	30	15	15	34	17	16
15-19	28	14	14	31	15	15	30	15	15	30	15	15
20-24	29	14	15	28	14	14	31	15	15	30	15	15
25-29	25	12	13	29	14	15	28	13	14	30	15	16
30-34	26	13	14	25	12	13	28	13	15	27	13	14
35-39	24	11	13	26	12	13	25	12	13	28	13	15
40-44	23	11	12	24	11	12	26	12	13	24	12	13
45-49	19	9	10	23	11	12	23	11	12	25	12	13
50-54	15	7	8	19	9	10	23	11	12	23	11	12
55-59	12	5	6	14	7	8	18	8	10	22	10	12
60-64	10	5	5	11	5	6	14	6	7	17	8	9
65-69	8	4	4	9	4	5	10	5	6	13	6	7
70-74	5	2	3	7	3	4	8	4	5	9	4	5
75-79	4	1	2	4	2	3	6	2	3	7	3	4
80-84	2	1	1	3	1	2	3	1	2	4	2	3
85-89	1	0	1	1	0	1	2	1	1	2	1	1
90-94	0	0	0	1	0	0	1	0	0	1	0	1
95-99	0	0	0	0	0	0	0	0	0	0	0	0
100 +	0	0	0	0	0	0	0	0	0	0	0	0

Age group	2025 Both sexes	2025 Males	2025 Females	2030 Both sexes	2030 Males	2030 Females	2035 Both sexes	2035 Males	2035 Females	2040 Both sexes	2040 Males	2040 Females
All ages	428	206	221	453	218	235	478	230	248	502	242	261
0-4	37	19	18	37	19	18	39	20	19	41	21	20
5-9	37	19	18	37	19	18	37	19	18	39	20	19
10-14	36	18	18	37	19	18	37	19	18	37	19	18
15-19	34	17	17	36	18	18	37	19	18	37	19	18
20-24	30	15	15	34	17	17	36	18	18	37	19	19
25-29	30	15	15	30	15	15	33	16	17	36	18	18
30-34	30	14	16	30	14	15	30	15	15	33	16	17
35-39	27	13	14	30	14	16	30	14	15	30	14	15
40-44	28	13	15	27	13	14	30	14	15	30	14	15
45-49	24	12	13	28	13	14	27	13	14	30	14	15
50-54	25	12	13	24	12	13	27	13	14	27	13	14
55-59	23	11	12	25	12	13	24	11	12	27	13	14
60-64	21	10	11	22	10	12	24	11	13	23	11	12
65-69	16	7	9	20	9	11	21	9	11	22	10	12
70-74	11	5	7	15	6	9	18	8	10	19	8	11
75-79	8	3	5	10	4	6	13	5	8	16	7	9
80-84	5	2	3	6	2	4	8	3	5	11	4	7
85-89	3	1	2	4	1	3	4	1	3	6	2	4
90-94	1	0	1	2	0	1	2	1	2	3	1	2
95-99	0	0	0	0	0	0	1	0	1	1	0	1
100 +	0	0	0	0	0	0	0	0	0	0	0	0

Age group	2045 Both sexes	2045 Males	2045 Females	2050 Both sexes	2050 Males	2050 Females
All ages	527	254	274	552	265	287
0-4	42	22	21	43	22	21
5-9	41	21	20	42	22	21
10-14	39	20	19	41	21	20
15-19	37	19	19	39	20	19
20-24	37	19	19	37	19	19
25-29	37	18	19	37	18	19
30-34	35	17	18	37	18	19
35-39	33	16	17	35	17	18
40-44	30	14	16	33	16	17
45-49	30	14	15	30	15	16
50-54	29	14	15	30	14	15
55-59	26	12	14	29	14	15
60-64	26	12	14	25	12	13
65-69	22	10	12	25	11	13
70-74	21	9	11	20	9	11
75-79	17	7	10	18	8	11
80-84	13	5	8	14	5	8
85-89	8	2	5	10	3	6
90-94	3	1	3	5	1	3
95-99	1	0	1	2	0	1
100 +	0	0	0	0	0	0

United Nations Department of Economic and Social Affairs/Population Division
World Population Prospects: The 2004 Revision, Volume II: Sex and Age Distribution of the World Population

POPULATION BY AGE AND SEX (in thousands)

Age group	2005 Both sexes	Males	Females	2010 Both sexes	Males	Females	2015 Both sexes	Males	Females	2020 Both sexes	Males	Females
All ages	333	157	166	341	165	170	356	172	184	369	177	191
0-4	30	15	15	27	14	13	24	12	12	22	11	11
5-9	30	15	15	30	15	15	27	14	13	24	12	12
10-14	31	16	15	30	15	15	30	15	15	27	14	13
15-19	28	14	14	31	15	15	30	15	15	30	15	15
20-24	29	14	15	28	14	14	31	15	15	30	15	15
25-29	25	12	13	29	14	15	28	13	14	30	15	16
30-34	26	13	14	25	12	13	28	13	15	27	13	14
35-39	24	11	13	26	12	13	25	12	13	28	13	15
40-44	23	11	12	24	11	12	26	12	13	24	12	13
45-49	19	9	10	23	11	12	23	11	12	25	12	13
50-54	15	7	8	19	9	10	23	11	12	23	11	12
55-59	12	5	6	14	7	8	18	8	10	22	10	12
60-64	10	5	5	11	5	6	14	6	7	17	8	9
65-69	8	4	4	9	4	5	10	5	6	13	6	7
70-74	5	2	3	7	3	4	8	4	5	9	4	5
75-79	4	1	2	4	2	3	6	2	3	7	3	4
80-84	2	1	1	3	1	2	3	1	2	4	2	3
85-89	1	0	1	1	0	1	2	1	1	2	1	1
90-94	0	0	0	1	0	0	1	0	0	1	0	1
95-99	0	0	0	0	0	0	0	0	0	0	0	0
100 +	0	0	0	0	0	0	0	0	0	0	0	0

Age group	2025 Both sexes	Males	Females	2030 Both sexes	Males	Females	2035 Both sexes	Males	Females	2040 Both sexes	Males	Females
All ages	379	182	198	388	185	203	392	186	206	394	186	208
0-4	22	11	11	20	10	10	19	10	9	17	9	9
5-9	22	11	11	22	11	11	20	10	10	19	10	9
10-14	24	12	12	22	11	11	22	11	11	20	10	10
15-19	27	13	13	24	12	12	22	11	11	22	11	11
20-24	30	15	15	27	13	13	24	12	12	23	11	11
25-29	30	15	15	30	15	15	27	13	14	24	12	12
30-34	30	14	16	30	14	15	30	15	15	26	13	14
35-39	27	13	14	30	14	16	30	14	15	30	14	15
40-44	20	10	15	27	13	14	30	14	15	30	14	15
45-49	24	12	13	28	13	14	27	13	14	30	14	15
50-54	25	12	13	24	12	13	27	13	14	27	13	14
55-59	23	11	12	25	12	13	24	11	12	27	13	14
60-64	21	10	11	22	10	12	24	11	13	23	11	12
65-69	16	7	9	20	9	11	21	9	11	22	10	12
70-74	11	5	7	15	6	9	18	8	10	19	8	11
75-79	8	3	5	10	4	6	13	5	8	16	7	9
80-84	5	2	3	6	2	4	8	3	5	11	4	7
85-89	3	1	2	4	1	3	4	1	3	6	2	4
90-94	1	0	1	2	0	1	2	1	2	3	1	2
95-99	0	0	0	0	0	0	1	0	1	1	0	1
100 +	0	0	0	0	0	0	0	0	0	0	0	0

Age group	2045 Both sexes	Males	Females	2050 Both sexes	Males	Females
All ages	393	185	208	390	183	207
0-4	16	8	8	15	8	7
5-9	17	9	9	16	8	8
10-14	19	10	9	17	9	9
15-19	20	10	10	19	9	9
20-24	22	11	11	20	10	10
25-29	22	11	12	22	11	11
30-34	24	12	13	22	11	12
35-39	27	13	14	24	12	13
40-44	30	14	16	27	13	14
45-49	30	14	15	30	15	16
50-54	29	14	15	30	14	15
55-59	26	12	14	29	14	15
60-64	26	12	14	25	12	13
65-69	22	10	12	25	11	13
70-74	21	9	11	20	9	11
75-79	17	7	10	18	8	11
80-84	13	5	8	14	5	8
85-89	8	2	5	10	3	6
90-94	3	1	3	5	1	3
95-99	1	0	1	2	0	1
100 +	0	0	0	0	0	0

POPULATION BY AGE AND SEX (in thousands)

Age group	1950 Both sexes	Males	Females	1955 Both sexes	Males	Females	1960 Both sexes	Males	Females	1965 Both sexes	Males	Females
All ages	116	62	53	134	72	62	156	84	72	191	96	95
0-4	20	10	10	24	12	12	28	14	14	40	20	20
5-9	16	8	8	19	9	9	22	11	11	33	17	17
10-14	13	7	6	15	8	7	18	9	9	24	12	11
15-19	11	6	5	13	7	6	15	8	7	17	8	9
20-24	11	6	5	12	7	5	14	8	6	15	7	8
25-29	10	6	4	12	7	5	14	8	6	13	6	7
30-34	8	5	3	9	5	4	11	6	4	11	6	6
35-39	6	4	3	7	4	3	9	5	4	10	5	5
40-44	5	3	2	6	3	3	7	4	3	8	4	4
45-49	4	2	2	5	3	2	5	3	2	6	3	3
50-54	3	2	2	4	2	2	4	2	2	5	2	2
55-59	3	1	1	3	1	1	3	2	2	3	2	2
60-64	2	1	1	2	1	1	3	1	1	2	1	1
65-69	1	1	1	2	1	1	2	1	1	2	1	1
70-74	1	0	1	1	1	1	1	1	1	1	1	1
75-79	1	0	0	1	0	0	1	0	0	1	0	0
80 +	0	0	0	0	0	0	0	0	0	1	0	0

Age group	1970 Both sexes	Males	Females	1975 Both sexes	Males	Females	1980 Both sexes	Males	Females	1985 Both sexes	Males	Females
All ages	220	118	102	272	149	123	347	202	145	413	244	170
0-4	38	19	19	41	20	20	44	22	22	49	26	23
5-9	34	17	17	40	20	20	40	20	20	44	23	21
10-14	29	15	14	36	19	17	36	18	18	38	20	18
15-19	23	12	11	35	20	15	34	17	17	30	15	14
20-24	17	10	7	30	18	12	40	24	16	37	21	17
25-29	16	9	7	20	12	8	42	29	13	50	31	19
30-34	13	8	6	15	8	6	31	21	9	53	35	18
35-39	12	7	5	13	7	6	21	14	7	40	28	12
40-44	10	6	4	11	6	5	17	11	6	24	17	7
45-49	8	5	3	9	5	4	13	8	5	14	9	5
50-54	6	4	3	8	4	3	10	6	4	11	6	4
55-59	4	2	2	6	3	2	7	4	3	8	5	3
60-64	3	2	1	4	2	2	5	3	2	6	3	3
65-69	2	1	1	3	1	1	3	2	1	4	2	2
70-74	1	1	1	2	1	1	2	1	1	3	1	1
75-79	1	1	1	1	1	1	1	1	1	1	1	1
80 +	1	0	0	1	0	0	1	0	0	1	1	1

Age group	1990 Both sexes	Males	Females	1995 Both sexes	Males	Females	2000 Both sexes	Males	Females	2005 Both sexes	Males	Females
All ages	493	286	207	584	337	247	672	387	285	727	414	313
0-4	58	30	28	68	35	33	66	34	32	65	33	32
5-9	52	27	25	56	29	27	67	34	33	66	34	32
10-14	45	23	22	53	27	26	57	29	27	67	34	33
15-19	35	18	17	46	23	22	53	27	26	57	29	27
20-24	45	24	21	49	28	21	59	33	26	53	27	26
25-29	61	37	24	67	41	26	73	45	28	59	33	26
30-34	63	42	21	72	45	27	78	49	29	73	45	27
35-39	47	32	15	60	39	21	68	41	26	78	48	29
40-44	29	20	9	41	28	13	53	34	19	67	41	26
45-49	17	11	6	25	17	8	38	25	12	53	34	19
50-54	13	8	5	14	8	6	22	14	7	37	25	12
55-59	9	5	4	11	6	5	11	6	5	21	14	7
60-64	7	4	3	8	4	4	9	5	5	11	6	5
65-69	5	3	2	6	3	3	7	4	4	9	4	4
70-74	3	2	1	4	2	2	6	3	3	6	3	3
75-79	2	1	1	2	1	1	3	2	1	4	2	2
80 +	1	1	1	2	1	1	2	1	1	3	1	1

194

United Nations Department of Economic and Social Affairs/Population Division
World Population Prospects: The 2004 Revision, Volume II: Sex and Age Distribution of the World Population

POPULATION BY AGE AND SEX (in thousands)

Age group	2005 Both sexes	2005 Males	2005 Females	2010 Both sexes	2010 Males	2010 Females	2015 Both sexes	2015 Males	2015 Females	2020 Both sexes	2020 Males	2020 Females
All ages	727	414	313	791	448	343	852	481	371	910	511	399
0-4	65	33	32	61	31	30	60	31	29	60	31	29
5-9	66	34	32	64	33	31	60	31	29	59	30	29
10-14	67	34	33	66	34	32	64	33	31	61	31	30
15-19	57	29	27	67	34	33	66	34	32	64	33	31
20-24	53	27	26	63	34	29	74	39	35	73	38	34
25-29	59	33	26	64	36	29	74	42	32	85	47	37
30-34	73	45	27	65	37	28	70	40	30	80	46	34
35-39	78	48	29	71	44	27	63	36	28	68	38	30
40-44	67	41	26	74	46	28	68	42	26	60	33	27
45-49	53	34	19	65	39	26	72	45	28	66	40	26
50-54	37	25	12	50	32	18	62	37	25	70	43	27
55-59	21	14	7	35	23	11	48	30	18	60	35	24
60-64	11	6	5	20	13	7	33	22	11	45	28	17
65-69	9	4	4	10	5	5	18	12	6	30	20	10
70-74	6	3	3	7	4	4	8	4	4	16	10	6
75-79	4	2	2	5	2	2	6	3	3	7	3	4
80-84	2	1	1	3	1	1	3	2	2	4	2	2
85-89	1	0	0	1	0	1	1	1	1	2	1	1
90-94	0	0	0	0	0	0	0	0	0	0	0	0
95-99	0	0	0	0	0	0	0	0	0	0	0	0
100 +	0	0	0	0	0	0	0	0	0	0	0	0

Age group	2025 Both sexes	2025 Males	2025 Females	2030 Both sexes	2030 Males	2030 Females	2035 Both sexes	2035 Males	2035 Females	2040 Both sexes	2040 Males	2040 Females
All ages	965	539	426	1 016	564	452	1 062	585	477	1 100	602	498
0-4	62	32	30	64	33	31	65	33	31	64	33	31
5-9	59	30	29	61	31	30	63	32	31	64	33	31
10-14	60	31	29	60	31	29	61	31	30	64	33	31
15-19	61	31	30	60	31	29	60	31	29	61	31	30
20-24	71	38	33	67	36	31	67	36	31	67	36	31
25-29	84	47	37	82	46	36	79	44	34	78	44	34
30-34	90	51	39	89	51	38	88	50	38	84	48	36
35-39	78	45	33	89	50	39	88	49	38	86	49	38
40-44	65	36	29	76	43	32	86	48	38	85	47	37
45-49	58	32	26	63	35	28	73	41	32	83	46	37
50-54	64	38	25	56	30	26	61	33	28	71	40	31
55-59	67	41	27	61	36	25	54	29	25	59	31	27
60-64	57	33	24	64	38	26	59	35	24	52	27	24
65-69	42	26	16	53	31	22	60	35	24	55	32	23
70-74	26	17	9	37	22	15	47	27	21	54	31	23
75-79	13	8	5	21	13	8	31	18	13	40	22	18
80-84	5	2	3	9	5	4	16	9	6	22	10	10
85-89	2	1	1	3	1	2	5	3	2	9	5	4
90-94	1	0	0	1	0	1	1	0	1	2	1	1
95-99	0	0	0	0	0	0	0	0	0	0	0	0
100 +	0	0	0	0	0	0	0	0	0	0	0	0

Age group	2045 Both sexes	2045 Males	2045 Females	2050 Both sexes	2050 Males	2050 Females
All ages	1 130	614	516	1 155	625	530
0-4	63	32	31	63	32	31
5-9	63	32	31	62	32	30
10-14	64	33	31	63	32	31
15-19	64	33	31	64	33	31
20-24	68	36	32	70	38	33
25-29	78	44	34	79	45	35
30-34	83	48	35	83	48	35
35-39	83	47	36	82	47	35
40-44	83	47	37	80	45	35
45-49	83	46	37	81	45	36
50-54	81	44	37	80	44	36
55-59	69	38	31	79	43	36
60-64	57	30	27	66	36	30
65-69	49	25	23	54	28	26
70-74	50	28	21	44	23	22
75-79	45	26	20	42	24	19
80-84	30	16	14	34	19	16
85-89	14	7	7	19	9	10
90-94	4	2	2	6	3	3
95-99	1	0	0	1	1	1
100 +	0	0	0	0	0	0

POPULATION BY AGE AND SEX (in thousands)

Age group	2005 Both sexes	2005 Males	2005 Females	2010 Both sexes	2010 Males	2010 Females	2015 Both sexes	2015 Males	2015 Females	2020 Both sexes	2020 Males	2020 Females
All ages	727	414	313	798	452	346	871	490	380	944	528	416
0-4	65	33	32	68	35	33	72	37	35	76	39	37
5-9	66	34	32	64	33	31	67	34	33	71	36	35
10-14	67	34	33	66	34	32	64	33	31	67	35	33
15-19	57	29	27	67	34	33	66	34	32	64	33	31
20-24	53	27	26	63	34	29	74	39	35	73	38	34
25-29	59	33	26	64	36	29	74	42	32	85	47	37
30-34	73	45	27	65	37	28	70	40	30	80	46	34
35-39	78	48	29	71	44	27	63	36	28	68	38	30
40-44	67	41	26	74	46	28	68	42	26	60	33	27
45-49	53	34	19	65	39	26	72	45	28	66	40	26
50-54	37	25	12	50	32	18	62	37	25	70	43	27
55-59	21	14	7	35	23	11	48	30	18	60	35	24
60-64	11	6	5	20	13	7	33	22	11	45	28	17
65-69	9	4	4	10	5	5	18	12	6	30	20	10
70-74	6	3	3	7	4	4	8	4	4	16	10	6
75-79	4	2	2	5	2	2	6	3	3	7	3	4
80-84	2	1	1	3	1	1	3	2	2	4	2	2
85-89	1	0	0	1	0	1	1	1	1	2	1	1
90-94	0	0	0	0	0	0	0	0	0	0	0	0
95-99	0	0	0	0	0	0	0	0	0	0	0	0
100 +	0	0	0	0	0	0	0	0	0	0	0	0

Age group	2025 Both sexes	2025 Males	2025 Females	2030 Both sexes	2030 Males	2030 Females	2035 Both sexes	2035 Males	2035 Females	2040 Both sexes	2040 Males	2040 Females
All ages	1 016	565	451	1 086	600	486	1 152	632	521	1 214	661	554
0-4	79	40	38	83	42	40	86	44	42	88	45	43
5-9	75	39	37	78	40	38	82	42	40	85	43	41
10-14	71	37	35	75	39	37	78	40	38	82	42	40
15-19	68	35	33	72	37	35	76	39	37	78	40	38
20-24	71	38	33	74	39	35	78	41	37	82	44	39
25-29	84	47	37	82	46	36	86	48	38	89	50	40
30-34	90	51	39	89	51	38	88	50	38	91	52	39
35-39	78	45	33	89	50	39	88	49	38	86	49	38
40-44	65	36	29	75	43	32	86	48	38	85	47	37
45-49	58	32	26	63	35	28	73	41	32	83	46	37
50-54	64	38	25	56	30	26	61	33	28	71	40	31
55-59	67	41	27	61	36	25	54	29	25	59	31	27
60-64	57	33	24	64	38	26	59	35	24	52	27	24
65-69	42	26	16	53	31	22	60	35	24	55	32	23
70-74	26	17	9	37	22	15	47	27	21	54	31	23
75-79	13	8	5	21	13	8	31	18	13	40	22	18
80-84	5	2	3	9	5	4	15	9	6	22	13	10
85-89	2	1	1	3	1	2	5	3	2	9	5	4
90-94	1	0	0	1	0	1	1	0	1	2	1	1
95-99	0	0	0	0	0	0	0	0	0	0	0	0
100 +	0	0	0	0	0	0	0	0	0	0	0	0

Age group	2045 Both sexes	2045 Males	2045 Females	2050 Both sexes	2050 Males	2050 Females
All ages	1 273	688	585	1 330	714	616
0-4	91	47	45	95	49	46
5-9	87	45	43	91	46	44
10-14	85	44	41	88	45	43
15-19	82	42	40	85	44	42
20-24	85	45	40	89	47	42
25-29	94	52	42	96	53	43
30-34	95	54	41	99	56	43
35-39	90	50	39	93	52	41
40-44	83	47	37	86	48	38
45-49	83	46	37	81	45	36
50-54	81	44	37	80	44	36
55-59	69	38	31	79	43	36
60-64	57	30	27	66	36	30
65-69	49	25	23	54	28	26
70-74	50	28	21	44	23	22
75-79	45	26	20	42	24	19
80-84	30	16	14	34	19	16
85-89	14	7	7	19	9	10
90-94	4	2	2	6	3	3
95-99	1	0	0	1	1	1
100 +	0	0	0	0	0	0

United Nations Department of Economic and Social Affairs/Population Division
World Population Prospects: The 2004 Revision, Volume II: Sex and Age Distribution of the World Population

196

POPULATION BY AGE AND SEX (in thousands)

Age group	2005 Both sexes	2005 Males	2005 Females	2010 Both sexes	2010 Males	2010 Females	2015 Both sexes	2015 Males	2015 Females	2020 Both sexes	2020 Males	2020 Females
All ages	727	414	313	784	445	339	834	471	362	876	493	382
0-4	65	33	32	54	28	26	49	25	24	44	23	22
5-9	66	34	32	64	33	31	54	27	26	48	24	23
10-14	67	34	33	66	34	32	64	33	31	54	28	26
15-19	57	29	27	67	34	33	66	34	32	64	33	31
20-24	53	27	26	63	34	29	74	39	35	73	38	34
25-29	59	33	26	64	36	29	74	42	32	85	47	37
30-34	73	45	27	65	37	28	70	40	30	80	46	34
35-39	78	48	29	71	44	27	63	36	28	68	38	30
40-44	67	41	26	74	46	28	68	42	26	60	33	27
45-49	53	34	19	65	39	26	72	45	28	66	40	26
50-54	37	25	12	50	32	18	62	37	25	70	43	27
55-59	21	14	7	35	23	11	48	30	18	60	35	24
60-64	11	6	5	20	13	7	33	22	11	45	28	17
65-69	9	4	4	10	5	5	18	12	6	30	20	10
70-74	6	3	3	7	4	4	8	4	4	16	10	6
75-79	4	2	2	5	2	2	6	3	3	7	3	4
80-84	2	1	1	3	1	1	3	2	2	4	2	2
85-89	1	0	0	1	0	1	1	1	1	2	1	1
90-94	0	0	0	0	0	0	0	0	0	0	0	0
95-99	0	0	0	0	0	0	0	0	0	0	0	0
100 +	0	0	0	0	0	0	0	0	0	0	0	0

Age group	2025 Both sexes	2025 Males	2025 Females	2030 Both sexes	2030 Males	2030 Females	2035 Both sexes	2035 Males	2035 Females	2040 Both sexes	2040 Males	2040 Females
All ages	914	513	401	947	529	419	973	540	433	990	545	444
0-4	45	23	22	46	24	22	45	23	22	42	22	21
5-9	44	22	21	44	23	22	45	23	22	44	23	22
10-14	48	25	23	44	23	21	44	23	22	45	23	22
15-19	54	28	26	48	25	24	44	23	22	45	23	22
20-24	71	38	33	61	32	28	55	30	25	51	27	23
25-29	84	47	37	82	46	36	72	41	31	66	38	28
30-34	90	51	39	89	51	38	88	50	38	77	45	33
35-39	78	45	33	89	50	39	88	49	38	86	49	38
40-44	65	36	29	75	43	32	86	48	38	85	47	37
45-49	58	32	26	63	35	28	73	41	32	83	46	37
50-54	64	38	25	56	30	26	61	33	28	71	40	31
55-59	67	41	27	61	36	25	54	29	25	59	31	27
60-64	57	33	24	64	38	26	59	35	24	52	27	24
65-69	42	26	16	53	31	22	60	35	24	55	32	23
70-74	26	17	9	37	22	15	47	27	21	54	31	23
75-79	13	8	5	21	13	8	31	18	13	40	22	18
80-84	5	2	3	9	5	4	15	9	6	22	13	10
85-89	2	1	1	3	1	2	5	3	2	9	5	4
90-94	1	0	0	1	0	1	1	0	1	2	1	1
95-99	0	0	0	0	0	0	0	0	0	0	0	0
100 +	0	0	0	0	0	0	0	0	0	0	0	0

Age group	2045 Both sexes	2045 Males	2045 Females	2050 Both sexes	2050 Males	2050 Females
All ages	997	546	451	996	543	453
0-4	39	20	19	37	10	18
5-9	42	21	20	39	20	19
10-14	45	23	22	42	22	20
15-19	46	23	22	45	23	22
20-24	51	28	24	52	28	24
25-29	62	36	26	63	36	26
30-34	72	42	30	68	40	28
35-39	76	44	33	70	41	30
40-44	83	47	37	73	41	32
45-49	83	46	37	81	45	36
50-54	81	44	37	80	44	36
55-59	69	38	31	79	43	36
60-64	57	30	27	66	36	30
65-69	49	25	23	54	28	26
70-74	50	28	21	44	23	22
75-79	45	26	20	42	24	19
80-84	30	16	14	34	19	16
85-89	14	7	7	19	9	10
90-94	4	2	2	6	3	3
95-99	1	0	0	1	1	1
100 +	0	0	0	0	0	0

POPULATION BY AGE AND SEX (in thousands)

Age group	1950 Both sexes	Males	Females	1955 Both sexes	Males	Females	1960 Both sexes	Males	Females	1965 Both sexes	Males	Females
All ages	41 783	22 227	19 556	46 041	24 381	21 660	51 224	26 985	24 239	57 549	30 151	27 398
0-4	6 116	3 037	3 079	7 786	4 007	3 780	8 868	4 556	4 311	10 184	5 226	4 958
5-9	5 091	2 541	2 550	5 520	2 767	2 753	7 090	3 678	3 412	8 139	4 212	3 928
10-14	4 512	2 281	2 231	4 946	2 478	2 468	5 375	2 703	2 672	6 918	3 599	3 319
15-19	4 036	2 110	1 926	4 373	2 220	2 153	4 805	2 416	2 389	5 230	2 639	2 592
20-24	3 547	1 894	1 653	3 868	2 029	1 839	4 203	2 140	2 063	4 625	2 330	2 295
25-29	3 021	1 647	1 374	3 368	1 804	1 565	3 686	1 939	1 748	4 011	2 044	1 967
30-34	2 667	1 481	1 187	2 852	1 560	1 292	3 192	1 714	1 478	3 500	1 844	1 656
35-39	2 676	1 568	1 109	2 497	1 390	1 108	2 682	1 471	1 212	3 010	1 618	1 392
40-44	2 655	1 519	1 137	2 480	1 452	1 028	2 326	1 294	1 033	2 507	1 373	1 135
45-49	1 835	1 028	807	2 432	1 385	1 047	2 284	1 332	952	2 152	1 191	961
50-54	1 689	971	717	1 647	916	731	2 196	1 242	955	2 073	1 200	873
55-59	1 366	790	576	1 467	837	630	1 442	795	647	1 935	1 084	851
60-64	1 057	600	457	1 127	646	481	1 222	690	532	1 212	661	551
65-69	730	390	340	805	453	352	869	493	376	953	532	421
70-74	445	215	230	496	262	234	555	309	247	608	340	268
75-79	239	105	134	251	120	131	286	149	137	326	178	148
80 +	100	50	50	125	56	69	142	65	77	165	81	84

Age group	1970 Both sexes	Males	Females	1975 Both sexes	Males	Females	1980 Both sexes	Males	Females	1985 Both sexes	Males	Females
All ages	64 907	33 809	31 099	73 178	37 990	35 188	82 185	42 534	39 651	92 818	47 909	44 909
0-4	11 321	5 787	5 534	12 379	6 347	6 032	13 343	6 834	6 508	15 003	7 686	7 317
5-9	9 433	4 864	4 568	10 559	5 429	5 130	11 619	5 989	5 630	12 656	6 514	6 142
10-14	7 960	4 128	3 833	9 242	4 777	4 465	10 363	5 339	5 024	11 434	5 903	5 530
15-19	6 750	3 520	3 231	7 784	4 046	3 737	9 051	4 688	4 363	10 174	5 251	4 924
20-24	5 053	2 552	2 500	6 543	3 418	3 125	7 557	3 933	3 624	8 814	4 568	4 246
25-29	4 434	2 235	2 199	4 864	2 461	2 404	6 311	3 299	3 012	7 314	3 807	3 507
30-34	3 827	1 953	1 875	4 250	2 146	2 103	4 671	2 365	2 306	6 087	3 183	2 904
35-39	3 319	1 749	1 570	3 646	1 863	1 784	4 059	2 051	2 008	4 483	2 269	2 213
40-44	2 831	1 519	1 312	3 137	1 652	1 486	3 457	1 763	1 694	3 870	1 952	1 918
45-49	2 334	1 271	1 063	2 649	1 415	1 234	2 946	1 544	1 402	3 267	1 659	1 608
50-54	1 967	1 080	887	2 146	1 161	985	2 447	1 298	1 149	2 741	1 426	1 315
55-59	1 841	1 055	785	1 760	957	802	1 930	1 034	896	2 220	1 166	1 054
60-64	1 643	909	733	1 575	894	681	1 516	815	701	1 681	889	792
65-69	959	515	444	1 313	717	596	1 268	710	559	1 239	656	584
70-74	678	372	306	691	365	326	957	513	443	940	516	424
75-79	365	200	165	415	223	191	429	222	207	607	318	289
80 +	193	100	94	224	118	107	260	135	125	288	145	143

Age group	1990 Both sexes	Males	Females	1995 Both sexes	Males	Females	2000 Both sexes	Males	Females	2005 Both sexes	Males	Females
All ages	104 047	53 602	50 444	116 455	59 800	56 654	128 916	66 034	62 881	141 822	72 459	69 363
0-4	15 681	8 036	7 645	16 893	8 625	8 268	16 852	8 619	8 233	17 399	8 889	8 510
5-9	14 371	7 392	6 979	15 164	7 784	7 381	16 488	8 432	8 056	16 545	8 470	8 075
10-14	12 486	6 435	6 051	14 213	7 315	6 898	15 035	7 721	7 314	16 375	8 376	8 000
15-19	11 254	5 818	5 436	12 316	6 349	5 967	14 057	7 234	6 824	14 896	7 645	7 251
20-24	9 936	5 130	4 806	11 014	5 688	5 326	12 095	6 223	5 872	13 839	7 104	6 734
25-29	8 560	4 437	4 123	9 672	4 985	4 687	10 766	5 545	5 221	11 855	6 079	5 775
30-34	7 082	3 689	3 394	8 312	4 304	4 008	9 437	4 854	4 583	10 538	5 413	5 125
35-39	5 870	3 071	2 799	6 855	3 566	3 289	8 090	4 181	3 909	9 220	4 732	4 488
40-44	4 296	2 172	2 124	5 653	2 950	2 703	6 642	3 447	3 195	7 874	4 059	3 815
45-49	3 678	1 848	1 830	4 102	2 064	2 038	5 436	2 826	2 610	6 418	3 318	3 100
50-54	3 060	1 544	1 516	3 465	1 728	1 736	3 893	1 946	1 947	5 188	2 682	2 506
55-59	2 506	1 292	1 214	2 819	1 407	1 412	3 220	1 591	1 630	3 642	1 803	1 838
60-64	1 952	1 013	939	2 226	1 131	1 095	2 533	1 246	1 286	2 917	1 420	1 497
65-69	1 392	724	667	1 637	833	804	1 894	945	949	2 179	1 051	1 127
70-74	933	484	450	1 065	541	524	1 276	635	641	1 497	728	768
75-79	608	326	282	617	311	307	721	356	365	879	424	455
80 +	382	192	190	431	218	213	479	233	246	562	265	297

United Nations Department of Economic and Social Affairs/Population Division
World Population Prospects: The 2004 Revision, Volume II: Sex and Age Distribution of the World Population

198

POPULATION BY AGE AND SEX (in thousands)

Age group	2005 Both sexes	Males	Females	2010 Both sexes	Males	Females	2015 Both sexes	Males	Females	2020 Both sexes	Males	Females
All ages	141 822	72 459	69 363	154 960	79 002	75 957	168 158	85 554	82 604	181 180	91 986	89 194
0-4	17 399	8 889	8 510	17 754	9 067	8 688	18 057	9 215	8 842	18 207	9 285	8 922
5-9	16 545	8 470	8 075	17 161	8 773	8 388	17 576	8 976	8 600	17 925	9 144	8 781
10-14	16 375	8 376	8 000	16 455	8 423	8 032	17 087	8 733	8 354	17 517	8 943	8 574
15-19	14 896	7 645	7 251	16 253	8 307	7 945	16 352	8 363	7 989	17 000	8 679	8 321
20-24	13 839	7 104	6 734	14 705	7 530	7 175	16 076	8 198	7 878	16 200	8 264	7 936
25-29	11 855	6 079	5 775	13 616	6 971	6 646	14 503	7 405	7 098	15 891	8 080	7 811
30-34	10 538	5 413	5 125	11 650	5 961	5 689	13 420	6 855	6 565	14 327	7 297	7 029
35-39	9 220	4 732	4 488	10 339	5 301	5 038	11 464	5 855	5 609	13 242	6 751	6 491
40-44	7 874	4 059	3 815	9 012	4 615	4 397	10 139	5 188	4 952	11 275	5 747	5 529
45-49	6 418	3 318	3 100	7 643	3 928	3 715	8 780	4 483	4 297	9 910	5 056	4 854
50-54	5 188	2 682	2 506	6 155	3 166	2 990	7 361	3 765	3 597	8 489	4 315	4 175
55-59	3 642	1 803	1 838	4 880	2 501	2 379	5 820	2 968	2 852	6 993	3 547	3 446
60-64	2 917	1 420	1 497	3 322	1 621	1 701	4 480	2 264	2 215	5 375	2 704	2 671
65-69	2 179	1 051	1 127	2 533	1 208	1 324	2 908	1 391	1 517	3 950	1 959	1 992
70-74	1 497	728	768	1 742	819	923	2 048	951	1 096	2 375	1 106	1 269
75-79	879	424	455	1 047	494	553	1 237	563	675	1 474	662	812
80-84	397	189	208	493	229	264	597	271	326	718	314	404
85-89	131	61	71	160	72	87	202	89	113	250	108	142
90-94	30	14	16	34	15	19	42	18	24	54	22	32
95-99	4	2	2	4	2	3	5	2	3	6	2	4
100 +	0	0	0	0	0	0	0	0	0	0	0	0

Age group	2025 Both sexes	Males	Females	2030 Both sexes	Males	Females	2035 Both sexes	Males	Females	2040 Both sexes	Males	Females
All ages	193 752	98 151	95 600	205 641	103 927	101 714	216 664	109 227	107 437	226 663	113 959	112 704
0-4	18 163	9 260	8 904	18 020	9 185	8 835	17 819	9 080	8 739	17 528	8 938	8 590
5-9	18 105	9 228	8 876	18 086	9 215	8 871	17 960	9 148	8 812	17 771	9 051	8 719
10-14	17 876	9 116	8 761	18 065	9 204	8 861	18 053	9 194	8 859	17 932	9 131	8 802
15-19	17 441	8 894	8 547	17 810	9 072	8 739	18 008	9 164	8 844	18 002	9 158	8 844
20-24	16 864	8 587	8 277	17 320	8 809	8 511	17 701	8 992	8 709	17 907	9 091	8 816
25-29	16 039	8 157	7 882	16 719	8 487	8 232	17 188	8 715	8 473	17 579	8 905	8 674
30-34	15 729	7 978	7 751	15 896	8 063	7 833	16 589	8 399	8 190	17 069	8 634	8 435
35-39	14 165	7 200	6 965	15 579	7 885	7 694	15 765	7 980	7 785	16 468	8 322	8 146
40-44	13 058	6 644	6 414	13 007	7 100	6 896	15 421	7 790	7 631	15 623	7 894	7 730
45-49	11 054	5 618	5 435	12 834	6 513	6 322	13 787	6 976	6 812	15 217	7 668	7 548
50-54	9 617	4 885	4 733	10 762	5 445	5 316	12 532	6 332	6 201	13 495	6 800	6 695
55-59	8 104	4 085	4 019	9 219	4 644	4 575	10 356	5 198	5 159	12 100	6 065	6 035
60-64	6 500	3 252	3 248	7 576	3 765	3 810	8 664	4 304	4 360	9 777	4 839	4 938
65-69	4 781	2 358	2 423	5 828	2 857	2 971	6 842	3 331	3 511	7 878	3 832	4 047
70-74	3 261	1 575	1 686	3 989	1 914	2 075	4 911	2 340	2 571	5 828	2 752	3 076
75-79	1 737	781	956	2 416	1 126	1 290	2 996	1 386	1 610	3 751	1 714	2 037
80-84	873	376	497	1 048	451	597	1 481	661	820	1 890	826	1 064
85-89	307	127	180	381	156	226	466	190	277	688	283	405
90-94	68	27	41	85	33	53	108	41	67	141	51	90
95-99	8	3	5	11	4	7	13	5	9	19	6	13
100 +	0	0	0	1	0	0	1	0	1	1	0	1

Age group	2045 Both sexes	Males	Females	2050 Both sexes	Males	Females
All ages	235 472	118 055	117 417	242 937	121 461	121 476
0-4	17 152	8 753	8 399	16 680	8 517	8 163
5-9	17 487	8 914	8 573	17 118	8 733	8 385
10-14	17 747	9 036	8 711	17 467	8 902	8 565
15-19	17 886	9 098	8 788	17 705	9 006	8 698
20-24	17 908	9 089	8 819	17 799	9 034	8 765
25-29	17 792	9 008	8 784	17 800	9 012	8 788
30-34	17 467	8 829	8 638	17 687	8 937	8 750
35-39	16 956	8 562	8 394	17 362	8 762	8 600
40-44	16 336	8 242	8 094	16 834	8 489	8 345
45-49	15 437	7 783	7 654	16 161	8 138	8 022
50-54	14 924	7 492	7 432	15 166	7 620	7 546
55-59	13 066	6 534	6 532	14 487	7 221	7 266
60-64	11 470	5 672	5 798	12 432	6 136	6 296
65-69	8 946	4 334	4 612	10 553	5 109	5 444
70-74	6 776	3 191	3 585	7 761	3 638	4 124
75-79	4 522	2 038	2 484	5 331	2 388	2 942
80-84	2 432	1 036	1 396	3 004	1 249	1 755
85-89	918	359	559	1 229	458	771
90-94	221	77	145	314	99	215
95-99	27	7	19	45	11	34
100 +	2	0	1	3	0	2

POPULATION BY AGE AND SEX (in thousands)

Age group	2005 Both sexes	Males	Females	2010 Both sexes	Males	Females	2015 Both sexes	Males	Females	2020 Both sexes	Males	Females
All ages	141 822	72 459	69 363	156 492	79 785	76 708	172 346	87 691	84 654	188 907	95 928	92 979
0-4	17 399	8 889	8 510	19 287	9 849	9 438	20 728	10 578	10 150	21 770	11 103	10 668
5-9	16 545	8 470	8 075	17 161	8 773	8 388	19 094	9 752	9 343	20 576	10 497	10 080
10-14	16 375	8 376	8 000	16 455	8 423	8 032	17 087	8 733	8 354	19 030	9 715	9 315
15-19	14 896	7 645	7 251	16 253	8 307	7 945	16 352	8 363	7 989	17 000	8 679	8 321
20-24	13 839	7 104	6 734	14 705	7 530	7 175	16 076	8 198	7 878	16 200	8 264	7 936
25-29	11 855	6 079	5 775	13 616	6 971	6 646	14 503	7 405	7 098	15 891	8 080	7 811
30-34	10 538	5 413	5 125	11 650	5 961	5 689	13 420	6 855	6 565	14 327	7 297	7 029
35-39	9 220	4 732	4 488	10 339	5 301	5 038	11 464	5 855	5 609	13 242	6 751	6 491
40-44	7 874	4 059	3 815	9 012	4 615	4 397	10 139	5 188	4 952	11 275	5 747	5 529
45-49	6 418	3 318	3 100	7 643	3 928	3 715	8 780	4 483	4 297	9 910	5 056	4 854
50-54	5 188	2 682	2 506	6 155	3 166	2 990	7 361	3 765	3 597	8 489	4 315	4 175
55-59	3 642	1 803	1 838	4 880	2 501	2 379	5 820	2 968	2 852	6 993	3 547	3 446
60-64	2 917	1 420	1 497	3 322	1 621	1 701	4 480	2 264	2 215	5 375	2 704	2 671
65-69	2 179	1 051	1 127	2 533	1 208	1 324	2 908	1 391	1 517	3 950	1 959	1 992
70-74	1 497	728	768	1 742	819	923	2 048	951	1 096	2 375	1 106	1 269
75-79	879	424	455	1 047	494	553	1 237	563	675	1 474	662	812
80-84	397	189	208	493	229	264	597	271	326	718	314	404
85-89	131	61	71	160	72	87	202	89	113	250	108	142
90-94	30	14	16	34	15	19	42	18	24	54	22	32
95-99	4	2	2	4	2	3	5	2	3	6	2	4
100 +	0	0	0	0	0	0	0	0	0	0	0	0

Age group	2025 Both sexes	Males	Females	2030 Both sexes	Males	Females	2035 Both sexes	Males	Females	2040 Both sexes	Males	Females
All ages	205 409	104 095	101 314	221 983	112 255	109 728	238 756	120 479	118 277	255 630	128 710	126 920
0-4	22 124	11 278	10 845	22 741	11 591	11 150	23 614	12 033	11 580	24 455	12 471	11 984
5-9	21 649	11 035	10 614	22 030	11 224	10 806	22 666	11 545	11 121	23 551	11 995	11 555
10-14	20 521	10 464	10 057	21 602	11 006	10 596	21 991	11 200	10 792	22 632	11 524	11 109
15-19	18 949	9 664	9 286	20 448	10 416	10 032	21 537	10 961	10 576	21 933	11 159	10 774
20-24	16 864	8 587	8 277	18 822	9 574	9 247	20 330	10 331	9 999	21 426	10 881	10 546
25-29	16 039	8 157	7 882	16 719	8 487	8 232	18 684	9 477	9 207	20 198	10 237	9 961
30-34	15 729	7 978	7 751	15 896	8 063	7 833	16 589	8 399	8 190	18 558	9 392	9 166
35-39	14 165	7 200	6 965	15 579	7 885	7 694	15 765	7 980	7 785	16 468	8 322	8 146
40-44	13 058	6 644	6 414	13 997	7 100	6 896	15 421	7 790	7 631	15 623	7 894	7 730
45-49	11 054	5 618	5 435	12 834	6 513	6 322	13 787	6 976	6 812	15 217	7 668	7 548
50-54	9 617	4 885	4 733	10 762	5 445	5 316	12 532	6 332	6 201	13 495	6 800	6 695
55-59	8 104	4 085	4 019	9 219	4 644	4 575	10 356	5 198	5 159	12 100	6 065	6 035
60-64	6 500	3 252	3 248	7 576	3 765	3 810	8 664	4 304	4 360	9 777	4 839	4 938
65-69	4 781	2 358	2 423	5 828	2 857	2 971	6 842	3 331	3 511	7 878	3 832	4 047
70-74	3 261	1 575	1 686	3 989	1 914	2 075	4 911	2 340	2 571	5 828	2 752	3 076
75-79	1 737	781	956	2 416	1 126	1 290	2 996	1 386	1 610	3 751	1 714	2 037
80-84	873	376	497	1 048	451	597	1 481	661	820	1 890	826	1 064
85-89	307	127	180	381	156	226	466	190	277	688	283	405
90-94	68	27	41	85	33	53	108	41	67	141	51	90
95-99	8	3	5	11	4	7	13	5	9	19	6	13
100 +	0	0	0	1	0	0	1	0	1	1	0	1

Age group	2045 Both sexes	Males	Females	2050 Both sexes	Males	Females
All ages	272 293	136 807	135 486	288 453	144 645	143 808
0-4	25 070	12 793	12 276	25 452	12 997	12 456
5-9	24 401	12 439	11 962	25 023	12 766	12 257
10-14	23 521	11 976	11 544	24 374	12 422	11 952
15-19	22 579	11 486	11 093	23 471	11 941	11 530
20-24	21 829	11 083	10 746	22 481	11 415	11 066
25-29	21 300	10 791	10 509	21 711	10 999	10 711
30-34	20 077	10 155	9 922	21 185	10 714	10 471
35-39	18 439	9 316	9 123	19 962	10 083	9 879
40-44	16 336	8 242	8 094	18 308	9 238	9 070
45-49	15 437	7 783	7 654	16 161	8 138	8 022
50-54	14 924	7 492	7 432	15 166	7 620	7 546
55-59	13 066	6 534	6 532	14 487	7 221	7 266
60-64	11 470	5 672	5 798	12 432	6 136	6 296
65-69	8 946	4 334	4 612	10 553	5 109	5 444
70-74	6 776	3 191	3 585	7 761	3 638	4 124
75-79	4 522	2 038	2 484	5 331	2 388	2 942
80-84	2 432	1 036	1 396	3 004	1 249	1 755
85-89	918	359	559	1 229	458	771
90-94	221	77	145	314	99	215
95-99	27	7	19	45	11	34
100 +	2	0	1	3	0	2

United Nations Department of Economic and Social Affairs/Population Division
World Population Prospects: The 2004 Revision, Volume II: Sex and Age Distribution of the World Population

POPULATION BY AGE AND SEX (in thousands)

Age group	2005 Both sexes	Males	Females	2010 Both sexes	Males	Females	2015 Both sexes	Males	Females	2020 Both sexes	Males	Females
All ages	141 822	72 459	69 363	153 432	78 222	75 210	163 980	83 421	80 559	173 459	88 047	85 412
0-4	17 399	8 889	8 510	16 227	8 286	7 940	15 393	7 856	7 537	14 640	7 466	7 174
5-9	16 545	8 470	8 075	17 161	8 773	8 388	16 063	8 204	7 860	15 279	7 795	7 485
10-14	16 375	8 376	8 000	16 455	8 423	8 032	17 087	8 733	8 354	16 009	8 173	7 836
15-19	14 896	7 645	7 251	16 253	8 307	7 945	16 352	8 363	7 989	17 000	8 679	8 321
20-24	13 839	7 104	6 734	14 705	7 530	7 175	16 076	8 198	7 878	16 200	8 264	7 936
25-29	11 855	6 079	5 775	13 616	6 971	6 646	14 503	7 405	7 098	15 891	8 080	7 811
30-34	10 538	5 413	5 125	11 650	5 961	5 689	13 420	6 855	6 565	14 327	7 297	7 029
35-39	9 220	4 732	4 488	10 339	5 301	5 038	11 464	5 855	5 609	13 242	6 751	6 491
40-44	7 874	4 059	3 815	9 012	4 615	4 397	10 139	5 188	4 952	11 275	5 747	5 529
45-49	6 418	3 318	3 100	7 643	3 928	3 715	8 780	4 483	4 297	9 910	5 056	4 854
50-54	5 188	2 682	2 506	6 155	3 166	2 990	7 361	3 765	3 597	8 489	4 315	4 175
55-59	3 642	1 803	1 838	4 880	2 501	2 379	5 820	2 968	2 852	6 993	3 547	3 446
60-64	2 917	1 420	1 497	3 322	1 621	1 701	4 480	2 264	2 215	5 375	2 704	2 671
65-69	2 179	1 051	1 127	2 533	1 208	1 324	2 908	1 391	1 517	3 950	1 959	1 992
70-74	1 497	728	768	1 742	819	923	2 048	951	1 096	2 375	1 106	1 269
75-79	879	424	455	1 047	494	553	1 237	563	675	1 474	662	812
80-84	397	189	208	493	229	264	597	271	326	718	314	404
85-89	131	61	71	160	72	87	202	89	113	250	108	142
90-94	30	14	16	34	15	19	42	18	24	54	22	32
95-99	4	2	2	4	2	3	5	2	3	6	2	4
100 +	0	0	0	0	0	0	0	0	0	0	0	0

Age group	2025 Both sexes	Males	Females	2030 Both sexes	Males	Females	2035 Both sexes	Males	Females	2040 Both sexes	Males	Females
All ages	182 201	92 262	89 939	189 764	95 837	93 928	195 734	98 567	97 167	199 935	100 349	99 586
0-4	14 303	7 292	7 012	13 658	6 961	6 696	12 725	6 484	6 240	11 679	5 956	5 723
5-9	14 557	7 420	7 137	14 241	7 256	6 985	13 611	6 933	6 678	12 688	6 463	6 226
10-14	15 237	7 770	7 467	14 524	7 400	7 124	14 214	7 239	6 975	13 589	6 919	6 670
15-19	15 938	8 127	7 811	15 178	7 730	7 448	14 474	7 365	7 109	14 170	7 207	6 963
20-24	16 864	8 587	8 277	15 823	8 046	7 777	15 078	7 667	7 421	14 384	7 299	7 086
25-29	16 039	8 157	7 882	16 719	8 487	8 232	15 697	7 956	7 741	14 965	7 576	7 389
30-34	15 729	7 978	7 751	15 896	8 063	7 833	16 589	8 399	8 190	15 584	7 879	7 705
35-39	14 165	7 200	6 965	15 579	7 885	7 694	15 765	7 980	7 785	16 468	8 322	8 146
40-44	13 058	6 644	6 414	13 997	7 100	6 896	15 421	7 790	7 631	15 623	7 894	7 730
45-49	11 064	5 618	5 405	12 004	6 513	6 322	13 787	6 976	6 812	15 217	7 668	7 548
50-54	9 617	4 885	4 733	10 762	5 445	5 316	12 532	6 332	6 201	13 495	6 800	6 695
55-59	8 104	4 085	4 019	9 219	4 644	4 575	10 356	5 198	5 159	12 100	6 065	6 035
60-64	6 500	3 252	3 248	7 576	3 765	3 810	8 664	4 304	4 360	9 777	4 839	4 938
65-69	4 781	2 358	2 423	5 828	2 857	2 971	6 842	3 331	3 511	7 878	3 832	4 047
70-74	3 261	1 575	1 686	3 989	1 914	2 075	4 911	2 340	2 571	5 828	2 752	3 076
75-79	1 737	781	956	2 416	1 126	1 290	2 996	1 386	1 610	3 751	1 714	2 037
80-84	873	376	497	1 048	451	597	1 481	661	820	1 890	826	1 064
85-89	307	127	180	381	156	226	466	190	277	688	283	405
90-94	68	27	41	85	33	53	108	41	67	141	51	90
95-99	8	3	5	11	4	7	13	5	9	19	6	13
100 +	0	0	0	1	0	0	1	0	1	1	0	1

Age group	2045 Both sexes	Males	Females	2050 Both sexes	Males	Females
All ages	202 368	101 198	101 169	203 069	101 157	101 912
0-4	10 715	5 468	5 247	9 844	5 027	4 817
5-9	11 650	5 939	5 711	10 692	5 455	5 237
10-14	12 670	6 451	6 219	11 635	5 930	5 706
15-19	13 549	6 891	6 659	12 635	6 426	6 209
20-24	14 086	7 145	6 941	13 472	6 833	6 639
25-29	14 280	7 223	7 057	13 988	7 074	6 914
30-34	14 862	7 505	7 357	14 186	7 158	7 028
35-39	15 478	7 811	7 667	14 768	7 444	7 324
40-44	16 336	8 242	8 094	15 364	7 742	7 622
45-49	15 437	7 783	7 654	16 161	8 138	8 022
50-54	14 924	7 492	7 432	15 166	7 620	7 546
55-59	13 066	6 534	6 532	14 487	7 221	7 266
60-64	11 470	5 672	5 798	12 432	6 136	6 296
65-69	8 946	4 334	4 612	10 553	5 109	5 444
70-74	6 776	3 191	3 585	7 761	3 638	4 124
75-79	4 522	2 038	2 484	5 331	2 388	2 942
80-84	2 432	1 036	1 396	3 004	1 249	1 755
85-89	918	359	559	1 229	458	771
90-94	221	77	145	314	99	215
95-99	27	7	19	45	11	34
100 +	2	0	1	3	0	2

POPULATION BY AGE AND SEX (in thousands)

Age group	1950 Both sexes	Males	Females	1955 Both sexes	Males	Females	1960 Both sexes	Males	Females	1965 Both sexes	Males	Females
All ages	211	97	114	227	104	123	231	103	127	235	108	127
0-4	26	13	13	31	15	16	32	16	17	33	16	16
5-9	22	11	11	27	13	13	29	14	15	31	15	16
10-14	22	11	11	22	10	11	27	13	14	28	14	14
15-19	20	10	10	20	9	10	20	9	11	24	12	12
20-24	17	8	9	18	8	9	16	7	9	15	7	8
25-29	15	7	8	15	7	8	14	6	8	12	6	7
30-34	16	8	8	13	6	7	13	6	8	11	5	7
35-39	15	7	8	14	7	7	12	5	7	12	5	7
40-44	13	6	7	13	6	7	13	6	7	11	5	6
45-49	12	5	7	13	6	7	12	5	6	12	5	6
50-54	9	4	5	11	5	6	11	5	6	11	5	6
55-59	6	2	4	8	3	5	10	5	6	10	5	5
60-64	6	2	4	6	2	4	8	3	5	9	4	5
65-69	4	1	3	5	2	3	6	2	5	6	2	4
70-74	3	1	3	4	1	3	4	1	3	5	1	4
75-79	3	1	2	3	1	2	3	1	2	3	1	2
80 +	2	0	1	3	1	2	2	1	2	2	1	2

Age group	1970 Both sexes	Males	Females	1975 Both sexes	Males	Females	1980 Both sexes	Males	Females	1985 Both sexes	Males	Females
All ages	239	112	127	246	118	128	249	118	131	253	121	132
0-4	26	13	13	22	11	11	22	11	11	21	11	11
5-9	32	16	16	25	12	12	26	13	13	21	11	11
10-14	31	15	15	31	16	15	26	13	13	26	13	13
15-19	26	13	13	28	13	15	28	14	14	25	13	13
20-24	20	10	10	23	12	11	26	13	13	26	13	13
25-29	12	6	6	17	8	9	21	10	11	24	12	12
30-34	11	5	6	13	6	7	16	8	8	19	10	10
35-39	10	4	6	11	5	5	11	5	6	15	7	8
40-44	11	5	6	10	4	6	10	5	6	10	5	5
45-49	10	4	6	12	5	6	9	4	5	9	4	5
50-54	11	5	6	10	4	6	10	4	6	8	4	5
55-59	10	5	6	10	5	5	9	4	5	9	4	5
60-64	9	4	5	9	5	5	9	4	5	8	4	5
65-69	8	3	5	11	5	6	9	4	5	9	4	5
70-74	5	2	3	7	3	4	8	3	4	8	3	5
75-79	3	1	2	4	1	3	5	2	3	6	3	4
80 +	3	1	2	3	1	2	4	1	3	6	2	4

Age group	1990 Both sexes	Males	Females	1995 Both sexes	Males	Females	2000 Both sexes	Males	Females	2005 Both sexes	Males	Females
All ages	257	123	134	262	126	136	266	128	138	270	130	139
0-4	20	10	10	18	9	9	17	9	8	16	8	8
5-9	21	11	11	20	10	10	18	9	9	17	9	8
10-14	21	11	11	21	11	11	20	10	10	18	9	9
15-19	25	13	12	21	11	10	21	11	10	20	10	10
20-24	24	12	12	25	12	12	21	10	10	21	11	10
25-29	25	13	12	24	12	12	24	12	12	20	10	10
30-34	22	11	11	24	12	12	23	12	12	24	12	12
35-39	18	9	9	22	11	11	24	12	12	23	11	11
40-44	14	7	7	18	9	9	22	11	11	23	12	12
45-49	10	4	5	14	7	7	18	9	9	21	10	11
50-54	9	4	5	9	4	5	14	7	7	17	8	9
55-59	8	3	5	8	4	5	9	4	5	13	6	7
60-64	9	4	5	8	3	5	8	3	5	9	4	5
65-69	8	3	5	8	3	5	7	3	4	7	3	4
70-74	8	3	5	7	3	4	7	3	4	6	2	4
75-79	7	3	4	6	2	4	6	2	3	6	2	4
80 +	7	2	5	8	2	5	8	2	5	7	2	5

United Nations Department of Economic and Social Affairs/Population Division
World Population Prospects: The 2004 Revision, Volume II: Sex and Age Distribution of the World Population

POPULATION BY AGE AND SEX (in thousands)

Age group	2005 Both sexes	Males	Females	2010 Both sexes	Males	Females	2015 Both sexes	Males	Females	2020 Both sexes	Males	Females
All ages	270	130	130	270	132	141	276	134	142	278	135	142
0-4	16	8	8	15	8	8	15	7	7	14	7	7
5-9	17	9	8	16	8	8	15	8	7	15	7	7
10-14	18	9	9	17	9	8	16	8	8	15	8	7
15-19	20	10	10	18	9	9	17	8	8	16	8	8
20-24	21	11	10	20	10	10	18	9	9	16	8	8
25-29	20	10	10	21	10	10	20	10	10	17	9	9
30-34	24	12	12	20	10	10	20	10	10	19	10	10
35-39	23	11	11	23	11	12	20	10	10	20	10	10
40-44	23	12	12	22	11	11	23	11	12	19	10	10
45-49	21	10	11	23	11	12	22	11	11	23	11	11
50-54	17	8	9	21	10	11	23	11	11	21	11	11
55-59	13	6	7	17	8	9	20	10	11	22	11	11
60-64	9	4	5	13	6	7	16	8	8	20	9	10
65-69	7	3	4	8	3	5	12	5	6	15	7	8
70-74	6	2	4	7	3	4	7	3	4	11	5	6
75-79	6	2	4	5	2	3	5	2	3	6	2	4
80-84	4	1	3	4	1	3	4	1	3	4	1	3
85-89	2	1	2	2	1	2	2	1	2	2	1	2
90-94	1	0	1	1	0	1	1	0	1	1	0	1
95-99	0	0	0	0	0	0	0	0	0	0	0	0
100 +	0	0	0	0	0	0	0	0	0	0	0	0

Age group	2025 Both sexes	Males	Females	2030 Both sexes	Males	Females	2035 Both sexes	Males	Females	2040 Both sexes	Males	Females
All ages	278	136	143	278	135	142	275	134	141	270	131	139
0-4	14	7	7	14	7	7	13	7	7	13	7	6
5-9	14	7	7	14	7	7	13	7	7	13	7	7
10-14	15	7	7	14	7	7	14	7	7	13	7	7
15-19	15	8	7	15	7	7	14	7	7	14	7	7
20-24	16	8	8	15	8	7	14	7	7	14	7	7
25-29	16	8	8	15	8	8	15	7	7	14	7	7
30-34	17	9	8	16	8	8	15	8	7	14	7	7
35-39	19	10	9	17	9	8	16	8	8	15	8	7
40-44	20	10	10	19	9	9	17	8	8	15	8	8
45-49	19	10	10	19	10	10	18	9	9	16	8	8
50-54	22	11	11	19	9	9	19	10	10	18	9	9
55-59	21	10	11	22	11	11	18	9	9	18	9	9
60-64	21	10	11	20	10	10	21	10	11	18	9	9
65-69	18	9	10	20	10	10	19	9	10	20	9	10
70-74	14	6	8	17	8	9	18	8	10	17	8	9
75-79	9	4	5	11	5	7	14	6	8	16	7	9
80-84	6	2	4	7	3	4	9	3	5	11	4	7
85-89	2	1	2	3	1	2	4	1	3	6	2	4
90-94	1	0	1	1	0	1	1	0	1	2	1	2
95-99	0	0	0	0	0	0	0	0	0	1	0	0
100 +	0	0	0	0	0	0	0	0	0	0	0	0

Age group	2045 Both sexes	Males	Females	2050 Both sexes	Males	Females
All ages	263	128	136	255	124	132
0-4	13	6	6	12	6	6
5-9	13	7	6	12	6	6
10-14	13	7	7	13	7	6
15-19	13	7	7	13	7	6
20-24	14	7	7	13	7	6
25-29	14	7	7	13	7	7
30-34	14	7	7	13	7	7
35-39	14	7	7	14	7	7
40-44	15	8	7	14	7	7
45-49	15	8	8	15	7	7
50-54	16	8	8	15	8	7
55-59	18	9	9	16	8	8
60-64	18	9	9	17	9	9
65-69	17	8	9	17	8	9
70-74	18	8	10	16	7	8
75-79	15	7	8	16	7	9
80-84	12	5	7	12	5	7
85-89	7	3	5	8	3	5
90-94	3	1	2	4	1	3
95-99	1	0	1	1	0	1
100 +	0	0	0	0	0	0

United Nations Department of Economic and Social Affairs/Population Division
World Population Prospects: The 2004 Revision, Volume II: Sex and Age Distribution of the World Population

203

POPULATION BY AGE AND SEX (in thousands)

Age group	2005 Both sexes	Males	Females	2010 Both sexes	Males	Females	2015 Both sexes	Males	Females	2020 Both sexes	Males	Females
All ages	270	130	139	275	134	142	282	137	145	289	141	148
0-4	16	8	8	18	9	9	19	9	9	19	10	9
5-9	17	9	8	16	8	8	18	9	9	18	9	9
10-14	18	9	9	17	9	8	16	8	8	18	9	9
15-19	20	10	10	18	9	9	17	8	8	16	8	8
20-24	21	11	10	20	10	10	18	9	9	16	8	8
25-29	20	10	10	21	10	10	20	10	10	17	9	9
30-34	24	12	12	20	10	10	20	10	10	19	10	10
35-39	23	11	11	23	11	12	20	10	10	20	10	10
40-44	23	12	12	22	11	11	23	11	12	19	10	10
45-49	21	10	11	23	11	12	22	11	11	23	11	11
50-54	17	8	9	21	10	11	23	11	11	21	11	11
55-59	13	6	7	17	8	9	20	10	11	22	11	11
60-64	9	4	5	13	6	7	16	8	8	20	9	10
65-69	7	3	4	8	3	5	12	5	6	15	7	8
70-74	6	2	4	7	3	4	7	3	4	11	5	6
75-79	6	2	4	5	2	3	5	2	3	6	2	4
80-84	4	1	3	4	1	3	4	1	3	4	1	3
85-89	2	1	2	2	1	2	2	1	2	2	1	2
90-94	1	0	1	1	0	1	1	0	1	1	0	1
95-99	0	0	0	0	0	0	0	0	0	0	0	0
100 +	0	0	0	0	0	0	0	0	0	0	0	0

Age group	2025 Both sexes	Males	Females	2030 Both sexes	Males	Females	2035 Both sexes	Males	Females	2040 Both sexes	Males	Females
All ages	294	143	150	297	145	152	300	147	154	302	148	155
0-4	18	9	9	18	9	9	19	10	9	20	10	10
5-9	19	10	9	18	9	9	18	9	9	19	10	9
10-14	18	9	9	19	9	9	18	9	9	18	9	9
15-19	18	9	9	18	9	9	19	9	9	18	9	9
20-24	16	8	8	17	9	9	18	9	9	18	9	9
25-29	16	8	8	15	8	8	17	9	8	18	9	9
30-34	17	9	8	16	8	8	15	8	7	17	9	8
35-39	19	10	9	17	9	8	16	8	8	15	8	7
40-44	20	10	10	19	9	9	17	8	8	15	8	8
45-49	19	10	10	19	10	10	18	9	9	16	8	8
50-54	22	11	11	19	9	9	19	10	10	18	9	9
55-59	21	10	11	22	11	11	18	9	9	19	9	9
60-64	21	10	11	20	10	10	21	10	11	18	9	9
65-69	18	9	10	20	10	10	19	9	10	20	9	10
70-74	14	6	8	17	8	9	18	8	10	17	8	9
75-79	9	4	5	11	5	7	14	6	8	16	7	9
80-84	4	2	3	7	3	4	9	3	5	11	4	7
85-89	2	1	2	3	1	2	4	1	3	6	2	4
90-94	1	0	1	1	0	1	1	0	1	2	1	2
95-99	0	0	0	0	0	0	0	0	0	1	0	0
100 +	0	0	0	0	0	0	0	0	0	0	0	0

Age group	2045 Both sexes	Males	Females	2050 Both sexes	Males	Females
All ages	304	148	155	304	148	155
0-4	20	10	10	20	10	10
5-9	20	10	10	20	10	10
10-14	19	10	9	20	10	10
15-19	18	9	9	19	10	9
20-24	18	9	9	18	9	9
25-29	18	9	9	18	9	9
30-34	18	9	9	18	9	9
35-39	17	8	8	17	9	9
40-44	15	8	7	16	8	8
45-49	15	8	8	15	7	7
50-54	16	8	8	15	8	7
55-59	18	9	9	16	8	8
60-64	18	9	9	17	9	9
65-69	17	8	9	17	8	9
70-74	18	8	10	16	7	8
75-79	15	7	8	16	7	9
80-84	12	5	7	12	5	7
85-89	7	3	5	8	3	5
90-94	3	1	2	4	1	3
95-99	1	0	1	1	0	1
100 +	0	0	0	0	0	0

United Nations Department of Economic and Social Affairs/Population Division
World Population Prospects: The 2004 Revision, Volume II: Sex and Age Distribution of the World Population

POPULATION BY AGE AND SEX (in thousands)

Age group	2005 Both sexes	Males	Females	2010 Both sexes	Males	Females	2015 Both sexes	Males	Females	2020 Both sexes	Males	Females
All ages	270	130	139	270	131	139	269	131	138	267	100	107
0-4	16	8	8	13	6	6	11	6	5	10	5	5
5-9	17	9	8	16	8	8	13	6	6	11	6	5
10-14	18	9	9	17	9	8	16	8	8	13	6	6
15-19	20	10	10	18	9	9	17	8	8	16	8	8
20-24	21	11	10	20	10	10	18	9	9	16	8	8
25-29	20	10	10	21	10	10	20	10	10	17	9	9
30-34	24	12	12	20	10	10	20	10	10	19	10	10
35-39	23	11	11	23	11	12	20	10	10	20	10	10
40-44	23	12	12	22	11	11	23	11	12	19	10	10
45-49	21	10	11	23	11	12	22	11	11	23	11	11
50-54	17	8	9	21	10	11	23	11	11	21	11	11
55-59	13	6	7	17	8	9	20	10	11	22	11	11
60-64	9	4	5	13	6	7	16	8	8	20	9	10
65-69	7	3	4	8	3	5	12	5	6	15	7	8
70-74	6	2	4	7	3	4	7	3	4	11	5	6
75-79	6	2	4	5	2	3	5	2	3	6	2	4
80-84	4	1	3	4	1	3	4	1	3	4	1	3
85-89	2	1	2	2	1	2	2	1	2	2	1	2
90-94	1	0	1	1	0	1	1	0	1	1	0	1
95-99	0	0	0	0	0	0	0	0	0	0	0	0
100 +	0	0	0	0	0	0	0	0	0	0	0	0

Age group	2025 Both sexes	Males	Females	2030 Both sexes	Males	Females	2035 Both sexes	Males	Females	2040 Both sexes	Males	Females
All ages	263	128	135	258	125	133	250	121	129	240	116	124
0-4	10	5	5	9	5	5	8	4	4	8	4	4
5-9	10	5	5	10	5	5	9	5	4	8	4	4
10-14	11	5	5	10	5	5	10	5	5	9	5	4
15-19	13	6	6	11	5	5	10	5	5	9	5	5
20-24	16	8	8	12	6	6	10	5	5	9	5	5
25-29	16	8	8	15	8	8	12	6	6	10	5	5
30-34	17	9	8	16	8	8	15	8	7	12	6	6
35-39	19	10	9	17	9	8	16	8	8	15	8	7
40-44	20	10	10	19	9	9	17	8	8	15	8	8
45-49	19	10	10	19	10	10	18	9	9	16	8	8
50-54	22	11	11	19	9	9	19	10	10	18	9	9
55-59	21	10	11	22	11	11	18	9	9	19	9	9
60-64	21	10	11	20	10	10	21	10	11	18	9	9
65-69	18	9	10	20	10	10	19	9	10	20	9	10
70-74	14	6	8	17	8	9	18	8	10	17	8	9
75-79	9	4	5	11	5	7	14	6	8	16	7	9
80-84	4	2	3	7	3	4	8	3	5	11	4	7
85-89	2	1	2	3	1	2	4	1	3	6	2	4
90-94	1	0	1	1	0	1	1	0	1	2	1	2
95-99	0	0	0	0	0	0	0	0	0	1	0	0
100 +	0	0	0	0	0	0	0	0	0	0	0	0

Age group	2045 Both sexes	Males	Females	2050 Both sexes	Males	Females
All ages	228	110	118	214	103	111
0-4	7	3	3	6	3	3
5-9	7	4	4	7	3	3
10-14	8	4	4	7	4	4
15-19	9	5	4	8	4	4
20-24	9	5	5	9	4	4
25-29	9	5	5	9	5	4
30-34	10	5	5	9	5	4
35-39	12	6	6	10	5	5
40-44	15	8	7	11	6	6
45-49	15	8	8	15	7	7
50-54	16	8	8	15	8	7
55-59	18	9	9	16	8	8
60-64	18	9	9	17	9	9
65-69	17	8	9	17	8	9
70-74	18	8	10	16	7	8
75-79	15	7	8	16	7	9
80-84	12	5	7	12	5	7
85-89	7	3	5	8	3	5
90-94	3	1	2	4	1	3
95-99	1	0	1	1	0	1
100 +	0	0	0	0	0	0

POPULATION BY AGE AND SEX (in thousands)

Age group	1950 Both sexes	1950 Males	1950 Females	1955 Both sexes	1955 Males	1955 Females	1960 Both sexes	1960 Males	1960 Females	1965 Both sexes	1965 Males	1965 Females
All ages	7 745	3 424	4 321	7 803	3 483	4 320	8 190	3 698	4 492	8 607	3 925	4 682
0-4	659	334	325	812	416	395	970	495	475	913	467	446
5-9	570	283	288	625	316	309	787	404	384	953	486	466
10-14	815	395	420	539	267	272	606	307	300	774	397	377
15-19	786	383	403	778	377	401	521	258	263	595	301	294
20-24	787	362	425	742	360	382	753	363	390	508	251	257
25-29	576	238	338	744	340	404	715	345	370	736	353	383
30-34	374	151	223	542	222	321	718	326	392	697	334	362
35-39	533	206	327	346	138	208	520	210	310	698	314	384
40-44	519	220	300	499	190	309	328	129	199	503	201	302
45-49	479	198	281	477	198	279	471	176	295	313	121	192
50-54	356	154	203	433	174	259	442	179	263	445	162	283
55-59	317	138	179	314	130	184	395	153	242	410	160	249
60-64	307	124	183	272	113	158	278	110	167	357	132	226
65-69	252	99	153	254	97	157	231	91	140	242	91	151
70-74	188	69	119	193	71	122	202	72	131	188	70	119
75-79	127	41	86	127	43	84	137	46	90	148	48	100
80 +	99	30	70	106	31	75	114	33	81	127	37	90

Age group	1970 Both sexes	1970 Males	1970 Females	1975 Both sexes	1975 Males	1975 Females	1980 Both sexes	1980 Males	1980 Females	1985 Both sexes	1985 Males	1985 Females
All ages	9 040	4 151	4 889	9 367	4 327	5 040	9 658	4 485	5 173	9 999	4 662	5 336
0-4	748	382	366	747	381	367	745	380	364	813	414	399
5-9	917	469	448	746	379	366	732	373	359	744	379	365
10-14	958	489	469	900	462	438	733	372	361	730	373	357
15-19	778	398	379	907	465	442	853	437	416	731	365	366
20-24	596	301	296	736	373	363	860	436	424	830	419	411
25-29	509	250	259	599	300	299	744	373	371	861	435	427
30-34	735	351	384	514	253	261	637	319	318	749	375	374
35-39	694	330	363	731	347	384	486	238	248	629	313	316
40-44	691	308	383	681	322	359	719	340	378	479	233	246
45-49	494	194	300	679	300	378	652	305	347	699	328	371
50-54	304	115	189	496	188	309	676	298	378	628	287	341
55-59	425	149	276	298	109	189	495	183	312	649	277	372
60-64	381	142	238	398	139	259	289	102	187	461	164	297
65-69	321	112	209	349	121	228	351	116	235	260	86	173
70-74	203	71	132	264	89	175	297	97	201	298	91	207
75-79	142	48	94	156	51	104	208	63	145	225	67	158
80 +	145	41	104	166	48	118	182	52	130	213	56	157

Age group	1990 Both sexes	1990 Males	1990 Females	1995 Both sexes	1995 Males	1995 Females	2000 Both sexes	2000 Males	2000 Females	2005 Both sexes	2005 Males	2005 Females
All ages	10 266	4 810	5 456	10 249	4 816	5 433	10 029	4 706	5 323	9 755	4 559	5 197
0-4	822	421	402	599	308	291	442	228	215	449	231	218
5-9	806	410	396	827	423	404	600	308	292	438	225	213
10-14	732	371	361	809	413	396	836	427	408	594	304	290
15-19	697	352	345	727	369	358	816	420	396	831	423	408
20-24	660	325	336	699	353	346	714	362	352	812	415	396
25-29	855	431	424	659	325	334	700	352	349	703	354	349
30-34	877	439	438	845	423	422	657	325	332	689	342	347
35-39	770	383	387	860	426	434	830	411	419	648	318	330
40-44	547	271	276	760	373	388	829	403	426	812	398	414
45-49	485	234	251	530	258	272	747	356	391	796	380	416
50-54	666	307	359	462	216	246	500	236	264	708	327	380
55-59	620	278	341	623	276	346	426	189	236	462	209	253
60-64	639	261	379	556	238	318	564	234	330	382	160	223
65-69	412	141	271	557	211	346	470	187	284	490	186	304
70-74	205	62	144	343	106	237	452	155	296	381	135	246
75-79	238	66	172	151	40	111	258	72	186	328	99	229
80 +	236	61	175	242	58	184	187	41	145	231	52	179

206

United Nations Department of Economic and Social Affairs/Population Division
World Population Prospects: The 2004 Revision, Volume II: Sex and Age Distribution of the World Population

POPULATION BY AGE AND SEX (in thousands)

Age group	2005 Both sexes	Males	Females	2010 Both sexes	Males	Females	2015 Both sexes	Males	Females	2020 Both sexes	Males	Females
All ages	9 755	4 559	5 197	9 484	4 418	5 066	9 218	4 284	4 933	8 939	4 145	4 795
0-4	449	231	218	454	234	220	447	230	217	414	213	201
5-9	438	225	213	445	229	216	450	231	218	443	228	215
10-14	594	304	290	432	222	211	439	225	214	444	228	216
15-19	831	423	408	590	301	290	429	218	211	436	222	214
20-24	812	415	396	827	419	408	588	298	290	428	217	212
25-29	703	354	349	800	406	394	817	411	406	580	291	288
30-34	689	342	347	693	345	348	790	397	392	807	403	405
35-39	648	318	330	680	335	345	685	339	346	782	391	391
40-44	812	398	414	635	309	327	668	327	342	674	331	343
45-49	796	380	416	781	376	405	612	293	319	646	311	334
50-54	708	327	380	756	351	406	745	350	395	586	274	312
55-59	462	209	253	656	291	365	705	315	390	697	316	381
60-64	382	160	223	416	177	239	595	250	346	642	272	371
65-69	490	186	304	335	128	207	366	143	223	526	203	322
70-74	381	135	246	401	136	265	276	94	182	303	107	197
75-79	328	99	229	278	87	192	297	88	209	206	62	145
80-84	161	39	122	205	53	152	177	48	129	193	49	144
85-89	43	9	34	78	16	62	101	22	79	90	20	69
90-94	23	4	19	14	2	12	27	5	22	36	7	30
95-99	4	1	3	5	1	4	3	0	3	6	1	5
100 +	0	0	0	1	0	0	1	0	0	0	0	0

Age group	2025 Both sexes	Males	Females	2030 Both sexes	Males	Females	2035 Both sexes	Males	Females	2040 Both sexes	Males	Females
All ages	8 635	3 991	4 645	8 314	3 828	4 486	7 990	3 668	4 322	7 667	3 515	4 152
0-4	368	190	179	337	174	164	331	171	161	338	174	164
5-9	410	211	199	364	187	177	334	172	162	328	169	159
10-14	437	224	213	405	207	197	359	184	175	328	168	160
15-19	441	225	217	435	221	213	402	205	197	356	181	175
20-24	435	220	215	441	223	217	434	220	214	402	204	198
25-29	421	211	210	428	215	213	434	218	216	428	216	213
30-34	573	285	288	416	207	210	424	211	213	430	214	215
35-39	800	397	403	569	282	287	414	205	209	422	210	212
40-44	770	383	387	789	390	400	563	279	284	411	204	207
45-49	652	317	336	748	368	380	769	376	392	548	270	278
50-54	620	293	327	629	299	329	723	350	373	745	360	386
55-59	550	249	301	585	268	317	596	277	319	688	325	363
60-64	638	275	363	506	219	288	541	238	303	554	247	307
65-69	570	223	347	569	228	341	456	184	272	489	201	288
70-74	439	153	286	480	170	310	483	177	306	389	144	246
75-79	229	71	158	337	104	233	372	117	255	378	123	255
80-84	136	35	102	154	41	113	229	61	169	257	70	187
85-89	101	21	80	73	15	58	85	18	66	129	28	101
90-94	34	6	27	39	7	33	30	5	25	35	6	29
95-99	9	1	7	8	1	7	10	1	9	8	1	7
100 +	1	0	1	1	0	1	1	0	1	2	0	1

Age group	2045 Both sexes	Males	Females	2050 Both sexes	Males	Females
All ages	7 342	3 368	3 975	7 017	3 223	3 794
0-4	338	174	164	327	168	158
5-9	334	172	162	334	172	162
10-14	322	165	157	329	169	160
15-19	326	166	160	320	163	157
20-24	356	180	176	326	165	161
25-29	396	199	197	351	177	175
30-34	424	212	212	392	196	196
35-39	429	214	215	423	211	212
40-44	419	209	211	426	213	213
45-49	400	198	202	409	203	206
50-54	533	259	274	390	191	199
55-59	712	336	376	511	244	267
60-64	642	293	349	667	305	362
65-69	503	211	292	585	252	332
70-74	421	159	261	435	169	266
75-79	308	102	206	335	114	221
80-84	265	75	190	219	63	156
85-89	148	33	115	155	36	119
90-94	56	9	47	66	11	55
95-99	10	1	9	17	2	15
100 +	1	0	1	2	0	2

United Nations Department of Economic and Social Affairs/Population Division
World Population Prospects: The 2004 Revision, Volume II: Sex and Age Distribution of the World Population

207

POPULATION BY AGE AND SEX (in thousands)

Age group	2005 Both sexes	2005 Males	2005 Females	2010 Both sexes	2010 Males	2010 Females	2015 Both sexes	2015 Males	2015 Females	2020 Both sexes	2020 Males	2020 Females
All ages	9 755	4 559	5 197	9 578	4 466	5 112	9 452	4 405	5 047	9 318	4 339	4 978
0-4	449	231	218	548	282	266	587	302	285	559	288	271
5-9	438	225	213	445	229	216	544	280	264	583	300	283
10-14	594	304	290	432	222	211	439	225	214	538	276	262
15-19	831	423	408	590	301	290	429	218	211	436	222	214
20-24	812	415	396	827	419	408	588	298	290	428	217	212
25-29	703	354	349	800	406	394	817	411	406	580	291	288
30-34	689	342	347	693	345	348	790	397	392	807	403	405
35-39	648	318	330	680	335	345	685	339	346	782	391	391
40-44	812	398	414	635	309	327	668	327	342	674	331	343
45-49	796	380	416	781	376	405	612	293	319	646	311	334
50-54	708	327	380	756	351	406	745	350	395	586	274	312
55-59	462	209	253	656	291	365	705	315	390	697	316	381
60-64	382	160	223	416	177	239	595	250	346	642	272	371
65-69	490	186	304	335	128	207	366	143	223	526	203	322
70-74	381	135	246	401	136	265	276	94	182	303	107	197
75-79	328	99	229	278	87	192	297	88	209	206	62	145
80-84	161	39	122	205	53	152	177	48	129	193	49	144
85-89	43	9	34	78	16	62	101	22	79	90	20	69
90-94	23	4	19	14	2	12	27	5	22	36	7	30
95-99	4	1	3	5	1	4	3	0	3	6	1	5
100 +	0	0	0	1	0	0	1	0	0	0	0	0

Age group	2025 Both sexes	2025 Males	2025 Females	2030 Both sexes	2030 Males	2030 Females	2035 Both sexes	2035 Males	2035 Females	2040 Both sexes	2040 Males	2040 Females
All ages	9 133	4 247	4 887	8 939	4 149	4 790	8 779	4 074	4 706	8 662	4 026	4 636
0-4	488	251	237	465	240	226	498	256	241	546	281	265
5-9	555	285	269	484	249	235	461	237	224	494	254	240
10-14	577	296	281	549	282	267	479	246	233	456	234	222
15-19	535	273	262	574	293	281	546	279	267	476	243	233
20-24	435	220	215	534	271	263	573	291	282	545	277	268
25-29	421	211	210	428	215	213	527	266	261	566	286	280
30-34	573	285	288	416	207	210	424	211	213	522	261	261
35-39	800	397	403	569	282	287	414	205	209	422	210	212
40-44	770	383	387	789	390	400	563	279	284	411	204	207
45-49	652	317	336	748	368	380	769	376	392	548	270	278
50-54	620	293	327	629	299	329	723	350	373	745	360	386
55-59	550	249	301	585	268	317	596	277	319	688	325	363
60-64	638	275	363	506	219	288	541	238	303	554	247	307
65-69	570	223	347	569	228	341	456	184	272	489	201	288
70-74	439	153	286	480	170	310	483	177	306	389	144	246
75-79	229	71	158	337	104	233	372	117	255	378	123	255
80-84	136	35	102	154	41	113	229	61	169	257	70	187
85-89	101	21	80	73	15	58	85	18	66	129	28	101
90-94	34	6	27	39	7	33	30	5	25	35	6	29
95-99	9	1	7	8	1	7	10	1	9	8	1	7
100 +	1	0	1	1	0	1	1	0	1	2	0	1

Age group	2045 Both sexes	2045 Males	2045 Females	2050 Both sexes	2050 Males	2050 Females
All ages	8 564	3 995	4 569	8 462	3 965	4 497
0-4	566	292	274	554	286	269
5-9	542	279	263	562	290	273
10-14	488	251	238	537	276	261
15-19	453	231	222	486	248	238
20-24	476	242	234	453	230	223
25-29	539	273	266	470	237	232
30-34	562	282	280	535	269	266
35-39	520	260	260	560	281	279
40-44	419	209	211	517	259	258
45-49	400	198	202	409	203	206
50-54	533	259	274	390	191	199
55-59	712	336	376	511	244	267
60-64	642	293	349	667	305	362
65-69	503	211	292	585	252	332
70-74	421	159	261	435	169	266
75-79	308	102	206	335	114	221
80-84	265	75	190	219	63	156
85-89	148	33	115	155	36	119
90-94	56	9	47	66	11	55
95-99	10	1	9	17	2	15
100 +	1	0	1	2	0	2

United Nations Department of Economic and Social Affairs/Population Division
World Population Prospects: The 2004 Revision, Volume II: Sex and Age Distribution of the World Population

208

POPULATION BY AGE AND SEX (in thousands)

Age group	2005 Both sexes	Males	Females	2010 Both sexes	Males	Females	2015 Both sexes	Males	Females	2020 Both sexes	Males	Females
All ages	9 755	4 559	5 197	9 390	4 370	5 021	8 900	4 103	4 819	8 554	3 946	4 607
0-4	449	231	218	361	186	175	306	157	148	263	135	128
5-9	438	225	213	445	229	216	356	183	173	302	155	147
10-14	594	304	290	432	222	211	439	225	214	351	180	171
15-19	831	423	408	590	301	290	429	218	211	436	222	214
20-24	812	415	396	827	419	408	588	298	290	428	217	212
25-29	703	354	349	800	406	394	817	411	406	580	291	288
30-34	689	342	347	693	345	348	790	397	392	807	403	405
35-39	648	318	330	680	335	345	685	339	346	782	391	391
40-44	812	398	414	635	309	327	668	327	342	674	331	343
45-49	796	380	416	781	376	405	612	293	319	646	311	334
50-54	708	327	380	756	351	406	745	350	395	586	274	312
55-59	462	209	253	656	291	365	705	315	390	697	316	381
60-64	382	160	223	416	177	239	595	250	346	642	272	371
65-69	490	186	304	335	128	207	366	143	223	526	203	322
70-74	381	135	246	401	136	265	276	94	182	303	107	197
75-79	328	99	229	278	87	192	297	88	209	206	62	145
80-84	161	39	122	205	53	152	177	48	129	193	49	144
85-89	43	9	34	78	16	62	101	22	79	90	20	69
90-94	23	4	19	14	2	12	27	5	22	36	7	30
95-99	4	1	3	5	1	4	3	0	3	6	1	5
100 +	0	0	0	1	0	0	1	0	0	0	0	0

Age group	2025 Both sexes	Males	Females	2030 Both sexes	Males	Females	2035 Both sexes	Males	Females	2040 Both sexes	Males	Females
All ages	8 125	3 728	4 397	7 688	3 506	4 181	7 236	3 281	3 955	6 765	3 052	3 713
0-4	243	125	118	220	113	107	202	104	98	188	97	91
5-9	259	133	126	239	123	116	217	112	105	199	102	96
10-14	297	152	145	254	130	124	234	120	114	212	108	103
15-19	348	177	171	294	149	145	251	127	124	232	117	115
20-24	435	220	215	348	176	172	294	148	146	252	127	125
25-29	421	211	210	428	215	213	342	171	171	289	144	144
30-34	573	285	288	416	207	210	424	211	213	338	168	170
35-39	800	397	403	569	282	287	414	205	209	422	210	212
40-44	770	383	387	790	390	400	563	279	284	411	204	207
45-49	652	317	336	748	368	380	769	376	392	548	270	278
50-54	620	293	327	629	299	329	723	350	373	745	360	386
55-59	550	249	301	585	268	317	596	277	319	688	325	363
60-64	638	275	363	506	219	288	541	238	303	554	247	307
65-69	570	223	347	569	228	341	456	184	272	489	201	288
70-74	439	153	286	480	170	310	483	177	306	389	144	246
75-79	229	71	158	337	104	233	372	117	255	378	123	255
80-84	136	35	102	154	41	113	229	61	169	257	70	187
85-89	101	21	80	73	15	58	85	18	66	129	28	101
90-94	34	6	27	39	7	33	30	5	25	35	6	29
95-99	9	1	7	8	1	7	10	1	9	8	1	7
100 +	1	0	1	1	0	1	1	0	1	2	0	1

Age group	2045 Both sexes	Males	Females	2050 Both sexes	Males	Females
All ages	6 277	2 821	3 456	5 787	2 592	3 194
0-4	171	88	83	158	82	77
5-9	184	95	89	168	86	81
10-14	194	99	94	179	92	87
15-19	209	106	104	191	97	95
20-24	232	117	116	210	105	105
25-29	246	123	124	227	113	114
30-34	285	141	144	244	120	124
35-39	338	167	170	285	141	144
40-44	419	209	211	336	167	169
45-49	400	198	202	409	203	206
50-54	533	259	274	390	191	199
55-59	712	336	376	511	244	267
60-64	642	293	349	667	305	362
65-69	503	211	292	585	252	332
70-74	421	159	261	435	169	266
75-79	308	102	206	335	114	221
80-84	265	75	190	219	63	156
85-89	148	33	115	155	36	119
90-94	56	9	47	66	11	55
95-99	10	1	9	17	2	15
100 +	1	0	1	2	0	2

United Nations Department of Economic and Social Affairs/Population Division
World Population Prospects: The 2004 Revision, Volume II: Sex and Age Distribution of the World Population

209

POPULATION BY AGE AND SEX (in thousands)

Age group	1950 Both sexes	1950 Males	1950 Females	1955 Both sexes	1955 Males	1955 Females	1960 Both sexes	1960 Males	1960 Females	1965 Both sexes	1965 Males	1965 Females
All ages	8 639	4 253	4 386	8 868	4 358	4 510	9 153	4 488	4 666	9 464	4 645	4 819
0-4	693	353	340	699	357	342	750	383	367	779	400	380
5-9	542	275	267	691	351	340	710	361	349	762	390	373
10-14	570	287	283	542	275	267	694	352	342	717	366	351
15-19	623	313	310	571	287	284	545	276	269	706	360	346
20-24	656	332	324	622	312	310	572	287	285	565	290	276
25-29	695	355	340	653	330	323	622	311	311	600	307	293
30-34	471	239	232	692	353	339	652	329	324	644	327	317
35-39	627	315	312	469	237	232	690	351	339	656	330	327
40-44	653	326	327	621	311	310	466	235	231	671	334	337
45-49	652	323	329	641	318	323	612	305	308	449	222	227
50-54	586	282	304	632	310	322	625	307	318	584	286	298
55-59	492	229	263	557	263	294	604	291	313	584	280	304
60-64	424	197	227	455	207	248	517	238	279	549	255	293
65-69	366	169	197	374	168	206	405	177	228	450	198	252
70-74	282	128	154	299	133	166	308	132	176	330	136	193
75-79	182	80	102	201	87	114	214	90	125	223	90	133
80 +	125	50	75	149	59	90	169	65	104	194	74	120

Age group	1970 Both sexes	1970 Males	1970 Females	1975 Both sexes	1975 Males	1975 Females	1980 Both sexes	1980 Males	1980 Females	1985 Both sexes	1985 Males	1985 Females
All ages	9 656	4 726	4 930	9 801	4 799	5 002	9 859	4 817	5 042	9 858	4 812	5 046
0-4	720	369	351	656	336	319	611	313	298	594	305	289
5-9	789	404	385	727	372	355	645	331	314	604	309	295
10-14	769	393	376	795	406	389	719	368	351	656	336	320
15-19	725	370	355	778	397	381	795	406	389	724	370	354
20-24	718	367	351	749	384	364	792	405	388	791	403	388
25-29	571	292	279	728	375	354	748	383	366	781	398	383
30-34	597	302	295	572	291	280	729	373	356	734	375	359
35-39	639	321	318	595	300	295	580	295	285	710	362	348
40-44	649	324	325	634	317	317	576	289	287	557	282	275
45-49	658	326	332	637	316	321	609	303	306	576	287	289
50-54	436	214	222	638	313	325	620	305	315	603	298	306
55-59	555	267	288	416	200	215	608	294	314	593	287	306
60-64	538	250	288	513	239	273	410	193	217	573	270	303
65-69	483	214	269	474	210	265	450	201	249	351	158	193
70-74	368	151	217	396	163	233	400	164	236	392	163	229
75-79	238	91	147	269	102	167	299	111	188	307	114	193
80 +	203	74	130	226	77	149	268	85	183	311	96	215

Age group	1990 Both sexes	1990 Males	1990 Females	1995 Both sexes	1995 Males	1995 Females	2000 Both sexes	2000 Males	2000 Females	2005 Both sexes	2005 Males	2005 Females
All ages	9 967	4 870	5 097	10 137	4 957	5 180	10 304	5 049	5 255	10 419	5 112	5 307
0-4	598	307	291	610	312	298	572	292	280	563	288	275
5-9	600	307	292	607	311	296	613	313	300	574	293	281
10-14	609	312	298	605	310	295	610	312	298	614	313	301
15-19	659	337	322	616	314	302	613	314	300	615	315	301
20-24	735	375	360	676	343	333	632	321	311	624	318	306
25-29	807	411	395	750	382	368	694	352	342	644	327	317
30-34	786	400	386	813	414	400	764	390	373	703	358	346
35-39	732	373	359	786	399	387	818	416	402	766	392	375
40-44	704	358	346	728	369	359	787	399	388	817	416	402
45-49	547	276	271	696	353	343	724	367	357	782	396	386
50-54	562	279	283	538	269	268	686	346	340	714	361	353
55-59	582	284	298	546	268	278	523	260	263	669	335	334
60-64	560	266	294	555	266	289	524	253	271	504	247	257
65-69	522	237	285	517	237	280	520	243	277	493	233	260
70-74	304	129	176	460	198	262	464	203	261	469	210	259
75-79	312	118	194	248	96	152	385	154	231	392	160	232
80 +	349	104	245	386	115	271	375	113	262	475	152	323

United Nations Department of Economic and Social Affairs/Population Division
World Population Prospects: The 2004 Revision, Volume II: Sex and Age Distribution of the World Population

210

POPULATION BY AGE AND SEX (in thousands)

Age group	2005 Both sexes	Males	Females	2010 Both sexes	Males	Females	2015 Both sexes	Males	Females	2020 Both sexes	Males	Females
All ages	10 419	5 112	5 307	10 406	5 154	5 041	10 540	5 182	5 358	10 573	5 206	5 366
0-4	563	288	275	539	275	263	531	272	259	534	273	261
5-9	574	293	281	565	288	276	541	276	265	533	272	261
10-14	614	313	301	576	293	282	566	289	278	542	277	266
15-19	615	315	301	620	316	304	581	296	285	572	292	281
20-24	624	318	306	626	319	307	631	320	311	592	301	292
25-29	644	327	317	637	324	313	639	325	314	644	327	317
30-34	703	358	346	653	332	321	646	330	317	649	331	318
35-39	766	392	375	707	360	347	657	334	323	650	332	318
40-44	817	416	402	766	392	375	707	360	347	659	335	323
45-49	782	396	386	813	413	400	763	390	373	705	359	347
50-54	714	361	353	772	390	382	804	407	397	755	385	371
55-59	669	335	334	698	350	348	756	379	377	788	397	391
60-64	504	247	257	645	319	326	675	335	340	733	364	369
65-69	493	233	260	476	228	248	611	297	315	642	313	329
70-74	469	210	259	448	203	244	434	201	233	561	264	297
75-79	392	160	232	400	168	232	385	165	220	376	165	210
80-84	288	104	185	299	111	188	309	119	190	301	119	182
85-89	112	33	79	182	56	126	193	62	131	204	69	135
90-94	59	13	46	53	12	40	89	22	67	98	26	72
95-99	14	2	12	18	3	15	17	3	14	31	6	25
100 +	2	0	1	2	0	2	3	0	3	4	0	3

Age group	2025 Both sexes	Males	Females	2030 Both sexes	Males	Females	2035 Both sexes	Males	Females	2040 Both sexes	Males	Females
All ages	10 590	5 219	5 371	10 588	5 218	5 370	10 555	5 196	5 358	10 489	5 158	5 331
0-4	537	275	262	535	274	261	527	270	258	522	267	255
5-9	537	274	263	540	276	264	537	274	263	530	271	259
10-14	535	273	262	538	275	264	541	276	265	539	275	264
15-19	548	279	269	541	275	265	544	277	267	547	279	269
20-24	584	296	287	560	284	276	552	280	272	556	282	274
25-29	606	307	298	597	303	294	573	291	282	566	287	278
30-34	654	333	321	616	313	302	607	309	298	583	297	286
35-39	653	333	319	658	335	323	620	316	304	612	312	300
40-44	652	333	319	655	335	320	660	336	324	622	317	305
45-49	657	334	323	651	332	318	654	334	320	659	336	323
50-54	699	354	344	652	331	321	646	329	317	649	331	318
55-59	741	376	366	687	347	340	641	324	317	636	322	313
60-64	765	382	383	721	362	359	669	335	334	625	313	312
65-69	698	341	357	731	359	372	690	341	348	641	316	325
70-74	591	280	311	645	307	338	677	324	353	642	310	332
75-79	488	219	269	517	234	283	568	259	309	599	276	324
80-84	297	121	176	009	102	226	416	176	240	461	197	264
85-89	202	71	131	202	73	129	269	101	169	293	111	182
90-94	106	30	76	108	31	76	111	34	77	151	47	104
95-99	35	7	28	39	8	31	42	9	33	44	10	34
100 +	6	1	6	8	1	7	9	1	8	11	1	9

Age group	2045 Both sexes	Males	Females	2050 Both sexes	Males	Females
All ages	10 400	5 110	5 291	10 302	5 060	5 241
0-4	521	266	254	522	267	255
5-9	524	267	256	523	267	256
10-14	532	271	260	526	268	258
15-19	545	278	267	538	274	264
20-24	559	284	275	557	283	274
25-29	570	289	280	573	291	282
30-34	576	293	283	580	296	285
35-39	588	300	288	581	296	285
40-44	614	313	301	591	302	289
45-49	622	317	305	614	313	301
50-54	655	333	322	619	315	304
55-59	640	325	315	646	327	319
60-64	621	312	308	626	315	310
65-69	601	297	304	598	297	301
70-74	598	289	310	562	272	290
75-79	571	265	305	535	249	286
80-84	491	212	279	471	206	265
85-89	330	127	203	356	139	217
90-94	169	54	115	195	63	132
95-99	63	15	48	73	18	55
100 +	12	2	10	17	3	14

United Nations Department of Economic and Social Affairs/Population Division
World Population Prospects: The 2004 Revision, Volume II: Sex and Age Distribution of the World Population
211

POPULATION BY AGE AND SEX (in thousands)

Age group	2005 Both sexes	Males	Females	2010 Both sexes	Males	Females	2015 Both sexes	Males	Females	2020 Both sexes	Males	Females
All ages	10 419	5 112	5 307	10 535	5 174	5 361	10 639	5 233	5 406	10 745	5 294	5 451
0-4	563	288	275	579	296	283	590	302	288	607	311	297
5-9	574	293	281	565	288	276	581	297	284	592	302	290
10-14	614	313	301	576	293	282	566	289	278	583	297	285
15-19	615	315	301	620	316	304	581	296	285	572	292	281
20-24	624	318	306	626	319	307	631	320	311	592	301	292
25-29	644	327	317	637	324	313	639	325	314	644	327	317
30-34	703	358	346	653	332	321	646	330	317	649	331	318
35-39	766	392	375	707	360	347	657	334	323	650	332	318
40-44	817	416	402	766	392	375	707	360	347	659	335	323
45-49	782	396	386	813	413	400	763	390	373	705	359	347
50-54	714	361	353	772	390	382	804	407	397	755	385	371
55-59	669	335	334	698	350	348	756	379	377	788	397	391
60-64	504	247	257	645	319	326	675	335	340	733	364	369
65-69	493	233	260	476	228	248	611	297	315	642	313	329
70-74	469	210	259	448	203	244	434	201	233	561	264	297
75-79	392	160	232	400	168	232	385	165	220	376	165	210
80-84	288	104	185	299	111	188	309	119	190	301	119	182
85-89	112	33	79	182	56	126	193	62	131	204	69	135
90-94	59	13	46	53	12	40	89	22	67	98	26	72
95-99	14	2	12	18	3	15	17	3	14	31	6	25
100 +	2	0	1	2	0	2	3	0	3	4	0	3

Age group	2025 Both sexes	Males	Females	2030 Both sexes	Males	Females	2035 Both sexes	Males	Females	2040 Both sexes	Males	Females
All ages	10 849	5 352	5 497	10 947	5 402	5 546	11 036	5 443	5 593	11 124	5 483	5 641
0-4	624	319	305	636	326	311	650	332	317	676	346	330
5-9	609	311	298	626	320	306	638	326	312	652	333	319
10-14	594	303	291	611	312	299	628	320	307	640	327	313
15-19	589	300	289	600	306	294	617	315	302	634	323	311
20-24	584	296	287	600	305	295	611	310	301	628	319	309
25-29	606	307	298	597	303	294	613	312	302	625	317	307
30-34	654	333	321	616	313	302	607	309	298	624	318	306
35-39	653	333	319	658	335	323	620	316	304	612	312	300
40-44	652	333	319	655	335	320	660	336	324	622	317	305
45-49	657	334	323	651	332	318	654	334	320	659	336	323
50-54	699	354	344	652	331	321	646	329	317	649	331	318
55-59	741	376	366	687	347	340	641	324	317	636	322	313
60-64	765	382	383	721	362	359	669	335	334	625	313	312
65-69	698	341	357	731	359	372	690	341	348	641	316	325
70-74	591	280	311	645	307	338	677	324	353	642	310	332
75-79	488	219	269	517	234	283	568	259	309	599	276	324
80-84	297	121	176	389	162	226	416	176	240	461	197	264
85-89	202	71	131	202	73	129	269	101	169	293	111	182
90-94	106	30	76	108	31	76	111	34	77	151	47	104
95-99	35	7	28	39	8	31	42	9	33	44	10	34
100 +	6	1	6	8	1	7	9	1	8	11	1	9

Age group	2045 Both sexes	Males	Females	2050 Both sexes	Males	Females
All ages	11 226	5 532	5 694	11 347	5 595	5 752
0-4	712	364	348	742	380	362
5-9	678	346	332	715	365	349
10-14	654	334	320	680	347	333
15-19	646	329	317	660	336	323
20-24	645	328	317	658	334	323
25-29	642	326	316	659	335	324
30-34	635	323	311	652	332	320
35-39	628	320	308	640	326	313
40-44	614	313	301	631	322	309
45-49	622	317	305	614	313	301
50-54	655	333	322	619	315	304
55-59	640	325	315	646	327	319
60-64	621	312	308	626	315	310
65-69	601	297	304	598	297	301
70-74	598	289	310	562	272	290
75-79	571	265	305	535	249	286
80-84	491	212	279	471	206	265
85-89	330	127	203	356	139	217
90-94	169	54	115	195	63	132
95-99	63	15	48	73	18	55
100 +	12	2	10	17	3	14

United Nations Department of Economic and Social Affairs/Population Division
World Population Prospects: The 2004 Revision, Volume II: Sex and Age Distribution of the World Population

212

POPULATION BY AGE AND SEX (in thousands)

Age group	2005 Both sexes	Males	Females	2010 Both sexes	Males	Females	2015 Both sexes	Males	Females	2020 Both sexes	Males	Females
All ages	10 419	5 112	5 307	10 454	5 133	5 321	10 440	5 131	5 309	10 401	5 118	5 282
0-4	563	288	275	498	255	244	471	241	230	462	236	226
5-9	574	293	281	565	288	276	501	256	245	474	242	232
10-14	614	313	301	576	293	282	566	289	278	502	256	246
15-19	615	315	301	620	316	304	581	296	285	572	292	281
20-24	624	318	306	626	319	307	631	320	311	592	301	292
25-29	644	327	317	637	324	313	639	325	314	644	327	317
30-34	703	358	346	653	332	321	646	330	317	649	331	318
35-39	766	392	375	707	360	347	657	334	323	650	332	318
40-44	817	416	402	766	392	375	707	360	347	659	335	323
45-49	782	396	386	813	413	400	763	390	373	705	359	347
50-54	714	361	353	772	390	382	804	407	397	755	385	371
55-59	669	335	334	698	350	348	756	379	377	788	397	391
60-64	504	247	257	645	319	326	675	335	340	733	364	369
65-69	493	233	260	476	228	248	611	297	315	642	313	329
70-74	469	210	259	448	203	244	434	201	233	561	264	297
75-79	392	160	232	400	168	232	385	165	220	376	165	210
80-84	288	104	185	299	111	188	309	119	190	301	119	182
85-89	112	33	79	182	56	126	193	62	131	204	69	135
90-94	59	13	46	53	12	40	89	22	67	98	26	72
95-99	14	2	12	18	3	15	17	3	14	31	6	25
100 +	2	0	1	2	0	2	3	0	3	4	0	3

Age group	2025 Both sexes	Males	Females	2030 Both sexes	Males	Females	2035 Both sexes	Males	Females	2040 Both sexes	Males	Females
All ages	10 332	5 087	5 245	10 229	5 034	5 195	10 078	4 953	5 126	9 871	4 842	5 029
0-4	451	231	220	435	222	212	409	209	200	380	194	186
5-9	464	237	227	453	231	222	437	223	214	412	210	202
10-14	475	242	233	466	237	228	455	232	223	439	224	215
15-19	508	259	249	481	245	236	472	240	232	461	235	226
20-24	584	296	287	520	264	256	493	250	243	483	245	238
25-29	606	307	298	597	303	294	533	271	263	507	257	250
30-34	654	333	321	616	313	302	607	309	298	544	277	267
35-39	653	333	319	658	335	323	620	316	304	612	312	300
40-44	652	333	310	655	335	320	660	336	324	622	317	305
45-49	657	334	323	651	332	318	654	334	320	659	336	323
50-54	699	354	344	652	331	321	646	329	317	649	331	318
55-59	741	376	366	687	347	340	641	324	317	636	322	313
60-64	765	382	383	721	362	359	669	335	334	625	313	312
65-69	698	341	357	731	359	372	690	341	348	641	316	325
70-74	591	280	311	645	307	338	677	324	353	642	310	332
75-79	488	219	269	517	234	283	568	259	309	599	276	324
80-84	297	121	176	380	160	220	418	178	240	461	197	264
85-89	202	71	131	202	73	129	269	101	169	293	111	182
90-94	106	30	76	108	31	76	111	34	77	151	47	104
95-99	35	7	28	39	8	31	42	9	33	44	10	34
100 +	6	1	6	8	1	7	9	1	8	11	1	9

Age group	2045 Both sexes	Males	Females	2050 Both sexes	Males	Females
All ages	9 615	4 708	4 907	9 331	4 564	4 767
0-4	353	180	172	336	172	164
5-9	382	195	187	355	181	174
10-14	414	211	203	384	196	188
15-19	445	226	219	420	214	206
20-24	473	240	233	457	231	225
25-29	497	252	245	487	247	240
30-34	517	263	254	508	259	249
35-39	549	280	269	522	266	256
40-44	614	313	301	551	281	270
45-49	622	317	305	614	313	301
50-54	655	333	322	619	315	304
55-59	640	325	315	646	327	319
60-64	621	312	308	626	315	310
65-69	601	297	304	598	297	301
70-74	598	289	310	562	272	290
75-79	571	265	305	535	249	286
80-84	491	212	279	471	206	265
85-89	330	127	203	356	139	217
90-94	169	54	115	195	63	132
95-99	63	15	48	73	18	55
100 +	12	2	10	17	3	14

POPULATION BY AGE AND SEX (in thousands)

Age group	1950 Both sexes	Males	Females	1955 Both sexes	Males	Females	1960 Both sexes	Males	Females	1965 Both sexes	Males	Females
All ages	69	34	35	80	39	41	93	46	47	107	53	54
0-4	11	5	5	16	8	8	18	9	9	19	10	9
5-9	8	4	4	10	5	5	14	7	7	18	9	9
10-14	8	4	4	8	4	4	10	5	5	13	7	7
15-19	7	3	4	7	4	4	8	4	4	10	5	5
20-24	6	3	3	6	3	3	7	3	4	7	4	4
25-29	5	3	3	6	3	3	6	3	3	6	3	3
30-34	4	2	2	5	2	2	6	3	3	6	3	3
35-39	4	2	2	4	2	2	5	2	2	5	3	3
40-44	4	2	2	4	2	2	4	2	2	4	2	2
45-49	3	1	1	3	2	2	4	2	2	4	2	2
50-54	3	1	1	3	1	1	3	2	2	4	2	2
55-59	2	1	1	2	1	1	3	1	1	3	2	2
60-64	2	1	1	2	1	1	2	1	1	2	1	1
65-69	1	1	1	1	1	1	2	1	1	2	1	1
70-74	1	0	0	1	0	0	1	1	1	1	1	1
75-79	0	0	0	0	0	0	1	0	0	1	0	0
80 +	0	0	0	0	0	0	0	0	0	1	0	0

Age group	1970 Both sexes	Males	Females	1975 Both sexes	Males	Females	1980 Both sexes	Males	Females	1985 Both sexes	Males	Females
All ages	123	61	62	134	67	67	144	73	71	163	83	80
0-4	22	11	11	24	12	12	24	12	12	27	14	13
5-9	19	9	9	21	11	10	23	11	11	25	13	12
10-14	18	9	9	18	9	9	20	10	10	22	11	11
15-19	13	7	7	17	8	8	17	9	9	19	9	9
20-24	10	5	5	12	6	6	13	7	6	15	7	7
25-29	7	3	3	8	4	4	9	4	4	11	6	6
30-34	6	3	3	5	3	3	7	3	3	9	4	4
35-39	5	2	3	5	2	2	5	3	3	7	3	3
40-44	5	2	3	4	2	2	5	3	2	6	3	3
45-49	4	2	2	4	2	2	5	2	2	5	2	2
50-54	3	2	2	4	2	2	4	2	2	5	2	2
55-59	3	2	2	3	1	2	3	2	2	4	2	2
60-64	3	1	1	3	1	2	3	1	1	3	2	1
65-69	2	1	1	2	1	1	2	1	1	3	1	1
70-74	1	1	1	2	1	1	2	1	1	2	1	1
75-79	1	0	1	1	1	1	1	1	1	1	1	1
80 +	1	0	0	1	0	0	1	1	1	2	1	1

Age group	1990 Both sexes	Males	Females	1995 Both sexes	Males	Females	2000 Both sexes	Males	Females	2005 Both sexes	Males	Females
All ages	186	94	91	214	109	105	242	123	120	270	136	134
0-4	30	15	15	33	17	16	33	17	16	34	17	17
5-9	28	14	14	30	15	15	33	17	16	33	17	16
10-14	24	12	12	28	14	14	29	15	14	32	16	16
15-19	21	10	10	24	12	12	27	14	14	29	15	14
20-24	17	8	8	20	10	10	24	12	12	27	14	13
25-29	14	7	7	17	8	8	20	10	10	24	12	12
30-34	11	6	6	14	7	7	16	8	8	20	10	10
35-39	9	5	4	11	6	5	14	7	7	16	8	8
40-44	7	4	3	9	4	4	11	6	5	13	7	7
45-49	5	3	2	7	3	3	8	4	4	11	5	5
50-54	5	2	2	5	3	2	6	3	3	8	4	4
55-59	4	2	2	4	2	2	5	2	2	6	3	3
60-64	3	2	2	4	2	2	4	2	2	4	2	2
65-69	3	1	1	3	2	2	3	2	2	4	2	2
70-74	2	1	1	2	1	1	3	1	1	3	2	1
75-79	1	1	1	2	1	1	2	1	1	2	1	1
80 +	2	1	1	2	1	1	2	1	1	2	1	1

United Nations Department of Economic and Social Affairs/Population Division
World Population Prospects: The 2004 Revision, Volume II: Sex and Age Distribution of the World Population

214

POPULATION BY AGE AND SEX (in thousands)

Age group	2005			2010			2015			2020		
	Both sexes	Males	Females	Both sexes	Males	Females	Both sexes	Males	Females	Both sexes	Males	Females
All ages	270	136	134	296	149	147	321	161	160	345	173	172
0-4	34	17	17	34	17	17	34	17	17	33	17	16
5-9	33	17	16	33	17	16	33	17	16	33	17	16
10-14	32	16	16	33	17	16	33	17	16	33	17	16
15-19	29	15	14	32	16	16	33	17	16	33	17	16
20-24	27	14	13	29	15	14	32	16	16	33	16	16
25-29	24	12	12	27	13	13	29	14	14	31	16	16
30-34	20	10	10	23	12	11	26	13	13	28	14	14
35-39	16	8	8	19	9	10	22	11	11	25	13	13
40-44	13	7	7	16	8	8	19	9	10	22	11	11
45-49	11	5	5	13	6	7	15	7	8	18	9	9
50-54	8	4	4	11	5	5	13	6	7	15	7	8
55-59	6	3	3	8	4	4	10	5	5	12	6	6
60-64	4	2	2	6	3	3	8	4	4	10	5	5
65-69	4	2	2	4	2	2	5	3	3	7	3	3
70-74	3	2	1	3	2	2	4	2	2	5	2	2
75-79	2	1	1	2	1	1	3	1	1	3	1	2
80-84	1	1	1	2	1	1	2	1	1	2	1	1
85-89	1	0	0	1	0	0	1	0	1	1	0	1
90-94	0	0	0	0	0	0	0	0	0	0	0	0
95-99	0	0	0	0	0	0	0	0	0	0	0	0
100 +	0	0	0	0	0	0	0	0	0	0	0	0

Age group	2025			2030			2035			2040		
	Both sexes	Males	Females	Both sexes	Males	Females	Both sexes	Males	Females	Both sexes	Males	Females
All ages	366	183	183	386	192	193	402	200	202	417	207	210
0-4	32	16	16	30	15	15	29	15	14	29	15	14
5-9	33	17	16	32	16	16	30	15	15	29	15	14
10-14	33	17	16	33	17	16	32	16	16	30	15	15
15-19	33	17	16	33	17	16	33	16	16	31	16	16
20-24	33	17	16	33	17	16	33	17	16	32	16	16
25-29	32	16	16	32	16	16	32	16	16	33	16	16
30-34	31	16	15	32	16	16	32	16	16	32	16	16
35-39	27	14	14	30	15	15	31	16	15	31	16	16
40-44	25	12	12	28	13	13	29	15	15	30	15	15
45-49	21	10	11	24	12	12	26	13	13	29	14	15
50-54	18	9	9	21	10	10	23	11	12	25	13	13
55-59	14	7	7	17	8	9	20	10	10	23	11	12
60-64	12	6	6	14	7	7	16	8	9	19	9	10
65-69	9	4	5	11	5	6	13	6	7	15	7	8
70-74	6	3	3	8	4	4	10	5	5	11	5	6
75-79	4	2	2	5	2	3	7	3	4	8	4	5
80-84	2	1	1	3	1	2	4	2	2	5	2	3
85-89	1	1	1	1	1	1	2	1	1	3	1	1
90-94	1	0	0	1	0	0	1	0	0	1	0	1
95-99	0	0	0	0	0	0	0	0	0	0	0	0
100 +	0	0	0	0	0	0	0	0	0	0	0	0

Age group	2045			2050		
	Both sexes	Males	Females	Both sexes	Males	Females
All ages	431	213	217	442	219	223
0-4	29	15	14	28	14	14
5-9	29	15	14	29	14	14
10-14	29	14	14	29	14	14
15-19	30	15	15	29	14	14
20-24	31	16	16	30	15	15
25-29	32	16	16	31	16	15
30-34	32	16	16	32	16	16
35-39	31	16	16	32	16	16
40-44	31	15	15	31	16	15
45-49	30	15	15	30	15	15
50-54	28	14	14	29	15	15
55-59	25	12	12	28	14	14
60-64	22	10	11	24	11	12
65-69	18	9	9	20	10	11
70-74	14	6	7	16	8	8
75-79	10	4	5	12	5	7
80-84	6	3	4	8	3	4
85-89	3	1	2	4	2	3
90-94	1	0	1	2	1	1
95-99	0	0	0	0	0	0
100 +	0	0	0	0	0	0

United Nations Department of Economic and Social Affairs/Population Division
World Population Prospects: The 2004 Revision, Volume II: Sex and Age Distribution of the World Population

215

POPULATION BY AGE AND SEX (in thousands)

Age group	2005 Both sexes	2005 Males	2005 Females	2010 Both sexes	2010 Males	2010 Females	2015 Both sexes	2015 Males	2015 Females	2020 Both sexes	2020 Males	2020 Females
All ages	270	136	134	299	151	148	330	166	164	360	180	180
0-4	34	17	17	37	19	18	39	20	19	40	20	20
5-9	33	17	16	33	17	16	36	18	18	39	20	19
10-14	32	16	16	33	17	16	33	17	16	36	18	18
15-19	29	15	14	32	16	16	33	17	16	33	17	16
20-24	27	14	13	29	15	14	32	16	16	33	16	16
25-29	24	12	12	27	13	13	29	14	14	31	16	16
30-34	20	10	10	23	12	11	26	13	13	28	14	14
35-39	16	8	8	19	9	10	22	11	11	25	13	13
40-44	13	7	7	16	8	8	19	9	10	22	11	11
45-49	11	5	5	13	6	7	15	7	8	18	9	9
50-54	8	4	4	11	5	5	13	6	7	15	7	8
55-59	6	3	3	8	4	4	10	5	5	12	6	6
60-64	4	2	2	6	3	3	8	4	4	10	5	5
65-69	4	2	2	4	2	2	5	3	3	7	3	3
70-74	3	2	1	3	2	2	4	2	2	5	2	2
75-79	2	1	1	2	1	1	3	1	1	3	1	2
80-84	1	1	1	2	1	1	2	1	1	2	1	1
85-89	1	0	0	1	0	0	1	0	1	1	0	1
90-94	0	0	0	0	0	0	0	0	0	0	0	0
95-99	0	0	0	0	0	0	0	0	0	0	0	0
100 +	0	0	0	0	0	0	0	0	0	0	0	0

Age group	2025 Both sexes	2025 Males	2025 Females	2030 Both sexes	2030 Males	2030 Females	2035 Both sexes	2035 Males	2035 Females	2040 Both sexes	2040 Males	2040 Females
All ages	389	195	195	417	208	209	444	221	223	472	235	237
0-4	40	20	20	39	20	19	39	20	20	41	21	20
5-9	40	20	20	39	20	19	39	20	19	39	20	19
10-14	38	19	19	40	20	20	39	20	19	39	20	19
15-19	36	18	18	38	19	19	40	20	20	39	20	19
20-24	33	17	16	36	18	18	38	19	19	39	20	20
25-29	32	16	16	32	16	16	35	18	17	38	19	19
30-34	31	16	15	32	16	16	32	16	16	35	18	17
35-39	27	14	14	30	15	15	31	16	15	31	16	16
40-44	25	12	12	26	13	13	29	15	15	30	15	15
45-49	21	10	11	24	12	12	26	13	13	29	14	15
50-54	18	9	9	21	10	10	23	11	12	25	13	13
55-59	14	7	7	17	8	9	20	10	10	23	11	12
60-64	12	6	6	14	7	7	16	8	9	19	9	10
65-69	9	4	5	11	5	6	13	6	7	15	7	8
70-74	6	3	3	8	4	4	10	5	5	11	5	6
75-79	4	2	2	5	2	3	7	3	4	8	4	5
80-84	2	1	1	3	1	2	4	2	2	5	2	3
85-89	1	1	1	1	1	1	2	1	1	3	1	1
90-94	1	0	0	1	0	0	1	0	0	1	0	1
95-99	0	0	0	0	0	0	0	0	0	0	0	0
100 +	0	0	0	0	0	0	0	0	0	0	0	0

Age group	2045 Both sexes	2045 Males	2045 Females	2050 Both sexes	2050 Males	2050 Females
All ages	499	248	251	526	261	265
0-4	43	22	21	44	22	22
5-9	41	21	20	43	22	21
10-14	39	20	19	41	21	20
15-19	39	20	19	39	20	19
20-24	39	20	19	39	19	19
25-29	39	20	19	39	20	19
30-34	37	19	18	39	20	19
35-39	34	17	17	37	18	18
40-44	31	15	15	34	17	17
45-49	30	15	15	30	15	15
50-54	28	14	14	29	15	15
55-59	25	12	12	28	14	14
60-64	22	10	11	24	11	12
65-69	18	9	9	20	10	11
70-74	14	6	7	16	8	8
75-79	10	4	5	12	5	7
80-84	6	3	4	8	3	4
85-89	3	1	2	4	2	3
90-94	1	0	1	2	1	1
95-99	0	0	0	0	0	0
100 +	0	0	0	0	0	0

United Nations Department of Economic and Social Affairs/Population Division
World Population Prospects: The 2004 Revision, Volume II: Sex and Age Distribution of the World Population

216

POPULATION BY AGE AND SEX (in thousands)

Age group	2005 Both sexes	Males	Females	2010 Both sexes	Males	Females	2015 Both sexes	Males	Females	2020 Both sexes	Males	Females
All ages	270	136	134	293	148	146	010	157	156	329	165	165
0-4	34	17	17	31	16	15	28	14	14	26	13	13
5-9	33	17	16	33	17	16	30	15	15	28	14	14
10-14	32	16	16	33	17	16	33	17	16	30	15	15
15-19	29	15	14	32	16	16	33	17	16	33	17	16
20-24	27	14	13	29	15	14	32	16	16	33	16	16
25-29	24	12	12	27	13	13	29	14	14	31	16	16
30-34	20	10	10	23	12	11	26	13	13	28	14	14
35-39	16	8	8	19	9	10	22	11	11	25	13	13
40-44	13	7	7	16	8	8	19	9	10	22	11	11
45-49	11	5	5	13	6	7	15	7	8	18	9	9
50-54	8	4	4	11	5	5	13	6	7	15	7	8
55-59	6	3	3	8	4	4	10	5	5	12	6	6
60-64	4	2	2	6	3	3	8	4	4	10	5	5
65-69	4	2	2	4	2	2	5	3	3	7	3	3
70-74	3	2	1	3	2	2	4	2	2	5	2	2
75-79	2	1	1	2	1	1	3	1	1	3	1	2
80-84	1	1	1	2	1	1	2	1	1	2	1	1
85-89	1	0	0	1	0	0	1	0	1	1	0	1
90-94	0	0	0	0	0	0	0	0	0	0	0	0
95-99	0	0	0	0	0	0	0	0	0	0	0	0
100 +	0	0	0	0	0	0	0	0	0	0	0	0

Age group	2025 Both sexes	Males	Females	2030 Both sexes	Males	Females	2035 Both sexes	Males	Females	2040 Both sexes	Males	Females
All ages	343	171	172	354	176	178	362	179	182	366	181	185
0-4	24	12	12	22	11	11	20	10	10	18	9	9
5-9	26	13	13	24	12	12	22	11	11	19	10	10
10-14	28	14	14	26	13	13	24	12	12	22	11	11
15-19	30	15	15	28	14	14	26	13	13	24	12	12
20-24	33	17	16	30	15	15	28	14	14	25	13	13
25-29	32	16	16	32	16	16	29	15	15	27	14	14
30-34	31	16	15	32	16	16	32	16	16	29	15	14
35-39	27	14	14	30	15	15	31	16	15	31	16	16
40-44	25	12	12	26	13	13	29	15	15	30	15	15
45-49	21	10	11	24	12	12	26	13	13	29	14	15
50-54	18	9	9	21	10	10	23	11	12	25	13	13
55-59	14	7	7	17	8	9	20	10	10	22	11	12
60-64	12	6	6	14	7	7	16	8	9	19	9	10
65-69	9	4	5	11	5	6	13	6	7	15	7	8
70-74	6	3	3	8	4	4	10	5	5	11	5	6
75-79	4	2	2	5	2	3	7	3	4	8	4	5
80-84	2	1	1	3	1	2	4	2	2	5	2	3
85-89	1	1	1	1	1	1	2	1	1	3	1	1
90-94	1	0	0	1	0	0	1	0	0	1	0	1
95-99	0	0	0	0	0	0	0	0	0	0	0	0
100 +	0	0	0	0	0	0	0	0	0	0	0	0

Age group	2045 Both sexes	Males	Females	2050 Both sexes	Males	Females
All ages	368	182	187	368	181	187
0-4	17	9	8	16	8	8
5-9	18	9	9	17	9	8
10-14	19	10	10	18	9	9
15-19	22	11	11	19	10	10
20-24	24	12	12	22	11	11
25-29	25	13	12	24	12	12
30-34	27	14	13	25	13	12
35-39	29	14	14	27	13	13
40-44	31	15	15	28	14	14
45-49	30	15	15	30	15	15
50-54	28	14	14	29	15	15
55-59	25	12	12	28	14	14
60-64	22	10	11	24	11	12
65-69	18	9	9	20	10	11
70-74	14	6	7	16	8	8
75-79	10	4	5	12	5	7
80-84	6	3	4	8	3	4
85-89	3	1	2	4	2	3
90-94	1	0	1	2	1	1
95-99	0	0	0	0	0	0
100 +	0	0	0	0	0	0

United Nations Department of Economic and Social Affairs/Population Division
World Population Prospects: The 2004 Revision, Volume II: Sex and Age Distribution of the World Population

217

POPULATION BY AGE AND SEX (in thousands)

Age group	1950 Both sexes	Males	Females	1955 Both sexes	Males	Females	1960 Both sexes	Males	Females	1965 Both sexes	Males	Females
All ages	2 005	961	1 044	2 130	1 024	1 106	2 316	1 117	1 199	2 533	1 226	1 307
0-4	302	145	157	356	179	177	407	205	202	430	217	213
5-9	226	109	117	265	127	138	316	159	157	366	184	182
10-14	197	95	102	219	106	113	258	124	134	309	155	153
15-19	169	81	87	191	92	99	212	102	110	251	120	131
20-24	148	72	76	159	76	83	181	86	94	202	97	105
25-29	127	62	65	137	66	72	148	70	78	170	80	90
30-34	112	54	57	118	57	61	128	61	67	139	65	74
35-39	95	47	48	104	50	54	110	52	58	120	56	64
40-44	85	42	43	88	43	45	97	46	51	103	48	55
45-49	79	39	40	78	38	40	82	40	42	91	43	48
50-54	84	39	45	72	35	38	72	35	37	76	36	40
55-59	109	51	58	75	34	41	65	31	34	65	31	34
60-64	96	44	52	93	43	51	65	29	36	57	26	30
65-69	77	36	41	76	34	42	75	34	41	53	23	30
70-74	53	25	29	53	24	29	53	23	30	54	24	30
75-79	31	13	17	30	13	16	30	14	17	31	13	18
80 +	16	7	9	15	7	9	15	7	9	16	7	9

Age group	1970 Both sexes	Males	Females	1975 Both sexes	Males	Females	1980 Both sexes	Males	Females	1985 Both sexes	Males	Females
All ages	2 828	1 374	1 454	3 212	1 567	1 645	3 709	1 816	1 893	4 393	2 162	2 231
0-4	497	251	246	582	294	288	685	346	339	873	442	431
5-9	392	198	194	458	231	227	542	273	269	640	323	317
10-14	359	181	178	385	194	191	451	227	223	534	269	265
15-19	301	152	150	351	177	174	378	190	187	444	224	220
20-24	241	115	126	290	145	145	340	171	170	369	185	183
25-29	191	90	100	229	108	121	279	139	140	330	165	165
30-34	160	75	85	181	85	96	220	103	117	270	134	136
35-39	131	60	71	152	70	82	173	81	93	212	99	113
40-44	113	52	61	124	56	68	145	66	79	167	77	90
45-49	97	45	52	107	49	58	118	53	65	139	63	76
50-54	85	39	45	91	41	49	101	45	55	112	50	62
55-59	69	32	37	77	35	42	84	37	46	94	41	52
60-64	57	27	31	61	28	33	69	31	38	75	33	42
65-69	46	21	25	47	21	26	51	23	28	58	25	33
70-74	39	16	22	34	15	19	36	16	20	39	17	22
75-79	32	14	19	24	10	14	22	9	12	23	10	13
80 +	17	7	10	18	7	11	16	6	10	15	6	9

Age group	1990 Both sexes	Males	Females	1995 Both sexes	Males	Females	2000 Both sexes	Males	Females	2005 Both sexes	Males	Females
All ages	5 178	2 561	2 617	6 201	3 098	3 103	7 197	3 602	3 594	8 439	4 253	4 186
0-4	988	501	487	1 133	576	557	1 276	649	627	1 441	733	708
5-9	821	416	406	938	476	462	1 077	548	530	1 220	621	599
10-14	632	319	313	814	412	402	928	471	457	1 068	543	525
15-19	527	265	261	632	320	312	804	407	397	926	471	455
20-24	434	218	216	533	271	263	616	311	305	807	410	397
25-29	359	180	179	444	226	218	512	259	253	619	315	303
30-34	321	160	161	367	186	180	424	215	209	507	260	247
35-39	262	129	133	325	164	161	351	177	173	417	214	203
40-44	205	95	110	263	131	132	311	156	155	343	175	168
45-49	160	74	87	203	95	108	251	124	127	302	152	150
50-54	132	59	73	157	72	85	193	89	104	242	119	123
55-59	104	46	59	126	57	70	146	66	80	183	84	99
60-64	84	37	48	96	42	54	115	50	64	135	61	75
65-69	64	27	37	74	32	42	83	35	48	101	43	57
70-74	45	19	26	50	21	29	58	24	34	66	28	39
75-79	25	10	15	29	12	17	33	13	20	39	16	23
80 +	15	6	9	16	6	10	19	7	12	23	9	14

United Nations Department of Economic and Social Affairs/Population Division
World Population Prospects: The 2004 Revision, Volume II: Sex and Age Distribution of the World Population

218

POPULATION BY AGE AND SEX (in thousands)

Age group	2005 Both sexes	2005 Males	2005 Females	2010 Both sexes	2010 Males	2010 Females	2015 Both sexes	2015 Males	2015 Females	2020 Both sexes	2020 Males	2020 Females
All ages	8 439	4 253	4 186	9 793	4 954	4 839	11 217	5 680	5 537	12 717	6 443	6 274
0-4	1 441	733	708	1 622	826	796	1 764	899	866	1 859	947	912
5-9	1 220	621	599	1 386	705	680	1 568	799	770	1 717	875	842
10-14	1 068	543	525	1 208	615	594	1 373	699	674	1 557	793	764
15-19	926	471	455	1 062	540	522	1 199	610	589	1 364	694	670
20-24	807	410	397	922	469	452	1 049	533	516	1 186	602	583
25-29	619	315	303	800	408	392	903	460	443	1 030	524	507
30-34	507	260	247	608	312	296	777	397	380	880	449	432
35-39	417	214	203	493	255	238	587	302	285	754	386	368
40-44	343	175	168	403	208	195	475	245	229	568	292	276
45-49	302	152	150	331	168	162	388	199	189	458	236	222
50-54	242	119	123	289	144	145	316	160	156	372	190	182
55-59	183	84	99	228	111	117	273	135	138	299	150	150
60-64	135	61	75	169	76	93	210	101	109	253	123	130
65-69	101	43	57	119	52	67	149	66	83	187	88	99
70-74	66	28	39	81	34	47	96	41	55	122	53	70
75-79	39	16	23	46	18	27	56	23	33	68	28	40
80-84	17	7	10	21	8	13	24	9	15	31	12	19
85-89	5	2	3	6	2	4	7	3	5	9	3	6
90-94	1	0	0	1	0	1	1	0	1	1	0	1
95-99	0	0	0	0	0	0	0	0	0	0	0	0
100 +	0	0	0	0	0	0	0	0	0	0	0	0

Age group	2025 Both sexes	2025 Males	2025 Females	2030 Both sexes	2030 Males	2030 Females	2035 Both sexes	2035 Males	2035 Females	2040 Both sexes	2040 Males	2040 Females
All ages	14 254	7 224	7 030	15 820	8 018	7 802	17 410	8 824	8 586	19 010	9 634	9 376
0-4	1 921	979	943	1 975	1 006	969	2 028	1 034	994	2 069	1 055	1 013
5-9	1 819	927	892	1 887	961	926	1 947	992	955	2 004	1 022	982
10-14	1 708	870	838	1 811	923	889	1 881	958	923	1 941	989	952
15-19	1 548	788	760	1 700	865	835	1 804	918	886	1 875	954	921
20-24	1 351	687	665	1 536	781	755	1 689	859	830	1 795	913	882
25-29	1 168	593	575	1 334	678	656	1 520	772	747	1 673	851	822
30-34	1 008	512	495	1 145	582	563	1 312	667	645	1 498	762	736
35-39	856	437	419	983	501	483	1 122	571	551	1 288	655	633
40-44	732	374	357	833	425	408	961	489	472	1 000	550	540
45-49	549	281	268	710	362	348	812	413	399	939	477	462
50-54	440	225	215	530	270	260	688	349	339	789	400	389
55-59	353	178	175	420	213	207	508	256	252	661	333	329
60-64	278	137	141	330	164	166	395	197	198	480	239	241
65-69	226	108	118	251	121	130	300	147	153	361	177	184
70-74	155	71	84	190	88	101	213	101	112	258	123	134
75-79	88	37	52	114	50	63	142	64	78	162	74	88
80-84	38	15	23	51	20	31	67	28	39	85	36	49
85-89	12	4	7	15	5	9	20	7	13	27	11	16
90-94	2	1	1	3	1	2	3	1	2	5	2	3
95-99	0	0	0	0	0	0	0	0	0	0	0	0
100 +	0	0	0	0	0	0	0	0	0	0	0	0

Age group	2045 Both sexes	2045 Males	2045 Females	2050 Both sexes	2050 Males	2050 Females
All ages	20 590	10 431	10 159	22 123	11 203	10 920
0-4	2 086	1 065	1 021	2 082	1 063	1 019
5-9	2 049	1 046	1 003	2 070	1 057	1 013
10-14	2 000	1 020	980	2 046	1 044	1 002
15-19	1 936	986	950	1 995	1 017	978
20-24	1 866	950	917	1 929	982	947
25-29	1 781	906	875	1 854	943	911
30-34	1 653	841	812	1 763	897	866
35-39	1 476	751	724	1 633	831	802
40-44	1 266	644	622	1 454	740	714
45-49	1 078	547	530	1 245	632	612
50-54	915	463	452	1 053	533	520
55-59	761	382	379	886	445	441
60-64	628	312	316	725	360	365
65-69	442	216	225	581	284	297
70-74	313	151	163	386	185	201
75-79	198	92	106	244	114	130
80-84	99	43	56	124	55	69
85-89	36	14	21	43	17	25
90-94	7	2	4	9	3	6
95-99	1	0	0	1	0	1
100 +	0	0	0	0	0	0

POPULATION BY AGE AND SEX (in thousands)

Age group	2005 Both sexes	2005 Males	2005 Females	2010 Both sexes	2010 Males	2010 Females	2015 Both sexes	2015 Males	2015 Females	2020 Both sexes	2020 Males	2020 Females
All ages	8 439	4 253	4 186	9 868	4 992	4 876	11 433	5 790	5 643	13 139	6 658	6 481
0-4	1 441	733	708	1 696	864	833	1 908	972	936	2 070	1 055	1 016
5-9	1 220	621	599	1 386	705	680	1 641	836	805	1 857	946	911
10-14	1 068	543	525	1 208	615	594	1 373	699	674	1 629	829	800
15-19	926	471	455	1 062	540	522	1 199	610	589	1 364	694	670
20-24	807	410	397	922	469	452	1 049	533	516	1 186	602	583
25-29	619	315	303	800	408	392	903	460	443	1 030	524	507
30-34	507	260	247	608	312	296	777	397	380	880	449	432
35-39	417	214	203	493	255	238	587	302	285	754	386	368
40-44	343	175	168	403	208	195	475	245	229	568	292	276
45-49	302	152	150	331	168	162	388	199	189	458	236	222
50-54	242	119	123	289	144	145	316	160	156	372	190	182
55-59	183	84	99	228	111	117	273	135	138	299	150	150
60-64	135	61	75	169	76	93	210	101	109	253	123	130
65-69	101	43	57	119	52	67	149	66	83	187	88	99
70-74	66	28	39	81	34	47	96	41	55	122	53	70
75-79	39	16	23	46	18	27	56	23	33	68	28	40
80-84	17	7	10	21	8	13	24	9	15	31	12	19
85-89	5	2	3	6	2	4	7	3	5	9	3	6
90-94	1	0	0	1	0	1	1	0	1	1	0	1
95-99	0	0	0	0	0	0	0	0	0	0	0	0
100 +	0	0	0	0	0	0	0	0	0	0	0	0

Age group	2025 Both sexes	2025 Males	2025 Females	2030 Both sexes	2030 Males	2030 Females	2035 Both sexes	2035 Males	2035 Females	2040 Both sexes	2040 Males	2040 Females
All ages	14 923	7 564	7 358	16 801	8 518	8 283	18 802	9 533	9 269	20 921	10 608	10 313
0-4	2 173	1 107	1 066	2 294	1 169	1 125	2 445	1 247	1 199	2 598	1 325	1 272
5-9	2 025	1 032	994	2 135	1 088	1 048	2 261	1 152	1 109	2 417	1 233	1 184
10-14	1 847	941	906	2 017	1 027	990	2 128	1 084	1 044	2 255	1 149	1 106
15-19	1 620	824	795	1 838	936	902	2 009	1 023	986	2 121	1 080	1 041
20-24	1 351	687	665	1 607	817	790	1 826	929	897	1 998	1 017	982
25-29	1 168	593	575	1 334	678	656	1 590	808	782	1 810	920	889
30-34	1 008	512	495	1 145	582	563	1 312	667	645	1 567	797	770
35-39	856	437	419	983	501	483	1 122	571	551	1 288	655	633
40-44	732	374	357	833	425	408	961	489	472	1 099	559	540
45-49	549	281	268	710	362	348	812	413	399	939	477	462
50-54	440	225	215	530	270	260	688	349	339	789	400	389
55-59	353	178	175	420	213	207	508	256	252	661	333	329
60-64	278	137	141	330	164	166	395	197	198	480	239	241
65-69	226	108	118	251	121	130	300	147	153	361	177	184
70-74	155	71	84	190	88	101	213	101	112	258	123	134
75-79	88	37	52	114	50	63	142	64	78	162	74	88
80-84	38	15	23	51	20	31	67	28	39	85	36	49
85-89	12	4	7	15	5	9	20	7	13	27	11	16
90-94	2	1	1	3	1	2	3	1	2	5	2	3
95-99	0	0	0	0	0	0	0	0	0	0	0	0
100 +	0	0	0	0	0	0	0	0	0	0	0	0

Age group	2045 Both sexes	2045 Males	2045 Females	2050 Both sexes	2050 Males	2050 Females
All ages	23 123	11 723	11 400	25 371	12 859	12 512
0-4	2 719	1 388	1 331	2 810	1 435	1 376
5-9	2 573	1 313	1 260	2 698	1 377	1 321
10-14	2 412	1 230	1 182	2 569	1 311	1 258
15-19	2 249	1 146	1 104	2 406	1 227	1 180
20-24	2 112	1 074	1 037	2 241	1 141	1 100
25-29	1 983	1 009	974	2 098	1 067	1 031
30-34	1 788	910	878	1 964	999	965
35-39	1 544	786	758	1 766	899	867
40-44	1 266	644	622	1 522	775	747
45-49	1 078	547	530	1 245	632	612
50-54	915	463	452	1 053	533	520
55-59	761	382	379	886	445	441
60-64	628	312	316	725	360	365
65-69	442	216	225	581	284	297
70-74	313	151	163	386	185	201
75-79	198	92	106	244	114	130
80-84	99	43	56	124	55	69
85-89	36	14	21	43	17	25
90-94	7	2	4	9	3	6
95-99	1	0	0	1	0	1
100 +	0	0	0	0	0	0

United Nations Department of Economic and Social Affairs/Population Division
World Population Prospects: The 2004 Revision, Volume II: Sex and Age Distribution of the World Population

220

POPULATION BY AGE AND SEX (in thousands)

Age group	2005			2010			2015			2020		
	Both sexes	Males	Females	Both sexes	Males	Females	Both sexes	Males	Females	Both sexes	Males	Females
All ages	8 439	4 253	4 186	9 719	4 916	4 802	11 001	5 570	5 401	12 295	6 228	6 067
0-4	1 441	733	708	1 547	788	759	1 621	826	795	1 649	840	809
5-9	1 220	621	599	1 386	705	680	1 496	762	734	1 578	804	774
10-14	1 068	543	525	1 208	615	594	1 373	699	674	1 485	756	729
15-19	926	471	455	1 062	540	522	1 199	610	589	1 364	694	670
20-24	807	410	397	922	469	452	1 049	533	516	1 186	602	583
25-29	619	315	303	800	408	392	903	460	443	1 030	524	507
30-34	507	260	247	608	312	296	777	397	380	880	449	432
35-39	417	214	203	493	255	238	587	302	285	754	386	368
40-44	343	175	168	403	208	195	475	245	229	568	292	276
45-49	302	152	150	331	168	162	388	199	189	458	236	222
50-54	242	119	123	289	144	145	316	160	156	372	190	182
55-59	183	84	99	228	111	117	273	135	138	299	150	150
60-64	135	61	75	169	76	93	210	101	109	253	123	130
65-69	101	43	57	119	52	67	149	66	83	187	88	99
70-74	66	28	39	81	34	47	96	41	55	122	53	70
75-79	39	16	23	46	18	27	56	23	33	68	28	40
80-84	17	7	10	21	8	13	24	9	15	31	12	19
85-89	5	2	3	6	2	4	7	3	5	9	3	6
90-94	1	0	0	1	0	1	1	0	1	1	0	1
95-99	0	0	0	0	0	0	0	0	0	0	0	0
100 +	0	0	0	0	0	0	0	0	0	0	0	0

Age group	2025			2030			2035			2040		
	Both sexes	Males	Females	Both sexes	Males	Females	Both sexes	Males	Females	Both sexes	Males	Females
All ages	13 587	6 884	6 703	14 849	7 523	7 325	16 055	8 134	7 921	17 185	8 704	8 481
0-4	1 671	851	820	1 665	848	816	1 636	834	802	1 590	811	779
5-9	1 613	822	791	1 641	836	805	1 641	836	805	1 617	825	792
10-14	1 569	799	770	1 606	818	788	1 636	833	803	1 636	834	803
15-19	1 477	752	725	1 562	795	767	1 600	814	785	1 631	830	801
20-24	1 351	687	665	1 465	745	720	1 551	789	762	1 591	809	782
25-29	1 168	593	575	1 334	678	656	1 449	737	713	1 537	782	755
30-34	1 008	512	495	1 145	582	563	1 312	667	645	1 429	727	702
35-39	856	437	419	983	501	483	1 122	571	551	1 288	655	633
40-44	732	374	357	833	425	400	961	489	472	1 099	559	540
45-49	549	281	268	710	362	348	812	413	399	939	477	462
50-54	440	225	215	530	270	260	688	349	339	789	400	389
55-59	353	178	175	420	213	207	508	256	252	661	333	329
60-64	278	137	141	330	164	166	395	197	198	480	239	241
65-69	226	108	118	251	121	130	300	147	153	361	177	184
70-74	155	71	84	190	88	101	213	101	112	258	123	134
75-79	88	37	52	114	50	63	142	64	78	162	74	88
80-84	38	15	23	51	20	31	67	28	39	85	36	49
85-89	12	4	7	15	5	9	20	7	13	27	11	16
90-94	2	1	1	3	1	2	3	1	2	5	2	3
95-99	0	0	0	0	0	0	0	0	0	0	0	0
100 +	0	0	0	0	0	0	0	0	0	0	0	0

Age group	2045			2050		
	Both sexes	Males	Females	Both sexes	Males	Females
All ages	18 220	9 223	8 997	19 143	9 683	9 460
0-4	1 530	781	749	1 460	745	715
5-9	1 575	804	771	1 518	775	743
10-14	1 614	823	791	1 572	802	770
15-19	1 632	831	801	1 610	821	789
20-24	1 623	826	797	1 625	827	798
25-29	1 578	803	776	1 612	820	792
30-34	1 519	773	746	1 563	795	768
35-39	1 407	716	691	1 500	763	736
40-44	1 266	644	622	1 387	706	681
45-49	1 078	547	530	1 245	632	612
50-54	915	463	452	1 053	533	520
55-59	761	382	379	886	445	441
60-64	628	312	316	725	360	365
65-69	442	216	225	581	284	297
70-74	313	151	163	386	185	201
75-79	198	92	106	244	114	130
80-84	99	43	56	124	55	69
85-89	36	14	21	43	17	25
90-94	7	2	4	9	3	6
95-99	1	0	0	1	0	1
100 +	0	0	0	0	0	0

United Nations Department of Economic and Social Affairs/Population Division
World Population Prospects: The 2004 Revision, Volume II: Sex and Age Distribution of the World Population

221

POPULATION BY AGE AND SEX (in thousands)

Age group	1950			1955			1960			1965		
	Both sexes	Males	Females	Both sexes	Males	Females	Both sexes	Males	Females	Both sexes	Males	Females
All ages	734	370	364	793	400	393	865	436	429	950	479	471
0-4	121	61	60	125	63	62	139	70	68	154	78	76
5-9	96	49	47	104	53	51	109	55	54	122	62	60
10-14	83	42	41	91	46	45	100	51	49	104	53	51
15-19	74	38	36	80	41	39	88	45	43	96	49	47
20-24	65	33	32	71	36	35	77	39	38	84	43	42
25-29	56	28	28	61	31	30	67	34	33	74	37	36
30-34	49	25	24	53	27	26	58	29	29	64	32	32
35-39	42	21	21	46	23	23	50	25	25	55	28	27
40-44	36	18	18	39	20	19	43	21	21	47	24	23
45-49	30	15	15	33	16	16	36	18	18	39	20	20
50-54	25	12	13	27	13	14	30	15	15	33	16	16
55-59	20	10	10	22	11	11	24	12	12	26	13	13
60-64	15	7	8	17	8	9	18	9	10	20	10	11
65-69	11	5	6	12	6	6	13	6	7	15	7	8
70-74	7	3	4	7	3	4	8	4	4	9	4	5
75-79	3	2	2	4	2	2	4	2	2	5	2	3
80 +	2	1	1	2	1	1	2	1	1	2	1	1

Age group	1970			1975			1980			1985		
	Both sexes	Males	Females	Both sexes	Males	Females	Both sexes	Males	Females	Both sexes	Males	Females
All ages	1 048	529	519	1 161	586	575	1 292	653	639	1 447	732	716
0-4	172	87	84	190	97	94	212	108	104	238	121	117
5-9	137	70	67	154	78	75	172	88	84	193	99	95
10-14	117	60	58	132	67	65	148	76	73	167	85	82
15-19	101	51	50	114	58	56	128	65	63	145	74	71
20-24	93	47	46	98	50	48	110	56	54	124	63	61
25-29	81	41	40	89	45	44	94	48	46	106	54	52
30-34	70	35	35	77	39	38	85	43	42	90	46	45
35-39	60	30	30	66	34	33	73	37	36	81	41	40
40-44	51	26	25	57	29	28	63	32	31	70	35	35
45-49	43	22	22	48	24	24	53	27	26	59	30	29
50-54	36	18	18	40	20	20	44	22	22	50	25	25
55-59	29	14	15	32	16	16	36	18	18	40	20	20
60-64	23	11	12	25	12	13	28	14	14	32	15	16
65-69	16	8	8	18	9	10	21	10	11	23	11	12
70-74	10	5	5	12	5	6	13	6	7	15	7	8
75-79	5	2	3	6	3	3	7	3	4	9	4	5
80 +	3	1	2	3	1	2	4	2	2	5	2	3

Age group	1990			1995			2000			2005		
	Both sexes	Males	Females	Both sexes	Males	Females	Both sexes	Males	Females	Both sexes	Males	Females
All ages	1 642	830	811	1 733	878	855	1 938	982	956	2 163	1 096	1 067
0-4	271	138	133	279	143	137	278	142	136	293	150	143
5-9	223	114	109	254	130	124	269	138	132	271	138	132
10-14	189	96	93	216	110	106	250	128	123	267	136	131
15-19	163	83	80	178	91	87	213	109	104	248	126	121
20-24	141	72	69	142	73	69	175	89	86	210	107	103
25-29	121	61	60	115	59	56	138	71	68	172	87	84
30-34	103	52	51	99	50	49	112	57	55	136	69	66
35-39	87	44	43	86	44	43	96	49	47	110	56	54
40-44	78	39	39	75	38	37	83	42	41	94	47	46
45-49	66	33	33	69	35	34	72	36	36	81	41	40
50-54	56	28	28	59	29	30	66	33	33	69	35	35
55-59	46	23	23	50	24	25	56	28	28	62	31	31
60-64	36	18	19	40	19	20	45	22	23	51	25	26
65-69	27	13	14	30	14	16	35	17	18	40	19	21
70-74	18	9	9	21	10	11	24	12	13	29	14	15
75-79	10	5	6	12	6	7	15	7	8	18	8	10
80 +	6	3	3	7	3	4	10	4	6	13	6	7

United Nations Department of Economic and Social Affairs/Population Division
World Population Prospects: The 2004 Revision, Volume II: Sex and Age Distribution of the World Population

222

POPULATION BY AGE AND SEX (in thousands)

Age group	2005 Both sexes	Males	Females	2010 Both sexes	Males	Females	2015 Both sexes	Males	Females	2020 Both sexes	Males	Females
All ages	2 163	1 096	1 067	2 414	1 223	1 191	2 684	1 360	1 324	2 950	1 494	1 455
0-4	293	150	143	314	160	153	335	171	164	345	176	169
5-9	271	138	132	287	147	141	309	158	151	331	169	162
10-14	267	136	131	269	137	131	286	146	140	308	157	151
15-19	248	126	121	265	135	130	267	136	131	284	145	139
20-24	210	107	103	246	125	121	264	134	130	265	135	130
25-29	172	87	84	209	106	103	245	124	121	261	132	128
30-34	136	69	66	170	87	84	207	105	102	242	123	119
35-39	110	56	54	134	69	66	169	86	83	205	103	101
40-44	94	47	46	108	55	53	133	68	65	166	84	82
45-49	81	41	40	92	46	45	106	54	52	130	66	64
50-54	69	35	35	78	39	39	89	45	44	103	52	51
55-59	62	31	31	66	33	33	75	37	38	85	43	43
60-64	51	25	26	58	29	30	62	31	31	71	35	36
65-69	40	19	21	46	22	24	52	25	27	56	27	29
70-74	29	14	15	33	16	17	39	19	20	44	21	23
75-79	18	8	10	21	10	11	25	12	13	30	14	16
80-84	9	4	5	11	5	6	13	6	7	16	7	9
85-89	3	1	2	4	2	2	5	2	3	6	3	4
90-94	1	0	0	1	0	1	1	1	1	2	1	1
95-99	0	0	0	0	0	0	0	0	0	0	0	0
100 +	0	0	0	0	0	0	0	0	0	0	0	0

Age group	2025 Both sexes	Males	Females	2030 Both sexes	Males	Females	2035 Both sexes	Males	Females	2040 Both sexes	Males	Females
All ages	3 209	1 626	1 583	3 460	1 752	1 707	3 706	1 876	1 829	3 948	1 998	1 950
0-4	343	176	168	340	174	166	342	175	167	347	177	169
5-9	342	175	167	341	174	167	338	173	165	341	174	167
10-14	330	169	162	341	174	167	340	174	166	338	172	165
15-19	306	156	150	329	168	161	340	173	166	339	173	166
20-24	282	143	138	304	155	149	327	166	160	338	172	166
25-29	262	133	129	279	142	137	302	153	148	325	165	160
30-34	258	131	127	260	132	128	277	141	136	300	152	147
35-39	239	121	118	255	129	126	257	130	127	275	139	136
40-44	202	102	100	236	119	117	252	128	125	255	129	126
45-49	163	82	81	198	100	98	233	117	115	249	126	123
50-54	126	64	62	159	80	79	194	97	96	228	114	113
55-59	99	50	49	122	61	60	154	77	77	188	94	94
60-64	80	40	40	94	47	47	116	58	58	146	73	73
65-69	64	31	33	73	36	37	86	43	44	107	53	54
70-74	48	23	25	55	27	29	64	31	33	75	37	39
75-79	34	16	18	37	18	20	44	21	23	51	24	27
80-84	19	9	10	23	10	12	25	12	13	30	14	16
85-89	8	4	4	10	4	5	11	5	6	13	6	7
90-94	2	1	1	3	1	2	3	1	2	4	2	2
95-99	0	0	0	0	0	0	1	0	0	1	0	0
100 +	0	0	0	0	0	0	0	0	0	0	0	0

Age group	2045 Both sexes	Males	Females	2050 Both sexes	Males	Females
All ages	4 180	2 114	2 066	4 393	2 220	2 173
0-4	347	178	170	341	174	166
5-9	346	177	169	346	177	169
10-14	340	174	166	345	176	169
15-19	337	172	165	339	173	166
20-24	338	172	166	335	171	164
25-29	336	171	165	336	171	165
30-34	323	164	159	334	170	164
35-39	297	151	147	321	163	158
40-44	272	138	134	295	149	146
45-49	252	127	125	269	136	133
50-54	244	123	121	247	124	123
55-59	221	111	110	238	119	118
60-64	180	89	90	212	106	106
65-69	136	67	69	167	82	85
70-74	94	46	48	121	59	62
75-79	61	29	32	77	37	40
80-84	35	17	19	43	20	23
85-89	16	7	9	19	9	11
90-94	5	2	3	6	3	4
95-99	1	0	1	1	0	1
100 +	0	0	0	0	0	0

United Nations Department of Economic and Social Affairs/Population Division
World Population Prospects: The 2004 Revision, Volume II: Sex and Age Distribution of the World Population

223

POPULATION BY AGE AND SEX (in thousands)

Age group	2005 Both sexes	Males	Females	2010 Both sexes	Males	Females	2015 Both sexes	Males	Females	2020 Both sexes	Males	Females
All ages	2 163	1 096	1 067	2 432	1 232	1 200	2 736	1 386	1 349	3 052	1 546	1 505
0-4	293	150	143	331	169	162	370	189	181	396	202	193
5-9	271	138	132	287	147	141	326	167	160	365	187	179
10-14	267	136	131	269	137	131	286	146	140	325	166	159
15-19	248	126	121	265	135	130	267	136	131	284	145	139
20-24	210	107	103	246	125	121	264	134	130	265	135	130
25-29	172	87	84	209	106	103	245	124	121	261	132	128
30-34	136	69	66	170	87	84	207	105	102	242	123	119
35-39	110	56	54	134	69	66	169	86	83	205	103	101
40-44	94	47	46	108	55	53	133	68	65	166	84	82
45-49	81	41	40	92	46	45	106	54	52	130	66	64
50-54	69	35	35	78	39	39	89	45	44	103	52	51
55-59	62	31	31	66	33	33	75	37	38	85	43	43
60-64	51	25	26	58	29	30	62	31	31	71	35	36
65-69	40	19	21	46	22	24	52	25	27	56	27	29
70-74	29	14	15	33	16	17	39	19	20	44	21	23
75-79	18	8	10	21	10	11	25	12	13	30	14	16
80-84	9	4	5	11	5	6	13	6	7	16	7	9
85-89	3	1	2	4	2	2	5	2	3	6	3	4
90-94	1	0	0	1	0	1	1	1	1	2	1	1
95-99	0	0	0	0	0	0	0	0	0	0	0	0
100 +	0	0	0	0	0	0	0	0	0	0	0	0

Age group	2025 Both sexes	Males	Females	2030 Both sexes	Males	Females	2035 Both sexes	Males	Females	2040 Both sexes	Males	Females
All ages	3 368	1 707	1 661	3 683	1 866	1 817	4 008	2 030	1 977	4 349	2 203	2 147
0-4	401	205	196	406	207	198	422	216	206	448	229	219
5-9	392	200	192	398	204	195	404	206	197	420	215	205
10-14	364	186	178	391	200	191	397	203	194	403	206	197
15-19	323	165	158	362	185	177	390	199	191	396	202	194
20-24	282	143	138	321	163	157	360	184	177	388	198	190
25-29	262	133	129	279	142	137	319	162	157	358	182	176
30-34	258	131	127	260	132	128	277	141	136	316	161	156
35-39	239	121	118	255	129	126	257	130	127	275	139	136
40-44	202	102	100	236	119	117	252	128	125	255	129	126
45-49	163	82	81	198	100	98	233	117	115	249	126	123
50-54	126	64	62	159	80	79	194	97	96	228	114	113
55-59	99	50	49	122	61	60	154	77	77	188	94	94
60-64	80	40	40	94	47	47	116	58	58	146	73	73
65-69	64	31	33	73	36	37	86	43	44	107	53	54
70-74	48	23	25	55	27	29	64	31	33	75	37	39
75-79	34	16	18	37	18	20	44	21	23	51	24	27
80-84	19	9	10	23	10	12	25	12	13	30	14	16
85-89	8	4	4	10	4	5	11	5	6	13	6	7
90-94	2	1	1	3	1	2	3	1	2	4	2	2
95-99	0	0	0	0	0	0	1	0	0	1	0	0
100 +	0	0	0	0	0	0	0	0	0	0	0	0

Age group	2045 Both sexes	Males	Females	2050 Both sexes	Males	Females
All ages	4 704	2 381	2 322	5 055	2 558	2 497
0-4	470	241	230	481	246	235
5-9	446	228	218	469	240	229
10-14	419	214	205	445	228	218
15-19	402	205	197	418	214	205
20-24	394	201	193	400	204	196
25-29	385	196	189	392	200	193
30-34	356	181	175	383	195	189
35-39	314	159	155	353	179	174
40-44	272	138	134	311	158	154
45-49	252	127	125	269	136	133
50-54	244	123	121	247	124	123
55-59	221	111	110	238	119	118
60-64	180	89	90	212	106	106
65-69	136	67	69	167	82	85
70-74	94	46	48	121	59	62
75-79	61	29	32	77	37	40
80-84	35	17	19	43	20	23
85-89	16	7	9	19	9	11
90-94	5	2	3	6	3	4
95-99	1	0	1	1	0	1
100 +	0	0	0	0	0	0

United Nations Department of Economic and Social Affairs/Population Division
World Population Prospects: The 2004 Revision, Volume II: Sex and Age Distribution of the World Population

224

POPULATION BY AGE AND SEX (in thousands)

Age group	2005 Both sexes	Males	Females	2010 Both sexes	Males	Females	2015 Both sexes	Males	Females	2020 Both sexes	Males	Females
All ages	2 163	1 096	1 067	2 396	1 214	1 182	2 631	1 333	1 298	2 846	1 442	1 405
0-4	293	150	143	296	151	145	300	154	147	294	150	144
5-9	271	138	132	287	147	141	292	149	143	297	152	145
10-14	267	136	131	269	137	131	286	146	140	290	148	142
15-19	248	126	121	265	135	130	267	136	131	284	145	139
20-24	210	107	103	246	125	121	264	134	130	265	135	130
25-29	172	87	84	209	106	103	245	124	121	261	132	128
30-34	136	69	66	170	87	84	207	105	102	242	123	119
35-39	110	56	54	134	69	66	169	86	83	205	103	101
40-44	94	47	46	108	55	53	133	68	65	166	84	82
45-49	81	41	40	92	46	45	106	54	52	130	66	64
50-54	69	35	35	78	39	39	89	45	44	103	52	51
55-59	62	31	31	66	33	33	75	37	38	85	43	43
60-64	51	25	26	58	29	30	62	31	31	71	35	36
65-69	40	19	21	46	22	24	52	25	27	56	27	29
70-74	29	14	15	33	16	17	39	19	20	44	21	23
75-79	18	8	10	21	10	11	25	12	13	30	14	16
80-84	9	4	5	11	5	6	13	6	7	16	7	9
85-89	3	1	2	4	2	2	5	2	3	6	3	4
90-94	1	0	0	1	0	1	1	1	1	2	1	1
95-99	0	0	0	0	0	0	0	0	0	0	0	0
100 +	0	0	0	0	0	0	0	0	0	0	0	0

Age group	2025 Both sexes	Males	Females	2030 Both sexes	Males	Females	2035 Both sexes	Males	Females	2040 Both sexes	Males	Females
All ages	3 048	1 543	1 505	3 233	1 637	1 597	3 401	1 721	1 681	3 549	1 794	1 755
0-4	285	146	139	274	140	134	263	135	129	251	128	123
5-9	291	149	142	283	145	138	273	139	133	262	134	128
10-14	296	151	145	290	148	142	282	144	138	272	139	133
15-19	289	147	141	294	150	144	289	148	142	282	144	138
20-24	282	143	138	287	146	141	293	149	144	288	147	141
25-29	262	133	129	279	142	137	284	145	140	291	148	143
30-34	258	131	127	260	132	128	277	141	136	283	143	139
35-39	239	121	118	255	129	126	257	130	127	275	139	136
40-44	202	102	100	236	119	117	252	128	125	255	129	126
45-49	163	82	81	198	100	98	233	117	115	240	126	123
50-54	126	64	62	159	80	79	194	97	96	228	114	113
55-59	99	50	49	122	61	60	154	77	77	188	94	94
60-64	80	40	40	94	47	47	116	58	58	146	73	73
65-69	64	31	33	73	36	37	86	43	44	107	53	54
70-74	48	23	25	55	27	29	64	31	33	75	37	39
75-79	34	16	18	37	18	20	44	21	23	51	24	27
80-84	19	9	10	23	10	12	25	12	13	30	14	16
85-89	8	4	4	10	4	5	11	5	6	13	6	7
90-94	2	1	1	3	1	2	3	1	2	4	2	2
95-99	0	0	0	0	0	0	1	0	0	1	0	0
100 +	0	0	0	0	0	0	0	0	0	0	0	0

Age group	2045 Both sexes	Males	Females	2050 Both sexes	Males	Females
All ages	3 672	1 855	1 817	3 765	1 900	1 865
0-4	236	121	115	220	113	107
5-9	250	128	122	236	121	115
10-14	262	134	128	250	128	122
15-19	271	139	133	261	133	128
20-24	280	143	137	270	138	133
25-29	286	146	141	279	142	137
30-34	289	147	142	284	145	140
35-39	281	142	138	287	146	141
40-44	272	138	134	278	141	137
45-49	252	127	125	269	136	133
50-54	244	123	121	247	124	123
55-59	221	111	110	238	119	118
60-64	180	89	90	212	106	106
65-69	136	67	69	167	82	85
70-74	94	46	48	121	59	62
75-79	61	29	32	77	37	40
80-84	35	17	19	43	20	23
85-89	16	7	9	19	9	11
90-94	5	2	3	6	3	4
95-99	1	0	1	1	0	1
100 +	0	0	0	0	0	0

POPULATION BY AGE AND SEX (in thousands)

Age group	1950 Both sexes	Males	Females	1955 Both sexes	Males	Females	1960 Both sexes	Males	Females	1965 Both sexes	Males	Females
All ages	2 714	1 353	1 360	3 006	1 493	1 513	3 351	1 660	1 692	3 748	1 852	1 896
0-4	458	231	227	512	257	255	575	289	286	638	320	317
5-9	351	177	174	409	205	204	461	230	231	522	260	262
10-14	314	158	156	339	171	168	396	198	198	447	222	225
15-19	277	139	138	303	152	151	328	164	163	384	191	192
20-24	247	124	123	261	130	131	286	142	144	311	155	156
25-29	193	96	97	231	115	116	245	121	124	270	133	137
30-34	163	81	82	182	91	92	219	109	111	234	115	119
35-39	151	75	76	154	76	78	173	85	88	209	103	106
40-44	129	64	65	142	70	72	145	71	74	164	80	83
45-49	110	55	55	121	59	62	134	65	68	137	66	70
50-54	93	46	47	102	50	52	112	55	58	125	60	64
55-59	75	36	39	84	41	43	92	45	48	102	49	53
60-64	57	27	30	65	31	34	73	35	38	81	38	42
65-69	42	20	22	46	21	25	52	24	28	59	28	32
70-74	29	13	16	30	13	16	33	15	18	38	17	21
75-79	16	7	9	17	7	9	17	8	10	20	9	11
80 +	8	3	4	9	4	5	9	4	5	10	4	6

Age group	1970 Both sexes	Males	Females	1975 Both sexes	Males	Females	1980 Both sexes	Males	Females	1985 Both sexes	Males	Females
All ages	4 212	2 077	2 134	4 759	2 345	2 414	5 355	2 641	2 714	5 964	2 947	3 017
0-4	717	361	357	817	411	406	865	437	428	940	477	463
5-9	584	291	293	662	330	332	766	383	382	816	411	405
10-14	508	253	255	569	283	286	648	323	325	742	371	371
15-19	434	215	219	495	245	250	556	276	280	626	312	314
20-24	365	181	184	415	204	211	476	235	241	525	259	265
25-29	294	145	149	347	171	177	398	195	203	449	221	228
30-34	258	126	131	281	138	143	334	164	171	377	183	193
35-39	223	109	114	246	120	126	270	132	138	320	155	164
40-44	198	97	102	212	103	109	236	114	121	257	125	132
45-49	155	75	79	188	91	97	202	97	105	224	108	116
50-54	128	62	66	145	70	75	177	85	92	190	91	99
55-59	114	55	59	117	56	61	134	64	69	164	78	85
60-64	90	43	47	100	48	53	104	49	55	120	57	63
65-69	66	31	35	74	35	40	85	39	45	90	42	48
70-74	43	20	24	49	22	27	57	26	31	66	30	36
75-79	23	10	13	27	12	15	32	14	18	38	17	21
80 +	11	5	7	14	6	8	17	7	10	21	9	12

Age group	1990 Both sexes	Males	Females	1995 Both sexes	Males	Females	2000 Both sexes	Males	Females	2005 Both sexes	Males	Females
All ages	6 669	3 304	3 365	7 482	3 716	3 765	8 317	4 138	4 178	9 182	4 575	4 607
0-4	1 038	528	510	1 157	590	567	1 190	607	583	1 239	632	607
5-9	899	455	443	1 003	510	493	1 124	573	551	1 159	591	568
10-14	793	399	394	875	443	432	979	498	482	1 100	560	540
15-19	720	360	360	770	387	383	853	431	422	957	486	471
20-24	594	295	299	688	343	345	740	371	369	822	415	408
25-29	498	246	252	568	281	286	661	329	332	713	357	357
30-34	428	210	218	477	235	243	547	270	277	640	317	323
35-39	362	175	186	412	201	211	462	226	236	531	261	270
40-44	306	148	158	347	168	180	398	193	204	446	218	229
45-49	245	119	126	292	141	151	333	160	173	382	185	197
50-54	211	101	109	231	111	120	277	133	144	316	151	165
55-59	176	84	92	196	94	103	216	103	113	260	124	136
60-64	149	70	78	161	76	85	181	85	96	200	94	106
65-69	105	49	56	132	61	71	144	66	78	162	75	87
70-74	72	33	39	86	39	47	109	49	60	120	54	66
75-79	46	20	26	51	22	29	62	27	35	80	35	45
80 +	27	11	16	34	14	20	42	17	25	53	21	32

United Nations Department of Economic and Social Affairs/Population Division
World Population Prospects: The 2004 Revision, Volume II: Sex and Age Distribution of the World Population

226

POPULATION BY AGE AND SEX (in thousands)

Age group	2005 Both sexes	Males	Females	2010 Both sexes	Males	Females	2015 Both sexes	Males	Females	2020 Both sexes	Males	Females
All ages	9 182	4 575	4 607	10 031	5 003	5 028	10 854	5 418	5 437	11 638	5 812	5 826
0-4	1 239	632	607	1 243	634	609	1 237	631	606	1 216	621	595
5-9	1 159	591	568	1 209	616	593	1 216	620	596	1 211	618	594
10-14	1 100	560	540	1 136	579	557	1 187	605	582	1 194	608	586
15-19	957	486	471	1 077	548	529	1 114	567	547	1 165	593	572
20-24	822	415	408	926	469	457	1 046	531	515	1 083	551	533
25-29	713	357	357	796	400	395	899	454	445	1 019	516	503
30-34	640	317	323	692	345	347	774	388	386	878	442	436
35-39	531	261	270	623	307	316	675	335	340	757	378	379
40-44	446	218	229	514	252	263	606	298	308	658	326	332
45-49	382	185	197	430	209	221	497	243	255	587	288	300
50-54	316	151	165	364	176	189	412	199	213	478	232	246
55-59	260	124	136	298	142	157	345	165	180	392	188	204
60-64	200	94	106	241	114	128	279	130	148	324	153	171
65-69	162	75	87	181	84	97	219	101	118	255	117	138
70-74	120	54	66	137	62	75	154	70	85	189	85	104
75-79	80	35	45	90	39	51	105	45	59	120	52	68
80-84	37	15	22	49	20	29	58	24	34	69	28	41
85-89	13	5	8	17	7	11	25	9	15	30	12	19
90-94	3	1	2	4	1	3	6	2	4	10	3	6
95-99	0	0	0	1	0	0	1	0	1	2	0	1
100 +	0	0	0	0	0	0	0	0	0	0	0	0

Age group	2025 Both sexes	Males	Females	2030 Both sexes	Males	Females	2035 Both sexes	Males	Females	2040 Both sexes	Males	Females
All ages	12 368	6 178	6 190	13 034	6 511	6 523	13 626	6 806	6 820	14 136	7 057	7 079
0-4	1 186	606	580	1 147	586	561	1 100	563	538	1 052	538	514
5-9	1 192	608	584	1 164	594	570	1 127	576	551	1 082	553	529
10-14	1 191	607	584	1 173	599	575	1 146	585	561	1 110	567	543
15-19	1 174	598	576	1 171	597	574	1 155	589	566	1 128	576	552
20-24	1 135	577	558	1 145	582	563	1 143	582	561	1 127	574	553
25-29	1 057	536	521	1 110	563	547	1 120	569	551	1 119	569	550
30-34	997	504	493	1 036	524	511	1 089	551	538	1 100	558	543
35-39	860	432	428	979	493	486	1 019	514	504	1 072	542	531
40-44	740	369	371	842	422	420	960	483	477	1 001	504	497
45-49	640	315	324	721	358	363	822	411	412	940	471	469
50-54	566	276	290	619	304	315	699	346	353	800	398	402
55-59	450	220	230	543	253	290	595	290	305	674	331	343
60-64	369	175	194	432	206	226	515	247	269	567	273	294
65-69	298	138	160	341	159	182	401	188	213	481	226	255
70-74	222	99	123	262	118	144	302	137	165	358	163	195
75-79	150	65	85	179	77	102	214	93	121	251	109	142
80-84	82	34	48	105	43	62	128	52	76	157	64	93
85-89	38	14	24	47	18	29	62	24	39	79	29	49
90-94	13	4	8	17	6	11	21	7	14	29	10	20
95-99	3	1	2	4	1	3	5	1	4	7	2	5
100 +	0	0	0	1	0	1	1	0	1	1	0	1

Age group	2045 Both sexes	Males	Females	2050 Both sexes	Males	Females
All ages	14 564	7 266	7 298	14 908	7 430	7 478
0-4	1 007	515	492	967	495	472
5-9	1 035	529	506	991	507	484
10-14	1 066	545	521	1 019	521	498
15-19	1 093	558	535	1 050	537	513
20-24	1 102	562	540	1 067	545	523
25-29	1 105	562	542	1 080	550	530
30-34	1 101	559	542	1 087	552	534
35-39	1 085	548	536	1 086	550	536
40-44	1 055	532	523	1 068	539	529
45-49	981	493	488	1 037	521	516
50-54	917	458	459	959	480	479
55-59	773	382	391	888	440	448
60-64	644	313	332	741	362	379
65-69	531	251	280	606	289	317
70-74	433	198	235	481	221	259
75-79	300	131	169	367	161	206
80-84	187	77	110	229	94	134
85-89	99	37	62	121	46	75
90-94	38	13	26	50	16	33
95-99	10	3	7	14	4	10
100 +	2	0	1	3	1	2

POPULATION BY AGE AND SEX (in thousands)

Age group	2005 Both sexes	Males	Females	2010 Both sexes	Males	Females	2015 Both sexes	Males	Females	2020 Both sexes	Males	Females
All ages	9 182	4 575	4 607	10 115	5 046	5 069	11 090	5 538	5 552	12 085	6 040	6 045
0-4	1 239	632	607	1 328	677	651	1 390	709	681	1 430	730	700
5-9	1 159	591	568	1 209	616	593	1 299	662	637	1 362	695	668
10-14	1 100	560	540	1 136	579	557	1 187	605	582	1 277	650	626
15-19	957	486	471	1 077	548	529	1 114	567	547	1 165	593	572
20-24	822	415	408	926	469	457	1 046	531	515	1 083	551	533
25-29	713	357	357	796	400	395	899	454	445	1 019	516	503
30-34	640	317	323	692	345	347	774	388	386	878	442	436
35-39	531	261	270	623	307	316	675	335	340	757	378	379
40-44	446	218	229	514	252	263	606	298	308	658	326	332
45-49	382	185	197	430	209	221	497	243	255	587	288	300
50-54	316	151	165	364	176	189	412	199	213	478	232	246
55-59	260	124	136	298	142	157	345	165	180	392	188	204
60-64	200	94	106	241	114	128	279	130	148	324	153	171
65-69	162	75	87	181	84	97	219	101	118	255	117	138
70-74	120	54	66	137	62	75	154	70	85	189	85	104
75-79	80	35	45	90	39	51	105	45	59	120	52	68
80-84	37	15	22	49	20	29	58	24	34	69	28	41
85-89	13	5	8	17	7	11	25	9	15	30	12	19
90-94	3	1	2	4	1	3	6	2	4	10	3	6
95-99	0	0	0	1	0	0	1	0	1	2	0	1
100 +	0	0	0	0	0	0	0	0	0	0	0	0

Age group	2025 Both sexes	Males	Females	2030 Both sexes	Males	Females	2035 Both sexes	Males	Females	2040 Both sexes	Males	Females
All ages	13 052	6 527	6 525	13 994	7 001	6 993	14 917	7 465	7 453	15 815	7 914	7 901
0-4	1 426	728	698	1 429	730	699	1 438	735	703	1 448	741	707
5-9	1 404	716	688	1 402	716	686	1 406	718	688	1 417	724	693
10-14	1 341	684	657	1 383	706	678	1 383	706	677	1 388	709	679
15-19	1 256	639	616	1 320	673	647	1 363	695	668	1 364	696	668
20-24	1 135	577	558	1 226	623	603	1 291	657	634	1 335	680	655
25-29	1 057	536	521	1 110	563	547	1 201	610	591	1 266	644	623
30-34	997	504	493	1 036	524	511	1 089	551	538	1 180	598	582
35-39	860	432	428	979	493	486	1 019	514	504	1 072	542	531
40-44	740	369	371	842	422	420	960	483	477	1 001	504	497
45-49	640	315	324	721	358	363	822	411	412	940	471	469
50-54	566	276	290	619	304	315	699	346	353	800	398	402
55-59	456	220	236	543	263	280	595	290	305	674	331	343
60-64	369	175	194	432	206	226	515	247	269	567	273	294
65-69	298	138	160	341	159	182	401	188	213	481	226	255
70-74	222	99	123	262	118	144	302	137	165	358	163	195
75-79	150	65	85	179	77	102	214	93	121	251	109	142
80-84	82	34	48	105	43	62	128	52	76	157	64	93
85-89	38	14	24	47	18	29	62	24	39	79	29	49
90-94	13	4	8	17	6	11	21	7	14	29	10	20
95-99	3	1	2	4	1	3	5	1	4	7	2	5
100 +	0	0	0	1	0	1	1	0	1	1	0	1

Age group	2045 Both sexes	Males	Females	2050 Both sexes	Males	Females
All ages	16 683	8 347	8 336	17 515	8 760	8 755
0-4	1 457	745	712	1 465	750	715
5-9	1 428	730	698	1 439	736	703
10-14	1 399	715	684	1 411	722	690
15-19	1 370	700	670	1 382	706	676
20-24	1 336	681	655	1 343	685	658
25-29	1 311	667	644	1 313	669	644
30-34	1 246	632	614	1 292	656	636
35-39	1 164	588	575	1 231	623	607
40-44	1 055	532	523	1 147	579	568
45-49	981	493	488	1 037	521	516
50-54	917	458	459	959	480	479
55-59	773	382	391	888	440	448
60-64	644	313	332	741	362	379
65-69	531	251	280	606	289	317
70-74	433	198	235	481	221	259
75-79	300	131	169	367	161	206
80-84	187	77	110	229	94	134
85-89	99	37	62	121	46	75
90-94	38	13	26	50	16	33
95-99	10	3	7	14	4	10
100 +	2	0	1	3	1	2

United Nations Department of Economic and Social Affairs/Population Division
World Population Prospects: The 2004 Revision, Volume II: Sex and Age Distribution of the World Population

228

POPULATION BY AGE AND SEX (in thousands)

Age group	2005 Both sexes	Males	Females	2010 Both sexes	Males	Females	2015 Both sexes	Males	Females	2020 Both sexes	Males	Females
All ages	9 182	4 576	4 607	9 046	4 560	4 486	10 616	5 296	5 320	11 186	5 582	5 605
0-4	1 239	632	607	1 158	591	568	1 082	552	530	1 000	511	490
5-9	1 159	591	568	1 209	616	593	1 132	577	555	1 059	540	519
10-14	1 100	560	540	1 136	579	557	1 187	605	582	1 111	566	545
15-19	957	486	471	1 077	548	529	1 114	567	547	1 165	593	572
20-24	822	415	408	926	469	457	1 046	531	515	1 083	551	533
25-29	713	357	357	796	400	395	899	454	445	1 019	516	503
30-34	640	317	323	692	345	347	774	388	386	878	442	436
35-39	531	261	270	623	307	316	675	335	340	757	378	379
40-44	446	218	229	514	252	263	606	298	308	658	326	332
45-49	382	185	197	430	209	221	497	243	255	587	288	300
50-54	316	151	165	364	176	189	412	199	213	478	232	246
55-59	260	124	136	298	142	157	345	165	180	392	188	204
60-64	200	94	106	241	114	128	279	130	148	324	153	171
65-69	162	75	87	181	84	97	219	101	118	255	117	138
70-74	120	54	66	137	62	75	154	70	85	189	85	104
75-79	80	35	45	90	39	51	105	45	59	120	52	68
80-84	37	15	22	49	20	29	58	24	34	69	28	41
85-89	13	5	8	17	7	11	25	9	15	30	12	19
90-94	3	1	2	4	1	3	6	2	4	10	3	6
95-99	0	0	0	1	0	0	1	0	1	2	0	1
100 +	0	0	0	0	0	0	0	0	0	0	0	0

Age group	2025 Both sexes	Males	Females	2030 Both sexes	Males	Females	2035 Both sexes	Males	Females	2040 Both sexes	Males	Females
All ages	11 680	5 827	5 853	12 078	6 023	6 054	12 364	6 162	6 202	12 534	6 240	6 294
0-4	945	483	462	873	446	427	789	403	386	704	360	344
5-9	979	499	479	925	472	453	856	437	419	773	395	378
10-14	1 040	530	510	961	490	471	909	464	445	840	429	411
15-19	1 091	556	536	1 021	520	501	944	481	462	892	455	437
20-24	1 135	577	558	1 063	540	522	994	506	488	918	468	450
25-29	1 057	536	521	1 110	563	547	1 039	527	511	971	494	477
30-34	997	504	493	1 036	524	511	1 089	551	538	1 019	517	503
35-39	860	432	428	979	493	486	1 019	514	504	1 072	542	531
40-44	740	369	371	842	422	420	900	423	477	1 001	504	497
45-49	640	315	324	721	358	363	822	411	412	940	471	469
50-54	566	276	290	619	304	315	699	346	353	800	398	402
55-59	456	220	236	543	263	280	595	290	305	674	331	343
60-64	369	175	194	432	206	226	515	247	269	567	273	294
65-69	298	138	160	341	159	182	401	188	213	481	226	255
70-74	222	99	123	262	118	144	302	137	165	358	163	195
75-79	150	65	85	179	77	102	214	93	121	251	109	142
80-84	92	52	40	105	43	62	120	50	70	157	67	90
85-89	38	14	24	47	18	29	62	24	39	79	29	49
90-94	13	4	8	17	6	11	21	7	14	29	10	20
95-99	3	1	2	4	1	3	5	1	4	7	2	5
100 +	0	0	0	1	0	1	1	0	1	1	0	1

Age group	2045 Both sexes	Males	Females	2050 Both sexes	Males	Females
All ages	12 594	6 261	6 333	12 550	6 227	6 323
0-4	630	322	308	568	291	277
5-9	689	352	337	616	315	301
10-14	758	387	371	675	345	330
15-19	824	421	403	743	380	363
20-24	867	442	425	800	408	392
25-29	896	456	440	846	431	415
30-34	953	484	469	879	447	432
35-39	1 005	508	497	940	476	464
40-44	1 055	532	523	989	499	490
45-49	981	493	488	1 037	521	516
50-54	917	458	459	959	480	479
55-59	773	382	391	888	440	448
60-64	644	313	332	741	362	379
65-69	531	251	280	606	289	317
70-74	433	198	235	481	221	259
75-79	300	131	169	367	161	206
80-84	187	77	110	229	94	134
85-89	99	37	62	121	46	75
90-94	38	13	26	50	16	33
95-99	10	3	7	14	4	10
100 +	2	0	1	3	1	2

United Nations Department of Economic and Social Affairs/Population Division
World Population Prospects: The 2004 Revision, Volume II: Sex and Age Distribution of the World Population

229

POPULATION BY AGE AND SEX (in thousands)

Age group	1950 Both sexes	Males	Females	1955 Both sexes	Males	Females	1960 Both sexes	Males	Females	1965 Both sexes	Males	Females
All ages	2 661	1 285	1 377	2 944	1 430	1 514	3 180	1 552	1 628	3 396	1 669	1 728
0-4	385	195	190	445	227	219	455	232	223	464	241	223
5-9	278	138	140	368	188	180	421	215	206	428	218	210
10-14	344	173	171	270	134	136	352	180	172	400	204	196
15-19	322	160	162	336	168	167	257	127	129	334	171	164
20-24	277	138	140	313	155	158	320	160	160	241	119	122
25-29	189	82	107	268	132	136	297	147	150	303	151	152
30-34	119	50	69	182	78	104	254	125	129	280	138	142
35-39	140	63	77	114	48	66	171	73	98	239	117	122
40-44	151	75	76	133	59	74	106	44	62	160	68	92
45-49	127	64	63	142	70	73	123	54	69	97	40	58
50-54	104	50	54	117	58	59	130	63	67	112	48	64
55-59	65	31	34	93	44	50	103	50	53	116	55	61
60-64	55	24	32	56	26	30	80	36	43	89	42	47
65-69	37	16	21	45	19	26	45	20	25	65	29	36
70-74	34	13	21	27	11	16	33	13	20	33	15	19
75-79	22	8	14	22	8	14	17	7	10	22	9	13
80 +	14	5	9	14	5	9	15	5	10	14	5	9

Age group	1970 Both sexes	Males	Females	1975 Both sexes	Males	Females	1980 Both sexes	Males	Females	1985 Both sexes	Males	Females
All ages	3 564	1 746	1 819	3 747	1 842	1 905	3 914	1 926	1 987	4 122	2 033	2 089
0-4	387	198	189	368	190	178	334	172	162	355	183	172
5-9	423	216	207	376	192	184	350	180	170	331	171	161
10-14	422	215	207	412	210	202	382	195	187	348	179	169
15-19	393	200	193	412	210	202	415	211	203	380	194	186
20-24	305	155	150	383	194	188	406	206	200	411	209	202
25-29	216	105	111	296	150	146	368	187	181	402	204	198
30-34	277	135	142	208	101	107	272	136	136	364	185	179
35-39	268	133	135	268	130	138	215	104	111	269	134	135
40-44	232	113	119	258	127	131	266	129	137	211	101	110
45-49	159	67	92	222	108	114	248	122	126	260	125	135
50-54	97	39	58	150	62	88	205	97	108	239	117	123
55-59	109	47	63	90	35	54	139	56	82	195	91	104
60-64	108	51	57	98	41	57	76	29	46	128	51	78
65-69	76	36	40	92	42	50	93	38	55	67	25	42
70-74	51	22	29	60	27	32	73	33	40	76	30	46
75-79	22	9	13	36	15	21	45	19	26	53	23	30
80 +	19	6	13	19	7	12	26	10	17	35	13	21

Age group	1990 Both sexes	Males	Females	1995 Both sexes	Males	Females	2000 Both sexes	Males	Females	2005 Both sexes	Males	Females
All ages	4 308	2 129	2 179	3 420	1 692	1 728	3 847	1 873	1 974	3 907	1 898	2 009
0-4	349	180	169	209	108	101	225	116	109	186	96	90
5-9	352	181	170	272	140	132	232	118	113	227	117	110
10-14	329	169	159	272	140	132	274	140	134	232	118	113
15-19	345	177	168	251	129	122	273	138	135	274	139	135
20-24	376	192	184	264	136	129	286	145	141	276	140	137
25-29	407	206	200	289	147	142	295	149	146	289	146	143
30-34	397	201	197	314	159	155	292	146	147	294	148	146
35-39	359	182	178	306	154	152	306	152	154	290	144	146
40-44	264	131	133	277	140	137	291	143	147	302	149	153
45-49	206	98	108	198	98	100	277	136	141	287	141	147
50-54	251	119	132	149	70	79	225	108	117	274	133	141
55-59	227	109	118	189	88	100	209	97	112	224	106	118
60-64	180	82	98	164	77	87	247	113	134	204	93	111
65-69	114	43	70	125	55	70	191	86	105	228	101	127
70-74	55	20	35	73	26	47	130	54	76	165	71	94
75-79	56	21	35	29	10	19	60	20	40	100	39	61
80 +	43	17	26	40	15	25	34	11	23	54	17	37

United Nations Department of Economic and Social Affairs/Population Division
World Population Prospects: The 2004 Revision, Volume II: Sex and Age Distribution of the World Population

230

POPULATION BY AGE AND SEX (in thousands)

Age group	2005 Both sexes	2005 Males	2005 Females	2010 Both sexes	2010 Males	2010 Females	2015 Both sexes	2015 Males	2015 Females	2020 Both sexes	2020 Males	2020 Females
All ages	3 907	1 898	2 009	3 935	1 906	2 028	3 893	1 886	2 007	3 827	1 855	1 972
0-4	186	96	90	180	93	87	175	91	85	171	88	83
5-9	227	117	110	189	97	91	180	93	87	175	90	84
10-14	232	118	113	227	117	111	189	97	91	180	93	87
15-19	274	139	135	231	118	114	227	117	111	188	97	91
20-24	276	140	137	277	141	137	231	117	113	227	116	110
25-29	289	146	143	279	141	138	277	140	136	230	117	113
30-34	294	148	146	288	145	143	278	140	138	276	140	136
35-39	290	144	146	292	147	145	287	144	143	277	139	138
40-44	302	149	153	286	141	145	290	145	145	285	143	142
45-49	287	141	147	299	146	152	283	139	144	287	143	144
50-54	274	133	141	285	138	147	293	143	150	278	136	142
55-59	224	106	118	272	131	142	275	132	143	284	137	147
60-64	204	93	111	219	101	118	257	121	136	261	123	138
65-69	228	101	127	190	84	106	200	90	110	236	108	128
70-74	165	71	94	198	84	114	164	69	95	173	75	98
75-79	100	39	61	128	52	76	155	62	94	130	52	78
80-84	39	12	27	67	24	43	87	32	55	107	39	68
85-89	9	3	6	21	6	15	36	11	25	48	15	32
90-94	5	1	3	3	1	2	8	2	6	15	4	11
95-99	1	0	1	1	0	1	1	0	1	2	0	2
100 +	0	0	0	0	0	0	0	0	0	0	0	0

Age group	2025 Both sexes	2025 Males	2025 Females	2030 Both sexes	2030 Males	2030 Females	2035 Both sexes	2035 Males	2035 Females	2040 Both sexes	2040 Males	2040 Females
All ages	3 741	1 815	1 926	3 639	1 767	1 872	3 526	1 713	1 814	3 408	1 657	1 752
0-4	163	85	79	155	80	75	148	77	71	145	75	70
5-9	171	88	82	163	85	79	155	80	75	148	76	71
10-14	175	90	84	171	88	82	163	84	79	155	80	75
15-19	179	93	87	175	90	84	171	88	82	163	84	79
20-24	188	97	91	179	92	87	174	90	84	170	88	82
25-29	226	116	110	188	97	91	179	92	87	174	90	84
30-34	230	117	113	225	115	110	187	96	91	178	92	86
35-39	275	139	136	229	116	113	225	115	110	187	96	91
40-44	275	138	137	273	138	135	228	115	112	224	114	109
45-49	282	141	141	273	137	136	271	137	134	226	114	112
50-54	282	140	142	278	138	139	269	134	135	267	134	133
55-59	269	130	139	274	135	139	270	133	137	261	129	132
60-64	269	127	142	256	122	134	261	126	135	258	125	133
65-69	240	110	130	248	114	134	237	110	127	242	115	128
70-74	205	90	115	210	92	117	218	97	122	210	94	116
75-79	138	56	82	164	68	96	169	70	99	178	74	104
80-84	90	32	58	97	36	61	110	44	73	122	46	76
85-89	60	19	41	51	16	35	56	17	38	69	22	47
90-94	20	5	14	25	6	19	22	5	17	25	6	19
95-99	4	1	3	5	1	4	7	1	6	7	1	5
100 +	0	0	0	1	0	1	1	0	1	1	0	1

Age group	2045 Both sexes	2045 Males	2045 Females	2050 Both sexes	2050 Males	2050 Females
All ages	3 289	1 600	1 689	3 170	1 545	1 626
0-4	145	75	70	145	75	70
5-9	145	75	70	145	75	70
10-14	148	76	71	145	75	70
15-19	154	80	74	148	76	71
20-24	163	84	79	154	80	74
25-29	170	88	82	163	84	79
30-34	174	90	84	170	88	82
35-39	178	92	86	173	89	84
40-44	186	95	90	177	91	86
45-49	222	113	109	184	95	90
50-54	223	112	110	219	111	108
55-59	260	130	131	217	109	109
60-64	250	122	128	250	123	127
65-69	240	114	126	234	112	122
70-74	215	98	117	215	99	116
75-79	173	73	100	179	77	101
80-84	130	49	80	127	49	78
85-89	73	24	50	80	26	54
90-94	31	8	23	35	9	26
95-99	8	1	6	10	2	8
100 +	1	0	1	2	0	1

POPULATION BY AGE AND SEX (in thousands)

Age group	2005 Both sexes	2005 Males	2005 Females	2010 Both sexes	2010 Males	2010 Females	2015 Both sexes	2015 Males	2015 Females	2020 Both sexes	2020 Males	2020 Females
All ages	3 907	1 898	2 009	3 969	1 924	2 045	3 979	1 931	2 048	3 971	1 930	2 042
0-4	186	96	90	214	110	103	227	117	109	230	119	111
5-9	227	117	110	189	97	91	214	110	103	226	117	109
10-14	232	118	113	227	117	111	189	97	91	213	110	103
15-19	274	139	135	231	118	114	227	117	111	188	97	91
20-24	276	140	137	277	141	137	231	117	113	227	116	110
25-29	289	146	143	279	141	138	277	140	136	230	117	113
30-34	294	148	146	288	145	143	278	140	138	276	140	136
35-39	290	144	146	292	147	145	287	144	143	277	139	138
40-44	302	149	153	286	141	145	290	145	145	285	143	142
45-49	287	141	147	299	146	152	283	139	144	287	143	144
50-54	274	133	141	285	138	147	293	143	150	278	136	142
55-59	224	106	118	272	131	142	275	132	143	284	137	147
60-64	204	93	111	219	101	118	257	121	136	261	123	138
65-69	228	101	127	190	84	106	200	90	110	236	108	128
70-74	165	71	94	198	84	114	164	69	95	173	75	98
75-79	100	39	61	128	52	76	155	62	94	130	52	78
80-84	39	12	27	67	24	43	87	32	55	107	39	68
85-89	9	3	6	21	6	15	36	11	25	48	15	32
90-94	5	1	3	3	1	2	8	2	6	15	4	11
95-99	1	0	1	1	0	1	1	0	1	2	0	2
100 +	0	0	0	0	0	0	0	0	0	0	0	0

Age group	2025 Both sexes	2025 Males	2025 Females	2030 Both sexes	2030 Males	2030 Females	2035 Both sexes	2035 Males	2035 Females	2040 Both sexes	2040 Males	2040 Females
All ages	3 939	1 917	2 022	3 892	1 897	1 994	3 844	1 877	1 967	3 808	1 864	1 945
0-4	217	112	105	209	108	101	214	111	103	227	118	110
5-9	230	119	111	217	112	105	209	108	101	214	111	103
10-14	226	117	109	229	119	111	217	112	105	209	108	101
15-19	213	110	103	226	117	109	229	119	111	217	112	105
20-24	188	97	91	213	110	103	226	117	109	229	118	111
25-29	226	116	110	188	97	91	212	110	103	225	116	109
30-34	230	117	113	225	115	110	187	96	91	212	109	103
35-39	275	139	136	229	116	113	225	115	110	187	96	91
40-44	275	138	137	273	138	135	228	115	112	224	114	109
45-49	282	141	141	273	137	136	271	137	134	226	114	112
50-54	282	140	142	278	138	139	269	134	135	267	134	133
55-59	269	130	139	274	135	139	270	133	137	261	129	132
60-64	269	127	142	256	122	134	261	126	135	258	125	133
65-69	240	110	130	248	114	134	237	110	127	242	115	128
70-74	205	90	115	210	92	117	218	97	122	210	94	116
75-79	138	56	82	164	68	96	169	70	99	178	74	104
80-84	90	32	58	97	36	61	116	44	73	122	46	76
85-89	60	19	41	51	16	35	56	17	38	69	22	47
90-94	20	5	14	25	6	19	22	5	17	25	6	19
95-99	4	1	3	5	1	4	7	1	6	7	1	5
100 +	0	0	0	1	0	1	1	0	1	1	0	1

Age group	2045 Both sexes	2045 Males	2045 Females	2050 Both sexes	2050 Males	2050 Females
All ages	3 783	1 856	1 928	3 764	1 852	1 912
0-4	240	124	116	244	127	118
5-9	227	118	110	240	124	116
10-14	213	111	103	227	118	110
15-19	209	108	101	213	110	103
20-24	216	112	104	209	108	101
25-29	229	118	110	216	112	104
30-34	225	116	109	228	118	110
35-39	211	109	102	224	116	109
40-44	186	95	90	210	108	102
45-49	222	113	109	184	95	90
50-54	223	112	110	219	111	108
55-59	260	130	131	217	109	109
60-64	250	122	128	250	123	127
65-69	240	114	126	234	112	122
70-74	215	98	117	215	99	116
75-79	173	73	100	179	77	101
80-84	130	49	80	127	49	78
85-89	73	24	50	80	26	54
90-94	31	8	23	35	9	26
95-99	8	1	6	10	2	8
100 +	1	0	1	2	0	1

United Nations Department of Economic and Social Affairs/Population Division
World Population Prospects: The 2004 Revision, Volume II: Sex and Age Distribution of the World Population

232

POPULATION BY AGE AND SEX (in thousands)

Age group	2005 Both sexes	Males	Females	2010 Both sexes	Males	Females	2015 Both sexes	Males	Females	2020 Both sexes	Males	Females
All ages	3 907	1 898	2 009	3 901	1 889	2 012	3 807	1 842	1 965	3 681	1 780	1 902
0-4	186	96	90	146	75	70	123	64	59	111	57	54
5-9	227	117	110	189	97	91	146	75	70	123	64	59
10-14	232	118	113	227	117	111	189	97	91	145	75	70
15-19	274	139	135	231	118	114	227	117	111	188	97	91
20-24	276	140	137	277	141	137	231	117	113	227	116	110
25-29	289	146	143	279	141	138	277	140	136	230	117	113
30-34	294	148	146	288	145	143	278	140	138	276	140	136
35-39	290	144	146	292	147	145	287	144	143	277	139	138
40-44	302	149	153	286	141	145	290	145	145	285	143	142
45-49	287	141	147	299	146	152	283	139	144	287	143	144
50-54	274	133	141	285	138	147	293	143	150	278	136	142
55-59	224	106	118	272	131	142	275	132	143	284	137	147
60-64	204	93	111	219	101	118	257	121	136	261	123	138
65-69	228	101	127	190	84	106	200	90	110	236	108	128
70-74	165	71	94	198	84	114	164	69	95	173	75	98
75-79	100	39	61	128	52	76	155	62	94	130	52	78
80-84	39	12	27	67	24	43	87	32	55	107	39	68
85-89	9	3	6	21	6	15	36	11	25	48	15	32
90-94	5	1	3	3	1	2	8	2	6	15	4	11
95-99	1	0	1	1	0	1	1	0	1	2	0	2
100 +	0	0	0	0	0	0	0	0	0	0	0	0

Age group	2025 Both sexes	Males	Females	2030 Both sexes	Males	Females	2035 Both sexes	Males	Females	2040 Both sexes	Males	Females
All ages	3 541	1 711	1 830	3 388	1 637	1 751	3 222	1 555	1 667	3 044	1 468	1 576
0-4	109	56	53	103	54	50	94	49	46	84	44	41
5-9	111	57	54	109	56	53	103	53	50	94	49	46
10-14	123	64	59	111	57	54	109	56	53	103	53	50
15-19	145	75	70	123	63	59	111	57	53	109	56	53
20-24	188	97	91	145	75	70	123	63	59	111	57	53
25-29	226	116	110	188	97	91	145	75	70	122	63	59
30-34	230	117	113	225	115	110	187	96	91	144	74	70
35-39	275	139	136	229	116	113	225	115	110	187	96	91
40-44	275	138	137	273	138	135	228	115	112	224	114	109
45-49	282	141	141	273	137	136	271	137	134	226	114	112
50-54	282	140	142	278	138	139	269	134	135	267	134	133
55-59	269	130	139	274	135	139	270	133	137	261	129	132
60-64	269	127	142	256	122	134	261	126	135	258	125	133
65-69	240	110	130	248	114	134	237	110	127	242	115	128
70-74	205	90	115	210	92	117	218	97	122	210	94	116
75-79	138	56	82	164	68	96	169	70	99	178	74	104
80-84	90	32	58	97	36	61	116	44	73	122	46	76
85-89	60	19	41	51	16	35	56	17	38	69	22	47
90-94	20	5	14	25	6	19	22	5	17	25	6	19
95-99	4	1	3	5	1	4	7	1	6	7	1	5
100 +	0	0	0	1	0	1	1	0	1	1	0	1

Age group	2045 Both sexes	Males	Females	2050 Both sexes	Males	Females
All ages	2 856	1 376	1 480	2 665	1 284	1 381
0-4	76	39	37	72	37	35
5-9	84	44	41	76	39	37
10-14	94	49	46	84	44	41
15-19	103	53	50	94	49	46
20-24	109	56	52	103	53	50
25-29	110	57	53	108	56	52
30-34	122	63	59	110	57	53
35-39	144	74	70	122	63	59
40-44	186	95	90	143	74	70
45-49	222	113	109	184	95	90
50-54	223	112	110	219	111	108
55-59	260	130	131	217	109	109
60-64	250	122	128	250	123	127
65-69	240	114	126	234	112	122
70-74	215	98	117	215	99	116
75-79	173	73	100	179	77	101
80-84	130	49	80	127	49	78
85-89	73	24	50	80	26	54
90-94	31	8	23	35	9	26
95-99	8	1	6	10	2	8
100 +	1	0	1	2	0	1

United Nations Department of Economic and Social Affairs/Population Division
World Population Prospects: The 2004 Revision, Volume II: Sex and Age Distribution of the World Population

233

POPULATION BY AGE AND SEX (in thousands)

Age group	1950			1955			1960			1965		
	Both sexes	Males	Females	Both sexes	Males	Females	Both sexes	Males	Females	Both sexes	Males	Females
All ages	449	214	235	511	245	266	572	274	298	650	312	338
0-4	78	39	39	97	48	48	111	56	56	126	63	63
5-9	63	32	32	73	37	36	91	45	46	106	53	53
10-14	58	29	29	62	31	31	71	36	35	89	44	45
15-19	48	23	25	56	28	29	59	29	30	68	34	34
20-24	38	18	20	45	21	23	50	24	26	54	26	28
25-29	35	17	18	35	16	19	38	17	21	44	20	24
30-34	25	12	13	32	15	17	29	13	16	33	14	19
35-39	19	9	10	23	11	12	28	12	15	26	11	15
40-44	15	7	8	17	8	9	20	9	11	25	11	14
45-49	15	7	8	14	6	7	15	7	8	18	8	10
50-54	12	5	7	14	6	8	13	6	7	14	6	8
55-59	12	5	7	11	5	6	13	6	7	12	6	6
60-64	11	4	7	11	4	6	10	4	5	12	6	6
65-69	9	3	6	9	3	6	9	4	5	8	4	5
70-74	6	2	4	7	2	4	7	3	5	7	3	4
75-79	3	1	2	4	1	3	4	2	3	5	2	3
80 +	2	1	1	2	1	1	2	1	2	3	1	2

Age group	1970			1975			1980			1985		
	Both sexes	Males	Females	Both sexes	Males	Females	Both sexes	Males	Females	Both sexes	Males	Females
All ages	750	361	389	885	428	456	1 049	510	539	1 236	604	632
0-4	145	73	72	174	87	86	202	102	100	224	113	111
5-9	121	60	60	140	70	70	169	85	84	198	100	98
10-14	104	52	52	119	60	60	138	69	69	168	84	84
15-19	86	43	44	102	51	51	117	58	59	137	68	68
20-24	64	31	32	83	41	42	98	49	50	114	57	57
25-29	48	23	26	60	29	31	79	39	41	95	47	48
30-34	40	18	22	45	21	24	57	27	30	76	37	39
35-39	30	13	17	37	17	21	43	20	23	55	26	29
40-44	24	10	14	28	12	17	36	16	20	41	19	23
45-49	23	10	13	22	9	13	27	11	16	34	15	19
50-54	17	7	10	22	9	13	21	8	13	25	10	15
55-59	13	6	7	16	7	9	20	9	12	20	8	12
60-64	11	5	5	12	5	6	14	6	8	19	8	11
65-69	10	5	5	9	4	5	10	5	6	13	5	7
70-74	7	3	4	8	4	4	7	3	4	8	4	5
75-79	5	2	3	5	2	3	5	2	3	5	2	3
80 +	3	1	2	4	1	2	4	1	2	4	2	3

Age group	1990			1995			2000			2005		
	Both sexes	Males	Females	Both sexes	Males	Females	Both sexes	Males	Females	Both sexes	Males	Females
All ages	1 429	700	729	1 616	793	823	1 754	859	895	1 765	867	898
0-4	230	116	114	231	116	114	233	118	115	218	110	108
5-9	220	111	109	227	115	113	227	114	112	222	112	110
10-14	197	99	98	219	110	109	226	114	112	224	113	111
15-19	166	83	83	195	98	97	217	109	108	225	113	112
20-24	133	66	67	162	81	81	185	93	93	206	104	103
25-29	110	54	56	129	63	65	146	72	74	148	75	73
30-34	92	45	47	107	52	55	114	55	59	104	52	52
35-39	74	35	38	89	43	46	96	46	50	83	40	43
40-44	53	25	28	72	34	37	82	39	43	75	35	40
45-49	40	18	22	51	24	27	67	31	36	68	31	36
50-54	33	14	19	38	17	21	48	22	26	58	26	32
55-59	24	10	14	31	13	18	36	16	20	43	19	24
60-64	18	7	11	22	9	13	29	12	17	32	14	18
65-69	17	7	10	16	6	10	20	8	12	25	10	15
70-74	10	4	6	14	5	8	13	5	8	16	6	10
75-79	6	2	3	7	3	4	10	4	6	10	4	6
80 +	4	2	3	5	2	3	6	2	4	8	3	5

234

United Nations Department of Economic and Social Affairs/Population Division
World Population Prospects: The 2004 Revision, Volume II: Sex and Age Distribution of the World Population

POPULATION BY AGE AND SEX (in thousands)

Age group	2005 Both sexes	Males	Females	2010 Both sexes	Males	Females	2015 Both sexes	Males	Females	2020 Both sexes	Males	Females
All ages	1 765	867	808	1 720	861	859	1 690	854	836	1 671	856	815
0-4	218	110	108	204	103	101	199	101	99	193	98	96
5-9	222	112	110	204	103	101	195	98	97	195	98	97
10-14	224	113	111	213	107	106	192	97	95	187	94	93
15-19	225	113	112	222	112	111	210	106	104	189	95	94
20-24	206	104	103	217	109	108	215	108	107	204	103	102
25-29	148	75	73	175	90	85	189	98	92	192	99	93
30-34	104	52	52	102	55	47	129	72	58	146	81	66
35-39	83	40	43	67	36	32	65	39	26	90	55	36
40-44	75	35	40	57	28	29	43	24	18	44	28	15
45-49	68	31	36	56	26	30	39	20	19	30	18	12
50-54	58	26	32	55	25	30	43	20	23	30	16	14
55-59	43	19	24	50	22	28	46	21	25	36	17	19
60-64	32	14	18	38	16	21	43	19	24	40	17	22
65-69	25	10	15	28	12	16	33	14	19	37	16	22
70-74	16	6	10	20	8	12	23	9	14	27	11	16
75-79	10	4	6	12	4	8	15	6	9	17	7	11
80-84	6	2	4	6	2	4	7	2	5	9	3	6
85-89	2	1	1	2	1	2	3	1	2	3	1	2
90-94	0	0	0	0	0	0	1	0	0	1	0	1
95-99	0	0	0	0	0	0	0	0	0	0	0	0
100 +	0	0	0	0	0	0	0	0	0	0	0	0

Age group	2025 Both sexes	Males	Females	2030 Both sexes	Males	Females	2035 Both sexes	Males	Females	2040 Both sexes	Males	Females
All ages	1 655	858	797	1 642	858	784	1 633	858	776	1 631	859	772
0-4	184	93	91	174	88	86	166	84	82	162	82	80
5-9	191	97	95	183	92	91	173	87	86	166	84	82
10-14	192	97	95	190	96	94	182	92	90	172	87	85
15-19	185	93	92	190	96	95	189	95	94	181	91	90
20-24	185	93	92	181	91	90	186	94	93	185	93	92
25-29	184	94	90	168	85	83	166	84	82	172	87	85
30-34	152	83	69	150	80	70	139	73	66	140	73	67
35-39	106	63	43	114	67	48	116	65	51	110	60	50
40-44	64	42	22	78	50	28	88	53	34	91	53	38
45-49	32	22	10	49	33	16	61	40	21	71	44	27
50-54	23	14	9	25	18	8	40	28	12	52	34	17
55-59	25	13	12	19	12	7	22	15	6	35	24	11
60-64	31	14	17	22	12	10	17	11	7	19	13	6
65-69	34	15	20	27	12	15	19	10	9	15	9	6
70-74	31	12	18	29	12	17	23	10	13	17	8	8
75-79	20	8	12	24	9	15	22	9	14	18	7	10
80-84	11	4	7	13	5	8	15	5	10	15	5	9
85-89	4	1	3	5	2	3	6	2	4	8	2	5
90-94	1	0	1	1	0	1	2	0	1	2	1	2
95-99	0	0	0	0	0	0	0	0	0	0	0	0
100 +	0	0	0	0	0	0	0	0	0	0	0	0

Age group	2045 Both sexes	Males	Females	2050 Both sexes	Males	Females
All ages	1 639	864	775	1 658	873	785
0-4	158	80	78	153	77	75
5-9	162	82	80	158	80	78
10-14	166	84	82	161	82	80
15-19	172	87	85	165	83	82
20-24	178	89	89	169	85	84
25-29	173	87	86	169	85	84
30-34	149	77	72	154	79	75
35-39	114	61	53	126	66	59
40-44	89	50	39	95	52	43
45-49	76	44	31	75	43	33
50-54	61	38	23	66	39	27
55-59	46	30	15	54	34	20
60-64	31	21	10	41	27	14
65-69	17	12	5	28	19	9
70-74	13	8	5	15	10	5
75-79	13	6	7	10	6	4
80-84	12	4	7	9	4	5
85-89	8	2	5	6	2	4
90-94	3	1	2	3	1	2
95-99	0	0	0	1	0	1
100 +	0	0	0	0	0	0

United Nations Department of Economic and Social Affairs/Population Division
World Population Prospects: The 2004 Revision, Volume II: Sex and Age Distribution of the World Population

235

POPULATION BY AGE AND SEX (in thousands)

Age group	2005 Both sexes	2005 Males	2005 Females	2010 Both sexes	2010 Males	2010 Females	2015 Both sexes	2015 Males	2015 Females	2020 Both sexes	2020 Males	2020 Females
All ages	1 765	867	898	1 747	870	877	1 737	878	859	1 755	898	857
0-4	218	110	108	222	112	110	229	115	113	232	117	115
5-9	222	112	110	204	103	101	212	107	105	224	113	111
10-14	224	113	111	213	107	106	192	97	95	203	102	101
15-19	225	113	112	222	112	111	210	106	104	189	95	94
20-24	206	104	103	217	109	108	215	108	107	204	103	102
25-29	148	75	73	175	90	85	189	98	92	192	99	93
30-34	104	52	52	102	55	47	129	72	58	146	81	66
35-39	83	40	43	67	36	32	65	39	26	90	55	36
40-44	75	35	40	57	28	29	43	24	18	44	28	15
45-49	68	31	36	56	26	30	39	20	19	30	18	12
50-54	58	26	32	55	25	30	43	20	23	30	16	14
55-59	43	19	24	50	22	28	46	21	25	36	17	19
60-64	32	14	18	38	16	21	43	19	24	40	17	22
65-69	25	10	15	28	12	16	33	14	19	37	16	22
70-74	16	6	10	20	8	12	23	9	14	27	11	16
75-79	10	4	6	12	4	8	15	6	9	17	7	11
80-84	6	2	4	6	2	4	7	2	5	9	3	6
85-89	2	1	1	2	1	2	3	1	2	3	1	2
90-94	0	0	0	0	0	0	1	0	0	1	0	1
95-99	0	0	0	0	0	0	0	0	0	0	0	0
100 +	0	0	0	0	0	0	0	0	0	0	0	0

Age group	2025 Both sexes	2025 Males	2025 Females	2030 Both sexes	2030 Males	2030 Females	2035 Both sexes	2035 Males	2035 Females	2040 Both sexes	2040 Males	2040 Females
All ages	1 777	920	858	1 809	942	866	1 851	968	883	1 910	1 000	910
0-4	224	113	111	218	110	108	220	111	109	227	115	112
5-9	229	116	114	223	112	110	217	110	108	220	111	109
10-14	220	111	109	228	115	113	222	112	110	217	110	107
15-19	201	101	100	219	110	109	227	114	112	221	111	110
20-24	185	93	92	196	99	98	214	108	107	222	112	111
25-29	184	94	90	168	85	83	180	91	89	198	100	98
30-34	152	83	69	150	80	70	139	73	66	152	79	73
35-39	106	63	43	114	67	48	116	65	51	110	60	50
40-44	64	42	22	78	50	28	88	53	34	91	53	38
45-49	32	22	10	49	33	16	61	40	21	71	44	27
50-54	23	14	9	25	18	8	40	28	12	52	34	17
55-59	25	13	12	19	12	7	22	15	6	35	24	11
60-64	31	14	17	22	12	10	17	11	7	19	13	6
65-69	34	15	20	27	12	15	19	10	9	15	9	6
70-74	31	12	18	29	12	17	23	10	13	17	8	8
75-79	20	8	12	24	9	15	22	9	14	18	7	10
80-84	11	4	7	13	5	8	15	5	10	15	5	9
85-89	4	1	3	5	2	3	6	2	4	8	2	5
90-94	1	0	1	1	0	1	2	0	1	2	1	2
95-99	0	0	0	0	0	0	0	0	0	0	0	0
100 +	0	0	0	0	0	0	0	0	0	0	0	0

Age group	2045 Both sexes	2045 Males	2045 Females	2050 Both sexes	2050 Males	2050 Females
All ages	1 983	1 039	945	2 073	1 084	989
0-4	233	118	115	234	119	115
5-9	227	115	112	232	118	115
10-14	219	111	108	226	115	112
15-19	216	109	107	218	110	108
20-24	217	109	108	213	107	106
25-29	208	105	103	206	104	102
30-34	172	88	83	185	95	90
35-39	124	66	58	145	76	69
40-44	89	50	39	104	56	47
45-49	76	44	31	75	43	33
50-54	61	38	23	66	39	27
55-59	46	30	15	54	34	20
60-64	31	21	10	41	27	14
65-69	17	12	5	28	19	9
70-74	13	8	5	15	10	5
75-79	13	6	7	10	6	4
80-84	12	4	7	9	4	5
85-89	8	2	5	6	2	4
90-94	3	1	2	3	1	2
95-99	0	0	0	1	0	1
100 +	0	0	0	0	0	0

United Nations Department of Economic and Social Affairs/Population Division
World Population Prospects: The 2004 Revision, Volume II: Sex and Age Distribution of the World Population

POPULATION BY AGE AND SEX (in thousands)

Age group	2005 Both sexes	Males	Females	2010 Both sexes	Males	Females	2015 Both sexes	Males	Females	2020 Both sexes	Males	Females
All ages	1 765	867	898	1 712	852	860	1 644	831	813	1 588	811	774
0-4	218	110	108	187	94	92	170	86	84	155	78	77
5-9	222	112	110	204	103	101	178	90	88	166	84	82
10-14	224	113	111	213	107	106	192	97	95	171	86	85
15-19	225	113	112	222	112	111	210	106	104	189	95	94
20-24	206	104	103	217	109	108	215	108	107	204	103	102
25-29	148	75	73	175	90	85	189	98	92	192	99	93
30-34	104	52	52	102	55	47	129	72	58	146	81	66
35-39	83	40	43	67	36	32	65	39	26	90	55	36
40-44	75	35	40	57	28	29	43	24	18	44	28	15
45-49	68	31	36	56	26	30	39	20	19	30	18	12
50-54	58	26	32	55	25	30	43	20	23	30	16	14
55-59	43	19	24	50	22	28	46	21	25	36	17	19
60-64	32	14	18	38	16	21	43	19	24	40	17	22
65-69	25	10	15	28	12	16	33	14	19	37	16	22
70-74	16	6	10	20	8	12	23	9	14	27	11	16
75-79	10	4	6	12	4	8	15	6	9	17	7	11
80-84	6	2	4	6	2	4	7	2	5	9	3	6
85-89	2	1	1	2	1	2	3	1	2	3	1	2
90-94	0	0	0	0	0	0	1	0	0	1	0	1
95-99	0	0	0	0	0	0	0	0	0	0	0	0
100 +	0	0	0	0	0	0	0	0	0	0	0	0

Age group	2025 Both sexes	Males	Females	2030 Both sexes	Males	Females	2035 Both sexes	Males	Females	2040 Both sexes	Males	Females
All ages	1 533	796	737	1 479	776	703	1 424	752	672	1 371	727	644
0-4	145	73	72	131	66	65	118	60	58	107	54	53
5-9	153	77	76	144	72	71	131	66	65	118	60	58
10-14	163	82	81	152	77	75	143	72	71	130	66	64
15-19	169	85	84	162	82	80	151	76	75	142	72	71
20-24	185	90	92	185	83	82	158	79	79	148	74	74
25-29	184	94	90	168	85	83	151	76	75	146	74	73
30-34	152	83	69	150	80	70	139	73	66	128	66	61
35-39	106	63	43	114	67	48	116	65	51	110	60	50
40-44	64	42	22	78	50	28	88	50	38	91	53	38
45-49	32	22	10	49	33	16	61	40	21	71	44	27
50-54	23	14	9	25	18	8	40	28	12	52	34	17
55-59	25	13	12	19	12	7	22	15	6	35	24	11
60-64	31	14	17	22	12	10	17	11	7	19	13	6
65-69	34	15	20	27	12	15	19	10	9	15	9	6
70-74	31	12	18	29	12	17	23	10	13	17	8	8
75-79	20	8	12	24	9	15	22	9	14	18	7	10
80-84	11	4	7	13	5	8	16	5	10	15	5	9
85-89	4	1	3	5	2	3	6	2	4	8	2	5
90-94	1	0	1	1	0	1	2	0	1	2	1	2
95-99	0	0	0	0	0	0	0	0	0	0	0	0
100 +	0	0	0	0	0	0	0	0	0	0	0	0

Age group	2045 Both sexes	Males	Females	2050 Both sexes	Males	Females
All ages	1 327	705	622	1 293	687	606
0-4	98	50	48	89	45	44
5-9	107	54	53	97	49	48
10-14	118	59	58	107	54	53
15-19	130	65	64	117	59	58
20-24	139	70	69	127	64	63
25-29	138	70	69	132	66	66
30-34	126	65	61	123	63	60
35-39	104	55	48	106	56	50
40-44	89	50	39	87	47	39
45-49	76	44	31	75	43	33
50-54	61	38	23	66	39	27
55-59	46	30	15	54	34	20
60-64	31	21	10	41	27	14
65-69	17	12	5	28	19	9
70-74	13	8	5	15	10	5
75-79	13	6	7	10	6	4
80-84	12	4	7	9	4	5
85-89	8	2	5	6	2	4
90-94	3	1	2	3	1	2
95-99	0	0	0	1	0	1
100 +	0	0	0	0	0	0

POPULATION BY AGE AND SEX (in thousands)

Age group	1950 Both sexes	1950 Males	1950 Females	1955 Both sexes	1955 Males	1955 Females	1960 Both sexes	1960 Males	1960 Females	1965 Both sexes	1965 Males	1965 Females
All ages	53 975	26 776	27 199	62 886	31 319	31 567	72 742	36 261	36 481	84 328	42 077	42 251
0-4	8 984	4 533	4 451	10 867	5 486	5 381	12 543	6 331	6 212	14 436	7 295	7 142
5-9	7 013	3 523	3 490	8 613	4 331	4 283	10 422	5 240	5 182	12 089	6 079	6 010
10-14	6 436	3 230	3 205	6 966	3 499	3 467	8 513	4 276	4 238	10 315	5 181	5 134
15-19	5 405	2 711	2 694	6 400	3 213	3 187	6 890	3 457	3 433	8 431	4 231	4 201
20-24	5 016	2 515	2 501	5 353	2 686	2 667	6 296	3 156	3 140	6 792	3 403	3 388
25-29	4 127	2 068	2 059	4 945	2 481	2 464	5 236	2 622	2 614	6 174	3 089	3 085
30-34	3 445	1 718	1 726	4 059	2 037	2 022	4 810	2 407	2 403	5 109	2 553	2 557
35-39	3 071	1 525	1 546	3 381	1 690	1 690	3 926	1 965	1 961	4 670	2 331	2 339
40-44	2 592	1 277	1 315	2 989	1 487	1 502	3 246	1 618	1 628	3 787	1 889	1 898
45-49	2 082	1 010	1 072	2 491	1 228	1 263	2 842	1 408	1 434	3 103	1 540	1 563
50-54	1 816	856	960	1 971	956	1 016	2 335	1 145	1 190	2 683	1 323	1 360
55-59	1 362	633	729	1 682	791	890	1 811	873	939	2 164	1 055	1 109
60-64	1 022	461	560	1 224	567	657	1 502	701	801	1 635	782	854
65-69	723	330	393	873	392	481	1 045	479	566	1 299	601	699
70-74	463	206	256	566	256	311	693	307	386	845	383	463
75-79	267	116	151	319	141	179	401	178	223	502	219	283
80 +	153	63	89	187	79	108	230	98	132	294	126	168

Age group	1970 Both sexes	1970 Males	1970 Females	1975 Both sexes	1975 Males	1975 Females	1980 Both sexes	1980 Males	1980 Females	1985 Both sexes	1985 Males	1985 Females
All ages	95 989	47 920	48 069	108 124	53 960	54 164	121 615	60 675	60 940	136 063	67 760	68 303
0-4	14 732	7 446	7 286	15 425	7 768	7 656	17 037	8 586	8 450	18 491	9 405	9 087
5-9	13 965	7 031	6 934	14 311	7 198	7 113	15 065	7 552	7 512	16 816	8 468	8 348
10-14	11 977	6 017	5 960	13 852	6 965	6 887	14 216	7 141	7 074	15 008	7 520	7 488
15-19	10 226	5 131	5 094	11 886	5 964	5 922	13 763	6 913	6 850	14 137	7 091	7 046
20-24	8 323	4 170	4 152	10 109	5 064	5 045	11 771	5 897	5 874	13 635	6 826	6 809
25-29	6 673	3 338	3 335	8 194	4 097	4 097	9 974	4 986	4 988	11 625	5 797	5 828
30-34	6 040	3 015	3 025	6 543	3 264	3 279	8 053	4 016	4 037	9 821	4 884	4 938
35-39	4 975	2 479	2 496	5 896	2 935	2 961	6 402	3 185	3 217	7 893	3 913	3 980
40-44	4 521	2 249	2 272	4 830	2 399	2 431	5 736	2 846	2 889	6 235	3 079	3 156
45-49	3 636	1 807	1 829	4 355	2 159	2 196	4 661	2 307	2 354	5 533	2 719	2 814
50-54	2 946	1 455	1 491	3 464	1 715	1 750	4 155	2 051	2 104	4 438	2 168	2 270
55-59	2 504	1 227	1 277	2 762	1 358	1 404	3 252	1 601	1 651	3 882	1 883	1 999
60-64	1 971	954	1 018	2 294	1 118	1 176	2 533	1 237	1 296	2 952	1 420	1 532
65-69	1 431	677	754	1 737	834	903	2 027	979	1 047	2 205	1 046	1 158
70-74	1 065	485	580	1 183	554	629	1 447	687	759	1 630	759	871
75-79	625	278	347	797	359	438	895	414	481	1 023	463	559
80 +	379	161	218	487	210	277	629	274	356	739	319	420

Age group	1990 Both sexes	1990 Males	1990 Females	1995 Both sexes	1995 Males	1995 Females	2000 Both sexes	2000 Males	2000 Females	2005 Both sexes	2005 Males	2005 Females
All ages	149 394	74 223	75 172	161 376	79 948	81 428	173 858	85 891	87 966	186 405	91 870	94 535
0-4	17 678	8 992	8 686	16 733	8 516	8 217	17 412	8 872	8 540	18 024	9 193	8 831
5-9	18 290	9 292	8 998	17 519	8 901	8 618	16 618	8 450	8 168	17 319	8 819	8 500
10-14	16 762	8 436	8 325	18 239	9 262	8 977	17 476	8 875	8 601	16 580	8 428	8 152
15-19	14 920	7 462	7 458	16 659	8 368	8 291	18 139	9 192	8 947	17 385	8 812	8 573
20-24	13 986	6 986	7 000	14 742	7 336	7 405	16 482	8 238	8 244	17 957	9 057	8 900
25-29	13 448	6 692	6 756	13 774	6 831	6 943	14 531	7 180	7 351	16 256	8 071	8 185
30-34	11 436	5 663	5 772	13 212	6 520	6 692	13 540	6 659	6 881	14 286	7 004	7 282
35-39	9 626	4 750	4 876	11 204	5 499	5 705	12 955	6 336	6 619	13 279	6 475	6 803
40-44	7 694	3 782	3 912	9 388	4 588	4 799	10 940	5 318	5 622	12 658	6 133	6 525
45-49	6 027	2 946	3 081	7 450	3 622	3 828	9 105	4 402	4 703	10 623	5 110	5 513
50-54	5 283	2 562	2 721	5 769	2 783	2 986	7 153	3 434	3 719	8 762	4 185	4 577
55-59	4 163	1 998	2 165	4 974	2 371	2 603	5 454	2 589	2 865	6 787	3 210	3 577
60-64	3 549	1 684	1 865	3 829	1 799	2 030	4 598	2 148	2 450	5 066	2 359	2 706
65-69	2 601	1 218	1 383	3 157	1 459	1 698	3 428	1 571	1 857	4 142	1 889	2 254
70-74	1 817	833	984	2 187	991	1 195	2 685	1 202	1 484	2 945	1 306	1 639
75-79	1 207	538	669	1 396	615	781	1 719	748	970	2 145	921	1 224
80 +	907	388	519	1 145	486	659	1 624	677	947	2 190	897	1 293

United Nations Department of Economic and Social Affairs/Population Division
World Population Prospects: The 2004 Revision, Volume II: Sex and Age Distribution of the World Population

238

POPULATION BY AGE AND SEX (in thousands)

Age group	2005 Both sexes	2005 Males	2005 Females	2010 Both sexes	2010 Males	2010 Females	2015 Both sexes	2015 Males	2015 Females	2020 Both sexes	2020 Males	2020 Females
All ages	106 405	91 070	94 535	198 497	97 669	100 827	209 401	102 873	106 528	219 193	107 539	111 654
0-4	18 024	9 193	8 831	17 986	9 177	8 809	17 421	8 892	8 530	16 883	8 619	8 263
5-9	17 319	8 819	8 500	17 941	9 145	8 796	17 911	9 134	8 777	17 356	8 854	8 502
10-14	16 580	8 428	8 152	17 284	8 799	8 485	17 907	9 126	8 782	17 880	9 116	8 764
15-19	17 385	8 812	8 573	16 501	8 373	8 128	17 209	8 747	8 462	17 836	9 077	8 759
20-24	17 957	9 057	8 900	17 226	8 695	8 531	16 361	8 272	8 090	17 076	8 651	8 425
25-29	16 256	8 071	8 185	17 745	8 901	8 844	17 039	8 558	8 481	16 200	8 154	8 046
30-34	14 286	7 004	7 282	16 026	7 907	8 118	17 507	8 733	8 774	16 836	8 415	8 422
35-39	13 279	6 475	6 803	14 051	6 841	7 209	15 767	7 732	8 036	17 254	8 561	8 694
40-44	12 658	6 133	6 525	13 011	6 297	6 715	13 775	6 659	7 116	15 485	7 545	7 939
45-49	10 623	5 110	5 513	12 330	5 921	6 409	12 688	6 088	6 600	13 458	6 456	7 002
50-54	8 762	4 185	4 577	10 261	4 883	5 377	11 931	5 671	6 260	12 306	5 849	6 457
55-59	6 787	3 210	3 577	8 352	3 935	4 416	9 809	4 607	5 202	11 441	5 371	6 070
60-64	5 066	2 359	2 706	6 342	2 947	3 395	7 838	3 630	4 207	9 246	4 273	4 973
65-69	4 142	1 889	2 254	4 599	2 093	2 505	5 794	2 633	3 162	7 203	3 265	3 938
70-74	2 945	1 306	1 639	3 596	1 590	2 007	4 029	1 778	2 250	5 119	2 257	2 862
75-79	2 145	921	1 224	2 390	1 018	1 372	2 955	1 253	1 702	3 349	1 419	1 930
80-84	1 245	518	727	1 582	649	934	1 790	726	1 064	2 245	905	1 340
85-89	625	252	373	807	319	488	1 042	404	638	1 196	457	739
90-94	240	95	145	340	130	210	444	165	278	579	209	370
95-99	66	26	40	104	39	64	147	53	94	192	67	125
100 +	14	6	8	25	10	15	38	14	23	52	19	34

Age group	2025 Both sexes	2025 Males	2025 Females	2030 Both sexes	2030 Males	2030 Females	2035 Both sexes	2035 Males	2035 Females	2040 Both sexes	2040 Males	2040 Females
All ages	227 930	111 678	116 252	235 505	115 231	120 274	241 726	118 106	123 620	246 766	120 404	126 362
0-4	16 489	8 420	8 068	16 089	8 219	7 871	15 581	7 961	7 620	15 300	7 820	7 481
5-9	16 825	8 587	8 239	16 438	8 391	8 046	16 044	8 193	7 851	15 541	7 938	7 603
10-14	17 328	8 838	8 490	16 801	8 572	8 229	16 415	8 378	8 037	16 024	8 181	7 843
15-19	17 815	9 072	8 743	17 269	8 798	8 471	16 746	8 536	8 211	16 366	8 345	8 021
20-24	17 710	8 986	8 724	17 697	8 987	8 709	17 161	8 722	8 440	16 649	8 467	8 182
25-29	16 922	8 539	8 383	17 562	8 879	8 683	17 560	8 888	8 672	17 038	8 633	8 405
30-34	16 024	8 029	7 995	16 752	8 419	8 333	17 399	8 764	8 635	17 409	8 782	8 627
35-39	16 619	8 266	8 353	15 833	7 898	7 935	16 567	8 292	8 275	17 222	8 642	8 580
40-44	16 975	8 374	8 601	16 372	8 100	8 272	15 614	7 751	7 863	16 356	8 149	8 207
45-49	15 159	7 335	7 824	16 644	8 158	8 486	16 075	7 905	8 170	15 052	7 577	7 774
50-54	13 083	6 221	6 862	14 766	7 086	7 680	16 239	7 897	8 341	15 710	7 668	8 042
55-59	11 833	5 558	6 275	12 613	5 920	6 692	14 297	6 773	7 404	15 701	7 500	8 154
60-64	10 823	5 002	5 822	11 230	5 194	6 036	12 007	5 561	6 446	13 621	6 372	7 248
65-69	8 540	3 863	4 677	10 039	4 542	5 497	10 457	4 736	5 721	11 225	5 091	6 134
70-74	6 407	2 818	3 589	7 643	3 354	4 289	9 034	3 965	5 069	9 458	4 154	5 304
75-79	4 297	1 817	2 480	5 426	2 287	3 139	6 524	2 741	3 783	7 767	3 261	4 506
80-84	2 574	1 035	1 540	3 338	1 336	2 002	4 257	1 695	2 562	5 166	2 046	3 120
85-89	1 518	574	944	1 761	661	1 100	2 307	859	1 449	2 971	1 095	1 876
90-94	671	237	434	859	298	561	1 004	344	660	1 324	447	877
95-99	250	83	167	290	93	196	371	116	254	432	133	299
100 +	67	23	44	84	28	57	96	30	66	115	36	80

Age group	2045 Both sexes	2045 Males	2045 Females	2050 Both sexes	2050 Males	2050 Females
All ages	250 571	122 110	128 461	253 105	123 223	129 883
0-4	14 999	7 668	7 330	14 646	7 489	7 157
5-9	15 265	7 799	7 465	14 967	7 650	7 317
10-14	15 523	7 927	7 596	15 248	7 789	7 459
15-19	15 978	8 150	7 828	15 481	7 900	7 582
20-24	16 276	8 282	7 994	15 896	8 093	7 803
25-29	16 537	8 387	8 150	16 176	8 211	7 965
30-34	16 903	8 538	8 365	16 418	8 303	8 115
35-39	17 246	8 670	8 576	16 757	8 438	8 320
40-44	17 018	8 504	8 515	17 058	8 542	8 516
45-49	16 100	7 978	8 122	16 772	8 338	8 434
50-54	15 025	7 363	7 662	15 780	7 766	8 013
55-59	15 238	7 363	7 875	14 600	7 086	7 515
60-64	15 043	7 138	7 905	14 615	6 964	7 651
65-69	12 778	5 856	6 922	14 150	6 579	7 572
70-74	10 204	4 488	5 716	11 666	5 187	6 480
75-79	8 186	3 437	4 749	8 888	3 735	5 152
80-84	6 201	2 450	3 751	6 582	2 597	3 985
85-89	3 639	1 330	2 309	4 402	1 600	2 803
90-94	1 716	571	1 145	2 112	693	1 419
95-99	567	171	396	732	216	516
100 +	130	40	90	160	48	111

POPULATION BY AGE AND SEX (in thousands)

Age group	2005 Both sexes	Males	Females	2010 Both sexes	Males	Females	2015 Both sexes	Males	Females	2020 Both sexes	Males	Females
All ages	186 405	91 870	94 535	200 436	98 659	101 777	214 549	105 500	109 049	228 392	112 233	116 159
0-4	18 024	9 193	8 831	19 926	10 167	9 759	20 638	10 533	10 105	20 948	10 695	10 253
5-9	17 319	8 819	8 500	17 941	9 145	8 796	19 843	10 119	9 723	20 561	10 489	10 072
10-14	16 580	8 428	8 152	17 284	8 799	8 485	17 907	9 126	8 782	19 809	10 100	9 709
15-19	17 385	8 812	8 573	16 501	8 373	8 128	17 209	8 747	8 462	17 836	9 077	8 759
20-24	17 957	9 057	8 900	17 226	8 695	8 531	16 361	8 272	8 090	17 076	8 651	8 425
25-29	16 256	8 071	8 185	17 745	8 901	8 844	17 039	8 558	8 481	16 200	8 154	8 046
30-34	14 286	7 004	7 282	16 026	7 907	8 118	17 507	8 733	8 774	16 836	8 415	8 422
35-39	13 279	6 475	6 803	14 051	6 841	7 209	15 767	7 732	8 036	17 254	8 561	8 694
40-44	12 658	6 133	6 525	13 011	6 297	6 715	13 775	6 659	7 116	15 485	7 545	7 939
45-49	10 623	5 110	5 513	12 330	5 921	6 409	12 688	6 088	6 600	13 458	6 456	7 002
50-54	8 762	4 185	4 577	10 261	4 883	5 377	11 931	5 671	6 260	12 306	5 849	6 457
55-59	6 787	3 210	3 577	8 352	3 935	4 416	9 809	4 607	5 202	11 441	5 371	6 070
60-64	5 066	2 359	2 706	6 342	2 947	3 395	7 838	3 630	4 207	9 246	4 273	4 973
65-69	4 142	1 889	2 254	4 599	2 093	2 505	5 794	2 633	3 162	7 203	3 265	3 938
70-74	2 945	1 306	1 639	3 596	1 590	2 007	4 029	1 778	2 250	5 119	2 257	2 862
75-79	2 145	921	1 224	2 390	1 018	1 372	2 955	1 253	1 702	3 349	1 419	1 930
80-84	1 245	518	727	1 582	649	934	1 790	726	1 064	2 245	905	1 340
85-89	625	252	373	807	319	488	1 042	404	638	1 196	457	739
90-94	240	95	145	340	130	210	444	165	278	579	209	370
95-99	66	26	40	104	39	64	147	53	94	192	67	125
100 +	14	6	8	25	10	15	38	14	23	52	19	34

Age group	2025 Both sexes	Males	Females	2030 Both sexes	Males	Females	2035 Both sexes	Males	Females	2040 Both sexes	Males	Females
All ages	241 425	118 563	122 862	253 993	124 662	129 331	266 247	130 609	135 638	278 366	136 509	141 857
0-4	20 808	10 626	10 182	21 119	10 788	10 331	21 668	11 071	10 597	22 457	11 478	10 980
5-9	20 877	10 654	10 223	20 744	10 590	10 155	21 060	10 754	10 306	21 613	11 039	10 574
10-14	20 529	10 471	10 058	20 847	10 637	10 211	20 717	10 573	10 143	21 034	10 739	10 296
15-19	19 738	10 051	9 687	20 461	10 424	10 037	20 784	10 593	10 190	20 658	10 533	10 124
20-24	17 710	8 986	8 724	19 611	9 959	9 651	20 339	10 337	10 002	20 670	10 512	10 158
25-29	16 922	8 539	8 383	17 562	8 879	8 683	19 462	9 851	9 610	20 198	10 235	9 963
30-34	16 024	8 029	7 995	16 752	8 419	8 333	17 399	8 764	8 635	19 297	9 735	9 562
35-39	16 619	8 266	8 353	15 833	7 898	7 935	16 567	8 292	8 275	17 222	8 642	8 580
40-44	16 975	8 374	8 601	16 372	8 100	8 272	15 614	7 751	7 863	16 356	8 149	8 207
45-49	15 159	7 335	7 824	16 644	8 158	8 486	16 075	7 905	8 170	15 352	7 577	7 774
50-54	13 083	6 221	6 862	14 766	7 086	7 680	16 239	7 897	8 341	15 710	7 668	8 042
55-59	11 833	5 558	6 275	12 613	5 930	6 683	14 267	6 773	7 494	15 721	7 566	8 154
60-64	10 823	5 002	5 822	11 230	5 194	6 036	12 007	5 561	6 446	13 621	6 372	7 248
65-69	8 540	3 863	4 677	10 039	4 542	5 497	10 457	4 736	5 721	11 225	5 091	6 134
70-74	6 407	2 818	3 589	7 643	3 354	4 289	9 034	3 965	5 069	9 458	4 154	5 304
75-79	4 297	1 817	2 480	5 426	2 287	3 139	6 524	2 741	3 783	7 767	3 261	4 506
80-84	2 574	1 035	1 540	3 338	1 336	2 002	4 257	1 695	2 562	5 166	2 046	3 120
85-89	1 518	574	944	1 761	661	1 100	2 307	859	1 449	2 971	1 095	1 876
90-94	671	237	434	859	298	561	1 004	344	660	1 324	447	877
95-99	250	83	167	290	93	196	371	116	254	432	133	299
100 +	67	23	44	84	28	57	96	30	66	115	36	80

Age group	2045 Both sexes	Males	Females	2050 Both sexes	Males	Females
All ages	290 116	142 257	147 860	301 352	147 792	153 559
0-4	23 050	11 785	11 265	23 484	12 009	11 476
5-9	22 406	11 448	10 958	23 002	11 757	11 245
10-14	21 588	11 025	10 564	22 383	11 434	10 949
15-19	20 979	10 701	10 278	21 536	10 989	10 547
20-24	20 553	10 459	10 094	20 880	10 632	10 249
25-29	20 538	10 417	10 121	20 433	10 373	10 060
30-34	20 041	10 124	9 917	20 394	10 315	10 079
35-39	19 117	9 611	9 506	19 871	10 006	9 865
40-44	17 018	8 504	8 515	18 909	9 469	9 440
45-49	16 100	7 978	8 122	16 772	8 338	8 434
50-54	15 025	7 363	7 662	15 780	7 766	8 013
55-59	15 238	7 363	7 875	14 600	7 086	7 515
60-64	15 043	7 138	7 905	14 615	6 964	7 651
65-69	12 778	5 856	6 922	14 150	6 579	7 572
70-74	10 204	4 488	5 716	11 666	5 187	6 480
75-79	8 186	3 437	4 749	8 888	3 735	5 152
80-84	6 201	2 450	3 751	6 582	2 597	3 985
85-89	3 639	1 330	2 309	4 402	1 600	2 803
90-94	1 716	571	1 145	2 112	693	1 419
95-99	567	171	396	732	216	516
100 +	130	40	90	160	48	111

United Nations Department of Economic and Social Affairs/Population Division
World Population Prospects: The 2004 Revision, Volume II: Sex and Age Distribution of the World Population

240

POPULATION BY AGE AND SEX (in thousands)

Age group	2005 Both sexes	2005 Males	2005 Females	2010 Both sexes	2010 Males	2010 Females	2015 Both sexes	2015 Males	2015 Females	2020 Both sexes	2020 Males	2020 Females
All ages	186 405	91 870	94 535	196 546	96 674	99 872	201 222	101 222	100 000	209 954	102 825	107 130
0-4	18 024	9 193	8 831	16 035	8 182	7 853	14 195	7 245	6 950	12 798	6 534	6 264
5-9	17 319	8 819	8 500	17 941	9 145	8 796	15 968	8 143	7 825	14 141	7 214	6 927
10-14	16 580	8 428	8 152	17 284	8 799	8 485	17 907	9 126	8 782	15 940	8 127	7 813
15-19	17 385	8 812	8 573	16 501	8 373	8 128	17 209	8 747	8 462	17 836	9 077	8 759
20-24	17 957	9 057	8 900	17 226	8 695	8 531	16 361	8 272	8 090	17 076	8 651	8 425
25-29	16 256	8 071	8 185	17 745	8 901	8 844	17 039	8 558	8 481	16 200	8 154	8 046
30-34	14 286	7 004	7 282	16 026	7 907	8 118	17 507	8 733	8 774	16 836	8 415	8 422
35-39	13 279	6 475	6 803	14 051	6 841	7 209	15 767	7 732	8 036	17 254	8 561	8 694
40-44	12 658	6 133	6 525	13 011	6 297	6 715	13 775	6 659	7 116	15 485	7 545	7 939
45-49	10 623	5 110	5 513	12 330	5 921	6 409	12 688	6 088	6 600	13 458	6 456	7 002
50-54	8 762	4 185	4 577	10 261	4 883	5 377	11 931	5 671	6 260	12 306	5 849	6 457
55-59	6 787	3 210	3 577	8 352	3 935	4 416	9 809	4 607	5 202	11 441	5 371	6 070
60-64	5 066	2 359	2 706	6 342	2 947	3 395	7 838	3 630	4 207	9 246	4 273	4 973
65-69	4 142	1 889	2 254	4 599	2 093	2 505	5 794	2 633	3 162	7 203	3 265	3 938
70-74	2 945	1 306	1 639	3 596	1 590	2 007	4 029	1 778	2 250	5 119	2 257	2 862
75-79	2 145	921	1 224	2 390	1 018	1 372	2 955	1 253	1 702	3 349	1 419	1 930
80-84	1 245	518	727	1 582	649	934	1 790	726	1 064	2 245	905	1 340
85-89	625	252	373	807	319	488	1 042	404	638	1 196	457	739
90-94	240	95	145	340	130	210	444	165	278	579	209	370
95-99	66	26	40	104	39	64	147	53	94	192	67	125
100 +	14	6	8	25	10	15	38	14	23	52	19	34

Age group	2025 Both sexes	2025 Males	2025 Females	2030 Both sexes	2030 Males	2030 Females	2035 Both sexes	2035 Males	2035 Females	2040 Both sexes	2040 Males	2040 Females
All ages	214 407	104 778	109 629	217 160	105 874	111 286	217 925	105 971	111 953	216 953	105 211	111 742
0-4	12 181	6 221	5 960	11 232	5 738	5 495	10 070	5 145	4 925	9 213	4 709	4 504
5-9	12 754	6 509	6 245	12 143	6 199	5 944	11 200	5 719	5 481	10 043	5 130	4 913
10-14	14 118	7 201	6 917	12 735	6 498	6 237	12 126	6 189	5 937	11 185	5 710	5 475
15-19	15 880	8 087	7 794	14 067	7 167	6 900	12 690	6 468	6 222	12 085	6 162	5 923
20-24	17 710	8 986	8 724	15 772	8 010	7 762	13 974	7 101	6 872	12 609	6 412	6 197
25-29	16 922	8 539	8 383	17 562	8 879	8 683	15 647	7 920	7 727	13 868	7 026	6 842
30-34	16 024	8 029	7 995	16 752	8 419	8 333	17 399	8 764	8 635	15 511	7 824	7 687
35-39	16 619	8 266	8 353	15 833	7 898	7 935	16 567	8 292	8 275	17 222	8 642	8 580
40-44	16 975	8 374	8 601	16 372	8 100	8 272	15 014	7 751	7 863	16 356	8 149	8 207
45-49	15 159	7 335	7 824	16 644	8 158	8 486	16 075	7 905	8 170	15 352	7 577	7 774
50-54	13 083	6 221	6 862	14 766	7 086	7 680	16 239	7 897	8 341	15 710	7 668	8 042
55-59	11 833	5 558	6 275	12 613	5 930	6 683	14 267	6 773	7 494	15 721	7 566	8 154
60-64	10 823	5 002	5 822	11 230	5 194	6 036	12 007	5 561	6 446	13 621	6 372	7 248
65-69	8 540	3 863	4 677	10 039	4 542	5 497	10 457	4 736	5 721	11 225	5 091	6 134
70-74	6 407	2 818	3 589	7 643	3 354	4 289	9 034	3 965	5 069	9 458	4 154	5 304
75-79	4 297	1 817	2 480	5 426	2 287	3 139	6 524	2 741	3 783	7 767	3 261	4 506
80-84	2 574	1 035	1 540	3 338	1 336	2 002	4 257	1 695	2 562	5 166	2 046	3 120
85-89	1 518	574	944	1 761	661	1 100	2 307	859	1 449	2 971	1 095	1 876
90-94	671	237	434	859	298	561	1 004	344	660	1 324	447	877
95-99	250	83	167	290	93	196	371	116	254	432	133	299
100 +	67	23	44	84	28	57	96	30	66	115	36	80

Age group	2045 Both sexes	2045 Males	2045 Females	2050 Both sexes	2050 Males	2050 Females
All ages	214 354	103 663	110 690	210 188	101 377	108 812
0-4	8 492	4 342	4 150	7 815	3 996	3 819
5-9	9 191	4 696	4 495	8 473	4 331	4 142
10-14	10 031	5 122	4 908	9 180	4 689	4 490
15-19	11 149	5 687	5 462	9 999	5 102	4 897
20-24	12 011	6 111	5 899	11 082	5 642	5 440
25-29	12 518	6 348	6 170	11 930	6 055	5 875
30-34	13 755	6 947	6 808	12 423	6 282	6 141
35-39	15 364	7 723	7 641	13 634	6 864	6 770
40-44	17 018	8 504	8 515	15 195	7 608	7 587
45-49	16 100	7 978	8 122	16 772	8 338	8 434
50-54	15 025	7 363	7 662	15 780	7 766	8 013
55-59	15 238	7 363	7 875	14 600	7 086	7 515
60-64	15 043	7 138	7 905	14 615	6 964	7 651
65-69	12 778	5 856	6 922	14 150	6 579	7 572
70-74	10 204	4 488	5 716	11 666	5 187	6 480
75-79	8 186	3 437	4 749	8 888	3 735	5 152
80-84	6 201	2 450	3 751	6 582	2 597	3 985
85-89	3 639	1 330	2 309	4 402	1 600	2 803
90-94	1 716	571	1 145	2 112	693	1 419
95-99	567	171	396	732	216	516
100 +	130	40	90	160	48	111

POPULATION BY AGE AND SEX (in thousands)

Age group	1950 Both sexes	1950 Males	1950 Females	1955 Both sexes	1955 Males	1955 Females	1960 Both sexes	1960 Males	1960 Females	1965 Both sexes	1965 Males	1965 Females
All ages	48	25	23	63	33	31	82	42	40	103	53	50
0-4	7	3	3	13	6	6	16	8	8	19	10	9
5-9	6	3	3	7	4	3	13	6	6	16	8	8
10-14	5	3	2	6	3	3	7	4	3	13	7	6
15-19	5	2	2	5	3	3	6	3	3	7	4	3
20-24	4	2	2	5	3	3	6	3	3	7	4	3
25-29	4	2	2	5	3	2	6	3	3	7	4	3
30-34	3	2	2	4	2	2	6	3	3	7	4	3
35-39	3	2	1	4	2	2	5	3	2	6	3	3
40-44	3	1	1	3	2	2	4	2	2	5	3	2
45-49	2	1	1	3	1	1	3	2	2	4	2	2
50-54	2	1	1	2	1	1	3	1	1	3	2	2
55-59	2	1	1	2	1	1	2	1	1	3	1	1
60-64	1	1	1	2	1	1	2	1	1	2	1	1
65-69	1	0	1	1	1	1	1	1	1	2	1	1
70-74	1	0	0	1	0	0	1	0	1	1	1	1
75-79	0	0	0	1	0	0	1	0	0	1	0	0
80 +	0	0	0	0	0	0	0	0	0	0	0	0

Age group	1970 Both sexes	1970 Males	1970 Females	1975 Both sexes	1975 Males	1975 Females	1980 Both sexes	1980 Males	1980 Females	1985 Both sexes	1985 Males	1985 Females
All ages	130	67	63	161	83	78	193	103	90	223	118	105
0-4	21	11	10	25	13	12	29	15	14	31	16	15
5-9	19	10	9	21	11	10	24	13	12	29	15	14
10-14	16	8	8	19	10	9	21	11	11	25	13	12
15-19	13	7	7	17	9	8	20	11	10	22	11	11
20-24	9	4	4	15	8	7	23	12	10	21	11	10
25-29	9	4	4	10	5	5	20	11	9	23	12	11
30-34	8	4	4	10	5	5	14	8	6	20	11	9
35-39	8	4	4	10	5	5	10	6	4	14	8	7
40-44	7	4	3	9	5	4	8	4	4	10	6	4
45-49	6	3	3	7	4	3	7	3	3	8	4	4
50-54	4	2	2	6	3	3	5	3	2	7	3	3
55-59	3	2	2	4	2	2	4	2	2	5	3	2
60-64	3	1	1	3	2	2	3	2	1	4	2	2
65-69	2	1	1	2	1	1	2	1	1	2	1	1
70-74	1	1	1	2	1	1	2	1	1	2	1	1
75-79	1	0	0	1	1	1	1	1	0	1	1	1
80 +	0	0	0	1	0	0	1	0	0	1	0	1

Age group	1990 Both sexes	1990 Males	1990 Females	1995 Both sexes	1995 Males	1995 Females	2000 Both sexes	2000 Males	2000 Females	2005 Both sexes	2005 Males	2005 Females
All ages	257	136	121	295	155	140	333	174	160	374	194	180
0-4	34	18	16	37	19	18	38	19	18	40	21	19
5-9	29	15	14	32	17	15	36	19	17	36	19	17
10-14	26	13	12	28	14	14	31	16	15	34	18	16
15-19	22	12	11	27	14	13	29	15	14	32	17	15
20-24	26	13	13	28	14	14	32	16	16	35	17	17
25-29	27	14	13	33	16	17	35	17	18	39	19	20
30-34	27	14	12	27	14	13	32	16	17	35	17	18
35-39	21	12	9	26	14	11	26	14	12	31	15	16
40-44	14	8	6	20	11	9	24	13	11	24	13	11
45-49	8	5	4	13	7	5	18	10	8	22	12	10
50-54	7	4	3	7	4	3	12	7	5	17	10	7
55-59	5	2	3	5	3	2	6	4	2	10	6	4
60-64	4	2	2	5	2	2	5	3	2	6	4	2
65-69	3	1	1	3	2	1	4	2	2	5	3	2
70-74	2	1	1	2	1	1	3	1	1	4	2	2
75-79	1	1	1	1	1	1	2	1	1	2	1	1
80 +	1	1	1	1	0	1	1	0	1	2	1	1

United Nations Department of Economic and Social Affairs/Population Division
World Population Prospects: The 2004 Revision, Volume II: Sex and Age Distribution of the World Population

242

POPULATION BY AGE AND SEX (in thousands)

Age group	2005 Both sexes	Males	Females	2010 Both sexes	Males	Females	2015 Both sexes	Males	Females	2020 Both sexes	Males	Females
All ages	374	194	180	414	214	201	453	233	221	491	251	240
0-4	40	21	19	41	21	20	41	21	20	40	21	19
5-9	36	19	17	39	20	19	39	20	19	39	20	19
10-14	34	18	16	35	18	17	37	19	18	38	20	18
15-19	32	17	15	36	18	17	36	19	18	39	20	19
20-24	35	17	17	38	19	18	41	21	20	42	21	20
25-29	39	19	20	42	20	21	44	22	22	48	24	24
30-34	35	17	18	39	19	20	41	20	21	44	22	22
35-39	31	15	16	34	16	17	38	19	20	40	20	21
40-44	24	13	11	30	15	15	32	16	16	37	18	19
45-49	22	12	10	22	12	11	28	14	14	30	15	15
50-54	17	10	7	21	12	9	21	11	10	27	13	14
55-59	10	6	4	15	9	6	19	11	8	20	11	9
60-64	6	4	2	10	6	4	15	9	6	19	11	8
65-69	5	3	2	5	3	2	9	6	3	14	8	6
70-74	4	2	2	4	2	2	5	3	2	8	5	3
75-79	2	1	1	3	1	2	3	2	1	4	2	1
80-84	1	0	1	1	1	1	2	1	1	2	1	1
85-89	0	0	0	1	0	0	1	0	0	1	0	1
90-94	0	0	0	0	0	0	0	0	0	0	0	0
95-99	0	0	0	0	0	0	0	0	0	0	0	0
100 +	0	0	0	0	0	0	0	0	0	0	0	0

Age group	2025 Both sexes	Males	Females	2030 Both sexes	Males	Females	2035 Both sexes	Males	Females	2040 Both sexes	Males	Females
All ages	526	268	259	561	284	277	595	299	295	626	313	312
0-4	40	21	19	42	22	20	43	22	21	43	22	21
5-9	39	20	19	39	20	19	40	21	19	41	22	20
10-14	38	20	18	37	19	18	37	19	18	39	20	19
15-19	39	20	19	39	20	19	39	20	19	39	20	19
20-24	44	23	22	45	23	22	45	23	22	44	23	22
25-29	49	24	24	51	25	25	52	26	26	52	26	26
30-34	48	23	24	48	24	25	51	25	26	52	25	26
35-39	43	21	22	47	23	24	47	23	24	50	25	25
40-44	39	19	20	42	21	21	45	22	23	46	23	23
45-49	35	17	18	37	18	19	40	20	20	43	21	22
50-54	29	14	15	33	16	17	36	17	18	39	19	19
55-59	20	10	10	28	14	14	32	16	16	34	17	17
60-64	19	10	9	24	12	12	26	13	13	31	15	16
65-69	17	10	7	18	10	8	23	11	12	25	12	13
70-74	12	7	5	16	9	7	16	9	8	21	10	11
75-79	6	4	3	10	5	4	13	7	6	13	7	7
80-84	2	1	1	4	2	2	7	4	3	9	5	5
85-89	1	0	1	1	1	1	3	1	1	4	2	2
90-94	0	0	0	1	0	0	1	0	0	1	0	1
95-99	0	0	0	0	0	0	0	0	0	0	0	0
100 +	0	0	0	0	0	0	0	0	0	0	0	0

Age group	2045 Both sexes	Males	Females	2050 Both sexes	Males	Females
All ages	654	326	328	681	338	342
0-4	44	22	21	44	23	21
5-9	42	22	20	42	22	20
10-14	40	21	19	41	21	19
15-19	40	21	19	41	21	20
20-24	44	23	22	46	23	22
25-29	51	25	26	51	25	26
30-34	51	25	26	51	25	26
35-39	50	25	25	50	25	25
40-44	48	24	24	49	24	25
45-49	44	22	22	46	23	23
50-54	42	21	21	43	21	21
55-59	37	19	18	40	20	20
60-64	33	16	17	36	18	18
65-69	29	14	15	31	15	16
70-74	23	11	12	27	13	14
75-79	18	8	10	19	9	11
80-84	10	5	5	13	5	8
85-89	6	2	3	6	2	4
90-94	2	1	1	3	1	2
95-99	0	0	0	1	0	1
100 +	0	0	0	0	0	0

POPULATION BY AGE AND SEX (in thousands)

Age group	2005 Both sexes	2005 Males	2005 Females	2010 Both sexes	2010 Males	2010 Females	2015 Both sexes	2015 Males	2015 Females	2020 Both sexes	2020 Males	2020 Females
All ages	374	194	180	419	216	203	466	239	227	514	263	251
0-4	40	21	19	45	23	22	49	25	24	51	26	25
5-9	36	19	17	39	20	19	44	23	21	47	24	23
10-14	34	18	16	35	18	17	37	19	18	43	22	20
15-19	32	17	15	36	18	17	36	19	18	39	20	19
20-24	35	17	17	38	19	18	41	21	20	42	21	20
25-29	39	19	20	42	20	21	44	22	22	48	24	24
30-34	35	17	18	39	19	20	41	20	21	44	22	22
35-39	31	15	16	34	16	17	38	19	20	40	20	21
40-44	24	13	11	30	15	15	32	16	16	37	18	19
45-49	22	12	10	22	12	11	28	14	14	30	15	15
50-54	17	10	7	21	12	9	21	11	10	27	13	14
55-59	10	6	4	15	9	6	19	11	8	20	11	9
60-64	6	4	2	10	6	4	15	9	6	19	11	8
65-69	5	3	2	5	3	2	9	6	3	14	8	6
70-74	4	2	2	4	2	2	5	3	2	8	5	3
75-79	2	1	1	3	1	2	3	2	1	4	2	1
80-84	1	0	1	1	1	1	2	1	1	2	1	1
85-89	0	0	0	1	0	0	1	0	0	1	0	1
90-94	0	0	0	0	0	0	0	0	0	0	0	0
95-99	0	0	0	0	0	0	0	0	0	0	0	0
100 +	0	0	0	0	0	0	0	0	0	0	0	0

Age group	2025 Both sexes	2025 Males	2025 Females	2030 Both sexes	2030 Males	2030 Females	2035 Both sexes	2035 Males	2035 Females	2040 Both sexes	2040 Males	2040 Females
All ages	561	285	275	608	308	300	657	331	326	706	355	352
0-4	51	26	25	54	28	26	58	30	28	62	32	30
5-9	49	26	24	50	26	24	53	27	25	56	29	27
10-14	46	24	22	48	25	23	49	25	23	51	27	25
15-19	44	23	21	47	24	23	49	25	24	50	26	24
20-24	44	23	22	49	25	24	53	27	26	55	28	27
25-29	49	24	24	51	25	25	56	28	28	59	30	30
30-34	48	23	24	48	24	25	51	25	26	56	28	28
35-39	43	21	22	47	23	24	47	23	24	50	25	25
40-44	39	19	20	42	21	21	45	22	23	46	23	23
45-49	35	17	18	37	18	19	40	20	20	43	21	22
50-54	29	14	15	33	16	17	36	17	18	39	19	19
55-59	25	13	13	27	14	14	32	16	16	34	17	17
60-64	19	10	9	24	12	12	26	13	13	31	15	16
65-69	17	10	7	18	10	8	23	11	12	25	12	13
70-74	12	7	5	16	9	7	16	9	8	21	10	11
75-79	6	4	3	10	5	4	13	7	6	13	7	7
80-84	2	1	1	4	2	2	7	4	3	9	5	5
85-89	1	0	1	1	1	1	3	1	1	4	2	2
90-94	0	0	0	1	0	0	1	0	0	1	0	1
95-99	0	0	0	0	0	0	0	0	0	0	0	0
100 +	0	0	0	0	0	0	0	0	0	0	0	0

Age group	2045 Both sexes	2045 Males	2045 Females	2050 Both sexes	2050 Males	2050 Females
All ages	756	378	378	806	403	403
0-4	65	34	32	68	35	33
5-9	60	31	29	64	33	31
10-14	55	29	26	59	31	28
15-19	53	27	26	56	29	27
20-24	55	28	27	58	30	28
25-29	62	31	31	62	31	31
30-34	59	29	30	61	31	31
35-39	55	27	28	58	29	29
40-44	48	24	24	53	27	27
45-49	44	22	22	46	23	23
50-54	42	21	21	43	21	21
55-59	37	19	18	40	20	20
60-64	33	16	17	36	18	18
65-69	29	14	15	31	15	16
70-74	23	11	12	27	13	14
75-79	18	8	10	19	9	11
80-84	10	5	5	13	5	8
85-89	6	2	3	6	2	4
90-94	2	1	1	3	1	2
95-99	0	0	0	1	0	1
100 +	0	0	0	0	0	0

United Nations Department of Economic and Social Affairs/Population Division
World Population Prospects: The 2004 Revision, Volume II: Sex and Age Distribution of the World Population

244

POPULATION BY AGE AND SEX (in thousands)

Age group	2005 Both sexes	2005 Males	2005 Females	2010 Both sexes	2010 Males	2010 Females	2015 Both sexes	2015 Males	2015 Females	2020 Both sexes	2020 Males	2020 Females
All ages	374	194	180	410	211	108	441	226	215	468	230	220
0-4	40	21	19	36	19	17	33	17	16	29	15	14
5-9	36	19	17	39	20	19	35	18	17	31	16	15
10-14	34	18	16	35	18	17	37	19	18	33	17	16
15-19	32	17	15	36	18	17	36	19	18	39	20	19
20-24	35	17	17	38	19	18	41	21	20	42	21	20
25-29	39	19	20	42	20	21	44	22	22	48	24	24
30-34	35	17	18	39	19	20	41	20	21	44	22	22
35-39	31	15	16	34	16	17	38	19	20	40	20	21
40-44	24	13	11	30	15	15	32	16	16	37	18	19
45-49	22	12	10	22	12	11	28	14	14	30	15	15
50-54	17	10	7	21	12	9	21	11	10	27	13	14
55-59	10	6	4	15	9	6	19	11	8	20	11	9
60-64	6	4	2	10	6	4	15	9	6	19	11	8
65-69	5	3	2	5	3	2	9	6	3	14	8	6
70-74	4	2	2	4	2	2	5	3	2	8	5	3
75-79	2	1	1	3	1	2	3	2	1	4	2	1
80-84	1	0	1	1	1	1	2	1	1	2	1	1
85-89	0	0	0	1	0	0	1	0	0	1	0	1
90-94	0	0	0	0	0	0	0	0	0	0	0	0
95-99	0	0	0	0	0	0	0	0	0	0	0	0
100 +	0	0	0	0	0	0	0	0	0	0	0	0

Age group	2025 Both sexes	2025 Males	2025 Females	2030 Both sexes	2030 Males	2030 Females	2035 Both sexes	2035 Males	2035 Females	2040 Both sexes	2040 Males	2040 Females
All ages	492	250	242	515	260	255	534	268	266	550	274	276
0-4	29	15	14	30	15	14	29	15	14	28	14	13
5-9	28	15	13	27	14	13	28	15	13	28	14	13
10-14	30	16	14	27	14	13	26	14	12	27	14	13
15-19	35	18	17	31	16	15	28	14	14	27	14	13
20-24	44	23	22	40	21	20	37	19	18	34	17	16
25-29	49	24	24	51	25	25	47	23	24	44	22	22
30-34	48	23	24	48	24	25	51	25	26	47	23	24
35-39	43	21	22	47	23	24	47	23	24	50	25	25
40-44	39	19	20	42	21	21	45	22	23	46	23	23
45-49	35	17	18	37	18	19	40	20	20	43	21	22
50-54	29	14	15	33	16	17	36	17	18	39	19	19
55-59	25	13	13	27	14	14	32	16	16	34	17	17
60-64	19	10	9	24	12	12	26	13	13	31	15	16
65-69	17	10	7	18	10	8	23	11	12	25	12	13
70-74	12	7	5	16	9	7	16	9	8	21	10	11
75-79	6	4	3	10	6	4	13	7	6	13	7	7
80-84	2	1	1	4	2	2	7	4	3	9	5	5
85-89	1	0	1	1	1	1	3	1	1	4	2	2
90-94	0	0	0	1	0	0	1	0	0	1	0	1
95-99	0	0	0	0	0	0	0	0	0	0	0	0
100 +	0	0	0	0	0	0	0	0	0	0	0	0

Age group	2045 Both sexes	2045 Males	2045 Females	2050 Both sexes	2050 Males	2050 Females
All ages	561	278	283	569	281	288
0-4	26	13	13	25	13	12
5-9	26	14	13	25	13	12
10-14	26	14	12	25	13	12
15-19	28	15	14	28	14	13
20-24	33	17	16	34	17	16
25-29	40	20	20	40	20	20
30-34	44	21	22	40	20	21
35-39	46	23	23	43	21	22
40-44	48	24	24	44	22	22
45-49	44	22	22	46	23	23
50-54	42	21	21	43	21	21
55-59	37	19	18	40	20	20
60-64	33	16	17	36	18	18
65-69	29	14	15	31	15	16
70-74	23	11	12	27	13	14
75-79	18	8	10	19	9	11
80-84	10	5	5	13	5	8
85-89	6	2	3	6	2	4
90-94	2	1	1	3	1	2
95-99	0	0	0	1	0	1
100 +	0	0	0	0	0	0

POPULATION BY AGE AND SEX (in thousands)

Age group	1950 Both sexes	Males	Females	1955 Both sexes	Males	Females	1960 Both sexes	Males	Females	1965 Both sexes	Males	Females
All ages	7 251	3 624	3 627	7 499	3 739	3 760	7 867	3 927	3 940	8 204	4 100	4 104
0-4	733	375	358	697	356	341	659	337	322	642	330	313
5-9	610	311	299	704	359	345	688	351	337	654	334	320
10-14	599	302	297	591	300	291	703	358	345	686	350	336
15-19	682	344	338	581	292	289	591	300	291	700	356	344
20-24	690	350	340	660	332	328	580	291	289	588	298	290
25-29	677	340	337	667	336	331	657	330	327	576	289	287
30-34	413	208	205	654	327	327	663	334	329	652	327	325
35-39	536	273	263	399	200	199	649	324	325	657	331	327
40-44	514	262	252	513	260	253	394	197	197	642	320	322
45-49	441	224	217	491	249	242	506	256	250	388	193	194
50-54	353	173	180	416	210	206	480	242	238	494	249	245
55-59	266	125	141	328	159	169	400	200	200	461	231	230
60-64	249	111	138	242	112	130	306	146	160	375	185	190
65-69	208	98	110	216	94	122	214	97	117	273	128	145
70-74	146	68	78	172	79	93	188	84	104	204	91	113
75-79	84	38	46	103	46	57	114	49	65	126	54	72
80 +	50	22	28	66	28	38	75	30	45	85	34	52

Age group	1970 Both sexes	Males	Females	1975 Both sexes	Males	Females	1980 Both sexes	Males	Females	1985 Both sexes	Males	Females
All ages	8 490	4 244	4 246	8 721	4 354	4 367	8 862	4 415	4 446	8 960	4 452	4 508
0-4	646	332	315	672	345	327	677	347	330	588	302	286
5-9	632	324	308	630	323	307	660	339	321	662	338	323
10-14	659	337	323	617	318	299	625	321	303	656	338	318
15-19	681	347	333	650	332	318	622	319	303	608	312	296
20-24	688	349	339	671	339	332	631	323	308	604	309	295
25-29	575	289	286	663	335	328	652	328	324	618	312	305
30-34	574	288	286	567	283	283	670	337	333	649	326	323
35-39	649	327	322	576	288	288	562	282	281	674	337	336
40-44	650	327	323	647	323	323	558	278	280	561	280	281
45-49	634	315	318	641	322	319	624	312	312	553	274	280
50-54	377	188	190	624	308	317	612	305	308	622	308	314
55-59	474	238	236	359	178	181	582	285	297	599	296	303
60-64	435	213	222	451	222	230	336	160	176	553	265	288
65-69	337	162	175	389	186	203	398	190	208	298	137	160
70-74	229	105	124	280	130	150	314	145	169	330	153	177
75-79	129	55	74	161	71	90	200	88	112	225	99	127
80 +	119	48	71	122	50	72	140	58	82	161	65	95

Age group	1990 Both sexes	Males	Females	1995 Both sexes	Males	Females	2000 Both sexes	Males	Females	2005 Both sexes	Males	Females
All ages	8 718	4 297	4 421	8 297	4 061	4 236	7 997	3 890	4 107	7 726	3 742	3 984
0-4	555	284	271	413	212	201	326	167	159	335	172	163
5-9	582	299	283	526	269	257	409	210	199	323	166	157
10-14	644	330	314	553	284	268	522	267	255	405	208	198
15-19	641	328	313	604	309	295	548	282	266	518	265	253
20-24	585	298	287	581	296	285	598	306	292	543	278	264
25-29	580	293	287	535	271	264	575	292	283	592	302	290
30-34	606	305	302	540	271	268	528	267	261	569	288	280
35-39	625	312	313	577	287	290	532	266	266	521	263	258
40-44	638	317	321	603	298	305	566	280	287	522	260	262
45-49	527	261	267	602	295	307	587	287	300	552	270	282
50-54	513	251	262	498	242	256	579	279	300	565	272	293
55-59	560	272	289	489	234	255	470	223	247	549	259	290
60-64	529	251	278	527	249	278	449	208	242	434	200	235
65-69	474	216	258	473	217	256	465	210	255	400	177	223
70-74	240	107	133	391	170	221	389	169	220	387	165	221
75-79	231	99	132	170	72	98	283	114	169	286	115	171
80 +	187	74	113	214	85	129	171	64	107	227	81	146

United Nations Department of Economic and Social Affairs/Population Division
World Population Prospects: The 2004 Revision, Volume II: Sex and Age Distribution of the World Population

POPULATION BY AGE AND SEX (in thousands)

Age group	2005			2010			2015			2020		
	Both sexes	Males	Females	Both sexes	Males	Females	Both sexes	Males	Females	Both sexes	Males	Females
All ages	7 726	3 742	3 984	7 446	3 594	3 852	7 156	3 448	3 708	6 850	3 001	3 557
0-4	335	172	163	316	163	154	295	152	143	272	140	132
5-9	323	166	157	332	170	161	313	161	152	292	150	142
10-14	405	208	198	320	164	156	329	169	160	311	160	151
15-19	518	265	253	402	206	196	317	163	154	326	168	159
20-24	543	278	264	513	262	251	398	204	194	314	161	153
25-29	592	302	290	537	275	262	508	259	249	394	202	193
30-34	569	288	280	586	299	287	531	272	259	503	256	247
35-39	521	263	258	561	284	277	579	294	284	525	268	257
40-44	522	260	262	512	257	255	553	279	274	570	289	281
45-49	552	270	282	510	252	258	501	250	251	541	271	270
50-54	565	272	293	533	258	275	494	242	252	486	240	246
55-59	549	259	290	538	254	284	508	241	267	472	227	245
60-64	434	200	235	509	233	276	501	230	271	475	220	256
65-69	400	177	223	389	172	217	459	202	257	453	201	253
70-74	387	165	221	336	141	195	329	138	191	391	164	228
75-79	286	115	171	289	114	174	254	98	156	252	97	155
80-84	168	62	107	174	63	111	181	64	117	163	56	107
85-89	41	14	27	75	24	51	81	25	56	87	25	62
90-94	15	5	11	12	3	8	23	5	17	26	6	20
95-99	2	0	2	2	0	2	2	0	2	4	1	4
100 +	0	0	0	0	0	0	0	0	0	0	0	0

Age group	2025			2030			2035			2040		
	Both sexes	Males	Females	Both sexes	Males	Females	Both sexes	Males	Females	Both sexes	Males	Females
All ages	6 552	3 152	3 401	6 243	3 001	3 241	5 936	2 853	3 083	5 638	2 710	2 928
0-4	249	128	121	234	121	114	229	118	111	226	117	110
5-9	269	138	131	246	127	120	232	119	113	227	117	110
10-14	290	149	141	267	137	130	244	126	119	230	118	112
15-19	308	158	150	287	148	140	265	136	129	242	124	118
20-24	323	166	157	305	157	149	285	146	138	262	135	127
25-29	311	159	152	320	164	156	302	155	147	282	145	137
30-34	390	199	191	307	157	150	317	162	154	299	153	146
35-39	497	253	244	385	197	189	304	155	148	313	160	153
40-44	517	264	253	490	240	241	300	194	180	299	153	146
45-49	559	282	276	507	258	250	482	244	238	373	190	183
50-54	526	261	264	544	273	271	494	250	245	470	237	233
55-59	465	226	239	505	248	257	524	259	264	477	238	239
60-64	443	208	235	438	208	229	476	229	247	496	241	254
65-69	432	193	239	404	184	220	401	185	216	438	205	233
70-74	389	164	225	373	158	215	351	152	199	351	155	196
75-79	303	117	186	305	118	187	296	116	180	281	113	168
80-84	165	56	109	202	60	134	207	71	137	205	71	134
85-89	81	23	58	85	23	62	108	29	79	114	31	84
90-94	29	6	23	29	5	24	32	6	26	43	7	36
95-99	5	1	5	7	1	6	7	1	6	8	1	8
100 +	1	0	0	1	0	1	1	0	1	1	0	1

Age group	2045			2050		
	Both sexes	Males	Females	Both sexes	Males	Females
All ages	5 349	2 574	2 775	5 065	2 440	2 625
0-4	220	113	107	212	109	103
5-9	224	115	109	218	112	106
10-14	225	116	109	222	114	108
15-19	228	117	111	222	114	108
20-24	239	123	116	225	116	109
25-29	259	133	126	237	122	115
30-34	278	143	136	256	132	125
35-39	295	151	144	275	141	134
40-44	309	158	151	291	149	142
45-49	294	150	144	304	155	149
50-54	365	185	180	287	146	141
55-59	454	226	228	352	177	176
60-64	452	222	230	432	212	220
65-69	458	217	241	419	201	218
70-74	386	173	213	406	185	221
75-79	284	117	167	316	133	183
80-84	199	71	128	205	75	129
85-89	117	32	85	117	34	83
90-94	48	9	40	52	10	42
95-99	12	1	11	14	1	13
100 +	1	0	1	2	0	2

United Nations Department of Economic and Social Affairs/Population Division
World Population Prospects: The 2004 Revision, Volume II: Sex and Age Distribution of the World Population

247

POPULATION BY AGE AND SEX (in thousands)

Age group	2005 Both sexes	Males	Females	2010 Both sexes	Males	Females	2015 Both sexes	Males	Females	2020 Both sexes	Males	Females
All ages	7 726	3 742	3 984	7 510	3 627	3 883	7 310	3 527	3 783	7 109	3 430	3 679
0-4	335	172	163	380	195	185	386	198	187	368	189	179
5-9	323	166	157	332	170	161	377	194	183	383	197	186
10-14	405	208	198	320	164	156	329	169	160	375	192	182
15-19	518	265	253	402	206	196	317	163	154	326	168	159
20-24	543	278	264	513	262	251	398	204	194	314	161	153
25-29	592	302	290	537	275	262	508	259	249	394	202	193
30-34	569	288	280	586	299	287	531	272	259	503	256	247
35-39	521	263	258	561	284	277	579	294	284	525	268	257
40-44	522	260	262	512	257	255	553	279	274	570	289	281
45-49	552	270	282	510	252	258	501	250	251	541	271	270
50-54	565	272	293	533	258	275	494	242	252	486	240	246
55-59	549	259	290	538	254	284	508	241	267	472	227	245
60-64	434	200	235	509	233	276	501	230	271	475	220	256
65-69	400	177	223	389	172	217	459	202	257	453	201	253
70-74	387	165	221	336	141	195	329	138	191	391	164	228
75-79	286	115	171	289	114	174	254	98	156	252	97	155
80-84	168	62	107	174	63	111	181	64	117	163	56	107
85-89	41	14	27	75	24	51	81	25	56	87	25	62
90-94	15	5	11	12	3	8	23	5	17	26	6	20
95-99	2	0	2	2	0	2	2	0	2	4	1	4
100 +	0	0	0	0	0	0	0	0	0	0	0	0

Age group	2025 Both sexes	Males	Females	2030 Both sexes	Males	Females	2035 Both sexes	Males	Females	2040 Both sexes	Males	Females
All ages	6 888	3 324	3 563	6 669	3 221	3 449	6 476	3 131	3 345	6 315	3 058	3 257
0-4	334	172	162	326	168	158	343	176	166	364	188	177
5-9	365	188	177	332	171	161	324	167	157	340	175	165
10-14	380	196	185	363	187	176	329	169	160	321	165	156
15-19	372	191	181	378	194	184	360	185	175	327	168	159
20-24	323	166	157	369	189	179	375	192	182	358	184	174
25-29	311	159	152	320	164	156	365	188	178	372	191	181
30-34	390	199	191	307	157	150	317	162	154	362	186	176
35-39	497	253	244	385	197	189	304	155	148	313	160	153
40-44	517	264	253	490	249	241	380	194	186	299	153	146
45-49	559	282	276	507	258	250	482	244	238	373	190	183
50-54	526	261	264	544	273	271	494	250	245	470	237	233
55-59	465	226	239	505	248	257	524	259	264	477	238	239
60-64	443	208	235	438	208	229	476	229	247	496	241	254
65-69	432	193	239	404	184	220	401	185	216	438	205	233
70-74	389	164	225	373	158	215	351	152	199	351	155	196
75-79	303	117	186	305	118	187	296	116	180	281	113	168
80-84	165	56	108	202	69	134	207	71	137	205	71	134
85-89	81	23	58	85	23	62	108	29	79	114	31	84
90-94	29	6	23	29	5	24	32	6	26	43	7	36
95-99	5	1	5	7	1	6	7	1	6	8	1	8
100 +	1	0	0	1	0	1	1	0	1	1	0	1

Age group	2045 Both sexes	Males	Females	2050 Both sexes	Males	Females
All ages	6 177	2 999	3 177	6 046	2 944	3 102
0-4	372	191	180	367	189	178
5-9	362	186	176	369	190	179
10-14	338	174	164	360	185	174
15-19	319	164	155	336	173	163
20-24	324	167	158	317	163	154
25-29	355	182	172	321	165	156
30-34	368	189	179	351	180	171
35-39	358	184	175	365	187	178
40-44	309	158	151	354	181	173
45-49	294	150	144	304	155	149
50-54	365	185	180	287	146	141
55-59	454	226	228	352	177	176
60-64	452	222	230	432	212	220
65-69	458	217	241	419	201	218
70-74	386	173	213	406	185	221
75-79	284	117	167	316	133	183
80-84	199	71	128	205	75	129
85-89	117	32	85	117	34	83
90-94	48	9	40	52	10	42
95-99	12	1	11	14	1	13
100 +	1	0	1	2	0	2

United Nations Department of Economic and Social Affairs/Population Division
World Population Prospects: The 2004 Revision, Volume II: Sex and Age Distribution of the World Population

POPULATION BY AGE AND SEX (in thousands)

Age group	2005 Both sexes	2005 Males	2005 Females	2010 Both sexes	2010 Males	2010 Females	2015 Both sexes	2015 Males	2015 Females	2020 Both sexes	2020 Males	2020 Females
All ages	7 726	3 742	3 984	7 382	3 561	3 820	7 000	3 367	3 632	6 603	3 170	3 433
0-4	335	172	163	252	130	123	203	104	98	172	89	84
5-9	323	166	157	332	170	161	249	128	121	200	103	97
10-14	405	208	198	320	164	156	329	169	160	247	127	120
15-19	518	265	253	402	206	196	317	163	154	326	168	159
20-24	543	278	264	513	262	251	398	204	194	314	161	153
25-29	592	302	290	537	275	262	508	259	249	394	202	193
30-34	569	288	280	586	299	287	531	272	259	503	256	247
35-39	521	263	258	561	284	277	579	294	284	525	268	257
40-44	522	260	262	512	257	255	553	279	274	570	289	281
45-49	552	270	282	510	252	258	501	250	251	541	271	270
50-54	565	272	293	533	258	275	494	242	252	486	240	246
55-59	549	259	290	538	254	284	508	241	267	472	227	245
60-64	434	200	235	509	233	276	501	230	271	475	220	256
65-69	400	177	223	389	172	217	459	202	257	453	201	253
70-74	387	165	221	336	141	195	329	138	191	391	164	228
75-79	286	115	171	289	114	174	254	98	156	252	97	155
80-84	168	62	107	174	63	111	181	64	117	163	56	107
85-89	41	14	27	75	24	51	81	25	56	87	25	62
90-94	15	5	11	12	3	8	23	5	17	26	6	20
95-99	2	0	2	2	0	2	2	0	2	4	1	4
100 +	0	0	0	0	0	0	0	0	0	0	0	0

Age group	2025 Both sexes	2025 Males	2025 Females	2030 Both sexes	2030 Males	2030 Females	2035 Both sexes	2035 Males	2035 Females	2040 Both sexes	2040 Males	2040 Females
All ages	6 210	2 976	3 234	5 818	2 783	3 035	5 422	2 589	2 833	5 024	2 395	2 630
0-4	162	83	79	151	78	73	139	72	68	126	65	61
5-9	170	87	83	160	82	78	149	77	72	137	71	67
10-14	198	102	96	168	86	81	158	81	77	147	75	71
15-19	244	125	119	195	100	95	165	85	80	155	80	76
20-24	323	166	157	241	124	118	193	99	94	163	84	79
25-29	311	159	152	320	164	156	239	122	116	190	98	92
30-34	390	199	191	307	157	150	317	162	154	235	121	115
35-39	497	253	244	385	197	189	304	155	148	313	160	153
40-44	517	264	253	490	249	241	380	194	186	299	153	146
45-49	559	282	276	507	258	250	482	244	238	373	190	183
50-54	526	261	264	544	273	271	494	250	245	470	237	233
55-59	465	226	239	505	248	257	524	259	264	477	238	239
60-64	443	208	235	438	208	229	476	229	247	496	241	254
65-69	432	193	239	404	184	220	401	185	216	438	205	233
70-74	389	164	225	373	158	215	351	152	199	351	155	196
75-79	303	117	186	305	118	187	296	116	180	281	113	168
80-84	165	56	108	202	60	104	207	71	107	205	71	134
85-89	81	23	58	85	23	62	108	29	79	114	31	84
90-94	29	6	23	29	5	24	32	6	26	43	7	36
95-99	5	1	5	7	1	6	7	1	6	8	1	8
100 +	1	0	0	1	0	1	1	0	1	1	0	1

Age group	2045 Both sexes	2045 Males	2045 Females	2050 Both sexes	2050 Males	2050 Females
All ages	4 626	2 202	2 424	4 230	2 011	2 220
0-4	110	57	53	99	51	48
5-9	124	64	60	108	56	52
10-14	135	70	66	122	63	59
15-19	144	74	70	133	68	65
20-24	153	79	74	142	73	69
25-29	160	82	78	151	77	73
30-34	187	96	91	157	81	77
35-39	232	119	113	184	94	90
40-44	309	158	151	228	117	111
45-49	294	150	144	304	155	149
50-54	365	185	180	287	146	141
55-59	454	226	228	352	177	176
60-64	452	222	230	432	212	220
65-69	458	217	241	419	201	218
70-74	386	173	213	406	185	221
75-79	284	117	167	316	133	183
80-84	199	71	128	205	75	129
85-89	117	32	85	117	34	83
90-94	48	9	40	52	10	42
95-99	12	1	11	14	1	13
100 +	1	0	1	2	0	2

United Nations Department of Economic and Social Affairs/Population Division
World Population Prospects: The 2004 Revision, Volume II: Sex and Age Distribution of the World Population

249

POPULATION BY AGE AND SEX (in thousands)

Age group	1950 Both sexes	Males	Females	1955 Both sexes	Males	Females	1960 Both sexes	Males	Females	1965 Both sexes	Males	Females
All ages	3 861	2 123	1 737	4 121	2 229	1 893	4 455	2 376	2 079	4 826	2 538	2 289
0-4	678	391	287	657	330	327	724	364	360	813	410	403
5-9	523	295	228	586	338	248	575	288	287	639	321	318
10-14	452	247	205	505	285	220	567	327	240	557	279	278
15-19	404	220	184	432	235	196	485	273	211	543	313	230
20-24	354	189	165	370	200	169	398	215	182	442	248	194
25-29	294	160	134	315	166	149	331	177	154	350	186	163
30-34	246	135	111	261	141	120	282	146	136	290	153	138
35-39	210	118	91	220	119	101	235	125	110	250	127	123
40-44	168	95	74	189	105	83	199	106	93	210	110	100
45-49	150	87	63	151	84	68	171	94	77	179	94	85
50-54	131	74	57	137	79	59	139	76	63	158	86	72
55-59	76	36	40	120	67	53	126	72	55	130	71	59
60-64	64	29	35	67	31	35	104	58	47	111	63	49
65-69	50	22	28	51	23	28	54	25	29	85	46	38
70-74	34	15	19	35	15	20	36	16	20	39	18	21
75-79	18	7	11	19	8	11	20	8	11	21	9	12
80 +	8	3	5	8	3	5	9	4	5	10	4	6

Age group	1970 Both sexes	Males	Females	1975 Both sexes	Males	Females	1980 Both sexes	Males	Females	1985 Both sexes	Males	Females
All ages	5 329	2 766	2 563	5 947	3 049	2 898	6 587	3 337	3 249	7 386	3 706	3 680
0-4	957	483	473	1 114	564	551	1 197	606	591	1 374	695	679
5-9	726	366	360	863	436	427	1 016	513	503	1 097	554	543
10-14	621	312	309	706	356	350	842	425	417	995	502	492
15-19	534	267	267	596	298	297	678	341	338	813	409	404
20-24	500	287	212	488	240	248	543	268	276	626	310	316
25-29	393	218	175	445	253	191	427	204	223	482	231	251
30-34	309	162	147	347	190	157	392	221	171	376	173	202
35-39	259	134	125	274	141	133	307	166	142	351	196	155
40-44	225	112	113	232	118	114	244	123	121	277	147	130
45-49	190	98	93	204	99	105	209	103	106	221	109	113
50-54	166	86	80	177	90	87	184	87	97	189	91	98
55-59	148	80	68	156	81	76	162	81	81	169	79	90
60-64	115	62	53	132	71	61	142	72	69	147	73	74
65-69	91	51	41	96	51	45	111	59	52	120	60	59
70-74	61	33	28	67	37	30	72	38	34	83	43	40
75-79	23	11	13	37	20	17	41	22	19	43	22	21
80 +	11	5	6	13	6	7	18	9	9	22	11	11

Age group	1990 Both sexes	Males	Females	1995 Both sexes	Males	Females	2000 Both sexes	Males	Females	2005 Both sexes	Males	Females
All ages	8 532	4 262	4 270	9 832	4 900	4 931	11 292	5 648	5 643	13 228	6 650	6 578
0-4	1 664	843	821	1 918	974	945	2 155	1 094	1 061	2 459	1 249	1 210
5-9	1 272	642	629	1 549	784	764	1 789	908	881	2 025	1 028	997
10-14	1 078	544	534	1 252	633	620	1 520	770	750	1 757	891	866
15-19	971	489	481	1 055	532	523	1 236	625	611	1 503	760	742
20-24	769	384	385	924	463	461	1 025	517	507	1 219	615	604
25-29	576	280	295	698	345	353	865	436	429	1 004	510	494
30-34	442	207	234	513	246	268	617	308	309	837	428	409
35-39	345	156	190	396	182	214	449	216	233	586	298	288
40-44	326	180	146	313	138	176	352	160	191	425	207	218
45-49	257	134	123	299	162	137	283	122	161	333	153	181
50-54	208	101	107	241	124	117	273	146	127	268	115	152
55-59	179	86	93	196	94	102	219	111	108	254	134	119
60-64	154	71	83	163	77	86	175	82	93	198	98	99
65-69	125	61	64	132	60	72	137	63	74	150	69	81
70-74	90	45	46	96	46	50	100	44	56	106	48	59
75-79	51	26	25	57	27	30	61	28	33	65	28	38
80 +	25	12	13	29	14	15	36	16	19	40	17	22

POPULATION BY AGE AND SEX (in thousands)

Age group	2005 Both sexes	2005 Males	2005 Females	2010 Both sexes	2010 Males	2010 Females	2015 Both sexes	2015 Males	2015 Females	2020 Both sexes	2020 Males	2020 Females
All ages	13 228	6 650	6 578	15 314	7 716	7 598	17 678	8 923	8 755	20 305	10 265	10 041
0-4	2 459	1 249	1 210	2 810	1 427	1 383	3 133	1 591	1 542	3 432	1 744	1 688
5-9	2 025	1 028	997	2 315	1 175	1 140	2 664	1 352	1 312	2 995	1 520	1 475
10-14	1 757	891	866	1 990	1 010	980	2 280	1 157	1 123	2 629	1 334	1 295
15-19	1 503	760	742	1 735	880	855	1 968	999	969	2 257	1 145	1 112
20-24	1 219	615	604	1 469	743	726	1 701	863	838	1 934	982	953
25-29	1 004	510	494	1 162	589	574	1 409	715	694	1 642	835	807
30-34	837	428	409	936	479	457	1 089	556	534	1 332	680	652
35-39	586	298	288	775	399	376	870	448	422	1 018	523	495
40-44	425	207	218	543	276	267	723	372	350	813	420	394
45-49	333	153	181	396	191	204	508	257	250	678	348	330
50-54	268	115	152	310	141	170	370	177	193	476	239	237
55-59	254	134	119	247	105	143	288	128	159	344	162	181
60-64	198	98	99	228	118	109	224	93	131	262	114	147
65-69	150	69	81	169	82	87	196	100	96	195	78	116
70-74	106	48	59	116	52	64	132	63	69	155	77	78
75-79	65	28	38	69	30	39	77	33	44	89	41	48
80-84	30	13	17	32	13	19	35	14	21	40	16	23
85-89	9	4	5	10	4	6	11	4	7	12	5	7
90-94	1	1	1	2	1	1	2	1	1	2	1	1
95-99	0	0	0	0	0	0	0	0	0	0	0	0
100 +	0	0	0	0	0	0	0	0	0	0	0	0

Age group	2025 Both sexes	2025 Males	2025 Females	2030 Both sexes	2030 Males	2030 Females	2035 Both sexes	2035 Males	2035 Females	2040 Both sexes	2040 Males	2040 Females
All ages	23 162	11 723	11 440	26 199	13 271	12 928	29 350	14 876	14 474	32 570	16 512	16 058
0-4	3 692	1 878	1 814	3 893	1 981	1 912	4 042	2 057	1 985	4 153	2 113	2 040
5-9	3 307	1 679	1 628	3 581	1 820	1 761	3 797	1 931	1 867	3 960	2 013	1 946
10-14	2 966	1 505	1 461	3 283	1 666	1 617	3 560	1 809	1 752	3 779	1 921	1 859
15-19	2 607	1 322	1 285	2 946	1 494	1 452	3 264	1 656	1 608	3 543	1 799	1 744
20-24	2 223	1 128	1 095	2 574	1 305	1 269	2 914	1 477	1 437	3 234	1 640	1 594
25-29	1 875	954	922	2 164	1 100	1 064	2 514	1 277	1 238	2 857	1 450	1 407
30-34	1 564	799	764	1 797	918	879	2 084	1 063	1 021	2 435	1 240	1 195
35-39	1 254	644	610	1 485	762	723	1 717	880	837	2 004	1 026	978
40-44	957	492	404	1 189	612	577	1 417	729	689	1 649	846	802
45-49	766	394	372	907	466	441	1 134	582	552	1 360	698	662
50-54	638	326	313	724	370	354	863	440	423	1 084	553	531
55-59	444	221	224	598	302	297	682	345	337	816	412	404
60-64	314	146	168	408	199	209	552	274	279	633	315	318
65-69	229	98	131	277	125	151	362	173	189	494	240	254
70-74	157	61	96	187	77	109	228	100	128	301	140	161
75-79	106	51	55	110	41	69	133	53	81	166	70	96
80-84	47	20	26	57	26	31	61	21	40	75	28	47
85-89	14	5	8	17	7	10	21	9	12	23	7	16
90-94	2	1	2	3	1	2	3	1	2	4	2	3
95-99	0	0	0	0	0	0	0	0	0	0	0	0
100 +	0	0	0	0	0	0	0	0	0	0	0	0

Age group	2045 Both sexes	2045 Males	2045 Females	2050 Both sexes	2050 Males	2050 Females
All ages	35 828	18 159	17 668	39 093	19 801	19 292
0-4	4 240	2 158	2 083	4 307	2 192	2 115
5-9	4 082	2 076	2 006	4 180	2 126	2 055
10-14	3 944	2 005	1 940	4 069	2 068	2 001
15-19	3 764	1 912	1 852	3 930	1 997	1 934
20-24	3 515	1 784	1 731	3 739	1 898	1 841
25-29	3 181	1 614	1 567	3 468	1 761	1 707
30-34	2 781	1 415	1 366	3 112	1 582	1 530
35-39	2 356	1 203	1 153	2 707	1 380	1 327
40-44	1 935	991	944	2 289	1 169	1 119
45-49	1 590	814	776	1 877	959	918
50-54	1 306	666	640	1 535	782	753
55-59	1 031	520	511	1 249	630	618
60-64	762	378	384	968	481	487
65-69	570	277	292	692	336	356
70-74	416	196	220	484	229	255
75-79	222	99	123	311	141	170
80-84	96	38	58	131	55	76
85-89	29	10	19	38	14	24
90-94	5	1	4	7	2	5
95-99	0	0	0	1	0	0
100 +	0	0	0	0	0	0

POPULATION BY AGE AND SEX (in thousands)

Age group	2005 Both sexes	Males	Females	2010 Both sexes	Males	Females	2015 Both sexes	Males	Females	2020 Both sexes	Males	Females
All ages	13 228	6 650	6 578	15 425	7 773	7 653	17 995	9 084	8 911	20 924	10 579	10 345
0-4	2 459	1 249	1 210	2 921	1 484	1 438	3 344	1 699	1 646	3 745	1 903	1 842
5-9	2 025	1 028	997	2 315	1 175	1 140	2 769	1 405	1 364	3 197	1 622	1 575
10-14	1 757	891	866	1 990	1 010	980	2 280	1 157	1 123	2 733	1 386	1 346
15-19	1 503	760	742	1 735	880	855	1 968	999	969	2 257	1 145	1 112
20-24	1 219	615	604	1 469	743	726	1 701	863	838	1 934	982	953
25-29	1 004	510	494	1 162	589	574	1 409	715	694	1 642	835	807
30-34	837	428	409	936	479	457	1 089	556	534	1 332	680	652
35-39	586	298	288	775	399	376	870	448	422	1 018	523	495
40-44	425	207	218	543	276	267	723	372	350	813	420	394
45-49	333	153	181	396	191	204	508	257	250	678	348	330
50-54	268	115	152	310	141	170	370	177	193	476	239	237
55-59	254	134	119	247	105	143	288	128	159	344	162	181
60-64	198	98	99	228	118	109	224	93	131	262	114	147
65-69	150	69	81	169	82	87	196	100	96	195	78	116
70-74	106	48	59	116	52	64	132	63	69	155	77	78
75-79	65	28	38	69	30	39	77	33	44	89	41	48
80-84	30	13	17	32	13	19	35	14	21	40	16	23
85-89	9	4	5	10	4	6	11	4	7	12	5	7
90-94	1	1	1	2	1	1	2	1	1	2	1	1
95-99	0	0	0	0	0	0	0	0	0	0	0	0
100 +	0	0	0	0	0	0	0	0	0	0	0	0

Age group	2025 Both sexes	Males	Females	2030 Both sexes	Males	Females	2035 Both sexes	Males	Females	2040 Both sexes	Males	Females
All ages	24 146	12 223	11 924	27 652	14 009	13 643	31 425	15 930	15 495	35 457	17 979	17 478
0-4	4 071	2 071	2 000	4 378	2 228	2 150	4 683	2 383	2 300	4 989	2 539	2 450
5-9	3 608	1 832	1 776	3 950	2 007	1 942	4 270	2 171	2 099	4 588	2 333	2 255
10-14	3 166	1 606	1 560	3 582	1 818	1 764	3 927	1 995	1 932	4 250	2 160	2 090
15-19	2 710	1 374	1 335	3 144	1 595	1 550	3 561	1 807	1 755	3 908	1 984	1 924
20-24	2 223	1 128	1 095	2 675	1 357	1 319	3 111	1 577	1 534	3 529	1 790	1 739
25-29	1 875	954	922	2 164	1 100	1 064	2 614	1 327	1 287	3 051	1 548	1 503
30-34	1 564	799	764	1 797	918	879	2 084	1 063	1 021	2 532	1 290	1 243
35-39	1 254	644	610	1 485	762	723	1 717	880	837	2 004	1 026	978
40-44	957	492	464	1 189	612	577	1 417	729	689	1 649	846	802
45-49	766	394	372	907	466	441	1 134	582	552	1 360	698	662
50-54	638	326	313	724	370	354	863	440	423	1 084	553	531
55-59	444	221	224	598	302	297	682	345	337	816	412	404
60-64	314	146	168	408	199	209	552	274	279	633	315	318
65-69	229	98	131	277	125	151	362	173	189	494	240	254
70-74	157	61	96	187	77	109	228	100	128	301	140	161
75-79	106	51	55	110	41	69	133	53	81	166	70	96
80-84	47	20	26	57	26	31	61	21	40	75	28	47
85-89	14	5	8	17	7	10	21	9	12	23	7	16
90-94	2	1	2	3	1	2	3	1	2	4	2	3
95-99	0	0	0	0	0	0	0	0	0	0	0	0
100 +	0	0	0	0	0	0	0	0	0	0	0	0

Age group	2045 Both sexes	Males	Females	2050 Both sexes	Males	Females
All ages	39 722	20 139	19 583	44 178	22 386	21 792
0-4	5 279	2 686	2 593	5 534	2 816	2 718
5-9	4 905	2 494	2 411	5 204	2 646	2 558
10-14	4 570	2 323	2 247	4 889	2 485	2 404
15-19	4 233	2 150	2 083	4 554	2 314	2 241
20-24	3 878	1 968	1 910	4 206	2 135	2 070
25-29	3 472	1 762	1 710	3 827	1 943	1 884
30-34	2 971	1 511	1 460	3 398	1 728	1 671
35-39	2 450	1 251	1 199	2 892	1 474	1 418
40-44	1 935	991	944	2 381	1 216	1 165
45-49	1 590	814	776	1 877	959	918
50-54	1 306	666	640	1 535	782	753
55-59	1 031	520	511	1 249	630	618
60-64	762	378	384	968	481	487
65-69	570	277	292	692	336	356
70-74	416	196	220	484	229	255
75-79	222	99	123	311	141	170
80-84	96	38	58	131	55	76
85-89	29	10	19	38	14	24
90-94	5	1	4	7	2	5
95-99	0	0	0	1	0	0
100 +	0	0	0	0	0	0

United Nations Department of Economic and Social Affairs/Population Division
World Population Prospects: The 2004 Revision, Volume II: Sex and Age Distribution of the World Population

252

POPULATION BY AGE AND SEX (in thousands)

Age group	2005 Both sexes	Males	Females	2010 Both sexes	Males	Females	2015 Both sexes	Males	Females	2020 Both sexes	Males	Females
All ages	13 228	6 650	6 578	15 204	7 660	7 544	17 362	8 763	8 599	19 687	9 951	9 737
0-4	2 459	1 249	1 210	2 699	1 371	1 328	2 922	1 484	1 438	3 120	1 586	1 534
5-9	2 025	1 028	997	2 315	1 175	1 140	2 559	1 298	1 260	2 793	1 417	1 376
10-14	1 757	891	866	1 990	1 010	980	2 280	1 157	1 123	2 525	1 281	1 244
15-19	1 503	760	742	1 735	880	855	1 968	999	969	2 257	1 145	1 112
20-24	1 219	615	604	1 469	743	726	1 701	863	838	1 934	982	953
25-29	1 004	510	494	1 162	589	574	1 409	715	694	1 642	835	807
30-34	837	428	409	936	479	457	1 089	556	534	1 332	680	652
35-39	586	298	288	775	399	376	870	448	422	1 018	523	495
40-44	425	207	218	543	276	267	723	372	350	813	420	394
45-49	333	153	181	396	191	204	508	257	250	678	348	330
50-54	268	115	152	310	141	170	370	177	193	476	239	237
55-59	254	134	119	247	105	143	288	128	159	344	162	181
60-64	198	98	99	228	118	109	224	93	131	262	114	147
65-69	150	69	81	169	82	87	196	100	96	195	78	116
70-74	106	48	59	116	52	64	132	63	69	155	77	78
75-79	65	28	38	69	30	39	77	33	44	89	41	48
80-84	30	13	17	32	13	19	35	14	21	40	16	23
85-89	9	4	5	10	4	6	11	4	7	12	5	7
90-94	1	1	1	2	1	1	2	1	1	2	1	1
95-99	0	0	0	0	0	0	0	0	0	0	0	0
100 +	0	0	0	0	0	0	0	0	0	0	0	0

Age group	2025 Both sexes	Males	Females	2030 Both sexes	Males	Females	2035 Both sexes	Males	Females	2040 Both sexes	Males	Females
All ages	22 180	11 224	10 957	24 758	12 539	12 219	27 317	13 843	13 474	29 787	15 098	14 690
0-4	3 314	1 686	1 628	3 419	1 740	1 679	3 431	1 746	1 685	3 379	1 719	1 659
5-9	3 006	1 526	1 480	3 214	1 634	1 581	3 334	1 695	1 639	3 361	1 709	1 652
10-14	2 766	1 403	1 363	2 984	1 514	1 469	3 196	1 623	1 572	3 318	1 687	1 632
15-19	2 504	1 270	1 234	2 747	1 393	1 354	2 966	1 505	1 461	3 180	1 615	1 565
20-24	2 223	1 128	1 095	2 472	1 253	1 218	2 717	1 377	1 340	2 939	1 490	1 448
25-29	1 875	954	922	2 164	1 100	1 064	2 414	1 226	1 188	2 663	1 351	1 311
30-34	1 564	799	764	1 797	918	879	2 084	1 063	1 021	2 337	1 191	1 147
35-39	1 254	644	610	1 485	762	723	1 717	880	837	2 004	1 026	978
40-44	957	492	464	1 189	612	577	1 417	729	689	1 649	846	802
45-49	766	394	372	907	466	441	1 134	582	552	1 360	698	662
50-54	638	326	313	724	370	354	863	440	423	1 084	553	531
55-59	444	221	224	598	302	297	682	345	337	816	412	404
60-64	314	146	168	408	199	209	552	274	279	633	315	318
65-69	229	98	131	277	125	151	362	173	189	494	240	254
70-74	157	61	96	187	77	109	228	100	128	301	140	161
75-79	106	51	55	110	41	69	133	53	81	166	70	96
80-84	47	20	26	57	26	31	61	21	40	75	28	47
85-89	14	5	8	17	7	10	21	9	12	23	7	16
90-94	2	1	2	3	1	2	3	1	2	4	2	3
95-99	0	0	0	0	0	0	0	0	0	0	0	0
100 +	0	0	0	0	0	0	0	0	0	0	0	0

Age group	2045 Both sexes	Males	Females	2050 Both sexes	Males	Females
All ages	32 138	16 284	15 854	34 357	17 394	16 962
0-4	3 304	1 681	1 623	3 225	1 641	1 584
5-9	3 321	1 689	1 632	3 257	1 656	1 601
10-14	3 348	1 701	1 646	3 310	1 682	1 627
15-19	3 305	1 679	1 626	3 336	1 695	1 641
20-24	3 155	1 601	1 554	3 282	1 667	1 616
25-29	2 890	1 467	1 423	3 111	1 580	1 531
30-34	2 591	1 318	1 273	2 826	1 437	1 389
35-39	2 261	1 155	1 106	2 522	1 285	1 236
40-44	1 935	991	944	2 196	1 122	1 074
45-49	1 590	814	776	1 877	959	918
50-54	1 306	666	640	1 535	782	753
55-59	1 031	520	511	1 249	630	618
60-64	762	378	384	968	481	487
65-69	570	277	292	692	336	356
70-74	416	196	220	484	229	255
75-79	222	99	123	311	141	170
80-84	96	38	58	131	55	76
85-89	29	10	19	38	14	24
90-94	5	1	4	7	2	5
95-99	0	0	0	1	0	0
100 +	0	0	0	0	0	0

United Nations Department of Economic and Social Affairs/Population Division
World Population Prospects: The 2004 Revision, Volume II: Sex and Age Distribution of the World Population

253

POPULATION BY AGE AND SEX (in thousands)

Age group	1950 Both sexes	1950 Males	1950 Females	1955 Both sexes	1955 Males	1955 Females	1960 Both sexes	1960 Males	1960 Females	1965 Both sexes	1965 Males	1965 Females
All ages	2 456	1 176	1 280	2 687	1 288	1 399	2 940	1 411	1 529	3 213	1 544	1 669
0-4	402	198	204	490	244	245	523	261	262	563	282	281
5-9	322	157	165	353	173	180	434	216	218	467	233	235
10-14	281	137	144	306	149	157	336	165	171	415	207	209
15-19	249	121	128	267	130	137	292	142	150	321	157	164
20-24	218	105	113	229	110	119	247	119	128	270	130	139
25-29	191	91	100	195	93	103	206	98	108	221	105	116
30-34	165	78	87	170	80	90	175	82	93	184	86	98
35-39	142	67	75	148	69	79	154	71	82	157	72	85
40-44	119	56	64	127	60	68	134	62	72	138	63	75
45-49	99	46	53	107	49	58	115	53	62	121	55	66
50-54	81	37	44	88	40	48	96	43	53	103	47	57
55-59	60	27	33	71	32	39	78	35	43	85	37	47
60-64	48	22	27	50	22	28	60	26	34	66	29	37
65-69	36	16	21	38	16	21	40	17	23	48	20	27
70-74	24	10	13	25	11	15	27	11	15	29	12	17
75-79	13	6	7	14	6	8	15	6	9	16	7	10
80 +	6	3	4	7	3	4	8	3	5	8	3	5

Age group	1970 Both sexes	1970 Males	1970 Females	1975 Both sexes	1975 Males	1975 Females	1980 Both sexes	1980 Males	1980 Females	1985 Both sexes	1985 Males	1985 Females
All ages	3 514	1 691	1 823	3 680	1 762	1 919	4 130	1 987	2 143	4 885	2 368	2 517
0-4	612	306	306	646	323	323	731	366	364	906	454	452
5-9	506	253	254	546	273	274	590	295	295	677	338	339
10-14	448	223	225	482	241	242	527	263	264	576	287	288
15-19	398	198	200	419	208	211	467	233	235	522	260	261
20-24	296	144	152	346	169	176	399	197	202	469	232	236
25-29	241	114	126	236	111	125	323	157	166	403	198	205
30-34	196	91	105	190	86	103	218	101	117	327	158	168
35-39	164	75	89	157	70	87	175	79	96	220	102	118
40-44	141	64	77	135	59	76	145	64	81	174	78	96
45-49	125	56	69	119	52	68	125	54	71	142	63	80
50-54	109	48	61	107	46	61	109	47	63	120	51	68
55-59	92	40	51	93	40	53	97	41	56	102	43	59
60-64	73	31	41	77	33	44	81	34	47	87	36	51
65-69	53	23	31	57	24	34	63	26	37	69	28	40
70-74	35	14	20	38	16	23	43	17	26	48	20	28
75-79	18	7	11	21	8	13	25	10	15	28	11	17
80 +	9	4	6	10	4	6	12	5	8	16	6	10

Age group	1990 Both sexes	1990 Males	1990 Females	1995 Both sexes	1995 Males	1995 Females	2000 Both sexes	2000 Males	2000 Females	2005 Both sexes	2005 Males	2005 Females
All ages	5 670	2 761	2 909	6 159	2 992	3 167	6 486	3 141	3 345	7 548	3 684	3 863
0-4	1 076	540	536	1 131	567	564	1 151	578	573	1 326	666	660
5-9	840	420	420	975	488	487	1 025	513	512	1 075	538	537
10-14	660	329	330	810	404	405	937	469	468	996	498	498
15-19	563	281	282	627	313	315	766	382	385	930	465	465
20-24	505	251	254	505	250	256	547	269	278	773	383	389
25-29	449	221	228	426	208	218	400	193	207	553	272	281
30-34	385	188	197	375	181	194	322	153	169	395	192	202
35-39	311	150	161	327	156	171	291	136	155	308	149	160
40-44	209	96	113	269	126	143	265	122	142	275	130	145
45-49	164	73	91	181	81	100	225	102	123	249	115	134
50-54	133	58	75	144	62	82	153	65	88	211	95	116
55-59	110	47	63	116	49	67	122	50	72	142	60	82
60-64	91	38	53	93	38	55	97	39	58	110	45	65
65-69	73	30	43	73	29	44	75	29	46	83	33	50
70-74	52	21	31	54	21	32	54	21	33	59	23	36
75-79	31	12	19	33	13	20	34	13	21	37	14	23
80 +	18	7	12	20	7	13	23	8	15	27	9	18

United Nations Department of Economic and Social Affairs/Population Division
World Population Prospects: The 2004 Revision, Volume II: Sex and Age Distribution of the World Population

POPULATION BY AGE AND SEX (in thousands)

Age group	2005 Both sexes	Males	Females	2010 Both sexes	Males	Females	2015 Both sexes	Males	Females	2020 Both sexes	Males	Females
All ages	7 548	3 684	3 863	9 099	4 472	4 628	10 617	5 239	5 378	12 263	6 070	6 193
0-4	1 326	666	660	1 730	869	861	2 084	1 046	1 038	2 260	1 135	1 126
5-9	1 075	538	537	1 252	626	626	1 628	814	814	1 980	990	990
10-14	996	498	498	1 050	525	525	1 216	607	608	1 588	793	795
15-19	930	465	465	997	497	500	1 029	514	515	1 194	596	598
20-24	773	383	389	953	474	479	969	482	487	1 002	499	504
25-29	553	272	281	793	393	400	906	450	456	924	459	465
30-34	395	192	202	560	277	283	734	365	368	842	420	422
35-39	308	149	160	394	194	200	511	254	256	672	337	335
40-44	275	130	145	303	147	156	359	177	182	467	233	234
45-49	249	115	134	267	126	141	278	135	144	330	162	167
50-54	211	95	116	238	110	129	245	115	130	256	123	133
55-59	142	60	82	198	89	109	217	99	119	224	104	121
60-64	110	45	65	131	55	76	177	78	99	195	87	108
65-69	83	33	50	96	39	57	111	46	66	152	65	86
70-74	59	23	36	66	26	40	75	30	46	88	35	53
75-79	37	14	23	41	15	25	45	17	28	52	20	32
80-84	19	7	12	21	7	13	23	8	15	26	9	16
85-89	7	2	4	8	3	5	8	3	6	9	3	6
90-94	1	0	1	2	1	1	2	1	1	2	1	2
95-99	0	0	0	0	0	0	0	0	0	0	0	0
100 +	0	0	0	0	0	0	0	0	0	0	0	0

Age group	2025 Both sexes	Males	Females	2030 Both sexes	Males	Females	2035 Both sexes	Males	Females	2040 Both sexes	Males	Females
All ages	14 003	6 946	7 057	15 930	7 914	8 016	18 156	9 030	9 125	20 646	10 277	10 369
0-4	2 393	1 201	1 191	2 607	1 310	1 297	2 944	1 480	1 464	3 258	1 639	1 619
5-9	2 163	1 081	1 081	2 303	1 152	1 151	2 523	1 263	1 260	2 864	1 435	1 429
10-14	1 940	969	971	2 128	1 063	1 065	2 272	1 135	1 137	2 495	1 248	1 248
15-19	1 562	779	783	1 913	954	959	2 101	1 048	1 053	2 248	1 121	1 126
20-24	1 165	579	586	1 528	760	768	1 875	932	943	2 064	1 026	1 038
25-29	959	476	483	1 119	555	563	1 473	731	742	1 813	900	913
30-34	864	431	433	902	449	453	1 056	526	530	1 397	696	702
35-39	775	389	386	801	402	400	841	421	420	991	495	495
40-44	617	310	307	717	361	356	746	375	371	787	395	393
45-49	430	215	216	572	287	285	669	336	333	700	351	349
50-54	304	149	156	399	198	202	534	266	268	627	313	314
55-59	235	111	123	280	136	145	370	181	189	497	246	252
60-64	202	92	110	212	99	113	255	122	133	338	164	175
65-69	168	73	94	175	78	97	185	85	100	224	105	119
70-74	121	51	70	135	58	77	142	62	80	152	68	84
75-79	62	24	38	86	35	51	97	40	57	104	44	60
80-84	30	11	19	36	13	23	51	20	31	59	23	35
85-89	11	4	7	13	4	9	16	5	10	23	8	14
90-94	3	1	2	3	1	2	4	1	3	5	1	3
95-99	0	0	0	0	0	0	1	0	0	1	0	1
100 +	0	0	0	0	0	0	0	0	0	0	0	0

Age group	2045 Both sexes	Males	Females	2050 Both sexes	Males	Females
All ages	23 236	11 572	11 664	25 812	12 856	12 956
0-4	3 407	1 714	1 693	3 437	1 730	1 707
5-9	3 184	1 596	1 588	3 343	1 676	1 666
10-14	2 837	1 420	1 418	3 159	1 582	1 578
15-19	2 471	1 234	1 238	2 813	1 406	1 408
20-24	2 211	1 100	1 111	2 436	1 212	1 223
25-29	2 003	994	1 009	2 154	1 069	1 085
30-34	1 730	860	869	1 922	955	967
35-39	1 318	659	660	1 644	820	824
40-44	932	467	465	1 249	625	624
45-49	743	372	371	884	442	442
50-54	659	329	331	703	350	353
55-59	587	291	297	620	306	314
60-64	457	223	234	543	265	277
65-69	299	142	157	408	196	212
70-74	186	85	101	250	116	134
75-79	112	49	63	139	62	77
80-84	63	26	38	70	29	40
85-89	27	10	17	30	11	18
90-94	7	2	5	8	3	5
95-99	1	0	1	1	0	1
100 +	0	0	0	0	0	0

United Nations Department of Economic and Social Affairs/Population Division
World Population Prospects: The 2004 Revision, Volume II: Sex and Age Distribution of the World Population

255

POPULATION BY AGE AND SEX (in thousands)

Age group	2005 Both sexes	2005 Males	2005 Females	2010 Both sexes	2010 Males	2010 Females	2015 Both sexes	2015 Males	2015 Females	2020 Both sexes	2020 Males	2020 Females
All ages	7 548	3 684	3 863	9 099	4 472	4 628	10 671	5 266	5 405	12 495	6 186	6 309
0-4	1 326	666	660	1 730	869	861	2 138	1 073	1 065	2 441	1 225	1 216
5-9	1 075	538	537	1 252	626	626	1 628	814	814	2 031	1 015	1 015
10-14	996	498	498	1 050	525	525	1 216	607	608	1 588	793	795
15-19	930	465	465	997	497	500	1 029	514	515	1 194	596	598
20-24	773	383	389	953	474	479	969	482	487	1 002	499	504
25-29	553	272	281	793	393	400	906	450	456	924	459	465
30-34	395	192	202	560	277	283	734	365	368	842	420	422
35-39	308	149	160	394	194	200	511	254	256	672	337	335
40-44	275	130	145	303	147	156	359	177	182	467	233	234
45-49	249	115	134	267	126	141	278	135	144	330	162	167
50-54	211	95	116	238	110	129	245	115	130	256	123	133
55-59	142	60	82	198	89	109	217	99	119	224	104	121
60-64	110	45	65	131	55	76	177	78	99	195	87	108
65-69	83	33	50	96	39	57	111	46	66	152	65	86
70-74	59	23	36	66	26	40	75	30	46	88	35	53
75-79	37	14	23	41	15	25	45	17	28	52	20	32
80-84	19	7	12	21	7	13	23	8	15	26	9	16
85-89	7	2	4	8	3	5	8	3	6	9	3	6
90-94	1	0	1	2	1	1	2	1	1	2	1	2
95-99	0	0	0	0	0	0	0	0	0	0	0	0
100 +	0	0	0	0	0	0	0	0	0	0	0	0

Age group	2025 Both sexes	2025 Males	2025 Females	2030 Both sexes	2030 Males	2030 Females	2035 Both sexes	2035 Males	2035 Females	2040 Both sexes	2040 Males	2040 Females
All ages	14 431	7 161	7 270	16 590	8 245	8 345	19 130	9 518	9 612	22 082	10 996	11 086
0-4	2 597	1 304	1 293	2 850	1 432	1 418	3 271	1 644	1 627	3 738	1 880	1 858
5-9	2 335	1 168	1 168	2 500	1 250	1 249	2 759	1 381	1 378	3 182	1 594	1 588
10-14	1 991	994	997	2 298	1 147	1 150	2 467	1 232	1 234	2 729	1 364	1 364
15-19	1 562	779	783	1 962	978	984	2 269	1 132	1 138	2 440	1 217	1 223
20-24	1 165	579	586	1 528	760	768	1 923	956	967	2 229	1 108	1 121
25-29	959	476	483	1 119	555	563	1 473	731	742	1 860	923	937
30-34	864	431	433	902	449	453	1 056	526	530	1 397	696	702
35-39	775	389	386	801	402	400	841	421	420	991	495	495
40-44	617	310	307	717	361	356	746	375	371	787	395	393
45-49	430	215	216	572	287	285	669	336	333	700	351	349
50-54	304	149	156	399	198	202	534	266	268	627	313	314
55-59	235	111	123	280	136	145	370	181	189	497	246	252
60-64	202	92	110	212	99	113	255	122	133	338	164	175
65-69	168	73	94	175	78	97	185	85	100	224	105	119
70-74	121	51	70	135	58	77	142	62	80	152	68	84
75-79	62	24	38	86	35	51	97	40	57	104	44	60
80-84	30	11	19	36	13	23	51	20	31	59	23	35
85-89	11	4	7	13	4	9	16	5	10	23	8	14
90-94	3	1	2	3	1	2	4	1	3	5	1	3
95-99	0	0	0	0	0	0	1	0	0	1	0	1
100 +	0	0	0	0	0	0	0	0	0	0	0	0

Age group	2045 Both sexes	2045 Males	2045 Females	2050 Both sexes	2050 Males	2050 Females
All ages	25 303	12 607	12 696	28 646	14 275	14 370
0-4	4 064	2 045	2 019	4 238	2 133	2 105
5-9	3 653	1 831	1 822	3 987	1 999	1 988
10-14	3 153	1 578	1 575	3 624	1 814	1 810
15-19	2 703	1 349	1 353	3 126	1 562	1 564
20-24	2 401	1 194	1 207	2 664	1 326	1 338
25-29	2 164	1 074	1 090	2 339	1 161	1 178
30-34	1 775	883	892	2 076	1 032	1 044
35-39	1 318	659	660	1 686	841	845
40-44	932	467	465	1 249	625	624
45-49	743	372	371	884	442	442
50-54	659	329	331	703	350	353
55-59	587	291	297	620	306	314
60-64	457	223	234	543	265	277
65-69	299	142	157	408	196	212
70-74	186	85	101	250	116	134
75-79	112	49	63	139	62	77
80-84	63	26	38	70	29	40
85-89	27	10	17	30	11	18
90-94	7	2	5	8	3	5
95-99	1	0	1	1	0	1
100 +	0	0	0	0	0	0

United Nations Department of Economic and Social Affairs/Population Division
World Population Prospects: The 2004 Revision, Volume II: Sex and Age Distribution of the World Population

256

POPULATION BY AGE AND SEX (in thousands)

Age group	2005 Both sexes	Males	Females	2010 Both sexes	Males	Females	2015 Both sexes	Males	Females	2020 Both sexes	Males	Females
All ages	7 548	3 684	3 863	9 036	4 440	4 596	10 432	5 146	5 286	11 905	5 891	6 015
0-4	1 326	666	660	1 667	837	830	1 958	983	975	2 080	1 044	1 036
5-9	1 075	538	537	1 252	626	626	1 568	784	784	1 860	930	930
10-14	996	498	498	1 050	525	525	1 216	607	608	1 530	764	766
15-19	930	465	465	997	497	500	1 029	514	515	1 194	596	598
20-24	773	383	389	953	474	479	969	482	487	1 002	499	504
25-29	553	272	281	793	393	400	906	450	456	924	459	465
30-34	395	192	202	560	277	283	734	365	368	842	420	422
35-39	308	149	160	394	194	200	511	254	256	672	337	335
40-44	275	130	145	303	147	156	359	177	182	467	233	234
45-49	249	115	134	267	126	141	278	135	144	330	162	167
50-54	211	95	116	238	110	129	245	115	130	256	123	133
55-59	142	60	82	198	89	109	217	99	119	224	104	121
60-64	110	45	65	131	55	76	177	78	99	195	87	108
65-69	83	33	50	96	39	57	111	46	66	152	65	86
70-74	59	23	36	66	26	40	75	30	46	88	35	53
75-79	37	14	23	41	15	25	45	17	28	52	20	32
80-84	19	7	12	21	7	13	23	8	15	26	9	16
85-89	7	2	4	8	3	5	8	3	6	9	3	6
90-94	1	0	1	2	1	1	2	1	1	2	1	2
95-99	0	0	0	0	0	0	0	0	0	0	0	0
100 +	0	0	0	0	0	0	0	0	0	0	0	0

Age group	2025 Both sexes	Males	Females	2030 Both sexes	Males	Females	2035 Both sexes	Males	Females	2040 Both sexes	Males	Females
All ages	13 449	6 669	6 780	15 123	7 511	7 613	16 988	8 446	8 542	18 982	9 444	9 537
0-4	2 186	1 098	1 088	2 341	1 176	1 165	2 565	1 289	1 276	2 737	1 377	1 361
5-9	1 990	995	995	2 104	1 052	1 052	2 266	1 134	1 132	2 495	1 250	1 245
10-14	1 823	910	913	1 958	978	980	2 076	1 037	1 039	2 241	1 121	1 121
15-19	1 505	751	754	1 797	896	901	1 933	964	969	2 053	1 024	1 029
20-24	1 165	579	586	1 472	732	740	1 761	876	886	1 898	944	955
25-29	959	476	483	1 119	555	563	1 419	704	714	1 703	845	858
30-34	864	431	433	902	449	453	1 056	526	530	1 346	670	676
35-39	775	009	000	001	402	400	841	421	420	991	495	495
40-44	617	310	307	717	361	356	746	375	371	787	395	393
45-49	430	215	216	572	287	285	669	336	333	700	351	349
50-54	304	149	156	399	198	202	534	266	268	627	313	314
55-59	235	111	123	280	136	145	370	181	189	497	246	252
60-64	202	92	110	212	99	113	255	122	133	338	164	175
65-69	168	73	94	175	78	97	185	85	100	224	105	119
70-74	121	51	70	135	58	77	142	62	80	152	68	84
75-79	62	24	00	06	05	51	97	40	57	104	44	00
80-84	30	11	19	36	13	23	51	20	31	59	23	35
85-89	11	4	7	13	4	9	16	5	10	23	8	14
90-94	3	1	2	3	1	2	4	1	3	5	1	3
95-99	0	0	0	0	0	0	1	0	0	1	0	1
100 +	0	0	0	0	0	0	0	0	0	0	0	0

Age group	2045 Both sexes	Males	Females	2050 Both sexes	Males	Females
All ages	20 959	10 432	10 527	22 830	11 363	11 467
0-4	2 762	1 390	1 372	2 692	1 355	1 337
5-9	2 675	1 341	1 334	2 710	1 359	1 351
10-14	2 472	1 237	1 235	2 654	1 329	1 325
15-19	2 219	1 108	1 111	2 451	1 225	1 227
20-24	2 020	1 004	1 015	2 187	1 089	1 098
25-29	1 842	914	928	1 967	976	991
30-34	1 625	808	817	1 767	878	889
35-39	1 270	634	635	1 544	770	774
40-44	932	467	465	1 203	602	601
45-49	743	372	371	884	442	442
50-54	659	329	331	703	350	353
55-59	587	291	297	620	306	314
60-64	457	223	234	543	265	277
65-69	299	142	157	408	196	212
70-74	186	85	101	250	116	134
75-79	112	49	63	139	62	77
80-84	63	26	38	70	29	40
85-89	27	10	17	30	11	18
90-94	7	2	5	8	3	5
95-99	1	0	1	1	0	1
100 +	0	0	0	0	0	0

United Nations Department of Economic and Social Affairs/Population Division
World Population Prospects: The 2004 Revision, Volume II: Sex and Age Distribution of the World Population
257

POPULATION BY AGE AND SEX (in thousands)

Age group	1950 Both sexes	Males	Females	1955 Both sexes	Males	Females	1960 Both sexes	Males	Females	1965 Both sexes	Males	Females
All ages	4 346	2 173	2 173	4 840	2 420	2 420	5 433	2 717	2 716	6 141	3 072	3 069
0-4	725	365	360	809	407	401	920	464	456	1 050	530	520
5-9	592	298	294	662	333	329	744	375	369	854	430	423
10-14	517	261	257	576	290	285	645	325	320	727	366	360
15-19	452	228	224	503	254	249	561	283	278	629	317	312
20-24	391	197	194	435	220	215	485	245	240	542	274	269
25-29	335	169	166	373	188	185	416	210	206	466	235	231
30-34	285	144	141	318	160	158	355	179	176	398	201	197
35-39	241	121	120	268	135	133	300	151	149	337	170	168
40-44	202	101	101	225	112	112	251	126	126	283	141	141
45-49	167	82	85	186	92	94	208	103	105	234	116	118
50-54	135	66	69	151	73	77	169	82	87	190	93	97
55-59	106	51	56	118	57	62	133	64	70	150	72	78
60-64	80	37	43	89	41	47	100	47	53	113	53	60
65-69	53	24	29	62	28	34	70	32	38	79	36	43
70-74	35	16	20	37	16	21	44	19	25	50	22	28
75-79	20	9	11	21	9	12	22	9	13	27	11	15
80 +	10	4	6	11	4	6	11	5	7	13	5	8

Age group	1970 Both sexes	Males	Females	1975 Both sexes	Males	Females	1980 Both sexes	Males	Females	1985 Both sexes	Males	Females
All ages	6 938	3 473	3 465	7 098	3 552	3 545	6 613	3 064	3 548	8 101	3 814	4 287
0-4	1 194	604	591	1 098	553	544	829	415	414	1 812	916	896
5-9	976	492	483	1 018	514	504	960	484	477	776	387	389
10-14	830	419	412	884	446	437	872	425	447	941	474	467
15-19	706	356	350	751	379	372	771	364	408	856	417	439
20-24	607	306	301	633	319	314	651	300	351	750	352	398
25-29	520	262	258	539	272	268	538	246	292	628	287	341
30-34	444	224	220	459	231	228	448	198	249	517	235	282
35-39	377	190	187	389	196	194	366	157	209	431	190	241
40-44	317	159	158	327	164	164	268	106	162	352	149	202
45-49	263	130	133	272	135	137	238	88	149	256	100	156
50-54	214	105	109	222	108	113	199	75	124	225	82	143
55-59	170	82	88	175	84	91	151	57	94	185	68	117
60-64	128	60	68	132	62	70	135	64	70	136	50	86
65-69	90	41	49	93	42	50	96	44	52	114	53	61
70-74	57	25	32	59	26	33	56	25	31	73	32	41
75-79	31	13	18	31	13	18	24	12	12	35	15	20
80 +	15	6	9	15	6	9	11	5	6	13	6	7

Age group	1990 Both sexes	Males	Females	1995 Both sexes	Males	Females	2000 Both sexes	Males	Females	2005 Both sexes	Males	Females
All ages	9 738	4 632	5 106	11 368	5 454	5 914	12 744	6 140	6 604	14 071	6 801	7 270
0-4	1 828	928	901	1 815	923	892	1 710	870	840	1 835	935	900
5-9	1 723	869	855	1 747	885	862	1 744	886	859	1 650	839	812
10-14	778	387	391	1 714	863	851	1 736	879	857	1 731	879	853
15-19	942	473	469	785	390	395	1 706	859	848	1 722	871	851
20-24	861	417	444	950	476	474	784	387	396	1 682	845	838
25-29	756	352	403	873	421	453	938	464	474	760	372	388
30-34	632	288	344	764	355	409	857	408	450	896	436	460
35-39	520	235	285	635	288	347	748	343	406	817	380	437
40-44	433	189	243	522	234	287	622	278	344	715	321	394
45-49	350	148	203	432	188	245	510	226	284	594	261	334
50-54	252	98	155	347	145	203	419	179	240	485	211	274
55-59	217	78	139	247	94	153	332	136	196	395	165	230
60-64	173	61	111	205	72	132	230	86	144	306	122	184
65-69	119	42	77	153	53	100	181	62	119	203	74	129
70-74	88	40	48	95	32	62	123	41	82	146	48	98
75-79	47	20	27	58	25	33	65	21	44	86	27	58
80 +	19	8	11	26	11	15	38	15	22	46	15	31

United Nations Department of Economic and Social Affairs/Population Division
World Population Prospects: The 2004 Revision, Volume II: Sex and Age Distribution of the World Population

POPULATION BY AGE AND SEX (in thousands)

Age group	2005 Both sexes	2005 Males	2005 Females	2010 Both sexes	2010 Males	2010 Females	2015 Both sexes	2015 Males	2015 Females	2020 Both sexes	2020 Males	2020 Females
All ages	14 071	6 801	7 270	15 530	7 536	7 994	17 066	8 315	8 751	18 580	9 087	9 493
0-4	1 835	935	900	1 996	1 018	978	2 103	1 073	1 030	2 116	1 080	1 036
5-9	1 650	839	812	1 780	906	874	1 946	992	955	2 060	1 050	1 010
10-14	1 731	879	853	1 638	832	806	1 768	899	869	1 935	986	950
15-19	1 722	871	851	1 720	872	847	1 629	827	802	1 759	894	865
20-24	1 682	845	838	1 701	859	842	1 702	862	840	1 615	819	796
25-29	760	372	388	1 645	821	823	1 669	840	830	1 676	847	829
30-34	896	436	460	732	355	378	1 597	792	805	1 627	814	813
35-39	817	380	437	858	410	447	705	338	368	1 546	760	786
40-44	715	321	394	782	357	425	825	389	436	681	322	359
45-49	594	261	334	684	301	383	752	338	414	795	370	425
50-54	485	211	274	567	244	323	656	284	372	722	320	402
55-59	395	165	230	458	195	263	538	227	311	624	266	358
60-64	306	122	184	365	149	216	426	177	248	503	208	295
65-69	203	74	129	271	105	166	326	130	196	384	156	228
70-74	146	48	98	166	58	108	225	85	140	274	106	169
75-79	86	27	58	104	33	71	120	40	80	166	60	106
80-84	34	10	24	47	14	33	58	17	41	69	22	47
85-89	10	4	6	12	3	9	17	5	13	23	6	16
90-94	1	0	1	2	1	1	3	1	2	4	1	3
95-99	0	0	0	0	0	0	0	0	0	0	0	0
100 +	0	0	0	0	0	0	0	0	0	0	0	0

Age group	2025 Both sexes	2025 Males	2025 Females	2030 Both sexes	2030 Males	2030 Females	2035 Both sexes	2035 Males	2035 Females	2040 Both sexes	2040 Males	2040 Females
All ages	19 993	9 813	10 179	21 313	10 491	10 822	22 574	11 137	11 437	23 792	11 762	12 030
0-4	2 059	1 052	1 007	2 010	1 027	983	2 008	1 025	983	2 028	1 036	992
5-9	2 082	1 062	1 019	2 032	1 039	994	1 988	1 015	973	1 990	1 016	974
10-14	2 050	1 045	1 005	2 073	1 058	1 015	2 025	1 035	991	1 982	1 012	970
15-19	1 927	981	946	2 043	1 041	1 002	2 067	1 054	1 013	2 020	1 031	989
20-24	1 747	887	859	1 916	974	941	2 032	1 034	998	2 057	1 048	1 009
25-29	1 592	806	786	1 724	874	850	1 893	961	932	2 011	1 022	989
30-34	1 638	825	813	1 558	786	772	1 690	855	836	1 858	941	917
35-39	1 580	786	794	1 594	799	796	1 519	763	756	1 650	831	819
40-44	1 407	730	767	1 535	759	776	1 552	773	779	1 481	740	741
45-49	658	308	350	1 452	702	750	1 492	732	760	1 512	748	763
50-54	766	353	413	636	295	341	1 408	674	733	1 449	705	744
55-59	680	301	309	704	303	401	611	290	322	1 357	642	715
60-64	586	244	342	652	279	372	696	310	385	581	261	320
65-69	457	184	273	537	219	318	601	251	349	645	281	364
70-74	327	129	198	394	154	240	468	185	283	527	214	313
75-79	206	76	129	250	94	155	306	114	191	368	139	229
80-84	98	33	64	125	43	81	154	55	100	193	68	125
85-89	28	8	20	40	13	28	53	17	36	67	22	46
90-94	5	1	4	7	2	5	10	3	7	13	4	10
95-99	0	0	0	1	0	1	1	0	1	1	0	1
100 +	0	0	0	0	0	0	0	0	0	0	0	0

Age group	2045 Both sexes	2045 Males	2045 Females	2050 Both sexes	2050 Males	2050 Females
All ages	24 941	12 351	12 589	25 972	12 879	13 093
0-4	2 022	1 033	989	1 968	1 005	963
5-9	2 013	1 028	985	2 009	1 026	983
10-14	1 985	1 013	972	2 008	1 025	983
15-19	1 978	1 009	969	1 981	1 010	970
20-24	2 011	1 026	985	1 971	1 005	966
25-29	2 038	1 037	1 001	1 994	1 016	978
30-34	1 977	1 002	975	2 007	1 019	988
35-39	1 818	918	901	1 938	980	958
40-44	1 612	808	804	1 779	894	885
45-49	1 445	718	727	1 576	786	790
50-54	1 471	723	749	1 410	696	714
55-59	1 401	674	727	1 425	693	732
60-64	1 295	603	692	1 341	636	705
65-69	541	238	303	1 211	553	658
70-74	570	242	328	480	205	275
75-79	420	163	257	458	186	272
80-84	237	84	153	277	100	177
85-89	87	28	59	111	35	76
90-94	18	5	13	24	6	18
95-99	2	0	1	3	1	2
100 +	0	0	0	0	0	0

POPULATION BY AGE AND SEX (in thousands)

Age group	2005 Both sexes	Males	Females	2010 Both sexes	Males	Females	2015 Both sexes	Males	Females	2020 Both sexes	Males	Females
All ages	14 071	6 801	7 270	15 581	7 562	8 019	17 305	8 437	8 868	19 130	9 368	9 762
0-4	1 835	935	900	2 048	1 044	1 004	2 292	1 169	1 123	2 431	1 241	1 190
5-9	1 650	839	812	1 780	906	874	1 997	1 017	980	2 246	1 145	1 101
10-14	1 731	879	853	1 638	832	806	1 768	899	869	1 986	1 011	974
15-19	1 722	871	851	1 720	872	847	1 629	827	802	1 759	894	865
20-24	1 682	845	838	1 701	859	842	1 702	862	840	1 615	819	796
25-29	760	372	388	1 645	821	823	1 669	840	830	1 676	847	829
30-34	896	436	460	732	355	378	1 597	792	805	1 627	814	813
35-39	817	380	437	858	410	447	705	338	368	1 546	760	786
40-44	715	321	394	782	357	425	825	389	436	681	322	359
45-49	594	261	334	684	301	383	752	338	414	795	370	425
50-54	485	211	274	567	244	323	656	284	372	722	320	402
55-59	395	165	230	458	195	263	538	227	311	624	266	358
60-64	306	122	184	365	149	216	426	177	248	503	208	295
65-69	203	74	129	271	105	166	326	130	196	384	156	228
70-74	146	48	98	166	58	108	225	85	140	274	106	169
75-79	86	27	58	104	33	71	120	40	80	166	60	106
80-84	34	10	24	47	14	33	58	17	41	69	22	47
85-89	10	4	6	12	3	9	17	5	13	23	6	16
90-94	1	0	1	2	1	1	3	1	2	4	1	3
95-99	0	0	0	0	0	0	0	0	0	0	0	0
100 +	0	0	0	0	0	0	0	0	0	0	0	0

Age group	2025 Both sexes	Males	Females	2030 Both sexes	Males	Females	2035 Both sexes	Males	Females	2040 Both sexes	Males	Females
All ages	20 894	10 273	10 621	22 602	11 149	11 453	24 320	12 028	12 292	26 110	12 944	13 166
0-4	2 417	1 235	1 182	2 405	1 228	1 176	2 472	1 262	1 210	2 610	1 333	1 277
5-9	2 391	1 220	1 171	2 385	1 219	1 166	2 379	1 215	1 164	2 450	1 251	1 200
10-14	2 235	1 139	1 096	2 381	1 215	1 166	2 377	1 214	1 163	2 372	1 211	1 161
15-19	1 977	1 006	971	2 227	1 134	1 092	2 374	1 211	1 164	2 371	1 210	1 160
20-24	1 747	887	859	1 965	999	966	2 215	1 127	1 088	2 363	1 204	1 159
25-29	1 592	806	786	1 724	874	850	1 942	986	956	2 192	1 114	1 078
30-34	1 638	825	813	1 558	786	772	1 690	855	836	1 907	965	941
35-39	1 580	786	794	1 594	799	796	1 519	763	756	1 650	831	819
40-44	1 497	730	767	1 535	759	776	1 552	773	779	1 481	740	741
45-49	658	308	350	1 452	702	750	1 492	732	760	1 512	748	763
50-54	766	353	413	636	295	341	1 408	674	733	1 449	705	744
55-59	690	301	389	734	333	401	611	280	332	1 357	642	715
60-64	586	244	342	652	279	372	696	310	385	581	261	320
65-69	457	184	273	537	219	318	601	251	349	645	281	364
70-74	327	129	198	394	154	240	468	185	283	527	214	313
75-79	206	76	129	250	94	155	306	114	191	368	139	229
80-84	98	33	64	125	43	81	154	55	100	193	68	125
85-89	28	8	20	40	13	28	53	17	36	67	22	46
90-94	5	1	4	7	2	5	10	3	7	13	4	10
95-99	0	0	0	1	0	1	1	0	1	1	0	1
100 +	0	0	0	0	0	0	0	0	0	0	0	0

Age group	2045 Both sexes	Males	Females	2050 Both sexes	Males	Females
All ages	27 963	13 893	14 070	29 801	14 831	14 970
0-4	2 739	1 399	1 340	2 794	1 427	1 367
5-9	2 591	1 323	1 268	2 723	1 390	1 333
10-14	2 444	1 247	1 197	2 585	1 319	1 266
15-19	2 367	1 208	1 159	2 439	1 244	1 195
20-24	2 361	1 205	1 156	2 358	1 203	1 156
25-29	2 341	1 191	1 150	2 341	1 193	1 148
30-34	2 156	1 093	1 063	2 306	1 171	1 135
35-39	1 865	941	924	2 113	1 068	1 045
40-44	1 612	808	804	1 826	918	908
45-49	1 445	718	727	1 576	786	790
50-54	1 471	723	749	1 410	696	714
55-59	1 401	674	727	1 425	693	732
60-64	1 295	603	692	1 341	636	705
65-69	541	238	303	1 211	553	658
70-74	570	242	328	480	205	275
75-79	420	163	257	458	186	272
80-84	237	84	153	277	100	177
85-89	87	28	59	111	35	76
90-94	18	5	13	24	6	18
95-99	2	0	1	3	1	2
100 +	0	0	0	0	0	0

United Nations Department of Economic and Social Affairs/Population Division
World Population Prospects: The 2004 Revision, Volume II: Sex and Age Distribution of the World Population

260

POPULATION BY AGE AND SEX (in thousands)

Age group	2005 Both sexes	Males	Females	2010 Both sexes	Males	Females	2015 Both sexes	Males	Females	2020 Both sexes	Males	Females
All ages	14 071	6 801	7 270	15 023	7 400	7 800	16 561	8 058	8 500	17 705	8 641	9 064
0-4	1 835	935	900	1 790	912	877	1 799	918	881	1 739	887	851
5-9	1 650	839	812	1 780	906	874	1 745	889	856	1 763	899	864
10-14	1 731	879	853	1 638	832	806	1 768	899	869	1 735	884	851
15-19	1 722	871	851	1 720	872	847	1 629	827	802	1 759	894	865
20-24	1 682	845	838	1 701	859	842	1 702	862	840	1 615	819	796
25-29	760	372	388	1 645	821	823	1 669	840	830	1 676	847	829
30-34	896	436	460	732	355	378	1 597	792	805	1 627	814	813
35-39	817	380	437	858	410	447	705	338	368	1 546	760	786
40-44	715	321	394	782	357	425	825	389	436	681	322	359
45-49	594	261	334	684	301	383	752	338	414	795	370	425
50-54	485	211	274	567	244	323	656	284	372	722	320	402
55-59	395	165	230	458	195	263	538	227	311	624	266	358
60-64	306	122	184	365	149	216	426	177	248	503	208	295
65-69	203	74	129	271	105	166	326	130	196	384	156	228
70-74	146	48	98	166	58	108	225	85	140	274	106	169
75-79	86	27	58	104	33	71	120	40	80	166	60	106
80-84	34	10	24	47	14	33	58	17	41	69	22	47
85-89	10	4	6	12	3	9	17	5	13	23	6	16
90-94	1	0	1	2	1	1	3	1	2	4	1	3
95-99	0	0	0	0	0	0	0	0	0	0	0	0
100 +	0	0	0	0	0	0	0	0	0	0	0	0

Age group	2025 Both sexes	Males	Females	2030 Both sexes	Males	Females	2035 Both sexes	Males	Females	2040 Both sexes	Males	Females
All ages	18 740	9 174	9 566	19 645	9 640	10 005	20 408	10 032	10 375	21 028	10 352	10 675
0-4	1 674	855	818	1 586	810	776	1 499	765	734	1 416	723	693
5-9	1 710	873	838	1 652	844	808	1 569	801	768	1 486	758	727
10-14	1 754	894	860	1 703	869	834	1 646	841	805	1 564	798	766
15-19	1 728	880	848	1 748	891	858	1 698	866	832	1 642	838	803
20-24	1 747	887	859	1 717	873	844	1 738	885	854	1 690	861	829
25-29	1 592	806	786	1 724	874	850	1 697	861	835	1 720	874	846
30-34	1 638	825	813	1 558	786	772	1 690	855	836	1 665	843	822
35-39	1 580	786	794	1 594	799	796	1 519	763	756	1 650	831	819
40-44	1 497	730	767	1 535	759	776	1 552	773	779	1 481	740	741
45-49	658	308	350	1 452	702	750	1 492	732	760	1 512	748	763
50-54	766	353	413	636	295	341	1 408	674	733	1 449	705	744
55-59	690	301	389	734	333	401	611	280	332	1 357	642	715
60-64	586	244	342	652	279	372	696	310	385	581	261	320
65-69	457	184	273	537	219	318	601	251	349	645	281	364
70-74	327	129	198	394	154	240	468	185	283	527	214	313
75-79	206	76	129	250	94	155	306	114	191	368	139	229
80-84	98	33	64	125	43	81	154	55	100	193	68	125
85-89	28	8	20	40	13	28	53	17	36	67	22	46
90-94	5	1	4	7	2	5	10	3	7	13	4	10
95-99	0	0	0	1	0	1	1	0	1	1	0	1
100 +	0	0	0	0	0	0	0	0	0	0	0	0

Age group	2045 Both sexes	Males	Females	2050 Both sexes	Males	Females
All ages	21 504	10 600	10 904	21 826	10 767	11 059
0-4	1 330	679	651	1 234	630	604
5-9	1 406	718	688	1 322	675	647
10-14	1 482	756	726	1 403	716	687
15-19	1 560	796	764	1 479	754	724
20-24	1 634	834	800	1 554	793	762
25-29	1 673	852	822	1 620	826	794
30-34	1 691	857	834	1 648	837	811
35-39	1 629	822	807	1 657	838	819
40-44	1 612	808	804	1 594	801	793
45-49	1 445	718	727	1 576	786	790
50-54	1 471	723	749	1 410	696	714
55-59	1 401	674	727	1 425	693	732
60-64	1 295	603	692	1 341	636	705
65-69	541	238	303	1 211	553	658
70-74	570	242	328	480	205	275
75-79	420	163	257	458	186	272
80-84	237	84	153	277	100	177
85-89	87	28	59	111	35	76
90-94	18	5	13	24	6	18
95-99	2	0	1	3	1	2
100 +	0	0	0	0	0	0

United Nations Department of Economic and Social Affairs/Population Division
World Population Prospects: The 2004 Revision, Volume II: Sex and Age Distribution of the World Population

261

POPULATION BY AGE AND SEX (in thousands)

Age group	1950			1955			1960			1965		
	Both sexes	Males	Females	Both sexes	Males	Females	Both sexes	Males	Females	Both sexes	Males	Females
All ages	4 466	2 189	2 277	4 846	2 375	2 470	5 302	2 601	2 701	5 891	2 893	2 998
0-4	708	352	355	776	387	390	860	429	431	997	499	498
5-9	567	281	285	613	304	309	681	338	343	765	381	384
10-14	497	247	250	540	268	272	586	291	295	655	325	329
15-19	442	220	223	479	238	241	522	259	263	569	282	287
20-24	391	194	198	424	210	214	460	228	232	503	249	254
25-29	343	169	174	372	183	189	404	199	205	440	217	223
30-34	300	147	153	325	159	165	353	173	180	385	189	196
35-39	260	127	133	282	138	144	306	150	156	334	164	170
40-44	224	109	115	242	118	124	263	128	135	287	140	147
45-49	190	92	98	206	99	106	224	108	115	245	119	126
50-54	159	76	83	172	82	90	187	89	98	205	98	107
55-59	130	61	69	140	66	75	153	72	81	168	79	89
60-64	101	46	54	109	50	59	119	55	64	131	61	71
65-69	72	33	40	78	35	43	86	39	47	96	43	52
70-74	46	20	26	50	22	28	55	24	31	61	27	34
75-79	24	10	14	26	11	15	29	12	17	33	14	19
80 +	12	5	7	13	5	8	14	5	9	16	6	10

Age group	1970			1975			1980			1985		
	Both sexes	Males	Females	Both sexes	Males	Females	Both sexes	Males	Females	Both sexes	Males	Females
All ages	6 631	3 262	3 369	7 563	3 728	3 835	8 754	4 323	4 430	10 067	4 981	5 086
0-4	1 156	579	577	1 353	679	674	1 587	797	789	1 830	921	909
5-9	899	449	450	1 057	529	529	1 261	632	629	1 477	741	736
10-14	739	368	371	873	435	437	1 036	518	518	1 225	614	611
15-19	637	316	320	722	359	362	860	429	431	1 011	505	506
20-24	550	272	278	619	307	312	707	351	356	834	415	419
25-29	484	239	246	532	262	270	603	298	306	683	338	345
30-34	422	207	214	466	229	237	517	254	263	581	286	295
35-39	367	180	187	404	198	206	451	221	230	496	243	252
40-44	316	154	162	349	171	178	388	190	198	430	210	219
45-49	269	131	139	298	145	153	333	162	171	368	179	189
50-54	227	109	118	251	121	130	281	135	146	312	150	161
55-59	186	88	98	207	98	109	232	110	122	258	123	135
60-64	146	68	78	163	76	87	185	86	98	206	97	110
65-69	107	49	59	121	55	66	138	63	75	155	72	84
70-74	70	31	39	80	36	45	93	41	51	106	47	58
75-79	38	16	22	45	19	26	53	23	30	61	26	35
80 +	19	8	12	23	9	14	29	11	17	35	14	21

Age group	1990			1995			2000			2005		
	Both sexes	Males	Females	Both sexes	Males	Females	Both sexes	Males	Females	Both sexes	Males	Females
All ages	11 651	5 774	5 877	13 302	6 598	6 705	14 856	7 373	7 483	16 322	8 119	8 203
0-4	2 059	1 037	1 022	2 251	1 133	1 118	2 333	1 175	1 158	2 453	1 236	1 217
5-9	1 734	871	863	1 947	979	968	2 127	1 069	1 059	2 196	1 104	1 092
10-14	1 451	728	723	1 698	853	845	1 907	959	948	2 079	1 044	1 035
15-19	1 206	604	602	1 425	714	711	1 669	838	831	1 876	943	933
20-24	990	493	497	1 175	587	588	1 384	692	692	1 626	814	811
25-29	813	403	410	954	473	481	1 109	553	556	1 303	653	650
30-34	664	327	336	781	385	396	889	440	449	1 006	506	500
35-39	563	276	286	637	313	324	729	358	371	801	399	402
40-44	478	234	244	538	263	275	596	291	305	662	325	337
45-49	411	200	211	455	221	234	505	245	260	547	266	282
50-54	348	168	180	388	187	200	425	204	220	465	223	242
55-59	290	138	151	323	154	168	357	171	187	388	184	204
60-64	233	110	123	261	123	138	289	137	153	319	150	169
65-69	177	82	95	199	92	107	222	103	119	246	114	132
70-74	122	55	67	138	63	75	156	71	85	174	79	95
75-79	72	31	41	83	36	46	94	42	53	106	47	59
80 +	42	17	25	50	20	30	63	26	37	74	31	43

United Nations Department of Economic and Social Affairs/Population Division
World Population Prospects: The 2004 Revision, Volume II: Sex and Age Distribution of the World Population

262

POPULATION BY AGE AND SEX (in thousands)

Age group	2005 Both sexes	Males	Females	2010 Both sexes	Males	Females	2015 Both sexes	Males	Females	2020 Both sexes	Males	Females
All ages	16 322	8 110	8 203	17 685	8 818	8 867	19 040	9 511	9 529	20 301	10 180	10 174
0-4	2 453	1 236	1 217	2 478	1 248	1 230	2 489	1 253	1 235	2 484	1 251	1 233
5-9	2 196	1 104	1 092	2 308	1 160	1 148	2 350	1 181	1 169	2 381	1 196	1 185
10-14	2 079	1 044	1 035	2 134	1 072	1 061	2 247	1 129	1 118	2 297	1 154	1 143
15-19	1 876	943	933	2 040	1 024	1 016	2 097	1 053	1 044	2 210	1 110	1 101
20-24	1 626	814	811	1 825	915	910	1 991	997	994	2 050	1 027	1 023
25-29	1 303	653	650	1 541	772	769	1 740	873	867	1 907	955	952
30-34	1 006	506	500	1 192	603	589	1 427	720	706	1 621	819	802
35-39	801	399	402	903	459	444	1 085	554	530	1 307	666	641
40-44	662	325	337	722	361	360	821	420	401	992	510	482
45-49	547	266	282	603	296	307	661	331	330	755	386	369
50-54	465	223	242	501	241	260	554	270	284	610	303	307
55-59	388	184	204	423	201	222	458	218	240	508	245	263
60-64	319	150	169	346	162	184	379	177	202	412	194	218
65-69	246	114	132	272	126	146	296	137	160	327	150	176
70-74	174	79	95	193	88	105	215	97	117	236	107	129
75-79	106	47	59	119	53	66	134	59	75	151	67	84
80-84	52	22	30	59	25	34	67	29	38	77	33	44
85-89	18	7	11	21	8	12	24	10	14	28	11	17
90-94	4	1	2	5	2	3	6	2	4	7	2	4
95-99	0	0	0	1	0	0	1	0	1	1	0	1
100 +	0	0	0	0	0	0	0	0	0	0	0	0

Age group	2025 Both sexes	Males	Females	2030 Both sexes	Males	Females	2035 Both sexes	Males	Females	2040 Both sexes	Males	Females
All ages	21 620	10 831	10 789	22 821	11 444	11 377	23 961	12 025	11 936	25 029	12 567	12 462
0-4	2 463	1 241	1 222	2 437	1 228	1 209	2 405	1 212	1 193	2 364	1 191	1 172
5-9	2 392	1 202	1 190	2 384	1 198	1 186	2 370	1 191	1 179	2 349	1 181	1 168
10-14	2 338	1 174	1 164	2 357	1 184	1 173	2 355	1 183	1 173	2 347	1 179	1 169
15-19	2 264	1 136	1 128	2 309	1 158	1 151	2 331	1 169	1 162	2 333	1 170	1 163
20-24	2 164	1 084	1 080	2 220	1 111	1 109	2 268	1 135	1 133	2 294	1 148	1 146
25-29	1 969	986	983	2 083	1 043	1 040	2 143	1 073	1 071	2 195	1 098	1 097
30-34	1 786	900	886	1 851	933	918	1 966	990	976	2 030	1 022	1 009
35-39	1 492	761	732	1 655	840	814	1 723	875	848	1 838	933	906
40-44	1 200	615	585	1 379	706	673	1 538	785	753	1 609	820	788
45-49	915	471	445	1 114	571	543	1 286	659	627	1 441	736	705
50-54	698	355	343	850	435	415	1 040	531	509	1 206	615	591
55-59	561	276	285	645	325	320	790	401	389	970	491	479
60-64	459	219	241	509	248	262	589	293	295	724	363	361
65-69	357	165	192	400	188	213	447	214	233	520	255	265
70-74	263	119	144	290	131	158	328	151	177	369	174	196
75-79	168	74	94	189	83	106	211	93	118	242	109	134
80-84	88	37	50	99	42	57	114	48	65	129	55	74
85-89	33	13	19	38	15	23	44	18	26	52	21	31
90-94	8	3	5	9	3	6	11	4	7	13	5	8
95-99	1	0	1	1	0	1	2	1	1	2	1	1
100 +	0	0	0	0	0	0	0	0	0	0	0	0

Age group	2045 Both sexes	Males	Females	2050 Both sexes	Males	Females
All ages	26 011	13 061	12 950	26 891	13 498	13 393
0-4	2 312	1 166	1 147	2 253	1 136	1 117
5-9	2 318	1 166	1 153	2 276	1 145	1 132
10-14	2 330	1 170	1 160	2 303	1 157	1 146
15-19	2 327	1 167	1 160	2 313	1 160	1 153
20-24	2 299	1 150	1 149	2 297	1 149	1 148
25-29	2 225	1 113	1 112	2 236	1 118	1 117
30-34	2 087	1 050	1 038	2 124	1 068	1 056
35-39	1 908	966	941	1 970	997	973
40-44	1 725	879	846	1 798	915	883
45-49	1 514	773	742	1 631	831	799
50-54	1 357	690	667	1 432	728	704
55-59	1 130	572	558	1 276	644	632
60-64	894	448	446	1 047	524	523
65-69	644	318	326	800	395	405
70-74	434	209	225	541	263	279
75-79	276	127	149	328	154	173
80-84	150	65	85	174	77	96
85-89	60	24	36	71	29	42
90-94	16	6	10	19	7	12
95-99	2	1	2	3	1	2
100 +	0	0	0	0	0	0

POPULATION BY AGE AND SEX (in thousands)

Age group	2005 Both sexes	2005 Males	2005 Females	2010 Both sexes	2010 Males	2010 Females	2015 Both sexes	2015 Males	2015 Females	2020 Both sexes	2020 Males	2020 Females
All ages	16 322	8 119	8 203	17 836	8 894	8 942	19 461	9 723	9 738	21 155	10 586	10 569
0-4	2 453	1 236	1 217	2 630	1 325	1 305	2 767	1 393	1 373	2 871	1 446	1 425
5-9	2 196	1 104	1 092	2 308	1 160	1 148	2 494	1 254	1 241	2 647	1 330	1 317
10-14	2 079	1 044	1 035	2 134	1 072	1 061	2 247	1 129	1 118	2 438	1 224	1 213
15-19	1 876	943	933	2 040	1 024	1 016	2 097	1 053	1 044	2 210	1 110	1 101
20-24	1 626	814	811	1 825	915	910	1 991	997	994	2 050	1 027	1 023
25-29	1 303	653	650	1 541	772	769	1 740	873	867	1 907	955	952
30-34	1 006	506	500	1 192	603	589	1 427	720	706	1 621	819	802
35-39	801	399	402	903	459	444	1 085	554	530	1 307	666	641
40-44	662	325	337	722	361	360	821	420	401	992	510	482
45-49	547	266	282	603	296	307	661	331	330	755	386	369
50-54	465	223	242	501	241	260	554	270	284	610	303	307
55-59	388	184	204	423	201	222	458	218	240	508	245	263
60-64	319	150	169	346	162	184	379	177	202	412	194	218
65-69	246	114	132	272	126	146	296	137	160	327	150	176
70-74	174	79	95	193	88	105	215	97	117	236	107	129
75-79	106	47	59	119	53	66	134	59	75	151	67	84
80-84	52	22	30	59	25	34	67	29	38	77	33	44
85-89	18	7	11	21	8	12	24	10	14	28	11	17
90-94	4	1	2	5	2	3	6	2	4	7	2	4
95-99	0	0	0	1	0	0	1	0	1	1	0	1
100 +	0	0	0	0	0	0	0	0	0	0	0	0

Age group	2025 Both sexes	2025 Males	2025 Females	2030 Both sexes	2030 Males	2030 Females	2035 Both sexes	2035 Males	2035 Females	2040 Both sexes	2040 Males	2040 Females
All ages	22 827	11 438	11 389	24 513	12 294	12 219	26 247	13 173	13 073	28 031	14 075	13 956
0-4	2 897	1 459	1 438	2 947	1 485	1 462	3 031	1 527	1 504	3 123	1 574	1 549
5-9	2 765	1 390	1 376	2 803	1 409	1 395	2 866	1 440	1 426	2 961	1 489	1 473
10-14	2 600	1 305	1 294	2 725	1 368	1 357	2 770	1 391	1 379	2 838	1 425	1 413
15-19	2 403	1 206	1 197	2 567	1 288	1 279	2 695	1 352	1 343	2 744	1 376	1 368
20-24	2 164	1 084	1 080	2 357	1 180	1 177	2 522	1 262	1 260	2 652	1 327	1 325
25-29	1 969	986	983	2 083	1 043	1 040	2 275	1 139	1 136	2 441	1 221	1 219
30-34	1 786	900	886	1 851	933	918	1 966	990	976	2 155	1 085	1 070
35-39	1 492	761	732	1 655	840	814	1 723	875	848	1 838	933	906
40-44	1 200	615	585	1 379	706	673	1 538	785	753	1 609	820	788
45-49	915	471	445	1 114	571	543	1 286	659	627	1 441	736	705
50-54	698	355	343	850	435	415	1 040	531	509	1 206	615	591
55-59	561	276	285	645	325	320	790	401	389	970	491	479
60-64	459	219	241	509	248	262	589	293	295	724	363	361
65-69	357	165	192	400	188	213	447	214	233	520	255	265
70-74	263	119	144	290	131	158	328	151	177	369	174	196
75-79	168	74	94	189	83	106	211	93	118	242	109	134
80-84	88	37	50	99	42	57	114	48	65	129	55	74
85-89	33	13	19	38	15	23	44	18	26	52	21	31
90-94	8	3	5	9	3	6	11	4	7	13	5	8
95-99	1	0	1	1	0	1	2	1	1	2	1	1
100 +	0	0	0	0	0	0	0	0	0	0	0	0

Age group	2045 Both sexes	2045 Males	2045 Females	2050 Both sexes	2050 Males	2050 Females
All ages	29 834	14 982	14 852	31 620	15 875	15 745
0-4	3 193	1 609	1 583	3 234	1 631	1 604
5-9	3 064	1 540	1 523	3 143	1 580	1 562
10-14	2 937	1 475	1 462	3 043	1 529	1 515
15-19	2 814	1 412	1 403	2 916	1 463	1 453
20-24	2 704	1 353	1 351	2 777	1 389	1 388
25-29	2 573	1 287	1 286	2 630	1 315	1 315
30-34	2 321	1 167	1 154	2 456	1 235	1 222
35-39	2 025	1 026	999	2 191	1 109	1 082
40-44	1 725	879	846	1 908	971	938
45-49	1 514	773	742	1 631	831	799
50-54	1 357	690	667	1 432	728	704
55-59	1 130	572	558	1 276	644	632
60-64	894	448	446	1 047	524	523
65-69	644	318	326	800	395	405
70-74	434	209	225	541	263	279
75-79	276	127	149	328	154	173
80-84	150	65	85	174	77	96
85-89	60	24	36	71	29	42
90-94	16	6	10	19	7	12
95-99	2	1	2	3	1	2
100 +	0	0	0	0	0	0

United Nations Department of Economic and Social Affairs/Population Division
World Population Prospects: The 2004 Revision, Volume II: Sex and Age Distribution of the World Population

264

POPULATION BY AGE AND SEX (in thousands)

Age group	2005 Both sexes	Males	Females	2010 Both sexes	Males	Females	2015 Both sexes	Males	Females	2020 Both sexes	Males	Females
All ages	16 322	8 119	8 203	17 533	8 741	8 791	18 618	9 298	9 319	19 566	9 787	9 780
0-4	2 453	1 236	1 217	2 326	1 172	1 155	2 211	1 114	1 097	2 096	1 056	1 040
5-9	2 196	1 104	1 092	2 308	1 160	1 148	2 206	1 109	1 097	2 115	1 063	1 052
10-14	2 079	1 044	1 035	2 134	1 072	1 061	2 247	1 129	1 118	2 156	1 083	1 073
15-19	1 876	943	933	2 040	1 024	1 016	2 097	1 053	1 044	2 210	1 110	1 101
20-24	1 626	814	811	1 825	915	910	1 991	997	994	2 050	1 027	1 023
25-29	1 303	653	650	1 541	772	769	1 740	873	867	1 907	955	952
30-34	1 006	506	500	1 192	603	589	1 427	720	706	1 621	819	802
35-39	801	399	402	903	459	444	1 085	554	530	1 307	666	641
40-44	662	325	337	722	361	360	821	420	401	992	510	482
45-49	547	266	282	603	296	307	661	331	330	755	386	369
50-54	465	223	242	501	241	260	554	270	284	610	303	307
55-59	388	184	204	423	201	222	458	218	240	508	245	263
60-64	319	150	169	346	162	184	379	177	202	412	194	218
65-69	246	114	132	272	126	146	296	137	160	327	150	176
70-74	174	79	95	193	88	105	215	97	117	236	107	129
75-79	106	47	59	119	53	66	134	59	75	151	67	84
80-84	52	22	30	59	25	34	67	29	38	77	33	44
85-89	18	7	11	21	8	12	24	10	14	28	11	17
90-94	4	1	2	5	2	3	6	2	4	7	2	4
95-99	0	0	0	1	0	0	1	0	1	1	0	1
100 +	0	0	0	0	0	0	0	0	0	0	0	0

Age group	2025 Both sexes	Males	Females	2030 Both sexes	Males	Females	2035 Both sexes	Males	Females	2040 Both sexes	Males	Females
All ages	20 416	10 226	10 190	21 151	10 605	10 546	21 745	10 912	10 833	22 188	11 140	11 048
0-4	2 033	1 024	1 009	1 946	980	966	1 828	921	907	1 696	855	841
5-9	2 018	1 014	1 004	1 967	989	979	1 892	951	941	1 786	898	888
10-14	2 077	1 043	1 034	1 989	999	990	1 944	976	968	1 874	941	933
15-19	2 125	1 066	1 059	2 051	1 029	1 022	1 967	987	980	1 925	965	960
20-24	2 104	1 084	1 080	2 084	1 043	1 041	2 015	1 008	1 007	1 935	968	967
25-29	1 969	986	983	2 083	1 043	1 040	2 012	1 007	1 005	1 950	976	974
30-34	1 786	900	886	1 851	933	918	1 966	990	976	1 906	959	947
35-39	1 492	761	732	1 655	840	814	1 723	875	848	1 838	933	906
40-44	1 200	615	585	1 379	706	673	1 538	785	753	1 600	820	788
45-49	915	471	445	1 114	571	543	1 286	659	627	1 441	736	705
50-54	698	355	343	850	435	415	1 040	531	509	1 206	615	591
55-59	561	276	285	645	325	320	790	401	389	970	491	479
60-64	459	219	241	509	248	262	589	293	295	724	363	361
65-69	357	165	192	400	188	213	447	214	233	520	255	265
70-74	263	119	144	290	131	158	328	151	177	369	174	196
75-79	168	74	94	189	83	106	211	93	118	242	109	134
80-84	99	39	60	99	42	57	114	49	66	129	55	74
85-89	33	13	19	38	15	23	44	18	26	52	21	31
90-94	8	3	5	9	3	6	11	4	7	13	5	8
95-99	1	0	1	1	0	1	2	1	1	2	1	1
100 +	0	0	0	0	0	0	0	0	0	0	0	0

Age group	2045 Both sexes	Males	Females	2050 Both sexes	Males	Females
All ages	22 481	11 287	11 194	22 631	11 357	11 274
0-4	1 567	790	777	1 450	731	719
5-9	1 663	836	827	1 542	776	767
10-14	1 771	890	882	1 652	830	822
15-19	1 858	932	926	1 758	882	876
20-24	1 897	949	948	1 833	917	916
25-29	1 877	939	938	1 845	923	922
30-34	1 854	932	922	1 792	901	891
35-39	1 791	907	883	1 750	886	864
40-44	1 725	879	846	1 687	858	829
45-49	1 514	773	742	1 631	831	799
50-54	1 357	690	667	1 432	728	704
55-59	1 130	572	558	1 276	644	632
60-64	894	448	446	1 047	524	523
65-69	644	318	326	800	395	405
70-74	434	209	225	541	263	279
75-79	276	127	149	328	154	173
80-84	150	65	85	174	77	96
85-89	60	24	36	71	29	42
90-94	16	6	10	19	7	12
95-99	2	1	2	3	1	2
100 +	0	0	0	0	0	0

POPULATION BY AGE AND SEX (in thousands)

Age group	1950 Both sexes	Males	Females	1955 Both sexes	Males	Females	1960 Both sexes	Males	Females	1965 Both sexes	Males	Females
All ages	13 737	6 969	6 768	15 736	7 978	7 758	17 909	9 076	8 833	19 678	9 896	9 782
0-4	1 636	835	801	1 944	993	951	2 236	1 144	1 092	2 265	1 161	1 104
5-9	1 316	671	645	1 735	886	849	2 027	1 032	995	2 260	1 155	1 105
10-14	1 125	571	554	1 372	700	672	1 744	892	852	2 044	1 045	999
15-19	1 078	544	534	1 140	576	564	1 383	705	678	1 769	895	875
20-24	1 110	552	558	1 124	564	560	1 224	619	605	1 385	691	694
25-29	1 114	550	564	1 195	601	594	1 221	628	593	1 209	603	606
30-34	1 034	513	521	1 185	586	599	1 276	645	631	1 241	630	611
35-39	966	488	478	1 098	549	549	1 225	609	616	1 284	646	638
40-44	843	432	411	1 000	510	490	1 121	562	559	1 235	612	623
45-49	731	378	353	855	443	412	999	510	489	1 072	535	537
50-54	656	338	318	723	375	348	837	433	404	968	490	478
55-59	572	296	276	622	317	305	700	358	342	793	403	391
60-64	502	263	239	524	266	258	573	285	288	644	322	323
65-69	418	221	197	460	237	223	474	235	239	521	251	269
70-74	303	156	147	363	184	179	393	193	200	413	194	218
75-79	184	92	92	221	110	111	270	131	139	306	141	164
80 +	149	69	80	175	81	94	206	95	111	269	122	147

Age group	1970 Both sexes	Males	Females	1975 Both sexes	Males	Females	1980 Both sexes	Males	Females	1985 Both sexes	Males	Females
All ages	21 717	10 912	10 805	23 142	11 580	11 563	24 516	12 211	12 305	25 843	12 831	13 012
0-4	1 852	946	906	1 769	908	861	1 792	919	872	1 847	948	899
5-9	2 349	1 200	1 148	1 935	990	945	1 813	931	882	1 816	932	884
10-14	2 336	1 194	1 143	2 353	1 203	1 149	1 970	1 010	960	1 841	942	898
15-19	2 122	1 078	1 044	2 348	1 196	1 153	2 418	1 234	1 184	2 018	1 037	982
20-24	1 927	966	961	2 190	1 103	1 086	2 425	1 224	1 201	2 498	1 275	1 224
25-29	1 572	803	769	1 997	1 012	985	2 206	1 107	1 099	2 441	1 230	1 211
30-34	1 285	657	628	1 609	821	788	2 021	1 021	1 000	2 226	1 113	1 113
35-39	1 273	656	617	1 321	673	647	1 602	817	785	2 012	1 016	997
40-44	1 284	655	629	1 288	659	629	1 328	676	652	1 594	809	785
45-49	1 250	620	630	1 264	637	627	1 268	644	624	1 305	659	646
50-54	1 036	513	523	1 215	595	620	1 241	619	622	1 250	628	622
55-59	952	475	478	996	485	511	1 175	566	610	1 218	598	620
60-64	762	376	386	899	435	464	953	451	502	1 127	529	598
65-69	608	291	317	701	331	370	831	386	445	890	406	485
70-74	448	201	247	524	238	286	615	274	342	732	322	410
75-79	322	139	182	354	147	207	421	176	245	500	206	294
80 +	338	141	197	379	146	233	438	156	282	527	182	345

Age group	1990 Both sexes	Males	Females	1995 Both sexes	Males	Females	2000 Both sexes	Males	Females	2005 Both sexes	Males	Females
All ages	27 701	13 733	13 967	29 302	14 503	14 799	30 689	15 197	15 492	32 268	15 994	16 275
0-4	1 931	989	943	1 984	1 017	967	1 761	903	858	1 698	871	827
5-9	1 924	987	937	1 992	1 020	971	2 045	1 048	997	1 849	948	901
10-14	1 878	963	914	1 997	1 025	972	2 052	1 053	999	2 132	1 095	1 037
15-19	1 938	995	943	1 980	1 018	962	2 067	1 061	1 006	2 155	1 106	1 049
20-24	2 124	1 081	1 043	2 009	1 022	987	2 061	1 055	1 006	2 186	1 116	1 070
25-29	2 583	1 308	1 275	2 185	1 104	1 081	2 096	1 061	1 035	2 189	1 114	1 075
30-34	2 537	1 275	1 261	2 625	1 325	1 300	2 266	1 143	1 124	2 217	1 121	1 097
35-39	2 289	1 144	1 145	2 571	1 287	1 283	2 686	1 353	1 333	2 363	1 189	1 173
40-44	2 055	1 033	1 022	2 306	1 149	1 157	2 606	1 303	1 303	2 745	1 382	1 364
45-49	1 600	808	792	2 058	1 029	1 030	2 316	1 153	1 163	2 630	1 315	1 315
50-54	1 302	655	647	1 584	791	793	2 047	1 019	1 028	2 314	1 148	1 166
55-59	1 237	616	620	1 294	641	652	1 560	773	787	2 025	1 002	1 023
60-64	1 182	571	611	1 208	594	614	1 256	616	641	1 526	748	777
65-69	1 071	489	582	1 112	524	588	1 141	550	592	1 200	578	622
70-74	800	349	451	956	420	536	1 005	458	547	1 044	489	555
75-79	608	249	358	661	270	391	808	336	473	862	375	488
80 +	643	220	423	780	266	514	916	313	603	1 132	397	735

266

United Nations Department of Economic and Social Affairs/Population Division
World Population Prospects: The 2004 Revision, Volume II: Sex and Age Distribution of the World Population

POPULATION BY AGE AND SEX (in thousands)

Age group	2005 Both sexes	2005 Males	2005 Females	2010 Both sexes	2010 Males	2010 Females	2015 Both sexes	2015 Males	2015 Females	2020 Both sexes	2020 Males	2020 Females
All ages	32 268	15 994	16 275	33 680	16 707	16 973	35 051	17 397	17 654	36 441	18 091	18 350
0-4	1 698	871	827	1 673	858	815	1 735	890	845	1 867	957	909
5-9	1 849	948	901	1 782	914	868	1 757	901	856	1 818	932	886
10-14	2 132	1 095	1 037	1 932	993	939	1 865	958	907	1 840	946	895
15-19	2 155	1 106	1 049	2 230	1 146	1 084	2 031	1 044	987	1 964	1 010	955
20-24	2 186	1 116	1 070	2 269	1 159	1 110	2 344	1 199	1 146	2 146	1 098	1 048
25-29	2 189	1 114	1 075	2 308	1 172	1 136	2 391	1 215	1 176	2 467	1 256	1 211
30-34	2 217	1 121	1 097	2 305	1 170	1 134	2 424	1 229	1 195	2 508	1 272	1 235
35-39	2 363	1 189	1 173	2 310	1 166	1 144	2 398	1 216	1 182	2 518	1 275	1 243
40-44	2 745	1 382	1 364	2 422	1 218	1 203	2 371	1 196	1 175	2 459	1 246	1 213
45-49	2 630	1 315	1 315	2 768	1 393	1 376	2 449	1 232	1 217	2 399	1 210	1 189
50-54	2 314	1 148	1 166	2 625	1 309	1 317	2 765	1 387	1 378	2 451	1 229	1 221
55-59	2 025	1 002	1 023	2 289	1 129	1 160	2 599	1 289	1 310	2 739	1 367	1 372
60-64	1 526	748	777	1 979	970	1 009	2 240	1 096	1 144	2 546	1 253	1 293
65-69	1 200	578	622	1 460	705	754	1 896	917	979	2 151	1 040	1 112
70-74	1 044	489	555	1 104	519	586	1 349	637	712	1 759	833	926
75-79	862	375	488	904	406	498	964	436	528	1 186	540	646
80-84	627	242	385	677	276	402	719	304	415	775	331	444
85-89	327	109	218	419	145	274	461	171	291	498	193	305
90-94	139	39	101	168	48	120	223	67	156	252	81	171
95-99	34	7	27	48	11	38	61	14	47	85	20	64
100 +	5	1	4	7	1	6	10	2	9	14	2	12

Age group	2025 Both sexes	2025 Males	2025 Females	2030 Both sexes	2030 Males	2030 Females	2035 Both sexes	2035 Males	2035 Females	2040 Both sexes	2040 Males	2040 Females
All ages	37 797	18 757	19 040	39 052	19 365	19 687	40 154	19 892	20 262	41 129	20 358	20 772
0-4	1 965	1 008	957	2 017	1 035	982	2 039	1 046	993	2 095	1 075	1 020
5-9	1 950	1 000	950	2 049	1 051	998	2 100	1 077	1 023	2 123	1 089	1 034
10-14	1 902	977	925	2 034	1 045	989	2 133	1 096	1 037	2 184	1 122	1 062
15-19	1 939	997	942	2 001	1 029	972	2 133	1 096	1 037	2 232	1 147	1 085
20-24	2 080	1 064	1 016	2 055	1 051	1 004	2 117	1 083	1 034	2 249	1 151	1 098
25-29	2 269	1 155	1 114	2 204	1 121	1 082	2 180	1 109	1 070	2 241	1 141	1 100
30-34	2 584	1 313	1 271	2 387	1 213	1 174	2 322	1 180	1 142	2 298	1 168	1 130
35-39	2 601	1 318	1 200	2 678	1 359	1 319	2 482	1 259	1 222	2 417	1 227	1 191
40-44	2 579	1 305	1 274	2 663	1 349	1 314	2 740	1 390	1 350	2 545	1 291	1 254
45-49	2 488	1 260	1 228	2 609	1 320	1 289	2 693	1 364	1 330	2 771	1 405	1 366
50-54	2 403	1 209	1 194	2 493	1 259	1 233	2 614	1 319	1 295	2 699	1 364	1 336
55-59	2 433	1 215	1 219	2 389	1 196	1 193	2 480	1 247	1 232	2 602	1 307	1 294
60-64	2 687	1 332	1 355	2 393	1 186	1 207	2 354	1 170	1 183	2 445	1 222	1 223
65-69	2 449	1 191	1 258	2 591	1 270	1 321	2 315	1 136	1 179	2 282	1 123	1 159
70-74	2 003	949	1 055	2 289	1 092	1 197	2 430	1 170	1 260	2 180	1 051	1 129
75-79	1 555	711	844	1 782	817	965	2 047	948	1 100	2 185	1 022	1 163
80-84	963	416	548	1 275	554	721	1 476	644	832	1 710	755	956
85-89	547	214	332	690	274	416	929	373	556	1 091	441	651
90-94	279	94	185	315	108	206	408	143	265	563	199	363
95-99	99	26	73	114	31	83	134	37	96	179	51	128
100 +	20	3	17	25	5	21	31	6	25	38	8	30

Age group	2045 Both sexes	2045 Males	2045 Females	2050 Both sexes	2050 Males	2050 Females
All ages	42 007	20 785	21 222	42 844	21 204	21 640
0-4	2 161	1 109	1 052	2 235	1 147	1 089
5-9	2 179	1 117	1 061	2 245	1 151	1 093
10-14	2 206	1 133	1 073	2 262	1 162	1 100
15-19	2 283	1 174	1 110	2 306	1 185	1 121
20-24	2 348	1 202	1 147	2 400	1 228	1 172
25-29	2 374	1 209	1 165	2 473	1 260	1 213
30-34	2 360	1 200	1 160	2 492	1 268	1 225
35-39	2 394	1 215	1 179	2 456	1 247	1 209
40-44	2 482	1 259	1 223	2 459	1 247	1 211
45-49	2 578	1 307	1 271	2 515	1 276	1 240
50-54	2 778	1 405	1 372	2 587	1 309	1 278
55-59	2 688	1 352	1 336	2 768	1 395	1 373
60-64	2 568	1 283	1 285	2 656	1 329	1 328
65-69	2 375	1 176	1 199	2 499	1 237	1 262
70-74	2 156	1 044	1 112	2 251	1 098	1 154
75-79	1 971	925	1 046	1 960	925	1 035
80-84	1 841	823	1 018	1 675	752	923
85-89	1 283	526	757	1 399	583	817
90-94	676	242	434	812	296	516
95-99	255	74	181	317	93	224
100 +	52	11	41	76	16	60

POPULATION BY AGE AND SEX (in thousands)

Age group	2005 Both sexes	Males	Females	2010 Both sexes	Males	Females	2015 Both sexes	Males	Females	2020 Both sexes	Males	Females
All ages	32 268	15 994	16 275	33 956	16 848	17 108	35 783	17 773	18 010	37 756	18 766	18 991
0-4	1 698	871	827	1 949	1 000	949	2 191	1 124	1 067	2 450	1 257	1 193
5-9	1 849	948	901	1 782	914	868	2 032	1 042	990	2 275	1 167	1 108
10-14	2 132	1 095	1 037	1 932	993	939	1 865	958	907	2 115	1 087	1 029
15-19	2 155	1 106	1 049	2 230	1 146	1 084	2 031	1 044	987	1 964	1 010	955
20-24	2 186	1 116	1 070	2 269	1 159	1 110	2 344	1 199	1 146	2 146	1 098	1 048
25-29	2 189	1 114	1 075	2 308	1 172	1 136	2 391	1 215	1 176	2 467	1 256	1 211
30-34	2 217	1 121	1 097	2 305	1 170	1 134	2 424	1 229	1 195	2 508	1 272	1 235
35-39	2 363	1 189	1 173	2 310	1 166	1 144	2 398	1 216	1 182	2 518	1 275	1 243
40-44	2 745	1 382	1 364	2 422	1 218	1 203	2 371	1 196	1 175	2 459	1 246	1 213
45-49	2 630	1 315	1 315	2 768	1 393	1 376	2 449	1 232	1 217	2 399	1 210	1 189
50-54	2 314	1 148	1 166	2 625	1 309	1 317	2 765	1 387	1 378	2 451	1 229	1 221
55-59	2 025	1 002	1 023	2 289	1 129	1 160	2 599	1 289	1 310	2 739	1 367	1 372
60-64	1 526	748	777	1 979	970	1 009	2 240	1 096	1 144	2 546	1 253	1 293
65-69	1 200	578	622	1 460	705	754	1 896	917	979	2 151	1 040	1 112
70-74	1 044	489	555	1 104	519	586	1 349	637	712	1 759	833	926
75-79	862	375	488	904	406	498	964	436	528	1 186	540	646
80-84	627	242	385	677	276	402	719	304	415	775	331	444
85-89	327	109	218	419	145	274	461	171	291	498	193	305
90-94	139	39	101	168	48	120	223	67	156	252	81	171
95-99	34	7	27	48	11	38	61	14	47	85	20	64
100 +	5	1	4	7	1	6	10	2	9	14	2	12

Age group	2025 Both sexes	Males	Females	2030 Both sexes	Males	Females	2035 Both sexes	Males	Females	2040 Both sexes	Males	Females
All ages	39 687	19 728	19 960	41 509	20 626	20 883	43 253	21 482	21 771	45 051	22 370	22 681
0-4	2 541	1 304	1 237	2 585	1 326	1 259	2 682	1 376	1 306	2 920	1 498	1 422
5-9	2 533	1 299	1 234	2 624	1 346	1 278	2 668	1 369	1 299	2 766	1 419	1 347
10-14	2 358	1 211	1 147	2 617	1 344	1 273	2 708	1 391	1 317	2 751	1 413	1 338
15-19	2 214	1 138	1 076	2 457	1 263	1 194	2 716	1 395	1 320	2 807	1 442	1 365
20-24	2 080	1 064	1 016	2 330	1 192	1 138	2 573	1 317	1 256	2 831	1 450	1 382
25-29	2 269	1 155	1 114	2 204	1 121	1 082	2 454	1 250	1 204	2 697	1 375	1 322
30-34	2 584	1 313	1 271	2 387	1 213	1 174	2 322	1 180	1 142	2 572	1 308	1 264
35-39	2 601	1 318	1 283	2 678	1 359	1 319	2 482	1 259	1 222	2 417	1 227	1 191
40-44	2 579	1 305	1 274	2 663	1 349	1 314	2 740	1 390	1 350	2 545	1 291	1 254
45-49	2 488	1 260	1 228	2 609	1 320	1 289	2 693	1 364	1 330	2 771	1 405	1 366
50-54	2 403	1 209	1 194	2 493	1 259	1 233	2 614	1 319	1 295	2 699	1 364	1 336
55-59	2 433	1 215	1 219	2 389	1 196	1 193	2 480	1 247	1 232	2 602	1 307	1 294
60-64	2 687	1 332	1 355	2 393	1 186	1 207	2 354	1 170	1 183	2 445	1 222	1 223
65-69	2 449	1 191	1 258	2 591	1 270	1 321	2 315	1 136	1 179	2 282	1 123	1 159
70-74	2 003	949	1 055	2 289	1 092	1 197	2 430	1 170	1 260	2 180	1 051	1 129
75-79	1 555	711	844	1 782	817	965	2 047	948	1 100	2 185	1 022	1 163
80-84	963	416	548	1 275	554	721	1 476	644	832	1 710	755	956
85-89	547	214	332	690	274	416	929	373	556	1 091	441	651
90-94	279	94	185	315	108	206	408	143	265	563	199	363
95-99	99	26	73	114	31	83	134	37	96	179	51	128
100 +	20	3	17	25	5	21	31	6	25	38	8	30

Age group	2045 Both sexes	Males	Females	2050 Both sexes	Males	Females
All ages	46 961	23 326	23 635	48 976	24 350	24 627
0-4	3 196	1 640	1 556	3 419	1 754	1 664
5-9	3 003	1 541	1 462	3 280	1 682	1 597
10-14	2 849	1 463	1 386	3 087	1 585	1 501
15-19	2 851	1 465	1 386	2 949	1 515	1 434
20-24	2 923	1 497	1 426	2 967	1 519	1 448
25-29	2 955	1 507	1 448	3 047	1 554	1 492
30-34	2 814	1 432	1 382	3 073	1 565	1 508
35-39	2 667	1 355	1 312	2 910	1 479	1 430
40-44	2 482	1 259	1 223	2 731	1 387	1 345
45-49	2 578	1 307	1 271	2 515	1 276	1 240
50-54	2 778	1 405	1 372	2 587	1 309	1 278
55-59	2 688	1 352	1 336	2 768	1 395	1 373
60-64	2 568	1 283	1 285	2 656	1 329	1 328
65-69	2 375	1 176	1 199	2 499	1 237	1 262
70-74	2 156	1 044	1 112	2 251	1 098	1 154
75-79	1 971	925	1 046	1 960	925	1 035
80-84	1 841	823	1 018	1 675	752	923
85-89	1 283	526	757	1 399	583	817
90-94	676	242	434	812	296	516
95-99	255	74	181	317	93	224
100 +	52	11	41	76	16	60

United Nations Department of Economic and Social Affairs/Population Division
World Population Prospects: The 2004 Revision, Volume II: Sex and Age Distribution of the World Population

268

POPULATION BY AGE AND SEX (in thousands)

Age group	2005 Both sexes	2005 Males	2005 Females	2010 Both sexes	2010 Males	2010 Females	2015 Both sexes	2015 Males	2015 Females	2020 Both sexes	2020 Males	2020 Females
All ages	32 268	15 994	16 275	33 405	16 565	16 839	34 318	17 021	17 297	35 120	17 413	17 707
0-4	1 698	871	827	1 397	717	681	1 277	655	622	1 279	656	623
5-9	1 849	948	901	1 782	914	868	1 481	759	722	1 361	698	663
10-14	2 132	1 095	1 037	1 932	993	939	1 865	958	907	1 565	804	761
15-19	2 155	1 106	1 049	2 230	1 146	1 084	2 031	1 044	987	1 964	1 010	955
20-24	2 186	1 116	1 070	2 269	1 159	1 110	2 344	1 199	1 146	2 146	1 098	1 048
25-29	2 189	1 114	1 075	2 308	1 172	1 136	2 391	1 215	1 176	2 467	1 256	1 211
30-34	2 217	1 121	1 097	2 305	1 170	1 134	2 424	1 229	1 195	2 508	1 272	1 235
35-39	2 363	1 189	1 173	2 310	1 166	1 144	2 398	1 216	1 182	2 518	1 275	1 243
40-44	2 745	1 382	1 364	2 422	1 218	1 203	2 371	1 196	1 175	2 459	1 246	1 213
45-49	2 630	1 315	1 315	2 768	1 393	1 376	2 449	1 232	1 217	2 399	1 210	1 189
50-54	2 314	1 148	1 166	2 625	1 309	1 317	2 765	1 387	1 378	2 451	1 229	1 221
55-59	2 025	1 002	1 023	2 289	1 129	1 160	2 599	1 289	1 310	2 739	1 367	1 372
60-64	1 526	748	777	1 979	970	1 009	2 240	1 096	1 144	2 546	1 253	1 293
65-69	1 200	578	622	1 460	705	754	1 896	917	979	2 151	1 040	1 112
70-74	1 044	489	555	1 104	519	586	1 349	637	712	1 759	833	926
75-79	862	375	488	904	406	498	964	436	528	1 186	540	646
80-84	627	242	385	677	276	402	719	304	415	775	331	444
85-89	327	109	218	419	145	274	461	171	291	498	193	305
90-94	139	39	101	168	48	120	223	67	156	252	81	171
95-99	34	7	27	48	11	38	61	14	47	85	20	64
100 +	5	1	4	7	1	6	10	2	9	14	2	12

Age group	2025 Both sexes	2025 Males	2025 Females	2030 Both sexes	2030 Males	2030 Females	2035 Both sexes	2035 Males	2035 Females	2040 Both sexes	2040 Males	2040 Females
All ages	35 891	17 779	18 112	36 576	18 094	18 481	37 093	18 321	18 772	37 401	18 445	18 956
0-4	1 379	707	672	1 445	741	704	1 452	745	707	1 426	731	695
5-9	1 363	699	664	1 463	750	713	1 529	784	745	1 536	788	749
10-14	1 444	742	702	1 447	744	703	1 547	795	752	1 613	829	784
15-19	1 664	856	808	1 544	794	750	1 546	795	751	1 646	847	800
20-24	2 080	1 064	1 016	1 781	910	870	1 661	849	812	1 663	850	813
25-29	2 269	1 155	1 114	2 204	1 121	1 082	1 905	969	936	1 785	907	878
30-34	2 584	1 313	1 271	2 387	1 213	1 174	2 322	1 180	1 142	2 024	1 027	997
35-39	2 601	1 318	1 283	2 678	1 359	1 319	2 482	1 259	1 222	2 417	1 227	1 191
40-44	2 579	1 305	1 274	2 000	1 040	1 314	2 740	1 390	1 350	2 545	1 291	1 254
45-49	2 488	1 260	1 228	2 609	1 320	1 289	2 693	1 364	1 330	2 771	1 405	1 366
50-54	2 403	1 209	1 194	2 493	1 259	1 233	2 614	1 319	1 295	2 699	1 364	1 336
55-59	2 433	1 215	1 219	2 389	1 196	1 193	2 400	1 247	1 200	2 603	1 307	1 294
60-64	2 687	1 332	1 355	2 393	1 186	1 207	2 354	1 170	1 183	2 445	1 222	1 223
65-69	2 449	1 191	1 258	2 591	1 270	1 321	2 315	1 136	1 179	2 282	1 123	1 159
70-74	2 003	949	1 055	2 289	1 092	1 197	2 430	1 170	1 260	2 180	1 051	1 129
75-79	1 555	711	844	1 782	817	965	2 047	948	1 100	2 185	1 022	1 163
80-84	963	416	548	1 275	554	721	1 476	644	832	1 710	755	956
85-89	547	214	332	690	274	416	929	373	556	1 091	441	651
90-94	279	94	185	315	108	206	408	143	265	563	199	363
95-99	99	26	73	114	31	83	134	37	96	179	51	128
100 +	20	3	17	25	5	21	31	6	25	38	8	30

Age group	2045 Both sexes	2045 Males	2045 Females	2050 Both sexes	2050 Males	2050 Females
All ages	37 486	18 466	19 020	37 418	18 421	18 996
0-4	1 364	700	665	1 326	680	646
5-9	1 510	774	736	1 448	743	706
10-14	1 620	833	787	1 594	819	775
15-19	1 713	881	832	1 720	885	835
20-24	1 763	902	862	1 830	936	894
25-29	1 788	909	879	1 889	960	928
30-34	1 905	966	938	1 908	968	940
35-39	2 120	1 075	1 045	2 002	1 015	987
40-44	2 482	1 259	1 223	2 186	1 108	1 078
45-49	2 578	1 307	1 271	2 515	1 276	1 240
50-54	2 778	1 405	1 372	2 587	1 309	1 278
55-59	2 688	1 352	1 336	2 768	1 395	1 373
60-64	2 568	1 283	1 285	2 656	1 329	1 328
65-69	2 375	1 176	1 199	2 499	1 237	1 262
70-74	2 156	1 044	1 112	2 251	1 098	1 154
75-79	1 971	925	1 046	1 960	925	1 035
80-84	1 841	823	1 018	1 675	752	923
85-89	1 283	526	757	1 399	583	817
90-94	676	242	434	812	296	516
95-99	255	74	181	317	93	224
100 +	52	11	41	76	16	60

POPULATION BY AGE AND SEX (in thousands)

Age group	1950 Both sexes	Males	Females	1955 Both sexes	Males	Females	1960 Both sexes	Males	Females	1965 Both sexes	Males	Females
All ages	146	66	80	169	78	92	196	91	105	229	108	121
0-4	15	8	8	25	13	13	38	19	19	40	20	20
5-9	15	7	8	22	11	11	31	15	15	37	18	19
10-14	20	10	10	19	9	10	16	8	8	27	13	14
15-19	19	9	10	17	8	9	14	7	7	21	10	11
20-24	16	7	8	16	7	9	17	7	9	16	8	8
25-29	9	4	5	12	5	6	14	6	8	13	6	7
30-34	9	4	5	10	5	6	13	6	7	13	6	7
35-39	10	4	5	9	4	5	8	4	4	11	5	6
40-44	10	5	5	9	4	5	8	4	4	10	4	5
45-49	6	3	4	7	3	4	9	4	5	8	4	4
50-54	5	2	3	7	3	4	10	5	5	9	4	5
55-59	3	1	2	4	2	3	6	2	3	7	3	4
60-64	4	1	3	4	1	3	4	2	3	6	3	4
65-69	2	1	1	3	1	2	3	1	2	4	2	2
70-74	2	1	1	2	1	2	3	1	2	3	1	2
75-79	1	0	1	2	1	1	2	1	2	3	1	2
80 +	1	0	0	1	0	1	1	0	1	2	1	1

Age group	1970 Both sexes	Males	Females	1975 Both sexes	Males	Females	1980 Both sexes	Males	Females	1985 Both sexes	Males	Females
All ages	267	127	140	278	130	148	289	133	157	319	148	171
0-4	42	21	21	45	22	23	49	24	25	59	29	29
5-9	45	22	22	43	21	22	41	20	20	48	23	25
10-14	40	20	20	42	21	21	43	21	22	40	20	20
15-19	30	15	15	34	17	17	39	19	20	40	20	20
20-24	15	8	7	21	10	11	26	11	15	33	16	17
25-29	11	5	6	13	5	8	15	6	9	20	8	12
30-34	14	6	8	11	4	6	7	3	4	13	5	8
35-39	14	6	8	11	4	7	8	3	5	8	3	5
40-44	12	5	6	11	5	7	11	4	7	8	3	5
45-49	8	4	4	9	4	5	11	4	6	11	4	7
50-54	7	3	4	8	4	5	10	4	5	10	4	6
55-59	8	4	4	7	3	4	6	3	3	9	4	5
60-64	8	4	5	8	3	4	6	3	3	5	2	3
65-69	5	2	3	6	2	3	6	3	3	5	2	3
70-74	3	1	2	4	2	3	6	3	3	5	2	3
75-79	3	1	2	4	1	2	4	1	3	4	2	2
80 +	2	1	1	2	1	1	2	1	1	3	1	2

Age group	1990 Both sexes	Males	Females	1995 Both sexes	Males	Females	2000 Both sexes	Males	Females	2005 Both sexes	Males	Females
All ages	355	167	189	401	190	211	451	215	236	507	243	264
0-4	65	32	32	65	33	32	65	33	32	72	36	36
5-9	58	29	29	64	32	32	65	32	32	64	32	32
10-14	47	23	24	57	29	28	63	32	32	64	32	32
15-19	36	18	18	45	22	23	56	28	28	62	31	31
20-24	33	16	17	33	16	16	43	21	22	54	27	27
25-29	27	13	14	30	15	15	31	15	16	41	20	21
30-34	18	7	11	26	12	13	29	14	15	30	15	15
35-39	13	5	8	18	7	11	26	12	13	29	14	15
40-44	8	3	5	13	5	8	18	7	11	25	12	13
45-49	7	3	5	8	3	5	13	5	8	18	7	11
50-54	10	4	7	7	2	5	7	3	5	13	5	8
55-59	10	4	6	10	4	6	7	2	4	7	3	4
60-64	8	3	5	9	3	5	9	3	6	6	2	4
65-69	5	2	3	7	3	4	8	3	5	8	3	5
70-74	4	2	2	4	2	2	6	2	4	7	2	4
75-79	3	1	2	3	1	2	3	1	2	4	2	3
80 +	3	1	2	3	1	2	3	1	2	3	1	2

United Nations Department of Economic and Social Affairs/Population Division
World Population Prospects: The 2004 Revision, Volume II: Sex and Age Distribution of the World Population

270

POPULATION BY AGE AND SEX (in thousands)

Age group	2005 Both sexes	Males	Females	2010 Both sexes	Males	Females	2015 Both sexes	Males	Females	2020 Both sexes	Males	Females
All ages	507	243	264	567	274	293	628	305	323	690	336	353
0-4	72	36	36	76	38	38	78	39	39	78	39	39
5-9	64	32	32	71	36	35	75	38	37	78	39	39
10-14	64	32	32	64	32	32	71	36	35	75	38	37
15-19	62	31	31	63	32	32	63	31	31	70	35	35
20-24	54	27	27	60	30	30	61	31	31	61	30	30
25-29	41	20	21	52	26	26	58	29	29	59	29	30
30-34	30	15	15	40	19	21	51	25	26	57	29	29
35-39	29	14	15	30	15	15	40	19	21	51	25	26
40-44	25	12	13	29	14	15	30	14	15	40	19	21
45-49	18	7	11	25	12	13	29	14	15	29	14	15
50-54	13	5	8	17	7	10	24	12	13	28	13	15
55-59	7	3	4	12	4	8	16	6	10	23	11	12
60-64	6	2	4	7	3	4	11	4	7	16	6	10
65-69	8	3	5	6	2	4	6	2	4	10	4	7
70-74	7	2	4	7	2	5	5	2	3	5	2	3
75-79	4	2	3	5	2	3	5	2	4	4	1	3
80-84	2	1	1	3	1	2	3	1	2	3	1	3
85-89	1	0	0	1	0	0	1	0	1	2	0	1
90-94	0	0	0	0	0	0	0	0	0	0	0	0
95-99	0	0	0	0	0	0	0	0	0	0	0	0
100 +	0	0	0	0	0	0	0	0	0	0	0	0

Age group	2025 Both sexes	Males	Females	2030 Both sexes	Males	Females	2035 Both sexes	Males	Females	2040 Both sexes	Males	Females
All ages	750	367	383	808	397	411	864	425	439	916	451	465
0-4	78	39	39	78	39	38	78	39	38	77	39	38
5-9	78	39	39	78	39	38	78	39	38	78	39	38
10-14	77	39	38	78	39	39	77	39	38	77	39	38
15-19	74	37	37	76	38	38	77	39	38	76	39	38
20-24	68	34	34	72	36	36	74	37	37	75	38	37
25-29	59	29	30	66	33	33	70	35	35	72	36	36
30-34	58	29	29	58	29	29	65	33	33	69	35	35
35-39	57	28	29	58	29	29	58	29	29	65	33	33
40-44	51	25	26	57	28	29	58	29	29	58	29	29
45-49	39	19	21	50	25	25	56	28	29	58	29	29
50-54	29	14	15	39	18	20	49	24	25	56	27	28
55-59	27	13	14	28	13	14	38	18	20	48	23	25
60-64	22	10	12	26	12	14	27	13	14	36	17	19
65-69	14	5	9	20	9	11	24	11	13	25	11	13
70-74	9	3	6	13	4	8	18	8	10	21	9	12
75-79	4	1	3	7	2	5	10	3	7	14	6	9
80-84	3	1	2	3	1	2	5	1	4	7	2	5
85-89	2	0	1	1	0	1	2	0	1	3	1	2
90-94	1	0	0	1	0	1	1	0	0	1	0	1
95-99	0	0	0	0	0	0	0	0	0	0	0	0
100 +	0	0	0	0	0	0	0	0	0	0	0	0

Age group	2045 Both sexes	Males	Females	2050 Both sexes	Males	Females
All ages	962	474	488	1 002	494	508
0-4	75	38	37	73	37	36
5-9	77	39	38	75	38	37
10-14	77	39	38	77	39	38
15-19	76	38	38	76	39	38
20-24	74	38	37	74	38	37
25-29	73	37	36	73	37	36
30-34	72	36	36	72	36	36
35-39	69	35	35	72	36	36
40-44	65	32	33	69	35	34
45-49	58	29	29	64	32	32
50-54	57	28	29	57	28	29
55-59	54	27	28	56	27	28
60-64	46	22	24	52	25	27
65-69	34	15	18	43	20	23
70-74	22	10	12	30	13	17
75-79	17	7	10	18	7	11
80-84	10	4	7	12	4	8
85-89	4	1	3	6	2	4
90-94	1	0	1	2	0	2
95-99	0	0	0	0	0	0
100 +	0	0	0	0	0	0

POPULATION BY AGE AND SEX (in thousands)

Age group	2005 Both sexes	Males	Females	2010 Both sexes	Males	Females	2015 Both sexes	Males	Females	2020 Both sexes	Males	Females
All ages	507	243	264	572	276	296	644	313	331	719	351	368
0-4	72	36	36	81	41	40	88	44	44	92	47	46
5-9	64	32	32	71	36	35	81	41	40	88	44	44
10-14	64	32	32	64	32	32	71	36	35	80	40	40
15-19	62	31	31	63	32	32	63	31	31	70	35	35
20-24	54	27	27	60	30	30	61	31	31	61	30	30
25-29	41	20	21	52	26	26	58	29	29	59	29	30
30-34	30	15	15	40	19	21	51	25	26	57	29	29
35-39	29	14	15	30	15	15	40	19	21	51	25	26
40-44	25	12	13	29	14	15	30	14	15	40	19	21
45-49	18	7	11	25	12	13	29	14	15	29	14	15
50-54	13	5	8	17	7	10	24	12	13	28	13	15
55-59	7	3	4	12	4	8	16	6	10	23	11	12
60-64	6	2	4	7	3	4	11	4	7	16	6	10
65-69	8	3	5	6	2	4	6	2	4	10	4	7
70-74	7	2	4	7	2	5	5	2	3	5	2	3
75-79	4	2	3	5	2	3	5	2	4	4	1	3
80-84	2	1	1	3	1	2	3	1	2	3	1	3
85-89	1	0	0	1	0	0	1	0	1	2	0	1
90-94	0	0	0	0	0	0	0	0	0	0	0	0
95-99	0	0	0	0	0	0	0	0	0	0	0	0
100 +	0	0	0	0	0	0	0	0	0	0	0	0

Age group	2025 Both sexes	Males	Females	2030 Both sexes	Males	Females	2035 Both sexes	Males	Females	2040 Both sexes	Males	Females
All ages	795	390	405	871	429	443	950	468	482	1 030	508	521
0-4	93	47	46	96	49	47	100	51	50	105	53	52
5-9	92	46	46	93	47	46	96	48	47	100	51	50
10-14	87	44	43	92	46	45	93	47	46	96	48	47
15-19	79	40	40	86	43	43	90	46	45	92	46	45
20-24	68	34	34	77	39	39	84	42	42	89	45	44
25-29	59	29	30	66	33	33	75	38	38	82	41	41
30-34	58	29	29	58	29	29	65	33	33	75	37	37
35-39	57	28	29	58	29	29	58	29	29	65	33	33
40-44	51	25	26	57	28	29	58	29	29	58	29	29
45-49	39	19	21	50	25	25	56	28	29	58	29	29
50-54	29	14	15	39	18	20	49	24	25	56	27	28
55-59	27	13	14	28	13	14	38	18	20	48	23	25
60-64	22	10	12	26	12	14	27	13	14	36	17	19
65-69	14	5	9	20	9	11	24	11	13	25	11	13
70-74	9	3	6	13	4	8	18	8	10	21	9	12
75-79	4	1	3	7	2	5	10	3	7	14	6	9
80-84	3	1	2	3	1	2	5	1	4	7	2	5
85-89	2	0	1	1	0	1	2	0	1	3	1	2
90-94	1	0	0	1	0	1	1	0	0	1	0	1
95-99	0	0	0	0	0	0	0	0	0	0	0	0
100 +	0	0	0	0	0	0	0	0	0	0	0	0

Age group	2045 Both sexes	Males	Females	2050 Both sexes	Males	Females
All ages	1 108	548	561	1 184	586	599
0-4	108	55	53	109	55	54
5-9	105	53	52	108	55	53
10-14	100	51	49	105	53	52
15-19	94	48	47	99	50	49
20-24	90	45	45	93	47	46
25-29	87	44	43	88	44	44
30-34	82	41	41	86	43	43
35-39	75	37	37	82	41	41
40-44	65	32	33	75	37	37
45-49	58	29	29	64	32	32
50-54	57	28	29	57	28	29
55-59	54	27	28	56	27	28
60-64	46	22	24	52	25	27
65-69	34	15	18	43	20	23
70-74	22	10	12	30	13	17
75-79	17	7	10	18	7	11
80-84	10	4	7	12	4	8
85-89	4	1	3	6	2	4
90-94	1	0	1	2	0	2
95-99	0	0	0	0	0	0
100 +	0	0	0	0	0	0

United Nations Department of Economic and Social Affairs/Population Division
World Population Prospects: The 2004 Revision, Volume II: Sex and Age Distribution of the World Population

272

POPULATION BY AGE AND SEX (in thousands)

Age group	2005 Both sexes	Males	Females	2010 Both sexes	Males	Females	2015 Both sexes	Males	Females	2020 Both sexes	Males	Females
All ages	507	240	204	561	271	290	613	297	315	660	321	339
0-4	72	36	36	70	35	35	68	34	34	64	32	32
5-9	64	32	32	71	36	35	70	35	35	67	34	33
10-14	64	32	32	64	32	32	71	36	35	69	35	35
15-19	62	31	31	63	32	32	63	31	31	70	35	35
20-24	54	27	27	60	30	30	61	31	31	61	30	30
25-29	41	20	21	52	26	26	58	29	29	59	29	30
30-34	30	15	15	40	19	21	51	25	26	57	29	29
35-39	29	14	15	30	15	15	40	19	21	51	25	26
40-44	25	12	13	29	14	15	30	14	15	40	19	21
45-49	18	7	11	25	12	13	29	14	15	29	14	15
50-54	13	5	8	17	7	10	24	12	13	28	13	15
55-59	7	3	4	12	4	8	16	6	10	23	11	12
60-64	6	2	4	7	3	4	11	4	7	16	6	10
65-69	8	3	5	6	2	4	6	2	4	10	4	7
70-74	7	2	4	7	2	5	5	2	3	5	2	3
75-79	4	2	3	5	2	3	5	2	4	4	1	3
80-84	2	1	1	3	1	2	3	1	2	3	1	3
85-89	1	0	0	1	0	0	1	0	1	2	0	1
90-94	0	0	0	0	0	0	0	0	0	0	0	0
95-99	0	0	0	0	0	0	0	0	0	0	0	0
100 +	0	0	0	0	0	0	0	0	0	0	0	0

Age group	2025 Both sexes	Males	Females	2030 Both sexes	Males	Females	2035 Both sexes	Males	Females	2040 Both sexes	Males	Females
All ages	705	344	361	746	365	381	781	383	398	809	397	412
0-4	63	32	31	60	30	30	57	29	28	53	27	26
5-9	64	32	32	62	32	31	60	30	30	57	29	28
10-14	67	34	33	64	32	32	62	31	31	60	30	30
15-19	68	34	34	66	33	33	63	32	31	61	31	30
20-24	68	34	34	66	33	33	64	32	32	61	31	30
25-29	59	29	30	66	33	33	64	32	32	62	31	31
30-34	58	29	29	58	29	29	65	33	33	64	32	32
35-39	57	28	29	58	29	29	58	29	29	65	33	33
40-44	51	25	26	57	28	29	58	29	29	58	29	29
45-49	39	19	21	50	25	25	56	28	29	58	29	29
50-54	29	14	15	39	18	20	49	24	25	56	27	28
55-59	27	13	14	28	13	14	39	19	20	48	23	26
60-64	22	10	12	26	12	14	27	13	14	36	17	19
65-69	14	5	9	20	9	11	24	11	13	25	11	13
70-74	9	3	6	13	4	8	18	8	10	21	9	12
75-79	4	1	3	7	2	5	10	3	7	14	6	9
80-84	3	1	2	3	1	2	5	1	4	7	2	5
85-89	2	0	1	1	0	1	2	0	1	3	1	2
90-94	1	0	0	1	0	1	1	0	0	1	0	1
95-99	0	0	0	0	0	0	0	0	0	0	0	0
100 +	0	0	0	0	0	0	0	0	0	0	0	0

Age group	2045 Both sexes	Males	Females	2050 Both sexes	Males	Females
All ages	828	406	422	840	412	428
0-4	49	25	24	44	22	22
5-9	53	27	26	49	25	24
10-14	57	29	28	53	27	26
15-19	59	30	29	56	28	27
20-24	59	30	29	57	29	28
25-29	59	30	29	57	29	28
30-34	62	31	31	58	29	29
35-39	64	32	32	62	31	31
40-44	65	32	33	64	32	32
45-49	58	29	29	64	32	32
50-54	57	28	29	57	28	29
55-59	54	27	28	56	27	28
60-64	46	22	24	52	25	27
65-69	34	15	18	43	20	23
70-74	22	10	12	30	13	17
75-79	17	7	10	18	7	11
80-84	10	4	7	12	4	8
85-89	4	1	3	6	2	4
90-94	1	0	1	2	0	2
95-99	0	0	0	0	0	0
100 +	0	0	0	0	0	0

POPULATION BY AGE AND SEX (in thousands)

Age group	1950 Both sexes	1950 Males	1950 Females	1955 Both sexes	1955 Males	1955 Females	1960 Both sexes	1960 Males	1960 Females	1965 Both sexes	1965 Males	1965 Females
All ages	1 314	629	685	1 412	674	738	1 530	730	800	1 685	805	880
0-4	187	91	96	225	111	114	246	122	125	272	135	138
5-9	151	73	78	162	78	84	197	96	101	218	107	111
10-14	136	66	70	144	70	74	154	74	80	189	92	97
15-19	124	60	64	131	63	67	139	67	72	150	72	78
20-24	113	55	58	119	57	62	125	60	65	136	65	71
25-29	101	48	53	107	51	56	113	54	59	122	58	64
30-34	91	42	48	96	45	50	101	48	53	109	52	57
35-39	81	38	43	85	40	45	90	42	48	97	46	51
40-44	71	34	37	75	35	40	79	37	43	85	40	45
45-49	62	29	33	65	31	35	69	32	37	74	34	40
50-54	54	26	28	56	26	30	60	27	32	64	29	35
55-59	43	20	23	47	22	25	50	23	27	53	24	29
60-64	37	17	20	36	17	20	40	18	22	43	19	24
65-69	29	13	15	29	13	16	29	13	16	32	14	18
70-74	19	9	10	20	9	11	20	9	11	20	9	12
75-79	11	5	6	11	5	6	11	5	6	12	5	7
80 +	5	2	3	5	2	3	6	2	4	6	2	4

Age group	1970 Both sexes	1970 Males	1970 Females	1975 Both sexes	1975 Males	1975 Females	1980 Both sexes	1980 Males	1980 Females	1985 Both sexes	1985 Males	1985 Females
All ages	1 871	896	976	2 060	988	1 072	2 329	1 120	1 209	2 677	1 292	1 386
0-4	306	152	154	343	170	173	404	201	203	454	226	228
5-9	244	120	124	275	135	140	315	155	160	375	185	190
10-14	211	103	108	235	115	120	267	131	136	307	151	156
15-19	185	90	95	204	99	104	230	112	117	264	129	135
20-24	147	70	77	176	85	90	198	96	102	229	112	118
25-29	133	63	69	138	66	72	169	82	88	199	96	103
30-34	119	56	62	124	59	65	133	63	70	170	81	88
35-39	105	50	55	111	52	58	119	56	62	132	62	70
40-44	93	44	49	98	46	52	105	50	56	116	55	61
45-49	80	37	43	86	40	46	93	43	49	102	48	54
50-54	69	31	38	74	34	40	80	37	43	88	41	47
55-59	58	26	32	62	27	34	67	30	37	74	34	40
60-64	46	21	26	50	22	28	55	24	31	60	27	34
65-69	35	15	19	38	16	21	42	18	24	46	20	26
70-74	23	10	13	25	11	15	28	12	16	32	13	19
75-79	12	5	7	14	6	8	16	7	10	19	7	11
80 +	7	3	5	8	3	5	9	3	6	11	4	7

Age group	1990 Both sexes	1990 Males	1990 Females	1995 Both sexes	1995 Males	1995 Females	2000 Both sexes	2000 Males	2000 Females	2005 Both sexes	2005 Males	2005 Females
All ages	3 000	1 450	1 550	3 414	1 654	1 761	3 777	1 834	1 944	4 038	1 969	2 069
0-4	517	258	259	576	288	288	620	310	310	640	320	320
5-9	423	209	214	486	241	244	538	267	271	575	286	289
10-14	365	180	185	414	204	209	474	235	239	521	258	262
15-19	298	147	152	361	178	183	407	201	206	463	229	234
20-24	251	122	128	294	144	150	350	172	178	387	190	197
25-29	213	103	110	243	118	125	271	133	138	311	153	157
30-34	184	88	96	204	98	106	215	105	111	223	111	112
35-39	158	75	83	176	83	92	181	86	95	174	86	88
40-44	122	57	65	150	71	79	158	74	84	150	72	79
45-49	108	51	58	116	54	63	137	63	73	135	63	73
50-54	94	44	51	102	47	55	107	48	58	120	55	65
55-59	80	37	44	87	40	47	93	42	51	95	42	53
60-64	66	30	36	72	32	40	78	35	43	81	36	45
65-69	51	22	29	56	25	31	61	27	34	65	28	37
70-74	35	15	21	39	17	23	44	19	25	47	20	27
75-79	21	8	13	24	9	14	27	11	16	30	12	17
80 +	13	5	8	15	5	9	18	7	12	21	8	13

United Nations Department of Economic and Social Affairs/Population Division
World Population Prospects: The 2004 Revision, Volume II: Sex and Age Distribution of the World Population

274

CENTRAL AFRICAN REPUBLIC

POPULATION BY AGE AND SEX (in thousands)

Age group	2005			2010			2015			2020		
	Both sexes	Males	Females	Both sexes	Males	Females	Both sexes	Males	Females	Both sexes	Males	Females
All ages	4 038	1 969	2 069	4 333	2 124	2 209	4 647	2 288	2 359	4 960	2 451	2 509
0-4	640	320	320	663	332	331	687	344	344	691	346	345
5-9	575	286	289	596	296	300	623	310	313	653	325	328
10-14	521	258	262	554	275	279	575	285	290	604	299	304
15-19	463	229	234	510	253	258	544	269	274	565	280	285
20-24	387	190	197	447	221	226	495	244	251	528	261	268
25-29	311	153	157	354	175	179	413	205	208	461	228	233
30-34	223	111	112	265	133	131	307	155	152	362	182	179
35-39	174	86	88	183	93	89	222	114	107	260	134	126
40-44	150	72	79	145	72	73	154	80	74	188	98	90
45-49	135	63	73	129	61	68	125	62	63	134	69	64
50-54	120	55	65	119	55	65	114	54	60	111	55	56
55-59	95	42	53	107	48	59	107	48	58	102	48	55
60-64	81	36	45	83	36	47	95	41	53	95	42	53
65-69	65	28	37	69	30	39	71	30	41	81	35	46
70-74	47	20	27	51	22	30	54	23	32	57	23	33
75-79	30	12	17	33	13	19	36	14	21	38	15	23
80-84	15	6	9	16	6	10	18	7	11	20	8	13
85-89	5	2	3	6	2	4	7	2	4	8	3	5
90-94	1	0	1	1	0	1	2	0	1	2	1	1
95-99	0	0	0	0	0	0	0	0	0	0	0	0
100 +	0	0	0	0	0	0	0	0	0	0	0	0

Age group	2025			2030			2035			2040		
	Both sexes	Males	Females	Both sexes	Males	Females	Both sexes	Males	Females	Both sexes	Males	Females
All ages	5 269	2 611	2 658	5 572	2 764	2 808	5 871	2 912	2 959	6 170	3 058	3 112
0-4	686	344	343	680	341	339	677	339	337	674	338	336
5-9	663	330	333	663	330	333	661	329	331	661	330	331
10-14	637	316	321	650	323	327	653	325	328	653	325	328
15-19	594	294	300	629	311	317	643	319	324	647	321	326
20-24	551	272	279	581	286	294	616	304	312	631	312	319
25-29	495	244	251	519	255	263	550	270	279	586	288	298
30-34	409	205	204	444	221	223	469	232	237	502	247	255
35-39	311	160	152	357	181	176	092	196	196	419	208	211
40-44	224	117	107	272	141	132	316	160	156	350	175	176
45-49	166	87	79	199	103	96	244	126	119	286	144	142
50-54	120	62	58	150	77	72	181	93	88	224	114	110
55-59	100	49	51	109	55	54	137	70	67	167	84	82
60-64	92	42	50	90	43	47	99	49	49	124	62	62
65-69	82	35	46	80	35	44	79	37	42	87	42	44
70-74	65	27	38	66	28	38	65	28	37	65	30	35
75-79	40	16	24	47	10	28	40	20	20	40	20	20
80-84	22	9	14	24	9	15	28	11	18	30	11	18
85-89	9	3	6	10	3	6	11	4	7	13	5	8
90-94	2	1	2	3	1	2	3	1	2	3	1	2
95-99	0	0	0	0	0	0	0	0	0	1	0	0
100 +	0	0	0	0	0	0	0	0	0	0	0	0

Age group	2045			2050		
	Both sexes	Males	Females	Both sexes	Males	Females
All ages	6 464	3 199	3 265	6 747	3 334	3 414
0-4	666	334	331	652	328	324
5-9	661	330	331	655	328	328
10-14	655	326	329	656	327	329
15-19	647	322	326	650	323	327
20-24	636	314	321	638	316	322
25-29	603	297	306	611	301	310
30-34	540	266	274	561	276	284
35-39	453	223	229	492	243	250
40-44	378	187	192	414	203	210
45-49	321	159	162	349	171	178
50-54	264	131	133	298	146	152
55-59	207	104	104	246	121	125
60-64	153	76	77	191	94	97
65-69	110	54	56	136	66	70
70-74	72	34	38	93	44	48
75-79	49	22	27	55	25	29
80-84	30	12	18	31	13	18
85-89	14	5	9	14	5	9
90-94	4	1	3	4	1	3
95-99	1	0	0	1	0	1
100 +	0	0	0	0	0	0

United Nations Department of Economic and Social Affairs/Population Division
World Population Prospects: The 2004 Revision, Volume II: Sex and Age Distribution of the World Population

275

POPULATION BY AGE AND SEX (in thousands)

Age group	2005 Both sexes	Males	Females	2010 Both sexes	Males	Females	2015 Both sexes	Males	Females	2020 Both sexes	Males	Females
All ages	4 038	1 969	2 069	4 370	2 142	2 227	4 748	2 338	2 409	5 150	2 546	2 604
0-4	640	320	320	699	350	350	754	377	377	786	393	392
5-9	575	286	289	596	296	300	657	326	330	716	356	360
10-14	521	258	262	554	275	279	575	285	290	636	316	321
15-19	463	229	234	510	253	258	544	269	274	565	280	285
20-24	387	190	197	447	221	226	495	244	251	528	261	268
25-29	311	153	157	354	175	179	413	205	208	461	228	233
30-34	223	111	112	265	133	131	307	155	152	362	182	179
35-39	174	86	88	183	93	89	222	114	107	260	134	126
40-44	150	72	79	145	72	73	154	80	74	188	98	90
45-49	135	63	73	129	61	68	125	62	63	134	69	64
50-54	120	55	65	119	55	65	114	54	60	111	55	56
55-59	95	42	53	107	48	59	107	48	58	102	48	55
60-64	81	36	45	83	36	47	95	41	53	95	42	53
65-69	65	28	37	69	30	39	71	30	41	81	35	46
70-74	47	20	27	51	22	30	54	23	32	57	23	33
75-79	30	12	17	33	13	19	36	14	21	38	15	23
80-84	15	6	9	16	6	10	18	7	11	20	8	13
85-89	5	2	3	6	2	4	7	2	4	8	3	5
90-94	1	0	1	1	0	1	2	0	1	2	1	1
95-99	0	0	0	0	0	0	0	0	0	0	0	0
100 +	0	0	0	0	0	0	0	0	0	0	0	0

Age group	2025 Both sexes	Males	Females	2030 Both sexes	Males	Females	2035 Both sexes	Males	Females	2040 Both sexes	Males	Females
All ages	5 561	2 756	2 805	5 985	2 970	3 015	6 437	3 194	3 243	6 921	3 432	3 490
0-4	794	397	396	808	405	403	838	420	418	873	438	435
5-9	753	375	378	766	382	385	785	392	394	819	409	410
10-14	699	347	352	739	367	372	755	375	380	776	387	390
15-19	627	310	316	690	342	348	730	362	368	747	371	376
20-24	551	272	279	612	302	310	675	333	342	717	354	363
25-29	495	244	251	519	255	263	580	285	295	643	316	326
30-34	409	205	204	444	221	223	469	232	237	529	261	269
35-39	311	160	152	357	181	176	392	196	196	419	208	211
40-44	224	117	107	272	141	132	316	160	156	350	175	176
45-49	166	87	79	199	103	96	244	126	119	286	144	142
50-54	120	62	58	150	77	72	181	93	88	224	114	110
55-59	100	49	51	109	55	54	137	70	67	167	84	82
60-64	92	42	50	90	43	47	99	49	49	124	62	62
65-69	82	35	46	80	35	44	79	37	42	87	42	44
70-74	65	27	38	66	28	38	65	28	37	65	30	35
75-79	40	16	24	47	19	28	48	20	29	48	20	28
80-84	22	9	14	24	9	15	28	11	18	30	11	18
85-89	9	3	6	10	3	6	11	4	7	13	5	8
90-94	2	1	2	3	1	2	3	1	2	3	1	2
95-99	0	0	0	0	0	0	0	0	0	1	0	0
100 +	0	0	0	0	0	0	0	0	0	0	0	0

Age group	2045 Both sexes	Males	Females	2050 Both sexes	Males	Females
All ages	7 428	3 679	3 749	7 948	3 932	4 016
0-4	898	451	447	912	458	454
5-9	856	428	429	884	442	442
10-14	811	404	407	850	424	426
15-19	770	383	387	805	401	405
20-24	735	363	371	758	375	383
25-29	685	338	348	706	348	358
30-34	592	292	300	637	314	323
35-39	478	236	242	540	266	274
40-44	378	187	192	436	215	222
45-49	321	159	162	349	171	178
50-54	264	131	133	298	146	152
55-59	207	104	104	246	121	125
60-64	153	76	77	191	94	97
65-69	110	54	56	136	66	70
70-74	72	34	38	93	44	48
75-79	49	22	27	55	25	29
80-84	30	12	18	31	13	18
85-89	14	5	9	14	5	9
90-94	4	1	3	4	1	3
95-99	1	0	0	1	0	1
100 +	0	0	0	0	0	0

United Nations Department of Economic and Social Affairs/Population Division
World Population Prospects: The 2004 Revision, Volume II: Sex and Age Distribution of the World Population

276

POPULATION BY AGE AND SEX (in thousands)

Age group	2005 Both sexes	Males	Females	2010 Both sexes	Males	Females	2015 Both sexes	Males	Females	2020 Both sexes	Males	Females
All ages	4 038	1 969	2 069	4 297	2 106	2 191	4 547	2 238	2 309	4 770	2 356	2 413
0-4	640	320	320	627	313	313	621	311	310	597	299	298
5-9	575	286	289	596	296	300	589	293	296	590	293	296
10-14	521	258	262	554	275	279	575	285	290	571	283	287
15-19	463	229	234	510	253	258	544	269	274	565	280	285
20-24	387	190	197	447	221	226	495	244	251	528	261	268
25-29	311	153	157	354	175	179	413	205	208	461	228	233
30-34	223	111	112	265	133	131	307	155	152	362	182	179
35-39	174	86	88	183	93	89	222	114	107	260	134	126
40-44	150	72	79	145	72	73	154	80	74	188	98	90
45-49	135	63	73	129	61	68	125	62	63	134	69	64
50-54	120	55	65	119	55	65	114	54	60	111	55	56
55-59	95	42	53	107	48	59	107	48	58	102	48	55
60-64	81	36	45	83	36	47	95	41	53	95	42	53
65-69	65	28	37	69	30	39	71	30	41	81	35	46
70-74	47	20	27	51	22	30	54	23	32	57	23	33
75-79	30	12	17	33	13	19	36	14	21	38	15	23
80-84	15	6	9	16	6	10	18	7	11	20	8	13
85-89	5	2	3	6	2	4	7	2	4	8	3	5
90-94	1	0	1	1	0	1	2	0	1	2	1	1
95-99	0	0	0	0	0	0	0	0	0	0	0	0
100 +	0	0	0	0	0	0	0	0	0	0	0	0

Age group	2025 Both sexes	Males	Females	2030 Both sexes	Males	Females	2035 Both sexes	Males	Females	2040 Both sexes	Males	Females
All ages	4 979	2 466	2 512	5 164	2 561	2 603	5 322	2 639	2 683	5 457	2 703	2 754
0-4	580	290	290	556	278	277	527	264	263	497	249	248
5-9	572	285	288	560	279	281	540	269	271	515	257	258
10-14	576	286	290	562	279	283	552	274	277	534	266	268
15-19	562	278	284	568	281	287	555	275	280	546	271	275
20-24	551	272	279	549	271	278	556	274	282	545	269	276
25-29	495	244	251	519	255	263	520	256	264	529	260	269
30-34	409	205	204	444	221	223	469	232	237	475	234	241
35-39	311	160	152	357	181	176	392	196	196	419	208	211
40-44	224	117	107	272	141	132	316	160	156	350	175	176
45-49	166	87	79	199	103	96	244	126	119	286	144	142
50-54	120	62	58	150	77	72	181	93	88	224	114	110
55-59	100	49	51	109	55	54	137	70	67	167	84	82
60-64	92	42	50	90	43	47	99	49	49	124	62	62
65-69	82	35	46	80	35	44	79	37	42	87	42	44
70-74	65	27	38	66	28	38	65	28	37	65	30	35
75-79	40	16	24	47	19	28	49	20	20	40	20	28
80-84	22	9	14	24	9	15	28	11	18	30	11	18
85-89	9	3	6	10	3	6	11	4	7	13	5	8
90-94	2	1	2	3	1	2	3	1	2	3	1	2
95-99	0	0	0	0	0	0	0	0	0	1	0	0
100 +	0	0	0	0	0	0	0	0	0	0	0	0

Age group	2045 Both sexes	Males	Females	2050 Both sexes	Males	Females
All ages	5 569	2 754	2 816	5 660	2 792	2 868
0-4	466	234	232	435	219	217
5-9	488	244	244	459	229	229
10-14	510	254	256	484	241	243
15-19	529	263	266	506	252	254
20-24	537	266	272	521	258	263
25-29	521	257	264	516	255	262
30-34	487	240	247	484	239	246
35-39	428	211	217	445	219	225
40-44	378	187	192	391	192	199
45-49	321	159	162	349	171	178
50-54	264	131	133	298	146	152
55-59	207	104	104	246	121	125
60-64	153	76	77	191	94	97
65-69	110	54	56	136	66	70
70-74	72	34	38	93	44	48
75-79	49	22	27	55	25	29
80-84	30	12	18	31	13	18
85-89	14	5	9	14	5	9
90-94	4	1	3	4	1	3
95-99	1	0	0	1	0	1
100 +	0	0	0	0	0	0

POPULATION BY AGE AND SEX (in thousands)

Age group	1950 Both sexes	1950 Males	1950 Females	1955 Both sexes	1955 Males	1955 Females	1960 Both sexes	1960 Males	1960 Females	1965 Both sexes	1965 Males	1965 Females
All ages	2 658	1 302	1 356	2 845	1 393	1 452	3 083	1 510	1 573	3 379	1 656	1 723
0-4	397	197	199	458	228	230	509	254	255	572	285	287
5-9	320	159	161	337	167	170	394	196	198	443	220	223
10-14	284	141	143	303	150	153	320	159	161	376	187	189
15-19	257	128	130	272	135	137	292	145	147	309	153	156
20-24	231	114	117	245	121	124	261	129	132	280	138	142
25-29	206	101	105	218	107	111	233	114	118	248	122	126
30-34	182	90	92	193	94	99	206	100	105	220	108	112
35-39	159	78	81	169	84	86	181	88	93	193	94	99
40-44	139	67	72	146	72	75	157	77	80	168	82	86
45-49	119	58	61	127	61	66	134	65	69	145	71	74
50-54	104	49	55	106	51	55	114	54	60	122	58	64
55-59	80	38	42	90	42	48	93	44	49	101	47	54
60-64	67	31	36	66	31	35	75	34	41	79	36	42
65-69	52	25	28	51	23	28	51	23	28	59	26	33
70-74	34	16	19	34	16	19	34	15	19	35	15	19
75-79	19	8	10	18	8	10	19	8	11	20	8	11
80 +	9	4	5	9	4	5	9	4	6	10	4	6

Age group	1970 Both sexes	1970 Males	1970 Females	1975 Both sexes	1975 Males	1975 Females	1980 Both sexes	1980 Males	1980 Females	1985 Both sexes	1985 Males	1985 Females
All ages	3 757	1 843	1 914	4 185	2 056	2 129	4 631	2 277	2 353	5 215	2 567	2 648
0-4	661	330	331	764	382	382	850	425	425	966	483	483
5-9	503	250	253	581	289	292	670	334	336	760	379	381
10-14	424	211	213	478	237	240	546	272	274	638	318	320
15-19	364	181	183	406	202	204	452	225	227	523	260	263
20-24	297	147	150	346	171	175	383	190	193	431	213	217
25-29	267	131	136	281	138	143	324	160	164	362	179	184
30-34	235	115	120	251	123	128	261	128	133	306	150	156
35-39	208	102	106	220	108	112	233	114	119	245	120	125
40-44	181	88	93	193	94	99	202	99	104	217	106	111
45-49	156	75	81	166	80	86	176	85	91	187	91	97
50-54	132	64	68	141	67	74	149	71	78	161	77	84
55-59	108	51	57	117	56	61	124	58	66	134	63	71
60-64	86	39	47	92	43	49	99	46	52	107	49	58
65-69	62	28	34	68	31	38	73	33	40	80	37	43
70-74	41	18	23	44	20	24	48	21	27	53	23	29
75-79	20	9	12	24	10	14	26	11	15	30	12	17
80 +	11	4	7	12	5	7	14	5	8	16	6	10

Age group	1990 Both sexes	1990 Males	1990 Females	1995 Both sexes	1995 Males	1995 Females	2000 Both sexes	2000 Males	2000 Females	2005 Both sexes	2005 Males	2005 Females
All ages	6 055	2 983	3 072	7 034	3 468	3 566	8 216	4 056	4 159	9 749	4 824	4 925
0-4	1 137	569	568	1 342	673	669	1 562	783	779	1 867	936	930
5-9	891	444	446	1 053	525	527	1 255	627	628	1 485	742	743
10-14	743	370	373	868	433	436	1 037	517	520	1 255	627	628
15-19	627	312	315	728	363	366	860	429	432	1 045	521	524
20-24	511	253	258	609	302	307	715	355	360	860	427	433
25-29	418	206	212	490	242	248	584	289	295	697	346	351
30-34	350	172	178	398	195	203	462	228	234	555	276	279
35-39	294	144	150	333	163	170	375	183	191	435	216	219
40-44	235	114	120	278	136	143	313	152	161	353	173	180
45-49	206	100	106	221	107	114	262	127	136	297	143	153
50-54	176	84	92	192	92	100	207	99	108	248	118	130
55-59	147	70	78	161	76	85	178	84	94	194	91	103
60-64	118	55	63	131	61	70	144	67	77	161	75	86
65-69	89	41	49	99	45	54	111	51	60	124	57	67
70-74	60	27	33	68	30	38	76	34	42	87	39	48
75-79	34	14	20	39	17	22	45	19	26	52	22	29
80 +	19	7	12	22	9	14	28	11	17	34	13	20

United Nations Department of Economic and Social Affairs/Population Division
World Population Prospects: The 2004 Revision, Volume II: Sex and Age Distribution of the World Population

278

POPULATION BY AGE AND SEX (in thousands)

Age group	2005			2010			2015			2020		
	Both sexes	Males	Females	Both sexes	Males	Females	Both sexes	Males	Females	Both sexes	Males	Females
All ages	9 749	4 824	4 925	11 130	5 519	5 611	12 832	6 374	6 458	14 881	7 402	7 479
0-4	1 867	936	930	2 162	1 085	1 077	2 482	1 246	1 236	2 779	1 396	1 383
5-9	1 485	742	743	1 703	852	852	2 001	1 001	1 000	2 339	1 170	1 169
10-14	1 255	627	628	1 419	709	710	1 640	820	821	1 951	975	976
15-19	1 045	521	524	1 211	604	606	1 379	688	690	1 610	804	806
20-24	860	427	433	1 001	498	503	1 168	581	587	1 344	669	675
25-29	697	346	351	806	400	406	946	470	476	1 118	556	562
30-34	555	276	279	637	318	319	745	371	374	886	442	444
35-39	435	216	219	500	250	249	581	291	289	688	345	343
40-44	353	173	180	392	195	197	455	229	227	536	270	267
45-49	297	143	153	319	156	164	358	177	181	421	211	210
50-54	248	118	130	268	128	140	292	141	151	331	162	168
55-59	194	91	103	222	105	117	242	115	128	267	127	139
60-64	161	75	86	169	78	91	195	91	105	216	101	116
65-69	124	57	67	133	61	72	141	64	77	166	76	90
70-74	87	39	48	94	42	52	102	46	56	110	49	61
75-79	52	22	29	57	25	32	62	27	35	70	30	39
80-84	24	10	14	27	11	16	30	13	18	34	14	20
85-89	8	3	5	9	3	6	10	4	6	12	5	7
90-94	2	1	1	2	1	1	2	1	2	3	1	2
95-99	0	0	0	0	0	0	0	0	0	0	0	0
100 +	0	0	0	0	0	0	0	0	0	0	0	0

Age group	2025			2030			2035			2040		
	Both sexes	Males	Females	Both sexes	Males	Females	Both sexes	Males	Females	Both sexes	Males	Females
All ages	17 189	8 560	8 629	19 751	9 845	9 906	22 532	11 240	11 292	25 460	12 707	12 753
0-4	3 078	1 547	1 530	3 374	1 698	1 677	3 643	1 834	1 809	3 843	1 935	1 907
5-9	2 642	1 323	1 319	2 948	1 478	1 470	3 252	1 632	1 620	3 530	1 773	1 758
10-14	2 289	1 144	1 145	2 594	1 298	1 296	2 903	1 454	1 449	3 211	1 610	1 601
15-19	1 918	958	961	2 255	1 126	1 129	2 561	1 280	1 281	2 870	1 436	1 434
20-24	1 573	783	790	1 878	935	943	2 212	1 102	1 110	2 516	1 254	1 262
25-29	1 291	642	650	1 515	753	762	1 815	902	913	2 145	1 067	1 078
30-34	1 053	525	528	1 221	609	613	1 439	717	722	1 732	863	869
35-39	824	413	411	985	493	492	1 149	575	574	1 000	680	680
40-44	630	321	310	769	386	383	925	464	461	1 084	543	541
45-49	498	250	249	598	299	298	723	362	361	874	437	437
50-54	391	194	197	465	232	234	560	279	281	681	339	342
55-59	304	148	156	361	178	184	432	213	219	523	258	265
60-64	240	113	127	275	132	143	329	160	169	395	192	202
65-69	185	85	100	207	96	111	239	113	126	288	138	150
70-74	131	59	73	148	66	81	167	76	91	195	90	105
75-79	76	33	43	92	40	52	105	46	60	121	53	67
80-84	39	16	23	44	18	25	54	22	31	62	26	36
85-89	14	5	9	16	6	10	19	7	11	24	9	14
90-94	3	1	2	4	1	3	5	2	3	5	2	4
95-99	0	0	0	1	0	0	1	0	0	1	0	1
100 +	0	0	0	0	0	0	0	0	0	0	0	0

Age group	2045			2050		
	Both sexes	Males	Females	Both sexes	Males	Females
All ages	28 461	14 208	14 253	31 497	15 722	15 775
0-4	3 967	1 999	1 969	4 057	2 045	2 013
5-9	3 742	1 880	1 862	3 881	1 950	1 931
10-14	3 493	1 752	1 740	3 709	1 862	1 847
15-19	3 178	1 592	1 587	3 461	1 734	1 727
20-24	2 825	1 409	1 415	3 133	1 565	1 568
25-29	2 447	1 218	1 229	2 756	1 373	1 383
30-34	2 057	1 025	1 032	2 357	1 175	1 182
35-39	1 647	823	824	1 966	982	985
40-44	1 291	646	645	1 571	785	786
45-49	1 030	515	515	1 232	615	617
50-54	827	412	416	979	487	492
55-59	639	315	324	779	384	395
60-64	481	234	246	591	288	302
65-69	348	167	181	427	205	222
70-74	237	111	126	289	136	153
75-79	143	64	78	176	80	95
80-84	73	31	42	87	38	49
85-89	28	11	17	33	14	20
90-94	7	3	4	9	3	5
95-99	1	0	1	1	0	1
100 +	0	0	0	0	0	0

CHAD   **HIGH VARIANT**

POPULATION BY AGE AND SEX (in thousands)

Age group	2005 Both sexes	Males	Females	2010 Both sexes	Males	Females	2015 Both sexes	Males	Females	2020 Both sexes	Males	Females
All ages	9 749	4 824	4 925	11 130	5 519	5 611	12 901	6 409	6 493	15 174	7 549	7 625
0-4	1 867	936	930	2 162	1 085	1 077	2 551	1 281	1 270	3 007	1 511	1 496
5-9	1 485	742	743	1 703	852	852	2 001	1 001	1 000	2 404	1 203	1 201
10-14	1 255	627	628	1 419	709	710	1 640	820	821	1 951	975	976
15-19	1 045	521	524	1 211	604	606	1 379	688	690	1 610	804	806
20-24	860	427	433	1 001	498	503	1 168	581	587	1 344	669	675
25-29	697	346	351	806	400	406	946	470	476	1 118	556	562
30-34	555	276	279	637	318	319	745	371	374	886	442	444
35-39	435	216	219	500	250	249	581	291	289	688	345	343
40-44	353	173	180	392	195	197	455	229	227	536	270	267
45-49	297	143	153	319	156	164	358	177	181	421	211	210
50-54	248	118	130	268	128	140	292	141	151	331	162	168
55-59	194	91	103	222	105	117	242	115	128	267	127	139
60-64	161	75	86	169	78	91	195	91	105	216	101	116
65-69	124	57	67	133	61	72	141	64	77	166	76	90
70-74	87	39	48	94	42	52	102	46	56	110	49	61
75-79	52	22	29	57	25	32	62	27	35	70	30	39
80-84	24	10	14	27	11	16	30	13	18	34	14	20
85-89	8	3	5	9	3	6	10	4	6	12	5	7
90-94	2	1	1	2	1	1	2	1	2	3	1	2
95-99	0	0	0	0	0	0	0	0	0	0	0	0
100 +	0	0	0	0	0	0	0	0	0	0	0	0

Age group	2025 Both sexes	Males	Females	2030 Both sexes	Males	Females	2035 Both sexes	Males	Females	2040 Both sexes	Males	Females
All ages	17 742	8 837	8 904	20 621	10 281	10 340	23 823	11 888	11 936	27 340	13 650	13 690
0-4	3 350	1 684	1 666	3 708	1 865	1 842	4 084	2 056	2 028	4 457	2 245	2 212
5-9	2 859	1 432	1 427	3 208	1 608	1 600	3 574	1 793	1 781	3 959	1 988	1 971
10-14	2 353	1 176	1 177	2 808	1 405	1 403	3 160	1 583	1 577	3 528	1 769	1 759
15-19	1 918	958	961	2 318	1 158	1 160	2 771	1 385	1 386	3 124	1 563	1 561
20-24	1 573	783	790	1 878	935	943	2 273	1 132	1 141	2 723	1 357	1 365
25-29	1 291	642	650	1 515	753	762	1 815	902	913	2 204	1 096	1 108
30-34	1 053	525	528	1 221	609	613	1 439	717	722	1 732	863	869
35-39	824	413	411	985	493	492	1 149	575	574	1 360	680	680
40-44	639	321	318	769	386	383	925	464	461	1 084	543	541
45-49	498	250	249	598	299	298	723	362	361	874	437	437
50-54	391	194	197	465	232	234	560	279	281	681	339	342
55-59	304	148	156	361	178	184	432	213	219	523	258	265
60-64	240	113	127	275	132	143	329	160	169	395	192	202
65-69	185	85	100	207	96	111	239	113	126	288	138	150
70-74	131	59	73	148	66	81	167	76	91	195	90	105
75-79	76	33	43	92	40	52	105	46	59	121	53	67
80-84	39	16	23	44	18	25	54	22	31	62	26	36
85-89	14	5	9	16	6	10	19	7	11	24	9	14
90-94	3	1	2	4	1	3	5	2	3	5	2	4
95-99	0	0	0	1	0	0	1	0	0	1	0	1
100 +	0	0	0	0	0	0	0	0	0	0	0	0

Age group	2045 Both sexes	Males	Females	2050 Both sexes	Males	Females
All ages	31 118	15 541	15 577	35 100	17 530	17 569
0-4	4 781	2 409	2 372	5 050	2 545	2 505
5-9	4 341	2 181	2 160	4 677	2 350	2 327
10-14	3 916	1 965	1 951	4 302	2 159	2 143
15-19	3 492	1 749	1 744	3 881	1 945	1 936
20-24	3 074	1 534	1 540	3 443	1 720	1 723
25-29	2 648	1 318	1 330	2 999	1 494	1 505
30-34	2 114	1 053	1 061	2 551	1 271	1 280
35-39	1 647	823	824	2 021	1 009	1 012
40-44	1 291	646	645	1 571	785	786
45-49	1 030	515	515	1 232	615	617
50-54	827	412	416	979	487	492
55-59	639	315	324	779	384	395
60-64	481	234	246	591	288	302
65-69	348	167	181	427	205	222
70-74	237	111	126	289	136	153
75-79	143	64	78	176	80	95
80-84	73	31	42	87	38	49
85-89	28	11	17	33	14	20
90-94	7	3	4	9	3	5
95-99	1	0	1	1	0	1
100 +	0	0	0	0	0	0

United Nations Department of Economic and Social Affairs/Population Division
World Population Prospects: The 2004 Revision, Volume II: Sex and Age Distribution of the World Population

280

POPULATION BY AGE AND SEX (in thousands)

Age group	2005 Both sexes	Males	Females	2010 Both sexes	Males	Females	2015 Both sexes	Males	Females	2020 Both sexes	Males	Females
All ages	9 749	4 824	4 925	11 049	5 478	5 570	12 602	6 259	6 343	14 433	7 178	7 255
0-4	1 867	936	930	2 080	1 044	1 037	2 328	1 169	1 159	2 551	1 282	1 269
5-9	1 485	742	743	1 703	852	852	1 925	962	962	2 194	1 098	1 096
10-14	1 255	627	628	1 419	709	710	1 640	820	821	1 876	938	939
15-19	1 045	521	524	1 211	604	606	1 379	688	690	1 610	804	806
20-24	860	427	433	1 001	498	503	1 168	581	587	1 344	669	675
25-29	697	346	351	806	400	406	946	470	476	1 118	556	562
30-34	555	276	279	637	318	319	745	371	374	886	442	444
35-39	435	216	219	500	250	249	581	291	289	688	345	343
40-44	353	173	180	392	195	197	455	229	227	536	270	267
45-49	297	143	153	319	156	164	358	177	181	421	211	210
50-54	248	118	130	268	128	140	292	141	151	331	162	168
55-59	194	91	103	222	105	117	242	115	128	267	127	139
60-64	161	75	86	169	78	91	195	91	105	216	101	116
65-69	124	57	67	133	61	72	141	64	77	166	76	90
70-74	87	39	48	94	42	52	102	46	56	110	49	61
75-79	52	22	29	57	25	32	62	27	35	70	30	39
80-84	24	10	14	27	11	16	30	13	18	34	14	20
85-89	8	3	5	9	3	6	10	4	6	12	5	7
90-94	2	1	1	2	1	1	2	1	2	3	1	2
95-99	0	0	0	0	0	0	0	0	0	0	0	0
100 +	0	0	0	0	0	0	0	0	0	0	0	0

Age group	2025 Both sexes	Males	Females	2030 Both sexes	Males	Females	2035 Both sexes	Males	Females	2040 Both sexes	Males	Females
All ages	16 475	8 202	8 273	18 686	9 311	9 375	20 990	10 467	10 523	23 304	11 626	11 678
0-4	2 796	1 406	1 390	3 003	1 511	1 492	3 141	1 582	1 560	3 194	1 609	1 585
5-9	2 425	1 214	1 210	2 678	1 342	1 336	2 895	1 452	1 442	3 045	1 529	1 516
10-14	2 147	1 073	1 074	2 381	1 192	1 190	2 638	1 321	1 317	2 858	1 433	1 425
15-19	1 845	921	924	2 115	1 057	1 059	2 350	1 175	1 175	2 607	1 304	1 303
20-24	1 573	783	790	1 806	899	907	2 075	1 033	1 041	2 309	1 151	1 158
25-29	1 291	642	650	1 515	753	762	1 746	868	878	2 012	1 001	1 011
30-34	1 053	525	528	1 221	609	613	1 439	717	722	1 666	830	836
35-39	824	413	411	985	493	492	1 149	575	574	1 360	680	680
40-44	639	321	318	769	386	383	925	464	461	1 084	543	541
45-49	498	250	249	598	299	298	723	362	361	874	437	437
50-54	391	194	197	465	232	234	560	279	281	681	339	342
55-59	304	148	156	361	178	184	432	213	219	523	258	265
60-64	240	113	127	275	132	143	329	160	169	395	192	202
65-69	185	85	100	207	96	111	239	113	126	288	138	150
70-74	131	59	73	148	66	81	167	76	91	195	90	105
75-79	76	33	43	92	40	52	105	46	60	121	50	07
80-84	39	16	23	44	18	25	54	22	31	62	26	36
85-89	14	5	9	16	6	10	19	7	11	24	9	14
90-94	3	1	2	4	1	3	5	2	3	5	2	4
95-99	0	0	0	1	0	0	1	0	0	1	0	1
100 +	0	0	0	0	0	0	0	0	0	0	0	0

Age group	2045 Both sexes	Males	Females	2050 Both sexes	Males	Females
All ages	25 560	12 753	12 807	27 726	13 831	13 895
0-4	3 178	1 601	1 577	3 133	1 579	1 554
5-9	3 111	1 563	1 548	3 109	1 562	1 547
10-14	3 012	1 511	1 501	3 083	1 547	1 536
15-19	2 829	1 417	1 412	2 985	1 496	1 489
20-24	2 566	1 280	1 286	2 789	1 393	1 396
25-29	2 246	1 118	1 128	2 504	1 247	1 257
30-34	1 929	961	968	2 164	1 078	1 085
35-39	1 584	791	793	1 844	921	924
40-44	1 291	646	645	1 511	755	756
45-49	1 030	515	515	1 232	615	617
50-54	827	412	416	979	487	492
55-59	639	315	324	779	384	395
60-64	481	234	246	591	288	302
65-69	348	167	181	427	205	222
70-74	237	111	126	289	136	153
75-79	143	64	78	176	80	95
80-84	73	31	42	87	38	49
85-89	28	11	17	33	14	20
90-94	7	3	4	9	3	5
95-99	1	0	1	1	0	1
100 +	0	0	0	0	0	0

POPULATION BY AGE AND SEX (in thousands)

Age group	1950 Both sexes	1950 Males	1950 Females	1955 Both sexes	1955 Males	1955 Females	1960 Both sexes	1960 Males	1960 Females	1965 Both sexes	1965 Males	1965 Females
All ages	102	49	53	106	51	55	110	53	57	116	56	60
0-4	9	4	4	8	4	4	8	4	4	8	4	4
5-9	6	3	3	7	3	3	7	4	4	8	4	4
10-14	7	4	3	8	4	4	8	4	4	8	4	4
15-19	7	3	3	7	3	3	6	3	3	7	3	4
20-24	7	3	4	7	3	4	8	4	4	9	4	4
25-29	8	4	4	8	4	4	8	4	4	8	4	4
30-34	7	3	3	7	3	4	7	4	4	8	4	4
35-39	8	4	4	8	4	4	7	4	4	7	4	4
40-44	8	4	4	7	4	4	7	3	4	7	3	4
45-49	7	4	4	7	4	4	8	4	4	8	4	4
50-54	6	3	3	7	3	4	8	4	4	7	4	4
55-59	5	2	3	6	3	3	7	3	4	7	4	4
60-64	5	2	3	6	2	3	6	3	3	7	3	4
65-69	4	2	3	5	2	3	5	2	3	6	2	3
70-74	4	2	2	4	2	2	4	2	2	4	2	3
75-79	2	1	1	3	1	2	3	1	2	3	1	2
80 +	2	1	1	2	1	2	3	1	2	3	1	2

Age group	1970 Both sexes	1970 Males	1970 Females	1975 Both sexes	1975 Males	1975 Females	1980 Both sexes	1980 Males	1980 Females	1985 Both sexes	1985 Males	1985 Females
All ages	122	59	63	127	62	66	129	62	67	135	65	70
0-4	9	4	4	7	4	4	7	3	3	7	4	4
5-9	9	5	5	9	4	4	8	4	4	7	4	4
10-14	8	4	4	10	5	5	9	5	4	8	4	4
15-19	7	4	4	9	5	5	10	5	5	10	5	5
20-24	10	5	5	10	5	5	10	5	5	12	6	6
25-29	8	4	4	11	6	5	10	5	5	11	6	6
30-34	8	4	4	8	4	4	10	5	5	10	5	5
35-39	7	4	4	8	4	4	8	4	4	11	5	5
40-44	7	4	4	8	4	4	8	4	4	8	4	4
45-49	8	4	4	7	4	4	8	4	4	8	4	4
50-54	7	3	4	8	4	4	7	4	4	8	4	4
55-59	8	4	4	6	3	3	7	3	4	7	3	4
60-64	7	3	4	7	3	4	7	3	4	7	3	4
65-69	6	3	3	6	3	4	6	3	3	6	3	3
70-74	5	2	3	5	2	3	5	2	3	6	2	3
75-79	3	1	2	4	1	2	4	1	2	4	2	3
80 +	3	1	2	4	1	3	4	1	3	5	1	3

Age group	1990 Both sexes	1990 Males	1990 Females	1995 Both sexes	1995 Males	1995 Females	2000 Both sexes	2000 Males	2000 Females	2005 Both sexes	2005 Males	2005 Females
All ages	142	69	73	144	70	74	147	72	75	149	73	76
0-4	8	4	4	8	4	4	8	4	4	8	4	4
5-9	7	4	4	8	4	4	8	4	4	8	4	4
10-14	7	4	4	8	4	4	9	4	4	9	5	4
15-19	9	4	4	8	4	4	8	4	4	9	5	5
20-24	13	6	7	10	5	5	9	4	5	9	5	5
25-29	13	6	7	13	6	7	11	5	5	9	5	5
30-34	11	6	6	13	6	6	13	6	6	10	5	5
35-39	11	5	5	11	6	6	13	6	7	13	6	7
40-44	11	5	5	10	5	5	11	6	6	13	6	7
45-49	8	4	4	11	5	5	10	5	5	11	6	6
50-54	8	4	4	8	4	4	11	5	5	10	5	5
55-59	7	4	4	8	4	4	8	4	4	11	5	5
60-64	7	3	4	7	3	3	7	4	4	7	4	4
65-69	6	3	3	6	3	3	6	3	3	7	3	3
70-74	5	2	3	5	2	3	5	2	3	5	2	3
75-79	4	2	3	4	2	2	4	2	2	4	2	2
80 +	5	2	4	6	2	4	5	2	4	5	2	4

(*) Including the islands of Guernsey and Jersey.

United Nations Department of Economic and Social Affairs/Population Division
World Population Prospects: The 2004 Revision, Volume II: Sex and Age Distribution of the World Population

282

POPULATION BY AGE AND SEX (in thousands)

Age group	2005 Both sexes	Males	Females	2010 Both sexes	Males	Females	2015 Both sexes	Males	Females	2020 Both sexes	Males	Females
All ages	149	73	76	152	75	77	155	76	70	168	77	80
0-4	8	4	4	7	4	3	7	4	4	8	4	4
5-9	8	4	4	8	4	4	7	4	4	7	4	4
10-14	9	5	4	9	4	4	8	4	4	8	4	4
15-19	9	5	5	9	5	4	9	5	4	8	4	4
20-24	9	5	5	10	5	5	10	5	5	10	5	5
25-29	9	5	5	10	5	5	11	5	5	11	5	5
30-34	10	5	5	9	5	5	9	5	5	11	5	5
35-39	13	6	7	11	5	6	9	5	5	10	5	5
40-44	13	6	7	13	6	7	11	5	6	10	5	5
45-49	11	6	6	13	6	7	13	6	7	11	5	6
50-54	10	5	5	11	6	6	13	6	7	13	6	7
55-59	11	5	5	10	5	5	11	6	6	13	6	6
60-64	7	4	4	10	5	5	9	5	5	11	5	5
65-69	7	3	3	7	3	3	9	5	5	9	4	4
70-74	5	2	3	6	3	3	6	3	3	8	4	4
75-79	4	2	2	4	2	2	5	2	3	5	2	3
80-84	3	1	2	3	1	2	3	1	2	4	2	2
85-89	2	0	1	2	1	1	2	1	1	2	1	1
90-94	1	0	0	1	0	0	1	0	1	1	0	1
95-99	0	0	0	0	0	0	0	0	0	0	0	0
100 +	0	0	0	0	0	0	0	0	0	0	0	0

Age group	2025 Both sexes	Males	Females	2030 Both sexes	Males	Females	2035 Both sexes	Males	Females	2040 Both sexes	Males	Females
All ages	161	79	82	164	80	83	166	81	85	168	82	85
0-4	8	4	4	9	4	4	9	4	4	9	5	4
5-9	8	4	4	8	4	4	9	5	4	9	5	4
10-14	8	4	4	8	4	4	9	5	4	9	5	4
15-19	8	4	4	8	4	4	9	4	4	9	5	5
20-24	10	5	5	9	5	5	9	5	5	10	5	5
25-29	11	5	5	10	5	5	10	5	5	10	5	5
30-34	11	5	5	10	5	5	10	5	5	9	5	5
35-39	11	5	5	11	5	5	11	5	5	10	5	5
40-44	10	5	5	11	6	5	11	6	5	11	5	5
45-49	9	5	5	10	5	5	11	5	6	11	5	5
50-54	11	5	5	9	5	5	10	5	5	11	5	5
55-59	13	6	7	11	5	5	9	5	5	10	5	5
60-64	12	6	6	12	6	6	10	5	5	9	4	5
65-69	10	5	5	11	5	6	11	5	6	9	4	5
70-74	8	4	4	9	4	5	10	5	5	10	5	6
75-79	7	3	4	7	3	4	8	4	4	9	4	5
80-84	4	2	2	5	2	3	6	2	3	6	2	4
85-89	2	1	2	3	1	2	4	1	2	4	1	2
90-94	1	0	1	1	0	1	1	0	1	2	1	1
95-99	0	0	0	0	0	0	0	0	0	1	0	0
100 +	0	0	0	0	0	0	0	0	0	0	0	0

Age group	2045 Both sexes	Males	Females	2050 Both sexes	Males	Females
All ages	170	83	86	171	84	87
0-4	9	5	4	9	5	4
5-9	9	5	4	9	5	4
10-14	9	5	4	9	5	4
15-19	10	5	5	10	5	5
20-24	10	5	5	11	5	5
25-29	10	5	5	11	5	5
30-34	10	5	5	10	5	5
35-39	10	5	5	10	5	5
40-44	10	5	5	10	5	5
45-49	11	5	5	10	5	5
50-54	11	6	5	11	5	5
55-59	11	5	5	11	6	5
60-64	9	5	5	10	5	5
65-69	8	4	4	9	4	4
70-74	9	4	5	8	4	4
75-79	9	4	5	8	4	4
80-84	8	3	4	8	3	4
85-89	5	2	3	5	2	3
90-94	2	1	1	3	1	2
95-99	1	0	1	1	0	1
100 +	0	0	0	0	0	0

United Nations Department of Economic and Social Affairs/Population Division
World Population Prospects: The 2004 Revision, Volume II: Sex and Age Distribution of the World Population

283

POPULATION BY AGE AND SEX (in thousands)

Age group	2005 Both sexes	Males	Females	2010 Both sexes	Males	Females	2015 Both sexes	Males	Females	2020 Both sexes	Males	Females
All ages	149	73	76	153	75	78	158	78	80	163	80	83
0-4	8	4	4	8	4	4	9	5	5	10	5	5
5-9	8	4	4	8	4	4	9	4	4	9	5	5
10-14	9	5	4	9	4	4	8	4	4	9	5	4
15-19	9	5	5	9	5	4	9	5	4	8	4	4
20-24	9	5	5	10	5	5	10	5	5	10	5	5
25-29	9	5	5	10	5	5	11	5	5	11	5	5
30-34	10	5	5	9	5	5	9	5	5	11	5	5
35-39	13	6	7	11	5	6	9	5	5	10	5	5
40-44	13	6	7	13	6	7	11	5	6	10	5	5
45-49	11	6	6	13	6	7	13	6	7	11	5	6
50-54	10	5	5	11	6	6	13	6	7	13	6	7
55-59	11	5	5	10	5	5	11	6	6	13	6	6
60-64	7	4	4	10	5	5	9	5	5	11	5	5
65-69	7	3	3	7	3	3	9	5	5	9	4	4
70-74	5	2	3	6	3	3	6	3	3	8	4	4
75-79	4	2	2	4	2	2	5	2	3	5	2	3
80-84	3	1	2	3	1	2	3	1	2	4	2	2
85-89	2	0	1	2	1	1	2	1	1	2	1	1
90-94	1	0	0	1	0	0	1	0	1	1	0	1
95-99	0	0	0	0	0	0	0	0	0	0	0	0
100 +	0	0	0	0	0	0	0	0	0	0	0	0

Age group	2025 Both sexes	Males	Females	2030 Both sexes	Males	Females	2035 Both sexes	Males	Females	2040 Both sexes	Males	Females
All ages	169	83	86	175	86	89	180	89	91	185	91	94
0-4	11	6	5	11	6	5	12	6	6	12	6	6
5-9	10	5	5	11	6	5	11	6	5	12	6	6
10-14	10	5	5	11	6	5	11	6	5	12	6	6
15-19	9	5	5	10	5	5	11	6	5	12	6	6
20-24	10	5	5	10	5	5	11	6	6	12	6	6
25-29	11	5	5	10	5	5	11	5	5	12	6	6
30-34	11	5	5	10	5	5	10	5	5	11	5	5
35-39	11	5	5	11	5	5	11	5	5	10	5	5
40-44	10	5	5	11	6	5	11	6	5	11	5	5
45-49	9	5	5	10	5	5	11	5	6	11	5	5
50-54	11	5	5	9	5	5	10	5	5	11	5	5
55-59	13	6	7	11	5	5	9	5	5	10	5	5
60-64	12	6	6	12	6	6	10	5	5	9	4	5
65-69	10	5	5	11	5	6	11	5	6	9	4	5
70-74	8	4	4	9	4	5	10	5	5	10	5	6
75-79	7	3	4	7	3	4	8	4	4	9	4	5
80-84	4	2	2	6	2	3	6	2	3	6	3	4
85-89	2	1	2	3	1	2	4	1	2	4	1	2
90-94	1	0	1	1	0	1	1	0	1	2	1	1
95-99	0	0	0	0	0	0	0	0	0	1	0	0
100 +	0	0	0	0	0	0	0	0	0	0	0	0

Age group	2045 Both sexes	Males	Females	2050 Both sexes	Males	Females
All ages	191	94	97	198	98	100
0-4	13	7	6	14	7	7
5-9	12	6	6	13	7	6
10-14	12	6	6	13	7	6
15-19	12	6	6	12	6	6
20-24	13	6	6	13	7	7
25-29	13	7	6	13	7	7
30-34	12	6	6	13	6	6
35-39	11	6	5	12	6	6
40-44	10	5	5	11	6	5
45-49	11	5	5	10	5	5
50-54	11	6	5	11	5	5
55-59	11	5	5	11	6	5
60-64	9	5	5	10	5	5
65-69	8	4	4	9	4	4
70-74	9	4	5	8	4	4
75-79	9	4	5	8	4	4
80-84	8	3	4	8	3	4
85-89	5	2	3	5	2	3
90-94	2	1	1	3	1	2
95-99	1	0	1	1	0	1
100 +	0	0	0	0	0	0

United Nations Department of Economic and Social Affairs/Population Division
World Population Prospects: The 2004 Revision, Volume II: Sex and Age Distribution of the World Population

284

POPULATION BY AGE AND SEX (in thousands)

Age group	2005 Both sexes	Males	Females	2010 Both sexes	Males	Females	2015 Both sexes	Males	Females	2020 Both sexes	Males	Females
All ages	149	73	76	151	74	77	151	74	77	152	74	77
0-4	8	4	4	6	3	3	5	3	3	5	3	3
5-9	8	4	4	8	4	4	6	3	3	5	3	3
10-14	9	5	4	9	4	4	8	4	4	6	3	3
15-19	9	5	5	9	5	4	9	5	4	8	4	4
20-24	9	5	5	10	5	5	10	5	5	10	5	5
25-29	9	5	5	10	5	5	11	5	5	11	5	5
30-34	10	5	5	9	5	5	9	5	5	11	5	5
35-39	13	6	7	11	5	6	9	5	5	10	5	5
40-44	13	6	7	13	6	7	11	5	6	10	5	5
45-49	11	6	6	13	6	7	13	6	7	11	5	6
50-54	10	5	5	11	6	6	13	6	7	13	6	7
55-59	11	5	5	10	5	5	11	6	6	13	6	6
60-64	7	4	4	10	5	5	9	5	5	11	5	5
65-69	7	3	3	7	3	3	9	5	5	9	4	4
70-74	5	2	3	6	3	3	6	3	3	8	4	4
75-79	4	2	2	4	2	2	5	2	3	5	2	3
80-84	3	1	2	3	1	2	3	1	2	4	2	2
85-89	2	0	1	2	1	1	2	1	1	2	1	1
90-94	1	0	0	1	0	0	1	0	1	1	0	1
95-99	0	0	0	0	0	0	0	0	0	0	0	0
100 +	0	0	0	0	0	0	0	0	0	0	0	0

Age group	2025 Both sexes	Males	Females	2030 Both sexes	Males	Females	2035 Both sexes	Males	Females	2040 Both sexes	Males	Females
All ages	152	75	78	153	75	78	152	75	78	151	74	77
0-4	6	3	3	6	3	3	6	3	3	6	3	3
5-9	5	3	3	6	3	3	6	3	3	6	3	3
10-14	6	3	3	6	3	3	6	3	3	6	3	3
15-19	7	3	3	6	3	3	6	3	3	7	3	3
20-24	10	5	5	8	4	4	7	4	4	7	4	4
25-29	11	5	5	10	5	5	8	4	4	8	4	4
30-34	11	5	5	10	5	5	10	5	5	8	4	4
35-39	11	5	5	11	5	5	11	5	5	10	5	5
40-44	10	5	5	11	6	5	11	6	5	11	5	5
45-49	9	5	5	10	5	5	11	5	6	11	5	6
50-54	11	5	5	9	5	5	10	5	5	11	5	5
55-59	13	6	7	11	5	5	9	5	5	10	5	5
60-64	12	6	6	12	6	6	10	5	5	9	4	5
65-69	10	5	5	11	5	6	11	5	6	9	4	5
70-74	8	4	4	9	4	5	10	5	5	10	5	6
75-79	7	3	4	7	3	4	8	4	4	9	4	5
80-84	4	2	2	6	2	3	6	2	3	6	3	4
85-89	2	1	2	3	1	2	4	1	2	4	1	2
90-94	1	0	1	1	0	1	1	0	1	2	1	1
95-99	0	0	0	0	0	0	0	0	0	1	0	0
100 +	0	0	0	0	0	0	0	0	0	0	0	0

Age group	2045 Both sexes	Males	Females	2050 Both sexes	Males	Females
All ages	149	73	76	147	72	75
0-4	5	3	3	5	3	3
5-9	6	3	3	5	3	3
10-14	6	3	3	6	3	3
15-19	7	4	3	7	4	3
20-24	8	4	4	8	4	4
25-29	8	4	4	8	4	4
30-34	8	4	4	8	4	4
35-39	8	4	4	8	4	4
40-44	10	5	5	9	4	4
45-49	11	5	5	10	5	5
50-54	11	6	5	11	5	5
55-59	11	5	5	11	6	5
60-64	9	5	5	10	5	5
65-69	8	4	4	9	4	4
70-74	9	4	5	8	4	4
75-79	9	4	5	8	4	4
80-84	8	3	4	8	3	4
85-89	5	2	3	5	2	3
90-94	2	1	1	3	1	2
95-99	1	0	1	1	0	1
100 +	0	0	0	0	0	0

United Nations Department of Economic and Social Affairs/Population Division
World Population Prospects: The 2004 Revision, Volume II: Sex and Age Distribution of the World Population

285

POPULATION BY AGE AND SEX (in thousands)

Age group	1950 Both sexes	1950 Males	1950 Females	1955 Both sexes	1955 Males	1955 Females	1960 Both sexes	1960 Males	1960 Females	1965 Both sexes	1965 Males	1965 Females
All ages	6 082	3 012	3 069	6 764	3 348	3 416	7 643	3 780	3 863	8 647	4 272	4 375
0-4	867	438	429	1 002	507	495	1 216	614	601	1 352	683	669
5-9	748	377	370	839	424	415	973	492	481	1 186	599	588
10-14	619	312	307	738	373	366	831	419	411	965	487	478
15-19	576	287	289	608	306	302	728	367	361	821	414	407
20-24	528	263	265	562	279	283	595	298	297	713	358	355
25-29	453	224	229	512	254	258	547	270	276	581	290	291
30-34	410	202	208	437	216	222	497	245	252	533	262	271
35-39	367	180	186	394	193	201	422	207	215	482	236	246
40-44	344	169	175	351	172	179	378	184	195	407	198	209
45-49	290	142	148	326	159	167	333	161	172	362	174	188
50-54	253	124	129	270	131	139	306	147	159	314	150	165
55-59	212	103	109	231	111	120	248	118	130	282	133	149
60-64	158	76	82	187	89	98	205	96	109	221	103	118
65-69	109	51	58	132	62	71	157	72	85	174	79	95
70-74	78	35	43	84	38	46	103	46	57	124	55	69
75-79	44	19	25	54	23	31	59	25	34	74	31	42
80 +	28	11	17	34	13	21	45	17	28	54	21	34

Age group	1970 Both sexes	1970 Males	1970 Females	1975 Both sexes	1975 Males	1975 Females	1980 Both sexes	1980 Males	1980 Females	1985 Both sexes	1985 Males	1985 Females
All ages	9 570	4 723	4 846	10 413	5 137	5 276	11 174	5 513	5 661	12 102	5 973	6 129
0-4	1 291	653	638	1 263	640	623	1 178	598	580	1 323	673	650
5-9	1 329	671	659	1 271	642	629	1 250	633	617	1 171	594	577
10-14	1 178	594	584	1 317	664	653	1 262	638	624	1 243	630	614
15-19	955	481	474	1 164	586	578	1 304	657	647	1 251	632	619
20-24	806	405	401	936	471	466	1 141	574	567	1 285	647	638
25-29	699	349	350	784	392	392	910	456	454	1 119	562	557
30-34	568	282	286	678	336	342	766	382	385	895	447	448
35-39	518	253	265	550	271	279	661	326	335	752	373	379
40-44	467	227	240	501	243	258	535	261	273	647	317	330
45-49	390	187	203	448	215	233	484	232	252	521	252	268
50-54	342	162	180	370	175	195	428	203	225	466	221	245
55-59	291	136	155	317	147	170	346	161	185	405	189	217
60-64	253	116	137	262	119	143	290	131	159	321	145	175
65-69	189	85	104	218	97	121	230	102	129	259	113	146
70-74	138	61	78	152	66	87	180	77	103	193	81	112
75-79	90	38	52	101	42	59	114	46	67	136	55	82
80 +	66	25	41	80	31	50	96	36	60	113	42	71

Age group	1990 Both sexes	1990 Males	1990 Females	1995 Both sexes	1995 Males	1995 Females	2000 Both sexes	2000 Males	2000 Females	2005 Both sexes	2005 Males	2005 Females
All ages	13 179	6 512	6 667	14 395	7 121	7 274	15 412	7 624	7 787	16 295	8 061	8 234
0-4	1 459	743	717	1 488	757	730	1 328	676	652	1 237	630	607
5-9	1 317	670	647	1 461	743	718	1 488	757	731	1 328	676	652
10-14	1 166	592	574	1 321	672	650	1 464	744	719	1 488	757	731
15-19	1 236	625	610	1 170	593	577	1 323	672	651	1 463	744	720
20-24	1 238	624	613	1 241	626	615	1 172	593	580	1 322	670	652
25-29	1 269	637	632	1 243	625	618	1 242	625	618	1 171	590	581
30-34	1 106	554	553	1 272	637	635	1 243	623	621	1 240	622	618
35-39	883	440	444	1 108	552	555	1 270	633	636	1 239	619	620
40-44	740	365	375	881	437	444	1 102	548	554	1 262	627	634
45-49	634	309	325	734	360	374	873	431	442	1 090	540	551
50-54	505	243	262	623	302	321	721	352	369	858	421	437
55-59	446	208	237	489	233	256	604	289	314	701	339	362
60-64	379	173	206	422	194	228	465	218	247	577	273	304
65-69	290	128	162	347	155	193	390	175	214	433	199	234
70-74	221	93	129	252	107	145	305	131	174	348	152	197
75-79	151	60	91	177	70	107	206	83	123	256	105	151
80 +	138	50	89	165	58	107	217	75	142	280	99	182

United Nations Department of Economic and Social Affairs/Population Division
World Population Prospects: The 2004 Revision, Volume II: Sex and Age Distribution of the World Population

286

POPULATION BY AGE AND SEX (in thousands)

Age group	2005 Both sexes	Males	Females	2010 Both sexes	Males	Females	2015 Both sexes	Males	Females	2020 Both sexes	Males	Females
All ages	16 295	8 061	8 234	17 134	8 474	8 660	17 926	8 861	9 065	18 639	9 205	9 435
0-4	1 237	630	607	1 248	636	613	1 260	642	618	1 249	636	613
5-9	1 328	676	652	1 237	630	607	1 249	636	613	1 261	642	619
10-14	1 488	757	731	1 329	676	653	1 238	630	608	1 250	636	613
15-19	1 463	744	720	1 488	757	732	1 329	676	653	1 239	630	609
20-24	1 322	670	652	1 462	742	721	1 488	755	733	1 330	675	655
25-29	1 171	590	581	1 321	668	653	1 461	739	722	1 487	753	734
30-34	1 240	622	618	1 170	588	581	1 319	665	654	1 459	737	722
35-39	1 239	619	620	1 236	618	618	1 167	585	582	1 316	662	654
40-44	1 262	627	634	1 232	613	619	1 230	613	617	1 161	581	580
45-49	1 090	540	551	1 249	619	631	1 221	605	615	1 219	606	614
50-54	858	421	437	1 073	528	545	1 230	606	624	1 203	593	610
55-59	701	339	362	835	406	429	1 046	510	536	1 200	586	614
60-64	577	273	304	672	320	351	802	385	417	1 006	484	522
65-69	433	199	234	539	250	290	630	294	336	754	355	399
70-74	348	152	197	389	173	216	488	219	269	572	259	313
75-79	256	105	151	295	123	173	333	141	191	420	180	240
80-84	156	59	97	197	76	121	230	89	140	261	104	157
85-89	84	28	56	103	36	68	132	47	86	156	56	101
90-94	31	9	22	44	13	31	55	17	38	71	22	49
95-99	8	2	6	12	3	9	17	4	12	21	6	15
100 +	1	0	1	2	0	1	3	1	2	4	1	3

Age group	2025 Both sexes	Males	Females	2030 Both sexes	Males	Females	2035 Both sexes	Males	Females	2040 Both sexes	Males	Females
All ages	19 266	9 502	9 765	19 779	9 737	10 041	20 167	9 908	10 259	20 437	10 019	10 418
0-4	1 235	629	606	1 202	613	590	1 168	595	573	1 147	584	562
5-9	1 249	636	613	1 236	629	606	1 203	613	590	1 169	596	574
10-14	1 262	642	619	1 250	637	614	1 237	630	607	1 204	613	591
15-19	1 250	636	614	1 263	643	620	1 251	637	614	1 238	630	608
20-24	1 240	630	610	1 251	636	616	1 264	642	622	1 253	637	616
25-29	1 329	674	656	1 240	629	612	1 252	635	617	1 265	642	623
30-34	1 485	751	735	1 329	672	657	1 240	628	613	1 252	634	618
35-39	1 456	733	722	1 482	748	735	1 327	670	657	1 239	626	613
40-44	1 310	657	652	1 449	728	721	1 476	743	733	1 322	665	656
45-49	1 152	574	578	1 299	650	650	1 438	720	718	1 405	705	700
50-54	1 202	594	608	1 137	564	573	1 283	638	645	1 420	708	713
55-59	1 175	575	600	1 176	576	600	1 113	547	565	1 257	621	636
60-64	1 157	558	599	1 135	548	587	1 137	550	587	1 077	523	554
65-69	949	448	501	1 094	517	577	1 075	509	566	1 080	513	567
70-74	688	314	374	869	398	471	1 006	462	544	991	456	535
75-79	496	215	281	600	262	338	761	333	428	885	388	496
80-84	333	134	199	396	161	235	483	197	285	617	253	363
85-89	180	65	114	231	85	146	278	103	175	341	127	214
90-94	85	27	58	99	32	67	129	42	87	156	51	105
95-99	27	8	20	33	9	24	39	11	28	51	14	36
100 +	5	1	4	6	2	5	8	2	6	9	2	6

Age group	2045 Both sexes	Males	Females	2050 Both sexes	Males	Females
All ages	20 598	10 077	10 521	20 657	10 090	10 567
0-4	1 135	578	557	1 123	572	551
5-9	1 148	585	563	1 136	579	557
10-14	1 171	596	574	1 149	585	564
15-19	1 206	614	592	1 172	597	575
20-24	1 240	630	610	1 207	614	593
25-29	1 254	636	618	1 241	630	611
30-34	1 265	641	624	1 254	636	619
35-39	1 251	632	619	1 264	639	625
40-44	1 234	622	612	1 247	629	618
45-49	1 312	659	654	1 226	616	610
50-54	1 448	722	725	1 298	648	649
55-59	1 393	689	704	1 420	703	717
60-64	1 218	594	624	1 351	660	691
65-69	1 025	489	536	1 160	556	605
70-74	998	460	538	950	440	510
75-79	876	385	491	885	390	495
80-84	721	296	424	717	295	422
85-89	439	164	275	517	194	323
90-94	193	64	130	251	83	168
95-99	61	17	44	76	22	55
100 +	11	3	8	13	4	10

United Nations Department of Economic and Social Affairs/Population Division
World Population Prospects: The 2004 Revision, Volume II: Sex and Age Distribution of the World Population

287

POPULATION BY AGE AND SEX (in thousands)

Age group	2005 Both sexes	Males	Females	2010 Both sexes	Males	Females	2015 Both sexes	Males	Females	2020 Both sexes	Males	Females
All ages	16 295	8 061	8 234	17 296	8 557	8 740	18 358	9 081	9 277	19 410	9 597	9 813
0-4	1 237	630	607	1 410	718	692	1 531	780	751	1 588	809	779
5-9	1 328	676	652	1 237	630	607	1 410	718	692	1 531	779	751
10-14	1 488	757	731	1 329	676	653	1 238	630	608	1 411	718	693
15-19	1 463	744	720	1 488	757	732	1 329	676	653	1 239	630	609
20-24	1 322	670	652	1 462	742	721	1 488	755	733	1 330	675	655
25-29	1 171	590	581	1 321	668	653	1 461	739	722	1 487	753	734
30-34	1 240	622	618	1 170	588	581	1 319	665	654	1 459	737	722
35-39	1 239	619	620	1 236	618	618	1 167	585	582	1 316	662	654
40-44	1 262	627	634	1 232	613	619	1 230	613	617	1 161	581	580
45-49	1 090	540	551	1 249	619	631	1 221	605	615	1 219	606	614
50-54	858	421	437	1 073	528	545	1 230	606	624	1 203	593	610
55-59	701	339	362	835	406	429	1 046	510	536	1 200	586	614
60-64	577	273	304	672	320	351	802	385	417	1 006	484	522
65-69	433	199	234	539	250	290	630	294	336	754	355	399
70-74	348	152	197	389	173	216	488	219	269	572	259	313
75-79	256	105	151	295	123	173	333	141	191	420	180	240
80-84	156	59	97	197	76	121	230	89	140	261	104	157
85-89	84	28	56	103	36	68	132	47	86	156	56	101
90-94	31	9	22	44	13	31	55	17	38	71	22	49
95-99	8	2	6	12	3	9	17	4	12	21	6	15
100 +	1	0	1	2	0	1	3	1	2	4	1	3

Age group	2025 Both sexes	Males	Females	2030 Both sexes	Males	Females	2035 Both sexes	Males	Females	2040 Both sexes	Males	Females
All ages	20 383	10 070	10 312	21 275	10 500	10 776	22 112	10 898	11 214	22 915	11 280	11 635
0-4	1 581	806	776	1 584	807	777	1 619	825	794	1 682	857	825
5-9	1 588	809	779	1 582	806	776	1 584	807	777	1 619	825	794
10-14	1 532	780	752	1 589	809	780	1 583	806	777	1 585	807	778
15-19	1 412	718	693	1 532	780	752	1 590	809	781	1 583	806	777
20-24	1 240	630	610	1 413	718	695	1 533	779	754	1 591	809	782
25-29	1 329	674	656	1 240	629	612	1 413	717	696	1 533	778	755
30-34	1 485	751	735	1 329	672	657	1 240	628	613	1 412	715	697
35-39	1 456	733	722	1 482	748	735	1 327	670	657	1 239	626	613
40-44	1 310	657	652	1 449	728	721	1 476	743	733	1 322	665	656
45-49	1 152	574	578	1 299	650	650	1 438	720	718	1 465	735	730
50-54	1 202	594	608	1 137	564	573	1 283	638	645	1 420	708	713
55-59	1 175	575	600	1 176	576	600	1 113	547	565	1 257	621	636
60-64	1 157	558	599	1 135	548	587	1 137	550	587	1 077	523	554
65-69	949	448	501	1 094	517	577	1 075	509	566	1 080	513	567
70-74	688	314	374	869	398	471	1 006	462	544	991	456	535
75-79	496	215	281	600	262	338	761	333	428	885	388	496
80-84	333	134	199	396	161	235	483	197	285	617	253	363
85-89	180	65	114	231	85	146	278	103	175	341	127	214
90-94	85	27	58	99	32	67	129	42	87	156	51	105
95-99	27	8	20	33	9	24	39	11	28	51	14	36
100 +	5	1	4	6	2	5	8	2	6	9	2	6

Age group	2045 Both sexes	Males	Females	2050 Both sexes	Males	Females
All ages	23 688	11 650	12 038	24 421	12 005	12 416
0-4	1 750	892	858	1 802	918	884
5-9	1 683	857	826	1 751	892	859
10-14	1 620	825	795	1 684	858	826
15-19	1 586	808	779	1 621	825	796
20-24	1 585	806	779	1 588	807	780
25-29	1 591	808	783	1 585	805	780
30-34	1 533	777	756	1 591	806	784
35-39	1 411	713	697	1 531	774	756
40-44	1 234	622	612	1 406	709	697
45-49	1 312	659	654	1 226	616	610
50-54	1 448	722	725	1 298	648	649
55-59	1 393	689	704	1 420	703	717
60-64	1 218	594	624	1 351	660	691
65-69	1 025	489	536	1 160	556	605
70-74	998	460	538	950	440	510
75-79	876	385	491	885	390	495
80-84	721	296	424	717	295	422
85-89	439	164	275	517	194	323
90-94	193	64	130	251	83	168
95-99	61	17	44	76	22	55
100 +	11	3	8	13	4	10

United Nations Department of Economic and Social Affairs/Population Division
World Population Prospects: The 2004 Revision, Volume II: Sex and Age Distribution of the World Population

288

POPULATION BY AGE AND SEX (in thousands)

Age group	2005 Both sexes	Males	Females	2010 Both sexes	Males	Females	2015 Both sexes	Males	Females	2020 Both sexes	Males	Females
All ages	16 295	8 061	8 234	16 973	8 392	8 581	17 496	8 642	8 854	17 871	8 814	9 058
0-4	1 237	630	607	1 087	554	533	992	505	487	910	463	446
5-9	1 328	676	652	1 237	630	607	1 087	554	534	993	506	487
10-14	1 488	757	731	1 329	676	653	1 238	630	608	1 089	554	534
15-19	1 463	744	720	1 488	757	732	1 329	676	653	1 239	630	609
20-24	1 322	670	652	1 462	742	721	1 488	755	733	1 330	675	655
25-29	1 171	590	581	1 321	668	653	1 461	739	722	1 487	753	734
30-34	1 240	622	618	1 170	588	581	1 319	665	654	1 459	737	722
35-39	1 239	619	620	1 236	618	618	1 167	585	582	1 316	662	654
40-44	1 262	627	634	1 232	613	619	1 230	613	617	1 161	581	580
45-49	1 090	540	551	1 249	619	631	1 221	605	615	1 219	606	614
50-54	858	421	437	1 073	528	545	1 230	606	624	1 203	593	610
55-59	701	339	362	835	406	429	1 046	510	536	1 200	586	614
60-64	577	273	304	672	320	351	802	385	417	1 006	484	522
65-69	433	199	234	539	250	290	630	294	336	754	355	399
70-74	348	152	197	389	173	216	488	219	269	572	259	313
75-79	256	105	151	295	123	173	333	141	191	420	180	240
80-84	156	59	97	197	76	121	230	89	140	261	104	157
85-89	84	28	56	103	36	68	132	47	86	156	56	101
90-94	31	9	22	44	13	31	55	17	38	71	22	49
95-99	8	2	6	12	3	9	17	4	12	21	6	15
100 +	1	0	1	2	0	1	3	1	2	4	1	3

Age group	2025 Both sexes	Males	Females	2030 Both sexes	Males	Females	2035 Both sexes	Males	Females	2040 Both sexes	Males	Females
All ages	18 159	8 938	9 221	18 319	8 994	9 325	18 323	8 969	9 354	18 165	8 862	9 302
0-4	895	456	439	848	432	416	782	398	384	716	365	351
5-9	911	464	447	896	456	440	849	432	417	783	399	384
10-14	994	506	488	912	464	448	898	457	441	851	433	418
15-19	1 090	554	535	996	507	489	914	465	449	899	457	441
20-24	1 240	630	610	1 091	554	537	997	507	491	915	465	450
25-29	1 329	674	656	1 240	629	612	1 092	554	538	999	507	492
30-34	1 485	751	735	1 329	672	657	1 240	628	613	1 093	553	540
35-39	1 456	733	722	1 482	748	735	1 327	670	657	1 239	626	613
40-44	1 310	657	652	1 449	728	721	1 476	743	733	1 322	665	656
45-49	1 152	574	578	1 299	650	650	1 438	720	718	1 465	735	730
50-54	1 202	594	608	1 137	564	573	1 283	638	645	1 420	708	713
55-59	1 175	575	600	1 176	576	600	1 113	547	565	1 257	621	636
60-64	1 157	558	599	1 135	548	587	1 137	550	587	1 077	523	554
65-69	949	448	501	1 094	517	577	1 075	509	566	1 080	513	567
70-74	688	314	374	869	398	471	1 006	462	544	991	456	535
75-79	496	215	281	600	262	338	761	333	428	885	388	496
80-84	333	134	199	396	161	235	483	197	285	617	253	363
85-89	180	65	114	231	85	146	278	103	175	341	127	214
90-94	85	27	58	99	32	67	129	42	87	156	51	105
95-99	27	8	20	33	9	24	39	11	28	51	14	36
100 +	5	1	4	6	2	5	8	2	6	9	2	6

Age group	2045 Both sexes	Males	Females	2050 Both sexes	Males	Females
All ages	17 855	8 682	9 173	17 413	8 440	8 973
0-4	661	337	324	617	314	303
5-9	717	365	352	662	337	325
10-14	785	400	385	719	366	353
15-19	852	434	419	787	400	386
20-24	901	458	443	855	434	420
25-29	917	465	452	903	458	445
30-34	1 000	506	494	919	465	453
35-39	1 092	552	540	1 000	505	494
40-44	1 234	622	612	1 089	549	540
45-49	1 312	659	654	1 226	616	610
50-54	1 448	722	725	1 298	648	649
55-59	1 393	689	704	1 420	703	717
60-64	1 218	594	624	1 351	660	691
65-69	1 025	489	536	1 160	556	605
70-74	998	460	538	950	440	510
75-79	876	385	491	885	390	495
80-84	721	296	424	717	295	422
85-89	439	164	275	517	194	323
90-94	193	64	130	251	83	168
95-99	61	17	44	76	22	55
100 +	11	3	8	13	4	10

United Nations Department of Economic and Social Affairs/Population Division
World Population Prospects: The 2004 Revision, Volume II: Sex and Age Distribution of the World Population

289

POPULATION BY AGE AND SEX (in thousands)

Age group	1950 Both sexes	Males	Females	1955 Both sexes	Males	Females	1960 Both sexes	Males	Females	1965 Both sexes	Males	Females
All ages	554 760	288 200	266 560	609 005	314 727	294 278	657 492	338 494	318 998	729 191	375 124	354 067
0-4	75 918	40 134	35 784	100 449	51 264	49 185	93 373	47 705	45 668	112 275	57 709	54 566
5-9	56 753	29 828	26 925	70 032	36 996	33 035	93 704	47 928	45 776	88 629	45 546	43 084
10-14	53 376	28 749	24 628	55 479	29 235	26 244	68 720	36 261	32 459	92 089	47 245	44 844
15-19	54 348	28 956	25 392	52 397	28 206	24 191	54 436	28 748	25 688	67 718	35 696	32 022
20-24	46 991	24 883	22 109	52 513	27 973	24 540	51 217	27 516	23 700	53 288	28 185	25 102
25-29	43 316	22 774	20 542	45 326	24 002	21 324	50 666	26 954	23 712	50 087	26 856	23 231
30-34	39 570	20 730	18 840	41 354	21 714	19 639	43 785	23 177	20 609	49 046	26 078	22 968
35-39	35 725	18 585	17 140	37 205	19 408	17 797	39 517	20 695	18 823	42 423	22 449	19 974
40-44	32 479	16 719	15 761	33 124	17 087	16 037	34 987	18 120	16 867	37 849	19 749	18 100
45-49	29 343	15 116	14 227	29 513	14 902	14 611	30 677	15 634	15 043	32 929	16 909	16 020
50-54	23 866	12 382	11 484	25 758	12 832	12 926	26 621	13 143	13 479	28 274	14 225	14 050
55-59	21 504	10 828	10 676	19 660	9 724	9 936	22 273	10 691	11 582	23 725	11 440	12 285
60-64	16 721	8 083	8 638	18 086	8 948	9 138	15 746	7 387	8 359	18 800	8 675	10 125
65-69	12 569	5 693	6 876	13 093	6 191	6 903	14 464	6 996	7 468	12 100	5 358	6 743
70-74	7 121	2 957	4 164	8 862	3 904	4 958	9 476	4 354	5 122	10 767	5 076	5 691
75-79	3 602	1 315	2 288	4 261	1 708	2 553	5 485	2 330	3 155	6 076	2 703	3 373
80 +	1 559	471	1 087	1 893	631	1 261	2 344	857	1 487	3 114	1 224	1 890

Age group	1970 Both sexes	Males	Females	1975 Both sexes	Males	Females	1980 Both sexes	Males	Females	1985 Both sexes	Males	Females
All ages	830 675	427 348	403 327	927 808	477 851	449 956	998 877	514 711	484 166	1 070 175	551 305	518 870
0-4	132 465	68 134	64 331	126 433	65 050	61 384	99 830	51 524	48 306	101 439	52 634	48 805
5-9	109 721	56 618	53 102	130 922	67 705	63 217	124 568	64 252	60 316	98 651	50 932	47 719
10-14	87 853	45 319	42 534	109 022	56 435	52 587	130 235	67 280	62 955	124 185	64 004	60 181
15-19	91 201	46 884	44 318	87 282	45 210	42 072	108 212	55 933	52 279	129 909	67 066	62 843
20-24	67 004	35 237	31 766	90 235	46 454	43 782	86 837	45 181	41 655	107 746	55 657	52 089
25-29	52 582	27 840	24 742	66 359	34 817	31 542	89 488	46 184	43 304	86 355	44 911	41 443
30-34	49 538	26 513	23 025	52 009	27 575	24 435	66 136	34 647	31 489	88 886	45 833	43 053
35-39	48 042	25 525	22 517	49 082	26 219	22 864	51 727	27 434	24 293	65 560	34 306	31 255
40-44	41 588	21 989	19 599	47 079	24 980	22 099	48 890	26 089	22 801	51 063	27 024	24 039
45-49	36 630	19 035	17 594	40 683	21 468	19 215	46 088	24 450	21 638	47 836	25 385	22 451
50-54	31 184	15 876	15 308	35 214	18 197	17 018	39 591	20 850	18 741	44 637	23 520	21 117
55-59	26 082	12 944	13 137	29 151	14 673	14 478	33 410	17 134	16 276	37 694	19 701	17 993
60-64	20 980	9 858	11 122	23 505	11 460	12 045	26 440	13 123	13 317	30 734	15 524	15 210
65-69	15 547	6 864	8 683	17 833	8 121	9 712	20 128	9 588	10 540	23 081	11 144	11 938
70-74	8 911	3 699	5 212	12 025	5 045	6 979	14 472	6 267	8 206	16 146	7 390	8 756
75-79	7 346	3 360	3 986	5 868	2 264	3 604	8 496	3 316	5 180	10 141	4 144	5 996
80 +	4 002	1 651	2 350	5 105	2 179	2 926	4 329	1 459	2 871	6 111	2 129	3 981

Age group	1990 Both sexes	Males	Females	1995 Both sexes	Males	Females	2000 Both sexes	Males	Females	2005 Both sexes	Males	Females
All ages	1 155 305	595 934	559 371	1 219 331	628 309	591 022	1 273 979	655 211	618 768	1 315 844	675 852	639 992
0-4	118 998	62 530	56 467	103 261	54 480	48 781	95 509	50 327	45 182	84 483	44 529	39 954
5-9	101 518	52 883	48 635	117 963	62 007	55 956	102 538	54 077	48 461	94 982	50 042	44 940
10-14	99 360	51 401	47 959	101 188	52 674	48 514	117 626	61 792	55 835	102 302	53 933	48 369
15-19	122 793	63 146	59 647	98 922	51 130	47 791	100 768	52 411	48 357	117 234	61 549	55 684
20-24	128 517	65 791	62 726	121 960	62 638	59 322	98 187	50 674	47 513	100 115	52 008	48 107
25-29	106 554	54 811	51 743	127 498	65 170	62 328	120 938	61 999	58 940	97 360	50 157	47 203
30-34	85 718	44 766	40 952	105 636	54 244	51 392	126 423	64 494	61 929	119 970	61 385	58 585
35-39	88 246	45 650	42 596	84 862	44 228	40 634	104 639	53 613	51 026	125 373	63 829	61 544
40-44	65 108	34 145	30 963	87 160	44 965	42 195	83 859	43 587	40 273	103 573	52 942	50 631
45-49	50 167	26 483	23 684	63 943	33 404	30 539	85 734	44 064	41 671	82 643	42 825	39 818
50-54	46 623	24 695	21 928	48 771	25 593	23 178	62 319	32 367	29 952	83 835	42 887	40 949
55-59	42 626	22 370	20 256	44 528	23 337	21 192	46 755	24 282	22 473	60 066	30 938	29 128
60-64	34 721	17 906	16 815	39 461	20 325	19 136	41 456	21 336	20 120	43 887	22 445	21 442
65-69	26 907	13 231	13 676	30 563	15 259	15 303	35 045	17 495	17 550	37 263	18 683	18 580
70-74	18 442	8 547	9 895	21 760	10 138	11 623	25 061	11 886	13 175	29 300	14 020	15 280
75-79	11 169	4 803	6 366	13 034	5 584	7 450	15 750	6 794	8 955	18 691	8 328	10 363
80 +	7 839	2 776	5 063	8 821	3 133	5 688	11 373	4 015	7 358	14 766	5 352	9 414

(*) For statistical purposes, the data for China do not include Hong Kong and Macao, Special Administrative Regions (SAR) of China.

United Nations Department of Economic and Social Affairs/Population Division
World Population Prospects: The 2004 Revision, Volume II: Sex and Age Distribution of the World Population

290

POPULATION BY AGE AND SEX (in thousands)

Age group	2005 Both sexes	Males	Females	2010 Both sexes	Males	Females	2015 Both sexes	Males	Females	2020 Both sexes	Males	Females
All ages	1 315 844	675 852	639 992	1 354 533	694 643	659 890	1 392 980	712 911	680 069	1 423 939	726 935	697 004
0-4	84 483	44 529	39 954	84 954	44 740	40 214	89 804	47 246	42 558	88 213	46 369	41 844
5-9	94 982	50 042	44 940	84 090	44 316	39 774	84 597	44 541	40 056	89 470	47 053	42 417
10-14	102 302	53 933	48 369	94 795	49 928	44 867	83 934	44 223	39 711	84 446	44 451	39 994
15-19	117 234	61 549	55 684	101 995	53 743	48 251	94 526	49 764	44 762	83 710	44 087	39 623
20-24	100 115	52 008	48 107	116 599	61 151	55 447	101 426	53 388	48 038	94 026	49 454	44 572
25-29	97 360	50 157	47 203	99 322	51 502	47 820	115 666	60 548	55 118	100 563	52 834	47 729
30-34	119 970	61 385	58 585	96 523	49 614	46 909	98 360	50 870	47 489	114 455	59 751	54 704
35-39	125 373	63 829	61 544	118 961	60 727	58 234	95 555	48 976	46 580	97 231	50 123	47 108
40-44	103 573	52 942	50 631	124 163	63 054	61 109	117 713	59 913	57 800	94 408	48 220	46 188
45-49	82 643	42 825	39 818	102 204	52 084	50 119	122 529	62 020	60 509	116 089	58 871	57 217
50-54	83 835	42 887	40 949	80 952	41 765	39 188	100 231	50 852	49 379	120 208	60 565	59 643
55-59	60 066	30 938	29 128	81 057	41 135	39 922	78 414	40 147	38 267	97 273	48 982	48 291
60-64	43 887	22 445	21 442	56 704	28 793	27 912	76 788	38 427	38 361	74 494	37 636	36 858
65-69	37 263	18 683	18 580	39 791	19 861	19 930	51 748	25 671	26 077	70 464	34 469	35 994
70-74	29 300	14 020	15 280	31 542	15 208	16 334	34 069	16 378	17 692	44 732	21 407	23 325
75-79	18 691	8 328	10 363	22 299	10 067	12 232	24 394	11 115	13 279	26 772	12 187	14 585
80-84	9 872	3 876	5 996	12 038	4 913	7 126	14 727	6 099	8 628	16 464	6 904	9 560
85-89	3 763	1 225	2 538	4 927	1 665	3 263	6 239	2 190	4 049	7 893	2 815	5 078
90-94	941	226	715	1 357	339	1 018	1 867	484	1 383	2 460	666	1 794
95-99	169	23	146	229	36	193	350	57	293	504	85	418
100 +	21	2	20	30	2	28	42	4	39	65	6	59

Age group	2025 Both sexes	Males	Females	2030 Both sexes	Males	Females	2035 Both sexes	Males	Females	2040 Both sexes	Males	Females
All ages	1 441 426	733 698	707 728	1 446 453	733 853	712 599	1 442 974	729 895	713 079	1 433 431	723 244	710 187
0-4	81 253	42 684	38 569	75 393	39 417	35 976	73 757	38 548	35 209	74 623	38 990	35 632
5-9	87 914	46 193	41 721	80 999	42 534	38 465	75 177	39 290	35 887	73 565	38 436	35 129
10-14	89 306	46 958	42 347	87 752	46 100	41 651	80 857	42 454	38 403	75 056	39 222	35 834
15-19	84 233	44 324	39 910	89 095	46 833	42 263	87 552	45 982	41 570	80 672	42 345	38 328
20-24	83 266	43 816	39 450	83 815	44 071	39 744	88 688	46 587	42 100	87 163	45 749	41 415
25-29	93 237	48 957	44 280	82 593	43 400	39 193	83 200	43 695	39 504	88 104	46 233	41 871
30-34	99 440	52 112	47 329	92 265	48 348	43 918	81 807	42 916	38 891	82 504	43 271	39 233
35-39	113 062	58 839	54 223	98 269	51 362	46 907	91 297	47 740	43 557	81 044	42 444	38 600
40-44	95 983	49 305	46 678	111 674	57 940	53 734	97 169	50 661	46 509	90 397	47 174	43 223
45-49	93 043	47 344	45 700	94 656	48 457	46 199	110 265	57 045	53 220	96 056	49 959	46 097
50-54	113 906	57 496	56 410	91 350	46 279	45 071	93 078	47 467	45 610	108 570	55 981	52 589
55-59	116 799	58 416	58 383	110 813	55 546	55 267	89 800	44 700	45 100	90 896	46 099	44 797
60-64	92 717	46 091	46 626	111 605	55 138	56 467	106 129	52 594	53 535	85 422	42 545	42 876
65-69	68 661	33 950	34 711	85 914	41 843	44 071	103 841	50 316	53 525	99 085	48 218	50 867
70-74	61 418	29 005	32 413	60 269	28 828	31 441	76 036	35 889	40 147	92 465	43 474	48 991
75-79	35 629	16 170	19 460	49 541	22 215	27 326	49 125	22 373	26 752	62 654	28 203	34 451
80-84	18 449	7 735	10 714	25 023	10 474	14 549	35 421	14 675	20 746	35 640	15 039	20 601
85-89	9 087	3 283	5 804	10 475	3 795	6 680	14 593	5 310	9 284	21 184	7 656	13 528
90-94	3 235	890	2 345	3 862	1 083	2 779	4 612	1 311	3 301	6 634	1 908	4 726
95-99	692	123	569	950	173	777	1 178	223	955	1 459	284	1 176
100 +	97	9	88	138	14	124	194	20	174	251	27	224

Age group	2045 Both sexes	Males	Females	2050 Both sexes	Males	Females
All ages	1 416 926	713 590	703 336	1 392 307	700 472	691 834
0-4	73 816	38 564	35 252	70 406	36 781	33 626
5-9	74 448	38 890	35 558	73 657	38 474	35 183
10-14	73 460	38 377	35 083	74 358	38 837	35 521
15-19	74 885	39 122	35 763	73 298	38 282	35 016
20-24	80 309	42 128	38 181	74 541	38 918	35 623
25-29	86 624	45 423	41 201	79 818	41 833	37 985
30-34	87 464	45 844	41 619	86 054	45 077	40 976
35-39	81 837	42 862	38 975	86 856	45 473	41 382
40-44	80 333	42 001	38 331	81 209	42 474	38 736
45-49	89 466	46 593	42 873	79 581	41 534	38 047
50-54	94 687	49 102	45 585	88 290	45 859	42 431
55-59	106 165	54 461	51 704	92 707	47 851	44 856
60-64	87 525	43 965	43 560	102 430	52 089	50 341
65-69	80 002	39 173	40 829	82 370	40 747	41 623
70-74	88 659	41 924	46 735	71 913	34 271	37 642
75-79	76 910	34 535	42 374	74 269	33 602	40 667
80-84	46 144	19 258	26 886	57 430	23 964	33 466
85-89	21 761	8 049	13 712	28 794	10 570	18 225
90-94	9 937	2 850	7 087	10 475	3 106	7 369
95-99	2 175	431	1 744	3 372	675	2 698
100 +	321	36	285	479	56	423

United Nations Department of Economic and Social Affairs/Population Division
World Population Prospects: The 2004 Revision, Volume II: Sex and Age Distribution of the World Population

291

POPULATION BY AGE AND SEX (in thousands)

Age group	2005 Both sexes	2005 Males	2005 Females	2010 Both sexes	2010 Males	2010 Females	2015 Both sexes	2015 Males	2015 Females	2020 Both sexes	2020 Males	2020 Females
All ages	1 315 844	675 852	639 992	1 366 745	701 074	665 671	1 425 006	729 764	695 242	1 479 739	756 279	723 460
0-4	84 483	44 529	39 954	97 167	51 171	45 995	109 659	57 692	51 967	112 066	58 907	53 159
5-9	94 982	50 042	44 940	84 090	44 316	39 774	96 767	50 948	45 819	109 264	57 462	51 802
10-14	102 302	53 933	48 369	94 795	49 928	44 867	83 934	44 223	39 711	96 599	50 848	45 750
15-19	117 234	61 549	55 684	101 995	53 743	48 251	94 526	49 764	44 762	83 710	44 087	39 623
20-24	100 115	52 008	48 107	116 599	61 151	55 447	101 426	53 388	48 038	94 026	49 454	44 572
25-29	97 360	50 157	47 203	99 322	51 502	47 820	115 666	60 548	55 118	100 563	52 834	47 729
30-34	119 970	61 385	58 585	96 523	49 614	46 909	98 360	50 870	47 489	114 455	59 751	54 704
35-39	125 373	63 829	61 544	118 961	60 727	58 234	95 555	48 976	46 580	97 231	50 123	47 108
40-44	103 573	52 942	50 631	124 163	63 054	61 109	117 713	59 913	57 800	94 408	48 220	46 188
45-49	82 643	42 825	39 818	102 204	52 084	50 119	122 529	62 020	60 509	116 089	58 871	57 217
50-54	83 835	42 887	40 949	80 952	41 765	39 188	100 231	50 852	49 379	120 208	60 565	59 643
55-59	60 066	30 938	29 128	81 057	41 135	39 922	78 414	40 147	38 267	97 273	48 982	48 291
60-64	43 887	22 445	21 442	56 704	28 793	27 912	76 788	38 427	38 361	74 494	37 636	36 858
65-69	37 263	18 683	18 580	39 791	19 861	19 930	51 748	25 671	26 077	70 464	34 469	35 994
70-74	29 300	14 020	15 280	31 542	15 208	16 334	34 069	16 378	17 692	44 732	21 407	23 325
75-79	18 691	8 328	10 363	22 299	10 067	12 232	24 394	11 115	13 279	26 772	12 187	14 585
80-84	9 872	3 876	5 996	12 038	4 913	7 126	14 727	6 099	8 628	16 464	6 904	9 560
85-89	3 763	1 225	2 538	4 927	1 665	3 263	6 239	2 190	4 049	7 893	2 815	5 078
90-94	941	226	715	1 357	339	1 018	1 867	484	1 383	2 460	666	1 794
95-99	169	23	146	229	36	193	350	57	293	504	85	418
100 +	21	2	20	30	2	28	42	4	39	65	6	59

Age group	2025 Both sexes	2025 Males	2025 Females	2030 Both sexes	2030 Males	2030 Females	2035 Both sexes	2035 Males	2035 Females	2040 Both sexes	2040 Males	2040 Females
All ages	1 519 180	774 565	744 615	1 547 562	786 919	760 644	1 574 273	798 721	775 552	1 602 869	811 970	790 899
0-4	103 317	54 274	49 042	98 886	51 699	47 187	104 131	54 422	49 709	113 030	59 057	53 972
5-9	111 701	58 690	53 011	103 010	54 092	48 918	98 621	51 542	47 079	103 885	54 276	49 608
10-14	109 071	57 351	51 721	111 503	58 578	52 926	102 837	53 994	48 843	98 471	51 458	47 014
15-19	96 371	50 711	45 660	108 838	57 210	51 627	111 278	58 443	52 835	102 631	53 871	48 760
20-24	83 266	43 816	39 450	95 927	50 442	45 486	108 394	56 942	51 452	110 851	58 185	52 665
25-29	93 237	48 957	44 280	82 593	43 400	39 193	95 268	50 038	45 230	107 749	56 550	51 199
30-34	99 440	52 112	47 329	92 265	48 348	43 918	81 807	42 916	38 891	94 509	49 575	44 934
35-39	113 062	58 839	54 223	98 269	51 362	46 907	91 297	47 740	43 557	81 044	42 444	38 600
40-44	95 983	49 305	46 678	111 674	57 940	53 734	97 169	50 661	46 509	90 397	47 174	43 223
45-49	93 043	47 344	45 700	94 656	48 457	46 199	110 265	57 045	53 220	96 056	49 959	46 097
50-54	113 906	57 496	56 410	91 350	46 279	45 071	93 078	47 467	45 610	108 570	55 981	52 589
55-59	116 799	58 416	58 383	110 815	55 548	55 267	88 999	44 799	44 199	90 885	46 088	44 797
60-64	92 717	46 091	46 626	111 605	55 138	56 467	106 129	52 594	53 535	85 422	42 545	42 876
65-69	68 661	33 950	34 711	85 914	41 843	44 071	103 841	50 316	53 525	99 085	48 218	50 867
70-74	61 418	29 005	32 413	60 269	28 828	31 441	76 036	35 889	40 147	92 465	43 474	48 991
75-79	35 629	16 170	19 460	49 541	22 215	27 326	49 125	22 373	26 752	62 654	28 203	34 451
80-84	18 449	7 735	10 714	25 023	10 474	14 549	35 421	14 675	20 746	35 640	15 039	20 601
85-89	9 087	3 283	5 804	10 475	3 795	6 680	14 593	5 310	9 284	21 184	7 656	13 528
90-94	3 235	890	2 345	3 862	1 083	2 779	4 612	1 311	3 301	6 634	1 908	4 726
95-99	692	123	569	950	173	777	1 178	223	955	1 459	284	1 176
100 +	97	9	88	138	14	124	194	20	174	251	27	224

Age group	2045 Both sexes	2045 Males	2045 Females	2050 Both sexes	2050 Males	2050 Females
All ages	1 628 749	824 426	804 323	1 647 189	833 760	813 428
0-4	116 562	60 895	55 667	113 909	59 506	54 403
5-9	112 794	58 920	53 874	116 345	60 770	55 574
10-14	103 749	54 199	49 549	112 675	58 849	53 827
15-19	98 280	51 345	46 936	103 563	54 090	49 473
20-24	102 235	53 634	48 601	97 905	51 121	46 784
25-29	110 248	57 820	52 428	101 694	53 308	48 386
30-34	107 024	56 109	50 915	109 594	57 423	52 170
35-39	93 772	49 123	44 649	106 322	55 680	50 642
40-44	80 333	42 001	38 331	93 071	48 689	44 382
45-49	89 466	46 593	42 873	79 581	41 534	38 047
50-54	94 687	49 102	45 585	88 290	45 859	42 431
55-59	106 165	54 461	51 704	92 707	47 851	44 856
60-64	87 525	43 965	43 560	102 430	52 089	50 341
65-69	80 002	39 173	40 829	82 370	40 747	41 623
70-74	88 659	41 924	46 735	71 913	34 271	37 642
75-79	76 910	34 535	42 374	74 269	33 602	40 667
80-84	46 144	19 258	26 886	57 430	23 964	33 466
85-89	21 761	8 049	13 712	28 794	10 570	18 225
90-94	9 937	2 850	7 087	10 475	3 106	7 369
95-99	2 175	431	1 744	3 372	675	2 698
100 +	321	36	285	479	56	423

POPULATION BY AGE AND SEX (in thousands)

Age group	2005 Both sexes	2005 Males	2005 Females	2010 Both sexes	2010 Males	2010 Females	2015 Both sexes	2015 Males	2015 Females	2020 Both sexes	2020 Males	2020 Females
All ages	1 315 844	675 852	639 992	1 342 320	688 212	654 109	1 360 954	696 058	664 896	1 368 138	697 591	670 548
0-4	84 483	44 529	39 954	72 742	38 309	34 433	69 948	36 800	33 148	64 361	33 831	30 530
5-9	94 982	50 042	44 940	84 090	44 316	39 774	72 427	38 133	34 294	69 675	36 643	33 032
10-14	102 302	53 933	48 369	94 795	49 928	44 867	83 934	44 223	39 711	72 292	38 055	34 238
15-19	117 234	61 549	55 684	101 995	53 743	48 251	94 526	49 764	44 762	83 710	44 087	39 623
20-24	100 115	52 008	48 107	116 599	61 151	55 447	101 426	53 388	48 038	94 026	49 454	44 572
25-29	97 360	50 157	47 203	99 322	51 502	47 820	115 666	60 548	55 118	100 563	52 834	47 729
30-34	119 970	61 385	58 585	96 523	49 614	46 909	98 360	50 870	47 489	114 455	59 751	54 704
35-39	125 373	63 829	61 544	118 961	60 727	58 234	95 555	48 976	46 580	97 231	50 123	47 108
40-44	103 573	52 942	50 631	124 163	63 054	61 109	117 713	59 913	57 800	94 408	48 220	46 188
45-49	82 643	42 825	39 818	102 204	52 084	50 119	122 529	62 020	60 509	116 089	58 871	57 217
50-54	83 835	42 887	40 949	80 952	41 765	39 188	100 231	50 852	49 379	120 208	60 565	59 643
55-59	60 066	30 938	29 128	81 057	41 135	39 922	78 414	40 147	38 267	97 273	48 982	48 291
60-64	43 887	22 445	21 442	56 704	28 793	27 912	76 788	38 427	38 361	74 494	37 636	36 858
65-69	37 263	18 683	18 580	39 791	19 861	19 930	51 748	25 671	26 077	70 464	34 469	35 994
70-74	29 300	14 020	15 280	31 542	15 208	16 334	34 069	16 378	17 692	44 732	21 407	23 325
75-79	18 691	8 328	10 363	22 299	10 067	12 232	24 394	11 115	13 279	26 772	12 187	14 585
80-84	9 872	3 876	5 996	12 038	4 913	7 126	14 727	6 099	8 628	16 464	6 904	9 560
85-89	3 763	1 225	2 538	4 927	1 665	3 263	6 239	2 190	4 049	7 893	2 815	5 078
90-94	941	226	715	1 357	339	1 018	1 867	484	1 383	2 460	666	1 794
95-99	169	23	146	229	36	193	350	57	293	504	85	418
100 +	21	2	20	30	2	28	42	4	39	65	6	59

Age group	2025 Both sexes	2025 Males	2025 Females	2030 Both sexes	2030 Males	2030 Females	2035 Both sexes	2035 Males	2035 Females	2040 Both sexes	2040 Males	2040 Females
All ages	1 363 712	692 851	670 861	1 346 703	681 499	665 205	1 317 471	664 099	653 372	1 277 536	641 593	635 943
0-4	59 229	31 114	28 114	53 222	27 826	25 396	47 821	24 993	22 828	43 972	22 976	20 997
5-9	64 127	33 695	30 432	59 028	30 997	28 031	53 052	27 728	25 325	47 676	24 910	22 766
10-14	69 540	36 566	32 974	64 000	33 623	30 377	58 915	30 934	27 981	52 957	27 674	25 283
15-19	72 096	37 937	34 159	69 353	36 455	32 898	63 826	33 520	30 305	58 753	30 839	27 914
20-24	83 266	43 816	39 450	71 702	37 700	34 003	68 981	36 232	32 749	63 476	33 312	30 164
25-29	93 237	48 957	44 280	82 593	43 400	39 193	71 131	37 352	33 779	68 459	35 917	32 542
30-34	99 440	52 112	47 329	92 265	48 348	43 918	81 807	42 916	38 891	70 499	36 967	33 532
35-39	113 062	58 839	54 223	98 269	51 362	40 907	91 297	47 740	40 557	81 044	42 444	38 600
40-44	95 983	49 305	46 678	111 674	57 940	53 734	97 169	50 661	46 509	90 397	47 174	43 223
45-49	93 043	47 344	45 700	94 656	48 457	46 199	110 265	57 045	53 220	96 056	49 959	46 097
50-54	113 906	57 496	56 410	91 350	46 279	45 071	93 078	47 467	45 610	108 570	55 981	52 589
55-59	116 799	58 416	58 383	110 815	55 548	55 267	88 999	44 799	44 199	90 885	46 088	44 797
60-64	92 717	46 091	46 626	111 605	55 138	56 467	106 129	52 594	53 535	85 422	42 545	42 876
65-69	68 661	33 950	34 711	85 914	41 843	44 071	103 841	50 316	53 525	99 085	48 218	50 867
70-74	61 418	29 005	32 413	60 269	28 828	31 441	76 036	35 889	40 147	92 465	43 474	48 991
75-79	35 629	16 170	19 460	49 541	22 215	27 020	49 125	22 070	26 762	62 654	28 203	34 451
80-84	18 449	7 735	10 714	25 023	10 474	14 549	35 421	14 675	20 746	35 640	15 039	20 601
85-89	9 087	3 283	5 804	10 475	3 795	6 680	14 593	5 310	9 284	21 184	7 656	13 528
90-94	3 235	890	2 345	3 862	1 083	2 779	4 612	1 311	3 301	6 634	1 908	4 726
95-99	692	123	569	950	173	777	1 178	223	955	1 459	284	1 176
100 +	97	9	88	138	14	124	194	20	174	251	27	224

Age group	2045 Both sexes	2045 Males	2045 Females	2050 Both sexes	2050 Males	2050 Females
All ages	1 228 335	614 890	613 445	1 171 259	584 857	586 402
0-4	40 777	21 304	19 474	37 530	19 606	17 924
5-9	43 846	22 905	20 941	40 664	21 241	19 422
10-14	47 596	24 866	22 730	43 779	22 867	20 913
15-19	52 806	27 587	25 220	47 454	24 784	22 671
20-24	58 421	30 642	27 779	52 491	27 400	25 090
25-29	63 000	33 025	29 974	57 980	30 378	27 602
30-34	67 903	35 580	32 323	62 514	32 732	29 782
35-39	69 902	36 601	33 301	67 389	35 266	32 123
40-44	80 333	42 001	38 331	69 347	36 258	33 089
45-49	89 466	46 593	42 873	79 581	41 534	38 047
50-54	94 687	49 102	45 585	88 290	45 859	42 431
55-59	106 165	54 461	51 704	92 707	47 851	44 856
60-64	87 525	43 965	43 560	102 430	52 089	50 341
65-69	80 002	39 173	40 829	82 370	40 747	41 623
70-74	88 659	41 924	46 735	71 913	34 271	37 642
75-79	76 910	34 535	42 374	74 269	33 602	40 667
80-84	46 144	19 258	26 886	57 430	23 964	33 466
85-89	21 761	8 049	13 712	28 794	10 570	18 225
90-94	9 937	2 850	7 087	10 475	3 106	7 369
95-99	2 175	431	1 744	3 372	675	2 698
100 +	321	36	285	479	56	423

POPULATION BY AGE AND SEX (in thousands)

Age group	1950 Both sexes	Males	Females	1955 Both sexes	Males	Females	1960 Both sexes	Males	Females	1965 Both sexes	Males	Females
All ages	1 974	1 014	960	2 490	1 279	1 211	3 075	1 578	1 497	3 692	1 873	1 818
0-4	316	167	149	410	212	197	492	253	239	527	271	256
5-9	125	67	58	326	172	154	419	217	202	523	272	251
10-14	158	84	75	146	79	67	346	183	163	444	231	213
15-19	214	115	99	173	93	81	161	88	73	381	202	179
20-24	234	127	108	235	127	108	195	106	89	199	106	93
25-29	212	114	99	248	134	114	249	134	115	209	113	96
30-34	187	101	85	224	119	105	259	138	120	242	128	115
35-39	156	83	73	195	104	91	232	122	110	257	131	127
40-44	116	59	57	162	85	77	200	106	94	231	117	114
45-49	82	38	44	121	60	61	165	86	80	190	97	93
50-54	61	25	36	85	38	47	122	60	63	164	83	82
55-59	40	15	25	63	25	38	86	37	49	115	53	63
60-64	24	8	16	42	14	27	63	23	39	90	35	55
65-69	20	6	14	25	8	17	40	13	27	56	18	38
70-74	16	4	12	20	5	15	26	8	18	32	10	23
75-79	9	2	7	10	3	7	12	3	9	23	7	16
80 +	6	2	4	7	2	6	8	2	6	9	2	7

Age group	1970 Both sexes	Males	Females	1975 Both sexes	Males	Females	1980 Both sexes	Males	Females	1985 Both sexes	Males	Females
All ages	3 942	2 004	1 937	4 396	2 249	2 147	5 039	2 625	2 414	5 456	2 816	2 641
0-4	426	219	207	394	203	191	412	213	199	422	219	204
5-9	528	273	254	409	210	200	414	215	200	418	217	201
10-14	506	263	243	531	271	260	460	237	223	438	229	209
15-19	429	225	204	526	269	256	563	292	271	471	245	226
20-24	348	184	164	439	226	213	576	303	273	581	297	284
25-29	192	104	88	357	191	166	479	257	222	600	310	290
30-34	219	119	101	215	122	93	386	213	173	491	258	232
35-39	250	131	119	226	125	101	246	139	107	391	211	181
40-44	247	125	122	250	134	116	257	144	113	241	134	107
45-49	218	112	107	250	130	120	266	144	122	266	145	121
50-54	177	88	89	226	116	110	258	137	121	273	147	126
55-59	149	73	76	184	93	91	214	110	104	250	130	120
60-64	98	42	56	151	74	77	181	91	90	208	104	104
65-69	78	28	50	98	42	56	136	64	72	162	78	84
70-74	41	11	30	68	24	45	92	37	55	119	53	66
75-79	27	7	20	41	13	28	57	19	38	66	25	41
80 +	10	1	8	30	7	23	40	10	30	60	16	45

Age group	1990 Both sexes	Males	Females	1995 Both sexes	Males	Females	2000 Both sexes	Males	Females	2005 Both sexes	Males	Females
All ages	5 704	2 922	2 782	6 187	3 074	3 113	6 637	3 206	3 431	7 041	3 313	3 728
0-4	376	195	181	358	183	175	325	166	159	295	150	144
5-9	426	221	205	391	201	191	373	189	185	341	172	169
10-14	424	221	203	435	225	210	400	204	196	382	192	190
15-19	434	226	208	443	225	219	454	228	226	419	208	212
20-24	462	235	227	476	232	244	485	231	254	496	234	261
25-29	607	302	305	515	244	271	529	241	288	538	240	299
30-34	608	310	298	658	311	346	566	253	313	580	250	330
35-39	495	256	239	643	316	327	693	317	376	601	259	343
40-44	390	209	182	513	258	255	661	317	343	711	319	392
45-49	240	133	107	400	208	192	522	258	264	669	317	353
50-54	259	142	118	244	131	113	403	206	197	524	255	269
55-59	263	140	124	258	138	120	244	129	116	401	202	199
60-64	236	121	115	256	133	123	253	132	121	241	124	116
65-69	186	90	96	223	111	112	243	123	120	242	124	118
70-74	136	62	73	167	78	89	203	98	105	225	111	114
75-79	92	39	53	113	49	64	143	63	80	177	81	96
80 +	69	21	49	95	33	62	141	52	89	198	75	123

(*) As of 1 July 1997, Hong Kong became a Special Administrative Region (SAR) of China.

United Nations Department of Economic and Social Affairs/Population Division
World Population Prospects: The 2004 Revision, Volume II: Sex and Age Distribution of the World Population

POPULATION BY AGE AND SEX (in thousands)

Age group	2005 Both sexes	2005 Males	2005 Females	2010 Both sexes	2010 Males	2010 Females	2015 Both sexes	2015 Males	2015 Females	2020 Both sexes	2020 Males	2020 Females
All ages	7 041	3 313	3 728	7 416	3 480	3 936	7 764	3 633	4 131	8 080	3 769	4 311
0-4	295	150	144	306	157	149	311	160	152	311	159	151
5-9	341	172	169	323	163	160	334	170	165	340	173	167
10-14	382	192	190	357	179	178	340	171	169	351	178	173
15-19	419	208	212	401	201	200	376	188	188	358	180	179
20-24	496	234	261	450	222	228	431	215	217	406	202	204
25-29	538	240	299	540	255	286	494	242	252	476	235	241
30-34	580	250	330	585	261	324	587	276	311	541	263	278
35-39	601	259	343	612	265	347	617	275	342	619	290	328
40-44	711	319	392	618	266	352	628	272	357	634	283	351
45-49	669	317	353	718	321	397	626	269	357	637	275	362
50-54	524	255	269	671	316	355	720	321	399	629	270	360
55-59	401	202	199	521	252	270	666	312	355	715	317	398
60-64	241	124	116	394	196	198	512	245	268	655	303	351
65-69	242	124	118	233	118	115	381	186	194	495	233	262
70-74	225	111	114	226	113	113	219	108	111	357	171	186
75-79	177	81	96	198	93	105	200	96	104	195	93	102
80-84	112	46	66	141	61	81	160	70	89	163	73	90
85-89	59	21	37	78	29	49	100	39	61	115	46	69
90-94	22	7	15	33	10	23	45	15	31	59	20	39
95-99	5	1	4	9	2	7	14	4	10	20	5	15
100 +	1	0	1	1	0	1	2	1	2	4	1	3

Age group	2025 Both sexes	2025 Males	2025 Females	2030 Both sexes	2030 Males	2030 Females	2035 Both sexes	2035 Males	2035 Females	2040 Both sexes	2040 Males	2040 Females
All ages	8 362	3 888	4 474	8 610	3 990	4 620	8 822	4 074	4 748	8 996	4 144	4 853
0-4	311	159	151	315	162	154	325	167	158	341	175	166
5-9	339	172	167	339	172	167	343	175	169	353	180	174
10-14	356	180	176	356	180	176	356	180	176	360	182	178
15-19	370	186	184	375	189	186	375	189	186	375	189	186
20-24	389	194	195	401	200	200	406	203	203	405	203	203
25-29	451	222	229	434	214	220	445	221	225	450	223	227
30-34	523	256	266	498	244	254	481	236	245	492	242	250
35-39	573	278	295	555	271	284	530	259	272	513	250	263
40-44	636	298	338	590	285	305	573	279	294	548	266	282
45-49	643	286	356	645	301	344	600	289	311	582	282	300
50-54	640	276	364	646	287	359	648	302	346	604	290	314
55-59	627	267	360	638	273	365	644	285	360	647	300	347
60-64	704	309	395	618	261	357	630	268	362	637	279	358
65-69	633	289	344	682	295	387	602	251	351	614	258	356
70-74	466	214	252	598	267	331	646	274	373	572	234	339
75-79	320	147	173	420	186	234	542	200	000	590	241	349
80-84	161	72	89	267	116	151	354	148	206	461	187	274
85-89	119	49	70	120	49	70	201	80	121	272	104	168
90-94	69	24	45	74	26	47	75	27	48	130	45	85
95-99	27	7	19	32	9	23	35	10	25	37	11	26
100 +	6	1	5	8	2	7	11	2	8	12	3	10

Age group	2045 Both sexes	2045 Males	2045 Females	2050 Both sexes	2050 Males	2050 Females
All ages	9 133	4 201	4 931	9 235	4 254	4 981
0-4	359	184	175	377	193	183
5-9	369	188	181	387	197	190
10-14	370	187	183	386	195	190
15-19	379	191	188	389	196	193
20-24	405	203	203	410	205	205
25-29	450	223	227	450	223	227
30-34	497	245	253	497	245	252
35-39	525	257	268	530	260	270
40-44	531	258	273	543	265	278
45-49	558	270	288	541	262	279
50-54	587	284	303	563	272	291
55-59	603	288	315	587	282	304
60-64	640	295	345	598	284	314
65-69	621	269	352	625	285	341
70-74	586	241	345	594	253	341
75-79	526	207	318	540	215	325
80-84	508	196	312	457	170	287
85-89	359	134	226	402	142	260
90-94	180	60	120	243	79	164
95-99	66	19	47	94	26	69
100 +	14	3	11	23	5	18

United Nations Department of Economic and Social Affairs/Population Division
World Population Prospects: The 2004 Revision, Volume II: Sex and Age Distribution of the World Population

295

POPULATION BY AGE AND SEX (in thousands)

Age group	2005 Both sexes	2005 Males	2005 Females	2010 Both sexes	2010 Males	2010 Females	2015 Both sexes	2015 Males	2015 Females	2020 Both sexes	2020 Males	2020 Females
All ages	7 041	3 313	3 728	7 491	3 519	3 972	7 953	3 730	4 222	8 401	3 935	4 466
0-4	295	150	144	381	196	185	425	218	207	443	228	216
5-9	341	172	169	323	163	160	409	209	201	453	231	222
10-14	382	192	190	357	179	178	340	171	169	426	216	210
15-19	419	208	212	401	201	200	376	188	188	358	180	179
20-24	496	234	261	450	222	228	431	215	217	406	202	204
25-29	538	240	299	540	255	286	494	242	252	476	235	241
30-34	580	250	330	585	261	324	587	276	311	541	263	278
35-39	601	259	343	612	265	347	617	275	342	619	290	328
40-44	711	319	392	618	266	352	628	272	357	634	283	351
45-49	669	317	353	718	321	397	626	269	357	637	275	362
50-54	524	255	269	671	316	355	720	321	399	629	270	360
55-59	401	202	199	521	252	270	666	312	355	715	317	398
60-64	241	124	116	394	196	198	512	245	268	655	303	351
65-69	242	124	118	233	118	115	381	186	194	495	233	262
70-74	225	111	114	226	113	113	219	108	111	357	171	186
75-79	177	81	96	198	93	105	200	96	104	195	93	102
80-84	112	46	66	141	61	81	160	70	89	163	73	90
85-89	59	21	37	78	29	49	100	39	61	115	46	69
90-94	22	7	15	33	10	23	45	15	31	59	20	39
95-99	5	1	4	9	2	7	14	4	10	20	5	15
100 +	1	0	1	1	0	1	2	1	2	4	1	3

Age group	2025 Both sexes	2025 Males	2025 Females	2030 Both sexes	2030 Males	2030 Females	2035 Both sexes	2035 Males	2035 Females	2040 Both sexes	2040 Males	2040 Females
All ages	8 809	4 119	4 690	9 183	4 285	4 898	9 540	4 445	5 095	9 893	4 606	5 287
0-4	436	224	212	442	227	215	470	242	229	520	267	252
5-9	472	241	231	465	237	228	470	240	230	499	255	244
10-14	469	239	231	488	248	240	481	245	237	487	248	239
15-19	445	225	220	488	247	241	507	257	250	500	253	247
20-24	389	194	195	475	239	236	519	261	258	538	271	267
25-29	451	222	229	434	214	220	520	259	261	564	282	282
30-34	523	256	266	498	244	254	481	236	245	567	281	286
35-39	573	278	295	555	271	284	530	259	272	513	250	263
40-44	636	298	338	590	285	305	573	279	294	548	266	282
45-49	643	286	356	645	301	344	600	289	311	582	282	300
50-54	640	276	364	646	287	359	648	302	346	604	290	314
55-59	627	267	360	638	273	365	644	285	360	647	300	347
60-64	704	309	395	618	261	357	630	268	362	637	279	358
65-69	633	289	344	682	295	387	602	251	351	614	258	356
70-74	466	214	252	598	267	331	646	274	373	572	234	339
75-79	320	147	173	420	186	234	542	233	309	590	241	349
80-84	161	72	89	267	116	151	354	148	206	461	187	274
85-89	119	49	70	120	49	70	201	80	121	272	104	168
90-94	69	24	45	74	26	47	75	27	48	130	45	85
95-99	27	7	19	32	9	23	35	10	25	37	11	26
100 +	6	1	5	8	2	7	11	2	8	12	3	10

Age group	2045 Both sexes	2045 Males	2045 Females	2050 Both sexes	2050 Males	2050 Females
All ages	10 242	4 773	5 468	10 578	4 947	5 631
0-4	572	294	278	612	315	297
5-9	548	280	268	600	307	293
10-14	515	262	253	564	288	277
15-19	506	256	249	534	271	263
20-24	531	267	263	536	270	266
25-29	582	291	291	576	288	288
30-34	610	303	307	629	313	316
35-39	599	295	304	643	318	325
40-44	531	258	273	617	303	314
45-49	558	270	288	541	262	279
50-54	587	284	303	563	272	291
55-59	603	288	315	587	282	304
60-64	640	295	345	598	284	314
65-69	621	269	352	625	285	341
70-74	586	241	345	594	253	341
75-79	526	207	318	540	215	325
80-84	508	196	312	457	170	287
85-89	359	134	226	402	142	260
90-94	180	60	120	243	79	164
95-99	66	19	47	94	26	69
100 +	14	3	11	23	5	18

United Nations Department of Economic and Social Affairs/Population Division
World Population Prospects: The 2004 Revision, Volume II: Sex and Age Distribution of the World Population

296

POPULATION BY AGE AND SEX (in thousands)

Age group	2005 Both sexes	Males	Females	2010 Both sexes	Males	Females	2015 Both sexes	Males	Females	2020 Both sexes	Males	Females
All ages	7 041	3 313	3 728	7 341	3 442	3 900	7 576	3 536	4 040	7 759	3 604	4 156
0-4	295	150	144	231	118	113	198	101	97	178	91	87
5-9	341	172	169	323	163	160	260	131	128	226	114	112
10-14	382	192	190	357	179	178	340	171	169	276	139	137
15-19	419	208	212	401	201	200	376	188	188	358	180	179
20-24	496	234	261	450	222	228	431	215	217	406	202	204
25-29	538	240	299	540	255	286	494	242	252	476	235	241
30-34	580	250	330	585	261	324	587	276	311	541	263	278
35-39	601	259	343	612	265	347	617	275	342	619	290	328
40-44	711	319	392	618	266	352	628	272	357	634	283	351
45-49	669	317	353	718	321	397	626	269	357	637	275	362
50-54	524	255	269	671	316	355	720	321	399	629	270	360
55-59	401	202	199	521	252	270	666	312	355	715	317	398
60-64	241	124	116	394	196	198	512	245	268	655	303	351
65-69	242	124	118	233	118	115	381	186	194	495	233	262
70-74	225	111	114	226	113	113	219	108	111	357	171	186
75-79	177	81	96	198	93	105	200	96	104	195	93	102
80-84	112	46	66	141	61	81	160	70	89	163	73	90
85-89	59	21	37	78	29	49	100	39	61	115	46	69
90-94	22	7	15	33	10	23	45	15	31	59	20	39
95-99	5	1	4	9	2	7	14	4	10	20	5	15
100 +	1	0	1	1	0	1	2	1	2	4	1	3

Age group	2025 Both sexes	Males	Females	2030 Both sexes	Males	Females	2035 Both sexes	Males	Females	2040 Both sexes	Males	Females
All ages	7 917	3 658	4 258	8 042	3 697	4 345	8 125	3 715	4 410	8 154	3 709	4 445
0-4	186	95	91	192	98	94	196	100	96	195	99	95
5-9	207	104	103	214	108	106	221	111	110	224	113	111
10-14	243	122	121	223	112	112	231	116	115	238	119	119
15-19	295	148	148	262	130	131	242	120	122	250	124	126
20-24	389	194	195	326	162	164	292	144	148	273	134	139
25-29	451	222	229	434	214	220	371	182	189	337	165	172
30-34	523	256	266	498	244	254	481	236	245	418	204	214
35-39	573	278	295	555	271	284	530	259	272	513	250	263
40 44	636	208	338	500	285	305	573	270	294	548	266	282
45-49	643	286	356	645	301	344	600	289	311	582	282	300
50-54	640	276	364	646	287	359	648	302	346	604	290	314
55-59	627	267	360	638	273	365	644	285	360	647	300	347
60-64	704	309	395	618	261	357	630	268	362	637	279	358
65-69	633	289	344	682	295	387	602	251	351	614	258	356
70-74	466	214	252	598	267	331	646	274	373	572	234	339
75-79	320	147	173	420	186	234	542	233	309	590	241	349
80 84	161	72	80	267	116	151	354	148	206	461	187	274
85-89	119	49	70	120	49	70	201	80	121	272	104	168
90-94	69	24	45	74	26	47	75	27	48	130	45	85
95-99	27	7	19	32	9	23	35	10	25	37	11	26
100 +	6	1	5	8	2	7	11	2	8	12	3	10

Age group	2045 Both sexes	Males	Females	2050 Both sexes	Males	Females
All ages	8 127	3 682	4 444	8 053	3 644	4 409
0-4	195	99	95	200	102	98
5-9	223	113	111	223	112	111
10-14	241	121	120	240	120	120
15-19	257	128	129	260	129	130
20-24	281	138	142	287	142	145
25-29	318	155	163	326	159	167
30-34	384	187	198	365	177	188
35-39	450	219	232	417	201	216
40-44	531	258	273	468	227	242
45-49	558	270	288	541	262	279
50-54	587	284	303	563	272	291
55-59	603	288	315	587	282	304
60-64	640	295	345	598	284	314
65-69	621	269	352	625	285	341
70-74	586	241	345	594	253	341
75-79	526	207	318	540	215	325
80-84	508	196	312	457	170	287
85-89	359	134	226	402	142	260
90-94	180	60	120	243	79	164
95-99	66	19	47	94	26	69
100 +	14	3	11	23	5	18

POPULATION BY AGE AND SEX (in thousands)

Age group	1950 Both sexes	Males	Females	1955 Both sexes	Males	Females	1960 Both sexes	Males	Females	1965 Both sexes	Males	Females
All ages	190	100	90	181	93	88	173	86	87	209	106	104
0-4	24	13	11	30	16	13	23	12	11	29	15	14
5-9	15	8	7	22	12	10	25	13	12	29	15	14
10-14	16	8	7	13	7	6	23	12	11	31	16	15
15-19	20	11	9	12	7	6	12	6	6	23	12	11
20-24	19	11	9	14	8	7	10	5	5	11	6	5
25-29	18	10	8	14	7	7	10	5	5	10	5	5
30-34	17	9	7	14	7	7	11	5	6	12	6	6
35-39	16	9	7	13	7	6	11	5	6	12	6	6
40-44	13	7	6	12	6	6	10	5	5	11	6	6
45-49	10	5	5	10	5	5	9	5	5	10	5	5
50-54	8	4	4	8	4	4	8	4	4	8	4	4
55-59	5	2	3	6	3	3	6	3	3	7	3	4
60-64	3	1	2	4	2	3	5	2	3	5	2	3
65-69	2	1	1	3	1	2	4	1	2	4	2	3
70-74	2	1	1	2	1	1	3	1	2	3	1	2
75-79	1	0	1	1	0	1	2	1	1	2	1	1
80 +	1	0	1	1	0	1	1	0	1	1	0	1

Age group	1970 Both sexes	Males	Females	1975 Both sexes	Males	Females	1980 Both sexes	Males	Females	1985 Both sexes	Males	Females
All ages	254	130	123	253	129	124	252	128	124	306	152	154
0-4	24	13	11	24	12	12	20	10	9	36	18	18
5-9	33	17	16	21	11	10	20	10	9	19	10	9
10-14	41	22	19	30	15	15	21	11	10	22	11	11
15-19	40	21	19	37	19	18	28	14	14	26	12	14
20-24	22	12	10	34	18	16	33	17	16	34	16	18
25-29	10	5	5	21	12	9	29	16	13	39	20	19
30-34	11	5	6	11	6	5	20	12	9	33	17	15
35-39	13	6	7	10	5	5	12	7	5	23	13	10
40-44	14	7	7	11	6	6	10	5	4	13	7	6
45-49	12	6	6	13	6	6	10	5	5	10	5	5
50-54	9	5	4	11	5	6	12	5	6	10	5	5
55-59	8	4	4	9	4	5	10	4	5	11	5	6
60-64	6	3	3	7	4	4	9	4	5	9	4	5
65-69	5	2	3	6	3	3	7	3	4	8	3	4
70-74	4	2	2	4	2	2	6	2	3	5	2	3
75-79	2	1	1	3	1	2	3	1	2	4	2	3
80 +	1	1	1	2	1	1	3	1	2	3	1	2

Age group	1990 Both sexes	Males	Females	1995 Both sexes	Males	Females	2000 Both sexes	Males	Females	2005 Both sexes	Males	Females
All ages	372	181	191	413	200	213	444	214	229	460	221	239
0-4	40	21	19	33	17	16	24	12	12	17	9	8
5-9	33	17	16	40	21	19	34	17	17	24	12	12
10-14	23	12	11	34	17	17	41	21	20	34	18	17
15-19	25	12	13	24	12	12	35	17	18	41	21	20
20-24	32	12	20	29	13	16	28	13	15	37	18	19
25-29	41	18	23	36	14	22	33	14	18	30	13	17
30-34	46	22	23	43	19	24	39	15	23	34	15	19
35-39	37	20	17	47	23	23	44	20	25	39	16	24
40-44	25	14	11	37	20	17	47	24	24	45	20	25
45-49	14	8	6	26	14	11	37	20	17	47	24	24
50-54	10	6	5	14	8	6	25	14	11	37	20	17
55-59	11	5	6	10	6	5	14	8	6	25	14	11
60-64	11	5	6	10	5	5	10	5	5	13	7	6
65-69	9	4	5	10	5	6	10	5	5	10	5	5
70-74	7	3	4	8	3	5	9	4	5	9	4	5
75-79	4	2	3	6	2	3	7	3	4	8	3	5
80 +	4	1	3	5	2	3	7	2	4	9	3	6

(*) As of 20 December 1999, Macao became a Special Administrative Region (SAR) of China.

298

United Nations Department of Economic and Social Affairs/Population Division
World Population Prospects: The 2004 Revision, Volume II: Sex and Age Distribution of the World Population

POPULATION BY AGE AND SEX (in thousands)

Age group	2005 Both sexes	2005 Males	2005 Females	2010 Both sexes	2010 Males	2010 Females	2015 Both sexes	2015 Males	2015 Females	2020 Both sexes	2020 Males	2020 Females
All ages	460	221	239	476	228	248	493	235	258	509	242	267
0-4	17	9	8	18	9	9	20	10	10	21	11	10
5-9	24	12	12	17	9	8	18	9	9	20	10	10
10-14	34	18	17	24	12	12	17	9	8	18	9	9
15-19	41	21	20	35	18	17	25	13	12	18	9	9
20-24	37	18	19	43	22	21	37	18	19	27	13	14
25-29	30	13	17	39	19	21	46	23	23	39	19	20
30-34	34	15	19	31	14	17	41	19	21	47	23	24
35-39	39	16	24	35	15	20	32	14	18	41	19	22
40-44	45	20	25	40	16	24	35	15	20	33	15	18
45-49	47	24	24	45	20	25	40	16	24	36	16	20
50-54	37	20	17	47	23	24	45	20	25	40	16	24
55-59	25	14	11	37	19	17	46	23	23	45	20	25
60-64	13	7	6	24	13	11	36	19	17	45	22	23
65-69	10	5	5	13	7	6	23	13	11	34	18	16
70-74	9	4	5	9	5	4	12	6	5	21	11	10
75-79	8	3	5	8	3	4	8	4	4	10	5	5
80-84	5	2	3	6	2	4	6	3	3	6	3	3
85-89	3	1	2	3	1	2	4	1	3	4	2	3
90-94	1	0	1	1	0	1	2	0	1	2	1	2
95-99	0	0	0	0	0	0	0	0	0	1	0	1
100 +	0	0	0	0	0	0	0	0	0	0	0	0

Age group	2025 Both sexes	2025 Males	2025 Females	2030 Both sexes	2030 Males	2030 Females	2035 Both sexes	2035 Males	2035 Females	2040 Both sexes	2040 Males	2040 Females
All ages	523	247	276	531	249	282	533	248	285	531	245	286
0-4	21	11	10	19	10	9	17	9	8	17	9	8
5-9	22	11	11	21	11	10	19	10	9	18	9	9
10-14	20	10	10	22	11	11	21	11	10	19	10	9
15-19	19	10	9	21	11	10	23	12	11	22	11	11
20-24	20	10	10	21	10	11	23	11	12	25	12	12
25-29	29	14	15	22	10	12	23	11	12	25	12	13
30-34	40	20	21	30	15	16	23	11	13	24	11	13
35-39	48	23	24	41	20	21	31	15	17	24	11	13
40-44	42	20	22	48	24	25	42	20	22	32	15	17
45-49	33	15	19	42	20	23	49	24	25	42	20	22
50-54	36	16	20	33	15	19	42	20	23	49	24	25
55-59	40	16	24	35	15	20	33	14	19	42	19	23
60-64	44	19	24	39	15	24	35	15	20	32	14	18
65-69	43	21	22	42	18	24	38	15	23	34	14	19
70-74	32	16	15	40	19	21	39	17	23	35	14	22
75-79	19	10	9	28	14	14	36	17	19	35	15	21
80-84	8	4	4	15	8	8	23	11	12	30	13	16
85-89	4	2	2	6	3	3	11	5	6	17	7	9
90-94	2	1	1	2	1	1	3	1	2	6	3	4
95-99	1	0	1	1	0	1	1	0	1	1	0	1
100 +	0	0	0	0	0	0	0	0	0	0	0	0

Age group	2045 Both sexes	2045 Males	2045 Females	2050 Both sexes	2050 Males	2050 Females
All ages	526	242	284	520	238	281
0-4	19	10	9	20	10	10
5-9	18	9	9	19	10	9
10-14	18	9	9	18	9	9
15-19	20	10	10	19	9	9
20-24	24	12	12	22	11	11
25-29	27	13	14	26	13	14
30-34	27	13	14	28	13	15
35-39	25	12	14	27	13	15
40-44	25	12	14	26	12	14
45-49	32	15	17	25	12	14
50-54	42	20	22	32	15	17
55-59	48	23	25	42	20	22
60-64	41	19	22	47	23	24
65-69	31	14	18	40	18	22
70-74	32	13	18	30	13	17
75-79	32	12	20	29	12	17
80-84	30	12	18	27	10	18
85-89	22	9	13	22	8	14
90-94	10	4	6	14	5	8
95-99	3	1	2	5	2	3
100 +	0	0	0	1	0	1

United Nations Department of Economic and Social Affairs/Population Division
World Population Prospects: The 2004 Revision, Volume II: Sex and Age Distribution of the World Population

299

POPULATION BY AGE AND SEX (in thousands)

Age group	2005 Both sexes	Males	Females	2010 Both sexes	Males	Females	2015 Both sexes	Males	Females	2020 Both sexes	Males	Females
All ages	460	221	239	481	231	250	506	242	264	532	254	278
0-4	17	9	8	22	11	11	28	14	14	31	16	15
5-9	24	12	12	17	9	8	23	12	11	28	14	14
10-14	34	18	17	24	12	12	17	9	8	23	12	11
15-19	41	21	20	35	18	17	25	13	12	18	9	9
20-24	37	18	19	43	22	21	37	18	19	27	13	14
25-29	30	13	17	39	19	21	46	23	23	39	19	20
30-34	34	15	19	31	14	17	41	19	21	47	23	24
35-39	39	16	24	35	15	20	32	14	18	41	19	22
40-44	45	20	25	40	16	24	35	15	20	33	15	18
45-49	47	24	24	45	20	25	40	16	24	36	16	20
50-54	37	20	17	47	23	24	45	20	25	40	16	24
55-59	25	14	11	37	19	17	46	23	23	45	20	25
60-64	13	7	6	24	13	11	36	19	17	45	22	23
65-69	10	5	5	13	7	6	23	13	11	34	18	16
70-74	9	4	5	9	5	4	12	6	5	21	11	10
75-79	8	3	5	8	3	4	8	4	4	10	5	5
80-84	5	2	3	6	2	4	6	3	3	6	3	3
85-89	3	1	2	3	1	2	4	1	3	4	2	3
90-94	1	0	1	1	0	1	2	0	1	2	1	2
95-99	0	0	0	0	0	0	0	0	0	1	0	1
100 +	0	0	0	0	0	0	0	0	0	0	0	0

Age group	2025 Both sexes	Males	Females	2030 Both sexes	Males	Females	2035 Both sexes	Males	Females	2040 Both sexes	Males	Females
All ages	555	263	291	571	270	301	582	273	309	591	276	315
0-4	30	15	15	27	14	13	26	13	13	28	14	14
5-9	32	16	16	30	16	15	27	14	13	26	13	13
10-14	28	15	14	32	16	16	31	16	15	28	14	14
15-19	24	12	12	29	15	14	33	17	16	31	16	15
20-24	20	10	10	26	13	13	31	15	16	35	17	17
25-29	29	14	15	22	10	12	28	13	14	33	16	17
30-34	40	20	21	30	15	16	23	11	13	29	14	15
35-39	48	23	24	41	20	21	31	15	17	24	11	13
40-44	42	20	22	48	24	25	42	20	22	32	15	17
45-49	33	15	19	42	20	23	49	24	25	42	20	22
50-54	36	16	20	33	15	19	42	20	23	49	24	25
55-59	40	16	24	35	15	20	33	14	18	42	19	22
60-64	44	19	24	39	15	24	35	15	20	32	14	18
65-69	43	21	22	42	18	24	38	15	23	34	14	19
70-74	32	16	15	40	19	21	39	17	23	35	14	22
75-79	19	10	9	28	14	14	36	17	19	35	15	21
80-84	8	4	4	15	8	8	23	11	12	30	13	16
85-89	4	2	2	6	3	3	11	5	6	17	7	9
90-94	2	1	1	2	1	1	3	1	2	6	3	4
95-99	1	0	1	1	0	1	1	0	1	1	0	1
100 +	0	0	0	0	0	0	0	0	0	0	0	0

Age group	2045 Both sexes	Males	Females	2050 Both sexes	Males	Females
All ages	599	279	320	607	283	324
0-4	32	16	16	35	18	17
5-9	28	15	14	32	17	16
10-14	27	14	13	29	15	14
15-19	28	14	14	27	14	13
20-24	33	17	17	30	15	15
25-29	37	18	19	35	17	18
30-34	35	17	18	38	18	20
35-39	30	14	16	35	17	19
40-44	25	12	14	31	14	16
45-49	32	15	17	25	12	14
50-54	42	20	22	32	15	17
55-59	48	23	25	42	20	22
60-64	41	19	22	47	23	24
65-69	31	14	18	40	18	22
70-74	32	13	18	30	13	17
75-79	32	12	20	29	12	17
80-84	30	12	18	27	10	18
85-89	22	9	13	22	8	14
90-94	10	4	6	14	5	8
95-99	3	1	2	5	2	3
100 +	0	0	0	1	0	1

United Nations Department of Economic and Social Affairs/Population Division
World Population Prospects: The 2004 Revision, Volume II: Sex and Age Distribution of the World Population

POPULATION BY AGE AND SEX (in thousands)

Age group	2005 Both sexes	Males	Females	2010 Both sexes	Males	Females	2015 Both sexes	Males	Females	2020 Both sexes	Males	Females
All ages	460	221	239	472	226	246	480	229	251	486	230	256
0-4	17	9	8	13	7	6	12	6	6	11	6	5
5-9	24	12	12	17	9	8	13	7	6	12	6	6
10-14	34	18	17	24	12	12	17	9	8	13	7	7
15-19	41	21	20	35	18	17	25	13	12	18	9	9
20-24	37	18	19	43	22	21	37	18	19	27	13	14
25-29	30	13	17	39	19	21	46	23	23	39	19	20
30-34	34	15	19	31	14	17	41	19	21	47	23	24
35-39	39	16	24	35	15	20	32	14	18	41	19	22
40-44	45	20	25	40	16	24	35	15	20	33	15	18
45-49	47	24	24	45	20	25	40	16	24	36	16	20
50-54	37	20	17	47	23	24	45	20	25	40	16	24
55-59	25	14	11	37	19	17	46	23	23	45	20	25
60-64	13	7	6	24	13	11	36	19	17	45	22	23
65-69	10	5	5	13	7	6	23	13	11	34	18	16
70-74	9	4	5	9	5	4	12	6	5	21	11	10
75-79	8	3	5	8	3	4	8	4	4	10	5	5
80-84	5	2	3	6	2	4	6	3	3	6	3	3
85-89	3	1	2	3	1	2	4	1	3	4	2	3
90-94	1	0	1	1	0	1	2	0	1	2	1	2
95-99	0	0	0	0	0	0	0	0	0	1	0	1
100 +	0	0	0	0	0	0	0	0	0	0	0	0

Age group	2025 Both sexes	Males	Females	2030 Both sexes	Males	Females	2035 Both sexes	Males	Females	2040 Both sexes	Males	Females
All ages	490	231	260	491	228	262	485	224	262	475	217	258
0-4	12	6	6	11	5	5	10	5	5	9	5	4
5-9	12	6	6	12	6	6	11	6	5	10	5	5
10-14	12	6	6	12	6	6	12	6	6	11	6	6
15-19	14	7	7	13	7	6	13	6	6	13	7	6
20-24	20	10	10	16	8	8	15	7	8	15	7	8
25-29	29	14	15	22	10	12	18	8	10	17	8	9
30-34	40	20	21	30	15	16	23	11	13	20	9	11
35-39	48	23	24	41	20	21	31	15	17	24	11	13
40-44	42	20	22	48	24	25	42	20	22	32	15	17
45-49	33	15	19	42	20	23	49	24	25	42	20	22
50-54	36	16	20	33	15	19	42	20	23	49	24	25
55-59	40	16	24	35	15	20	33	14	18	42	19	22
60-64	44	19	24	39	15	24	35	15	20	32	14	18
65-69	43	21	22	42	18	24	38	15	23	34	14	19
70-74	32	16	15	40	19	21	39	17	23	35	14	22
75-79	19	10	9	28	14	14	36	17	19	35	15	21
80-84	8	4	4	15	8	8	23	11	12	30	13	16
85-89	4	2	2	6	3	3	11	5	6	17	7	9
90-94	2	1	1	2	1	1	3	1	2	6	3	4
95-99	1	0	1	1	0	1	1	0	1	1	0	1
100 +	0	0	0	0	0	0	0	0	0	0	0	0

Age group	2045 Both sexes	Males	Females	2050 Both sexes	Males	Females
All ages	460	208	252	443	199	244
0-4	9	5	4	9	5	4
5-9	9	5	5	9	5	5
10-14	10	5	5	10	5	5
15-19	12	6	6	11	6	5
20-24	15	7	8	14	7	7
25-29	17	8	9	17	8	9
30-34	19	8	10	18	8	10
35-39	21	9	11	20	9	11
40-44	25	12	14	21	10	12
45-49	32	15	17	25	12	14
50-54	42	20	22	32	15	17
55-59	48	23	25	42	20	22
60-64	41	19	22	47	23	24
65-69	31	14	18	40	18	22
70-74	32	13	18	30	13	17
75-79	32	12	20	29	12	17
80-84	30	12	18	27	10	18
85-89	22	9	13	22	8	14
90-94	10	4	6	14	5	8
95-99	3	1	2	5	2	3
100 +	0	0	0	1	0	1

United Nations Department of Economic and Social Affairs/Population Division
World Population Prospects: The 2004 Revision, Volume II: Sex and Age Distribution of the World Population

301

POPULATION BY AGE AND SEX (in thousands)

Age group	1950 Both sexes	Males	Females	1955 Both sexes	Males	Females	1960 Both sexes	Males	Females	1965 Both sexes	Males	Females
All ages	12 568	6 220	6 349	14 527	7 200	7 327	16 857	8 365	8 492	19 591	9 733	9 858
0-4	2 252	1 137	1 114	2 728	1 383	1 345	3 114	1 581	1 533	3 584	1 821	1 763
5-9	1 686	849	837	2 120	1 067	1 053	2 609	1 319	1 289	3 002	1 522	1 480
10-14	1 421	714	707	1 648	829	819	2 082	1 047	1 035	2 568	1 298	1 270
15-19	1 243	623	620	1 383	694	688	1 610	809	800	2 039	1 025	1 014
20-24	1 083	541	542	1 187	592	595	1 323	661	662	1 542	771	771
25-29	953	475	478	1 021	505	516	1 119	551	568	1 245	614	632
30-34	789	392	397	902	445	457	967	473	495	1 059	514	545
35-39	702	347	354	750	370	380	861	421	440	924	447	477
40-44	599	296	302	669	329	339	718	352	366	826	402	424
45-49	504	252	252	567	278	289	637	311	325	686	334	352
50-54	399	189	210	472	233	239	535	260	275	603	292	310
55-59	314	144	170	365	170	195	436	212	224	495	238	258
60-64	230	101	129	277	124	153	326	149	177	391	187	203
65-69	168	70	98	192	82	110	234	103	132	277	124	153
70-74	115	47	68	127	52	76	149	62	87	184	78	106
75-79	71	28	43	73	29	44	85	33	52	102	41	61
80 +	41	16	26	44	17	28	53	20	33	66	25	41

Age group	1970 Both sexes	Males	Females	1975 Both sexes	Males	Females	1980 Both sexes	Males	Females	1985 Both sexes	Males	Females
All ages	22 561	11 218	11 343	25 381	12 623	12 758	28 447	14 151	14 295	31 659	15 728	15 931
0-4	3 895	1 979	1 916	3 800	1 931	1 869	4 090	2 083	2 008	4 237	2 158	2 079
5-9	3 472	1 761	1 711	3 789	1 922	1 867	3 723	1 890	1 833	4 036	2 053	1 984
10-14	2 954	1 494	1 460	3 424	1 733	1 691	3 754	1 901	1 853	3 701	1 876	1 825
15-19	2 505	1 259	1 246	2 892	1 455	1 437	3 373	1 701	1 671	3 710	1 874	1 837
20-24	1 950	968	981	2 415	1 201	1 214	2 814	1 406	1 408	3 300	1 654	1 646
25-29	1 471	733	738	1 875	929	946	2 336	1 153	1 183	2 731	1 350	1 381
30-34	1 193	586	607	1 416	704	713	1 807	889	918	2 261	1 104	1 157
35-39	1 018	492	526	1 151	562	588	1 363	673	690	1 747	851	896
40-44	889	429	460	982	474	509	1 103	536	567	1 311	642	669
45-49	792	384	408	854	410	444	939	450	489	1 058	511	547
50-54	651	315	336	754	363	391	810	387	423	894	425	469
55-59	561	269	291	607	291	316	704	337	368	761	360	401
60-64	447	212	235	507	241	267	551	261	290	646	304	341
65-69	335	157	177	384	178	206	439	204	234	484	225	259
70-74	219	95	124	266	121	145	309	140	169	362	164	198
75-79	128	53	75	155	65	90	191	84	106	231	101	130
80 +	83	32	51	108	43	65	141	56	85	189	76	113

Age group	1990 Both sexes	Males	Females	1995 Both sexes	Males	Females	2000 Both sexes	Males	Females	2005 Both sexes	Males	Females
All ages	34 970	17 340	17 630	38 542	19 049	19 492	42 120	20 804	21 316	45 600	22 530	23 070
0-4	4 406	2 245	2 161	4 751	2 422	2 329	4 757	2 428	2 329	4 726	2 414	2 312
5-9	4 184	2 129	2 055	4 358	2 219	2 139	4 710	2 402	2 308	4 721	2 411	2 310
10-14	4 012	2 037	1 975	4 161	2 116	2 045	4 336	2 208	2 129	4 688	2 391	2 297
15-19	3 654	1 845	1 809	3 966	2 007	1 959	4 120	2 092	2 028	4 299	2 187	2 112
20-24	3 626	1 815	1 811	3 565	1 780	1 786	3 888	1 954	1 934	4 050	2 048	2 003
25-29	3 211	1 592	1 619	3 518	1 733	1 786	3 476	1 717	1 758	3 805	1 900	1 905
30-34	2 655	1 299	1 356	3 124	1 525	1 599	3 443	1 679	1 764	3 410	1 673	1 737
35-39	2 200	1 064	1 136	2 589	1 250	1 339	3 064	1 483	1 581	3 387	1 642	1 745
40-44	1 695	819	876	2 147	1 027	1 120	2 539	1 217	1 322	3 013	1 451	1 562
45-49	1 267	616	651	1 651	790	860	2 099	998	1 102	2 489	1 187	1 302
50-54	1 014	486	528	1 224	590	634	1 602	762	840	2 044	966	1 078
55-59	846	399	447	966	458	508	1 171	560	612	1 539	726	813
60-64	703	328	375	788	366	421	904	423	481	1 101	520	581
65-69	573	265	308	630	289	342	711	325	386	821	378	444
70-74	404	183	221	485	219	266	538	240	298	612	272	340
75-79	275	120	155	312	137	175	379	165	214	425	183	242
80 +	245	98	147	306	121	185	382	151	232	469	182	287

United Nations Department of Economic and Social Affairs/Population Division
World Population Prospects: The 2004 Revision, Volume II: Sex and Age Distribution of the World Population

302

POPULATION BY AGE AND SEX (in thousands)

Age group	2005 Both sexes	Males	Females	2010 Both sexes	Males	Females	2015 Both sexes	Males	Females	2020 Both sexes	Males	Females
All ages	45 600	22 530	23 070	48 930	24 184	24 746	52 086	25 742	26 344	55 046	27 193	27 854
0-4	4 726	2 414	2 312	4 682	2 392	2 290	4 657	2 380	2 277	4 626	2 365	2 261
5-9	4 721	2 411	2 310	4 695	2 400	2 295	4 653	2 379	2 274	4 631	2 368	2 263
10-14	4 688	2 391	2 297	4 701	2 401	2 300	4 675	2 390	2 285	4 634	2 370	2 264
15-19	4 299	2 187	2 112	4 652	2 372	2 280	4 666	2 383	2 283	4 642	2 373	2 269
20-24	4 050	2 048	2 003	4 233	2 147	2 086	4 587	2 332	2 255	4 605	2 346	2 259
25-29	3 805	1 900	1 905	3 973	1 998	1 975	4 157	2 098	2 059	4 513	2 285	2 228
30-34	3 410	1 673	1 737	3 742	1 858	1 884	3 911	1 957	1 954	4 099	2 060	2 039
35-39	3 387	1 642	1 745	3 360	1 640	1 719	3 691	1 824	1 867	3 862	1 925	1 937
40-44	3 013	1 451	1 562	3 336	1 610	1 726	3 312	1 611	1 702	3 644	1 794	1 849
45-49	2 489	1 187	1 302	2 959	1 418	1 541	3 280	1 576	1 704	3 259	1 578	1 682
50-54	2 044	966	1 078	2 427	1 151	1 277	2 889	1 377	1 513	3 207	1 531	1 676
55-59	1 539	726	813	1 968	922	1 046	2 341	1 100	1 241	2 791	1 318	1 474
60-64	1 101	520	581	1 452	676	775	1 861	860	1 001	2 219	1 028	1 192
65-69	821	378	444	1 005	465	540	1 329	606	723	1 710	772	939
70-74	612	272	340	710	317	393	873	391	482	1 161	510	651
75-79	425	183	242	487	207	280	569	242	327	704	299	405
80-84	266	110	156	300	121	179	347	138	209	407	161	246
85-89	130	50	80	160	60	99	181	66	115	209	75	134
90-94	53	18	35	63	21	42	77	25	52	86	27	59
95-99	16	4	12	20	5	15	23	6	17	27	7	20
100+	5	1	4	6	1	5	7	1	5	7	1	6

Age group	2025 Both sexes	Males	Females	2030 Both sexes	Males	Females	2035 Both sexes	Males	Females	2040 Both sexes	Males	Females
All ages	57 738	28 499	29 239	60 153	29 684	30 468	62 146	30 652	31 493	63 705	31 397	32 307
0-4	4 545	2 324	2 221	4 412	2 256	2 156	4 260	2 178	2 082	4 101	2 097	2 004
5-9	4 603	2 355	2 249	4 517	2 310	2 207	4 387	2 243	2 143	4 237	2 167	2 070
10-14	4 613	2 359	2 253	4 584	2 345	2 239	4 499	2 301	2 198	4 369	2 235	2 135
15-19	4 604	2 355	2 249	4 578	2 340	2 238	4 551	2 327	2 224	4 468	2 285	2 183
20-24	4 586	2 340	2 246	4 537	2 312	2 225	4 515	2 300	2 214	4 491	2 290	2 201
25-29	4 537	2 304	2 233	4 504	2 285	2 219	4 459	2 260	2 199	4 440	2 252	2 189
30-34	4 457	2 249	2 209	4 468	2 256	2 212	4 438	2 240	2 199	4 397	2 218	2 179
35-39	4 053	2 000	2 020	4 390	2 207	2 191	4 411	2 216	2 195	4 386	2 203	2 183
40-44	3 817	1 897	1 921	3 998	1 993	2 005	4 342	2 170	2 172	4 359	2 181	2 178
45-49	3 590	1 760	1 829	3 758	1 859	1 899	3 940	1 956	1 984	4 283	2 131	2 151
50-54	3 191	1 535	1 656	3 516	1 715	1 801	3 685	1 813	1 871	3 867	1 910	1 957
55-59	3 104	1 468	1 637	3 094	1 478	1 616	3 414	1 655	1 760	3 584	1 752	1 832
60-64	2 654	1 233	1 421	2 964	1 388	1 576	2 961	1 400	1 560	3 275	1 571	1 703
65-69	2 047	924	1 124	2 471	1 131	1 339	2 770	1 278	1 492	2 775	1 293	1 483
70-74	1 503	651	852	1 833	809	1 023	2 223	996	1 227	2 505	1 129	1 376
75-79	911	361	550	1 290	532	734	1 556	665	890	1 902	824	1 078
80-84	508	199	308	724	287	437	981	393	588	1 218	496	722
85-89	247	87	160	340	124	216	490	180	310	672	250	422
90-94	99	30	69	137	43	94	189	61	128	275	89	186
95-99	30	8	22	43	11	32	59	15	44	81	21	60
100+	7	1	6	11	2	9	15	3	13	20	4	16

Age group	2045 Both sexes	Males	Females	2050 Both sexes	Males	Females
All ages	64 852	31 934	32 918	65 679	32 310	33 369
0-4	3 967	2 029	1 938	3 902	1 996	1 907
5-9	4 080	2 087	1 993	3 948	2 019	1 928
10-14	4 220	2 159	2 061	4 063	2 079	1 985
15-19	4 340	2 220	2 120	4 192	2 145	2 047
20-24	4 410	2 250	2 161	4 285	2 187	2 098
25-29	4 420	2 244	2 176	4 343	2 207	2 136
30-34	4 382	2 212	2 170	4 365	2 207	2 158
35-39	4 348	2 184	2 164	4 335	2 180	2 155
40-44	4 337	2 170	2 166	4 302	2 154	2 149
45-49	4 302	2 144	2 158	4 284	2 136	2 148
50-54	4 208	2 084	2 124	4 231	2 099	2 133
55-59	3 766	1 848	1 919	4 105	2 019	2 086
60-64	3 444	1 666	1 778	3 627	1 761	1 866
65-69	3 079	1 455	1 625	3 249	1 547	1 701
70-74	2 523	1 148	1 375	2 812	1 297	1 515
75-79	2 159	940	1 219	2 190	960	1 229
80-84	1 503	618	884	1 722	710	1 012
85-89	842	317	525	1 050	398	651
90-94	380	124	255	479	158	320
95-99	117	31	86	160	43	117
100+	26	5	21	35	7	28

POPULATION BY AGE AND SEX (in thousands)

Age group	2005 Both sexes	Males	Females	2010 Both sexes	Males	Females	2015 Both sexes	Males	Females	2020 Both sexes	Males	Females
All ages	45 600	22 530	23 070	49 413	24 431	24 982	53 378	26 402	26 976	57 386	28 388	28 998
0-4	4 726	2 414	2 312	5 165	2 639	2 526	5 468	2 795	2 674	5 678	2 902	2 775
5-9	4 721	2 411	2 310	4 695	2 400	2 295	5 134	2 625	2 509	5 439	2 781	2 658
10-14	4 688	2 391	2 297	4 701	2 401	2 300	4 675	2 390	2 285	5 114	2 615	2 499
15-19	4 299	2 187	2 112	4 652	2 372	2 280	4 666	2 383	2 283	4 642	2 373	2 269
20-24	4 050	2 048	2 003	4 233	2 147	2 086	4 587	2 332	2 255	4 605	2 346	2 259
25-29	3 805	1 900	1 905	3 973	1 998	1 975	4 157	2 098	2 059	4 513	2 285	2 228
30-34	3 410	1 673	1 737	3 742	1 858	1 884	3 911	1 957	1 954	4 099	2 060	2 039
35-39	3 387	1 642	1 745	3 360	1 640	1 719	3 691	1 824	1 867	3 862	1 925	1 937
40-44	3 013	1 451	1 562	3 336	1 610	1 726	3 312	1 611	1 702	3 644	1 794	1 849
45-49	2 489	1 187	1 302	2 959	1 418	1 541	3 280	1 576	1 704	3 259	1 578	1 682
50-54	2 044	966	1 078	2 427	1 151	1 277	2 889	1 377	1 513	3 207	1 531	1 676
55-59	1 539	726	813	1 968	922	1 046	2 341	1 100	1 241	2 791	1 318	1 474
60-64	1 101	520	581	1 452	676	775	1 861	860	1 001	2 219	1 028	1 192
65-69	821	378	444	1 005	465	540	1 329	606	723	1 710	772	939
70-74	612	272	340	710	317	393	873	391	482	1 161	510	651
75-79	425	183	242	487	207	280	569	242	327	704	299	405
80-84	266	110	156	300	121	179	347	138	209	407	161	246
85-89	130	50	80	160	60	99	181	66	115	209	75	134
90-94	53	18	35	63	21	42	77	25	52	86	27	59
95-99	16	4	12	20	5	15	23	6	17	27	7	20
100 +	5	1	4	6	1	5	7	1	5	7	1	6

Age group	2025 Both sexes	Males	Females	2030 Both sexes	Males	Females	2035 Both sexes	Males	Females	2040 Both sexes	Males	Females
All ages	61 194	30 265	30 928	64 884	32 101	32 783	68 399	33 843	34 556	71 739	35 494	36 245
0-4	5 667	2 897	2 769	5 700	2 914	2 786	5 800	2 966	2 835	5 906	3 020	2 886
5-9	5 651	2 890	2 761	5 634	2 881	2 753	5 670	2 899	2 771	5 772	2 952	2 820
10-14	5 420	2 772	2 648	5 631	2 880	2 751	5 615	2 871	2 743	5 651	2 890	2 761
15-19	5 083	2 599	2 484	5 383	2 751	2 632	5 595	2 860	2 735	5 580	2 853	2 728
20-24	4 586	2 340	2 246	5 013	2 554	2 459	5 314	2 707	2 607	5 528	2 818	2 711
25-29	4 537	2 304	2 233	4 504	2 285	2 219	4 932	2 499	2 432	5 235	2 654	2 581
30-34	4 457	2 249	2 209	4 468	2 256	2 212	4 438	2 240	2 199	4 866	2 454	2 412
35-39	4 053	2 030	2 023	4 398	2 207	2 191	4 411	2 216	2 195	4 386	2 203	2 183
40-44	3 817	1 897	1 921	3 998	1 993	2 005	4 342	2 170	2 172	4 359	2 181	2 178
45-49	3 590	1 760	1 829	3 758	1 859	1 899	3 940	1 956	1 984	4 283	2 131	2 151
50-54	3 191	1 535	1 656	3 516	1 715	1 801	3 685	1 813	1 871	3 867	1 910	1 957
55-59	3 104	1 468	1 637	3 094	1 478	1 616	3 414	1 655	1 760	3 584	1 752	1 832
60-64	2 654	1 233	1 421	2 964	1 388	1 576	2 961	1 400	1 560	3 275	1 571	1 703
65-69	2 047	924	1 124	2 471	1 131	1 339	2 770	1 278	1 492	2 775	1 293	1 483
70-74	1 503	651	852	1 833	809	1 023	2 223	996	1 227	2 505	1 129	1 376
75-79	944	391	553	1 266	532	734	1 556	665	890	1 902	824	1 078
80-84	508	199	308	724	287	437	981	393	588	1 218	496	722
85-89	247	87	160	340	124	216	490	180	310	672	250	422
90-94	99	30	69	137	43	94	189	61	128	275	89	186
95-99	30	8	22	43	11	32	59	15	44	81	21	60
100 +	7	1	6	11	2	9	15	3	13	20	4	16

Age group	2045 Both sexes	Males	Females	2050 Both sexes	Males	Females
All ages	74 890	37 048	37 842	77 922	38 543	39 379
0-4	6 002	3 069	2 933	6 145	3 142	3 003
5-9	5 879	3 007	2 873	5 977	3 057	2 920
10-14	5 753	2 942	2 811	5 861	2 998	2 863
15-19	5 618	2 872	2 746	5 722	2 926	2 796
20-24	5 517	2 813	2 704	5 558	2 835	2 723
25-29	5 451	2 767	2 684	5 444	2 766	2 679
30-34	5 171	2 610	2 561	5 390	2 725	2 665
35-39	4 813	2 418	2 396	5 119	2 574	2 545
40-44	4 337	2 170	2 166	4 764	2 385	2 379
45-49	4 302	2 144	2 158	4 284	2 136	2 148
50-54	4 208	2 084	2 124	4 231	2 099	2 133
55-59	3 766	1 848	1 919	4 105	2 019	2 086
60-64	3 444	1 666	1 778	3 627	1 761	1 866
65-69	3 079	1 455	1 625	3 249	1 547	1 701
70-74	2 523	1 148	1 375	2 812	1 297	1 515
75-79	2 159	940	1 219	2 190	960	1 229
80-84	1 503	618	884	1 722	710	1 012
85-89	842	317	525	1 050	398	651
90-94	380	124	255	479	158	320
95-99	117	31	86	160	43	117
100 +	26	5	21	35	7	28

United Nations Department of Economic and Social Affairs/Population Division
World Population Prospects: The 2004 Revision, Volume II: Sex and Age Distribution of the World Population

304

POPULATION BY AGE AND SEX (in thousands)

Age group	2005			2010			2015			2020		
	Both sexes	Males	Females	Both sexes	Males	Females	Both sexes	Males	Females	Both sexes	Males	Females
All ages	45 600	22 530	23 070	48 451	23 939	24 512	50 802	25 086	25 716	52 715	26 001	26 714
0-4	4 726	2 414	2 312	4 203	2 148	2 055	3 850	1 968	1 882	3 575	1 828	1 747
5-9	4 721	2 411	2 310	4 695	2 400	2 295	4 176	2 135	2 041	3 827	1 957	1 870
10-14	4 688	2 391	2 297	4 701	2 401	2 300	4 675	2 390	2 285	4 158	2 126	2 031
15-19	4 299	2 187	2 112	4 652	2 372	2 280	4 666	2 383	2 283	4 642	2 373	2 269
20-24	4 050	2 048	2 003	4 233	2 147	2 086	4 587	2 332	2 255	4 605	2 346	2 259
25-29	3 805	1 900	1 905	3 973	1 998	1 975	4 157	2 098	2 059	4 513	2 285	2 228
30-34	3 410	1 673	1 737	3 742	1 858	1 884	3 911	1 957	1 954	4 099	2 060	2 039
35-39	3 387	1 642	1 745	3 360	1 640	1 719	3 691	1 824	1 867	3 862	1 925	1 937
40-44	3 013	1 451	1 562	3 336	1 610	1 726	3 312	1 611	1 702	3 644	1 794	1 849
45-49	2 489	1 187	1 302	2 959	1 418	1 541	3 280	1 576	1 704	3 259	1 578	1 682
50-54	2 044	966	1 078	2 427	1 151	1 277	2 889	1 377	1 513	3 207	1 531	1 676
55-59	1 539	726	813	1 968	922	1 046	2 341	1 100	1 241	2 791	1 318	1 474
60-64	1 101	520	581	1 452	676	775	1 861	860	1 001	2 219	1 028	1 192
65-69	821	378	444	1 005	465	540	1 329	606	723	1 710	772	939
70-74	612	272	340	710	317	393	873	391	482	1 161	510	651
75-79	425	183	242	487	207	280	569	242	327	704	299	405
80-84	266	110	156	300	121	179	347	138	209	407	161	246
85-89	130	50	80	160	60	99	181	66	115	209	75	134
90-94	53	18	35	63	21	42	77	25	52	86	27	59
95-99	16	4	12	20	5	15	23	6	17	27	7	20
100 +	5	1	4	6	1	5	7	1	5	7	1	6

Age group	2025			2030			2035			2040		
	Both sexes	Males	Females	Both sexes	Males	Females	Both sexes	Males	Females	Both sexes	Males	Females
All ages	54 315	26 750	27 565	55 547	27 332	28 215	56 218	27 628	28 590	56 311	27 629	28 682
0-4	3 448	1 763	1 685	3 218	1 645	1 572	2 921	1 494	1 427	2 611	1 336	1 276
5-9	3 555	1 819	1 737	3 425	1 752	1 673	3 197	1 635	1 562	2 902	1 485	1 417
10-14	3 810	1 949	1 861	3 538	1 810	1 728	3 408	1 744	1 664	3 181	1 627	1 553
15-19	4 129	2 112	2 017	3 778	1 932	1 846	3 508	1 795	1 713	3 380	1 730	1 650
20-24	4 588	2 340	2 246	4 065	2 072	1 993	3 719	1 896	1 823	3 453	1 762	1 691
25-29	4 537	2 304	2 233	4 504	2 285	2 219	3 991	2 023	1 967	3 651	1 852	1 799
30-34	4 457	2 249	2 209	4 468	2 256	2 212	4 438	2 240	2 199	3 932	1 984	1 949
35-39	4 053	2 030	2 023	4 398	2 207	2 191	4 411	2 216	2 195	4 386	2 203	2 183
40-44	3 817	1 807	1 021	3 008	1 000	2 005	4 042	2 170	2 172	4 359	2 181	2 178
45-49	3 590	1 760	1 829	3 758	1 859	1 899	3 940	1 956	1 984	4 283	2 131	2 151
50-54	3 191	1 535	1 656	3 516	1 715	1 801	3 685	1 813	1 871	3 867	1 910	1 957
55-59	3 104	1 468	1 637	3 094	1 478	1 616	3 414	1 655	1 760	3 584	1 752	1 832
60-64	2 654	1 233	1 421	2 964	1 388	1 576	2 961	1 400	1 560	3 275	1 571	1 703
65-69	2 047	924	1 124	2 471	1 131	1 339	2 770	1 278	1 492	2 775	1 293	1 483
70-74	1 503	651	852	1 833	809	1 023	2 223	996	1 227	2 505	1 129	1 376
75-79	944	391	553	1 266	532	734	1 556	665	890	1 902	824	1 078
80-84	509	199	308	724	287	407	901	390	500	1 218	496	722
85-89	247	87	160	340	124	216	490	180	310	672	250	422
90-94	99	30	69	137	43	94	189	61	128	275	89	186
95-99	30	8	22	43	11	32	59	15	44	81	21	60
100 +	7	1	6	11	2	9	15	3	13	20	4	16

Age group	2045			2050		
	Both sexes	Males	Females	Both sexes	Males	Females
All ages	55 878	27 363	28 514	55 034	26 893	28 141
0-4	2 357	1 206	1 152	2 197	1 124	1 073
5-9	2 595	1 328	1 267	2 342	1 199	1 144
10-14	2 886	1 477	1 409	2 580	1 321	1 259
15-19	3 154	1 614	1 540	2 861	1 465	1 396
20-24	3 328	1 699	1 629	3 105	1 586	1 519
25-29	3 389	1 721	1 667	3 266	1 661	1 606
30-34	3 597	1 816	1 781	3 339	1 689	1 650
35-39	3 886	1 952	1 934	3 556	1 788	1 768
40-44	4 337	2 170	2 166	3 844	1 925	1 920
45-49	4 302	2 144	2 158	4 284	2 136	2 148
50-54	4 208	2 084	2 124	4 231	2 099	2 133
55-59	3 766	1 848	1 919	4 105	2 019	2 086
60-64	3 444	1 666	1 778	3 627	1 761	1 866
65-69	3 079	1 455	1 625	3 249	1 547	1 701
70-74	2 523	1 148	1 375	2 812	1 297	1 515
75-79	2 159	940	1 219	2 190	960	1 229
80-84	1 503	618	884	1 722	710	1 012
85-89	842	317	525	1 050	398	651
90-94	380	124	255	479	158	320
95-99	117	31	86	160	43	117
100 +	26	5	21	35	7	28

POPULATION BY AGE AND SEX (in thousands)

Age group	1950 Both sexes	1950 Males	1950 Females	1955 Both sexes	1955 Males	1955 Females	1960 Both sexes	1960 Males	1960 Females	1965 Both sexes	1965 Males	1965 Females
All ages	173	85	87	194	96	98	215	106	108	240	119	121
0-4	31	15	15	34	17	17	39	20	19	46	23	23
5-9	24	12	12	28	14	14	30	15	15	35	18	17
10-14	20	10	10	24	12	12	27	13	13	28	14	14
15-19	18	9	9	20	10	10	22	11	11	25	13	13
20-24	15	7	8	17	8	9	19	9	9	21	10	10
25-29	13	6	6	14	7	7	16	8	8	17	9	9
30-34	11	5	5	12	6	6	13	7	7	15	7	7
35-39	9	4	5	10	5	5	11	5	6	12	6	6
40-44	8	4	4	8	4	4	9	5	5	10	5	5
45-49	6	3	3	7	3	4	8	4	4	8	4	4
50-54	5	2	3	6	3	3	6	3	3	7	3	3
55-59	4	2	2	5	2	2	5	2	3	5	3	3
60-64	3	2	2	4	2	2	4	2	2	4	2	2
65-69	3	1	1	3	1	1	3	1	1	3	1	2
70-74	2	1	1	2	1	1	2	1	1	2	1	1
75-79	1	0	1	1	0	1	1	0	1	1	0	1
80 +	1	0	0	1	0	0	1	0	0	1	0	0

Age group	1970 Both sexes	1970 Males	1970 Females	1975 Both sexes	1975 Males	1975 Females	1980 Both sexes	1980 Males	1980 Females	1985 Both sexes	1985 Males	1985 Females
All ages	275	137	138	318	158	159	387	193	194	456	228	228
0-4	53	27	26	61	31	30	75	38	37	89	45	44
5-9	42	21	21	50	25	25	60	30	30	71	36	35
10-14	34	17	17	40	20	20	50	25	25	59	30	29
15-19	27	14	13	32	16	16	41	21	20	49	25	24
20-24	24	12	12	26	13	13	32	16	16	40	20	20
25-29	20	10	10	23	11	11	26	13	13	31	16	16
30-34	16	8	8	19	9	9	23	11	11	25	13	12
35-39	14	7	7	15	8	8	18	9	9	22	11	11
40-44	11	6	6	13	6	6	15	7	8	17	9	9
45-49	9	5	5	10	5	5	12	6	6	14	7	7
50-54	8	4	4	8	4	4	10	5	5	12	6	6
55-59	6	3	3	7	3	4	8	4	4	9	4	5
60-64	4	2	2	5	2	3	6	3	3	7	3	4
65-69	3	1	2	4	2	2	4	2	2	5	2	3
70-74	2	1	1	2	1	1	3	1	2	3	1	2
75-79	1	0	1	1	1	1	2	1	1	2	1	1
80 +	1	0	0	1	0	0	1	0	1	1	0	1

Age group	1990 Both sexes	1990 Males	1990 Females	1995 Both sexes	1995 Males	1995 Females	2000 Both sexes	2000 Males	2000 Females	2005 Both sexes	2005 Males	2005 Females
All ages	527	263	263	607	304	303	699	350	349	798	400	398
0-4	92	47	46	101	51	50	115	59	57	127	65	62
5-9	85	43	42	89	45	44	98	50	48	112	57	55
10-14	70	35	35	84	43	42	88	44	43	96	49	47
15-19	57	29	29	68	34	34	83	42	41	86	43	43
20-24	48	24	24	56	28	28	67	34	33	81	41	40
25-29	38	19	19	46	23	23	55	28	27	65	33	32
30-34	30	15	15	37	19	19	45	23	22	53	27	27
35-39	24	12	12	29	15	15	36	18	18	44	22	22
40-44	21	10	10	23	12	11	28	14	14	35	17	17
45-49	17	8	8	20	10	10	22	11	11	27	13	14
50-54	13	6	7	16	8	8	19	9	10	21	10	10
55-59	11	5	5	12	6	6	14	7	8	17	8	9
60-64	8	4	4	9	4	5	11	5	6	13	6	7
65-69	6	3	3	7	3	4	8	4	4	9	4	5
70-74	4	2	2	4	2	2	5	2	3	6	3	3
75-79	2	1	1	3	1	1	3	1	2	4	2	2
80 +	1	0	1	1	1	1	2	1	1	2	1	1

(*) Including the island of Mayotte.

306

United Nations Department of Economic and Social Affairs/Population Division
World Population Prospects: The 2004 Revision, Volume II: Sex and Age Distribution of the World Population

POPULATION BY AGE AND SEX (in thousands)

Age group	2005 Both sexes	Males	Females	2010 Both sexes	Males	Females	2015 Both sexes	Males	Females	2020 Both sexes	Males	Females
All ages	798	400	398	907	455	452	1 019	511	507	1 130	567	560
0-4	127	65	62	134	68	66	137	70	67	138	70	68
5-9	112	57	55	125	63	61	132	67	65	135	69	67
10-14	96	49	47	111	56	55	124	63	61	131	67	65
15-19	86	43	43	95	48	47	110	56	54	122	62	60
20-24	81	41	40	85	43	42	93	47	46	109	55	54
25-29	65	33	32	79	40	39	83	42	41	92	47	46
30-34	53	27	27	64	32	32	78	39	39	82	41	41
35-39	44	22	22	52	26	26	63	31	31	77	39	38
40-44	35	17	17	43	21	21	51	25	26	62	31	31
45-49	27	13	14	34	17	17	41	21	21	50	25	25
50-54	21	10	10	26	13	13	32	16	16	40	20	20
55-59	17	8	9	19	10	10	24	12	12	31	15	16
60-64	13	6	7	16	7	8	18	9	9	22	11	12
65-69	9	4	5	11	5	6	14	6	7	16	7	8
70-74	6	3	3	7	3	4	9	4	5	11	5	6
75-79	4	2	2	4	2	3	5	2	3	7	3	4
80-84	2	1	1	2	1	1	2	1	1	3	1	2
85-89	1	0	0	1	0	0	1	0	1	1	0	1
90-94	0	0	0	0	0	0	0	0	0	0	0	0
95-99	0	0	0	0	0	0	0	0	0	0	0	0
100 +	0	0	0	0	0	0	0	0	0	0	0	0

Age group	2025 Both sexes	Males	Females	2030 Both sexes	Males	Females	2035 Both sexes	Males	Females	2040 Both sexes	Males	Females
All ages	1 242	623	619	1 357	681	677	1 472	738	734	1 583	793	790
0-4	142	72	70	147	75	72	150	77	74	150	77	74
5-9	137	70	67	141	72	69	146	74	72	149	76	73
10-14	134	68	66	136	69	67	140	71	69	145	74	71
15-19	130	66	64	133	68	66	136	69	67	140	71	69
20-24	121	61	60	129	65	64	133	67	65	135	68	66
25-29	107	54	53	120	61	60	128	65	63	132	67	65
30-34	91	46	45	106	54	53	119	60	59	127	64	63
35-39	81	41	41	90	45	45	105	53	52	118	60	59
40-44	76	38	38	80	40	40	80	45	44	104	52	52
45-49	60	30	30	74	37	37	79	39	39	88	44	44
50-54	48	24	24	59	29	30	72	36	37	77	38	39
55-59	38	19	19	46	23	24	56	28	29	70	34	36
60-64	28	14	15	35	17	18	43	21	22	53	26	27
65-69	20	9	11	26	12	14	32	15	17	39	18	21
70-74	13	6	7	17	8	9	22	10	12	27	12	15
75-79	8	4	5	10	4	5	13	5	7	17	7	9
80-84	4	2	2	5	2	3	6	2	4	8	3	5
85-89	1	0	1	2	1	1	2	1	1	3	1	2
90-94	0	0	0	0	0	0	1	0	0	1	0	1
95-99	0	0	0	0	0	0	0	0	0	0	0	0
100 +	0	0	0	0	0	0	0	0	0	0	0	0

Age group	2045 Both sexes	Males	Females	2050 Both sexes	Males	Females
All ages	1 686	844	842	1 781	890	891
0-4	148	76	72	145	74	71
5-9	149	76	73	147	75	72
10-14	149	76	73	149	76	73
15-19	145	74	71	148	75	73
20-24	139	70	68	144	73	71
25-29	134	68	66	138	70	68
30-34	131	66	65	133	67	66
35-39	126	64	63	130	66	64
40-44	117	59	58	125	63	62
45-49	103	52	51	116	58	58
50-54	86	43	43	101	50	50
55-59	74	37	38	83	41	42
60-64	66	32	34	71	34	36
65-69	48	23	26	61	29	32
70-74	34	15	19	42	19	23
75-79	21	9	12	27	11	15
80-84	11	4	7	14	6	9
85-89	4	1	3	6	2	4
90-94	1	0	1	1	0	1
95-99	0	0	0	0	0	0
100 +	0	0	0	0	0	0

United Nations Department of Economic and Social Affairs/Population Division
World Population Prospects: The 2004 Revision, Volume II: Sex and Age Distribution of the World Population

307

POPULATION BY AGE AND SEX (in thousands)

Age group	2005 Both sexes	2005 Males	2005 Females	2010 Both sexes	2010 Males	2010 Females	2015 Both sexes	2015 Males	2015 Females	2020 Both sexes	2020 Males	2020 Females
All ages	798	400	398	915	459	456	1 041	523	518	1 173	589	584
0-4	127	65	62	142	72	70	151	77	74	159	81	78
5-9	112	57	55	125	63	61	140	71	69	150	76	74
10-14	96	49	47	111	56	55	124	63	61	139	70	68
15-19	86	43	43	95	48	47	110	56	54	122	62	60
20-24	81	41	40	85	43	42	93	47	46	109	55	54
25-29	65	33	32	79	40	39	83	42	41	92	47	46
30-34	53	27	27	64	32	32	78	39	39	82	41	41
35-39	44	22	22	52	26	26	63	31	31	77	39	38
40-44	35	17	17	43	21	21	51	25	26	62	31	31
45-49	27	13	14	34	17	17	41	21	21	50	25	25
50-54	21	10	10	26	13	13	32	16	16	40	20	20
55-59	17	8	9	19	10	10	24	12	12	31	15	16
60-64	13	6	7	16	7	8	18	9	9	22	11	12
65-69	9	4	5	11	5	6	14	6	7	16	7	8
70-74	6	3	3	7	3	4	9	4	5	11	5	6
75-79	4	2	2	4	2	3	5	2	3	7	3	4
80-84	2	1	1	2	1	1	2	1	1	3	1	2
85-89	1	0	0	1	0	0	1	0	1	1	0	1
90-94	0	0	0	0	0	0	0	0	0	0	0	0
95-99	0	0	0	0	0	0	0	0	0	0	0	0
100 +	0	0	0	0	0	0	0	0	0	0	0	0

Age group	2025 Both sexes	2025 Males	2025 Females	2030 Both sexes	2030 Males	2030 Females	2035 Both sexes	2035 Males	2035 Females	2040 Both sexes	2040 Males	2040 Females
All ages	1 309	657	652	1 453	729	723	1 603	805	799	1 759	882	876
0-4	166	84	81	176	89	86	186	95	91	195	100	96
5-9	158	80	78	165	84	81	175	89	86	185	94	91
10-14	149	75	73	157	80	77	164	83	81	174	88	86
15-19	138	70	68	148	75	73	156	79	77	163	83	80
20-24	121	61	60	137	69	68	147	74	73	155	79	77
25-29	107	54	53	120	61	60	136	69	67	146	74	72
30-34	91	46	45	106	54	53	119	60	59	135	68	67
35-39	81	41	41	90	45	45	105	53	52	118	60	59
40-44	76	38	38	80	40	40	89	45	44	104	52	52
45-49	60	30	30	74	37	37	79	39	39	88	44	44
50-54	48	24	24	59	29	30	72	36	37	77	38	39
55-59	38	19	19	46	23	24	56	28	29	70	34	36
60-64	28	14	15	35	17	18	43	21	22	53	26	27
65-69	20	9	11	26	12	14	32	15	17	39	18	21
70-74	13	6	7	17	8	9	22	10	12	27	12	15
75-79	8	4	5	10	4	5	13	5	7	17	7	9
80-84	4	2	2	5	2	3	6	2	4	8	3	5
85-89	1	0	1	2	1	1	2	1	1	3	1	2
90-94	0	0	0	0	0	0	1	0	0	1	0	1
95-99	0	0	0	0	0	0	0	0	0	0	0	0
100 +	0	0	0	0	0	0	0	0	0	0	0	0

Age group	2045 Both sexes	2045 Males	2045 Females	2050 Both sexes	2050 Males	2050 Females
All ages	1 915	960	955	2 070	1 037	1 032
0-4	201	103	99	206	105	101
5-9	194	99	95	201	102	98
10-14	185	94	91	194	99	95
15-19	173	88	85	184	94	90
20-24	162	82	80	172	88	85
25-29	154	78	76	162	82	80
30-34	145	73	72	153	78	76
35-39	134	67	66	144	73	71
40-44	117	59	58	133	67	66
45-49	103	52	51	116	58	58
50-54	86	43	43	101	50	50
55-59	74	37	38	83	41	42
60-64	66	32	34	71	34	36
65-69	48	23	26	61	29	32
70-74	34	15	19	42	19	23
75-79	21	9	12	27	11	15
80-84	11	4	7	14	6	9
85-89	4	1	3	6	2	4
90-94	1	0	1	1	0	1
95-99	0	0	0	0	0	0
100 +	0	0	0	0	0	0

United Nations Department of Economic and Social Affairs/Population Division
World Population Prospects: The 2004 Revision, Volume II: Sex and Age Distribution of the World Population

308

POPULATION BY AGE AND SEX (in thousands)

Age group	2005 Both sexes	Males	Females	2010 Both sexes	Males	Females	2015 Both sexes	Males	Females	2020 Both sexes	Males	Females
All ages	798	400	398	900	451	448	996	500	496	1 087	545	542
0-4	127	66	62	126	64	62	122	62	60	118	60	58
5-9	112	57	55	125	63	61	124	63	61	121	61	59
10-14	96	49	47	111	56	55	124	63	61	123	63	61
15-19	86	43	43	95	48	47	110	56	54	122	62	60
20-24	81	41	40	85	43	42	93	47	46	109	55	54
25-29	65	33	32	79	40	39	83	42	41	92	47	46
30-34	53	27	27	64	32	32	78	39	39	82	41	41
35-39	44	22	22	52	26	26	63	31	31	77	39	38
40-44	35	17	17	43	21	21	51	25	26	62	31	31
45-49	27	13	14	34	17	17	41	21	21	50	25	25
50-54	21	10	10	26	13	13	32	16	16	40	20	20
55-59	17	8	9	19	10	10	24	12	12	31	15	16
60-64	13	6	7	16	7	8	18	9	9	22	11	12
65-69	9	4	5	11	5	6	14	6	7	16	7	8
70-74	6	3	3	7	3	4	9	4	5	11	5	6
75-79	4	2	2	4	2	3	5	2	3	7	3	4
80-84	2	1	1	2	1	1	2	1	1	3	1	2
85-89	1	0	0	1	0	0	1	0	1	1	0	1
90-94	0	0	0	0	0	0	0	0	0	0	0	0
95-99	0	0	0	0	0	0	0	0	0	0	0	0
100 +	0	0	0	0	0	0	0	0	0	0	0	0

Age group	2025 Both sexes	Males	Females	2030 Both sexes	Males	Females	2035 Both sexes	Males	Females	2040 Both sexes	Males	Females
All ages	1 176	590	586	1 263	633	630	1 344	673	671	1 415	707	708
0-4	118	60	58	119	61	58	116	59	57	110	56	54
5-9	116	59	57	117	60	58	118	60	58	116	59	57
10-14	120	61	59	116	59	57	117	59	57	117	60	58
15-19	122	62	60	119	60	59	115	58	57	116	59	57
20-24	121	61	60	121	61	60	118	60	58	114	58	56
25-29	107	54	53	120	61	60	121	61	60	117	59	58
30-34	91	46	45	106	54	53	119	60	59	120	60	59
35-39	81	41	41	90	45	45	105	53	52	118	60	59
40-44	76	38	38	80	40	40	89	45	44	104	52	52
45-49	60	30	30	74	37	37	79	39	39	88	44	44
50-54	48	24	24	59	29	30	72	36	37	77	38	39
55-59	38	19	19	46	23	24	56	28	29	70	34	36
60-64	28	14	15	35	17	18	43	21	22	53	26	27
65-69	20	9	11	26	12	14	32	15	17	39	18	21
70-74	13	6	7	17	8	9	22	10	12	27	12	15
75-79	8	4	5	10	4	5	13	5	7	17	7	9
80-84	4	2	2	5	2	3	6	2	4	8	3	5
85-89	1	0	1	2	1	1	2	1	1	3	1	2
90-94	0	0	0	0	0	0	1	0	0	1	0	1
95-99	0	0	0	0	0	0	0	0	0	0	0	0
100 +	0	0	0	0	0	0	0	0	0	0	0	0

Age group	2045 Both sexes	Males	Females	2050 Both sexes	Males	Females
All ages	1 473	735	738	1 518	756	761
0-4	102	52	50	95	49	46
5-9	109	56	54	102	52	50
10-14	115	59	57	109	55	53
15-19	117	59	57	115	58	56
20-24	115	58	57	116	59	57
25-29	113	57	56	114	58	56
30-34	116	59	58	113	57	56
35-39	119	60	59	116	58	57
40-44	117	59	58	118	59	58
45-49	103	52	51	116	58	58
50-54	86	43	43	101	50	50
55-59	74	37	38	83	41	42
60-64	66	32	34	71	34	36
65-69	48	23	26	61	29	32
70-74	34	15	19	42	19	23
75-79	21	9	12	27	11	15
80-84	11	4	7	14	6	9
85-89	4	1	3	6	2	4
90-94	1	0	1	1	0	1
95-99	0	0	0	0	0	0
100 +	0	0	0	0	0	0

POPULATION BY AGE AND SEX (in thousands)

Age group	1950 Both sexes	1950 Males	1950 Females	1955 Both sexes	1955 Males	1955 Females	1960 Both sexes	1960 Males	1960 Females	1965 Both sexes	1965 Males	1965 Females
All ages	808	397	411	895	438	456	1 003	491	512	1 143	560	583
0-4	129	64	65	144	71	73	166	82	83	197	98	99
5-9	104	52	52	119	59	60	134	66	68	156	77	79
10-14	91	45	46	102	50	51	117	58	59	132	65	67
15-19	80	40	40	88	44	44	99	49	50	114	57	58
20-24	71	35	36	78	39	39	86	43	43	97	48	49
25-29	62	30	31	68	34	34	75	37	38	83	41	42
30-34	54	26	27	59	29	30	65	32	33	72	36	36
35-39	46	23	24	51	25	26	56	28	29	62	31	32
40-44	40	19	20	44	21	22	48	23	25	53	26	27
45-49	34	16	17	37	18	19	41	20	21	45	22	24
50-54	28	14	15	31	15	16	34	16	18	38	18	20
55-59	23	11	12	25	12	13	28	13	15	31	14	16
60-64	18	8	10	19	9	11	21	10	12	24	11	13
65-69	13	6	7	14	6	8	16	7	9	17	8	10
70-74	8	4	5	9	4	5	10	4	6	12	5	7
75-79	4	2	3	5	2	3	6	2	3	6	3	4
80 +	2	1	1	3	1	2	3	1	2	4	1	2

Age group	1970 Both sexes	1970 Males	1970 Females	1975 Both sexes	1975 Males	1975 Females	1980 Both sexes	1980 Males	1980 Females	1985 Both sexes	1985 Males	1985 Females
All ages	1 323	649	674	1 544	759	785	1 803	888	915	2 114	1 043	1 071
0-4	236	118	118	279	140	139	325	163	162	383	192	191
5-9	188	93	94	227	113	114	270	135	135	314	157	157
10-14	154	76	78	186	92	93	225	112	113	267	133	134
15-19	130	64	66	152	75	77	183	91	92	222	111	112
20-24	112	55	56	127	63	65	149	74	76	180	89	91
25-29	94	47	47	109	54	55	124	61	63	146	72	74
30-34	80	40	41	92	45	46	107	53	54	121	60	62
35-39	70	34	35	78	39	40	89	44	45	104	51	53
40-44	60	29	31	67	33	34	75	37	38	86	42	44
45-49	51	25	26	57	28	29	64	31	33	72	35	37
50-54	42	20	22	48	23	25	54	26	28	61	29	31
55-59	35	16	18	39	18	21	44	21	23	50	24	26
60-64	27	12	15	31	14	17	35	16	19	39	18	21
65-69	20	9	11	23	10	13	26	11	14	29	13	16
70-74	13	6	8	15	6	9	17	7	10	20	9	11
75-79	7	3	4	9	4	5	10	4	6	12	5	7
80 +	4	2	3	5	2	3	6	2	4	7	3	4

Age group	1990 Both sexes	1990 Males	1990 Females	1995 Both sexes	1995 Males	1995 Females	2000 Both sexes	2000 Males	2000 Females	2005 Both sexes	2005 Males	2005 Females
All ages	2 484	1 226	1 258	2 916	1 439	1 477	3 438	1 701	1 737	3 999	1 983	2 016
0-4	455	228	227	540	271	269	640	321	319	750	376	373
5-9	372	186	186	442	221	221	525	263	262	620	310	309
10-14	312	156	156	369	184	185	437	219	219	516	258	258
15-19	264	132	132	309	154	155	368	184	184	432	216	216
20-24	218	108	110	261	130	131	310	155	156	359	179	180
25-29	175	86	89	209	103	105	257	128	129	296	148	149
30-34	142	69	72	165	81	84	197	98	99	238	120	119
35-39	117	57	60	134	65	69	154	75	78	178	90	88
40-44	100	49	51	111	54	58	125	60	64	139	68	71
45-49	82	40	42	95	46	49	104	50	55	114	55	59
50-54	68	33	35	78	37	40	89	42	46	96	45	51
55-59	56	27	29	63	30	33	72	34	38	81	38	43
60-64	45	21	24	51	24	27	57	27	31	64	29	34
65-69	33	15	18	38	17	21	43	20	24	48	22	27
70-74	23	10	13	26	11	15	30	13	17	34	15	19
75-79	13	5	8	16	6	9	18	8	11	20	9	12
80 +	8	3	5	9	4	6	12	5	7	14	5	9

United Nations Department of Economic and Social Affairs/Population Division
World Population Prospects: The 2004 Revision, Volume II: Sex and Age Distribution of the World Population

310

POPULATION BY AGE AND SEX (in thousands)

Age group	2005			2010			2015			2020		
	Both sexes	Males	Females	Both sexes	Males	Females	Both sexes	Males	Females	Both sexes	Males	Females
All ages	3 999	1 983	2 016	4 633	2 302	2 331	5 441	2 708	2 733	6 363	3 172	3 191
0-4	750	376	373	874	439	435	1 011	508	503	1 142	574	569
5-9	620	310	309	726	364	362	853	427	426	991	496	495
10-14	516	258	258	609	305	304	716	358	358	843	422	421
15-19	432	216	216	507	253	253	604	302	302	710	355	355
20-24	359	179	180	416	208	208	499	249	250	595	297	298
25-29	296	148	149	335	167	168	401	201	201	483	242	242
30-34	238	120	119	270	135	134	315	159	157	379	191	188
35-39	178	90	88	215	109	106	250	127	124	294	149	145
40-44	139	68	71	161	81	80	200	101	99	233	118	115
45-49	114	55	59	127	62	65	150	75	75	187	95	92
50-54	96	45	51	104	49	55	118	57	61	140	70	70
55-59	81	38	43	87	40	47	96	45	51	109	52	57
60-64	64	29	34	72	33	39	78	35	43	87	40	47
65-69	48	22	27	54	24	30	61	27	34	67	30	38
70-74	34	15	19	38	16	21	43	19	24	49	21	28
75-79	20	9	12	23	10	13	26	11	15	30	12	18
80-84	10	4	6	11	4	7	13	5	8	15	6	9
85-89	3	1	2	4	1	2	4	2	3	5	2	3
90-94	1	0	0	1	0	1	1	0	1	1	0	1
95-99	0	0	0	0	0	0	0	0	0	0	0	0
100 +	0	0	0	0	0	0	0	0	0	0	0	0

Age group	2025			2030			2035			2040		
	Both sexes	Males	Females	Both sexes	Males	Females	Both sexes	Males	Females	Both sexes	Males	Females
All ages	7 404	3 695	3 709	8 551	4 271	4 280	9 777	4 887	4 890	11 057	5 529	5 528
0-4	1 275	641	635	1 397	702	695	1 495	752	743	1 570	790	780
5-9	1 125	564	561	1 261	632	629	1 384	695	690	1 485	746	739
10-14	983	492	491	1 118	560	558	1 255	629	626	1 379	691	688
15-19	837	418	419	977	488	489	1 113	556	556	1 250	625	624
20-24	702	350	351	828	413	415	968	483	485	1 104	551	553
25-29	578	289	289	683	341	342	809	404	405	949	473	476
30-34	459	231	228	552	277	275	655	329	327	780	391	389
35-39	356	180	175	433	219	214	524	265	259	626	315	310
40-44	275	140	135	335	170	165	411	209	202	500	253	247
45-49	219	111	108	260	132	128	318	162	157	392	100	104
50-54	176	88	87	207	104	103	246	124	122	303	153	150
55-59	130	64	66	164	81	83	194	96	98	232	116	116
60-64	99	46	53	119	57	62	150	70	77	179	87	82
65-69	75	34	42	87	40	47	105	49	56	133	63	70
70-74	54	23	31	61	26	35	71	31	40	86	39	47
75-79	35	14	20	39	16	23	44	18	26	52	22	30
80-84	17	7	10	20	8	12	23	9	14	26	10	16
85-89	6	2	4	7	3	4	8	3	5	10	3	6
90-94	1	0	1	2	1	1	2	1	1	2	1	2
95-99	0	0	0	0	0	0	0	0	0	0	0	0
100 +	0	0	0	0	0	0	0	0	0	0	0	0

Age group	2045			2050		
	Both sexes	Males	Females	Both sexes	Males	Females
All ages	12 375	6 189	6 186	13 721	6 862	6 859
0-4	1 630	821	809	1 684	849	835
5-9	1 562	785	777	1 623	817	807
10-14	1 480	743	737	1 558	783	775
15-19	1 375	688	686	1 476	740	736
20-24	1 241	620	621	1 367	683	683
25-29	1 085	541	544	1 223	611	612
30-34	919	460	459	1 056	528	527
35-39	749	377	372	887	446	442
40-44	600	303	297	722	364	358
45-49	479	242	237	578	292	287
50-54	375	189	186	460	231	229
55-59	287	143	144	357	178	179
60-64	215	105	110	267	131	136
65-69	159	75	84	192	92	101
70-74	110	50	60	133	61	72
75-79	63	27	36	82	36	46
80-84	31	12	19	38	16	23
85-89	11	4	7	14	5	9
90-94	3	1	2	3	1	2
95-99	0	0	0	0	0	0
100 +	0	0	0	0	0	0

POPULATION BY AGE AND SEX (in thousands)

Age group	2005 Both sexes	2005 Males	2005 Females	2010 Both sexes	2010 Males	2010 Females	2015 Both sexes	2015 Males	2015 Females	2020 Both sexes	2020 Males	2020 Females
All ages	3 999	1 983	2 016	4 633	2 302	2 331	5 474	2 725	2 749	6 496	3 238	3 257
0-4	750	376	373	874	439	435	1 044	524	520	1 243	624	619
5-9	620	310	309	726	364	362	853	427	426	1 024	513	511
10-14	516	258	258	609	305	304	716	358	358	843	422	421
15-19	432	216	216	507	253	253	604	302	302	710	355	355
20-24	359	179	180	416	208	208	499	249	250	595	297	298
25-29	296	148	149	335	167	168	401	201	201	483	242	242
30-34	238	120	119	270	135	134	315	159	157	379	191	188
35-39	178	90	88	215	109	106	250	127	124	294	149	145
40-44	139	68	71	161	81	80	200	101	99	233	118	115
45-49	114	55	59	127	62	65	150	75	75	187	95	92
50-54	96	45	51	104	49	55	118	57	61	140	70	70
55-59	81	38	43	87	40	47	96	45	51	109	52	57
60-64	64	29	34	72	33	39	78	35	43	87	40	47
65-69	48	22	27	54	24	30	61	27	34	67	30	38
70-74	34	15	19	38	16	21	43	19	24	49	21	28
75-79	20	9	12	23	10	13	26	11	15	30	12	18
80-84	10	4	6	11	4	7	13	5	8	15	6	9
85-89	3	1	2	4	1	2	4	2	3	5	2	3
90-94	1	0	0	1	0	1	1	0	1	1	0	1
95-99	0	0	0	0	0	0	0	0	0	0	0	0
100 +	0	0	0	0	0	0	0	0	0	0	0	0

Age group	2025 Both sexes	2025 Males	2025 Females	2030 Both sexes	2030 Males	2030 Females	2035 Both sexes	2035 Males	2035 Females	2040 Both sexes	2040 Males	2040 Females
All ages	7 658	3 822	3 836	8 955	4 474	4 481	10 380	5 189	5 191	11 937	5 971	5 967
0-4	1 398	703	696	1 549	779	770	1 697	854	843	1 850	932	919
5-9	1 225	613	611	1 382	693	689	1 536	770	765	1 685	846	839
10-14	1 015	508	507	1 217	609	608	1 376	689	687	1 530	767	763
15-19	837	418	419	1 009	504	505	1 211	605	606	1 370	686	685
20-24	702	350	351	828	413	415	1 000	499	501	1 201	600	602
25-29	578	289	289	683	341	342	809	404	405	980	489	491
30-34	459	231	228	552	277	275	655	329	327	780	391	389
35-39	356	180	175	433	219	214	524	265	259	626	315	310
40-44	275	140	135	335	170	165	411	209	202	500	253	247
45-49	219	111	108	260	132	128	318	162	157	392	199	194
50-54	176	88	87	207	104	103	246	124	122	303	153	150
55-59	130	64	66	164	81	83	194	96	98	232	116	116
60-64	99	46	53	119	57	62	150	73	77	179	87	92
65-69	75	34	42	87	40	47	105	49	56	133	63	70
70-74	54	23	31	61	26	35	71	31	40	86	39	47
75-79	35	14	20	39	16	23	44	18	26	52	22	30
80-84	17	7	10	20	8	12	23	9	14	26	10	16
85-89	6	2	4	7	3	4	8	3	5	10	3	6
90-94	1	0	1	2	1	1	2	1	1	2	1	2
95-99	0	0	0	0	0	0	0	0	0	0	0	0
100 +	0	0	0	0	0	0	0	0	0	0	0	0

Age group	2045 Both sexes	2045 Males	2045 Females	2050 Both sexes	2050 Males	2050 Females
All ages	13 621	6 815	6 806	15 411	7 711	7 700
0-4	2 001	1 008	993	2 138	1 078	1 060
5-9	1 840	925	915	1 993	1 003	990
10-14	1 680	843	837	1 836	922	914
15-19	1 525	764	761	1 675	840	835
20-24	1 361	680	681	1 516	758	758
25-29	1 181	589	592	1 341	670	671
30-34	949	475	474	1 149	575	574
35-39	749	377	372	916	461	456
40-44	600	303	297	722	364	358
45-49	479	242	237	578	292	287
50-54	375	189	186	460	231	229
55-59	287	143	144	357	178	179
60-64	215	105	110	267	131	136
65-69	159	75	84	192	92	101
70-74	110	50	60	133	61	72
75-79	63	27	36	82	36	46
80-84	31	12	19	38	16	23
85-89	11	4	7	14	5	9
90-94	3	1	2	3	1	2
95-99	0	0	0	0	0	0
100 +	0	0	0	0	0	0

United Nations Department of Economic and Social Affairs/Population Division
World Population Prospects: The 2004 Revision, Volume II: Sex and Age Distribution of the World Population

312

POPULATION BY AGE AND SEX (in thousands)

Age group	2005 Both sexes	Males	Females	2010 Both sexes	Males	Females	2015 Both sexes	Males	Females	2020 Both sexes	Males	Females
All ages	3 999	1 983	2 016	4 598	2 284	2 314	5 340	2 658	2 683	6 160	3 071	3 092
0-4	750	376	373	839	421	418	945	474	470	1 042	523	518
5-9	620	310	309	726	364	362	819	410	409	926	464	462
10-14	516	258	258	609	305	304	716	358	358	810	405	405
15-19	432	216	216	507	253	253	604	302	302	710	355	355
20-24	359	179	180	416	208	208	499	249	250	595	297	298
25-29	296	148	149	335	167	168	401	201	201	483	242	242
30-34	238	120	119	270	135	134	315	159	157	379	191	188
35-39	178	90	88	215	109	106	250	127	124	294	149	145
40-44	139	68	71	161	81	80	200	101	99	233	118	115
45-49	114	55	59	127	62	65	150	75	75	187	95	92
50-54	96	45	51	104	49	55	118	57	61	140	70	70
55-59	81	38	43	87	40	47	96	45	51	109	52	57
60-64	64	29	34	72	33	39	78	35	43	87	40	47
65-69	48	22	27	54	24	30	61	27	34	67	30	38
70-74	34	15	19	38	16	21	43	19	24	49	21	28
75-79	20	9	12	23	10	13	26	11	15	30	12	18
80-84	10	4	6	11	4	7	13	5	8	15	6	9
85-89	3	1	2	4	1	2	4	2	3	5	2	3
90-94	1	0	0	1	0	1	1	0	1	1	0	1
95-99	0	0	0	0	0	0	0	0	0	0	0	0
100 +	0	0	0	0	0	0	0	0	0	0	0	0

Age group	2025 Both sexes	Males	Females	2030 Both sexes	Males	Females	2035 Both sexes	Males	Females	2040 Both sexes	Males	Females
All ages	7 080	3 533	3 548	8 063	4 026	4 036	9 067	4 531	4 536	10 063	5 030	5 032
0-4	1 149	577	572	1 229	618	611	1 270	639	631	1 279	644	635
5-9	1 026	514	512	1 136	569	566	1 219	611	607	1 261	633	628
10-14	918	459	459	1 019	510	509	1 130	566	564	1 214	609	605
15-19	804	402	402	913	456	457	1 015	507	507	1 126	563	563
20-24	702	350	351	795	397	399	905	451	453	1 006	502	504
25-29	578	289	289	683	341	342	777	388	389	887	442	444
30-34	459	231	228	552	277	275	655	329	327	749	375	374
35-39	356	180	175	433	219	214	524	265	259	626	315	310
40-44	275	140	135	335	170	165	411	209	202	500	253	247
45-49	219	111	108	260	132	128	318	162	157	392	199	194
50-54	176	88	87	207	104	103	246	124	122	303	153	150
55-59	130	64	66	164	81	83	194	96	98	232	116	116
60-64	99	46	53	119	57	62	150	73	77	179	87	92
65-69	75	34	42	87	40	47	105	49	56	133	63	70
70-74	54	23	31	61	26	35	71	31	40	86	39	47
75-79	35	14	20	39	16	23	44	18	26	52	22	30
80-84	17	7	10	20	8	12	23	9	14	28	10	18
85-89	6	2	4	7	3	4	8	3	5	10	3	6
90-94	1	0	1	2	1	1	2	1	1	2	1	2
95-99	0	0	0	0	0	0	0	0	0	0	0	0
100 +	0	0	0	0	0	0	0	0	0	0	0	0

Age group	2045 Both sexes	Males	Females	2050 Both sexes	Males	Females
All ages	11 035	5 516	5 518	11 975	5 985	5 990
0-4	1 275	642	633	1 267	639	628
5-9	1 272	640	633	1 270	639	631
10-14	1 257	631	626	1 269	638	632
15-19	1 210	606	604	1 254	629	625
20-24	1 118	559	560	1 203	601	602
25-29	989	494	496	1 102	550	552
30-34	859	430	429	962	482	481
35-39	719	362	357	829	417	413
40-44	600	303	297	694	350	344
45-49	479	242	237	578	292	287
50-54	375	189	186	460	231	229
55-59	287	143	144	357	178	179
60-64	215	105	110	267	131	136
65-69	159	75	84	192	92	101
70-74	110	50	60	133	61	72
75-79	63	27	36	82	36	46
80-84	31	12	19	38	16	23
85-89	11	4	7	14	5	9
90-94	3	1	2	3	1	2
95-99	0	0	0	0	0	0
100 +	0	0	0	0	0	0

POPULATION BY AGE AND SEX (in thousands)

Age group	1950			1955			1960			1965		
	Both sexes	Males	Females	Both sexes	Males	Females	Both sexes	Males	Females	Both sexes	Males	Females
All ages	966	493	473	1 129	575	554	1 334	679	655	1 582	804	778
0-4	155	79	76	207	105	102	249	127	122	293	149	144
5-9	117	59	58	149	76	73	201	102	99	243	123	120
10-14	100	50	49	116	58	58	148	75	73	199	101	98
15-19	86	43	43	99	50	49	115	58	57	147	75	73
20-24	79	41	39	85	43	43	98	49	49	114	57	57
25-29	64	33	31	78	40	38	84	42	42	97	49	48
30-34	68	36	32	63	32	31	77	39	38	83	41	42
35-39	57	31	26	66	35	31	62	32	30	76	39	37
40-44	49	26	23	55	30	26	65	34	30	61	31	29
45-49	44	23	21	48	25	22	54	29	25	63	34	30
50-54	40	21	20	42	22	20	46	24	21	52	28	24
55-59	33	16	16	37	19	18	39	20	19	43	23	20
60-64	27	13	14	29	15	15	34	17	17	36	19	17
65-69	20	9	11	23	11	12	25	12	13	30	15	15
70-74	14	6	7	16	7	8	18	9	10	21	10	11
75-79	8	4	4	9	4	5	11	5	6	13	6	7
80 +	5	2	3	6	3	3	8	3	4	10	4	5

Age group	1970			1975			1980			1985		
	Both sexes	Males	Females	Both sexes	Males	Females	Both sexes	Males	Females	Both sexes	Males	Females
All ages	1 821	924	897	2 051	1 039	1 011	2 347	1 196	1 151	2 697	1 373	1 323
0-4	285	145	140	279	142	137	318	163	156	367	188	179
5-9	288	147	142	283	144	139	276	141	135	321	164	157
10-14	242	123	119	287	146	141	292	150	142	280	143	137
15-19	199	101	98	241	122	119	288	149	140	296	153	144
20-24	147	74	72	197	100	97	247	128	120	292	151	141
25-29	113	57	57	145	74	72	195	100	95	250	129	121
30-34	96	48	48	112	56	56	146	74	72	196	100	96
35-39	82	41	41	95	48	47	113	56	57	147	74	73
40-44	75	38	37	81	40	41	95	48	48	113	56	57
45-49	59	30	29	73	37	36	81	40	41	95	47	48
50-54	61	32	29	58	29	28	72	37	36	80	40	40
55-59	49	26	23	58	31	28	56	29	28	71	36	35
60-64	40	21	19	46	24	22	56	29	27	54	27	27
65-69	32	16	16	36	18	17	42	22	20	51	26	25
70-74	25	12	13	27	13	13	31	15	15	37	18	18
75-79	15	7	8	18	9	10	21	10	11	24	12	13
80 +	12	5	7	14	6	8	18	8	10	21	9	12

Age group	1990			1995			2000			2005		
	Both sexes	Males	Females	Both sexes	Males	Females	Both sexes	Males	Females	Both sexes	Males	Females
All ages	3 076	1 565	1 511	3 475	1 768	1 707	3 929	1 998	1 931	4 327	2 200	2 127
0-4	411	211	201	404	207	197	397	203	193	393	201	191
5-9	370	189	181	418	215	203	419	216	203	406	209	198
10-14	323	165	158	376	193	183	432	222	210	428	220	208
15-19	284	145	139	333	170	163	398	204	194	446	229	217
20-24	300	154	145	293	150	143	353	181	173	411	211	200
25-29	293	151	142	305	157	148	306	156	150	361	185	177
30-34	250	129	121	296	152	144	313	160	153	311	158	153
35-39	196	100	96	251	129	122	301	154	147	316	162	155
40-44	147	74	73	197	100	97	255	131	124	303	155	148
45-49	112	56	57	146	73	73	197	100	97	254	130	124
50-54	94	47	47	112	55	56	146	73	73	196	99	97
55-59	78	38	39	92	46	46	110	54	56	144	72	72
60-64	68	34	34	75	37	38	89	44	45	107	52	54
65-69	50	25	25	63	31	32	71	34	37	84	41	43
70-74	45	22	23	44	21	23	57	27	30	64	30	34
75-79	30	14	15	37	18	19	37	17	20	48	22	26
80 +	26	11	14	33	15	18	46	21	26	55	24	31

United Nations Department of Economic and Social Affairs/Population Division
World Population Prospects: The 2004 Revision, Volume II: Sex and Age Distribution of the World Population

POPULATION BY AGE AND SEX (in thousands)

Age group	2005			2010			2015			2020		
	Both sexes	Males	Females	Both sexes	Males	Females	Both sexes	Males	Females	Both sexes	Males	Females
All ages	4 327	2 200	2 127	4 665	2 369	2 296	4 983	2 527	2 456	5 276	2 672	2 604
0-4	393	201	191	396	203	193	388	199	190	379	194	185
5-9	406	209	198	396	203	193	399	204	195	392	201	191
10-14	428	220	208	409	210	199	399	205	194	402	206	196
15-19	446	229	217	433	223	210	414	213	201	404	207	197
20-24	411	211	200	450	231	219	437	225	212	418	215	203
25-29	361	185	177	413	211	201	451	232	220	439	226	213
30-34	311	158	153	362	185	177	413	211	202	452	232	220
35-39	316	162	155	311	158	153	362	184	178	413	211	202
40-44	303	155	148	315	161	155	310	157	153	361	183	177
45-49	254	130	124	300	153	147	313	159	154	308	156	152
50-54	196	99	97	250	127	123	296	150	146	309	156	152
55-59	144	72	72	191	96	95	245	124	121	290	146	143
60-64	107	52	54	139	68	70	185	92	93	237	119	118
65-69	84	41	43	101	49	52	131	64	67	175	86	89
70-74	64	30	34	76	36	40	92	43	48	120	57	63
75-79	48	22	26	55	25	30	66	30	36	79	36	43
80-84	29	13	16	37	17	21	43	19	24	52	23	29
85-89	18	8	10	19	8	11	25	11	14	29	12	17
90-94	6	3	4	9	4	6	10	4	6	13	5	8
95-99	2	1	1	2	1	1	4	1	2	4	1	2
100 +	0	0	0	0	0	0	1	0	0	1	0	1

Age group	2025			2030			2035			2040		
	Both sexes	Males	Females	Both sexes	Males	Females	Both sexes	Males	Females	Both sexes	Males	Females
All ages	5 549	2 806	2 743	5 795	2 925	2 870	6 008	3 026	2 982	6 185	3 108	3 077
0-4	378	193	185	374	191	182	369	189	180	364	186	177
5-9	383	196	187	381	195	186	377	193	184	372	191	181
10-14	395	202	192	386	198	188	385	197	187	380	195	185
15-19	407	209	198	400	205	195	391	200	190	390	200	190
20-24	408	209	199	411	211	200	404	207	197	395	203	193
25-29	421	216	205	410	210	200	414	212	202	407	209	198
30-34	440	226	214	422	216	205	412	211	201	415	212	203
35-39	452	231	221	440	225	214	422	216	206	412	211	201
40-44	412	210	202	451	230	220	438	224	214	421	215	206
45-49	358	182	177	409	208	201	447	228	220	436	222	213
50-54	305	153	151	354	179	175	404	205	200	442	224	218
55-59	303	152	150	299	148	149	347	174	173	397	200	197
60-64	280	140	140	293	146	147	289	144	146	337	168	169
65-69	224	111	113	266	131	135	279	137	142	276	135	141
70-74	160	77	83	206	100	107	245	118	127	257	124	134
75-79	104	48	56	140	65	75	181	84	96	216	101	115
80-84	63	27	36	83	37	47	113	50	63	146	65	81
85-89	36	15	21	44	18	26	58	24	34	79	33	47
90-94	16	6	10	19	7	12	24	9	15	32	12	20
95-99	5	2	3	6	2	4	7	3	5	9	3	6
100 +	1	0	1	1	0	1	1	0	1	2	1	1

Age group	2045			2050		
	Both sexes	Males	Females	Both sexes	Males	Females
All ages	6 324	3 170	3 154	6 426	3 215	3 211
0-4	359	184	175	356	182	174
5-9	367	188	179	363	186	177
10-14	375	192	183	370	190	180
15-19	385	198	188	380	195	185
20-24	394	202	192	390	200	190
25-29	398	204	194	397	204	193
30-34	408	209	199	400	205	195
35-39	415	212	203	409	209	200
40-44	411	210	201	415	212	203
45-49	418	213	205	408	208	200
50-54	431	219	212	414	210	203
55-59	434	219	215	423	214	209
60-64	385	192	193	422	211	211
65-69	321	157	164	367	180	187
70-74	255	122	133	298	143	155
75-79	228	106	122	226	104	122
80-84	176	78	98	186	82	104
85-89	104	43	61	125	52	73
90-94	44	17	28	58	22	36
95-99	12	4	8	17	6	11
100 +	2	1	1	3	1	2

United Nations Department of Economic and Social Affairs/Population Division
World Population Prospects: The 2004 Revision, Volume II: Sex and Age Distribution of the World Population

315

POPULATION BY AGE AND SEX (in thousands)

Age group	2005			2010			2015			2020		
	Both sexes	Males	Females	Both sexes	Males	Females	Both sexes	Males	Females	Both sexes	Males	Females
All ages	4 327	2 200	2 127	4 711	2 392	2 319	5 107	2 591	2 517	5 502	2 787	2 714
0-4	393	201	191	442	226	216	467	239	228	481	246	235
5-9	406	209	198	396	203	193	445	228	217	470	241	229
10-14	428	220	208	409	210	199	399	205	194	448	229	218
15-19	446	229	217	433	223	210	414	213	201	404	207	197
20-24	411	211	200	450	231	219	437	225	212	418	215	203
25-29	361	185	177	413	211	201	451	232	220	439	226	213
30-34	311	158	153	362	185	177	413	211	202	452	232	220
35-39	316	162	155	311	158	153	362	184	178	413	211	202
40-44	303	155	148	315	161	155	310	157	153	361	183	177
45-49	254	130	124	300	153	147	313	159	154	308	156	152
50-54	196	99	97	250	127	123	296	150	146	309	156	152
55-59	144	72	72	191	96	95	245	124	121	290	146	143
60-64	107	52	54	139	68	70	185	92	93	237	119	118
65-69	84	41	43	101	49	52	131	64	67	175	86	89
70-74	64	30	34	76	36	40	92	43	48	120	57	63
75-79	48	22	26	55	25	30	66	30	36	79	36	43
80-84	29	13	16	37	17	21	43	19	24	52	23	29
85-89	18	8	10	19	8	11	25	11	14	29	12	17
90-94	6	3	4	9	4	6	10	4	6	13	5	8
95-99	2	1	1	2	1	1	4	1	2	4	1	2
100 +	0	0	0	0	0	0	1	0	0	1	0	1

Age group	2025			2030			2035			2040		
	Both sexes	Males	Females	Both sexes	Males	Females	Both sexes	Males	Females	Both sexes	Males	Females
All ages	5 881	2 976	2 906	6 247	3 156	3 091	6 603	3 330	3 273	6 948	3 498	3 450
0-4	485	248	237	494	253	241	512	262	250	533	273	260
5-9	484	248	236	488	250	238	498	255	243	515	264	251
10-14	473	242	231	487	249	237	491	252	239	501	256	244
15-19	453	232	221	478	245	233	492	252	240	496	254	242
20-24	408	209	199	457	234	223	482	247	235	496	254	242
25-29	421	216	205	410	210	200	459	235	224	485	248	237
30-34	440	226	214	422	216	205	412	211	201	461	236	225
35-39	452	231	221	440	225	214	422	216	206	412	211	201
40-44	412	210	202	451	230	220	438	224	214	421	215	206
45-49	358	182	177	409	208	201	447	228	220	436	222	213
50-54	305	153	151	354	179	175	404	205	200	442	224	218
55-59	303	152	150	299	149	149	347	174	173	397	200	197
60-64	280	140	140	293	146	147	289	144	146	337	168	169
65-69	224	111	113	266	131	135	279	137	142	276	135	141
70-74	160	77	83	206	100	107	245	118	127	257	124	134
75-79	104	48	56	140	65	75	181	84	96	216	101	115
80-84	63	27	36	83	37	47	113	50	63	146	65	81
85-89	36	15	21	44	18	26	58	24	34	79	33	47
90-94	16	6	10	19	7	12	24	9	15	32	12	20
95-99	5	2	3	6	2	4	7	3	5	9	3	6
100 +	1	0	1	1	0	1	1	0	1	2	1	1

Age group	2045			2050		
	Both sexes	Males	Females	Both sexes	Males	Females
All ages	7 279	3 658	3 620	7 591	3 810	3 781
0-4	552	283	269	568	291	277
5-9	536	275	261	555	284	271
10-14	518	265	253	539	276	263
15-19	506	259	246	523	268	255
20-24	500	256	244	510	261	249
25-29	499	255	243	503	258	245
30-34	486	249	237	500	256	244
35-39	461	235	225	486	248	238
40-44	411	210	201	460	234	225
45-49	418	213	205	408	208	200
50-54	431	219	212	414	210	203
55-59	434	219	215	423	214	209
60-64	385	192	193	422	211	211
65-69	321	157	164	367	180	187
70-74	255	122	133	298	143	155
75-79	228	106	122	226	104	122
80-84	176	78	98	186	82	104
85-89	104	43	61	125	52	73
90-94	44	17	28	58	22	36
95-99	12	4	8	17	6	11
100 +	2	1	1	3	1	2

316

United Nations Department of Economic and Social Affairs/Population Division
World Population Prospects: The 2004 Revision, Volume II: Sex and Age Distribution of the World Population

POPULATION BY AGE AND SEX (in thousands)

Age group	2005 Both sexes	Males	Females	2010 Both sexes	Males	Females	2015 Both sexes	Males	Females	2020 Both sexes	Males	Females
All ages	4 327	2 200	2 127	4 619	2 345	2 274	4 858	2 463	2 395	5 049	2 550	2 403
0-4	393	201	191	349	179	171	310	158	151	277	142	135
5-9	406	209	198	396	203	193	353	181	172	313	160	153
10-14	428	220	208	409	210	199	399	205	194	356	182	173
15-19	446	229	217	433	223	210	414	213	201	404	207	197
20-24	411	211	200	450	231	219	437	225	212	418	215	203
25-29	361	185	177	413	211	201	451	232	220	439	226	213
30-34	311	158	153	362	185	177	413	211	202	452	232	220
35-39	316	162	155	311	158	153	362	184	178	413	211	202
40-44	303	155	148	315	161	155	310	157	153	361	183	177
45-49	254	130	124	300	153	147	313	159	154	308	156	152
50-54	196	99	97	250	127	123	296	150	146	309	156	152
55-59	144	72	72	191	96	95	245	124	121	290	146	143
60-64	107	52	54	139	68	70	185	92	93	237	119	118
65-69	84	41	43	101	49	52	131	64	67	175	86	89
70-74	64	30	34	76	36	40	92	43	48	120	57	63
75-79	48	22	26	55	25	30	66	30	36	79	36	43
80-84	29	13	16	37	17	21	43	19	24	52	23	29
85-89	18	8	10	19	8	11	25	11	14	29	12	17
90-94	6	3	4	9	4	6	10	4	6	13	5	8
95-99	2	1	1	2	1	1	4	1	2	4	1	2
100 +	0	0	0	0	0	0	1	0	0	1	0	1

Age group	2025 Both sexes	Males	Females	2030 Both sexes	Males	Females	2035 Both sexes	Males	Females	2040 Both sexes	Males	Females
All ages	5 218	2 636	2 582	5 351	2 698	2 654	5 439	2 735	2 704	5 476	2 745	2 731
0-4	273	140	133	261	134	127	243	124	118	223	114	109
5-9	281	144	137	277	142	135	265	136	129	246	126	120
10-14	316	162	154	284	146	138	280	144	136	268	137	130
15-19	361	185	176	321	165	156	289	148	141	285	146	139
20-24	408	209	199	365	187	178	326	167	159	294	151	143
25-29	421	216	205	410	210	200	368	188	179	328	168	160
30-34	440	226	214	422	216	205	412	211	201	369	189	180
35-39	452	231	221	440	225	214	422	216	206	412	211	201
40-44	412	210	202	451	230	220	438	224	214	421	215	206
45-49	358	182	177	409	208	201	447	228	220	436	222	213
50-54	305	153	151	354	179	175	404	205	200	442	224	218
55-59	303	152	150	299	149	148	347	174	172	397	200	197
60-64	280	140	140	293	146	147	289	144	146	337	168	169
65-69	224	111	113	266	131	135	279	137	142	276	135	141
70-74	160	77	83	206	100	107	245	118	127	257	124	134
75-79	104	48	56	140	65	75	181	84	96	216	101	115
80-84	63	27	36	83	37	47	113	50	63	146	65	81
85-89	36	15	21	44	18	26	58	24	34	79	33	47
90-94	16	6	10	19	7	12	24	9	15	32	12	20
95-99	5	2	3	6	2	4	7	3	5	9	3	6
100 +	1	0	1	1	0	1	1	0	1	2	1	1

Age group	2045 Both sexes	Males	Females	2050 Both sexes	Males	Females
All ages	5 463	2 730	2 733	5 405	2 693	2 712
0-4	207	106	101	194	99	95
5-9	227	116	110	210	108	102
10-14	249	128	121	230	118	112
15-19	273	140	133	255	131	124
20-24	290	149	141	278	143	135
25-29	297	152	144	293	150	142
30-34	330	169	161	299	153	145
35-39	370	189	181	331	169	161
40-44	411	210	201	369	188	181
45-49	418	213	205	408	208	200
50-54	431	219	212	414	210	203
55-59	434	219	215	423	214	209
60-64	385	192	193	422	211	211
65-69	321	157	164	367	180	187
70-74	255	122	133	298	143	155
75-79	228	106	122	226	104	122
80-84	176	78	98	186	82	104
85-89	104	43	61	125	52	73
90-94	44	17	28	58	22	36
95-99	12	4	8	17	6	11
100 +	2	1	1	3	1	2

POPULATION BY AGE AND SEX (in thousands)

Age group	1950 Both sexes	1950 Males	1950 Females	1955 Both sexes	1955 Males	1955 Females	1960 Both sexes	1960 Males	1960 Females	1965 Both sexes	1965 Males	1965 Females
All ages	2 505	1 270	1 235	2 969	1 507	1 461	3 557	1 811	1 746	4 290	2 190	2 101
0-4	431	220	211	559	278	281	674	336	338	812	405	407
5-9	346	176	169	386	197	189	506	251	255	619	308	311
10-14	302	154	148	338	173	165	379	193	186	498	248	251
15-19	263	135	129	303	156	147	342	176	166	386	198	188
20-24	227	116	111	269	139	129	313	163	150	358	187	171
25-29	194	99	95	231	120	111	278	146	132	327	173	154
30-34	164	84	80	196	101	94	237	125	112	286	152	133
35-39	137	70	67	164	85	79	198	104	94	240	128	112
40-44	114	58	56	135	69	66	163	85	78	197	104	93
45-49	93	47	47	111	56	55	132	68	64	160	84	76
50-54	75	37	38	89	44	45	106	54	52	128	66	62
55-59	58	28	30	69	34	35	83	41	42	100	50	49
60-64	42	20	22	51	24	27	62	30	32	74	37	38
65-69	28	13	15	34	16	19	42	20	22	52	25	27
70-74	17	7	10	20	9	11	25	12	14	32	15	17
75-79	9	4	5	10	4	6	12	5	7	16	7	9
80 +	4	2	2	4	2	3	5	2	3	7	3	4

Age group	1970 Both sexes	1970 Males	1970 Females	1975 Both sexes	1975 Males	1975 Females	1980 Both sexes	1980 Males	1980 Females	1985 Both sexes	1985 Males	1985 Females
All ages	5 310	2 728	2 582	6 592	3 398	3 194	8 344	4 322	4 022	10 503	5 445	5 058
0-4	999	499	500	1 274	637	636	1 625	814	811	2 080	1 041	1 038
5-9	756	377	379	939	469	471	1 212	605	606	1 549	774	775
10-14	612	305	307	749	374	376	935	467	468	1 206	603	603
15-19	518	261	257	633	319	314	787	398	389	972	491	481
20-24	426	225	201	560	289	271	705	366	339	859	445	414
25-29	394	212	183	466	252	214	627	334	293	772	410	361
30-34	352	191	161	421	230	191	514	284	230	674	365	308
35-39	301	163	137	368	202	165	451	251	200	543	305	239
40-44	247	134	114	308	169	139	383	214	170	466	262	204
45-49	199	106	93	248	135	113	314	174	140	388	217	171
50-54	158	83	75	196	105	91	248	135	113	311	172	139
55-59	122	63	59	151	79	72	190	102	88	240	130	109
60-64	92	46	46	113	58	55	141	74	67	177	94	83
65-69	64	31	33	79	39	40	99	50	49	125	64	60
70-74	40	19	21	50	24	26	63	31	32	79	39	39
75-79	20	9	11	26	12	14	34	16	18	42	20	22
80 +	9	4	5	12	6	6	16	8	8	21	10	11

Age group	1990 Both sexes	1990 Males	1990 Females	1995 Both sexes	1995 Males	1995 Females	2000 Both sexes	2000 Males	2000 Females	2005 Both sexes	2005 Males	2005 Females
All ages	12 657	6 529	6 128	14 755	7 569	7 186	16 735	8 549	8 186	18 154	9 230	8 924
0-4	2 345	1 175	1 170	2 521	1 263	1 258	2 654	1 330	1 324	2 773	1 389	1 384
5-9	1 985	992	993	2 231	1 115	1 115	2 386	1 193	1 193	2 489	1 244	1 245
10-14	1 538	768	769	1 968	983	985	2 203	1 101	1 101	2 336	1 168	1 168
15-19	1 221	614	608	1 544	774	770	1 964	983	981	2 136	1 068	1 067
20-24	1 004	513	491	1 236	626	610	1 542	776	766	1 848	925	923
25-29	882	461	420	995	514	482	1 207	616	591	1 397	706	691
30-34	783	419	364	858	452	407	939	491	448	1 061	548	513
35-39	677	368	309	757	405	352	801	424	376	817	431	386
40-44	541	303	238	653	354	299	708	379	329	707	375	331
45-49	459	257	202	521	290	231	613	331	283	637	339	298
50-54	377	210	167	438	243	195	489	270	219	557	297	260
55-59	296	163	133	354	195	159	407	223	184	442	241	202
60-64	221	119	102	270	146	124	320	173	147	360	194	166
65-69	155	81	74	191	101	90	232	123	109	270	143	127
70-74	98	50	48	121	62	59	149	77	72	178	91	86
75-79	52	25	27	64	32	33	80	39	40	96	47	49
80 +	26	12	13	31	15	17	41	19	22	50	23	27

United Nations Department of Economic and Social Affairs/Population Division
World Population Prospects: The 2004 Revision, Volume II: Sex and Age Distribution of the World Population

318

POPULATION BY AGE AND SEX (in thousands)

Age group	2005			2010			2015			2020		
	Both sexes	Males	Females	Both sexes	Males	Females	Both sexes	Males	Females	Both sexes	Males	Females
All ages	18 154	9 230	8 924	19 777	10 018	9 759	21 553	10 890	10 663	23 339	11 775	11 564
0-4	2 773	1 389	1 384	2 870	1 437	1 433	2 950	1 478	1 472	2 978	1 494	1 484
5-9	2 489	1 244	1 245	2 609	1 303	1 306	2 722	1 360	1 363	2 827	1 413	1 414
10-14	2 336	1 168	1 168	2 441	1 220	1 221	2 562	1 279	1 283	2 679	1 338	1 342
15-19	2 136	1 068	1 067	2 293	1 146	1 147	2 415	1 206	1 209	2 540	1 268	1 272
20-24	1 848	925	923	2 062	1 031	1 031	2 253	1 125	1 128	2 383	1 190	1 193
25-29	1 397	706	691	1 729	869	860	1 973	990	983	2 174	1 089	1 085
30-34	1 061	548	513	1 264	646	618	1 596	811	785	1 843	934	908
35-39	817	431	386	948	495	454	1 148	594	554	1 463	753	710
40-44	707	375	331	735	389	345	864	453	411	1 053	548	505
45-49	637	339	298	644	341	303	676	358	319	800	419	380
50-54	557	297	260	585	308	276	596	313	283	629	330	299
55-59	442	241	202	509	268	241	539	280	259	552	286	266
60-64	360	194	166	395	211	184	459	237	222	489	249	239
65-69	270	143	127	307	161	146	341	178	163	399	201	198
70-74	178	91	86	209	107	102	241	123	118	271	137	134
75-79	96	47	49	116	58	59	140	69	70	164	81	83
80-84	38	18	20	47	22	25	59	28	31	72	34	38
85-89	10	4	6	12	5	7	16	7	9	20	9	11
90-94	1	1	1	2	1	1	2	1	1	3	1	2
95-99	0	0	0	0	0	0	0	0	0	0	0	0
100 +	0	0	0	0	0	0	0	0	0	0	0	0

Age group	2025			2030			2035			2040		
	Both sexes	Males	Females	Both sexes	Males	Females	Both sexes	Males	Females	Both sexes	Males	Females
All ages	25 114	12 656	12 459	26 883	13 534	13 349	28 654	14 411	14 243	30 437	15 290	15 147
0-4	2 975	1 494	1 482	2 966	1 490	1 477	2 959	1 486	1 473	2 947	1 481	1 467
5-9	2 877	1 440	1 437	2 894	1 450	1 444	2 900	1 454	1 446	2 906	1 457	1 449
10-14	2 794	1 396	1 398	2 853	1 427	1 426	2 876	1 440	1 436	2 887	1 446	1 440
15-19	2 660	1 328	1 333	2 778	1 387	1 391	2 840	1 420	1 420	2 866	1 434	1 431
20-24	2 512	1 253	1 259	2 636	1 315	1 321	2 758	1 376	1 381	2 824	1 411	1 413
25-29	2 310	1 157	1 153	2 446	1 223	1 222	2 579	1 289	1 290	2 712	1 356	1 356
30-34	2 050	1 037	1 013	2 195	1 108	1 087	2 343	1 180	1 163	2 493	1 253	1 240
35-39	1 708	875	833	1 920	980	940	2 075	1 056	1 019	2 238	1 135	1 104
40-44	1 355	701	654	1 599	823	775	1 813	929	884	1 980	1 011	969
45-49	982	511	471	1 274	659	615	1 515	779	736	1 732	887	845
50-54	748	389	358	925	478	447	1 207	620	587	1 445	739	706
55-59	565	304	262	700	360	340	870	445	426	1 143	581	562
60-64	504	256	247	538	274	264	648	327	320	810	407	403
65-69	428	213	215	445	221	224	479	239	241	582	288	294
70-74	322	157	164	349	169	180	368	178	190	402	194	207
75-79	188	91	96	227	107	121	251	116	135	269	125	145
80-84	87	41	46	102	47	55	127	56	71	143	63	81
85-89	25	11	14	31	14	18	38	16	22	49	20	29
90-94	4	2	2	5	2	3	7	3	4	8	3	5
95-99	0	0	0	0	0	0	1	0	0	1	0	0
100 +	0	0	0	0	0	0	0	0	0	0	0	0

Age group	2045			2050		
	Both sexes	Males	Females	Both sexes	Males	Females
All ages	32 216	16 159	16 057	33 959	16 998	16 961
0-4	2 918	1 466	1 452	2 872	1 443	1 429
5-9	2 904	1 457	1 447	2 883	1 447	1 436
10-14	2 895	1 451	1 444	2 896	1 452	1 444
15-19	2 879	1 442	1 437	2 890	1 448	1 442
20-24	2 854	1 428	1 426	2 871	1 437	1 433
25-29	2 790	1 395	1 394	2 830	1 417	1 414
30-34	2 643	1 327	1 317	2 740	1 374	1 366
35-39	2 407	1 215	1 191	2 577	1 297	1 280
40-44	2 156	1 096	1 060	2 340	1 183	1 157
45-49	1 907	972	935	2 093	1 062	1 031
50-54	1 664	847	817	1 843	934	909
55-59	1 377	696	680	1 594	802	791
60-64	1 070	535	536	1 296	645	651
65-69	733	360	373	976	477	499
70-74	494	237	257	628	299	329
75-79	299	139	160	373	171	202
80-84	157	68	89	178	78	101
85-89	57	23	34	64	25	38
90-94	11	4	7	13	5	9
95-99	1	0	1	1	0	1
100 +	0	0	0	0	0	0

United Nations Department of Economic and Social Affairs/Population Division
World Population Prospects: The 2004 Revision, Volume II: Sex and Age Distribution of the World Population

319

POPULATION BY AGE AND SEX (in thousands)

Age group	2005			2010			2015			2020		
	Both sexes	Males	Females	Both sexes	Males	Females	Both sexes	Males	Females	Both sexes	Males	Females
All ages	18 154	9 230	8 924	19 939	10 099	9 840	22 008	11 117	10 890	24 211	12 211	12 000
0-4	2 773	1 389	1 384	3 031	1 518	1 513	3 253	1 630	1 623	3 410	1 710	1 700
5-9	2 489	1 244	1 245	2 609	1 303	1 306	2 875	1 436	1 439	3 116	1 558	1 559
10-14	2 336	1 168	1 168	2 441	1 220	1 221	2 562	1 279	1 283	2 830	1 413	1 417
15-19	2 136	1 068	1 067	2 293	1 146	1 147	2 415	1 206	1 209	2 540	1 268	1 272
20-24	1 848	925	923	2 062	1 031	1 031	2 253	1 125	1 128	2 383	1 190	1 193
25-29	1 397	706	691	1 729	869	860	1 973	990	983	2 174	1 089	1 085
30-34	1 061	548	513	1 264	646	618	1 596	811	785	1 843	934	908
35-39	817	431	386	948	495	454	1 148	594	554	1 463	753	710
40-44	707	375	331	735	389	345	864	453	411	1 053	548	505
45-49	637	339	298	644	341	303	676	358	319	800	419	380
50-54	557	297	260	585	308	276	596	313	283	629	330	299
55-59	442	241	202	509	268	241	539	280	259	552	286	266
60-64	360	194	166	395	211	184	459	237	222	489	249	239
65-69	270	143	127	307	161	146	341	178	163	399	201	198
70-74	178	91	86	209	107	102	241	123	118	271	137	134
75-79	96	47	49	116	58	59	140	69	70	164	81	83
80-84	38	18	20	47	22	25	59	28	31	72	34	38
85-89	10	4	6	12	5	7	16	7	9	20	9	11
90-94	1	1	1	2	1	1	2	1	1	3	1	2
95-99	0	0	0	0	0	0	0	0	0	0	0	0
100 +	0	0	0	0	0	0	0	0	0	0	0	0

Age group	2025			2030			2035			2040		
	Both sexes	Males	Females	Both sexes	Males	Females	Both sexes	Males	Females	Both sexes	Males	Females
All ages	26 459	13 329	13 130	28 792	14 490	14 303	31 270	15 721	15 548	33 920	17 035	16 885
0-4	3 467	1 740	1 726	3 552	1 784	1 768	3 690	1 854	1 837	3 846	1 932	1 914
5-9	3 295	1 649	1 646	3 372	1 689	1 682	3 473	1 741	1 732	3 624	1 817	1 806
10-14	3 080	1 539	1 541	3 266	1 634	1 633	3 350	1 678	1 673	3 456	1 732	1 724
15-19	2 810	1 402	1 408	3 063	1 529	1 533	3 252	1 626	1 626	3 338	1 671	1 667
20-24	2 512	1 253	1 259	2 783	1 388	1 395	3 039	1 517	1 522	3 232	1 615	1 617
25-29	2 310	1 157	1 153	2 446	1 223	1 222	2 723	1 361	1 362	2 988	1 494	1 495
30-34	2 050	1 037	1 013	2 195	1 108	1 087	2 343	1 180	1 163	2 632	1 323	1 309
35-39	1 708	875	833	1 920	980	940	2 075	1 056	1 019	2 238	1 135	1 104
40-44	1 355	701	654	1 599	823	775	1 813	929	884	1 980	1 011	969
45-49	982	511	471	1 274	659	615	1 515	779	736	1 732	887	845
50-54	748	389	358	925	478	447	1 207	620	587	1 445	739	706
55-59	585	304	282	700	360	340	870	445	426	1 143	581	562
60-64	504	256	247	538	274	264	648	327	320	810	407	403
65-69	428	213	215	445	221	224	479	239	241	582	288	294
70-74	322	157	164	349	169	180	368	178	190	402	194	207
75-79	188	91	96	227	107	121	251	116	135	269	125	145
80-84	87	41	46	102	47	55	127	56	71	143	63	81
85-89	25	11	14	31	14	18	38	16	22	49	20	29
90-94	4	2	2	5	2	3	7	3	4	8	3	5
95-99	0	0	0	0	0	0	1	0	0	1	0	0
100 +	0	0	0	0	0	0	0	0	0	0	0	0

Age group	2045			2050		
	Both sexes	Males	Females	Both sexes	Males	Females
All ages	36 712	18 412	18 300	39 595	19 825	19 771
0-4	3 971	1 995	1 976	4 057	2 039	2 018
5-9	3 790	1 901	1 889	3 923	1 969	1 954
10-14	3 611	1 810	1 801	3 779	1 895	1 884
15-19	3 447	1 726	1 720	3 602	1 805	1 798
20-24	3 323	1 662	1 661	3 435	1 720	1 716
25-29	3 192	1 597	1 596	3 295	1 649	1 646
30-34	2 912	1 461	1 451	3 135	1 572	1 563
35-39	2 541	1 283	1 258	2 839	1 429	1 410
40-44	2 156	1 096	1 060	2 470	1 249	1 221
45-49	1 907	972	935	2 093	1 062	1 031
50-54	1 664	847	817	1 843	934	909
55-59	1 377	696	680	1 594	802	791
60-64	1 070	535	536	1 296	645	651
65-69	733	360	373	976	477	499
70-74	494	237	257	628	299	329
75-79	299	139	160	373	171	202
80-84	157	68	89	178	78	101
85-89	57	23	34	64	25	38
90-94	11	4	7	13	5	9
95-99	1	0	1	1	0	1
100 +	0	0	0	0	0	0

United Nations Department of Economic and Social Affairs/Population Division
World Population Prospects: The 2004 Revision, Volume II: Sex and Age Distribution of the World Population

320

POPULATION BY AGE AND SEX (in thousands)

Age group	2005 Both sexes	Males	Females	2010 Both sexes	Males	Females	2015 Both sexes	Males	Females	2020 Both sexes	Males	Females
All ages	18 154	9 230	8 924	19 616	9 937	9 679	21 097	10 662	10 436	22 467	11 338	11 129
0-4	2 773	1 389	1 384	2 709	1 356	1 352	2 648	1 327	1 321	2 546	1 277	1 269
5-9	2 489	1 244	1 245	2 609	1 303	1 306	2 570	1 283	1 286	2 537	1 268	1 269
10-14	2 336	1 168	1 168	2 441	1 220	1 221	2 562	1 279	1 283	2 529	1 262	1 266
15-19	2 136	1 068	1 067	2 293	1 146	1 147	2 415	1 206	1 209	2 540	1 268	1 272
20-24	1 848	925	923	2 062	1 031	1 031	2 253	1 125	1 128	2 383	1 190	1 193
25-29	1 397	706	691	1 729	869	860	1 973	990	983	2 174	1 089	1 085
30-34	1 061	548	513	1 264	646	618	1 596	811	785	1 843	934	908
35-39	817	431	386	948	495	454	1 148	594	554	1 463	753	710
40-44	707	375	331	735	389	345	864	453	411	1 053	548	505
45-49	637	339	298	644	341	303	676	358	319	800	419	380
50-54	557	297	260	585	308	276	596	313	283	629	330	299
55-59	442	241	202	509	268	241	539	280	259	552	286	266
60-64	360	194	166	395	211	184	459	237	222	489	249	239
65-69	270	143	127	307	161	146	341	178	163	399	201	198
70-74	178	91	86	209	107	102	241	123	118	271	137	134
75-79	96	47	49	116	58	59	140	69	70	164	81	83
80-84	38	18	20	47	22	25	59	28	31	72	34	38
85-89	10	4	6	12	5	7	16	7	9	20	9	11
90-94	1	1	1	2	1	1	2	1	1	3	1	2
95-99	0	0	0	0	0	0	0	0	0	0	0	0
100 +	0	0	0	0	0	0	0	0	0	0	0	0

Age group	2025 Both sexes	Males	Females	2030 Both sexes	Males	Females	2035 Both sexes	Males	Females	2040 Both sexes	Males	Females
All ages	23 773	11 984	11 789	24 996	12 589	12 407	26 115	13 139	12 975	27 132	13 634	13 497
0-4	2 487	1 249	1 239	2 400	1 205	1 195	2 282	1 146	1 136	2 151	1 080	1 070
5-9	2 460	1 231	1 229	2 419	1 212	1 207	2 346	1 176	1 170	2 241	1 124	1 117
10-14	2 507	1 253	1 255	2 439	1 220	1 219	2 404	1 204	1 200	2 335	1 170	1 165
15-19	2 511	1 253	1 258	2 494	1 245	1 249	2 429	1 214	1 214	2 396	1 199	1 197
20-24	2 512	1 253	1 259	2 488	1 241	1 247	2 476	1 236	1 240	2 416	1 207	1 208
25-29	2 310	1 157	1 153	2 446	1 223	1 222	2 435	1 217	1 218	2 436	1 218	1 218
30-34	2 050	1 037	1 013	2 195	1 108	1 087	2 343	1 180	1 163	2 354	1 183	1 171
35-39	1 708	875	833	1 920	980	940	2 075	1 056	1 019	2 238	1 135	1 104
40-44	1 355	701	654	1 599	823	775	1 813	929	884	1 980	1 011	969
45-49	982	511	471	1 274	659	615	1 515	779	736	1 732	887	845
50-54	748	389	358	925	478	447	1 207	620	587	1 445	739	706
55-59	585	304	282	700	360	340	870	445	426	1 143	581	562
60-64	504	256	247	538	274	264	648	327	320	810	407	403
65-69	428	213	215	445	221	224	479	239	241	582	288	294
70-74	322	157	164	349	169	180	368	178	190	402	194	207
75-79	188	91	96	227	107	121	251	116	135	269	125	145
80-84	87	41	46	102	47	55	127	56	71	143	63	81
85-89	25	11	14	31	14	18	38	16	22	49	20	29
90-94	4	2	2	5	2	3	7	3	4	8	3	5
95-99	0	0	0	0	0	0	1	0	0	1	0	0
100 +	0	0	0	0	0	0	0	0	0	0	0	0

Age group	2045 Both sexes	Males	Females	2050 Both sexes	Males	Females
All ages	28 048	14 069	13 979	28 851	14 437	14 414
0-4	2 018	1 014	1 004	1 891	950	941
5-9	2 119	1 063	1 056	1 994	1 001	993
10-14	2 233	1 120	1 114	2 114	1 060	1 054
15-19	2 330	1 167	1 163	2 230	1 117	1 112
20-24	2 387	1 195	1 193	2 324	1 164	1 160
25-29	2 387	1 194	1 193	2 369	1 186	1 183
30-34	2 374	1 192	1 182	2 345	1 177	1 169
35-39	2 273	1 148	1 125	2 315	1 166	1 149
40-44	2 156	1 096	1 060	2 210	1 118	1 092
45-49	1 907	972	935	2 093	1 062	1 031
50-54	1 664	847	817	1 843	934	909
55-59	1 377	696	680	1 594	802	791
60-64	1 070	535	536	1 296	645	651
65-69	733	360	373	976	477	499
70-74	494	237	257	628	299	329
75-79	299	139	160	373	171	202
80-84	157	68	89	178	78	101
85-89	57	23	34	64	25	38
90-94	11	4	7	13	5	9
95-99	1	0	1	1	0	1
100 +	0	0	0	0	0	0

United Nations Department of Economic and Social Affairs/Population Division
World Population Prospects: The 2004 Revision, Volume II: Sex and Age Distribution of the World Population

321

POPULATION BY AGE AND SEX (in thousands)

Age group	1950 Both sexes	Males	Females	1955 Both sexes	Males	Females	1960 Both sexes	Males	Females	1965 Both sexes	Males	Females
All ages	3 850	1 834	2 016	3 966	1 891	2 075	4 045	1 932	2 114	4 122	1 974	2 147
0-4	389	197	192	388	197	191	352	179	173	345	178	167
5-9	298	150	148	380	193	188	378	192	186	343	175	169
10-14	343	175	168	292	147	145	372	189	183	370	189	182
15-19	366	186	181	337	172	165	285	144	141	364	185	180
20-24	353	175	178	358	181	177	328	167	161	278	140	138
25-29	303	133	170	345	170	175	349	176	173	320	162	158
30-34	196	88	109	295	129	166	335	165	170	339	171	169
35-39	253	116	137	190	84	106	285	124	162	325	159	166
40-44	288	138	150	242	110	132	182	80	102	275	118	157
45-49	255	123	132	273	129	144	230	103	127	173	75	98
50-54	217	102	115	238	112	125	255	118	137	217	95	121
55-59	154	68	86	198	91	107	218	101	117	235	107	129
60-64	133	56	76	136	58	78	176	78	98	195	88	107
65-69	111	49	62	112	45	67	115	47	68	151	64	86
70-74	86	38	48	85	35	50	87	33	54	91	35	56
75-79	62	26	37	56	23	33	57	22	35	59	21	39
80 +	45	17	27	42	16	26	41	15	26	42	15	27

Age group	1970 Both sexes	Males	Females	1975 Both sexes	Males	Females	1980 Both sexes	Males	Females	1985 Both sexes	Males	Females
All ages	4 169	2 015	2 155	4 263	2 061	2 202	4 377	2 118	2 258	4 471	2 164	2 308
0-4	296	150	145	308	158	150	316	162	153	320	164	156
5-9	315	161	154	295	150	145	304	156	148	317	163	154
10-14	339	173	166	314	160	154	304	154	149	305	156	148
15-19	371	189	182	338	172	166	320	163	157	305	155	150
20-24	348	181	167	370	188	182	348	177	172	320	163	157
25-29	262	134	128	346	180	166	369	188	181	348	176	172
30-34	314	160	153	260	133	127	322	167	155	368	187	181
35-39	336	170	166	311	158	153	268	136	132	321	165	156
40-44	319	157	162	331	166	165	312	158	154	266	134	132
45-49	270	116	154	311	151	160	328	163	165	307	153	153
50-54	169	73	96	260	110	150	293	138	155	318	155	163
55-59	208	91	117	160	68	93	247	102	145	280	129	151
60-64	219	97	122	192	81	110	136	56	80	231	91	139
65-69	171	74	97	193	82	111	185	76	109	122	48	74
70-74	122	49	73	139	57	82	159	64	95	153	58	95
75-79	63	23	40	87	32	55	103	38	65	115	41	73
80 +	49	16	33	51	16	35	64	21	43	78	25	53

Age group	1990 Both sexes	Males	Females	1995 Both sexes	Males	Females	2000 Both sexes	Males	Females	2005 Both sexes	Males	Females
All ages	4 517	2 185	2 332	4 669	2 250	2 419	4 505	2 170	2 336	4 551	2 191	2 361
0-4	290	149	142	264	135	129	234	120	114	207	106	101
5-9	319	164	156	287	147	141	255	131	125	239	122	116
10-14	317	162	154	320	164	156	278	142	136	261	133	127
15-19	305	156	149	324	165	159	309	158	151	283	145	139
20-24	304	154	150	310	157	153	312	159	153	315	161	154
25-29	319	162	157	314	157	156	298	150	148	318	162	156
30-34	347	175	172	341	171	170	302	151	151	304	153	151
35-39	366	185	181	358	180	178	328	164	164	307	153	154
40-44	317	162	155	358	182	175	343	172	172	332	165	167
45-49	261	130	131	320	160	160	341	172	168	346	172	174
50-54	297	146	151	247	119	128	302	149	153	339	170	170
55-59	303	145	158	304	144	160	228	107	121	296	144	153
60-64	260	116	145	299	135	163	276	127	150	220	101	119
65-69	207	78	130	251	106	145	262	113	148	257	113	144
70-74	102	37	65	180	62	117	207	82	125	229	93	136
75-79	112	38	74	89	32	58	134	43	92	165	60	105
80 +	91	28	63	104	34	70	96	30	66	133	38	95

United Nations Department of Economic and Social Affairs/Population Division
World Population Prospects: The 2004 Revision, Volume II: Sex and Age Distribution of the World Population

322

POPULATION BY AGE AND SEX (in thousands)

Age group	2005 Both sexes	Males	Females	2010 Both sexes	Males	Females	2015 Both sexes	Males	Females	2020 Both sexes	Males	Females
All ages	4 551	2 191	2 361	4 532	2 182	2 350	4 454	2 147	2 307	4 007	2 107	2 260
0-4	207	106	101	204	105	99	206	106	100	201	103	98
5-9	239	122	116	209	107	102	204	105	99	205	106	100
10-14	261	133	127	241	124	117	209	107	102	204	105	99
15-19	283	145	139	263	135	129	241	123	117	209	107	101
20-24	315	161	154	286	146	140	263	134	129	240	123	117
25-29	318	162	156	317	162	156	285	145	140	262	134	128
30-34	304	153	151	321	163	158	316	161	155	284	144	140
35-39	307	153	154	306	154	152	319	162	157	315	160	155
40-44	332	165	167	308	153	155	304	152	152	317	160	157
45-49	346	172	174	331	164	167	304	151	154	300	150	151
50-54	339	170	170	342	168	174	325	159	165	299	147	152
55-59	296	144	153	331	163	168	331	161	170	315	153	162
60-64	220	101	119	283	134	149	314	152	163	316	150	166
65-69	257	113	144	204	90	114	261	119	142	291	136	155
70-74	229	93	136	225	93	131	179	75	104	230	100	130
75-79	165	60	105	183	69	114	181	70	111	145	57	89
80-84	91	26	65	113	37	76	128	44	84	128	45	83
85-89	29	8	21	50	12	37	63	18	45	73	21	51
90-94	10	3	7	11	3	8	20	4	16	26	6	20
95-99	2	1	2	2	1	2	3	1	2	6	1	5
100 +	0	0	0	0	0	0	0	0	0	0	0	0

Age group	2025 Both sexes	Males	Females	2030 Both sexes	Males	Females	2035 Both sexes	Males	Females	2040 Both sexes	Males	Females
All ages	4 271	2 062	2 208	4 164	2 012	2 152	4 047	1 957	2 091	3 926	1 899	2 027
0-4	193	99	94	184	94	89	177	91	86	177	91	86
5-9	201	103	98	193	99	94	183	94	89	177	91	86
10-14	205	106	100	201	103	98	193	99	94	183	94	89
15-19	204	105	99	205	105	100	201	103	98	192	99	94
20-24	208	107	101	203	104	99	205	105	100	200	103	98
25-29	239	122	117	208	106	101	203	104	99	204	105	100
30-34	261	133	128	239	122	117	207	106	101	203	104	99
35-39	283	144	140	260	132	128	238	122	117	207	106	101
40-44	313	159	154	282	142	139	259	132	128	237	121	116
45-49	314	158	156	310	157	154	270	141	138	257	130	127
50-54	295	146	149	309	155	154	306	153	152	275	138	137
55-59	291	141	150	288	141	147	302	149	152	299	149	150
60-64	301	143	158	279	133	146	277	133	143	290	142	149
65-69	293	135	158	281	130	151	261	121	140	260	122	138
70-74	258	115	143	262	116	146	252	112	140	235	105	130
75-79	189	77	112	214	90	124	219	91	127	212	89	123
80-84	105	37	68	138	52	87	158	61	97	164	63	101
85-89	75	23	53	63	20	44	85	28	57	99	34	65
90-94	32	8	24	34	9	26	30	8	22	41	11	30
95-99	8	1	6	10	2	8	11	2	9	10	2	8
100 +	1	0	1	1	0	1	2	0	2	2	0	2

Age group	2045 Both sexes	Males	Females	2050 Both sexes	Males	Females
All ages	3 806	1 844	1 962	3 686	1 790	1 896
0-4	179	92	87	176	91	86
5-9	177	91	86	179	92	87
10-14	177	91	86	176	91	86
15-19	183	94	89	177	91	86
20-24	192	99	93	183	94	89
25-29	200	103	97	192	99	93
30-34	204	105	99	200	102	97
35-39	202	103	99	204	104	99
40-44	206	105	101	201	103	98
45-49	235	120	116	204	104	100
50-54	254	128	126	232	118	115
55-59	269	134	135	249	124	124
60-64	288	141	147	260	128	132
65-69	273	131	143	272	131	141
70-74	235	107	128	248	115	134
75-79	199	85	115	200	87	114
80-84	161	63	98	153	60	93
85-89	105	36	69	105	36	68
90-94	49	14	35	53	15	38
95-99	14	3	11	17	4	13
100 +	2	0	2	3	0	3

United Nations Department of Economic and Social Affairs/Population Division
World Population Prospects: The 2004 Revision, Volume II: Sex and Age Distribution of the World Population

323

POPULATION BY AGE AND SEX (in thousands)

Age group	2005 Both sexes	Males	Females	2010 Both sexes	Males	Females	2015 Both sexes	Males	Females	2020 Both sexes	Males	Females
All ages	4 551	2 191	2 361	4 569	2 201	2 368	4 549	2 195	2 353	4 528	2 190	2 338
0-4	207	106	101	242	124	118	263	135	128	267	137	130
5-9	239	122	116	209	107	102	242	124	117	263	135	128
10-14	261	133	127	241	124	117	209	107	102	242	124	117
15-19	283	145	139	263	135	129	241	123	117	209	107	101
20-24	315	161	154	286	146	140	263	134	129	240	123	117
25-29	318	162	156	317	162	156	285	145	140	262	134	128
30-34	304	153	151	321	163	158	316	161	155	284	144	140
35-39	307	153	154	306	154	152	319	162	157	315	160	155
40-44	332	165	167	308	153	155	304	152	152	317	160	157
45-49	346	172	174	331	164	167	304	151	154	300	150	151
50-54	339	170	170	342	168	174	325	159	165	299	147	152
55-59	296	144	153	331	163	168	331	161	170	315	153	162
60-64	220	101	119	283	134	149	314	152	163	316	150	166
65-69	257	113	144	204	90	114	261	119	142	291	136	155
70-74	229	93	136	225	93	131	179	75	104	230	100	130
75-79	165	60	105	183	69	114	181	70	111	145	57	89
80-84	91	26	65	113	37	76	128	44	84	128	45	83
85-89	29	8	21	50	12	37	63	18	45	73	21	51
90-94	10	3	7	11	3	8	20	4	16	26	6	20
95-99	2	1	2	2	1	2	3	1	2	6	1	5
100 +	0	0	0	0	0	0	0	0	0	0	0	0

Age group	2025 Both sexes	Males	Females	2030 Both sexes	Males	Females	2035 Both sexes	Males	Females	2040 Both sexes	Males	Females
All ages	4 491	2 176	2 316	4 445	2 156	2 288	4 400	2 138	2 262	4 370	2 128	2 243
0-4	253	130	123	244	125	118	250	128	121	269	139	131
5-9	267	137	130	253	130	123	244	125	118	249	128	121
10-14	263	135	128	267	137	130	253	130	123	243	125	118
15-19	241	124	117	262	135	128	266	137	130	252	130	123
20-24	208	107	101	241	124	117	262	134	127	266	137	129
25-29	239	122	117	208	106	101	240	123	117	261	134	127
30-34	261	133	128	239	122	117	207	106	101	240	123	117
35-39	283	144	140	260	132	128	238	122	117	207	106	101
40-44	313	159	154	282	142	139	259	132	128	237	121	116
45-49	314	158	156	310	157	154	279	141	138	257	130	127
50-54	295	146	149	309	155	154	306	153	152	275	138	137
55-59	291	141	150	288	141	147	302	149	152	299	149	150
60-64	301	143	158	279	133	146	277	133	143	290	142	149
65-69	293	135	158	281	130	151	261	121	140	260	122	138
70-74	258	115	143	262	116	146	252	112	140	235	105	130
75-79	189	77	112	214	90	124	219	91	127	212	89	123
80-84	105	37	68	138	52	87	158	61	97	164	63	101
85-89	75	23	53	63	20	44	85	28	57	99	34	65
90-94	32	8	24	34	9	26	30	8	22	41	11	30
95-99	8	1	6	10	2	8	11	2	9	10	2	8
100 +	1	0	1	1	0	1	2	0	2	2	0	2

Age group	2045 Both sexes	Males	Females	2050 Both sexes	Males	Females
All ages	4 359	2 128	2 231	4 353	2 133	2 221
0-4	288	148	140	291	150	141
5-9	269	138	131	288	148	140
10-14	249	128	121	269	138	131
15-19	243	125	118	249	128	121
20-24	252	129	123	243	125	118
25-29	266	136	129	252	129	122
30-34	261	134	127	265	136	129
35-39	239	123	117	260	133	127
40-44	206	105	101	238	122	116
45-49	235	120	116	204	104	100
50-54	254	128	126	232	118	115
55-59	269	134	135	249	124	124
60-64	288	141	147	260	128	132
65-69	273	131	143	272	131	141
70-74	235	107	128	248	115	134
75-79	199	85	115	200	87	114
80-84	161	63	98	153	60	93
85-89	105	36	69	105	36	68
90-94	49	14	35	53	15	38
95-99	14	3	11	17	4	13
100 +	2	0	2	3	0	3

United Nations Department of Economic and Social Affairs/Population Division
World Population Prospects: The 2004 Revision, Volume II: Sex and Age Distribution of the World Population

324

POPULATION BY AGE AND SEX (in thousands)

Age group	2005 Both sexes	2005 Males	2005 Females	2010 Both sexes	2010 Males	2010 Females	2015 Both sexes	2015 Males	2015 Females	2020 Both sexes	2020 Males	2020 Females
All ages	4 551	2 191	2 361	4 494	2 163	2 332	4 359	2 098	2 261	4 205	2 024	2 181
0-4	207	106	101	167	86	81	148	76	72	134	69	65
5-9	239	122	116	209	107	102	167	86	81	148	76	72
10-14	261	133	127	241	124	117	209	107	102	166	86	81
15-19	283	145	139	263	135	129	241	123	117	209	107	101
20-24	315	161	154	286	146	140	263	134	129	240	123	117
25-29	318	162	156	317	162	156	285	145	140	262	134	128
30-34	304	153	151	321	163	158	316	161	155	284	144	140
35-39	307	153	154	306	154	152	319	162	157	315	160	155
40-44	332	165	167	308	153	155	304	152	152	317	160	157
45-49	346	172	174	331	164	167	304	151	154	300	150	151
50-54	339	170	170	342	168	174	325	159	165	299	147	152
55-59	296	144	153	331	163	168	331	161	170	315	153	162
60-64	220	101	119	283	134	149	314	152	163	316	150	166
65-69	257	113	144	204	90	114	261	119	142	291	136	155
70-74	229	93	136	225	93	131	179	75	104	230	100	130
75-79	165	60	105	183	69	114	181	70	111	145	57	89
80-84	91	26	65	113	37	76	128	44	84	128	45	83
85-89	29	8	21	50	12	37	63	18	45	73	21	51
90-94	10	3	7	11	3	8	20	4	16	26	6	20
95-99	2	1	2	2	1	2	3	1	2	6	1	5
100 +	0	0	0	0	0	0	0	0	0	0	0	0

Age group	2025 Both sexes	2025 Males	2025 Females	2030 Both sexes	2030 Males	2030 Females	2035 Both sexes	2035 Males	2035 Females	2040 Both sexes	2040 Males	2040 Females
All ages	4 048	1 948	2 100	3 884	1 868	2 016	3 708	1 782	1 926	3 518	1 689	1 828
0-4	132	68	64	126	65	61	118	60	57	108	55	52
5-9	134	69	65	132	68	64	126	65	61	117	60	57
10-14	148	76	72	134	69	65	132	68	64	126	65	61
15-19	166	85	81	148	76	72	134	69	65	132	68	64
20-24	208	107	101	166	85	81	147	76	72	134	69	65
25-29	239	122	117	208	106	101	166	85	81	147	75	72
30-34	261	133	128	239	122	117	207	106	101	165	85	81
35-39	283	144	140	260	132	128	238	122	117	207	106	101
40-44	313	159	154	282	142	130	259	132	128	237	121	116
45-49	314	158	156	310	157	154	279	141	138	257	130	127
50-54	295	146	149	309	155	154	306	153	152	275	138	137
55-59	291	141	150	288	141	147	300	149	152	299	149	150
60-64	301	143	158	279	133	146	277	133	143	290	142	149
65-69	293	135	158	281	130	151	261	121	140	260	122	138
70-74	258	115	143	262	116	146	252	112	140	235	105	130
75-79	180	77	112	214	90	124	219	91	127	212	89	123
80-84	105	37	68	138	52	87	158	61	97	164	63	101
85-89	75	23	53	63	20	44	85	28	57	99	34	65
90-94	32	8	24	34	9	26	30	8	22	41	11	30
95-99	8	1	6	10	2	8	11	2	9	10	2	8
100 +	1	0	1	1	0	1	2	0	2	2	0	2

Age group	2045 Both sexes	2045 Males	2045 Females	2050 Both sexes	2050 Males	2050 Females
All ages	3 318	1 593	1 724	3 113	1 496	1 617
0-4	99	51	48	91	47	44
5-9	108	55	52	99	51	48
10-14	117	60	57	107	55	52
15-19	126	65	61	117	60	57
20-24	132	68	64	126	65	61
25-29	134	69	65	131	67	64
30-34	147	75	72	133	68	65
35-39	165	84	80	146	75	71
40-44	206	105	101	164	84	80
45-49	235	120	116	204	104	100
50-54	254	128	126	232	118	115
55-59	269	134	135	249	124	124
60-64	288	141	147	260	128	132
65-69	273	131	143	272	131	141
70-74	235	107	128	248	115	134
75-79	199	85	115	200	87	114
80-84	161	63	98	153	60	93
85-89	105	36	69	105	36	68
90-94	49	14	35	53	15	38
95-99	14	3	11	17	4	13
100 +	2	0	2	3	0	3

POPULATION BY AGE AND SEX (in thousands)

Age group	1950 Both sexes	1950 Males	1950 Females	1955 Both sexes	1955 Males	1955 Females	1960 Both sexes	1960 Males	1960 Females	1965 Both sexes	1965 Males	1965 Females
All ages	5 850	3 053	2 797	6 416	3 323	3 094	6 976	3 587	3 389	7 738	3 955	3 783
0-4	784	390	394	827	420	407	833	423	410	1 187	602	585
5-9	695	347	348	761	378	383	804	407	397	801	403	398
10-14	617	310	307	688	344	345	750	372	379	786	395	391
15-19	508	255	254	611	306	304	683	341	342	734	363	371
20-24	483	243	240	501	251	250	605	303	301	662	331	331
25-29	415	216	199	474	238	236	492	246	246	582	292	290
30-34	424	219	206	407	211	196	466	234	232	468	235	233
35-39	394	204	190	414	213	201	397	206	191	441	222	219
40-44	356	191	165	382	198	185	403	207	196	372	194	178
45-49	326	187	139	343	183	160	369	190	179	375	193	182
50-54	236	138	98	310	177	133	328	174	154	342	177	165
55-59	185	109	77	221	129	92	292	166	126	300	159	141
60-64	143	83	60	169	98	71	202	117	86	263	149	114
65-69	114	67	47	125	72	53	148	85	63	181	103	78
70-74	84	48	35	91	53	38	101	57	44	122	69	53
75-79	53	30	23	55	32	23	62	36	26	72	40	32
80 +	33	16	17	38	20	18	42	23	19	49	27	22

Age group	1970 Both sexes	1970 Males	1970 Females	1975 Both sexes	1975 Males	1975 Females	1980 Both sexes	1980 Males	1980 Females	1985 Both sexes	1985 Males	1985 Females
All ages	8 483	4 325	4 158	9 251	4 694	4 556	9 645	4 880	4 765	10 041	5 062	4 979
0-4	1 206	616	590	1 127	576	551	789	404	384	779	399	380
5-9	1 155	585	570	1 187	607	580	1 117	571	546	776	398	378
10-14	776	389	387	1 141	576	565	1 174	600	574	1 107	564	543
15-19	770	386	384	763	381	382	1 121	566	556	1 163	593	569
20-24	716	355	361	756	377	379	735	367	368	1 108	558	550
25-29	635	318	316	702	347	355	731	364	368	724	360	364
30-34	554	279	275	618	308	310	680	335	345	718	356	362
35-39	443	222	221	541	271	270	602	300	302	668	328	340
40-44	417	211	206	430	215	215	528	265	263	591	294	297
45-49	345	180	165	403	204	199	418	209	209	514	258	257
50-54	347	180	167	329	171	158	389	197	192	403	200	202
55-59	316	164	152	327	169	158	314	163	152	370	186	184
60-64	272	143	129	293	151	142	305	156	149	293	151	143
65-69	230	130	100	242	126	116	264	134	129	276	140	136
70-74	152	85	67	197	110	87	210	107	103	231	115	115
75-79	91	50	41	117	64	53	157	85	72	170	84	86
80 +	60	32	28	78	41	37	110	57	52	152	79	73

Age group	1990 Both sexes	1990 Males	1990 Females	1995 Both sexes	1995 Males	1995 Females	2000 Both sexes	2000 Males	2000 Females	2005 Both sexes	2005 Males	2005 Females
All ages	10 537	5 298	5 239	10 867	5 454	5 413	11 125	5 571	5 554	11 269	5 639	5 630
0-4	882	452	430	787	404	384	711	363	348	682	351	332
5-9	770	395	375	873	447	426	776	396	380	701	358	343
10-14	769	394	375	760	389	371	865	442	423	765	391	375
15-19	1 098	559	539	757	386	370	752	385	368	854	436	418
20-24	1 152	587	565	1 082	550	532	747	382	365	736	377	359
25-29	1 097	551	546	1 136	578	558	1 069	542	527	728	373	355
30-34	713	354	360	1 083	543	540	1 121	570	551	1 046	530	515
35-39	708	350	358	700	347	353	1 067	534	532	1 097	557	540
40-44	658	322	336	693	342	351	684	339	346	1 040	520	520
45-49	578	287	291	640	312	327	674	332	342	659	325	334
50-54	499	249	250	557	276	282	619	301	318	650	319	331
55-59	385	190	195	475	236	240	533	262	271	590	285	305
60-64	347	173	174	361	177	184	448	220	228	501	244	257
65-69	267	135	131	319	157	162	333	161	172	416	201	214
70-74	242	120	122	234	116	118	282	136	146	297	140	156
75-79	188	91	97	197	95	102	192	93	100	235	110	125
80 +	184	90	94	213	101	112	251	114	137	271	121	150

United Nations Department of Economic and Social Affairs/Population Division
World Population Prospects: The 2004 Revision, Volume II: Sex and Age Distribution of the World Population

326

POPULATION BY AGE AND SEX (in thousands)

Age group	2005			2010			2015			2020		
	Both sexes	Males	Females	Both sexes	Males	Females	Both sexes	Males	Females	Both sexes	Males	Females
All ages	11 269	5 639	5 630	11 379	5 693	5 686	11 437	5 720	5 717	11 402	5 716	5 717
0-4	682	351	332	635	326	308	607	312	295	582	300	283
5-9	701	358	343	673	346	327	626	322	304	598	308	291
10-14	765	391	375	692	354	338	664	342	323	617	318	300
15-19	854	436	418	756	386	370	683	349	334	655	337	318
20-24	736	377	359	839	429	410	742	379	363	669	343	326
25-29	728	373	355	720	370	350	823	422	401	727	373	354
30-34	1 046	530	515	710	364	346	701	361	341	805	413	392
35-39	1 097	557	540	1 026	519	506	692	354	337	684	351	332
40-44	1 040	520	520	1 074	544	530	1 004	507	497	673	344	329
45-49	659	325	334	1 014	506	508	1 049	530	519	980	495	486
50-54	650	319	331	639	314	325	989	491	497	1 024	516	508
55-59	590	285	305	624	304	320	614	300	314	957	473	484
60-64	501	244	257	560	268	291	594	287	307	587	284	302
65-69	416	201	214	469	226	244	527	249	277	561	268	293
70-74	297	140	156	375	178	197	427	201	225	481	224	258
75-79	235	110	125	252	116	136	322	149	173	370	170	200
80-84	142	66	76	179	80	98	195	87	109	253	113	140
85-89	87	38	49	90	40	50	117	50	67	131	55	76
90-94	34	14	20	41	17	24	45	19	26	60	24	36
95-99	7	3	4	10	4	6	13	5	8	15	6	9
100 +	1	0	0	1	0	1	2	1	1	2	1	1

Age group	2025			2030			2035			2040		
	Both sexes	Males	Females	Both sexes	Males	Females	Both sexes	Males	Females	Both sexes	Males	Females
All ages	11 348	5 671	5 677	11 182	5 587	5 596	10 934	5 461	5 473	10 608	5 297	5 311
0-4	553	284	269	521	268	253	492	253	239	469	241	228
5-9	574	295	278	544	280	264	512	264	249	483	249	235
10-14	590	304	286	565	291	274	536	276	260	504	260	244
15-19	608	313	295	581	299	282	556	287	270	527	272	255
20-24	642	331	311	595	307	288	568	293	274	543	281	262
25-29	654	337	317	627	325	302	580	301	279	553	287	266
30-34	708	364	344	636	328	308	609	316	293	563	293	270
35-39	787	403	384	691	355	336	619	319	300	593	307	285
40-44	665	341	324	700	363	376	673	345	328	601	309	292
45-49	652	333	319	645	331	315	747	382	365	653	334	319
50-54	957	482	476	635	323	311	628	321	307	729	372	357
55-59	993	498	495	928	465	464	610	311	299	607	309	298
60-64	918	451	468	954	475	479	893	444	449	589	297	292
65-69	555	266	289	871	423	449	907	446	460	850	418	432
70-74	515	241	274	511	240	271	804	383	421	839	406	433
75-79	420	189	230	451	206	246	450	206	244	710	329	381
80-84	293	130	164	336	146	190	364	160	205	365	161	204
85-89	172	73	99	202	85	117	234	97	138	255	106	149
90-94	68	27	41	91	36	55	109	43	66	127	49	78
95-99	21	8	13	24	9	15	33	12	21	39	15	25
100 +	3	1	2	4	2	2	5	2	3	6	2	4

Age group	2045			2050		
	Both sexes	Males	Females	Both sexes	Males	Females
All ages	10 212	5 098	5 114	9 749	4 867	4 882
0-4	448	231	218	431	222	209
5-9	460	237	223	440	227	213
10-14	475	245	230	452	233	219
15-19	495	255	240	466	241	226
20-24	514	266	248	482	250	233
25-29	529	275	254	500	260	240
30-34	536	279	257	512	267	245
35-39	546	284	262	520	270	249
40-44	575	298	277	529	275	254
45-49	583	300	283	557	288	268
50-54	637	325	312	567	291	276
55-59	707	359	348	616	314	303
60-64	583	295	288	680	343	337
65-69	561	279	282	556	278	278
70-74	788	380	408	521	255	266
75-79	743	349	393	699	328	371
80-84	579	258	321	607	275	332
85-89	258	108	150	410	174	237
90-94	140	55	86	143	56	87
95-99	47	17	30	52	19	33
100 +	8	3	5	9	4	6

POPULATION BY AGE AND SEX (in thousands)

Age group	2005 Both sexes	2005 Males	2005 Females	2010 Both sexes	2010 Males	2010 Females	2015 Both sexes	2015 Males	2015 Females	2020 Both sexes	2020 Males	2020 Females
All ages	11 269	5 639	5 630	11 478	5 743	5 734	11 684	5 847	5 837	11 856	5 933	5 923
0-4	682	351	332	734	377	356	756	389	367	759	390	369
5-9	701	358	343	673	346	327	724	373	352	747	384	363
10-14	765	391	375	692	354	338	664	342	323	716	368	348
15-19	854	436	418	756	386	370	683	349	334	655	337	318
20-24	736	377	359	839	429	410	742	379	363	669	343	326
25-29	728	373	355	720	370	350	823	422	401	727	373	354
30-34	1 046	530	515	710	364	346	701	361	341	805	413	392
35-39	1 097	557	540	1 026	519	506	692	354	337	684	351	332
40-44	1 040	520	520	1 074	544	530	1 004	507	497	673	344	329
45-49	659	325	334	1 014	506	508	1 049	530	519	980	495	486
50-54	650	319	331	639	314	325	989	491	497	1 024	516	508
55-59	590	285	305	624	304	320	614	300	314	957	473	484
60-64	501	244	257	560	268	291	594	287	307	587	284	302
65-69	416	201	214	469	226	244	527	249	277	561	268	293
70-74	297	140	156	375	178	197	427	201	225	481	224	258
75-79	235	110	125	252	116	136	322	149	173	370	170	200
80-84	142	66	76	179	80	98	195	87	109	253	113	140
85-89	87	38	49	90	40	50	117	50	67	131	55	76
90-94	34	14	20	41	17	24	45	19	26	60	24	36
95-99	7	3	4	10	4	6	13	5	8	15	6	9
100 +	1	0	0	1	0	1	2	1	1	2	1	1

Age group	2025 Both sexes	2025 Males	2025 Females	2030 Both sexes	2030 Males	2030 Females	2035 Both sexes	2035 Males	2035 Females	2040 Both sexes	2040 Males	2040 Females
All ages	11 946	5 978	5 967	11 970	5 991	5 979	11 948	5 982	5 966	11 888	5 955	5 933
0-4	727	374	353	712	366	346	719	370	349	736	378	357
5-9	750	386	364	718	370	349	703	362	341	711	366	345
10-14	738	380	358	741	382	360	710	365	344	694	358	337
15-19	707	364	343	730	376	354	733	377	355	701	361	340
20-24	642	331	311	693	358	336	716	370	347	719	371	348
25-29	654	337	317	627	325	302	678	352	327	701	363	338
30-34	708	364	344	636	328	308	609	316	293	661	343	318
35-39	787	403	384	691	355	336	619	319	300	593	307	285
40-44	665	341	324	768	393	375	673	345	328	601	309	292
45-49	652	333	319	645	331	315	747	382	365	653	334	319
50-54	957	482	476	635	323	311	628	321	307	729	372	357
55-59	993	498	495	928	465	464	613	311	302	607	309	298
60-64	918	451	468	954	475	479	893	444	449	589	297	292
65-69	555	266	289	871	423	449	907	446	460	850	418	432
70-74	515	241	274	511	240	271	804	383	421	839	406	433
75-79	420	189	230	451	206	246	450	206	244	710	329	381
80-84	293	130	164	336	146	190	364	160	205	365	161	204
85-89	172	73	99	202	85	117	234	97	138	255	106	149
90-94	68	27	41	91	36	55	109	43	66	127	49	78
95-99	21	8	13	24	9	15	33	12	21	39	15	25
100 +	3	1	2	4	2	2	5	2	3	6	2	4

Age group	2045 Both sexes	2045 Males	2045 Females	2050 Both sexes	2050 Males	2050 Females
All ages	11 787	5 907	5 880	11 638	5 838	5 800
0-4	745	383	362	747	384	363
5-9	727	374	353	736	379	357
10-14	702	361	341	719	370	349
15-19	686	353	332	693	357	336
20-24	688	355	333	673	347	325
25-29	705	365	339	673	349	324
30-34	684	355	329	687	357	330
35-39	644	334	310	667	346	321
40-44	575	298	277	626	324	302
45-49	583	300	283	557	288	268
50-54	637	325	312	567	291	276
55-59	707	359	348	616	314	303
60-64	583	295	288	680	343	337
65-69	561	279	282	556	278	278
70-74	788	380	408	521	255	266
75-79	743	349	393	699	328	371
80-84	579	258	321	607	275	332
85-89	258	108	150	410	174	237
90-94	140	55	86	143	56	87
95-99	47	17	30	52	19	33
100 +	8	3	5	9	4	6

United Nations Department of Economic and Social Affairs/Population Division
World Population Prospects: The 2004 Revision, Volume II: Sex and Age Distribution of the World Population

328

POPULATION BY AGE AND SEX (in thousands)

Age group	2005			2010			2015			2020		
	Both sexes	Males	Females	Both sexes	Males	Females	Both sexes	Males	Females	Both sexes	Males	Females
All ages	11 269	5 639	5 630	11 280	5 042	5 608	11 189	5 592	5 596	11 007	5 497	5 510
0-4	682	351	332	536	276	260	458	235	222	405	208	197
5-9	701	358	343	673	346	327	527	271	256	449	231	218
10-14	765	391	375	692	354	338	664	342	323	519	267	252
15-19	854	436	418	756	386	370	683	349	334	655	337	318
20-24	736	377	359	839	429	410	742	379	363	669	343	326
25-29	728	373	355	720	370	350	823	422	401	727	373	354
30-34	1 046	530	515	710	364	346	701	361	341	805	413	392
35-39	1 097	557	540	1 026	519	506	692	354	337	684	351	332
40-44	1 040	520	520	1 074	544	530	1 004	507	497	673	344	329
45-49	659	325	334	1 014	506	508	1 049	530	519	980	495	486
50-54	650	319	331	639	314	325	989	491	497	1 024	516	508
55-59	590	285	305	624	304	320	614	300	314	957	473	484
60-64	501	244	257	560	268	291	594	287	307	587	284	302
65-69	416	201	214	469	226	244	527	249	277	561	268	293
70-74	297	140	156	375	178	197	427	201	225	481	224	258
75-79	235	110	125	252	116	136	322	149	173	370	170	200
80-84	142	66	76	179	80	98	195	87	109	253	113	140
85-89	87	38	49	90	40	50	117	50	67	131	55	76
90-94	34	14	20	41	17	24	45	19	26	60	24	36
95-99	7	3	4	10	4	6	13	5	8	15	6	9
100 +	1	0	0	1	0	1	2	1	1	2	1	1

Age group	2025			2030			2035			2040		
	Both sexes	Males	Females	Both sexes	Males	Females	Both sexes	Males	Females	Both sexes	Males	Females
All ages	10 753	5 365	5 387	10 413	5 191	5 221	9 975	4 968	5 007	9 441	4 697	4 744
0-4	382	197	186	346	178	168	302	155	147	260	134	126
5-9	397	204	192	374	193	181	338	174	164	294	151	142
10-14	441	227	214	388	200	188	365	188	177	329	170	159
15-19	510	262	247	432	223	209	380	196	184	357	184	173
20-24	642	331	311	497	257	240	419	217	202	367	190	177
25-29	654	337	317	627	325	302	482	251	231	405	211	193
30-34	708	364	344	636	328	308	609	316	293	465	242	222
35-39	787	403	384	691	355	336	619	319	300	593	307	285
40-44	665	341	324	768	393	375	673	345	328	601	309	292
45-49	652	333	319	645	331	315	747	382	365	653	334	319
50-54	957	482	476	635	323	311	628	321	307	729	372	357
55-59	993	499	495	928	465	464	613	311	302	607	309	298
60-64	918	451	468	954	475	479	893	444	449	589	297	292
65-69	555	266	289	871	423	449	907	446	460	850	418	432
70-74	515	241	274	511	240	271	804	383	421	839	406	433
75-79	420	189	230	451	206	246	450	206	244	710	329	381
80-84	293	130	164	336	146	190	364	160	205	365	161	204
85-89	172	73	99	202	85	117	234	97	138	255	106	149
90-94	68	27	41	91	36	55	109	43	66	127	49	78
95-99	21	8	13	24	9	15	33	12	21	39	15	25
100 +	3	1	2	4	2	2	5	2	3	6	2	4

Age group	2045			2050		
	Both sexes	Males	Females	Both sexes	Males	Females
All ages	8 825	4 385	4 440	8 137	4 039	4 098
0-4	227	117	110	203	105	99
5-9	252	130	122	219	113	106
10-14	285	147	138	243	126	118
15-19	321	166	155	277	143	134
20-24	344	179	166	308	160	148
25-29	352	184	168	330	173	157
30-34	388	203	185	336	176	159
35-39	449	234	215	372	195	177
40-44	575	298	277	432	225	207
45-49	583	300	283	557	288	268
50-54	637	325	312	567	291	276
55-59	707	359	348	616	314	303
60-64	583	295	288	680	343	337
65-69	561	279	282	556	278	278
70-74	788	380	408	521	255	266
75-79	743	349	393	699	328	371
80-84	579	258	321	607	275	332
85-89	258	108	150	410	174	237
90-94	140	55	86	143	56	87
95-99	47	17	30	52	19	33
100 +	8	3	5	9	4	6

United Nations Department of Economic and Social Affairs/Population Division
World Population Prospects: The 2004 Revision, Volume II: Sex and Age Distribution of the World Population

329

POPULATION BY AGE AND SEX (in thousands)

Age group	1950 Both sexes	Males	Females	1955 Both sexes	Males	Females	1960 Both sexes	Males	Females	1965 Both sexes	Males	Females
All ages	494	244	250	530	260	270	573	282	291	582	286	297
0-4	67	34	32	65	33	32	75	38	37	70	36	35
5-9	53	27	26	65	33	31	68	35	33	66	33	32
10-14	51	26	25	52	26	25	67	34	33	65	33	32
15-19	46	23	23	47	24	24	48	23	24	59	30	30
20-24	42	20	22	41	20	22	47	23	24	47	23	24
25-29	37	17	19	39	18	21	38	18	20	40	19	21
30-34	33	16	17	35	16	19	37	17	20	36	17	19
35-39	31	15	16	32	15	17	31	15	15	33	15	18
40-44	28	13	15	30	14	15	32	15	17	31	15	16
45-49	24	12	12	28	13	14	28	14	14	26	13	13
50-54	22	11	11	23	11	12	28	13	15	28	14	15
55-59	17	8	9	21	10	11	19	10	9	23	11	12
60-64	15	7	8	17	8	8	21	9	11	21	10	11
65-69	12	6	6	14	7	7	11	6	5	13	6	7
70-74	9	4	5	11	5	6	12	6	6	13	6	7
75-79	5	3	3	7	3	3	7	3	4	7	3	4
80 +	3	1	2	4	2	2	4	2	2	5	2	3

Age group	1970 Both sexes	Males	Females	1975 Both sexes	Males	Females	1980 Both sexes	Males	Females	1985 Both sexes	Males	Females
All ages	615	304	311	609	303	306	611	305	306	647	322	325
0-4	59	30	28	47	24	23	57	29	28	62	32	30
5-9	65	34	32	51	26	25	44	22	22	51	26	25
10-14	67	35	33	60	31	29	48	25	23	50	25	25
15-19	58	29	28	66	34	33	56	29	27	53	27	26
20-24	51	25	25	58	30	28	60	31	30	60	31	29
25-29	42	20	21	53	27	27	54	28	26	56	29	27
30-34	38	18	19	37	19	19	50	25	25	48	24	24
35-39	35	16	18	40	20	20	35	18	18	47	23	23
40-44	33	15	17	31	15	16	38	19	19	37	18	19
45-49	29	14	15	30	14	16	29	14	15	35	17	18
50-54	26	13	13	26	13	13	29	14	15	29	14	15
55-59	26	12	14	25	12	13	25	12	12	27	13	14
60-64	24	12	12	25	12	13	23	11	12	24	11	13
65-69	21	10	11	23	10	12	22	10	12	22	10	12
70-74	17	8	9	16	8	9	19	8	10	20	9	11
75-79	12	5	7	9	4	6	12	6	6	15	6	8
80 +	11	5	6	11	6	6	10	4	6	12	5	6

Age group	1990 Both sexes	Males	Females	1995 Both sexes	Males	Females	2000 Both sexes	Males	Females	2005 Both sexes	Males	Females
All ages	681	339	341	731	365	366	786	387	399	835	406	429
0-4	62	32	30	61	32	30	53	27	26	49	25	24
5-9	60	31	29	61	32	30	62	32	30	54	27	26
10-14	55	28	27	61	32	30	63	32	30	63	33	31
15-19	50	25	24	56	29	27	63	32	30	64	33	31
20-24	52	27	26	51	26	25	59	30	29	65	33	32
25-29	53	27	26	54	27	27	54	26	28	62	30	32
30-34	54	27	27	55	28	27	57	27	30	57	27	31
35-39	49	25	24	57	29	28	59	29	30	60	28	32
40-44	45	22	22	50	25	25	59	29	30	61	29	32
45-49	40	20	20	46	23	23	51	25	26	61	29	31
50-54	33	16	17	40	20	20	46	23	24	52	25	27
55-59	29	14	15	32	15	16	40	20	20	46	23	24
60-64	26	12	14	29	14	15	32	15	17	40	19	20
65-69	24	11	13	25	11	14	29	13	15	32	15	17
70-74	19	9	10	21	10	12	23	10	13	27	12	15
75-79	15	7	8	16	7	9	18	8	10	20	9	11
80 +	16	7	9	16	7	9	19	8	11	22	9	13

United Nations Department of Economic and Social Affairs/Population Division
World Population Prospects: The 2004 Revision, Volume II: Sex and Age Distribution of the World Population

330

POPULATION BY AGE AND SEX (in thousands)

Age group	2005 Both sexes	Males	Females	2010 Both sexes	Males	Females	2015 Both sexes	Males	Females	2020 Both sexes	Males	Females
All ages	835	406	429	881	429	452	927	452	475	972	475	497
0-4	49	25	24	53	27	25	55	29	27	57	30	28
5-9	54	27	26	50	26	24	54	28	26	56	29	27
10-14	63	33	31	54	28	27	51	26	25	54	28	26
15-19	64	33	31	65	33	32	56	28	27	52	27	25
20-24	65	33	32	68	35	33	69	35	34	60	30	29
25-29	62	30	32	70	35	34	72	37	36	73	37	36
30-34	57	27	31	66	32	34	73	37	36	76	39	38
35-39	60	28	32	60	28	32	68	33	35	76	38	38
40-44	61	29	32	62	29	33	61	29	33	70	34	36
45-49	61	29	31	62	29	33	63	29	34	62	29	33
50-54	52	25	27	61	29	31	62	29	33	63	29	34
55-59	46	23	24	51	25	26	60	29	31	62	29	33
60-64	40	19	20	45	22	23	50	24	26	59	28	31
65-69	32	15	17	38	18	20	43	21	23	48	23	25
70-74	27	12	15	29	13	16	35	16	18	40	18	21
75-79	20	9	11	23	10	13	25	11	14	30	13	17
80-84	14	6	8	15	6	9	17	7	10	19	8	11
85-89	6	3	4	8	3	5	9	3	6	10	4	6
90-94	2	1	1	2	1	2	3	1	2	4	1	3
95-99	0	0	0	0	0	0	1	0	0	1	0	1
100 +	0	0	0	0	0	0	0	0	0	0	0	0

Age group	2025 Both sexes	Males	Females	2030 Both sexes	Males	Females	2035 Both sexes	Males	Females	2040 Both sexes	Males	Females
All ages	1 014	495	518	1 051	514	537	1 086	532	554	1 118	548	570
0-4	57	30	28	57	29	28	58	30	28	60	31	29
5-9	58	30	28	59	30	28	58	30	28	59	31	29
10-14	57	29	28	59	30	29	59	31	29	59	30	28
15-19	56	29	27	59	30	28	60	31	29	61	31	29
20-24	56	28	27	60	30	29	62	32	30	64	33	31
25-29	64	32	32	60	31	30	64	33	31	67	34	33
30-34	77	39	38	68	34	34	64	33	32	68	35	33
35-39	79	40	39	80	40	39	71	36	35	67	34	33
40-44	78	39	38	81	41	40	81	41	40	72	36	36
45-49	71	35	36	79	40	39	81	41	40	82	41	41
50-54	63	29	33	71	35	36	79	40	39	82	41	40
55-59	60	29	31	62	29	33	70	34	36	78	39	39
60-64	60	28	32	61	28	33	61	28	33	69	33	36
65-69	56	26	30	58	27	31	59	27	32	59	27	32
70-74	44	21	24	52	24	28	54	24	30	55	24	31
75-79	34	15	19	39	17	21	46	20	26	47	21	27
80-84	23	10	13	27	11	16	30	13	18	36	15	21
85-89	12	4	7	14	5	9	17	6	11	20	7	13
90-94	5	1	3	6	2	4	7	2	5	9	3	6
95-99	1	0	1	2	0	1	2	0	1	3	1	2
100 +	0	0	0	0	0	0	0	0	0	0	0	0

Age group	2045 Both sexes	Males	Females	2050 Both sexes	Males	Females
All ages	1 147	563	584	1 174	578	597
0-4	61	32	30	62	32	30
5-9	61	31	29	62	32	30
10-14	60	31	29	61	32	30
15-19	60	31	29	62	32	30
20-24	65	33	31	64	33	31
25-29	69	35	34	69	35	34
30-34	71	36	35	73	37	36
35-39	71	36	35	74	37	36
40-44	69	35	34	73	37	36
45-49	73	37	36	70	35	35
50-54	82	42	41	74	37	37
55-59	81	41	40	82	41	41
60-64	77	38	38	80	40	40
65-69	67	32	35	74	37	37
70-74	55	25	30	62	29	33
75-79	49	21	28	49	21	28
80-84	38	16	23	40	16	24
85-89	25	9	15	26	10	17
90-94	11	3	7	13	4	9
95-99	3	1	3	4	1	3
100 +	1	0	1	1	0	1

United Nations Department of Economic and Social Affairs/Population Division
World Population Prospects: The 2004 Revision, Volume II: Sex and Age Distribution of the World Population

331

POPULATION BY AGE AND SEX (in thousands)

Age group	2005 Both sexes	2005 Males	2005 Females	2010 Both sexes	2010 Males	2010 Females	2015 Both sexes	2015 Males	2015 Females	2020 Both sexes	2020 Males	2020 Females
All ages	835	406	429	889	433	456	949	463	485	1 011	495	516
0-4	49	25	24	61	31	29	69	36	33	74	38	36
5-9	54	27	26	50	26	24	62	32	30	70	36	34
10-14	63	33	31	54	28	27	51	26	25	62	32	30
15-19	64	33	31	65	33	32	56	28	27	52	27	25
20-24	65	33	32	68	35	33	69	35	34	60	30	29
25-29	62	30	32	70	35	34	72	37	36	73	37	36
30-34	57	27	31	66	32	34	73	37	36	76	39	38
35-39	60	28	32	60	28	32	68	33	35	76	38	38
40-44	61	29	32	62	29	33	61	29	33	70	34	36
45-49	61	29	31	62	29	33	63	29	34	62	29	33
50-54	52	25	27	61	29	31	62	29	33	63	29	34
55-59	46	23	24	51	25	26	60	29	31	62	29	33
60-64	40	19	20	45	22	23	50	24	26	59	28	31
65-69	32	15	17	38	18	20	43	21	23	48	23	25
70-74	27	12	15	29	13	16	35	16	18	40	18	21
75-79	20	9	11	23	10	13	25	11	14	30	13	17
80-84	14	6	8	15	6	9	17	7	10	19	8	11
85-89	6	3	4	8	3	5	9	3	6	10	4	6
90-94	2	1	1	2	1	2	3	1	2	4	1	3
95-99	0	0	0	0	0	0	1	0	0	1	0	1
100 +	0	0	0	0	0	0	0	0	0	0	0	0

Age group	2025 Both sexes	2025 Males	2025 Females	2030 Both sexes	2030 Males	2030 Females	2035 Both sexes	2035 Males	2035 Females	2040 Both sexes	2040 Males	2040 Females
All ages	1 069	524	545	1 124	552	572	1 180	580	600	1 239	610	628
0-4	74	38	36	74	38	36	80	41	38	87	45	42
5-9	76	39	37	75	39	36	75	39	36	81	42	39
10-14	71	36	34	76	39	37	76	39	37	76	39	37
15-19	64	33	31	72	37	35	78	40	38	77	40	38
20-24	56	28	27	68	35	33	76	39	37	81	42	40
25-29	64	32	32	60	31	30	72	37	35	80	41	39
30-34	77	39	38	68	34	34	64	33	32	76	39	37
35-39	79	40	39	80	40	39	71	36	35	67	34	33
40-44	78	39	38	81	41	40	81	41	40	72	36	36
45-49	71	35	36	79	40	39	81	41	40	82	41	41
50-54	63	29	33	71	35	36	79	40	39	82	41	40
55-59	63	29	34	62	29	33	70	34	36	78	39	39
60-64	60	28	32	61	28	33	61	28	33	69	33	36
65-69	56	26	30	58	27	31	59	27	32	59	27	32
70-74	44	21	24	52	24	28	54	24	30	55	24	31
75-79	34	15	19	39	17	21	46	20	26	47	21	27
80-84	23	10	13	27	11	16	30	13	18	36	15	21
85-89	12	4	7	14	5	9	17	6	11	20	7	13
90-94	5	1	3	6	2	4	7	2	5	9	3	6
95-99	1	0	1	2	0	1	2	0	1	3	1	2
100 +	0	0	0	0	0	0	0	0	0	0	0	0

Age group	2045 Both sexes	2045 Males	2045 Females	2050 Both sexes	2050 Males	2050 Females
All ages	1 300	642	658	1 362	675	687
0-4	93	48	45	97	50	47
5-9	88	45	43	95	49	46
10-14	81	42	39	89	46	43
15-19	78	40	38	83	43	40
20-24	81	42	40	81	42	40
25-29	86	44	42	86	44	42
30-34	84	43	41	90	46	44
35-39	79	40	39	87	44	43
40-44	69	35	34	81	41	40
45-49	73	37	36	70	35	35
50-54	82	42	41	74	37	37
55-59	81	41	40	82	41	41
60-64	77	38	38	80	40	40
65-69	67	32	35	74	37	37
70-74	55	25	30	62	29	33
75-79	49	21	28	49	21	28
80-84	38	16	23	40	16	24
85-89	25	9	15	26	10	17
90-94	11	3	7	13	4	9
95-99	3	1	3	4	1	3
100 +	1	0	1	1	0	1

332

United Nations Department of Economic and Social Affairs/Population Division
World Population Prospects: The 2004 Revision, Volume II: Sex and Age Distribution of the World Population

POPULATION BY AGE AND SEX (in thousands)

Age group	2005 Both sexes	2005 Males	2005 Females	2010 Both sexes	2010 Males	2010 Females	2015 Both sexes	2015 Males	2015 Females	2020 Both sexes	2020 Males	2020 Females
All ages	835	406	429	873	425	448	905	441	465	933	454	470
0-4	49	25	24	45	23	22	42	22	20	40	21	19
5-9	54	27	26	50	26	24	46	24	22	43	22	21
10-14	63	33	31	54	28	27	51	26	25	46	24	22
15-19	64	33	31	65	33	32	56	28	27	52	27	25
20-24	65	33	32	68	35	33	69	35	34	60	30	29
25-29	62	30	32	70	35	34	72	37	36	73	37	36
30-34	57	27	31	66	32	34	73	37	36	76	39	38
35-39	60	28	32	60	28	32	68	33	35	76	38	38
40-44	61	29	32	62	29	33	61	29	33	70	34	36
45-49	61	29	31	62	29	33	63	29	34	62	29	33
50-54	52	25	27	61	29	31	62	29	33	63	29	34
55-59	46	23	24	51	25	26	60	29	31	62	29	33
60-64	40	19	20	45	22	23	50	24	26	59	28	31
65-69	32	15	17	38	18	20	43	21	23	48	23	25
70-74	27	12	15	29	13	16	35	16	18	40	18	21
75-79	20	9	11	23	10	13	25	11	14	30	13	17
80-84	14	6	8	15	6	9	17	7	10	19	8	11
85-89	6	3	4	8	3	5	9	3	6	10	4	6
90-94	2	1	1	2	1	2	3	1	2	4	1	3
95-99	0	0	0	0	0	0	1	0	0	1	0	1
100 +	0	0	0	0	0	0	0	0	0	0	0	0

Age group	2025 Both sexes	2025 Males	2025 Females	2030 Both sexes	2030 Males	2030 Females	2035 Both sexes	2035 Males	2035 Females	2040 Both sexes	2040 Males	2040 Females
All ages	958	467	491	979	477	502	995	485	510	1 004	489	515
0-4	41	21	20	40	21	20	39	20	19	37	19	18
5-9	41	21	20	42	22	20	41	21	20	41	21	20
10-14	43	22	21	42	21	20	42	22	21	42	22	20
15-19	48	25	23	45	23	22	43	22	21	44	23	21
20-24	56	28	27	52	26	25	49	25	24	47	24	23
25-29	64	32	32	60	31	30	56	29	28	53	27	26
30-34	77	39	38	68	34	34	64	33	32	60	30	30
35-39	79	40	39	80	40	39	71	36	35	67	34	33
40-44	78	39	38	81	41	40	81	41	40	72	36	30
45-49	71	35	36	79	40	39	81	41	40	82	41	41
50-54	63	29	33	71	35	36	79	40	39	82	41	40
55-59	63	29	34	62	29	33	70	34	36	78	39	39
60-64	60	28	32	61	28	33	61	28	33	69	33	36
65-69	56	26	30	58	27	31	59	27	32	59	27	32
70-74	44	21	24	52	24	28	54	24	30	55	24	31
75-79	34	15	19	39	17	21	46	20	26	47	21	27
80-84	23	10	13	27	11	16	30	13	18	36	15	21
85-89	12	4	7	14	5	9	17	6	11	20	7	13
90-94	5	1	3	6	2	4	7	2	5	9	3	6
95-99	1	0	1	2	0	1	2	0	1	3	1	2
100 +	0	0	0	0	0	0	0	0	0	0	0	0

Age group	2045 Both sexes	2045 Males	2045 Females	2050 Both sexes	2050 Males	2050 Females
All ages	1 009	492	517	1 009	492	517
0-4	36	19	17	35	18	17
5-9	39	20	19	37	19	18
10-14	41	21	20	39	20	19
15-19	44	22	21	43	22	21
20-24	48	24	23	47	24	23
25-29	52	26	25	53	27	26
30-34	57	29	28	56	28	27
35-39	63	32	31	60	30	30
40-44	69	35	34	65	33	32
45-49	73	37	36	70	35	35
50-54	82	42	41	74	37	37
55-59	81	41	40	82	41	41
60-64	77	38	38	80	40	40
65-69	67	32	35	74	37	37
70-74	55	25	30	62	29	33
75-79	49	21	28	49	21	28
80-84	38	16	23	40	16	24
85-89	25	9	15	26	10	17
90-94	11	3	7	13	4	9
95-99	3	1	3	4	1	3
100 +	1	0	1	1	0	1

United Nations Department of Economic and Social Affairs/Population Division
World Population Prospects: The 2004 Revision, Volume II: Sex and Age Distribution of the World Population

333

POPULATION BY AGE AND SEX (in thousands)

Age group	1950 Both sexes	Males	Females	1955 Both sexes	Males	Females	1960 Both sexes	Males	Females	1965 Both sexes	Males	Females
All ages	8 925	4 340	4 585	9 302	4 528	4 774	9 552	4 654	4 899	9 717	4 735	4 982
0-4	882	450	432	872	445	427	735	375	360	695	355	340
5-9	712	362	350	881	449	432	871	444	427	733	374	359
10-14	553	279	274	713	362	351	881	448	433	869	443	427
15-19	635	322	313	553	279	274	712	362	351	879	447	432
20-24	707	358	349	634	320	314	551	277	274	709	359	350
25-29	744	364	380	705	356	349	632	318	314	549	275	274
30-34	425	209	217	741	361	380	702	353	349	628	315	313
35-39	731	359	372	423	206	217	736	357	379	697	349	348
40-44	729	359	370	719	351	368	418	203	215	726	351	375
45-49	678	331	347	710	347	363	704	341	363	408	196	212
50-54	570	265	305	649	313	337	683	330	354	678	324	354
55-59	448	201	246	531	242	290	611	289	322	643	304	339
60-64	373	165	208	400	175	225	481	213	268	553	254	299
65-69	297	130	167	310	133	177	339	143	196	409	175	234
70-74	218	94	124	221	94	127	237	98	138	260	106	154
75-79	136	58	78	137	59	78	143	61	83	154	63	91
80 +	88	35	52	105	39	66	117	42	75	127	44	83

Age group	1970 Both sexes	Males	Females	1975 Both sexes	Males	Females	1980 Both sexes	Males	Females	1985 Both sexes	Males	Females
All ages	9 805	4 748	5 057	9 997	4 857	5 140	10 283	4 983	5 300	10 305	5 014	5 291
0-4	689	353	336	847	432	415	866	443	423	703	358	344
5-9	695	356	338	688	352	336	861	440	420	866	443	423
10-14	699	358	341	694	355	338	687	351	335	860	440	420
15-19	831	425	406	698	357	341	688	352	336	686	351	336
20-24	878	447	430	828	423	406	699	356	342	687	351	336
25-29	715	362	353	874	444	430	829	420	408	697	354	342
30-34	563	283	280	712	359	353	862	437	425	826	418	408
35-39	590	294	296	559	280	280	699	352	347	858	432	425
40-44	647	316	331	582	288	294	549	273	276	691	345	345
45-49	689	330	359	632	306	326	571	281	290	538	265	273
50-54	411	195	216	663	313	351	613	294	320	551	267	284
55-59	603	285	319	387	180	207	630	291	339	579	271	308
60-64	605	279	326	546	250	296	356	160	196	573	256	317
65-69	487	211	276	512	228	285	489	212	277	305	132	173
70-74	350	135	215	373	155	218	422	170	252	378	157	221
75-79	206	71	135	228	86	142	270	95	174	278	109	168
80 +	148	47	100	174	50	124	193	54	139	231	65	166

Age group	1990 Both sexes	Males	Females	1995 Both sexes	Males	Females	2000 Both sexes	Males	Females	2005 Both sexes	Males	Females
All ages	10 306	5 009	5 297	10 331	5 020	5 311	10 267	4 996	5 271	10 220	4 975	5 245
0-4	648	332	316	586	301	285	450	230	219	453	232	221
5-9	692	354	338	645	330	315	588	302	286	452	231	220
10-14	871	445	426	690	353	337	647	331	316	591	303	288
15-19	839	429	410	870	445	425	692	354	338	650	332	317
20-24	684	350	334	842	430	412	871	445	427	694	355	340
25-29	684	350	334	684	350	335	843	430	413	873	445	428
30-34	707	360	347	679	346	333	685	349	336	844	430	414
35-39	818	413	405	699	353	346	679	345	334	686	349	337
40-44	834	419	414	808	405	403	696	351	346	677	343	334
45-49	668	332	336	820	408	412	799	398	401	690	346	344
50-54	513	250	263	653	320	333	803	395	408	785	387	398
55-59	528	250	278	494	235	259	629	302	327	777	376	401
60-64	532	239	293	494	226	268	465	215	250	596	279	317
65-69	502	210	292	478	204	273	449	197	252	426	189	237
70-74	246	97	149	420	163	257	410	165	245	389	161	228
75-79	288	104	184	186	67	119	326	116	210	324	120	204
80 +	253	74	179	282	84	198	233	70	163	313	95	218

United Nations Department of Economic and Social Affairs/Population Division
World Population Prospects: The 2004 Revision, Volume II: Sex and Age Distribution of the World Population

334

POPULATION BY AGE AND SEX (in thousands)

Age group	2005 Both sexes	Males	Females	2010 Both sexes	Males	Females	2015 Both sexes	Males	Females	2020 Both sexes	Males	Females
All ages	10 220	4 975	5 245	10 158	4 945	5 214	10 066	4 898	5 168	9 932	4 829	5 103
0-4	453	232	221	454	233	221	441	226	215	419	215	204
5-9	452	231	220	455	233	222	456	234	222	443	227	216
10-14	591	303	288	454	232	221	457	234	223	458	235	223
15-19	650	332	317	593	304	289	456	233	222	459	235	224
20-24	694	355	340	651	333	318	595	305	290	457	234	223
25-29	873	445	428	696	355	341	653	333	320	596	306	291
30-34	844	430	414	874	445	429	698	356	342	655	334	321
35-39	686	349	337	845	430	415	876	445	430	700	357	343
40-44	677	343	334	685	348	337	844	429	415	875	445	431
45-49	690	346	344	673	339	333	681	345	337	840	426	415
50-54	785	387	398	680	338	342	664	333	331	674	339	335
55-59	777	376	401	763	371	392	662	325	337	648	321	327
60-64	596	279	317	739	349	389	728	347	381	635	306	329
65-69	426	189	237	549	248	301	684	313	371	677	312	365
70-74	389	161	228	372	157	216	483	207	276	606	263	342
75-79	324	120	204	311	119	192	301	117	184	395	156	238
80-84	220	70	150	223	73	149	218	74	144	215	74	141
85-89	62	17	45	117	31	85	122	33	89	123	34	89
90-94	27	7	21	21	5	16	43	9	34	48	10	38
95-99	3	1	3	5	1	4	4	1	4	9	1	8
100 +	0	0	0	0	0	0	0	0	0	0	0	0

Age group	2025 Both sexes	Males	Females	2030 Both sexes	Males	Females	2035 Both sexes	Males	Females	2040 Both sexes	Males	Females
All ages	9 753	4 737	5 016	9 525	4 621	4 905	9 263	4 490	4 773	8 988	4 356	4 632
0-4	391	201	191	370	190	180	361	185	176	365	187	178
5-9	420	216	205	393	202	191	371	191	181	363	186	177
10-14	445	228	217	422	217	206	395	203	192	373	191	182
15-19	460	236	224	447	229	218	424	218	207	397	204	193
20-24	461	236	225	461	236	225	449	230	219	426	219	208
25-29	459	235	224	462	237	226	463	237	226	451	231	220
30-34	598	306	292	461	236	225	464	237	226	465	238	227
35-39	656	335	322	600	307	293	462	230	226	465	238	227
40-44	700	356	344	657	335	322	600	307	293	463	236	227
45-49	872	442	430	698	355	344	656	333	322	599	306	294
50-54	832	419	413	804	406	429	693	350	343	651	329	322
55-59	659	328	331	815	407	408	849	424	424	682	342	340
60-64	623	304	320	636	312	324	788	388	401	822	405	417
65-69	594	278	316	585	278	308	600	287	313	746	359	387
70-74	605	266	338	534	239	295	530	242	288	546	252	294
75-79	501	203	298	505	208	297	451	190	261	451	194	257
80-84	287	101	186	370	135	236	380	141	238	344	132	212
85-89	126	36	90	173	51	122	230	71	159	241	77	165
90-94	51	11	41	55	12	43	79	18	61	109	26	83
95-99	12	1	10	14	2	12	16	2	14	24	4	21
100 +	1	0	1	1	0	1	2	0	2	2	0	2

Age group	2045 Both sexes	Males	Females	2050 Both sexes	Males	Females
All ages	8 718	4 227	4 492	8 452	4 097	4 355
0-4	372	191	181	373	191	182
5-9	367	188	179	374	192	182
10-14	365	187	178	369	189	180
15-19	375	192	183	367	188	179
20-24	399	204	194	377	193	184
25-29	428	219	209	401	205	195
30-34	453	232	221	430	220	210
35-39	466	239	228	454	232	222
40-44	466	238	228	467	239	229
45-49	463	236	227	466	238	228
50-54	595	303	293	461	234	227
55-59	642	322	319	588	296	291
60-64	663	328	335	625	310	315
65-69	781	377	404	632	307	325
70-74	683	318	365	718	336	382
75-79	469	205	264	591	261	330
80-84	348	137	211	367	148	220
85-89	223	74	149	231	79	152
90-94	119	30	89	114	30	84
95-99	36	6	30	41	7	34
100 +	4	0	4	6	0	6

United Nations Department of Economic and Social Affairs/Population Division
World Population Prospects: The 2004 Revision, Volume II: Sex and Age Distribution of the World Population

335

POPULATION BY AGE AND SEX (in thousands)

Age group	2005 Both sexes	Males	Females	2010 Both sexes	Males	Females	2015 Both sexes	Males	Females	2020 Both sexes	Males	Females
All ages	10 220	4 975	5 245	10 251	4 992	5 259	10 293	5 015	5 278	10 308	5 022	5 286
0-4	453	232	221	546	280	266	575	295	280	568	291	277
5-9	452	231	220	455	233	222	548	281	267	577	296	281
10-14	591	303	288	454	232	221	457	234	223	550	282	268
15-19	650	332	317	593	304	289	456	233	222	459	235	224
20-24	694	355	340	651	333	318	595	305	290	457	234	223
25-29	873	445	428	696	355	341	653	333	320	596	306	291
30-34	844	430	414	874	445	429	698	356	342	655	334	321
35-39	686	349	337	845	430	415	876	445	430	700	357	343
40-44	677	343	334	685	348	337	844	429	415	875	445	431
45-49	690	346	344	673	339	333	681	345	337	840	426	415
50-54	785	387	398	680	338	342	664	333	331	674	339	335
55-59	777	376	401	763	371	392	662	325	337	648	321	327
60-64	596	279	317	739	349	389	728	347	381	635	306	329
65-69	426	189	237	549	248	301	684	313	371	677	312	365
70-74	389	161	228	372	157	216	483	207	276	606	263	342
75-79	324	120	204	311	119	192	301	117	184	395	156	238
80-84	220	70	150	223	73	149	218	74	144	215	74	141
85-89	62	17	45	117	31	85	122	33	89	123	34	89
90-94	27	7	21	21	5	16	43	9	34	48	10	38
95-99	3	1	3	5	1	4	4	1	4	9	1	8
100 +	0	0	0	0	0	0	0	0	0	0	0	0

Age group	2025 Both sexes	Males	Females	2030 Both sexes	Males	Females	2035 Both sexes	Males	Females	2040 Both sexes	Males	Females
All ages	10 260	4 997	5 263	10 160	4 946	5 214	10 049	4 893	5 156	9 969	4 859	5 110
0-4	523	268	255	498	255	242	513	263	250	560	287	273
5-9	570	292	277	525	269	256	499	256	243	515	264	251
10-14	579	297	282	571	293	278	527	270	256	501	257	244
15-19	552	283	269	581	298	283	573	294	279	528	271	257
20-24	461	236	225	554	284	270	583	299	284	575	295	280
25-29	459	235	224	462	237	226	555	284	271	584	299	285
30-34	598	306	292	461	236	225	464	237	226	557	285	272
35-39	656	335	322	600	307	293	462	236	226	465	238	227
40-44	700	356	344	657	335	322	600	307	293	463	236	227
45-49	872	442	430	698	355	344	656	333	322	599	306	294
50-54	832	419	413	864	436	428	693	350	343	651	329	322
55-59	659	328	331	815	407	408	849	424	424	682	342	340
60-64	623	304	320	636	312	324	788	388	401	822	405	417
65-69	594	278	316	585	278	308	600	287	313	746	359	387
70-74	605	266	338	534	239	295	530	242	288	546	252	294
75-79	501	203	298	505	208	297	451	190	261	451	194	257
80-84	287	101	186	370	135	236	380	141	238	344	132	212
85-89	126	36	90	173	51	122	230	71	159	241	77	165
90-94	51	11	41	55	12	43	79	18	61	109	26	83
95-99	12	1	10	14	2	12	16	2	14	24	4	21
100 +	1	0	1	1	0	1	2	0	2	2	0	2

Age group	2045 Both sexes	Males	Females	2050 Both sexes	Males	Females
All ages	9 929	4 847	5 082	9 909	4 844	5 065
0-4	603	310	294	621	318	302
5-9	562	288	274	605	310	295
10-14	517	265	252	564	289	275
15-19	503	258	245	519	266	253
20-24	530	272	258	505	259	246
25-29	577	295	281	532	273	259
30-34	586	300	286	578	296	282
35-39	558	286	273	587	301	287
40-44	466	238	228	559	286	273
45-49	463	236	227	466	238	228
50-54	595	303	293	461	234	227
55-59	642	322	319	588	296	291
60-64	663	328	335	625	310	315
65-69	781	377	404	632	307	325
70-74	683	318	365	718	336	382
75-79	469	205	264	591	261	330
80-84	348	137	211	367	148	220
85-89	223	74	149	231	79	152
90-94	119	30	89	114	30	84
95-99	36	6	30	41	7	34
100 +	4	0	4	6	0	6

United Nations Department of Economic and Social Affairs/Population Division
World Population Prospects: The 2004 Revision, Volume II: Sex and Age Distribution of the World Population

336

POPULATION BY AGE AND SEX (in thousands)

Age group	2005 Both sexes	Males	Females	2010 Both sexes	Males	Females	2015 Both sexes	Males	Females	2020 Both sexes	Males	Females
All ages	10 220	4 975	5 245	10 065	4 897	5 168	9 837	4 781	5 056	9 552	4 534	5 018
0-4	453	232	221	361	185	176	306	157	149	267	137	130
5-9	452	231	220	455	233	222	363	186	177	308	158	150
10-14	591	303	288	454	232	221	457	234	223	365	187	178
15-19	650	332	317	593	304	289	456	233	222	459	235	224
20-24	694	355	340	651	333	318	595	305	290	457	234	223
25-29	873	445	428	696	355	341	653	333	320	596	306	291
30-34	844	430	414	874	445	429	698	356	342	655	334	321
35-39	686	349	337	845	430	415	876	445	430	700	357	343
40-44	677	343	334	685	348	337	844	429	415	875	445	431
45-49	690	346	344	673	339	333	681	345	337	840	426	415
50-54	785	387	398	680	338	342	664	333	331	674	339	335
55-59	777	376	401	763	371	392	662	325	337	648	321	327
60-64	596	279	317	739	349	389	728	347	381	635	306	329
65-69	426	189	237	549	248	301	684	313	371	677	312	365
70-74	389	161	228	372	157	216	483	207	276	606	263	342
75-79	324	120	204	311	119	192	301	117	184	395	156	238
80-84	220	70	150	223	73	149	218	74	144	215	74	141
85-89	62	17	45	117	31	85	122	33	89	123	34	89
90-94	27	7	21	21	5	16	43	9	34	48	10	38
95-99	3	1	3	5	1	4	4	1	4	9	1	8
100 +	0	0	0	0	0	0	0	0	0	0	0	0

Age group	2025 Both sexes	Males	Females	2030 Both sexes	Males	Females	2035 Both sexes	Males	Females	2040 Both sexes	Males	Females
All ages	9 238	4 473	4 765	8 887	4 293	4 594	8 495	4 096	4 399	8 074	3 887	4 186
0-4	257	132	125	245	126	119	232	119	113	218	112	106
5-9	269	138	131	259	133	126	247	127	120	234	120	114
10-14	310	159	151	271	139	132	261	134	127	249	128	121
15-19	367	188	179	312	160	152	273	140	133	263	135	128
20-24	461	236	225	369	189	180	314	161	153	275	141	134
25-29	459	235	224	462	237	226	370	190	181	316	162	154
30-34	598	306	292	461	236	225	464	237	226	372	191	182
35-39	656	335	322	600	307	293	462	236	226	465	238	227
40-44	700	356	344	657	335	322	600	307	293	463	236	227
45-49	872	442	430	698	355	344	656	333	322	599	306	294
50-54	832	419	413	864	436	428	693	350	343	651	329	322
55-59	659	328	331	815	407	408	849	424	424	682	342	340
60-64	623	304	320	636	312	324	788	388	401	822	405	417
65-69	594	278	316	585	278	308	600	287	313	746	359	387
70-74	605	266	338	534	239	295	530	242	288	546	252	294
75-79	501	203	298	505	208	297	451	190	261	451	194	257
80-84	287	101	186	370	135	236	380	141	238	344	132	212
85-89	126	36	90	173	51	122	230	71	159	241	77	165
90-94	51	11	41	55	12	43	79	18	61	109	26	83
95-99	12	1	10	14	2	12	16	2	14	24	4	21
100 +	1	0	1	1	0	1	2	0	2	2	0	2

Age group	2045 Both sexes	Males	Females	2050 Both sexes	Males	Females
All ages	7 636	3 672	3 964	7 188	3 450	3 738
0-4	203	104	99	190	97	93
5-9	220	113	107	205	105	100
10-14	236	121	115	222	114	108
15-19	251	129	122	238	122	116
20-24	265	136	129	253	130	123
25-29	277	142	135	267	137	130
30-34	318	163	155	279	143	136
35-39	374	191	183	320	164	156
40-44	466	238	228	375	192	184
45-49	463	236	227	466	238	228
50-54	595	303	293	461	234	227
55-59	642	322	319	588	296	291
60-64	663	328	335	625	310	315
65-69	781	377	404	632	307	325
70-74	683	318	365	718	336	382
75-79	469	205	264	591	261	330
80-84	348	137	211	367	148	220
85-89	223	74	149	231	79	152
90-94	119	30	89	114	30	84
95-99	36	6	30	41	7	34
100 +	4	0	4	6	0	6

POPULATION BY AGE AND SEX (in thousands)

Age group	1950 Both sexes	Males	Females	1955 Both sexes	Males	Females	1960 Both sexes	Males	Females	1965 Both sexes	Males	Females
All ages	10 815	5 463	5 353	10 342	5 227	5 115	11 430	5 784	5 647	12 688	6 427	6 260
0-4	1 553	799	754	1 041	532	509	1 629	835	794	1 802	924	878
5-9	1 478	744	734	1 456	750	706	1 014	519	495	1 595	818	777
10-14	1 374	700	674	1 435	722	713	1 441	742	699	1 006	514	491
15-19	1 104	561	544	1 292	660	632	1 418	713	705	1 427	734	693
20-24	939	472	467	939	482	458	1 267	647	619	1 395	702	694
25-29	818	416	402	740	375	365	915	470	445	1 241	634	606
30-34	687	355	331	645	331	314	718	365	354	893	459	434
35-39	621	322	299	554	288	266	622	319	303	697	354	343
40-44	517	267	250	517	267	250	528	274	254	598	306	292
45-49	423	217	207	434	222	212	485	249	236	500	258	242
50-54	368	183	185	352	177	175	397	200	196	448	228	220
55-59	335	161	174	299	145	154	310	153	157	354	176	178
60-64	264	128	136	261	121	140	250	118	132	263	126	137
65-69	181	78	103	190	87	103	202	89	113	197	88	109
70-74	82	34	49	116	46	71	132	56	76	144	59	85
75-79	47	19	28	45	16	29	71	25	46	82	32	50
80 +	24	9	15	27	9	18	31	10	21	45	14	31

Age group	1970 Both sexes	Males	Females	1975 Both sexes	Males	Females	1980 Both sexes	Males	Females	1985 Both sexes	Males	Females
All ages	14 397	7 303	7 094	16 018	8 123	7 895	17 196	8 705	8 491	18 438	9 318	9 120
0-4	2 251	1 155	1 096	2 124	1 089	1 035	1 641	840	801	1 790	916	874
5-9	1 772	909	863	2 226	1 142	1 084	2 109	1 080	1 029	1 628	833	796
10-14	1 585	812	773	1 764	905	860	2 220	1 138	1 082	2 103	1 076	1 026
15-19	998	510	488	1 576	807	769	1 758	901	857	2 211	1 133	1 078
20-24	1 408	725	684	989	505	484	1 567	802	766	1 747	894	853
25-29	1 372	690	682	1 392	716	676	981	500	481	1 554	794	760
30-34	1 216	622	594	1 352	680	673	1 379	708	671	971	495	477
35-39	871	448	423	1 194	610	583	1 336	670	665	1 361	698	663
40-44	673	341	332	849	435	414	1 172	597	575	1 311	656	655
45-49	570	290	279	649	327	321	826	421	405	1 139	578	562
50-54	466	238	228	539	272	267	621	310	311	789	399	390
55-59	405	203	202	428	216	213	503	250	253	580	285	294
60-64	305	148	157	356	174	182	385	189	196	452	219	233
65-69	211	97	114	251	116	135	303	141	162	326	153	173
70-74	143	60	83	159	68	91	197	85	112	236	103	133
75-79	92	35	58	97	37	60	113	44	69	139	55	84
80 +	58	19	39	72	24	49	85	28	58	100	32	67

Age group	1990 Both sexes	Males	Females	1995 Both sexes	Males	Females	2000 Both sexes	Males	Females	2005 Both sexes	Males	Females
All ages	19 690	9 933	9 757	20 918	10 530	10 389	21 862	10 964	10 898	22 488	11 233	11 255
0-4	1 897	971	926	2 035	1 041	994	1 919	980	939	1 723	879	843
5-9	1 776	909	868	1 880	962	918	2 012	1 028	984	1 897	967	930
10-14	1 623	830	794	1 770	905	865	1 871	956	915	2 003	1 022	981
15-19	2 095	1 071	1 023	1 616	825	791	1 760	899	861	1 861	950	911
20-24	2 197	1 125	1 073	2 079	1 062	1 017	1 601	816	785	1 744	889	855
25-29	1 733	886	847	2 175	1 112	1 064	2 054	1 047	1 007	1 582	805	777
30-34	1 538	785	754	1 712	874	838	2 145	1 094	1 051	2 025	1 030	995
35-39	958	487	471	1 515	771	743	1 681	856	825	2 106	1 071	1 035
40-44	1 335	682	652	937	475	462	1 476	748	728	1 638	830	808
45-49	1 273	634	639	1 291	656	635	903	454	449	1 422	715	707
50-54	1 088	547	542	1 210	596	614	1 220	612	608	853	423	430
55-59	735	366	370	1 007	497	510	1 112	537	576	1 121	551	570
60-64	520	249	271	653	316	337	887	424	463	979	457	523
65-69	382	176	205	434	198	236	539	247	292	731	331	400
70-74	254	111	143	293	126	167	328	138	190	407	172	235
75-79	165	66	100	174	69	105	197	76	121	221	84	138
80 +	119	39	80	139	46	93	155	51	104	174	56	118

338
United Nations Department of Economic and Social Affairs/Population Division
World Population Prospects: The 2004 Revision, Volume II: Sex and Age Distribution of the World Population

POPULATION BY AGE AND SEX (in thousands)

Age group	2005 Both sexes	Males	Females	2010 Both sexes	Males	Females	2015 Both sexes	Males	Females	2020 Both sexes	Males	Females
All ages	22 488	11 233	11 255	22 907	11 402	11 505	23 299	11 562	11 737	23 722	11 744	11 978
0-4	1 723	879	843	1 557	795	761	1 564	799	764	1 636	837	799
5-9	1 897	967	930	1 706	870	836	1 545	788	756	1 554	794	760
10-14	2 003	1 022	981	1 890	963	927	1 701	866	834	1 540	786	755
15-19	1 861	950	911	1 994	1 016	977	1 882	958	924	1 695	863	832
20-24	1 744	889	855	1 847	941	906	1 981	1 008	972	1 872	951	920
25-29	1 582	805	777	1 726	878	848	1 831	931	899	1 966	999	967
30-34	2 025	1 030	995	1 563	794	769	1 708	868	841	1 814	922	893
35-39	2 106	1 071	1 035	1 993	1 012	982	1 542	781	761	1 689	856	833
40-44	1 638	830	808	2 058	1 043	1 016	1 954	988	966	1 515	765	750
45-49	1 422	715	707	1 584	797	787	1 998	1 006	992	1 903	957	946
50-54	853	423	430	1 350	671	679	1 512	752	759	1 916	955	961
55-59	1 121	551	570	789	384	405	1 257	613	643	1 416	693	723
60-64	979	457	523	994	474	521	706	334	373	1 135	538	597
65-69	731	331	400	817	361	456	839	380	459	603	271	332
70-74	407	172	235	561	235	326	638	262	376	663	280	384
75-79	221	84	138	279	106	173	393	148	245	456	169	287
80-84	113	38	75	130	43	87	167	56	111	241	80	161
85-89	44	13	31	52	15	37	61	17	44	81	23	58
90-94	14	3	10	15	4	11	18	4	14	22	5	17
95-99	2	1	2	3	1	2	3	1	3	4	1	3
100 +	0	0	0	0	0	0	0	0	0	0	0	0

Age group	2025 Both sexes	Males	Females	2030 Both sexes	Males	Females	2035 Both sexes	Males	Females	2040 Both sexes	Males	Females
All ages	24 118	11 918	12 200	24 375	12 022	12 353	24 458	12 038	12 420	24 414	11 989	12 425
0-4	1 656	847	808	1 569	803	766	1 450	742	707	1 386	710	676
5-9	1 627	832	795	1 648	843	805	1 563	800	763	1 445	740	705
10-14	1 550	791	759	1 624	830	794	1 645	841	804	1 561	798	763
15-19	1 536	783	753	1 546	789	757	1 620	827	793	1 642	839	803
20-24	1 687	858	829	1 530	779	751	1 541	785	756	1 616	824	791
25-29	1 860	944	916	1 678	852	826	1 523	775	749	1 535	781	753
30-34	1 951	990	961	1 848	937	912	1 669	846	823	1 516	770	746
35-39	1 796	911	886	1 934	980	954	1 834	928	906	1 658	840	818
40-44	1 000	041	823	1 773	896	876	1 912	966	945	1 815	917	899
45-49	1 480	744	736	1 829	819	809	1 740	876	863	1 880	947	933
50-54	1 832	913	919	1 430	713	717	1 579	788	790	1 690	846	845
55-59	1 804	885	818	1 734	851	880	1 360	669	691	1 506	743	763
60-64	1 288	613	675	1 652	790	862	1 597	765	832	1 259	605	654
65-69	979	443	535	1 121	511	610	1 449	665	785	1 411	650	761
70-74	483	203	280	794	337	457	919	393	525	1 200	518	681
75-79	482	184	298	357	136	221	594	230	365	697	273	424
80-84	287	93	193	308	104	204	233	79	154	393	135	258
85-89	120	34	86	146	41	105	160	46	114	123	36	87
90-94	30	7	23	46	11	35	57	13	44	64	15	49
95-99	5	1	4	8	1	6	12	2	10	15	3	13
100 +	1	0	1	1	0	1	1	0	1	2	0	2

Age group	2045 Both sexes	Males	Females	2050 Both sexes	Males	Females
All ages	24 318	11 918	12 400	24 192	11 843	12 349
0-4	1 399	717	682	1 426	731	695
5-9	1 382	708	674	1 395	715	681
10-14	1 443	739	705	1 380	707	674
15-19	1 559	797	762	1 441	737	704
20-24	1 638	836	802	1 555	795	760
25-29	1 610	821	789	1 633	833	800
30-34	1 528	777	751	1 604	817	787
35-39	1 507	765	742	1 520	773	747
40-44	1 642	830	812	1 494	757	737
45-49	1 787	900	888	1 619	816	803
50-54	1 831	916	914	1 745	873	871
55-59	1 618	800	818	1 758	870	887
60-64	1 401	676	725	1 512	732	780
65-69	1 120	518	602	1 254	584	671
70-74	1 180	513	667	944	413	531
75-79	921	365	556	916	366	549
80-84	468	163	305	628	222	406
85-89	214	63	151	260	78	182
90-94	51	12	39	90	21	69
95-99	18	3	15	14	2	12
100 +	2	0	2	3	0	3

United Nations Department of Economic and Social Affairs/Population Division
World Population Prospects: The 2004 Revision, Volume II: Sex and Age Distribution of the World Population

339

POPULATION BY AGE AND SEX (in thousands)

Age group	2005 Both sexes	2005 Males	2005 Females	2010 Both sexes	2010 Males	2010 Females	2015 Both sexes	2015 Males	2015 Females	2020 Both sexes	2020 Males	2020 Females
All ages	22 488	11 233	11 255	23 109	11 505	11 604	23 834	11 835	11 999	24 696	12 241	12 454
0-4	1 723	879	843	1 758	898	860	1 898	970	928	2 078	1 063	1 015
5-9	1 897	967	930	1 706	870	836	1 745	891	854	1 886	963	922
10-14	2 003	1 022	981	1 890	963	927	1 701	866	834	1 740	887	852
15-19	1 861	950	911	1 994	1 016	977	1 882	958	924	1 695	863	832
20-24	1 744	889	855	1 847	941	906	1 981	1 008	972	1 872	951	920
25-29	1 582	805	777	1 726	878	848	1 831	931	899	1 966	999	967
30-34	2 025	1 030	995	1 563	794	769	1 708	868	841	1 814	922	893
35-39	2 106	1 071	1 035	1 993	1 012	982	1 542	781	761	1 689	856	833
40-44	1 638	830	808	2 058	1 043	1 016	1 954	988	966	1 515	765	750
45-49	1 422	715	707	1 584	797	787	1 998	1 006	992	1 903	957	946
50-54	853	423	430	1 350	671	679	1 512	752	759	1 916	955	961
55-59	1 121	551	570	789	384	405	1 257	613	643	1 416	693	723
60-64	979	457	523	994	474	521	706	334	373	1 135	538	597
65-69	731	331	400	817	361	456	839	380	459	603	271	332
70-74	407	172	235	561	235	326	638	262	376	663	280	384
75-79	221	84	138	279	106	173	393	148	245	456	169	287
80-84	113	38	75	130	43	87	167	56	111	241	80	161
85-89	44	13	31	52	15	37	61	17	44	81	23	58
90-94	14	3	10	15	4	11	18	4	14	22	5	17
95-99	2	1	2	3	1	2	3	1	3	4	1	3
100 +	0	0	0	0	0	0	0	0	0	0	0	0

Age group	2025 Both sexes	2025 Males	2025 Females	2030 Both sexes	2030 Males	2030 Females	2035 Both sexes	2035 Males	2035 Females	2040 Both sexes	2040 Males	2040 Females
All ages	25 536	12 642	12 894	26 230	12 970	13 260	26 813	13 241	13 572	27 405	13 517	13 888
0-4	2 103	1 076	1 027	2 011	1 029	982	1 955	1 001	954	2 028	1 039	989
5-9	2 067	1 056	1 010	2 094	1 071	1 023	2 003	1 025	978	1 949	997	951
10-14	1 882	961	921	2 063	1 054	1 009	2 091	1 069	1 022	2 001	1 023	977
15-19	1 735	884	851	1 877	958	919	2 058	1 051	1 007	2 087	1 066	1 021
20-24	1 687	858	829	1 728	880	848	1 871	953	917	2 052	1 047	1 005
25-29	1 860	944	916	1 678	852	826	1 720	875	845	1 863	949	915
30-34	1 951	990	961	1 848	937	912	1 669	846	823	1 712	870	842
35-39	1 796	911	886	1 934	980	954	1 834	928	906	1 658	840	818
40-44	1 663	841	823	1 773	896	876	1 912	966	945	1 815	917	899
45-49	1 480	744	736	1 629	819	809	1 740	876	863	1 880	947	933
50-54	1 832	913	919	1 430	713	717	1 579	788	790	1 690	846	845
55-59	1 804	885	919	1 734	851	883	1 359	668	691	1 506	743	763
60-64	1 288	613	675	1 652	790	862	1 597	765	832	1 259	605	654
65-69	979	443	535	1 121	511	610	1 449	665	785	1 411	650	761
70-74	483	203	280	794	337	457	919	393	525	1 200	518	681
75-79	482	184	298	357	136	221	594	230	365	697	273	424
80-84	287	93	193	308	104	204	233	79	154	393	135	258
85-89	120	34	86	146	41	105	160	46	114	123	36	87
90-94	30	7	23	46	11	35	57	13	44	64	15	49
95-99	5	1	4	8	1	6	12	2	10	15	3	13
100 +	1	0	1	1	0	1	1	0	1	2	0	2

Age group	2045 Both sexes	2045 Males	2045 Females	2050 Both sexes	2050 Males	2050 Females
All ages	28 079	13 840	14 239	28 800	14 197	14 602
0-4	2 176	1 115	1 061	2 284	1 170	1 114
5-9	2 023	1 036	987	2 171	1 112	1 059
10-14	1 946	996	950	2 021	1 034	986
15-19	1 997	1 021	976	1 943	994	949
20-24	2 081	1 063	1 019	1 993	1 018	975
25-29	2 045	1 042	1 003	2 075	1 059	1 016
30-34	1 855	944	911	2 037	1 038	1 000
35-39	1 702	864	838	1 845	938	907
40-44	1 642	830	812	1 687	855	832
45-49	1 787	900	888	1 619	816	803
50-54	1 831	916	914	1 745	873	871
55-59	1 618	800	818	1 758	870	887
60-64	1 401	676	725	1 512	732	780
65-69	1 120	518	602	1 254	584	671
70-74	1 180	513	667	944	413	531
75-79	921	365	556	916	366	549
80-84	468	163	305	628	222	406
85-89	214	63	151	260	78	182
90-94	51	12	39	90	21	69
95-99	18	3	15	14	2	12
100 +	2	0	2	3	0	3

United Nations Department of Economic and Social Affairs/Population Division
World Population Prospects: The 2004 Revision, Volume II: Sex and Age Distribution of the World Population

340

POPULATION BY AGE AND SEX (in thousands)

Age group	2005 Both sexes	2005 Males	2005 Females	2010 Both sexes	2010 Males	2010 Females	2015 Both sexes	2015 Males	2015 Females	2020 Both sexes	2020 Males	2020 Females
All ages	22 488	11 233	11 255	22 706	11 299	11 407	22 765	11 280	11 476	22 748	11 246	11 502
0-4	1 723	879	843	1 355	693	663	1 229	628	601	1 194	611	583
5-9	1 897	967	930	1 706	870	836	1 345	686	658	1 221	624	597
10-14	2 003	1 022	981	1 890	963	927	1 701	866	834	1 341	684	657
15-19	1 861	950	911	1 994	1 016	977	1 882	958	924	1 695	863	832
20-24	1 744	889	855	1 847	941	906	1 981	1 008	972	1 872	951	920
25-29	1 582	805	777	1 726	878	848	1 831	931	899	1 966	999	967
30-34	2 025	1 030	995	1 563	794	769	1 708	868	841	1 814	922	893
35-39	2 106	1 071	1 035	1 993	1 012	982	1 542	781	761	1 689	856	833
40-44	1 638	830	808	2 058	1 043	1 016	1 954	988	966	1 515	765	750
45-49	1 422	715	707	1 584	797	787	1 998	1 006	992	1 903	957	946
50-54	853	423	430	1 350	671	679	1 512	752	759	1 916	955	961
55-59	1 121	551	570	789	384	405	1 257	613	643	1 416	693	723
60-64	979	457	523	994	474	521	706	334	373	1 135	538	597
65-69	731	331	400	817	361	456	839	380	459	603	271	332
70-74	407	172	235	561	235	326	638	262	376	663	280	384
75-79	221	84	138	279	106	173	393	148	245	456	169	287
80-84	113	38	75	130	43	87	167	56	111	241	80	161
85-89	44	13	31	52	15	37	61	17	44	81	23	58
90-94	14	3	10	15	4	11	18	4	14	22	5	17
95-99	2	1	2	3	1	2	3	1	3	4	1	3
100 +	0	0	0	0	0	0	0	0	0	0	0	0

Age group	2025 Both sexes	2025 Males	2025 Females	2030 Both sexes	2030 Males	2030 Females	2035 Both sexes	2035 Males	2035 Females	2040 Both sexes	2040 Males	2040 Females
All ages	22 700	11 193	11 507	22 527	11 078	11 449	22 158	10 863	11 296	21 592	10 547	11 045
0-4	1 208	618	590	1 135	581	554	993	508	484	857	439	418
5-9	1 187	607	580	1 202	615	587	1 131	579	552	989	506	483
10-14	1 218	622	596	1 185	605	580	1 200	614	587	1 129	577	552
15-19	1 337	682	656	1 216	620	595	1 182	604	579	1 198	612	586
20-24	1 687	858	829	1 332	678	654	1 211	617	594	1 179	601	578
25-29	1 860	944	916	1 678	852	826	1 326	674	652	1 207	614	592
30-34	1 951	990	961	1 848	937	912	1 669	846	823	1 320	670	649
35-39	1 796	911	886	1 934	980	954	1 834	928	906	1 658	840	818
40-44	1 663	841	823	1 773	896	876	1 912	900	945	1 815	917	899
45-49	1 480	744	736	1 629	819	809	1 740	876	863	1 880	947	933
50-54	1 832	913	919	1 430	713	717	1 579	788	790	1 690	846	845
55-59	1 904	885	919	1 734	851	883	1 359	668	691	1 506	743	763
60-64	1 288	613	675	1 652	790	862	1 597	765	832	1 259	605	654
65-69	979	443	535	1 121	511	610	1 449	665	785	1 411	650	761
70-74	483	203	280	794	337	457	919	393	525	1 200	518	681
75-79	482	184	298	357	136	221	594	230	365	697	273	424
80-84	287	93	193	308	104	204	233	79	154	303	135	269
85-89	120	34	86	146	41	105	160	46	114	123	36	87
90-94	30	7	23	46	11	35	57	13	44	64	15	49
95-99	5	1	4	8	1	6	12	2	10	15	3	13
100 +	1	0	1	1	0	1	1	0	1	2	0	2

Age group	2045 Both sexes	2045 Males	2045 Females	2050 Both sexes	2050 Males	2050 Females
All ages	20 897	10 171	10 727	20 125	9 765	10 360
0-4	791	405	386	770	394	375
5-9	855	438	417	789	404	385
10-14	988	506	483	854	437	417
15-19	1 127	576	551	987	505	482
20-24	1 195	610	585	1 125	575	550
25-29	1 175	599	576	1 191	608	584
30-34	1 201	611	590	1 170	596	574
35-39	1 312	666	646	1 195	607	588
40-44	1 642	830	812	1 301	659	642
45-49	1 787	900	888	1 619	816	803
50-54	1 831	916	914	1 745	873	871
55-59	1 618	800	818	1 758	870	887
60-64	1 401	676	725	1 512	732	780
65-69	1 120	518	602	1 254	584	671
70-74	1 180	513	667	944	413	531
75-79	921	365	556	916	366	549
80-84	468	163	305	628	222	406
85-89	214	63	151	260	78	182
90-94	51	12	39	90	21	69
95-99	18	3	15	14	2	12
100 +	2	0	2	3	0	3

POPULATION BY AGE AND SEX (in thousands)

Age group	1950 Both sexes	1950 Males	1950 Females	1955 Both sexes	1955 Males	1955 Females	1960 Both sexes	1960 Males	1960 Females	1965 Both sexes	1965 Males	1965 Females
All ages	12 184	5 707	6 477	13 601	6 436	7 165	15 451	7 376	8 075	17 661	8 496	9 165
0-4	2 170	1 071	1 099	2 409	1 203	1 206	2 798	1 399	1 400	3 247	1 625	1 623
5-9	1 708	832	876	1 916	942	973	2 156	1 073	1 082	2 518	1 255	1 263
10-14	1 444	696	748	1 638	798	840	1 852	911	941	2 084	1 037	1 047
15-19	1 236	590	646	1 398	674	724	1 597	778	819	1 805	888	917
20-24	1 055	497	558	1 190	566	624	1 356	651	704	1 548	752	797
25-29	891	413	478	1 008	472	536	1 146	543	603	1 305	624	681
30-34	754	345	409	847	392	456	967	452	515	1 099	519	580
35-39	633	286	347	713	326	387	807	373	435	922	430	492
40-44	526	235	291	594	267	326	674	307	367	764	351	413
45-49	435	189	246	488	216	272	556	248	308	632	286	346
50-54	357	154	204	398	171	227	451	198	254	515	227	288
55-59	292	123	169	319	135	184	359	152	207	408	176	232
60-64	219	89	129	250	103	147	276	115	161	312	130	183
65-69	165	66	99	174	70	104	202	82	120	225	91	133
70-74	123	49	74	116	45	71	125	49	76	147	58	89
75-79	88	35	53	73	28	45	70	26	44	77	29	48
80 +	85	35	50	69	27	42	58	21	37	53	19	34

Age group	1970 Both sexes	1970 Males	1970 Females	1975 Both sexes	1975 Males	1975 Females	1980 Both sexes	1980 Males	1980 Females	1985 Both sexes	1985 Males	1985 Females
All ages	20 543	9 948	10 595	23 912	11 646	12 266	27 996	13 702	14 294	32 346	15 891	16 455
0-4	3 817	1 911	1 905	4 506	2 259	2 247	5 352	2 686	2 665	6 202	3 113	3 089
5-9	2 980	1 487	1 493	3 509	1 753	1 756	4 174	2 089	2 086	4 891	2 450	2 441
10-14	2 466	1 229	1 237	2 906	1 450	1 456	3 425	1 711	1 714	4 019	2 010	2 009
15-19	2 056	1 023	1 033	2 420	1 206	1 214	2 851	1 422	1 429	3 315	1 655	1 660
20-24	1 771	868	902	2 007	996	1 011	2 362	1 174	1 189	2 744	1 364	1 380
25-29	1 510	730	780	1 718	839	879	1 949	963	986	2 260	1 117	1 142
30-34	1 268	605	663	1 460	704	756	1 663	810	853	1 858	915	943
35-39	1 062	500	561	1 220	581	639	1 407	677	730	1 579	767	812
40-44	884	411	473	1 015	477	538	1 168	554	614	1 328	637	691
45-49	727	332	395	839	387	451	965	451	514	1 095	516	578
50-54	594	265	328	681	308	373	788	360	427	893	413	480
55-59	473	206	267	545	240	304	627	280	347	715	323	392
60-64	361	153	208	419	180	239	485	211	274	550	242	308
65-69	259	106	154	301	125	176	352	148	204	402	172	230
70-74	168	67	101	196	78	118	229	93	136	264	108	156
75-79	94	36	58	109	42	67	128	49	79	148	58	90
80 +	54	19	35	62	21	40	72	25	47	83	29	54

Age group	1990 Both sexes	1990 Males	1990 Females	1995 Both sexes	1995 Males	1995 Females	2000 Both sexes	2000 Males	2000 Females	2005 Both sexes	2005 Males	2005 Females
All ages	37 764	18 600	19 164	44 999	22 210	22 789	50 052	24 761	25 291	57 549	28 542	29 007
0-4	7 215	3 621	3 593	8 600	4 316	4 284	9 534	4 778	4 756	11 209	5 625	5 585
5-9	5 745	2 877	2 867	6 853	3 432	3 421	7 596	3 803	3 794	8 693	4 346	4 347
10-14	4 773	2 390	2 383	5 750	2 880	2 871	6 431	3 220	3 211	7 302	3 655	3 648
15-19	3 943	1 971	1 972	4 804	2 405	2 399	5 440	2 724	2 717	6 242	3 125	3 118
20-24	3 226	1 606	1 620	3 932	1 961	1 972	4 510	2 251	2 259	5 239	2 616	2 623
25-29	2 642	1 306	1 335	3 147	1 562	1 585	3 609	1 797	1 812	4 258	2 122	2 135
30-34	2 167	1 066	1 100	2 545	1 255	1 290	2 813	1 401	1 412	3 329	1 665	1 664
35-39	1 776	871	905	2 083	1 021	1 062	2 256	1 115	1 141	2 557	1 281	1 276
40-44	1 503	726	777	1 708	832	875	1 849	904	945	2 048	1 014	1 035
45-49	1 257	598	659	1 443	691	752	1 520	735	785	1 684	819	865
50-54	1 026	479	547	1 199	563	635	1 281	606	675	1 382	662	721
55-59	821	375	446	962	443	519	1 049	486	563	1 151	537	614
60-64	636	283	353	746	336	411	816	369	447	916	417	498
65-69	462	200	262	546	239	307	597	264	333	674	300	375
70-74	305	127	178	360	152	208	394	169	226	449	194	255
75-79	172	68	105	204	82	123	222	90	131	255	106	150
80 +	98	35	63	117	42	75	135	49	86	159	59	99

342

United Nations Department of Economic and Social Affairs/Population Division
World Population Prospects: The 2004 Revision, Volume II: Sex and Age Distribution of the World Population

POPULATION BY AGE AND SEX (in thousands)

Age group	2005 Both sexes	2005 Males	2005 Females	2010 Both sexes	2010 Males	2010 Females	2015 Both sexes	2015 Males	2015 Females	2020 Both sexes	2020 Males	2020 Females
All ages	57 549	28 542	29 007	67 129	33 358	33 771	78 016	38 820	39 196	90 022	44 906	45 100
0-4	11 209	5 625	5 585	13 225	6 638	6 587	15 056	7 558	7 498	16 538	8 306	8 233
5-9	8 693	4 346	4 347	10 381	5 195	5 186	12 299	6 153	6 146	14 113	7 060	7 054
10-14	7 302	3 655	3 648	8 438	4 217	4 221	10 074	5 038	5 035	11 963	5 981	5 983
15-19	6 242	3 125	3 118	7 150	3 577	3 573	8 254	4 123	4 132	9 871	4 933	4 938
20-24	5 239	2 616	2 623	6 067	3 029	3 038	6 944	3 464	3 480	8 034	4 001	4 033
25-29	4 258	2 122	2 135	4 992	2 489	2 503	5 784	2 883	2 901	6 639	3 307	3 332
30-34	3 329	1 665	1 664	3 972	1 988	1 984	4 661	2 333	2 328	5 418	2 710	2 707
35-39	2 557	1 281	1 276	3 070	1 543	1 527	3 667	1 844	1 823	4 316	2 171	2 145
40-44	2 048	1 014	1 035	2 353	1 180	1 173	2 829	1 424	1 405	3 389	1 707	1 682
45-49	1 684	819	865	1 889	931	958	2 173	1 086	1 087	2 620	1 314	1 306
50-54	1 382	662	721	1 550	747	803	1 740	850	890	2 007	994	1 013
55-59	1 151	537	614	1 256	594	663	1 410	671	739	1 589	767	822
60-64	916	417	498	1 017	467	550	1 113	518	595	1 256	589	667
65-69	674	300	375	767	344	424	855	386	469	942	431	511
70-74	449	194	255	516	224	292	590	258	332	664	293	371
75-79	255	106	150	297	124	173	344	145	199	399	170	230
80-84	114	44	70	134	53	81	158	63	95	187	75	112
85-89	37	13	24	43	16	28	52	19	33	62	23	39
90-94	7	2	5	9	3	6	11	3	7	13	4	9
95-99	1	0	1	1	0	1	1	0	1	2	0	1
100 +	0	0	0	0	0	0	0	0	0	0	0	0

Age group	2025 Both sexes	2025 Males	2025 Females	2030 Both sexes	2030 Males	2030 Females	2035 Both sexes	2035 Males	2035 Females	2040 Both sexes	2040 Males	2040 Females
All ages	103 224	51 447	51 776	117 494	58 591	58 903	132 437	66 070	66 367	147 586	73 647	73 939
0-4	18 027	9 059	8 968	19 371	9 741	9 630	20 341	10 236	10 106	20 870	10 508	10 362
5-9	15 644	7 829	7 815	17 192	8 611	8 580	18 608	9 329	9 278	19 656	9 865	9 792
10-14	13 773	6 884	6 889	15 325	7 663	7 662	16 896	8 456	8 440	18 337	9 185	9 151
15-19	11 744	5 866	5 878	13 548	6 765	6 783	15 103	7 544	7 559	16 679	8 338	8 341
20-24	9 627	4 797	4 830	11 478	5 717	5 761	13 267	6 606	6 661	14 818	7 381	7 436
25-29	7 704	3 831	3 873	9 258	4 607	4 652	11 072	5 506	5 566	12 835	6 381	6 454
30-34	6 243	3 120	3 123	7 272	3 627	3 645	8 774	4 378	4 396	10 537	5 253	5 283
35-39	5 037	2 531	2 505	5 831	2 926	2 905	6 823	3 416	3 406	8 272	4 142	4 130
40-44	4 004	2 017	1 987	4 695	2 363	2 332	5 461	2 744	2 717	6 420	3 219	3 202
45-49	3 149	1 581	1 568	3 738	1 878	1 860	4 403	2 210	2 193	5 145	2 580	2 566
50-54	2 429	1 209	1 220	2 932	1 462	1 470	3 496	1 745	1 751	4 137	2 064	2 073
55-59	1 841	902	939	2 238	1 102	1 136	2 715	1 341	1 375	3 253	1 608	1 645
60-64	1 423	677	746	1 658	802	856	2 027	986	1 041	2 474	1 207	1 268
65-69	1 071	494	577	1 222	572	650	1 436	683	753	1 769	847	922
70-74	739	331	408	849	383	466	980	449	530	1 163	543	620
75-79	456	195	260	515	224	291	601	264	337	703	314	389
80-84	221	90	131	257	106	151	290	124	172	353	149	203
85-89	75	28	47	91	35	57	109	42	67	129	51	78
90-94	16	5	11	21	7	14	26	9	17	31	11	20
95-99	2	1	2	3	1	2	3	1	2	4	1	3
100 +	0	0	0	0	0	0	0	0	0	0	0	0

Age group	2045 Both sexes	2045 Males	2045 Females	2050 Both sexes	2050 Males	2050 Females
All ages	162 598	81 144	81 454	177 271	88 454	88 817
0-4	21 076	10 616	10 461	21 113	10 637	10 476
5-9	20 273	10 180	10 092	20 568	10 333	10 236
10-14	19 415	9 735	9 680	20 064	10 066	9 998
15-19	18 129	9 071	9 058	19 222	9 626	9 596
20-24	16 393	8 173	8 220	17 846	8 905	8 941
25-29	14 376	7 151	7 225	15 944	7 937	8 007
30-34	12 263	6 111	6 153	13 786	6 870	6 916
35-39	9 980	4 991	4 989	11 667	5 828	5 839
40-44	7 821	3 920	3 901	9 480	4 744	4 736
45-49	6 077	3 040	3 038	7 436	3 719	3 717
50-54	4 855	2 420	2 436	5 759	2 864	2 895
55-59	3 868	1 912	1 956	4 560	2 253	2 307
60-64	2 981	1 456	1 525	3 564	1 742	1 822
65-69	2 175	1 044	1 131	2 638	1 269	1 369
70-74	1 447	680	767	1 797	847	950
75-79	847	385	461	1 067	489	578
80-84	420	181	239	515	227	288
85-89	157	63	94	191	78	113
90-94	38	14	24	47	17	30
95-99	6	2	4	7	2	5
100 +	0	0	0	1	0	0

POPULATION BY AGE AND SEX (in thousands)

Age group	2005 Both sexes	2005 Males	2005 Females	2010 Both sexes	2010 Males	2010 Females	2015 Both sexes	2015 Males	2015 Females	2020 Both sexes	2020 Males	2020 Females
All ages	57 549	28 542	29 007	67 129	33 358	33 771	78 508	39 067	39 441	91 855	45 756	46 099
0-4	11 209	5 625	5 585	13 225	6 638	6 587	15 548	7 805	7 743	17 909	8 994	8 915
5-9	8 693	4 346	4 347	10 381	5 195	5 186	12 299	6 153	6 146	14 575	7 291	7 284
10-14	7 302	3 655	3 648	8 438	4 217	4 221	10 074	5 038	5 035	11 963	5 981	5 983
15-19	6 242	3 125	3 118	7 150	3 577	3 573	8 254	4 123	4 132	9 871	4 933	4 938
20-24	5 239	2 616	2 623	6 067	3 029	3 038	6 944	3 464	3 480	8 034	4 001	4 033
25-29	4 258	2 122	2 135	4 992	2 489	2 503	5 784	2 883	2 901	6 639	3 307	3 332
30-34	3 329	1 665	1 664	3 972	1 988	1 984	4 661	2 333	2 328	5 418	2 710	2 707
35-39	2 557	1 281	1 276	3 070	1 543	1 527	3 667	1 844	1 823	4 316	2 171	2 145
40-44	2 048	1 014	1 035	2 353	1 180	1 173	2 829	1 424	1 405	3 389	1 707	1 682
45-49	1 684	819	865	1 889	931	958	2 173	1 086	1 087	2 620	1 314	1 306
50-54	1 382	662	721	1 550	747	803	1 740	850	890	2 007	994	1 013
55-59	1 151	537	614	1 256	594	663	1 410	671	739	1 589	767	822
60-64	916	417	498	1 017	467	550	1 113	518	595	1 256	589	667
65-69	674	300	375	767	344	424	855	386	469	942	431	511
70-74	449	194	255	516	224	292	590	258	332	664	293	371
75-79	255	106	150	297	124	173	344	145	199	399	170	230
80-84	114	44	70	134	53	81	158	63	95	187	75	112
85-89	37	13	24	43	16	28	52	19	33	62	23	39
90-94	7	2	5	9	3	6	11	3	7	13	4	9
95-99	1	0	1	1	0	1	1	0	1	2	0	1
100 +	0	0	0	0	0	0	0	0	0	0	0	0

Age group	2025 Both sexes	2025 Males	2025 Females	2030 Both sexes	2030 Males	2030 Females	2035 Both sexes	2035 Males	2035 Females	2040 Both sexes	2040 Males	2040 Females
All ages	106 607	53 144	53 463	122 792	61 246	61 545	140 278	70 000	70 277	158 890	79 315	79 575
0-4	19 661	9 880	9 781	21 393	10 757	10 636	23 015	11 581	11 434	24 505	12 338	12 167
5-9	16 942	8 479	8 463	18 751	9 393	9 359	20 551	10 304	10 247	22 242	11 162	11 080
10-14	14 224	7 110	7 115	16 598	8 299	8 298	18 429	9 223	9 206	20 253	10 145	10 108
15-19	11 744	5 866	5 878	13 992	6 986	7 005	16 358	8 171	8 187	18 194	9 095	9 098
20-24	9 627	4 797	4 830	11 478	5 717	5 761	13 701	6 822	6 879	16 049	7 995	8 054
25-29	7 704	3 831	3 873	9 258	4 607	4 652	11 072	5 506	5 566	13 256	6 591	6 665
30-34	6 243	3 120	3 123	7 272	3 627	3 645	8 774	4 378	4 396	10 537	5 253	5 283
35-39	5 037	2 531	2 505	5 831	2 926	2 905	6 823	3 416	3 406	8 272	4 142	4 130
40-44	4 004	2 017	1 987	4 695	2 363	2 332	5 461	2 744	2 717	6 420	3 219	3 202
45-49	3 149	1 581	1 568	3 738	1 878	1 860	4 403	2 210	2 193	5 145	2 580	2 566
50-54	2 429	1 209	1 220	2 932	1 462	1 470	3 496	1 745	1 751	4 137	2 064	2 073
55-59	1 841	902	939	2 238	1 102	1 136	2 715	1 341	1 375	3 253	1 608	1 645
60-64	1 423	677	746	1 658	802	856	2 027	986	1 041	2 474	1 207	1 268
65-69	1 071	494	577	1 222	572	650	1 436	683	753	1 769	847	922
70-74	739	331	408	849	383	466	980	449	530	1 163	543	620
75-79	456	195	260	515	224	291	601	264	337	703	314	389
80-84	221	90	131	257	106	151	296	124	172	353	149	203
85-89	75	28	47	91	35	57	109	42	67	129	51	78
90-94	16	5	11	21	7	14	26	9	17	31	11	20
95-99	2	1	2	3	1	2	3	1	2	4	1	3
100 +	0	0	0	0	0	0	0	0	0	0	0	0

Age group	2045 Both sexes	2045 Males	2045 Females	2050 Both sexes	2050 Males	2050 Females
All ages	178 355	89 046	89 310	198 342	99 023	99 319
0-4	25 764	12 977	12 787	26 733	13 468	13 265
5-9	23 805	11 954	11 851	25 145	12 632	12 513
10-14	21 970	11 016	10 954	23 561	11 821	11 740
15-19	20 025	10 019	10 005	21 752	10 893	10 859
20-24	17 882	8 916	8 967	19 712	9 837	9 876
25-29	15 571	7 745	7 826	17 394	8 659	8 735
30-34	12 666	6 311	6 355	14 933	7 442	7 491
35-39	9 980	4 991	4 989	12 050	6 020	6 030
40-44	7 821	3 920	3 901	9 480	4 744	4 736
45-49	6 077	3 040	3 038	7 436	3 719	3 717
50-54	4 855	2 420	2 436	5 759	2 864	2 895
55-59	3 868	1 912	1 956	4 560	2 253	2 307
60-64	2 981	1 456	1 525	3 564	1 742	1 822
65-69	2 175	1 044	1 131	2 638	1 269	1 369
70-74	1 447	680	767	1 797	847	950
75-79	847	385	461	1 067	489	578
80-84	420	181	239	515	227	288
85-89	157	63	94	191	78	113
90-94	38	14	24	47	17	30
95-99	6	2	4	7	2	5
100 +	0	0	0	1	0	0

POPULATION BY AGE AND SEX (in thousands)

Age group	2005 Both sexes	Males	Females	2010 Both sexes	Males	Females	2015 Both sexes	Males	Females	2020 Both sexes	Males	Females
All ages	57 549	28 542	29 007	66 636	33 111	33 525	76 628	38 124	38 504	87 302	43 400	43 044
0-4	11 209	5 625	5 585	12 732	6 391	6 342	14 127	7 092	7 035	15 167	7 617	7 550
5-9	8 693	4 346	4 347	10 381	5 195	5 186	11 839	5 923	5 916	13 242	6 624	6 618
10-14	7 302	3 655	3 648	8 438	4 217	4 221	10 074	5 038	5 035	11 516	5 757	5 759
15-19	6 242	3 125	3 118	7 150	3 577	3 573	8 254	4 123	4 132	9 871	4 933	4 938
20-24	5 239	2 616	2 623	6 067	3 029	3 038	6 944	3 464	3 480	8 034	4 001	4 033
25-29	4 258	2 122	2 135	4 992	2 489	2 503	5 784	2 883	2 901	6 639	3 307	3 332
30-34	3 329	1 665	1 664	3 972	1 988	1 984	4 661	2 333	2 328	5 418	2 710	2 707
35-39	2 557	1 281	1 276	3 070	1 543	1 527	3 667	1 844	1 823	4 316	2 171	2 145
40-44	2 048	1 014	1 035	2 353	1 180	1 173	2 829	1 424	1 405	3 389	1 707	1 682
45-49	1 684	819	865	1 889	931	958	2 173	1 086	1 087	2 620	1 314	1 306
50-54	1 382	662	721	1 550	747	803	1 740	850	890	2 007	994	1 013
55-59	1 151	537	614	1 256	594	663	1 410	671	739	1 589	767	822
60-64	916	417	498	1 017	467	550	1 113	518	595	1 256	589	667
65-69	674	300	375	767	344	424	855	386	469	942	431	511
70-74	449	194	255	516	224	292	590	258	332	664	293	371
75-79	255	106	150	297	124	173	344	145	199	399	170	230
80-84	114	44	70	134	53	81	158	63	95	187	75	112
85-89	37	13	24	43	16	28	52	19	33	62	23	39
90-94	7	2	5	9	3	6	11	3	7	13	4	9
95-99	1	0	1	1	0	1	1	0	1	2	0	1
100 +	0	0	0	0	0	0	0	0	0	0	0	0

Age group	2025 Both sexes	Males	Females	2030 Both sexes	Males	Females	2035 Both sexes	Males	Females	2040 Both sexes	Males	Females
All ages	98 937	49 300	49 638	111 102	55 388	55 714	123 247	61 465	61 782	134 863	67 270	67 592
0-4	16 329	8 206	8 123	17 139	8 619	8 521	17 380	8 746	8 634	17 119	8 619	8 500
5-9	14 346	7 180	7 166	15 571	7 800	7 772	16 463	8 254	8 209	16 793	8 428	8 366
10-14	12 922	6 459	6 464	14 053	7 027	7 026	15 302	7 658	7 644	16 222	8 126	8 096
15-19	11 305	5 647	5 658	12 710	6 346	6 364	13 848	6 917	6 931	15 105	7 551	7 554
20-24	9 627	4 797	4 830	11 048	5 503	5 545	12 446	6 197	6 249	13 586	6 768	6 818
25-29	7 704	3 831	3 873	9 258	4 607	4 652	10 657	5 300	5 357	12 041	5 986	6 054
30-34	6 243	3 120	3 123	7 272	3 627	3 645	8 774	4 378	4 396	10 142	5 057	5 085
35-39	5 037	2 531	2 505	5 831	2 926	2 905	6 823	3 416	3 406	8 272	4 142	4 130
40-44	4 004	2 017	1 987	4 695	2 363	2 332	5 461	2 744	2 717	6 420	3 219	3 202
45-49	3 149	1 581	1 568	3 738	1 878	1 860	4 403	2 210	2 193	5 145	2 580	2 566
50-54	2 429	1 209	1 220	2 932	1 462	1 470	3 496	1 745	1 751	4 137	2 064	2 073
55-59	1 841	902	939	2 238	1 102	1 136	2 715	1 341	1 375	3 253	1 608	1 645
60-64	1 423	677	746	1 658	802	856	2 027	986	1 041	2 474	1 207	1 268
65-69	1 071	494	577	1 222	572	650	1 436	683	753	1 769	847	922
70-74	739	331	408	849	383	466	980	449	530	1 163	543	620
75-79	456	195	260	515	224	291	601	264	337	703	314	389
80-84	221	90	131	257	106	151	296	124	172	353	149	203
85-89	75	28	47	91	35	57	109	42	67	129	51	78
90-94	16	5	11	21	7	14	26	9	17	31	11	20
95-99	2	1	2	3	1	2	3	1	2	4	1	3
100 +	0	0	0	0	0	0	0	0	0	0	0	0

Age group	2045 Both sexes	Males	Females	2050 Both sexes	Males	Females
All ages	145 668	72 656	73 012	155 514	77 545	77 969
0-4	16 590	8 356	8 234	15 938	8 030	7 908
5-9	16 628	8 350	8 278	16 188	8 132	8 056
10-14	16 586	8 316	8 270	16 455	8 255	8 199
15-19	16 037	8 024	8 013	16 420	8 223	8 197
20-24	14 845	7 401	7 444	15 786	7 877	7 908
25-29	13 180	6 556	6 624	14 439	7 188	7 251
30-34	11 504	5 732	5 772	12 639	6 299	6 340
35-39	9 606	4 804	4 802	10 944	5 467	5 477
40-44	7 821	3 920	3 901	9 125	4 566	4 558
45-49	6 077	3 040	3 038	7 436	3 719	3 717
50-54	4 855	2 420	2 436	5 759	2 864	2 895
55-59	3 868	1 912	1 956	4 560	2 253	2 307
60-64	2 981	1 456	1 525	3 564	1 742	1 822
65-69	2 175	1 044	1 131	2 638	1 269	1 369
70-74	1 447	680	767	1 797	847	950
75-79	847	385	461	1 067	489	578
80-84	420	181	239	515	227	288
85-89	157	63	94	191	78	113
90-94	38	14	24	47	17	30
95-99	6	2	4	7	2	5
100 +	0	0	0	1	0	0

United Nations Department of Economic and Social Affairs/Population Division
World Population Prospects: The 2004 Revision, Volume II: Sex and Age Distribution of the World Population

345

POPULATION BY AGE AND SEX (in thousands)

Age group	1950 Both sexes	1950 Males	1950 Females	1955 Both sexes	1955 Males	1955 Females	1960 Both sexes	1960 Males	1960 Females	1965 Both sexes	1965 Males	1965 Females
All ages	433	219	214	462	234	228	501	254	246	549	279	270
0-4	71	36	35	76	39	37	83	42	41	92	47	45
5-9	55	28	27	61	31	30	66	34	33	74	37	36
10-14	50	25	25	53	27	26	58	30	29	64	32	31
15-19	44	23	22	48	24	24	51	26	25	56	29	28
20-24	41	21	20	42	21	20	45	23	22	48	25	24
25-29	34	18	17	38	19	18	39	20	19	43	22	21
30-34	30	16	14	31	16	15	35	18	17	36	19	18
35-39	24	13	11	28	15	13	29	15	14	32	17	16
40-44	20	11	9	21	11	10	25	13	12	27	14	13
45-49	19	9	10	17	10	8	19	10	9	23	12	11
50-54	14	6	8	16	8	8	15	8	7	17	9	8
55-59	9	4	5	11	5	6	13	6	7	13	7	6
60-64	10	4	5	7	3	4	9	4	5	11	5	6
65-69	7	3	4	7	3	4	5	2	3	7	3	4
70-74	4	2	3	4	2	2	5	2	3	4	2	2
75-79	2	1	1	2	1	1	2	1	1	3	1	2
80 +	1	0	1	1	0	1	1	1	1	1	1	1

Age group	1970 Both sexes	1970 Males	1970 Females	1975 Both sexes	1975 Males	1975 Females	1980 Both sexes	1980 Males	1980 Females	1985 Both sexes	1985 Males	1985 Females
All ages	604	308	297	672	342	330	581	296	285	659	335	324
0-4	99	51	49	111	57	55	78	42	36	117	60	57
5-9	83	42	41	91	46	44	78	41	37	71	38	33
10-14	71	36	35	81	41	39	75	37	38	76	40	36
15-19	62	31	30	69	35	34	75	37	38	73	36	37
20-24	54	27	26	59	30	29	62	31	31	72	35	37
25-29	46	23	22	51	26	25	47	24	23	59	30	29
30-34	40	20	20	43	22	21	39	18	20	45	23	22
35-39	34	18	17	38	19	19	34	18	16	36	17	19
40-44	30	16	15	32	16	16	26	14	12	31	16	15
45-49	24	13	12	28	14	14	19	10	9	24	13	11
50-54	20	10	10	22	11	11	16	8	8	17	9	8
55-59	15	8	7	18	9	9	11	6	5	14	7	7
60-64	11	6	5	12	6	6	8	4	4	9	5	4
65-69	8	4	5	8	4	4	7	3	4	6	3	3
70-74	5	2	3	6	3	3	4	2	2	5	2	2
75-79	2	1	1	3	1	2	2	1	1	2	1	1
80 +	1	1	1	1	1	1	1	0	1	1	0	1

Age group	1990 Both sexes	1990 Males	1990 Females	1995 Both sexes	1995 Males	1995 Females	2000 Both sexes	2000 Males	2000 Females	2005 Both sexes	2005 Males	2005 Females
All ages	740	383	357	848	436	412	722	383	339	947	492	455
0-4	133	68	65	124	63	61	100	51	49	179	91	88
5-9	106	55	51	126	65	61	109	56	53	100	51	49
10-14	68	37	31	105	55	50	120	62	58	110	56	54
15-19	73	39	34	68	37	31	90	48	42	123	63	60
20-24	69	35	34	74	39	35	37	24	13	100	53	48
25-29	68	34	34	71	36	36	35	22	13	51	29	21
30-34	55	28	27	69	34	35	38	21	17	47	27	19
35-39	42	22	20	56	28	27	44	23	21	46	24	22
40-44	34	16	17	41	21	20	38	20	18	49	25	24
45-49	29	15	14	33	16	17	30	16	14	41	21	20
50-54	22	12	10	27	14	13	24	12	13	30	16	14
55-59	15	8	7	20	11	10	21	11	10	24	11	13
60-64	12	6	6	13	7	7	15	8	7	20	10	10
65-69	7	4	3	10	5	5	9	5	5	13	7	6
70-74	4	2	2	5	3	3	6	3	3	8	4	4
75-79	2	1	1	3	1	2	3	1	1	4	2	2
80 +	1	1	0	1	1	1	1	1	1	2	1	1

United Nations Department of Economic and Social Affairs/Population Division
World Population Prospects: The 2004 Revision, Volume II: Sex and Age Distribution of the World Population

POPULATION BY AGE AND SEX (in thousands)

Age group	2005 Both sexes	2005 Males	2005 Females	2010 Both sexes	2010 Males	2010 Females	2015 Both sexes	2015 Males	2015 Females	2020 Both sexes	2020 Males	2020 Females
All ages	947	492	455	1 244	638	607	1 486	759	727	1 713	873	839
0-4	179	91	88	257	131	126	265	135	130	272	139	133
5-9	100	51	49	177	90	87	252	129	124	260	133	127
10-14	110	56	54	101	52	50	176	90	87	251	128	123
15-19	123	63	60	114	58	56	102	52	50	175	89	86
20-24	100	53	48	133	67	66	115	58	57	101	51	49
25-29	51	29	21	113	58	55	135	68	67	114	57	56
30-34	47	27	19	62	34	28	114	58	56	133	67	66
35-39	46	24	22	55	31	24	63	34	28	112	57	55
40-44	49	25	24	50	26	24	55	30	24	61	34	28
45-49	41	21	20	51	26	25	50	26	24	53	29	23
50-54	30	16	14	41	21	20	49	25	24	47	24	23
55-59	24	11	13	30	15	14	39	20	19	46	23	23
60-64	20	10	10	23	10	12	27	14	13	35	17	18
65-69	13	7	6	17	9	9	19	9	11	23	12	12
70-74	8	4	4	11	5	5	14	7	7	15	7	9
75-79	4	2	2	5	2	3	7	4	4	9	4	5
80-84	2	1	1	3	1	1	3	1	2	4	2	2
85-89	0	0	0	1	0	0	1	0	1	1	0	1
90-94	0	0	0	0	0	0	0	0	0	0	0	0
95-99	0	0	0	0	0	0	0	0	0	0	0	0
100 +	0	0	0	0	0	0	0	0	0	0	0	0

Age group	2025 Both sexes	2025 Males	2025 Females	2030 Both sexes	2030 Males	2030 Females	2035 Both sexes	2035 Males	2035 Females	2040 Both sexes	2040 Males	2040 Females
All ages	1 938	987	951	2 173	1 105	1 068	2 435	1 237	1 198	2 720	1 379	1 340
0-4	273	139	134	285	146	140	316	161	155	343	175	168
5-9	268	137	132	270	138	132	283	144	139	314	160	154
10-14	259	132	127	267	136	131	269	137	132	283	144	139
15-19	249	127	122	257	131	126	266	136	131	268	137	132
20-24	173	88	85	247	126	121	256	130	126	265	135	130
25-29	99	50	49	172	87	84	245	125	120	254	129	125
30-34	112	56	56	98	50	48	170	86	84	243	124	120
35-39	131	66	65	111	56	55	97	49	48	169	86	83
40-44	110	56	54	128	64	64	109	55	54	96	49	47
45-49	60	33	27	107	54	53	126	63	63	107	54	53
50-54	51	28	23	58	31	26	104	52	51	122	61	61
55-59	45	23	22	49	26	23	55	29	25	99	50	50
60-64	42	21	21	41	21	20	44	24	20	51	27	24
65-69	30	15	16	37	18	19	36	18	18	39	21	18
70-74	19	9	10	25	12	13	30	14	16	30	14	16
75-79	11	5	6	13	6	7	18	8	10	22	10	12
80-84	5	2	3	6	3	4	8	3	4	10	5	6
85-89	2	1	1	2	1	1	3	1	2	3	1	2
90-94	0	0	0	0	0	0	1	0	0	1	0	0
95-99	0	0	0	0	0	0	0	0	0	0	0	0
100 +	0	0	0	0	0	0	0	0	0	0	0	0

Age group	2045 Both sexes	2045 Males	2045 Females	2050 Both sexes	2050 Males	2050 Females
All ages	3 002	1 520	1 482	3 265	1 651	1 614
0-4	346	176	170	332	169	163
5-9	341	174	167	345	176	169
10-14	313	160	154	341	174	167
15-19	282	143	138	313	159	154
20-24	267	136	131	281	143	138
25-29	263	134	130	266	135	131
30-34	253	128	124	262	133	129
35-39	242	123	119	251	127	124
40-44	167	85	82	239	121	118
45-49	95	48	47	165	83	81
50-54	104	52	52	92	46	46
55-59	117	58	59	101	50	51
60-64	93	46	47	110	53	57
65-69	46	24	22	84	40	43
70-74	33	17	16	38	19	19
75-79	22	10	12	25	12	12
80-84	13	6	8	14	6	8
85-89	5	2	3	6	2	4
90-94	1	0	1	1	0	1
95-99	0	0	0	0	0	0
100 +	0	0	0	0	0	0

United Nations Department of Economic and Social Affairs/Population Division
World Population Prospects: The 2004 Revision, Volume II: Sex and Age Distribution of the World Population

347

POPULATION BY AGE AND SEX (in thousands)

Age group	2005 Both sexes	2005 Males	2005 Females	2010 Both sexes	2010 Males	2010 Females	2015 Both sexes	2015 Males	2015 Females	2020 Both sexes	2020 Males	2020 Females
All ages	947	492	455	1 253	642	611	1 514	773	741	1 767	901	866
0-4	179	91	88	266	136	130	284	145	139	299	153	146
5-9	100	51	49	177	90	87	261	133	128	279	142	137
10-14	110	56	54	101	52	50	176	90	87	259	132	127
15-19	123	63	60	114	58	56	102	52	50	175	89	86
20-24	100	53	48	133	67	66	115	58	57	101	51	49
25-29	51	29	21	113	58	55	135	68	67	114	57	56
30-34	47	27	19	62	34	28	114	58	56	133	67	66
35-39	46	24	22	55	31	24	63	34	28	112	57	55
40-44	49	25	24	50	26	24	55	30	24	61	34	28
45-49	41	21	20	51	26	25	50	26	24	53	29	23
50-54	30	16	14	41	21	20	49	25	24	47	24	23
55-59	24	11	13	30	15	14	39	20	19	46	23	23
60-64	20	10	10	23	10	12	27	14	13	35	17	18
65-69	13	7	6	17	9	9	19	9	11	23	12	12
70-74	8	4	4	11	5	5	14	7	7	15	7	9
75-79	4	2	2	5	2	3	7	4	4	9	4	5
80-84	2	1	1	3	1	1	3	1	2	4	2	2
85-89	0	0	0	1	0	0	1	0	1	1	0	1
90-94	0	0	0	0	0	0	0	0	0	0	0	0
95-99	0	0	0	0	0	0	0	0	0	0	0	0
100 +	0	0	0	0	0	0	0	0	0	0	0	0

Age group	2025 Both sexes	2025 Males	2025 Females	2030 Both sexes	2030 Males	2030 Females	2035 Both sexes	2035 Males	2035 Females	2040 Both sexes	2040 Males	2040 Females
All ages	2 024	1 031	993	2 298	1 169	1 129	2 606	1 324	1 282	2 954	1 498	1 455
0-4	304	155	149	326	166	160	363	185	178	406	207	199
5-9	295	150	145	301	153	148	323	165	159	361	184	177
10-14	278	142	136	294	150	144	300	153	147	323	164	158
15-19	258	131	126	276	141	135	292	149	144	299	152	147
20-24	173	88	85	256	130	125	274	140	135	291	148	143
25-29	99	50	49	172	87	84	253	129	125	273	139	134
30-34	112	56	56	98	50	48	170	86	84	252	128	124
35-39	131	66	65	111	56	55	97	49	48	169	86	83
40-44	110	56	54	128	64	64	109	55	54	96	49	47
45-49	60	33	27	107	54	53	126	63	63	107	54	53
50-54	51	28	23	58	31	26	104	52	51	122	61	61
55-59	45	23	22	48	26	22	55	29	25	99	50	50
60-64	42	21	21	41	21	20	44	24	20	51	27	24
65-69	30	15	16	37	18	19	36	18	18	39	21	18
70-74	19	9	10	25	12	13	30	14	16	30	14	16
75-79	11	5	6	13	6	7	18	8	10	22	10	12
80-84	5	2	3	6	3	4	8	3	4	10	5	6
85-89	2	1	1	2	1	1	3	1	2	3	1	2
90-94	0	0	0	0	0	0	1	0	0	1	0	0
95-99	0	0	0	0	0	0	0	0	0	0	0	0
100 +	0	0	0	0	0	0	0	0	0	0	0	0

Age group	2045 Both sexes	2045 Males	2045 Females	2050 Both sexes	2050 Males	2050 Females
All ages	3 320	1 682	1 638	3 682	1 863	1 819
0-4	430	219	211	432	220	212
5-9	405	206	198	429	218	210
10-14	360	183	177	404	206	198
15-19	322	164	158	359	183	176
20-24	298	151	146	321	163	158
25-29	289	147	142	297	151	146
30-34	271	138	133	288	146	142
35-39	250	127	123	269	137	133
40-44	167	85	82	248	126	122
45-49	95	48	47	165	83	81
50-54	104	52	52	92	46	46
55-59	117	58	59	101	50	51
60-64	93	46	47	110	53	57
65-69	46	24	22	84	40	43
70-74	33	17	16	38	19	19
75-79	22	10	12	25	12	12
80-84	13	6	8	14	6	8
85-89	5	2	3	6	2	4
90-94	1	0	1	1	0	1
95-99	0	0	0	0	0	0
100 +	0	0	0	0	0	0

United Nations Department of Economic and Social Affairs/Population Division
World Population Prospects: The 2004 Revision, Volume II: Sex and Age Distribution of the World Population

348

LOW VARIANT   **DEMOCRATIC REPUBLIC OF TIMOR-LESTE**

POPULATION BY AGE AND SEX (in thousands)

Age group	2005 Both sexes	Males	Females	2010 Both sexes	Males	Females	2015 Both sexes	Males	Females	2020 Both sexes	Males	Females
All ages	947	492	455	1 233	632	601	1 455	743	712	1 657	845	812
0-4	179	91	88	246	126	121	245	125	120	246	126	121
5-9	100	51	49	177	90	87	241	123	118	241	123	118
10-14	110	56	54	101	52	50	176	90	87	240	122	118
15-19	123	63	60	114	58	56	102	52	50	175	89	86
20-24	100	53	48	133	67	66	115	58	57	101	51	49
25-29	51	29	21	113	58	55	135	68	67	114	57	56
30-34	47	27	19	62	34	28	114	58	56	133	67	66
35-39	46	24	22	55	31	24	63	34	28	112	57	55
40-44	49	25	24	50	26	24	55	30	24	61	34	28
45-49	41	21	20	51	26	25	50	26	24	53	29	23
50-54	30	16	14	41	21	20	49	25	24	47	24	23
55-59	24	11	13	30	15	14	39	20	19	46	23	23
60-64	20	10	10	23	10	12	27	14	13	35	17	18
65-69	13	7	6	17	9	9	19	9	11	23	12	12
70-74	8	4	4	11	5	5	14	7	7	15	7	9
75-79	4	2	2	5	2	3	7	4	4	9	4	5
80-84	2	1	1	3	1	1	3	1	2	4	2	2
85-89	0	0	0	1	0	0	1	0	1	1	0	1
90-94	0	0	0	0	0	0	0	0	0	0	0	0
95-99	0	0	0	0	0	0	0	0	0	0	0	0
100 +	0	0	0	0	0	0	0	0	0	0	0	0

Age group	2025 Both sexes	Males	Females	2030 Both sexes	Males	Females	2035 Both sexes	Males	Females	2040 Both sexes	Males	Females
All ages	1 852	943	909	2 052	1 043	1 009	2 268	1 152	1 117	2 491	1 263	1 228
0-4	242	124	119	249	127	122	269	137	132	281	143	138
5-9	243	124	119	240	122	118	247	126	121	268	137	131
10-14	240	122	117	242	123	119	239	122	117	247	126	121
15-19	238	121	117	238	121	117	241	123	118	238	121	117
20-24	173	88	85	236	120	116	237	121	116	240	122	118
25-29	99	50	49	172	87	84	235	119	115	235	120	116
30-34	112	56	56	98	50	48	170	86	84	233	118	115
35-39	131	66	65	111	56	55	97	49	48	169	86	83
40-44	110	56	54	128	64	64	109	55	54	96	49	47
45-49	60	33	27	107	54	53	126	63	63	107	54	53
50-54	51	28	23	50	24	26	104	52	51	122	61	61
55-59	45	23	22	48	26	22	55	29	25	99	50	50
60-64	42	21	21	41	21	20	44	24	20	51	27	24
65-69	30	15	16	37	18	19	36	18	18	39	21	18
70-74	19	9	10	25	12	13	30	14	16	30	14	16
75-79	11	5	6	13	6	7	18	8	10	22	10	12
80-84	5	2	3	6	3	4	8	3	4	10	5	6
85-89	2	1	1	2	1	1	3	1	2	3	1	2
90-94	0	0	0	0	0	0	1	0	0	1	0	0
95-99	0	0	0	0	0	0	0	0	0	0	0	0
100 +	0	0	0	0	0	0	0	0	0	0	0	0

Age group	2045 Both sexes	Males	Females	2050 Both sexes	Males	Females
All ages	2 696	1 364	1 331	2 870	1 450	1 420
0-4	267	136	131	242	124	119
5-9	280	142	137	266	135	130
10-14	267	136	131	279	142	137
15-19	246	125	121	267	136	131
20-24	237	121	117	245	125	121
25-29	238	121	117	236	120	116
30-34	234	119	115	237	120	117
35-39	231	117	114	233	118	115
40-44	167	85	82	229	116	113
45-49	95	48	47	165	83	81
50-54	104	52	52	92	46	46
55-59	117	58	59	101	50	51
60-64	93	46	47	110	53	57
65-69	46	24	22	84	40	43
70-74	33	17	16	38	19	19
75-79	22	10	12	25	12	12
80-84	13	6	8	14	6	8
85-89	5	2	3	6	2	4
90-94	1	0	1	1	0	1
95-99	0	0	0	0	0	0
100 +	0	0	0	0	0	0

United Nations Department of Economic and Social Affairs/Population Division
World Population Prospects: The 2004 Revision, Volume II: Sex and Age Distribution of the World Population

349

POPULATION BY AGE AND SEX (in thousands)

Age group	1950 Both sexes	1950 Males	1950 Females	1955 Both sexes	1955 Males	1955 Females	1960 Both sexes	1960 Males	1960 Females	1965 Both sexes	1965 Males	1965 Females
All ages	4 271	2 118	2 153	4 439	2 203	2 236	4 581	2 272	2 309	4 758	2 359	2 399
0-4	416	213	203	375	193	182	368	189	179	392	201	191
5-9	393	200	193	419	214	205	371	190	181	368	188	180
10-14	315	160	155	384	196	188	417	213	204	371	190	181
15-19	292	148	144	311	158	153	381	195	186	415	213	202
20-24	295	148	147	287	144	143	303	153	150	378	193	185
25-29	315	156	159	292	145	147	279	139	140	301	152	149
30-34	310	154	156	316	156	160	287	142	145	279	139	140
35-39	314	156	158	304	151	153	311	153	158	287	142	145
40-44	307	152	155	311	154	157	299	148	151	310	153	157
45-49	277	136	141	300	148	152	305	151	154	297	147	150
50-54	251	121	130	269	131	138	293	144	149	297	146	151
55-59	214	103	111	239	114	125	258	125	133	281	137	144
60-64	182	87	95	199	95	104	224	106	118	242	115	127
65-69	151	72	79	163	77	86	180	84	96	201	92	109
70-74	115	55	60	125	59	66	137	63	74	151	68	83
75-79	72	34	38	83	39	44	94	43	51	103	46	57
80 +	52	23	29	62	29	33	74	34	40	85	37	48

Age group	1970 Both sexes	1970 Males	1970 Females	1975 Both sexes	1975 Males	1975 Females	1980 Both sexes	1980 Males	1980 Females	1985 Both sexes	1985 Males	1985 Females
All ages	4 929	2 446	2 483	5 060	2 506	2 554	5 123	2 529	2 594	5 114	2 519	2 595
0-4	388	199	189	362	185	177	314	161	153	265	135	130
5-9	392	200	192	389	199	189	364	186	178	314	161	153
10-14	368	189	180	393	201	192	390	200	190	364	186	178
15-19	373	191	181	370	190	180	396	202	193	392	201	191
20-24	416	214	202	375	192	183	372	190	181	398	204	194
25-29	375	193	183	416	214	202	374	191	182	371	190	181
30-34	302	153	149	375	192	183	413	212	202	371	190	182
35-39	279	140	139	301	153	149	373	191	182	410	210	201
40-44	285	142	143	277	138	139	299	151	148	369	188	181
45-49	306	151	155	281	139	142	272	136	137	294	148	146
50-54	289	142	146	298	146	152	273	135	139	265	131	134
55-59	287	140	147	277	135	142	286	139	147	262	128	134
60-64	264	126	138	270	129	140	260	124	135	267	127	140
65-69	219	100	118	239	110	129	239	111	128	235	109	126
70-74	170	75	95	186	81	105	205	90	115	210	92	118
75-79	115	49	66	131	53	78	146	59	88	160	64	97
80 +	101	42	60	122	47	75	148	52	96	166	56	110

Age group	1990 Both sexes	1990 Males	1990 Females	1995 Both sexes	1995 Males	1995 Females	2000 Both sexes	2000 Males	2000 Females	2005 Both sexes	2005 Males	2005 Females
All ages	5 140	2 533	2 607	5 228	2 580	2 648	5 340	2 639	2 700	5 431	2 688	2 743
0-4	291	150	142	339	174	165	339	174	165	326	167	158
5-9	267	136	131	297	152	144	347	178	169	345	177	168
10-14	317	162	155	272	139	133	301	155	147	351	180	171
15-19	368	188	180	322	165	158	281	143	138	308	158	150
20-24	396	203	193	375	191	184	333	169	164	289	147	143
25-29	401	206	195	403	207	196	385	195	191	341	172	169
30-34	371	190	181	404	207	197	408	209	199	389	196	193
35-39	369	188	181	373	190	183	408	209	199	410	209	201
40-44	408	208	200	368	187	181	375	191	185	408	208	200
45-49	364	185	179	403	205	199	366	185	181	373	189	184
50-54	286	143	143	356	180	176	396	200	196	361	182	179
55-59	255	125	130	277	138	139	345	173	172	385	194	191
60-64	245	118	128	240	116	124	263	129	134	329	164	165
65-69	241	111	130	224	105	119	219	103	115	241	116	125
70-74	203	90	114	208	91	116	194	87	106	190	87	103
75-79	167	68	99	161	66	95	167	69	98	157	66	91
80 +	190	62	128	205	67	138	212	70	142	227	75	152

United Nations Department of Economic and Social Affairs/Population Division
World Population Prospects: The 2004 Revision, Volume II: Sex and Age Distribution of the World Population

350

POPULATION BY AGE AND SEX (in thousands)

Age group	2005 Both sexes	Males	Females	2010 Both sexes	Males	Females	2015 Both sexes	Males	Females	2020 Both sexes	Males	Females
All ages	5 431	2 688	2 743	5 502	2 725	2 776	5 560	2 755	2 806	5 624	2 784	2 839
0-4	326	167	158	306	157	149	297	153	145	310	159	151
5-9	345	177	168	332	171	161	313	161	152	304	156	148
10-14	351	180	171	349	180	170	336	173	163	317	163	154
15-19	308	158	150	357	183	174	355	183	173	342	176	166
20-24	289	147	143	316	161	154	365	186	178	363	186	177
25-29	341	172	169	297	149	147	323	164	159	372	189	183
30-34	389	196	193	345	174	172	301	151	150	328	166	162
35-39	410	209	201	392	197	195	348	175	173	305	153	152
40-44	408	208	200	411	209	202	393	197	196	350	175	175
45-49	373	189	184	406	207	200	410	208	201	392	196	196
50-54	361	182	179	368	186	182	401	203	198	405	205	200
55-59	385	194	191	352	176	175	359	181	179	392	198	194
60-64	329	164	165	368	184	185	337	168	169	346	172	173
65-69	241	116	125	303	148	155	341	167	174	314	153	160
70-74	190	87	103	212	99	113	268	127	141	304	145	159
75-79	157	66	91	156	67	89	175	77	98	224	100	123
80-84	122	45	78	117	44	73	118	45	72	133	53	80
85-89	69	21	47	75	24	52	74	24	50	76	25	50
90-94	29	7	21	31	8	23	35	9	26	35	9	26
95-99	7	1	5	8	2	6	9	2	7	11	2	9
100 +	1	0	1	1	0	1	1	0	1	2	0	1

Age group	2025 Both sexes	Males	Females	2030 Both sexes	Males	Females	2035 Both sexes	Males	Females	2040 Both sexes	Males	Females
All ages	5 691	2 814	2 876	5 752	2 841	2 911	5 795	2 859	2 936	5 819	2 868	2 951
0-4	326	168	158	335	172	163	332	171	161	322	165	156
5-9	317	163	154	333	171	162	342	176	166	338	174	164
10-14	308	159	149	321	165	156	337	173	163	346	178	168
15-19	323	166	157	314	162	153	327	168	159	343	176	166
20-24	350	180	171	331	170	161	323	165	157	335	172	163
25-29	371	189	182	358	183	176	339	173	166	331	168	162
30-34	377	191	186	376	191	185	363	185	179	344	175	169
35-39	331	167	164	380	192	188	379	192	187	366	186	180
40-44	307	154	153	333	168	165	382	193	189	381	193	188
45-49	349	175	175	307	153	154	333	168	165	382	193	189
50-54	388	194	194	346	173	174	305	152	153	331	166	165
55-59	396	200	196	381	189	191	340	169	171	300	149	151
60-64	378	189	189	383	192	191	368	182	186	330	163	167
65-69	323	158	164	354	175	179	360	178	182	348	169	178
70-74	281	134	147	290	139	152	321	154	166	327	157	170
75-79	256	115	140	238	108	131	249	113	136	276	127	150
80-84	172	70	102	198	82	116	187	77	109	197	82	114
85-89	87	30	57	113	41	73	133	49	84	127	47	81
90-94	37	10	27	44	13	31	59	18	41	70	22	49
95-99	11	2	9	13	3	10	15	3	12	21	5	16
100 +	2	0	2	2	0	2	3	0	2	3	0	3

Age group	2045 Both sexes	Males	Females	2050 Both sexes	Males	Females
All ages	5 834	2 874	2 960	5 851	2 883	2 969
0-4	316	163	154	320	164	155
5-9	329	169	160	323	166	157
10-14	342	176	166	333	171	161
15-19	352	181	171	349	179	169
20-24	351	180	171	360	185	176
25-29	343	175	168	359	183	176
30-34	335	170	165	348	177	171
35-39	347	176	171	339	172	167
40-44	369	187	182	350	177	173
45-49	382	193	189	369	187	182
50-54	379	191	188	379	191	188
55-59	326	163	163	374	188	186
60-64	291	144	148	317	158	159
65-69	312	152	160	276	134	142
70-74	318	151	167	286	136	150
75-79	284	130	153	277	126	151
80-84	220	93	127	229	97	131
85-89	136	51	85	154	59	96
90-94	69	21	48	75	24	52
95-99	26	6	20	27	6	20
100 +	5	1	4	6	1	5

POPULATION BY AGE AND SEX (in thousands)

Age group	2005			2010			2015			2020		
	Both sexes	Males	Females	Both sexes	Males	Females	Both sexes	Males	Females	Both sexes	Males	Females
All ages	5 431	2 688	2 743	5 543	2 747	2 797	5 666	2 809	2 857	5 812	2 881	2 931
0-4	326	167	158	347	179	169	361	186	175	393	202	191
5-9	345	177	168	332	171	161	354	182	172	368	189	179
10-14	351	180	171	349	180	170	336	173	163	358	184	174
15-19	308	158	150	357	183	174	355	183	173	342	176	166
20-24	289	147	143	316	161	154	365	186	178	363	186	177
25-29	341	172	169	297	149	147	323	164	159	372	189	183
30-34	389	196	193	345	174	172	301	151	150	328	166	162
35-39	410	209	201	392	197	195	348	175	173	305	153	152
40-44	408	208	200	411	209	202	393	197	196	350	175	175
45-49	373	189	184	406	207	200	410	208	201	392	196	196
50-54	361	182	179	368	186	182	401	203	198	405	205	200
55-59	385	194	191	352	176	175	359	181	179	392	198	194
60-64	329	164	165	368	184	185	337	168	169	346	172	173
65-69	241	116	125	303	148	155	341	167	174	314	153	160
70-74	190	87	103	212	99	113	268	127	141	304	145	159
75-79	157	66	91	156	67	89	175	77	98	224	100	123
80-84	122	45	78	117	44	73	118	45	72	133	53	80
85-89	69	21	47	75	24	52	74	24	50	76	25	50
90-94	29	7	21	31	8	23	35	9	26	35	9	26
95-99	7	1	5	8	2	6	9	2	7	11	2	9
100 +	1	0	1	1	0	1	1	0	1	2	0	1

Age group	2025			2030			2035			2040		
	Both sexes	Males	Females	Both sexes	Males	Females	Both sexes	Males	Females	Both sexes	Males	Females
All ages	5 968	2 957	3 011	6 121	3 031	3 090	6 266	3 101	3 165	6 413	3 174	3 239
0-4	415	213	201	427	220	208	433	223	210	445	229	216
5-9	400	206	194	421	217	205	434	223	211	440	226	214
10-14	372	191	180	404	208	196	425	219	206	438	225	212
15-19	364	187	177	378	194	183	410	211	199	432	222	209
20-24	350	180	171	372	191	182	386	198	188	418	215	204
25-29	371	189	182	358	183	176	380	194	186	394	201	193
30-34	377	191	186	376	191	185	363	185	179	385	196	189
35-39	331	167	164	380	192	188	379	192	187	366	186	180
40-44	307	154	153	333	168	165	382	193	189	381	193	188
45-49	349	175	175	307	153	154	333	168	165	382	193	189
50-54	388	194	194	346	173	174	305	152	153	331	166	165
55-59	396	200	196	381	189	191	340	169	171	300	149	151
60-64	378	189	189	383	192	191	368	182	186	330	163	167
65-69	323	158	164	354	175	179	360	178	182	348	169	178
70-74	281	134	147	290	139	152	321	154	166	327	157	170
75-79	256	115	140	238	108	131	249	113	136	276	127	150
80-84	172	70	102	198	82	116	187	77	109	197	82	114
85-89	87	30	57	113	41	73	133	49	84	127	47	81
90-94	37	10	27	44	13	31	59	18	41	70	22	49
95-99	11	2	9	13	3	10	15	3	12	21	5	16
100 +	2	0	2	2	0	2	3	0	2	3	0	3

Age group	2045			2050		
	Both sexes	Males	Females	Both sexes	Males	Females
All ages	6 577	3 256	3 321	6 767	3 353	3 413
0-4	467	240	227	492	253	239
5-9	452	233	219	473	244	230
10-14	444	229	215	456	235	221
15-19	444	229	216	450	232	218
20-24	440	226	214	452	232	220
25-29	426	218	209	448	229	219
30-34	399	203	196	431	220	211
35-39	388	197	191	402	205	198
40-44	369	187	182	391	198	193
45-49	382	193	189	369	187	182
50-54	379	191	188	379	191	188
55-59	326	163	163	374	188	186
60-64	291	144	148	317	158	159
65-69	312	152	160	276	134	142
70-74	318	151	167	286	136	150
75-79	284	130	153	277	126	151
80-84	220	93	127	229	97	131
85-89	136	51	85	154	59	96
90-94	69	21	48	75	24	52
95-99	26	6	20	27	6	20
100 +	5	1	4	6	1	5

United Nations Department of Economic and Social Affairs/Population Division
World Population Prospects: The 2004 Revision, Volume II: Sex and Age Distribution of the World Population

352

POPULATION BY AGE AND SEX (in thousands)

Age group	2005 Both sexes	Males	Females	2010 Both sexes	Males	Females	2015 Both sexes	Males	Females	2020 Both sexes	Males	Females
All ages	5 431	2 688	2 743	5 460	2 704	2 756	5 455	2 700	2 754	5 435	2 696	2 740
0-4	326	167	158	264	136	128	233	120	113	227	117	111
5-9	345	177	168	332	171	161	271	139	132	240	124	117
10-14	351	180	171	349	180	170	336	173	163	275	142	133
15-19	308	158	150	357	183	174	355	183	173	342	176	166
20-24	289	147	143	316	161	154	365	186	178	363	186	177
25-29	341	172	169	297	149	147	323	164	159	372	189	183
30-34	389	196	193	345	174	172	301	151	150	328	166	162
35-39	410	209	201	392	197	195	348	175	173	305	153	152
40-44	408	208	200	411	209	202	393	197	196	350	175	175
45-49	373	189	184	406	207	200	410	208	201	392	196	196
50-54	361	182	179	368	186	182	401	203	198	405	205	200
55-59	385	194	191	352	176	175	359	181	179	392	198	194
60-64	329	164	165	368	184	185	337	168	169	346	172	173
65-69	241	116	125	303	148	155	341	167	174	314	153	160
70-74	190	87	103	212	99	113	268	127	141	304	145	159
75-79	157	66	91	156	67	89	175	77	98	224	100	123
80-84	122	45	78	117	44	73	118	45	72	133	53	80
85-89	69	21	47	75	24	52	74	24	50	76	25	50
90-94	29	7	21	31	8	23	35	9	26	35	9	26
95-99	7	1	5	8	2	6	9	2	7	11	2	9
100 +	1	0	1	1	0	1	1	0	1	2	0	1

Age group	2025 Both sexes	Males	Females	2030 Both sexes	Males	Females	2035 Both sexes	Males	Females	2040 Both sexes	Males	Females
All ages	5 414	2 672	2 742	5 385	2 652	2 733	5 337	2 623	2 714	5 260	2 580	2 679
0-4	238	122	116	245	126	119	239	123	116	221	113	107
5-9	234	121	114	245	126	119	251	129	122	246	127	119
10-14	244	126	118	238	123	116	249	128	121	255	132	124
15-19	281	145	136	250	129	122	245	126	119	255	131	124
20-24	350	180	171	289	148	141	259	132	126	253	129	123
25-29	371	189	182	358	183	176	297	151	146	267	136	131
30-34	377	191	186	376	191	185	363	185	179	302	153	149
35-39	331	167	164	380	192	188	379	192	187	366	186	180
40-44	307	154	153	333	168	165	382	193	189	381	193	188
45-49	349	175	175	307	153	154	333	168	165	382	193	189
50-54	388	194	194	346	173	174	305	152	153	331	166	165
55-59	400	200	100	361	180	181	340	169	171	300	149	151
60-64	378	189	189	383	192	191	368	182	186	330	163	167
65-69	323	158	164	354	175	179	360	178	182	348	169	178
70-74	281	134	147	290	139	152	321	154	166	327	157	170
75-79	256	115	140	238	108	131	249	113	136	276	127	150
80-84	172	70	102	198	82	116	187	77	109	197	82	114
85-89	87	30	57	113	41	73	133	49	84	127	47	81
90-94	37	10	27	44	13	31	59	18	41	70	22	49
95-99	11	2	9	13	3	10	15	3	12	21	5	16
100 +	2	0	2	2	0	2	3	0	2	3	0	3

Age group	2045 Both sexes	Males	Females	2050 Both sexes	Males	Females
All ages	5 159	2 527	2 632	5 046	2 469	2 578
0-4	200	103	97	189	97	92
5-9	228	117	110	207	107	101
10-14	250	129	121	231	119	112
15-19	262	135	127	256	132	124
20-24	263	135	129	270	138	132
25-29	261	133	128	272	138	134
30-34	272	138	134	266	135	131
35-39	306	155	151	276	140	136
40-44	369	187	182	309	156	153
45-49	382	193	189	369	187	182
50-54	379	191	188	379	191	188
55-59	326	163	163	374	188	186
60-64	291	144	148	317	158	159
65-69	312	152	160	276	134	142
70-74	318	151	167	286	136	150
75-79	284	130	153	277	126	151
80-84	220	93	127	229	97	131
85-89	136	51	85	154	59	96
90-94	69	21	48	75	24	52
95-99	26	6	20	27	6	20
100 +	5	1	4	6	1	5

United Nations Department of Economic and Social Affairs/Population Division
World Population Prospects: The 2004 Revision, Volume II: Sex and Age Distribution of the World Population

353

POPULATION BY AGE AND SEX (in thousands)

Age group	1950 Both sexes	1950 Males	1950 Females	1955 Both sexes	1955 Males	1955 Females	1960 Both sexes	1960 Males	1960 Females	1965 Both sexes	1965 Males	1965 Females
All ages	62	31	31	70	35	35	85	42	43	117	58	59
0-4	12	6	6	12	6	6	15	8	8	22	11	11
5-9	9	5	5	11	6	5	12	6	6	17	8	8
10-14	8	4	4	9	5	5	11	6	6	14	7	7
15-19	6	3	3	8	4	4	9	5	5	13	7	7
20-24	5	3	3	6	3	3	8	4	4	11	5	5
25-29	5	2	2	5	3	3	6	3	3	9	4	4
30-34	4	2	2	4	2	2	5	3	3	7	4	4
35-39	3	2	2	4	2	2	4	2	2	6	3	3
40-44	3	1	1	3	1	1	4	2	2	5	2	2
45-49	2	1	1	2	1	1	3	1	1	4	2	2
50-54	2	1	1	2	1	1	2	1	1	3	1	2
55-59	1	1	1	1	1	1	2	1	1	2	1	1
60-64	1	0	0	1	0	1	1	1	1	2	1	1
65-69	1	0	0	1	0	0	1	0	0	1	1	1
70-74	0	0	0	0	0	0	1	0	0	1	0	0
75-79	0	0	0	0	0	0	0	0	0	0	0	0
80 +	0	0	0	0	0	0	0	0	0	0	0	0

Age group	1970 Both sexes	1970 Males	1970 Females	1975 Both sexes	1975 Males	1975 Females	1980 Both sexes	1980 Males	1980 Females	1985 Both sexes	1985 Males	1985 Females
All ages	162	80	81	224	111	113	340	169	171	403	201	202
0-4	30	15	15	41	20	20	60	30	30	70	35	35
5-9	24	12	12	34	17	17	50	25	25	58	29	29
10-14	20	10	10	28	14	14	44	22	22	51	26	25
15-19	16	8	8	23	12	12	37	18	18	44	22	22
20-24	15	8	8	19	10	10	30	15	15	37	18	18
25-29	12	6	6	17	9	9	25	12	12	30	15	15
30-34	10	5	5	14	7	7	22	11	11	24	12	12
35-39	8	4	4	12	6	6	18	9	9	22	11	11
40-44	7	3	3	9	5	5	14	7	7	18	9	9
45-49	5	3	3	8	4	4	12	6	6	14	7	7
50-54	4	2	2	6	3	3	9	4	5	11	5	6
55-59	3	2	2	5	2	2	7	3	4	9	4	4
60-64	2	1	1	3	2	2	5	2	3	6	3	3
65-69	2	1	1	2	1	1	4	2	2	4	2	2
70-74	1	0	1	1	1	1	2	1	1	3	1	2
75-79	1	0	0	1	0	0	1	0	1	1	1	1
80 +	0	0	0	0	0	0	1	0	0	1	0	0

Age group	1990 Both sexes	1990 Males	1990 Females	1995 Both sexes	1995 Males	1995 Females	2000 Both sexes	2000 Males	2000 Females	2005 Both sexes	2005 Males	2005 Females
All ages	558	278	280	609	304	305	715	357	358	793	396	397
0-4	97	49	48	103	52	51	115	58	57	120	61	60
5-9	80	40	40	87	44	43	102	51	51	109	55	54
10-14	69	35	34	75	38	37	89	45	44	99	50	49
15-19	60	30	30	64	32	32	76	38	38	87	44	43
20-24	52	26	26	56	28	28	65	33	32	74	37	37
25-29	43	21	21	47	24	24	56	28	28	62	31	31
30-34	35	17	17	39	20	20	47	24	23	52	26	26
35-39	28	14	14	32	16	16	39	19	19	44	22	22
40-44	25	12	12	26	13	13	31	15	16	36	18	18
45-49	20	10	10	22	11	11	25	12	13	29	14	15
50-54	16	8	8	18	9	9	22	11	11	23	11	12
55-59	12	6	6	14	7	7	17	8	9	20	10	10
60-64	9	4	5	10	5	5	12	6	7	15	7	8
65-69	6	3	3	7	3	4	9	4	5	10	5	6
70-74	4	2	2	4	2	3	6	2	3	7	3	4
75-79	2	1	1	2	1	1	3	1	2	4	2	2
80 +	1	0	1	1	0	1	2	1	1	2	1	1

United Nations Department of Economic and Social Affairs/Population Division
World Population Prospects: The 2004 Revision, Volume II: Sex and Age Distribution of the World Population

354

POPULATION BY AGE AND SEX (in thousands)

Age group	2005 Both sexes	Males	Females	2010 Both sexes	Males	Females	2015 Both sexes	Males	Females	2020 Both sexes	Males	Females
All ages	793	396	397	859	430	429	930	466	464	1 015	509	506
0-4	120	61	60	121	61	60	121	61	60	124	63	61
5-9	109	55	54	113	57	56	115	58	57	118	60	59
10-14	99	50	49	105	53	52	110	56	55	114	58	56
15-19	87	44	43	96	48	48	103	52	51	109	55	54
20-24	74	37	37	83	42	41	93	47	46	101	51	50
25-29	62	31	31	70	35	35	79	40	39	91	46	45
30-34	52	26	26	58	29	29	66	33	33	77	39	38
35-39	44	22	22	48	25	24	54	27	27	63	32	31
40-44	36	18	18	41	20	20	45	23	22	52	26	25
45-49	29	14	15	33	17	17	38	19	19	43	22	21
50-54	23	11	12	26	13	13	31	15	16	36	18	18
55-59	20	10	10	21	10	11	24	12	12	29	14	15
60-64	15	7	8	17	8	9	18	9	10	22	10	11
65-69	10	5	6	12	6	7	14	7	8	16	7	8
70-74	7	3	4	8	3	4	9	4	5	11	5	6
75-79	4	2	2	4	2	2	5	2	3	6	3	4
80-84	2	1	1	2	1	1	2	1	1	3	1	2
85-89	0	0	0	1	0	0	1	0	0	1	0	1
90-94	0	0	0	0	0	0	0	0	0	0	0	0
95-99	0	0	0	0	0	0	0	0	0	0	0	0
100 +	0	0	0	0	0	0	0	0	0	0	0	0

Age group	2025 Both sexes	Males	Females	2030 Both sexes	Males	Females	2035 Both sexes	Males	Females	2040 Both sexes	Males	Females
All ages	1 107	555	551	1 200	602	598	1 292	648	644	1 381	693	688
0-4	127	65	63	130	66	64	131	67	65	131	67	65
5-9	122	62	60	126	64	62	129	65	64	131	66	65
10-14	118	60	58	122	62	60	126	64	62	129	65	64
15-19	114	57	56	118	59	58	122	62	60	126	64	62
20-24	108	55	54	113	57	56	117	59	58	121	61	60
25-29	100	50	49	107	54	53	112	56	55	116	58	58
30-34	88	45	44	98	49	48	105	53	52	110	56	55
35-39	74	38	37	86	43	42	95	48	47	103	52	51
40-44	61	31	30	72	37	35	84	42	41	93	47	46
45-49	49	25	24	59	30	29	70	35	34	82	41	40
50-54	41	21	20	47	24	23	56	28	28	67	34	33
55-59	34	17	17	39	19	19	45	22	22	57	27	27
60-64	26	12	14	31	15	16	36	17	18	41	20	21
65-69	19	9	10	23	11	12	27	13	14	31	15	16
70-74	12	6	7	15	7	8	18	8	10	22	10	12
75-79	8	3	4	9	4	5	11	5	6	13	6	7
80-84	4	1	2	4	2	3	5	2	3	6	3	4
85-89	1	0	1	1	1	1	2	1	1	2	1	1
90-94	0	0	0	0	0	0	0	0	0	0	0	0
95-99	0	0	0	0	0	0	0	0	0	0	0	0
100 +	0	0	0	0	0	0	0	0	0	0	0	0

Age group	2045 Both sexes	Males	Females	2050 Both sexes	Males	Females
All ages	1 466	735	731	1 547	774	773
0-4	131	66	65	131	66	64
5-9	131	66	65	131	66	65
10-14	131	66	65	131	66	65
15-19	129	65	64	131	66	65
20-24	126	63	62	129	65	64
25-29	121	61	60	125	63	62
30-34	115	58	57	120	60	59
35-39	109	55	54	114	57	56
40-44	101	51	50	107	54	53
45-49	91	46	45	99	50	49
50-54	79	40	39	89	44	44
55-59	64	32	32	75	38	38
60-64	50	24	25	60	29	30
65-69	36	18	19	44	21	23
70-74	26	12	14	30	14	16
75-79	16	7	9	19	8	10
80-84	8	3	5	9	4	5
85-89	3	1	2	3	1	2
90-94	1	0	0	1	0	0
95-99	0	0	0	0	0	0
100 +	0	0	0	0	0	0

POPULATION BY AGE AND SEX (in thousands)

Age group	2005 Both sexes	Males	Females	2010 Both sexes	Males	Females	2015 Both sexes	Males	Females	2020 Both sexes	Males	Females
All ages	793	396	397	866	434	433	949	475	473	1 051	528	524
0-4	120	61	60	127	64	63	134	68	66	142	72	70
5-9	109	55	54	113	57	56	122	62	60	131	66	65
10-14	99	50	49	105	53	52	110	56	55	121	61	60
15-19	87	44	43	96	48	48	103	52	51	109	55	54
20-24	74	37	37	83	42	41	93	47	46	101	51	50
25-29	62	31	31	70	35	35	79	40	39	91	46	45
30-34	52	26	26	58	29	29	66	33	33	77	39	38
35-39	44	22	22	48	25	24	54	27	27	63	32	31
40-44	36	18	18	41	20	20	45	23	22	52	26	25
45-49	29	14	15	33	17	17	38	19	19	43	22	21
50-54	23	11	12	26	13	13	31	15	16	36	18	18
55-59	20	10	10	21	10	11	24	12	12	29	14	15
60-64	15	7	8	17	8	9	18	9	10	22	10	11
65-69	10	5	6	12	6	7	14	7	8	16	7	8
70-74	7	3	4	8	3	4	9	4	5	11	5	6
75-79	4	2	2	4	2	2	5	2	3	6	3	4
80-84	2	1	1	2	1	1	2	1	1	3	1	2
85-89	0	0	0	1	0	0	1	0	0	1	0	1
90-94	0	0	0	0	0	0	0	0	0	0	0	0
95-99	0	0	0	0	0	0	0	0	0	0	0	0
100 +	0	0	0	0	0	0	0	0	0	0	0	0

Age group	2025 Both sexes	Males	Females	2030 Both sexes	Males	Females	2035 Both sexes	Males	Females	2040 Both sexes	Males	Females
All ages	1 164	584	580	1 281	643	638	1 402	704	698	1 528	767	761
0-4	148	75	73	155	78	76	162	82	80	169	86	83
5-9	140	71	69	147	74	72	154	78	76	161	81	79
10-14	130	66	64	140	71	69	146	74	72	153	78	76
15-19	120	61	60	130	65	64	139	70	69	146	74	72
20-24	108	55	54	119	60	59	129	65	64	139	70	69
25-29	100	50	49	107	54	53	118	59	59	128	64	63
30-34	88	45	44	98	49	48	105	53	52	116	59	58
35-39	74	38	37	86	43	42	95	48	47	103	52	51
40-44	61	31	30	72	37	35	84	42	41	93	47	46
45-49	49	25	24	59	30	29	70	35	34	82	41	40
50-54	41	21	20	47	24	23	56	28	28	67	34	33
55-59	34	17	17	39	19	19	45	22	22	53	27	27
60-64	26	12	14	31	15	16	36	17	18	41	20	21
65-69	19	9	10	23	11	12	27	13	14	31	15	16
70-74	12	6	7	15	7	8	18	8	10	22	10	12
75-79	8	3	4	9	4	5	11	5	6	13	6	7
80-84	4	1	2	4	2	3	5	2	3	6	3	4
85-89	1	0	1	1	1	1	2	1	1	2	1	1
90-94	0	0	0	0	0	0	0	0	0	0	0	0
95-99	0	0	0	0	0	0	0	0	0	0	0	0
100 +	0	0	0	0	0	0	0	0	0	0	0	0

Age group	2045 Both sexes	Males	Females	2050 Both sexes	Males	Females
All ages	1 658	832	826	1 790	897	893
0-4	176	89	87	183	93	90
5-9	168	85	83	176	89	87
10-14	161	81	79	168	85	83
15-19	153	77	76	161	81	80
20-24	146	73	72	153	77	76
25-29	138	69	68	145	73	72
30-34	126	64	63	136	69	68
35-39	115	58	57	125	63	62
40-44	101	51	50	113	57	56
45-49	91	46	45	99	50	49
50-54	79	40	39	89	44	44
55-59	64	32	32	75	38	38
60-64	50	24	25	60	29	30
65-69	36	18	19	44	21	23
70-74	26	12	14	30	14	16
75-79	16	7	9	19	8	10
80-84	8	3	5	9	4	5
85-89	3	1	2	3	1	2
90-94	1	0	0	1	0	0
95-99	0	0	0	0	0	0
100 +	0	0	0	0	0	0

United Nations Department of Economic and Social Affairs/Population Division
World Population Prospects: The 2004 Revision, Volume II: Sex and Age Distribution of the World Population

356

POPULATION BY AGE AND SEX (in thousands)

Age group	2005 Both sexes	Males	Females	2010 Both sexes	Males	Females	2015 Both sexes	Males	Females	2020 Both sexes	Males	Females
All ages	793	396	397	853	427	426	911	456	454	978	491	488
0-4	120	61	60	114	58	56	109	55	54	106	54	52
5-9	109	55	54	113	57	56	109	55	54	106	54	53
10-14	99	50	49	105	53	52	110	56	55	108	54	53
15-19	87	44	43	96	48	48	103	52	51	109	55	54
20-24	74	37	37	83	42	41	93	47	46	101	51	50
25-29	62	31	31	70	35	35	79	40	39	91	46	45
30-34	52	26	26	58	29	29	66	33	33	77	39	38
35-39	44	22	22	48	25	24	54	27	27	63	32	31
40-44	36	18	18	41	20	20	45	23	22	52	26	25
45-49	29	14	15	33	17	17	38	19	19	43	22	21
50-54	23	11	12	26	13	13	31	15	16	36	18	18
55-59	20	10	10	21	10	11	24	12	12	29	14	15
60-64	15	7	8	17	8	9	18	9	10	22	10	11
65-69	10	5	6	12	6	7	14	7	8	16	7	8
70-74	7	3	4	8	3	4	9	4	5	11	5	6
75-79	4	2	2	4	2	2	5	2	3	6	3	4
80-84	2	1	1	2	1	1	2	1	1	3	1	2
85-89	0	0	0	1	0	0	1	0	0	1	0	1
90-94	0	0	0	0	0	0	0	0	0	0	0	0
95-99	0	0	0	0	0	0	0	0	0	0	0	0
100 +	0	0	0	0	0	0	0	0	0	0	0	0

Age group	2025 Both sexes	Males	Females	2030 Both sexes	Males	Females	2035 Both sexes	Males	Females	2040 Both sexes	Males	Females
All ages	1 050	527	523	1 120	562	558	1 184	594	590	1 239	621	618
0-4	107	54	53	106	54	52	103	52	51	98	49	48
5-9	105	53	52	106	54	52	105	53	52	102	52	51
10-14	106	54	52	105	53	52	106	54	52	105	53	52
15-19	107	54	53	106	53	52	105	53	52	106	53	52
20-24	108	55	54	106	54	53	105	53	52	104	53	52
25-29	100	50	49	107	54	53	105	53	52	104	53	52
30-34	88	45	44	98	49	48	105	53	52	104	52	52
35-39	74	38	37	86	43	42	95	48	47	103	52	51
40-44	61	31	30	72	37	35	84	42	41	93	47	46
45-49	49	25	24	59	30	29	70	35	34	82	41	40
50-54	41	21	20	47	24	23	56	28	28	67	34	33
55-59	34	17	17	39	19	19	45	22	22	53	27	27
60-64	26	12	14	31	15	16	36	17	18	41	20	21
65-69	19	9	10	23	11	12	27	13	14	31	15	16
70-74	12	6	7	15	7	8	18	8	10	22	10	12
75-79	8	3	4	9	4	5	11	5	6	13	6	7
80-84	4	1	2	4	2	3	5	2	3	6	3	4
85-89	1	0	1	1	1	1	2	1	1	2	1	1
90-94	0	0	0	0	0	0	0	0	0	0	0	0
95-99	0	0	0	0	0	0	0	0	0	0	0	0
100 +	0	0	0	0	0	0	0	0	0	0	0	0

Age group	2045 Both sexes	Males	Females	2050 Both sexes	Males	Females
All ages	1 287	644	643	1 326	662	663
0-4	92	47	45	87	44	43
5-9	97	49	48	92	47	45
10-14	102	52	51	98	49	48
15-19	106	53	52	103	52	51
20-24	106	53	52	105	53	52
25-29	104	52	51	105	53	52
30-34	103	52	51	103	52	51
35-39	103	52	51	102	51	51
40-44	101	51	50	101	51	50
45-49	91	46	45	99	50	49
50-54	79	40	39	89	44	44
55-59	64	32	32	75	38	38
60-64	50	24	25	60	29	30
65-69	36	18	19	44	21	23
70-74	26	12	14	30	14	16
75-79	16	7	9	19	8	10
80-84	8	3	5	9	4	5
85-89	3	1	2	3	1	2
90-94	1	0	0	1	0	0
95-99	0	0	0	0	0	0
100 +	0	0	0	0	0	0

United Nations Department of Economic and Social Affairs/Population Division
World Population Prospects: The 2004 Revision, Volume II: Sex and Age Distribution of the World Population

357

POPULATION BY AGE AND SEX (in thousands)

Age group	1950			1955			1960			1965		
	Both sexes	Males	Females	Both sexes	Males	Females	Both sexes	Males	Females	Both sexes	Males	Females
All ages	2 353	1 199	1 154	2 737	1 391	1 346	3 231	1 638	1 593	3 804	1 928	1 877
0-4	438	222	216	518	263	255	626	318	308	741	376	365
5-9	330	166	164	403	204	199	485	246	239	593	301	293
10-14	280	141	139	324	163	161	397	200	197	477	241	235
15-19	238	119	119	275	138	137	319	161	159	389	196	193
20-24	215	110	105	233	116	116	270	136	134	309	155	153
25-29	155	79	76	209	106	102	227	113	114	260	131	129
30-34	138	71	67	150	76	74	203	103	100	218	109	109
35-39	121	65	56	133	69	64	145	74	71	195	99	96
40-44	99	53	46	116	62	54	128	66	62	138	70	68
45-49	86	45	41	94	50	44	111	59	52	121	63	59
50-54	72	37	36	81	42	39	89	47	42	103	55	48
55-59	59	31	28	66	33	33	75	39	36	81	43	38
60-64	46	23	23	52	26	25	59	29	30	66	34	32
65-69	34	17	17	38	19	19	43	22	21	49	24	25
70-74	23	11	11	25	12	13	29	14	15	33	16	17
75-79	12	6	6	14	7	7	16	8	9	19	9	10
80 +	7	3	4	8	4	4	10	4	5	11	5	6

Age group	1970			1975			1980			1985		
	Both sexes	Males	Females	Both sexes	Males	Females	Both sexes	Males	Females	Both sexes	Males	Females
All ages	4 424	2 242	2 182	5 058	2 563	2 496	5 718	2 897	2 821	6 443	3 264	3 179
0-4	807	410	397	825	419	406	859	437	422	964	490	474
5-9	710	360	350	782	396	386	806	409	397	839	427	412
10-14	585	296	289	702	356	346	774	392	382	796	404	393
15-19	467	237	230	575	291	284	691	350	341	762	386	376
20-24	376	190	186	453	230	223	559	284	276	672	340	332
25-29	297	149	147	363	183	179	439	223	216	542	274	268
30-34	249	125	124	285	144	142	350	177	173	423	214	209
35-39	208	104	104	239	120	119	274	138	136	336	170	167
40-44	186	95	91	199	99	100	229	115	114	262	132	130
45-49	130	66	64	177	90	86	190	95	95	217	109	108
50-54	113	59	55	122	62	60	167	85	82	178	89	89
55-59	95	51	44	104	54	50	113	58	55	153	78	75
60-64	72	38	34	85	45	40	94	48	46	100	51	49
65-69	56	28	27	62	32	30	73	38	35	80	41	39
70-74	38	18	20	44	22	22	50	25	25	58	30	28
75-79	22	11	12	26	12	14	31	15	16	35	18	17
80 +	14	6	8	16	7	9	19	8	11	24	11	13

Age group	1990			1995			2000			2005		
	Both sexes	Males	Females	Both sexes	Males	Females	Both sexes	Males	Females	Both sexes	Males	Females
All ages	7 090	3 595	3 495	7 672	3 892	3 780	8 265	4 185	4 080	8 895	4 490	4 405
0-4	993	505	488	980	499	481	973	495	478	1 003	511	492
5-9	942	479	463	971	494	477	962	489	472	957	487	470
10-14	825	420	406	926	471	455	958	487	471	951	484	467
15-19	780	396	385	807	410	397	910	463	447	945	481	465
20-24	738	373	365	753	381	372	783	397	386	891	452	438
25-29	638	323	315	696	352	344	714	360	354	750	379	371
30-34	513	259	253	601	304	297	659	331	328	679	340	339
35-39	395	201	194	478	242	236	566	285	281	624	311	313
40-44	312	158	154	366	186	179	449	227	222	537	268	269
45-49	243	123	120	290	147	143	344	174	169	426	214	213
50-54	199	100	99	223	113	110	270	136	133	324	163	161
55-59	161	81	81	181	91	90	206	103	102	252	126	126
60-64	135	69	67	143	71	72	163	82	82	188	93	94
65-69	84	43	41	115	58	57	124	61	63	144	71	73
70-74	62	32	30	66	34	32	94	47	47	103	50	53
75-79	40	21	19	44	23	21	49	24	24	71	35	36
80 +	28	13	15	33	16	17	42	21	21	51	24	26

United Nations Department of Economic and Social Affairs/Population Division
World Population Prospects: The 2004 Revision, Volume II: Sex and Age Distribution of the World Population

POPULATION BY AGE AND SEX (in thousands)

Age group	2005 Both sexes	Males	Females	2010 Both sexes	Males	Females	2015 Both sexes	Males	Females	2020 Both sexes	Males	Females
All ages	8 895	4 490	4 405	9 522	4 794	4 728	10 124	5 086	5 038	10 676	5 353	5 323
0-4	1 003	511	492	1 016	518	498	1 005	513	492	979	500	480
5-9	957	487	470	989	504	485	1 003	512	492	994	507	487
10-14	951	484	467	946	482	464	978	499	480	993	506	487
15-19	945	481	465	938	477	461	934	475	458	966	492	474
20-24	891	452	438	926	471	456	920	468	452	916	466	450
25-29	750	379	371	859	435	424	896	455	442	891	453	439
30-34	679	340	339	718	361	357	829	418	410	867	439	428
35-39	624	311	313	645	321	324	686	344	342	797	401	396
40-44	537	268	269	594	294	300	617	305	312	659	328	330
45-49	426	214	213	512	254	258	569	280	290	593	291	302
50-54	324	163	161	404	201	203	489	240	249	546	266	280
55-59	252	126	126	305	152	153	383	188	194	465	226	239
60-64	188	93	94	232	115	117	282	139	143	357	173	184
65-69	144	71	73	167	82	85	208	101	107	256	123	132
70-74	103	50	53	121	58	62	142	68	74	179	84	94
75-79	71	35	36	79	37	42	94	44	50	112	51	61
80-84	32	15	16	47	22	25	54	24	30	65	29	36
85-89	14	7	8	17	8	9	26	11	15	30	12	18
90-94	4	2	2	5	2	3	7	3	4	10	4	6
95-99	1	0	0	1	0	1	1	1	1	2	1	1
100 +	0	0	0	0	0	0	0	0	0	0	0	0

Age group	2025 Both sexes	Males	Females	2030 Both sexes	Males	Females	2035 Both sexes	Males	Females	2040 Both sexes	Males	Females
All ages	11 174	5 592	5 582	11 626	5 808	5 818	12 008	5 990	6 018	12 311	6 132	6 179
0-4	954	487	467	930	475	455	902	461	441	866	443	423
5-9	969	495	474	943	481	462	920	470	450	892	456	436
10-14	984	502	482	959	490	470	933	476	457	910	465	445
15-19	981	500	481	972	496	476	947	484	464	922	470	451
20-24	949	483	466	964	491	473	955	487	468	931	475	456
25-29	888	452	436	921	469	452	936	477	459	928	473	455
30-34	863	437	426	860	437	424	893	454	439	910	463	447
35-39	836	422	414	833	421	412	831	421	410	865	439	426
40-44	769	385	383	808	406	402	805	406	399	805	407	398
45-49	635	315	320	743	371	373	783	382	301	782	303	380
50-54	569	278	292	611	301	310	718	356	362	758	377	381
55-59	521	251	270	545	263	282	586	286	300	691	339	351
60-64	400	209	227	491	233	257	515	245	270	556	268	288
65-69	326	154	171	401	188	212	453	211	242	477	223	254
70-74	221	103	118	286	132	154	355	162	193	404	183	220
75-79	143	64	78	182	82	100	239	106	133	299	131	168
80-84	78	34	45	106	45	61	137	58	79	183	77	106
85-89	37	15	22	49	20	30	68	27	41	90	35	55
90-94	12	5	8	18	6	12	25	9	16	35	12	23
95-99	3	1	2	4	1	3	6	2	4	9	3	6
100 +	0	0	0	1	0	0	1	0	1	1	0	1

Age group	2045 Both sexes	Males	Females	2050 Both sexes	Males	Females
All ages	12 526	6 230	6 296	12 668	6 293	6 375
0-4	823	421	402	794	406	388
5-9	857	438	419	815	416	398
10-14	883	451	432	848	433	415
15-19	899	459	440	872	445	426
20-24	905	462	443	883	451	432
25-29	905	462	443	880	450	431
30-34	903	460	443	882	450	432
35-39	883	449	434	878	447	431
40-44	840	426	415	859	436	423
45-49	783	394	388	819	414	405
50-54	758	378	379	760	381	379
55-59	730	360	370	732	363	369
60-64	657	319	338	696	339	357
65-69	516	245	272	613	292	321
70-74	427	195	233	465	214	251
75-79	343	149	194	366	160	206
80-84	231	96	135	268	110	158
85-89	121	47	75	156	59	97
90-94	47	16	31	64	22	42
95-99	13	4	9	17	5	12
100 +	2	0	1	3	1	2

POPULATION BY AGE AND SEX (in thousands)

Age group	2005 Both sexes	Males	Females	2010 Both sexes	Males	Females	2015 Both sexes	Males	Females	2020 Both sexes	Males	Females
All ages	8 895	4 490	4 405	9 615	4 841	4 774	10 374	5 213	5 161	11 133	5 586	5 547
0-4	1 003	511	492	1 109	565	544	1 163	593	570	1 187	606	581
5-9	957	487	470	989	504	485	1 096	559	537	1 151	587	564
10-14	951	484	467	946	482	464	978	499	480	1 085	553	532
15-19	945	481	465	938	477	461	934	475	458	966	492	474
20-24	891	452	438	926	471	456	920	468	452	916	466	450
25-29	750	379	371	859	435	424	896	455	442	891	453	439
30-34	679	340	339	718	361	357	829	418	410	867	439	428
35-39	624	311	313	645	321	324	686	344	342	797	401	396
40-44	537	268	269	594	294	300	617	305	312	659	328	330
45-49	426	214	213	512	254	258	569	280	290	593	291	302
50-54	324	163	161	404	201	203	489	240	249	546	266	280
55-59	252	126	126	305	152	153	383	188	194	465	226	239
60-64	188	93	94	232	115	117	282	139	143	357	173	184
65-69	144	71	73	167	82	85	208	101	107	256	123	132
70-74	103	50	53	121	58	62	142	68	74	179	84	94
75-79	71	35	36	79	37	42	94	44	50	112	51	61
80-84	32	15	16	47	22	25	54	24	30	65	29	36
85-89	14	7	8	17	8	9	26	11	15	30	12	18
90-94	4	2	2	5	2	3	7	3	4	10	4	6
95-99	1	0	0	1	0	1	1	1	1	2	1	1
100 +	0	0	0	0	0	0	0	0	0	0	0	0

Age group	2025 Both sexes	Males	Females	2030 Both sexes	Males	Females	2035 Both sexes	Males	Females	2040 Both sexes	Males	Females
All ages	11 852	5 938	5 914	12 565	6 287	6 278	13 270	6 634	6 636	13 953	6 969	6 983
0-4	1 177	601	576	1 195	610	584	1 228	628	601	1 252	640	612
5-9	1 175	600	575	1 165	595	570	1 182	604	578	1 217	622	595
10-14	1 140	582	559	1 165	594	570	1 154	589	565	1 172	599	573
15-19	1 073	547	526	1 128	575	553	1 153	588	564	1 142	583	559
20-24	949	483	466	1 055	537	518	1 111	566	544	1 135	579	556
25-29	888	452	436	921	469	452	1 027	523	504	1 083	552	531
30-34	863	437	426	860	437	424	893	454	439	1 000	508	491
35-39	836	422	414	833	421	412	831	421	410	865	439	426
40-44	769	385	383	808	406	402	805	406	399	805	407	398
45-49	635	315	320	743	371	373	783	392	391	782	393	389
50-54	569	278	292	611	301	310	718	356	362	758	377	381
55-59	521	251	270	545	263	282	586	286	300	691	339	351
60-64	436	209	227	491	233	257	515	245	270	556	268	288
65-69	326	154	171	401	188	212	453	211	242	477	223	254
70-74	221	103	118	286	132	154	355	162	193	404	183	220
75-79	143	64	78	182	82	100	239	106	133	299	131	168
80-84	78	34	45	106	45	61	137	58	79	183	77	106
85-89	37	15	22	49	20	30	68	27	41	90	35	55
90-94	12	5	8	18	6	12	25	9	16	35	12	23
95-99	3	1	2	4	1	3	6	2	4	9	3	6
100 +	0	0	0	1	0	0	1	0	1	1	0	1

Age group	2045 Both sexes	Males	Females	2050 Both sexes	Males	Females
All ages	14 592	7 284	7 308	15 196	7 582	7 614
0-4	1 254	641	613	1 264	646	618
5-9	1 241	634	607	1 243	635	608
10-14	1 207	617	590	1 231	629	602
15-19	1 160	593	568	1 195	611	585
20-24	1 125	574	551	1 144	584	560
25-29	1 108	565	543	1 099	561	538
30-34	1 057	538	519	1 084	552	531
35-39	972	494	478	1 030	524	506
40-44	840	426	415	947	481	467
45-49	783	394	388	819	414	405
50-54	758	378	379	760	381	379
55-59	730	360	370	732	363	369
60-64	657	319	338	696	339	357
65-69	516	245	272	613	292	321
70-74	427	195	233	465	214	251
75-79	343	149	194	366	160	206
80-84	231	96	135	268	110	158
85-89	121	47	75	156	59	97
90-94	47	16	31	64	22	42
95-99	13	4	9	17	5	12
100 +	2	0	1	3	1	2

360

United Nations Department of Economic and Social Affairs/Population Division
World Population Prospects: The 2004 Revision, Volume II: Sex and Age Distribution of the World Population

POPULATION BY AGE AND SEX (in thousands)

Age group	2005 Both sexes	Males	Females	2010 Both sexes	Males	Females	2015 Both sexes	Males	Females	2020 Both sexes	Males	Females
All ages	8 895	4 490	4 405	9 428	4 746	4 682	9 868	4 956	4 913	10 212	5 116	5 096
0-4	1 003	511	492	922	470	452	844	430	413	769	392	376
5-9	957	487	470	989	504	485	910	464	446	833	425	408
10-14	951	484	467	946	482	464	978	499	480	900	459	441
15-19	945	481	465	938	477	461	934	475	458	966	492	474
20-24	891	452	438	926	471	456	920	468	452	916	466	450
25-29	750	379	371	859	435	424	896	455	442	891	453	439
30-34	679	340	339	718	361	357	829	418	410	867	439	428
35-39	624	311	313	645	321	324	686	344	342	797	401	396
40-44	537	268	269	594	294	300	617	305	312	659	328	330
45-49	426	214	213	512	254	258	569	280	290	593	291	302
50-54	324	163	161	404	201	203	489	240	249	546	266	280
55-59	252	126	126	305	152	153	383	188	194	465	226	239
60-64	188	93	94	232	115	117	282	139	143	357	173	184
65-69	144	71	73	167	82	85	208	101	107	256	123	132
70-74	103	50	53	121	58	62	142	68	74	179	84	94
75-79	71	35	36	79	37	42	94	44	50	112	51	61
80-84	32	15	16	47	22	25	54	24	30	65	29	36
85-89	14	7	8	17	8	9	26	11	15	30	12	18
90-94	4	2	2	5	2	3	7	3	4	10	4	6
95-99	1	0	0	1	0	1	1	1	1	2	1	1
100 +	0	0	0	0	0	0	0	0	0	0	0	0

Age group	2025 Both sexes	Males	Females	2030 Both sexes	Males	Females	2035 Both sexes	Males	Females	2040 Both sexes	Males	Females
All ages	10 488	5 242	5 246	10 689	5 330	5 359	10 781	5 364	5 417	10 760	5 341	5 419
0-4	731	373	358	677	346	331	607	310	297	537	274	262
5-9	760	388	372	721	368	353	668	341	327	599	306	293
10-14	824	420	403	750	383	367	712	363	348	659	337	322
15-19	888	453	435	812	414	398	739	377	362	701	358	343
20-24	949	483	466	871	444	427	796	406	390	723	369	354
25-29	888	452	436	921	469	452	844	430	414	770	393	377
30-34	863	437	426	860	437	424	893	454	439	819	417	402
35-39	830	422	414	833	421	412	831	421	410	865	439	426
40-44	769	385	383	808	406	402	805	406	399	805	407	398
45-49	635	315	320	743	371	373	783	392	391	782	393	389
50-54	569	278	292	611	301	310	718	356	362	758	377	381
55-59	521	251	270	545	263	282	606	296	300	691	339	351
60-64	436	209	227	491	233	257	515	245	270	556	268	288
65-69	326	154	171	401	188	212	453	211	242	477	223	254
70-74	221	103	118	286	132	154	355	162	193	404	183	220
75-79	140	61	78	182	82	100	239	106	133	299	131	168
80-84	78	34	45	106	45	61	137	58	79	100	77	106
85-89	37	15	22	49	20	30	68	27	41	90	35	55
90-94	12	5	8	18	6	12	25	9	16	35	12	23
95-99	3	1	2	4	1	3	6	2	4	9	3	6
100 +	0	0	0	1	0	0	1	0	1	1	0	1

Age group	2045 Both sexes	Males	Females	2050 Both sexes	Males	Females
All ages	10 633	5 265	5 368	10 420	5 148	5 272
0-4	474	242	232	431	220	211
5-9	529	271	259	467	239	228
10-14	591	302	289	521	266	255
15-19	648	331	317	580	297	284
20-24	685	350	335	633	324	309
25-29	698	357	341	661	338	323
30-34	746	381	366	676	346	331
35-39	793	403	389	723	369	354
40-44	840	426	415	770	391	379
45-49	783	394	388	819	414	405
50-54	758	378	379	760	381	379
55-59	730	360	370	732	363	369
60-64	657	319	338	696	339	357
65-69	516	245	272	613	292	321
70-74	427	195	233	465	214	251
75-79	343	149	194	366	160	206
80-84	231	96	135	268	110	158
85-89	121	47	75	156	59	97
90-94	47	16	31	64	22	42
95-99	13	4	9	17	5	12
100 +	2	0	1	3	1	2

POPULATION BY AGE AND SEX (in thousands)

Age group	1950 Both sexes	Males	Females	1955 Both sexes	Males	Females	1960 Both sexes	Males	Females	1965 Both sexes	Males	Females
All ages	3 387	1 684	1 704	3 862	1 926	1 937	4 439	2 219	2 220	5 144	2 578	2 566
0-4	535	271	264	688	348	340	786	398	388	907	460	447
5-9	430	217	212	501	254	248	650	329	322	748	379	370
10-14	374	189	185	419	212	207	492	249	243	642	324	317
15-19	323	163	161	367	185	181	413	209	204	486	246	240
20-24	278	140	139	316	159	157	360	182	178	407	206	202
25-29	237	119	118	271	136	135	309	156	154	353	178	175
30-34	205	102	103	229	115	114	264	132	131	302	152	150
35-39	191	95	96	198	99	99	222	111	111	257	129	128
40-44	161	79	82	182	91	92	190	95	95	215	108	107
45-49	142	69	73	152	75	77	174	86	88	183	91	92
50-54	125	61	64	132	64	68	144	70	73	166	82	84
55-59	111	54	58	114	55	59	123	59	64	135	66	69
60-64	96	45	51	98	47	51	102	49	53	112	54	58
65-69	77	35	42	80	37	43	84	39	44	89	42	47
70-74	54	24	30	58	26	32	62	28	34	68	31	36
75-79	31	13	18	34	15	20	39	17	22	44	19	25
80 +	19	8	11	20	8	12	24	10	14	29	12	18

Age group	1970 Both sexes	Males	Females	1975 Both sexes	Males	Females	1980 Both sexes	Males	Females	1985 Both sexes	Males	Females
All ages	5 970	2 997	2 973	6 907	3 471	3 436	7 961	4 004	3 958	9 099	4 576	4 523
0-4	1 039	527	512	1 162	590	572	1 284	652	632	1 367	695	672
5-9	870	440	429	1 003	508	495	1 129	573	557	1 257	638	619
10-14	739	374	365	861	436	425	995	504	491	1 122	568	553
15-19	635	321	314	733	371	363	854	432	422	988	500	488
20-24	480	243	238	628	317	311	726	367	359	847	428	419
25-29	401	202	199	473	239	235	620	312	308	718	362	356
30-34	346	174	172	394	198	195	466	235	231	612	308	305
35-39	295	148	147	339	170	169	386	194	192	459	230	229
40-44	249	125	125	287	144	143	331	166	165	378	189	189
45-49	207	104	104	241	120	121	279	139	140	322	161	162
50-54	175	87	88	198	99	100	232	115	117	269	133	136
55-59	156	77	79	165	81	84	188	93	95	220	109	112
60-64	123	60	64	143	70	73	152	74	78	175	85	89
65-69	97	46	51	108	51	56	126	61	66	136	65	71
70-74	72	34	39	79	37	43	89	42	47	106	50	56
75-79	48	22	27	52	24	28	58	26	32	67	31	37
80 +	35	15	21	40	17	23	46	20	26	55	23	31

Age group	1990 Both sexes	Males	Females	1995 Both sexes	Males	Females	2000 Both sexes	Males	Females	2005 Both sexes	Males	Females
All ages	10 272	5 165	5 107	11 396	5 727	5 669	12 306	6 178	6 127	13 228	6 633	6 595
0-4	1 404	715	690	1 418	722	696	1 458	744	714	1 445	737	708
5-9	1 346	684	663	1 389	706	683	1 403	714	689	1 447	737	709
10-14	1 251	634	616	1 340	680	660	1 378	700	678	1 393	709	684
15-19	1 116	565	551	1 238	627	611	1 297	658	640	1 341	681	661
20-24	981	496	485	1 095	554	542	1 156	584	572	1 227	620	607
25-29	839	423	416	961	485	477	1 023	515	508	1 094	550	544
30-34	710	357	353	822	413	409	907	454	452	975	488	487
35-39	603	302	301	694	348	347	778	389	389	867	433	435
40-44	450	225	225	590	294	296	664	331	333	750	373	377
45-49	369	184	186	438	218	220	567	281	286	642	318	324
50-54	312	155	158	358	177	181	421	208	213	548	270	278
55-59	257	126	131	299	147	152	342	168	174	405	199	206
60-64	207	101	106	242	118	124	282	138	145	325	158	167
65-69	158	76	82	189	91	98	225	108	117	264	127	137
70-74	117	55	62	138	66	73	169	80	89	204	96	108
75-79	83	38	45	95	44	51	117	54	63	147	68	79
80 +	68	29	39	88	38	50	118	51	67	155	68	87

United Nations Department of Economic and Social Affairs/Population Division
World Population Prospects: The 2004 Revision, Volume II: Sex and Age Distribution of the World Population

362

POPULATION BY AGE AND SEX (in thousands)

Age group	2005 Both sexes	Males	Females	2010 Both sexes	Males	Females	2015 Both sexes	Males	Females	2020 Both sexes	Males	Females
All ages	13 228	6 633	6 595	14 192	7 109	7 083	15 144	7 576	7 568	16 026	8 006	8 020
0-4	1 445	737	708	1 423	727	696	1 406	718	688	1 383	707	676
5-9	1 447	737	709	1 435	732	703	1 415	722	693	1 399	714	684
10-14	1 393	709	684	1 439	734	706	1 430	729	701	1 409	719	690
15-19	1 341	681	661	1 370	697	673	1 422	725	698	1 413	720	693
20-24	1 227	620	607	1 295	656	639	1 337	679	658	1 389	706	683
25-29	1 094	550	544	1 185	596	589	1 264	638	626	1 306	661	645
30-34	975	488	487	1 059	529	530	1 158	579	579	1 237	621	616
35-39	867	433	435	950	473	477	1 038	516	522	1 136	566	570
40-44	750	373	377	846	420	426	930	461	469	1 018	504	514
45-49	642	318	324	731	362	369	827	408	419	911	449	462
50-54	548	270	278	623	307	316	712	350	361	807	396	411
55-59	405	199	206	528	259	269	603	295	308	689	337	352
60-64	325	158	167	386	188	198	505	245	259	577	280	297
65-69	264	127	137	304	146	158	362	174	188	475	227	247
70-74	204	96	108	240	113	127	278	131	147	331	156	175
75-79	147	68	79	177	82	95	209	97	113	243	112	131
80-84	92	41	50	115	52	63	140	63	77	167	74	92
85-89	46	20	26	59	26	34	76	33	43	94	40	54
90-94	15	6	9	21	8	12	28	11	17	36	14	22
95-99	2	1	2	4	1	2	5	2	4	7	2	5
100 +	0	0	0	0	0	0	0	0	0	0	0	0

Age group	2025 Both sexes	Males	Females	2030 Both sexes	Males	Females	2035 Both sexes	Males	Females	2040 Both sexes	Males	Females
All ages	16 819	8 390	8 429	17 520	8 726	8 794	18 116	9 008	9 108	18 597	9 231	9 366
0-4	1 347	689	658	1 308	670	639	1 264	647	617	1 219	624	595
5-9	1 376	703	673	1 341	686	655	1 303	666	636	1 259	644	615
10-14	1 393	712	682	1 371	701	671	1 336	683	653	1 298	664	634
15-19	1 393	711	682	1 378	703	674	1 356	693	663	1 321	676	646
20-24	1 380	702	678	1 361	694	668	1 347	687	660	1 326	677	649
25-29	1 358	688	670	1 350	685	665	1 333	677	655	1 319	671	648
30-34	1 279	644	635	1 332	672	660	1 325	669	656	1 308	662	646
35-39	1 215	607	607	1 257	631	627	1 311	659	652	1 305	657	648
40-44	1 116	553	563	1 194	594	600	1 207	618	619	1 291	647	644
45-49	998	492	506	1 095	540	555	1 174	582	592	1 217	606	612
50-54	890	436	453	976	478	498	1 072	526	546	1 150	567	583
55-59	782	381	401	864	421	443	949	462	487	1 044	500	545
60-64	661	320	341	751	362	388	830	401	430	913	440	473
65-69	543	260	284	624	297	326	710	338	372	787	374	413
70-74	435	204	231	499	233	265	574	268	306	655	304	351
75-79	290	133	157	382	174	208	440	200	240	507	229	278
80-84	194	86	108	233	103	130	309	135	174	357	155	202
85-89	113	47	65	132	55	77	161	66	94	215	88	127
90-94	46	18	28	56	21	35	68	25	42	83	31	52
95-99	10	3	7	13	4	9	17	6	12	21	7	14
100 +	1	0	1	1	0	1	1	0	1	2	1	1

Age group	2045 Both sexes	Males	Females	2050 Both sexes	Males	Females
All ages	18 957	9 394	9 563	10 214	9 506	9 708
0-4	1 172	600	572	1 147	587	560
5-9	1 214	621	593	1 168	598	570
10-14	1 255	642	613	1 210	619	591
15-19	1 284	657	627	1 241	635	606
20-24	1 292	660	632	1 255	642	613
25-29	1 299	661	637	1 265	645	620
30-34	1 295	657	638	1 276	648	628
35-39	1 289	651	638	1 276	645	631
40-44	1 286	645	641	1 271	640	631
45-49	1 271	634	637	1 267	633	633
50-54	1 194	591	603	1 248	620	628
55-59	1 121	549	572	1 164	573	592
60-64	1 006	486	520	1 082	525	557
65-69	867	411	456	956	454	502
70-74	727	337	390	802	372	431
75-79	580	261	319	646	289	356
80-84	414	179	235	475	203	271
85-89	250	101	149	292	117	175
90-94	113	42	72	134	49	85
95-99	27	9	19	38	12	26
100 +	3	1	2	4	1	3

POPULATION BY AGE AND SEX (in thousands)

Age group	2005 Both sexes	Males	Females	2010 Both sexes	Males	Females	2015 Both sexes	Males	Females	2020 Both sexes	Males	Females
All ages	13 228	6 633	6 595	14 322	7 175	7 147	15 500	7 757	7 742	16 680	8 340	8 340
0-4	1 445	737	708	1 553	793	760	1 632	834	798	1 683	861	823
5-9	1 447	737	709	1 435	732	703	1 544	788	756	1 624	829	794
10-14	1 393	709	684	1 439	734	706	1 430	729	701	1 539	785	753
15-19	1 341	681	661	1 370	697	673	1 422	725	698	1 413	720	693
20-24	1 227	620	607	1 295	656	639	1 337	679	658	1 389	706	683
25-29	1 094	550	544	1 185	596	589	1 264	638	626	1 306	661	645
30-34	975	488	487	1 059	529	530	1 158	579	579	1 237	621	616
35-39	867	433	435	950	473	477	1 038	516	522	1 136	566	570
40-44	750	373	377	846	420	426	930	461	469	1 018	504	514
45-49	642	318	324	731	362	369	827	408	419	911	449	462
50-54	548	270	278	623	307	316	712	350	361	807	396	411
55-59	405	199	206	528	259	269	603	295	308	689	337	352
60-64	325	158	167	386	188	198	505	245	259	577	280	297
65-69	264	127	137	304	146	158	362	174	188	475	227	247
70-74	204	96	108	240	113	127	278	131	147	331	156	175
75-79	147	68	79	177	82	95	209	97	113	243	112	131
80-84	92	41	50	115	52	63	140	63	77	167	74	92
85-89	46	20	26	59	26	34	76	33	43	94	40	54
90-94	15	6	9	21	8	12	28	11	17	36	14	22
95-99	2	1	2	4	1	2	5	2	4	7	2	5
100 +	0	0	0	0	0	0	0	0	0	0	0	0

Age group	2025 Both sexes	Males	Females	2030 Both sexes	Males	Females	2035 Both sexes	Males	Females	2040 Both sexes	Males	Females
All ages	17 798	8 890	8 908	18 874	9 417	9 456	19 916	9 927	9 989	20 917	10 415	10 501
0-4	1 674	856	818	1 686	863	823	1 715	878	837	1 745	893	852
5-9	1 675	856	819	1 666	852	814	1 680	859	820	1 708	874	834
10-14	1 618	826	792	1 670	853	817	1 661	849	812	1 674	856	818
15-19	1 522	777	745	1 601	817	784	1 654	845	809	1 645	841	804
20-24	1 380	702	678	1 489	759	731	1 569	800	769	1 622	828	794
25-29	1 358	688	670	1 350	685	665	1 460	741	718	1 540	783	757
30-34	1 279	644	635	1 332	672	660	1 325	669	656	1 434	726	708
35-39	1 215	607	607	1 257	631	627	1 311	659	652	1 305	657	648
40-44	1 116	553	563	1 194	594	600	1 237	618	619	1 291	647	644
45-49	998	492	506	1 095	540	555	1 174	582	592	1 217	606	612
50-54	890	436	453	976	478	498	1 072	526	546	1 150	567	583
55-59	782	381	401	864	421	443	949	462	487	1 044	509	535
60-64	661	320	341	751	362	388	830	401	430	913	440	473
65-69	543	260	284	624	297	326	710	338	372	787	374	413
70-74	435	204	231	499	233	265	574	268	306	655	304	351
75-79	290	133	157	382	174	208	440	200	240	507	229	278
80-84	194	86	108	233	103	130	309	135	174	357	155	202
85-89	113	47	65	132	55	77	161	66	94	215	88	127
90-94	46	18	28	56	21	35	68	25	42	83	31	52
95-99	10	3	7	13	4	9	17	6	12	21	7	14
100 +	1	0	1	1	0	1	1	0	1	2	1	1

Age group	2045 Both sexes	Males	Females	2050 Both sexes	Males	Females
All ages	21 861	10 875	10 986	22 764	11 316	11 448
0-4	1 766	903	862	1 804	923	881
5-9	1 739	889	849	1 760	900	859
10-14	1 703	871	832	1 734	887	847
15-19	1 659	849	810	1 688	864	825
20-24	1 614	824	790	1 629	832	796
25-29	1 593	811	782	1 586	808	778
30-34	1 515	768	747	1 568	796	772
35-39	1 414	714	700	1 494	756	739
40-44	1 286	645	641	1 395	702	693
45-49	1 271	634	637	1 267	633	633
50-54	1 194	591	603	1 248	620	628
55-59	1 121	549	572	1 164	573	592
60-64	1 006	486	520	1 082	525	557
65-69	867	411	456	956	454	502
70-74	727	337	390	802	372	431
75-79	580	261	319	646	289	356
80-84	414	179	235	475	203	271
85-89	250	101	149	292	117	175
90-94	113	42	72	134	49	85
95-99	27	9	19	38	12	26
100 +	3	1	2	4	1	3

United Nations Department of Economic and Social Affairs/Population Division
World Population Prospects: The 2004 Revision, Volume II: Sex and Age Distribution of the World Population

364

POPULATION BY AGE AND SEX (in thousands)

Age group	2005 Both sexes	Males	Females	2010 Both sexes	Males	Females	2015 Both sexes	Males	Females	2020 Both sexes	Males	Females
All ages	13 228	6 633	6 595	14 060	7 041	7 019	14 785	7 392	7 392	15 363	7 667	7 695
0-4	1 445	737	708	1 291	659	632	1 177	602	576	1 079	552	527
5-9	1 447	737	709	1 435	732	703	1 284	655	628	1 171	598	573
10-14	1 393	709	684	1 439	734	706	1 430	729	701	1 278	653	626
15-19	1 341	681	661	1 370	697	673	1 422	725	698	1 413	720	693
20-24	1 227	620	607	1 295	656	639	1 337	679	658	1 389	706	683
25-29	1 094	550	544	1 185	596	589	1 264	638	626	1 306	661	645
30-34	975	488	487	1 059	529	530	1 158	579	579	1 237	621	616
35-39	867	433	435	950	473	477	1 038	516	522	1 136	566	570
40-44	750	373	377	846	420	426	930	461	469	1 018	504	514
45-49	642	318	324	731	362	369	827	408	419	911	449	462
50-54	548	270	278	623	307	316	712	350	361	807	396	411
55-59	405	199	206	528	259	269	603	295	308	689	337	352
60-64	325	158	167	386	188	198	505	245	259	577	280	297
65-69	264	127	137	304	146	158	362	174	188	475	227	247
70-74	204	96	108	240	113	127	278	131	147	331	156	175
75-79	147	68	79	177	82	95	209	97	113	243	112	131
80-84	92	41	50	115	52	63	140	63	77	167	74	92
85-89	46	20	26	59	26	34	76	33	43	94	40	54
90-94	15	6	9	21	8	12	28	11	17	36	14	22
95-99	2	1	2	4	1	2	5	2	4	7	2	5
100 +	0	0	0	0	0	0	0	0	0	0	0	0

Age group	2025 Both sexes	Males	Females	2030 Both sexes	Males	Females	2035 Both sexes	Males	Females	2040 Both sexes	Males	Females
All ages	15 830	7 885	7 945	16 170	8 037	8 133	16 360	8 112	8 248	16 395	8 108	8 287
0-4	1 019	521	498	944	483	461	854	437	417	766	392	374
5-9	1 073	549	525	1 013	518	495	939	481	459	850	435	415
10-14	1 166	596	571	1 069	546	523	1 009	516	493	936	479	457
15-19	1 263	644	618	1 151	588	563	1 055	539	516	996	509	486
20-24	1 380	702	678	1 232	628	604	1 121	572	549	1 026	524	502
25-29	1 358	688	670	1 350	685	665	1 204	612	592	1 095	557	538
30-34	1 279	644	635	1 332	672	660	1 325	669	656	1 180	598	582
35-39	1 215	607	607	1 257	631	627	1 311	659	652	1 305	657	648
40-44	1 116	553	563	1 194	594	600	1 237	618	619	1 291	647	644
45-49	998	492	506	1 095	540	555	1 174	582	592	1 217	606	612
50-54	890	436	453	976	478	498	1 072	526	546	1 150	567	583
55-59	782	381	401	864	421	443	949	462	487	1 044	509	535
60-64	661	320	341	751	362	388	830	401	430	913	440	473
65-69	543	260	284	624	297	326	710	338	372	787	374	413
70-74	435	204	231	499	233	265	574	268	306	655	304	351
75-79	290	133	157	382	174	208	440	200	240	507	229	278
80-84	194	86	108	233	103	130	309	135	174	357	155	202
85-89	113	47	65	132	55	77	161	66	94	215	88	127
90-94	46	18	28	56	21	35	68	25	42	83	31	52
95-99	10	3	7	13	4	9	17	6	12	21	7	14
100 +	1	0	1	1	0	1	1	0	1	2	1	1

Age group	2045 Both sexes	Males	Females	2050 Both sexes	Males	Females
All ages	16 277	8 027	8 250	16 031	7 884	8 147
0-4	687	352	335	633	324	309
5-9	762	390	372	683	350	333
10-14	846	433	413	759	388	370
15-19	922	472	450	833	427	406
20-24	967	495	473	895	458	437
25-29	1 000	510	490	943	481	462
30-34	1 072	544	528	979	498	482
35-39	1 162	587	575	1 055	534	521
40-44	1 286	645	641	1 145	576	569
45-49	1 271	634	637	1 267	633	633
50-54	1 194	591	603	1 248	620	628
55-59	1 121	549	572	1 164	573	592
60-64	1 006	486	520	1 082	525	557
65-69	867	411	456	956	454	502
70-74	727	337	390	802	372	431
75-79	580	261	319	646	289	356
80-84	414	179	235	475	203	271
85-89	250	101	149	292	117	175
90-94	113	42	72	134	49	85
95-99	27	9	19	38	12	26
100 +	3	1	2	4	1	3

POPULATION BY AGE AND SEX (in thousands)

Age group	1950 Both sexes	1950 Males	1950 Females	1955 Both sexes	1955 Males	1955 Females	1960 Both sexes	1960 Males	1960 Females	1965 Both sexes	1965 Males	1965 Females
All ages	21 834	10 857	10 977	24 692	12 346	12 346	27 840	14 004	13 837	31 563	15 908	15 655
0-4	3 531	1 786	1 745	4 238	2 155	2 083	4 761	2 433	2 327	5 266	2 704	2 561
5-9	2 696	1 358	1 337	3 221	1 633	1 587	3 843	1 960	1 884	4 534	2 324	2 210
10-14	2 437	1 226	1 211	2 636	1 334	1 302	3 216	1 639	1 577	3 944	2 006	1 938
15-19	2 234	1 123	1 111	2 398	1 211	1 186	2 539	1 291	1 248	3 045	1 548	1 496
20-24	1 979	992	987	2 171	1 094	1 077	2 290	1 161	1 129	2 299	1 167	1 131
25-29	1 700	847	853	1 909	957	951	2 061	1 041	1 020	2 092	1 062	1 030
30-34	1 470	731	739	1 637	817	820	1 831	922	909	1 908	966	942
35-39	1 266	629	637	1 411	703	708	1 562	782	780	1 688	853	836
40-44	1 084	536	548	1 208	600	609	1 338	668	671	1 466	732	733
45-49	921	452	470	1 026	505	521	1 139	564	575	1 226	606	619
50-54	770	372	398	858	417	442	954	467	488	1 066	523	543
55-59	623	296	327	697	333	364	781	376	405	934	452	482
60-64	475	221	255	535	250	285	611	288	323	787	374	413
65-69	328	149	179	374	171	203	440	203	237	590	273	317
70-74	194	86	108	225	101	124	277	125	152	387	174	213
75-79	89	38	51	106	46	60	139	61	79	203	90	113
80 +	36	15	21	42	18	25	58	24	34	127	52	76

Age group	1970 Both sexes	1970 Males	1970 Females	1975 Both sexes	1975 Males	1975 Females	1980 Both sexes	1980 Males	1980 Females	1985 Both sexes	1985 Males	1985 Females
All ages	35 285	17 854	17 431	39 295	19 817	19 478	43 860	22 025	21 836	49 612	24 932	24 681
0-4	5 351	2 760	2 591	6 274	3 183	3 091	7 088	3 605	3 483	7 909	4 028	3 881
5-9	4 762	2 467	2 296	5 106	2 634	2 472	6 018	3 055	2 963	6 857	3 490	3 367
10-14	4 488	2 302	2 186	4 695	2 432	2 263	5 038	2 599	2 439	5 955	3 023	2 931
15-19	3 907	1 988	1 919	4 344	2 224	2 120	4 533	2 331	2 203	4 956	2 548	2 409
20-24	3 000	1 525	1 475	3 623	1 813	1 810	3 986	1 988	1 998	4 336	2 215	2 120
25-29	2 258	1 146	1 112	2 727	1 346	1 381	3 257	1 575	1 681	3 724	1 866	1 858
30-34	2 051	1 041	1 011	2 115	1 066	1 049	2 543	1 246	1 298	3 206	1 584	1 622
35-39	1 866	944	922	2 006	1 026	981	2 080	1 060	1 020	2 592	1 287	1 305
40-44	1 644	828	816	1 848	935	913	2 008	1 029	979	2 038	1 031	1 007
45-49	1 417	704	713	1 622	817	805	1 838	930	908	1 921	959	962
50-54	1 171	575	597	1 355	669	686	1 556	777	779	1 708	832	876
55-59	999	484	515	1 067	514	553	1 236	599	637	1 426	696	730
60-64	847	403	443	877	416	461	939	443	496	1 102	524	578
65-69	674	314	361	697	325	372	726	337	389	789	364	425
70-74	458	207	251	499	227	272	521	236	284	552	250	302
75-79	245	107	138	286	126	160	315	139	176	337	149	188
80 +	146	60	86	155	65	90	178	75	103	203	86	117

Age group	1990 Both sexes	1990 Males	1990 Females	1995 Both sexes	1995 Males	1995 Females	2000 Both sexes	2000 Males	2000 Females	2005 Both sexes	2005 Males	2005 Females
All ages	55 673	28 021	27 653	61 225	30 800	30 425	67 285	33 804	33 482	74 033	37 120	36 913
0-4	8 306	4 245	4 061	7 852	4 010	3 842	8 203	4 186	4 016	8 933	4 558	4 374
5-9	7 742	3 946	3 796	8 184	4 183	4 001	7 782	3 972	3 809	8 149	4 157	3 992
10-14	6 807	3 464	3 343	7 699	3 923	3 776	8 152	4 165	3 987	7 757	3 958	3 799
15-19	5 690	2 888	2 803	6 624	3 400	3 224	7 599	3 856	3 743	8 057	4 100	3 957
20-24	4 528	2 295	2 234	5 278	2 682	2 595	6 379	3 250	3 129	7 385	3 706	3 678
25-29	4 120	2 068	2 053	4 218	2 072	2 146	5 030	2 531	2 499	6 159	3 098	3 061
30-34	3 722	1 882	1 840	4 075	2 011	2 064	4 110	2 010	2 100	4 923	2 469	2 454
35-39	3 231	1 625	1 606	3 747	1 904	1 843	4 053	2 010	2 043	4 095	2 012	2 083
40-44	2 591	1 297	1 294	3 238	1 633	1 605	3 740	1 902	1 839	4 049	2 011	2 039
45-49	2 036	1 035	1 002	2 589	1 297	1 291	3 212	1 617	1 595	3 713	1 885	1 828
50-54	1 861	924	937	1 983	1 001	982	2 518	1 253	1 265	3 134	1 567	1 567
55-59	1 593	764	829	1 746	854	892	1 875	933	942	2 397	1 175	1 221
60-64	1 288	616	672	1 451	682	769	1 608	770	838	1 739	847	892
65-69	943	437	505	1 115	519	595	1 277	583	694	1 429	665	764
70-74	615	276	339	747	336	411	903	407	496	1 052	463	589
75-79	369	162	207	420	182	239	527	227	299	651	281	370
80 +	230	98	132	261	110	151	320	132	188	412	168	243

366

United Nations Department of Economic and Social Affairs/Population Division
World Population Prospects: The 2004 Revision, Volume II: Sex and Age Distribution of the World Population

POPULATION BY AGE AND SEX (in thousands)

Age group	2005 Both sexes	Males	Females	2010 Both sexes	Males	Females	2015 Both sexes	Males	Females	2020 Both sexes	Males	Females
All ages	74 033	37 120	36 913	81 133	40 616	40 517	88 175	44 075	44 100	94 004	47 027	47 507
0-4	8 933	4 558	4 374	9 382	4 788	4 594	9 505	4 853	4 653	9 318	4 761	4 557
5-9	8 149	4 157	3 992	8 889	4 534	4 355	9 346	4 768	4 578	9 474	4 835	4 638
10-14	7 757	3 958	3 799	8 128	4 144	3 983	8 870	4 522	4 347	9 328	4 757	4 571
15-19	8 057	4 100	3 957	7 675	3 902	3 774	8 049	4 089	3 959	8 792	4 468	4 324
20-24	7 385	3 706	3 678	7 865	3 964	3 900	7 489	3 770	3 719	7 865	3 960	3 906
25-29	6 159	3 098	3 061	7 185	3 567	3 618	7 669	3 827	3 842	7 299	3 637	3 663
30-34	4 923	2 469	2 454	6 056	3 035	3 021	7 083	3 504	3 579	7 569	3 766	3 803
35-39	4 095	2 012	2 083	4 902	2 463	2 439	6 034	3 028	3 006	7 060	3 497	3 563
40-44	4 049	2 011	2 039	4 096	2 016	2 080	4 902	2 466	2 437	6 031	3 029	3 002
45-49	3 713	1 885	1 828	4 029	2 001	2 028	4 083	2 010	2 073	4 885	2 457	2 428
50-54	3 134	1 567	1 567	3 635	1 836	1 799	3 953	1 954	2 000	4 015	1 968	2 047
55-59	2 397	1 175	1 221	2 999	1 479	1 520	3 491	1 740	1 751	3 810	1 859	1 951
60-64	1 739	847	892	2 239	1 075	1 164	2 816	1 360	1 456	3 293	1 609	1 684
65-69	1 429	665	764	1 560	738	822	2 025	944	1 080	2 564	1 204	1 360
70-74	1 052	463	589	1 192	535	658	1 315	600	715	1 727	775	952
75-79	651	281	370	773	325	448	890	381	510	999	433	566
80-84	301	124	177	381	157	225	463	185	278	551	221	331
85-89	92	37	55	122	48	74	159	62	97	205	75	130
90-94	17	7	10	22	9	14	30	12	19	43	15	28
95-99	2	1	1	2	1	1	3	1	2	4	1	3
100 +	0	0	0	0	0	0	0	0	0	0	0	0

Age group	2025 Both sexes	Males	Females	2030 Both sexes	Males	Females	2035 Both sexes	Males	Females	2040 Both sexes	Males	Females
All ages	101 092	50 364	50 728	107 056	53 248	53 808	112 689	55 963	56 726	117 803	58 416	59 387
0-4	9 170	4 689	4 481	9 188	4 701	4 487	9 221	4 721	4 500	9 099	4 662	4 438
5-9	9 291	4 747	4 545	9 146	4 677	4 470	9 166	4 690	4 476	9 201	4 712	4 490
10-14	9 458	4 826	4 632	9 277	4 738	4 539	9 133	4 669	4 464	9 154	4 684	4 470
15-19	9 252	4 704	4 548	9 383	4 774	4 609	9 204	4 688	4 517	9 062	4 620	4 442
20-24	8 610	4 339	4 271	9 072	4 577	4 495	9 205	4 648	4 557	9 029	4 564	4 465
25-29	7 678	3 828	3 850	8 423	4 209	4 214	8 886	4 448	4 439	9 022	4 521	4 501
30-34	7 204	3 579	3 626	7 584	3 772	3 813	8 330	4 153	4 178	8 795	4 393	4 402
35-39	7 549	3 761	3 788	7 189	3 577	3 612	7 571	3 771	3 800	8 318	4 153	4 164
40-44	7 056	3 498	3 558	7 547	3 763	3 784	7 193	3 584	3 610	7 578	3 780	3 798
45-49	6 008	3 017	2 991	7 030	3 486	3 544	7 523	3 752	3 771	7 178	3 579	3 600
50-54	4 809	2 409	2 400	5 920	2 961	2 959	6 935	3 426	3 509	7 429	3 694	3 736
55-59	4 079	1 070	2 001	4 668	2 307	2 361	5 749	2 846	2 903	6 748	3 302	3 447
60-64	3 608	1 726	1 882	3 686	1 751	1 935	4 439	2 160	2 278	5 494	2 675	2 819
65-69	3 014	1 433	1 581	3 322	1 546	1 775	3 410	1 578	1 832	4 121	1 957	2 164
70-74	2 208	997	1 211	2 617	1 197	1 420	2 909	1 302	1 607	3 007	1 338	1 669
75-79	1 335	566	769	1 732	738	994	2 080	897	1 183	2 341	986	1 355
80-84	638	255	383	876	340	537	1 163	450	713	1 424	555	869
85-89	257	92	165	311	109	203	447	147	299	614	199	415
90-94	61	19	42	82	24	58	106	29	78	162	40	123
95-99	7	2	5	11	3	9	17	3	13	23	4	19
100 +	0	0	0	1	0	1	1	0	1	2	0	2

Age group	2045 Both sexes	Males	Females	2050 Both sexes	Males	Females
All ages	122 234	60 531	61 703	125 916	62 277	63 639
0-4	8 803	4 511	4 293	8 442	4 325	4 117
5-9	9 081	4 653	4 428	8 785	4 502	4 284
10-14	9 189	4 705	4 484	9 069	4 646	4 423
15-19	9 084	4 635	4 449	9 120	4 657	4 463
20-24	8 888	4 498	4 391	8 911	4 514	4 398
25-29	8 848	4 438	4 410	8 709	4 373	4 336
30-34	8 933	4 467	4 465	8 760	4 385	4 374
35-39	8 783	4 394	4 389	8 922	4 469	4 453
40-44	8 324	4 161	4 162	8 789	4 402	4 387
45-49	7 564	3 775	3 789	8 308	4 156	4 152
50-54	7 097	3 528	3 569	7 484	3 725	3 758
55-59	7 242	3 568	3 673	6 929	3 416	3 513
60-64	6 469	3 116	3 353	6 960	3 382	3 579
65-69	5 123	2 438	2 686	6 059	2 856	3 203
70-74	3 657	1 675	1 982	4 579	2 106	2 472
75-79	2 450	1 027	1 423	3 012	1 306	1 706
80-84	1 640	624	1 016	1 755	669	1 087
85-89	779	254	525	935	301	634
90-94	237	57	180	319	78	240
95-99	39	6	33	62	9	53
100 +	3	0	3	5	0	5

POPULATION BY AGE AND SEX (in thousands)

Age group	2005 Both sexes	Males	Females	2010 Both sexes	Males	Females	2015 Both sexes	Males	Females	2020 Both sexes	Males	Females
All ages	74 033	37 120	36 913	81 919	41 017	40 902	90 341	45 181	45 160	98 812	49 358	49 454
0-4	8 933	4 558	4 374	10 168	5 189	4 979	10 888	5 558	5 329	11 134	5 689	5 446
5-9	8 149	4 157	3 992	8 889	4 534	4 355	10 129	5 168	4 962	10 853	5 539	5 314
10-14	7 757	3 958	3 799	8 128	4 144	3 983	8 870	4 522	4 347	10 111	5 156	4 954
15-19	8 057	4 100	3 957	7 675	3 902	3 774	8 049	4 089	3 959	8 792	4 468	4 324
20-24	7 385	3 706	3 678	7 865	3 964	3 900	7 489	3 770	3 719	7 865	3 960	3 906
25-29	6 159	3 098	3 061	7 185	3 567	3 618	7 669	3 827	3 842	7 299	3 637	3 663
30-34	4 923	2 469	2 454	6 056	3 035	3 021	7 083	3 504	3 579	7 569	3 766	3 803
35-39	4 095	2 012	2 083	4 902	2 463	2 439	6 034	3 028	3 006	7 060	3 497	3 563
40-44	4 049	2 011	2 039	4 096	2 016	2 080	4 902	2 466	2 437	6 031	3 029	3 002
45-49	3 713	1 885	1 828	4 029	2 001	2 028	4 083	2 010	2 073	4 885	2 457	2 428
50-54	3 134	1 567	1 567	3 635	1 836	1 799	3 953	1 954	2 000	4 015	1 968	2 047
55-59	2 397	1 175	1 221	2 999	1 479	1 520	3 491	1 740	1 751	3 810	1 859	1 951
60-64	1 739	847	892	2 239	1 075	1 164	2 816	1 360	1 456	3 293	1 609	1 684
65-69	1 429	665	764	1 560	738	822	2 025	944	1 080	2 564	1 204	1 360
70-74	1 052	463	589	1 192	535	658	1 315	600	715	1 727	775	952
75-79	651	281	370	773	325	448	890	381	510	999	433	566
80-84	301	124	177	381	157	225	463	185	278	551	221	331
85-89	92	37	55	122	48	74	159	62	97	205	75	130
90-94	17	7	10	22	9	14	30	12	19	43	15	28
95-99	2	1	1	2	1	1	3	1	2	4	1	3
100 +	0	0	0	0	0	0	0	0	0	0	0	0

Age group	2025 Both sexes	Males	Females	2030 Both sexes	Males	Females	2035 Both sexes	Males	Females	2040 Both sexes	Males	Females
All ages	106 990	53 376	53 613	115 188	57 402	57 785	123 642	61 560	62 082	132 237	65 795	66 442
0-4	11 095	5 674	5 422	11 429	5 848	5 581	12 053	6 171	5 882	12 594	6 452	6 142
5-9	11 104	5 673	5 432	11 069	5 660	5 409	11 405	5 836	5 569	12 031	6 160	5 870
10-14	10 836	5 529	5 307	11 088	5 663	5 425	11 054	5 651	5 403	11 392	5 828	5 563
15-19	10 034	5 103	4 931	10 760	5 476	5 284	11 014	5 611	5 402	10 981	5 601	5 380
20-24	8 610	4 339	4 271	9 851	4 974	4 877	10 579	5 348	5 230	10 835	5 486	5 349
25-29	7 678	3 828	3 850	8 423	4 209	4 214	9 664	4 843	4 821	10 393	5 219	5 174
30-34	7 204	3 579	3 626	7 584	3 772	3 813	8 330	4 153	4 178	9 571	4 788	4 784
35-39	7 549	3 761	3 788	7 189	3 577	3 612	7 571	3 771	3 800	8 318	4 153	4 164
40-44	7 056	3 498	3 558	7 547	3 763	3 784	7 193	3 584	3 610	7 578	3 780	3 798
45-49	6 008	3 017	2 991	7 030	3 486	3 544	7 523	3 752	3 771	7 178	3 579	3 600
50-54	4 809	2 409	2 400	5 920	2 961	2 959	6 935	3 426	3 509	7 429	3 694	3 736
55-59	3 879	1 878	2 001	4 658	2 307	2 351	5 748	2 846	2 903	6 748	3 302	3 447
60-64	3 608	1 726	1 882	3 686	1 751	1 935	4 439	2 160	2 278	5 494	2 675	2 819
65-69	3 014	1 433	1 581	3 322	1 546	1 775	3 410	1 578	1 832	4 121	1 957	2 164
70-74	2 208	997	1 211	2 617	1 197	1 420	2 909	1 302	1 607	3 007	1 338	1 669
75-79	1 335	566	769	1 732	738	994	2 080	897	1 183	2 341	986	1 355
80-84	638	255	383	876	340	537	1 163	450	713	1 424	555	869
85-89	257	92	165	311	109	203	447	147	299	614	199	415
90-94	61	19	42	82	24	58	106	29	78	162	40	123
95-99	7	2	5	11	3	9	17	3	13	23	4	19
100 +	0	0	0	1	0	1	1	0	1	2	0	2

Age group	2045 Both sexes	Males	Females	2050 Both sexes	Males	Females
All ages	140 653	69 950	70 702	148 649	73 905	74 744
0-4	12 806	6 562	6 245	12 780	6 548	6 233
5-9	12 572	6 441	6 131	12 785	6 551	6 234
10-14	12 017	6 153	5 865	12 559	6 434	6 125
15-19	11 320	5 779	5 541	11 946	6 103	5 843
20-24	10 805	5 477	5 328	11 144	5 655	5 489
25-29	10 651	5 358	5 293	10 622	5 349	5 272
30-34	10 300	5 164	5 137	10 559	5 303	5 256
35-39	9 557	4 788	4 770	10 286	5 163	5 123
40-44	8 324	4 161	4 162	9 560	4 794	4 766
45-49	7 564	3 775	3 789	8 308	4 156	4 152
50-54	7 097	3 528	3 569	7 484	3 725	3 758
55-59	7 242	3 568	3 673	6 929	3 416	3 513
60-64	6 469	3 116	3 353	6 960	3 382	3 579
65-69	5 123	2 438	2 686	6 059	2 856	3 203
70-74	3 657	1 675	1 982	4 579	2 106	2 472
75-79	2 450	1 027	1 423	3 012	1 306	1 706
80-84	1 640	624	1 016	1 755	669	1 087
85-89	779	254	525	935	301	634
90-94	237	57	180	319	78	240
95-99	39	6	33	62	9	53
100 +	3	0	3	5	0	5

United Nations Department of Economic and Social Affairs/Population Division
World Population Prospects: The 2004 Revision, Volume II: Sex and Age Distribution of the World Population

POPULATION BY AGE AND SEX (in thousands)

Age group	2005 Both sexes	Males	Females	2010 Both sexes	Males	Females	2015 Both sexes	Males	Females	2020 Both sexes	Males	Females
All ages	74 033	37 120	36 913	80 347	40 215	40 132	86 009	42 970	43 039	90 856	45 296	45 560
0-4	8 933	4 558	4 374	8 597	4 387	4 209	8 123	4 147	3 976	7 502	3 833	3 669
5-9	8 149	4 157	3 992	8 889	4 534	4 355	8 562	4 368	4 194	8 094	4 131	3 963
10-14	7 757	3 958	3 799	8 128	4 144	3 983	8 870	4 522	4 347	8 545	4 358	4 187
15-19	8 057	4 100	3 957	7 675	3 902	3 774	8 049	4 089	3 959	8 792	4 468	4 324
20-24	7 385	3 706	3 678	7 865	3 964	3 900	7 489	3 770	3 719	7 865	3 960	3 906
25-29	6 159	3 098	3 061	7 185	3 567	3 618	7 669	3 827	3 842	7 299	3 637	3 663
30-34	4 923	2 469	2 454	6 056	3 035	3 021	7 083	3 504	3 579	7 569	3 766	3 803
35-39	4 095	2 012	2 083	4 902	2 463	2 439	6 034	3 028	3 006	7 060	3 497	3 563
40-44	4 049	2 011	2 039	4 096	2 016	2 080	4 902	2 466	2 437	6 031	3 029	3 002
45-49	3 713	1 885	1 828	4 029	2 001	2 028	4 083	2 010	2 073	4 885	2 457	2 428
50-54	3 134	1 567	1 567	3 635	1 836	1 799	3 953	1 954	2 000	4 015	1 968	2 047
55-59	2 397	1 175	1 221	2 999	1 479	1 520	3 491	1 740	1 751	3 810	1 859	1 951
60-64	1 739	847	892	2 239	1 075	1 164	2 816	1 360	1 456	3 293	1 609	1 684
65-69	1 429	665	764	1 560	738	822	2 025	944	1 080	2 564	1 204	1 360
70-74	1 052	463	589	1 192	535	658	1 315	600	715	1 727	775	952
75-79	651	281	370	773	325	448	890	381	510	999	433	566
80-84	301	124	177	381	157	225	463	185	278	551	221	331
85-89	92	37	55	122	48	74	159	62	97	205	75	130
90-94	17	7	10	22	9	14	30	12	19	43	15	28
95-99	2	1	1	2	1	1	3	1	2	4	1	3
100 +	0	0	0	0	0	0	0	0	0	0	0	0

Age group	2025 Both sexes	Males	Females	2030 Both sexes	Males	Females	2035 Both sexes	Males	Females	2040 Both sexes	Males	Females
All ages	95 204	47 357	47 847	99 019	49 142	49 877	102 099	50 551	51 548	104 241	51 483	52 758
0-4	7 255	3 710	3 545	7 031	3 598	3 433	6 658	3 409	3 249	6 114	3 132	2 982
5-9	7 478	3 820	3 658	7 233	3 699	3 535	7 012	3 588	3 424	6 640	3 400	3 240
10-14	8 080	4 123	3 957	7 465	3 813	3 652	7 221	3 692	3 529	7 000	3 582	3 419
15-19	8 470	4 306	4 165	8 007	4 072	3 935	7 395	3 764	3 631	7 152	3 644	3 508
20-24	8 610	4 339	4 271	8 292	4 180	4 112	7 831	3 948	3 883	7 222	3 642	3 580
25-29	7 678	3 828	3 850	8 423	4 209	4 214	8 109	4 052	4 057	7 652	3 823	3 829
30-34	7 204	3 579	3 626	7 584	3 772	3 813	8 330	4 153	4 178	8 019	3 998	4 021
35-39	7 549	3 761	3 788	7 189	3 577	3 612	7 571	3 771	3 800	8 318	4 153	4 164
40-44	7 056	3 498	3 558	7 547	3 763	3 784	7 193	3 584	3 610	7 578	3 780	3 798
45-49	6 008	3 017	2 991	7 030	3 486	3 544	7 523	3 752	3 771	7 178	3 579	3 600
50-54	4 809	2 409	2 400	5 920	2 961	2 959	6 935	3 426	3 509	7 429	3 694	3 736
55-59	3 870	1 878	1 991	4 658	2 307	2 351	5 748	2 846	2 903	6 748	3 300	3 447
60-64	3 608	1 726	1 882	3 686	1 751	1 935	4 439	2 160	2 278	5 494	2 675	2 819
65-69	3 014	1 433	1 581	3 322	1 546	1 775	3 410	1 578	1 832	4 121	1 957	2 164
70-74	2 208	997	1 211	2 617	1 197	1 420	2 909	1 302	1 607	3 007	1 338	1 669
75-79	1 335	566	769	1 732	738	994	2 080	897	1 183	2 341	986	1 355
80-84	638	255	383	876	340	537	1 163	450	713	1 424	555	869
85-89	257	92	165	311	109	203	447	147	299	614	199	415
90-94	61	19	42	82	24	58	106	29	78	162	40	123
95-99	7	2	5	11	3	9	17	3	13	23	4	19
100 +	0	0	0	1	0	1	1	0	1	2	0	2

Age group	2045 Both sexes	Males	Females	2050 Both sexes	Males	Females
All ages	105 410	51 928	53 482	105 679	51 928	53 751
0-4	5 525	2 831	2 694	5 006	2 565	2 441
5-9	6 098	3 124	2 974	5 510	2 823	2 686
10-14	6 630	3 394	3 235	6 088	3 119	2 969
15-19	6 932	3 534	3 398	6 562	3 348	3 215
20-24	6 982	3 524	3 458	6 763	3 415	3 348
25-29	7 045	3 519	3 526	6 806	3 401	3 405
30-34	7 565	3 771	3 794	6 961	3 468	3 493
35-39	8 009	4 001	4 009	7 558	3 775	3 783
40-44	8 324	4 161	4 162	8 018	4 010	4 008
45-49	7 564	3 775	3 789	8 308	4 156	4 152
50-54	7 097	3 528	3 569	7 484	3 725	3 758
55-59	7 242	3 568	3 673	6 929	3 416	3 513
60-64	6 469	3 116	3 353	6 960	3 382	3 579
65-69	5 123	2 438	2 686	6 059	2 856	3 203
70-74	3 657	1 675	1 982	4 579	2 106	2 472
75-79	2 450	1 027	1 423	3 012	1 306	1 706
80-84	1 640	624	1 016	1 755	669	1 087
85-89	779	254	525	935	301	634
90-94	237	57	180	319	78	240
95-99	39	6	33	62	9	53
100 +	3	0	3	5	0	5

POPULATION BY AGE AND SEX (in thousands)

Age group	1950 Both sexes	1950 Males	1950 Females	1955 Both sexes	1955 Males	1955 Females	1960 Both sexes	1960 Males	1960 Females	1965 Both sexes	1965 Males	1965 Females
All ages	1 951	975	976	2 224	1 113	1 111	2 578	1 293	1 285	3 012	1 512	1 500
0-4	350	177	173	410	208	202	489	248	241	566	287	279
5-9	263	133	130	325	164	160	384	194	189	462	234	228
10-14	227	115	113	256	129	126	317	161	156	376	191	185
15-19	204	103	101	220	111	109	249	126	123	311	158	153
20-24	175	88	88	196	99	97	213	108	105	243	123	120
25-29	147	74	74	167	84	84	189	95	94	206	104	102
30-34	127	63	64	140	70	70	160	80	80	182	91	90
35-39	101	50	51	120	60	60	133	66	67	153	76	77
40-44	90	45	46	94	46	48	113	56	57	126	63	64
45-49	73	36	37	83	41	43	88	43	45	106	52	54
50-54	57	28	29	66	32	34	77	37	40	81	39	42
55-59	43	21	22	50	24	26	59	28	31	70	33	36
60-64	33	16	17	36	17	19	43	20	23	52	24	27
65-69	25	12	13	26	12	14	29	14	16	36	17	19
70-74	17	8	9	18	8	10	19	9	10	22	10	12
75-79	11	5	6	10	5	6	11	5	6	13	6	7
80 +	7	3	4	7	3	4	7	3	4	8	3	4

Age group	1970 Both sexes	1970 Males	1970 Females	1975 Both sexes	1975 Males	1975 Females	1980 Both sexes	1980 Males	1980 Females	1985 Both sexes	1985 Males	1985 Females
All ages	3 598	1 810	1 788	4 120	2 070	2 049	4 586	2 288	2 298	4 769	2 345	2 424
0-4	658	334	324	720	365	354	772	392	380	702	357	345
5-9	547	278	270	626	317	309	685	347	338	729	370	359
10-14	463	235	228	533	270	263	605	306	299	647	327	320
15-19	377	191	186	446	226	220	501	252	249	531	261	270
20-24	310	157	153	354	179	176	401	200	202	396	188	207
25-29	241	122	119	293	148	145	321	158	162	337	159	177
30-34	205	103	102	229	115	114	269	134	135	280	135	145
35-39	179	90	90	195	98	97	212	106	107	241	117	123
40-44	150	75	76	172	86	86	182	90	92	192	94	98
45-49	123	61	62	144	71	73	161	79	82	167	81	86
50-54	102	50	52	117	57	59	135	66	69	149	72	77
55-59	77	37	40	96	47	49	108	52	56	124	59	65
60-64	64	30	34	70	34	37	87	41	46	98	46	52
65-69	45	21	24	56	26	30	61	28	33	76	35	41
70-74	29	13	16	37	17	20	46	20	25	50	22	28
75-79	16	7	9	21	9	11	27	11	15	33	14	19
80 +	10	4	6	11	5	7	14	6	9	19	7	12

Age group	1990 Both sexes	1990 Males	1990 Females	1995 Both sexes	1995 Males	1995 Females	2000 Both sexes	2000 Males	2000 Females	2005 Both sexes	2005 Males	2005 Females
All ages	5 110	2 502	2 608	5 669	2 776	2 892	6 280	3 082	3 198	6 881	3 382	3 499
0-4	703	358	345	759	387	372	797	407	390	805	411	394
5-9	677	344	333	693	352	341	751	382	369	789	402	387
10-14	704	357	348	668	339	329	686	348	338	744	379	366
15-19	599	299	301	690	349	342	658	333	325	676	343	334
20-24	465	222	243	581	288	293	676	340	336	644	325	319
25-29	356	165	191	450	213	237	569	281	288	663	332	331
30-34	310	145	165	344	158	186	440	207	233	557	274	284
35-39	261	125	136	300	139	161	336	153	183	430	201	229
40-44	227	110	117	252	119	133	292	135	158	328	149	179
45-49	181	88	93	218	105	114	245	115	130	284	130	154
50-54	158	76	82	173	83	90	210	100	110	236	110	126
55-59	139	66	73	149	71	78	165	78	87	201	94	106
60-64	114	54	61	129	61	69	139	65	74	155	73	82
65-69	87	40	47	103	47	56	117	54	63	127	59	69
70-74	64	29	36	74	33	41	89	40	49	102	46	57
75-79	38	16	22	50	21	29	59	25	34	71	30	41
80 +	25	10	16	34	13	22	51	19	33	68	25	43

United Nations Department of Economic and Social Affairs/Population Division
World Population Prospects: The 2004 Revision, Volume II: Sex and Age Distribution of the World Population

370

POPULATION BY AGE AND SEX (in thousands)

Age group	2005 Both sexes	2005 Males	2005 Females	2010 Both sexes	2010 Males	2010 Females	2015 Both sexes	2015 Males	2015 Females	2020 Both sexes	2020 Males	2020 Females
All ages	6 881	3 382	3 499	7 461	3 671	3 790	8 017	3 948	4 069	8 550	4 212	4 337
0-4	805	411	394	805	411	393	800	409	391	795	407	388
5-9	789	402	387	797	407	390	797	407	390	793	405	388
10-14	744	379	366	782	398	384	790	403	387	791	403	387
15-19	676	343	334	734	373	361	772	393	379	780	397	383
20-24	644	325	319	662	334	328	720	364	356	758	384	374
25-29	663	332	331	631	317	314	650	327	323	708	357	351
30-34	557	274	284	650	325	326	620	311	309	639	320	319
35-39	430	201	229	546	267	279	639	317	321	609	304	305
40-44	328	149	179	421	196	225	535	260	275	627	310	317
45-49	284	130	154	319	144	176	410	190	220	523	253	270
50-54	236	110	126	275	125	150	310	138	171	399	183	216
55-59	201	94	106	226	104	122	264	118	146	298	132	166
60-64	155	73	82	189	88	101	214	97	116	250	111	140
65-69	127	59	69	142	65	77	174	79	95	198	88	109
70-74	102	46	57	111	50	62	125	56	69	155	68	86
75-79	71	30	41	83	35	48	91	39	52	104	44	60
80-84	42	16	25	51	20	31	60	24	36	68	27	41
85-89	20	7	13	25	9	16	31	11	20	38	13	24
90-94	5	2	4	9	3	6	11	3	8	15	4	10
95-99	1	0	1	2	0	1	3	1	2	4	1	3
100 +	0	0	0	0	0	0	0	0	0	0	0	0

Age group	2025 Both sexes	2025 Males	2025 Females	2030 Both sexes	2030 Males	2030 Females	2035 Both sexes	2035 Males	2035 Females	2040 Both sexes	2040 Males	2040 Females
All ages	9 052	4 461	4 591	9 517	4 690	4 827	9 935	4 896	5 039	10 297	5 072	5 225
0-4	786	402	384	771	395	377	752	384	367	728	372	356
5-9	788	403	385	780	399	381	765	391	374	746	381	365
10-14	787	402	385	782	399	383	774	395	379	760	388	372
15-19	781	398	383	777	396	381	773	394	379	765	390	375
20-24	766	389	377	768	390	378	764	389	376	760	387	374
25-29	746	377	369	755	382	373	757	384	373	754	382	372
30-34	697	350	346	735	371	365	745	376	369	747	378	369
35-39	629	314	315	686	344	342	725	365	361	735	370	365
40-44	598	297	301	618	308	311	676	337	339	715	358	357
45-49	613	302	312	587	290	297	607	300	306	664	330	334
50-54	509	244	265	598	292	306	573	281	292	593	292	302
55-59	505	176	210	400	231	258	570	280	290	556	270	285
60-64	284	124	160	367	165	202	470	221	249	554	265	289
65-69	233	101	132	264	113	152	343	151	192	441	203	238
70-74	177	76	100	209	88	121	239	99	140	312	133	179
75-79	129	54	75	149	61	88	178	71	107	205	81	125
80-84	78	31	47	98	38	60	115	44	71	139	52	87
85-89	43	15	28	50	18	32	65	23	42	77	26	50
90-94	18	5	13	21	6	15	26	8	18	34	10	24
95-99	5	1	4	6	1	5	7	2	6	9	2	7
100 +	1	0	1	1	0	1	1	0	1	2	0	1

Age group	2045 Both sexes	2045 Males	2045 Females	2050 Both sexes	2050 Males	2050 Females
All ages	10 595	5 216	5 379	10 823	5 323	5 500
0-4	701	359	342	674	345	329
5-9	723	370	353	696	356	340
10-14	741	378	362	718	367	351
15-19	751	383	368	732	374	359
20-24	753	383	370	739	376	363
25-29	750	381	370	743	377	366
30-34	745	377	368	742	376	366
35-39	738	372	366	736	372	365
40-44	726	364	362	729	367	363
45-49	704	351	353	715	357	358
50-54	651	321	329	690	342	348
55-59	577	281	295	633	310	323
60-64	533	256	277	554	267	287
65-69	521	245	277	503	237	265
70-74	402	179	222	477	217	259
75-79	269	109	160	348	148	200
80-84	162	59	103	214	81	133
85-89	94	31	63	111	36	75
90-94	41	12	29	51	14	37
95-99	12	3	9	15	4	11
100 +	2	0	1	2	1	2

POPULATION BY AGE AND SEX (in thousands)

Age group	2005 Both sexes	Males	Females	2010 Both sexes	Males	Females	2015 Both sexes	Males	Females	2020 Both sexes	Males	Females
All ages	6 881	3 382	3 499	7 536	3 709	3 826	8 219	4 051	4 168	8 918	4 400	4 517
0-4	805	411	394	879	449	430	927	474	453	962	492	470
5-9	789	402	387	797	407	390	871	445	427	919	470	450
10-14	744	379	366	782	398	384	790	403	387	865	441	423
15-19	676	343	334	734	373	361	772	393	379	780	397	383
20-24	644	325	319	662	334	328	720	364	356	758	384	374
25-29	663	332	331	631	317	314	650	327	323	708	357	351
30-34	557	274	284	650	325	326	620	311	309	639	320	319
35-39	430	201	229	546	267	279	639	317	321	609	304	305
40-44	328	149	179	421	196	225	535	260	275	627	310	317
45-49	284	130	154	319	144	176	410	190	220	523	253	270
50-54	236	110	126	275	125	150	310	138	171	399	183	216
55-59	201	94	106	226	104	122	264	118	146	298	132	166
60-64	155	73	82	189	88	101	214	97	116	250	111	140
65-69	127	59	69	142	65	77	174	79	95	198	88	109
70-74	102	46	57	111	50	62	125	56	69	155	68	86
75-79	71	30	41	83	35	48	91	39	52	104	44	60
80-84	42	16	25	51	20	31	60	24	36	68	27	41
85-89	20	7	13	25	9	16	31	11	20	38	13	24
90-94	5	2	4	9	3	6	11	3	8	15	4	10
95-99	1	0	1	2	0	1	3	1	2	4	1	3
100 +	0	0	0	0	0	0	0	0	0	0	0	0

Age group	2025 Both sexes	Males	Females	2030 Both sexes	Males	Females	2035 Both sexes	Males	Females	2040 Both sexes	Males	Females
All ages	9 600	4 741	4 859	10 274	5 077	5 197	10 943	5 411	5 532	11 600	5 738	5 863
0-4	967	495	473	982	502	480	1 006	514	491	1 026	525	501
5-9	955	488	467	960	491	470	975	499	477	999	511	488
10-14	913	466	447	948	484	464	954	487	467	969	495	474
15-19	855	436	419	903	460	443	939	479	460	945	482	463
20-24	766	389	377	841	427	414	889	452	437	925	471	455
25-29	746	377	369	755	382	373	830	421	409	878	446	433
30-34	697	350	346	735	371	365	745	376	369	820	414	405
35-39	629	314	315	686	344	342	725	365	361	735	370	365
40-44	598	297	301	618	308	311	676	337	339	715	358	357
45-49	613	302	312	587	290	297	607	300	306	664	330	334
50-54	509	244	265	598	292	306	573	281	292	593	292	302
55-59	385	175	210	492	234	258	579	280	299	556	270	285
60-64	284	124	160	367	165	202	470	221	249	554	265	289
65-69	233	101	132	264	113	152	343	151	192	441	203	238
70-74	177	76	100	209	88	121	239	99	140	312	133	179
75-79	129	54	75	149	61	88	178	71	107	205	81	125
80-84	78	31	47	98	38	60	115	44	71	139	52	87
85-89	43	15	28	50	18	32	65	23	42	77	26	50
90-94	18	5	13	21	6	15	26	8	18	34	10	24
95-99	5	1	4	6	1	5	7	2	6	9	2	7
100 +	1	0	1	1	0	1	1	0	1	2	0	1

Age group	2045 Both sexes	Males	Females	2050 Both sexes	Males	Females
All ages	12 230	6 050	6 180	12 823	6 344	6 479
0-4	1 038	531	507	1 045	535	510
5-9	1 021	522	499	1 033	528	505
10-14	993	508	486	1 015	519	496
15-19	960	490	470	984	502	482
20-24	932	474	457	947	482	465
25-29	915	465	450	921	468	453
30-34	868	440	429	905	459	446
35-39	810	409	401	859	434	425
40-44	726	364	362	800	402	398
45-49	704	351	353	715	357	358
50-54	651	321	329	690	342	348
55-59	577	281	295	633	310	323
60-64	533	256	277	554	267	287
65-69	521	245	277	503	237	265
70-74	402	179	222	477	217	259
75-79	269	109	160	348	148	200
80-84	162	59	103	214	81	133
85-89	94	31	63	111	36	75
90-94	41	12	29	51	14	37
95-99	12	3	9	15	4	11
100 +	2	0	1	2	1	2

United Nations Department of Economic and Social Affairs/Population Division
World Population Prospects: The 2004 Revision, Volume II: Sex and Age Distribution of the World Population

372

POPULATION BY AGE AND SEX (in thousands)

Age group	2005			2010			2015			2020		
	Both sexes	Males	Females	Both sexes	Males	Females	Both sexes	Males	Females	Both sexes	Males	Females
All ages	6 881	3 382	3 499	7 386	3 633	3 753	7 816	3 845	3 971	8 182	4 024	4 158
0-4	805	411	394	730	373	357	673	344	329	627	321	306
5-9	789	402	387	797	407	390	723	369	354	666	340	326
10-14	744	379	366	782	398	384	790	403	387	717	366	351
15-19	676	343	334	734	373	361	772	393	379	780	397	383
20-24	644	325	319	662	334	328	720	364	356	758	384	374
25-29	663	332	331	631	317	314	650	327	323	708	357	351
30-34	557	274	284	650	325	326	620	311	309	639	320	319
35-39	430	201	229	546	267	279	639	317	321	609	304	305
40-44	328	149	179	421	196	225	535	260	275	627	310	317
45-49	284	130	154	319	144	176	410	190	220	523	253	270
50-54	236	110	126	275	125	150	310	138	171	399	183	216
55-59	201	94	106	226	104	122	264	118	146	298	132	166
60-64	155	73	82	189	88	101	214	97	116	250	111	140
65-69	127	59	69	142	65	77	174	79	95	198	88	109
70-74	102	46	57	111	50	62	125	56	69	155	68	86
75-79	71	30	41	83	35	48	91	39	52	104	44	60
80-84	42	16	25	51	20	31	60	24	36	68	27	41
85-89	20	7	13	25	9	16	31	11	20	38	13	24
90-94	5	2	4	9	3	6	11	3	8	15	4	10
95-99	1	0	1	2	0	1	3	1	2	4	1	3
100 +	0	0	0	0	0	0	0	0	0	0	0	0

Age group	2025			2030			2035			2040		
	Both sexes	Males	Females	Both sexes	Males	Females	Both sexes	Males	Females	Both sexes	Males	Females
All ages	8 507	4 183	4 325	8 775	4 311	4 463	8 969	4 402	4 567	9 081	4 451	4 630
0-4	607	310	297	572	293	279	525	269	257	475	243	232
5-9	622	318	304	602	308	294	567	290	277	521	266	255
10-14	660	337	323	616	315	301	596	305	292	562	287	275
15-19	708	360	347	652	332	320	607	310	298	588	300	288
20-24	766	389	377	695	353	342	639	325	314	595	303	293
25-29	746	377	369	755	382	373	684	347	338	629	319	310
30-34	697	350	346	735	371	365	745	376	369	675	341	334
35-39	629	314	315	686	344	342	725	365	361	735	370	365
40-44	598	297	301	618	308	311	676	337	339	715	358	357
45-49	613	302	312	587	290	297	607	300	306	664	330	334
50-54	509	244	265	598	292	306	573	281	292	593	292	302
55-59	385	176	210	492	234	258	578	280	299	555	270	285
60-64	284	124	160	367	165	202	470	221	249	554	265	289
65-69	233	101	132	264	113	152	343	151	192	441	203	238
70-74	177	76	100	209	88	121	239	99	140	312	133	179
75-79	129	54	75	149	61	88	178	71	107	205	81	125
80-84	78	31	47	98	38	60	115	44	71	139	52	87
85-89	43	15	28	50	18	32	65	23	42	77	26	50
90-94	18	5	13	21	6	15	26	8	18	34	10	24
95-99	5	1	4	6	1	5	7	2	6	9	2	7
100 +	1	0	1	1	0	1	1	0	1	2	0	1

Age group	2045			2050		
	Both sexes	Males	Females	Both sexes	Males	Females
All ages	9 111	4 458	4 653	9 057	4 422	4 635
0-4	428	219	209	386	198	189
5-9	471	241	230	424	217	207
10-14	516	263	252	466	238	228
15-19	554	282	271	508	259	249
20-24	576	293	283	542	276	267
25-29	586	297	289	567	288	280
30-34	621	314	307	579	293	286
35-39	667	336	331	614	310	304
40-44	726	364	362	658	331	328
45-49	704	351	353	715	357	358
50-54	651	321	329	690	342	348
55-59	577	281	295	633	310	323
60-64	533	256	277	554	267	287
65-69	521	245	277	503	237	265
70-74	402	179	222	477	217	259
75-79	269	109	160	348	148	200
80-84	162	59	103	214	81	133
85-89	94	31	63	111	36	75
90-94	41	12	29	51	14	37
95-99	12	3	9	15	4	11
100 +	2	0	1	2	1	2

POPULATION BY AGE AND SEX (in thousands)

Age group	1950 Both sexes	1950 Males	1950 Females	1955 Both sexes	1955 Males	1955 Females	1960 Both sexes	1960 Males	1960 Females	1965 Both sexes	1965 Males	1965 Females
All ages	226	111	115	238	117	121	254	124	129	272	133	139
0-4	30	15	15	36	18	18	39	19	19	42	21	21
5-9	25	12	13	26	13	13	32	16	16	34	17	17
10-14	22	11	11	23	11	12	25	12	13	30	15	15
15-19	21	10	11	21	11	11	23	11	12	24	12	12
20-24	19	9	10	20	10	10	21	10	10	22	11	11
25-29	17	8	9	18	9	9	19	9	10	20	10	10
30-34	16	8	8	16	8	8	17	8	9	18	9	9
35-39	14	7	7	15	7	7	15	7	8	16	8	8
40-44	12	6	6	13	6	6	14	7	7	14	7	7
45-49	11	5	6	11	5	6	12	6	6	13	6	6
50-54	10	5	5	10	5	5	10	5	5	11	5	6
55-59	9	4	4	9	4	4	9	4	5	9	4	5
60-64	7	3	4	7	3	4	7	3	4	7	3	4
65-69	6	3	3	6	3	3	6	3	3	6	3	3
70-74	4	2	2	4	2	2	4	2	2	4	2	2
75-79	2	1	1	2	1	1	2	1	1	2	1	1
80 +	1	0	1	1	0	1	1	0	1	1	0	1

Age group	1970 Both sexes	1970 Males	1970 Females	1975 Both sexes	1975 Males	1975 Females	1980 Both sexes	1980 Males	1980 Females	1985 Both sexes	1985 Males	1985 Females
All ages	294	144	150	228	112	116	219	108	112	314	154	159
0-4	46	23	23	37	18	18	36	18	18	53	26	26
5-9	37	18	18	29	15	15	29	14	14	41	21	21
10-14	32	16	16	25	12	12	25	12	12	35	18	18
15-19	29	14	15	22	11	11	21	10	11	31	15	16
20-24	23	11	12	20	10	10	19	9	9	26	13	13
25-29	21	10	11	15	8	8	17	9	9	23	11	12
30-34	19	9	9	14	7	7	13	6	7	21	10	11
35-39	17	8	9	12	6	6	11	5	6	16	8	8
40-44	15	7	8	11	6	6	10	5	5	14	7	7
45-49	13	6	7	10	5	5	9	4	5	12	6	6
50-54	12	6	6	9	4	4	8	4	4	11	5	6
55-59	10	5	5	7	3	4	7	3	4	9	4	5
60-64	8	4	4	6	3	3	6	3	3	8	4	4
65-69	6	3	3	4	2	2	4	2	2	6	3	3
70-74	4	2	2	3	1	2	3	1	2	4	2	2
75-79	2	1	1	2	1	1	2	1	1	2	1	1
80 +	1	1	1	1	0	1	1	0	1	1	1	1

Age group	1990 Both sexes	1990 Males	1990 Females	1995 Both sexes	1995 Males	1995 Females	2000 Both sexes	2000 Males	2000 Females	2005 Both sexes	2005 Males	2005 Females
All ages	353	173	179	398	196	202	449	221	228	504	249	254
0-4	61	31	30	69	35	34	78	39	39	88	45	44
5-9	48	24	24	56	28	28	64	32	32	73	36	36
10-14	40	20	20	47	23	23	55	27	27	62	31	31
15-19	35	17	17	39	19	20	46	23	23	54	27	27
20-24	30	15	15	33	17	17	38	19	19	44	22	22
25-29	25	12	13	29	14	14	32	16	16	35	17	18
30-34	22	11	11	24	12	12	26	13	13	28	14	14
35-39	20	10	10	21	10	11	22	11	11	24	12	12
40-44	15	7	8	19	9	10	19	9	10	20	10	10
45-49	13	6	7	14	7	7	17	8	9	17	8	9
50-54	12	6	6	13	6	7	13	6	7	16	8	8
55-59	10	5	5	11	5	6	12	5	6	12	6	6
60-64	8	4	4	9	4	5	9	4	5	10	5	6
65-69	6	3	3	7	3	4	8	3	4	8	4	4
70-74	4	2	2	5	2	3	5	2	3	6	3	3
75-79	2	1	1	3	1	2	3	1	2	4	2	2
80 +	1	1	1	2	1	1	2	1	1	2	1	1

United Nations Department of Economic and Social Affairs/Population Division
World Population Prospects: The 2004 Revision, Volume II: Sex and Age Distribution of the World Population

374

POPULATION BY AGE AND SEX (in thousands)

Age group	2005 Both sexes	2005 Males	2005 Females	2010 Both sexes	2010 Males	2010 Females	2015 Both sexes	2015 Males	2015 Females	2020 Both sexes	2020 Males	2020 Females
All ages	504	249	254	563	280	283	627	313	314	693	348	345
0-4	88	45	44	101	51	50	111	56	55	118	59	58
5-9	73	36	36	83	41	41	94	47	47	106	53	52
10-14	62	31	31	71	35	35	80	40	40	92	46	46
15-19	54	27	27	61	31	31	69	35	35	79	39	39
20-24	44	22	22	52	26	26	59	30	30	67	34	34
25-29	35	17	18	40	20	20	47	24	24	54	27	27
30-34	28	14	14	30	15	15	35	18	17	40	21	20
35-39	24	12	12	24	12	12	25	13	12	29	15	13
40-44	20	10	10	21	10	10	21	11	10	21	11	10
45-49	17	8	9	18	9	9	18	9	9	18	9	8
50-54	16	8	8	16	8	8	16	8	8	16	8	8
55-59	12	6	6	14	7	8	14	7	7	14	7	7
60-64	10	5	6	11	5	6	13	6	7	13	6	7
65-69	8	4	4	9	4	5	9	4	5	11	5	6
70-74	6	3	3	6	3	3	7	3	4	7	3	4
75-79	4	2	2	4	2	2	4	2	2	5	2	3
80-84	2	1	1	2	1	1	2	1	1	2	1	1
85-89	1	0	0	1	0	0	1	0	0	1	0	1
90-94	0	0	0	0	0	0	0	0	0	0	0	0
95-99	0	0	0	0	0	0	0	0	0	0	0	0
100 +	0	0	0	0	0	0	0	0	0	0	0	0

Age group	2025 Both sexes	2025 Males	2025 Females	2030 Both sexes	2030 Males	2030 Females	2035 Both sexes	2035 Males	2035 Females	2040 Both sexes	2040 Males	2040 Females
All ages	762	384	378	836	422	414	913	461	452	991	500	491
0-4	123	62	61	128	65	63	132	67	65	135	68	67
5-9	113	57	56	119	60	59	125	63	62	129	65	64
10-14	103	52	51	111	56	55	117	59	58	123	62	61
15-19	90	45	45	102	51	51	109	55	54	116	58	58
20-24	77	38	38	88	44	44	99	50	50	107	54	54
25-29	62	31	31	71	36	36	83	41	41	94	47	47
30-34	47	24	23	54	28	27	63	32	31	74	37	37
35-39	34	18	16	39	21	19	47	24	23	55	28	27
40-44	24	13	11	28	15	13	34	18	16	41	21	20
45-49	18	10	8	21	11	9	25	13	12	30	16	14
50-54	16	8	8	16	9	8	19	10	9	23	12	11
55-59	14	7	7	14	7	7	15	8	7	17	9	8
60-64	13	6	7	13	6	7	13	6	6	13	7	6
65-69	11	5	6	11	5	6	11	5	6	11	6	6
70-74	9	4	5	9	4	5	9	4	5	9	4	5
75-79	5	2	3	6	3	4	7	3	4	7	3	4
80-84	3	1	2	3	1	2	4	2	2	4	2	2
85-89	1	0	1	1	1	1	1	1	1	2	1	1
90-94	0	0	0	0	0	0	0	0	0	0	0	0
95-99	0	0	0	0	0	0	0	0	0	0	0	0
100 +	0	0	0	0	0	0	0	0	0	0	0	0

Age group	2045 Both sexes	2045 Males	2045 Females	2050 Both sexes	2050 Males	2050 Females
All ages	1 069	538	531	1 146	577	570
0-4	136	69	67	136	69	68
5-9	132	67	66	134	67	67
10-14	128	64	64	131	66	65
15-19	122	61	61	127	64	63
20-24	114	57	57	120	60	60
25-29	102	51	51	109	55	55
30-34	85	43	42	93	47	46
35-39	65	33	32	76	38	38
40-44	49	25	24	59	30	29
45-49	37	19	18	44	22	22
50-54	28	14	13	34	17	17
55-59	21	11	10	26	13	12
60-64	16	8	7	19	10	9
65-69	12	6	6	14	7	7
70-74	9	5	5	10	5	5
75-79	7	3	4	7	3	4
80-84	4	2	2	4	2	2
85-89	2	1	1	2	1	1
90-94	1	0	0	1	0	0
95-99	0	0	0	0	0	0
100 +	0	0	0	0	0	0

POPULATION BY AGE AND SEX (in thousands)

Age group	2005 Both sexes	2005 Males	2005 Females	2010 Both sexes	2010 Males	2010 Females	2015 Both sexes	2015 Males	2015 Females	2020 Both sexes	2020 Males	2020 Females
All ages	504	249	254	563	280	283	631	315	316	708	355	353
0-4	88	45	44	101	51	50	116	58	57	129	65	64
5-9	73	36	36	83	41	41	94	47	47	110	55	55
10-14	62	31	31	71	35	35	80	40	40	92	46	46
15-19	54	27	27	61	31	31	69	35	35	79	39	39
20-24	44	22	22	52	26	26	59	30	30	67	34	34
25-29	35	17	18	40	20	20	47	24	24	54	27	27
30-34	28	14	14	30	15	15	35	18	17	40	21	20
35-39	24	12	12	24	12	12	25	13	12	29	15	13
40-44	20	10	10	21	10	10	21	11	10	21	11	10
45-49	17	8	9	18	9	9	18	9	9	18	9	8
50-54	16	8	8	16	8	8	16	8	8	16	8	8
55-59	12	6	6	14	7	8	14	7	7	14	7	7
60-64	10	5	6	11	5	6	13	6	7	13	6	7
65-69	8	4	4	9	4	5	9	4	5	11	5	6
70-74	6	3	3	6	3	3	7	3	4	7	3	4
75-79	4	2	2	4	2	2	4	2	2	5	2	3
80-84	2	1	1	2	1	1	2	1	1	2	1	1
85-89	1	0	0	1	0	0	1	0	0	1	0	1
90-94	0	0	0	0	0	0	0	0	0	0	0	0
95-99	0	0	0	0	0	0	0	0	0	0	0	0
100 +	0	0	0	0	0	0	0	0	0	0	0	0

Age group	2025 Both sexes	2025 Males	2025 Females	2030 Both sexes	2030 Males	2030 Females	2035 Both sexes	2035 Males	2035 Females	2040 Both sexes	2040 Males	2040 Females
All ages	790	398	392	879	444	436	976	492	483	1 079	544	535
0-4	136	69	68	144	73	71	152	77	75	162	82	80
5-9	124	62	61	132	66	66	140	70	70	149	75	74
10-14	107	54	53	121	61	60	130	65	65	138	70	69
15-19	90	45	45	105	53	53	120	60	60	129	65	64
20-24	77	38	38	88	44	44	103	52	52	118	59	59
25-29	62	31	31	71	36	36	83	41	41	98	49	49
30-34	47	24	23	54	28	27	63	32	31	74	37	37
35-39	34	18	16	39	21	19	47	24	23	55	28	27
40-44	24	13	11	28	15	13	34	18	16	41	21	20
45-49	18	10	8	21	11	9	25	13	12	30	16	14
50-54	16	8	8	16	9	8	19	10	9	23	12	11
55-59	14	7	7	14	7	7	15	8	7	17	9	8
60-64	13	6	7	13	6	7	13	6	6	13	7	6
65-69	11	5	6	11	5	6	11	5	6	11	6	6
70-74	9	4	5	9	4	5	9	4	5	9	4	5
75-79	5	2	3	6	3	4	7	3	4	7	3	4
80-84	3	1	2	3	1	2	4	2	2	4	2	2
85-89	1	0	1	1	1	1	1	1	1	2	1	1
90-94	0	0	0	0	0	0	0	0	0	0	0	0
95-99	0	0	0	0	0	0	0	0	0	0	0	0
100 +	0	0	0	0	0	0	0	0	0	0	0	0

Age group	2045 Both sexes	2045 Males	2045 Females	2050 Both sexes	2050 Males	2050 Females
All ages	1 190	599	591	1 305	656	649
0-4	170	86	84	177	89	88
5-9	159	80	79	168	85	83
10-14	148	74	73	158	79	78
15-19	137	69	68	147	74	73
20-24	126	63	63	135	68	67
25-29	112	56	56	121	60	60
30-34	88	44	44	102	51	51
35-39	65	33	32	79	40	39
40-44	49	25	24	59	30	29
45-49	37	19	18	44	22	22
50-54	28	14	13	34	17	17
55-59	21	11	10	26	13	12
60-64	16	8	7	19	10	9
65-69	12	6	6	14	7	7
70-74	9	5	5	10	5	5
75-79	7	3	4	7	3	4
80-84	4	2	2	4	2	2
85-89	2	1	1	2	1	1
90-94	1	0	0	1	0	0
95-99	0	0	0	0	0	0
100 +	0	0	0	0	0	0

United Nations Department of Economic and Social Affairs/Population Division
World Population Prospects: The 2004 Revision, Volume II: Sex and Age Distribution of the World Population

376

POPULATION BY AGE AND SEX (in thousands)

Age group	2005 Both sexes	Males	Females	2010 Both sexes	Males	Females	2015 Both sexes	Males	Females	2020 Both sexes	Males	Females
All ages	504	249	254	559	278	281	615	307	308	670	336	334
0-4	88	45	44	96	49	48	103	52	51	106	54	53
5-9	73	36	36	83	41	41	90	45	45	98	49	49
10-14	62	31	31	71	35	35	80	40	40	88	44	44
15-19	54	27	27	61	31	31	69	35	35	79	39	39
20-24	44	22	22	52	26	26	59	30	30	67	34	34
25-29	35	17	18	40	20	20	47	24	24	54	27	27
30-34	28	14	14	30	15	15	35	18	17	40	21	20
35-39	24	12	12	24	12	12	25	13	12	29	15	13
40-44	20	10	10	21	10	10	21	11	10	21	11	10
45-49	17	8	9	18	9	9	18	9	9	18	9	8
50-54	16	8	8	16	8	8	16	8	8	16	8	8
55-59	12	6	6	14	7	8	14	7	7	14	7	7
60-64	10	5	6	11	5	6	13	6	7	13	6	7
65-69	8	4	4	9	4	5	9	4	5	11	5	6
70-74	6	3	3	6	3	3	7	3	4	7	3	4
75-79	4	2	2	4	2	2	4	2	2	5	2	3
80-84	2	1	1	2	1	1	2	1	1	2	1	1
85-89	1	0	0	1	0	0	1	0	0	1	0	1
90-94	0	0	0	0	0	0	0	0	0	0	0	0
95-99	0	0	0	0	0	0	0	0	0	0	0	0
100 +	0	0	0	0	0	0	0	0	0	0	0	0

Age group	2025 Both sexes	Males	Females	2030 Both sexes	Males	Females	2035 Both sexes	Males	Females	2040 Both sexes	Males	Females
All ages	727	366	361	784	396	388	840	424	416	892	450	442
0-4	110	55	54	111	56	55	110	55	54	107	54	53
5-9	102	51	51	106	53	53	108	54	54	107	54	53
10-14	96	48	48	100	50	50	104	53	52	107	54	53
15-19	86	43	43	94	47	47	99	50	49	104	52	52
20-24	77	38	38	84	42	42	92	46	46	97	49	48
25-29	62	31	31	71	36	36	79	40	40	87	44	44
30-34	47	24	23	54	28	27	63	32	31	71	36	35
35-39	34	18	16	39	21	19	47	24	23	55	28	27
40-44	24	13	11	28	15	13	34	18	16	41	21	20
45-49	18	10	8	21	11	9	25	13	12	30	16	14
50-54	16	8	8	16	9	8	19	10	9	23	12	11
55-59	14	7	7	14	7	7	15	8	7	17	9	8
60-64	13	6	7	13	6	7	13	6	6	13	7	6
65-69	11	5	6	11	5	6	11	5	6	11	6	6
70-74	9	4	5	9	4	5	9	4	5	9	4	5
75-79	5	2	3	6	3	4	7	3	4	7	3	4
80-84	3	1	2	3	1	2	4	2	2	4	2	2
85-89	1	0	1	1	1	1	1	1	1	2	1	1
90-94	0	0	0	0	0	0	0	0	0	0	0	0
95-99	0	0	0	0	0	0	0	0	0	0	0	0
100 +	0	0	0	0	0	0	0	0	0	0	0	0

Age group	2045 Both sexes	Males	Females	2050 Both sexes	Males	Females
All ages	940	474	466	984	495	489
0-4	103	52	51	100	50	49
5-9	105	53	52	102	51	51
10-14	106	53	53	104	52	52
15-19	106	53	53	106	53	53
20-24	102	51	51	104	52	52
25-29	92	46	46	97	49	49
30-34	79	40	39	84	42	42
35-39	63	32	31	71	36	35
40-44	49	25	24	56	28	28
45-49	37	19	18	44	22	22
50-54	28	14	13	34	17	17
55-59	21	11	10	26	13	12
60-64	16	8	7	19	10	9
65-69	12	6	6	14	7	7
70-74	9	5	5	10	5	5
75-79	7	3	4	7	3	4
80-84	4	2	2	4	2	2
85-89	2	1	1	2	1	1
90-94	1	0	0	1	0	0
95-99	0	0	0	0	0	0
100 +	0	0	0	0	0	0

POPULATION BY AGE AND SEX (in thousands)

Age group	1950 Both sexes	Males	Females	1955 Both sexes	Males	Females	1960 Both sexes	Males	Females	1965 Both sexes	Males	Females
All ages	1 140	565	575	1 262	625	637	1 419	703	717	1 608	796	812
0-4	213	109	105	222	111	111	258	129	129	293	146	147
5-9	165	83	81	185	94	91	195	97	98	230	114	115
10-14	138	70	69	156	79	77	177	90	87	187	93	94
15-19	118	59	58	134	67	66	151	77	75	171	87	84
20-24	99	50	50	113	57	56	128	65	64	146	74	72
25-29	83	41	42	94	47	47	108	54	54	123	62	61
30-34	68	33	35	78	39	40	90	45	45	103	51	51
35-39	56	27	29	64	31	33	74	36	37	85	42	43
40-44	46	22	24	52	25	27	60	29	31	69	34	35
45-49	37	18	20	42	20	22	48	23	25	56	27	29
50-54	32	15	17	34	16	18	38	18	20	44	21	23
55-59	27	12	14	28	13	15	30	14	16	34	16	18
60-64	22	10	12	22	10	12	24	11	13	26	12	14
65-69	17	7	9	17	7	10	18	8	10	19	8	11
70-74	11	5	6	11	5	6	12	5	7	13	5	7
75-79	6	3	4	6	3	4	7	3	4	7	3	4
80 +	3	1	2	3	1	2	3	1	2	4	1	2

Age group	1970 Both sexes	Males	Females	1975 Both sexes	Males	Females	1980 Both sexes	Males	Females	1985 Both sexes	Males	Females
All ages	1 831	907	924	2 089	1 035	1 054	2 382	1 156	1 226	2 682	1 301	1 381
0-4	333	167	166	374	187	187	450	226	225	489	245	244
5-9	264	131	132	303	151	152	361	181	181	425	212	213
10-14	221	110	111	254	127	128	266	133	134	354	176	177
15-19	182	90	92	215	107	108	203	99	105	260	129	130
20-24	165	84	82	176	87	89	181	81	100	195	95	100
25-29	140	70	70	159	80	79	163	72	91	172	77	95
30-34	117	59	59	134	67	67	152	71	81	154	68	86
35-39	97	49	49	112	56	56	133	64	69	142	66	76
40-44	80	40	40	92	46	47	106	53	53	123	59	64
45-49	65	32	33	75	37	38	87	43	44	96	47	49
50-54	51	25	27	60	29	31	77	38	39	76	37	39
55-59	40	19	21	46	22	25	62	30	32	64	31	34
60-64	30	14	16	35	16	19	48	23	25	48	23	26
65-69	21	9	12	24	11	13	36	17	19	34	15	19
70-74	14	6	8	16	7	9	26	12	14	23	10	13
75-79	8	3	5	9	4	5	18	8	9	14	6	8
80 +	4	2	3	5	2	3	13	6	7	12	5	7

Age group	1990 Both sexes	Males	Females	1995 Both sexes	Males	Females	2000 Both sexes	Males	Females	2005 Both sexes	Males	Females
All ages	3 038	1 476	1 562	3 097	1 509	1 588	3 557	1 738	1 818	4 401	2 161	2 241
0-4	536	269	267	546	275	271	621	313	307	759	384	375
5-9	465	232	233	458	229	229	528	265	263	650	327	322
10-14	417	208	209	408	203	205	453	226	227	561	281	280
15-19	346	172	174	366	182	184	402	200	203	482	240	242
20-24	251	125	126	300	149	151	357	177	180	425	211	214
25-29	187	91	96	214	107	108	287	143	145	371	184	187
30-34	164	74	90	158	77	81	203	101	102	292	145	146
35-39	145	64	81	139	62	77	149	72	77	205	101	103
40-44	132	61	71	121	53	68	130	57	72	150	72	78
45-49	112	53	59	109	50	59	112	48	64	130	57	73
50-54	85	41	44	90	41	49	99	44	55	111	47	64
55-59	65	30	34	65	30	35	79	35	44	94	41	54
60-64	51	24	28	47	21	26	55	24	30	72	31	41
65-69	35	15	20	34	15	20	36	15	21	47	20	27
70-74	22	9	13	21	8	13	24	10	15	28	11	17
75-79	13	5	8	12	4	7	13	5	8	16	6	11
80 +	10	4	6	9	3	6	9	3	6	11	3	8

United Nations Department of Economic and Social Affairs/Population Division
World Population Prospects: The 2004 Revision, Volume II: Sex and Age Distribution of the World Population
378

POPULATION BY AGE AND SEX (in thousands)

Age group	2005 Both sexes	Males	Females	2010 Both sexes	Males	Females	2015 Both sexes	Males	Females	2020 Both sexes	Males	Females
All ages	4 401	2 161	2 241	5 128	2 528	2 600	5 840	2 890	2 951	6 584	3 268	3 316
0-4	759	384	375	848	429	419	907	459	448	950	481	469
5-9	650	327	322	754	381	373	833	421	412	895	453	442
10-14	561	281	280	652	328	324	747	377	370	827	418	409
15-19	482	240	242	564	282	282	647	325	322	742	374	368
20-24	425	211	214	481	240	242	557	278	278	640	321	318
25-29	371	184	187	420	208	211	469	234	236	545	273	272
30-34	292	145	146	361	180	181	404	201	203	454	226	227
35-39	205	101	103	280	140	140	345	172	173	387	193	194
40-44	150	72	78	195	97	99	266	133	134	329	164	165
45-49	130	57	73	142	68	75	184	91	94	252	125	127
50-54	111	47	64	121	52	69	132	62	70	172	84	89
55-59	94	41	54	101	41	59	110	46	64	121	56	65
60-64	72	31	41	83	34	48	88	35	53	97	39	58
65-69	47	20	27	59	24	35	68	27	41	73	27	46
70-74	28	11	17	35	13	21	44	17	28	51	19	33
75-79	16	6	11	19	6	12	23	8	15	30	10	20
80-84	7	2	5	9	3	6	10	3	7	13	4	9
85-89	3	1	2	3	1	2	4	1	3	5	1	3
90-94	1	0	1	1	0	1	1	0	1	1	0	1
95-99	0	0	0	0	0	0	0	0	0	0	0	0
100 +	0	0	0	0	0	0	0	0	0	0	0	0

Age group	2025 Both sexes	Males	Females	2030 Both sexes	Males	Females	2035 Both sexes	Males	Females	2040 Both sexes	Males	Females
All ages	7 352	3 659	3 693	8 138	4 058	4 080	8 933	4 461	4 472	9 722	4 859	4 863
0-4	987	500	486	1 021	518	503	1 050	532	517	1 067	541	526
5-9	940	476	464	978	495	482	1 013	514	500	1 043	529	514
10-14	889	450	439	935	473	462	974	493	481	1 010	512	498
15-19	822	415	407	885	447	438	931	471	460	970	491	479
20-24	734	370	365	815	411	404	878	443	435	925	468	458
25-29	628	315	312	722	363	359	803	405	398	867	438	429
30-34	529	265	264	611	307	303	704	355	349	785	397	388
35-39	436	218	218	511	257	254	591	298	293	684	346	338
40-44	371	185	186	420	210	210	493	248	245	573	289	284
45-49	313	155	158	355	176	179	403	201	202	475	238	237
50-54	237	116	121	296	146	151	337	166	171	385	190	195
55-59	160	78	82	220	106	114	276	134	143	316	153	163
60-64	107	48	59	142	66	76	199	93	105	251	118	133
65-69	81	31	50	91	39	52	122	54	68	172	77	94
70-74	57	20	37	64	23	41	72	29	44	98	41	57
75-79	36	12	24	40	13	28	46	15	31	53	19	34
80-84	18	5	13	22	6	16	25	7	18	30	9	21
85-89	6	2	5	8	2	6	11	3	8	13	3	10
90-94	2	0	1	2	0	2	3	1	2	4	1	3
95-99	0	0	0	0	0	0	1	0	0	1	0	1
100 +	0	0	0	0	0	0	0	0	0	0	0	0

Age group	2045 Both sexes	Males	Females	2050 Both sexes	Males	Females
All ages	10 491	5 245	5 246	11 229	5 613	5 616
0-4	1 073	545	529	1 072	544	528
5-9	1 062	539	523	1 069	542	527
10-14	1 041	527	513	1 059	537	522
15-19	1 007	510	497	1 038	526	512
20-24	965	488	477	1 003	507	495
25-29	915	462	453	956	483	472
30-34	850	430	420	899	455	444
35-39	765	387	378	831	421	410
40-44	665	336	329	746	378	368
45-49	554	279	275	646	326	320
50-54	456	227	229	534	267	267
55-59	363	177	186	432	212	220
60-64	289	137	152	334	159	175
65-69	219	99	120	254	115	138
70-74	140	59	81	180	77	103
75-79	73	28	45	105	41	64
80-84	34	11	23	47	16	31
85-89	15	4	12	18	5	13
90-94	5	1	4	6	1	5
95-99	1	0	1	1	0	1
100 +	0	0	0	0	0	0

United Nations Department of Economic and Social Affairs/Population Division
World Population Prospects: The 2004 Revision, Volume II: Sex and Age Distribution of the World Population

379

POPULATION BY AGE AND SEX (in thousands)

Age group	2005 Both sexes	Males	Females	2010 Both sexes	Males	Females	2015 Both sexes	Males	Females	2020 Both sexes	Males	Females
All ages	4 401	2 161	2 241	5 160	2 544	2 616	5 938	2 939	2 999	6 780	3 367	3 412
0-4	759	384	375	880	445	435	973	493	480	1 050	532	518
5-9	650	327	322	754	381	373	865	437	428	959	485	474
10-14	561	281	280	652	328	324	747	377	370	858	433	425
15-19	482	240	242	564	282	282	647	325	322	742	374	368
20-24	425	211	214	481	240	242	557	278	278	640	321	318
25-29	371	184	187	420	208	211	469	234	236	545	273	272
30-34	292	145	146	361	180	181	404	201	203	454	226	227
35-39	205	101	103	280	140	140	345	172	173	387	193	194
40-44	150	72	78	195	97	99	266	133	134	329	164	165
45-49	130	57	73	142	68	75	184	91	94	252	125	127
50-54	111	47	64	121	52	69	132	62	70	172	84	89
55-59	94	41	54	101	41	59	110	46	64	121	56	65
60-64	72	31	41	83	34	48	88	35	53	97	39	58
65-69	47	20	27	59	24	35	68	27	41	73	27	46
70-74	28	11	17	35	13	21	44	17	28	51	19	33
75-79	16	6	11	19	6	12	23	8	15	30	10	20
80-84	7	2	5	9	3	6	10	3	7	13	4	9
85-89	3	1	2	3	1	2	4	1	3	5	1	3
90-94	1	0	1	1	0	1	1	0	1	1	0	1
95-99	0	0	0	0	0	0	0	0	0	0	0	0
100 +	0	0	0	0	0	0	0	0	0	0	0	0

Age group	2025 Both sexes	Males	Females	2030 Both sexes	Males	Females	2035 Both sexes	Males	Females	2040 Both sexes	Males	Females
All ages	7 668	3 819	3 849	8 609	4 297	4 312	9 604	4 801	4 803	10 647	5 328	5 319
0-4	1 109	562	547	1 177	597	580	1 253	636	617	1 325	672	652
5-9	1 038	526	512	1 099	557	542	1 168	592	576	1 245	632	614
10-14	953	482	471	1 033	523	510	1 095	554	540	1 165	590	575
15-19	853	431	423	949	479	469	1 029	520	509	1 091	552	539
20-24	734	370	365	846	427	419	942	475	466	1 023	517	506
25-29	628	315	312	722	363	359	833	420	413	930	469	460
30-34	529	265	264	611	307	303	704	355	349	815	412	403
35-39	436	218	218	511	257	254	591	298	293	684	346	338
40-44	371	185	186	420	210	210	493	248	245	573	289	284
45-49	313	155	158	355	176	179	403	201	202	475	238	237
50-54	237	116	121	296	146	151	337	166	171	385	190	195
55-59	159	76	83	220	106	114	276	134	143	316	153	163
60-64	107	48	59	142	66	76	199	93	105	251	118	133
65-69	81	31	50	91	39	52	122	54	68	172	77	94
70-74	57	20	37	64	23	41	72	29	44	98	41	57
75-79	36	12	24	40	13	28	46	15	31	53	19	34
80-84	18	5	13	22	6	16	25	7	18	30	8	21
85-89	6	2	5	8	2	6	11	3	8	13	3	10
90-94	2	0	1	2	0	2	3	1	2	4	1	3
95-99	0	0	0	0	0	0	1	0	0	1	0	1
100 +	0	0	0	0	0	0	0	0	0	0	0	0

Age group	2045 Both sexes	Males	Females	2050 Both sexes	Males	Females
All ages	11 722	5 869	5 853	12 816	6 418	6 398
0-4	1 385	703	682	1 436	729	707
5-9	1 318	669	649	1 380	700	680
10-14	1 242	630	612	1 315	667	648
15-19	1 161	588	573	1 239	628	611
20-24	1 085	549	536	1 156	585	571
25-29	1 011	511	500	1 075	543	531
30-34	911	461	450	994	503	491
35-39	794	402	392	891	452	440
40-44	665	336	329	775	392	382
45-49	554	279	275	646	326	320
50-54	456	227	229	534	267	267
55-59	363	177	186	432	212	220
60-64	289	137	152	334	159	175
65-69	219	99	120	254	115	138
70-74	140	59	81	180	77	103
75-79	73	28	45	105	41	64
80-84	34	11	23	47	16	31
85-89	15	4	12	18	5	13
90-94	5	1	4	6	1	5
95-99	1	0	1	1	0	1
100 +	0	0	0	0	0	0

United Nations Department of Economic and Social Affairs/Population Division
World Population Prospects: The 2004 Revision, Volume II: Sex and Age Distribution of the World Population

380

POPULATION BY AGE AND SEX (in thousands)

Age group	2005 Both sexes	Males	Females	2010 Both sexes	Males	Females	2015 Both sexes	Males	Females	2020 Both sexes	Males	Females
All ages	4 401	2 161	2 241	5 095	2 511	2 583	5 740	2 839	2 901	6 381	3 165	3 216
0-4	759	384	375	815	412	403	840	425	414	846	429	418
5-9	650	327	322	754	381	373	801	405	396	828	419	409
10-14	561	281	280	652	328	324	747	377	370	794	401	393
15-19	482	240	242	564	282	282	647	325	322	742	374	368
20-24	425	211	214	481	240	242	557	278	278	640	321	318
25-29	371	184	187	420	208	211	469	234	236	545	273	272
30-34	292	145	146	361	180	181	404	201	203	454	226	227
35-39	205	101	103	280	140	140	345	172	173	387	193	194
40-44	150	72	78	195	97	99	266	133	134	329	164	165
45-49	130	57	73	142	68	75	184	91	94	252	125	127
50-54	111	47	64	121	52	69	132	62	70	172	84	89
55-59	94	41	54	101	41	59	110	46	64	121	56	65
60-64	72	31	41	83	34	48	88	35	53	97	39	58
65-69	47	20	27	59	24	35	68	27	41	73	27	46
70-74	28	11	17	35	13	21	44	17	28	51	19	33
75-79	16	6	11	19	6	12	23	8	15	30	10	20
80-84	7	2	5	9	3	6	10	3	7	13	4	9
85-89	3	1	2	3	1	2	4	1	3	5	1	3
90-94	1	0	1	1	0	1	1	0	1	1	0	1
95-99	0	0	0	0	0	0	0	0	0	0	0	0
100 +	0	0	0	0	0	0	0	0	0	0	0	0

Age group	2025 Both sexes	Males	Females	2030 Both sexes	Males	Females	2035 Both sexes	Males	Females	2040 Both sexes	Males	Females
All ages	7 024	3 493	3 531	7 654	3 813	3 841	8 252	4 116	4 136	8 798	4 391	4 407
0-4	860	436	424	863	437	425	849	431	418	821	417	404
5-9	837	424	413	852	432	420	856	434	422	844	428	416
10-14	822	416	407	833	421	411	849	430	419	853	432	421
15-19	790	399	391	819	414	405	829	419	410	846	428	418
20-24	734	370	365	783	395	388	813	410	402	824	416	408
25-29	628	315	312	722	363	359	771	389	382	802	405	397
30-34	529	265	264	611	307	303	704	355	349	754	381	373
35-39	436	218	218	511	257	254	501	208	293	684	346	338
40-44	371	185	186	420	210	210	493	248	245	573	289	284
45-49	313	155	158	355	176	179	403	201	202	475	238	237
50-54	237	116	121	296	146	151	337	166	171	385	190	195
55-59	159	76	83	220	106	114	276	134	143	316	153	163
60-64	107	48	59	142	66	76	199	93	105	251	118	133
65-69	81	31	50	91	39	52	122	54	68	172	77	94
70-74	57	20	37	64	23	41	72	29	44	98	41	57
75-79	36	12	24	40	13	20	46	15	31	53	19	34
80-84	18	5	13	22	6	16	25	7	18	30	8	21
85-89	6	2	5	8	2	6	11	3	8	13	3	10
90-94	2	0	1	2	0	2	3	1	2	4	1	3
95-99	0	0	0	0	0	0	1	0	0	1	0	1
100 +	0	0	0	0	0	0	0	0	0	0	0	0

Age group	2045 Both sexes	Males	Females	2050 Both sexes	Males	Females
All ages	9 285	4 634	4 651	9 704	4 840	4 864
0-4	785	398	387	746	379	367
5-9	817	414	402	782	397	385
10-14	842	427	415	815	413	402
15-19	851	431	420	839	425	414
20-24	841	426	416	847	429	418
25-29	815	412	403	833	421	412
30-34	786	398	389	801	405	396
35-39	735	372	363	769	390	379
40-44	665	336	329	717	363	354
45-49	554	279	275	646	326	320
50-54	456	227	229	534	267	267
55-59	363	177	186	432	212	220
60-64	289	137	152	334	159	175
65-69	219	99	120	254	115	138
70-74	140	59	81	180	77	103
75-79	73	28	45	105	41	64
80-84	34	11	23	47	16	31
85-89	15	4	12	18	5	13
90-94	5	1	4	6	1	5
95-99	1	0	1	1	0	1
100 +	0	0	0	0	0	0

POPULATION BY AGE AND SEX (in thousands)

Age group	1950 Both sexes	Males	Females	1955 Both sexes	Males	Females	1960 Both sexes	Males	Females	1965 Both sexes	Males	Females
All ages	1 101	470	631	1 160	504	656	1 216	534	682	1 291	574	717
0-4	92	49	43	91	46	45	97	50	47	98	50	48
5-9	87	45	43	94	50	44	95	49	46	99	50	49
10-14	102	51	51	90	46	44	84	42	41	98	50	48
15-19	97	48	49	104	52	52	87	44	43	92	48	45
20-24	97	45	52	99	48	50	100	50	50	92	46	46
25-29	76	31	45	99	46	53	105	50	55	106	52	53
30-34	56	24	32	78	32	46	100	43	57	105	50	55
35-39	75	31	44	57	24	33	77	30	47	102	45	57
40-44	73	29	44	76	31	45	63	26	37	79	31	48
45-49	70	27	43	74	29	45	79	32	47	61	25	36
50-54	60	21	38	70	27	43	75	30	44	78	31	47
55-59	52	18	34	58	20	38	70	27	43	73	28	45
60-64	46	16	31	49	16	33	56	20	36	66	24	42
65-69	40	13	27	42	14	28	47	16	32	51	17	35
70-74	33	10	22	34	10	23	33	10	23	40	12	28
75-79	24	7	17	24	7	17	28	8	20	26	7	19
80 +	20	5	15	21	5	16	19	5	14	24	6	18

Age group	1970 Both sexes	Males	Females	1975 Both sexes	Males	Females	1980 Both sexes	Males	Females	1985 Both sexes	Males	Females
All ages	1 365	624	741	1 432	661	771	1 473	681	792	1 525	710	815
0-4	97	49	47	111	57	54	110	56	54	117	60	58
5-9	103	53	50	99	50	49	110	56	54	113	58	56
10-14	102	52	50	102	53	50	99	50	49	106	54	52
15-19	101	53	48	107	55	51	103	53	50	110	58	52
20-24	101	53	48	113	59	54	117	61	56	108	56	52
25-29	96	49	47	105	54	51	116	59	57	118	60	59
30-34	112	55	56	97	48	48	104	51	52	112	55	57
35-39	105	51	54	111	55	56	95	46	48	109	54	56
40-44	105	48	57	103	50	54	109	52	56	98	47	51
45-49	81	32	49	102	46	56	100	47	53	99	47	52
50-54	58	24	34	80	31	49	98	43	55	97	44	54
55-59	75	30	46	56	22	34	76	28	47	85	36	49
60-64	69	26	43	71	27	44	52	20	32	73	28	44
65-69	60	21	39	62	22	40	63	22	41	60	21	39
70-74	44	13	31	51	16	34	52	17	35	45	15	30
75-79	29	8	21	33	9	24	37	11	27	39	11	28
80 +	26	6	20	29	7	22	31	7	24	36	8	27

Age group	1990 Both sexes	Males	Females	1995 Both sexes	Males	Females	2000 Both sexes	Males	Females	2005 Both sexes	Males	Females
All ages	1 584	741	843	1 447	670	777	1 367	630	737	1 330	611	718
0-4	124	63	61	80	41	39	61	31	29	64	33	31
5-9	117	60	57	111	57	54	78	40	38	60	31	29
10-14	113	58	56	107	54	52	108	55	52	77	40	38
15-19	113	59	53	99	50	48	104	53	51	107	55	52
20-24	102	52	50	99	50	49	94	48	46	103	52	50
25-29	120	60	60	92	46	46	95	47	47	93	47	46
30-34	125	62	63	102	50	52	89	44	45	93	46	47
35-39	116	57	59	107	52	55	96	47	50	86	42	44
40-44	92	44	48	103	49	53	99	47	52	93	44	49
45-49	96	46	50	93	43	49	95	44	51	95	45	51
50-54	99	46	53	82	38	44	86	39	47	90	41	49
55-59	98	44	53	92	41	51	73	32	41	80	35	45
60-64	90	36	54	82	35	47	83	35	48	67	28	39
65-69	58	19	38	76	28	47	69	27	42	72	28	44
70-74	40	13	27	52	16	37	61	21	40	58	21	37
75-79	41	12	29	29	8	20	40	11	29	47	15	33
80 +	40	10	31	42	10	32	36	8	28	42	9	33

United Nations Department of Economic and Social Affairs/Population Division
World Population Prospects: The 2004 Revision, Volume II: Sex and Age Distribution of the World Population

382

POPULATION BY AGE AND SEX (in thousands)

Age group	2005 Both sexes	Males	Females	2010 Both sexes	Males	Females	2015 Both sexes	Males	Females	2020 Both sexes	Males	Females
All ages	1 330	611	718	1 309	602	707	1 292	595	697	1 272	588	684
0-4	64	33	31	68	35	33	70	36	34	67	34	32
5-9	60	31	29	64	33	31	68	35	33	70	36	34
10-14	77	40	38	60	31	29	64	33	31	68	35	33
15-19	107	55	52	77	40	38	60	31	29	64	33	31
20-24	103	52	50	106	54	52	77	39	38	60	31	29
25-29	93	47	46	102	52	50	106	54	52	77	39	37
30-34	93	46	47	92	47	46	102	51	50	105	54	52
35-39	86	42	44	92	46	47	92	46	46	101	51	50
40-44	93	44	49	85	41	44	91	45	46	90	45	45
45-49	95	45	51	91	43	48	83	40	44	89	43	46
50-54	90	41	49	92	42	50	88	40	47	81	38	43
55-59	80	35	45	86	37	48	87	39	49	84	38	46
60-64	67	28	39	74	31	43	80	33	46	82	35	47
65-69	72	28	44	60	23	37	67	26	41	72	29	44
70-74	58	21	37	62	22	40	51	18	33	58	21	37
75-79	47	15	33	45	14	31	49	15	34	41	13	28
80-84	27	6	21	32	8	24	31	8	23	35	9	26
85-89	9	2	7	15	3	12	18	4	15	18	4	14
90-94	5	1	4	4	1	3	6	1	5	8	1	7
95-99	1	0	1	1	0	1	1	0	1	2	0	2
100 +	0	0	0	0	0	0	0	0	0	0	0	0

Age group	2025 Both sexes	Males	Females	2030 Both sexes	Males	Females	2035 Both sexes	Males	Females	2040 Both sexes	Males	Females
All ages	1 248	579	669	1 221	568	652	1 194	558	635	1 170	550	620
0-4	61	31	30	57	29	28	57	29	28	60	31	29
5-9	67	34	32	61	31	30	57	29	28	57	29	28
10-14	70	36	34	67	34	32	61	31	30	57	29	28
15-19	68	35	33	70	36	34	67	34	32	61	31	30
20-24	64	33	31	68	35	33	70	36	34	66	34	32
25-29	60	31	29	64	33	31	68	35	33	69	35	34
30-34	76	39	37	59	30	29	64	32	31	68	34	33
35-39	105	53	52	76	39	37	59	30	29	63	32	31
40-44	100	50	50	104	52	51	75	38	37	59	30	29
45-49	89	44	45	98	49	49	103	52	51	75	38	37
50-54	87	42	45	87	43	44	96	48	49	100	50	50
55-59	78	35	42	84	39	44	84	40	44	93	45	48
60-64	79	34	45	73	32	41	79	36	43	80	37	42
65-69	75	30	45	72	30	42	67	29	39	73	32	41
70-74	63	23	40	65	25	41	64	25	39	60	24	36
75-79	47	15	32	52	17	35	54	18	36	53	19	34
80-84	30	8	22	34	9	25	38	11	27	40	12	28
85-89	21	4	16	18	4	14	21	4	16	23	5	18
90-94	8	1	7	9	1	8	8	1	7	10	1	9
95-99	2	0	2	2	0	2	3	0	3	3	0	3
100 +	0	0	0	0	0	0	0	0	0	1	0	1

Age group	2045 Both sexes	Males	Females	2050 Both sexes	Males	Females
All ages	1 145	541	604	1 119	531	588
0-4	60	31	29	57	30	28
5-9	60	31	29	60	31	29
10-14	57	29	28	60	31	29
15-19	57	29	28	57	29	28
20-24	61	31	30	56	29	27
25-29	66	34	32	60	31	29
30-34	69	35	34	66	34	32
35-39	67	34	33	69	35	34
40-44	63	32	31	67	34	33
45-49	58	30	29	62	32	31
50-54	73	37	36	57	29	28
55-59	98	48	50	71	35	36
60-64	89	42	47	93	45	48
65-69	74	33	40	83	38	45
70-74	65	27	38	66	28	38
75-79	50	18	32	55	21	34
80-84	39	12	27	37	12	25
85-89	25	6	19	25	6	19
90-94	11	2	10	12	2	10
95-99	3	0	3	4	0	4
100 +	1	0	1	1	0	1

POPULATION BY AGE AND SEX (in thousands)

Age group	2005 Both sexes	Males	Females	2010 Both sexes	Males	Females	2015 Both sexes	Males	Females	2020 Both sexes	Males	Females
All ages	1 330	611	718	1 321	608	713	1 322	611	711	1 323	614	709
0-4	64	33	31	80	41	39	88	45	43	87	45	42
5-9	60	31	29	64	33	31	80	41	39	88	45	43
10-14	77	40	38	60	31	29	64	33	31	80	41	39
15-19	107	55	52	77	40	38	60	31	29	64	33	31
20-24	103	52	50	106	54	52	77	39	38	60	31	29
25-29	93	47	46	102	52	50	106	54	52	77	39	37
30-34	93	46	47	92	47	46	102	51	50	105	54	52
35-39	86	42	44	92	46	47	92	46	46	101	51	50
40-44	93	44	49	85	41	44	91	45	46	90	45	45
45-49	95	45	51	91	43	48	83	40	44	89	43	46
50-54	90	41	49	92	42	50	88	40	47	81	38	43
55-59	80	35	45	86	37	48	87	39	49	84	38	46
60-64	67	28	39	74	31	43	80	33	46	82	35	47
65-69	72	28	44	60	23	37	67	26	41	72	29	44
70-74	58	21	37	62	22	40	51	18	33	58	21	37
75-79	47	15	33	45	14	31	49	15	34	41	13	28
80-84	27	6	21	32	8	24	31	8	23	35	9	26
85-89	9	2	7	15	3	12	18	4	15	18	4	14
90-94	5	1	4	4	1	3	6	1	5	8	1	7
95-99	1	0	1	1	0	1	1	0	1	2	0	2
100 +	0	0	0	0	0	0	0	0	0	0	0	0

Age group	2025 Both sexes	Males	Females	2030 Both sexes	Males	Females	2035 Both sexes	Males	Females	2040 Both sexes	Males	Females
All ages	1 316	614	702	1 306	613	694	1 303	615	689	1 310	622	688
0-4	78	40	38	75	38	36	81	41	39	91	46	44
5-9	87	45	42	78	40	38	75	38	36	81	41	39
10-14	88	45	43	87	45	42	78	40	38	75	38	36
15-19	80	41	39	88	45	43	87	44	42	78	40	38
20-24	64	33	31	80	41	39	88	45	43	87	44	42
25-29	60	31	29	64	33	31	80	41	39	88	45	43
30-34	76	39	37	59	30	29	64	32	31	79	41	39
35-39	105	53	52	76	39	37	59	30	29	63	32	31
40-44	100	50	50	104	52	51	75	38	37	59	30	29
45-49	89	44	45	98	49	49	103	52	51	75	38	37
50-54	87	42	45	87	43	44	96	48	49	100	50	50
55-59	78	35	42	84	39	44	84	40	44	93	45	48
60-64	79	34	45	73	32	41	79	36	43	80	37	42
65-69	75	30	45	72	30	42	67	29	39	73	32	41
70-74	63	23	40	65	25	41	64	25	39	60	24	36
75-79	47	15	32	52	17	35	54	18	36	53	19	34
80-84	30	8	22	34	9	25	38	11	27	40	12	28
85-89	21	4	16	18	4	14	21	4	16	23	5	18
90-94	8	1	7	9	1	8	8	1	7	10	1	9
95-99	2	0	2	2	0	2	3	0	3	3	0	3
100 +	0	0	0	0	0	0	0	0	0	1	0	1

Age group	2045 Both sexes	Males	Females	2050 Both sexes	Males	Females
All ages	1 320	631	690	1 330	639	690
0-4	95	49	46	93	48	45
5-9	90	46	44	95	49	46
10-14	81	41	39	90	46	44
15-19	75	38	36	80	41	39
20-24	78	40	38	74	38	36
25-29	86	44	42	78	40	38
30-34	88	45	43	86	44	42
35-39	79	40	39	87	45	43
40-44	63	32	31	79	40	39
45-49	58	30	29	62	32	31
50-54	73	37	36	57	29	28
55-59	98	48	50	71	35	36
60-64	89	42	47	93	45	48
65-69	74	33	40	83	38	45
70-74	65	27	38	66	28	38
75-79	50	18	32	55	21	34
80-84	39	12	27	37	12	25
85-89	25	6	19	25	6	19
90-94	11	2	10	12	2	10
95-99	3	0	3	4	0	4
100 +	1	0	1	1	0	1

United Nations Department of Economic and Social Affairs/Population Division
World Population Prospects: The 2004 Revision, Volume II: Sex and Age Distribution of the World Population

384

POPULATION BY AGE AND SEX (in thousands)

Age group	2005 Both sexes	Males	Females	2010 Both sexes	Males	Females	2015 Both sexes	Males	Females	2020 Both sexes	Males	Females
All ages	1 330	611	718	1 297	596	702	1 261	579	682	1 221	562	659
0-4	64	33	31	56	29	27	51	26	25	46	24	22
5-9	60	31	29	64	33	31	56	29	27	51	26	25
10-14	77	40	38	60	31	29	64	33	31	56	29	27
15-19	107	55	52	77	40	38	60	31	29	64	33	31
20-24	103	52	50	106	54	52	77	39	38	60	31	29
25-29	93	47	46	102	52	50	106	54	52	77	39	37
30-34	93	46	47	92	47	46	102	51	50	105	54	52
35-39	86	42	44	92	46	47	92	46	46	101	51	50
40-44	93	44	49	85	41	44	91	45	46	90	45	45
45-49	95	45	51	91	43	48	83	40	44	89	43	46
50-54	90	41	49	92	42	50	88	40	47	81	38	43
55-59	80	35	45	86	37	48	87	39	49	84	38	46
60-64	67	28	39	74	31	43	80	33	46	82	35	47
65-69	72	28	44	60	23	37	67	26	41	72	29	44
70-74	58	21	37	62	22	40	51	18	33	58	21	37
75-79	47	15	33	45	14	31	49	15	34	41	13	28
80-84	27	6	21	32	8	24	31	8	23	35	9	26
85-89	9	2	7	15	3	12	18	4	15	18	4	14
90-94	5	1	4	4	1	3	6	1	5	8	1	7
95-99	1	0	1	1	0	1	1	0	1	2	0	2
100 +	0	0	0	0	0	0	0	0	0	0	0	0

Age group	2025 Both sexes	Males	Females	2030 Both sexes	Males	Females	2035 Both sexes	Males	Females	2040 Both sexes	Males	Females
All ages	1 179	543	635	1 135	524	610	1 089	505	584	1 042	484	558
0-4	43	22	21	40	20	19	38	19	18	36	19	18
5-9	46	24	22	43	22	21	40	20	19	38	19	18
10-14	51	26	25	46	23	22	43	22	21	40	20	19
15-19	56	29	27	51	26	25	46	23	22	43	22	21
20-24	64	33	31	56	29	27	51	26	25	46	23	22
25-29	60	31	29	64	33	31	56	29	27	51	26	25
30-34	76	39	37	59	30	29	64	32	31	56	28	27
35-39	105	53	52	76	39	37	59	30	29	63	32	31
40-44	100	50	50	104	52	51	75	38	37	60	30	29
45-49	89	44	45	98	49	49	103	52	51	75	38	37
50-54	87	42	45	87	43	44	96	48	49	100	50	50
55-59	78	35	42	84	39	44	84	40	44	83	45	40
60-64	79	34	45	73	32	41	79	36	43	80	37	42
65-69	75	30	45	72	30	42	67	29	39	73	32	41
70-74	63	23	40	65	25	41	64	25	39	60	24	36
75-79	47	16	32	52	17	35	54	18	36	53	19	34
80-84	30	8	22	34	9	25	38	11	27	40	12	28
85-89	21	4	16	18	4	14	21	4	16	23	5	18
90-94	8	1	7	9	1	8	8	1	7	10	1	9
95-99	2	0	2	2	0	2	3	0	3	3	0	3
100 +	0	0	0	0	0	0	0	0	0	1	0	1

Age group	2045 Both sexes	Males	Females	2050 Both sexes	Males	Females
All ages	991	462	529	930	430	500
0-4	34	17	16	31	16	15
5-9	36	19	18	33	17	16
10-14	38	19	18	36	19	18
15-19	40	20	19	38	19	18
20-24	43	22	21	40	20	19
25-29	46	23	22	43	22	21
30-34	51	26	25	46	23	22
35-39	55	28	27	51	26	25
40-44	63	32	31	55	28	27
45-49	58	30	29	62	32	31
50-54	73	37	36	57	29	28
55-59	98	48	50	71	35	36
60-64	89	42	47	93	45	48
65-69	74	33	40	83	38	45
70-74	65	27	38	66	28	38
75-79	50	18	32	55	21	34
80-84	39	12	27	37	12	25
85-89	25	6	19	25	6	19
90-94	11	2	10	12	2	10
95-99	3	0	3	4	0	4
100 +	1	0	1	1	0	1

POPULATION BY AGE AND SEX (in thousands)

Age group	1950 Both sexes	Males	Females	1955 Both sexes	Males	Females	1960 Both sexes	Males	Females	1965 Both sexes	Males	Females
All ages	18 434	9 131	9 303	20 474	10 145	10 329	22 943	11 371	11 572	26 090	12 933	13 157
0-4	3 387	1 710	1 677	3 756	1 873	1 883	4 193	2 093	2 100	4 854	2 426	2 428
5-9	2 577	1 295	1 282	2 894	1 458	1 437	3 266	1 624	1 641	3 719	1 851	1 868
10-14	2 172	1 090	1 082	2 444	1 229	1 215	2 760	1 390	1 370	3 134	1 559	1 576
15-19	1 870	942	928	2 086	1 048	1 038	2 357	1 185	1 171	2 673	1 346	1 327
20-24	1 603	805	798	1 784	896	888	1 999	1 001	998	2 269	1 138	1 131
25-29	1 367	683	685	1 516	757	758	1 696	847	848	1 910	952	958
30-34	1 159	579	581	1 286	641	645	1 433	714	719	1 614	804	809
35-39	984	494	491	1 082	539	542	1 207	601	607	1 355	674	681
40-44	826	414	412	909	454	455	1 006	500	506	1 132	562	571
45-49	690	340	350	754	375	379	837	415	422	935	461	474
50-54	500	226	274	620	301	318	684	335	348	767	376	391
55-59	415	184	231	437	194	243	547	262	285	611	295	315
60-64	334	144	189	345	150	195	368	160	208	469	221	248
65-69	254	106	148	256	108	147	270	115	155	295	126	169
70-74	167	70	97	170	69	101	176	73	103	192	80	112
75-79	89	35	54	91	36	54	97	38	59	105	42	63
80 +	41	16	25	44	16	28	48	18	30	55	20	35

Age group	1970 Both sexes	Males	Females	1975 Both sexes	Males	Females	1980 Both sexes	Males	Females	1985 Both sexes	Males	Females
All ages	29 823	14 788	15 035	34 114	16 922	17 193	37 062	18 390	18 673	43 361	21 518	21 843
0-4	5 543	2 775	2 769	6 329	3 171	3 157	6 876	3 448	3 428	8 065	4 045	4 020
5-9	4 353	2 171	2 183	4 995	2 495	2 500	5 429	2 715	2 714	6 361	3 184	3 177
10-14	3 582	1 783	1 799	4 192	2 090	2 102	4 565	2 280	2 285	5 339	2 670	2 669
15-19	3 043	1 513	1 530	3 475	1 729	1 745	3 859	1 924	1 935	4 519	2 257	2 262
20-24	2 581	1 296	1 285	2 936	1 456	1 480	3 179	1 578	1 601	3 799	1 888	1 911
25-29	2 176	1 086	1 090	2 474	1 237	1 237	2 671	1 318	1 352	3 112	1 538	1 574
30-34	1 824	907	917	2 078	1 035	1 043	2 242	1 119	1 123	2 604	1 282	1 322
35-39	1 532	763	770	1 733	860	873	1 873	931	942	2 175	1 084	1 092
40-44	1 277	634	644	1 445	717	728	1 551	768	784	1 805	895	910
45-49	1 058	521	537	1 194	588	606	1 283	633	650	1 483	729	754
50-54	862	420	441	976	476	500	1 047	511	536	1 211	591	619
55-59	690	334	356	777	374	403	837	403	434	967	466	500
60-64	528	252	277	599	285	314	642	305	337	745	354	391
65-69	379	175	204	430	201	229	465	218	247	537	251	286
70-74	214	89	125	278	126	152	301	138	163	349	160	189
75-79	118	47	71	133	54	80	166	73	93	190	84	106
80 +	62	23	40	72	26	45	78	29	49	100	39	61

Age group	1990 Both sexes	Males	Females	1995 Both sexes	Males	Females	2000 Both sexes	Males	Females	2005 Both sexes	Males	Females
All ages	51 040	25 333	25 707	60 007	29 788	30 219	68 525	34 039	34 486	77 431	38 514	38 917
0-4	9 532	4 786	4 746	11 143	5 600	5 542	12 096	6 085	6 011	13 063	6 577	6 486
5-9	7 536	3 773	3 763	8 972	4 497	4 474	10 374	5 204	5 170	11 314	5 681	5 634
10-14	6 283	3 144	3 139	7 455	3 733	3 722	8 739	4 380	4 359	10 095	5 063	5 032
15-19	5 304	2 652	2 651	6 246	3 125	3 121	7 297	3 652	3 645	8 558	4 287	4 270
20-24	4 461	2 221	2 240	5 229	2 608	2 621	6 063	3 026	3 037	7 085	3 538	3 548
25-29	3 724	1 843	1 882	4 345	2 154	2 191	4 980	2 479	2 502	5 773	2 878	2 895
30-34	3 041	1 498	1 543	3 609	1 778	1 831	4 080	2 022	2 059	4 646	2 320	2 326
35-39	2 534	1 245	1 289	2 939	1 442	1 497	3 379	1 662	1 717	3 776	1 876	1 900
40-44	2 104	1 044	1 059	2 440	1 193	1 247	2 752	1 344	1 408	3 130	1 538	1 592
45-49	1 733	854	879	2 015	993	1 022	2 283	1 108	1 175	2 555	1 242	1 314
50-54	1 407	686	721	1 644	802	842	1 873	914	959	2 113	1 016	1 097
55-59	1 125	543	582	1 310	631	679	1 504	725	779	1 712	826	887
60-64	868	413	455	1 014	483	531	1 164	553	611	1 339	637	702
65-69	630	295	335	739	346	393	854	400	453	984	460	524
70-74	410	187	223	487	223	264	568	261	307	661	304	357
75-79	227	100	127	272	119	153	324	144	180	383	171	211
80 +	122	49	72	149	61	88	196	80	115	243	101	142

United Nations Department of Economic and Social Affairs/Population Division
World Population Prospects: The 2004 Revision, Volume II: Sex and Age Distribution of the World Population

386

POPULATION BY AGE AND SEX (in thousands)

Age group	2005 Both sexes	2005 Males	2005 Females	2010 Both sexes	2010 Males	2010 Females	2015 Both sexes	2015 Males	2015 Females	2020 Both sexes	2020 Males	2020 Females
All ages	77 431	38 514	38 917	86 998	43 338	43 660	97 155	48 478	48 677	107 681	53 819	53 862
0-4	13 063	6 577	6 486	14 110	7 108	7 002	15 069	7 595	7 474	15 741	7 939	7 802
5-9	11 314	5 681	5 634	12 305	6 183	6 122	13 395	6 735	6 660	14 427	7 259	7 168
10-14	10 095	5 063	5 032	11 029	5 536	5 494	12 017	6 036	5 981	13 110	6 589	6 521
15-19	8 558	4 287	4 270	9 907	4 966	4 941	10 848	5 441	5 407	11 836	5 940	5 896
20-24	7 085	3 538	3 548	8 329	4 163	4 166	9 674	4 838	4 836	10 616	5 312	5 304
25-29	5 773	2 878	2 895	6 749	3 369	3 380	7 957	3 978	3 980	9 294	4 646	4 647
30-34	4 646	2 320	2 326	5 383	2 696	2 687	6 290	3 159	3 132	7 456	3 750	3 705
35-39	3 776	1 876	1 900	4 291	2 153	2 138	4 964	2 503	2 462	5 815	2 942	2 872
40-44	3 130	1 538	1 592	3 490	1 736	1 754	3 963	1 994	1 969	4 590	2 323	2 267
45-49	2 555	1 242	1 314	2 904	1 422	1 483	3 239	1 607	1 632	3 682	1 850	1 832
50-54	2 113	1 016	1 097	2 368	1 141	1 227	2 696	1 310	1 386	3 012	1 485	1 527
55-59	1 712	826	887	1 938	921	1 016	2 179	1 039	1 140	2 488	1 198	1 290
60-64	1 339	637	702	1 532	729	803	1 744	818	925	1 970	928	1 042
65-69	984	460	524	1 141	534	607	1 316	617	699	1 508	697	811
70-74	661	304	357	771	354	417	904	415	488	1 053	485	569
75-79	383	171	211	453	203	250	537	240	296	639	287	352
80-84	175	75	100	211	91	120	255	110	145	308	134	175
85-89	56	22	34	70	28	42	87	35	51	108	44	64
90-94	11	4	7	15	5	10	19	7	12	24	9	15
95-99	1	0	1	2	0	1	2	1	2	3	1	2
100 +	0	0	0	0	0	0	0	0	0	0	0	0

Age group	2025 Both sexes	2025 Males	2025 Females	2030 Both sexes	2030 Males	2030 Females	2035 Both sexes	2035 Males	2035 Females	2040 Both sexes	2040 Males	2040 Females
All ages	118 354	59 232	59 122	128 979	64 611	64 368	139 490	69 922	69 568	149 904	75 168	74 735
0-4	16 070	8 108	7 962	16 185	8 167	8 018	16 279	8 215	8 063	16 407	8 281	8 126
5-9	15 185	7 646	7 539	15 600	7 857	7 742	15 793	7 956	7 837	15 951	8 035	7 915
10-14	14 175	7 129	7 046	14 971	7 533	7 437	15 421	7 763	7 658	15 645	7 876	7 769
15-19	12 934	6 495	6 439	14 009	7 039	6 970	14 818	7 449	7 368	15 284	7 686	7 598
20-24	11 607	5 812	5 795	12 706	6 366	6 340	13 786	6 911	6 875	14 607	7 326	7 281
25-29	10 236	5 120	5 116	11 230	5 620	5 610	12 327	6 173	6 155	13 419	6 722	6 697
30-34	8 774	4 408	4 366	9 716	4 881	4 835	10 708	5 379	5 329	11 809	5 933	5 876
35-39	6 947	3 517	3 429	8 239	4 162	4 077	9 176	4 632	4 545	10 166	5 129	5 038
40-44	5 409	2 748	2 662	6 514	3 308	3 206	7 773	3 936	3 837	8 703	4 402	4 300
45-49	4 286	2 168	2 118	5 000	2 501	2 505	6 158	3 125	3 034	7 386	3 737	3 649
50-54	3 439	1 719	1 720	4 025	2 025	2 000	4 800	2 424	2 376	5 840	2 950	2 890
55-59	2 792	1 305	1 420	3 205	1 500	1 617	3 771	1 883	1 999	4 517	2 265	2 253
60-64	2 262	1 076	1 186	2 554	1 235	1 320	2 948	1 446	1 502	3 485	1 722	1 763
65-69	1 717	797	920	1 986	931	1 055	2 257	1 076	1 182	2 623	1 268	1 355
70-74	1 221	554	666	1 404	640	763	1 639	755	884	1 879	880	999
75-79	755	340	416	888	394	494	1 034	461	573	1 222	551	672
80-84	374	163	212	451	197	254	539	232	307	639	276	362
85-89	134	55	79	166	69	97	204	85	119	250	103	147
90-94	31	12	19	39	15	24	50	19	31	63	24	39
95-99	4	1	3	5	2	4	7	2	5	9	3	6
100 +	0	0	0	0	0	0	1	0	0	1	0	1

Age group	2045 Both sexes	2045 Males	2045 Females	2050 Both sexes	2050 Males	2050 Females
All ages	160 195	80 326	79 870	170 190	85 304	84 887
0-4	16 515	8 335	8 180	16 496	8 326	8 171
5-9	16 135	8 128	8 007	16 293	8 207	8 086
10-14	15 829	7 968	7 861	16 035	8 071	7 964
15-19	15 524	7 806	7 717	15 722	7 905	7 817
20-24	15 086	7 568	7 518	15 343	7 697	7 646
25-29	14 258	7 144	7 114	14 762	7 398	7 364
30-34	12 919	6 488	6 431	13 782	6 920	6 862
35-39	11 277	5 685	5 592	12 403	6 246	6 157
40-44	9 696	4 900	4 796	10 812	5 457	5 354
45-49	8 310	4 200	4 111	9 302	4 696	4 607
50-54	7 035	3 544	3 491	7 948	4 000	3 948
55-59	5 519	2 768	2 752	6 675	3 339	3 336
60-64	4 197	2 083	2 114	5 150	2 557	2 593
65-69	3 118	1 519	1 599	3 776	1 848	1 928
70-74	2 202	1 047	1 155	2 635	1 262	1 373
75-79	1 417	649	768	1 676	779	897
80-84	766	335	431	899	400	499
85-89	301	125	176	367	154	213
90-94	79	30	49	96	37	59
95-99	12	4	8	15	5	10
100 +	1	0	1	1	0	1

United Nations Department of Economic and Social Affairs/Population Division
World Population Prospects: The 2004 Revision, Volume II: Sex and Age Distribution of the World Population

387

POPULATION BY AGE AND SEX (in thousands)

Age group	2005 Both sexes	Males	Females	2010 Both sexes	Males	Females	2015 Both sexes	Males	Females	2020 Both sexes	Males	Females
All ages	77 431	38 514	38 917	87 650	43 666	43 983	98 997	49 406	49 591	111 240	55 612	55 628
0-4	13 063	6 577	6 486	14 762	7 436	7 325	16 292	8 212	8 080	17 523	8 837	8 686
5-9	11 314	5 681	5 634	12 305	6 183	6 122	14 014	7 046	6 968	15 599	7 849	7 750
10-14	10 095	5 063	5 032	11 029	5 536	5 494	12 017	6 036	5 981	13 716	6 893	6 822
15-19	8 558	4 287	4 270	9 907	4 966	4 941	10 848	5 441	5 407	11 836	5 940	5 896
20-24	7 085	3 538	3 548	8 329	4 163	4 166	9 674	4 838	4 836	10 616	5 312	5 304
25-29	5 773	2 878	2 895	6 749	3 369	3 380	7 957	3 978	3 980	9 294	4 646	4 647
30-34	4 646	2 320	2 326	5 383	2 696	2 687	6 290	3 159	3 132	7 456	3 750	3 705
35-39	3 776	1 876	1 900	4 291	2 153	2 138	4 964	2 503	2 462	5 815	2 942	2 872
40-44	3 130	1 538	1 592	3 490	1 736	1 754	3 963	1 994	1 969	4 590	2 323	2 267
45-49	2 555	1 242	1 314	2 904	1 422	1 483	3 239	1 607	1 632	3 682	1 850	1 832
50-54	2 113	1 016	1 097	2 368	1 141	1 227	2 696	1 310	1 386	3 012	1 485	1 527
55-59	1 712	826	887	1 938	921	1 016	2 179	1 039	1 140	2 488	1 198	1 290
60-64	1 339	637	702	1 532	729	803	1 744	818	925	1 970	928	1 042
65-69	984	460	524	1 141	534	607	1 316	617	699	1 508	697	811
70-74	661	304	357	771	354	417	904	415	488	1 053	485	569
75-79	383	171	211	453	203	250	537	240	296	639	287	352
80-84	175	75	100	211	91	120	255	110	145	308	134	175
85-89	56	22	34	70	28	42	87	35	51	108	44	64
90-94	11	4	7	15	5	10	19	7	12	24	9	15
95-99	1	0	1	2	0	1	2	1	2	3	1	2
100 +	0	0	0	0	0	0	0	0	0	0	0	0

Age group	2025 Both sexes	Males	Females	2030 Both sexes	Males	Females	2035 Both sexes	Males	Females	2040 Both sexes	Males	Females
All ages	123 905	62 028	61 877	136 941	68 620	68 321	150 475	75 452	75 024	164 676	82 603	82 072
0-4	18 152	9 158	8 994	18 703	9 438	9 265	19 437	9 809	9 628	20 373	10 282	10 091
5-9	16 905	8 511	8 393	17 622	8 876	8 746	18 251	9 194	9 057	19 047	9 595	9 452
10-14	15 327	7 708	7 619	16 667	8 387	8 280	17 421	8 769	8 651	18 080	9 102	8 978
15-19	13 531	6 795	6 736	15 147	7 611	7 536	16 497	8 294	8 204	17 266	8 682	8 584
20-24	11 607	5 812	5 795	13 293	6 660	6 633	14 907	7 473	7 434	16 262	8 156	8 106
25-29	10 236	5 120	5 116	11 230	5 620	5 610	12 897	6 458	6 439	14 510	7 269	7 241
30-34	8 774	4 408	4 366	9 716	4 881	4 835	10 708	5 379	5 329	12 355	6 207	6 147
35-39	6 947	3 517	3 429	8 239	4 162	4 077	9 176	4 632	4 545	10 166	5 129	5 038
40-44	5 409	2 748	2 662	6 514	3 308	3 206	7 773	3 936	3 837	8 703	4 402	4 300
45-49	4 286	2 168	2 118	5 086	2 581	2 505	6 158	3 125	3 034	7 386	3 737	3 649
50-54	3 439	1 719	1 720	4 025	2 025	2 000	4 800	2 424	2 376	5 840	2 950	2 890
55-59	2 792	1 365	1 428	3 205	1 589	1 617	3 771	1 882	1 888	4 517	2 265	2 253
60-64	2 262	1 076	1 186	2 554	1 235	1 320	2 948	1 446	1 502	3 485	1 722	1 763
65-69	1 717	797	920	1 986	931	1 055	2 257	1 076	1 182	2 623	1 268	1 355
70-74	1 221	554	666	1 404	640	763	1 639	755	884	1 879	880	999
75-79	755	340	416	888	394	494	1 034	461	573	1 222	551	672
80-84	374	163	212	451	197	254	539	232	307	639	276	362
85-89	134	55	79	166	69	97	204	85	119	250	103	147
90-94	31	12	19	39	15	24	50	19	31	63	24	39
95-99	4	1	3	5	2	4	7	2	5	9	3	6
100 +	0	0	0	0	0	0	1	0	0	1	0	1

Age group	2045 Both sexes	Males	Females	2050 Both sexes	Males	Females
All ages	179 537	90 060	89 476	194 792	97 685	97 107
0-4	21 319	10 759	10 559	22 049	11 128	10 921
5-9	20 036	10 093	9 943	21 033	10 594	10 439
10-14	18 902	9 515	9 387	19 913	10 022	9 890
15-19	17 941	9 022	8 919	18 775	9 440	9 335
20-24	17 043	8 550	8 493	17 733	8 896	8 837
25-29	15 875	7 954	7 921	16 678	8 358	8 320
30-34	13 970	7 016	6 954	15 345	7 705	7 641
35-39	11 799	5 948	5 850	13 411	6 754	6 658
40-44	9 696	4 900	4 796	11 312	5 710	5 602
45-49	8 310	4 200	4 111	9 302	4 696	4 607
50-54	7 035	3 544	3 491	7 948	4 000	3 948
55-59	5 519	2 768	2 752	6 675	3 339	3 336
60-64	4 197	2 083	2 114	5 150	2 557	2 593
65-69	3 118	1 519	1 599	3 776	1 848	1 928
70-74	2 202	1 047	1 155	2 635	1 262	1 373
75-79	1 417	649	768	1 676	779	897
80-84	766	335	431	899	400	499
85-89	301	125	176	367	154	213
90-94	79	30	49	96	37	59
95-99	12	4	8	15	5	10
100 +	1	0	1	1	0	1

388

United Nations Department of Economic and Social Affairs/Population Division
World Population Prospects: The 2004 Revision, Volume II: Sex and Age Distribution of the World Population

POPULATION BY AGE AND SEX (in thousands)

Age group	2005 Both sexes	2005 Males	2005 Females	2010 Both sexes	2010 Males	2010 Females	2015 Both sexes	2015 Males	2015 Females	2020 Both sexes	2020 Males	2020 Females
All ages	77 431	38 514	38 917	86 347	43 010	43 337	95 313	47 551	47 763	104 122	52 027	52 095
0-4	13 063	6 577	6 486	13 459	6 780	6 679	13 846	6 979	6 867	13 959	7 040	6 919
5-9	11 314	5 681	5 634	12 305	6 183	6 122	12 777	6 424	6 353	13 256	6 670	6 586
10-14	10 095	5 063	5 032	11 029	5 536	5 494	12 017	6 036	5 981	12 505	6 285	6 220
15-19	8 558	4 287	4 270	9 907	4 966	4 941	10 848	5 441	5 407	11 836	5 940	5 896
20-24	7 085	3 538	3 548	8 329	4 163	4 166	9 674	4 838	4 836	10 616	5 312	5 304
25-29	5 773	2 878	2 895	6 749	3 369	3 380	7 957	3 978	3 980	9 294	4 646	4 647
30-34	4 646	2 320	2 326	5 383	2 696	2 687	6 290	3 159	3 132	7 456	3 750	3 705
35-39	3 776	1 876	1 900	4 291	2 153	2 138	4 964	2 503	2 462	5 815	2 942	2 872
40-44	3 130	1 538	1 592	3 490	1 736	1 754	3 963	1 994	1 969	4 590	2 323	2 267
45-49	2 555	1 242	1 314	2 904	1 422	1 483	3 239	1 607	1 632	3 682	1 850	1 832
50-54	2 113	1 016	1 097	2 368	1 141	1 227	2 696	1 310	1 386	3 012	1 485	1 527
55-59	1 712	826	887	1 938	921	1 016	2 179	1 039	1 140	2 488	1 198	1 290
60-64	1 339	637	702	1 532	729	803	1 744	818	925	1 970	928	1 042
65-69	984	460	524	1 141	534	607	1 316	617	699	1 508	697	811
70-74	661	304	357	771	354	417	904	415	488	1 053	485	569
75-79	383	171	211	453	203	250	537	240	296	639	287	352
80-84	175	75	100	211	91	120	255	110	145	308	134	175
85-89	56	22	34	70	28	42	87	35	51	108	44	64
90-94	11	4	7	15	5	10	19	7	12	24	9	15
95-99	1	0	1	2	0	1	2	1	2	3	1	2
100 +	0	0	0	0	0	0	0	0	0	0	0	0

Age group	2025 Both sexes	2025 Males	2025 Females	2030 Both sexes	2030 Males	2030 Females	2035 Both sexes	2035 Males	2035 Females	2040 Both sexes	2040 Males	2040 Females
All ages	112 810	56 440	56 370	121 075	60 631	60 443	128 717	64 499	64 218	135 670	68 005	67 665
0-4	13 995	7 061	6 934	13 717	6 922	6 795	13 277	6 700	6 576	12 771	6 445	6 325
5-9	13 465	6 780	6 685	13 585	6 843	6 742	13 384	6 742	6 642	13 008	6 553	6 455
10-14	13 024	6 550	6 474	13 274	6 680	6 594	13 429	6 760	6 669	13 258	6 674	6 584
15-19	12 336	6 195	6 141	12 871	6 467	6 404	13 138	6 605	6 533	13 309	6 692	6 617
20-24	11 607	5 812	5 795	12 119	6 072	6 047	12 666	6 349	6 316	12 951	6 495	6 455
25-29	10 236	5 120	5 116	11 230	5 620	5 610	11 757	5 887	5 870	12 328	6 175	6 152
30-34	8 774	4 408	4 366	9 716	4 881	4 835	10 708	5 379	5 329	11 262	5 658	5 604
35-39	6 947	3 517	3 429	8 239	4 162	4 077	9 176	4 632	4 545	10 166	5 129	5 038
40-44	5 409	2 748	2 662	6 514	3 308	3 206	7 773	3 936	3 837	8 703	4 402	4 300
45-49	4 286	2 168	2 118	5 086	2 581	2 505	6 158	3 125	3 034	7 386	3 737	3 649
50-54	3 439	1 719	1 720	4 025	2 025	2 000	4 800	2 424	2 376	5 840	2 950	2 890
55-59	2 792	1 365	1 428	3 205	1 589	1 617	3 771	1 882	1 888	4 517	2 265	2 253
60-64	2 262	1 076	1 186	2 554	1 235	1 320	2 948	1 446	1 502	3 485	1 722	1 763
65-69	1 717	797	920	1 986	931	1 055	2 257	1 076	1 182	2 623	1 268	1 355
70-74	1 221	554	666	1 404	640	763	1 639	755	884	1 879	880	999
75-79	755	340	416	888	394	494	1 034	461	573	1 222	551	672
80-84	374	163	212	451	197	254	509	202	307	639	276	362
85-89	134	55	79	166	69	97	204	85	119	250	103	147
90-94	31	12	19	39	15	24	50	19	31	63	24	39
95-99	4	1	3	5	2	4	7	2	5	9	3	6
100 +	0	0	0	0	0	0	1	0	0	1	0	1

Age group	2045 Both sexes	2045 Males	2045 Females	2050 Both sexes	2050 Males	2050 Females
All ages	141 926	71 132	70 794	147 410	73 840	73 570
0-4	12 251	6 183	6 068	11 704	5 907	5 797
5-9	12 558	6 326	6 232	12 086	6 087	5 998
10-14	12 908	6 498	6 411	12 479	6 281	6 198
15-19	13 155	6 615	6 540	12 820	6 446	6 375
20-24	13 136	6 590	6 546	13 001	6 522	6 479
25-29	12 642	6 334	6 307	12 853	6 441	6 412
30-34	11 868	5 961	5 908	12 219	6 135	6 084
35-39	10 755	5 422	5 333	11 394	5 738	5 656
40-44	9 696	4 900	4 796	10 311	5 205	5 107
45-49	8 310	4 200	4 111	9 302	4 696	4 607
50-54	7 035	3 544	3 491	7 948	4 000	3 948
55-59	5 519	2 768	2 752	6 675	3 339	3 336
60-64	4 197	2 083	2 114	5 150	2 557	2 593
65-69	3 118	1 519	1 599	3 776	1 848	1 928
70-74	2 202	1 047	1 155	2 635	1 262	1 373
75-79	1 417	649	768	1 676	779	897
80-84	766	335	431	899	400	499
85-89	301	125	176	367	154	213
90-94	79	30	49	96	37	59
95-99	12	4	8	15	5	10
100 +	1	0	1	1	0	1

United Nations Department of Economic and Social Affairs/Population Division
World Population Prospects: The 2004 Revision, Volume II: Sex and Age Distribution of the World Population

389

POPULATION BY AGE AND SEX (in thousands)

Age group	1950 Both sexes	Males	Females	1955 Both sexes	Males	Females	1960 Both sexes	Males	Females	1965 Both sexes	Males	Females
All ages	289	151	138	336	171	165	394	203	191	464	237	227
0-4	55	28	27	65	33	32	76	39	37	80	41	39
5-9	44	22	22	52	26	26	63	32	31	75	38	37
10-14	36	18	18	43	21	22	50	25	25	62	31	30
15-19	30	15	15	36	18	18	41	20	21	50	25	25
20-24	25	13	12	29	15	14	34	17	17	41	20	20
25-29	21	11	10	24	12	12	27	14	13	33	17	17
30-34	19	10	9	20	10	10	23	12	11	27	14	13
35-39	15	8	7	17	9	8	19	10	9	22	11	11
40-44	11	6	5	14	7	7	17	9	8	19	10	9
45-49	8	4	4	10	5	5	13	7	6	16	8	8
50-54	7	4	3	7	4	3	9	5	4	13	7	6
55-59	5	3	2	5	3	2	7	4	3	9	5	4
60-64	5	3	2	4	2	2	5	3	2	6	3	3
65-69	3	2	1	3	2	1	3	2	1	4	2	2
70-74	2	2	1	3	2	1	3	2	1	3	2	1
75-79	1	1	0	2	1	1	2	1	1	2	1	1
80 +	1	1	0	2	1	1	2	1	1	2	1	1

Age group	1970 Both sexes	Males	Females	1975 Both sexes	Males	Females	1980 Both sexes	Males	Females	1985 Both sexes	Males	Females
All ages	520	265	256	576	291	285	634	321	313	709	359	350
0-4	75	38	37	77	39	38	87	45	43	102	53	50
5-9	78	40	38	75	38	37	82	42	40	94	48	46
10-14	73	37	36	78	40	38	78	40	38	78	40	38
15-19	60	31	30	73	37	36	73	37	36	73	37	36
20-24	48	24	24	57	28	29	64	32	32	75	37	38
25-29	39	20	20	45	23	23	53	27	27	64	32	32
30-34	32	16	16	37	19	19	43	21	22	50	25	25
35-39	26	13	13	32	16	16	36	18	18	40	20	20
40-44	22	11	10	25	13	12	29	15	14	34	17	17
45-49	18	9	9	21	11	10	24	12	12	28	14	14
50-54	15	8	7	17	9	8	19	10	9	22	11	11
55-59	12	6	6	14	7	7	15	8	7	17	9	8
60-64	8	4	4	11	6	5	11	6	5	12	6	6
65-69	5	3	3	6	3	3	8	4	4	9	5	4
70-74	4	2	2	5	2	2	5	3	3	6	3	3
75-79	2	1	1	3	1	1	3	2	2	4	2	2
80 +	2	1	1	2	1	1	2	1	1	1	1	1

Age group	1990 Both sexes	Males	Females	1995 Both sexes	Males	Females	2000 Both sexes	Males	Females	2005 Both sexes	Males	Females
All ages	724	367	356	768	390	378	811	412	399	848	431	417
0-4	95	49	46	95	49	46	96	49	46	92	47	45
5-9	92	47	45	88	45	43	90	46	43	90	46	44
10-14	87	44	42	91	47	44	85	44	41	87	44	42
15-19	71	36	35	83	42	40	87	45	43	81	42	39
20-24	66	33	33	68	35	33	78	40	38	83	43	40
25-29	66	33	33	62	31	31	63	33	31	74	38	36
30-34	56	28	27	60	30	30	58	30	29	60	31	29
35-39	45	22	22	54	28	26	57	29	28	56	28	27
40-44	37	19	18	43	22	21	52	26	25	55	28	27
45-49	31	16	15	36	18	18	41	20	20	49	25	24
50-54	25	12	12	28	14	14	33	16	17	38	19	19
55-59	18	9	9	22	11	11	25	12	13	30	15	15
60-64	13	7	6	15	7	8	18	9	10	21	10	11
65-69	9	4	4	11	5	5	12	6	6	15	7	8
70-74	7	3	3	6	3	3	8	4	4	9	4	5
75-79	4	2	2	5	2	3	4	2	2	5	2	3
80 +	3	1	2	2	1	1	3	1	2	4	1	2

United Nations Department of Economic and Social Affairs/Population Division
World Population Prospects: The 2004 Revision, Volume II: Sex and Age Distribution of the World Population

POPULATION BY AGE AND SEX (in thousands)

Age group	2005 Both sexes	2005 Males	2005 Females	2010 Both sexes	2010 Males	2010 Females	2015 Both sexes	2015 Males	2015 Females	2020 Both sexes	2020 Males	2020 Females
All ages	848	431	417	878	446	432	903	458	444	920	467	453
0-4	92	47	45	88	45	43	84	43	41	79	41	38
5-9	90	46	44	86	44	42	82	42	40	78	40	38
10-14	87	44	42	87	45	42	83	43	41	79	41	39
15-19	81	42	39	83	43	40	83	43	41	80	41	39
20-24	83	43	40	77	40	37	78	40	38	79	41	38
25-29	74	38	36	79	41	38	72	37	35	74	38	36
30-34	60	31	29	70	36	34	75	39	36	69	36	33
35-39	56	28	27	57	30	28	68	35	33	72	38	35
40-44	55	28	27	54	27	26	55	29	27	65	34	32
45-49	49	25	24	52	26	26	51	26	25	53	27	26
50-54	38	19	19	46	23	23	49	25	25	48	24	24
55-59	30	15	15	34	17	17	42	21	21	45	22	23
60-64	21	10	11	26	12	14	30	14	16	38	18	19
65-69	15	7	8	18	8	9	22	10	12	25	12	14
70-74	9	4	5	11	5	6	14	6	8	17	7	10
75-79	5	2	3	6	3	4	8	3	5	10	4	6
80-84	2	1	1	3	1	2	4	1	2	5	2	3
85-89	1	0	1	1	0	1	1	0	1	2	1	1
90-94	0	0	0	0	0	0	0	0	0	0	0	0
95-99	0	0	0	0	0	0	0	0	0	0	0	0
100 +	0	0	0	0	0	0	0	0	0	0	0	0

Age group	2025 Both sexes	2025 Males	2025 Females	2030 Both sexes	2030 Males	2030 Females	2035 Both sexes	2035 Males	2035 Females	2040 Both sexes	2040 Males	2040 Females
All ages	939	476	463	952	482	470	958	485	474	958	484	474
0-4	76	39	37	72	37	35	68	35	33	64	33	31
5-9	75	39	37	72	37	35	69	35	33	65	33	31
10-14	76	39	37	73	38	35	70	36	34	66	34	32
15-19	77	39	37	74	38	36	70	36	34	67	35	33
20-24	77	39	37	74	38	36	71	36	34	67	35	33
25-29	76	39	37	73	38	36	71	36	34	68	35	33
30-34	72	37	34	73	38	36	71	37	34	68	35	33
35-39	67	35	32	70	36	34	72	37	35	69	36	33
40-44	71	37	34	66	34	31	68	35	33	70	36	34
45-49	63	33	31	69	36	33	64	33	31	66	34	32
50-54	50	26	24	61	31	30	66	34	32	61	32	30
55-59	45	22	23	47	24	23	57	29	28	63	32	31
60-64	41	20	21	41	20	21	43	21	22	53	26	27
65-69	32	15	17	35	16	19	36	17	19	38	18	20
70-74	20	9	11	26	12	15	29	13	16	30	13	16
75-79	12	5	7	15	6	9	20	8	12	22	9	13
80-84	6	2	4	8	3	5	10	3	6	10	5	8
85-89	2	1	2	3	1	2	4	1	3	5	2	4
90-94	1	0	0	1	0	1	1	0	1	1	0	1
95-99	0	0	0	0	0	0	0	0	0	0	0	0
100 +	0	0	0	0	0	0	0	0	0	0	0	0

Age group	2045 Both sexes	2045 Males	2045 Females	2050 Both sexes	2050 Males	2050 Females
All ages	950	479	471	934	471	464
0-4	59	30	28	54	28	26
5-9	60	31	29	55	28	27
10-14	63	32	30	58	30	28
15-19	64	33	31	60	31	29
20-24	64	33	31	61	31	29
25-29	65	33	31	61	32	30
30-34	65	34	31	62	32	30
35-39	66	34	32	64	33	30
40-44	68	35	33	65	34	31
45-49	69	35	33	66	34	32
50-54	64	33	31	66	34	32
55-59	58	30	28	61	31	30
60-64	58	29	29	54	27	27
65-69	47	23	24	52	26	27
70-74	32	15	17	40	19	22
75-79	23	10	14	25	11	15
80-84	15	6	10	16	6	10
85-89	7	2	5	9	3	6
90-94	2	0	2	3	1	2
95-99	0	0	0	1	0	0
100 +	0	0	0	0	0	0

POPULATION BY AGE AND SEX (in thousands)

Age group	2005 Both sexes	2005 Males	2005 Females	2010 Both sexes	2010 Males	2010 Females	2015 Both sexes	2015 Males	2015 Females	2020 Both sexes	2020 Males	2020 Females
All ages	848	431	417	887	451	436	925	470	455	959	487	472
0-4	92	47	45	96	50	47	98	50	47	96	50	47
5-9	90	46	44	86	44	42	91	47	44	92	47	45
10-14	87	44	42	87	45	42	83	43	41	88	45	43
15-19	81	42	39	83	43	40	83	43	41	80	41	39
20-24	83	43	40	77	40	37	78	40	38	79	41	38
25-29	74	38	36	79	41	38	72	37	35	74	38	36
30-34	60	31	29	70	36	34	75	39	36	69	36	33
35-39	56	28	27	57	30	28	68	35	33	72	38	35
40-44	55	28	27	54	27	26	55	29	27	65	34	32
45-49	49	25	24	52	26	26	51	26	25	53	27	26
50-54	38	19	19	46	23	23	49	25	25	48	24	24
55-59	30	15	15	34	17	17	42	21	21	45	22	23
60-64	21	10	11	26	12	14	30	14	16	38	18	19
65-69	15	7	8	18	8	9	22	10	12	25	12	14
70-74	9	4	5	11	5	6	14	6	8	17	7	10
75-79	5	2	3	6	3	4	8	3	5	10	4	6
80-84	2	1	1	3	1	2	4	1	2	5	2	3
85-89	1	0	1	1	0	1	1	0	1	2	1	1
90-94	0	0	0	0	0	0	0	0	0	0	0	0
95-99	0	0	0	0	0	0	0	0	0	0	0	0
100 +	0	0	0	0	0	0	0	0	0	0	0	0

Age group	2025 Both sexes	2025 Males	2025 Females	2030 Both sexes	2030 Males	2030 Females	2035 Both sexes	2035 Males	2035 Females	2040 Both sexes	2040 Males	2040 Females
All ages	995	505	490	1 026	520	506	1 053	533	520	1 077	545	532
0-4	93	48	45	90	46	44	89	46	43	88	45	43
5-9	92	48	45	89	46	43	86	44	42	85	44	41
10-14	90	46	44	90	46	44	87	45	42	84	43	41
15-19	85	44	41	87	45	42	88	45	43	84	43	41
20-24	77	39	37	82	42	40	84	43	41	85	44	41
25-29	76	39	37	73	38	36	79	41	38	81	42	39
30-34	72	37	34	73	38	36	71	37	34	76	40	37
35-39	67	35	32	70	36	34	72	37	35	69	36	33
40-44	71	37	34	65	34	31	68	35	33	70	36	34
45-49	63	33	31	69	36	33	64	33	31	66	34	32
50-54	50	26	24	61	31	30	66	34	32	61	32	30
55-59	45	22	23	47	24	23	57	29	28	63	32	31
60-64	41	20	21	41	20	21	43	21	22	53	26	27
65-69	32	15	17	35	16	19	36	17	19	38	18	20
70-74	20	9	11	26	12	15	29	13	16	30	13	16
75-79	12	5	7	15	6	9	20	8	12	22	9	13
80-84	6	2	4	8	3	5	10	3	6	13	5	8
85-89	2	1	2	3	1	2	4	1	3	5	2	4
90-94	1	0	0	1	0	1	1	0	1	1	0	1
95-99	0	0	0	0	0	0	0	0	0	0	0	0
100 +	0	0	0	0	0	0	0	0	0	0	0	0

Age group	2045 Both sexes	2045 Males	2045 Females	2050 Both sexes	2050 Males	2050 Females
All ages	1 098	555	543	1 115	563	551
0-4	88	45	43	86	44	42
5-9	85	44	41	84	43	41
10-14	83	43	40	82	42	40
15-19	82	42	40	80	41	39
20-24	81	42	39	79	41	38
25-29	82	42	39	78	41	38
30-34	79	41	38	79	41	38
35-39	75	39	36	77	40	37
40-44	68	35	33	73	38	35
45-49	69	35	33	66	34	32
50-54	64	33	31	66	34	32
55-59	58	30	28	61	31	30
60-64	58	29	29	54	27	27
65-69	47	23	24	52	26	27
70-74	32	15	17	40	19	22
75-79	23	10	14	25	11	15
80-84	15	6	10	16	6	10
85-89	7	2	5	9	3	6
90-94	2	0	2	3	1	2
95-99	0	0	0	1	0	0
100 +	0	0	0	0	0	0

United Nations Department of Economic and Social Affairs/Population Division
World Population Prospects: The 2004 Revision, Volume II: Sex and Age Distribution of the World Population

POPULATION BY AGE AND SEX (in thousands)

Age group	2005 Both sexes	Males	Females	2010 Both sexes	Males	Females	2015 Both sexes	Males	Females	2020 Both sexes	Males	Females
All ages	848	431	417	870	442	428	000	447	434	880	446	434
0-4	92	47	45	79	41	38	70	36	34	62	32	30
5-9	90	46	44	86	44	42	74	38	36	65	33	31
10-14	87	44	42	87	45	42	83	43	41	71	36	35
15-19	81	42	39	83	43	40	83	43	41	80	41	39
20-24	83	43	40	77	40	37	78	40	38	79	41	38
25-29	74	38	36	79	41	38	72	37	35	74	38	36
30-34	60	31	29	70	36	34	75	39	36	69	36	33
35-39	56	28	27	57	30	28	68	35	33	72	38	35
40-44	55	28	27	54	27	26	55	29	27	65	34	32
45-49	49	25	24	52	26	26	51	26	25	53	27	26
50-54	38	19	19	46	23	23	49	25	25	48	24	24
55-59	30	15	15	34	17	17	42	21	21	45	22	23
60-64	21	10	11	26	12	14	30	14	16	38	18	19
65-69	15	7	8	18	8	9	22	10	12	25	12	14
70-74	9	4	5	11	5	6	14	6	8	17	7	10
75-79	5	2	3	6	3	4	8	3	5	10	4	6
80-84	2	1	1	3	1	2	4	1	2	5	2	3
85-89	1	0	1	1	0	1	1	0	1	2	1	1
90-94	0	0	0	0	0	0	0	0	0	0	0	0
95-99	0	0	0	0	0	0	0	0	0	0	0	0
100 +	0	0	0	0	0	0	0	0	0	0	0	0

Age group	2025 Both sexes	Males	Females	2030 Both sexes	Males	Females	2035 Both sexes	Males	Females	2040 Both sexes	Males	Females
All ages	882	447	435	877	444	434	865	437	428	844	425	419
0-4	58	30	28	55	28	26	49	25	24	42	22	21
5-9	58	30	28	55	28	27	51	26	25	46	24	22
10-14	62	32	30	56	29	27	52	27	25	49	25	24
15-19	68	35	33	60	31	29	53	27	26	50	26	24
20-24	77	39	37	65	34	32	57	29	28	50	26	24
25-29	76	39	37	73	38	36	62	32	30	54	28	26
30-34	72	37	34	73	38	36	71	37	34	60	31	29
35-39	67	35	32	70	36	34	72	37	35	69	36	33
40-44	71	37	34	65	34	31	68	35	33	70	36	34
45-49	63	33	31	60	36	33	64	33	31	66	34	32
50-54	50	26	24	61	31	30	66	34	32	61	32	30
55-59	45	22	23	47	24	23	57	29	28	63	32	31
60-64	41	20	21	41	20	21	43	21	22	53	26	27
65-69	32	15	17	35	16	19	36	17	19	38	18	20
70-74	20	9	11	26	12	15	29	13	16	30	13	16
75-79	12	5	7	15	6	9	20	8	12	22	9	13
80-84	6	2	4	8	3	5	10	3	6	13	5	8
85-89	2	1	2	3	1	2	4	1	3	5	2	4
90-94	1	0	0	1	0	1	1	0	1	1	0	1
95-99	0	0	0	0	0	0	0	0	0	0	0	0
100 +	0	0	0	0	0	0	0	0	0	0	0	0

Age group	2045 Both sexes	Males	Females	2050 Both sexes	Males	Females
All ages	812	408	404	772	387	385
0-4	35	18	17	29	15	14
5-9	39	20	19	31	16	15
10-14	44	22	21	37	19	18
15-19	46	24	22	41	21	20
20-24	47	24	23	43	22	21
25-29	47	25	23	44	23	21
30-34	52	27	25	45	23	22
35-39	58	30	28	50	26	24
40-44	68	35	33	57	30	27
45-49	69	35	33	66	34	32
50-54	64	33	31	66	34	32
55-59	58	30	28	61	31	30
60-64	58	29	29	54	27	27
65-69	47	23	24	52	26	27
70-74	32	15	17	40	19	22
75-79	23	10	14	25	11	15
80-84	15	6	10	16	6	10
85-89	7	2	5	9	3	6
90-94	2	0	2	3	1	2
95-99	0	0	0	1	0	0
100 +	0	0	0	0	0	0

POPULATION BY AGE AND SEX (in thousands)

Age group	1950 Both sexes	1950 Males	1950 Females	1955 Both sexes	1955 Males	1955 Females	1960 Both sexes	1960 Males	1960 Females	1965 Both sexes	1965 Males	1965 Females
All ages	4 009	1 916	2 093	4 235	2 030	2 205	4 430	2 134	2 296	4 564	2 203	2 361
0-4	500	255	245	445	227	218	413	211	202	392	200	192
5-9	375	192	183	494	252	242	442	225	217	406	207	199
10-14	327	166	161	359	183	176	492	251	241	438	223	215
15-19	310	157	153	327	166	161	357	182	175	484	247	237
20-24	326	165	161	306	155	151	319	162	157	350	178	172
25-29	307	147	160	317	159	158	296	150	146	307	156	151
30-34	266	123	143	301	142	159	310	155	155	285	145	140
35-39	287	135	152	259	119	140	294	139	155	300	150	150
40-44	288	136	152	284	133	151	253	116	137	286	134	152
45-49	245	115	130	278	130	148	276	128	148	244	111	133
50-54	206	93	113	233	107	126	266	123	143	263	120	143
55-59	165	73	92	193	85	108	218	98	120	250	112	138
60-64	140	59	81	148	63	85	175	74	101	199	86	113
65-69	109	43	66	119	47	72	127	52	75	151	60	91
70-74	78	29	49	86	32	54	94	35	59	101	38	63
75-79	50	18	32	53	19	34	57	20	37	64	22	42
80 +	30	10	20	33	11	22	41	13	28	44	14	30

Age group	1970 Both sexes	1970 Males	1970 Females	1975 Both sexes	1975 Males	1975 Females	1980 Both sexes	1980 Males	1980 Females	1985 Both sexes	1985 Males	1985 Females
All ages	4 606	2 225	2 381	4 711	2 278	2 433	4 780	2 311	2 469	4 902	2 374	2 529
0-4	348	178	170	302	155	148	320	164	156	325	166	159
5-9	383	195	188	350	179	172	300	153	146	324	166	158
10-14	402	205	197	385	196	189	351	179	172	302	155	148
15-19	426	218	208	399	204	195	382	195	187	351	179	172
20-24	448	230	218	421	215	205	384	197	187	378	193	185
25-29	319	163	156	451	232	219	407	209	198	385	197	187
30-34	291	147	144	323	165	157	442	228	214	409	210	199
35-39	277	140	137	291	148	144	318	163	155	442	228	215
40-44	294	146	148	275	138	136	287	145	142	316	161	155
45-49	279	130	149	289	142	147	270	135	135	283	142	141
50-54	236	105	131	270	123	147	280	136	144	263	130	133
55-59	250	111	139	224	97	127	258	115	143	269	128	141
60-64	231	100	131	231	98	133	209	87	122	243	104	138
65-69	175	71	104	204	82	122	200	80	120	190	75	115
70-74	124	46	78	144	54	90	173	65	108	178	66	112
75-79	72	25	47	90	30	60	112	37	74	133	44	89
80 +	51	15	36	62	18	44	88	25	63	111	30	81

Age group	1990 Both sexes	1990 Males	1990 Females	1995 Both sexes	1995 Males	1995 Females	2000 Both sexes	2000 Males	2000 Females	2005 Both sexes	2005 Males	2005 Females
All ages	4 986	2 419	2 567	5 108	2 487	2 621	5 177	2 526	2 651	5 249	2 570	2 679
0-4	311	159	152	326	166	160	295	150	144	279	143	137
5-9	327	167	160	315	161	154	327	167	161	297	152	145
10-14	325	166	159	330	169	161	317	162	155	331	169	163
15-19	302	155	148	328	167	160	332	170	162	321	164	157
20-24	349	178	171	304	155	149	328	168	161	335	171	163
25-29	377	193	185	352	180	173	305	156	149	331	169	161
30-34	385	197	188	381	195	186	353	180	173	307	158	150
35-39	408	209	199	387	197	190	380	194	186	353	180	173
40-44	439	225	214	407	207	200	384	195	189	379	193	186
45-49	312	158	154	434	221	213	402	203	199	382	193	189
50-54	277	137	139	306	154	152	426	215	211	397	199	198
55-59	254	123	131	269	132	137	297	147	150	416	208	208
60-64	254	117	137	242	115	127	258	124	134	287	140	147
65-69	222	91	131	235	104	131	226	104	123	243	113	130
70-74	164	60	104	195	75	120	210	88	122	205	90	115
75-79	140	47	93	133	44	89	162	57	105	177	69	108
80 +	141	39	102	163	45	118	175	47	127	208	59	149

(*) Including Åland Islands.

United Nations Department of Economic and Social Affairs/Population Division
World Population Prospects: The 2004 Revision, Volume II: Sex and Age Distribution of the World Population

POPULATION BY AGE AND SEX (in thousands)

Age group	2005 Both sexes	Males	Females	2010 Both sexes	Males	Females	2015 Both sexes	Males	Females	2020 Both sexes	Males	Females
All ages	5 240	2 570	2 670	5 307	2 605	2 702	5 359	2 636	2 723	5 409	2 664	2 745
0-4	279	143	137	275	141	135	282	144	138	293	150	143
5-9	297	152	145	282	144	138	277	142	136	284	145	139
10-14	331	169	163	301	154	147	286	146	140	281	144	138
15-19	321	164	157	335	171	164	305	156	149	290	148	141
20-24	335	171	163	324	166	158	338	173	165	308	158	150
25-29	331	169	161	337	173	164	326	168	158	341	175	166
30-34	307	158	150	333	171	162	340	175	165	329	170	159
35-39	353	180	173	309	158	150	335	172	162	341	176	165
40-44	379	193	186	353	180	174	309	158	151	335	172	163
45-49	382	193	189	378	191	186	352	179	174	309	158	151
50-54	397	199	198	378	190	188	374	188	186	350	176	173
55-59	416	208	208	389	194	196	372	185	187	369	184	184
60-64	287	140	147	403	198	204	377	185	192	361	178	184
65-69	243	113	130	272	129	143	382	184	198	360	173	187
70-74	205	90	115	222	99	123	249	114	135	351	163	188
75-79	177	69	108	175	72	103	191	80	110	215	94	122
80-84	121	38	82	134	48	86	134	51	84	149	58	91
85-89	58	15	43	75	21	55	86	27	59	88	29	59
90-94	24	5	19	26	5	21	36	8	28	43	11	32
95-99	5	1	4	7	1	5	8	1	7	12	2	10
100 +	0	0	0	1	0	1	1	0	1	1	0	1

Age group	2025 Both sexes	Males	Females	2030 Both sexes	Males	Females	2035 Both sexes	Males	Females	2040 Both sexes	Males	Females
All ages	5 444	2 683	2 761	5 453	2 688	2 765	5 435	2 680	2 755	5 399	2 665	2 734
0-4	294	150	144	284	145	139	273	140	134	267	137	131
5-9	296	151	145	296	151	145	287	146	140	276	141	135
10-14	288	147	141	300	153	147	300	153	147	291	149	142
15-19	285	146	139	292	150	143	304	155	148	304	156	148
20-24	292	150	142	288	148	140	295	151	144	307	157	149
25-29	311	160	151	295	152	143	291	150	141	298	154	145
30-34	344	177	167	314	162	151	299	155	144	295	153	142
35-39	331	171	160	345	178	167	315	163	152	301	156	145
40-44	342	176	166	332	171	160	346	178	168	317	164	153
45-49	335	171	163	342	176	166	332	171	161	347	178	168
50-54	307	156	151	333	170	163	341	175	166	331	170	161
55-59	345	173	172	304	154	150	330	168	163	338	172	165
60-64	359	178	182	337	167	170	297	149	148	323	163	161
65-69	345	167	179	344	167	177	324	158	166	287	142	145
70-74	332	155	177	321	151	170	321	152	169	304	145	159
75-79	306	136	170	292	130	162	284	128	156	286	130	156
80-84	170	69	102	244	101	143	206	68	138	232	98	134
85-89	100	35	65	116	42	74	170	63	107	168	63	105
90-94	45	13	33	53	16	38	64	20	45	97	31	66
95-99	15	3	12	16	4	13	20	5	16	26	6	20
100 +	2	0	2	3	0	3	4	1	3	5	1	4

Age group	2045 Both sexes	Males	Females	2050 Both sexes	Males	Females
All ages	5 360	2 651	2 709	5 329	2 642	2 687
0-4	269	137	132	273	140	134
5-9	270	138	132	271	139	133
10-14	280	143	137	274	140	134
15-19	295	151	144	284	145	139
20-24	307	158	149	298	153	145
25-29	310	160	150	310	160	150
30-34	302	156	145	313	162	151
35-39	297	154	143	304	158	146
40-44	302	157	145	298	155	144
45-49	317	164	153	303	157	146
50-54	346	177	169	317	164	154
55-59	329	168	160	344	176	168
60-64	331	168	164	323	164	159
65-69	312	155	157	321	160	160
70-74	270	130	139	295	144	151
75-79	272	125	147	243	113	130
80-84	237	102	135	228	99	129
85-89	168	65	104	174	68	106
90-94	99	32	67	102	34	68
95-99	41	10	31	43	11	32
100 +	7	1	6	11	2	9

POPULATION BY AGE AND SEX (in thousands)

Age group	2005 Both sexes	Males	Females	2010 Both sexes	Males	Females	2015 Both sexes	Males	Females	2020 Both sexes	Males	Females
All ages	5 249	2 570	2 679	5 347	2 626	2 721	5 463	2 689	2 774	5 594	2 759	2 835
0-4	279	143	137	315	161	154	346	177	169	374	191	183
5-9	297	152	145	282	144	138	317	162	155	348	178	170
10-14	331	169	163	301	154	147	286	146	140	321	164	157
15-19	321	164	157	335	171	164	305	156	149	290	148	141
20-24	335	171	163	324	166	158	338	173	165	308	158	150
25-29	331	169	161	337	173	164	326	168	158	341	175	166
30-34	307	158	150	333	171	162	340	175	165	329	170	159
35-39	353	180	173	309	158	150	335	172	162	341	176	165
40-44	379	193	186	353	180	174	309	158	151	335	172	163
45-49	382	193	189	378	191	186	352	179	174	309	158	151
50-54	397	199	198	378	190	188	374	188	186	350	176	173
55-59	416	208	208	389	194	196	372	185	187	369	184	184
60-64	287	140	147	403	198	204	377	185	192	361	178	184
65-69	243	113	130	272	129	143	382	184	198	360	173	187
70-74	205	90	115	222	99	123	249	114	135	351	163	188
75-79	177	69	108	175	72	103	191	80	110	215	94	122
80-84	121	38	82	134	48	86	134	51	84	149	58	91
85-89	58	15	43	75	21	55	86	27	59	88	29	59
90-94	24	5	19	26	5	21	36	8	28	43	11	32
95-99	5	1	4	7	1	5	8	1	7	12	2	10
100 +	0	0	0	1	0	1	1	0	1	1	0	1

Age group	2025 Both sexes	Males	Females	2030 Both sexes	Males	Females	2035 Both sexes	Males	Females	2040 Both sexes	Males	Females
All ages	5 709	2 819	2 890	5 800	2 866	2 934	5 869	2 902	2 967	5 937	2 940	2 997
0-4	374	191	183	366	187	179	361	184	176	372	190	182
5-9	376	192	184	376	192	184	368	188	180	363	186	178
10-14	352	180	172	380	194	186	380	194	186	372	190	182
15-19	325	167	159	356	182	174	384	197	188	384	197	188
20-24	292	150	142	328	168	160	359	184	175	387	198	189
25-29	311	160	151	295	152	143	331	171	161	362	186	176
30-34	344	177	167	314	162	151	299	155	144	335	173	161
35-39	331	171	160	345	178	167	315	163	152	301	156	145
40-44	342	176	166	332	171	160	346	178	168	317	164	153
45-49	335	171	163	342	176	166	332	171	161	347	178	168
50-54	307	156	151	333	170	163	341	175	166	331	170	161
55-59	345	173	172	304	154	150	330	168	163	338	172	165
60-64	359	178	182	337	167	170	297	149	148	323	163	161
65-69	345	167	179	344	167	177	324	158	166	287	142	145
70-74	332	155	177	321	151	170	321	152	169	304	145	159
75-79	306	136	170	292	130	162	284	128	156	286	130	156
80-84	170	69	102	244	101	143	236	98	138	232	98	134
85-89	100	35	65	116	42	74	170	63	107	168	63	105
90-94	45	13	33	53	16	38	64	20	45	97	31	66
95-99	15	3	12	16	4	13	20	5	16	26	6	20
100 +	2	0	2	3	0	3	4	1	3	5	1	4

Age group	2045 Both sexes	Males	Females	2050 Both sexes	Males	Females
All ages	6 026	2 992	3 034	6 146	3 060	3 085
0-4	398	203	194	424	217	207
5-9	374	191	183	400	204	196
10-14	367	188	179	378	193	185
15-19	377	193	184	371	190	181
20-24	387	199	189	380	195	185
25-29	390	201	189	391	201	190
30-34	365	189	176	393	203	190
35-39	336	174	162	367	190	177
40-44	302	157	145	338	175	163
45-49	317	164	153	303	157	146
50-54	346	177	169	317	164	154
55-59	329	168	160	344	176	168
60-64	331	168	164	323	164	159
65-69	312	155	157	321	160	160
70-74	270	130	139	295	144	151
75-79	272	125	147	243	113	130
80-84	237	102	135	228	99	129
85-89	168	65	104	174	68	106
90-94	99	32	67	102	34	68
95-99	41	10	31	43	11	32
100 +	7	1	6	11	2	9

United Nations Department of Economic and Social Affairs/Population Division
World Population Prospects: The 2004 Revision, Volume II: Sex and Age Distribution of the World Population

POPULATION BY AGE AND SEX (in thousands)

Age group	2005 Both sexes	Males	Females	2010 Both sexes	Males	Females	2015 Both sexes	Males	Females	2020 Both sexes	Males	Females
All ages	5 249	2 570	2 679	5 267	2 585	2 682	5 255	2 583	2 672	5 225	2 570	2 655
0-4	279	143	137	235	120	115	218	111	106	213	109	104
5-9	297	152	145	282	144	138	238	121	116	220	112	108
10-14	331	169	163	301	154	147	286	146	140	242	123	118
15-19	321	164	157	335	171	164	305	156	149	290	148	141
20-24	335	171	163	324	166	158	338	173	165	308	158	150
25-29	331	169	161	337	173	164	326	168	158	341	175	166
30-34	307	158	150	333	171	162	340	175	165	329	170	159
35-39	353	180	173	309	158	150	335	172	162	341	176	165
40-44	379	193	186	353	180	174	309	158	151	335	172	163
45-49	382	193	189	378	191	186	352	179	174	309	158	151
50-54	397	199	198	378	190	188	374	188	186	350	176	173
55-59	416	208	208	389	194	196	372	185	187	369	184	184
60-64	287	140	147	403	198	204	377	185	192	361	178	184
65-69	243	113	130	272	129	143	382	184	198	360	173	187
70-74	205	90	115	222	99	123	249	114	135	351	163	188
75-79	177	69	108	175	72	103	191	80	110	215	94	122
80-84	121	38	82	134	48	86	134	51	84	149	58	91
85-89	58	15	43	75	21	55	86	27	59	88	29	59
90-94	24	5	19	26	5	21	36	8	28	43	11	32
95-99	5	1	4	7	1	5	8	1	7	12	2	10
100 +	0	0	0	1	0	1	1	0	1	1	0	1

Age group	2025 Both sexes	Males	Females	2030 Both sexes	Males	Females	2035 Both sexes	Males	Females	2040 Both sexes	Males	Females
All ages	5 182	2 549	2 633	5 114	2 515	2 599	5 018	2 467	2 551	4 893	2 406	2 487
0-4	215	110	105	208	106	102	195	100	96	178	91	87
5-9	216	110	106	217	111	106	210	107	103	198	101	97
10-14	224	114	110	220	112	107	221	113	108	214	109	105
15-19	246	126	120	228	117	111	224	114	109	225	115	110
20-24	292	150	142	249	128	121	231	119	112	227	116	110
25-29	311	160	151	295	152	143	252	130	122	234	121	113
30-34	344	177	167	314	162	151	299	155	144	255	133	123
35-39	331	171	160	345	178	167	315	163	152	301	156	145
40-44	342	176	166	332	171	160	346	178	168	317	164	153
45-49	335	171	163	342	176	166	332	171	161	347	178	168
50-54	307	156	151	333	170	163	341	175	166	331	170	161
55-59	345	173	172	304	154	150	330	168	163	338	172	165
60-64	359	178	182	337	167	170	297	149	148	323	160	163
65-69	345	167	179	344	167	177	324	158	166	287	142	145
70-74	332	155	177	321	151	170	321	152	169	304	145	159
75-79	306	136	170	292	130	162	284	128	156	286	130	156
80-84	170	69	102	244	101	143	236	98	138	232	98	134
85-89	100	35	65	116	42	74	170	63	107	168	63	105
90-94	45	13	33	53	16	38	64	20	45	97	31	66
95-99	15	3	12	16	4	13	20	5	16	26	6	20
100 +	2	0	2	3	0	3	4	1	3	5	1	4

Age group	2045 Both sexes	Males	Females	2050 Both sexes	Males	Females
All ages	4 749	2 338	2 411	4 600	2 270	2 331
0-4	164	84	80	155	79	76
5-9	181	92	89	166	85	81
10-14	202	103	99	185	94	90
15-19	218	112	107	206	105	101
20-24	228	117	111	221	114	108
25-29	230	119	111	232	120	112
30-34	238	124	114	233	121	112
35-39	257	134	123	240	125	115
40-44	302	157	145	259	135	124
45-49	317	164	153	303	157	146
50-54	346	177	169	317	164	154
55-59	329	168	160	344	176	168
60-64	331	168	164	323	164	159
65-69	312	155	157	321	160	160
70-74	270	130	139	295	144	151
75-79	272	125	147	243	113	130
80-84	237	102	135	228	99	129
85-89	168	65	104	174	68	106
90-94	99	32	67	102	34	68
95-99	41	10	31	43	11	32
100 +	7	1	6	11	2	9

United Nations Department of Economic and Social Affairs/Population Division
World Population Prospects: The 2004 Revision, Volume II: Sex and Age Distribution of the World Population

397

POPULATION BY AGE AND SEX (in thousands)

Age group	1950 Both sexes	1950 Males	1950 Females	1955 Both sexes	1955 Males	1955 Females	1960 Both sexes	1960 Males	1960 Females	1965 Both sexes	1965 Males	1965 Females
All ages	41 829	20 105	21 723	43 428	20 971	22 457	45 684	22 162	23 522	48 758	23 737	25 021
0-4	3 962	2 018	1 943	3 922	1 998	1 924	4 005	2 041	1 964	4 222	2 154	2 068
5-9	2 714	1 379	1 335	3 966	2 020	1 946	4 010	2 040	1 970	4 123	2 100	2 023
10-14	2 822	1 421	1 401	2 733	1 392	1 341	4 032	2 054	1 978	4 140	2 108	2 032
15-19	3 136	1 592	1 544	2 836	1 433	1 403	2 782	1 421	1 361	4 151	2 122	2 029
20-24	3 219	1 640	1 580	3 133	1 593	1 540	2 883	1 478	1 405	2 912	1 500	1 412
25-29	3 281	1 649	1 633	3 206	1 634	1 572	3 194	1 633	1 561	3 017	1 554	1 463
30-34	1 975	988	987	3 265	1 641	1 624	3 266	1 659	1 607	3 306	1 690	1 616
35-39	2 897	1 442	1 455	1 965	984	981	3 298	1 652	1 646	3 362	1 704	1 658
40-44	3 083	1 538	1 544	2 861	1 422	1 439	1 978	985	993	3 346	1 668	1 678
45-49	3 041	1 514	1 526	3 009	1 492	1 517	2 842	1 399	1 443	1 996	984	1 012
50-54	2 681	1 257	1 424	2 924	1 439	1 485	2 928	1 434	1 494	2 814	1 368	1 446
55-59	2 227	934	1 293	2 532	1 165	1 367	2 791	1 345	1 446	2 837	1 361	1 476
60-64	2 028	848	1 181	2 055	837	1 218	2 358	1 052	1 306	2 628	1 222	1 406
65-69	1 752	714	1 038	1 793	720	1 073	1 839	720	1 119	2 142	907	1 235
70-74	1 376	564	812	1 439	554	885	1 496	568	928	1 578	580	998
75-79	935	370	565	1 014	385	629	1 068	382	686	1 146	397	749
80 +	699	238	461	775	262	513	914	299	615	1 038	318	720

Age group	1970 Both sexes	1970 Males	1970 Females	1975 Both sexes	1975 Males	1975 Females	1980 Both sexes	1980 Males	1980 Females	1985 Both sexes	1985 Males	1985 Females
All ages	50 772	24 792	25 980	52 699	25 807	26 892	53 880	26 312	27 568	55 284	26 956	28 329
0-4	4 205	2 148	2 057	4 118	2 107	2 011	3 699	1 889	1 810	3 796	1 944	1 852
5-9	4 240	2 161	2 079	4 179	2 135	2 044	4 122	2 103	2 019	3 710	1 900	1 809
10-14	4 160	2 117	2 043	4 297	2 194	2 104	4 185	2 132	2 053	4 217	2 165	2 052
15-19	4 201	2 139	2 062	4 236	2 155	2 080	4 299	2 187	2 112	4 274	2 184	2 090
20-24	4 117	2 113	2 004	4 247	2 160	2 087	4 228	2 140	2 088	4 305	2 164	2 141
25-29	3 042	1 578	1 464	4 278	2 208	2 069	4 248	2 153	2 095	4 216	2 111	2 105
30-34	3 087	1 595	1 492	3 017	1 574	1 443	4 272	2 197	2 076	4 278	2 152	2 126
35-39	3 338	1 707	1 631	3 057	1 571	1 486	3 006	1 561	1 445	4 265	2 170	2 095
40-44	3 341	1 688	1 653	3 298	1 672	1 626	3 029	1 545	1 484	2 981	1 520	1 461
45-49	3 310	1 640	1 670	3 288	1 645	1 643	3 243	1 626	1 617	2 976	1 502	1 474
50-54	1 904	925	979	3 201	1 563	1 638	3 200	1 576	1 624	3 137	1 556	1 581
55-59	2 662	1 270	1 392	1 855	892	964	3 076	1 469	1 607	3 061	1 480	1 581
60-64	2 633	1 221	1 412	2 526	1 168	1 358	1 750	815	935	2 910	1 353	1 557
65-69	2 347	1 036	1 310	2 391	1 061	1 330	2 065	914	1 151	1 617	724	893
70-74	1 798	706	1 092	2 016	837	1 180	2 131	888	1 243	2 034	844	1 190
75-79	1 218	410	807	1 395	504	891	1 667	631	1 036	1 690	638	1 051
80 +	1 172	339	833	1 299	361	939	1 662	488	1 174	1 818	548	1 270

Age group	1990 Both sexes	1990 Males	1990 Females	1995 Both sexes	1995 Males	1995 Females	2000 Both sexes	2000 Males	2000 Females	2005 Both sexes	2005 Males	2005 Females
All ages	56 735	27 622	29 113	58 203	28 300	29 903	59 278	28 847	30 431	60 496	29 463	31 033
0-4	3 798	1 941	1 856	3 576	1 829	1 747	3 646	1 868	1 778	3 727	1 910	1 817
5-9	3 834	1 962	1 872	3 806	1 947	1 859	3 587	1 834	1 753	3 662	1 876	1 786
10-14	3 855	1 973	1 882	3 861	1 976	1 885	3 817	1 952	1 865	3 603	1 842	1 761
15-19	4 232	2 161	2 071	3 810	1 948	1 863	3 870	1 980	1 890	3 831	1 959	1 872
20-24	4 285	2 168	2 116	4 133	2 083	2 050	3 813	1 946	1 867	3 879	1 982	1 897
25-29	4 313	2 154	2 159	4 207	2 101	2 105	4 131	2 079	2 053	3 819	1 947	1 873
30-34	4 287	2 138	2 150	4 361	2 172	2 188	4 203	2 095	2 107	4 136	2 078	2 058
35-39	4 290	2 151	2 139	4 292	2 132	2 160	4 350	2 161	2 188	4 202	2 091	2 111
40-44	4 138	2 095	2 043	4 243	2 112	2 131	4 269	2 112	2 156	4 338	2 149	2 188
45-49	2 949	1 492	1 457	4 291	2 159	2 133	4 200	2 079	2 121	4 239	2 089	2 151
50-54	2 900	1 441	1 458	2 899	1 457	1 442	4 219	2 105	2 114	4 147	2 039	2 108
55-59	3 006	1 459	1 547	2 783	1 370	1 413	2 828	1 404	1 424	4 129	2 039	2 091
60-64	2 913	1 368	1 545	2 874	1 370	1 505	2 677	1 293	1 384	2 734	1 335	1 399
65-69	2 543	1 141	1 402	2 743	1 252	1 490	2 707	1 251	1 456	2 535	1 192	1 343
70-74	1 614	685	929	2 464	1 057	1 406	2 499	1 090	1 409	2 482	1 101	1 381
75-79	1 642	630	1 012	1 366	550	816	2 122	851	1 271	2 169	889	1 280
80 +	2 136	663	1 474	2 494	784	1 710	2 341	745	1 596	2 863	946	1 917

398

United Nations Department of Economic and Social Affairs/Population Division
World Population Prospects: The 2004 Revision, Volume II: Sex and Age Distribution of the World Population

POPULATION BY AGE AND SEX (in thousands)

Age group	2005 Both sexes	2005 Males	2005 Females	2010 Both sexes	2010 Males	2010 Females	2015 Both sexes	2015 Males	2015 Females	2020 Both sexes	2020 Males	2020 Females
All ages	60 496	29 463	31 033	61 535	29 986	31 549	62 339	30 387	31 952	62 954	30 694	32 260
0-4	3 727	1 910	1 817	3 646	1 869	1 778	3 535	1 812	1 723	3 464	1 775	1 689
5-9	3 662	1 876	1 786	3 742	1 918	1 825	3 662	1 876	1 785	3 550	1 819	1 731
10-14	3 603	1 842	1 761	3 678	1 884	1 794	3 758	1 926	1 833	3 677	1 884	1 793
15-19	3 831	1 959	1 872	3 617	1 849	1 768	3 692	1 891	1 801	3 773	1 933	1 840
20-24	3 879	1 982	1 897	3 841	1 962	1 879	3 628	1 853	1 775	3 703	1 895	1 808
25-29	3 819	1 947	1 873	3 886	1 983	1 903	3 849	1 964	1 885	3 636	1 855	1 781
30-34	4 136	2 078	2 058	3 825	1 947	1 878	3 892	1 984	1 908	3 856	1 965	1 891
35-39	4 202	2 091	2 111	4 136	2 074	2 061	3 827	1 945	1 882	3 895	1 982	1 912
40-44	4 338	2 149	2 188	4 193	2 081	2 112	4 129	2 066	2 063	3 823	1 938	1 885
45-49	4 239	2 089	2 151	4 312	2 128	2 184	4 172	2 063	2 109	4 111	2 049	2 061
50-54	4 147	2 039	2 108	4 191	2 052	2 139	4 268	2 094	2 174	4 135	2 033	2 101
55-59	4 129	2 039	2 091	4 069	1 981	2 088	4 120	1 999	2 120	4 201	2 044	2 157
60-64	2 734	1 335	1 399	4 000	1 945	2 055	3 953	1 898	2 056	4 011	1 921	2 090
65-69	2 535	1 192	1 343	2 599	1 238	1 360	3 810	1 811	1 999	3 779	1 776	2 003
70-74	2 482	1 101	1 381	2 334	1 057	1 277	2 403	1 106	1 297	3 534	1 627	1 908
75-79	2 169	889	1 280	2 166	907	1 259	2 048	879	1 169	2 120	928	1 192
80-84	1 663	606	1 056	1 717	644	1 073	1 731	666	1 064	1 651	655	997
85-89	686	217	469	1 101	350	750	1 159	381	778	1 190	403	787
90-94	386	96	290	338	88	250	564	147	417	614	165	449
95-99	111	22	89	124	25	99	116	24	92	203	41	163
100 +	16	3	12	21	4	17	26	4	21	26	4	22

Age group	2025 Both sexes	2025 Males	2025 Females	2030 Both sexes	2030 Males	2030 Females	2035 Both sexes	2035 Males	2035 Females	2040 Both sexes	2040 Males	2040 Females
All ages	63 407	30 913	32 494	63 712	31 043	32 670	63 850	31 082	32 768	63 787	31 033	32 754
0-4	3 406	1 745	1 660	3 374	1 729	1 645	3 374	1 729	1 645	3 358	1 721	1 637
5-9	3 479	1 783	1 696	3 420	1 752	1 667	3 388	1 736	1 652	3 388	1 736	1 652
10-14	3 565	1 827	1 738	3 494	1 790	1 704	3 435	1 760	1 675	3 403	1 744	1 659
15-19	3 692	1 891	1 801	3 580	1 834	1 746	3 508	1 797	1 711	3 449	1 767	1 682
20-24	3 785	1 937	1 847	3 704	1 897	1 808	3 592	1 839	1 753	3 521	1 803	1 718
25-29	3 713	1 898	1 815	3 795	1 941	1 854	3 715	1 900	1 815	3 603	1 844	1 760
30-34	3 644	1 857	1 787	3 721	1 900	1 820	3 804	1 944	1 860	3 725	1 904	1 821
35-39	3 650	1 964	1 895	3 649	1 857	1 792	3 727	1 901	1 826	3 811	1 945	1 866
40-44	3 892	1 977	1 916	3 858	1 959	1 899	3 650	1 854	1 796	3 729	1 898	1 830
45-49	3 810	1 925	1 885	3 880	1 964	1 916	3 849	1 949	1 900	3 644	1 846	1 798
50-54	4 078	2 023	2 055	3 783	1 903	1 881	3 856	1 944	1 913	3 828	1 930	1 898
55-59	4 076	1 989	2 087	4 025	1 982	2 043	3 739	1 868	1 871	3 815	1 911	1 904
60-64	4 098	1 970	2 128	3 983	1 922	2 061	3 939	1 920	2 019	3 666	1 814	1 852
65-69	3 845	1 805	2 040	3 938	1 858	2 080	3 837	1 820	2 017	3 803	1 824	1 978
70-74	3 521	1 605	1 916	3 596	1 640	1 955	3 694	1 697	1 997	3 612	1 671	1 941
75-79	3 133	1 375	1 758	3 142	1 368	1 774	3 225	1 409	1 816	3 329	1 468	1 861
80-84	1 725	700	1 025	2 572	1 050	1 522	2 604	1 057	1 547	2 696	1 101	1 595
85-89	1 155	405	750	1 227	443	785	1 859	676	1 183	1 914	693	1 221
90-94	651	181	470	652	188	464	712	212	500	1 107	333	774
95-99	234	48	186	260	55	205	272	59	213	309	69	240
100 +	46	7	38	59	9	50	71	11	60	80	12	67

Age group	2045 Both sexes	2045 Males	2045 Females	2050 Both sexes	2050 Males	2050 Females
All ages	63 523	30 914	32 609	63 116	30 753	32 363
0-4	3 302	1 692	1 610	3 233	1 657	1 576
5-9	3 372	1 728	1 644	3 316	1 699	1 617
10-14	3 403	1 744	1 659	3 387	1 736	1 652
15-19	3 418	1 751	1 667	3 418	1 751	1 667
20-24	3 462	1 773	1 689	3 431	1 757	1 674
25-29	3 532	1 807	1 725	3 474	1 778	1 696
30-34	3 613	1 847	1 766	3 543	1 811	1 731
35-39	3 732	1 905	1 827	3 622	1 849	1 772
40-44	3 813	1 943	1 871	3 737	1 904	1 832
45-49	3 724	1 891	1 833	3 810	1 936	1 874
50-54	3 627	1 830	1 797	3 709	1 877	1 833
55-59	3 791	1 901	1 890	3 596	1 805	1 791
60-64	3 745	1 860	1 886	3 727	1 853	1 874
65-69	3 546	1 730	1 816	3 630	1 778	1 852
70-74	3 589	1 682	1 907	3 357	1 602	1 755
75-79	3 270	1 455	1 815	3 264	1 474	1 789
80-84	2 806	1 159	1 646	2 778	1 162	1 616
85-89	2 012	736	1 276	2 124	789	1 334
90-94	1 172	353	819	1 263	385	877
95-99	498	113	385	549	125	425
100 +	94	15	79	150	24	126

POPULATION BY AGE AND SEX (in thousands)

Age group	2005 Both sexes	Males	Females	2010 Both sexes	Males	Females	2015 Both sexes	Males	Females	2020 Both sexes	Males	Females
All ages	60 496	29 463	31 033	62 027	30 238	31 789	63 593	31 030	32 563	65 141	31 815	33 326
0-4	3 727	1 910	1 817	4 138	2 121	2 017	4 297	2 202	2 095	4 398	2 254	2 144
5-9	3 662	1 876	1 786	3 742	1 918	1 825	4 153	2 128	2 025	4 312	2 209	2 102
10-14	3 603	1 842	1 761	3 678	1 884	1 794	3 758	1 926	1 833	4 168	2 136	2 033
15-19	3 831	1 959	1 872	3 617	1 849	1 768	3 692	1 891	1 801	3 773	1 933	1 840
20-24	3 879	1 982	1 897	3 841	1 962	1 879	3 628	1 853	1 775	3 703	1 895	1 808
25-29	3 819	1 947	1 873	3 886	1 983	1 903	3 849	1 964	1 885	3 636	1 855	1 781
30-34	4 136	2 078	2 058	3 825	1 947	1 878	3 892	1 984	1 908	3 856	1 965	1 891
35-39	4 202	2 091	2 111	4 136	2 074	2 061	3 827	1 945	1 882	3 895	1 982	1 912
40-44	4 338	2 149	2 188	4 193	2 081	2 112	4 129	2 066	2 063	3 823	1 938	1 885
45-49	4 239	2 089	2 151	4 312	2 128	2 184	4 172	2 063	2 109	4 111	2 049	2 061
50-54	4 147	2 039	2 108	4 191	2 052	2 139	4 268	2 094	2 174	4 135	2 033	2 101
55-59	4 129	2 039	2 091	4 069	1 981	2 088	4 120	1 999	2 120	4 201	2 044	2 157
60-64	2 734	1 335	1 399	4 000	1 945	2 055	3 953	1 898	2 056	4 011	1 921	2 090
65-69	2 535	1 192	1 343	2 599	1 238	1 360	3 810	1 811	1 999	3 779	1 776	2 003
70-74	2 482	1 101	1 381	2 334	1 057	1 277	2 403	1 106	1 297	3 534	1 627	1 908
75-79	2 169	889	1 280	2 166	907	1 259	2 048	879	1 169	2 120	928	1 192
80-84	1 663	606	1 056	1 717	644	1 073	1 731	666	1 064	1 651	655	997
85-89	686	217	469	1 101	350	750	1 159	381	778	1 190	403	787
90-94	386	96	290	338	88	250	564	147	417	614	165	449
95-99	111	22	89	124	25	99	116	24	92	203	41	163
100 +	16	3	12	21	4	17	26	4	21	26	4	22

Age group	2025 Both sexes	Males	Females	2030 Both sexes	Males	Females	2035 Both sexes	Males	Females	2040 Both sexes	Males	Females
All ages	66 512	32 504	34 008	67 748	33 110	34 638	68 922	33 680	35 242	70 131	34 282	35 849
0-4	4 325	2 216	2 109	4 306	2 207	2 099	4 413	2 262	2 151	4 634	2 375	2 259
5-9	4 412	2 261	2 151	4 339	2 223	2 115	4 320	2 214	2 106	4 427	2 268	2 158
10-14	4 327	2 217	2 110	4 427	2 268	2 159	4 353	2 231	2 123	4 335	2 221	2 114
15-19	4 183	2 143	2 040	4 341	2 224	2 117	4 441	2 275	2 166	4 367	2 237	2 130
20-24	3 785	1 937	1 847	4 194	2 147	2 047	4 353	2 229	2 124	4 452	2 280	2 173
25-29	3 713	1 898	1 815	3 795	1 941	1 854	4 204	2 151	2 054	4 362	2 232	2 130
30-34	3 644	1 857	1 787	3 721	1 900	1 820	3 804	1 944	1 860	4 213	2 153	2 060
35-39	3 859	1 964	1 895	3 649	1 857	1 792	3 727	1 901	1 826	3 811	1 945	1 866
40-44	3 892	1 977	1 916	3 858	1 959	1 899	3 650	1 854	1 796	3 729	1 898	1 830
45-49	3 810	1 925	1 885	3 880	1 964	1 916	3 849	1 949	1 900	3 644	1 846	1 798
50-54	4 078	2 023	2 055	3 783	1 903	1 881	3 856	1 944	1 913	3 828	1 930	1 898
55-59	4 076	1 989	2 087	4 025	1 982	2 043	3 739	1 868	1 871	3 815	1 911	1 904
60-64	4 098	1 970	2 128	3 983	1 922	2 061	3 939	1 920	2 019	3 666	1 814	1 852
65-69	3 845	1 805	2 040	3 938	1 858	2 080	3 837	1 820	2 017	3 803	1 824	1 978
70-74	3 521	1 605	1 916	3 596	1 640	1 955	3 694	1 697	1 997	3 612	1 671	1 941
75-79	3 133	1 375	1 758	3 142	1 368	1 774	3 225	1 409	1 816	3 329	1 468	1 861
80-84	1 725	700	1 025	2 572	1 050	1 522	2 604	1 057	1 547	2 696	1 101	1 595
85-89	1 155	405	750	1 227	443	785	1 859	676	1 183	1 914	693	1 221
90-94	651	181	470	652	188	464	712	212	500	1 107	333	774
95-99	234	48	186	260	55	205	272	59	213	309	69	240
100 +	46	7	38	59	9	50	71	11	60	80	12	67

Age group	2045 Both sexes	Males	Females	2050 Both sexes	Males	Females
All ages	71 424	34 960	36 464	72 785	35 703	37 083
0-4	4 866	2 494	2 372	5 010	2 567	2 442
5-9	4 647	2 381	2 266	4 879	2 500	2 379
10-14	4 442	2 276	2 166	4 662	2 389	2 273
15-19	4 349	2 228	2 121	4 456	2 283	2 173
20-24	4 379	2 243	2 137	4 361	2 234	2 128
25-29	4 462	2 283	2 179	4 390	2 247	2 143
30-34	4 371	2 234	2 137	4 471	2 286	2 185
35-39	4 219	2 154	2 065	4 377	2 235	2 142
40-44	3 813	1 943	1 871	4 222	2 151	2 070
45-49	3 724	1 891	1 833	3 810	1 936	1 874
50-54	3 627	1 830	1 797	3 709	1 877	1 833
55-59	3 791	1 901	1 890	3 596	1 805	1 791
60-64	3 745	1 860	1 886	3 727	1 853	1 874
65-69	3 546	1 730	1 816	3 630	1 778	1 852
70-74	3 589	1 682	1 907	3 357	1 602	1 755
75-79	3 270	1 455	1 815	3 264	1 474	1 789
80-84	2 806	1 159	1 646	2 778	1 162	1 616
85-89	2 012	736	1 276	2 124	789	1 334
90-94	1 172	353	819	1 263	385	877
95-99	498	113	385	549	125	425
100 +	94	15	79	150	24	126

United Nations Department of Economic and Social Affairs/Population Division
World Population Prospects: The 2004 Revision, Volume II: Sex and Age Distribution of the World Population

400

POPULATION BY AGE AND SEX (in thousands)

Age group	2005 Both sexes	Males	Females	2010 Both sexes	Males	Females	2015 Both sexes	Males	Females	2020 Both sexes	Males	Females
All ages	60 496	29 463	31 033	61 043	29 734	31 309	61 086	29 745	31 341	60 767	29 573	31 194
0-4	3 727	1 910	1 817	3 155	1 617	1 538	2 773	1 421	1 352	2 530	1 297	1 233
5-9	3 662	1 876	1 786	3 742	1 918	1 825	3 170	1 625	1 546	2 788	1 429	1 359
10-14	3 603	1 842	1 761	3 678	1 884	1 794	3 758	1 926	1 833	3 186	1 633	1 554
15-19	3 831	1 959	1 872	3 617	1 849	1 768	3 692	1 891	1 801	3 773	1 933	1 840
20-24	3 879	1 982	1 897	3 841	1 962	1 879	3 628	1 853	1 775	3 703	1 895	1 808
25-29	3 819	1 947	1 873	3 886	1 983	1 903	3 849	1 964	1 885	3 636	1 855	1 781
30-34	4 136	2 078	2 058	3 825	1 947	1 878	3 892	1 984	1 908	3 856	1 965	1 891
35-39	4 202	2 091	2 111	4 136	2 074	2 061	3 827	1 945	1 882	3 895	1 982	1 912
40-44	4 338	2 149	2 188	4 193	2 081	2 112	4 129	2 066	2 063	3 823	1 938	1 885
45-49	4 239	2 089	2 151	4 312	2 128	2 184	4 172	2 063	2 109	4 111	2 049	2 061
50-54	4 147	2 039	2 108	4 191	2 052	2 139	4 268	2 094	2 174	4 135	2 033	2 101
55-59	4 129	2 039	2 091	4 069	1 981	2 088	4 120	1 999	2 120	4 201	2 044	2 157
60-64	2 734	1 335	1 399	4 000	1 945	2 055	3 953	1 898	2 056	4 011	1 921	2 090
65-69	2 535	1 192	1 343	2 599	1 238	1 360	3 810	1 811	1 999	3 779	1 776	2 003
70-74	2 482	1 101	1 381	2 334	1 057	1 277	2 403	1 106	1 297	3 534	1 627	1 908
75-79	2 169	889	1 280	2 166	907	1 259	2 048	879	1 169	2 120	928	1 192
80-84	1 663	606	1 056	1 717	644	1 073	1 731	666	1 064	1 651	655	997
85-89	686	217	469	1 101	350	750	1 159	381	778	1 190	403	787
90-94	386	96	290	338	88	250	564	147	417	614	165	449
95-99	111	22	89	124	25	99	116	24	92	203	41	163
100 +	16	3	12	21	4	17	26	4	21	26	4	22

Age group	2025 Both sexes	Males	Females	2030 Both sexes	Males	Females	2035 Both sexes	Males	Females	2040 Both sexes	Males	Females
All ages	60 302	29 322	30 980	59 687	28 980	30 707	58 844	28 517	30 326	57 667	27 899	29 769
0-4	2 487	1 274	1 212	2 451	1 256	1 195	2 390	1 225	1 165	2 240	1 148	1 092
5-9	2 545	1 304	1 241	2 502	1 282	1 220	2 466	1 263	1 202	2 404	1 232	1 172
10-14	2 804	1 437	1 367	2 561	1 312	1 249	2 517	1 290	1 227	2 481	1 271	1 210
15-19	3 202	1 640	1 562	2 819	1 444	1 375	2 576	1 319	1 256	2 532	1 297	1 235
20-24	3 785	1 937	1 847	3 215	1 646	1 569	2 832	1 450	1 382	2 589	1 326	1 263
25-29	3 713	1 898	1 815	3 795	1 941	1 854	3 226	1 650	1 576	2 844	1 455	1 389
30-34	3 644	1 857	1 787	3 721	1 900	1 820	3 804	1 944	1 860	3 237	1 654	1 582
35-39	3 859	1 964	1 895	3 649	1 857	1 792	3 727	1 901	1 826	3 811	1 945	1 866
40-44	3 892	1 977	1 916	3 868	1 959	1 899	3 650	1 854	1 796	3 728	1 898	1 830
45-49	3 810	1 925	1 885	3 880	1 964	1 916	3 849	1 949	1 900	3 644	1 846	1 798
50-54	4 078	2 023	2 055	3 783	1 903	1 881	3 856	1 944	1 913	3 828	1 930	1 898
55-59	4 078	1 989	2 087	4 025	1 982	2 042	3 739	1 868	1 871	3 815	1 911	1 904
60-64	4 098	1 970	2 128	3 983	1 922	2 061	3 939	1 920	2 019	3 666	1 814	1 852
65-69	3 845	1 805	2 040	3 938	1 858	2 080	3 837	1 820	2 017	3 803	1 824	1 978
70-74	3 521	1 605	1 916	3 596	1 640	1 955	3 694	1 697	1 997	3 612	1 671	1 941
75-79	3 133	1 375	1 758	3 142	1 368	1 774	3 225	1 409	1 816	3 329	1 468	1 861
80-84	1 725	700	1 025	2 572	1 050	1 522	2 604	1 057	1 547	2 606	1 101	1 595
85-89	1 155	405	750	1 227	443	785	1 859	676	1 183	1 914	693	1 221
90-94	651	181	470	652	188	464	712	212	500	1 107	333	774
95-99	234	48	186	260	55	205	272	59	213	309	69	240
100 +	46	7	38	59	9	50	71	11	60	80	12	67

Age group	2045 Both sexes	Males	Females	2050 Both sexes	Males	Females
All ages	56 132	27 130	29 002	54 342	26 261	28 081
0-4	2 025	1 038	987	1 841	943	898
5-9	2 254	1 155	1 099	2 040	1 045	994
10-14	2 420	1 240	1 180	2 270	1 163	1 107
15-19	2 496	1 279	1 217	2 435	1 247	1 187
20-24	2 546	1 304	1 242	2 510	1 285	1 225
25-29	2 602	1 332	1 271	2 559	1 309	1 249
30-34	2 856	1 460	1 396	2 614	1 337	1 278
35-39	3 246	1 657	1 589	2 866	1 464	1 403
40-44	3 813	1 943	1 871	3 252	1 657	1 595
45-49	3 724	1 891	1 833	3 810	1 936	1 874
50-54	3 627	1 830	1 797	3 709	1 877	1 833
55-59	3 791	1 901	1 890	3 596	1 805	1 791
60-64	3 745	1 860	1 886	3 727	1 853	1 874
65-69	3 546	1 730	1 816	3 630	1 778	1 852
70-74	3 589	1 682	1 907	3 357	1 602	1 755
75-79	3 270	1 455	1 815	3 264	1 474	1 789
80-84	2 806	1 159	1 646	2 778	1 162	1 616
85-89	2 012	736	1 276	2 124	789	1 334
90-94	1 172	353	819	1 263	385	877
95-99	498	113	385	549	125	425
100 +	94	15	79	150	24	126

POPULATION BY AGE AND SEX (in thousands)

Age group	1950 Both sexes	1950 Males	1950 Females	1955 Both sexes	1955 Males	1955 Females	1960 Both sexes	1960 Males	1960 Females	1965 Both sexes	1965 Males	1965 Females
All ages	25	13	12	29	15	14	32	16	16	40	21	19
0-4	4	2	2	4	2	2	5	2	2	6	3	3
5-9	2	1	1	3	2	2	4	2	2	5	3	3
10-14	2	1	1	2	1	1	3	2	2	4	2	2
15-19	2	1	1	2	1	1	2	1	1	3	2	2
20-24	2	1	1	2	1	1	2	1	1	3	2	1
25-29	2	1	1	2	1	1	2	1	1	3	1	1
30-34	2	1	1	2	1	1	2	1	1	2	1	1
35-39	2	1	1	2	1	1	2	1	1	3	1	1
40-44	2	1	1	2	1	1	2	1	1	2	1	1
45-49	1	1	1	2	1	1	2	1	1	2	1	1
50-54	1	1	1	1	1	1	2	1	1	2	1	1
55-59	1	0	0	1	1	1	1	1	1	1	1	1
60-64	1	0	0	1	0	0	1	1	1	1	1	1
65-69	1	0	0	1	0	0	1	0	0	1	0	0
70-74	0	0	0	1	0	0	1	0	0	1	0	0
75-79	0	0	0	0	0	0	0	0	0	0	0	0
80 +	0	0	0	0	0	0	0	0	0	0	0	0

Age group	1970 Both sexes	1970 Males	1970 Females	1975 Both sexes	1975 Males	1975 Females	1980 Both sexes	1980 Males	1980 Females	1985 Both sexes	1985 Males	1985 Females
All ages	48	25	23	56	28	28	68	35	33	88	46	42
0-4	7	3	3	8	4	4	8	4	4	9	5	5
5-9	6	3	3	7	4	4	8	4	4	10	5	5
10-14	5	3	3	7	3	3	8	4	4	9	5	5
15-19	5	2	2	6	3	3	7	3	3	8	4	4
20-24	4	2	2	4	2	2	6	4	3	8	5	4
25-29	3	2	2	5	2	2	6	3	3	8	4	4
30-34	3	2	1	4	2	2	6	3	3	8	4	4
35-39	3	2	1	3	2	2	4	2	2	6	3	3
40-44	3	1	1	3	2	1	4	2	2	5	3	2
45-49	2	1	1	2	1	1	3	1	1	4	2	2
50-54	2	1	1	2	1	1	2	1	1	3	2	1
55-59	1	1	1	2	1	1	2	1	1	2	1	1
60-64	1	1	1	1	1	1	2	1	1	2	1	1
65-69	1	0	0	1	0	0	1	1	1	1	1	1
70-74	1	0	0	1	0	0	1	0	0	1	1	1
75-79	0	0	0	0	0	0	0	0	0	1	0	0
80 +	0	0	0	0	0	0	1	0	0	1	0	0

Age group	1990 Both sexes	1990 Males	1990 Females	1995 Both sexes	1995 Males	1995 Females	2000 Both sexes	2000 Males	2000 Females	2005 Both sexes	2005 Males	2005 Females
All ages	116	61	56	139	72	67	164	85	80	187	96	91
0-4	15	8	7	20	10	10	22	11	11	22	11	11
5-9	14	7	7	15	8	8	21	11	10	22	11	11
10-14	11	6	6	15	8	7	16	9	8	21	11	10
15-19	11	5	5	12	6	6	15	8	7	17	9	8
20-24	10	5	5	10	6	5	11	6	5	16	8	7
25-29	11	6	5	11	6	6	12	6	6	12	7	5
30-34	10	5	5	13	6	6	14	6	7	13	6	6
35-39	9	5	4	11	6	5	13	7	7	14	6	8
40-44	7	4	3	9	5	4	11	6	5	13	7	7
45-49	5	3	2	7	4	3	9	5	4	11	6	5
50-54	4	2	2	5	3	2	7	4	3	9	5	4
55-59	3	2	1	4	2	2	5	3	2	7	4	3
60-64	2	1	1	3	1	1	3	2	2	5	2	2
65-69	2	1	1	2	1	1	2	1	1	3	2	2
70-74	1	1	1	1	1	1	2	1	1	2	1	1
75-79	1	0	0	1	0	0	1	0	1	1	1	1
80 +	1	0	0	1	0	0	1	0	1	1	0	1

402

United Nations Department of Economic and Social Affairs/Population Division
World Population Prospects: The 2004 Revision, Volume II: Sex and Age Distribution of the World Population

POPULATION BY AGE AND SEX (in thousands)

Age group	2005 Both sexes	Males	Females	2010 Both sexes	Males	Females	2015 Both sexes	Males	Females	2020 Both sexes	Males	Females
All ages	187	96	91	209	107	102	232	118	114	254	129	125
0-4	22	11	11	22	11	11	23	12	11	24	12	12
5-9	22	11	11	22	11	11	22	11	11	23	12	11
10-14	21	11	10	22	11	11	22	11	11	22	11	11
15-19	17	9	8	21	11	10	22	11	11	22	11	11
20-24	16	8	7	17	9	8	22	11	11	23	12	11
25-29	12	7	5	16	9	8	18	9	9	22	11	11
30-34	13	6	6	13	7	6	17	9	8	19	10	9
35-39	14	6	8	13	7	7	13	7	6	17	9	8
40-44	13	7	7	14	7	8	13	7	7	13	7	6
45-49	11	6	5	13	7	7	14	7	8	14	7	7
50-54	9	5	4	11	6	5	13	7	7	14	7	8
55-59	7	4	3	9	5	4	11	6	5	13	6	7
60-64	5	2	2	6	3	3	9	4	4	10	5	5
65-69	3	2	2	4	2	2	6	3	3	8	4	4
70-74	2	1	1	3	1	1	4	2	2	5	3	3
75-79	1	1	1	2	1	1	2	1	1	3	1	2
80-84	1	0	0	1	0	0	1	0	1	2	1	1
85-89	0	0	0	0	0	0	0	0	0	1	0	0
90-94	0	0	0	0	0	0	0	0	0	0	0	0
95-99	0	0	0	0	0	0	0	0	0	0	0	0
100 +	0	0	0	0	0	0	0	0	0	0	0	0

Age group	2025 Both sexes	Males	Females	2030 Both sexes	Males	Females	2035 Both sexes	Males	Females	2040 Both sexes	Males	Females
All ages	276	140	136	296	149	147	314	158	156	330	165	164
0-4	24	12	12	23	12	11	22	11	11	22	11	11
5-9	24	12	12	24	12	12	23	12	11	22	11	11
10-14	23	12	11	24	12	12	24	12	12	24	12	11
15-19	22	11	11	20	12	11	24	12	12	24	12	12
20-24	23	12	11	23	12	11	24	12	12	25	13	12
25-29	23	12	12	24	12	12	23	12	12	24	12	12
30-34	23	12	11	24	12	12	24	12	12	24	12	12
35-39	19	10	9	23	12	11	24	12	12	25	12	12
40-44	17	9	8	19	10	9	23	12	12	25	12	12
45-49	13	7	6	18	9	8	19	10	9	23	12	12
50-54	14	7	7	13	7	6	18	9	8	19	10	9
55-59	14	6	8	12	7	7	13	7	6	17	9	8
60-64	13	6	6	14	6	7	13	6	7	13	7	6
65-69	10	5	5	12	6	6	13	6	7	12	6	6
70-74	7	3	4	9	4	4	11	5	6	12	5	7
75-79	4	2	2	6	3	3	7	3	4	9	4	5
80-84	2	1	1	3	1	2	4	2	3	5	2	3
85-89	1	0	1	1	0	1	2	1	1	3	1	2
90-94	0	0	0	0	0	0	1	0	0	1	0	1
95-99	0	0	0	0	0	0	0	0	0	0	0	0
100 +	0	0	0	0	0	0	0	0	0	0	0	0

Age group	2045 Both sexes	Males	Females	2050 Both sexes	Males	Females
All ages	345	173	172	359	179	179
0-4	22	11	11	23	12	11
5-9	22	11	11	23	12	11
10-14	23	12	11	22	11	11
15-19	24	12	12	23	12	11
20-24	25	13	12	24	12	12
25-29	25	13	12	26	13	13
30-34	25	13	12	26	13	13
35-39	24	12	12	25	13	13
40-44	25	13	12	25	13	12
45-49	25	12	12	25	13	12
50-54	23	12	12	25	12	12
55-59	19	10	9	23	12	11
60-64	17	9	8	18	9	9
65-69	12	6	6	16	8	8
70-74	11	5	6	11	6	5
75-79	10	4	6	10	4	5
80-84	7	3	4	8	3	5
85-89	3	1	2	5	2	3
90-94	1	0	1	2	1	1
95-99	0	0	0	0	0	0
100 +	0	0	0	0	0	0

POPULATION BY AGE AND SEX (in thousands)

Age group	2005 Both sexes	2005 Males	2005 Females	2010 Both sexes	2010 Males	2010 Females	2015 Both sexes	2015 Males	2015 Females	2020 Both sexes	2020 Males	2020 Females
All ages	187	96	91	211	108	103	237	121	116	264	134	130
0-4	22	11	11	23	12	11	26	13	13	28	15	14
5-9	22	11	11	22	11	11	24	12	12	26	13	13
10-14	21	11	10	22	11	11	22	11	11	24	12	12
15-19	17	9	8	21	11	10	22	11	11	22	11	11
20-24	16	8	7	17	9	8	22	11	11	23	12	11
25-29	12	7	5	16	9	8	18	9	9	22	11	11
30-34	13	6	6	13	7	6	17	9	8	19	10	9
35-39	14	6	8	13	7	7	13	7	6	17	9	8
40-44	13	7	7	14	7	8	13	7	7	13	7	6
45-49	11	6	5	13	7	7	14	7	8	14	7	7
50-54	9	5	4	11	6	5	13	7	7	14	7	8
55-59	7	4	3	9	5	4	11	6	5	13	6	7
60-64	5	2	2	6	3	3	9	4	4	10	5	5
65-69	3	2	2	4	2	2	6	3	3	8	4	4
70-74	2	1	1	3	1	1	4	2	2	5	3	3
75-79	1	1	1	2	1	1	2	1	1	3	1	2
80-84	1	0	0	1	0	0	1	0	1	2	1	1
85-89	0	0	0	0	0	0	0	0	0	1	0	0
90-94	0	0	0	0	0	0	0	0	0	0	0	0
95-99	0	0	0	0	0	0	0	0	0	0	0	0
100 +	0	0	0	0	0	0	0	0	0	0	0	0

Age group	2025 Both sexes	2025 Males	2025 Females	2030 Both sexes	2030 Males	2030 Females	2035 Both sexes	2035 Males	2035 Females	2040 Both sexes	2040 Males	2040 Females
All ages	291	147	144	317	160	157	343	173	170	367	185	183
0-4	29	15	14	30	15	14	30	15	15	31	16	15
5-9	29	15	14	29	15	14	30	15	15	30	15	15
10-14	26	13	13	29	15	14	30	15	14	30	15	15
15-19	24	12	12	26	13	13	29	15	14	30	15	15
20-24	23	12	11	25	12	12	27	14	13	29	15	14
25-29	23	12	12	24	12	12	25	13	12	28	14	14
30-34	23	12	11	24	12	12	24	12	12	26	13	13
35-39	19	10	9	23	12	11	24	12	12	25	12	12
40-44	17	9	8	19	10	9	23	12	12	25	12	12
45-49	13	7	6	18	9	8	19	10	9	23	12	12
50-54	14	7	7	13	7	6	18	9	8	19	10	9
55-59	14	6	8	13	7	7	13	7	6	17	9	8
60-64	13	6	6	14	6	7	13	6	7	13	7	6
65-69	10	5	5	12	6	6	13	6	7	12	6	6
70-74	7	3	4	9	4	4	11	5	6	12	5	7
75-79	4	2	2	6	3	3	7	3	4	9	4	5
80-84	2	1	1	3	1	2	4	2	3	5	2	3
85-89	1	0	1	1	0	1	2	1	1	3	1	2
90-94	0	0	0	0	0	0	1	0	0	1	0	1
95-99	0	0	0	0	0	0	0	0	0	0	0	0
100 +	0	0	0	0	0	0	0	0	0	0	0	0

Age group	2045 Both sexes	2045 Males	2045 Females	2050 Both sexes	2050 Males	2050 Females
All ages	393	197	196	419	210	209
0-4	33	17	16	34	18	17
5-9	31	16	15	33	17	16
10-14	30	15	15	31	16	15
15-19	30	15	15	30	15	15
20-24	30	15	15	31	16	15
25-29	30	15	15	31	16	15
30-34	28	14	14	31	16	15
35-39	26	13	13	29	15	14
40-44	25	13	12	26	13	13
45-49	25	12	12	25	13	12
50-54	23	12	12	25	12	12
55-59	19	10	9	23	12	11
60-64	17	9	8	18	9	9
65-69	12	6	6	16	8	8
70-74	11	5	6	11	6	5
75-79	10	4	6	10	4	5
80-84	7	3	4	8	3	5
85-89	3	1	2	5	2	3
90-94	1	0	1	2	1	1
95-99	0	0	0	0	0	0
100 +	0	0	0	0	0	0

United Nations Department of Economic and Social Affairs/Population Division
World Population Prospects: The 2004 Revision, Volume II: Sex and Age Distribution of the World Population

POPULATION BY AGE AND SEX (in thousands)

Age group	2005 Both sexes	Males	Females	2010 Both sexes	Males	Females	2015 Both sexes	Males	Females	2020 Both sexes	Males	Females
All ages	187	96	91	207	106	101	227	115	111	244	124	120
0-4	22	11	11	20	10	10	19	10	9	19	10	9
5-9	22	11	11	22	11	11	20	10	10	19	10	10
10-14	21	11	10	22	11	11	22	11	11	20	10	10
15-19	17	9	8	21	11	10	22	11	11	22	11	11
20-24	16	8	7	17	9	8	22	11	11	23	12	11
25-29	12	7	5	16	9	8	18	9	9	22	11	11
30-34	13	6	6	13	7	6	17	9	8	19	10	9
35-39	14	6	8	13	7	7	13	7	6	17	9	8
40-44	13	7	7	14	7	8	13	7	7	13	7	6
45-49	11	6	5	13	7	7	14	7	8	14	7	7
50-54	9	5	4	11	6	5	13	7	7	14	7	8
55-59	7	4	3	9	5	4	11	6	5	13	6	7
60-64	5	2	2	6	3	3	9	4	4	10	5	5
65-69	3	2	2	4	2	2	6	3	3	8	4	4
70-74	2	1	1	3	1	1	4	2	2	5	3	3
75-79	1	1	1	2	1	1	2	1	1	3	1	2
80-84	1	0	0	1	0	0	1	0	1	2	1	1
85-89	0	0	0	0	0	0	0	0	0	1	0	0
90-94	0	0	0	0	0	0	0	0	0	0	0	0
95-99	0	0	0	0	0	0	0	0	0	0	0	0
100 +	0	0	0	0	0	0	0	0	0	0	0	0

Age group	2025 Both sexes	Males	Females	2030 Both sexes	Males	Females	2035 Both sexes	Males	Females	2040 Both sexes	Males	Females
All ages	261	132	129	275	138	136	286	143	142	294	147	147
0-4	19	9	9	17	9	8	16	8	8	14	7	7
5-9	19	10	9	19	10	9	17	9	9	16	8	8
10-14	20	10	10	19	10	9	19	10	9	18	9	9
15-19	20	10	10	20	10	10	19	10	9	19	10	9
20-24	23	12	11	21	11	10	20	10	10	20	10	10
25-29	23	12	12	24	12	12	22	11	11	21	11	10
30-34	23	12	11	24	12	12	24	12	12	22	11	11
35-39	19	10	9	23	12	11	24	12	12	25	12	12
40-44	17	9	8	19	10	9	23	12	12	25	12	12
45-49	13	7	6	18	9	8	19	10	9	23	12	12
50-54	14	7	7	13	7	6	18	9	8	19	10	9
55-59	14	6	8	13	7	7	13	7	6	17	9	8
60-64	13	6	6	14	6	7	13	6	7	13	7	6
65-69	10	5	5	12	6	6	13	6	7	12	6	6
70-74	7	3	4	9	4	4	11	5	6	12	5	7
75-79	4	2	2	6	3	3	7	3	4	9	4	5
80-84	2	1	1	3	1	2	4	2	3	5	2	3
85-89	1	0	1	1	0	1	2	1	1	3	1	2
90-94	0	0	0	0	0	0	1	0	0	1	0	1
95-99	0	0	0	0	0	0	0	0	0	0	0	0
100 +	0	0	0	0	0	0	0	0	0	0	0	0

Age group	2045 Both sexes	Males	Females	2050 Both sexes	Males	Females
All ages	301	150	151	305	152	153
0-4	14	7	7	13	7	7
5-9	14	7	7	14	7	7
10-14	16	8	8	15	7	7
15-19	18	9	9	16	8	8
20-24	20	10	10	18	9	9
25-29	21	11	10	20	10	10
30-34	22	11	11	21	11	10
35-39	23	12	11	22	11	11
40-44	25	13	12	23	12	11
45-49	25	12	12	25	13	12
50-54	23	12	12	25	12	12
55-59	19	10	9	23	12	11
60-64	17	9	8	18	9	9
65-69	12	6	6	16	8	8
70-74	11	5	6	11	6	5
75-79	10	4	6	10	4	5
80-84	7	3	4	8	3	5
85-89	3	1	2	5	2	3
90-94	1	0	1	2	1	1
95-99	0	0	0	0	0	0
100 +	0	0	0	0	0	0

United Nations Department of Economic and Social Affairs/Population Division
World Population Prospects: The 2004 Revision, Volume II: Sex and Age Distribution of the World Population

405

POPULATION BY AGE AND SEX (in thousands)

Age group	1950 Both sexes	1950 Males	1950 Females	1955 Both sexes	1955 Males	1955 Females	1960 Both sexes	1960 Males	1960 Females	1965 Both sexes	1965 Males	1965 Females
All ages	61	31	30	69	36	34	79	41	39	93	48	45
0-4	11	5	5	12	6	6	14	7	7	16	8	8
5-9	9	5	5	11	5	5	12	6	6	14	7	7
10-14	7	4	3	8	4	4	9	5	5	12	6	6
15-19	6	3	3	7	3	3	8	4	4	9	5	5
20-24	5	2	3	6	3	3	6	3	3	7	3	3
25-29	4	2	2	5	3	2	6	3	3	6	3	3
30-34	4	2	2	4	2	2	5	3	2	6	3	3
35-39	3	2	2	4	2	2	4	2	2	5	3	3
40-44	3	1	1	3	2	1	3	2	2	4	2	2
45-49	2	1	1	3	1	1	3	2	2	3	2	2
50-54	2	1	1	2	1	1	3	1	1	3	1	1
55-59	2	1	1	2	1	1	2	1	1	2	1	1
60-64	1	1	0	1	1	1	1	1	1	2	1	1
65-69	1	0	0	1	0	0	1	1	0	1	1	1
70-74	0	0	0	1	0	0	1	0	0	1	0	0
75-79	0	0	0	0	0	0	0	0	0	0	0	0
80 +	0	0	0	0	0	0	0	0	0	0	0	0

Age group	1970 Both sexes	1970 Males	1970 Females	1975 Both sexes	1975 Males	1975 Females	1980 Both sexes	1980 Males	1980 Females	1985 Both sexes	1985 Males	1985 Females
All ages	111	57	54	130	68	62	151	79	72	174	91	83
0-4	19	10	9	18	9	9	21	11	10	24	12	11
5-9	17	8	8	19	10	9	20	10	10	21	11	10
10-14	15	8	7	17	9	9	20	10	10	21	11	10
15-19	11	6	6	14	7	7	17	9	8	20	10	10
20-24	8	4	4	12	7	6	14	8	7	17	9	8
25-29	7	4	4	9	5	4	12	6	5	15	8	7
30-34	7	4	3	8	4	4	10	5	5	12	7	6
35-39	6	3	3	7	4	3	9	5	4	10	5	5
40-44	5	3	2	6	3	3	7	4	3	9	5	4
45-49	4	2	2	5	3	2	6	3	3	7	4	3
50-54	3	2	1	4	2	2	5	3	2	6	3	3
55-59	3	1	1	3	1	1	3	2	2	4	2	2
60-64	2	1	1	3	1	1	3	1	1	3	2	1
65-69	1	1	1	2	1	1	2	1	1	2	1	1
70-74	1	0	0	1	1	1	1	1	1	2	1	1
75-79	0	0	0	0	0	0	1	0	0	1	0	0
80 +	0	0	0	1	0	0	1	0	0	1	0	0

Age group	1990 Both sexes	1990 Males	1990 Females	1995 Both sexes	1995 Males	1995 Females	2000 Both sexes	2000 Males	2000 Females	2005 Both sexes	2005 Males	2005 Females
All ages	195	102	94	216	112	104	236	122	114	257	131	125
0-4	25	13	12	22	11	11	24	12	12	24	12	12
5-9	23	12	11	28	14	13	22	12	11	25	13	12
10-14	21	11	10	24	12	12	28	15	14	23	12	11
15-19	21	11	10	20	10	9	23	12	12	27	14	13
20-24	19	10	9	19	10	9	19	10	9	22	11	11
25-29	17	9	8	21	11	10	19	10	9	19	10	9
30-34	15	8	7	18	9	9	21	11	10	20	10	10
35-39	12	7	6	15	8	7	19	10	9	22	11	11
40-44	10	6	5	13	7	6	15	8	7	19	10	9
45-49	8	5	4	9	5	4	13	7	6	15	8	7
50-54	7	4	3	8	5	4	9	5	4	13	7	6
55-59	5	3	3	6	3	3	8	4	4	8	4	4
60-64	4	2	2	5	3	2	6	3	3	8	4	4
65-69	3	1	1	3	2	2	5	2	2	5	3	3
70-74	2	1	1	2	1	1	3	1	1	4	2	2
75-79	1	1	1	1	1	1	2	1	1	2	1	1
80 +	1	0	0	1	0	1	1	0	1	2	1	1

United Nations Department of Economic and Social Affairs/Population Division
World Population Prospects: The 2004 Revision, Volume II: Sex and Age Distribution of the World Population

406

POPULATION BY AGE AND SEX (in thousands)

Age group	2005 Both sexes	2005 Males	2005 Females	2010 Both sexes	2010 Males	2010 Females	2015 Both sexes	2015 Males	2015 Females	2020 Both sexes	2020 Males	2020 Females
All ages	257	131	125	274	140	134	291	148	143	307	156	152
0-4	24	12	12	24	12	12	25	13	12	24	12	12
5-9	25	13	12	24	12	11	24	12	12	24	13	12
10-14	23	12	11	25	13	12	24	12	11	24	12	12
15-19	27	14	13	23	12	11	25	13	12	23	12	11
20-24	22	11	11	27	14	13	23	12	11	25	13	12
25-29	19	10	9	22	11	11	27	14	13	23	12	11
30-34	20	10	10	19	10	9	22	11	11	27	14	13
35-39	22	11	11	20	10	10	19	10	9	22	11	11
40-44	19	10	9	22	11	10	20	10	10	19	9	9
45-49	15	8	7	19	10	9	21	11	10	19	10	9
50-54	13	7	6	14	8	7	18	9	9	21	11	10
55-59	8	4	4	12	6	6	14	7	7	18	9	9
60-64	8	4	4	8	4	4	12	6	6	13	7	6
65-69	5	3	3	7	3	3	7	4	4	11	5	5
70-74	4	2	2	4	2	2	6	3	3	6	3	3
75-79	2	1	1	3	1	2	3	2	2	4	2	2
80-84	1	0	1	1	1	1	2	1	1	2	1	1
85-89	0	0	0	1	0	0	1	0	0	1	0	1
90-94	0	0	0	0	0	0	0	0	0	0	0	0
95-99	0	0	0	0	0	0	0	0	0	0	0	0
100 +	0	0	0	0	0	0	0	0	0	0	0	0

Age group	2025 Both sexes	2025 Males	2025 Females	2030 Both sexes	2030 Males	2030 Females	2035 Both sexes	2035 Males	2035 Females	2040 Both sexes	2040 Males	2040 Females
All ages	321	162	159	333	167	165	342	171	170	350	175	175
0-4	23	12	11	22	11	11	22	11	11	22	11	11
5-9	24	12	12	23	12	11	22	11	11	22	11	11
10-14	24	13	12	24	12	12	23	12	11	22	11	11
15-19	24	12	12	24	13	12	24	12	12	23	12	11
20-24	23	12	11	24	12	12	24	12	12	24	12	12
25-29	24	13	12	23	12	11	24	12	12	24	12	12
30-34	23	12	11	24	12	12	23	12	11	24	12	12
35-39	27	14	13	23	12	11	24	12	12	23	12	11
40-44	22	11	11	27	14	13	23	12	11	24	12	12
45-49	18	9	9	22	11	11	27	14	13	23	12	11
50-54	19	10	9	18	9	9	21	10	11	26	13	13
55-59	20	10	10	19	9	9	18	9	9	21	10	11
60-64	17	8	8	19	10	10	18	9	9	17	8	9
65-69	12	6	6	15	8	8	18	9	9	16	8	8
70-74	9	4	5	10	5	5	14	6	7	16	8	8
75-79	5	2	3	7	3	4	9	4	5	11	5	6
80-84	3	1	2	3	1	2	5	2	3	6	3	4
85-89	1	0	1	2	1	1	2	1	1	3	1	2
90-94	0	0	0	1	0	0	1	0	1	1	0	1
95-99	0	0	0	0	0	0	0	0	0	0	0	0
100 +	0	0	0	0	0	0	0	0	0	0	0	0

Age group	2045 Both sexes	2045 Males	2045 Females	2050 Both sexes	2050 Males	2050 Females
All ages	356	177	178	360	179	181
0-4	22	11	11	21	11	10
5-9	22	11	10	22	11	10
10-14	22	11	11	22	11	10
15-19	22	11	11	22	11	11
20-24	23	12	11	22	11	11
25-29	24	12	12	23	12	11
30-34	24	12	12	24	12	12
35-39	24	12	12	24	12	12
40-44	23	12	11	24	12	12
45-49	24	12	12	23	12	11
50-54	22	11	11	24	12	12
55-59	26	13	13	22	11	11
60-64	20	10	10	25	12	12
65-69	16	8	8	19	9	10
70-74	15	7	8	14	7	8
75-79	13	6	7	12	6	7
80-84	8	3	5	10	4	6
85-89	4	1	3	5	2	3
90-94	2	0	1	2	1	1
95-99	0	0	0	1	0	0
100 +	0	0	0	0	0	0

POPULATION BY AGE AND SEX (in thousands)

Age group	2005 Both sexes	Males	Females	2010 Both sexes	Males	Females	2015 Both sexes	Males	Females	2020 Both sexes	Males	Females
All ages	257	131	125	277	141	136	299	152	147	320	162	158
0-4	24	12	12	27	14	13	29	15	14	30	15	15
5-9	25	13	12	24	12	11	27	14	13	29	15	14
10-14	23	12	11	25	13	12	24	12	11	27	14	13
15-19	27	14	13	23	12	11	25	13	12	23	12	11
20-24	22	11	11	27	14	13	23	12	11	25	13	12
25-29	19	10	9	22	11	11	27	14	13	23	12	11
30-34	20	10	10	19	10	9	22	11	11	27	14	13
35-39	22	11	11	20	10	10	19	10	9	22	11	11
40-44	19	10	9	22	11	10	20	10	10	19	9	9
45-49	15	8	7	19	10	9	21	11	10	19	10	9
50-54	13	7	6	14	8	7	18	9	9	21	11	10
55-59	8	4	4	12	6	6	14	7	7	18	9	9
60-64	8	4	4	8	4	4	12	6	6	13	7	6
65-69	5	3	3	7	3	3	7	4	4	11	5	5
70-74	4	2	2	4	2	2	6	3	3	6	3	3
75-79	2	1	1	3	1	2	3	2	2	4	2	2
80-84	1	0	1	1	1	1	2	1	1	2	1	1
85-89	0	0	0	1	0	0	1	0	0	1	0	1
90-94	0	0	0	0	0	0	0	0	0	0	0	0
95-99	0	0	0	0	0	0	0	0	0	0	0	0
100 +	0	0	0	0	0	0	0	0	0	0	0	0

Age group	2025 Both sexes	Males	Females	2030 Both sexes	Males	Females	2035 Both sexes	Males	Females	2040 Both sexes	Males	Females
All ages	340	172	168	358	180	178	375	188	186	391	196	195
0-4	29	15	14	29	15	14	29	15	14	31	16	15
5-9	30	15	15	29	15	14	29	15	14	29	15	14
10-14	29	15	14	30	15	15	29	15	14	29	15	14
15-19	27	14	13	29	15	14	30	15	15	29	15	14
20-24	23	12	11	27	14	13	29	15	14	30	15	15
25-29	24	13	12	23	12	11	27	14	13	29	15	14
30-34	23	12	11	24	12	12	23	12	11	26	14	13
35-39	27	14	13	23	12	11	24	12	12	23	12	11
40-44	22	11	11	27	14	13	23	12	11	24	12	12
45-49	18	9	9	22	11	11	27	14	13	23	12	11
50-54	19	10	9	18	9	9	21	10	11	26	13	13
55-59	20	10	10	19	9	9	18	9	9	21	10	11
60-64	17	8	8	19	10	10	18	9	9	17	8	9
65-69	12	6	6	15	8	8	18	9	9	16	8	8
70-74	9	4	5	10	5	5	14	6	7	16	8	8
75-79	5	2	3	7	3	4	9	4	5	11	5	6
80-84	3	1	2	3	1	2	5	2	3	6	3	4
85-89	1	0	1	2	1	1	2	1	1	3	1	2
90-94	0	0	0	1	0	0	1	0	1	1	0	1
95-99	0	0	0	0	0	0	0	0	0	0	0	0
100 +	0	0	0	0	0	0	0	0	0	0	0	0

Age group	2045 Both sexes	Males	Females	2050 Both sexes	Males	Females
All ages	408	204	204	425	212	212
0-4	33	17	16	33	17	16
5-9	31	16	15	32	17	16
10-14	29	15	14	31	16	15
15-19	29	15	14	29	15	14
20-24	29	15	14	28	15	14
25-29	30	15	15	29	15	14
30-34	29	15	14	30	15	15
35-39	26	13	13	29	15	14
40-44	23	12	11	26	13	13
45-49	24	12	12	23	12	11
50-54	22	11	11	24	12	12
55-59	26	13	13	22	11	11
60-64	20	10	10	25	12	12
65-69	16	8	8	19	9	10
70-74	15	7	8	14	7	8
75-79	13	6	7	12	6	7
80-84	8	3	5	10	4	6
85-89	4	1	3	5	2	3
90-94	2	0	1	2	1	1
95-99	0	0	0	1	0	0
100 +	0	0	0	0	0	0

United Nations Department of Economic and Social Affairs/Population Division
World Population Prospects: The 2004 Revision, Volume II: Sex and Age Distribution of the World Population

POPULATION BY AGE AND SEX (in thousands)

Age group	2005 Both sexes	Males	Females	2010 Both sexes	Males	Females	2015 Both sexes	Males	Females	2020 Both sexes	Males	Females
All ages	257	101	125	272	138	133	284	144	140	294	149	145
0-4	24	12	12	21	11	10	20	10	10	18	9	9
5-9	25	13	12	24	12	11	21	11	10	20	10	10
10-14	23	12	11	25	13	12	24	12	11	21	11	10
15-19	27	14	13	23	12	11	25	13	12	23	12	11
20-24	22	11	11	27	14	13	23	12	11	25	13	12
25-29	19	10	9	22	11	11	27	14	13	23	12	11
30-34	20	10	10	19	10	9	22	11	11	27	14	13
35-39	22	11	11	20	10	10	19	10	9	22	11	11
40-44	19	10	9	22	11	10	20	10	10	19	9	9
45-49	15	8	7	19	10	9	21	11	10	19	10	9
50-54	13	7	6	14	8	7	18	9	9	21	11	10
55-59	8	4	4	12	6	6	14	7	7	18	9	9
60-64	8	4	4	8	4	4	12	6	6	13	7	6
65-69	5	3	3	7	3	3	7	4	4	11	5	5
70-74	4	2	2	4	2	2	6	3	3	6	3	3
75-79	2	1	1	3	1	2	3	2	2	4	2	2
80-84	1	0	1	1	1	1	2	1	1	2	1	1
85-89	0	0	0	1	0	0	1	0	0	1	0	1
90-94	0	0	0	0	0	0	0	0	0	0	0	0
95-99	0	0	0	0	0	0	0	0	0	0	0	0
100 +	0	0	0	0	0	0	0	0	0	0	0	0

Age group	2025 Both sexes	Males	Females	2030 Both sexes	Males	Females	2035 Both sexes	Males	Females	2040 Both sexes	Males	Females
All ages	302	152	150	308	155	153	310	155	155	310	155	155
0-4	17	9	8	16	8	8	15	8	7	14	7	7
5-9	18	9	9	17	9	8	16	8	8	15	8	7
10-14	20	10	10	18	9	9	17	9	8	16	8	8
15-19	21	11	10	20	10	10	18	9	9	17	9	8
20-24	23	12	11	21	11	10	20	10	10	18	9	9
25-29	24	13	12	23	12	11	21	11	10	20	10	10
30-34	23	12	11	24	12	12	23	12	11	21	11	10
35-39	27	14	13	23	12	11	24	12	12	23	12	11
40-44	22	11	11	27	14	10	23	12	11	24	12	12
45-49	18	9	9	22	11	11	27	14	13	23	12	11
50-54	19	10	9	18	9	9	21	10	11	26	13	13
55-59	20	10	10	19	9	9	18	9	9	21	10	11
60-64	17	8	8	19	10	10	18	9	9	17	8	9
65-69	12	6	6	15	8	8	18	9	9	16	8	8
70-74	9	4	5	10	5	5	14	6	7	16	8	8
75-79	5	2	3	7	3	4	9	4	5	11	5	6
80-84	3	1	2	3	1	2	5	2	3	6	3	4
85-89	1	0	1	2	1	1	2	1	1	3	1	2
90-94	0	0	0	1	0	0	1	0	1	1	0	1
95-99	0	0	0	0	0	0	0	0	0	0	0	0
100 +	0	0	0	0	0	0	0	0	0	0	0	0

Age group	2045 Both sexes	Males	Females	2050 Both sexes	Males	Females
All ages	307	153	155	302	150	153
0-4	13	7	6	12	6	6
5-9	14	7	7	13	7	6
10-14	15	8	7	14	7	7
15-19	16	8	8	15	8	7
20-24	17	9	8	16	8	8
25-29	18	9	9	17	9	8
30-34	20	10	10	18	9	9
35-39	21	11	10	20	10	10
40-44	23	12	11	21	11	10
45-49	24	12	12	23	12	11
50-54	22	11	11	24	12	12
55-59	26	13	13	22	11	11
60-64	20	10	10	25	12	12
65-69	16	8	8	19	9	10
70-74	15	7	8	14	7	8
75-79	13	6	7	12	6	7
80-84	8	3	5	10	4	6
85-89	4	1	3	5	2	3
90-94	2	0	1	2	1	1
95-99	0	0	0	1	0	0
100 +	0	0	0	0	0	0

POPULATION BY AGE AND SEX (in thousands)

Age group	1950 Both sexes	1950 Males	1950 Females	1955 Both sexes	1955 Males	1955 Females	1960 Both sexes	1960 Males	1960 Females	1965 Both sexes	1965 Males	1965 Females
All ages	469	229	240	476	232	244	486	237	249	502	245	257
0-4	49	25	25	56	28	28	57	29	29	62	31	31
5-9	43	21	22	43	21	22	49	24	25	51	25	26
10-14	41	20	21	41	20	21	41	20	21	47	24	24
15-19	39	20	20	40	20	20	40	20	20	40	20	20
20-24	38	19	19	38	19	19	38	19	19	38	19	19
25-29	36	18	18	36	18	18	36	18	18	36	18	18
30-34	34	17	17	34	17	17	34	17	17	34	17	18
35-39	32	16	16	32	16	16	32	16	16	32	16	16
40-44	30	15	15	30	15	15	30	15	15	30	15	15
45-49	27	13	14	27	13	14	28	13	14	28	14	14
50-54	25	12	13	25	12	13	25	12	13	25	12	13
55-59	22	10	12	22	10	12	22	10	12	22	11	12
60-64	19	9	10	19	9	10	19	9	10	19	9	10
65-69	15	7	8	15	7	8	15	7	8	15	7	8
70-74	10	5	6	10	4	6	10	5	6	11	5	6
75-79	6	3	3	6	2	3	6	3	3	6	3	4
80 +	3	1	2	3	1	2	3	1	2	4	1	2

Age group	1970 Both sexes	1970 Males	1970 Females	1975 Both sexes	1975 Males	1975 Females	1980 Both sexes	1980 Males	1980 Females	1985 Both sexes	1985 Males	1985 Females
All ages	529	259	271	601	295	306	696	343	354	813	402	412
0-4	69	35	35	92	46	46	115	58	57	136	69	67
5-9	56	28	28	66	33	33	89	45	44	112	56	56
10-14	49	24	25	57	28	29	67	33	34	90	45	45
15-19	46	23	23	52	25	27	60	29	31	70	34	36
20-24	39	19	19	50	25	26	56	27	29	64	31	33
25-29	37	18	19	43	21	22	55	27	28	61	29	31
30-34	35	17	18	39	20	19	45	23	22	56	29	28
35-39	33	16	17	32	16	16	36	19	16	42	22	20
40-44	31	15	16	30	14	16	29	14	15	33	17	15
45-49	28	14	15	29	14	15	28	13	15	27	13	14
50-54	26	12	13	27	13	14	27	13	14	26	12	14
55-59	23	11	12	24	11	12	25	12	13	25	12	13
60-64	20	9	10	20	10	11	21	10	11	22	11	12
65-69	16	7	9	16	8	9	17	8	9	18	9	10
70-74	11	5	6	12	5	7	13	6	7	14	6	8
75-79	7	3	4	7	3	4	8	4	5	9	4	5
80 +	4	2	2	5	2	3	5	2	3	6	2	4

Age group	1990 Both sexes	1990 Males	1990 Females	1995 Both sexes	1995 Males	1995 Females	2000 Both sexes	2000 Males	2000 Females	2005 Both sexes	2005 Males	2005 Females
All ages	957	474	484	1 119	555	564	1 272	632	640	1 384	689	695
0-4	163	82	81	185	93	92	191	96	94	193	98	96
5-9	134	67	66	160	81	80	181	91	90	184	93	91
10-14	113	56	56	135	68	67	160	81	80	177	90	88
15-19	93	46	47	116	57	58	136	68	68	156	79	77
20-24	75	36	38	97	47	50	117	58	60	129	64	65
25-29	69	33	36	79	38	40	98	48	50	107	53	54
30-34	62	31	31	70	34	35	77	38	39	88	43	46
35-39	53	28	26	59	30	29	65	33	33	72	35	37
40-44	39	20	19	49	25	24	55	27	27	62	31	31
45-49	31	16	15	37	19	18	47	23	23	52	26	26
50-54	26	13	14	30	15	14	35	18	17	44	22	22
55-59	25	11	14	25	12	13	28	14	14	33	16	16
60-64	23	11	12	23	10	13	23	11	12	26	13	13
65-69	20	9	10	20	9	11	20	9	11	20	9	11
70-74	15	7	8	16	7	9	17	8	9	17	7	9
75-79	10	4	6	11	5	6	12	5	7	12	5	7
80 +	7	3	4	8	3	5	10	4	6	11	5	6

United Nations Department of Economic and Social Affairs/Population Division
World Population Prospects: The 2004 Revision, Volume II: Sex and Age Distribution of the World Population

POPULATION BY AGE AND SEX (in thousands)

Age group	2005 Both sexes	Males	Females	2010 Both sexes	Males	Females	2015 Both sexes	Males	Females	2020 Both sexes	Males	Females
All ages	1 384	689	695	1 498	748	749	1 605	805	800	1 709	860	849
0-4	193	98	96	193	98	96	197	100	98	200	101	99
5-9	184	93	91	187	94	93	188	95	93	194	98	96
10-14	177	90	88	181	91	90	184	93	91	185	94	92
15-19	156	79	77	176	89	87	179	90	89	182	92	91
20-24	129	64	65	153	77	76	173	87	86	177	89	88
25-29	107	53	54	122	61	61	145	73	72	165	84	82
30-34	88	43	46	98	49	49	111	56	55	132	68	64
35-39	72	35	37	80	39	41	87	44	43	99	51	48
40-44	62	31	31	66	33	34	72	36	37	78	40	38
45-49	52	26	26	58	29	29	61	30	31	65	32	33
50-54	44	22	22	48	24	24	53	27	27	56	27	28
55-59	33	16	16	41	20	21	45	22	23	49	25	25
60-64	26	13	13	30	15	15	38	18	19	41	20	21
65-69	20	9	11	23	11	12	27	13	14	34	16	18
70-74	17	7	9	17	8	9	19	9	10	23	11	12
75-79	12	5	7	12	5	7	13	6	7	15	7	8
80-84	7	3	4	8	3	4	8	3	5	8	4	4
85-89	3	1	2	3	1	2	4	1	2	4	2	2
90-94	1	0	0	1	0	1	1	0	1	1	0	1
95-99	0	0	0	0	0	0	0	0	0	0	0	0
100 +	0	0	0	0	0	0	0	0	0	0	0	0

Age group	2025 Both sexes	Males	Females	2030 Both sexes	Males	Females	2035 Both sexes	Males	Females	2040 Both sexes	Males	Females
All ages	1 809	914	895	1 907	966	941	2 002	1 016	985	2 095	1 065	1 030
0-4	200	101	99	197	100	98	195	99	96	193	98	95
5-9	198	100	98	198	100	98	196	99	97	194	98	96
10-14	192	97	95	197	99	97	197	100	98	196	99	97
15-19	184	93	91	191	96	95	196	99	97	197	99	97
20-24	180	91	89	182	92	90	189	95	94	194	98	96
25-29	170	86	84	174	88	86	177	89	88	185	93	92
30-34	153	78	74	159	81	78	164	84	80	168	86	83
35-39	119	62	57	139	72	67	146	76	71	153	79	74
40-44	88	46	42	108	57	50	128	67	60	136	71	65
45-49	70	36	34	81	43	38	100	53	46	120	63	56
50-54	60	30	30	65	34	31	75	40	35	93	50	44
55-59	52	25	26	55	27	28	61	31	29	71	37	33
60-64	46	23	23	48	23	25	52	25	27	57	29	28
65-69	37	18	19	41	20	21	43	21	23	47	23	25
70-74	29	14	15	32	15	17	35	17	18	38	18	20
75-79	18	8	9	22	10	12	25	12	13	28	13	15
80-84	9	4	5	11	5	6	15	7	8	16	8	9
85-89	4	2	2	5	2	3	6	3	3	7	3	4
90-94	1	0	1	1	1	1	2	1	1	2	1	1
95-99	0	0	0	0	0	0	0	0	0	0	0	0
100 +	0	0	0	0	0	0	0	0	0	0	0	0

Age group	2045 Both sexes	Males	Females	2050 Both sexes	Males	Females
All ages	2 188	1 113	1 075	2 279	1 159	1 119
0-4	190	96	94	187	95	92
5-9	192	97	95	190	96	94
10-14	193	98	96	192	97	95
15-19	195	98	97	193	97	95
20-24	195	98	97	194	98	96
25-29	190	96	94	192	97	95
30-34	177	90	87	184	93	91
35-39	159	82	77	170	87	83
40-44	144	75	69	152	78	73
45-49	129	68	61	138	72	66
50-54	113	60	53	123	65	59
55-59	89	47	42	108	57	51
60-64	66	35	32	84	44	40
65-69	52	26	26	61	32	30
70-74	41	20	22	46	23	23
75-79	30	14	16	33	15	18
80-84	19	9	10	20	9	11
85-89	9	4	5	10	4	6
90-94	3	1	2	3	1	2
95-99	0	0	0	1	0	0
100 +	0	0	0	0	0	0

United Nations Department of Economic and Social Affairs/Population Division
World Population Prospects: The 2004 Revision, Volume II: Sex and Age Distribution of the World Population

411

POPULATION BY AGE AND SEX (in thousands)

Age group	2005 Both sexes	Males	Females	2010 Both sexes	Males	Females	2015 Both sexes	Males	Females	2020 Both sexes	Males	Females
All ages	1 384	689	695	1 511	755	756	1 643	824	819	1 781	897	884
0-4	193	98	96	207	105	102	222	112	110	235	119	116
5-9	184	93	91	187	94	93	202	102	100	218	110	108
10-14	177	90	88	181	91	90	184	93	91	198	100	98
15-19	156	79	77	176	89	87	179	90	89	182	92	91
20-24	129	64	65	153	77	76	173	87	86	177	89	88
25-29	107	53	54	122	61	61	145	73	72	165	84	82
30-34	88	43	46	98	49	49	111	56	55	132	68	64
35-39	72	35	37	80	39	41	87	44	43	99	51	48
40-44	62	31	31	66	33	34	72	36	37	78	40	38
45-49	52	26	26	58	29	29	61	30	31	65	32	33
50-54	44	22	22	48	24	24	53	27	27	56	27	28
55-59	33	16	16	41	20	21	45	22	23	49	25	25
60-64	26	13	13	30	15	15	38	18	19	41	20	21
65-69	20	9	11	23	11	12	27	13	14	34	16	18
70-74	17	7	9	17	8	9	19	9	10	23	11	12
75-79	12	5	7	12	5	7	13	6	7	15	7	8
80-84	7	3	4	8	3	4	8	3	5	8	4	4
85-89	3	1	2	3	1	2	4	1	2	4	2	2
90-94	1	0	0	1	0	1	1	0	1	1	0	1
95-99	0	0	0	0	0	0	0	0	0	0	0	0
100 +	0	0	0	0	0	0	0	0	0	0	0	0

Age group	2025 Both sexes	Males	Females	2030 Both sexes	Males	Females	2035 Both sexes	Males	Females	2040 Both sexes	Males	Females
All ages	1 919	969	949	2 061	1 044	1 017	2 210	1 122	1 088	2 369	1 204	1 165
0-4	238	120	118	242	123	120	250	127	124	260	132	129
5-9	232	117	115	236	119	117	241	122	119	249	126	123
10-14	217	109	107	231	116	114	235	119	116	240	121	119
15-19	197	99	98	215	109	107	230	116	114	234	118	116
20-24	180	91	89	195	98	97	213	107	106	228	115	113
25-29	170	86	84	174	88	86	189	95	94	208	105	103
30-34	153	78	74	159	81	78	164	84	80	180	92	89
35-39	119	62	57	139	72	67	146	76	71	153	79	74
40-44	88	46	42	108	57	50	128	67	60	136	71	65
45-49	70	36	34	81	43	38	100	53	46	120	63	56
50-54	60	30	30	65	34	31	75	40	35	93	50	44
55-59	52	25	26	56	27	28	61	31	29	71	37	33
60-64	46	23	23	48	23	25	52	25	27	57	29	28
65-69	37	18	19	41	20	21	43	21	23	47	23	25
70-74	29	14	15	32	15	17	35	17	18	38	18	20
75-79	18	8	9	22	10	12	25	12	13	28	13	15
80-84	9	4	5	11	5	6	15	7	8	16	8	9
85-89	4	2	2	5	2	3	6	3	3	7	3	4
90-94	1	0	1	1	1	1	2	1	1	2	1	1
95-99	0	0	0	0	0	0	0	0	0	0	0	0
100 +	0	0	0	0	0	0	0	0	0	0	0	0

Age group	2045 Both sexes	Males	Females	2050 Both sexes	Males	Females
All ages	2 537	1 290	1 247	2 711	1 378	1 333
0-4	269	136	133	274	139	135
5-9	259	131	128	268	135	132
10-14	248	125	123	259	131	128
15-19	239	121	119	248	125	123
20-24	233	117	115	238	120	118
25-29	223	112	111	229	115	114
30-34	200	101	98	216	109	107
35-39	170	87	83	191	98	93
40-44	144	75	69	162	84	78
45-49	129	68	61	138	72	66
50-54	113	60	53	123	65	59
55-59	89	47	42	108	57	51
60-64	66	35	32	84	44	40
65-69	52	26	26	61	32	30
70-74	41	20	22	46	23	23
75-79	30	14	16	33	15	18
80-84	19	9	10	20	9	11
85-89	9	4	5	10	4	6
90-94	3	1	2	3	1	2
95-99	0	0	0	1	0	0
100 +	0	0	0	0	0	0

United Nations Department of Economic and Social Affairs/Population Division
World Population Prospects: The 2004 Revision, Volume II: Sex and Age Distribution of the World Population

412

POPULATION BY AGE AND SEX (in thousands)

Age group	2005 Both sexes	Males	Females	2010 Both sexes	Males	Females	2015 Both sexes	Males	Females	2020 Both sexes	Males	Females
All ages	1 384	689	695	1 484	741	743	1 567	785	781	1 636	824	813
0-4	193	98	96	180	91	89	172	87	85	165	84	82
5-9	184	93	91	187	94	93	175	88	87	169	86	84
10-14	177	90	88	181	91	90	184	93	91	172	87	85
15-19	156	79	77	176	89	87	179	90	89	182	92	91
20-24	129	64	65	153	77	76	173	87	86	177	89	88
25-29	107	53	54	122	61	61	145	73	72	165	84	82
30-34	88	43	46	98	49	49	111	56	55	132	68	64
35-39	72	35	37	80	39	41	87	44	43	99	51	48
40-44	62	31	31	66	33	34	72	36	37	78	40	38
45-49	52	26	26	58	29	29	61	30	31	65	32	33
50-54	44	22	22	48	24	24	53	27	27	56	27	28
55-59	33	16	16	41	20	21	45	22	23	49	25	25
60-64	26	13	13	30	15	15	38	18	19	41	20	21
65-69	20	9	11	23	11	12	27	13	14	34	16	18
70-74	17	7	9	17	8	9	19	9	10	23	11	12
75-79	12	5	7	12	5	7	13	6	7	15	7	8
80-84	7	3	4	8	3	4	8	3	5	8	4	4
85-89	3	1	2	3	1	2	4	1	2	4	2	2
90-94	1	0	0	1	0	1	1	0	1	1	0	1
95-99	0	0	0	0	0	0	0	0	0	0	0	0
100 +	0	0	0	0	0	0	0	0	0	0	0	0

Age group	2025 Both sexes	Males	Females	2030 Both sexes	Males	Females	2035 Both sexes	Males	Females	2040 Both sexes	Males	Females
All ages	1 699	859	841	1 755	889	866	1 801	915	886	1 838	935	902
0-4	162	82	80	154	78	76	144	73	71	134	68	66
5-9	163	83	81	160	81	79	153	78	76	144	73	71
10-14	168	85	83	163	82	81	160	81	79	153	77	76
15-19	171	86	85	167	84	83	162	82	80	159	80	79
20-24	180	91	89	169	85	84	165	83	82	160	81	80
25-29	170	86	84	174	88	86	164	83	81	161	81	80
30-34	153	78	74	159	81	78	164	84	80	156	80	77
35-39	119	62	57	139	72	67	146	76	71	153	79	74
40-44	88	46	42	108	57	50	128	67	60	130	71	65
45-49	70	36	34	81	43	38	100	53	46	120	63	56
50-54	60	30	30	65	34	31	75	40	35	93	50	44
55-59	52	25	26	56	27	28	61	31	29	71	37	33
60-64	46	23	23	48	23	25	52	25	27	57	29	28
65-69	37	18	19	41	20	21	43	21	23	47	23	25
70-74	29	14	15	32	15	17	35	17	18	38	18	20
75-79	18	8	9	22	10	12	25	12	13	28	13	15
80-84	9	4	5	11	5	6	15	7	8	16	8	9
85-89	4	2	2	5	2	3	6	3	3	7	3	4
90-94	1	0	1	1	1	1	2	1	1	2	1	1
95-99	0	0	0	0	0	0	0	0	0	0	0	0
100 +	0	0	0	0	0	0	0	0	0	0	0	0

Age group	2045 Both sexes	Males	Females	2050 Both sexes	Males	Females
All ages	1 868	952	916	1 892	964	928
0-4	125	63	62	116	59	57
5-9	134	68	66	125	63	62
10-14	143	72	71	133	67	66
15-19	152	77	75	143	72	71
20-24	158	80	78	151	76	75
25-29	157	79	78	155	78	77
30-34	155	79	76	152	77	75
35-39	148	76	72	148	76	72
40-44	144	75	69	141	73	68
45-49	129	68	61	138	72	66
50-54	113	60	53	123	65	59
55-59	89	47	42	108	57	51
60-64	66	35	32	84	44	40
65-69	52	26	26	61	32	30
70-74	41	20	22	46	23	23
75-79	30	14	16	33	15	18
80-84	19	9	10	20	9	11
85-89	9	4	5	10	4	6
90-94	3	1	2	3	1	2
95-99	0	0	0	1	0	0
100 +	0	0	0	0	0	0

United Nations Department of Economic and Social Affairs/Population Division
World Population Prospects: The 2004 Revision, Volume II: Sex and Age Distribution of the World Population

413

POPULATION BY AGE AND SEX (in thousands)

Age group	1950 Both sexes	1950 Males	1950 Females	1955 Both sexes	1955 Males	1955 Females	1960 Both sexes	1960 Males	1960 Females	1965 Both sexes	1965 Males	1965 Females
All ages	294	143	151	314	153	161	355	173	182	408	199	209
0-4	49	24	25	51	26	26	61	30	31	73	36	37
5-9	38	19	19	41	20	21	44	22	22	52	26	26
10-14	33	16	17	36	18	18	39	19	20	42	21	21
15-19	29	15	15	32	16	16	35	17	18	38	19	19
20-24	26	13	13	28	14	14	32	16	16	36	17	18
25-29	23	11	12	24	12	12	29	14	15	33	16	17
30-34	20	10	10	21	10	11	25	12	13	29	14	15
35-39	17	8	9	18	9	9	21	10	11	25	12	13
40-44	14	7	7	15	7	8	18	9	9	20	10	10
45-49	12	6	6	13	6	7	15	7	8	17	8	9
50-54	10	5	5	11	5	6	12	6	6	14	6	7
55-59	8	4	4	9	4	5	9	4	5	11	5	6
60-64	6	3	3	6	3	4	7	3	4	8	4	4
65-69	4	2	2	4	2	2	5	2	3	6	2	3
70-74	2	1	1	3	1	1	3	1	2	3	1	2
75-79	1	0	1	1	0	1	1	1	1	2	1	1
80 +	0	0	0	0	0	0	1	0	0	1	0	0

Age group	1970 Both sexes	1970 Males	1970 Females	1975 Both sexes	1975 Males	1975 Females	1980 Both sexes	1980 Males	1980 Females	1985 Both sexes	1985 Males	1985 Females
All ages	469	229	240	555	272	283	652	320	332	773	380	392
0-4	84	42	42	99	49	50	118	59	59	140	70	70
5-9	63	31	32	75	37	38	89	44	45	108	54	54
10-14	50	25	25	61	30	31	72	36	36	87	43	44
15-19	41	20	21	50	25	25	61	30	31	72	36	36
20-24	39	19	20	44	21	22	52	25	26	63	31	32
25-29	37	18	19	42	21	22	46	22	23	54	27	28
30-34	33	16	17	39	19	20	44	21	22	48	23	25
35-39	29	14	15	34	17	18	39	19	20	44	22	23
40-44	24	12	12	29	14	15	34	17	17	39	19	20
45-49	19	9	10	23	11	12	28	14	14	33	16	17
50-54	16	7	8	19	9	10	22	11	12	27	13	14
55-59	12	6	6	14	7	8	17	8	9	21	10	11
60-64	9	4	5	11	5	6	13	6	7	15	7	8
65-69	6	3	3	7	3	4	9	4	5	11	5	6
70-74	4	2	2	5	2	3	5	2	3	7	3	4
75-79	2	1	1	2	1	1	3	1	2	3	1	2
80 +	1	0	1	1	0	1	1	1	1	2	1	1

Age group	1990 Both sexes	1990 Males	1990 Females	1995 Both sexes	1995 Males	1995 Females	2000 Both sexes	2000 Males	2000 Females	2005 Both sexes	2005 Males	2005 Females
All ages	936	462	474	1 115	551	564	1 316	652	664	1 517	752	765
0-4	165	83	82	185	93	92	210	106	104	231	116	115
5-9	131	66	66	157	79	78	177	89	88	203	102	101
10-14	106	53	53	129	65	65	155	78	77	175	88	87
15-19	88	44	44	107	53	54	130	65	65	155	78	77
20-24	77	38	39	92	46	47	111	55	56	132	66	66
25-29	69	34	35	83	41	42	98	48	50	114	56	57
30-34	59	29	30	74	36	38	87	43	44	99	49	50
35-39	51	25	26	62	31	32	76	37	39	87	43	45
40-44	46	22	23	52	26	27	63	31	32	76	37	39
45-49	39	19	20	46	22	23	52	26	27	62	30	32
50-54	32	16	17	38	19	20	45	22	23	51	25	26
55-59	26	12	13	31	15	16	37	18	19	42	20	22
60-64	19	9	10	23	11	12	29	14	15	34	16	18
65-69	13	6	7	16	8	9	20	10	11	25	12	13
70-74	8	4	4	10	5	6	13	6	7	17	8	9
75-79	4	2	2	6	2	3	7	3	4	9	4	5
80 +	2	1	1	3	1	2	4	2	2	6	2	3

United Nations Department of Economic and Social Affairs/Population Division
World Population Prospects: The 2004 Revision, Volume II: Sex and Age Distribution of the World Population

414

POPULATION BY AGE AND SEX (in thousands)

Age group	2005 Both sexes	Males	Females	2010 Both sexes	Males	Females	2015 Both sexes	Males	Females	2020 Both sexes	Males	Females
All ages	1 517	752	765	1 706	847	859	1 889	939	950	2 070	1 031	1 040
0-4	231	116	115	239	120	118	243	123	120	248	126	123
5-9	203	102	101	223	112	111	232	117	115	237	120	117
10-14	175	88	87	200	101	99	221	111	110	230	116	114
15-19	155	78	77	174	87	87	198	100	99	219	110	109
20-24	132	66	66	154	77	77	172	86	86	196	98	98
25-29	114	56	57	132	65	66	153	76	77	170	85	85
30-34	99	49	50	112	56	57	130	64	65	150	74	75
35-39	87	43	45	98	48	49	110	54	56	127	63	64
40-44	76	37	39	85	42	43	95	47	48	107	53	54
45-49	62	30	32	73	36	37	82	40	42	92	45	47
50-54	51	25	26	59	29	31	70	34	36	79	39	41
55-59	42	20	22	48	23	25	56	27	29	66	32	34
60-64	34	16	18	39	19	20	44	21	23	52	25	27
65-69	25	12	13	30	14	16	34	16	18	39	18	21
70-74	17	8	9	20	9	11	24	11	13	28	13	15
75-79	9	4	5	12	5	6	15	7	8	18	8	10
80-84	4	2	2	5	2	3	7	3	4	9	4	5
85-89	1	1	1	2	1	1	2	1	1	3	1	2
90-94	0	0	0	0	0	0	1	0	0	1	0	0
95-99	0	0	0	0	0	0	0	0	0	0	0	0
100 +	0	0	0	0	0	0	0	0	0	0	0	0

Age group	2025 Both sexes	Males	Females	2030 Both sexes	Males	Females	2035 Both sexes	Males	Females	2040 Both sexes	Males	Females
All ages	2 254	1 124	1 131	2 439	1 217	1 222	2 620	1 308	1 312	2 792	1 394	1 398
0-4	255	129	126	261	132	129	262	133	129	260	132	128
5-9	244	123	120	251	127	124	257	130	127	259	131	128
10-14	235	119	116	242	122	120	250	127	123	256	130	127
15-19	228	115	113	234	118	116	241	122	119	249	126	123
20-24	217	109	108	226	114	112	232	117	115	239	121	118
25-29	193	97	97	214	107	107	223	112	111	229	115	114
30-34	167	83	83	190	95	95	211	105	105	221	111	110
35-39	146	73	74	163	81	82	187	93	94	208	104	104
40-44	124	61	62	143	71	72	160	80	80	184	92	92
45-49	104	51	53	120	60	61	140	69	70	157	78	79
50-54	89	43	45	100	49	51	117	57	59	136	67	69
55-59	76	37	38	85	41	44	96	47	49	112	55	57
60-64	62	30	32	70	34	37	79	38	41	90	44	46
65-69	47	22	24	56	26	29	64	30	33	72	34	37
70-74	33	15	17	39	18	21	47	22	25	54	25	29
75-79	21	10	11	25	11	13	30	14	16	36	17	20
80-84	11	5	6	13	6	7	16	7	9	19	9	11
85-89	4	2	2	5	2	3	6	3	4	8	3	4
90-94	1	0	1	1	1	1	2	1	1	2	1	1
95-99	0	0	0	0	0	0	0	0	0	0	0	0
100 +	0	0	0	0	0	0	0	0	0	0	0	0

Age group	2045 Both sexes	Males	Females	2050 Both sexes	Males	Females
All ages	2 955	1 475	1 479	3 106	1 550	1 556
0-4	257	130	127	254	129	126
5-9	258	131	128	256	129	126
10-14	259	131	128	257	130	127
15-19	255	129	126	258	130	127
20-24	247	125	122	254	128	126
25-29	237	119	118	246	124	122
30-34	227	114	113	235	118	117
35-39	218	109	109	225	113	112
40-44	205	102	103	215	108	108
45-49	181	90	91	202	100	101
50-54	153	76	77	176	87	89
55-59	130	64	66	147	73	75
60-64	105	51	54	123	60	63
65-69	82	39	43	96	46	50
70-74	61	29	32	71	34	37
75-79	42	19	23	48	22	26
80-84	24	11	13	28	12	15
85-89	9	4	5	12	5	7
90-94	3	1	1	3	1	2
95-99	0	0	0	0	0	0
100 +	0	0	0	0	0	0

POPULATION BY AGE AND SEX (in thousands)

Age group	2005 Both sexes	2005 Males	2005 Females	2010 Both sexes	2010 Males	2010 Females	2015 Both sexes	2015 Males	2015 Females	2020 Both sexes	2020 Males	2020 Females
All ages	1 517	752	765	1 720	854	866	1 930	960	970	2 148	1 070	1 078
0-4	231	116	115	253	128	125	269	136	133	286	145	141
5-9	203	102	101	223	112	111	246	124	122	263	133	130
10-14	175	88	87	200	101	99	221	111	110	243	123	121
15-19	155	78	77	174	87	87	198	100	99	219	110	109
20-24	132	66	66	154	77	77	172	86	86	196	98	98
25-29	114	56	57	132	65	66	153	76	77	170	85	85
30-34	99	49	50	112	56	57	130	64	65	150	74	75
35-39	87	43	45	98	48	49	110	54	56	127	63	64
40-44	76	37	39	85	42	43	95	47	48	107	53	54
45-49	62	30	32	73	36	37	82	40	42	92	45	47
50-54	51	25	26	59	29	31	70	34	36	79	39	41
55-59	42	20	22	48	23	25	56	27	29	66	32	34
60-64	34	16	18	39	19	20	44	21	23	52	25	27
65-69	25	12	13	30	14	16	34	16	18	39	18	21
70-74	17	8	9	20	9	11	24	11	13	28	13	15
75-79	9	4	5	12	5	6	15	7	8	18	8	10
80-84	4	2	2	5	2	3	7	3	4	9	4	5
85-89	1	1	1	2	1	1	2	1	1	3	1	2
90-94	0	0	0	0	0	0	1	0	0	1	0	0
95-99	0	0	0	0	0	0	0	0	0	0	0	0
100 +	0	0	0	0	0	0	0	0	0	0	0	0

Age group	2025 Both sexes	2025 Males	2025 Females	2030 Both sexes	2030 Males	2030 Females	2035 Both sexes	2035 Males	2035 Females	2040 Both sexes	2040 Males	2040 Females
All ages	2 375	1 185	1 190	2 613	1 305	1 308	2 859	1 429	1 430	3 113	1 556	1 556
0-4	300	152	148	315	159	155	329	167	163	343	174	169
5-9	281	142	139	295	149	146	311	157	153	326	165	161
10-14	261	132	129	279	141	138	294	149	145	309	157	153
15-19	242	122	120	259	131	128	277	140	137	292	148	144
20-24	217	109	108	239	120	119	257	129	127	275	139	136
25-29	193	97	97	214	107	107	237	119	118	254	128	126
30-34	167	83	83	190	95	95	211	105	105	234	117	117
35-39	146	73	74	163	81	82	187	93	94	208	104	104
40-44	124	61	62	143	71	72	160	80	80	184	92	92
45-49	104	51	53	120	60	61	140	69	70	157	78	79
50-54	89	43	45	100	49	51	117	57	59	136	67	69
55-59	75	37	39	85	41	43	96	47	49	112	55	57
60-64	62	30	32	70	34	37	79	38	41	90	44	46
65-69	47	22	24	56	26	29	64	30	33	72	34	37
70-74	33	15	17	39	18	21	47	22	25	54	25	29
75-79	21	10	11	25	11	13	30	14	16	36	17	20
80-84	11	5	6	13	6	7	16	7	9	19	9	11
85-89	4	2	2	5	2	3	6	3	4	8	3	4
90-94	1	0	1	1	1	1	2	1	1	2	1	1
95-99	0	0	0	0	0	0	0	0	0	0	0	0
100 +	0	0	0	0	0	0	0	0	0	0	0	0

Age group	2045 Both sexes	2045 Males	2045 Females	2050 Both sexes	2050 Males	2050 Females
All ages	3 370	1 685	1 685	3 629	1 814	1 815
0-4	354	179	175	365	184	180
5-9	340	172	168	352	178	174
10-14	325	164	161	339	171	168
15-19	308	156	152	324	164	160
20-24	290	147	144	306	155	152
25-29	273	138	136	288	145	143
30-34	252	127	125	271	136	135
35-39	231	116	115	249	125	124
40-44	205	102	103	228	114	114
45-49	181	90	91	202	100	101
50-54	153	76	77	176	87	89
55-59	130	64	66	147	73	75
60-64	105	51	54	123	60	63
65-69	82	39	43	96	46	50
70-74	61	29	32	71	34	37
75-79	42	19	23	48	22	26
80-84	24	11	13	28	12	15
85-89	9	4	5	12	5	7
90-94	3	1	1	3	1	2
95-99	0	0	0	0	0	0
100 +	0	0	0	0	0	0

United Nations Department of Economic and Social Affairs/Population Division
World Population Prospects: The 2004 Revision, Volume II: Sex and Age Distribution of the World Population

416

POPULATION BY AGE AND SEX (in thousands)

Age group	2005 Both sexes	Males	Females	2010 Both sexes	Males	Females	2015 Both sexes	Males	Females	2020 Both sexes	Males	Females
All ages	1 517	752	765	1 692	840	852	1 849	919	930	1 993	991	1 001
0-4	231	116	115	224	113	111	216	109	107	210	106	104
5-9	203	102	101	223	112	111	218	110	108	211	107	104
10-14	175	88	87	200	101	99	221	111	110	216	109	107
15-19	155	78	77	174	87	87	198	100	99	219	110	109
20-24	132	66	66	154	77	77	172	86	86	196	98	98
25-29	114	56	57	132	65	66	153	76	77	170	85	85
30-34	99	49	50	112	56	57	130	64	65	150	74	75
35-39	87	43	45	98	48	49	110	54	56	127	63	64
40-44	76	37	39	85	42	43	95	47	48	107	53	54
45-49	62	30	32	73	36	37	82	40	42	92	45	47
50-54	51	25	26	59	29	31	70	34	36	79	39	41
55-59	42	20	22	48	23	25	56	27	29	66	32	34
60-64	34	16	18	39	19	20	44	21	23	52	25	27
65-69	25	12	13	30	14	16	34	16	18	39	18	21
70-74	17	8	9	20	9	11	24	11	13	28	13	15
75-79	9	4	5	12	5	6	15	7	8	18	8	10
80-84	4	2	2	5	2	3	7	3	4	9	4	5
85-89	1	1	1	2	1	1	2	1	1	3	1	2
90-94	0	0	0	0	0	0	1	0	0	1	0	0
95-99	0	0	0	0	0	0	0	0	0	0	0	0
100 +	0	0	0	0	0	0	0	0	0	0	0	0

Age group	2025 Both sexes	Males	Females	2030 Both sexes	Males	Females	2035 Both sexes	Males	Females	2040 Both sexes	Males	Females
All ages	2 134	1 063	1 071	2 268	1 130	1 137	2 388	1 190	1 197	2 489	1 241	1 248
0-4	211	107	104	208	106	103	200	101	99	187	95	93
5-9	206	104	102	208	105	103	206	104	102	198	100	98
10-14	209	106	104	205	104	101	207	105	102	205	104	101
15-19	214	108	106	208	105	103	204	103	101	206	104	102
20-24	217	109	108	212	107	106	206	104	102	202	102	100
25-29	193	97	97	214	107	107	210	105	105	205	103	102
30-34	167	83	83	190	95	95	211	105	105	208	104	104
35-39	146	73	74	163	81	82	187	93	94	208	104	104
40-44	124	61	62	140	71	72	160	80	80	184	92	92
45-49	104	51	53	120	60	61	140	69	70	157	78	79
50-54	89	43	45	100	49	51	117	57	59	136	67	69
55-59	75	37	39	85	41	43	90	47	49	112	55	57
60-64	62	30	32	70	34	37	79	38	41	90	44	46
65-69	47	22	24	56	26	29	64	30	33	72	34	37
70-74	33	15	17	39	18	21	47	22	25	54	25	29
75-79	21	10	11	25	11	13	30	14	16	36	17	20
80-84	11	5	6	13	6	7	16	7	9	19	9	11
85-89	4	2	2	5	2	3	6	3	4	8	3	4
90-94	1	0	1	1	1	1	2	1	1	2	1	1
95-99	0	0	0	0	0	0	0	0	0	0	0	0
100 +	0	0	0	0	0	0	0	0	0	0	0	0

Age group	2045 Both sexes	Males	Females	2050 Both sexes	Males	Females
All ages	2 571	1 282	1 290	2 635	1 313	1 323
0-4	175	88	86	164	83	81
5-9	186	94	92	174	88	86
10-14	197	100	97	185	94	92
15-19	204	103	101	197	99	97
20-24	205	103	101	203	103	101
25-29	201	101	100	203	102	101
30-34	203	102	101	199	100	99
35-39	205	103	103	201	101	100
40-44	205	102	103	203	101	101
45-49	181	90	91	202	100	101
50-54	153	76	77	176	87	89
55-59	130	64	66	147	73	75
60-64	105	51	54	123	60	63
65-69	82	39	43	96	46	50
70-74	61	29	32	71	34	37
75-79	42	19	23	48	22	26
80-84	24	11	13	28	12	15
85-89	9	4	5	12	5	7
90-94	3	1	1	3	1	2
95-99	0	0	0	0	0	0
100 +	0	0	0	0	0	0

United Nations Department of Economic and Social Affairs/Population Division
World Population Prospects: The 2004 Revision, Volume II: Sex and Age Distribution of the World Population

417

POPULATION BY AGE AND SEX (in thousands)

Age group	1950 Both sexes	1950 Males	1950 Females	1955 Both sexes	1955 Males	1955 Females	1960 Both sexes	1960 Males	1960 Females	1965 Both sexes	1965 Males	1965 Females
All ages	3 527	1 629	1 898	3 839	1 779	2 061	4 159	1 937	2 223	4 477	2 096	2 381
0-4	287	141	146	399	204	195	491	251	240	520	265	255
5-9	266	123	143	296	145	151	402	205	197	490	250	240
10-14	394	190	204	277	128	149	300	147	153	403	205	198
15-19	340	170	170	409	197	212	280	130	151	300	147	153
20-24	370	185	184	351	175	175	411	197	214	280	129	151
25-29	232	104	129	379	189	190	352	175	177	408	195	213
30-34	176	73	103	238	105	133	379	188	191	348	172	176
35-39	239	96	142	179	74	105	237	104	133	373	183	190
40-44	216	95	121	242	96	146	178	72	106	233	101	132
45-49	193	86	107	216	93	123	237	92	145	173	69	104
50-54	149	69	80	189	82	107	208	87	121	227	86	142
55-59	140	70	70	143	64	79	179	75	104	196	79	117
60-64	169	81	89	130	63	67	130	56	74	163	66	97
65-69	139	61	78	149	68	81	113	52	60	114	47	67
70-74	103	43	60	113	47	67	120	52	68	91	40	51
75-79	65	25	40	73	29	44	81	32	49	86	36	51
80 +	50	17	33	57	20	37	64	23	41	72	26	46

Age group	1970 Both sexes	1970 Males	1970 Females	1975 Both sexes	1975 Males	1975 Females	1980 Both sexes	1980 Males	1980 Females	1985 Both sexes	1985 Males	1985 Females
All ages	4 707	2 211	2 496	4 908	2 306	2 602	5 073	2 381	2 692	5 287	2 497	2 790
0-4	436	222	214	443	226	218	433	220	214	459	234	225
5-9	517	264	254	442	224	219	434	220	215	434	220	214
10-14	490	250	240	506	258	248	438	222	216	437	222	215
15-19	402	205	197	476	242	234	480	243	237	421	215	205
20-24	299	146	153	393	192	200	437	216	220	462	228	234
25-29	278	128	150	295	140	154	381	183	198	436	212	224
30-34	404	192	212	272	125	147	311	148	163	381	183	197
35-39	344	169	175	397	190	207	251	116	135	310	148	162
40-44	366	178	188	329	161	167	394	187	207	250	117	133
45-49	226	96	130	351	169	181	317	155	162	382	181	201
50-54	166	65	102	232	92	140	343	164	179	309	147	161
55-59	215	78	136	163	61	103	233	92	142	330	153	177
60-64	180	70	110	191	70	121	158	55	103	214	83	131
65-69	143	55	88	155	58	98	166	59	107	140	47	93
70-74	93	37	57	114	42	72	128	45	83	139	47	92
75-79	67	28	39	67	26	42	88	30	58	95	32	63
80 +	81	30	51	82	30	52	80	27	53	90	28	63

Age group	1990 Both sexes	1990 Males	1990 Females	1995 Both sexes	1995 Males	1995 Females	2000 Both sexes	2000 Males	2000 Females	2005 Both sexes	2005 Males	2005 Females
All ages	5 460	2 595	2 865	5 033	2 391	2 642	4 720	2 238	2 482	4 474	2 114	2 360
0-4	457	235	222	360	186	175	269	141	128	242	127	115
5-9	454	231	223	421	216	205	349	179	169	261	137	124
10-14	432	220	212	406	206	201	401	205	196	344	176	168
15-19	413	213	199	381	191	190	375	188	187	388	198	190
20-24	405	204	200	364	185	179	347	171	177	351	175	177
25-29	461	222	239	354	176	178	330	164	166	321	154	167
30-34	433	209	224	411	195	215	319	155	164	302	146	156
35-39	377	182	195	386	185	201	376	176	200	291	137	154
40-44	305	146	159	334	160	174	353	168	185	348	160	188
45-49	245	114	131	269	127	142	304	143	160	327	154	173
50-54	365	172	194	210	96	114	243	113	130	278	129	149
55-59	295	138	158	320	147	173	184	83	102	220	100	120
60-64	308	138	170	247	113	135	282	126	155	162	71	91
65-69	189	71	118	253	109	143	206	91	115	242	105	137
70-74	118	37	80	143	50	93	199	81	117	163	68	95
75-79	105	33	72	79	23	57	100	32	68	143	54	88
80 +	98	29	69	95	27	68	84	21	62	92	25	68

United Nations Department of Economic and Social Affairs/Population Division
World Population Prospects: The 2004 Revision, Volume II: Sex and Age Distribution of the World Population

418

POPULATION BY AGE AND SEX (in thousands)

Age group	2005			2010			2015			2020		
	Both sexes	Males	Females	Both sexes	Males	Females	Both sexes	Males	Females	Both sexes	Males	Females
All ages	4 474	2 114	2 360	4 299	2 026	2 274	4 183	1 970	2 213	4 059	1 911	2 148
0-4	242	127	115	221	116	105	213	111	101	205	107	99
5-9	261	137	124	235	123	112	217	114	103	209	110	99
10-14	344	176	168	257	135	122	233	122	111	215	113	102
15-19	388	198	190	333	171	163	251	132	120	227	119	108
20-24	351	175	177	364	185	179	321	164	157	239	125	114
25-29	321	154	167	321	158	163	348	176	172	305	155	150
30-34	302	146	156	294	139	155	307	150	157	334	168	166
35-39	291	137	154	282	134	148	283	132	151	296	143	152
40-44	348	160	188	276	128	148	273	128	144	274	126	147
45-49	327	154	173	334	151	183	267	122	145	264	123	141
50-54	278	129	149	312	144	168	323	143	179	258	116	142
55-59	220	100	120	264	120	144	299	135	164	309	135	175
60-64	162	71	91	205	91	114	248	109	138	281	124	158
65-69	242	105	137	145	61	84	185	79	106	225	96	129
70-74	163	68	95	204	83	120	123	48	74	158	64	94
75-79	143	54	88	123	47	75	156	59	97	95	35	60
80-84	60	17	42	91	31	60	80	28	52	103	35	68
85-89	21	5	17	30	8	22	46	14	32	41	13	29
90-94	9	2	7	8	1	6	11	2	8	17	4	13
95-99	2	0	2	2	0	2	2	0	2	3	0	2
100 +	0	0	0	0	0	0	0	0	0	0	0	0

Age group	2025			2030			2035			2040		
	Both sexes	Males	Females	Both sexes	Males	Females	Both sexes	Males	Females	Both sexes	Males	Females
All ages	3 917	1 842	2 075	3 755	1 764	1 991	3 576	1 678	1 898	3 384	1 588	1 796
0-4	187	97	91	167	86	81	152	78	74	145	75	70
5-9	202	105	97	184	95	89	163	84	79	149	77	72
10-14	207	109	98	200	104	96	182	94	88	162	83	78
15-19	210	110	100	202	106	96	195	101	94	177	91	86
20-24	215	113	103	198	104	94	190	99	90	183	95	88
25-29	224	117	107	200	105	96	183	96	87	175	91	84
30-34	291	147	144	211	109	101	187	97	90	170	88	82
35-39	320	161	161	280	141	139	201	104	97	177	92	86
40-44	286	138	149	313	150	150	272	136	136	193	99	94
45-49	266	121	144	278	132	146	305	150	155	264	131	134
50-54	256	117	139	257	116	142	270	127	143	297	144	152
55-59	247	109	138	245	110	135	248	100	138	260	120	140
60-64	292	124	168	234	101	133	232	102	130	235	102	133
65-69	256	109	147	267	110	158	214	89	125	214	91	123
70-74	193	78	115	221	89	132	232	91	142	187	74	113
75-79	120	46	77	152	57	95	176	66	110	187	68	119
80-84	64	21	42	84	28	55	105	36	69	123	42	81
85-89	55	16	38	35	10	25	47	14	33	60	18	42
90-94	16	4	12	22	5	16	14	3	11	20	5	15
95-99	4	1	4	4	1	3	6	1	5	4	1	3
100 +	0	0	0	1	0	1	1	0	1	1	0	1

Age group	2045			2050		
	Both sexes	Males	Females	Both sexes	Males	Females
All ages	3 186	1 497	1 690	2 985	1 406	1 579
0-4	142	73	69	136	70	66
5-9	142	73	69	139	72	67
10-14	147	76	71	140	72	68
15-19	157	81	76	142	73	69
20-24	165	85	80	145	74	70
25-29	168	87	81	150	77	74
30-34	162	84	78	155	80	75
35-39	160	83	77	153	79	74
40-44	170	87	83	153	79	75
45-49	187	95	92	164	84	81
50-54	257	126	131	181	91	90
55-59	286	137	149	248	120	128
60-64	248	112	135	273	129	144
65-69	217	91	126	229	101	128
70-74	188	76	111	192	77	115
75-79	152	56	95	153	59	95
80-84	133	44	89	109	37	72
85-89	72	21	50	79	23	56
90-94	26	6	20	32	8	24
95-99	6	1	5	8	2	7
100 +	1	0	1	1	0	1

POPULATION BY AGE AND SEX (in thousands)

Age group	2005 Both sexes	Males	Females	2010 Both sexes	Males	Females	2015 Both sexes	Males	Females	2020 Both sexes	Males	Females
All ages	4 474	2 114	2 360	4 340	2 047	2 293	4 286	2 024	2 262	4 232	2 001	2 230
0-4	242	127	115	262	137	124	275	144	131	275	143	132
5-9	261	137	124	235	123	112	258	135	123	271	142	129
10-14	344	176	168	257	135	122	233	122	111	256	134	122
15-19	388	198	190	333	171	163	251	132	120	227	119	108
20-24	351	175	177	364	185	179	321	164	157	239	125	114
25-29	321	154	167	321	158	163	348	176	172	305	155	150
30-34	302	146	156	294	139	155	307	150	157	334	168	166
35-39	291	137	154	282	134	148	283	132	151	296	143	152
40-44	348	160	188	276	128	148	273	128	144	274	126	147
45-49	327	154	173	334	151	183	267	122	145	264	123	141
50-54	278	129	149	312	144	168	323	143	179	258	116	142
55-59	220	100	120	264	120	144	299	135	164	309	135	175
60-64	162	71	91	205	91	114	248	109	138	281	124	158
65-69	242	105	137	145	61	84	185	79	106	225	96	129
70-74	163	68	95	204	83	120	123	48	74	158	64	94
75-79	143	54	88	123	47	75	156	59	97	95	35	60
80-84	60	17	42	91	31	60	80	28	52	103	35	68
85-89	21	5	17	30	8	22	46	14	32	41	13	29
90-94	9	2	7	8	1	6	11	2	8	17	4	13
95-99	2	0	2	2	0	2	2	0	2	3	0	2
100 +	0	0	0	0	0	0	0	0	0	0	0	0

Age group	2025 Both sexes	Males	Females	2030 Both sexes	Males	Females	2035 Both sexes	Males	Females	2040 Both sexes	Males	Females
All ages	4 149	1 963	2 186	4 046	1 915	2 131	3 938	1 866	2 073	3 838	1 822	2 016
0-4	247	127	120	226	116	110	224	115	109	237	122	115
5-9	271	141	130	244	125	118	222	115	108	221	114	107
10-14	269	141	128	269	140	129	242	124	117	221	114	107
15-19	250	131	119	264	138	126	264	137	127	237	122	115
20-24	215	113	103	238	125	114	252	132	120	252	131	121
25-29	224	117	107	200	105	96	223	117	107	237	124	113
30-34	291	147	144	211	109	101	187	97	90	210	109	101
35-39	323	161	161	280	141	139	201	104	97	177	92	86
40-44	286	138	149	313	156	158	272	136	136	193	99	94
45-49	266	121	144	278	132	146	305	150	155	264	131	134
50-54	256	117	139	257	116	142	270	127	143	297	144	152
55-59	247	109	138	245	110	135	248	109	138	260	120	140
60-64	292	124	168	234	101	133	232	102	130	235	102	133
65-69	256	109	147	267	110	158	214	89	125	214	91	123
70-74	193	78	115	221	89	132	232	91	142	187	74	113
75-79	123	46	77	152	57	95	176	66	110	187	68	119
80-84	64	21	42	84	28	55	105	36	69	123	42	81
85-89	55	16	38	35	10	25	47	14	33	60	18	42
90-94	16	4	12	22	5	16	14	3	11	20	5	15
95-99	4	1	4	4	1	3	6	1	5	4	1	3
100 +	0	0	0	1	0	1	1	0	1	1	0	1

Age group	2045 Both sexes	Males	Females	2050 Both sexes	Males	Females
All ages	3 744	1 785	1 959	3 647	1 747	1 900
0-4	247	127	120	242	125	118
5-9	233	120	113	244	126	118
10-14	219	113	106	232	119	112
15-19	215	111	105	214	110	104
20-24	225	115	109	204	105	99
25-29	237	123	114	210	107	102
30-34	224	116	107	224	116	109
35-39	200	104	97	214	111	103
40-44	170	87	83	193	99	94
45-49	187	95	92	164	84	81
50-54	257	126	131	181	91	90
55-59	286	137	149	248	120	128
60-64	248	112	135	273	129	144
65-69	217	91	126	229	101	128
70-74	188	76	111	192	77	115
75-79	152	56	95	153	59	95
80-84	133	44	89	109	37	72
85-89	72	21	50	79	23	56
90-94	26	6	20	32	8	24
95-99	6	1	5	8	2	7
100 +	1	0	1	1	0	1

United Nations Department of Economic and Social Affairs/Population Division
World Population Prospects: The 2004 Revision, Volume II: Sex and Age Distribution of the World Population

420

POPULATION BY AGE AND SEX (in thousands)

Age group	2005			2010			2015			2020		
	Both sexes	Males	Females	Both sexes	Males	Females	Both sexes	Males	Females	Both sexes	Males	Females
All ages	4 474	2 114	2 360	4 259	2 004	2 254	4 000	1 916	2 164	3 885	1 820	2 065
0-4	242	127	115	180	95	86	150	79	71	134	70	65
5-9	261	137	124	235	123	112	177	93	84	147	77	70
10-14	344	176	168	257	135	122	233	122	111	175	92	83
15-19	388	198	190	333	171	163	251	132	120	227	119	108
20-24	351	175	177	364	185	179	321	164	157	239	125	114
25-29	321	154	167	321	158	163	348	176	172	305	155	150
30-34	302	146	156	294	139	155	307	150	157	334	168	166
35-39	291	137	154	282	134	148	283	132	151	296	143	152
40-44	348	160	188	276	128	148	273	128	144	274	126	147
45-49	327	154	173	334	151	183	267	122	145	264	123	141
50-54	278	129	149	312	144	168	323	143	179	258	116	142
55-59	220	100	120	264	120	144	299	135	164	309	135	175
60-64	162	71	91	205	91	114	248	109	138	281	124	158
65-69	242	105	137	145	61	84	185	79	106	225	96	129
70-74	163	68	95	204	83	120	123	48	74	158	64	94
75-79	143	54	88	123	47	75	156	59	97	95	35	60
80-84	60	17	42	91	31	60	80	28	52	103	35	68
85-89	21	5	17	30	8	22	46	14	32	41	13	29
90-94	9	2	7	8	1	6	11	2	8	17	4	13
95-99	2	0	2	2	0	2	2	0	2	3	0	2
100 +	0	0	0	0	0	0	0	0	0	0	0	0

Age group	2025			2030			2035			2040		
	Both sexes	Males	Females	Both sexes	Males	Females	Both sexes	Males	Females	Both sexes	Males	Females
All ages	3 683	1 721	1 962	3 466	1 614	1 852	3 231	1 500	1 732	2 976	1 377	1 599
0-4	126	65	61	112	58	54	96	49	46	80	41	39
5-9	131	68	63	123	63	60	109	56	53	93	48	45
10-14	145	76	69	129	67	62	121	62	59	107	55	52
15-19	169	89	81	140	73	66	124	64	60	116	60	56
20-24	215	113	103	158	83	75	128	67	61	112	58	54
25-29	224	117	107	200	105	96	143	75	68	113	59	54
30-34	291	147	144	211	109	101	187	97	90	130	68	62
35-39	323	161	161	280	141	139	201	104	97	177	92	86
40-44	288	130	140	313	156	158	272	106	136	193	99	94
45-49	266	121	144	278	132	146	305	150	155	264	131	134
50-54	256	117	139	257	116	142	270	127	143	297	144	152
55-59	247	109	138	246	110	135	248	109	138	260	120	140
60-64	292	124	168	234	101	133	232	102	130	235	102	133
65-69	256	109	147	267	110	158	214	89	125	214	91	123
70-74	193	78	115	221	89	132	232	91	142	187	74	113
75-79	123	46	77	152	57	95	176	66	110	187	68	119
80-84	64	21	42	84	28	55	105	36	69	123	42	81
85-89	55	16	38	35	10	25	47	14	33	60	18	42
90-94	16	4	12	22	5	16	14	3	11	20	5	15
95-99	4	1	4	4	1	3	6	1	5	4	1	3
100 +	0	0	0	1	0	1	1	0	1	1	0	1

Age group	2045			2050		
	Both sexes	Males	Females	Both sexes	Males	Females
All ages	2 705	1 248	1 457	2 428	1 119	1 309
0-4	68	35	33	60	31	29
5-9	77	40	37	65	34	31
10-14	91	47	44	76	39	37
15-19	102	53	50	86	44	42
20-24	105	54	51	90	46	44
25-29	98	50	47	90	46	44
30-34	101	52	48	85	44	42
35-39	121	62	58	92	47	44
40-44	170	87	83	114	58	56
45-49	187	95	92	164	84	81
50-54	257	126	131	181	91	90
55-59	286	137	149	248	120	128
60-64	248	112	135	273	129	144
65-69	217	91	126	229	101	128
70-74	188	76	111	192	77	115
75-79	152	56	95	153	59	95
80-84	133	44	89	109	37	72
85-89	72	21	50	79	23	56
90-94	26	6	20	32	8	24
95-99	6	1	5	8	2	7
100 +	1	0	1	1	0	1

United Nations Department of Economic and Social Affairs/Population Division
World Population Prospects: The 2004 Revision, Volume II: Sex and Age Distribution of the World Population

421

POPULATION BY AGE AND SEX (in thousands)

Age group	1950 Both sexes	1950 Males	1950 Females	1955 Both sexes	1955 Males	1955 Females	1960 Both sexes	1960 Males	1960 Females	1965 Both sexes	1965 Males	1965 Females
All ages	68 376	31 493	36 883	70 326	32 573	37 753	72 815	33 866	38 949	75 964	35 763	40 200
0-4	4 529	2 321	2 208	5 180	2 660	2 520	5 698	2 925	2 773	6 455	3 311	3 144
5-9	5 131	2 619	2 512	4 475	2 286	2 189	5 255	2 694	2 561	5 680	2 916	2 764
10-14	6 194	3 153	3 041	5 251	2 676	2 575	4 538	2 318	2 220	5 223	2 679	2 545
15-19	4 934	2 500	2 434	6 176	3 143	3 033	5 316	2 707	2 609	4 598	2 362	2 236
20-24	4 874	2 352	2 522	4 934	2 505	2 429	6 179	3 154	3 025	5 390	2 768	2 623
25-29	4 779	1 989	2 790	4 866	2 343	2 523	4 849	2 463	2 387	6 234	3 240	2 994
30-34	3 369	1 389	1 980	4 784	1 994	2 790	4 820	2 317	2 504	4 995	2 591	2 404
35-39	5 062	2 126	2 936	3 330	1 375	1 955	4 772	1 987	2 785	4 971	2 443	2 528
40-44	5 556	2 446	3 110	5 031	2 118	2 913	3 322	1 371	1 952	4 819	2 029	2 790
45-49	5 415	2 530	2 885	5 479	2 414	3 065	5 002	2 098	2 904	3 288	1 362	1 926
50-54	4 690	2 082	2 608	5 260	2 444	2 816	5 399	2 362	3 037	4 896	2 044	2 851
55-59	3 860	1 618	2 242	4 457	1 944	2 513	5 086	2 326	2 760	5 169	2 228	2 941
60-64	3 338	1 435	1 903	3 586	1 474	2 112	4 191	1 778	2 413	4 732	2 104	2 628
65-69	2 683	1 184	1 499	2 959	1 241	1 718	3 222	1 275	1 947	3 728	1 514	2 214
70-74	2 080	931	1 149	2 194	942	1 252	2 449	983	1 466	2 671	995	1 676
75-79	1 200	535	665	1 463	634	829	1 573	644	929	1 772	666	1 106
80 +	682	283	399	901	380	521	1 142	465	677	1 343	512	831

Age group	1970 Both sexes	1970 Males	1970 Females	1975 Both sexes	1975 Males	1975 Females	1980 Both sexes	1980 Males	1980 Females	1985 Both sexes	1985 Males	1985 Females
All ages	78 169	36 935	41 234	78 674	37 319	41 354	78 289	37 257	41 032	77 685	37 059	40 626
0-4	5 988	3 069	2 919	4 367	2 236	2 131	4 015	2 059	1 956	4 145	2 124	2 021
5-9	6 458	3 308	3 150	6 039	3 095	2 944	4 364	2 231	2 133	3 953	2 021	1 932
10-14	5 704	2 927	2 777	6 526	3 344	3 182	6 095	3 125	2 970	4 343	2 217	2 126
15-19	5 334	2 731	2 603	5 841	3 000	2 841	6 643	3 417	3 226	6 130	3 147	2 982
20-24	4 678	2 392	2 286	5 550	2 812	2 739	5 984	3 088	2 895	6 712	3 451	3 261
25-29	5 492	2 829	2 662	4 946	2 551	2 395	5 603	2 865	2 738	5 987	3 086	2 901
30-34	6 308	3 269	3 039	5 545	2 869	2 676	4 874	2 506	2 369	5 542	2 822	2 720
35-39	5 021	2 597	2 424	6 288	3 252	3 036	5 446	2 791	2 655	4 778	2 440	2 338
40-44	4 945	2 415	2 529	4 974	2 558	2 417	6 177	3 162	3 014	5 340	2 711	2 630
45-49	4 756	1 985	2 771	4 849	2 353	2 496	4 860	2 472	2 388	6 043	3 060	2 983
50-54	3 161	1 297	1 865	4 608	1 903	2 704	4 707	2 255	2 451	4 715	2 365	2 350
55-59	4 791	1 969	2 822	3 071	1 237	1 833	4 423	1 792	2 631	4 518	2 127	2 392
60-64	4 830	2 023	2 807	4 397	1 752	2 645	2 887	1 129	1 759	4 167	1 638	2 530
65-69	4 202	1 785	2 418	4 319	1 726	2 592	3 734	1 424	2 310	2 633	983	1 649
70-74	3 050	1 152	1 898	3 450	1 359	2 091	3 657	1 348	2 309	3 414	1 211	2 203
75-79	1 931	661	1 270	2 199	746	1 453	2 654	953	1 701	2 768	924	1 844
80 +	1 520	526	994	1 706	527	1 179	2 165	639	1 527	2 497	732	1 764

Age group	1990 Both sexes	1990 Males	1990 Females	1995 Both sexes	1995 Males	1995 Females	2000 Both sexes	2000 Males	2000 Females	2005 Both sexes	2005 Males	2005 Females
All ages	79 433	38 309	41 124	81 661	39 731	41 930	82 344	40 159	42 185	82 689	40 388	42 301
0-4	4 409	2 263	2 146	4 114	2 111	2 003	3 927	2 016	1 911	3 545	1 820	1 725
5-9	4 271	2 191	2 080	4 653	2 388	2 265	4 207	2 159	2 048	4 013	2 060	1 953
10-14	4 095	2 103	1 992	4 497	2 307	2 190	4 719	2 422	2 297	4 267	2 190	2 077
15-19	4 472	2 296	2 176	4 323	2 223	2 100	4 681	2 403	2 278	4 873	2 501	2 372
20-24	6 391	3 275	3 117	4 903	2 516	2 387	4 482	2 287	2 195	4 926	2 514	2 411
25-29	6 926	3 571	3 354	6 807	3 528	3 279	5 064	2 592	2 472	4 635	2 362	2 273
30-34	6 135	3 156	2 979	7 198	3 730	3 469	6 917	3 569	3 348	5 171	2 636	2 536
35-39	5 623	2 857	2 765	6 327	3 259	3 068	7 239	3 726	3 514	6 960	3 570	3 390
40-44	4 893	2 499	2 393	5 731	2 911	2 820	6 270	3 210	3 060	7 187	3 682	3 506
45-49	5 341	2 725	2 616	4 882	2 482	2 400	5 753	2 895	2 858	6 291	3 197	3 094
50-54	6 032	3 055	2 977	5 310	2 685	2 626	4 652	2 343	2 309	5 754	2 864	2 890
55-59	4 628	2 305	2 323	5 877	2 934	2 943	5 278	2 631	2 647	4 345	2 165	2 180
60-64	4 335	2 008	2 327	4 403	2 140	2 263	5 671	2 777	2 894	5 197	2 548	2 649
65-69	3 859	1 465	2 394	4 012	1 786	2 226	4 016	1 896	2 119	5 235	2 499	2 736
70-74	2 322	821	1 501	3 423	1 225	2 198	3 586	1 518	2 067	3 605	1 635	1 969
75-79	2 714	883	1 831	1 886	613	1 274	3 023	979	2 044	3 038	1 223	1 815
80 +	2 987	836	2 151	3 313	893	2 419	2 859	736	2 123	3 647	922	2 725

United Nations Department of Economic and Social Affairs/Population Division
World Population Prospects: The 2004 Revision, Volume II: Sex and Age Distribution of the World Population

422

POPULATION BY AGE AND SEX (in thousands)

Age group	2005 Both sexes	2005 Males	2005 Females	2010 Both sexes	2010 Males	2010 Females	2015 Both sexes	2015 Males	2015 Females	2020 Both sexes	2020 Males	2020 Females
All ages	82 689	40 388	42 301	82 701	40 410	42 290	82 513	40 309	42 204	82 283	40 150	42 134
0-4	3 545	1 820	1 725	3 390	1 741	1 649	3 514	1 804	1 710	3 680	1 890	1 791
5-9	4 013	2 060	1 953	3 632	1 865	1 767	3 469	1 781	1 688	3 593	1 845	1 748
10-14	4 267	2 190	2 077	4 073	2 091	1 982	3 687	1 893	1 794	3 524	1 810	1 714
15-19	4 873	2 501	2 372	4 422	2 269	2 153	4 214	2 163	2 051	3 828	1 966	1 863
20-24	4 926	2 514	2 411	5 118	2 612	2 506	4 646	2 371	2 275	4 440	2 266	2 173
25-29	4 635	2 362	2 273	5 078	2 589	2 489	5 257	2 680	2 576	4 786	2 440	2 345
30-34	5 171	2 636	2 536	4 745	2 407	2 338	5 176	2 629	2 547	5 355	2 720	2 635
35-39	6 960	3 570	3 390	5 222	2 641	2 581	4 792	2 413	2 379	5 224	2 635	2 589
40-44	7 187	3 682	3 506	6 913	3 529	3 384	5 188	2 610	2 578	4 761	2 383	2 378
45-49	6 291	3 197	3 094	7 205	3 666	3 539	6 930	3 516	3 415	5 223	2 607	2 615
50-54	5 754	2 864	2 890	6 291	3 165	3 127	7 192	3 628	3 564	6 928	3 484	3 444
55-59	4 345	2 165	2 180	5 431	2 676	2 754	5 983	2 984	2 999	6 876	3 442	3 434
60-64	5 197	2 548	2 649	4 316	2 117	2 199	5 363	2 606	2 757	5 910	2 910	3 000
65-69	5 235	2 499	2 736	4 817	2 309	2 508	4 013	1 929	2 085	5 020	2 393	2 627
70-74	3 605	1 635	1 969	4 727	2 176	2 552	4 378	2 028	2 350	3 671	1 710	1 961
75-79	3 038	1 223	1 815	3 078	1 334	1 743	4 055	1 782	2 273	3 793	1 685	2 108
80-84	2 270	620	1 649	2 295	803	1 492	2 353	902	1 451	3 142	1 239	1 903
85-89	756	184	572	1 425	328	1 097	1 460	440	1 020	1 527	510	1 017
90-94	490	95	395	353	69	284	699	128	571	734	180	554
95-99	119	20	99	151	23	128	116	17	98	245	34	211
100 +	12	2	10	20	3	17	28	3	25	26	3	23

Age group	2025 Both sexes	2025 Males	2025 Females	2030 Both sexes	2030 Males	2030 Females	2035 Both sexes	2035 Males	2035 Females	2040 Both sexes	2040 Males	2040 Females
All ages	81 967	39 928	42 040	81 512	39 624	41 888	80 884	39 234	41 650	80 159	38 792	41 367
0-4	3 756	1 929	1 828	3 741	1 921	1 820	3 686	1 893	1 793	3 705	1 902	1 803
5-9	3 759	1 930	1 829	3 835	1 969	1 866	3 820	1 961	1 859	3 765	1 933	1 832
10-14	3 648	1 873	1 775	3 814	1 958	1 856	3 891	1 998	1 893	3 875	1 990	1 886
15-19	3 666	1 882	1 783	3 700	1 946	1 844	3 956	2 031	1 925	4 033	2 071	1 962
20-24	4 055	2 070	1 985	3 893	1 987	1 906	4 018	2 051	1 967	4 184	2 136	2 048
25-29	4 580	2 336	2 244	4 196	2 140	2 057	4 035	2 058	1 978	4 160	2 122	2 039
30-34	4 886	2 481	2 405	4 682	2 378	2 304	4 299	2 182	2 117	4 139	2 100	2 038
35-39	5 403	2 726	2 677	4 936	2 489	2 447	4 733	2 386	2 347	4 352	2 191	2 160
40-44	5 193	2 605	2 588	5 373	2 697	2 676	4 909	2 461	2 448	4 708	2 360	2 348
45-49	4 802	2 385	2 418	5 233	2 606	2 627	5 414	2 698	2 716	4 955	2 485	2 470
50-54	5 246	2 594	2 652	4 982	2 443	2 539	5 264	2 597	2 667	5 446	2 690	2 756
55-59	6 620	3 402	3 218	4 834	2 376	2 458	4 582	2 234	2 348	5 009	2 453	2 557
60-64	6 787	3 357	3 430	6 558	3 237	3 320	4 970	2 411	2 559	4 588	2 214	2 373
65-69	5 555	2 687	2 868	6 406	3 116	3 289	6 204	3 016	3 188	4 702	2 249	2 454
70-74	4 614	2 135	2 479	5 126	2 412	2 714	5 932	2 812	3 119	5 767	2 736	3 031
75-79	3 214	1 442	1 772	4 060	1 810	2 250	4 531	2 058	2 474	5 267	2 412	2 854
80-84	2 980	1 192	1 788	2 558	1 033	1 525	3 263	1 322	1 941	3 672	1 526	2 146
85-89	2 086	723	1 363	2 019	714	1 306	1 763	632	1 131	2 287	826	1 461
90-94	792	218	574	1 115	320	794	1 107	326	781	992	297	694
95-99	267	50	217	298	63	235	434	96	338	447	101	345
100 +	51	5	46	63	8	54	73	11	62	107	17	90

Age group	2045 Both sexes	2045 Males	2045 Females	2050 Both sexes	2050 Males	2050 Females
All ages	79 455	38 362	41 092	78 765	37 968	40 797
0-4	3 847	1 975	1 872	3 965	2 036	1 929
5-9	3 784	1 943	1 841	3 926	2 015	1 910
10-14	3 821	1 962	1 859	3 840	1 972	1 868
15-19	4 018	2 063	1 955	3 963	2 035	1 928
20-24	4 261	2 176	2 085	4 246	2 168	2 078
25-29	4 327	2 207	2 120	4 404	2 247	2 157
30-34	4 264	2 165	2 099	4 430	2 250	2 180
35-39	4 192	2 110	2 082	4 317	2 174	2 143
40-44	4 329	2 167	2 162	4 171	2 086	2 085
45-49	4 756	2 366	2 390	4 381	2 175	2 206
50-54	4 994	2 462	2 532	4 799	2 364	2 435
55-59	5 193	2 547	2 647	4 751	2 326	2 426
60-64	5 010	2 430	2 580	5 196	2 525	2 671
65-69	4 347	2 070	2 277	4 762	2 280	2 481
70-74	4 391	2 052	2 339	4 074	1 898	2 176
75-79	5 151	2 365	2 785	3 955	1 796	2 160
80-84	4 305	1 816	2 489	4 248	1 801	2 447
85-89	2 612	973	1 639	3 106	1 180	1 926
90-94	1 319	400	919	1 539	485	1 054
95-99	414	96	318	569	134	435
100 +	122	19	103	123	20	103

POPULATION BY AGE AND SEX (in thousands)

Age group	2005 Both sexes	2005 Males	2005 Females	2010 Both sexes	2010 Males	2010 Females	2015 Both sexes	2015 Males	2015 Females	2020 Both sexes	2020 Males	2020 Females
All ages	82 689	40 388	42 301	83 302	40 721	42 581	84 090	41 119	42 972	85 069	41 580	43 489
0-4	3 545	1 820	1 725	3 991	2 049	1 942	4 491	2 306	2 185	4 889	2 510	2 379
5-9	4 013	2 060	1 953	3 632	1 865	1 767	4 069	2 089	1 980	4 569	2 346	2 223
10-14	4 267	2 190	2 077	4 073	2 091	1 982	3 687	1 893	1 794	4 124	2 118	2 006
15-19	4 873	2 501	2 372	4 422	2 269	2 153	4 214	2 163	2 051	3 828	1 966	1 863
20-24	4 926	2 514	2 411	5 118	2 612	2 506	4 646	2 371	2 275	4 440	2 266	2 173
25-29	4 635	2 362	2 273	5 078	2 589	2 489	5 257	2 680	2 576	4 786	2 440	2 345
30-34	5 171	2 636	2 536	4 745	2 407	2 338	5 176	2 629	2 547	5 355	2 720	2 635
35-39	6 960	3 570	3 390	5 222	2 641	2 581	4 792	2 413	2 379	5 224	2 635	2 589
40-44	7 187	3 682	3 506	6 913	3 529	3 384	5 188	2 610	2 578	4 761	2 383	2 378
45-49	6 291	3 197	3 094	7 205	3 666	3 539	6 930	3 516	3 415	5 223	2 607	2 615
50-54	5 754	2 864	2 890	6 291	3 165	3 127	7 192	3 628	3 564	6 928	3 484	3 444
55-59	4 345	2 165	2 180	5 431	2 676	2 754	5 983	2 984	2 999	6 876	3 442	3 434
60-64	5 197	2 548	2 649	4 316	2 117	2 199	5 363	2 606	2 757	5 910	2 910	3 000
65-69	5 235	2 499	2 736	4 817	2 309	2 508	4 013	1 929	2 085	5 020	2 393	2 627
70-74	3 605	1 635	1 969	4 727	2 176	2 552	4 378	2 028	2 350	3 671	1 710	1 961
75-79	3 038	1 223	1 815	3 078	1 334	1 743	4 055	1 782	2 273	3 793	1 685	2 108
80-84	2 270	620	1 649	2 295	803	1 492	2 353	902	1 451	3 142	1 239	1 903
85-89	756	184	572	1 425	328	1 097	1 460	440	1 020	1 527	510	1 017
90-94	490	95	395	353	69	284	699	128	571	734	180	554
95-99	119	20	99	151	23	128	116	17	98	245	34	211
100 +	12	2	10	20	3	17	28	3	25	26	3	23

Age group	2025 Both sexes	2025 Males	2025 Females	2030 Both sexes	2030 Males	2030 Females	2035 Both sexes	2035 Males	2035 Females	2040 Both sexes	2040 Males	2040 Females
All ages	85 897	41 945	43 952	86 546	42 207	44 338	87 156	42 452	44 703	88 021	42 826	45 195
0-4	4 902	2 517	2 385	4 847	2 489	2 359	4 927	2 530	2 397	5 300	2 721	2 579
5-9	4 967	2 550	2 417	4 980	2 557	2 423	4 926	2 529	2 397	5 005	2 570	2 436
10-14	4 624	2 374	2 250	5 022	2 579	2 444	5 035	2 585	2 450	4 981	2 557	2 424
15-19	4 265	2 190	2 075	4 766	2 447	2 319	5 164	2 651	2 513	5 177	2 658	2 519
20-24	4 055	2 070	1 985	4 492	2 294	2 198	4 992	2 551	2 442	5 390	2 755	2 635
25-29	4 580	2 336	2 244	4 196	2 140	2 057	4 634	2 364	2 269	5 134	2 621	2 513
30-34	4 886	2 481	2 405	4 682	2 378	2 304	4 299	2 182	2 117	4 736	2 406	2 329
35-39	5 403	2 726	2 677	4 936	2 489	2 447	4 733	2 386	2 347	4 352	2 191	2 160
40-44	5 193	2 605	2 588	5 373	2 697	2 676	4 909	2 461	2 448	4 708	2 360	2 348
45-49	4 802	2 385	2 418	5 233	2 606	2 627	5 414	2 698	2 716	4 955	2 466	2 489
50-54	5 246	2 594	2 652	4 834	2 376	2 458	5 264	2 597	2 667	5 446	2 690	2 756
55-59	6 626	3 308	3 318	4 982	2 443	2 539	4 582	2 234	2 348	5 009	2 453	2 557
60-64	6 787	3 357	3 430	6 558	3 237	3 320	4 970	2 411	2 559	4 588	2 214	2 373
65-69	5 555	2 687	2 868	6 406	3 116	3 289	6 204	3 016	3 188	4 702	2 249	2 454
70-74	4 614	2 135	2 479	5 126	2 412	2 714	5 932	2 812	3 119	5 767	2 736	3 031
75-79	3 214	1 442	1 772	4 060	1 810	2 250	4 531	2 058	2 474	5 267	2 412	2 854
80-84	2 980	1 192	1 788	2 558	1 033	1 525	3 263	1 322	1 941	3 672	1 526	2 146
85-89	2 086	723	1 363	2 019	714	1 306	1 763	632	1 131	2 287	826	1 461
90-94	792	218	574	1 115	320	794	1 107	326	781	992	297	694
95-99	267	50	217	298	63	235	434	96	338	447	101	345
100 +	51	5	46	63	8	54	73	11	62	107	17	90

Age group	2045 Both sexes	2045 Males	2045 Females	2050 Both sexes	2050 Males	2050 Females
All ages	89 327	43 427	45 900	90 909	44 197	46 712
0-4	5 864	3 011	2 854	6 247	3 207	3 040
5-9	5 378	2 761	2 617	5 942	3 051	2 892
10-14	5 061	2 598	2 463	5 434	2 790	2 644
15-19	5 123	2 630	2 493	5 203	2 671	2 532
20-24	5 404	2 762	2 642	5 350	2 735	2 616
25-29	5 531	2 825	2 707	5 545	2 832	2 713
30-34	5 235	2 663	2 573	5 633	2 867	2 766
35-39	4 788	2 415	2 373	5 287	2 671	2 616
40-44	4 329	2 167	2 162	4 764	2 390	2 375
45-49	4 756	2 366	2 390	4 381	2 175	2 206
50-54	4 994	2 462	2 532	4 799	2 364	2 435
55-59	5 193	2 547	2 647	4 751	2 326	2 426
60-64	5 010	2 430	2 580	5 196	2 525	2 671
65-69	4 347	2 070	2 277	4 762	2 280	2 481
70-74	4 391	2 052	2 339	4 074	1 898	2 176
75-79	5 151	2 365	2 785	3 955	1 796	2 160
80-84	4 305	1 816	2 489	4 248	1 801	2 447
85-89	2 612	973	1 639	3 106	1 180	1 926
90-94	1 319	400	919	1 539	485	1 054
95-99	414	96	318	569	134	435
100 +	122	19	103	123	20	103

United Nations Department of Economic and Social Affairs/Population Division
World Population Prospects: The 2004 Revision, Volume II: Sex and Age Distribution of the World Population

424

POPULATION BY AGE AND SEX (in thousands)

Age group	2005 Both sexes	Males	Females	2010 Both sexes	Males	Females	2015 Both sexes	Males	Females	2020 Both sexes	Males	Females
All ages	82 689	40 388	42 301	82 097	40 102	41 995	80 931	39 497	41 404	79 481	38 711	40 769
0-4	3 545	1 820	1 725	2 786	1 431	1 355	2 536	1 302	1 234	2 459	1 263	1 196
5-9	4 013	2 060	1 953	3 632	1 865	1 767	2 865	1 471	1 394	2 615	1 343	1 272
10-14	4 267	2 190	2 077	4 073	2 091	1 982	3 687	1 893	1 794	2 920	1 500	1 421
15-19	4 873	2 501	2 372	4 422	2 269	2 153	4 214	2 163	2 051	3 828	1 966	1 863
20-24	4 926	2 514	2 411	5 118	2 612	2 506	4 646	2 371	2 275	4 440	2 266	2 173
25-29	4 635	2 362	2 273	5 078	2 589	2 489	5 257	2 680	2 576	4 786	2 440	2 345
30-34	5 171	2 636	2 536	4 745	2 407	2 338	5 176	2 629	2 547	5 355	2 720	2 635
35-39	6 960	3 570	3 390	5 222	2 641	2 581	4 792	2 413	2 379	5 224	2 635	2 589
40-44	7 187	3 682	3 506	6 913	3 529	3 384	5 188	2 610	2 578	4 761	2 383	2 378
45-49	6 291	3 197	3 094	7 205	3 666	3 539	6 930	3 516	3 415	5 223	2 607	2 615
50-54	5 754	2 864	2 890	6 291	3 165	3 127	7 192	3 628	3 564	6 928	3 484	3 444
55-59	4 345	2 165	2 180	5 431	2 676	2 754	5 983	2 984	2 999	6 876	3 442	3 434
60-64	5 197	2 548	2 649	4 316	2 117	2 199	5 363	2 606	2 757	5 910	2 910	3 000
65-69	5 235	2 499	2 736	4 817	2 309	2 508	4 013	1 929	2 085	5 020	2 393	2 627
70-74	3 605	1 635	1 969	4 727	2 176	2 552	4 378	2 028	2 350	3 671	1 710	1 961
75-79	3 038	1 223	1 815	3 078	1 334	1 743	4 055	1 782	2 273	3 793	1 685	2 108
80-84	2 270	620	1 649	2 295	803	1 492	2 353	902	1 451	3 142	1 239	1 903
85-89	756	184	572	1 425	328	1 097	1 460	440	1 020	1 527	510	1 017
90-94	490	95	395	353	69	284	699	128	571	734	180	554
95-99	119	20	99	151	23	128	116	17	98	245	34	211
100 +	12	2	10	20	3	17	28	3	25	26	3	23

Age group	2025 Both sexes	Males	Females	2030 Both sexes	Males	Females	2035 Both sexes	Males	Females	2040 Both sexes	Males	Females
All ages	77 993	37 888	40 105	76 428	37 015	39 413	74 687	36 054	38 633	72 704	34 967	37 737
0-4	2 583	1 327	1 257	2 630	1 350	1 279	2 568	1 319	1 249	2 443	1 254	1 188
5-9	2 538	1 303	1 235	2 663	1 367	1 295	2 709	1 391	1 318	2 648	1 359	1 288
10-14	2 671	1 372	1 299	2 594	1 332	1 262	2 718	1 396	1 322	2 765	1 420	1 345
15-19	3 062	1 573	1 490	2 813	1 445	1 369	2 737	1 406	1 331	2 861	1 469	1 392
20-24	4 055	2 070	1 985	3 290	1 678	1 613	3 042	1 550	1 492	2 966	1 511	1 455
25-29	4 580	2 336	2 244	4 196	2 140	2 057	3 434	1 749	1 685	3 186	1 622	1 564
30-34	4 886	2 481	2 405	4 682	2 378	2 304	4 299	2 182	2 117	3 538	1 792	1 745
35-39	5 403	2 726	2 077	4 936	2 489	2 447	4 733	2 386	2 347	4 352	2 191	2 160
40-44	5 193	2 605	2 588	5 373	2 697	2 676	4 909	2 461	2 448	4 708	2 360	2 348
45-49	4 802	2 385	2 418	5 233	2 606	2 627	5 414	2 698	2 716	4 955	2 466	2 489
50-54	5 246	2 594	2 652	4 834	2 376	2 458	5 264	2 597	2 667	5 446	2 690	2 756
55-59	6 626	3 308	3 318	4 982	2 443	2 539	4 500	2 224	2 348	5 009	2 453	2 557
60-64	6 787	3 357	3 430	6 558	3 237	3 320	4 970	2 411	2 559	4 588	2 214	2 373
65-69	5 555	2 687	2 868	6 406	3 116	3 289	6 204	3 016	3 188	4 702	2 249	2 454
70-74	4 614	2 135	2 479	5 126	2 412	2 714	5 932	2 812	3 119	5 767	2 736	3 031
75-79	3 214	1 442	1 772	4 060	1 810	2 250	4 531	2 058	2 474	5 267	2 412	2 854
80-84	2 980	1 192	1 788	2 558	1 033	1 525	3 263	1 322	1 941	3 672	1 526	2 146
85-89	2 086	723	1 363	2 019	714	1 306	1 763	632	1 131	2 287	826	1 461
90-94	792	218	574	1 115	320	794	1 107	326	781	992	297	694
95-99	267	50	217	298	63	235	434	96	338	447	101	345
100 +	51	5	46	63	8	54	73	11	62	107	17	90

Age group	2045 Both sexes	Males	Females	2050 Both sexes	Males	Females
All ages	70 491	33 764	36 727	68 006	32 490	35 596
0-4	2 332	1 197	1 134	2 241	1 151	1 090
5-9	2 522	1 295	1 227	2 411	1 238	1 173
10-14	2 703	1 388	1 315	2 578	1 324	1 254
15-19	2 908	1 493	1 415	2 846	1 462	1 385
20-24	3 090	1 575	1 515	3 137	1 599	1 538
25-29	3 110	1 583	1 527	3 234	1 647	1 587
30-34	3 291	1 666	1 625	3 215	1 627	1 588
35-39	3 593	1 803	1 789	3 346	1 677	1 669
40-44	4 329	2 167	2 162	3 573	1 780	1 793
45-49	4 756	2 366	2 390	4 381	2 175	2 206
50-54	4 994	2 462	2 532	4 799	2 364	2 435
55-59	5 193	2 547	2 647	4 751	2 326	2 426
60-64	5 010	2 430	2 580	5 196	2 525	2 671
65-69	4 347	2 070	2 277	4 762	2 280	2 481
70-74	4 391	2 052	2 339	4 074	1 898	2 176
75-79	5 151	2 365	2 785	3 955	1 796	2 160
80-84	4 305	1 816	2 489	4 248	1 801	2 447
85-89	2 612	973	1 639	3 106	1 180	1 926
90-94	1 319	400	919	1 539	485	1 054
95-99	414	96	318	569	134	435
100 +	122	19	103	123	20	103

POPULATION BY AGE AND SEX (in thousands)

Age group	1950 Both sexes	Males	Females	1955 Both sexes	Males	Females	1960 Both sexes	Males	Females	1965 Both sexes	Males	Females
All ages	5 243	2 650	2 593	6 110	3 084	3 026	7 131	3 596	3 534	8 186	4 126	4 060
0-4	974	498	476	1 088	551	537	1 281	649	632	1 473	747	726
5-9	756	385	370	901	460	441	1 010	511	499	1 174	594	580
10-14	636	324	312	748	382	366	889	454	435	980	495	484
15-19	544	277	267	634	323	311	744	379	364	868	443	425
20-24	461	234	227	539	274	265	627	319	308	722	367	355
25-29	389	197	192	454	230	224	530	268	262	605	307	299
30-34	325	164	161	382	193	189	445	225	220	510	258	252
35-39	272	137	135	318	160	157	372	188	185	426	215	211
40-44	225	113	112	263	132	131	307	155	153	354	178	176
45-49	183	91	92	216	108	108	253	126	126	290	145	145
50-54	148	72	75	173	85	88	204	101	103	236	117	119
55-59	115	56	60	137	66	71	161	78	83	187	91	95
60-64	87	42	45	103	49	54	122	58	64	142	68	74
65-69	61	28	32	72	34	38	86	41	46	101	48	54
70-74	38	18	21	46	21	25	55	25	29	65	30	35
75-79	20	9	12	24	11	14	29	13	16	35	16	19
80 +	10	4	5	12	5	7	15	6	9	18	8	11

Age group	1970 Both sexes	Males	Females	1975 Both sexes	Males	Females	1980 Both sexes	Males	Females	1985 Both sexes	Males	Females
All ages	8 983	4 526	4 457	10 241	5 159	5 081	11 302	5 695	5 607	13 399	6 753	6 646
0-4	1 597	810	787	1 861	945	916	2 024	1 029	995	2 438	1 241	1 197
5-9	1 300	658	642	1 464	742	722	1 666	845	821	1 948	989	959
10-14	1 091	552	539	1 248	632	616	1 364	691	673	1 659	842	818
15-19	914	462	452	1 052	532	520	1 167	591	576	1 362	690	672
20-24	807	411	396	877	442	435	979	494	485	1 159	585	574
25-29	667	338	329	770	391	379	810	407	403	968	487	481
30-34	558	282	276	635	321	314	711	360	351	800	401	399
35-39	468	236	232	528	267	262	584	295	289	699	353	346
40-44	388	195	193	440	222	219	483	243	240	571	288	283
45-49	320	160	160	363	182	181	400	200	200	469	235	234
50-54	259	129	131	296	147	149	326	162	164	384	191	193
55-59	206	101	105	235	115	119	261	128	133	307	151	156
60-64	158	76	82	181	88	93	200	97	103	239	116	123
65-69	113	53	60	131	62	69	146	70	76	174	83	91
70-74	73	34	40	85	40	46	97	45	51	116	54	62
75-79	41	18	22	48	22	26	55	25	30	67	30	37
80 +	21	9	12	26	11	15	30	13	18	38	16	22

Age group	1990 Both sexes	Males	Females	1995 Both sexes	Males	Females	2000 Both sexes	Males	Females	2005 Both sexes	Males	Females
All ages	15 479	7 806	7 674	17 725	8 944	8 781	19 867	10 038	9 829	22 113	11 191	10 921
0-4	2 670	1 362	1 309	2 843	1 451	1 392	2 919	1 492	1 426	3 102	1 586	1 516
5-9	2 323	1 182	1 142	2 573	1 311	1 261	2 738	1 398	1 340	2 825	1 445	1 380
10-14	1 911	970	941	2 294	1 167	1 127	2 532	1 291	1 241	2 701	1 379	1 322
15-19	1 631	827	804	1 890	959	931	2 261	1 150	1 111	2 505	1 277	1 228
20-24	1 331	673	659	1 602	811	792	1 849	937	912	2 223	1 128	1 094
25-29	1 127	567	560	1 297	653	643	1 546	781	764	1 790	907	883
30-34	939	471	468	1 094	549	545	1 239	625	615	1 471	747	725
35-39	774	387	387	910	455	455	1 044	523	521	1 174	594	580
40-44	673	339	334	748	372	375	868	433	435	990	497	493
45-49	547	274	272	648	325	322	713	354	359	825	411	414
50-54	444	221	223	521	260	261	613	306	307	675	333	342
55-59	358	176	181	417	206	211	487	241	246	575	285	290
60-64	278	136	143	327	160	167	381	187	194	447	219	228
65-69	206	99	107	242	117	126	285	138	147	335	162	172
70-74	138	65	73	165	78	87	196	93	103	233	111	122
75-79	80	36	44	97	45	53	118	55	63	142	66	76
80 +	47	20	27	58	25	33	79	35	44	101	45	56

United Nations Department of Economic and Social Affairs/Population Division
World Population Prospects: The 2004 Revision, Volume II: Sex and Age Distribution of the World Population

426

POPULATION BY AGE AND SEX (in thousands)

Age group	2005 Both sexes	Males	Females	2010 Both sexes	Males	Females	2015 Both sexes	Males	Females	2020 Both sexes	Males	Females
All ages	22 113	11 191	10 921	24 312	12 322	11 991	26 562	13 474	13 088	28 789	14 611	14 178
0-4	3 102	1 586	1 516	3 191	1 631	1 560	3 268	1 670	1 599	3 303	1 686	1 616
5-9	2 825	1 445	1 380	3 006	1 536	1 470	3 112	1 590	1 522	3 203	1 635	1 568
10-14	2 701	1 379	1 322	2 779	1 421	1 358	2 965	1 515	1 450	3 076	1 571	1 505
15-19	2 505	1 277	1 228	2 667	1 361	1 306	2 751	1 406	1 345	2 938	1 500	1 438
20-24	2 223	1 128	1 094	2 459	1 251	1 208	2 627	1 338	1 289	2 713	1 384	1 329
25-29	1 790	907	883	2 155	1 094	1 061	2 393	1 217	1 176	2 564	1 306	1 259
30-34	1 471	747	725	1 708	869	839	2 069	1 053	1 016	2 306	1 176	1 130
35-39	1 174	594	580	1 392	710	682	1 627	831	796	1 979	1 011	968
40-44	990	497	493	1 111	563	548	1 325	677	648	1 555	796	759
45-49	825	411	414	939	471	468	1 058	536	522	1 267	647	620
50-54	675	333	342	780	387	393	892	445	446	1 009	509	500
55-59	575	285	290	632	310	322	735	362	373	843	418	425
60-64	447	219	228	528	259	269	584	284	300	682	333	349
65-69	335	162	172	394	191	203	469	228	241	522	251	271
70-74	233	111	122	275	131	143	327	156	171	392	188	205
75-79	142	66	76	170	80	90	204	96	108	245	115	130
80-84	70	32	38	85	39	46	104	48	57	127	58	69
85-89	25	11	14	31	14	18	39	17	22	49	22	27
90-94	5	2	3	7	3	4	10	4	6	12	5	7
95-99	1	0	0	1	0	1	1	0	1	2	1	1
100 +	0	0	0	0	0	0	0	0	0	0	0	0

Age group	2025 Both sexes	Males	Females	2030 Both sexes	Males	Females	2035 Both sexes	Males	Females	2040 Both sexes	Males	Females
All ages	30 964	15 717	15 247	33 075	16 786	16 289	35 115	17 813	17 301	37 065	18 790	18 275
0-4	3 304	1 686	1 618	3 296	1 682	1 614	3 289	1 677	1 611	3 270	1 668	1 602
5-9	3 251	1 658	1 593	3 262	1 663	1 599	3 264	1 663	1 601	3 263	1 662	1 601
10-14	3 174	1 619	1 555	3 228	1 645	1 582	3 244	1 653	1 592	3 249	1 654	1 595
15-19	3 052	1 557	1 495	3 152	1 607	1 546	3 208	1 634	1 575	3 227	1 642	1 585
20-24	2 902	1 479	1 423	3 018	1 536	1 481	3 121	1 587	1 533	3 180	1 616	1 564
25-29	2 655	1 353	1 302	2 846	1 449	1 397	2 966	1 508	1 458	3 074	1 561	1 512
30-34	2 481	1 266	1 215	2 577	1 316	1 262	2 772	1 413	1 359	2 899	1 475	1 424
35-39	2 210	1 108	1 083	2 395	1 224	1 170	2 498	1 277	1 221	2 698	1 377	1 321
40-44	1 899	972	927	2 136	1 093	1 042	2 317	1 100	1 131	2 427	1 241	1 185
45-49	1 492	763	729	1 830	936	894	2 065	1 056	1 009	2 249	1 149	1 000
50-54	1 212	617	595	1 432	730	703	1 762	898	864	1 994	1 016	978
55-59	957	480	477	1 154	583	570	1 367	692	675	1 607	804	803
60-64	786	386	399	896	445	450	1 083	543	540	1 288	646	641
65-69	613	295	317	709	344	365	812	398	413	986	488	498
70-74	440	208	232	520	247	273	606	289	316	697	337	360
75-79	297	140	168	337	156	181	401	187	215	471	221	251
80-84	155	71	84	190	87	103	218	98	119	262	119	143
85-89	60	27	34	75	33	42	93	41	52	108	47	61
90-94	15	6	9	19	8	11	24	10	14	31	13	18
95-99	2	1	1	3	1	2	4	1	2	5	2	3
100 +	0	0	0	0	0	0	0	0	0	0	0	0

Age group	2045 Both sexes	Males	Females	2050 Both sexes	Males	Females
All ages	38 896	19 699	19 197	40 573	20 524	20 049
0-4	3 229	1 648	1 582	3 169	1 617	1 552
5-9	3 249	1 655	1 593	3 212	1 637	1 575
10-14	3 251	1 655	1 596	3 238	1 649	1 590
15-19	3 234	1 645	1 589	3 238	1 646	1 591
20-24	3 202	1 626	1 576	3 212	1 630	1 582
25-29	3 139	1 593	1 546	3 167	1 606	1 562
30-34	3 015	1 532	1 483	3 090	1 567	1 522
35-39	2 832	1 442	1 390	2 958	1 503	1 455
40-44	2 631	1 343	1 288	2 773	1 411	1 361
45-49	2 363	1 207	1 156	2 570	1 310	1 261
50-54	2 178	1 109	1 069	2 295	1 168	1 127
55-59	1 915	970	945	2 097	1 062	1 035
60-64	1 594	800	794	1 815	912	904
65-69	1 177	583	594	1 464	725	738
70-74	852	415	437	1 022	499	524
75-79	547	259	288	674	322	352
80-84	311	142	169	366	169	197
85-89	132	58	74	159	70	89
90-94	37	15	22	46	19	27
95-99	6	2	4	7	3	5
100 +	1	0	0	1	0	0

United Nations Department of Economic and Social Affairs/Population Division
World Population Prospects: The 2004 Revision, Volume II: Sex and Age Distribution of the World Population

427

POPULATION BY AGE AND SEX (in thousands)

Age group	2005 Both sexes	2005 Males	2005 Females	2010 Both sexes	2010 Males	2010 Females	2015 Both sexes	2015 Males	2015 Females	2020 Both sexes	2020 Males	2020 Females
All ages	22 113	11 191	10 921	24 521	12 428	12 093	27 151	13 775	13 376	29 908	15 183	14 726
0-4	3 102	1 586	1 516	3 400	1 737	1 662	3 654	1 866	1 787	3 843	1 962	1 881
5-9	2 825	1 445	1 380	3 006	1 536	1 470	3 315	1 693	1 622	3 581	1 828	1 753
10-14	2 701	1 379	1 322	2 779	1 421	1 358	2 965	1 515	1 450	3 277	1 674	1 604
15-19	2 505	1 277	1 228	2 667	1 361	1 306	2 751	1 406	1 345	2 938	1 500	1 438
20-24	2 223	1 128	1 094	2 459	1 251	1 208	2 627	1 338	1 289	2 713	1 384	1 329
25-29	1 790	907	883	2 155	1 094	1 061	2 393	1 217	1 176	2 564	1 306	1 259
30-34	1 471	747	725	1 708	869	839	2 069	1 053	1 016	2 306	1 176	1 130
35-39	1 174	594	580	1 392	710	682	1 627	831	796	1 979	1 011	968
40-44	990	497	493	1 111	563	548	1 325	677	648	1 555	796	759
45-49	825	411	414	939	471	468	1 058	536	522	1 267	647	620
50-54	675	333	342	780	387	393	892	445	446	1 009	509	500
55-59	575	285	290	632	310	322	735	362	373	843	418	425
60-64	447	219	228	528	259	269	584	284	300	682	333	349
65-69	335	162	172	394	191	203	469	228	241	522	251	271
70-74	233	111	122	275	131	143	327	156	171	392	188	205
75-79	142	66	76	170	80	90	204	96	108	245	115	130
80-84	70	32	38	85	39	46	104	48	57	127	58	69
85-89	25	11	14	31	14	18	39	17	22	49	22	27
90-94	5	2	3	7	3	4	10	4	6	12	5	7
95-99	1	0	0	1	0	1	1	0	1	2	1	1
100 +	0	0	0	0	0	0	0	0	0	0	0	0

Age group	2025 Both sexes	2025 Males	2025 Females	2030 Both sexes	2030 Males	2030 Females	2035 Both sexes	2035 Males	2035 Females	2040 Both sexes	2040 Males	2040 Females
All ages	32 667	16 586	16 081	35 448	17 996	17 453	38 307	19 440	18 868	41 273	20 932	20 341
0-4	3 901	1 991	1 910	3 981	2 031	1 950	4 127	2 105	2 022	4 310	2 199	2 111
5-9	3 782	1 929	1 853	3 852	1 964	1 889	3 942	2 008	1 934	4 095	2 086	2 009
10-14	3 549	1 811	1 738	3 756	1 915	1 841	3 831	1 952	1 880	3 925	1 998	1 927
15-19	3 251	1 659	1 593	3 525	1 797	1 728	3 734	1 901	1 832	3 811	1 939	1 872
20-24	2 902	1 479	1 423	3 215	1 637	1 578	3 490	1 775	1 715	3 701	1 881	1 820
25-29	2 655	1 353	1 302	2 846	1 449	1 397	3 160	1 607	1 553	3 438	1 746	1 691
30-34	2 481	1 266	1 215	2 577	1 316	1 262	2 772	1 413	1 359	3 089	1 572	1 517
35-39	2 216	1 133	1 083	2 395	1 224	1 170	2 498	1 277	1 221	2 698	1 377	1 321
40-44	1 899	972	927	2 136	1 093	1 042	2 317	1 186	1 131	2 427	1 241	1 185
45-49	1 492	763	729	1 830	936	894	2 065	1 056	1 009	2 249	1 149	1 099
50-54	1 212	617	595	1 432	730	703	1 762	898	864	1 994	1 016	978
55-59	957	480	477	1 154	583	570	1 367	692	675	1 687	854	833
60-64	786	386	399	896	445	450	1 083	543	540	1 288	646	641
65-69	613	295	317	709	344	365	812	398	413	986	488	498
70-74	440	208	232	520	247	273	606	289	316	697	337	360
75-79	297	140	158	337	156	181	401	187	215	471	221	251
80-84	155	71	84	190	87	103	218	98	119	262	119	143
85-89	60	27	34	75	33	42	93	41	52	108	47	61
90-94	15	6	9	19	8	11	24	10	14	31	13	18
95-99	2	1	1	3	1	2	4	1	2	5	2	3
100 +	0	0	0	0	0	0	0	0	0	0	0	0

Age group	2045 Both sexes	2045 Males	2045 Females	2050 Both sexes	2050 Males	2050 Females
All ages	44 306	22 453	21 853	47 331	23 963	23 368
0-4	4 465	2 278	2 187	4 558	2 326	2 232
5-9	4 283	2 182	2 101	4 441	2 263	2 178
10-14	4 081	2 077	2 003	4 270	2 174	2 096
15-19	3 907	1 987	1 920	4 064	2 067	1 998
20-24	3 782	1 920	1 862	3 881	1 969	1 911
25-29	3 654	1 854	1 800	3 741	1 896	1 845
30-34	3 372	1 714	1 659	3 597	1 824	1 772
35-39	3 018	1 537	1 481	3 308	1 681	1 627
40-44	2 631	1 343	1 288	2 955	1 504	1 451
45-49	2 363	1 207	1 156	2 570	1 310	1 261
50-54	2 178	1 109	1 069	2 295	1 168	1 127
55-59	1 915	970	945	2 097	1 062	1 035
60-64	1 594	800	794	1 815	912	904
65-69	1 177	583	594	1 464	725	738
70-74	852	415	437	1 022	499	524
75-79	547	259	288	674	322	352
80-84	311	142	169	366	169	197
85-89	132	58	74	159	70	89
90-94	37	15	22	46	19	27
95-99	6	2	4	7	3	5
100 +	1	0	0	1	0	0

United Nations Department of Economic and Social Affairs/Population Division
World Population Prospects: The 2004 Revision, Volume II: Sex and Age Distribution of the World Population

POPULATION BY AGE AND SEX (in thousands)

Age group	2005 Both sexes	Males	Females	2010 Both sexes	Males	Females	2015 Both sexes	Males	Females	2020 Both sexes	Males	Females
All ages	22 113	11 191	10 921	24 104	12 215	11 889	26 073	13 173	12 900	27 670	14 040	13 630
0-4	3 102	1 586	1 516	2 983	1 524	1 459	2 883	1 473	1 410	2 763	1 411	1 352
5-9	2 825	1 445	1 380	3 006	1 536	1 470	2 909	1 486	1 423	2 825	1 442	1 383
10-14	2 701	1 379	1 322	2 779	1 421	1 358	2 965	1 515	1 450	2 875	1 468	1 407
15-19	2 505	1 277	1 228	2 667	1 361	1 306	2 751	1 406	1 345	2 938	1 500	1 438
20-24	2 223	1 128	1 094	2 459	1 251	1 208	2 627	1 338	1 289	2 713	1 384	1 329
25-29	1 790	907	883	2 155	1 094	1 061	2 393	1 217	1 176	2 564	1 306	1 259
30-34	1 471	747	725	1 708	869	839	2 069	1 053	1 016	2 306	1 176	1 130
35-39	1 174	594	580	1 392	710	682	1 627	831	796	1 979	1 011	968
40-44	990	497	493	1 111	563	548	1 325	677	648	1 555	796	759
45-49	825	411	414	939	471	468	1 058	536	522	1 267	647	620
50-54	675	333	342	780	387	393	892	445	446	1 009	509	500
55-59	575	285	290	632	310	322	735	362	373	843	418	425
60-64	447	219	228	528	259	269	584	284	300	682	333	349
65-69	335	162	172	394	191	203	469	228	241	522	251	271
70-74	233	111	122	275	131	143	327	156	171	392	188	205
75-79	142	66	76	170	80	90	204	96	108	245	115	130
80-84	70	32	38	85	39	46	104	48	57	127	58	69
85-89	25	11	14	31	14	18	39	17	22	49	22	27
90-94	5	2	3	7	3	4	10	4	6	12	5	7
95-99	1	0	0	1	0	1	1	0	1	2	1	1
100 +	0	0	0	0	0	0	0	0	0	0	0	0

Age group	2025 Both sexes	Males	Females	2030 Both sexes	Males	Females	2035 Both sexes	Males	Females	2040 Both sexes	Males	Females
All ages	29 263	14 849	14 414	30 722	15 586	15 136	31 999	16 226	15 773	33 054	16 748	16 306
0-4	2 710	1 383	1 327	2 629	1 341	1 287	2 507	1 279	1 228	2 349	1 198	1 151
5-9	2 719	1 387	1 332	2 675	1 364	1 312	2 602	1 326	1 277	2 487	1 267	1 220
10-14	2 799	1 428	1 371	2 699	1 376	1 323	2 660	1 355	1 305	2 590	1 319	1 272
15-19	2 852	1 455	1 397	2 780	1 417	1 363	2 683	1 366	1 317	2 646	1 346	1 300
20-24	2 902	1 479	1 423	2 820	1 436	1 384	2 752	1 399	1 352	2 659	1 351	1 308
25-29	2 655	1 353	1 302	2 846	1 449	1 397	2 771	1 409	1 362	2 710	1 377	1 333
30-34	2 481	1 266	1 215	2 577	1 316	1 262	2 772	1 413	1 359	2 709	1 379	1 330
35-39	2 216	1 133	1 083	2 395	1 224	1 170	2 498	1 277	1 221	2 698	1 377	1 321
40-44	1 899	972	927	2 136	1 093	1 042	2 317	1 186	1 131	2 427	1 241	1 185
45-49	1 492	763	720	1 830	936	894	2 065	1 056	1 009	2 249	1 149	1 099
50-54	1 212	617	595	1 432	730	703	1 762	898	864	1 994	1 016	978
55-59	877	400	477	1 154	583	570	1 367	692	675	1 687	854	833
60-64	786	386	399	896	445	450	1 083	543	540	1 288	646	641
65-69	613	295	317	709	344	365	812	398	413	986	488	498
70-74	440	208	232	520	247	273	606	289	316	697	337	360
75-79	297	140	158	337	156	181	401	187	215	471	221	251
80-84	155	71	84	190	87	103	210	91	119	262	119	143
85-89	60	27	34	75	33	42	93	41	52	108	47	61
90-94	15	6	9	19	8	11	24	10	14	31	13	18
95-99	2	1	1	3	1	2	4	1	2	5	2	3
100 +	0	0	0	0	0	0	0	0	0	0	0	0

Age group	2045 Both sexes	Males	Females	2050 Both sexes	Males	Females
All ages	33 868	17 140	16 728	34 443	17 405	17 038
0-4	2 181	1 113	1 068	2 028	1 035	993
5-9	2 333	1 189	1 144	2 168	1 105	1 063
10-14	2 478	1 261	1 217	2 325	1 184	1 141
15-19	2 578	1 311	1 267	2 467	1 255	1 213
20-24	2 625	1 333	1 292	2 560	1 299	1 261
25-29	2 624	1 331	1 293	2 596	1 316	1 280
30-34	2 658	1 351	1 308	2 583	1 310	1 273
35-39	2 647	1 348	1 299	2 607	1 325	1 282
40-44	2 631	1 343	1 288	2 591	1 319	1 272
45-49	2 363	1 207	1 156	2 570	1 310	1 261
50-54	2 178	1 109	1 069	2 295	1 168	1 127
55-59	1 915	970	945	2 097	1 062	1 035
60-64	1 594	800	794	1 815	912	904
65-69	1 177	583	594	1 464	725	738
70-74	852	415	437	1 022	499	524
75-79	547	259	288	674	322	352
80-84	311	142	169	366	169	197
85-89	132	58	74	159	70	89
90-94	37	15	22	46	19	27
95-99	6	2	4	7	3	5
100 +	1	0	0	1	0	0

POPULATION BY AGE AND SEX (in thousands)

Age group	1950 Both sexes	Males	Females	1955 Both sexes	Males	Females	1960 Both sexes	Males	Females	1965 Both sexes	Males	Females
All ages	7 566	3 687	3 879	7 966	3 889	4 077	8 334	4 067	4 266	8 551	4 158	4 393
0-4	744	382	362	735	378	357	755	389	365	720	371	349
5-9	647	333	314	732	376	356	722	372	349	740	380	360
10-14	777	395	382	642	330	312	732	373	358	717	370	347
15-19	784	389	395	768	389	379	626	315	311	723	368	355
20-24	719	350	369	762	373	389	738	360	377	591	294	297
25-29	585	280	305	698	336	362	726	349	376	687	325	362
30-34	504	240	264	560	270	290	682	328	353	686	320	366
35-39	513	246	267	489	234	255	532	258	274	662	315	347
40-44	488	238	250	502	240	262	461	222	239	514	245	269
45-49	424	206	218	477	232	245	495	238	257	448	212	236
50-54	344	163	181	413	200	213	459	226	233	489	236	253
55-59	283	129	154	329	154	175	400	193	207	442	216	226
60-64	240	107	133	266	119	147	318	146	172	375	179	196
65-69	198	89	109	217	94	123	240	105	135	287	129	158
70-74	147	67	80	171	75	96	196	83	113	200	85	115
75-79	91	41	50	114	50	64	140	59	81	143	60	83
80 +	78	32	46	91	39	52	111	48	63	127	53	74

Age group	1970 Both sexes	Males	Females	1975 Both sexes	Males	Females	1980 Both sexes	Males	Females	1985 Both sexes	Males	Females
All ages	8 793	4 292	4 501	9 047	4 432	4 615	9 643	4 733	4 909	9 934	4 887	5 047
0-4	770	391	379	690	356	334	718	371	347	688	356	332
5-9	700	360	340	759	391	368	703	363	340	711	368	343
10-14	716	369	347	711	366	345	779	402	377	716	369	347
15-19	660	337	323	705	361	343	725	374	351	775	402	373
20-24	634	328	306	639	333	306	698	354	343	726	378	348
25-29	503	245	258	614	303	311	650	329	320	684	338	346
30-34	606	287	320	519	250	269	657	324	333	660	331	329
35-39	653	315	338	616	291	325	564	273	291	668	333	335
40-44	664	322	343	656	318	338	652	311	341	565	271	294
45-49	513	245	269	637	308	328	681	329	352	678	326	352
50-54	444	205	239	500	241	259	645	311	334	684	328	356
55-59	497	242	255	429	201	229	488	236	253	609	294	315
60-64	451	219	232	465	219	246	416	191	224	449	213	236
65-69	367	173	194	402	189	212	427	197	231	445	203	243
70-74	281	120	161	316	142	173	356	164	192	371	169	202
75-79	153	67	86	201	85	116	258	113	145	269	116	153
80 +	179	69	110	189	75	113	226	91	135	236	93	142

Age group	1990 Both sexes	Males	Females	1995 Both sexes	Males	Females	2000 Both sexes	Males	Females	2005 Both sexes	Males	Females
All ages	10 160	5 006	5 154	10 657	5 264	5 393	10 975	5 423	5 552	11 120	5 494	5 626
0-4	552	283	268	523	270	253	524	269	255	514	264	250
5-9	657	338	319	570	294	276	543	280	263	531	273	258
10-14	747	384	363	697	362	335	601	312	290	547	282	265
15-19	759	391	368	806	419	387	738	387	352	612	317	295
20-24	784	396	388	819	424	395	846	442	405	763	399	364
25-29	715	356	359	841	426	415	852	440	412	877	457	420
30-34	722	358	364	763	381	382	868	438	429	877	453	425
35-39	675	339	336	761	378	383	784	390	394	884	447	438
40-44	667	333	334	706	354	352	776	383	393	793	395	398
45-49	555	276	279	686	341	345	715	357	359	778	383	394
50-54	651	316	335	562	276	286	686	337	348	710	352	358
55-59	649	319	329	654	312	342	556	269	288	674	329	345
60-64	639	306	333	650	313	338	642	300	342	539	257	282
65-69	449	208	241	610	284	326	618	290	329	606	276	330
70-74	341	149	192	397	177	220	545	246	299	557	252	305
75-79	293	128	165	276	116	161	324	140	184	454	196	258
80 +	307	127	181	337	140	197	356	144	212	403	162	241

United Nations Department of Economic and Social Affairs/Population Division
World Population Prospects: The 2004 Revision, Volume II: Sex and Age Distribution of the World Population

430

POPULATION BY AGE AND SEX (in thousands)

Age group	2005 Both sexes	2005 Males	2005 Females	2010 Both sexes	2010 Males	2010 Females	2015 Both sexes	2015 Males	2015 Females	2020 Both sexes	2020 Males	2020 Females
All ages	11 120	5 494	5 626	11 205	5 538	5 667	11 233	5 557	5 676	11 217	5 556	5 661
0-4	514	264	250	499	257	242	481	248	234	467	240	227
5-9	531	273	258	521	268	253	506	260	246	488	251	237
10-14	547	282	265	534	275	260	524	269	255	509	262	248
15-19	612	317	295	557	287	270	545	280	265	535	275	260
20-24	763	399	364	637	330	307	583	300	283	571	293	278
25-29	877	457	420	794	415	379	669	346	323	615	317	298
30-34	877	453	425	902	470	432	820	428	391	695	360	335
35-39	884	447	438	894	461	433	919	479	440	837	437	399
40-44	793	395	398	892	451	442	902	465	437	928	483	445
45-49	778	383	394	794	395	400	893	450	443	903	465	438
50-54	710	352	358	772	379	393	789	390	398	887	445	442
55-59	674	329	345	698	344	354	759	370	390	777	382	395
60-64	539	257	282	653	314	339	677	329	348	738	355	383
65-69	606	276	330	510	237	273	619	291	327	643	306	337
70-74	557	252	305	549	242	307	463	209	254	563	257	306
75-79	454	196	258	467	202	265	464	195	268	393	170	224
80-84	232	96	137	330	135	195	344	141	203	346	137	208
85-89	110	42	68	135	53	82	196	76	120	209	80	128
90-94	47	19	28	49	18	31	62	23	39	92	33	59
95-99	12	5	7	14	5	9	15	5	10	20	7	13
100 +	2	1	1	2	1	1	3	1	2	3	1	2

Age group	2025 Both sexes	2025 Males	2025 Females	2030 Both sexes	2030 Males	2030 Females	2035 Both sexes	2035 Males	2035 Females	2040 Both sexes	2040 Males	2040 Females
All ages	11 173	5 543	5 630	11 119	5 523	5 596	11 055	5 495	5 560	10 973	5 457	5 516
0-4	455	234	221	457	235	222	465	239	226	475	244	231
5-9	473	243	230	462	238	225	464	238	225	472	243	229
10-14	492	253	239	477	245	232	466	239	226	467	240	227
15-19	520	267	253	503	258	244	488	251	237	477	245	232
20-24	561	288	273	546	281	265	529	272	257	514	264	250
25-29	603	310	293	593	305	288	578	298	281	561	289	272
30-34	641	331	310	630	324	305	620	319	300	605	312	293
35-39	713	370	343	659	341	319	648	334	314	638	329	309
40-44	846	442	404	723	375	348	670	346	324	659	340	319
45-49	929	483	446	849	442	406	727	376	350	674	348	326
50-54	897	460	437	923	478	445	844	439	406	724	374	350
55-59	874	435	438	884	451	404	910	469	442	834	431	403
60-64	755	367	388	850	419	431	861	434	427	887	452	435
65-69	701	331	370	719	343	376	810	392	418	822	408	414
70-74	587	271	316	642	294	348	660	306	354	745	352	394
75-79	480	210	270	503	223	280	553	243	310	571	254	317
80-84	296	121	175	365	151	214	386	162	224	429	178	251
85-89	214	80	135	187	71	116	235	90	144	252	98	154
90-94	100	36	64	106	36	70	95	33	62	122	43	79
95-99	31	10	20	35	11	23	38	12	26	35	11	24
100 +	4	1	3	6	2	4	7	2	5	9	2	6

Age group	2045 Both sexes	2045 Males	2045 Females	2050 Both sexes	2050 Males	2050 Females
All ages	10 868	5 407	5 461	10 742	5 346	5 396
0-4	483	248	235	491	253	238
5-9	482	248	234	490	252	238
10-14	476	245	231	486	250	236
15-19	479	246	233	487	250	237
20-24	503	259	244	505	260	245
25-29	547	282	265	536	276	260
30-34	588	303	285	574	296	278
35-39	624	322	302	607	314	293
40-44	650	335	314	635	328	307
45-49	664	342	322	655	338	317
50-54	673	347	326	663	341	322
55-59	716	368	348	666	341	325
60-64	813	417	397	700	356	343
65-69	848	426	422	778	393	385
70-74	758	366	391	783	384	400
75-79	648	294	354	661	308	353
80-84	447	188	259	510	219	291
85-89	284	109	175	300	117	183
90-94	133	47	86	153	53	100
95-99	46	14	32	51	16	35
100 +	8	2	6	11	3	8

United Nations Department of Economic and Social Affairs/Population Division
World Population Prospects: The 2004 Revision, Volume II: Sex and Age Distribution of the World Population

431

POPULATION BY AGE AND SEX (in thousands)

Age group	2005 Both sexes	Males	Females	2010 Both sexes	Males	Females	2015 Both sexes	Males	Females	2020 Both sexes	Males	Females
All ages	11 120	5 494	5 626	11 302	5 590	5 712	11 472	5 683	5 789	11 616	5 766	5 850
0-4	514	264	250	596	308	289	624	322	302	626	323	303
5-9	531	273	258	521	268	252	603	311	292	630	325	305
10-14	547	282	265	534	275	259	524	270	254	607	313	294
15-19	612	317	295	557	287	270	545	281	265	535	276	259
20-24	763	399	364	637	330	307	583	300	283	571	294	277
25-29	877	457	420	794	415	379	669	346	323	615	317	298
30-34	877	453	425	902	470	432	820	428	391	695	360	335
35-39	884	447	438	894	461	433	919	479	440	837	437	399
40-44	793	395	398	892	451	442	902	465	437	928	483	445
45-49	778	383	394	794	395	400	893	450	443	903	465	438
50-54	710	352	358	772	379	393	789	390	398	887	445	442
55-59	674	329	345	698	344	354	759	370	390	777	382	395
60-64	539	257	282	653	314	339	677	329	348	738	355	383
65-69	606	276	330	510	237	273	619	291	327	643	306	337
70-74	557	252	305	549	242	307	463	209	254	563	257	306
75-79	454	196	258	467	202	265	464	195	268	393	170	224
80-84	232	96	137	330	135	195	344	141	203	346	137	208
85-89	110	42	68	135	53	82	196	76	120	209	80	128
90-94	47	19	28	49	18	31	62	23	39	92	33	59
95-99	12	5	7	14	5	9	15	5	10	20	7	13
100 +	2	1	1	2	1	1	3	1	2	3	1	2

Age group	2025 Both sexes	Males	Females	2030 Both sexes	Males	Females	2035 Both sexes	Males	Females	2040 Both sexes	Males	Females
All ages	11 720	5 830	5 890	11 814	5 887	5 927	11 922	5 949	5 973	12 058	6 024	6 034
0-4	603	311	292	606	312	293	638	329	309	693	358	336
5-9	633	326	307	610	315	295	612	316	297	645	333	312
10-14	634	327	307	637	328	308	614	316	297	616	318	298
15-19	617	318	299	645	332	312	648	334	314	625	322	303
20-24	561	289	272	643	332	312	671	346	325	673	347	326
25-29	603	311	292	593	306	287	675	348	327	703	363	340
30-34	641	331	310	630	325	305	620	320	300	702	363	339
35-39	713	370	343	659	341	319	648	335	313	638	330	308
40-44	846	442	404	723	375	348	670	346	324	659	341	318
45-49	929	483	446	849	442	406	727	376	350	674	348	326
50-54	897	460	437	923	478	445	844	439	406	724	374	350
55-59	874	435	438	884	451	434	910	469	442	834	431	403
60-64	755	367	388	850	419	431	861	434	427	887	452	435
65-69	701	331	370	719	343	376	810	392	418	822	408	414
70-74	587	271	316	642	294	348	660	306	354	745	352	394
75-79	480	210	270	503	223	280	553	243	310	571	254	317
80-84	296	121	175	365	151	214	386	162	224	429	178	251
85-89	214	80	135	187	71	116	235	90	144	252	98	154
90-94	100	36	64	106	36	70	95	33	62	122	43	79
95-99	31	10	20	35	11	23	38	12	26	35	11	24
100 +	4	1	3	6	2	4	7	2	5	9	2	6

Age group	2045 Both sexes	Males	Females	2050 Both sexes	Males	Females
All ages	12 214	6 109	6 105	12 373	6 195	6 177
0-4	746	385	361	778	402	377
5-9	700	361	339	752	388	364
10-14	649	334	314	704	363	341
15-19	627	323	304	660	340	319
20-24	651	336	315	653	337	316
25-29	706	364	341	683	353	330
30-34	730	377	353	733	379	354
35-39	720	373	348	748	387	361
40-44	650	336	313	731	378	353
45-49	663	343	321	654	339	316
50-54	673	347	326	663	342	321
55-59	716	368	348	666	341	325
60-64	813	417	397	700	356	343
65-69	848	426	422	778	393	385
70-74	758	366	391	783	384	400
75-79	648	294	354	661	308	353
80-84	447	188	259	510	219	291
85-89	284	109	175	300	117	183
90-94	133	47	86	153	53	100
95-99	46	14	32	51	16	35
100 +	8	2	6	11	3	8

United Nations Department of Economic and Social Affairs/Population Division
World Population Prospects: The 2004 Revision, Volume II: Sex and Age Distribution of the World Population

432

POPULATION BY AGE AND SEX (in thousands)

Age group	2005 Both sexes	2005 Males	2005 Females	2010 Both sexes	2010 Males	2010 Females	2015 Both sexes	2015 Males	2015 Females	2020 Both sexes	2020 Males	2020 Females
All ages	11 120	5 494	5 626	11 107	5 490	5 617	10 989	5 434	5 555	10 808	5 349	5 459
0-4	514	264	250	401	207	194	336	173	163	301	155	146
5-9	531	273	258	521	268	252	408	210	198	343	177	166
10-14	547	282	265	534	275	259	524	270	254	412	212	199
15-19	612	317	295	557	287	270	545	281	265	535	276	259
20-24	763	399	364	637	330	307	583	300	283	571	294	277
25-29	877	457	420	794	415	379	669	346	323	615	317	298
30-34	877	453	425	902	470	432	820	428	391	695	360	335
35-39	884	447	438	894	461	433	919	479	440	837	437	399
40-44	793	395	398	892	451	442	902	465	437	928	483	445
45-49	778	383	394	794	395	400	893	450	443	903	465	438
50-54	710	352	358	772	379	393	789	390	398	887	445	442
55-59	674	329	345	698	344	354	759	370	390	777	382	395
60-64	539	257	282	653	314	339	677	329	348	738	355	383
65-69	606	276	330	510	237	273	619	291	327	643	306	337
70-74	557	252	305	549	242	307	463	209	254	563	257	306
75-79	454	196	258	467	202	265	464	195	268	393	170	224
80-84	232	96	137	330	135	195	344	141	203	346	137	208
85-89	110	42	68	135	53	82	196	76	120	209	80	128
90-94	47	19	28	49	18	31	62	23	39	92	33	59
95-99	12	5	7	14	5	9	15	5	10	20	7	13
100 +	2	1	1	2	1	1	3	1	2	3	1	2

Age group	2025 Both sexes	2025 Males	2025 Females	2030 Both sexes	2030 Males	2030 Females	2035 Both sexes	2035 Males	2035 Females	2040 Both sexes	2040 Males	2040 Females
All ages	10 612	5 258	5 354	10 409	5 162	5 247	10 190	5 055	5 135	9 935	4 929	5 006
0-4	302	156	146	308	159	149	310	160	150	300	155	145
5-9	308	159	149	309	159	150	315	162	153	317	163	153
10-14	347	179	168	312	161	151	313	161	152	319	164	154
15-19	423	218	205	358	184	173	323	166	157	324	167	157
20-24	561	289	272	449	231	217	384	198	186	349	180	169
25-29	603	311	292	593	306	287	481	248	233	417	215	201
30-34	641	331	310	630	325	305	620	320	300	508	263	245
35-39	713	370	343	659	341	319	648	335	313	638	330	308
40-44	840	442	404	723	375	348	670	346	324	659	341	318
45-49	929	483	446	849	442	406	727	376	350	674	348	326
50-54	897	460	437	923	478	445	844	439	406	724	374	350
55-59	874	435	438	884	451	434	910	469	442	834	431	403
60-64	755	367	388	850	419	431	861	434	427	887	452	435
65-69	701	331	370	719	343	376	810	392	418	822	408	414
70-74	587	271	316	642	294	348	660	306	354	745	352	394
75-79	480	210	270	503	223	280	553	243	310	571	254	317
80-84	296	121	175	365	151	214	386	162	224	429	178	251
85-89	214	80	135	187	71	116	235	90	144	252	98	154
90-94	100	36	64	106	36	70	95	33	62	122	43	79
95-99	31	10	20	35	11	23	38	12	26	35	11	24
100 +	4	1	3	6	2	4	7	2	5	9	2	6

Age group	2045 Both sexes	2045 Males	2045 Females	2050 Both sexes	2050 Males	2050 Females
All ages	9 630	4 776	4 854	9 284	4 603	4 681
0-4	282	145	136	270	139	131
5-9	307	158	149	289	149	140
10-14	321	165	155	311	160	151
15-19	330	170	160	332	171	161
20-24	351	181	170	356	184	173
25-29	382	197	185	383	198	185
30-34	444	230	214	409	212	197
35-39	527	273	254	463	240	223
40-44	650	336	313	539	280	259
45-49	663	343	321	654	339	316
50-54	673	347	326	663	342	321
55-59	716	368	348	666	341	325
60-64	813	417	397	700	356	343
65-69	848	426	422	778	393	385
70-74	758	366	391	783	384	400
75-79	648	294	354	661	308	353
80-84	447	188	259	510	219	291
85-89	284	109	175	300	117	183
90-94	133	47	86	153	53	100
95-99	46	14	32	51	16	35
100 +	8	2	6	11	3	8

GUADELOUPE   ESTIMATES

POPULATION BY AGE AND SEX (in thousands)

Age group	1950 Both sexes	1950 Males	1950 Females	1955 Both sexes	1955 Males	1955 Females	1960 Both sexes	1960 Males	1960 Females	1965 Both sexes	1965 Males	1965 Females
All ages	210	101	109	236	115	121	275	135	140	300	148	153
0-4	36	18	18	39	20	19	45	23	22	49	25	24
5-9	25	13	12	34	17	17	39	20	19	44	23	21
10-14	22	11	11	24	12	12	34	17	17	40	20	19
15-19	19	9	10	20	10	10	23	11	12	33	16	16
20-24	17	8	9	19	9	10	19	9	10	23	12	12
25-29	16	8	8	17	8	9	17	8	9	16	8	9
30-34	14	7	7	16	8	8	17	8	9	15	7	8
35-39	14	7	7	14	7	7	16	8	8	15	7	8
40-44	11	5	6	12	6	6	14	7	7	15	7	8
45-49	9	4	5	10	5	5	12	6	6	12	6	6
50-54	7	3	4	8	4	4	10	5	5	11	5	6
55-59	6	3	3	7	3	4	8	4	4	10	5	5
60-64	5	2	3	5	2	3	6	3	3	7	3	4
65-69	3	1	2	5	2	3	5	2	3	5	2	3
70-74	3	1	2	3	1	2	5	2	3	3	1	2
75-79	2	1	1	2	1	1	3	1	2	3	1	2
80 +	1	0	1	1	0	1	1	0	1	2	1	1

Age group	1970 Both sexes	1970 Males	1970 Females	1975 Both sexes	1975 Males	1975 Females	1980 Both sexes	1980 Males	1980 Females	1985 Both sexes	1985 Males	1985 Females
All ages	320	157	163	329	161	168	327	160	167	355	174	181
0-4	50	25	24	45	23	22	30	15	15	32	16	16
5-9	46	23	22	47	24	24	37	19	18	36	18	18
10-14	42	21	21	46	23	23	42	21	21	38	19	19
15-19	36	18	18	37	19	18	40	20	20	41	21	20
20-24	27	14	14	23	12	12	30	15	14	33	16	16
25-29	18	8	10	19	9	10	23	11	12	28	14	14
30-34	15	7	8	16	8	9	21	10	11	25	12	13
35-39	15	7	8	15	7	8	18	8	9	22	10	11
40-44	15	7	8	15	7	8	15	7	8	19	9	10
45-49	14	7	7	14	7	7	14	7	7	16	8	8
50-54	12	6	6	13	6	7	13	6	7	14	7	7
55-59	11	5	6	10	5	5	12	6	6	13	6	7
60-64	8	4	4	10	5	5	10	5	5	11	5	6
65-69	6	3	3	7	3	4	8	4	4	9	4	5
70-74	4	2	2	5	2	3	6	3	3	7	3	4
75-79	3	1	2	3	1	2	4	2	3	5	2	3
80 +	3	1	2	4	1	2	4	1	3	5	2	4

Age group	1990 Both sexes	1990 Males	1990 Females	1995 Both sexes	1995 Males	1995 Females	2000 Both sexes	2000 Males	2000 Females	2005 Both sexes	2005 Males	2005 Females
All ages	391	191	200	409	199	210	430	208	222	448	216	232
0-4	35	18	17	37	19	18	37	19	18	36	18	18
5-9	34	17	17	36	18	18	38	19	18	38	19	19
10-14	35	18	17	35	17	17	36	18	17	38	19	19
15-19	42	21	21	31	16	15	30	15	15	33	17	16
20-24	36	18	18	33	17	17	22	11	11	25	13	12
25-29	36	18	18	38	18	20	37	17	20	24	11	13
30-34	32	16	16	37	18	19	40	19	22	37	17	20
35-39	27	13	14	32	16	16	36	18	19	40	19	22
40-44	23	11	12	27	13	14	31	15	16	36	17	19
45-49	18	9	9	23	11	12	26	13	14	31	15	16
50-54	16	8	8	18	9	9	22	11	12	26	12	14
55-59	14	7	7	15	7	8	17	8	9	22	10	11
60-64	12	6	7	14	6	7	15	7	8	17	8	9
65-69	11	5	6	12	5	6	13	6	7	14	6	7
70-74	8	4	4	10	4	5	10	4	6	11	5	6
75-79	6	2	4	7	3	4	8	3	5	9	4	5
80 +	7	2	4	8	3	5	9	3	6	11	4	7

United Nations Department of Economic and Social Affairs/Population Division
World Population Prospects: The 2004 Revision, Volume II: Sex and Age Distribution of the World Population

POPULATION BY AGE AND SEX (in thousands)

Age group	2005 Both sexes	2005 Males	2005 Females	2010 Both sexes	2010 Males	2010 Females	2015 Both sexes	2015 Males	2015 Females	2020 Both sexes	2020 Males	2020 Females
All ages	448	216	232	462	222	240	472	226	246	480	229	251
0-4	36	18	18	32	16	15	29	15	14	28	14	14
5-9	38	19	19	36	18	18	32	16	16	29	15	14
10-14	38	19	19	38	19	19	36	18	18	32	16	16
15-19	33	17	16	35	18	17	35	18	17	34	17	17
20-24	25	13	12	28	14	14	30	15	15	30	15	15
25-29	24	11	13	27	13	14	30	15	15	32	16	16
30-34	37	17	20	25	12	13	27	13	14	30	15	16
35-39	40	19	22	38	17	20	25	12	13	28	13	15
40-44	36	17	19	40	19	22	37	17	20	25	12	13
45-49	31	15	16	36	17	19	40	18	22	37	17	20
50-54	26	12	14	31	15	16	35	17	18	40	18	21
55-59	22	10	11	25	12	13	30	15	15	35	17	18
60-64	17	8	9	21	10	11	25	11	13	29	14	15
65-69	14	6	7	16	7	8	20	9	11	23	11	13
70-74	11	5	6	13	6	7	14	6	8	18	8	10
75-79	9	4	5	10	4	6	11	5	6	12	5	7
80-84	6	2	4	7	3	4	8	3	5	8	3	5
85-89	3	1	2	4	1	3	5	2	3	5	2	3
90-94	1	0	1	2	1	1	2	1	2	3	1	2
95-99	0	0	0	1	0	0	1	0	1	1	0	1
100 +	0	0	0	0	0	0	0	0	0	0	0	0

Age group	2025 Both sexes	2025 Males	2025 Females	2030 Both sexes	2030 Males	2030 Females	2035 Both sexes	2035 Males	2035 Females	2040 Both sexes	2040 Males	2040 Females
All ages	487	232	255	492	234	258	494	234	260	491	231	259
0-4	29	15	14	29	15	14	28	14	14	26	13	13
5-9	29	15	14	29	15	14	29	15	14	28	14	14
10-14	29	15	14	29	15	14	30	15	15	30	15	14
15-19	30	15	15	27	14	13	26	13	13	27	14	13
20-24	29	15	14	25	12	12	22	11	11	21	11	10
25-29	32	16	16	30	15	16	26	13	14	24	11	12
30-34	33	16	17	33	16	17	31	15	16	27	13	14
35-39	31	15	16	33	16	17	33	16	17	31	15	16
40-44	20	10	15	31	15	16	33	16	17	33	16	17
45-49	25	12	13	28	13	14	31	15	16	33	16	17
50-54	37	17	20	24	11	13	27	13	14	30	15	16
55-59	39	18	21	36	16	20	24	11	13	27	13	14
60-64	34	16	18	38	17	21	35	16	19	23	11	13
65-69	28	13	14	32	15	17	36	16	20	34	15	19
70-74	21	10	12	25	12	14	30	14	16	34	15	19
75-79	16	7	9	19	8	11	22	10	12	26	12	15
80-84	10	4	6	10	5	8	15	6	9	18	8	11
85-89	6	2	4	7	3	4	9	3	6	11	4	7
90-94	3	1	2	3	1	2	4	1	3	5	2	4
95-99	1	0	1	1	0	1	1	0	1	2	0	1
100 +	0	0	0	0	0	0	0	0	0	0	0	0

Age group	2045 Both sexes	2045 Males	2045 Females	2050 Both sexes	2050 Males	2050 Females
All ages	484	227	257	474	222	252
0-4	24	12	12	23	12	11
5-9	26	13	13	24	12	12
10-14	28	14	14	26	13	13
15-19	27	14	13	26	13	13
20-24	22	11	11	22	11	11
25-29	23	11	12	24	11	12
30-34	24	12	13	24	11	12
35-39	27	13	14	25	12	13
40-44	31	15	16	27	13	14
45-49	33	16	17	31	15	16
50-54	33	16	17	33	16	17
55-59	30	14	16	32	15	17
60-64	26	12	14	29	14	15
65-69	23	10	12	25	12	14
70-74	32	14	18	21	9	12
75-79	30	13	17	28	12	16
80-84	22	9	13	25	10	15
85-89	13	5	8	16	6	10
90-94	7	2	5	8	3	5
95-99	2	1	2	3	1	2
100 +	1	0	0	1	0	1

POPULATION BY AGE AND SEX (in thousands)

Age group	2005 Both sexes	2005 Males	2005 Females	2010 Both sexes	2010 Males	2010 Females	2015 Both sexes	2015 Males	2015 Females	2020 Both sexes	2020 Males	2020 Females
All ages	448	216	232	466	224	242	482	231	251	497	238	259
0-4	36	18	18	35	18	17	35	18	17	36	18	18
5-9	38	19	19	36	18	18	36	18	18	35	18	17
10-14	38	19	19	38	19	19	36	18	18	36	18	18
15-19	33	17	16	35	18	17	35	18	17	34	17	17
20-24	25	13	12	28	14	14	30	15	15	30	15	15
25-29	24	11	13	27	13	14	30	15	15	32	16	16
30-34	37	17	20	25	12	13	27	13	14	30	15	16
35-39	40	19	22	38	17	20	25	12	13	28	13	15
40-44	36	17	19	40	19	22	37	17	20	25	12	13
45-49	31	15	16	36	17	19	40	18	22	37	17	20
50-54	26	12	14	31	15	16	35	17	18	40	18	21
55-59	22	10	11	25	12	13	30	15	15	35	17	18
60-64	17	8	9	21	10	11	25	11	13	29	14	15
65-69	14	6	7	16	7	8	20	9	11	23	11	13
70-74	11	5	6	13	6	7	14	6	8	18	8	10
75-79	9	4	5	10	4	6	11	5	6	12	5	7
80-84	6	2	4	7	3	4	8	3	5	8	3	5
85-89	3	1	2	4	1	3	5	2	3	5	2	3
90-94	1	0	1	2	1	1	2	1	2	3	1	2
95-99	0	0	0	1	0	0	1	0	1	1	0	1
100 +	0	0	0	0	0	0	0	0	0	0	0	0

Age group	2025 Both sexes	2025 Males	2025 Females	2030 Both sexes	2030 Males	2030 Females	2035 Both sexes	2035 Males	2035 Females	2040 Both sexes	2040 Males	2040 Females
All ages	512	245	267	526	251	275	537	256	281	545	259	286
0-4	37	19	18	37	19	18	37	19	18	37	19	18
5-9	36	18	18	37	19	18	38	19	19	37	19	18
10-14	35	18	17	36	19	18	37	19	18	38	19	19
15-19	33	17	16	33	17	16	34	17	17	35	18	17
20-24	29	15	14	28	14	14	28	14	14	29	15	14
25-29	32	16	16	30	15	16	30	15	15	30	14	15
30-34	33	16	17	33	16	17	31	15	16	31	15	16
35-39	31	15	16	33	16	17	33	16	17	31	15	16
40-44	28	13	15	31	15	16	33	16	17	33	16	17
45-49	25	12	13	28	13	14	31	15	16	33	16	17
50-54	37	17	20	24	11	13	27	13	14	30	15	16
55-59	39	18	21	36	16	20	24	11	13	27	13	14
60-64	34	16	18	38	17	21	35	16	19	23	11	13
65-69	28	13	14	32	15	17	36	16	20	34	15	19
70-74	21	10	12	25	12	14	30	14	16	34	15	19
75-79	16	7	9	19	8	11	22	10	12	26	12	15
80-84	10	4	6	13	5	8	15	6	9	18	8	11
85-89	6	2	4	7	3	4	9	3	6	11	4	7
90-94	3	1	2	3	1	2	4	1	3	5	2	4
95-99	1	0	1	1	0	1	1	0	1	2	0	1
100 +	0	0	0	0	0	0	0	0	0	0	0	0

Age group	2045 Both sexes	2045 Males	2045 Females	2050 Both sexes	2050 Males	2050 Females
All ages	551	261	289	555	263	291
0-4	37	19	18	37	19	18
5-9	37	19	18	37	19	18
10-14	38	19	18	37	19	18
15-19	35	18	17	35	18	17
20-24	30	15	15	30	16	15
25-29	31	15	16	32	15	16
30-34	30	15	16	31	15	16
35-39	31	15	16	30	15	16
40-44	31	15	16	31	15	16
45-49	33	16	17	31	15	16
50-54	33	16	17	33	16	17
55-59	30	14	16	32	15	17
60-64	26	12	14	29	14	15
65-69	23	10	12	25	12	14
70-74	32	14	18	21	9	12
75-79	30	13	17	28	12	16
80-84	22	9	13	25	10	15
85-89	13	5	8	16	6	10
90-94	7	2	5	8	3	5
95-99	2	1	2	3	1	2
100 +	1	0	0	1	0	1

United Nations Department of Economic and Social Affairs/Population Division
World Population Prospects: The 2004 Revision, Volume II: Sex and Age Distribution of the World Population

436

POPULATION BY AGE AND SEX (in thousands)

Age group	2005 Both sexes	2005 Males	2005 Females	2010 Both sexes	2010 Males	2010 Females	2015 Both sexes	2015 Males	2015 Females	2020 Both sexes	2020 Males	2020 Females
All ages	448	216	232	458	220	238	462	221	241	463	220	242
0-4	36	18	18	28	14	14	23	12	11	21	11	10
5-9	38	19	19	36	18	18	28	14	14	23	12	11
10-14	38	19	19	38	19	19	36	18	18	28	14	14
15-19	33	17	16	35	18	17	35	18	17	34	17	17
20-24	25	13	12	28	14	14	30	15	15	30	15	15
25-29	24	11	13	27	13	14	30	15	15	32	16	16
30-34	37	17	20	25	12	13	27	13	14	30	15	16
35-39	40	19	22	38	17	20	25	12	13	28	13	15
40-44	36	17	19	40	19	22	37	17	20	25	12	13
45-49	31	15	16	36	17	19	40	18	22	37	17	20
50-54	26	12	14	31	15	16	35	17	18	40	18	21
55-59	22	10	11	25	12	13	30	15	15	35	17	18
60-64	17	8	9	21	10	11	25	11	13	29	14	15
65-69	14	6	7	16	7	8	20	9	11	23	11	13
70-74	11	5	6	13	6	7	14	6	8	18	8	10
75-79	9	4	5	10	4	6	11	5	6	12	5	7
80-84	6	2	4	7	3	4	8	3	5	8	3	5
85-89	3	1	2	4	1	3	5	2	3	5	2	3
90-94	1	0	1	2	1	1	2	1	2	3	1	2
95-99	0	0	0	1	0	0	1	0	1	1	0	1
100 +	0	0	0	0	0	0	0	0	0	0	0	0

Age group	2025 Both sexes	2025 Males	2025 Females	2030 Both sexes	2030 Males	2030 Females	2035 Both sexes	2035 Males	2035 Females	2040 Both sexes	2040 Males	2040 Females
All ages	462	219	243	459	217	242	452	212	239	440	205	234
0-4	21	11	10	21	11	10	19	10	9	17	8	8
5-9	21	11	10	22	11	11	21	11	10	19	10	10
10-14	23	12	11	21	11	10	22	11	11	21	11	10
15-19	26	13	13	21	11	10	19	10	9	19	10	9
20-24	29	15	14	21	10	10	16	8	8	14	7	7
25-29	32	16	16	30	15	16	22	11	12	18	8	9
30-34	33	16	17	33	16	17	31	15	16	23	11	12
35-39	31	15	16	33	16	17	33	16	17	31	15	16
40-44	28	13	15	31	15	16	33	16	17	33	16	17
45-49	25	12	13	28	13	14	31	15	16	33	16	17
50-54	37	17	20	24	11	13	27	13	14	30	15	16
55-59	39	18	21	36	16	20	24	11	13	27	13	14
60-64	34	16	18	38	17	21	35	16	19	23	11	13
65-69	28	13	14	32	15	17	36	16	20	34	15	19
70-74	21	10	12	25	12	14	30	14	16	34	15	19
75-79	16	7	9	19	8	11	22	10	12	26	12	15
80-84	10	4	6	13	5	8	15	6	9	18	8	11
85-89	6	2	4	7	3	4	9	3	6	11	4	7
90-94	3	1	2	3	1	2	4	1	3	5	2	4
95-99	1	0	1	1	0	1	1	0	1	2	0	1
100 +	0	0	0	0	0	0	0	0	0	0	0	0

Age group	2045 Both sexes	2045 Males	2045 Females	2050 Both sexes	2050 Males	2050 Females
All ages	423	196	227	402	186	217
0-4	14	7	7	12	6	6
5-9	17	9	8	14	7	7
10-14	20	10	10	17	9	8
15-19	19	10	9	17	9	8
20-24	14	7	7	14	7	7
25-29	16	7	8	16	7	8
30-34	18	9	10	16	8	9
35-39	23	11	12	19	9	10
40-44	31	15	16	23	11	12
45-49	33	16	17	31	15	16
50-54	33	16	17	33	16	17
55-59	30	14	16	32	15	17
60-64	26	12	14	29	14	15
65-69	23	10	12	25	12	14
70-74	32	14	18	21	9	12
75-79	30	13	17	28	12	16
80-84	22	9	13	25	10	15
85-89	13	5	8	16	6	10
90-94	7	2	5	8	3	5
95-99	2	1	2	3	1	2
100 +	1	0	0	1	0	1

POPULATION BY AGE AND SEX (in thousands)

Age group	1950 Both sexes	Males	Females	1955 Both sexes	Males	Females	1960 Both sexes	Males	Females	1965 Both sexes	Males	Females
All ages	60	40	19	63	40	23	67	39	28	76	43	33
0-4	8	4	4	9	5	4	11	6	5	11	6	6
5-9	4	2	2	7	3	3	9	5	5	10	5	5
10-14	4	2	2	6	3	3	7	4	4	9	4	4
15-19	7	6	2	6	4	2	5	3	2	6	4	3
20-24	11	10	2	9	7	2	7	5	2	8	6	3
25-29	7	5	2	6	4	2	6	3	2	6	4	3
30-34	5	4	2	6	4	2	7	5	2	6	4	2
35-39	4	3	1	5	3	1	5	3	2	5	3	2
40-44	3	2	1	3	2	1	3	2	1	4	3	1
45-49	2	1	1	2	2	1	3	2	1	3	2	1
50-54	1	1	0	1	1	1	2	1	1	2	1	1
55-59	1	0	0	1	1	0	1	1	1	1	1	1
60-64	0	0	0	1	0	0	1	0	0	1	0	0
65-69	0	0	0	0	0	0	0	0	0	1	0	0
70-74	0	0	0	0	0	0	0	0	0	0	0	0
75-79	0	0	0	0	0	0	0	0	0	0	0	0
80 +	0	0	0	0	0	0	0	0	0	0	0	0

Age group	1970 Both sexes	Males	Females	1975 Both sexes	Males	Females	1980 Both sexes	Males	Females	1985 Both sexes	Males	Females
All ages	85	48	38	95	51	44	107	56	51	119	63	56
0-4	12	6	6	12	6	6	13	7	6	14	7	7
5-9	12	6	6	12	6	6	13	6	6	13	7	6
10-14	10	5	5	11	6	5	11	6	6	12	6	6
15-19	8	4	4	9	5	5	11	6	5	12	6	5
20-24	10	7	4	11	6	4	11	6	5	13	7	6
25-29	6	4	3	8	4	4	10	5	5	12	6	6
30-34	6	4	3	8	4	3	9	5	4	11	6	5
35-39	6	3	2	6	3	3	6	3	3	8	4	4
40-44	5	3	2	5	3	2	5	3	2	6	3	3
45-49	4	2	1	4	2	2	4	2	2	5	3	2
50-54	2	1	1	3	2	1	4	2	2	4	2	2
55-59	2	1	1	2	1	1	3	2	1	3	2	2
60-64	1	1	0	1	1	1	2	1	1	3	1	1
65-69	1	0	0	1	1	1	1	1	1	2	1	1
70-74	0	0	0	1	0	0	1	0	0	1	1	1
75-79	0	0	0	0	0	0	0	0	0	1	0	0
80 +	0	0	0	0	0	0	0	0	0	0	0	0

Age group	1990 Both sexes	Males	Females	1995 Both sexes	Males	Females	2000 Both sexes	Males	Females	2005 Both sexes	Males	Females
All ages	134	71	63	146	76	70	155	79	76	170	86	83
0-4	15	8	8	18	9	9	17	9	8	18	9	9
5-9	13	7	6	15	8	7	16	8	8	17	9	8
10-14	12	6	6	13	6	6	14	7	7	16	8	8
15-19	12	7	6	12	6	6	12	6	6	14	7	7
20-24	14	8	6	12	7	6	12	6	6	12	6	6
25-29	14	7	6	14	8	6	13	7	6	12	6	6
30-34	12	6	5	13	7	6	14	7	6	13	7	6
35-39	10	6	5	11	6	5	12	6	6	13	7	6
40-44	8	4	4	10	5	5	11	6	5	12	6	6
45-49	5	3	2	8	4	4	9	5	4	11	6	5
50-54	5	3	2	5	3	2	7	4	4	9	4	4
55-59	4	2	2	5	2	2	5	3	2	7	4	4
60-64	4	2	2	4	2	2	4	2	2	5	2	2
65-69	2	1	1	3	2	1	4	2	2	4	2	2
70-74	1	1	1	2	1	1	3	1	1	3	1	2
75-79	1	0	0	1	0	1	1	1	1	2	1	1
80 +	1	0	0	1	0	0	1	0	0	1	1	1

United Nations Department of Economic and Social Affairs/Population Division
World Population Prospects: The 2004 Revision, Volume II: Sex and Age Distribution of the World Population

438

POPULATION BY AGE AND SEX (in thousands)

Age group	2005 Both sexes	Males	Females	2010 Both sexes	Males	Females	2015 Both sexes	Males	Females	2020 Both sexes	Males	Females
All ages	170	86	83	182	93	90	194	98	96	206	104	102
0-4	18	9	9	17	9	8	17	9	8	17	9	8
5-9	17	9	8	18	9	9	17	9	8	17	9	8
10-14	16	8	8	17	9	8	18	9	9	17	9	8
15-19	14	7	7	16	8	8	17	9	8	18	9	9
20-24	12	6	6	14	7	7	16	8	8	17	9	8
25-29	12	6	6	12	6	6	14	7	7	15	8	7
30-34	13	7	6	12	6	6	12	6	6	14	7	7
35-39	13	7	6	13	7	6	12	6	6	12	6	6
40-44	12	6	6	13	7	6	13	6	6	12	6	6
45-49	11	6	5	12	6	6	13	7	6	13	6	6
50-54	9	4	4	11	6	5	12	6	6	13	7	6
55-59	7	4	4	9	4	4	10	5	5	12	6	6
60-64	5	2	2	7	3	3	8	4	4	10	5	5
65-69	4	2	2	4	2	2	6	3	3	8	4	4
70-74	3	1	2	4	2	2	4	2	2	6	3	3
75-79	2	1	1	3	1	1	3	1	2	3	1	2
80-84	1	0	0	1	1	1	2	1	1	2	1	1
85-89	0	0	0	0	0	0	1	0	0	1	0	1
90-94	0	0	0	0	0	0	0	0	0	0	0	0
95-99	0	0	0	0	0	0	0	0	0	0	0	0
100 +	0	0	0	0	0	0	0	0	0	0	0	0

Age group	2025 Both sexes	Males	Females	2030 Both sexes	Males	Females	2035 Both sexes	Males	Females	2040 Both sexes	Males	Females
All ages	217	110	107	227	115	113	236	119	117	243	122	121
0-4	18	9	9	18	9	9	17	9	8	16	8	8
5-9	17	9	8	18	9	9	18	9	9	17	9	8
10-14	17	9	8	17	9	8	18	9	9	18	9	9
15-19	17	9	8	17	9	8	17	9	8	18	9	9
20-24	18	9	9	17	9	8	17	9	8	17	9	8
25-29	17	9	8	18	9	9	17	9	8	17	9	8
30-34	15	8	7	17	9	8	18	9	9	17	9	8
35-39	14	7	7	15	8	7	17	9	8	18	9	9
40-44	12	6	6	14	7	7	15	8	7	17	9	8
45-49	11	6	6	12	6	6	14	7	7	15	8	7
50-54	12	6	6	11	6	6	12	6	6	14	7	7
55-59	13	7	6	12	6	6	11	6	6	12	6	6
60-64	11	5	6	12	6	6	12	6	6	11	5	5
65-69	9	5	5	10	5	5	12	6	6	11	5	6
70-74	7	3	4	8	4	4	9	4	5	11	5	5
75-79	5	2	3	6	3	3	7	3	4	8	4	4
80-84	2	1	1	3	1	2	4	2	2	5	2	3
85-89	1	0	1	1	0	1	2	1	1	2	1	2
90-94	0	0	0	0	0	0	0	0	0	1	0	1
95-99	0	0	0	0	0	0	0	0	0	0	0	0
100 +	0	0	0	0	0	0	0	0	0	0	0	0

Age group	2045 Both sexes	Males	Females	2050 Both sexes	Males	Females
All ages	249	125	124	254	127	126
0-4	16	8	8	16	8	8
5-9	16	8	8	16	8	8
10-14	17	9	8	16	8	8
15-19	18	9	9	17	9	8
20-24	18	9	9	17	9	9
25-29	17	9	8	18	9	9
30-34	17	9	8	17	9	8
35-39	17	8	8	17	9	8
40-44	18	9	9	17	8	8
45-49	17	9	8	17	9	9
50-54	15	8	7	17	9	8
55-59	13	7	7	15	8	7
60-64	11	6	6	13	6	7
65-69	10	5	5	11	5	6
70-74	10	5	5	9	4	5
75-79	9	4	5	9	4	5
80-84	6	2	4	7	3	4
85-89	3	1	2	4	1	2
90-94	1	0	1	1	0	1
95-99	0	0	0	0	0	0
100 +	0	0	0	0	0	0

United Nations Department of Economic and Social Affairs/Population Division
World Population Prospects: The 2004 Revision, Volume II: Sex and Age Distribution of the World Population

439

POPULATION BY AGE AND SEX (in thousands)

Age group	2005 Both sexes	2005 Males	2005 Females	2010 Both sexes	2010 Males	2010 Females	2015 Both sexes	2015 Males	2015 Females	2020 Both sexes	2020 Males	2020 Females
All ages	170	86	83	184	93	90	198	101	98	214	108	106
0-4	18	9	9	18	9	9	20	10	10	21	11	10
5-9	17	9	8	18	9	9	18	9	9	20	10	10
10-14	16	8	8	17	9	8	18	9	9	18	9	9
15-19	14	7	7	16	8	8	17	9	8	18	9	9
20-24	12	6	6	14	7	7	16	8	8	17	9	8
25-29	12	6	6	12	6	6	14	7	7	15	8	7
30-34	13	7	6	12	6	6	12	6	6	14	7	7
35-39	13	7	6	13	7	6	12	6	6	12	6	6
40-44	12	6	6	13	7	6	13	6	6	12	6	6
45-49	11	6	5	12	6	6	13	7	6	13	6	6
50-54	9	4	4	11	6	5	12	6	6	13	7	6
55-59	7	4	4	9	4	4	10	5	5	12	6	6
60-64	5	2	2	7	3	3	8	4	4	10	5	5
65-69	4	2	2	4	2	2	6	3	3	8	4	4
70-74	3	1	2	4	2	2	4	2	2	6	3	3
75-79	2	1	1	3	1	1	3	1	2	3	1	2
80-84	1	0	0	1	1	1	2	1	1	2	1	1
85-89	0	0	0	0	0	0	1	0	0	1	0	1
90-94	0	0	0	0	0	0	0	0	0	0	0	0
95-99	0	0	0	0	0	0	0	0	0	0	0	0
100 +	0	0	0	0	0	0	0	0	0	0	0	0

Age group	2025 Both sexes	2025 Males	2025 Females	2030 Both sexes	2030 Males	2030 Females	2035 Both sexes	2035 Males	2035 Females	2040 Both sexes	2040 Males	2040 Females
All ages	229	116	113	244	123	121	258	130	128	272	137	135
0-4	22	11	11	22	11	11	23	12	11	23	12	11
5-9	21	11	10	22	11	11	22	11	11	23	12	11
10-14	20	10	10	21	11	10	22	11	11	22	11	11
15-19	18	9	9	20	10	9	21	11	10	22	11	11
20-24	18	9	9	18	9	9	19	10	9	21	11	10
25-29	17	9	8	18	9	9	18	9	9	19	10	9
30-34	15	8	7	17	9	8	18	9	9	18	9	9
35-39	14	7	7	15	8	7	17	9	8	18	9	9
40-44	12	6	6	14	7	7	15	8	7	17	9	8
45-49	11	6	6	12	6	6	14	7	7	15	8	7
50-54	12	6	6	11	6	6	12	6	6	14	7	7
55-59	13	7	6	12	6	6	11	6	6	12	6	6
60-64	11	5	6	12	6	6	12	6	6	11	5	5
65-69	9	5	5	10	5	5	12	6	6	11	5	6
70-74	7	3	4	8	4	4	9	4	5	11	5	5
75-79	5	2	3	6	3	3	7	3	4	8	4	4
80-84	2	1	1	3	1	2	4	2	2	5	2	3
85-89	1	0	1	1	0	1	2	1	1	2	1	2
90-94	0	0	0	0	0	0	0	0	0	1	0	1
95-99	0	0	0	0	0	0	0	0	0	0	0	0
100 +	0	0	0	0	0	0	0	0	0	0	0	0

Age group	2045 Both sexes	2045 Males	2045 Females	2050 Both sexes	2050 Males	2050 Females
All ages	286	144	142	299	150	148
0-4	24	12	12	24	12	12
5-9	23	12	11	24	12	12
10-14	23	12	11	23	12	11
15-19	22	11	11	23	12	11
20-24	22	11	11	22	11	11
25-29	21	11	10	22	11	11
30-34	19	10	9	21	11	10
35-39	18	9	9	19	10	9
40-44	18	9	9	18	9	9
45-49	17	9	8	17	9	9
50-54	15	8	7	17	9	8
55-59	13	7	7	15	8	7
60-64	11	6	6	13	6	7
65-69	10	5	5	11	5	6
70-74	10	5	5	9	4	5
75-79	9	4	5	9	4	5
80-84	6	2	4	7	3	4
85-89	3	1	2	4	1	2
90-94	1	0	1	1	0	1
95-99	0	0	0	0	0	0
100 +	0	0	0	0	0	0

United Nations Department of Economic and Social Affairs/Population Division
World Population Prospects: The 2004 Revision, Volume II: Sex and Age Distribution of the World Population

440

POPULATION BY AGE AND SEX (in thousands)

Age group	2005 Both sexes	Males	Females	2010 Both sexes	Males	Females	2015 Both sexes	Males	Females	2020 Both sexes	Males	Females
All ages	170	86	83	181	92	89	190	96	94	198	100	98
0-4	18	9	9	15	8	7	14	7	7	14	7	7
5-9	17	9	8	18	9	9	15	8	7	14	7	7
10-14	16	8	8	17	9	8	18	9	9	15	8	7
15-19	14	7	7	16	8	8	17	9	8	18	9	9
20-24	12	6	6	14	7	7	16	8	8	17	9	8
25-29	12	6	6	12	6	6	14	7	7	15	8	7
30-34	13	7	6	12	6	6	12	6	6	14	7	7
35-39	13	7	6	13	7	6	12	6	6	12	6	6
40-44	12	6	6	13	7	6	13	6	6	12	6	6
45-49	11	6	5	12	6	6	13	7	6	13	6	6
50-54	9	4	4	11	6	5	12	6	6	13	7	6
55-59	7	4	4	9	4	4	10	5	5	12	6	6
60-64	5	2	2	7	3	3	8	4	4	10	5	5
65-69	4	2	2	4	2	2	6	3	3	8	4	4
70-74	3	1	2	4	2	2	4	2	2	6	3	3
75-79	2	1	1	3	1	1	3	1	2	3	1	2
80-84	1	0	0	1	1	1	2	1	1	2	1	1
85-89	0	0	0	0	0	0	1	0	0	1	0	1
90-94	0	0	0	0	0	0	0	0	0	0	0	0
95-99	0	0	0	0	0	0	0	0	0	0	0	0
100 +	0	0	0	0	0	0	0	0	0	0	0	0

Age group	2025 Both sexes	Males	Females	2030 Both sexes	Males	Females	2035 Both sexes	Males	Females	2040 Both sexes	Males	Females
All ages	205	104	102	211	106	105	215	108	107	216	108	108
0-4	14	7	7	13	7	6	12	6	6	11	5	5
5-9	14	7	7	14	7	7	13	7	6	12	6	6
10-14	14	7	7	14	7	7	14	7	7	13	7	6
15-19	15	8	7	14	7	7	14	7	7	14	7	7
20-24	18	9	9	15	8	7	14	7	7	14	7	7
25-29	17	9	8	18	9	9	15	8	7	14	7	7
30-34	15	8	7	17	9	8	18	9	9	15	8	7
35-39	14	7	7	15	8	7	17	9	8	18	9	9
40-44	12	6	6	14	7	7	16	8	7	17	9	8
45-49	11	6	6	12	6	6	14	7	7	15	8	7
50-54	12	6	6	11	6	6	12	6	6	14	7	7
55-59	13	7	6	12	6	6	11	6	6	12	6	6
60-64	11	5	6	12	6	6	12	6	6	11	5	5
65-69	9	5	5	10	5	5	12	6	6	11	5	6
70-74	7	3	4	8	4	4	9	4	5	11	5	5
75-79	5	2	3	6	3	3	7	3	4	8	4	4
80-84	2	1	1	3	1	2	4	2	2	5	2	3
85-89	1	0	1	1	0	1	2	1	1	2	1	2
90-94	0	0	0	0	0	0	0	0	0	1	0	1
95-99	0	0	0	0	0	0	0	0	0	0	0	0
100 +	0	0	0	0	0	0	0	0	0	0	0	0

Age group	2045 Both sexes	Males	Females	2050 Both sexes	Males	Females
All ages	216	108	108	214	107	107
0-4	10	5	5	9	5	4
5-9	11	5	5	10	5	5
10-14	12	6	6	11	5	5
15-19	13	7	6	12	6	6
20-24	14	7	7	13	7	6
25-29	14	7	7	14	7	7
30-34	14	7	7	14	7	7
35-39	15	8	7	14	7	7
40-44	18	9	9	15	8	7
45-49	17	9	8	17	9	9
50-54	15	8	7	17	9	8
55-59	13	7	7	15	8	7
60-64	11	6	6	13	6	7
65-69	10	5	5	11	5	6
70-74	10	5	5	9	4	5
75-79	9	4	5	9	4	5
80-84	6	2	4	7	3	4
85-89	3	1	2	4	1	2
90-94	1	0	1	1	0	1
95-99	0	0	0	0	0	0
100 +	0	0	0	0	0	0

GUATEMALA   ESTIMATES

POPULATION BY AGE AND SEX (in thousands)

Age group	1950 Both sexes	Males	Females	1955 Both sexes	Males	Females	1960 Both sexes	Males	Females	1965 Both sexes	Males	Females
All ages	3 146	1 589	1 557	3 619	1 831	1 787	4 139	2 097	2 043	4 736	2 399	2 337
0-4	602	305	296	689	350	339	750	381	369	851	432	419
5-9	431	219	212	538	273	264	624	317	307	686	349	338
10-14	370	188	183	416	211	205	521	265	256	604	307	297
15-19	339	171	168	361	183	178	407	206	200	508	258	250
20-24	292	147	145	328	165	162	350	178	172	392	199	193
25-29	238	121	117	280	142	139	316	160	156	336	171	165
30-34	185	94	91	227	116	111	269	137	133	303	153	150
35-39	156	79	76	176	90	86	217	111	106	257	130	127
40-44	124	63	62	147	75	72	167	85	82	206	105	101
45-49	115	57	58	116	58	58	137	70	68	157	80	77
50-54	92	46	47	105	52	53	107	53	53	127	64	63
55-59	69	34	35	82	41	42	94	47	48	96	48	48
60-64	54	26	27	60	29	30	71	35	36	82	40	42
65-69	36	18	18	43	21	22	49	24	25	58	29	30
70-74	23	11	12	27	13	14	32	16	17	37	18	19
75-79	13	6	7	15	7	8	18	9	9	22	11	11
80 +	8	3	4	9	4	5	11	5	6	13	6	7

Age group	1970 Both sexes	Males	Females	1975 Both sexes	Males	Females	1980 Both sexes	Males	Females	1985 Both sexes	Males	Females
All ages	5 418	2 743	2 675	6 203	3 138	3 064	7 012	3 545	3 466	7 929	4 004	3 924
0-4	963	490	474	1 109	564	544	1 265	645	620	1 416	722	693
5-9	789	401	388	906	460	446	1 046	532	513	1 199	611	588
10-14	666	338	328	766	388	378	873	443	431	1 012	514	498
15-19	588	298	290	646	327	318	733	371	362	837	423	414
20-24	487	247	240	558	282	276	589	296	292	669	336	334
25-29	373	189	184	460	233	227	508	256	251	534	267	266
30-34	320	162	158	353	178	175	423	212	211	467	233	234
35-39	289	146	143	304	154	150	326	164	161	392	196	196
40-44	245	124	121	276	139	137	286	144	142	306	154	152
45-49	195	99	96	232	117	115	259	130	129	268	136	133
50-54	146	74	72	182	92	90	216	109	107	242	121	120
55-59	116	58	58	134	67	67	166	83	82	198	99	99
60-64	84	42	43	103	51	51	118	59	59	148	74	74
65-69	68	33	35	71	35	36	86	43	44	101	50	51
70-74	45	22	23	53	25	27	55	27	28	68	34	34
75-79	26	12	13	31	15	16	36	18	19	39	19	20
80 +	17	8	9	21	10	12	27	12	15	33	15	18

Age group	1990 Both sexes	Males	Females	1995 Both sexes	Males	Females	2000 Both sexes	Males	Females	2005 Both sexes	Males	Females
All ages	8 894	4 483	4 411	9 970	4 954	5 017	11 166	5 478	5 688	12 599	6 139	6 460
0-4	1 519	775	744	1 702	866	836	1 852	941	911	2 020	1 027	993
5-9	1 353	690	663	1 464	742	722	1 651	834	816	1 811	915	895
10-14	1 162	591	571	1 312	663	649	1 421	714	707	1 616	812	804
15-19	970	491	479	1 110	556	554	1 256	626	631	1 375	683	692
20-24	763	382	381	880	428	452	1 014	488	526	1 176	569	607
25-29	605	302	303	688	332	355	799	374	424	942	441	501
30-34	487	241	247	549	261	287	625	288	338	743	335	408
35-39	431	214	217	451	217	234	508	235	273	588	264	324
40-44	369	183	186	405	197	208	423	199	224	482	218	264
45-49	287	144	143	347	170	177	381	183	198	402	187	216
50-54	251	126	125	268	133	135	326	157	168	362	172	190
55-59	222	111	111	231	115	116	249	122	127	308	147	161
60-64	178	88	90	201	98	102	211	103	107	232	112	120
65-69	128	63	65	154	75	79	178	86	92	192	93	99
70-74	81	40	41	104	51	54	131	62	68	156	74	81
75-79	50	24	25	60	29	32	82	39	43	107	50	57
80 +	37	17	20	44	20	24	61	27	34	88	39	49

United Nations Department of Economic and Social Affairs/Population Division
World Population Prospects: The 2004 Revision, Volume II: Sex and Age Distribution of the World Population

442

POPULATION BY AGE AND SEX (in thousands)

Age group	2005 Both sexes	2005 Males	2005 Females	2010 Both sexes	2010 Males	2010 Females	2015 Both sexes	2015 Males	2015 Females	2020 Both sexes	2020 Males	2020 Females
All ages	12 599	6 139	6 460	14 213	6 916	7 297	15 869	7 715	8 154	17 527	8 514	9 013
0-4	2 020	1 027	993	2 143	1 091	1 052	2 225	1 133	1 092	2 261	1 152	1 109
5-9	1 811	915	895	1 987	1 008	979	2 111	1 072	1 039	2 195	1 115	1 080
10-14	1 616	812	804	1 784	899	885	1 960	991	969	2 084	1 056	1 028
15-19	1 375	683	692	1 582	790	792	1 749	877	873	1 925	969	956
20-24	1 176	569	607	1 317	644	673	1 523	750	773	1 690	837	853
25-29	942	441	501	1 120	534	587	1 262	608	653	1 467	714	753
30-34	743	335	408	895	409	486	1 072	501	571	1 214	575	639
35-39	588	264	324	708	314	394	858	387	471	1 033	477	556
40-44	482	218	264	564	249	315	681	298	383	829	369	460
45-49	402	187	216	462	207	255	542	236	305	657	284	373
50-54	362	172	190	385	177	208	443	196	247	521	225	296
55-59	308	147	161	344	162	183	367	167	200	424	186	238
60-64	232	112	120	289	137	152	324	151	174	347	156	191
65-69	192	93	99	213	102	111	266	125	142	300	138	162
70-74	156	74	81	169	81	88	188	89	99	237	109	128
75-79	107	50	57	128	60	68	140	66	74	158	73	85
80-84	59	27	32	78	35	42	95	43	52	105	47	57
85-89	23	10	13	34	15	19	46	20	27	58	24	33
90-94	6	2	4	9	3	6	14	5	9	20	8	13
95-99	1	0	0	1	0	1	2	1	2	4	1	3
100 +	0	0	0	0	0	0	0	0	0	0	0	0

Age group	2025 Both sexes	2025 Males	2025 Females	2030 Both sexes	2030 Males	2030 Females	2035 Both sexes	2035 Males	2035 Females	2040 Both sexes	2040 Males	2040 Females
All ages	19 149	9 294	9 855	20 698	10 038	10 660	22 140	10 728	11 412	23 453	11 354	12 099
0-4	2 255	1 150	1 105	2 216	1 130	1 085	2 150	1 097	1 052	2 064	1 054	1 010
5-9	2 231	1 134	1 097	2 227	1 133	1 094	2 189	1 114	1 075	2 124	1 082	1 043
10-14	2 169	1 099	1 070	2 206	1 119	1 087	2 203	1 118	1 085	2 165	1 100	1 066
15-19	2 049	1 034	1 016	2 135	1 077	1 057	2 173	1 097	1 075	2 170	1 097	1 073
20-24	1 866	929	937	1 991	994	997	2 077	1 038	1 039	2 116	1 059	1 057
25-29	1 634	800	834	1 810	892	918	1 935	958	978	2 023	1 003	1 020
30-34	1 419	680	738	1 586	767	819	1 762	859	903	1 889	925	964
35-39	1 176	552	625	1 380	655	724	1 547	742	805	1 723	833	890
40-44	1 003	458	545	1 140	528	613	1 348	635	713	1 515	721	794
45-49	803	354	449	975	441	533	1 117	515	602	1 317	616	701
50-54	635	272	363	778	340	438	947	425	522	1 088	498	590
55-59	500	214	286	611	259	352	751	325	426	917	408	609
60-64	402	174	228	476	201	275	583	244	339	719	307	412
65-69	322	143	179	375	160	215	446	185	260	548	226	323
70-74	268	121	147	290	126	164	339	142	198	406	165	241
75-79	200	90	110	228	100	129	249	104	144	293	118	175
80-84	119	53	66	153	66	88	177	74	103	195	78	117
85-89	66	28	38	76	31	45	100	40	60	118	45	73
90-94	26	10	17	31	11	20	37	13	24	50	17	33
95-99	6	2	4	8	2	6	10	3	7	12	3	9
100 +	1	0	0	1	0	1	1	0	1	2	0	1

Age group	2045 Both sexes	2045 Males	2045 Females	2050 Both sexes	2050 Males	2050 Females
All ages	24 615	11 906	12 710	25 612	12 375	13 237
0-4	1 966	1 005	961	1 863	952	911
5-9	2 040	1 039	1 001	1 943	991	953
10-14	2 101	1 067	1 034	2 017	1 025	992
15-19	2 134	1 079	1 055	2 070	1 048	1 023
20-24	2 115	1 059	1 055	2 080	1 043	1 037
25-29	2 064	1 025	1 039	2 064	1 027	1 038
30-34	1 977	971	1 007	2 020	994	1 026
35-39	1 851	900	951	1 940	947	994
40-44	1 690	812	878	1 818	879	940
45-49	1 483	701	782	1 658	792	866
50-54	1 285	597	688	1 450	681	769
55-59	1 055	478	576	1 249	575	674
60-64	880	387	493	1 014	454	560
65-69	677	285	393	831	359	472
70-74	501	201	300	621	254	367
75-79	353	138	215	439	169	270
80-84	233	88	144	283	104	179
85-89	132	48	84	159	55	104
90-94	60	20	40	69	22	47
95-99	17	5	12	21	6	15
100 +	2	0	2	3	1	2

POPULATION BY AGE AND SEX (in thousands)

Age group	2005 Both sexes	2005 Males	2005 Females	2010 Both sexes	2010 Males	2010 Females	2015 Both sexes	2015 Males	2015 Females	2020 Both sexes	2020 Males	2020 Females
All ages	12 599	6 139	6 460	14 335	6 979	7 357	16 221	7 894	8 327	18 208	8 861	9 347
0-4	2 020	1 027	993	2 265	1 153	1 112	2 456	1 251	1 205	2 592	1 321	1 271
5-9	1 811	915	895	1 987	1 008	979	2 232	1 134	1 098	2 423	1 231	1 192
10-14	1 616	812	804	1 784	899	885	1 960	991	969	2 205	1 117	1 088
15-19	1 375	683	692	1 582	790	792	1 749	877	873	1 925	969	956
20-24	1 176	569	607	1 317	644	673	1 523	750	773	1 690	837	853
25-29	942	441	501	1 120	534	587	1 262	608	653	1 467	714	753
30-34	743	335	408	895	409	486	1 072	501	571	1 214	575	639
35-39	588	264	324	708	314	394	858	387	471	1 033	477	556
40-44	482	218	264	564	249	315	681	298	383	829	369	460
45-49	402	187	216	462	207	255	542	236	305	657	284	373
50-54	362	172	190	385	177	208	443	196	247	521	225	296
55-59	308	147	161	344	162	183	367	167	200	424	186	238
60-64	232	112	120	289	137	152	324	151	174	347	156	191
65-69	192	93	99	213	102	111	266	125	142	300	138	162
70-74	156	74	81	169	81	88	188	89	99	237	109	128
75-79	107	50	57	128	60	68	140	66	74	158	73	85
80-84	59	27	32	78	35	42	95	43	52	105	47	57
85-89	23	10	13	34	15	19	46	20	27	58	24	33
90-94	6	2	4	9	3	6	14	5	9	20	8	13
95-99	1	0	0	1	0	1	2	1	2	4	1	3
100 +	0	0	0	0	0	0	0	0	0	0	0	0

Age group	2025 Both sexes	2025 Males	2025 Females	2030 Both sexes	2030 Males	2030 Females	2035 Both sexes	2035 Males	2035 Females	2040 Both sexes	2040 Males	2040 Females
All ages	20 216	9 838	10 378	22 237	10 822	11 415	24 264	11 810	12 454	26 274	12 791	13 483
0-4	2 645	1 348	1 296	2 693	1 374	1 319	2 741	1 400	1 342	2 772	1 416	1 356
5-9	2 560	1 302	1 259	2 615	1 330	1 284	2 664	1 357	1 308	2 714	1 383	1 331
10-14	2 397	1 215	1 181	2 534	1 286	1 248	2 589	1 315	1 274	2 640	1 341	1 298
15-19	2 170	1 095	1 075	2 362	1 193	1 169	2 500	1 264	1 236	2 555	1 293	1 262
20-24	1 866	929	937	2 110	1 054	1 056	2 302	1 152	1 150	2 441	1 224	1 217
25-29	1 634	800	834	1 810	892	918	2 053	1 017	1 036	2 246	1 115	1 130
30-34	1 419	680	738	1 586	767	819	1 762	859	903	2 005	983	1 022
35-39	1 176	552	625	1 380	655	724	1 547	742	805	1 723	833	890
40-44	1 003	458	545	1 146	532	613	1 348	635	713	1 515	721	794
45-49	803	354	449	975	441	533	1 117	515	602	1 317	616	701
50-54	635	272	363	778	340	438	947	425	522	1 088	498	590
55-59	500	214	286	611	259	352	751	325	426	917	408	509
60-64	402	174	228	476	201	275	583	244	339	719	307	412
65-69	322	143	179	375	160	215	446	185	260	548	226	323
70-74	268	121	147	290	126	164	339	142	198	406	165	241
75-79	200	90	110	228	100	129	249	104	144	293	118	175
80-84	119	53	66	153	66	88	177	74	103	195	78	117
85-89	66	28	38	76	31	45	100	40	60	118	45	73
90-94	26	10	17	31	11	20	37	13	24	50	17	33
95-99	6	2	4	8	2	6	10	3	7	12	3	9
100 +	1	0	0	1	0	1	1	0	1	2	0	1

Age group	2045 Both sexes	2045 Males	2045 Females	2050 Both sexes	2050 Males	2050 Females
All ages	28 235	13 748	14 487	30 118	14 667	15 451
0-4	2 780	1 420	1 359	2 768	1 415	1 353
5-9	2 746	1 400	1 346	2 754	1 405	1 349
10-14	2 689	1 368	1 322	2 722	1 385	1 337
15-19	2 606	1 320	1 286	2 657	1 347	1 310
20-24	2 498	1 254	1 244	2 550	1 282	1 268
25-29	2 386	1 187	1 198	2 444	1 219	1 225
30-34	2 198	1 081	1 116	2 339	1 154	1 185
35-39	1 966	957	1 008	2 158	1 055	1 103
40-44	1 690	812	878	1 932	935	997
45-49	1 483	701	782	1 658	792	866
50-54	1 285	597	688	1 450	681	769
55-59	1 055	478	576	1 249	575	674
60-64	880	387	493	1 014	454	560
65-69	677	285	393	831	359	472
70-74	501	201	300	621	254	367
75-79	353	138	215	439	169	270
80-84	233	88	144	283	104	179
85-89	132	48	84	159	55	104
90-94	60	20	40	69	22	47
95-99	17	5	12	21	6	15
100 +	2	0	2	3	1	2

United Nations Department of Economic and Social Affairs/Population Division
World Population Prospects: The 2004 Revision, Volume II: Sex and Age Distribution of the World Population

444

POPULATION BY AGE AND SEX (in thousands)

Age group	2005 Both sexes	Males	Females	2010 Both sexes	Males	Females	2015 Both sexes	Males	Females	2020 Both sexes	Males	Females
All ages	12 599	6 139	6 460	14 090	6 854	7 236	15 516	7 535	7 981	16 840	8 164	8 676
0-4	2 020	1 027	993	2 020	1 028	991	1 994	1 015	979	1 925	981	944
5-9	1 811	915	895	1 987	1 008	979	1 988	1 010	979	1 965	998	967
10-14	1 616	812	804	1 784	899	885	1 960	991	969	1 962	994	968
15-19	1 375	683	692	1 582	790	792	1 749	877	873	1 925	969	956
20-24	1 176	569	607	1 317	644	673	1 523	750	773	1 690	837	853
25-29	942	441	501	1 120	534	587	1 262	608	653	1 467	714	753
30-34	743	335	408	895	409	486	1 072	501	571	1 214	575	639
35-39	588	264	324	708	314	394	858	387	471	1 033	477	556
40-44	482	218	264	564	249	315	681	298	383	829	369	460
45-49	402	187	216	462	207	255	542	236	305	657	284	373
50-54	362	172	190	385	177	208	443	196	247	521	225	296
55-59	308	147	161	344	162	183	367	167	200	424	186	238
60-64	232	112	120	289	137	152	324	151	174	347	156	191
65-69	192	93	99	213	102	111	266	125	142	300	138	162
70-74	156	74	81	169	81	88	188	89	99	237	109	128
75-79	107	50	57	128	60	68	140	66	74	158	73	85
80-84	59	27	32	78	35	42	95	43	52	105	47	57
85-89	23	10	13	34	15	19	46	20	27	58	24	33
90-94	6	2	4	9	3	6	14	5	9	20	8	13
95-99	1	0	0	1	0	1	2	1	2	4	1	3
100 +	0	0	0	0	0	0	0	0	0	0	0	0

Age group	2025 Both sexes	Males	Females	2030 Both sexes	Males	Females	2035 Both sexes	Males	Females	2040 Both sexes	Males	Females
All ages	18 076	8 748	9 329	19 166	9 257	9 908	20 066	9 672	10 394	20 760	9 983	10 777
0-4	1 866	951	915	1 752	893	858	1 600	816	783	1 434	732	702
5-9	1 898	964	934	1 840	936	905	1 727	879	849	1 577	803	775
10-14	1 940	982	957	1 874	949	924	1 817	921	896	1 704	864	840
15-19	1 928	972	956	1 906	961	945	1 842	929	913	1 786	901	885
20-24	1 866	929	937	1 870	933	937	1 850	923	927	1 787	892	895
25-29	1 634	800	834	1 810	892	918	1 816	898	919	1 798	889	909
30-34	1 419	680	738	1 586	767	819	1 762	859	903	1 771	866	905
35-39	1 176	552	625	1 380	655	724	1 547	742	805	1 723	833	890
40-44	1 003	458	545	1 146	532	613	1 348	635	710	1 516	721	794
45-49	803	354	449	975	441	533	1 117	515	602	1 317	616	701
50-54	635	272	363	778	340	438	947	425	522	1 088	498	590
55-59	500	214	286	611	259	352	751	325	426	900	400	500
60-64	402	174	228	476	201	275	583	244	339	719	307	412
65-69	322	143	179	375	160	215	446	185	260	548	226	323
70-74	268	121	147	290	126	164	339	142	198	406	165	241
75-79	200	90	110	228	100	129	249	104	144	293	118	175
80-84	119	53	66	153	66	88	177	74	103	195	78	117
85-89	66	28	38	76	31	45	100	40	60	118	45	73
90-94	26	10	17	31	11	20	37	13	24	50	17	33
95-99	6	2	4	8	2	6	10	3	7	12	3	9
100 +	1	0	0	1	0	1	1	0	1	2	0	1

Age group	2045 Both sexes	Males	Females	2050 Both sexes	Males	Females
All ages	21 246	10 191	11 055	21 526	10 297	11 229
0-4	1 275	651	624	1 128	576	552
5-9	1 413	719	694	1 255	639	616
10-14	1 555	789	766	1 392	706	686
15-19	1 674	845	829	1 526	770	756
20-24	1 732	865	867	1 623	810	812
25-29	1 737	860	878	1 685	834	850
30-34	1 755	859	896	1 697	831	866
35-39	1 735	842	893	1 721	837	884
40-44	1 690	812	878	1 704	822	882
45-49	1 483	701	782	1 658	792	866
50-54	1 285	597	688	1 450	681	769
55-59	1 055	478	576	1 249	575	674
60-64	880	387	493	1 014	454	560
65-69	677	285	393	831	359	472
70-74	501	201	300	621	254	367
75-79	353	138	215	439	169	270
80-84	233	88	144	283	104	179
85-89	132	48	84	159	55	104
90-94	60	20	40	69	22	47
95-99	17	5	12	21	6	15
100 +	2	0	2	3	1	2

POPULATION BY AGE AND SEX (in thousands)

Age group	1950 Both sexes	Males	Females	1955 Both sexes	Males	Females	1960 Both sexes	Males	Females	1965 Both sexes	Males	Females
All ages	2 758	1 376	1 382	2 985	1 496	1 488	3 248	1 635	1 613	3 591	1 814	1 778
0-4	488	248	240	461	235	226	510	261	249	606	310	296
5-9	365	184	181	414	211	203	394	202	192	440	226	214
10-14	316	159	156	352	178	174	399	204	195	380	195	185
15-19	279	141	138	306	155	151	341	173	168	387	198	189
20-24	245	123	122	267	135	132	292	148	144	326	165	161
25-29	213	107	106	232	117	115	253	128	125	277	140	137
30-34	183	91	92	201	101	101	219	111	109	239	121	118
35-39	156	78	78	173	86	87	190	95	95	207	104	103
40-44	131	65	66	146	73	74	162	81	81	178	89	89
45-49	109	53	56	122	60	62	136	67	69	151	75	76
50-54	88	42	46	100	48	51	112	54	57	125	61	64
55-59	69	32	37	78	37	41	89	42	46	100	48	52
60-64	51	23	27	58	27	31	66	31	35	75	35	40
65-69	34	15	19	39	18	21	45	20	24	51	24	28
70-74	19	8	11	22	10	12	26	12	14	30	14	16
75-79	8	3	5	10	4	6	11	5	6	14	6	8
80 +	3	1	2	3	1	2	4	2	2	5	2	3

Age group	1970 Both sexes	Males	Females	1975 Both sexes	Males	Females	1980 Both sexes	Males	Females	1985 Both sexes	Males	Females
All ages	4 008	2 030	1 978	4 212	2 139	2 073	4 798	2 442	2 356	5 386	2 746	2 640
0-4	701	359	342	718	368	350	837	429	408	933	478	454
5-9	528	271	257	584	300	284	648	333	315	746	384	362
10-14	426	219	207	484	249	235	574	295	278	629	324	305
15-19	368	190	179	390	201	189	476	246	231	558	288	270
20-24	370	190	181	332	171	161	380	196	184	459	237	222
25-29	310	157	153	334	171	163	322	166	156	364	187	176
30-34	263	133	130	279	141	137	323	165	158	307	158	149
35-39	227	115	112	236	119	116	269	136	133	308	158	150
40-44	195	98	97	202	102	100	226	114	112	255	129	126
45-49	167	83	84	173	86	86	193	97	96	213	107	106
50-54	139	68	71	145	72	74	162	80	82	179	89	90
55-59	112	54	58	118	57	61	133	65	69	147	72	75
60-64	85	40	45	91	43	48	104	49	54	116	56	60
65-69	59	27	31	64	30	34	74	35	39	84	39	44
70-74	35	16	19	39	18	21	46	21	25	52	24	28
75-79	16	7	9	19	8	10	23	10	12	26	12	14
80 +	6	3	3	7	3	4	9	4	5	11	5	6

Age group	1990 Both sexes	Males	Females	1995 Both sexes	Males	Females	2000 Both sexes	Males	Females	2005 Both sexes	Males	Females
All ages	6 217	3 174	3 043	7 525	3 846	3 678	8 434	4 316	4 118	9 402	4 818	4 584
0-4	1 091	560	531	1 347	692	654	1 450	746	704	1 590	819	771
5-9	859	442	417	1 060	546	514	1 234	636	598	1 338	690	648
10-14	740	381	359	888	457	430	1 020	525	494	1 185	611	574
15-19	625	323	303	765	394	370	854	440	414	979	505	474
20-24	549	283	266	642	331	311	730	377	354	814	420	394
25-29	449	231	218	559	288	271	607	313	294	687	355	332
30-34	356	183	173	455	234	221	527	272	255	566	293	273
35-39	300	154	146	360	185	175	428	221	208	490	253	237
40-44	299	153	146	304	156	148	338	173	165	399	205	194
45-49	246	124	122	300	152	147	283	145	139	314	160	153
50-54	203	101	102	244	122	122	277	140	138	261	132	128
55-59	167	82	85	197	97	100	222	109	112	252	126	126
60-64	132	64	68	156	76	81	174	84	89	196	95	101
65-69	97	46	51	116	55	61	130	62	68	146	70	76
70-74	61	28	33	76	35	41	87	41	47	100	46	53
75-79	31	14	17	39	18	22	48	21	26	57	26	31
80 +	13	6	7	17	7	10	23	10	13	30	13	17

United Nations Department of Economic and Social Affairs/Population Division
World Population Prospects: The 2004 Revision, Volume II: Sex and Age Distribution of the World Population

446

POPULATION BY AGE AND SEX (in thousands)

Age group	2005 Both sexes	2005 Males	2005 Females	2010 Both sexes	2010 Males	2010 Females	2015 Both sexes	2015 Males	2015 Females	2020 Both sexes	2020 Males	2020 Females
All ages	9 402	4 818	4 584	10 485	5 382	5 103	11 890	6 113	5 777	13 071	6 604	6 467
0-4	1 590	819	771	1 710	881	829	1 868	962	906	1 978	1 018	960
5-9	1 338	690	648	1 490	769	721	1 651	852	799	1 817	937	880
10-14	1 185	611	574	1 293	667	626	1 474	760	713	1 634	843	791
15-19	979	505	474	1 148	592	556	1 283	662	621	1 464	755	709
20-24	814	420	394	942	486	456	1 133	584	549	1 269	655	614
25-29	687	355	332	769	398	372	913	472	441	1 103	570	532
30-34	566	293	273	640	333	307	730	381	350	869	454	416
35-39	490	253	237	524	273	252	603	316	287	688	362	326
40-44	399	205	194	456	236	220	495	259	237	568	299	269
45-49	314	160	153	371	191	181	432	224	209	469	245	224
50-54	261	132	128	291	148	143	352	180	173	410	211	199
55-59	252	126	126	238	120	119	274	137	136	332	168	164
60-64	196	95	101	225	111	115	219	108	111	253	125	128
65-69	146	70	76	168	80	88	199	96	103	195	95	100
70-74	100	46	53	114	53	61	136	64	73	164	77	87
75-79	57	26	31	67	30	36	80	36	44	98	44	53
80-84	23	10	13	29	13	16	36	16	20	44	19	25
85-89	6	2	4	8	3	5	10	4	6	13	5	8
90-94	1	0	0	1	0	1	2	1	1	2	1	1
95-99	0	0	0	0	0	0	0	0	0	0	0	0
100 +	0	0	0	0	0	0	0	0	0	0	0	0

Age group	2025 Both sexes	2025 Males	2025 Females	2030 Both sexes	2030 Males	2030 Females	2035 Both sexes	2035 Males	2035 Females	2040 Both sexes	2040 Males	2040 Females
All ages	14 911	7 684	7 227	16 492	8 501	7 991	18 105	9 330	8 774	19 741	10 168	9 574
0-4	2 055	1 058	998	2 109	1 085	1 025	2 155	1 108	1 047	2 195	1 128	1 067
5-9	1 937	998	939	2 022	1 041	981	2 083	1 071	1 012	2 135	1 097	1 038
10-14	1 803	929	873	1 926	992	934	2 014	1 036	977	2 076	1 068	1 009
15-19	1 625	838	787	1 795	925	870	1 918	988	931	2 008	1 033	975
20-24	1 450	748	702	1 613	831	781	1 783	919	865	1 909	982	926
25-29	1 240	641	599	1 422	735	687	1 586	819	767	1 759	907	852
30-34	1 056	550	506	1 194	621	573	1 377	715	662	1 544	800	744
35-39	823	433	390	1 007	529	479	1 146	600	546	1 330	694	636
40-44	651	345	307	785	415	370	967	509	458	1 107	581	526
45-49	510	285	256	623	330	293	755	399	356	935	492	443
50-54	447	232	214	517	271	246	599	315	283	729	384	345
55-59	389	199	190	424	219	206	494	257	237	574	300	274
60-64	308	154	155	363	182	181	400	203	197	467	240	227
65-69	227	110	117	280	137	143	332	164	168	368	183	184
70-74	163	77	86	193	92	101	241	115	126	288	139	150
75-79	120	55	65	122	56	66	147	68	80	187	86	101
80-84	56	24	32	71	31	40	74	32	42	91	40	52
85-89	17	7	10	22	9	13	29	12	17	31	13	19
90-94	3	1	2	4	1	2	5	2	3	7	3	5
95-99	0	0	0	0	0	0	0	0	0	1	0	0
100 +	0	0	0	0	0	0	0	0	0	0	0	0

Age group	2045 Both sexes	2045 Males	2045 Females	2050 Both sexes	2050 Males	2050 Females
All ages	21 378	11 000	10 377	22 987	11 814	11 172
0-4	2 219	1 140	1 079	2 221	1 140	1 081
5-9	2 178	1 119	1 059	2 205	1 132	1 073
10-14	2 129	1 094	1 035	2 174	1 116	1 057
15-19	2 071	1 065	1 007	2 125	1 091	1 033
20-24	1 999	1 028	971	2 064	1 060	1 004
25-29	1 887	972	915	1 981	1 019	962
30-34	1 721	890	831	1 853	957	896
35-39	1 501	780	720	1 681	872	809
40-44	1 292	675	617	1 465	763	702
45-49	1 076	564	512	1 261	658	603
50-54	907	475	432	1 047	547	500
55-59	703	367	336	877	456	421
60-64	546	282	265	671	346	325
65-69	433	218	215	509	258	251
70-74	323	157	166	383	188	195
75-79	227	105	122	258	121	137
80-84	118	51	67	147	64	83
85-89	40	16	24	54	21	32
90-94	8	3	5	11	4	7
95-99	1	0	1	1	0	1
100 +	0	0	0	0	0	0

POPULATION BY AGE AND SEX (in thousands)

Age group	2005 Both sexes	2005 Males	2005 Females	2010 Both sexes	2010 Males	2010 Females	2015 Both sexes	2015 Males	2015 Females	2020 Both sexes	2020 Males	2020 Females
All ages	9 402	4 818	4 584	10 565	5 423	5 141	12 116	6 230	5 886	13 812	7 111	6 701
0-4	1 590	819	771	1 790	922	868	2 017	1 039	978	2 198	1 131	1 066
5-9	1 338	690	648	1 490	769	721	1 728	891	837	1 962	1 012	951
10-14	1 185	611	574	1 293	667	626	1 474	760	713	1 710	882	828
15-19	979	505	474	1 148	592	556	1 283	662	621	1 464	755	709
20-24	814	420	394	942	486	456	1 133	584	549	1 269	655	614
25-29	687	355	332	769	398	372	913	472	441	1 103	570	532
30-34	566	293	273	640	333	307	730	381	350	869	454	416
35-39	490	253	237	524	273	252	603	316	287	688	362	326
40-44	399	205	194	456	236	220	495	259	237	568	299	269
45-49	314	160	153	371	191	181	432	224	209	469	245	224
50-54	261	132	128	291	148	143	352	180	173	410	211	199
55-59	252	126	126	238	120	119	274	137	136	332	168	164
60-64	196	95	101	225	111	115	219	108	111	253	125	128
65-69	146	70	76	168	80	88	199	96	103	195	95	100
70-74	100	46	53	114	53	61	136	64	73	164	77	87
75-79	57	26	31	67	30	36	80	36	44	98	44	53
80-84	23	10	13	29	13	16	36	16	20	44	19	25
85-89	6	2	4	8	3	5	10	4	6	13	5	8
90-94	1	0	0	1	0	1	2	1	1	2	1	1
95-99	0	0	0	0	0	0	0	0	0	0	0	0
100 +	0	0	0	0	0	0	0	0	0	0	0	0

Age group	2025 Both sexes	2025 Males	2025 Females	2030 Both sexes	2030 Males	2030 Females	2035 Both sexes	2035 Males	2035 Females	2040 Both sexes	2040 Males	2040 Females
All ages	15 612	8 045	7 567	17 525	9 033	8 493	19 571	10 085	9 486	21 754	11 203	10 551
0-4	2 321	1 195	1 127	2 448	1 259	1 189	2 596	1 335	1 262	2 751	1 414	1 338
5-9	2 152	1 109	1 043	2 284	1 176	1 109	2 418	1 244	1 174	2 571	1 321	1 250
10-14	1 947	1 004	943	2 140	1 102	1 038	2 275	1 170	1 104	2 410	1 239	1 171
15-19	1 701	877	824	1 938	999	939	2 132	1 098	1 034	2 268	1 166	1 101
20-24	1 450	748	702	1 688	870	818	1 926	992	934	2 121	1 091	1 029
25-29	1 240	641	599	1 422	735	687	1 660	857	803	1 900	980	920
30-34	1 056	550	506	1 194	621	573	1 377	715	662	1 616	838	779
35-39	823	433	390	1 007	529	479	1 146	600	546	1 330	694	636
40-44	651	345	307	785	415	370	967	509	458	1 107	581	526
45-49	540	285	256	623	330	293	755	399	356	935	492	443
50-54	447	232	214	517	271	246	599	315	283	729	384	345
55-59	388	198	190	424	219	206	494	257	237	574	300	274
60-64	308	154	155	363	182	181	400	203	197	467	240	227
65-69	227	110	117	280	137	143	332	164	168	368	183	184
70-74	163	77	86	193	92	101	241	115	126	288	139	150
75-79	120	55	65	122	56	66	147	68	80	187	86	101
80-84	56	24	32	71	31	40	74	32	42	91	40	52
85-89	17	7	10	22	9	13	29	12	17	31	13	19
90-94	3	1	2	4	1	2	5	2	3	7	3	5
95-99	0	0	0	0	0	0	0	0	0	1	0	0
100 +	0	0	0	0	0	0	0	0	0	0	0	0

Age group	2045 Both sexes	2045 Males	2045 Females	2050 Both sexes	2050 Males	2050 Females
All ages	24 044	12 371	11 672	26 407	13 573	12 834
0-4	2 886	1 482	1 403	2 992	1 536	1 456
5-9	2 731	1 403	1 328	2 868	1 473	1 395
10-14	2 565	1 318	1 247	2 725	1 400	1 326
15-19	2 404	1 236	1 169	2 560	1 315	1 245
20-24	2 258	1 161	1 097	2 396	1 231	1 165
25-29	2 097	1 080	1 017	2 238	1 151	1 086
30-34	1 859	962	897	2 060	1 064	996
35-39	1 571	817	754	1 816	942	874
40-44	1 292	675	617	1 533	799	735
45-49	1 076	564	512	1 261	658	603
50-54	907	475	432	1 047	547	500
55-59	703	367	336	877	456	421
60-64	546	282	265	671	346	325
65-69	433	218	215	509	258	251
70-74	323	157	166	383	188	195
75-79	227	105	122	258	121	137
80-84	118	51	67	147	64	83
85-89	40	16	24	54	21	32
90-94	8	3	5	11	4	7
95-99	1	0	1	1	0	1
100 +	0	0	0	0	0	0

United Nations Department of Economic and Social Affairs/Population Division
World Population Prospects: The 2004 Revision, Volume II: Sex and Age Distribution of the World Population

448

POPULATION BY AGE AND SEX (in thousands)

Age group	2005			2010			2015			2020		
	Both sexes	Males	Females	Both sexes	Males	Females	Both sexes	Males	Females	Both sexes	Males	Females
All ages	9 402	4 818	4 584	10 405	5 341	5 064	11 664	5 997	5 667	12 930	6 657	6 273
0-4	1 590	819	771	1 630	840	790	1 719	885	833	1 758	905	853
5-9	1 338	690	648	1 490	769	721	1 574	812	762	1 672	862	810
10-14	1 185	611	574	1 293	667	626	1 474	760	713	1 558	804	754
15-19	979	505	474	1 148	592	556	1 283	662	621	1 464	755	709
20-24	814	420	394	942	486	456	1 133	584	549	1 269	655	614
25-29	687	355	332	769	398	372	913	472	441	1 103	570	532
30-34	566	293	273	640	333	307	730	381	350	869	454	416
35-39	490	253	237	524	273	252	603	316	287	688	362	326
40-44	399	205	194	456	236	220	495	259	237	568	299	269
45-49	314	160	153	371	191	181	432	224	209	469	245	224
50-54	261	132	128	291	148	143	352	180	173	410	211	199
55-59	252	126	126	238	120	119	274	137	136	332	168	164
60-64	196	95	101	225	111	115	219	108	111	253	125	128
65-69	146	70	76	168	80	88	199	96	103	195	95	100
70-74	100	46	53	114	53	61	136	64	73	164	77	87
75-79	57	26	31	67	30	36	80	36	44	98	44	53
80-84	23	10	13	29	13	16	36	16	20	44	19	25
85-89	6	2	4	8	3	5	10	4	6	13	5	8
90-94	1	0	0	1	0	1	2	1	1	2	1	1
95-99	0	0	0	0	0	0	0	0	0	0	0	0
100 +	0	0	0	0	0	0	0	0	0	0	0	0

Age group	2025			2030			2035			2040		
	Both sexes	Males	Females	Both sexes	Males	Females	Both sexes	Males	Females	Both sexes	Males	Females
All ages	14 212	7 323	6 888	15 471	7 975	7 496	16 679	8 597	8 082	17 822	9 180	8 641
0-4	1 791	922	870	1 781	916	865	1 743	896	847	1 691	869	822
5-9	1 722	887	835	1 763	907	855	1 759	905	854	1 726	887	839
10-14	1 659	855	804	1 711	881	830	1 755	903	852	1 753	901	852
15-19	1 549	799	750	1 651	851	800	1 705	878	827	1 749	900	850
20-24	1 450	748	702	1 537	792	745	1 641	845	795	1 696	873	823
25-29	1 240	641	599	1 422	735	687	1 512	780	731	1 618	835	784
30-34	1 056	550	506	1 194	621	573	1 377	715	662	1 472	763	709
35-39	823	433	390	1 007	529	479	1 146	600	546	1 330	694	636
40-44	651	345	307	785	415	370	967	509	458	1 107	581	526
45-49	540	285	256	623	330	293	755	399	356	935	492	443
50-54	447	232	214	517	271	246	599	315	283	729	384	345
55-59	388	198	190	424	219	206	494	257	237	574	300	274
60-64	308	154	155	363	182	181	400	203	197	467	240	227
65-69	227	110	117	280	137	143	332	164	168	368	183	184
70-74	163	77	86	193	92	101	241	115	126	288	139	150
75-79	120	55	65	122	56	66	147	68	80	187	86	101
80-84	56	24	32	71	31	40	74	32	42	91	40	52
85-89	17	7	10	22	9	13	29	12	17	31	13	19
90-94	3	1	2	4	1	2	5	2	3	7	3	5
95-99	0	0	0	0	0	0	0	0	0	1	0	0
100 +	0	0	0	0	0	0	0	0	0	0	0	0

Age group	2045			2050		
	Both sexes	Males	Females	Both sexes	Males	Females
All ages	18 885	9 719	9 167	19 853	10 203	9 650
0-4	1 632	838	794	1 563	803	761
5-9	1 678	862	816	1 622	833	789
10-14	1 721	884	837	1 675	860	815
15-19	1 749	899	850	1 717	882	835
20-24	1 742	895	846	1 742	895	847
25-29	1 677	864	813	1 726	888	838
30-34	1 583	819	764	1 647	850	796
35-39	1 430	744	686	1 547	802	744
40-44	1 292	675	617	1 396	727	669
45-49	1 076	564	512	1 261	658	603
50-54	907	475	432	1 047	547	500
55-59	703	367	336	877	456	421
60-64	546	282	265	671	346	325
65-69	433	218	215	509	258	251
70-74	323	157	166	383	188	195
75-79	227	105	122	258	121	137
80-84	118	51	67	147	64	83
85-89	40	16	24	54	21	32
90-94	8	3	5	11	4	7
95-99	1	0	1	1	0	1
100 +	0	0	0	0	0	0

POPULATION BY AGE AND SEX (in thousands)

Age group	1950 Both sexes	1950 Males	1950 Females	1955 Both sexes	1955 Males	1955 Females	1960 Both sexes	1960 Males	1960 Females	1965 Both sexes	1965 Males	1965 Females
All ages	505	250	255	528	261	267	554	273	281	558	275	283
0-4	74	37	37	82	41	41	86	43	43	91	45	46
5-9	60	30	30	62	31	31	69	34	35	68	34	34
10-14	54	27	27	55	28	28	57	29	29	61	30	31
15-19	50	25	25	50	25	25	52	26	26	51	26	26
20-24	45	23	23	46	23	23	47	24	24	46	23	23
25-29	41	20	21	42	21	21	43	21	22	42	21	21
30-34	37	19	19	38	19	19	39	19	19	38	19	19
35-39	34	17	17	34	17	17	35	17	17	34	17	17
40-44	27	14	14	30	15	15	31	15	16	30	15	15
45-49	21	10	11	24	12	12	27	13	14	26	13	13
50-54	18	9	10	19	9	10	22	10	11	23	11	12
55-59	14	6	7	16	7	8	16	8	8	18	8	9
60-64	11	5	6	11	5	6	13	6	7	12	6	7
65-69	9	4	5	8	4	5	8	4	5	9	4	5
70-74	6	3	3	6	2	3	5	2	3	5	2	3
75-79	3	1	2	3	1	2	3	1	2	3	1	2
80 +	2	1	1	1	1	1	1	1	1	1	1	1

Age group	1970 Both sexes	1970 Males	1970 Females	1975 Both sexes	1975 Males	1975 Females	1980 Both sexes	1980 Males	1980 Females	1985 Both sexes	1985 Males	1985 Females
All ages	584	287	297	651	320	331	793	390	403	891	439	452
0-4	101	50	50	119	60	60	144	72	72	163	81	81
5-9	75	37	38	87	43	44	114	57	57	127	63	64
10-14	62	31	31	71	35	36	91	45	46	109	54	55
15-19	56	28	28	60	30	30	75	37	38	88	44	44
20-24	47	23	23	54	26	27	63	31	32	72	36	37
25-29	42	21	21	44	22	22	56	27	28	60	29	30
30-34	37	19	19	40	20	20	46	23	23	53	26	27
35-39	34	17	17	35	17	18	41	20	21	44	22	22
40-44	30	15	15	31	15	16	36	18	18	38	19	19
45-49	26	13	13	27	13	14	32	15	16	33	16	17
50-54	23	11	12	24	11	12	27	13	14	29	14	15
55-59	19	9	10	20	9	10	23	11	12	24	11	13
60-64	14	7	7	16	8	9	18	9	10	19	9	10
65-69	9	4	5	11	5	6	14	6	8	15	7	8
70-74	6	3	3	6	3	4	8	4	5	10	4	5
75-79	3	1	2	3	1	2	4	2	2	5	2	3
80 +	1	1	1	1	1	1	2	1	1	2	1	1

Age group	1990 Both sexes	1990 Males	1990 Females	1995 Both sexes	1995 Males	1995 Females	2000 Both sexes	2000 Males	2000 Females	2005 Both sexes	2005 Males	2005 Females
All ages	1 016	500	515	1 189	586	603	1 366	674	692	1 586	784	803
0-4	190	95	95	227	114	114	265	133	132	310	156	155
5-9	146	73	73	175	87	88	206	103	103	244	122	122
10-14	123	61	62	143	71	72	168	84	84	200	100	100
15-19	106	53	53	122	60	61	139	69	70	164	82	82
20-24	85	42	43	105	52	53	117	58	59	134	67	68
25-29	69	34	35	83	41	42	99	49	50	111	55	56
30-34	57	28	29	67	33	34	79	38	40	93	46	47
35-39	50	25	26	55	27	28	63	31	32	73	36	37
40-44	41	20	21	48	24	25	52	25	27	59	29	30
45-49	36	17	18	39	19	20	45	22	23	48	23	25
50-54	31	15	16	34	16	17	36	17	19	42	20	22
55-59	26	12	14	28	13	15	30	14	16	33	16	17
60-64	21	10	11	23	11	12	25	12	13	27	13	14
65-69	16	7	9	17	8	9	19	9	10	21	9	11
70-74	10	5	6	12	5	6	13	6	7	14	6	8
75-79	6	2	3	7	3	4	7	3	4	8	4	5
80 +	3	1	2	3	1	2	4	2	3	5	2	3

United Nations Department of Economic and Social Affairs/Population Division
World Population Prospects: The 2004 Revision, Volume II: Sex and Age Distribution of the World Population

450

POPULATION BY AGE AND SEX (in thousands)

Age group	2005 Both sexes	Males	Females	2010 Both sexes	Males	Females	2015 Both sexes	Males	Females	2020 Both sexes	Males	Females
All ages	1 586	784	803	1 835	908	927	2 133	1 058	1 076	2 479	1 231	1 248
0-4	310	156	155	361	181	180	411	206	204	463	233	230
5-9	244	122	122	285	142	143	337	168	168	387	193	193
10-14	200	100	100	235	117	118	277	138	138	328	164	164
15-19	164	82	82	194	97	97	230	115	115	271	135	136
20-24	134	67	68	158	79	80	189	94	95	224	111	112
25-29	111	55	56	127	63	64	151	75	76	181	90	91
30-34	93	46	47	103	51	52	120	59	60	143	71	72
35-39	73	36	37	85	42	43	95	47	48	112	56	56
40-44	59	29	30	67	33	34	79	39	40	89	44	45
45-49	48	23	25	54	26	28	62	30	32	74	36	37
50-54	42	20	22	44	21	23	50	24	26	58	28	30
55-59	33	16	17	38	18	20	40	19	21	46	22	24
60-64	27	13	14	29	14	15	34	16	18	36	17	19
65-69	21	9	11	22	10	12	24	11	13	28	13	15
70-74	14	6	8	16	7	9	17	8	9	19	9	10
75-79	8	4	5	9	4	5	10	5	6	12	5	7
80-84	4	2	2	4	2	3	5	2	3	6	2	3
85-89	1	0	1	1	1	1	2	1	1	2	1	1
90-94	0	0	0	0	0	0	0	0	0	0	0	0
95-99	0	0	0	0	0	0	0	0	0	0	0	0
100 +	0	0	0	0	0	0	0	0	0	0	0	0

Age group	2025 Both sexes	Males	Females	2030 Both sexes	Males	Females	2035 Both sexes	Males	Females	2040 Both sexes	Males	Females
All ages	2 875	1 429	1 446	3 317	1 650	1 667	3 793	1 888	1 905	4 288	2 135	2 153
0-4	518	261	258	570	287	283	610	307	303	635	320	315
5-9	440	220	220	496	249	247	549	275	273	591	297	294
10-14	378	189	189	432	216	216	488	244	244	541	271	270
15-19	322	161	161	372	186	186	425	213	213	482	241	241
20-24	264	132	133	315	157	158	365	182	183	418	208	210
25-29	216	107	109	256	127	129	306	152	154	356	177	179
30-34	173	86	87	207	103	104	247	122	124	297	147	149
35-39	135	67	68	164	82	82	198	98	99	237	118	119
40-44	105	52	53	128	64	64	150	78	79	190	94	95
45-49	83	41	42	99	49	50	122	60	61	150	74	75
50-54	69	34	35	78	39	40	94	46	48	116	57	59
55-59	54	26	28	64	31	33	73	36	37	88	43	45
60-64	42	19	22	49	23	26	58	28	30	67	32	35
65-69	31	14	17	36	16	19	42	20	23	51	24	27
70-74	22	10	12	25	11	14	29	13	16	34	16	19
75-79	13	6	7	16	7	9	18	8	10	21	9	12
80-84	7	3	4	7	3	4	9	4	5	10	4	6
85-89	2	1	1	3	1	2	3	1	2	4	2	2
90-94	1	0	0	1	0	0	1	0	0	1	0	1
95-99	0	0	0	0	0	0	0	0	0	0	0	0
100 +	0	0	0	0	0	0	0	0	0	0	0	0

Age group	2045 Both sexes	Males	Females	2050 Both sexes	Males	Females
All ages	4 794	2 387	2 407	5 312	2 644	2 668
0-4	652	328	323	669	337	332
5-9	618	310	307	637	320	317
10-14	584	293	291	612	307	305
15-19	535	268	267	578	290	289
20-24	474	237	238	528	264	264
25-29	409	203	206	466	232	234
30-34	346	172	174	400	198	201
35-39	287	142	145	337	167	170
40-44	229	114	115	279	138	141
45-49	182	90	92	221	109	112
50-54	143	70	72	175	86	89
55-59	109	53	56	135	66	69
60-64	81	39	42	101	49	52
65-69	59	28	31	72	34	38
70-74	42	19	22	49	23	26
75-79	25	11	14	31	14	17
80-84	13	5	7	15	7	9
85-89	5	2	3	6	2	3
90-94	1	0	1	1	1	1
95-99	0	0	0	0	0	0
100 +	0	0	0	0	0	0

POPULATION BY AGE AND SEX (in thousands)

Age group	2005			2010			2015			2020		
	Both sexes	Males	Females	Both sexes	Males	Females	Both sexes	Males	Females	Both sexes	Males	Females
All ages	1 586	784	803	1 837	909	928	2 156	1 069	1 087	2 537	1 260	1 277
0-4	310	156	155	363	182	181	432	217	215	500	251	249
5-9	244	122	122	285	142	143	338	169	169	407	204	203
10-14	200	100	100	235	117	118	277	138	138	329	165	165
15-19	164	82	82	194	97	97	230	115	115	271	135	136
20-24	134	67	68	158	79	80	189	94	95	224	111	112
25-29	111	55	56	127	63	64	151	75	76	181	90	91
30-34	93	46	47	103	51	52	120	59	60	143	71	72
35-39	73	36	37	85	42	43	95	47	48	112	56	56
40-44	59	29	30	67	33	34	79	39	40	89	44	45
45-49	48	23	25	54	26	28	62	30	32	74	36	37
50-54	42	20	22	44	21	23	50	24	26	58	28	30
55-59	33	16	17	38	18	20	40	19	21	46	22	24
60-64	27	13	14	29	14	15	34	16	18	36	17	19
65-69	21	9	11	22	10	12	24	11	13	28	13	15
70-74	14	6	8	16	7	9	17	8	9	19	9	10
75-79	8	4	5	9	4	5	10	5	6	12	5	7
80-84	4	2	2	4	2	3	5	2	3	6	2	3
85-89	1	0	1	1	1	1	2	1	1	2	1	1
90-94	0	0	0	0	0	0	0	0	0	0	0	0
95-99	0	0	0	0	0	0	0	0	0	0	0	0
100 +	0	0	0	0	0	0	0	0	0	0	0	0

Age group	2025			2030			2035			2040		
	Both sexes	Males	Females	Both sexes	Males	Females	Both sexes	Males	Females	Both sexes	Males	Females
All ages	2 976	1 480	1 496	3 472	1 728	1 744	4 023	2 004	2 020	4 622	2 302	2 319
0-4	563	283	280	627	316	312	689	347	342	743	374	369
5-9	475	238	237	539	270	269	604	303	301	667	335	332
10-14	398	199	199	466	233	233	530	266	265	596	299	297
15-19	323	161	162	392	196	196	459	230	230	524	262	262
20-24	264	132	133	316	158	159	384	191	193	451	225	226
25-29	216	107	109	256	127	129	308	153	155	375	186	189
30-34	173	86	87	207	103	104	247	122	124	298	148	150
35-39	135	67	68	164	82	82	198	98	99	237	118	119
40-44	105	52	53	128	64	64	156	78	79	190	94	95
45-49	83	41	42	99	49	50	122	60	61	150	74	75
50-54	69	34	35	78	39	40	94	46	48	116	57	59
55-59	54	26	28	64	31	33	73	36	37	88	43	45
60-64	42	19	22	49	23	26	58	28	30	67	32	35
65-69	31	14	17	36	16	19	42	20	23	51	24	27
70-74	22	10	12	25	11	14	29	13	16	34	16	19
75-79	13	6	7	16	7	9	18	8	10	21	9	12
80-84	7	3	4	7	3	4	9	4	5	10	4	6
85-89	2	1	1	3	1	2	3	1	2	4	2	2
90-94	1	0	0	1	0	0	1	0	0	1	0	1
95-99	0	0	0	0	0	0	0	0	0	0	0	0
100 +	0	0	0	0	0	0	0	0	0	0	0	0

Age group	2045			2050		
	Both sexes	Males	Females	Both sexes	Males	Females
All ages	5 261	2 621	2 640	5 939	2 958	2 981
0-4	791	398	392	837	422	415
5-9	723	363	360	773	388	384
10-14	659	331	329	716	359	357
15-19	589	295	294	653	327	326
20-24	515	257	258	581	290	291
25-29	442	220	222	506	252	254
30-34	365	181	184	432	214	217
35-39	288	143	145	355	176	179
40-44	229	114	115	280	139	141
45-49	182	90	92	221	109	112
50-54	143	70	72	175	86	89
55-59	109	53	56	135	66	69
60-64	81	39	42	101	49	52
65-69	59	28	31	72	34	38
70-74	42	19	22	49	23	26
75-79	25	11	14	31	14	17
80-84	13	5	7	15	7	9
85-89	5	2	3	6	2	3
90-94	1	0	1	1	1	1
95-99	0	0	0	0	0	0
100 +	0	0	0	0	0	0

United Nations Department of Economic and Social Affairs/Population Division
World Population Prospects: The 2004 Revision, Volume II: Sex and Age Distribution of the World Population

452

POPULATION BY AGE AND SEX (in thousands)

Age group	2005 Both sexes	Males	Females	2010 Both sexes	Males	Females	2015 Both sexes	Males	Females	2020 Both sexes	Males	Females
All ages	1 588	784	804	1 822	902	920	2 097	1 040	1 057	2 408	1 195	1 213
0-4	310	156	155	349	175	174	386	194	192	426	214	212
5-9	244	122	122	285	142	143	325	162	162	364	182	182
10-14	200	100	100	235	117	118	277	138	138	316	158	158
15-19	164	82	82	194	97	97	230	115	115	271	135	136
20-24	134	67	68	158	79	80	189	94	95	224	111	112
25-29	111	55	56	127	63	64	151	75	76	181	90	91
30-34	93	46	47	103	51	52	120	59	60	143	71	72
35-39	73	36	37	85	42	43	95	47	48	112	56	56
40-44	59	29	30	67	33	34	79	39	40	89	44	45
45-49	48	23	25	54	26	28	62	30	32	74	36	37
50-54	42	20	22	44	21	23	50	24	26	58	28	30
55-59	33	16	17	38	18	20	40	19	21	46	22	24
60-64	27	13	14	29	14	15	34	16	18	36	17	19
65-69	21	9	11	22	10	12	24	11	13	28	13	15
70-74	14	6	8	16	7	9	17	8	9	19	9	10
75-79	8	4	5	9	4	5	10	5	6	12	5	7
80-84	4	2	2	4	2	3	5	2	3	6	2	3
85-89	1	0	1	1	1	1	2	1	1	2	1	1
90-94	0	0	0	0	0	0	0	0	0	0	0	0
95-99	0	0	0	0	0	0	0	0	0	0	0	0
100 +	0	0	0	0	0	0	0	0	0	0	0	0

Age group	2025 Both sexes	Males	Females	2030 Both sexes	Males	Females	2035 Both sexes	Males	Females	2040 Both sexes	Males	Females
All ages	2 760	1 371	1 389	3 144	1 563	1 581	3 542	1 762	1 780	3 936	1 958	1 977
0-4	472	238	235	509	256	253	528	266	262	528	266	262
5-9	405	203	202	452	227	225	490	246	244	511	257	254
10-14	355	178	178	397	199	198	445	223	222	483	242	241
15-19	310	155	155	350	175	175	392	196	196	439	220	219
20-24	264	132	133	304	151	153	343	171	172	385	192	193
25-29	216	107	109	256	127	129	295	147	149	335	166	168
30-34	173	86	87	207	103	104	247	122	124	286	142	144
35-39	135	67	68	164	82	82	198	98	99	237	118	119
40-44	105	52	53	128	64	64	156	78	79	190	94	95
45-49	83	41	42	99	49	50	122	60	61	150	74	76
50-54	69	34	35	78	39	40	94	46	48	116	57	59
55-59	54	26	28	64	31	33	73	36	37	88	43	45
60-64	42	19	22	49	23	26	58	28	30	67	32	35
65-69	31	14	17	36	16	19	42	20	23	51	24	27
70-74	22	10	12	25	11	14	29	13	16	34	16	19
75-79	13	6	7	16	7	9	18	8	10	21	9	12
80-84	7	3	4	7	3	4	9	4	5	10	4	6
85-89	2	1	1	3	1	2	3	1	2	4	2	2
90-94	1	0	0	1	0	0	1	0	0	1	0	1
95-99	0	0	0	0	0	0	0	0	0	0	0	0
100 +	0	0	0	0	0	0	0	0	0	0	0	0

Age group	2045 Both sexes	Males	Females	2050 Both sexes	Males	Females
All ages	4 318	2 148	2 170	4 690	2 332	2 358
0-4	522	263	259	516	260	256
5-9	514	258	256	510	256	254
10-14	505	253	252	509	255	254
15-19	478	239	239	500	251	249
20-24	432	216	216	471	235	236
25-29	377	187	189	424	211	213
30-34	325	162	164	368	183	185
35-39	277	137	140	317	157	160
40-44	229	114	115	269	133	136
45-49	182	90	92	221	109	112
50-54	143	70	72	175	86	89
55-59	109	53	56	135	66	69
60-64	81	39	42	101	49	52
65-69	59	28	31	72	34	38
70-74	42	19	22	49	23	26
75-79	25	11	14	31	14	17
80-84	13	5	7	15	7	9
85-89	5	2	3	6	2	3
90-94	1	0	1	1	1	1
95-99	0	0	0	0	0	0
100 +	0	0	0	0	0	0

POPULATION BY AGE AND SEX (in thousands)

Age group	1950			1955			1960			1965		
	Both sexes	Males	Females	Both sexes	Males	Females	Both sexes	Males	Females	Both sexes	Males	Females
All ages	423	206	217	486	237	249	569	278	291	645	322	323
0-4	77	37	40	97	48	49	115	57	58	117	59	58
5-9	54	26	28	71	34	37	92	45	47	99	50	49
10-14	43	20	23	52	25	27	69	33	36	87	44	43
15-19	40	19	20	41	20	22	50	23	26	67	34	33
20-24	36	18	18	38	19	20	39	19	20	49	24	25
25-29	32	16	16	34	16	17	37	18	19	40	20	20
30-34	27	14	14	31	15	15	33	16	17	34	16	18
35-39	26	14	12	26	13	13	28	15	14	31	15	15
40-44	19	10	9	23	12	11	24	13	12	27	14	14
45-49	18	9	9	17	9	9	22	12	11	23	12	11
50-54	12	7	6	17	9	9	16	8	7	20	10	10
55-59	11	5	7	11	6	5	15	7	7	16	8	8
60-64	9	5	5	10	4	5	11	5	5	13	7	6
65-69	8	3	5	8	3	4	8	3	5	9	4	5
70-74	6	2	3	5	2	3	5	2	3	6	2	4
75-79	3	1	2	3	1	2	3	1	2	3	1	2
80 +	2	1	1	2	1	1	2	1	1	3	1	2

Age group	1970			1975			1980			1985		
	Both sexes	Males	Females	Both sexes	Males	Females	Both sexes	Males	Females	Both sexes	Males	Females
All ages	709	353	357	734	364	370	761	377	384	754	370	383
0-4	122	62	61	110	55	55	105	52	52	101	51	50
5-9	114	57	57	110	55	55	104	52	52	97	48	48
10-14	102	51	51	104	52	52	104	52	51	97	49	48
15-19	80	40	40	88	44	45	97	48	49	92	46	46
20-24	57	28	29	67	33	35	78	38	40	80	38	41
25-29	40	20	21	49	24	25	58	29	29	63	30	33
30-34	33	16	17	39	19	20	44	22	23	48	24	25
35-39	32	15	16	33	16	17	34	16	17	38	18	20
40-44	28	14	14	28	14	14	28	14	14	29	14	15
45-49	25	13	12	25	13	13	26	13	13	24	11	12
50-54	20	10	10	22	11	11	23	12	12	21	10	11
55-59	18	10	9	18	9	9	18	9	9	19	9	9
60-64	13	6	6	13	7	7	14	7	7	15	8	8
65-69	11	5	6	12	6	6	13	6	6	11	6	6
70-74	6	3	3	7	3	4	8	4	4	10	5	5
75-79	4	2	3	5	2	3	5	2	3	5	2	3
80 +	3	1	2	3	1	2	4	2	3	4	2	3

Age group	1990			1995			2000			2005		
	Both sexes	Males	Females	Both sexes	Males	Females	Both sexes	Males	Females	Both sexes	Males	Females
All ages	729	355	374	732	355	377	744	361	383	751	364	387
0-4	84	43	41	81	41	40	80	41	40	75	38	37
5-9	93	47	46	77	39	38	75	38	37	75	38	37
10-14	90	45	45	88	44	43	73	37	36	70	36	35
15-19	86	42	43	85	42	43	83	42	41	68	34	34
20-24	75	36	38	80	39	40	79	39	40	77	39	38
25-29	64	30	34	67	32	35	73	36	37	73	36	37
30-34	53	24	29	57	26	31	59	28	31	66	32	34
35-39	42	20	22	46	21	25	51	23	28	53	26	28
40-44	33	16	17	36	17	19	42	19	23	47	21	26
45-49	24	11	13	29	13	15	32	15	17	38	17	21
50-54	19	9	10	21	10	11	26	12	14	30	14	16
55-59	17	8	9	17	8	9	19	8	10	23	10	13
60-64	15	7	8	15	7	8	15	7	8	17	7	9
65-69	13	6	7	13	6	7	13	6	7	13	6	7
70-74	9	4	5	10	5	6	11	5	6	11	4	6
75-79	7	3	4	6	3	4	7	3	4	8	3	5
80 +	5	2	3	6	2	3	6	3	4	7	3	5

United Nations Department of Economic and Social Affairs/Population Division
World Population Prospects: The 2004 Revision, Volume II: Sex and Age Distribution of the World Population

POPULATION BY AGE AND SEX (in thousands)

Age group	2005 Both sexes	2005 Males	2005 Females	2010 Both sexes	2010 Males	2010 Females	2015 Both sexes	2015 Males	2015 Females	2020 Both sexes	2020 Males	2020 Females
All ages	751	364	387	751	364	387	742	360	382	725	351	374
0-4	75	38	37	66	34	33	57	29	28	50	25	24
5-9	75	38	37	70	36	35	61	31	30	52	27	26
10-14	70	36	35	71	36	35	66	33	32	57	29	28
15-19	68	34	34	66	33	33	66	33	33	61	31	30
20-24	77	39	38	63	32	31	60	30	30	60	31	30
25-29	73	36	37	71	36	35	57	29	28	55	28	27
30-34	66	32	34	66	33	34	64	32	32	51	26	25
35-39	53	26	28	61	30	31	61	30	31	59	30	29
40-44	47	21	26	50	24	26	57	28	29	57	28	29
45-49	38	17	21	43	19	24	46	22	24	53	26	28
50-54	30	14	16	35	15	20	40	18	22	43	20	23
55-59	23	10	13	27	12	15	33	14	19	37	16	21
60-64	17	7	9	21	9	12	25	11	14	30	13	18
65-69	13	6	7	15	6	9	19	8	11	22	10	13
70-74	11	4	6	11	4	6	12	5	8	16	7	10
75-79	8	3	5	8	3	5	8	3	5	10	4	6
80-84	5	2	3	5	2	3	5	2	3	6	2	4
85-89	2	1	1	2	1	2	3	1	2	3	1	2
90-94	1	0	0	1	0	0	1	0	1	1	0	1
95-99	0	0	0	0	0	0	0	0	0	0	0	0
100 +	0	0	0	0	0	0	0	0	0	0	0	0

Age group	2025 Both sexes	2025 Males	2025 Females	2030 Both sexes	2030 Males	2030 Females	2035 Both sexes	2035 Males	2035 Females	2040 Both sexes	2040 Males	2040 Females
All ages	703	341	363	676	328	349	641	311	331	598	290	309
0-4	46	24	23	43	22	21	38	19	18	31	16	15
5-9	45	23	22	42	21	21	38	20	19	33	17	16
10-14	48	24	24	41	21	20	38	19	19	34	18	17
15-19	52	27	26	44	22	21	37	19	18	33	17	16
20-24	56	28	27	47	24	23	38	20	19	32	16	15
25-29	55	28	27	50	26	25	42	21	21	33	17	16
30-34	49	25	24	49	25	24	44	23	22	36	19	18
35-39	46	23	23	44	22	22	44	23	22	40	20	20
40-44	56	28	20	43	22	21	41	21	20	42	21	20
45-49	54	26	27	52	26	26	40	20	20	38	19	19
50-54	50	24	26	51	25	26	49	24	25	37	19	19
55-59	40	19	22	47	22	25	48	23	25	46	23	24
60-64	35	15	20	38	17	21	44	20	24	45	21	24
65-69	28	11	16	32	13	19	34	15	19	40	18	22
70-74	19	8	11	24	9	15	28	11	17	30	13	17
75-79	13	5	8	15	6	9	19	7	12	23	8	14
80-84	7	2	4	9	3	6	11	4	7	14	5	9
85-89	3	1	2	4	1	3	5	2	4	7	2	4
90-94	1	0	1	1	0	1	2	0	1	2	1	2
95-99	0	0	0	0	0	0	0	0	0	1	0	0
100 +	0	0	0	0	0	0	0	0	0	0	0	0

Age group	2045 Both sexes	2045 Males	2045 Females	2050 Both sexes	2050 Males	2050 Females
All ages	547	265	282	488	236	252
0-4	25	13	12	20	10	10
5-9	27	14	13	21	11	10
10-14	29	15	14	23	12	11
15-19	30	15	14	25	13	12
20-24	28	15	14	25	13	12
25-29	26	14	13	23	12	11
30-34	28	14	13	21	11	10
35-39	32	17	16	24	12	11
40-44	37	19	18	30	15	14
45-49	39	20	19	35	18	17
50-54	36	18	18	36	18	18
55-59	35	17	18	34	17	17
60-64	44	21	22	33	16	17
65-69	41	19	22	40	19	21
70-74	36	15	20	36	16	20
75-79	25	10	15	29	12	17
80-84	16	6	11	18	7	11
85-89	8	2	6	10	3	7
90-94	3	1	2	4	1	3
95-99	1	0	1	1	0	1
100 +	0	0	0	0	0	0

United Nations Department of Economic and Social Affairs/Population Division
World Population Prospects: The 2004 Revision, Volume II: Sex and Age Distribution of the World Population

455

POPULATION BY AGE AND SEX (in thousands)

Age group	2005			2010			2015			2020		
	Both sexes	Males	Females	Both sexes	Males	Females	Both sexes	Males	Females	Both sexes	Males	Females
All ages	751	364	387	759	368	391	762	370	392	759	368	390
0-4	75	38	37	74	38	36	69	35	34	64	33	31
5-9	75	38	37	70	36	35	69	35	34	64	33	32
10-14	70	36	35	71	36	35	66	33	32	65	33	32
15-19	68	34	34	66	33	33	66	33	33	61	31	30
20-24	77	39	38	63	32	31	60	30	30	60	31	30
25-29	73	36	37	71	36	35	57	29	28	55	28	27
30-34	66	32	34	66	33	34	64	32	32	51	26	25
35-39	53	26	28	61	30	31	61	30	31	59	30	29
40-44	47	21	26	50	24	26	57	28	29	57	28	29
45-49	38	17	21	43	19	24	46	22	24	53	26	28
50-54	30	14	16	35	15	20	40	18	22	43	20	23
55-59	23	10	13	27	12	15	33	14	19	37	16	21
60-64	17	7	9	21	9	12	25	11	14	30	13	18
65-69	13	6	7	15	6	9	19	8	11	22	10	13
70-74	11	4	6	11	4	6	12	5	8	16	7	10
75-79	8	3	5	8	3	5	8	3	5	10	4	6
80-84	5	2	3	5	2	3	5	2	3	6	2	4
85-89	2	1	1	2	1	2	3	1	2	3	1	2
90-94	1	0	0	1	0	0	1	0	1	1	0	1
95-99	0	0	0	0	0	0	0	0	0	0	0	0
100 +	0	0	0	0	0	0	0	0	0	0	0	0

Age group	2025			2030			2035			2040		
	Both sexes	Males	Females	Both sexes	Males	Females	Both sexes	Males	Females	Both sexes	Males	Females
All ages	750	365	386	737	359	379	718	350	369	693	338	355
0-4	60	30	29	57	29	28	54	27	26	50	25	24
5-9	59	30	29	55	28	27	52	27	26	49	25	24
10-14	60	31	29	55	28	27	51	26	25	48	25	24
15-19	60	31	30	55	28	27	51	26	25	47	24	23
20-24	56	28	27	55	28	27	50	26	25	45	23	22
25-29	55	28	27	50	26	25	50	25	24	45	23	22
30-34	49	25	24	49	25	24	44	23	22	44	22	22
35-39	46	23	23	44	22	22	44	23	22	40	20	20
40-44	56	28	28	43	22	21	41	21	20	42	21	20
45-49	54	26	27	52	26	26	40	20	20	38	19	19
50-54	50	24	26	51	25	26	49	24	25	37	19	19
55-59	40	19	22	47	22	25	48	23	25	46	23	24
60-64	35	15	20	38	17	21	44	20	24	45	21	24
65-69	28	11	16	32	13	19	34	15	19	40	18	22
70-74	19	8	11	24	9	15	28	11	17	30	13	17
75-79	13	5	8	15	6	9	19	7	12	23	8	14
80-84	7	2	4	9	3	6	11	4	7	14	5	9
85-89	3	1	2	4	1	3	5	2	4	7	2	4
90-94	1	0	1	1	0	1	2	0	1	2	1	2
95-99	0	0	0	0	0	0	0	0	0	1	0	0
100 +	0	0	0	0	0	0	0	0	0	0	0	0

Age group	2045			2050		
	Both sexes	Males	Females	Both sexes	Males	Females
All ages	661	323	338	623	305	318
0-4	45	23	22	41	21	20
5-9	46	23	22	41	21	20
10-14	45	23	22	42	21	20
15-19	44	22	21	41	21	20
20-24	42	21	20	39	20	19
25-29	40	20	20	36	19	18
30-34	39	20	19	35	18	17
35-39	40	20	19	35	18	17
40-44	37	19	18	37	19	18
45-49	39	20	19	35	18	17
50-54	36	18	18	36	18	18
55-59	35	17	18	34	17	17
60-64	44	21	22	33	16	17
65-69	41	19	22	40	19	21
70-74	36	15	20	36	16	20
75-79	25	10	15	29	12	17
80-84	16	6	11	18	7	11
85-89	8	2	6	10	3	7
90-94	3	1	2	4	1	3
95-99	1	0	1	1	0	1
100 +	0	0	0	0	0	0

United Nations Department of Economic and Social Affairs/Population Division
World Population Prospects: The 2004 Revision, Volume II: Sex and Age Distribution of the World Population

456

POPULATION BY AGE AND SEX (in thousands)

Age group	2005 Both sexes	Males	Females	2010 Both sexes	Males	Females	2015 Both sexes	Males	Females	2020 Both sexes	Males	Females
All ages	751	364	387	743	360	383	722	350	372	691	334	357
0-4	75	38	37	58	30	29	45	23	22	36	18	18
5-9	75	38	37	70	36	35	53	27	26	40	21	20
10-14	70	36	35	71	36	35	66	33	32	49	25	24
15-19	68	34	34	66	33	33	66	33	33	61	31	30
20-24	77	39	38	63	32	31	60	30	30	60	31	30
25-29	73	36	37	71	36	35	57	29	28	55	28	27
30-34	66	32	34	66	33	34	64	32	32	51	26	25
35-39	53	26	28	61	30	31	61	30	31	59	30	29
40-44	47	21	26	50	24	26	57	28	29	57	28	29
45-49	38	17	21	43	19	24	46	22	24	53	26	28
50-54	30	14	16	35	15	20	40	18	22	43	20	23
55-59	23	10	13	27	12	15	33	14	19	37	16	21
60-64	17	7	9	21	9	12	25	11	14	30	13	18
65-69	13	6	7	15	6	9	19	8	11	22	10	13
70-74	11	4	6	11	4	6	12	5	8	16	7	10
75-79	8	3	5	8	3	5	8	3	5	10	4	6
80-84	5	2	3	5	2	3	5	2	3	6	2	4
85-89	2	1	1	2	1	2	3	1	2	3	1	2
90-94	1	0	0	1	0	0	1	0	1	1	0	1
95-99	0	0	0	0	0	0	0	0	0	0	0	0
100 +	0	0	0	0	0	0	0	0	0	0	0	0

Age group	2025 Both sexes	Males	Females	2030 Both sexes	Males	Females	2035 Both sexes	Males	Females	2040 Both sexes	Males	Females
All ages	656	317	339	616	297	319	568	273	295	511	245	265
0-4	33	17	16	29	15	14	24	12	12	17	9	8
5-9	32	16	15	29	15	14	25	13	12	20	10	10
10-14	36	18	18	27	14	13	25	13	12	21	11	10
15-19	45	23	22	32	16	15	23	12	11	20	10	10
20-24	56	28	27	39	20	19	27	14	13	18	9	9
25-29	55	28	27	50	26	25	34	17	17	21	11	10
30-34	49	25	24	49	25	24	44	23	22	29	15	14
35-39	46	23	23	44	22	22	44	23	22	40	20	20
40-44	56	28	28	43	22	21	41	21	20	42	21	20
45-49	54	26	27	52	26	26	40	20	20	38	19	19
50-54	50	24	26	51	25	26	49	24	25	37	19	19
55-59	40	19	22	47	22	25	48	23	25	46	23	24
60-64	35	15	20	38	17	21	44	20	24	45	21	24
65-69	28	11	16	32	13	19	34	15	19	40	18	22
70-74	19	8	11	24	9	15	28	11	17	30	13	17
75-79	13	5	8	15	6	9	19	7	12	23	8	14
80-84	7	2	4	9	3	6	11	4	7	14	5	9
85-89	3	1	2	4	1	3	6	2	4	7	2	4
90-94	1	0	1	1	0	1	2	0	1	2	1	2
95-99	0	0	0	0	0	0	0	0	0	1	0	0
100 +	0	0	0	0	0	0	0	0	0	0	0	0

Age group	2045 Both sexes	Males	Females	2050 Both sexes	Males	Females
All ages	445	213	232	373	178	196
0-4	11	6	5	6	3	3
5-9	13	7	6	7	4	3
10-14	16	8	8	9	5	4
15-19	17	9	8	11	6	5
20-24	15	8	7	12	6	5
25-29	13	7	6	10	5	5
30-34	16	8	8	8	4	4
35-39	25	13	12	12	7	6
40-44	37	19	18	22	12	11
45-49	39	20	19	35	18	17
50-54	36	18	18	36	18	18
55-59	35	17	18	34	17	17
60-64	44	21	22	33	16	17
65-69	41	19	22	40	19	21
70-74	36	15	20	36	16	20
75-79	25	10	15	29	12	17
80-84	16	6	11	18	7	11
85-89	8	2	6	10	3	7
90-94	3	1	2	4	1	3
95-99	1	0	1	1	0	1
100 +	0	0	0	0	0	0

POPULATION BY AGE AND SEX (in thousands)

Age group	1950 Both sexes	Males	Females	1955 Both sexes	Males	Females	1960 Both sexes	Males	Females	1965 Both sexes	Males	Females
All ages	3 261	1 586	1 675	3 508	1 710	1 798	3 803	1 857	1 946	4 143	2 025	2 118
0-4	477	240	237	539	271	267	595	300	295	659	333	327
5-9	385	193	192	428	214	214	491	246	245	549	275	274
10-14	339	169	170	371	184	186	413	206	207	474	236	238
15-19	301	149	152	325	160	164	355	176	180	395	195	200
20-24	262	129	133	285	140	145	308	151	157	336	165	171
25-29	235	115	121	246	120	126	268	131	137	288	140	148
30-34	214	103	111	221	107	114	231	112	119	251	122	130
35-39	195	93	101	202	97	105	208	100	108	217	105	113
40-44	175	83	92	183	87	96	189	90	99	195	93	102
45-49	156	73	82	163	77	86	170	81	90	176	83	93
50-54	137	64	73	143	67	76	150	70	80	156	73	83
55-59	118	55	63	122	57	65	128	59	68	134	62	72
60-64	98	45	52	101	47	54	105	48	56	109	51	59
65-69	73	33	40	79	36	43	81	37	44	84	39	46
70-74	50	22	28	53	24	29	57	26	31	59	27	32
75-79	28	12	16	31	14	17	33	15	18	36	16	20
80 +	18	7	11	19	8	11	21	9	12	22	10	13

Age group	1970 Both sexes	Males	Females	1975 Both sexes	Males	Females	1980 Both sexes	Males	Females	1985 Both sexes	Males	Females
All ages	4 520	2 214	2 306	4 920	2 410	2 510	5 453	2 672	2 781	6 129	3 007	3 122
0-4	703	355	348	762	385	377	908	459	449	1 068	542	526
5-9	616	309	307	662	332	329	725	364	361	865	435	430
10-14	532	266	266	598	299	299	647	325	322	711	357	354
15-19	456	226	230	510	253	257	577	289	289	626	314	312
20-24	375	184	191	427	209	218	475	233	242	541	267	274
25-29	316	154	162	347	168	179	394	189	205	441	212	229
30-34	271	131	140	294	142	152	322	154	169	368	174	194
35-39	237	114	123	254	122	132	276	131	144	304	143	161
40-44	204	97	106	221	105	116	237	113	125	258	122	137
45-49	181	86	96	190	90	100	206	97	109	222	104	118
50-54	162	76	86	166	78	88	174	82	92	190	89	101
55-59	140	65	74	145	67	77	149	70	79	157	73	83
60-64	115	53	62	120	56	64	125	58	67	129	60	69
65-69	88	41	48	93	43	50	98	45	52	102	47	55
70-74	62	28	34	65	30	35	69	31	37	73	33	39
75-79	37	17	20	39	18	21	42	19	23	44	20	24
80 +	25	11	14	27	12	15	29	13	16	31	14	17

Age group	1990 Both sexes	Males	Females	1995 Both sexes	Males	Females	2000 Both sexes	Males	Females	2005 Both sexes	Males	Females
All ages	6 867	3 369	3 498	7 391	3 625	3 767	7 939	3 900	4 038	8 528	4 202	4 326
0-4	1 180	600	580	1 066	542	524	1 099	560	540	1 147	584	563
5-9	1 019	515	504	1 124	569	555	1 019	517	503	1 054	535	519
10-14	850	427	422	1 001	506	495	1 099	556	543	997	505	492
15-19	691	347	344	827	415	411	977	493	484	1 074	543	531
20-24	588	292	296	651	324	328	784	391	393	933	468	465
25-29	496	240	256	534	261	272	603	297	306	728	361	367
30-34	405	190	215	438	208	230	480	234	247	547	269	278
35-39	342	158	183	361	166	195	389	183	206	434	211	223
40-44	282	131	151	307	139	168	321	146	175	350	164	186
45-49	240	112	128	256	116	140	277	124	153	293	131	161
50-54	204	95	109	217	99	118	231	103	128	252	111	141
55-59	171	80	91	182	84	98	194	88	106	208	92	116
60-64	136	63	73	148	68	80	158	72	86	171	76	94
65-69	106	49	57	112	51	60	123	56	67	133	60	73
70-74	76	35	42	80	36	43	86	39	47	96	43	53
75-79	47	21	26	50	22	28	54	24	30	60	26	33
80 +	34	15	19	38	17	21	45	19	26	52	22	30

458

United Nations Department of Economic and Social Affairs/Population Division
World Population Prospects: The 2004 Revision, Volume II: Sex and Age Distribution of the World Population

POPULATION BY AGE AND SEX (in thousands)

Age group	2005			2010			2015			2020		
	Both sexes	Males	Females	Both sexes	Males	Females	Both sexes	Males	Females	Both sexes	Males	Females
All ages	8 628	4 202	4 326	9 145	4 522	4 623	9 751	4 838	4 913	10 328	5 140	5 188
0-4	1 147	584	563	1 184	603	581	1 180	601	579	1 155	589	566
5-9	1 054	535	519	1 103	560	543	1 143	581	562	1 145	582	563
10-14	997	505	492	1 032	524	509	1 081	549	532	1 122	570	552
15-19	1 074	543	531	974	493	481	1 010	512	498	1 059	538	522
20-24	933	468	465	1 030	518	512	935	471	464	972	490	482
25-29	728	361	367	875	437	438	975	488	487	887	445	442
30-34	547	269	278	666	331	335	811	406	405	913	458	455
35-39	434	211	223	497	245	252	611	305	306	752	379	373
40-44	350	164	186	395	192	203	456	225	231	564	283	282
45-49	293	131	161	322	150	172	365	177	188	423	209	214
50-54	252	111	141	269	120	149	297	138	160	339	163	175
55-59	208	92	116	229	101	129	247	109	137	275	126	148
60-64	171	76	94	185	81	104	207	90	117	224	98	126
65-69	133	60	73	146	65	82	161	70	91	182	78	104
70-74	96	43	53	107	47	60	120	52	68	134	57	77
75-79	60	26	33	69	30	39	80	34	45	91	39	53
80-84	32	14	18	37	16	21	45	19	26	54	22	31
85-89	14	6	8	17	7	10	20	8	12	26	10	15
90-94	5	2	3	6	2	4	7	3	4	9	3	6
95-99	1	0	1	1	0	1	2	1	1	2	1	2
100 +	0	0	0	0	0	0	0	0	0	0	0	0

Age group	2025			2030			2035			2040		
	Both sexes	Males	Females	Both sexes	Males	Females	Both sexes	Males	Females	Both sexes	Males	Females
All ages	10 868	5 423	5 445	11 371	5 688	5 683	11 837	5 933	5 904	12 268	6 158	6 110
0-4	1 124	573	551	1 093	558	536	1 066	544	522	1 041	531	509
5-9	1 125	573	553	1 098	559	539	1 071	546	526	1 047	534	513
10-14	1 126	573	553	1 108	564	544	1 083	552	531	1 058	539	519
15-19	1 101	560	542	1 107	563	544	1 090	555	535	1 066	543	523
20-24	1 022	516	506	1 066	539	527	1 072	543	529	1 057	536	521
25-29	925	465	460	976	491	485	1 021	515	506	1 030	520	510
30-34	833	418	415	872	439	433	923	466	457	971	490	480
35-39	853	430	422	780	394	386	820	415	405	873	443	430
40-44	700	354	346	799	405	395	734	372	362	775	394	382
45-49	528	264	264	659	333	326	756	383	373	697	353	344
50-54	396	195	201	497	248	249	624	314	309	719	363	356
55-59	315	151	164	371	181	189	468	232	235	591	296	294
60-64	251	115	137	291	138	152	344	167	177	438	216	222
65-69	199	86	113	226	102	124	264	124	140	315	151	164
70-74	154	65	89	171	73	99	197	87	110	232	107	125
75-79	105	43	62	123	50	73	140	57	82	163	69	93
80-84	64	26	38	75	30	46	91	35	55	105	41	64
85-89	32	12	19	39	15	24	47	17	30	58	21	37
90-94	12	4	8	15	5	10	19	7	13	24	8	16
95-99	3	1	2	4	1	3	5	2	4	7	2	5
100 +	1	0	0	1	0	1	1	0	1	1	0	1

Age group	2045			2050		
	Both sexes	Males	Females	Both sexes	Males	Females
All ages	12 658	6 360	6 298	12 996	6 530	6 466
0-4	1 012	517	495	976	499	477
5-9	1 025	523	502	998	509	488
10-14	1 035	528	507	1 014	517	496
15-19	1 042	531	511	1 020	520	499
20-24	1 034	525	510	1 011	513	498
25-29	1 018	514	504	998	504	493
30-34	983	497	486	975	493	482
35-39	923	469	454	940	477	463
40-44	830	422	408	882	449	433
45-49	740	376	364	796	405	391
50-54	666	336	330	710	359	350
55-59	684	344	340	636	320	316
60-64	556	276	279	647	322	324
65-69	403	196	207	515	253	262
70-74	279	131	148	360	171	189
75-79	194	87	108	236	107	129
80-84	124	50	74	150	64	86
85-89	69	25	44	83	31	52
90-94	30	10	21	37	12	25
95-99	9	3	6	12	3	8
100 +	2	0	1	2	1	2

United Nations Department of Economic and Social Affairs/Population Division
World Population Prospects: The 2004 Revision, Volume II: Sex and Age Distribution of the World Population

459

POPULATION BY AGE AND SEX (in thousands)

Age group	2005 Both sexes	2005 Males	2005 Females	2010 Both sexes	2010 Males	2010 Females	2015 Both sexes	2015 Males	2015 Females	2020 Both sexes	2020 Males	2020 Females
All ages	8 528	4 202	4 326	9 226	4 563	4 663	9 976	4 953	5 023	10 744	5 352	5 392
0-4	1 147	584	563	1 265	645	621	1 325	675	650	1 351	689	662
5-9	1 054	535	519	1 103	560	543	1 223	621	601	1 287	654	632
10-14	997	505	492	1 032	524	509	1 081	549	532	1 200	610	590
15-19	1 074	543	531	974	493	481	1 010	512	498	1 059	538	522
20-24	933	468	465	1 030	518	512	935	471	464	972	490	482
25-29	728	361	367	875	437	438	975	488	487	887	445	442
30-34	547	269	278	666	331	335	811	406	405	913	458	455
35-39	434	211	223	497	245	252	611	305	306	752	379	373
40-44	350	164	186	395	192	203	456	225	231	564	283	282
45-49	293	131	161	322	150	172	365	177	188	423	209	214
50-54	252	111	141	269	120	149	297	138	160	339	163	175
55-59	208	92	116	229	101	129	247	109	137	275	126	148
60-64	171	76	94	185	81	104	207	90	117	224	98	126
65-69	133	60	73	146	65	82	161	70	91	182	78	104
70-74	96	43	53	107	47	60	120	52	68	134	57	77
75-79	60	26	33	69	30	39	80	34	45	91	39	53
80-84	32	14	18	37	16	21	45	19	26	54	22	31
85-89	14	6	8	17	7	10	20	8	12	26	10	15
90-94	5	2	3	6	2	4	7	3	4	9	3	6
95-99	1	0	1	1	0	1	2	1	1	2	1	2
100 +	0	0	0	0	0	0	0	0	0	0	0	0

Age group	2025 Both sexes	2025 Males	2025 Females	2030 Both sexes	2030 Males	2030 Females	2035 Both sexes	2035 Males	2035 Females	2040 Both sexes	2040 Males	2040 Females
All ages	11 488	5 739	5 749	12 222	6 121	6 101	12 959	6 504	6 455	13 711	6 894	6 817
0-4	1 335	681	654	1 332	679	653	1 347	687	660	1 376	702	673
5-9	1 317	670	647	1 305	665	641	1 306	665	641	1 324	675	649
10-14	1 266	644	622	1 298	661	637	1 289	656	632	1 291	658	633
15-19	1 179	599	580	1 246	633	612	1 279	651	628	1 270	647	623
20-24	1 022	516	506	1 142	578	564	1 210	613	597	1 244	631	613
25-29	925	465	460	976	491	485	1 096	553	543	1 165	589	576
30-34	833	418	415	872	439	433	923	466	457	1 043	527	515
35-39	853	430	422	780	394	386	820	415	405	873	443	430
40-44	700	354	346	799	405	395	734	372	362	775	394	382
45-49	528	264	264	659	333	326	756	383	373	697	353	344
50-54	396	195	201	497	248	249	624	314	309	719	363	356
55-59	315	151	164	371	181	189	468	232	235	591	296	294
60-64	251	115	137	291	138	152	344	167	177	438	216	222
65-69	199	86	113	226	102	124	264	124	140	315	151	164
70-74	154	65	89	171	73	99	197	87	110	232	107	125
75-79	105	43	62	123	50	73	140	57	82	163	69	93
80-84	64	26	38	75	30	46	91	35	55	105	41	64
85-89	32	12	19	39	15	24	47	17	30	58	21	37
90-94	12	4	8	15	5	10	19	7	13	24	8	16
95-99	3	1	2	4	1	3	5	2	4	7	2	5
100 +	1	0	0	1	0	1	1	0	1	1	0	1

Age group	2045 Both sexes	2045 Males	2045 Females	2050 Both sexes	2050 Males	2050 Females
All ages	14 470	7 284	7 186	15 218	7 666	7 553
0-4	1 400	715	685	1 410	721	689
5-9	1 356	692	664	1 382	706	676
10-14	1 311	668	642	1 343	685	657
15-19	1 273	649	624	1 294	660	634
20-24	1 237	628	609	1 241	631	611
25-29	1 201	608	594	1 198	606	591
30-34	1 114	564	550	1 154	585	569
35-39	992	504	488	1 066	542	524
40-44	830	422	408	949	483	465
45-49	740	376	364	796	405	391
50-54	666	336	330	710	359	350
55-59	684	344	340	636	320	316
60-64	556	276	279	647	322	324
65-69	403	196	207	515	253	262
70-74	279	131	148	360	171	189
75-79	194	87	108	236	107	129
80-84	124	50	74	150	64	86
85-89	69	25	44	83	31	52
90-94	30	10	21	37	12	25
95-99	9	3	6	12	3	8
100 +	2	0	1	2	1	2

United Nations Department of Economic and Social Affairs/Population Division
World Population Prospects: The 2004 Revision, Volume II: Sex and Age Distribution of the World Population

460

POPULATION BY AGE AND SEX (in thousands)

Age group	2005 Both sexes	Males	Females	2010 Both sexes	Males	Females	2015 Both sexes	Males	Females	2020 Both sexes	Males	Females
All ages	8 528	4 202	4 326	9 063	4 480	4 583	9 526	4 724	4 803	9 911	4 928	4 983
0-4	1 147	584	563	1 102	561	541	1 034	527	507	959	489	470
5-9	1 054	535	519	1 103	560	543	1 064	541	524	1 003	510	493
10-14	997	505	492	1 032	524	509	1 081	549	532	1 044	531	514
15-19	1 074	543	531	974	493	481	1 010	512	498	1 059	538	522
20-24	933	468	465	1 030	518	512	935	471	464	972	490	482
25-29	728	361	367	875	437	438	975	488	487	887	445	442
30-34	547	269	278	666	331	335	811	406	405	913	458	455
35-39	434	211	223	497	245	252	611	305	306	752	379	373
40-44	350	164	186	395	192	203	456	225	231	564	283	282
45-49	293	131	161	322	150	172	365	177	188	423	209	214
50-54	252	111	141	269	120	149	297	138	160	339	163	175
55-59	208	92	116	229	101	129	247	109	137	275	126	148
60-64	171	76	94	185	81	104	207	90	117	224	98	126
65-69	133	60	73	146	65	82	161	70	91	182	78	104
70-74	96	43	53	107	47	60	120	52	68	134	57	77
75-79	60	26	33	69	30	39	80	34	45	91	39	53
80-84	32	14	18	37	16	21	45	19	26	54	22	31
85-89	14	6	8	17	7	10	20	8	12	26	10	15
90-94	5	2	3	6	2	4	7	3	4	9	3	6
95-99	1	0	1	1	0	1	2	1	1	2	1	2
100 +	0	0	0	0	0	0	0	0	0	0	0	0

Age group	2025 Both sexes	Males	Females	2030 Both sexes	Males	Females	2035 Both sexes	Males	Females	2040 Both sexes	Males	Females
All ages	10 248	5 108	5 140	10 528	5 259	5 269	10 742	5 375	5 366	10 889	5 455	5 433
0-4	914	466	448	862	440	422	804	411	394	744	380	364
5-9	933	475	458	892	454	438	844	430	414	789	402	387
10-14	985	501	484	918	467	451	879	448	431	832	424	408
15-19	1 024	520	504	967	492	475	901	459	442	863	440	423
20-24	1 022	516	506	989	500	489	934	473	461	870	441	429
25-29	925	465	460	976	491	485	946	477	469	895	451	443
30-34	833	418	415	872	439	433	923	466	457	898	454	445
35-39	853	430	422	780	394	386	820	415	405	873	443	430
40-44	700	354	346	799	405	395	734	372	362	775	394	382
45-49	528	264	264	659	333	320	750	377	373	697	353	344
50-54	396	195	201	497	248	249	624	314	309	719	363	356
55-59	315	151	164	371	181	189	468	232	235	591	296	294
60-64	251	115	137	291	138	152	344	167	177	438	210	222
65-69	199	86	113	226	102	124	264	124	140	315	151	164
70-74	154	65	89	171	73	99	197	87	110	232	107	125
75-79	105	43	62	123	50	73	140	57	82	163	69	93
80-84	64	26	38	75	30	46	91	35	55	105	41	64
85-89	32	12	19	39	15	24	47	17	30	58	21	37
90-94	12	4	8	15	5	10	19	7	13	24	8	16
95-99	3	1	2	4	1	3	5	2	4	7	2	5
100 +	1	0	0	1	0	1	1	0	1	1	0	1

Age group	2045 Both sexes	Males	Females	2050 Both sexes	Males	Females
All ages	10 966	5 497	5 470	10 972	5 496	5 475
0-4	681	348	333	620	317	303
5-9	731	373	358	671	342	328
10-14	779	397	381	721	368	353
15-19	817	417	400	764	390	374
20-24	833	422	411	788	400	388
25-29	834	420	413	799	403	396
30-34	852	430	422	796	402	395
35-39	854	433	421	813	412	401
40-44	830	422	408	816	415	401
45-49	740	376	364	796	405	391
50-54	666	336	330	710	359	350
55-59	684	344	340	636	320	316
60-64	556	276	279	647	322	324
65-69	403	196	207	515	253	262
70-74	279	131	148	360	171	189
75-79	194	87	108	236	107	129
80-84	124	50	74	150	64	86
85-89	69	25	44	83	31	52
90-94	30	10	21	37	12	25
95-99	9	3	6	12	3	8
100 +	2	0	1	2	1	2

POPULATION BY AGE AND SEX (in thousands)

Age group	1950 Both sexes	1950 Males	1950 Females	1955 Both sexes	1955 Males	1955 Females	1960 Both sexes	1960 Males	1960 Females	1965 Both sexes	1965 Males	1965 Females
All ages	1 380	695	685	1 610	812	799	1 894	955	939	2 244	1 130	1 114
0-4	253	129	124	315	160	154	374	190	184	441	224	217
5-9	197	100	97	226	115	111	286	145	141	346	175	171
10-14	173	88	85	192	98	95	221	112	109	281	142	139
15-19	151	77	74	170	86	84	189	96	93	219	111	108
20-24	121	61	59	147	75	73	167	85	82	186	94	92
25-29	100	51	49	117	59	58	143	73	71	163	82	81
30-34	85	43	42	96	49	48	113	57	56	139	70	69
35-39	70	35	35	81	41	40	93	47	46	109	55	54
40-44	60	30	30	67	33	33	77	39	38	89	45	44
45-49	49	24	25	56	28	28	63	31	32	74	37	37
50-54	39	19	20	45	22	23	53	26	27	59	29	30
55-59	29	14	15	35	17	18	41	20	21	48	24	25
60-64	22	10	11	24	12	13	30	14	16	36	17	19
65-69	15	7	8	17	8	9	20	9	11	25	12	13
70-74	10	4	5	11	5	6	13	6	7	15	7	8
75-79	5	2	3	6	3	3	7	3	4	9	4	5
80 +	3	1	2	3	1	2	4	2	2	5	2	3

Age group	1970 Both sexes	1970 Males	1970 Females	1975 Both sexes	1975 Males	1975 Females	1980 Both sexes	1980 Males	1980 Females	1985 Both sexes	1985 Males	1985 Females
All ages	2 592	1 302	1 289	3 016	1 515	1 501	3 568	1 793	1 775	4 182	2 103	2 079
0-4	509	258	251	572	290	282	663	337	326	753	383	370
5-9	407	206	202	479	242	237	549	278	271	640	324	316
10-14	333	168	165	396	200	196	473	239	234	540	273	267
15-19	272	137	135	323	163	160	392	197	194	465	235	230
20-24	208	105	103	262	132	130	318	160	158	383	193	190
25-29	175	88	87	197	100	98	256	129	127	309	155	153
30-34	152	77	76	165	83	82	192	96	95	247	124	123
35-39	129	65	64	143	72	72	160	80	80	184	92	92
40-44	101	51	50	122	61	61	138	69	69	153	76	77
45-49	82	41	41	94	47	47	117	58	59	132	66	66
50-54	67	33	34	76	38	38	90	44	45	110	55	56
55-59	53	26	27	61	30	31	71	35	36	84	41	43
60-64	41	20	21	46	22	24	55	27	28	64	31	33
65-69	29	14	16	35	16	18	40	19	21	48	23	25
70-74	19	9	10	23	11	13	28	13	15	33	15	18
75-79	10	5	6	14	6	8	17	8	10	22	10	12
80 +	6	2	3	7	3	4	10	4	6	13	6	8

Age group	1990 Both sexes	1990 Males	1990 Females	1995 Both sexes	1995 Males	1995 Females	2000 Both sexes	2000 Males	2000 Females	2005 Both sexes	2005 Males	2005 Females
All ages	4 867	2 450	2 417	5 625	2 833	2 792	6 424	3 236	3 188	7 205	3 631	3 573
0-4	834	424	410	921	469	452	962	490	472	979	499	480
5-9	735	373	361	818	416	402	907	462	445	947	483	465
10-14	631	320	311	726	369	357	811	413	399	898	457	441
15-19	532	269	263	622	315	306	719	365	354	803	409	395
20-24	455	230	225	521	264	257	614	311	303	710	360	349
25-29	372	187	185	442	223	219	508	257	251	600	304	296
30-34	298	149	149	359	180	179	427	215	212	490	248	243
35-39	238	119	119	287	143	144	346	173	173	410	206	203
40-44	177	88	89	229	114	115	277	138	139	332	166	166
45-49	147	73	74	170	84	85	221	109	111	266	132	134
50-54	126	62	64	140	69	71	163	81	83	212	104	108
55-59	104	51	53	119	58	61	133	65	68	155	76	79
60-64	77	37	40	97	47	50	111	54	57	125	60	65
65-69	57	27	30	70	33	36	88	42	46	102	49	53
70-74	41	19	22	49	23	26	61	28	32	77	36	41
75-79	26	12	14	33	15	18	40	18	22	50	23	27
80 +	18	7	10	23	10	13	36	15	21	48	20	28

United Nations Department of Economic and Social Affairs/Population Division
World Population Prospects: The 2004 Revision, Volume II: Sex and Age Distribution of the World Population

POPULATION BY AGE AND SEX (in thousands)

Age group	2005 Both sexes	2005 Males	2005 Females	2010 Both sexes	2010 Males	2010 Females	2015 Both sexes	2015 Males	2015 Females	2020 Both sexes	2020 Males	2020 Females
All ages	7 205	3 631	3 573	7 997	4 032	3 965	8 780	4 429	4 351	9 500	4 800	4 724
0-4	979	499	480	1 006	513	493	1 017	519	498	1 012	517	496
5-9	947	483	465	965	492	473	993	506	486	1 005	513	492
10-14	898	457	441	938	478	460	956	487	469	984	502	482
15-19	803	409	395	890	453	437	930	474	456	948	484	465
20-24	710	360	349	794	404	390	880	448	432	920	469	452
25-29	600	304	296	696	353	343	780	396	383	866	441	425
30-34	490	248	243	582	295	287	678	344	334	761	387	374
35-39	410	206	203	474	239	234	565	286	279	658	334	324
40-44	332	166	166	395	199	197	458	231	227	547	277	270
45-49	266	132	134	321	159	161	383	192	191	444	224	221
50-54	212	104	108	256	126	130	309	153	156	370	184	185
55-59	155	76	79	202	99	104	245	120	125	297	146	151
60-64	125	60	65	146	71	75	191	92	99	232	112	120
65-69	102	49	53	115	55	60	135	64	71	177	84	93
70-74	77	36	41	90	42	48	102	48	55	121	56	65
75-79	50	23	27	64	29	35	76	34	42	87	39	48
80-84	30	13	17	37	16	21	49	21	28	58	25	33
85-89	14	6	8	18	7	11	23	9	14	31	12	19
90-94	4	1	2	6	2	4	8	3	5	11	4	7
95-99	1	0	0	1	0	1	2	1	1	2	1	2
100 +	0	0	0	0	0	0	0	0	0	0	0	0

Age group	2025 Both sexes	2025 Males	2025 Females	2030 Both sexes	2030 Males	2030 Females	2035 Both sexes	2035 Males	2035 Females	2040 Both sexes	2040 Males	2040 Females
All ages	10 239	5 165	5 074	10 883	5 489	5 394	11 455	5 775	5 680	11 948	6 020	5 929
0-4	990	505	485	955	488	468	911	465	446	862	440	422
5-9	1 001	511	490	980	500	480	946	483	463	904	462	442
10-14	997	509	488	994	507	487	973	497	476	940	480	460
15-19	977	498	478	990	505	485	987	504	483	967	494	473
20-24	939	479	460	968	494	474	982	501	481	979	500	479
25-29	907	462	445	926	472	454	956	487	468	970	495	475
30-34	847	431	416	889	453	436	910	464	446	940	479	460
35-39	741	376	364	827	421	406	869	443	427	892	455	437
40-44	640	324	315	721	366	355	807	410	397	851	433	418
45-49	531	268	263	622	315	307	704	357	347	789	400	389
50-54	430	215	215	516	259	256	605	305	300	686	346	339
55-59	356	176	170	414	209	209	499	249	249	586	293	293
60-64	282	137	145	339	166	173	396	195	201	477	236	241
65-69	216	103	113	263	126	137	317	153	164	371	180	191
70-74	159	74	85	195	91	104	239	111	127	288	136	152
75-79	103	46	57	136	61	75	168	75	93	207	93	114
80-84	67	28	38	80	34	46	107	45	62	133	56	77
85-89	37	15	23	44	17	27	53	21	32	72	28	44
90-94	15	5	10	18	6	12	22	8	14	27	10	18
95-99	3	1	2	5	1	3	6	2	4	7	2	5
100 +	0	0	0	0	0	0	1	0	1	1	0	1

Age group	2045 Both sexes	2045 Males	2045 Females	2050 Both sexes	2050 Males	2050 Females
All ages	12 388	6 236	6 153	12 776	6 423	6 353
0-4	844	431	413	835	427	409
5-9	855	437	418	838	428	410
10-14	898	459	439	850	434	415
15-19	934	477	457	892	456	436
20-24	960	490	469	927	474	453
25-29	969	495	474	950	486	464
30-34	956	488	468	956	488	468
35-39	923	471	452	941	480	460
40-44	874	446	429	907	463	444
45-49	833	424	410	858	437	422
50-54	770	390	381	815	413	402
55-59	665	334	331	749	376	372
60-64	562	279	283	640	318	322
65-69	449	219	230	531	259	272
70-74	340	161	179	412	196	216
75-79	251	114	137	297	136	161
80-84	165	70	95	202	87	115
85-89	91	36	55	114	45	69
90-94	38	13	25	48	17	31
95-99	9	3	7	13	4	9
100 +	1	0	1	1	0	1

POPULATION BY AGE AND SEX (in thousands)

Age group	2005 Both sexes	Males	Females	2010 Both sexes	Males	Females	2015 Both sexes	Males	Females	2020 Both sexes	Males	Females
All ages	7 205	3 631	3 573	8 070	4 070	4 000	8 987	4 534	4 453	9 924	5 009	4 916
0-4	979	499	480	1 079	550	529	1 151	587	564	1 199	612	587
5-9	947	483	465	965	492	473	1 065	543	522	1 138	580	557
10-14	898	457	441	938	478	460	956	487	469	1 056	539	518
15-19	803	409	395	890	453	437	930	474	456	948	484	465
20-24	710	360	349	794	404	390	880	448	432	920	469	452
25-29	600	304	296	696	353	343	780	396	383	866	441	425
30-34	490	248	243	582	295	287	678	344	334	761	387	374
35-39	410	206	203	474	239	234	565	286	279	658	334	324
40-44	332	166	166	395	199	197	458	231	227	547	277	270
45-49	266	132	134	321	159	161	383	192	191	444	224	221
50-54	212	104	108	256	126	130	309	153	156	370	184	185
55-59	155	76	79	202	99	104	245	120	125	297	146	151
60-64	125	60	65	146	71	75	191	92	99	232	112	120
65-69	102	49	53	115	55	60	135	64	71	177	84	93
70-74	77	36	41	90	42	48	102	48	55	121	56	65
75-79	50	23	27	64	29	35	76	34	42	87	39	48
80-84	30	13	17	37	16	21	49	21	28	58	25	33
85-89	14	6	8	18	7	11	23	9	14	31	12	19
90-94	4	1	2	6	2	4	8	3	5	11	4	7
95-99	1	0	0	1	0	1	2	1	1	2	1	2
100 +	0	0	0	0	0	0	0	0	0	0	0	0

Age group	2025 Both sexes	Males	Females	2030 Both sexes	Males	Females	2035 Both sexes	Males	Females	2040 Both sexes	Males	Females
All ages	10 836	5 470	5 366	11 722	5 917	5 805	12 585	6 351	6 234	13 416	6 768	6 648
0-4	1 199	612	587	1 200	613	588	1 206	616	590	1 205	615	590
5-9	1 186	605	581	1 187	606	581	1 190	608	582	1 196	611	585
10-14	1 129	576	553	1 178	601	577	1 180	602	577	1 183	604	579
15-19	1 048	535	514	1 121	572	549	1 170	597	573	1 173	599	574
20-24	939	479	460	1 039	530	509	1 112	568	545	1 162	593	569
25-29	907	462	445	926	472	454	1 027	524	503	1 100	561	539
30-34	847	431	416	889	453	436	910	464	446	1 010	515	495
35-39	741	376	364	827	421	406	869	443	427	892	455	437
40-44	640	324	315	721	366	355	807	410	397	851	433	418
45-49	531	268	263	622	315	307	704	357	347	789	400	389
50-54	430	215	215	516	259	256	605	305	300	686	346	339
55-59	356	176	179	414	206	208	498	249	249	586	293	293
60-64	282	137	145	339	166	173	396	195	201	477	236	241
65-69	216	103	113	263	126	137	317	153	164	371	180	191
70-74	159	74	85	195	91	104	239	111	127	288	136	152
75-79	103	46	57	136	61	75	168	75	93	207	93	114
80-84	67	28	38	80	34	46	107	45	62	133	56	77
85-89	37	15	23	44	17	27	53	21	32	72	28	44
90-94	15	5	10	18	6	12	22	8	14	27	10	18
95-99	3	1	2	5	1	3	6	2	4	7	2	5
100 +	0	0	0	0	0	0	1	0	1	1	0	1

Age group	2045 Both sexes	Males	Females	2050 Both sexes	Males	Females
All ages	14 239	7 180	7 059	15 053	7 585	7 468
0-4	1 235	631	604	1 271	649	622
5-9	1 197	611	586	1 227	627	600
10-14	1 190	608	582	1 191	608	582
15-19	1 176	601	575	1 183	605	579
20-24	1 165	595	570	1 169	597	572
25-29	1 150	587	563	1 154	590	564
30-34	1 084	553	531	1 135	580	556
35-39	992	506	486	1 067	545	522
40-44	874	446	429	975	497	478
45-49	833	424	410	858	437	422
50-54	770	390	381	815	413	402
55-59	665	334	331	749	376	372
60-64	562	279	283	640	318	322
65-69	449	219	230	531	259	272
70-74	340	161	179	412	196	216
75-79	251	114	137	297	136	161
80-84	165	70	95	202	87	115
85-89	91	36	55	114	45	69
90-94	38	13	25	48	17	31
95-99	9	3	7	13	4	9
100 +	1	0	1	1	0	1

United Nations Department of Economic and Social Affairs/Population Division
World Population Prospects: The 2004 Revision, Volume II: Sex and Age Distribution of the World Population

464

POPULATION BY AGE AND SEX (in thousands)

Age group	2005 Both sexes	Males	Females	2010 Both sexes	Males	Females	2015 Both sexes	Males	Females	2020 Both sexes	Males	Females
All ages	7 205	3 631	3 573	7 923	3 995	3 928	8 572	4 323	4 250	9 139	4 608	4 531
0-4	979	499	480	932	475	457	882	450	432	825	421	404
5-9	947	483	465	965	492	473	920	469	451	871	445	427
10-14	898	457	441	938	478	460	956	487	469	912	465	447
15-19	803	409	395	890	453	437	930	474	456	948	484	465
20-24	710	360	349	794	404	390	880	448	432	920	469	452
25-29	600	304	296	696	353	343	780	396	383	866	441	425
30-34	490	248	243	582	295	287	678	344	334	761	387	374
35-39	410	206	203	474	239	234	565	286	279	658	334	324
40-44	332	166	166	395	199	197	458	231	227	547	277	270
45-49	266	132	134	321	159	161	383	192	191	444	224	221
50-54	212	104	108	256	126	130	309	153	156	370	184	185
55-59	155	76	79	202	99	104	245	120	125	297	146	151
60-64	125	60	65	146	71	75	191	92	99	232	112	120
65-69	102	49	53	115	55	60	135	64	71	177	84	93
70-74	77	36	41	90	42	48	102	48	55	121	56	65
75-79	50	23	27	64	29	35	76	34	42	87	39	48
80-84	30	13	17	37	16	21	49	21	28	58	25	33
85-89	14	6	8	18	7	11	23	9	14	31	12	19
90-94	4	1	2	6	2	4	8	3	5	11	4	7
95-99	1	0	0	1	0	1	2	1	1	2	1	2
100 +	0	0	0	0	0	0	0	0	0	0	0	0

Age group	2025 Both sexes	Males	Females	2030 Both sexes	Males	Females	2035 Both sexes	Males	Females	2040 Both sexes	Males	Females
All ages	9 639	4 859	4 780	10 051	5 064	4 986	10 359	5 216	5 143	10 560	5 311	5 248
0-4	782	399	383	719	367	352	643	328	315	564	288	276
5-9	815	416	399	774	395	379	712	364	348	637	325	312
10-14	864	441	423	808	413	396	768	392	375	706	361	345
15-19	904	461	443	857	438	420	802	410	392	762	389	372
20-24	939	479	460	896	457	439	850	434	416	795	406	389
25-29	907	462	445	926	472	454	884	451	433	839	429	411
30-34	847	431	416	889	453	436	910	464	446	870	444	426
35-39	741	376	364	827	421	406	869	443	427	892	455	437
40-44	640	324	315	721	366	355	807	410	397	851	433	418
45-49	531	268	263	622	315	307	704	357	347	789	400	389
50-54	430	215	215	516	259	256	605	305	300	686	346	339
55-59	356	176	179	414	206	208	498	249	249	586	293	293
60-64	282	137	145	339	166	173	396	195	201	477	236	241
65-69	216	103	113	263	126	137	317	153	164	371	180	191
70-74	159	74	85	195	91	104	239	111	127	288	136	152
75-79	103	46	57	136	61	75	168	75	93	207	93	114
80-84	67	28	38	80	34	46	107	45	62	133	56	77
85-89	37	15	23	44	17	27	53	21	32	72	28	44
90-94	15	5	10	18	6	12	22	8	14	27	10	18
95-99	3	1	2	5	1	3	6	2	4	7	2	5
100 +	0	0	0	0	0	0	1	0	1	1	0	1

Age group	2045 Both sexes	Males	Females	2050 Both sexes	Males	Females
All ages	10 684	5 366	5 318	10 735	5 382	5 352
0-4	520	266	255	490	250	240
5-9	559	286	273	516	264	252
10-14	632	323	309	554	284	271
15-19	701	358	342	627	321	306
20-24	755	386	369	695	355	339
25-29	786	402	384	747	382	365
30-34	826	422	404	775	396	379
35-39	854	436	418	813	415	398
40-44	874	446	429	839	428	411
45-49	833	424	410	858	437	422
50-54	770	390	381	815	413	402
55-59	665	334	331	749	376	372
60-64	562	279	283	640	318	322
65-69	449	219	230	531	259	272
70-74	340	161	179	412	196	216
75-79	251	114	137	297	136	161
80-84	165	70	95	202	87	115
85-89	91	36	55	114	45	69
90-94	38	13	25	48	17	31
95-99	9	3	7	13	4	9
100 +	1	0	1	1	0	1

POPULATION BY AGE AND SEX (in thousands)

Age group	1950 Both sexes	Males	Females	1955 Both sexes	Males	Females	1960 Both sexes	Males	Females	1965 Both sexes	Males	Females
All ages	9 338	4 490	4 848	9 825	4 745	5 080	9 984	4 816	5 168	10 153	4 904	5 249
0-4	832	426	406	938	481	457	800	410	390	643	331	312
5-9	773	392	381	814	416	398	924	472	452	796	408	388
10-14	739	373	366	767	389	378	804	409	395	917	467	450
15-19	765	384	381	733	370	363	750	377	373	803	407	396
20-24	788	389	399	756	379	377	684	333	351	745	375	370
25-29	794	379	415	777	383	394	714	350	364	683	331	352
30-34	497	233	264	782	373	409	752	367	385	710	348	362
35-39	733	346	387	489	229	260	757	361	396	744	361	383
40-44	705	337	368	718	338	380	475	223	252	747	356	391
45-49	640	309	331	685	326	359	692	326	366	467	218	249
50-54	570	265	305	614	294	320	659	313	346	673	316	357
55-59	445	197	248	537	247	290	578	275	303	633	297	336
60-64	372	162	210	409	178	231	492	223	269	539	250	289
65-69	305	133	172	326	139	187	358	152	206	435	191	244
70-74	194	85	109	247	105	142	265	110	155	293	120	173
75-79	113	50	63	143	61	82	170	70	100	187	74	113
80 +	73	30	43	90	37	53	110	45	65	133	52	81

Age group	1970 Both sexes	Males	Females	1975 Both sexes	Males	Females	1980 Both sexes	Males	Females	1985 Both sexes	Males	Females
All ages	10 337	5 011	5 326	10 532	5 109	5 423	10 707	5 188	5 520	10 579	5 105	5 474
0-4	712	367	345	790	406	384	844	434	410	650	332	318
5-9	643	331	313	709	366	344	793	408	385	837	430	407
10-14	796	409	387	642	330	312	711	367	344	786	404	382
15-19	927	475	452	793	407	386	645	333	313	705	363	342
20-24	797	405	392	922	471	450	786	401	385	639	328	311
25-29	738	371	367	792	402	390	901	457	444	777	395	382
30-34	676	329	347	732	367	365	773	390	383	889	449	440
35-39	704	345	359	670	325	345	716	357	359	759	381	378
40-44	735	358	377	694	338	356	656	316	340	698	345	353
45-49	734	348	386	719	347	371	676	326	350	633	300	332
50-54	454	212	242	711	334	377	691	329	362	643	304	339
55-59	644	299	345	432	199	233	675	310	365	644	298	346
60-64	584	268	316	596	270	326	401	179	222	611	270	341
65-69	473	212	261	516	227	288	492	214	279	348	147	201
70-74	356	148	208	385	163	222	441	183	257	424	171	253
75-79	210	80	130	253	98	155	279	108	172	298	112	187
80 +	155	56	99	177	60	117	226	75	150	237	77	161

Age group	1990 Both sexes	Males	Females	1995 Both sexes	Males	Females	2000 Both sexes	Males	Females	2005 Both sexes	Males	Females
All ages	10 365	4 979	5 386	10 329	4 942	5 387	10 226	4 878	5 348	10 098	4 808	5 290
0-4	616	315	301	598	306	292	504	258	246	477	245	233
5-9	647	331	316	621	317	303	603	309	294	506	259	247
10-14	834	427	407	653	334	319	626	320	306	605	310	295
15-19	790	405	385	841	430	410	659	336	322	628	321	307
20-24	689	352	337	794	407	387	846	433	413	661	337	323
25-29	615	311	304	692	353	339	799	409	390	847	433	415
30-34	750	376	373	615	310	305	695	353	341	799	408	391
35-39	855	427	428	745	372	373	615	309	306	692	351	341
40-44	732	363	369	843	417	427	738	365	373	609	304	305
45-49	671	326	344	714	348	365	824	401	423	723	353	369
50-54	601	279	321	643	305	338	688	328	360	797	381	416
55-59	599	276	324	565	253	312	608	279	329	654	304	350
60-64	583	259	325	548	240	308	521	223	298	565	249	316
65-69	530	222	309	512	213	299	486	199	286	467	188	279
70-74	284	112	171	437	168	269	428	163	264	412	156	256
75-79	305	113	193	213	77	137	332	116	216	332	115	217
80 +	264	84	180	295	92	203	255	77	178	325	95	230

466

United Nations Department of Economic and Social Affairs/Population Division
World Population Prospects: The 2004 Revision, Volume II: Sex and Age Distribution of the World Population

POPULATION BY AGE AND SEX (in thousands)

Age group	2005 Both sexes	2005 Males	2005 Females	2010 Both sexes	2010 Males	2010 Females	2015 Both sexes	2015 Males	2015 Females	2020 Both sexes	2020 Males	2020 Females
All ages	10 098	4 808	5 290	9 961	4 739	5 222	9 802	4 664	5 138	9 628	4 585	5 043
0-4	477	245	233	456	234	222	434	223	212	420	215	205
5-9	506	259	247	479	246	234	458	235	223	436	224	213
10-14	605	310	295	509	260	248	481	247	235	460	236	224
15-19	628	321	307	607	311	296	511	261	249	483	248	236
20-24	661	337	323	630	322	308	609	311	298	513	262	250
25-29	847	433	415	662	338	325	632	322	310	611	312	299
30-34	799	408	391	848	432	415	664	338	326	633	323	311
35-39	692	351	341	797	406	391	847	431	416	664	338	326
40-44	609	304	305	687	347	340	793	402	391	843	428	415
45-49	723	353	369	599	296	303	678	340	338	784	396	389
50-54	797	381	416	702	338	364	585	286	299	664	329	335
55-59	654	304	350	762	356	406	675	319	357	565	271	294
60-64	565	249	316	611	274	337	716	324	393	638	293	346
65-69	467	188	279	510	213	297	556	238	319	656	283	373
70-74	412	156	256	401	150	251	442	172	269	485	194	292
75-79	332	115	217	324	112	213	321	109	212	356	127	230
80-84	222	68	154	227	69	158	227	68	159	228	67	161
85-89	71	19	52	119	30	88	126	31	95	129	31	98
90-94	28	6	22	24	5	19	43	8	35	48	8	40
95-99	3	1	2	5	1	4	4	1	4	9	1	8
100 +	0	0	0	0	0	0	0	0	0	0	0	0

Age group	2025 Both sexes	2025 Males	2025 Females	2030 Both sexes	2030 Males	2030 Females	2035 Both sexes	2035 Males	2035 Females	2040 Both sexes	2040 Males	2040 Females
All ages	9 436	4 498	4 938	9 221	4 398	4 823	8 985	4 290	4 696	8 742	4 180	4 562
0-4	405	208	197	390	200	190	380	195	185	376	193	183
5-9	422	216	206	407	209	198	392	201	191	382	196	186
10-14	438	225	214	424	217	207	409	210	199	394	202	192
15-19	462	237	225	440	226	215	426	218	208	411	211	200
20-24	485	248	237	464	238	226	442	227	216	428	219	209
25-29	514	263	251	487	249	238	466	238	227	444	227	217
30-34	612	313	300	516	264	252	489	250	239	468	239	228
35-39	634	323	311	613	313	300	517	264	253	490	251	240
40-44	662	336	326	633	322	311	613	313	300	510	264	253
45-49	836	422	413	658	333	325	630	319	310	610	310	300
50-54	770	385	385	823	413	410	650	327	323	623	314	309
55-59	643	314	329	749	369	379	802	397	404	635	316	320
60-64	537	251	286	613	292	321	716	346	371	770	374	396
65-69	588	259	329	497	224	274	570	263	308	670	313	356
70-74	576	234	342	520	215	304	443	188	254	511	224	287
75-79	396	144	251	474	176	298	431	164	267	371	146	225
80-84	257	79	177	289	92	197	350	114	236	324	109	215
85-89	133	31	102	153	37	116	176	44	132	218	57	161
90-94	52	8	44	56	8	48	67	10	57	80	13	67
95-99	11	1	10	13	1	12	15	1	14	20	2	18
100 +	1	0	1	1	0	1	2	0	2	2	0	2

Age group	2045 Both sexes	2045 Males	2045 Females	2050 Both sexes	2050 Males	2050 Females
All ages	8 499	4 072	4 428	8 262	3 964	4 298
0-4	375	192	183	376	193	183
5-9	378	194	184	377	193	184
10-14	384	197	187	380	195	185
15-19	396	203	193	386	198	188
20-24	413	212	201	398	204	194
25-29	430	220	210	415	213	202
30-34	446	228	218	432	221	211
35-39	469	240	229	447	229	219
40-44	491	250	240	469	240	230
45-49	516	263	253	489	249	240
50-54	604	305	299	511	259	252
55-59	610	304	306	593	297	296
60-64	612	299	313	589	289	300
65-69	723	341	381	578	275	303
70-74	603	270	334	655	297	358
75-79	432	176	255	514	215	298
80-84	282	99	183	332	122	210
85-89	206	57	149	183	53	130
90-94	103	19	85	101	20	81
95-99	25	2	23	34	3	30
100 +	3	0	3	4	0	4

United Nations Department of Economic and Social Affairs/Population Division
World Population Prospects: The 2004 Revision, Volume II: Sex and Age Distribution of the World Population

467

POPULATION BY AGE AND SEX (in thousands)

Age group	2005 Both sexes	Males	Females	2010 Both sexes	Males	Females	2015 Both sexes	Males	Females	2020 Both sexes	Males	Females
All ages	10 098	4 808	5 290	10 049	4 784	5 265	10 019	4 775	5 243	9 991	4 771	5 220
0-4	477	245	233	544	279	265	563	289	274	567	291	276
5-9	506	259	247	479	246	234	546	280	266	565	289	275
10-14	605	310	295	509	260	248	481	247	235	548	281	267
15-19	628	321	307	607	311	296	511	261	249	483	248	236
20-24	661	337	323	630	322	308	609	311	298	513	262	250
25-29	847	433	415	662	338	325	632	322	310	611	312	299
30-34	799	408	391	848	432	415	664	338	326	633	323	311
35-39	692	351	341	797	406	391	847	431	416	664	338	326
40-44	609	304	305	687	347	340	793	402	391	843	428	415
45-49	723	353	369	599	296	303	678	340	338	784	396	389
50-54	797	381	416	702	338	364	585	286	299	664	329	335
55-59	654	304	350	762	356	406	675	319	357	565	271	294
60-64	565	249	316	611	274	337	716	324	393	638	293	346
65-69	467	188	279	510	213	297	556	238	319	656	283	373
70-74	412	156	256	401	150	251	442	172	269	485	194	292
75-79	332	115	217	324	112	213	321	109	212	356	127	230
80-84	222	68	154	227	69	158	227	68	159	228	67	161
85-89	71	19	52	119	30	88	126	31	95	129	31	98
90-94	28	6	22	24	5	19	43	8	35	48	8	40
95-99	3	1	2	5	1	4	4	1	4	9	1	8
100 +	0	0	0	0	0	0	0	0	0	0	0	0

Age group	2025 Both sexes	Males	Females	2030 Both sexes	Males	Females	2035 Both sexes	Males	Females	2040 Both sexes	Males	Females
All ages	9 934	4 753	5 181	9 855	4 723	5 132	9 782	4 698	5 084	9 741	4 692	5 049
0-4	540	277	263	526	270	256	542	278	264	579	297	282
5-9	569	291	277	542	278	264	528	271	257	544	279	265
10-14	567	290	276	571	292	278	544	279	265	530	272	258
15-19	550	282	268	569	291	277	572	293	279	546	280	266
20-24	485	248	237	552	282	269	570	292	278	574	294	280
25-29	514	263	251	487	249	238	553	283	270	572	293	279
30-34	612	313	300	516	264	252	489	250	239	555	284	271
35-39	634	323	311	613	313	300	517	264	253	490	251	240
40-44	662	336	326	633	322	311	613	313	300	518	264	253
45-49	836	422	413	658	333	325	630	319	310	610	310	300
50-54	770	385	385	823	413	410	650	327	323	623	314	309
55-59	643	314	329	749	369	379	802	397	404	635	316	320
60-64	537	251	286	613	292	321	716	346	371	770	374	396
65-69	588	259	329	497	224	274	570	263	308	670	313	356
70-74	576	234	342	520	215	304	443	188	254	511	224	287
75-79	396	144	251	474	176	298	431	164	267	371	146	225
80-84	257	79	177	289	92	197	350	114	236	324	109	215
85-89	133	31	102	153	37	116	176	44	132	218	57	161
90-94	52	8	44	56	8	48	67	10	57	80	13	67
95-99	11	1	10	13	1	12	15	1	14	20	2	18
100 +	1	0	1	1	0	1	2	0	2	2	0	2

Age group	2045 Both sexes	Males	Females	2050 Both sexes	Males	Females
All ages	9 733	4 704	5 029	9 746	4 725	5 021
0-4	611	314	298	627	322	305
5-9	581	298	283	613	315	299
10-14	546	280	266	583	299	284
15-19	532	273	259	548	281	267
20-24	548	281	267	534	274	260
25-29	576	295	281	549	282	268
30-34	574	294	280	578	296	282
35-39	556	284	272	575	294	281
40-44	491	250	240	556	284	272
45-49	516	263	253	489	249	240
50-54	604	305	299	511	259	252
55-59	610	304	306	593	297	296
60-64	612	299	313	589	289	300
65-69	723	341	381	578	275	303
70-74	603	270	334	655	297	358
75-79	432	176	255	514	215	298
80-84	282	99	183	332	122	210
85-89	206	57	149	183	53	130
90-94	103	19	85	101	20	81
95-99	25	2	23	34	3	30
100 +	3	0	3	4	0	4

United Nations Department of Economic and Social Affairs/Population Division
World Population Prospects: The 2004 Revision, Volume II: Sex and Age Distribution of the World Population

POPULATION BY AGE AND SEX (in thousands)

Age group	2005 Both sexes	Males	Females	2010 Both sexes	Males	Females	2015 Both sexes	Males	Females	2020 Both sexes	Males	Females
All ages	10 098	4 808	5 290	9 872	4 693	5 179	9 584	4 552	5 031	9 261	4 397	4 864
0-4	477	245	233	368	188	179	304	156	148	271	139	132
5-9	506	259	247	479	246	234	370	189	180	306	157	149
10-14	605	310	295	509	260	248	481	247	235	372	190	181
15-19	628	321	307	607	311	296	511	261	249	483	248	236
20-24	661	337	323	630	322	308	609	311	298	513	262	250
25-29	847	433	415	662	338	325	632	322	310	611	312	299
30-34	799	408	391	848	432	415	664	338	326	633	323	311
35-39	692	351	341	797	406	391	847	431	416	664	338	326
40-44	609	304	305	687	347	340	793	402	391	843	428	415
45-49	723	353	369	599	296	303	678	340	338	784	396	389
50-54	797	381	416	702	338	364	585	286	299	664	329	335
55-59	654	304	350	762	356	406	675	319	357	565	271	294
60-64	565	249	316	611	274	337	716	324	393	638	293	346
65-69	467	188	279	510	213	297	556	238	319	656	283	373
70-74	412	156	256	401	150	251	442	172	269	485	194	292
75-79	332	115	217	324	112	213	321	109	212	356	127	230
80-84	222	68	154	227	69	158	227	68	159	228	67	161
85-89	71	19	52	119	30	88	126	31	95	129	31	98
90-94	28	6	22	24	5	19	43	8	35	48	8	40
95-99	3	1	2	5	1	4	4	1	4	9	1	8
100 +	0	0	0	0	0	0	0	0	0	0	0	0

Age group	2025 Both sexes	Males	Females	2030 Both sexes	Males	Females	2035 Both sexes	Males	Females	2040 Both sexes	Males	Females
All ages	8 932	4 240	4 693	8 587	4 073	4 514	8 218	3 896	4 322	7 824	3 709	4 115
0-4	268	137	131	260	133	127	245	126	119	224	115	109
5-9	273	140	133	270	138	132	262	134	128	247	127	120
10-14	308	158	150	275	141	134	272	140	133	264	135	129
15-19	374	191	182	311	159	151	277	142	135	274	141	134
20-24	485	248	237	376	192	183	313	160	152	279	143	136
25-29	514	263	251	487	249	238	378	193	184	315	161	154
30-34	612	313	300	516	264	252	489	250	239	380	194	185
35-39	634	323	311	613	313	300	517	264	253	490	251	240
40-44	662	336	326	633	322	311	613	313	300	518	264	253
45-49	836	422	413	658	333	325	630	319	310	610	310	300
50-54	770	385	385	823	413	410	650	327	323	623	314	309
55-59	643	314	329	749	369	379	802	397	404	635	316	320
60-64	537	251	286	613	292	321	716	346	371	770	374	396
65-69	588	259	329	497	224	274	570	263	308	670	313	356
70-74	576	234	342	520	215	304	443	188	254	511	224	287
75-79	396	144	251	474	176	298	431	164	267	371	146	225
80-84	257	79	177	289	92	197	350	114	236	324	109	215
85-89	133	31	102	153	37	116	176	44	132	218	57	161
90-94	52	8	44	56	8	48	67	10	57	80	13	67
95-99	11	1	10	13	1	12	15	1	14	20	2	18
100 +	1	0	1	1	0	1	2	0	2	2	0	2

Age group	2045 Both sexes	Males	Females	2050 Both sexes	Males	Females
All ages	7 409	3 513	3 896	6 989	3 312	3 677
0-4	203	104	99	191	98	93
5-9	226	116	110	205	105	100
10-14	249	128	121	228	117	111
15-19	266	137	130	251	129	122
20-24	276	142	135	268	138	131
25-29	282	144	137	278	143	136
30-34	317	162	155	284	145	138
35-39	381	195	186	318	163	156
40-44	491	250	240	382	195	187
45-49	516	263	253	489	249	240
50-54	604	305	299	511	259	252
55-59	610	304	306	593	297	296
60-64	612	299	313	589	289	300
65-69	723	341	381	578	275	303
70-74	603	270	334	655	297	358
75-79	432	176	255	514	215	298
80-84	282	99	183	332	122	210
85-89	206	57	149	183	53	130
90-94	103	19	85	101	20	81
95-99	25	2	23	34	3	30
100 +	3	0	3	4	0	4

United Nations Department of Economic and Social Affairs/Population Division
World Population Prospects: The 2004 Revision, Volume II: Sex and Age Distribution of the World Population

469

POPULATION BY AGE AND SEX (in thousands)

Age group	1950 Both sexes	Males	Females	1955 Both sexes	Males	Females	1960 Both sexes	Males	Females	1965 Both sexes	Males	Females
All ages	143	71	72	158	80	78	176	89	87	192	97	95
0-4	18	9	9	21	11	10	23	12	11	23	12	11
5-9	14	7	7	18	9	9	20	10	10	23	12	11
10-14	12	6	6	14	7	7	18	9	9	20	10	10
15-19	12	6	6	12	6	6	14	7	7	18	9	9
20-24	12	6	6	12	6	6	12	6	6	14	7	7
25-29	12	6	6	12	6	6	12	6	6	11	6	5
30-34	10	5	5	11	6	5	12	6	6	12	6	6
35-39	9	5	4	10	5	5	11	6	5	12	6	6
40-44	8	4	4	9	5	4	10	5	5	11	6	5
45-49	8	4	4	8	4	4	8	4	4	10	5	5
50-54	7	3	4	8	4	4	8	4	4	8	4	4
55-59	6	3	3	6	3	3	8	4	4	8	4	4
60-64	4	2	2	6	3	3	6	3	3	6	3	3
65-69	4	2	2	4	2	2	6	3	3	6	3	3
70-74	3	1	2	3	1	2	4	2	2	5	2	3
75-79	2	1	1	2	1	1	2	1	1	3	1	2
80 +	2	1	1	2	1	1	2	1	1	2	1	1

Age group	1970 Both sexes	Males	Females	1975 Both sexes	Males	Females	1980 Both sexes	Males	Females	1985 Both sexes	Males	Females
All ages	204	103	101	218	110	108	228	115	113	241	121	120
0-4	21	11	10	21	11	10	21	11	10	22	11	11
5-9	23	12	11	21	11	10	21	11	10	21	11	10
10-14	23	12	11	23	12	11	21	11	10	21	11	10
15-19	20	10	10	22	12	11	23	12	11	22	11	11
20-24	17	9	8	20	10	9	21	11	10	22	11	11
25-29	14	7	7	17	9	8	19	10	9	21	11	10
30-34	11	6	5	13	7	7	16	9	8	19	10	9
35-39	11	6	6	11	5	5	13	7	6	16	8	8
40-44	11	6	6	11	6	6	11	5	5	12	6	6
45-49	10	5	5	11	6	5	11	6	6	11	5	5
50-54	9	5	5	10	5	5	11	5	5	11	6	6
55-59	8	4	4	9	4	4	10	5	5	10	5	5
60-64	7	4	4	8	4	4	8	4	4	9	5	5
65-69	6	3	3	7	3	3	7	3	4	8	4	4
70-74	5	2	3	5	3	3	6	3	3	6	3	3
75-79	4	2	2	4	2	2	4	2	2	5	2	3
80 +	3	1	2	4	2	2	5	2	3	6	2	3

Age group	1990 Both sexes	Males	Females	1995 Both sexes	Males	Females	2000 Both sexes	Males	Females	2005 Both sexes	Males	Females
All ages	255	128	127	267	134	133	281	141	140	295	147	147
0-4	21	11	10	23	12	11	21	11	10	21	11	10
5-9	21	11	10	21	11	10	23	12	11	21	11	11
10-14	21	11	10	21	11	10	21	11	10	23	12	11
15-19	21	11	10	21	11	10	21	11	11	22	11	11
20-24	21	11	10	21	11	10	21	11	11	22	11	11
25-29	22	11	11	20	10	10	21	11	10	22	11	11
30-34	21	11	10	21	11	11	20	10	10	21	11	10
35-39	19	10	9	21	11	10	21	11	11	20	10	10
40-44	16	8	8	19	10	9	21	11	10	22	11	11
45-49	13	7	6	16	8	8	19	10	9	21	11	10
50-54	10	5	5	13	6	6	16	8	8	19	9	9
55-59	11	5	5	10	5	5	12	6	6	16	8	8
60-64	10	5	5	10	5	5	10	5	5	12	6	6
65-69	9	4	5	10	5	5	10	5	5	9	4	5
70-74	7	3	4	8	4	4	9	4	5	9	4	5
75-79	5	2	3	6	3	3	7	3	4	7	3	4
80 +	6	2	4	7	3	4	8	3	5	9	4	6

470

United Nations Department of Economic and Social Affairs/Population Division
World Population Prospects: The 2004 Revision, Volume II: Sex and Age Distribution of the World Population

POPULATION BY AGE AND SEX (in thousands)

Age group	2005 Both sexes	Males	Females	2010 Both sexes	Males	Females	2015 Both sexes	Males	Females	2020 Both sexes	Males	Females
All ages	295	147	147	307	153	154	319	159	160	330	164	165
0-4	21	11	10	21	11	10	20	10	10	21	11	10
5-9	21	11	11	21	11	10	21	10	10	20	10	10
10-14	23	12	11	21	11	11	21	11	10	21	10	10
15-19	22	11	11	23	12	11	22	11	11	21	11	10
20-24	22	11	11	22	11	11	23	12	12	22	11	11
25-29	22	11	11	22	11	11	22	11	11	24	12	12
30-34	21	11	10	22	11	11	22	11	11	22	11	11
35-39	20	10	10	21	11	10	22	11	11	22	11	11
40-44	22	11	11	20	10	10	21	11	11	22	11	11
45-49	21	11	10	22	11	11	20	10	10	21	11	11
50-54	19	9	9	21	10	10	21	11	11	20	10	10
55-59	16	8	8	18	9	9	21	10	10	21	11	11
60-64	12	6	6	15	8	7	18	9	9	20	10	10
65-69	9	4	5	11	6	6	15	7	7	17	9	8
70-74	9	4	5	8	4	4	11	5	5	14	7	7
75-79	7	3	4	8	4	4	7	3	4	9	4	5
80-84	5	2	3	6	2	3	6	3	3	6	3	3
85-89	3	1	2	3	1	2	4	2	2	4	2	2
90-94	1	0	1	1	0	1	2	1	1	2	1	1
95-99	0	0	0	0	0	0	0	0	0	1	0	0
100 +	0	0	0	0	0	0	0	0	0	0	0	0

Age group	2025 Both sexes	Males	Females	2030 Both sexes	Males	Females	2035 Both sexes	Males	Females	2040 Both sexes	Males	Females
All ages	340	169	171	349	174	176	357	177	180	363	179	183
0-4	21	11	10	21	11	10	20	10	10	20	10	10
5-9	21	10	10	21	11	10	21	11	10	20	10	10
10-14	20	10	10	21	10	10	21	11	10	21	11	10
15-19	21	11	10	21	10	10	21	11	10	21	11	10
20-24	21	11	11	21	11	11	21	11	11	21	11	11
25-29	22	11	11	22	11	11	22	11	11	21	11	11
30-34	24	12	12	22	11	11	22	11	11	22	11	11
35-39	22	11	11	24	12	12	22	11	11	22	11	11
40-44	22	11	11	22	11	11	24	12	12	22	11	11
45-49	22	11	11	22	11	11	22	11	11	24	12	12
50-54	21	11	10	22	11	11	22	11	11	22	11	11
55-59	20	10	10	21	11	10	21	11	11	22	11	11
60-64	21	10	10	20	10	10	20	10	10	21	10	11
65-69	19	10	10	20	10	10	19	9	10	20	10	10
70-74	16	8	8	18	9	9	19	9	10	18	9	9
75-79	12	6	6	14	7	7	16	8	8	17	8	9
80-84	8	3	4	10	5	5	12	5	6	13	6	7
85-89	4	2	2	5	2	3	7	3	4	9	4	5
90-94	2	1	1	2	1	1	3	1	2	4	2	3
95-99	1	0	1	1	0	1	1	0	1	1	0	1
100 +	0	0	0	0	0	0	0	0	0	0	0	0

Age group	2045 Both sexes	Males	Females	2050 Both sexes	Males	Females
All ages	367	181	186	370	182	188
0-4	20	10	10	20	10	10
5-9	20	10	10	20	10	10
10-14	20	10	10	20	10	10
15-19	21	11	10	21	10	10
20-24	22	11	11	22	11	11
25-29	22	11	11	22	11	11
30-34	21	11	11	22	11	11
35-39	22	11	11	21	11	11
40-44	22	11	11	22	11	11
45-49	23	11	11	22	11	11
50-54	24	12	12	22	11	11
55-59	22	11	11	24	12	12
60-64	22	11	11	22	11	11
65-69	20	10	10	21	10	11
70-74	19	9	10	19	9	10
75-79	16	8	9	17	8	9
80-84	14	6	8	14	6	8
85-89	10	4	6	11	5	6
90-94	5	2	3	6	2	4
95-99	2	1	1	2	1	2
100 +	0	0	0	1	0	0

POPULATION BY AGE AND SEX (in thousands)

Age group	2005 Both sexes	2005 Males	2005 Females	2010 Both sexes	2010 Males	2010 Females	2015 Both sexes	2015 Males	2015 Females	2020 Both sexes	2020 Males	2020 Females
All ages	295	147	147	310	155	155	326	163	163	342	171	172
0-4	21	11	10	23	12	11	25	13	12	26	13	13
5-9	21	11	11	21	11	10	23	12	11	25	13	12
10-14	23	12	11	21	11	11	21	11	10	23	12	11
15-19	22	11	11	23	12	11	22	11	11	21	11	10
20-24	22	11	11	22	11	11	23	12	12	22	11	11
25-29	22	11	11	22	11	11	22	11	11	24	12	12
30-34	21	11	10	22	11	11	22	11	11	22	11	11
35-39	20	10	10	21	11	10	22	11	11	22	11	11
40-44	22	11	11	20	10	10	21	11	11	22	11	11
45-49	21	11	10	22	11	11	20	10	10	21	11	11
50-54	19	9	9	21	10	10	21	11	11	20	10	10
55-59	16	8	8	18	9	9	21	10	10	21	11	11
60-64	12	6	6	15	8	7	18	9	9	20	10	10
65-69	9	4	5	11	6	6	15	7	7	17	9	8
70-74	9	4	5	8	4	4	11	5	5	14	7	7
75-79	7	3	4	8	4	4	7	3	4	9	4	5
80-84	5	2	3	6	2	3	6	3	3	6	3	3
85-89	3	1	2	3	1	2	4	2	2	4	2	2
90-94	1	0	1	1	0	1	2	1	1	2	1	1
95-99	0	0	0	0	0	0	0	0	0	1	0	0
100 +	0	0	0	0	0	0	0	0	0	0	0	0

Age group	2025 Both sexes	2025 Males	2025 Females	2030 Both sexes	2030 Males	2030 Females	2035 Both sexes	2035 Males	2035 Females	2040 Both sexes	2040 Males	2040 Females
All ages	358	179	180	373	186	188	387	193	195	401	199	202
0-4	26	14	13	26	14	13	27	14	13	28	14	14
5-9	26	13	13	27	13	13	27	14	13	27	14	13
10-14	25	13	12	26	13	13	27	13	13	27	14	13
15-19	24	12	12	25	13	12	27	13	13	27	14	13
20-24	21	11	11	24	12	12	26	13	13	27	14	13
25-29	22	11	11	22	11	11	24	12	12	26	13	13
30-34	24	12	12	22	11	11	22	11	11	24	12	12
35-39	22	11	11	24	12	12	22	11	11	22	11	11
40-44	22	11	11	22	11	11	24	12	12	22	11	11
45-49	22	11	11	22	11	11	22	11	11	24	12	12
50-54	21	11	10	22	11	11	22	11	11	22	11	11
55-59	20	10	10	21	11	10	21	11	11	22	11	11
60-64	21	10	10	20	10	10	20	10	10	21	10	11
65-69	19	10	10	20	10	10	19	9	10	20	10	10
70-74	16	8	8	18	9	9	19	9	10	18	9	9
75-79	12	6	6	14	7	7	16	8	8	17	8	9
80-84	8	3	4	10	5	5	12	5	6	13	6	7
85-89	4	2	2	5	2	3	7	3	4	9	4	5
90-94	2	1	1	2	1	1	3	1	2	4	2	3
95-99	1	0	1	1	0	1	1	0	1	1	0	1
100 +	0	0	0	0	0	0	0	0	0	0	0	0

Age group	2045 Both sexes	2045 Males	2045 Females	2050 Both sexes	2050 Males	2050 Females
All ages	415	206	209	430	213	217
0-4	30	15	15	31	16	15
5-9	28	14	14	30	15	15
10-14	27	14	13	28	14	14
15-19	27	14	13	27	14	13
20-24	27	14	13	27	14	13
25-29	27	14	13	27	14	14
30-34	26	13	13	27	14	13
35-39	24	12	12	26	13	13
40-44	22	11	11	24	12	12
45-49	23	11	11	22	11	11
50-54	24	12	12	22	11	11
55-59	22	11	11	24	12	12
60-64	22	11	11	22	11	11
65-69	20	10	10	21	10	11
70-74	19	9	10	19	9	10
75-79	16	8	9	17	8	9
80-84	14	6	8	14	6	8
85-89	10	4	6	11	5	6
90-94	5	2	3	6	2	4
95-99	2	1	1	2	1	2
100 +	0	0	0	1	0	0

United Nations Department of Economic and Social Affairs/Population Division
World Population Prospects: The 2004 Revision, Volume II: Sex and Age Distribution of the World Population

POPULATION BY AGE AND SEX (in thousands)

Age group	2005 Both sexes	Males	Females	2010 Both sexes	Males	Females	2015 Both sexes	Males	Females	2020 Both sexes	Males	Females
All ages	295	147	147	304	152	152	312	155	156	317	158	159
0-4	21	11	10	18	9	9	16	8	8	15	8	7
5-9	21	11	11	21	11	10	18	9	9	16	8	8
10-14	23	12	11	21	11	11	21	11	10	18	9	9
15-19	22	11	11	23	12	11	22	11	11	21	11	10
20-24	22	11	11	22	11	11	23	12	12	22	11	11
25-29	22	11	11	22	11	11	22	11	11	24	12	12
30-34	21	11	10	22	11	11	22	11	11	22	11	11
35-39	20	10	10	21	11	10	22	11	11	22	11	11
40-44	22	11	11	20	10	10	21	11	11	22	11	11
45-49	21	11	10	22	11	11	20	10	10	21	11	11
50-54	19	9	9	21	10	10	21	11	11	20	10	10
55-59	16	8	8	18	9	9	21	10	10	21	11	11
60-64	12	6	6	15	8	7	18	9	9	20	10	10
65-69	9	4	5	11	6	6	15	7	7	17	9	8
70-74	9	4	5	8	4	4	11	5	5	14	7	7
75-79	7	3	4	8	4	4	7	3	4	9	4	5
80-84	5	2	3	6	2	3	6	3	3	6	3	3
85-89	3	1	2	3	1	2	4	2	2	4	2	2
90-94	1	0	1	1	0	1	2	1	1	2	1	1
95-99	0	0	0	0	0	0	0	0	0	1	0	0
100 +	0	0	0	0	0	0	0	0	0	0	0	0

Age group	2025 Both sexes	Males	Females	2030 Both sexes	Males	Females	2035 Both sexes	Males	Females	2040 Both sexes	Males	Females
All ages	322	160	162	326	161	164	327	162	166	327	161	166
0-4	15	8	7	15	8	7	15	7	7	14	7	7
5-9	15	8	7	15	8	8	15	8	8	15	7	7
10-14	16	8	8	15	8	7	15	8	8	15	8	8
15-19	18	9	9	16	8	8	15	8	8	16	8	8
20-24	21	11	11	19	9	9	17	8	8	16	8	8
25-29	22	11	11	22	11	11	19	9	9	17	8	9
30-34	24	12	12	22	11	11	22	11	11	19	9	9
35-39	22	11	11	24	12	12	22	11	11	22	11	11
40-44	22	11	11	22	11	11	24	12	12	22	11	11
45-49	22	11	11	22	11	11	22	11	11	24	12	12
50-54	21	11	10	22	11	11	22	11	11	22	11	11
55-59	20	10	10	21	11	10	21	11	11	22	11	11
60-64	21	10	10	20	10	10	20	10	10	21	10	11
65-69	19	10	10	20	10	10	19	9	10	20	10	10
70-74	16	8	8	18	9	9	19	9	10	18	9	9
75-79	12	6	6	14	7	7	16	8	8	17	8	9
80-84	8	3	4	10	5	5	12	5	6	13	6	7
85-89	4	2	2	5	2	3	7	3	4	9	4	5
90-94	2	1	1	2	1	1	3	1	2	4	2	3
95-99	1	0	1	1	0	1	1	0	1	1	0	1
100 +	0	0	0	0	0	0	0	0	0	0	0	0

Age group	2045 Both sexes	Males	Females	2050 Both sexes	Males	Females
All ages	323	159	165	318	156	162
0-4	12	6	6	12	6	6
5-9	14	7	7	12	6	6
10-14	15	7	7	14	7	7
15-19	16	8	8	15	8	7
20-24	16	8	8	16	8	8
25-29	16	8	8	16	8	8
30-34	17	8	9	16	8	8
35-39	19	9	10	17	8	9
40-44	22	11	11	19	10	10
45-49	23	11	11	22	11	11
50-54	24	12	12	22	11	11
55-59	22	11	11	24	12	12
60-64	22	11	11	22	11	11
65-69	20	10	10	21	10	11
70-74	19	9	10	19	9	10
75-79	16	8	9	17	8	9
80-84	14	6	8	14	6	8
85-89	10	4	6	11	5	6
90-94	5	2	3	6	2	4
95-99	2	1	1	2	1	2
100 +	0	0	0	1	0	0

POPULATION BY AGE AND SEX (in thousands)

Age group	1950 Both sexes	Males	Females	1955 Both sexes	Males	Females	1960 Both sexes	Males	Females	1965 Both sexes	Males	Females
All ages	357 561	183 306	174 255	395 096	203 241	191 855	442 344	228 225	214 119	495 157	255 886	239 270
0-4	55 003	27 834	27 168	62 562	32 218	30 344	71 485	36 913	34 572	78 964	40 744	38 220
5-9	44 001	22 194	21 807	48 769	24 923	23 846	56 729	29 512	27 217	65 608	34 175	31 434
10-14	40 152	20 294	19 859	42 824	21 678	21 146	47 710	24 464	23 246	55 528	28 967	26 561
15-19	36 848	18 851	17 998	39 341	19 930	19 411	42 114	21 366	20 748	46 820	24 064	22 756
20-24	32 430	16 776	15 654	35 832	18 343	17 490	38 448	19 498	18 950	41 005	20 838	20 167
25-29	27 990	14 566	13 424	31 298	16 213	15 085	34 784	17 840	16 943	37 246	18 917	18 330
30-34	24 208	12 650	11 558	26 919	14 056	12 864	30 280	15 739	14 541	33 637	17 287	16 350
35-39	21 007	11 044	9 962	23 173	12 145	11 028	25 929	13 576	12 352	29 200	15 200	13 999
40-44	17 969	9 550	8 419	19 984	10 512	9 472	22 192	11 638	10 553	24 881	13 024	11 856
45-49	14 987	8 034	6 953	16 946	8 975	7 971	18 981	9 956	9 025	21 137	11 048	10 089
50-54	12 560	6 472	6 089	13 925	7 422	6 503	15 874	8 364	7 510	17 837	9 300	8 538
55-59	10 308	5 526	4 782	11 354	5 799	5 554	12 715	6 723	5 992	14 574	7 615	6 959
60-64	8 127	4 188	3 940	8 873	4 718	4 155	9 924	5 025	4 899	11 201	5 867	5 334
65-69	5 339	2 187	3 152	6 451	3 306	3 145	7 200	3 804	3 397	8 163	4 098	4 065
70-74	3 776	1 770	2 006	3 723	1 524	2 200	4 644	2 371	2 273	5 282	2 773	2 509
75-79	1 934	914	1 021	2 134	1 004	1 130	2 203	900	1 303	2 822	1 433	1 389
80 +	922	457	466	989	476	513	1 135	537	597	1 251	536	716

Age group	1970 Both sexes	Males	Females	1975 Both sexes	Males	Females	1980 Both sexes	Males	Females	1985 Both sexes	Males	Females
All ages	554 911	287 006	267 905	620 701	321 451	299 250	688 856	356 665	332 191	766 053	396 019	370 034
0-4	86 621	44 700	41 921	93 693	48 461	45 232	96 705	49 857	46 848	108 688	55 890	52 797
5-9	73 333	38 140	35 193	81 206	42 263	38 943	88 726	46 173	42 553	91 848	47 657	44 191
10-14	64 409	33 629	30 779	72 163	37 621	34 542	80 119	41 767	38 352	87 460	45 564	41 896
15-19	54 623	28 551	26 072	63 480	33 209	30 270	71 273	37 207	34 066	79 288	41 379	37 909
20-24	45 740	23 543	22 197	53 509	28 014	25 495	62 367	32 659	29 708	70 281	36 760	33 521
25-29	39 878	20 293	19 585	44 625	23 008	21 617	52 385	27 453	24 932	61 369	32 197	29 173
30-34	36 157	18 397	17 760	38 836	19 804	19 032	43 612	22 514	21 099	51 458	27 007	24 451
35-39	32 564	16 757	15 807	35 118	17 896	17 222	37 855	19 318	18 537	42 732	22 056	20 676
40-44	28 134	14 642	13 492	31 484	16 204	15 280	34 081	17 359	16 722	36 892	18 787	18 105
45-49	23 799	12 419	11 379	27 009	14 022	12 987	30 345	15 573	14 772	32 893	16 671	16 222
50-54	19 958	10 373	9 585	22 563	11 717	10 846	25 721	13 282	12 439	28 766	14 640	14 125
55-59	16 474	8 518	7 956	18 526	9 557	8 969	21 061	10 847	10 214	23 751	12 112	11 639
60-64	12 947	6 700	6 247	14 740	7 554	7 186	16 709	8 530	8 179	18 550	9 401	9 150
65-69	9 323	4 841	4 483	10 890	5 590	5 301	12 547	6 361	6 186	13 777	6 885	6 892
70-74	6 096	3 036	3 059	7 065	3 644	3 421	8 394	4 263	4 131	9 487	4 678	4 810
75-79	3 288	1 714	1 574	3 874	1 918	1 957	4 596	2 343	2 253	5 597	2 753	2 844
80 +	1 570	753	817	1 920	970	950	2 359	1 161	1 199	3 215	1 582	1 633

Age group	1990 Both sexes	Males	Females	1995 Both sexes	Males	Females	2000 Both sexes	Males	Females	2005 Both sexes	Males	Females
All ages	849 415	438 573	410 841	935 572	482 255	453 317	1 021 084	525 068	496 016	1 103 371	565 778	537 593
0-4	116 016	59 649	56 367	120 508	61 900	58 608	120 837	62 017	58 820	120 011	61 561	58 451
5-9	103 943	53 760	50 183	111 735	57 701	54 034	116 832	60 192	56 640	117 788	60 576	57 211
10-14	90 743	47 120	43 623	102 820	53 198	49 623	110 730	57 185	53 545	115 950	59 729	56 221
15-19	86 678	45 191	41 487	89 968	46 735	43 233	102 090	52 824	49 266	110 072	56 839	53 233
20-24	78 331	40 933	37 397	85 654	44 685	40 970	89 020	46 239	42 781	101 182	52 337	48 845
25-29	69 294	36 285	33 009	77 217	40 349	36 867	84 460	43 998	40 462	87 787	45 499	42 288
30-34	60 418	31 722	28 696	68 224	35 699	32 524	76 000	39 613	36 386	82 999	43 062	39 937
35-39	50 547	26 516	24 031	59 391	31 131	28 260	67 058	34 972	32 086	74 572	38 671	35 901
40-44	41 770	21 515	20 254	49 484	25 886	23 598	58 187	30 377	27 810	65 646	34 045	31 601
45-49	35 743	18 119	17 623	40 572	20 798	19 774	48 160	25 057	23 103	56 669	29 393	27 276
50-54	31 344	15 763	15 581	34 198	17 201	16 998	38 961	19 812	19 149	46 368	23 921	22 448
55-59	26 746	13 452	13 294	29 317	14 568	14 748	32 162	15 984	16 178	36 816	18 499	18 317
60-64	21 125	10 605	10 519	24 002	11 881	12 121	26 532	12 971	13 561	29 341	14 345	14 996
65-69	15 499	7 693	7 806	17 870	8 785	9 085	20 548	9 953	10 595	22 979	10 990	11 989
70-74	10 589	5 151	5 438	12 103	5 848	6 255	14 169	6 778	7 391	16 542	7 795	8 747
75-79	6 460	3 086	3 374	7 356	3 467	3 889	8 576	4 012	4 564	10 243	4 742	5 501
80 +	4 171	2 011	2 160	5 154	2 424	2 730	6 761	3 084	3 678	8 404	3 774	4 630

United Nations Department of Economic and Social Affairs/Population Division
World Population Prospects: The 2004 Revision, Volume II: Sex and Age Distribution of the World Population

474

POPULATION BY AGE AND SEX (in thousands)

Age group	2005 Both sexes	2005 Males	2005 Females	2010 Both sexes	2010 Males	2010 Females	2015 Both sexes	2015 Males	2015 Females	2020 Both sexes	2020 Males	2020 Females
All ages	1 103 371	565 778	537 593	1 183 293	605 060	578 232	1 260 066	642 792	617 574	1 332 032	677 661	654 371
0-4	120 011	61 561	58 451	119 667	61 350	58 316	118 706	60 821	57 884	115 685	59 244	56 441
5-9	117 788	60 576	57 211	117 522	60 364	57 157	117 635	60 351	57 284	117 054	59 987	57 066
10-14	115 950	59 729	56 221	117 030	60 171	56 859	116 862	60 005	56 857	117 072	60 038	57 034
15-19	110 072	56 839	53 233	115 383	59 423	55 959	116 539	59 899	56 640	116 431	59 762	56 669
20-24	101 182	52 337	48 845	109 275	56 403	52 871	114 682	59 033	55 649	115 922	59 550	56 372
25-29	87 787	45 499	42 288	100 009	51 636	48 373	108 214	55 774	52 441	113 711	58 460	55 251
30-34	82 999	43 062	39 937	86 338	44 579	41 759	98 606	50 767	47 839	106 884	54 966	51 918
35-39	74 572	38 671	35 901	81 433	42 030	39 403	84 867	43 632	41 235	97 125	49 838	47 287
40-44	65 646	34 045	31 601	73 015	37 641	35 375	79 874	41 012	38 863	83 405	42 693	40 712
45-49	56 669	29 393	27 276	64 010	32 973	31 037	71 354	36 556	34 798	78 235	39 950	38 286
50-54	46 368	23 921	22 448	54 712	28 135	26 576	61 999	31 677	30 322	69 326	35 249	34 077
55-59	36 816	18 499	18 317	44 012	22 444	21 569	52 171	26 529	25 641	59 372	30 010	29 362
60-64	29 341	14 345	14 996	33 839	16 730	17 109	40 731	20 444	20 287	48 585	24 321	24 264
65-69	22 979	10 990	11 989	25 691	12 287	13 404	29 929	14 478	15 451	36 346	17 854	18 492
70-74	16 542	7 795	8 747	18 770	8 731	10 040	21 275	9 893	11 382	25 093	11 804	13 289
75-79	10 243	4 742	5 501	12 194	5 555	6 639	14 095	6 329	7 766	16 251	7 289	8 962
80-84	5 340	2 415	2 925	6 532	2 920	3 612	7 959	3 493	4 466	9 403	4 058	5 344
85-89	2 254	997	1 257	2 764	1 213	1 551	3 466	1 500	1 966	4 327	1 833	2 494
90-94	661	294	368	889	384	505	1 117	476	640	1 435	601	834
95-99	132	60	72	184	80	104	251	106	145	322	133	188
100 +	17	8	9	25	11	14	35	15	20	48	20	28

Age group	2025 Both sexes	2025 Males	2025 Females	2030 Both sexes	2030 Males	2030 Females	2035 Both sexes	2035 Males	2035 Females	2040 Both sexes	2040 Males	2040 Females
All ages	1 395 496	708 226	687 270	1 449 078	733 643	715 435	1 494 269	754 685	739 584	1 534 402	773 136	761 267
0-4	110 526	56 580	53 946	104 239	53 347	50 892	100 096	51 203	48 893	99 815	51 032	48 784
5-9	114 348	58 554	55 794	109 445	56 008	53 437	103 371	52 880	50 490	99 371	50 804	48 567
10-14	116 578	59 716	56 862	113 939	58 313	55 626	109 099	55 802	53 297	103 074	52 704	50 370
15-19	116 692	59 819	56 873	116 240	59 519	56 721	113 634	58 134	55 500	108 822	55 641	53 181
20-24	115 887	59 449	56 438	116 204	59 535	56 669	115 797	59 261	56 536	113 229	57 902	55 327
25-29	115 049	59 037	56 012	115 112	58 992	56 120	115 516	59 129	56 387	115 194	58 909	56 286
30-34	112 465	57 719	54 747	113 934	58 380	55 553	114 134	58 417	55 717	114 675	58 637	56 038
35-39	105 452	54 088	51 363	111 135	56 918	54 217	112 752	57 675	55 076	113 115	57 814	55 301
40-44	95 632	40 006	46 736	104 019	53 198	50 822	109 801	56 007	53 704	111 567	56 954	54 613
45-49	81 861	41 701	40 160	94 050	47 892	46 166	102 490	52 229	50 261	108 358	55 192	50 165
50-54	76 221	38 651	37 570	79 950	40 470	39 480	92 070	46 613	45 457	100 509	50 961	49 548
55-59	66 639	33 538	33 100	70 610	35 914	35 596	77 318	38 782	38 536	89 267	44 818	44 449
60-64	55 601	27 671	27 930	62 717	31 087	31 629	69 465	34 375	35 090	73 303	36 258	37 046
65-69	43 698	21 407	22 291	50 365	24 531	25 833	57 162	27 741	29 421	63 643	30 852	32 792
70-74	30 799	14 714	16 085	37 388	17 810	19 578	43 462	20 583	22 879	49 712	23 463	26 249
75-79	19 457	8 822	10 635	24 197	11 142	13 055	29 728	13 640	16 088	34 941	15 931	19 009
80-84	11 050	4 753	6 296	13 461	5 849	7 612	16 996	7 492	9 504	21 194	9 296	11 898
85-89	5 225	2 170	3 056	6 270	2 589	3 681	7 795	3 237	4 559	10 052	4 210	5 841
90-94	1 833	748	1 085	2 265	901	1 363	2 782	1 093	1 689	3 546	1 388	2 158
95-99	421	170	250	548	215	333	693	262	431	875	322	553
100 +	62	25	37	82	32	50	108	40	68	139	49	90

Age group	2045 Both sexes	2045 Males	2045 Females	2050 Both sexes	2050 Males	2050 Females
All ages	1 567 734	788 199	779 535	1 592 704	799 063	793 641
0-4	98 235	50 200	48 035	95 174	48 626	46 549
5-9	99 186	50 676	48 510	97 691	49 886	47 805
10-14	99 108	50 646	48 461	98 944	50 530	48 413
15-19	102 821	52 557	50 264	98 873	50 511	48 362
20-24	108 452	55 432	53 021	102 484	52 370	50 114
25-29	112 698	57 594	55 104	107 998	55 172	52 826
30-34	114 483	58 494	55 989	112 110	57 254	54 857
35-39	113 811	58 128	55 683	113 768	58 075	55 693
40-44	112 091	57 195	54 896	112 935	57 603	55 332
45-49	110 264	56 145	54 120	110 936	56 484	54 452
50-54	106 442	53 975	52 468	108 484	55 020	53 465
55-59	97 656	49 138	48 518	103 622	52 176	51 446
60-64	84 924	42 081	42 843	93 170	46 299	46 871
65-69	67 457	32 707	34 750	78 519	38 165	40 354
70-74	55 728	26 284	29 444	59 416	28 035	31 381
75-79	40 361	18 342	22 019	45 663	20 731	24 932
80-84	25 246	10 996	14 250	29 550	12 803	16 747
85-89	12 777	5 301	7 476	15 502	6 353	9 149
90-94	4 673	1 833	2 841	6 081	2 339	3 742
95-99	1 143	414	729	1 545	552	993
100 +	179	61	118	238	78	160

United Nations Department of Economic and Social Affairs/Population Division
World Population Prospects: The 2004 Revision, Volume II: Sex and Age Distribution of the World Population

475

POPULATION BY AGE AND SEX (in thousands)

Age group	2005 Both sexes	2005 Males	2005 Females	2010 Both sexes	2010 Males	2010 Females	2015 Both sexes	2015 Males	2015 Females	2020 Both sexes	2020 Males	2020 Females
All ages	1 103 371	565 778	537 593	1 194 144	610 624	583 520	1 290 027	657 998	632 029	1 386 693	705 671	681 022
0-4	120 011	61 561	58 451	130 518	66 914	63 604	137 690	70 549	67 141	140 975	72 196	68 779
5-9	117 788	60 576	57 211	117 522	60 364	57 157	128 311	65 829	62 482	135 789	69 591	66 199
10-14	115 950	59 729	56 221	117 030	60 171	56 859	116 862	60 005	56 857	127 707	65 493	62 214
15-19	110 072	56 839	53 233	115 383	59 423	55 959	116 539	59 899	56 640	116 431	59 762	56 669
20-24	101 182	52 337	48 845	109 275	56 403	52 871	114 682	59 033	55 649	115 922	59 550	56 372
25-29	87 787	45 499	42 288	100 009	51 636	48 373	108 214	55 774	52 441	113 711	58 460	55 251
30-34	82 999	43 062	39 937	86 338	44 579	41 759	98 606	50 767	47 839	106 884	54 966	51 918
35-39	74 572	38 671	35 901	81 433	42 030	39 403	84 867	43 632	41 235	97 125	49 838	47 287
40-44	65 646	34 045	31 601	73 015	37 641	35 375	79 874	41 012	38 863	83 405	42 693	40 712
45-49	56 669	29 393	27 276	64 010	32 973	31 037	71 354	36 556	34 798	78 235	39 950	38 286
50-54	46 368	23 921	22 448	54 712	28 135	26 576	61 999	31 677	30 322	69 326	35 249	34 077
55-59	36 816	18 499	18 317	44 012	22 444	21 569	52 171	26 529	25 641	59 372	30 010	29 362
60-64	29 341	14 345	14 996	33 839	16 730	17 109	40 731	20 444	20 287	48 585	24 321	24 264
65-69	22 979	10 990	11 989	25 691	12 287	13 404	29 929	14 478	15 451	36 346	17 854	18 492
70-74	16 542	7 795	8 747	18 770	8 731	10 040	21 275	9 893	11 382	25 093	11 804	13 289
75-79	10 243	4 742	5 501	12 194	5 555	6 639	14 095	6 329	7 766	16 251	7 289	8 962
80-84	5 340	2 415	2 925	6 532	2 920	3 612	7 959	3 493	4 466	9 403	4 058	5 344
85-89	2 254	997	1 257	2 764	1 213	1 551	3 466	1 500	1 966	4 327	1 833	2 494
90-94	661	294	368	889	384	505	1 117	476	640	1 435	601	834
95-99	132	60	72	184	80	104	251	106	145	322	133	188
100 +	17	8	9	25	11	14	35	15	20	48	20	28

Age group	2025 Both sexes	2025 Males	2025 Females	2030 Both sexes	2030 Males	2030 Females	2035 Both sexes	2035 Males	2035 Females	2040 Both sexes	2040 Males	2040 Females
All ages	1 476 570	749 753	726 816	1 560 357	790 615	769 742	1 642 527	830 551	811 976	1 727 110	871 696	855 413
0-4	137 289	70 281	67 008	134 808	68 992	65 816	137 481	70 327	67 154	144 765	74 013	70 751
5-9	139 367	71 367	68 000	135 971	69 585	66 386	133 713	68 405	65 308	136 522	69 801	66 721
10-14	135 256	69 286	65 970	138 893	71 088	67 805	135 568	69 345	66 223	133 363	68 196	65 167
15-19	127 305	65 261	62 044	134 885	69 069	65 816	138 551	70 886	67 665	135 257	69 162	66 095
20-24	115 887	59 449	56 438	126 789	64 960	61 829	134 401	68 786	65 615	138 098	70 624	67 474
25-29	115 049	59 037	56 012	115 112	58 992	56 120	126 056	64 527	61 529	133 733	68 394	65 339
30-34	112 465	57 719	54 747	113 934	58 380	55 553	114 134	58 417	55 717	125 151	63 999	61 153
35-39	105 452	54 088	51 363	111 135	56 918	54 217	112 752	57 675	55 076	113 115	57 814	55 301
40-44	95 632	48 896	46 736	104 019	53 198	50 822	109 801	56 097	53 704	111 567	56 954	54 613
45-49	81 861	41 701	40 160	94 059	47 892	46 166	102 490	52 229	50 261	108 358	55 192	53 165
50-54	76 221	38 651	37 570	79 950	40 470	39 480	92 070	46 613	45 457	100 509	50 961	49 548
55-59	66 639	33 536	33 103	73 510	36 914	36 596	77 318	38 782	38 536	89 267	44 818	44 449
60-64	55 601	27 671	27 930	62 717	31 087	31 629	69 465	34 375	35 090	73 303	36 258	37 046
65-69	43 698	21 407	22 291	50 365	24 531	25 833	57 162	27 741	29 421	63 643	30 852	32 792
70-74	30 799	14 714	16 085	37 388	17 810	19 578	43 462	20 583	22 879	49 712	23 463	26 249
75-79	19 457	8 822	10 635	24 197	11 142	13 055	29 728	13 640	16 088	34 941	15 931	19 009
80-84	11 050	4 753	6 296	13 461	5 849	7 612	16 996	7 492	9 504	21 194	9 296	11 898
85-89	5 225	2 170	3 056	6 270	2 589	3 681	7 795	3 237	4 559	10 052	4 210	5 841
90-94	1 833	748	1 085	2 265	901	1 363	2 782	1 093	1 689	3 546	1 388	2 158
95-99	421	170	250	548	215	333	693	262	431	875	322	553
100 +	62	25	37	82	32	50	108	40	68	139	49	90

Age group	2045 Both sexes	2045 Males	2045 Females	2050 Both sexes	2050 Males	2050 Females
All ages	1 810 622	912 362	898 260	1 889 631	950 786	938 845
0-4	149 025	76 156	72 869	149 919	76 597	73 322
5-9	143 896	73 523	70 374	148 251	75 709	72 542
10-14	136 203	69 609	66 594	143 596	73 342	70 254
15-19	133 074	68 027	65 047	135 930	69 450	66 479
20-24	134 842	68 925	65 917	132 693	67 813	64 880
25-29	137 493	70 272	67 220	134 325	68 629	65 696
30-34	132 930	67 928	65 003	136 808	69 878	66 930
35-39	124 218	63 450	60 768	132 116	67 452	64 664
40-44	112 091	57 195	54 896	123 267	62 880	60 387
45-49	110 264	56 145	54 120	110 936	56 484	54 452
50-54	106 442	53 975	52 468	108 484	55 020	53 465
55-59	97 656	49 138	48 518	103 622	52 176	51 446
60-64	84 924	42 081	42 843	93 170	46 299	46 871
65-69	67 457	32 707	34 750	78 519	38 165	40 354
70-74	55 728	26 284	29 444	59 416	28 035	31 381
75-79	40 361	18 342	22 019	45 663	20 731	24 932
80-84	25 246	10 996	14 250	29 550	12 803	16 747
85-89	12 777	5 301	7 476	15 502	6 353	9 149
90-94	4 673	1 833	2 841	6 081	2 339	3 742
95-99	1 143	414	729	1 545	552	993
100 +	179	61	118	238	78	160

POPULATION BY AGE AND SEX (in thousands)

Age group	2005 Both sexes	Males	Females	2010 Both sexes	Males	Females	2015 Both sexes	Males	Females	2020 Both sexes	Males	Females
All ages	1 103 371	565 778	537 593	1 172 441	599 497	572 944	1 230 700	627 507	603 110	1 277 372	649 651	627 721
0-4	120 011	61 561	58 451	108 816	55 787	53 029	99 722	51 094	48 627	90 395	46 292	44 103
5-9	117 788	60 576	57 211	117 522	60 364	57 157	106 959	54 873	52 086	98 318	50 384	47 933
10-14	115 950	59 729	56 221	117 030	60 171	56 859	116 862	60 005	56 857	106 437	54 582	51 855
15-19	110 072	56 839	53 233	115 383	59 423	55 959	116 539	59 899	56 640	116 431	59 762	56 669
20-24	101 182	52 337	48 845	109 275	56 403	52 871	114 682	59 033	55 649	115 922	59 550	56 372
25-29	87 787	45 499	42 288	100 009	51 636	48 373	108 214	55 774	52 441	113 711	58 460	55 251
30-34	82 999	43 062	39 937	86 338	44 579	41 759	98 606	50 767	47 839	106 884	54 966	51 918
35-39	74 572	38 671	35 901	81 433	42 030	39 403	84 867	43 632	41 235	97 125	49 838	47 287
40-44	65 646	34 045	31 601	73 015	37 641	35 375	79 874	41 012	38 863	83 405	42 693	40 712
45-49	56 669	29 393	27 276	64 010	32 973	31 037	71 354	36 556	34 798	78 235	39 950	38 286
50-54	46 368	23 921	22 448	54 712	28 135	26 576	61 999	31 677	30 322	69 326	35 249	34 077
55-59	36 816	18 499	18 317	44 012	22 444	21 569	52 171	26 529	25 641	59 372	30 010	29 362
60-64	29 341	14 345	14 996	33 839	16 730	17 109	40 731	20 444	20 287	48 585	24 321	24 264
65-69	22 979	10 990	11 989	25 691	12 287	13 404	29 929	14 478	15 451	36 346	17 854	18 492
70-74	16 542	7 795	8 747	18 770	8 731	10 040	21 275	9 893	11 382	25 093	11 804	13 289
75-79	10 243	4 742	5 501	12 194	5 555	6 639	14 095	6 329	7 766	16 251	7 289	8 962
80-84	5 340	2 415	2 925	6 532	2 920	3 612	7 959	3 493	4 466	9 403	4 058	5 344
85-89	2 254	997	1 257	2 764	1 213	1 551	3 466	1 500	1 966	4 327	1 833	2 494
90-94	661	294	368	889	384	505	1 117	476	640	1 435	601	834
95-99	132	60	72	184	80	104	251	106	145	322	133	188
100 +	17	8	9	25	11	14	35	15	20	48	20	28

Age group	2025 Both sexes	Males	Females	2030 Both sexes	Males	Females	2035 Both sexes	Males	Females	2040 Both sexes	Males	Females
All ages	1 314 620	666 800	647 820	1 339 548	677 566	661 982	1 352 153	681 960	670 192	1 355 453	681 610	673 843
0-4	83 959	42 979	40 980	75 224	38 497	36 727	67 116	34 332	32 784	62 513	31 960	30 554
5-9	89 329	45 741	43 589	83 115	42 531	40 583	74 570	38 144	36 425	66 597	34 045	32 552
10-14	97 900	50 146	47 755	88 984	45 538	43 446	82 824	42 359	40 465	74 324	37 999	36 325
15-19	106 079	54 377	51 703	97 595	49 969	47 626	88 717	45 382	43 335	82 582	42 219	40 363
20-24	115 887	59 449	56 438	105 619	54 110	51 509	97 193	49 737	47 456	88 361	45 180	43 181
25-29	115 049	59 037	56 012	115 112	58 992	56 120	104 976	53 731	51 245	96 656	49 424	47 233
30-34	112 465	57 719	54 747	113 934	58 380	55 553	114 134	58 417	55 717	104 198	53 275	50 923
35-39	105 452	54 088	51 363	111 135	56 918	54 217	112 752	57 675	55 076	113 115	57 814	55 301
40-44	95 632	48 896	46 736	104 019	53 198	50 822	109 801	56 097	53 704	111 567	56 954	54 613
45-49	81 861	41 701	40 160	94 050	47 892	46 166	102 490	52 229	50 261	108 358	55 192	53 165
50-54	76 221	38 651	37 570	79 950	40 470	39 480	92 070	46 613	45 457	100 509	50 961	49 548
55-59	66 638	33 538	33 100	70 510	35 914	35 596	77 318	38 782	38 536	89 267	44 818	44 449
60-64	55 601	27 671	27 930	62 717	31 087	31 629	69 465	34 375	35 090	73 303	36 258	37 046
65-69	43 698	21 407	22 291	50 365	24 531	25 833	57 162	27 741	29 421	63 643	30 852	32 792
70-74	30 799	14 714	16 085	37 388	17 810	19 578	43 462	20 583	22 879	49 712	23 463	26 249
75-79	19 457	8 822	10 635	24 197	11 142	13 055	29 728	13 640	16 088	34 941	15 931	19 009
80-84	11 050	4 753	6 296	13 461	5 849	7 612	16 996	7 492	9 504	21 104	9 296	11 898
85-89	5 225	2 170	3 056	6 270	2 589	3 681	7 795	3 237	4 559	10 052	4 210	5 841
90-94	1 833	748	1 085	2 265	901	1 363	2 782	1 093	1 689	3 546	1 388	2 158
95-99	421	170	250	548	215	333	693	262	431	875	322	553
100 +	62	25	37	82	32	50	108	40	68	139	49	90

Age group	2045 Both sexes	Males	Females	2050 Both sexes	Males	Females
All ages	1 348 929	676 344	672 585	1 332 527	666 115	666 412
0-4	57 819	29 546	28 273	53 161	27 160	26 001
5-9	62 082	31 715	30 367	57 458	29 338	28 121
10-14	66 383	33 918	32 465	61 888	31 600	30 288
15-19	74 104	37 873	36 232	66 182	33 803	32 378
20-24	82 257	42 037	40 219	73 810	37 711	36 099
25-29	87 903	44 916	42 987	81 865	41 814	40 051
30-34	96 036	49 060	46 975	87 413	44 630	42 783
35-39	103 405	52 807	50 597	95 421	48 699	46 722
40-44	112 091	57 195	54 896	102 603	52 326	50 277
45-49	110 264	56 145	54 120	110 936	56 484	54 452
50-54	106 442	53 975	52 468	108 484	55 020	53 465
55-59	97 656	49 138	48 518	103 622	52 176	51 446
60-64	84 924	42 081	42 843	93 170	46 299	46 871
65-69	67 457	32 707	34 750	78 519	38 165	40 354
70-74	55 728	26 284	29 444	59 416	28 035	31 381
75-79	40 361	18 342	22 019	45 663	20 731	24 932
80-84	25 246	10 996	14 250	29 550	12 803	16 747
85-89	12 777	5 301	7 476	15 502	6 353	9 149
90-94	4 673	1 833	2 841	6 081	2 339	3 742
95-99	1 143	414	729	1 545	552	993
100 +	179	61	118	238	78	160

United Nations Department of Economic and Social Affairs/Population Division
World Population Prospects: The 2004 Revision, Volume II: Sex and Age Distribution of the World Population

477

POPULATION BY AGE AND SEX (in thousands)

Age group	1950 Both sexes	1950 Males	1950 Females	1955 Both sexes	1955 Males	1955 Females	1960 Both sexes	1960 Males	1960 Females	1965 Both sexes	1965 Males	1965 Females
All ages	79 538	39 455	40 083	86 446	42 983	43 463	95 931	47 797	48 134	106 552	53 186	53 366
0-4	11 392	5 559	5 834	13 476	6 839	6 637	16 035	8 136	7 899	17 281	8 772	8 509
5-9	10 116	4 896	5 220	10 285	5 033	5 252	12 304	6 256	6 047	14 798	7 520	7 278
10-14	9 648	4 722	4 926	9 829	4 767	5 062	10 021	4 912	5 109	12 022	6 121	5 901
15-19	8 583	4 240	4 343	9 353	4 590	4 763	9 556	4 645	4 911	9 768	4 797	4 972
20-24	7 358	3 710	3 648	8 227	4 070	4 157	9 000	4 422	4 578	9 222	4 486	4 737
25-29	5 926	3 040	2 886	6 989	3 525	3 463	7 851	3 885	3 966	8 618	4 233	4 385
30-34	5 053	2 575	2 479	5 594	2 872	2 722	6 632	3 347	3 286	7 481	3 702	3 780
35-39	4 671	2 390	2 281	4 730	2 409	2 322	5 268	2 702	2 566	6 278	3 164	3 113
40-44	4 017	2 041	1 975	4 328	2 205	2 123	4 413	2 238	2 176	4 943	2 526	2 418
45-49	3 173	1 579	1 594	3 680	1 852	1 827	3 993	2 017	1 977	4 099	2 061	2 038
50-54	2 483	1 241	1 242	2 849	1 399	1 450	3 331	1 656	1 675	3 643	1 818	1 825
55-59	2 166	1 061	1 105	2 159	1 062	1 098	2 503	1 210	1 293	2 953	1 447	1 507
60-64	1 803	894	909	1 790	861	929	1 807	873	934	2 120	1 006	1 114
65-69	1 389	669	719	1 376	668	708	1 390	654	736	1 425	673	752
70-74	948	459	489	945	444	501	957	452	504	986	451	535
75-79	538	252	286	537	252	284	551	251	300	572	262	311
80 +	276	128	147	299	135	165	318	142	176	341	148	193

Age group	1970 Both sexes	1970 Males	1970 Females	1975 Both sexes	1975 Males	1975 Females	1980 Both sexes	1980 Males	1980 Females	1985 Both sexes	1985 Males	1985 Females
All ages	119 936	59 975	59 961	134 395	67 281	67 114	150 072	75 218	74 855	166 180	83 290	82 891
0-4	19 848	10 080	9 768	20 917	10 620	10 297	22 138	11 258	10 880	22 528	11 439	11 089
5-9	16 157	8 210	7 947	18 779	9 542	9 237	20 021	10 167	9 854	21 407	10 871	10 536
10-14	14 509	7 380	7 129	15 891	8 080	7 811	18 524	9 416	9 108	19 803	10 054	9 749
15-19	11 763	5 997	5 766	14 244	7 251	6 992	15 645	7 959	7 687	18 291	9 296	8 995
20-24	9 476	4 655	4 821	11 461	5 842	5 619	13 923	7 086	6 837	15 355	7 803	7 552
25-29	8 888	4 321	4 567	9 180	4 506	4 674	11 144	5 677	5 467	13 607	6 915	6 691
30-34	8 271	4 062	4 209	8 579	4 169	4 410	8 899	4 366	4 533	10 863	5 528	5 335
35-39	7 138	3 528	3 610	7 942	3 895	4 047	8 281	4 020	4 261	8 641	4 233	4 409
40-44	5 943	2 985	2 958	6 805	3 351	3 454	7 619	3 725	3 894	7 996	3 868	4 127
45-49	4 633	2 350	2 283	5 613	2 799	2 813	6 471	3 168	3 303	7 294	3 545	3 748
50-54	3 778	1 880	1 898	4 306	2 162	2 143	5 256	2 598	2 657	6 106	2 963	3 143
55-59	3 269	1 609	1 660	3 424	1 680	1 743	3 936	1 952	1 984	4 848	2 366	2 482
60-64	2 539	1 222	1 317	2 845	1 375	1 470	3 012	1 453	1 559	3 501	1 705	1 795
65-69	1 706	791	915	2 075	975	1 100	2 357	1 113	1 244	2 531	1 191	1 340
70-74	1 036	476	560	1 265	569	696	1 565	714	851	1 810	828	981
75-79	610	269	341	658	291	367	822	356	466	1 040	456	584
80 +	372	160	212	411	172	239	458	190	268	561	228	333

Age group	1990 Both sexes	1990 Males	1990 Females	1995 Both sexes	1995 Males	1995 Females	2000 Both sexes	2000 Males	2000 Females	2005 Both sexes	2005 Males	2005 Females
All ages	181 414	90 903	90 511	195 649	97 986	97 664	209 174	104 599	104 575	222 781	111 231	111 551
0-4	21 782	11 080	10 702	21 247	10 818	10 429	20 914	10 648	10 266	21 571	10 983	10 588
5-9	21 995	11 155	10 840	21 379	10 863	10 516	20 933	10 646	10 288	20 664	10 508	10 156
10-14	21 217	10 768	10 449	21 841	11 065	10 776	21 245	10 789	10 457	20 818	10 580	10 238
15-19	19 577	9 929	9 648	20 957	10 620	10 337	21 635	10 948	10 687	21 058	10 679	10 378
20-24	17 972	9 117	8 855	19 187	9 708	9 479	20 592	10 390	10 202	21 277	10 717	10 560
25-29	15 027	7 621	7 406	17 591	8 899	8 692	18 761	9 424	9 336	20 162	10 096	10 066
30-34	13 298	6 749	6 549	14 700	7 438	7 262	17 210	8 657	8 553	18 384	9 179	9 205
35-39	10 581	5 375	5 207	12 990	6 579	6 411	14 390	7 256	7 133	16 889	8 467	8 422
40-44	8 376	4 089	4 287	10 297	5 217	5 080	12 692	6 411	6 281	14 095	7 089	7 006
45-49	7 696	3 703	3 992	8 092	3 933	4 160	9 987	5 043	4 945	12 348	6 217	6 131
50-54	6 931	3 342	3 588	7 345	3 508	3 837	7 751	3 744	4 007	9 597	4 819	4 779
55-59	5 683	2 724	2 959	6 487	3 092	3 395	6 906	3 263	3 643	7 314	3 496	3 818
60-64	4 363	2 092	2 270	5 153	2 428	2 726	5 920	2 773	3 147	6 334	2 941	3 393
65-69	2 985	1 420	1 565	3 758	1 760	1 998	4 478	2 059	2 419	5 178	2 367	2 811
70-74	1 981	904	1 077	2 364	1 091	1 273	3 009	1 366	1 643	3 617	1 611	2 006
75-79	1 232	542	690	1 370	601	769	1 658	735	922	2 134	930	1 204
80 +	719	294	425	890	365	525	1 092	446	646	1 339	551	789

United Nations Department of Economic and Social Affairs/Population Division
World Population Prospects: The 2004 Revision, Volume II: Sex and Age Distribution of the World Population

POPULATION BY AGE AND SEX (in thousands)

Age group	2005 Both sexes	Males	Females	2010 Both sexes	Males	Females	2015 Both sexes	Males	Females	2020 Both sexes	Males	Females
All ages	222 781	111 231	111 551	235 755	117 632	118 123	246 813	123 100	123 713	255 853	127 592	128 261
0-4	21 571	10 983	10 588	21 172	10 800	10 371	19 873	10 149	9 725	18 495	9 443	9 051
5-9	20 664	10 508	10 156	21 387	10 881	10 506	21 021	10 718	10 303	19 750	10 080	9 670
10-14	20 818	10 580	10 238	20 575	10 458	10 117	21 307	10 836	10 471	20 955	10 680	10 276
15-19	21 058	10 679	10 378	20 666	10 490	10 175	20 437	10 376	10 061	21 196	10 769	10 427
20-24	21 277	10 717	10 560	20 760	10 484	10 275	20 391	10 309	10 082	20 221	10 244	9 977
25-29	20 162	10 096	10 066	20 909	10 463	10 446	20 421	10 247	10 174	20 124	10 149	9 975
30-34	18 384	9 179	9 205	19 835	9 882	9 953	20 602	10 260	10 342	20 166	10 098	10 068
35-39	16 889	8 467	8 422	18 106	9 016	9 091	19 571	9 727	9 844	20 343	10 113	10 230
40-44	14 095	7 089	7 006	16 608	8 311	8 298	17 841	8 870	8 971	19 295	9 572	9 723
45-49	12 348	6 217	6 131	13 770	6 909	6 862	16 269	8 124	8 145	17 507	8 680	8 826
50-54	9 597	4 819	4 779	11 928	5 978	5 950	13 344	6 668	6 676	15 806	7 857	7 949
55-59	7 314	3 496	3 818	9 110	4 534	4 576	11 370	5 653	5 717	12 759	6 323	6 436
60-64	6 334	2 941	3 393	6 757	3 179	3 578	8 455	4 150	4 305	10 597	5 195	5 403
65-69	5 178	2 367	2 811	5 594	2 539	3 055	6 006	2 767	3 239	7 552	3 631	3 921
70-74	3 617	1 611	2 006	4 235	1 880	2 356	4 618	2 037	2 581	4 993	2 234	2 758
75-79	2 134	930	1 204	2 609	1 119	1 490	3 093	1 323	1 769	3 407	1 447	1 960
80-84	945	399	546	1 242	518	725	1 543	633	909	1 853	758	1 095
85-89	317	124	193	397	158	238	530	209	321	669	259	409
90-94	69	25	44	85	31	54	108	40	68	146	53	93
95-99	8	2	5	10	3	7	13	4	9	17	5	11
100 +	0	0	0	1	0	0	1	0	1	1	0	1

Age group	2025 Both sexes	Males	Females	2030 Both sexes	Males	Females	2035 Both sexes	Males	Females	2040 Both sexes	Males	Females
All ages	263 746	131 478	132 268	270 844	134 903	135 941	276 850	137 654	139 197	281 211	139 540	141 672
0-4	18 171	9 280	8 890	18 216	9 302	8 914	17 974	9 186	8 789	17 392	8 896	8 496
5-9	18 393	9 387	9 006	18 085	9 231	8 854	18 141	9 260	8 881	17 908	9 149	8 759
10-14	19 694	10 047	9 647	18 346	9 359	8 987	18 044	9 207	8 837	18 103	9 238	8 865
15-19	20 854	10 618	10 236	19 605	9 992	9 613	18 266	9 309	8 956	17 968	9 161	8 807
20-24	20 990	10 642	10 349	20 664	10 499	10 164	19 428	9 882	9 546	18 100	9 208	8 893
25-29	19 970	10 093	9 877	20 753	10 497	10 256	20 440	10 363	10 077	19 218	9 756	9 462
30-34	19 888	10 010	9 878	19 754	9 963	9 791	20 547	10 373	10 173	20 246	10 248	9 998
35-39	19 932	9 963	9 969	19 677	9 885	9 792	19 560	9 849	9 711	20 362	10 266	10 096
40-44	20 085	9 967	10 118	19 705	9 832	9 873	19 474	9 767	9 707	19 376	9 743	9 633
45-49	18 967	9 386	9 581	19 781	9 792	9 990	19 437	9 676	9 761	19 236	9 630	9 606
50-54	17 048	8 416	8 632	18 519	9 125	9 394	19 360	9 544	9 815	19 061	9 455	9 606
55-59	15 161	7 476	7 685	16 410	8 036	8 374	17 885	8 744	9 141	18 753	9 178	9 574
60-64	11 941	5 835	6 106	14 258	6 933	7 325	15 506	7 488	8 018	16 973	8 188	8 785
65-69	9 519	4 572	4 948	10 797	5 169	5 629	12 985	6 180	6 805	14 214	6 721	7 494
70-74	6 319	2 954	3 365	8 036	3 752	4 284	9 217	4 277	4 940	11 200	5 162	6 038
75-79	3 719	1 603	2 116	4 759	2 145	2 614	6 160	2 754	3 406	7 182	3 181	4 001
80-84	2 068	840	1 228	2 292	944	1 348	3 021	1 282	1 740	4 022	1 674	2 348
85-89	815	315	500	925	355	570	1 079	405	674	1 484	561	922
90-94	187	67	120	231	83	149	284	95	189	354	110	244
95-99	23	7	15	30	9	20	41	12	29	55	14	41
100 +	1	0	1	2	0	1	3	1	2	4	1	3

Age group	2045 Both sexes	Males	Females	2050 Both sexes	Males	Females
All ages	283 756	140 466	143 290	284 640	140 594	144 045
0-4	16 734	8 563	8 170	16 257	8 325	7 932
5-9	17 333	8 864	8 469	16 680	8 536	8 144
10-14	17 873	9 130	8 743	17 301	8 846	8 455
15-19	18 031	9 195	8 837	17 805	9 089	8 716
20-24	17 810	9 064	8 746	17 878	9 101	8 776
25-29	17 901	9 088	8 813	17 617	8 950	8 667
30-34	19 036	9 648	9 388	17 730	8 988	8 742
35-39	20 074	10 148	9 926	18 878	9 557	9 321
40-44	20 189	10 167	10 022	19 915	10 058	9 856
45-49	19 161	9 618	9 542	19 986	10 051	9 935
50-54	18 896	9 429	9 468	18 850	9 436	9 415
55-59	18 509	9 118	9 391	18 388	9 118	9 271
60-64	17 863	8 630	9 233	17 685	8 607	9 078
65-69	15 648	7 390	8 257	16 546	7 831	8 715
70-74	12 373	5 657	6 717	13 724	6 266	7 458
75-79	8 857	3 879	4 978	9 907	4 294	5 613
80-84	4 810	1 960	2 850	6 055	2 423	3 632
85-89	2 060	745	1 316	2 549	885	1 664
90-94	518	155	363	760	209	551
95-99	75	16	59	118	23	95
100 +	6	1	5	9	1	8

United Nations Department of Economic and Social Affairs/Population Division
World Population Prospects: The 2004 Revision, Volume II: Sex and Age Distribution of the World Population

479

POPULATION BY AGE AND SEX (in thousands)

Age group	2005 Both sexes	Males	Females	2010 Both sexes	Males	Females	2015 Both sexes	Males	Females	2020 Both sexes	Males	Females
All ages	222 781	111 231	111 551	238 015	118 785	119 231	252 881	126 197	126 684	266 777	133 166	133 611
0-4	21 571	10 983	10 588	23 431	11 953	11 478	23 694	12 100	11 594	23 374	11 934	11 439
5-9	20 664	10 508	10 156	21 387	10 881	10 506	23 268	11 863	11 405	23 553	12 021	11 532
10-14	20 818	10 580	10 238	20 575	10 458	10 117	21 307	10 836	10 471	23 198	11 823	11 375
15-19	21 058	10 679	10 378	20 666	10 490	10 175	20 437	10 376	10 061	21 196	10 769	10 427
20-24	21 277	10 717	10 560	20 760	10 484	10 275	20 391	10 309	10 082	20 221	10 244	9 977
25-29	20 162	10 096	10 066	20 909	10 463	10 446	20 421	10 247	10 174	20 124	10 149	9 975
30-34	18 384	9 179	9 205	19 835	9 882	9 953	20 602	10 260	10 342	20 166	10 098	10 068
35-39	16 889	8 467	8 422	18 106	9 016	9 091	19 571	9 727	9 844	20 343	10 113	10 230
40-44	14 095	7 089	7 006	16 608	8 311	8 298	17 841	8 870	8 971	19 295	9 572	9 723
45-49	12 348	6 217	6 131	13 770	6 909	6 862	16 269	8 124	8 145	17 507	8 680	8 826
50-54	9 597	4 819	4 779	11 928	5 978	5 950	13 344	6 668	6 676	15 806	7 857	7 949
55-59	7 314	3 496	3 818	9 110	4 534	4 576	11 370	5 653	5 717	12 759	6 323	6 436
60-64	6 334	2 941	3 393	6 757	3 179	3 578	8 455	4 150	4 305	10 597	5 195	5 403
65-69	5 178	2 367	2 811	5 594	2 539	3 055	6 006	2 767	3 239	7 552	3 631	3 921
70-74	3 617	1 611	2 006	4 235	1 880	2 356	4 618	2 037	2 581	4 993	2 234	2 758
75-79	2 134	930	1 204	2 609	1 119	1 490	3 093	1 323	1 769	3 407	1 447	1 960
80-84	945	399	546	1 242	518	725	1 543	633	909	1 853	758	1 095
85-89	317	124	193	397	158	238	530	209	321	669	259	409
90-94	69	25	44	85	31	54	108	40	68	146	53	93
95-99	8	2	5	10	3	7	13	4	9	17	5	11
100 +	0	0	0	1	0	0	1	0	1	1	0	1

Age group	2025 Both sexes	Males	Females	2030 Both sexes	Males	Females	2035 Both sexes	Males	Females	2040 Both sexes	Males	Females
All ages	279 692	139 615	140 077	292 429	145 914	146 515	305 187	152 109	153 078	317 543	158 077	159 466
0-4	23 224	11 861	11 363	23 891	12 200	11 692	24 773	12 660	12 113	25 443	13 014	12 430
5-9	23 254	11 867	11 387	23 124	11 803	11 320	23 804	12 150	11 654	24 694	12 616	12 078
10-14	23 490	11 984	11 506	23 200	11 835	11 365	23 076	11 775	11 301	23 760	12 125	11 635
15-19	23 091	11 757	11 334	23 393	11 923	11 469	23 111	11 779	11 331	22 993	11 724	11 269
20-24	20 990	10 642	10 349	22 893	11 633	11 260	23 205	11 806	11 399	22 933	11 670	11 264
25-29	19 970	10 093	9 877	20 753	10 497	10 256	22 661	11 492	11 169	22 983	11 672	11 311
30-34	19 888	10 010	9 878	19 754	9 963	9 791	20 547	10 373	10 173	22 460	11 373	11 087
35-39	19 932	9 963	9 969	19 677	9 885	9 792	19 560	9 849	9 711	20 362	10 266	10 096
40-44	20 085	9 967	10 118	19 705	9 832	9 873	19 474	9 767	9 707	19 376	9 743	9 633
45-49	18 967	9 386	9 581	19 781	9 792	9 990	19 437	9 676	9 761	19 236	9 630	9 606
50-54	17 048	8 416	8 632	18 519	9 125	9 394	19 360	9 544	9 815	19 061	9 455	9 606
55-59	15 161	7 476	7 685	16 410	8 036	8 374	17 885	8 744	9 141	18 753	9 178	9 574
60-64	11 941	5 835	6 106	14 258	6 933	7 325	15 506	7 488	8 018	16 973	8 188	8 785
65-69	9 519	4 572	4 948	10 797	5 169	5 629	12 985	6 180	6 805	14 214	6 721	7 494
70-74	6 319	2 954	3 365	8 036	3 752	4 284	9 217	4 277	4 940	11 200	5 162	6 038
75-79	3 719	1 603	2 116	4 759	2 145	2 614	6 160	2 754	3 406	7 182	3 181	4 001
80-84	2 068	840	1 228	2 292	944	1 348	3 021	1 282	1 740	4 022	1 674	2 348
85-89	815	315	500	925	355	570	1 079	405	674	1 484	561	922
90-94	187	67	120	231	83	149	284	95	189	354	110	244
95-99	23	7	15	30	9	20	41	12	29	55	14	41
100 +	1	0	1	2	0	1	3	1	2	4	1	3

Age group	2045 Both sexes	Males	Females	2050 Both sexes	Males	Females
All ages	329 109	163 614	165 495	339 817	168 769	171 048
0-4	25 822	13 215	12 608	26 162	13 397	12 764
5-9	25 372	12 975	12 397	25 757	13 181	12 577
10-14	24 653	12 593	12 060	25 334	12 954	12 380
15-19	23 681	12 076	11 605	24 578	12 547	12 031
20-24	22 824	11 620	11 204	23 517	11 977	11 541
25-29	22 722	11 543	11 179	22 620	11 499	11 121
30-34	22 791	11 559	11 232	22 539	11 436	11 103
35-39	22 280	11 269	11 011	22 621	11 462	11 159
40-44	20 189	10 167	10 022	22 110	11 173	10 937
45-49	19 161	9 618	9 542	19 986	10 051	9 935
50-54	18 896	9 429	9 468	18 850	9 436	9 415
55-59	18 509	9 118	9 391	18 388	9 118	9 271
60-64	17 863	8 630	9 233	17 685	8 607	9 078
65-69	15 648	7 390	8 257	16 546	7 831	8 715
70-74	12 373	5 657	6 717	13 724	6 266	7 458
75-79	8 857	3 879	4 978	9 907	4 294	5 613
80-84	4 810	1 960	2 850	6 055	2 423	3 632
85-89	2 060	745	1 316	2 549	885	1 664
90-94	518	155	363	760	209	551
95-99	75	16	59	118	23	95
100 +	6	1	5	9	1	8

United Nations Department of Economic and Social Affairs/Population Division
World Population Prospects: The 2004 Revision, Volume II: Sex and Age Distribution of the World Population

480

POPULATION BY AGE AND SEX (in thousands)

Age group	2005 Both sexes	Males	Females	2010 Both sexes	Males	Females	2015 Both sexes	Males	Females	2020 Both sexes	Males	Females
All ages	222 781	111 231	111 551	233 393	116 427	116 966	240 542	119 899	120 642	244 090	121 000	123 790
0-4	21 571	10 983	10 588	18 809	9 595	9 214	15 951	8 146	7 805	13 588	6 938	6 650
5-9	20 664	10 508	10 156	21 387	10 881	10 506	18 671	9 520	9 152	15 845	8 087	7 758
10-14	20 818	10 580	10 238	20 575	10 458	10 117	21 307	10 836	10 471	18 612	9 485	9 126
15-19	21 058	10 679	10 378	20 666	10 490	10 175	20 437	10 376	10 061	21 196	10 769	10 427
20-24	21 277	10 717	10 560	20 760	10 484	10 275	20 391	10 309	10 082	20 221	10 244	9 977
25-29	20 162	10 096	10 066	20 909	10 463	10 446	20 421	10 247	10 174	20 124	10 149	9 975
30-34	18 384	9 179	9 205	19 835	9 882	9 953	20 602	10 260	10 342	20 166	10 098	10 068
35-39	16 889	8 467	8 422	18 106	9 016	9 091	19 571	9 727	9 844	20 343	10 113	10 230
40-44	14 095	7 089	7 006	16 608	8 311	8 298	17 841	8 870	8 971	19 295	9 572	9 723
45-49	12 348	6 217	6 131	13 770	6 909	6 862	16 269	8 124	8 145	17 507	8 680	8 826
50-54	9 597	4 819	4 779	11 928	5 978	5 950	13 344	6 668	6 676	15 806	7 857	7 949
55-59	7 314	3 496	3 818	9 110	4 534	4 576	11 370	5 653	5 717	12 759	6 323	6 436
60-64	6 334	2 941	3 393	6 757	3 179	3 578	8 455	4 150	4 305	10 597	5 195	5 403
65-69	5 178	2 367	2 811	5 594	2 539	3 055	6 006	2 767	3 239	7 552	3 631	3 921
70-74	3 617	1 611	2 006	4 235	1 880	2 356	4 618	2 037	2 581	4 993	2 234	2 758
75-79	2 134	930	1 204	2 609	1 119	1 490	3 093	1 323	1 769	3 407	1 447	1 960
80-84	945	399	546	1 242	518	725	1 543	633	909	1 853	758	1 095
85-89	317	124	193	397	158	238	530	209	321	669	259	409
90-94	69	25	44	85	31	54	108	40	68	146	53	93
95-99	8	2	5	10	3	7	13	4	9	17	5	11
100 +	0	0	0	1	0	0	1	0	1	1	0	1

Age group	2025 Both sexes	Males	Females	2030 Both sexes	Males	Females	2035 Both sexes	Males	Females	2040 Both sexes	Males	Females
All ages	247 615	123 247	124 368	249 344	123 935	125 409	249 328	123 615	125 713	247 020	122 096	124 924
0-4	13 163	6 723	6 440	12 809	6 541	6 268	11 906	6 085	5 821	10 668	5 456	5 211
5-9	13 505	6 892	6 613	13 092	6 683	6 409	12 747	6 506	6 240	11 851	6 055	5 796
10-14	15 797	8 059	7 738	13 465	6 869	6 596	13 056	6 662	6 394	12 714	6 488	6 226
15-19	18 516	9 427	9 089	15 715	8 009	7 706	13 393	6 825	6 568	12 988	6 621	6 367
20-24	20 990	10 642	10 349	18 333	9 314	9 020	15 550	7 907	7 643	13 240	6 731	6 508
25-29	19 970	10 093	9 877	20 753	10 497	10 256	18 117	9 183	8 935	15 351	7 788	7 564
30-34	19 888	10 010	9 878	19 754	9 963	9 791	20 547	10 373	10 173	17 931	9 072	8 859
35-39	19 932	9 963	9 969	19 677	9 885	9 792	19 560	9 849	9 711	20 362	10 266	10 096
40-44	20 085	9 967	10 118	19 705	9 832	9 873	19 474	9 767	9 707	19 376	9 743	9 633
45-49	18 967	9 386	9 581	19 781	9 792	9 990	19 437	9 676	9 761	19 236	9 630	9 606
50-54	17 048	8 416	8 632	18 519	9 125	9 394	19 360	9 544	9 815	19 061	9 455	9 606
55-59	15 161	7 476	7 685	16 410	8 036	8 374	17 005	8 744	9 141	18 753	9 178	9 574
60-64	11 941	5 835	6 106	14 258	6 933	7 325	15 506	7 488	8 018	16 973	8 188	8 785
65-69	9 519	4 572	4 948	10 797	5 169	5 629	12 985	6 180	6 805	14 214	6 721	7 494
70-74	6 319	2 954	3 365	8 036	3 752	4 284	9 217	4 277	4 940	11 200	5 162	6 038
75-79	3 719	1 603	2 116	4 759	2 145	2 614	6 160	2 754	3 406	7 182	3 181	4 001
80-84	2 068	840	1 228	2 292	944	1 348	3 021	1 282	1 740	4 022	1 674	2 040
85-89	815	315	500	925	355	570	1 079	405	674	1 484	561	922
90-94	187	67	120	231	83	149	284	95	189	354	110	244
95-99	23	7	15	30	9	20	41	12	29	55	14	41
100 +	1	0	1	2	0	1	3	1	2	4	1	3

Age group	2045 Both sexes	Males	Females	2050 Both sexes	Males	Females
All ages	242 431	119 378	123 053	235 866	115 697	120 169
0-4	9 535	4 880	4 655	8 731	4 471	4 260
5-9	10 618	5 430	5 188	9 490	4 857	4 633
10-14	11 822	6 039	5 783	10 592	5 416	5 176
15-19	12 649	6 449	6 200	11 760	6 002	5 758
20-24	12 840	6 531	6 309	12 506	6 363	6 143
25-29	13 053	6 620	6 433	12 659	6 424	6 235
30-34	15 181	7 686	7 494	12 894	6 526	6 368
35-39	17 768	8 977	8 791	15 035	7 602	7 433
40-44	20 189	10 167	10 022	17 620	8 893	8 727
45-49	19 161	9 618	9 542	19 986	10 051	9 935
50-54	18 896	9 429	9 468	18 850	9 436	9 415
55-59	18 509	9 118	9 391	18 388	9 118	9 271
60-64	17 863	8 630	9 233	17 685	8 607	9 078
65-69	15 648	7 390	8 257	16 546	7 831	8 715
70-74	12 373	5 657	6 717	13 724	6 266	7 458
75-79	8 857	3 879	4 978	9 907	4 294	5 613
80-84	4 810	1 960	2 850	6 055	2 423	3 632
85-89	2 060	745	1 316	2 549	885	1 664
90-94	518	155	363	760	209	551
95-99	75	16	59	118	23	95
100 +	6	1	5	9	1	8

POPULATION BY AGE AND SEX (in thousands)

Age group	1950 Both sexes	1950 Males	1950 Females	1955 Both sexes	1955 Males	1955 Females	1960 Both sexes	1960 Males	1960 Females	1965 Both sexes	1965 Males	1965 Females
All ages	16 913	8 586	8 327	19 090	9 698	9 392	21 704	11 039	10 665	24 886	12 674	12 211
0-4	2 816	1 418	1 398	3 337	1 705	1 632	3 781	1 936	1 846	4 372	2 240	2 131
5-9	2 061	1 041	1 020	2 628	1 330	1 298	3 142	1 613	1 529	3 587	1 844	1 743
10-14	1 734	876	858	2 024	1 024	1 000	2 586	1 311	1 275	3 097	1 592	1 505
15-19	1 550	784	766	1 704	862	842	1 992	1 010	983	2 549	1 293	1 256
20-24	1 368	694	674	1 511	765	746	1 665	843	822	1 950	988	962
25-29	1 213	619	594	1 326	674	653	1 469	744	725	1 621	821	800
30-34	1 070	550	520	1 173	600	573	1 286	655	631	1 427	724	703
35-39	940	483	457	1 029	530	499	1 132	580	552	1 244	634	610
40-44	857	440	417	898	461	437	987	508	479	1 089	558	531
45-49	758	388	370	811	415	397	854	437	417	942	483	459
50-54	618	300	318	706	358	348	759	385	374	801	407	395
55-59	532	265	267	560	269	291	643	323	320	694	348	346
60-64	493	257	236	461	227	233	488	232	256	564	280	284
65-69	381	199	182	396	205	191	374	182	191	400	188	212
70-74	271	143	128	272	141	131	286	147	139	273	132	141
75-79	161	83	78	160	84	76	164	84	79	175	89	86
80 +	90	46	44	94	48	46	97	50	46	101	52	49

Age group	1970 Both sexes	1970 Males	1970 Females	1975 Both sexes	1975 Males	1975 Females	1980 Both sexes	1980 Males	1980 Females	1985 Both sexes	1985 Males	1985 Females
All ages	28 805	14 697	14 108	33 344	17 040	16 303	39 330	20 118	19 212	48 418	24 847	23 571
0-4	5 103	2 621	2 482	5 762	2 965	2 798	7 079	3 634	3 445	9 043	4 626	4 417
5-9	4 189	2 155	2 033	4 927	2 541	2 386	5 609	2 894	2 715	6 971	3 582	3 389
10-14	3 544	1 824	1 720	4 147	2 136	2 011	4 890	2 524	2 366	5 600	2 890	2 709
15-19	3 059	1 574	1 485	3 482	1 781	1 701	4 121	2 124	1 997	4 947	2 558	2 389
20-24	2 502	1 270	1 233	2 847	1 386	1 461	3 462	1 772	1 690	4 301	2 230	2 071
25-29	1 906	966	940	2 129	972	1 158	2 835	1 383	1 452	3 681	1 896	1 785
30-34	1 582	802	779	1 635	786	849	2 120	972	1 148	2 997	1 469	1 528
35-39	1 387	705	682	1 523	783	739	1 622	783	839	2 210	1 025	1 185
40-44	1 203	613	590	1 525	833	692	1 498	772	726	1 632	803	829
45-49	1 044	533	511	1 426	808	618	1 482	808	674	1 488	778	710
50-54	889	453	436	1 198	672	527	1 364	769	595	1 493	813	680
55-59	738	371	367	911	484	427	1 119	622	497	1 373	775	599
60-64	614	305	309	658	327	331	819	430	389	1 101	617	484
65-69	467	229	238	515	252	263	557	272	285	734	385	349
70-74	298	138	160	353	171	182	395	190	205	432	207	226
75-79	171	82	89	191	87	103	231	110	121	262	123	139
80 +	110	56	54	114	56	59	127	59	68	151	70	81

Age group	1990 Both sexes	1990 Males	1990 Females	1995 Both sexes	1995 Males	1995 Females	2000 Both sexes	2000 Males	2000 Females	2005 Both sexes	2005 Males	2005 Females
All ages	56 674	29 042	27 632	62 324	31 753	30 571	66 365	33 719	32 645	69 515	35 250	34 266
0-4	9 467	4 850	4 618	8 357	4 286	4 071	5 982	3 066	2 915	6 035	3 091	2 944
5-9	8 918	4 568	4 350	9 130	4 683	4 448	8 288	4 253	4 035	5 815	2 981	2 833
10-14	6 941	3 567	3 374	9 006	4 610	4 396	9 097	4 665	4 432	8 102	4 157	3 946
15-19	5 580	2 880	2 700	6 961	3 568	3 393	8 945	4 575	4 370	8 892	4 557	4 335
20-24	4 934	2 550	2 384	5 202	2 643	2 559	6 850	3 502	3 347	8 737	4 462	4 274
25-29	4 294	2 227	2 067	4 491	2 273	2 218	5 075	2 568	2 508	6 677	3 409	3 269
30-34	3 671	1 893	1 779	3 997	2 050	1 947	4 379	2 208	2 172	4 937	2 494	2 443
35-39	2 980	1 463	1 516	3 467	1 781	1 686	3 903	1 995	1 907	4 254	2 141	2 113
40-44	2 186	1 015	1 171	2 848	1 400	1 448	3 386	1 734	1 652	3 784	1 932	1 852
45-49	1 601	787	814	2 085	966	1 119	2 771	1 356	1 415	3 267	1 669	1 598
50-54	1 438	747	690	1 534	749	786	2 009	923	1 086	2 650	1 290	1 359
55-59	1 409	760	649	1 379	704	674	1 453	700	753	1 890	858	1 032
60-64	1 252	696	556	1 331	704	627	1 273	640	634	1 330	629	701
65-69	950	523	428	1 141	620	521	1 176	610	566	1 116	548	568
70-74	579	297	282	782	420	362	928	494	435	954	482	472
75-79	294	137	157	403	201	202	554	290	264	660	341	319
80 +	179	82	97	210	95	115	296	141	155	416	208	208

United Nations Department of Economic and Social Affairs/Population Division
World Population Prospects: The 2004 Revision, Volume II: Sex and Age Distribution of the World Population

482

POPULATION BY AGE AND SEX (in thousands)

Age group	2005 Both sexes	Males	Females	2010 Both sexes	Males	Females	2015 Both sexes	Males	Females	2020 Both sexes	Males	Females
All ages	69 515	35 250	34 266	74 283	37 597	36 686	79 917	40 382	39 535	85 036	42 900	42 136
0-4	6 035	3 091	2 944	7 003	3 584	3 419	7 496	3 833	3 662	7 107	3 637	3 471
5-9	5 815	2 981	2 833	5 959	3 052	2 907	6 984	3 574	3 410	7 479	3 824	3 654
10-14	8 102	4 157	3 946	5 738	2 942	2 797	5 950	3 046	2 903	6 975	3 568	3 406
15-19	8 892	4 557	4 335	8 010	4 106	3 903	5 721	2 931	2 791	5 934	3 036	2 898
20-24	8 737	4 462	4 274	8 784	4 495	4 288	7 969	4 080	3 889	5 690	2 911	2 780
25-29	6 677	3 409	3 269	8 632	4 402	4 230	8 731	4 461	4 270	7 923	4 050	3 873
30-34	4 937	2 494	2 443	6 591	3 360	3 231	8 579	4 369	4 211	8 682	4 431	4 251
35-39	4 254	2 141	2 113	4 862	2 453	2 410	6 545	3 332	3 213	8 529	4 338	4 191
40-44	3 784	1 932	1 852	4 181	2 101	2 080	4 818	2 426	2 392	6 494	3 302	3 192
45-49	3 267	1 669	1 598	3 703	1 886	1 817	4 126	2 068	2 058	4 761	2 392	2 369
50-54	2 650	1 290	1 359	3 169	1 611	1 557	3 622	1 835	1 787	4 044	2 017	2 027
55-59	1 890	858	1 032	2 533	1 220	1 313	3 054	1 537	1 518	3 501	1 755	1 746
60-64	1 330	629	701	1 766	786	980	2 390	1 130	1 260	2 892	1 429	1 462
65-69	1 116	548	568	1 191	549	642	1 608	697	911	2 188	1 008	1 180
70-74	954	482	472	928	442	485	1 012	451	560	1 384	577	807
75-79	660	341	319	699	341	357	697	320	377	777	330	447
80-84	312	159	153	385	193	192	420	198	223	437	188	248
85-89	88	42	46	127	63	64	161	79	83	189	82	106
90-94	14	6	8	22	10	12	32	15	16	45	20	25
95-99	1	1	1	2	1	1	3	1	2	5	2	3
100 +	0	0	0	0	0	0	0	0	0	0	0	0

Age group	2025 Both sexes	Males	Females	2030 Both sexes	Males	Females	2035 Both sexes	Males	Females	2040 Both sexes	Males	Females
All ages	89 042	44 847	44 195	92 253	46 382	45 872	95 204	47 767	47 437	98 023	49 068	48 956
0-4	6 199	3 173	3 026	5 705	2 921	2 784	5 844	2 994	2 850	6 164	3 158	3 006
5-9	7 094	3 630	3 464	6 189	3 168	3 021	5 696	2 917	2 779	5 836	2 990	2 846
10-14	7 471	3 820	3 651	7 087	3 626	3 461	6 183	3 165	3 018	5 691	2 914	2 777
15-19	6 959	3 558	3 401	7 456	3 810	3 645	7 073	3 617	3 456	6 171	3 157	3 014
20-24	5 905	3 018	2 887	6 929	3 540	3 390	7 427	3 792	3 635	7 047	3 601	3 446
25-29	5 654	2 888	2 766	5 870	2 996	2 874	6 894	3 518	3 376	7 392	3 771	3 622
30-34	7 881	4 025	3 857	5 622	2 868	2 753	5 839	2 977	2 862	6 862	3 499	3 364
35-39	8 636	4 403	4 233	7 842	4 001	3 841	5 592	2 851	2 741	5 810	2 961	2 850
40-44	8 472	4 305	4 167	8 564	4 070	4 211	7 798	3 976	3 822	5 561	2 833	2 728
45-49	6 427	3 261	3 165	8 394	4 258	4 136	8 512	4 331	4 182	7 738	3 940	3 798
50-54	4 675	2 338	2 337	6 322	3 194	3 127	8 269	4 179	4 090	8 395	4 256	4 139
55-59	3 921	1 935	1 985	4 543	2 250	2 293	6 166	3 083	3 079	8 066	4 042	4 024
60-64	3 327	1 640	1 687	3 739	1 815	1 924	4 345	2 118	2 227	5 902	2 912	2 990
65-69	2 660	1 282	1 378	3 076	1 479	1 597	3 474	1 646	1 828	4 054	1 931	2 123
70-74	1 899	842	1 056	2 325	1 081	1 244	2 710	1 256	1 454	3 084	1 409	1 675
75-79	1 085	428	657	1 508	631	876	1 867	818	1 048	2 204	964	1 240
80-84	505	198	307	729	261	468	1 033	390	642	1 304	517	707
85-89	208	80	128	255	86	169	386	115	271	567	178	388
90-94	57	21	36	69	21	48	92	23	69	150	33	118
95-99	7	3	5	11	3	8	15	3	12	22	3	19
100 +	0	0	0	1	0	1	1	0	1	2	0	2

Age group	2045 Both sexes	Males	Females	2050 Both sexes	Males	Females
All ages	100 403	50 132	50 271	101 944	50 760	51 185
0-4	6 188	3 170	3 018	5 850	2 996	2 854
5-9	6 156	3 154	3 002	6 181	3 166	3 014
10-14	5 831	2 987	2 844	6 151	3 152	3 000
15-19	5 680	2 908	2 773	5 821	2 981	2 840
20-24	6 147	3 142	3 005	5 657	2 893	2 764
25-29	7 014	3 580	3 434	6 117	3 124	2 993
30-34	7 360	3 752	3 609	6 983	3 562	3 422
35-39	6 832	3 481	3 351	7 330	3 733	3 596
40-44	5 780	2 943	2 837	6 799	3 461	3 338
45-49	5 519	2 808	2 711	5 738	2 918	2 821
50-54	7 638	3 876	3 762	5 451	2 764	2 687
55-59	8 203	4 126	4 077	7 474	3 766	3 708
60-64	7 757	3 834	3 923	7 908	3 927	3 980
65-69	5 530	2 670	2 860	7 295	3 534	3 761
70-74	3 626	1 669	1 957	4 976	2 327	2 649
75-79	2 543	1 098	1 445	3 023	1 318	1 705
80-84	1 578	626	952	1 861	731	1 130
85-89	743	248	495	933	314	619
90-94	235	55	180	323	81	242
95-99	40	5	35	68	10	58
100 +	3	0	3	6	0	6

POPULATION BY AGE AND SEX (in thousands)

Age group	2005 Both sexes	2005 Males	2005 Females	2010 Both sexes	2010 Males	2010 Females	2015 Both sexes	2015 Males	2015 Females	2020 Both sexes	2020 Males	2020 Females
All ages	69 515	35 250	34 266	75 144	38 038	37 106	82 302	41 602	40 700	89 288	45 075	44 213
0-4	6 035	3 091	2 944	7 864	4 025	3 839	9 021	4 614	4 408	8 978	4 594	4 384
5-9	5 815	2 981	2 833	5 959	3 052	2 907	7 843	4 013	3 830	9 002	4 603	4 398
10-14	8 102	4 157	3 946	5 738	2 942	2 797	5 950	3 046	2 903	7 833	4 008	3 826
15-19	8 892	4 557	4 335	8 010	4 106	3 903	5 721	2 931	2 791	5 934	3 036	2 898
20-24	8 737	4 462	4 274	8 784	4 495	4 288	7 969	4 080	3 889	5 690	2 911	2 780
25-29	6 677	3 409	3 269	8 632	4 402	4 230	8 731	4 461	4 270	7 923	4 050	3 873
30-34	4 937	2 494	2 443	6 591	3 360	3 231	8 579	4 369	4 211	8 682	4 431	4 251
35-39	4 254	2 141	2 113	4 862	2 453	2 410	6 545	3 332	3 213	8 529	4 338	4 191
40-44	3 784	1 932	1 852	4 181	2 101	2 080	4 818	2 426	2 392	6 494	3 302	3 192
45-49	3 267	1 669	1 598	3 703	1 886	1 817	4 126	2 068	2 058	4 761	2 392	2 369
50-54	2 650	1 290	1 359	3 169	1 611	1 557	3 622	1 835	1 787	4 044	2 017	2 027
55-59	1 890	858	1 032	2 533	1 220	1 313	3 054	1 537	1 518	3 501	1 755	1 746
60-64	1 330	629	701	1 766	786	980	2 390	1 130	1 260	2 892	1 429	1 462
65-69	1 116	548	568	1 191	549	642	1 608	697	911	2 188	1 008	1 180
70-74	954	482	472	928	442	485	1 012	451	560	1 384	577	807
75-79	660	341	319	699	341	357	697	320	377	777	330	447
80-84	312	159	153	385	193	192	420	198	223	437	188	248
85-89	88	42	46	127	63	64	161	79	83	189	82	106
90-94	14	6	8	22	10	12	32	15	16	45	20	25
95-99	1	1	1	2	1	1	3	1	2	5	2	3
100 +	0	0	0	0	0	0	0	0	0	0	0	0

Age group	2025 Both sexes	2025 Males	2025 Females	2030 Both sexes	2030 Males	2030 Females	2035 Both sexes	2035 Males	2035 Females	2040 Both sexes	2040 Males	2040 Females
All ages	94 975	47 882	47 093	99 885	50 286	49 599	105 020	52 789	52 231	110 719	55 564	55 155
0-4	7 885	4 036	3 849	7 411	3 795	3 616	8 036	4 117	3 919	9 056	4 640	4 416
5-9	8 962	4 585	4 377	7 872	4 029	3 843	7 400	3 790	3 611	8 026	4 112	3 914
10-14	8 992	4 598	4 394	8 954	4 581	4 373	7 865	4 026	3 840	7 395	3 787	3 608
15-19	7 816	3 997	3 820	8 975	4 587	4 388	8 939	4 571	4 368	7 852	4 017	3 835
20-24	5 905	3 018	2 887	7 785	3 977	3 808	8 944	4 567	4 377	8 909	4 552	4 357
25-29	5 654	2 888	2 766	5 870	2 996	2 874	7 748	3 954	3 794	8 907	4 544	4 363
30-34	7 881	4 025	3 857	5 622	2 868	2 753	5 839	2 977	2 862	7 714	3 934	3 781
35-39	8 636	4 403	4 233	7 842	4 001	3 841	5 592	2 851	2 741	5 810	2 961	2 850
40-44	8 472	4 305	4 167	8 584	4 373	4 211	7 798	3 976	3 822	5 561	2 833	2 728
45-49	6 427	3 261	3 165	8 394	4 258	4 136	8 512	4 331	4 182	7 738	3 940	3 798
50-54	4 675	2 338	2 337	6 322	3 194	3 127	8 269	4 179	4 090	8 395	4 256	4 139
55-59	3 921	1 935	1 985	4 543	2 250	2 293	6 155	3 082	3 073	8 066	4 042	4 024
60-64	3 327	1 640	1 687	3 739	1 815	1 924	4 345	2 118	2 227	5 902	2 912	2 990
65-69	2 660	1 282	1 378	3 076	1 479	1 597	3 474	1 646	1 828	4 054	1 931	2 123
70-74	1 899	842	1 056	2 325	1 081	1 244	2 710	1 256	1 454	3 084	1 409	1 675
75-79	1 085	428	657	1 508	631	876	1 867	818	1 048	2 204	964	1 240
80-84	505	198	307	729	261	468	1 033	390	642	1 304	517	787
85-89	208	80	128	255	86	169	386	115	271	567	178	388
90-94	57	21	36	69	21	48	92	23	69	150	33	118
95-99	7	3	5	11	3	8	15	3	12	22	3	19
100 +	0	0	0	1	0	1	1	0	1	2	0	2

Age group	2045 Both sexes	2045 Males	2045 Females	2050 Both sexes	2050 Males	2050 Females
All ages	116 452	58 345	58 107	121 459	60 745	60 714
0-4	9 558	4 896	4 662	9 335	4 781	4 554
5-9	9 046	4 635	4 411	9 548	4 891	4 657
10-14	8 021	4 109	3 912	9 040	4 632	4 409
15-19	7 382	3 779	3 603	8 009	4 101	3 907
20-24	7 826	4 001	3 825	7 357	3 763	3 594
25-29	8 873	4 530	4 343	7 792	3 980	3 812
30-34	8 871	4 523	4 349	8 839	4 510	4 329
35-39	7 682	3 914	3 767	8 837	4 502	4 335
40-44	5 780	2 943	2 837	7 645	3 893	3 752
45-49	5 519	2 808	2 711	5 738	2 918	2 821
50-54	7 638	3 876	3 762	5 451	2 764	2 687
55-59	8 203	4 126	4 077	7 474	3 766	3 708
60-64	7 757	3 834	3 923	7 908	3 927	3 980
65-69	5 530	2 670	2 860	7 295	3 534	3 761
70-74	3 626	1 669	1 957	4 976	2 327	2 649
75-79	2 543	1 098	1 445	3 023	1 318	1 705
80-84	1 578	626	952	1 861	731	1 130
85-89	743	248	495	933	314	619
90-94	235	55	180	323	81	242
95-99	40	5	35	68	10	58
100 +	3	0	3	6	0	6

United Nations Department of Economic and Social Affairs/Population Division
World Population Prospects: The 2004 Revision, Volume II: Sex and Age Distribution of the World Population

484

POPULATION BY AGE AND SEX (in thousands)

Age group	2005 Both sexes	Males	Females	2010 Both sexes	Males	Females	2015 Both sexes	Males	Females	2020 Both sexes	Males	Females
All ages	69 515	35 250	34 266	73 422	37 156	36 265	77 532	39 162	38 370	80 700	40 721	40 059
0-4	6 035	3 091	2 944	6 142	3 143	2 998	5 970	3 053	2 917	5 236	2 679	2 557
5-9	5 815	2 981	2 833	5 959	3 052	2 907	6 124	3 134	2 990	5 956	3 046	2 910
10-14	8 102	4 157	3 946	5 738	2 942	2 797	5 950	3 046	2 903	6 116	3 129	2 987
15-19	8 892	4 557	4 335	8 010	4 106	3 903	5 721	2 931	2 791	5 934	3 036	2 898
20-24	8 737	4 462	4 274	8 784	4 495	4 288	7 969	4 080	3 889	5 690	2 911	2 780
25-29	6 677	3 409	3 269	8 632	4 402	4 230	8 731	4 461	4 270	7 923	4 050	3 873
30-34	4 937	2 494	2 443	6 591	3 360	3 231	8 579	4 369	4 211	8 682	4 431	4 251
35-39	4 254	2 141	2 113	4 862	2 453	2 410	6 545	3 332	3 213	8 529	4 338	4 191
40-44	3 784	1 932	1 852	4 181	2 101	2 080	4 818	2 426	2 392	6 494	3 302	3 192
45-49	3 267	1 669	1 598	3 703	1 886	1 817	4 126	2 068	2 058	4 761	2 392	2 369
50-54	2 650	1 290	1 359	3 169	1 611	1 557	3 622	1 835	1 787	4 044	2 017	2 027
55-59	1 890	858	1 032	2 533	1 220	1 313	3 054	1 537	1 518	3 501	1 755	1 746
60-64	1 330	629	701	1 766	786	980	2 390	1 130	1 260	2 892	1 429	1 462
65-69	1 116	548	568	1 191	549	642	1 608	697	911	2 188	1 008	1 180
70-74	954	482	472	928	442	485	1 012	451	560	1 384	577	807
75-79	660	341	319	699	341	357	697	320	377	777	330	447
80-84	312	159	153	385	193	192	420	198	223	437	188	248
85-89	88	42	46	127	63	64	161	79	83	189	82	106
90-94	14	6	8	22	10	12	32	15	16	45	20	25
95-99	1	1	1	2	1	1	3	1	2	5	2	3
100 +	0	0	0	0	0	0	0	0	0	0	0	0

Age group	2025 Both sexes	Males	Females	2030 Both sexes	Males	Females	2035 Both sexes	Males	Females	2040 Both sexes	Males	Females
All ages	83 114	41 815	41 300	84 696	42 515	42 180	85 724	42 917	42 807	86 184	43 010	43 174
0-4	4 519	2 313	2 206	4 068	2 083	1 985	3 912	2 004	1 908	3 794	1 944	1 850
5-9	5 225	2 674	2 552	4 510	2 309	2 202	4 061	2 080	1 981	3 906	2 001	1 905
10-14	5 949	3 042	2 907	5 220	2 670	2 549	4 506	2 306	2 200	4 057	2 077	1 979
15-19	6 102	3 120	2 982	5 936	3 033	2 902	5 208	2 663	2 545	4 495	2 300	2 196
20-24	5 905	3 018	2 887	6 074	3 102	2 971	5 910	3 017	2 893	5 184	2 649	2 536
25-29	5 654	2 888	2 766	5 870	2 996	2 874	6 041	3 082	2 959	5 878	2 998	2 880
30-34	7 881	4 025	3 857	5 622	2 868	2 753	5 839	2 977	2 862	6 010	3 064	2 947
35-39	8 636	4 403	4 233	7 842	4 001	3 841	5 592	2 851	2 741	5 810	2 961	2 850
40-44	8 472	4 305	4 167	8 584	4 373	4 211	7 790	3 976	3 822	5 561	2 833	2 728
45-49	6 427	3 261	3 165	8 394	4 258	4 136	8 512	4 331	4 182	7 738	3 940	3 798
50-54	4 675	2 338	2 337	6 322	3 194	3 127	8 269	4 179	4 090	8 395	4 256	4 139
55-59	3 921	1 935	1 985	4 543	2 250	2 293	6 155	3 082	3 073	8 066	4 042	4 024
60-64	3 327	1 640	1 687	3 739	1 815	1 924	4 345	2 118	2 227	5 902	2 912	2 990
65-69	2 660	1 282	1 378	3 076	1 479	1 597	3 474	1 646	1 828	4 054	1 931	2 123
70-74	1 899	842	1 056	2 325	1 081	1 244	2 710	1 256	1 454	3 084	1 409	1 675
75-79	1 085	428	657	1 508	631	876	1 867	818	1 048	2 204	964	1 240
80-84	505	198	307	729	261	468	1 033	390	642	1 304	517	787
85-89	208	80	128	255	86	169	386	115	271	567	178	388
90-94	57	21	36	69	21	48	92	23	69	150	33	118
95-99	7	3	5	11	3	8	15	3	12	22	3	19
100 +	0	0	0	1	0	1	1	0	1	2	0	2

Age group	2045 Both sexes	Males	Females	2050 Both sexes	Males	Females
All ages	85 931	42 728	43 204	84 827	42 002	42 825
0-4	3 542	1 814	1 727	3 185	1 631	1 554
5-9	3 787	1 941	1 847	3 536	1 811	1 724
10-14	3 902	1 999	1 903	3 784	1 939	1 845
15-19	4 047	2 072	1 976	3 893	1 993	1 899
20-24	4 473	2 286	2 187	4 026	2 059	1 967
25-29	5 155	2 631	2 524	4 446	2 270	2 176
30-34	5 849	2 980	2 869	5 128	2 614	2 514
35-39	5 982	3 047	2 935	5 822	2 964	2 858
40-44	5 780	2 943	2 837	5 952	3 029	2 923
45-49	5 519	2 808	2 711	5 738	2 918	2 821
50-54	7 638	3 876	3 762	5 451	2 764	2 687
55-59	8 203	4 126	4 077	7 474	3 766	3 708
60-64	7 757	3 834	3 923	7 908	3 927	3 980
65-69	5 530	2 670	2 860	7 295	3 534	3 761
70-74	3 626	1 669	1 957	4 976	2 327	2 649
75-79	2 543	1 098	1 445	3 023	1 318	1 705
80-84	1 578	626	952	1 861	731	1 130
85-89	743	248	495	933	314	619
90-94	235	55	180	323	81	242
95-99	40	5	35	68	10	58
100 +	3	0	3	6	0	6

POPULATION BY AGE AND SEX (in thousands)

Age group	1950 Both sexes	1950 Males	1950 Females	1955 Both sexes	1955 Males	1955 Females	1960 Both sexes	1960 Males	1960 Females	1965 Both sexes	1965 Males	1965 Females
All ages	5 340	2 671	2 670	6 264	3 139	3 126	7 332	3 682	3 650	8 589	4 322	4 267
0-4	835	421	413	1 263	642	621	1 422	724	698	1 619	825	794
5-9	725	364	360	777	393	384	1 192	607	585	1 355	691	665
10-14	605	304	302	710	357	353	764	387	377	1 174	598	576
15-19	498	249	249	592	297	294	696	351	345	751	381	371
20-24	486	243	243	483	242	241	576	290	286	680	343	337
25-29	405	202	203	468	234	234	467	234	233	560	281	278
30-34	369	184	185	388	194	194	451	226	226	453	227	226
35-39	303	151	151	352	175	176	372	186	186	435	217	218
40-44	252	126	126	286	142	144	335	166	168	356	177	179
45-49	236	118	118	236	117	119	270	133	136	318	157	160
50-54	195	97	99	217	107	110	219	107	111	252	124	128
55-59	141	70	71	175	85	89	196	96	100	199	97	103
60-64	109	53	56	121	59	62	152	73	79	172	82	89
65-69	80	39	41	87	41	45	98	47	51	125	59	66
70-74	61	30	31	58	27	31	64	30	34	74	34	39
75-79	30	14	15	37	18	19	36	17	20	41	19	23
80 +	11	5	6	17	7	9	22	10	12	25	11	14

Age group	1970 Both sexes	1970 Males	1970 Females	1975 Both sexes	1975 Males	1975 Females	1980 Both sexes	1980 Males	1980 Females	1985 Both sexes	1985 Males	1985 Females
All ages	10 112	5 100	5 012	11 972	6 051	5 921	14 093	7 132	6 961	16 288	8 246	8 042
0-4	1 898	968	929	2 278	1 163	1 115	2 560	1 308	1 252	2 803	1 431	1 372
5-9	1 557	794	763	1 877	958	919	2 221	1 135	1 086	2 480	1 267	1 213
10-14	1 338	682	656	1 579	805	774	1 857	948	909	2 178	1 113	1 065
15-19	1 157	590	567	1 216	622	595	1 560	796	764	1 818	928	891
20-24	736	373	363	984	503	481	1 192	607	584	1 517	771	746
25-29	663	334	329	721	365	356	961	489	471	1 156	588	568
30-34	545	274	271	692	349	343	705	357	348	931	473	457
35-39	438	219	219	554	279	275	675	340	335	682	345	337
40-44	419	209	210	443	222	222	537	270	267	651	328	323
45-49	340	168	171	421	209	212	427	213	214	514	258	257
50-54	299	147	152	340	168	173	400	198	202	403	200	203
55-59	231	112	119	295	144	151	316	154	162	370	181	189
60-64	176	84	92	215	103	112	265	127	138	283	136	147
65-69	143	67	76	149	70	79	183	86	97	226	106	120
70-74	95	44	52	110	51	60	116	53	63	143	65	78
75-79	48	22	27	63	28	35	75	33	42	79	35	44
80 +	29	12	16	34	14	19	44	18	25	53	22	31

Age group	1990 Both sexes	1990 Males	1990 Females	1995 Both sexes	1995 Males	1995 Females	2000 Both sexes	2000 Males	2000 Females	2005 Both sexes	2005 Males	2005 Females
All ages	18 515	9 378	9 137	21 632	10 956	10 676	25 075	12 700	12 375	28 807	14 587	14 221
0-4	3 210	1 638	1 572	3 596	1 832	1 765	4 021	2 048	1 973	4 322	2 201	2 121
5-9	2 667	1 361	1 306	3 158	1 610	1 547	3 528	1 796	1 731	3 955	2 014	1 941
10-14	2 382	1 216	1 165	2 668	1 361	1 307	3 152	1 607	1 545	3 532	1 798	1 734
15-19	2 091	1 068	1 023	2 379	1 214	1 164	2 663	1 358	1 305	3 155	1 608	1 547
20-24	1 737	884	853	2 078	1 060	1 018	2 362	1 204	1 158	2 653	1 351	1 302
25-29	1 448	735	713	1 721	875	846	2 059	1 048	1 011	2 348	1 195	1 153
30-34	1 098	558	540	1 431	726	705	1 703	865	838	2 043	1 039	1 004
35-39	882	449	434	1 083	550	533	1 412	715	697	1 685	855	830
40-44	643	325	318	865	439	426	1 063	539	525	1 390	703	687
45-49	614	308	306	625	315	310	843	426	417	1 039	524	515
50-54	478	238	240	588	293	295	601	300	301	812	407	405
55-59	366	180	186	448	221	227	552	272	280	566	279	287
60-64	328	158	170	332	160	172	407	197	210	501	243	259
65-69	238	112	126	281	132	149	284	135	150	349	165	184
70-74	175	80	95	188	86	102	218	100	118	222	102	120
75-79	97	43	55	120	53	67	125	55	69	145	65	80
80 +	59	25	35	71	29	42	83	35	48	89	38	51

United Nations Department of Economic and Social Affairs/Population Division
World Population Prospects: The 2004 Revision, Volume II: Sex and Age Distribution of the World Population

POPULATION BY AGE AND SEX (in thousands)

Age group	2005 Both sexes	Males	Females	2010 Both sexes	Males	Females	2015 Both sexes	Males	Females	2020 Both sexes	Males	Females
All ages	28 807	14 587	14 221	32 534	16 471	16 063	36 473	18 461	18 012	40 522	20 498	20 020
0-4	4 322	2 201	2 121	4 501	2 296	2 205	4 709	2 406	2 302	4 882	2 494	2 388
5-9	3 955	2 014	1 941	4 248	2 164	2 085	4 460	2 274	2 185	4 677	2 389	2 288
10-14	3 532	1 798	1 734	3 940	2 006	1 934	4 236	2 157	2 079	4 445	2 266	2 179
15-19	3 155	1 608	1 547	3 517	1 790	1 727	3 925	1 997	1 928	4 218	2 146	2 072
20-24	2 653	1 351	1 302	3 129	1 592	1 537	3 492	1 775	1 718	3 900	1 981	1 919
25-29	2 348	1 195	1 153	2 625	1 335	1 290	3 102	1 576	1 526	3 466	1 758	1 708
30-34	2 043	1 039	1 004	2 320	1 179	1 140	2 601	1 321	1 280	3 077	1 561	1 515
35-39	1 685	855	830	2 013	1 023	990	2 293	1 165	1 129	2 575	1 306	1 269
40-44	1 390	703	687	1 653	837	816	1 983	1 006	977	2 263	1 148	1 116
45-49	1 039	524	515	1 353	681	672	1 616	816	801	1 945	984	961
50-54	812	407	405	998	500	499	1 307	654	653	1 568	786	782
55-59	566	279	287	764	378	386	946	468	478	1 245	615	630
60-64	501	243	259	515	249	266	702	341	361	877	426	451
65-69	349	165	184	432	204	227	451	213	237	622	295	328
70-74	222	102	120	274	126	147	346	159	187	369	169	200
75-79	145	65	80	149	67	82	190	85	105	247	110	138
80-84	64	28	36	76	33	43	81	35	46	107	46	61
85-89	21	9	13	23	9	13	28	12	16	31	13	18
90-94	4	1	2	5	2	3	5	2	3	7	3	4
95-99	0	0	0	0	0	0	1	0	0	1	0	0
100 +	0	0	0	0	0	0	0	0	0	0	0	0

Age group	2025 Both sexes	Males	Females	2030 Both sexes	Males	Females	2035 Both sexes	Males	Females	2040 Both sexes	Males	Females
All ages	44 664	22 571	22 093	48 797	24 633	24 164	52 833	26 639	26 194	56 694	28 549	28 145
0-4	5 037	2 573	2 464	5 143	2 628	2 515	5 188	2 651	2 537	5 188	2 653	2 534
5-9	4 859	2 481	2 378	5 019	2 563	2 456	5 129	2 620	2 509	5 176	2 645	2 531
10-14	4 665	2 383	2 283	4 849	2 475	2 374	5 010	2 558	2 452	5 121	2 615	2 506
15-19	4 430	2 257	2 173	4 652	2 374	2 278	4 837	2 468	2 370	5 000	2 551	2 449
20-24	4 197	2 132	2 065	4 412	2 244	2 167	4 635	2 363	2 273	4 822	2 457	2 365
25-29	3 877	1 966	1 910	4 176	2 118	2 058	4 393	2 232	2 161	4 618	2 351	2 267
30-34	3 444	1 745	1 699	3 856	1 953	1 903	4 156	2 106	2 051	4 375	2 220	2 154
35-39	3 052	1 547	1 505	3 421	1 731	1 690	3 834	1 940	1 894	4 136	2 094	2 042
40-44	2 548	1 290	1 257	3 025	1 531	1 494	3 394	1 715	1 679	3 807	1 924	1 883
45-49	2 227	1 126	1 101	2 511	1 268	1 243	2 987	1 508	1 479	3 356	1 692	1 664
50-54	1 894	952	942	2 174	1 093	1 081	2 458	1 235	1 223	2 929	1 471	1 458
55-59	1 502	744	758	1 821	905	916	2 097	1 043	1 055	2 377	1 181	1 196
60-64	1 164	564	599	1 411	686	725	1 718	838	880	1 986	969	1 016
65-69	786	372	414	1 051	496	555	1 283	607	675	1 571	746	825
70-74	518	237	280	661	302	359	894	407	486	1 102	503	599
75-79	270	119	151	385	169	216	500	218	282	687	298	390
80-84	144	61	83	160	67	93	235	98	137	315	128	187
85-89	43	18	25	59	24	35	69	27	42	107	41	67
90-94	8	3	5	11	4	6	16	6	10	20	7	13
95-99	1	0	1	1	0	1	1	1	1	2	1	2
100 +	0	0	0	0	0	0	0	0	0	0	0	0

Age group	2045 Both sexes	Males	Females	2050 Both sexes	Males	Females
All ages	60 328	30 339	29 989	63 693	31 989	31 703
0-4	5 167	2 645	2 523	5 128	2 626	2 502
5-9	5 178	2 648	2 530	5 159	2 640	2 519
10-14	5 169	2 641	2 528	5 172	2 645	2 527
15-19	5 112	2 609	2 503	5 161	2 636	2 525
20-24	4 986	2 542	2 444	5 099	2 601	2 498
25-29	4 806	2 447	2 359	4 971	2 532	2 439
30-34	4 601	2 341	2 260	4 790	2 437	2 353
35-39	4 355	2 209	2 146	4 583	2 330	2 252
40-44	4 110	2 079	2 031	4 331	2 195	2 135
45-49	3 769	1 901	1 867	4 072	2 057	2 016
50-54	3 296	1 654	1 642	3 707	1 863	1 844
55-59	2 839	1 412	1 427	3 202	1 592	1 610
60-64	2 258	1 103	1 155	2 706	1 323	1 383
65-69	1 826	869	957	2 086	994	1 092
70-74	1 361	623	738	1 595	732	863
75-79	860	372	488	1 078	467	611
80-84	446	178	268	573	226	346
85-89	151	54	97	224	77	146
90-94	33	10	23	50	14	36
95-99	3	1	2	6	1	5
100 +	0	0	0	0	0	0

POPULATION BY AGE AND SEX (in thousands)

Age group	2005 Both sexes	Males	Females	2010 Both sexes	Males	Females	2015 Both sexes	Males	Females	2020 Both sexes	Males	Females
All ages	28 807	14 587	14 221	32 799	16 606	16 192	37 242	18 854	18 389	42 028	21 265	20 763
0-4	4 322	2 201	2 121	4 767	2 431	2 335	5 216	2 665	2 551	5 622	2 872	2 750
5-9	3 955	2 014	1 941	4 248	2 164	2 085	4 722	2 408	2 314	5 181	2 647	2 534
10-14	3 532	1 798	1 734	3 940	2 006	1 934	4 236	2 157	2 079	4 707	2 400	2 307
15-19	3 155	1 608	1 547	3 517	1 790	1 727	3 925	1 997	1 928	4 218	2 146	2 072
20-24	2 653	1 351	1 302	3 129	1 592	1 537	3 492	1 775	1 718	3 900	1 981	1 919
25-29	2 348	1 195	1 153	2 625	1 335	1 290	3 102	1 576	1 526	3 466	1 758	1 708
30-34	2 043	1 039	1 004	2 320	1 179	1 140	2 601	1 321	1 280	3 077	1 561	1 515
35-39	1 685	855	830	2 013	1 023	990	2 293	1 165	1 129	2 575	1 306	1 269
40-44	1 390	703	687	1 653	837	816	1 983	1 006	977	2 263	1 148	1 116
45-49	1 039	524	515	1 353	681	672	1 616	816	801	1 945	984	961
50-54	812	407	405	998	500	499	1 307	654	653	1 568	786	782
55-59	566	279	287	764	378	386	946	468	478	1 245	615	630
60-64	501	243	259	515	249	266	702	341	361	877	426	451
65-69	349	165	184	432	204	227	451	213	237	622	295	328
70-74	222	102	120	274	126	147	346	159	187	369	169	200
75-79	145	65	80	149	67	82	190	85	105	247	110	138
80-84	64	28	36	76	33	43	81	35	46	107	46	61
85-89	21	9	13	23	9	13	28	12	16	31	13	18
90-94	4	1	2	5	2	3	5	2	3	7	3	4
95-99	0	0	0	0	0	0	1	0	0	1	0	0
100 +	0	0	0	0	0	0	0	0	0	0	0	0

Age group	2025 Both sexes	Males	Females	2030 Both sexes	Males	Females	2035 Both sexes	Males	Females	2040 Both sexes	Males	Females
All ages	47 018	23 773	23 245	52 150	26 345	25 805	57 423	28 982	28 441	62 833	31 683	31 150
0-4	5 889	3 008	2 881	6 147	3 141	3 007	6 432	3 287	3 145	6 745	3 450	3 295
5-9	5 596	2 858	2 739	5 869	2 997	2 872	6 131	3 131	3 000	6 419	3 280	3 139
10-14	5 169	2 640	2 529	5 585	2 851	2 734	5 859	2 991	2 868	6 122	3 126	2 996
15-19	4 692	2 390	2 301	5 155	2 631	2 524	5 572	2 843	2 729	5 847	2 984	2 864
20-24	4 197	2 132	2 065	4 672	2 377	2 295	5 136	2 618	2 518	5 555	2 831	2 724
25-29	3 877	1 966	1 910	4 176	2 118	2 058	4 652	2 363	2 288	5 117	2 605	2 512
30-34	3 444	1 745	1 699	3 856	1 953	1 903	4 156	2 106	2 051	4 633	2 352	2 281
35-39	3 052	1 547	1 505	3 421	1 731	1 690	3 834	1 940	1 894	4 136	2 094	2 042
40-44	2 548	1 290	1 257	3 025	1 531	1 494	3 394	1 715	1 679	3 807	1 924	1 883
45-49	2 227	1 126	1 101	2 511	1 268	1 243	2 987	1 508	1 479	3 356	1 692	1 664
50-54	1 894	952	942	2 174	1 093	1 081	2 458	1 235	1 223	2 929	1 471	1 458
55-59	1 502	744	758	1 821	905	916	2 097	1 043	1 055	2 377	1 181	1 196
60-64	1 164	564	599	1 411	686	725	1 718	838	880	1 986	969	1 016
65-69	786	372	414	1 051	496	555	1 283	607	675	1 571	746	825
70-74	518	237	280	661	302	359	894	407	486	1 102	503	599
75-79	270	119	151	385	169	216	500	218	282	687	298	390
80-84	144	61	83	160	67	93	235	98	137	315	128	187
85-89	43	18	25	59	24	35	69	27	42	107	41	67
90-94	8	3	5	11	4	6	16	6	10	20	7	13
95-99	1	0	1	1	0	1	1	1	1	2	1	2
100 +	0	0	0	0	0	0	0	0	0	0	0	0

Age group	2045 Both sexes	Males	Females	2050 Both sexes	Males	Females
All ages	68 326	34 423	33 903	73 813	37 159	36 654
0-4	7 039	3 602	3 437	7 264	3 719	3 544
5-9	6 733	3 444	3 289	7 029	3 597	3 431
10-14	6 411	3 275	3 135	6 726	3 440	3 286
15-19	6 112	3 119	2 992	6 401	3 269	3 132
20-24	5 831	2 973	2 858	6 097	3 110	2 987
25-29	5 537	2 819	2 718	5 814	2 962	2 852
30-34	5 098	2 594	2 505	5 519	2 808	2 711
35-39	4 612	2 340	2 273	5 078	2 582	2 496
40-44	4 110	2 079	2 031	4 587	2 325	2 262
45-49	3 769	1 901	1 867	4 072	2 057	2 016
50-54	3 296	1 654	1 642	3 707	1 863	1 844
55-59	2 839	1 412	1 427	3 202	1 592	1 610
60-64	2 258	1 103	1 155	2 706	1 323	1 383
65-69	1 826	869	957	2 086	994	1 092
70-74	1 361	623	738	1 595	732	863
75-79	860	372	488	1 078	467	611
80-84	446	178	268	573	226	346
85-89	151	54	97	224	77	146
90-94	33	10	23	50	14	36
95-99	3	1	2	6	1	5
100 +	0	0	0	0	0	0

POPULATION BY AGE AND SEX (in thousands)

Age group	2005 Both sexes	Males	Females	2010 Both sexes	Males	Females	2015 Both sexes	Males	Females	2020 Both sexes	Males	Females
All ages	28 807	14 507	14 301	32 260	16 336	15 923	35 703	18 068	17 636	39 016	19 727	19 289
0-4	4 322	2 201	2 121	4 236	2 161	2 076	4 201	2 147	2 054	4 141	2 116	2 026
5-9	3 955	2 014	1 941	4 248	2 164	2 085	4 197	2 141	2 057	4 173	2 132	2 041
10-14	3 532	1 798	1 734	3 940	2 006	1 934	4 236	2 157	2 079	4 183	2 133	2 051
15-19	3 155	1 608	1 547	3 517	1 790	1 727	3 925	1 997	1 928	4 218	2 146	2 072
20-24	2 653	1 351	1 302	3 129	1 592	1 537	3 492	1 775	1 718	3 900	1 981	1 919
25-29	2 348	1 195	1 153	2 625	1 335	1 290	3 102	1 576	1 526	3 466	1 758	1 708
30-34	2 043	1 039	1 004	2 320	1 179	1 140	2 601	1 321	1 280	3 077	1 561	1 515
35-39	1 685	855	830	2 013	1 023	990	2 293	1 165	1 129	2 575	1 306	1 269
40-44	1 390	703	687	1 653	837	816	1 983	1 006	977	2 263	1 148	1 116
45-49	1 039	524	515	1 353	681	672	1 616	816	801	1 945	984	961
50-54	812	407	405	998	500	499	1 307	654	653	1 568	786	782
55-59	566	279	287	764	378	386	946	468	478	1 245	615	630
60-64	501	243	259	515	249	266	702	341	361	877	426	451
65-69	349	165	184	432	204	227	451	213	237	622	295	328
70-74	222	102	120	274	126	147	346	159	187	369	169	200
75-79	145	65	80	149	67	82	190	85	105	247	110	138
80-84	64	28	36	76	33	43	81	35	46	107	46	61
85-89	21	9	13	23	9	13	28	12	16	31	13	18
90-94	4	1	2	5	2	3	5	2	3	7	3	4
95-99	0	0	0	0	0	0	1	0	0	1	0	0
100 +	0	0	0	0	0	0	0	0	0	0	0	0

Age group	2025 Both sexes	Males	Females	2030 Both sexes	Males	Females	2035 Both sexes	Males	Females	2040 Both sexes	Males	Females
All ages	42 313	21 370	20 942	45 469	22 934	22 535	48 344	24 348	23 997	50 823	25 552	25 271
0-4	4 187	2 139	2 048	4 160	2 126	2 035	4 020	2 055	1 966	3 797	1 942	1 855
5-9	4 122	2 105	2 017	4 172	2 131	2 041	4 148	2 119	2 030	4 011	2 049	1 961
10-14	4 162	2 126	2 037	4 113	2 100	2 013	4 164	2 126	2 038	4 142	2 115	2 027
15-19	4 169	2 124	2 045	4 150	2 118	2 032	4 103	2 093	2 010	4 155	2 120	2 035
20-24	4 197	2 132	2 065	4 151	2 112	2 039	4 135	2 107	2 027	4 089	2 084	2 005
25-29	3 877	1 966	1 910	4 176	2 118	2 058	4 133	2 100	2 033	4 119	2 097	2 022
30-34	3 444	1 745	1 699	3 856	1 953	1 903	4 156	2 106	2 051	4 116	2 089	2 027
35-39	3 052	1 547	1 505	3 421	1 731	1 690	3 834	1 940	1 894	4 136	2 094	2 042
40-44	2 548	1 290	1 257	3 025	1 531	1 494	3 394	1 716	1 679	3 807	1 924	1 883
45-49	2 227	1 126	1 101	2 511	1 268	1 243	2 987	1 508	1 479	3 356	1 692	1 664
50-54	1 894	952	942	2 174	1 093	1 081	2 458	1 235	1 223	2 929	1 471	1 458
55-59	1 502	744	758	1 821	905	916	2 097	1 043	1 055	2 377	1 181	1 196
60-64	1 164	564	599	1 411	686	725	1 718	838	880	1 986	969	1 018
65-69	786	372	414	1 051	496	555	1 283	607	675	1 571	746	825
70-74	518	237	280	661	302	359	894	407	486	1 102	503	599
75-79	270	119	151	385	169	216	500	218	282	687	298	390
80-84	144	61	83	187	80	107	235	98	137	315	128	187
85-89	43	18	25	59	24	35	69	27	42	107	41	67
90-94	8	3	5	11	4	6	16	6	10	20	7	13
95-99	1	0	1	1	0	1	1	1	1	2	1	2
100 +	0	0	0	0	0	0	0	0	0	0	0	0

Age group	2045 Both sexes	Males	Females	2050 Both sexes	Males	Females
All ages	52 864	26 528	26 336	54 470	27 279	27 190
0-4	3 564	1 824	1 740	3 356	1 718	1 637
5-9	3 789	1 938	1 851	3 557	1 821	1 737
10-14	4 005	2 046	1 959	3 784	1 935	1 849
15-19	4 134	2 110	2 024	3 998	2 042	1 956
20-24	4 143	2 112	2 031	4 123	2 103	2 020
25-29	4 075	2 075	2 000	4 130	2 104	2 026
30-34	4 103	2 088	2 016	4 061	2 067	1 995
35-39	4 098	2 079	2 019	4 087	2 078	2 009
40-44	4 110	2 079	2 031	4 075	2 066	2 009
45-49	3 769	1 901	1 867	4 072	2 057	2 016
50-54	3 296	1 654	1 642	3 707	1 863	1 844
55-59	2 839	1 412	1 427	3 202	1 592	1 610
60-64	2 258	1 103	1 155	2 706	1 323	1 383
65-69	1 826	869	957	2 086	994	1 092
70-74	1 361	623	738	1 595	732	863
75-79	860	372	488	1 078	467	611
80-84	446	178	268	573	226	346
85-89	151	54	97	224	77	146
90-94	33	10	23	50	14	36
95-99	3	1	2	6	1	5
100 +	0	0	0	0	0	0

United Nations Department of Economic and Social Affairs/Population Division
World Population Prospects: The 2004 Revision, Volume II: Sex and Age Distribution of the World Population

489

POPULATION BY AGE AND SEX (in thousands)

Age group	1950 Both sexes	1950 Males	1950 Females	1955 Both sexes	1955 Males	1955 Females	1960 Both sexes	1960 Males	1960 Females	1965 Both sexes	1965 Males	1965 Females
All ages	2 969	1 511	1 458	2 921	1 475	1 446	2 834	1 424	1 410	2 876	1 446	1 430
0-4	314	161	153	300	152	148	302	154	148	315	161	154
5-9	282	144	138	298	153	145	289	148	141	298	152	146
10-14	262	133	129	278	141	137	290	149	141	284	145	139
15-19	242	126	116	234	122	112	235	121	114	259	133	126
20-24	203	106	97	181	93	88	159	81	78	185	95	90
25-29	199	100	99	172	85	87	148	74	74	149	75	74
30-34	192	97	95	177	87	90	154	76	78	147	74	73
35-39	202	103	99	184	90	94	168	82	86	154	76	78
40-44	180	94	86	187	95	92	171	85	86	163	81	82
45-49	162	83	79	175	90	85	175	89	86	166	83	83
50-54	163	83	80	148	76	72	158	82	76	164	84	80
55-59	129	65	64	153	78	75	137	69	68	147	76	71
60-64	122	61	61	117	58	59	131	64	67	123	61	62
65-69	108	54	54	109	55	54	104	51	53	114	55	59
70-74	100	49	51	94	46	48	94	45	49	89	42	47
75-79	65	32	33	66	32	34	64	30	34	63	29	34
80 +	44	20	24	48	22	26	55	24	31	56	24	32

Age group	1970 Both sexes	1970 Males	1970 Females	1975 Both sexes	1975 Males	1975 Females	1980 Both sexes	1980 Males	1980 Females	1985 Both sexes	1985 Males	1985 Females
All ages	2 954	1 484	1 469	3 177	1 591	1 587	3 401	1 710	1 691	3 539	1 777	1 762
0-4	311	159	152	348	178	170	347	178	169	353	181	171
5-9	314	160	153	326	167	159	354	181	173	348	178	170
10-14	296	151	145	318	162	156	340	174	166	350	179	170
15-19	258	132	126	292	149	143	321	164	157	329	169	160
20-24	211	108	104	244	125	119	269	137	132	289	147	142
25-29	171	86	85	208	106	102	241	123	118	261	132	129
30-34	151	76	74	175	88	86	223	115	108	242	123	120
35-39	150	76	74	155	78	77	180	92	88	218	111	107
40-44	154	77	77	153	78	75	160	82	78	183	94	89
45-49	161	81	81	155	77	78	155	79	76	159	81	77
50-54	160	81	79	158	78	80	150	75	74	149	75	73
55-59	154	78	75	154	76	77	156	77	79	146	72	74
60-64	133	67	66	142	71	72	139	68	71	139	67	72
65-69	111	54	58	121	58	63	134	65	69	130	62	68
70-74	97	45	53	100	46	54	99	46	52	108	50	58
75-79	66	30	36	69	29	40	70	29	41	71	31	41
80 +	56	24	33	60	23	37	63	24	39	64	23	41

Age group	1990 Both sexes	1990 Males	1990 Females	1995 Both sexes	1995 Males	1995 Females	2000 Both sexes	2000 Males	2000 Females	2005 Both sexes	2005 Males	2005 Females
All ages	3 515	1 755	1 759	3 609	1 792	1 817	3 801	1 888	1 913	4 148	2 063	2 085
0-4	283	145	137	255	132	124	266	137	129	303	156	148
5-9	333	171	162	287	147	140	267	137	130	265	136	129
10-14	345	177	168	333	171	162	291	149	142	268	137	131
15-19	333	171	162	338	173	165	333	171	162	291	149	143
20-24	268	138	130	291	148	143	329	165	163	327	167	161
25-29	240	120	120	253	127	126	305	154	151	326	161	165
30-34	241	120	121	257	125	132	272	135	136	353	177	176
35-39	235	119	116	251	124	127	268	132	137	346	174	172
40-44	225	114	111	238	119	119	259	129	130	302	150	152
45-49	180	92	88	223	113	111	236	118	119	272	136	135
50-54	157	80	77	180	92	88	227	115	112	240	120	120
55-59	143	71	71	152	77	76	174	88	87	230	117	113
60-64	134	65	69	137	68	69	150	75	75	172	86	86
65-69	132	62	70	126	59	66	128	62	66	139	69	70
70-74	108	49	59	113	50	63	111	50	60	115	54	61
75-79	84	35	49	83	35	48	89	37	52	91	39	52
80 +	74	27	48	90	32	58	98	34	64	108	37	71

United Nations Department of Economic and Social Affairs/Population Division
World Population Prospects: The 2004 Revision, Volume II: Sex and Age Distribution of the World Population

490

POPULATION BY AGE AND SEX (in thousands)

Age group	2005 Both sexes	2005 Males	2005 Females	2010 Both sexes	2010 Males	2010 Females	2015 Both sexes	2015 Males	2015 Females	2020 Both sexes	2020 Males	2020 Females
All ages	4 148	2 063	2 085	4 422	2 202	2 220	4 674	2 329	2 345	4 893	2 438	2 455
0-4	303	156	148	328	169	159	315	162	153	292	150	142
5-9	265	136	129	303	155	148	328	168	159	314	161	153
10-14	268	137	131	266	136	130	304	155	148	328	169	160
15-19	291	149	143	268	137	131	266	136	130	304	155	149
20-24	327	167	161	288	146	142	265	135	130	263	134	129
25-29	326	161	165	326	164	161	287	144	142	264	133	131
30-34	353	177	176	350	172	178	350	176	174	311	156	155
35-39	346	174	172	391	196	195	388	192	196	388	195	192
40-44	302	150	152	362	183	180	407	205	202	404	201	203
45-49	272	136	135	308	153	154	368	186	182	412	208	204
50-54	240	120	120	272	136	135	308	153	154	367	185	182
55-59	230	117	113	239	119	120	270	135	135	306	152	154
60-64	172	86	86	223	113	111	233	116	117	264	131	132
65-69	139	69	70	161	79	81	209	104	105	219	107	112
70-74	115	54	61	125	60	65	145	69	75	190	91	98
75-79	91	39	52	95	42	53	104	47	57	122	55	67
80-84	62	23	39	65	25	40	69	28	42	77	32	46
85-89	31	10	21	36	11	25	39	13	26	43	15	28
90-94	12	3	9	14	3	10	16	4	12	19	5	14
95-99	2	0	2	3	1	3	4	1	3	5	1	4
100 +	0	0	0	0	0	0	1	0	0	1	0	1

Age group	2025 Both sexes	2025 Males	2025 Females	2030 Both sexes	2030 Males	2030 Females	2035 Both sexes	2035 Males	2035 Females	2040 Both sexes	2040 Males	2040 Females
All ages	5 082	2 529	2 553	5 249	2 608	2 641	5 406	2 682	2 724	5 553	2 750	2 802
0-4	277	142	134	275	141	133	287	148	139	300	155	146
5-9	292	150	142	276	142	135	274	141	134	287	147	140
10-14	315	162	153	292	150	142	277	142	135	275	141	134
15-19	328	168	160	315	162	153	293	150	143	277	142	135
20-24	301	153	148	326	167	159	312	160	153	290	148	142
25-29	262	132	130	300	151	149	324	165	160	311	158	153
30-34	288	145	144	286	143	143	324	163	162	349	176	173
35-39	349	175	174	327	164	162	325	163	161	362	182	180
40-44	405	204	200	366	185	182	344	174	170	342	173	169
45-49	410	204	206	410	207	202	372	188	184	350	177	173
50-54	411	207	204	409	204	205	410	208	202	373	188	184
55-59	365	184	181	409	206	203	407	202	205	408	206	202
60-64	299	148	151	356	179	178	400	200	200	399	197	202
65-69	249	123	127	284	138	145	339	168	171	382	189	193
70-74	200	95	105	228	109	119	261	124	137	313	151	162
75-79	161	74	88	172	77	94	197	90	108	227	103	124
80-84	92	38	54	124	52	72	134	56	78	156	66	90
85-89	49	18	31	60	22	38	82	31	52	91	34	58
90-94	21	6	15	25	7	18	32	9	22	45	14	31
95-99	6	1	5	7	2	6	9	2	7	12	3	10
100 +	1	0	1	1	0	1	2	0	1	2	0	2

Age group	2045 Both sexes	2045 Males	2045 Females	2050 Both sexes	2050 Males	2050 Females
All ages	5 675	2 806	2 868	5 762	2 845	2 917
0-4	301	155	146	290	149	141
5-9	300	154	146	300	154	146
10-14	288	148	140	301	154	146
15-19	275	141	134	288	148	140
20-24	275	140	135	273	139	134
25-29	289	146	143	274	138	135
30-34	336	169	167	314	158	156
35-39	387	196	191	374	189	185
40-44	380	192	188	405	205	199
45-49	348	176	172	386	195	191
50-54	351	178	173	349	177	172
55-59	372	188	184	351	178	173
60-64	401	202	199	366	184	182
65-69	382	187	195	384	191	193
70-74	354	171	183	356	170	186
75-79	275	127	148	313	145	168
80-84	182	77	105	223	96	127
85-89	108	41	68	129	49	80
90-94	51	16	35	63	20	43
95-99	18	4	14	21	5	17
100 +	3	0	3	5	1	4

POPULATION BY AGE AND SEX (in thousands)

Age group	2005 Both sexes	2005 Males	2005 Females	2010 Both sexes	2010 Males	2010 Females	2015 Both sexes	2015 Males	2015 Females	2020 Both sexes	2020 Males	2020 Females
All ages	4 148	2 063	2 085	4 464	2 224	2 240	4 783	2 385	2 397	5 080	2 534	2 546
0-4	303	156	148	370	191	179	381	196	185	371	191	180
5-9	265	136	129	303	155	148	370	190	180	380	196	185
10-14	268	137	131	266	136	130	304	155	148	370	190	180
15-19	291	149	143	268	137	131	266	136	130	304	155	149
20-24	327	167	161	288	146	142	265	135	130	263	134	129
25-29	326	161	165	326	164	161	287	144	142	264	133	131
30-34	353	177	176	350	172	178	350	176	174	311	156	155
35-39	346	174	172	391	196	195	388	192	196	388	195	192
40-44	302	150	152	362	183	180	407	205	202	404	201	203
45-49	272	136	135	308	153	154	368	186	182	412	208	204
50-54	240	120	120	272	136	135	308	153	154	367	185	182
55-59	230	117	113	239	119	120	270	135	135	306	152	154
60-64	172	86	86	223	113	111	233	116	117	264	131	132
65-69	139	69	70	161	79	81	209	104	105	219	107	112
70-74	115	54	61	125	60	65	145	69	75	190	91	98
75-79	91	39	52	95	42	53	104	47	57	122	55	67
80-84	62	23	39	65	25	40	69	28	42	77	32	46
85-89	31	10	21	36	11	25	39	13	26	43	15	28
90-94	12	3	9	14	3	10	16	4	12	19	5	14
95-99	2	0	2	3	1	3	4	1	3	5	1	4
100 +	0	0	0	0	0	0	1	0	0	1	0	1

Age group	2025 Both sexes	2025 Males	2025 Females	2030 Both sexes	2030 Males	2030 Females	2035 Both sexes	2035 Males	2035 Females	2040 Both sexes	2040 Males	2040 Females
All ages	5 343	2 664	2 679	5 587	2 783	2 804	5 836	2 904	2 932	6 100	3 033	3 067
0-4	352	181	171	351	181	170	379	195	184	418	215	202
5-9	370	190	180	351	180	171	351	180	171	378	194	184
10-14	381	196	185	371	191	180	352	181	171	352	181	171
15-19	370	190	180	381	196	185	371	191	181	352	181	171
20-24	301	153	148	368	188	180	379	194	185	369	189	180
25-29	262	132	130	300	151	149	366	186	180	377	192	185
30-34	288	145	144	286	143	143	324	163	162	391	198	193
35-39	349	175	174	327	164	162	325	163	161	362	182	180
40-44	405	204	200	366	185	182	344	174	170	342	173	169
45-49	410	204	206	410	207	202	372	188	184	350	177	173
50-54	411	208	204	409	204	205	410	208	202	373	188	184
55-59	365	184	181	409	206	203	407	202	205	408	206	202
60-64	299	148	151	356	179	178	400	200	200	399	197	202
65-69	249	123	127	284	138	145	339	168	171	382	189	193
70-74	200	95	105	228	109	119	261	124	137	313	151	162
75-79	161	74	88	172	77	94	197	90	108	227	103	124
80-84	92	38	54	124	52	72	134	56	78	156	66	90
85-89	49	18	31	60	22	38	82	31	52	91	34	58
90-94	21	6	15	25	7	18	32	9	22	45	14	31
95-99	6	1	5	7	2	6	9	2	7	12	3	10
100 +	1	0	1	1	0	1	2	0	1	2	0	2

Age group	2045 Both sexes	2045 Males	2045 Females	2050 Both sexes	2050 Males	2050 Females
All ages	6 364	3 163	3 202	6 608	3 282	3 326
0-4	444	229	215	447	230	216
5-9	417	215	203	443	228	215
10-14	379	195	184	418	215	203
15-19	352	181	171	379	195	184
20-24	350	179	171	350	179	171
25-29	367	187	181	349	177	171
30-34	402	203	198	392	198	194
35-39	429	217	212	440	223	217
40-44	380	192	188	446	227	219
45-49	348	176	172	386	195	191
50-54	351	178	173	349	177	172
55-59	372	188	184	351	178	173
60-64	401	202	199	366	184	182
65-69	382	187	195	384	191	193
70-74	354	171	183	356	170	186
75-79	275	127	148	313	145	168
80-84	182	77	105	223	96	127
85-89	108	41	68	129	49	80
90-94	51	16	35	63	20	43
95-99	18	4	14	21	5	17
100 +	3	0	3	5	1	4

United Nations Department of Economic and Social Affairs/Population Division
World Population Prospects: The 2004 Revision, Volume II: Sex and Age Distribution of the World Population

POPULATION BY AGE AND SEX (in thousands)

Age group	2005 Both sexes	Males	Females	2010 Both sexes	Males	Females	2015 Both sexes	Males	Females	2020 Both sexes	Males	Females
All ages	4 148	2 063	2 085	4 380	2 180	2 199	4 500	2 270	2 203	4 706	2 341	2 365
0-4	303	156	148	286	147	139	248	128	121	213	110	104
5-9	265	136	129	303	155	148	286	146	139	248	127	121
10-14	268	137	131	266	136	130	304	155	148	286	147	139
15-19	291	149	143	268	137	131	266	136	130	304	155	149
20-24	327	167	161	288	146	142	265	135	130	263	134	129
25-29	326	161	165	326	164	161	287	144	142	264	133	131
30-34	353	177	176	350	172	178	350	176	174	311	156	155
35-39	346	174	172	391	196	195	388	192	196	388	195	192
40-44	302	150	152	362	183	180	407	205	202	404	201	203
45-49	272	136	135	308	153	154	368	186	182	412	208	204
50-54	240	120	120	272	136	135	308	153	154	367	185	182
55-59	230	117	113	239	119	120	270	135	135	306	152	154
60-64	172	86	86	223	113	111	233	116	117	264	131	132
65-69	139	69	70	161	79	81	209	104	105	219	107	112
70-74	115	54	61	125	60	65	145	69	75	190	91	98
75-79	91	39	52	95	42	53	104	47	57	122	55	67
80-84	62	23	39	65	25	40	69	28	42	77	32	46
85-89	31	10	21	36	11	25	39	13	26	43	15	28
90-94	12	3	9	14	3	10	16	4	12	19	5	14
95-99	2	0	2	3	1	3	4	1	3	5	1	4
100 +	0	0	0	0	0	0	1	0	0	1	0	1

Age group	2025 Both sexes	Males	Females	2030 Both sexes	Males	Females	2035 Both sexes	Males	Females	2040 Both sexes	Males	Females
All ages	4 820	2 394	2 426	4 912	2 434	2 478	4 984	2 464	2 520	5 029	2 480	2 549
0-4	202	104	98	199	102	97	202	104	98	198	102	96
5-9	213	109	104	202	103	99	199	102	97	201	103	98
10-14	249	127	121	214	109	104	202	104	99	200	102	98
15-19	286	147	140	249	127	121	214	109	105	203	104	99
20-24	301	153	148	284	145	139	246	125	121	212	108	104
25-29	262	132	130	300	151	149	283	143	140	245	124	122
30-34	288	145	144	286	143	143	324	163	162	307	154	153
35-39	349	175	174	327	164	162	325	163	161	362	182	180
40-44	405	204	200	366	185	182	344	174	170	342	173	160
45-49	410	204	206	410	207	202	372	188	184	350	177	173
50-54	411	208	204	409	204	205	410	208	202	373	188	184
55-59	365	184	181	409	206	203	407	202	205	408	206	202
60-64	299	148	151	356	179	178	400	200	200	399	197	202
65-69	249	123	127	284	138	145	339	168	171	382	189	193
70-74	200	95	105	228	109	119	261	124	137	313	151	162
75-79	161	74	88	172	77	94	197	90	108	227	103	124
80-84	92	38	54	124	52	72	134	50	70	156	66	90
85-89	49	18	31	60	22	38	82	31	52	91	34	58
90-94	21	6	15	25	7	18	32	9	22	45	14	31
95-99	6	1	5	7	2	6	9	2	7	12	3	10
100 +	1	0	1	1	0	1	2	0	1	2	0	2

Age group	2045 Both sexes	Males	Females	2050 Both sexes	Males	Females
All ages	5 034	2 476	2 559	4 999	2 451	2 548
0-4	184	94	89	167	86	81
5-9	198	101	97	184	94	90
10-14	202	103	99	199	102	97
15-19	200	102	98	202	103	99
20-24	200	102	99	197	100	97
25-29	210	106	105	199	100	99
30-34	270	135	135	235	117	118
35-39	345	174	171	308	155	153
40-44	380	192	188	363	184	179
45-49	348	176	172	386	195	191
50-54	351	178	173	349	177	172
55-59	372	188	184	351	178	173
60-64	401	202	199	366	184	182
65-69	382	187	195	384	191	193
70-74	354	171	183	356	170	186
75-79	275	127	148	313	145	168
80-84	182	77	105	223	96	127
85-89	108	41	68	129	49	80
90-94	51	16	35	63	20	43
95-99	18	4	14	21	5	17
100 +	3	0	3	5	1	4

POPULATION BY AGE AND SEX (in thousands)

Age group	1950 Both sexes	Males	Females	1955 Both sexes	Males	Females	1960 Both sexes	Males	Females	1965 Both sexes	Males	Females
All ages	1 258	647	611	1 748	888	860	2 114	1 073	1 041	2 563	1 296	1 266
0-4	176	91	85	250	129	121	264	136	128	303	156	147
5-9	114	59	55	207	107	100	269	139	130	290	150	141
10-14	109	56	53	146	75	71	229	118	111	296	152	144
15-19	109	57	52	139	72	67	162	84	78	264	137	127
20-24	110	55	55	138	71	67	153	79	74	180	92	87
25-29	114	59	54	130	64	66	147	75	72	160	80	80
30-34	89	45	44	129	65	64	137	67	70	152	74	78
35-39	107	53	53	101	49	52	139	69	69	147	69	77
40-44	93	49	44	124	61	63	110	53	56	151	74	77
45-49	70	38	32	110	57	53	131	64	67	120	59	61
50-54	54	29	25	84	44	40	116	60	56	141	70	71
55-59	36	19	17	67	35	33	87	45	41	121	63	58
60-64	29	14	15	43	22	21	67	34	33	90	47	43
65-69	21	10	11	35	16	19	40	21	20	66	33	33
70-74	16	8	8	26	12	14	34	16	18	45	22	23
75-79	8	4	4	14	6	7	19	8	10	25	12	13
80 +	4	2	2	7	3	4	10	4	6	14	6	7

Age group	1970 Both sexes	Males	Females	1975 Both sexes	Males	Females	1980 Both sexes	Males	Females	1985 Both sexes	Males	Females
All ages	2 898	1 461	1 437	3 358	1 682	1 676	3 764	1 881	1 883	4 103	2 047	2 056
0-4	348	179	169	425	218	207	455	233	221	464	239	225
5-9	312	160	152	356	183	173	433	222	211	449	231	219
10-14	300	154	145	322	166	156	362	186	176	422	216	206
15-19	304	157	148	316	163	153	326	168	158	363	187	176
20-24	271	140	132	323	164	159	321	163	158	330	170	160
25-29	182	92	90	276	139	138	324	163	161	315	158	157
30-34	161	80	81	181	90	91	283	141	142	314	156	158
35-39	153	74	79	168	83	85	184	92	93	273	135	138
40-44	148	70	79	162	79	83	168	82	85	181	89	92
45-49	152	74	78	156	73	83	160	78	82	171	83	87
50-54	120	58	61	157	76	81	154	72	82	160	77	83
55-59	138	68	70	120	58	62	152	72	80	151	70	82
60-64	115	59	56	135	65	70	118	56	62	149	69	80
65-69	82	42	40	110	55	55	122	57	65	109	50	59
70-74	56	27	29	74	37	38	99	47	51	114	53	62
75-79	30	14	15	45	21	24	57	28	30	78	37	40
80 +	25	12	14	32	15	17	47	21	26	60	27	33

Age group	1990 Both sexes	Males	Females	1995 Both sexes	Males	Females	2000 Both sexes	Males	Females	2005 Both sexes	Males	Females
All ages	4 514	2 248	2 266	5 374	2 651	2 723	6 084	3 004	3 080	6 725	3 327	3 398
0-4	488	250	238	538	276	262	622	320	302	666	342	323
5-9	470	242	229	522	267	255	558	286	272	633	325	307
10-14	454	233	221	510	262	248	542	277	264	569	292	277
15-19	426	218	208	499	257	241	527	271	256	551	282	269
20-24	366	187	179	462	235	227	513	264	249	535	274	261
25-29	329	167	162	383	191	192	478	242	236	522	267	254
30-34	319	158	161	354	174	180	403	200	203	489	247	242
35-39	318	158	160	350	170	180	376	184	192	415	205	210
40-44	277	137	141	347	168	178	370	179	191	387	189	198
45-49	180	89	92	315	153	162	361	175	186	377	182	195
50-54	171	83	88	198	97	101	324	157	168	364	176	188
55-59	157	75	82	193	91	101	208	100	108	326	156	170
60-64	148	67	81	173	80	94	201	93	107	210	100	110
65-69	141	64	77	167	73	94	179	80	99	199	91	108
70-74	96	43	53	150	65	85	162	69	93	170	74	96
75-79	91	41	51	91	40	51	134	55	78	144	58	85
80 +	81	37	45	122	51	71	128	52	76	169	66	103

United Nations Department of Economic and Social Affairs/Population Division
World Population Prospects: The 2004 Revision, Volume II: Sex and Age Distribution of the World Population

POPULATION BY AGE AND SEX (in thousands)

Age group	2005 Both sexes	Males	Females	2010 Both sexes	Males	Females	2015 Both sexes	Males	Females	2020 Both sexes	Males	Females
All ages	6 725	3 327	3 398	7 315	3 627	3 688	7 838	3 897	3 942	8 296	4 135	4 160
0-4	666	342	323	672	346	326	664	342	322	656	338	319
5-9	633	325	307	674	346	327	677	348	329	666	343	324
10-14	569	292	277	641	329	311	679	349	330	679	349	330
15-19	551	282	269	576	295	281	645	331	313	681	350	331
20-24	535	274	261	557	284	272	579	297	283	646	332	314
25-29	522	267	254	541	276	264	560	285	275	580	297	284
30-34	489	247	242	529	270	259	545	278	267	562	286	276
35-39	415	205	210	497	251	247	534	272	262	547	278	268
40-44	387	189	198	422	208	214	501	252	249	535	272	263
45-49	377	182	195	391	191	200	424	209	215	500	251	249
50-54	364	176	188	378	182	196	391	190	201	422	207	215
55-59	326	156	170	364	174	189	376	180	196	387	187	199
60-64	210	100	110	323	153	170	358	170	188	368	175	193
65-69	199	91	108	206	96	110	313	146	166	344	162	183
70-74	170	74	96	188	83	104	193	88	105	291	134	158
75-79	144	58	85	151	63	88	166	71	95	171	76	95
80-84	107	42	65	116	45	71	122	49	73	135	56	79
85-89	45	18	28	68	25	43	76	28	48	82	31	51
90-94	15	5	10	18	6	12	30	10	20	35	11	24
95-99	2	1	1	3	1	2	5	1	3	9	2	6
100 +	0	0	0	0	0	0	0	0	0	1	0	0

Age group	2025 Both sexes	Males	Females	2030 Both sexes	Males	Females	2035 Both sexes	Males	Females	2040 Both sexes	Males	Females
All ages	8 734	4 363	4 371	9 156	4 581	4 575	9 545	4 782	4 764	9 884	4 956	4 928
0-4	660	339	320	667	343	324	666	343	323	649	334	315
5-9	659	339	320	662	341	321	669	344	325	668	344	324
10-14	669	344	325	661	340	321	664	342	323	672	346	326
15-19	681	350	331	670	345	326	663	341	322	666	343	324
20-24	682	350	331	682	351	332	672	345	327	664	341	323
25-29	647	332	315	682	350	332	683	351	333	673	345	327
30-34	582	297	285	648	332	316	684	351	333	685	351	334
35-39	563	286	277	583	297	286	650	332	317	685	351	335
40-44	547	278	269	564	286	278	584	297	287	650	332	318
45-49	534	271	263	546	277	269	563	285	278	583	297	287
50-54	497	249	249	531	269	262	544	275	268	560	283	277
55-59	417	204	213	492	245	247	526	265	260	539	272	267
60-64	379	182	197	410	199	211	483	239	244	516	259	257
65-69	355	167	188	366	174	192	396	190	206	468	230	238
70-74	322	148	173	333	154	179	344	161	183	373	176	197
75-79	258	115	143	280	120	160	298	134	164	309	141	168
80-84	140	60	80	213	91	121	238	103	135	249	108	141
85-89	92	36	56	97	39	58	150	60	90	171	69	101
90-94	39	13	26	46	16	30	51	18	33	81	29	52
95-99	11	3	8	13	3	10	16	5	12	19	5	13
100 +	1	0	1	2	0	1	2	0	2	3	1	3

Age group	2045 Both sexes	Males	Females	2050 Both sexes	Males	Females
All ages	10 167	5 103	5 065	10 403	5 225	5 178
0-4	625	322	304	606	312	294
5-9	652	335	316	628	323	305
10-14	670	345	325	654	336	318
15-19	674	346	327	672	346	327
20-24	668	343	324	675	347	328
25-29	665	342	324	669	343	325
30-34	674	346	329	667	342	325
35-39	686	351	335	676	346	330
40-44	686	351	335	687	351	336
45-49	649	331	318	685	350	335
50-54	581	295	286	647	329	318
55-59	556	280	276	576	291	285
60-64	530	266	264	547	274	273
65-69	500	249	251	514	256	258
70-74	441	213	228	473	232	241
75-79	337	155	181	400	189	211
80-84	260	115	146	285	127	158
85-89	181	74	107	192	80	113
90-94	95	34	61	105	38	67
95-99	32	9	22	39	11	27
100 +	4	1	3	7	1	6

POPULATION BY AGE AND SEX (in thousands)

Age group	2005 Both sexes	Males	Females	2010 Both sexes	Males	Females	2015 Both sexes	Males	Females	2020 Both sexes	Males	Females
All ages	6 725	3 327	3 398	7 378	3 659	3 719	8 007	3 984	4 023	8 603	4 294	4 310
0-4	666	342	323	735	378	357	770	396	374	795	409	386
5-9	633	325	307	674	346	327	740	381	359	772	397	375
10-14	569	292	277	641	329	311	679	349	330	742	382	360
15-19	551	282	269	576	295	281	645	331	313	681	350	331
20-24	535	274	261	557	284	272	579	297	283	646	332	314
25-29	522	267	254	541	276	264	560	285	275	580	297	284
30-34	489	247	242	529	270	259	545	278	267	562	286	276
35-39	415	205	210	497	251	247	534	272	262	547	278	268
40-44	387	189	198	422	208	214	501	252	249	535	272	263
45-49	377	182	195	391	191	200	424	209	215	500	251	249
50-54	364	176	188	378	182	196	391	190	201	422	207	215
55-59	326	156	170	364	174	189	376	180	196	387	187	199
60-64	210	100	110	323	153	170	358	170	188	368	175	193
65-69	199	91	108	206	96	110	313	146	166	344	162	183
70-74	170	74	96	188	83	104	193	88	105	291	134	158
75-79	144	58	85	151	63	88	166	71	95	171	76	95
80-84	107	42	65	116	45	71	122	49	73	135	56	79
85-89	45	18	28	68	25	43	76	28	48	82	31	51
90-94	15	5	10	18	6	12	30	10	20	35	11	24
95-99	2	1	1	3	1	2	5	1	3	9	2	6
100 +	0	0	0	0	0	0	0	0	0	1	0	0

Age group	2025 Both sexes	Males	Females	2030 Both sexes	Males	Females	2035 Both sexes	Males	Females	2040 Both sexes	Males	Females
All ages	9 190	4 597	4 592	9 778	4 901	4 877	10 367	5 204	5 163	10 949	5 504	5 445
0-4	808	416	392	834	429	405	866	445	420	893	459	434
5-9	798	410	387	810	417	393	836	430	406	868	446	421
10-14	775	398	376	800	411	388	812	418	394	838	431	407
15-19	744	382	361	776	399	377	802	412	389	814	419	395
20-24	682	350	331	745	383	362	777	400	378	803	413	390
25-29	647	332	315	682	350	332	746	383	363	778	400	379
30-34	582	297	285	648	332	316	684	351	333	747	383	364
35-39	563	286	277	583	297	286	650	332	317	685	351	335
40-44	547	278	269	564	286	278	584	297	287	650	332	318
45-49	534	271	263	546	277	269	563	285	278	583	297	287
50-54	497	249	249	531	269	262	544	275	268	560	283	277
55-59	417	204	213	492	245	247	526	265	260	539	272	267
60-64	379	182	197	410	199	211	483	239	244	516	259	257
65-69	355	167	188	366	174	192	396	190	206	468	230	238
70-74	322	148	173	333	154	179	344	161	183	373	176	197
75-79	258	115	143	286	128	158	298	134	164	309	141	168
80-84	140	60	80	213	91	121	238	103	135	249	108	141
85-89	92	36	56	97	39	58	150	60	90	171	69	101
90-94	39	13	26	46	16	30	51	18	33	81	29	52
95-99	11	3	8	13	3	10	16	5	12	19	5	13
100 +	1	0	1	2	0	1	2	0	2	3	1	3

Age group	2045 Both sexes	Males	Females	2050 Both sexes	Males	Females
All ages	11 515	5 796	5 719	12 063	6 079	5 985
0-4	910	468	442	919	473	446
5-9	895	460	435	912	469	443
10-14	870	448	423	897	462	436
15-19	840	432	408	872	449	424
20-24	815	419	396	841	432	409
25-29	804	413	391	816	419	397
30-34	780	400	380	805	413	392
35-39	749	383	365	781	400	381
40-44	686	351	335	749	383	366
45-49	649	331	318	685	350	335
50-54	581	295	286	647	329	318
55-59	556	280	276	576	291	285
60-64	530	266	264	547	274	273
65-69	500	249	251	514	256	258
70-74	441	213	228	473	232	241
75-79	337	155	181	400	189	211
80-84	260	115	146	285	127	158
85-89	181	74	107	192	80	113
90-94	95	34	61	105	38	67
95-99	32	9	22	39	11	27
100 +	4	1	3	7	1	6

496

United Nations Department of Economic and Social Affairs/Population Division
World Population Prospects: The 2004 Revision, Volume II: Sex and Age Distribution of the World Population

ISRAEL

POPULATION BY AGE AND SEX (in thousands)

Age group	2005 Both sexes	Males	Females	2010 Both sexes	Males	Females	2015 Both sexes	Males	Females	2020 Both sexes	Males	Females
All ages	6 725	3 327	3 398	7 252	3 595	3 658	7 670	3 810	3 860	7 988	3 977	4 011
0-4	666	342	323	609	313	296	558	287	271	517	266	251
5-9	633	325	307	674	346	327	614	316	298	560	288	272
10-14	569	292	277	641	329	311	679	349	330	617	317	299
15-19	551	282	269	576	295	281	645	331	313	681	350	331
20-24	535	274	261	557	284	272	579	297	283	646	332	314
25-29	522	267	254	541	276	264	560	285	275	580	297	284
30-34	489	247	242	529	270	259	545	278	267	562	286	276
35-39	415	205	210	497	251	247	534	272	262	547	278	268
40-44	387	189	198	422	208	214	501	252	249	535	272	263
45-49	377	182	195	391	191	200	424	209	215	500	251	249
50-54	364	176	188	378	182	196	391	190	201	422	207	215
55-59	326	156	170	364	174	189	376	180	196	387	187	199
60-64	210	100	110	323	153	170	358	170	188	368	175	193
65-69	199	91	108	206	96	110	313	146	166	344	162	183
70-74	170	74	96	188	83	104	193	88	105	291	134	158
75-79	144	58	85	151	63	88	166	71	95	171	76	95
80-84	107	42	65	116	45	71	122	49	73	135	56	79
85-89	45	18	28	68	25	43	76	28	48	82	31	51
90-94	15	5	10	18	6	12	30	10	20	35	11	24
95-99	2	1	1	3	1	2	5	1	3	9	2	6
100 +	0	0	0	0	0	0	0	0	0	1	0	0

Age group	2025 Both sexes	Males	Females	2030 Both sexes	Males	Females	2035 Both sexes	Males	Females	2040 Both sexes	Males	Females
All ages	8 279	4 129	4 150	8 539	4 263	4 275	8 744	4 369	4 374	8 872	4 436	4 436
0-4	512	264	249	505	260	245	481	247	233	438	225	213
5-9	520	267	252	515	265	250	507	261	246	483	249	235
10-14	563	289	273	522	268	254	517	266	251	509	262	247
15-19	618	318	300	564	290	274	524	269	255	519	267	252
20-24	682	350	331	620	318	301	566	291	275	525	270	255
25-29	647	332	315	682	350	332	621	319	302	567	291	276
30-34	582	297	285	648	332	316	684	351	333	623	319	303
35-39	563	286	277	583	297	286	650	332	317	685	351	335
40-44	547	278	260	564	286	278	584	297	287	650	332	318
45-49	534	271	263	546	277	269	563	285	278	583	297	287
50-54	497	249	248	531	269	262	544	275	268	560	283	277
55-59	417	204	213	492	245	247	526	265	260	509	272	267
60-64	379	182	197	410	199	211	483	239	244	516	259	257
65-69	355	167	188	366	174	192	396	190	206	468	230	238
70-74	322	148	173	333	154	179	344	161	183	373	176	197
75-79	258	115	143	286	128	158	298	134	164	309	141	168
80-84	140	60	80	213	91	121	238	103	135	249	108	141
85-89	92	36	56	97	39	58	150	60	90	171	69	101
90-94	39	13	26	46	16	30	51	18	33	81	29	52
95-99	11	3	8	13	3	10	16	5	12	19	5	13
100 +	1	0	1	2	0	1	2	0	2	3	1	3

Age group	2045 Both sexes	Males	Females	2050 Both sexes	Males	Females
All ages	8 922	4 462	4 459	8 910	4 458	4 452
0-4	391	201	190	357	184	173
5-9	440	227	214	394	203	191
10-14	485	250	236	443	228	215
15-19	512	263	248	488	251	237
20-24	520	267	253	513	264	249
25-29	527	270	256	522	268	254
30-34	569	292	277	529	271	258
35-39	624	320	305	571	292	278
40-44	686	351	335	625	320	305
45-49	649	331	318	685	350	335
50-54	581	295	286	647	329	318
55-59	556	280	276	576	291	285
60-64	530	266	264	547	274	273
65-69	500	249	251	514	256	258
70-74	441	213	228	473	232	241
75-79	337	155	181	400	189	211
80-84	260	115	146	285	127	158
85-89	181	74	107	192	80	113
90-94	95	34	61	105	38	67
95-99	32	9	22	39	11	27
100 +	4	1	3	7	1	6

United Nations Department of Economic and Social Affairs/Population Division
World Population Prospects: The 2004 Revision, Volume II: Sex and Age Distribution of the World Population

497

POPULATION BY AGE AND SEX (in thousands)

Age group	1950 Both sexes	Males	Females	1955 Both sexes	Males	Females	1960 Both sexes	Males	Females	1965 Both sexes	Males	Females
All ages	47 104	22 934	24 170	48 633	23 815	24 818	50 200	24 584	25 616	52 112	25 508	26 605
0-4	4 327	2 216	2 111	4 059	2 074	1 985	4 192	2 143	2 049	4 628	2 368	2 260
5-9	3 865	1 977	1 888	4 305	2 200	2 105	3 975	2 026	1 949	4 118	2 104	2 014
10-14	4 205	2 136	2 069	3 816	1 945	1 872	4 266	2 176	2 090	3 916	1 996	1 920
15-19	4 000	2 010	1 990	4 130	2 091	2 039	3 774	1 916	1 858	4 190	2 131	2 059
20-24	4 027	2 011	2 015	3 996	2 007	1 989	4 025	2 030	1 995	3 668	1 849	1 819
25-29	3 894	1 884	2 009	3 972	1 982	1 990	3 861	1 929	1 931	3 939	1 974	1 965
30-34	2 814	1 343	1 471	3 877	1 887	1 990	3 858	1 917	1 942	3 771	1 877	1 894
35-39	3 386	1 634	1 752	2 591	1 251	1 339	3 797	1 844	1 953	3 777	1 871	1 907
40-44	3 341	1 631	1 710	3 512	1 718	1 794	2 537	1 224	1 313	3 717	1 799	1 917
45-49	2 862	1 388	1 474	3 195	1 568	1 628	3 425	1 671	1 754	2 471	1 187	1 284
50-54	2 497	1 171	1 325	2 702	1 307	1 394	3 086	1 506	1 580	3 315	1 608	1 707
55-59	2 122	944	1 178	2 319	1 061	1 258	2 573	1 231	1 342	2 976	1 433	1 543
60-64	1 874	834	1 040	1 936	856	1 080	2 156	968	1 188	2 431	1 136	1 295
65-69	1 530	688	842	1 624	717	908	1 734	749	986	1 913	824	1 089
70-74	1 119	515	604	1 239	549	690	1 364	581	783	1 444	598	845
75-79	731	333	398	785	353	432	913	395	518	1 018	419	599
80 +	510	220	290	575	248	327	662	278	384	821	333	488

Age group	1970 Both sexes	Males	Females	1975 Both sexes	Males	Females	1980 Both sexes	Males	Females	1985 Both sexes	Males	Females
All ages	53 822	26 325	27 497	55 441	27 072	28 369	56 434	27 472	28 962	56 593	27 500	29 093
0-4	4 589	2 351	2 238	4 318	2 218	2 101	3 617	1 858	1 759	3 026	1 553	1 472
5-9	4 556	2 335	2 222	4 563	2 336	2 228	4 339	2 226	2 113	3 674	1 885	1 789
10-14	4 080	2 085	1 995	4 555	2 329	2 226	4 614	2 357	2 257	4 382	2 245	2 138
15-19	3 857	1 966	1 890	4 058	2 065	1 992	4 569	2 327	2 242	4 696	2 391	2 305
20-24	4 097	2 077	2 019	3 818	1 934	1 885	4 043	2 044	1 998	4 574	2 320	2 253
25-29	3 535	1 767	1 768	4 045	2 038	2 007	3 791	1 901	1 889	4 029	2 027	2 002
30-34	3 859	1 918	1 941	3 501	1 743	1 758	4 018	2 009	2 009	3 772	1 884	1 888
35-39	3 696	1 832	1 864	3 807	1 885	1 922	3 503	1 739	1 763	3 906	1 946	1 960
40-44	3 703	1 829	1 874	3 654	1 804	1 850	3 760	1 856	1 905	3 521	1 742	1 779
45-49	3 625	1 745	1 880	3 643	1 788	1 855	3 612	1 772	1 840	3 657	1 796	1 861
50-54	2 385	1 136	1 249	3 536	1 686	1 850	3 567	1 732	1 835	3 535	1 718	1 817
55-59	3 160	1 511	1 648	2 293	1 077	1 217	3 413	1 600	1 813	3 406	1 627	1 779
60-64	2 818	1 325	1 492	2 971	1 388	1 583	2 169	993	1 176	3 207	1 463	1 744
65-69	2 161	975	1 187	2 521	1 142	1 379	2 619	1 172	1 447	1 923	849	1 074
70-74	1 625	673	952	1 868	797	1 071	2 133	911	1 221	2 304	978	1 326
75-79	1 090	427	663	1 221	471	750	1 429	564	865	1 582	619	963
80 +	986	373	613	1 068	374	694	1 239	411	828	1 399	456	944

Age group	1990 Both sexes	Males	Females	1995 Both sexes	Males	Females	2000 Both sexes	Males	Females	2005 Both sexes	Males	Females
All ages	56 719	27 529	29 190	57 301	27 804	29 497	57 715	28 004	29 710	58 093	28 195	29 898
0-4	2 746	1 412	1 334	2 755	1 415	1 340	2 649	1 364	1 284	2 662	1 371	1 291
5-9	2 882	1 480	1 403	2 789	1 428	1 361	2 781	1 428	1 352	2 674	1 377	1 297
10-14	3 371	1 726	1 645	3 025	1 546	1 479	2 816	1 442	1 374	2 808	1 442	1 366
15-19	4 294	2 188	2 106	3 605	1 839	1 766	3 053	1 560	1 494	2 843	1 455	1 388
20-24	4 530	2 301	2 229	4 409	2 243	2 166	3 633	1 851	1 782	3 079	1 571	1 508
25-29	4 640	2 340	2 300	4 669	2 360	2 308	4 439	2 254	2 184	3 661	1 863	1 799
30-34	4 105	2 062	2 043	4 556	2 287	2 268	4 699	2 371	2 327	4 469	2 266	2 203
35-39	3 806	1 900	1 906	4 014	2 006	2 007	4 580	2 295	2 285	4 727	2 382	2 345
40-44	3 922	1 950	1 973	3 761	1 871	1 889	4 032	2 012	2 020	4 603	2 302	2 300
45-49	3 432	1 697	1 735	3 940	1 954	1 986	3 767	1 870	1 897	4 043	2 013	2 031
50-54	3 647	1 784	1 863	3 398	1 668	1 730	3 922	1 937	1 985	3 760	1 859	1 901
55-59	3 367	1 620	1 747	3 556	1 722	1 835	3 356	1 635	1 721	3 881	1 903	1 977
60-64	3 286	1 545	1 741	3 303	1 562	1 741	3 462	1 653	1 810	3 282	1 579	1 703
65-69	2 995	1 338	1 657	3 067	1 399	1 669	3 137	1 447	1 691	3 307	1 544	1 763
70-74	1 908	804	1 104	2 674	1 137	1 538	2 795	1 220	1 576	2 886	1 280	1 606
75-79	1 836	731	1 105	1 452	574	878	2 283	908	1 375	2 421	995	1 426
80 +	1 953	654	1 299	2 329	792	1 537	2 309	758	1 551	2 986	992	1 995

United Nations Department of Economic and Social Affairs/Population Division
World Population Prospects: The 2004 Revision, Volume II: Sex and Age Distribution of the World Population

POPULATION BY AGE AND SEX (in thousands)

Age group	2005 Both sexes	2005 Males	2005 Females	2010 Both sexes	2010 Males	2010 Females	2015 Both sexes	2015 Males	2015 Females	2020 Both sexes	2020 Males	2020 Females
All ages	58 093	28 195	29 898	58 176	28 246	29 930	57 818	28 082	29 706	57 132	27 760	29 372
0-4	2 662	1 371	1 291	2 578	1 328	1 250	2 325	1 198	1 128	2 162	1 114	1 048
5-9	2 674	1 377	1 297	2 687	1 384	1 303	2 602	1 340	1 262	2 349	1 210	1 139
10-14	2 808	1 442	1 366	2 701	1 391	1 310	2 714	1 398	1 316	2 628	1 354	1 275
15-19	2 843	1 455	1 388	2 833	1 455	1 379	2 727	1 404	1 323	2 740	1 411	1 329
20-24	3 079	1 571	1 508	2 867	1 466	1 401	2 857	1 466	1 392	2 751	1 415	1 336
25-29	3 661	1 863	1 799	3 104	1 582	1 522	2 891	1 476	1 414	2 881	1 476	1 405
30-34	4 469	2 266	2 203	3 689	1 874	1 815	3 128	1 592	1 536	2 914	1 487	1 427
35-39	4 727	2 382	2 345	4 497	2 277	2 220	3 715	1 884	1 830	3 152	1 602	1 550
40-44	4 603	2 302	2 300	4 752	2 390	2 362	4 521	2 285	2 236	3 738	1 893	1 845
45-49	4 043	2 013	2 031	4 616	2 304	2 312	4 768	2 393	2 375	4 538	2 289	2 249
50-54	3 760	1 859	1 901	4 038	2 003	2 035	4 612	2 294	2 318	4 768	2 385	2 383
55-59	3 881	1 903	1 977	3 727	1 831	1 896	4 008	1 976	2 032	4 581	2 265	2 315
60-64	3 282	1 579	1 703	3 798	1 842	1 957	3 658	1 778	1 880	3 940	1 923	2 017
65-69	3 307	1 544	1 763	3 147	1 483	1 664	3 648	1 736	1 913	3 526	1 684	1 842
70-74	2 886	1 280	1 606	3 055	1 376	1 679	2 923	1 333	1 590	3 400	1 569	1 832
75-79	2 421	995	1 426	2 517	1 056	1 461	2 682	1 146	1 535	2 585	1 123	1 463
80-84	1 768	641	1 127	1 899	715	1 184	2 000	772	1 227	2 156	852	1 303
85-89	709	221	487	1 166	370	796	1 281	424	857	1 378	471	907
90-94	409	108	300	357	92	265	610	160	450	693	190	503
95-99	92	20	73	133	27	106	125	25	101	225	45	181
100 +	8	1	7	15	2	13	25	3	21	27	3	23

Age group	2025 Both sexes	2025 Males	2025 Females	2030 Both sexes	2030 Males	2030 Females	2035 Both sexes	2035 Males	2035 Females	2040 Both sexes	2040 Males	2040 Females
All ages	56 307	27 371	28 936	55 423	26 945	28 479	54 483	26 483	28 001	53 443	25 965	27 479
0-4	2 151	1 108	1 043	2 191	1 129	1 063	2 237	1 152	1 085	2 248	1 158	1 090
5-9	2 184	1 125	1 059	2 173	1 119	1 054	2 214	1 140	1 074	2 261	1 165	1 097
10-14	2 373	1 222	1 151	2 207	1 137	1 070	2 196	1 131	1 065	2 238	1 153	1 086
15-19	2 654	1 366	1 287	2 397	1 234	1 163	2 231	1 149	1 082	2 220	1 143	1 077
20-24	2 765	1 422	1 342	2 679	1 378	1 300	2 421	1 246	1 175	2 254	1 160	1 094
25-29	2 775	1 426	1 349	2 789	1 434	1 355	2 703	1 390	1 313	2 445	1 257	1 188
30-34	2 905	1 487	1 418	2 800	1 437	1 362	2 814	1 445	1 369	2 728	1 401	1 326
35-39	2 937	1 496	1 440	2 928	1 497	1 431	2 823	1 448	1 375	2 838	1 456	1 382
40-44	3 174	1 611	1 563	2 958	1 505	1 453	2 949	1 506	1 444	2 846	1 458	1 388
45-49	3 756	1 899	1 858	3 191	1 616	1 575	2 976	1 511	1 464	2 968	1 512	1 455
50-54	4 542	2 284	2 258	3 764	1 897	1 867	3 200	1 617	1 584	2 986	1 513	1 474
55-59	4 742	2 359	2 382	4 521	2 262	2 260	3 753	1 883	1 870	3 195	1 607	1 588
60-64	4 509	2 210	2 299	4 675	2 307	2 368	4 465	2 216	2 248	3 713	1 849	1 864
65-69	3 808	1 828	1 980	4 368	2 108	2 260	4 540	2 208	2 331	4 344	2 129	2 216
70-74	3 303	1 533	1 770	3 581	1 675	1 907	4 122	1 941	2 181	4 300	2 044	2 256
75-79	3 024	1 333	1 691	2 959	1 315	1 644	3 227	1 449	1 778	3 734	1 692	2 042
80-84	2 104	848	1 255	2 485	1 021	1 464	2 458	1 022	1 436	2 707	1 141	1 567
85-89	1 514	532	982	1 506	542	964	1 809	666	1 143	1 821	682	1 140
90-94	770	219	551	872	255	616	892	269	623	1 099	341	757
95-99	269	56	213	314	67	247	371	82	289	395	91	304
100 +	48	6	42	65	8	57	82	11	71	104	14	89

Age group	2045 Both sexes	2045 Males	2045 Females	2050 Both sexes	2050 Males	2050 Females
All ages	52 256	25 371	26 885	50 912	24 706	26 206
0-4	2 210	1 138	1 072	2 150	1 108	1 043
5-9	2 273	1 171	1 102	2 235	1 151	1 084
10-14	2 286	1 177	1 109	2 299	1 184	1 115
15-19	2 263	1 165	1 098	2 312	1 190	1 121
20-24	2 243	1 155	1 089	2 288	1 178	1 110
25-29	2 277	1 171	1 106	2 267	1 166	1 101
30-34	2 469	1 269	1 200	2 300	1 182	1 118
35-39	2 752	1 413	1 340	2 493	1 280	1 213
40-44	2 862	1 467	1 395	2 776	1 423	1 353
45-49	2 866	1 465	1 400	2 883	1 475	1 408
50-54	2 979	1 515	1 465	2 880	1 469	1 411
55-59	2 984	1 505	1 479	2 979	1 509	1 470
60-64	3 166	1 581	1 585	2 961	1 484	1 477
65-69	3 623	1 782	1 841	3 097	1 529	1 568
70-74	4 129	1 980	2 149	3 457	1 667	1 790
75-79	3 916	1 796	2 120	3 780	1 752	2 028
80-84	3 161	1 348	1 813	3 345	1 448	1 897
85-89	2 038	776	1 262	2 414	934	1 479
90-94	1 136	360	775	1 301	422	879
95-99	504	120	384	541	132	409
100 +	120	17	103	157	23	133

POPULATION BY AGE AND SEX (in thousands)

Age group	2005 Both sexes	Males	Females	2010 Both sexes	Males	Females	2015 Both sexes	Males	Females	2020 Both sexes	Males	Females
All ages	58 093	28 195	29 898	58 624	28 476	30 147	58 889	28 634	30 255	58 917	28 680	30 237
0-4	2 662	1 371	1 291	3 025	1 558	1 467	2 949	1 519	1 430	2 877	1 482	1 395
5-9	2 674	1 377	1 297	2 687	1 384	1 303	3 050	1 571	1 479	2 972	1 531	1 441
10-14	2 808	1 442	1 366	2 701	1 391	1 310	2 714	1 398	1 316	3 075	1 584	1 491
15-19	2 843	1 455	1 388	2 833	1 455	1 379	2 727	1 404	1 323	2 740	1 411	1 329
20-24	3 079	1 571	1 508	2 867	1 466	1 401	2 857	1 466	1 392	2 751	1 415	1 336
25-29	3 661	1 863	1 799	3 104	1 582	1 522	2 891	1 476	1 414	2 881	1 476	1 405
30-34	4 469	2 266	2 203	3 689	1 874	1 815	3 128	1 592	1 536	2 914	1 487	1 427
35-39	4 727	2 382	2 345	4 497	2 277	2 220	3 715	1 884	1 830	3 152	1 602	1 550
40-44	4 603	2 302	2 300	4 752	2 390	2 362	4 521	2 285	2 236	3 738	1 893	1 845
45-49	4 043	2 013	2 031	4 616	2 304	2 312	4 768	2 393	2 375	4 538	2 289	2 249
50-54	3 760	1 859	1 901	4 038	2 003	2 035	4 612	2 294	2 318	4 768	2 385	2 383
55-59	3 881	1 903	1 977	3 727	1 831	1 896	4 008	1 976	2 032	4 581	2 265	2 315
60-64	3 282	1 579	1 703	3 798	1 842	1 957	3 658	1 778	1 880	3 940	1 923	2 017
65-69	3 307	1 544	1 763	3 147	1 483	1 664	3 648	1 736	1 913	3 526	1 684	1 842
70-74	2 886	1 280	1 606	3 055	1 376	1 679	2 923	1 333	1 590	3 400	1 569	1 832
75-79	2 421	995	1 426	2 517	1 056	1 461	2 682	1 146	1 535	2 585	1 123	1 463
80-84	1 768	641	1 127	1 899	715	1 184	2 000	772	1 227	2 156	852	1 303
85-89	709	221	487	1 166	370	796	1 281	424	857	1 378	471	907
90-94	409	108	300	357	92	265	610	160	450	693	190	503
95-99	92	20	73	133	27	106	125	25	101	225	45	181
100 +	8	1	7	15	2	13	25	3	21	27	3	23

Age group	2025 Both sexes	Males	Females	2030 Both sexes	Males	Females	2035 Both sexes	Males	Females	2040 Both sexes	Males	Females
All ages	58 779	28 645	30 135	58 599	28 580	30 019	58 473	28 537	29 936	58 439	28 536	29 902
0-4	2 839	1 462	1 377	2 896	1 492	1 404	3 053	1 573	1 480	3 258	1 678	1 580
5-9	2 898	1 493	1 405	2 861	1 474	1 387	2 919	1 503	1 415	3 077	1 585	1 492
10-14	2 996	1 543	1 453	2 921	1 504	1 417	2 884	1 485	1 399	2 943	1 515	1 427
15-19	3 101	1 596	1 504	3 020	1 555	1 465	2 944	1 516	1 428	2 907	1 497	1 410
20-24	2 765	1 422	1 342	3 125	1 608	1 517	3 043	1 566	1 477	2 967	1 527	1 440
25-29	2 775	1 426	1 349	2 789	1 434	1 355	3 149	1 619	1 530	3 066	1 577	1 489
30-34	2 905	1 487	1 418	2 800	1 437	1 362	2 814	1 445	1 369	3 173	1 630	1 543
35-39	2 937	1 496	1 440	2 928	1 497	1 431	2 823	1 448	1 375	2 838	1 456	1 382
40-44	3 174	1 611	1 563	2 958	1 505	1 453	2 949	1 506	1 444	2 846	1 458	1 388
45-49	3 756	1 899	1 858	3 191	1 616	1 575	2 976	1 511	1 464	2 968	1 512	1 455
50-54	4 542	2 284	2 258	3 764	1 897	1 867	3 200	1 617	1 584	2 986	1 513	1 474
55-59	4 742	2 359	2 382	4 521	2 262	2 259	3 753	1 883	1 870	3 195	1 607	1 588
60-64	4 509	2 210	2 299	4 675	2 307	2 368	4 465	2 216	2 248	3 713	1 849	1 864
65-69	3 808	1 828	1 980	4 368	2 108	2 260	4 540	2 208	2 331	4 344	2 129	2 216
70-74	3 303	1 533	1 770	3 581	1 675	1 907	4 122	1 941	2 181	4 300	2 044	2 256
75-79	3 024	1 333	1 691	2 959	1 315	1 644	3 227	1 449	1 778	3 734	1 692	2 042
80-84	2 104	848	1 255	2 485	1 021	1 464	2 458	1 022	1 436	2 707	1 141	1 567
85-89	1 514	532	982	1 506	542	964	1 809	666	1 143	1 821	682	1 140
90-94	770	219	551	872	255	616	892	269	623	1 099	341	757
95-99	269	56	213	314	67	247	371	82	289	395	91	304
100 +	48	6	42	65	8	57	82	11	71	104	14	89

Age group	2045 Both sexes	Males	Females	2050 Both sexes	Males	Females
All ages	58 436	28 552	29 885	58 382	28 550	29 832
0-4	3 399	1 751	1 648	3 446	1 775	1 671
5-9	3 282	1 690	1 591	3 424	1 763	1 660
10-14	3 102	1 597	1 504	3 307	1 703	1 604
15-19	2 967	1 528	1 439	3 127	1 610	1 517
20-24	2 930	1 508	1 422	2 991	1 540	1 451
25-29	2 989	1 537	1 452	2 953	1 519	1 434
30-34	3 089	1 587	1 502	3 011	1 548	1 463
35-39	3 196	1 640	1 556	3 111	1 597	1 514
40-44	2 862	1 467	1 395	3 219	1 650	1 569
45-49	2 866	1 465	1 400	2 883	1 475	1 408
50-54	2 979	1 515	1 465	2 880	1 469	1 411
55-59	2 984	1 505	1 479	2 979	1 509	1 470
60-64	3 166	1 581	1 585	2 961	1 484	1 477
65-69	3 623	1 782	1 841	3 097	1 529	1 568
70-74	4 129	1 980	2 149	3 457	1 667	1 790
75-79	3 916	1 796	2 120	3 780	1 752	2 028
80-84	3 161	1 348	1 813	3 345	1 448	1 897
85-89	2 038	776	1 262	2 414	934	1 479
90-94	1 136	360	775	1 301	422	879
95-99	504	120	384	541	132	409
100 +	120	17	103	157	23	133

United Nations Department of Economic and Social Affairs/Population Division
World Population Prospects: The 2004 Revision, Volume II: Sex and Age Distribution of the World Population

500

POPULATION BY AGE AND SEX (in thousands)

Age group	2005 Both sexes	Males	Females	2010 Both sexes	Males	Females	2015 Both sexes	Males	Females	2020 Both sexes	Males	Females
All ages	58 093	28 195	29 898	57 723	28 012	29 710	56 720	27 521	29 209	55 316	26 825	28 491
0-4	2 662	1 371	1 291	2 125	1 094	1 030	1 689	870	819	1 434	739	696
5-9	2 674	1 377	1 297	2 687	1 384	1 303	2 149	1 107	1 042	1 713	882	830
10-14	2 808	1 442	1 366	2 701	1 391	1 310	2 714	1 398	1 316	2 175	1 120	1 055
15-19	2 843	1 455	1 388	2 833	1 455	1 379	2 727	1 404	1 323	2 740	1 411	1 329
20-24	3 079	1 571	1 508	2 867	1 466	1 401	2 857	1 466	1 392	2 751	1 415	1 336
25-29	3 661	1 863	1 799	3 104	1 582	1 522	2 891	1 476	1 414	2 881	1 476	1 405
30-34	4 469	2 266	2 203	3 689	1 874	1 815	3 128	1 592	1 536	2 914	1 487	1 427
35-39	4 727	2 382	2 345	4 497	2 277	2 220	3 715	1 884	1 830	3 152	1 602	1 550
40-44	4 603	2 302	2 300	4 752	2 390	2 362	4 521	2 285	2 236	3 738	1 893	1 845
45-49	4 043	2 013	2 031	4 616	2 304	2 312	4 768	2 393	2 375	4 538	2 289	2 249
50-54	3 760	1 859	1 901	4 038	2 003	2 035	4 612	2 294	2 318	4 768	2 385	2 383
55-59	3 881	1 903	1 977	3 727	1 831	1 896	4 008	1 976	2 032	4 581	2 265	2 315
60-64	3 282	1 579	1 703	3 798	1 842	1 957	3 658	1 778	1 880	3 940	1 923	2 017
65-69	3 307	1 544	1 763	3 147	1 483	1 664	3 648	1 736	1 913	3 526	1 684	1 842
70-74	2 886	1 280	1 606	3 055	1 376	1 679	2 923	1 333	1 590	3 400	1 569	1 832
75-79	2 421	995	1 426	2 517	1 056	1 461	2 682	1 146	1 535	2 585	1 123	1 463
80-84	1 768	641	1 127	1 899	715	1 184	2 000	772	1 227	2 156	852	1 303
85-89	709	221	487	1 166	370	796	1 281	424	857	1 378	471	907
90-94	409	108	300	357	92	265	610	160	450	693	190	503
95-99	92	20	73	133	27	106	125	25	101	225	45	181
100 +	8	1	7	15	2	13	25	3	21	27	3	23

Age group	2025 Both sexes	Males	Females	2030 Both sexes	Males	Females	2035 Both sexes	Males	Females	2040 Both sexes	Males	Females
All ages	53 796	26 078	27 718	52 227	25 298	26 928	50 570	24 468	26 102	48 735	23 541	25 194
0-4	1 455	750	706	1 504	775	729	1 519	782	736	1 450	747	703
5-9	1 457	750	706	1 478	761	717	1 527	786	741	1 543	795	748
10-14	1 737	895	842	1 480	762	718	1 501	773	728	1 551	799	752
15-19	2 201	1 133	1 068	1 762	907	855	1 504	774	730	1 525	785	740
20-24	2 765	1 422	1 342	2 227	1 146	1 081	1 786	919	867	1 528	786	742
25-29	2 775	1 426	1 349	2 789	1 434	1 355	2 252	1 158	1 094	1 811	931	880
30-34	2 905	1 487	1 418	2 800	1 437	1 362	2 814	1 445	1 369	2 278	1 170	1 108
35-39	2 937	1 496	1 440	2 928	1 497	1 431	2 823	1 448	1 375	2 838	1 456	1 382
40-44	3 174	1 611	1 563	2 958	1 505	1 453	2 949	1 500	1 444	2 846	1 458	1 388
45-49	3 766	1 899	1 858	3 191	1 616	1 575	2 976	1 511	1 464	2 968	1 512	1 455
50-54	4 542	2 284	2 258	3 764	1 897	1 867	3 200	1 617	1 584	2 986	1 513	1 474
55-59	4 742	2 369	2 372	4 521	2 262	2 259	3 753	1 883	1 870	3 195	1 607	1 588
60-64	4 509	2 210	2 299	4 675	2 307	2 368	4 465	2 216	2 248	3 713	1 849	1 864
65-69	3 808	1 828	1 980	4 368	2 108	2 260	4 540	2 208	2 331	4 344	2 129	2 216
70-74	3 303	1 533	1 770	3 581	1 675	1 907	4 122	1 941	2 181	4 300	2 044	2 256
75-79	3 024	1 333	1 691	2 959	1 315	1 644	3 227	1 449	1 778	3 734	1 692	2 042
80-84	2 104	848	1 255	2 485	1 021	1 464	2 458	1 022	1 436	2 707	1 141	1 567
85-89	1 514	532	982	1 506	542	964	1 809	666	1 143	1 821	682	1 140
90-94	770	219	551	872	255	616	892	269	623	1 099	341	757
95-99	269	56	213	314	67	247	371	82	289	395	91	304
100 +	48	6	42	65	8	57	82	11	71	104	14	89

Age group	2045 Both sexes	Males	Females	2050 Both sexes	Males	Females
All ages	46 655	22 489	24 167	44 344	21 327	23 017
0-4	1 313	676	636	1 178	607	571
5-9	1 475	760	715	1 338	689	649
10-14	1 568	808	760	1 501	773	728
15-19	1 576	812	765	1 594	821	773
20-24	1 549	797	752	1 601	824	777
25-29	1 552	798	754	1 574	810	764
30-34	1 836	943	893	1 577	810	766
35-39	2 303	1 182	1 121	1 861	956	906
40-44	2 862	1 467	1 395	2 328	1 194	1 135
45-49	2 866	1 465	1 400	2 883	1 475	1 408
50-54	2 979	1 515	1 465	2 880	1 469	1 411
55-59	2 984	1 505	1 479	2 979	1 509	1 470
60-64	3 166	1 581	1 585	2 961	1 484	1 477
65-69	3 623	1 782	1 841	3 097	1 529	1 568
70-74	4 129	1 980	2 149	3 457	1 667	1 790
75-79	3 916	1 796	2 120	3 780	1 752	2 028
80-84	3 161	1 348	1 813	3 345	1 448	1 897
85-89	2 038	776	1 262	2 414	934	1 479
90-94	1 136	360	775	1 301	422	879
95-99	504	120	384	541	132	409
100 +	120	17	103	157	23	133

POPULATION BY AGE AND SEX (in thousands)

Age group	1950 Both sexes	1950 Males	1950 Females	1955 Both sexes	1955 Males	1955 Females	1960 Both sexes	1960 Males	1960 Females	1965 Both sexes	1965 Males	1965 Females
All ages	1 403	682	720	1 542	750	792	1 629	783	846	1 760	841	919
0-4	189	95	94	227	114	113	283	143	140	319	159	160
5-9	167	84	83	183	92	91	222	112	110	256	128	128
10-14	150	75	75	162	81	81	174	87	87	189	88	101
15-19	143	72	71	149	75	74	146	69	77	170	79	91
20-24	120	59	61	133	67	66	125	57	68	129	59	69
25-29	110	51	58	113	54	58	112	50	62	100	47	54
30-34	104	48	56	101	46	55	94	43	51	93	43	50
35-39	99	47	51	102	47	55	90	41	49	88	42	46
40-44	79	38	41	86	40	46	82	40	42	77	37	40
45-49	72	36	36	78	38	40	78	39	39	73	35	38
50-54	51	25	26	64	32	33	67	33	34	64	32	32
55-59	40	18	21	48	23	25	48	23	25	60	29	31
60-64	27	12	15	33	15	18	38	18	20	47	23	24
65-69	24	11	14	27	12	15	25	10	15	35	16	18
70-74	18	7	11	21	9	12	23	10	13	28	12	16
75-79	9	3	5	10	4	6	14	5	9	18	7	11
80 +	3	1	2	7	2	5	8	3	6	14	5	9

Age group	1970 Both sexes	1970 Males	1970 Females	1975 Both sexes	1975 Males	1975 Females	1980 Both sexes	1980 Males	1980 Females	1985 Both sexes	1985 Males	1985 Females
All ages	1 869	912	957	2 013	984	1 029	2 133	1 052	1 081	2 297	1 137	1 160
0-4	322	162	160	297	150	147	283	143	140	274	138	136
5-9	307	154	153	313	158	155	289	147	143	278	142	135
10-14	249	125	124	300	151	149	286	145	141	290	147	143
15-19	165	80	85	236	118	117	248	123	125	279	139	140
20-24	126	59	67	141	67	73	197	96	101	239	118	121
25-29	100	48	52	103	47	56	146	71	75	184	90	94
30-34	83	40	43	86	41	45	111	54	57	133	64	68
35-39	81	38	43	79	37	42	92	45	47	104	51	53
40-44	79	38	41	78	36	42	80	39	41	88	44	45
45-49	71	34	37	77	37	40	74	36	38	78	38	40
50-54	69	33	36	68	32	35	68	32	35	71	34	36
55-59	59	29	30	65	31	34	61	29	32	63	30	33
60-64	54	26	28	54	27	28	55	27	29	55	26	29
65-69	41	20	21	47	22	25	50	24	26	48	23	25
70-74	28	13	15	33	15	18	40	20	21	45	22	23
75-79	20	8	12	20	9	11	22	12	10	33	16	17
80 +	15	5	10	17	6	11	31	10	21	35	14	22

Age group	1990 Both sexes	1990 Males	1990 Females	1995 Both sexes	1995 Males	1995 Females	2000 Both sexes	2000 Males	2000 Females	2005 Both sexes	2005 Males	2005 Females
All ages	2 369	1 161	1 208	2 484	1 224	1 260	2 585	1 275	1 309	2 651	1 310	1 341
0-4	281	142	139	295	151	144	284	146	139	258	132	126
5-9	283	143	140	278	140	138	294	150	144	279	143	136
10-14	269	135	134	271	136	135	275	139	137	291	149	142
15-19	254	127	128	247	123	123	253	126	127	268	135	133
20-24	229	111	118	234	115	118	210	102	108	235	117	118
25-29	205	98	107	210	100	111	212	103	109	188	91	97
30-34	167	79	88	191	90	102	201	95	106	191	92	99
35-39	126	61	65	160	77	83	177	82	94	184	87	97
40-44	100	50	50	117	58	60	149	73	76	165	76	89
45-49	84	42	42	95	48	47	106	54	53	140	68	72
50-54	71	35	36	81	41	40	89	45	44	99	50	50
55-59	63	30	32	67	33	34	76	39	37	83	42	41
60-64	63	30	33	59	29	30	60	29	31	70	36	34
65-69	55	26	29	56	28	27	61	28	33	54	26	28
70-74	44	21	24	46	22	24	54	27	27	53	24	29
75-79	35	16	19	35	16	19	36	18	18	43	21	23
80 +	40	16	24	43	17	26	47	19	28	50	22	28

United Nations Department of Economic and Social Affairs/Population Division
World Population Prospects: The 2004 Revision, Volume II: Sex and Age Distribution of the World Population

POPULATION BY AGE AND SEX (in thousands)

Age group	2005			2010			2015			2020		
	Both sexes	Males	Females	Both sexes	Males	Females	Both sexes	Males	Females	Both sexes	Males	Females
All ages	2 651	1 310	1 341	2 703	1 337	1 366	2 748	1 301	1 087	2 785	1 380	1 404
0-4	258	132	126	248	127	121	243	124	119	235	120	115
5-9	279	143	136	252	129	123	242	124	118	238	122	116
10-14	291	149	142	275	141	134	249	127	121	239	123	117
15-19	268	135	133	284	145	138	268	137	131	242	124	118
20-24	235	117	118	251	126	124	267	137	130	251	129	123
25-29	188	91	97	213	106	107	229	115	114	245	126	120
30-34	191	92	99	167	81	87	193	96	97	210	106	104
35-39	184	87	97	174	84	90	152	73	79	178	89	90
40-44	165	76	89	172	80	91	162	78	84	141	67	74
45-49	140	68	72	155	71	84	162	75	86	153	73	80
50-54	99	50	50	132	64	68	147	67	80	154	71	83
55-59	83	42	41	93	46	47	124	60	64	139	63	76
60-64	70	36	34	76	38	38	86	43	44	116	56	61
65-69	54	26	28	63	32	31	69	34	35	79	38	40
70-74	53	24	29	47	22	25	55	27	28	61	29	31
75-79	43	21	23	43	19	24	38	17	21	45	22	23
80-84	26	12	13	31	14	17	31	13	18	28	12	16
85-89	15	6	9	16	7	9	19	8	11	20	8	12
90-94	7	3	4	7	3	4	8	3	4	9	4	6
95-99	2	1	1	2	1	2	2	1	2	3	1	2
100 +	0	0	0	0	0	0	1	0	0	1	0	0

Age group	2025			2030			2035			2040		
	Both sexes	Males	Females	Both sexes	Males	Females	Both sexes	Males	Females	Both sexes	Males	Females
All ages	2 804	1 391	1 413	2 801	1 390	1 410	2 775	1 378	1 397	2 729	1 356	1 373
0-4	220	113	107	202	103	99	185	95	90	173	89	84
5-9	230	118	112	215	110	105	197	101	96	180	92	88
10-14	235	120	114	227	116	111	212	109	104	194	100	95
15-19	232	119	113	227	117	111	220	113	107	205	105	100
20-24	225	116	110	216	111	105	211	109	103	204	105	99
25-29	230	118	112	204	105	99	195	101	95	191	98	93
30-34	226	116	110	211	109	103	186	96	90	177	92	86
35-39	195	98	97	211	108	103	197	101	96	173	89	84
40-44	167	83	84	184	92	92	200	103	90	187	96	91
45-49	133	63	70	159	78	81	176	88	88	192	98	94
50-54	145	69	77	126	59	67	152	74	77	168	84	85
55-59	146	67	79	138	65	73	120	56	64	145	71	74
60-64	130	58	72	137	62	75	130	61	69	113	52	61
65-69	106	50	56	120	53	67	127	57	70	120	56	65
70-74	69	33	36	94	44	51	107	46	60	113	50	63
75-79	50	24	26	57	27	31	79	35	43	89	38	52
80-84	33	15	18	37	17	20	43	19	24	59	25	34
85-89	18	7	10	21	9	12	24	10	14	28	11	16
90-94	10	3	6	9	3	5	10	4	6	12	4	7
95-99	3	1	2	3	1	2	3	1	2	4	1	2
100 +	1	0	0	1	0	1	1	0	1	1	0	1

Age group	2045			2050		
	Both sexes	Males	Females	Both sexes	Males	Females
All ages	2 666	1 327	1 340	2 586	1 289	1 297
0-4	164	84	80	153	78	75
5-9	168	86	82	159	82	78
10-14	178	91	87	166	85	81
15-19	188	96	91	171	88	83
20-24	189	97	92	172	88	83
25-29	184	95	89	169	88	82
30-34	173	89	84	166	86	80
35-39	164	85	79	160	83	77
40-44	163	84	79	154	80	75
45-49	179	92	87	155	80	76
50-54	185	94	91	172	88	84
55-59	161	80	81	177	90	87
60-64	137	66	71	153	75	78
65-69	105	48	57	128	61	66
70-74	108	49	59	94	42	52
75-79	95	41	55	91	40	51
80-84	68	27	41	73	30	43
85-89	39	15	23	45	17	28
90-94	14	5	9	20	7	13
95-99	4	1	3	5	2	3
100 +	1	0	1	1	0	1

United Nations Department of Economic and Social Affairs/Population Division
World Population Prospects: The 2004 Revision, Volume II: Sex and Age Distribution of the World Population

503

POPULATION BY AGE AND SEX (in thousands)

Age group	2005 Both sexes	Males	Females	2010 Both sexes	Males	Females	2015 Both sexes	Males	Females	2020 Both sexes	Males	Females
All ages	2 651	1 310	1 341	2 730	1 351	1 379	2 820	1 398	1 422	2 913	1 446	1 467
0-4	258	132	126	275	141	134	287	147	140	291	149	142
5-9	279	143	136	252	129	123	269	138	132	282	144	138
10-14	291	149	142	275	141	134	249	127	121	266	136	130
15-19	268	135	133	284	145	138	268	137	131	242	124	118
20-24	235	117	118	251	126	124	267	137	130	251	129	123
25-29	188	91	97	213	106	107	229	115	114	245	126	120
30-34	191	92	99	167	81	87	193	96	97	210	106	104
35-39	184	87	97	174	84	90	152	73	79	178	89	90
40-44	165	76	89	172	80	91	162	78	84	141	67	74
45-49	140	68	72	155	71	84	162	75	86	153	73	80
50-54	99	50	50	132	64	68	147	67	80	154	71	83
55-59	83	42	41	93	46	47	124	60	64	139	63	76
60-64	70	36	34	76	38	38	86	43	44	116	56	61
65-69	54	26	28	63	32	31	69	34	35	79	38	40
70-74	53	24	29	47	22	25	55	27	28	61	29	31
75-79	43	21	23	43	19	24	38	17	21	45	22	23
80-84	26	12	13	31	14	17	31	13	18	28	12	16
85-89	15	6	9	16	7	9	19	8	11	20	8	12
90-94	7	3	4	7	3	4	8	3	4	9	4	6
95-99	2	1	1	2	1	2	2	1	2	3	1	2
100 +	0	0	0	0	0	0	1	0	0	1	0	0

Age group	2025 Both sexes	Males	Females	2030 Both sexes	Males	Females	2035 Both sexes	Males	Females	2040 Both sexes	Males	Females
All ages	2 989	1 486	1 503	3 048	1 517	1 531	3 097	1 543	1 554	3 139	1 566	1 573
0-4	278	142	135	265	136	130	261	133	127	262	134	128
5-9	286	146	140	272	139	133	260	133	127	256	131	125
10-14	279	143	136	283	145	138	270	138	132	258	132	126
15-19	259	133	126	272	139	133	276	141	135	262	135	128
20-24	225	116	110	243	124	118	255	131	124	260	133	126
25-29	230	118	112	204	105	99	222	114	108	235	121	114
30-34	226	116	110	211	109	103	186	96	90	204	105	99
35-39	195	98	97	211	108	103	197	101	96	173	89	84
40-44	167	83	84	184	92	92	200	103	98	187	96	91
45-49	133	63	70	159	78	81	176	88	88	192	98	94
50-54	145	69	77	126	59	67	152	74	77	168	84	85
55-59	146	67	79	138	65	73	120	56	64	145	71	74
60-64	130	58	72	137	62	75	130	61	69	113	52	61
65-69	106	50	56	120	53	67	127	57	70	120	56	65
70-74	69	33	36	94	44	51	107	46	60	113	50	63
75-79	50	24	26	57	27	31	79	35	43	89	38	52
80-84	33	15	18	37	17	20	43	19	24	59	25	34
85-89	18	7	10	21	9	12	24	10	14	28	11	16
90-94	10	3	6	9	3	5	10	4	6	12	4	7
95-99	3	1	2	3	1	2	3	1	2	4	1	2
100 +	1	0	0	1	0	1	1	0	1	1	0	1

Age group	2045 Both sexes	Males	Females	2050 Both sexes	Males	Females
All ages	3 175	1 586	1 588	3 198	1 601	1 597
0-4	264	135	129	259	133	126
5-9	257	132	125	259	133	126
10-14	253	130	123	254	130	124
15-19	251	128	122	246	126	120
20-24	246	126	120	235	121	114
25-29	239	123	116	226	116	110
30-34	217	112	105	221	114	107
35-39	190	98	92	203	105	98
40-44	163	84	79	180	93	87
45-49	179	92	87	155	80	76
50-54	185	94	91	172	88	84
55-59	161	80	81	177	90	87
60-64	137	66	71	153	75	78
65-69	105	48	57	128	61	66
70-74	108	49	59	94	42	52
75-79	95	41	55	91	40	51
80-84	68	27	41	73	30	43
85-89	39	15	23	45	17	28
90-94	14	5	9	20	7	13
95-99	4	1	3	5	2	3
100 +	1	0	1	1	0	1

United Nations Department of Economic and Social Affairs/Population Division
World Population Prospects: The 2004 Revision, Volume II: Sex and Age Distribution of the World Population

POPULATION BY AGE AND SEX (in thousands)

Age group	2005			2010			2015			2020		
	Both sexes	Males	Females	Both sexes	Males	Females	Both sexes	Males	Females	Both sexes	Males	Females
All ages	2 651	1 310	1 341	2 675	1 323	1 352	2 677	1 324	1 352	2 657	1 315	1 342
0-4	258	132	126	221	113	108	198	101	97	178	91	87
5-9	279	143	136	252	129	123	215	110	105	193	99	94
10-14	291	149	142	275	141	134	249	127	121	212	109	104
15-19	268	135	133	284	145	138	268	137	131	242	124	118
20-24	235	117	118	251	126	124	267	137	130	251	129	123
25-29	188	91	97	213	106	107	229	115	114	245	126	120
30-34	191	92	99	167	81	87	193	96	97	210	106	104
35-39	184	87	97	174	84	90	152	73	79	178	89	90
40-44	165	76	89	172	80	91	162	78	84	141	67	74
45-49	140	68	72	155	71	84	162	75	86	153	73	80
50-54	99	50	50	132	64	68	147	67	80	154	71	83
55-59	83	42	41	93	46	47	124	60	64	139	63	76
60-64	70	36	34	76	38	38	86	43	44	116	56	61
65-69	54	26	28	63	32	31	69	34	35	79	38	40
70-74	53	24	29	47	22	25	55	27	28	61	29	31
75-79	43	21	23	43	19	24	38	17	21	45	22	23
80-84	26	12	13	31	14	17	31	13	18	28	12	16
85-89	15	6	9	16	7	9	19	8	11	20	8	12
90-94	7	3	4	7	3	4	8	3	4	9	4	6
95-99	2	1	1	2	1	2	2	1	2	3	1	2
100 +	0	0	0	0	0	0	1	0	0	1	0	0

Age group	2025			2030			2035			2040		
	Both sexes	Males	Females	Both sexes	Males	Females	Both sexes	Males	Females	Both sexes	Males	Females
All ages	2 620	1 297	1 323	2 558	1 266	1 292	2 468	1 221	1 247	2 352	1 164	1 189
0-4	164	84	80	143	73	70	121	62	59	102	52	50
5-9	173	89	85	159	81	77	138	71	67	116	59	56
10-14	190	97	93	171	87	83	156	80	76	136	70	66
15-19	205	105	100	183	94	89	164	84	80	149	77	73
20-24	225	116	110	189	97	92	167	86	81	148	76	72
25-29	230	118	112	204	105	99	169	87	82	147	76	71
30-34	226	116	110	211	109	103	186	96	90	151	78	73
35-39	195	98	97	211	108	103	197	101	96	173	89	84
40-44	167	83	84	184	92	92	200	103	98	187	96	91
45-49	133	63	70	159	78	81	176	88	88	192	98	94
50-54	145	69	77	126	59	67	152	74	77	168	84	85
55-59	146	67	79	138	65	73	120	56	64	145	71	74
60-64	130	58	72	137	62	75	130	61	69	113	52	61
65-69	106	50	56	120	53	67	127	57	70	120	56	65
70-74	69	33	36	94	44	51	107	46	60	113	50	63
75-79	50	24	26	57	27	31	79	35	43	89	38	52
80-84	33	16	18	37	17	20	43	10	24	50	25	34
85-89	18	7	10	21	9	12	24	10	14	28	11	16
90-94	10	3	6	9	3	5	10	4	6	12	4	7
95-99	3	1	2	3	1	2	3	1	2	4	1	2
100 +	1	0	0	1	0	1	1	0	1	1	0	1

Age group	2045			2050		
	Both sexes	Males	Females	Both sexes	Males	Females
All ages	2 215	1 096	1 119	2 059	1 020	1 039
0-4	88	45	43	76	39	37
5-9	97	50	47	83	43	41
10-14	113	58	55	95	49	46
15-19	129	66	63	107	55	52
20-24	134	69	65	113	59	55
25-29	128	66	62	114	59	55
30-34	130	67	62	111	58	53
35-39	138	71	67	117	61	56
40-44	163	84	79	129	67	62
45-49	179	92	87	155	80	76
50-54	185	94	91	172	88	84
55-59	161	80	81	177	90	87
60-64	137	66	71	153	75	78
65-69	105	48	57	128	61	66
70-74	108	49	59	94	42	52
75-79	95	41	55	91	40	51
80-84	68	27	41	73	30	43
85-89	39	15	23	45	17	28
90-94	14	5	9	20	7	13
95-99	4	1	3	5	2	3
100 +	1	0	1	1	0	1

United Nations Department of Economic and Social Affairs/Population Division
World Population Prospects: The 2004 Revision, Volume II: Sex and Age Distribution of the World Population

505

POPULATION BY AGE AND SEX (in thousands)

Age group	1950 Both sexes	Males	Females	1955 Both sexes	Males	Females	1960 Both sexes	Males	Females	1965 Both sexes	Males	Females
All ages	83 625	41 003	42 622	89 815	44 111	45 704	94 096	46 176	47 920	98 881	48 531	50 350
0-4	11 175	5 699	5 476	9 519	4 864	4 655	8 007	4 079	3 928	8 203	4 185	4 018
5-9	9 672	4 901	4 771	10 993	5 608	5 385	9 499	4 842	4 657	7 998	4 071	3 927
10-14	8 796	4 452	4 344	9 641	4 883	4 758	10 920	5 548	5 372	9 445	4 802	4 643
15-19	8 637	4 354	4 283	8 703	4 383	4 320	9 390	4 742	4 648	10 776	5 437	5 339
20-24	7 759	3 844	3 915	8 451	4 220	4 231	8 361	4 134	4 227	9 169	4 545	4 624
25-29	6 186	2 807	3 379	7 621	3 775	3 846	8 274	4 122	4 152	8 421	4 187	4 234
30-34	5 215	2 372	2 843	6 108	2 778	3 330	7 519	3 761	3 758	8 293	4 166	4 127
35-39	5 081	2 394	2 687	5 120	2 327	2 793	6 028	2 742	3 286	7 505	3 743	3 762
40-44	4 492	2 205	2 287	4 971	2 340	2 631	5 041	2 296	2 745	5 944	2 707	3 237
45-49	4 029	2 031	1 998	4 368	2 138	2 230	4 833	2 258	2 575	4 920	2 229	2 691
50-54	3 391	1 720	1 671	3 864	1 937	1 927	4 204	2 057	2 147	4 676	2 184	2 492
55-59	2 755	1 380	1 375	3 203	1 606	1 597	3 680	1 806	1 874	3 997	1 930	2 067
60-64	2 302	1 107	1 195	2 499	1 225	1 274	2 943	1 446	1 497	3 355	1 630	1 725
65-69	1 779	799	980	1 962	915	1 047	2 166	1 030	1 136	2 557	1 216	1 341
70-74	1 290	543	747	1 396	595	801	1 584	703	881	1 745	787	958
75-79	690	269	421	880	344	536	968	382	586	1 097	451	646
80 +	376	126	250	516	173	343	679	228	451	780	261	519

Age group	1970 Both sexes	Males	Females	1975 Both sexes	Males	Females	1980 Both sexes	Males	Females	1985 Both sexes	Males	Females
All ages	104 331	51 205	53 126	111 524	54 880	56 644	116 807	57 468	59 339	120 837	59 393	61 444
0-4	8 879	4 550	4 329	9 944	5 099	4 845	8 593	4 407	4 186	7 449	3 814	3 634
5-9	8 240	4 212	4 028	8 902	4 566	4 336	9 985	5 120	4 865	8 520	4 367	4 153
10-14	7 953	4 054	3 899	8 263	4 227	4 036	8 934	4 582	4 352	10 028	5 141	4 888
15-19	9 138	4 608	4 530	8 007	4 069	3 938	8 265	4 220	4 045	8 968	4 594	4 373
20-24	10 693	5 328	5 365	9 155	4 604	4 551	7 907	3 993	3 913	8 190	4 161	4 029
25-29	9 119	4 531	4 588	10 713	5 383	5 330	9 132	4 592	4 540	7 812	3 943	3 869
30-34	8 414	4 202	4 212	9 206	4 606	4 600	10 701	5 386	5 316	9 041	4 552	4 489
35-39	8 246	4 141	4 105	8 415	4 210	4 205	9 171	4 581	4 590	10 723	5 391	5 332
40-44	7 370	3 679	3 691	8 183	4 104	4 079	8 341	4 163	4 178	9 122	4 546	4 576
45-49	5 901	2 688	3 213	7 290	3 609	3 681	8 061	4 019	4 042	8 225	4 087	4 138
50-54	4 826	2 166	2 660	5 735	2 595	3 140	7 128	3 498	3 630	7 922	3 921	4 001
55-59	4 441	2 049	2 392	4 663	2 072	2 591	5 568	2 491	3 078	6 989	3 405	3 585
60-64	3 740	1 761	1 979	4 258	1 928	2 330	4 461	1 948	2 513	5 398	2 377	3 021
65-69	2 996	1 403	1 593	3 427	1 563	1 864	3 941	1 737	2 204	4 187	1 779	2 408
70-74	2 144	965	1 179	2 555	1 140	1 415	3 002	1 310	1 692	3 559	1 502	2 057
75-79	1 277	535	742	1 622	680	942	2 017	841	1 176	2 489	1 016	1 474
80 +	954	333	621	1 186	425	761	1 600	581	1 019	2 215	797	1 418

Age group	1990 Both sexes	Males	Females	1995 Both sexes	Males	Females	2000 Both sexes	Males	Females	2005 Both sexes	Males	Females
All ages	123 537	60 658	62 879	125 472	61 526	63 946	127 034	62 178	64 856	128 085	62 578	65 506
0-4	6 561	3 364	3 197	5 997	3 072	2 925	6 055	3 109	2 946	5 871	3 015	2 857
5-9	7 543	3 865	3 678	6 542	3 352	3 190	5 998	3 072	2 926	6 057	3 110	2 948
10-14	8 627	4 425	4 202	7 480	3 829	3 650	6 544	3 352	3 192	6 001	3 073	2 928
15-19	9 988	5 117	4 871	8 560	4 389	4 172	7 503	3 839	3 664	6 568	3 363	3 206
20-24	8 800	4 472	4 328	9 898	5 045	4 853	8 597	4 402	4 195	7 542	3 855	3 688
25-29	8 086	4 090	3 996	8 791	4 455	4 336	9 924	5 053	4 871	8 628	4 413	4 214
30-34	7 874	3 972	3 902	8 129	4 117	4 012	8 803	4 457	4 346	9 936	5 054	4 882
35-39	9 115	4 585	4 530	7 824	3 948	3 876	8 123	4 109	4 014	8 798	4 449	4 348
40-44	10 613	5 330	5 283	9 009	4 530	4 478	7 797	3 929	3 868	8 099	4 090	4 008
45-49	9 008	4 481	4 527	10 621	5 332	5 289	8 939	4 484	4 455	7 747	3 893	3 853
50-54	8 108	4 011	4 097	8 924	4 425	4 500	10 472	5 232	5 240	8 831	4 410	4 422
55-59	7 713	3 780	3 933	7 956	3 909	4 046	8 726	4 290	4 436	10 269	5 091	5 178
60-64	6 693	3 201	3 491	7 477	3 614	3 863	7 690	3 725	3 964	8 470	4 112	4 359
65-69	5 071	2 181	2 889	6 398	3 001	3 397	7 086	3 347	3 739	7 334	3 480	3 854
70-74	3 817	1 564	2 253	4 696	1 943	2 753	5 870	2 652	3 219	6 566	2 998	3 568
75-79	2 999	1 193	1 806	3 290	1 261	2 028	4 095	1 591	2 503	5 181	2 217	2 964
80 +	2 922	1 026	1 896	3 881	1 304	2 577	4 812	1 535	3 277	6 187	1 956	4 231

United Nations Department of Economic and Social Affairs/Population Division
World Population Prospects: The 2004 Revision, Volume II: Sex and Age Distribution of the World Population

506

POPULATION BY AGE AND SEX (in thousands)

Age group	2005 Both sexes	2005 Males	2005 Females	2010 Both sexes	2010 Males	2010 Females	2015 Both sexes	2015 Males	2015 Females	2020 Both sexes	2020 Males	2020 Females
All ages	128 085	62 578	65 506	128 457	62 619	65 838	127 993	62 219	65 774	126 713	61 398	65 315
0-4	5 871	3 015	2 857	5 726	2 940	2 786	5 440	2 793	2 647	5 137	2 637	2 499
5-9	6 057	3 110	2 948	5 874	3 016	2 859	5 729	2 941	2 788	5 444	2 795	2 650
10-14	6 001	3 073	2 928	6 060	3 111	2 950	5 878	3 017	2 861	5 733	2 943	2 791
15-19	6 568	3 363	3 206	6 026	3 084	2 942	6 086	3 122	2 964	5 905	3 029	2 876
20-24	7 542	3 855	3 688	6 611	3 381	3 231	6 072	3 104	2 968	6 133	3 143	2 990
25-29	8 628	4 413	4 214	7 578	3 869	3 709	6 650	3 397	3 253	6 112	3 122	2 991
30-34	9 936	5 054	4 882	8 645	4 418	4 227	7 599	3 876	3 723	6 675	3 407	3 269
35-39	8 798	4 449	4 348	9 930	5 045	4 885	8 647	4 414	4 233	7 606	3 875	3 731
40-44	8 099	4 090	4 008	8 776	4 431	4 344	9 908	5 026	4 882	8 633	4 400	4 234
45-49	7 747	3 893	3 853	8 053	4 057	3 996	8 733	4 398	4 335	9 865	4 991	4 874
50-54	8 831	4 410	4 422	7 666	3 836	3 830	7 979	4 003	3 977	8 661	4 344	4 317
55-59	10 269	5 091	5 178	8 679	4 302	4 377	7 548	3 751	3 798	7 869	3 921	3 948
60-64	8 470	4 112	4 359	9 993	4 896	5 097	8 467	4 151	4 316	7 380	3 630	3 750
65-69	7 334	3 480	3 854	8 108	3 861	4 247	9 596	4 619	4 978	8 156	3 932	4 223
70-74	6 566	2 998	3 568	6 831	3 141	3 690	7 588	3 509	4 079	9 018	4 224	4 795
75-79	5 181	2 217	2 964	5 840	2 535	3 305	6 120	2 682	3 437	6 845	3 024	3 821
80-84	3 318	1 174	2 144	4 241	1 666	2 575	4 844	1 936	2 908	5 140	2 081	3 059
85-89	1 805	538	1 267	2 380	724	1 656	3 100	1 056	2 044	3 623	1 259	2 363
90-94	822	202	621	1 042	244	798	1 440	342	1 098	1 936	520	1 416
95-99	214	39	175	343	58	285	469	74	395	692	110	582
100 +	28	3	25	55	6	49	97	9	88	150	13	137

Age group	2025 Both sexes	2025 Males	2025 Females	2030 Both sexes	2030 Males	2030 Females	2035 Both sexes	2035 Males	2035 Females	2040 Both sexes	2040 Males	2040 Females
All ages	124 819	60 284	64 535	122 566	59 021	63 546	120 140	57 711	62 429	117 621	56 416	61 205
0-4	4 979	2 556	2 423	4 987	2 560	2 427	5 064	2 599	2 464	5 116	2 627	2 490
5-9	5 141	2 639	2 502	4 984	2 558	2 426	4 992	2 562	2 430	5 069	2 602	2 467
10-14	5 448	2 796	2 652	5 146	2 641	2 505	4 989	2 560	2 429	4 996	2 564	2 432
15-19	5 761	2 955	2 806	5 476	2 809	2 667	5 174	2 654	2 520	5 017	2 573	2 444
20-24	5 952	3 050	2 902	5 809	2 977	2 832	5 525	2 831	2 694	5 223	2 677	2 547
25-29	6 175	3 161	3 014	5 995	3 069	2 926	5 852	2 996	2 856	5 569	2 852	2 718
30-34	6 139	3 133	3 007	6 202	3 172	3 030	6 024	3 081	2 942	5 882	3 009	2 873
35-39	6 686	3 408	3 277	6 153	3 130	3 017	6 216	3 176	3 040	6 039	3 086	2 953
40-44	7 599	3 865	3 733	6 683	3 402	3 281	6 153	3 132	3 021	6 218	3 170	3 046
45-49	8 601	4 373	4 228	7 576	3 845	3 731	6 667	3 386	3 280	6 140	3 119	3 021
50-54	9 792	4 935	4 857	8 545	4 328	4 216	7 531	3 809	3 722	6 632	3 358	3 274
55-59	8 552	4 263	4 289	9 679	4 850	4 829	8 455	4 260	4 195	7 459	3 754	3 705
60-64	7 707	3 804	3 903	8 390	4 145	4 245	9 507	4 725	4 783	8 315	4 157	4 158
65-69	7 127	3 451	3 676	7 461	3 629	3 831	8 139	3 966	4 173	9 240	4 533	4 707
70-74	7 695	3 616	4 079	6 749	3 190	3 560	7 089	3 370	3 718	7 755	3 698	4 057
75-79	8 183	3 671	4 512	7 024	3 107	3 057	6 192	2 814	3 379	6 533	2 992	3 542
80-84	5 813	2 379	3 434	7 016	2 925	4 091	6 076	2 553	3 522	5 399	2 293	3 106
85-89	3 922	1 387	2 535	4 514	1 620	2 893	5 527	2 032	3 496	4 852	1 807	3 046
90-94	2 341	645	1 697	2 608	734	1 874	3 077	884	2 193	3 845	1 142	2 704
95-99	968	176	792	1 220	229	991	1 410	272	1 138	1 716	342	1 375
100 +	236	20	216	352	34	318	481	47	434	603	60	543

Age group	2045 Both sexes	2045 Males	2045 Females	2050 Both sexes	2050 Males	2050 Females
All ages	114 983	55 137	59 846	112 198	53 833	58 365
0-4	5 058	2 596	2 461	4 878	2 504	2 374
5-9	5 122	2 629	2 493	5 063	2 599	2 465
10-14	5 074	2 604	2 470	5 127	2 631	2 496
15-19	5 025	2 577	2 448	5 102	2 617	2 485
20-24	5 067	2 597	2 470	5 075	2 601	2 474
25-29	5 268	2 698	2 571	5 113	2 618	2 495
30-34	5 600	2 865	2 735	5 300	2 711	2 588
35-39	5 898	3 015	2 883	5 617	2 871	2 746
40-44	6 042	3 084	2 958	5 902	3 013	2 889
45-49	6 206	3 161	3 045	6 032	3 074	2 959
50-54	6 112	3 095	3 016	6 180	3 139	3 041
55-59	6 573	3 313	3 261	6 062	3 057	3 005
60-64	7 344	3 669	3 675	6 479	3 243	3 236
65-69	8 095	3 998	4 096	7 160	3 537	3 624
70-74	8 827	4 242	4 585	7 750	3 754	3 996
75-79	7 178	3 302	3 876	8 199	3 807	4 392
80-84	5 736	2 462	3 274	6 341	2 741	3 600
85-89	4 361	1 650	2 712	4 680	1 798	2 882
90-94	3 438	1 043	2 395	3 136	975	2 161
95-99	2 197	459	1 738	2 005	434	1 571
100 +	763	79	684	997	111	886

United Nations Department of Economic and Social Affairs/Population Division
World Population Prospects: The 2004 Revision, Volume II: Sex and Age Distribution of the World Population

507

POPULATION BY AGE AND SEX (in thousands)

Age group	2005 Both sexes	Males	Females	2010 Both sexes	Males	Females	2015 Both sexes	Males	Females	2020 Both sexes	Males	Females
All ages	128 085	62 578	65 506	129 462	63 135	66 327	130 419	63 464	66 955	130 734	63 462	67 271
0-4	5 871	3 015	2 857	6 731	3 456	3 275	6 862	3 523	3 339	6 733	3 457	3 276
5-9	6 057	3 110	2 948	5 874	3 016	2 859	6 734	3 457	3 277	6 865	3 524	3 341
10-14	6 001	3 073	2 928	6 060	3 111	2 950	5 878	3 017	2 861	6 738	3 458	3 279
15-19	6 568	3 363	3 206	6 026	3 084	2 942	6 086	3 122	2 964	5 905	3 029	2 876
20-24	7 542	3 855	3 688	6 611	3 381	3 231	6 072	3 104	2 968	6 133	3 143	2 990
25-29	8 628	4 413	4 214	7 578	3 869	3 709	6 650	3 397	3 253	6 112	3 122	2 991
30-34	9 936	5 054	4 882	8 645	4 418	4 227	7 599	3 876	3 723	6 675	3 407	3 269
35-39	8 798	4 449	4 348	9 930	5 045	4 885	8 647	4 414	4 233	7 606	3 875	3 731
40-44	8 099	4 090	4 008	8 776	4 431	4 344	9 908	5 026	4 882	8 633	4 400	4 234
45-49	7 747	3 893	3 853	8 053	4 057	3 996	8 733	4 398	4 335	9 865	4 991	4 874
50-54	8 831	4 410	4 422	7 666	3 836	3 830	7 979	4 003	3 977	8 661	4 344	4 317
55-59	10 269	5 091	5 178	8 679	4 302	4 377	7 548	3 751	3 798	7 869	3 921	3 948
60-64	8 470	4 112	4 359	9 993	4 896	5 097	8 467	4 151	4 316	7 380	3 630	3 750
65-69	7 334	3 480	3 854	8 108	3 861	4 247	9 596	4 619	4 978	8 156	3 932	4 223
70-74	6 566	2 998	3 568	6 831	3 141	3 690	7 588	3 509	4 079	9 018	4 224	4 795
75-79	5 181	2 217	2 964	5 840	2 535	3 305	6 120	2 682	3 437	6 845	3 024	3 821
80-84	3 318	1 174	2 144	4 241	1 666	2 575	4 844	1 936	2 908	5 140	2 081	3 059
85-89	1 805	538	1 267	2 380	724	1 656	3 100	1 056	2 044	3 623	1 259	2 363
90-94	822	202	621	1 042	244	798	1 440	342	1 098	1 936	520	1 416
95-99	214	39	175	343	58	285	469	74	395	692	110	582
100 +	28	3	25	55	6	49	97	9	88	150	13	137

Age group	2025 Both sexes	Males	Females	2030 Both sexes	Males	Females	2035 Both sexes	Males	Females	2040 Both sexes	Males	Females
All ages	130 340	63 118	67 222	129 628	62 645	66 983	129 009	62 263	66 746	128 780	62 142	66 638
0-4	6 482	3 328	3 154	6 529	3 352	3 177	6 875	3 530	3 346	7 411	3 804	3 606
5-9	6 737	3 458	3 279	6 486	3 329	3 157	6 533	3 354	3 180	6 880	3 531	3 349
10-14	6 869	3 525	3 343	6 741	3 460	3 281	6 490	3 331	3 159	6 538	3 355	3 183
15-19	6 764	3 470	3 294	6 896	3 537	3 358	6 768	3 472	3 296	6 518	3 344	3 174
20-24	5 952	3 050	2 902	6 812	3 491	3 320	6 944	3 559	3 385	6 817	3 494	3 323
25-29	6 175	3 161	3 014	5 995	3 069	2 926	6 854	3 510	3 344	6 987	3 578	3 408
30-34	6 139	3 133	3 007	6 202	3 172	3 030	6 024	3 081	2 942	6 883	3 522	3 361
35-39	6 686	3 408	3 277	6 153	3 136	3 017	6 216	3 176	3 040	6 039	3 086	2 953
40-44	7 599	3 865	3 733	6 683	3 402	3 281	6 153	3 132	3 021	6 218	3 173	3 045
45-49	8 601	4 373	4 228	7 576	3 845	3 731	6 667	3 386	3 280	6 140	3 119	3 021
50-54	9 792	4 935	4 857	8 545	4 328	4 216	7 531	3 809	3 722	6 632	3 358	3 274
55-59	8 552	4 263	4 289	9 679	4 850	4 829	8 455	4 260	4 195	7 459	3 754	3 705
60-64	7 707	3 804	3 903	8 390	4 145	4 245	9 507	4 725	4 783	8 315	4 157	4 158
65-69	7 127	3 451	3 676	7 461	3 629	3 831	8 139	3 966	4 173	9 240	4 533	4 707
70-74	7 695	3 616	4 079	6 749	3 190	3 560	7 089	3 370	3 718	7 755	3 698	4 057
75-79	8 183	3 671	4 512	7 024	3 167	3 857	6 192	2 814	3 379	6 533	2 992	3 542
80-84	5 813	2 379	3 434	7 016	2 925	4 091	6 076	2 553	3 522	5 399	2 293	3 106
85-89	3 922	1 387	2 535	4 514	1 620	2 893	5 527	2 032	3 496	4 852	1 807	3 046
90-94	2 341	645	1 697	2 608	734	1 874	3 077	884	2 193	3 845	1 142	2 704
95-99	968	176	792	1 220	229	991	1 410	272	1 138	1 716	342	1 375
100 +	236	20	216	352	34	318	481	47	434	603	60	543

Age group	2045 Both sexes	Males	Females	2050 Both sexes	Males	Females
All ages	128 870	62 261	66 609	129 013	62 458	66 555
0-4	7 793	4 000	3 792	7 816	4 012	3 804
5-9	7 415	3 806	3 609	7 798	4 002	3 795
10-14	6 884	3 533	3 351	7 420	3 808	3 612
15-19	6 566	3 368	3 198	6 912	3 546	3 366
20-24	6 567	3 366	3 201	6 615	3 391	3 224
25-29	6 861	3 514	3 347	6 611	3 386	3 225
30-34	7 016	3 591	3 425	6 890	3 527	3 363
35-39	6 897	3 526	3 371	7 031	3 595	3 435
40-44	6 042	3 084	2 958	6 899	3 523	3 376
45-49	6 206	3 161	3 045	6 032	3 074	2 959
50-54	6 112	3 095	3 016	6 180	3 139	3 041
55-59	6 573	3 313	3 261	6 062	3 057	3 005
60-64	7 344	3 669	3 675	6 479	3 243	3 236
65-69	8 095	3 998	4 096	7 160	3 537	3 624
70-74	8 827	4 242	4 585	7 750	3 754	3 996
75-79	7 178	3 302	3 876	8 199	3 807	4 392
80-84	5 736	2 462	3 274	6 341	2 741	3 600
85-89	4 361	1 650	2 712	4 680	1 798	2 882
90-94	3 438	1 043	2 395	3 136	975	2 161
95-99	2 197	459	1 738	2 005	434	1 571
100 +	763	79	684	997	111	886

United Nations Department of Economic and Social Affairs/Population Division
World Population Prospects: The 2004 Revision, Volume II: Sex and Age Distribution of the World Population

508

POPULATION BY AGE AND SEX (in thousands)

Age group	2005 Both sexes	2005 Males	2005 Females	2010 Both sexes	2010 Males	2010 Females	2015 Both sexes	2015 Males	2015 Females	2020 Both sexes	2020 Males	2020 Females
All ages	128 085	62 578	65 506	127 436	62 095	65 341	125 514	60 946	64 568	122 593	59 283	63 310
0-4	5 871	3 015	2 857	4 705	2 416	2 289	3 981	2 044	1 937	3 495	1 794	1 701
5-9	6 057	3 110	2 948	5 874	3 016	2 859	4 709	2 417	2 292	3 986	2 046	1 940
10-14	6 001	3 073	2 928	6 060	3 111	2 950	5 878	3 017	2 861	4 713	2 419	2 294
15-19	6 568	3 363	3 206	6 026	3 084	2 942	6 086	3 122	2 964	5 905	3 029	2 876
20-24	7 542	3 855	3 688	6 611	3 381	3 231	6 072	3 104	2 968	6 133	3 143	2 990
25-29	8 628	4 413	4 214	7 578	3 869	3 709	6 650	3 397	3 253	6 112	3 122	2 991
30-34	9 936	5 054	4 882	8 645	4 418	4 227	7 599	3 876	3 723	6 675	3 407	3 269
35-39	8 798	4 449	4 348	9 930	5 045	4 885	8 647	4 414	4 233	7 606	3 875	3 731
40-44	8 099	4 090	4 008	8 776	4 431	4 344	9 908	5 026	4 882	8 633	4 400	4 234
45-49	7 747	3 893	3 853	8 053	4 057	3 996	8 733	4 398	4 335	9 865	4 991	4 874
50-54	8 831	4 410	4 422	7 666	3 836	3 830	7 979	4 003	3 977	8 661	4 344	4 317
55-59	10 269	5 091	5 178	8 679	4 302	4 377	7 548	3 751	3 798	7 869	3 921	3 948
60-64	8 470	4 112	4 359	9 993	4 896	5 097	8 467	4 151	4 316	7 380	3 630	3 750
65-69	7 334	3 480	3 854	8 108	3 861	4 247	9 596	4 619	4 978	8 156	3 932	4 223
70-74	6 566	2 998	3 568	6 831	3 141	3 690	7 588	3 509	4 079	9 018	4 224	4 795
75-79	5 181	2 217	2 964	5 840	2 535	3 305	6 120	2 682	3 437	6 845	3 024	3 821
80-84	3 318	1 174	2 144	4 241	1 666	2 575	4 844	1 936	2 908	5 140	2 081	3 059
85-89	1 805	538	1 267	2 380	724	1 656	3 100	1 056	2 044	3 623	1 259	2 363
90-94	822	202	621	1 042	244	798	1 440	342	1 098	1 936	520	1 416
95-99	214	39	175	343	58	285	469	74	395	692	110	582
100 +	28	3	25	55	6	49	97	9	88	150	13	137

Age group	2025 Both sexes	2025 Males	2025 Females	2030 Both sexes	2030 Males	2030 Females	2035 Both sexes	2035 Males	2035 Females	2040 Both sexes	2040 Males	2040 Females
All ages	119 172	57 385	61 787	115 420	55 353	60 068	111 414	53 233	58 181	107 101	51 018	56 083
0-4	3 451	1 772	1 679	3 485	1 789	1 696	3 481	1 787	1 694	3 318	1 703	1 615
5-9	3 500	1 797	1 704	3 457	1 774	1 683	3 491	1 792	1 699	3 486	1 789	1 697
10-14	3 991	2 048	1 943	3 505	1 799	1 706	3 462	1 776	1 685	3 496	1 794	1 702
15-19	4 741	2 432	2 309	4 019	2 061	1 958	3 534	1 812	1 722	3 490	1 790	1 701
20-24	5 952	3 050	2 902	4 790	2 454	2 336	4 069	2 084	1 985	3 584	1 836	1 748
25-29	6 175	3 161	3 014	5 995	3 069	2 926	4 834	2 475	2 360	4 115	2 106	2 009
30-34	6 139	3 133	3 007	6 202	3 172	3 030	6 024	3 081	2 942	4 865	2 488	2 377
35-39	6 686	3 408	3 277	6 153	3 136	3 017	6 216	3 176	3 040	6 039	3 086	2 953
40-44	7 599	3 865	3 733	6 683	3 402	3 281	6 153	3 132	3 021	6 218	3 173	3 045
45-49	8 601	4 373	4 228	7 576	3 845	3 731	6 667	3 386	3 280	6 140	3 119	3 021
50-54	9 792	4 935	4 857	8 545	4 328	4 216	7 531	3 809	3 722	6 632	3 358	3 274
55-59	8 552	4 263	4 289	9 679	4 850	4 829	8 455	4 260	4 195	7 459	3 754	3 705
60-64	7 707	3 804	3 903	8 390	4 145	4 245	9 507	4 725	4 783	8 315	4 157	4 158
65-69	7 127	3 451	3 676	7 461	3 629	3 831	8 139	3 966	4 173	9 240	4 533	4 707
70-74	7 695	3 616	4 079	6 749	3 190	3 560	7 089	3 370	3 718	7 755	3 698	4 057
75-79	8 183	3 671	4 512	7 024	3 167	3 857	6 192	2 814	3 379	6 533	2 992	3 542
80-84	5 813	2 379	3 434	7 016	2 925	4 091	6 076	2 553	3 522	5 399	2 293	3 106
85-89	3 922	1 387	2 535	4 514	1 620	2 893	5 527	2 032	3 496	4 852	1 807	3 046
90-94	2 341	645	1 697	2 608	734	1 874	3 077	884	2 193	3 845	1 142	2 704
95-99	968	176	792	1 220	229	991	1 410	272	1 138	1 716	342	1 375
100 +	236	20	216	352	34	318	481	47	434	603	60	543

Age group	2045 Both sexes	2045 Males	2045 Females	2050 Both sexes	2050 Males	2050 Females
All ages	102 406	48 685	53 721	97 410	46 249	51 161
0-4	2 994	1 537	1 457	2 658	1 364	1 294
5-9	3 324	1 706	1 618	3 000	1 540	1 460
10-14	3 491	1 792	1 700	3 329	1 708	1 621
15-19	3 524	1 807	1 717	3 520	1 805	1 715
20-24	3 541	1 814	1 727	3 575	1 831	1 744
25-29	3 631	1 858	1 773	3 588	1 836	1 752
30-34	4 147	2 120	2 026	3 664	1 873	1 791
35-39	4 883	2 495	2 388	4 166	2 128	2 037
40-44	6 042	3 084	2 958	4 889	2 495	2 394
45-49	6 206	3 161	3 045	6 032	3 074	2 959
50-54	6 112	3 095	3 016	6 180	3 139	3 041
55-59	6 573	3 313	3 261	6 062	3 057	3 005
60-64	7 344	3 669	3 675	6 479	3 243	3 236
65-69	8 095	3 998	4 096	7 160	3 537	3 624
70-74	8 827	4 242	4 585	7 750	3 754	3 996
75-79	7 178	3 302	3 876	8 199	3 807	4 392
80-84	5 736	2 462	3 274	6 341	2 741	3 600
85-89	4 361	1 650	2 712	4 680	1 798	2 882
90-94	3 438	1 043	2 395	3 136	975	2 161
95-99	2 197	459	1 738	2 005	434	1 571
100 +	763	79	684	997	111	886

POPULATION BY AGE AND SEX (in thousands)

Age group	1950 Both sexes	1950 Males	1950 Females	1955 Both sexes	1955 Males	1955 Females	1960 Both sexes	1960 Males	1960 Females	1965 Both sexes	1965 Males	1965 Females
All ages	472	245	227	665	345	320	896	465	431	1 106	571	536
0-4	88	47	41	116	61	55	156	81	74	208	106	102
5-9	70	36	34	100	53	47	127	67	61	156	81	75
10-14	58	30	28	84	44	40	115	61	54	132	69	63
15-19	46	24	23	71	37	34	97	50	47	119	64	55
20-24	36	18	18	57	29	27	82	42	39	101	52	48
25-29	30	14	16	44	22	22	66	34	32	84	43	40
30-34	24	12	12	36	18	19	52	26	25	67	35	33
35-39	20	10	10	29	14	15	42	21	22	53	27	26
40-44	19	10	9	24	13	12	33	17	17	43	21	22
45-49	16	9	7	22	12	11	27	14	13	33	16	17
50-54	15	9	7	19	10	9	25	13	12	27	14	14
55-59	15	8	7	17	9	8	20	11	10	24	12	12
60-64	12	7	6	16	9	8	18	9	8	19	10	9
65-69	10	5	4	12	6	6	16	8	8	16	8	8
70-74	7	4	3	9	5	5	12	6	6	11	6	5
75-79	4	2	2	5	3	2	6	3	3	9	4	4
80 +	2	1	1	2	1	1	3	1	1	5	3	3

Age group	1970 Both sexes	1970 Males	1970 Females	1975 Both sexes	1975 Males	1975 Females	1980 Both sexes	1980 Males	1980 Females	1985 Both sexes	1985 Males	1985 Females
All ages	1 623	833	789	1 937	991	946	2 225	1 152	1 074	2 706	1 414	1 292
0-4	308	157	152	379	193	186	416	215	200	480	246	234
5-9	244	124	120	294	150	145	368	192	176	417	216	200
10-14	192	100	92	241	122	118	315	165	151	376	203	173
15-19	163	85	77	190	99	91	253	136	118	321	174	147
20-24	145	78	67	159	83	76	178	92	86	237	125	112
25-29	123	64	59	142	76	66	123	63	60	178	92	86
30-34	102	53	49	121	63	58	108	55	52	135	68	67
35-39	82	42	40	99	51	48	99	51	49	111	56	56
40-44	64	32	32	80	41	39	91	45	46	103	53	50
45-49	51	25	26	61	31	31	73	37	36	87	45	42
50-54	40	19	20	50	24	26	57	30	27	67	34	33
55-59	32	16	16	37	18	19	42	21	21	55	28	27
60-64	26	13	13	29	14	15	33	17	16	41	21	21
65-69	20	10	10	22	10	11	23	12	11	28	14	14
70-74	15	8	7	16	8	8	22	10	12	33	18	15
75-79	9	4	4	10	5	5	15	7	7	22	12	9
80 +	7	3	4	7	3	4	10	5	5	15	9	7

Age group	1990 Both sexes	1990 Males	1990 Females	1995 Both sexes	1995 Males	1995 Females	2000 Both sexes	2000 Males	2000 Females	2005 Both sexes	2005 Males	2005 Females
All ages	3 254	1 696	1 558	4 288	2 242	2 046	4 972	2 590	2 382	5 703	2 964	2 739
0-4	579	299	280	634	325	309	736	377	359	732	374	357
5-9	503	258	245	582	298	284	635	326	309	745	382	364
10-14	441	229	212	544	279	265	583	298	285	642	329	313
15-19	391	211	180	497	258	239	544	279	265	588	301	288
20-24	318	173	145	473	254	219	497	258	239	550	282	268
25-29	222	118	104	402	223	179	474	255	219	508	265	243
30-34	164	86	78	289	155	134	403	224	179	484	261	222
35-39	125	63	62	198	104	94	289	155	134	407	226	181
40-44	106	52	53	146	76	70	197	103	94	290	155	135
45-49	100	51	49	131	65	66	144	75	69	197	103	94
50-54	85	43	41	119	64	55	128	63	65	143	74	69
55-59	65	33	32	96	51	45	114	61	53	125	62	63
60-64	51	26	26	71	37	34	89	47	42	108	57	51
65-69	37	18	19	43	23	20	63	32	31	80	42	39
70-74	23	11	12	30	14	16	36	19	17	53	27	26
75-79	25	13	11	15	8	7	23	10	13	27	14	13
80 +	18	10	8	18	9	10	18	9	9	23	10	13

United Nations Department of Economic and Social Affairs/Population Division
World Population Prospects: The 2004 Revision, Volume II: Sex and Age Distribution of the World Population

510

POPULATION BY AGE AND SEX (in thousands)

Age group	2005 Both sexes	Males	Females	2010 Both sexes	Males	Females	2015 Both sexes	Males	Females	2020 Both sexes	Males	Females
All ages	5 703	2 964	2 739	6 338	3 283	3 056	6 956	3 592	3 365	7 556	3 890	3 666
0-4	732	374	357	740	379	362	736	376	360	734	376	359
5-9	745	382	364	729	373	356	739	378	361	735	376	359
10-14	642	329	313	744	381	363	728	372	356	738	377	361
15-19	588	301	288	641	328	312	742	380	362	727	372	355
20-24	550	282	268	586	300	287	639	327	311	740	378	362
25-29	508	265	243	548	281	267	584	298	286	636	326	311
30-34	484	261	222	505	264	241	545	279	266	582	297	285
35-39	407	226	181	480	259	221	502	262	240	542	277	265
40-44	290	155	135	403	224	179	476	257	219	498	259	238
45-49	197	103	94	286	152	133	397	220	177	470	253	217
50-54	143	74	69	192	100	92	279	148	131	389	214	174
55-59	125	62	63	137	70	67	184	95	89	269	142	127
60-64	108	57	51	117	57	60	129	65	64	174	89	85
65-69	80	42	39	96	50	46	105	50	55	117	58	59
70-74	53	27	26	67	34	33	81	41	40	90	42	48
75-79	27	14	13	40	19	21	51	25	26	63	31	32
80-84	15	6	9	18	9	9	26	12	14	34	16	18
85-89	5	2	3	8	3	5	9	4	5	14	6	8
90-94	2	1	1	2	1	1	3	1	2	4	2	2
95-99	0	0	0	1	0	0	0	0	0	1	0	1
100 +	0	0	0	0	0	0	0	0	0	0	0	0

Age group	2025 Both sexes	Males	Females	2030 Both sexes	Males	Females	2035 Both sexes	Males	Females	2040 Both sexes	Males	Females
All ages	8 134	4 176	3 957	8 672	4 441	4 231	9 149	4 672	4 477	9 556	4 866	4 691
0-4	733	375	358	719	368	351	688	352	335	656	336	320
5-9	733	375	358	732	375	358	718	368	350	687	352	335
10-14	734	375	359	732	375	358	732	374	357	718	367	350
15-19	736	376	360	733	375	358	732	374	357	731	374	357
20-24	725	371	355	735	375	360	732	374	358	730	373	357
25-29	738	377	361	723	369	354	733	374	359	730	373	357
30-34	634	324	310	736	376	360	721	368	353	731	373	358
35-39	579	295	284	632	323	309	733	374	359	719	367	352
40-44	538	275	263	575	293	282	628	321	307	729	372	357
45-49	492	256	236	533	272	261	570	290	280	623	318	305
50-54	461	247	213	484	251	233	524	267	257	562	285	276
55-59	376	206	170	447	238	208	470	243	228	511	250	260
60-64	255	133	122	357	194	163	426	225	201	450	229	220
65-69	159	79	80	234	120	114	329	175	154	395	205	190
70-74	101	49	52	138	67	71	204	101	103	290	150	140
75-79	71	31	40	80	37	43	111	51	60	166	79	87
80-84	43	20	23	49	20	29	57	24	32	80	34	45
85-89	19	8	11	24	10	14	28	10	18	33	13	21
90-94	6	2	3	8	3	5	10	4	7	13	4	9
95-99	1	0	1	2	1	1	2	1	2	3	1	2
100 +	0	0	0	0	0	0	0	0	0	0	0	0

Age group	2045 Both sexes	Males	Females	2050 Both sexes	Males	Females
All ages	9 917	5 033	4 884	10 225	5 172	5 053
0-4	654	335	319	651	333	318
5-9	655	336	320	653	334	319
10-14	686	352	335	655	335	319
15-19	717	367	350	686	351	335
20-24	730	373	357	716	366	350
25-29	729	372	356	729	373	356
30-34	728	372	357	727	372	356
35-39	729	372	357	726	371	356
40-44	716	365	350	726	370	356
45-49	724	369	355	710	362	348
50-54	614	313	301	714	364	351
55-59	548	277	271	600	304	296
60-64	490	246	244	527	264	263
65-69	419	210	209	459	226	232
70-74	350	177	174	375	183	192
75-79	238	118	120	291	141	150
80-84	121	54	67	176	82	93
85-89	48	19	29	75	30	45
90-94	15	5	10	23	8	15
95-99	4	1	3	5	1	4
100 +	1	0	0	1	0	1

POPULATION BY AGE AND SEX (in thousands)

Age group	2005 Both sexes	2005 Males	2005 Females	2010 Both sexes	2010 Males	2010 Females	2015 Both sexes	2015 Males	2015 Females	2020 Both sexes	2020 Males	2020 Females
All ages	5 703	2 964	2 739	6 398	3 313	3 084	7 120	3 676	3 445	7 864	4 048	3 816
0-4	732	374	357	799	409	391	841	430	411	879	450	429
5-9	745	382	364	729	373	356	798	408	390	839	429	410
10-14	642	329	313	744	381	363	728	372	356	796	407	389
15-19	588	301	288	641	328	312	742	380	362	727	372	355
20-24	550	282	268	586	300	287	639	327	311	740	378	362
25-29	508	265	243	548	281	267	584	298	286	636	326	311
30-34	484	261	222	505	264	241	545	279	266	582	297	285
35-39	407	226	181	480	259	221	502	262	240	542	277	265
40-44	290	155	135	403	224	179	476	257	219	498	259	238
45-49	197	103	94	286	152	133	397	220	177	470	253	217
50-54	143	74	69	192	100	92	279	148	131	389	214	174
55-59	125	62	63	137	70	67	184	95	89	269	142	127
60-64	108	57	51	117	57	60	129	65	64	174	89	85
65-69	80	42	39	96	50	46	105	50	55	117	58	59
70-74	53	27	26	67	34	33	81	41	40	90	42	48
75-79	27	14	13	40	19	21	51	25	26	63	31	32
80-84	15	6	9	18	9	9	26	12	14	34	16	18
85-89	5	2	3	8	3	5	9	4	5	14	6	8
90-94	2	1	1	2	1	1	3	1	2	4	2	2
95-99	0	0	0	1	0	0	0	0	0	1	0	1
100 +	0	0	0	0	0	0	0	0	0	0	0	0

Age group	2025 Both sexes	2025 Males	2025 Females	2030 Both sexes	2030 Males	2030 Females	2035 Both sexes	2035 Males	2035 Females	2040 Both sexes	2040 Males	2040 Females
All ages	8 601	4 415	4 186	9 320	4 773	4 548	10 010	5 113	4 898	10 674	5 437	5 237
0-4	893	457	436	900	461	439	902	462	440	913	468	445
5-9	877	449	429	892	456	435	899	460	439	901	462	439
10-14	839	429	410	877	448	428	891	456	435	898	460	438
15-19	795	406	389	838	428	410	876	448	428	890	455	435
20-24	725	371	355	794	405	388	836	427	409	874	447	427
25-29	738	377	361	723	369	354	792	404	388	834	426	408
30-34	634	324	310	736	376	360	721	368	353	790	403	387
35-39	579	295	284	632	323	309	733	374	359	719	367	352
40-44	538	275	263	575	293	282	628	321	307	729	372	357
45-49	492	256	236	533	272	261	570	290	280	623	318	305
50-54	461	247	213	484	251	233	524	267	257	562	285	276
55-59	376	206	170	447	238	208	470	243	228	511	259	252
60-64	255	133	122	357	194	163	426	225	201	450	229	220
65-69	159	79	80	234	120	114	329	175	154	395	205	190
70-74	101	49	52	138	67	71	204	101	103	290	150	140
75-79	71	31	40	80	37	43	111	51	60	166	79	87
80-84	43	20	23	49	20	29	57	24	32	80	34	45
85-89	19	8	11	24	10	14	28	10	18	33	13	21
90-94	6	2	3	8	3	5	10	4	7	13	4	9
95-99	1	0	1	2	1	1	2	1	2	3	1	2
100 +	0	0	0	0	0	0	0	0	0	0	0	0

Age group	2045 Both sexes	2045 Males	2045 Females	2050 Both sexes	2050 Males	2050 Females
All ages	11 334	5 758	5 576	11 979	6 069	5 909
0-4	955	489	466	989	506	482
5-9	912	467	445	954	489	465
10-14	900	461	439	911	467	445
15-19	898	460	438	900	461	439
20-24	889	455	434	896	459	438
25-29	872	446	427	887	454	434
30-34	832	425	407	870	445	426
35-39	787	402	386	830	424	406
40-44	716	365	350	784	400	384
45-49	724	369	355	710	362	348
50-54	614	313	301	714	364	351
55-59	548	277	271	600	304	296
60-64	490	246	244	527	264	263
65-69	419	210	209	459	226	232
70-74	350	177	174	375	183	192
75-79	238	118	120	291	141	150
80-84	121	54	67	176	82	93
85-89	48	19	29	75	30	45
90-94	15	5	10	23	8	15
95-99	4	1	3	5	1	4
100 +	1	0	0	1	0	1

United Nations Department of Economic and Social Affairs/Population Division
World Population Prospects: The 2004 Revision, Volume II: Sex and Age Distribution of the World Population

512

POPULATION BY AGE AND SEX (in thousands)

Age group	2005 Both sexes	2005 Males	2005 Females	2010 Both sexes	2010 Males	2010 Females	2015 Both sexes	2015 Males	2015 Females	2020 Both sexes	2020 Males	2020 Females
All ages	5 703	2 964	2 739	6 279	3 253	3 027	6 792	3 508	3 284	7 247	3 732	3 515
0-4	732	374	357	681	348	333	631	323	309	590	302	288
5-9	745	382	364	729	373	356	680	347	332	630	322	308
10-14	642	329	313	744	381	363	728	372	356	679	347	332
15-19	588	301	288	641	328	312	742	380	362	727	372	355
20-24	550	282	268	586	300	287	639	327	311	740	378	362
25-29	508	265	243	548	281	267	584	298	286	636	326	311
30-34	484	261	222	505	264	241	545	279	266	582	297	285
35-39	407	226	181	480	259	221	502	262	240	542	277	265
40-44	290	155	135	403	224	179	476	257	219	498	259	238
45-49	197	103	94	286	152	133	397	220	177	470	253	217
50-54	143	74	69	192	100	92	279	148	131	389	214	174
55-59	125	62	63	137	70	67	184	95	89	269	142	127
60-64	108	57	51	117	57	60	129	65	64	174	89	85
65-69	80	42	39	96	50	46	105	50	55	117	58	59
70-74	53	27	26	67	34	33	81	41	40	90	42	48
75-79	27	14	13	40	19	21	51	25	26	63	31	32
80-84	15	6	9	18	9	9	26	12	14	34	16	18
85-89	5	2	3	8	3	5	9	4	5	14	6	8
90-94	2	1	1	2	1	1	3	1	2	4	2	2
95-99	0	0	0	1	0	0	0	0	0	1	0	1
100 +	0	0	0	0	0	0	0	0	0	0	0	0

Age group	2025 Both sexes	2025 Males	2025 Females	2030 Both sexes	2030 Males	2030 Females	2035 Both sexes	2035 Males	2035 Females	2040 Both sexes	2040 Males	2040 Females
All ages	7 667	3 938	3 729	8 030	4 112	3 917	8 309	4 242	4 067	8 495	4 322	4 173
0-4	574	294	280	543	278	265	489	251	239	433	222	211
5-9	589	301	288	573	293	280	542	278	265	489	250	238
10-14	629	322	308	588	301	287	573	293	280	542	277	264
15-19	678	346	331	628	321	307	588	300	287	572	293	280
20-24	725	371	355	676	345	331	627	320	307	587	300	287
25-29	738	377	361	723	369	354	675	344	330	626	320	306
30-34	634	324	310	736	376	360	721	368	353	673	344	330
35-39	570	295	284	632	323	309	733	374	359	719	367	352
40-44	538	275	263	575	293	282	628	321	307	729	372	357
45-49	492	256	236	533	272	261	570	290	280	623	318	305
50-54	461	247	210	484	251	232	524	267	257	562	285	276
55-59	376	206	170	447	238	208	470	243	228	511	259	252
60-64	255	133	122	357	194	163	426	225	201	450	229	220
65-69	159	79	80	234	120	114	329	175	154	395	205	190
70-74	101	49	52	138	67	71	204	101	103	290	150	140
75-79	71	31	40	80	37	43	111	51	60	166	79	87
80-84	43	20	23	49	20	29	57	24	32	80	34	45
85-89	19	8	11	24	10	14	28	10	18	33	13	21
90-94	6	2	3	8	3	5	10	4	7	13	4	9
95-99	1	0	1	2	1	1	2	1	2	3	1	2
100 +	0	0	0	0	0	0	0	0	0	0	0	0

Age group	2045 Both sexes	2045 Males	2045 Females	2050 Both sexes	2050 Males	2050 Females
All ages	8 609	4 363	4 245	8 651	4 366	4 284
0-4	405	208	198	383	196	187
5-9	433	222	211	405	207	198
10-14	489	250	238	433	222	211
15-19	541	277	264	488	250	238
20-24	572	292	279	540	277	264
25-29	585	299	286	570	292	279
30-34	625	319	306	584	298	286
35-39	671	342	329	623	318	305
40-44	716	365	350	668	341	327
45-49	724	369	355	710	362	348
50-54	614	313	301	714	364	351
55-59	548	277	271	600	304	296
60-64	490	246	244	527	264	263
65-69	419	210	209	459	226	232
70-74	350	177	174	375	183	192
75-79	238	118	120	291	141	150
80-84	121	54	67	176	82	93
85-89	48	19	29	75	30	45
90-94	15	5	10	23	8	15
95-99	4	1	3	5	1	4
100 +	1	0	0	1	0	1

POPULATION BY AGE AND SEX (in thousands)

Age group	1950 Both sexes	1950 Males	1950 Females	1955 Both sexes	1955 Males	1955 Females	1960 Both sexes	1960 Males	1960 Females	1965 Both sexes	1965 Males	1965 Females
All ages	6 703	3 244	3 459	7 992	3 853	4 139	9 996	4 813	5 183	11 909	5 736	6 173
0-4	741	382	359	1 096	568	529	1 521	777	744	1 756	893	862
5-9	572	287	285	799	411	388	1 208	624	585	1 597	814	783
10-14	990	514	476	635	319	317	893	458	435	1 282	660	622
15-19	572	304	268	1 054	546	508	724	363	361	949	485	464
20-24	745	367	378	628	332	296	1 138	587	551	773	387	386
25-29	415	178	237	785	383	402	706	369	337	1 178	604	574
30-34	318	140	179	448	191	257	845	407	437	747	386	361
35-39	437	183	254	343	148	195	495	209	286	870	414	456
40-44	387	171	216	457	188	269	378	160	218	516	215	301
45-49	351	144	206	401	172	229	483	194	289	390	161	229
50-54	264	124	140	354	141	213	419	173	246	482	187	294
55-59	228	119	109	261	117	144	360	137	223	409	161	248
60-64	245	126	120	214	106	108	255	108	148	339	121	217
65-69	180	89	91	215	103	112	198	91	107	229	90	139
70-74	130	61	69	147	67	80	182	81	101	164	70	94
75-79	76	34	43	93	39	53	110	46	64	132	53	79
80 +	52	21	31	63	25	38	80	30	50	96	35	61

Age group	1970 Both sexes	1970 Males	1970 Females	1975 Both sexes	1975 Males	1975 Females	1980 Both sexes	1980 Males	1980 Females	1985 Both sexes	1985 Males	1985 Females
All ages	13 110	6 315	6 795	14 136	6 816	7 320	14 919	7 186	7 733	15 780	7 612	8 168
0-4	1 559	791	768	1 639	832	807	1 709	866	842	1 819	925	894
5-9	1 757	892	865	1 541	778	762	1 615	819	797	1 657	838	819
10-14	1 609	818	791	1 716	870	846	1 509	763	746	1 581	800	780
15-19	1 290	663	627	1 579	805	774	1 584	803	782	1 427	724	704
20-24	951	485	466	1 314	671	643	1 481	755	727	1 544	780	763
25-29	773	384	389	959	487	471	1 268	634	634	1 445	724	721
30-34	1 169	593	575	743	368	375	966	480	486	1 210	600	610
35-39	742	379	363	1 100	554	547	649	317	331	912	448	463
40-44	856	402	454	690	349	341	1 048	515	533	611	295	316
45-49	504	206	298	801	367	434	645	318	327	978	472	506
50-54	374	149	225	491	188	303	752	339	413	596	286	311
55-59	450	168	283	355	134	221	468	176	293	689	299	389
60-64	370	137	233	406	145	261	315	112	202	416	148	267
65-69	292	97	195	316	109	207	343	114	229	268	89	179
70-74	183	66	117	231	73	158	253	81	172	275	84	191
75-79	117	45	72	130	44	86	172	50	122	183	53	130
80 +	114	40	74	124	42	83	142	44	99	169	45	124

Age group	1990 Both sexes	1990 Males	1990 Females	1995 Both sexes	1995 Males	1995 Females	2000 Both sexes	2000 Males	2000 Females	2005 Both sexes	2005 Males	2005 Females
All ages	16 500	8 024	8 476	15 866	7 693	8 173	15 033	7 238	7 795	14 825	7 102	7 723
0-4	1 943	986	956	1 385	708	678	1 139	581	558	1 075	547	528
5-9	1 702	862	841	1 783	905	878	1 330	678	652	1 089	554	535
10-14	1 599	806	793	1 531	776	754	1 667	846	821	1 268	645	622
15-19	1 436	743	693	1 429	716	713	1 390	706	684	1 596	808	787
20-24	1 271	646	625	1 307	667	640	1 275	635	640	1 319	666	653
25-29	1 534	767	767	1 137	571	566	1 192	596	595	1 213	597	616
30-34	1 408	704	704	1 366	676	691	1 032	510	523	1 126	557	569
35-39	1 196	590	606	1 240	611	629	1 217	592	625	957	466	491
40-44	775	381	394	1 082	524	558	1 073	516	557	1 136	543	593
45-49	646	307	339	672	324	347	956	447	509	999	470	529
50-54	934	446	489	563	259	304	560	260	300	878	398	480
55-59	541	255	286	823	381	441	479	209	270	500	223	277
60-64	653	270	382	444	202	241	680	297	382	409	168	240
65-69	331	110	221	538	212	325	336	143	193	565	231	334
70-74	215	66	150	255	80	175	393	143	250	256	101	155
75-79	203	56	147	149	42	107	164	47	118	277	90	187
80 +	112	28	84	163	39	124	151	34	117	162	36	126

United Nations Department of Economic and Social Affairs/Population Division
World Population Prospects: The 2004 Revision, Volume II: Sex and Age Distribution of the World Population

514

POPULATION BY AGE AND SEX (in thousands)

Age group	2005 Both sexes	Males	Females	2010 Both sexes	Males	Females	2015 Both sexes	Males	Females	2020 Both sexes	Males	Females
All ages	14 825	7 102	7 723	14 802	7 062	7 740	14 877	7 075	7 803	14 883	7 057	7 826
0-4	1 075	547	528	1 083	551	532	1 101	561	540	1 038	529	509
5-9	1 089	554	535	1 039	527	512	1 054	536	519	1 073	546	527
10-14	1 268	645	622	1 047	532	515	1 007	511	496	1 023	519	504
15-19	1 596	808	787	1 220	620	600	1 012	514	498	972	492	480
20-24	1 319	666	653	1 544	778	765	1 182	598	583	976	494	483
25-29	1 213	597	616	1 273	638	636	1 505	753	751	1 148	577	571
30-34	1 126	557	569	1 165	568	597	1 234	613	621	1 464	728	737
35-39	957	466	491	1 070	523	546	1 119	540	579	1 188	585	604
40-44	1 136	543	593	901	432	469	1 022	494	528	1 073	511	562
45-49	999	470	529	1 075	504	571	855	403	453	975	463	512
50-54	878	398	480	931	426	505	1 011	462	549	805	370	435
55-59	500	223	277	804	351	453	860	380	481	940	415	525
60-64	409	168	240	436	184	252	718	298	421	774	326	448
65-69	565	231	334	342	131	211	371	147	224	621	242	380
70-74	256	101	155	448	168	280	274	97	177	300	110	190
75-79	277	90	187	182	65	117	328	110	217	203	64	138
80-84	99	24	75	171	49	123	113	35	78	210	62	148
85-89	39	8	31	50	10	40	88	21	67	59	16	43
90-94	21	4	18	15	2	12	19	3	16	34	7	27
95-99	3	0	2	5	1	5	4	1	3	5	1	4
100 +	0	0	0	1	0	0	1	0	1	1	0	1

Age group	2025 Both sexes	Males	Females	2030 Both sexes	Males	Females	2035 Both sexes	Males	Females	2040 Both sexes	Males	Females
All ages	14 774	6 986	7 788	14 556	6 866	7 691	14 267	6 715	7 552	13 932	6 549	7 383
0-4	934	477	457	845	432	413	805	412	393	794	407	387
5-9	1 013	516	497	911	464	446	823	421	403	784	401	383
10-14	1 042	530	512	982	500	482	881	449	431	793	406	388
15-19	988	501	487	1 008	512	496	949	483	466	848	432	415
20-24	938	473	465	955	483	472	975	494	481	916	465	451
25-29	945	475	471	908	455	453	926	465	461	947	477	470
30-34	1 113	556	557	914	456	458	878	437	441	897	448	449
35-39	1 418	708	710	1 073	532	541	877	434	443	842	417	425
40-44	1 143	557	586	1 372	670	701	1 033	508	525	841	413	428
45-49	1 028	482	546	1 099	529	571	1 325	641	685	996	484	511
50-54	923	429	494	977	449	527	1 049	496	553	1 271	605	666
55-59	750	334	415	865	391	473	919	412	507	1 002	469	533
60-64	851	360	491	680	291	389	789	343	446	844	365	479
65-69	674	267	407	747	298	448	598	242	356	699	289	409
70-74	512	184	327	559	206	353	624	232	392	502	190	312
75-79	224	74	150	390	127	263	430	143	286	484	163	321
80-84	132	37	95	148	43	105	262	74	187	292	85	207
85-89	111	28	84	71	17	55	81	20	61	146	35	111
90-94	23	5	18	45	9	36	29	6	24	34	7	27
95-99	9	2	8	6	1	5	13	2	11	9	1	7
100 +	1	0	1	2	0	1	1	0	1	2	0	2

Age group	2045 Both sexes	Males	Females	2050 Both sexes	Males	Females
All ages	13 543	6 364	7 179	13 086	6 151	6 935
0-4	772	396	376	721	370	351
5-9	773	396	377	752	386	366
10-14	754	386	368	744	382	362
15-19	761	389	372	722	370	352
20-24	816	415	401	730	372	358
25-29	889	449	441	790	399	390
30-34	918	460	458	861	432	428
35-39	862	428	433	884	441	443
40-44	808	397	411	828	409	419
45-49	809	394	415	777	379	399
50-54	954	458	496	773	372	402
55-59	1 206	562	644	905	426	479
60-64	913	408	505	1 117	505	612
65-69	751	309	442	817	349	468
70-74	590	229	361	640	247	392
75-79	392	135	257	465	165	300
80-84	334	99	235	273	83	190
85-89	166	41	126	193	48	145
90-94	63	12	51	74	14	59
95-99	10	2	9	19	3	17
100 +	2	0	2	2	0	2

POPULATION BY AGE AND SEX (in thousands)

Age group	2005 Both sexes	Males	Females	2010 Both sexes	Males	Females	2015 Both sexes	Males	Females	2020 Both sexes	Males	Females
All ages	14 825	7 102	7 723	14 954	7 140	7 815	15 274	7 277	7 998	15 556	7 399	8 157
0-4	1 075	547	528	1 236	629	607	1 347	686	661	1 317	671	646
5-9	1 089	554	535	1 039	527	512	1 206	612	593	1 317	670	647
10-14	1 268	645	622	1 047	532	515	1 007	511	496	1 174	596	578
15-19	1 596	808	787	1 220	620	600	1 012	514	498	972	492	480
20-24	1 319	666	653	1 544	778	765	1 182	598	583	976	494	483
25-29	1 213	597	616	1 273	638	636	1 505	753	751	1 148	577	571
30-34	1 126	557	569	1 165	568	597	1 234	613	621	1 464	728	737
35-39	957	466	491	1 070	523	546	1 119	540	579	1 188	585	604
40-44	1 136	543	593	901	432	469	1 022	494	528	1 073	511	562
45-49	999	470	529	1 075	504	571	855	403	453	975	463	512
50-54	878	398	480	931	426	505	1 011	462	549	805	370	435
55-59	500	223	277	804	351	453	860	380	481	940	415	525
60-64	409	168	240	436	184	252	718	298	421	774	326	448
65-69	565	231	334	342	131	211	371	147	224	621	242	380
70-74	256	101	155	448	168	280	274	97	177	300	110	190
75-79	277	90	187	182	65	117	328	110	217	203	64	138
80-84	99	24	75	171	49	123	113	35	78	210	62	148
85-89	39	8	31	50	10	40	88	21	67	59	16	43
90-94	21	4	18	15	2	12	19	3	16	34	7	27
95-99	3	0	2	5	1	5	4	1	3	5	1	4
100 +	0	0	0	1	0	0	1	0	1	1	0	1

Age group	2025 Both sexes	Males	Females	2030 Both sexes	Males	Females	2035 Both sexes	Males	Females	2040 Both sexes	Males	Females
All ages	15 691	7 453	8 239	15 733	7 464	8 269	15 779	7 484	8 295	15 866	7 533	8 333
0-4	1 182	603	578	1 109	567	542	1 144	586	558	1 223	627	596
5-9	1 290	656	633	1 156	590	567	1 085	554	531	1 121	573	547
10-14	1 286	654	632	1 259	641	618	1 126	574	552	1 055	539	516
15-19	1 139	578	561	1 251	635	615	1 224	623	602	1 092	557	536
20-24	938	473	465	1 104	558	546	1 217	616	600	1 191	604	587
25-29	945	475	471	908	455	453	1 075	540	535	1 187	598	589
30-34	1 113	556	557	914	456	458	878	437	441	1 044	522	522
35-39	1 418	699	719	1 073	532	541	877	434	443	842	417	425
40-44	1 143	557	586	1 372	670	701	1 033	508	525	841	413	428
45-49	1 028	482	546	1 099	529	571	1 325	641	685	996	484	511
50-54	923	429	494	977	449	527	1 049	496	553	1 271	605	666
55-59	750	334	415	865	391	473	919	412	507	990	458	533
60-64	851	360	491	680	291	389	789	343	446	844	365	479
65-69	674	267	407	747	298	448	598	242	356	699	289	409
70-74	512	184	327	559	206	353	624	232	392	502	190	312
75-79	224	74	150	390	127	263	430	143	286	484	163	321
80-84	132	37	95	148	43	105	262	74	187	292	85	207
85-89	111	28	84	71	17	55	81	20	61	146	35	111
90-94	23	5	18	45	9	36	29	6	24	34	7	27
95-99	9	2	8	6	1	5	13	2	11	9	1	7
100 +	1	0	1	2	0	1	1	0	1	2	0	2

Age group	2045 Both sexes	Males	Females	2050 Both sexes	Males	Females
All ages	15 946	7 588	8 359	15 957	7 612	8 345
0-4	1 248	640	608	1 198	615	583
5-9	1 200	615	585	1 226	629	597
10-14	1 091	558	533	1 170	600	571
15-19	1 022	522	500	1 058	541	517
20-24	1 060	539	521	990	504	485
25-29	1 162	587	576	1 033	523	510
30-34	1 157	581	576	1 133	570	563
35-39	1 008	502	507	1 121	560	561
40-44	808	397	411	973	481	492
45-49	809	394	415	777	379	399
50-54	954	458	496	773	372	402
55-59	1 206	562	644	905	426	479
60-64	913	408	505	1 117	505	612
65-69	751	309	442	817	349	468
70-74	590	229	361	640	247	392
75-79	392	135	257	465	165	300
80-84	334	99	235	273	83	190
85-89	166	41	126	193	48	145
90-94	63	12	51	74	14	59
95-99	10	2	9	19	3	17
100 +	2	0	2	2	0	2

United Nations Department of Economic and Social Affairs/Population Division
World Population Prospects: The 2004 Revision, Volume II: Sex and Age Distribution of the World Population

POPULATION BY AGE AND SEX (in thousands)

Age group	2005 Both sexes	Males	Females	2010 Both sexes	Males	Females	2015 Both sexes	Males	Females	2020 Both sexes	Males	Females
All ages	14 825	7 102	7 723	14 649	6 985	7 665	14 481	6 873	7 608	14 206	6 712	7 493
0-4	1 075	547	528	931	474	457	856	436	420	755	385	370
5-9	1 089	554	535	1 039	527	512	904	459	445	830	422	408
10-14	1 268	645	622	1 047	532	515	1 007	511	496	873	443	430
15-19	1 596	808	787	1 220	620	600	1 012	514	498	972	492	480
20-24	1 319	666	653	1 544	778	765	1 182	598	583	976	494	483
25-29	1 213	597	616	1 273	638	636	1 505	753	751	1 148	577	571
30-34	1 126	557	569	1 165	568	597	1 234	613	621	1 464	728	737
35-39	957	466	491	1 070	523	546	1 119	540	579	1 188	585	604
40-44	1 136	543	593	901	432	469	1 022	494	528	1 073	511	562
45-49	999	470	529	1 075	504	571	855	403	453	975	463	512
50-54	878	398	480	931	426	505	1 011	462	549	805	370	435
55-59	500	223	277	804	351	453	860	380	481	940	415	525
60-64	409	168	240	436	184	252	718	298	421	774	326	448
65-69	565	231	334	342	131	211	371	147	224	621	242	380
70-74	256	101	155	448	168	280	274	97	177	300	110	190
75-79	277	90	187	182	65	117	328	110	217	203	64	138
80-84	99	24	75	171	49	123	113	35	78	210	62	148
85-89	39	8	31	50	10	40	88	21	67	59	16	43
90-94	21	4	18	15	2	12	19	3	16	34	7	27
95-99	3	0	2	5	1	5	4	1	3	5	1	4
100 +	0	0	0	1	0	0	1	0	1	1	0	1

Age group	2025 Both sexes	Males	Females	2030 Both sexes	Males	Females	2035 Both sexes	Males	Females	2040 Both sexes	Males	Females
All ages	13 848	6 515	7 333	13 390	6 273	7 118	12 833	5 986	6 847	12 184	5 660	6 524
0-4	683	349	334	602	308	294	533	273	260	475	244	231
5-9	731	372	359	661	337	324	581	297	284	512	262	250
10-14	800	407	393	701	357	344	631	322	309	552	282	269
15-19	839	426	413	766	390	377	668	340	328	599	306	293
20-24	938	473	465	806	407	398	734	372	362	637	323	314
25-29	945	475	471	908	455	453	778	391	388	707	356	352
30-34	1 113	556	557	914	456	458	878	437	441	749	374	375
35-39	1 418	699	719	1 073	532	541	877	434	443	842	417	425
40-44	1 143	557	586	1 372	670	701	1 033	508	525	841	413	428
45-49	1 028	482	546	1 099	529	571	1 325	641	685	996	484	511
50-54	923	429	494	977	449	527	1 049	496	553	1 271	605	666
55-59	750	334	415	865	391	473	919	412	507	950	450	500
60-64	851	360	491	680	291	389	789	343	446	844	365	479
65-69	674	267	407	747	298	448	598	242	356	699	289	409
70-74	512	184	327	559	206	353	624	232	392	502	190	312
75-79	224	74	150	390	127	263	430	143	286	484	163	321
80-84	132	37	95	148	43	105	262	74	187	292	85	207
85-89	111	28	84	71	17	55	81	20	61	146	35	111
90-94	23	5	18	45	9	36	29	6	24	34	7	27
95-99	9	2	8	6	1	5	13	2	11	9	1	7
100 +	1	0	1	2	0	1	1	0	1	2	0	2

Age group	2045 Both sexes	Males	Females	2050 Both sexes	Males	Females
All ages	11 448	5 299	6 150	10 643	4 908	5 735
0-4	419	215	204	366	188	178
5-9	455	233	222	399	205	194
10-14	483	248	235	426	219	207
15-19	519	266	253	451	232	220
20-24	568	289	279	489	249	240
25-29	611	308	303	542	274	269
30-34	680	340	340	584	293	291
35-39	716	355	360	647	322	325
40-44	808	397	411	683	337	347
45-49	809	394	415	777	379	399
50-54	954	458	496	773	372	402
55-59	1 206	562	644	905	426	479
60-64	913	408	505	1 117	505	612
65-69	751	309	442	817	349	468
70-74	590	229	361	640	247	392
75-79	392	135	257	465	165	300
80-84	334	99	235	273	83	190
85-89	166	41	126	193	48	145
90-94	63	12	51	74	14	59
95-99	10	2	9	19	3	17
100 +	2	0	2	2	0	2

United Nations Department of Economic and Social Affairs/Population Division
World Population Prospects: The 2004 Revision, Volume II: Sex and Age Distribution of the World Population

517

POPULATION BY AGE AND SEX (in thousands)

Age group	1950 Both sexes	Males	Females	1955 Both sexes	Males	Females	1960 Both sexes	Males	Females	1965 Both sexes	Males	Females
All ages	6 077	3 065	3 012	6 984	3 511	3 473	8 115	4 070	4 045	9 524	4 762	4 763
0-4	1 056	530	526	1 366	682	684	1 617	809	808	1 925	963	963
5-9	707	354	353	949	474	474	1 242	618	624	1 492	743	749
10-14	654	327	327	681	341	340	918	459	459	1 207	600	607
15-19	623	316	307	635	318	318	664	332	332	896	447	449
20-24	526	272	255	602	305	298	616	307	309	643	320	322
25-29	438	231	208	505	259	246	580	292	288	592	293	299
30-34	379	200	179	419	220	199	485	248	237	556	279	277
35-39	335	180	155	360	190	171	400	209	190	463	236	227
40-44	300	160	141	316	169	147	341	179	162	380	198	182
45-49	263	132	131	281	148	132	297	158	139	322	168	154
50-54	226	110	116	243	121	122	260	136	124	277	146	131
55-59	184	87	97	204	98	106	220	108	112	238	123	115
60-64	146	68	78	160	74	85	178	84	94	195	94	100
65-69	108	48	60	119	54	65	131	60	71	149	69	80
70-74	69	29	40	78	34	45	88	39	49	100	44	55
75-79	41	15	26	42	17	25	50	21	29	57	25	33
80 +	21	7	14	24	8	16	27	9	18	32	12	20

Age group	1970 Both sexes	Males	Females	1975 Both sexes	Males	Females	1980 Both sexes	Males	Females	1985 Both sexes	Males	Females
All ages	11 273	5 623	5 650	13 512	6 731	6 781	16 282	8 109	8 174	19 673	9 800	9 873
0-4	2 285	1 145	1 140	2 792	1 402	1 391	3 338	1 679	1 659	3 975	2 003	1 972
5-9	1 799	896	903	2 162	1 079	1 083	2 667	1 335	1 332	3 218	1 615	1 603
10-14	1 457	725	732	1 763	877	886	2 125	1 060	1 065	2 631	1 316	1 315
15-19	1 182	587	595	1 431	711	720	1 737	863	874	2 099	1 046	1 053
20-24	871	433	438	1 154	571	583	1 403	695	708	1 708	847	862
25-29	620	307	313	845	418	427	1 126	555	571	1 375	679	696
30-34	570	281	289	599	296	303	823	406	417	1 102	542	560
35-39	534	267	267	549	270	279	582	287	295	803	395	408
40-44	442	225	217	512	255	257	531	260	271	565	278	288
45-49	360	187	174	422	213	209	492	244	248	512	250	262
50-54	302	156	146	340	175	165	401	201	200	470	231	239
55-59	255	132	122	280	143	137	317	162	156	376	187	189
60-64	212	108	104	229	118	111	254	128	125	290	146	144
65-69	164	78	86	181	91	90	197	100	97	221	110	111
70-74	115	52	63	129	60	69	144	71	73	159	79	80
75-79	67	29	38	78	34	44	90	41	49	102	49	53
80 +	38	15	24	46	18	28	56	23	33	67	28	39

Age group	1990 Both sexes	Males	Females	1995 Both sexes	Males	Females	2000 Both sexes	Males	Females	2005 Both sexes	Males	Females
All ages	23 430	11 667	11 764	27 226	13 545	13 681	30 689	15 296	15 393	34 256	17 153	17 103
0-4	4 441	2 238	2 204	4 482	2 259	2 223	4 949	2 495	2 455	5 736	2 891	2 846
5-9	3 839	1 930	1 909	4 317	2 170	2 147	4 312	2 168	2 143	4 716	2 371	2 344
10-14	3 176	1 592	1 584	3 800	1 909	1 891	4 262	2 141	2 121	4 211	2 116	2 095
15-19	2 599	1 298	1 301	3 155	1 580	1 575	3 757	1 885	1 872	4 198	2 105	2 092
20-24	2 062	1 024	1 038	2 572	1 281	1 290	3 073	1 537	1 536	3 649	1 826	1 824
25-29	1 670	824	847	2 020	999	1 021	2 381	1 196	1 185	2 853	1 439	1 414
30-34	1 342	660	682	1 631	800	831	1 817	908	910	2 063	1 066	997
35-39	1 074	526	548	1 310	640	670	1 474	725	749	1 549	794	755
40-44	780	382	397	1 046	509	537	1 201	585	616	1 281	639	642
45-49	546	267	279	758	369	389	971	469	502	1 069	522	548
50-54	490	237	252	527	256	271	707	341	366	880	422	458
55-59	442	216	226	465	223	242	489	235	255	644	307	337
60-64	345	170	175	409	197	212	424	201	223	440	208	232
65-69	254	126	128	305	148	157	358	170	188	368	171	197
70-74	179	88	91	208	102	106	249	118	130	289	135	155
75-79	114	55	58	130	62	68	151	72	79	178	83	96
80 +	78	34	44	91	41	50	112	51	61	131	59	72

518

United Nations Department of Economic and Social Affairs/Population Division
World Population Prospects: The 2004 Revision, Volume II: Sex and Age Distribution of the World Population

POPULATION BY AGE AND SEX (in thousands)

Age group	2005 Both sexes	Males	Females	2010 Both sexes	Males	Females	2015 Both sexes	Males	Females	2020 Both sexes	Males	Females
All ages	34 256	17 153	17 103	38 956	19 590	19 366	44 194	22 262	21 932	49 563	24 974	24 589
0-4	5 736	2 891	2 846	6 649	3 349	3 299	7 029	3 540	3 489	7 064	3 557	3 507
5-9	4 716	2 371	2 344	5 501	2 765	2 736	6 437	3 234	3 203	6 857	3 444	3 413
10-14	4 211	2 116	2 095	4 586	2 304	2 282	5 378	2 701	2 677	6 338	3 181	3 157
15-19	4 198	2 105	2 092	4 154	2 085	2 069	4 525	2 271	2 254	5 316	2 666	2 650
20-24	3 649	1 826	1 824	4 120	2 062	2 058	4 087	2 046	2 041	4 459	2 232	2 227
25-29	2 853	1 439	1 414	3 508	1 762	1 746	3 999	2 004	1 995	3 990	1 996	1 994
30-34	2 063	1 066	997	2 633	1 355	1 278	3 332	1 691	1 641	3 852	1 940	1 912
35-39	1 549	794	755	1 841	980	861	2 454	1 284	1 170	3 171	1 624	1 547
40-44	1 281	639	642	1 383	725	659	1 704	920	785	2 323	1 225	1 098
45-49	1 069	522	548	1 161	585	576	1 286	679	607	1 612	874	739
50-54	880	422	458	980	479	502	1 082	545	537	1 213	639	574
55-59	644	307	337	808	385	423	910	441	469	1 013	507	506
60-64	440	208	232	584	275	309	739	348	390	837	402	435
65-69	368	171	197	384	178	206	513	238	275	654	303	350
70-74	289	135	155	299	136	163	315	143	172	425	193	232
75-79	178	83	96	209	95	115	218	97	121	233	103	130
80-84	88	41	48	106	48	58	126	55	71	133	57	76
85-89	33	15	19	39	17	22	47	20	27	57	24	33
90-94	8	3	5	10	4	6	11	5	7	14	6	9
95-99	1	0	1	1	0	1	2	1	1	2	1	1
100 +	0	0	0	0	0	0	0	0	0	0	0	0

Age group	2025 Both sexes	Males	Females	2030 Both sexes	Males	Females	2035 Both sexes	Males	Females	2040 Both sexes	Males	Females
All ages	54 997	27 696	27 301	60 606	30 489	30 116	66 393	33 362	33 031	72 188	36 226	35 962
0-4	7 133	3 591	3 542	7 384	3 718	3 666	7 691	3 873	3 817	7 854	3 957	3 898
5-9	6 916	3 472	3 444	7 006	3 517	3 489	7 277	3 654	3 624	7 601	3 817	3 784
10-14	6 786	3 405	3 381	6 861	3 441	3 421	6 962	3 491	3 471	7 240	3 631	3 610
15-19	6 278	3 147	3 131	6 731	3 372	3 359	6 813	3 412	3 402	6 919	3 464	3 455
20-24	5 243	2 623	2 621	6 199	3 099	3 100	6 654	3 325	3 330	6 743	3 367	3 376
25-29	4 365	2 181	2 184	5 140	2 567	2 573	6 089	3 039	3 050	6 547	3 266	3 282
30-34	3 871	1 941	1 930	4 247	2 126	2 121	5 012	2 507	2 505	5 952	2 974	2 979
35-39	3 707	1 876	1 831	3 740	1 878	1 862	4 122	2 068	2 054	4 879	2 445	2 434
40-44	3 037	1 563	1 475	3 576	1 814	1 762	3 627	1 827	1 800	4 003	2 011	1 992
45-49	2 220	1 173	1 047	2 923	1 504	1 419	3 455	1 752	1 703	3 516	1 770	1 746
50-54	1 533	829	704	2 123	1 119	1 005	2 808	1 440	1 367	3 329	1 682	1 646
55-59	1 143	599	544	1 451	780	671	2 018	1 057	962	2 678	1 365	1 313
60-64	936	464	472	1 061	551	511	1 354	721	633	1 891	981	910
65-69	744	352	393	837	409	428	953	488	466	1 223	642	581
70-74	544	247	296	624	289	335	706	338	368	809	407	403
75-79	316	140	176	409	181	228	473	214	260	540	253	288
80-84	143	61	82	197	84	113	258	111	148	303	132	170
85-89	61	25	36	67	27	40	94	38	56	125	51	74
90-94	18	7	11	19	7	12	21	8	13	30	11	19
95-99	3	1	2	3	1	2	4	1	2	4	1	3
100 +	0	0	0	0	0	0	0	0	0	0	0	0

Age group	2045 Both sexes	Males	Females	2050 Both sexes	Males	Females
All ages	77 783	38 973	38 810	83 073	41 548	41 525
0-4	7 836	3 949	3 887	7 752	3 908	3 843
5-9	7 782	3 910	3 872	7 777	3 910	3 867
10-14	7 569	3 797	3 773	7 755	3 891	3 863
15-19	7 202	3 606	3 596	7 534	3 773	3 760
20-24	6 854	3 422	3 432	7 141	3 566	3 575
25-29	6 645	3 312	3 332	6 763	3 371	3 392
30-34	6 416	3 202	3 214	6 523	3 253	3 271
35-39	5 811	2 906	2 904	6 278	3 135	3 142
40-44	4 751	2 383	2 369	5 674	2 839	2 835
45-49	3 890	1 953	1 938	4 629	2 319	2 310
50-54	3 396	1 704	1 693	3 768	1 884	1 883
55-59	3 185	1 599	1 586	3 258	1 623	1 634
60-64	2 518	1 271	1 247	3 004	1 493	1 510
65-69	1 716	877	838	2 295	1 142	1 154
70-74	1 043	539	505	1 474	740	734
75-79	624	306	318	811	409	402
80-84	349	158	191	407	194	214
85-89	148	62	86	173	75	98
90-94	41	16	25	50	19	30
95-99	6	2	4	8	3	5
100 +	0	0	0	1	0	0

POPULATION BY AGE AND SEX (in thousands)

Age group	2005 Both sexes	2005 Males	2005 Females	2010 Both sexes	2010 Males	2010 Females	2015 Both sexes	2015 Males	2015 Females	2020 Both sexes	2020 Males	2020 Females
All ages	34 256	17 153	17 103	39 291	19 758	19 532	45 138	22 737	22 401	51 362	25 878	25 484
0-4	5 736	2 891	2 846	6 984	3 518	3 466	7 648	3 852	3 796	7 939	3 997	3 941
5-9	4 716	2 371	2 344	5 501	2 765	2 736	6 761	3 397	3 364	7 461	3 748	3 714
10-14	4 211	2 116	2 095	4 586	2 304	2 282	5 378	2 701	2 677	6 658	3 342	3 316
15-19	4 198	2 105	2 092	4 154	2 085	2 069	4 525	2 271	2 254	5 316	2 666	2 650
20-24	3 649	1 826	1 824	4 120	2 062	2 058	4 087	2 046	2 041	4 459	2 232	2 227
25-29	2 853	1 439	1 414	3 508	1 762	1 746	3 999	2 004	1 995	3 990	1 996	1 994
30-34	2 063	1 066	997	2 633	1 355	1 278	3 332	1 691	1 641	3 852	1 940	1 912
35-39	1 549	794	755	1 841	980	861	2 454	1 284	1 170	3 171	1 624	1 547
40-44	1 281	639	642	1 383	725	659	1 704	920	785	2 323	1 225	1 098
45-49	1 069	522	548	1 161	585	576	1 286	679	607	1 612	874	739
50-54	880	422	458	980	479	502	1 082	545	537	1 213	639	574
55-59	644	307	337	808	385	423	910	441	469	1 013	507	506
60-64	440	208	232	584	275	309	739	348	390	837	402	435
65-69	368	171	197	384	178	206	513	238	275	654	303	350
70-74	289	135	155	299	136	163	315	143	172	425	193	232
75-79	178	83	96	209	95	115	218	97	121	233	103	130
80-84	88	41	48	106	48	58	126	55	71	133	57	76
85-89	33	15	19	39	17	22	47	20	27	57	24	33
90-94	8	3	5	10	4	6	11	5	7	14	6	9
95-99	1	0	1	1	0	1	2	1	1	2	1	1
100 +	0	0	0	0	0	0	0	0	0	0	0	0

Age group	2025 Both sexes	2025 Males	2025 Females	2030 Both sexes	2030 Males	2030 Females	2035 Both sexes	2035 Males	2035 Females	2040 Both sexes	2040 Males	2040 Females
All ages	57 790	29 099	28 691	64 661	32 525	32 136	72 112	36 232	35 880	79 998	40 144	39 854
0-4	8 154	4 105	4 048	8 681	4 371	4 310	9 397	4 733	4 664	10 002	5 039	4 963
5-9	7 773	3 902	3 871	8 009	4 020	3 989	8 555	4 295	4 260	9 288	4 664	4 623
10-14	7 384	3 705	3 679	7 712	3 867	3 845	7 958	3 990	3 968	8 511	4 268	4 243
15-19	6 594	3 305	3 289	7 324	3 669	3 655	7 658	3 834	3 823	7 910	3 960	3 950
20-24	5 243	2 623	2 621	6 512	3 255	3 257	7 241	3 618	3 623	7 579	3 785	3 794
25-29	4 365	2 181	2 184	5 140	2 567	2 573	6 396	3 192	3 204	7 125	3 554	3 571
30-34	3 871	1 941	1 930	4 247	2 126	2 121	5 012	2 507	2 505	6 253	3 124	3 129
35-39	3 707	1 876	1 831	3 746	1 884	1 862	4 122	2 068	2 054	4 879	2 445	2 434
40-44	3 037	1 563	1 475	3 576	1 814	1 762	3 627	1 827	1 800	4 003	2 011	1 992
45-49	2 220	1 173	1 047	2 923	1 504	1 419	3 455	1 752	1 703	3 516	1 770	1 746
50-54	1 533	829	704	2 123	1 119	1 005	2 808	1 440	1 367	3 329	1 682	1 646
55-59	1 143	599	544	1 451	780	671	2 018	1 057	962	2 678	1 365	1 313
60-64	936	464	472	1 061	551	511	1 354	721	633	1 891	981	910
65-69	744	352	393	837	409	428	953	488	466	1 223	642	581
70-74	544	247	296	624	289	335	706	338	368	809	407	403
75-79	316	140	176	409	181	228	473	214	260	540	253	288
80-84	143	61	82	197	84	113	258	111	148	303	132	170
85-89	61	25	36	67	27	40	94	38	56	125	51	74
90-94	18	7	11	19	7	12	21	8	13	30	11	19
95-99	3	1	2	3	1	2	4	1	2	4	1	3
100 +	0	0	0	0	0	0	0	0	0	0	0	0

Age group	2045 Both sexes	2045 Males	2045 Females	2050 Both sexes	2050 Males	2050 Females
All ages	88 059	44 127	43 932	96 153	48 109	48 043
0-4	10 374	5 228	5 146	10 646	5 368	5 279
5-9	9 910	4 979	4 931	10 295	5 176	5 119
10-14	9 249	4 639	4 610	9 875	4 956	4 920
15-19	8 466	4 239	4 227	9 206	4 611	4 595
20-24	7 836	3 913	3 923	8 395	4 193	4 202
25-29	7 469	3 723	3 746	7 732	3 854	3 878
30-34	6 982	3 484	3 498	7 332	3 656	3 676
35-39	6 104	3 053	3 051	6 832	3 412	3 420
40-44	4 751	2 383	2 369	5 961	2 982	2 978
45-49	3 890	1 953	1 938	4 629	2 319	2 310
50-54	3 396	1 704	1 693	3 768	1 884	1 883
55-59	3 185	1 599	1 586	3 258	1 623	1 634
60-64	2 518	1 271	1 247	3 004	1 493	1 510
65-69	1 716	877	838	2 295	1 142	1 154
70-74	1 043	539	505	1 474	740	734
75-79	624	306	318	811	409	402
80-84	349	158	191	407	194	214
85-89	148	62	86	173	75	98
90-94	41	16	25	50	19	30
95-99	6	2	4	8	3	5
100 +	0	0	0	1	0	0

United Nations Department of Economic and Social Affairs/Population Division
World Population Prospects: The 2004 Revision, Volume II: Sex and Age Distribution of the World Population

520

POPULATION BY AGE AND SEX (in thousands)

Age group	2005 Both sexes	2005 Males	2005 Females	2010 Both sexes	2010 Males	2010 Females	2015 Both sexes	2015 Males	2015 Females	2020 Both sexes	2020 Males	2020 Females
All ages	34 256	17 153	17 103	38 620	19 421	19 200	43 250	21 787	21 463	47 764	24 069	23 695
0-4	5 736	2 891	2 846	6 313	3 180	3 133	6 410	3 228	3 182	6 189	3 116	3 072
5-9	4 716	2 371	2 344	5 501	2 765	2 736	6 112	3 071	3 041	6 253	3 140	3 112
10-14	4 211	2 116	2 095	4 586	2 304	2 282	5 378	2 701	2 677	6 018	3 021	2 998
15-19	4 198	2 105	2 092	4 154	2 085	2 069	4 525	2 271	2 254	5 316	2 666	2 650
20-24	3 649	1 826	1 824	4 120	2 062	2 058	4 087	2 046	2 041	4 459	2 232	2 227
25-29	2 853	1 439	1 414	3 508	1 762	1 746	3 999	2 004	1 995	3 990	1 996	1 994
30-34	2 063	1 066	997	2 633	1 355	1 278	3 332	1 691	1 641	3 852	1 940	1 912
35-39	1 549	794	755	1 841	980	861	2 454	1 284	1 170	3 171	1 624	1 547
40-44	1 281	639	642	1 383	725	659	1 704	920	785	2 323	1 225	1 098
45-49	1 069	522	548	1 161	585	576	1 286	679	607	1 612	874	739
50-54	880	422	458	980	479	502	1 082	545	537	1 213	639	574
55-59	644	307	337	808	385	423	910	441	469	1 013	507	506
60-64	440	208	232	584	275	309	739	348	390	837	402	435
65-69	368	171	197	384	178	206	513	238	275	654	303	350
70-74	289	135	155	299	136	163	315	143	172	425	193	232
75-79	178	83	96	209	95	115	218	97	121	233	103	130
80-84	88	41	48	106	48	58	126	55	71	133	57	76
85-89	33	15	19	39	17	22	47	20	27	57	24	33
90-94	8	3	5	10	4	6	11	5	7	14	6	9
95-99	1	0	1	1	0	1	2	1	1	2	1	1
100 +	0	0	0	0	0	0	0	0	0	0	0	0

Age group	2025 Both sexes	2025 Males	2025 Females	2030 Both sexes	2030 Males	2030 Females	2035 Both sexes	2035 Males	2035 Females	2040 Both sexes	2040 Males	2040 Females
All ages	52 211	26 296	25 915	56 597	28 477	28 120	60 835	30 573	30 262	64 755	32 498	32 257
0-4	6 119	3 081	3 038	6 128	3 086	3 043	6 099	3 072	3 027	5 925	2 985	2 940
5-9	6 059	3 042	3 017	6 009	3 017	2 993	6 039	3 032	3 007	6 028	3 027	3 001
10-14	6 188	3 104	3 083	6 011	3 014	2 997	5 972	2 994	2 977	6 009	3 013	2 996
15-19	5 961	2 988	2 973	6 138	3 075	3 063	5 969	2 989	2 980	5 935	2 971	2 964
20-24	5 243	2 623	2 621	5 886	2 942	2 944	6 067	3 031	3 036	5 907	2 950	2 957
25-29	4 365	2 181	2 184	5 140	2 567	2 573	5 781	2 885	2 896	5 970	2 978	2 992
30-34	3 871	1 941	1 930	4 247	2 126	2 121	5 012	2 507	2 505	5 652	2 823	2 829
35-39	3 707	1 876	1 831	3 746	1 884	1 862	4 122	2 068	2 054	4 879	2 445	2 434
40-44	3 037	1 563	1 475	3 576	1 814	1 762	3 627	1 827	1 800	4 003	2 011	1 992
45-49	2 220	1 173	1 047	2 923	1 504	1 419	3 455	1 752	1 703	3 516	1 770	1 746
50-54	1 533	829	704	2 123	1 119	1 005	2 808	1 440	1 367	3 329	1 682	1 646
55-59	1 143	599	544	1 451	780	671	2 018	1 057	962	2 678	1 365	1 313
60-64	936	464	472	1 061	551	511	1 354	721	633	1 891	981	910
65-69	744	352	393	837	409	428	953	488	466	1 223	642	581
70-74	544	247	296	624	289	335	706	338	368	809	407	403
75-79	316	140	176	409	181	228	473	214	260	540	253	288
80-84	140	61	80	197	84	113	258	111	148	303	132	170
85-89	61	25	36	67	27	40	94	38	56	125	51	74
90-94	18	7	11	19	7	12	21	8	13	30	11	19
95-99	3	1	2	3	1	2	4	1	2	4	1	3
100 +	0	0	0	0	0	0	0	0	0	0	0	0

Age group	2045 Both sexes	2045 Males	2045 Females	2050 Both sexes	2050 Males	2050 Females
All ages	68 212	34 173	34 039	71 148	35 568	35 580
0-4	5 628	2 836	2 792	5 310	2 677	2 633
5-9	5 870	2 949	2 921	5 585	2 808	2 777
10-14	6 003	3 011	2 992	5 849	2 935	2 914
15-19	5 976	2 992	2 984	5 975	2 992	2 982
20-24	5 879	2 935	2 943	5 926	2 959	2 966
25-29	5 821	2 901	2 919	5 800	2 891	2 909
30-34	5 849	2 919	2 930	5 714	2 849	2 865
35-39	5 517	2 760	2 758	5 723	2 859	2 865
40-44	4 751	2 383	2 369	5 387	2 696	2 692
45-49	3 890	1 953	1 938	4 629	2 319	2 310
50-54	3 396	1 704	1 693	3 768	1 884	1 883
55-59	3 185	1 599	1 586	3 258	1 623	1 634
60-64	2 518	1 271	1 247	3 004	1 493	1 510
65-69	1 716	877	838	2 295	1 142	1 154
70-74	1 043	539	505	1 474	740	734
75-79	624	306	318	811	409	402
80-84	349	158	191	407	194	214
85-89	148	62	86	173	75	98
90-94	41	16	25	50	19	30
95-99	6	2	4	8	3	5
100 +	0	0	0	1	0	0

POPULATION BY AGE AND SEX (in thousands)

Age group	1950 Both sexes	Males	Females	1955 Both sexes	Males	Females	1960 Both sexes	Males	Females	1965 Both sexes	Males	Females
All ages	152	90	62	199	120	80	278	174	104	471	287	183
0-4	23	12	11	34	18	16	44	22	22	81	41	40
5-9	17	9	9	22	12	10	32	16	16	60	31	29
10-14	15	8	7	17	9	7	22	12	10	39	21	18
15-19	16	9	7	18	10	8	22	13	9	40	23	16
20-24	18	12	6	24	16	9	35	25	11	56	38	19
25-29	16	11	5	22	16	7	37	27	10	59	41	18
30-34	13	9	4	15	11	4	25	19	7	42	31	11
35-39	9	7	3	14	10	4	20	14	5	30	22	8
40-44	6	4	2	8	6	3	11	8	3	20	14	6
45-49	6	3	2	6	4	2	9	6	3	14	9	5
50-54	5	3	2	5	3	2	6	3	2	10	7	4
55-59	3	2	1	5	3	2	5	3	2	7	4	3
60-64	2	1	1	3	1	1	4	2	2	4	2	2
65-69	2	1	1	2	1	1	3	1	1	3	2	2
70-74	1	1	1	2	1	1	2	1	1	2	1	1
75-79	1	0	0	1	1	1	1	1	1	1	1	0
80 +	0	0	0	1	0	0	0	0	0	2	1	1

Age group	1970 Both sexes	Males	Females	1975 Both sexes	Males	Females	1980 Both sexes	Males	Females	1985 Both sexes	Males	Females
All ages	744	422	322	1 007	551	456	1 375	788	587	1 720	977	743
0-4	138	70	68	182	93	89	215	110	106	250	127	123
5-9	111	56	54	155	79	77	186	95	91	214	108	106
10-14	75	39	36	110	56	54	153	78	75	175	89	86
15-19	62	33	29	88	45	42	122	65	56	146	73	73
20-24	73	42	32	90	49	41	126	73	52	150	78	72
25-29	78	47	31	91	50	41	140	87	53	189	116	73
30-34	61	40	21	78	46	31	122	77	45	176	112	64
35-39	49	33	16	68	43	25	98	64	34	139	90	50
40-44	32	22	10	48	31	17	78	53	25	99	65	34
45-49	21	15	7	34	22	12	51	35	16	72	49	24
50-54	16	10	6	23	14	9	35	24	11	47	32	15
55-59	10	6	4	14	8	6	19	12	7	28	18	9
60-64	6	3	3	11	6	5	12	7	5	15	9	6
65-69	5	3	3	6	3	3	9	5	4	9	5	4
70-74	4	2	2	5	2	2	5	2	2	5	3	3
75-79	2	1	1	3	1	1	3	1	2	3	1	2
80 +	2	1	1	2	1	1	2	1	1	3	2	2

Age group	1990 Both sexes	Males	Females	1995 Both sexes	Males	Females	2000 Both sexes	Males	Females	2005 Both sexes	Males	Females
All ages	2 143	1 218	925	1 696	1 019	677	2 230	1 355	874	2 687	1 612	1 075
0-4	304	154	149	182	93	88	211	107	104	241	122	119
5-9	264	134	130	172	88	84	192	99	93	216	110	106
10-14	217	110	107	144	73	70	178	91	87	196	101	95
15-19	182	91	91	114	58	56	157	82	75	189	98	91
20-24	187	97	91	153	88	64	174	95	79	226	123	103
25-29	238	146	92	232	153	78	262	167	95	306	182	124
30-34	221	141	80	215	143	71	312	213	98	369	246	122
35-39	175	112	63	175	117	58	248	166	83	331	230	101
40-44	125	82	42	123	84	39	193	133	60	219	145	74
45-49	92	62	30	75	51	24	126	88	38	160	107	53
50-54	58	40	19	45	29	15	74	50	24	95	62	33
55-59	34	23	11	30	19	11	43	28	15	57	36	21
60-64	19	11	8	16	10	7	28	18	10	35	22	13
65-69	11	6	5	9	5	4	15	9	6	24	14	9
70-74	7	4	3	6	3	3	8	4	4	13	7	6
75-79	4	2	2	3	2	1	4	2	2	6	3	3
80 +	4	2	2	3	2	2	4	2	2	5	2	3

United Nations Department of Economic and Social Affairs/Population Division
World Population Prospects: The 2004 Revision, Volume II: Sex and Age Distribution of the World Population

522

POPULATION BY AGE AND SEX (in thousands)

Age group	2005 Both sexes	Males	Females	2010 Both sexes	Males	Females	2015 Both sexes	Males	Females	2020 Both sexes	Males	Females
All ages	2 687	1 612	1 075	3 047	1 800	1 247	3 381	1 979	1 401	3 698	2 148	1 549
0-4	241	122	119	268	136	132	268	136	132	263	133	130
5-9	216	110	106	245	124	121	270	137	133	271	137	134
10-14	196	101	95	219	111	108	247	125	122	272	138	134
15-19	189	98	91	204	106	98	224	115	110	252	128	124
20-24	226	123	103	233	125	108	233	124	109	254	132	121
25-29	306	182	124	308	179	129	287	162	125	288	161	127
30-34	369	246	122	365	227	138	348	209	139	327	192	135
35-39	331	230	101	367	244	123	367	229	139	350	211	139
40-44	219	145	74	302	207	95	352	233	118	352	218	134
45-49	160	107	53	195	126	69	289	198	91	339	224	114
50-54	95	62	33	140	91	49	185	120	65	278	190	88
55-59	57	36	21	80	51	30	131	84	47	176	113	63
60-64	35	22	13	51	32	19	75	47	28	124	79	45
65-69	24	14	9	32	20	12	47	29	18	70	43	27
70-74	13	7	6	21	12	8	29	17	11	42	26	16
75-79	6	3	3	11	6	5	17	10	7	24	14	10
80-84	3	1	2	4	2	2	8	4	4	12	7	6
85-89	1	0	1	2	1	1	3	1	2	5	2	3
90-94	0	0	0	1	0	0	1	0	1	1	0	1
95-99	0	0	0	0	0	0	0	0	0	0	0	0
100 +	0	0	0	0	0	0	0	0	0	0	0	0

Age group	2025 Both sexes	Males	Females	2030 Both sexes	Males	Females	2035 Both sexes	Males	Females	2040 Both sexes	Males	Females
All ages	4 002	2 308	1 694	4 296	2 459	1 837	4 577	2 599	1 978	4 840	2 724	2 116
0-4	265	134	130	274	139	135	284	144	140	294	149	145
5-9	266	135	131	267	136	132	277	140	136	287	146	142
10-14	273	138	135	267	136	132	269	137	133	279	141	137
15-19	278	141	136	278	142	137	273	139	134	275	140	135
20-24	281	146	135	307	159	148	307	160	148	302	157	145
25-29	308	170	139	336	183	152	361	196	165	362	197	165
30-34	328	191	137	348	199	148	375	213	162	401	226	175
35-39	329	194	135	330	193	137	350	201	149	377	215	162
40-44	335	200	135	314	183	131	315	182	133	335	191	144
45-49	339	209	130	322	191	131	301	174	127	302	174	129
50-54	327	217	111	328	201	127	311	184	127	291	167	124
55-59	266	182	85	315	208	108	310	198	103	300	176	124
60-64	167	106	61	254	172	82	302	198	105	304	184	120
65-69	115	73	42	156	99	58	239	161	78	286	186	100
70-74	63	38	25	104	65	39	142	89	53	218	145	73
75-79	35	21	14	53	31	21	88	54	34	121	74	47
80-84	17	10	8	26	15	12	40	22	18	68	39	28
85-89	8	4	4	11	5	6	17	9	8	26	13	13
90-94	2	1	1	4	1	2	6	2	3	9	4	5
95-99	0	0	0	1	0	1	1	0	1	2	1	2
100 +	0	0	0	0	0	0	0	0	0	0	0	0

Age group	2045 Both sexes	Males	Females	2050 Both sexes	Males	Females
All ages	5 076	2 831	2 245	5 279	2 916	2 363
0-4	299	152	147	301	153	148
5-9	297	151	146	302	153	149
10-14	289	146	142	299	151	147
15-19	284	145	139	294	150	144
20-24	304	158	146	313	162	151
25-29	357	194	163	359	195	164
30-34	402	226	175	396	224	172
35-39	403	228	175	404	228	175
40-44	362	204	158	388	217	171
45-49	322	182	140	350	196	154
50-54	292	167	125	312	175	137
55-59	281	160	121	282	160	122
60-64	289	168	121	271	153	117
65-69	289	173	115	275	159	116
70-74	262	168	94	266	158	108
75-79	187	122	65	227	143	84
80-84	94	55	40	146	92	55
85-89	45	24	21	64	34	30
90-94	14	6	8	24	11	13
95-99	3	1	2	5	2	4
100 +	1	0	1	1	0	1

United Nations Department of Economic and Social Affairs/Population Division
World Population Prospects: The 2004 Revision, Volume II: Sex and Age Distribution of the World Population

523

POPULATION BY AGE AND SEX (in thousands)

Age group	2005			2010			2015			2020		
	Both sexes	Males	Females	Both sexes	Males	Females	Both sexes	Males	Females	Both sexes	Males	Females
All ages	2 687	1 612	1 075	3 073	1 813	1 260	3 452	2 016	1 437	3 831	2 216	1 615
0-4	241	122	119	294	149	145	314	159	155	325	165	160
5-9	216	110	106	245	124	121	296	150	146	317	161	156
10-14	196	101	95	219	111	108	247	125	122	298	151	147
15-19	189	98	91	204	106	98	224	115	110	252	128	124
20-24	226	123	103	233	125	108	233	124	109	254	132	121
25-29	306	182	124	308	179	129	287	162	125	288	161	127
30-34	369	246	122	365	227	138	348	209	139	327	192	135
35-39	331	230	101	367	244	123	367	229	139	350	211	139
40-44	219	145	74	302	207	95	352	233	118	352	218	134
45-49	160	107	53	195	126	69	289	198	91	339	224	114
50-54	95	62	33	140	91	49	185	120	65	278	190	88
55-59	57	36	21	80	51	30	131	84	47	176	113	63
60-64	35	22	13	51	32	19	75	47	28	124	79	45
65-69	24	14	9	32	20	12	47	29	18	70	43	27
70-74	13	7	6	21	12	8	29	17	11	42	26	16
75-79	6	3	3	11	6	5	17	10	7	24	14	10
80-84	3	1	2	4	2	2	8	4	4	12	7	6
85-89	1	0	1	2	1	1	3	1	2	5	2	3
90-94	0	0	0	1	0	0	1	0	1	1	0	1
95-99	0	0	0	0	0	0	0	0	0	0	0	0
100 +	0	0	0	0	0	0	0	0	0	0	0	0

Age group	2025			2030			2035			2040		
	Both sexes	Males	Females	Both sexes	Males	Females	Both sexes	Males	Females	Both sexes	Males	Females
All ages	4 201	2 409	1 792	4 571	2 598	1 973	4 944	2 785	2 159	5 319	2 967	2 352
0-4	331	168	163	349	177	172	376	191	185	407	206	201
5-9	327	166	161	334	169	165	352	179	174	379	192	187
10-14	319	162	157	329	167	162	336	170	165	354	179	175
15-19	303	154	149	324	165	159	334	170	164	341	173	167
20-24	281	146	135	333	172	160	353	183	170	364	188	176
25-29	308	170	139	336	183	152	387	209	178	408	220	188
30-34	328	191	137	348	199	148	375	213	162	427	239	187
35-39	329	194	135	330	193	137	350	201	149	377	215	162
40-44	335	200	135	314	183	131	315	182	133	335	191	144
45-49	339	209	130	322	191	131	301	174	127	302	174	129
50-54	327	217	111	328	201	127	311	184	127	291	167	124
55-59	266	182	85	315	208	108	316	193	123	300	176	124
60-64	167	106	61	254	172	82	302	198	105	304	184	120
65-69	115	73	42	156	99	58	239	161	78	286	186	100
70-74	63	38	25	104	65	39	142	89	53	218	145	73
75-79	35	21	14	53	31	21	88	54	34	121	74	47
80-84	17	10	8	26	15	12	40	22	18	68	39	28
85-89	8	4	4	11	5	6	17	9	8	26	13	13
90-94	2	1	1	4	1	2	6	2	3	9	4	5
95-99	0	0	0	1	0	1	1	0	1	2	1	2
100 +	0	0	0	0	0	0	0	0	0	0	0	0

Age group	2045			2050		
	Both sexes	Males	Females	Both sexes	Males	Females
All ages	5 687	3 141	2 546	6 038	3 301	2 737
0-4	431	219	213	449	228	221
5-9	410	208	202	434	220	214
10-14	381	193	188	411	209	203
15-19	359	183	176	386	196	190
20-24	370	191	179	388	201	188
25-29	418	225	193	425	229	196
30-34	447	250	198	457	255	203
35-39	429	241	188	449	251	198
40-44	362	204	158	414	230	183
45-49	322	182	140	350	196	154
50-54	292	167	125	312	175	137
55-59	281	160	121	282	160	122
60-64	289	168	121	271	153	117
65-69	289	173	115	275	159	116
70-74	262	168	94	266	158	108
75-79	187	122	65	227	143	84
80-84	94	55	40	146	92	55
85-89	45	24	21	64	34	30
90-94	14	6	8	24	11	13
95-99	3	1	2	5	2	4
100 +	1	0	1	1	0	1

United Nations Department of Economic and Social Affairs/Population Division
World Population Prospects: The 2004 Revision, Volume II: Sex and Age Distribution of the World Population

524

POPULATION BY AGE AND SEX (in thousands)

Age group	2005 Both sexes	Males	Females	2010 Both sexes	Males	Females	2015 Both sexes	Males	Females	2020 Both sexes	Males	Females
All ages	2 687	1 612	1 075	3 019	1 786	1 234	3 304	1 941	1 364	3 558	2 078	1 481
0-4	241	122	119	240	122	118	219	111	108	200	101	99
5-9	216	110	106	245	124	121	243	123	120	222	113	110
10-14	196	101	95	219	111	108	247	125	122	245	124	121
15-19	189	98	91	204	106	98	224	115	110	252	128	124
20-24	226	123	103	233	125	108	233	124	109	254	132	121
25-29	306	182	124	308	179	129	287	162	125	288	161	127
30-34	369	246	122	365	227	138	348	209	139	327	192	135
35-39	331	230	101	367	244	123	367	229	139	350	211	139
40-44	219	145	74	302	207	95	352	233	118	352	218	134
45-49	160	107	53	195	126	69	289	198	91	339	224	114
50-54	95	62	33	140	91	49	185	120	65	278	190	88
55-59	57	36	21	80	51	30	131	84	47	176	113	63
60-64	35	22	13	51	32	19	75	47	28	124	79	45
65-69	24	14	9	32	20	12	47	29	18	70	43	27
70-74	13	7	6	21	12	8	29	17	11	42	26	16
75-79	6	3	3	11	6	5	17	10	7	24	14	10
80-84	3	1	2	4	2	2	8	4	4	12	7	6
85-89	1	0	1	2	1	1	3	1	2	5	2	3
90-94	0	0	0	1	0	0	1	0	1	1	0	1
95-99	0	0	0	0	0	0	0	0	0	0	0	0
100 +	0	0	0	0	0	0	0	0	0	0	0	0

Age group	2025 Both sexes	Males	Females	2030 Both sexes	Males	Females	2035 Both sexes	Males	Females	2040 Both sexes	Males	Females
All ages	3 796	2 204	1 592	4 017	2 317	1 700	4 212	2 414	1 798	4 374	2 488	1 886
0-4	198	101	98	200	102	99	198	100	98	193	98	95
5-9	203	103	100	201	102	99	203	103	100	201	102	99
10-14	224	114	111	205	104	101	203	103	100	205	104	101
15-19	250	127	123	229	117	112	210	107	103	209	106	102
20-24	281	146	135	279	145	134	259	135	124	239	125	114
25-29	308	170	139	336	183	152	334	183	151	313	172	141
30-34	328	191	137	348	199	148	375	213	162	373	212	161
35-39	329	194	135	330	193	137	350	201	149	377	215	162
40-44	335	200	135	314	183	131	315	182	133	335	191	144
45-49	339	209	130	322	191	131	301	174	127	302	174	129
50-54	327	217	111	328	201	127	311	184	127	291	167	124
55-59	266	182	85	315	208	108	316	193	123	300	176	124
60-64	167	106	61	254	172	82	302	198	105	304	184	120
65-69	115	73	42	156	99	58	239	161	78	286	186	100
70-74	63	38	25	104	65	39	142	89	53	218	145	73
75-79	35	21	14	53	31	21	88	54	34	121	74	47
80-84	17	10	8	26	15	12	40	22	18	68	39	28
85-89	8	4	4	11	5	6	17	9	8	26	13	13
90-94	2	1	1	4	1	2	6	2	3	9	4	5
95-99	0	0	0	1	0	1	1	0	1	2	1	2
100 +	0	0	0	0	0	0	0	0	0	0	0	0

Age group	2045 Both sexes	Males	Females	2050 Both sexes	Males	Females
All ages	4 498	2 538	1 960	4 581	2 563	2 018
0-4	186	94	92	180	91	89
5-9	196	99	97	189	96	93
10-14	203	103	100	198	100	98
15-19	210	107	103	208	106	102
20-24	238	124	114	240	125	114
25-29	294	162	132	293	162	131
30-34	353	202	151	334	192	142
35-39	376	214	162	355	204	151
40-44	362	204	158	361	203	157
45-49	322	182	140	350	196	154
50-54	292	167	125	312	175	137
55-59	281	160	121	282	160	122
60-64	289	168	121	271	153	117
65-69	289	173	115	275	159	116
70-74	262	168	94	266	158	108
75-79	187	122	65	227	143	84
80-84	94	55	40	146	92	55
85-89	45	24	21	64	34	30
90-94	14	6	8	24	11	13
95-99	3	1	2	5	2	4
100 +	1	0	1	1	0	1

POPULATION BY AGE AND SEX (in thousands)

Age group	1950 Both sexes	Males	Females	1955 Both sexes	Males	Females	1960 Both sexes	Males	Females	1965 Both sexes	Males	Females
All ages	1 740	829	911	1 903	900	1 002	2 173	1 031	1 142	2 573	1 226	1 347
0-4	167	80	87	264	131	133	362	184	178	428	217	211
5-9	132	67	65	164	78	86	262	130	132	370	188	182
10-14	204	103	100	133	67	65	166	79	87	272	135	138
15-19	174	89	85	204	103	101	134	68	66	173	82	91
20-24	186	92	93	173	88	85	204	103	101	140	71	69
25-29	117	52	65	183	91	93	172	87	85	208	104	104
30-34	82	36	47	115	50	65	181	88	92	176	88	88
35-39	108	45	63	81	34	46	113	49	64	182	88	94
40-44	99	42	57	104	43	61	79	33	46	115	49	66
45-49	103	43	60	95	39	56	100	40	60	79	32	47
50-54	81	39	42	96	38	58	90	36	54	98	38	60
55-59	70	37	33	74	34	39	89	34	55	86	33	53
60-64	75	39	36	62	31	30	66	30	36	83	31	52
65-69	58	29	30	62	31	31	52	26	27	59	25	34
70-74	41	19	22	45	20	24	49	22	26	43	19	23
75-79	25	11	15	28	12	16	31	13	18	35	15	20
80 +	17	7	10	19	8	12	22	9	13	26	10	16

Age group	1970 Both sexes	Males	Females	1975 Both sexes	Males	Females	1980 Both sexes	Males	Females	1985 Both sexes	Males	Females
All ages	2 964	1 417	1 548	3 299	1 594	1 705	3 627	1 759	1 868	4 013	1 951	2 063
0-4	417	211	206	470	237	233	488	247	241	565	287	279
5-9	436	221	215	416	209	207	450	227	223	476	240	236
10-14	382	194	188	430	217	212	409	206	203	444	224	220
15-19	281	139	142	371	191	180	409	206	203	389	196	193
20-24	179	85	94	276	139	137	354	180	174	399	198	201
25-29	144	72	72	180	88	92	276	138	139	349	175	174
30-34	211	105	106	139	71	69	194	97	97	270	134	136
35-39	179	89	90	204	102	102	125	63	62	187	93	94
40-44	183	87	95	169	83	86	199	98	101	121	61	60
45-49	115	48	67	175	82	93	160	78	82	190	92	98
50-54	78	31	47	115	45	70	172	79	92	153	73	80
55-59	94	35	59	75	28	47	112	43	68	161	73	88
60-64	81	30	51	84	31	53	71	25	46	101	38	63
65-69	75	26	48	69	24	45	73	25	48	62	21	41
70-74	49	19	29	57	20	38	55	18	37	60	20	41
75-79	31	13	18	35	13	22	43	14	29	41	13	28
80 +	30	12	19	35	13	22	39	14	25	46	14	32

Age group	1990 Both sexes	Males	Females	1995 Both sexes	Males	Females	2000 Both sexes	Males	Females	2005 Both sexes	Males	Females
All ages	4 395	2 149	2 245	4 588	2 257	2 331	4 952	2 439	2 514	5 264	2 592	2 671
0-4	629	319	310	597	304	292	539	275	264	541	277	265
5-9	549	277	272	601	304	297	588	300	288	530	270	260
10-14	473	238	234	527	265	261	597	302	295	585	298	287
15-19	430	216	214	452	227	224	523	263	259	590	298	292
20-24	366	187	179	409	205	204	447	224	222	508	256	253
25-29	376	186	190	343	175	169	403	201	202	429	215	214
30-34	337	167	170	349	171	178	337	171	166	387	192	194
35-39	261	129	132	309	152	157	341	166	175	324	163	161
40-44	177	87	90	235	115	120	300	146	154	329	159	170
45-49	113	56	56	157	76	81	226	109	117	288	138	150
50-54	178	85	93	93	46	47	149	71	78	215	102	113
55-59	141	66	75	151	71	80	86	42	44	139	64	75
60-64	145	64	81	115	52	62	137	63	75	78	37	41
65-69	85	31	54	116	50	66	100	44	56	121	53	68
70-74	49	16	33	64	22	42	95	38	57	83	34	49
75-79	42	13	29	32	9	22	48	15	33	71	26	45
80 +	43	12	31	39	11	28	36	10	27	46	12	34

United Nations Department of Economic and Social Affairs/Population Division
World Population Prospects: The 2004 Revision, Volume II: Sex and Age Distribution of the World Population

526

POPULATION BY AGE AND SEX (in thousands)

Age group	2005 Both sexes	2005 Males	2005 Females	2010 Both sexes	2010 Males	2010 Females	2015 Both sexes	2015 Males	2015 Females	2020 Both sexes	2020 Males	2020 Females
All ages	5 264	2 592	2 671	5 567	2 742	2 826	5 852	2 881	2 971	6 094	2 999	3 096
0-4	541	277	265	545	278	267	539	275	263	506	259	247
5-9	530	270	260	533	272	261	538	274	263	532	271	260
10-14	585	298	287	527	268	259	530	270	260	535	273	262
15-19	590	298	292	578	294	284	521	265	256	524	267	257
20-24	508	256	253	575	291	285	564	287	277	507	258	249
25-29	429	215	214	490	246	244	557	281	276	546	277	269
30-34	387	192	194	412	206	207	473	237	237	540	272	269
35-39	324	163	161	373	184	189	399	198	201	460	229	231
40-44	329	159	170	312	156	156	361	177	184	387	190	197
45-49	288	138	150	316	150	166	300	148	152	349	169	180
50-54	215	102	113	274	129	145	303	142	161	288	140	148
55-59	139	64	75	202	93	108	259	119	140	287	131	155
60-64	78	37	41	128	57	70	186	83	103	240	108	133
65-69	121	53	68	69	31	38	114	49	65	167	72	95
70-74	83	34	49	101	41	60	58	24	33	96	39	57
75-79	71	26	45	63	23	40	78	29	49	44	17	27
80-84	31	8	23	47	15	32	42	14	28	52	17	35
85-89	10	2	8	16	4	12	25	7	18	23	7	16
90-94	4	1	3	4	1	3	6	1	5	10	3	7
95-99	1	0	1	1	0	1	1	0	1	1	0	1
100 +	0	0	0	0	0	0	0	0	0	0	0	0

Age group	2025 Both sexes	2025 Males	2025 Females	2030 Both sexes	2030 Males	2030 Females	2035 Both sexes	2035 Males	2035 Females	2040 Both sexes	2040 Males	2040 Females
All ages	6 282	3 088	3 194	6 431	3 157	3 275	6 553	3 212	3 341	6 637	3 250	3 387
0-4	463	237	226	439	225	214	435	223	212	426	218	208
5-9	500	255	244	457	234	223	434	222	212	430	220	210
10-14	529	270	259	497	254	243	455	232	222	432	221	211
15-19	528	270	259	523	267	256	491	251	240	449	230	219
20-24	511	260	250	515	263	252	510	260	250	479	245	234
25-29	490	249	241	494	252	242	499	254	245	494	252	242
30-34	530	268	262	475	241	234	479	244	236	484	246	238
35-39	527	263	263	517	261	256	463	234	229	467	237	230
40-44	448	221	227	514	256	259	505	254	252	452	228	224
45-49	375	183	193	435	213	222	502	248	254	493	246	247
50-54	336	160	176	362	174	188	422	204	218	487	238	249
55-59	274	130	143	321	150	170	347	164	183	405	193	212
60-64	267	119	148	256	119	137	301	138	163	326	151	175
65-69	217	93	123	242	104	138	233	105	128	275	122	153
70-74	142	58	85	186	76	110	210	85	124	202	86	116
75-79	75	28	47	113	42	71	149	58	90	160	64	105
80-84	30	11	20	52	17	35	79	27	52	106	36	70
85-89	29	9	20	17	5	12	30	9	21	46	14	32
90-94	9	2	7	12	3	9	7	2	5	13	3	10
95-99	2	1	2	2	1	2	3	1	2	2	1	2
100 +	0	0	0	0	0	0	0	0	0	1	0	0

Age group	2045 Both sexes	2045 Males	2045 Females	2050 Both sexes	2050 Males	2050 Females
All ages	6 675	3 266	3 408	6 664	3 260	3 404
0-4	408	209	199	386	198	188
5-9	421	215	206	404	207	197
10-14	427	219	209	419	214	205
15-19	426	218	208	422	216	206
20-24	437	223	213	414	212	202
25-29	463	237	226	421	215	205
30-34	479	244	235	449	229	220
35-39	472	240	233	468	238	230
40-44	457	231	226	463	234	228
45-49	441	221	221	447	224	222
50-54	480	237	243	430	213	216
55-59	468	226	243	462	225	237
60-64	382	178	204	444	210	234
65-69	299	134	165	352	160	192
70-74	240	102	139	263	113	150
75-79	164	65	98	196	78	118
80-84	121	42	80	119	43	75
85-89	63	19	44	73	22	51
90-94	21	5	15	29	8	21
95-99	4	1	3	6	1	5
100 +	0	0	0	1	0	0

POPULATION BY AGE AND SEX (in thousands)

Age group	2005 Both sexes	Males	Females	2010 Both sexes	Males	Females	2015 Both sexes	Males	Females	2020 Both sexes	Males	Females
All ages	5 264	2 592	2 671	5 623	2 770	2 853	6 003	2 958	3 045	6 367	3 138	3 229
0-4	541	277	265	601	307	294	634	324	310	628	321	307
5-9	530	270	260	533	272	261	593	302	290	627	320	307
10-14	585	298	287	527	268	259	530	270	260	590	301	289
15-19	590	298	292	578	294	284	521	265	256	524	267	257
20-24	508	256	253	575	291	285	564	287	277	507	258	249
25-29	429	215	214	490	246	244	557	281	276	546	277	269
30-34	387	192	194	412	206	207	473	237	237	540	272	269
35-39	324	163	161	373	184	189	399	198	201	460	229	231
40-44	329	159	170	312	156	156	361	177	184	387	190	197
45-49	288	138	150	316	150	166	300	148	152	349	169	180
50-54	215	102	113	274	129	145	303	142	161	288	140	148
55-59	139	64	75	202	93	108	259	119	140	287	131	155
60-64	78	37	41	128	57	70	186	83	103	240	108	133
65-69	121	53	68	69	31	38	114	49	65	167	72	95
70-74	83	34	49	101	41	60	58	24	33	96	39	57
75-79	71	26	45	63	23	40	78	29	49	44	17	27
80-84	31	8	23	47	15	32	42	14	28	52	17	35
85-89	10	2	8	16	4	12	25	7	18	23	7	16
90-94	4	1	3	4	1	3	6	1	5	10	3	7
95-99	1	0	1	1	0	1	1	0	1	1	0	1
100 +	0	0	0	0	0	0	0	0	0	0	0	0

Age group	2025 Both sexes	Males	Females	2030 Both sexes	Males	Females	2035 Both sexes	Males	Females	2040 Both sexes	Males	Females
All ages	6 677	3 289	3 387	6 960	3 426	3 533	7 243	3 564	3 679	7 522	3 701	3 820
0-4	586	300	286	575	294	281	599	306	292	622	318	304
5-9	621	318	304	579	296	283	569	291	278	593	303	290
10-14	624	318	305	619	316	303	577	295	282	566	290	277
15-19	583	298	286	618	315	302	613	313	300	571	292	279
20-24	511	260	250	570	291	279	605	309	296	600	306	293
25-29	490	249	241	494	252	242	553	282	271	588	300	288
30-34	530	268	262	475	241	234	479	244	236	538	274	264
35-39	527	263	263	517	261	256	463	234	229	467	237	230
40-44	448	221	227	514	256	259	505	254	252	452	228	224
45-49	375	183	193	435	213	222	502	248	254	493	246	247
50-54	336	160	176	362	174	188	422	204	218	487	238	249
55-59	274	130	143	321	150	170	347	164	183	405	193	212
60-64	267	119	148	256	119	137	301	138	163	326	151	175
65-69	217	93	123	242	104	138	233	105	128	275	122	153
70-74	142	58	85	186	76	110	210	85	124	202	86	116
75-79	75	28	47	113	42	71	149	56	93	169	64	105
80-84	30	11	20	52	17	35	79	27	52	106	36	70
85-89	29	9	20	17	5	12	30	9	21	46	14	32
90-94	9	2	7	12	3	9	7	2	5	13	3	10
95-99	2	1	2	2	1	2	3	1	2	2	1	2
100 +	0	0	0	0	0	0	0	0	0	1	0	0

Age group	2045 Both sexes	Males	Females	2050 Both sexes	Males	Females
All ages	7 776	3 829	3 948	7 996	3 940	4 056
0-4	628	321	306	620	317	303
5-9	616	315	301	623	319	304
10-14	591	302	288	614	314	300
15-19	561	287	274	585	299	286
20-24	558	285	273	548	280	267
25-29	583	298	285	542	277	265
30-34	573	292	281	568	290	279
35-39	526	267	259	561	285	276
40-44	457	231	226	516	261	255
45-49	441	221	221	447	224	222
50-54	480	237	243	430	213	216
55-59	468	226	243	462	225	237
60-64	382	178	204	444	210	234
65-69	299	134	165	352	160	192
70-74	240	102	139	263	113	150
75-79	164	65	98	196	78	118
80-84	121	42	80	119	43	75
85-89	63	19	44	73	22	51
90-94	21	5	15	29	8	21
95-99	4	1	3	6	1	5
100 +	0	0	0	1	0	0

United Nations Department of Economic and Social Affairs/Population Division
World Population Prospects: The 2004 Revision, Volume II: Sex and Age Distribution of the World Population

528

POPULATION BY AGE AND SEX (in thousands)

Age group	2005 Both sexes	Males	Females	2010 Both sexes	Males	Females	2015 Both sexes	Males	Females	2020 Both sexes	Males	Females
All ages	5 264	2 592	2 672	5 509	2 710	2 799	5 701	2 803	2 898	5 806	2 843	2 963
0-4	541	277	265	490	250	239	443	226	216	384	196	188
5-9	530	270	260	533	272	261	482	246	236	436	223	214
10-14	585	298	287	527	268	259	530	270	260	480	245	235
15-19	590	298	292	578	294	284	521	265	256	524	267	257
20-24	508	256	253	575	291	285	564	287	277	507	258	249
25-29	429	215	214	490	246	244	557	281	276	546	277	269
30-34	387	192	194	412	206	207	473	237	237	540	272	269
35-39	324	163	161	373	184	189	399	198	201	460	229	231
40-44	329	159	170	312	156	156	361	177	184	387	190	197
45-49	288	138	150	316	150	166	300	148	152	349	169	180
50-54	215	102	113	274	129	145	303	142	161	288	140	148
55-59	139	64	75	202	93	108	259	119	140	287	131	155
60-64	78	37	41	128	57	70	186	83	103	240	108	133
65-69	121	53	68	69	31	38	114	49	65	167	72	95
70-74	83	34	49	101	41	60	58	24	33	96	39	57
75-79	71	26	45	63	23	40	78	29	49	44	17	27
80-84	31	8	23	47	15	32	42	14	28	52	17	35
85-89	10	2	8	16	4	12	25	7	18	23	7	16
90-94	4	1	3	4	1	3	6	1	5	10	3	7
95-99	1	0	1	1	0	1	1	0	1	1	0	1
100 +	0	0	0	0	0	0	0	0	0	0	0	0

Age group	2025 Both sexes	Males	Females	2030 Both sexes	Males	Females	2035 Both sexes	Males	Females	2040 Both sexes	Males	Females
All ages	5 889	2 887	3 002	5 910	2 891	3 020	5 889	2 873	3 016	5 813	2 829	2 984
0-4	341	174	166	311	159	152	290	149	142	264	135	129
5-9	378	193	185	336	172	164	306	157	149	286	146	140
10-14	434	221	212	376	192	184	334	171	163	304	155	148
15-19	474	242	232	428	219	210	370	189	181	328	168	160
20-24	511	260	250	461	235	226	415	212	203	358	183	175
25-29	490	249	241	494	252	242	444	227	218	399	204	195
30-34	530	268	262	475	241	234	479	244	236	430	219	211
35-39	527	263	263	517	261	256	463	234	229	467	237	230
40-44	448	221	227	514	256	259	505	254	252	452	228	224
45-49	375	183	193	435	213	222	502	248	254	493	246	247
50-54	336	160	176	362	174	188	422	204	218	487	238	249
55-59	274	130	143	321	150	170	347	164	183	405	193	212
60-64	267	119	148	256	119	137	301	138	163	326	151	175
65-69	217	93	123	242	104	138	233	105	128	275	122	153
70-74	142	58	85	186	76	110	210	85	124	202	86	116
75-79	75	28	47	113	42	71	149	56	93	169	64	105
80-84	30	11	20	52	17	35	79	27	52	106	36	70
85-89	29	9	20	17	5	12	30	9	21	46	14	32
90-94	9	2	7	12	3	9	7	2	5	13	3	10
95-99	2	1	2	2	1	2	3	1	2	2	1	2
100 +	0	0	0	0	0	0	0	0	0	1	0	0

Age group	2045 Both sexes	Males	Females	2050 Both sexes	Males	Females
All ages	5 680	2 759	2 922	5 495	2 664	2 832
0-4	235	120	115	208	107	102
5-9	260	133	127	231	118	113
10-14	284	145	139	258	132	126
15-19	298	153	146	278	143	136
20-24	316	162	154	286	147	140
25-29	342	175	167	301	154	146
30-34	386	197	189	329	168	161
35-39	419	213	206	375	191	184
40-44	457	231	226	409	207	202
45-49	441	221	221	447	224	222
50-54	480	237	243	430	213	216
55-59	468	226	243	462	225	237
60-64	382	178	204	444	210	234
65-69	299	134	165	352	160	192
70-74	240	102	139	263	113	150
75-79	164	65	98	196	78	118
80-84	121	42	80	119	43	75
85-89	63	19	44	73	22	51
90-94	21	5	15	29	8	21
95-99	4	1	3	6	1	5
100 +	0	0	0	1	0	0

POPULATION BY AGE AND SEX (in thousands)

Age group	1950 Both sexes	1950 Males	1950 Females	1955 Both sexes	1955 Males	1955 Females	1960 Both sexes	1960 Males	1960 Females	1965 Both sexes	1965 Males	1965 Females
All ages	1 755	897	858	1 944	990	955	2 177	1 105	1 072	2 432	1 231	1 202
0-4	286	146	141	323	162	160	367	185	182	406	205	201
5-9	239	123	116	259	132	127	296	149	147	337	170	167
10-14	210	108	102	232	119	113	252	129	124	288	145	143
15-19	181	90	91	204	105	99	225	116	109	246	125	120
20-24	164	85	79	174	86	87	196	101	95	217	112	105
25-29	140	72	68	156	80	75	166	83	83	187	97	91
30-34	121	62	59	132	68	64	148	76	72	158	78	79
35-39	100	52	48	113	58	55	124	64	60	140	72	68
40-44	82	42	40	93	48	45	106	54	52	116	59	57
45-49	68	36	32	75	38	37	86	44	42	98	49	48
50-54	50	26	23	62	32	30	68	34	34	78	39	38
55-59	34	17	17	43	22	21	54	28	27	60	30	30
60-64	32	15	16	28	14	15	36	18	18	45	23	23
65-69	23	11	12	24	11	13	22	11	12	28	14	14
70-74	14	6	8	16	7	8	17	8	9	16	7	8
75-79	8	4	5	8	4	5	9	4	5	10	4	6
80 +	4	2	3	4	2	3	5	2	3	5	2	3

Age group	1970 Both sexes	1970 Males	1970 Females	1975 Both sexes	1975 Males	1975 Females	1980 Both sexes	1980 Males	1980 Females	1985 Both sexes	1985 Males	1985 Females
All ages	2 713	1 369	1 343	3 024	1 523	1 501	3 205	1 613	1 593	3 621	1 793	1 828
0-4	449	226	222	500	252	248	533	269	264	626	318	309
5-9	372	187	185	411	207	204	436	220	216	506	256	250
10-14	328	165	162	362	183	179	379	191	188	434	220	214
15-19	280	141	139	319	161	158	334	169	165	367	179	188
20-24	237	121	116	270	136	134	292	147	144	315	155	160
25-29	207	107	101	226	115	111	245	123	121	277	137	140
30-34	178	92	86	197	101	96	204	104	100	205	100	105
35-39	149	74	75	168	86	82	176	90	86	180	88	91
40-44	130	67	64	139	69	70	149	76	73	132	61	71
45-49	107	54	53	120	61	59	122	59	62	144	70	74
50-54	88	44	44	97	49	49	104	52	52	95	47	49
55-59	68	34	34	78	38	40	82	40	41	112	54	57
60-64	50	24	26	57	28	29	63	30	33	64	33	32
65-69	35	17	18	39	19	21	43	21	22	66	33	33
70-74	20	10	10	25	12	13	27	12	14	41	19	23
75-79	9	4	5	12	5	6	14	7	8	25	12	13
80 +	6	2	3	5	2	3	6	2	3	31	13	18

Age group	1990 Both sexes	1990 Males	1990 Females	1995 Both sexes	1995 Males	1995 Females	2000 Both sexes	2000 Males	2000 Females	2005 Both sexes	2005 Males	2005 Females
All ages	4 132	2 053	2 079	4 686	2 334	2 351	5 279	2 636	2 643	5 924	2 964	2 960
0-4	738	375	363	792	403	389	836	426	410	895	456	439
5-9	579	293	286	689	350	339	746	379	366	793	404	389
10-14	493	249	243	565	286	279	674	343	332	731	372	359
15-19	424	215	210	482	244	238	554	281	273	663	337	326
20-24	357	174	183	412	208	204	470	237	233	542	274	268
25-29	305	149	155	344	167	177	400	201	198	457	230	227
30-34	267	132	136	293	143	150	333	161	172	388	195	193
35-39	197	96	101	256	126	130	283	138	144	322	156	166
40-44	171	84	87	188	91	97	246	121	125	272	133	139
45-49	125	58	67	163	79	83	179	87	93	235	115	120
50-54	135	65	70	117	54	64	153	74	79	170	81	88
55-59	87	42	45	124	59	65	108	49	59	142	68	74
60-64	99	47	51	78	37	40	112	53	59	98	44	54
65-69	54	27	27	83	39	44	66	31	35	96	44	51
70-74	50	24	25	41	20	21	65	30	35	52	24	28
75-79	27	12	15	33	16	17	28	13	15	45	20	24
80 +	24	10	14	23	9	13	25	11	14	24	11	13

United Nations Department of Economic and Social Affairs/Population Division
World Population Prospects: The 2004 Revision, Volume II: Sex and Age Distribution of the World Population

530

POPULATION BY AGE AND SEX (in thousands)

Age group	2005 Both sexes	Males	Females	2010 Both sexes	Males	Females	2015 Both sexes	Males	Females	2020 Both sexes	Males	Females
All ages	5 924	2 964	2 960	6 604	3 310	3 294	7 306	3 667	3 639	8 014	4 028	3 986
0-4	895	456	439	938	478	460	965	492	472	975	498	477
5-9	793	404	389	856	436	420	904	461	443	936	477	459
10-14	731	372	359	780	397	383	843	430	414	893	455	438
15-19	663	337	326	720	366	354	770	391	378	834	424	409
20-24	542	274	268	649	329	320	707	359	348	757	384	373
25-29	457	230	227	528	266	262	634	321	314	693	351	342
30-34	388	195	193	444	223	221	515	259	256	621	313	308
35-39	322	156	166	376	189	187	432	217	216	503	253	250
40-44	272	133	139	311	150	161	364	182	182	421	211	210
45-49	235	115	120	261	127	134	300	144	155	353	176	176
50-54	170	81	88	223	109	115	249	120	129	287	137	150
55-59	142	68	74	158	75	83	210	101	108	235	113	122
60-64	98	44	54	129	61	68	145	68	76	193	92	101
65-69	96	44	51	84	37	47	113	53	60	127	59	68
70-74	52	24	28	76	35	41	68	30	38	92	43	49
75-79	45	20	24	36	16	20	54	24	30	49	21	28
80-84	15	7	8	25	11	14	21	9	12	32	14	18
85-89	7	3	4	6	3	4	11	5	6	9	4	5
90-94	2	1	1	2	1	1	2	1	1	3	1	2
95-99	0	0	0	0	0	0	0	0	0	0	0	0
100 +	0	0	0	0	0	0	0	0	0	0	0	0

Age group	2025 Both sexes	Males	Females	2030 Both sexes	Males	Females	2035 Both sexes	Males	Females	2040 Both sexes	Males	Females
All ages	8 712	4 381	4 331	9 389	4 722	4 667	10 032	5 046	4 987	10 624	5 341	5 284
0-4	973	496	476	964	492	472	947	483	464	919	469	450
5-9	952	485	466	955	487	468	951	484	466	937	478	460
10-14	927	473	454	944	481	463	949	483	466	946	482	464
15-19	885	450	434	919	468	451	938	478	460	943	480	463
20-24	822	417	404	873	444	430	909	462	447	928	472	457
25-29	744	377	367	809	410	399	861	437	425	898	455	443
30-34	680	343	337	731	370	362	798	403	394	851	430	420
35-39	608	306	302	668	337	331	720	363	357	787	397	390
40-44	491	246	245	590	290	296	656	330	326	709	356	352
45-49	409	204	205	478	239	239	582	292	290	642	322	320
50-54	339	169	171	395	196	199	463	231	233	565	282	283
55-59	272	130	143	323	160	164	377	186	191	445	220	225
60-64	218	104	114	254	120	134	303	148	155	355	174	181
65-69	171	81	90	195	92	103	229	107	122	275	133	142
70-74	105	48	57	143	67	77	165	76	89	195	89	106
75-79	68	31	37	79	36	43	109	50	59	127	57	69
80-84	30	12	18	42	19	24	50	22	28	70	31	39
85-89	15	6	8	14	6	8	20	9	12	24	10	14
90-94	3	1	2	5	2	3	4	2	3	7	3	4
95-99	1	0	0	1	0	0	1	0	1	1	0	1
100 +	0	0	0	0	0	0	0	0	0	0	0	0

Age group	2045 Both sexes	Males	Females	2050 Both sexes	Males	Females
All ages	11 146	5 598	5 548	11 586	5 814	5 773
0-4	879	448	431	832	425	408
5-9	911	464	447	874	445	429
10-14	934	475	458	908	462	446
15-19	941	479	463	930	473	457
20-24	935	475	460	934	474	460
25-29	918	466	453	926	469	457
30-34	888	449	439	909	460	449
35-39	840	424	416	879	443	435
40-44	775	390	385	830	417	412
45-49	695	349	347	762	382	380
50-54	625	312	313	678	339	340
55-59	544	270	274	603	299	304
60-64	420	206	214	516	253	262
65-69	324	156	167	385	186	199
70-74	236	112	124	280	133	147
75-79	152	68	84	185	86	99
80-84	83	36	46	100	44	57
85-89	35	15	20	42	18	24
90-94	8	3	5	12	5	7
95-99	1	0	1	2	1	1
100 +	0	0	0	0	0	0

United Nations Department of Economic and Social Affairs/Population Division
World Population Prospects: The 2004 Revision, Volume II: Sex and Age Distribution of the World Population

531

POPULATION BY AGE AND SEX (in thousands)

Age group	2005 Both sexes	Males	Females	2010 Both sexes	Males	Females	2015 Both sexes	Males	Females	2020 Both sexes	Males	Females
All ages	5 924	2 964	2 960	6 652	3 334	3 318	7 444	3 737	3 706	8 283	4 165	4 118
0-4	895	456	439	986	503	483	1 056	539	517	1 109	566	543
5-9	793	404	389	856	436	420	950	484	466	1 025	523	502
10-14	731	372	359	780	397	383	843	430	414	939	478	460
15-19	663	337	326	720	366	354	770	391	378	834	424	409
20-24	542	274	268	649	329	320	707	359	348	757	384	373
25-29	457	230	227	528	266	262	634	321	314	693	351	342
30-34	388	195	193	444	223	221	515	259	256	621	313	308
35-39	322	156	166	376	189	187	432	217	216	503	253	250
40-44	272	133	139	311	150	161	364	182	182	421	211	210
45-49	235	115	120	261	127	134	300	144	155	353	176	176
50-54	170	81	88	223	109	115	249	120	129	287	137	150
55-59	142	68	74	158	75	83	210	101	108	235	113	122
60-64	98	44	54	129	61	68	145	68	76	193	92	101
65-69	96	44	51	84	37	47	113	53	60	127	59	68
70-74	52	24	28	76	35	41	68	30	38	92	43	49
75-79	45	20	24	36	16	20	54	24	30	49	21	28
80-84	15	7	8	25	11	14	21	9	12	32	14	18
85-89	7	3	4	6	3	4	11	5	6	9	4	5
90-94	2	1	1	2	1	1	2	1	1	3	1	2
95-99	0	0	0	0	0	0	0	0	0	0	0	0
100 +	0	0	0	0	0	0	0	0	0	0	0	0

Age group	2025 Both sexes	Males	Females	2030 Both sexes	Males	Females	2035 Both sexes	Males	Females	2040 Both sexes	Males	Females
All ages	9 133	4 596	4 538	9 998	5 032	4 965	10 875	5 475	5 400	11 752	5 914	5 837
0-4	1 131	577	554	1 156	590	566	1 187	606	581	1 210	617	593
5-9	1 082	552	530	1 109	565	544	1 140	581	559	1 174	598	576
10-14	1 015	518	498	1 074	548	527	1 103	562	541	1 135	578	557
15-19	930	474	456	1 007	513	494	1 067	543	523	1 096	558	539
20-24	822	417	404	918	467	452	996	506	490	1 056	537	520
25-29	744	377	367	809	410	399	906	459	447	984	499	485
30-34	680	343	337	731	370	362	798	403	394	894	452	442
35-39	608	306	302	668	337	331	720	363	357	787	397	390
40-44	491	246	245	596	299	296	656	330	326	709	356	352
45-49	409	204	205	478	239	239	582	292	290	642	322	320
50-54	339	169	171	395	196	199	463	231	233	565	282	283
55-59	272	130	143	323	160	164	377	186	191	445	220	225
60-64	218	104	114	254	120	134	303	148	155	355	174	181
65-69	171	81	90	195	92	103	229	107	122	275	133	142
70-74	105	48	57	143	67	77	165	76	89	195	89	106
75-79	68	31	37	79	36	43	109	50	59	127	57	69
80-84	30	12	18	42	19	24	50	22	28	70	31	39
85-89	15	6	8	14	6	8	20	9	12	24	10	14
90-94	3	1	2	5	2	3	4	2	3	7	3	4
95-99	1	0	0	1	0	0	1	0	1	1	0	1
100 +	0	0	0	0	0	0	0	0	0	0	0	0

Age group	2045 Both sexes	Males	Females	2050 Both sexes	Males	Females
All ages	12 605	6 340	6 265	13 417	6 744	6 673
0-4	1 219	621	597	1 213	619	594
5-9	1 201	611	589	1 211	617	594
10-14	1 170	596	574	1 197	609	588
15-19	1 129	574	555	1 165	592	572
20-24	1 087	552	535	1 120	569	552
25-29	1 045	530	515	1 077	545	532
30-34	973	492	481	1 035	523	512
35-39	884	446	438	963	486	477
40-44	775	390	385	872	439	433
45-49	695	349	347	762	382	380
50-54	625	312	313	678	339	340
55-59	544	270	274	603	299	304
60-64	420	206	214	516	253	262
65-69	324	156	167	385	186	199
70-74	236	112	124	280	133	147
75-79	152	68	84	185	86	99
80-84	83	36	46	100	44	57
85-89	35	15	20	42	18	24
90-94	8	3	5	12	5	7
95-99	1	0	1	2	1	1
100 +	0	0	0	0	0	0

United Nations Department of Economic and Social Affairs/Population Division
World Population Prospects: The 2004 Revision, Volume II: Sex and Age Distribution of the World Population

532

POPULATION BY AGE AND SEX (in thousands)

Age group	2005 Both sexes	Males	Females	2010 Both sexes	Males	Females	2015 Both sexes	Males	Females	2020 Both sexes	Males	Females
All ages	5 924	2 964	2 960	6 555	3 285	3 270	7 165	3 595	3 570	7 739	3 887	3 852
0-4	895	456	439	890	454	436	871	444	426	837	428	410
5-9	793	404	389	856	436	420	857	437	420	845	431	414
10-14	731	372	359	780	397	383	843	430	414	847	432	415
15-19	663	337	326	720	366	354	770	391	378	834	424	409
20-24	542	274	268	649	329	320	707	359	348	757	384	373
25-29	457	230	227	528	266	262	634	321	314	693	351	342
30-34	388	195	193	444	223	221	515	259	256	621	313	308
35-39	322	156	166	376	189	187	432	217	216	503	253	250
40-44	272	133	139	311	150	161	364	182	182	421	211	210
45-49	235	115	120	261	127	134	300	144	155	353	176	176
50-54	170	81	88	223	109	115	249	120	129	287	137	150
55-59	142	68	74	158	75	83	210	101	108	235	113	122
60-64	98	44	54	129	61	68	145	68	76	193	92	101
65-69	96	44	51	84	37	47	113	53	60	127	59	68
70-74	52	24	28	76	35	41	68	30	38	92	43	49
75-79	45	20	24	36	16	20	54	24	30	49	21	28
80-84	15	7	8	25	11	14	21	9	12	32	14	18
85-89	7	3	4	6	3	4	11	5	6	9	4	5
90-94	2	1	1	2	1	1	2	1	1	3	1	2
95-99	0	0	0	0	0	0	0	0	0	0	0	0
100 +	0	0	0	0	0	0	0	0	0	0	0	0

Age group	2025 Both sexes	Males	Females	2030 Both sexes	Males	Females	2035 Both sexes	Males	Females	2040 Both sexes	Males	Females
All ages	8 281	4 161	4 120	8 773	4 408	4 365	9 192	4 618	4 575	9 523	4 780	4 743
0-4	813	415	398	774	395	379	717	366	351	651	332	319
5-9	817	417	400	797	406	391	763	389	374	710	362	348
10-14	837	427	410	811	413	397	793	404	389	759	387	373
15-19	839	427	412	830	423	407	805	410	395	788	401	387
20-24	822	417	404	828	421	407	821	417	403	797	405	392
25-29	744	377	367	809	410	399	817	414	403	811	411	400
30-34	680	343	337	731	370	362	798	403	394	806	408	398
35-39	608	306	302	668	337	331	720	363	357	787	397	390
40-44	491	246	245	596	299	296	656	330	326	709	356	352
45-49	409	204	205	478	239	239	582	292	290	642	322	320
50-54	340	169	171	395	196	199	463	231	233	565	282	283
55-59	272	130	143	323	160	164	377	186	191	445	220	225
60-64	218	104	114	254	120	134	303	148	155	355	174	181
65-69	171	81	90	195	92	103	229	107	122	275	133	142
70-74	105	48	57	143	67	77	165	76	89	195	89	106
75-79	68	31	37	70	36	43	109	50	59	127	57	69
80-84	30	12	18	42	19	24	50	22	28	70	31	39
85-89	15	6	8	14	6	8	20	9	12	24	10	14
90-94	3	1	2	5	2	3	4	2	3	7	3	4
95-99	1	0	0	1	0	0	1	0	1	1	0	1
100 +	0	0	0	0	0	0	0	0	0	0	0	0

Age group	2045 Both sexes	Males	Females	2050 Both sexes	Males	Females
All ages	9 755	4 891	4 864	9 888	4 950	4 907
0-4	582	297	285	516	263	253
5-9	645	329	317	578	295	284
10-14	707	360	347	643	327	316
15-19	755	384	371	704	358	346
20-24	781	396	384	749	380	369
25-29	788	400	389	773	392	382
30-34	801	405	396	780	395	386
35-39	796	402	395	793	400	393
40-44	775	390	385	786	396	391
45-49	695	349	347	762	382	380
50-54	625	312	313	678	339	340
55-59	544	270	274	603	299	304
60-64	420	206	214	516	253	262
65-69	324	156	167	385	186	199
70-74	236	112	124	280	133	147
75-79	152	68	84	185	86	99
80-84	83	36	46	100	44	57
85-89	35	15	20	42	18	24
90-94	8	3	5	12	5	7
95-99	1	0	1	2	1	1
100 +	0	0	0	0	0	0

United Nations Department of Economic and Social Affairs/Population Division
World Population Prospects: The 2004 Revision, Volume II: Sex and Age Distribution of the World Population

533

POPULATION BY AGE AND SEX (in thousands)

Age group	1950 Both sexes	Males	Females	1955 Both sexes	Males	Females	1960 Both sexes	Males	Females	1965 Both sexes	Males	Females
All ages	1 949	843	1 106	2 015	884	1 131	2 121	931	1 190	2 266	1 022	1 244
0-4	150	78	72	155	78	77	165	84	81	170	86	83
5-9	163	82	80	151	78	73	155	79	76	171	87	84
10-14	181	90	90	164	83	81	145	74	72	163	84	79
15-19	167	82	85	182	91	91	170	85	85	161	83	78
20-24	169	76	93	169	83	86	173	83	90	175	88	87
25-29	134	53	81	170	76	94	180	86	93	193	96	97
30-34	96	41	56	135	53	82	175	72	103	178	87	91
35-39	133	55	78	97	40	56	134	51	82	179	80	99
40-44	135	58	77	132	55	77	108	44	64	142	56	86
45-49	126	52	74	134	57	77	140	58	82	101	42	59
50-54	100	36	64	123	50	73	138	60	78	135	55	80
55-59	91	33	57	96	34	62	120	47	73	133	55	78
60-64	86	32	54	85	30	54	95	33	62	117	46	71
65-69	75	27	48	77	27	49	79	27	51	86	28	58
70-74	61	21	39	62	21	40	58	20	39	68	22	45
75-79	45	15	30	44	15	30	48	16	32	50	16	34
80 +	37	11	26	39	12	27	38	11	27	45	13	32

Age group	1970 Both sexes	Males	Females	1975 Both sexes	Males	Females	1980 Both sexes	Males	Females	1985 Both sexes	Males	Females
All ages	2 359	1 078	1 281	2 456	1 129	1 327	2 512	1 156	1 356	2 579	1 191	1 388
0-4	160	82	78	178	91	87	173	88	84	192	98	94
5-9	176	90	86	163	83	80	177	90	87	175	89	86
10-14	174	89	85	176	90	86	164	83	80	180	92	88
15-19	166	87	79	186	95	91	188	97	91	170	89	82
20-24	164	84	80	183	95	88	199	102	97	198	100	98
25-29	178	89	89	170	86	84	186	94	92	202	101	101
30-34	196	97	99	179	89	90	169	83	86	185	91	94
35-39	181	88	93	196	96	100	176	85	91	166	80	86
40-44	182	81	101	177	85	92	192	92	100	171	82	90
45-49	143	55	87	176	77	99	172	81	91	186	88	99
50-54	100	41	59	140	52	88	170	72	97	166	76	90
55-59	132	53	80	96	38	58	132	48	84	162	67	95
60-64	127	51	76	124	48	76	88	33	55	122	43	80
65-69	107	40	67	113	43	70	110	40	70	78	28	51
70-74	74	23	51	90	31	59	94	33	61	92	30	62
75-79	51	16	36	56	15	40	67	21	46	70	22	48
80 +	48	13	35	54	14	40	57	14	43	65	17	48

Age group	1990 Both sexes	Males	Females	1995 Both sexes	Males	Females	2000 Both sexes	Males	Females	2005 Both sexes	Males	Females
All ages	2 713	1 263	1 450	2 498	1 151	1 347	2 373	1 087	1 286	2 307	1 055	1 252
0-4	215	110	106	139	71	68	97	50	47	101	52	49
5-9	194	99	95	195	100	95	142	73	70	96	49	47
10-14	172	87	85	182	93	89	186	95	91	142	72	70
15-19	191	98	93	163	83	81	178	91	87	185	95	90
20-24	180	93	87	172	87	85	160	81	79	175	89	86
25-29	213	107	106	164	82	82	164	83	81	157	79	78
30-34	207	103	104	187	92	95	157	78	79	161	81	80
35-39	192	94	98	185	90	95	175	85	90	154	75	78
40-44	151	73	78	167	80	87	175	84	91	171	82	89
45-49	175	83	92	144	67	77	155	72	83	169	80	89
50-54	176	81	95	154	70	84	138	62	76	148	67	81
55-59	162	74	87	160	70	90	140	61	79	130	57	73
60-64	161	63	98	139	59	80	145	60	85	129	54	75
65-69	116	38	78	132	49	84	119	46	73	129	51	78
70-74	62	20	42	91	27	64	106	35	71	100	35	65
75-79	71	21	50	46	14	32	68	18	51	82	24	58
80 +	74	20	55	76	18	58	67	13	54	80	13	67

United Nations Department of Economic and Social Affairs/Population Division
World Population Prospects: The 2004 Revision, Volume II: Sex and Age Distribution of the World Population

POPULATION BY AGE AND SEX (in thousands)

Age group	2005 Both sexes	2005 Males	2005 Females	2010 Both sexes	2010 Males	2010 Females	2015 Both sexes	2015 Males	2015 Females	2020 Both sexes	2020 Males	2020 Females
All ages	2 307	1 055	1 252	2 248	1 029	1 219	2 191	1 005	1 185	2 129	981	1 149
0-4	101	52	49	104	53	51	104	54	51	99	51	48
5-9	96	49	47	100	52	49	104	53	50	104	53	51
10-14	142	72	70	96	49	46	100	51	49	103	53	50
15-19	185	95	90	141	72	69	95	49	46	99	51	48
20-24	175	89	86	182	93	89	138	71	68	92	48	45
25-29	157	79	78	172	88	85	179	92	88	136	69	67
30-34	161	81	80	154	78	77	170	86	84	177	90	87
35-39	154	75	78	158	78	79	152	76	76	167	84	83
40-44	171	82	89	150	73	77	155	76	79	149	74	75
45-49	169	80	89	166	79	87	146	70	76	151	74	78
50-54	148	67	81	163	75	87	160	75	86	142	67	75
55-59	130	57	73	140	62	78	155	70	85	154	70	83
60-64	129	54	75	120	51	69	131	56	75	145	64	81
65-69	129	51	78	115	46	70	108	44	65	119	49	70
70-74	100	35	65	109	39	70	99	36	62	94	35	58
75-79	82	24	58	78	24	54	86	27	59	79	26	53
80-84	47	9	38	57	13	44	55	13	41	62	16	46
85-89	17	3	15	28	4	25	35	5	30	34	6	28
90-94	11	1	10	8	1	8	14	1	13	18	1	16
95-99	4	0	4	4	0	4	3	0	3	6	0	6
100 +	1	0	1	1	0	1	1	0	1	1	0	1

Age group	2025 Both sexes	2025 Males	2025 Females	2030 Both sexes	2030 Males	2030 Females	2035 Both sexes	2035 Males	2035 Females	2040 Both sexes	2040 Males	2040 Females
All ages	2 059	952	1 107	1 981	920	1 061	1 902	886	1 016	1 826	853	973
0-4	88	45	43	78	40	38	75	39	37	77	40	37
5-9	99	51	48	88	45	43	78	40	38	75	38	36
10-14	104	53	50	99	51	48	88	45	43	78	40	38
15-19	102	52	50	102	53	50	97	50	47	86	44	42
20-24	97	50	47	100	51	49	100	52	49	95	49	46
25-29	90	46	44	95	49	46	98	50	48	98	51	48
30-34	134	68	66	88	45	43	93	48	45	96	49	47
35-39	174	80	86	132	67	65	87	45	42	91	47	45
40-44	165	83	82	172	87	85	130	66	64	86	44	42
45-49	146	72	74	162	81	81	169	85	84	128	64	64
50-54	147	71	76	142	69	73	158	78	80	166	83	83
55-59	136	63	73	142	67	74	138	66	71	153	75	78
60-64	145	64	80	129	58	70	134	62	72	131	62	69
65-69	132	56	77	132	57	76	119	52	67	124	56	68
70-74	103	40	63	116	46	70	117	47	70	105	43	62
75-79	75	25	50	84	29	55	95	34	61	96	35	61
80-84	57	15	42	55	15	40	62	18	44	71	22	49
85-89	38	7	31	36	7	29	35	7	28	40	9	31
90-94	17	2	16	20	2	18	19	2	17	19	2	16
95-99	7	0	7	7	0	7	8	0	8	8	0	7
100 +	2	0	2	2	0	2	2	0	2	3	0	3

Age group	2045 Both sexes	2045 Males	2045 Females	2050 Both sexes	2050 Males	2050 Females
All ages	1 752	821	931	1 678	788	890
0-4	78	40	38	77	39	37
5-9	77	39	37	78	40	38
10-14	75	38	36	76	39	37
15-19	77	39	37	73	38	36
20-24	84	43	41	75	38	36
25-29	93	48	45	82	42	40
30-34	97	50	47	92	47	44
35-39	95	49	46	95	49	46
40-44	90	46	44	94	48	46
45-49	84	43	41	89	45	44
50-54	126	63	63	83	42	41
55-59	161	79	82	122	60	62
60-64	146	70	76	154	75	79
65-69	121	55	66	136	63	73
70-74	110	47	63	108	47	61
75-79	87	33	54	93	36	56
80-84	73	23	50	66	22	45
85-89	46	10	36	48	11	36
90-94	21	3	19	25	4	21
95-99	8	0	7	9	1	8
100 +	3	0	3	3	0	3

United Nations Department of Economic and Social Affairs/Population Division
World Population Prospects: The 2004 Revision, Volume II: Sex and Age Distribution of the World Population

535

POPULATION BY AGE AND SEX (in thousands)

Age group	2005 Both sexes	Males	Females	2010 Both sexes	Males	Females	2015 Both sexes	Males	Females	2020 Both sexes	Males	Females
All ages	2 307	1 055	1 252	2 269	1 040	1 229	2 243	1 032	1 211	2 216	1 025	1 191
0-4	101	52	49	125	64	61	136	70	66	134	69	65
5-9	96	49	47	100	52	49	124	64	60	135	70	66
10-14	142	72	70	96	49	46	100	51	49	124	64	60
15-19	185	95	90	141	72	69	95	49	46	99	51	48
20-24	175	89	86	182	93	89	138	71	68	92	48	45
25-29	157	79	78	172	88	85	179	92	88	136	69	67
30-34	161	81	80	154	78	77	170	86	84	177	90	87
35-39	154	75	78	158	78	79	152	76	76	167	84	83
40-44	171	82	89	150	73	77	155	76	79	149	74	75
45-49	169	80	89	166	79	87	146	70	76	151	74	78
50-54	148	67	81	163	75	87	160	75	86	142	67	75
55-59	130	57	73	140	62	78	155	70	85	154	70	83
60-64	129	54	75	120	51	69	131	56	75	145	64	81
65-69	129	51	78	115	46	70	108	44	65	119	49	70
70-74	100	35	65	109	39	70	99	36	62	94	35	58
75-79	82	24	58	78	24	54	86	27	59	79	26	53
80-84	47	9	38	57	13	44	55	13	41	62	16	46
85-89	17	3	15	28	4	25	35	5	30	34	6	28
90-94	11	1	10	8	1	8	14	1	13	18	1	16
95-99	4	0	4	4	0	4	3	0	3	6	0	6
100 +	1	0	1	1	0	1	1	0	1	1	0	1

Age group	2025 Both sexes	Males	Females	2030 Both sexes	Males	Females	2035 Both sexes	Males	Females	2040 Both sexes	Males	Females
All ages	2 173	1 011	1 162	2 123	993	1 130	2 079	977	1 102	2 048	967	1 081
0-4	116	60	57	106	54	51	110	57	54	123	63	60
5-9	133	68	65	116	60	56	105	54	51	110	56	53
10-14	135	69	66	133	68	65	116	59	56	105	54	51
15-19	122	63	60	134	69	65	132	68	64	114	59	56
20-24	97	50	47	120	62	58	132	68	64	129	67	63
25-29	90	46	44	95	49	46	118	61	57	130	67	63
30-34	134	68	66	88	45	43	93	48	45	116	60	57
35-39	174	89	86	132	67	65	87	45	42	91	47	45
40-44	165	83	82	172	87	85	130	66	64	86	44	42
45-49	146	72	74	162	81	81	169	85	84	128	64	64
50-54	147	71	76	142	69	73	158	78	80	166	83	83
55-59	136	63	73	142	67	74	138	66	71	153	75	78
60-64	145	64	80	129	58	70	134	62	72	131	62	69
65-69	132	56	77	132	57	76	119	52	67	124	56	68
70-74	103	40	63	116	46	70	117	47	70	105	43	62
75-79	75	25	50	84	29	55	95	34	61	96	35	61
80-84	57	15	42	55	15	40	62	18	44	71	22	49
85-89	38	7	31	36	7	29	35	7	28	40	9	31
90-94	17	2	16	20	2	18	19	2	17	19	2	16
95-99	7	0	7	7	0	7	8	0	8	8	0	7
100 +	2	0	2	2	0	2	2	0	2	3	0	3

Age group	2045 Both sexes	Males	Females	2050 Both sexes	Males	Females
All ages	2 027	962	1 065	2 006	957	1 050
0-4	132	68	64	131	67	63
5-9	123	63	60	131	68	64
10-14	110	56	53	122	63	59
15-19	104	53	50	108	56	53
20-24	112	58	54	102	52	49
25-29	127	66	62	110	57	53
30-34	128	66	62	126	65	61
35-39	115	59	56	126	65	62
40-44	90	46	44	114	58	55
45-49	84	43	41	89	45	44
50-54	126	63	63	83	42	41
55-59	161	79	82	122	60	62
60-64	146	70	76	154	75	79
65-69	121	55	66	136	63	73
70-74	110	47	63	108	47	61
75-79	87	33	54	93	36	56
80-84	73	23	50	66	22	45
85-89	46	10	36	48	11	36
90-94	21	3	19	25	4	21
95-99	8	0	7	9	1	8
100 +	3	0	3	3	0	3

United Nations Department of Economic and Social Affairs/Population Division
World Population Prospects: The 2004 Revision, Volume II: Sex and Age Distribution of the World Population

POPULATION BY AGE AND SEX (in thousands)

Age group	2005 Both sexes	Males	Females	2010 Both sexes	Males	Females	2015 Both sexes	Males	Females	2020 Both sexes	Males	Females
All ages	2 307	1 055	1 252	2 228	1 019	1 209	2 139	979	1 160	2 042	936	1 106
0-4	101	52	49	84	43	41	73	37	35	64	33	31
5-9	96	49	47	100	52	49	83	43	41	72	37	35
10-14	142	72	70	96	49	46	100	51	49	83	43	40
15-19	185	95	90	141	72	69	95	49	46	99	51	48
20-24	175	89	86	182	93	89	138	71	68	92	48	45
25-29	157	79	78	172	88	85	179	92	88	136	69	67
30-34	161	81	80	154	78	77	170	86	84	177	90	87
35-39	154	75	78	158	78	79	152	76	76	167	84	83
40-44	171	82	89	150	73	77	155	76	79	149	74	75
45-49	169	80	89	166	79	87	146	70	76	151	74	78
50-54	148	67	81	163	75	87	160	75	86	142	67	75
55-59	130	57	73	140	62	78	155	70	85	154	70	83
60-64	129	54	75	120	51	69	131	56	75	145	64	81
65-69	129	51	78	115	46	70	108	44	65	119	49	70
70-74	100	35	65	109	39	70	99	36	62	94	35	58
75-79	82	24	58	78	24	54	86	27	59	79	26	53
80-84	47	9	38	57	13	44	55	13	41	62	16	46
85-89	17	3	15	28	4	25	35	5	30	34	6	28
90-94	11	1	10	8	1	8	14	1	13	18	1	16
95-99	4	0	4	4	0	4	3	0	3	6	0	6
100 +	1	0	1	1	0	1	1	0	1	1	0	1

Age group	2025 Both sexes	Males	Females	2030 Both sexes	Males	Females	2035 Both sexes	Males	Females	2040 Both sexes	Males	Females
All ages	1 943	893	1 050	1 839	847	992	1 733	799	934	1 623	749	874
0-4	59	30	29	53	27	26	47	24	23	44	22	21
5-9	64	33	31	59	30	29	52	27	25	47	24	23
10-14	72	37	35	63	33	31	58	30	28	52	27	25
15-19	82	42	40	71	36	34	62	32	30	57	29	28
20-24	97	50	47	80	41	39	69	35	33	60	31	29
25-29	90	46	44	95	49	46	78	40	38	67	34	32
30-34	134	68	66	88	45	43	93	48	45	76	39	37
35-39	174	89	86	132	67	65	87	45	42	91	47	45
40-44	165	83	82	172	87	85	130	66	64	86	44	42
45-49	146	72	74	162	81	81	169	85	84	128	64	64
50-54	147	71	76	142	69	73	158	78	80	166	83	83
55-59	136	63	73	142	67	74	138	66	71	153	75	78
60-64	145	64	80	129	58	70	134	62	72	131	62	69
65-69	132	56	77	132	57	76	119	52	67	124	56	68
70-74	103	40	63	116	46	70	117	47	70	105	43	62
75-79	75	25	50	84	29	55	95	34	61	96	35	61
80-84	57	15	42	55	15	40	62	18	44	71	22	49
85-89	38	7	31	36	7	29	35	7	28	40	9	31
90-94	17	2	16	20	2	18	19	2	17	19	2	16
95-99	7	0	7	7	0	7	8	0	8	8	0	7
100 +	2	0	2	2	0	2	2	0	2	3	0	3

Age group	2045 Both sexes	Males	Females	2050 Both sexes	Males	Females
All ages	1 511	697	814	1 398	644	753
0-4	40	21	19	37	19	18
5-9	43	22	21	40	20	19
10-14	47	24	23	43	22	21
15-19	51	26	25	46	23	22
20-24	55	29	27	49	25	24
25-29	58	30	28	53	28	26
30-34	65	34	32	57	29	27
35-39	75	38	36	64	33	31
40-44	90	46	44	74	38	36
45-49	84	43	41	89	45	44
50-54	126	63	63	83	42	41
55-59	161	79	82	122	60	62
60-64	146	70	76	154	75	79
65-69	121	55	66	136	63	73
70-74	110	47	63	108	47	61
75-79	87	33	54	93	36	56
80-84	73	23	50	66	22	45
85-89	46	10	36	48	11	36
90-94	21	3	19	25	4	21
95-99	8	0	7	9	1	8
100 +	3	0	3	3	0	3

United Nations Department of Economic and Social Affairs/Population Division
World Population Prospects: The 2004 Revision, Volume II: Sex and Age Distribution of the World Population

537

POPULATION BY AGE AND SEX (in thousands)

Age group	1950 Both sexes	Males	Females	1955 Both sexes	Males	Females	1960 Both sexes	Males	Females	1965 Both sexes	Males	Females
All ages	1 443	726	717	1 613	812	801	1 888	950	939	2 163	1 088	1 076
0-4	196	100	95	255	131	124	322	164	158	358	182	176
5-9	151	74	77	186	95	91	255	131	124	316	161	156
10-14	147	72	74	149	73	76	189	97	92	253	130	124
15-19	143	73	71	145	72	74	151	74	77	187	96	92
20-24	133	68	65	141	71	70	147	72	74	150	73	76
25-29	105	53	52	130	66	64	142	72	70	144	71	73
30-34	74	38	36	103	52	51	130	66	64	140	70	69
35-39	90	46	44	72	37	35	103	52	51	128	65	63
40-44	77	39	38	87	44	43	72	37	35	100	51	50
45-49	67	34	33	75	38	37	86	43	42	70	35	34
50-54	57	29	28	63	32	32	73	37	36	82	41	41
55-59	54	27	27	53	27	27	60	30	30	68	34	34
60-64	45	22	23	45	22	23	49	24	25	55	27	28
65-69	40	20	21	42	20	22	39	19	20	42	20	22
70-74	31	15	16	31	15	16	34	16	18	31	14	16
75-79	20	10	10	21	10	11	22	10	12	23	10	13
80 +	13	6	7	14	6	7	16	7	9	17	7	10

Age group	1970 Both sexes	Males	Females	1975 Both sexes	Males	Females	1980 Both sexes	Males	Females	1985 Both sexes	Males	Females
All ages	2 390	1 202	1 188	2 678	1 346	1 332	2 698	1 332	1 366	2 793	1 362	1 431
0-4	364	185	179	377	192	185	371	189	182	381	193	187
5-9	343	174	169	358	182	176	337	171	166	344	174	169
10-14	306	155	151	341	173	168	321	163	159	314	160	155
15-19	245	125	120	304	154	150	300	149	151	294	147	147
20-24	180	92	88	242	124	118	258	126	133	269	129	140
25-29	144	70	73	178	91	87	207	101	106	232	108	125
30-34	139	68	71	141	69	72	157	76	81	186	86	99
35-39	134	67	66	136	67	69	124	58	67	141	66	75
40-44	122	62	60	131	66	65	121	58	63	113	51	62
45-49	95	48	47	118	60	59	117	58	59	109	51	58
50-54	65	33	32	91	46	45	105	53	53	105	52	53
55-59	75	37	38	61	30	31	79	39	40	92	46	47
60-64	60	30	31	69	34	35	52	26	27	68	33	35
65-69	46	22	24	53	25	27	59	28	31	45	21	23
70-74	33	15	17	37	17	20	43	20	23	48	22	26
75-79	21	9	12	23	10	13	26	12	15	30	13	17
80 +	18	8	10	18	8	11	19	8	11	21	9	13

Age group	1990 Both sexes	Males	Females	1995 Both sexes	Males	Females	2000 Both sexes	Males	Females	2005 Both sexes	Males	Females
All ages	2 741	1 322	1 419	3 177	1 557	1 620	3 398	1 665	1 732	3 577	1 753	1 824
0-4	335	170	165	355	181	174	355	181	174	322	164	158
5-9	332	169	164	337	171	166	352	179	173	352	179	173
10-14	304	154	150	335	170	165	335	170	165	351	179	172
15-19	281	141	140	311	158	153	332	168	164	332	168	164
20-24	257	125	132	292	147	145	305	154	151	325	165	161
25-29	230	105	125	266	130	137	284	142	142	296	149	147
30-34	197	86	110	240	111	129	259	126	134	277	138	138
35-39	156	70	86	206	92	114	234	108	126	254	123	131
40-44	121	56	64	164	74	89	201	89	112	229	105	124
45-49	100	45	55	133	63	70	159	72	87	196	87	109
50-54	100	46	53	117	55	62	128	60	68	154	69	85
55-59	95	46	49	115	56	59	111	52	59	122	57	65
60-64	81	40	42	106	53	53	107	51	56	104	48	56
65-69	59	28	31	85	42	43	95	46	49	96	45	51
70-74	36	17	20	56	28	28	70	34	36	79	37	42
75-79	34	15	19	30	14	16	41	20	21	52	24	28
80 +	24	10	14	29	12	17	29	12	17	35	16	20

United Nations Department of Economic and Social Affairs/Population Division
World Population Prospects: The 2004 Revision, Volume II: Sex and Age Distribution of the World Population

538

POPULATION BY AGE AND SEX (in thousands)

Age group	2005 Both sexes	2005 Males	2005 Females	2010 Both sexes	2010 Males	2010 Females	2015 Both sexes	2015 Males	2015 Females	2020 Both sexes	2020 Males	2020 Females
All ages	3 577	1 753	1 824	3 773	1 850	1 923	3 965	1 944	2 020	4 140	2 031	2 108
0-4	322	164	158	324	165	159	325	166	159	323	165	158
5-9	352	179	173	321	163	157	322	164	158	324	165	159
10-14	351	179	172	351	179	172	320	163	157	322	164	158
15-19	332	168	164	349	178	172	349	178	172	318	162	156
20-24	325	165	161	329	166	162	346	176	171	345	175	170
25-29	296	149	147	321	162	159	325	164	161	341	173	168
30-34	277	138	138	293	147	145	318	160	158	320	162	159
35-39	254	123	131	273	136	137	290	146	144	314	158	156
40-44	229	105	124	251	121	130	270	135	136	286	144	143
45-49	196	87	109	225	103	122	247	119	128	267	132	134
50-54	154	69	85	191	84	107	220	100	120	242	116	126
55-59	122	57	65	148	66	82	185	81	104	213	96	117
60-64	104	48	56	115	53	62	140	61	79	176	75	100
65-69	96	45	51	94	42	52	105	47	58	129	55	74
70-74	79	37	42	81	37	45	81	35	46	91	39	52
75-79	52	24	28	60	27	33	63	27	36	63	26	37
80-84	25	11	13	32	14	18	38	16	22	41	16	25
85-89	8	3	5	11	5	6	15	6	9	19	7	12
90-94	2	1	2	2	1	1	3	1	2	5	2	3
95-99	0	0	0	0	0	0	0	0	0	1	0	0
100 +	0	0	0	0	0	0	0	0	0	0	0	0

Age group	2025 Both sexes	2025 Males	2025 Females	2030 Both sexes	2030 Males	2030 Females	2035 Both sexes	2035 Males	2035 Females	2040 Both sexes	2040 Males	2040 Females
All ages	4 297	2 111	2 186	4 428	2 178	2 251	4 531	2 230	2 301	4 611	2 272	2 339
0-4	314	161	153	299	153	146	286	146	140	281	144	137
5-9	322	164	157	313	160	153	298	152	145	285	146	139
10-14	323	165	158	321	164	157	312	160	153	297	152	145
15-19	320	163	157	321	164	158	319	163	156	311	159	152
20-24	314	160	155	316	161	155	318	162	156	316	161	155
25-29	340	173	168	310	157	152	311	158	153	313	159	154
30-34	337	170	166	336	170	166	305	155	151	307	156	151
35-39	317	160	157	333	168	165	333	168	164	302	153	149
40-44	311	156	155	314	158	156	330	167	164	330	167	163
45-49	283	141	141	307	154	153	310	156	154	327	165	162
50-54	261	129	132	278	138	139	302	151	151	305	153	152
55-59	234	111	123	254	125	129	270	134	136	295	146	148
60-64	203	90	113	224	105	119	243	118	125	259	127	132
65-69	162	68	94	188	81	107	208	95	113	227	108	119
70-74	112	46	66	143	57	85	167	69	97	185	82	103
75-79	72	29	43	90	35	56	116	44	72	137	54	83
80-84	42	16	27	49	18	31	63	22	42	83	28	55
85-89	21	7	14	23	7	16	27	8	19	36	10	26
90-94	7	2	5	8	2	6	9	2	7	11	3	9
95-99	1	0	1	2	0	1	2	0	2	2	0	2
100 +	0	0	0	0	0	0	0	0	0	0	0	0

Age group	2045 Both sexes	2045 Males	2045 Females	2050 Both sexes	2050 Males	2050 Females
All ages	4 669	2 303	2 366	4 702	2 321	2 381
0-4	278	143	136	273	140	133
5-9	280	144	137	277	142	135
10-14	284	145	139	280	143	137
15-19	296	151	144	283	145	138
20-24	307	157	150	292	149	143
25-29	311	158	153	302	154	148
30-34	309	157	152	307	156	151
35-39	304	154	150	306	155	151
40-44	299	151	148	301	153	149
45-49	326	165	162	296	150	147
50-54	322	162	160	322	162	160
55-59	298	149	150	315	157	158
60-64	283	139	144	288	142	146
65-69	243	117	126	267	129	138
70-74	203	93	110	219	102	117
75-79	154	64	89	170	74	96
80-84	100	36	64	114	44	70
85-89	50	14	35	61	19	43
90-94	16	3	13	23	5	18
95-99	3	0	3	5	1	4
100 +	0	0	0	1	0	1

United Nations Department of Economic and Social Affairs/Population Division
World Population Prospects: The 2004 Revision, Volume II: Sex and Age Distribution of the World Population

539

POPULATION BY AGE AND SEX (in thousands)

Age group	2005 Both sexes	2005 Males	2005 Females	2010 Both sexes	2010 Males	2010 Females	2015 Both sexes	2015 Males	2015 Females	2020 Both sexes	2020 Males	2020 Females
All ages	3 577	1 753	1 824	3 810	1 868	1 941	4 063	1 994	2 068	4 317	2 122	2 195
0-4	322	164	158	360	184	177	387	198	189	403	206	197
5-9	352	179	173	321	163	157	359	183	176	385	197	189
10-14	351	179	172	351	179	172	320	163	157	358	183	176
15-19	332	168	164	349	178	172	349	178	172	318	162	156
20-24	325	165	161	329	166	162	346	176	171	345	175	170
25-29	296	149	147	321	162	159	325	164	161	341	173	168
30-34	277	138	138	293	147	145	318	160	158	320	162	159
35-39	254	123	131	273	136	137	290	146	144	314	158	156
40-44	229	105	124	251	121	130	270	135	136	286	144	143
45-49	196	87	109	225	103	122	247	119	128	267	132	134
50-54	154	69	85	191	84	107	220	100	120	242	116	126
55-59	122	57	65	148	66	82	185	81	104	213	96	117
60-64	104	48	56	115	53	62	140	61	79	176	75	100
65-69	96	45	51	94	42	52	105	47	58	129	55	74
70-74	79	37	42	81	37	45	81	35	46	91	39	52
75-79	52	24	28	60	27	33	63	27	36	63	26	37
80-84	25	11	13	32	14	18	38	16	22	41	16	25
85-89	8	3	5	11	5	6	15	6	9	19	7	12
90-94	2	1	2	2	1	1	3	1	2	5	2	3
95-99	0	0	0	0	0	0	0	0	0	1	0	0
100 +	0	0	0	0	0	0	0	0	0	0	0	0

Age group	2025 Both sexes	2025 Males	2025 Females	2030 Both sexes	2030 Males	2030 Females	2035 Both sexes	2035 Males	2035 Females	2040 Both sexes	2040 Males	2040 Females
All ages	4 556	2 243	2 313	4 774	2 354	2 420	4 978	2 458	2 519	5 181	2 564	2 618
0-4	396	202	193	386	197	188	388	198	189	406	208	198
5-9	401	205	196	394	202	193	385	197	188	386	198	189
10-14	385	196	188	401	205	196	394	201	192	384	196	188
15-19	356	182	175	383	195	188	399	204	195	392	200	192
20-24	314	160	155	353	179	173	379	193	186	395	201	194
25-29	340	173	168	310	157	152	348	177	171	374	190	184
30-34	337	170	166	336	170	166	305	155	151	344	174	169
35-39	317	160	157	333	168	165	333	168	164	302	153	149
40-44	311	156	155	314	158	156	330	167	164	330	167	163
45-49	283	141	141	307	154	153	310	156	154	327	165	162
50-54	261	129	132	278	138	139	302	151	151	305	153	152
55-59	234	111	123	254	125	129	270	134	136	295	146	148
60-64	203	90	113	224	105	119	243	118	125	259	127	132
65-69	162	68	94	188	81	107	208	95	113	227	108	119
70-74	112	46	66	143	57	85	167	69	97	185	82	103
75-79	72	29	43	90	35	56	116	44	72	137	54	83
80-84	42	16	27	49	18	31	63	22	42	83	28	55
85-89	21	7	14	23	7	16	27	8	19	36	10	26
90-94	7	2	5	8	2	6	9	2	7	11	3	9
95-99	1	0	1	2	0	1	2	0	2	2	0	2
100 +	0	0	0	0	0	0	0	0	0	0	0	0

Age group	2045 Both sexes	2045 Males	2045 Females	2050 Both sexes	2050 Males	2050 Females
All ages	5 384	2 669	2 715	5 576	2 768	2 808
0-4	424	217	207	433	222	211
5-9	404	207	197	423	216	206
10-14	386	197	188	404	207	197
15-19	382	196	187	384	197	188
20-24	388	198	190	379	193	185
25-29	390	199	191	383	195	188
30-34	370	188	182	386	196	190
35-39	340	173	168	367	186	180
40-44	299	151	148	337	171	167
45-49	326	165	162	296	150	147
50-54	322	162	160	322	162	160
55-59	298	149	150	315	157	158
60-64	283	139	144	288	142	146
65-69	243	117	126	267	129	138
70-74	203	93	110	219	102	117
75-79	154	64	89	170	74	96
80-84	100	36	64	114	44	70
85-89	50	14	35	61	19	43
90-94	16	3	13	23	5	18
95-99	3	0	3	5	1	4
100 +	0	0	0	1	0	1

United Nations Department of Economic and Social Affairs/Population Division
World Population Prospects: The 2004 Revision, Volume II: Sex and Age Distribution of the World Population

540

POPULATION BY AGE AND SEX (in thousands)

Age group	2005 Both sexes	Males	Females	2010 Both sexes	Males	Females	2015 Both sexes	Males	Females	2020 Both sexes	Males	Females
All ages	3 577	1 753	1 824	3 736	1 831	1 905	3 880	1 908	1 972	3 962	1 941	2 021
0-4	322	164	158	287	146	141	264	135	129	243	124	119
5-9	352	179	173	321	163	157	286	146	140	262	134	128
10-14	351	179	172	351	179	172	320	163	157	285	145	140
15-19	332	168	164	349	178	172	349	178	172	318	162	156
20-24	325	165	161	329	166	162	346	176	171	345	175	170
25-29	296	149	147	321	162	159	325	164	161	341	173	168
30-34	277	138	138	293	147	145	318	160	158	320	162	159
35-39	254	123	131	273	136	137	290	146	144	314	158	156
40-44	229	105	124	251	121	130	270	135	136	286	144	143
45-49	196	87	109	225	103	122	247	119	128	267	132	134
50-54	154	69	85	191	84	107	220	100	120	242	116	126
55-59	122	57	65	148	66	82	185	81	104	213	96	117
60-64	104	48	56	115	53	62	140	61	79	176	75	100
65-69	96	45	51	94	42	52	105	47	58	129	55	74
70-74	79	37	42	81	37	45	81	35	46	91	39	52
75-79	52	24	28	60	27	33	63	27	36	63	26	37
80-84	25	11	13	32	14	18	38	16	22	41	16	25
85-89	8	3	5	11	5	6	15	6	9	19	7	12
90-94	2	1	2	2	1	1	3	1	2	5	2	3
95-99	0	0	0	0	0	0	0	0	0	1	0	0
100 +	0	0	0	0	0	0	0	0	0	0	0	0

Age group	2025 Both sexes	Males	Females	2030 Both sexes	Males	Females	2035 Both sexes	Males	Females	2040 Both sexes	Males	Females
All ages	4 039	1 979	2 060	4 086	2 003	2 083	4 098	2 009	2 089	4 075	1 998	2 077
0-4	233	119	114	215	110	105	195	100	95	178	91	87
5-9	242	124	118	232	119	113	214	110	105	194	99	94
10-14	262	134	128	242	123	118	231	118	113	214	109	104
15-19	283	144	139	260	133	127	240	123	118	230	117	112
20-24	314	160	155	280	142	137	256	131	126	236	121	116
25-29	340	173	168	310	157	152	275	140	135	252	128	124
30-34	337	170	166	336	170	166	305	155	151	271	137	134
35-39	317	160	157	333	168	165	333	168	164	302	153	149
40-44	311	156	155	314	158	156	330	167	164	330	167	163
45-49	283	141	141	307	154	153	310	156	154	327	165	162
50-54	261	129	132	278	138	139	302	151	151	305	153	152
55-59	234	111	123	254	125	129	270	134	136	295	146	148
60-64	203	90	113	224	105	119	243	118	125	259	127	132
65-69	162	68	94	188	81	107	208	95	113	227	108	119
70-74	112	46	66	143	57	85	167	69	97	185	82	103
75-79	72	29	43	90	35	56	116	44	72	137	54	83
80-84	42	16	27	49	18	31	63	22	42	83	28	55
85-89	21	7	14	23	7	16	27	8	19	36	10	26
90-94	7	2	5	8	2	6	9	2	7	11	3	9
95-99	1	0	1	2	0	1	2	0	2	2	0	2
100 +	0	0	0	0	0	0	0	0	0	0	0	0

Age group	2045 Both sexes	Males	Females	2050 Both sexes	Males	Females
All ages	4 018	1 971	2 048	3 929	1 926	2 003
0-4	163	83	79	151	77	73
5-9	177	91	86	162	83	79
10-14	193	99	94	176	90	86
15-19	212	108	104	192	98	94
20-24	226	116	111	209	107	102
25-29	232	118	114	222	113	109
30-34	248	126	122	228	116	112
35-39	268	136	132	245	124	121
40-44	299	151	148	265	134	131
45-49	326	165	162	296	150	147
50-54	322	162	160	322	162	160
55-59	298	149	150	315	157	158
60-64	283	139	144	288	142	146
65-69	243	117	126	267	129	138
70-74	203	93	110	219	102	117
75-79	154	64	89	170	74	96
80-84	100	36	64	114	44	70
85-89	50	14	35	61	19	43
90-94	16	3	13	23	5	18
95-99	3	0	3	5	1	4
100 +	0	0	0	1	0	1

United Nations Department of Economic and Social Affairs/Population Division
World Population Prospects: The 2004 Revision, Volume II: Sex and Age Distribution of the World Population

541

POPULATION BY AGE AND SEX (in thousands)

Age group	1950 Both sexes	Males	Females	1955 Both sexes	Males	Females	1960 Both sexes	Males	Females	1965 Both sexes	Males	Females
All ages	734	344	390	788	369	418	851	396	455	933	430	503
0-4	119	59	61	128	64	64	142	71	71	158	79	79
5-9	96	47	49	109	54	56	118	59	59	133	66	67
10-14	83	41	42	93	46	48	107	52	54	116	58	58
15-19	72	35	37	78	38	41	88	42	46	102	49	53
20-24	61	30	32	63	29	35	70	32	38	76	34	43
25-29	54	26	28	52	23	29	55	23	32	60	25	35
30-34	46	22	25	47	22	26	46	19	27	50	20	30
35-39	40	19	21	42	20	23	42	19	24	42	17	26
40-44	35	17	19	38	18	19	38	17	21	40	17	23
45-49	29	13	16	33	16	17	34	16	18	36	15	21
50-54	25	10	15	27	12	15	31	15	16	32	14	18
55-59	22	8	13	23	9	13	25	11	13	28	13	15
60-64	18	7	11	19	7	12	20	8	12	22	10	12
65-69	14	5	9	14	5	9	15	6	10	17	7	10
70-74	10	4	6	10	4	7	11	4	7	12	4	7
75-79	6	2	4	6	2	4	7	2	4	7	2	4
80 +	3	1	2	3	1	2	4	1	3	4	1	3

Age group	1970 Both sexes	Males	Females	1975 Both sexes	Males	Females	1980 Both sexes	Males	Females	1985 Both sexes	Males	Females
All ages	1 030	476	554	1 145	528	617	1 292	596	696	1 469	680	789
0-4	174	87	87	197	99	98	226	114	113	253	127	126
5-9	149	74	74	164	82	82	188	94	94	218	109	109
10-14	130	65	65	146	73	73	163	81	81	188	94	94
15-19	111	54	57	125	61	64	142	70	72	159	78	81
20-24	91	41	50	101	47	54	114	53	62	128	58	70
25-29	64	25	39	79	32	47	88	36	51	99	40	59
30-34	53	21	32	56	19	37	69	25	44	77	29	48
35-39	48	20	28	48	19	30	51	17	34	65	24	40
40-44	41	16	24	46	19	26	47	19	28	53	20	32
45-49	38	16	22	39	16	23	46	20	25	50	22	28
50-54	34	15	20	37	16	21	40	17	23	47	21	25
55-59	29	13	16	33	14	19	36	16	20	40	17	22
60-64	25	11	14	26	11	15	29	12	17	34	15	19
65-69	18	8	10	21	9	12	22	9	13	25	10	15
70-74	13	5	8	14	6	8	16	7	9	17	7	10
75-79	7	3	5	8	3	5	9	4	5	11	4	6
80 +	5	1	3	5	2	3	6	2	4	6	2	4

Age group	1990 Both sexes	Males	Females	1995 Both sexes	Males	Females	2000 Both sexes	Males	Females	2005 Both sexes	Males	Females
All ages	1 593	739	854	1 692	788	904	1 788	829	958	1 795	835	960
0-4	259	131	129	248	125	123	237	120	118	231	116	114
5-9	244	122	121	252	126	125	241	121	120	224	113	111
10-14	215	108	107	241	121	120	249	125	124	238	119	118
15-19	178	87	91	205	101	104	235	117	118	244	121	122
20-24	133	61	72	147	68	79	185	88	97	217	105	112
25-29	102	42	60	102	43	58	120	51	69	142	65	78
30-34	86	33	52	89	35	54	82	32	51	81	32	48
35-39	70	26	44	79	30	49	77	29	48	58	22	37
40-44	59	22	37	64	25	40	73	27	46	61	22	38
45-49	50	20	30	55	22	33	61	23	38	62	22	39
50-54	48	22	26	47	20	27	53	22	31	55	21	34
55-59	45	21	24	45	21	24	44	19	25	48	20	29
60-64	37	16	20	41	19	22	41	18	23	40	16	23
65-69	29	12	17	32	14	18	35	16	19	35	15	20
70-74	20	8	12	23	10	13	25	11	15	28	12	16
75-79	12	5	7	14	5	9	16	7	10	18	7	11
80 +	7	3	5	8	3	5	11	4	7	13	5	8

United Nations Department of Economic and Social Affairs/Population Division
World Population Prospects: The 2004 Revision, Volume II: Sex and Age Distribution of the World Population

542

POPULATION BY AGE AND SEX (in thousands)

Age group	2005 Both sexes	2005 Males	2005 Females	2010 Both sexes	2010 Males	2010 Females	2015 Both sexes	2015 Males	2015 Females	2020 Both sexes	2020 Males	2020 Females
All ages	1 795	835	960	1 768	831	937	1 744	830	914	1 718	828	890
0-4	231	116	114	224	113	111	221	111	109	211	106	105
5-9	224	113	111	217	109	108	212	107	105	212	107	105
10-14	238	119	118	215	108	107	206	104	102	203	102	101
15-19	244	121	122	232	115	117	208	104	105	200	99	100
20-24	217	105	112	226	110	116	216	105	111	194	94	100
25-29	142	65	78	180	85	95	188	90	98	181	87	95
30-34	81	32	48	96	44	52	132	64	68	139	69	71
35-39	58	22	37	50	21	30	65	31	34	93	48	45
40-44	61	22	38	41	15	25	35	15	20	47	24	23
45-49	62	22	39	47	17	30	32	12	19	28	13	15
50-54	55	21	34	52	19	33	40	15	25	28	12	16
55-59	48	20	29	48	18	30	46	17	29	36	14	22
60-64	40	16	23	42	17	26	42	16	27	41	15	26
65-69	35	15	20	34	14	20	36	14	22	37	13	24
70-74	28	12	16	28	12	16	28	11	17	30	11	19
75-79	18	7	11	20	8	12	20	8	12	20	8	13
80-84	9	4	6	10	4	6	11	5	7	12	5	7
85-89	3	1	2	4	1	2	4	2	3	5	2	3
90-94	1	0	0	1	0	1	1	0	1	1	0	1
95-99	0	0	0	0	0	0	0	0	0	0	0	0
100 +	0	0	0	0	0	0	0	0	0	0	0	0

Age group	2025 Both sexes	2025 Males	2025 Females	2030 Both sexes	2030 Males	2030 Females	2035 Both sexes	2035 Males	2035 Females	2040 Both sexes	2040 Males	2040 Females
All ages	1 690	823	867	1 663	816	847	1 639	807	831	1 620	800	820
0-4	195	99	97	181	92	90	172	87	85	166	84	82
5-9	205	103	102	191	96	95	178	90	88	170	86	84
10-14	205	103	102	200	101	100	188	95	93	176	89	87
15-19	197	98	99	200	99	101	195	97	98	183	91	92
20-24	186	90	96	183	88	95	187	90	97	182	88	94
25-29	164	77	86	157	74	84	156	73	83	161	75	86
30-34	138	68	71	126	60	66	123	58	65	124	57	67
35-39	101	53	48	104	53	51	96	48	49	96	46	50
40-44	70	38	32	79	43	35	83	44	39	78	40	38
45-49	38	21	18	58	32	25	66	37	29	70	38	32
50-54	25	12	13	34	19	15	52	29	22	59	34	26
55-59	20	11	16	24	12	12	32	18	14	47	27	20
60-64	32	12	20	23	10	13	22	11	11	29	16	13
65-69	36	13	23	29	11	18	21	9	12	19	9	10
70-74	31	11	20	30	10	20	24	9	15	18	7	10
75-79	22	8	14	23	8	15	23	7	15	18	6	12
80-84	12	4	8	13	5	8	14	4	10	14	4	10
85-89	5	2	3	5	2	3	6	2	4	6	2	4
90-94	1	0	1	1	0	1	1	0	1	2	0	1
95-99	0	0	0	0	0	0	0	0	0	0	0	0
100 +	0	0	0	0	0	0	0	0	0	0	0	0

Age group	2045 Both sexes	2045 Males	2045 Females	2050 Both sexes	2050 Males	2050 Females
All ages	1 608	795	813	1 601	790	811
0-4	160	81	79	152	77	75
5-9	164	83	81	158	80	78
10-14	168	85	83	163	82	81
15-19	172	85	86	164	81	82
20-24	171	82	89	160	77	83
25-29	159	74	85	150	69	80
30-34	130	60	70	131	60	71
35-39	99	47	52	107	50	56
40-44	79	39	40	83	40	43
45-49	68	35	33	70	35	35
50-54	64	35	29	62	33	30
55-59	55	31	24	60	33	27
60-64	43	24	19	51	28	22
65-69	26	14	12	39	21	18
70-74	17	8	9	22	12	11
75-79	14	5	8	13	6	7
80-84	11	4	8	9	3	5
85-89	7	2	5	6	2	4
90-94	2	0	1	2	0	2
95-99	0	0	0	0	0	0
100 +	0	0	0	0	0	0

United Nations Department of Economic and Social Affairs/Population Division
World Population Prospects: The 2004 Revision, Volume II: Sex and Age Distribution of the World Population

543

POPULATION BY AGE AND SEX (in thousands)

Age group	2005 Both sexes	2005 Males	2005 Females	2010 Both sexes	2010 Males	2010 Females	2015 Both sexes	2015 Males	2015 Females	2020 Both sexes	2020 Males	2020 Females
All ages	1 795	835	960	1 785	840	945	1 790	853	937	1 801	870	932
0-4	231	116	114	241	121	119	250	126	124	250	126	124
5-9	224	113	111	217	109	108	228	115	113	241	121	120
10-14	238	119	118	215	108	107	206	104	102	219	110	109
15-19	244	121	122	232	115	117	208	104	105	200	99	100
20-24	217	105	112	226	110	116	216	105	111	194	94	100
25-29	142	65	78	180	85	95	188	90	98	181	87	95
30-34	81	32	48	96	44	52	132	64	68	139	69	71
35-39	58	22	37	50	21	30	65	31	34	93	48	45
40-44	61	22	38	41	15	25	35	15	20	47	24	23
45-49	62	22	39	47	17	30	32	12	19	28	13	15
50-54	55	21	34	52	19	33	40	15	25	28	12	16
55-59	48	20	29	48	18	30	46	17	29	36	14	22
60-64	40	16	23	42	17	26	42	16	27	41	15	26
65-69	35	15	20	34	14	20	36	14	22	37	13	24
70-74	28	12	16	28	12	16	28	11	17	30	11	19
75-79	18	7	11	20	8	12	20	8	12	20	8	13
80-84	9	4	6	10	4	6	11	5	7	12	5	7
85-89	3	1	2	4	1	2	4	2	3	5	2	3
90-94	1	0	0	1	0	1	1	0	1	1	0	1
95-99	0	0	0	0	0	0	0	0	0	0	0	0
100 +	0	0	0	0	0	0	0	0	0	0	0	0

Age group	2025 Both sexes	2025 Males	2025 Females	2030 Both sexes	2030 Males	2030 Females	2035 Both sexes	2035 Males	2035 Females	2040 Both sexes	2040 Males	2040 Females
All ages	1 810	883	927	1 823	896	927	1 845	911	934	1 882	932	950
0-4	234	118	116	223	113	110	222	112	110	227	115	112
5-9	243	122	120	229	116	114	219	111	109	219	110	109
10-14	233	117	116	237	119	118	226	114	112	217	109	108
15-19	212	106	107	228	113	114	232	116	117	221	110	111
20-24	186	90	96	198	96	102	214	104	110	219	106	112
25-29	164	77	86	157	74	84	170	80	90	186	88	98
30-34	138	68	71	126	60	66	123	58	65	136	63	72
35-39	101	53	48	104	53	51	96	48	49	96	46	50
40-44	70	38	32	79	43	35	83	44	39	78	40	38
45-49	38	21	18	58	32	25	66	37	29	70	38	32
50-54	25	12	13	34	19	15	52	29	22	59	34	26
55-59	26	11	15	24	12	12	32	18	14	47	27	20
60-64	32	12	20	23	10	13	22	11	11	29	16	13
65-69	36	13	23	29	11	18	21	9	12	19	9	10
70-74	31	11	20	30	10	20	24	9	15	18	7	10
75-79	22	8	14	23	8	15	23	7	15	18	6	12
80-84	12	4	8	13	5	9	14	4	10	14	4	10
85-89	5	2	3	5	2	3	6	2	4	6	2	4
90-94	1	0	1	1	0	1	1	0	1	2	0	1
95-99	0	0	0	0	0	0	0	0	0	0	0	0
100 +	0	0	0	0	0	0	0	0	0	0	0	0

Age group	2045 Both sexes	2045 Males	2045 Females	2050 Both sexes	2050 Males	2050 Females
All ages	1 931	958	973	1 988	986	1 002
0-4	231	117	114	228	115	113
5-9	225	113	111	229	115	113
10-14	217	109	108	223	113	111
15-19	212	106	107	213	106	107
20-24	208	101	107	200	97	103
25-29	192	91	102	185	87	98
30-34	152	71	81	161	75	86
35-39	108	52	57	125	60	65
40-44	79	39	40	92	45	47
45-49	68	35	33	70	35	35
50-54	64	35	29	62	33	30
55-59	55	31	24	60	33	27
60-64	43	24	19	51	28	22
65-69	26	14	12	39	21	18
70-74	17	8	9	22	12	11
75-79	14	5	8	13	6	7
80-84	11	4	8	9	3	5
85-89	7	2	5	6	2	4
90-94	2	0	1	2	0	2
95-99	0	0	0	0	0	0
100 +	0	0	0	0	0	0

United Nations Department of Economic and Social Affairs/Population Division
World Population Prospects: The 2004 Revision, Volume II: Sex and Age Distribution of the World Population

544

POPULATION BY AGE AND SEX (in thousands)

Age group	2005 Both sexes	Males	Females	2010 Both sexes	Males	Females	2015 Both sexes	Males	Females	2020 Both sexes	Males	Females
All ages	1 795	835	960	1 750	822	928	1 698	807	892	1 635	786	849
0-4	231	116	114	206	104	102	191	96	95	172	87	85
5-9	224	113	111	217	109	108	196	99	97	183	92	91
10-14	238	119	118	215	108	107	206	104	102	187	94	93
15-19	244	121	122	232	115	117	208	104	105	200	99	100
20-24	217	105	112	226	110	116	216	105	111	194	94	100
25-29	142	65	78	180	85	95	188	90	98	181	87	95
30-34	81	32	48	96	44	52	132	64	68	139	69	71
35-39	58	22	37	50	21	30	65	31	34	93	48	45
40-44	61	22	38	41	15	25	35	15	20	47	24	23
45-49	62	22	39	47	17	30	32	12	19	28	13	15
50-54	55	21	34	52	19	33	40	15	25	28	12	16
55-59	48	20	29	48	18	30	46	17	29	36	14	22
60-64	40	16	23	42	17	26	42	16	27	41	15	26
65-69	35	15	20	34	14	20	36	14	22	37	13	24
70-74	28	12	16	28	12	16	28	11	17	30	11	19
75-79	18	7	11	20	8	12	20	8	12	20	8	13
80-84	9	4	6	10	4	6	11	5	7	12	5	7
85-89	3	1	2	4	1	2	4	2	3	5	2	3
90-94	1	0	0	1	0	1	1	0	1	1	0	1
95-99	0	0	0	0	0	0	0	0	0	0	0	0
100 +	0	0	0	0	0	0	0	0	0	0	0	0

Age group	2025 Both sexes	Males	Females	2030 Both sexes	Males	Females	2035 Both sexes	Males	Females	2040 Both sexes	Males	Females
All ages	1 570	762	808	1 505	736	769	1 438	706	732	1 372	675	697
0-4	157	79	78	141	71	70	127	64	63	114	57	56
5-9	167	84	83	153	77	76	138	70	69	125	63	62
10-14	177	89	88	163	82	81	150	76	75	137	69	68
15-19	181	90	91	172	86	87	159	79	80	146	72	74
20-24	186	90	96	168	81	87	159	76	83	146	70	76
25-29	164	77	86	157	74	84	142	66	77	136	62	73
30-34	138	68	71	126	60	66	123	58	65	112	51	61
35-39	101	53	48	104	53	51	96	48	49	96	46	50
40-44	70	38	32	79	43	35	83	44	39	78	40	38
45-49	38	21	18	58	32	25	66	37	29	70	38	32
50-54	26	12	13	34	19	15	52	29	22	59	34	26
55-59	26	11	15	24	12	12	32	18	14	47	27	20
60-64	32	12	20	23	10	13	22	11	11	29	16	13
65-69	36	13	23	29	11	18	21	9	12	19	9	10
70-74	31	11	20	30	10	20	24	9	15	18	7	10
75-79	22	8	14	20	8	15	23	7	15	18	6	12
80-84	12	4	8	13	5	9	14	4	10	14	4	10
85-89	5	2	3	5	2	3	6	2	4	6	2	4
90-94	1	0	1	1	0	1	1	0	1	2	0	1
95-99	0	0	0	0	0	0	0	0	0	0	0	0
100 +	0	0	0	0	0	0	0	0	0	0	0	0

Age group	2045 Both sexes	Males	Females	2050 Both sexes	Males	Females
All ages	1 311	645	667	1 255	615	641
0-4	102	52	50	91	46	45
5-9	112	57	56	101	51	50
10-14	123	62	61	111	56	55
15-19	132	66	67	119	59	60
20-24	134	64	70	121	57	64
25-29	125	57	68	115	52	63
30-34	108	49	60	101	45	57
35-39	89	42	47	88	40	48
40-44	79	39	40	75	36	39
45-49	68	35	33	70	35	35
50-54	64	35	29	62	33	30
55-59	55	31	24	60	33	27
60-64	43	24	19	51	28	22
65-69	26	14	12	39	21	18
70-74	17	8	9	22	12	11
75-79	14	5	8	13	6	7
80-84	11	4	8	9	3	5
85-89	7	2	5	6	2	4
90-94	2	0	1	2	0	2
95-99	0	0	0	0	0	0
100 +	0	0	0	0	0	0

POPULATION BY AGE AND SEX (in thousands)

Age group	1950 Both sexes	1950 Males	1950 Females	1955 Both sexes	1955 Males	1955 Females	1960 Both sexes	1960 Males	1960 Females	1965 Both sexes	1965 Males	1965 Females
All ages	824	408	416	925	457	467	1 052	521	532	1 203	596	607
0-4	138	69	69	164	82	82	189	94	95	218	109	109
5-9	109	55	55	125	63	62	150	75	76	174	87	87
10-14	95	47	47	106	53	53	123	62	61	148	74	74
15-19	83	42	42	92	46	46	104	52	52	121	61	60
20-24	73	36	36	80	40	40	89	45	44	101	51	50
25-29	63	31	32	69	34	35	77	38	38	86	43	43
30-34	54	27	27	60	30	30	66	33	33	73	37	37
35-39	46	23	24	51	25	26	57	28	29	63	31	32
40-44	39	19	20	43	21	22	48	23	24	53	26	27
45-49	33	16	17	36	18	19	40	19	21	45	22	23
50-54	27	13	14	30	14	15	33	16	17	37	18	19
55-59	22	10	12	24	11	13	26	12	14	29	14	15
60-64	17	8	9	18	8	10	20	9	11	22	10	12
65-69	12	5	6	13	6	7	14	6	8	16	7	9
70-74	7	3	4	8	4	5	9	4	5	10	4	6
75-79	4	2	2	4	2	2	5	2	3	5	2	3
80 +	2	1	1	2	1	1	2	1	1	3	1	2

Age group	1970 Both sexes	1970 Males	1970 Females	1975 Both sexes	1975 Males	1975 Females	1980 Both sexes	1980 Males	1980 Females	1985 Both sexes	1985 Males	1985 Females
All ages	1 387	688	698	1 605	799	806	1 868	931	937	2 171	1 083	1 088
0-4	255	128	127	298	150	148	351	177	175	413	207	205
5-9	202	101	101	237	119	118	279	140	138	327	164	163
10-14	171	86	86	199	100	99	234	118	116	273	138	135
15-19	145	72	73	168	84	84	196	98	97	228	115	113
20-24	117	59	58	141	71	71	164	82	82	190	95	94
25-29	98	49	49	113	57	56	137	68	68	158	79	79
30-34	82	41	41	94	47	47	109	55	54	131	65	66
35-39	70	35	35	79	39	39	90	45	45	104	52	52
40-44	59	29	30	66	33	33	75	37	37	85	42	42
45-49	50	24	25	56	27	28	62	31	32	70	34	35
50-54	41	20	21	46	22	24	51	25	26	57	28	29
55-59	33	15	17	37	17	19	41	20	22	46	22	24
60-64	25	11	13	28	13	15	31	15	17	35	16	19
65-69	18	8	10	20	9	11	22	10	12	25	11	14
70-74	11	5	6	13	6	7	14	6	8	16	7	9
75-79	6	3	3	7	3	4	8	3	4	9	4	5
80 +	3	1	2	4	1	2	4	2	2	5	2	3

Age group	1990 Both sexes	1990 Males	1990 Females	1995 Both sexes	1995 Males	1995 Females	2000 Both sexes	2000 Males	2000 Females	2005 Both sexes	2005 Males	2005 Females
All ages	2 136	1 067	1 069	2 141	1 068	1 073	3 065	1 528	1 537	3 283	1 638	1 645
0-4	409	205	203	398	200	199	579	291	289	631	317	314
5-9	325	163	162	329	165	163	458	230	229	499	251	249
10-14	270	136	134	278	140	138	399	201	198	415	208	207
15-19	225	114	111	230	116	114	337	170	167	362	182	180
20-24	187	94	93	190	96	94	276	139	137	302	152	150
25-29	154	77	77	155	78	77	223	113	111	241	122	119
30-34	128	64	64	127	63	64	179	90	90	191	97	95
35-39	105	53	53	105	52	53	146	72	74	152	76	76
40-44	83	41	41	86	43	44	120	59	61	124	61	63
45-49	67	33	34	67	33	34	98	48	50	102	49	52
50-54	54	26	28	53	26	27	76	37	39	83	40	43
55-59	43	21	23	42	20	22	59	28	31	62	30	33
60-64	33	16	18	32	15	17	44	21	23	47	22	25
65-69	24	11	13	23	10	12	32	15	17	33	15	18
70-74	15	7	9	15	6	8	20	9	11	21	10	12
75-79	8	4	5	8	3	5	11	5	6	12	5	7
80 +	5	2	3	4	2	3	6	2	4	7	3	4

United Nations Department of Economic and Social Affairs/Population Division
World Population Prospects: The 2004 Revision, Volume II: Sex and Age Distribution of the World Population

546

POPULATION BY AGE AND SEX (in thousands)

Age group	2005 Both sexes	2005 Males	2005 Females	2010 Both sexes	2010 Males	2010 Females	2015 Both sexes	2015 Males	2015 Females	2020 Both sexes	2020 Males	2020 Females
All ages	3 283	1 638	1 645	3 800	1 899	1 900	4 381	2 194	2 186	5 042	2 530	2 511
0-4	631	317	314	735	369	366	827	416	412	924	464	459
5-9	499	251	249	590	296	293	691	347	344	785	394	391
10-14	415	208	207	489	245	243	576	290	287	677	340	337
15-19	362	182	180	407	204	203	480	241	239	567	285	282
20-24	302	152	150	350	176	174	395	198	197	467	235	232
25-29	241	122	119	283	143	140	331	167	163	376	189	187
30-34	191	97	95	220	112	108	258	132	126	304	156	149
35-39	152	76	76	173	88	85	197	102	96	233	121	112
40-44	124	61	63	137	69	69	155	79	76	178	92	86
45-49	102	49	52	112	55	58	124	62	63	141	72	69
50-54	83	40	43	92	44	48	102	49	53	113	56	57
55-59	62	30	33	74	35	39	82	39	43	91	43	48
60-64	47	22	25	54	25	29	64	29	34	72	33	38
65-69	33	15	18	38	17	21	44	20	24	52	24	29
70-74	21	10	12	24	11	14	28	13	16	33	15	18
75-79	12	5	7	14	6	8	16	7	9	18	8	10
80-84	5	2	3	6	2	3	7	3	4	8	3	5
85-89	2	1	1	2	1	1	2	1	1	2	1	2
90-94	0	0	0	0	0	0	0	0	0	0	0	0
95-99	0	0	0	0	0	0	0	0	0	0	0	0
100 +	0	0	0	0	0	0	0	0	0	0	0	0

Age group	2025 Both sexes	2025 Males	2025 Females	2030 Both sexes	2030 Males	2030 Females	2035 Both sexes	2035 Males	2035 Females	2040 Both sexes	2040 Males	2040 Females
All ages	5 800	2 915	2 885	6 655	3 348	3 307	7 590	3 821	3 769	8 577	4 320	4 257
0-4	1 030	518	512	1 137	573	564	1 228	619	609	1 292	652	640
5-9	884	444	440	993	499	494	1 102	555	548	1 197	603	594
10-14	772	388	384	872	438	434	982	493	488	1 092	550	543
15-19	666	335	331	761	383	379	861	433	429	972	488	483
20-24	553	278	275	652	328	325	747	375	372	848	426	422
25-29	447	225	222	532	268	264	631	317	313	726	365	361
30-34	350	178	172	420	213	207	504	255	249	602	305	298
35-39	278	144	135	324	166	158	393	201	192	476	243	233
40-44	212	111	102	257	133	124	302	155	147	370	190	180
45-49	163	84	78	196	102	94	239	124	115	284	146	138
50-54	129	65	64	150	77	73	182	94	88	224	115	109
55-59	102	49	52	117	58	59	137	69	67	167	85	82
60-64	80	37	43	90	43	47	104	51	53	122	61	61
65-69	59	27	33	67	30	36	76	35	40	88	42	46
70-74	40	17	23	46	20	26	52	23	29	59	27	32
75-79	22	9	12	26	11	15	31	13	18	35	15	20
80-84	9	4	6	11	5	7	14	6	9	17	7	10
85-89	3	1	2	4	1	2	4	2	3	6	2	3
90-94	1	0	0	1	0	0	1	0	1	1	0	1
95-99	0	0	0	0	0	0	0	0	0	0	0	0
100 +	0	0	0	0	0	0	0	0	0	0	0	0

Age group	2045 Both sexes	2045 Males	2045 Females	2050 Both sexes	2050 Males	2050 Females
All ages	9 600	4 836	4 764	10 653	5 364	5 289
0-4	1 336	674	662	1 373	693	680
5-9	1 266	638	628	1 314	662	652
10-14	1 188	598	590	1 258	634	624
15-19	1 083	545	538	1 179	594	586
20-24	958	481	477	1 070	538	532
25-29	827	416	412	940	472	468
30-34	699	353	346	803	404	398
35-39	574	292	282	673	341	332
40-44	452	231	221	550	280	270
45-49	350	179	171	431	220	211
50-54	267	136	131	332	169	163
55-59	207	105	102	249	126	123
60-64	151	76	75	188	94	94
65-69	105	51	54	130	64	66
70-74	69	32	37	83	39	44
75-79	41	18	23	48	22	27
80-84	19	8	12	23	9	13
85-89	7	2	4	8	3	5
90-94	1	0	1	2	1	1
95-99	0	0	0	0	0	0
100 +	0	0	0	0	0	0

POPULATION BY AGE AND SEX (in thousands)

Age group	2005 Both sexes	2005 Males	2005 Females	2010 Both sexes	2010 Males	2010 Females	2015 Both sexes	2015 Males	2015 Females	2020 Both sexes	2020 Males	2020 Females
All ages	3 283	1 638	1 645	3 803	1 901	1 902	4 423	2 216	2 208	5 158	2 589	2 569
0-4	631	317	314	738	371	367	867	436	432	999	502	497
5-9	499	251	249	590	296	293	694	349	345	823	413	410
10-14	415	208	207	489	245	243	576	290	287	679	341	338
15-19	362	182	180	407	204	203	480	241	239	567	285	282
20-24	302	152	150	350	176	174	395	198	197	467	235	232
25-29	241	122	119	283	143	140	331	167	163	376	189	187
30-34	191	97	95	220	112	108	258	132	126	304	156	149
35-39	152	76	76	173	88	85	197	102	96	233	121	112
40-44	124	61	63	137	69	69	155	79	76	178	92	86
45-49	102	49	52	112	55	58	124	62	63	141	72	69
50-54	83	40	43	92	44	48	102	49	53	113	56	57
55-59	62	30	33	74	35	39	82	39	43	91	43	48
60-64	47	22	25	54	25	29	64	29	34	72	33	38
65-69	33	15	18	38	17	21	44	20	24	52	24	29
70-74	21	10	12	24	11	14	28	13	16	33	15	18
75-79	12	5	7	14	6	8	16	7	9	18	8	10
80-84	5	2	3	6	2	3	7	3	4	8	3	5
85-89	2	1	1	2	1	1	2	1	1	2	1	2
90-94	0	0	0	0	0	0	0	0	0	0	0	0
95-99	0	0	0	0	0	0	0	0	0	0	0	0
100 +	0	0	0	0	0	0	0	0	0	0	0	0

Age group	2025 Both sexes	2025 Males	2025 Females	2030 Both sexes	2030 Males	2030 Females	2035 Both sexes	2035 Males	2035 Females	2040 Both sexes	2040 Males	2040 Females
All ages	6 003	3 017	2 986	6 970	3 506	3 463	8 055	4 055	4 000	9 252	4 660	4 592
0-4	1 121	564	557	1 253	631	622	1 385	698	687	1 509	761	748
5-9	956	480	476	1 080	543	537	1 215	611	603	1 351	680	670
10-14	809	406	403	943	474	469	1 068	537	531	1 204	606	598
15-19	669	336	333	798	401	397	932	468	464	1 058	532	526
20-24	553	278	275	655	329	326	783	393	390	917	460	457
25-29	447	225	222	532	268	264	633	319	315	761	383	379
30-34	350	178	172	420	213	207	504	255	249	605	306	299
35-39	278	144	135	324	166	158	393	201	192	476	243	233
40-44	212	111	102	257	133	124	302	155	147	370	190	180
45-49	163	84	78	196	102	94	239	124	115	284	146	138
50-54	129	65	64	150	77	73	182	94	88	224	115	109
55-59	102	49	52	117	58	59	137	69	67	167	85	82
60-64	80	37	43	90	43	47	104	51	53	122	61	61
65-69	59	27	33	67	30	36	76	35	40	88	42	46
70-74	40	17	23	46	20	26	52	23	29	59	27	32
75-79	22	9	12	26	11	15	31	13	18	35	15	20
80-84	9	4	6	11	5	7	14	6	9	17	7	10
85-89	3	1	2	4	1	2	4	2	3	6	2	3
90-94	1	0	0	1	0	0	1	0	1	1	0	1
95-99	0	0	0	0	0	0	0	0	0	0	0	0
100 +	0	0	0	0	0	0	0	0	0	0	0	0

Age group	2045 Both sexes	2045 Males	2045 Females	2050 Both sexes	2050 Males	2050 Females
All ages	10 544	5 311	5 233	11 923	6 004	5 919
0-4	1 616	815	801	1 713	864	848
5-9	1 478	745	733	1 589	801	788
10-14	1 341	675	666	1 469	740	729
15-19	1 193	600	593	1 331	670	661
20-24	1 043	524	519	1 179	592	587
25-29	895	450	446	1 023	514	509
30-34	733	370	363	869	438	431
35-39	576	293	283	705	357	348
40-44	452	231	221	552	281	271
45-49	350	179	171	431	220	211
50-54	267	136	131	332	169	163
55-59	207	105	102	249	126	123
60-64	151	76	75	188	94	94
65-69	105	51	54	130	64	66
70-74	69	32	37	83	39	44
75-79	41	18	23	48	22	27
80-84	19	8	12	23	9	13
85-89	7	2	4	8	3	5
90-94	1	0	1	2	1	1
95-99	0	0	0	0	0	0
100 +	0	0	0	0	0	0

United Nations Department of Economic and Social Affairs/Population Division
World Population Prospects: The 2004 Revision, Volume II: Sex and Age Distribution of the World Population

548

POPULATION BY AGE AND SEX (in thousands)

Age group	2005 Both sexes	Males	Females	2010 Both sexes	Males	Females	2015 Both sexes	Males	Females	2020 Both sexes	Males	Females
All ages	3 283	1 638	1 645	3 772	1 886	1 887	4 304	2 156	2 148	4 893	2 455	2 437
0-4	631	317	314	708	356	352	776	390	386	848	426	422
5-9	499	251	249	590	296	293	666	334	331	737	370	367
10-14	415	208	207	489	245	243	576	290	287	652	328	324
15-19	362	182	180	407	204	203	480	241	239	567	285	282
20-24	302	152	150	350	176	174	395	198	197	467	235	232
25-29	241	122	119	283	143	140	331	167	163	376	189	187
30-34	191	97	95	220	112	108	258	132	126	304	156	149
35-39	152	76	76	173	88	85	197	102	96	233	121	112
40-44	124	61	63	137	69	69	155	79	76	178	92	86
45-49	102	49	52	112	55	58	124	62	63	141	72	69
50-54	83	40	43	92	44	48	102	49	53	113	56	57
55-59	62	30	33	74	35	39	82	39	43	91	43	48
60-64	47	22	25	54	25	29	64	29	34	72	33	38
65-69	33	15	18	38	17	21	44	20	24	52	24	29
70-74	21	10	12	24	11	14	28	13	16	33	15	18
75-79	12	5	7	14	6	8	16	7	9	18	8	10
80-84	5	2	3	6	2	3	7	3	4	8	3	5
85-89	2	1	1	2	1	1	2	1	1	2	1	2
90-94	0	0	0	0	0	0	0	0	0	0	0	0
95-99	0	0	0	0	0	0	0	0	0	0	0	0
100 +	0	0	0	0	0	0	0	0	0	0	0	0

Age group	2025 Both sexes	Males	Females	2030 Both sexes	Males	Females	2035 Both sexes	Males	Females	2040 Both sexes	Males	Females
All ages	5 561	2 795	2 766	6 297	3 168	3 129	7 071	3 560	3 511	7 852	3 955	3 897
0-4	936	471	465	1 012	510	502	1 060	534	526	1 075	542	533
5-9	811	408	404	902	453	448	981	494	488	1 034	521	513
10-14	724	364	360	800	402	398	892	448	443	972	489	483
15-19	642	323	319	714	359	355	791	397	394	883	444	439
20-24	553	278	275	628	316	313	701	352	349	778	391	388
25-29	447	225	222	532	268	264	607	306	302	681	342	339
30-34	350	178	172	420	213	207	504	255	249	580	293	287
35-39	278	144	135	324	166	158	393	201	192	476	243	233
40-44	212	111	102	257	133	124	302	155	147	370	190	180
45-49	163	84	78	196	102	94	239	124	115	284	146	138
50-54	129	65	64	150	77	73	182	94	88	224	115	109
55-59	102	49	52	117	58	59	137	69	67	167	85	82
60-64	80	37	43	90	43	47	104	51	53	122	61	61
65-69	59	27	33	67	30	36	76	35	40	88	42	46
70-74	40	17	23	46	20	26	52	23	29	59	27	32
75-79	22	9	12	26	11	15	31	13	18	35	15	20
80-84	9	4	6	11	5	7	14	6	9	17	7	10
85-89	3	1	2	4	1	2	4	2	3	6	2	3
90-94	1	0	0	1	0	0	1	0	1	1	0	1
95-99	0	0	0	0	0	0	0	0	0	0	0	0
100 +	0	0	0	0	0	0	0	0	0	0	0	0

Age group	2045 Both sexes	Males	Females	2050 Both sexes	Males	Females
All ages	8 622	4 343	4 279	9 378	4 722	4 657
0-4	1 071	540	531	1 061	536	526
5-9	1 054	531	523	1 054	531	523
10-14	1 026	517	509	1 047	528	520
15-19	964	485	479	1 018	513	506
20-24	871	437	433	953	479	474
25-29	760	382	378	854	429	425
30-34	656	331	325	737	371	366
35-39	553	281	272	631	320	312
40-44	452	231	221	530	270	260
45-49	350	179	171	431	220	211
50-54	267	136	131	332	169	163
55-59	207	105	102	249	126	123
60-64	151	76	75	188	94	94
65-69	105	51	54	130	64	66
70-74	69	32	37	83	39	44
75-79	41	18	23	48	22	27
80-84	19	8	12	23	9	13
85-89	7	2	4	8	3	5
90-94	1	0	1	2	1	1
95-99	0	0	0	0	0	0
100 +	0	0	0	0	0	0

POPULATION BY AGE AND SEX (in thousands)

Age group	1950 Both sexes	1950 Males	1950 Females	1955 Both sexes	1955 Males	1955 Females	1960 Both sexes	1960 Males	1960 Females	1965 Both sexes	1965 Males	1965 Females
All ages	1 029	531	498	1 126	575	551	1 349	692	657	1 623	842	781
0-4	172	90	83	196	99	97	238	121	117	292	149	144
5-9	140	72	68	155	80	75	189	96	93	226	114	111
10-14	119	59	60	133	68	65	157	82	75	187	94	92
15-19	103	50	53	113	56	57	135	70	65	158	82	75
20-24	88	43	45	97	47	50	116	58	58	138	73	65
25-29	74	36	38	82	40	42	99	49	50	120	62	57
30-34	62	31	31	69	33	35	84	42	42	103	53	50
35-39	53	27	26	58	29	29	71	36	35	88	46	42
40-44	45	24	21	48	25	24	59	30	29	73	38	35
45-49	36	19	17	41	22	19	49	25	24	60	32	28
50-54	32	18	14	32	16	16	41	22	19	49	26	23
55-59	31	18	13	28	15	12	31	16	15	40	22	18
60-64	26	15	11	26	15	11	26	14	12	30	16	14
65-69	20	12	8	20	12	8	23	13	10	23	13	10
70-74	16	9	6	16	9	7	18	10	8	20	11	9
75-79	8	5	3	8	5	3	9	5	4	10	6	4
80 +	4	3	1	4	3	1	4	3	2	5	3	2

Age group	1970 Both sexes	1970 Males	1970 Females	1975 Both sexes	1975 Males	1975 Females	1980 Both sexes	1980 Males	1980 Females	1985 Both sexes	1985 Males	1985 Females
All ages	1 986	1 041	945	2 446	1 297	1 150	3 043	1 610	1 433	3 786	1 995	1 791
0-4	378	193	185	481	245	237	573	291	281	703	358	345
5-9	281	144	137	369	189	180	473	240	232	571	290	281
10-14	234	120	114	276	142	134	375	192	183	483	246	238
15-19	200	103	97	239	124	116	284	146	138	386	197	188
20-24	172	92	81	215	114	102	251	130	121	296	153	144
25-29	148	81	67	189	104	85	228	122	106	264	138	125
30-34	125	68	57	156	88	68	198	112	87	238	130	109
35-39	105	57	48	128	73	54	163	94	69	206	117	88
40-44	87	48	39	107	62	44	133	78	55	168	99	70
45-49	70	38	32	83	47	35	108	64	44	136	80	55
50-54	56	30	26	64	36	28	83	48	35	108	64	44
55-59	43	23	20	48	26	22	63	35	28	81	46	34
60-64	33	18	16	36	19	17	45	24	21	59	32	27
65-69	23	12	11	25	13	12	32	16	15	40	21	19
70-74	16	8	7	16	8	8	20	10	10	26	13	13
75-79	11	6	5	8	4	4	11	5	6	14	7	7
80 +	5	3	2	6	3	3	6	3	3	8	4	4

Age group	1990 Both sexes	1990 Males	1990 Females	1995 Both sexes	1995 Males	1995 Females	2000 Both sexes	2000 Males	2000 Females	2005 Both sexes	2005 Males	2005 Females
All ages	4 334	2 268	2 066	4 808	2 503	2 305	5 306	2 749	2 557	5 853	3 020	2 834
0-4	623	318	305	550	281	269	575	294	281	636	326	310
5-9	699	356	343	621	317	304	549	281	268	574	294	280
10-14	570	290	280	699	356	343	621	317	304	549	281	268
15-19	482	245	237	569	289	280	698	355	343	620	317	304
20-24	385	197	188	482	245	237	569	289	280	698	355	343
25-29	296	153	143	384	197	188	482	245	237	569	289	280
30-34	263	138	125	296	153	143	385	197	188	482	245	237
35-39	236	129	108	262	137	124	295	152	143	384	197	187
40-44	203	116	87	234	127	107	260	136	124	293	151	142
45-49	164	96	68	199	113	86	230	125	105	257	134	122
50-54	130	76	53	158	92	66	193	109	84	225	122	103
55-59	101	59	42	122	71	51	151	87	64	185	104	81
60-64	72	41	32	92	53	39	113	65	48	141	80	61
65-69	50	26	23	62	34	28	81	46	35	101	56	44
70-74	31	15	16	40	20	20	51	27	25	68	37	31
75-79	18	8	10	23	10	12	30	14	16	39	19	20
80 +	11	5	6	15	6	9	22	9	13	31	13	18

United Nations Department of Economic and Social Affairs/Population Division
World Population Prospects: The 2004 Revision, Volume II: Sex and Age Distribution of the World Population

550

POPULATION BY AGE AND SEX (in thousands)

Age group	2005 Both sexes	2005 Males	2005 Females	2010 Both sexes	2010 Males	2010 Females	2015 Both sexes	2015 Males	2015 Females	2020 Both sexes	2020 Males	2020 Females
All ages	5 853	3 020	2 834	6 439	3 308	3 130	7 018	3 593	3 425	7 538	3 846	3 692
0-4	636	326	310	689	353	336	701	359	342	663	340	323
5-9	574	294	280	636	326	310	689	353	336	700	359	342
10-14	549	281	268	575	294	281	636	326	310	689	353	336
15-19	620	317	304	549	281	268	575	294	281	636	326	310
20-24	698	355	343	621	317	304	550	281	269	575	295	281
25-29	569	289	280	698	355	343	621	317	304	550	281	269
30-34	482	245	237	569	289	280	698	355	343	621	318	304
35-39	384	197	187	481	245	236	568	289	279	697	355	342
40-44	293	151	142	382	195	186	479	243	235	566	288	278
45-49	257	134	122	290	149	141	378	193	185	474	241	233
50-54	225	122	103	251	131	120	285	146	139	372	189	182
55-59	185	104	81	217	116	101	243	126	117	276	141	135
60-64	141	80	61	174	96	78	205	108	96	230	118	113
65-69	101	56	44	127	70	56	158	85	73	187	96	91
70-74	68	37	31	85	46	39	108	58	51	136	71	66
75-79	39	19	20	53	27	26	67	34	33	87	44	43
80-84	20	9	11	27	12	15	37	17	19	48	22	25
85-89	8	3	5	11	4	7	16	6	9	22	9	13
90-94	2	1	1	3	1	2	5	2	3	7	2	5
95-99	0	0	0	1	0	0	1	0	1	2	0	1
100 +	0	0	0	0	0	0	0	0	0	0	0	0

Age group	2025 Both sexes	2025 Males	2025 Females	2030 Both sexes	2030 Males	2030 Females	2035 Both sexes	2035 Males	2035 Females	2040 Both sexes	2040 Males	2040 Females
All ages	7 976	4 057	3 919	8 345	4 232	4 113	8 685	4 392	4 293	9 015	4 547	4 467
0-4	604	310	295	563	289	275	564	289	275	590	302	288
5-9	662	339	323	604	310	294	563	289	275	564	289	275
10-14	701	359	342	663	340	323	604	310	295	564	289	275
15-19	689	353	336	701	359	342	663	340	323	605	310	295
20-24	637	326	311	690	353	336	701	359	342	664	340	324
25-29	576	295	281	637	327	311	691	354	337	702	360	342
30-34	551	282	269	577	296	281	638	327	311	691	354	337
35-39	621	317	303	551	282	269	577	296	281	638	327	311
40-44	694	353	341	618	316	302	549	281	268	575	295	280
45-49	561	285	276	688	350	338	614	314	300	545	279	266
50-54	467	238	229	552	280	273	679	345	335	606	309	297
55-59	361	183	178	455	229	226	540	272	268	664	335	329
60-64	263	132	131	345	172	173	436	217	219	518	258	260
65-69	212	105	106	243	119	124	321	157	164	407	198	209
70-74	163	81	82	187	90	97	216	102	114	287	136	151
75-79	110	54	56	134	63	71	155	70	85	181	82	100
80-84	62	29	33	81	37	44	100	43	56	117	49	68
85-89	29	12	17	38	16	22	51	20	30	64	25	39
90-94	10	3	6	14	5	9	19	6	12	25	9	17
95-99	2	1	2	3	1	2	5	1	3	7	2	5
100 +	0	0	0	0	0	0	1	0	1	1	0	1

Age group	2045 Both sexes	2045 Males	2045 Females	2050 Both sexes	2050 Males	2050 Females
All ages	9 313	4 687	4 626	9 553	4 797	4 756
0-4	598	307	292	583	299	285
5-9	590	302	288	599	307	292
10-14	565	289	275	590	302	288
15-19	564	289	275	565	290	276
20-24	606	310	295	565	290	275
25-29	665	341	324	607	311	296
30-34	703	360	342	665	341	324
35-39	691	354	337	703	360	342
40-44	636	326	310	689	353	336
45-49	571	292	279	632	324	308
50-54	539	275	264	565	289	276
55-59	593	301	293	528	268	260
60-64	639	319	320	573	288	285
65-69	486	238	248	602	296	306
70-74	366	173	193	440	209	231
75-79	243	109	133	312	141	171
80-84	138	58	81	188	79	109
85-89	76	29	48	92	34	58
90-94	33	11	22	40	13	28
95-99	9	2	7	12	3	9
100 +	1	0	1	2	0	2

United Nations Department of Economic and Social Affairs/Population Division
World Population Prospects: The 2004 Revision, Volume II: Sex and Age Distribution of the World Population

551

POPULATION BY AGE AND SEX (in thousands)

Age group	2005			2010			2015			2020		
	Both sexes	Males	Females	Both sexes	Males	Females	Both sexes	Males	Females	Both sexes	Males	Females
All ages	5 853	3 020	2 834	6 502	3 341	3 161	7 194	3 683	3 511	7 861	4 012	3 849
0-4	636	326	310	753	385	367	814	417	397	809	415	394
5-9	574	294	280	636	326	310	752	385	367	813	417	397
10-14	549	281	268	575	294	281	636	326	310	752	385	367
15-19	620	317	304	549	281	268	575	294	281	636	326	310
20-24	698	355	343	621	317	304	550	281	269	575	295	281
25-29	569	289	280	698	355	343	621	317	304	550	281	269
30-34	482	245	237	569	289	280	698	355	343	621	318	304
35-39	384	197	187	481	245	236	568	289	279	697	355	342
40-44	293	151	142	382	195	186	479	243	235	566	288	278
45-49	257	134	122	290	149	141	378	193	185	474	241	233
50-54	225	122	103	251	131	120	285	146	139	372	189	182
55-59	185	104	81	217	116	101	243	126	117	276	141	135
60-64	141	80	61	174	96	78	205	108	96	230	118	113
65-69	101	56	44	127	70	56	158	85	73	187	96	91
70-74	68	37	31	85	46	39	108	58	51	136	71	66
75-79	39	19	20	53	27	26	67	34	33	87	44	43
80-84	20	9	11	27	12	15	37	17	19	48	22	25
85-89	8	3	5	11	4	7	16	6	9	22	9	13
90-94	2	1	1	3	1	2	5	2	3	7	2	5
95-99	0	0	0	1	0	0	1	0	1	2	0	1
100 +	0	0	0	0	0	0	0	0	0	0	0	0

Age group	2025			2030			2035			2040		
	Both sexes	Males	Females	Both sexes	Males	Females	Both sexes	Males	Females	Both sexes	Males	Females
All ages	8 443	4 296	4 147	8 967	4 550	4 416	9 487	4 803	4 684	10 042	5 074	4 968
0-4	750	384	365	717	368	350	746	382	364	816	418	398
5-9	809	414	394	750	384	365	717	368	350	746	382	364
10-14	814	417	397	809	414	394	750	384	366	718	368	350
15-19	752	385	367	814	417	397	809	415	394	750	384	366
20-24	637	326	311	753	386	367	814	417	397	810	415	395
25-29	576	295	281	637	327	311	753	386	367	815	418	397
30-34	551	282	269	577	296	281	638	327	311	754	386	367
35-39	621	317	303	551	282	269	577	296	281	638	327	311
40-44	694	353	341	618	316	302	549	281	268	575	295	280
45-49	561	285	276	688	350	338	614	314	300	545	279	266
50-54	467	236	230	553	280	273	679	345	335	606	309	297
55-59	361	183	178	455	229	226	540	272	268	664	335	329
60-64	263	132	131	345	172	173	436	217	219	518	258	260
65-69	212	105	106	243	119	124	321	157	164	407	198	209
70-74	163	81	82	187	90	97	216	102	114	287	136	151
75-79	110	54	56	134	63	71	155	70	85	181	82	100
80-84	62	29	33	81	37	44	100	43	56	117	49	68
85-89	29	12	17	38	16	22	51	20	30	64	25	39
90-94	10	3	6	14	5	9	19	6	12	25	9	17
95-99	2	1	2	3	1	2	5	1	3	7	2	5
100 +	0	0	0	0	0	0	1	0	1	1	0	1

Age group	2045			2050		
	Both sexes	Males	Females	Both sexes	Males	Females
All ages	10 610	5 351	5 259	11 147	5 613	5 534
0-4	868	445	424	882	452	430
5-9	816	418	398	868	445	424
10-14	746	382	364	816	418	398
15-19	718	368	350	746	382	364
20-24	751	385	366	719	368	350
25-29	810	415	395	752	385	366
30-34	815	418	397	811	416	395
35-39	753	386	367	815	418	397
40-44	636	326	310	751	385	366
45-49	571	292	279	632	324	308
50-54	539	275	264	565	289	276
55-59	593	301	293	528	268	260
60-64	639	319	320	573	288	285
65-69	486	238	248	602	296	306
70-74	366	173	193	440	209	231
75-79	243	109	133	312	141	171
80-84	138	58	81	188	79	109
85-89	76	29	48	92	34	58
90-94	33	11	22	40	13	28
95-99	9	2	7	12	3	9
100 +	1	0	1	2	0	2

United Nations Department of Economic and Social Affairs/Population Division
World Population Prospects: The 2004 Revision, Volume II: Sex and Age Distribution of the World Population

POPULATION BY AGE AND SEX (in thousands)

Age group	2005 Both sexes	2005 Males	2005 Females	2010 Both sexes	2010 Males	2010 Females	2015 Both sexes	2015 Males	2015 Females	2020 Both sexes	2020 Males	2020 Females
All ages	5 853	3 020	2 834	6 375	3 276	3 099	6 841	3 503	0 000	7 216	3 681	3 535
0-4	636	326	310	626	321	305	587	301	286	516	265	252
5-9	574	294	280	636	326	310	626	321	305	587	301	286
10-14	549	281	268	575	294	281	636	326	310	626	321	305
15-19	620	317	304	549	281	268	575	294	281	636	326	310
20-24	698	355	343	621	317	304	550	281	269	575	295	281
25-29	569	289	280	698	355	343	621	317	304	550	281	269
30-34	482	245	237	569	289	280	698	355	343	621	318	304
35-39	384	197	187	481	245	236	568	289	279	697	355	342
40-44	293	151	142	382	195	186	479	243	235	566	288	278
45-49	257	134	122	290	149	141	378	193	185	474	241	233
50-54	225	122	103	251	131	120	285	146	139	372	189	182
55-59	185	104	81	217	116	101	243	126	117	276	141	135
60-64	141	80	61	174	96	78	205	108	96	230	118	113
65-69	101	56	44	127	70	56	158	85	73	187	96	91
70-74	68	37	31	85	46	39	108	58	51	136	71	66
75-79	39	19	20	53	27	26	67	34	33	87	44	43
80-84	20	9	11	27	12	15	37	17	19	48	22	25
85-89	8	3	5	11	4	7	16	6	9	22	9	13
90-94	2	1	1	3	1	2	5	2	3	7	2	5
95-99	0	0	0	1	0	0	1	0	1	2	0	1
100 +	0	0	0	0	0	0	0	0	0	0	0	0

Age group	2025 Both sexes	2025 Males	2025 Females	2030 Both sexes	2030 Males	2030 Females	2035 Both sexes	2035 Males	2035 Females	2040 Both sexes	2040 Males	2040 Females
All ages	7 508	3 817	3 691	7 728	3 915	3 812	7 898	3 989	3 909	8 032	4 044	3 988
0-4	459	235	224	413	212	201	395	202	193	392	201	191
5-9	516	265	252	459	235	224	413	212	201	395	202	193
10-14	588	301	287	517	265	252	459	235	224	413	212	202
15-19	626	321	305	588	301	287	517	265	252	460	236	224
20-24	637	326	311	627	321	306	589	302	287	518	265	252
25-29	576	295	281	637	327	311	628	322	306	590	302	287
30-34	551	282	269	577	296	281	638	327	311	628	322	306
35-39	621	317	303	551	282	269	577	296	281	638	327	311
40-44	694	353	341	618	316	302	549	281	268	575	295	280
45-49	561	285	276	688	350	338	614	314	300	545	279	266
50-54	467	236	230	553	280	273	679	345	335	606	309	297
55-59	361	183	178	455	229	226	540	272	268	664	335	329
60-64	263	132	131	345	172	173	436	217	219	518	258	260
65-69	212	105	106	243	119	124	321	157	164	407	198	209
70-74	163	81	82	187	90	97	216	102	114	287	136	151
75-79	110	54	56	134	63	71	155	70	85	181	82	100
80-84	62	29	33	81	37	44	100	43	50	117	49	68
85-89	29	12	17	38	16	22	51	20	30	64	25	39
90-94	10	3	6	14	5	9	19	6	12	25	9	17
95-99	2	1	2	3	1	2	5	1	3	7	2	5
100 +	0	0	0	0	0	0	1	0	1	1	0	1

Age group	2045 Both sexes	2045 Males	2045 Females	2050 Both sexes	2050 Males	2050 Females
All ages	8 107	4 069	4 038	8 110	4 057	4 052
0-4	374	192	183	345	177	168
5-9	392	201	191	375	192	183
10-14	396	203	193	393	201	192
15-19	414	212	202	396	203	193
20-24	461	236	225	415	213	202
25-29	519	266	253	462	237	225
30-34	590	303	288	520	267	253
35-39	628	322	306	590	303	288
40-44	636	326	310	627	321	305
45-49	571	292	279	632	324	308
50-54	539	275	264	565	289	276
55-59	593	301	293	528	268	260
60-64	639	319	320	573	288	285
65-69	486	238	248	602	296	306
70-74	366	173	193	440	209	231
75-79	243	109	133	312	141	171
80-84	138	58	81	188	79	109
85-89	76	29	48	92	34	58
90-94	33	11	22	40	13	28
95-99	9	2	7	12	3	9
100 +	1	0	1	2	0	2

POPULATION BY AGE AND SEX (in thousands)

Age group	1950 Both sexes	Males	Females	1955 Both sexes	Males	Females	1960 Both sexes	Males	Females	1965 Both sexes	Males	Females
All ages	2 567	1 158	1 409	2 629	1 200	1 429	2 779	1 275	1 503	2 971	1 384	1 588
0-4	222	112	111	262	133	130	270	137	132	286	146	141
5-9	233	116	117	214	107	107	249	126	123	284	144	140
10-14	247	120	127	226	112	114	229	115	113	248	126	122
15-19	245	117	127	239	116	123	242	119	123	216	108	108
20-24	234	106	128	237	113	123	240	114	126	228	113	115
25-29	186	80	106	226	102	124	245	115	130	240	116	124
30-34	120	52	69	180	77	103	225	97	128	237	113	124
35-39	153	61	92	115	49	66	171	73	98	226	101	125
40-44	186	91	95	147	58	89	122	50	71	178	76	103
45-49	162	72	90	177	86	90	146	59	88	114	48	65
50-54	129	54	75	152	67	85	173	88	85	142	56	87
55-59	110	51	59	119	49	69	138	57	80	166	79	87
60-64	99	39	60	98	44	54	116	48	68	136	58	79
65-69	85	33	52	85	32	53	84	34	50	100	39	61
70-74	68	26	42	67	25	42	56	20	36	73	31	42
75-79	49	17	32	47	17	30	40	14	26	52	18	34
80 +	39	13	27	40	12	27	34	10	24	45	14	31

Age group	1970 Both sexes	Males	Females	1975 Both sexes	Males	Females	1980 Both sexes	Males	Females	1985 Both sexes	Males	Females
All ages	3 140	1 473	1 666	3 302	1 555	1 747	3 413	1 607	1 807	3 545	1 669	1 875
0-4	269	137	132	274	139	135	259	132	127	277	142	135
5-9	298	151	146	272	138	134	272	138	134	264	134	130
10-14	283	143	139	295	150	144	273	138	134	277	141	136
15-19	236	121	115	281	143	137	293	150	143	277	143	134
20-24	219	109	110	242	124	119	279	142	138	298	150	148
25-29	230	113	116	226	112	114	247	124	123	287	143	144
30-34	242	117	126	231	114	118	227	111	116	247	122	125
35-39	239	113	125	241	115	126	228	111	118	224	108	116
40-44	227	101	126	234	110	124	237	112	125	223	106	116
45-49	178	75	103	220	97	122	229	106	122	230	107	123
50-54	112	47	65	177	72	104	212	92	120	219	99	120
55-59	138	53	85	110	45	65	168	67	101	202	85	116
60-64	157	73	84	131	50	82	103	40	62	156	60	96
65-69	124	51	73	139	62	77	120	44	76	91	34	57
70-74	85	32	53	103	40	63	117	49	68	102	35	67
75-79	55	22	33	64	22	42	80	29	51	89	34	55
80 +	49	15	34	60	20	40	69	22	47	83	26	57

Age group	1990 Both sexes	Males	Females	1995 Both sexes	Males	Females	2000 Both sexes	Males	Females	2005 Both sexes	Males	Females
All ages	3 698	1 749	1 949	3 628	1 709	1 919	3 500	1 637	1 862	3 431	1 600	1 831
0-4	290	148	142	236	121	115	185	95	90	150	77	73
5-9	281	143	138	278	142	136	235	120	115	176	91	86
10-14	263	133	130	270	137	133	273	139	134	247	127	121
15-19	275	140	135	255	129	126	258	131	127	284	144	139
20-24	279	144	135	267	136	132	235	118	117	255	131	125
25-29	304	155	149	268	137	131	250	124	126	220	111	109
30-34	293	146	148	289	146	144	255	127	128	245	122	123
35-39	246	121	125	277	136	141	274	135	138	245	120	125
40-44	223	107	116	232	112	120	261	126	135	277	134	143
45-49	218	103	115	209	98	112	216	103	114	246	117	130
50-54	220	101	119	204	93	111	194	88	106	209	97	113
55-59	209	92	117	203	90	114	188	83	105	167	74	93
60-64	192	79	114	189	79	110	185	78	107	178	75	103
65-69	146	53	93	170	65	105	167	66	101	165	65	100
70-74	81	28	53	123	41	82	143	51	93	144	53	91
75-79	78	24	54	62	20	42	95	29	66	117	37	80
80 +	99	33	67	95	28	67	84	23	61	105	27	77

United Nations Department of Economic and Social Affairs/Population Division
World Population Prospects: The 2004 Revision, Volume II: Sex and Age Distribution of the World Population

POPULATION BY AGE AND SEX (in thousands)

Age group	2005 Both sexes	Males	Females	2010 Both sexes	Males	Females	2015 Both sexes	Males	Females	2020 Both sexes	Males	Females
All ages	3 431	1 600	1 831	3 358	1 563	1 795	3 288	1 531	1 757	3 214	1 499	1 716
0-4	150	77	73	151	78	74	155	80	76	154	79	75
5-9	176	91	86	149	77	72	151	77	73	155	79	75
10-14	247	127	121	176	90	85	149	77	72	150	77	73
15-19	284	144	139	245	125	119	173	89	84	146	75	71
20-24	255	131	125	278	141	137	240	123	117	169	87	82
25-29	220	111	109	250	127	123	273	138	135	235	120	115
30-34	245	122	123	216	108	107	245	125	121	269	136	133
35-39	245	120	125	241	119	122	212	106	106	242	122	120
40-44	277	134	143	240	116	123	236	116	120	208	103	105
45-49	246	117	130	269	128	141	233	112	122	231	112	119
50-54	209	97	113	237	110	127	260	122	138	226	107	120
55-59	167	74	93	199	89	110	226	102	124	249	114	135
60-64	178	75	103	155	66	90	186	80	106	213	93	120
65-69	165	65	100	161	64	98	142	57	85	171	70	101
70-74	144	53	91	142	51	91	140	51	89	124	46	78
75-79	117	37	80	114	38	76	113	37	76	113	37	76
80-84	65	17	48	83	22	60	81	24	58	82	23	59
85-89	24	6	18	39	9	30	50	12	38	50	13	37
90-94	12	3	9	10	2	8	18	4	14	23	5	19
95-99	3	1	2	3	1	3	3	1	2	5	1	4
100 +	0	0	0	0	0	0	0	0	0	0	0	0

Age group	2025 Both sexes	Males	Females	2030 Both sexes	Males	Females	2035 Both sexes	Males	Females	2040 Both sexes	Males	Females
All ages	3 129	1 461	1 668	3 029	1 416	1 613	2 917	1 364	1 553	2 800	1 309	1 491
0-4	141	72	68	124	64	60	113	58	55	111	57	54
5-9	153	78	74	140	72	68	123	63	60	112	58	55
10-14	154	79	75	152	78	74	139	72	68	123	63	60
15-19	148	76	72	152	78	74	150	77	73	137	70	67
20-24	142	73	69	143	74	70	147	76	72	146	75	71
25-29	164	84	80	138	71	67	139	72	68	143	74	70
30-34	231	118	113	161	82	79	135	69	65	136	70	66
35-39	265	133	132	220	116	112	158	81	77	132	68	64
40-44	238	120	118	262	131	131	225	114	111	156	80	76
45-49	204	100	104	234	117	117	258	128	129	222	112	110
50-54	224	107	117	199	96	102	228	113	115	252	124	128
55-59	217	100	117	216	101	115	192	92	100	221	108	110
60-64	235	104	131	206	92	114	205	94	111	183	85	98
65-69	196	82	114	217	92	125	191	82	109	191	84	107
70-74	150	57	92	173	67	106	193	77	116	170	69	101
75-79	101	34	67	123	43	80	143	51	92	160	58	102
80-84	83	24	59	75	22	53	92	28	64	108	33	75
85-89	51	12	39	53	13	40	48	12	36	60	15	45
90-94	24	5	19	25	5	20	26	5	22	24	4	20
95-99	7	1	6	8	1	7	8	1	7	9	1	8
100 +	1	0	1	1	0	1	1	0	1	2	0	1

Age group	2045 Both sexes	Males	Females	2050 Both sexes	Males	Females
All ages	2 682	1 254	1 428	2 565	1 201	1 363
0-4	114	59	55	114	59	56
5-9	111	57	54	114	58	55
10-14	112	58	54	110	57	54
15-19	120	62	58	110	56	53
20-24	133	68	65	116	60	56
25-29	142	73	69	129	66	63
30-34	140	72	68	139	71	67
35-39	134	69	65	138	71	67
40-44	130	67	63	132	68	64
45-49	154	78	76	128	66	63
50-54	217	109	109	151	76	75
55-59	245	119	126	211	105	107
60-64	211	101	111	235	112	123
65-69	171	77	94	198	91	107
70-74	171	71	100	154	66	88
75-79	143	53	90	144	55	89
80-84	122	38	83	109	35	74
85-89	71	18	53	81	21	60
90-94	31	6	25	38	7	31
95-99	9	1	8	11	1	10
100 +	2	0	2	2	0	2

United Nations Department of Economic and Social Affairs/Population Division
World Population Prospects: The 2004 Revision, Volume II: Sex and Age Distribution of the World Population

555

POPULATION BY AGE AND SEX (in thousands)

Age group	2005 Both sexes	Males	Females	2010 Both sexes	Males	Females	2015 Both sexes	Males	Females	2020 Both sexes	Males	Females
All ages	3 431	1 600	1 831	3 389	1 579	1 810	3 367	1 571	1 796	3 349	1 568	1 782
0-4	150	77	73	182	93	89	204	105	99	209	107	102
5-9	176	91	86	149	77	72	181	93	88	203	104	99
10-14	247	127	121	176	90	85	149	77	72	180	93	88
15-19	284	144	139	245	125	119	173	89	84	146	75	71
20-24	255	131	125	278	141	137	240	123	117	169	87	82
25-29	220	111	109	250	127	123	273	138	135	235	120	115
30-34	245	122	123	216	108	107	245	125	121	269	136	133
35-39	245	120	125	241	119	122	212	106	106	242	122	120
40-44	277	134	143	240	116	123	236	116	120	208	103	105
45-49	246	117	130	269	128	141	233	112	122	231	112	119
50-54	209	97	113	237	110	127	260	122	138	226	107	120
55-59	167	74	93	199	89	110	226	102	124	249	114	135
60-64	178	75	103	155	66	90	186	80	106	213	93	120
65-69	165	65	100	161	64	98	142	57	85	171	70	101
70-74	144	53	91	142	51	91	140	51	89	124	46	78
75-79	117	37	80	114	38	76	113	37	76	113	37	76
80-84	65	17	48	83	22	60	81	24	58	82	23	59
85-89	24	6	18	39	9	30	50	12	38	50	13	37
90-94	12	3	9	10	2	8	18	4	14	23	5	19
95-99	3	1	2	3	1	3	3	1	2	5	1	4
100 +	0	0	0	0	0	0	0	0	0	0	0	0

Age group	2025 Both sexes	Males	Females	2030 Both sexes	Males	Females	2035 Both sexes	Males	Females	2040 Both sexes	Males	Females
All ages	3 311	1 554	1 756	3 253	1 530	1 722	3 192	1 505	1 687	3 144	1 486	1 658
0-4	187	96	91	167	86	81	165	85	80	180	93	88
5-9	208	107	101	186	96	91	166	85	81	165	85	80
10-14	203	104	99	208	107	101	186	95	90	166	85	81
15-19	178	91	87	200	103	97	205	106	100	183	94	89
20-24	142	73	69	174	89	84	196	101	95	201	103	98
25-29	164	84	80	138	71	67	169	87	82	192	98	93
30-34	231	118	113	161	82	79	135	69	65	166	85	81
35-39	265	133	132	228	116	112	158	81	77	132	68	64
40-44	238	120	118	262	131	131	225	114	111	156	80	76
45-49	204	100	104	234	117	117	258	128	129	222	112	110
50-54	224	107	117	199	96	102	228	113	115	252	124	128
55-59	217	100	117	216	101	115	192	92	100	221	108	113
60-64	235	104	131	206	92	114	205	94	111	183	85	98
65-69	196	82	114	217	92	125	191	82	109	191	84	107
70-74	150	57	92	173	67	106	193	77	116	170	69	101
75-79	101	34	67	123	43	80	143	51	92	160	58	102
80-84	83	24	59	75	22	53	92	28	64	108	33	75
85-89	51	12	39	53	13	40	48	12	36	60	15	45
90-94	24	5	19	25	5	20	26	5	22	24	4	20
95-99	7	1	6	8	1	7	8	1	7	9	1	8
100 +	1	0	1	1	0	1	1	0	1	2	0	1

Age group	2045 Both sexes	Males	Females	2050 Both sexes	Males	Females
All ages	3 108	1 473	1 635	3 075	1 463	1 612
0-4	196	101	95	199	102	97
5-9	180	92	87	196	101	95
10-14	164	84	80	179	92	87
15-19	163	84	79	162	83	79
20-24	179	92	87	159	82	77
25-29	197	101	96	175	90	85
30-34	188	97	92	194	100	94
35-39	164	84	80	186	95	91
40-44	130	67	63	162	83	79
45-49	154	78	76	128	66	63
50-54	217	109	109	151	76	75
55-59	245	119	126	211	105	107
60-64	211	101	111	235	112	123
65-69	171	77	94	198	91	107
70-74	171	71	100	154	66	88
75-79	143	53	90	144	55	89
80-84	122	38	83	109	35	74
85-89	71	18	53	81	21	60
90-94	31	6	25	38	7	31
95-99	9	1	8	11	1	10
100 +	2	0	2	2	0	2

United Nations Department of Economic and Social Affairs/Population Division
World Population Prospects: The 2004 Revision, Volume II: Sex and Age Distribution of the World Population

556

POPULATION BY AGE AND SEX (in thousands)

Age group	2005			2010			2015			2020		
	Both sexes	Males	Females	Both sexes	Males	Females	Both sexes	Males	Females	Both sexes	Males	Females
All ages	3 431	1 600	1 831	3 328	1 548	1 780	3 209	1 490	1 719	3 079	1 429	1 650
0-4	150	77	73	121	62	59	107	55	52	97	50	47
5-9	176	91	86	149	77	72	120	62	59	106	54	52
10-14	247	127	121	176	90	85	149	77	72	120	62	58
15-19	284	144	139	245	125	119	173	89	84	146	75	71
20-24	255	131	125	278	141	137	240	123	117	169	87	82
25-29	220	111	109	250	127	123	273	138	135	235	120	115
30-34	245	122	123	216	108	107	245	125	121	269	136	133
35-39	245	120	125	241	119	122	212	106	106	242	122	120
40-44	277	134	143	240	116	123	236	116	120	208	103	105
45-49	246	117	130	269	128	141	233	112	122	231	112	119
50-54	209	97	113	237	110	127	260	122	138	226	107	120
55-59	167	74	93	199	89	110	226	102	124	249	114	135
60-64	178	75	103	155	66	90	186	80	106	213	93	120
65-69	165	65	100	161	64	98	142	57	85	171	70	101
70-74	144	53	91	142	51	91	140	51	89	124	46	78
75-79	117	37	80	114	38	76	113	37	76	113	37	76
80-84	65	17	48	83	22	60	81	24	58	82	23	59
85-89	24	6	18	39	9	30	50	12	38	50	13	37
90-94	12	3	9	10	2	8	18	4	14	23	5	19
95-99	3	1	2	3	1	3	3	1	2	5	1	4
100 +	0	0	0	0	0	0	0	0	0	0	0	0

Age group	2025			2030			2035			2040		
	Both sexes	Males	Females	Both sexes	Males	Females	Both sexes	Males	Females	Both sexes	Males	Females
All ages	2 946	1 367	1 579	2 804	1 300	1 504	2 651	1 227	1 424	2 486	1 148	1 338
0-4	93	48	45	82	42	40	71	37	35	63	32	30
5-9	97	50	47	92	47	45	82	42	40	71	36	34
10-14	106	54	51	96	49	47	91	47	44	81	42	40
15-19	117	60	57	103	53	50	94	48	46	89	46	43
20-24	142	73	69	113	58	55	99	51	48	90	46	43
25-29	164	84	80	138	71	67	109	56	53	95	49	46
30-34	231	118	113	161	82	79	135	69	65	106	55	52
35-39	265	133	132	228	116	112	158	81	77	132	68	64
40-44	238	120	118	262	131	131	225	114	111	156	80	76
45-49	204	100	104	234	117	117	258	128	129	222	112	110
50-54	224	107	117	199	96	102	228	113	115	252	124	128
55-59	217	100	117	216	101	115	192	92	100	221	100	110
60-64	235	104	131	206	92	114	205	94	111	183	85	98
65-69	196	82	114	217	92	125	191	82	109	191	84	107
70-74	150	57	92	173	67	106	193	77	116	170	69	101
75-79	101	34	67	123	43	80	143	51	92	160	58	102
80-84	83	24	59	75	22	53	92	28	64	108	33	75
85-89	51	12	39	53	13	40	48	12	36	60	15	45
90-94	24	5	19	25	5	20	26	5	22	24	4	20
95-99	7	1	6	8	1	7	8	1	7	9	1	8
100 +	1	0	1	1	0	1	1	0	1	2	0	1

Age group	2045			2050		
	Both sexes	Males	Females	Both sexes	Males	Females
All ages	2 311	1 064	1 247	2 132	980	1 152
0-4	56	29	27	53	27	26
5-9	62	32	30	56	29	27
10-14	70	36	34	61	32	30
15-19	79	41	38	68	35	33
20-24	85	44	41	75	39	36
25-29	86	44	42	81	42	39
30-34	92	47	45	83	43	40
35-39	104	53	51	90	46	44
40-44	130	67	63	102	52	50
45-49	154	78	76	128	66	63
50-54	217	109	109	151	76	75
55-59	245	119	126	211	105	107
60-64	211	101	111	235	112	123
65-69	171	77	94	198	91	107
70-74	171	71	100	154	66	88
75-79	143	53	90	144	55	89
80-84	122	38	83	109	35	74
85-89	71	18	53	81	21	60
90-94	31	6	25	38	7	31
95-99	9	1	8	11	1	10
100 +	2	0	2	2	0	2

United Nations Department of Economic and Social Affairs/Population Division
World Population Prospects: The 2004 Revision, Volume II: Sex and Age Distribution of the World Population

557

LUXEMBOURG

ESTIMATES

POPULATION BY AGE AND SEX (in thousands)

Age group	1950 Both sexes	Males	Females	1955 Both sexes	Males	Females	1960 Both sexes	Males	Females	1965 Both sexes	Males	Females
All ages	296	148	148	305	153	152	314	155	159	332	163	169
0-4	19	10	9	21	11	10	25	13	12	26	13	13
5-9	20	10	10	19	10	9	22	11	11	25	13	12
10-14	20	10	10	20	10	10	20	10	10	24	12	12
15-19	24	13	11	20	10	10	20	10	10	22	11	11
20-24	24	12	12	23	12	11	21	11	10	22	11	10
25-29	21	10	11	25	13	12	23	12	11	23	12	11
30-34	20	10	10	22	11	11	25	13	12	23	12	11
35-39	24	12	12	20	10	10	22	10	12	26	13	12
40-44	24	12	12	23	12	11	18	9	9	22	10	12
45-49	22	11	11	24	12	12	22	11	11	19	9	10
50-54	19	9	10	22	11	11	24	12	12	21	10	10
55-59	16	8	8	19	9	10	21	10	11	22	11	11
60-64	14	7	7	15	7	8	17	8	9	20	9	10
65-69	12	6	6	12	6	6	13	6	7	16	7	9
70-74	8	4	4	9	4	5	10	4	5	10	5	6
75-79	5	2	3	6	3	3	6	3	4	7	3	4
80 +	4	2	2	5	2	3	5	2	3	6	2	4

Age group	1970 Both sexes	Males	Females	1975 Both sexes	Males	Females	1980 Both sexes	Males	Females	1985 Both sexes	Males	Females
All ages	339	167	173	359	178	181	364	178	186	367	178	188
0-4	24	12	12	23	12	11	21	11	10	21	11	10
5-9	26	13	13	27	14	13	22	11	11	20	11	10
10-14	25	13	12	28	14	14	27	14	13	22	11	11
15-19	24	12	12	27	14	13	28	14	14	26	13	13
20-24	23	12	11	26	13	13	29	15	15	30	15	15
25-29	23	12	11	28	15	13	29	15	14	30	15	15
30-34	23	12	11	25	13	12	27	14	13	29	15	14
35-39	24	12	12	25	13	12	25	13	12	27	14	13
40-44	25	13	12	25	13	12	24	12	12	24	12	12
45-49	21	10	12	23	12	11	24	13	12	24	12	12
50-54	18	9	9	21	9	11	24	12	12	24	12	12
55-59	21	10	11	16	8	8	20	9	11	23	11	12
60-64	20	9	11	20	9	11	15	7	8	18	8	11
65-69	17	7	9	18	7	10	17	7	10	13	6	7
70-74	12	5	7	13	6	8	15	6	9	15	6	9
75-79	7	3	4	8	4	5	10	4	6	11	4	7
80 +	6	2	4	8	3	5	8	2	5	9	3	6

Age group	1990 Both sexes	Males	Females	1995 Both sexes	Males	Females	2000 Both sexes	Males	Females	2005 Both sexes	Males	Females
All ages	378	186	192	405	200	205	435	214	221	465	229	236
0-4	23	12	11	27	14	13	28	14	14	29	15	14
5-9	22	11	11	24	12	12	28	14	14	29	15	14
10-14	21	11	10	24	12	12	26	13	13	30	15	15
15-19	22	11	10	26	13	13	25	13	12	26	13	13
20-24	29	14	14	27	14	13	26	13	13	25	13	12
25-29	34	17	17	32	16	16	31	16	16	31	15	16
30-34	33	17	16	35	18	17	38	19	19	37	19	19
35-39	30	16	15	33	17	17	39	20	19	41	21	21
40-44	28	15	14	30	15	15	35	18	17	40	20	20
45-49	23	12	11	28	14	13	30	16	15	35	18	17
50-54	23	11	11	23	12	11	27	14	13	30	15	15
55-59	21	11	11	22	11	11	22	11	11	27	14	13
60-64	22	11	11	20	10	10	20	10	11	21	10	10
65-69	16	6	10	20	10	11	19	9	10	19	9	10
70-74	12	5	7	14	5	9	18	8	10	16	7	9
75-79	11	4	7	10	4	6	12	4	8	15	6	9
80 +	7	2	5	10	3	7	12	3	9	14	4	11

United Nations Department of Economic and Social Affairs/Population Division
World Population Prospects: The 2004 Revision, Volume II: Sex and Age Distribution of the World Population

558

POPULATION BY AGE AND SEX (in thousands)

Age group	2005 Both sexes	Males	Females	2010 Both sexes	Males	Females	2015 Both sexes	Males	Females	2020 Both sexes	Males	Females
All ages	465	229	236	494	244	251	523	258	265	552	272	280
0-4	29	15	14	29	15	14	30	15	15	31	16	15
5-9	29	15	14	30	15	15	30	16	15	31	16	15
10-14	30	15	15	31	16	15	32	16	15	32	16	16
15-19	26	13	13	30	15	15	31	16	15	32	16	15
20-24	25	13	12	26	14	13	30	16	15	31	16	15
25-29	31	15	16	29	15	15	31	16	16	35	18	17
30-34	37	19	19	37	18	19	36	18	18	37	19	19
35-39	41	21	21	41	21	21	41	20	21	39	20	20
40-44	40	20	20	43	22	21	43	21	21	42	21	21
45-49	35	18	17	40	21	20	43	22	21	43	22	21
50-54	30	15	15	35	18	17	40	20	20	43	22	21
55-59	27	14	13	29	15	14	34	17	17	39	20	19
60-64	21	10	10	25	13	13	28	14	14	33	16	16
65-69	19	9	10	19	9	10	23	12	12	26	13	13
70-74	16	7	9	17	7	9	17	8	9	21	10	11
75-79	15	6	9	14	6	8	14	6	8	15	6	8
80-84	8	2	6	11	4	7	10	4	6	11	4	7
85-89	4	1	3	5	1	4	7	2	5	7	2	5
90-94	2	0	2	2	0	2	3	0	2	3	1	3
95-99	0	0	0	1	0	1	1	0	1	1	0	1
100 +	0	0	0	0	0	0	0	0	0	0	0	0

Age group	2025 Both sexes	Males	Females	2030 Both sexes	Males	Females	2035 Both sexes	Males	Females	2040 Both sexes	Males	Females
All ages	582	287	295	612	302	310	642	317	325	670	330	340
0-4	33	17	16	35	18	17	37	19	18	38	19	18
5-9	32	17	16	34	18	17	36	19	18	38	19	18
10-14	33	17	16	34	17	17	36	19	18	38	20	19
15-19	32	17	16	33	17	16	34	18	17	36	19	18
20-24	32	16	16	32	17	16	33	17	16	34	18	17
25-29	36	18	18	37	18	18	37	19	18	38	19	19
30-34	41	21	20	42	21	21	43	22	21	43	22	22
35-39	41	21	21	45	23	22	46	23	23	47	24	23
40-44	41	21	20	43	22	21	47	24	23	48	24	23
45-49	43	21	21	41	21	21	43	22	21	47	24	23
50-54	43	21	21	42	21	21	41	21	20	40	22	21
55-59	42	21	21	42	21	21	42	21	21	41	20	20
60-64	38	19	19	41	20	21	40	20	20	40	20	21
65-69	31	15	16	35	17	18	38	19	20	38	19	20
70-74	24	11	13	28	13	15	32	15	17	35	17	19
75-79	18	8	10	20	9	11	24	11	14	28	13	16
80-84	11	4	7	14	6	8	16	6	10	19	8	11
85-89	7	2	5	7	2	5	10	3	6	11	4	7
90-94	3	1	3	4	1	3	4	1	3	5	1	4
95-99	1	0	1	1	0	1	1	0	1	2	0	1
100 +	0	0	0	0	0	0	0	0	0	0	0	0

Age group	2045 Both sexes	Males	Females	2050 Both sexes	Males	Females
All ages	696	342	354	721	355	367
0-4	39	20	19	40	21	19
5-9	39	20	19	40	20	19
10-14	40	20	19	40	21	20
15-19	38	20	19	40	20	19
20-24	36	19	18	39	20	19
25-29	39	20	19	41	21	20
30-34	44	22	22	45	23	22
35-39	47	24	23	48	24	24
40-44	48	25	24	49	25	24
45-49	48	24	24	49	25	24
50-54	47	24	23	48	24	24
55-59	42	21	21	46	23	23
60-64	39	19	20	41	20	21
65-69	38	18	20	37	18	19
70-74	35	17	19	35	16	19
75-79	31	14	17	31	14	17
80-84	23	9	13	25	10	15
85-89	13	5	9	16	6	10
90-94	6	2	5	8	2	6
95-99	2	0	2	3	0	2
100 +	0	0	0	1	0	1

United Nations Department of Economic and Social Affairs/Population Division
World Population Prospects: The 2004 Revision, Volume II: Sex and Age Distribution of the World Population

559

POPULATION BY AGE AND SEX (in thousands)

Age group	2005 Both sexes	Males	Females	2010 Both sexes	Males	Females	2015 Both sexes	Males	Females	2020 Both sexes	Males	Females
All ages	465	229	236	497	245	252	528	261	268	561	277	284
0-4	29	15	14	32	16	15	33	17	16	35	18	17
5-9	29	15	14	30	15	15	33	17	16	34	17	16
10-14	30	15	15	31	16	15	32	16	15	34	18	17
15-19	26	13	13	30	15	15	31	16	15	32	16	15
20-24	25	13	12	26	14	13	30	16	15	31	16	15
25-29	31	15	16	29	15	15	31	16	16	35	18	17
30-34	37	19	19	37	18	19	36	18	18	37	19	19
35-39	41	21	21	41	21	21	41	20	21	39	20	20
40-44	40	20	20	43	22	21	43	21	21	42	21	21
45-49	35	18	17	40	21	20	43	22	21	43	22	21
50-54	30	15	15	35	18	17	40	20	20	43	22	21
55-59	27	14	13	29	15	14	34	17	17	39	20	19
60-64	21	10	10	25	13	13	28	14	14	33	16	16
65-69	19	9	10	19	9	10	23	12	12	26	13	13
70-74	16	7	9	17	7	9	17	8	9	21	10	11
75-79	15	6	9	14	6	8	14	6	8	15	6	8
80-84	8	2	6	11	4	7	10	4	6	11	4	7
85-89	4	1	3	5	1	4	7	2	5	7	2	5
90-94	2	0	2	2	0	2	3	0	2	3	1	3
95-99	0	0	0	1	0	1	1	0	1	1	0	1
100 +	0	0	0	0	0	0	0	0	0	0	0	0

Age group	2025 Both sexes	Males	Females	2030 Both sexes	Males	Females	2035 Both sexes	Males	Females	2040 Both sexes	Males	Females
All ages	596	295	301	633	313	320	671	331	339	709	350	359
0-4	38	20	19	42	22	20	45	23	22	48	25	23
5-9	36	19	18	39	20	19	43	22	21	46	24	22
10-14	35	18	17	38	19	18	41	21	20	45	23	22
15-19	35	18	17	36	18	17	38	20	18	41	21	20
20-24	32	16	16	35	18	17	36	18	17	38	20	19
25-29	36	18	18	37	18	18	39	20	19	40	20	20
30-34	41	21	20	42	21	21	43	22	21	46	23	23
35-39	41	21	21	45	23	22	46	23	23	47	24	23
40-44	41	21	20	43	22	21	47	24	23	48	24	23
45-49	43	21	21	41	21	21	43	22	21	47	24	23
50-54	43	21	21	42	21	21	41	21	20	43	22	21
55-59	42	21	21	42	21	21	42	21	21	41	20	20
60-64	38	19	19	41	20	21	40	20	20	40	20	21
65-69	31	15	16	35	17	18	38	19	20	38	19	20
70-74	24	11	13	28	13	15	32	15	17	35	17	19
75-79	18	8	10	20	9	11	24	11	14	28	13	16
80-84	11	4	7	14	6	8	16	6	10	19	8	11
85-89	7	2	5	7	2	5	10	3	6	11	4	7
90-94	3	1	3	4	1	3	4	1	3	5	1	4
95-99	1	0	1	1	0	1	1	0	1	2	0	1
100 +	0	0	0	0	0	0	0	0	0	0	0	0

Age group	2045 Both sexes	Males	Females	2050 Both sexes	Males	Females
All ages	748	369	379	788	389	399
0-4	52	27	25	55	28	27
5-9	49	25	24	53	27	26
10-14	48	25	23	51	26	25
15-19	45	23	22	48	25	23
20-24	41	21	20	45	23	22
25-29	43	22	21	46	23	23
30-34	47	24	23	49	25	24
35-39	50	25	24	51	26	25
40-44	48	25	24	51	26	25
45-49	48	24	24	49	25	24
50-54	47	24	23	48	24	24
55-59	42	21	21	46	23	23
60-64	39	19	20	41	20	21
65-69	38	18	20	37	18	19
70-74	35	17	19	35	16	19
75-79	31	14	17	31	14	17
80-84	23	9	13	25	10	15
85-89	13	5	9	16	6	10
90-94	6	2	5	8	2	6
95-99	2	0	2	3	0	2
100 +	0	0	0	1	0	1

United Nations Department of Economic and Social Affairs/Population Division
World Population Prospects: The 2004 Revision, Volume II: Sex and Age Distribution of the World Population

560

POPULATION BY AGE AND SEX (in thousands)

Age group	2005			2010			2015			2020		
	Both sexes	Males	Females	Both sexes	Males	Females	Both sexes	Males	Females	Both sexes	Males	Females
All ages	465	229	236	492	242	249	518	255	263	543	268	275
0-4	29	15	14	27	14	13	27	14	13	28	14	13
5-9	29	15	14	30	15	15	28	14	14	28	14	14
10-14	30	15	15	31	16	15	32	16	15	30	15	14
15-19	26	13	13	30	15	15	31	16	15	32	16	15
20-24	25	13	12	26	14	13	30	16	15	31	16	15
25-29	31	15	16	29	15	15	31	16	16	35	18	17
30-34	37	19	19	37	18	19	36	18	18	37	19	19
35-39	41	21	21	41	21	21	41	20	21	39	20	20
40-44	40	20	20	43	22	21	43	21	21	42	21	21
45-49	35	18	17	40	21	20	43	22	21	43	22	21
50-54	30	15	15	35	18	17	40	20	20	43	22	21
55-59	27	14	13	29	15	14	34	17	17	39	20	19
60-64	21	10	10	25	13	13	28	14	14	33	16	16
65-69	19	9	10	19	9	10	23	12	12	26	13	13
70-74	16	7	9	17	7	9	17	8	9	21	10	11
75-79	15	6	9	14	6	8	14	6	8	15	6	8
80-84	8	2	6	11	4	7	10	4	6	11	4	7
85-89	4	1	3	5	1	4	7	2	5	7	2	5
90-94	2	0	2	2	0	2	3	0	2	3	1	3
95-99	0	0	0	1	0	1	1	0	1	1	0	1
100 +	0	0	0	0	0	0	0	0	0	0	0	0

Age group	2025			2030			2035			2040		
	Both sexes	Males	Females	Both sexes	Males	Females	Both sexes	Males	Females	Both sexes	Males	Females
All ages	568	280	288	592	292	300	614	302	312	632	310	321
0-4	28	15	14	29	15	14	29	15	14	28	14	14
5-9	29	15	14	29	15	14	30	15	15	30	15	14
10-14	30	15	15	30	16	15	31	16	15	32	16	15
15-19	30	15	15	30	15	15	31	16	15	31	16	15
20-24	32	16	16	30	16	15	30	16	15	31	16	15
25-29	36	18	18	37	18	18	35	17	17	35	18	17
30-34	41	21	20	42	21	21	43	22	21	41	21	20
35-39	41	21	21	45	23	22	46	23	23	47	24	23
40-44	41	21	20	43	22	21	47	24	23	48	24	23
45-49	43	21	21	41	21	21	43	22	21	47	24	23
50-54	43	21	21	42	21	21	41	21	20	43	22	21
55-59	42	21	21	42	21	21	42	21	21	41	20	20
60-64	38	19	19	41	20	21	40	20	20	40	20	21
65-69	31	15	16	35	17	18	38	19	20	38	19	20
70-74	24	11	13	28	13	15	32	15	17	35	17	19
75-79	10	8	10	20	9	11	24	11	14	28	13	16
80-84	11	4	7	14	6	8	16	6	10	19	8	11
85-89	7	2	5	7	2	5	10	3	6	11	4	7
90-94	3	1	3	4	1	3	4	1	3	5	1	4
95-99	1	0	1	1	0	1	1	0	1	2	0	1
100 +	0	0	0	0	0	0	0	0	0	0	0	0

Age group	2045			2050		
	Both sexes	Males	Females	Both sexes	Males	Females
All ages	646	317	330	658	322	336
0-4	27	14	13	27	14	13
5-9	29	15	14	28	14	14
10-14	31	16	15	31	16	15
15-19	32	16	16	32	16	15
20-24	32	16	15	32	17	16
25-29	35	18	18	36	18	18
30-34	41	21	20	42	21	21
35-39	45	23	22	45	23	22
40-44	48	25	24	47	24	23
45-49	48	24	24	49	25	24
50-54	47	24	23	48	24	24
55-59	42	21	21	46	23	23
60-64	39	19	20	41	20	21
65-69	38	18	20	37	18	19
70-74	35	17	19	35	16	19
75-79	31	14	17	31	14	17
80-84	23	9	13	25	10	15
85-89	13	5	9	16	6	10
90-94	6	2	5	8	2	6
95-99	2	0	2	3	0	2
100 +	0	0	0	1	0	1

POPULATION BY AGE AND SEX (in thousands)

Age group	1950 Both sexes	1950 Males	1950 Females	1955 Both sexes	1955 Males	1955 Females	1960 Both sexes	1960 Males	1960 Females	1965 Both sexes	1965 Males	1965 Females
All ages	4 230	2 076	2 153	4 752	2 342	2 410	5 368	2 653	2 715	6 089	3 016	3 074
0-4	705	347	357	875	439	436	990	496	494	1 116	559	557
5-9	568	279	288	613	304	309	771	388	383	882	443	439
10-14	495	244	251	542	267	274	588	292	296	742	374	368
15-19	434	214	220	478	236	242	524	259	265	570	283	287
20-24	377	186	191	416	205	211	460	227	233	506	249	256
25-29	324	160	164	358	176	182	397	195	202	440	216	224
30-34	278	138	141	307	151	155	340	167	173	379	186	193
35-39	237	117	120	261	129	132	290	143	147	323	159	164
40-44	200	99	102	221	109	112	245	121	124	272	134	138
45-49	167	82	86	184	90	94	205	101	104	228	112	116
50-54	138	66	71	152	73	78	169	82	87	188	92	96
55-59	109	52	57	121	58	64	135	65	71	151	73	79
60-64	82	39	44	92	43	49	104	49	55	116	55	61
65-69	57	27	31	64	30	34	73	34	39	83	39	44
70-74	34	16	19	39	18	21	45	21	24	52	24	28
75-79	17	8	9	19	9	11	23	10	13	27	12	15
80 +	8	4	4	9	4	5	10	5	6	13	5	7

Age group	1970 Both sexes	1970 Males	1970 Females	1975 Both sexes	1975 Males	1975 Females	1980 Both sexes	1980 Males	1980 Females	1985 Both sexes	1985 Males	1985 Females
All ages	6 931	3 439	3 492	7 909	3 926	3 983	9 066	4 503	4 562	10 447	5 193	5 254
0-4	1 266	634	631	1 438	719	719	1 654	828	826	1 886	945	941
5-9	1 005	505	501	1 151	577	574	1 320	661	659	1 535	769	766
10-14	851	428	423	973	489	484	1 117	560	556	1 285	644	642
15-19	721	363	357	828	417	412	948	476	472	1 092	548	544
20-24	550	273	277	696	350	346	800	402	399	922	462	459
25-29	484	238	246	526	260	266	667	334	332	774	387	386
30-34	420	206	214	462	227	235	502	248	254	642	322	321
35-39	360	177	183	399	196	204	440	215	224	482	237	244
40-44	304	149	155	340	166	173	378	185	193	419	205	214
45-49	255	125	130	285	139	146	320	156	164	358	174	184
50-54	210	103	108	236	115	121	265	129	137	299	145	155
55-59	170	82	88	191	92	99	215	104	112	244	117	127
60-64	131	62	69	148	71	78	168	80	88	191	91	100
65-69	95	44	50	108	51	57	123	58	65	141	66	75
70-74	61	28	33	70	32	38	81	37	44	94	43	50
75-79	32	15	18	38	17	21	45	20	25	53	24	29
80 +	15	7	9	19	8	11	24	10	14	29	12	17

Age group	1990 Both sexes	1990 Males	1990 Females	1995 Both sexes	1995 Males	1995 Females	2000 Both sexes	2000 Males	2000 Females	2005 Both sexes	2005 Males	2005 Females
All ages	12 045	5 989	6 055	13 946	6 935	7 010	16 195	8 053	8 142	18 606	9 255	9 351
0-4	2 170	1 087	1 083	2 493	1 249	1 244	2 877	1 442	1 436	3 106	1 560	1 546
5-9	1 753	878	874	2 043	1 023	1 020	2 367	1 185	1 182	2 753	1 378	1 375
10-14	1 496	750	746	1 715	860	855	2 004	1 003	1 001	2 328	1 165	1 163
15-19	1 258	630	628	1 468	736	732	1 686	845	841	1 975	988	987
20-24	1 063	532	531	1 227	613	614	1 435	718	718	1 651	826	826
25-29	892	446	446	1 031	515	517	1 193	594	599	1 393	695	699
30-34	746	373	373	863	430	433	999	497	502	1 152	573	579
35-39	617	309	308	720	359	361	833	415	419	963	478	484
40-44	460	226	234	592	296	297	692	344	348	801	397	403
45-49	398	194	204	439	215	224	566	281	285	662	328	334
50-54	336	162	173	375	181	194	415	202	213	536	265	272
55-59	275	132	143	311	149	162	349	167	182	387	187	201
60-64	217	103	114	247	117	130	281	133	148	316	150	166
65-69	161	75	85	184	86	98	212	99	113	243	113	129
70-74	108	50	58	125	57	67	145	67	78	169	78	91
75-79	62	28	34	72	32	40	86	39	47	102	46	56
80 +	35	15	20	42	18	24	55	23	32	69	29	40

562

United Nations Department of Economic and Social Affairs/Population Division
World Population Prospects: The 2004 Revision, Volume II: Sex and Age Distribution of the World Population

POPULATION BY AGE AND SEX (in thousands)

Age group	2005			2010			2015			2020		
	Both sexes	Males	Females	Both sexes	Males	Females	Both sexes	Males	Females	Both sexes	Males	Females
All ages	18 606	9 255	9 351	21 151	10 531	10 619	23 813	11 874	11 939	26 584	13 271	13 314
0-4	3 106	1 560	1 546	3 329	1 677	1 652	3 533	1 784	1 749	3 706	1 872	1 834
5-9	2 753	1 378	1 375	2 988	1 499	1 489	3 219	1 620	1 599	3 435	1 733	1 702
10-14	2 328	1 165	1 163	2 712	1 357	1 355	2 945	1 477	1 468	3 177	1 598	1 579
15-19	1 975	988	987	2 297	1 149	1 148	2 680	1 340	1 340	2 913	1 460	1 453
20-24	1 651	826	826	1 937	967	970	2 258	1 127	1 131	2 638	1 316	1 322
25-29	1 393	695	699	1 601	799	802	1 882	938	944	2 201	1 097	1 104
30-34	1 152	573	579	1 339	668	671	1 536	768	768	1 813	905	907
35-39	963	478	484	1 104	549	555	1 278	639	640	1 469	736	733
40-44	801	397	403	921	457	464	1 053	524	530	1 221	610	610
45-49	662	328	334	765	378	387	878	435	444	1 005	499	506
50-54	536	265	272	628	309	319	725	357	369	834	411	424
55-59	387	187	201	502	246	256	588	287	301	682	333	349
60-64	316	150	166	353	169	185	460	223	237	541	262	280
65-69	243	113	129	276	129	147	310	146	164	406	194	212
70-74	169	78	91	195	90	106	224	103	121	255	118	137
75-79	102	46	56	120	54	66	141	63	77	164	74	90
80-84	49	21	27	59	26	33	71	31	40	85	37	48
85-89	17	7	10	21	9	12	26	11	15	32	13	18
90-94	3	1	2	5	2	3	6	2	4	8	3	5
95-99	0	0	0	1	0	0	1	0	1	1	0	1
100 +	0	0	0	0	0	0	0	0	0	0	0	0

Age group	2025			2030			2035			2040		
	Both sexes	Males	Females	Both sexes	Males	Females	Both sexes	Males	Females	Both sexes	Males	Females
All ages	29 434	14 703	14 731	32 317	16 148	16 169	35 195	17 586	17 609	38 038	19 001	19 037
0-4	3 835	1 937	1 898	3 922	1 981	1 941	3 983	2 011	1 971	4 025	2 033	1 993
5-9	3 622	1 827	1 795	3 764	1 898	1 865	3 862	1 948	1 915	3 934	1 983	1 950
10-14	3 399	1 714	1 685	3 591	1 810	1 780	3 738	1 884	1 854	3 841	1 935	1 905
15-19	3 147	1 581	1 565	3 370	1 698	1 673	3 565	1 795	1 769	3 714	1 870	1 844
20-24	2 872	1 436	1 436	3 107	1 558	1 549	3 332	1 674	1 657	3 528	1 773	1 755
25-29	2 578	1 284	1 294	2 814	1 405	1 410	3 051	1 527	1 524	3 278	1 644	1 634
30-34	2 130	1 062	1 067	2 505	1 248	1 257	2 742	1 369	1 373	2 982	1 492	1 490
35-39	1 742	872	871	2 057	1 027	1 030	2 429	1 211	1 218	2 669	1 332	1 337
40-44	1 409	707	702	1 679	840	839	1 991	993	997	2 359	1 175	1 184
45-49	1 169	584	580	1 356	679	677	1 622	810	812	1 930	961	969
50-54	958	473	485	1 119	556	563	1 302	649	653	1 563	777	786
55-59	787	385	403	908	445	463	1 064	525	539	1 242	615	627
60-64	630	305	326	732	354	378	847	412	436	997	487	510
65-69	481	229	251	563	268	295	657	314	343	765	367	398
70-74	336	158	178	402	189	213	474	222	252	557	262	296
75-79	188	85	103	252	116	136	304	140	164	362	166	196
80-84	100	44	56	117	52	65	158	71	87	194	87	107
85-89	39	16	22	47	20	27	55	23	32	76	33	43
90-94	10	4	6	12	5	7	15	6	9	18	7	11
95-99	1	0	1	2	1	1	2	1	1	3	1	2
100 +	0	0	0	0	0	0	0	0	0	0	0	0

Age group	2045			2050		
	Both sexes	Males	Females	Both sexes	Males	Females
All ages	40 821	20 382	20 440	43 508	21 709	21 800
0-4	4 051	2 045	2 005	4 049	2 045	2 004
5-9	3 986	2 009	1 977	4 019	2 026	1 993
10-14	3 916	1 973	1 943	3 972	2 000	1 971
15-19	3 820	1 923	1 897	3 897	1 961	1 936
20-24	3 680	1 848	1 832	3 788	1 902	1 886
25-29	3 477	1 744	1 734	3 634	1 821	1 812
30-34	3 213	1 611	1 602	3 417	1 712	1 705
35-39	2 912	1 456	1 455	3 147	1 577	1 570
40-44	2 601	1 297	1 304	2 846	1 422	1 424
45-49	2 294	1 141	1 153	2 536	1 263	1 274
50-54	1 865	925	940	2 223	1 101	1 122
55-59	1 496	739	757	1 790	882	908
60-64	1 168	573	595	1 411	690	721
65-69	904	436	468	1 064	515	549
70-74	653	308	345	776	368	408
75-79	429	197	232	507	234	273
80-84	233	104	129	280	125	155
85-89	94	41	54	115	50	66
90-94	25	10	15	31	13	19
95-99	3	1	2	5	2	3
100 +	0	0	0	0	0	0

United Nations Department of Economic and Social Affairs/Population Division
World Population Prospects: The 2004 Revision, Volume II: Sex and Age Distribution of the World Population
563

POPULATION BY AGE AND SEX (in thousands)

Age group	2005 Both sexes	Males	Females	2010 Both sexes	Males	Females	2015 Both sexes	Males	Females	2020 Both sexes	Males	Females
All ages	18 606	9 255	9 351	21 321	10 617	10 704	24 300	12 120	12 180	27 536	13 751	13 785
0-4	3 106	1 560	1 546	3 499	1 763	1 737	3 855	1 947	1 908	4 182	2 112	2 070
5-9	2 753	1 378	1 375	2 988	1 499	1 489	3 383	1 702	1 681	3 749	1 891	1 858
10-14	2 328	1 165	1 163	2 712	1 357	1 355	2 945	1 477	1 468	3 339	1 680	1 660
15-19	1 975	988	987	2 297	1 149	1 148	2 680	1 340	1 340	2 913	1 460	1 453
20-24	1 651	826	826	1 937	967	970	2 258	1 127	1 131	2 638	1 316	1 322
25-29	1 393	695	699	1 601	799	802	1 882	938	944	2 201	1 097	1 104
30-34	1 152	573	579	1 339	668	671	1 536	768	768	1 813	905	907
35-39	963	478	484	1 104	549	555	1 278	639	640	1 469	736	733
40-44	801	397	403	921	457	464	1 053	524	530	1 221	610	610
45-49	662	328	334	765	378	387	878	435	444	1 005	499	506
50-54	536	265	272	628	309	319	725	357	369	834	411	424
55-59	387	187	201	502	246	256	588	287	301	682	333	349
60-64	316	150	166	353	169	185	460	223	237	541	262	280
65-69	243	113	129	276	129	147	310	146	164	406	194	212
70-74	169	78	91	195	90	106	224	103	121	255	118	137
75-79	102	46	56	120	54	66	141	63	77	164	74	90
80-84	49	21	27	59	26	33	71	31	40	85	37	48
85-89	17	7	10	21	9	12	26	11	15	32	13	18
90-94	3	1	2	5	2	3	6	2	4	8	3	5
95-99	0	0	0	1	0	0	1	0	1	1	0	1
100 +	0	0	0	0	0	0	0	0	0	0	0	0

Age group	2025 Both sexes	Males	Females	2030 Both sexes	Males	Females	2035 Both sexes	Males	Females	2040 Both sexes	Males	Females
All ages	30 941	15 464	15 478	34 519	17 259	17 261	38 289	19 145	19 144	42 250	21 123	21 127
0-4	4 406	2 225	2 180	4 637	2 342	2 295	4 900	2 474	2 425	5 175	2 613	2 561
5-9	4 087	2 062	2 025	4 323	2 181	2 143	4 566	2 302	2 263	4 839	2 440	2 400
10-14	3 709	1 870	1 839	4 052	2 043	2 009	4 293	2 164	2 129	4 540	2 288	2 252
15-19	3 308	1 662	1 645	3 678	1 853	1 825	4 023	2 026	1 997	4 267	2 148	2 118
20-24	2 872	1 436	1 436	3 266	1 637	1 628	3 636	1 827	1 809	3 981	2 001	1 981
25-29	2 578	1 284	1 294	2 814	1 405	1 410	3 206	1 605	1 602	3 577	1 794	1 783
30-34	2 130	1 062	1 067	2 505	1 248	1 257	2 742	1 369	1 373	3 134	1 568	1 566
35-39	1 742	872	871	2 057	1 027	1 030	2 429	1 211	1 218	2 669	1 332	1 337
40-44	1 409	707	702	1 679	840	839	1 991	993	997	2 359	1 175	1 184
45-49	1 169	584	586	1 356	679	677	1 622	810	812	1 930	961	969
50-54	958	473	485	1 119	556	563	1 302	649	653	1 563	777	786
55-59	787	385	403	908	445	463	1 064	525	539	1 242	615	627
60-64	630	305	326	732	354	378	847	412	436	997	487	510
65-69	481	229	251	563	268	295	657	314	343	765	367	398
70-74	336	158	178	402	189	213	474	222	252	557	262	296
75-79	188	85	103	252	116	136	304	140	164	362	166	196
80-84	100	44	56	117	52	65	158	71	87	194	87	107
85-89	39	16	22	47	20	27	55	23	32	76	33	43
90-94	10	4	6	12	5	7	15	6	9	18	7	11
95-99	1	0	1	2	1	1	2	1	1	3	1	2
100 +	0	0	0	0	0	0	0	0	0	0	0	0

Age group	2045 Both sexes	Males	Females	2050 Both sexes	Males	Females
All ages	46 369	23 175	23 194	50 596	25 275	25 320
0-4	5 427	2 740	2 687	5 637	2 847	2 791
5-9	5 124	2 583	2 541	5 385	2 714	2 671
10-14	4 818	2 427	2 391	5 106	2 571	2 534
15-19	4 516	2 273	2 243	4 795	2 413	2 382
20-24	4 227	2 123	2 104	4 478	2 249	2 230
25-29	3 924	1 968	1 956	4 174	2 092	2 081
30-34	3 506	1 758	1 748	3 856	1 932	1 924
35-39	3 061	1 531	1 530	3 435	1 721	1 714
40-44	2 601	1 297	1 304	2 992	1 495	1 497
45-49	2 294	1 141	1 153	2 536	1 263	1 274
50-54	1 865	925	940	2 223	1 101	1 122
55-59	1 496	739	757	1 790	882	908
60-64	1 168	573	595	1 411	690	721
65-69	904	436	468	1 064	515	549
70-74	653	308	345	776	368	408
75-79	429	197	232	507	234	273
80-84	233	104	129	280	125	155
85-89	94	41	54	115	50	66
90-94	25	10	15	31	13	19
95-99	3	1	2	5	2	3
100 +	0	0	0	0	0	0

United Nations Department of Economic and Social Affairs/Population Division
World Population Prospects: The 2004 Revision, Volume II: Sex and Age Distribution of the World Population

564

POPULATION BY AGE AND SEX (in thousands)

Age group	2005 Both sexes	2005 Males	2005 Females	2010 Both sexes	2010 Males	2010 Females	2015 Both sexes	2015 Males	2015 Females	2020 Both sexes	2020 Males	2020 Females
All ages	18 600	9 255	9 051	20 081	10 446	10 535	23 326	11 628	11 698	25 632	12 790	12 842
0-4	3 106	1 560	1 546	3 159	1 591	1 568	3 210	1 621	1 589	3 230	1 631	1 598
5-9	2 753	1 378	1 375	2 988	1 499	1 489	3 054	1 537	1 518	3 122	1 575	1 547
10-14	2 328	1 165	1 163	2 712	1 357	1 355	2 945	1 477	1 468	3 015	1 516	1 498
15-19	1 975	988	987	2 297	1 149	1 148	2 680	1 340	1 340	2 913	1 460	1 453
20-24	1 651	826	826	1 937	967	970	2 258	1 127	1 131	2 638	1 316	1 322
25-29	1 393	695	699	1 601	799	802	1 882	938	944	2 201	1 097	1 104
30-34	1 152	573	579	1 339	668	671	1 536	768	768	1 813	905	907
35-39	963	478	484	1 104	549	555	1 278	639	640	1 469	736	733
40-44	801	397	403	921	457	464	1 053	524	530	1 221	610	610
45-49	662	328	334	765	378	387	878	435	444	1 005	499	506
50-54	536	265	272	628	309	319	725	357	369	834	411	424
55-59	387	187	201	502	246	256	588	287	301	682	333	349
60-64	316	150	166	353	169	185	460	223	237	541	262	280
65-69	243	113	129	276	129	147	310	146	164	406	194	212
70-74	169	78	91	195	90	106	224	103	121	255	118	137
75-79	102	46	56	120	54	66	141	63	77	164	74	90
80-84	49	21	27	59	26	33	71	31	40	85	37	48
85-89	17	7	10	21	9	12	26	11	15	32	13	18
90-94	3	1	2	5	2	3	6	2	4	8	3	5
95-99	0	0	0	1	0	0	1	0	1	1	0	1
100 +	0	0	0	0	0	0	0	0	0	0	0	0

Age group	2025 Both sexes	2025 Males	2025 Females	2030 Both sexes	2030 Males	2030 Females	2035 Both sexes	2035 Males	2035 Females	2040 Both sexes	2040 Males	2040 Females
All ages	27 932	13 946	13 986	30 144	15 052	15 091	32 194	16 073	16 120	34 043	16 989	17 054
0-4	3 269	1 651	1 618	3 232	1 632	1 599	3 131	1 581	1 550	3 000	1 515	1 485
5-9	3 156	1 592	1 564	3 208	1 618	1 590	3 182	1 605	1 578	3 093	1 559	1 533
10-14	3 088	1 557	1 531	3 129	1 578	1 552	3 186	1 606	1 580	3 165	1 595	1 570
15-19	2 986	1 501	1 485	3 063	1 543	1 520	3 107	1 565	1 542	3 166	1 594	1 572
20-24	2 872	1 436	1 436	2 948	1 478	1 470	3 028	1 522	1 506	3 075	1 545	1 530
25-29	2 578	1 284	1 294	2 814	1 405	1 410	2 895	1 449	1 446	2 979	1 494	1 485
30-34	2 130	1 062	1 067	2 505	1 248	1 257	2 742	1 369	1 373	2 829	1 416	1 414
35-39	1 742	872	871	2 057	1 027	1 030	2 429	1 211	1 218	2 669	1 332	1 337
40-44	1 409	707	702	1 679	840	839	1 991	993	997	2 359	1 175	1 184
45-49	1 169	584	586	1 356	679	677	1 622	810	812	1 930	961	969
50-54	958	473	485	1 119	556	563	1 302	649	653	1 563	777	786
55-59	787	385	403	908	445	463	1 064	525	539	1 242	615	627
60-64	630	305	326	732	354	378	847	412	436	997	487	510
65-69	481	229	251	563	268	295	657	314	343	765	367	398
70-74	336	158	178	402	189	213	474	222	252	557	262	296
75-79	188	85	103	252	116	136	304	140	164	362	166	196
80-84	100	44	56	117	52	65	158	71	87	194	87	107
85-89	39	16	22	47	20	27	55	23	32	76	33	43
90-94	10	4	6	12	5	7	15	6	9	18	7	11
95-99	1	0	1	2	1	1	2	1	1	3	1	2
100 +	0	0	0	0	0	0	0	0	0	0	0	0

Age group	2045 Both sexes	2045 Males	2045 Females	2050 Both sexes	2050 Males	2050 Females
All ages	35 679	17 793	17 886	37 088	18 478	18 610
0-4	2 865	1 446	1 418	2 725	1 376	1 349
5-9	2 971	1 498	1 473	2 842	1 433	1 410
10-14	3 079	1 551	1 528	2 960	1 491	1 469
15-19	3 147	1 584	1 563	3 064	1 542	1 522
20-24	3 137	1 576	1 561	3 121	1 567	1 554
25-29	3 031	1 520	1 511	3 097	1 553	1 545
30-34	2 920	1 464	1 456	2 978	1 492	1 486
35-39	2 763	1 382	1 381	2 860	1 433	1 427
40-44	2 601	1 297	1 304	2 701	1 349	1 351
45-49	2 294	1 141	1 153	2 536	1 263	1 274
50-54	1 865	925	940	2 223	1 101	1 122
55-59	1 496	739	757	1 790	882	908
60-64	1 168	573	595	1 411	690	721
65-69	904	436	468	1 064	515	549
70-74	653	308	345	776	368	408
75-79	429	197	232	507	234	273
80-84	233	104	129	280	125	155
85-89	94	41	54	115	50	66
90-94	25	10	15	31	13	19
95-99	3	1	2	5	2	3
100 +	0	0	0	0	0	0

POPULATION BY AGE AND SEX (in thousands)

Age group	1950 Both sexes	1950 Males	1950 Females	1955 Both sexes	1955 Males	1955 Females	1960 Both sexes	1960 Males	1960 Females	1965 Both sexes	1965 Males	1965 Females
All ages	2 881	1 389	1 491	3 169	1 524	1 645	3 529	1 695	1 834	3 975	1 910	2 065
0-4	556	271	284	585	282	303	670	325	345	769	375	394
5-9	416	202	213	471	229	242	501	240	260	580	280	300
10-14	345	168	178	389	189	199	442	215	227	471	226	245
15-19	293	143	150	328	159	169	370	180	190	422	205	217
20-24	246	119	127	276	135	142	311	150	160	351	170	181
25-29	207	99	108	230	111	120	259	126	134	292	141	152
30-34	189	91	97	192	92	100	215	103	112	243	117	126
35-39	141	67	74	174	84	90	178	85	93	200	96	104
40-44	104	50	54	129	61	68	160	77	83	164	78	86
45-49	97	46	51	94	44	49	117	55	62	146	70	76
50-54	79	37	42	87	41	46	83	39	44	106	49	57
55-59	67	31	36	68	32	37	75	35	40	73	34	39
60-64	54	25	29	55	25	30	57	26	31	63	28	34
65-69	41	18	22	41	18	22	42	19	23	44	20	24
70-74	27	12	15	27	12	15	28	12	15	29	13	16
75-79	14	6	8	15	6	8	15	6	9	16	7	9
80 +	7	3	4	7	3	4	7	3	4	8	3	5

Age group	1970 Both sexes	1970 Males	1970 Females	1975 Both sexes	1975 Males	1975 Females	1980 Both sexes	1980 Males	1980 Females	1985 Both sexes	1985 Males	1985 Females
All ages	4 518	2 173	2 345	5 244	2 527	2 717	6 183	2 992	3 191	7 250	3 532	3 718
0-4	888	434	454	1 035	508	527	1 244	626	618	1 416	713	703
5-9	673	327	346	796	388	408	919	452	467	1 134	571	563
10-14	547	265	283	646	314	332	773	377	396	901	443	458
15-19	450	216	234	532	257	275	631	306	325	759	371	388
20-24	401	195	207	435	208	227	517	248	269	613	297	316
25-29	331	160	171	385	186	199	423	199	223	499	239	260
30-34	275	132	143	317	153	164	374	178	196	407	192	216
35-39	227	109	117	261	125	136	307	146	161	359	171	189
40-44	185	88	97	214	103	111	252	119	133	294	139	155
45-49	150	71	79	173	82	91	205	97	108	239	112	127
50-54	132	62	70	138	64	74	164	76	87	192	90	102
55-59	93	42	51	119	55	63	128	59	70	150	69	81
60-64	61	28	34	80	36	44	106	49	58	113	51	62
65-69	49	22	27	49	22	27	68	30	38	88	39	48
70-74	31	13	17	36	15	20	38	16	21	49	21	28
75-79	17	7	10	19	8	11	23	10	13	22	9	13
80 +	9	3	5	9	4	6	11	5	7	12	5	7

Age group	1990 Both sexes	1990 Males	1990 Females	1995 Both sexes	1995 Males	1995 Females	2000 Both sexes	2000 Males	2000 Females	2005 Both sexes	2005 Males	2005 Females
All ages	9 459	4 641	4 819	10 111	4 981	5 130	11 512	5 685	5 827	12 884	6 397	6 487
0-4	1 771	892	879	1 868	938	930	2 201	1 110	1 091	2 340	1 180	1 160
5-9	1 421	713	708	1 398	699	699	1 739	873	866	2 059	1 037	1 021
10-14	1 222	616	606	1 241	618	623	1 378	689	689	1 701	854	847
15-19	928	456	472	1 143	572	571	1 224	610	614	1 362	681	682
20-24	847	408	439	907	439	467	1 102	550	552	1 190	593	598
25-29	742	356	386	765	365	401	816	395	420	1 007	507	499
30-34	583	279	304	616	296	320	660	314	345	680	338	342
35-39	452	215	237	484	232	252	533	254	279	538	261	277
40-44	377	181	197	393	189	204	427	202	225	446	213	233
45-49	293	140	153	336	165	172	353	168	186	371	174	197
50-54	238	114	125	262	130	132	306	148	158	315	147	168
55-59	190	92	98	216	107	109	238	116	121	275	130	145
60-64	151	70	80	172	86	86	192	94	98	211	101	111
65-69	110	49	60	134	64	70	146	71	74	164	78	86
70-74	77	35	42	92	43	50	104	48	55	114	54	60
75-79	40	18	22	55	25	30	60	27	33	69	31	38
80 +	16	7	9	28	12	16	35	15	20	41	17	24

United Nations Department of Economic and Social Affairs/Population Division
World Population Prospects: The 2004 Revision, Volume II: Sex and Age Distribution of the World Population

566

POPULATION BY AGE AND SEX (in thousands)

Age group	2005 Both sexes	Males	Females	2010 Both sexes	Males	Females	2015 Both sexes	Males	Females	2020 Both sexes	Males	Females
All ages	12 884	6 397	6 487	14 348	7 103	7 105	16 008	8 034	7 973	17 816	8 974	8 843
0-4	2 340	1 180	1 160	2 475	1 250	1 226	2 679	1 353	1 326	2 890	1 460	1 429
5-9	2 059	1 037	1 021	2 205	1 112	1 094	2 355	1 188	1 167	2 577	1 301	1 276
10-14	1 701	854	847	2 002	1 009	993	2 149	1 083	1 066	2 304	1 162	1 142
15-19	1 362	681	682	1 681	843	837	1 979	997	983	2 127	1 071	1 056
20-24	1 190	593	598	1 328	663	665	1 644	824	819	1 942	977	965
25-29	1 007	507	499	1 101	553	549	1 234	622	612	1 539	778	761
30-34	680	338	342	867	448	420	960	493	467	1 083	558	524
35-39	538	261	277	560	286	274	731	388	344	815	430	385
40-44	446	213	233	448	220	227	474	246	228	626	337	288
45-49	371	174	197	384	184	201	390	192	198	416	217	199
50-54	315	147	168	329	152	176	344	163	181	350	172	179
55-59	275	130	145	283	130	154	298	136	162	312	146	167
60-64	211	101	111	246	114	132	255	114	141	269	120	149
65-69	164	78	86	182	85	97	214	96	118	223	97	126
70-74	114	54	60	130	60	70	146	66	80	174	76	98
75-79	69	31	38	77	35	42	90	40	50	103	45	59
80-84	30	13	18	36	15	21	41	18	23	49	21	28
85-89	9	4	5	10	4	6	13	5	8	15	6	9
90-94	1	1	1	2	1	1	2	1	1	3	1	2
95-99	0	0	0	0	0	0	0	0	0	0	0	0
100 +	0	0	0	0	0	0	0	0	0	0	0	0

Age group	2025 Both sexes	Males	Females	2030 Both sexes	Males	Females	2035 Both sexes	Males	Females	2040 Both sexes	Males	Females
All ages	19 737	9 972	9 765	21 687	10 975	10 711	23 625	11 960	11 665	25 561	12 935	12 627
0-4	3 032	1 532	1 500	3 093	1 563	1 530	3 120	1 576	1 543	3 156	1 595	1 561
5-9	2 804	1 416	1 388	2 963	1 496	1 467	3 037	1 534	1 504	3 074	1 552	1 522
10-14	2 536	1 280	1 256	2 773	1 400	1 373	2 939	1 484	1 456	3 020	1 524	1 496
15-19	2 285	1 151	1 133	2 519	1 270	1 249	2 758	1 391	1 367	2 926	1 476	1 450
20-24	2 091	1 052	1 039	2 250	1 132	1 118	2 485	1 251	1 234	2 725	1 373	1 352
25-29	1 831	926	905	1 983	1 000	983	2 144	1 080	1 064	2 378	1 198	1 180
30-34	1 368	704	663	1 647	844	803	1 800	915	885	1 962	995	968
35-39	930	491	439	1 194	625	568	1 456	754	702	1 608	824	785
40-44	703	377	326	814	435	379	1 059	558	501	1 305	677	628
45-49	552	299	253	628	337	291	735	392	343	965	506	459
50-54	375	195	181	503	270	232	576	307	269	679	358	321
55-59	330	164	165	345	176	168	464	246	218	535	281	254
60-64	284	130	154	292	138	154	317	159	158	429	223	206
65-69	238	103	135	253	112	140	262	121	141	286	140	146
70-74	184	78	107	199	83	115	213	92	121	223	100	123
75-79	125	52	73	135	54	80	148	59	88	161	66	95
80-84	58	24	34	71	28	40	70	30	49	88	33	55
85-89	18	7	11	22	8	14	28	10	18	32	11	21
90-94	3	1	2	4	1	3	5	2	3	7	2	4
95-99	0	0	0	0	0	0	0	0	0	1	0	0
100 +	0	0	0	0	0	0	0	0	0	0	0	0

Age group	2045 Both sexes	Males	Females	2050 Both sexes	Males	Females
All ages	27 508	13 908	13 601	29 452	14 873	14 579
0-4	3 198	1 616	1 582	3 216	1 625	1 591
5-9	3 119	1 575	1 544	3 167	1 599	1 568
10-14	3 061	1 545	1 516	3 109	1 569	1 540
15-19	3 009	1 518	1 491	3 052	1 539	1 513
20-24	2 896	1 459	1 437	2 981	1 502	1 479
25-29	2 621	1 321	1 300	2 798	1 411	1 388
30-34	2 196	1 113	1 083	2 444	1 238	1 206
35-39	1 772	903	869	2 007	1 022	985
40-44	1 457	746	711	1 623	827	796
45-49	1 199	619	581	1 351	688	663
50-54	898	466	432	1 125	574	550
55-59	635	330	305	845	432	413
60-64	498	256	241	594	303	291
65-69	390	198	191	455	229	226
70-74	246	117	129	338	167	171
75-79	171	73	98	190	87	103
80-84	98	38	60	106	42	63
85-89	37	13	24	42	15	27
90-94	8	2	5	9	3	6
95-99	1	0	1	1	0	1
100 +	0	0	0	0	0	0

POPULATION BY AGE AND SEX (in thousands)

Age group	2005 Both sexes	2005 Males	2005 Females	2010 Both sexes	2010 Males	2010 Females	2015 Both sexes	2015 Males	2015 Females	2020 Both sexes	2020 Males	2020 Females
All ages	12 884	6 397	6 487	14 457	7 218	7 239	16 308	8 181	8 127	18 424	9 280	9 143
0-4	2 340	1 180	1 160	2 585	1 305	1 280	2 885	1 458	1 428	3 197	1 615	1 582
5-9	2 059	1 037	1 021	2 205	1 112	1 094	2 459	1 240	1 219	2 775	1 401	1 374
10-14	1 701	854	847	2 002	1 009	993	2 149	1 083	1 066	2 406	1 213	1 193
15-19	1 362	681	682	1 681	843	837	1 979	997	983	2 127	1 071	1 056
20-24	1 190	593	598	1 328	663	665	1 644	824	819	1 942	977	965
25-29	1 007	507	499	1 101	553	549	1 234	622	612	1 539	778	761
30-34	680	338	342	867	448	420	960	493	467	1 083	558	524
35-39	538	261	277	560	286	274	731	388	344	815	430	385
40-44	446	213	233	448	220	227	474	246	228	626	337	288
45-49	371	174	197	384	184	201	390	192	198	416	217	199
50-54	315	147	168	329	152	176	344	163	181	350	172	179
55-59	275	130	145	283	130	154	298	136	162	312	146	167
60-64	211	101	111	246	114	132	255	114	141	269	120	149
65-69	164	78	86	182	85	97	214	96	118	223	97	126
70-74	114	54	60	130	60	70	146	66	80	174	76	98
75-79	69	31	38	77	35	42	90	40	50	103	45	59
80-84	30	13	18	36	15	21	41	18	23	49	21	28
85-89	9	4	5	10	4	6	13	5	8	15	6	9
90-94	1	1	1	2	1	1	2	1	1	3	1	2
95-99	0	0	0	0	0	0	0	0	0	0	0	0
100 +	0	0	0	0	0	0	0	0	0	0	0	0

Age group	2025 Both sexes	2025 Males	2025 Females	2030 Both sexes	2030 Males	2030 Females	2035 Both sexes	2035 Males	2035 Females	2040 Both sexes	2040 Males	2040 Females
All ages	20 707	10 462	10 245	23 119	11 698	11 421	25 654	12 985	12 670	28 339	14 337	14 002
0-4	3 408	1 722	1 686	3 570	1 804	1 766	3 736	1 888	1 848	3 936	1 989	1 947
5-9	3 103	1 567	1 536	3 330	1 681	1 648	3 505	1 770	1 735	3 682	1 859	1 823
10-14	2 731	1 378	1 353	3 068	1 549	1 520	3 304	1 667	1 636	3 486	1 759	1 726
15-19	2 385	1 202	1 183	2 713	1 368	1 345	3 052	1 539	1 513	3 289	1 659	1 630
20-24	2 091	1 052	1 039	2 350	1 182	1 167	2 677	1 348	1 329	3 016	1 519	1 497
25-29	1 831	926	905	1 983	1 000	983	2 239	1 128	1 111	2 562	1 291	1 271
30-34	1 368	704	663	1 647	844	803	1 800	915	885	2 049	1 039	1 011
35-39	930	491	439	1 194	625	568	1 456	754	702	1 608	824	785
40-44	703	377	326	814	435	379	1 059	558	501	1 305	677	628
45-49	552	299	253	628	337	291	735	392	343	965	506	459
50-54	375	195	181	503	270	232	576	307	269	679	358	321
55-59	320	154	165	345	176	168	464	246	218	535	281	254
60-64	284	130	154	292	138	154	317	159	158	429	223	206
65-69	238	103	135	253	112	140	262	121	141	286	140	146
70-74	184	78	107	199	83	115	213	92	121	223	100	123
75-79	125	52	73	135	54	80	148	59	88	161	66	95
80-84	58	24	34	71	28	43	79	30	49	88	33	55
85-89	18	7	11	22	8	14	28	10	18	32	11	21
90-94	3	1	2	4	1	3	5	2	3	7	2	4
95-99	0	0	0	0	0	0	0	0	0	1	0	0
100 +	0	0	0	0	0	0	0	0	0	0	0	0

Age group	2045 Both sexes	2045 Males	2045 Females	2050 Both sexes	2050 Males	2050 Females
All ages	31 180	15 762	15 418	34 154	17 248	16 906
0-4	4 141	2 092	2 049	4 314	2 180	2 134
5-9	3 889	1 964	1 926	4 101	2 071	2 030
10-14	3 667	1 851	1 816	3 877	1 957	1 920
15-19	3 473	1 752	1 721	3 656	1 844	1 812
20-24	3 255	1 640	1 615	3 442	1 734	1 708
25-29	2 901	1 462	1 439	3 146	1 586	1 560
30-34	2 366	1 199	1 167	2 705	1 370	1 335
35-39	1 851	943	907	2 163	1 101	1 061
40-44	1 457	746	711	1 696	864	831
45-49	1 199	619	581	1 351	688	663
50-54	898	466	432	1 125	574	550
55-59	635	330	305	845	432	413
60-64	498	256	241	594	303	291
65-69	390	198	191	455	229	226
70-74	246	117	129	338	167	171
75-79	171	73	98	190	87	103
80-84	98	38	60	106	42	63
85-89	37	13	24	42	15	27
90-94	8	2	5	9	3	6
95-99	1	0	1	1	0	1
100 +	0	0	0	0	0	0

POPULATION BY AGE AND SEX (in thousands)

Age group	2005 Both sexes	Males	Females	2010 Both sexes	Males	Females	2015 Both sexes	Males	Females	2020 Both sexes	Males	Females
All ages	12 884	6 397	6 487	14 239	7 108	7 131	15 688	7 868	7 820	17 209	8 667	0 542
0-4	2 340	1 180	1 160	2 366	1 195	1 172	2 473	1 249	1 224	2 582	1 305	1 277
5-9	2 059	1 037	1 021	2 205	1 112	1 094	2 251	1 136	1 116	2 379	1 201	1 178
10-14	1 701	854	847	2 002	1 009	993	2 149	1 083	1 066	2 203	1 111	1 092
15-19	1 362	681	682	1 681	843	837	1 979	997	983	2 127	1 071	1 056
20-24	1 190	593	598	1 328	663	665	1 644	824	819	1 942	977	965
25-29	1 007	507	499	1 101	553	549	1 234	622	612	1 539	778	761
30-34	680	338	342	867	448	420	960	493	467	1 083	558	524
35-39	538	261	277	560	286	274	731	388	344	815	430	385
40-44	446	213	233	448	220	227	474	246	228	626	337	288
45-49	371	174	197	384	184	201	390	192	198	416	217	199
50-54	315	147	168	329	152	176	344	163	181	350	172	179
55-59	275	130	145	283	130	154	298	136	162	312	146	167
60-64	211	101	111	246	114	132	255	114	141	269	120	149
65-69	164	78	86	182	85	97	214	96	118	223	97	126
70-74	114	54	60	130	60	70	146	66	80	174	76	98
75-79	69	31	38	77	35	42	90	40	50	103	45	59
80-84	30	13	18	36	15	21	41	18	23	49	21	28
85-89	9	4	5	10	4	6	13	5	8	15	6	9
90-94	1	1	1	2	1	1	2	1	1	3	1	2
95-99	0	0	0	0	0	0	0	0	0	0	0	0
100 +	0	0	0	0	0	0	0	0	0	0	0	0

Age group	2025 Both sexes	Males	Females	2030 Both sexes	Males	Females	2035 Both sexes	Males	Females	2040 Both sexes	Males	Females
All ages	18 770	9 484	9 286	20 271	10 261	10 011	21 651	10 964	10 687	22 912	11 597	11 315
0-4	2 659	1 344	1 316	2 631	1 329	1 301	2 541	1 284	1 257	2 449	1 237	1 212
5-9	2 506	1 265	1 240	2 598	1 312	1 286	2 583	1 304	1 279	2 504	1 264	1 240
10-14	2 341	1 181	1 160	2 478	1 251	1 227	2 578	1 301	1 277	2 568	1 296	1 272
15-19	2 184	1 100	1 083	2 325	1 172	1 153	2 464	1 243	1 221	2 567	1 294	1 272
20-24	2 091	1 052	1 039	2 151	1 082	1 068	2 294	1 155	1 139	2 435	1 226	1 208
25-29	1 831	926	905	1 983	1 000	983	2 049	1 032	1 017	2 194	1 106	1 089
30-34	1 368	704	663	1 647	844	803	1 800	915	885	1 875	950	925
35-39	900	401	439	1 194	625	568	1 456	754	702	1 608	824	785
40-44	703	377	326	814	435	379	1 059	558	501	1 305	677	628
45-49	552	299	253	628	337	291	735	392	343	965	506	459
50-54	375	195	181	503	270	232	576	307	269	679	358	321
55-59	320	154	165	345	176	168	464	240	218	535	281	254
60-64	284	130	154	292	138	154	317	159	158	429	223	206
65-69	238	103	135	253	112	140	262	121	141	286	140	146
70-74	184	78	107	199	83	115	213	92	121	223	100	123
75-79	125	52	73	135	54	80	148	59	88	161	66	95
80-84	58	24	34	71	28	43	79	30	49	88	33	55
85-89	18	7	11	22	8	14	28	10	18	32	11	21
90-94	3	1	2	4	1	3	5	2	3	7	2	4
95-99	0	0	0	0	0	0	0	0	0	1	0	0
100 +	0	0	0	0	0	0	0	0	0	0	0	0

Age group	2045 Both sexes	Males	Females	2050 Both sexes	Males	Females
All ages	24 077	12 175	11 902	25 148	12 699	12 450
0-4	2 368	1 196	1 171	2 278	1 151	1 127
5-9	2 420	1 222	1 198	2 345	1 184	1 161
10-14	2 494	1 259	1 235	2 412	1 217	1 195
15-19	2 559	1 291	1 268	2 486	1 254	1 232
20-24	2 539	1 279	1 260	2 535	1 277	1 258
25-29	2 341	1 180	1 161	2 453	1 237	1 217
30-34	2 026	1 027	1 000	2 182	1 105	1 077
35-39	1 694	863	830	1 852	943	909
40-44	1 457	746	711	1 551	791	761
45-49	1 199	619	581	1 351	688	663
50-54	898	466	432	1 125	574	550
55-59	635	330	305	845	432	413
60-64	498	256	241	594	303	291
65-69	390	198	191	455	229	226
70-74	246	117	129	338	167	171
75-79	171	73	98	190	87	103
80-84	98	38	60	106	42	63
85-89	37	13	24	42	15	27
90-94	8	2	5	9	3	6
95-99	1	0	1	1	0	1
100 +	0	0	0	0	0	0

POPULATION BY AGE AND SEX (in thousands)

Age group	1950 Both sexes	Males	Females	1955 Both sexes	Males	Females	1960 Both sexes	Males	Females	1965 Both sexes	Males	Females
All ages	6 110	3 144	2 966	7 000	3 569	3 432	8 140	4 138	4 003	9 502	4 819	4 683
0-4	1 020	509	511	1 278	635	642	1 515	770	745	1 714	876	838
5-9	752	379	373	964	480	483	1 222	607	615	1 465	744	721
10-14	727	369	358	738	372	366	949	473	476	1 207	600	607
15-19	580	287	293	713	362	351	727	367	360	937	467	470
20-24	517	262	255	564	279	285	697	354	344	713	360	354
25-29	440	221	219	500	254	247	549	272	278	682	346	336
30-34	403	209	194	424	213	211	485	246	239	535	265	271
35-39	342	186	156	386	200	187	409	205	204	471	238	233
40-44	323	177	147	325	176	149	370	191	180	395	198	198
45-49	227	132	95	305	165	139	309	166	143	354	182	173
50-54	195	107	88	210	121	89	285	153	132	291	155	136
55-59	138	74	64	176	95	81	191	109	82	262	139	123
60-64	139	72	67	119	63	57	154	82	72	169	95	74
65-69	109	59	50	102	52	51	98	51	48	129	67	62
70-74	98	52	46	91	50	41	75	41	34	75	38	38
75-79	63	32	31	64	32	33	62	32	30	57	30	27
80 +	39	19	19	40	20	20	42	20	22	45	21	24

Age group	1970 Both sexes	Males	Females	1975 Both sexes	Males	Females	1980 Both sexes	Males	Females	1985 Both sexes	Males	Females
All ages	10 853	5 477	5 375	12 258	6 169	6 089	13 763	6 929	6 835	15 677	7 897	7 780
0-4	1 776	907	869	1 873	957	916	1 868	958	910	2 398	1 233	1 165
5-9	1 646	830	816	1 703	870	833	1 851	945	906	1 836	942	894
10-14	1 418	706	712	1 583	787	796	1 694	865	829	1 829	933	896
15-19	1 173	582	590	1 364	664	700	1 574	782	792	1 674	854	820
20-24	921	464	457	1 131	560	572	1 352	657	694	1 552	770	781
25-29	702	357	345	927	471	456	1 119	553	566	1 330	646	684
30-34	663	337	325	710	365	345	915	465	450	1 099	543	557
35-39	518	257	261	662	340	323	700	359	340	897	455	442
40-44	458	232	226	505	252	253	649	332	317	682	349	332
45-49	376	188	189	449	227	222	492	244	247	628	320	308
50-54	337	170	166	353	175	178	431	217	215	469	231	238
55-59	263	138	125	311	155	156	333	164	169	400	198	202
60-64	232	121	111	229	117	112	284	139	145	298	144	154
65-69	145	79	66	193	99	95	199	100	99	237	113	124
70-74	114	57	57	115	60	54	155	77	78	154	74	80
75-79	58	28	30	88	42	46	81	41	39	117	55	62
80 +	53	24	29	61	27	33	68	31	38	76	34	42

Age group	1990 Both sexes	Males	Females	1995 Both sexes	Males	Females	2000 Both sexes	Males	Females	2005 Both sexes	Males	Females
All ages	17 845	9 056	8 789	20 362	10 338	10 024	22 997	11 680	11 317	25 347	12 865	12 483
0-4	2 276	1 172	1 105	2 734	1 404	1 330	2 736	1 405	1 331	2 734	1 405	1 329
5-9	2 265	1 164	1 102	2 280	1 173	1 107	2 741	1 407	1 334	2 736	1 404	1 332
10-14	1 972	1 008	964	2 274	1 167	1 106	2 284	1 174	1 109	2 740	1 406	1 334
15-19	1 780	900	880	1 984	1 013	971	2 292	1 176	1 116	2 288	1 176	1 112
20-24	1 634	822	812	1 802	910	892	2 034	1 038	996	2 306	1 181	1 124
25-29	1 580	796	785	1 664	836	827	1 866	943	923	2 052	1 046	1 006
30-34	1 426	724	702	1 603	807	796	1 716	865	851	1 880	950	931
35-39	1 182	603	579	1 437	729	708	1 635	824	811	1 722	867	855
40-44	941	484	458	1 184	604	580	1 452	737	715	1 631	821	810
45-49	679	353	326	934	479	455	1 184	602	581	1 438	728	711
50-54	617	314	303	666	345	322	922	470	452	1 160	587	573
55-59	454	227	227	593	299	294	646	331	315	889	449	440
60-64	378	183	194	423	208	215	556	276	280	605	305	300
65-69	246	118	128	332	158	175	376	180	196	496	240	256
70-74	197	92	106	200	93	107	274	126	148	312	145	168
75-79	117	54	63	143	64	79	147	66	81	204	90	114
80 +	100	44	56	110	49	62	136	59	77	152	65	87

United Nations Department of Economic and Social Affairs/Population Division
World Population Prospects: The 2004 Revision, Volume II: Sex and Age Distribution of the World Population

570

POPULATION BY AGE AND SEX (in thousands)

Age group	2005 Both sexes	Males	Females	2010 Both sexes	Males	Females	2015 Both sexes	Males	Females	2020 Both sexes	Males	Females
All ages	25 347	12 865	12 483	27 532	13 963	13 569	29 558	14 972	14 586	31 474	15 922	15 552
0-4	2 734	1 405	1 329	2 675	1 375	1 300	2 642	1 359	1 284	2 629	1 352	1 277
5-9	2 736	1 404	1 332	2 732	1 403	1 329	2 672	1 373	1 299	2 640	1 358	1 283
10-14	2 740	1 406	1 334	2 734	1 403	1 331	2 730	1 402	1 328	2 671	1 372	1 298
15-19	2 288	1 176	1 112	2 741	1 405	1 336	2 733	1 401	1 331	2 730	1 401	1 329
20-24	2 306	1 181	1 124	2 295	1 178	1 117	2 740	1 403	1 337	2 733	1 400	1 333
25-29	2 052	1 046	1 006	2 316	1 186	1 130	2 297	1 178	1 119	2 742	1 403	1 338
30-34	1 880	950	931	2 060	1 050	1 010	2 315	1 185	1 130	2 297	1 178	1 119
35-39	1 722	867	855	1 881	950	931	2 055	1 047	1 008	2 311	1 182	1 129
40-44	1 631	821	810	1 716	863	853	1 872	944	928	2 046	1 042	1 005
45-49	1 438	728	711	1 615	811	804	1 699	852	846	1 855	934	921
50-54	1 160	587	573	1 411	710	701	1 586	793	793	1 671	835	836
55-59	889	449	440	1 121	562	559	1 366	682	684	1 539	763	776
60-64	605	305	300	837	416	421	1 059	523	536	1 296	637	659
65-69	496	240	256	544	268	277	758	367	390	966	465	501
70-74	312	145	168	417	195	222	462	219	243	650	303	346
75-79	204	90	114	237	105	132	321	143	178	361	162	199
80-84	93	40	53	133	55	77	158	65	93	218	90	128
85-89	44	19	26	48	19	29	70	27	44	86	32	54
90-94	12	5	7	16	6	10	18	7	12	28	9	19
95-99	3	1	1	3	1	2	4	1	3	5	1	3
100 +	0	0	0	0	0	0	0	0	0	1	0	0

Age group	2025 Both sexes	Males	Females	2030 Both sexes	Males	Females	2035 Both sexes	Males	Females	2040 Both sexes	Males	Females
All ages	33 223	16 783	16 440	34 720	17 514	17 206	36 037	18 155	17 882	37 180	18 711	18 469
0-4	2 577	1 326	1 251	2 455	1 264	1 192	2 415	1 243	1 172	2 391	1 230	1 161
5-9	2 628	1 352	1 276	2 576	1 326	1 251	2 455	1 263	1 192	2 415	1 243	1 172
10-14	2 639	1 357	1 282	2 627	1 351	1 276	2 576	1 325	1 251	2 455	1 263	1 192
15-19	2 671	1 372	1 299	2 640	1 357	1 283	2 628	1 351	1 276	2 577	1 326	1 251
20-24	2 731	1 401	1 330	2 673	1 373	1 301	2 643	1 358	1 285	2 631	1 353	1 278
25-29	2 736	1 401	1 334	2 734	1 402	1 332	2 677	1 374	1 303	2 647	1 360	1 287
30-34	2 742	1 403	1 339	2 737	1 402	1 335	2 736	1 403	1 333	2 679	1 376	1 304
35-39	2 295	1 177	1 118	2 709	1 402	1 337	2 734	1 400	1 334	2 734	1 402	1 332
40-44	2 302	1 177	1 125	2 287	1 173	1 115	2 730	1 397	1 333	2 726	1 396	1 331
45-49	2 030	1 032	998	2 285	1 167	1 118	2 272	1 163	1 109	2 713	1 386	1 327
50-54	1 828	917	911	2 002	1 015	988	2 256	1 149	1 107	2 244	1 146	1 098
55-59	1 625	806	819	1 782	888	894	1 955	984	971	2 206	1 117	1 000
60-64	1 466	716	749	1 553	760	793	1 707	840	867	1 878	935	943
65-69	1 188	570	618	1 352	646	706	1 440	690	750	1 590	767	823
70-74	835	387	448	1 037	479	558	1 190	549	642	1 278	592	686
75-79	515	227	287	670	294	377	844	370	474	980	429	551
80-84	249	103	146	362	147	216	482	195	288	618	250	368
85-89	122	44	78	143	52	91	215	77	138	294	105	189
90-94	36	11	25	52	16	37	64	19	45	100	30	70
95-99	8	2	6	10	2	8	16	4	12	20	5	16
100 +	1	0	1	1	0	1	2	0	2	3	1	2

Age group	2045 Both sexes	Males	Females	2050 Both sexes	Males	Females
All ages	38 144	19 180	18 964	38 924	19 559	19 366
0-4	2 362	1 216	1 147	2 323	1 195	1 127
5-9	2 391	1 230	1 161	2 362	1 216	1 147
10-14	2 415	1 243	1 172	2 391	1 230	1 161
15-19	2 456	1 264	1 192	2 416	1 243	1 173
20-24	2 581	1 327	1 253	2 460	1 266	1 195
25-29	2 636	1 355	1 281	2 586	1 330	1 256
30-34	2 650	1 361	1 288	2 639	1 357	1 282
35-39	2 678	1 375	1 303	2 649	1 361	1 288
40-44	2 727	1 398	1 329	2 671	1 371	1 300
45-49	2 710	1 386	1 324	2 712	1 389	1 323
50-54	2 682	1 367	1 315	2 681	1 368	1 313
55-59	2 198	1 116	1 082	2 629	1 333	1 296
60-64	2 124	1 064	1 060	2 121	1 067	1 055
65-69	1 757	859	898	1 995	982	1 013
70-74	1 421	665	756	1 580	750	830
75-79	1 063	470	594	1 194	534	661
80-84	730	297	433	803	330	473
85-89	386	139	247	466	169	297
90-94	141	42	99	191	57	133
95-99	33	7	25	48	11	37
100 +	4	1	3	7	1	6

United Nations Department of Economic and Social Affairs/Population Division
World Population Prospects: The 2004 Revision, Volume II: Sex and Age Distribution of the World Population

571

POPULATION BY AGE AND SEX (in thousands)

Age group	2005			2010			2015			2020		
	Both sexes	Males	Females	Both sexes	Males	Females	Both sexes	Males	Females	Both sexes	Males	Females
All ages	25 347	12 865	12 483	27 771	14 086	13 686	30 216	15 310	14 906	32 700	16 552	16 148
0-4	2 734	1 405	1 329	2 914	1 498	1 416	3 061	1 574	1 487	3 198	1 645	1 553
5-9	2 736	1 404	1 332	2 732	1 403	1 329	2 912	1 496	1 415	3 059	1 573	1 486
10-14	2 740	1 406	1 334	2 734	1 403	1 331	2 730	1 402	1 328	2 910	1 495	1 415
15-19	2 288	1 176	1 112	2 741	1 405	1 336	2 733	1 401	1 331	2 730	1 401	1 329
20-24	2 306	1 181	1 124	2 295	1 178	1 117	2 740	1 403	1 337	2 733	1 400	1 333
25-29	2 052	1 046	1 006	2 316	1 186	1 130	2 297	1 178	1 119	2 742	1 403	1 338
30-34	1 880	950	931	2 060	1 050	1 010	2 315	1 185	1 130	2 297	1 178	1 119
35-39	1 722	867	855	1 881	950	931	2 055	1 047	1 008	2 311	1 182	1 129
40-44	1 631	821	810	1 716	863	853	1 872	944	928	2 046	1 042	1 005
45-49	1 438	728	711	1 615	811	804	1 699	852	846	1 855	934	921
50-54	1 160	587	573	1 411	710	701	1 586	793	793	1 671	835	836
55-59	889	449	440	1 121	562	559	1 366	682	684	1 539	763	776
60-64	605	305	300	837	416	421	1 059	523	536	1 296	637	659
65-69	496	240	256	544	268	277	758	367	390	966	465	501
70-74	312	145	168	417	195	222	462	219	243	650	303	346
75-79	204	90	114	237	105	132	321	143	178	361	162	199
80-84	93	40	53	133	55	77	158	65	93	218	90	128
85-89	44	19	26	48	19	29	70	27	44	86	32	54
90-94	12	5	7	16	6	10	18	7	12	28	9	19
95-99	3	1	1	3	1	2	4	1	3	5	1	3
100 +	0	0	0	0	0	0	0	0	0	1	0	0

Age group	2025			2030			2035			2040		
	Both sexes	Males	Females	Both sexes	Males	Females	Both sexes	Males	Females	Both sexes	Males	Females
All ages	35 068	17 732	17 336	37 250	18 815	18 435	39 367	19 868	19 500	41 472	20 918	20 554
0-4	3 197	1 645	1 552	3 143	1 618	1 526	3 219	1 656	1 562	3 356	1 727	1 629
5-9	3 196	1 644	1 552	3 195	1 644	1 551	3 142	1 617	1 525	3 218	1 656	1 562
10-14	3 057	1 572	1 486	3 195	1 643	1 552	3 194	1 643	1 551	3 142	1 617	1 525
15-19	2 909	1 494	1 415	3 057	1 571	1 486	3 195	1 643	1 552	3 195	1 643	1 551
20-24	2 731	1 401	1 330	2 911	1 495	1 416	3 059	1 572	1 488	3 197	1 644	1 554
25-29	2 736	1 401	1 334	2 734	1 402	1 332	2 915	1 496	1 418	3 063	1 573	1 490
30-34	2 742	1 403	1 339	2 737	1 402	1 335	2 736	1 403	1 333	2 916	1 497	1 419
35-39	2 295	1 177	1 118	2 739	1 402	1 337	2 734	1 400	1 334	2 734	1 402	1 332
40-44	2 302	1 177	1 125	2 287	1 173	1 115	2 730	1 397	1 333	2 726	1 396	1 331
45-49	2 030	1 032	998	2 285	1 167	1 118	2 272	1 163	1 109	2 713	1 386	1 327
50-54	1 828	917	911	2 002	1 015	988	2 256	1 149	1 107	2 244	1 146	1 098
55-59	1 625	806	819	1 782	888	894	1 955	984	971	2 206	1 117	1 089
60-64	1 466	716	749	1 553	760	793	1 707	840	867	1 878	935	943
65-69	1 188	570	618	1 352	646	706	1 440	690	750	1 590	767	823
70-74	835	387	448	1 037	479	558	1 190	549	642	1 278	592	686
75-79	515	227	287	670	294	377	844	370	474	980	429	551
80-84	249	103	146	362	147	216	482	195	288	618	250	368
85-89	122	44	78	143	52	91	215	77	138	294	105	189
90-94	36	11	25	52	16	37	64	19	45	100	30	70
95-99	8	2	6	10	2	8	16	4	12	20	5	16
100 +	1	0	1	1	0	1	2	0	2	3	1	2

Age group	2045			2050		
	Both sexes	Males	Females	Both sexes	Males	Females
All ages	43 555	21 962	21 593	45 576	22 979	22 597
0-4	3 487	1 794	1 692	3 571	1 837	1 733
5-9	3 355	1 727	1 629	3 486	1 794	1 692
10-14	3 217	1 655	1 562	3 355	1 726	1 629
15-19	3 142	1 617	1 526	3 218	1 656	1 562
20-24	3 198	1 645	1 553	3 146	1 618	1 528
25-29	3 201	1 645	1 556	3 202	1 647	1 555
30-34	3 065	1 574	1 490	3 203	1 646	1 557
35-39	2 914	1 496	1 418	3 063	1 573	1 490
40-44	2 727	1 398	1 329	2 907	1 492	1 415
45-49	2 710	1 386	1 324	2 712	1 389	1 323
50-54	2 682	1 367	1 315	2 681	1 368	1 313
55-59	2 198	1 116	1 082	2 629	1 333	1 296
60-64	2 124	1 064	1 060	2 121	1 067	1 055
65-69	1 757	859	898	1 995	982	1 013
70-74	1 421	665	756	1 580	750	830
75-79	1 063	470	594	1 194	534	661
80-84	730	297	433	803	330	473
85-89	386	139	247	466	169	297
90-94	141	42	99	191	57	133
95-99	33	7	25	48	11	37
100 +	4	1	3	7	1	6

United Nations Department of Economic and Social Affairs/Population Division
World Population Prospects: The 2004 Revision, Volume II: Sex and Age Distribution of the World Population

572

POPULATION BY AGE AND SEX (in thousands)

Age group	2005 Both sexes	Males	Females	2010 Both sexes	Males	Females	2015 Both sexes	Males	Females	2020 Both sexes	Males	Females
All ages	25 347	12 865	12 483	27 290	13 838	13 451	28 886	14 626	14 259	30 207	15 270	14 937
0-4	2 734	1 405	1 329	2 433	1 250	1 182	2 212	1 137	1 074	2 033	1 046	987
5-9	2 736	1 404	1 332	2 732	1 403	1 329	2 431	1 249	1 181	2 211	1 137	1 074
10-14	2 740	1 406	1 334	2 734	1 403	1 331	2 730	1 402	1 328	2 429	1 248	1 181
15-19	2 288	1 176	1 112	2 741	1 405	1 336	2 733	1 401	1 331	2 730	1 401	1 329
20-24	2 306	1 181	1 124	2 295	1 178	1 117	2 740	1 403	1 337	2 733	1 400	1 333
25-29	2 052	1 046	1 006	2 316	1 186	1 130	2 297	1 178	1 119	2 742	1 403	1 338
30-34	1 880	950	931	2 060	1 050	1 010	2 315	1 185	1 130	2 297	1 178	1 119
35-39	1 722	867	855	1 881	950	931	2 055	1 047	1 008	2 311	1 182	1 129
40-44	1 631	821	810	1 716	863	853	1 872	944	928	2 046	1 042	1 005
45-49	1 438	728	711	1 615	811	804	1 699	852	846	1 855	934	921
50-54	1 160	587	573	1 411	710	701	1 586	793	793	1 671	835	836
55-59	889	449	440	1 121	562	559	1 366	682	684	1 539	763	776
60-64	605	305	300	837	416	421	1 059	523	536	1 296	637	659
65-69	496	240	256	544	268	277	758	367	390	966	465	501
70-74	312	145	168	417	195	222	462	219	243	650	303	346
75-79	204	90	114	237	105	132	321	143	178	361	162	199
80-84	93	40	53	133	55	77	158	65	93	218	90	128
85-89	44	19	26	48	19	29	70	27	44	86	32	54
90-94	12	5	7	16	6	10	18	7	12	28	9	19
95-99	3	1	1	3	1	2	4	1	3	5	1	3
100 +	0	0	0	0	0	0	0	0	0	1	0	0

Age group	2025 Both sexes	Males	Females	2030 Both sexes	Males	Females	2035 Both sexes	Males	Females	2040 Both sexes	Males	Females
All ages	31 317	15 803	15 514	32 136	16 185	15 951	32 711	16 444	16 266	33 019	16 571	16 448
0-4	1 937	996	940	1 777	914	862	1 670	860	811	1 551	798	753
5-9	2 032	1 045	987	1 937	996	940	1 777	915	863	1 671	860	811
10-14	2 210	1 136	1 074	2 032	1 045	987	1 936	996	940	1 777	914	863
15-19	2 429	1 248	1 182	2 211	1 136	1 074	2 033	1 045	988	1 938	997	941
20-24	2 731	1 401	1 330	2 432	1 249	1 183	2 214	1 138	1 077	2 038	1 048	990
25-29	2 736	1 401	1 334	2 734	1 402	1 332	2 437	1 251	1 186	2 220	1 141	1 079
30-34	2 742	1 403	1 339	2 737	1 402	1 335	2 736	1 403	1 333	2 440	1 253	1 187
35-39	2 295	1 177	1 118	2 730	1 402	1 337	2 734	1 400	1 334	2 734	1 402	1 332
40-44	2 302	1 177	1 125	2 287	1 173	1 115	2 730	1 397	1 333	2 726	1 396	1 331
45-49	2 030	1 032	998	2 285	1 167	1 118	2 272	1 163	1 109	2 713	1 386	1 327
50-54	1 828	917	911	2 002	1 015	988	2 256	1 149	1 107	2 244	1 146	1 098
55-59	1 625	806	819	1 782	888	894	1 955	984	971	2 206	1 117	1 089
60-64	1 466	716	749	1 553	760	793	1 707	840	867	1 878	935	943
65-69	1 188	570	618	1 352	646	706	1 440	690	750	1 590	767	823
70-74	835	387	448	1 037	479	558	1 190	549	642	1 278	592	686
75-79	515	227	287	670	294	377	844	370	474	980	429	551
80-84	249	103	146	362	147	216	482	195	288	618	250	368
85-89	122	44	78	143	52	91	215	77	138	294	105	189
90-94	36	11	25	52	16	37	64	19	45	100	30	70
95-99	8	2	6	10	2	8	16	4	12	20	5	16
100 +	1	0	1	1	0	1	2	0	2	3	1	2

Age group	2045 Both sexes	Males	Females	2050 Both sexes	Males	Females
All ages	33 056	16 564	16 492	32 845	16 433	16 412
0-4	1 430	736	694	1 326	682	644
5-9	1 552	799	753	1 431	736	695
10-14	1 671	860	811	1 552	799	754
15-19	1 779	915	864	1 673	861	812
20-24	1 943	999	943	1 784	918	866
25-29	2 043	1 051	993	1 949	1 003	946
30-34	2 223	1 143	1 081	2 048	1 053	994
35-39	2 439	1 252	1 186	2 223	1 143	1 081
40-44	2 727	1 398	1 329	2 433	1 249	1 184
45-49	2 710	1 386	1 324	2 712	1 389	1 323
50-54	2 682	1 367	1 315	2 681	1 368	1 313
55-59	2 198	1 116	1 082	2 629	1 333	1 296
60-64	2 124	1 064	1 060	2 121	1 067	1 055
65-69	1 757	859	898	1 995	982	1 013
70-74	1 421	665	756	1 580	750	830
75-79	1 063	470	594	1 194	534	661
80-84	730	297	433	803	330	473
85-89	386	139	247	466	169	297
90-94	141	42	99	191	57	133
95-99	33	7	25	48	11	37
100 +	4	1	3	7	1	6

POPULATION BY AGE AND SEX (in thousands)

Age group	1950 Both sexes	Males	Females	1955 Both sexes	Males	Females	1960 Both sexes	Males	Females	1965 Both sexes	Males	Females
All ages	82	44	38	90	48	42	99	53	46	109	58	51
0-4	10	5	5	15	8	7	16	8	8	17	9	8
5-9	9	5	4	10	5	4	14	7	7	15	8	7
10-14	8	4	4	8	4	4	9	5	4	14	7	6
15-19	7	4	3	8	4	4	8	4	4	9	5	4
20-24	7	4	3	7	4	3	7	4	3	8	4	4
25-29	6	3	3	7	4	3	7	4	3	7	4	3
30-34	6	3	3	6	3	3	6	3	3	7	4	3
35-39	5	3	2	6	3	2	6	3	3	6	3	3
40-44	5	3	2	5	3	2	5	3	2	5	3	2
45-49	4	2	2	4	2	2	5	3	2	5	3	2
50-54	4	2	2	4	2	2	4	2	2	4	2	2
55-59	3	2	1	3	2	2	3	2	2	4	2	2
60-64	3	1	1	3	1	1	3	2	1	3	2	1
65-69	2	1	1	2	1	1	2	1	1	2	1	1
70-74	1	1	1	1	1	1	1	1	1	2	1	1
75-79	1	0	0	1	0	0	1	0	0	1	0	0
80 +	0	0	0	0	0	0	0	0	0	0	0	0

Age group	1970 Both sexes	Males	Females	1975 Both sexes	Males	Females	1980 Both sexes	Males	Females	1985 Both sexes	Males	Females
All ages	121	64	57	137	72	65	158	83	75	184	95	88
0-4	19	10	9	23	12	11	28	14	13	35	18	17
5-9	16	9	8	18	10	9	22	11	11	27	14	13
10-14	15	8	7	16	8	8	18	9	9	22	11	10
15-19	13	7	6	14	8	7	16	8	8	18	9	9
20-24	9	5	4	13	7	6	14	7	7	16	8	7
25-29	8	4	4	9	5	4	13	7	6	14	7	7
30-34	7	4	3	7	4	3	8	4	4	12	6	6
35-39	6	3	3	7	4	3	7	4	3	8	4	4
40-44	6	3	3	6	3	3	6	4	3	7	4	3
45-49	5	3	2	5	3	2	6	3	3	6	3	3
50-54	4	2	2	5	3	2	5	3	2	5	3	2
55-59	4	2	2	4	2	2	4	2	2	5	3	2
60-64	3	2	1	3	2	2	4	2	2	4	2	2
65-69	2	1	1	3	1	1	3	1	1	3	1	2
70-74	2	1	1	2	1	1	2	1	1	2	1	1
75-79	1	0	0	1	1	1	1	1	1	1	0	0
80 +	1	0	0	1	0	0	1	0	0	0	0	0

Age group	1990 Both sexes	Males	Females	1995 Both sexes	Males	Females	2000 Both sexes	Males	Females	2005 Both sexes	Males	Females
All ages	216	111	105	252	129	123	290	149	141	329	169	160
0-4	40	20	20	43	22	21	46	23	22	46	24	23
5-9	34	17	17	39	20	19	43	22	21	45	23	22
10-14	26	13	13	34	17	17	39	20	19	42	22	20
15-19	22	11	10	26	13	13	33	17	17	39	20	19
20-24	18	9	9	21	11	10	26	13	13	33	17	16
25-29	15	8	7	18	9	8	21	11	10	26	13	12
30-34	13	6	6	15	8	7	17	9	8	21	11	10
35-39	11	5	6	13	6	6	15	8	7	17	9	8
40-44	7	4	4	11	5	5	12	6	6	15	8	7
45-49	7	4	3	7	3	4	10	5	5	12	6	6
50-54	6	3	3	6	3	3	7	3	3	10	5	5
55-59	5	3	2	6	3	3	6	3	3	6	3	3
60-64	4	2	2	5	3	2	5	3	2	5	3	2
65-69	3	2	2	4	2	2	4	2	2	4	2	2
70-74	2	1	1	3	1	1	3	2	1	3	2	2
75-79	1	1	0	2	1	1	2	1	1	2	1	1
80 +	1	0	0	1	0	0	1	0	1	1	1	1

United Nations Department of Economic and Social Affairs/Population Division
World Population Prospects: The 2004 Revision, Volume II: Sex and Age Distribution of the World Population

574

POPULATION BY AGE AND SEX (in thousands)

Age group	2005 Both sexes	2005 Males	2005 Females	2010 Both sexes	2010 Males	2010 Females	2015 Both sexes	2015 Males	2015 Females	2020 Both sexes	2020 Males	2020 Females
All ages	329	169	160	371	191	181	416	213	203	461	236	225
0-4	46	24	23	50	26	24	53	27	26	54	27	26
5-9	45	23	22	46	24	22	50	25	24	53	27	26
10-14	42	22	20	45	23	22	46	24	22	50	25	24
15-19	39	20	19	42	22	20	45	23	22	46	24	22
20-24	33	17	16	38	20	19	42	22	20	45	23	22
25-29	26	13	12	33	17	16	38	20	19	42	22	20
30-34	21	11	10	25	13	12	33	17	16	38	19	19
35-39	17	9	8	21	11	10	25	13	12	32	16	16
40-44	15	8	7	17	9	8	20	11	10	25	13	12
45-49	12	6	6	14	8	7	17	9	8	20	10	10
50-54	10	5	5	12	6	6	14	7	7	16	8	8
55-59	6	3	3	10	5	5	11	6	6	13	7	6
60-64	5	3	2	6	3	3	9	4	5	10	5	5
65-69	4	2	2	5	3	2	5	2	3	8	4	4
70-74	3	2	2	4	2	2	4	2	2	4	2	2
75-79	2	1	1	2	1	1	3	1	1	3	2	1
80-84	1	0	1	1	1	1	1	1	1	2	1	1
85-89	0	0	0	0	0	0	1	0	0	1	0	0
90-94	0	0	0	0	0	0	0	0	0	0	0	0
95-99	0	0	0	0	0	0	0	0	0	0	0	0
100 +	0	0	0	0	0	0	0	0	0	0	0	0

Age group	2025 Both sexes	2025 Males	2025 Females	2030 Both sexes	2030 Males	2030 Females	2035 Both sexes	2035 Males	2035 Females	2040 Both sexes	2040 Males	2040 Females
All ages	506	258	247	547	279	268	586	298	288	622	316	306
0-4	53	27	26	52	26	26	51	26	25	49	25	24
5-9	54	27	26	53	27	26	52	26	25	51	26	25
10-14	52	27	26	54	27	26	53	27	26	52	26	25
15-19	50	25	24	52	27	26	54	27	26	53	27	26
20-24	46	23	22	49	25	24	52	27	26	53	27	26
25-29	45	23	22	46	23	22	49	25	24	52	27	26
30-34	42	22	20	44	23	22	45	23	22	49	25	24
35-39	38	10	18	41	21	20	44	23	21	45	23	22
40-44	32	16	16	38	19	18	41	21	20	44	23	21
45-49	25	13	12	32	16	16	37	19	18	41	21	20
50-54	20	10	9	24	12	12	31	16	16	37	19	18
55-59	16	8	7	19	10	9	23	12	11	30	15	15
60-64	13	7	6	15	8	7	18	9	9	22	11	11
65-69	9	5	5	12	6	6	14	7	7	17	8	8
70-74	7	3	4	8	4	4	10	5	5	12	6	6
75-79	0	2	2	5	2	3	6	3	3	8	4	4
80-84	2	1	1	2	1	1	3	1	2	4	2	2
85-89	1	0	0	1	0	0	1	0	1	2	1	1
90-94	0	0	0	0	0	0	0	0	0	0	0	0
95-99	0	0	0	0	0	0	0	0	0	0	0	0
100 +	0	0	0	0	0	0	0	0	0	0	0	0

Age group	2045 Both sexes	2045 Males	2045 Females	2050 Both sexes	2050 Males	2050 Females
All ages	654	331	322	682	345	337
0-4	48	24	23	47	24	23
5-9	49	25	24	48	24	23
10-14	51	26	25	49	25	24
15-19	52	26	25	51	26	25
20-24	53	27	26	52	26	25
25-29	53	27	26	53	27	26
30-34	52	27	26	53	27	26
35-39	49	25	24	52	26	25
40-44	45	23	22	49	25	24
45-49	44	22	21	45	23	22
50-54	40	21	19	43	22	21
55-59	36	18	18	39	20	19
60-64	29	15	15	34	17	17
65-69	21	10	10	27	13	14
70-74	15	7	7	18	9	9
75-79	9	5	5	12	6	6
80-84	5	2	3	7	3	4
85-89	2	1	1	3	1	2
90-94	1	0	0	1	0	1
95-99	0	0	0	0	0	0
100 +	0	0	0	0	0	0

United Nations Department of Economic and Social Affairs/Population Division
World Population Prospects: The 2004 Revision, Volume II: Sex and Age Distribution of the World Population

575

POPULATION BY AGE AND SEX (in thousands)

Age group	2005 Both sexes	Males	Females	2010 Both sexes	Males	Females	2015 Both sexes	Males	Females	2020 Both sexes	Males	Females
All ages	329	169	160	375	192	182	425	218	207	479	245	234
0-4	46	24	23	53	27	26	59	30	29	63	32	31
5-9	45	23	22	46	24	22	53	27	26	59	30	29
10-14	42	22	20	45	23	22	46	24	22	53	27	26
15-19	39	20	19	42	22	20	45	23	22	46	24	22
20-24	33	17	16	38	20	19	42	22	20	45	23	22
25-29	26	13	12	33	17	16	38	20	19	42	22	20
30-34	21	11	10	25	13	12	33	17	16	38	19	19
35-39	17	9	8	21	11	10	25	13	12	32	16	16
40-44	15	8	7	17	9	8	20	11	10	25	13	12
45-49	12	6	6	14	8	7	17	9	8	20	10	10
50-54	10	5	5	12	6	6	14	7	7	16	8	8
55-59	6	3	3	10	5	5	11	6	6	13	7	6
60-64	5	3	2	6	3	3	9	4	5	10	5	5
65-69	4	2	2	5	3	2	5	2	3	8	4	4
70-74	3	2	2	4	2	2	4	2	2	4	2	2
75-79	2	1	1	2	1	1	3	1	1	3	2	1
80-84	1	0	1	1	1	1	1	1	1	2	1	1
85-89	0	0	0	0	0	0	1	0	0	1	0	0
90-94	0	0	0	0	0	0	0	0	0	0	0	0
95-99	0	0	0	0	0	0	0	0	0	0	0	0
100 +	0	0	0	0	0	0	0	0	0	0	0	0

Age group	2025 Both sexes	Males	Females	2030 Both sexes	Males	Females	2035 Both sexes	Males	Females	2040 Both sexes	Males	Females
All ages	533	272	261	586	299	287	639	325	314	691	351	340
0-4	63	32	31	63	32	31	65	33	32	66	34	33
5-9	62	32	31	63	32	31	63	32	31	64	33	32
10-14	58	30	29	62	32	31	63	32	31	63	32	31
15-19	53	27	26	58	30	29	62	32	31	63	32	31
20-24	46	23	22	53	27	26	58	30	29	62	32	31
25-29	45	23	22	46	23	22	52	27	26	58	30	29
30-34	42	22	20	44	23	22	45	23	22	52	27	26
35-39	38	19	18	41	21	20	44	23	21	45	23	22
40-44	32	16	16	38	19	18	41	21	20	44	23	21
45-49	25	13	12	32	16	16	37	19	18	41	21	20
50-54	20	10	9	24	12	12	31	16	16	37	19	18
55-59	16	8	7	19	10	9	23	12	11	30	15	15
60-64	13	7	6	15	8	7	18	9	9	22	11	11
65-69	9	5	5	12	6	6	14	7	7	17	8	8
70-74	7	3	4	8	4	4	10	5	5	12	6	6
75-79	3	2	2	5	2	3	6	3	3	8	4	4
80-84	2	1	1	2	1	1	3	1	2	4	2	2
85-89	1	0	0	1	0	0	1	0	1	2	1	1
90-94	0	0	0	0	0	0	0	0	0	0	0	0
95-99	0	0	0	0	0	0	0	0	0	0	0	0
100 +	0	0	0	0	0	0	0	0	0	0	0	0

Age group	2045 Both sexes	Males	Females	2050 Both sexes	Males	Females
All ages	743	377	366	794	402	392
0-4	68	34	33	70	35	34
5-9	66	34	33	68	34	33
10-14	64	33	32	66	34	33
15-19	63	32	31	64	33	32
20-24	63	32	31	63	32	31
25-29	62	31	30	63	32	31
30-34	58	30	28	62	31	30
35-39	52	27	25	58	29	28
40-44	45	23	22	52	26	25
45-49	44	22	21	45	23	22
50-54	40	21	19	43	22	21
55-59	36	18	18	39	20	19
60-64	29	15	15	34	17	17
65-69	21	10	10	27	13	14
70-74	15	7	7	18	9	9
75-79	9	5	5	12	6	6
80-84	5	2	3	7	3	4
85-89	2	1	1	3	1	2
90-94	1	0	0	1	0	1
95-99	0	0	0	0	0	0
100 +	0	0	0	0	0	0

United Nations Department of Economic and Social Affairs/Population Division
World Population Prospects: The 2004 Revision, Volume II: Sex and Age Distribution of the World Population

576

POPULATION BY AGE AND SEX (in thousands)

Age group	2005 Both sexes	Males	Females	2010 Both sexes	Males	Females	2015 Both sexes	Males	Females	2020 Both sexes	Males	Females
All ages	329	169	160	368	189	179	407	208	198	443	227	217
0-4	46	24	23	47	24	23	47	24	23	45	23	22
5-9	45	23	22	46	24	22	47	24	23	46	24	23
10-14	42	22	20	45	23	22	46	24	22	46	24	23
15-19	39	20	19	42	22	20	45	23	22	46	24	22
20-24	33	17	16	38	20	19	42	22	20	45	23	22
25-29	26	13	12	33	17	16	38	20	19	42	22	20
30-34	21	11	10	25	13	12	33	17	16	38	19	19
35-39	17	9	8	21	11	10	25	13	12	32	16	16
40-44	15	8	7	17	9	8	20	11	10	25	13	12
45-49	12	6	6	14	8	7	17	9	8	20	10	10
50-54	10	5	5	12	6	6	14	7	7	16	8	8
55-59	6	3	3	10	5	5	11	6	6	13	7	6
60-64	5	3	2	6	3	3	9	4	5	10	5	5
65-69	4	2	2	5	3	2	5	2	3	8	4	4
70-74	3	2	2	4	2	2	4	2	2	4	2	2
75-79	2	1	1	2	1	1	3	1	1	3	2	1
80-84	1	0	1	1	1	1	1	1	1	2	1	1
85-89	0	0	0	0	0	0	1	0	0	1	0	0
90-94	0	0	0	0	0	0	0	0	0	0	0	0
95-99	0	0	0	0	0	0	0	0	0	0	0	0
100 +	0	0	0	0	0	0	0	0	0	0	0	0

Age group	2025 Both sexes	Males	Females	2030 Both sexes	Males	Females	2035 Both sexes	Males	Females	2040 Both sexes	Males	Females
All ages	478	244	234	508	259	249	534	272	262	555	282	273
0-4	43	22	21	41	21	20	38	19	19	34	17	17
5-9	45	23	22	43	22	21	41	21	20	38	19	19
10-14	46	24	23	45	23	22	43	22	21	41	21	20
15-19	46	24	23	46	24	23	45	23	22	43	22	21
20-24	46	23	22	46	24	23	46	24	23	45	23	22
25-29	45	23	22	46	23	22	46	24	23	46	23	23
30-34	43	22	20	44	23	22	45	23	22	46	23	23
35-39	38	19	18	41	21	20	44	23	21	45	23	22
40-44	32	16	16	38	19	18	41	21	20	44	23	21
45-49	25	13	12	32	16	16	37	19	18	41	21	20
50-54	20	10	9	24	12	12	31	16	16	37	19	18
55-59	16	8	7	19	10	9	23	12	11	30	15	15
60-64	13	7	6	15	8	7	18	9	9	22	11	11
65-69	9	5	5	12	6	6	14	7	7	17	8	8
70-74	7	3	4	8	4	4	10	5	5	12	6	6
75-79	3	2	2	5	2	3	6	3	3	8	4	4
80-84	2	1	1	2	1	1	3	1	2	4	2	2
85-89	1	0	0	1	0	0	1	0	1	2	1	1
90-94	0	0	0	0	0	0	0	0	0	0	0	0
95-99	0	0	0	0	0	0	0	0	0	0	0	0
100 +	0	0	0	0	0	0	0	0	0	0	0	0

Age group	2045 Both sexes	Males	Females	2050 Both sexes	Males	Females
All ages	570	289	281	580	293	287
0-4	31	16	15	29	15	14
5-9	34	17	17	31	16	15
10-14	38	19	19	34	17	17
15-19	41	21	20	38	19	18
20-24	43	22	21	41	21	20
25-29	45	23	22	43	22	21
30-34	46	23	23	45	23	22
35-39	46	23	22	46	23	23
40-44	45	23	22	46	23	22
45-49	44	22	21	45	23	22
50-54	40	21	19	43	22	21
55-59	36	18	18	39	20	19
60-64	29	15	15	34	17	17
65-69	21	10	10	27	13	14
70-74	15	7	7	18	9	9
75-79	9	5	5	12	6	6
80-84	5	2	3	7	3	4
85-89	2	1	1	3	1	2
90-94	1	0	0	1	0	1
95-99	0	0	0	0	0	0
100 +	0	0	0	0	0	0

POPULATION BY AGE AND SEX (in thousands)

Age group	1950 Both sexes	Males	Females	1955 Both sexes	Males	Females	1960 Both sexes	Males	Females	1965 Both sexes	Males	Females
All ages	3 449	1 725	1 725	3 841	1 920	1 921	4 317	2 159	2 159	4 805	2 398	2 407
0-4	636	319	317	689	348	341	791	400	391	889	450	440
5-9	499	249	250	535	268	266	586	296	290	678	343	335
10-14	430	214	216	480	240	240	516	260	256	565	287	279
15-19	369	183	186	415	207	208	465	233	232	496	250	246
20-24	313	155	158	351	174	177	396	198	199	435	217	218
25-29	262	130	133	295	146	149	332	164	168	363	180	184
30-34	218	108	110	247	122	125	279	138	141	304	149	155
35-39	180	89	91	205	101	104	233	115	118	256	125	130
40-44	146	73	73	168	83	85	192	95	97	214	105	109
45-49	118	59	58	135	67	69	156	76	80	176	85	90
50-54	92	47	45	107	53	54	124	60	64	141	68	73
55-59	70	36	34	82	41	40	95	47	48	109	52	57
60-64	50	27	24	58	30	28	68	34	35	79	38	41
65-69	33	18	15	38	20	18	45	23	22	52	25	27
70-74	19	11	9	21	11	10	25	13	12	29	15	15
75-79	9	5	4	10	5	4	11	6	5	13	7	6
80 +	4	2	2	4	2	2	4	2	2	4	2	2

Age group	1970 Both sexes	Males	Females	1975 Both sexes	Males	Females	1980 Both sexes	Males	Females	1985 Both sexes	Males	Females
All ages	5 431	2 711	2 720	6 211	3 105	3 107	6 975	3 479	3 496	7 878	3 922	3 956
0-4	1 029	521	508	1 193	604	589	1 343	681	662	1 539	781	758
5-9	772	391	381	903	458	445	1 054	535	519	1 198	608	590
10-14	656	333	323	750	380	369	876	445	431	1 026	521	505
15-19	547	277	269	638	324	314	721	366	355	843	428	415
20-24	469	236	234	522	264	258	589	297	292	665	334	330
25-29	405	201	204	443	222	221	468	234	234	525	261	264
30-34	338	166	172	382	189	193	397	196	201	414	204	211
35-39	283	138	145	319	156	162	345	169	177	355	172	183
40-44	237	116	122	266	129	137	289	140	149	313	150	163
45-49	198	96	102	222	107	115	242	116	126	263	125	138
50-54	160	77	84	182	87	95	201	95	106	219	102	117
55-59	125	59	66	144	68	76	161	76	86	179	83	96
60-64	92	43	49	107	50	58	122	56	66	138	63	75
65-69	62	29	33	73	34	39	85	38	46	100	45	55
70-74	35	17	18	43	20	23	50	23	28	61	27	34
75-79	16	8	8	19	9	10	24	11	13	29	13	16
80 +	5	3	3	7	3	3	8	4	4	11	5	6

Age group	1990 Both sexes	Males	Females	1995 Both sexes	Males	Females	2000 Both sexes	Males	Females	2005 Both sexes	Males	Females
All ages	8 894	4 421	4 473	10 147	5 042	5 105	11 647	5 791	5 856	13 518	6 737	6 782
0-4	1 696	862	834	1 976	1 005	971	2 300	1 171	1 130	2 602	1 324	1 278
5-9	1 389	706	683	1 548	788	761	1 818	926	892	2 132	1 086	1 046
10-14	1 170	594	576	1 360	692	668	1 518	773	745	1 786	910	876
15-19	991	503	488	1 133	575	558	1 320	671	649	1 483	755	728
20-24	782	394	388	924	465	459	1 060	535	526	1 264	639	625
25-29	595	295	300	704	350	354	835	416	419	999	499	499
30-34	467	228	239	530	258	272	627	307	320	782	387	395
35-39	370	178	192	418	200	218	472	226	247	585	284	301
40-44	321	152	168	334	157	176	376	176	200	441	208	232
45-49	285	134	151	292	136	156	302	139	163	351	162	189
50-54	239	111	128	260	119	140	265	120	145	280	127	153
55-59	196	90	107	215	97	118	234	105	129	243	108	135
60-64	156	70	86	174	78	96	191	85	106	207	91	116
65-69	115	51	64	132	58	74	149	66	83	160	69	91
70-74	73	33	40	86	38	48	100	44	56	111	48	63
75-79	36	16	20	44	19	25	54	23	31	62	26	36
80 +	14	6	8	18	7	10	25	10	15	31	13	19

United Nations Department of Economic and Social Affairs/Population Division
World Population Prospects: The 2004 Revision, Volume II: Sex and Age Distribution of the World Population

578

POPULATION BY AGE AND SEX (in thousands)

Age group	2005			2010			2015			2020		
	Both sexes	Males	Females	Both sexes	Males	Females	Both sexes	Males	Females	Both sexes	Males	Females
All ages	13 518	6 737	6 782	15 017	7 800	7 814	18 093	9 067	9 025	20 904	10 504	10 400
0-4	2 602	1 324	1 278	2 942	1 498	1 444	3 302	1 682	1 620	3 669	1 870	1 798
5-9	2 132	1 086	1 046	2 426	1 236	1 190	2 768	1 411	1 357	3 132	1 597	1 535
10-14	1 786	910	876	2 095	1 068	1 027	2 389	1 217	1 171	2 731	1 392	1 339
15-19	1 483	755	728	1 749	891	858	2 060	1 050	1 010	2 354	1 199	1 155
20-24	1 264	639	625	1 422	721	701	1 694	861	833	2 004	1 020	985
25-29	999	499	499	1 187	597	590	1 354	685	670	1 625	824	801
30-34	782	387	395	926	462	465	1 119	562	557	1 286	649	636
35-39	585	284	301	723	356	367	870	433	437	1 059	531	528
40-44	441	208	232	542	261	281	679	333	346	822	408	415
45-49	351	162	189	408	191	218	508	243	266	641	312	329
50-54	280	127	153	324	147	177	382	176	206	478	226	252
55-59	243	108	135	256	114	142	299	133	166	354	160	193
60-64	207	91	116	215	94	122	229	100	130	270	118	152
65-69	160	69	91	174	74	100	183	78	106	197	83	114
70-74	111	48	63	121	51	70	134	56	78	143	59	84
75-79	62	26	36	70	29	41	78	32	46	88	35	53
80-84	25	10	15	29	12	17	34	14	20	39	15	24
85-89	6	2	4	8	3	5	9	3	6	11	4	7
90-94	1	0	0	1	0	1	1	0	1	2	1	1
95-99	0	0	0	0	0	0	0	0	0	0	0	0
100 +	0	0	0	0	0	0	0	0	0	0	0	0

Age group	2025			2030			2035			2040		
	Both sexes	Males	Females	Both sexes	Males	Females	Both sexes	Males	Females	Both sexes	Males	Females
All ages	24 031	12 102	11 929	27 413	13 830	13 583	30 962	15 639	15 323	34 600	17 488	17 112
0-4	4 010	2 046	1 964	4 292	2 191	2 101	4 489	2 292	2 197	4 616	2 357	2 260
5-9	3 508	1 790	1 718	3 862	1 972	1 890	4 160	2 125	2 035	4 374	2 235	2 140
10-14	3 099	1 580	1 518	3 477	1 775	1 703	3 834	1 958	1 877	4 135	2 112	2 023
15-19	2 697	1 374	1 322	3 065	1 563	1 502	3 444	1 757	1 687	3 803	1 941	1 862
20-24	2 298	1 169	1 129	2 641	1 344	1 297	3 010	1 532	1 478	3 392	1 728	1 664
25-29	1 934	982	952	2 227	1 131	1 097	2 572	1 306	1 266	2 943	1 496	1 447
30-34	1 554	787	767	1 861	944	917	2 156	1 094	1 062	2 502	1 270	1 232
35-39	1 224	618	606	1 490	754	736	1 796	910	886	2 091	1 060	1 031
40-44	1 008	504	503	1 172	590	582	1 435	725	710	1 740	880	859
45-49	781	385	396	963	480	484	1 126	564	562	1 386	697	689
50-54	606	292	314	742	363	380	920	454	465	1 080	537	543
55-59	446	208	238	568	270	298	700	338	362	871	426	446
60-64	322	143	179	408	186	221	523	245	279	648	307	340
65-69	234	100	134	281	122	159	359	161	199	465	213	252
70-74	156	64	92	187	78	110	228	96	132	295	129	167
75-79	96	38	58	107	42	64	131	52	79	162	66	96
80-84	45	17	28	50	19	31	57	21	36	72	27	44
85-89	13	5	8	16	6	10	18	6	11	21	7	13
90-94	2	1	1	3	1	2	3	1	2	4	1	3
95-99	0	0	0	0	0	0	0	0	0	0	0	0
100 +	0	0	0	0	0	0	0	0	0	0	0	0

Age group	2045			2050		
	Both sexes	Males	Females	Both sexes	Males	Females
All ages	38 281	19 352	18 929	41 976	21 214	20 761
0-4	4 708	2 403	2 305	4 789	2 443	2 345
5-9	4 518	2 307	2 211	4 625	2 361	2 264
10-14	4 352	2 223	2 129	4 499	2 297	2 202
15-19	4 106	2 096	2 010	4 325	2 208	2 117
20-24	3 753	1 912	1 841	4 058	2 068	1 990
25-29	3 328	1 692	1 635	3 692	1 878	1 814
30-34	2 876	1 460	1 416	3 265	1 658	1 606
35-39	2 439	1 237	1 203	2 816	1 428	1 388
40-44	2 036	1 030	1 006	2 384	1 207	1 178
45-49	1 688	851	837	1 983	1 000	984
50-54	1 336	667	668	1 633	818	815
55-59	1 028	506	522	1 276	631	645
60-64	811	390	421	962	466	496
65-69	580	269	310	732	345	387
70-74	386	173	214	487	221	266
75-79	214	90	124	284	122	162
80-84	91	35	56	123	49	74
85-89	27	9	17	35	13	23
90-94	4	1	3	6	2	4
95-99	0	0	0	1	0	0
100 +	0	0	0	0	0	0

POPULATION BY AGE AND SEX (in thousands)

Age group	2005 Both sexes	Males	Females	2010 Both sexes	Males	Females	2015 Both sexes	Males	Females	2020 Both sexes	Males	Females
All ages	13 518	6 737	6 782	15 729	7 860	7 869	18 411	9 229	9 182	21 528	10 822	10 706
0-4	2 602	1 324	1 278	3 054	1 555	1 499	3 514	1 790	1 724	3 985	2 032	1 954
5-9	2 132	1 086	1 046	2 426	1 236	1 190	2 873	1 464	1 409	3 334	1 700	1 634
10-14	1 786	910	876	2 095	1 068	1 027	2 389	1 217	1 171	2 836	1 446	1 390
15-19	1 483	755	728	1 749	891	858	2 060	1 050	1 010	2 354	1 199	1 155
20-24	1 264	639	625	1 422	721	701	1 694	861	833	2 004	1 020	985
25-29	999	499	499	1 187	597	590	1 354	685	670	1 625	824	801
30-34	782	387	395	926	462	465	1 119	562	557	1 286	649	636
35-39	585	284	301	723	356	367	870	433	437	1 059	531	528
40-44	441	208	232	542	261	281	679	333	346	822	408	415
45-49	351	162	189	408	191	218	508	243	266	641	312	329
50-54	280	127	153	324	147	177	382	176	206	478	226	252
55-59	243	108	135	256	114	142	299	133	166	354	160	193
60-64	207	91	116	215	94	122	229	100	130	270	118	152
65-69	160	69	91	174	74	100	183	78	106	197	83	114
70-74	111	48	63	121	51	70	134	56	78	143	59	84
75-79	62	26	36	70	29	41	78	32	46	88	35	53
80-84	25	10	15	29	12	17	34	14	20	39	15	24
85-89	6	2	4	8	3	5	9	3	6	11	4	7
90-94	1	0	0	1	0	1	1	0	1	2	1	1
95-99	0	0	0	0	0	0	0	0	0	0	0	0
100 +	0	0	0	0	0	0	0	0	0	0	0	0

Age group	2025 Both sexes	Males	Females	2030 Both sexes	Males	Females	2035 Both sexes	Males	Females	2040 Both sexes	Males	Females
All ages	25 029	12 611	12 417	28 898	14 588	14 310	33 095	16 728	16 367	37 579	19 009	18 570
0-4	4 401	2 245	2 156	4 798	2 449	2 349	5 160	2 635	2 525	5 489	2 802	2 687
5-9	3 811	1 945	1 866	4 239	2 164	2 075	4 652	2 376	2 276	5 029	2 569	2 460
10-14	3 299	1 683	1 616	3 778	1 928	1 850	4 209	2 149	2 060	4 624	2 362	2 262
15-19	2 800	1 427	1 373	3 263	1 664	1 599	3 743	1 909	1 834	4 175	2 131	2 045
20-24	2 298	1 169	1 129	2 743	1 396	1 347	3 207	1 633	1 574	3 688	1 879	1 809
25-29	1 934	982	952	2 227	1 131	1 097	2 672	1 358	1 315	3 137	1 595	1 542
30-34	1 554	787	767	1 861	944	917	2 156	1 094	1 062	2 601	1 320	1 280
35-39	1 224	618	606	1 490	754	736	1 796	910	886	2 091	1 060	1 031
40-44	1 008	504	503	1 172	590	582	1 435	725	710	1 740	880	859
45-49	781	385	396	963	480	484	1 126	564	562	1 386	697	689
50-54	606	292	314	742	363	380	920	454	465	1 080	537	543
55-59	446	208	238	568	270	298	700	338	362	871	426	446
60-64	322	143	179	408	186	221	523	245	279	648	307	340
65-69	234	100	134	281	122	159	359	161	199	465	213	252
70-74	156	64	92	187	78	110	228	96	132	295	129	167
75-79	96	38	58	107	42	64	131	52	79	162	66	96
80-84	45	17	28	50	19	31	57	21	36	72	27	44
85-89	13	5	8	16	6	10	18	6	11	21	7	13
90-94	2	1	1	3	1	2	3	1	2	4	1	3
95-99	0	0	0	0	0	0	0	0	0	0	0	0
100 +	0	0	0	0	0	0	0	0	0	0	0	0

Age group	2045 Both sexes	Males	Females	2050 Both sexes	Males	Females
All ages	42 311	21 409	20 902	47 262	23 912	23 350
0-4	5 794	2 957	2 837	6 082	3 103	2 979
5-9	5 374	2 744	2 629	5 692	2 906	2 786
10-14	5 004	2 556	2 448	5 351	2 732	2 619
15-19	4 592	2 344	2 248	4 974	2 539	2 435
20-24	4 122	2 101	2 022	4 542	2 315	2 227
25-29	3 621	1 842	1 779	4 059	2 065	1 993
30-34	3 067	1 558	1 509	3 554	1 806	1 748
35-39	2 536	1 286	1 250	3 005	1 524	1 481
40-44	2 036	1 030	1 006	2 480	1 255	1 225
45-49	1 688	851	837	1 983	1 000	984
50-54	1 336	667	668	1 633	818	815
55-59	1 028	506	522	1 276	631	645
60-64	811	390	421	962	466	496
65-69	580	269	310	732	345	387
70-74	386	173	214	487	221	266
75-79	214	90	124	284	122	162
80-84	91	35	56	123	49	74
85-89	27	9	17	35	13	23
90-94	4	1	3	6	2	4
95-99	0	0	0	1	0	0
100 +	0	0	0	0	0	0

United Nations Department of Economic and Social Affairs/Population Division
World Population Prospects: The 2004 Revision, Volume II: Sex and Age Distribution of the World Population

580

POPULATION BY AGE AND SEX (in thousands)

Age group	2005 Both sexes	2005 Males	2005 Females	2010 Both sexes	2010 Males	2010 Females	2015 Both sexes	2015 Males	2015 Females	2020 Both sexes	2020 Males	2020 Females
All ages	13 518	6 737	6 780	15 506	7 746	7 759	17 774	8 905	8 869	20 281	10 187	10 095
0-4	2 602	1 324	1 278	2 830	1 441	1 389	3 089	1 574	1 515	3 352	1 709	1 643
5-9	2 132	1 086	1 046	2 426	1 236	1 190	2 662	1 357	1 305	2 930	1 494	1 436
10-14	1 786	910	876	2 095	1 068	1 027	2 389	1 217	1 171	2 627	1 339	1 288
15-19	1 483	755	728	1 749	891	858	2 060	1 050	1 010	2 354	1 199	1 155
20-24	1 264	639	625	1 422	721	701	1 694	861	833	2 004	1 020	985
25-29	999	499	499	1 187	597	590	1 354	685	670	1 625	824	801
30-34	782	387	395	926	462	465	1 119	562	557	1 286	649	636
35-39	585	284	301	723	356	367	870	433	437	1 059	531	528
40-44	441	208	232	542	261	281	679	333	346	822	408	415
45-49	351	162	189	408	191	218	508	243	266	641	312	329
50-54	280	127	153	324	147	177	382	176	206	478	226	252
55-59	243	108	135	256	114	142	299	133	166	354	160	193
60-64	207	91	116	215	94	122	229	100	130	270	118	152
65-69	160	69	91	174	74	100	183	78	106	197	83	114
70-74	111	48	63	121	51	70	134	56	78	143	59	84
75-79	62	26	36	70	29	41	78	32	46	88	35	53
80-84	25	10	15	29	12	17	34	14	20	39	15	24
85-89	6	2	4	8	3	5	9	3	6	11	4	7
90-94	1	0	0	1	0	1	1	0	1	2	1	1
95-99	0	0	0	0	0	0	0	0	0	0	0	0
100 +	0	0	0	0	0	0	0	0	0	0	0	0

Age group	2025 Both sexes	2025 Males	2025 Females	2030 Both sexes	2030 Males	2030 Females	2035 Both sexes	2035 Males	2035 Females	2040 Both sexes	2040 Males	2040 Females
All ages	23 036	11 595	11 441	25 942	13 079	12 863	28 874	14 573	14 301	31 729	16 023	15 707
0-4	3 622	1 848	1 774	3 797	1 938	1 859	3 849	1 965	1 884	3 806	1 943	1 863
5-9	3 205	1 635	1 569	3 488	1 781	1 707	3 680	1 880	1 800	3 750	1 916	1 834
10-14	2 898	1 478	1 420	3 176	1 621	1 555	3 462	1 768	1 695	3 658	1 868	1 790
15-19	2 593	1 322	1 272	2 866	1 461	1 405	3 146	1 605	1 541	3 433	1 752	1 681
20-24	2 298	1 169	1 129	2 539	1 292	1 247	2 814	1 432	1 381	3 096	1 577	1 519
25-29	1 934	982	952	2 227	1 131	1 097	2 471	1 255	1 216	2 749	1 397	1 352
30-34	1 554	787	767	1 861	944	917	2 156	1 094	1 062	2 403	1 219	1 184
35-39	1 224	618	606	1 490	754	736	1 796	910	886	2 091	1 060	1 031
40-44	1 008	504	503	1 172	590	582	1 435	725	710	1 740	880	859
45-49	781	385	396	963	480	484	1 126	564	562	1 386	697	689
50-54	606	292	314	742	363	380	920	454	465	1 080	537	543
55-59	446	208	238	568	270	298	700	338	362	871	426	446
60-64	322	143	179	408	186	221	523	245	279	648	307	340
65-69	234	100	134	281	122	159	359	161	199	465	213	252
70-74	156	64	92	187	78	110	228	96	132	295	129	167
75-79	96	38	58	107	42	64	131	52	79	162	66	96
80-84	45	17	28	50	10	31	57	21	36	72	27	44
85-89	13	5	8	16	6	10	18	6	11	21	7	13
90-94	2	1	1	3	1	2	3	1	2	4	1	3
95-99	0	0	0	0	0	0	0	0	0	0	0	0
100 +	0	0	0	0	0	0	0	0	0	0	0	0

Age group	2045 Both sexes	2045 Males	2045 Females	2050 Both sexes	2050 Males	2050 Females
All ages	34 458	17 401	17 057	37 044	18 698	18 346
0-4	3 726	1 901	1 824	3 644	1 859	1 785
5-9	3 724	1 902	1 822	3 658	1 867	1 791
10-14	3 731	1 906	1 825	3 708	1 893	1 815
15-19	3 630	1 853	1 777	3 706	1 892	1 814
20-24	3 385	1 725	1 661	3 586	1 827	1 758
25-29	3 035	1 543	1 492	3 328	1 693	1 635
30-34	2 685	1 363	1 322	2 975	1 510	1 464
35-39	2 342	1 187	1 155	2 628	1 332	1 296
40-44	2 036	1 030	1 006	2 289	1 158	1 131
45-49	1 688	851	837	1 983	1 000	984
50-54	1 336	667	668	1 633	818	815
55-59	1 028	506	522	1 276	631	645
60-64	811	390	421	962	466	496
65-69	580	269	310	732	345	387
70-74	386	173	214	487	221	266
75-79	214	90	124	284	122	162
80-84	91	35	56	123	49	74
85-89	27	9	17	35	13	23
90-94	4	1	3	6	2	4
95-99	0	0	0	1	0	0
100 +	0	0	0	0	0	0

POPULATION BY AGE AND SEX (in thousands)

Age group	1950 Both sexes	Males	Females	1955 Both sexes	Males	Females	1960 Both sexes	Males	Females	1965 Both sexes	Males	Females
All ages	312	154	158	314	152	162	312	151	161	305	147	158
0-4	47	24	23	43	21	22	42	21	21	32	17	16
5-9	30	15	15	45	22	23	42	21	21	36	19	18
10-14	32	16	16	31	15	16	31	15	16	35	19	17
15-19	28	14	14	29	14	15	28	14	14	35	18	18
20-24	26	13	13	23	10	13	21	10	11	20	10	11
25-29	23	11	12	18	8	10	21	9	12	18	8	11
30-34	18	9	9	18	9	9	18	8	10	19	8	12
35-39	18	9	9	16	8	8	18	9	9	17	8	10
40-44	19	9	10	16	8	8	15	8	7	17	8	10
45-49	16	8	8	18	9	9	15	7	8	14	7	8
50-54	14	7	7	14	7	7	16	7	9	13	7	7
55-59	12	6	6	12	6	6	13	6	7	14	7	8
60-64	11	5	6	10	5	5	11	5	6	11	6	5
65-69	7	3	4	8	4	4	10	5	5	8	4	4
70-74	6	3	3	7	3	4	7	3	4	8	4	4
75-79	3	1	2	4	2	2	4	2	2	5	2	3
80 +	2	1	1	2	1	1	2	1	1	3	1	2

Age group	1970 Both sexes	Males	Females	1975 Both sexes	Males	Females	1980 Both sexes	Males	Females	1985 Both sexes	Males	Females
All ages	303	146	157	304	147	157	324	158	166	344	169	175
0-4	23	12	11	25	13	12	27	14	13	28	14	14
5-9	28	15	14	23	12	11	25	13	12	28	15	14
10-14	32	17	16	27	14	13	23	12	11	27	14	13
15-19	32	16	16	27	13	14	27	14	13	24	12	12
20-24	31	15	16	27	14	14	30	15	15	27	14	13
25-29	21	9	11	30	14	16	29	14	15	29	15	14
30-34	19	8	10	20	9	11	30	14	16	28	14	14
35-39	18	8	10	20	9	10	20	9	11	30	15	15
40-44	17	8	9	17	8	9	19	9	10	22	11	11
45-49	17	8	9	17	8	9	17	8	9	19	9	10
50-54	13	6	7	18	9	9	16	8	8	18	8	10
55-59	13	6	7	13	6	7	16	8	8	16	7	9
60-64	13	6	7	11	5	6	12	6	6	15	7	8
65-69	11	5	6	12	6	6	10	5	6	11	5	6
70-74	8	3	4	8	4	5	10	5	6	10	4	5
75-79	5	2	3	5	2	3	7	3	4	7	3	4
80 +	4	2	2	4	2	2	5	2	3	6	2	4

Age group	1990 Both sexes	Males	Females	1995 Both sexes	Males	Females	2000 Both sexes	Males	Females	2005 Both sexes	Males	Females
All ages	360	178	182	378	187	191	392	194	198	402	199	202
0-4	27	14	13	26	13	13	24	12	11	20	10	10
5-9	28	14	14	28	14	14	26	14	13	24	12	12
10-14	29	15	14	29	15	14	29	15	14	27	14	13
15-19	26	14	13	29	15	14	29	15	14	29	15	14
20-24	24	12	12	27	14	13	30	15	14	30	15	15
25-29	28	14	13	23	12	11	27	14	13	30	15	15
30-34	29	15	14	26	14	13	23	12	11	27	14	13
35-39	28	14	14	30	15	15	27	14	13	23	12	11
40-44	30	15	15	28	14	14	30	15	15	27	14	13
45-49	21	10	11	31	15	15	28	14	14	30	15	15
50-54	19	9	10	22	11	11	31	15	15	29	14	14
55-59	17	8	10	19	9	10	22	11	11	30	15	15
60-64	15	7	8	17	8	9	18	9	10	21	10	11
65-69	14	6	8	14	6	8	16	7	9	17	8	9
70-74	9	4	5	12	5	7	13	6	7	14	6	8
75-79	7	3	4	8	3	4	10	4	6	11	4	6
80 +	7	3	4	8	3	5	9	3	6	12	4	8

United Nations Department of Economic and Social Affairs/Population Division
World Population Prospects: The 2004 Revision, Volume II: Sex and Age Distribution of the World Population

582

POPULATION BY AGE AND SEX (in thousands)

Age group	2005 Both sexes	Males	Females	2010 Both sexes	Males	Females	2015 Both sexes	Males	Females	2020 Both sexes	Males	Females
All ages	402	199	202	411	204	207	419	208	211	426	212	214
0-4	20	10	10	21	11	10	22	11	11	23	12	11
5-9	24	12	12	20	10	10	21	11	10	22	11	11
10-14	27	14	13	24	12	12	21	11	10	21	11	10
15-19	29	15	14	27	14	13	24	13	12	21	11	10
20-24	30	15	15	29	15	14	27	14	13	25	13	12
25-29	30	15	15	30	15	15	29	15	14	28	14	13
30-34	27	14	13	30	16	15	30	16	15	30	15	15
35-39	23	12	11	27	14	13	31	16	15	31	16	15
40-44	27	14	13	24	12	12	28	14	13	31	16	15
45-49	30	15	15	27	14	13	24	12	12	28	14	14
50-54	29	14	14	30	15	15	27	14	13	24	12	12
55-59	30	15	15	28	14	14	30	15	15	27	14	13
60-64	21	10	11	30	15	15	28	14	14	29	15	15
65-69	17	8	9	20	10	11	28	14	14	27	13	14
70-74	14	6	8	16	7	9	18	9	10	26	12	14
75-79	11	4	6	12	5	7	13	6	8	16	7	9
80-84	7	3	5	8	3	5	9	3	6	10	4	6
85-89	3	1	2	4	1	3	5	1	3	6	2	4
90-94	1	0	1	1	0	1	2	0	2	2	1	2
95-99	0	0	0	0	0	0	0	0	0	1	0	1
100 +	0	0	0	0	0	0	0	0	0	0	0	0

Age group	2025 Both sexes	Males	Females	2030 Both sexes	Males	Females	2035 Both sexes	Males	Females	2040 Both sexes	Males	Females
All ages	432	215	217	434	216	218	434	216	218	432	215	217
0-4	22	11	11	22	11	10	21	11	10	20	11	10
5-9	23	12	11	23	12	11	22	11	11	21	11	10
10-14	22	12	11	23	12	11	23	12	11	22	11	11
15-19	22	11	11	23	12	11	23	12	11	23	12	11
20-24	21	11	10	22	11	11	23	12	11	24	12	11
25-29	25	13	12	21	11	10	22	11	11	23	12	11
30-34	28	14	14	25	13	12	21	11	10	22	11	11
35-39	30	15	15	28	14	14	25	13	12	22	11	11
40-44	31	16	15	30	15	15	28	15	14	26	13	12
45-49	31	16	15	31	16	15	30	16	15	29	15	14
50-54	28	14	14	31	16	15	31	16	15	31	16	15
55-59	24	12	10	28	14	14	31	16	15	31	16	15
60-64	27	13	13	23	12	12	27	14	14	31	16	15
65-69	28	14	14	26	13	13	23	11	11	27	13	13
70-74	25	12	13	26	13	14	24	12	12	21	11	11
75-79	22	10	12	21	10	12	23	11	12	21	10	11
80-84	12	5	7	18	7	10	17	7	10	19	8	11
85-89	7	2	4	8	3	5	12	5	7	12	5	7
90-94	3	1	2	3	1	3	4	1	3	7	2	5
95-99	1	0	1	1	0	1	1	0	1	2	0	1
100 +	0	0	0	0	0	0	0	0	0	0	0	0

Age group	2045 Both sexes	Males	Females	2050 Both sexes	Males	Females
All ages	430	214	216	428	213	215
0-4	21	11	10	21	11	10
5-9	21	11	10	21	11	10
10-14	21	11	10	21	11	10
15-19	22	11	11	21	11	10
20-24	23	12	11	23	12	11
25-29	24	12	12	24	12	11
30-34	23	12	11	24	12	12
35-39	23	12	11	24	12	11
40-44	22	11	11	23	12	11
45-49	26	13	13	22	11	11
50-54	29	15	14	26	13	13
55-59	31	16	15	29	15	14
60-64	31	16	15	30	15	15
65-69	30	15	15	30	15	15
70-74	25	12	13	28	14	14
75-79	19	9	10	23	11	12
80-84	17	8	10	16	7	9
85-89	13	5	8	13	5	8
90-94	7	2	5	8	3	5
95-99	3	1	2	3	1	2
100 +	0	0	0	1	0	1

United Nations Department of Economic and Social Affairs/Population Division
World Population Prospects: The 2004 Revision, Volume II: Sex and Age Distribution of the World Population

583

POPULATION BY AGE AND SEX (in thousands)

Age group	2005 Both sexes	Males	Females	2010 Both sexes	Males	Females	2015 Both sexes	Males	Females	2020 Both sexes	Males	Females
All ages	402	199	202	414	206	208	428	213	215	442	220	222
0-4	20	10	10	25	13	12	28	14	13	29	15	14
5-9	24	12	12	20	10	10	25	13	12	28	14	14
10-14	27	14	13	24	12	12	21	11	10	25	13	12
15-19	29	15	14	27	14	13	24	13	12	21	11	10
20-24	30	15	15	29	15	14	27	14	13	25	13	12
25-29	30	15	15	30	15	15	29	15	14	28	14	13
30-34	27	14	13	30	16	15	30	16	15	30	15	15
35-39	23	12	11	27	14	13	31	16	15	31	16	15
40-44	27	14	13	24	12	12	28	14	13	31	16	15
45-49	30	15	15	27	14	13	24	12	12	28	14	14
50-54	29	14	14	30	15	15	27	14	13	24	12	12
55-59	30	15	15	28	14	14	30	15	15	27	14	13
60-64	21	10	11	30	15	15	28	14	14	29	15	15
65-69	17	8	9	20	10	11	28	14	14	27	13	14
70-74	14	6	8	16	7	9	18	9	10	26	12	14
75-79	11	4	6	12	5	7	13	6	8	16	7	9
80-84	7	3	5	8	3	5	9	3	6	10	4	6
85-89	3	1	2	4	1	3	5	1	3	6	2	4
90-94	1	0	1	1	0	1	2	0	2	2	1	2
95-99	0	0	0	0	0	0	0	0	0	1	0	1
100 +	0	0	0	0	0	0	0	0	0	0	0	0

Age group	2025 Both sexes	Males	Females	2030 Both sexes	Males	Females	2035 Both sexes	Males	Females	2040 Both sexes	Males	Females
All ages	454	226	227	462	231	232	469	234	235	476	237	239
0-4	29	15	14	27	14	13	27	14	13	29	15	14
5-9	30	15	14	29	15	14	28	14	13	28	14	13
10-14	28	14	14	30	15	14	29	15	14	28	14	14
15-19	25	13	12	28	15	14	30	15	15	29	15	14
20-24	21	11	10	25	13	12	29	15	14	30	16	15
25-29	25	13	12	21	11	10	26	13	12	29	15	14
30-34	28	14	14	25	13	12	21	11	10	26	13	13
35-39	30	15	15	28	14	14	25	13	12	22	11	11
40-44	31	16	15	30	15	15	28	15	14	26	13	12
45-49	31	16	15	31	16	15	30	16	15	29	15	14
50-54	28	14	14	31	16	15	31	16	15	31	16	15
55-59	24	12	12	28	14	14	31	16	15	31	16	15
60-64	27	13	13	23	12	12	27	14	14	31	16	15
65-69	28	14	14	26	13	13	23	11	11	27	13	13
70-74	25	12	13	26	13	14	24	12	12	21	11	11
75-79	22	10	12	21	10	12	23	11	12	21	10	11
80-84	12	5	7	18	7	10	17	7	10	19	8	11
85-89	7	2	4	8	3	5	12	5	7	12	5	7
90-94	3	1	2	3	1	3	4	1	3	7	2	5
95-99	1	0	1	1	0	1	1	0	1	2	0	1
100 +	0	0	0	0	0	0	0	0	0	0	0	0

Age group	2045 Both sexes	Males	Females	2050 Both sexes	Males	Females
All ages	485	242	243	496	248	248
0-4	32	17	16	34	17	16
5-9	30	15	14	32	17	16
10-14	28	14	14	30	15	15
15-19	28	14	14	28	14	14
20-24	30	15	14	28	15	14
25-29	31	16	15	30	15	15
30-34	29	15	14	31	16	15
35-39	26	13	13	29	15	14
40-44	22	11	11	26	13	13
45-49	26	13	13	22	11	11
50-54	29	15	14	26	13	13
55-59	31	16	15	29	15	14
60-64	31	16	15	30	15	15
65-69	30	15	15	30	15	15
70-74	25	12	13	28	14	14
75-79	19	9	10	23	11	12
80-84	17	8	10	16	7	9
85-89	13	5	8	13	5	8
90-94	7	2	5	8	3	5
95-99	3	1	2	3	1	2
100 +	0	0	0	1	0	1

United Nations Department of Economic and Social Affairs/Population Division
World Population Prospects: The 2004 Revision, Volume II: Sex and Age Distribution of the World Population

584

POPULATION BY AGE AND SEX (in thousands)

Age group	2005 Both sexes	2005 Males	2005 Females	2010 Both sexes	2010 Males	2010 Females	2015 Both sexes	2015 Males	2015 Females	2020 Both sexes	2020 Males	2020 Females
All ages	402	199	202	407	202	205	410	204	206	410	204	206
0-4	20	10	10	17	9	8	16	8	8	16	8	8
5-9	24	12	12	20	10	10	18	9	9	16	8	8
10-14	27	14	13	24	12	12	21	11	10	18	9	9
15-19	29	15	14	27	14	13	24	13	12	21	11	10
20-24	30	15	15	29	15	14	27	14	13	25	13	12
25-29	30	15	15	30	15	15	29	15	14	28	14	13
30-34	27	14	13	30	16	15	30	16	15	30	15	15
35-39	23	12	11	27	14	13	31	16	15	31	16	15
40-44	27	14	13	24	12	12	28	14	13	31	16	15
45-49	30	15	15	27	14	13	24	12	12	28	14	14
50-54	29	14	14	30	15	15	27	14	13	24	12	12
55-59	30	15	15	28	14	14	30	15	15	27	14	13
60-64	21	10	11	30	15	15	28	14	14	29	15	15
65-69	17	8	9	20	10	11	28	14	14	27	13	14
70-74	14	6	8	16	7	9	18	9	10	26	12	14
75-79	11	4	6	12	5	7	13	6	8	16	7	9
80-84	7	3	5	8	3	5	9	3	6	10	4	6
85-89	3	1	2	4	1	3	5	1	3	6	2	4
90-94	1	0	1	1	0	1	2	0	2	2	1	2
95-99	0	0	0	0	0	0	0	0	0	1	0	1
100 +	0	0	0	0	0	0	0	0	0	0	0	0

Age group	2025 Both sexes	2025 Males	2025 Females	2030 Both sexes	2030 Males	2030 Females	2035 Both sexes	2035 Males	2035 Females	2040 Both sexes	2040 Males	2040 Females
All ages	409	203	206	406	201	204	400	198	201	391	194	197
0-4	16	8	8	16	8	8	15	8	7	13	7	7
5-9	16	8	8	16	8	8	16	8	8	15	8	7
10-14	17	9	8	16	8	8	16	8	8	16	8	8
15-19	18	9	9	17	9	8	16	8	8	17	9	8
20-24	21	11	10	18	9	9	17	9	8	17	9	8
25-29	25	13	12	21	11	10	19	10	9	17	9	8
30-34	28	14	14	25	13	12	21	11	10	19	10	9
35-39	30	15	15	28	14	14	25	13	12	22	11	11
40-44	31	16	15	30	15	15	28	15	14	26	13	12
45-49	31	16	15	31	16	15	30	16	15	29	15	14
50-54	28	14	14	31	16	15	31	16	15	31	16	15
55-59	24	12	12	28	14	14	31	16	15	31	16	15
60-64	27	13	13	23	12	12	27	14	14	31	16	15
65-69	28	14	14	26	13	13	23	11	11	27	13	13
70-74	25	12	13	26	13	14	24	12	12	21	11	11
75-79	22	10	12	21	10	12	23	11	12	21	10	11
80-84	12	5	7	18	7	10	17	7	10	19	8	11
85-89	7	2	4	8	3	5	12	5	7	12	5	7
90-94	3	1	2	3	1	3	4	1	3	7	2	5
95-99	1	0	1	1	0	1	1	0	1	2	0	1
100 +	0	0	0	0	0	0	0	0	0	0	0	0

Age group	2045 Both sexes	2045 Males	2045 Females	2050 Both sexes	2050 Males	2050 Females
All ages	380	188	192	369	183	187
0-4	12	6	6	12	6	6
5-9	14	7	7	13	6	6
10-14	15	8	7	14	7	7
15-19	16	8	8	15	8	8
20-24	17	9	8	17	9	8
25-29	17	9	8	17	9	8
30-34	18	9	9	17	9	8
35-39	19	10	9	18	9	9
40-44	22	11	11	19	10	9
45-49	26	13	13	22	11	11
50-54	29	15	14	26	13	13
55-59	31	16	15	29	15	14
60-64	31	16	15	30	15	15
65-69	30	15	15	30	15	15
70-74	25	12	13	28	14	14
75-79	19	9	10	23	11	12
80-84	17	8	10	16	7	9
85-89	13	5	8	13	5	8
90-94	7	2	5	8	3	5
95-99	3	1	2	3	1	2
100 +	0	0	0	1	0	1

POPULATION BY AGE AND SEX (in thousands)

Age group	1950 Both sexes	1950 Males	1950 Females	1955 Both sexes	1955 Males	1955 Females	1960 Both sexes	1960 Males	1960 Females	1965 Both sexes	1965 Males	1965 Females
All ages	222	106	116	246	118	128	282	138	144	311	150	161
0-4	34	17	17	42	21	21	45	23	23	51	25	25
5-9	25	12	13	32	16	16	42	21	21	47	23	23
10-14	24	12	12	25	13	12	32	17	16	41	20	20
15-19	21	10	11	24	12	12	26	14	12	30	15	15
20-24	18	8	10	19	9	10	24	12	12	19	9	10
25-29	17	8	9	17	8	9	19	9	10	18	8	10
30-34	15	7	8	15	7	8	16	7	9	17	8	9
35-39	14	7	7	14	7	7	15	7	8	17	8	9
40-44	12	6	6	14	7	7	13	6	7	15	7	8
45-49	10	5	5	11	5	6	13	6	7	12	6	6
50-54	8	4	4	9	4	5	11	5	6	12	6	6
55-59	7	3	4	7	3	4	8	4	4	10	5	5
60-64	5	2	3	5	2	3	7	3	4	7	3	4
65-69	5	2	3	5	2	3	5	2	3	5	2	3
70-74	3	1	2	3	1	2	3	1	2	5	2	3
75-79	2	1	1	2	1	1	3	1	2	3	1	2
80 +	1	0	1	2	1	1	2	1	1	2	1	1

Age group	1970 Both sexes	1970 Males	1970 Females	1975 Both sexes	1975 Males	1975 Females	1980 Both sexes	1980 Males	1980 Females	1985 Both sexes	1985 Males	1985 Females
All ages	325	159	166	328	159	169	326	158	168	341	165	176
0-4	49	25	23	40	20	20	26	14	13	29	14	14
5-9	45	22	22	45	23	23	32	16	16	30	15	15
10-14	41	21	21	47	24	24	41	21	20	35	18	17
15-19	34	17	18	40	20	20	42	21	21	38	20	19
20-24	25	12	14	24	12	12	31	16	15	33	17	16
25-29	19	9	10	17	8	9	22	10	12	27	13	14
30-34	18	9	9	15	7	8	20	9	11	23	11	12
35-39	17	8	9	16	8	9	17	8	9	20	9	11
40-44	15	7	8	15	7	8	16	7	8	18	8	9
45-49	15	7	8	15	7	8	16	7	8	16	8	9
50-54	12	6	6	13	6	7	14	7	7	15	7	8
55-59	12	6	6	11	5	5	13	6	7	14	6	7
60-64	9	4	5	10	5	5	11	5	6	12	6	7
65-69	7	3	4	8	4	4	9	4	5	10	5	6
70-74	5	2	3	6	2	3	7	3	4	8	3	4
75-79	3	1	2	4	1	2	5	2	3	6	2	3
80 +	2	1	1	4	1	2	5	2	3	6	2	4

Age group	1990 Both sexes	1990 Males	1990 Females	1995 Both sexes	1995 Males	1995 Females	2000 Both sexes	2000 Males	2000 Females	2005 Both sexes	2005 Males	2005 Females
All ages	360	174	186	375	180	195	386	183	203	396	188	208
0-4	31	16	15	31	16	15	28	14	14	27	14	13
5-9	29	15	14	31	16	15	30	15	15	28	14	14
10-14	29	15	14	29	15	14	32	16	16	30	15	15
15-19	35	18	17	26	13	13	29	15	14	31	15	15
20-24	34	17	17	31	15	16	22	11	11	26	13	13
25-29	33	16	17	34	16	17	27	13	14	20	10	10
30-34	28	14	14	34	17	18	33	15	18	27	13	14
35-39	24	11	13	29	14	15	34	16	18	33	15	18
40-44	20	10	11	24	11	13	29	13	15	34	16	18
45-49	17	8	9	20	10	11	24	11	13	29	13	15
50-54	16	8	9	17	8	9	21	9	11	24	11	13
55-59	15	7	8	16	7	8	17	8	9	20	9	11
60-64	14	6	7	15	7	8	15	7	8	16	7	9
65-69	12	5	6	13	6	7	14	6	8	15	7	8
70-74	9	4	5	10	5	6	12	5	7	13	6	7
75-79	7	3	4	7	3	4	9	4	5	10	4	6
80 +	8	3	5	9	3	6	11	4	7	13	5	8

586

United Nations Department of Economic and Social Affairs/Population Division
World Population Prospects: The 2004 Revision, Volume II: Sex and Age Distribution of the World Population

POPULATION BY AGE AND SEX (in thousands)

Age group	2005			2010			2015			2020		
	Both sexes	Males	Females	Both sexes	Males	Females	Both sexes	Males	Females	Both sexes	Males	Females
All ages	396	188	208	401	190	211	404	192	213	405	192	213
0-4	27	14	13	24	12	12	22	11	11	22	11	11
5-9	28	14	14	27	14	13	24	12	12	22	11	11
10-14	30	15	15	28	14	14	27	14	13	24	12	12
15-19	31	15	15	29	15	14	27	14	13	26	13	13
20-24	26	13	13	27	14	14	25	13	13	23	12	11
25-29	20	10	10	24	12	12	25	13	13	24	12	12
30-34	27	13	14	20	10	10	24	12	12	26	13	13
35-39	33	15	18	27	13	14	20	10	10	24	12	12
40-44	34	16	18	33	15	18	28	13	15	21	10	11
45-49	29	13	15	34	16	18	33	15	18	28	13	15
50-54	24	11	13	29	13	15	34	16	18	33	15	18
55-59	20	9	11	24	11	13	28	13	15	34	15	18
60-64	16	7	9	20	9	11	23	10	13	27	13	15
65-69	15	7	8	15	7	9	19	8	11	22	10	12
70-74	13	6	7	13	6	8	14	6	8	17	7	10
75-79	10	4	6	11	5	6	12	5	7	12	5	7
80-84	7	3	4	8	3	5	9	3	5	9	4	6
85-89	4	1	2	5	2	3	5	2	3	6	2	4
90-94	2	1	1	2	1	1	3	1	2	3	1	2
95-99	1	0	0	1	0	1	1	0	1	1	0	1
100 +	0	0	0	0	0	0	0	0	0	0	0	0

Age group	2025			2030			2035			2040		
	Both sexes	Males	Females	Both sexes	Males	Females	Both sexes	Males	Females	Both sexes	Males	Females
All ages	404	192	212	399	190	210	392	186	206	381	181	200
0-4	21	11	10	19	10	9	18	9	9	16	8	8
5-9	21	11	10	21	10	10	19	10	9	17	9	8
10-14	22	11	11	22	11	11	21	11	10	20	10	10
15-19	23	12	11	21	11	10	21	10	10	20	10	10
20-24	22	11	11	19	10	9	18	9	9	17	9	8
25-29	21	11	10	21	11	10	17	9	8	16	8	8
30-34	24	12	12	22	11	11	21	11	10	18	9	9
35-39	26	13	13	24	12	12	22	11	11	21	11	10
40-44	25	13	12	26	13	13	24	12	12	22	11	11
45-49	21	10	11	25	13	12	26	13	13	25	12	12
50-54	28	13	15	21	10	11	25	13	12	26	13	13
55-59	33	15	18	27	12	15	21	10	11	25	12	12
60-64	33	15	18	32	14	18	27	12	15	21	10	11
65-69	26	12	15	31	14	17	31	14	17	26	12	14
70-74	20	9	12	24	11	14	29	13	17	29	12	17
75-79	15	6	9	18	7	11	22	9	13	26	11	15
80-84	10	4	6	12	5	8	15	6	9	18	7	11
85-89	7	2	4	7	3	5	9	3	6	11	4	7
90-94	3	1	2	4	1	3	4	1	3	6	2	4
95-99	1	0	1	2	0	1	2	0	1	2	1	1
100 +	0	0	0	0	0	0	1	0	0	1	0	0

Age group	2045			2050		
	Both sexes	Males	Females	Both sexes	Males	Females
All ages	367	174	192	350	167	184
0-4	15	8	7	14	7	7
5-9	16	8	8	14	7	7
10-14	18	9	9	16	8	8
15-19	18	9	9	16	8	8
20-24	16	8	8	15	8	7
25-29	15	8	7	14	7	7
30-34	16	8	8	16	8	8
35-39	18	9	9	16	8	8
40-44	21	11	10	18	9	9
45-49	23	11	11	22	11	11
50-54	25	12	12	23	11	11
55-59	26	13	13	25	12	12
60-64	24	12	12	26	13	13
65-69	20	10	10	24	12	12
70-74	24	11	14	19	9	10
75-79	26	11	15	22	9	13
80-84	22	9	13	22	8	13
85-89	13	5	9	16	6	11
90-94	7	2	5	8	3	6
95-99	3	1	2	3	1	2
100 +	1	0	1	1	0	1

United Nations Department of Economic and Social Affairs/Population Division
World Population Prospects: The 2004 Revision, Volume II: Sex and Age Distribution of the World Population

587

POPULATION BY AGE AND SEX (in thousands)

Age group	2005 Both sexes	2005 Males	2005 Females	2010 Both sexes	2010 Males	2010 Females	2015 Both sexes	2015 Males	2015 Females	2020 Both sexes	2020 Males	2020 Females
All ages	396	188	208	405	192	213	412	196	217	419	199	220
0-4	27	14	13	27	14	13	27	14	13	28	14	14
5-9	28	14	14	27	14	13	27	14	13	27	14	13
10-14	30	15	15	28	14	14	27	14	13	27	14	13
15-19	31	15	15	29	15	14	27	14	13	26	13	13
20-24	26	13	13	27	14	14	25	13	13	23	12	11
25-29	20	10	10	24	12	12	25	13	13	24	12	12
30-34	27	13	14	20	10	10	24	12	12	26	13	13
35-39	33	15	18	27	13	14	20	10	10	24	12	12
40-44	34	16	18	33	15	18	28	13	15	21	10	11
45-49	29	13	15	34	16	18	33	15	18	28	13	15
50-54	24	11	13	29	13	15	34	16	18	33	15	18
55-59	20	9	11	24	11	13	28	13	15	34	15	18
60-64	16	7	9	20	9	11	23	10	13	27	13	15
65-69	15	7	8	15	7	9	19	8	11	22	10	12
70-74	13	6	7	13	6	8	14	6	8	17	7	10
75-79	10	4	6	11	5	6	12	5	7	12	5	7
80-84	7	3	4	8	3	5	9	3	5	9	4	6
85-89	4	1	2	5	2	3	5	2	3	6	2	4
90-94	2	1	1	2	1	1	3	1	2	3	1	2
95-99	1	0	0	1	0	1	1	0	1	1	0	1
100 +	0	0	0	0	0	0	0	0	0	0	0	0

Age group	2025 Both sexes	2025 Males	2025 Females	2030 Both sexes	2030 Males	2030 Females	2035 Both sexes	2035 Males	2035 Females	2040 Both sexes	2040 Males	2040 Females
All ages	424	202	222	426	203	223	425	203	222	422	202	220
0-4	27	14	13	26	13	13	25	13	12	24	12	12
5-9	27	14	13	26	13	13	25	13	12	24	12	12
10-14	27	14	13	28	14	14	27	14	13	26	13	13
15-19	26	13	13	26	13	13	27	14	13	26	13	13
20-24	22	11	11	22	11	11	23	12	11	23	12	11
25-29	21	11	10	21	11	10	21	11	10	21	11	10
30-34	24	12	12	22	11	11	21	11	10	21	11	10
35-39	26	13	13	24	12	12	22	11	11	21	11	10
40-44	25	13	12	26	13	13	24	12	12	22	11	11
45-49	21	10	11	25	13	12	26	13	13	25	12	12
50-54	28	13	15	21	10	11	25	13	12	26	13	13
55-59	33	15	18	27	13	15	21	10	11	25	12	12
60-64	33	15	18	32	14	18	27	12	15	21	10	11
65-69	26	12	15	31	14	17	31	14	17	26	12	14
70-74	20	9	12	24	11	14	29	13	17	29	12	17
75-79	15	6	9	18	7	11	22	9	13	26	11	15
80-84	10	4	6	12	5	8	15	6	9	18	7	11
85-89	7	2	4	7	3	5	9	3	6	11	4	7
90-94	3	1	2	4	1	3	4	1	3	6	2	4
95-99	1	0	1	2	0	1	2	0	1	2	1	1
100 +	0	0	0	0	0	0	1	0	0	1	0	0

Age group	2045 Both sexes	2045 Males	2045 Females	2050 Both sexes	2050 Males	2050 Females
All ages	418	200	217	411	198	214
0-4	24	12	12	24	12	12
5-9	24	12	12	24	12	12
10-14	25	13	12	24	12	12
15-19	24	12	12	24	12	12
20-24	22	11	11	21	11	10
25-29	21	11	10	20	10	10
30-34	21	11	10	22	11	11
35-39	21	11	10	21	11	10
40-44	21	11	10	21	11	11
45-49	23	11	11	22	11	11
50-54	25	12	12	23	11	11
55-59	26	13	13	25	12	12
60-64	24	12	12	26	13	13
65-69	20	10	10	24	12	12
70-74	24	11	14	19	9	10
75-79	26	11	15	22	9	13
80-84	22	9	13	22	8	13
85-89	13	5	9	16	6	11
90-94	7	2	5	8	3	6
95-99	3	1	2	3	1	2
100 +	1	0	1	1	0	1

United Nations Department of Economic and Social Affairs/Population Division
World Population Prospects: The 2004 Revision, Volume II: Sex and Age Distribution of the World Population

POPULATION BY AGE AND SEX (in thousands)

Age group	2005 Both sexes	2005 Males	2005 Females	2010 Both sexes	2010 Males	2010 Females	2015 Both sexes	2015 Males	2015 Females	2020 Both sexes	2020 Males	2020 Females
All ages	396	188	208	398	189	210	396	187	209	391	185	206
0-4	27	14	13	21	11	10	17	9	9	16	8	8
5-9	28	14	14	27	14	13	20	10	10	17	9	8
10-14	30	15	15	28	14	14	27	14	13	21	11	10
15-19	31	15	15	29	15	14	27	14	13	26	13	13
20-24	26	13	13	27	14	14	25	13	13	23	12	11
25-29	20	10	10	24	12	12	25	13	13	24	12	12
30-34	27	13	14	20	10	10	24	12	12	26	13	13
35-39	33	15	18	27	13	14	20	10	10	24	12	12
40-44	34	16	18	33	15	18	28	13	15	21	10	11
45-49	29	13	15	34	16	18	33	15	18	28	13	15
50-54	24	11	13	29	13	15	34	16	18	33	15	18
55-59	20	9	11	24	11	13	28	13	15	34	15	18
60-64	16	7	9	20	9	11	23	10	13	27	13	15
65-69	15	7	8	15	7	9	19	8	11	22	10	12
70-74	13	6	7	13	6	8	14	6	8	17	7	10
75-79	10	4	6	11	5	6	12	5	7	12	5	7
80-84	7	3	4	8	3	5	9	3	5	9	4	6
85-89	4	1	2	5	2	3	5	2	3	6	2	4
90-94	2	1	1	2	1	1	3	1	2	3	1	2
95-99	1	0	0	1	0	1	1	0	1	1	0	1
100 +	0	0	0	0	0	0	0	0	0	0	0	0

Age group	2025 Both sexes	2025 Males	2025 Females	2030 Both sexes	2030 Males	2030 Females	2035 Both sexes	2035 Males	2035 Females	2040 Both sexes	2040 Males	2040 Females
All ages	384	181	202	374	176	197	360	170	190	342	161	181
0-4	15	8	7	14	7	7	12	6	6	9	5	5
5-9	15	8	8	15	7	7	13	7	6	11	6	5
10-14	18	9	9	16	8	8	15	8	7	14	7	7
15-19	20	10	10	16	8	8	15	7	7	14	7	7
20-24	22	11	11	16	8	8	13	7	6	11	6	5
25-29	21	11	10	21	11	10	14	7	7	11	6	5
30-34	24	12	12	22	11	11	21	11	10	15	7	7
35-39	26	13	13	24	12	12	22	11	11	21	11	10
40-44	25	13	12	26	13	13	24	12	12	22	11	11
45-49	21	10	11	25	13	12	26	13	13	25	12	12
50-54	28	13	15	21	10	11	25	13	12	26	13	13
55-59	33	15	18	27	13	15	21	10	11	25	12	12
60-64	33	15	18	32	14	18	27	12	16	21	10	11
65-69	26	12	15	31	14	17	31	14	17	26	12	14
70-74	20	9	12	24	11	14	29	13	17	29	12	17
75-79	15	6	9	18	7	11	22	9	13	26	11	15
80-84	10	4	6	12	5	8	15	6	9	18	7	11
85-89	7	2	4	7	3	5	9	3	6	11	4	7
90-94	3	1	2	4	1	3	4	1	3	6	2	4
95-99	1	0	1	2	0	1	2	0	1	2	1	1
100 +	0	0	0	0	0	0	1	0	0	1	0	0

Age group	2045 Both sexes	2045 Males	2045 Females	2050 Both sexes	2050 Males	2050 Females
All ages	321	151	170	297	140	158
0-4	8	4	4	6	3	3
5-9	9	5	4	7	4	4
10-14	12	6	6	10	5	5
15-19	12	6	6	10	5	5
20-24	10	5	5	9	5	4
25-29	9	5	4	9	4	4
30-34	11	6	5	10	5	5
35-39	15	8	7	12	6	6
40-44	21	11	10	15	8	7
45-49	23	11	11	22	11	11
50-54	25	12	12	23	11	11
55-59	26	13	13	25	12	12
60-64	24	12	12	26	13	13
65-69	20	10	10	24	12	12
70-74	24	11	14	19	9	10
75-79	26	11	15	22	9	13
80-84	22	9	13	22	8	13
85-89	13	5	9	16	6	11
90-94	7	2	5	8	3	6
95-99	3	1	2	3	1	2
100 +	1	0	1	1	0	1

POPULATION BY AGE AND SEX (in thousands)

Age group	1950 Both sexes	Males	Females	1955 Both sexes	Males	Females	1960 Both sexes	Males	Females	1965 Both sexes	Males	Females
All ages	825	422	403	900	456	445	1 001	503	498	1 122	561	561
0-4	145	73	72	146	73	73	172	86	86	197	98	98
5-9	115	58	57	125	63	62	128	63	64	153	76	77
10-14	101	51	50	110	55	54	120	60	60	122	61	62
15-19	87	44	43	97	49	48	106	53	52	116	58	58
20-24	75	38	37	83	42	41	93	47	46	102	51	51
25-29	63	32	31	71	36	35	78	39	39	89	44	44
30-34	53	27	26	59	30	29	67	33	33	74	37	37
35-39	45	23	22	49	25	24	56	28	28	63	31	31
40-44	37	19	18	42	21	20	46	23	23	52	26	26
45-49	30	16	14	34	17	17	38	19	19	43	22	21
50-54	24	13	11	27	14	13	31	15	15	35	18	18
55-59	19	10	9	21	11	10	24	12	12	28	14	14
60-64	13	7	6	16	8	8	18	9	8	20	10	10
65-69	9	5	4	10	5	5	12	6	6	14	7	7
70-74	5	3	2	6	3	3	7	4	3	9	4	4
75-79	3	2	1	3	2	1	3	2	2	4	2	2
80 +	1	1	0	1	1	0	1	1	1	2	1	1

Age group	1970 Both sexes	Males	Females	1975 Both sexes	Males	Females	1980 Both sexes	Males	Females	1985 Both sexes	Males	Females
All ages	1 262	628	634	1 423	705	718	1 609	795	814	1 812	894	919
0-4	223	111	111	251	125	125	283	142	141	313	157	156
5-9	176	88	88	201	100	101	228	114	114	260	130	130
10-14	147	73	74	170	85	85	195	97	98	221	111	111
15-19	119	59	60	143	71	72	165	82	83	189	94	95
20-24	111	55	56	114	56	58	137	68	69	158	78	80
25-29	97	48	49	106	52	54	108	53	55	129	63	66
30-34	84	41	42	90	44	46	100	49	51	101	49	53
35-39	70	35	35	78	38	40	85	41	44	94	45	48
40-44	59	30	30	66	33	33	74	36	38	80	39	42
45-49	49	24	24	56	28	28	62	30	31	69	33	36
50-54	39	20	20	45	22	23	51	25	26	57	28	29
55-59	32	16	16	36	18	18	41	20	21	47	23	24
60-64	24	12	12	27	13	14	31	15	16	36	17	19
65-69	16	8	8	19	9	10	23	11	12	26	12	14
70-74	10	5	5	12	6	6	14	7	8	17	8	9
75-79	5	3	3	6	3	3	8	4	4	9	4	5
80 +	2	1	1	3	1	2	4	2	2	5	2	3

Age group	1990 Both sexes	Males	Females	1995 Both sexes	Males	Females	2000 Both sexes	Males	Females	2005 Both sexes	Males	Females
All ages	2 030	999	1 031	2 300	1 131	1 169	2 645	1 304	1 341	3 069	1 518	1 551
0-4	350	176	174	396	199	197	457	230	227	526	265	261
5-9	289	145	144	324	163	162	370	185	184	432	217	215
10-14	253	126	126	281	141	140	317	159	158	362	182	181
15-19	215	107	108	247	123	123	276	138	138	313	157	156
20-24	179	89	91	207	103	104	242	121	121	274	137	137
25-29	147	72	75	171	84	87	202	100	102	241	120	121
30-34	120	58	62	140	68	72	167	82	85	201	100	102
35-39	94	45	49	113	54	59	136	66	70	165	81	84
40-44	87	42	46	89	42	47	109	52	57	133	64	68
45-49	74	35	39	82	39	43	85	40	45	106	51	55
50-54	63	30	33	69	33	37	78	36	41	81	38	43
55-59	52	25	27	58	27	31	64	30	34	72	34	39
60-64	41	20	21	46	22	24	52	24	28	58	27	31
65-69	30	14	16	34	16	18	39	18	21	44	20	24
70-74	19	9	10	23	10	12	26	12	14	30	14	17
75-79	11	5	6	13	6	7	15	7	8	18	8	10
80 +	6	3	4	8	3	4	9	4	5	11	5	7

United Nations Department of Economic and Social Affairs/Population Division
World Population Prospects: The 2004 Revision, Volume II: Sex and Age Distribution of the World Population

590

POPULATION BY AGE AND SEX (in thousands)

Age group	2005 Both sexes	2005 Males	2005 Females	2010 Both sexes	2010 Males	2010 Females	2015 Both sexes	2015 Males	2015 Females	2020 Both sexes	2020 Males	2020 Females
All ages	3 069	1 518	1 551	3 520	1 744	1 776	3 988	1 978	2 009	4 473	2 222	2 250
0-4	526	265	261	582	293	289	615	310	305	640	323	317
5-9	432	217	215	500	251	249	556	280	277	592	298	294
10-14	362	182	181	424	212	211	491	247	245	548	276	273
15-19	313	157	156	357	179	178	417	209	208	485	243	242
20-24	274	137	137	308	154	154	350	175	175	410	205	205
25-29	241	120	121	269	134	135	301	150	151	343	171	172
30-34	201	100	102	236	117	119	263	131	132	294	146	148
35-39	165	81	84	196	97	99	229	114	116	256	127	129
40-44	133	64	68	160	78	81	190	93	96	222	110	112
45-49	106	51	55	128	62	66	153	75	79	183	90	93
50-54	81	38	43	101	48	53	121	58	63	146	71	75
55-59	72	34	39	76	35	41	94	44	50	114	54	60
60-64	58	27	31	66	30	35	69	32	37	86	40	46
65-69	44	20	24	50	23	27	57	26	31	60	27	33
70-74	30	14	17	35	16	19	40	18	22	46	20	25
75-79	18	8	10	21	9	12	24	11	14	28	12	16
80-84	8	4	5	10	4	6	12	5	7	14	6	8
85-89	3	1	2	3	1	2	4	2	2	5	2	3
90-94	1	0	0	1	0	0	1	0	1	1	0	1
95-99	0	0	0	0	0	0	0	0	0	0	0	0
100 +	0	0	0	0	0	0	0	0	0	0	0	0

Age group	2025 Both sexes	2025 Males	2025 Females	2030 Both sexes	2030 Males	2030 Females	2035 Both sexes	2035 Males	2035 Females	2040 Both sexes	2040 Males	2040 Females
All ages	4 973	2 472	2 501	5 482	2 727	2 755	5 996	2 984	3 012	6 510	3 241	3 269
0-4	661	334	327	679	343	336	692	350	342	702	355	347
5-9	620	312	308	644	324	319	664	335	329	680	343	337
10-14	585	294	291	613	309	304	638	321	317	660	333	327
15-19	542	272	270	579	291	288	608	306	302	633	319	314
20-24	477	239	238	534	268	267	572	287	285	601	302	299
25-29	402	201	202	469	234	235	526	263	263	564	282	282
30-34	336	167	169	395	196	199	461	230	232	519	259	260
35-39	287	142	146	329	163	166	388	192	195	454	226	228
40-44	249	123	126	280	139	142	322	159	163	380	188	192
45-49	215	106	109	241	119	122	273	135	138	314	155	159
50-54	175	85	90	207	101	105	233	114	118	264	130	134
55-59	138	66	72	166	80	85	186	90	101	222	108	114
60-64	105	49	55	127	61	67	154	74	80	183	89	95
65-69	75	35	41	92	43	49	113	53	60	138	66	73
70-74	49	22	27	62	28	34	77	35	42	95	44	51
75-79	30	14	18	36	16	20	46	20	26	58	26	32
80-84	17	7	10	20	8	11	22	9	13	29	12	16
85-89	6	2	4	7	3	4	9	4	5	10	4	6
90-94	1	1	1	2	1	1	2	1	1	3	1	2
95-99	0	0	0	0	0	0	0	0	0	0	0	0
100 +	0	0	0	0	0	0	0	0	0	0	0	0

Age group	2045 Both sexes	2045 Males	2045 Females	2050 Both sexes	2050 Males	2050 Females
All ages	7 013	3 494	3 520	7 497	3 736	3 761
0-4	706	357	349	704	357	348
5-9	693	350	343	699	354	345
10-14	677	341	335	690	348	341
15-19	656	330	325	673	339	334
20-24	627	315	312	650	327	323
25-29	594	298	297	621	311	309
30-34	557	278	279	587	294	294
35-39	511	254	257	550	274	276
40-44	446	221	225	504	250	253
45-49	372	184	188	438	217	221
50-54	305	150	155	362	178	184
55-59	252	123	129	292	143	149
60-64	208	101	107	238	115	122
65-69	166	79	86	189	91	98
70-74	117	55	62	141	67	75
75-79	73	33	40	90	41	49
80-84	37	16	21	47	21	26
85-89	14	6	8	18	8	10
90-94	3	1	2	4	2	3
95-99	1	0	0	1	0	0
100 +	0	0	0	0	0	0

POPULATION BY AGE AND SEX (in thousands)

Age group	2005			2010			2015			2020		
	Both sexes	Males	Females	Both sexes	Males	Females	Both sexes	Males	Females	Both sexes	Males	Females
All ages	3 069	1 518	1 551	3 566	1 767	1 799	4 093	2 031	2 062	4 647	2 309	2 338
0-4	526	265	261	627	316	311	677	341	336	712	359	353
5-9	432	217	215	500	251	249	600	302	298	652	328	324
10-14	362	182	181	424	212	211	491	247	245	591	297	294
15-19	313	157	156	357	179	178	417	209	208	485	243	242
20-24	274	137	137	308	154	154	350	175	175	410	205	205
25-29	241	120	121	269	134	135	301	150	151	343	171	172
30-34	201	100	102	236	117	119	263	131	132	294	146	148
35-39	165	81	84	196	97	99	229	114	116	256	127	129
40-44	133	64	68	160	78	81	190	93	96	222	110	112
45-49	106	51	55	128	62	66	153	75	79	183	90	93
50-54	81	38	43	101	48	53	121	58	63	146	71	75
55-59	72	34	39	76	35	41	94	44	50	114	54	60
60-64	58	27	31	66	30	35	69	32	37	86	40	46
65-69	44	20	24	50	23	27	57	26	31	60	27	33
70-74	30	14	17	35	16	19	40	18	22	46	20	25
75-79	18	8	10	21	9	12	24	11	14	28	12	16
80-84	8	4	5	10	4	6	12	5	7	14	6	8
85-89	3	1	2	3	1	2	4	2	2	5	2	3
90-94	1	0	0	1	0	0	1	0	1	1	0	1
95-99	0	0	0	0	0	0	0	0	0	0	0	0
100 +	0	0	0	0	0	0	0	0	0	0	0	0

Age group	2025			2030			2035			2040		
	Both sexes	Males	Females	Both sexes	Males	Females	Both sexes	Males	Females	Both sexes	Males	Females
All ages	5 230	2 601	2 628	5 847	2 911	2 936	6 503	3 239	3 264	7 198	3 587	3 611
0-4	748	378	370	791	399	391	840	424	415	889	449	440
5-9	689	347	342	728	367	361	774	390	383	826	417	409
10-14	643	324	320	682	343	339	722	364	358	768	387	381
15-19	584	293	291	637	320	317	676	340	336	716	361	356
20-24	477	239	238	576	289	287	629	315	314	669	336	333
25-29	402	201	202	469	234	235	567	283	284	621	310	310
30-34	336	167	169	395	196	199	461	230	232	559	279	280
35-39	287	142	145	329	163	166	388	192	195	454	226	228
40-44	249	123	126	280	139	142	322	159	163	380	188	192
45-49	215	106	109	241	119	122	273	135	138	314	155	159
50-54	175	85	90	207	101	105	233	114	118	264	130	134
55-59	138	66	72	166	80	85	196	96	101	222	108	114
60-64	105	49	55	127	61	67	154	74	80	183	89	95
65-69	75	35	41	92	43	49	113	53	60	138	66	73
70-74	49	22	27	62	28	34	77	35	42	95	44	51
75-79	33	14	18	36	16	20	46	20	26	58	26	32
80-84	17	7	10	20	8	11	22	9	13	29	12	16
85-89	6	2	4	7	3	4	9	4	5	10	4	6
90-94	1	1	1	2	1	1	2	1	1	3	1	2
95-99	0	0	0	0	0	0	0	0	0	0	0	0
100 +	0	0	0	0	0	0	0	0	0	0	0	0

Age group	2045			2050		
	Both sexes	Males	Females	Both sexes	Males	Females
All ages	7 915	3 948	3 967	8 640	4 312	4 328
0-4	926	469	457	954	483	471
5-9	877	443	434	917	464	453
10-14	821	414	407	873	441	432
15-19	763	385	379	817	412	405
20-24	709	356	353	757	381	376
25-29	661	331	330	702	352	350
30-34	613	306	307	653	326	327
35-39	551	274	277	605	301	304
40-44	446	221	225	543	270	273
45-49	372	184	188	438	217	221
50-54	305	150	155	362	178	184
55-59	252	123	129	292	143	149
60-64	208	101	107	238	115	122
65-69	166	79	86	189	91	98
70-74	117	55	62	141	67	75
75-79	73	33	40	90	41	49
80-84	37	16	21	47	21	26
85-89	14	6	8	18	8	10
90-94	3	1	2	4	2	3
95-99	1	0	0	1	0	0
100 +	0	0	0	0	0	0

United Nations Department of Economic and Social Affairs/Population Division
World Population Prospects: The 2004 Revision, Volume II: Sex and Age Distribution of the World Population

592

POPULATION BY AGE AND SEX (in thousands)

Age group	2005			2010			2015			2020		
	Both sexes	Males	Females	Both sexes	Males	Females	Both sexes	Males	Females	Both sexes	Males	Females
All ages	3 069	1 518	1 551	3 475	1 721	1 754	3 882	1 925	1 957	4 299	2 134	2 165
0-4	526	265	261	537	270	266	554	279	275	569	287	282
5-9	432	217	215	500	251	249	513	258	255	533	268	265
10-14	362	182	181	424	212	211	491	247	245	506	254	251
15-19	313	157	156	357	179	178	417	209	208	485	243	242
20-24	274	137	137	308	154	154	350	175	175	410	205	205
25-29	241	120	121	269	134	135	301	150	151	343	171	172
30-34	201	100	102	236	117	119	263	131	132	294	146	148
35-39	165	81	84	196	97	99	229	114	116	256	127	129
40-44	133	64	68	160	78	81	190	93	96	222	110	112
45-49	106	51	55	128	62	66	153	75	79	183	90	93
50-54	81	38	43	101	48	53	121	58	63	146	71	75
55-59	72	34	39	76	35	41	94	44	50	114	54	60
60-64	58	27	31	66	30	35	69	32	37	86	40	46
65-69	44	20	24	50	23	27	57	26	31	60	27	33
70-74	30	14	17	35	16	19	40	18	22	46	20	25
75-79	18	8	10	21	9	12	24	11	14	28	12	16
80-84	8	4	5	10	4	6	12	5	7	14	6	8
85-89	3	1	2	3	1	2	4	2	2	5	2	3
90-94	1	0	0	1	0	0	1	0	1	1	0	1
95-99	0	0	0	0	0	0	0	0	0	0	0	0
100 +	0	0	0	0	0	0	0	0	0	0	0	0

Age group	2025			2030			2035			2040		
	Both sexes	Males	Females	Both sexes	Males	Females	Both sexes	Males	Females	Both sexes	Males	Females
All ages	4 717	2 343	2 374	5 122	2 546	2 577	5 504	2 736	2 768	5 855	2 911	2 944
0-4	575	290	285	571	289	283	554	280	274	534	270	264
5-9	550	277	273	560	282	278	559	282	277	545	275	270
10-14	526	265	261	545	274	270	555	280	275	555	280	275
15-19	500	251	249	521	262	259	540	272	268	551	277	274
20-24	477	239	238	493	247	246	514	258	256	534	268	266
25-29	402	201	202	469	234	235	485	242	243	507	254	254
30-34	336	167	169	395	196	199	461	230	232	478	238	240
35-39	287	142	145	329	163	166	388	192	195	454	226	228
40-44	249	123	126	280	139	142	322	160	162	380	188	192
45-49	215	106	109	241	119	122	273	135	138	314	155	159
50-54	175	85	90	207	101	105	233	114	118	264	130	134
55-59	138	66	72	166	80	85	196	96	101	222	108	114
60-64	105	49	55	127	61	67	154	74	80	183	89	95
65-69	75	35	41	92	43	49	113	53	60	138	66	73
70-74	49	22	27	62	28	34	77	35	42	95	44	51
75-79	33	14	18	36	16	20	46	20	26	58	26	32
80-84	17	7	10	20	8	11	22	9	13	29	12	16
85-89	6	2	4	7	3	4	9	4	5	10	4	6
90-94	1	1	1	2	1	1	2	1	1	3	1	2
95-99	0	0	0	0	0	0	0	0	0	0	0	0
100 +	0	0	0	0	0	0	0	0	0	0	0	0

Age group	2045			2050		
	Both sexes	Males	Females	Both sexes	Males	Females
All ages	6 172	3 070	3 102	6 450	3 208	3 241
0-4	513	260	253	491	249	243
5-9	527	266	261	508	257	251
10-14	542	273	268	525	265	260
15-19	551	278	274	539	272	267
20-24	546	274	272	547	275	272
25-29	528	264	263	540	271	269
30-34	501	250	251	522	261	261
35-39	471	235	237	495	246	248
40-44	446	221	225	464	231	234
45-49	372	184	188	438	217	221
50-54	305	150	155	362	178	184
55-59	252	123	129	292	143	149
60-64	208	101	107	238	115	122
65-69	166	79	86	189	91	98
70-74	117	55	62	141	67	75
75-79	73	33	40	90	41	49
80-84	37	16	21	47	21	26
85-89	14	6	8	18	8	10
90-94	3	1	2	4	2	3
95-99	1	0	0	1	0	0
100 +	0	0	0	0	0	0

United Nations Department of Economic and Social Affairs/Population Division
World Population Prospects: The 2004 Revision, Volume II: Sex and Age Distribution of the World Population

593

POPULATION BY AGE AND SEX (in thousands)

Age group	1950 Both sexes	Males	Females	1955 Both sexes	Males	Females	1960 Both sexes	Males	Females	1965 Both sexes	Males	Females
All ages	493	246	248	571	284	286	660	329	331	753	377	377
0-4	89	45	44	107	55	52	123	63	60	135	69	66
5-9	73	37	36	85	43	42	102	52	50	117	60	57
10-14	61	31	30	71	36	36	82	42	41	99	51	48
15-19	51	26	26	58	29	29	68	34	34	78	40	39
20-24	43	22	21	49	24	25	56	28	28	64	32	32
25-29	36	18	18	42	21	21	47	23	24	53	26	27
30-34	30	15	15	35	17	17	40	20	20	45	22	23
35-39	25	12	13	29	14	15	33	16	17	38	19	19
40-44	21	10	10	24	12	12	28	13	14	32	16	16
45-49	17	8	9	19	9	10	22	11	11	26	12	13
50-54	14	7	7	16	8	8	18	9	9	21	10	11
55-59	11	5	6	12	6	6	14	7	7	16	8	8
60-64	9	4	4	9	4	5	10	5	6	12	5	7
65-69	6	3	3	7	3	4	7	3	4	8	4	5
70-74	4	2	2	4	2	3	5	2	3	5	2	3
75-79	2	1	1	2	1	1	3	1	2	3	1	2
80 +	2	1	1	2	1	1	2	1	1	2	1	1

Age group	1970 Both sexes	Males	Females	1975 Both sexes	Males	Females	1980 Both sexes	Males	Females	1985 Both sexes	Males	Females
All ages	826	413	413	892	440	452	966	476	490	1 016	506	510
0-4	115	59	56	102	52	50	109	55	54	111	56	55
5-9	132	67	65	118	59	58	115	58	57	108	54	53
10-14	114	58	56	134	68	66	120	61	60	103	52	51
15-19	92	48	44	103	53	50	110	56	54	112	57	55
20-24	73	36	37	82	40	42	96	47	49	107	54	53
25-29	62	31	31	71	35	37	84	42	43	96	48	48
30-34	51	25	25	61	30	30	73	36	36	84	42	41
35-39	43	21	22	50	24	26	57	28	29	63	31	32
40-44	37	18	19	44	21	23	46	22	24	47	23	24
45-49	30	15	15	36	17	18	39	19	20	41	21	21
50-54	24	12	13	29	14	15	32	16	16	35	17	17
55-59	19	9	10	22	11	12	28	14	15	35	17	18
60-64	14	6	8	16	7	9	21	10	12	27	13	14
65-69	10	4	6	11	5	7	16	7	9	21	10	11
70-74	6	2	4	7	3	5	10	4	6	13	6	8
75-79	3	1	2	4	1	3	6	2	4	8	3	5
80 +	2	1	1	2	1	2	4	1	3	6	2	5

Age group	1990 Both sexes	Males	Females	1995 Both sexes	Males	Females	2000 Both sexes	Males	Females	2005 Both sexes	Males	Females
All ages	1 057	528	529	1 125	561	563	1 186	590	596	1 245	618	627
0-4	97	49	48	109	55	54	100	51	49	98	50	48
5-9	103	53	51	96	48	48	108	55	53	100	51	49
10-14	113	57	56	103	52	51	96	48	47	108	55	53
15-19	97	49	48	113	57	56	103	52	51	96	48	47
20-24	103	52	50	96	49	47	112	56	55	102	52	51
25-29	106	54	52	101	51	49	95	48	47	111	56	55
30-34	94	48	46	104	53	51	100	51	49	94	48	47
35-39	81	41	40	92	47	45	102	52	51	99	50	49
40-44	60	30	30	79	40	39	90	46	45	101	51	50
45-49	45	22	23	59	29	30	77	39	39	88	44	44
50-54	38	18	20	43	21	22	56	27	29	75	37	38
55-59	32	16	16	36	17	19	40	19	21	53	26	28
60-64	31	15	16	29	14	15	33	15	18	37	17	20
65-69	24	11	13	27	12	15	25	12	14	29	13	16
70-74	15	6	8	20	9	11	22	9	12	21	9	12
75-79	10	4	6	11	4	6	15	6	9	17	7	10
80 +	8	2	5	10	3	7	12	4	8	16	5	10

(*) Including Agalega, Rodrigues, and Saint Brandon.

United Nations Department of Economic and Social Affairs/Population Division
World Population Prospects: The 2004 Revision, Volume II: Sex and Age Distribution of the World Population

POPULATION BY AGE AND SEX (in thousands)

Age group	2005			2010			2015			2020		
	Both sexes	Males	Females	Both sexes	Males	Females	Both sexes	Males	Females	Both sexes	Males	Females
All ages	1 245	618	627	1 298	643	655	1 344	665	679	1 384	683	701
0-4	98	50	48	96	49	47	93	47	46	92	47	45
5-9	100	51	49	98	50	48	96	49	47	93	47	45
10-14	108	55	53	99	51	49	98	50	48	96	49	47
15-19	96	48	47	108	55	53	99	50	49	98	50	48
20-24	102	52	51	95	48	47	108	55	53	99	50	49
25-29	111	56	55	102	52	50	95	48	47	107	54	53
30-34	94	48	47	111	56	55	101	51	50	95	47	47
35-39	99	50	49	93	47	46	110	55	55	101	51	50
40-44	101	51	50	98	49	48	92	46	46	109	54	54
45-49	88	44	44	99	50	49	96	48	48	91	45	46
50-54	75	37	38	86	42	43	96	48	49	93	47	47
55-59	53	26	28	71	35	36	82	40	42	92	45	47
60-64	37	17	20	49	23	26	66	31	35	76	37	40
65-69	29	13	16	33	15	18	44	20	24	59	27	32
70-74	21	9	12	24	10	14	28	12	16	38	16	22
75-79	17	7	10	16	7	10	19	7	11	22	9	13
80-84	10	4	6	11	4	7	11	4	7	13	5	8
85-89	4	1	3	6	2	4	7	2	4	7	2	5
90-94	1	0	1	2	0	1	2	1	2	3	1	2
95-99	0	0	0	0	0	0	1	0	0	1	0	1
100 +	0	0	0	0	0	0	0	0	0	0	0	0

Age group	2025			2030			2035			2040		
	Both sexes	Males	Females	Both sexes	Males	Females	Both sexes	Males	Females	Both sexes	Males	Females
All ages	1 417	698	719	1 443	709	734	1 459	715	744	1 468	718	750
0-4	90	46	44	89	45	43	87	44	42	85	43	41
5-9	91	47	45	90	46	44	89	45	43	87	44	42
10-14	93	47	45	91	47	45	90	46	44	89	45	43
15-19	96	49	47	93	47	45	91	47	45	90	46	44
20-24	98	50	48	96	49	47	92	47	45	91	46	45
25-29	99	50	49	97	49	48	96	49	47	92	47	45
30-34	107	54	53	98	50	49	97	49	48	95	49	47
35-39	94	47	47	106	54	53	98	50	48	97	49	48
40-44	100	50	50	93	47	47	106	53	52	97	49	48
45-49	107	53	54	99	49	49	92	46	46	105	53	52
50-54	89	44	45	105	52	53	97	48	49	90	45	46
55-59	90	44	45	86	42	44	101	49	52	94	46	47
60-64	86	41	45	84	41	44	81	39	42	96	46	50
65-69	69	32	37	79	36	42	77	36	41	74	35	40
70-74	51	22	29	60	26	33	68	30	38	68	30	37
75-79	30	12	18	41	17	24	48	20	28	56	23	33
80-84	16	6	10	21	8	14	30	11	19	36	13	22
85-89	8	2	5	9	3	7	13	4	9	19	6	13
90-94	3	1	2	4	1	3	5	1	3	7	2	5
95-99	1	0	1	1	0	1	1	0	1	2	0	1
100 +	0	0	0	0	0	0	0	0	0	0	0	0

Age group	2045			2050		
	Both sexes	Males	Females	Both sexes	Males	Females
All ages	1 469	718	752	1 465	715	750
0-4	83	42	41	81	42	40
5-9	84	43	41	83	42	41
10-14	87	44	42	84	43	41
15-19	88	45	43	86	44	42
20-24	90	46	44	88	45	43
25-29	91	46	45	90	46	44
30-34	92	47	45	91	46	45
35-39	95	48	47	92	47	45
40-44	96	49	47	95	48	47
45-49	96	49	48	95	48	47
50-54	103	51	51	95	48	47
55-59	88	43	45	100	50	50
60-64	89	43	46	84	41	43
65-69	89	41	47	83	39	44
70-74	66	29	36	79	35	43
75-79	56	24	32	55	23	32
80-84	42	16	26	42	16	26
85-89	23	7	15	27	9	18
90-94	9	2	7	12	3	9
95-99	2	0	2	4	1	3
100 +	0	0	0	1	0	1

POPULATION BY AGE AND SEX (in thousands)

Age group	2005 Both sexes	Males	Females	2010 Both sexes	Males	Females	2015 Both sexes	Males	Females	2020 Both sexes	Males	Females
All ages	1 245	618	627	1 311	650	661	1 377	681	695	1 441	712	729
0-4	98	50	48	109	55	53	113	57	55	116	59	57
5-9	100	51	49	98	50	48	109	55	53	112	57	55
10-14	108	55	53	99	51	49	98	50	48	109	55	53
15-19	96	48	47	108	55	53	99	50	49	98	50	48
20-24	102	52	51	95	48	47	108	55	53	99	50	49
25-29	111	56	55	102	52	50	95	48	47	107	54	53
30-34	94	48	47	111	56	55	101	51	50	95	47	47
35-39	99	50	49	93	47	46	110	55	55	101	51	50
40-44	101	51	50	98	49	48	92	46	46	109	54	54
45-49	88	44	44	99	50	49	96	48	48	91	45	46
50-54	75	37	38	86	42	43	96	48	49	93	47	47
55-59	53	26	28	71	35	36	82	40	42	92	45	47
60-64	37	17	20	49	23	26	66	31	35	76	37	40
65-69	29	13	16	33	15	18	44	20	24	59	27	32
70-74	21	9	12	24	10	14	28	12	16	38	16	22
75-79	17	7	10	16	7	10	19	7	11	22	9	13
80-84	10	4	6	11	4	7	11	4	7	13	5	8
85-89	4	1	3	6	2	4	7	2	4	7	2	5
90-94	1	0	1	2	0	1	2	1	2	3	1	2
95-99	0	0	0	0	0	0	1	0	0	1	0	1
100 +	0	0	0	0	0	0	0	0	0	0	0	0

Age group	2025 Both sexes	Males	Females	2030 Both sexes	Males	Females	2035 Both sexes	Males	Females	2040 Both sexes	Males	Females
All ages	1 499	740	759	1 552	764	787	1 602	788	814	1 650	811	839
0-4	115	59	57	116	59	57	120	61	59	125	64	61
5-9	116	59	57	115	59	56	116	59	57	120	61	59
10-14	112	57	55	116	59	57	115	59	56	116	59	57
15-19	108	55	53	112	57	55	116	59	57	115	59	56
20-24	98	50	48	108	55	53	112	57	55	116	59	57
25-29	99	50	49	97	49	48	108	55	53	112	57	55
30-34	107	54	53	98	50	49	97	49	48	108	55	53
35-39	94	47	47	106	54	53	98	50	48	97	49	48
40-44	100	50	50	93	47	47	106	53	52	97	49	48
45-49	107	53	54	99	49	49	92	46	46	105	53	52
50-54	89	44	45	105	52	53	97	48	49	90	45	46
55-59	90	44	45	86	42	44	101	49	52	94	46	47
60-64	86	41	45	84	41	44	81	39	42	96	46	50
65-69	69	32	37	79	36	42	77	36	41	74	35	40
70-74	51	22	29	60	26	33	68	30	38	68	30	37
75-79	30	12	18	41	17	24	48	20	28	56	23	33
80-84	16	6	10	21	8	14	30	11	19	36	13	22
85-89	8	2	5	9	3	7	13	4	9	19	6	13
90-94	3	1	2	4	1	3	5	1	3	7	2	5
95-99	1	0	1	1	0	1	1	0	1	2	0	1
100 +	0	0	0	0	0	0	0	0	0	0	0	0

Age group	2045 Both sexes	Males	Females	2050 Both sexes	Males	Females
All ages	1 697	834	863	1 742	856	886
0-4	129	66	63	131	67	64
5-9	125	64	61	129	66	63
10-14	120	61	59	125	64	61
15-19	116	59	57	120	61	59
20-24	115	59	56	116	59	57
25-29	116	59	57	115	58	56
30-34	112	57	55	115	59	57
35-39	107	55	53	111	57	55
40-44	96	49	47	107	54	53
45-49	96	49	48	95	48	47
50-54	103	51	51	95	48	47
55-59	88	43	45	100	50	50
60-64	89	43	46	84	41	43
65-69	89	41	47	83	39	44
70-74	66	29	36	79	35	43
75-79	56	24	32	55	23	32
80-84	42	16	26	42	16	26
85-89	23	7	15	27	9	18
90-94	9	2	7	12	3	9
95-99	2	0	2	4	1	3
100 +	0	0	0	1	0	1

United Nations Department of Economic and Social Affairs/Population Division
World Population Prospects: The 2004 Revision, Volume II: Sex and Age Distribution of the World Population

POPULATION BY AGE AND SEX (in thousands)

Age group	2005 Both sexes	Males	Females	2010 Both sexes	Males	Females	2015 Both sexes	Males	Females	2020 Both sexes	Males	Females
All ages	1 245	618	627	1 286	637	649	1 312	649	664	1 327	654	673
0-4	98	50	48	84	43	41	73	37	36	67	34	33
5-9	100	51	49	98	50	48	84	43	41	73	37	36
10-14	108	55	53	99	51	49	98	50	48	84	43	41
15-19	96	48	47	108	55	53	99	50	49	98	50	48
20-24	102	52	51	95	48	47	108	55	53	99	50	49
25-29	111	56	55	102	52	50	95	48	47	107	54	53
30-34	94	48	47	111	56	55	101	51	50	95	47	47
35-39	99	50	49	93	47	46	110	55	55	101	51	50
40-44	101	51	50	98	49	48	92	46	46	109	54	54
45-49	88	44	44	99	50	49	96	48	48	91	45	46
50-54	75	37	38	86	42	43	96	48	49	93	47	47
55-59	53	26	28	71	35	36	82	40	42	92	45	47
60-64	37	17	20	49	23	26	66	31	35	76	37	40
65-69	29	13	16	33	15	18	44	20	24	59	27	32
70-74	21	9	12	24	10	14	28	12	16	38	16	22
75-79	17	7	10	16	7	10	19	7	11	22	9	13
80-84	10	4	6	11	4	7	11	4	7	13	5	8
85-89	4	1	3	6	2	4	7	2	4	7	2	5
90-94	1	0	1	2	0	1	2	1	2	3	1	2
95-99	0	0	0	0	0	0	1	0	0	1	0	1
100 +	0	0	0	0	0	0	0	0	0	0	0	0

Age group	2025 Both sexes	Males	Females	2030 Both sexes	Males	Females	2035 Both sexes	Males	Females	2040 Both sexes	Males	Females
All ages	1 336	656	679	1 335	654	681	1 323	646	677	1 299	632	667
0-4	66	34	32	63	32	31	58	29	28	52	26	25
5-9	67	34	33	66	33	32	63	32	31	58	29	28
10-14	73	37	36	67	34	33	66	33	32	63	32	31
15-19	84	43	41	73	37	36	67	34	33	66	33	32
20-24	98	50	48	84	43	41	73	37	36	67	34	33
25-29	99	50	49	97	49	48	83	42	41	72	37	36
30-34	107	54	53	98	50	49	97	49	48	83	42	41
35-39	94	47	47	100	54	53	98	50	48	97	49	48
40-44	100	50	50	93	47	47	106	53	52	97	49	48
45-49	107	53	54	99	49	49	92	46	46	105	53	52
50-54	89	44	45	105	52	53	97	48	49	90	45	46
55-59	90	44	45	86	42	44	101	49	52	94	46	47
60-64	86	41	45	84	41	44	81	39	42	96	46	50
65-69	69	32	37	79	36	42	77	36	41	74	35	40
70-74	51	22	29	60	26	33	68	30	38	68	30	37
75-79	30	12	18	41	17	24	48	20	28	56	23	33
80-84	16	6	10	21	8	14	30	11	19	36	13	22
85-89	8	2	5	9	3	7	13	4	9	19	6	13
90-94	3	1	2	4	1	3	5	1	3	7	2	5
95-99	1	0	1	1	0	1	1	0	1	2	0	1
100 +	0	0	0	0	0	0	0	0	0	0	0	0

Age group	2045 Both sexes	Males	Females	2050 Both sexes	Males	Females
All ages	1 265	613	651	1 224	592	632
0-4	47	24	23	44	22	21
5-9	52	26	25	47	24	23
10-14	58	29	28	52	26	25
15-19	63	32	31	57	29	28
20-24	66	33	32	63	32	31
25-29	66	34	33	65	33	32
30-34	72	37	36	66	34	33
35-39	83	42	41	72	37	35
40-44	96	49	47	82	42	41
45-49	96	49	48	95	48	47
50-54	103	51	51	95	48	47
55-59	88	43	45	100	50	50
60-64	89	43	46	84	41	43
65-69	89	41	47	83	39	44
70-74	66	29	36	79	35	43
75-79	56	24	32	55	23	32
80-84	42	16	26	42	16	26
85-89	23	7	15	27	9	18
90-94	9	2	7	12	3	9
95-99	2	0	2	4	1	3
100 +	0	0	0	1	0	1

United Nations Department of Economic and Social Affairs/Population Division
World Population Prospects: The 2004 Revision, Volume II: Sex and Age Distribution of the World Population

597

POPULATION BY AGE AND SEX (in thousands)

Age group	1950 Both sexes	Males	Females	1955 Both sexes	Males	Females	1960 Both sexes	Males	Females	1965 Both sexes	Males	Females
All ages	27 737	13 860	13 877	31 737	15 842	15 895	36 940	18 433	18 507	43 141	21 522	21 619
0-4	4 715	2 388	2 327	5 698	2 884	2 814	6 829	3 455	3 374	7 946	4 020	3 926
5-9	3 776	1 916	1 860	4 427	2 245	2 182	5 434	2 751	2 682	6 549	3 309	3 241
10-14	3 152	1 614	1 539	3 702	1 878	1 824	4 359	2 209	2 150	5 352	2 706	2 647
15-19	2 722	1 394	1 328	3 079	1 569	1 510	3 633	1 835	1 797	4 287	2 166	2 120
20-24	2 284	1 158	1 126	2 620	1 328	1 292	2 984	1 508	1 476	3 542	1 782	1 759
25-29	1 976	992	983	2 192	1 101	1 090	2 533	1 274	1 258	2 887	1 449	1 438
30-34	1 482	739	743	1 895	944	951	2 116	1 056	1 060	2 447	1 223	1 224
35-39	1 347	667	680	1 417	701	715	1 826	904	922	2 043	1 012	1 031
40-44	1 253	614	640	1 282	630	652	1 358	668	691	1 755	862	893
45-49	1 136	552	584	1 186	576	610	1 222	596	626	1 300	635	666
50-54	1 027	493	534	1 061	510	551	1 118	538	580	1 156	559	597
55-59	904	430	474	941	446	495	982	467	515	1 040	496	544
60-64	732	344	387	801	376	425	846	396	450	889	418	471
65-69	536	248	288	616	286	330	690	320	370	734	339	395
70-74	350	159	191	419	191	228	498	227	270	565	259	306
75-79	216	97	119	246	110	136	308	138	170	375	169	206
80 +	130	56	74	156	68	89	204	89	115	273	120	154

Age group	1970 Both sexes	Males	Females	1975 Both sexes	Males	Females	1980 Both sexes	Males	Females	1985 Both sexes	Males	Females
All ages	50 611	25 241	25 370	59 287	29 521	29 766	68 046	33 799	34 247	76 117	37 666	38 452
0-4	9 434	4 783	4 652	11 019	5 590	5 429	11 240	5 708	5 531	11 023	5 610	5 413
5-9	7 660	3 868	3 792	9 135	4 622	4 513	10 766	5 451	5 315	11 010	5 579	5 431
10-14	6 454	3 254	3 200	7 539	3 798	3 741	9 001	4 543	4 458	10 608	5 354	5 254
15-19	5 248	2 641	2 607	6 286	3 149	3 137	7 339	3 669	3 670	8 685	4 326	4 359
20-24	4 154	2 083	2 072	5 025	2 495	2 530	6 014	2 964	3 050	6 935	3 397	3 538
25-29	3 426	1 712	1 714	3 987	1 975	2 012	4 840	2 373	2 467	5 759	2 798	2 961
30-34	2 795	1 394	1 401	3 303	1 636	1 667	3 859	1 891	1 968	4 680	2 273	2 407
35-39	2 371	1 178	1 193	2 703	1 337	1 366	3 208	1 576	1 632	3 748	1 821	1 927
40-44	1 974	973	1 001	2 290	1 130	1 160	2 617	1 285	1 333	3 109	1 515	1 594
45-49	1 682	820	861	1 897	928	968	2 207	1 081	1 126	2 528	1 231	1 297
50-54	1 233	597	636	1 599	772	827	1 815	881	934	2 112	1 022	1 090
55-59	1 078	515	563	1 155	554	601	1 505	719	786	1 715	824	891
60-64	943	443	499	983	464	518	1 062	502	561	1 388	655	734
65-69	776	360	416	830	384	446	872	404	468	951	440	511
70-74	604	275	329	646	294	352	699	316	383	743	336	407
75-79	429	193	236	464	207	258	505	224	281	554	243	311
80 +	349	153	197	426	185	241	497	213	284	570	242	328

Age group	1990 Both sexes	Males	Females	1995 Both sexes	Males	Females	2000 Both sexes	Males	Females	2005 Both sexes	Males	Females
All ages	84 296	41 566	42 729	92 523	45 485	47 038	100 088	49 060	51 028	107 029	52 308	54 722
0-4	11 416	5 803	5 613	11 704	5 954	5 750	11 264	5 728	5 536	10 857	5 522	5 335
5-9	10 782	5 473	5 309	11 169	5 662	5 508	11 455	5 812	5 643	11 027	5 592	5 435
10-14	10 852	5 490	5 362	10 616	5 379	5 237	10 991	5 561	5 430	11 277	5 711	5 567
15-19	10 292	5 155	5 136	10 510	5 275	5 235	10 246	5 147	5 099	10 623	5 330	5 293
20-24	8 196	3 994	4 203	9 753	4 789	4 964	9 929	4 881	5 048	9 672	4 757	4 915
25-29	6 633	3 198	3 435	7 869	3 779	4 091	9 400	4 558	4 843	9 582	4 653	4 929
30-34	5 572	2 678	2 893	6 437	3 073	3 364	7 661	3 647	4 014	9 186	4 420	4 766
35-39	4 559	2 197	2 362	5 446	2 599	2 847	6 307	2 991	3 315	7 524	3 560	3 965
40-44	3 644	1 757	1 887	4 449	2 129	2 320	5 330	2 528	2 801	6 185	2 916	3 269
45-49	3 014	1 459	1 556	3 546	1 699	1 846	4 344	2 068	2 276	5 216	2 461	2 755
50-54	2 429	1 170	1 259	2 910	1 395	1 515	3 438	1 634	1 804	4 224	1 996	2 228
55-59	1 997	953	1 044	2 310	1 099	1 211	2 785	1 322	1 463	3 302	1 555	1 747
60-64	1 593	757	836	1 869	884	985	2 179	1 031	1 148	2 637	1 244	1 393
65-69	1 253	580	673	1 451	679	772	1 720	804	916	2 015	943	1 072
70-74	818	370	448	1 091	495	596	1 281	591	690	1 528	704	824
75-79	596	262	334	667	294	373	904	403	502	1 070	484	585
80 +	650	272	378	728	302	425	854	354	500	1 104	460	644

United Nations Department of Economic and Social Affairs/Population Division
World Population Prospects: The 2004 Revision, Volume II: Sex and Age Distribution of the World Population

598

POPULATION BY AGE AND SEX (in thousands)

Age group	2005 Both sexes	2005 Males	2005 Females	2010 Both sexes	2010 Males	2010 Females	2015 Both sexes	2015 Males	2015 Females	2020 Both sexes	2020 Males	2020 Females
All ages	107 029	52 308	54 722	113 271	55 255	58 016	119 146	58 034	61 111	124 652	60 647	64 005
0-4	10 857	5 522	5 335	10 147	5 181	4 966	9 865	5 039	4 826	9 645	4 929	4 717
5-9	11 027	5 592	5 435	10 639	5 405	5 234	9 955	5 078	4 877	9 698	4 950	4 748
10-14	11 277	5 711	5 567	10 875	5 504	5 370	10 505	5 328	5 177	9 838	5 011	4 827
15-19	10 623	5 330	5 293	10 968	5 509	5 459	10 601	5 326	5 275	10 265	5 172	5 093
20-24	9 672	4 757	4 915	10 115	4 989	5 126	10 516	5 206	5 310	10 206	5 062	5 144
25-29	9 582	4 653	4 929	9 355	4 560	4 795	9 832	4 813	5 019	10 266	5 051	5 216
30-34	9 186	4 420	4 766	9 389	4 533	4 856	9 185	4 454	4 731	9 680	4 718	4 962
35-39	7 524	3 560	3 965	9 051	4 335	4 717	9 267	4 455	4 812	9 077	4 386	4 691
40-44	6 185	2 916	3 269	7 409	3 484	3 924	8 932	4 256	4 675	9 157	4 383	4 774
45-49	5 216	2 461	2 755	6 069	2 848	3 221	7 287	3 412	3 875	8 801	4 177	4 624
50-54	4 224	1 996	2 228	5 088	2 384	2 704	5 935	2 767	3 168	7 141	3 324	3 817
55-59	3 302	1 555	1 747	4 075	1 909	2 166	4 925	2 290	2 636	5 761	2 666	3 095
60-64	2 637	1 244	1 393	3 141	1 469	1 672	3 892	1 810	2 082	4 719	2 177	2 543
65-69	2 015	943	1 072	2 453	1 144	1 310	2 936	1 356	1 579	3 652	1 677	1 975
70-74	1 528	704	824	1 804	831	973	2 212	1 014	1 198	2 662	1 208	1 454
75-79	1 070	484	585	1 291	582	708	1 539	692	847	1 902	850	1 052
80-84	673	292	381	811	356	455	994	434	560	1 200	521	680
85-89	299	122	176	423	174	249	523	217	306	654	269	385
90-94	107	39	68	136	50	86	202	75	127	258	97	161
95-99	23	7	17	30	9	21	41	12	29	64	20	44
100 +	2	0	2	3	1	3	4	1	3	6	1	5

Age group	2025 Both sexes	2025 Males	2025 Females	2030 Both sexes	2030 Males	2030 Females	2035 Both sexes	2035 Males	2035 Females	2040 Both sexes	2040 Males	2040 Females
All ages	129 381	62 869	66 512	133 221	64 645	68 576	136 175	65 981	70 194	138 160	66 840	71 320
0-4	9 264	4 735	4 529	8 846	4 522	4 324	8 518	4 354	4 163	8 191	4 188	4 003
5-9	9 482	4 842	4 640	9 103	4 649	4 453	8 688	4 438	4 250	8 361	4 272	4 089
10-14	9 582	4 884	4 699	9 368	4 777	4 591	8 990	4 585	4 405	8 576	4 374	4 202
15-19	9 602	4 858	4 744	9 348	4 732	4 616	9 135	4 626	4 509	8 759	4 435	4 323
20-24	9 874	4 911	4 964	9 215	4 600	4 615	8 964	4 476	4 488	8 752	4 371	4 381
25-29	9 962	4 910	5 051	9 635	4 763	4 872	8 979	4 455	4 524	8 731	4 334	4 397
30-34	10 117	4 958	5 159	9 817	4 822	4 995	9 495	4 678	4 817	8 845	4 374	4 470
35-39	9 574	4 652	4 922	10 014	4 894	5 120	9 720	4 762	4 958	9 402	4 622	4 780
40-44	8 975	4 319	4 656	9 473	4 586	4 887	9 914	4 830	5 084	9 626	4 702	4 924
45-49	9 031	4 307	4 724	8 857	4 248	4 609	9 356	4 515	4 840	9 796	4 759	5 038
50-54	8 637	4 077	4 559	8 871	4 210	4 662	8 707	4 156	4 551	9 203	4 421	4 782
55-59	6 945	3 210	3 735	8 414	3 945	4 468	8 651	4 078	4 573	8 498	4 031	4 468
60-64	5 533	2 540	2 993	6 685	3 064	3 620	8 110	3 772	4 338	8 350	3 905	4 445
65-69	4 443	2 023	2 420	5 223	2 367	2 857	6 324	2 861	3 463	7 686	3 528	4 157
70-74	3 327	1 500	1 827	4 064	1 815	2 249	4 793	2 130	2 663	5 819	2 581	3 238
75-79	2 305	1 018	1 287	2 897	1 270	1 627	3 555	1 542	2 013	4 209	1 815	2 394
80-84	1 498	644	854	1 832	777	1 055	2 318	974	1 344	2 862	1 188	1 673
85-89	803	328	475	1 017	411	606	1 257	501	757	1 606	632	974
90-94	332	123	209	416	154	263	536	196	340	673	242	431
95-99	85	27	58	112	36	77	145	46	99	190	60	130
100 +	10	3	8	14	4	10	19	5	14	26	7	18

Age group	2045 Both sexes	2045 Males	2045 Females	2050 Both sexes	2050 Males	2050 Females
All ages	139 123	67 203	71 920	139 015	67 051	71 963
0-4	7 882	4 030	3 852	7 574	3 873	3 702
5-9	8 036	4 106	3 930	7 729	3 949	3 780
10-14	8 250	4 209	4 042	7 926	4 044	3 883
15-19	8 346	4 226	4 120	8 021	4 061	3 961
20-24	8 378	4 182	4 196	7 967	3 974	3 993
25-29	8 522	4 231	4 291	8 150	4 044	4 106
30-34	8 599	4 255	4 344	8 392	4 154	4 238
35-39	8 757	4 322	4 435	8 515	4 205	4 310
40-44	9 313	4 565	4 748	8 675	4 270	4 406
45-49	9 515	4 635	4 880	9 209	4 502	4 706
50-54	9 643	4 663	4 979	9 369	4 545	4 825
55-59	8 990	4 292	4 698	9 425	4 530	4 894
60-64	8 210	3 863	4 347	8 692	4 117	4 575
65-69	7 924	3 657	4 266	7 800	3 623	4 177
70-74	7 085	3 188	3 896	7 316	3 310	4 006
75-79	5 125	2 204	2 921	6 253	2 728	3 525
80-84	3 404	1 403	2 001	4 160	1 709	2 451
85-89	1 998	776	1 221	2 389	921	1 468
90-94	869	309	560	1 091	383	708
95-99	242	75	167	317	98	219
100 +	34	10	24	45	13	32

POPULATION BY AGE AND SEX (in thousands)

Age group	2005			2010			2015			2020		
	Both sexes	Males	Females	Both sexes	Males	Females	Both sexes	Males	Females	Both sexes	Males	Females
All ages	107 029	52 308	54 722	114 455	55 861	58 595	122 283	59 638	62 645	130 261	63 515	66 747
0-4	10 857	5 522	5 335	11 331	5 786	5 545	11 821	6 039	5 782	12 124	6 196	5 927
5-9	11 027	5 592	5 435	10 639	5 405	5 234	11 136	5 682	5 454	11 649	5 947	5 702
10-14	11 277	5 711	5 567	10 875	5 504	5 370	10 505	5 328	5 177	11 017	5 613	5 404
15-19	10 623	5 330	5 293	10 968	5 509	5 459	10 601	5 326	5 275	10 265	5 172	5 093
20-24	9 672	4 757	4 915	10 115	4 989	5 126	10 516	5 206	5 310	10 206	5 062	5 144
25-29	9 582	4 653	4 929	9 355	4 560	4 795	9 832	4 813	5 019	10 266	5 051	5 216
30-34	9 186	4 420	4 766	9 389	4 533	4 856	9 185	4 454	4 731	9 680	4 718	4 962
35-39	7 524	3 560	3 965	9 051	4 335	4 717	9 267	4 455	4 812	9 077	4 386	4 691
40-44	6 185	2 916	3 269	7 409	3 484	3 924	8 932	4 256	4 675	9 157	4 383	4 774
45-49	5 216	2 461	2 755	6 069	2 848	3 221	7 287	3 412	3 875	8 801	4 177	4 624
50-54	4 224	1 996	2 228	5 088	2 384	2 704	5 935	2 767	3 168	7 141	3 324	3 817
55-59	3 302	1 555	1 747	4 075	1 909	2 166	4 925	2 290	2 636	5 761	2 666	3 095
60-64	2 637	1 244	1 393	3 141	1 469	1 672	3 892	1 810	2 082	4 719	2 177	2 543
65-69	2 015	943	1 072	2 453	1 144	1 310	2 936	1 356	1 579	3 652	1 677	1 975
70-74	1 528	704	824	1 804	831	973	2 212	1 014	1 198	2 662	1 208	1 454
75-79	1 070	484	585	1 291	582	708	1 539	692	847	1 902	850	1 052
80-84	673	292	381	811	356	455	994	434	560	1 200	521	680
85-89	299	122	176	423	174	249	523	217	306	654	269	385
90-94	107	39	68	136	50	86	202	75	127	258	97	161
95-99	23	7	17	30	9	21	41	12	29	64	20	44
100 +	2	0	2	3	1	3	4	1	3	6	1	5

Age group	2025			2030			2035			2040		
	Both sexes	Males	Females	Both sexes	Males	Females	Both sexes	Males	Females	Both sexes	Males	Females
All ages	137 551	67 046	70 505	144 256	70 286	73 969	150 578	73 343	77 235	156 513	76 221	80 292
0-4	11 834	6 050	5 785	11 723	5 994	5 729	11 904	6 087	5 817	12 165	6 222	5 944
5-9	11 954	6 106	5 848	11 668	5 962	5 707	11 559	5 907	5 652	11 742	6 002	5 740
10-14	11 531	5 880	5 652	11 838	6 039	5 798	11 553	5 896	5 657	11 445	5 842	5 603
15-19	10 779	5 459	5 320	11 295	5 726	5 568	11 602	5 887	5 715	11 319	5 744	5 575
20-24	9 874	4 911	4 964	10 390	5 199	5 191	10 906	5 467	5 439	11 215	5 629	5 586
25-29	9 962	4 910	5 051	9 635	4 763	4 872	10 151	5 052	5 099	10 669	5 322	5 347
30-34	10 117	4 958	5 159	9 817	4 822	4 995	9 495	4 678	4 817	10 012	4 968	5 044
35-39	9 574	4 652	4 922	10 014	4 894	5 120	9 720	4 762	4 958	9 402	4 622	4 780
40-44	8 975	4 319	4 656	9 473	4 586	4 887	9 914	4 830	5 084	9 626	4 702	4 924
45-49	9 031	4 307	4 724	8 857	4 248	4 609	9 356	4 515	4 840	9 796	4 759	5 038
50-54	8 637	4 077	4 559	8 871	4 210	4 662	8 707	4 156	4 551	9 203	4 421	4 782
55-59	6 945	3 210	3 735	8 414	3 945	4 468	8 651	4 078	4 573	8 498	4 031	4 468
60-64	5 533	2 540	2 993	6 685	3 064	3 620	8 110	3 772	4 338	8 350	3 905	4 445
65-69	4 443	2 023	2 420	5 223	2 367	2 857	6 324	2 861	3 463	7 686	3 528	4 157
70-74	3 327	1 500	1 827	4 064	1 815	2 249	4 793	2 130	2 663	5 819	2 581	3 238
75-79	2 305	1 018	1 287	2 897	1 270	1 627	3 555	1 542	2 013	4 209	1 815	2 394
80-84	1 498	644	854	1 832	777	1 055	2 318	974	1 344	2 862	1 188	1 673
85-89	803	328	475	1 017	411	606	1 257	501	757	1 606	632	974
90-94	332	123	209	416	154	263	536	196	340	673	242	431
95-99	85	27	58	112	36	77	145	46	99	190	60	130
100 +	10	3	8	14	4	10	19	5	14	26	7	18

Age group	2045			2050		
	Both sexes	Males	Females	Both sexes	Males	Females
All ages	161 928	78 857	83 071	166 660	81 176	85 484
0-4	12 367	6 326	6 042	12 460	6 373	6 087
5-9	12 005	6 137	5 868	12 207	6 241	5 966
10-14	11 629	5 937	5 692	11 892	6 073	5 819
15-19	11 212	5 691	5 521	11 396	5 787	5 609
20-24	10 934	5 488	5 446	10 829	5 436	5 392
25-29	10 979	5 485	5 494	10 700	5 346	5 355
30-34	10 531	5 239	5 292	10 842	5 403	5 439
35-39	9 920	4 912	5 007	10 438	5 183	5 255
40-44	9 313	4 565	4 748	9 830	4 855	4 975
45-49	9 515	4 635	4 880	9 209	4 502	4 706
50-54	9 643	4 663	4 979	9 369	4 545	4 825
55-59	8 990	4 292	4 698	9 425	4 530	4 894
60-64	8 210	3 863	4 347	8 692	4 117	4 575
65-69	7 924	3 657	4 266	7 800	3 623	4 177
70-74	7 085	3 188	3 896	7 316	3 310	4 006
75-79	5 125	2 204	2 921	6 253	2 728	3 525
80-84	3 404	1 403	2 001	4 160	1 709	2 451
85-89	1 998	776	1 221	2 389	921	1 468
90-94	869	309	560	1 091	383	708
95-99	242	75	167	317	98	219
100 +	34	10	24	45	13	32

United Nations Department of Economic and Social Affairs/Population Division
World Population Prospects: The 2004 Revision, Volume II: Sex and Age Distribution of the World Population

600

POPULATION BY AGE AND SEX (in thousands)

Age group	2005			2010			2015			2020		
	Both sexes	Males	Females	Both sexes	Males	Females	Both sexes	Males	Females	Both sexes	Males	Females
All ages	107 029	52 308	54 722	112 088	54 650	57 437	116 007	56 430	59 577	119 031	57 773	61 257
0-4	10 857	5 522	5 335	8 963	4 576	4 387	7 905	4 037	3 868	7 157	3 656	3 501
5-9	11 027	5 592	5 435	10 639	5 405	5 234	8 775	4 475	4 300	7 743	3 951	3 792
10-14	11 277	5 711	5 567	10 875	5 504	5 370	10 505	5 328	5 177	8 660	4 409	4 250
15-19	10 623	5 330	5 293	10 968	5 509	5 459	10 601	5 326	5 275	10 265	5 172	5 093
20-24	9 672	4 757	4 915	10 115	4 989	5 126	10 516	5 206	5 310	10 206	5 062	5 144
25-29	9 582	4 653	4 929	9 355	4 560	4 795	9 832	4 813	5 019	10 266	5 051	5 216
30-34	9 186	4 420	4 766	9 389	4 533	4 856	9 185	4 454	4 731	9 680	4 718	4 962
35-39	7 524	3 560	3 965	9 051	4 335	4 717	9 267	4 455	4 812	9 077	4 386	4 691
40-44	6 185	2 916	3 269	7 409	3 484	3 924	8 932	4 256	4 675	9 157	4 383	4 774
45-49	5 216	2 461	2 755	6 069	2 848	3 221	7 287	3 412	3 875	8 801	4 177	4 624
50-54	4 224	1 996	2 228	5 088	2 384	2 704	5 935	2 767	3 168	7 141	3 324	3 817
55-59	3 302	1 555	1 747	4 075	1 909	2 166	4 925	2 290	2 636	5 761	2 666	3 095
60-64	2 637	1 244	1 393	3 141	1 469	1 672	3 892	1 810	2 082	4 719	2 177	2 543
65-69	2 015	943	1 072	2 453	1 144	1 310	2 936	1 356	1 579	3 652	1 677	1 975
70-74	1 528	704	824	1 804	831	973	2 212	1 014	1 198	2 662	1 208	1 454
75-79	1 070	484	585	1 291	582	708	1 539	692	847	1 902	850	1 052
80-84	673	292	381	811	356	455	994	434	560	1 200	521	680
85-89	299	122	176	423	174	249	523	217	306	654	269	385
90-94	107	39	68	136	50	86	202	75	127	258	97	161
95-99	23	7	17	30	9	21	41	12	29	64	20	44
100 +	2	0	2	3	1	3	4	1	3	6	1	5

Age group	2025			2030			2035			2040		
	Both sexes	Males	Females	Both sexes	Males	Females	Both sexes	Males	Females	Both sexes	Males	Females
All ages	121 225	58 699	62 525	122 384	59 105	63 279	122 381	58 931	63 451	121 102	58 123	62 979
0-4	6 719	3 433	3 286	6 152	3 144	3 009	5 544	2 833	2 711	4 904	2 505	2 398
5-9	6 998	3 572	3 426	6 563	3 350	3 213	5 999	3 062	2 936	5 392	2 752	2 640
10-14	7 630	3 886	3 744	6 887	3 508	3 379	6 453	3 288	3 166	5 890	3 000	2 889
15-19	8 425	4 257	4 168	7 399	3 736	3 662	6 657	3 360	3 298	6 225	3 140	3 085
20-24	9 874	4 911	4 964	8 041	4 001	4 040	7 018	3 483	3 535	6 279	3 108	3 171
25-29	9 962	4 910	5 051	9 635	4 763	4 872	7 809	3 859	3 950	6 790	3 344	3 446
30-34	10 117	4 958	5 159	9 817	4 822	4 995	9 495	4 678	4 817	7 678	3 781	3 897
35-39	9 574	4 652	4 922	10 014	4 894	5 120	9 720	4 762	4 958	9 402	4 622	4 780
40-44	8 975	4 319	4 656	9 473	4 586	4 887	9 914	4 830	5 084	9 626	4 702	4 924
45-49	9 031	4 307	4 724	8 857	4 248	4 609	9 356	4 515	4 840	9 796	4 759	5 038
50-54	8 637	4 077	4 559	8 871	4 210	4 662	8 707	4 156	4 551	9 203	4 421	4 782
55-59	6 945	3 210	3 735	8 414	3 945	4 468	8 651	4 078	4 573	8 498	4 031	4 468
60-64	5 533	2 540	2 993	6 685	3 064	3 620	8 110	3 772	4 338	8 350	3 905	4 445
65-69	4 443	2 023	2 420	5 223	2 367	2 857	6 324	2 861	3 463	7 686	3 528	4 157
70-74	3 327	1 500	1 827	4 064	1 815	2 249	4 793	2 130	2 663	5 819	2 581	3 238
75-79	2 305	1 018	1 287	2 897	1 270	1 627	3 555	1 542	2 013	4 209	1 815	2 394
80-84	1 498	644	854	1 832	777	1 055	2 318	974	1 344	2 862	1 188	1 673
85-89	803	328	475	1 017	411	606	1 257	501	757	1 606	632	974
90-94	332	123	209	416	154	263	536	196	340	673	242	431
95-99	85	27	58	112	36	77	145	46	99	190	60	130
100 +	10	3	8	14	4	10	19	5	14	26	7	18

Age group	2045			2050		
	Both sexes	Males	Females	Both sexes	Males	Females
All ages	118 567	56 700	61 867	114 830	54 697	60 133
0-4	4 353	2 224	2 129	3 903	1 993	1 909
5-9	4 754	2 426	2 328	4 204	2 145	2 059
10-14	5 284	2 691	2 593	4 646	2 365	2 281
15-19	5 662	2 853	2 809	5 058	2 545	2 513
20-24	5 848	2 889	2 958	5 287	2 604	2 683
25-29	6 054	2 972	3 082	5 625	2 755	2 870
30-34	6 665	3 270	3 395	5 933	2 901	3 032
35-39	7 596	3 732	3 864	6 589	3 226	3 363
40-44	9 313	4 565	4 748	7 521	3 685	3 836
45-49	9 515	4 635	4 880	9 209	4 502	4 706
50-54	9 643	4 663	4 979	9 369	4 545	4 825
55-59	8 990	4 292	4 698	9 425	4 530	4 894
60-64	8 210	3 863	4 347	8 692	4 117	4 575
65-69	7 924	3 657	4 266	7 800	3 623	4 177
70-74	7 085	3 188	3 896	7 316	3 310	4 006
75-79	5 125	2 204	2 921	6 253	2 728	3 525
80-84	3 404	1 403	2 001	4 160	1 709	2 451
85-89	1 998	776	1 221	2 389	921	1 468
90-94	869	309	560	1 091	383	708
95-99	242	75	167	317	98	219
100 +	34	10	24	45	13	32

POPULATION BY AGE AND SEX (in thousands)

Age group	1950 Both sexes	Males	Females	1955 Both sexes	Males	Females	1960 Both sexes	Males	Females	1965 Both sexes	Males	Females
All ages	32	16	16	38	20	18	45	23	22	52	27	25
0-4	5	3	2	7	4	4	8	4	4	9	5	5
5-9	4	2	2	5	2	2	7	4	3	8	4	4
10-14	4	2	2	4	2	2	5	2	2	7	4	3
15-19	3	2	2	4	2	2	4	2	2	5	2	2
20-24	3	1	1	3	2	2	4	2	2	4	2	2
25-29	2	1	1	3	1	1	3	2	1	4	2	2
30-34	2	1	1	2	1	1	3	1	1	3	2	1
35-39	2	1	1	2	1	1	2	1	1	3	1	1
40-44	2	1	1	2	1	1	2	1	1	2	1	1
45-49	1	1	1	1	1	1	2	1	1	2	1	1
50-54	1	1	1	1	1	1	1	1	1	2	1	1
55-59	1	0	0	1	1	0	1	1	1	1	1	1
60-64	1	0	0	1	0	0	1	0	0	1	1	1
65-69	1	0	0	1	0	0	1	0	0	1	0	0
70-74	0	0	0	0	0	0	0	0	0	1	0	0
75-79	0	0	0	0	0	0	0	0	0	0	0	0
80 +	0	0	0	0	0	0	0	0	0	0	0	0

Age group	1970 Both sexes	Males	Females	1975 Both sexes	Males	Females	1980 Both sexes	Males	Females	1985 Both sexes	Males	Females
All ages	61	32	30	63	33	30	73	37	36	86	44	42
0-4	11	6	5	11	6	6	13	7	6	15	8	7
5-9	9	5	4	10	5	5	12	6	6	13	7	6
10-14	8	4	4	8	4	4	10	5	5	12	6	6
15-19	7	4	3	7	4	3	8	4	4	10	5	5
20-24	5	2	2	6	3	3	6	3	3	8	4	4
25-29	4	2	2	3	2	2	5	3	3	6	3	3
30-34	3	2	2	3	1	1	4	2	2	5	3	3
35-39	3	2	1	2	1	1	3	2	1	3	2	2
40-44	3	1	1	2	1	1	2	1	1	3	2	1
45-49	2	1	1	2	1	1	2	1	1	2	1	1
50-54	2	1	1	2	1	1	2	1	1	2	1	1
55-59	1	1	1	2	1	1	2	1	1	2	1	1
60-64	1	1	1	1	1	1	1	1	1	2	1	1
65-69	1	0	0	1	1	1	1	1	1	1	1	1
70-74	1	0	0	1	0	0	1	0	0	1	0	0
75-79	0	0	0	1	0	0	0	0	0	0	0	0
80 +	0	0	0	0	0	0	0	0	0	0	0	0

Age group	1990 Both sexes	Males	Females	1995 Both sexes	Males	Females	2000 Both sexes	Males	Females	2005 Both sexes	Males	Females
All ages	96	49	47	107	55	52	107	54	53	110	56	55
0-4	15	8	7	16	8	8	15	8	7	16	8	8
5-9	15	8	7	16	8	7	14	7	7	14	7	7
10-14	12	6	6	15	8	7	14	7	7	13	7	6
15-19	11	6	5	13	7	6	13	7	7	13	7	6
20-24	9	5	4	9	4	4	10	5	5	11	6	6
25-29	7	4	3	7	3	4	7	3	4	7	4	4
30-34	6	3	3	7	4	3	7	3	4	6	3	3
35-39	5	3	3	6	3	3	6	3	3	6	3	3
40-44	3	2	2	5	3	2	5	3	3	6	3	3
45-49	3	1	1	4	2	2	5	2	2	5	2	2
50-54	2	1	1	2	1	1	3	2	2	4	2	2
55-59	2	1	1	2	1	1	2	1	1	3	1	1
60-64	2	1	1	2	1	1	2	1	1	2	1	1
65-69	1	1	1	1	1	1	2	1	1	1	1	1
70-74	1	0	1	1	1	1	1	0	0	1	1	1
75-79	1	0	0	1	0	0	1	0	0	1	0	0
80 +	0	0	0	0	0	0	1	0	0	1	0	0

United Nations Department of Economic and Social Affairs/Population Division
World Population Prospects: The 2004 Revision, Volume II: Sex and Age Distribution of the World Population

MEDIUM VARIANT   **MICRONESIA (FED. STATES OF)**

POPULATION BY AGE AND SEX (in thousands)

Age group	2005 Both sexes	Males	Females	2010 Both sexes	Males	Females	2015 Both sexes	Males	Females	2020 Both sexes	Males	Females
All ages	110	56	55	114	57	57	116	58	58	117	58	59
0-4	16	8	8	16	8	8	15	8	7	14	7	7
5-9	14	7	7	15	8	7	15	8	7	14	7	7
10-14	13	7	6	13	7	7	14	7	7	14	7	7
15-19	13	7	6	12	6	6	12	6	6	13	7	7
20-24	11	6	6	11	6	5	10	5	5	10	5	5
25-29	7	4	4	9	4	5	9	5	4	8	4	4
30-34	6	3	3	6	3	3	8	4	4	8	4	4
35-39	6	3	3	5	3	3	6	3	3	7	3	4
40-44	6	3	3	6	3	3	5	2	3	5	2	3
45-49	5	2	2	5	3	3	5	3	3	5	2	2
50-54	4	2	2	4	2	2	5	2	2	5	2	3
55-59	3	1	1	4	2	2	4	2	2	4	2	2
60-64	2	1	1	3	1	1	3	2	2	4	2	2
65-69	1	1	1	1	1	1	2	1	1	3	1	1
70-74	1	1	1	1	0	1	1	0	1	2	1	1
75-79	1	0	0	1	0	0	1	0	0	1	0	0
80-84	1	0	0	0	0	0	0	0	0	0	0	0
85-89	0	0	0	0	0	0	0	0	0	0	0	0
90-94	0	0	0	0	0	0	0	0	0	0	0	0
95-99	0	0	0	0	0	0	0	0	0	0	0	0
100 +	0	0	0	0	0	0	0	0	0	0	0	0

Age group	2025 Both sexes	Males	Females	2030 Both sexes	Males	Females	2035 Both sexes	Males	Females	2040 Both sexes	Males	Females
All ages	117	57	59	115	56	59	112	54	58	109	52	57
0-4	12	6	6	11	6	5	11	6	5	10	5	5
5-9	13	7	6	11	6	6	11	5	5	10	5	5
10-14	13	7	7	12	6	6	11	5	5	10	5	5
15-19	13	7	6	13	6	6	11	6	5	10	5	5
20-24	11	6	6	11	6	6	11	5	5	9	5	5
25-29	8	4	4	9	4	5	9	4	5	8	4	4
30-34	7	3	4	7	3	4	8	4	4	8	4	4
35-39	7	4	4	6	3	3	7	3	4	7	3	4
40-44	7	3	4	7	3	3	6	3	3	6	3	3
45-49	5	2	3	7	3	4	6	3	3	5	2	3
50-54	4	2	2	4	2	2	6	3	3	6	3	3
55-59	5	2	2	4	2	2	4	2	2	6	3	3
60-64	4	2	2	4	2	2	3	1	2	4	2	2
65-69	3	1	2	3	2	2	4	2	2	3	1	2
70-74	2	1	1	2	1	1	3	1	1	3	1	2
75-79	1	0	1	2	1	1	2	1	1	2	1	1
80-84	0	0	0	1	0	0	1	0	1	1	0	1
85-89	0	0	0	0	0	0	0	0	0	0	0	0
90-94	0	0	0	0	0	0	0	0	0	0	0	0
95-99	0	0	0	0	0	0	0	0	0	0	0	0
100 +	0	0	0	0	0	0	0	0	0	0	0	0

Age group	2045 Both sexes	Males	Females	2050 Both sexes	Males	Females
All ages	105	50	55	99	46	52
0-4	9	5	4	8	4	4
5-9	9	5	5	8	4	4
10-14	9	5	5	9	4	4
15-19	9	4	4	8	4	4
20-24	8	4	4	7	3	3
25-29	7	3	4	6	3	3
30-34	7	3	4	6	3	3
35-39	7	3	4	7	3	4
40-44	7	3	4	7	3	4
45-49	6	3	3	7	3	4
50-54	5	2	3	5	2	3
55-59	6	3	3	5	2	3
60-64	5	2	3	5	2	3
65-69	3	1	2	5	2	3
70-74	2	1	2	3	1	2
75-79	2	1	1	2	1	1
80-84	1	1	1	1	1	1
85-89	1	0	0	1	0	0
90-94	0	0	0	0	0	0
95-99	0	0	0	0	0	0
100 +	0	0	0	0	0	0

MICRONESIA (FED. STATES OF)　　　　　　　　　　　　　　　　　**HIGH VARIANT**

POPULATION BY AGE AND SEX (in thousands)

Age group	2005 Both sexes	Males	Females	2010 Both sexes	Males	Females	2015 Both sexes	Males	Females	2020 Both sexes	Males	Females
All ages	110	56	55	115	57	57	119	59	60	122	61	62
0-4	16	8	8	17	9	8	17	9	8	16	8	8
5-9	14	7	7	15	8	7	16	8	8	16	8	8
10-14	13	7	6	13	7	7	14	7	7	15	8	7
15-19	13	7	6	12	6	6	12	6	6	13	7	7
20-24	11	6	6	11	6	5	10	5	5	10	5	5
25-29	7	4	4	9	4	5	9	5	4	8	4	4
30-34	6	3	3	6	3	3	8	4	4	8	4	4
35-39	6	3	3	5	3	3	6	3	3	7	3	4
40-44	6	3	3	6	3	3	5	2	3	5	2	3
45-49	5	2	2	5	3	3	5	3	3	5	2	2
50-54	4	2	2	4	2	2	5	2	2	5	2	3
55-59	3	1	1	4	2	2	4	2	2	4	2	2
60-64	2	1	1	3	1	1	3	2	2	4	2	2
65-69	1	1	1	1	1	1	2	1	1	3	1	1
70-74	1	1	1	1	0	1	1	0	1	2	1	1
75-79	1	0	0	1	0	0	1	0	0	1	0	0
80-84	1	0	0	0	0	0	0	0	0	0	0	0
85-89	0	0	0	0	0	0	0	0	0	0	0	0
90-94	0	0	0	0	0	0	0	0	0	0	0	0
95-99	0	0	0	0	0	0	0	0	0	0	0	0
100 +	0	0	0	0	0	0	0	0	0	0	0	0

Age group	2025 Both sexes	Males	Females	2030 Both sexes	Males	Females	2035 Both sexes	Males	Females	2040 Both sexes	Males	Females
All ages	124	61	63	125	61	64	125	61	64	126	61	65
0-4	14	7	7	14	7	7	14	7	7	14	7	7
5-9	15	8	7	14	7	7	13	7	6	13	7	6
10-14	15	8	7	14	7	7	13	7	6	12	6	6
15-19	14	7	7	14	7	7	13	7	7	12	6	6
20-24	11	6	6	12	6	6	12	6	6	11	6	6
25-29	8	4	4	9	4	5	10	5	5	10	5	5
30-34	7	3	4	7	3	4	8	4	4	9	4	5
35-39	7	4	4	6	3	3	7	3	4	7	3	4
40-44	7	3	4	7	3	3	6	3	3	6	3	3
45-49	5	2	3	7	3	4	6	3	3	5	2	3
50-54	4	2	2	4	2	2	6	3	3	6	3	3
55-59	5	2	2	4	2	2	4	2	2	6	3	3
60-64	4	2	2	4	2	2	3	1	2	4	2	2
65-69	3	1	2	3	2	2	4	2	2	3	1	2
70-74	2	1	1	2	1	1	3	1	1	3	1	2
75-79	1	0	1	2	1	1	2	1	1	2	1	1
80-84	0	0	0	1	0	0	1	0	1	1	0	1
85-89	0	0	0	0	0	0	0	0	0	0	0	0
90-94	0	0	0	0	0	0	0	0	0	0	0	0
95-99	0	0	0	0	0	0	0	0	0	0	0	0
100 +	0	0	0	0	0	0	0	0	0	0	0	0

Age group	2045 Both sexes	Males	Females	2050 Both sexes	Males	Females
All ages	126	61	65	124	59	65
0-4	13	7	6	12	6	6
5-9	13	7	6	13	6	6
10-14	12	6	6	12	6	6
15-19	11	6	6	12	6	6
20-24	10	5	5	9	5	5
25-29	9	4	5	8	4	4
30-34	9	4	5	8	4	4
35-39	8	4	4	9	4	5
40-44	7	3	4	8	4	4
45-49	6	3	3	7	3	4
50-54	5	2	3	5	2	3
55-59	6	3	3	5	2	3
60-64	5	2	3	5	2	3
65-69	3	1	2	5	2	3
70-74	2	1	2	3	1	2
75-79	2	1	1	2	1	1
80-84	1	1	1	1	1	1
85-89	1	0	0	1	0	0
90-94	0	0	0	0	0	0
95-99	0	0	0	0	0	0
100 +	0	0	0	0	0	0

United Nations Department of Economic and Social Affairs/Population Division
World Population Prospects: The 2004 Revision, Volume II: Sex and Age Distribution of the World Population

604

POPULATION BY AGE AND SEX (in thousands)

Age group	2005 Both sexes	2005 Males	2005 Females	2010 Both sexes	2010 Males	2010 Females	2015 Both sexes	2015 Males	2015 Females	2020 Both sexes	2020 Males	2020 Females
All ages	110	56	55	113	56	56	113	56	57	112	55	57
0-4	16	8	8	15	8	7	13	7	6	11	6	6
5-9	14	7	7	15	8	7	14	7	7	12	6	6
10-14	13	7	6	13	7	7	14	7	7	13	7	6
15-19	13	7	6	12	6	6	12	6	6	13	7	7
20-24	11	6	6	11	6	5	10	5	5	10	5	5
25-29	7	4	4	9	4	5	9	5	4	8	4	4
30-34	6	3	3	6	3	3	8	4	4	8	4	4
35-39	6	3	3	5	3	3	6	3	3	7	3	4
40-44	6	3	3	6	3	3	5	2	3	5	2	3
45-49	5	2	2	5	3	3	5	3	3	5	2	2
50-54	4	2	2	4	2	2	5	2	2	5	2	3
55-59	3	1	1	4	2	2	4	2	2	4	2	2
60-64	2	1	1	3	1	1	3	2	2	4	2	2
65-69	1	1	1	1	1	1	2	1	1	3	1	1
70-74	1	1	1	1	0	1	1	0	1	2	1	1
75-79	1	0	0	1	0	0	1	0	0	1	0	0
80-84	1	0	0	0	0	0	0	0	0	0	0	0
85-89	0	0	0	0	0	0	0	0	0	0	0	0
90-94	0	0	0	0	0	0	0	0	0	0	0	0
95-99	0	0	0	0	0	0	0	0	0	0	0	0
100 +	0	0	0	0	0	0	0	0	0	0	0	0

Age group	2025 Both sexes	2025 Males	2025 Females	2030 Both sexes	2030 Males	2030 Females	2035 Both sexes	2035 Males	2035 Females	2040 Both sexes	2040 Males	2040 Females
All ages	109	54	56	105	51	54	100	48	52	94	45	49
0-4	10	5	5	9	5	4	8	4	4	7	4	4
5-9	11	5	5	9	5	5	8	4	4	8	4	4
10-14	12	6	6	10	5	5	9	4	4	7	4	4
15-19	12	6	6	11	5	5	9	5	4	8	4	4
20-24	11	6	6	10	5	5	9	4	4	7	3	4
25-29	8	4	4	9	4	5	8	4	4	7	3	3
30-34	7	3	4	7	3	4	8	4	4	7	3	4
35-39	7	4	4	6	3	3	7	3	4	7	3	4
40-44	7	3	4	7	3	3	6	3	3	6	3	3
45-49	5	2	3	7	3	4	6	3	3	5	2	3
50-54	4	2	2	4	2	2	6	3	3	6	3	3
55-59	5	2	2	4	2	2	4	2	2	6	3	3
60-64	4	2	2	4	2	2	3	1	2	4	2	2
65-69	3	1	2	3	2	2	4	2	2	3	1	2
70-74	2	1	1	2	1	1	3	1	1	3	1	2
75-79	1	0	1	2	1	1	2	1	1	2	1	1
80-84	0	0	0	1	0	0	1	0	1	1	0	1
85-89	0	0	0	0	0	0	0	0	0	0	0	0
90-94	0	0	0	0	0	0	0	0	0	0	0	0
95-99	0	0	0	0	0	0	0	0	0	0	0	0
100 +	0	0	0	0	0	0	0	0	0	0	0	0

Age group	2045 Both sexes	2045 Males	2045 Females	2050 Both sexes	2050 Males	2050 Females
All ages	86	40	46	77	35	42
0-4	6	3	3	4	2	2
5-9	7	3	3	5	3	3
10-14	7	3	3	6	3	3
15-19	7	3	3	6	3	3
20-24	6	3	3	5	2	2
25-29	5	2	3	4	2	2
30-34	5	2	3	4	2	2
35-39	6	3	3	5	2	3
40-44	7	3	4	6	3	3
45-49	6	3	3	7	3	4
50-54	5	2	3	5	2	3
55-59	6	3	3	5	2	3
60-64	5	2	3	5	2	3
65-69	3	1	2	5	2	3
70-74	2	1	2	3	1	2
75-79	2	1	1	2	1	1
80-84	1	1	1	1	1	1
85-89	1	0	0	1	0	0
90-94	0	0	0	0	0	0
95-99	0	0	0	0	0	0
100 +	0	0	0	0	0	0

POPULATION BY AGE AND SEX (in thousands)

Age group	1950 Both sexes	Males	Females	1955 Both sexes	Males	Females	1960 Both sexes	Males	Females	1965 Both sexes	Males	Females
All ages	761	373	389	850	418	432	959	474	485	1 094	543	551
0-4	127	63	64	143	72	71	164	83	81	189	96	93
5-9	103	51	52	117	58	59	134	67	66	154	78	76
10-14	88	44	45	101	50	51	114	57	57	131	66	65
15-19	76	38	38	86	43	43	99	49	50	113	56	56
20-24	66	33	33	74	37	37	84	42	42	96	48	48
25-29	57	28	29	63	31	32	71	35	36	81	40	41
30-34	49	24	25	54	27	27	60	30	30	68	34	34
35-39	41	20	21	46	23	23	52	26	26	58	29	29
40-44	35	17	18	39	19	20	44	21	22	49	24	25
45-49	30	14	15	32	15	17	36	17	19	41	20	21
50-54	25	12	13	27	13	14	29	14	15	33	16	17
55-59	21	10	11	22	10	12	24	11	13	26	12	14
60-64	16	7	9	18	8	10	19	9	10	20	9	11
65-69	12	5	7	13	6	7	14	6	8	15	7	8
70-74	8	3	4	8	3	5	9	4	5	10	4	6
75-79	4	2	2	4	2	3	5	2	3	6	2	3
80 +	2	1	1	2	1	2	3	1	2	3	1	2

Age group	1970 Both sexes	Males	Females	1975 Both sexes	Males	Females	1980 Both sexes	Males	Females	1985 Both sexes	Males	Females
All ages	1 256	625	630	1 447	723	724	1 663	834	830	1 909	959	950
0-4	216	110	107	248	126	122	273	139	134	305	156	149
5-9	180	91	89	208	106	102	239	122	117	266	135	130
10-14	152	77	75	178	90	88	205	104	101	237	121	116
15-19	129	65	64	150	76	74	176	89	87	204	103	100
20-24	110	55	55	127	64	63	148	75	73	174	88	86
25-29	93	47	47	108	54	54	124	63	62	146	73	72
30-34	79	39	39	91	45	46	105	52	53	122	61	61
35-39	66	33	33	76	38	38	89	44	44	103	51	52
40-44	55	27	28	63	31	32	74	37	37	86	43	43
45-49	46	23	24	53	26	27	61	30	31	71	35	36
50-54	38	18	20	43	21	22	50	24	25	57	28	29
55-59	30	14	16	34	16	18	40	19	21	46	22	24
60-64	22	10	12	26	12	14	30	14	16	35	17	19
65-69	16	7	9	18	8	10	22	10	12	26	12	14
70-74	11	5	6	12	5	7	14	6	8	17	7	9
75-79	6	3	4	7	3	4	8	3	5	9	4	6
80 +	4	2	2	5	2	3	6	2	3	7	3	4

Age group	1990 Both sexes	Males	Females	1995 Both sexes	Males	Females	2000 Both sexes	Males	Females	2005 Both sexes	Males	Females
All ages	2 216	1 106	1 110	2 389	1 195	1 195	2 497	1 250	1 247	2 646	1 326	1 321
0-4	354	179	175	303	155	148	268	137	131	270	138	132
5-9	299	151	148	337	170	166	286	146	140	258	132	126
10-14	271	137	134	290	146	143	324	164	160	279	143	137
15-19	245	124	121	263	133	131	278	140	138	317	160	157
20-24	214	107	107	237	120	117	252	127	125	271	137	134
25-29	197	98	99	207	104	103	227	115	112	246	123	122
30-34	151	75	76	190	94	96	197	99	99	220	111	109
35-39	101	50	51	144	72	73	180	89	91	191	95	96
40-44	72	36	36	96	48	48	136	67	69	174	86	88
45-49	71	36	35	68	34	34	89	44	45	130	64	66
50-54	58	30	29	66	33	32	62	30	31	84	41	43
55-59	55	27	28	52	26	26	59	29	29	56	27	29
60-64	40	19	21	47	22	25	45	22	23	52	25	27
65-69	34	15	18	33	15	17	39	18	21	38	18	20
70-74	27	11	16	26	11	14	25	11	14	30	13	17
75-79	18	7	11	18	7	11	17	7	10	17	7	10
80 +	11	4	7	13	4	8	14	5	9	15	5	9

606

United Nations Department of Economic and Social Affairs/Population Division
World Population Prospects: The 2004 Revision, Volume II: Sex and Age Distribution of the World Population

POPULATION BY AGE AND SEX (in thousands)

Age group	2005 Both sexes	2005 Males	2005 Females	2010 Both sexes	2010 Males	2010 Females	2015 Both sexes	2015 Males	2015 Females	2020 Both sexes	2020 Males	2020 Females
All ages	2 646	1 326	1 321	2 813	1 409	1 404	2 988	1 498	1 490	3 137	1 573	1 565
0-4	270	138	132	269	137	131	262	134	128	242	124	118
5-9	258	132	126	263	134	128	264	135	129	258	132	126
10-14	279	143	137	254	130	124	261	133	128	263	135	129
15-19	317	160	157	275	140	135	252	129	124	260	133	127
20-24	271	137	134	313	158	155	273	139	134	251	128	123
25-29	246	123	122	267	134	132	310	156	154	271	138	133
30-34	220	111	109	241	121	120	264	133	131	308	155	153
35-39	191	95	96	216	109	107	238	119	119	261	131	130
40-44	174	86	88	186	93	93	212	107	105	234	117	117
45-49	130	64	66	168	82	85	181	90	91	207	104	103
50-54	84	41	43	123	60	63	161	79	82	175	86	89
55-59	56	27	29	78	37	40	116	56	60	153	74	79
60-64	52	25	27	51	24	27	71	33	37	107	51	56
65-69	38	18	20	44	21	23	44	20	24	62	29	34
70-74	30	13	17	30	14	16	36	17	20	37	16	20
75-79	17	7	10	22	9	13	22	10	13	27	12	15
80-84	10	4	6	10	4	6	13	5	8	14	6	8
85-89	4	1	3	4	1	3	5	2	3	6	2	4
90-94	1	0	1	1	0	1	1	0	1	1	0	1
95-99	0	0	0	0	0	0	0	0	0	0	0	0
100 +	0	0	0	0	0	0	0	0	0	0	0	0

Age group	2025 Both sexes	2025 Males	2025 Females	2030 Both sexes	2030 Males	2030 Females	2035 Both sexes	2035 Males	2035 Females	2040 Both sexes	2040 Males	2040 Females
All ages	3 266	1 637	1 630	3 381	1 693	1 688	3 478	1 740	1 739	3 554	1 775	1 779
0-4	230	118	112	227	116	111	224	115	109	219	112	107
5-9	239	123	117	228	117	111	225	115	110	222	114	108
10-14	257	132	125	238	122	116	227	116	111	224	115	109
15-19	262	134	128	256	131	125	237	121	116	226	116	110
20-24	258	132	126	260	133	127	255	130	124	236	121	115
25-29	249	127	122	257	131	126	259	132	127	253	130	124
30-34	269	137	132	247	126	121	255	130	125	257	131	126
35-39	305	153	151	266	136	131	245	125	121	253	129	124
40-44	257	129	128	301	151	150	264	134	130	240	123	119
45-49	230	115	115	253	127	126	296	148	148	260	132	128
50-54	201	100	100	223	111	112	246	123	123	289	144	145
55-59	166	81	85	192	95	97	214	105	109	237	117	120
60-64	141	67	74	155	74	81	180	87	92	201	98	104
65-69	95	44	51	127	59	68	140	66	74	163	78	86
70-74	52	23	29	81	36	45	109	49	60	121	55	66
75-79	28	12	16	41	17	23	64	27	36	87	37	49
80-84	18	7	10	19	7	11	27	11	10	44	18	26
85-89	7	3	4	9	3	5	9	3	6	15	5	9
90-94	2	1	1	2	1	1	3	1	2	3	1	2
95-99	0	0	0	0	0	0	0	0	0	1	0	0
100 +	0	0	0	0	0	0	0	0	0	0	0	0

Age group	2045 Both sexes	2045 Males	2045 Females	2050 Both sexes	2050 Males	2050 Females
All ages	3 602	1 797	1 806	3 625	1 805	1 820
0-4	211	108	103	204	104	100
5-9	217	111	106	210	108	103
10-14	221	113	108	217	111	106
15-19	223	114	109	221	113	108
20-24	225	115	110	222	114	108
25-29	235	120	115	224	115	109
30-34	252	129	123	233	119	114
35-39	256	130	125	250	128	122
40-44	251	128	123	253	129	124
45-49	239	121	118	247	126	122
50-54	254	128	126	235	119	116
55-59	279	138	141	246	123	122
60-64	224	109	115	265	129	135
65-69	184	87	97	206	98	108
70-74	142	66	77	162	74	87
75-79	98	43	55	116	51	65
80-84	61	24	36	70	28	41
85-89	24	9	15	34	12	22
90-94	6	2	4	10	3	7
95-99	1	0	1	1	0	1
100 +	0	0	0	0	0	0

United Nations Department of Economic and Social Affairs/Population Division
World Population Prospects: The 2004 Revision, Volume II: Sex and Age Distribution of the World Population

607

POPULATION BY AGE AND SEX (in thousands)

Age group	2005 Both sexes	2005 Males	2005 Females	2010 Both sexes	2010 Males	2010 Females	2015 Both sexes	2015 Males	2015 Females	2020 Both sexes	2020 Males	2020 Females
All ages	2 646	1 326	1 321	2 843	1 425	1 418	3 070	1 540	1 530	3 282	1 647	1 636
0-4	270	138	132	299	153	146	313	160	153	306	157	149
5-9	258	132	126	263	134	128	294	151	144	309	158	151
10-14	279	143	137	254	130	124	261	133	128	293	150	143
15-19	317	160	157	275	140	135	253	129	124	260	133	127
20-24	271	137	134	313	158	155	273	139	134	251	128	123
25-29	246	123	122	267	134	132	310	156	154	271	138	133
30-34	220	111	109	241	121	120	264	133	131	308	155	153
35-39	191	95	96	216	109	107	238	119	119	261	131	130
40-44	174	86	88	186	93	93	212	107	105	234	117	117
45-49	130	64	66	168	82	85	181	90	91	207	104	103
50-54	84	41	43	123	60	63	161	79	82	175	86	89
55-59	56	27	29	78	37	40	116	56	60	153	74	79
60-64	52	25	27	51	24	27	71	33	37	107	51	56
65-69	38	18	20	44	21	23	44	20	24	62	29	34
70-74	30	13	17	30	14	16	36	17	20	37	16	20
75-79	17	7	10	22	9	13	22	10	13	27	12	15
80-84	10	4	6	10	4	6	13	5	8	14	6	8
85-89	4	1	3	4	1	3	5	2	3	6	2	4
90-94	1	0	1	1	0	1	1	0	1	1	0	1
95-99	0	0	0	0	0	0	0	0	0	0	0	0
100 +	0	0	0	0	0	0	0	0	0	0	0	0

Age group	2025 Both sexes	2025 Males	2025 Females	2030 Both sexes	2030 Males	2030 Females	2035 Both sexes	2035 Males	2035 Females	2040 Both sexes	2040 Males	2040 Females
All ages	3 475	1 744	1 731	3 660	1 836	1 824	3 844	1 927	1 917	4 021	2 014	2 007
0-4	294	151	144	298	153	146	311	159	152	322	165	157
5-9	302	155	147	292	150	142	296	152	144	309	158	150
10-14	308	157	150	301	154	147	291	149	142	295	151	144
15-19	291	149	142	306	157	149	300	153	146	289	148	141
20-24	258	132	126	290	148	142	305	156	149	298	153	146
25-29	249	127	122	257	131	126	288	147	141	303	155	148
30-34	269	137	132	247	126	121	255	130	125	287	146	140
35-39	305	153	151	267	136	131	245	125	121	253	129	124
40-44	257	129	128	301	151	150	264	134	130	243	123	120
45-49	230	115	115	253	127	126	296	149	148	260	132	128
50-54	201	100	101	223	111	112	246	123	123	289	144	145
55-59	167	81	85	192	95	97	214	105	109	237	117	120
60-64	141	67	74	155	75	81	180	87	92	202	98	104
65-69	95	44	51	127	59	68	140	66	75	164	78	86
70-74	52	23	29	81	36	45	109	49	60	121	55	66
75-79	28	12	16	41	17	23	64	27	36	87	37	49
80-84	18	7	10	19	7	11	27	11	16	44	18	26
85-89	7	3	4	9	3	5	9	3	6	15	5	9
90-94	2	1	1	2	1	1	3	1	2	3	1	2
95-99	0	0	0	0	0	0	0	0	0	1	0	0
100 +	0	0	0	0	0	0	0	0	0	0	0	0

Age group	2045 Both sexes	2045 Males	2045 Females	2050 Both sexes	2050 Males	2050 Females
All ages	4 185	2 095	2 090	4 330	2 166	2 164
0-4	327	167	160	328	168	160
5-9	320	164	156	325	166	159
10-14	307	157	150	319	163	156
15-19	294	151	143	306	157	150
20-24	288	148	141	293	150	143
25-29	297	152	145	287	147	140
30-34	302	154	147	295	151	144
35-39	285	145	140	300	153	147
40-44	251	128	123	282	144	139
45-49	240	122	118	248	126	122
50-54	254	128	126	235	119	116
55-59	279	138	141	246	123	123
60-64	224	109	115	265	130	136
65-69	185	88	97	206	98	108
70-74	142	66	77	162	75	87
75-79	98	43	55	116	51	65
80-84	61	25	36	70	28	41
85-89	24	9	15	34	12	22
90-94	6	2	4	10	3	7
95-99	1	0	1	1	0	1
100 +	0	0	0	0	0	0

United Nations Department of Economic and Social Affairs/Population Division
World Population Prospects: The 2004 Revision, Volume II: Sex and Age Distribution of the World Population

608

POPULATION BY AGE AND SEX (in thousands)

Age group	2005 Both sexes	Males	Females	2010 Both sexes	Males	Females	2015 Both sexes	Males	Females	2020 Both sexes	Males	Females
All ages	2 646	1 326	1 321	2 783	1 394	1 389	2 907	1 456	1 451	2 992	1 498	1 494
0-4	270	138	132	238	122	116	210	108	103	178	91	87
5-9	258	132	126	263	134	129	235	120	115	208	106	101
10-14	279	143	137	254	130	124	261	133	128	233	119	114
15-19	317	160	157	275	140	135	252	129	124	260	133	127
20-24	271	137	134	313	158	155	273	139	134	251	128	123
25-29	246	123	122	267	134	132	310	156	154	271	138	133
30-34	220	111	109	241	121	120	264	133	131	307	155	153
35-39	191	95	96	216	109	107	238	119	119	261	131	130
40-44	174	86	88	186	93	93	212	107	105	234	117	117
45-49	130	64	66	167	82	85	181	90	91	207	104	103
50-54	84	41	43	123	60	63	161	79	82	175	86	89
55-59	56	27	29	78	37	40	116	56	60	153	74	79
60-64	52	25	27	51	24	27	71	33	37	107	51	56
65-69	38	18	20	44	21	23	44	20	24	62	29	34
70-74	30	13	17	30	14	16	36	17	20	37	16	20
75-79	17	7	10	22	9	13	22	10	13	27	12	15
80-84	10	4	6	10	4	6	13	5	8	14	6	8
85-89	4	1	3	4	1	3	5	2	3	6	2	4
90-94	1	0	1	1	0	1	1	0	1	1	0	1
95-99	0	0	0	0	0	0	0	0	0	0	0	0
100 +	0	0	0	0	0	0	0	0	0	0	0	0

Age group	2025 Both sexes	Males	Females	2030 Both sexes	Males	Females	2035 Both sexes	Males	Females	2040 Both sexes	Males	Females
All ages	3 059	1 530	1 528	3 107	1 553	1 554	3 129	1 561	1 568	3 121	1 553	1 567
0-4	167	86	81	159	82	78	148	76	72	134	69	66
5-9	176	90	86	165	85	81	158	81	77	147	75	72
10-14	207	106	101	175	90	85	164	84	80	157	81	77
15-19	232	119	113	206	105	100	174	89	85	164	84	80
20-24	258	132	126	231	118	113	204	105	100	173	89	85
25-29	249	127	122	257	131	126	229	117	112	203	104	99
30-34	269	137	132	247	126	121	255	130	125	228	116	112
35-39	304	153	151	266	136	131	245	125	120	253	129	124
40-44	257	129	128	301	151	150	263	134	129	242	123	119
45-49	229	115	115	252	127	126	296	148	147	259	131	128
50-54	201	100	100	223	111	112	246	123	123	289	144	145
55-59	166	81	85	192	95	97	214	105	109	237	117	120
60-64	141	67	74	155	74	81	179	87	92	201	97	104
65-69	95	44	51	127	59	68	140	66	74	163	78	86
70-74	52	23	29	81	36	45	109	49	60	121	55	66
75-79	28	12	16	41	17	23	63	27	36	87	37	49
80-84	18	7	10	18	7	11	27	11	16	44	18	26
85-89	7	3	4	9	3	5	9	3	6	15	5	9
90-94	2	1	1	2	1	1	3	1	2	3	1	2
95-99	0	0	0	0	0	0	0	0	0	1	0	0
100 +	0	0	0	0	0	0	0	0	0	0	0	0

Age group	2045 Both sexes	Males	Females	2050 Both sexes	Males	Females
All ages	3 080	1 529	1 550	3 010	1 491	1 519
0-4	121	62	59	110	56	54
5-9	133	68	65	120	61	59
10-14	146	75	71	133	68	65
15-19	157	80	76	146	75	71
20-24	163	83	79	156	80	76
25-29	172	88	84	162	83	79
30-34	202	103	99	171	88	84
35-39	226	115	111	201	102	98
40-44	250	127	123	224	114	110
45-49	239	121	118	247	126	122
50-54	253	128	125	234	118	116
55-59	279	138	141	245	123	122
60-64	223	109	114	264	129	135
65-69	184	87	97	205	98	107
70-74	142	66	76	161	74	87
75-79	97	42	55	116	51	64
80-84	61	24	36	69	28	41
85-89	24	9	15	34	12	22
90-94	6	2	4	10	3	7
95-99	1	0	1	1	0	1
100 +	0	0	0	0	0	0

United Nations Department of Economic and Social Affairs/Population Division
World Population Prospects: The 2004 Revision, Volume II: Sex and Age Distribution of the World Population

609

POPULATION BY AGE AND SEX (in thousands)

Age group	1950 Both sexes	1950 Males	1950 Females	1955 Both sexes	1955 Males	1955 Females	1960 Both sexes	1960 Males	1960 Females	1965 Both sexes	1965 Males	1965 Females
All ages	8 953	4 481	4 472	10 132	5 067	5 065	11 626	5 812	5 814	13 323	6 659	6 664
0-4	1 598	807	792	1 814	914	900	2 096	1 055	1 041	2 455	1 242	1 213
5-9	1 284	645	639	1 463	736	727	1 686	848	838	2 063	1 062	1 001
10-14	1 091	548	544	1 245	625	619	1 429	719	710	1 599	807	792
15-19	930	466	463	1 057	531	526	1 216	611	604	1 247	611	637
20-24	785	394	391	891	447	444	1 023	513	510	1 071	506	565
25-29	659	330	329	747	375	372	855	428	427	945	449	496
30-34	554	277	277	625	313	312	715	359	357	836	408	428
35-39	466	233	233	523	261	262	596	299	298	701	347	354
40-44	391	196	195	437	218	219	496	247	249	557	285	272
45-49	324	162	163	362	180	182	412	204	208	467	241	225
50-54	265	131	134	295	146	149	335	165	170	356	186	170
55-59	196	96	100	234	114	120	265	129	136	325	160	164
60-64	153	74	79	166	80	86	203	97	106	241	122	120
65-69	116	57	59	121	57	64	134	63	71	201	99	101
70-74	84	39	45	92	43	49	101	47	54	116	59	57
75-79	41	19	22	44	20	24	48	22	26	103	53	50
80 +	16	7	9	17	8	10	18	8	10	43	22	20

Age group	1970 Both sexes	1970 Males	1970 Females	1975 Both sexes	1975 Males	1975 Females	1980 Both sexes	1980 Males	1980 Females	1985 Both sexes	1985 Males	1985 Females
All ages	15 310	7 672	7 638	17 305	8 647	8 658	19 527	9 761	9 766	22 193	11 088	11 104
0-4	2 828	1 438	1 390	3 208	1 631	1 577	3 199	1 634	1 566	3 438	1 751	1 687
5-9	2 456	1 250	1 206	2 603	1 323	1 280	2 776	1 410	1 366	3 095	1 579	1 516
10-14	1 998	1 051	947	2 354	1 198	1 156	2 412	1 230	1 182	2 751	1 397	1 355
15-19	1 489	755	734	1 910	1 004	906	2 091	1 023	1 068	2 388	1 217	1 171
20-24	1 071	509	562	1 406	710	696	1 860	927	933	2 059	1 006	1 053
25-29	930	412	518	1 000	470	530	1 447	727	720	1 824	907	916
30-34	861	387	475	871	381	490	1 068	528	540	1 416	710	707
35-39	803	381	422	806	358	448	801	377	424	1 043	515	529
40-44	675	330	345	752	353	399	838	377	461	780	365	415
45-49	513	268	245	630	306	325	687	338	349	812	363	449
50-54	432	233	199	474	245	228	681	324	357	659	321	338
55-59	304	166	138	392	209	183	432	228	204	642	302	341
60-64	311	154	157	266	143	123	420	222	198	395	206	190
65-69	217	113	103	257	125	132	321	168	153	365	189	176
70-74	196	100	96	162	83	79	220	113	108	256	131	125
75-79	98	54	45	124	62	63	163	82	82	150	74	76
80 +	129	72	57	90	48	41	110	56	55	119	57	62

Age group	1990 Both sexes	1990 Males	1990 Females	1995 Both sexes	1995 Males	1995 Females	2000 Both sexes	2000 Males	2000 Females	2005 Both sexes	2005 Males	2005 Females
All ages	24 696	12 328	12 368	27 004	13 462	13 541	29 231	14 549	14 681	31 478	15 646	15 833
0-4	3 381	1 723	1 658	3 293	1 679	1 614	3 221	1 638	1 582	3 378	1 719	1 659
5-9	3 351	1 706	1 646	3 318	1 690	1 628	3 247	1 653	1 594	3 181	1 616	1 565
10-14	3 071	1 566	1 505	3 329	1 693	1 636	3 299	1 679	1 620	3 229	1 643	1 586
15-19	2 722	1 380	1 341	3 035	1 546	1 490	3 296	1 674	1 622	3 262	1 657	1 605
20-24	2 338	1 188	1 150	2 654	1 341	1 313	2 970	1 507	1 462	3 217	1 628	1 589
25-29	2 001	973	1 028	2 258	1 142	1 116	2 576	1 296	1 280	2 874	1 451	1 423
30-34	1 771	878	894	1 931	934	998	2 190	1 103	1 088	2 493	1 247	1 246
35-39	1 374	686	689	1 715	845	870	1 877	902	975	2 125	1 064	1 061
40-44	1 010	496	515	1 330	660	670	1 669	818	850	1 824	871	953
45-49	752	349	402	973	474	499	1 289	636	653	1 620	789	830
50-54	778	344	434	718	330	388	935	451	484	1 241	607	634
55-59	622	299	323	736	321	415	681	308	372	889	423	465
60-64	590	272	318	572	271	302	683	292	391	632	281	351
65-69	345	176	169	521	235	286	508	234	273	610	254	356
70-74	293	148	145	280	139	141	428	187	241	420	188	232
75-79	177	88	90	206	101	105	200	96	104	311	130	181
80 +	119	56	63	134	62	72	163	75	88	173	77	96

United Nations Department of Economic and Social Affairs/Population Division
World Population Prospects: The 2004 Revision, Volume II: Sex and Age Distribution of the World Population

610

POPULATION BY AGE AND SEX (in thousands)

Age group	2005 Both sexes	2005 Males	2005 Females	2010 Both sexes	2010 Males	2010 Females	2015 Both sexes	2015 Males	2015 Females	2020 Both sexes	2020 Males	2020 Females
All ages	31 478	15 646	15 833	33 832	16 804	17 028	36 152	17 951	18 201	38 327	19 025	19 302
0-4	3 378	1 719	1 659	3 486	1 774	1 711	3 493	1 779	1 714	3 398	1 732	1 667
5-9	3 181	1 616	1 565	3 345	1 700	1 645	3 458	1 758	1 700	3 470	1 765	1 705
10-14	3 229	1 643	1 586	3 166	1 607	1 559	3 332	1 692	1 639	3 447	1 751	1 695
15-19	3 262	1 657	1 605	3 198	1 624	1 573	3 138	1 590	1 547	3 306	1 677	1 629
20-24	3 217	1 628	1 589	3 194	1 617	1 577	3 136	1 588	1 548	3 082	1 557	1 525
25-29	2 874	1 451	1 423	3 133	1 578	1 555	3 118	1 571	1 546	3 067	1 547	1 520
30-34	2 493	1 247	1 246	2 800	1 407	1 393	3 065	1 537	1 528	3 056	1 535	1 521
35-39	2 125	1 064	1 061	2 434	1 212	1 222	2 745	1 374	1 371	3 014	1 507	1 507
40-44	1 824	871	953	2 076	1 035	1 041	2 388	1 184	1 204	2 702	1 348	1 354
45-49	1 620	789	830	1 779	844	934	2 032	1 008	1 024	2 344	1 158	1 186
50-54	1 241	607	634	1 569	759	810	1 730	815	915	1 982	977	1 004
55-59	889	423	465	1 187	574	613	1 508	722	786	1 668	778	890
60-64	632	281	351	830	389	441	1 116	531	585	1 424	671	754
65-69	610	254	356	568	246	322	751	343	408	1 016	472	544
70-74	420	188	232	511	206	306	480	201	279	640	283	357
75-79	311	130	181	310	133	177	383	147	237	365	145	220
80-84	115	53	63	184	73	111	187	76	111	239	85	153
85-89	47	21	27	48	20	28	79	29	50	83	31	53
90-94	9	4	6	12	5	7	12	5	8	22	7	15
95-99	1	0	1	1	0	1	2	1	1	2	1	1
100 +	0	0	0	0	0	0	0	0	0	0	0	0

Age group	2025 Both sexes	2025 Males	2025 Females	2030 Both sexes	2030 Males	2030 Females	2035 Both sexes	2035 Males	2035 Females	2040 Both sexes	2040 Males	2040 Females
All ages	40 280	19 982	20 298	42 016	20 821	21 195	43 538	21 547	21 992	44 801	22 138	22 663
0-4	3 274	1 670	1 604	3 192	1 630	1 562	3 149	1 609	1 540	3 086	1 579	1 508
5-9	3 378	1 720	1 658	3 255	1 660	1 596	3 175	1 621	1 554	3 133	1 601	1 532
10-14	3 459	1 759	1 700	3 368	1 714	1 654	3 246	1 655	1 592	3 167	1 616	1 550
15-19	3 422	1 737	1 685	3 435	1 744	1 690	3 344	1 700	1 644	3 223	1 641	1 582
20-24	3 251	1 644	1 607	3 368	1 705	1 663	3 382	1 713	1 669	3 292	1 670	1 622
25-29	3 014	1 517	1 497	3 184	1 605	1 579	3 302	1 666	1 636	3 317	1 675	1 642
30-34	3 007	1 511	1 496	2 956	1 483	1 474	3 127	1 571	1 556	3 245	1 632	1 612
35-39	3 007	1 505	1 502	2 960	1 483	1 477	2 911	1 456	1 455	3 082	1 545	1 537
40-44	2 971	1 481	1 490	2 966	1 481	1 485	2 921	1 460	1 461	2 873	1 434	1 440
45-49	2 657	1 321	1 336	2 926	1 454	1 472	2 925	1 456	1 469	2 882	1 437	1 446
50-54	2 292	1 126	1 166	2 803	1 390	1 413	2 873	1 421	1 451	2 874	1 425	1 449
55-59	1 916	936	980	2 222	1 082	1 140	2 529	1 241	1 288	2 796	1 373	1 423
60-64	1 592	726	866	1 823	877	945	2 120	1 018	1 103	2 421	1 172	1 248
65-69	1 305	600	705	1 458	653	805	1 686	794	892	1 970	925	1 045
70-74	874	392	482	1 133	503	631	1 277	551	726	1 484	674	810
75-79	494	207	287	684	290	394	899	376	523	1 026	416	610
80-84	234	85	148	324	124	200	459	176	282	616	232	384
85-89	113	35	78	115	36	79	166	53	113	243	77	166
90-94	25	7	18	37	9	28	40	9	31	61	14	47
95-99	4	1	3	5	1	4	8	1	7	9	1	8
100 +	0	0	0	0	0	0	1	0	0	1	0	1

Age group	2045 Both sexes	2045 Males	2045 Females	2050 Both sexes	2050 Males	2050 Females
All ages	45 746	22 569	23 177	46 397	22 861	23 536
0-4	2 974	1 522	1 452	2 862	1 465	1 397
5-9	3 071	1 571	1 500	2 960	1 515	1 445
10-14	3 125	1 596	1 528	3 063	1 566	1 497
15-19	3 144	1 603	1 541	3 103	1 584	1 519
20-24	3 172	1 611	1 560	3 093	1 574	1 520
25-29	3 228	1 632	1 596	3 109	1 575	1 534
30-34	3 261	1 642	1 618	3 173	1 600	1 573
35-39	3 201	1 607	1 594	3 217	1 617	1 600
40-44	3 045	1 523	1 522	3 164	1 585	1 579
45-49	2 837	1 412	1 425	3 009	1 502	1 507
50-54	2 836	1 408	1 427	2 793	1 385	1 408
55-59	2 802	1 380	1 422	2 769	1 366	1 402
60-64	2 683	1 301	1 382	2 695	1 312	1 383
65-69	2 257	1 070	1 187	2 512	1 194	1 318
70-74	1 745	790	954	2 013	923	1 090
75-79	1 203	514	689	1 432	613	819
80-84	717	259	457	856	330	525
85-89	336	103	233	408	121	287
90-94	93	20	73	138	30	108
95-99	15	2	13	25	3	22
100 +	1	0	1	2	0	2

POPULATION BY AGE AND SEX (in thousands)

Age group	2005 Both sexes	Males	Females	2010 Both sexes	Males	Females	2015 Both sexes	Males	Females	2020 Both sexes	Males	Females
All ages	31 478	15 646	15 833	34 129	16 955	17 174	36 969	18 366	18 602	39 841	19 796	20 045
0-4	3 378	1 719	1 659	3 783	1 926	1 857	4 014	2 044	1 970	4 099	2 088	2 010
5-9	3 181	1 616	1 565	3 345	1 700	1 645	3 754	1 909	1 845	3 989	2 029	1 960
10-14	3 229	1 643	1 586	3 166	1 607	1 559	3 332	1 692	1 639	3 742	1 901	1 840
15-19	3 262	1 657	1 605	3 198	1 624	1 573	3 138	1 590	1 547	3 306	1 677	1 629
20-24	3 217	1 628	1 589	3 194	1 617	1 577	3 136	1 588	1 548	3 082	1 557	1 525
25-29	2 874	1 451	1 423	3 133	1 578	1 555	3 118	1 571	1 546	3 067	1 547	1 520
30-34	2 493	1 247	1 246	2 800	1 407	1 393	3 065	1 537	1 528	3 056	1 535	1 521
35-39	2 125	1 064	1 061	2 434	1 212	1 222	2 745	1 374	1 371	3 014	1 507	1 507
40-44	1 824	871	953	2 076	1 035	1 041	2 388	1 184	1 204	2 702	1 348	1 354
45-49	1 620	789	830	1 779	844	934	2 032	1 008	1 024	2 344	1 158	1 186
50-54	1 241	607	634	1 569	759	810	1 730	815	915	1 982	977	1 004
55-59	889	423	465	1 187	574	613	1 508	722	786	1 668	778	890
60-64	632	281	351	830	389	441	1 116	531	585	1 424	671	754
65-69	610	254	356	568	246	322	751	343	408	1 016	472	544
70-74	420	188	232	511	206	306	480	201	279	640	283	357
75-79	311	130	181	310	133	177	383	147	237	365	145	220
80-84	115	53	63	184	73	111	187	76	111	239	85	153
85-89	47	21	27	48	20	28	79	29	50	83	31	53
90-94	9	4	6	12	5	7	12	5	8	22	7	15
95-99	1	0	1	1	0	1	2	1	1	2	1	1
100 +	0	0	0	0	0	0	0	0	0	0	0	0

Age group	2025 Both sexes	Males	Females	2030 Both sexes	Males	Females	2035 Both sexes	Males	Females	2040 Both sexes	Males	Females
All ages	42 533	21 129	21 405	45 077	22 380	22 697	47 555	23 593	23 962	49 986	24 782	25 205
0-4	4 016	2 049	1 967	4 003	2 044	1 959	4 110	2 100	2 009	4 261	2 180	2 082
5-9	4 076	2 075	2 001	3 996	2 037	1 959	3 985	2 034	1 951	4 092	2 091	2 001
10-14	3 977	2 022	1 955	4 066	2 069	1 996	3 986	2 032	1 954	3 975	2 029	1 947
15-19	3 716	1 886	1 830	3 952	2 007	1 945	4 041	2 055	1 986	3 962	2 018	1 944
20-24	3 251	1 644	1 607	3 661	1 854	1 808	3 898	1 975	1 923	3 988	2 023	1 964
25-29	3 014	1 517	1 497	3 184	1 605	1 579	3 595	1 814	1 780	3 832	1 936	1 895
30-34	3 007	1 511	1 496	2 956	1 483	1 474	3 127	1 571	1 556	3 537	1 780	1 757
35-39	3 007	1 505	1 502	2 960	1 483	1 477	2 911	1 456	1 455	3 082	1 545	1 537
40-44	2 971	1 481	1 490	2 966	1 481	1 485	2 921	1 460	1 461	2 873	1 434	1 440
45-49	2 657	1 321	1 336	2 926	1 454	1 472	2 925	1 456	1 469	2 882	1 437	1 446
50-54	2 292	1 126	1 166	2 603	1 288	1 315	2 872	1 421	1 451	2 874	1 425	1 449
55-59	1 916	936	980	2 222	1 082	1 140	2 529	1 241	1 288	2 796	1 373	1 423
60-64	1 582	726	856	1 823	877	945	2 120	1 018	1 103	2 421	1 172	1 248
65-69	1 305	600	705	1 458	653	805	1 686	794	892	1 970	925	1 045
70-74	874	392	482	1 133	503	631	1 277	551	726	1 484	674	810
75-79	494	207	287	684	290	394	899	376	523	1 026	416	610
80-84	234	85	148	324	124	200	459	176	282	616	232	384
85-89	113	35	78	115	36	79	166	53	113	243	77	166
90-94	25	7	18	37	9	28	40	9	31	61	14	47
95-99	4	1	3	5	1	4	8	1	7	9	1	8
100 +	0	0	0	0	0	0	1	0	0	1	0	1

Age group	2045 Both sexes	Males	Females	2050 Both sexes	Males	Females
All ages	52 300	25 912	26 387	54 460	26 976	27 485
0-4	4 350	2 227	2 123	4 381	2 243	2 139
5-9	4 245	2 171	2 074	4 334	2 218	2 116
10-14	4 083	2 086	1 997	4 236	2 166	2 070
15-19	3 952	2 015	1 937	4 060	2 073	1 988
20-24	3 910	1 987	1 923	3 900	1 985	1 915
25-29	3 922	1 985	1 937	3 845	1 949	1 896
30-34	3 775	1 903	1 872	3 866	1 952	1 914
35-39	3 492	1 754	1 738	3 730	1 877	1 853
40-44	3 045	1 523	1 522	3 455	1 732	1 722
45-49	2 837	1 412	1 425	3 009	1 502	1 507
50-54	2 836	1 408	1 427	2 793	1 385	1 408
55-59	2 802	1 380	1 422	2 769	1 366	1 402
60-64	2 683	1 301	1 382	2 695	1 312	1 383
65-69	2 257	1 070	1 187	2 512	1 194	1 318
70-74	1 745	790	954	2 013	923	1 090
75-79	1 203	514	689	1 432	613	819
80-84	717	259	457	856	330	525
85-89	336	103	233	408	121	287
90-94	93	20	73	138	30	108
95-99	15	2	13	25	3	22
100 +	1	0	1	2	0	2

United Nations Department of Economic and Social Affairs/Population Division
World Population Prospects: The 2004 Revision, Volume II: Sex and Age Distribution of the World Population

POPULATION BY AGE AND SEX (in thousands)

Age group	2005 Both sexes	2005 Males	2005 Females	2010 Both sexes	2010 Males	2010 Females	2015 Both sexes	2015 Males	2015 Females	2020 Both sexes	2020 Males	2020 Females
All ages	31 478	15 646	15 833	33 528	16 649	16 879	35 306	17 520	17 785	36 753	18 224	18 529
0-4	3 378	1 719	1 659	3 182	1 620	1 562	2 949	1 502	1 447	2 669	1 360	1 309
5-9	3 181	1 616	1 565	3 345	1 700	1 645	3 156	1 604	1 551	2 928	1 489	1 439
10-14	3 229	1 643	1 586	3 166	1 607	1 559	3 332	1 692	1 639	3 144	1 598	1 547
15-19	3 262	1 657	1 605	3 198	1 624	1 573	3 138	1 590	1 547	3 306	1 677	1 629
20-24	3 217	1 628	1 589	3 194	1 617	1 577	3 136	1 588	1 548	3 082	1 557	1 525
25-29	2 874	1 451	1 423	3 133	1 578	1 555	3 118	1 571	1 546	3 067	1 547	1 520
30-34	2 493	1 247	1 246	2 800	1 407	1 393	3 065	1 537	1 528	3 056	1 535	1 521
35-39	2 125	1 064	1 061	2 434	1 212	1 222	2 745	1 374	1 371	3 014	1 507	1 507
40-44	1 824	871	953	2 076	1 035	1 041	2 388	1 184	1 204	2 702	1 348	1 354
45-49	1 620	789	830	1 779	844	934	2 032	1 008	1 024	2 344	1 158	1 186
50-54	1 241	607	634	1 569	759	810	1 730	815	915	1 982	977	1 004
55-59	889	423	465	1 187	574	613	1 508	722	786	1 668	778	890
60-64	632	281	351	830	389	441	1 116	531	585	1 424	671	754
65-69	610	254	356	568	246	322	751	343	408	1 016	472	544
70-74	420	188	232	511	206	306	480	201	279	640	283	357
75-79	311	130	181	310	133	177	383	147	237	365	145	220
80-84	115	53	63	184	73	111	187	76	111	239	85	153
85-89	47	21	27	48	20	28	79	29	50	83	31	53
90-94	9	4	6	12	5	7	12	5	8	22	7	15
95-99	1	0	1	1	0	1	2	1	1	2	1	1
100 +	0	0	0	0	0	0	0	0	0	0	0	0

Age group	2025 Both sexes	2025 Males	2025 Females	2030 Both sexes	2030 Males	2030 Females	2035 Both sexes	2035 Males	2035 Females	2040 Both sexes	2040 Males	2040 Females
All ages	37 959	18 800	19 159	38 900	19 234	19 666	39 514	19 496	20 018	39 729	19 553	20 176
0-4	2 523	1 287	1 236	2 393	1 222	1 171	2 237	1 143	1 094	2 032	1 040	993
5-9	2 650	1 349	1 301	2 507	1 278	1 229	2 377	1 214	1 164	2 222	1 136	1 087
10-14	2 918	1 483	1 434	2 641	1 344	1 297	2 498	1 273	1 225	2 369	1 209	1 160
15-19	3 120	1 583	1 537	2 894	1 470	1 425	2 618	1 331	1 287	2 476	1 261	1 215
20-24	3 251	1 644	1 607	3 066	1 552	1 515	2 842	1 439	1 403	2 567	1 301	1 266
25-29	3 014	1 517	1 497	3 184	1 605	1 579	3 001	1 513	1 488	2 778	1 402	1 376
30-34	3 007	1 511	1 496	2 956	1 483	1 474	3 127	1 571	1 556	2 945	1 480	1 465
35-39	3 007	1 505	1 502	2 960	1 483	1 477	2 911	1 456	1 455	3 082	1 545	1 537
40-44	2 971	1 481	1 490	2 966	1 481	1 485	2 921	1 460	1 461	2 873	1 434	1 440
45-49	2 657	1 321	1 336	2 926	1 454	1 472	2 925	1 456	1 469	2 882	1 437	1 446
50-54	2 292	1 126	1 166	2 603	1 288	1 315	2 872	1 421	1 451	2 874	1 425	1 449
55-59	1 916	936	980	2 222	1 082	1 140	2 529	1 241	1 288	2 796	1 373	1 423
60-64	1 582	726	856	1 823	877	945	2 120	1 018	1 103	2 421	1 172	1 248
65-69	1 305	600	705	1 458	653	805	1 686	794	892	1 970	925	1 045
70-74	874	392	482	1 133	503	631	1 277	551	726	1 484	674	810
75-79	494	207	287	684	290	394	899	376	523	1 026	416	610
80-84	234	85	148	324	124	200	459	176	282	616	232	384
85-89	113	35	78	115	36	79	166	53	113	243	77	166
90-94	25	7	18	37	9	28	40	9	31	61	14	47
95-99	4	1	3	5	1	4	8	1	7	9	1	8
100 +	0	0	0	0	0	0	1	0	0	1	0	1

Age group	2045 Both sexes	2045 Males	2045 Females	2050 Both sexes	2050 Males	2050 Females
All ages	39 518	19 393	20 125	38 956	19 064	19 892
0-4	1 811	927	884	1 640	839	800
5-9	2 019	1 033	986	1 798	920	878
10-14	2 215	1 131	1 083	2 011	1 029	983
15-19	2 347	1 197	1 151	2 193	1 119	1 074
20-24	2 426	1 232	1 194	2 298	1 168	1 130
25-29	2 505	1 265	1 240	2 364	1 195	1 168
30-34	2 724	1 370	1 354	2 451	1 233	1 218
35-39	2 902	1 455	1 447	2 681	1 345	1 336
40-44	3 045	1 523	1 522	2 867	1 435	1 432
45-49	2 837	1 412	1 425	3 009	1 502	1 507
50-54	2 836	1 408	1 427	2 793	1 385	1 408
55-59	2 802	1 380	1 422	2 769	1 366	1 402
60-64	2 683	1 301	1 382	2 695	1 312	1 383
65-69	2 257	1 070	1 187	2 512	1 194	1 318
70-74	1 745	790	954	2 013	923	1 090
75-79	1 203	514	689	1 432	613	819
80-84	717	259	457	856	330	525
85-89	336	103	233	408	121	287
90-94	93	20	73	138	30	108
95-99	15	2	13	25	3	22
100 +	1	0	1	2	0	2

POPULATION BY AGE AND SEX (in thousands)

Age group	1950 Both sexes	Males	Females	1955 Both sexes	Males	Females	1960 Both sexes	Males	Females	1965 Both sexes	Males	Females
All ages	6 442	3 149	3 294	6 954	3 397	3 557	7 609	3 717	3 892	8 416	4 112	4 303
0-4	1 100	547	554	1 179	587	592	1 318	657	661	1 478	737	741
5-9	850	421	430	922	457	465	1 006	500	506	1 143	568	575
10-14	736	364	372	802	397	405	874	433	441	959	476	483
15-19	650	322	328	703	348	355	770	381	389	841	417	424
20-24	569	281	288	614	302	312	668	328	339	734	361	373
25-29	494	242	252	531	259	272	577	281	296	630	307	323
30-34	427	209	218	459	223	235	496	241	255	542	262	279
35-39	365	178	187	393	191	202	425	206	219	463	223	239
40-44	309	150	159	333	162	171	361	175	187	394	190	204
45-49	258	124	134	279	134	145	303	145	158	331	159	173
50-54	212	100	112	229	108	121	250	118	132	274	129	145
55-59	169	78	91	182	84	98	199	92	107	220	102	118
60-64	127	58	69	138	62	75	151	68	82	167	76	91
65-69	88	39	49	95	42	53	105	47	58	117	52	65
70-74	52	23	30	57	25	32	63	27	36	72	31	41
75-79	25	10	15	27	11	16	31	13	18	36	15	21
80 +	11	4	7	11	4	7	13	5	8	15	6	9

Age group	1970 Both sexes	Males	Females	1975 Both sexes	Males	Females	1980 Both sexes	Males	Females	1985 Both sexes	Males	Females
All ages	9 384	4 588	4 796	10 569	5 173	5 397	12 048	5 892	6 156	13 219	6 445	6 774
0-4	1 660	829	831	1 901	950	950	2 126	1 064	1 062	2 348	1 176	1 172
5-9	1 300	647	653	1 478	736	742	1 714	854	859	1 904	951	953
10-14	1 094	544	550	1 249	621	628	1 427	711	717	1 647	821	826
15-19	926	460	466	1 060	526	533	1 223	607	617	1 364	677	687
20-24	806	397	408	890	439	450	1 041	512	530	1 126	552	574
25-29	696	340	356	767	375	392	873	425	448	930	448	482
30-34	595	288	307	660	320	340	754	365	389	775	370	405
35-39	508	245	263	561	270	290	640	308	331	675	321	354
40-44	431	207	224	476	228	248	531	254	277	576	273	303
45-49	363	173	190	400	190	210	447	212	235	479	225	254
50-54	302	142	159	333	157	176	371	174	197	401	186	215
55-59	243	113	130	270	125	144	301	140	161	327	150	177
60-64	186	85	102	209	95	113	235	107	127	257	116	140
65-69	132	59	73	150	67	83	170	76	94	188	84	104
70-74	82	36	46	95	41	53	109	48	62	122	53	69
75-79	42	17	24	50	21	29	59	25	34	66	28	38
80 +	18	7	11	23	9	14	28	11	17	34	13	21

Age group	1990 Both sexes	Males	Females	1995 Both sexes	Males	Females	2000 Both sexes	Males	Females	2005 Both sexes	Males	Females
All ages	13 429	6 418	7 012	15 854	7 563	8 291	17 911	8 602	9 308	19 792	9 580	10 212
0-4	2 349	1 177	1 172	2 831	1 421	1 410	3 080	1 548	1 532	3 291	1 656	1 635
5-9	2 074	1 037	1 038	2 272	1 137	1 135	2 617	1 311	1 306	2 864	1 436	1 427
10-14	1 810	903	907	1 947	973	974	2 215	1 108	1 107	2 549	1 277	1 272
15-19	1 514	747	767	1 683	803	880	1 910	955	956	2 172	1 086	1 086
20-24	1 120	535	585	1 462	646	817	1 632	776	856	1 843	918	925
25-29	837	380	457	1 151	506	645	1 378	605	772	1 492	711	781
30-34	683	301	383	943	436	507	1 069	466	602	1 204	532	671
35-39	590	259	331	775	367	407	875	401	474	932	407	525
40-44	538	240	299	639	307	332	722	340	383	775	353	422
45-49	474	212	262	536	252	284	598	285	313	650	302	348
50-54	401	178	222	450	205	245	498	231	267	543	255	288
55-59	335	148	187	371	167	204	411	184	227	451	206	245
60-64	267	117	150	298	133	166	329	146	183	365	161	204
65-69	198	86	112	223	98	125	250	109	141	278	121	157
70-74	130	55	75	148	63	85	170	73	97	194	83	111
75-79	71	29	42	82	34	48	98	40	57	115	48	67
80 +	37	13	23	43	16	27	58	22	36	73	28	45

614

United Nations Department of Economic and Social Affairs/Population Division
World Population Prospects: The 2004 Revision, Volume II: Sex and Age Distribution of the World Population

POPULATION BY AGE AND SEX (in thousands)

Age group	2005 Both sexes	Males	Females	2010 Both sexes	Males	Females	2015 Both sexes	Males	Females	2020 Both sexes	Males	Females
All ages	19 792	9 580	10 212	21 620	10 557	11 063	23 513	11 567	11 945	25 508	12 624	12 884
0-4	3 291	1 656	1 635	3 432	1 728	1 704	3 552	1 789	1 763	3 676	1 853	1 823
5-9	2 864	1 436	1 427	3 078	1 545	1 533	3 240	1 628	1 613	3 392	1 705	1 687
10-14	2 549	1 277	1 272	2 777	1 392	1 385	2 979	1 494	1 485	3 151	1 582	1 569
15-19	2 172	1 086	1 086	2 503	1 252	1 251	2 727	1 366	1 362	2 930	1 468	1 462
20-24	1 843	918	925	2 105	1 049	1 056	2 433	1 213	1 219	2 658	1 327	1 331
25-29	1 492	711	781	1 704	851	852	1 962	980	982	2 285	1 142	1 143
30-34	1 204	532	671	1 293	627	666	1 505	764	740	1 751	888	863
35-39	932	407	525	1 019	459	560	1 106	548	558	1 307	676	630
40-44	775	353	422	801	352	449	876	400	477	963	483	480
45-49	650	302	348	683	310	373	705	310	395	777	355	422
50-54	543	255	288	584	268	315	613	276	337	636	278	358
55-59	451	206	245	489	226	263	527	239	288	556	247	309
60-64	365	161	204	401	180	221	436	199	237	472	211	261
65-69	278	121	157	310	134	176	343	151	192	376	168	208
70-74	194	83	111	218	93	126	246	104	142	275	119	156
75-79	115	48	67	134	56	78	153	63	90	175	72	103
80-84	53	21	32	64	26	38	76	30	46	89	35	53
85-89	17	6	11	22	8	14	27	10	17	33	12	20
90-94	3	1	2	5	1	3	6	2	4	8	3	5
95-99	0	0	0	1	0	0	1	0	1	1	0	1
100 +	0	0	0	0	0	0	0	0	0	0	0	0

Age group	2025 Both sexes	Males	Females	2030 Both sexes	Males	Females	2035 Both sexes	Males	Females	2040 Both sexes	Males	Females
All ages	27 556	13 696	13 860	29 604	14 751	14 852	31 631	15 781	15 850	33 646	16 793	16 854
0-4	3 755	1 894	1 862	3 789	1 911	1 878	3 799	1 917	1 883	3 807	1 920	1 886
5-9	3 542	1 782	1 760	3 645	1 834	1 810	3 698	1 862	1 837	3 726	1 876	1 850
10-14	3 320	1 668	1 652	3 485	1 752	1 733	3 599	1 810	1 789	3 662	1 842	1 820
15-19	3 105	1 557	1 548	3 279	1 645	1 634	3 448	1 731	1 717	3 566	1 791	1 775
20-24	2 861	1 428	1 432	3 039	1 518	1 521	3 216	1 608	1 608	3 388	1 695	1 693
25-29	2 507	1 252	1 256	2 711	1 352	1 359	2 894	1 442	1 452	3 077	1 534	1 542
30-34	2 060	1 041	1 019	2 278	1 145	1 133	2 483	1 243	1 240	2 673	1 335	1 338
35-39	1 539	702	746	1 831	934	896	2 044	1 033	1 010	2 251	1 130	1 121
40-44	1 151	601	549	1 370	710	661	1 646	842	804	1 855	938	918
45-49	861	433	429	1 039	543	496	1 248	644	604	1 511	769	742
50-54	706	321	385	787	393	394	956	495	460	1 155	591	564
55-59	581	251	330	648	291	357	726	359	368	886	454	432
60-64	502	220	282	527	224	303	592	262	330	666	325	342
65-69	410	180	230	439	189	250	465	194	271	525	229	297
70-74	304	134	171	336	145	191	363	153	210	388	159	229
75-79	198	83	115	222	95	127	240	104	144	272	112	160
80-84	103	41	62	119	48	71	136	56	80	154	63	92
85-89	39	15	24	46	17	29	54	21	33	63	25	38
90-94	9	3	6	12	4	8	14	5	9	17	6	11
95-99	1	0	1	2	0	1	2	1	1	3	1	2
100 +	0	0	0	0	0	0	0	0	0	0	0	0

Age group	2045 Both sexes	Males	Females	2050 Both sexes	Males	Females
All ages	35 644	17 789	17 855	37 604	18 760	18 845
0-4	3 804	1 919	1 885	3 782	1 908	1 874
5-9	3 748	1 887	1 861	3 757	1 891	1 866
10-14	3 697	1 860	1 838	3 725	1 874	1 851
15-19	3 633	1 825	1 809	3 672	1 844	1 828
20-24	3 510	1 756	1 753	3 581	1 792	1 789
25-29	3 256	1 624	1 631	3 387	1 691	1 697
30-34	2 865	1 431	1 435	3 056	1 526	1 530
35-39	2 448	1 225	1 223	2 649	1 325	1 325
40-44	2 063	1 034	1 029	2 265	1 131	1 134
45-49	1 718	863	854	1 925	960	966
50-54	1 409	710	698	1 612	803	808
55-59	1 078	546	532	1 321	659	662
60-64	817	414	404	999	499	499
65-69	595	285	310	733	365	368
70-74	442	188	253	503	236	266
75-79	294	117	177	338	140	197
80-84	171	68	103	188	72	115
85-89	73	28	45	83	31	51
90-94	20	7	13	24	9	15
95-99	3	1	2	4	1	3
100 +	0	0	0	0	0	0

POPULATION BY AGE AND SEX (in thousands)

Age group	2005 Both sexes	Males	Females	2010 Both sexes	Males	Females	2015 Both sexes	Males	Females	2020 Both sexes	Males	Females
All ages	19 792	9 580	10 212	21 788	10 641	11 146	23 980	11 802	12 177	26 405	13 076	13 330
0-4	3 291	1 656	1 635	3 600	1 812	1 788	3 860	1 945	1 916	4 125	2 079	2 046
5-9	2 864	1 436	1 427	3 078	1 545	1 533	3 399	1 707	1 692	3 687	1 853	1 833
10-14	2 549	1 277	1 272	2 777	1 392	1 385	2 979	1 494	1 485	3 305	1 659	1 646
15-19	2 172	1 086	1 086	2 503	1 252	1 251	2 727	1 366	1 362	2 930	1 468	1 462
20-24	1 843	918	925	2 105	1 049	1 056	2 433	1 213	1 219	2 658	1 327	1 331
25-29	1 492	711	781	1 704	851	852	1 962	980	982	2 285	1 142	1 143
30-34	1 204	532	671	1 293	627	666	1 505	764	740	1 751	888	863
35-39	932	407	525	1 019	459	560	1 106	548	558	1 307	676	630
40-44	775	353	422	801	352	449	876	400	477	963	483	480
45-49	650	302	348	683	310	373	705	310	395	777	355	422
50-54	543	255	288	584	268	315	613	276	337	636	278	358
55-59	451	206	245	489	226	263	527	239	288	556	247	309
60-64	365	161	204	401	180	221	436	199	237	472	211	261
65-69	278	121	157	310	134	176	343	151	192	376	168	208
70-74	194	83	111	218	93	126	246	104	142	275	119	156
75-79	115	48	67	134	56	78	153	63	90	175	72	103
80-84	53	21	32	64	26	38	76	30	46	89	35	53
85-89	17	6	11	22	8	14	27	10	17	33	12	20
90-94	3	1	2	5	1	3	6	2	4	8	3	5
95-99	0	0	0	1	0	0	1	0	1	1	0	1
100 +	0	0	0	0	0	0	0	0	0	0	0	0

Age group	2025 Both sexes	Males	Females	2030 Both sexes	Males	Females	2035 Both sexes	Males	Females	2040 Both sexes	Males	Females
All ages	28 960	14 402	14 558	31 635	15 773	15 862	34 458	17 202	17 255	37 455	18 708	18 747
0-4	4 287	2 162	2 125	4 445	2 242	2 203	4 633	2 337	2 296	4 845	2 444	2 401
5-9	3 975	1 999	1 975	4 161	2 094	2 067	4 339	2 184	2 155	4 543	2 287	2 256
10-14	3 609	1 813	1 796	3 910	1 966	1 945	4 108	2 066	2 042	4 297	2 161	2 136
15-19	3 257	1 633	1 624	3 565	1 788	1 776	3 869	1 943	1 927	4 071	2 045	2 027
20-24	2 861	1 428	1 432	3 187	1 592	1 595	3 496	1 748	1 748	3 802	1 902	1 900
25-29	2 507	1 252	1 256	2 711	1 352	1 359	3 036	1 513	1 523	3 345	1 668	1 677
30-34	2 060	1 041	1 019	2 278	1 145	1 133	2 483	1 243	1 240	2 805	1 401	1 404
35-39	1 539	792	746	1 831	934	896	2 044	1 033	1 010	2 251	1 130	1 121
40-44	1 151	601	549	1 370	710	661	1 646	842	804	1 855	938	918
45-49	861	433	429	1 039	543	496	1 248	644	604	1 511	769	742
50-54	706	321	385	787	393	394	956	495	460	1 155	591	564
55-59	581	251	330	648	291	357	726	359	368	886	454	432
60-64	502	220	282	527	224	303	592	262	330	666	325	342
65-69	410	180	230	439	189	250	465	194	271	525	229	297
70-74	304	134	171	336	145	191	363	153	210	388	159	229
75-79	198	83	115	222	95	127	248	104	144	272	112	160
80-84	103	41	62	119	48	71	136	56	80	154	63	92
85-89	39	15	24	46	17	29	54	21	33	63	25	38
90-94	9	3	6	12	4	8	14	5	9	17	6	11
95-99	1	0	1	2	0	1	2	1	1	3	1	2
100 +	0	0	0	0	0	0	0	0	0	0	0	0

Age group	2045 Both sexes	Males	Females	2050 Both sexes	Males	Females
All ages	40 610	20 286	20 325	43 889	21 919	21 970
0-4	5 041	2 543	2 498	5 203	2 625	2 578
5-9	4 770	2 401	2 369	4 979	2 506	2 473
10-14	4 508	2 268	2 241	4 741	2 384	2 356
15-19	4 263	2 141	2 122	4 478	2 249	2 229
20-24	4 007	2 005	2 002	4 203	2 104	2 099
25-29	3 654	1 824	1 831	3 868	1 931	1 937
30-34	3 116	1 556	1 559	3 430	1 714	1 716
35-39	2 568	1 285	1 283	2 881	1 441	1 440
40-44	2 063	1 034	1 029	2 377	1 187	1 190
45-49	1 718	863	854	1 925	960	966
50-54	1 409	710	698	1 612	803	808
55-59	1 078	546	532	1 321	659	662
60-64	817	414	404	999	499	499
65-69	595	285	310	733	365	368
70-74	442	188	253	503	236	266
75-79	294	117	177	338	140	197
80-84	171	68	103	188	72	115
85-89	73	28	45	83	31	51
90-94	20	7	13	24	9	15
95-99	3	1	2	4	1	3
100 +	0	0	0	0	0	0

United Nations Department of Economic and Social Affairs/Population Division
World Population Prospects: The 2004 Revision, Volume II: Sex and Age Distribution of the World Population

616

POPULATION BY AGE AND SEX (in thousands)

Age group	2005 Both sexes	2005 Males	2005 Females	2010 Both sexes	2010 Males	2010 Females	2015 Both sexes	2015 Males	2015 Females	2020 Both sexes	2020 Males	2020 Females
All ages	19 792	9 580	10 212	21 452	10 472	10 980	23 046	11 332	11 713	24 611	12 173	12 438
0-4	3 291	1 656	1 635	3 264	1 643	1 621	3 243	1 634	1 610	3 228	1 627	1 601
5-9	2 864	1 436	1 427	3 078	1 545	1 533	3 082	1 548	1 534	3 097	1 557	1 540
10-14	2 549	1 277	1 272	2 777	1 392	1 385	2 979	1 494	1 485	2 996	1 504	1 492
15-19	2 172	1 086	1 086	2 503	1 252	1 251	2 727	1 366	1 362	2 930	1 468	1 462
20-24	1 843	918	925	2 105	1 049	1 056	2 433	1 213	1 219	2 658	1 327	1 331
25-29	1 492	711	781	1 704	851	852	1 962	980	982	2 285	1 142	1 143
30-34	1 204	532	671	1 293	627	666	1 505	764	740	1 751	888	863
35-39	932	407	525	1 019	459	560	1 106	548	558	1 307	676	630
40-44	775	353	422	801	352	449	876	400	477	963	483	480
45-49	650	302	348	683	310	373	705	310	395	777	355	422
50-54	543	255	288	584	268	315	613	276	337	636	278	358
55-59	451	206	245	489	226	263	527	239	288	556	247	309
60-64	365	161	204	401	180	221	436	199	237	472	211	261
65-69	278	121	157	310	134	176	343	151	192	376	168	208
70-74	194	83	111	218	93	126	246	104	142	275	119	156
75-79	115	48	67	134	56	78	153	63	90	175	72	103
80-84	53	21	32	64	26	38	76	30	46	89	35	53
85-89	17	6	11	22	8	14	27	10	17	33	12	20
90-94	3	1	2	5	1	3	6	2	4	8	3	5
95-99	0	0	0	1	0	0	1	0	1	1	0	1
100 +	0	0	0	0	0	0	0	0	0	0	0	0

Age group	2025 Both sexes	2025 Males	2025 Females	2030 Both sexes	2030 Males	2030 Females	2035 Both sexes	2035 Males	2035 Females	2040 Both sexes	2040 Males	2040 Females
All ages	26 155	12 991	13 164	27 596	13 741	13 854	28 884	14 399	14 484	30 021	14 970	15 051
0-4	3 228	1 627	1 600	3 152	1 590	1 562	3 022	1 524	1 498	2 875	1 450	1 425
5-9	3 110	1 565	1 546	3 132	1 576	1 556	3 077	1 549	1 528	2 963	1 492	1 472
10-14	3 032	1 523	1 509	3 060	1 538	1 522	3 093	1 555	1 538	3 047	1 532	1 514
15-19	2 953	1 481	1 473	2 994	1 502	1 492	3 028	1 520	1 508	3 065	1 539	1 526
20-24	2 861	1 428	1 432	2 890	1 443	1 446	2 936	1 468	1 468	2 974	1 487	1 486
25-29	2 507	1 252	1 256	2 711	1 352	1 359	2 752	1 371	1 381	2 808	1 400	1 408
30-34	2 060	1 041	1 019	2 278	1 145	1 133	2 483	1 243	1 240	2 542	1 269	1 273
35-39	1 539	792	740	1 801	994	806	2 044	1 033	1 010	2 251	1 130	1 121
40-44	1 151	601	549	1 370	710	661	1 646	842	804	1 855	938	916
45-49	861	433	429	1 039	543	496	1 248	644	604	1 511	769	742
50-54	706	321	385	787	393	394	956	495	460	1 155	591	564
55-59	581	251	330	648	291	357	726	359	368	886	454	432
60-64	502	220	282	527	224	303	592	262	330	666	325	342
65-69	410	180	230	439	189	250	465	194	271	525	229	297
70-74	304	134	171	336	145	191	363	153	210	388	159	229
75-79	198	83	115	222	96	127	248	104	144	272	112	160
80-84	103	41	62	119	48	71	136	56	80	154	63	92
85-89	39	15	24	46	17	29	54	21	33	63	25	38
90-94	9	3	6	12	4	8	14	5	9	17	6	11
95-99	1	0	1	2	0	1	2	1	1	3	1	2
100 +	0	0	0	0	0	0	0	0	0	0	0	0

Age group	2045 Both sexes	2045 Males	2045 Females	2050 Both sexes	2050 Males	2050 Females
All ages	31 021	15 465	15 557	31 887	15 886	16 001
0-4	2 730	1 377	1 353	2 587	1 305	1 282
5-9	2 830	1 425	1 405	2 696	1 357	1 339
10-14	2 941	1 479	1 462	2 813	1 415	1 398
15-19	3 022	1 518	1 505	2 920	1 466	1 454
20-24	3 016	1 509	1 507	2 979	1 490	1 488
25-29	2 857	1 425	1 432	2 910	1 452	1 458
30-34	2 615	1 306	1 310	2 682	1 339	1 343
35-39	2 328	1 164	1 163	2 418	1 209	1 209
40-44	2 063	1 034	1 029	2 154	1 075	1 079
45-49	1 718	863	854	1 925	960	966
50-54	1 409	710	698	1 612	803	808
55-59	1 078	546	532	1 321	659	662
60-64	817	414	404	999	499	499
65-69	595	285	310	733	365	368
70-74	442	188	253	503	236	266
75-79	294	117	177	338	140	197
80-84	171	68	103	188	72	115
85-89	73	28	45	83	31	51
90-94	20	7	13	24	9	15
95-99	3	1	2	4	1	3
100 +	0	0	0	0	0	0

United Nations Department of Economic and Social Affairs/Population Division
World Population Prospects: The 2004 Revision, Volume II: Sex and Age Distribution of the World Population

617

POPULATION BY AGE AND SEX (in thousands)

Age group	1950 Both sexes	1950 Males	1950 Females	1955 Both sexes	1955 Males	1955 Females	1960 Both sexes	1960 Males	1960 Females	1965 Both sexes	1965 Males	1965 Females
All ages	17 832	8 890	8 942	19 497	9 720	9 776	21 595	10 770	10 825	23 984	11 961	12 023
0-4	2 850	1 435	1 416	3 177	1 587	1 590	3 479	1 747	1 732	3 804	1 913	1 891
5-9	2 138	1 076	1 062	2 508	1 262	1 246	2 885	1 440	1 444	3 195	1 603	1 591
10-14	1 750	881	869	2 060	1 037	1 023	2 439	1 227	1 212	2 815	1 405	1 410
15-19	1 616	815	801	1 700	857	843	2 015	1 014	1 001	2 392	1 203	1 189
20-24	1 593	804	790	1 548	782	767	1 646	829	817	1 958	984	973
25-29	1 470	741	729	1 509	761	747	1 485	749	736	1 586	797	788
30-34	1 331	670	661	1 382	697	685	1 438	725	713	1 423	717	706
35-39	1 111	558	553	1 242	625	617	1 309	659	649	1 370	690	680
40-44	965	482	484	1 029	515	514	1 168	586	582	1 237	621	616
45-49	834	412	422	886	438	448	959	476	483	1 094	545	549
50-54	668	324	343	754	368	386	813	398	415	885	435	450
55-59	528	252	276	588	282	306	675	326	349	733	354	378
60-64	399	186	212	445	210	235	505	239	266	585	279	306
65-69	275	125	150	314	145	169	359	167	192	411	192	219
70-74	170	75	95	195	87	107	229	104	125	265	121	144
75-79	88	37	51	104	45	59	124	55	69	148	66	82
80 +	45	17	28	56	23	34	70	29	41	85	36	49

Age group	1970 Both sexes	1970 Males	1970 Females	1975 Both sexes	1975 Males	1975 Females	1980 Both sexes	1980 Males	1980 Females	1985 Both sexes	1985 Males	1985 Females
All ages	26 838	13 381	13 457	30 138	15 022	15 116	33 678	16 778	16 900	37 237	18 558	18 679
0-4	4 312	2 171	2 141	4 813	2 426	2 388	5 165	2 603	2 562	5 275	2 668	2 607
5-9	3 528	1 772	1 756	4 036	2 029	2 007	4 528	2 277	2 251	4 889	2 463	2 426
10-14	3 126	1 568	1 558	3 462	1 738	1 724	3 966	1 992	1 974	4 460	2 242	2 218
15-19	2 767	1 380	1 387	3 079	1 543	1 536	3 414	1 712	1 702	3 915	1 964	1 951
20-24	2 331	1 171	1 161	2 705	1 347	1 358	3 016	1 508	1 508	3 344	1 673	1 671
25-29	1 894	950	944	2 264	1 134	1 130	2 633	1 307	1 326	2 935	1 464	1 472
30-34	1 527	766	761	1 832	917	915	2 195	1 096	1 098	2 554	1 265	1 289
35-39	1 362	684	677	1 468	735	733	1 765	881	884	2 119	1 056	1 063
40-44	1 302	653	649	1 300	651	650	1 405	701	705	1 694	843	852
45-49	1 165	580	585	1 232	613	618	1 234	613	621	1 338	663	675
50-54	1 015	501	515	1 087	536	551	1 153	569	584	1 159	571	588
55-59	802	390	413	926	451	475	995	485	510	1 061	517	543
60-64	640	305	334	706	338	368	818	393	425	885	426	459
65-69	481	226	255	531	249	281	589	277	311	689	326	363
70-74	308	141	167	364	168	196	405	187	218	455	211	245
75-79	174	78	96	206	92	113	246	111	135	278	125	153
80 +	105	45	60	127	55	72	153	66	87	186	81	105

Age group	1990 Both sexes	1990 Males	1990 Females	1995 Both sexes	1995 Males	1995 Females	2000 Both sexes	2000 Males	2000 Females	2005 Both sexes	2005 Males	2005 Females
All ages	40 753	20 310	20 444	44 500	22 167	22 332	47 724	23 745	23 979	50 519	25 083	25 436
0-4	5 357	2 713	2 644	5 632	2 854	2 778	4 987	2 529	2 457	4 657	2 364	2 293
5-9	5 023	2 538	2 485	5 132	2 595	2 537	5 438	2 751	2 687	4 844	2 453	2 391
10-14	4 823	2 428	2 395	4 963	2 506	2 457	5 083	2 568	2 515	5 394	2 727	2 667
15-19	4 404	2 211	2 192	4 770	2 399	2 371	4 927	2 485	2 442	5 053	2 550	2 503
20-24	3 832	1 918	1 914	4 322	2 165	2 157	4 717	2 366	2 351	4 881	2 455	2 426
25-29	3 249	1 621	1 629	3 735	1 863	1 873	4 254	2 121	2 132	4 642	2 315	2 327
30-34	2 843	1 414	1 430	3 157	1 569	1 588	3 663	1 818	1 845	4 164	2 062	2 101
35-39	2 465	1 217	1 248	2 754	1 364	1 390	3 083	1 525	1 558	3 571	1 759	1 812
40-44	2 035	1 010	1 025	2 377	1 168	1 209	2 675	1 318	1 357	2 993	1 469	1 524
45-49	1 616	798	817	1 949	961	988	2 292	1 119	1 173	2 582	1 262	1 320
50-54	1 260	619	641	1 529	749	780	1 858	908	950	2 191	1 059	1 132
55-59	1 071	522	549	1 170	568	602	1 431	693	738	1 746	843	903
60-64	949	456	492	964	463	501	1 063	509	554	1 308	624	684
65-69	751	356	395	812	384	428	833	394	440	928	436	491
70-74	538	250	289	594	275	318	650	301	349	675	312	363
75-79	317	143	174	380	172	208	427	193	234	475	214	261
80 +	221	96	125	259	112	147	343	148	195	416	178	239

United Nations Department of Economic and Social Affairs/Population Division
World Population Prospects: The 2004 Revision, Volume II: Sex and Age Distribution of the World Population

POPULATION BY AGE AND SEX (in thousands)

Age group	2005 Both sexes	2005 Males	2005 Females	2010 Both sexes	2010 Males	2010 Females	2015 Both sexes	2015 Males	2015 Females	2020 Both sexes	2020 Males	2020 Females
All ages	50 519	25 083	25 436	52 801	26 149	26 652	54 970	27 164	27 807	57 054	28 141	28 912
0-4	4 657	2 364	2 293	4 318	2 194	2 124	4 256	2 164	2 092	4 241	2 158	2 084
5-9	4 844	2 453	2 391	4 541	2 302	2 240	4 229	2 145	2 084	4 185	2 124	2 061
10-14	5 394	2 727	2 667	4 809	2 433	2 376	4 512	2 285	2 227	4 206	2 132	2 074
15-19	5 053	2 550	2 503	5 362	2 708	2 654	4 784	2 418	2 366	4 493	2 273	2 219
20-24	4 881	2 455	2 426	5 003	2 519	2 484	5 318	2 680	2 639	4 751	2 397	2 355
25-29	4 642	2 315	2 327	4 798	2 402	2 396	4 936	2 476	2 460	5 257	2 640	2 616
30-34	4 164	2 062	2 101	4 530	2 244	2 286	4 701	2 342	2 360	4 853	2 425	2 428
35-39	3 571	1 759	1 812	4 047	1 988	2 058	4 416	2 174	2 243	4 601	2 280	2 321
40-44	2 993	1 469	1 524	3 460	1 690	1 770	3 932	1 917	2 015	4 307	2 106	2 201
45-49	2 582	1 262	1 320	2 888	1 405	1 483	3 349	1 622	1 727	3 819	1 848	1 971
50-54	2 191	1 059	1 132	2 471	1 195	1 276	2 774	1 336	1 439	3 230	1 550	1 680
55-59	1 746	843	903	2 066	986	1 080	2 341	1 118	1 223	2 641	1 257	1 385
60-64	1 308	624	684	1 605	763	842	1 911	898	1 013	2 179	1 025	1 155
65-69	928	436	491	1 152	540	612	1 426	665	760	1 713	789	924
70-74	675	312	363	762	350	412	959	439	520	1 201	547	654
75-79	475	214	261	502	225	277	577	257	320	739	327	412
80-84	267	116	151	304	132	172	329	141	187	386	164	222
85-89	114	48	66	134	56	79	157	65	93	175	71	104
90-94	30	12	18	42	16	26	51	19	32	62	23	39
95-99	5	2	3	7	2	5	10	3	7	13	4	9
100 +	0	0	0	1	0	0	1	0	1	1	0	1

Age group	2025 Both sexes	2025 Males	2025 Females	2030 Both sexes	2030 Males	2030 Females	2035 Both sexes	2035 Males	2035 Females	2040 Both sexes	2040 Males	2040 Females
All ages	59 002	29 059	29 944	60 629	29 822	30 807	61 862	30 396	31 466	62 746	30 805	31 942
0-4	4 215	2 146	2 070	4 041	2 058	1 983	3 836	1 954	1 881	3 700	1 885	1 814
5-9	4 183	2 125	2 058	4 168	2 119	2 049	4 003	2 036	1 967	3 805	1 937	1 869
10-14	4 166	2 113	2 052	4 167	2 115	2 051	4 154	2 110	2 044	3 991	2 029	1 962
15-19	4 190	2 122	2 068	4 153	2 105	2 048	4 156	2 108	2 048	4 144	2 104	2 040
20-24	4 466	2 255	2 211	4 169	2 108	2 061	4 134	2 092	2 042	4 139	2 097	2 042
25-29	4 704	2 366	2 338	4 427	2 231	2 197	4 138	2 088	2 050	4 107	2 075	2 032
30-34	5 181	2 594	2 587	4 645	2 331	2 314	4 379	2 202	2 177	4 098	2 064	2 033
35-39	4 765	2 372	2 393	5 100	2 546	2 554	4 581	2 293	2 288	4 325	2 171	2 154
40-44	4 503	2 220	2 282	4 676	2 318	2 358	5 016	2 496	2 520	4 514	2 254	2 260
45-49	4 198	2 040	2 158	4 402	2 159	2 243	4 583	2 262	2 321	4 926	2 442	2 484
50-54	3 698	1 775	1 923	4 078	1 967	2 111	4 288	2 090	2 199	4 475	2 196	2 279
55-59	3 089	1 466	1 623	3 551	1 687	1 864	3 929	1 877	2 052	4 142	2 000	2 142
60-64	2 474	1 159	1 314	2 908	1 360	1 548	3 357	1 572	1 785	3 727	1 756	1 970
65-69	1 968	908	1 060	2 250	1 034	1 216	2 661	1 221	1 440	3 087	1 419	1 668
70-74	1 459	656	803	1 693	761	931	1 952	875	1 077	2 326	1 041	1 285
75-79	940	413	527	1 158	502	656	1 359	589	770	1 584	684	900
80-84	504	213	292	653	273	380	818	337	482	975	401	574
85-89	211	84	127	282	111	171	372	145	227	478	182	296
90-94	71	26	45	88	31	56	120	42	78	164	56	108
95-99	16	5	11	19	6	13	25	7	17	35	10	25
100 +	2	0	1	3	1	2	3	1	2	4	1	3

Age group	2045 Both sexes	2045 Males	2045 Females	2050 Both sexes	2050 Males	2050 Females
All ages	63 338	31 077	32 262	63 657	31 221	32 437
0-4	3 643	1 857	1 787	3 612	1 841	1 771
5-9	3 675	1 870	1 804	3 623	1 844	1 779
10-14	3 796	1 931	1 865	3 667	1 866	1 802
15-19	3 983	2 024	1 959	3 789	1 926	1 863
20-24	4 129	2 094	2 035	3 970	2 015	1 955
25-29	4 115	2 082	2 034	4 109	2 081	2 028
30-34	4 073	2 055	2 017	4 086	2 065	2 022
35-39	4 054	2 040	2 014	4 035	2 034	2 002
40-44	4 269	2 139	2 131	4 008	2 013	1 995
45-49	4 441	2 210	2 231	4 208	2 102	2 106
50-54	4 819	2 377	2 443	4 352	2 156	2 196
55-59	4 333	2 109	2 224	4 676	2 288	2 388
60-64	3 941	1 879	2 062	4 134	1 988	2 146
65-69	3 442	1 593	1 848	3 654	1 713	1 941
70-74	2 717	1 219	1 498	3 045	1 377	1 669
75-79	1 906	822	1 084	2 244	971	1 274
80-84	1 151	471	679	1 401	573	828
85-89	580	220	361	698	262	436
90-94	215	71	144	268	88	180
95-99	49	14	36	67	18	49
100 +	6	1	5	9	2	7

POPULATION BY AGE AND SEX (in thousands)

Age group	2005 Both sexes	2005 Males	2005 Females	2010 Both sexes	2010 Males	2010 Females	2015 Both sexes	2015 Males	2015 Females	2020 Both sexes	2020 Males	2020 Females
All ages	50 519	25 083	25 436	53 321	26 414	26 907	56 366	27 873	28 493	59 578	29 424	30 154
0-4	4 657	2 364	2 293	4 838	2 458	2 380	5 142	2 614	2 528	5 388	2 741	2 647
5-9	4 844	2 453	2 391	4 541	2 302	2 240	4 739	2 404	2 335	5 056	2 567	2 490
10-14	5 394	2 727	2 667	4 809	2 433	2 376	4 512	2 285	2 227	4 713	2 389	2 324
15-19	5 053	2 550	2 503	5 362	2 708	2 654	4 784	2 418	2 366	4 493	2 273	2 219
20-24	4 881	2 455	2 426	5 003	2 519	2 484	5 318	2 680	2 639	4 751	2 397	2 355
25-29	4 642	2 315	2 327	4 798	2 402	2 396	4 936	2 476	2 460	5 257	2 640	2 616
30-34	4 164	2 062	2 101	4 530	2 244	2 286	4 701	2 342	2 360	4 853	2 425	2 428
35-39	3 571	1 759	1 812	4 047	1 988	2 058	4 416	2 174	2 243	4 601	2 280	2 321
40-44	2 993	1 469	1 524	3 460	1 690	1 770	3 932	1 917	2 015	4 307	2 106	2 201
45-49	2 582	1 262	1 320	2 888	1 405	1 483	3 349	1 622	1 727	3 819	1 848	1 971
50-54	2 191	1 059	1 132	2 471	1 195	1 276	2 774	1 336	1 439	3 230	1 550	1 680
55-59	1 746	843	903	2 066	986	1 080	2 341	1 118	1 223	2 641	1 257	1 385
60-64	1 308	624	684	1 605	763	842	1 911	898	1 013	2 179	1 025	1 155
65-69	928	436	491	1 152	540	612	1 426	665	760	1 713	789	924
70-74	675	312	363	762	350	412	959	439	520	1 201	547	654
75-79	475	214	261	502	225	277	577	257	320	739	327	412
80-84	267	116	151	304	132	172	329	141	187	386	164	222
85-89	114	48	66	134	56	79	157	65	93	175	71	104
90-94	30	12	18	42	16	26	51	19	32	62	23	39
95-99	5	2	3	7	2	5	10	3	7	13	4	9
100 +	0	0	0	1	0	0	1	0	1	1	0	1

Age group	2025 Both sexes	2025 Males	2025 Females	2030 Both sexes	2030 Males	2030 Females	2035 Both sexes	2035 Males	2035 Females	2040 Both sexes	2040 Males	2040 Females
All ages	62 655	30 914	31 741	65 442	32 266	33 176	68 010	33 518	34 492	70 521	34 752	35 769
0-4	5 365	2 731	2 634	5 224	2 661	2 564	5 194	2 646	2 548	5 357	2 730	2 627
5-9	5 314	2 699	2 615	5 304	2 696	2 608	5 175	2 632	2 543	5 153	2 622	2 531
10-14	5 033	2 553	2 480	5 293	2 687	2 606	5 287	2 686	2 601	5 161	2 624	2 537
15-19	4 695	2 378	2 318	5 017	2 543	2 474	5 279	2 678	2 601	5 274	2 678	2 597
20-24	4 466	2 255	2 211	4 671	2 362	2 310	4 995	2 528	2 467	5 259	2 664	2 595
25-29	4 704	2 366	2 338	4 427	2 231	2 197	4 636	2 339	2 297	4 963	2 507	2 455
30-34	5 181	2 594	2 587	4 645	2 331	2 314	4 379	2 202	2 177	4 592	2 313	2 279
35-39	4 765	2 372	2 393	5 100	2 546	2 554	4 581	2 293	2 288	4 325	2 171	2 154
40-44	4 503	2 220	2 282	4 676	2 318	2 358	5 016	2 496	2 520	4 514	2 254	2 260
45-49	4 198	2 040	2 158	4 402	2 159	2 243	4 583	2 262	2 321	4 926	2 442	2 484
50-54	3 698	1 775	1 923	4 078	1 967	2 111	4 288	2 090	2 199	4 475	2 196	2 279
55-59	3 089	1 466	1 623	3 551	1 687	1 864	3 929	1 877	2 052	4 142	2 000	2 142
60-64	2 474	1 159	1 314	2 908	1 360	1 548	3 357	1 572	1 785	3 727	1 756	1 970
65-69	1 968	908	1 060	2 250	1 034	1 216	2 661	1 221	1 440	3 087	1 419	1 668
70-74	1 459	656	803	1 693	761	931	1 952	875	1 077	2 326	1 041	1 285
75-79	940	413	527	1 158	502	656	1 359	589	770	1 584	684	900
80-84	504	213	292	653	273	380	818	337	482	975	401	574
85-89	211	84	127	282	111	171	372	145	227	478	182	296
90-94	71	26	45	88	31	56	120	42	78	164	56	108
95-99	16	5	11	19	6	13	25	7	17	35	10	25
100 +	2	0	1	3	1	2	3	1	2	4	1	3

Age group	2045 Both sexes	2045 Males	2045 Females	2050 Both sexes	2050 Males	2050 Females
All ages	73 027	35 996	37 031	75 445	37 205	38 240
0-4	5 595	2 851	2 744	5 756	2 934	2 823
5-9	5 322	2 709	2 613	5 564	2 832	2 732
10-14	5 141	2 615	2 526	5 311	2 702	2 609
15-19	5 150	2 616	2 533	5 131	2 609	2 523
20-24	5 256	2 665	2 591	5 134	2 606	2 528
25-29	5 229	2 645	2 584	5 230	2 649	2 582
30-34	4 921	2 483	2 438	5 192	2 624	2 569
35-39	4 543	2 286	2 257	4 877	2 458	2 419
40-44	4 269	2 139	2 131	4 492	2 256	2 236
45-49	4 441	2 210	2 231	4 208	2 102	2 106
50-54	4 819	2 377	2 443	4 352	2 156	2 196
55-59	4 333	2 109	2 224	4 676	2 288	2 388
60-64	3 941	1 879	2 062	4 134	1 988	2 146
65-69	3 442	1 593	1 848	3 654	1 713	1 941
70-74	2 717	1 219	1 498	3 045	1 377	1 669
75-79	1 906	822	1 084	2 244	971	1 274
80-84	1 151	471	679	1 401	573	828
85-89	580	220	361	698	262	436
90-94	215	71	144	268	88	180
95-99	49	14	36	67	18	49
100 +	6	1	5	9	2	7

United Nations Department of Economic and Social Affairs/Population Division
World Population Prospects: The 2004 Revision, Volume II: Sex and Age Distribution of the World Population

POPULATION BY AGE AND SEX (in thousands)

Age group	2005 Both sexes	Males	Females	2010 Both sexes	Males	Females	2015 Both sexes	Males	Females	2020 Both sexes	Males	Females
All ages	50 519	25 083	25 436	52 281	25 885	26 396	53 575	26 455	27 120	54 530	26 859	27 671
0-4	4 657	2 364	2 293	3 798	1 929	1 868	3 371	1 714	1 657	3 095	1 574	1 520
5-9	4 844	2 453	2 391	4 541	2 302	2 240	3 720	1 887	1 833	3 314	1 682	1 632
10-14	5 394	2 727	2 667	4 809	2 433	2 376	4 512	2 285	2 227	3 699	1 875	1 824
15-19	5 053	2 550	2 503	5 362	2 708	2 654	4 784	2 418	2 366	4 493	2 273	2 219
20-24	4 881	2 455	2 426	5 003	2 519	2 484	5 318	2 680	2 639	4 751	2 397	2 355
25-29	4 642	2 315	2 327	4 798	2 402	2 396	4 936	2 476	2 460	5 257	2 640	2 616
30-34	4 164	2 062	2 101	4 530	2 244	2 286	4 701	2 342	2 360	4 853	2 425	2 428
35-39	3 571	1 759	1 812	4 047	1 988	2 058	4 416	2 174	2 243	4 601	2 280	2 321
40-44	2 993	1 469	1 524	3 460	1 690	1 770	3 932	1 917	2 015	4 307	2 106	2 201
45-49	2 582	1 262	1 320	2 888	1 405	1 483	3 349	1 622	1 727	3 819	1 848	1 971
50-54	2 191	1 059	1 132	2 471	1 195	1 276	2 774	1 336	1 439	3 230	1 550	1 680
55-59	1 746	843	903	2 066	986	1 080	2 341	1 118	1 223	2 641	1 257	1 385
60-64	1 308	624	684	1 605	763	842	1 911	898	1 013	2 179	1 025	1 155
65-69	928	436	491	1 152	540	612	1 426	665	760	1 713	789	924
70-74	675	312	363	762	350	412	959	439	520	1 201	547	654
75-79	475	214	261	502	225	277	577	257	320	739	327	412
80-84	267	116	151	304	132	172	329	141	187	386	164	222
85-89	114	48	66	134	56	79	157	65	93	175	71	104
90-94	30	12	18	42	16	26	51	19	32	62	23	39
95-99	5	2	3	7	2	5	10	3	7	13	4	9
100 +	0	0	0	1	0	0	1	0	1	1	0	1

Age group	2025 Both sexes	Males	Females	2030 Both sexes	Males	Females	2035 Both sexes	Males	Females	2040 Both sexes	Males	Females
All ages	55 355	27 206	28 149	55 859	27 399	28 459	55 895	27 366	28 529	55 430	27 091	28 340
0-4	3 070	1 563	1 507	2 896	1 475	1 421	2 614	1 332	1 282	2 322	1 183	1 139
5-9	3 052	1 551	1 502	3 035	1 543	1 492	2 869	1 459	1 410	2 593	1 320	1 274
10-14	3 299	1 673	1 625	3 040	1 544	1 497	3 025	1 537	1 488	2 861	1 454	1 406
15-19	3 686	1 866	1 819	3 288	1 667	1 621	3 032	1 538	1 494	3 018	1 532	1 486
20-24	4 466	2 255	2 211	3 667	1 854	1 813	3 273	1 656	1 617	3 020	1 530	1 490
25-29	4 704	2 366	2 338	4 427	2 231	2 197	3 639	1 836	1 803	3 251	1 643	1 608
30-34	5 181	2 594	2 587	4 645	2 331	2 314	4 379	2 202	2 177	3 603	1 815	1 788
35-39	4 765	2 372	2 393	5 100	2 546	2 554	4 581	2 293	2 288	4 325	2 171	2 154
40-44	4 503	2 220	2 282	4 676	2 318	2 358	5 016	2 496	2 520	4 514	2 254	2 260
45-49	4 198	2 040	2 158	4 402	2 159	2 243	4 583	2 262	2 321	4 926	2 442	2 484
50-54	3 698	1 778	1 920	4 078	1 967	2 111	4 288	2 090	2 199	4 475	2 196	2 279
55-59	3 089	1 466	1 623	3 551	1 687	1 864	3 929	1 877	2 052	4 142	2 000	2 142
60-64	2 474	1 159	1 314	2 908	1 360	1 548	3 357	1 572	1 785	3 727	1 756	1 970
65-69	1 968	908	1 060	2 250	1 034	1 216	2 661	1 221	1 440	3 087	1 419	1 668
70-74	1 459	656	803	1 693	761	931	1 952	875	1 077	2 326	1 041	1 285
75-79	940	413	527	1 158	502	650	1 360	589	770	1 584	684	900
80-84	504	213	292	653	273	380	818	337	482	975	401	574
85-89	211	84	127	282	111	171	372	145	227	478	182	296
90-94	71	26	45	88	31	56	120	42	78	164	56	108
95-99	16	5	11	19	6	13	25	7	17	35	10	25
100 +	2	0	1	3	1	2	3	1	2	4	1	3

Age group	2045 Both sexes	Males	Females	2050 Both sexes	Males	Females
All ages	54 518	26 600	27 918	53 238	25 933	27 304
0-4	2 104	1 072	1 032	1 970	1 004	966
5-9	2 306	1 174	1 132	2 092	1 065	1 027
10-14	2 587	1 316	1 271	2 301	1 171	1 131
15-19	2 854	1 450	1 404	2 582	1 313	1 269
20-24	3 007	1 525	1 482	2 845	1 444	1 401
25-29	3 002	1 518	1 483	2 991	1 515	1 476
30-34	3 224	1 627	1 597	2 980	1 506	1 474
35-39	3 565	1 793	1 771	3 194	1 610	1 584
40-44	4 269	2 139	2 131	3 525	1 770	1 755
45-49	4 441	2 210	2 231	4 208	2 102	2 106
50-54	4 819	2 377	2 443	4 352	2 156	2 196
55-59	4 333	2 109	2 224	4 676	2 288	2 388
60-64	3 941	1 879	2 062	4 134	1 988	2 146
65-69	3 442	1 593	1 848	3 654	1 713	1 941
70-74	2 717	1 219	1 498	3 045	1 377	1 669
75-79	1 906	822	1 084	2 244	971	1 274
80-84	1 151	471	679	1 401	573	828
85-89	580	220	361	698	262	436
90-94	215	71	144	268	88	180
95-99	49	14	36	67	18	49
100 +	6	1	5	9	2	7

POPULATION BY AGE AND SEX (in thousands)

Age group	1950 Both sexes	Males	Females	1955 Both sexes	Males	Females	1960 Both sexes	Males	Females	1965 Both sexes	Males	Females
All ages	485	241	244	536	266	270	599	298	301	677	337	340
0-4	76	39	37	87	43	43	98	49	49	112	56	56
5-9	61	31	30	70	36	34	81	41	40	93	47	46
10-14	51	26	25	59	30	29	69	35	34	80	40	40
15-19	47	24	23	50	25	25	58	30	28	67	34	33
20-24	44	22	22	45	23	22	48	25	24	56	29	28
25-29	38	19	19	42	21	21	43	22	21	47	24	23
30-34	33	16	17	36	18	18	40	20	20	42	21	21
35-39	28	14	15	31	15	16	34	17	17	39	20	19
40-44	24	11	12	26	13	14	29	14	15	33	17	16
45-49	21	10	11	22	11	12	25	12	13	28	13	14
50-54	17	8	9	19	9	10	20	10	11	23	11	12
55-59	14	6	7	15	7	8	17	8	9	18	9	10
60-64	12	5	7	11	5	6	13	6	7	15	7	8
65-69	9	4	5	9	4	5	9	4	5	11	5	6
70-74	6	3	3	6	3	4	7	3	4	7	3	4
75-79	3	2	2	4	2	2	4	2	2	4	2	3
80 +	2	1	1	2	1	1	2	1	1	2	1	1

Age group	1970 Both sexes	Males	Females	1975 Both sexes	Males	Females	1980 Both sexes	Males	Females	1985 Both sexes	Males	Females
All ages	771	385	386	891	445	446	987	487	500	1 119	549	569
0-4	130	66	65	158	80	79	176	89	87	197	99	98
5-9	107	54	53	125	63	62	152	77	75	171	86	85
10-14	91	46	45	106	53	53	123	62	61	150	76	75
15-19	78	39	39	90	45	45	102	51	51	120	60	60
20-24	66	33	32	76	38	38	81	40	42	96	47	48
25-29	55	28	27	63	32	31	66	32	34	74	36	39
30-34	45	23	22	53	27	26	55	27	28	60	28	32
35-39	40	20	20	43	22	21	46	22	24	50	24	26
40-44	37	19	18	38	19	19	38	19	20	42	20	22
45-49	31	16	16	35	18	18	34	17	18	36	17	19
50-54	26	12	14	29	14	15	32	15	16	32	15	16
55-59	21	10	11	24	11	13	26	12	13	29	14	15
60-64	16	7	9	18	8	10	21	9	11	23	11	12
65-69	12	5	7	13	6	7	15	7	8	17	8	10
70-74	8	4	5	9	4	5	10	4	6	12	5	7
75-79	4	2	3	5	2	3	6	2	4	7	3	4
80 +	3	1	2	3	1	2	3	1	2	4	1	3

Age group	1990 Both sexes	Males	Females	1995 Both sexes	Males	Females	2000 Both sexes	Males	Females	2005 Both sexes	Males	Females
All ages	1 398	690	708	1 652	818	834	1 894	938	956	2 031	1 007	1 024
0-4	245	124	122	296	149	147	292	148	145	268	135	133
5-9	196	99	97	241	122	120	292	147	145	285	144	141
10-14	172	86	85	195	98	97	241	121	119	290	146	144
15-19	154	77	76	171	86	85	195	98	97	239	120	119
20-24	130	65	65	152	76	76	169	85	84	189	95	94
25-29	108	53	55	128	64	64	148	74	74	151	77	75
30-34	85	41	44	106	52	54	123	61	62	126	63	62
35-39	67	32	36	83	40	44	103	50	53	106	52	54
40-44	54	26	28	66	31	35	81	38	43	90	43	47
45-49	45	21	23	53	25	28	64	30	34	73	34	39
50-54	36	17	19	43	20	22	51	24	27	59	27	32
55-59	31	15	16	34	16	18	41	19	22	47	22	25
60-64	27	13	14	28	13	15	32	15	17	37	17	20
65-69	20	9	11	23	11	13	25	12	13	28	13	15
70-74	14	6	8	16	7	9	19	9	10	20	9	11
75-79	8	3	5	10	4	6	11	5	6	14	6	8
80 +	5	2	3	6	2	4	8	3	5	10	4	6

United Nations Department of Economic and Social Affairs/Population Division
World Population Prospects: The 2004 Revision, Volume II: Sex and Age Distribution of the World Population

622

POPULATION BY AGE AND SEX (in thousands)

Age group	2005 Both sexes	Males	Females	2010 Both sexes	Males	Females	2015 Both sexes	Males	Females	2020 Both sexes	Males	Females
All ages	2 031	1 007	1 024	2 132	1 063	1 069	2 248	1 129	1 120	2 384	1 204	1 180
0-4	268	135	133	261	132	129	275	139	136	295	149	146
5-9	285	144	141	258	130	128	254	128	126	272	137	135
10-14	290	146	144	279	141	138	250	126	124	249	125	123
15-19	239	120	119	289	145	143	277	140	137	249	125	123
20-24	189	95	94	234	118	116	285	144	142	274	138	136
25-29	151	77	75	173	88	85	220	112	108	271	137	133
30-34	126	63	62	126	66	60	151	79	72	196	102	94
35-39	106	52	54	102	53	49	103	56	47	128	69	58
40-44	90	43	47	88	44	44	84	45	40	87	48	38
45-49	73	34	39	79	38	41	76	38	38	73	39	34
50-54	59	27	32	66	30	35	70	33	36	67	34	33
55-59	47	22	25	53	24	29	59	27	32	63	30	33
60-64	37	17	20	42	19	23	48	21	27	54	24	30
65-69	28	13	15	32	15	18	37	16	21	43	18	24
70-74	20	9	11	23	10	13	27	12	15	31	13	18
75-79	14	6	8	15	6	8	17	7	10	20	8	12
80-84	7	3	4	8	3	5	9	4	5	10	4	6
85-89	2	1	1	3	1	2	4	1	2	4	2	2
90-94	0	0	0	1	0	0	1	0	0	1	0	1
95-99	0	0	0	0	0	0	0	0	0	0	0	0
100 +	0	0	0	0	0	0	0	0	0	0	0	0

Age group	2025 Both sexes	Males	Females	2030 Both sexes	Males	Females	2035 Both sexes	Males	Females	2040 Both sexes	Males	Females
All ages	2 519	1 279	1 241	2 641	1 345	1 296	2 747	1 401	1 346	2 849	1 453	1 396
0-4	298	150	148	284	143	141	270	136	133	266	134	131
5-9	293	148	145	297	150	147	283	143	140	269	136	133
10-14	270	136	134	292	147	145	296	149	147	283	143	140
15-19	248	125	123	269	135	134	291	147	145	296	149	147
20-24	247	124	123	246	124	122	267	134	133	290	146	144
25-29	262	133	129	237	119	117	237	119	117	258	130	128
30-34	243	126	117	239	123	116	217	111	106	218	111	107
35-39	168	90	78	213	113	100	212	110	101	194	100	94
40-44	109	61	48	146	80	66	188	101	87	189	99	90
45-49	75	43	33	96	54	42	131	72	59	170	92	79
50-54	65	35	30	68	38	29	87	49	38	120	66	54
55-59	61	30	30	59	31	27	62	35	27	81	45	36
60-64	57	27	31	55	27	28	54	28	26	57	32	26
65-69	48	21	27	51	23	28	50	24	26	49	25	24
70-74	36	15	21	41	17	23	44	19	25	43	20	23
75-79	23	10	14	27	11	17	31	12	19	34	14	20
80-84	12	5	7	15	6	9	18	7	11	20	8	13
85-89	5	2	3	6	2	4	7	2	5	9	3	6
90-94	1	0	1	1	0	1	2	1	1	2	1	2
95-99	0	0	0	0	0	0	0	0	0	0	0	0
100 +	0	0	0	0	0	0	0	0	0	0	0	0

Age group	2045 Both sexes	Males	Females	2050 Both sexes	Males	Females
All ages	2 953	1 506	1 448	3 060	1 558	1 502
0-4	269	136	133	269	136	133
5-9	265	134	131	269	136	133
10-14	269	136	133	265	134	131
15-19	283	143	140	269	136	133
20-24	294	148	146	282	142	140
25-29	281	141	139	287	144	142
30-34	240	122	118	263	134	130
35-39	197	101	96	219	112	107
40-44	175	91	84	180	93	87
45-49	172	91	82	161	84	77
50-54	157	84	73	160	84	76
55-59	112	61	51	147	78	69
60-64	75	41	34	104	56	48
65-69	52	28	24	68	37	31
70-74	42	21	21	45	24	21
75-79	33	15	19	33	16	17
80-84	23	9	14	23	9	13
85-89	10	3	7	12	4	8
90-94	3	1	2	4	1	3
95-99	0	0	0	1	0	1
100 +	0	0	0	0	0	0

POPULATION BY AGE AND SEX (in thousands)

Age group	2005 Both sexes	2005 Males	2005 Females	2010 Both sexes	2010 Males	2010 Females	2015 Both sexes	2015 Males	2015 Females	2020 Both sexes	2020 Males	2020 Females
All ages	2 031	1 007	1 024	2 151	1 072	1 078	2 302	1 156	1 146	2 488	1 257	1 232
0-4	268	135	133	280	141	139	311	157	154	346	175	172
5-9	285	144	141	258	130	128	273	137	135	307	155	152
10-14	290	146	144	279	141	138	250	126	124	266	134	132
15-19	239	120	119	289	145	143	277	140	137	249	125	123
20-24	189	95	94	234	118	116	285	144	142	274	138	136
25-29	151	77	75	173	88	85	220	112	108	271	137	133
30-34	126	63	62	126	66	60	151	79	72	196	102	94
35-39	106	52	54	102	53	49	103	56	47	128	69	58
40-44	90	43	47	88	44	44	84	45	40	87	48	38
45-49	73	34	39	79	38	41	76	38	38	73	39	34
50-54	59	27	32	66	30	35	70	33	36	67	34	33
55-59	47	22	25	53	24	29	59	27	32	63	30	33
60-64	37	17	20	42	19	23	48	21	27	54	24	30
65-69	28	13	15	32	15	18	37	16	21	43	18	24
70-74	20	9	11	23	10	13	27	12	15	31	13	18
75-79	14	6	8	15	6	8	17	7	10	20	8	12
80-84	7	3	4	8	3	5	9	4	5	10	4	6
85-89	2	1	1	3	1	2	4	1	2	4	2	2
90-94	0	0	0	1	0	0	1	0	0	1	0	1
95-99	0	0	0	0	0	0	0	0	0	0	0	0
100 +	0	0	0	0	0	0	0	0	0	0	0	0

Age group	2025 Both sexes	2025 Males	2025 Females	2030 Both sexes	2030 Males	2030 Females	2035 Both sexes	2035 Males	2035 Females	2040 Both sexes	2040 Males	2040 Females
All ages	2 680	1 360	1 320	2 862	1 456	1 406	3 040	1 548	1 491	3 229	1 645	1 584
0-4	355	179	176	346	174	171	342	173	169	356	180	176
5-9	344	173	171	353	178	175	345	174	171	342	173	169
10-14	304	153	151	343	173	170	353	178	175	345	174	171
15-19	265	134	132	303	153	151	342	172	170	352	177	175
20-24	247	124	123	263	132	131	301	152	150	340	171	169
25-29	262	133	129	237	119	117	254	128	126	291	147	144
30-34	243	126	117	239	123	116	217	111	106	234	119	115
35-39	168	90	78	213	113	100	212	110	101	194	100	94
40-44	109	61	48	146	80	66	188	101	87	189	99	90
45-49	75	43	33	96	54	42	131	72	59	170	92	79
50-54	65	35	30	68	38	29	87	49	38	120	66	54
55-59	61	30	30	59	31	27	62	35	27	81	45	36
60-64	57	27	31	55	27	28	54	28	26	57	32	26
65-69	48	21	27	51	23	28	50	24	26	49	25	24
70-74	36	15	21	41	17	23	44	19	25	43	20	23
75-79	23	10	14	27	11	17	31	12	19	34	14	20
80-84	12	5	7	15	6	9	18	7	11	20	8	13
85-89	5	2	3	6	2	4	7	2	5	9	3	6
90-94	1	0	1	1	0	1	2	1	1	2	1	2
95-99	0	0	0	0	0	0	0	0	0	0	0	0
100 +	0	0	0	0	0	0	0	0	0	0	0	0

Age group	2045 Both sexes	2045 Males	2045 Females	2050 Both sexes	2050 Males	2050 Females
All ages	3 436	1 750	1 687	3 658	1 861	1 797
0-4	378	191	187	393	199	194
5-9	356	180	176	378	191	187
10-14	342	172	169	355	180	176
15-19	344	174	171	341	172	169
20-24	350	176	174	343	173	170
25-29	330	166	164	341	172	169
30-34	270	137	133	309	157	152
35-39	211	109	103	247	127	120
40-44	175	91	84	192	99	93
45-49	172	91	82	161	84	77
50-54	157	84	73	160	84	76
55-59	112	61	51	147	78	69
60-64	75	41	34	104	56	48
65-69	52	28	24	68	37	31
70-74	42	21	21	45	24	21
75-79	33	15	19	33	16	17
80-84	23	9	14	23	9	13
85-89	10	3	7	12	4	8
90-94	3	1	2	4	1	3
95-99	0	0	0	1	0	1
100 +	0	0	0	0	0	0

United Nations Department of Economic and Social Affairs/Population Division
World Population Prospects: The 2004 Revision, Volume II: Sex and Age Distribution of the World Population

624

POPULATION BY AGE AND SEX (in thousands)

Age group	2005 Both sexes	Males	Females	2010 Both sexes	Males	Females	2015 Both sexes	Males	Females	2020 Both sexes	Males	Females
All ages	2 031	1 007	1 024	2 113	1 054	1 060	2 195	1 102	1 093	2 280	1 151	1 128
0-4	268	135	133	242	122	120	240	121	119	243	123	120
5-9	285	144	141	258	130	128	236	119	117	237	120	118
10-14	290	146	144	279	141	138	250	126	124	231	116	114
15-19	239	120	119	289	145	143	277	140	137	249	125	123
20-24	189	95	94	234	118	116	285	144	142	274	138	136
25-29	151	77	75	173	88	85	220	112	108	271	137	133
30-34	126	63	62	126	66	60	151	79	72	196	102	94
35-39	106	52	54	102	53	49	103	56	47	128	69	58
40-44	90	43	47	88	44	44	84	45	40	87	48	38
45-49	73	34	39	79	38	41	76	38	38	73	39	34
50-54	59	27	32	66	30	35	70	33	36	67	34	33
55-59	47	22	25	53	24	29	59	27	32	63	30	33
60-64	37	17	20	42	19	23	48	21	27	54	24	30
65-69	28	13	15	32	15	18	37	16	21	43	18	24
70-74	20	9	11	23	10	13	27	12	15	31	13	18
75-79	14	6	8	15	6	8	17	7	10	20	8	12
80-84	7	3	4	8	3	5	9	4	5	10	4	6
85-89	2	1	1	3	1	2	4	1	2	4	2	2
90-94	0	0	0	1	0	0	1	0	0	1	0	1
95-99	0	0	0	0	0	0	0	0	0	0	0	0
100 +	0	0	0	0	0	0	0	0	0	0	0	0

Age group	2025 Both sexes	Males	Females	2030 Both sexes	Males	Females	2035 Both sexes	Males	Females	2040 Both sexes	Males	Females
All ages	2 359	1 198	1 161	2 421	1 234	1 187	2 462	1 257	1 205	2 488	1 271	1 217
0-4	241	122	119	224	113	111	202	102	100	187	94	92
5-9	242	122	120	240	121	119	223	113	111	202	102	100
10-14	235	118	117	241	121	119	240	121	119	223	112	111
15-19	230	116	114	235	118	117	240	121	119	240	121	119
20-24	247	124	123	228	115	113	233	117	116	239	120	119
25-29	262	133	129	237	119	117	220	111	109	225	114	112
30-34	243	126	117	239	123	116	217	111	106	203	103	100
35-39	168	90	78	213	113	100	212	110	101	194	100	94
40-44	109	61	48	146	80	66	188	101	87	189	99	90
45-49	75	43	33	96	54	42	131	72	59	170	92	79
50-54	65	35	30	68	39	29	87	49	38	120	66	54
55-59	61	30	30	59	31	27	62	35	27	81	45	36
60-64	57	27	31	55	27	28	54	28	26	57	32	26
65-69	48	21	27	51	23	28	50	24	26	49	25	24
70-74	36	15	21	41	17	23	44	19	25	43	20	23
75-79	23	10	14	27	11	17	31	12	19	34	14	20
80-84	12	5	7	15	6	9	18	7	11	20	8	13
85-89	5	2	3	6	2	4	7	2	5	9	3	6
90-94	1	0	1	1	0	1	2	1	1	2	1	2
95-99	0	0	0	0	0	0	0	0	0	0	0	0
100 +	0	0	0	0	0	0	0	0	0	0	0	0

Age group	2045 Both sexes	Males	Females	2050 Both sexes	Males	Females
All ages	2 507	1 280	1 227	2 522	1 286	1 236
0-4	177	89	87	168	85	83
5-9	187	94	92	177	89	87
10-14	202	102	100	186	94	92
15-19	223	112	111	202	102	100
20-24	239	120	119	222	112	110
25-29	232	117	115	233	117	115
30-34	209	106	103	218	110	107
35-39	183	94	89	191	98	93
40-44	175	91	84	167	86	81
45-49	172	91	82	161	84	77
50-54	157	84	73	160	84	76
55-59	112	61	51	147	78	69
60-64	75	41	34	104	56	48
65-69	52	28	24	68	37	31
70-74	42	21	21	45	24	21
75-79	33	15	19	33	16	17
80-84	23	9	14	23	9	13
85-89	10	3	7	12	4	8
90-94	3	1	2	4	1	3
95-99	0	0	0	1	0	1
100 +	0	0	0	0	0	0

POPULATION BY AGE AND SEX (in thousands)

Age group	1950 Both sexes	Males	Females	1955 Both sexes	Males	Females	1960 Both sexes	Males	Females	1965 Both sexes	Males	Females
All ages	8 643	4 320	4 323	9 311	4 678	4 633	10 070	5 058	5 011	11 001	5 527	5 474
0-4	1 299	652	647	1 476	759	717	1 614	828	786	1 783	913	870
5-9	1 067	539	528	1 165	590	575	1 333	691	642	1 469	759	711
10-14	950	481	469	1 034	524	510	1 132	575	557	1 298	674	624
15-19	846	429	417	917	465	452	998	506	492	1 095	556	538
20-24	748	379	368	803	406	397	866	435	430	948	477	471
25-29	657	334	323	700	353	347	747	372	375	812	403	409
30-34	580	295	286	612	309	303	648	322	326	697	343	354
35-39	512	260	253	537	271	265	564	281	283	602	295	306
40-44	447	225	221	470	237	233	491	245	246	520	256	264
45-49	382	190	192	406	202	203	427	212	215	449	221	228
50-54	313	154	160	340	167	173	362	177	184	383	187	196
55-59	270	130	140	270	131	140	295	142	152	316	152	163
60-64	216	101	115	221	105	116	222	106	117	245	116	129
65-69	159	72	87	163	75	88	168	78	90	171	80	92
70-74	105	45	60	107	48	59	111	50	61	116	53	63
75-79	59	23	36	58	25	34	60	26	34	64	28	36
80 +	32	10	22	33	12	21	33	13	21	35	14	21

Age group	1970 Both sexes	Males	Females	1975 Both sexes	Males	Females	1980 Both sexes	Males	Females	1985 Both sexes	Males	Females
All ages	12 155	6 099	6 056	13 548	6 825	6 723	15 159	7 659	7 500	17 003	8 584	8 419
0-4	1 968	1 007	960	2 195	1 127	1 069	2 455	1 261	1 194	2 756	1 417	1 339
5-9	1 640	844	796	1 827	940	886	2 059	1 063	996	2 325	1 201	1 124
10-14	1 435	742	693	1 605	828	777	1 792	924	868	2 025	1 047	978
15-19	1 259	654	605	1 400	726	674	1 569	811	759	1 753	903	849
20-24	1 048	528	520	1 216	631	585	1 353	700	653	1 513	775	737
25-29	902	447	456	1 006	505	501	1 166	603	563	1 291	659	632
30-34	772	377	395	864	426	437	960	480	480	1 110	566	543
35-39	659	319	339	734	357	377	820	403	417	911	450	461
40-44	563	273	290	621	299	321	693	335	358	775	376	399
45-49	481	233	247	525	253	273	581	278	303	650	310	339
50-54	408	197	210	441	212	229	484	230	254	537	253	284
55-59	338	162	176	363	174	190	396	188	208	437	205	232
60-64	265	126	140	288	136	152	313	147	165	343	160	183
65-69	191	89	103	211	98	113	232	108	124	255	118	137
70-74	120	55	66	137	62	75	154	70	84	172	78	94
75-79	69	30	38	73	32	40	85	38	47	97	43	54
80 +	38	16	22	42	18	25	47	20	27	55	23	32

Age group	1990 Both sexes	Males	Females	1995 Both sexes	Males	Females	2000 Both sexes	Males	Females	2005 Both sexes	Males	Females
All ages	19 114	9 633	9 482	21 682	10 788	10 894	24 431	12 132	12 298	27 133	13 446	13 687
0-4	3 073	1 582	1 492	3 485	1 791	1 695	3 643	1 869	1 774	3 639	1 867	1 772
5-9	2 636	1 362	1 274	2 980	1 539	1 441	3 402	1 752	1 650	3 573	1 836	1 736
10-14	2 292	1 185	1 107	2 610	1 349	1 261	2 956	1 527	1 429	3 378	1 740	1 638
15-19	1 983	1 024	960	2 242	1 151	1 091	2 575	1 327	1 247	2 921	1 505	1 416
20-24	1 690	862	828	1 907	956	951	2 188	1 110	1 078	2 520	1 284	1 236
25-29	1 443	727	716	1 628	789	839	1 852	909	943	2 132	1 060	1 072
30-34	1 229	617	612	1 403	670	733	1 581	749	832	1 804	866	938
35-39	1 055	530	524	1 192	573	619	1 360	637	722	1 538	715	823
40-44	862	420	442	1 014	493	521	1 150	544	606	1 317	607	709
45-49	729	349	380	820	388	432	971	466	505	1 106	516	590
50-54	603	284	320	683	319	364	775	361	414	922	437	486
55-59	488	226	262	552	253	299	632	290	342	722	331	390
60-64	382	176	206	431	195	236	495	223	272	570	257	313
65-69	283	129	154	318	142	176	365	161	204	423	186	237
70-74	191	86	105	215	95	120	248	107	140	287	123	164
75-79	111	49	62	126	54	71	145	62	83	169	71	99
80 +	65	27	38	76	31	45	93	38	55	112	45	67

United Nations Department of Economic and Social Affairs/Population Division
World Population Prospects: The 2004 Revision, Volume II: Sex and Age Distribution of the World Population

626

POPULATION BY AGE AND SEX (in thousands)

Age group	2005 Both sexes	Males	Females	2010 Both sexes	Males	Females	2015 Both sexes	Males	Females	2020 Both sexes	Males	Females
All ages	27 133	13 446	13 687	29 891	14 015	15 076	32 747	16 232	16 515	35 679	17 667	18 013
0-4	3 639	1 867	1 772	3 720	1 907	1 813	3 855	1 974	1 880	3 980	2 037	1 943
5-9	3 573	1 836	1 736	3 583	1 841	1 743	3 679	1 888	1 791	3 825	1 960	1 865
10-14	3 378	1 740	1 638	3 551	1 826	1 726	3 567	1 832	1 735	3 666	1 880	1 786
15-19	2 921	1 505	1 416	3 345	1 719	1 626	3 522	1 807	1 715	3 541	1 813	1 728
20-24	2 520	1 284	1 236	2 869	1 467	1 402	3 295	1 682	1 613	3 475	1 768	1 707
25-29	2 132	1 060	1 072	2 466	1 241	1 225	2 817	1 424	1 393	3 244	1 636	1 608
30-34	1 804	866	938	2 086	1 024	1 062	2 421	1 205	1 216	2 774	1 386	1 389
35-39	1 538	715	823	1 762	837	926	2 045	994	1 051	2 382	1 173	1 209
40-44	1 317	607	709	1 497	689	808	1 722	810	912	2 005	966	1 039
45-49	1 106	516	590	1 273	582	691	1 453	663	790	1 677	783	895
50-54	922	437	486	1 056	488	568	1 221	553	668	1 400	633	767
55-59	722	331	390	864	404	460	995	454	541	1 157	517	639
60-64	570	257	313	656	296	360	790	364	427	916	411	505
65-69	423	186	237	492	217	276	571	252	319	694	312	382
70-74	287	123	164	337	144	193	396	169	226	464	199	265
75-79	169	71	99	200	83	117	237	98	140	283	117	166
80-84	79	32	47	94	38	56	113	45	68	137	54	83
85-89	26	10	16	32	12	20	38	15	24	47	18	29
90-94	5	2	3	7	2	4	8	3	5	10	4	7
95-99	1	0	0	1	0	1	1	0	1	1	0	1
100 +	0	0	0	0	0	0	0	0	0	0	0	0

Age group	2025 Both sexes	Males	Females	2030 Both sexes	Males	Females	2035 Both sexes	Males	Females	2040 Both sexes	Males	Females
All ages	38 600	19 091	19 509	41 424	20 463	20 961	44 116	21 765	22 351	46 658	22 989	23 669
0-4	4 030	2 060	1 969	4 011	2 050	1 961	3 975	2 031	1 944	3 946	2 015	1 930
5-9	3 958	2 025	1 933	4 014	2 052	1 963	4 001	2 043	1 957	3 968	2 026	1 942
10-14	3 815	1 954	1 861	3 950	2 020	1 930	4 008	2 047	1 961	3 996	2 040	1 956
15-19	3 644	1 863	1 780	3 795	1 937	1 857	3 932	2 005	1 927	3 991	2 033	1 958
20-24	3 499	1 776	1 723	3 605	1 828	1 777	3 758	1 903	1 855	3 898	1 971	1 926
25-29	3 429	1 724	1 705	3 457	1 734	1 723	3 567	1 787	1 779	3 722	1 864	1 859
30-34	3 204	1 598	1 606	3 392	1 687	1 705	3 424	1 699	1 725	3 536	1 753	1 783
35-39	2 737	1 354	1 383	3 167	1 566	1 601	3 359	1 657	1 702	3 395	1 671	1 724
40-44	2 042	1 145	1 197	2 698	1 326	1 372	3 129	1 538	1 591	3 324	1 630	1 694
45-49	1 960	938	1 022	2 296	1 115	1 181	2 652	1 296	1 356	3 083	1 507	1 575
50-54	1 622	751	872	1 903	904	999	2 237	1 079	1 158	2 591	1 258	1 333
55-59	1 332	595	737	1 551	710	841	1 826	858	968	2 155	1 030	1 125
60-64	1 072	471	600	1 242	546	696	1 454	655	799	1 720	796	924
65-69	812	356	456	958	412	546	1 119	480	639	1 318	580	738
70-74	570	249	321	674	287	387	805	335	469	949	395	554
75-79	337	139	198	420	177	243	504	207	298	610	244	366
80-84	166	66	100	201	80	122	255	103	152	313	122	191
85-89	58	22	36	72	27	45	89	33	56	115	44	72
90-94	13	4	8	16	6	10	20	7	13	26	9	17
95-99	2	0	1	2	1	1	3	1	2	3	1	2
100 +	0	0	0	0	0	0	0	0	0	0	0	0

Age group	2045 Both sexes	Males	Females	2050 Both sexes	Males	Females
All ages	49 029	24 119	24 910	51 172	25 131	26 041
0-4	3 906	1 997	1 909	3 838	1 963	1 875
5-9	3 940	2 012	1 928	3 902	1 994	1 908
10-14	3 964	2 023	1 941	3 937	2 010	1 928
15-19	3 980	2 026	1 954	3 949	2 010	1 939
20-24	3 958	2 000	1 958	3 949	1 995	1 954
25-29	3 863	1 933	1 930	3 926	1 963	1 962
30-34	3 694	1 831	1 863	3 836	1 901	1 935
35-39	3 509	1 726	1 782	3 667	1 805	1 863
40-44	3 363	1 646	1 717	3 479	1 703	1 776
45-49	3 280	1 601	1 679	3 322	1 619	1 704
50-54	3 018	1 468	1 551	3 218	1 562	1 655
55-59	2 503	1 204	1 299	2 925	1 410	1 515
60-64	2 038	959	1 079	2 377	1 127	1 250
65-69	1 570	710	860	1 870	861	1 009
70-74	1 130	481	649	1 357	593	764
75-79	732	290	442	885	358	527
80-84	391	146	245	483	177	306
85-89	149	53	96	195	64	131
90-94	36	12	24	50	14	35
95-99	5	1	3	7	2	5
100 +	0	0	0	0	0	0

POPULATION BY AGE AND SEX (in thousands)

Age group	2005			2010			2015			2020		
	Both sexes	Males	Females	Both sexes	Males	Females	Both sexes	Males	Females	Both sexes	Males	Females
All ages	27 133	13 446	13 687	30 180	14 963	15 216	33 558	16 647	16 910	37 210	18 451	18 759
0-4	3 639	1 867	1 772	4 009	2 055	1 954	4 380	2 243	2 136	4 706	2 408	2 298
5-9	3 573	1 836	1 736	3 583	1 841	1 743	3 964	2 034	1 930	4 346	2 227	2 119
10-14	3 378	1 740	1 638	3 551	1 826	1 726	3 567	1 832	1 735	3 950	2 026	1 924
15-19	2 921	1 505	1 416	3 345	1 719	1 626	3 522	1 807	1 715	3 541	1 813	1 728
20-24	2 520	1 284	1 236	2 869	1 467	1 402	3 295	1 682	1 613	3 475	1 768	1 707
25-29	2 132	1 060	1 072	2 466	1 241	1 225	2 817	1 424	1 393	3 244	1 636	1 608
30-34	1 804	866	938	2 086	1 024	1 062	2 421	1 205	1 216	2 774	1 386	1 389
35-39	1 538	715	823	1 762	837	926	2 045	994	1 051	2 382	1 173	1 209
40-44	1 317	607	709	1 497	689	808	1 722	810	912	2 005	966	1 039
45-49	1 106	516	590	1 273	582	691	1 453	663	790	1 677	783	895
50-54	922	437	486	1 056	488	568	1 221	553	668	1 400	633	767
55-59	722	331	390	864	404	460	995	454	541	1 157	517	639
60-64	570	257	313	656	296	360	790	364	427	916	411	505
65-69	423	186	237	492	217	276	571	252	319	694	312	382
70-74	287	123	164	337	144	193	396	169	226	464	199	265
75-79	169	71	99	200	83	117	237	98	140	283	117	166
80-84	79	32	47	94	38	56	113	45	68	137	54	83
85-89	26	10	16	32	12	20	38	15	24	47	18	29
90-94	5	2	3	7	2	4	8	3	5	10	4	7
95-99	1	0	0	1	0	1	1	0	1	1	0	1
100 +	0	0	0	0	0	0	0	0	0	0	0	0

Age group	2025			2030			2035			2040		
	Both sexes	Males	Females	Both sexes	Males	Females	Both sexes	Males	Females	Both sexes	Males	Females
All ages	40 934	20 286	20 648	44 718	22 148	22 571	48 601	24 057	24 544	52 592	26 019	26 572
0-4	4 841	2 475	2 366	4 979	2 544	2 434	5 177	2 645	2 532	5 406	2 762	2 645
5-9	4 680	2 394	2 285	4 822	2 464	2 357	4 964	2 536	2 428	5 166	2 638	2 528
10-14	4 334	2 220	2 114	4 670	2 388	2 282	4 814	2 459	2 355	4 958	2 531	2 427
15-19	3 927	2 008	1 918	4 312	2 202	2 110	4 650	2 372	2 278	4 795	2 443	2 352
20-24	3 499	1 776	1 723	3 887	1 972	1 915	4 274	2 167	2 107	4 613	2 337	2 277
25-29	3 429	1 724	1 705	3 457	1 734	1 723	3 847	1 931	1 916	4 236	2 126	2 110
30-34	3 204	1 598	1 606	3 392	1 687	1 705	3 424	1 699	1 725	3 815	1 896	1 919
35-39	2 737	1 354	1 383	3 167	1 566	1 601	3 359	1 657	1 702	3 395	1 671	1 724
40-44	2 342	1 145	1 197	2 698	1 326	1 372	3 129	1 538	1 591	3 324	1 630	1 694
45-49	1 960	938	1 022	2 296	1 115	1 181	2 652	1 296	1 356	3 083	1 507	1 575
50-54	1 622	751	872	1 903	904	999	2 237	1 079	1 158	2 591	1 258	1 333
55-59	1 332	595	737	1 551	710	841	1 826	858	968	2 155	1 030	1 125
60-64	1 072	471	600	1 242	546	696	1 454	655	799	1 720	796	924
65-69	812	356	456	958	412	546	1 119	480	639	1 318	580	738
70-74	570	249	321	674	287	387	805	335	469	949	395	554
75-79	337	139	198	420	177	243	504	207	298	610	244	366
80-84	166	66	100	201	80	122	255	103	152	313	122	191
85-89	58	22	36	72	27	45	89	33	56	115	44	72
90-94	13	4	8	16	6	10	20	7	13	26	9	17
95-99	2	0	1	2	1	1	3	1	2	3	1	2
100 +	0	0	0	0	0	0	0	0	0	0	0	0

Age group	2045			2050		
	Both sexes	Males	Females	Both sexes	Males	Females
All ages	56 639	28 006	28 634	60 651	29 971	30 680
0-4	5 596	2 861	2 735	5 723	2 928	2 796
5-9	5 398	2 756	2 641	5 589	2 857	2 733
10-14	5 161	2 634	2 527	5 393	2 753	2 640
15-19	4 941	2 516	2 424	5 144	2 620	2 524
20-24	4 760	2 410	2 351	4 907	2 484	2 424
25-29	4 577	2 297	2 280	4 725	2 371	2 354
30-34	4 205	2 092	2 113	4 547	2 264	2 283
35-39	3 786	1 868	1 918	4 177	2 065	2 112
40-44	3 363	1 646	1 717	3 755	1 844	1 911
45-49	3 280	1 601	1 679	3 322	1 619	1 704
50-54	3 018	1 468	1 551	3 218	1 562	1 655
55-59	2 503	1 204	1 299	2 925	1 410	1 515
60-64	2 038	959	1 079	2 377	1 127	1 250
65-69	1 570	710	860	1 870	861	1 009
70-74	1 130	481	649	1 357	593	764
75-79	732	290	442	885	358	527
80-84	391	146	245	483	177	306
85-89	149	53	96	195	64	131
90-94	36	12	24	50	14	35
95-99	5	1	3	7	2	5
100 +	0	0	0	0	0	0

United Nations Department of Economic and Social Affairs/Population Division
World Population Prospects: The 2004 Revision, Volume II: Sex and Age Distribution of the World Population

POPULATION BY AGE AND SEX (in thousands)

Age group	2005			2010			2015			2020		
	Both sexes	Males	Females	Both sexes	Males	Females	Both sexes	Males	Females	Both sexes	Males	Females
All ages	27 133	13 446	13 687	29 603	14 668	14 900	31 040	15 918	16 122	34 153	16 885	17 268
0-4	3 639	1 867	1 772	3 433	1 760	1 673	3 332	1 707	1 625	3 255	1 666	1 589
5-9	3 573	1 836	1 736	3 583	1 841	1 743	3 395	1 742	1 653	3 307	1 694	1 613
10-14	3 378	1 740	1 638	3 551	1 826	1 726	3 567	1 832	1 735	3 383	1 735	1 648
15-19	2 921	1 505	1 416	3 345	1 719	1 626	3 522	1 807	1 715	3 541	1 813	1 728
20-24	2 520	1 284	1 236	2 869	1 467	1 402	3 295	1 682	1 613	3 475	1 768	1 707
25-29	2 132	1 060	1 072	2 466	1 241	1 225	2 817	1 424	1 393	3 244	1 636	1 608
30-34	1 804	866	938	2 086	1 024	1 062	2 421	1 205	1 216	2 774	1 386	1 389
35-39	1 538	715	823	1 762	837	926	2 045	994	1 051	2 382	1 173	1 209
40-44	1 317	607	709	1 497	689	808	1 722	810	912	2 005	966	1 039
45-49	1 106	516	590	1 273	582	691	1 453	663	790	1 677	783	895
50-54	922	437	486	1 056	488	568	1 221	553	668	1 400	633	767
55-59	722	331	390	864	404	460	995	454	541	1 157	517	639
60-64	570	257	313	656	296	360	790	364	427	916	411	505
65-69	423	186	237	492	217	276	571	252	319	694	312	382
70-74	287	123	164	337	144	193	396	169	226	464	199	265
75-79	169	71	99	200	83	117	237	98	140	283	117	166
80-84	79	32	47	94	38	56	113	45	68	137	54	83
85-89	26	10	16	32	12	20	38	15	24	47	18	29
90-94	5	2	3	7	2	4	8	3	5	10	4	7
95-99	1	0	0	1	0	1	1	0	1	1	0	1
100 +	0	0	0	0	0	0	0	0	0	0	0	0

Age group	2025			2030			2035			2040		
	Both sexes	Males	Females	Both sexes	Males	Females	Both sexes	Males	Females	Both sexes	Males	Females
All ages	36 282	17 905	18 377	38 204	18 816	19 388	39 834	19 576	20 258	41 141	20 171	20 970
0-4	3 231	1 652	1 579	3 101	1 585	1 516	2 904	1 483	1 420	2 700	1 379	1 321
5-9	3 238	1 657	1 581	3 220	1 646	1 574	3 093	1 580	1 513	2 899	1 480	1 419
10-14	3 298	1 689	1 609	3 232	1 652	1 579	3 215	1 642	1 573	3 090	1 577	1 512
15-19	3 361	1 718	1 643	3 279	1 674	1 606	3 215	1 638	1 577	3 199	1 628	1 571
20-24	3 499	1 776	1 723	3 324	1 684	1 640	3 245	1 640	1 604	3 183	1 606	1 577
25-29	3 429	1 724	1 705	3 457	1 734	1 723	3 287	1 644	1 643	3 211	1 602	1 609
30-34	3 204	1 598	1 606	3 392	1 687	1 705	3 424	1 699	1 725	3 258	1 611	1 647
35-39	2 737	1 354	1 383	3 167	1 566	1 601	3 359	1 657	1 702	3 395	1 671	1 724
40-44	2 342	1 145	1 197	2 698	1 326	1 372	3 129	1 538	1 591	3 324	1 630	1 694
45-49	1 960	938	1 022	2 296	1 115	1 181	2 652	1 296	1 356	3 083	1 507	1 575
50-54	1 622	751	872	1 903	904	999	2 237	1 079	1 158	2 591	1 258	1 333
55-59	1 332	585	707	1 551	710	841	1 826	858	968	2 155	1 030	1 125
60-64	1 072	471	600	1 242	546	696	1 454	655	799	1 720	796	824
65-69	812	356	456	958	412	546	1 119	480	639	1 318	580	738
70-74	570	249	321	674	287	387	805	335	469	949	395	554
75-79	337	139	198	420	177	243	504	207	298	610	244	366
80-84	166	66	100	201	80	122	255	103	152	313	122	191
85-89	58	22	36	72	27	45	89	33	56	115	44	72
90-94	13	4	8	16	6	10	20	7	13	26	9	17
95-99	2	0	1	2	1	1	3	1	2	3	1	2
100 +	0	0	0	0	0	0	0	0	0	0	0	0

Age group	2045			2050		
	Both sexes	Males	Females	Both sexes	Males	Females
All ages	42 135	20 599	21 536	42 798	20 855	21 943
0-4	2 515	1 286	1 229	2 342	1 198	1 144
5-9	2 697	1 377	1 320	2 514	1 285	1 229
10-14	2 897	1 478	1 418	2 695	1 376	1 320
15-19	3 075	1 564	1 511	2 883	1 466	1 417
20-24	3 169	1 598	1 571	3 046	1 535	1 512
25-29	3 151	1 570	1 581	3 138	1 562	1 577
30-34	3 184	1 571	1 613	3 126	1 539	1 587
35-39	3 232	1 585	1 647	3 160	1 546	1 614
40-44	3 363	1 646	1 717	3 204	1 562	1 642
45-49	3 280	1 601	1 679	3 322	1 619	1 704
50-54	3 018	1 468	1 551	3 218	1 562	1 655
55-59	2 503	1 204	1 299	2 925	1 410	1 515
60-64	2 038	959	1 079	2 377	1 127	1 250
65-69	1 570	710	860	1 870	861	1 009
70-74	1 130	481	649	1 357	593	764
75-79	732	290	442	885	358	527
80-84	391	146	245	483	177	306
85-89	149	53	96	195	64	131
90-94	36	12	24	50	14	35
95-99	5	1	3	7	2	5
100 +	0	0	0	0	0	0

United Nations Department of Economic and Social Affairs/Population Division
World Population Prospects: The 2004 Revision, Volume II: Sex and Age Distribution of the World Population

629

POPULATION BY AGE AND SEX (in thousands)

Age group	1950 Both sexes	Males	Females	1955 Both sexes	Males	Females	1960 Both sexes	Males	Females	1965 Both sexes	Males	Females
All ages	10 114	5 041	5 073	10 751	5 356	5 395	11 487	5 720	5 766	12 295	6 134	6 160
0-4	1 207	620	587	1 110	570	540	1 155	591	563	1 215	622	593
5-9	932	478	454	1 186	609	577	1 107	568	538	1 152	590	562
10-14	825	421	404	918	470	448	1 184	607	576	1 107	568	539
15-19	811	414	397	817	416	401	914	467	446	1 183	606	577
20-24	800	404	396	790	401	389	806	410	396	912	468	444
25-29	796	395	401	767	383	384	771	390	381	808	417	391
30-34	689	341	348	773	380	393	756	376	380	774	395	379
35-39	683	335	348	675	333	342	765	375	390	757	378	379
40-44	650	317	333	670	328	342	669	329	340	763	375	388
45-49	593	289	304	637	310	327	662	323	339	663	325	338
50-54	520	252	268	579	281	298	625	303	322	650	316	334
55-59	449	218	231	503	242	261	561	270	291	604	289	315
60-64	376	183	193	424	204	220	475	225	250	529	249	280
65-69	305	148	157	343	165	178	387	182	205	431	198	233
70-74	231	111	120	259	124	135	293	138	155	331	151	180
75-79	145	69	76	173	82	91	196	91	105	224	102	122
80 +	102	46	56	127	58	69	158	72	86	189	84	105

Age group	1970 Both sexes	Males	Females	1975 Both sexes	Males	Females	1980 Both sexes	Males	Females	1985 Both sexes	Males	Females
All ages	13 039	6 507	6 531	13 666	6 804	6 862	14 150	7 021	7 128	14 492	7 167	7 325
0-4	1 188	608	580	1 028	526	502	885	453	432	873	446	427
5-9	1 214	621	593	1 204	616	588	1 051	537	514	889	455	434
10-14	1 155	591	564	1 231	630	601	1 223	626	598	1 056	540	517
15-19	1 111	569	542	1 172	599	573	1 255	642	613	1 232	630	602
20-24	1 185	609	577	1 131	577	553	1 201	612	589	1 272	648	624
25-29	917	477	440	1 201	620	581	1 151	589	562	1 210	616	594
30-34	813	423	390	925	482	443	1 206	623	584	1 149	587	562
35-39	775	397	378	818	425	393	924	480	445	1 199	616	582
40-44	754	377	378	774	394	380	815	420	395	916	473	443
45-49	754	369	385	747	371	376	766	387	379	804	411	393
50-54	650	317	333	741	360	381	732	361	372	751	377	374
55-59	627	301	326	628	302	326	717	344	373	709	345	364
60-64	569	266	303	593	277	315	594	279	315	680	319	361
65-69	480	218	262	511	227	284	536	242	294	545	246	299
70-74	367	160	206	413	174	239	442	186	256	472	198	273
75-79	254	109	145	280	120	160	326	127	199	357	135	222
80 +	225	96	129	271	105	165	324	115	209	377	124	253

Age group	1990 Both sexes	Males	Females	1995 Both sexes	Males	Females	2000 Both sexes	Males	Females	2005 Both sexes	Males	Females
All ages	14 952	7 389	7 563	15 459	7 645	7 814	15 898	7 879	8 019	16 299	8 091	8 208
0-4	937	479	459	985	504	481	971	497	474	973	499	475
5-9	887	453	434	955	488	467	997	510	487	983	503	479
10-14	902	462	440	904	462	442	967	494	473	1 009	516	493
15-19	1 078	550	528	923	472	451	916	468	448	978	500	479
20-24	1 265	646	620	1 113	564	548	935	477	458	927	472	455
25-29	1 299	665	634	1 300	665	635	1 134	576	559	955	488	467
30-34	1 222	623	599	1 318	675	643	1 328	682	647	1 161	591	570
35-39	1 151	587	564	1 229	625	604	1 334	683	651	1 343	690	654
40-44	1 194	612	582	1 150	585	565	1 233	627	607	1 337	684	653
45-49	908	466	441	1 185	605	580	1 145	581	564	1 228	623	606
50-54	789	400	389	892	456	436	1 168	594	574	1 130	571	559
55-59	727	360	367	766	385	381	870	441	429	1 140	576	564
60-64	674	321	353	693	338	355	733	363	370	834	416	417
65-69	627	284	343	624	289	336	644	306	339	683	330	354
70-74	478	203	275	554	238	317	554	245	310	574	261	313
75-79	382	146	236	390	151	239	456	180	276	459	188	271
80 +	432	133	299	479	144	334	511	156	355	582	183	399

United Nations Department of Economic and Social Affairs/Population Division
World Population Prospects: The 2004 Revision, Volume II: Sex and Age Distribution of the World Population

630

POPULATION BY AGE AND SEX (in thousands)

Age group	2005 Both sexes	Males	Females	2010 Both sexes	Males	Females	2015 Both sexes	Males	Females	2020 Both sexes	Males	Females
All ages	16 299	8 091	8 208	16 592	8 244	8 348	16 812	8 354	8 458	17 007	8 446	8 561
0-4	973	499	475	889	456	434	853	437	416	871	446	425
5-9	983	503	479	985	505	481	901	462	440	865	443	422
10-14	1 009	516	493	995	509	485	997	511	486	913	468	445
15-19	978	500	479	1 021	522	499	1 006	515	491	1 009	516	492
20-24	927	472	455	990	504	485	1 032	527	505	1 017	520	498
25-29	955	488	467	948	483	464	1 010	515	495	1 053	538	515
30-34	1 161	591	570	983	504	479	976	499	476	1 038	531	507
35-39	1 343	690	654	1 177	600	577	1 000	513	487	993	509	484
40-44	1 337	684	653	1 347	691	656	1 182	602	580	1 006	516	490
45-49	1 228	623	606	1 332	680	652	1 343	687	655	1 180	599	581
50-54	1 130	571	559	1 213	613	601	1 317	670	647	1 328	677	651
55-59	1 140	576	564	1 105	555	551	1 188	596	592	1 291	653	638
60-64	834	416	417	1 097	547	550	1 065	528	538	1 148	569	579
65-69	683	330	354	780	381	399	1 031	503	527	1 005	488	517
70-74	574	261	313	613	284	329	704	332	373	935	441	494
75-79	459	188	271	480	204	276	516	225	291	598	266	332
80-84	333	117	216	340	125	215	361	138	222	393	156	237
85-89	166	48	118	202	61	142	212	67	145	229	77	153
90-94	67	15	51	74	17	57	94	23	71	101	26	75
95-99	15	3	12	18	3	15	22	4	18	29	6	24
100 +	2	0	1	2	0	2	3	0	3	4	1	3

Age group	2025 Both sexes	Males	Females	2030 Both sexes	Males	Females	2035 Both sexes	Males	Females	2040 Both sexes	Males	Females
All ages	17 178	8 519	8 659	17 303	8 567	8 737	17 356	8 578	8 778	17 329	8 554	8 775
0-4	901	462	439	918	470	448	913	468	445	891	456	434
5-9	883	452	430	913	468	445	930	477	454	925	474	451
10-14	877	449	428	895	458	436	925	474	451	942	483	460
15-19	925	474	451	889	455	434	907	464	442	937	480	457
20-24	1 020	521	499	937	479	458	901	460	441	919	470	449
25-29	1 038	531	507	1 041	533	509	958	490	468	922	472	450
30-34	1 081	554	527	1 066	547	519	1 070	549	521	987	506	480
35-39	1 055	541	515	1 098	563	535	1 084	556	527	1 087	558	529
40-44	999	511	488	1 062	543	518	1 104	566	538	1 091	559	531
45-49	1 005	514	491	999	510	489	1 062	542	520	1 104	565	540
50-54	1 168	591	577	997	508	489	991	504	487	1 054	536	518
55-59	1 304	661	643	1 148	577	571	981	496	484	976	494	482
60-64	1 250	625	625	1 264	634	630	1 115	555	560	954	478	475
65-69	1 086	529	557	1 186	583	603	1 203	594	609	1 064	521	542
70-74	917	431	485	995	470	525	1 091	522	569	1 111	534	576
75-79	800	358	442	790	353	437	864	389	475	953	436	517
80-84	461	188	273	624	257	367	623	258	366	688	288	401
85-89	255	89	166	305	110	195	420	154	266	428	158	270
90-94	114	31	82	130	38	92	160	48	112	227	70	157
95-99	33	7	27	39	8	31	47	11	36	60	14	46
100 +	5	1	5	7	1	6	8	1	7	11	2	9

Age group	2045 Both sexes	Males	Females	2050 Both sexes	Males	Females
All ages	17 243	8 506	8 737	17 139	8 456	8 684
0-4	873	447	426	873	447	426
5-9	903	463	440	885	454	432
10-14	937	480	457	915	469	446
15-19	954	489	466	949	486	463
20-24	949	485	464	966	494	472
25-29	940	481	459	971	497	474
30-34	951	488	463	969	497	471
35-39	1 004	516	488	969	498	471
40-44	1 094	561	533	1 012	519	492
45-49	1 091	558	533	1 095	561	534
50-54	1 096	559	538	1 084	553	531
55-59	1 039	525	513	1 082	548	534
60-64	950	476	474	1 013	508	505
65-69	912	450	461	911	450	461
70-74	986	472	515	848	409	439
75-79	976	450	526	872	400	471
80-84	767	327	440	793	342	451
85-89	480	180	300	543	209	334
90-94	237	74	163	273	87	186
95-99	88	21	67	96	24	73
100 +	14	2	12	21	4	18

United Nations Department of Economic and Social Affairs/Population Division
World Population Prospects: The 2004 Revision, Volume II: Sex and Age Distribution of the World Population

631

POPULATION BY AGE AND SEX (in thousands)

Age group	2005			2010			2015			2020		
	Both sexes	Males	Females	Both sexes	Males	Females	Both sexes	Males	Females	Both sexes	Males	Females
All ages	16 299	8 091	8 208	16 703	8 300	8 402	17 057	8 480	8 578	17 403	8 648	8 755
0-4	973	499	475	1 000	512	488	988	506	482	1 022	524	499
5-9	983	503	479	985	505	481	1 012	518	493	1 000	512	488
10-14	1 009	516	493	995	509	485	997	511	486	1 024	524	499
15-19	978	500	479	1 021	522	499	1 006	515	491	1 009	516	492
20-24	927	472	455	990	504	485	1 032	527	505	1 017	520	498
25-29	955	488	467	948	483	464	1 010	515	495	1 053	538	515
30-34	1 161	591	570	983	504	479	976	499	476	1 038	531	507
35-39	1 343	690	654	1 177	600	577	1 000	513	487	993	509	484
40-44	1 337	684	653	1 347	691	656	1 182	602	580	1 006	516	490
45-49	1 228	623	606	1 332	680	652	1 343	687	655	1 180	599	581
50-54	1 130	571	559	1 213	613	601	1 317	670	647	1 328	677	651
55-59	1 140	576	564	1 105	555	551	1 188	596	592	1 291	653	638
60-64	834	416	417	1 097	547	550	1 065	528	538	1 148	569	579
65-69	683	330	354	780	381	399	1 031	503	527	1 005	488	517
70-74	574	261	313	613	284	329	704	332	373	935	441	494
75-79	459	188	271	480	204	276	516	225	291	598	266	332
80-84	333	117	216	340	125	215	361	138	222	393	156	237
85-89	166	48	118	202	61	142	212	67	145	229	77	153
90-94	67	15	51	74	17	57	94	23	71	101	26	75
95-99	15	3	12	18	3	15	22	4	18	29	6	24
100 +	2	0	1	2	0	2	3	0	3	4	1	3

Age group	2025			2030			2035			2040		
	Both sexes	Males	Females	Both sexes	Males	Females	Both sexes	Males	Females	Both sexes	Males	Females
All ages	17 747	8 811	8 936	18 070	8 960	9 111	18 361	9 093	9 268	18 631	9 221	9 410
0-4	1 074	550	524	1 116	572	544	1 151	590	561	1 189	609	580
5-9	1 034	530	504	1 086	556	530	1 128	578	550	1 163	596	567
10-14	1 012	518	493	1 046	536	510	1 098	563	536	1 140	584	556
15-19	1 035	530	505	1 023	524	499	1 058	542	516	1 110	568	542
20-24	1 020	521	499	1 047	535	512	1 035	529	506	1 070	547	523
25-29	1 038	531	507	1 041	533	509	1 068	546	522	1 056	540	516
30-34	1 081	554	527	1 066	547	519	1 070	549	521	1 096	562	534
35-39	1 055	541	515	1 098	563	535	1 084	556	527	1 087	558	529
40-44	999	511	488	1 062	543	518	1 104	566	538	1 091	559	531
45-49	1 005	514	491	999	510	489	1 062	542	520	1 104	565	540
50-54	1 168	591	577	997	508	489	991	504	487	1 054	536	518
55-59	1 304	661	643	1 148	577	571	981	496	484	976	494	482
60-64	1 250	625	625	1 264	634	630	1 115	555	560	954	478	475
65-69	1 086	529	557	1 186	583	603	1 203	594	609	1 064	521	542
70-74	917	431	485	995	470	525	1 091	522	569	1 111	534	576
75-79	800	358	442	790	353	437	864	389	475	953	436	517
80-84	461	188	273	624	257	367	623	258	366	688	288	401
85-89	255	89	166	305	110	195	420	154	266	428	158	270
90-94	114	31	82	130	38	92	160	48	112	227	70	157
95-99	33	7	27	39	8	31	47	11	36	60	14	46
100 +	5	1	5	7	1	6	8	1	7	11	2	9

Age group	2045			2050		
	Both sexes	Males	Females	Both sexes	Males	Females
All ages	18 903	9 356	9 547	19 200	9 511	9 689
0-4	1 232	631	601	1 275	653	622
5-9	1 201	615	586	1 244	637	607
10-14	1 175	602	573	1 213	621	591
15-19	1 152	590	562	1 187	608	579
20-24	1 122	574	548	1 164	595	569
25-29	1 091	558	533	1 143	585	558
30-34	1 085	557	528	1 120	575	545
35-39	1 114	572	542	1 102	566	536
40-44	1 094	561	533	1 121	575	546
45-49	1 091	558	533	1 095	561	534
50-54	1 096	559	538	1 084	553	531
55-59	1 039	525	513	1 082	548	534
60-64	950	476	474	1 013	508	505
65-69	912	450	461	911	450	461
70-74	986	472	515	848	409	439
75-79	976	450	526	872	400	471
80-84	767	327	440	793	342	451
85-89	480	180	300	543	209	334
90-94	237	74	163	273	87	186
95-99	88	21	67	96	24	73
100 +	14	2	12	21	4	18

United Nations Department of Economic and Social Affairs/Population Division
World Population Prospects: The 2004 Revision, Volume II: Sex and Age Distribution of the World Population

632

POPULATION BY AGE AND SEX (in thousands)

Age group	2005 Both sexes	Males	Females	2010 Both sexes	Males	Females	2015 Both sexes	Males	Females	2020 Both sexes	Males	Females
All ages	16 299	8 091	8 208	16 446	8 169	8 277	16 509	8 199	8 310	16 531	8 202	8 329
0-4	973	499	475	744	381	363	695	356	339	698	358	340
5-9	983	503	479	985	505	481	756	387	369	708	363	345
10-14	1 009	516	493	995	509	485	997	511	486	768	393	374
15-19	978	500	479	1 021	522	499	1 006	515	491	1 009	516	492
20-24	927	472	455	990	504	485	1 032	527	505	1 017	520	498
25-29	955	488	467	948	483	464	1 010	515	495	1 053	538	515
30-34	1 161	591	570	983	504	479	976	499	476	1 038	531	507
35-39	1 343	690	654	1 177	600	577	1 000	513	487	993	509	484
40-44	1 337	684	653	1 347	691	656	1 182	602	580	1 006	516	490
45-49	1 228	623	606	1 332	680	652	1 343	687	655	1 180	599	581
50-54	1 130	571	559	1 213	613	601	1 317	670	647	1 328	677	651
55-59	1 140	576	564	1 105	555	551	1 188	596	592	1 291	653	638
60-64	834	416	417	1 097	547	550	1 065	528	538	1 148	569	579
65-69	683	330	354	780	381	399	1 031	503	527	1 005	488	517
70-74	574	261	313	613	284	329	704	332	373	935	441	494
75-79	459	188	271	480	204	276	516	225	291	598	266	332
80-84	333	117	216	340	125	215	361	138	222	393	156	237
85-89	166	48	118	202	61	142	212	67	145	229	77	153
90-94	67	15	51	74	17	57	94	23	71	101	26	75
95-99	15	3	12	18	3	15	22	4	18	29	6	24
100 +	2	0	1	2	0	2	3	0	3	4	1	3

Age group	2025 Both sexes	Males	Females	2030 Both sexes	Males	Females	2035 Both sexes	Males	Females	2040 Both sexes	Males	Females
All ages	16 513	8 179	8 334	16 428	8 118	8 309	16 240	8 007	8 233	15 930	7 838	8 092
0-4	711	364	347	707	362	345	671	344	327	608	311	296
5-9	710	364	346	724	371	353	720	369	351	683	350	333
10-14	720	369	351	722	370	352	736	377	359	732	375	357
15-19	779	399	380	732	375	357	734	376	358	748	383	365
20-24	1 020	521	499	792	404	387	744	380	364	747	381	365
25-29	1 038	531	507	1 041	533	509	813	416	397	765	392	374
30-34	1 081	554	527	1 066	547	519	1 070	549	521	842	432	409
35-39	1 055	541	515	1 098	563	535	1 084	556	527	1 087	558	529
40-44	999	511	488	1 002	540	518	1 104	566	538	1 091	559	531
45-49	1 005	514	491	999	510	489	1 062	542	520	1 104	565	540
50-54	1 168	591	577	997	508	489	991	504	487	1 054	536	518
55-59	1 304	661	643	1 148	577	571	981	496	484	976	494	482
60-64	1 250	625	625	1 264	634	630	1 115	555	560	954	478	475
65-69	1 086	529	557	1 186	583	603	1 203	594	609	1 064	521	542
70-74	917	431	485	995	470	525	1 091	522	569	1 111	534	576
75-79	800	358	442	700	353	437	864	389	475	953	436	517
80-84	461	188	273	624	257	367	623	258	366	688	288	401
85-89	255	89	166	305	110	195	420	154	266	428	158	270
90-94	114	31	82	130	38	92	160	48	112	227	70	157
95-99	33	7	27	39	8	31	47	11	36	60	14	46
100 +	5	1	5	7	1	6	8	1	7	11	2	9

Age group	2045 Both sexes	Males	Females	2050 Both sexes	Males	Females
All ages	15 525	7 626	7 898	15 078	7 401	7 677
0-4	552	283	269	528	271	258
5-9	620	318	302	564	289	275
10-14	696	356	339	632	324	308
15-19	744	381	363	707	362	345
20-24	760	388	372	756	386	370
25-29	768	393	375	782	400	382
30-34	794	408	386	797	410	387
35-39	860	442	417	813	418	394
40-44	1 094	561	533	868	446	422
45-49	1 091	558	533	1 095	561	534
50-54	1 096	559	538	1 084	553	531
55-59	1 039	525	513	1 082	548	534
60-64	950	476	474	1 013	508	505
65-69	912	450	461	911	450	461
70-74	986	472	515	848	409	439
75-79	976	450	526	872	400	471
80-84	767	327	440	793	342	451
85-89	480	180	300	543	209	334
90-94	237	74	163	273	87	186
95-99	88	21	67	96	24	73
100 +	14	2	12	21	4	18

POPULATION BY AGE AND SEX (in thousands)

Age group	1950 Both sexes	Males	Females	1955 Both sexes	Males	Females	1960 Both sexes	Males	Females	1965 Both sexes	Males	Females
All ages	112	54	58	123	60	63	135	66	68	146	72	74
0-4	16	8	8	22	11	11	22	11	11	20	10	10
5-9	12	6	6	16	8	8	18	9	9	21	11	10
10-14	11	5	5	12	6	6	16	8	8	18	9	9
15-19	10	5	5	10	5	5	12	6	6	15	8	7
20-24	10	5	5	9	5	5	10	5	5	11	6	6
25-29	9	4	4	8	4	4	9	4	5	9	4	5
30-34	8	4	4	8	4	4	8	4	4	8	4	4
35-39	7	4	3	7	4	4	8	4	4	8	4	4
40-44	7	4	3	6	3	3	7	4	4	7	4	4
45-49	5	3	3	6	3	3	6	3	3	7	3	3
50-54	4	2	2	5	2	2	6	3	3	6	3	3
55-59	3	1	2	4	2	2	4	2	2	5	3	3
60-64	3	1	2	3	1	2	3	1	2	4	2	2
65-69	2	1	2	2	1	1	2	1	1	3	1	2
70-74	2	1	2	2	1	1	2	1	1	2	1	1
75-79	1	0	1	1	0	1	1	0	1	1	0	1
80 +	1	0	1	1	0	1	1	0	1	1	0	1

Age group	1970 Both sexes	Males	Females	1975 Both sexes	Males	Females	1980 Both sexes	Males	Females	1985 Both sexes	Males	Females
All ages	159	79	80	166	82	84	174	84	90	182	87	94
0-4	18	9	9	18	9	9	16	8	8	17	9	8
5-9	19	10	10	18	9	9	18	9	9	17	9	9
10-14	21	11	10	19	10	10	19	9	9	17	9	8
15-19	18	9	9	20	10	10	20	10	10	17	9	9
20-24	15	8	7	17	9	9	17	8	9	15	7	8
25-29	11	6	6	14	7	7	15	7	8	16	8	8
30-34	9	4	5	10	5	5	14	6	7	16	7	8
35-39	8	4	4	8	4	4	11	5	6	14	6	7
40-44	8	4	4	8	4	4	9	4	5	11	5	6
45-49	7	3	4	7	3	4	8	4	4	9	4	5
50-54	6	3	3	7	3	3	7	3	3	8	4	4
55-59	5	3	3	6	3	3	6	3	3	6	3	3
60-64	5	2	2	5	2	2	5	2	3	5	2	3
65-69	3	2	2	4	2	2	4	2	2	4	2	2
70-74	2	1	1	3	1	1	3	2	2	4	2	2
75-79	1	0	1	2	1	1	2	1	1	2	1	1
80 +	1	0	1	1	0	1	2	1	2	3	1	2

Age group	1990 Both sexes	Males	Females	1995 Both sexes	Males	Females	2000 Both sexes	Males	Females	2005 Both sexes	Males	Females
All ages	191	91	99	187	89	98	176	83	93	183	86	97
0-4	17	9	9	18	9	9	13	7	6	13	7	6
5-9	17	9	8	16	8	8	16	8	8	13	7	6
10-14	16	8	8	15	7	7	15	7	7	16	8	8
15-19	15	8	8	12	6	6	12	6	6	15	7	7
20-24	14	7	7	13	7	7	8	4	4	12	6	6
25-29	19	9	10	14	7	8	11	5	6	8	4	4
30-34	18	9	10	17	8	9	14	6	8	11	5	6
35-39	15	7	8	17	8	9	16	8	9	14	6	8
40-44	13	6	7	14	6	8	15	7	8	16	7	9
45-49	11	5	6	12	6	7	13	6	7	15	7	8
50-54	8	4	4	10	4	5	11	5	6	12	6	7
55-59	7	3	4	7	3	4	9	4	5	11	5	6
60-64	6	3	3	6	3	3	6	3	4	8	4	5
65-69	4	2	2	5	2	3	6	3	3	6	3	3
70-74	4	2	2	4	2	2	4	2	2	5	2	3
75-79	2	1	1	3	1	2	3	1	2	3	1	2
80 +	3	1	2	3	1	2	3	1	2	3	1	2

United Nations Department of Economic and Social Affairs/Population Division
World Population Prospects: The 2004 Revision, Volume II: Sex and Age Distribution of the World Population

634

POPULATION BY AGE AND SEX (in thousands)

Age group	2005 Both sexes	2005 Males	2005 Females	2010 Both sexes	2010 Males	2010 Females	2015 Both sexes	2015 Males	2015 Females	2020 Both sexes	2020 Males	2020 Females
All ages	183	86	97	199	99	99	193	91	102	198	94	104
0-4	13	7	6	12	6	6	12	6	6	13	6	6
5-9	13	7	6	13	7	6	12	6	6	12	6	6
10-14	16	8	8	13	7	6	13	7	6	12	6	6
15-19	15	7	7	16	8	8	13	7	6	13	7	6
20-24	12	6	6	15	7	7	16	8	8	13	7	6
25-29	8	4	4	12	6	6	15	7	7	16	8	8
30-34	11	5	6	8	4	4	12	6	6	15	7	7
35-39	14	6	8	11	5	6	8	4	4	12	6	6
40-44	16	7	9	14	6	8	11	5	6	8	4	4
45-49	15	7	8	16	7	9	14	6	8	11	5	6
50-54	12	6	7	15	7	8	16	7	9	14	6	8
55-59	11	5	6	12	5	7	15	6	8	15	7	8
60-64	8	4	5	11	5	6	12	5	7	14	6	8
65-69	6	3	3	8	3	4	10	4	6	11	5	6
70-74	5	2	3	5	2	3	7	3	4	9	4	5
75-79	3	1	2	4	2	2	4	2	3	6	2	3
80-84	2	1	1	2	1	1	3	1	2	3	1	2
85-89	1	0	1	1	0	1	1	0	1	2	0	1
90-94	0	0	0	0	0	0	0	0	0	1	0	0
95-99	0	0	0	0	0	0	0	0	0	0	0	0
100 +	0	0	0	0	0	0	0	0	0	0	0	0

Age group	2025 Both sexes	2025 Males	2025 Females	2030 Both sexes	2030 Males	2030 Females	2035 Both sexes	2035 Males	2035 Females	2040 Both sexes	2040 Males	2040 Females
All ages	202	96	106	205	97	108	206	98	108	205	98	107
0-4	13	7	6	13	6	6	12	6	6	11	6	5
5-9	13	6	6	13	7	6	13	6	6	12	6	6
10-14	12	6	6	13	6	6	13	7	6	13	6	6
15-19	12	6	6	12	6	6	13	6	6	13	7	6
20-24	13	7	6	12	6	6	12	6	6	13	6	6
25-29	13	7	6	13	7	6	12	6	6	12	6	6
30-34	16	8	8	13	7	6	13	7	6	12	6	6
35-39	15	7	7	15	8	8	13	7	6	13	7	6
40-44	12	6	6	15	7	7	15	8	8	13	7	6
45-49	8	4	4	12	6	6	14	7	7	15	8	8
50-54	11	5	6	8	4	4	12	6	6	14	7	7
55-59	14	6	7	11	5	6	8	4	4	12	6	6
60-64	15	7	8	13	6	7	10	5	6	7	4	4
65-69	13	6	8	14	6	8	12	5	7	10	4	5
70-74	10	4	6	12	5	7	13	5	7	11	5	7
75-79	7	3	4	8	3	5	10	4	6	11	4	7
80-84	4	1	3	5	2	4	6	2	4	8	3	5
85-89	2	1	1	3	1	2	3	1	2	4	1	3
90-94	1	0	1	1	0	1	1	0	1	2	0	1
95-99	0	0	0	0	0	0	0	0	0	0	0	0
100 +	0	0	0	0	0	0	0	0	0	0	0	0

Age group	2045 Both sexes	2045 Males	2045 Females	2050 Both sexes	2050 Males	2050 Females
All ages	204	98	106	203	98	105
0-4	11	6	5	11	6	5
5-9	11	6	5	11	6	5
10-14	12	6	6	11	6	5
15-19	13	6	6	12	6	6
20-24	13	7	6	13	6	6
25-29	13	6	6	13	7	6
30-34	12	6	6	13	6	6
35-39	12	6	6	12	6	6
40-44	13	7	6	12	6	6
45-49	13	6	6	13	7	6
50-54	15	8	8	13	6	6
55-59	14	7	7	15	7	8
60-64	12	6	6	14	7	7
65-69	7	3	4	11	5	6
70-74	9	4	5	6	3	3
75-79	10	4	6	8	3	5
80-84	8	3	5	8	3	5
85-89	5	2	4	6	2	4
90-94	2	0	2	3	1	2
95-99	1	0	1	1	0	1
100 +	0	0	0	0	0	0

United Nations Department of Economic and Social Affairs/Population Division
World Population Prospects: The 2004 Revision, Volume II: Sex and Age Distribution of the World Population

635

POPULATION BY AGE AND SEX (in thousands)

Age group	2005 Both sexes	2005 Males	2005 Females	2010 Both sexes	2010 Males	2010 Females	2015 Both sexes	2015 Males	2015 Females	2020 Both sexes	2020 Males	2020 Females
All ages	183	86	97	190	90	100	197	93	104	205	97	108
0-4	13	7	6	13	7	7	15	7	7	16	8	8
5-9	13	7	6	13	7	6	13	7	7	15	7	7
10-14	16	8	8	13	7	6	13	7	6	13	7	7
15-19	15	7	7	16	8	8	13	7	6	13	7	6
20-24	12	6	6	15	7	7	16	8	8	13	7	6
25-29	8	4	4	12	6	6	15	7	7	16	8	8
30-34	11	5	6	8	4	4	12	6	6	15	7	7
35-39	14	6	8	11	5	6	8	4	4	12	6	6
40-44	16	7	9	14	6	8	11	5	6	8	4	4
45-49	15	7	8	16	7	9	14	6	8	11	5	6
50-54	12	6	7	15	7	8	16	7	9	14	6	8
55-59	11	5	6	12	5	7	15	6	8	15	7	8
60-64	8	4	5	11	5	6	12	5	7	14	6	8
65-69	6	3	3	8	3	4	10	4	6	11	5	6
70-74	5	2	3	5	2	3	7	3	4	9	4	5
75-79	3	1	2	4	2	2	4	2	3	6	2	3
80-84	2	1	1	2	1	1	3	1	2	3	1	2
85-89	1	0	1	1	0	1	1	0	1	2	0	1
90-94	0	0	0	0	0	0	0	0	0	1	0	0
95-99	0	0	0	0	0	0	0	0	0	0	0	0
100 +	0	0	0	0	0	0	0	0	0	0	0	0

Age group	2025 Both sexes	2025 Males	2025 Females	2030 Both sexes	2030 Males	2030 Females	2035 Both sexes	2035 Males	2035 Females	2040 Both sexes	2040 Males	2040 Females
All ages	213	101	112	219	105	115	224	107	117	228	110	118
0-4	16	8	8	16	8	8	15	8	7	16	8	8
5-9	16	8	8	16	8	8	16	8	8	15	8	7
10-14	15	7	7	16	8	8	16	8	8	16	8	8
15-19	13	7	7	15	7	7	16	8	8	16	8	8
20-24	13	7	6	13	7	7	15	7	7	16	8	8
25-29	13	7	6	13	7	6	13	7	7	15	7	7
30-34	16	8	8	13	7	6	13	7	6	13	7	7
35-39	15	7	7	15	8	8	13	7	6	13	7	6
40-44	12	6	6	15	7	7	13	7	6	13	7	6
45-49	8	4	4	12	6	6	14	7	7	15	8	8
50-54	11	5	6	8	4	4	12	6	6	14	7	7
55-59	14	6	7	11	5	6	8	4	4	12	6	6
60-64	15	7	8	13	6	7	10	5	6	7	4	4
65-69	13	6	8	14	6	8	12	5	7	10	4	5
70-74	10	4	6	12	5	7	13	5	7	11	5	7
75-79	7	3	4	8	3	5	10	4	6	11	4	7
80-84	4	1	3	5	2	4	6	2	4	8	3	5
85-89	2	1	1	3	1	2	3	1	2	4	1	3
90-94	1	0	1	1	0	1	1	0	1	2	0	1
95-99	0	0	0	0	0	0	0	0	0	0	0	0
100 +	0	0	0	0	0	0	0	0	0	0	0	0

Age group	2045 Both sexes	2045 Males	2045 Females	2050 Both sexes	2050 Males	2050 Females
All ages	232	113	120	238	116	122
0-4	17	9	8	18	9	9
5-9	16	8	8	17	9	8
10-14	15	8	7	16	8	8
15-19	16	8	8	15	8	7
20-24	16	8	8	16	8	8
25-29	16	8	8	16	8	8
30-34	15	7	7	16	8	8
35-39	13	7	7	14	7	7
40-44	13	7	6	13	7	6
45-49	13	6	6	13	7	6
50-54	15	8	8	13	6	6
55-59	14	7	7	15	7	8
60-64	12	6	6	14	7	7
65-69	7	3	4	11	5	6
70-74	9	4	5	6	3	3
75-79	10	4	6	8	3	5
80-84	8	3	5	6	2	4
85-89	5	2	4	6	2	4
90-94	2	0	2	3	1	2
95-99	1	0	1	1	0	1
100 +	0	0	0	0	0	0

United Nations Department of Economic and Social Affairs/Population Division
World Population Prospects: The 2004 Revision, Volume II: Sex and Age Distribution of the World Population

636

POPULATION BY AGE AND SEX (in thousands)

Age group	2005 Both sexes	2005 Males	2005 Females	2010 Both sexes	2010 Males	2010 Females	2015 Both sexes	2015 Males	2015 Females	2020 Both sexes	2020 Males	2020 Females
All ages	183	86	97	187	88	99	189	89	100	190	90	101
0-4	13	7	6	11	5	5	9	5	5	9	5	4
5-9	13	7	6	13	7	6	11	5	5	9	5	5
10-14	16	8	8	13	7	6	13	7	6	11	5	5
15-19	15	7	7	16	8	8	13	7	6	13	7	6
20-24	12	6	6	15	7	7	16	8	8	13	7	6
25-29	8	4	4	12	6	6	15	7	7	16	8	8
30-34	11	5	6	8	4	4	12	6	6	15	7	7
35-39	14	6	8	11	5	6	8	4	4	12	6	6
40-44	16	7	9	14	6	8	11	5	6	8	4	4
45-49	15	7	8	16	7	9	14	6	8	11	5	6
50-54	12	6	7	15	7	8	16	7	9	14	6	8
55-59	11	5	6	12	5	7	15	6	8	15	7	8
60-64	8	4	5	11	5	6	12	5	7	14	6	8
65-69	6	3	3	8	3	4	10	4	6	11	5	6
70-74	5	2	3	5	2	3	7	3	4	9	4	5
75-79	3	1	2	4	2	2	4	2	3	6	2	3
80-84	2	1	1	2	1	1	3	1	2	3	1	2
85-89	1	0	1	1	0	1	1	0	1	2	0	1
90-94	0	0	0	0	0	0	0	0	0	1	0	0
95-99	0	0	0	0	0	0	0	0	0	0	0	0
100 +	0	0	0	0	0	0	0	0	0	0	0	0

Age group	2025 Both sexes	2025 Males	2025 Females	2030 Both sexes	2030 Males	2030 Females	2035 Both sexes	2035 Males	2035 Females	2040 Both sexes	2040 Males	2040 Females
All ages	191	90	101	191	90	101	188	89	99	184	87	97
0-4	9	5	5	9	5	4	8	4	4	8	4	4
5-9	9	5	4	9	5	5	9	5	4	8	4	4
10-14	9	5	5	9	5	4	9	5	5	9	5	4
15-19	11	5	5	9	5	5	9	5	4	9	5	5
20-24	13	7	6	11	5	5	9	5	5	9	5	4
25-29	13	7	6	13	7	6	10	5	5	9	5	5
30-34	16	8	8	13	7	6	13	7	6	10	5	5
35-39	15	7	7	15	8	8	13	7	6	13	7	6
40-44	12	6	6	15	7	7	15	8	8	13	7	6
45-49	8	4	4	12	6	6	14	7	7	15	8	8
50-54	11	5	6	8	4	4	12	6	6	14	7	7
55-59	14	6	7	11	5	6	8	4	4	13	6	6
60-64	15	7	8	13	6	7	10	5	6	7	4	4
65-69	13	6	8	14	6	8	12	5	7	10	4	5
70-74	10	4	6	12	5	7	13	5	7	11	5	7
75-79	7	3	4	8	3	5	10	4	6	11	4	7
80-84	4	1	3	5	2	4	6	2	4	8	3	5
85-89	2	1	1	3	1	2	3	1	2	4	1	3
90-94	1	0	1	1	0	1	1	0	1	2	0	1
95-99	0	0	0	0	0	0	0	0	0	0	0	0
100 +	0	0	0	0	0	0	0	0	0	0	0	0

Age group	2045 Both sexes	2045 Males	2045 Females	2050 Both sexes	2050 Males	2050 Females
All ages	179	85	94	173	83	90
0-4	7	3	3	6	3	3
5-9	8	4	4	7	3	3
10-14	8	4	4	8	4	4
15-19	9	5	4	8	4	4
20-24	9	5	5	9	5	4
25-29	9	5	4	9	5	5
30-34	9	5	5	9	5	4
35-39	10	5	5	9	5	5
40-44	13	7	6	10	5	5
45-49	13	6	6	13	7	6
50-54	15	8	8	13	6	6
55-59	14	7	7	15	7	8
60-64	12	6	6	14	7	7
65-69	7	3	4	11	5	6
70-74	9	4	5	6	3	3
75-79	10	4	6	8	3	5
80-84	8	3	5	8	3	5
85-89	5	2	4	6	2	4
90-94	2	0	2	3	1	2
95-99	1	0	1	1	0	1
100 +	0	0	0	0	0	0

POPULATION BY AGE AND SEX (in thousands)

Age group	1950 Both sexes	1950 Males	1950 Females	1955 Both sexes	1955 Males	1955 Females	1960 Both sexes	1960 Males	1960 Females	1965 Both sexes	1965 Males	1965 Females
All ages	65	34	31	68	36	32	78	41	37	91	48	43
0-4	9	5	4	9	5	5	12	6	6	14	7	7
5-9	8	4	4	8	4	4	10	5	5	12	6	6
10-14	7	3	3	7	4	3	8	4	4	10	5	5
15-19	6	3	3	6	3	3	7	4	3	8	4	4
20-24	5	3	3	6	3	3	6	3	3	8	4	3
25-29	5	3	2	5	3	2	6	3	3	7	3	3
30-34	4	2	2	5	3	2	5	3	2	6	3	3
35-39	4	2	2	4	2	2	5	3	2	6	3	3
40-44	4	3	2	5	3	2	5	3	2	5	3	2
45-49	3	2	1	4	2	2	4	2	2	4	2	2
50-54	3	1	1	3	1	1	3	2	1	4	2	2
55-59	2	1	1	2	1	1	2	1	1	3	2	1
60-64	1	1	1	2	1	1	2	1	1	2	1	1
65-69	1	1	1	1	1	1	1	1	1	1	1	1
70-74	1	0	0	1	0	0	1	0	0	1	0	0
75-79	0	0	0	0	0	0	0	0	0	1	0	0
80 +	0	0	0	0	0	0	0	0	0	0	0	0

Age group	1970 Both sexes	1970 Males	1970 Females	1975 Both sexes	1975 Males	1975 Females	1980 Both sexes	1980 Males	1980 Females	1985 Both sexes	1985 Males	1985 Females
All ages	105	55	50	129	67	62	143	73	69	155	79	76
0-4	16	8	8	18	9	9	18	9	9	18	9	9
5-9	14	7	7	17	8	8	18	9	9	18	9	9
10-14	12	6	6	15	8	7	17	9	9	18	9	9
15-19	10	5	5	13	7	6	15	8	7	17	9	8
20-24	9	5	4	11	6	5	12	6	6	14	7	7
25-29	8	4	4	10	5	5	11	6	5	12	6	6
30-34	7	4	3	9	5	4	10	5	5	11	6	6
35-39	7	3	3	8	4	4	9	5	4	10	5	5
40-44	6	3	3	7	4	3	8	4	4	9	5	4
45-49	5	2	2	6	3	3	6	3	3	7	4	3
50-54	4	2	2	4	2	2	5	3	2	6	3	3
55-59	3	2	2	3	2	2	4	2	2	5	2	2
60-64	2	1	1	3	2	1	3	2	1	3	2	2
65-69	2	1	1	2	1	1	2	1	1	3	1	1
70-74	1	0	0	1	1	1	2	1	1	2	1	1
75-79	1	0	0	1	0	0	1	0	1	1	1	1
80 +	0	0	0	1	0	0	1	0	0	1	0	0

Age group	1990 Both sexes	1990 Males	1990 Females	1995 Both sexes	1995 Males	1995 Females	2000 Both sexes	2000 Males	2000 Females	2005 Both sexes	2005 Males	2005 Females
All ages	171	87	84	193	99	94	215	110	105	237	122	115
0-4	19	10	9	21	11	10	22	11	11	22	11	11
5-9	18	9	9	20	11	10	21	11	10	23	12	11
10-14	18	9	9	19	10	9	21	11	10	22	12	11
15-19	18	9	9	18	9	9	19	10	9	21	11	10
20-24	16	8	8	18	9	9	17	9	9	18	9	9
25-29	14	7	7	17	8	8	18	9	9	18	9	9
30-34	13	6	6	16	8	8	18	9	9	20	10	9
35-39	11	6	5	13	7	7	17	9	8	19	10	9
40-44	10	5	5	11	6	6	14	7	7	17	9	8
45-49	9	5	4	10	6	5	12	6	6	14	7	7
50-54	7	4	3	8	5	4	10	6	5	11	6	5
55-59	6	3	3	7	3	3	8	4	4	10	5	5
60-64	4	2	2	5	3	2	6	3	3	8	4	4
65-69	3	1	2	4	2	2	4	2	2	6	3	3
70-74	2	1	1	2	1	1	3	2	2	4	2	2
75-79	2	1	1	2	1	1	2	1	1	3	1	1
80 +	1	0	1	2	1	1	2	1	1	2	1	1

United Nations Department of Economic and Social Affairs/Population Division
World Population Prospects: The 2004 Revision, Volume II: Sex and Age Distribution of the World Population

638

POPULATION BY AGE AND SEX (in thousands)

Age group	2005 Both sexes	2005 Males	2005 Females	2010 Both sexes	2010 Males	2010 Females	2015 Both sexes	2015 Males	2015 Females	2020 Both sexes	2020 Males	2020 Females
All ages	237	122	115	257	132	125	277	142	135	290	152	144
0-4	22	11	11	22	11	11	22	11	11	22	11	11
5-9	23	12	11	23	12	11	22	12	11	23	12	11
10-14	22	12	11	23	12	11	23	12	11	23	12	11
15-19	21	11	10	22	12	11	24	12	11	23	12	11
20-24	18	9	9	21	11	10	22	11	10	23	12	11
25-29	18	9	9	19	10	9	21	11	10	22	12	11
30-34	20	10	9	19	10	9	20	10	10	22	12	11
35-39	19	10	9	20	11	10	20	10	10	21	11	10
40-44	17	9	8	19	10	9	21	11	10	20	10	10
45-49	14	7	7	17	9	8	19	10	9	21	11	10
50-54	11	6	5	14	7	7	17	9	8	19	10	9
55-59	10	5	5	11	6	5	13	7	7	17	9	8
60-64	8	4	4	9	5	4	11	5	5	13	6	6
65-69	6	3	3	7	4	3	9	4	4	10	5	5
70-74	4	2	2	5	2	3	6	3	3	8	4	4
75-79	3	1	1	3	1	2	4	2	2	5	2	3
80-84	1	1	1	2	1	1	2	1	1	3	1	2
85-89	1	0	0	1	0	0	1	0	1	1	0	1
90-94	0	0	0	0	0	0	0	0	0	0	0	0
95-99	0	0	0	0	0	0	0	0	0	0	0	0
100 +	0	0	0	0	0	0	0	0	0	0	0	0

Age group	2025 Both sexes	2025 Males	2025 Females	2030 Both sexes	2030 Males	2030 Females	2035 Both sexes	2035 Males	2035 Females	2040 Both sexes	2040 Males	2040 Females
All ages	314	161	153	331	169	162	346	177	169	359	183	176
0-4	22	11	11	22	11	11	22	11	11	22	11	10
5-9	23	12	11	23	12	11	23	12	11	23	12	11
10-14	23	12	11	24	12	11	24	12	12	24	12	11
15-19	23	12	11	23	12	11	24	12	11	24	12	12
20-24	23	12	11	23	12	11	23	12	11	23	12	11
25-29	24	12	11	23	12	11	23	12	11	23	12	11
30-34	23	12	11	25	13	12	25	13	12	24	13	12
35-39	23	12	11	24	13	11	26	13	12	25	13	12
40-44	21	11	10	23	12	11	25	13	12	26	13	12
45-49	20	10	10	21	11	10	24	12	11	25	13	12
50-54	21	11	10	20	10	10	21	11	10	23	12	11
55-59	19	10	9	20	10	10	20	10	10	21	11	10
60-64	16	8	8	18	9	9	19	10	9	19	10	9
65-69	12	6	6	15	7	7	17	8	8	18	9	9
70-74	9	4	4	11	5	6	13	7	7	15	7	8
75-79	6	3	3	7	3	4	9	4	5	11	5	6
80-84	4	2	2	5	2	3	6	2	3	7	3	4
85-89	2	1	1	2	1	1	3	1	2	4	1	2
90-94	1	0	0	1	0	1	1	0	1	2	0	1
95-99	0	0	0	0	0	0	0	0	0	0	0	0
100 +	0	0	0	0	0	0	0	0	0	0	0	0

Age group	2045 Both sexes	2045 Males	2045 Females	2050 Both sexes	2050 Males	2050 Females
All ages	371	189	182	382	195	187
0-4	22	11	11	22	11	11
5-9	22	11	11	22	12	11
10-14	23	12	11	23	12	11
15-19	24	12	11	23	12	11
20-24	24	12	11	24	12	11
25-29	24	12	12	24	12	12
30-34	25	13	12	25	13	12
35-39	25	13	12	25	13	12
40-44	26	13	12	26	13	12
45-49	26	14	12	26	13	12
50-54	25	13	12	26	14	12
55-59	23	12	11	24	13	11
60-64	20	10	10	22	12	11
65-69	18	9	9	19	10	9
70-74	17	8	8	17	8	8
75-79	13	6	7	15	7	8
80-84	9	4	5	10	5	6
85-89	5	2	3	6	2	4
90-94	2	1	1	3	1	2
95-99	1	0	0	1	0	1
100 +	0	0	0	0	0	0

POPULATION BY AGE AND SEX (in thousands)

Age group	2005 Both sexes	Males	Females	2010 Both sexes	Males	Females	2015 Both sexes	Males	Females	2020 Both sexes	Males	Females
All ages	237	122	115	260	133	126	283	145	138	307	158	150
0-4	22	11	11	24	12	12	26	13	13	27	14	13
5-9	23	12	11	23	12	11	25	13	12	26	14	13
10-14	22	12	11	23	12	11	23	12	11	25	13	12
15-19	21	11	10	22	12	11	24	12	11	23	12	11
20-24	18	9	9	21	11	10	22	11	10	23	12	11
25-29	18	9	9	19	10	9	21	11	10	22	12	11
30-34	20	10	9	19	10	9	20	10	10	22	12	11
35-39	19	10	9	20	11	10	20	10	10	21	11	10
40-44	17	9	8	19	10	9	21	11	10	20	10	10
45-49	14	7	7	17	9	8	19	10	9	21	11	10
50-54	11	6	5	14	7	7	17	9	8	19	10	9
55-59	10	5	5	11	6	5	13	7	7	17	9	8
60-64	8	4	4	9	5	4	11	5	5	13	6	6
65-69	6	3	3	7	4	3	9	4	4	10	5	5
70-74	4	2	2	5	2	3	6	3	3	8	4	4
75-79	3	1	1	3	1	2	4	2	2	5	2	3
80-84	1	1	1	2	1	1	2	1	1	3	1	2
85-89	1	0	0	1	0	0	1	0	1	1	0	1
90-94	0	0	0	0	0	0	0	0	0	0	0	0
95-99	0	0	0	0	0	0	0	0	0	0	0	0
100 +	0	0	0	0	0	0	0	0	0	0	0	0

Age group	2025 Both sexes	Males	Females	2030 Both sexes	Males	Females	2035 Both sexes	Males	Females	2040 Both sexes	Males	Females
All ages	331	170	162	354	181	173	376	192	184	399	204	195
0-4	28	14	14	28	15	14	29	15	14	30	16	15
5-9	28	14	14	29	15	14	29	15	14	30	15	15
10-14	27	14	13	29	15	14	29	15	14	30	15	14
15-19	26	13	12	27	14	13	29	15	14	29	15	14
20-24	23	12	11	25	13	12	27	14	13	29	15	14
25-29	24	12	11	23	12	11	26	13	12	27	14	13
30-34	23	12	11	25	13	12	25	13	12	27	14	13
35-39	23	12	11	24	13	11	26	13	12	25	13	12
40-44	21	11	10	23	12	11	25	13	12	26	13	12
45-49	20	10	10	21	11	10	24	12	11	25	13	12
50-54	21	11	10	20	10	10	21	11	10	23	12	11
55-59	19	10	9	20	10	10	20	10	10	21	11	10
60-64	16	8	8	18	9	9	19	10	9	19	10	9
65-69	12	6	6	15	7	7	17	8	8	18	9	9
70-74	9	4	4	11	5	6	13	7	7	15	7	8
75-79	6	3	3	7	3	4	9	4	5	11	5	6
80-84	4	2	2	5	2	3	6	2	3	7	3	4
85-89	2	1	1	2	1	1	3	1	2	4	1	2
90-94	1	0	0	1	0	1	1	0	1	2	0	1
95-99	0	0	0	0	0	0	0	0	0	0	0	0
100 +	0	0	0	0	0	0	0	0	0	0	0	0

Age group	2045 Both sexes	Males	Females	2050 Both sexes	Males	Females
All ages	421	215	206	443	226	217
0-4	32	16	16	33	17	16
5-9	31	16	15	33	17	16
10-14	31	16	15	32	16	15
15-19	30	15	15	31	16	15
20-24	29	15	14	30	15	14
25-29	29	15	14	30	15	14
30-34	28	15	14	30	16	14
35-39	28	14	13	29	15	14
40-44	26	13	12	28	15	13
45-49	26	14	12	26	13	12
50-54	25	13	12	26	14	12
55-59	23	12	11	24	13	11
60-64	20	10	10	22	12	11
65-69	18	9	9	19	10	9
70-74	17	8	8	17	8	8
75-79	13	6	7	15	7	8
80-84	9	4	5	10	5	6
85-89	5	2	3	6	2	4
90-94	2	1	1	3	1	2
95-99	1	0	0	1	0	1
100 +	0	0	0	0	0	0

United Nations Department of Economic and Social Affairs/Population Division
World Population Prospects: The 2004 Revision, Volume II: Sex and Age Distribution of the World Population

640

POPULATION BY AGE AND SEX (in thousands)

Age group	2005 Both sexes	2005 Males	2005 Females	2010 Both sexes	2010 Males	2010 Females	2015 Both sexes	2015 Males	2015 Females	2020 Both sexes	2020 Males	2020 Females
All ages	237	122	115	255	131	124	271	139	132	285	146	139
0-4	22	11	11	19	10	9	18	9	9	17	9	8
5-9	23	12	11	23	12	11	20	10	10	19	10	9
10-14	22	12	11	23	12	11	23	12	11	21	11	10
15-19	21	11	10	22	12	11	24	12	11	23	12	11
20-24	18	9	9	21	11	10	22	11	10	23	12	11
25-29	18	9	9	19	10	9	21	11	10	22	12	11
30-34	20	10	9	19	10	9	20	10	10	22	12	11
35-39	19	10	9	20	11	10	20	10	10	21	11	10
40-44	17	9	8	19	10	9	21	11	10	20	10	10
45-49	14	7	7	17	9	8	19	10	9	21	11	10
50-54	11	6	5	14	7	7	17	9	8	19	10	9
55-59	10	5	5	11	6	5	13	7	7	17	9	8
60-64	8	4	4	9	5	4	11	5	5	13	6	6
65-69	6	3	3	7	4	3	9	4	4	10	5	5
70-74	4	2	2	5	2	3	6	3	3	8	4	4
75-79	3	1	1	3	1	2	4	2	2	5	2	3
80-84	1	1	1	2	1	1	2	1	1	3	1	2
85-89	1	0	0	1	0	0	1	0	1	1	0	1
90-94	0	0	0	0	0	0	0	0	0	0	0	0
95-99	0	0	0	0	0	0	0	0	0	0	0	0
100 +	0	0	0	0	0	0	0	0	0	0	0	0

Age group	2025 Both sexes	2025 Males	2025 Females	2030 Both sexes	2030 Males	2030 Females	2035 Both sexes	2035 Males	2035 Females	2040 Both sexes	2040 Males	2040 Females
All ages	297	152	145	308	158	151	316	162	155	322	165	158
0-4	17	9	8	16	8	8	15	8	7	14	7	7
5-9	18	9	9	18	9	9	17	9	8	16	8	8
10-14	19	10	9	18	9	9	18	9	9	18	9	9
15-19	21	11	10	19	10	9	18	10	9	18	9	9
20-24	23	12	11	21	11	10	19	10	9	18	9	9
25-29	24	12	11	23	12	11	21	11	10	20	10	9
30-34	23	12	11	25	13	12	25	13	12	22	12	11
35-39	23	12	11	24	13	11	26	13	12	25	13	12
40-44	21	11	10	23	12	11	25	13	12	26	13	12
45-49	20	10	10	21	11	10	24	12	11	25	13	12
50-54	21	11	10	20	10	10	21	11	10	23	12	11
55-59	19	10	9	20	10	10	20	10	10	21	11	10
60-64	16	8	8	18	9	9	19	10	9	19	10	9
65-69	12	6	6	15	7	7	17	8	8	18	9	9
70-74	9	4	4	11	5	6	13	7	7	15	7	8
75-79	6	3	3	7	3	4	9	4	5	11	5	6
80-84	4	2	2	5	2	3	6	2	3	7	3	4
85-89	2	1	1	2	1	1	3	1	2	4	1	2
90-94	1	0	0	1	0	1	1	0	1	2	0	1
95-99	0	0	0	0	0	0	0	0	0	0	0	0
100 +	0	0	0	0	0	0	0	0	0	0	0	0

Age group	2045 Both sexes	2045 Males	2045 Females	2050 Both sexes	2050 Males	2050 Females
All ages	326	166	160	328	167	161
0-4	13	7	6	13	7	6
5-9	15	8	7	14	7	7
10-14	17	9	8	16	8	7
15-19	18	9	9	17	9	8
20-24	18	9	9	18	9	8
25-29	19	10	9	19	10	9
30-34	21	11	10	20	10	9
35-39	23	12	11	22	11	10
40-44	26	13	12	23	12	11
45-49	26	14	12	26	13	12
50-54	25	13	12	26	14	12
55-59	23	12	11	24	13	11
60-64	20	10	10	22	12	11
65-69	18	9	9	19	10	9
70-74	17	8	8	17	8	8
75-79	13	6	7	15	7	8
80-84	9	4	5	10	5	6
85-89	5	2	3	6	2	4
90-94	2	1	1	3	1	2
95-99	1	0	0	1	0	1
100 +	0	0	0	0	0	0

POPULATION BY AGE AND SEX (in thousands)

Age group	1950			1955			1960			1965		
	Both sexes	Males	Females	Both sexes	Males	Females	Both sexes	Males	Females	Both sexes	Males	Females
All ages	1 908	959	949	2 136	1 075	1 061	2 372	1 192	1 180	2 628	1 318	1 310
0-4	232	119	113	253	130	123	289	148	141	303	155	148
5-9	177	90	87	232	118	114	254	129	125	293	149	144
10-14	146	74	72	182	93	89	237	121	116	261	134	127
15-19	133	68	65	149	76	73	183	94	89	243	124	119
20-24	140	72	68	138	71	67	152	77	75	187	96	91
25-29	143	71	72	153	80	73	146	75	71	164	83	81
30-34	136	67	69	153	78	75	158	82	76	148	76	72
35-39	137	69	68	140	69	71	154	78	76	162	84	78
40-44	127	65	62	140	70	70	143	71	72	158	80	78
45-49	109	56	53	126	64	62	139	70	69	143	71	72
50-54	95	47	48	110	56	54	124	63	61	136	68	68
55-59	83	40	43	90	44	46	103	52	51	119	60	59
60-64	79	39	40	78	37	41	85	41	44	97	48	49
65-69	69	34	35	70	33	37	69	31	38	78	36	42
70-74	52	25	27	57	26	31	58	26	32	57	23	34
75-79	29	14	15	38	18	20	43	19	24	41	16	25
80 +	21	9	12	27	12	15	35	15	20	38	15	23

Age group	1970			1975			1980			1985		
	Both sexes	Males	Females	Both sexes	Males	Females	Both sexes	Males	Females	Both sexes	Males	Females
All ages	2 820	1 409	1 410	3 083	1 538	1 545	3 113	1 549	1 564	3 247	1 609	1 638
0-4	297	151	145	303	154	148	248	126	121	248	127	121
5-9	304	155	148	304	155	149	284	145	139	253	129	124
10-14	295	150	145	318	162	156	300	153	147	290	148	142
15-19	262	134	128	298	152	146	302	154	147	299	152	146
20-24	230	118	112	256	131	125	268	137	131	281	142	139
25-29	183	92	91	242	122	120	237	118	119	266	132	133
30-34	164	82	81	199	101	98	235	118	117	245	121	124
35-39	148	75	73	167	85	83	189	95	94	239	119	120
40-44	160	83	78	156	80	77	167	84	83	190	96	95
45-49	156	79	77	159	81	78	146	74	72	165	83	82
50-54	139	69	71	156	78	78	153	79	75	144	73	71
55-59	131	64	66	132	64	68	146	73	73	148	76	73
60-64	112	55	57	124	60	65	127	60	67	138	67	71
65-69	88	42	46	101	47	54	113	52	61	114	52	62
70-74	66	28	37	75	33	42	87	38	49	95	42	53
75-79	43	16	27	48	19	29	57	23	34	67	27	40
80 +	43	15	27	44	15	30	53	17	36	64	21	43

Age group	1990			1995			2000			2005		
	Both sexes	Males	Females	Both sexes	Males	Females	Both sexes	Males	Females	Both sexes	Males	Females
All ages	3 411	1 682	1 728	3 658	1 802	1 856	3 818	1 872	1 946	4 028	1 980	2 049
0-4	278	142	136	283	146	137	281	145	137	274	141	133
5-9	255	131	124	291	150	142	292	151	141	286	147	139
10-14	265	135	130	267	138	130	300	154	146	299	155	145
15-19	292	149	144	266	135	130	267	137	130	311	159	151
20-24	278	139	138	275	137	138	245	121	124	277	142	135
25-29	276	135	141	276	134	142	259	123	136	251	124	127
30-34	273	134	139	297	144	152	290	139	152	265	126	140
35-39	250	124	126	288	141	147	309	150	159	296	141	155
40-44	234	117	117	258	127	131	287	140	147	313	152	162
45-49	187	94	93	244	122	122	255	126	130	289	141	148
50-54	160	80	80	189	95	94	241	120	121	254	125	129
55-59	142	71	70	160	80	80	185	92	93	237	118	119
60-64	143	71	71	137	68	68	154	76	78	179	89	90
65-69	127	60	67	134	66	68	127	63	65	145	71	74
70-74	100	44	56	115	52	62	120	57	63	115	55	60
75-79	76	31	45	83	34	49	96	42	54	102	47	55
80 +	77	25	51	95	32	63	111	38	73	133	48	85

United Nations Department of Economic and Social Affairs/Population Division
World Population Prospects: The 2004 Revision, Volume II: Sex and Age Distribution of the World Population

642

POPULATION BY AGE AND SEX (in thousands)

Age group	2005 Both sexes	Males	Females	2010 Both sexes	Males	Females	2015 Both sexes	Males	Females	2020 Both sexes	Males	Females
All ages	4 020	1 900	2 049	4 172	2 054	2 118	4 302	2 121	2 181	4 425	2 183	2 241
0-4	274	141	133	269	138	131	265	137	129	268	138	130
5-9	286	147	139	276	142	134	271	139	131	267	137	130
10-14	299	155	145	289	148	140	278	143	135	273	140	133
15-19	311	159	151	302	156	146	292	150	142	281	145	137
20-24	277	142	135	313	161	153	305	158	147	295	151	143
25-29	251	124	127	278	142	136	315	161	154	307	159	148
30-34	265	126	140	253	125	128	280	143	137	317	162	155
35-39	296	141	155	267	126	140	254	125	129	282	143	138
40-44	313	152	162	297	141	155	267	126	141	255	126	130
45-49	289	141	148	312	151	161	296	141	155	267	126	141
50-54	254	125	129	286	139	147	309	149	160	294	140	154
55-59	237	118	119	250	122	127	281	136	145	305	147	158
60-64	179	89	90	229	113	116	242	118	124	273	131	142
65-69	145	71	74	169	83	86	217	106	111	230	111	119
70-74	115	55	60	132	63	69	154	74	80	199	95	104
75-79	102	47	55	99	45	53	114	52	62	134	62	72
80-84	73	29	44	78	33	45	77	33	44	90	39	51
85-89	39	13	26	47	17	30	52	20	32	52	20	31
90-94	16	5	12	19	6	14	24	8	16	27	9	18
95-99	4	1	3	5	1	4	7	2	5	9	2	6
100 +	1	0	0	1	0	1	1	0	1	2	0	1

Age group	2025 Both sexes	Males	Females	2030 Both sexes	Males	Females	2035 Both sexes	Males	Females	2040 Both sexes	Males	Females
All ages	4 539	2 241	2 298	4 635	2 289	2 346	4 704	2 324	2 380	4 749	2 348	2 401
0-4	272	140	132	269	138	130	262	135	127	256	132	124
5-9	269	139	131	273	141	133	270	139	131	263	135	128
10-14	269	139	131	272	140	132	276	142	134	273	140	132
15-19	276	142	134	273	140	132	275	142	134	279	144	136
20-24	285	146	138	279	144	136	276	142	134	278	143	135
25-29	297	152	144	286	147	139	281	145	137	278	143	135
30-34	309	159	150	299	153	146	288	148	140	283	146	138
35-39	318	162	156	310	160	151	300	154	147	290	149	141
40-44	282	144	139	319	163	156	311	160	151	301	154	147
45-49	255	125	130	282	144	139	319	162	156	311	160	151
50-54	265	125	140	254	125	129	281	143	138	317	161	156
55-59	290	137	152	262	123	139	251	123	128	278	141	137
60-64	296	142	155	282	133	149	256	120	136	245	119	126
65-69	260	124	136	283	134	149	271	126	144	245	114	132
70-74	212	100	112	241	113	129	263	122	141	253	116	137
75-79	174	80	94	187	85	102	214	97	117	234	105	129
80-84	107	47	60	140	61	79	152	66	86	175	75	100
85-89	62	24	37	75	30	45	99	40	59	109	43	66
90-94	28	10	18	34	12	22	42	15	27	57	21	37
95-99	10	3	7	11	3	8	14	4	10	17	5	12
100 +	2	0	2	3	1	2	3	1	2	4	1	3

Age group	2045 Both sexes	Males	Females	2050 Both sexes	Males	Females
All ages	4 775	2 364	2 411	4 790	2 376	2 414
0-4	253	130	123	253	130	123
5-9	258	133	125	255	131	124
10-14	266	137	129	260	134	126
15-19	276	142	134	269	139	131
20-24	283	145	137	279	144	136
25-29	281	144	136	285	147	138
30-34	280	144	136	283	145	137
35-39	285	146	139	282	145	137
40-44	291	149	142	286	147	140
45-49	301	154	147	292	149	142
50-54	310	159	151	300	153	147
55-59	314	159	154	307	157	150
60-64	272	137	135	307	155	152
65-69	236	114	122	262	131	131
70-74	230	105	125	221	105	116
75-79	226	100	125	206	91	115
80-84	193	83	111	188	79	109
85-89	127	50	77	142	56	86
90-94	64	23	41	77	27	50
95-99	24	7	17	28	8	20
100 +	5	1	4	7	2	5

United Nations Department of Economic and Social Affairs/Population Division
World Population Prospects: The 2004 Revision, Volume II: Sex and Age Distribution of the World Population

643

POPULATION BY AGE AND SEX (in thousands)

Age group	2005 Both sexes	2005 Males	2005 Females	2010 Both sexes	2010 Males	2010 Females	2015 Both sexes	2015 Males	2015 Females	2020 Both sexes	2020 Males	2020 Females
All ages	4 028	1 980	2 049	4 206	2 071	2 134	4 393	2 167	2 225	4 589	2 268	2 321
0-4	274	141	133	303	156	147	322	166	157	342	176	166
5-9	286	147	139	276	142	134	304	157	148	324	167	157
10-14	299	155	145	289	148	140	278	143	135	307	158	149
15-19	311	159	151	302	156	146	292	150	142	281	145	137
20-24	277	142	135	313	161	153	305	158	147	295	151	143
25-29	251	124	127	278	142	136	315	161	154	307	159	148
30-34	265	126	140	253	125	128	280	143	137	317	162	155
35-39	296	141	155	267	126	140	254	125	129	282	143	138
40-44	313	152	162	297	141	155	267	126	141	255	126	130
45-49	289	141	148	312	151	161	296	141	155	267	126	141
50-54	254	125	129	286	139	147	309	149	160	294	140	154
55-59	237	118	119	250	122	127	281	136	145	305	147	158
60-64	179	89	90	229	113	116	242	118	124	273	131	142
65-69	145	71	74	169	83	86	217	106	111	230	111	119
70-74	115	55	60	132	63	69	154	74	80	199	95	104
75-79	102	47	55	99	45	53	114	52	62	134	62	72
80-84	73	29	44	78	33	45	77	33	44	90	39	51
85-89	39	13	26	47	17	30	52	20	32	52	20	31
90-94	16	5	12	19	6	14	24	8	16	27	9	18
95-99	4	1	3	5	1	4	7	2	5	9	2	6
100 +	1	0	0	1	0	1	1	0	1	2	0	1

Age group	2025 Both sexes	2025 Males	2025 Females	2030 Both sexes	2030 Males	2030 Females	2035 Both sexes	2035 Males	2035 Females	2040 Both sexes	2040 Males	2040 Females
All ages	4 777	2 363	2 413	4 945	2 449	2 496	5 097	2 526	2 571	5 245	2 603	2 642
0-4	345	178	168	342	176	166	344	177	167	360	185	175
5-9	343	176	167	347	178	168	343	177	167	346	178	168
10-14	326	168	158	345	178	168	349	180	169	346	178	168
15-19	310	159	151	329	170	160	349	179	169	353	181	171
20-24	285	146	138	313	161	152	333	171	161	352	181	171
25-29	297	152	144	286	147	139	315	162	153	335	172	162
30-34	309	159	150	299	153	146	288	148	140	317	163	154
35-39	318	162	156	310	160	151	300	154	147	290	149	141
40-44	282	144	139	319	163	156	311	160	151	301	154	147
45-49	255	125	130	282	144	139	319	162	156	311	160	151
50-54	265	125	140	254	125	129	281	143	138	317	161	156
55-59	290	137	152	262	123	139	251	123	128	278	141	137
60-64	296	142	155	282	133	149	256	120	136	245	119	126
65-69	260	124	136	283	134	149	271	126	144	245	114	132
70-74	212	100	112	241	113	129	263	122	141	253	116	137
75-79	174	80	94	187	85	102	214	97	117	234	105	129
80-84	107	47	60	140	61	79	152	66	86	175	75	100
85-89	62	24	37	75	30	45	99	40	59	109	43	66
90-94	28	10	18	34	12	22	42	15	27	57	21	37
95-99	10	3	7	11	3	8	14	4	10	17	5	12
100 +	2	0	2	3	1	2	3	1	2	4	1	3

Age group	2045 Both sexes	2045 Males	2045 Females	2050 Both sexes	2050 Males	2050 Females
All ages	5 397	2 684	2 713	5 555	2 769	2 785
0-4	380	196	184	396	204	192
5-9	361	186	175	382	196	185
10-14	348	179	169	363	187	176
15-19	349	180	169	352	181	171
20-24	356	183	173	352	181	171
25-29	354	182	172	358	184	174
30-34	337	173	164	356	183	173
35-39	319	164	155	338	174	165
40-44	291	149	142	320	164	156
45-49	301	154	147	292	149	142
50-54	310	159	151	300	153	147
55-59	314	159	154	307	157	150
60-64	272	137	135	307	155	152
65-69	236	114	122	262	131	131
70-74	230	105	125	221	105	116
75-79	226	100	125	206	91	115
80-84	193	83	111	188	79	109
85-89	127	50	77	142	56	86
90-94	64	23	41	77	27	50
95-99	24	7	17	28	8	20
100 +	5	1	4	7	2	5

United Nations Department of Economic and Social Affairs/Population Division
World Population Prospects: The 2004 Revision, Volume II: Sex and Age Distribution of the World Population

POPULATION BY AGE AND SEX (in thousands)

Age group	2005 Both sexes	2005 Males	2005 Females	2010 Both sexes	2010 Males	2010 Females	2015 Both sexes	2015 Males	2015 Females	2020 Both sexes	2020 Males	2020 Females
All ages	4 020	1 900	2 049	4 130	2 030	2 102	4 212	2 075	2 138	4 202	2 099	2 102
0-4	274	141	133	235	121	114	209	108	102	195	100	95
5-9	286	147	139	276	142	134	237	122	115	211	108	102
10-14	299	155	145	289	148	140	278	143	135	239	123	116
15-19	311	159	151	302	156	146	292	150	142	281	145	137
20-24	277	142	135	313	161	153	305	158	147	295	151	143
25-29	251	124	127	278	142	136	315	161	154	307	159	148
30-34	265	126	140	253	125	128	280	143	137	317	162	155
35-39	296	141	155	267	126	140	254	125	129	282	143	138
40-44	313	152	162	297	141	155	267	126	141	255	126	130
45-49	289	141	148	312	151	161	296	141	155	267	126	141
50-54	254	125	129	286	139	147	309	149	160	294	140	154
55-59	237	118	119	250	122	127	281	136	145	305	147	158
60-64	179	89	90	229	113	116	242	118	124	273	131	142
65-69	145	71	74	169	83	86	217	106	111	230	111	119
70-74	115	55	60	132	63	69	154	74	80	199	95	104
75-79	102	47	55	99	45	53	114	52	62	134	62	72
80-84	73	29	44	78	33	45	77	33	44	90	39	51
85-89	39	13	26	47	17	30	52	20	32	52	20	31
90-94	16	5	12	19	6	14	24	8	16	27	9	18
95-99	4	1	3	5	1	4	7	2	5	9	2	6
100 +	1	0	0	1	0	1	1	0	1	2	0	1

Age group	2025 Both sexes	2025 Males	2025 Females	2030 Both sexes	2030 Males	2030 Females	2035 Both sexes	2035 Males	2035 Females	2040 Both sexes	2040 Males	2040 Females
All ages	4 303	2 119	2 183	4 326	2 130	2 196	4 321	2 127	2 194	4 283	2 108	2 175
0-4	198	102	96	196	101	95	187	96	91	173	89	84
5-9	196	101	95	200	103	97	198	102	96	189	97	92
10-14	213	110	104	199	102	97	202	104	98	200	103	97
15-19	243	125	118	217	111	105	202	104	98	206	106	100
20-24	285	146	138	246	126	119	220	113	107	206	106	100
25-29	297	152	144	286	147	139	248	127	120	222	114	108
30-34	309	159	150	299	153	146	288	148	140	250	128	122
35-39	318	162	156	310	160	151	300	154	147	290	149	141
40-44	282	144	139	319	163	156	311	160	151	301	154	147
45-49	255	125	130	282	144	139	319	162	156	311	160	151
50-54	265	125	140	254	125	129	281	143	138	317	161	156
55-59	290	137	152	262	123	139	251	123	128	278	141	137
60-64	296	142	155	282	133	149	256	120	136	245	119	126
65-69	260	124	136	283	134	149	271	126	144	245	114	132
70-74	212	100	112	241	113	129	263	122	141	253	116	137
75-79	174	80	94	187	85	102	214	97	117	234	105	129
80-84	107	47	60	140	61	79	152	66	86	175	75	100
85-89	62	24	37	75	30	45	99	40	59	109	43	66
90-94	28	10	18	34	12	22	42	15	27	57	21	37
95-99	10	3	7	11	3	8	14	4	10	17	5	12
100 +	2	0	2	3	1	2	3	1	2	4	1	3

Age group	2045 Both sexes	2045 Males	2045 Females	2050 Both sexes	2050 Males	2050 Females
All ages	4 213	2 075	2 138	4 120	2 032	2 089
0-4	157	81	76	146	75	71
5-9	174	90	85	159	82	77
10-14	191	98	93	177	91	86
15-19	204	105	99	195	100	94
20-24	209	108	101	207	107	101
25-29	208	107	101	211	109	103
30-34	224	115	109	210	108	102
35-39	252	129	123	226	116	110
40-44	291	149	142	253	130	123
45-49	301	154	147	292	149	142
50-54	310	159	151	300	153	147
55-59	314	159	154	307	157	150
60-64	272	137	135	307	155	152
65-69	236	114	122	262	131	131
70-74	230	105	125	221	105	116
75-79	226	100	125	206	91	115
80-84	193	83	111	188	79	109
85-89	127	50	77	142	56	86
90-94	64	23	41	77	27	50
95-99	24	7	17	28	8	20
100 +	5	1	4	7	2	5

United Nations Department of Economic and Social Affairs/Population Division
World Population Prospects: The 2004 Revision, Volume II: Sex and Age Distribution of the World Population

645

POPULATION BY AGE AND SEX (in thousands)

Age group	1950 Both sexes	1950 Males	1950 Females	1955 Both sexes	1955 Males	1955 Females	1960 Both sexes	1960 Males	1960 Females	1965 Both sexes	1965 Males	1965 Females
All ages	1 190	591	599	1 383	687	696	1 617	805	813	1 898	945	953
0-4	217	110	107	278	141	137	321	163	158	372	189	183
5-9	167	85	82	200	101	98	259	131	128	302	153	149
10-14	145	73	71	162	82	80	195	99	96	253	128	125
15-19	125	62	63	140	71	69	157	80	78	190	96	94
20-24	110	54	56	120	59	60	134	67	67	151	76	75
25-29	92	45	47	105	51	53	114	56	58	128	64	64
30-34	71	35	36	87	43	44	99	48	51	109	53	55
35-39	64	31	32	67	33	34	82	40	42	94	46	49
40-44	48	24	25	59	29	31	62	30	32	78	38	40
45-49	41	20	21	44	21	23	55	26	29	58	28	30
50-54	34	16	18	37	18	19	40	19	21	51	24	27
55-59	24	11	13	30	14	16	33	15	18	37	17	19
60-64	23	11	12	20	9	11	26	12	14	29	13	16
65-69	11	5	6	18	8	10	16	7	9	21	10	12
70-74	10	4	5	8	3	4	13	6	7	12	5	7
75-79	6	2	3	6	2	3	5	2	3	8	4	5
80 +	5	2	3	4	2	2	4	2	2	4	1	2

Age group	1970 Both sexes	1970 Males	1970 Females	1975 Both sexes	1975 Males	1975 Females	1980 Both sexes	1980 Males	1980 Females	1985 Both sexes	1985 Males	1985 Females
All ages	2 228	1 110	1 118	2 622	1 309	1 313	3 067	1 531	1 535	3 526	1 756	1 770
0-4	429	218	211	502	255	247	577	293	284	655	332	322
5-9	353	179	174	410	208	202	481	244	237	550	278	272
10-14	297	150	146	347	176	171	402	204	198	467	236	230
15-19	247	124	122	289	146	143	337	170	167	384	193	192
20-24	182	91	91	237	119	118	278	139	138	318	158	159
25-29	145	72	73	174	87	87	226	113	113	260	129	131
30-34	123	61	62	138	68	70	165	82	83	211	104	107
35-39	104	50	53	117	58	59	131	65	66	153	75	78
40-44	90	43	47	99	48	51	111	54	56	122	60	62
45-49	73	35	38	85	41	44	92	45	48	102	50	52
50-54	54	26	28	68	33	36	79	38	42	85	41	44
55-59	46	22	25	50	24	26	63	30	33	71	33	38
60-64	32	15	17	41	19	22	45	21	24	56	26	30
65-69	24	11	13	28	12	15	36	16	20	38	18	21
70-74	16	7	9	19	8	11	22	10	12	28	13	16
75-79	8	3	5	11	5	7	13	6	8	16	7	9
80 +	6	2	3	7	2	4	9	3	6	11	4	7

Age group	1990 Both sexes	1990 Males	1990 Females	1995 Both sexes	1995 Males	1995 Females	2000 Both sexes	2000 Males	2000 Females	2005 Both sexes	2005 Males	2005 Females
All ages	3 960	1 971	1 988	4 477	2 232	2 245	4 959	2 476	2 483	5 487	2 742	2 745
0-4	686	349	337	717	365	352	731	373	359	731	373	358
5-9	629	318	310	669	340	330	698	355	343	717	365	352
10-14	533	269	264	617	312	305	654	332	322	688	349	338
15-19	444	224	220	517	261	256	596	302	294	639	324	315
20-24	354	176	178	423	212	210	489	246	243	576	291	285
25-29	290	143	147	334	165	169	396	198	198	470	236	234
30-34	238	117	121	273	133	139	312	153	159	380	189	191
35-39	194	95	99	224	109	115	255	124	131	298	145	153
40-44	140	69	71	183	89	94	210	102	108	244	118	126
45-49	112	55	57	131	64	67	171	83	88	200	97	103
50-54	93	45	48	104	50	53	121	59	62	162	78	84
55-59	77	36	41	86	41	45	95	46	49	113	54	59
60-64	63	29	34	69	32	37	77	36	40	87	41	45
65-69	47	21	26	54	25	30	60	27	32	68	32	36
70-74	30	13	17	38	17	21	44	20	25	50	22	28
75-79	19	8	11	22	9	13	28	12	16	34	15	20
80 +	12	5	8	16	6	10	21	8	13	29	12	18

United Nations Department of Economic and Social Affairs/Population Division
World Population Prospects: The 2004 Revision, Volume II: Sex and Age Distribution of the World Population

646

POPULATION BY AGE AND SEX (in thousands)

Age group	2005 Both sexes	2005 Males	2005 Females	2010 Both sexes	2010 Males	2010 Females	2015 Both sexes	2015 Males	2015 Females	2020 Both sexes	2020 Males	2020 Females
All ages	5 487	2 742	2 745	6 066	3 032	3 035	6 637	3 316	3 321	7 179	3 585	3 594
0-4	731	373	358	752	384	368	756	386	370	740	378	362
5-9	717	365	352	722	368	354	743	379	364	748	382	366
10-14	688	349	338	711	362	349	716	365	351	738	376	361
15-19	639	324	315	677	343	334	701	356	345	706	359	347
20-24	576	291	285	624	316	309	663	335	328	687	347	339
25-29	470	236	234	561	282	279	610	307	303	648	326	322
30-34	380	189	191	458	228	230	548	274	274	597	299	298
35-39	298	145	153	369	183	186	447	222	225	537	267	270
40-44	244	118	126	290	140	149	359	177	182	436	216	221
45-49	200	97	103	236	113	122	281	135	146	350	171	178
50-54	162	78	84	192	92	100	227	108	118	271	130	141
55-59	113	54	59	154	74	80	183	87	96	217	103	114
60-64	87	41	45	105	50	55	144	68	76	172	81	91
65-69	68	32	36	78	37	41	95	45	51	132	61	70
70-74	50	22	28	58	27	31	68	31	37	84	39	45
75-79	34	15	20	40	18	23	47	21	26	56	25	31
80-84	19	8	11	24	10	14	29	12	17	35	15	20
85-89	8	3	5	11	4	7	14	6	9	18	7	11
90-94	2	1	1	3	1	2	5	2	3	6	2	4
95-99	0	0	0	0	0	0	1	0	1	1	0	1
100 +	0	0	0	0	0	0	0	0	0	0	0	0

Age group	2025 Both sexes	2025 Males	2025 Females	2030 Both sexes	2030 Males	2030 Females	2035 Both sexes	2035 Males	2035 Females	2040 Both sexes	2040 Males	2040 Females
All ages	7 674	3 830	3 845	8 116	4 047	4 070	8 497	4 231	4 266	8 836	4 394	4 442
0-4	712	364	348	677	346	331	640	327	313	627	321	306
5-9	733	374	359	705	360	345	670	343	328	634	324	310
10-14	742	379	363	727	371	356	699	357	342	665	340	325
15-19	728	370	357	733	373	360	718	366	352	690	352	338
20-24	692	351	341	714	362	352	719	365	354	705	358	347
25-29	672	339	333	678	342	336	700	354	346	706	357	348
30-34	636	318	317	660	332	329	666	335	331	689	347	342
35-39	585	292	293	624	311	313	649	325	324	655	329	327
40-44	526	261	265	574	285	289	613	305	308	638	318	320
45-49	426	209	216	514	254	261	563	270	264	602	298	304
50-54	339	165	174	414	202	211	501	246	255	549	270	279
55-59	260	124	137	326	158	168	399	194	205	485	236	249
60-64	205	96	109	247	116	131	310	148	162	381	183	198
65-69	158	73	85	190	88	102	229	106	123	290	136	153
70-74	117	53	63	141	64	77	170	77	94	207	94	114
75-79	70	31	39	98	43	55	120	53	68	146	64	83
80-84	42	18	24	53	23	31	76	32	44	94	39	55
85-89	22	9	13	27	11	16	35	14	21	50	20	31
90-94	8	3	5	10	4	7	13	5	8	17	6	11
95-99	2	1	1	2	1	2	3	1	2	4	1	3
100 +	0	0	0	0	0	0	0	0	0	0	0	0

Age group	2045 Both sexes	2045 Males	2045 Females	2050 Both sexes	2050 Males	2050 Females
All ages	9 134	4 535	4 599	9 371	4 645	4 726
0-4	618	316	302	599	306	292
5-9	621	318	304	612	313	299
10-14	629	322	308	616	315	301
15-19	657	335	322	621	317	304
20-24	678	344	333	644	328	317
25-29	692	351	341	665	337	328
30-34	695	351	344	681	344	337
35-39	678	341	337	684	344	340
40-44	645	323	323	668	335	333
45-49	627	312	315	634	316	318
50-54	588	290	298	613	303	310
55-59	532	260	272	571	279	292
60-64	464	224	240	510	247	264
65-69	357	169	188	436	207	229
70-74	263	121	142	325	150	175
75-79	179	78	101	228	101	127
80-84	115	47	68	142	58	83
85-89	63	24	39	78	30	49
90-94	26	9	17	33	11	22
95-99	6	2	4	9	3	6
100 +	1	0	0	1	0	1

POPULATION BY AGE AND SEX (in thousands)

Age group	2005			2010			2015			2020		
	Both sexes	Males	Females	Both sexes	Males	Females	Both sexes	Males	Females	Both sexes	Males	Females
All ages	5 487	2 742	2 745	6 126	3 062	3 064	6 804	3 401	3 403	7 493	3 745	3 747
0-4	731	373	358	811	414	397	864	441	423	889	454	435
5-9	717	365	352	722	368	354	802	409	393	855	436	419
10-14	688	349	338	711	362	349	716	365	351	796	406	390
15-19	639	324	315	677	343	334	701	356	345	706	359	347
20-24	576	291	285	624	316	309	663	335	328	687	347	339
25-29	470	236	234	561	282	279	610	307	303	648	326	322
30-34	380	189	191	458	228	230	548	274	274	597	299	298
35-39	298	145	153	369	183	186	447	222	225	537	267	270
40-44	244	118	126	290	140	149	359	177	182	436	216	221
45-49	200	97	103	236	113	122	281	135	146	350	171	178
50-54	162	78	84	192	92	100	227	108	118	271	130	141
55-59	113	54	59	154	74	80	183	87	96	217	103	114
60-64	87	41	45	105	50	55	144	68	76	172	81	91
65-69	68	32	36	78	37	41	95	45	51	132	61	70
70-74	50	22	28	58	27	31	68	31	37	84	39	45
75-79	34	15	20	40	18	23	47	21	26	56	25	31
80-84	19	8	11	24	10	14	29	12	17	35	15	20
85-89	8	3	5	11	4	7	14	6	9	18	7	11
90-94	2	1	1	3	1	2	5	2	3	6	2	4
95-99	0	0	0	0	0	0	1	0	1	1	0	1
100 +	0	0	0	0	0	0	0	0	0	0	0	0

Age group	2025			2030			2035			2040		
	Both sexes	Males	Females	Both sexes	Males	Females	Both sexes	Males	Females	Both sexes	Males	Females
All ages	8 152	4 074	4 078	8 787	4 389	4 398	9 401	4 693	4 708	10 014	4 995	5 019
0-4	876	448	428	872	446	426	876	448	428	904	463	442
5-9	880	449	431	868	444	425	865	442	423	869	444	425
10-14	849	433	416	874	446	428	863	441	422	859	439	420
15-19	787	400	386	839	428	412	865	441	424	853	435	418
20-24	692	351	341	772	392	380	825	419	406	851	433	418
25-29	672	339	333	678	342	336	758	384	375	811	411	400
30-34	636	318	317	660	332	329	666	335	331	747	376	370
35-39	585	292	293	624	311	313	649	325	324	655	329	327
40-44	526	261	265	574	285	289	613	305	308	638	318	320
45-49	426	209	216	514	254	261	563	278	284	602	298	304
50-54	339	165	174	414	202	211	501	246	255	549	270	279
55-59	260	124	137	326	158	169	399	194	206	485	236	249
60-64	205	96	109	247	116	131	310	148	162	381	183	198
65-69	158	73	85	190	88	102	229	106	123	290	136	153
70-74	117	53	63	141	64	77	170	77	94	207	94	114
75-79	70	31	39	98	43	55	120	53	68	146	64	83
80-84	42	18	24	53	23	31	76	32	44	94	39	55
85-89	22	9	13	27	11	16	35	14	21	50	20	31
90-94	8	3	5	10	4	7	13	5	8	17	6	11
95-99	2	1	1	2	1	2	3	1	2	4	1	3
100 +	0	0	0	0	0	0	0	0	0	0	0	0

Age group	2045			2050		
	Both sexes	Males	Females	Both sexes	Males	Females
All ages	10 622	5 295	5 327	11 200	5 579	5 621
0-4	932	477	455	945	484	461
5-9	898	459	439	925	473	452
10-14	863	441	422	892	456	436
15-19	850	434	416	854	436	418
20-24	840	427	413	837	426	411
25-29	837	425	413	827	419	407
30-34	800	404	396	826	418	408
35-39	736	370	366	789	397	391
40-44	645	323	323	725	364	362
45-49	627	312	315	634	316	318
50-54	588	290	298	613	303	310
55-59	532	260	272	571	279	292
60-64	464	224	240	510	247	264
65-69	357	169	188	436	207	229
70-74	263	121	142	325	150	175
75-79	179	78	101	228	101	127
80-84	115	47	68	142	58	83
85-89	63	24	39	78	30	49
90-94	26	9	17	33	11	22
95-99	6	2	4	9	3	6
100 +	1	0	0	1	0	1

United Nations Department of Economic and Social Affairs/Population Division
World Population Prospects: The 2004 Revision, Volume II: Sex and Age Distribution of the World Population

648

POPULATION BY AGE AND SEX (in thousands)

Age group	2005 Both sexes	Males	Females	2010 Both sexes	Males	Females	2015 Both sexes	Males	Females	2020 Both sexes	Males	Females
All ages	5 487	2 742	2 745	6 006	3 001	3 005	6 407	3 229	3 239	6 859	3 422	3 437
0-4	731	373	358	692	353	339	646	330	316	590	301	289
5-9	717	365	352	722	368	354	684	349	335	638	326	313
10-14	688	349	338	711	362	349	716	365	351	678	346	332
15-19	639	324	315	677	343	334	701	356	345	706	359	347
20-24	576	291	285	624	316	309	663	335	328	687	347	339
25-29	470	236	234	561	282	279	610	307	303	648	326	322
30-34	380	189	191	458	228	230	548	274	274	597	299	298
35-39	298	145	153	369	183	186	447	222	225	537	267	270
40-44	244	118	126	290	140	149	359	177	182	436	216	221
45-49	200	97	103	236	113	122	281	135	146	350	171	178
50-54	162	78	84	192	92	100	227	108	118	271	130	141
55-59	113	54	59	154	74	80	183	87	96	217	103	114
60-64	87	41	45	105	50	55	144	68	76	172	81	91
65-69	68	32	36	78	37	41	95	45	51	132	61	70
70-74	50	22	28	58	27	31	68	31	37	84	39	45
75-79	34	15	20	40	18	23	47	21	26	56	25	31
80-84	19	8	11	24	10	14	29	12	17	35	15	20
85-89	8	3	5	11	4	7	14	6	9	18	7	11
90-94	2	1	1	3	1	2	5	2	3	6	2	4
95-99	0	0	0	0	0	0	1	0	1	1	0	1
100 +	0	0	0	0	0	0	0	0	0	0	0	0

Age group	2025 Both sexes	Males	Females	2030 Both sexes	Males	Females	2035 Both sexes	Males	Females	2040 Both sexes	Males	Females
All ages	7 192	3 584	3 608	7 451	3 707	3 744	7 622	3 785	3 838	7 729	3 829	3 900
0-4	548	280	268	492	252	240	429	219	210	392	200	191
5-9	583	298	285	541	277	265	486	249	238	424	217	207
10-14	633	323	310	578	295	283	536	274	262	481	246	235
15-19	669	340	328	624	318	306	569	290	279	528	269	259
20-24	692	351	341	655	332	323	611	310	301	557	283	274
25-29	672	339	333	678	342	336	642	324	317	598	302	295
30-34	636	318	317	660	332	329	666	335	331	631	318	313
35-39	585	292	293	624	311	313	649	325	324	655	329	327
40-44	526	261	265	574	285	289	613	305	308	638	318	320
45-49	426	209	210	514	254	261	563	278	284	602	298	304
50-54	339	165	174	414	202	211	501	246	255	549	270	279
55-59	231	124	107	326	158	169	399	194	206	485	236	249
60-64	205	96	109	247	116	131	310	148	162	381	183	198
65-69	158	73	85	190	88	102	229	106	123	290	136	153
70-74	117	53	63	141	64	77	170	77	94	207	94	114
75-79	70	31	39	98	43	55	120	53	68	146	64	83
80-84	42	18	24	53	23	31	70	32	44	94	39	55
85-89	22	9	13	27	11	16	35	14	21	50	20	31
90-94	8	3	5	10	4	7	13	5	8	17	6	11
95-99	2	1	1	2	1	2	3	1	2	4	1	3
100 +	0	0	0	0	0	0	0	0	0	0	0	0

Age group	2045 Both sexes	Males	Females	2050 Both sexes	Males	Females
All ages	7 776	3 842	3 934	7 750	3 818	3 932
0-4	363	186	177	331	170	162
5-9	387	198	189	358	183	175
10-14	419	214	205	382	195	187
15-19	473	241	232	411	210	202
20-24	516	262	254	461	234	227
25-29	544	275	269	504	255	249
30-34	587	296	291	534	269	265
35-39	620	312	309	578	290	287
40-44	645	323	323	611	306	305
45-49	627	312	315	634	316	318
50-54	588	290	298	613	303	310
55-59	532	260	272	571	279	292
60-64	464	224	240	510	247	264
65-69	357	169	188	436	207	229
70-74	263	121	142	325	150	175
75-79	179	78	101	228	101	127
80-84	115	47	68	142	58	83
85-89	63	24	39	78	30	49
90-94	26	9	17	33	11	22
95-99	6	2	4	9	3	6
100 +	1	0	0	1	0	1

POPULATION BY AGE AND SEX (in thousands)

Age group	1950 Both sexes	Males	Females	1955 Both sexes	Males	Females	1960 Both sexes	Males	Females	1965 Both sexes	Males	Females
All ages	2 612	1 264	1 348	3 019	1 479	1 541	3 446	1 699	1 748	3 969	1 970	1 999
0-4	477	235	243	600	306	294	681	347	334	787	402	386
5-9	363	177	185	415	205	210	524	268	255	596	305	291
10-14	309	151	158	352	172	179	401	199	203	508	261	247
15-19	268	131	137	301	148	153	340	167	173	390	193	197
20-24	231	113	119	259	127	132	284	138	145	324	159	166
25-29	198	96	102	221	108	113	240	116	124	268	130	138
30-34	168	81	87	189	92	97	205	99	106	226	109	117
35-39	141	68	73	160	77	82	175	84	91	193	93	100
40-44	117	56	61	133	64	69	148	71	77	165	79	86
45-49	96	46	51	110	52	58	125	60	65	139	66	73
50-54	78	36	41	89	42	47	103	49	54	116	55	61
55-59	61	28	33	70	32	38	81	38	43	93	44	49
60-64	45	20	25	52	23	28	60	28	33	70	32	37
65-69	31	13	17	35	16	20	41	18	23	48	22	26
70-74	18	8	10	21	9	12	24	11	14	28	13	16
75-79	8	3	5	10	4	6	11	5	6	13	6	7
80 +	4	1	2	4	1	2	4	2	3	5	2	3

Age group	1970 Both sexes	Males	Females	1975 Both sexes	Males	Females	1980 Both sexes	Males	Females	1985 Both sexes	Males	Females
All ages	4 587	2 290	2 297	5 325	2 673	2 653	6 205	3 128	3 078	7 245	3 664	3 581
0-4	915	467	448	1 076	549	526	1 270	649	621	1 495	763	731
5-9	692	355	337	806	414	393	950	488	462	1 119	575	544
10-14	579	297	282	673	346	327	784	403	381	924	476	449
15-19	494	254	240	563	290	273	654	337	318	763	393	370
20-24	373	185	188	473	243	230	539	277	262	627	322	305
25-29	307	150	157	354	174	179	448	229	219	511	261	249
30-34	253	122	131	291	141	149	334	164	170	424	217	208
35-39	213	103	111	239	115	124	274	133	141	315	154	161
40-44	182	87	95	201	96	105	225	108	117	258	124	134
45-49	155	74	81	171	81	89	189	90	99	210	100	110
50-54	129	61	68	144	68	76	159	75	84	175	83	93
55-59	105	49	56	117	55	62	131	61	70	145	68	77
60-64	80	37	43	91	42	49	101	47	55	113	52	61
65-69	55	25	30	64	29	34	72	33	39	81	37	44
70-74	33	15	18	38	17	21	44	20	24	50	23	27
75-79	16	7	9	18	8	10	21	10	12	24	11	13
80 +	6	3	3	7	3	4	8	4	5	10	4	5

Age group	1990 Both sexes	Males	Females	1995 Both sexes	Males	Females	2000 Both sexes	Males	Females	2005 Both sexes	Males	Females
All ages	8 472	4 299	4 174	9 929	5 055	4 874	11 782	6 013	5 770	13 957	7 136	6 821
0-4	1 747	893	854	2 011	1 028	983	2 456	1 256	1 199	2 851	1 459	1 392
5-9	1 315	676	639	1 545	794	751	1 802	926	876	2 227	1 145	1 082
10-14	1 089	561	528	1 282	660	622	1 511	778	733	1 766	909	857
15-19	900	464	436	1 064	549	515	1 255	648	607	1 483	765	718
20-24	732	377	355	871	449	422	1 031	532	499	1 218	629	589
25-29	595	305	290	704	362	341	837	432	405	991	512	479
30-34	485	248	237	572	293	278	675	347	327	802	414	388
35-39	402	205	197	464	237	227	547	281	266	644	332	312
40-44	297	145	152	383	195	188	442	226	216	521	267	254
45-49	243	116	127	281	136	145	362	183	179	419	213	206
50-54	196	93	104	227	108	119	263	126	137	339	170	169
55-59	160	75	85	179	83	95	207	97	110	241	114	127
60-64	126	58	68	139	64	75	157	72	85	183	84	98
65-69	91	42	49	101	46	55	113	51	62	129	58	70
70-74	56	25	30	63	29	35	72	32	40	82	37	45
75-79	27	12	15	31	14	17	36	16	20	42	19	24
80 +	11	5	6	13	6	7	16	7	9	20	9	11

United Nations Department of Economic and Social Affairs/Population Division
World Population Prospects: The 2004 Revision, Volume II: Sex and Age Distribution of the World Population

650

POPULATION BY AGE AND SEX (in thousands)

Age group	2005 Both sexes	2005 Males	2005 Females	2010 Both sexes	2010 Males	2010 Females	2015 Both sexes	2015 Males	2015 Females	2020 Both sexes	2020 Males	2020 Females
All ages	13 957	7 136	6 821	16 430	8 414	8 016	19 283	9 889	9 394	22 585	11 596	10 990
0-4	2 851	1 459	1 392	3 232	1 655	1 577	3 696	1 893	1 803	4 226	2 166	2 060
5-9	2 227	1 145	1 082	2 609	1 342	1 267	2 983	1 534	1 449	3 439	1 769	1 670
10-14	1 766	909	857	2 186	1 126	1 060	2 563	1 320	1 243	2 934	1 511	1 423
15-19	1 483	765	718	1 735	895	840	2 151	1 109	1 042	2 526	1 302	1 224
20-24	1 218	629	589	1 442	744	698	1 693	873	820	2 104	1 085	1 019
25-29	991	512	479	1 171	605	566	1 391	718	673	1 639	846	793
30-34	802	414	388	947	490	456	1 119	580	539	1 334	692	643
35-39	644	332	312	764	395	369	900	468	433	1 067	555	512
40-44	521	267	254	612	315	297	725	375	350	856	445	411
45-49	419	213	206	493	251	242	580	297	283	687	354	333
50-54	339	170	169	393	198	195	463	234	229	546	278	268
55-59	241	114	127	312	155	157	362	180	182	428	214	214
60-64	183	84	98	214	100	114	278	136	142	324	159	165
65-69	129	58	70	152	69	83	179	82	96	234	113	121
70-74	82	37	45	95	42	52	113	51	62	135	61	74
75-79	42	19	24	49	22	28	58	25	33	71	31	40
80-84	16	7	9	19	8	11	23	10	13	27	12	16
85-89	4	2	2	4	2	3	6	2	3	7	3	4
90-94	0	0	0	1	0	0	1	0	0	1	0	1
95-99	0	0	0	0	0	0	0	0	0	0	0	0
100 +	0	0	0	0	0	0	0	0	0	0	0	0

Age group	2025 Both sexes	2025 Males	2025 Females	2030 Both sexes	2030 Males	2030 Females	2035 Both sexes	2035 Males	2035 Females	2040 Both sexes	2040 Males	2040 Females
All ages	26 376	13 552	12 824	30 637	15 750	14 888	35 274	18 139	17 136	40 144	20 644	19 500
0-4	4 786	2 454	2 332	5 319	2 729	2 590	5 752	2 953	2 800	6 039	3 101	2 938
5-9	3 967	2 041	1 926	4 531	2 332	2 199	5 076	2 613	2 463	5 529	2 848	2 682
10-14	3 388	1 744	1 644	3 917	2 017	1 900	4 485	2 310	2 175	5 033	2 593	2 440
15-19	2 896	1 493	1 404	3 349	1 726	1 623	3 878	1 998	1 880	4 446	2 291	2 155
20-24	2 477	1 277	1 200	2 846	1 467	1 379	3 298	1 700	1 599	3 827	1 972	1 855
25-29	2 045	1 055	990	2 417	1 247	1 170	2 786	1 437	1 349	3 240	1 670	1 569
30-34	1 580	818	762	1 981	1 025	956	2 352	1 216	1 136	2 724	1 407	1 317
35-39	1 270	664	614	1 523	790	732	1 919	995	925	2 290	1 185	1 105
40-44	1 019	530	488	1 227	638	589	1 469	763	707	1 862	965	897
45-49	815	422	393	974	506	468	1 179	612	567	1 419	736	684
50-54	649	332	317	772	398	375	928	479	449	1 128	582	546
55-59	507	255	251	606	307	298	724	369	355	874	447	427
60-64	385	190	195	459	228	231	552	276	276	663	334	329
65-69	275	133	142	331	161	170	397	194	203	482	237	244
70-74	179	85	94	214	102	112	260	124	136	316	152	164
75-79	87	38	48	117	54	63	142	66	76	176	82	94
80-84	34	15	20	43	18	24	59	27	32	73	33	40
85-89	8	3	5	11	4	6	14	6	8	20	9	11
90-94	1	0	1	2	1	1	2	1	1	3	1	2
95-99	0	0	0	0	0	0	0	0	0	0	0	0
100 +	0	0	0	0	0	0	0	0	0	0	0	0

Age group	2045 Both sexes	2045 Males	2045 Females	2050 Both sexes	2050 Males	2050 Females
All ages	45 122	23 199	21 923	50 156	25 774	24 382
0-4	6 199	3 183	3 016	6 313	3 241	3 072
5-9	5 843	3 010	2 834	6 033	3 106	2 927
10-14	5 491	2 829	2 662	5 811	2 993	2 817
15-19	4 996	2 575	2 421	5 457	2 812	2 645
20-24	4 396	2 266	2 131	4 949	2 550	2 399
25-29	3 770	1 943	1 827	4 342	2 238	2 104
30-34	3 179	1 641	1 538	3 712	1 915	1 798
35-39	2 663	1 377	1 287	3 121	1 611	1 510
40-44	2 231	1 154	1 076	2 605	1 346	1 259
45-49	1 804	933	872	2 171	1 121	1 050
50-54	1 363	702	661	1 740	895	845
55-59	1 067	546	522	1 295	661	634
60-64	805	407	399	989	499	489
65-69	583	289	294	714	355	359
70-74	389	188	200	476	232	244
75-79	218	102	116	273	129	144
80-84	93	42	51	118	53	64
85-89	25	11	14	33	14	19
90-94	4	2	2	5	2	3
95-99	0	0	0	0	0	0
100 +	0	0	0	0	0	0

United Nations Department of Economic and Social Affairs/Population Division
World Population Prospects: The 2004 Revision, Volume II: Sex and Age Distribution of the World Population

651

POPULATION BY AGE AND SEX (in thousands)

Age group	2005 Both sexes	Males	Females	2010 Both sexes	Males	Females	2015 Both sexes	Males	Females	2020 Both sexes	Males	Females
All ages	13 957	7 136	6 821	16 601	8 502	8 099	19 833	10 171	9 662	23 419	12 024	11 395
0-4	2 851	1 459	1 392	3 403	1 742	1 660	4 089	2 094	1 994	4 539	2 326	2 213
5-9	2 227	1 145	1 082	2 609	1 342	1 267	3 140	1 615	1 525	3 804	1 957	1 848
10-14	1 766	909	857	2 186	1 126	1 060	2 563	1 320	1 243	3 089	1 591	1 498
15-19	1 483	765	718	1 735	895	840	2 151	1 109	1 042	2 526	1 302	1 224
20-24	1 218	629	589	1 442	744	698	1 693	873	820	2 104	1 085	1 019
25-29	991	512	479	1 171	605	566	1 391	718	673	1 639	846	793
30-34	802	414	388	947	490	456	1 119	580	539	1 334	692	643
35-39	644	332	312	764	395	369	900	468	433	1 067	555	512
40-44	521	267	254	612	315	297	725	375	350	856	445	411
45-49	419	213	206	493	251	242	580	297	283	687	354	333
50-54	339	170	169	393	198	195	463	234	229	546	278	268
55-59	241	114	127	312	155	157	362	180	182	428	214	214
60-64	183	84	98	214	100	114	278	136	142	324	159	165
65-69	129	58	70	152	69	83	179	82	96	234	113	121
70-74	82	37	45	95	42	52	113	51	62	135	61	74
75-79	42	19	24	49	22	28	58	25	33	71	31	40
80-84	16	7	9	19	8	11	23	10	13	27	12	16
85-89	4	2	2	4	2	3	6	2	3	7	3	4
90-94	0	0	0	1	0	0	1	0	0	1	0	1
95-99	0	0	0	0	0	0	0	0	0	0	0	0
100 +	0	0	0	0	0	0	0	0	0	0	0	0

Age group	2025 Both sexes	Males	Females	2030 Both sexes	Males	Females	2035 Both sexes	Males	Females	2040 Both sexes	Males	Females
All ages	27 590	14 176	13 413	32 398	16 656	15 743	37 810	19 444	18 367	43 703	22 477	21 227
0-4	5 193	2 662	2 530	5 899	3 026	2 872	6 569	3 372	3 197	7 114	3 653	3 461
5-9	4 261	2 192	2 068	4 916	2 530	2 386	5 629	2 898	2 731	6 314	3 252	3 062
10-14	3 748	1 930	1 818	4 207	2 166	2 041	4 866	2 506	2 360	5 582	2 876	2 706
15-19	3 049	1 571	1 478	3 705	1 909	1 796	4 165	2 146	2 019	4 824	2 486	2 338
20-24	2 477	1 277	1 200	2 996	1 544	1 452	3 649	1 881	1 769	4 111	2 118	1 992
25-29	2 045	1 055	990	2 417	1 247	1 170	2 933	1 513	1 421	3 585	1 848	1 736
30-34	1 580	818	762	1 981	1 025	956	2 352	1 216	1 136	2 868	1 481	1 387
35-39	1 278	664	614	1 523	790	732	1 919	995	925	2 290	1 185	1 105
40-44	1 019	530	488	1 227	638	589	1 469	763	707	1 862	965	897
45-49	815	422	393	974	506	468	1 179	612	567	1 419	735	684
50-54	649	332	317	772	398	375	928	479	449	1 128	582	546
55-59	507	255	251	606	307	298	724	369	355	874	447	427
60-64	385	190	195	459	228	231	552	276	276	663	334	329
65-69	275	133	142	331	161	170	397	194	203	482	237	244
70-74	179	85	94	214	102	112	260	124	136	316	152	164
75-79	87	38	48	117	54	63	142	66	76	176	82	94
80-84	34	15	20	43	18	24	59	27	32	73	33	40
85-89	8	3	5	11	4	6	14	6	8	20	9	11
90-94	1	0	1	2	1	1	2	1	1	3	1	2
95-99	0	0	0	0	0	0	0	0	0	0	0	0
100 +	0	0	0	0	0	0	0	0	0	0	0	0

Age group	2045 Both sexes	Males	Females	2050 Both sexes	Males	Females
All ages	49 922	25 671	24 251	56 402	28 990	27 412
0-4	7 501	3 852	3 649	7 827	4 019	3 809
5-9	6 884	3 546	3 339	7 301	3 758	3 542
10-14	6 271	3 231	3 040	6 846	3 527	3 319
15-19	5 541	2 855	2 685	6 232	3 211	3 020
20-24	4 770	2 458	2 312	5 489	2 829	2 660
25-29	4 049	2 087	1 962	4 711	2 428	2 283
30-34	3 518	1 816	1 702	3 988	2 057	1 931
35-39	2 804	1 450	1 355	3 454	1 783	1 671
40-44	2 231	1 154	1 076	2 743	1 417	1 326
45-49	1 804	933	872	2 171	1 121	1 050
50-54	1 363	702	661	1 740	895	845
55-59	1 067	546	522	1 295	661	634
60-64	805	407	399	989	499	489
65-69	583	289	294	714	355	359
70-74	389	188	200	476	232	244
75-79	218	102	116	273	129	144
80-84	93	42	51	118	53	64
85-89	25	11	14	33	14	19
90-94	4	2	2	5	2	3
95-99	0	0	0	0	0	0
100 +	0	0	0	0	0	0

United Nations Department of Economic and Social Affairs/Population Division
World Population Prospects: The 2004 Revision, Volume II: Sex and Age Distribution of the World Population

POPULATION BY AGE AND SEX (in thousands)

Age group	2005 Both sexes	2005 Males	2005 Females	2010 Both sexes	2010 Males	2010 Females	2015 Both sexes	2015 Males	2015 Females	2020 Both sexes	2020 Males	2020 Females
All ages	13 957	7 136	6 821	16 322	8 359	7 963	18 977	9 732	9 245	21 902	11 200	10 606
0-4	2 851	1 459	1 392	3 125	1 600	1 525	3 489	1 787	1 702	3 913	2 005	1 908
5-9	2 227	1 145	1 082	2 609	1 342	1 267	2 884	1 483	1 401	3 246	1 670	1 576
10-14	1 766	909	857	2 186	1 126	1 060	2 563	1 320	1 243	2 837	1 461	1 376
15-19	1 483	765	718	1 735	895	840	2 151	1 109	1 042	2 526	1 302	1 224
20-24	1 218	629	589	1 442	744	698	1 693	873	820	2 104	1 085	1 019
25-29	991	512	479	1 171	605	566	1 391	718	673	1 639	846	793
30-34	802	414	388	947	490	456	1 119	580	539	1 334	692	643
35-39	644	332	312	764	395	369	900	468	433	1 067	555	512
40-44	521	267	254	612	315	297	725	375	350	856	445	411
45-49	419	213	206	493	251	242	580	297	283	687	354	333
50-54	339	170	169	393	198	195	463	234	229	546	278	268
55-59	241	114	127	312	155	157	362	180	182	428	214	214
60-64	183	84	98	214	100	114	278	136	142	324	159	165
65-69	129	58	70	152	69	83	179	82	96	234	113	121
70-74	82	37	45	95	42	52	113	51	62	135	61	74
75-79	42	19	24	49	22	28	58	25	33	71	31	40
80-84	16	7	9	19	8	11	23	10	13	27	12	16
85-89	4	2	2	4	2	3	6	2	3	7	3	4
90-94	0	0	0	1	0	0	1	0	0	1	0	1
95-99	0	0	0	0	0	0	0	0	0	0	0	0
100 +	0	0	0	0	0	0	0	0	0	0	0	0

Age group	2025 Both sexes	2025 Males	2025 Females	2030 Both sexes	2030 Males	2030 Females	2035 Both sexes	2035 Males	2035 Females	2040 Both sexes	2040 Males	2040 Females
All ages	25 403	13 052	12 351	29 177	14 999	14 178	33 165	17 053	16 111	37 193	19 125	18 068
0-4	4 393	2 252	2 140	4 803	2 464	2 339	5 069	2 602	2 467	5 155	2 647	2 508
5-9	3 673	1 890	1 783	4 159	2 140	2 018	4 584	2 360	2 224	4 872	2 509	2 363
10-14	3 198	1 647	1 552	3 627	1 868	1 759	4 116	2 120	1 996	4 545	2 342	2 204
15-19	2 800	1 443	1 357	3 161	1 629	1 532	3 591	1 850	1 740	4 080	2 103	1 978
20-24	2 477	1 277	1 200	2 751	1 418	1 333	3 113	1 604	1 509	3 544	1 826	1 718
25-29	2 045	1 055	990	2 417	1 247	1 170	2 693	1 389	1 304	3 058	1 577	1 481
30-34	1 580	818	762	1 981	1 025	956	2 352	1 216	1 136	2 633	1 360	1 273
35-39	1 278	664	614	1 523	790	732	1 919	995	925	2 290	1 185	1 105
40-44	1 019	530	488	1 227	638	589	1 469	763	707	1 862	965	897
45-49	815	422	393	974	506	468	1 170	612	567	1 419	735	684
50-54	649	332	317	772	398	375	928	479	449	1 128	582	546
55-59	507	255	251	606	307	298	724	369	355	874	447	427
60-64	385	190	195	459	228	231	552	276	276	663	334	329
65-69	275	133	142	331	161	170	397	194	203	482	237	244
70-74	179	85	94	214	102	112	260	124	136	316	152	164
75-79	87	38	48	117	54	63	142	66	76	176	82	94
80-84	34	15	20	43	18	24	59	27	32	73	33	40
85-89	8	3	5	11	4	6	14	6	8	20	9	11
90-94	1	0	1	2	1	1	2	1	1	3	1	2
95-99	0	0	0	0	0	0	0	0	0	0	0	0
100 +	0	0	0	0	0	0	0	0	0	0	0	0

Age group	2045 Both sexes	2045 Males	2045 Females	2050 Both sexes	2050 Males	2050 Females
All ages	41 129	21 144	19 986	44 925	23 081	21 844
0-4	5 108	2 623	2 485	5 019	2 577	2 442
5-9	4 988	2 569	2 419	4 971	2 559	2 412
10-14	4 839	2 493	2 345	4 960	2 555	2 405
15-19	4 512	2 325	2 187	4 808	2 478	2 330
20-24	4 035	2 079	1 956	4 469	2 303	2 166
25-29	3 491	1 799	1 691	3 984	2 054	1 931
30-34	3 001	1 549	1 452	3 437	1 773	1 664
35-39	2 574	1 331	1 244	2 946	1 521	1 425
40-44	2 231	1 154	1 076	2 518	1 301	1 217
45-49	1 804	933	872	2 171	1 121	1 050
50-54	1 363	702	661	1 740	895	845
55-59	1 067	546	522	1 295	661	634
60-64	805	407	399	989	499	489
65-69	583	289	294	714	355	359
70-74	389	188	200	476	232	244
75-79	218	102	116	273	129	144
80-84	93	42	51	118	53	64
85-89	25	11	14	33	14	19
90-94	4	2	2	5	2	3
95-99	0	0	0	0	0	0
100 +	0	0	0	0	0	0

United Nations Department of Economic and Social Affairs/Population Division
World Population Prospects: The 2004 Revision, Volume II: Sex and Age Distribution of the World Population

653

POPULATION BY AGE AND SEX (in thousands)

Age group	1950			1955			1960			1965		
	Both sexes	Males	Females	Both sexes	Males	Females	Both sexes	Males	Females	Both sexes	Males	Females
All ages	32 769	16 069	16 699	36 520	17 978	18 542	40 866	20 185	20 682	45 935	22 757	23 178
0-4	5 476	2 747	2 729	6 559	3 319	3 240	7 358	3 728	3 630	8 265	4 192	4 073
5-9	4 397	2 198	2 200	4 755	2 377	2 378	5 747	2 899	2 849	6 505	3 286	3 219
10-14	3 796	1 894	1 902	4 195	2 096	2 099	4 549	2 273	2 276	5 514	2 780	2 733
15-19	3 296	1 642	1 654	3 662	1 827	1 835	4 054	2 026	2 028	4 405	2 201	2 204
20-24	2 865	1 423	1 442	3 160	1 569	1 591	3 518	1 750	1 768	3 904	1 944	1 959
25-29	2 487	1 230	1 258	2 724	1 346	1 378	3 012	1 488	1 524	3 362	1 664	1 698
30-34	2 133	1 048	1 084	2 353	1 160	1 193	2 584	1 273	1 311	2 865	1 412	1 453
35-39	1 781	868	913	2 003	983	1 020	2 217	1 091	1 126	2 443	1 201	1 241
40-44	1 512	731	782	1 657	804	853	1 870	915	956	2 078	1 019	1 059
45-49	1 281	610	671	1 392	667	726	1 532	737	795	1 736	842	894
50-54	1 140	538	603	1 162	546	616	1 269	599	669	1 402	667	736
55-59	929	428	502	1 006	466	540	1 031	477	554	1 132	527	605
60-64	696	310	385	782	353	429	854	388	465	881	400	481
65-69	478	205	273	543	237	306	617	273	344	680	303	376
70-74	292	120	172	328	137	191	378	161	217	436	188	248
75-79	145	56	89	165	65	100	190	76	114	224	92	132
80 +	64	23	42	74	26	48	87	31	56	103	37	66

Age group	1970			1975			1980			1985		
	Both sexes	Males	Females	Both sexes	Males	Females	Both sexes	Males	Females	Both sexes	Males	Females
All ages	51 857	25 759	26 098	58 950	29 357	29 592	68 447	34 256	34 191	78 435	39 260	39 175
0-4	9 345	4 746	4 599	10 708	5 444	5 263	12 519	6 372	6 148	14 819	7 548	7 271
5-9	7 373	3 729	3 643	8 414	4 262	4 151	9 780	4 961	4 819	11 403	5 791	5 612
10-14	6 256	3 160	3 097	7 112	3 597	3 515	8 192	4 149	4 043	9 442	4 789	4 653
15-19	5 346	2 695	2 651	6 080	3 070	3 010	7 011	3 554	3 457	7 928	4 008	3 920
20-24	4 244	2 114	2 130	5 164	2 595	2 569	6 023	3 046	2 976	6 700	3 375	3 325
25-29	3 733	1 850	1 883	4 070	2 017	2 053	5 117	2 575	2 542	5 695	2 858	2 838
30-34	3 201	1 579	1 622	3 565	1 762	1 804	4 038	2 016	2 022	4 815	2 402	2 413
35-39	2 713	1 334	1 379	3 042	1 497	1 545	3 493	1 737	1 756	3 794	1 879	1 915
40-44	2 296	1 125	1 171	2 560	1 254	1 306	2 928	1 442	1 486	3 284	1 624	1 660
45-49	1 936	942	993	2 148	1 046	1 103	2 438	1 190	1 248	2 736	1 337	1 399
50-54	1 596	765	831	1 787	861	927	2 017	974	1 043	2 252	1 087	1 165
55-59	1 258	589	669	1 440	681	759	1 633	777	856	1 831	873	958
60-64	975	446	529	1 092	504	588	1 263	589	674	1 434	673	761
65-69	709	316	393	793	357	437	899	408	491	1 044	479	565
70-74	489	213	276	518	226	292	588	259	329	671	297	374
75-79	264	110	154	302	127	175	327	138	189	375	158	217
80 +	125	46	78	152	58	94	183	70	112	211	82	129

Age group	1990			1995			2000			2005		
	Both sexes	Males	Females	Both sexes	Males	Females	Both sexes	Males	Females	Both sexes	Males	Females
All ages	90 557	45 417	45 140	103 914	52 236	51 677	117 608	59 290	58 318	131 530	66 558	64 971
0-4	16 901	8 625	8 276	18 961	9 699	9 263	20 588	10 545	10 043	22 257	11 412	10 845
5-9	13 619	6 928	6 691	15 586	7 955	7 631	17 506	8 958	8 548	18 995	9 738	9 257
10-14	11 070	5 622	5 448	13 235	6 735	6 500	15 148	7 736	7 412	16 972	8 692	8 281
15-19	9 214	4 672	4 542	10 811	5 490	5 321	12 934	6 582	6 352	14 803	7 561	7 242
20-24	7 681	3 871	3 810	8 912	4 507	4 406	10 449	5 295	5 154	12 513	6 354	6 158
25-29	6 441	3 228	3 213	7 330	3 679	3 652	8 397	4 243	4 154	9 830	4 987	4 843
30-34	5 456	2 727	2 729	6 111	3 051	3 060	6 798	3 415	3 383	7 660	3 901	3 759
35-39	4 596	2 285	2 311	5 165	2 572	2 594	5 658	2 823	2 835	6 151	3 111	3 040
40-44	3 602	1 778	1 824	4 339	2 148	2 191	4 793	2 378	2 414	5 145	2 572	2 573
45-49	3 097	1 522	1 575	3 386	1 659	1 726	4 031	1 982	2 049	4 386	2 168	2 218
50-54	2 550	1 234	1 316	2 882	1 403	1 479	3 129	1 518	1 611	3 689	1 798	1 892
55-59	2 058	982	1 075	2 330	1 115	1 215	2 624	1 262	1 362	2 834	1 359	1 474
60-64	1 617	761	856	1 819	857	962	2 058	972	1 086	2 313	1 098	1 214
65-69	1 194	552	642	1 349	626	723	1 520	706	814	1 720	801	919
70-74	786	352	433	902	409	494	1 025	467	558	1 158	529	629
75-79	433	184	249	510	221	289	591	261	330	675	301	374
80 +	245	96	149	284	112	172	359	145	214	429	177	252

United Nations Department of Economic and Social Affairs/Population Division
World Population Prospects: The 2004 Revision, Volume II: Sex and Age Distribution of the World Population

654

POPULATION BY AGE AND SEX (in thousands)

Age group	2005 Both sexes	2005 Males	2005 Females	2010 Both sexes	2010 Males	2010 Females	2015 Both sexes	2015 Males	2015 Females	2020 Both sexes	2020 Males	2020 Females
All ages	131 530	66 558	64 971	145 991	74 119	71 872	160 931	81 909	79 022	175 798	89 667	86 131
0-4	22 257	11 412	10 845	23 536	12 067	11 469	24 429	12 528	11 901	24 674	12 660	12 013
5-9	18 995	9 738	9 257	20 633	10 584	10 049	21 999	11 278	10 721	23 058	11 822	11 236
10-14	16 972	8 692	8 281	18 396	9 436	8 959	20 021	10 274	9 747	21 424	10 987	10 438
15-19	14 803	7 561	7 242	16 598	8 500	8 098	18 011	9 238	8 774	19 638	10 075	9 563
20-24	12 513	6 354	6 158	14 348	7 313	7 035	16 126	8 241	7 885	17 542	8 978	8 564
25-29	9 830	4 987	4 843	11 847	6 018	5 828	13 638	6 953	6 685	15 401	7 871	7 530
30-34	7 660	3 901	3 759	9 038	4 622	4 416	10 978	5 615	5 363	12 714	6 524	6 190
35-39	6 151	3 111	3 040	6 935	3 567	3 368	8 259	4 260	3 999	10 097	5 208	4 889
40-44	5 145	2 572	2 573	5 578	2 836	2 742	6 333	3 274	3 059	7 589	3 935	3 655
45-49	4 386	2 168	2 218	4 697	2 344	2 352	5 119	2 600	2 519	5 842	3 019	2 823
50-54	3 689	1 798	1 892	4 009	1 967	2 042	4 311	2 138	2 173	4 720	2 384	2 336
55-59	2 834	1 359	1 474	3 342	1 612	1 731	3 647	1 772	1 875	3 941	1 937	2 004
60-64	2 313	1 098	1 214	2 503	1 186	1 318	2 968	1 414	1 554	3 257	1 564	1 693
65-69	1 720	801	919	1 939	908	1 032	2 114	987	1 127	2 525	1 187	1 339
70-74	1 158	529	629	1 319	604	715	1 500	691	809	1 654	760	894
75-79	675	301	374	770	344	426	889	398	491	1 026	462	564
80-84	309	132	177	357	154	204	415	179	236	489	212	277
85-89	99	39	60	118	47	71	139	57	83	166	68	98
90-94	19	6	13	25	9	16	30	11	19	36	13	23
95-99	2	1	2	3	1	2	4	1	3	5	1	3
100 +	0	0	0	0	0	0	0	0	0	0	0	0

Age group	2025 Both sexes	2025 Males	2025 Females	2030 Both sexes	2030 Males	2030 Females	2035 Both sexes	2035 Males	2035 Females	2040 Both sexes	2040 Males	2040 Females
All ages	190 287	97 235	93 052	204 465	104 645	99 820	218 436	111 937	106 499	232 180	119 072	113 108
0-4	24 509	12 584	11 925	24 368	12 520	11 847	24 348	12 516	11 832	24 300	12 492	11 808
5-9	23 496	12 054	11 442	23 514	12 074	11 440	23 521	12 088	11 433	23 626	12 145	11 481
10-14	22 555	11 567	10 988	23 068	11 836	11 231	23 155	11 891	11 264	23 220	11 933	11 286
15-19	21 058	10 795	10 263	22 214	11 387	10 826	22 759	11 673	11 086	22 880	11 743	11 137
20-24	19 168	9 814	9 355	20 599	10 539	10 060	21 776	11 141	10 635	22 352	11 441	10 911
25-29	16 823	8 609	8 213	18 453	9 447	9 005	19 907	10 183	9 724	21 124	10 803	10 321
30-34	14 455	7 430	7 025	15 884	8 171	7 713	17 526	9 014	8 512	19 019	9 766	9 253
35-39	11 782	6 093	5 690	13 500	6 986	6 514	14 936	7 730	7 206	16 596	8 580	8 017
40-44	9 342	4 842	4 500	10 985	5 705	5 280	12 674	6 585	6 089	14 119	7 333	6 787
45-49	7 042	3 651	3 391	8 728	4 524	4 204	10 329	5 366	4 963	11 991	6 231	5 760
50-54	5 415	2 784	2 630	6 567	3 390	3 177	8 186	4 227	3 959	9 741	5 042	4 699
55-59	4 337	2 172	2 164	5 004	2 554	2 449	6 102	3 129	2 973	7 648	3 925	3 723
60-64	3 540	1 721	1 819	3 921	1 945	1 976	4 553	2 304	2 249	5 585	2 839	2 746
65-69	2 792	1 324	1 468	3 059	1 469	1 590	3 414	1 675	1 740	3 995	1 999	1 996
70-74	1 997	924	1 073	2 231	1 043	1 188	2 471	1 171	1 300	2 786	1 349	1 437
75-79	1 149	517	631	1 408	639	768	1 595	732	863	1 791	834	957
80-84	576	252	324	658	289	369	822	364	458	949	426	523
85-89	200	83	118	242	101	141	284	119	164	363	155	208
90-94	45	17	28	56	21	34	69	27	42	83	32	51
95-99	6	2	4	7	2	5	9	3	6	12	4	8
100 +	0	0	0	1	0	0	1	0	1	1	0	1

Age group	2045 Both sexes	2045 Males	2045 Females	2050 Both sexes	2050 Males	2050 Females
All ages	245 493	125 924	119 569	258 108	132 337	125 771
0-4	24 050	12 361	11 689	23 574	12 112	11 462
5-9	23 691	12 176	11 515	23 546	12 095	11 451
10-14	23 373	12 013	11 359	23 479	12 064	11 415
15-19	22 976	11 800	11 176	23 156	11 892	11 264
20-24	22 511	11 530	10 981	22 644	11 604	11 040
25-29	21 757	11 129	10 628	21 986	11 250	10 736
30-34	20 298	10 411	9 887	21 021	10 775	10 246
35-39	18 134	9 350	8 784	19 481	10 023	9 458
40-44	15 795	8 188	7 607	17 369	8 974	8 396
45-49	13 439	6 979	6 460	15 120	7 836	7 284
50-54	11 369	5 888	5 481	12 806	6 628	6 178
55-59	9 148	4 707	4 441	10 730	5 524	5 206
60-64	7 042	3 583	3 458	8 469	4 321	4 148
65-69	4 935	2 481	2 454	6 265	3 152	3 113
70-74	3 292	1 626	1 666	4 103	2 035	2 068
75-79	2 046	974	1 072	2 449	1 188	1 260
80-84	1 084	493	591	1 259	585	673
85-89	428	185	243	499	219	280
90-94	109	43	66	131	53	78
95-99	15	5	10	20	7	13
100 +	1	0	1	1	0	1

United Nations Department of Economic and Social Affairs/Population Division
World Population Prospects: The 2004 Revision, Volume II: Sex and Age Distribution of the World Population

655

POPULATION BY AGE AND SEX (in thousands)

Age group	2005 Both sexes	Males	Females	2010 Both sexes	Males	Females	2015 Both sexes	Males	Females	2020 Both sexes	Males	Females
All ages	131 530	66 558	64 971	147 096	74 686	72 411	164 029	83 498	80 531	181 729	92 709	89 020
0-4	22 257	11 412	10 845	24 642	12 634	12 008	26 493	13 586	12 906	27 648	14 186	13 462
5-9	18 995	9 738	9 257	20 633	10 584	10 049	23 033	11 808	11 225	25 007	12 822	12 185
10-14	16 972	8 692	8 281	18 396	9 436	8 959	20 021	10 274	9 747	22 432	11 503	10 928
15-19	14 803	7 561	7 242	16 598	8 500	8 098	18 011	9 238	8 774	19 638	10 075	9 563
20-24	12 513	6 354	6 158	14 348	7 313	7 035	16 126	8 241	7 885	17 542	8 978	8 564
25-29	9 830	4 987	4 843	11 847	6 018	5 828	13 638	6 953	6 685	15 401	7 871	7 530
30-34	7 660	3 901	3 759	9 038	4 622	4 416	10 978	5 615	5 363	12 714	6 524	6 190
35-39	6 151	3 111	3 040	6 935	3 567	3 368	8 259	4 260	3 999	10 097	5 208	4 889
40-44	5 145	2 572	2 573	5 578	2 836	2 742	6 333	3 274	3 059	7 589	3 935	3 655
45-49	4 386	2 168	2 218	4 697	2 344	2 352	5 119	2 600	2 519	5 842	3 019	2 823
50-54	3 689	1 798	1 892	4 009	1 967	2 042	4 311	2 138	2 173	4 720	2 384	2 336
55-59	2 834	1 359	1 474	3 342	1 612	1 731	3 647	1 772	1 875	3 941	1 937	2 004
60-64	2 313	1 098	1 214	2 503	1 186	1 318	2 968	1 414	1 554	3 257	1 564	1 693
65-69	1 720	801	919	1 939	908	1 032	2 114	987	1 127	2 525	1 187	1 339
70-74	1 158	529	629	1 319	604	715	1 500	691	809	1 654	760	894
75-79	675	301	374	770	344	426	889	398	491	1 026	462	564
80-84	309	132	177	357	154	204	415	179	236	489	212	277
85-89	99	39	60	118	47	71	139	57	83	166	68	98
90-94	19	6	13	25	9	16	30	11	19	36	13	23
95-99	2	1	2	3	1	2	4	1	3	5	1	3
100 +	0	0	0	0	0	0	0	0	0	0	0	0

Age group	2025 Both sexes	Males	Females	2030 Both sexes	Males	Females	2035 Both sexes	Males	Females	2040 Both sexes	Males	Females
All ages	199 457	101 940	97 517	217 491	111 331	106 161	236 254	121 084	115 170	255 938	131 272	124 666
0-4	27 947	14 349	13 598	28 461	14 624	13 837	29 431	15 129	14 302	30 614	15 738	14 876
5-9	26 330	13 508	12 822	26 814	13 768	13 046	27 473	14 119	13 355	28 561	14 681	13 879
10-14	24 462	12 545	11 917	25 851	13 265	12 587	26 406	13 560	12 846	27 123	13 939	13 184
15-19	22 048	11 303	10 746	24 093	12 351	11 742	25 507	13 082	12 425	26 095	13 393	12 702
20-24	19 168	9 814	9 355	21 570	11 035	10 534	23 620	12 085	11 535	25 053	12 824	12 229
25-29	16 823	8 609	8 213	18 453	9 447	9 005	20 846	10 664	10 182	22 915	11 719	11 195
30-34	14 455	7 430	7 025	15 884	8 171	7 713	17 526	9 014	8 512	19 917	10 228	9 690
35-39	11 782	6 093	5 690	13 500	6 986	6 514	14 936	7 730	7 206	16 596	8 580	8 017
40-44	9 342	4 842	4 500	10 985	5 705	5 280	12 674	6 585	6 089	14 119	7 333	6 787
45-49	7 042	3 651	3 391	8 728	4 524	4 204	10 329	5 366	4 963	11 991	6 231	5 760
50-54	5 415	2 784	2 630	6 567	3 390	3 177	8 186	4 227	3 959	9 741	5 042	4 699
55-59	4 337	2 172	2 164	5 004	2 554	2 449	6 102	3 129	2 973	7 648	3 925	3 723
60-64	3 540	1 721	1 819	3 921	1 945	1 976	4 553	2 304	2 249	5 585	2 839	2 746
65-69	2 792	1 324	1 468	3 059	1 469	1 590	3 414	1 675	1 740	3 995	1 999	1 996
70-74	1 997	924	1 073	2 231	1 043	1 188	2 471	1 171	1 300	2 786	1 349	1 437
75-79	1 149	517	631	1 408	639	768	1 595	732	863	1 791	834	957
80-84	576	252	324	658	289	369	822	364	458	949	426	523
85-89	200	83	118	242	101	141	284	119	164	363	155	208
90-94	45	17	28	56	21	34	69	27	42	83	32	51
95-99	6	2	4	7	2	5	9	3	6	12	4	8
100 +	0	0	0	1	0	0	1	0	1	1	0	1

Age group	2045 Both sexes	Males	Females	2050 Both sexes	Males	Females
All ages	276 289	141 741	134 548	296 848	152 232	144 615
0-4	31 559	16 221	15 338	32 079	16 482	15 598
5-9	29 850	15 341	14 509	30 901	15 873	15 028
10-14	28 256	14 523	13 733	29 585	15 201	14 384
15-19	26 841	13 785	13 056	27 998	14 379	13 619
20-24	25 677	13 152	12 525	26 457	13 559	12 898
25-29	24 390	12 477	11 913	25 081	12 834	12 247
30-34	22 021	11 296	10 725	23 568	12 081	11 486
35-39	18 991	9 793	9 199	21 136	10 875	10 261
40-44	15 795	8 188	7 607	18 191	9 399	8 792
45-49	13 439	6 979	6 460	15 120	7 836	7 284
50-54	11 369	5 888	5 481	12 806	6 628	6 178
55-59	9 148	4 707	4 441	10 730	5 524	5 206
60-64	7 042	3 583	3 458	8 469	4 321	4 148
65-69	4 935	2 481	2 454	6 265	3 152	3 113
70-74	3 292	1 626	1 666	4 103	2 035	2 068
75-79	2 046	974	1 072	2 449	1 188	1 260
80-84	1 084	493	591	1 259	585	673
85-89	428	185	243	499	219	280
90-94	109	43	66	131	53	78
95-99	15	5	10	20	7	13
100 +	1	0	1	1	0	1

United Nations Department of Economic and Social Affairs/Population Division
World Population Prospects: The 2004 Revision, Volume II: Sex and Age Distribution of the World Population

656

POPULATION BY AGE AND SEX (in thousands)

Age group	2005 Both sexes	2005 Males	2005 Females	2010 Both sexes	2010 Males	2010 Females	2015 Both sexes	2015 Males	2015 Females	2020 Both sexes	2020 Males	2020 Females
All ages	131 530	66 558	64 971	144 885	73 552	71 333	157 833	80 321	77 512	169 967	86 626	83 242
0-4	22 257	11 412	10 845	22 430	11 500	10 930	22 365	11 470	10 896	21 699	11 134	10 565
5-9	18 995	9 738	9 257	20 633	10 584	10 049	20 964	10 748	10 217	21 109	10 823	10 286
10-14	16 972	8 692	8 281	18 396	9 436	8 959	20 021	10 274	9 747	20 417	10 470	9 947
15-19	14 803	7 561	7 242	16 598	8 500	8 098	18 011	9 238	8 774	19 638	10 075	9 563
20-24	12 513	6 354	6 158	14 348	7 313	7 035	16 126	8 241	7 885	17 542	8 978	8 564
25-29	9 830	4 987	4 843	11 847	6 018	5 828	13 638	6 953	6 685	15 401	7 871	7 530
30-34	7 660	3 901	3 759	9 038	4 622	4 416	10 978	5 615	5 363	12 714	6 524	6 190
35-39	6 151	3 111	3 040	6 935	3 567	3 368	8 259	4 260	3 999	10 097	5 208	4 889
40-44	5 145	2 572	2 573	5 578	2 836	2 742	6 333	3 274	3 059	7 589	3 935	3 655
45-49	4 386	2 168	2 218	4 697	2 344	2 352	5 119	2 600	2 519	5 842	3 019	2 823
50-54	3 689	1 798	1 892	4 009	1 967	2 042	4 311	2 138	2 173	4 720	2 384	2 336
55-59	2 834	1 359	1 474	3 342	1 612	1 731	3 647	1 772	1 875	3 941	1 937	2 004
60-64	2 313	1 098	1 214	2 503	1 186	1 318	2 968	1 414	1 554	3 257	1 564	1 693
65-69	1 720	801	919	1 939	908	1 032	2 114	987	1 127	2 525	1 187	1 339
70-74	1 158	529	629	1 319	604	715	1 500	691	809	1 654	760	894
75-79	675	301	374	770	344	426	889	398	491	1 026	462	564
80-84	309	132	177	357	154	204	415	179	236	489	212	277
85-89	99	39	60	118	47	71	139	57	83	166	68	98
90-94	19	6	13	25	9	16	30	11	19	36	13	23
95-99	2	1	2	3	1	2	4	1	3	5	1	3
100 +	0	0	0	0	0	0	0	0	0	0	0	0

Age group	2025 Both sexes	2025 Males	2025 Females	2030 Both sexes	2030 Males	2030 Females	2035 Both sexes	2035 Males	2035 Females	2040 Both sexes	2040 Males	2040 Females
All ages	181 133	92 538	88 595	191 544	98 013	93 531	200 997	102 983	98 013	209 366	107 357	102 009
0-4	21 088	10 827	10 260	20 364	10 463	9 901	19 541	10 045	9 496	18 560	9 542	9 019
5-9	20 662	10 600	10 062	20 230	10 387	9 843	19 655	10 101	9 554	18 960	9 746	9 214
10-14	20 648	10 589	10 059	20 284	10 408	9 876	19 920	10 229	9 690	19 402	9 971	9 431
15-19	20 067	10 287	9 780	20 334	10 424	9 910	20 011	10 263	9 748	19 681	10 101	9 580
20-24	19 168	9 814	9 355	19 629	10 042	9 587	19 931	10 197	9 734	19 650	10 058	9 592
25-29	16 823	8 609	8 213	18 453	9 447	9 005	18 968	9 702	9 265	19 332	9 886	9 446
30-34	14 455	7 430	7 025	15 884	8 171	7 713	17 526	9 014	8 512	18 121	9 305	8 816
35-39	11 782	6 093	5 690	13 500	6 986	6 514	14 936	7 730	7 206	16 596	8 580	8 017
40-44	9 342	4 842	4 500	10 985	5 705	5 280	12 674	6 586	6 080	14 119	7 033	5 760
45-49	7 042	3 651	3 391	8 728	4 524	4 204	10 329	5 366	4 963	11 991	6 231	5 760
50-54	5 415	2 784	2 630	6 567	3 390	3 177	8 186	4 227	3 959	9 741	5 042	4 699
55-59	4 337	2 172	2 164	5 004	2 554	2 449	6 102	3 129	2 973	7 648	3 925	3 723
60-64	3 540	1 721	1 819	3 921	1 945	1 976	4 553	2 304	2 249	5 585	2 839	2 746
65-69	2 792	1 324	1 468	3 059	1 469	1 590	3 414	1 675	1 740	3 995	1 999	1 996
70-74	1 997	924	1 073	2 231	1 043	1 188	2 471	1 171	1 300	2 786	1 349	1 437
75-79	1 149	517	631	1 408	639	768	1 595	732	863	1 791	834	957
80-84	576	252	324	658	289	369	822	364	458	940	420	520
85-89	200	83	118	242	101	141	284	119	164	363	155	208
90-94	45	17	28	56	21	34	69	27	42	83	32	51
95-99	6	2	4	7	2	5	9	3	6	12	4	8
100 +	0	0	0	1	0	0	1	0	1	1	0	1

Age group	2045 Both sexes	2045 Males	2045 Females	2050 Both sexes	2050 Males	2050 Females
All ages	216 541	111 055	105 486	222 444	114 022	108 422
0-4	17 459	8 973	8 485	16 328	8 389	7 939
5-9	18 093	9 299	8 794	17 090	8 778	8 311
10-14	18 755	9 640	9 115	17 929	9 212	8 717
15-19	19 196	9 858	9 337	18 578	9 541	9 037
20-24	19 361	9 916	9 445	18 914	9 693	9 222
25-29	19 125	9 782	9 343	18 905	9 673	9 233
30-34	18 575	9 527	9 048	18 474	9 469	9 006
35-39	17 277	8 908	8 369	17 826	9 170	8 655
40-44	15 795	8 188	7 607	16 548	8 549	7 999
45-49	13 439	6 979	6 460	15 120	7 836	7 284
50-54	11 369	5 888	5 481	12 806	6 628	6 178
55-59	9 148	4 707	4 441	10 730	5 524	5 206
60-64	7 042	3 583	3 458	8 469	4 321	4 148
65-69	4 935	2 481	2 454	6 265	3 152	3 113
70-74	3 292	1 626	1 666	4 103	2 035	2 068
75-79	2 046	974	1 072	2 449	1 188	1 260
80-84	1 084	493	591	1 259	585	673
85-89	428	185	243	499	219	280
90-94	109	43	66	131	53	78
95-99	15	5	10	20	7	13
100 +	1	0	1	1	0	1

POPULATION BY AGE AND SEX (in thousands)

Age group	1950 Both sexes	Males	Females	1955 Both sexes	Males	Females	1960 Both sexes	Males	Females	1965 Both sexes	Males	Females
All ages	3 265	1 618	1 647	3 427	1 705	1 722	3 581	1 784	1 797	3 723	1 855	1 868
0-4	319	164	155	304	156	148	308	158	150	312	160	152
5-9	265	136	129	317	163	154	302	155	147	308	158	150
10-14	214	109	105	258	132	126	317	163	154	302	155	147
15-19	204	104	100	210	107	103	262	134	128	317	163	154
20-24	229	117	112	206	105	101	208	106	102	256	132	124
25-29	260	132	128	230	118	112	199	101	98	205	104	101
30-34	261	131	130	265	134	131	223	113	110	199	101	98
35-39	248	125	123	257	129	128	257	130	127	223	113	110
40-44	232	115	117	247	124	123	256	128	128	258	130	128
45-49	215	104	111	228	113	115	243	122	121	251	125	126
50-54	198	96	102	210	102	108	224	111	113	239	119	120
55-59	167	80	87	191	92	99	203	98	105	216	105	111
60-64	137	64	73	156	74	82	181	86	95	192	91	101
65-69	110	50	60	124	57	67	145	68	77	164	76	88
70-74	89	41	48	94	42	52	109	49	60	123	56	67
75-79	61	27	34	69	31	38	75	32	43	83	36	47
80 +	56	23	33	61	26	35	69	30	39	75	31	44

Age group	1970 Both sexes	Males	Females	1975 Both sexes	Males	Females	1980 Both sexes	Males	Females	1985 Both sexes	Males	Females
All ages	3 877	1 929	1 949	4 007	1 991	2 017	4 086	2 025	2 061	4 153	2 053	2 099
0-4	330	169	160	310	158	151	261	134	127	254	130	124
5-9	311	160	152	331	170	161	312	159	152	263	135	129
10-14	308	158	150	313	160	152	333	171	162	313	160	153
15-19	302	155	147	309	158	151	314	161	153	335	172	163
20-24	315	162	152	302	155	147	310	158	151	316	162	154
25-29	253	130	123	315	163	152	304	156	148	313	160	153
30-34	204	103	100	253	130	123	316	163	153	306	157	149
35-39	199	101	98	204	103	100	253	130	123	317	164	153
40-44	222	112	109	198	100	98	203	103	100	253	130	123
45-49	255	128	127	219	111	109	196	99	97	201	102	100
50-54	245	122	124	250	125	125	215	108	107	192	96	96
55-59	230	113	117	237	116	121	242	119	123	208	103	105
60-64	204	98	107	218	105	113	225	108	117	229	110	119
65-69	176	81	96	187	86	101	198	92	106	207	96	111
70-74	141	62	79	152	66	86	164	72	92	175	77	98
75-79	96	41	55	110	45	65	120	48	72	131	53	78
80 +	86	34	52	100	38	61	121	44	78	140	48	92

Age group	1990 Both sexes	Males	Females	1995 Both sexes	Males	Females	2000 Both sexes	Males	Females	2005 Both sexes	Males	Females
All ages	4 241	2 097	2 144	4 359	2 156	2 204	4 502	2 231	2 271	4 620	2 295	2 326
0-4	280	144	137	304	156	148	300	154	146	283	145	138
5-9	258	132	125	285	146	139	311	160	151	307	157	150
10-14	266	136	130	261	134	127	289	148	141	315	162	153
15-19	315	161	154	269	138	132	265	136	129	292	150	143
20-24	338	173	165	320	163	157	275	140	135	270	138	132
25-29	323	166	157	344	176	168	328	166	162	282	143	139
30-34	317	163	155	327	168	159	352	180	173	335	169	166
35-39	307	157	149	319	163	156	332	170	162	356	181	175
40-44	315	163	153	306	157	150	320	163	157	333	170	163
45-49	250	128	122	313	160	152	305	155	149	319	162	157
50-54	197	99	99	246	125	121	309	158	151	301	153	148
55-59	186	92	94	193	96	97	240	121	119	302	154	148
60-64	197	96	102	178	87	91	186	91	94	232	116	116
65-69	211	98	113	183	86	97	168	80	88	176	85	91
70-74	182	80	102	187	83	104	167	76	90	154	72	82
75-79	141	57	84	149	61	89	160	68	92	143	63	81
80 +	158	53	105	175	58	117	196	65	131	219	76	143

(*) Including Svalbard and Jan Mayen Islands.

658

United Nations Department of Economic and Social Affairs/Population Division
World Population Prospects: The 2004 Revision, Volume II: Sex and Age Distribution of the World Population

POPULATION BY AGE AND SEX (in thousands)

Age group	2005 Both sexes	Males	Females	2010 Both sexes	Males	Females	2015 Both sexes	Males	Females	2020 Both sexes	Males	Females
All ages	4 620	2 295	2 326	4 730	2 354	2 376	4 841	2 412	2 429	4 960	2 472	2 487
0-4	283	145	138	272	140	132	274	140	133	285	146	139
5-9	307	157	150	290	148	141	279	143	136	281	144	137
10-14	315	162	153	310	159	151	294	150	143	283	145	138
15-19	292	150	143	319	164	155	314	161	153	297	152	145
20-24	270	138	132	298	152	146	324	166	158	320	163	157
25-29	282	143	139	278	141	137	305	155	150	332	169	163
30-34	335	169	166	289	146	143	285	144	141	313	158	154
35-39	356	181	175	339	171	169	294	148	146	290	147	144
40-44	333	170	163	358	182	176	341	171	170	296	149	147
45-49	319	162	157	332	169	163	357	181	176	341	171	170
50-54	301	153	148	316	160	156	329	167	162	354	179	175
55-59	302	154	148	296	150	146	310	156	154	324	164	160
60-64	232	116	116	293	148	145	287	144	143	302	151	150
65-69	176	85	91	221	109	112	279	139	140	275	136	138
70-74	154	72	82	162	77	86	204	99	106	259	126	132
75-79	143	63	81	134	60	74	142	65	77	179	84	96
80-84	122	47	74	111	45	66	105	44	62	113	48	65
85-89	68	22	46	76	26	50	71	26	46	69	26	44
90-94	24	6	18	30	8	22	36	10	25	35	11	24
95-99	5	1	4	6	1	5	9	2	7	11	2	9
100 +	1	0	0	1	0	1	1	0	1	2	0	1

Age group	2025 Both sexes	Males	Females	2030 Both sexes	Males	Females	2035 Both sexes	Males	Females	2040 Both sexes	Males	Females
All ages	5 080	2 530	2 550	5 190	2 581	2 609	5 276	2 619	2 657	5 339	2 646	2 693
0-4	296	152	144	300	154	146	295	152	144	288	148	140
5-9	292	150	142	303	156	148	307	158	149	302	155	147
10-14	285	146	139	296	152	144	307	158	150	311	160	151
15-19	287	147	140	289	148	141	300	154	146	311	160	152
20-24	303	155	148	293	150	143	294	150	144	306	156	149
25-29	327	166	161	311	158	153	301	153	148	302	154	148
30-34	339	172	167	335	170	165	319	162	157	308	157	152
35-39	010	161	157	344	175	170	340	172	168	324	164	160
40-44	292	147	145	320	162	158	347	176	171	342	173	169
45-49	296	149	147	292	147	145	320	161	159	347	176	171
50-54	338	169	169	294	147	147	291	146	145	318	160	158
55-59	348	176	173	333	166	167	290	145	145	287	144	143
60-64	316	159	157	340	170	170	326	162	164	284	141	143
65-69	289	144	146	303	151	152	327	162	165	315	154	160
70-74	255	124	131	270	131	139	284	139	145	308	150	158
75-79	229	108	121	227	107	120	241	114	128	255	121	134
80-84	144	63	81	185	82	103	186	83	103	199	89	111
85-89	76	29	47	99	39	60	129	52	77	132	53	79
90-94	35	11	24	40	13	27	54	18	36	73	25	48
95-99	12	3	9	13	3	10	15	4	11	21	6	16
100 +	2	0	2	3	0	2	3	0	2	4	1	3

Age group	2045 Both sexes	Males	Females	2050 Both sexes	Males	Females
All ages	5 388	2 667	2 721	5 435	2 689	2 746
0-4	287	148	140	292	150	142
5-9	296	152	144	295	151	143
10-14	306	157	149	300	154	146
15-19	315	161	153	310	159	151
20-24	317	162	155	321	164	157
25-29	314	160	154	325	165	159
30-34	310	157	153	322	163	158
35-39	314	159	155	315	160	155
40-44	326	165	161	316	160	156
45-49	343	173	170	327	165	161
50-54	345	174	171	341	172	169
55-59	315	158	157	341	172	169
60-64	282	140	141	309	155	154
65-69	275	136	140	273	135	138
70-74	296	143	153	260	126	134
75-79	278	131	146	269	126	143
80-84	213	95	117	233	105	129
85-89	145	59	86	157	64	92
90-94	77	27	51	87	30	56
95-99	30	8	22	33	9	24
100 +	5	1	5	8	2	7

United Nations Department of Economic and Social Affairs/Population Division
World Population Prospects: The 2004 Revision, Volume II: Sex and Age Distribution of the World Population

659

POPULATION BY AGE AND SEX (in thousands)

Age group	2005 Both sexes	Males	Females	2010 Both sexes	Males	Females	2015 Both sexes	Males	Females	2020 Both sexes	Males	Females
All ages	4 620	2 295	2 326	4 767	2 373	2 394	4 935	2 461	2 474	5 131	2 560	2 570
0-4	283	145	138	308	158	150	332	170	161	361	186	176
5-9	307	157	150	290	148	141	316	162	154	339	174	165
10-14	315	162	153	310	159	151	294	150	143	320	164	156
15-19	292	150	143	319	164	155	314	161	153	297	152	145
20-24	270	138	132	298	152	146	324	166	158	320	163	157
25-29	282	143	139	278	141	137	305	155	150	332	169	163
30-34	335	169	166	289	146	143	285	144	141	313	158	154
35-39	356	181	175	339	171	169	294	148	146	290	147	144
40-44	333	170	163	358	182	176	341	171	170	296	149	147
45-49	319	162	157	332	169	163	357	181	176	341	171	170
50-54	301	153	148	316	160	156	329	167	162	354	179	175
55-59	302	154	148	296	150	146	310	156	154	324	164	160
60-64	232	116	116	293	148	145	287	144	143	302	151	150
65-69	176	85	91	221	109	112	279	139	140	275	136	138
70-74	154	72	82	162	77	86	204	99	106	259	126	132
75-79	143	63	81	134	60	74	142	65	77	179	84	96
80-84	122	47	74	111	45	66	105	44	62	113	48	65
85-89	68	22	46	76	26	50	71	26	46	69	26	44
90-94	24	6	18	30	8	22	36	10	25	35	11	24
95-99	5	1	4	6	1	5	9	2	7	11	2	9
100 +	1	0	0	1	0	1	1	0	1	2	0	1

Age group	2025 Both sexes	Males	Females	2030 Both sexes	Males	Females	2035 Both sexes	Males	Females	2040 Both sexes	Males	Females
All ages	5 331	2 659	2 672	5 522	2 752	2 770	5 698	2 836	2 862	5 872	2 920	2 952
0-4	376	193	183	381	196	185	385	198	187	400	205	194
5-9	368	189	179	383	196	186	388	199	189	392	201	191
10-14	343	176	167	372	191	181	387	198	188	392	201	191
15-19	323	166	158	347	178	169	376	193	183	391	200	190
20-24	303	155	148	329	168	161	352	180	172	382	195	186
25-29	327	166	161	311	158	153	337	171	165	360	184	177
30-34	339	172	167	335	170	165	319	162	157	345	175	170
35-39	318	161	157	344	175	170	340	172	168	324	164	160
40-44	292	147	145	320	162	158	347	176	171	342	173	169
45-49	296	149	147	292	147	145	320	161	159	347	176	171
50-54	338	169	169	294	147	147	291	146	145	318	160	158
55-59	348	176	173	333	166	167	290	145	145	287	144	143
60-64	316	159	157	340	170	170	326	162	164	284	141	143
65-69	289	144	146	303	151	152	327	162	165	315	154	160
70-74	255	124	131	270	131	139	284	139	145	308	150	158
75-79	228	108	121	227	107	120	241	114	128	255	121	134
80-84	144	63	81	185	82	103	186	83	103	199	89	111
85-89	76	29	47	99	39	60	129	52	77	132	53	79
90-94	35	11	24	40	13	27	54	18	36	73	25	48
95-99	12	3	9	13	3	10	15	4	11	21	6	16
100 +	2	0	2	3	0	2	3	0	2	4	1	3

Age group	2045 Both sexes	Males	Females	2050 Both sexes	Males	Females
All ages	6 058	3 011	3 046	6 261	3 113	3 148
0-4	425	218	206	450	231	219
5-9	407	209	198	432	222	210
10-14	396	203	193	411	211	200
15-19	396	203	193	400	205	195
20-24	396	203	193	402	206	196
25-29	390	199	191	404	206	198
30-34	368	187	181	398	202	195
35-39	350	178	172	373	190	183
40-44	326	165	161	352	179	174
45-49	343	173	170	327	165	161
50-54	345	174	171	341	172	169
55-59	315	158	157	341	172	169
60-64	282	140	141	309	155	154
65-69	275	136	140	273	135	138
70-74	296	143	153	260	126	134
75-79	278	131	146	269	126	143
80-84	213	95	117	233	105	129
85-89	145	59	86	157	64	92
90-94	77	27	51	87	30	56
95-99	30	8	22	33	9	24
100 +	5	1	5	8	2	7

United Nations Department of Economic and Social Affairs/Population Division
World Population Prospects: The 2004 Revision, Volume II: Sex and Age Distribution of the World Population

660

POPULATION BY AGE AND SEX (in thousands)

Age group	2005 Both sexes	2005 Males	2005 Females	2010 Both sexes	2010 Males	2010 Females	2015 Both sexes	2015 Males	2015 Females	2020 Both sexes	2020 Males	2020 Females
All ages	4 620	2 295	2 326	4 694	2 335	2 358	4 746	2 364	2 382	4 789	2 385	2 404
0-4	283	145	138	236	121	115	215	111	105	209	107	102
5-9	307	157	150	290	148	141	243	124	118	223	114	108
10-14	315	162	153	310	159	151	294	150	143	247	126	120
15-19	292	150	143	319	164	155	314	161	153	297	152	145
20-24	270	138	132	298	152	146	324	166	158	320	163	157
25-29	282	143	139	278	141	137	305	155	150	332	169	163
30-34	335	169	166	289	146	143	285	144	141	313	158	154
35-39	356	181	175	339	171	169	294	148	146	290	147	144
40-44	333	170	163	358	182	176	341	171	170	296	149	147
45-49	319	162	157	332	169	163	357	181	176	341	171	170
50-54	301	153	148	316	160	156	329	167	162	354	179	175
55-59	302	154	148	296	150	146	310	156	154	324	164	160
60-64	232	116	116	293	148	145	287	144	143	302	151	150
65-69	176	85	91	221	109	112	279	139	140	275	136	138
70-74	154	72	82	162	77	86	204	99	106	259	126	132
75-79	143	63	81	134	60	74	142	65	77	179	84	96
80-84	122	47	74	111	45	66	105	44	62	113	48	65
85-89	68	22	46	76	26	50	71	26	46	69	26	44
90-94	24	6	18	30	8	22	36	10	25	35	11	24
95-99	5	1	4	6	1	5	9	2	7	11	2	9
100 +	1	0	0	1	0	1	1	0	1	2	0	1

Age group	2025 Both sexes	2025 Males	2025 Females	2030 Both sexes	2030 Males	2030 Females	2035 Both sexes	2035 Males	2035 Females	2040 Both sexes	2040 Males	2040 Females
All ages	4 830	2 402	2 428	4 860	2 412	2 448	4 865	2 408	2 457	4 837	2 388	2 449
0-4	217	111	105	219	113	107	213	109	104	198	101	96
5-9	216	111	105	224	115	109	227	116	110	220	113	107
10-14	227	116	110	220	113	107	228	117	111	231	118	112
15-19	251	128	122	230	118	112	224	115	109	232	119	113
20-24	303	155	148	256	131	125	236	121	116	230	117	112
25-29	327	166	161	311	158	153	264	134	130	244	124	120
30-34	339	172	167	335	170	165	319	162	157	272	138	134
35-39	318	161	157	344	175	170	340	172	168	324	164	160
40-44	292	147	145	320	162	158	347	176	171	342	173	169
45-49	296	149	147	292	147	145	320	161	150	347	176	171
50-54	338	169	169	294	147	147	291	146	145	318	160	158
55-59	348	176	173	333	166	167	290	145	145	287	144	143
60-64	316	159	157	340	170	170	326	162	164	284	141	143
65-69	289	144	146	303	151	152	327	162	165	315	154	160
70-74	255	124	131	270	131	139	284	139	145	308	150	158
75-79	228	108	121	227	107	120	241	114	128	255	121	134
80-84	144	63	81	185	82	103	186	83	103	199	89	111
85-89	76	29	47	99	39	60	129	52	77	132	53	79
90-94	35	11	24	40	13	27	54	18	36	73	25	48
95-99	12	3	9	13	3	10	15	4	11	21	6	16
100 +	2	0	2	3	0	2	3	0	2	4	1	3

Age group	2045 Both sexes	2045 Males	2045 Females	2050 Both sexes	2050 Males	2050 Females
All ages	4 781	2 355	2 425	4 708	2 316	2 392
0-4	182	93	88	173	89	84
5-9	205	105	100	189	97	92
10-14	224	115	109	209	107	102
15-19	235	120	114	228	117	111
20-24	238	121	116	240	123	118
25-29	238	121	117	246	125	121
30-34	252	128	124	246	125	121
35-39	277	141	137	258	130	127
40-44	326	165	161	280	142	138
45-49	343	173	170	327	165	161
50-54	345	174	171	341	172	169
55-59	315	158	157	341	172	169
60-64	282	140	141	309	155	154
65-69	275	136	140	273	135	138
70-74	296	143	153	260	126	134
75-79	278	131	146	269	126	143
80-84	213	95	117	233	105	129
85-89	145	59	86	157	64	92
90-94	77	27	51	87	30	56
95-99	30	8	22	33	9	24
100 +	5	1	5	8	2	7

United Nations Department of Economic and Social Affairs/Population Division
World Population Prospects: The 2004 Revision, Volume II: Sex and Age Distribution of the World Population

661

POPULATION BY AGE AND SEX (in thousands)

Age group	1950 Both sexes	Males	Females	1955 Both sexes	Males	Females	1960 Both sexes	Males	Females	1965 Both sexes	Males	Females
All ages	1 005	521	483	1 042	540	501	1 101	571	530	1 199	618	580
0-4	187	99	88	182	95	86	191	100	91	225	114	110
5-9	148	77	71	157	83	74	156	82	74	169	88	81
10-14	124	64	60	132	68	63	141	75	66	143	75	68
15-19	99	51	48	111	57	54	119	62	57	129	69	60
20-24	77	38	39	88	46	43	100	52	48	109	57	52
25-29	63	30	33	69	35	35	80	42	39	91	47	44
30-34	51	25	26	57	28	30	63	32	31	73	38	35
35-39	43	22	21	45	23	23	52	25	26	57	29	28
40-44	40	21	19	38	20	18	41	21	20	46	23	24
45-49	35	19	16	35	18	16	34	17	16	36	18	18
50-54	33	18	14	30	16	14	30	16	15	30	15	15
55-59	32	17	15	27	15	12	25	13	12	26	13	13
60-64	26	14	12	25	13	12	22	12	10	20	11	10
65-69	20	11	9	19	10	9	19	10	9	17	9	8
70-74	16	8	7	15	8	7	15	7	7	12	6	6
75-79	8	5	4	8	4	4	8	4	4	9	5	5
80 +	4	2	2	4	2	2	4	2	2	6	3	3

Age group	1970 Both sexes	Males	Females	1975 Both sexes	Males	Females	1980 Both sexes	Males	Females	1985 Both sexes	Males	Females
All ages	1 096	562	534	1 255	641	614	1 476	762	714	1 783	917	866
0-4	203	103	100	239	122	117	273	143	130	320	162	158
5-9	161	82	79	186	95	91	237	125	112	271	141	131
10-14	128	67	62	153	78	75	193	101	91	240	128	112
15-19	110	58	53	123	64	59	170	92	78	195	104	91
20-24	98	53	46	104	54	50	126	66	60	163	86	77
25-29	82	42	39	93	49	44	96	50	46	125	65	60
30-34	68	35	33	77	40	37	73	37	36	101	51	49
35-39	55	28	27	64	33	31	60	29	31	74	36	38
40-44	44	22	22	52	27	26	54	25	29	62	29	32
45-49	36	18	19	41	20	21	48	24	25	52	25	28
50-54	28	14	14	34	16	18	41	20	21	46	22	23
55-59	24	12	12	26	12	13	32	16	17	39	18	21
60-64	20	10	10	21	10	11	23	12	11	31	15	16
65-69	15	7	7	16	8	8	18	9	9	20	10	10
70-74	11	6	5	12	6	6	16	7	8	22	11	10
75-79	6	3	3	8	4	4	10	5	5	14	7	7
80 +	5	2	3	5	2	3	7	4	3	10	5	5

Age group	1990 Both sexes	Males	Females	1995 Both sexes	Males	Females	2000 Both sexes	Males	Females	2005 Both sexes	Males	Females
All ages	2 154	1 104	1 050	2 610	1 326	1 284	3 150	1 601	1 549	3 702	1 883	1 819
0-4	396	201	195	466	239	227	587	300	287	646	330	316
5-9	328	166	162	413	212	201	465	238	227	578	295	283
10-14	282	146	136	318	163	154	413	212	202	459	235	224
15-19	246	131	115	272	140	132	318	164	154	408	209	199
20-24	194	104	90	237	122	114	272	140	132	313	161	152
25-29	156	83	74	191	99	92	236	122	114	268	138	130
30-34	118	62	57	166	87	80	191	99	92	232	120	112
35-39	96	49	47	127	66	61	166	86	80	187	97	91
40-44	71	35	36	94	47	47	126	65	61	162	84	78
45-49	60	29	32	74	38	36	93	46	47	123	64	59
50-54	51	24	27	59	28	31	72	37	36	90	45	45
55-59	44	21	23	46	19	26	57	26	30	69	35	34
60-64	37	17	20	45	20	25	43	18	25	53	24	28
65-69	28	13	15	38	16	21	40	18	23	38	16	22
70-74	17	8	9	28	12	16	31	13	18	34	14	19
75-79	16	8	8	16	7	9	21	9	12	23	9	14
80 +	12	6	6	19	9	10	17	8	10	19	8	11

United Nations Department of Economic and Social Affairs/Population Division
World Population Prospects: The 2004 Revision, Volume II: Sex and Age Distribution of the World Population

662

POPULATION BY AGE AND SEX (in thousands)

Age group	2005 Both sexes	Males	Females	2010 Both sexes	Males	Females	2015 Both sexes	Males	Females	2020 Both sexes	Males	Females
All ages	3 702	1 883	1 819	4 330	2 204	2 126	4 996	2 544	2 452	5 694	2 900	2 794
0-4	646	330	316	698	356	341	741	379	362	779	399	381
5-9	578	295	283	643	328	315	695	355	340	738	377	361
10-14	459	235	224	576	294	282	641	327	314	693	354	339
15-19	408	209	199	457	234	223	574	293	281	639	326	313
20-24	313	161	152	406	208	198	455	233	222	572	291	280
25-29	268	138	130	311	160	151	403	206	197	453	231	221
30-34	232	120	112	266	137	129	309	159	151	401	205	196
35-39	187	97	91	231	119	112	264	136	128	307	158	150
40-44	162	84	78	186	96	90	228	118	111	262	135	127
45-49	123	64	59	160	83	77	183	94	89	226	116	109
50-54	90	45	45	120	62	58	156	81	76	179	92	87
55-59	69	35	34	86	43	44	116	59	57	151	78	74
60-64	53	24	28	65	32	33	81	40	42	110	56	54
65-69	38	16	22	48	21	26	59	29	30	75	36	39
70-74	34	14	19	32	13	19	41	18	23	51	24	27
75-79	23	9	14	25	10	15	25	10	15	32	13	19
80-84	13	5	7	14	6	9	16	6	10	16	6	11
85-89	4	2	3	6	2	3	7	2	4	8	3	5
90-94	2	1	1	1	0	1	2	1	1	2	1	2
95-99	0	0	0	0	0	0	0	0	0	0	0	0
100 +	0	0	0	0	0	0	0	0	0	0	0	0

Age group	2025 Both sexes	Males	Females	2030 Both sexes	Males	Females	2035 Both sexes	Males	Females	2040 Both sexes	Males	Females
All ages	6 422	3 270	3 151	7 171	3 651	3 520	7 923	4 032	3 892	8 661	4 404	4 257
0-4	820	420	400	855	438	417	875	448	427	883	452	431
5-9	777	397	379	817	418	399	853	437	416	873	447	426
10-14	736	376	360	775	397	379	816	418	398	851	436	415
15-19	691	353	338	734	375	359	773	396	378	814	417	398
20-24	636	325	312	688	351	337	732	374	358	771	394	377
25-29	569	290	279	634	323	311	686	350	336	730	373	357
30-34	450	230	220	567	289	278	632	322	310	684	349	335
35-39	399	204	195	448	229	219	565	288	277	629	321	308
40-44	305	156	149	307	203	194	446	228	218	562	286	276
45-49	259	133	126	302	155	147	393	201	192	442	226	216
50-54	222	114	108	255	131	124	298	152	145	388	198	190
55-59	174	89	85	216	110	105	248	127	122	290	148	143
60-64	144	73	71	166	84	82	207	104	102	238	120	118
65-69	101	50	51	133	66	67	154	77	78	193	96	97
70-74	65	30	35	89	43	46	118	57	61	137	66	71
75-79	40	18	22	52	23	29	72	33	39	96	45	52
80-84	21	8	13	27	11	16	36	15	22	51	22	29
85-89	8	3	6	11	4	8	15	5	10	21	7	13
90-94	3	1	2	3	1	2	4	1	3	6	2	4
95-99	0	0	0	1	0	1	1	0	1	1	0	1
100 +	0	0	0	0	0	0	0	0	0	0	0	0

Age group	2045 Both sexes	Males	Females	2050 Both sexes	Males	Females
All ages	9 375	4 763	4 612	10 058	5 105	4 953
0-4	884	453	431	883	452	431
5-9	881	451	430	882	452	430
10-14	872	446	425	879	450	429
15-19	850	435	415	870	446	425
20-24	812	416	397	848	434	414
25-29	769	393	376	810	414	396
30-34	727	371	356	767	392	375
35-39	681	347	334	725	370	355
40-44	626	319	307	678	346	332
45-49	557	284	274	621	317	305
50-54	436	222	214	550	280	271
55-59	379	192	187	427	217	210
60-64	280	141	139	366	184	182
65-69	224	111	112	263	131	132
70-74	173	84	89	201	98	104
75-79	114	53	61	145	67	77
80-84	70	30	40	84	36	48
85-89	30	11	19	42	16	26
90-94	9	3	6	13	4	9
95-99	2	0	1	3	1	2
100 +	0	0	0	0	0	0

POPULATION BY AGE AND SEX (in thousands)

Age group	2005 Both sexes	2005 Males	2005 Females	2010 Both sexes	2010 Males	2010 Females	2015 Both sexes	2015 Males	2015 Females	2020 Both sexes	2020 Males	2020 Females
All ages	3 702	1 883	1 819	4 365	2 222	2 143	5 098	2 596	2 502	5 897	3 004	2 893
0-4	646	330	316	732	374	358	808	413	395	881	451	430
5-9	578	295	283	643	328	315	729	373	357	805	412	393
10-14	459	235	224	576	294	282	641	327	314	727	371	356
15-19	408	209	199	457	234	223	574	293	281	639	326	313
20-24	313	161	152	406	208	198	455	233	222	572	291	280
25-29	268	138	130	311	160	151	403	206	197	453	231	221
30-34	232	120	112	266	137	129	309	159	151	401	205	196
35-39	187	97	91	231	119	112	264	136	128	307	158	150
40-44	162	84	78	186	96	90	228	118	111	262	135	127
45-49	123	64	59	160	83	77	183	94	89	226	116	109
50-54	90	45	45	120	62	58	156	81	76	179	92	87
55-59	69	35	34	86	43	44	116	59	57	151	78	74
60-64	53	24	28	65	32	33	81	40	42	110	56	54
65-69	38	16	22	48	21	26	59	29	30	75	36	39
70-74	34	14	19	32	13	19	41	18	23	51	24	27
75-79	23	9	14	25	10	15	25	10	15	32	13	19
80-84	13	5	7	14	6	9	16	6	10	16	6	11
85-89	4	2	3	6	2	3	7	2	4	8	3	5
90-94	2	1	1	1	0	1	2	1	1	2	1	2
95-99	0	0	0	0	0	0	0	0	0	0	0	0
100 +	0	0	0	0	0	0	0	0	0	0	0	0

Age group	2025 Both sexes	2025 Males	2025 Females	2030 Both sexes	2030 Males	2030 Females	2035 Both sexes	2035 Males	2035 Females	2040 Both sexes	2040 Males	2040 Females
All ages	6 747	3 437	3 310	7 647	3 895	3 753	8 590	4 373	4 217	9 568	4 868	4 700
0-4	942	482	460	1 006	515	491	1 067	546	520	1 123	575	548
5-9	878	449	429	940	481	459	1 004	514	490	1 064	545	519
10-14	803	411	393	876	448	428	938	480	458	1 002	513	489
15-19	725	370	355	801	409	392	874	447	427	936	479	457
20-24	636	325	312	723	369	354	799	408	391	872	446	426
25-29	569	290	279	634	323	311	721	368	353	797	407	390
30-34	450	230	220	567	289	278	632	322	310	718	366	352
35-39	399	204	195	448	229	219	565	288	277	629	321	308
40-44	305	156	149	397	203	194	446	228	218	562	286	276
45-49	259	133	126	302	155	147	393	201	192	442	226	216
50-54	222	114	108	255	131	124	298	152	145	388	198	190
55-59	174	89	85	216	110	105	248	127	122	290	148	143
60-64	144	73	71	166	84	82	207	104	102	238	120	118
65-69	101	50	51	133	66	67	154	77	78	193	96	97
70-74	65	30	35	89	43	46	118	57	61	137	66	71
75-79	40	18	22	52	23	29	72	33	39	96	45	52
80-84	21	8	13	27	11	16	36	15	22	51	22	29
85-89	8	3	6	11	4	8	15	5	10	21	7	13
90-94	3	1	2	3	1	2	4	1	3	6	2	4
95-99	0	0	0	1	0	1	1	0	1	1	0	1
100 +	0	0	0	0	0	0	0	0	0	0	0	0

Age group	2045 Both sexes	2045 Males	2045 Females	2050 Both sexes	2050 Males	2050 Females
All ages	10 571	5 375	5 196	11 587	5 888	5 699
0-4	1 174	601	573	1 217	623	594
5-9	1 121	574	547	1 172	600	572
10-14	1 063	544	519	1 119	573	546
15-19	1 000	512	488	1 061	543	518
20-24	934	478	456	998	511	487
25-29	870	445	425	932	477	455
30-34	794	405	389	867	443	424
35-39	716	365	351	791	404	387
40-44	626	319	307	712	363	349
45-49	557	284	274	621	317	305
50-54	436	222	214	550	280	271
55-59	379	192	187	427	217	210
60-64	280	141	139	366	184	182
65-69	224	111	112	263	131	132
70-74	173	84	89	201	98	104
75-79	114	53	61	145	67	77
80-84	70	30	40	84	36	48
85-89	30	11	19	42	16	26
90-94	9	3	6	13	4	9
95-99	2	0	1	3	1	2
100 +	0	0	0	0	0	0

United Nations Department of Economic and Social Affairs/Population Division
World Population Prospects: The 2004 Revision, Volume II: Sex and Age Distribution of the World Population

664

POPULATION BY AGE AND SEX (in thousands)

Age group	2005 Both sexes	Males	Females	2010 Both sexes	Males	Females	2015 Both sexes	Males	Females	2020 Both sexes	Males	Females
All ages	3 702	1 883	1 819	4 295	2 186	2 109	4 894	2 492	2 402	5 490	2 796	2 694
0-4	646	330	316	663	339	324	673	344	329	678	347	331
5-9	578	295	283	643	328	315	660	337	323	671	343	328
10-14	459	235	224	576	294	282	641	327	314	658	336	322
15-19	408	209	199	457	234	223	574	293	281	639	326	313
20-24	313	161	152	406	208	198	455	233	222	572	291	280
25-29	268	138	130	311	160	151	403	206	197	453	231	221
30-34	232	120	112	266	137	129	309	159	151	401	205	196
35-39	187	97	91	231	119	112	264	136	128	307	158	150
40-44	162	84	78	186	96	90	228	118	111	262	135	127
45-49	123	64	59	160	83	77	183	94	89	226	116	109
50-54	90	45	45	120	62	58	156	81	76	179	92	87
55-59	69	35	34	86	43	44	116	59	57	151	78	74
60-64	53	24	28	65	32	33	81	40	42	110	56	54
65-69	38	16	22	48	21	26	59	29	30	75	36	39
70-74	34	14	19	32	13	19	41	18	23	51	24	27
75-79	23	9	14	25	10	15	25	10	15	32	13	19
80-84	13	5	7	14	6	9	16	6	10	16	6	11
85-89	4	2	3	6	2	3	7	2	4	8	3	5
90-94	2	1	1	1	0	1	2	1	1	2	1	2
95-99	0	0	0	0	0	0	0	0	0	0	0	0
100 +	0	0	0	0	0	0	0	0	0	0	0	0

Age group	2025 Both sexes	Males	Females	2030 Both sexes	Males	Females	2035 Both sexes	Males	Females	2040 Both sexes	Males	Females
All ages	6 097	3 104	2 992	6 699	3 409	3 289	7 271	3 698	3 573	7 792	3 959	3 833
0-4	698	357	341	707	362	345	695	356	339	665	341	325
5-9	676	346	330	696	356	340	705	361	344	693	355	338
10-14	669	342	327	674	345	329	694	355	339	704	360	343
15-19	656	335	321	667	341	326	672	344	329	693	354	338
20-24	636	325	312	654	334	320	665	340	325	671	343	328
25-29	569	290	279	634	323	311	651	332	319	663	338	324
30-34	450	230	220	567	289	278	632	322	310	649	331	318
35-39	399	204	195	448	229	219	565	288	277	629	321	308
40-44	305	156	149	397	203	194	446	228	218	562	286	276
45-49	259	133	126	302	155	147	393	201	192	442	226	216
50-54	222	114	108	255	131	124	298	152	145	388	198	190
55-59	174	89	85	216	110	105	248	127	122	290	148	143
60-64	144	73	71	166	84	82	207	104	102	238	120	118
65-69	101	50	51	133	66	67	154	77	78	193	96	97
70-74	65	30	35	89	43	46	118	57	61	137	66	71
75-79	40	18	22	52	23	29	72	33	39	96	45	52
80-84	21	8	13	27	11	16	36	15	22	51	22	29
85-89	8	3	6	11	4	8	15	5	10	21	7	13
90-94	3	1	2	3	1	2	4	1	3	6	2	4
95-99	0	0	0	1	0	1	1	0	1	1	0	1
100 +	0	0	0	0	0	0	0	0	0	0	0	0

Age group	2045 Both sexes	Males	Females	2050 Both sexes	Males	Females
All ages	8 254	4 189	4 065	8 656	4 388	4 269
0-4	631	323	308	600	307	293
5-9	664	340	324	630	323	307
10-14	692	354	337	662	339	323
15-19	702	359	343	690	353	337
20-24	691	353	337	700	358	342
25-29	669	342	327	689	352	337
30-34	661	337	323	666	341	326
35-39	647	330	317	658	336	322
40-44	626	319	307	644	328	315
45-49	557	284	274	621	317	305
50-54	436	222	214	550	280	271
55-59	379	192	187	427	217	210
60-64	280	141	139	366	184	182
65-69	224	111	112	263	131	132
70-74	173	84	89	201	98	104
75-79	114	53	61	145	67	77
80-84	70	30	40	84	36	48
85-89	30	11	19	42	16	26
90-94	9	3	6	13	4	9
95-99	2	0	1	3	1	2
100 +	0	0	0	0	0	0

United Nations Department of Economic and Social Affairs/Population Division
World Population Prospects: The 2004 Revision, Volume II: Sex and Age Distribution of the World Population

665

OMAN ESTIMATES

POPULATION BY AGE AND SEX (in thousands)

Age group	1950 Both sexes	Males	Females	1955 Both sexes	Males	Females	1960 Both sexes	Males	Females	1965 Both sexes	Males	Females
All ages	456	232	225	505	253	252	565	280	286	642	315	327
0-4	78	40	38	94	48	46	107	54	53	123	62	60
5-9	62	31	30	70	36	34	86	44	42	99	50	49
10-14	53	27	26	60	31	29	69	35	34	84	43	41
15-19	46	24	23	51	26	25	58	29	28	67	34	33
20-24	40	20	20	44	22	22	48	24	24	55	28	27
25-29	34	17	17	35	17	18	39	19	21	44	21	23
30-34	29	15	14	29	14	16	31	13	17	34	15	19
35-39	25	13	12	26	13	13	26	12	14	27	11	16
40-44	21	11	11	23	11	11	23	11	12	24	10	13
45-49	18	9	9	19	10	10	20	10	10	21	10	11
50-54	15	8	7	16	8	8	17	8	9	19	9	10
55-59	11	6	6	13	6	6	14	7	7	15	7	8
60-64	9	4	4	9	5	5	11	5	6	12	6	6
65-69	6	3	3	7	3	3	7	4	4	9	4	4
70-74	4	2	2	4	2	2	5	2	2	5	3	3
75-79	2	1	1	2	1	1	3	1	1	3	1	2
80 +	1	0	1	1	1	1	1	1	1	2	1	1

Age group	1970 Both sexes	Males	Females	1975 Both sexes	Males	Females	1980 Both sexes	Males	Females	1985 Both sexes	Males	Females
All ages	747	367	380	917	462	455	1 187	625	562	1 527	825	702
0-4	145	74	71	179	91	88	229	117	112	292	149	143
5-9	115	58	57	139	70	68	174	88	86	225	114	110
10-14	97	49	48	114	58	56	138	70	68	173	88	85
15-19	82	42	40	96	49	47	115	59	56	140	72	68
20-24	64	33	32	83	43	40	102	54	48	122	65	57
25-29	52	26	26	69	37	31	100	59	41	121	72	49
30-34	41	19	22	58	32	26	90	57	33	123	80	43
35-39	32	14	18	43	22	22	69	41	28	102	67	35
40-44	26	10	15	33	15	18	48	25	23	74	45	29
45-49	22	9	13	26	11	15	35	17	19	51	27	23
50-54	20	9	11	21	9	12	25	11	14	34	17	18
55-59	17	8	9	18	8	10	19	8	11	23	10	13
60-64	13	6	7	15	7	8	15	7	9	17	7	10
65-69	10	5	5	11	5	6	12	5	7	13	5	8
70-74	6	3	3	7	3	4	8	4	5	9	4	5
75-79	3	2	2	4	2	2	5	2	3	6	2	3
80 +	2	1	1	2	1	1	3	1	2	4	1	2

Age group	1990 Both sexes	Males	Females	1995 Both sexes	Males	Females	2000 Both sexes	Males	Females	2005 Both sexes	Males	Females
All ages	1 843	1 026	817	2 177	1 285	893	2 442	1 423	1 019	2 567	1 443	1 124
0-4	321	164	157	322	164	157	319	163	156	301	154	147
5-9	274	140	134	294	150	144	296	151	144	296	152	144
10-14	218	111	107	264	135	129	276	141	135	288	147	140
15-19	164	84	80	204	104	100	251	128	123	278	142	136
20-24	147	83	65	159	93	66	249	141	108	260	134	126
25-29	146	89	56	197	139	58	243	158	85	256	148	108
30-34	143	93	50	202	146	57	221	156	66	218	141	77
35-39	131	89	42	162	112	50	178	127	51	179	121	58
40-44	97	65	32	126	88	38	129	89	40	150	102	49
45-49	69	43	26	84	60	25	91	61	30	109	70	39
50-54	46	25	20	59	37	21	58	37	22	76	47	29
55-59	31	16	15	37	22	15	47	27	20	50	29	21
60-64	21	9	11	26	15	11	33	18	14	41	22	19
65-69	14	6	8	18	9	8	22	12	10	28	15	13
70-74	10	4	6	11	5	6	14	7	7	19	10	9
75-79	7	3	4	8	3	5	8	3	5	11	5	5
80 +	4	2	3	5	2	3	7	3	4	8	3	5

United Nations Department of Economic and Social Affairs/Population Division
World Population Prospects: The 2004 Revision, Volume II: Sex and Age Distribution of the World Population

OMAN

POPULATION BY AGE AND SEX (in thousands)

Age group	2005			2010			2015			2020		
	Both sexes	Males	Females	Both sexes	Males	Females	Both sexes	Males	Females	Both sexes	Males	Females
All ages	2 567	1 443	1 124	2 863	1 592	1 270	3 173	1 748	1 424	3 481	1 902	1 579
0-4	301	154	147	325	166	158	345	177	168	352	180	172
5-9	296	152	144	301	154	147	324	166	158	345	177	168
10-14	288	147	140	296	152	144	300	154	147	324	166	158
15-19	278	142	136	287	147	140	296	152	144	300	154	147
20-24	260	134	126	281	146	136	291	151	140	299	155	144
25-29	256	148	108	267	141	126	288	153	135	298	158	140
30-34	218	141	77	260	151	108	271	145	126	292	156	135
35-39	179	121	58	217	141	77	259	151	108	270	145	125
40-44	150	102	49	175	118	58	214	138	76	256	148	108
45-49	109	70	39	144	96	48	169	112	57	207	131	76
50-54	76	47	29	103	65	38	138	90	48	163	106	56
55-59	50	29	21	73	44	28	99	62	37	133	87	47
60-64	41	22	19	47	27	20	69	42	27	95	59	36
65-69	28	15	13	37	20	18	43	25	19	64	38	26
70-74	19	10	9	24	13	11	33	17	16	38	21	17
75-79	11	5	5	14	7	7	19	10	9	26	13	13
80-84	5	2	3	7	3	4	9	5	5	13	6	7
85-89	2	1	1	2	1	2	4	2	2	5	2	3
90-94	1	0	0	1	0	1	1	0	1	1	0	1
95-99	0	0	0	0	0	0	0	0	0	0	0	0
100 +	0	0	0	0	0	0	0	0	0	0	0	0

Age group	2025			2030			2035			2040		
	Both sexes	Males	Females	Both sexes	Males	Females	Both sexes	Males	Females	Both sexes	Males	Females
All ages	3 776	2 048	1 728	4 053	2 181	1 872	4 313	2 303	2 009	4 554	2 413	2 140
0-4	350	179	170	345	177	168	344	176	168	345	177	168
5-9	352	180	172	349	179	170	345	176	168	344	176	168
10-14	345	177	168	352	180	172	349	179	170	344	176	168
15-19	324	166	158	345	176	168	352	180	172	349	179	170
20-24	304	157	147	324	166	158	345	177	168	352	181	172
25-29	306	162	144	305	159	147	326	168	158	347	179	168
30-34	302	162	140	307	163	144	306	159	147	327	169	158
35-39	292	156	135	301	162	140	307	163	144	306	159	146
40-44	267	142	125	290	155	135	300	161	139	306	162	144
45-49	249	142	107	265	141	124	288	154	134	298	159	139
50-54	201	126	75	245	140	106	262	139	123	285	152	133
55-59	158	102	55	196	122	74	240	136	104	256	135	121
60-64	127	82	45	151	97	54	189	117	72	232	130	101
65-69	88	54	34	119	76	43	141	90	51	177	109	68
70-74	56	33	23	78	47	31	106	66	39	127	79	47
75-79	30	16	14	46	26	20	64	37	27	88	54	34
80-84	18	8	10	22	11	11	33	18	15	47	26	21
85-89	7	3	4	10	4	6	12	6	7	19	10	10
90-94	2	1	1	3	1	2	4	1	3	5	2	3
95-99	0	0	0	0	0	0	1	0	1	1	0	1
100 +	0	0	0	0	0	0	0	0	0	0	0	0

Age group	2045			2050		
	Both sexes	Males	Females	Both sexes	Males	Females
All ages	4 771	2 508	2 263	4 958	2 585	2 372
0-4	343	176	167	335	172	164
5-9	344	176	168	343	175	167
10-14	343	176	168	344	176	168
15-19	344	176	168	343	176	168
20-24	350	179	170	345	177	168
25-29	354	182	172	351	181	170
30-34	348	179	168	355	183	172
35-39	326	168	158	347	179	168
40-44	305	158	146	325	168	158
45-49	304	161	143	303	157	145
50-54	295	157	137	300	159	142
55-59	279	149	131	289	154	136
60-64	248	130	118	271	143	128
65-69	219	122	97	235	122	113
70-74	160	97	63	199	109	90
75-79	106	65	41	135	80	56
80-84	65	38	27	80	47	33
85-89	28	14	14	40	22	18
90-94	9	4	5	13	6	7
95-99	2	0	1	3	1	2
100 +	0	0	0	0	0	0

United Nations Department of Economic and Social Affairs/Population Division
World Population Prospects: The 2004 Revision, Volume II: Sex and Age Distribution of the World Population

667

POPULATION BY AGE AND SEX (in thousands)

Age group	2005			2010			2015			2020		
	Both sexes	Males	Females	Both sexes	Males	Females	Both sexes	Males	Females	Both sexes	Males	Females
All ages	2 567	1 443	1 124	2 888	1 605	1 282	3 245	1 786	1 459	3 618	1 973	1 646
0-4	301	154	147	350	179	171	392	201	191	417	214	204
5-9	296	152	144	301	154	147	349	179	170	392	201	191
10-14	288	147	140	296	152	144	300	154	147	349	179	170
15-19	278	142	136	287	147	140	296	152	144	300	154	147
20-24	260	134	126	281	146	136	291	151	140	299	155	144
25-29	256	148	108	267	141	126	288	153	135	298	158	140
30-34	218	141	77	260	151	108	271	145	126	292	156	135
35-39	179	121	58	217	141	77	259	151	108	270	145	125
40-44	150	102	49	175	118	58	214	138	76	256	148	108
45-49	109	70	39	144	96	48	169	112	57	207	131	76
50-54	76	47	29	103	65	38	138	90	48	163	106	56
55-59	50	29	21	73	44	28	99	62	37	133	87	47
60-64	41	22	19	47	27	20	69	42	27	95	59	36
65-69	28	15	13	37	20	18	43	25	19	64	38	26
70-74	19	10	9	24	13	11	33	17	16	38	21	17
75-79	11	5	5	14	7	7	19	10	9	26	13	13
80-84	5	2	3	7	3	4	9	5	5	13	6	7
85-89	2	1	1	2	1	2	4	2	2	5	2	3
90-94	1	0	0	1	0	1	1	0	1	1	0	1
95-99	0	0	0	0	0	0	0	0	0	0	0	0
100 +	0	0	0	0	0	0	0	0	0	0	0	0

Age group	2025			2030			2035			2040		
	Both sexes	Males	Females	Both sexes	Males	Females	Both sexes	Males	Females	Both sexes	Males	Females
All ages	3 983	2 154	1 829	4 340	2 328	2 011	4 697	2 500	2 196	5 059	2 672	2 387
0-4	420	215	205	424	217	207	442	226	215	467	239	228
5-9	417	214	203	419	215	204	424	217	207	441	226	215
10-14	392	201	191	417	213	203	419	215	204	424	217	207
15-19	349	178	170	392	201	191	417	213	203	419	215	204
20-24	304	157	147	349	179	170	392	201	191	417	214	203
25-29	306	162	144	305	159	147	351	180	170	394	203	191
30-34	302	162	140	307	163	144	306	159	147	352	181	170
35-39	292	156	135	301	162	140	307	163	144	306	159	146
40-44	267	142	125	290	155	135	300	161	139	306	162	144
45-49	249	142	107	265	141	124	288	154	134	298	159	139
50-54	201	126	75	245	140	106	262	139	123	285	152	133
55-59	158	102	55	196	122	74	240	136	104	256	135	121
60-64	127	82	45	151	97	54	189	117	72	232	130	101
65-69	88	54	34	119	76	43	141	90	51	177	109	68
70-74	56	33	23	78	47	31	106	66	39	127	79	47
75-79	30	16	14	46	26	20	64	37	27	88	54	34
80-84	18	8	10	22	11	11	33	18	15	47	26	21
85-89	7	3	4	10	4	6	12	6	7	19	10	10
90-94	2	1	1	3	1	2	4	1	3	5	2	3
95-99	0	0	0	0	0	0	1	0	1	1	0	1
100 +	0	0	0	0	0	0	0	0	0	0	0	0

Age group	2045			2050		
	Both sexes	Males	Females	Both sexes	Males	Females
All ages	5 421	2 841	2 580	5 767	3 000	2 767
0-4	487	250	238	496	254	242
5-9	466	239	227	487	249	238
10-14	441	226	215	466	239	227
15-19	424	217	207	441	226	215
20-24	420	215	204	424	218	207
25-29	418	215	203	421	217	204
30-34	394	203	191	419	216	203
35-39	351	181	170	394	203	191
40-44	305	158	146	350	180	170
45-49	304	161	143	303	157	145
50-54	295	157	137	300	159	142
55-59	279	149	131	289	154	136
60-64	248	130	118	271	143	128
65-69	219	122	97	235	122	113
70-74	160	97	63	199	109	90
75-79	106	65	41	135	80	56
80-84	65	38	27	80	47	33
85-89	28	14	14	40	22	18
90-94	9	4	5	13	6	7
95-99	2	0	1	3	1	2
100 +	0	0	0	0	0	0

United Nations Department of Economic and Social Affairs/Population Division
World Population Prospects: The 2004 Revision, Volume II: Sex and Age Distribution of the World Population

668

POPULATION BY AGE AND SEX (in thousands)

Age group	2005 Both sexes	Males	Females	2010 Both sexes	Males	Females	2015 Both sexes	Males	Females	2020 Both sexes	Males	Females
All ages	2 567	1 443	1 124	2 837	1 580	1 258	3 100	1 711	1 389	3 344	1 832	1 512
0-4	301	154	147	299	153	146	298	153	145	287	147	140
5-9	296	152	144	301	154	147	299	153	146	298	152	145
10-14	288	147	140	296	152	144	300	154	147	299	153	146
15-19	278	142	136	287	147	140	296	152	144	300	154	147
20-24	260	134	126	281	146	136	291	151	140	299	155	144
25-29	256	148	108	267	141	126	288	153	135	298	158	140
30-34	218	141	77	260	151	108	271	145	126	292	156	135
35-39	179	121	58	217	141	77	259	151	108	270	145	125
40-44	150	102	49	175	118	58	214	138	76	256	148	108
45-49	109	70	39	144	96	48	169	112	57	207	131	76
50-54	76	47	29	103	65	38	138	90	48	163	106	56
55-59	50	29	21	73	44	28	99	62	37	133	87	47
60-64	41	22	19	47	27	20	69	42	27	95	59	36
65-69	28	15	13	37	20	18	43	25	19	64	38	26
70-74	19	10	9	24	13	11	33	17	16	38	21	17
75-79	11	5	5	14	7	7	19	10	9	26	13	13
80-84	5	2	3	7	3	4	9	5	5	13	6	7
85-89	2	1	1	2	1	2	4	2	2	5	2	3
90-94	1	0	0	1	0	1	1	0	1	1	0	1
95-99	0	0	0	0	0	0	0	0	0	0	0	0
100 +	0	0	0	0	0	0	0	0	0	0	0	0

Age group	2025 Both sexes	Males	Females	2030 Both sexes	Males	Females	2035 Both sexes	Males	Females	2040 Both sexes	Males	Females
All ages	3 569	1 942	1 627	3 769	2 036	1 733	3 939	2 112	1 827	4 075	2 168	1 907
0-4	280	143	136	268	137	131	254	130	124	239	122	116
5-9	287	147	140	280	143	136	268	137	131	254	130	124
10-14	298	152	145	287	147	140	279	143	136	268	137	131
15-19	299	153	146	298	152	145	287	147	140	279	143	136
20-24	304	157	147	299	153	146	298	153	145	288	148	140
25-29	306	162	144	305	159	147	301	155	146	300	154	145
30-34	302	162	140	307	163	144	306	159	147	302	156	146
35-39	292	156	135	301	162	140	307	163	144	306	159	146
40-44	267	142	126	290	155	135	300	161	139	306	162	144
45-49	249	142	107	265	141	124	288	154	134	298	159	139
50-54	201	126	75	245	140	106	262	139	123	285	152	133
55-59	158	102	55	196	122	74	240	136	104	256	135	121
60-64	127	82	45	151	97	54	189	117	72	232	130	101
65-69	88	54	34	119	76	43	141	90	51	177	109	68
70-74	56	33	23	78	47	31	106	66	39	127	79	47
75-79	30	16	14	46	26	20	64	37	27	88	54	34
80-84	18	8	10	22	11	11	33	18	15	47	26	21
85-89	7	3	4	10	4	6	12	6	7	19	10	10
90-94	2	1	1	3	1	2	4	1	3	5	2	3
95-99	0	0	0	0	0	0	1	0	1	1	0	1
100 +	0	0	0	0	0	0	0	0	0	0	0	0

Age group	2045 Both sexes	Males	Females	2050 Both sexes	Males	Females
All ages	4 172	2 202	1 971	4 230	2 213	2 017
0-4	222	114	109	206	105	100
5-9	239	122	116	222	114	108
10-14	254	130	124	238	122	116
15-19	268	137	131	254	130	124
20-24	280	144	136	268	138	131
25-29	289	149	140	282	145	136
30-34	301	155	145	290	150	140
35-39	301	156	146	301	155	145
40-44	305	158	146	300	155	145
45-49	304	161	143	303	157	145
50-54	295	157	137	300	159	142
55-59	279	149	131	289	154	136
60-64	248	130	118	271	143	128
65-69	219	122	97	235	122	113
70-74	160	97	63	199	109	90
75-79	106	65	41	135	80	56
80-84	65	38	27	80	47	33
85-89	28	14	14	40	22	18
90-94	9	4	5	13	6	7
95-99	2	0	1	3	1	2
100 +	0	0	0	0	0	0

POPULATION BY AGE AND SEX (in thousands)

Age group	1950 Both sexes	1950 Males	1950 Females	1955 Both sexes	1955 Males	1955 Females	1960 Both sexes	1960 Males	1960 Females	1965 Both sexes	1965 Males	1965 Females
All ages	36 944	19 365	17 579	41 127	21 508	19 619	46 259	24 133	22 126	52 327	27 238	25 089
0-4	5 559	2 825	2 735	6 795	3 507	3 288	7 809	4 026	3 783	8 852	4 560	4 292
5-9	4 428	2 216	2 213	5 006	2 571	2 435	6 190	3 223	2 967	7 185	3 732	3 453
10-14	4 028	2 028	2 000	4 325	2 170	2 155	4 902	2 524	2 379	6 074	3 169	2 906
15-19	3 625	1 843	1 782	3 964	2 002	1 962	4 263	2 145	2 118	4 832	2 493	2 339
20-24	3 331	1 657	1 673	3 550	1 815	1 736	3 890	1 973	1 917	4 176	2 108	2 067
25-29	2 725	1 421	1 304	3 252	1 627	1 625	3 474	1 783	1 691	3 802	1 935	1 867
30-34	2 363	1 268	1 094	2 652	1 389	1 263	3 173	1 594	1 580	3 391	1 746	1 645
35-39	2 089	1 148	942	2 288	1 233	1 056	2 576	1 353	1 222	3 085	1 554	1 532
40-44	1 783	987	796	2 008	1 104	904	2 206	1 189	1 017	2 487	1 308	1 180
45-49	1 437	815	622	1 692	935	757	1 913	1 049	863	2 107	1 133	974
50-54	1 355	785	570	1 334	753	581	1 579	868	711	1 791	978	813
55-59	1 181	631	550	1 215	700	515	1 204	676	528	1 431	783	649
60-64	1 065	585	480	1 005	535	470	1 042	598	444	1 039	580	459
65-69	913	542	370	838	459	380	799	423	376	835	476	359
70-74	557	321	237	643	381	262	599	326	273	578	304	274
75-79	330	191	139	337	195	141	395	235	160	373	204	169
80 +	175	102	73	220	132	89	247	149	98	289	177	112

Age group	1970 Both sexes	1970 Males	1970 Females	1975 Both sexes	1975 Males	1975 Females	1980 Both sexes	1980 Males	1980 Females	1985 Both sexes	1985 Males	1985 Females
All ages	59 565	30 941	28 624	68 294	35 404	32 889	79 297	41 029	38 269	94 719	48 906	45 814
0-4	10 029	5 162	4 866	11 537	5 935	5 603	13 718	7 054	6 664	16 710	8 592	8 118
5-9	8 225	4 264	3 962	9 405	4 866	4 539	10 919	5 639	5 279	13 154	6 786	6 368
10-14	7 068	3 677	3 391	8 110	4 208	3 901	9 296	4 813	4 483	10 855	5 609	5 247
15-19	6 002	3 136	2 866	6 999	3 645	3 354	8 066	4 188	3 878	9 443	4 884	4 559
20-24	4 752	2 458	2 293	5 927	3 103	2 823	6 970	3 635	3 335	8 405	4 361	4 044
25-29	4 097	2 074	2 023	4 682	2 427	2 255	5 892	3 090	2 802	7 248	3 785	3 463
30-34	3 724	1 900	1 824	4 027	2 043	1 985	4 636	2 407	2 229	6 017	3 161	2 856
35-39	3 309	1 707	1 602	3 647	1 863	1 783	3 968	2 015	1 953	4 690	2 435	2 255
40-44	2 991	1 506	1 485	3 220	1 660	1 559	3 569	1 822	1 747	3 980	2 016	1 964
45-49	2 386	1 251	1 135	2 881	1 447	1 435	3 120	1 604	1 516	3 536	1 797	1 739
50-54	1 982	1 061	922	2 256	1 177	1 080	2 744	1 370	1 374	3 032	1 548	1 484
55-59	1 634	887	747	1 821	968	853	2 089	1 082	1 007	2 590	1 283	1 307
60-64	1 245	677	569	1 433	772	661	1 612	850	762	1 889	969	920
65-69	842	467	375	1 020	549	471	1 188	634	554	1 367	713	654
70-74	611	346	265	625	343	282	769	410	359	918	484	434
75-79	366	193	173	394	223	171	411	225	186	521	276	245
80 +	302	178	124	310	175	135	333	191	141	364	207	158

Age group	1990 Both sexes	1990 Males	1990 Females	1995 Both sexes	1995 Males	1995 Females	2000 Both sexes	2000 Males	2000 Females	2005 Both sexes	2005 Males	2005 Females
All ages	111 698	57 613	54 086	126 075	64 962	61 113	142 648	73 423	69 226	157 935	81 283	76 653
0-4	19 619	10 092	9 527	20 352	10 441	9 911	20 462	10 501	9 961	21 115	10 853	10 262
5-9	16 064	8 286	7 779	18 857	9 715	9 142	19 702	10 122	9 580	19 811	10 186	9 625
10-14	13 056	6 738	6 317	15 876	8 191	7 685	18 723	9 646	9 077	19 531	10 036	9 494
15-19	10 872	5 617	5 255	12 693	6 563	6 130	15 794	8 150	7 644	18 436	9 507	8 929
20-24	9 531	4 931	4 600	10 229	5 297	4 932	12 606	6 520	6 085	15 309	7 910	7 400
25-29	8 466	4 397	4 069	8 969	4 638	4 331	10 146	5 256	4 890	12 184	6 302	5 882
30-34	7 246	3 788	3 458	8 110	4 209	3 902	8 885	4 596	4 290	9 873	5 112	4 761
35-39	5 983	3 143	2 839	6 981	3 653	3 328	8 015	4 159	3 856	8 670	4 486	4 184
40-44	4 638	2 405	2 233	5 749	3 024	2 724	6 867	3 590	3 277	7 804	4 051	3 753
45-49	3 900	1 970	1 930	4 423	2 293	2 130	5 611	2 945	2 667	6 647	3 471	3 175
50-54	3 409	1 723	1 686	3 676	1 850	1 826	4 258	2 197	2 061	5 365	2 807	2 558
55-59	2 849	1 444	1 405	3 151	1 583	1 568	3 461	1 729	1 732	3 985	2 045	1 941
60-64	2 337	1 147	1 189	2 543	1 277	1 266	2 859	1 421	1 437	3 131	1 550	1 581
65-69	1 603	813	790	1 975	956	1 019	2 181	1 080	1 100	2 452	1 204	1 248
70-74	1 062	547	515	1 245	622	623	1 559	742	816	1 727	843	884
75-79	628	329	299	728	371	358	870	429	441	1 098	516	581
80 +	435	240	194	518	280	238	652	341	311	797	404	393

United Nations Department of Economic and Social Affairs/Population Division
World Population Prospects: The 2004 Revision, Volume II: Sex and Age Distribution of the World Population

670

POPULATION BY AGE AND SEX (in thousands)

Age group	2005 Both sexes	Males	Females	2010 Both sexes	Males	Females	2015 Both sexes	Males	Females	2020 Both sexes	Males	Females
All ages	157 935	81 283	76 653	175 178	90 147	85 031	193 419	99 518	93 901	211 703	108 891	102 811
0-4	21 115	10 853	10 262	22 409	11 526	10 883	23 500	12 091	11 410	23 887	12 290	11 598
5-9	19 811	10 186	9 625	20 584	10 599	9 985	21 942	11 304	10 638	23 087	11 895	11 192
10-14	19 531	10 036	9 494	19 683	10 122	9 561	20 474	10 544	9 930	21 841	11 253	10 588
15-19	18 436	9 507	8 929	19 354	9 950	9 404	19 538	10 051	9 487	20 336	10 476	9 860
20-24	15 309	7 910	7 400	18 147	9 364	8 783	19 114	9 831	9 283	19 309	9 937	9 372
25-29	12 184	6 302	5 882	15 051	7 776	7 275	17 922	9 247	8 675	18 898	9 718	9 179
30-34	9 873	5 112	4 761	12 003	6 207	5 796	14 884	7 689	7 195	17 754	9 159	8 595
35-39	8 670	4 486	4 184	9 722	5 035	4 687	11 860	6 134	5 727	14 735	7 612	7 123
40-44	7 804	4 051	3 753	8 511	4 403	4 108	9 575	4 957	4 618	11 706	6 052	5 654
45-49	6 647	3 471	3 175	7 617	3 949	3 669	8 336	4 307	4 029	9 400	4 861	4 539
50-54	5 365	2 807	2 558	6 413	3 338	3 075	7 382	3 815	3 568	8 103	4 174	3 929
55-59	3 985	2 045	1 941	5 075	2 640	2 434	6 101	3 159	2 942	7 053	3 626	3 427
60-64	3 131	1 550	1 581	3 647	1 855	1 792	4 679	2 414	2 264	5 659	2 907	2 753
65-69	2 452	1 204	1 248	2 722	1 331	1 391	3 202	1 610	1 592	4 143	2 114	2 029
70-74	1 727	843	884	1 975	956	1 019	2 223	1 072	1 151	2 644	1 311	1 333
75-79	1 098	516	581	1 242	599	643	1 447	692	755	1 655	788	867
80-84	522	258	264	677	319	359	784	378	406	932	444	488
85-89	207	108	99	256	129	127	341	164	178	404	198	207
90-94	57	32	25	74	40	34	95	49	46	129	64	66
95-99	10	6	4	13	8	6	18	10	8	23	13	11
100 +	1	1	0	1	1	1	2	1	1	2	1	1

Age group	2025 Both sexes	Males	Females	2030 Both sexes	Males	Females	2035 Both sexes	Males	Females	2040 Both sexes	Males	Females
All ages	229 353	117 909	111 444	246 322	126 517	119 805	262 612	134 703	127 908	277 995	142 360	135 635
0-4	23 685	12 183	11 502	23 515	12 085	11 429	23 450	12 038	11 411	23 308	11 956	11 351
5-9	23 529	12 119	11 410	23 382	12 036	11 346	23 259	11 958	11 302	23 231	11 927	11 304
10-14	22 995	11 848	11 147	23 448	12 077	11 371	23 311	11 999	11 313	23 196	11 924	11 272
15-19	21 708	11 187	10 521	22 867	11 784	11 083	23 326	12 015	11 310	23 195	11 940	11 255
20-24	20 114	10 364	9 750	21 492	11 078	10 414	22 657	11 677	10 980	23 121	11 910	11 211
25-29	19 103	9 828	9 274	19 916	10 259	9 657	21 299	10 974	10 325	22 469	11 575	10 894
30-34	18 738	9 634	9 105	18 954	9 749	9 206	19 775	10 182	9 593	21 163	10 899	10 264
35-39	17 602	9 080	8 522	18 595	9 558	9 037	18 823	9 678	9 145	19 651	10 114	9 537
40-44	14 570	7 524	7 046	17 431	8 087	8 443	18 434	9 470	8 964	18 675	9 596	9 080
45-49	11 517	5 948	5 569	14 364	7 408	6 955	17 213	8 863	8 350	18 226	9 350	8 876
50-54	9 161	4 724	4 437	11 255	5 796	5 459	14 070	7 235	6 835	16 895	8 672	8 223
55-59	7 770	3 983	3 787	8 816	4 523	4 293	10 868	5 566	5 302	13 628	6 968	6 660
60-64	6 579	3 355	3 224	7 286	3 702	3 583	8 307	4 223	4 084	10 285	5 217	5 068
65-69	5 052	2 565	2 487	5 917	2 980	2 937	6 600	3 309	3 291	7 572	3 795	3 777
70-74	3 459	1 741	1 718	4 263	2 132	2 131	5 047	2 499	2 547	5 680	2 797	2 884
75-79	1 999	978	1 021	2 654	1 315	1 340	3 321	1 629	1 692	3 983	1 929	2 054
80-84	1 087	514	572	1 338	648	690	1 812	885	927	2 306	1 110	1 196
85-89	492	237	255	587	279	307	740	358	382	1 023	496	527
90-94	157	79	79	197	96	100	241	115	126	312	150	162
95-99	33	17	16	41	21	20	53	26	27	67	32	35
100 +	3	2	2	5	2	2	6	3	3	8	4	4

Age group	2045 Both sexes	Males	Females	2050 Both sexes	Males	Females
All ages	292 208	149 370	142 839	304 700	155 459	149 242
0-4	23 045	11 811	11 234	22 384	11 462	10 921
5-9	23 118	11 857	11 261	22 881	11 723	11 158
10-14	23 174	11 896	11 278	23 066	11 829	11 237
15-19	23 084	11 867	11 217	23 065	11 841	11 224
20-24	22 995	11 837	11 159	22 887	11 766	11 121
25-29	22 938	11 811	11 127	22 816	11 740	11 075
30-34	22 336	11 501	10 835	22 809	11 740	11 069
35-39	21 042	10 833	10 210	22 218	11 437	10 781
40-44	19 510	10 035	9 474	20 902	10 755	10 147
45-49	18 480	9 483	8 997	19 320	9 926	9 393
50-54	17 915	9 163	8 752	18 185	9 307	8 878
55-59	16 402	8 373	8 029	17 424	8 865	8 559
60-64	12 943	6 555	6 389	15 625	7 902	7 724
65-69	9 427	4 713	4 714	11 921	5 950	5 971
70-74	6 571	3 231	3 340	8 241	4 040	4 201
75-79	4 538	2 181	2 357	5 306	2 543	2 763
80-84	2 812	1 332	1 480	3 251	1 523	1 728
85-89	1 332	632	701	1 661	768	893
90-94	443	212	232	593	274	320
95-99	89	42	47	131	60	71
100 +	11	5	6	15	6	8

United Nations Department of Economic and Social Affairs/Population Division
World Population Prospects: The 2004 Revision, Volume II: Sex and Age Distribution of the World Population

671

POPULATION BY AGE AND SEX (in thousands)

Age group	2005 Both sexes	Males	Females	2010 Both sexes	Males	Females	2015 Both sexes	Males	Females	2020 Both sexes	Males	Females
All ages	157 935	81 283	76 653	176 475	90 814	85 661	197 214	101 471	95 742	219 121	112 711	106 411
0-4	21 115	10 853	10 262	23 705	12 193	11 513	26 024	13 389	12 635	27 556	14 177	13 379
5-9	19 811	10 186	9 625	20 584	10 599	9 985	23 213	11 959	11 254	25 569	13 174	12 396
10-14	19 531	10 036	9 494	19 683	10 122	9 561	20 474	10 544	9 930	23 108	11 906	11 202
15-19	18 436	9 507	8 929	19 354	9 950	9 404	19 538	10 051	9 487	20 336	10 476	9 860
20-24	15 309	7 910	7 400	18 147	9 364	8 783	19 114	9 831	9 283	19 309	9 937	9 372
25-29	12 184	6 302	5 882	15 051	7 776	7 275	17 922	9 247	8 675	18 898	9 718	9 179
30-34	9 873	5 112	4 761	12 003	6 207	5 796	14 884	7 689	7 195	17 754	9 159	8 595
35-39	8 670	4 486	4 184	9 722	5 035	4 687	11 860	6 134	5 727	14 735	7 612	7 123
40-44	7 804	4 051	3 753	8 511	4 403	4 108	9 575	4 957	4 618	11 706	6 052	5 654
45-49	6 647	3 471	3 175	7 617	3 949	3 669	8 336	4 307	4 029	9 400	4 861	4 539
50-54	5 365	2 807	2 558	6 413	3 338	3 075	7 382	3 815	3 568	8 103	4 174	3 929
55-59	3 985	2 045	1 941	5 075	2 640	2 434	6 101	3 159	2 942	7 053	3 626	3 427
60-64	3 131	1 550	1 581	3 647	1 855	1 792	4 679	2 414	2 264	5 659	2 907	2 753
65-69	2 452	1 204	1 248	2 722	1 331	1 391	3 202	1 610	1 592	4 143	2 114	2 029
70-74	1 727	843	884	1 975	956	1 019	2 223	1 072	1 151	2 644	1 311	1 333
75-79	1 098	516	581	1 242	599	643	1 447	692	755	1 655	788	867
80-84	522	258	264	677	319	359	784	378	406	932	444	488
85-89	207	108	99	256	129	127	341	164	178	404	198	207
90-94	57	32	25	74	40	34	95	49	46	129	64	66
95-99	10	6	4	13	8	6	18	10	8	23	13	11
100 +	1	1	0	1	1	1	2	1	1	2	1	1

Age group	2025 Both sexes	Males	Females	2030 Both sexes	Males	Females	2035 Both sexes	Males	Females	2040 Both sexes	Males	Females
All ages	240 880	123 843	117 037	262 697	134 944	127 752	284 997	146 216	138 782	307 783	157 668	150 115
0-4	27 853	14 327	13 527	28 426	14 609	13 817	29 530	15 160	14 370	30 786	15 792	14 994
5-9	27 148	13 983	13 166	27 503	14 157	13 346	28 125	14 459	13 666	29 263	15 024	14 240
10-14	25 470	13 123	12 347	27 058	13 936	13 122	27 424	14 115	13 309	28 053	14 420	13 633
15-19	22 972	11 839	11 134	25 338	13 057	12 281	26 930	13 871	13 059	27 302	14 053	13 249
20-24	20 114	10 364	9 750	22 753	11 727	11 026	25 123	12 947	12 176	26 720	13 763	12 957
25-29	19 103	9 828	9 274	19 916	10 259	9 657	22 557	11 622	10 935	24 930	12 842	12 088
30-34	18 738	9 634	9 105	18 954	9 749	9 206	19 775	10 182	9 593	22 418	11 545	10 873
35-39	17 602	9 080	8 522	18 595	9 558	9 037	18 823	9 678	9 145	19 651	10 114	9 537
40-44	14 570	7 524	7 046	17 431	8 987	8 443	18 434	9 470	8 964	18 675	9 596	9 080
45-49	11 517	5 948	5 569	14 364	7 408	6 955	17 213	8 863	8 350	18 226	9 350	8 876
50-54	9 161	4 724	4 437	11 255	5 796	5 459	14 070	7 235	6 835	16 895	8 672	8 223
55-59	7 770	3 983	3 787	8 816	4 523	4 293	10 868	5 566	5 302	13 628	6 968	6 660
60-64	6 579	3 355	3 224	7 286	3 702	3 583	8 307	4 223	4 084	10 285	5 217	5 068
65-69	5 052	2 565	2 487	5 917	2 980	2 937	6 600	3 309	3 291	7 572	3 795	3 777
70-74	3 459	1 741	1 718	4 263	2 132	2 131	5 047	2 499	2 547	5 680	2 797	2 884
75-79	1 999	978	1 021	2 654	1 315	1 340	3 321	1 629	1 692	3 983	1 929	2 054
80-84	1 087	514	572	1 338	648	690	1 812	885	927	2 306	1 110	1 196
85-89	492	237	255	587	279	307	740	358	382	1 023	496	527
90-94	157	79	79	197	96	100	241	115	126	312	150	162
95-99	33	17	16	41	21	20	53	26	27	67	32	35
100 +	3	2	2	5	2	2	6	3	3	8	4	4

Age group	2045 Both sexes	Males	Females	2050 Both sexes	Males	Females
All ages	330 704	169 136	161 568	352 982	180 231	172 751
0-4	31 840	16 319	15 521	32 270	16 525	15 745
5-9	30 547	15 667	14 880	31 626	16 204	15 423
10-14	29 197	14 987	14 209	30 485	15 633	14 852
15-19	27 935	14 360	13 575	29 081	14 928	14 153
20-24	27 096	13 946	13 150	27 732	14 255	13 477
25-29	26 530	13 659	12 870	26 909	13 846	13 064
30-34	24 791	12 765	12 027	26 393	13 584	12 809
35-39	22 293	11 476	10 817	24 666	12 697	11 969
40-44	19 510	10 035	9 474	22 147	11 395	10 751
45-49	18 480	9 483	8 997	19 320	9 926	9 393
50-54	17 915	9 163	8 752	18 185	9 307	8 878
55-59	16 402	8 373	8 029	17 424	8 865	8 559
60-64	12 943	6 555	6 389	15 625	7 902	7 724
65-69	9 427	4 713	4 714	11 921	5 950	5 971
70-74	6 571	3 231	3 340	8 241	4 040	4 201
75-79	4 538	2 181	2 357	5 306	2 543	2 763
80-84	2 812	1 332	1 480	3 251	1 523	1 728
85-89	1 332	632	701	1 661	768	893
90-94	443	212	232	593	274	320
95-99	89	42	47	131	60	71
100 +	11	5	6	15	6	8

United Nations Department of Economic and Social Affairs/Population Division
World Population Prospects: The 2004 Revision, Volume II: Sex and Age Distribution of the World Population

672

POPULATION BY AGE AND SEX (in thousands)

Age group	2005 Both sexes	Males	Females	2010 Both sexes	Males	Females	2015 Both sexes	Males	Females	2020 Both sexes	Males	Females
All ages	157 935	81 283	76 653	173 856	89 467	84 389	189 529	97 516	92 013	204 100	104 977	99 123
0-4	21 115	10 853	10 262	21 086	10 846	10 241	20 908	10 757	10 151	20 128	10 355	9 772
5-9	19 811	10 186	9 625	20 584	10 599	9 985	20 644	10 636	10 009	20 536	10 581	9 955
10-14	19 531	10 036	9 494	19 683	10 122	9 561	20 474	10 544	9 930	20 549	10 587	9 961
15-19	18 436	9 507	8 929	19 354	9 950	9 404	19 538	10 051	9 487	20 336	10 476	9 860
20-24	15 309	7 910	7 400	18 147	9 364	8 783	19 114	9 831	9 283	19 309	9 937	9 372
25-29	12 184	6 302	5 882	15 051	7 776	7 275	17 922	9 247	8 675	18 898	9 718	9 179
30-34	9 873	5 112	4 761	12 003	6 207	5 796	14 884	7 689	7 195	17 754	9 159	8 595
35-39	8 670	4 486	4 184	9 722	5 035	4 687	11 860	6 134	5 727	14 735	7 612	7 123
40-44	7 804	4 051	3 753	8 511	4 403	4 108	9 575	4 957	4 618	11 706	6 052	5 654
45-49	6 647	3 471	3 175	7 617	3 949	3 669	8 336	4 307	4 029	9 400	4 861	4 539
50-54	5 365	2 807	2 558	6 413	3 338	3 075	7 382	3 815	3 568	8 103	4 174	3 929
55-59	3 985	2 045	1 941	5 075	2 640	2 434	6 101	3 159	2 942	7 053	3 626	3 427
60-64	3 131	1 550	1 581	3 647	1 855	1 792	4 679	2 414	2 264	5 659	2 907	2 753
65-69	2 452	1 204	1 248	2 722	1 331	1 391	3 202	1 610	1 592	4 143	2 114	2 029
70-74	1 727	843	884	1 975	956	1 019	2 223	1 072	1 151	2 644	1 311	1 333
75-79	1 098	516	581	1 242	599	643	1 447	692	755	1 655	788	867
80-84	522	258	264	677	319	359	784	378	406	932	444	488
85-89	207	108	99	256	129	127	341	164	178	404	198	207
90-94	57	32	25	74	40	34	95	49	46	129	64	66
95-99	10	6	4	13	8	6	18	10	8	23	13	11
100 +	1	1	0	1	1	1	2	1	1	2	1	1

Age group	2025 Both sexes	Males	Females	2030 Both sexes	Males	Females	2035 Both sexes	Males	Females	2040 Both sexes	Males	Females
All ages	217 592	111 854	105 738	229 765	117 996	111 768	240 321	123 239	117 081	248 961	127 439	121 521
0-4	19 465	10 012	9 453	18 654	9 587	9 067	17 648	9 060	8 588	16 489	8 459	8 031
5-9	19 820	10 209	9 612	19 210	9 889	9 321	18 444	9 482	8 962	17 474	8 972	8 503
10-14	20 452	10 538	9 914	19 749	10 172	9 577	19 148	9 856	9 292	18 390	9 453	8 936
15-19	20 418	10 523	9 895	20 329	10 477	9 852	19 632	10 114	9 519	19 037	9 800	9 237
20-24	20 114	10 364	9 750	20 205	10 415	9 790	20 124	10 372	9 752	19 434	10 012	9 422
25-29	19 103	9 828	9 274	19 916	10 259	9 657	20 015	10 313	9 702	19 941	10 273	9 668
30-34	18 738	9 634	9 105	18 954	9 749	9 206	19 775	10 182	9 593	19 883	10 240	9 643
35-39	17 002	9 000	8 522	18 595	9 558	9 037	18 823	9 678	9 145	19 051	10 114	9 537
40-44	14 570	7 524	7 046	17 431	8 987	8 443	18 434	9 470	8 964	18 675	9 596	9 080
45-49	11 517	5 948	5 569	14 364	7 408	6 955	17 213	8 863	8 350	18 226	9 350	8 876
50-54	9 161	4 724	4 437	11 255	5 796	5 459	14 070	7 235	6 835	16 895	8 672	8 223
55-59	7 770	3 983	3 787	8 816	4 523	4 293	10 868	5 566	5 302	13 628	6 968	6 660
60-64	6 579	3 355	3 224	7 286	3 702	3 583	8 307	4 223	4 084	10 285	5 217	5 068
65-69	5 052	2 565	2 487	5 917	2 980	2 937	6 600	3 309	3 291	7 572	3 795	3 777
70-74	3 459	1 741	1 718	4 263	2 132	2 131	5 047	2 499	2 547	5 680	2 797	2 884
75-79	1 999	970	1 021	2 054	1 015	1 040	3 321	1 029	1 092	3 903	1 929	2 054
80-84	1 087	514	572	1 338	648	690	1 812	885	927	2 306	1 110	1 196
85-89	492	237	255	587	279	307	740	358	382	1 023	496	527
90-94	157	79	79	197	96	100	241	115	126	312	150	162
95-99	33	17	16	41	21	20	53	26	27	67	32	35
100 +	3	2	2	5	2	2	6	3	3	8	4	4

Age group	2045 Both sexes	Males	Females	2050 Both sexes	Males	Females
All ages	255 586	130 563	125 023	259 909	132 474	127 435
0-4	15 375	7 880	7 495	14 121	7 231	6 890
5-9	16 345	8 384	7 962	15 254	7 816	7 438
10-14	17 426	8 946	8 480	16 302	8 360	7 942
15-19	18 283	9 400	8 883	17 323	8 894	8 429
20-24	18 844	9 701	9 143	18 093	9 303	8 790
25-29	19 257	9 917	9 341	18 671	9 608	9 062
30-34	19 814	10 203	9 611	19 136	9 850	9 286
35-39	19 766	10 176	9 590	19 703	10 143	9 560
40-44	19 510	10 035	9 474	19 632	10 102	9 530
45-49	18 480	9 483	8 997	19 320	9 926	9 393
50-54	17 915	9 163	8 752	18 185	9 307	8 878
55-59	16 402	8 373	8 029	17 424	8 865	8 559
60-64	12 943	6 555	6 389	15 625	7 902	7 724
65-69	9 427	4 713	4 714	11 921	5 950	5 971
70-74	6 571	3 231	3 340	8 241	4 040	4 201
75-79	4 538	2 181	2 357	5 306	2 543	2 763
80-84	2 812	1 332	1 480	3 251	1 523	1 728
85-89	1 332	632	701	1 661	768	893
90-94	443	212	232	593	274	320
95-99	89	42	47	131	60	71
100 +	11	5	6	15	6	8

POPULATION BY AGE AND SEX (in thousands)

Age group	1950 Both sexes	1950 Males	1950 Females	1955 Both sexes	1955 Males	1955 Females	1960 Both sexes	1960 Males	1960 Females	1965 Both sexes	1965 Males	1965 Females
All ages	860	441	419	977	500	478	1 126	575	551	1 303	665	638
0-4	139	71	68	163	83	80	194	98	95	226	115	111
5-9	114	58	56	134	68	65	158	80	78	188	96	92
10-14	93	47	46	112	57	56	132	67	65	156	79	77
15-19	81	41	40	92	46	46	111	56	55	130	66	64
20-24	72	36	35	78	40	39	90	45	45	109	55	54
25-29	64	33	32	69	35	34	76	39	37	87	44	43
30-34	55	29	26	61	31	30	66	34	33	74	38	36
35-39	51	27	24	53	28	25	59	30	29	65	33	32
40-44	41	22	19	49	26	23	51	27	24	56	29	27
45-49	35	19	16	39	21	18	46	25	22	49	26	23
50-54	32	17	15	33	17	15	37	19	18	44	23	21
55-59	27	14	13	30	16	14	30	16	14	34	18	16
60-64	21	11	10	24	12	12	27	14	13	28	15	13
65-69	15	7	8	17	9	9	21	10	10	23	12	11
70-74	10	5	5	12	6	6	14	7	7	17	8	9
75-79	6	3	3	7	3	4	8	4	4	10	5	5
80 +	4	2	2	5	2	2	6	3	3	7	3	4

Age group	1970 Both sexes	1970 Males	1970 Females	1975 Both sexes	1975 Males	1975 Females	1980 Both sexes	1980 Males	1980 Females	1985 Both sexes	1985 Males	1985 Females
All ages	1 506	769	737	1 723	878	845	1 949	991	959	2 176	1 104	1 071
0-4	256	130	125	272	138	133	272	139	133	283	144	139
5-9	220	112	108	250	127	123	269	137	132	269	137	132
10-14	185	94	91	217	110	107	249	127	122	267	136	131
15-19	153	78	76	182	92	90	216	109	107	247	125	121
20-24	127	65	63	151	76	74	180	90	89	212	107	105
25-29	106	54	52	125	63	61	149	75	74	177	89	88
30-34	85	43	41	104	53	51	123	63	60	146	74	72
35-39	72	37	35	83	42	40	102	52	50	120	61	59
40-44	63	32	31	71	36	34	82	42	40	100	51	49
45-49	54	28	26	61	31	30	69	36	34	80	41	39
50-54	47	25	22	52	27	25	60	30	29	67	34	33
55-59	41	22	19	45	24	21	51	26	25	57	29	28
60-64	32	16	15	38	20	18	42	22	20	47	24	23
65-69	24	13	12	28	14	14	35	18	17	38	20	18
70-74	19	9	9	20	10	10	24	12	12	30	15	15
75-79	12	6	6	14	7	7	16	8	8	19	9	10
80 +	9	4	5	11	5	6	14	6	7	16	7	9

Age group	1990 Both sexes	1990 Males	1990 Females	1995 Both sexes	1995 Males	1995 Females	2000 Both sexes	2000 Males	2000 Females	2005 Both sexes	2005 Males	2005 Females
All ages	2 411	1 220	1 190	2 670	1 349	1 321	2 950	1 489	1 461	3 232	1 630	1 601
0-4	302	154	148	309	158	152	331	169	162	343	175	168
5-9	280	143	137	300	153	147	309	157	151	330	168	161
10-14	267	136	131	280	143	137	300	153	147	308	157	151
15-19	264	134	130	266	135	131	280	142	137	300	153	147
20-24	242	123	120	264	133	130	266	135	131	279	142	137
25-29	208	105	103	242	122	120	263	133	130	265	134	131
30-34	173	87	86	207	104	103	241	121	119	262	132	130
35-39	143	72	71	172	86	86	206	103	103	239	120	119
40-44	118	60	58	142	71	71	171	85	86	205	102	102
45-49	98	50	48	117	59	57	140	70	70	169	84	85
50-54	78	39	38	96	49	48	115	58	57	138	69	69
55-59	65	33	32	75	38	37	94	47	46	111	56	55
60-64	54	27	27	62	31	31	72	36	36	90	45	45
65-69	43	22	22	50	25	25	57	29	29	67	33	34
70-74	33	17	16	38	19	19	44	22	23	52	25	26
75-79	24	12	12	27	13	14	31	15	16	37	18	19
80 +	19	9	10	24	11	13	31	14	16	38	17	21

United Nations Department of Economic and Social Affairs/Population Division
World Population Prospects: The 2004 Revision, Volume II: Sex and Age Distribution of the World Population

674

POPULATION BY AGE AND SEX (in thousands)

Age group	2005 Both sexes	2005 Males	2005 Females	2010 Both sexes	2010 Males	2010 Females	2015 Both sexes	2015 Males	2015 Females	2020 Both sexes	2020 Males	2020 Females
All ages	3 232	1 630	1 601	3 509	1 769	1 740	3 774	1 900	1 873	4 027	2 026	2 001
0-4	343	175	168	344	176	168	342	175	167	342	175	167
5-9	330	168	161	342	175	167	344	176	168	342	175	167
10-14	308	157	151	330	168	161	342	175	167	344	176	168
15-19	300	153	147	308	157	151	330	168	161	342	175	167
20-24	279	142	137	300	152	147	308	157	151	329	168	161
25-29	265	134	131	278	141	137	299	152	147	308	156	151
30-34	262	132	130	264	133	131	278	141	137	299	151	147
35-39	239	120	119	260	131	130	263	133	130	277	140	137
40-44	205	102	102	238	119	118	259	130	129	261	132	130
45-49	169	84	85	202	101	101	235	118	117	256	128	128
50-54	138	69	69	166	82	84	199	99	100	231	115	116
55-59	111	56	55	134	66	68	162	80	82	194	96	98
60-64	90	45	45	107	53	54	129	63	66	156	76	80
65-69	67	33	34	84	41	43	101	49	51	122	59	63
70-74	52	25	26	61	30	31	76	37	39	91	44	47
75-79	37	18	19	43	21	23	51	24	27	65	30	34
80-84	23	10	12	27	12	15	33	15	18	39	18	21
85-89	11	5	6	14	6	8	17	7	9	20	9	12
90-94	3	1	2	5	2	3	6	2	4	7	3	5
95-99	1	0	0	1	0	0	1	0	1	2	1	1
100 +	0	0	0	0	0	0	0	0	0	0	0	0

Age group	2025 Both sexes	2025 Males	2025 Females	2030 Both sexes	2030 Males	2030 Females	2035 Both sexes	2035 Males	2035 Females	2040 Both sexes	2040 Males	2040 Females
All ages	4 267	2 144	2 123	4 488	2 252	2 237	4 684	2 346	2 338	4 850	2 425	2 425
0-4	343	175	167	340	174	166	332	170	162	323	165	157
5-9	342	175	167	342	175	167	339	174	166	332	170	162
10-14	342	175	167	342	175	167	343	175	167	340	174	166
15-19	344	176	168	342	175	167	342	175	167	343	175	167
20-24	342	174	168	344	175	168	342	175	167	342	175	167
25-29	329	168	162	342	174	168	344	175	168	342	175	167
30-34	307	156	151	328	167	161	341	174	168	343	175	168
35-39	297	151	147	306	155	151	327	166	161	340	173	167
40-44	275	139	136	296	150	146	304	154	150	326	165	161
45-49	259	130	129	272	137	135	293	148	145	302	152	149
50-54	252	126	126	255	128	128	269	135	134	289	145	144
55-59	226	112	114	246	122	124	249	124	126	263	131	132
60-64	187	91	96	218	107	111	238	116	121	241	119	123
65-69	147	71	76	177	85	92	206	100	107	226	109	117
70-74	111	53	58	134	63	71	162	76	86	190	89	100
75-79	78	37	42	96	44	52	117	53	64	141	64	77
80-84	50	22	28	61	27	34	75	32	42	92	39	53
85-89	25	10	14	32	13	19	40	16	24	50	20	30
90-94	9	4	6	12	5	7	16	6	10	20	7	13
95-99	2	1	1	3	1	2	4	1	2	5	2	3
100 +	0	0	0	0	0	0	0	0	0	1	0	0

Age group	2045 Both sexes	2045 Males	2045 Females	2050 Both sexes	2050 Males	2050 Females
All ages	4 985	2 488	2 496	5 093	2 538	2 554
0-4	312	160	152	307	157	150
5-9	323	165	157	312	160	152
10-14	333	170	162	323	165	157
15-19	340	174	166	333	170	162
20-24	343	175	168	340	174	166
25-29	342	175	167	343	175	168
30-34	342	174	167	342	175	168
35-39	342	174	168	341	174	167
40-44	339	172	167	341	173	168
45-49	323	163	160	336	170	166
50-54	298	150	148	319	161	158
55-59	283	141	142	292	146	146
60-64	254	125	129	274	135	139
65-69	229	111	118	242	117	125
70-74	208	98	110	212	100	112
75-79	166	75	91	183	83	100
80-84	113	48	64	133	57	76
85-89	62	25	38	77	30	47
90-94	26	9	17	33	12	21
95-99	7	2	5	9	3	6
100 +	1	0	1	1	0	1

POPULATION BY AGE AND SEX (in thousands)

Age group	2005			2010			2015			2020		
	Both sexes	Males	Females	Both sexes	Males	Females	Both sexes	Males	Females	Both sexes	Males	Females
All ages	3 232	1 630	1 601	3 541	1 785	1 756	3 860	1 945	1 916	4 185	2 106	2 079
0-4	343	175	168	377	192	184	397	203	194	414	212	202
5-9	330	168	161	342	175	167	376	192	184	396	202	194
10-14	308	157	151	330	168	161	342	175	167	376	192	184
15-19	300	153	147	308	157	151	330	168	161	342	175	167
20-24	279	142	137	300	152	147	308	157	151	329	168	161
25-29	265	134	131	278	141	137	299	152	147	308	156	151
30-34	262	132	130	264	133	131	278	141	137	299	151	147
35-39	239	120	119	260	131	130	263	133	130	277	140	137
40-44	205	102	102	238	119	118	259	130	129	261	132	130
45-49	169	84	85	202	101	101	235	118	117	256	128	128
50-54	138	69	69	166	82	84	199	99	100	231	115	116
55-59	111	56	55	134	66	68	162	80	82	194	96	98
60-64	90	45	45	107	53	54	129	63	66	156	76	80
65-69	67	33	34	84	41	43	101	49	51	122	59	63
70-74	52	25	26	61	30	31	76	37	39	91	44	47
75-79	37	18	19	43	21	23	51	24	27	65	30	34
80-84	23	10	12	27	12	15	33	15	18	39	18	21
85-89	11	5	6	14	6	8	17	7	9	20	9	12
90-94	3	1	2	5	2	3	6	2	4	7	3	5
95-99	1	0	0	1	0	0	1	0	1	2	1	1
100 +	0	0	0	0	0	0	0	0	0	0	0	0

Age group	2025			2030			2035			2040		
	Both sexes	Males	Females	Both sexes	Males	Females	Both sexes	Males	Females	Both sexes	Males	Females
All ages	4 504	2 264	2 239	4 817	2 420	2 398	5 127	2 572	2 555	5 428	2 720	2 708
0-4	422	216	206	433	221	211	447	229	218	459	235	224
5-9	413	211	202	421	215	206	432	221	211	446	228	218
10-14	396	202	193	414	212	202	421	215	206	433	221	211
15-19	376	192	184	396	202	194	413	211	202	421	215	206
20-24	342	174	168	376	192	184	396	202	194	413	211	202
25-29	329	168	162	342	174	168	375	191	184	395	202	194
30-34	307	156	151	328	167	161	341	174	168	375	191	184
35-39	297	151	147	306	155	151	327	166	161	340	173	167
40-44	275	139	136	296	150	146	304	154	150	326	165	161
45-49	259	130	129	272	137	135	293	148	145	302	152	149
50-54	252	126	126	255	128	128	269	135	134	289	145	144
55-59	226	112	114	246	122	124	249	124	126	263	131	132
60-64	187	91	96	218	107	111	238	116	121	241	119	123
65-69	147	71	76	177	85	92	206	100	107	226	109	117
70-74	111	53	58	134	63	71	162	76	86	190	89	100
75-79	78	37	42	96	44	52	117	53	64	141	64	77
80-84	50	22	28	61	27	34	75	32	42	92	39	53
85-89	25	10	14	32	13	19	40	16	24	50	20	30
90-94	9	4	6	12	5	7	16	6	10	20	7	13
95-99	2	1	1	3	1	2	4	1	2	5	2	3
100 +	0	0	0	0	0	0	0	0	0	1	0	0

Age group	2045			2050		
	Both sexes	Males	Females	Both sexes	Males	Females
All ages	5 717	2 862	2 855	5 993	2 998	2 996
0-4	467	239	228	478	245	233
5-9	459	235	224	467	239	228
10-14	446	229	218	459	235	224
15-19	433	221	211	446	229	218
20-24	421	215	206	433	221	211
25-29	413	211	202	421	215	206
30-34	395	201	194	413	211	202
35-39	374	190	184	394	201	193
40-44	339	172	167	372	189	183
45-49	323	163	160	336	170	166
50-54	298	150	148	319	161	158
55-59	283	141	142	292	146	146
60-64	254	125	129	274	135	139
65-69	229	111	118	242	117	125
70-74	208	98	110	212	100	112
75-79	166	75	91	183	83	100
80-84	113	48	64	133	57	76
85-89	62	25	38	77	30	47
90-94	26	9	17	33	12	21
95-99	7	2	5	9	3	6
100 +	1	0	1	1	0	1

United Nations Department of Economic and Social Affairs/Population Division
World Population Prospects: The 2004 Revision, Volume II: Sex and Age Distribution of the World Population

POPULATION BY AGE AND SEX (in thousands)

Age group	2005			2010			2015			2020		
	Both sexes	Males	Females	Both sexes	Males	Females	Both sexes	Males	Females	Both sexes	Males	Females
All ages	3 232	1 630	1 601	3 476	1 752	1 724	3 686	1 856	1 000	3 866	1 944	1 923
0-4	343	175	168	312	159	152	287	147	140	269	138	131
5-9	330	168	161	342	175	167	311	159	152	287	147	140
10-14	308	157	151	330	168	161	342	175	167	311	159	152
15-19	300	153	147	308	157	151	330	168	161	342	175	167
20-24	279	142	137	300	152	147	308	157	151	329	168	161
25-29	265	134	131	278	141	137	299	152	147	308	156	151
30-34	262	132	130	264	133	131	278	141	137	299	151	147
35-39	239	120	119	260	131	130	263	133	130	277	140	137
40-44	205	102	102	238	119	118	259	130	129	261	132	130
45-49	169	84	85	202	101	101	235	118	117	256	128	128
50-54	138	69	69	166	82	84	199	99	100	231	115	116
55-59	111	56	55	134	66	68	162	80	82	194	96	98
60-64	90	45	45	107	53	54	129	63	66	156	76	80
65-69	67	33	34	84	41	43	101	49	51	122	59	63
70-74	52	25	26	61	30	31	76	37	39	91	44	47
75-79	37	18	19	43	21	23	51	24	27	65	30	34
80-84	23	10	12	27	12	15	33	15	18	39	18	21
85-89	11	5	6	14	6	8	17	7	9	20	9	12
90-94	3	1	2	5	2	3	6	2	4	7	3	5
95-99	1	0	0	1	0	0	1	0	1	2	1	1
100 +	0	0	0	0	0	0	0	0	0	0	0	0

Age group	2025			2030			2035			2040		
	Both sexes	Males	Females	Both sexes	Males	Females	Both sexes	Males	Females	Both sexes	Males	Females
All ages	4 028	2 022	2 006	4 160	2 084	2 076	4 253	2 126	2 127	4 302	2 145	2 156
0-4	264	135	129	250	128	122	228	117	111	204	105	100
5-9	269	138	131	264	135	129	250	128	122	228	117	111
10-14	287	147	140	269	138	131	264	135	129	251	128	122
15-19	311	159	152	287	147	140	269	138	131	265	135	129
20-24	342	174	168	311	159	152	287	147	140	270	138	132
25-29	329	168	162	342	174	168	312	159	153	287	147	141
30-34	307	156	151	328	167	161	341	174	168	311	159	153
35-39	297	151	147	306	155	151	327	166	161	340	173	167
40-44	275	139	136	296	150	146	304	154	150	326	165	161
45-49	259	130	129	272	137	135	293	148	145	302	152	149
50-54	252	126	126	255	128	128	269	135	134	289	145	144
55-59	226	112	114	248	122	104	249	124	126	263	131	132
60-64	187	91	96	218	107	111	238	116	121	241	119	123
65-69	147	71	76	177	85	92	206	100	107	226	109	117
70-74	111	53	58	134	63	71	162	76	86	190	89	100
75-79	78	37	42	96	44	52	117	53	64	141	64	77
80-84	50	22	28	61	27	34	75	32	42	92	39	53
85-89	25	10	14	32	13	19	40	16	24	50	20	30
90-94	9	4	6	12	5	7	16	6	10	20	7	13
95-99	2	1	1	3	1	2	4	1	2	5	2	3
100 +	0	0	0	0	0	0	0	0	0	1	0	0

Age group	2045			2050		
	Both sexes	Males	Females	Both sexes	Males	Females
All ages	4 310	2 144	2 166	4 286	2 127	2 159
0-4	185	95	90	173	88	84
5-9	204	105	100	185	95	90
10-14	229	117	111	205	105	100
15-19	251	129	122	229	117	112
20-24	265	136	129	252	129	123
25-29	270	138	132	265	136	130
30-34	287	147	141	270	138	132
35-39	311	158	152	287	146	141
40-44	339	172	167	309	157	152
45-49	323	163	160	336	170	166
50-54	298	150	148	319	161	158
55-59	283	141	142	292	146	146
60-64	254	125	129	274	135	139
65-69	229	111	118	242	117	125
70-74	208	98	110	212	100	112
75-79	166	75	91	183	83	100
80-84	113	48	64	133	57	76
85-89	62	25	38	77	30	47
90-94	26	9	17	33	12	21
95-99	7	2	5	9	3	6
100 +	1	0	1	1	0	1

POPULATION BY AGE AND SEX (in thousands)

Age group	1950 Both sexes	1950 Males	1950 Females	1955 Both sexes	1955 Males	1955 Females	1960 Both sexes	1960 Males	1960 Females	1965 Both sexes	1965 Males	1965 Females
All ages	1 798	947	851	1 922	1 002	920	2 080	1 077	1 003	2 289	1 175	1 114
0-4	275	142	133	321	162	159	349	177	172	457	233	224
5-9	227	119	108	251	129	122	295	149	146	314	160	154
10-14	205	108	97	219	114	105	243	124	118	274	139	136
15-19	184	97	87	197	103	93	211	110	101	242	122	120
20-24	163	87	77	172	92	80	185	98	87	195	100	94
25-29	143	76	67	150	81	70	159	85	74	164	86	78
30-34	124	66	57	130	70	60	138	75	64	141	75	66
35-39	106	57	49	111	60	52	118	64	55	119	64	55
40-44	89	48	42	94	50	44	99	53	46	101	54	46
45-49	75	40	35	77	41	37	82	43	39	83	44	39
50-54	60	32	28	62	32	30	65	34	32	66	34	32
55-59	40	21	19	48	25	23	50	25	25	50	25	25
60-64	34	18	16	29	15	14	36	18	18	36	17	19
65-69	33	17	15	23	11	11	20	10	10	23	11	13
70-74	23	12	11	19	9	10	14	6	7	14	6	8
75-79	13	7	6	11	5	6	10	4	5	6	2	3
80 +	6	3	3	7	3	3	6	3	4	4	2	3

Age group	1970 Both sexes	1970 Males	1970 Females	1975 Both sexes	1975 Males	1975 Females	1980 Both sexes	1980 Males	1980 Females	1985 Both sexes	1985 Males	1985 Females
All ages	2 554	1 311	1 243	2 866	1 468	1 398	3 241	1 658	1 583	3 655	1 869	1 786
0-4	431	220	211	488	249	238	550	282	268	592	304	288
5-9	364	185	179	408	208	200	466	238	228	530	272	258
10-14	318	161	157	356	181	175	401	204	197	458	234	224
15-19	280	141	139	310	157	153	348	177	171	394	201	193
20-24	225	116	109	269	136	133	300	152	148	338	172	166
25-29	190	100	90	214	111	104	258	131	127	289	147	142
30-34	163	87	76	179	95	85	204	106	98	247	126	122
35-39	138	75	64	153	82	71	169	90	80	194	101	93
40-44	117	63	54	128	69	59	142	76	66	159	84	75
45-49	96	51	45	106	56	49	117	62	54	131	70	62
50-54	77	40	37	85	44	40	94	49	44	105	55	50
55-59	58	29	29	64	33	32	72	37	35	81	42	39
60-64	42	20	21	46	22	24	52	25	26	58	29	29
65-69	27	12	15	30	14	16	34	16	18	38	18	21
70-74	16	7	9	17	7	10	20	8	11	23	10	13
75-79	7	3	4	9	3	5	10	4	6	11	4	7
80 +	5	2	3	4	2	3	5	2	3	6	2	4

Age group	1990 Both sexes	1990 Males	1990 Females	1995 Both sexes	1995 Males	1995 Females	2000 Both sexes	2000 Males	2000 Females	2005 Both sexes	2005 Males	2005 Females
All ages	4 114	2 156	1 958	4 687	2 435	2 252	5 299	2 739	2 560	5 887	3 035	2 852
0-4	644	343	301	776	400	376	827	426	401	815	421	394
5-9	566	300	267	625	333	292	756	390	366	808	417	391
10-14	489	247	242	560	296	264	619	330	289	749	386	363
15-19	468	229	239	483	244	239	553	293	260	612	326	286
20-24	405	201	204	458	224	234	473	239	234	543	288	255
25-29	352	177	175	394	196	198	446	219	227	462	234	228
30-34	273	140	134	341	172	169	382	191	191	434	213	221
35-39	221	117	104	263	134	128	328	166	162	369	185	184
40-44	175	94	81	210	111	99	250	128	122	314	158	156
45-49	134	75	59	164	87	76	197	104	93	236	120	116
50-54	121	68	53	122	68	54	149	79	70	181	95	86
55-59	89	52	37	106	59	47	107	59	49	132	69	63
60-64	67	41	26	73	42	32	88	48	40	90	48	42
65-69	50	32	18	50	30	21	56	31	25	68	36	33
70-74	32	21	11	33	21	13	34	19	15	39	20	19
75-79	18	12	6	19	11	7	20	11	8	21	11	10
80 +	9	6	3	11	7	4	13	7	5	14	8	6

United Nations Department of Economic and Social Affairs/Population Division
World Population Prospects: The 2004 Revision, Volume II: Sex and Age Distribution of the World Population

678

POPULATION BY AGE AND SEX (in thousands)

Age group	2005 Both sexes	2005 Males	2005 Females	2010 Both sexes	2010 Males	2010 Females	2015 Both sexes	2015 Males	2015 Females	2020 Both sexes	2020 Males	2020 Females
All ages	5 887	3 035	2 852	6 450	3 319	3 131	7 010	3 605	3 406	7 602	3 905	3 697
0-4	815	421	394	796	411	385	806	417	389	845	437	408
5-9	808	417	391	799	413	386	783	405	378	795	411	383
10-14	749	386	363	801	414	388	794	410	383	778	403	376
15-19	612	326	286	742	382	359	795	411	384	788	408	381
20-24	543	288	255	602	322	281	732	378	354	786	406	380
25-29	462	234	228	532	282	250	592	316	276	721	372	349
30-34	434	213	221	451	229	222	522	277	244	582	311	271
35-39	369	185	184	421	207	214	440	223	216	510	271	239
40-44	314	158	156	355	178	178	407	200	207	427	217	210
45-49	236	120	116	298	150	148	339	169	170	390	192	199
50-54	181	95	86	219	110	108	278	139	139	318	157	160
55-59	132	69	63	162	84	78	197	98	99	253	125	128
60-64	90	48	42	113	57	55	139	70	69	172	84	88
65-69	68	36	33	71	36	34	90	44	46	113	55	58
70-74	39	20	19	48	24	25	51	25	26	66	31	35
75-79	21	11	10	24	12	12	31	14	17	33	15	18
80-84	10	5	4	11	5	5	13	6	7	17	7	10
85-89	3	2	2	4	2	2	4	2	2	5	2	3
90-94	1	0	0	1	0	0	1	1	1	1	1	1
95-99	0	0	0	0	0	0	0	0	0	0	0	0
100 +	0	0	0	0	0	0	0	0	0	0	0	0

Age group	2025 Both sexes	2025 Males	2025 Females	2030 Both sexes	2030 Males	2030 Females	2035 Both sexes	2035 Males	2035 Females	2040 Both sexes	2040 Males	2040 Females
All ages	8 205	4 213	3 993	8 784	4 507	4 277	9 311	4 774	4 538	9 787	5 013	4 775
0-4	876	453	423	872	450	421	845	436	408	820	424	397
5-9	835	432	403	868	449	419	865	447	418	839	434	405
10-14	791	409	382	832	431	402	865	447	417	863	446	416
15-19	774	400	374	787	407	380	829	429	400	862	446	416
20-24	781	404	377	768	397	371	782	405	378	824	426	398
25-29	777	401	375	773	400	373	761	394	367	777	402	375
30-34	711	367	343	767	397	370	765	396	369	755	390	364
35-39	571	306	265	699	362	338	757	391	365	756	391	365
40-44	497	264	233	558	299	259	686	354	331	744	384	359
45-49	411	208	203	481	255	226	542	290	252	668	345	323
50-54	369	180	189	390	197	194	459	242	217	520	276	243
55-59	292	143	149	341	165	176	364	182	182	430	225	205
60-64	222	108	115	259	124	135	306	145	161	328	161	167
65-69	141	67	75	185	86	99	219	101	117	261	119	142
70-74	85	39	46	108	48	60	144	64	80	173	76	96
75-79	44	19	25	58	25	33	75	31	44	102	42	60
80-84	19	8	11	25	10	15	34	13	21	45	17	28
85-89	7	3	4	8	3	5	12	4	7	16	6	10
90-94	2	1	1	2	1	2	3	1	2	4	1	3
95-99	0	0	0	0	0	0	1	0	0	1	0	0
100 +	0	0	0	0	0	0	0	0	0	0	0	0

Age group	2045 Both sexes	2045 Males	2045 Females	2050 Both sexes	2050 Males	2050 Females
All ages	10 223	5 230	4 993	10 619	5 425	5 194
0-4	810	418	392	806	416	390
5-9	816	422	394	807	417	390
10-14	837	433	404	814	421	394
15-19	860	445	415	835	432	404
20-24	858	444	414	857	443	414
25-29	819	424	396	854	441	412
30-34	771	399	372	814	421	393
35-39	747	386	361	764	395	369
40-44	745	385	360	737	381	356
45-49	727	375	352	730	377	353
50-54	643	330	313	702	361	341
55-59	490	258	232	609	310	299
60-64	391	201	190	448	232	216
65-69	283	134	149	339	169	170
70-74	209	91	118	229	104	125
75-79	125	51	73	153	62	91
80-84	63	24	39	79	30	49
85-89	22	8	14	32	11	21
90-94	6	2	4	8	2	6
95-99	1	0	1	1	0	1
100 +	0	0	0	0	0	0

POPULATION BY AGE AND SEX (in thousands)

Age group	2005 Both sexes	Males	Females	2010 Both sexes	Males	Females	2015 Both sexes	Males	Females	2020 Both sexes	Males	Females
All ages	5 887	3 035	2 852	6 505	3 348	3 157	7 168	3 685	3 483	7 900	4 059	3 840
0-4	815	421	394	851	440	412	906	468	438	990	512	478
5-9	808	417	391	799	413	386	837	433	404	894	463	431
10-14	749	386	363	801	414	388	794	410	383	832	431	402
15-19	612	326	286	742	382	359	795	411	384	788	408	381
20-24	543	288	255	602	322	281	732	378	354	786	406	380
25-29	462	234	228	532	282	250	592	316	276	721	372	349
30-34	434	213	221	451	229	222	522	277	244	582	311	271
35-39	369	185	184	421	207	214	440	223	216	510	271	239
40-44	314	158	156	355	178	178	407	200	207	427	217	210
45-49	236	120	116	298	150	148	339	169	170	390	192	199
50-54	181	95	86	219	110	108	278	139	139	318	157	160
55-59	132	69	63	162	84	78	197	98	99	253	125	128
60-64	90	48	42	113	57	55	139	70	69	172	84	88
65-69	68	36	33	71	36	34	90	44	46	113	55	58
70-74	39	20	19	48	24	25	51	25	26	66	31	35
75-79	21	11	10	24	12	12	31	14	17	33	15	18
80-84	10	5	4	11	5	5	13	6	7	17	7	10
85-89	3	2	2	4	2	2	4	2	2	5	2	3
90-94	1	0	0	1	0	0	1	1	1	1	1	1
95-99	0	0	0	0	0	0	0	0	0	0	0	0
100 +	0	0	0	0	0	0	0	0	0	0	0	0

Age group	2025 Both sexes	Males	Females	2030 Both sexes	Males	Females	2035 Both sexes	Males	Females	2040 Both sexes	Males	Females
All ages	8 664	4 450	4 214	9 425	4 839	4 587	10 172	5 219	4 953	10 917	5 597	5 320
0-4	1 040	537	502	1 058	547	511	1 068	552	516	1 094	565	529
5-9	978	506	472	1 030	533	497	1 049	543	507	1 061	548	512
10-14	890	460	429	974	504	470	1 026	531	495	1 047	541	505
15-19	828	428	400	885	458	427	971	502	468	1 023	529	494
20-24	781	404	377	821	425	396	880	455	425	965	499	466
25-29	777	401	375	773	400	373	814	421	393	873	452	422
30-34	711	367	343	767	397	370	765	396	369	807	418	389
35-39	571	306	265	699	362	338	757	391	365	756	391	365
40-44	497	264	233	558	299	259	686	354	331	744	384	359
45-49	411	208	203	481	255	226	542	290	252	668	345	323
50-54	369	180	189	390	197	194	459	242	217	520	276	243
55-59	292	143	149	341	165	176	364	182	182	430	225	205
60-64	222	108	115	259	124	135	306	145	161	328	161	167
65-69	141	67	75	185	86	99	219	101	117	261	119	142
70-74	85	39	46	108	48	60	144	64	80	173	76	96
75-79	44	19	25	58	25	33	75	31	44	102	42	60
80-84	19	8	11	25	10	15	34	13	21	45	17	28
85-89	7	3	4	8	3	5	12	4	7	16	6	10
90-94	2	1	1	2	1	2	3	1	2	4	1	3
95-99	0	0	0	0	0	0	1	0	0	1	0	0
100 +	0	0	0	0	0	0	0	0	0	0	0	0

Age group	2045 Both sexes	Males	Females	2050 Both sexes	Males	Females
All ages	11 672	5 979	5 693	12 429	6 360	6 069
0-4	1 135	586	549	1 173	606	568
5-9	1 088	562	526	1 130	584	546
10-14	1 058	547	511	1 086	561	525
15-19	1 044	540	504	1 056	546	510
20-24	1 018	527	492	1 040	537	502
25-29	959	496	463	1 013	524	489
30-34	867	448	418	953	493	460
35-39	799	413	386	859	444	415
40-44	745	385	360	789	408	381
45-49	727	375	352	730	377	353
50-54	643	330	313	702	361	341
55-59	490	258	232	609	310	299
60-64	391	201	190	448	232	216
65-69	283	134	149	339	169	170
70-74	209	91	118	229	104	125
75-79	125	51	73	153	62	91
80-84	63	24	39	79	30	49
85-89	22	8	14	32	11	21
90-94	6	2	4	8	2	6
95-99	1	0	1	1	0	1
100 +	0	0	0	0	0	0

United Nations Department of Economic and Social Affairs/Population Division
World Population Prospects: The 2004 Revision, Volume II: Sex and Age Distribution of the World Population

680

POPULATION BY AGE AND SEX (in thousands)

Age group	2005 Both sexes	Males	Females	2010 Both sexes	Males	Females	2015 Both sexes	Males	Females	2020 Both sexes	Males	Females
All ages	5 887	3 035	2 852	6 395	3 291	0 104	6 858	3 525	3 333	7 305	3 751	3 553
0-4	815	421	394	741	383	358	706	365	341	701	362	339
5-9	808	417	391	799	413	386	728	377	351	696	360	336
10-14	749	386	363	801	414	388	794	410	383	724	375	350
15-19	612	326	286	742	382	359	795	411	384	788	408	381
20-24	543	288	255	602	322	281	732	378	354	786	406	380
25-29	462	234	228	532	282	250	592	316	276	721	372	349
30-34	434	213	221	451	229	222	522	277	244	582	311	271
35-39	369	185	184	421	207	214	440	223	216	510	271	239
40-44	314	158	156	355	178	178	407	200	207	427	217	210
45-49	236	120	116	298	150	148	339	169	170	390	192	199
50-54	181	95	86	219	110	108	278	139	139	318	157	160
55-59	132	69	63	162	84	78	197	98	99	253	125	128
60-64	90	48	42	113	57	55	139	70	69	172	84	88
65-69	68	36	33	71	36	34	90	44	46	113	55	58
70-74	39	20	19	48	24	25	51	25	26	66	31	35
75-79	21	11	10	24	12	12	31	14	17	33	15	18
80-84	10	5	4	11	5	5	13	6	7	17	7	10
85-89	3	2	2	4	2	2	4	2	2	5	2	3
90-94	1	0	0	1	0	0	1	1	1	1	1	1
95-99	0	0	0	0	0	0	0	0	0	0	0	0
100 +	0	0	0	0	0	0	0	0	0	0	0	0

Age group	2025 Both sexes	Males	Females	2030 Both sexes	Males	Females	2035 Both sexes	Males	Females	2040 Both sexes	Males	Females
All ages	7 747	3 976	3 771	8 147	4 177	3 970	8 471	4 339	4 132	8 712	4 457	4 255
0-4	713	369	344	690	357	334	638	329	308	581	300	281
5-9	693	358	334	706	365	341	685	354	331	634	328	306
10-14	693	358	334	690	357	333	704	364	340	683	353	330
15-19	720	373	348	689	357	333	687	356	332	702	363	339
20-24	781	404	377	715	370	345	685	354	331	683	354	330
25-29	777	401	375	773	400	373	708	366	342	680	352	328
30-34	711	367	343	767	397	370	765	396	369	702	363	339
35-39	571	306	265	699	362	338	757	391	365	756	391	365
40-44	497	264	233	558	299	259	606	354	331	744	384	359
45-49	411	208	203	481	255	226	542	290	252	668	345	323
50-54	369	180	189	390	197	194	459	242	217	520	276	243
55-59	292	143	140	341	165	176	364	182	182	430	225	205
60-64	222	108	115	259	124	135	306	145	161	328	161	167
65-69	141	67	75	185	86	99	219	101	117	261	119	142
70-74	85	39	46	108	48	60	144	64	80	173	76	96
75-79	44	19	25	58	25	33	75	31	44	102	42	60
80-84	19	8	11	25	10	15	34	13	21	45	17	28
85-89	7	3	4	8	3	5	12	4	7	16	6	10
90-94	2	1	1	2	1	2	3	1	2	4	1	3
95-99	0	0	0	0	0	0	1	0	0	1	0	0
100 +	0	0	0	0	0	0	0	0	0	0	0	0

Age group	2045 Both sexes	Males	Females	2050 Both sexes	Males	Females
All ages	8 879	4 535	4 344	8 982	4 579	4 403
0-4	537	277	260	507	262	245
5-9	577	298	279	535	276	259
10-14	632	327	305	576	298	279
15-19	681	352	329	631	326	305
20-24	698	361	337	678	351	328
25-29	679	351	328	695	359	336
30-34	675	349	326	675	349	326
35-39	695	360	335	669	346	323
40-44	745	385	360	686	355	331
45-49	727	375	352	730	377	353
50-54	643	330	313	702	361	341
55-59	490	258	232	609	310	299
60-64	391	201	190	448	232	216
65-69	283	134	149	339	169	170
70-74	209	91	118	229	104	125
75-79	125	51	73	153	62	91
80-84	63	24	39	79	30	49
85-89	22	8	14	32	11	21
90-94	6	2	4	8	2	6
95-99	1	0	1	1	0	1
100 +	0	0	0	0	0	0

United Nations Department of Economic and Social Affairs/Population Division
World Population Prospects: The 2004 Revision, Volume II: Sex and Age Distribution of the World Population

681

POPULATION BY AGE AND SEX (in thousands)

Age group	1950 Both sexes	1950 Males	1950 Females	1955 Both sexes	1955 Males	1955 Females	1960 Both sexes	1960 Males	1960 Females	1965 Both sexes	1965 Males	1965 Females
All ages	1 488	723	765	1 659	810	848	1 842	905	938	2 081	1 026	1 055
0-4	215	109	105	302	154	148	322	164	158	357	182	175
5-9	191	97	94	206	105	101	291	148	144	313	159	154
10-14	174	88	86	185	94	90	200	102	98	286	145	141
15-19	143	71	72	164	84	80	174	90	84	192	99	93
20-24	118	57	62	122	60	63	143	73	70	160	82	77
25-29	94	45	49	103	48	55	107	51	56	132	67	65
30-34	83	39	44	84	40	45	93	43	51	100	47	53
35-39	76	35	41	78	36	42	80	37	43	90	41	49
40-44	69	31	37	72	34	38	74	35	40	77	36	41
45-49	68	32	37	65	30	35	68	32	37	71	33	38
50-54	68	32	36	64	30	35	61	28	34	65	30	35
55-59	57	27	30	63	29	34	60	27	32	57	26	32
60-64	47	22	24	52	24	27	57	26	31	55	25	30
65-69	36	17	19	40	19	21	45	21	24	50	22	28
70-74	25	11	14	29	13	16	32	15	18	36	16	20
75-79	15	6	9	18	8	10	20	9	11	23	10	13
80 +	10	3	7	12	4	8	14	6	9	17	7	10

Age group	1970 Both sexes	1970 Males	1970 Females	1975 Both sexes	1975 Males	1975 Females	1980 Both sexes	1980 Males	1980 Females	1985 Both sexes	1985 Males	1985 Females
All ages	2 350	1 164	1 186	2 659	1 327	1 332	3 114	1 563	1 550	3 609	1 813	1 796
0-4	393	200	193	428	218	210	492	250	241	608	310	299
5-9	348	177	171	386	197	190	430	219	211	486	247	239
10-14	308	156	151	345	176	169	391	200	192	427	217	210
15-19	279	142	136	302	154	147	349	178	171	388	198	190
20-24	178	91	87	264	136	127	305	156	149	344	175	169
25-29	149	76	73	166	85	81	266	138	128	299	153	147
30-34	125	63	62	143	73	69	168	86	81	260	134	126
35-39	96	45	51	122	61	61	144	74	70	162	83	79
40-44	87	39	47	94	44	50	123	62	61	140	72	68
45-49	74	34	40	84	38	46	94	44	50	118	59	59
50-54	68	31	36	71	33	38	83	38	45	89	41	48
55-59	61	28	33	64	29	35	69	32	37	78	35	43
60-64	53	23	29	56	25	31	60	27	33	63	28	35
65-69	48	21	27	46	20	26	50	22	28	53	23	30
70-74	40	18	23	39	17	22	38	16	22	41	18	24
75-79	26	11	15	29	12	17	28	12	17	28	11	16
80 +	19	8	11	21	8	13	24	9	15	25	9	15

Age group	1990 Both sexes	1990 Males	1990 Females	1995 Both sexes	1995 Males	1995 Females	2000 Both sexes	2000 Males	2000 Females	2005 Both sexes	2005 Males	2005 Females
All ages	4 219	2 126	2 093	4 829	2 433	2 396	5 470	2 756	2 714	6 158	3 102	3 056
0-4	679	346	333	735	374	360	771	393	378	825	421	405
5-9	605	308	298	673	342	331	728	370	358	765	389	375
10-14	487	248	239	602	306	296	669	340	329	725	369	356
15-19	428	218	210	483	245	238	599	304	295	666	338	328
20-24	388	198	191	423	215	208	478	242	236	593	301	293
25-29	344	175	169	383	194	188	417	211	206	473	239	234
30-34	299	153	146	338	171	167	376	191	186	411	207	203
35-39	259	134	126	292	149	144	331	167	164	370	186	183
40-44	161	83	79	253	130	123	286	145	141	325	164	161
45-49	138	71	67	156	79	77	246	126	120	279	140	138
50-54	115	57	58	132	67	65	149	75	74	238	121	117
55-59	85	39	46	109	53	55	125	63	62	142	71	71
60-64	73	32	41	79	36	43	101	49	52	117	58	59
65-69	56	25	31	65	28	37	71	31	40	91	43	48
70-74	44	19	25	47	20	27	54	23	32	60	26	34
75-79	30	12	18	32	13	19	35	14	21	42	17	25
80 +	25	9	16	27	10	17	31	12	20	37	14	23

United Nations Department of Economic and Social Affairs/Population Division
World Population Prospects: The 2004 Revision, Volume II: Sex and Age Distribution of the World Population

POPULATION BY AGE AND SEX (in thousands)

Age group	2005 Both sexes	2005 Males	2005 Females	2010 Both sexes	2010 Males	2010 Females	2015 Both sexes	2015 Males	2015 Females	2020 Both sexes	2020 Males	2020 Females
All ages	6 158	3 102	3 056	6 882	3 466	3 416	7 613	3 832	3 781	8 041	4 195	4 146
0-4	825	421	405	872	445	428	896	457	439	912	465	447
5-9	765	389	375	819	417	402	867	441	425	891	454	437
10-14	725	369	356	762	388	374	816	415	401	864	440	424
15-19	666	338	328	721	366	355	758	386	373	813	413	400
20-24	593	301	293	661	335	326	716	363	353	753	382	371
25-29	473	239	234	587	297	291	654	331	323	710	359	351
30-34	411	207	203	466	235	231	581	293	288	647	327	321
35-39	370	186	183	404	203	201	459	231	228	573	288	285
40-44	325	164	161	363	183	180	397	199	198	452	227	226
45-49	279	140	138	317	159	158	355	178	177	389	194	195
50-54	238	121	117	270	135	135	308	153	155	345	172	173
55-59	142	71	71	228	114	113	259	129	131	297	146	150
60-64	117	58	59	134	66	68	215	106	109	246	120	126
65-69	91	43	48	106	51	55	122	59	63	198	96	102
70-74	60	26	34	79	36	42	92	43	49	107	50	57
75-79	42	17	25	47	20	28	62	28	35	74	34	41
80-84	23	9	14	28	11	18	33	13	20	44	19	25
85-89	10	4	7	12	4	8	16	5	10	19	7	12
90-94	3	1	2	4	1	3	5	1	3	6	2	4
95-99	0	0	0	1	0	0	1	0	1	1	0	1
100 +	0	0	0	0	0	0	0	0	0	0	0	0

Age group	2025 Both sexes	2025 Males	2025 Females	2030 Both sexes	2030 Males	2030 Females	2035 Both sexes	2035 Males	2035 Females	2040 Both sexes	2040 Males	2040 Females
All ages	9 055	4 550	4 505	9 747	4 893	4 854	10 407	5 218	5 189	11 025	5 521	5 504
0-4	922	470	451	927	473	454	928	474	454	922	471	451
5-9	907	463	445	917	468	449	923	471	452	924	471	452
10-14	888	452	436	905	461	444	915	466	448	921	469	451
15-19	860	438	423	885	450	434	901	459	442	912	464	447
20-24	808	410	398	855	435	421	880	447	432	897	456	440
25-29	747	379	368	802	407	395	849	431	418	874	444	430
30-34	703	355	348	740	375	366	795	402	393	843	427	416
35-39	640	322	318	695	350	345	733	370	363	787	398	389
40-44	565	283	282	632	317	314	687	346	341	724	365	359
45-49	444	222	222	556	278	278	622	311	311	677	339	338
50-54	379	188	191	433	215	218	543	270	273	609	303	306
55-59	334	164	169	367	181	186	420	207	213	528	260	268
60-64	282	137	145	318	155	163	350	170	180	402	196	207
65-69	227	109	118	261	125	137	296	142	154	328	156	171
70-74	174	82	92	201	94	107	234	109	125	266	124	142
75-79	87	39	48	144	66	78	168	76	92	197	88	108
80-84	53	23	30	64	27	36	106	46	60	126	54	72
85-89	26	10	16	32	13	19	39	16	24	67	27	40
90-94	8	3	5	11	4	7	15	5	9	18	7	12
95-99	2	0	1	2	1	2	3	1	2	5	1	3
100 +	0	0	0	0	0	0	0	0	0	1	0	0

Age group	2045 Both sexes	2045 Males	2045 Females	2050 Both sexes	2050 Males	2050 Females
All ages	11 590	5 797	5 793	12 095	6 042	6 053
0-4	909	464	445	890	455	435
5-9	918	469	449	906	462	443
10-14	922	470	451	916	467	448
15-19	918	468	450	919	468	450
20-24	907	462	445	913	465	448
25-29	891	453	438	902	458	443
30-34	867	440	428	885	449	436
35-39	835	422	413	859	435	424
40-44	779	393	386	826	417	410
45-49	714	359	356	768	386	382
50-54	663	331	333	701	350	351
55-59	592	292	300	646	320	326
60-64	507	247	260	569	278	291
65-69	377	180	197	476	228	248
70-74	296	138	158	342	159	182
75-79	226	101	124	253	113	139
80-84	150	64	86	174	74	100
85-89	81	32	49	98	39	59
90-94	32	12	21	40	14	26
95-99	6	2	4	11	3	8
100 +	1	0	1	1	0	1

United Nations Department of Economic and Social Affairs/Population Division
World Population Prospects: The 2004 Revision, Volume II: Sex and Age Distribution of the World Population

683

POPULATION BY AGE AND SEX (in thousands)

Age group	2005 Both sexes	Males	Females	2010 Both sexes	Males	Females	2015 Both sexes	Males	Females	2020 Both sexes	Males	Females
All ages	6 158	3 102	3 056	6 941	3 496	3 445	7 779	3 917	3 863	8 658	4 357	4 301
0-4	825	421	405	931	475	457	1 004	512	492	1 064	543	521
5-9	765	389	375	819	417	402	925	471	454	998	508	489
10-14	725	369	356	762	388	374	816	415	401	922	470	453
15-19	666	338	328	721	366	355	758	386	373	813	413	400
20-24	593	301	293	661	335	326	716	363	353	753	382	371
25-29	473	239	234	587	297	291	654	331	323	710	359	351
30-34	411	207	203	466	235	231	581	293	288	647	327	321
35-39	370	186	183	404	203	201	459	231	228	573	288	285
40-44	325	164	161	363	183	180	397	199	198	452	227	226
45-49	279	140	138	317	159	158	355	178	177	389	194	195
50-54	238	121	117	270	135	135	308	153	155	345	172	173
55-59	142	71	71	228	114	113	259	129	131	297	146	150
60-64	117	58	59	134	66	68	215	106	109	246	120	126
65-69	91	43	48	106	51	55	122	59	63	198	96	102
70-74	60	26	34	79	36	42	92	43	49	107	50	57
75-79	42	17	25	47	20	28	62	28	35	74	34	41
80-84	23	9	14	28	11	18	33	13	20	44	19	25
85-89	10	4	7	12	4	8	16	5	10	19	7	12
90-94	3	1	2	4	1	3	5	1	3	6	2	4
95-99	0	0	0	1	0	0	1	0	1	1	0	1
100 +	0	0	0	0	0	0	0	0	0	0	0	0

Age group	2025 Both sexes	Males	Females	2030 Both sexes	Males	Females	2035 Both sexes	Males	Females	2040 Both sexes	Males	Females
All ages	9 542	4 799	4 743	10 434	5 243	5 191	11 339	5 694	5 646	12 255	6 149	6 107
0-4	1 093	557	535	1 129	576	553	1 175	600	575	1 222	624	598
5-9	1 058	539	519	1 087	554	533	1 124	573	550	1 170	597	573
10-14	995	507	488	1 055	538	517	1 084	553	531	1 121	572	549
15-19	919	467	451	991	505	487	1 052	536	516	1 081	551	530
20-24	808	410	398	914	464	449	986	501	485	1 047	533	514
25-29	747	379	368	802	407	395	907	460	447	980	498	482
30-34	703	355	348	740	375	366	795	402	393	900	456	444
35-39	640	322	318	695	350	345	733	370	363	787	398	389
40-44	565	283	282	632	317	314	687	346	341	724	365	359
45-49	444	222	222	556	278	278	622	311	311	677	339	338
50-54	379	188	191	433	215	218	543	270	273	609	303	306
55-59	334	164	169	367	181	186	420	207	213	528	260	268
60-64	282	137	145	318	155	163	350	170	180	402	196	207
65-69	227	109	118	261	125	137	296	142	154	328	156	171
70-74	174	82	92	201	94	107	234	109	125	266	124	142
75-79	87	39	48	144	66	78	168	76	92	197	88	108
80-84	53	23	30	64	27	36	106	46	60	126	54	72
85-89	26	10	16	32	13	19	39	16	24	67	27	40
90-94	8	3	5	11	4	7	15	5	9	18	7	12
95-99	2	0	1	2	1	2	3	1	2	5	1	3
100 +	0	0	0	0	0	0	0	0	0	1	0	0

Age group	2045 Both sexes	Males	Females	2050 Both sexes	Males	Females
All ages	13 170	6 603	6 567	14 069	7 049	7 020
0-4	1 261	644	617	1 288	658	630
5-9	1 218	622	596	1 257	642	615
10-14	1 167	596	572	1 215	620	595
15-19	1 118	570	548	1 164	594	571
20-24	1 076	548	528	1 113	567	546
25-29	1 041	529	512	1 070	544	526
30-34	973	493	479	1 033	525	509
35-39	892	451	441	965	488	476
40-44	779	393	386	884	446	438
45-49	714	359	356	768	386	382
50-54	663	331	333	701	350	351
55-59	592	292	300	646	320	326
60-64	507	247	260	569	278	291
65-69	377	180	197	476	228	248
70-74	296	138	158	342	159	182
75-79	226	101	124	253	113	139
80-84	150	64	86	174	74	100
85-89	81	32	49	98	39	59
90-94	32	12	21	40	14	26
95-99	6	2	4	11	3	8
100 +	1	0	1	1	0	1

United Nations Department of Economic and Social Affairs/Population Division
World Population Prospects: The 2004 Revision, Volume II: Sex and Age Distribution of the World Population

684

POPULATION BY AGE AND SEX (in thousands)

Age group	2005 Both sexes	Males	Females	2010 Both sexes	Males	Females	2015 Both sexes	Males	Females	2020 Both sexes	Males	Females
All ages	6 158	3 102	3 056	6 822	3 435	3 387	7 446	3 747	3 699	8 021	4 032	3 989
0-4	825	421	405	813	414	399	787	401	386	759	387	372
5-9	765	389	375	819	417	402	808	411	396	783	399	384
10-14	725	369	356	762	388	374	816	415	401	805	410	395
15-19	666	338	328	721	366	355	758	386	373	813	413	400
20-24	593	301	293	661	335	326	716	363	353	753	382	371
25-29	473	239	234	587	297	291	654	331	323	710	359	351
30-34	411	207	203	466	235	231	581	293	288	647	327	321
35-39	370	186	183	404	203	201	459	231	228	573	288	285
40-44	325	164	161	363	183	180	397	199	198	452	227	226
45-49	279	140	138	317	159	158	355	178	177	389	194	195
50-54	238	121	117	270	135	135	308	153	155	345	172	173
55-59	142	71	71	228	114	113	259	129	131	297	146	150
60-64	117	58	59	134	66	68	215	106	109	246	120	126
65-69	91	43	48	106	51	55	122	59	63	198	96	102
70-74	60	26	34	79	36	42	92	43	49	107	50	57
75-79	42	17	25	47	20	28	62	28	35	74	34	41
80-84	23	9	14	28	11	18	33	13	20	44	19	25
85-89	10	4	7	12	4	8	16	5	10	19	7	12
90-94	3	1	2	4	1	3	5	1	3	6	2	4
95-99	0	0	0	1	0	0	1	0	1	1	0	1
100 +	0	0	0	0	0	0	0	0	0	0	0	0

Age group	2025 Both sexes	Males	Females	2030 Both sexes	Males	Females	2035 Both sexes	Males	Females	2040 Both sexes	Males	Females
All ages	8 565	4 300	4 264	9 062	4 544	4 518	9 494	4 753	4 741	9 845	4 920	4 925
0-4	751	383	368	731	373	358	697	356	341	653	333	320
5-9	754	385	370	747	381	366	728	371	357	694	354	340
10-14	780	397	383	752	383	369	745	380	365	726	370	356
15-19	802	408	394	777	395	381	749	381	368	742	378	364
20-24	808	410	398	797	405	392	772	393	380	745	379	366
25-29	747	379	368	802	407	395	791	401	390	767	389	378
30-34	703	355	348	740	375	366	795	402	393	785	397	387
35-39	640	322	318	695	350	345	733	370	363	787	398	389
40-44	565	283	282	632	317	314	687	346	341	724	365	359
45-49	444	222	222	556	278	278	622	311	311	677	339	338
50-54	379	188	191	433	215	218	543	270	273	609	303	306
55-59	334	164	169	367	181	186	420	207	213	528	260	268
60-64	282	137	145	318	155	163	350	170	180	402	196	207
65-69	227	109	118	261	125	137	296	142	154	328	156	171
70-74	174	82	92	201	94	107	234	109	125	266	124	142
75-79	87	39	48	144	66	78	168	76	92	197	88	108
80-84	53	23	30	64	27	36	106	46	60	126	54	72
85-89	26	10	16	32	13	19	39	16	24	67	27	40
90-94	8	3	5	11	4	7	15	5	9	18	7	12
95-99	2	0	1	2	1	2	3	1	2	5	1	3
100 +	0	0	0	0	0	0	0	0	0	1	0	0

Age group	2045 Both sexes	Males	Females	2050 Both sexes	Males	Females
All ages	10 110	5 043	5 068	10 291	5 122	5 169
0-4	606	310	297	562	287	275
5-9	650	332	318	604	308	296
10-14	692	353	339	648	331	318
15-19	723	369	355	690	352	338
20-24	738	375	362	719	366	353
25-29	740	376	364	733	372	360
30-34	761	386	375	734	372	361
35-39	777	393	384	753	381	372
40-44	779	393	386	769	388	381
45-49	714	359	356	768	386	382
50-54	663	331	333	701	350	351
55-59	592	292	300	646	320	326
60-64	507	247	260	569	278	291
65-69	377	180	197	476	228	248
70-74	296	138	158	342	159	182
75-79	226	101	124	253	113	139
80-84	150	64	86	174	74	100
85-89	81	32	49	98	39	59
90-94	32	12	21	40	14	26
95-99	6	2	4	11	3	8
100 +	1	0	1	1	0	1

POPULATION BY AGE AND SEX (in thousands)

Age group	1950 Both sexes	1950 Males	1950 Females	1955 Both sexes	1955 Males	1955 Females	1960 Both sexes	1960 Males	1960 Females	1965 Both sexes	1965 Males	1965 Females
All ages	7 632	3 842	3 790	8 672	4 368	4 304	9 931	5 004	4 927	11 467	5 779	5 688
0-4	1 282	651	632	1 519	771	748	1 758	893	865	2 046	1 040	1 007
5-9	1 003	509	495	1 168	593	575	1 399	710	689	1 640	833	808
10-14	887	450	437	980	497	483	1 144	581	564	1 376	698	677
15-19	779	396	384	869	441	428	963	489	474	1 127	572	555
20-24	653	331	322	757	384	373	847	430	418	942	478	464
25-29	544	276	268	631	320	312	735	372	363	825	418	407
30-34	464	235	229	525	266	259	611	309	302	714	361	353
35-39	419	212	207	447	226	221	507	256	251	593	299	294
40-44	368	186	182	401	202	199	429	216	213	489	246	243
45-49	307	154	153	350	175	174	383	192	191	411	206	205
50-54	271	134	137	287	143	145	329	163	166	362	180	182
55-59	220	108	112	248	121	127	265	129	135	305	149	156
60-64	169	82	88	193	93	100	219	105	114	236	114	122
65-69	114	54	60	139	66	73	160	75	84	184	86	97
70-74	81	37	44	83	38	45	102	47	55	120	56	65
75-79	44	19	24	49	22	27	51	23	28	65	29	36
80 +	25	10	15	25	11	15	28	12	16	31	13	18

Age group	1970 Both sexes	1970 Males	1970 Females	1975 Both sexes	1975 Males	1975 Females	1980 Both sexes	1980 Males	1980 Females	1985 Both sexes	1985 Males	1985 Females
All ages	13 193	6 649	6 544	15 161	7 640	7 521	17 324	8 721	8 603	19 516	9 822	9 694
0-4	2 261	1 150	1 112	2 488	1 265	1 222	2 724	1 386	1 338	2 807	1 427	1 380
5-9	1 928	979	949	2 161	1 098	1 064	2 397	1 217	1 180	2 643	1 342	1 300
10-14	1 616	821	796	1 907	968	939	2 142	1 087	1 055	2 374	1 205	1 169
15-19	1 357	689	668	1 600	812	788	1 889	958	931	2 121	1 075	1 045
20-24	1 106	561	545	1 337	678	659	1 576	797	778	1 860	942	918
25-29	920	466	454	1 086	550	536	1 310	661	648	1 542	779	763
30-34	805	407	398	902	456	446	1 062	536	526	1 280	646	634
35-39	695	351	344	788	397	390	882	444	438	1 037	522	516
40-44	574	289	285	677	341	336	768	386	382	858	431	427
45-49	470	236	235	555	278	278	656	328	328	744	373	372
50-54	391	194	197	450	223	227	533	264	269	630	313	317
55-59	337	165	172	367	180	187	424	208	216	503	247	256
60-64	274	132	142	307	148	159	336	162	175	390	188	201
65-69	200	94	106	236	111	125	268	126	142	295	139	156
70-74	141	65	76	157	72	85	189	87	102	217	100	117
75-79	78	35	43	94	42	52	107	47	60	135	60	75
80 +	39	16	22	49	21	28	62	26	36	80	33	47

Age group	1990 Both sexes	1990 Males	1990 Females	1995 Both sexes	1995 Males	1995 Females	2000 Both sexes	2000 Males	2000 Females	2005 Both sexes	2005 Males	2005 Females
All ages	21 753	10 944	10 809	23 837	11 995	11 842	25 952	13 055	12 897	27 968	14 060	13 908
0-4	2 965	1 507	1 458	3 100	1 576	1 523	3 083	1 570	1 512	2 997	1 528	1 469
5-9	2 735	1 388	1 346	2 886	1 466	1 421	3 029	1 539	1 490	3 020	1 537	1 483
10-14	2 613	1 327	1 287	2 687	1 363	1 323	2 846	1 444	1 402	2 993	1 519	1 473
15-19	2 346	1 189	1 157	2 564	1 300	1 264	2 646	1 341	1 305	2 810	1 425	1 385
20-24	2 079	1 052	1 027	2 269	1 148	1 120	2 500	1 265	1 235	2 590	1 310	1 279
25-29	1 809	914	896	1 983	1 000	982	2 189	1 105	1 084	2 429	1 226	1 203
30-34	1 499	757	742	1 727	874	854	1 914	966	948	2 126	1 073	1 053
35-39	1 246	626	619	1 438	723	715	1 674	844	830	1 865	938	926
40-44	1 006	504	501	1 194	598	595	1 391	697	694	1 628	818	810
45-49	830	416	415	967	484	482	1 155	578	577	1 351	675	676
50-54	714	355	358	791	394	396	927	462	465	1 112	553	559
55-59	594	293	302	670	332	338	747	370	377	880	436	445
60-64	462	224	238	544	266	279	618	303	315	694	340	354
65-69	343	163	180	407	195	212	483	232	251	553	267	287
70-74	242	112	130	282	132	150	339	159	180	408	192	216
75-79	160	71	89	182	82	100	216	98	118	264	120	144
80 +	110	46	65	147	61	86	196	82	114	249	103	145

United Nations Department of Economic and Social Affairs/Population Division
World Population Prospects: The 2004 Revision, Volume II: Sex and Age Distribution of the World Population

686

MEDIUM VARIANT   PERU

POPULATION BY AGE AND SEX (in thousands)

Age group	2005 Both sexes	Males	Females	2010 Both sexes	Males	Females	2015 Both sexes	Males	Females	2020 Both sexes	Males	Females
All ages	27 968	14 060	13 908	30 063	15 099	14 965	32 172	16 141	16 031	34 250	17 162	17 088
0-4	2 997	1 528	1 469	3 037	1 550	1 487	3 068	1 566	1 502	3 066	1 566	1 500
5-9	3 020	1 537	1 483	2 946	1 501	1 446	2 994	1 526	1 467	3 031	1 546	1 485
10-14	2 993	1 519	1 473	2 993	1 522	1 471	2 925	1 489	1 436	2 977	1 517	1 460
15-19	2 810	1 425	1 385	2 967	1 505	1 461	2 972	1 511	1 461	2 909	1 480	1 429
20-24	2 590	1 310	1 279	2 769	1 402	1 367	2 933	1 486	1 447	2 946	1 496	1 450
25-29	2 429	1 226	1 203	2 539	1 283	1 256	2 727	1 379	1 348	2 900	1 468	1 432
30-34	2 126	1 073	1 053	2 378	1 199	1 180	2 497	1 260	1 238	2 694	1 360	1 334
35-39	1 865	938	926	2 088	1 051	1 036	2 343	1 179	1 165	2 467	1 242	1 225
40-44	1 628	818	810	1 825	916	909	2 051	1 030	1 021	2 309	1 158	1 151
45-49	1 351	675	676	1 588	795	793	1 786	893	894	2 013	1 007	1 006
50-54	1 112	553	559	1 308	649	658	1 543	767	776	1 741	865	876
55-59	880	436	445	1 062	523	539	1 255	617	638	1 487	733	754
60-64	694	340	354	823	402	421	999	486	513	1 187	576	611
65-69	553	267	287	627	301	325	750	359	391	918	438	480
70-74	408	192	216	473	222	251	543	254	289	658	307	351
75-79	264	120	144	324	146	177	383	173	210	446	200	246
80-84	149	65	85	188	81	107	235	101	135	283	121	163
85-89	70	29	42	89	36	53	115	46	69	147	58	89
90-94	24	9	15	32	12	20	42	15	27	56	20	36
95-99	5	2	3	7	2	5	10	3	7	14	4	10
100	1	0	0	1	0	1	1	0	1	2	1	1

Age group	2025 Both sexes	Males	Females	2030 Both sexes	Males	Females	2035 Both sexes	Males	Females	2040 Both sexes	Males	Females
All ages	36 191	18 111	18 081	37 931	18 954	18 977	39 452	19 684	19 768	40 739	20 293	20 446
0-4	3 017	1 541	1 476	2 942	1 503	1 438	2 859	1 461	1 397	2 773	1 418	1 355
5-9	3 033	1 547	1 485	2 986	1 524	1 462	2 913	1 488	1 426	2 833	1 447	1 386
10-14	3 015	1 537	1 478	3 017	1 539	1 478	2 972	1 517	1 455	2 900	1 481	1 419
15-19	2 961	1 508	1 453	3 000	1 529	1 471	3 003	1 531	1 472	2 958	1 509	1 449
20-24	2 885	1 467	1 418	2 938	1 495	1 443	2 977	1 516	1 461	2 981	1 519	1 462
25-29	2 915	1 478	1 437	2 855	1 450	1 405	2 909	1 479	1 430	2 949	1 500	1 449
30-34	2 867	1 449	1 418	2 883	1 460	1 423	2 824	1 433	1 392	2 879	1 462	1 417
35-39	2 664	1 342	1 321	2 837	1 431	1 406	2 855	1 443	1 411	2 798	1 417	1 381
40-44	2 434	1 222	1 212	2 630	1 322	1 308	2 803	1 411	1 392	2 822	1 424	1 398
45-49	2 270	1 134	1 135	2 395	1 198	1 196	2 590	1 297	1 292	2 763	1 386	1 377
50-54	1 958	970	988	2 219	1 103	1 117	2 344	1 166	1 178	2 538	1 264	1 273
55-59	1 682	828	854	1 902	938	964	2 151	1 060	1 091	2 275	1 123	1 150
60-64	1 412	687	725	1 602	778	823	1 815	884	932	2 057	1 001	1 056
65-69	1 097	523	575	1 310	625	685	1 490	711	779	1 695	810	885
70-74	812	377	435	977	453	524	1 172	544	627	1 340	622	718
75-79	547	245	303	682	303	370	826	367	459	997	444	553
80-84	336	142	194	417	176	241	524	220	304	641	268	373
85-89	182	71	110	219	85	133	274	106	168	349	135	215
90-94	73	26	47	92	32	60	113	39	73	143	49	94
95-99	19	6	13	26	8	18	33	10	23	40	12	28
100 +	3	1	2	4	1	3	5	2	4	7	2	5

Age group	2045 Both sexes	Males	Females	2050 Both sexes	Males	Females
All ages	41 774	20 774	21 000	42 552	21 125	21 427
0-4	2 682	1 372	1 311	2 592	1 326	1 267
5-9	2 750	1 405	1 344	2 661	1 360	1 301
10-14	2 820	1 440	1 380	2 737	1 399	1 338
15-19	2 887	1 473	1 413	2 808	1 434	1 374
20-24	2 937	1 497	1 440	2 866	1 462	1 404
25-29	2 954	1 504	1 450	2 911	1 483	1 428
30-34	2 920	1 484	1 436	2 926	1 488	1 438
35-39	2 853	1 447	1 406	2 895	1 469	1 426
40-44	2 767	1 398	1 369	2 823	1 429	1 395
45-49	2 783	1 399	1 384	2 731	1 375	1 355
50-54	2 710	1 352	1 358	2 732	1 367	1 365
55-59	2 467	1 219	1 248	2 638	1 306	1 332
60-64	2 181	1 063	1 118	2 369	1 157	1 212
65-69	1 927	921	1 006	2 048	981	1 067
70-74	1 531	712	819	1 748	813	935
75-79	1 148	511	637	1 320	589	731
80-84	781	327	453	906	380	526
85-89	432	166	266	532	205	327
90-94	185	63	121	231	79	152
95-99	52	16	36	68	20	48
100 +	8	2	6	10	3	7

POPULATION BY AGE AND SEX (in thousands)

Age group	2005 Both sexes	Males	Females	2010 Both sexes	Males	Females	2015 Both sexes	Males	Females	2020 Both sexes	Males	Females
All ages	27 968	14 060	13 908	30 344	15 242	15 102	32 933	16 529	16 404	35 648	17 875	17 773
0-4	2 997	1 528	1 469	3 318	1 693	1 625	3 552	1 813	1 738	3 709	1 894	1 815
5-9	3 020	1 537	1 483	2 946	1 501	1 446	3 271	1 667	1 603	3 510	1 790	1 720
10-14	2 993	1 519	1 473	2 993	1 522	1 471	2 925	1 489	1 436	3 253	1 658	1 595
15-19	2 810	1 425	1 385	2 967	1 505	1 461	2 972	1 511	1 461	2 909	1 480	1 429
20-24	2 590	1 310	1 279	2 769	1 402	1 367	2 933	1 486	1 447	2 946	1 496	1 450
25-29	2 429	1 226	1 203	2 539	1 283	1 256	2 727	1 379	1 348	2 900	1 468	1 432
30-34	2 126	1 073	1 053	2 378	1 199	1 180	2 497	1 260	1 238	2 694	1 360	1 334
35-39	1 865	938	926	2 088	1 051	1 036	2 343	1 179	1 165	2 467	1 242	1 225
40-44	1 628	818	810	1 825	916	909	2 051	1 030	1 021	2 309	1 158	1 151
45-49	1 351	675	676	1 588	795	793	1 786	893	894	2 013	1 007	1 006
50-54	1 112	553	559	1 308	649	658	1 543	767	776	1 741	865	876
55-59	880	436	445	1 062	523	539	1 255	617	638	1 487	733	754
60-64	694	340	354	823	402	421	999	486	513	1 187	576	611
65-69	553	267	287	627	301	325	750	359	391	918	438	480
70-74	408	192	216	473	222	251	543	254	289	658	307	351
75-79	264	120	144	324	146	177	383	173	210	446	200	246
80-84	149	65	85	188	81	107	235	101	135	283	121	163
85-89	70	29	42	89	36	53	115	46	69	147	58	89
90-94	24	9	15	32	12	20	42	15	27	56	20	36
95-99	5	2	3	7	2	5	10	3	7	14	4	10
100 +	1	0	0	1	0	1	1	0	1	2	1	1

Age group	2025 Both sexes	Males	Females	2030 Both sexes	Males	Females	2035 Both sexes	Males	Females	2040 Both sexes	Males	Females
All ages	38 268	19 170	19 098	40 772	20 403	20 369	43 200	21 595	21 604	45 558	22 751	22 807
0-4	3 703	1 892	1 812	3 715	1 898	1 817	3 777	1 931	1 846	3 859	1 973	1 886
5-9	3 670	1 873	1 797	3 667	1 872	1 795	3 681	1 880	1 801	3 745	1 913	1 832
10-14	3 492	1 780	1 712	3 653	1 863	1 790	3 651	1 863	1 788	3 666	1 871	1 794
15-19	3 237	1 649	1 588	3 476	1 771	1 705	3 637	1 854	1 783	3 636	1 855	1 781
20-24	2 885	1 467	1 418	3 213	1 635	1 578	3 452	1 758	1 694	3 613	1 841	1 772
25-29	2 915	1 478	1 437	2 855	1 450	1 405	3 182	1 618	1 565	3 422	1 741	1 681
30-34	2 867	1 449	1 418	2 883	1 460	1 423	2 824	1 433	1 392	3 151	1 600	1 551
35-39	2 664	1 342	1 321	2 837	1 431	1 406	2 855	1 443	1 411	2 798	1 417	1 381
40-44	2 434	1 222	1 212	2 630	1 322	1 308	2 803	1 411	1 392	2 822	1 424	1 398
45-49	2 270	1 134	1 135	2 395	1 198	1 196	2 590	1 297	1 292	2 763	1 386	1 377
50-54	1 966	978	988	2 219	1 103	1 117	2 344	1 166	1 178	2 538	1 264	1 273
55-59	1 682	828	854	1 902	938	964	2 151	1 060	1 091	2 275	1 123	1 153
60-64	1 412	687	725	1 602	778	823	1 815	884	932	2 057	1 001	1 056
65-69	1 097	523	575	1 310	625	685	1 490	711	779	1 695	810	885
70-74	812	377	435	977	453	524	1 172	544	627	1 340	622	718
75-79	547	245	303	682	303	378	825	367	459	997	444	553
80-84	336	142	194	417	176	241	524	220	304	641	268	373
85-89	182	71	110	219	85	133	274	106	168	349	135	215
90-94	73	26	47	92	32	60	113	39	73	143	49	94
95-99	19	6	13	26	8	18	33	10	23	40	12	28
100 +	3	1	2	4	1	3	5	2	4	7	2	5

Age group	2045 Both sexes	Males	Females	2050 Both sexes	Males	Females
All ages	47 816	23 855	23 961	49 942	24 894	25 048
0-4	3 924	2 006	1 917	3 963	2 027	1 936
5-9	3 829	1 957	1 872	3 895	1 991	1 904
10-14	3 730	1 905	1 825	3 815	1 949	1 865
15-19	3 651	1 863	1 788	3 716	1 897	1 819
20-24	3 613	1 842	1 771	3 629	1 851	1 778
25-29	3 584	1 824	1 759	3 584	1 826	1 758
30-34	3 391	1 723	1 668	3 553	1 807	1 746
35-39	3 123	1 584	1 540	3 363	1 706	1 656
40-44	2 767	1 398	1 369	3 092	1 564	1 527
45-49	2 783	1 399	1 384	2 731	1 375	1 355
50-54	2 710	1 352	1 358	2 732	1 367	1 365
55-59	2 467	1 219	1 248	2 638	1 306	1 332
60-64	2 181	1 063	1 118	2 369	1 157	1 212
65-69	1 927	921	1 006	2 048	981	1 067
70-74	1 531	712	819	1 748	813	935
75-79	1 148	511	637	1 320	589	731
80-84	781	327	453	906	380	526
85-89	432	166	266	532	205	327
90-94	185	63	121	231	79	152
95-99	52	16	36	68	20	48
100 +	8	2	6	10	3	7

United Nations Department of Economic and Social Affairs/Population Division
World Population Prospects: The 2004 Revision, Volume II: Sex and Age Distribution of the World Population

688

POPULATION BY AGE AND SEX (in thousands)

Age group	2005 Both sexes	Males	Females	2010 Both sexes	Males	Females	2015 Both sexes	Males	Females	2020 Both sexes	Males	Females
All ages	27 068	14 060	13 008	29 792	14 966	14 827	31 406	15 750	15 656	32 843	16 444	16 399
0-4	2 997	1 528	1 469	2 756	1 407	1 350	2 580	1 317	1 263	2 419	1 236	1 184
5-9	3 020	1 537	1 483	2 946	1 501	1 446	2 716	1 384	1 331	2 548	1 300	1 248
10-14	2 993	1 519	1 473	2 993	1 522	1 471	2 925	1 489	1 436	2 700	1 376	1 324
15-19	2 810	1 425	1 385	2 967	1 505	1 461	2 972	1 511	1 461	2 909	1 480	1 429
20-24	2 590	1 310	1 279	2 769	1 402	1 367	2 933	1 486	1 447	2 946	1 496	1 450
25-29	2 429	1 226	1 203	2 539	1 283	1 256	2 727	1 379	1 348	2 900	1 468	1 432
30-34	2 126	1 073	1 053	2 378	1 199	1 180	2 497	1 260	1 238	2 694	1 360	1 334
35-39	1 865	938	926	2 088	1 051	1 036	2 343	1 179	1 165	2 467	1 242	1 225
40-44	1 628	818	810	1 825	916	909	2 051	1 030	1 021	2 309	1 158	1 151
45-49	1 351	675	676	1 588	795	793	1 786	893	894	2 013	1 007	1 006
50-54	1 112	553	559	1 308	649	658	1 543	767	776	1 741	865	876
55-59	880	436	445	1 062	523	539	1 255	617	638	1 487	733	754
60-64	694	340	354	823	402	421	999	486	513	1 187	576	611
65-69	553	267	287	627	301	325	750	359	391	918	438	480
70-74	408	192	216	473	222	251	543	254	289	658	307	351
75-79	264	120	144	324	146	177	383	173	210	446	200	246
80-84	149	65	85	188	81	107	235	101	135	283	121	163
85-89	70	29	42	89	36	53	115	46	69	147	58	89
90-94	24	9	15	32	12	20	42	15	27	56	20	36
95-99	5	2	3	7	2	5	10	3	7	14	4	10
100 +	1	0	0	1	0	1	1	0	1	2	1	1

Age group	2025 Both sexes	Males	Females	2030 Both sexes	Males	Females	2035 Both sexes	Males	Females	2040 Both sexes	Males	Females
All ages	34 109	17 049	17 061	35 113	17 517	17 596	35 807	17 825	17 982	36 168	17 962	18 206
0-4	2 334	1 192	1 142	2 196	1 122	1 074	2 021	1 033	988	1 834	938	896
5-9	2 392	1 220	1 171	2 309	1 179	1 130	2 173	1 110	1 063	2 001	1 022	978
10-14	2 534	1 292	1 242	2 378	1 213	1 165	2 296	1 172	1 124	2 161	1 104	1 058
15-19	2 685	1 368	1 317	2 520	1 284	1 236	2 365	1 206	1 159	2 284	1 165	1 119
20-24	2 885	1 467	1 418	2 662	1 355	1 307	2 499	1 272	1 226	2 345	1 195	1 150
25-29	2 915	1 478	1 437	2 855	1 450	1 405	2 635	1 340	1 295	2 472	1 258	1 214
30-34	2 867	1 449	1 418	2 883	1 460	1 423	2 824	1 433	1 392	2 606	1 324	1 283
35-39	2 664	1 342	1 321	2 837	1 431	1 406	2 855	1 443	1 411	2 798	1 417	1 381
40-44	2 434	1 222	1 212	2 630	1 322	1 308	2 803	1 411	1 392	2 822	1 424	1 398
45-49	2 270	1 134	1 135	2 395	1 198	1 196	2 590	1 297	1 292	2 763	1 386	1 377
50-54	1 966	978	988	2 219	1 103	1 117	2 344	1 166	1 178	2 538	1 264	1 273
55-59	1 682	828	854	1 902	938	964	2 151	1 060	1 091	2 275	1 123	1 153
60-64	1 412	687	725	1 602	778	823	1 815	884	932	2 057	1 001	1 056
65-69	1 097	523	575	1 310	625	685	1 490	711	779	1 695	810	885
70-74	812	377	435	977	453	524	1 172	544	627	1 340	622	718
75-79	547	245	303	682	303	378	825	367	459	997	444	553
80-84	330	142	194	417	176	241	524	220	304	641	268	373
85-89	182	71	110	219	85	133	274	106	168	349	135	215
90-94	73	26	47	92	32	60	113	39	73	143	49	94
95-99	19	6	13	26	8	18	33	10	23	40	12	28
100 +	3	1	2	4	1	3	5	2	4	7	2	5

Age group	2045 Both sexes	Males	Females	2050 Both sexes	Males	Females
All ages	36 196	17 930	18 267	35 909	17 739	18 170
0-4	1 658	848	810	1 507	771	736
5-9	1 816	928	888	1 643	840	803
10-14	1 989	1 016	973	1 805	923	883
15-19	2 150	1 097	1 052	1 978	1 010	968
20-24	2 264	1 155	1 110	2 131	1 088	1 044
25-29	2 320	1 181	1 138	2 240	1 142	1 099
30-34	2 446	1 243	1 202	2 295	1 168	1 127
35-39	2 582	1 309	1 272	2 423	1 230	1 193
40-44	2 767	1 398	1 369	2 554	1 293	1 262
45-49	2 783	1 399	1 384	2 731	1 375	1 355
50-54	2 710	1 352	1 358	2 732	1 367	1 365
55-59	2 467	1 219	1 248	2 638	1 306	1 332
60-64	2 181	1 063	1 118	2 369	1 157	1 212
65-69	1 927	921	1 006	2 048	981	1 067
70-74	1 531	712	819	1 748	813	935
75-79	1 148	511	637	1 320	589	731
80-84	781	327	453	906	380	526
85-89	432	166	266	532	205	327
90-94	185	63	121	231	79	152
95-99	52	16	36	68	20	48
100 +	8	2	6	10	3	7

United Nations Department of Economic and Social Affairs/Population Division
World Population Prospects: The 2004 Revision, Volume II: Sex and Age Distribution of the World Population

689

POPULATION BY AGE AND SEX (in thousands)

Age group	1950 Both sexes	Males	Females	1955 Both sexes	Males	Females	1960 Both sexes	Males	Females	1965 Both sexes	Males	Females
All ages	19 996	9 943	10 053	23 222	11 596	11 626	27 054	13 558	13 496	31 567	15 861	15 706
0-4	3 500	1 813	1 687	4 378	2 222	2 156	4 988	2 536	2 451	5 666	2 885	2 780
5-9	2 841	1 458	1 383	3 293	1 703	1 590	4 173	2 115	2 058	4 804	2 439	2 365
10-14	2 376	1 204	1 171	2 791	1 432	1 359	3 245	1 678	1 567	4 123	2 089	2 034
15-19	2 022	1 038	984	2 329	1 181	1 148	2 745	1 409	1 336	3 202	1 656	1 546
20-24	1 561	772	789	1 967	1 009	958	2 275	1 153	1 122	2 692	1 380	1 312
25-29	1 424	685	739	1 509	745	764	1 911	979	932	2 221	1 124	1 097
30-34	1 222	593	630	1 372	659	713	1 462	721	741	1 861	952	908
35-39	1 132	558	574	1 171	566	604	1 322	634	688	1 417	698	720
40-44	981	502	479	1 076	528	548	1 121	540	581	1 274	608	666
45-49	747	389	358	924	469	455	1 020	497	523	1 071	512	558
50-54	608	305	303	691	356	336	862	433	429	960	463	497
55-59	479	207	272	548	270	278	630	319	310	793	393	400
60-64	386	154	232	416	175	241	480	232	248	557	278	280
65-69	302	116	187	315	122	193	344	141	203	401	189	212
70-74	213	81	132	224	82	141	237	88	149	263	104	159
75-79	130	47	83	135	49	86	145	51	94	157	56	101
80 +	73	25	48	84	28	56	94	31	63	104	34	71

Age group	1970 Both sexes	Males	Females	1975 Both sexes	Males	Females	1980 Both sexes	Males	Females	1985 Both sexes	Males	Females
All ages	36 551	18 395	18 156	42 019	21 172	20 847	48 088	24 241	23 847	54 266	27 338	26 928
0-4	6 341	3 233	3 108	7 000	3 574	3 425	7 816	3 992	3 824	8 433	4 306	4 127
5-9	5 477	2 785	2 692	6 154	3 134	3 020	6 823	3 479	3 343	7 637	3 894	3 743
10-14	4 750	2 411	2 339	5 421	2 755	2 665	6 096	3 103	2 993	6 758	3 445	3 314
15-19	4 065	2 059	2 006	4 685	2 376	2 308	5 346	2 716	2 630	5 995	3 048	2 946
20-24	3 127	1 615	1 512	3 968	2 007	1 961	4 564	2 311	2 253	5 158	2 613	2 545
25-29	2 611	1 336	1 275	3 026	1 560	1 466	3 833	1 933	1 900	4 343	2 190	2 153
30-34	2 149	1 086	1 063	2 521	1 288	1 233	2 911	1 497	1 414	3 640	1 827	1 813
35-39	1 795	917	878	2 070	1 043	1 027	2 424	1 234	1 189	2 762	1 414	1 348
40-44	1 361	667	694	1 724	877	847	1 986	996	990	2 303	1 166	1 137
45-49	1 215	576	639	1 297	631	666	1 645	832	813	1 882	937	945
50-54	1 007	477	530	1 145	537	607	1 223	590	633	1 545	773	771
55-59	884	421	464	930	434	495	1 060	490	569	1 128	536	593
60-64	704	343	361	789	368	421	833	382	452	950	430	520
65-69	467	227	240	594	282	312	671	305	366	711	316	395
70-74	308	141	167	361	170	191	463	213	250	527	231	296
75-79	175	66	109	206	90	116	245	111	134	317	140	178
80 +	115	37	78	129	44	86	150	57	93	177	71	106

Age group	1990 Both sexes	Males	Females	1995 Both sexes	Males	Females	2000 Both sexes	Males	Females	2005 Both sexes	Males	Females
All ages	61 104	30 775	30 330	68 396	34 443	33 953	75 766	38 151	37 615	83 054	41 814	41 241
0-4	9 150	4 675	4 475	9 721	4 970	4 750	9 841	5 036	4 805	9 863	5 050	4 813
5-9	8 279	4 221	4 058	9 022	4 603	4 418	9 615	4 910	4 704	9 753	4 986	4 767
10-14	7 577	3 862	3 716	8 224	4 190	4 034	8 973	4 576	4 397	9 570	4 885	4 685
15-19	6 661	3 391	3 269	7 479	3 807	3 672	8 132	4 139	3 993	8 885	4 526	4 359
20-24	5 809	2 946	2 863	6 469	3 285	3 184	7 293	3 703	3 590	7 952	4 037	3 914
25-29	4 940	2 493	2 447	5 581	2 820	2 761	6 246	3 161	3 086	7 075	3 581	3 494
30-34	4 154	2 086	2 068	4 741	2 383	2 358	5 387	2 712	2 675	6 057	3 055	3 002
35-39	3 487	1 743	1 745	3 995	1 997	1 998	4 587	2 296	2 290	5 236	2 627	2 609
40-44	2 641	1 345	1 296	3 357	1 669	1 688	3 868	1 925	1 942	4 461	2 225	2 236
45-49	2 196	1 105	1 092	2 531	1 282	1 250	3 241	1 603	1 638	3 751	1 858	1 893
50-54	1 779	877	902	2 088	1 041	1 046	2 420	1 216	1 204	3 118	1 531	1 587
55-59	1 436	710	727	1 664	810	854	1 966	969	997	2 293	1 140	1 153
60-64	1 019	474	545	1 307	634	673	1 527	730	797	1 817	880	937
65-69	819	360	459	885	400	485	1 146	542	604	1 352	630	722
70-74	565	242	323	658	279	379	720	314	405	943	431	512
75-79	367	154	213	399	163	236	473	192	281	525	219	306
80 +	226	92	134	275	108	166	332	127	206	404	151	253

United Nations Department of Economic and Social Affairs/Population Division
World Population Prospects: The 2004 Revision, Volume II: Sex and Age Distribution of the World Population

690

POPULATION BY AGE AND SEX (in thousands)

Age group	2005 Both sexes	2005 Males	2005 Females	2010 Both sexes	2010 Males	2010 Females	2015 Both sexes	2015 Males	2015 Females	2020 Both sexes	2020 Males	2020 Females
All ages	83 054	41 814	41 241	90 048	45 313	44 735	96 840	48 696	48 143	103 266	51 880	51 387
0-4	9 863	5 050	4 813	9 712	4 974	4 738	9 700	4 969	4 731	9 565	4 905	4 660
5-9	9 753	4 986	4 767	9 787	5 007	4 780	9 646	4 936	4 710	9 640	4 935	4 705
10-14	9 570	4 885	4 685	9 713	4 963	4 750	9 751	4 986	4 765	9 613	4 917	4 696
15-19	8 885	4 526	4 359	9 486	4 837	4 649	9 634	4 918	4 716	9 675	4 943	4 732
20-24	7 952	4 037	3 914	8 709	4 426	4 282	9 315	4 740	4 575	9 466	4 823	4 643
25-29	7 075	3 581	3 494	7 739	3 917	3 822	8 500	4 308	4 192	9 109	4 624	4 485
30-34	6 057	3 055	3 002	6 889	3 476	3 413	7 557	3 814	3 743	8 320	4 207	4 114
35-39	5 236	2 627	2 609	5 909	2 971	2 939	6 744	3 393	3 351	7 414	3 732	3 681
40-44	4 461	2 225	2 236	5 113	2 556	2 557	5 788	2 901	2 888	6 623	3 323	3 300
45-49	3 751	1 858	1 893	4 344	2 157	2 187	4 996	2 487	2 509	5 671	2 832	2 839
50-54	3 118	1 531	1 587	3 626	1 784	1 841	4 215	2 080	2 135	4 863	2 408	2 455
55-59	2 293	1 140	1 153	2 973	1 444	1 529	3 472	1 691	1 781	4 053	1 980	2 072
60-64	1 817	880	937	2 132	1 042	1 090	2 783	1 329	1 454	3 268	1 565	1 702
65-69	1 352	630	722	1 623	767	856	1 919	915	1 004	2 526	1 176	1 350
70-74	943	431	512	1 126	507	619	1 364	623	741	1 632	751	881
75-79	525	219	306	698	305	392	845	364	481	1 043	453	590
80-84	280	107	173	316	125	191	428	177	251	536	215	321
85-89	99	36	63	122	44	79	141	52	89	201	75	126
90-94	22	7	15	27	9	18	35	11	24	44	14	30
95-99	3	1	2	3	1	2	4	1	3	6	2	5
100 +	0	0	0	0	0	0	0	0	0	0	0	0

Age group	2025 Both sexes	2025 Males	2025 Females	2030 Both sexes	2030 Males	2030 Females	2035 Both sexes	2035 Males	2035 Females	2040 Both sexes	2040 Males	2040 Females
All ages	109 084	54 743	54 341	114 080	57 182	56 898	118 189	59 164	59 025	121 750	60 865	60 885
0-4	9 248	4 747	4 501	8 772	4 506	4 266	8 292	4 262	4 030	8 202	4 219	3 984
5-9	9 510	4 875	4 635	9 197	4 720	4 478	8 724	4 480	4 243	8 246	4 239	4 008
10-14	9 609	4 918	4 691	9 481	4 859	4 622	9 169	4 705	4 465	8 698	4 466	4 231
15-19	9 539	4 876	4 663	9 537	4 878	4 659	9 411	4 820	4 591	9 102	4 667	4 434
20-24	9 511	4 851	4 660	9 379	4 787	4 593	9 380	4 791	4 589	9 256	4 735	4 521
25-29	9 265	4 710	4 555	9 313	4 741	4 572	9 185	4 679	4 506	9 189	4 686	4 503
30-34	8 931	4 524	4 408	9 090	4 613	4 478	9 142	4 646	4 497	9 018	4 587	4 431
35-39	8 178	4 126	4 052	8 792	4 445	4 347	8 954	4 537	4 418	9 010	4 572	4 438
40-44	7 294	3 664	3 630	8 060	4 059	4 001	8 676	4 380	4 296	8 843	4 474	4 369
45-49	6 504	3 254	3 250	7 176	3 595	3 581	7 942	3 991	3 951	8 560	4 313	4 247
50-54	5 535	2 750	2 785	6 363	3 169	3 194	7 035	3 511	3 524	7 799	3 906	3 894
55-59	4 691	2 301	2 390	5 355	2 638	2 717	6 172	3 050	3 122	6 839	3 389	3 451
60-64	3 831	1 842	1 989	4 452	2 151	2 301	5 099	2 477	2 623	5 897	2 875	3 022
65-69	2 984	1 394	1 590	3 518	1 652	1 867	4 109	1 940	2 169	4 728	2 245	2 482
70-74	2 171	974	1 197	2 587	1 164	1 423	3 074	1 390	1 684	3 614	1 644	1 970
75-79	1 266	552	714	1 710	724	986	2 063	875	1 188	2 477	1 054	1 423
80-84	679	271	407	843	335	508	1 165	446	719	1 431	546	885
85-89	263	92	171	346	119	228	445	149	296	636	201	434
90-94	66	20	46	92	25	67	128	33	95	172	42	130
95-99	8	2	7	14	3	11	21	4	18	32	5	27
100 +	1	0	1	1	0	1	2	0	2	3	0	3

Age group	2045 Both sexes	2045 Males	2045 Females	2050 Both sexes	2050 Males	2050 Females
All ages	124 754	62 295	62 459	127 068	63 379	63 689
0-4	8 107	4 170	3 937	7 915	4 071	3 844
5-9	8 158	4 196	3 962	8 063	4 147	3 916
10-14	8 221	4 225	3 996	8 133	4 183	3 950
15-19	8 631	4 430	4 201	8 156	4 190	3 966
20-24	8 949	4 584	4 365	8 481	4 348	4 132
25-29	9 067	4 631	4 436	8 761	4 481	4 281
30-34	9 023	4 594	4 429	8 902	4 540	4 362
35-39	8 888	4 514	4 373	8 894	4 522	4 372
40-44	8 901	4 511	4 390	8 781	4 454	4 327
45-49	8 731	4 410	4 321	8 792	4 448	4 344
50-54	8 416	4 227	4 189	8 592	4 326	4 266
55-59	7 597	3 779	3 818	8 212	4 099	4 113
60-64	6 553	3 207	3 346	7 299	3 590	3 710
65-69	5 493	2 623	2 870	6 130	2 943	3 187
70-74	4 191	1 922	2 268	4 904	2 267	2 636
75-79	2 950	1 268	1 682	3 460	1 505	1 955
80-84	1 756	677	1 079	2 133	836	1 297
85-89	810	259	552	1 028	336	692
90-94	262	61	201	350	84	267
95-99	46	7	39	75	11	64
100 +	5	0	4	7	1	7

POPULATION BY AGE AND SEX (in thousands)

Age group	2005 Both sexes	Males	Females	2010 Both sexes	Males	Females	2015 Both sexes	Males	Females	2020 Both sexes	Males	Females
All ages	83 054	41 814	41 241	90 907	45 752	45 154	99 212	49 911	49 301	107 682	54 141	53 541
0-4	9 863	5 050	4 813	10 571	5 414	5 157	11 217	5 746	5 471	11 613	5 955	5 658
5-9	9 753	4 986	4 767	9 787	5 007	4 780	10 502	5 374	5 128	11 153	5 710	5 443
10-14	9 570	4 885	4 685	9 713	4 963	4 750	9 751	4 986	4 765	10 468	5 354	5 114
15-19	8 885	4 526	4 359	9 486	4 837	4 649	9 634	4 918	4 716	9 675	4 943	4 732
20-24	7 952	4 037	3 914	8 709	4 426	4 282	9 315	4 740	4 575	9 466	4 823	4 643
25-29	7 075	3 581	3 494	7 739	3 917	3 822	8 500	4 308	4 192	9 109	4 624	4 485
30-34	6 057	3 055	3 002	6 889	3 476	3 413	7 557	3 814	3 743	8 320	4 207	4 114
35-39	5 236	2 627	2 609	5 909	2 971	2 939	6 744	3 393	3 351	7 414	3 732	3 681
40-44	4 461	2 225	2 236	5 113	2 556	2 557	5 788	2 901	2 888	6 623	3 323	3 300
45-49	3 751	1 858	1 893	4 344	2 157	2 187	4 996	2 487	2 509	5 671	2 832	2 839
50-54	3 118	1 531	1 587	3 626	1 784	1 841	4 215	2 080	2 135	4 863	2 408	2 455
55-59	2 293	1 140	1 153	2 973	1 444	1 529	3 472	1 691	1 781	4 053	1 980	2 072
60-64	1 817	880	937	2 132	1 042	1 090	2 783	1 329	1 454	3 268	1 565	1 702
65-69	1 352	630	722	1 623	767	856	1 919	915	1 004	2 526	1 176	1 350
70-74	943	431	512	1 126	507	619	1 364	623	741	1 632	751	881
75-79	525	219	306	698	305	392	845	364	481	1 043	453	590
80-84	280	107	173	316	125	191	428	177	251	536	215	321
85-89	99	36	63	122	44	79	141	52	89	201	75	126
90-94	22	7	15	27	9	18	35	11	24	44	14	30
95-99	3	1	2	3	1	2	4	1	3	6	2	5
100 +	0	0	0	0	0	0	0	0	0	0	0	0

Age group	2025 Both sexes	Males	Females	2030 Both sexes	Males	Females	2035 Both sexes	Males	Females	2040 Both sexes	Males	Females
All ages	115 677	58 122	57 556	123 067	61 789	61 278	129 975	65 208	64 767	136 915	68 644	68 270
0-4	11 433	5 868	5 565	11 176	5 741	5 435	11 103	5 707	5 396	11 596	5 964	5 632
5-9	11 554	5 922	5 631	11 378	5 838	5 539	11 124	5 713	5 411	11 054	5 682	5 373
10-14	11 120	5 691	5 429	11 523	5 905	5 618	11 348	5 822	5 526	11 097	5 698	5 398
15-19	10 393	5 312	5 081	11 046	5 650	5 396	11 450	5 865	5 586	11 278	5 784	5 495
20-24	9 511	4 851	4 660	10 231	5 222	5 009	10 886	5 561	5 325	11 292	5 777	5 515
25-29	9 265	4 710	4 555	9 313	4 741	4 572	10 034	5 113	4 922	10 691	5 453	5 238
30-34	8 931	4 524	4 408	9 090	4 613	4 478	9 142	4 646	4 497	9 865	5 019	4 846
35-39	8 178	4 126	4 052	8 792	4 445	4 347	8 954	4 537	4 418	9 010	4 572	4 438
40-44	7 294	3 664	3 630	8 060	4 059	4 001	8 676	4 380	4 296	8 843	4 474	4 369
45-49	6 504	3 254	3 250	7 176	3 595	3 581	7 942	3 991	3 951	8 560	4 313	4 247
50-54	5 535	2 750	2 785	6 363	3 169	3 194	7 035	3 511	3 524	7 799	3 906	3 894
55-59	4 691	2 301	2 390	5 355	2 638	2 717	6 172	3 050	3 122	6 839	3 389	3 451
60-64	3 831	1 842	1 989	4 452	2 151	2 301	5 099	2 477	2 623	5 897	2 875	3 022
65-69	2 984	1 394	1 590	3 518	1 652	1 867	4 109	1 940	2 169	4 728	2 245	2 482
70-74	2 171	974	1 197	2 587	1 164	1 423	3 074	1 390	1 684	3 614	1 644	1 970
75-79	1 266	552	714	1 710	724	986	2 063	875	1 188	2 477	1 054	1 423
80-84	679	271	407	843	335	508	1 165	446	719	1 431	546	885
85-89	263	92	171	346	119	228	445	149	296	636	201	434
90-94	66	20	46	92	25	67	128	33	95	172	42	130
95-99	8	2	7	14	3	11	21	4	18	32	5	27
100 +	1	0	1	1	0	1	2	0	2	3	0	3

Age group	2045 Both sexes	Males	Females	2050 Both sexes	Males	Females
All ages	143 866	72 102	71 764	150 537	75 425	75 112
0-4	12 076	6 211	5 865	12 298	6 326	5 973
5-9	11 548	5 939	5 609	12 028	6 186	5 842
10-14	11 028	5 667	5 360	11 522	5 925	5 597
15-19	11 028	5 661	5 367	10 960	5 630	5 329
20-24	11 123	5 698	5 425	10 874	5 576	5 298
25-29	11 099	5 671	5 428	10 931	5 592	5 339
30-34	10 522	5 360	5 163	10 930	5 577	5 353
35-39	9 732	4 945	4 787	10 389	5 285	5 104
40-44	8 901	4 511	4 390	9 623	4 883	4 739
45-49	8 731	4 410	4 321	8 792	4 448	4 344
50-54	8 416	4 227	4 189	8 592	4 326	4 266
55-59	7 597	3 779	3 818	8 212	4 099	4 113
60-64	6 553	3 207	3 346	7 299	3 590	3 710
65-69	5 493	2 623	2 870	6 130	2 943	3 187
70-74	4 191	1 922	2 268	4 904	2 267	2 636
75-79	2 950	1 268	1 682	3 460	1 505	1 955
80-84	1 756	677	1 079	2 133	836	1 297
85-89	810	259	552	1 028	336	692
90-94	262	61	201	350	84	267
95-99	46	7	39	75	11	64
100 +	5	0	4	7	1	7

United Nations Department of Economic and Social Affairs/Population Division
World Population Prospects: The 2004 Revision, Volume II: Sex and Age Distribution of the World Population

692

POPULATION BY AGE AND SEX (in thousands)

Age group	2005 Both sexes	Males	Females	2010 Both sexes	Males	Females	2015 Both sexes	Males	Females	2020 Both sexes	Males	Females
All ages	83 054	41 814	41 241	89 189	44 873	44 316	94 467	47 481	46 986	98 851	49 618	49 233
0-4	9 863	5 050	4 813	8 853	4 534	4 319	8 184	4 192	3 991	7 517	3 855	3 662
5-9	9 753	4 986	4 767	9 787	5 007	4 780	8 790	4 498	4 292	8 127	4 161	3 966
10-14	9 570	4 885	4 685	9 713	4 963	4 750	9 751	4 986	4 765	8 758	4 480	4 278
15-19	8 885	4 526	4 359	9 486	4 837	4 649	9 634	4 918	4 716	9 675	4 943	4 732
20-24	7 952	4 037	3 914	8 709	4 426	4 282	9 315	4 740	4 575	9 466	4 823	4 643
25-29	7 075	3 581	3 494	7 739	3 917	3 822	8 500	4 308	4 192	9 109	4 624	4 485
30-34	6 057	3 055	3 002	6 889	3 476	3 413	7 557	3 814	3 743	8 320	4 207	4 114
35-39	5 236	2 627	2 609	5 909	2 971	2 939	6 744	3 393	3 351	7 414	3 732	3 681
40-44	4 461	2 225	2 236	5 113	2 556	2 557	5 788	2 901	2 888	6 623	3 323	3 300
45-49	3 751	1 858	1 893	4 344	2 157	2 187	4 996	2 487	2 509	5 671	2 832	2 839
50-54	3 118	1 531	1 587	3 626	1 784	1 841	4 215	2 080	2 135	4 863	2 408	2 455
55-59	2 293	1 140	1 153	2 973	1 444	1 529	3 472	1 691	1 781	4 053	1 980	2 072
60-64	1 817	880	937	2 132	1 042	1 090	2 783	1 329	1 454	3 268	1 565	1 702
65-69	1 352	630	722	1 623	767	856	1 919	915	1 004	2 526	1 176	1 350
70-74	943	431	512	1 126	507	619	1 364	623	741	1 632	751	881
75-79	525	219	306	698	305	392	845	364	481	1 043	453	590
80-84	280	107	173	316	125	191	428	177	251	536	215	321
85-89	99	36	63	122	44	79	141	52	89	201	75	126
90-94	22	7	15	27	9	18	35	11	24	44	14	30
95-99	3	1	2	3	1	2	4	1	3	6	2	5
100 +	0	0	0	0	0	0	0	0	0	0	0	0

Age group	2025 Both sexes	Males	Females	2030 Both sexes	Males	Females	2035 Both sexes	Males	Females	2040 Both sexes	Males	Females
All ages	102 502	51 370	51 132	105 180	52 620	52 560	106 736	53 292	53 444	107 418	53 514	53 904
0-4	7 075	3 632	3 443	6 445	3 310	3 134	5 726	2 943	2 783	5 306	2 729	2 577
5-9	7 466	3 827	3 639	7 027	3 606	3 421	6 400	3 287	3 113	5 684	2 922	2 762
10-14	8 098	4 145	3 953	7 438	3 812	3 626	7 001	3 592	3 409	6 375	3 274	3 101
15-19	8 686	4 440	4 246	8 028	4 106	3 922	7 371	3 775	3 596	6 936	3 557	3 379
20-24	9 511	4 851	4 660	8 528	4 352	4 176	7 874	4 021	3 853	7 220	3 693	3 527
25-29	9 265	4 710	4 555	9 313	4 741	4 572	8 336	4 245	4 090	7 686	3 918	3 768
30-34	8 931	4 524	4 408	9 090	4 613	4 478	9 142	4 646	4 497	8 170	4 154	4 016
35-39	8 178	4 126	4 052	8 792	4 445	4 047	8 951	4 537	4 418	9 010	4 572	4 438
40-44	7 294	3 664	3 630	8 060	4 059	4 001	8 676	4 380	4 296	8 843	4 474	4 369
45-49	6 504	3 254	3 250	7 176	3 595	3 581	7 942	3 991	3 951	8 560	4 313	4 247
50-54	5 525	2 750	2 785	6 363	3 169	3 194	7 035	3 511	3 524	7 799	3 906	3 894
55-59	4 691	2 301	2 390	5 355	2 638	2 717	6 172	3 050	3 122	6 839	3 389	3 451
60-64	3 831	1 842	1 989	4 452	2 151	2 301	5 099	2 477	2 623	5 897	2 875	3 022
65-69	2 984	1 394	1 590	3 518	1 652	1 867	4 109	1 940	2 169	4 728	2 245	2 482
70-74	2 171	974	1 197	2 587	1 164	1 423	3 074	1 390	1 684	3 614	1 644	1 970
75-79	1 266	552	714	1 710	724	986	2 063	875	1 188	2 477	1 054	1 423
80-84	679	271	407	843	335	508	1 165	446	719	1 431	546	885
85-89	263	92	171	346	119	228	445	149	296	636	201	434
90-94	66	20	46	92	25	67	128	33	95	172	42	130
95-99	8	2	7	14	3	11	21	4	18	32	5	27
100 +	1	0	1	1	0	1	2	0	2	3	0	3

Age group	2045 Both sexes	Males	Females	2050 Both sexes	Males	Females
All ages	107 228	53 303	53 925	106 150	52 645	53 505
0-4	4 894	2 517	2 377	4 496	2 313	2 183
5-9	5 265	2 708	2 557	4 853	2 497	2 357
10-14	5 660	2 909	2 751	5 242	2 696	2 546
15-19	6 311	3 240	3 071	5 597	2 875	2 721
20-24	6 787	3 476	3 311	6 164	3 160	3 004
25-29	7 034	3 591	3 444	6 603	3 375	3 228
30-34	7 523	3 828	3 696	6 874	3 502	3 372
35-39	8 043	4 083	3 960	7 399	3 758	3 641
40-44	8 901	4 511	4 390	7 940	4 025	3 915
45-49	8 731	4 410	4 321	8 792	4 448	4 344
50-54	8 416	4 227	4 189	8 592	4 326	4 266
55-59	7 597	3 779	3 818	8 212	4 099	4 113
60-64	6 553	3 207	3 346	7 299	3 590	3 710
65-69	5 493	2 623	2 870	6 130	2 943	3 187
70-74	4 191	1 922	2 268	4 904	2 267	2 636
75-79	2 950	1 268	1 682	3 460	1 505	1 955
80-84	1 756	677	1 079	2 133	836	1 297
85-89	810	259	552	1 028	336	692
90-94	262	61	201	350	84	267
95-99	46	7	39	75	11	64
100 +	5	0	4	7	1	7

POPULATION BY AGE AND SEX (in thousands)

Age group	1950 Both sexes	1950 Males	1950 Females	1955 Both sexes	1955 Males	1955 Females	1960 Both sexes	1960 Males	1960 Females	1965 Both sexes	1965 Males	1965 Females
All ages	24 824	11 830	12 994	27 281	13 123	14 158	29 638	14 338	15 300	31 445	15 262	16 183
0-4	2 950	1 500	1 450	3 525	1 807	1 718	3 511	1 795	1 716	2 830	1 454	1 377
5-9	2 022	1 022	1 000	2 923	1 486	1 437	3 499	1 785	1 714	3 448	1 762	1 686
10-14	2 323	1 171	1 152	2 000	1 014	986	2 908	1 479	1 429	3 482	1 775	1 707
15-19	2 412	1 204	1 208	2 297	1 158	1 139	1 954	988	966	2 887	1 469	1 419
20-24	2 369	1 159	1 210	2 393	1 200	1 193	2 226	1 127	1 099	1 935	978	956
25-29	2 108	1 000	1 108	2 322	1 128	1 194	2 337	1 171	1 166	2 212	1 109	1 103
30-34	1 355	623	732	2 079	989	1 090	2 313	1 124	1 189	2 324	1 156	1 168
35-39	1 766	810	956	1 334	614	720	2 023	942	1 081	2 303	1 113	1 190
40-44	1 793	850	943	1 724	788	936	1 313	609	705	2 002	924	1 077
45-49	1 554	725	829	1 740	819	921	1 686	779	907	1 307	602	705
50-54	1 227	549	678	1 484	686	798	1 680	791	889	1 631	748	884
55-59	900	392	508	1 149	503	646	1 412	645	767	1 626	757	870
60-64	747	312	435	807	344	463	1 065	455	610	1 314	590	724
65-69	531	218	313	645	260	385	714	289	425	940	389	551
70-74	354	140	214	426	166	260	491	180	311	584	226	358
75-79	230	90	140	245	97	148	289	105	183	366	130	237
80 +	183	65	118	188	64	124	217	75	141	251	80	171

Age group	1970 Both sexes	1970 Males	1970 Females	1975 Both sexes	1975 Males	1975 Females	1980 Both sexes	1980 Males	1980 Females	1985 Both sexes	1985 Males	1985 Females
All ages	32 664	15 863	16 801	34 015	16 549	17 467	35 574	17 332	18 242	37 202	18 143	19 059
0-4	2 549	1 305	1 244	2 866	1 473	1 393	3 242	1 659	1 583	3 423	1 755	1 668
5-9	2 804	1 434	1 370	2 534	1 294	1 239	2 865	1 465	1 399	3 224	1 649	1 575
10-14	3 455	1 763	1 692	2 774	1 419	1 356	2 522	1 290	1 232	2 852	1 458	1 394
15-19	3 466	1 765	1 701	3 422	1 746	1 676	2 773	1 425	1 348	2 509	1 282	1 227
20-24	2 845	1 438	1 407	3 423	1 740	1 683	3 340	1 709	1 630	2 750	1 410	1 340
25-29	1 918	963	955	2 799	1 415	1 384	3 350	1 699	1 651	3 305	1 688	1 617
30-34	2 182	1 089	1 093	1 889	946	943	2 768	1 396	1 373	3 310	1 674	1 636
35-39	2 290	1 145	1 145	2 143	1 066	1 077	1 855	924	931	2 731	1 371	1 360
40-44	2 243	1 084	1 159	2 241	1 113	1 129	2 102	1 038	1 064	1 820	900	920
45-49	1 948	899	1 050	2 184	1 047	1 137	2 173	1 068	1 105	2 047	1 000	1 047
50-54	1 242	567	675	1 879	857	1 022	2 105	995	1 109	2 091	1 012	1 079
55-59	1 545	694	851	1 180	530	650	1 783	797	986	1 991	919	1 072
60-64	1 485	668	817	1 438	630	808	1 097	478	618	1 647	711	936
65-69	1 142	485	657	1 314	567	747	1 212	507	705	976	406	570
70-74	769	296	473	958	383	575	1 114	453	661	1 074	419	655
75-79	479	169	311	571	202	369	732	268	464	810	297	513
80 +	302	100	202	401	121	280	541	161	380	642	192	450

Age group	1990 Both sexes	1990 Males	1990 Females	1995 Both sexes	1995 Males	1995 Females	2000 Both sexes	2000 Males	2000 Females	2005 Both sexes	2005 Males	2005 Females
All ages	38 111	18 574	19 537	38 595	18 782	19 813	38 649	18 779	19 870	38 530	18 685	19 844
0-4	2 953	1 513	1 440	2 485	1 273	1 211	2 020	1 038	983	1 811	931	881
5-9	3 389	1 731	1 658	2 937	1 505	1 433	2 477	1 269	1 208	2 013	1 034	979
10-14	3 231	1 652	1 579	3 378	1 725	1 653	2 929	1 500	1 429	2 469	1 265	1 204
15-19	2 848	1 456	1 392	3 216	1 642	1 574	3 366	1 717	1 648	2 918	1 494	1 424
20-24	2 467	1 263	1 204	2 826	1 441	1 385	3 198	1 630	1 568	3 349	1 706	1 643
25-29	2 678	1 360	1 318	2 447	1 250	1 197	2 808	1 428	1 380	3 180	1 617	1 562
30-34	3 267	1 652	1 615	2 652	1 343	1 310	2 428	1 236	1 192	2 789	1 415	1 375
35-39	3 244	1 628	1 616	3 227	1 624	1 603	2 624	1 322	1 302	2 406	1 221	1 185
40-44	2 671	1 330	1 341	3 186	1 587	1 599	3 175	1 586	1 589	2 590	1 298	1 292
45-49	1 766	864	902	2 602	1 280	1 321	3 108	1 531	1 577	3 111	1 541	1 570
50-54	1 961	942	1 018	1 698	815	883	2 507	1 214	1 294	3 013	1 464	1 549
55-59	1 972	930	1 042	1 852	865	987	1 609	753	856	2 394	1 134	1 260
60-64	1 831	815	1 015	1 813	820	992	1 714	770	944	1 502	680	823
65-69	1 462	601	860	1 620	681	939	1 618	693	924	1 548	661	886
70-74	812	318	494	1 221	466	755	1 367	535	833	1 384	554	830
75-79	793	283	510	615	219	396	940	328	613	1 075	384	691
80 +	765	234	531	822	247	574	760	229	531	977	287	690

United Nations Department of Economic and Social Affairs/Population Division
World Population Prospects: The 2004 Revision, Volume II: Sex and Age Distribution of the World Population

694

POPULATION BY AGE AND SEX (in thousands)

Age group	2005 Both sexes	Males	Females	2010 Both sexes	Males	Females	2015 Both sexes	Males	Females	2020 Both sexes	Males	Females
All ages	38 530	18 685	19 844	38 359	18 580	19 779	38 110	18 443	19 667	37 712	18 236	19 476
0-4	1 811	931	881	1 837	944	893	1 827	939	888	1 745	897	848
5-9	2 013	1 034	979	1 805	927	878	1 831	941	890	1 822	936	886
10-14	2 469	1 265	1 204	2 008	1 031	977	1 800	925	876	1 826	938	888
15-19	2 918	1 494	1 424	2 461	1 260	1 201	2 001	1 027	974	1 795	921	873
20-24	3 349	1 706	1 643	2 905	1 485	1 420	2 450	1 253	1 197	1 993	1 022	971
25-29	3 180	1 617	1 562	3 332	1 695	1 637	2 891	1 476	1 415	2 439	1 246	1 193
30-34	2 789	1 415	1 375	3 161	1 605	1 556	3 314	1 683	1 631	2 876	1 467	1 409
35-39	2 406	1 221	1 185	2 768	1 400	1 368	3 139	1 591	1 549	3 293	1 670	1 623
40-44	2 590	1 298	1 292	2 378	1 202	1 176	2 739	1 381	1 358	3 111	1 572	1 538
45-49	3 111	1 541	1 570	2 542	1 266	1 277	2 339	1 176	1 164	2 700	1 355	1 345
50-54	3 013	1 464	1 549	3 025	1 481	1 544	2 478	1 221	1 257	2 286	1 139	1 147
55-59	2 394	1 134	1 260	2 887	1 376	1 511	2 908	1 400	1 508	2 390	1 160	1 230
60-64	1 502	680	823	2 245	1 031	1 214	2 720	1 260	1 459	2 751	1 291	1 460
65-69	1 548	661	886	1 363	589	775	2 049	902	1 148	2 496	1 112	1 384
70-74	1 384	554	830	1 335	534	801	1 184	480	704	1 793	743	1 050
75-79	1 075	384	691	1 099	402	696	1 072	393	679	960	357	603
80-84	640	197	443	743	234	508	771	249	522	764	246	518
85-89	218	60	157	355	93	262	423	111	311	449	120	329
90-94	99	24	74	86	20	66	147	31	117	182	37	145
95-99	19	4	15	24	5	19	22	4	18	40	6	34
100	1	0	1	2	0	2	3	0	3	3	0	3

Age group	2025 Both sexes	Males	Females	2030 Both sexes	Males	Females	2035 Both sexes	Males	Females	2040 Both sexes	Males	Females
All ages	37 095	17 916	19 180	36 254	17 477	18 777	35 257	16 971	18 286	34 173	16 439	17 735
0-4	1 596	820	775	1 465	753	711	1 405	723	683	1 410	725	685
5-9	1 740	894	845	1 591	818	773	1 460	751	709	1 401	720	681
10-14	1 817	934	883	1 735	892	843	1 587	816	771	1 456	749	707
15-19	1 821	935	886	1 812	931	881	1 730	889	841	1 582	813	769
20-24	1 788	917	870	1 814	931	883	1 805	927	878	1 724	886	838
25-29	1 984	1 017	967	1 780	913	867	1 807	927	880	1 798	923	875
30-34	2 428	1 240	1 188	1 975	1 012	964	1 773	908	864	1 799	923	877
35-39	2 860	1 457	1 403	2 415	1 232	1 183	1 905	1 006	959	1 763	903	860
40-44	3 267	1 654	1 613	2 838	1 444	1 394	2 398	1 222	1 176	1 951	997	954
45-49	3 070	1 546	1 524	3 229	1 629	1 599	2 807	1 424	1 383	2 372	1 205	1 167
50-54	2 644	1 317	1 326	3 012	1 507	1 505	3 171	1 591	1 580	2 759	1 392	1 367
55-59	2 210	1 086	1 124	2 563	1 262	1 301	2 926	1 448	1 478	3 086	1 533	1 554
60-64	2 268	1 076	1 193	2 104	1 012	1 091	2 448	1 182	1 266	2 802	1 362	1 440
65-69	2 536	1 147	1 389	2 099	962	1 137	1 955	912	1 043	2 285	1 072	1 213
70-74	2 196	924	1 272	2 243	961	1 282	1 869	815	1 054	1 751	781	970
75-79	1 465	559	907	1 809	701	1 107	1 866	741	1 124	1 568	638	930
80-84	693	226	467	1 070	357	713	1 342	460	882	1 404	498	906
85-89	455	119	336	420	111	310	665	182	483	852	243	610
90-94	200	40	160	209	40	170	200	39	162	328	67	260
95-99	52	7	45	61	8	53	67	8	59	67	9	59
100 +	6	1	6	9	1	8	11	1	10	13	1	12

Age group	2045 Both sexes	Males	Females	2050 Both sexes	Males	Females
All ages	33 053	15 906	17 147	31 916	15 373	16 543
0-4	1 426	733	693	1 414	727	687
5-9	1 405	723	683	1 422	731	691
10-14	1 397	718	679	1 402	721	681
15-19	1 452	747	705	1 393	716	677
20-24	1 576	810	766	1 447	744	703
25-29	1 717	882	836	1 570	806	764
30-34	1 791	919	872	1 710	877	833
35-39	1 791	917	873	1 782	913	869
40-44	1 751	896	856	1 779	910	869
45-49	1 931	985	947	1 734	885	849
50-54	2 334	1 180	1 154	1 902	965	937
55-59	2 689	1 345	1 345	2 278	1 142	1 136
60-64	2 963	1 448	1 515	2 587	1 274	1 313
65-69	2 625	1 243	1 382	2 786	1 329	1 457
70-74	2 058	926	1 132	2 377	1 083	1 294
75-79	1 480	618	861	1 753	742	1 011
80-84	1 194	437	757	1 140	431	708
85-89	908	270	638	786	244	543
90-94	432	93	339	472	108	365
95-99	115	16	99	157	23	135
100 +	14	1	13	24	2	22

United Nations Department of Economic and Social Affairs/Population Division
World Population Prospects: The 2004 Revision, Volume II: Sex and Age Distribution of the World Population

695

POPULATION BY AGE AND SEX (in thousands)

Age group	2005 Both sexes	2005 Males	2005 Females	2010 Both sexes	2010 Males	2010 Females	2015 Both sexes	2015 Males	2015 Females	2020 Both sexes	2020 Males	2020 Females
All ages	38 530	18 685	19 844	38 734	18 773	19 961	39 054	18 928	20 125	39 280	19 042	20 238
0-4	1 811	931	881	2 212	1 136	1 075	2 397	1 232	1 165	2 370	1 218	1 152
5-9	2 013	1 034	979	1 805	927	878	2 206	1 133	1 072	2 391	1 229	1 162
10-14	2 469	1 265	1 204	2 008	1 031	977	1 800	925	876	2 200	1 130	1 070
15-19	2 918	1 494	1 424	2 461	1 260	1 201	2 001	1 027	974	1 795	921	873
20-24	3 349	1 706	1 643	2 905	1 485	1 420	2 450	1 253	1 197	1 993	1 022	971
25-29	3 180	1 617	1 562	3 332	1 695	1 637	2 891	1 476	1 415	2 439	1 246	1 193
30-34	2 789	1 415	1 375	3 161	1 605	1 556	3 314	1 683	1 631	2 876	1 467	1 409
35-39	2 406	1 221	1 185	2 768	1 400	1 368	3 139	1 591	1 549	3 293	1 670	1 623
40-44	2 590	1 298	1 292	2 378	1 202	1 176	2 739	1 381	1 358	3 111	1 572	1 538
45-49	3 111	1 541	1 570	2 542	1 266	1 277	2 339	1 176	1 164	2 700	1 355	1 345
50-54	3 013	1 464	1 549	3 025	1 481	1 544	2 478	1 221	1 257	2 286	1 139	1 147
55-59	2 394	1 134	1 260	2 887	1 376	1 511	2 908	1 400	1 508	2 390	1 160	1 230
60-64	1 502	680	823	2 245	1 031	1 214	2 720	1 260	1 459	2 751	1 291	1 460
65-69	1 548	661	886	1 363	589	775	2 049	902	1 148	2 496	1 112	1 384
70-74	1 384	554	830	1 335	534	801	1 184	480	704	1 793	743	1 050
75-79	1 075	384	691	1 099	402	696	1 072	393	679	960	357	603
80-84	640	197	443	743	234	508	771	249	522	764	246	518
85-89	218	60	157	355	93	262	423	111	311	449	120	329
90-94	99	24	74	86	20	66	147	31	117	182	37	145
95-99	19	4	15	24	5	19	22	4	18	40	6	34
100 +	1	0	1	2	0	2	3	0	3	3	0	3

Age group	2025 Both sexes	2025 Males	2025 Females	2030 Both sexes	2030 Males	2030 Females	2035 Both sexes	2035 Males	2035 Females	2040 Both sexes	2040 Males	2040 Females
All ages	39 196	18 995	20 201	38 878	18 825	20 052	38 523	18 650	19 873	38 267	18 542	19 725
0-4	2 130	1 095	1 035	1 989	1 023	966	2 050	1 054	996	2 241	1 152	1 089
5-9	2 364	1 215	1 149	2 125	1 093	1 032	1 985	1 021	964	2 045	1 052	994
10-14	2 386	1 226	1 160	2 359	1 213	1 147	2 121	1 090	1 030	1 981	1 018	962
15-19	2 195	1 127	1 067	2 380	1 223	1 157	2 354	1 210	1 144	2 115	1 087	1 028
20-24	1 788	917	870	2 187	1 123	1 065	2 373	1 218	1 154	2 347	1 205	1 141
25-29	1 984	1 017	967	1 780	913	867	2 180	1 118	1 061	2 365	1 214	1 151
30-34	2 428	1 240	1 188	1 975	1 012	964	1 773	908	864	2 171	1 113	1 058
35-39	2 860	1 457	1 403	2 415	1 232	1 183	1 965	1 006	959	1 763	903	860
40-44	3 267	1 654	1 613	2 838	1 444	1 394	2 398	1 222	1 176	1 951	997	954
45-49	3 070	1 546	1 524	3 229	1 629	1 599	2 807	1 424	1 383	2 372	1 205	1 167
50-54	2 644	1 317	1 326	3 012	1 507	1 505	3 171	1 591	1 580	2 759	1 392	1 367
55-59	2 210	1 086	1 124	2 563	1 262	1 301	2 926	1 448	1 478	3 086	1 533	1 554
60-64	2 268	1 076	1 193	2 104	1 012	1 091	2 448	1 182	1 266	2 802	1 362	1 440
65-69	2 536	1 147	1 389	2 099	962	1 137	1 955	912	1 043	2 285	1 072	1 213
70-74	2 196	924	1 272	2 243	961	1 282	1 869	815	1 054	1 751	781	970
75-79	1 465	559	907	1 809	701	1 107	1 866	741	1 124	1 568	638	930
80-84	693	226	467	1 070	357	713	1 342	460	882	1 404	498	906
85-89	455	119	336	420	111	310	665	182	483	852	243	610
90-94	200	40	160	209	40	170	200	39	162	328	67	260
95-99	52	7	45	61	8	53	67	8	59	67	9	59
100 +	6	1	6	9	1	8	11	1	10	13	1	12

Age group	2045 Both sexes	2045 Males	2045 Females	2050 Both sexes	2050 Males	2050 Females
All ages	38 107	18 502	19 605	37 956	18 475	19 481
0-4	2 390	1 229	1 161	2 406	1 237	1 169
5-9	2 237	1 150	1 087	2 386	1 227	1 159
10-14	2 041	1 049	992	2 232	1 148	1 085
15-19	1 976	1 016	960	2 036	1 047	990
20-24	2 109	1 084	1 026	1 970	1 013	958
25-29	2 339	1 201	1 138	2 102	1 080	1 023
30-34	2 356	1 208	1 148	2 331	1 196	1 135
35-39	2 161	1 107	1 054	2 346	1 202	1 143
40-44	1 751	896	856	2 148	1 099	1 049
45-49	1 931	985	947	1 734	885	849
50-54	2 334	1 180	1 154	1 902	965	937
55-59	2 689	1 345	1 345	2 278	1 142	1 136
60-64	2 963	1 448	1 515	2 587	1 274	1 313
65-69	2 625	1 243	1 382	2 786	1 329	1 457
70-74	2 058	926	1 132	2 377	1 083	1 294
75-79	1 480	618	861	1 753	742	1 011
80-84	1 194	437	757	1 140	431	708
85-89	908	270	638	786	244	543
90-94	432	93	339	472	108	365
95-99	115	16	99	157	23	135
100 +	14	1	13	24	2	22

United Nations Department of Economic and Social Affairs/Population Division
World Population Prospects: The 2004 Revision, Volume II: Sex and Age Distribution of the World Population

696

POPULATION BY AGE AND SEX (in thousands)

Age group	2005 Both sexes	2005 Males	2005 Females	2010 Both sexes	2010 Males	2010 Females	2015 Both sexes	2015 Males	2015 Females	2020 Both sexes	2020 Males	2020 Females
All ages	38 530	18 685	19 844	37 985	18 388	19 597	37 163	17 956	19 206	36 125	17 421	18 705
0-4	1 811	931	881	1 463	752	711	1 254	644	609	1 105	568	537
5-9	2 013	1 034	979	1 805	927	878	1 458	749	709	1 249	642	607
10-14	2 469	1 265	1 204	2 008	1 031	977	1 800	925	876	1 453	746	706
15-19	2 918	1 494	1 424	2 461	1 260	1 201	2 001	1 027	974	1 795	921	873
20-24	3 349	1 706	1 643	2 905	1 485	1 420	2 450	1 253	1 197	1 993	1 022	971
25-29	3 180	1 617	1 562	3 332	1 695	1 637	2 891	1 476	1 415	2 439	1 246	1 193
30-34	2 789	1 415	1 375	3 161	1 605	1 556	3 314	1 683	1 631	2 876	1 467	1 409
35-39	2 406	1 221	1 185	2 768	1 400	1 368	3 139	1 591	1 549	3 293	1 670	1 623
40-44	2 590	1 298	1 292	2 378	1 202	1 176	2 739	1 381	1 358	3 111	1 572	1 538
45-49	3 111	1 541	1 570	2 542	1 266	1 277	2 339	1 176	1 164	2 700	1 355	1 345
50-54	3 013	1 464	1 549	3 025	1 481	1 544	2 478	1 221	1 257	2 286	1 139	1 147
55-59	2 394	1 134	1 260	2 887	1 376	1 511	2 908	1 400	1 508	2 390	1 160	1 230
60-64	1 502	680	823	2 245	1 031	1 214	2 720	1 260	1 459	2 751	1 291	1 460
65-69	1 548	661	886	1 363	589	775	2 049	902	1 148	2 496	1 112	1 384
70-74	1 384	554	830	1 335	534	801	1 184	480	704	1 793	743	1 050
75-79	1 075	384	691	1 099	402	696	1 072	393	679	960	357	603
80-84	640	197	443	743	234	508	771	249	522	764	246	518
85-89	218	60	157	355	93	262	423	111	311	449	120	329
90-94	99	24	74	86	20	66	147	31	117	182	37	145
95-99	19	4	15	24	5	19	22	4	18	40	6	34
100 +	1	0	1	2	0	2	3	0	3	3	0	3

Age group	2025 Both sexes	2025 Males	2025 Females	2030 Both sexes	2030 Males	2030 Females	2035 Both sexes	2035 Males	2035 Females	2040 Both sexes	2040 Males	2040 Females
All ages	34 960	16 818	18 142	33 620	16 123	17 497	32 104	15 351	16 753	30 419	14 510	15 909
0-4	1 046	538	508	965	496	469	883	454	429	806	414	391
5-9	1 100	565	535	1 041	535	506	961	494	467	879	452	427
10-14	1 244	639	605	1 096	563	533	1 037	533	504	958	492	465
15-19	1 448	744	704	1 239	637	603	1 091	561	530	1 033	531	502
20-24	1 788	917	870	1 442	740	702	1 234	633	600	1 086	558	528
25-29	1 984	1 017	967	1 780	913	867	1 435	736	699	1 228	630	598
30-34	2 428	1 240	1 188	1 975	1 012	964	1 773	908	864	1 428	732	696
35-39	2 860	1 457	1 403	2 415	1 232	1 183	1 965	1 006	959	1 763	903	860
40-44	3 267	1 654	1 613	2 838	1 444	1 394	2 398	1 222	1 176	1 951	997	954
45-49	3 070	1 546	1 524	3 229	1 629	1 599	2 807	1 424	1 383	2 372	1 205	1 167
50-54	2 644	1 317	1 326	3 012	1 507	1 505	3 171	1 591	1 580	2 750	1 392	1 367
55-59	2 210	1 086	1 124	2 563	1 262	1 301	2 926	1 448	1 478	3 086	1 533	1 554
60-64	2 268	1 076	1 193	2 104	1 012	1 091	2 448	1 182	1 266	2 802	1 362	1 440
65-69	2 536	1 147	1 389	2 099	962	1 137	1 955	912	1 043	2 285	1 072	1 213
70-74	2 196	924	1 272	2 243	961	1 282	1 869	815	1 054	1 751	781	970
75-79	1 465	559	907	1 809	701	1 107	1 866	741	1 124	1 568	638	930
80-84	693	226	467	1 070	357	713	1 342	460	882	1 404	498	906
85-89	455	119	336	420	111	310	665	182	483	852	243	610
90-94	200	40	160	209	40	170	200	39	162	328	67	260
95-99	52	7	45	61	8	53	67	8	59	67	9	59
100 +	6	1	6	9	1	8	11	1	10	13	1	12

Age group	2045 Both sexes	2045 Males	2045 Females	2050 Both sexes	2050 Males	2050 Females
All ages	28 610	13 623	14 987	26 749	12 719	14 030
0-4	733	377	356	684	352	332
5-9	802	412	390	729	375	354
10-14	875	450	425	798	410	388
15-19	953	490	463	871	448	423
20-24	1 028	528	500	949	488	461
25-29	1 080	554	526	1 023	525	498
30-34	1 221	626	595	1 074	551	523
35-39	1 420	728	693	1 214	622	592
40-44	1 751	896	856	1 410	722	688
45-49	1 931	985	947	1 734	885	849
50-54	2 334	1 180	1 154	1 902	965	937
55-59	2 689	1 345	1 345	2 278	1 142	1 136
60-64	2 963	1 448	1 515	2 587	1 274	1 313
65-69	2 625	1 243	1 382	2 786	1 329	1 457
70-74	2 058	926	1 132	2 377	1 083	1 294
75-79	1 480	618	861	1 753	742	1 011
80-84	1 194	437	757	1 140	431	708
85-89	908	270	638	786	244	543
90-94	432	93	339	472	108	365
95-99	115	16	99	157	23	135
100 +	14	1	13	24	2	22

POPULATION BY AGE AND SEX (in thousands)

Age group	1950			1955			1960			1965		
	Both sexes	Males	Females	Both sexes	Males	Females	Both sexes	Males	Females	Both sexes	Males	Females
All ages	8 405	4 043	4 362	8 610	4 142	4 468	8 858	4 239	4 619	8 999	4 293	4 706
0-4	885	452	433	885	453	432	898	461	438	952	489	463
5-9	796	405	391	816	414	402	848	433	415	845	432	412
10-14	796	404	392	767	388	379	836	422	414	817	415	402
15-19	808	403	405	770	388	382	744	364	379	792	393	399
20-24	758	378	380	772	382	390	703	335	367	680	325	355
25-29	678	333	345	720	356	364	670	323	347	643	300	343
30-34	539	262	277	635	309	326	635	304	331	622	295	328
35-39	565	272	293	512	247	265	589	284	305	590	278	313
40-44	522	247	275	539	257	282	498	239	259	556	263	293
45-49	458	210	248	491	229	262	509	243	266	461	218	243
50-54	389	175	214	426	192	234	480	224	256	488	229	259
55-59	331	146	185	354	156	198	407	184	224	436	200	236
60-64	293	125	168	296	127	169	333	145	189	374	164	210
65-69	228	94	134	250	103	147	264	111	153	272	115	157
70-74	169	69	100	174	71	103	206	83	122	218	88	130
75-79	107	41	66	109	41	68	130	50	80	153	58	95
80 +	83	27	56	94	29	65	107	35	72	101	32	68

Age group	1970			1975			1980			1985		
	Both sexes	Males	Females	Both sexes	Males	Females	Both sexes	Males	Females	Both sexes	Males	Females
All ages	8 680	4 118	4 563	9 093	4 299	4 795	9 766	4 723	5 043	10 011	4 831	5 180
0-4	856	440	416	820	420	400	838	433	405	702	362	340
5-9	860	441	419	846	434	412	832	431	401	799	408	390
10-14	780	398	382	873	446	427	864	449	415	855	436	419
15-19	749	376	373	797	403	394	905	469	436	848	431	416
20-24	693	337	355	735	363	373	820	421	399	843	424	418
25-29	564	261	303	637	298	339	753	378	376	746	373	373
30-34	542	244	298	530	237	293	654	310	344	667	329	338
35-39	550	254	296	537	240	296	535	241	293	618	299	319
40-44	532	244	289	555	252	303	540	244	296	552	262	290
45-49	506	235	271	541	246	296	560	256	303	569	269	300
50-54	421	196	225	499	229	270	545	249	296	571	268	303
55-59	442	205	238	419	193	226	498	230	269	545	253	293
60-64	387	173	213	406	185	222	401	184	217	498	229	270
65-69	310	132	178	356	154	202	375	170	205	388	173	215
70-74	223	88	135	265	105	159	308	132	176	354	150	204
75-79	160	61	99	148	53	95	203	81	122	252	98	154
80 +	106	33	73	130	42	88	135	45	90	205	67	139

Age group	1990			1995			2000			2005		
	Both sexes	Males	Females	Both sexes	Males	Females	Both sexes	Males	Females	Both sexes	Males	Females
All ages	9 983	4 813	5 170	10 030	4 834	5 197	10 225	4 934	5 292	10 495	5 072	5 422
0-4	562	288	274	545	280	266	557	286	270	561	289	273
5-9	671	344	327	557	285	272	539	277	262	556	286	270
10-14	804	410	394	674	345	330	562	287	274	550	282	268
15-19	849	430	419	791	402	389	689	352	337	585	299	287
20-24	775	391	384	815	411	404	800	405	395	704	358	347
25-29	743	368	375	749	375	374	813	408	405	801	403	397
30-34	702	345	357	736	362	374	745	371	374	811	405	406
35-39	666	325	341	700	342	358	744	365	380	762	378	384
40-44	636	307	328	668	325	343	715	349	366	773	379	393
45-49	566	270	296	633	305	328	676	328	347	733	359	374
50-54	569	270	299	561	266	295	633	304	329	683	332	351
55-59	567	265	301	559	263	296	556	261	294	633	302	331
60-64	535	246	290	550	254	296	545	252	293	549	256	294
65-69	470	212	258	499	224	275	525	237	288	530	241	288
70-74	341	147	194	415	180	235	452	195	257	485	212	273
75-79	276	111	165	274	112	163	341	140	201	379	155	224
80 +	252	84	168	304	104	200	333	116	218	399	135	264

United Nations Department of Economic and Social Affairs/Population Division
World Population Prospects: The 2004 Revision, Volume II: Sex and Age Distribution of the World Population

POPULATION BY AGE AND SEX (in thousands)

Age group	2005 Both sexes	Males	Females	2010 Both sexes	Males	Females	2015 Both sexes	Males	Females	2020 Both sexes	Males	Females
All ages	10 495	5 072	5 422	10 712	5 186	5 526	10 827	5 248	5 579	10 902	5 294	5 608
0-4	561	289	273	542	279	263	519	267	252	501	258	243
5-9	556	286	270	561	288	272	542	279	263	519	267	252
10-14	550	282	268	567	291	276	569	293	277	550	283	267
15-19	585	299	287	573	293	280	586	300	285	588	302	286
20-24	704	358	347	601	305	296	586	298	287	598	306	293
25-29	801	403	397	706	357	349	603	305	298	588	298	290
30-34	811	405	406	800	401	398	705	355	350	602	304	299
35-39	762	378	384	828	413	415	813	407	406	720	362	358
40-44	773	379	393	791	394	397	851	425	426	836	419	417
45-49	733	359	374	791	389	401	805	401	404	864	432	432
50-54	683	332	351	740	363	378	795	391	404	809	403	406
55-59	633	302	331	683	330	353	737	359	378	791	387	404
60-64	549	256	294	625	295	330	671	320	351	724	349	376
65-69	530	241	288	536	246	290	604	280	324	649	305	344
70-74	485	212	273	491	217	274	496	220	275	560	252	308
75-79	379	155	224	409	170	239	416	174	242	423	179	245
80-84	247	92	155	278	102	175	302	112	190	313	118	195
85-89	109	34	75	139	42	97	160	47	113	180	55	125
90-94	36	9	28	42	9	33	56	12	45	69	14	55
95-99	6	1	5	9	1	7	11	1	9	16	2	14
100 +	0	0	0	1	0	1	1	0	1	2	0	2

Age group	2025 Both sexes	Males	Females	2030 Both sexes	Males	Females	2035 Both sexes	Males	Females	2040 Both sexes	Males	Females
All ages	10 924	5 312	5 612	10 933	5 323	5 610	10 930	5 326	5 604	10 903	5 317	5 586
0-4	493	254	240	504	259	245	519	267	252	526	270	255
5-9	500	257	243	493	254	239	503	259	244	519	267	252
10-14	526	271	256	508	261	247	501	257	243	511	263	248
15-19	567	291	276	543	279	264	524	269	255	517	266	252
20-24	599	306	293	578	296	282	554	283	271	536	274	262
25-29	600	305	295	601	306	295	580	295	284	556	283	273
30-34	587	297	290	600	304	295	601	305	296	580	295	285
35-39	615	309	306	600	303	297	613	310	302	614	311	303
40-44	740	373	367	636	321	316	621	314	307	634	322	312
45-49	848	426	422	753	380	373	650	328	322	636	322	313
50-54	867	433	434	851	427	424	757	382	376	656	331	325
55-59	804	398	406	862	428	434	847	423	424	756	380	377
60-64	776	376	401	791	388	403	848	418	430	835	414	421
65-69	700	332	368	751	358	393	766	371	395	823	400	423
70-74	602	275	327	651	300	351	700	326	375	717	339	378
75-79	481	206	275	520	226	294	566	250	316	613	273	340
80-84	322	123	199	371	145	226	406	162	244	446	181	265
85-89	192	60	132	203	65	138	239	79	160	267	91	176
90-94	81	18	64	90	20	70	99	23	76	121	30	90
95-99	21	3	18	26	3	22	30	4	26	35	5	30
100 +	3	0	3	4	0	4	5	0	5	7	0	6

Age group	2045 Both sexes	Males	Females	2050 Both sexes	Males	Females
All ages	10 832	5 285	5 546	10 723	5 235	5 487
0-4	512	263	248	498	256	242
5-9	525	270	255	511	263	248
10-14	527	271	256	533	274	259
15-19	528	271	257	543	279	264
20-24	529	271	258	539	276	263
25-29	538	274	264	531	271	260
30-34	556	283	274	538	273	265
35-39	593	301	292	570	289	281
40-44	635	323	313	615	312	303
45-49	648	330	319	650	331	319
50-54	642	326	317	655	333	322
55-59	657	331	327	644	325	319
60-64	747	372	375	652	326	326
65-69	812	397	415	730	360	370
70-74	772	367	405	765	367	398
75-79	631	287	344	683	313	370
80-84	488	201	287	508	214	293
85-89	299	105	195	334	119	214
90-94	139	36	103	161	44	117
95-99	44	7	37	53	9	44
100 +	8	1	8	11	1	10

POPULATION BY AGE AND SEX (in thousands)

Age group	2005 Both sexes	Males	Females	2010 Both sexes	Males	Females	2015 Both sexes	Males	Females	2020 Both sexes	Males	Females
All ages	10 495	5 072	5 422	10 803	5 233	5 570	11 050	5 363	5 687	11 275	5 486	5 790
0-4	561	289	273	633	326	307	651	335	316	651	335	316
5-9	556	286	270	561	288	272	633	325	307	651	335	316
10-14	550	282	268	567	291	276	569	293	277	641	330	312
15-19	585	299	287	573	293	280	586	300	285	588	302	286
20-24	704	358	347	601	305	296	586	298	287	598	306	293
25-29	801	403	397	706	357	349	603	305	298	588	298	290
30-34	811	405	406	800	401	398	705	355	350	602	304	299
35-39	762	378	384	828	413	415	813	407	406	720	362	358
40-44	773	379	393	791	394	397	851	425	426	836	419	417
45-49	733	359	374	791	389	401	805	401	404	864	432	432
50-54	683	332	351	740	363	378	795	391	404	809	403	406
55-59	633	302	331	683	330	353	737	359	378	791	387	404
60-64	549	256	294	625	295	330	671	320	351	724	349	376
65-69	530	241	288	536	246	290	604	280	324	649	305	344
70-74	485	212	273	491	217	274	496	220	275	560	252	308
75-79	379	155	224	409	170	239	416	174	242	423	179	245
80-84	247	92	155	278	102	175	302	112	190	313	118	195
85-89	109	34	75	139	42	97	160	47	113	180	55	125
90-94	36	9	28	42	9	33	56	12	45	69	14	55
95-99	6	1	5	9	1	7	11	1	9	16	2	14
100 +	0	0	0	1	0	1	1	0	1	2	0	2

Age group	2025 Both sexes	Males	Females	2030 Both sexes	Males	Females	2035 Both sexes	Males	Females	2040 Both sexes	Males	Females
All ages	11 443	5 579	5 864	11 604	5 668	5 936	11 778	5 762	6 016	11 973	5 867	6 106
0-4	639	329	310	656	337	318	697	359	339	749	385	364
5-9	651	335	316	639	329	310	655	337	318	697	359	338
10-14	658	339	320	658	339	320	646	332	314	663	341	322
15-19	657	338	320	675	346	328	675	347	328	663	340	322
20-24	599	306	293	669	342	326	686	351	335	686	351	335
25-29	600	305	295	601	306	295	670	342	328	687	351	337
30-34	587	297	290	600	304	295	601	305	296	670	341	329
35-39	615	309	306	600	303	297	613	310	302	614	311	303
40-44	740	373	367	636	321	316	621	314	307	634	322	312
45-49	848	426	422	753	380	373	650	328	322	636	322	313
50-54	867	433	434	851	427	424	757	382	376	656	331	325
55-59	804	398	406	862	428	434	847	423	424	756	380	377
60-64	776	376	401	791	388	403	848	418	430	835	414	421
65-69	700	332	368	751	358	393	766	371	395	823	400	423
70-74	602	275	327	651	300	351	700	326	375	717	339	378
75-79	481	206	275	520	226	294	566	250	316	613	273	340
80-84	322	123	199	371	145	226	406	162	244	446	181	265
85-89	192	60	132	203	65	138	239	79	160	267	91	176
90-94	81	18	64	90	20	70	99	23	76	121	30	90
95-99	21	3	18	26	3	22	30	4	26	35	5	30
100 +	3	0	3	4	0	4	5	0	5	7	0	6

Age group	2045 Both sexes	Males	Females	2050 Both sexes	Males	Females
All ages	12 166	5 971	6 195	12 343	6 068	6 275
0-4	777	400	377	786	404	381
5-9	749	385	363	777	400	377
10-14	705	362	342	756	389	367
15-19	679	349	330	721	370	351
20-24	674	345	329	691	354	337
25-29	688	351	337	676	345	331
30-34	687	350	338	688	350	338
35-39	683	347	336	701	356	345
40-44	635	323	313	704	358	346
45-49	648	330	319	650	331	319
50-54	642	326	317	655	333	322
55-59	657	331	327	644	325	319
60-64	747	372	375	652	326	326
65-69	812	397	415	730	360	370
70-74	772	367	405	765	367	398
75-79	631	287	344	683	313	370
80-84	488	201	287	508	214	293
85-89	299	105	195	334	119	214
90-94	139	36	103	161	44	117
95-99	44	7	37	53	9	44
100 +	8	1	8	11	1	10

United Nations Department of Economic and Social Affairs/Population Division
World Population Prospects: The 2004 Revision, Volume II: Sex and Age Distribution of the World Population

700

LOW VARIANT

PORTUGAL

POPULATION BY AGE AND SEX (in thousands)

Age group	2005 Both sexes	Males	Females	2010 Both sexes	Males	Females	2015 Both sexes	Males	Females	2020 Both sexes	Males	Females
All ages	10 495	5 072	5 422	10 621	5 139	5 482	10 601	5 132	5 469	10 521	5 098	5 424
0-4	561	289	273	451	232	219	384	198	186	346	178	168
5-9	556	286	270	561	288	272	450	232	219	384	198	186
10-14	550	282	268	567	291	276	569	293	277	459	236	223
15-19	585	299	287	573	293	280	586	300	285	588	302	286
20-24	704	358	347	601	305	296	586	298	287	598	306	293
25-29	801	403	397	706	357	349	603	305	298	588	298	290
30-34	811	405	406	800	401	398	705	355	350	602	304	299
35-39	762	378	384	828	413	415	813	407	406	720	362	358
40-44	773	379	393	791	394	397	851	425	426	836	419	417
45-49	733	359	374	791	389	401	805	401	404	864	432	432
50-54	683	332	351	740	363	378	795	391	404	809	403	406
55-59	633	302	331	683	330	353	737	359	378	791	387	404
60-64	549	256	294	625	295	330	671	320	351	724	349	376
65-69	530	241	288	536	246	290	604	280	324	649	305	344
70-74	485	212	273	491	217	274	496	220	275	560	252	308
75-79	379	155	224	409	170	239	416	174	242	423	179	245
80-84	247	92	155	278	102	175	302	112	190	313	118	195
85-89	109	34	75	139	42	97	160	47	113	180	55	125
90-94	36	9	28	42	9	33	56	12	45	69	14	55
95-99	6	1	5	9	1	7	11	1	9	16	2	14
100 +	0	0	0	1	0	1	1	0	1	2	0	2

Age group	2025 Both sexes	Males	Females	2030 Both sexes	Males	Females	2035 Both sexes	Males	Females	2040 Both sexes	Males	Females
All ages	10 397	5 041	5 356	10 260	4 976	5 283	10 100	4 900	5 201	9 896	4 799	5 097
0-4	347	178	168	356	183	173	363	187	176	348	179	169
5-9	346	178	168	346	178	168	356	183	173	362	186	176
10-14	392	201	190	354	182	172	354	182	172	364	187	177
15-19	476	244	232	408	209	199	370	190	180	371	190	181
20-24	599	306	293	487	249	238	420	214	205	382	195	187
25-29	600	305	295	601	306	295	489	249	240	422	214	207
30-34	587	297	290	600	304	295	601	305	296	489	248	241
35-39	615	309	306	600	303	297	613	310	302	614	311	303
40-44	740	373	367	636	321	316	621	314	307	634	322	312
45-49	848	426	422	753	380	373	650	328	322	636	322	313
50-54	867	433	434	851	427	424	757	382	376	656	331	325
55-59	804	398	406	862	428	434	847	423	424	756	380	377
60-64	776	376	401	791	388	403	848	418	430	835	414	421
65-69	700	332	368	751	358	393	766	371	395	823	400	423
70-74	602	275	327	651	300	351	700	326	375	717	339	378
75-79	481	206	275	520	226	294	566	250	316	613	273	340
80-84	322	123	199	371	145	226	406	162	244	446	181	265
85-89	192	60	132	203	65	138	239	79	160	267	91	176
90-94	81	18	64	90	20	70	99	23	76	121	30	90
95-99	21	3	18	26	3	22	30	4	26	35	5	30
100 +	3	0	3	4	0	4	5	0	5	7	0	6

Age group	2045 Both sexes	Males	Females	2050 Both sexes	Males	Females
All ages	9 625	4 665	4 960	9 298	4 503	4 795
0-4	310	159	150	279	143	135
5-9	348	179	169	310	159	150
10-14	370	190	180	356	183	173
15-19	381	195	185	387	198	188
20-24	383	195	187	392	200	192
25-29	384	195	189	385	195	189
30-34	422	214	209	385	195	190
35-39	503	255	248	436	221	216
40-44	635	323	313	525	266	259
45-49	648	330	319	650	331	319
50-54	642	326	317	655	333	322
55-59	657	331	327	644	325	319
60-64	747	372	375	652	326	326
65-69	812	397	415	730	360	370
70-74	772	367	405	765	367	398
75-79	631	287	344	683	313	370
80-84	488	201	287	508	214	293
85-89	299	105	195	334	119	214
90-94	139	36	103	161	44	117
95-99	44	7	37	53	9	44
100 +	8	1	8	11	1	10

United Nations Department of Economic and Social Affairs/Population Division
World Population Prospects: The 2004 Revision, Volume II: Sex and Age Distribution of the World Population

701

POPULATION BY AGE AND SEX (in thousands)

Age group	1950 Both sexes	Males	Females	1955 Both sexes	Males	Females	1960 Both sexes	Males	Females	1965 Both sexes	Males	Females
All ages	2 218	1 114	1 104	2 250	1 121	1 129	2 360	1 167	1 193	2 583	1 266	1 318
0-4	367	185	181	355	180	175	356	181	175	360	182	177
5-9	319	162	157	318	161	157	329	167	162	328	165	162
10-14	273	140	133	293	149	144	322	163	159	314	159	154
15-19	221	110	112	230	114	116	251	125	126	246	119	128
20-24	193	91	102	179	84	95	171	79	92	206	98	109
25-29	158	76	82	145	68	77	135	61	74	178	81	98
30-34	132	67	65	128	62	66	127	58	68	158	71	88
35-39	133	67	66	130	63	67	130	61	69	142	66	77
40-44	92	48	44	98	50	48	108	53	55	135	66	70
45-49	77	40	36	90	46	44	106	54	52	121	61	60
50-54	72	37	35	72	38	34	77	40	36	105	54	51
55-59	47	25	22	56	29	27	67	35	32	80	41	39
60-64	50	26	24	53	27	26	58	29	29	65	32	33
65-69	33	17	17	40	20	20	48	24	24	52	26	26
70-74	22	11	11	27	14	13	31	16	15	40	20	20
75-79	20	8	12	17	8	9	22	11	11	27	15	12
80 +	11	6	5	20	8	12	23	10	13	28	12	16

Age group	1970 Both sexes	Males	Females	1975 Both sexes	Males	Females	1980 Both sexes	Males	Females	1985 Both sexes	Males	Females
All ages	2 716	1 332	1 384	2 939	1 438	1 501	3 197	1 557	1 640	3 378	1 650	1 728
0-4	319	162	157	329	166	163	341	173	167	327	166	161
5-9	339	171	168	329	167	162	330	168	162	330	168	162
10-14	335	170	165	329	166	163	338	172	166	344	175	169
15-19	292	144	148	328	166	162	337	168	169	339	170	169
20-24	234	108	126	292	142	150	272	129	143	284	136	148
25-29	183	85	98	242	112	130	236	111	125	255	122	133
30-34	157	74	83	185	86	99	230	107	122	244	116	128
35-39	145	68	77	155	73	82	194	91	103	215	102	113
40-44	129	62	67	141	66	75	166	78	88	191	91	100
45-49	122	60	63	124	59	65	145	68	77	167	80	87
50-54	106	53	53	116	56	60	130	61	69	144	70	75
55-59	97	49	47	98	48	50	120	57	62	132	63	69
60-64	82	41	41	87	44	44	105	51	54	114	54	60
65-69	67	33	34	70	34	36	95	46	49	103	49	53
70-74	44	22	22	53	26	28	65	32	34	75	36	40
75-79	28	14	15	30	14	16	45	22	24	57	27	30
80 +	39	17	22	31	13	18	47	21	26	57	25	31

Age group	1990 Both sexes	Males	Females	1995 Both sexes	Males	Females	2000 Both sexes	Males	Females	2005 Both sexes	Males	Females
All ages	3 528	1 708	1 819	3 696	1 784	1 912	3 835	1 846	1 989	3 955	1 898	2 057
0-4	303	154	149	316	162	154	295	151	144	277	142	135
5-9	317	162	155	301	153	148	309	158	151	294	151	144
10-14	340	173	167	320	163	157	305	155	150	309	158	151
15-19	327	166	161	337	171	166	317	162	156	304	155	149
20-24	288	141	146	299	149	150	302	151	151	316	160	155
25-29	271	129	142	260	125	135	274	135	140	299	149	150
30-34	255	119	135	262	124	139	260	124	136	271	132	139
35-39	237	111	126	256	120	137	267	126	141	257	122	135
40-44	226	106	121	236	110	127	251	116	134	263	123	140
45-49	194	92	103	226	104	121	236	109	127	246	113	133
50-54	162	76	86	197	92	105	228	105	124	230	105	126
55-59	141	66	75	164	77	88	199	92	107	221	100	121
60-64	125	58	67	140	65	75	162	75	88	189	86	103
65-69	113	52	60	121	55	66	135	61	74	150	67	83
70-74	87	40	46	102	46	56	109	48	61	120	52	68
75-79	68	32	36	72	32	40	85	37	48	91	38	53
80 +	74	32	42	86	37	49	100	41	59	117	45	72

United Nations Department of Economic and Social Affairs/Population Division
World Population Prospects: The 2004 Revision, Volume II: Sex and Age Distribution of the World Population

702

POPULATION BY AGE AND SEX (in thousands)

Age group	2005			2010			2015			2020		
	Both sexes	Males	Females	Both sexes	Males	Females	Both sexes	Males	Females	Both sexes	Males	Females
All ages	3 955	1 898	2 057	4 060	1 944	2 116	4 157	1 988	2 169	4 242	2 028	2 214
0-4	277	142	135	272	139	133	274	140	133	272	140	133
5-9	294	151	144	277	142	135	271	139	132	273	140	133
10-14	309	158	151	294	150	144	276	141	135	271	139	132
15-19	304	155	149	308	158	151	293	150	143	276	141	135
20-24	316	160	155	303	154	149	307	157	150	292	149	143
25-29	299	149	150	313	159	155	300	152	148	305	155	150
30-34	271	132	139	296	147	149	311	157	154	298	151	148
35-39	257	122	135	268	130	138	293	145	148	308	155	153
40-44	263	123	140	253	119	134	265	128	137	290	143	147
45-49	246	113	133	259	120	139	249	116	133	262	125	136
50-54	230	105	126	241	109	131	254	116	137	245	113	132
55-59	221	100	121	223	100	123	234	105	129	247	112	135
60-64	189	86	103	211	93	118	214	94	120	224	99	126
65-69	150	67	83	176	77	98	197	84	112	200	85	115
70-74	120	52	68	134	57	77	158	66	91	177	73	104
75-79	91	38	53	100	41	59	113	45	67	133	53	81
80-84	64	25	38	68	26	42	76	28	47	86	32	55
85-89	34	13	21	40	14	26	44	15	29	49	16	33
90-94	15	5	9	17	5	11	20	6	14	23	6	16
95-99	4	1	3	5	2	4	6	2	5	8	2	6
100 +	1	0	1	1	0	1	1	0	1	2	0	1

Age group	2025			2030			2035			2040		
	Both sexes	Males	Females	Both sexes	Males	Females	Both sexes	Males	Females	Both sexes	Males	Females
All ages	4 311	2 061	2 249	4 361	2 087	2 274	4 391	2 105	2 286	4 406	2 118	2 288
0-4	268	137	131	261	134	127	251	129	123	245	125	119
5-9	272	139	133	268	137	130	261	134	127	251	129	122
10-14	273	140	133	272	130	133	268	137	130	261	134	127
15-19	271	139	132	273	140	133	271	139	132	267	137	130
20-24	275	140	134	270	138	132	272	139	133	270	138	132
25-29	290	148	142	273	139	134	268	137	131	270	138	132
30-34	303	154	149	289	147	142	272	138	133	267	136	131
35-39	296	149	147	301	153	148	287	146	141	270	137	133
40-44	305	153	152	294	147	146	299	151	148	285	144	141
45-49	287	140	146	302	151	151	291	145	145	296	149	147
50-54	237	122	135	282	137	145	297	147	150	287	142	144
55-59	239	109	130	251	118	133	276	133	143	291	143	148
60-64	237	105	132	230	103	126	242	112	130	266	126	140
65-69	211	90	121	223	96	127	217	95	122	229	104	125
70-74	181	74	107	191	78	113	203	84	119	198	83	115
75-79	151	58	93	155	59	96	104	63	101	176	69	107
80-84	103	37	66	117	40	77	121	42	80	130	45	85
85-89	57	18	39	68	20	48	79	23	56	83	24	59
90-94	26	7	19	30	7	23	37	9	29	44	10	34
95-99	9	2	7	10	2	8	12	2	10	16	3	13
100 +	2	0	2	3	0	2	3	0	3	4	0	3

Age group	2045			2050		
	Both sexes	Males	Females	Both sexes	Males	Females
All ages	4 410	2 126	2 284	4 405	2 130	2 275
0-4	242	124	118	240	123	117
5-9	244	125	119	242	124	118
10-14	251	129	122	244	125	119
15-19	260	133	127	251	129	122
20-24	266	136	130	260	133	127
25-29	269	138	132	265	136	129
30-34	269	137	132	268	137	131
35-39	266	135	130	268	136	131
40-44	268	136	132	264	134	130
45-49	282	143	140	266	135	131
50-54	292	146	146	279	140	139
55-59	281	138	142	286	142	144
60-64	282	136	145	272	132	140
65-69	253	117	135	268	127	140
70-74	210	92	118	233	104	128
75-79	172	69	104	184	76	108
80-84	140	50	91	139	50	89
85-89	91	27	64	99	30	69
90-94	47	11	37	52	12	40
95-99	19	3	16	21	3	17
100 +	5	1	4	6	1	5

POPULATION BY AGE AND SEX (in thousands)

Age group	2005 Both sexes	Males	Females	2010 Both sexes	Males	Females	2015 Both sexes	Males	Females	2020 Both sexes	Males	Females
All ages	3 955	1 898	2 057	4 097	1 963	2 134	4 254	2 038	2 216	4 412	2 115	2 297
0-4	277	142	135	309	158	151	333	171	162	346	177	168
5-9	294	151	144	277	142	135	309	158	151	333	171	162
10-14	309	158	151	294	150	144	276	141	135	309	158	151
15-19	304	155	149	308	158	151	293	150	143	276	141	135
20-24	316	160	155	303	154	149	307	157	150	292	149	143
25-29	299	149	150	313	159	155	300	152	148	305	155	150
30-34	271	132	139	296	147	149	311	157	154	298	151	148
35-39	257	122	135	268	130	138	293	145	148	308	155	153
40-44	263	123	140	253	119	134	265	128	137	290	143	147
45-49	246	113	133	259	120	139	249	116	133	262	125	136
50-54	230	105	126	241	109	131	254	116	137	245	113	132
55-59	221	100	121	223	100	123	234	105	129	247	112	135
60-64	189	86	103	211	93	118	214	94	120	224	99	126
65-69	150	67	83	176	77	98	197	84	112	200	85	115
70-74	120	52	68	134	57	77	158	66	91	177	73	104
75-79	91	38	53	100	41	59	113	45	67	133	53	81
80-84	64	25	38	68	26	42	76	28	47	86	32	55
85-89	34	13	21	40	14	26	44	15	29	49	16	33
90-94	15	5	9	17	5	11	20	6	14	23	6	16
95-99	4	1	3	5	2	4	6	2	5	8	2	6
100 +	1	0	1	1	0	1	1	0	1	2	0	1

Age group	2025 Both sexes	Males	Females	2030 Both sexes	Males	Females	2035 Both sexes	Males	Females	2040 Both sexes	Males	Females
All ages	4 553	2 186	2 368	4 675	2 248	2 427	4 787	2 308	2 479	4 904	2 373	2 531
0-4	340	174	166	333	171	162	333	171	162	348	178	170
5-9	345	177	168	340	174	166	333	171	162	333	171	162
10-14	333	170	162	345	177	168	340	174	166	332	170	162
15-19	308	158	150	332	170	162	345	177	168	339	174	165
20-24	275	140	134	307	157	150	331	169	162	344	176	168
25-29	290	148	142	273	139	134	306	156	149	330	168	161
30-34	303	154	149	289	147	142	272	138	133	304	155	149
35-39	296	149	147	301	153	148	287	146	141	270	137	133
40-44	305	153	152	294	147	146	299	151	148	285	144	141
45-49	287	140	146	302	151	151	291	145	145	296	149	147
50-54	257	122	135	282	137	145	297	147	150	287	142	144
55-59	239	109	130	251	118	133	276	133	143	291	143	148
60-64	237	105	132	230	103	126	242	112	130	266	126	140
65-69	211	90	121	223	96	127	217	95	122	229	104	125
70-74	181	74	107	191	78	113	203	84	119	198	83	115
75-79	151	58	93	155	59	96	164	63	101	176	69	107
80-84	103	37	66	117	40	77	121	42	80	130	45	85
85-89	57	18	39	68	20	48	79	23	56	83	24	59
90-94	26	7	19	30	7	23	37	9	29	44	10	34
95-99	9	2	7	10	2	8	12	2	10	16	3	13
100 +	2	0	2	3	0	2	3	0	3	4	0	3

Age group	2045 Both sexes	Males	Females	2050 Both sexes	Males	Females
All ages	5 033	2 445	2 588	5 167	2 520	2 647
0-4	368	189	179	380	195	185
5-9	348	178	169	368	189	179
10-14	333	170	162	347	178	169
15-19	332	170	162	332	170	162
20-24	338	173	165	331	170	161
25-29	342	175	167	337	172	165
30-34	328	167	161	341	174	167
35-39	302	154	148	326	166	160
40-44	268	136	132	301	153	148
45-49	282	143	140	266	135	131
50-54	292	146	146	279	140	139
55-59	281	138	142	286	142	144
60-64	282	136	145	272	132	140
65-69	253	117	135	268	127	140
70-74	210	92	118	233	104	128
75-79	172	69	104	184	76	108
80-84	140	50	91	139	50	89
85-89	91	27	64	99	30	69
90-94	47	11	37	52	12	40
95-99	19	3	16	21	3	17
100 +	5	1	4	6	1	5

United Nations Department of Economic and Social Affairs/Population Division
World Population Prospects: The 2004 Revision, Volume II: Sex and Age Distribution of the World Population

704

POPULATION BY AGE AND SEX (in thousands)

Age group	2005 Both sexes	Males	Females	2010 Both sexes	Males	Females	2015 Both sexes	Males	Females	2020 Both sexes	Males	Females
All ages	3 955	1 898	2 057	4 022	1 925	2 098	4 060	1 938	2 121	4 071	1 940	2 131
0-4	277	142	135	235	120	114	214	110	104	199	102	97
5-9	294	151	144	277	142	135	234	120	114	214	109	104
10-14	309	158	151	294	150	144	276	141	135	234	120	114
15-19	304	155	149	308	158	151	293	150	143	276	141	135
20-24	316	160	155	303	154	149	307	157	150	292	149	143
25-29	299	149	150	313	159	155	300	152	148	305	155	150
30-34	271	132	139	296	147	149	311	157	154	298	151	148
35-39	257	122	135	268	130	138	293	145	148	308	155	153
40-44	263	123	140	253	119	134	265	128	137	290	143	147
45-49	246	113	133	259	120	139	249	116	133	262	125	136
50-54	230	105	126	241	109	131	254	116	137	245	113	132
55-59	221	100	121	223	100	123	234	105	129	247	112	135
60-64	189	86	103	211	93	118	214	94	120	224	99	126
65-69	150	67	83	176	77	98	197	84	112	200	85	115
70-74	120	52	68	134	57	77	158	66	91	177	73	104
75-79	91	38	53	100	41	59	113	45	67	133	53	81
80-84	64	25	38	68	26	42	76	28	47	86	32	55
85-89	34	13	21	40	14	26	44	15	29	49	16	33
90-94	15	5	9	17	5	11	20	6	14	23	6	16
95-99	4	1	3	5	2	4	6	2	5	8	2	6
100 +	1	0	1	1	0	1	1	0	1	2	0	1

Age group	2025 Both sexes	Males	Females	2030 Both sexes	Males	Females	2035 Both sexes	Males	Females	2040 Both sexes	Males	Females
All ages	4 068	1 937	2 131	4 048	1 927	2 121	4 007	1 908	2 098	3 940	1 879	2 061
0-4	196	100	95	191	98	93	179	92	87	163	83	79
5-9	198	102	97	195	100	95	191	98	93	179	92	87
10-14	213	109	104	198	102	97	195	100	95	190	98	93
15-19	234	120	114	213	109	104	198	101	97	195	100	95
20-24	275	140	134	233	119	114	212	109	104	197	101	96
25-29	290	148	142	273	139	134	231	118	113	211	108	103
30-34	303	154	149	289	147	142	272	138	133	230	117	113
35-39	296	149	147	301	153	140	287	146	141	270	137	133
40-44	305	153	152	294	147	146	299	151	148	285	144	141
45-49	287	140	146	302	151	151	291	145	145	296	149	147
50-54	257	122	135	282	137	145	297	147	150	287	142	144
55-59	239	109	130	251	118	133	276	133	143	291	143	148
60-64	237	105	132	230	103	126	242	112	130	266	126	140
65-69	211	90	121	223	96	127	217	95	122	229	104	125
70-74	181	74	107	191	78	113	203	84	119	198	83	115
75-79	151	58	93	155	59	96	164	63	101	176	69	107
80-84	103	37	66	117	40	77	121	42	80	130	45	85
85-89	57	18	39	68	20	48	79	23	56	83	24	59
90-94	26	7	19	30	7	23	37	9	29	44	10	34
95-99	9	2	7	10	2	8	12	2	10	16	3	13
100 +	2	0	2	3	0	2	3	0	3	4	0	3

Age group	2045 Both sexes	Males	Females	2050 Both sexes	Males	Females
All ages	3 849	1 839	2 010	3 740	1 789	1 950
0-4	147	75	71	135	69	66
5-9	163	83	79	146	75	71
10-14	179	92	87	162	83	79
15-19	190	97	93	178	91	87
20-24	194	99	95	189	97	92
25-29	196	100	96	193	99	94
30-34	210	107	103	195	100	95
35-39	229	117	112	209	106	102
40-44	268	136	132	227	116	112
45-49	282	143	140	266	135	131
50-54	292	146	146	279	140	139
55-59	281	138	142	286	142	144
60-64	282	136	145	272	132	140
65-69	253	117	135	268	127	140
70-74	210	92	118	233	104	128
75-79	172	69	104	184	76	108
80-84	140	50	91	139	50	89
85-89	91	27	64	99	30	69
90-94	47	11	37	52	12	40
95-99	19	3	16	21	3	17
100 +	5	1	4	6	1	5

POPULATION BY AGE AND SEX (in thousands)

Age group	1950 Both sexes	Males	Females	1955 Both sexes	Males	Females	1960 Both sexes	Males	Females	1965 Both sexes	Males	Females
All ages	25	13	12	35	19	16	45	26	19	70	43	27
0-4	4	2	2	6	3	3	7	4	4	11	5	5
5-9	3	2	2	5	2	2	6	3	3	8	4	4
10-14	3	1	1	4	2	2	5	2	2	6	3	3
15-19	2	1	1	3	2	2	4	2	2	7	4	2
20-24	2	1	1	3	2	1	4	3	2	7	5	2
25-29	2	1	1	3	2	1	4	3	2	8	6	2
30-34	2	1	1	3	2	1	4	2	1	6	5	2
35-39	1	1	1	2	1	1	3	2	1	5	4	2
40-44	1	1	1	2	1	1	2	1	1	4	2	1
45-49	1	0	0	1	1	1	2	1	1	3	2	1
50-54	1	0	0	1	1	0	1	1	1	2	1	1
55-59	1	0	0	1	0	0	1	1	0	1	1	1
60-64	1	0	0	1	0	0	1	0	0	1	1	0
65-69	0	0	0	0	0	0	1	0	0	1	0	0
70-74	0	0	0	0	0	0	0	0	0	0	0	0
75-79	0	0	0	0	0	0	0	0	0	0	0	0
80 +	0	0	0	0	0	0	0	0	0	0	0	0

Age group	1970 Both sexes	Males	Females	1975 Both sexes	Males	Females	1980 Both sexes	Males	Females	1985 Both sexes	Males	Females
All ages	111	72	39	171	115	56	229	146	83	361	243	118
0-4	16	8	8	22	11	11	27	14	13	40	20	20
5-9	14	7	7	18	9	9	25	12	12	34	17	16
10-14	10	5	5	16	9	8	22	12	10	26	13	12
15-19	9	6	3	16	10	6	19	10	9	22	12	10
20-24	11	8	3	19	14	4	25	17	8	33	23	10
25-29	13	10	3	18	14	4	29	22	8	53	42	11
30-34	11	8	3	18	14	4	26	19	7	53	40	13
35-39	9	6	2	14	11	3	19	13	6	39	29	10
40-44	6	5	1	10	8	2	14	10	4	24	19	6
45-49	4	3	1	7	5	2	9	6	2	16	12	4
50-54	3	2	1	4	3	1	7	5	2	10	7	2
55-59	1	1	0	3	2	1	3	2	1	5	4	1
60-64	1	1	1	2	1	1	3	2	1	3	2	1
65-69	1	0	0	2	1	1	1	1	0	2	1	1
70-74	1	0	0	1	1	0	1	0	0	1	1	0
75-79	0	0	0	1	0	0	0	0	0	0	0	0
80 +	0	0	0	0	0	0	0	0	0	1	0	0

Age group	1990 Both sexes	Males	Females	1995 Both sexes	Males	Females	2000 Both sexes	Males	Females	2005 Both sexes	Males	Females
All ages	467	313	154	526	346	179	606	388	218	813	547	265
0-4	52	26	25	51	26	25	59	30	29	67	34	33
5-9	42	21	21	49	25	24	51	26	25	59	30	29
10-14	35	18	17	40	21	20	49	25	24	51	26	25
15-19	26	14	12	30	16	14	41	21	20	47	24	22
20-24	33	21	12	43	31	12	38	21	17	66	45	21
25-29	50	37	13	61	46	16	56	39	17	98	71	27
30-34	64	51	14	68	46	21	73	53	20	105	73	32
35-39	61	46	15	65	47	18	74	50	23	91	66	25
40-44	43	33	10	49	37	12	66	48	18	78	59	19
45-49	26	20	6	29	22	7	46	35	11	66	52	14
50-54	17	13	4	18	14	4	25	19	6	42	34	8
55-59	8	6	2	10	8	3	14	11	3	22	17	5
60-64	5	3	1	6	4	2	7	5	2	11	9	3
65-69	3	2	1	3	2	1	4	3	1	5	3	2
70-74	1	1	0	2	1	1	3	2	1	3	2	1
75-79	1	0	0	1	1	0	1	1	0	1	1	1
80 +	1	0	0	1	0	0	1	0	0	1	1	0

United Nations Department of Economic and Social Affairs/Population Division
World Population Prospects: The 2004 Revision, Volume II: Sex and Age Distribution of the World Population

706

POPULATION BY AGE AND SEX (in thousands)

Age group	2005 Both sexes	Males	Females	2010 Both sexes	Males	Females	2015 Both sexes	Males	Females	2020 Both sexes	Males	Females
All ages	813	547	265	894	589	305	972	628	344	1 036	659	377
0-4	67	34	33	73	37	36	71	36	35	70	36	34
5-9	59	30	29	67	34	33	73	37	36	71	36	35
10-14	51	26	25	59	30	29	67	34	33	73	38	36
15-19	47	24	22	52	27	25	61	31	29	68	35	33
20-24	66	45	21	60	35	25	65	38	28	67	37	31
25-29	98	71	27	90	66	24	84	56	28	77	48	29
30-34	105	73	32	118	89	29	111	84	26	95	65	29
35-39	91	66	25	113	80	33	126	96	30	116	89	27
40-44	78	59	19	85	61	25	107	74	33	127	97	30
45-49	66	52	14	67	48	18	74	50	24	101	69	32
50-54	42	34	8	53	40	13	54	36	17	63	40	23
55-59	22	17	5	30	23	7	40	29	11	44	28	16
60-64	11	9	3	12	8	4	20	14	6	33	22	11
65-69	5	3	2	7	5	2	8	5	3	16	11	5
70-74	3	2	1	4	3	2	6	4	2	7	4	3
75-79	1	1	1	2	1	1	3	2	1	5	3	2
80-84	1	0	0	1	1	0	1	1	1	2	1	1
85-89	0	0	0	0	0	0	1	0	0	1	0	0
90-94	0	0	0	0	0	0	0	0	0	0	0	0
95-99	0	0	0	0	0	0	0	0	0	0	0	0
100 +	0	0	0	0	0	0	0	0	0	0	0	0

Age group	2025 Both sexes	Males	Females	2030 Both sexes	Males	Females	2035 Both sexes	Males	Females	2040 Both sexes	Males	Females
All ages	1 098	688	410	1 158	715	443	1 214	739	475	1 263	759	505
0-4	71	36	34	73	38	36	75	39	37	75	38	37
5-9	70	36	34	71	36	35	73	38	36	76	39	37
10-14	71	36	35	70	36	34	71	36	35	73	38	36
15-19	74	38	36	72	37	35	70	36	34	71	37	35
20-24	74	40	34	80	43	37	78	42	36	77	41	35
25-29	78	46	32	85	49	36	91	52	39	88	51	38
30-34	84	54	30	85	52	33	92	55	37	98	58	40
35-39	98	68	30	88	57	31	88	54	34	95	58	38
40-44	118	91	27	99	70	30	89	59	31	90	56	34
45-49	123	93	30	114	87	26	96	66	29	86	55	30
50-54	93	62	31	114	85	29	105	80	26	88	60	29
55-59	55	33	22	85	55	30	105	78	28	97	72	25
60-64	37	22	15	48	27	21	77	48	29	96	70	26
65-69	28	18	10	32	18	14	43	23	20	70	42	27
70-74	14	9	5	24	16	9	29	16	13	38	20	18
75-79	5	3	2	11	7	4	20	12	8	24	13	11
80-84	3	2	1	4	2	2	8	5	3	15	8	6
85-89	1	1	1	2	1	1	2	1	1	5	3	2
90-94	0	0	0	1	0	0	1	0	0	1	0	1
95-99	0	0	0	0	0	0	0	0	0	0	0	0
100 +	0	0	0	0	0	0	0	0	0	0	0	0

Age group	2045 Both sexes	Males	Females	2050 Both sexes	Males	Females
All ages	1 302	772	530	1 330	778	552
0-4	73	37	36	71	36	35
5-9	75	39	37	73	37	36
10-14	76	39	37	75	39	37
15-19	74	38	36	76	39	37
20-24	78	42	36	80	43	37
25-29	87	50	37	88	51	38
30-34	95	57	39	94	56	38
35-39	101	61	41	99	59	39
40-44	97	59	38	103	62	41
45-49	87	53	33	93	56	37
50-54	78	49	30	79	47	33
55-59	80	53	28	71	42	29
60-64	89	65	24	73	46	26
65-69	88	63	25	81	59	22
70-74	62	37	25	79	55	23
75-79	32	16	16	52	30	22
80-84	18	9	9	25	12	13
85-89	9	5	4	11	5	6
90-94	2	1	1	4	2	2
95-99	0	0	0	1	0	1
100 +	0	0	0	0	0	0

United Nations Department of Economic and Social Affairs/Population Division
World Population Prospects: The 2004 Revision, Volume II: Sex and Age Distribution of the World Population

707

POPULATION BY AGE AND SEX (in thousands)

Age group	2005 Both sexes	Males	Females	2010 Both sexes	Males	Females	2015 Both sexes	Males	Females	2020 Both sexes	Males	Females
All ages	813	547	265	901	592	309	989	637	352	1 068	675	393
0-4	67	34	33	80	41	39	82	42	40	84	43	41
5-9	59	30	29	67	34	33	80	41	39	82	42	40
10-14	51	26	25	59	30	29	67	34	33	80	41	39
15-19	47	24	22	52	27	25	61	31	29	68	35	33
20-24	66	45	21	60	35	25	65	38	28	67	37	31
25-29	98	71	27	90	66	24	84	56	28	77	48	29
30-34	105	73	32	118	89	29	111	84	26	95	65	29
35-39	91	66	25	113	80	33	126	96	30	116	89	27
40-44	78	59	19	85	61	25	107	74	33	127	97	30
45-49	66	52	14	67	48	18	74	50	24	101	69	32
50-54	42	34	8	53	40	13	54	36	17	63	40	23
55-59	22	17	5	30	23	7	40	29	11	44	28	16
60-64	11	9	3	12	8	4	20	14	6	33	22	11
65-69	5	3	2	7	5	2	8	5	3	16	11	5
70-74	3	2	1	4	3	2	6	4	2	7	4	3
75-79	1	1	1	2	1	1	3	2	1	5	3	2
80-84	1	0	0	1	1	0	1	1	1	2	1	1
85-89	0	0	0	0	0	0	1	0	0	1	0	0
90-94	0	0	0	0	0	0	0	0	0	0	0	0
95-99	0	0	0	0	0	0	0	0	0	0	0	0
100 +	0	0	0	0	0	0	0	0	0	0	0	0

Age group	2025 Both sexes	Males	Females	2030 Both sexes	Males	Females	2035 Both sexes	Males	Females	2040 Both sexes	Males	Females
All ages	1 145	712	433	1 223	748	475	1 302	784	518	1 378	818	561
0-4	86	44	42	91	47	45	98	50	48	103	53	50
5-9	84	43	41	86	44	42	91	47	45	98	50	48
10-14	82	42	40	84	43	41	86	44	42	91	47	45
15-19	81	41	39	82	42	40	85	43	41	87	45	42
20-24	74	40	34	87	46	40	88	47	41	91	48	42
25-29	78	46	32	85	49	36	97	55	42	99	56	43
30-34	84	54	30	85	52	33	92	55	37	104	61	43
35-39	98	68	30	88	57	31	88	54	34	95	58	38
40-44	118	91	27	99	70	30	89	59	31	90	56	34
45-49	123	93	30	114	87	26	96	66	29	86	55	30
50-54	93	62	31	114	85	29	105	80	26	88	60	29
55-59	55	33	22	85	55	30	105	78	28	97	72	25
60-64	37	22	15	48	27	21	77	48	29	96	70	26
65-69	28	18	10	32	18	14	43	23	20	70	42	27
70-74	14	9	5	24	16	9	29	16	13	38	20	18
75-79	5	3	2	11	7	4	20	12	8	24	13	11
80-84	3	2	1	4	2	2	8	5	3	15	8	6
85-89	1	1	1	2	1	1	2	1	1	5	3	2
90-94	0	0	0	1	0	0	1	0	0	1	0	1
95-99	0	0	0	0	0	0	0	0	0	0	0	0
100 +	0	0	0	0	0	0	0	0	0	0	0	0

Age group	2045 Both sexes	Males	Females	2050 Both sexes	Males	Females
All ages	1 449	847	602	1 511	871	640
0-4	105	54	51	106	54	52
5-9	103	53	50	105	54	51
10-14	98	50	48	103	53	50
15-19	92	47	45	99	51	48
20-24	93	49	43	98	52	46
25-29	101	57	44	104	58	45
30-34	106	62	44	108	63	45
35-39	108	64	44	109	65	45
40-44	97	59	38	109	66	44
45-49	87	53	33	93	56	37
50-54	78	49	30	79	47	33
55-59	80	53	28	71	42	29
60-64	89	65	24	73	46	26
65-69	88	63	25	81	59	22
70-74	62	37	25	79	55	23
75-79	32	16	16	52	30	22
80-84	18	9	9	25	12	13
85-89	9	5	4	11	5	6
90-94	2	1	1	4	2	2
95-99	0	0	0	1	0	1
100 +	0	0	0	0	0	0

United Nations Department of Economic and Social Affairs/Population Division
World Population Prospects: The 2004 Revision, Volume II: Sex and Age Distribution of the World Population

708

POPULATION BY AGE AND SEX (in thousands)

Age group	2005 Both sexes	Males	Females	2010 Both sexes	Males	Females	2015 Both sexes	Males	Females	2020 Both sexes	Males	Females
All ages	813	547	265	887	585	302	954	619	335	1 004	643	362
0-4	67	34	33	67	34	33	60	31	29	55	28	27
5-9	59	30	29	67	34	33	67	34	33	60	31	29
10-14	51	26	25	59	30	29	67	34	33	67	34	33
15-19	47	24	22	52	27	25	61	31	29	68	35	33
20-24	66	45	21	60	35	25	65	38	28	67	37	31
25-29	98	71	27	90	66	24	84	56	28	77	48	29
30-34	105	73	32	118	89	29	111	84	26	95	65	29
35-39	91	66	25	113	80	33	126	96	30	116	89	27
40-44	78	59	19	85	61	25	107	74	33	127	97	30
45-49	66	52	14	67	48	18	74	50	24	101	69	32
50-54	42	34	8	53	40	13	54	36	17	63	40	23
55-59	22	17	5	30	23	7	40	29	11	44	28	16
60-64	11	9	3	12	8	4	20	14	6	33	22	11
65-69	5	3	2	7	5	2	8	5	3	16	11	5
70-74	3	2	1	4	3	2	6	4	2	7	4	3
75-79	1	1	1	2	1	1	3	2	1	5	3	2
80-84	1	0	0	1	1	0	1	1	1	2	1	1
85-89	0	0	0	0	0	0	1	0	0	1	0	0
90-94	0	0	0	0	0	0	0	0	0	0	0	0
95-99	0	0	0	0	0	0	0	0	0	0	0	0
100 +	0	0	0	0	0	0	0	0	0	0	0	0

Age group	2025 Both sexes	Males	Females	2030 Both sexes	Males	Females	2035 Both sexes	Males	Females	2040 Both sexes	Males	Females
All ages	1 051	664	387	1 094	682	412	1 130	696	434	1 155	703	451
0-4	55	28	27	56	29	27	55	28	27	51	26	25
5-9	55	28	27	55	28	27	56	29	27	55	28	27
10-14	60	31	29	56	28	27	55	28	27	56	29	27
15-19	68	35	33	61	31	30	56	29	27	56	29	27
20-24	74	40	34	74	40	34	67	36	31	62	34	29
25-29	78	46	32	85	49	36	84	49	36	77	45	32
30-34	84	54	30	85	52	33	92	55	37	91	55	37
35-39	98	68	30	88	57	31	88	54	34	95	58	38
40-44	118	91	27	99	70	30	89	59	31	90	56	34
45-49	123	93	30	114	87	28	90	60	29	86	55	30
50-54	93	62	31	114	85	29	105	80	26	88	60	29
55-59	55	33	22	85	55	30	105	78	28	97	72	25
60-64	37	22	15	48	27	21	77	48	29	95	70	26
65-69	28	18	10	32	18	14	43	23	20	70	42	27
70-74	14	9	5	24	16	9	29	16	13	38	20	18
75-79	5	3	2	11	7	4	20	12	8	24	13	11
80-84	3	2	1	4	2	2	8	5	3	15	8	6
85-89	1	1	1	2	1	1	2	1	1	5	3	2
90-94	0	0	0	1	0	0	1	0	0	1	0	1
95-99	0	0	0	0	0	0	0	0	0	0	0	0
100 +	0	0	0	0	0	0	0	0	0	0	0	0

Age group	2045 Both sexes	Males	Females	2050 Both sexes	Males	Females
All ages	1 167	703	464	1 167	695	472
0-4	46	24	23	43	22	21
5-9	51	26	25	47	24	23
10-14	55	28	27	51	26	25
15-19	57	29	28	56	29	27
20-24	62	34	28	63	34	29
25-29	73	43	30	73	43	30
30-34	85	51	33	80	49	31
35-39	95	57	37	88	54	34
40-44	97	59	38	96	59	37
45-49	87	53	33	93	56	37
50-54	78	49	30	79	47	33
55-59	80	53	28	71	42	29
60-64	89	65	24	73	46	26
65-69	88	63	25	81	59	22
70-74	62	37	25	79	55	23
75-79	32	16	16	52	30	22
80-84	18	9	9	25	12	13
85-89	9	5	4	11	5	6
90-94	2	1	1	4	2	2
95-99	0	0	0	1	0	1
100 +	0	0	0	0	0	0

POPULATION BY AGE AND SEX (in thousands)

Age group	1950 Both sexes	Males	Females	1955 Both sexes	Males	Females	1960 Both sexes	Males	Females	1965 Both sexes	Males	Females
All ages	18 859	9 528	9 330	21 422	10 497	10 925	25 003	12 403	12 600	28 530	14 273	14 256
0-4	2 961	1 524	1 437	3 344	1 706	1 638	4 656	2 414	2 242	4 704	2 441	2 263
5-9	2 537	1 277	1 260	2 672	1 377	1 295	3 201	1 631	1 569	4 481	2 321	2 161
10-14	2 358	1 201	1 157	2 417	1 234	1 183	2 630	1 356	1 275	3 151	1 606	1 545
15-19	1 896	963	933	2 376	1 204	1 172	2 377	1 214	1 163	2 587	1 333	1 254
20-24	1 612	810	802	2 033	1 006	1 027	2 323	1 177	1 146	2 325	1 186	1 138
25-29	1 405	714	690	1 623	771	852	1 978	978	1 000	2 263	1 145	1 118
30-34	1 179	610	569	1 455	719	735	1 573	747	826	1 921	949	972
35-39	1 066	552	513	1 196	602	594	1 404	693	711	1 521	721	800
40-44	887	458	429	1 045	513	532	1 146	575	571	1 349	664	685
45-49	726	372	355	874	414	461	993	484	509	1 092	544	547
50-54	631	314	317	640	284	356	818	383	435	932	450	482
55-59	574	276	298	554	230	324	585	256	329	751	347	404
60-64	453	220	233	408	156	251	488	198	290	518	222	295
65-69	310	133	177	325	119	206	339	126	213	408	161	247
70-74	142	58	84	232	84	147	247	87	159	260	94	166
75-79	81	32	48	144	49	94	152	53	99	164	55	109
80 +	42	16	26	87	29	58	94	30	64	103	33	70

Age group	1970 Both sexes	Males	Females	1975 Both sexes	Males	Females	1980 Both sexes	Males	Females	1985 Both sexes	Males	Females
All ages	31 922	16 057	15 865	35 281	17 775	17 506	38 124	19 259	18 865	40 806	20 576	20 230
0-4	4 385	2 269	2 116	4 472	2 274	2 199	4 292	2 203	2 089	3 718	1 943	1 775
5-9	4 593	2 380	2 213	4 291	2 218	2 073	4 269	2 207	2 062	3 975	2 063	1 913
10-14	4 453	2 305	2 148	4 555	2 359	2 195	4 400	2 280	2 120	4 536	2 358	2 177
15-19	3 129	1 595	1 535	4 412	2 283	2 129	4 659	2 417	2 242	4 348	2 270	2 078
20-24	2 557	1 317	1 241	3 088	1 572	1 517	4 103	2 120	1 983	4 256	2 209	2 047
25-29	2 290	1 167	1 123	2 516	1 294	1 222	3 119	1 598	1 521	4 094	2 044	2 050
30-34	2 223	1 124	1 099	2 248	1 145	1 103	2 432	1 231	1 201	3 153	1 621	1 532
35-39	1 880	928	952	2 175	1 098	1 077	2 237	1 139	1 098	2 594	1 340	1 255
40-44	1 481	700	781	1 830	901	929	2 124	1 079	1 045	2 230	1 129	1 100
45-49	1 302	637	664	1 430	673	757	1 738	842	896	2 132	1 081	1 051
50-54	1 038	514	525	1 240	603	637	1 372	644	728	1 715	826	890
55-59	867	413	453	968	473	495	1 102	515	587	1 279	575	704
60-64	674	306	368	782	366	415	824	385	439	1 026	456	570
65-69	441	184	256	577	256	322	637	288	349	722	309	413
70-74	319	122	197	347	141	207	433	178	255	504	197	307
75-79	177	61	116	220	80	139	231	86	145	314	106	209
80 +	115	36	79	129	41	89	152	47	105	210	50	159

Age group	1990 Both sexes	Males	Females	1995 Both sexes	Males	Females	2000 Both sexes	Males	Females	2005 Both sexes	Males	Females
All ages	42 869	21 568	21 301	45 007	22 668	22 339	46 779	23 525	23 254	47 817	23 973	23 844
0-4	3 280	1 733	1 547	3 438	1 824	1 614	3 076	1 613	1 463	2 412	1 248	1 165
5-9	3 836	1 984	1 852	3 262	1 721	1 541	3 423	1 815	1 608	3 065	1 607	1 458
10-14	3 962	2 044	1 918	3 819	1 974	1 845	3 250	1 714	1 536	3 412	1 809	1 603
15-19	4 464	2 297	2 167	3 930	2 026	1 904	3 788	1 955	1 834	3 222	1 697	1 525
20-24	4 289	2 205	2 083	4 386	2 250	2 136	3 867	1 986	1 881	3 730	1 918	1 812
25-29	4 276	2 181	2 095	4 203	2 152	2 052	4 300	2 198	2 102	3 787	1 939	1 849
30-34	4 096	2 089	2 007	4 221	2 144	2 077	4 129	2 107	2 022	4 230	2 157	2 073
35-39	3 018	1 554	1 464	4 048	2 056	1 992	4 172	2 113	2 060	4 089	2 082	2 007
40-44	2 504	1 284	1 219	2 969	1 519	1 450	3 996	2 019	1 977	4 130	2 083	2 047
45-49	2 202	1 122	1 080	2 447	1 243	1 203	2 917	1 480	1 437	3 942	1 978	1 964
50-54	2 039	1 021	1 018	2 154	1 084	1 070	2 400	1 205	1 195	2 873	1 444	1 429
55-59	1 604	749	856	1 978	973	1 006	2 109	1 043	1 066	2 362	1 168	1 194
60-64	1 156	496	659	1 520	689	831	1 909	914	995	2 050	990	1 060
65-69	904	380	524	1 061	439	622	1 425	624	801	1 801	836	965
70-74	596	234	362	780	312	468	939	370	569	1 276	533	743
75-79	368	124	244	459	168	291	619	230	389	768	279	489
80 +	276	71	206	331	94	237	458	141	318	665	204	462

710

United Nations Department of Economic and Social Affairs/Population Division
World Population Prospects: The 2004 Revision, Volume II: Sex and Age Distribution of the World Population

POPULATION BY AGE AND SEX (in thousands)

Age group	2005 Both sexes	Males	Females	2010 Both sexes	Males	Females	2015 Both sexes	Males	Females	2020 Both sexes	Males	Females
All ages	47 817	23 973	23 844	48 566	24 260	24 306	49 092	24 426	24 666	49 393	24 472	24 921
0-4	2 412	1 248	1 165	2 224	1 139	1 085	2 176	1 114	1 061	2 139	1 096	1 044
5-9	3 065	1 607	1 458	2 409	1 246	1 163	2 221	1 138	1 084	2 173	1 113	1 060
10-14	3 412	1 809	1 603	3 063	1 606	1 457	2 407	1 245	1 162	2 220	1 137	1 083
15-19	3 222	1 697	1 525	3 407	1 805	1 601	3 058	1 603	1 455	2 403	1 242	1 161
20-24	3 730	1 918	1 812	3 211	1 689	1 522	3 396	1 798	1 598	3 049	1 597	1 452
25-29	3 787	1 939	1 849	3 715	1 908	1 807	3 198	1 681	1 518	3 384	1 790	1 594
30-34	4 230	2 157	2 073	3 771	1 928	1 843	3 701	1 899	1 802	3 186	1 673	1 514
35-39	4 089	2 082	2 007	4 208	2 143	2 066	3 754	1 917	1 838	3 686	1 889	1 797
40-44	4 130	2 083	2 047	4 058	2 060	1 998	4 182	2 124	2 058	3 733	1 901	1 832
45-49	3 942	1 978	1 964	4 084	2 049	2 035	4 020	2 032	1 988	4 147	2 098	2 049
50-54	2 873	1 444	1 429	3 876	1 929	1 946	4 024	2 005	2 019	3 967	1 992	1 974
55-59	2 362	1 168	1 194	2 794	1 385	1 409	3 782	1 860	1 921	3 937	1 941	1 996
60-64	2 050	990	1 060	2 257	1 092	1 165	2 683	1 305	1 378	3 648	1 763	1 884
65-69	1 801	836	965	1 914	897	1 017	2 121	998	1 123	2 536	1 202	1 333
70-74	1 276	533	743	1 608	711	897	1 726	773	953	1 930	871	1 059
75-79	768	279	489	1 054	406	649	1 347	552	795	1 469	612	856
80-84	436	143	293	559	178	382	788	265	523	1 032	374	658
85-89	173	48	125	260	69	190	352	89	262	517	141	376
90-94	47	10	37	77	16	61	126	24	102	185	34	151
95-99	8	1	7	14	2	12	26	4	23	47	6	42
100 +	1	0	1	1	0	1	3	0	3	6	0	5

Age group	2025 Both sexes	Males	Females	2030 Both sexes	Males	Females	2035 Both sexes	Males	Females	2040 Both sexes	Males	Females
All ages	49 457	24 391	25 065	49 161	24 128	25 032	48 450	23 660	24 790	47 405	23 027	24 378
0-4	2 107	1 079	1 028	1 985	1 017	969	1 845	945	900	1 779	911	868
5-9	2 137	1 094	1 043	2 104	1 078	1 027	1 983	1 015	968	1 843	944	899
10-14	2 172	1 112	1 060	2 136	1 094	1 042	2 103	1 077	1 026	1 982	1 015	967
15-19	2 216	1 134	1 082	2 169	1 110	1 059	2 133	1 092	1 041	2 100	1 075	1 025
20-24	2 396	1 237	1 159	2 209	1 130	1 080	2 162	1 106	1 056	2 126	1 087	1 039
25-29	3 038	1 589	1 449	2 387	1 231	1 156	2 201	1 124	1 077	2 154	1 100	1 054
30-34	3 373	1 782	1 591	3 028	1 582	1 446	2 378	1 225	1 153	2 192	1 118	1 074
35-39	3 174	1 664	1 510	3 360	1 773	1 587	3 017	1 574	1 443	2 369	1 219	1 150
40-44	3 667	1 875	1 792	3 158	1 652	1 506	3 345	1 762	1 500	3 004	1 564	1 439
45-49	3 704	1 880	1 824	3 641	1 855	1 786	3 137	1 636	1 501	3 324	1 745	1 578
50-54	4 098	2 061	2 037	3 664	1 849	1 814	3 604	1 827	1 776	3 106	1 613	1 493
55-59	3 889	1 935	1 954	4 024	2 006	2 018	3 602	1 804	1 798	3 547	1 785	1 762
60-64	3 811	1 849	1 962	3 773	1 851	1 923	3 912	1 925	1 987	3 508	1 735	1 772
65-69	3 465	1 636	1 829	3 633	1 725	1 908	3 606	1 734	1 873	3 748	1 810	1 938
70-74	2 325	1 061	1 264	3 197	1 456	1 741	3 367	1 546	1 821	3 356	1 564	1 792
75-79	1 665	703	962	2 026	868	1 158	2 808	1 205	1 602	2 977	1 293	1 684
80-84	1 150	427	723	1 326	502	824	1 632	632	1 001	2 289	892	1 397
85-89	698	208	490	799	247	553	938	298	640	1 175	385	789
90-94	285	56	229	399	87	311	468	108	360	563	136	427
95-99	75	8	67	123	15	107	176	25	151	213	32	181
100 +	12	1	11	20	1	19	34	2	32	52	4	48

Age group	2045 Both sexes	Males	Females	2050 Both sexes	Males	Females
All ages	46 111	22 280	23 831	44 629	21 467	23 161
0-4	1 779	911	868	1 800	922	878
5-9	1 778	910	867	1 778	910	867
10-14	1 842	943	899	1 777	910	867
15-19	1 979	1 013	966	1 839	941	898
20-24	2 094	1 071	1 023	1 973	1 009	964
25-29	2 118	1 082	1 036	2 086	1 065	1 021
30-34	2 145	1 094	1 051	2 110	1 076	1 034
35-39	2 184	1 112	1 072	2 138	1 089	1 049
40-44	2 359	1 211	1 148	2 175	1 106	1 069
45-49	2 986	1 551	1 435	2 345	1 201	1 144
50-54	3 293	1 722	1 571	2 960	1 532	1 429
55-59	3 060	1 578	1 482	3 247	1 688	1 559
60-64	3 460	1 722	1 738	2 988	1 526	1 463
65-69	3 369	1 638	1 731	3 330	1 631	1 699
70-74	3 501	1 642	1 859	3 158	1 494	1 664
75-79	2 985	1 320	1 664	3 133	1 400	1 734
80-84	2 452	972	1 480	2 482	1 008	1 474
85-89	1 675	558	1 118	1 823	623	1 200
90-94	720	181	539	1 051	272	779
95-99	264	42	222	348	59	289
100 +	68	6	63	89	8	81

POPULATION BY AGE AND SEX (in thousands)

Age group	2005 Both sexes	Males	Females	2010 Both sexes	Males	Females	2015 Both sexes	Males	Females	2020 Both sexes	Males	Females
All ages	47 817	23 973	23 844	49 027	24 496	24 531	50 236	25 012	25 224	51 332	25 465	25 867
0-4	2 412	1 248	1 165	2 685	1 375	1 310	2 858	1 464	1 394	2 935	1 503	1 432
5-9	3 065	1 607	1 458	2 409	1 246	1 163	2 682	1 374	1 309	2 855	1 462	1 393
10-14	3 412	1 809	1 603	3 063	1 606	1 457	2 407	1 245	1 162	2 681	1 373	1 308
15-19	3 222	1 697	1 525	3 407	1 805	1 601	3 058	1 603	1 455	2 403	1 242	1 161
20-24	3 730	1 918	1 812	3 211	1 689	1 522	3 396	1 798	1 598	3 049	1 597	1 452
25-29	3 787	1 939	1 849	3 715	1 908	1 807	3 198	1 681	1 518	3 384	1 790	1 594
30-34	4 230	2 157	2 073	3 771	1 928	1 843	3 701	1 899	1 802	3 186	1 673	1 514
35-39	4 089	2 082	2 007	4 208	2 143	2 066	3 754	1 917	1 838	3 686	1 889	1 797
40-44	4 130	2 083	2 047	4 058	2 060	1 998	4 182	2 124	2 058	3 733	1 901	1 832
45-49	3 942	1 978	1 964	4 084	2 049	2 035	4 020	2 032	1 988	4 147	2 098	2 049
50-54	2 873	1 444	1 429	3 876	1 929	1 946	4 024	2 005	2 019	3 967	1 992	1 974
55-59	2 362	1 168	1 194	2 794	1 385	1 409	3 782	1 860	1 921	3 937	1 941	1 996
60-64	2 050	990	1 060	2 257	1 092	1 165	2 683	1 305	1 378	3 648	1 763	1 884
65-69	1 801	836	965	1 914	897	1 017	2 121	998	1 123	2 536	1 202	1 333
70-74	1 276	533	743	1 608	711	897	1 726	773	953	1 930	871	1 059
75-79	768	279	489	1 054	406	649	1 347	552	795	1 469	612	856
80-84	436	143	293	559	178	382	788	265	523	1 032	374	658
85-89	173	48	125	260	69	190	352	89	262	517	141	376
90-94	47	10	37	77	16	61	126	24	102	185	34	151
95-99	8	1	7	14	2	12	26	4	23	47	6	42
100 +	1	0	1	1	0	1	3	0	3	6	0	5

Age group	2025 Both sexes	Males	Females	2030 Both sexes	Males	Females	2035 Both sexes	Males	Females	2040 Both sexes	Males	Females
All ages	52 145	25 768	26 377	52 574	25 876	26 698	52 687	25 829	26 858	52 671	25 722	26 949
0-4	2 857	1 463	1 394	2 712	1 389	1 323	2 671	1 368	1 303	2 811	1 439	1 372
5-9	2 932	1 502	1 431	2 854	1 462	1 393	2 710	1 387	1 322	2 669	1 366	1 302
10-14	2 854	1 461	1 392	2 931	1 501	1 430	2 853	1 461	1 392	2 708	1 387	1 322
15-19	2 677	1 370	1 307	2 850	1 459	1 391	2 927	1 498	1 429	2 850	1 459	1 391
20-24	2 396	1 237	1 159	2 670	1 365	1 304	2 843	1 454	1 389	2 920	1 494	1 427
25-29	3 038	1 589	1 449	2 387	1 231	1 156	2 660	1 359	1 301	2 834	1 448	1 386
30-34	3 373	1 782	1 591	3 028	1 582	1 446	2 378	1 225	1 153	2 651	1 353	1 298
35-39	3 174	1 664	1 510	3 360	1 773	1 587	3 017	1 574	1 443	2 369	1 219	1 150
40-44	3 667	1 875	1 792	3 158	1 652	1 506	3 345	1 762	1 583	3 004	1 564	1 439
45-49	3 704	1 880	1 824	3 641	1 855	1 786	3 137	1 636	1 501	3 324	1 745	1 578
50-54	4 098	2 061	2 037	3 664	1 849	1 814	3 604	1 827	1 776	3 106	1 613	1 493
55-59	3 889	1 935	1 954	4 024	2 006	2 018	3 602	1 804	1 798	3 547	1 785	1 762
60-64	3 811	1 849	1 962	3 773	1 851	1 923	3 912	1 925	1 987	3 508	1 735	1 772
65-69	3 465	1 636	1 829	3 633	1 725	1 908	3 606	1 734	1 873	3 748	1 810	1 938
70-74	2 325	1 061	1 264	3 197	1 456	1 741	3 367	1 546	1 821	3 356	1 564	1 792
75-79	1 665	703	962	2 026	868	1 158	2 808	1 205	1 602	2 977	1 293	1 684
80-84	1 150	427	723	1 326	502	824	1 632	632	1 001	2 289	892	1 397
85-89	698	208	490	799	247	553	938	298	640	1 175	385	789
90-94	285	56	229	399	87	311	468	108	360	563	136	427
95-99	75	8	67	123	15	107	176	25	151	213	32	181
100 +	12	1	11	20	1	19	34	2	32	52	4	48

Age group	2045 Both sexes	Males	Females	2050 Both sexes	Males	Females
All ages	52 586	25 593	26 993	52 409	25 448	26 961
0-4	2 994	1 533	1 461	3 111	1 593	1 518
5-9	2 809	1 438	1 371	2 992	1 532	1 460
10-14	2 667	1 366	1 302	2 808	1 437	1 370
15-19	2 705	1 385	1 321	2 664	1 364	1 301
20-24	2 843	1 454	1 389	2 699	1 380	1 319
25-29	2 911	1 487	1 424	2 834	1 448	1 386
30-34	2 825	1 441	1 383	2 902	1 481	1 421
35-39	2 642	1 346	1 296	2 815	1 435	1 380
40-44	2 359	1 211	1 148	2 631	1 338	1 293
45-49	2 986	1 551	1 435	2 345	1 201	1 144
50-54	3 293	1 722	1 571	2 960	1 532	1 429
55-59	3 060	1 578	1 482	3 247	1 688	1 559
60-64	3 460	1 722	1 738	2 988	1 526	1 463
65-69	3 369	1 638	1 731	3 330	1 631	1 699
70-74	3 501	1 642	1 859	3 158	1 494	1 664
75-79	2 985	1 320	1 664	3 133	1 400	1 734
80-84	2 452	972	1 480	2 482	1 008	1 474
85-89	1 675	558	1 118	1 823	623	1 200
90-94	720	181	539	1 051	272	779
95-99	264	42	222	348	59	289
100 +	68	6	63	89	8	81

United Nations Department of Economic and Social Affairs/Population Division
World Population Prospects: The 2004 Revision, Volume II: Sex and Age Distribution of the World Population

POPULATION BY AGE AND SEX (in thousands)

Age group	2005 Both sexes	Males	Females	2010 Both sexes	Males	Females	2015 Both sexes	Males	Females	2020 Both sexes	Males	Females
All ages	47 817	23 973	23 844	48 104	24 024	24 000	47 948	23 840	24 108	47 454	23 479	23 975
0-4	2 412	1 248	1 165	1 762	903	860	1 493	765	728	1 344	688	656
5-9	3 065	1 607	1 458	2 409	1 246	1 163	1 760	901	859	1 491	764	727
10-14	3 412	1 809	1 603	3 063	1 606	1 457	2 407	1 245	1 162	1 759	901	858
15-19	3 222	1 697	1 525	3 407	1 805	1 601	3 058	1 603	1 455	2 403	1 242	1 161
20-24	3 730	1 918	1 812	3 211	1 689	1 522	3 396	1 798	1 598	3 049	1 597	1 452
25-29	3 787	1 939	1 849	3 715	1 908	1 807	3 198	1 681	1 518	3 384	1 790	1 594
30-34	4 230	2 157	2 073	3 771	1 928	1 843	3 701	1 899	1 802	3 186	1 673	1 514
35-39	4 089	2 082	2 007	4 208	2 143	2 066	3 754	1 917	1 838	3 686	1 889	1 797
40-44	4 130	2 083	2 047	4 058	2 060	1 998	4 182	2 124	2 058	3 733	1 901	1 832
45-49	3 942	1 978	1 964	4 084	2 049	2 035	4 020	2 032	1 988	4 147	2 098	2 049
50-54	2 873	1 444	1 429	3 876	1 929	1 946	4 024	2 005	2 019	3 967	1 992	1 974
55-59	2 362	1 168	1 194	2 794	1 385	1 409	3 782	1 860	1 921	3 937	1 941	1 996
60-64	2 050	990	1 060	2 257	1 092	1 165	2 683	1 305	1 378	3 648	1 763	1 884
65-69	1 801	836	965	1 914	897	1 017	2 121	998	1 123	2 536	1 202	1 333
70-74	1 276	533	743	1 608	711	897	1 726	773	953	1 930	871	1 059
75-79	768	279	489	1 054	406	649	1 347	552	795	1 469	612	856
80-84	436	143	293	559	178	382	788	265	523	1 032	374	658
85-89	173	48	125	260	69	190	352	89	262	517	141	376
90-94	47	10	37	77	16	61	126	24	102	185	34	151
95-99	8	1	7	14	2	12	26	4	23	47	6	42
100 +	1	0	1	1	0	1	3	0	3	6	0	5

Age group	2025 Both sexes	Males	Females	2030 Both sexes	Males	Females	2035 Both sexes	Males	Females	2040 Both sexes	Males	Females
All ages	46 772	23 017	23 755	45 779	22 397	23 382	44 359	21 566	22 793	42 513	20 523	21 990
0-4	1 359	696	663	1 288	659	628	1 132	580	552	975	499	476
5-9	1 342	687	655	1 357	695	662	1 286	659	628	1 131	579	552
10-14	1 490	763	727	1 341	687	654	1 356	695	662	1 285	658	627
15-19	1 756	899	857	1 487	761	726	1 339	685	653	1 354	693	661
20-24	2 396	1 237	1 159	1 749	894	855	1 481	757	724	1 333	681	652
25-29	3 038	1 589	1 449	2 387	1 231	1 156	1 741	889	852	1 473	752	721
30-34	3 373	1 782	1 591	3 028	1 582	1 446	2 378	1 225	1 153	1 733	884	850
35-39	3 174	1 664	1 510	3 360	1 773	1 587	3 017	1 574	1 443	2 369	1 219	1 150
40-44	3 667	1 875	1 792	3 158	1 652	1 506	3 045	1 762	1 583	3 004	1 564	1 439
45-49	3 704	1 880	1 824	3 641	1 855	1 786	3 137	1 636	1 501	3 324	1 745	1 578
50-54	4 098	2 061	2 037	3 664	1 849	1 814	3 604	1 827	1 776	3 106	1 613	1 493
55-59	3 889	1 935	1 954	4 024	2 006	2 018	3 602	1 804	1 798	3 547	1 785	1 762
60-64	3 811	1 849	1 962	3 773	1 851	1 923	3 912	1 925	1 987	3 508	1 735	1 772
65-69	3 465	1 636	1 829	3 033	1 705	2 008	3 606	1 734	1 873	3 748	1 810	1 938
70-74	2 325	1 061	1 264	3 197	1 456	1 741	3 367	1 546	1 821	3 356	1 564	1 792
75-79	1 665	703	962	2 026	868	1 158	2 808	1 205	1 602	2 977	1 293	1 684
80-84	1 150	427	723	1 326	502	824	1 602	632	1 001	2 289	892	1 397
85-89	698	208	490	799	247	553	938	298	640	1 175	385	789
90-94	285	56	229	399	87	311	468	108	360	563	136	427
95-99	75	8	67	123	15	107	176	25	151	213	32	181
100 +	12	1	11	20	1	19	34	2	32	52	4	48

Age group	2045 Both sexes	Males	Females	2050 Both sexes	Males	Females
All ages	40 323	19 318	21 005	37 894	18 022	19 872
0-4	880	450	429	847	434	413
5-9	974	499	475	878	450	429
10-14	1 130	578	551	973	498	475
15-19	1 283	656	626	1 128	577	551
20-24	1 348	689	659	1 277	653	624
25-29	1 325	676	649	1 341	684	657
30-34	1 466	747	719	1 319	672	647
35-39	1 726	878	848	1 460	743	717
40-44	2 359	1 211	1 148	1 718	873	846
45-49	2 986	1 551	1 435	2 345	1 201	1 144
50-54	3 293	1 722	1 571	2 960	1 532	1 429
55-59	3 060	1 578	1 482	3 247	1 688	1 559
60-64	3 460	1 722	1 738	2 988	1 526	1 463
65-69	3 369	1 638	1 731	3 330	1 631	1 699
70-74	3 501	1 642	1 859	3 158	1 494	1 664
75-79	2 985	1 320	1 664	3 133	1 400	1 734
80-84	2 452	972	1 480	2 482	1 008	1 474
85-89	1 675	558	1 118	1 823	623	1 200
90-94	720	181	539	1 051	272	779
95-99	264	42	222	348	59	289
100 +	68	6	63	89	8	81

POPULATION BY AGE AND SEX (in thousands)

Age group	1950 Both sexes	Males	Females	1955 Both sexes	Males	Females	1960 Both sexes	Males	Females	1965 Both sexes	Males	Females
All ages	2 341	1 093	1 248	2 627	1 227	1 400	3 004	1 405	1 598	3 335	1 561	1 774
0-4	203	103	100	321	163	158	398	203	196	393	200	193
5-9	205	104	101	211	107	104	334	170	164	407	207	200
10-14	250	127	123	214	109	106	222	113	109	343	174	169
15-19	223	109	114	261	123	138	225	105	120	230	106	123
20-24	225	106	118	232	113	119	270	127	144	230	107	123
25-29	201	92	109	232	109	123	240	115	125	275	128	147
30-34	132	62	70	207	94	113	240	111	129	245	116	128
35-39	183	84	98	135	63	72	212	95	117	242	111	131
40-44	143	68	76	185	84	101	139	64	75	213	94	119
45-49	137	61	75	143	66	77	185	82	102	139	63	76
50-54	99	43	56	133	58	75	140	63	77	178	77	100
55-59	78	35	44	93	40	54	126	53	72	132	58	74
60-64	82	34	49	71	30	41	86	35	51	114	47	67
65-69	68	27	41	71	28	43	62	25	37	74	29	45
70-74	52	19	33	54	20	34	57	21	36	50	19	31
75-79	35	11	24	36	12	24	38	13	25	40	14	26
80 +	26	8	18	27	8	19	28	9	20	30	10	21

Age group	1970 Both sexes	Males	Females	1975 Both sexes	Males	Females	1980 Both sexes	Males	Females	1985 Both sexes	Males	Females
All ages	3 595	1 681	1 914	3 839	1 804	2 035	4 010	1 896	2 114	4 215	2 001	2 214
0-4	340	173	167	371	187	183	378	192	186	419	213	206
5-9	399	203	196	339	171	168	360	182	178	376	191	185
10-14	415	211	204	398	202	197	333	168	165	352	179	173
15-19	349	167	182	399	201	198	379	189	190	336	167	169
20-24	233	108	126	353	170	184	367	179	188	352	172	179
25-29	233	108	126	244	116	128	346	168	178	373	183	190
30-34	277	128	149	233	108	125	266	129	137	346	169	177
35-39	246	116	130	273	126	147	218	103	116	262	127	135
40-44	242	110	132	240	113	127	265	123	142	212	99	113
45-49	209	91	118	237	107	130	232	109	123	251	116	136
50-54	134	59	75	209	88	121	232	104	128	221	101	120
55-59	167	71	96	129	55	74	197	81	117	219	95	123
60-64	120	51	69	153	64	89	124	51	73	178	71	107
65-69	99	39	60	106	42	64	130	52	78	106	42	64
70-74	60	22	38	76	29	47	85	33	53	104	40	65
75-79	36	13	23	43	15	28	55	20	35	61	22	39
80 +	33	11	23	37	12	25	40	13	28	47	15	33

Age group	1990 Both sexes	Males	Females	1995 Both sexes	Males	Females	2000 Both sexes	Males	Females	2005 Both sexes	Males	Females
All ages	4 364	2 080	2 284	4 339	2 073	2 266	4 275	2 043	2 232	4 206	2 010	2 195
0-4	427	218	209	328	168	160	248	127	121	207	106	101
5-9	415	211	204	418	213	205	321	164	157	245	126	119
10-14	376	191	185	408	207	201	411	209	202	318	162	155
15-19	340	171	170	366	185	181	400	203	198	406	207	199
20-24	292	147	145	319	159	160	358	181	177	395	199	195
25-29	340	164	176	279	140	139	311	154	157	352	177	175
30-34	375	182	193	328	158	171	271	135	136	305	151	155
35-39	344	167	177	360	174	187	318	151	167	264	131	133
40-44	254	122	132	327	157	170	346	165	181	308	145	163
45-49	202	94	109	237	112	125	311	147	164	332	156	176
50-54	236	107	129	188	85	103	221	102	119	293	136	157
55-59	204	91	113	213	94	119	170	75	95	204	92	112
60-64	197	83	114	177	77	101	187	80	107	151	64	87
65-69	152	59	94	163	66	97	147	61	87	158	64	94
70-74	83	31	52	116	42	74	125	47	78	116	45	71
75-79	73	26	47	56	20	36	78	26	52	87	31	57
80 +	53	17	37	57	18	39	51	15	35	64	19	45

United Nations Department of Economic and Social Affairs/Population Division
World Population Prospects: The 2004 Revision, Volume II: Sex and Age Distribution of the World Population

714

POPULATION BY AGE AND SEX (in thousands)

Age group	2005			2010			2015			2020		
	Both sexes	Males	Females	Both sexes	Males	Females	Both sexes	Males	Females	Both sexes	Males	Females
All ages	4 206	2 010	2 195	4 160	1 990	2 170	4 114	1 970	2 144	4 054	1 943	2 111
0-4	207	106	101	214	110	104	214	110	104	202	104	98
5-9	245	126	119	204	105	99	211	108	103	211	109	103
10-14	318	162	155	242	124	118	202	104	98	209	107	102
15-19	406	207	199	314	160	154	239	123	117	200	102	97
20-24	395	199	195	401	204	197	310	158	152	236	121	115
25-29	352	177	175	389	196	193	396	200	195	306	155	150
30-34	305	151	155	346	173	173	383	192	191	390	197	193
35-39	264	131	133	299	147	152	339	169	170	376	188	188
40-44	308	145	163	257	126	131	292	142	150	332	164	167
45-49	332	156	176	298	138	159	248	121	128	283	137	146
50-54	293	136	157	316	146	170	285	131	154	238	114	124
55-59	204	92	112	274	124	149	297	135	162	268	121	147
60-64	151	64	87	184	80	104	249	110	140	272	120	152
65-69	158	64	94	131	53	78	161	67	93	219	93	127
70-74	116	45	71	128	49	79	107	41	66	133	53	80
75-79	87	31	57	84	30	54	95	34	61	81	29	52
80-84	45	14	31	53	17	37	53	17	36	61	20	42
85-89	13	4	9	21	6	16	26	7	19	27	7	19
90-94	5	1	4	4	1	3	7	2	6	10	2	7
95-99	1	0	1	1	0	1	1	0	1	2	0	2
100 +	0	0	0	0	0	0	0	0	0	0	0	0

Age group	2025			2030			2035			2040		
	Both sexes	Males	Females	Both sexes	Males	Females	Both sexes	Males	Females	Both sexes	Males	Females
All ages	3 967	1 902	2 065	3 856	1 849	2 007	3 729	1 789	1 940	3 595	1 726	1 869
0-4	181	93	88	161	83	78	152	78	74	152	78	74
5-9	200	103	97	178	92	87	159	82	77	150	77	73
10-14	209	107	102	198	102	96	176	91	86	157	81	76
15-19	206	106	100	207	106	101	196	100	95	174	89	85
20-24	197	101	96	204	104	99	204	105	99	193	99	94
25-29	233	119	114	194	99	95	201	103	98	201	103	98
30-34	301	153	148	229	117	112	191	98	94	198	101	97
35-39	383	193	190	290	150	146	226	115	111	188	96	92
40-44	368	183	185	375	188	187	290	146	144	221	112	109
45-49	322	158	164	358	177	181	366	183	184	283	142	141
50-54	272	130	142	310	151	159	346	169	176	355	175	179
55-59	224	106	118	258	121	137	295	142	153	330	160	170
60-64	247	108	139	208	96	112	240	110	130	276	130	146
65-69	241	102	139	221	93	127	186	83	103	217	97	120
70-74	184	74	110	204	82	122	188	76	112	160	69	91
75-79	101	38	64	143	54	89	161	61	100	150	57	93
80-84	53	17	36	68	23	45	98	34	64	113	39	74
85-89	32	9	23	29	8	21	38	11	27	56	17	40
90-94	10	2	8	13	3	10	12	3	9	17	4	13
95-99	3	0	2	3	0	2	4	1	3	4	1	3
100 +	0	0	0	0	0	0	1	0	0	1	0	1

Age group	2045			2050		
	Both sexes	Males	Females	Both sexes	Males	Females
All ages	3 456	1 662	1 794	3 312	1 594	1 718
0-4	153	79	74	149	76	72
5-9	150	77	73	151	78	73
10-14	148	76	72	148	76	72
15-19	155	80	75	146	75	71
20-24	172	88	84	153	78	74
25-29	191	98	93	170	87	83
30-34	199	102	97	188	96	92
35-39	195	100	95	195	100	96
40-44	185	94	91	191	98	94
45-49	216	109	107	180	91	89
50-54	274	137	138	209	105	104
55-59	339	166	173	262	129	133
60-64	309	147	162	319	153	166
65-69	250	115	136	282	130	152
70-74	188	80	107	218	96	122
75-79	129	52	77	153	62	91
80-84	107	37	70	93	34	58
85-89	66	20	46	64	19	45
90-94	25	6	19	31	7	23
95-99	5	1	4	8	1	7
100 +	1	0	1	1	0	1

POPULATION BY AGE AND SEX (in thousands)

Age group	2005 Both sexes	Males	Females	2010 Both sexes	Males	Females	2015 Both sexes	Males	Females	2020 Both sexes	Males	Females
All ages	4 206	2 010	2 195	4 205	2 013	2 192	4 228	2 028	2 199	4 241	2 039	2 202
0-4	207	106	101	258	133	126	283	145	137	276	142	134
5-9	245	126	119	204	105	99	256	131	124	280	144	136
10-14	318	162	155	242	124	118	202	104	98	253	130	123
15-19	406	207	199	314	160	154	239	123	117	200	102	97
20-24	395	199	195	401	204	197	310	158	152	236	121	115
25-29	352	177	175	389	196	193	396	200	195	306	155	150
30-34	305	151	155	346	173	173	383	192	191	390	197	193
35-39	264	131	133	299	147	152	339	169	170	376	188	188
40-44	308	145	163	257	126	131	292	142	150	332	164	167
45-49	332	156	176	298	138	159	248	121	128	283	137	146
50-54	293	136	157	316	146	170	285	131	154	238	114	124
55-59	204	92	112	274	124	149	297	135	162	268	121	147
60-64	151	64	87	184	80	104	249	110	140	272	120	152
65-69	158	64	94	131	53	78	161	67	93	219	93	127
70-74	116	45	71	128	49	79	107	41	66	133	53	80
75-79	87	31	57	84	30	54	95	34	61	81	29	52
80-84	45	14	31	53	17	37	53	17	36	61	20	42
85-89	13	4	9	21	6	16	26	7	19	27	7	19
90-94	5	1	4	4	1	3	7	2	6	10	2	7
95-99	1	0	1	1	0	1	1	0	1	2	0	2
100 +	0	0	0	0	0	0	0	0	0	0	0	0

Age group	2025 Both sexes	Males	Females	2030 Both sexes	Males	Females	2035 Both sexes	Males	Females	2040 Both sexes	Males	Females
All ages	4 216	2 030	2 186	4 165	2 008	2 157	4 115	1 987	2 128	4 079	1 974	2 104
0-4	242	124	118	222	114	108	229	118	111	251	129	122
5-9	274	141	133	240	123	116	220	113	107	227	117	110
10-14	277	143	135	272	140	132	237	122	115	218	112	106
15-19	251	129	122	275	141	134	269	138	131	235	121	114
20-24	197	101	96	248	127	121	272	140	133	267	137	130
25-29	233	119	114	194	99	95	245	126	120	269	138	131
30-34	301	153	148	229	117	112	191	98	94	242	124	118
35-39	383	193	190	296	150	146	226	115	111	188	96	92
40-44	368	183	185	375	188	187	290	146	144	221	112	109
45-49	322	158	164	358	177	181	366	183	184	283	142	141
50-54	272	130	142	310	151	159	346	169	176	355	175	179
55-59	224	106	118	258	121	137	295	142	153	330	160	170
60-64	247	108	139	208	96	112	240	110	130	276	130	146
65-69	241	102	139	221	93	127	186	83	103	217	97	120
70-74	184	74	110	204	82	122	188	76	112	160	69	91
75-79	101	38	64	143	54	89	161	61	100	150	57	93
80-84	53	17	36	68	23	45	98	34	64	113	39	74
85-89	32	9	23	29	8	21	38	11	27	56	17	40
90-94	10	2	8	13	3	10	12	3	9	17	4	13
95-99	3	0	2	3	0	2	4	1	3	4	1	3
100 +	0	0	0	0	0	0	1	0	0	1	0	1

Age group	2045 Both sexes	Males	Females	2050 Both sexes	Males	Females
All ages	4 050	1 966	2 084	4 016	1 955	2 060
0-4	264	136	128	260	133	126
5-9	249	128	121	262	135	127
10-14	225	116	109	247	127	120
15-19	216	111	105	223	115	108
20-24	233	120	113	214	110	104
25-29	264	135	129	230	118	112
30-34	266	136	130	261	134	127
35-39	239	122	117	263	134	129
40-44	185	94	91	235	120	115
45-49	216	109	107	180	91	89
50-54	274	137	138	209	105	104
55-59	339	166	173	262	129	133
60-64	309	147	162	319	153	166
65-69	250	115	136	282	130	152
70-74	188	80	107	218	96	122
75-79	129	52	77	153	62	91
80-84	107	37	70	93	34	58
85-89	66	20	46	64	19	45
90-94	25	6	19	31	7	23
95-99	5	1	4	8	1	7
100 +	1	0	1	1	0	1

United Nations Department of Economic and Social Affairs/Population Division
World Population Prospects: The 2004 Revision, Volume II: Sex and Age Distribution of the World Population

716

POPULATION BY AGE AND SEX (in thousands)

Age group	2005			2010			2015			2020		
	Both sexes	Males	Females	Both sexes	Males	Females	Both sexes	Males	Females	Both sexes	Males	Females
All ages	4 206	2 010	2 195	4 116	1 967	2 149	4 001	1 912	2 089	3 865	1 845	2 019
0-4	207	106	101	169	87	82	145	74	70	126	65	61
5-9	245	126	119	204	105	99	166	85	81	142	73	69
10-14	318	162	155	242	124	118	202	104	98	164	84	80
15-19	406	207	199	314	160	154	239	123	117	200	102	97
20-24	395	199	195	401	204	197	310	158	152	236	121	115
25-29	352	177	175	389	196	193	396	200	195	306	155	150
30-34	305	151	155	346	173	173	383	192	191	390	197	193
35-39	264	131	133	299	147	152	339	169	170	376	188	188
40-44	308	145	163	257	126	131	292	142	150	332	164	167
45-49	332	156	176	298	138	159	248	121	128	283	137	146
50-54	293	136	157	316	146	170	285	131	154	238	114	124
55-59	204	92	112	274	124	149	297	135	162	268	121	147
60-64	151	64	87	184	80	104	249	110	140	272	120	152
65-69	158	64	94	131	53	78	161	67	93	219	93	127
70-74	116	45	71	128	49	79	107	41	66	133	53	80
75-79	87	31	57	84	30	54	95	34	61	81	29	52
80-84	45	14	31	53	17	37	53	17	36	61	20	42
85-89	13	4	9	21	6	16	26	7	19	27	7	19
90-94	5	1	4	4	1	3	7	2	6	10	2	7
95-99	1	0	1	1	0	1	1	0	1	2	0	2
100 +	0	0	0	0	0	0	0	0	0	0	0	0

Age group	2025			2030			2035			2040		
	Both sexes	Males	Females	Both sexes	Males	Females	Both sexes	Males	Females	Both sexes	Males	Females
All ages	3 715	1 773	1 943	3 548	1 691	1 857	3 361	1 600	1 761	3 158	1 502	1 656
0-4	117	60	57	104	53	51	92	47	45	82	42	40
5-9	124	64	60	115	59	56	102	53	50	90	46	44
10-14	140	72	68	122	63	59	113	58	55	100	52	49
15-19	162	83	79	138	71	67	120	62	58	111	57	54
20-24	197	101	96	159	82	78	136	70	66	118	60	57
25-29	233	119	114	194	99	95	157	80	77	133	68	65
30-34	301	153	148	229	117	112	191	98	94	154	79	75
35-39	383	193	190	296	150	146	226	115	111	188	96	92
40-44	360	180	185	375	188	187	290	146	144	221	112	109
45-49	322	158	164	358	177	181	366	183	184	283	142	141
50-54	272	130	142	310	151	159	346	169	176	355	175	179
55-59	224	106	118	258	121	137	295	142	153	330	160	170
60-64	247	108	139	208	96	112	240	110	130	276	130	146
65-69	241	102	139	221	93	127	186	83	103	217	97	120
70-74	184	74	110	204	82	122	188	76	112	160	69	91
75-79	101	38	64	143	54	89	161	61	100	150	57	93
80-84	53	17	36	68	23	45	98	34	64	113	39	74
85-89	32	9	23	29	8	21	38	11	27	56	17	40
90-94	10	2	8	13	3	10	12	3	9	17	4	13
95-99	3	0	2	3	0	2	4	1	3	4	1	3
100 +	0	0	0	0	0	0	1	0	0	1	0	1

Age group	2045			2050		
	Both sexes	Males	Females	Both sexes	Males	Females
All ages	2 941	1 397	1 543	2 717	1 289	1 428
0-4	74	38	36	68	35	33
5-9	80	41	39	72	37	35
10-14	88	45	43	78	40	38
15-19	98	51	48	86	44	42
20-24	109	56	53	96	50	47
25-29	115	59	56	107	55	52
30-34	130	67	64	113	58	55
35-39	151	77	74	128	65	62
40-44	185	94	91	148	75	73
45-49	216	109	107	180	91	89
50-54	274	137	138	209	105	104
55-59	339	166	173	262	129	133
60-64	309	147	162	319	153	166
65-69	250	115	136	282	130	152
70-74	188	80	107	218	96	122
75-79	129	52	77	153	62	91
80-84	107	37	70	93	34	58
85-89	66	20	46	64	19	45
90-94	25	6	19	31	7	23
95-99	5	1	4	8	1	7
100 +	1	0	1	1	0	1

United Nations Department of Economic and Social Affairs/Population Division
World Population Prospects: The 2004 Revision, Volume II: Sex and Age Distribution of the World Population

717

POPULATION BY AGE AND SEX (in thousands)

Age group	1950 Both sexes	1950 Males	1950 Females	1955 Both sexes	1955 Males	1955 Females	1960 Both sexes	1960 Males	1960 Females	1965 Both sexes	1965 Males	1965 Females
All ages	248	119	129	291	141	150	335	163	172	390	190	199
0-4	42	21	21	56	28	28	57	29	29	65	32	32
5-9	31	16	16	40	20	20	54	27	27	59	29	30
10-14	25	11	14	31	15	15	40	20	20	54	27	27
15-19	24	12	13	25	11	14	30	15	15	40	20	20
20-24	21	11	11	24	12	12	24	11	14	27	13	14
25-29	21	10	10	21	10	10	23	11	12	24	12	13
30-34	17	8	8	20	10	10	20	10	10	24	12	12
35-39	15	7	7	16	8	8	19	10	10	20	10	10
40-44	12	6	6	14	7	7	16	8	8	18	9	9
45-49	10	5	5	12	6	6	14	7	7	15	7	8
50-54	8	4	4	10	5	5	11	5	6	12	6	6
55-59	7	3	4	7	3	4	9	4	5	10	5	5
60-64	5	2	3	6	2	4	6	3	4	8	3	4
65-69	4	1	3	5	2	3	5	2	3	5	2	3
70-74	3	1	2	3	1	2	3	1	2	4	1	2
75-79	2	1	1	2	0	1	2	1	1	2	1	2
80 +	1	0	1	1	0	1	1	0	1	2	0	1

Age group	1970 Both sexes	1970 Males	1970 Females	1975 Both sexes	1975 Males	1975 Females	1980 Both sexes	1980 Males	1980 Females	1985 Both sexes	1985 Males	1985 Females
All ages	461	222	238	483	235	248	506	248	259	555	271	283
0-4	76	38	39	62	31	31	58	29	29	63	32	31
5-9	70	34	36	71	36	36	63	32	31	61	31	30
10-14	64	32	32	69	34	34	67	34	33	61	31	30
15-19	47	23	24	56	28	29	66	33	33	60	29	31
20-24	32	15	17	39	18	21	44	21	23	57	28	29
25-29	29	14	15	31	15	16	37	18	19	47	23	24
30-34	28	14	14	28	14	14	32	16	16	41	20	21
35-39	23	11	12	26	13	13	27	14	14	32	16	16
40-44	22	11	11	22	11	11	24	12	12	27	14	14
45-49	18	9	9	19	10	10	21	10	11	24	12	12
50-54	15	7	8	17	8	9	18	9	9	20	9	11
55-59	12	6	6	13	6	7	15	7	8	17	8	9
60-64	9	4	5	11	5	6	12	5	6	14	7	8
65-69	6	2	4	8	3	4	9	4	5	10	4	6
70-74	4	2	3	5	2	3	6	2	4	8	3	5
75-79	3	1	2	3	1	2	4	1	2	6	2	4
80 +	2	1	2	3	1	2	3	1	3	5	1	4

Age group	1990 Both sexes	1990 Males	1990 Females	1995 Both sexes	1995 Males	1995 Females	2000 Both sexes	2000 Males	2000 Females	2005 Both sexes	2005 Males	2005 Females
All ages	604	296	308	664	325	339	724	354	370	785	384	402
0-4	64	32	32	67	34	33	69	35	34	75	38	37
5-9	63	31	31	65	33	32	68	34	34	69	35	34
10-14	61	31	31	66	33	33	68	34	34	70	35	35
15-19	62	31	31	62	31	31	66	33	32	68	35	34
20-24	59	29	30	56	28	28	56	28	28	62	31	31
25-29	57	28	29	59	28	31	56	27	29	56	27	28
30-34	47	23	24	63	31	32	65	31	34	59	28	31
35-39	41	20	21	48	24	24	64	32	32	66	32	34
40-44	32	16	16	41	21	21	49	25	24	64	32	32
45-49	27	13	13	32	16	16	41	20	21	48	24	24
50-54	24	12	12	26	13	13	31	15	16	40	19	21
55-59	19	9	10	23	11	12	25	12	13	30	14	16
60-64	16	8	9	18	8	10	21	10	11	24	11	13
65-69	13	6	7	14	6	8	16	7	9	19	9	11
70-74	9	3	5	11	5	6	12	5	7	14	6	8
75-79	6	2	4	7	2	4	9	3	5	10	4	6
80 +	6	2	4	7	2	5	8	2	6	11	3	7

United Nations Department of Economic and Social Affairs/Population Division
World Population Prospects: The 2004 Revision, Volume II: Sex and Age Distribution of the World Population

POPULATION BY AGE AND SEX (in thousands)

Age group	2005 Both sexes	Males	Females	2010 Both sexes	Males	Females	2015 Both sexes	Males	Females	2020 Both sexes	Males	Females
All ages	785	384	402	838	409	429	886	432	454	931	453	478
0-4	75	38	37	75	38	37	73	37	36	72	37	36
5-9	69	35	34	75	38	37	75	38	37	73	37	36
10-14	70	35	35	69	35	34	75	38	37	75	38	37
15-19	68	35	34	70	35	35	69	35	34	75	38	37
20-24	62	31	31	68	34	34	70	35	35	69	35	34
25-29	56	27	28	62	31	31	68	34	34	70	35	34
30-34	59	28	31	55	27	28	62	31	31	68	34	33
35-39	66	32	34	59	28	31	55	27	28	61	31	31
40-44	64	32	32	65	31	34	58	28	30	55	27	28
45-49	48	24	24	63	32	32	64	31	34	58	27	30
50-54	40	19	21	47	23	24	62	31	31	63	30	33
55-59	30	14	16	39	18	20	45	22	23	60	29	31
60-64	24	11	13	28	13	15	37	17	20	43	21	23
65-69	19	9	11	22	10	12	26	11	15	34	15	19
70-74	14	6	8	17	7	10	19	8	11	23	9	13
75-79	10	4	6	11	4	7	14	5	9	15	6	10
80-84	6	2	4	7	2	5	8	3	6	10	3	7
85-89	3	1	2	4	1	3	4	1	3	5	1	4
90-94	1	0	1	1	0	1	2	0	1	2	0	2
95-99	0	0	0	0	0	0	0	0	0	1	0	1
100 +	0	0	0	0	0	0	0	0	0	0	0	0

Age group	2025 Both sexes	Males	Females	2030 Both sexes	Males	Females	2035 Both sexes	Males	Females	2040 Both sexes	Males	Females
All ages	972	472	500	1 007	488	519	1 038	502	536	1 061	513	549
0-4	72	36	36	71	36	35	70	35	35	68	34	34
5-9	72	36	36	72	36	36	71	36	35	70	35	35
10-14	73	37	36	72	36	36	72	36	36	71	36	35
15-19	75	38	37	73	37	36	72	36	36	72	36	36
20-24	74	37	37	75	37	37	73	37	36	72	36	36
25-29	69	35	34	74	37	37	74	37	37	73	37	36
30-34	69	35	34	69	35	34	74	37	37	74	37	37
35-39	67	34	33	69	35	34	69	34	34	74	37	37
40-44	61	31	30	67	34	33	69	35	34	68	34	34
45-49	54	26	28	60	30	30	66	33	33	68	34	34
50-54	57	27	30	53	26	27	59	30	30	65	33	33
55-59	61	29	33	55	26	29	52	25	27	58	29	29
60-64	57	27	30	59	27	32	53	24	29	50	23	26
65-69	40	18	22	53	25	28	54	24	30	49	22	27
70-74	30	13	17	35	15	20	47	21	26	49	20	28
75-79	19	7	12	25	9	15	29	12	18	40	16	23
80-84	11	4	8	14	5	9	19	6	12	22	8	14
85-89	6	2	5	7	2	5	9	2	7	12	3	9
90-94	2	1	2	3	1	3	4	1	3	5	1	4
95-99	1	0	1	1	0	1	1	0	1	1	0	1
100 +	0	0	0	0	0	0	0	0	0	0	0	0

Age group	2045 Both sexes	Males	Females	2050 Both sexes	Males	Females
All ages	1 079	521	558	1 092	527	565
0-4	66	33	33	66	33	33
5-9	68	34	34	66	33	33
10-14	70	35	35	68	34	34
15-19	71	36	35	70	35	35
20-24	72	36	36	71	36	35
25-29	72	36	36	72	36	36
30-34	72	36	36	72	36	36
35-39	74	37	37	72	36	36
40-44	73	37	37	74	37	37
45-49	68	34	34	73	36	36
50-54	67	33	34	67	33	33
55-59	64	32	32	66	32	33
60-64	56	27	29	61	30	31
65-69	46	21	25	52	25	28
70-74	44	19	26	42	18	24
75-79	41	16	25	38	15	23
80-84	30	11	19	32	11	21
85-89	15	4	10	20	6	14
90-94	6	1	5	8	2	6
95-99	2	0	2	2	0	2
100 +	0	0	0	0	0	0

United Nations Department of Economic and Social Affairs/Population Division
World Population Prospects: The 2004 Revision, Volume II: Sex and Age Distribution of the World Population

719

POPULATION BY AGE AND SEX (in thousands)

Age group	2005 Both sexes	Males	Females	2010 Both sexes	Males	Females	2015 Both sexes	Males	Females	2020 Both sexes	Males	Females
All ages	785	384	402	846	413	433	907	442	465	968	471	496
0-4	75	38	37	82	42	41	86	43	42	89	45	44
5-9	69	35	34	75	38	37	82	41	41	86	43	42
10-14	70	35	35	69	35	34	75	38	37	82	41	41
15-19	68	35	34	70	35	35	69	35	34	75	38	37
20-24	62	31	31	68	34	34	70	35	35	69	35	34
25-29	56	27	28	62	31	31	68	34	34	70	35	34
30-34	59	28	31	55	27	28	62	31	31	68	34	33
35-39	66	32	34	59	28	31	55	27	28	61	31	31
40-44	64	32	32	65	31	34	58	28	30	55	27	28
45-49	48	24	24	63	32	32	64	31	34	58	27	30
50-54	40	19	21	47	23	24	62	31	31	63	30	33
55-59	30	14	16	39	18	20	45	22	23	60	29	31
60-64	24	11	13	28	13	15	37	17	20	43	21	23
65-69	19	9	11	22	10	12	26	11	15	34	15	19
70-74	14	6	8	17	7	10	19	8	11	23	9	13
75-79	10	4	6	11	4	7	14	5	9	15	6	10
80-84	6	2	4	7	2	5	8	3	6	10	3	7
85-89	3	1	2	4	1	3	4	1	3	5	1	4
90-94	1	0	1	1	0	1	2	0	1	2	0	2
95-99	0	0	0	0	0	0	0	0	0	1	0	1
100 +	0	0	0	0	0	0	0	0	0	0	0	0

Age group	2025 Both sexes	Males	Females	2030 Both sexes	Males	Females	2035 Both sexes	Males	Females	2040 Both sexes	Males	Females
All ages	1 026	499	527	1 081	525	556	1 134	551	584	1 186	576	611
0-4	89	45	44	91	46	45	94	47	46	97	49	48
5-9	89	45	44	89	45	44	91	46	45	94	47	46
10-14	86	43	42	89	45	44	89	45	44	91	46	45
15-19	82	41	41	85	43	42	89	45	44	89	45	44
20-24	74	37	37	82	41	41	85	43	42	89	45	44
25-29	69	35	34	74	37	37	82	41	41	85	43	42
30-34	69	35	34	69	35	34	74	37	37	82	41	41
35-39	67	34	33	69	35	34	69	34	34	74	37	37
40-44	61	31	30	67	34	33	69	35	34	68	34	34
45-49	54	26	28	60	30	30	66	33	33	68	34	34
50-54	57	27	30	53	26	27	59	30	30	65	33	33
55-59	61	29	33	55	26	29	52	25	27	58	29	29
60-64	57	27	30	59	27	32	53	24	29	50	23	26
65-69	40	18	22	53	25	28	54	24	30	49	22	27
70-74	30	13	17	35	15	20	47	21	26	49	20	28
75-79	19	7	12	25	9	15	29	12	18	40	16	23
80-84	11	4	8	14	5	9	19	6	12	22	8	14
85-89	6	2	5	7	2	5	9	2	7	12	3	9
90-94	2	1	2	3	1	3	4	1	3	5	1	4
95-99	1	0	1	1	0	1	1	0	1	1	0	1
100 +	0	0	0	0	0	0	0	0	0	0	0	0

Age group	2045 Both sexes	Males	Females	2050 Both sexes	Males	Females
All ages	1 236	600	636	1 285	624	661
0-4	99	50	49	102	51	51
5-9	96	49	48	99	50	49
10-14	93	47	46	96	49	48
15-19	91	46	45	93	47	46
20-24	89	45	44	91	46	45
25-29	88	44	44	89	45	44
30-34	85	43	42	88	44	44
35-39	82	41	41	85	43	42
40-44	73	37	37	81	41	40
45-49	68	34	34	73	36	36
50-54	67	33	34	67	33	33
55-59	64	32	32	66	32	33
60-64	56	27	29	61	30	31
65-69	46	21	25	52	25	28
70-74	44	19	26	42	18	24
75-79	41	16	25	38	15	23
80-84	30	11	19	32	11	21
85-89	15	4	10	20	6	14
90-94	6	1	5	8	2	6
95-99	2	0	2	2	0	2
100 +	0	0	0	0	0	0

United Nations Department of Economic and Social Affairs/Population Division
World Population Prospects: The 2004 Revision, Volume II: Sex and Age Distribution of the World Population

720

POPULATION BY AGE AND SEX (in thousands)

Age group	2005 Both sexes	Males	Females	2010 Both sexes	Males	Females	2015 Both sexes	Males	Females	2020 Both sexes	Males	Females
All ages	785	384	402	830	405	425	866	422	444	894	434	460
0-4	75	38	37	67	34	33	60	30	30	56	28	28
5-9	69	35	34	75	38	37	67	34	33	60	30	30
10-14	70	35	35	69	35	34	75	38	37	67	34	33
15-19	68	35	34	70	35	35	69	35	34	75	38	37
20-24	62	31	31	68	34	34	70	35	35	69	35	34
25-29	56	27	28	62	31	31	68	34	34	70	35	34
30-34	59	28	31	55	27	28	62	31	31	68	34	33
35-39	66	32	34	59	28	31	55	27	28	61	31	31
40-44	64	32	32	65	31	34	58	28	30	55	27	28
45-49	48	24	24	63	32	32	64	31	34	58	27	30
50-54	40	19	21	47	23	24	62	31	31	63	30	33
55-59	30	14	16	39	18	20	45	22	23	60	29	31
60-64	24	11	13	28	13	15	37	17	20	43	21	23
65-69	19	9	11	22	10	12	26	11	15	34	15	19
70-74	14	6	8	17	7	10	19	8	11	23	9	13
75-79	10	4	6	11	4	7	14	5	9	15	6	10
80-84	6	2	4	7	2	5	8	3	6	10	3	7
85-89	3	1	2	4	1	3	4	1	3	5	1	4
90-94	1	0	1	1	0	1	2	0	1	2	0	2
95-99	0	0	0	0	0	0	0	0	0	1	0	1
100 +	0	0	0	0	0	0	0	0	0	0	0	0

Age group	2025 Both sexes	Males	Females	2030 Both sexes	Males	Females	2035 Both sexes	Males	Females	2040 Both sexes	Males	Females
All ages	918	445	473	935	452	483	944	455	489	944	454	490
0-4	55	28	27	53	27	26	49	25	24	44	22	22
5-9	56	28	28	55	28	27	53	27	26	49	25	24
10-14	60	30	30	56	28	28	55	28	27	53	27	26
15-19	67	34	33	60	30	30	56	28	28	55	28	27
20-24	74	37	37	67	34	33	60	30	30	56	28	28
25-29	69	35	34	74	37	37	67	34	33	60	30	30
30-34	69	35	34	69	35	34	74	37	37	67	33	33
35-39	67	34	33	69	35	34	69	34	34	74	37	37
40-44	61	31	30	67	34	33	69	35	34	68	34	34
45-49	54	26	28	60	30	30	66	33	33	68	34	34
50-54	57	27	30	53	26	27	59	30	30	65	33	33
55-59	61	29	33	55	26	29	52	25	27	58	29	29
60-64	57	27	30	59	27	32	53	24	29	50	23	26
65-69	40	18	22	53	25	28	54	24	30	49	22	27
70-74	30	13	17	35	15	20	47	21	26	49	20	28
75-79	19	7	12	25	9	15	29	12	18	40	16	23
80-84	11	4	8	14	5	9	19	6	12	22	8	14
85-89	6	2	5	7	2	5	9	2	7	12	3	9
90-94	2	1	2	3	1	3	4	1	3	5	1	4
95-99	1	0	1	1	0	1	1	0	1	1	0	1
100 +	0	0	0	0	0	0	0	0	0	0	0	0

Age group	2045 Both sexes	Males	Females	2050 Both sexes	Males	Females
All ages	935	448	487	920	440	480
0-4	40	20	20	37	19	19
5-9	44	22	22	40	20	20
10-14	49	25	24	44	22	22
15-19	53	27	26	49	25	24
20-24	55	28	27	53	26	26
25-29	56	28	28	55	27	27
30-34	60	30	30	56	28	28
35-39	66	33	33	60	30	30
40-44	73	37	37	66	33	33
45-49	68	34	34	73	36	36
50-54	67	33	34	67	33	33
55-59	64	32	32	66	32	33
60-64	56	27	29	61	30	31
65-69	46	21	25	52	25	28
70-74	44	19	26	42	18	24
75-79	41	16	25	38	15	23
80-84	30	11	19	32	11	21
85-89	15	4	10	20	6	14
90-94	6	1	5	8	2	6
95-99	2	0	2	2	0	2
100 +	0	0	0	0	0	0

POPULATION BY AGE AND SEX (in thousands)

Age group	1950 Both sexes	Males	Females	1955 Both sexes	Males	Females	1960 Both sexes	Males	Females	1965 Both sexes	Males	Females
All ages	16 311	7 867	8 444	17 486	8 490	8 996	18 407	8 981	9 426	19 032	9 318	9 714
0-4	1 626	828	798	1 859	949	910	1 811	927	884	1 440	739	701
5-9	1 378	699	679	1 581	803	778	1 815	926	889	1 779	910	869
10-14	1 630	807	823	1 365	692	673	1 562	794	768	1 796	916	880
15-19	1 638	826	812	1 613	799	814	1 348	683	665	1 546	785	761
20-24	1 589	798	791	1 611	811	800	1 587	785	802	1 330	673	657
25-29	1 380	659	721	1 560	782	778	1 585	798	787	1 565	773	792
30-34	854	387	467	1 355	646	709	1 532	768	764	1 560	784	776
35-39	1 205	567	638	837	379	458	1 327	632	695	1 506	754	752
40-44	1 135	557	578	1 170	548	622	816	369	447	1 300	618	682
45-49	975	482	493	1 096	536	560	1 140	534	606	794	358	436
50-54	832	381	451	934	462	472	1 053	512	541	1 098	511	587
55-59	653	286	367	783	360	423	879	428	451	998	481	517
60-64	547	235	312	603	262	341	716	320	396	811	390	421
65-69	313	132	181	475	199	276	521	220	301	633	277	356
70-74	296	123	173	338	142	196	371	154	217	439	183	256
75-79	166	66	100	193	78	115	215	85	130	265	105	160
80 +	94	34	60	113	42	71	129	46	83	172	61	111

Age group	1970 Both sexes	Males	Females	1975 Both sexes	Males	Females	1980 Both sexes	Males	Females	1985 Both sexes	Males	Females
All ages	20 253	9 945	10 308	21 245	10 460	10 785	22 201	10 954	11 248	22 725	11 214	11 511
0-4	2 040	1 043	997	1 928	988	940	2 006	1 027	979	1 723	881	841
5-9	1 419	728	691	2 020	1 032	988	1 909	977	932	1 984	1 015	969
10-14	1 793	916	877	1 413	724	689	2 007	1 024	983	1 896	970	926
15-19	1 807	922	886	1 785	911	874	1 429	731	698	1 994	1 017	977
20-24	1 502	765	737	1 795	914	880	1 756	894	862	1 414	724	690
25-29	1 283	645	638	1 490	758	732	1 773	898	875	1 736	883	853
30-34	1 573	786	787	1 270	638	633	1 487	750	737	1 751	885	866
35-39	1 553	779	774	1 554	775	779	1 259	629	630	1 466	738	729
40-44	1 486	740	746	1 528	765	764	1 543	766	777	1 234	613	621
45-49	1 303	614	689	1 454	721	733	1 491	743	748	1 503	740	763
50-54	749	335	414	1 264	591	672	1 400	689	711	1 436	707	729
55-59	1 066	490	576	715	316	399	1 198	556	642	1 326	642	685
60-64	939	440	499	991	447	544	662	288	373	1 108	502	606
65-69	740	341	399	833	379	454	836	366	471	588	248	340
70-74	495	209	286	606	269	338	706	311	395	732	309	423
75-79	292	115	177	352	143	209	447	192	255	491	205	286
80 +	214	79	135	248	91	157	291	112	179	342	136	206

Age group	1990 Both sexes	Males	Females	1995 Both sexes	Males	Females	2000 Both sexes	Males	Females	2005 Both sexes	Males	Females
All ages	23 207	11 449	11 758	22 681	11 124	11 557	22 117	10 806	11 311	21 711	10 581	11 130
0-4	1 805	921	884	1 230	631	600	1 105	567	538	1 054	541	513
5-9	1 698	868	830	1 746	890	856	1 209	619	589	1 094	561	533
10-14	1 966	1 005	961	1 669	852	817	1 732	883	850	1 203	616	587
15-19	1 879	960	919	1 964	1 003	960	1 640	837	803	1 718	875	843
20-24	1 974	1 006	968	1 822	926	895	1 900	971	929	1 611	822	789
25-29	1 394	714	681	1 861	946	915	1 746	887	859	1 864	951	913
30-34	1 708	868	841	1 305	660	645	1 794	909	885	1 713	868	845
35-39	1 720	867	853	1 629	817	813	1 252	629	622	1 761	889	872
40-44	1 437	720	717	1 641	818	823	1 574	782	792	1 222	610	612
45-49	1 197	589	608	1 380	683	697	1 579	777	802	1 530	752	778
50-54	1 441	699	742	1 128	548	580	1 312	637	675	1 519	736	783
55-59	1 354	654	700	1 347	638	708	1 055	499	556	1 241	588	653
60-64	1 219	574	646	1 240	578	662	1 234	564	669	976	446	530
65-69	981	430	551	1 077	487	590	1 095	488	607	1 102	483	619
70-74	488	197	291	807	336	471	891	382	509	917	388	529
75-79	534	214	320	357	135	223	596	233	363	667	269	398
80 +	410	164	246	479	178	301	403	141	262	519	184	335

United Nations Department of Economic and Social Affairs/Population Division
World Population Prospects: The 2004 Revision, Volume II: Sex and Age Distribution of the World Population

POPULATION BY AGE AND SEX (in thousands)

Age group	2005			2010			2015			2020		
	Both sexes	Males	Females	Both sexes	Males	Females	Both sexes	Males	Females	Both sexes	Males	Females
All ages	21 711	10 581	11 130	21 287	10 350	10 937	20 871	10 130	10 741	20 396	9 887	10 509
0-4	1 054	541	513	1 010	518	492	960	493	467	897	461	436
5-9	1 094	561	533	1 047	537	510	1 006	516	490	956	491	466
10-14	1 203	616	587	1 090	559	531	1 044	535	509	1 004	515	489
15-19	1 718	875	843	1 193	611	582	1 086	557	530	1 041	533	508
20-24	1 611	822	789	1 697	864	833	1 186	607	579	1 080	553	527
25-29	1 864	951	913	1 586	808	778	1 687	857	829	1 178	602	576
30-34	1 713	868	845	1 839	936	902	1 574	801	774	1 676	851	825
35-39	1 761	889	872	1 688	853	836	1 823	926	897	1 562	792	769
40-44	1 222	610	612	1 730	868	862	1 667	838	829	1 802	911	891
45-49	1 530	752	778	1 192	590	602	1 697	845	852	1 638	817	820
50-54	1 519	736	783	1 478	716	762	1 156	564	591	1 650	812	838
55-59	1 241	588	653	1 444	684	760	1 411	670	741	1 107	531	576
60-64	976	446	530	1 154	530	624	1 349	620	729	1 324	611	712
65-69	1 102	483	619	876	385	492	1 043	461	582	1 225	543	683
70-74	917	388	529	931	387	543	746	311	435	894	376	519
75-79	667	269	398	696	277	419	716	279	437	580	226	354
80-84	370	135	234	422	158	264	450	164	285	472	167	304
85-89	100	33	67	175	59	117	206	69	137	227	73	154
90-94	42	14	29	31	9	22	58	17	41	71	20	51
95-99	6	2	4	7	2	5	6	1	5	12	3	9
100 +	0	0	0	1	0	0	1	0	1	1	0	1

Age group	2025			2030			2035			2040		
	Both sexes	Males	Females	Both sexes	Males	Females	Both sexes	Males	Females	Both sexes	Males	Females
All ages	19 858	9 616	10 243	19 285	9 325	9 960	18 691	9 023	9 668	18 073	8 712	9 361
0-4	827	425	402	782	402	380	767	394	373	763	393	371
5-9	894	459	435	824	423	401	780	401	379	765	393	372
10-14	955	490	465	893	458	434	823	423	400	779	400	378
15-19	1 001	513	488	952	488	464	890	457	433	820	421	399
20-24	1 035	530	505	995	510	485	946	485	461	885	454	431
25-29	1 072	548	524	1 028	526	502	988	506	482	939	481	458
30-34	1 170	597	573	1 065	544	521	1 021	522	499	982	502	479
35-39	1 664	843	821	1 161	592	570	1 058	540	518	1 014	518	496
40-44	1 546	782	764	1 649	833	816	1 151	585	566	1 049	535	514
45-49	1 773	892	882	1 523	767	757	1 628	819	809	1 138	577	561
50-54	1 596	789	807	1 733	863	869	1 492	745	747	1 597	798	799
55-59	1 585	767	818	1 538	748	790	1 675	823	852	1 446	713	733
60-64	1 042	487	555	1 498	708	790	1 459	694	764	1 594	768	826
65-69	1 208	538	670	955	431	524	1 380	631	748	1 350	623	726
70-74	1 058	446	612	1 050	445	605	836	360	476	1 215	531	684
75-79	702	275	427	840	330	510	844	333	510	678	272	406
80-84	389	137	252	479	169	310	584	205	379	595	210	386
85-89	245	75	170	208	62	146	264	78	187	330	95	235
90-94	81	21	60	92	22	70	82	18	64	108	23	85
95-99	15	3	12	19	3	15	23	4	19	22	3	19
100 +	1	0	1	2	0	2	2	0	2	3	0	3

Age group	2045			2050		
	Both sexes	Males	Females	Both sexes	Males	Females
All ages	17 425	8 386	9 039	16 757	8 059	8 698
0-4	751	387	365	733	377	356
5-9	761	392	370	750	386	364
10-14	764	393	371	760	391	369
15-19	776	399	377	762	392	370
20-24	815	419	397	771	396	375
25-29	878	451	428	809	415	394
30-34	934	478	455	873	448	425
35-39	976	499	477	928	475	453
40-44	1 007	514	493	969	495	474
45-49	1 038	528	510	997	507	490
50-54	1 118	563	555	1 021	516	505
55-59	1 552	767	785	1 088	543	545
60-64	1 380	668	712	1 486	722	764
65-69	1 480	693	787	1 287	607	680
70-74	1 195	528	668	1 320	593	727
75-79	994	405	589	988	409	579
80-84	485	173	312	724	264	460
85-89	345	99	246	289	85	204
90-94	141	29	112	154	32	123
95-99	30	4	27	42	5	37
100 +	4	0	3	5	0	5

POPULATION BY AGE AND SEX (in thousands)

Age group	2005 Both sexes	Males	Females	2010 Both sexes	Males	Females	2015 Both sexes	Males	Females	2020 Both sexes	Males	Females
All ages	21 711	10 581	11 130	21 487	10 453	11 034	21 363	10 383	10 980	21 201	10 300	10 901
0-4	1 054	541	513	1 210	621	589	1 251	642	609	1 211	622	589
5-9	1 094	561	533	1 047	537	510	1 206	619	588	1 247	640	607
10-14	1 203	616	587	1 090	559	531	1 044	535	509	1 204	617	587
15-19	1 718	875	843	1 193	611	582	1 086	557	530	1 041	533	508
20-24	1 611	822	789	1 697	864	833	1 186	607	579	1 080	553	527
25-29	1 864	951	913	1 586	808	778	1 687	857	829	1 178	602	576
30-34	1 713	868	845	1 839	936	902	1 574	801	774	1 676	851	825
35-39	1 761	889	872	1 688	853	836	1 823	926	897	1 562	792	769
40-44	1 222	610	612	1 730	868	862	1 667	838	829	1 802	911	891
45-49	1 530	752	778	1 192	590	602	1 697	845	852	1 638	817	820
50-54	1 519	736	783	1 478	716	762	1 156	564	591	1 650	812	838
55-59	1 241	588	653	1 444	684	760	1 411	670	741	1 107	531	576
60-64	976	446	530	1 154	530	624	1 349	620	729	1 324	611	712
65-69	1 102	483	619	876	385	492	1 043	461	582	1 225	543	683
70-74	917	388	529	931	387	543	746	311	435	894	376	519
75-79	667	269	398	696	277	419	716	279	437	580	226	354
80-84	370	135	234	422	158	264	450	164	285	472	167	304
85-89	100	33	67	175	59	117	206	69	137	227	73	154
90-94	42	14	29	31	9	22	58	17	41	71	20	51
95-99	6	2	4	7	2	5	6	1	5	12	3	9
100 +	0	0	0	1	0	0	1	0	1	1	0	1

Age group	2025 Both sexes	Males	Females	2030 Both sexes	Males	Females	2035 Both sexes	Males	Females	2040 Both sexes	Males	Females
All ages	20 941	10 171	10 770	20 662	10 031	10 631	20 434	9 918	10 516	20 266	9 837	10 429
0-4	1 105	568	537	1 078	554	524	1 135	584	551	1 216	625	591
5-9	1 208	620	588	1 102	566	536	1 075	553	523	1 132	582	550
10-14	1 245	639	606	1 206	619	587	1 101	565	535	1 074	552	522
15-19	1 200	615	585	1 242	637	605	1 203	617	586	1 098	564	534
20-24	1 035	530	505	1 194	612	582	1 236	633	602	1 197	614	583
25-29	1 072	548	524	1 028	526	502	1 187	608	579	1 228	629	599
30-34	1 170	597	573	1 065	544	521	1 021	522	499	1 180	604	576
35-39	1 664	843	821	1 161	592	570	1 058	540	518	1 014	518	496
40-44	1 546	782	764	1 649	833	816	1 151	585	566	1 049	535	514
45-49	1 773	892	882	1 523	767	757	1 628	819	809	1 138	577	561
50-54	1 596	789	807	1 733	863	869	1 492	745	747	1 597	798	799
55-59	1 585	767	818	1 538	748	790	1 675	823	852	1 446	713	733
60-64	1 042	487	555	1 498	708	790	1 459	694	764	1 594	768	826
65-69	1 208	538	670	955	431	524	1 380	631	748	1 350	623	726
70-74	1 058	446	612	1 050	445	605	836	360	476	1 215	531	684
75-79	702	275	427	840	330	510	844	333	510	678	272	406
80-84	389	137	252	479	169	310	584	205	379	595	210	386
85-89	245	75	170	208	62	146	264	78	187	330	95	235
90-94	81	21	60	92	22	70	82	18	64	108	23	85
95-99	15	3	12	19	3	15	23	4	19	22	3	19
100 +	1	0	1	2	0	2	2	0	2	3	0	3

Age group	2045 Both sexes	Males	Females	2050 Both sexes	Males	Females
All ages	20 119	9 770	10 349	19 964	9 705	10 258
0-4	1 255	646	609	1 249	643	607
5-9	1 214	624	589	1 253	645	608
10-14	1 131	581	550	1 212	624	589
15-19	1 071	550	521	1 129	580	548
20-24	1 093	561	532	1 066	548	518
25-29	1 190	610	580	1 086	557	529
30-34	1 222	626	596	1 184	607	577
35-39	1 174	600	573	1 216	622	593
40-44	1 007	514	493	1 166	596	570
45-49	1 038	528	510	997	507	490
50-54	1 118	563	555	1 021	516	505
55-59	1 552	767	785	1 088	543	545
60-64	1 380	668	712	1 486	722	764
65-69	1 480	693	787	1 287	607	680
70-74	1 195	528	668	1 320	593	727
75-79	994	405	589	988	409	579
80-84	485	173	312	724	264	460
85-89	345	99	246	289	85	204
90-94	141	29	112	154	32	123
95-99	30	4	27	42	5	37
100 +	4	0	3	5	0	5

United Nations Department of Economic and Social Affairs/Population Division
World Population Prospects: The 2004 Revision, Volume II: Sex and Age Distribution of the World Population

724

POPULATION BY AGE AND SEX (in thousands)

Age group	2005 Both sexes	Males	Females	2010 Both sexes	Males	Females	2015 Both sexes	Males	Females	2020 Both sexes	Males	Females
All ages	21 711	10 581	11 130	21 086	10 247	10 839	20 376	9 876	10 500	19 579	9 468	10 111
0-4	1 054	541	513	809	415	394	665	341	324	574	295	279
5-9	1 094	561	533	1 047	537	510	806	413	392	662	340	322
10-14	1 203	616	587	1 090	559	531	1 044	535	509	804	412	392
15-19	1 718	875	843	1 193	611	582	1 086	557	530	1 041	533	508
20-24	1 611	822	789	1 697	864	833	1 186	607	579	1 080	553	527
25-29	1 864	951	913	1 586	808	778	1 687	857	829	1 178	602	576
30-34	1 713	868	845	1 839	936	902	1 574	801	774	1 676	851	825
35-39	1 761	889	872	1 688	853	836	1 823	926	897	1 562	792	769
40-44	1 222	610	612	1 730	868	862	1 667	838	829	1 802	911	891
45-49	1 530	752	778	1 192	590	602	1 697	845	852	1 638	817	820
50-54	1 519	736	783	1 478	716	762	1 156	564	591	1 650	812	838
55-59	1 241	588	653	1 444	684	760	1 411	670	741	1 107	531	576
60-64	976	446	530	1 154	530	624	1 349	620	729	1 324	611	712
65-69	1 102	483	619	876	385	492	1 043	461	582	1 225	543	683
70-74	917	388	529	931	387	543	746	311	435	894	376	519
75-79	667	269	398	696	277	419	716	279	437	580	226	354
80-84	370	135	234	422	158	264	450	164	285	472	167	304
85-89	100	33	67	175	59	117	206	69	137	227	73	154
90-94	42	14	29	31	9	22	58	17	41	71	20	51
95-99	6	2	4	7	2	5	6	1	5	12	3	9
100 +	0	0	0	1	0	0	1	0	1	1	0	1

Age group	2025 Both sexes	Males	Females	2030 Both sexes	Males	Females	2035 Both sexes	Males	Females	2040 Both sexes	Males	Females
All ages	18 759	9 051	9 708	17 916	8 622	9 294	17 032	8 172	8 860	16 085	7 691	8 394
0-4	544	279	264	510	262	248	475	244	231	433	223	210
5-9	572	294	278	542	278	263	509	261	247	473	243	230
10-14	661	339	322	570	293	278	541	278	263	508	261	247
15-19	801	411	390	658	338	321	568	292	277	538	277	262
20-24	1 035	530	505	795	408	388	653	335	318	563	289	274
25-29	1 072	548	524	1 028	526	502	789	404	385	647	332	315
30-34	1 170	597	573	1 065	544	521	1 021	522	499	783	401	382
35-39	1 664	843	821	1 161	592	570	1 058	540	518	1 014	518	496
40-44	1 546	782	764	1 649	833	816	1 151	585	566	1 049	535	514
45-49	1 773	892	882	1 523	767	757	1 628	819	809	1 138	577	561
50-54	1 600	760	807	1 722	863	869	1 492	745	747	1 597	798	799
55-59	1 585	767	818	1 538	748	790	1 675	823	852	1 446	713	733
60-64	1 042	487	555	1 498	708	790	1 459	694	764	1 594	768	826
65-69	1 208	538	670	955	431	524	1 380	631	748	1 350	623	726
70-74	1 058	446	612	1 050	445	605	836	360	476	1 215	531	684
75-79	702	275	427	840	330	510	844	333	510	678	272	406
80-84	389	137	252	479	169	310	584	205	379	595	210	386
85-89	245	75	170	208	62	146	264	78	187	330	95	235
90-94	81	21	60	92	22	70	82	18	64	108	23	85
95-99	15	3	12	19	3	15	23	4	19	22	3	19
100 +	1	0	1	2	0	2	2	0	2	3	0	3

Age group	2045 Both sexes	Males	Females	2050 Both sexes	Males	Females
All ages	15 074	7 180	7 895	14 033	6 661	7 372
0-4	385	198	187	355	183	172
5-9	431	222	209	384	197	186
10-14	472	243	230	430	221	209
15-19	505	260	246	470	242	229
20-24	534	274	260	501	257	243
25-29	558	286	271	528	271	257
30-34	642	329	313	553	283	269
35-39	778	398	380	637	326	311
40-44	1 007	514	493	772	395	378
45-49	1 038	528	510	997	507	490
50-54	1 118	563	555	1 021	516	505
55-59	1 552	767	785	1 088	543	545
60-64	1 380	668	712	1 486	722	764
65-69	1 480	693	787	1 287	607	680
70-74	1 195	528	668	1 320	593	727
75-79	994	405	589	988	409	579
80-84	485	173	312	724	264	460
85-89	345	99	246	289	85	204
90-94	141	29	112	154	32	123
95-99	30	4	27	42	5	37
100 +	4	0	3	5	0	5

POPULATION BY AGE AND SEX (in thousands)

Age group	1950 Both sexes	Males	Females	1955 Both sexes	Males	Females	1960 Both sexes	Males	Females	1965 Both sexes	Males	Females
All ages	102 702	44 078	58 624	111 402	48 826	62 576	119 906	53 472	66 434	126 749	57 261	69 488
0-4	10 041	5 181	4 859	12 637	6 487	6 150	13 462	6 856	6 606	12 125	6 183	5 942
5-9	7 405	3 742	3 662	10 005	5 161	4 844	12 522	6 425	6 097	13 344	6 792	6 552
10-14	12 244	6 157	6 087	7 398	3 737	3 662	9 937	5 123	4 815	12 434	6 376	6 058
15-19	9 911	4 980	4 931	12 221	6 139	6 082	7 333	3 700	3 633	9 856	5 076	4 780
20-24	11 715	5 559	6 156	9 851	4 934	4 917	12 085	6 051	6 035	7 238	3 640	3 598
25-29	7 326	2 889	4 437	11 616	5 479	6 137	9 707	4 835	4 872	11 927	5 940	5 987
30-34	5 952	2 357	3 596	7 258	2 839	4 419	11 439	5 359	6 080	9 550	4 728	4 822
35-39	8 134	3 094	5 040	5 872	2 302	3 570	7 119	2 756	4 363	11 230	5 219	6 011
40-44	7 007	2 630	4 377	7 977	2 995	4 982	5 723	2 216	3 507	6 950	2 658	4 293
45-49	5 824	1 962	3 861	6 796	2 505	4 291	7 702	2 840	4 861	5 530	2 105	3 425
50-54	4 287	1 467	2 820	5 571	1 827	3 744	6 463	2 322	4 141	7 349	2 643	4 707
55-59	3 417	1 226	2 191	4 022	1 329	2 693	5 208	1 648	3 560	6 054	2 103	3 952
60-64	3 086	1 059	2 028	3 108	1 066	2 043	3 651	1 151	2 500	4 758	1 433	3 325
65-69	2 422	764	1 658	2 696	871	1 824	2 705	874	1 831	3 205	948	2 257
70-74	1 782	510	1 272	1 982	583	1 399	2 198	662	1 535	2 222	667	1 555
75-79	1 183	299	884	1 315	342	972	1 457	390	1 067	1 630	446	1 185
80 +	967	202	765	1 076	232	844	1 195	266	929	1 345	306	1 039

Age group	1970 Both sexes	Males	Females	1975 Both sexes	Males	Females	1980 Both sexes	Males	Females	1985 Both sexes	Males	Females
All ages	130 392	59 368	71 024	134 233	61 362	72 870	138 660	63 895	74 765	143 329	66 497	76 832
0-4	9 363	4 767	4 595	10 102	5 132	4 970	10 676	5 427	5 249	11 640	5 925	5 715
5-9	12 022	6 125	5 897	9 353	4 746	4 607	10 078	5 118	4 960	10 719	5 443	5 276
10-14	13 254	6 740	6 514	11 825	6 033	5 792	9 263	4 703	4 560	10 119	5 148	4 971
15-19	12 338	6 319	6 019	12 880	6 540	6 340	11 510	5 860	5 650	9 342	4 762	4 580
20-24	9 744	5 001	4 743	12 157	6 164	5 993	13 022	6 673	6 349	11 682	5 929	5 753
25-29	7 130	3 565	3 565	9 647	4 896	4 751	12 207	6 177	6 030	13 039	6 623	6 417
30-34	11 754	5 815	5 939	7 086	3 512	3 574	10 045	5 047	4 997	12 125	6 084	6 041
35-39	9 364	4 598	4 766	11 556	5 649	5 907	6 447	3 159	3 288	9 848	4 894	4 953
40-44	10 968	5 039	5 928	9 088	4 391	4 697	11 313	5 446	5 867	6 303	3 047	3 256
45-49	6 724	2 523	4 202	10 615	4 810	5 805	8 596	4 072	4 525	10 885	5 146	5 740
50-54	5 274	1 955	3 319	6 613	2 379	4 234	10 236	4 574	5 662	8 179	3 762	4 417
55-59	6 901	2 393	4 508	5 058	1 794	3 264	6 548	2 292	4 256	9 567	4 099	5 468
60-64	5 531	1 827	3 705	6 369	2 124	4 246	4 558	1 526	3 032	5 972	1 973	4 000
65-69	4 197	1 179	3 018	4 887	1 486	3 401	5 535	1 710	3 825	3 995	1 234	2 761
70-74	2 653	723	1 930	3 428	878	2 550	4 126	1 137	2 989	4 551	1 263	3 287
75-79	1 655	449	1 207	1 904	461	1 443	2 607	586	2 021	3 015	728	2 287
80 +	1 520	350	1 170	1 664	367	1 297	1 891	385	1 506	2 348	439	1 909

Age group	1990 Both sexes	Males	Females	1995 Both sexes	Males	Females	2000 Both sexes	Males	Females	2005 Both sexes	Males	Females
All ages	148 370	69 480	78 890	148 189	69 583	78 607	146 560	68 290	78 270	143 202	66 447	76 754
0-4	11 551	5 895	5 656	7 909	4 059	3 850	6 595	3 377	3 217	7 225	3 709	3 517
5-9	11 727	5 959	5 768	11 686	5 966	5 720	8 093	4 139	3 954	6 579	3 367	3 213
10-14	10 788	5 473	5 315	11 856	6 024	5 831	12 016	6 121	5 894	8 081	4 129	3 952
15-19	10 216	5 196	5 020	10 860	5 509	5 351	12 363	6 277	6 087	12 004	6 102	5 902
20-24	9 554	4 895	4 659	10 270	5 269	5 001	11 075	5 578	5 497	12 299	6 204	6 095
25-29	11 761	5 974	5 787	9 545	4 887	4 658	10 375	5 217	5 157	10 937	5 448	5 488
30-34	12 991	6 543	6 449	11 720	5 902	5 818	9 605	4 792	4 812	10 192	5 058	5 134
35-39	12 060	6 012	6 048	12 866	6 399	6 467	11 591	5 706	5 885	9 383	4 608	4 776
40-44	9 683	4 768	4 915	11 832	5 802	6 031	12 515	6 065	6 450	11 231	5 418	5 813
45-49	6 147	2 928	3 218	9 372	4 512	4 859	11 257	5 330	5 927	11 983	5 653	6 329
50-54	10 453	4 843	5 610	5 816	2 675	3 140	8 873	4 095	4 778	10 614	4 847	5 767
55-59	7 737	3 443	4 294	9 736	4 309	5 427	5 317	2 304	3 013	8 198	3 606	4 592
60-64	8 816	3 591	5 225	6 973	2 918	4 055	8 806	3 622	5 184	4 758	1 930	2 829
65-69	5 309	1 637	3 672	7 640	2 867	4 773	5 920	2 269	3 651	7 503	2 831	4 672
70-74	3 327	936	2 391	4 370	1 213	3 156	6 066	2 045	4 021	4 700	1 618	3 082
75-79	3 407	835	2 572	2 457	611	1 846	3 160	765	2 395	4 348	1 288	3 061
80 +	2 842	552	2 290	3 282	659	2 622	2 935	588	2 347	3 165	632	2 534

726

United Nations Department of Economic and Social Affairs/Population Division
World Population Prospects: The 2004 Revision, Volume II: Sex and Age Distribution of the World Population

POPULATION BY AGE AND SEX (in thousands)

Age group	2005 Both sexes	Males	Females	2010 Both sexes	Males	Females	2015 Both sexes	Males	Females	2020 Both sexes	Males	Females
All ages	143 202	66 447	76 754	140 028	64 660	75 369	136 696	62 867	73 829	133 101	61 033	72 069
0-4	7 225	3 709	3 517	7 772	3 989	3 782	7 490	3 845	3 644	6 840	3 513	3 328
5-9	6 579	3 367	3 213	7 199	3 692	3 507	7 745	3 972	3 773	7 469	3 832	3 637
10-14	8 081	4 129	3 952	6 570	3 360	3 210	7 186	3 684	3 502	7 733	3 964	3 768
15-19	12 004	6 102	5 902	8 075	4 118	3 957	6 574	3 356	3 218	7 192	3 681	3 511
20-24	12 299	6 204	6 095	11 919	6 023	5 896	8 051	4 085	3 965	6 573	3 342	3 231
25-29	10 937	5 448	5 488	12 073	6 025	6 048	11 734	5 880	5 854	7 969	4 017	3 951
30-34	10 192	5 058	5 134	10 647	5 228	5 419	11 739	5 790	5 949	11 462	5 694	5 768
35-39	9 383	4 608	4 776	9 877	4 817	5 060	10 283	4 971	5 312	11 369	5 541	5 828
40-44	11 231	5 418	5 813	9 050	4 351	4 699	9 503	4 545	4 958	9 913	4 715	5 199
45-49	11 983	5 653	6 329	10 732	5 039	5 693	8 650	4 056	4 595	9 109	4 263	4 846
50-54	10 614	4 847	5 767	11 303	5 146	6 157	10 146	4 608	5 537	8 210	3 738	4 472
55-59	8 198	3 606	4 592	9 833	4 284	5 550	10 513	4 581	5 932	9 481	4 137	5 344
60-64	4 758	1 930	2 829	7 375	3 046	4 329	8 897	3 652	5 246	9 569	3 944	5 624
65-69	7 503	2 831	4 672	4 083	1 522	2 561	6 392	2 441	3 951	7 772	2 960	4 812
70-74	4 700	1 618	3 082	6 013	2 039	3 974	3 312	1 114	2 198	5 253	1 822	3 432
75-79	4 348	1 288	3 061	3 415	1 034	2 381	4 434	1 323	3 111	2 482	737	1 745
80-84	1 962	409	1 553	2 723	701	2 022	2 183	574	1 609	2 888	746	2 143
85-89	749	142	607	993	180	813	1 400	314	1 087	1 155	261	894
90-94	372	65	306	277	48	229	378	61	317	551	108	443
95-99	74	13	61	90	16	74	70	12	58	100	15	85
100 +	8	2	6	11	2	9	14	3	11	12	2	10

Age group	2025 Both sexes	Males	Females	2030 Both sexes	Males	Females	2035 Both sexes	Males	Females	2040 Both sexes	Males	Females
All ages	129 230	59 128	70 102	125 325	57 285	68 040	121 679	55 678	66 000	118 334	54 338	63 997
0-4	6 162	3 165	2 997	5 903	3 033	2 870	6 084	3 126	2 957	6 337	3 257	3 079
5-9	6 825	3 502	3 323	6 151	3 157	2 994	5 894	3 027	2 868	6 076	3 121	2 955
10-14	7 461	3 826	3 635	6 821	3 499	3 322	6 149	3 155	2 994	5 894	3 025	2 868
15-19	7 740	3 963	3 777	7 472	3 827	3 644	6 835	3 503	3 332	6 166	3 161	3 005
20-24	7 192	3 669	3 523	7 742	3 953	3 789	7 481	3 823	3 658	6 852	3 504	3 348
25-29	6 523	3 299	3 224	7 140	3 628	3 511	7 691	3 916	3 775	7 441	3 795	3 647
30-34	7 819	3 917	3 902	6 412	3 229	3 183	7 023	3 559	3 463	7 575	3 851	3 724
35-39	11 148	5 489	5 659	7 626	3 796	3 830	6 265	3 142	3 123	6 873	3 474	3 399
40-44	11 004	5 295	5 709	10 821	5 275	5 546	7 420	3 665	3 754	6 110	3 047	3 063
45-49	9 542	4 456	5 086	10 629	5 040	5 590	10 476	5 045	5 431	7 203	3 523	3 680
50-54	8 688	3 964	4 724	9 137	4 174	4 964	10 212	4 752	5 460	10 088	4 780	5 309
55-59	7 715	3 389	4 326	8 205	3 627	4 578	8 662	3 845	4 817	9 716	4 410	5 306
60-64	8 681	3 599	5 082	7 106	2 979	4 127	7 598	3 219	4 380	8 053	3 436	4 617
65-69	8 419	3 235	5 185	7 688	2 983	4 705	6 335	2 497	3 838	6 817	2 726	4 090
70-74	6 451	2 239	4 212	7 047	2 477	4 570	6 483	2 311	4 172	5 385	1 960	3 425
75-79	4 000	1 231	2 769	4 974	1 536	3 438	5 488	1 723	3 764	5 093	1 628	3 464
80-84	1 649	424	1 225	2 708	723	1 985	3 421	918	2 503	3 822	1 045	2 777
85-89	1 574	346	1 228	921	200	721	1 543	346	1 197	1 989	446	1 543
90-94	471	91	380	663	122	541	400	72	328	687	126	562
95-99	151	27	124	134	23	111	196	30	165	122	18	104
100 +	16	3	14	25	4	21	25	4	21	35	5	30

Age group	2045 Both sexes	Males	Females	2050 Both sexes	Males	Females
All ages	115 098	53 134	61 964	111 752	51 903	59 849
0-4	6 298	3 238	3 060	5 915	3 042	2 874
5-9	6 330	3 252	3 078	6 292	3 234	3 059
10-14	6 076	3 120	2 956	6 330	3 252	3 079
15-19	5 912	3 032	2 880	6 095	3 128	2 968
20-24	6 190	3 168	3 022	5 940	3 042	2 898
25-29	6 829	3 486	3 343	6 181	3 158	3 023
30-34	7 345	3 742	3 604	6 758	3 447	3 311
35-39	7 429	3 770	3 659	7 223	3 675	3 548
40-44	6 718	3 382	3 336	7 280	3 682	3 598
45-49	5 950	2 943	3 006	6 559	3 279	3 280
50-54	6 958	3 355	3 602	5 766	2 818	2 949
55-59	9 623	4 457	5 166	6 658	3 146	3 512
60-64	9 074	3 974	5 100	9 007	4 036	4 972
65-69	7 258	2 933	4 325	8 225	3 428	4 797
70-74	5 840	2 166	3 674	6 254	2 353	3 902
75-79	4 272	1 401	2 871	4 680	1 572	3 108
80-84	3 585	999	2 585	3 046	875	2 171
85-89	2 261	515	1 745	2 154	501	1 653
90-94	908	164	744	1 054	192	862
95-99	216	31	185	293	41	252
100 +	26	3	23	41	5	36

United Nations Department of Economic and Social Affairs/Population Division
World Population Prospects: The 2004 Revision, Volume II: Sex and Age Distribution of the World Population

727

POPULATION BY AGE AND SEX (in thousands)

Age group	2005 Both sexes	2005 Males	2005 Females	2010 Both sexes	2010 Males	2010 Females	2015 Both sexes	2015 Males	2015 Females	2020 Both sexes	2020 Males	2020 Females
All ages	143 202	66 447	76 754	141 420	65 374	76 046	140 132	64 630	75 501	138 654	63 882	74 772
0-4	7 225	3 709	3 517	9 164	4 704	4 460	9 539	4 897	4 642	8 967	4 605	4 362
5-9	6 579	3 367	3 213	7 199	3 692	3 507	9 132	4 684	4 448	9 511	4 879	4 632
10-14	8 081	4 129	3 952	6 570	3 360	3 210	7 186	3 684	3 502	9 116	4 674	4 442
15-19	12 004	6 102	5 902	8 075	4 118	3 957	6 574	3 356	3 218	7 192	3 681	3 511
20-24	12 299	6 204	6 095	11 919	6 023	5 896	8 051	4 085	3 965	6 573	3 342	3 231
25-29	10 937	5 448	5 488	12 073	6 025	6 048	11 734	5 880	5 854	7 969	4 017	3 951
30-34	10 192	5 058	5 134	10 647	5 228	5 419	11 739	5 790	5 949	11 462	5 694	5 768
35-39	9 383	4 608	4 776	9 877	4 817	5 060	10 283	4 971	5 312	11 369	5 541	5 828
40-44	11 231	5 418	5 813	9 050	4 351	4 699	9 503	4 545	4 958	9 913	4 715	5 199
45-49	11 983	5 653	6 329	10 732	5 039	5 693	8 650	4 056	4 595	9 109	4 263	4 846
50-54	10 614	4 847	5 767	11 303	5 146	6 157	10 146	4 608	5 537	8 210	3 738	4 472
55-59	8 198	3 606	4 592	9 833	4 284	5 550	10 513	4 581	5 932	9 481	4 137	5 344
60-64	4 758	1 930	2 829	7 375	3 046	4 329	8 897	3 652	5 246	9 569	3 944	5 624
65-69	7 503	2 831	4 672	4 083	1 522	2 561	6 392	2 441	3 951	7 772	2 960	4 812
70-74	4 700	1 618	3 082	6 013	2 039	3 974	3 312	1 114	2 198	5 253	1 822	3 432
75-79	4 348	1 288	3 061	3 415	1 034	2 381	4 434	1 323	3 111	2 482	737	1 745
80-84	1 962	409	1 553	2 723	701	2 022	2 183	574	1 609	2 888	746	2 143
85-89	749	142	607	993	180	813	1 400	314	1 087	1 155	261	894
90-94	372	65	306	277	48	229	378	61	317	551	108	443
95-99	74	13	61	90	16	74	70	12	58	100	15	85
100 +	8	2	6	11	2	9	14	3	11	12	2	10

Age group	2025 Both sexes	2025 Males	2025 Females	2030 Both sexes	2030 Males	2030 Females	2035 Both sexes	2035 Males	2035 Females	2040 Both sexes	2040 Males	2040 Females
All ages	136 611	62 915	73 696	134 772	62 130	72 642	133 858	61 922	71 936	133 885	62 308	71 577
0-4	8 004	4 111	3 893	7 990	4 105	3 885	8 856	4 551	4 305	9 780	5 027	4 753
5-9	8 946	4 591	4 355	7 988	4 101	3 888	7 977	4 096	3 881	8 842	4 542	4 300
10-14	9 499	4 872	4 628	8 939	4 585	4 353	7 984	4 097	3 887	7 974	4 093	3 880
15-19	9 119	4 670	4 450	9 505	4 869	4 636	8 948	4 586	4 362	7 998	4 101	3 897
20-24	7 192	3 669	3 523	9 113	4 654	4 459	9 504	4 858	4 646	8 955	4 581	4 375
25-29	6 523	3 299	3 224	7 140	3 628	3 511	9 045	4 606	4 439	9 441	4 815	4 626
30-34	7 819	3 917	3 902	6 412	3 229	3 183	7 023	3 559	3 463	8 903	4 526	4 376
35-39	11 148	5 489	5 659	7 626	3 796	3 830	6 265	3 142	3 123	6 873	3 474	3 399
40-44	11 004	5 295	5 709	10 821	5 275	5 546	7 420	3 665	3 754	6 110	3 047	3 063
45-49	9 542	4 456	5 086	10 629	5 040	5 590	10 476	5 045	5 431	7 203	3 523	3 680
50-54	8 688	3 964	4 724	9 137	4 174	4 964	10 212	4 752	5 460	10 088	4 780	5 309
55-59	7 715	3 389	4 326	8 205	3 627	4 578	8 662	3 845	4 817	9 716	4 410	5 306
60-64	8 681	3 599	5 082	7 106	2 979	4 127	7 598	3 219	4 380	8 053	3 436	4 617
65-69	8 419	3 235	5 185	7 688	2 983	4 705	6 335	2 497	3 838	6 817	2 726	4 090
70-74	6 451	2 239	4 212	7 047	2 477	4 570	6 483	2 311	4 172	5 385	1 960	3 425
75-79	4 000	1 231	2 769	4 974	1 536	3 438	5 488	1 723	3 764	5 093	1 628	3 464
80-84	1 649	424	1 225	2 708	723	1 985	3 421	918	2 503	3 822	1 045	2 777
85-89	1 574	346	1 228	921	200	721	1 543	346	1 197	1 989	446	1 543
90-94	471	91	380	663	122	541	400	72	328	687	126	562
95-99	151	27	124	134	23	111	196	30	165	122	18	104
100 +	16	3	14	25	4	21	25	4	21	35	5	30

Age group	2045 Both sexes	2045 Males	2045 Females	2050 Both sexes	2050 Males	2050 Females
All ages	134 282	62 966	71 316	134 532	63 577	70 956
0-4	10 037	5 160	4 877	9 648	4 961	4 687
5-9	9 766	5 018	4 748	10 024	5 152	4 872
10-14	8 839	4 539	4 300	9 763	5 015	4 748
15-19	7 989	4 098	3 891	8 855	4 544	4 311
20-24	8 014	4 102	3 912	8 009	4 102	3 907
25-29	8 911	4 550	4 361	7 989	4 083	3 906
30-34	9 310	4 744	4 567	8 808	4 494	4 314
35-39	8 727	4 430	4 298	9 149	4 656	4 493
40-44	6 718	3 382	3 336	8 549	4 324	4 225
45-49	5 950	2 943	3 006	6 559	3 279	3 280
50-54	6 958	3 355	3 602	5 766	2 818	2 949
55-59	9 623	4 457	5 166	6 658	3 146	3 512
60-64	9 074	3 974	5 100	9 007	4 036	4 972
65-69	7 258	2 933	4 325	8 225	3 428	4 797
70-74	5 840	2 166	3 674	6 254	2 353	3 902
75-79	4 272	1 401	2 871	4 680	1 572	3 108
80-84	3 585	999	2 585	3 046	875	2 171
85-89	2 261	515	1 745	2 154	501	1 653
90-94	908	164	744	1 054	192	862
95-99	216	31	185	293	41	252
100 +	26	3	23	41	5	36

United Nations Department of Economic and Social Affairs/Population Division
World Population Prospects: The 2004 Revision, Volume II: Sex and Age Distribution of the World Population

728

POPULATION BY AGE AND SEX (in thousands)

Age group	2005 Both sexes	Males	Females	2010 Both sexes	Males	Females	2015 Both sexes	Males	Females	2020 Both sexes	Males	Females
All ages	143 202	66 447	76 754	138 639	63 946	74 692	133 243	61 095	72 149	127 458	58 137	69 321
0-4	7 225	3 709	3 517	6 382	3 276	3 106	5 421	2 783	2 638	4 639	2 382	2 257
5-9	6 579	3 367	3 213	7 199	3 692	3 507	6 362	3 263	3 099	5 408	2 774	2 634
10-14	8 081	4 129	3 952	6 570	3 360	3 210	7 186	3 684	3 502	6 352	3 257	3 096
15-19	12 004	6 102	5 902	8 075	4 118	3 957	6 574	3 356	3 218	7 192	3 681	3 511
20-24	12 299	6 204	6 095	11 919	6 023	5 896	8 051	4 085	3 965	6 573	3 342	3 231
25-29	10 937	5 448	5 488	12 073	6 025	6 048	11 734	5 880	5 854	7 969	4 017	3 951
30-34	10 192	5 058	5 134	10 647	5 228	5 419	11 739	5 790	5 949	11 462	5 694	5 768
35-39	9 383	4 608	4 776	9 877	4 817	5 060	10 283	4 971	5 312	11 369	5 541	5 828
40-44	11 231	5 418	5 813	9 050	4 351	4 699	9 503	4 545	4 958	9 913	4 715	5 199
45-49	11 983	5 653	6 329	10 732	5 039	5 693	8 650	4 056	4 595	9 109	4 263	4 846
50-54	10 614	4 847	5 767	11 303	5 146	6 157	10 146	4 608	5 537	8 210	3 738	4 472
55-59	8 198	3 606	4 592	9 833	4 284	5 550	10 513	4 581	5 932	9 481	4 137	5 344
60-64	4 758	1 930	2 829	7 375	3 046	4 329	8 897	3 652	5 246	9 569	3 944	5 624
65-69	7 503	2 831	4 672	4 083	1 522	2 561	6 392	2 441	3 951	7 772	2 960	4 812
70-74	4 700	1 618	3 082	6 013	2 039	3 974	3 312	1 114	2 198	5 253	1 822	3 432
75-79	4 348	1 288	3 061	3 415	1 034	2 381	4 434	1 323	3 111	2 482	737	1 745
80-84	1 962	409	1 553	2 723	701	2 022	2 183	574	1 609	2 888	746	2 143
85-89	749	142	607	993	180	813	1 400	314	1 087	1 155	261	894
90-94	372	65	306	277	48	229	378	61	317	551	108	443
95-99	74	13	61	90	16	74	70	12	58	100	15	85
100 +	8	2	6	11	2	9	14	3	11	12	2	10

Age group	2025 Both sexes	Males	Females	2030 Both sexes	Males	Females	2035 Both sexes	Males	Females	2040 Both sexes	Males	Females
All ages	121 721	55 276	66 445	115 953	52 479	63 474	110 156	49 772	60 384	104 314	47 154	57 160
0-4	4 281	2 199	2 082	4 018	2 065	1 954	3 894	2 001	1 893	3 769	1 937	1 832
5-9	4 631	2 376	2 255	4 276	2 195	2 081	4 015	2 061	1 953	3 891	1 999	1 893
10-14	5 404	2 771	2 633	4 630	2 375	2 255	4 276	2 194	2 082	4 016	2 061	1 955
15-19	6 363	3 258	3 105	5 419	2 775	2 644	4 648	2 381	2 267	4 296	2 202	2 094
20-24	7 192	3 669	3 523	6 374	3 254	3 120	5 439	2 779	2 660	4 675	2 390	2 285
25-29	6 523	3 299	3 224	7 140	3 628	3 511	6 339	3 227	3 112	5 423	2 764	2 659
30-34	7 819	3 917	3 902	6 412	3 229	3 183	7 023	3 559	3 463	6 250	3 177	3 074
35-39	11 148	5 489	5 659	7 626	3 796	3 830	6 265	3 142	3 123	6 873	3 474	3 399
40-44	11 004	5 295	5 709	10 821	5 275	5 546	7 420	3 665	3 754	6 110	3 047	3 063
45-49	9 542	4 456	5 086	10 629	5 040	5 590	10 476	5 045	5 431	7 203	3 523	3 680
50-54	8 688	3 964	4 724	9 137	4 174	4 964	10 212	4 752	5 460	10 088	4 780	5 309
55-59	7 715	3 389	4 326	8 205	3 627	4 578	8 662	3 845	4 817	9 716	4 410	5 306
60-64	8 681	3 599	5 082	7 106	2 979	4 127	7 598	3 219	4 380	8 053	3 436	4 617
65-69	8 419	3 235	5 185	7 688	2 983	4 705	6 335	2 497	3 838	6 817	2 726	4 090
70-74	6 451	2 239	4 212	7 047	2 477	4 570	6 483	2 311	4 172	5 385	1 960	3 425
75-79	4 000	1 231	2 769	4 974	1 536	3 438	5 488	1 723	3 764	5 093	1 628	3 464
80-84	1 649	424	1 225	2 708	723	1 985	3 421	918	2 503	3 822	1 045	2 777
85-89	1 574	346	1 228	921	200	721	1 543	346	1 197	1 989	446	1 543
90-94	471	91	380	663	122	541	400	72	328	687	126	562
95-99	151	27	124	134	23	111	196	30	165	122	18	104
100 +	16	3	14	25	4	21	25	4	21	35	5	30

Age group	2045 Both sexes	Males	Females	2050 Both sexes	Males	Females
All ages	98 371	44 564	53 807	92 358	41 969	50 389
0-4	3 487	1 792	1 694	3 113	1 601	1 513
5-9	3 768	1 936	1 832	3 487	1 792	1 695
10-14	3 893	1 999	1 894	3 770	1 936	1 834
15-19	4 038	2 070	1 967	3 916	2 009	1 907
20-24	4 328	2 214	2 114	4 072	2 084	1 988
25-29	4 674	2 385	2 289	4 335	2 214	2 121
30-34	5 362	2 730	2 632	4 636	2 364	2 272
35-39	6 134	3 112	3 022	5 279	2 685	2 594
40-44	6 718	3 382	3 336	6 013	3 041	2 973
45-49	5 950	2 943	3 006	6 559	3 279	3 280
50-54	6 958	3 355	3 602	5 766	2 818	2 949
55-59	9 623	4 457	5 166	6 658	3 146	3 512
60-64	9 074	3 974	5 100	9 007	4 036	4 972
65-69	7 258	2 933	4 325	8 225	3 428	4 797
70-74	5 840	2 166	3 674	6 254	2 353	3 902
75-79	4 272	1 401	2 871	4 680	1 572	3 108
80-84	3 585	999	2 585	3 046	875	2 171
85-89	2 261	515	1 745	2 154	501	1 653
90-94	908	164	744	1 054	192	862
95-99	216	31	185	293	41	252
100 +	26	3	23	41	5	36

United Nations Department of Economic and Social Affairs/Population Division
World Population Prospects: The 2004 Revision, Volume II: Sex and Age Distribution of the World Population

729

POPULATION BY AGE AND SEX (in thousands)

Age group	1950 Both sexes	1950 Males	1950 Females	1955 Both sexes	1955 Males	1955 Females	1960 Both sexes	1960 Males	1960 Females	1965 Both sexes	1965 Males	1965 Females
All ages	2 162	1 069	1 093	2 485	1 227	1 258	2 887	1 426	1 462	3 202	1 581	1 621
0-4	414	207	207	479	239	241	573	285	287	642	320	322
5-9	320	160	161	368	183	184	429	213	216	490	243	246
10-14	268	134	134	308	153	154	354	176	178	392	195	198
15-19	226	113	114	260	129	130	299	149	150	326	163	164
20-24	190	94	96	218	108	110	251	125	126	274	136	138
25-29	158	78	80	182	90	92	209	103	106	229	113	116
30-34	131	65	67	151	74	76	174	86	88	190	94	96
35-39	108	53	55	124	61	63	143	70	73	157	77	80
40-44	89	44	45	102	50	52	117	57	60	128	63	65
45-49	72	35	37	82	40	42	95	46	49	104	51	53
50-54	57	28	30	66	32	34	76	37	39	83	40	43
55-59	45	21	24	51	24	27	59	28	31	65	31	34
60-64	33	16	18	38	18	20	44	21	24	49	23	26
65-69	23	11	13	27	12	14	31	14	17	34	16	19
70-74	14	6	8	17	7	9	19	9	11	21	10	12
75-79	7	3	4	9	4	5	10	4	6	11	5	6
80 +	4	2	2	4	2	3	5	2	3	6	2	4

Age group	1970 Both sexes	1970 Males	1970 Females	1975 Both sexes	1975 Males	1975 Females	1980 Both sexes	1980 Males	1980 Females	1985 Both sexes	1985 Males	1985 Females
All ages	3 776	1 864	1 912	4 410	2 178	2 232	5 197	2 567	2 630	6 061	2 988	3 073
0-4	761	380	381	890	444	446	1 060	529	531	1 279	635	644
5-9	585	291	294	686	342	345	801	399	402	951	473	478
10-14	476	236	239	562	279	283	657	327	330	750	373	377
15-19	384	190	193	460	229	232	562	279	282	627	312	315
20-24	318	158	160	370	183	187	462	229	233	534	264	270
25-29	265	131	134	304	150	154	352	173	179	435	214	221
30-34	220	109	112	252	125	128	289	142	146	331	162	169
35-39	182	90	92	209	103	106	239	117	121	270	132	137
40-44	149	73	76	171	84	87	196	96	100	222	109	113
45-49	121	59	62	139	68	71	159	78	82	181	88	93
50-54	97	47	50	112	54	58	128	62	66	145	70	75
55-59	76	36	40	87	42	46	100	48	53	114	55	60
60-64	57	27	30	66	31	35	76	36	40	87	41	46
65-69	40	18	22	47	21	25	54	25	29	62	29	33
70-74	25	11	14	30	13	16	34	15	19	40	18	22
75-79	14	6	8	16	7	9	19	8	10	22	9	12
80 +	7	3	4	9	3	5	10	4	6	12	5	7

Age group	1990 Both sexes	1990 Males	1990 Females	1995 Both sexes	1995 Males	1995 Females	2000 Both sexes	2000 Males	2000 Females	2005 Both sexes	2005 Males	2005 Females
All ages	7 096	3 484	3 612	5 439	2 636	2 803	8 025	3 879	4 146	9 038	4 379	4 658
0-4	1 463	728	735	971	485	487	1 361	678	684	1 500	746	754
5-9	1 180	584	597	981	486	495	1 209	601	609	1 268	629	639
10-14	904	449	455	771	380	391	1 220	604	616	1 162	577	585
15-19	724	359	365	572	281	291	984	485	499	1 191	589	602
20-24	599	296	304	443	209	234	727	351	376	960	471	489
25-29	501	245	256	368	172	195	546	251	294	694	333	361
30-34	405	196	209	313	150	163	440	203	237	507	233	274
35-39	307	148	159	254	120	134	369	173	195	403	185	218
40-44	251	121	129	191	90	101	300	140	160	338	158	180
45-49	206	99	106	156	75	82	230	106	123	276	128	149
50-54	166	80	86	127	60	67	187	87	100	211	97	115
55-59	131	62	69	101	47	53	151	70	81	171	78	92
60-64	100	47	53	76	35	41	116	53	63	133	61	73
65-69	72	33	39	53	23	30	84	37	46	98	44	54
70-74	47	21	26	33	13	20	54	22	31	65	28	36
75-79	26	11	15	18	6	11	29	11	18	36	15	22
80 +	15	6	9	10	3	7	18	6	12	23	8	15

United Nations Department of Economic and Social Affairs/Population Division
World Population Prospects: The 2004 Revision, Volume II: Sex and Age Distribution of the World Population

POPULATION BY AGE AND SEX (in thousands)

Age group	2005 Both sexes	Males	Females	2010 Both sexes	Males	Females	2015 Both sexes	Males	Females	2020 Both sexes	Males	Females
All ages	9 038	4 379	4 658	10 125	4 919	5 206	11 262	5 483	5 779	12 352	6 023	6 329
0-4	1 500	746	754	1 681	834	847	1 782	883	898	1 769	875	893
5-9	1 268	629	639	1 386	687	700	1 561	772	790	1 668	826	842
10-14	1 162	577	585	1 221	605	616	1 339	663	677	1 514	748	767
15-19	1 191	589	602	1 132	561	571	1 194	591	603	1 312	648	663
20-24	960	471	489	1 154	569	585	1 099	543	556	1 162	573	589
25-29	694	333	361	909	445	464	1 100	541	559	1 052	519	534
30-34	507	233	274	644	310	335	846	415	431	1 033	509	524
35-39	403	185	218	466	214	251	592	286	307	783	386	397
40-44	338	158	180	370	169	200	428	197	231	546	264	283
45-49	276	128	149	311	144	166	340	155	185	395	181	214
50-54	211	97	115	253	116	138	286	131	154	314	142	172
55-59	171	78	92	191	86	105	231	104	127	261	118	143
60-64	133	61	73	151	68	82	170	75	94	205	91	114
65-69	98	44	54	112	50	62	127	56	70	144	62	81
70-74	65	28	36	75	33	42	86	38	48	98	43	56
75-79	36	15	22	43	18	25	50	21	29	58	25	33
80-84	16	6	10	19	8	12	23	9	14	27	11	16
85-89	5	2	4	6	2	4	8	3	5	10	4	6
90-94	1	0	1	1	0	1	2	1	1	2	1	1
95-99	0	0	0	0	0	0	0	0	0	0	0	0
100 +	0	0	0	0	0	0	0	0	0	0	0	0

Age group	2025 Both sexes	Males	Females	2030 Both sexes	Males	Females	2035 Both sexes	Males	Females	2040 Both sexes	Males	Females
All ages	13 374	6 529	6 845	14 368	7 021	7 347	15 366	7 517	7 849	16 358	8 009	8 348
0-4	1 716	852	865	1 709	850	859	1 746	869	877	1 775	884	891
5-9	1 673	825	848	1 638	809	828	1 641	813	829	1 687	837	851
10-14	1 626	804	822	1 638	807	831	1 608	794	815	1 616	799	817
15-19	1 486	733	753	1 600	790	810	1 614	794	820	1 587	782	805
20-24	1 279	630	649	1 452	713	738	1 565	771	795	1 583	776	807
25-29	1 116	549	567	1 230	605	625	1 400	687	713	1 514	744	770
30-34	993	490	503	1 055	520	535	1 166	574	591	1 331	655	677
35-39	962	470	407	920	460	469	990	489	500	1 097	542	555
40-44	726	358	368	898	444	454	869	431	438	929	460	469
45-49	507	244	263	677	333	344	841	414	426	816	403	413
50-54	366	166	200	471	225	247	632	308	324	788	386	402
55-59	288	128	160	337	151	186	436	206	230	587	283	304
60-64	233	104	129	259	114	146	305	135	170	397	185	212
65-69	175	76	99	200	88	113	225	97	128	266	115	151
70-74	113	48	65	139	59	80	161	69	92	182	77	106
75-79	67	20	00	70	32	46	98	40	58	115	48	68
80-84	33	13	19	39	15	23	46	18	28	59	23	35
85-89	12	4	7	14	5	9	17	7	11	21	8	13
90-94	3	1	2	3	1	2	4	1	3	5	2	3
95-99	0	0	0	1	0	0	1	0	0	1	0	1
100 +	0	0	0	0	0	0	0	0	0	0	0	0

Age group	2045 Both sexes	Males	Females	2050 Both sexes	Males	Females
All ages	17 299	8 477	8 823	18 153	8 899	9 254
0-4	1 758	876	883	1 707	851	856
5-9	1 724	856	869	1 716	852	864
10-14	1 665	824	841	1 705	845	860
15-19	1 597	789	808	1 648	815	833
20-24	1 559	766	793	1 572	774	798
25-29	1 535	752	784	1 516	744	772
30-34	1 446	712	734	1 471	721	750
35-39	1 259	621	638	1 373	678	695
40-44	1 034	512	522	1 192	588	604
45-49	876	433	443	980	484	496
50-54	768	377	391	828	407	421
55-59	735	356	379	720	350	370
60-64	537	256	281	676	324	352
65-69	349	160	189	475	223	253
70-74	218	92	126	289	129	159
75-79	133	54	79	161	66	95
80-84	70	28	42	82	32	50
85-89	27	10	17	33	13	21
90-94	7	2	4	9	3	6
95-99	1	0	1	1	0	1
100 +	0	0	0	0	0	0

United Nations Department of Economic and Social Affairs/Population Division
World Population Prospects: The 2004 Revision, Volume II: Sex and Age Distribution of the World Population

731

POPULATION BY AGE AND SEX (in thousands)

Age group	2005 Both sexes	Males	Females	2010 Both sexes	Males	Females	2015 Both sexes	Males	Females	2020 Both sexes	Males	Females
All ages	9 038	4 379	4 658	10 206	4 960	5 247	11 492	5 597	5 895	12 790	6 240	6 550
0-4	1 500	746	754	1 762	874	888	1 936	960	976	1 988	984	1 004
5-9	1 268	629	639	1 386	687	700	1 637	809	828	1 813	898	915
10-14	1 162	577	585	1 221	605	616	1 339	663	677	1 587	784	804
15-19	1 191	589	602	1 132	561	571	1 194	591	603	1 312	648	663
20-24	960	471	489	1 154	569	585	1 099	543	556	1 162	573	589
25-29	694	333	361	909	445	464	1 100	541	559	1 052	519	534
30-34	507	233	274	644	310	335	846	415	431	1 033	509	524
35-39	403	185	218	466	214	251	592	286	307	783	386	397
40-44	338	158	180	370	169	200	428	197	231	546	264	283
45-49	276	128	149	311	144	166	340	155	185	395	181	214
50-54	211	97	115	253	116	138	286	131	154	314	142	172
55-59	171	78	92	191	86	105	231	104	127	261	118	143
60-64	133	61	73	151	68	82	170	75	94	205	91	114
65-69	98	44	54	112	50	62	127	56	70	144	62	81
70-74	65	28	36	75	33	42	86	38	48	98	43	56
75-79	36	15	22	43	18	25	50	21	29	58	25	33
80-84	16	6	10	19	8	12	23	9	14	27	11	16
85-89	5	2	4	6	2	4	8	3	5	10	4	6
90-94	1	0	1	1	0	1	2	1	1	2	1	1
95-99	0	0	0	0	0	0	0	0	0	0	0	0
100 +	0	0	0	0	0	0	0	0	0	0	0	0

Age group	2025 Both sexes	Males	Females	2030 Both sexes	Males	Females	2035 Both sexes	Males	Females	2040 Both sexes	Males	Females
All ages	14 040	6 859	7 182	15 310	7 487	7 823	16 666	8 160	8 507	18 112	8 878	9 235
0-4	1 961	973	988	2 003	996	1 007	2 128	1 059	1 069	2 260	1 125	1 135
5-9	1 881	928	953	1 872	925	947	1 924	953	971	2 056	1 020	1 037
10-14	1 768	874	894	1 842	907	935	1 838	907	931	1 895	937	958
15-19	1 558	768	790	1 739	859	880	1 815	893	922	1 815	894	920
20-24	1 279	630	649	1 522	748	774	1 702	838	864	1 780	873	907
25-29	1 116	549	567	1 230	605	625	1 468	720	748	1 647	809	837
30-34	993	490	503	1 055	520	535	1 166	574	591	1 396	686	710
35-39	962	476	487	929	460	469	990	489	500	1 097	542	555
40-44	726	358	368	898	444	454	869	431	438	929	460	469
45-49	507	244	263	677	333	344	841	414	426	816	403	413
50-54	366	166	200	471	225	247	632	308	324	788	386	402
55-59	288	128	160	337	151	186	436	206	230	587	283	304
60-64	233	104	129	259	114	146	305	135	170	397	185	212
65-69	175	76	99	200	88	113	225	97	128	266	115	151
70-74	113	48	65	139	59	80	161	69	92	182	77	106
75-79	67	28	39	79	32	46	98	40	58	115	48	68
80-84	33	13	19	39	15	23	46	18	28	59	23	35
85-89	12	4	7	14	5	9	17	7	11	21	8	13
90-94	3	1	2	3	1	2	4	1	3	5	2	3
95-99	0	0	0	1	0	0	1	0	0	1	0	1
100 +	0	0	0	0	0	0	0	0	0	0	0	0

Age group	2045 Both sexes	Males	Females	2050 Both sexes	Males	Females
All ages	19 588	9 609	9 979	21 032	10 324	10 708
0-4	2 332	1 162	1 170	2 346	1 169	1 177
5-9	2 196	1 090	1 106	2 277	1 131	1 146
10-14	2 030	1 005	1 025	2 172	1 076	1 095
15-19	1 873	925	948	2 009	993	1 016
20-24	1 783	876	907	1 843	908	936
25-29	1 727	845	882	1 733	850	883
30-34	1 572	774	798	1 655	812	843
35-39	1 320	651	669	1 493	737	756
40-44	1 034	512	522	1 250	617	633
45-49	876	433	443	980	484	496
50-54	768	377	391	828	407	421
55-59	735	356	379	720	350	370
60-64	537	256	281	676	324	352
65-69	349	160	189	475	223	253
70-74	218	92	126	289	129	159
75-79	133	54	79	161	66	95
80-84	70	28	42	82	32	50
85-89	27	10	17	33	13	21
90-94	7	2	4	9	3	6
95-99	1	0	1	1	0	1
100 +	0	0	0	0	0	0

United Nations Department of Economic and Social Affairs/Population Division
World Population Prospects: The 2004 Revision, Volume II: Sex and Age Distribution of the World Population

732

POPULATION BY AGE AND SEX (in thousands)

Age group	2005 Both sexes	Males	Females	2010 Both sexes	Males	Females	2015 Both sexes	Males	Females	2020 Both sexes	Males	Females
All ages	9 038	4 379	4 658	10 045	4 879	5 165	11 032	5 369	5 663	11 914	5 807	6 108
0-4	1 500	746	754	1 600	794	806	1 627	807	820	1 549	767	782
5-9	1 268	629	639	1 386	687	700	1 486	734	752	1 523	754	769
10-14	1 162	577	585	1 221	605	616	1 339	663	677	1 441	711	730
15-19	1 191	589	602	1 132	561	571	1 194	591	603	1 312	648	663
20-24	960	471	489	1 154	569	585	1 099	543	556	1 162	573	589
25-29	694	333	361	909	445	464	1 100	541	559	1 052	519	534
30-34	507	233	274	644	310	335	846	415	431	1 033	509	524
35-39	403	185	218	466	214	251	592	286	307	783	386	397
40-44	338	158	180	370	169	200	428	197	231	546	264	283
45-49	276	128	149	311	144	166	340	155	185	395	181	214
50-54	211	97	115	253	116	138	286	131	154	314	142	172
55-59	171	78	92	191	86	105	231	104	127	261	118	143
60-64	133	61	73	151	68	82	170	75	94	205	91	114
65-69	98	44	54	112	50	62	127	56	70	144	62	81
70-74	65	28	36	75	33	42	86	38	48	98	43	56
75-79	36	15	22	43	18	25	50	21	29	58	25	33
80-84	16	6	10	19	8	12	23	9	14	27	11	16
85-89	5	2	4	6	2	4	8	3	5	10	4	6
90-94	1	0	1	1	0	1	2	1	1	2	1	1
95-99	0	0	0	0	0	0	0	0	0	0	0	0
100 +	0	0	0	0	0	0	0	0	0	0	0	0

Age group	2025 Both sexes	Males	Females	2030 Both sexes	Males	Females	2035 Both sexes	Males	Females	2040 Both sexes	Males	Females
All ages	12 708	6 200	6 508	13 433	6 559	6 874	14 096	6 889	7 207	14 681	7 180	7 501
0-4	1 472	731	742	1 422	707	715	1 388	691	697	1 338	666	672
5-9	1 465	723	743	1 404	694	710	1 365	676	689	1 341	665	676
10-14	1 485	734	751	1 434	707	728	1 379	681	698	1 344	665	679
15-19	1 414	697	717	1 460	721	739	1 413	695	718	1 361	671	690
20-24	1 279	630	649	1 381	679	702	1 429	703	725	1 385	679	706
25-29	1 116	549	567	1 230	605	625	1 332	653	679	1 382	679	703
30-34	993	490	503	1 055	520	535	1 166	574	591	1 267	623	644
35-39	962	476	487	929	460	469	990	489	500	1 097	542	555
40-44	726	358	368	808	354	454	869	431	438	929	460	469
45-49	507	244	263	677	333	344	841	414	426	816	403	413
50-54	366	166	200	471	225	247	632	308	324	788	386	402
55-59	288	128	160	337	151	180	400	200	200	607	303	304
60-64	233	104	129	259	114	146	305	135	170	397	185	212
65-69	175	76	99	200	88	113	225	97	128	266	115	151
70-74	113	48	65	139	59	80	161	69	92	182	77	106
75-79	67	28	39	79	32	46	98	40	58	115	48	68
80-84	33	13	19	39	15	23	46	18	28	59	23	35
85-89	12	4	7	14	5	9	17	7	11	21	8	13
90-94	3	1	2	3	1	2	4	1	3	5	2	3
95-99	0	0	0	1	0	0	1	0	0	1	0	1
100 +	0	0	0	0	0	0	0	0	0	0	0	0

Age group	2045 Both sexes	Males	Females	2050 Both sexes	Males	Females
All ages	15 161	7 419	7 742	15 521	7 596	7 925
0-4	1 259	627	632	1 167	581	585
5-9	1 300	645	655	1 229	610	619
10-14	1 323	655	668	1 284	637	648
15-19	1 328	656	672	1 309	647	662
20-24	1 336	657	680	1 306	643	663
25-29	1 343	658	686	1 299	637	662
30-34	1 319	650	670	1 287	631	656
35-39	1 197	591	607	1 253	618	634
40-44	1 034	512	522	1 134	560	574
45-49	876	433	443	980	484	496
50-54	768	377	391	828	407	421
55-59	735	356	379	720	350	370
60-64	537	256	281	676	324	352
65-69	349	160	189	475	223	253
70-74	218	92	126	289	129	159
75-79	133	54	79	161	66	95
80-84	70	28	42	82	32	50
85-89	27	10	17	33	13	21
90-94	7	2	4	9	3	6
95-99	1	0	1	1	0	1
100 +	0	0	0	0	0	0

POPULATION BY AGE AND SEX (in thousands)

Age group	1950 Both sexes	Males	Females	1955 Both sexes	Males	Females	1960 Both sexes	Males	Females	1965 Both sexes	Males	Females
All ages	83	41	42	87	43	43	90	43	47	96	46	50
0-4	12	6	6	13	7	6	16	8	8	18	9	9
5-9	11	5	5	12	6	6	13	7	6	15	8	8
10-14	10	5	5	10	5	5	11	6	5	13	7	6
15-19	8	4	4	8	4	4	9	4	4	9	5	5
20-24	8	4	4	8	4	4	7	3	4	7	3	4
25-29	7	3	3	7	3	3	5	2	3	5	2	3
30-34	5	3	3	5	3	3	5	2	3	4	2	2
35-39	5	3	3	5	3	3	5	2	3	4	2	2
40-44	4	2	2	4	2	2	4	2	2	4	2	2
45-49	4	2	2	4	2	2	4	2	2	4	2	2
50-54	3	1	2	3	1	2	3	1	2	3	2	2
55-59	2	1	1	2	1	1	2	1	1	3	1	1
60-64	2	1	1	1	1	1	2	1	1	2	1	1
65-69	1	0	1	1	0	0	1	1	1	2	1	1
70-74	1	0	1	1	0	1	1	0	1	1	0	1
75-79	1	0	0	1	0	0	1	0	0	1	0	1
80 +	1	0	0	1	0	0	1	0	0	1	0	0

Age group	1970 Both sexes	Males	Females	1975 Both sexes	Males	Females	1980 Both sexes	Males	Females	1985 Both sexes	Males	Females
All ages	104	50	54	110	53	57	118	58	60	127	62	65
0-4	19	10	9	17	9	9	17	8	8	17	8	8
5-9	18	10	9	18	9	9	18	9	9	18	9	9
10-14	14	7	7	16	8	8	17	9	8	17	9	8
15-19	10	5	5	12	6	6	15	7	7	15	8	7
20-24	7	3	4	9	4	5	10	5	5	12	6	6
25-29	5	2	3	6	3	3	7	4	4	9	4	5
30-34	4	2	2	5	2	3	6	3	3	7	3	4
35-39	4	2	2	4	2	2	5	2	2	6	3	3
40-44	4	2	2	4	2	2	4	2	2	5	2	3
45-49	4	2	2	4	2	2	4	2	2	4	2	2
50-54	3	2	2	3	2	2	4	2	2	4	2	2
55-59	3	1	2	3	1	2	3	1	2	3	2	2
60-64	3	1	1	3	1	2	3	1	2	3	1	2
65-69	2	1	1	2	1	1	2	1	1	3	1	1
70-74	1	1	1	2	1	1	2	1	1	2	1	1
75-79	1	0	1	1	0	1	1	0	1	1	1	1
80 +	1	0	0	1	0	0	1	0	0	1	0	1

Age group	1990 Both sexes	Males	Females	1995 Both sexes	Males	Females	2000 Both sexes	Males	Females	2005 Both sexes	Males	Females
All ages	138	68	70	148	73	75	154	76	78	161	79	82
0-4	17	9	8	18	9	9	14	7	7	14	7	7
5-9	17	9	9	17	9	8	18	9	9	14	7	7
10-14	16	8	8	17	8	9	17	8	8	18	9	9
15-19	15	7	7	15	8	8	16	8	8	16	8	8
20-24	13	6	7	14	7	7	13	7	7	16	8	8
25-29	12	6	6	12	5	6	12	6	6	13	6	6
30-34	8	4	4	11	5	5	11	6	6	12	6	6
35-39	8	4	4	8	4	4	11	5	6	11	5	6
40-44	5	2	3	8	4	4	9	4	5	11	5	5
45-49	5	2	2	5	2	3	7	4	3	8	4	4
50-54	5	2	3	5	2	2	5	3	3	7	3	3
55-59	4	2	2	5	2	3	5	2	2	5	3	3
60-64	3	2	2	4	2	2	4	2	2	4	2	2
65-69	4	2	2	3	1	2	3	2	2	4	2	2
70-74	3	1	2	3	1	2	3	1	1	3	1	1
75-79	2	1	1	2	1	1	2	1	1	2	1	1
80 +	2	1	1	2	1	1	3	1	2	3	1	2

United Nations Department of Economic and Social Affairs/Population Division
World Population Prospects: The 2004 Revision, Volume II: Sex and Age Distribution of the World Population

POPULATION BY AGE AND SEX (in thousands)

Age group	2005 Both sexes	Males	Females	2010 Both sexes	Males	Females	2015 Both sexes	Males	Females	2020 Both sexes	Males	Females
All ages	161	79	82	168	83	85	174	86	88	180	89	91
0-4	14	7	7	15	8	7	15	8	7	14	7	7
5-9	14	7	7	14	7	7	15	8	7	15	8	7
10-14	18	9	9	14	7	7	14	7	7	15	8	7
15-19	16	8	8	18	9	9	14	7	7	14	7	7
20-24	16	8	8	16	8	8	17	9	8	13	7	7
25-29	13	6	6	15	8	8	15	8	8	16	8	8
30-34	12	6	6	12	6	6	15	7	7	15	7	7
35-39	11	5	6	11	6	6	12	6	6	14	7	7
40-44	11	5	5	11	5	5	11	5	6	11	6	6
45-49	8	4	4	10	5	5	10	5	5	11	5	6
50-54	7	3	3	8	4	4	10	5	5	10	5	5
55-59	5	3	3	6	3	3	8	4	4	9	5	5
60-64	4	2	2	5	2	2	6	3	3	7	3	4
65-69	4	2	2	4	2	2	4	2	2	5	3	3
70-74	3	1	1	3	1	2	3	1	2	4	2	2
75-79	2	1	1	2	1	1	2	1	1	2	1	1
80-84	2	1	1	1	1	1	2	1	1	2	1	1
85-89	1	0	1	1	0	1	1	0	0	1	0	1
90-94	0	0	0	0	0	0	0	0	0	0	0	0
95-99	0	0	0	0	0	0	0	0	0	0	0	0
100 +	0	0	0	0	0	0	0	0	0	0	0	0

Age group	2025 Both sexes	Males	Females	2030 Both sexes	Males	Females	2035 Both sexes	Males	Females	2040 Both sexes	Males	Females
All ages	184	91	93	187	93	94	189	93	95	190	94	96
0-4	13	7	7	12	6	6	12	6	6	12	6	6
5-9	14	7	7	13	7	6	12	6	6	12	6	6
10-14	15	7	7	14	7	7	13	7	6	12	6	6
15-19	15	7	7	15	7	7	14	7	7	13	7	6
20-24	13	7	7	14	7	7	14	7	7	13	7	7
25-29	13	6	6	13	7	6	13	7	7	13	7	7
30-34	16	8	8	12	6	6	12	6	6	13	7	6
35-39	14	7	7	15	8	8	12	6	6	12	6	6
40-44	14	7	7	14	7	7	15	8	7	11	6	6
45-49	11	6	6	14	7	7	14	7	7	15	7	7
50-54	10	5	5	11	5	5	13	7	7	13	7	7
55-59	10	5	5	10	5	5	10	5	5	13	6	7
60-64	9	4	5	9	4	5	9	4	5	10	5	5
65-69	6	3	3	8	4	4	8	4	4	9	4	5
70-74	5	2	2	6	2	3	7	3	4	7	3	4
75-79	3	1	2	4	2	2	5	2	3	6	3	3
80-84	2	1	1	2	1	1	3	1	1	3	1	2
85-89	1	0	1	1	0	1	1	0	1	2	1	1
90-94	0	0	0	0	0	0	0	0	0	1	0	0
95-99	0	0	0	0	0	0	0	0	0	0	0	0
100 +	0	0	0	0	0	0	0	0	0	0	0	0

Age group	2045 Both sexes	Males	Females	2050 Both sexes	Males	Females
All ages	190	94	96	188	93	95
0-4	11	6	6	11	6	5
5-9	12	6	6	11	6	6
10-14	12	6	6	12	6	6
15-19	12	6	6	12	6	6
20-24	12	6	6	11	6	6
25-29	13	7	6	12	6	6
30-34	13	7	6	12	6	6
35-39	13	6	6	13	6	6
40-44	12	6	6	12	6	6
45-49	11	6	5	11	6	6
50-54	14	7	7	11	6	5
55-59	13	6	6	14	7	7
60-64	12	6	6	12	6	6
65-69	9	4	5	11	5	6
70-74	8	3	4	8	4	4
75-79	6	3	3	6	3	4
80-84	4	2	2	4	2	3
85-89	2	1	1	3	1	2
90-94	1	0	1	1	0	1
95-99	0	0	0	0	0	0
100 +	0	0	0	0	0	0

United Nations Department of Economic and Social Affairs/Population Division
World Population Prospects: The 2004 Revision, Volume II: Sex and Age Distribution of the World Population

735

POPULATION BY AGE AND SEX (in thousands)

Age group	2005 Both sexes	Males	Females	2010 Both sexes	Males	Females	2015 Both sexes	Males	Females	2020 Both sexes	Males	Females
All ages	161	79	82	169	84	86	179	88	90	188	93	95
0-4	14	7	7	17	9	8	18	9	9	18	9	9
5-9	14	7	7	14	7	7	17	8	8	18	9	9
10-14	18	9	9	14	7	7	14	7	7	17	8	8
15-19	16	8	8	18	9	9	14	7	7	14	7	7
20-24	16	8	8	16	8	8	17	9	8	13	7	7
25-29	13	6	6	15	8	8	15	8	8	16	8	8
30-34	12	6	6	12	6	6	15	7	7	15	7	7
35-39	11	5	6	11	6	6	12	6	6	14	7	7
40-44	11	5	5	11	5	5	11	5	6	11	6	6
45-49	8	4	4	10	5	5	10	5	5	11	5	6
50-54	7	3	3	8	4	4	10	5	5	10	5	5
55-59	5	3	3	6	3	3	8	4	4	9	5	5
60-64	4	2	2	5	2	2	6	3	3	7	3	4
65-69	4	2	2	4	2	2	4	2	2	5	3	3
70-74	3	1	1	3	1	2	3	1	2	4	2	2
75-79	2	1	1	2	1	1	2	1	1	2	1	1
80-84	2	1	1	1	1	1	2	1	1	2	1	1
85-89	1	0	1	1	0	1	1	0	0	1	0	1
90-94	0	0	0	0	0	0	0	0	0	0	0	0
95-99	0	0	0	0	0	0	0	0	0	0	0	0
100 +	0	0	0	0	0	0	0	0	0	0	0	0

Age group	2025 Both sexes	Males	Females	2030 Both sexes	Males	Females	2035 Both sexes	Males	Females	2040 Both sexes	Males	Females
All ages	196	97	99	202	100	102	209	104	105	216	107	108
0-4	17	9	8	16	8	8	17	8	8	18	9	9
5-9	18	9	9	17	8	8	16	8	8	17	8	8
10-14	18	9	9	18	9	9	17	8	8	16	8	8
15-19	16	8	8	17	9	9	17	9	9	16	8	8
20-24	13	7	7	16	8	8	17	9	8	17	9	8
25-29	13	6	6	13	7	6	15	8	7	16	8	8
30-34	16	8	8	12	6	6	12	6	6	15	7	7
35-39	14	7	7	15	8	8	12	6	6	12	6	6
40-44	14	7	7	14	7	7	15	8	7	11	6	6
45-49	11	6	6	14	7	7	14	7	7	15	7	7
50-54	10	5	5	11	5	5	13	7	7	13	7	7
55-59	10	5	5	10	5	5	10	5	5	13	6	7
60-64	9	4	5	9	4	5	9	4	5	10	5	5
65-69	6	3	3	8	4	4	8	4	4	9	4	5
70-74	5	2	2	6	2	3	7	3	4	7	3	4
75-79	3	1	2	4	2	2	5	2	3	6	3	3
80-84	2	1	1	2	1	1	3	1	1	3	1	2
85-89	1	0	1	1	0	1	1	0	1	2	1	1
90-94	0	0	0	0	0	0	0	0	0	1	0	0
95-99	0	0	0	0	0	0	0	0	0	0	0	0
100 +	0	0	0	0	0	0	0	0	0	0	0	0

Age group	2045 Both sexes	Males	Females	2050 Both sexes	Males	Females
All ages	222	111	112	228	113	114
0-4	18	9	9	18	9	9
5-9	17	9	9	18	9	9
10-14	17	8	8	17	9	9
15-19	16	8	8	16	8	8
20-24	16	8	8	15	8	8
25-29	16	8	8	15	8	8
30-34	16	8	8	16	8	8
35-39	14	7	7	15	8	8
40-44	12	6	6	14	7	7
45-49	11	6	5	11	6	6
50-54	14	7	7	11	6	5
55-59	13	6	6	14	7	7
60-64	12	6	6	12	6	6
65-69	9	4	5	11	5	6
70-74	8	3	4	8	4	4
75-79	6	3	3	6	3	4
80-84	4	2	2	4	2	3
85-89	2	1	1	3	1	2
90-94	1	0	1	1	0	1
95-99	0	0	0	0	0	0
100 +	0	0	0	0	0	0

United Nations Department of Economic and Social Affairs/Population Division
World Population Prospects: The 2004 Revision, Volume II: Sex and Age Distribution of the World Population

736

LOW VARIANT   **SAINT LUCIA**

POPULATION BY AGE AND SEX (in thousands)

Age group	2005 Both sexes	Males	Females	2010 Both sexes	Males	Females	2015 Both sexes	Males	Females	2020 Both sexes	Males	Females
All ages	161	79	82	166	82	84	169	84	86	171	85	87
0-4	14	7	7	13	7	7	12	6	6	11	5	5
5-9	14	7	7	14	7	7	13	7	6	12	6	6
10-14	18	9	9	14	7	7	14	7	7	13	7	6
15-19	16	8	8	18	9	9	14	7	7	14	7	7
20-24	16	8	8	16	8	8	17	9	8	13	7	7
25-29	13	6	6	15	8	8	15	8	8	16	8	8
30-34	12	6	6	12	6	6	15	7	7	15	7	7
35-39	11	5	6	11	6	6	12	6	6	14	7	7
40-44	11	5	5	11	5	5	11	5	6	11	6	6
45-49	8	4	4	10	5	5	10	5	5	11	5	6
50-54	7	3	3	8	4	4	10	5	5	10	5	5
55-59	5	3	3	6	3	3	8	4	4	9	5	5
60-64	4	2	2	5	2	2	6	3	3	7	3	4
65-69	4	2	2	4	2	2	4	2	2	5	3	3
70-74	3	1	1	3	1	2	3	1	2	4	2	2
75-79	2	1	1	2	1	1	2	1	1	2	1	1
80-84	2	1	1	1	1	1	2	1	1	2	1	1
85-89	1	0	1	1	0	1	1	0	0	1	0	1
90-94	0	0	0	0	0	0	0	0	0	0	0	0
95-99	0	0	0	0	0	0	0	0	0	0	0	0
100 +	0	0	0	0	0	0	0	0	0	0	0	0

Age group	2025 Both sexes	Males	Females	2030 Both sexes	Males	Females	2035 Both sexes	Males	Females	2040 Both sexes	Males	Females
All ages	172	85	87	171	85	87	169	84	85	166	82	84
0-4	10	5	5	9	4	4	8	4	4	7	4	4
5-9	11	5	5	10	5	5	9	4	4	8	4	4
10-14	12	6	6	11	5	5	10	5	5	9	4	4
15-19	13	7	6	12	6	6	10	5	5	9	5	5
20-24	13	7	7	12	6	6	11	6	5	10	5	5
25-29	13	6	6	13	7	6	12	6	6	11	5	5
30-34	16	8	8	12	6	6	12	6	6	11	6	6
35-39	14	7	7	15	8	8	12	6	6	12	6	6
40-44	14	7	7	14	7	7	15	8	7	11	6	6
45-49	11	6	6	14	7	7	14	7	7	15	7	7
50-54	10	5	5	11	5	5	10	7	7	13	7	7
55-59	10	5	5	10	5	5	10	5	5	13	6	7
60-64	9	4	5	9	4	5	9	4	5	10	5	5
65-69	6	3	3	8	4	4	8	4	4	9	4	5
70-74	5	2	2	6	2	3	7	3	4	7	3	4
75-79	3	1	2	4	2	2	5	2	3	6	3	3
80-84	2	1	1	2	1	1	3	1	1	3	1	2
85-89	1	0	1	1	0	1	1	0	1	2	1	1
90-94	0	0	0	0	0	0	0	0	0	1	0	0
95-99	0	0	0	0	0	0	0	0	0	0	0	0
100 +	0	0	0	0	0	0	0	0	0	0	0	0

Age group	2045 Both sexes	Males	Females	2050 Both sexes	Males	Females
All ages	161	79	81	154	76	78
0-4	6	3	3	6	3	3
5-9	7	4	3	6	3	3
10-14	8	4	4	7	4	3
15-19	8	4	4	7	4	4
20-24	9	5	4	8	4	4
25-29	9	5	5	8	4	4
30-34	10	5	5	9	4	4
35-39	11	6	5	10	5	5
40-44	12	6	6	11	5	5
45-49	11	6	5	11	6	6
50-54	14	7	7	11	6	5
55-59	13	6	6	14	7	7
60-64	12	6	6	12	6	6
65-69	9	4	5	11	5	6
70-74	8	3	4	8	4	4
75-79	6	3	3	6	3	4
80-84	4	2	2	4	2	3
85-89	2	1	1	3	1	2
90-94	1	0	1	1	0	1
95-99	0	0	0	0	0	0
100 +	0	0	0	0	0	0

POPULATION BY AGE AND SEX (in thousands)

Age group	1950 Both sexes	Males	Females	1955 Both sexes	Males	Females	1960 Both sexes	Males	Females	1965 Both sexes	Males	Females
All ages	67	32	35	74	35	39	81	38	43	86	40	46
0-4	14	7	7	15	7	7	16	8	8	17	9	8
5-9	11	6	5	12	6	6	13	7	7	15	7	7
10-14	9	4	4	10	5	5	11	5	5	12	6	6
15-19	6	3	3	8	4	4	7	4	4	9	4	5
20-24	5	2	3	5	2	3	6	3	3	6	3	3
25-29	4	2	2	4	2	2	4	2	2	5	2	3
30-34	3	1	2	3	1	2	4	2	2	3	1	2
35-39	3	1	2	3	1	2	3	1	2	3	1	2
40-44	3	1	2	3	1	1	3	1	2	3	1	2
45-49	2	1	1	2	1	1	3	1	2	3	1	2
50-54	2	1	1	2	1	1	3	1	2	3	1	2
55-59	2	1	1	2	1	1	2	1	1	3	1	1
60-64	1	1	1	2	1	1	2	1	1	2	1	1
65-69	1	0	1	1	0	1	1	0	1	2	1	1
70-74	1	0	1	1	0	0	1	0	1	1	0	1
75-79	1	0	0	1	0	0	1	0	0	1	0	0
80 +	0	0	0	0	0	0	1	0	0	1	0	0

Age group	1970 Both sexes	Males	Females	1975 Both sexes	Males	Females	1980 Both sexes	Males	Females	1985 Both sexes	Males	Females
All ages	90	43	48	96	46	50	100	49	52	104	51	53
0-4	17	8	8	16	8	8	15	7	7	14	7	7
5-9	15	8	8	15	8	8	15	8	7	14	7	7
10-14	13	7	6	14	7	7	14	7	7	14	7	7
15-19	10	5	5	12	6	6	13	7	6	13	7	6
20-24	7	4	4	8	4	4	10	5	5	11	6	6
25-29	5	2	3	5	2	3	6	3	3	8	4	4
30-34	4	1	2	4	2	2	4	2	2	5	2	3
35-39	3	1	2	3	1	2	3	2	2	4	2	2
40-44	2	1	1	2	1	1	3	2	2	3	2	2
45-49	2	1	1	2	1	1	3	1	2	4	2	2
50-54	3	1	2	2	1	1	3	1	2	3	1	2
55-59	3	1	2	3	1	1	2	1	1	3	1	1
60-64	3	1	1	3	1	2	2	1	1	2	1	1
65-69	2	1	1	2	1	1	2	1	1	2	1	1
70-74	1	0	1	2	1	1	2	1	1	2	1	1
75-79	1	0	0	1	0	1	1	0	1	1	1	1
80 +	1	0	0	1	0	0	1	0	1	1	0	1

Age group	1990 Both sexes	Males	Females	1995 Both sexes	Males	Females	2000 Both sexes	Males	Females	2005 Both sexes	Males	Females
All ages	109	54	55	113	56	57	116	58	58	119	59	60
0-4	14	7	7	13	7	6	11	6	6	12	6	6
5-9	14	7	7	15	7	7	13	6	6	11	6	6
10-14	14	7	7	14	7	7	14	7	7	12	6	6
15-19	12	6	6	13	7	6	13	7	7	13	7	6
20-24	10	5	5	11	5	5	12	6	6	12	6	6
25-29	10	5	5	9	5	5	10	5	5	11	6	6
30-34	8	4	4	9	5	4	9	4	4	9	5	4
35-39	5	3	3	6	3	3	8	4	4	8	4	4
40-44	4	2	2	4	2	2	5	3	3	8	4	4
45-49	3	1	2	4	2	2	4	2	2	5	3	2
50-54	3	1	2	3	1	1	4	2	2	3	2	2
55-59	3	1	1	3	1	2	3	1	1	3	2	2
60-64	3	1	1	3	1	1	3	1	2	3	1	1
65-69	2	1	1	3	1	1	3	1	1	3	1	1
70-74	2	1	1	2	1	1	2	1	1	2	1	1
75-79	1	1	1	1	1	1	1	1	1	2	1	1
80 +	1	0	1	1	0	1	1	0	1	1	0	1

United Nations Department of Economic and Social Affairs/Population Division
World Population Prospects: The 2004 Revision, Volume II: Sex and Age Distribution of the World Population

MEDIUM VARIANT   **SAINT VINCENT AND THE GRENADINES**

POPULATION BY AGE AND SEX (in thousands)

Age group	2005 Both sexes	Males	Females	2010 Both sexes	Males	Females	2015 Both sexes	Males	Females	2020 Both sexes	Males	Females
All ages	119	59	60	122	61	61	124	62	62	125	62	63
0-4	12	6	6	12	6	6	11	6	5	10	5	5
5-9	11	6	6	11	6	6	11	6	6	11	5	5
10-14	12	6	6	11	5	5	11	5	5	11	5	5
15-19	13	7	7	11	6	6	10	5	5	10	5	5
20-24	12	6	6	12	6	6	10	5	5	9	4	4
25-29	11	6	6	12	6	6	11	6	6	10	5	5
30-34	9	5	4	10	5	5	11	5	5	11	5	5
35-39	8	4	4	8	4	4	10	5	5	10	5	5
40-44	8	4	4	8	4	4	8	4	4	9	5	5
45-49	5	3	2	7	4	4	7	4	3	8	4	4
50-54	3	2	2	5	3	2	7	4	3	7	4	3
55-59	3	2	2	3	2	2	5	2	2	7	4	3
60-64	3	1	1	3	2	2	3	2	2	5	2	2
65-69	3	1	1	3	1	1	3	1	2	3	1	2
70-74	2	1	1	2	1	1	2	1	1	3	1	2
75-79	2	1	1	2	1	1	2	1	1	2	1	1
80-84	1	0	1	1	0	1	1	0	1	1	0	1
85-89	0	0	0	0	0	0	0	0	0	0	0	0
90-94	0	0	0	0	0	0	0	0	0	0	0	0
95-99	0	0	0	0	0	0	0	0	0	0	0	0
100 +	0	0	0	0	0	0	0	0	0	0	0	0

Age group	2025 Both sexes	Males	Females	2030 Both sexes	Males	Females	2035 Both sexes	Males	Females	2040 Both sexes	Males	Females
All ages	125	62	63	123	61	62	121	60	61	117	57	60
0-4	9	4	4	8	4	4	7	4	4	7	4	3
5-9	10	5	5	8	4	4	8	4	4	7	4	4
10-14	10	5	5	9	5	4	8	4	4	7	4	4
15-19	10	5	5	9	5	5	8	4	4	7	4	4
20-24	9	4	5	9	4	5	8	4	4	7	4	4
25-29	8	4	4	8	4	4	8	4	4	8	4	4
30-34	9	4	4	7	4	4	7	4	4	7	4	4
35-39	10	5	5	8	4	4	7	3	3	7	3	3
40-44	10	5	5	10	5	5	8	4	4	6	3	3
45-49	9	4	4	9	5	5	9	5	5	7	4	4
50-54	7	4	4	9	4	4	9	5	5	9	4	4
55-59	7	3	3	7	4	4	8	4	4	9	4	5
60-64	7	3	3	7	3	3	7	4	3	8	4	4
65-69	4	2	2	6	3	3	6	3	3	7	3	3
70-74	3	1	2	4	2	2	6	3	3	5	3	3
75-79	2	1	1	2	1	1	3	1	2	4	2	2
80-84	1	0	1	1	1	1	1	1	1	2	1	1
85-89	1	0	0	1	0	0	1	0	1	1	0	1
90-94	0	0	0	0	0	0	0	0	0	0	0	0
95-99	0	0	0	0	0	0	0	0	0	0	0	0
100 +	0	0	0	0	0	0	0	0	0	0	0	0

Age group	2045 Both sexes	Males	Females	2050 Both sexes	Males	Females
All ages	112	55	57	105	51	54
0-4	6	3	3	6	3	3
5-9	7	3	3	6	3	3
10-14	7	3	3	6	3	3
15-19	6	3	3	6	3	3
20-24	6	3	3	6	3	3
25-29	7	3	3	5	3	3
30-34	7	3	3	6	3	3
35-39	7	3	3	6	3	3
40-44	6	3	3	6	3	3
45-49	6	3	3	6	3	3
50-54	7	4	4	6	3	3
55-59	9	4	4	7	4	4
60-64	9	4	4	9	4	4
65-69	8	4	4	8	4	4
70-74	6	3	3	7	3	4
75-79	4	2	2	5	2	3
80-84	3	1	2	3	1	2
85-89	1	0	1	2	1	1
90-94	0	0	0	0	0	0
95-99	0	0	0	0	0	0
100 +	0	0	0	0	0	0

United Nations Department of Economic and Social Affairs/Population Division
World Population Prospects: The 2004 Revision, Volume II: Sex and Age Distribution of the World Population

739

POPULATION BY AGE AND SEX (in thousands)

Age group	2005 Both sexes	Males	Females	2010 Both sexes	Males	Females	2015 Both sexes	Males	Females	2020 Both sexes	Males	Females
All ages	119	59	60	123	61	62	128	64	64	131	65	66
0-4	12	6	6	13	7	6	13	7	6	12	6	6
5-9	11	6	6	11	6	6	13	6	6	13	6	6
10-14	12	6	6	11	5	5	11	5	5	12	6	6
15-19	13	7	7	11	6	6	10	5	5	10	5	5
20-24	12	6	6	12	6	6	10	5	5	9	4	4
25-29	11	6	6	12	6	6	11	6	6	10	5	5
30-34	9	5	4	10	5	5	11	5	5	11	5	5
35-39	8	4	4	8	4	4	10	5	5	10	5	5
40-44	8	4	4	8	4	4	8	4	4	9	5	5
45-49	5	3	2	7	4	4	7	4	3	8	4	4
50-54	3	2	2	5	3	2	7	4	3	7	4	3
55-59	3	2	2	3	2	2	5	2	2	7	4	3
60-64	3	1	1	3	2	2	3	2	2	5	2	2
65-69	3	1	1	3	1	1	3	1	2	3	1	2
70-74	2	1	1	2	1	1	2	1	1	3	1	2
75-79	2	1	1	2	1	1	2	1	1	2	1	1
80-84	1	0	1	1	0	1	1	0	1	1	0	1
85-89	0	0	0	0	0	0	0	0	0	0	0	0
90-94	0	0	0	0	0	0	0	0	0	0	0	0
95-99	0	0	0	0	0	0	0	0	0	0	0	0
100 +	0	0	0	0	0	0	0	0	0	0	0	0

Age group	2025 Both sexes	Males	Females	2030 Both sexes	Males	Females	2035 Both sexes	Males	Females	2040 Both sexes	Males	Females
All ages	133	66	67	134	67	68	135	67	68	135	67	68
0-4	11	6	6	11	5	5	11	5	5	11	5	5
5-9	12	6	6	11	6	5	10	5	5	10	5	5
10-14	12	6	6	12	6	6	10	5	5	10	5	5
15-19	11	6	6	11	6	6	11	5	5	10	5	5
20-24	9	4	5	10	5	5	11	5	5	10	5	5
25-29	8	4	4	8	4	4	10	5	5	10	5	5
30-34	9	4	4	7	4	4	7	4	4	9	4	4
35-39	10	5	5	8	4	4	7	3	3	7	3	3
40-44	10	5	5	10	5	5	8	4	4	6	3	3
45-49	9	4	4	9	5	5	9	5	5	7	4	4
50-54	7	4	4	9	4	4	9	5	5	9	4	4
55-59	7	3	3	7	4	4	8	4	4	9	4	5
60-64	7	3	3	7	3	3	7	4	3	8	4	4
65-69	4	2	2	6	3	3	6	3	3	7	3	3
70-74	3	1	2	4	2	2	6	3	3	5	3	3
75-79	2	1	1	2	1	1	3	1	2	4	2	2
80-84	1	0	1	1	1	1	1	1	1	2	1	1
85-89	1	0	0	1	0	0	1	0	1	1	0	1
90-94	0	0	0	0	0	0	0	0	0	0	0	0
95-99	0	0	0	0	0	0	0	0	0	0	0	0
100 +	0	0	0	0	0	0	0	0	0	0	0	0

Age group	2045 Both sexes	Males	Females	2050 Both sexes	Males	Females
All ages	134	66	68	132	65	67
0-4	10	5	5	10	5	5
5-9	10	5	5	10	5	5
10-14	10	5	5	10	5	5
15-19	9	5	4	9	5	5
20-24	9	4	4	8	4	4
25-29	9	4	5	8	4	4
30-34	9	4	4	8	4	4
35-39	8	4	4	8	4	4
40-44	6	3	3	8	4	4
45-49	6	3	3	6	3	3
50-54	7	4	4	6	3	3
55-59	9	4	4	7	4	4
60-64	9	4	4	9	4	4
65-69	8	4	4	8	4	4
70-74	6	3	3	7	3	4
75-79	4	2	2	5	2	3
80-84	3	1	2	3	1	2
85-89	1	0	1	2	1	1
90-94	0	0	0	0	0	0
95-99	0	0	0	0	0	0
100 +	0	0	0	0	0	0

United Nations Department of Economic and Social Affairs/Population Division
World Population Prospects: The 2004 Revision, Volume II: Sex and Age Distribution of the World Population

POPULATION BY AGE AND SEX (in thousands)

Age group	2005 Both sexes	Males	Females	2010 Both sexes	Males	Females	2015 Both sexes	Males	Females	2020 Both sexes	Males	Females
All ages	119	59	60	121	60	61	121	60	61	119	59	60
0-4	12	6	6	10	5	5	9	4	4	7	4	4
5-9	11	6	6	11	6	6	10	5	5	8	4	4
10-14	12	6	6	11	5	5	11	5	5	9	5	5
15-19	13	7	7	11	6	6	10	5	5	10	5	5
20-24	12	6	6	12	6	6	10	5	5	9	4	4
25-29	11	6	6	12	6	6	11	6	6	10	5	5
30-34	9	5	4	10	5	5	11	5	5	11	5	5
35-39	8	4	4	8	4	4	10	5	5	10	5	5
40-44	8	4	4	8	4	4	8	4	4	9	5	5
45-49	5	3	2	7	4	4	7	4	3	8	4	4
50-54	3	2	2	5	3	2	7	4	3	7	4	3
55-59	3	2	2	3	2	2	5	2	2	7	4	3
60-64	3	1	1	3	2	2	3	2	2	5	2	2
65-69	3	1	1	3	1	1	3	1	2	3	1	2
70-74	2	1	1	2	1	1	2	1	1	3	1	2
75-79	2	1	1	2	1	1	2	1	1	2	1	1
80-84	1	0	1	1	0	1	1	0	1	1	0	1
85-89	0	0	0	0	0	0	0	0	0	0	0	0
90-94	0	0	0	0	0	0	0	0	0	0	0	0
95-99	0	0	0	0	0	0	0	0	0	0	0	0
100 +	0	0	0	0	0	0	0	0	0	0	0	0

Age group	2025 Both sexes	Males	Females	2030 Both sexes	Males	Females	2035 Both sexes	Males	Females	2040 Both sexes	Males	Females
All ages	116	58	59	112	56	57	107	53	54	101	49	51
0-4	6	3	3	6	3	3	5	2	2	4	2	2
5-9	7	4	3	6	3	3	5	3	3	4	2	2
10-14	8	4	4	7	3	3	6	3	3	5	2	2
15-19	9	4	4	7	3	4	6	3	3	5	2	2
20-24	9	4	5	8	4	4	6	3	3	5	2	2
25-29	8	4	4	8	4	4	7	3	3	5	3	3
30-34	9	4	4	7	4	4	7	4	4	6	3	3
35-39	10	5	5	8	4	4	7	3	3	7	3	3
40-44	10	5	5	10	5	5	8	4	4	6	3	3
45-49	9	4	4	9	5	5	9	5	5	7	4	4
50-54	7	4	4	9	4	4	9	5	5	9	4	4
55-59	7	3	3	7	4	4	8	4	4	9	4	5
60-64	7	3	3	7	3	3	7	4	3	8	4	4
65-69	4	2	2	6	3	3	6	3	3	7	3	3
70-74	3	1	2	4	2	2	6	3	3	5	3	3
75-79	2	1	1	2	1	1	3	1	2	4	2	2
80-84	1	0	1	1	1	1	1	1	1	2	1	1
85-89	1	0	0	1	0	0	1	0	1	1	0	1
90-94	0	0	0	0	0	0	0	0	0	0	0	0
95-99	0	0	0	0	0	0	0	0	0	0	0	0
100 +	0	0	0	0	0	0	0	0	0	0	0	0

Age group	2045 Both sexes	Males	Females	2050 Both sexes	Males	Females
All ages	92	45	48	83	40	43
0-4	3	2	2	2	1	1
5-9	4	2	2	3	1	1
10-14	4	2	2	3	2	2
15-19	4	2	2	3	2	2
20-24	4	2	2	3	1	2
25-29	4	2	2	3	1	2
30-34	5	2	2	3	2	2
35-39	6	3	3	4	2	2
40-44	6	3	3	5	3	3
45-49	6	3	3	6	3	3
50-54	7	4	4	6	3	3
55-59	9	4	4	7	4	4
60-64	9	4	4	9	4	4
65-69	8	4	4	8	4	4
70-74	6	3	3	7	3	4
75-79	4	2	2	5	2	3
80-84	3	1	2	3	1	2
85-89	1	0	1	2	1	1
90-94	0	0	0	0	0	0
95-99	0	0	0	0	0	0
100 +	0	0	0	0	0	0

POPULATION BY AGE AND SEX (in thousands)

Age group	1950 Both sexes	Males	Females	1955 Both sexes	Males	Females	1960 Both sexes	Males	Females	1965 Both sexes	Males	Females
All ages	82	42	40	94	48	46	110	56	54	127	64	63
0-4	15	8	7	19	10	10	22	11	11	25	13	12
5-9	13	7	6	14	7	7	18	9	9	21	10	10
10-14	11	6	5	12	6	6	13	7	6	18	9	9
15-19	8	4	4	10	6	5	12	6	6	13	7	6
20-24	7	3	4	8	4	4	10	5	5	11	6	5
25-29	7	3	3	7	3	4	7	4	4	9	5	4
30-34	5	3	2	6	3	3	6	3	3	7	3	3
35-39	4	2	2	5	2	2	6	3	3	6	3	3
40-44	3	2	1	4	2	2	4	2	2	5	2	3
45-49	3	1	1	3	1	1	3	2	2	4	2	2
50-54	2	1	1	2	1	1	2	1	1	3	2	2
55-59	1	1	1	2	1	1	2	1	1	2	1	1
60-64	1	1	1	1	0	0	1	1	1	1	1	1
65-69	1	0	0	1	0	1	1	0	0	1	0	1
70-74	1	0	0	0	0	0	1	0	0	0	0	0
75-79	0	0	0	0	0	0	0	0	0	0	0	0
80 +	0	0	0	0	0	0	0	0	0	0	0	0

Age group	1970 Both sexes	Males	Females	1975 Both sexes	Males	Females	1980 Both sexes	Males	Females	1985 Both sexes	Males	Females
All ages	142	72	70	150	76	74	155	79	76	157	81	75
0-4	25	13	12	24	12	12	23	12	11	25	13	12
5-9	23	12	11	22	11	11	21	11	10	19	10	9
10-14	20	10	10	22	11	11	20	10	10	19	10	9
15-19	17	9	9	19	9	9	20	10	10	18	10	9
20-24	12	6	6	16	8	8	17	9	8	18	9	9
25-29	11	6	5	11	6	5	14	7	7	15	8	7
30-34	9	5	4	9	5	4	9	5	4	12	6	6
35-39	6	3	3	7	4	3	8	4	3	7	4	3
40-44	5	2	3	5	3	3	6	4	3	6	3	3
45-49	5	2	2	4	2	2	4	2	2	5	3	2
50-54	3	2	2	4	2	2	4	2	2	3	2	2
55-59	3	1	1	3	1	1	3	1	2	3	1	2
60-64	2	1	1	2	1	1	2	1	1	3	1	1
65-69	1	1	1	1	1	1	2	1	1	2	1	1
70-74	1	0	0	1	0	0	1	0	1	1	0	1
75-79	0	0	0	0	0	0	0	0	0	1	0	0
80 +	0	0	0	0	0	0	0	0	0	0	0	0

Age group	1990 Both sexes	Males	Females	1995 Both sexes	Males	Females	2000 Both sexes	Males	Females	2005 Both sexes	Males	Females
All ages	161	85	77	168	88	81	177	92	85	185	96	89
0-4	23	12	11	24	13	12	27	14	13	26	13	12
5-9	21	11	10	22	12	11	24	12	11	27	14	13
10-14	22	11	10	19	10	9	21	11	10	23	12	11
15-19	21	12	10	18	10	9	18	9	8	20	10	9
20-24	15	9	7	17	9	8	15	8	7	14	8	6
25-29	12	7	6	14	7	6	14	7	6	11	6	5
30-34	10	5	5	12	6	6	12	6	6	12	6	6
35-39	7	4	4	9	5	4	11	6	6	12	6	6
40-44	6	3	3	7	3	3	8	5	4	10	6	5
45-49	5	3	3	5	3	3	6	3	3	8	4	4
50-54	5	2	2	5	2	2	5	2	2	6	3	3
55-59	4	2	2	4	2	2	4	2	2	4	2	2
60-64	3	2	2	3	2	2	4	2	2	4	2	2
65-69	3	2	1	3	1	1	3	1	1	3	2	2
70-74	2	1	1	2	1	1	2	1	1	2	1	1
75-79	1	0	1	1	1	1	2	1	1	2	1	1
80 +	1	0	0	1	0	1	1	0	1	2	1	1

United Nations Department of Economic and Social Affairs/Population Division
World Population Prospects: The 2004 Revision, Volume II: Sex and Age Distribution of the World Population

POPULATION BY AGE AND SEX (in thousands)

Age group	2005 Both sexes	Males	Females	2010 Both sexes	Males	Females	2015 Both sexes	Males	Females	2020 Both sexes	Males	Females
All ages	185	96	89	189	98	91	190	99	91	190	99	91
0-4	26	13	12	22	11	11	19	10	9	18	10	9
5-9	27	14	13	25	13	12	22	11	10	19	10	9
10-14	23	12	11	26	13	12	24	13	11	21	11	10
15-19	20	10	9	21	11	10	24	13	11	22	12	11
20-24	14	8	6	16	9	8	18	9	8	21	11	10
25-29	11	6	5	10	6	5	12	7	6	14	7	7
30-34	12	6	6	10	5	5	9	5	5	11	6	6
35-39	12	6	6	12	6	6	10	5	5	9	5	4
40-44	10	6	5	11	6	5	11	6	5	9	5	4
45-49	8	4	4	10	5	5	11	6	5	11	6	5
50-54	6	3	3	7	4	3	9	5	4	10	5	5
55-59	4	2	2	5	3	2	7	4	3	9	5	4
60-64	4	2	2	4	2	2	5	2	2	6	3	3
65-69	3	2	2	3	1	2	3	2	2	4	2	2
70-74	2	1	1	2	1	1	2	1	1	3	1	1
75-79	2	1	1	2	1	1	2	1	1	2	1	1
80-84	1	0	1	1	0	1	1	0	1	1	0	1
85-89	0	0	0	1	0	0	1	0	0	1	0	0
90-94	0	0	0	0	0	0	0	0	0	0	0	0
95-99	0	0	0	0	0	0	0	0	0	0	0	0
100 +	0	0	0	0	0	0	0	0	0	0	0	0

Age group	2025 Both sexes	Males	Females	2030 Both sexes	Males	Females	2035 Both sexes	Males	Females	2040 Both sexes	Males	Females
All ages	190	99	91	189	98	91	186	97	90	179	93	87
0-4	19	10	9	18	10	9	17	9	8	14	7	7
5-9	18	9	9	18	9	9	18	9	9	16	8	8
10-14	18	9	9	17	9	8	17	9	8	17	9	8
15-19	19	10	9	16	9	8	15	8	7	15	8	7
20-24	19	10	9	16	8	7	13	7	6	12	6	5
25-29	17	9	8	15	8	7	12	6	6	9	5	4
30-34	13	6	6	16	8	8	14	7	7	11	5	5
35-39	11	5	5	12	6	6	15	8	8	14	7	7
40-44	8	4	4	10	5	5	12	6	6	15	8	7
45-49	8	4	4	8	4	4	10	5	5	11	6	5
50-54	10	5	5	8	4	4	7	4	3	9	5	4
55-59	9	5	4	9	5	4	7	4	3	7	4	3
60-64	8	4	4	9	5	4	9	5	4	7	4	3
65-69	5	3	2	7	4	3	8	4	4	8	4	4
70-74	3	2	2	5	2	2	6	3	3	7	3	3
75-79	2	1	1	3	1	1	4	2	2	5	2	3
80-84	1	1	1	1	1	1	2	1	1	3	1	1
85-89	1	0	0	1	0	1	1	0	1	1	0	1
90-94	0	0	0	0	0	0	0	0	0	0	0	0
95-99	0	0	0	0	0	0	0	0	0	0	0	0
100 +	0	0	0	0	0	0	0	0	0	0	0	0

Age group	2045 Both sexes	Males	Females	2050 Both sexes	Males	Females
All ages	169	87	82	157	81	76
0-4	11	6	5	9	4	4
5-9	13	7	6	10	5	5
10-14	15	8	7	12	6	6
15-19	15	8	7	14	7	6
20-24	12	7	5	12	6	5
25-29	8	4	4	8	4	4
30-34	8	4	4	7	3	4
35-39	10	5	5	8	4	4
40-44	13	7	6	10	5	5
45-49	14	7	7	12	7	6
50-54	11	6	5	14	7	6
55-59	9	5	4	10	5	5
60-64	6	3	3	8	4	4
65-69	6	3	3	6	3	3
70-74	7	3	3	5	3	3
75-79	5	3	3	6	3	3
80-84	4	2	2	4	2	2
85-89	2	1	1	2	1	1
90-94	1	0	0	1	0	1
95-99	0	0	0	0	0	0
100 +	0	0	0	0	0	0

POPULATION BY AGE AND SEX (in thousands)

Age group	2005 Both sexes	Males	Females	2010 Both sexes	Males	Females	2015 Both sexes	Males	Females	2020 Both sexes	Males	Females
All ages	185	96	89	190	99	91	194	101	93	198	103	95
0-4	26	13	12	24	12	11	22	11	11	22	11	11
5-9	27	14	13	25	13	12	23	12	11	21	11	10
10-14	23	12	11	26	13	12	24	13	11	22	12	11
15-19	20	10	9	21	11	10	24	13	11	22	12	11
20-24	14	8	6	16	9	8	18	9	8	21	11	10
25-29	11	6	5	10	6	5	12	7	6	14	7	7
30-34	12	6	6	10	5	5	9	5	5	11	6	6
35-39	12	6	6	12	6	6	10	5	5	9	5	4
40-44	10	6	5	11	6	5	11	6	5	9	5	4
45-49	8	4	4	10	5	5	11	6	5	11	6	5
50-54	6	3	3	7	4	3	9	5	4	10	5	5
55-59	4	2	2	5	3	2	7	4	3	9	5	4
60-64	4	2	2	4	2	2	5	2	2	6	3	3
65-69	3	2	2	3	1	2	3	2	2	4	2	2
70-74	2	1	1	2	1	1	2	1	1	3	1	1
75-79	2	1	1	2	1	1	2	1	1	2	1	1
80-84	1	0	1	1	0	1	1	0	1	1	0	1
85-89	0	0	0	1	0	0	1	0	0	1	0	0
90-94	0	0	0	0	0	0	0	0	0	0	0	0
95-99	0	0	0	0	0	0	0	0	0	0	0	0
100 +	0	0	0	0	0	0	0	0	0	0	0	0

Age group	2025 Both sexes	Males	Females	2030 Both sexes	Males	Females	2035 Both sexes	Males	Females	2040 Both sexes	Males	Females
All ages	201	105	97	205	106	98	206	107	99	204	106	98
0-4	23	12	11	23	12	11	21	11	10	18	9	9
5-9	21	11	10	22	11	11	22	11	11	20	11	10
10-14	20	11	10	20	11	10	21	11	10	21	11	10
15-19	20	11	10	19	10	9	19	10	9	19	10	9
20-24	19	10	9	17	9	8	15	8	7	15	8	7
25-29	17	9	8	15	8	7	13	7	6	12	6	6
30-34	13	6	6	16	8	8	14	7	7	12	6	6
35-39	11	5	5	12	6	6	15	8	8	14	7	7
40-44	8	4	4	10	5	5	12	6	6	15	8	7
45-49	8	4	4	8	4	4	10	5	5	11	6	5
50-54	10	5	5	8	4	4	7	4	3	9	5	4
55-59	9	5	4	9	5	4	7	4	3	7	4	3
60-64	8	4	4	9	5	4	9	5	4	7	4	3
65-69	5	3	2	7	4	3	8	4	4	8	4	4
70-74	3	2	2	5	2	2	6	3	3	7	3	3
75-79	2	1	1	3	1	1	4	2	2	5	2	3
80-84	1	1	1	1	1	1	2	1	1	3	1	1
85-89	1	0	0	1	0	1	1	0	1	1	0	1
90-94	0	0	0	0	0	0	0	0	0	0	0	0
95-99	0	0	0	0	0	0	0	0	0	0	0	0
100 +	0	0	0	0	0	0	0	0	0	0	0	0

Age group	2045 Both sexes	Males	Females	2050 Both sexes	Males	Females
All ages	199	103	96	192	99	93
0-4	16	8	8	15	8	7
5-9	18	9	8	15	8	7
10-14	19	10	9	17	9	8
15-19	19	10	9	18	9	8
20-24	16	9	7	16	9	7
25-29	12	6	6	12	6	6
30-34	10	5	5	11	5	5
35-39	12	6	6	10	5	5
40-44	13	7	6	11	6	5
45-49	14	7	7	12	7	6
50-54	11	6	5	14	7	6
55-59	9	5	4	10	5	5
60-64	6	3	3	8	4	4
65-69	6	3	3	6	3	3
70-74	7	3	3	5	3	3
75-79	5	3	3	6	3	3
80-84	4	2	2	4	2	2
85-89	2	1	1	2	1	1
90-94	1	0	0	1	0	1
95-99	0	0	0	0	0	0
100 +	0	0	0	0	0	0

744

United Nations Department of Economic and Social Affairs/Population Division
World Population Prospects: The 2004 Revision, Volume II: Sex and Age Distribution of the World Population

LOW VARIANT   **SAMOA**

POPULATION BY AGE AND SEX (in thousands)

Age group	2005 Both sexes	Males	Females	2010 Both sexes	Males	Females	2015 Both sexes	Males	Females	2020 Both sexes	Males	Females
All ages	185	96	89	187	98	90	180	07	99	183	95	88
0-4	26	13	12	21	11	10	17	9	8	15	8	7
5-9	27	14	13	25	13	12	20	10	10	17	9	8
10-14	23	12	11	26	13	12	24	13	11	19	10	9
15-19	20	10	9	21	11	10	24	13	11	22	12	11
20-24	14	8	6	16	9	8	18	9	8	21	11	10
25-29	11	6	5	10	6	5	12	7	6	14	7	7
30-34	12	6	6	10	5	5	9	5	5	11	6	6
35-39	12	6	6	12	6	6	10	5	5	9	5	4
40-44	10	6	5	11	6	5	11	6	5	9	5	4
45-49	8	4	4	10	5	5	11	6	5	11	6	5
50-54	6	3	3	7	4	3	9	5	4	10	5	5
55-59	4	2	2	5	3	2	7	4	3	9	5	4
60-64	4	2	2	4	2	2	5	2	2	6	3	3
65-69	3	2	2	3	1	2	3	2	2	4	2	2
70-74	2	1	1	2	1	1	2	1	1	3	1	1
75-79	2	1	1	2	1	1	2	1	1	2	1	1
80-84	1	0	1	1	0	1	1	0	1	1	0	1
85-89	0	0	0	1	0	0	1	0	0	1	0	0
90-94	0	0	0	0	0	0	0	0	0	0	0	0
95-99	0	0	0	0	0	0	0	0	0	0	0	0
100 +	0	0	0	0	0	0	0	0	0	0	0	0

Age group	2025 Both sexes	Males	Females	2030 Both sexes	Males	Females	2035 Both sexes	Males	Females	2040 Both sexes	Males	Females
All ages	179	93	86	174	91	84	168	87	81	157	81	76
0-4	15	8	7	14	8	7	13	7	6	10	5	5
5-9	15	8	7	14	7	7	14	7	7	12	7	6
10-14	16	8	7	14	7	6	13	7	6	13	7	6
15-19	17	9	8	14	7	7	12	6	6	12	6	5
20-24	19	10	9	14	8	7	11	6	5	9	5	4
25-29	17	9	8	15	8	7	10	5	5	7	4	3
30-34	13	6	6	16	8	8	14	7	7	9	5	5
35-39	11	5	5	12	6	6	15	8	8	14	7	7
40-44	8	4	4	10	5	5	12	6	6	15	8	7
45-49	8	4	4	8	4	4	10	5	5	11	6	5
50-54	10	5	5	8	4	4	7	4	3	9	5	4
55-59	9	5	4	9	5	4	7	4	3	7	4	3
60-64	8	4	4	9	5	4	9	5	4	7	4	3
65-69	5	3	2	7	4	3	8	4	4	8	4	4
70-74	3	2	2	5	2	2	6	3	3	7	3	3
75-79	2	1	1	3	1	1	4	2	2	5	2	3
80-84	1	1	1	1	1	1	2	1	1	3	1	1
85-89	1	0	0	1	0	1	1	0	1	1	0	1
90-94	0	0	0	0	0	0	0	0	0	0	0	0
95-99	0	0	0	0	0	0	0	0	0	0	0	0
100 +	0	0	0	0	0	0	0	0	0	0	0	0

Age group	2045 Both sexes	Males	Females	2050 Both sexes	Males	Females
All ages	143	74	69	127	65	61
0-4	7	4	3	4	2	2
5-9	9	5	5	6	3	3
10-14	11	6	5	8	5	4
15-19	11	6	5	10	5	5
20-24	8	5	4	8	4	4
25-29	5	3	2	5	2	2
30-34	6	3	3	4	2	2
35-39	9	4	4	5	3	3
40-44	13	7	6	8	4	4
45-49	14	7	7	12	7	6
50-54	11	6	5	14	7	6
55-59	9	5	4	10	5	5
60-64	6	3	3	8	4	4
65-69	6	3	3	6	3	3
70-74	7	3	3	5	3	3
75-79	5	3	3	6	3	3
80-84	4	2	2	4	2	2
85-89	2	1	1	2	1	1
90-94	1	0	0	1	0	1
95-99	0	0	0	0	0	0
100 +	0	0	0	0	0	0

United Nations Department of Economic and Social Affairs/Population Division
World Population Prospects: The 2004 Revision, Volume II: Sex and Age Distribution of the World Population

745

POPULATION BY AGE AND SEX (in thousands)

Age group	1950			1955			1960			1965		
	Both sexes	Males	Females	Both sexes	Males	Females	Both sexes	Males	Females	Both sexes	Males	Females
All ages	60	33	27	59	33	26	64	36	29	65	34	31
0-4	10	5	5	10	5	5	10	5	5	12	6	6
5-9	6	3	3	6	3	3	7	3	3	8	4	4
10-14	4	2	2	4	2	2	4	2	2	6	3	3
15-19	3	2	2	3	2	1	4	2	2	5	3	2
20-24	8	5	3	7	5	3	8	5	3	7	4	3
25-29	7	4	3	7	4	3	8	5	3	6	3	3
30-34	6	4	2	6	4	2	6	4	2	4	3	2
35-39	4	2	2	4	2	2	4	2	2	3	2	2
40-44	3	2	1	3	2	1	3	2	1	3	2	1
45-49	2	1	1	2	1	1	3	1	1	3	1	1
50-54	2	1	1	2	1	1	2	1	1	2	1	1
55-59	2	1	1	1	1	1	2	1	1	2	1	1
60-64	3	2	2	3	2	2	4	2	2	2	1	1
65-69	0	0	0	0	0	0	0	0	0	1	0	0
70-74	0	0	0	0	0	0	0	0	0	0	0	0
75-79	0	0	0	0	0	0	0	0	0	0	0	0
80 +	0	0	0	0	0	0	0	0	0	0	0	0

Age group	1970			1975			1980			1985		
	Both sexes	Males	Females	Both sexes	Males	Females	Both sexes	Males	Females	Both sexes	Males	Females
All ages	74	37	36	82	41	41	94	47	47	104	51	52
0-4	14	7	7	16	8	8	18	9	9	19	10	9
5-9	11	6	5	12	6	6	14	7	7	16	8	8
10-14	9	5	4	10	5	5	12	6	6	14	7	7
15-19	8	4	4	9	5	4	10	5	5	11	6	6
20-24	6	3	3	7	3	3	8	4	4	9	4	4
25-29	4	2	2	5	2	3	6	3	3	7	3	3
30-34	3	1	2	3	2	2	4	2	2	5	2	2
35-39	2	1	1	3	1	1	3	2	2	4	2	2
40-44	3	1	1	3	2	2	4	2	2	4	2	2
45-49	3	1	1	3	2	2	4	2	2	3	2	2
50-54	2	1	1	3	1	1	3	2	2	3	2	2
55-59	2	1	1	2	1	1	3	1	1	3	1	1
60-64	2	1	1	2	1	1	2	1	1	2	1	1
65-69	1	1	1	1	1	1	2	1	1	2	1	1
70-74	2	1	1	1	0	1	1	1	1	1	1	1
75-79	0	0	0	1	0	0	1	0	1	1	0	1
80 +	0	0	0	0	0	0	1	0	1	1	0	1

Age group	1990			1995			2000			2005		
	Both sexes	Males	Females	Both sexes	Males	Females	Both sexes	Males	Females	Both sexes	Males	Females
All ages	117	58	59	128	63	64	140	69	70	157	78	79
0-4	19	10	10	19	10	10	21	11	10	23	12	11
5-9	20	10	10	19	9	9	19	10	9	20	10	10
10-14	17	8	8	20	10	10	18	9	9	19	9	9
15-19	12	6	6	16	8	8	19	10	10	18	9	9
20-24	10	5	5	11	6	5	15	8	8	19	10	9
25-29	8	4	4	9	4	4	10	5	5	15	7	7
30-34	6	3	3	7	3	4	8	4	4	10	5	5
35-39	5	2	3	5	2	3	6	3	3	7	4	4
40-44	3	2	2	4	2	2	5	2	3	6	3	3
45-49	3	1	2	3	1	2	4	2	2	5	2	3
50-54	4	2	2	3	1	1	3	1	2	4	2	2
55-59	3	2	1	3	2	2	2	1	1	3	1	1
60-64	3	1	1	3	1	1	3	1	2	2	1	1
65-69	2	1	1	2	1	1	2	1	1	3	1	1
70-74	1	1	1	2	1	1	2	1	1	2	1	1
75-79	1	0	0	1	0	0	1	1	1	1	1	1
80 +	1	0	1	1	0	0	1	0	0	1	0	0

United Nations Department of Economic and Social Affairs/Population Division
World Population Prospects: The 2004 Revision, Volume II: Sex and Age Distribution of the World Population

POPULATION BY AGE AND SEX (in thousands)

Age group	2005 Both sexes	2005 Males	2005 Females	2010 Both sexes	2010 Males	2010 Females	2015 Both sexes	2015 Males	2015 Females	2020 Both sexes	2020 Males	2020 Females
All ages	157	78	79	174	87	88	192	96	96	209	104	105
0-4	23	12	11	24	12	12	24	12	12	23	12	11
5-9	20	10	10	22	11	11	24	12	12	24	12	12
10-14	19	9	9	20	10	10	22	11	11	23	12	12
15-19	18	9	9	18	9	9	20	10	10	22	11	11
20-24	19	10	9	18	9	9	18	9	9	20	10	10
25-29	15	7	7	18	9	9	17	9	8	17	9	9
30-34	10	5	5	14	7	7	18	9	9	17	8	8
35-39	7	4	4	9	5	5	14	7	7	17	9	9
40-44	6	3	3	7	3	4	9	5	4	14	7	7
45-49	5	2	3	6	3	3	7	3	4	9	4	4
50-54	4	2	2	4	2	2	6	3	3	7	3	3
55-59	3	1	1	3	1	2	4	2	2	5	3	3
60-64	2	1	1	2	1	1	3	1	2	4	2	2
65-69	3	1	1	2	1	1	2	1	1	3	1	2
70-74	2	1	1	2	1	1	2	1	1	2	1	1
75-79	1	1	1	1	1	1	2	1	1	1	0	1
80-84	1	0	0	1	0	0	1	0	0	1	0	1
85-89	0	0	0	0	0	0	0	0	0	0	0	0
90-94	0	0	0	0	0	0	0	0	0	0	0	0
95-99	0	0	0	0	0	0	0	0	0	0	0	0
100 +	0	0	0	0	0	0	0	0	0	0	0	0

Age group	2025 Both sexes	2025 Males	2025 Females	2030 Both sexes	2030 Males	2030 Females	2035 Both sexes	2035 Males	2035 Females	2040 Both sexes	2040 Males	2040 Females
All ages	225	112	113	241	120	121	257	128	129	272	135	136
0-4	23	12	11	23	12	11	23	12	11	23	12	11
5-9	23	12	11	23	11	11	23	12	11	23	12	11
10-14	23	12	12	23	12	11	22	11	11	23	11	11
15-19	23	12	11	23	12	11	23	11	11	22	11	11
20-24	22	11	11	23	12	11	23	12	11	22	11	11
25-29	19	10	9	21	11	10	22	11	11	22	11	11
30-34	17	9	8	19	9	9	21	10	10	22	11	11
35-39	16	8	8	17	8	8	18	9	9	20	10	10
40-44	17	9	9	16	8	8	16	8	8	18	9	9
45-49	13	7	7	17	8	8	16	8	8	16	8	8
50-54	8	4	4	13	6	7	16	8	8	15	8	8
55-59	6	3	3	8	4	4	12	6	6	16	8	8
60-64	5	2	3	6	3	3	8	4	4	12	6	6
65-69	3	1	2	5	2	3	6	3	3	7	3	4
70-74	2	1	2	3	1	2	4	2	2	5	2	3
75-79	1	1	1	2	1	1	2	1	1	3	1	2
80-84	1	0	0	1	0	1	1	0	1	1	1	1
85-89	0	0	0	0	0	0	0	0	0	0	0	0
90-94	0	0	0	0	0	0	0	0	0	0	0	0
95-99	0	0	0	0	0	0	0	0	0	0	0	0
100 +	0	0	0	0	0	0	0	0	0	0	0	0

Age group	2045 Both sexes	2045 Males	2045 Females	2050 Both sexes	2050 Males	2050 Females
All ages	285	142	143	295	147	148
0-4	22	11	11	21	11	11
5-9	23	12	11	22	11	11
10-14	23	12	11	23	12	11
15-19	22	11	11	23	12	11
20-24	22	11	11	22	11	11
25-29	22	11	11	21	11	11
30-34	22	11	11	21	11	11
35-39	22	11	11	22	11	11
40-44	20	10	10	21	11	11
45-49	18	9	9	20	10	10
50-54	16	8	8	17	9	9
55-59	15	7	8	15	8	8
60-64	15	7	8	14	7	7
65-69	11	5	6	14	7	7
70-74	6	3	3	10	4	5
75-79	4	2	2	5	2	3
80-84	2	1	1	2	1	1
85-89	1	0	0	1	0	1
90-94	0	0	0	0	0	0
95-99	0	0	0	0	0	0
100 +	0	0	0	0	0	0

United Nations Department of Economic and Social Affairs/Population Division
World Population Prospects: The 2004 Revision, Volume II: Sex and Age Distribution of the World Population

747

POPULATION BY AGE AND SEX (in thousands)

Age group	2005 Both sexes	2005 Males	2005 Females	2010 Both sexes	2010 Males	2010 Females	2015 Both sexes	2015 Males	2015 Females	2020 Both sexes	2020 Males	2020 Females
All ages	157	78	79	176	88	89	197	98	99	217	108	109
0-4	23	12	11	26	13	13	27	14	13	27	14	13
5-9	20	10	10	22	11	11	25	13	12	27	13	13
10-14	19	9	9	20	10	10	22	11	11	25	13	12
15-19	18	9	9	18	9	9	20	10	10	22	11	11
20-24	19	10	9	18	9	9	18	9	9	20	10	10
25-29	15	7	7	18	9	9	17	9	8	17	9	9
30-34	10	5	5	14	7	7	18	9	9	17	8	8
35-39	7	4	4	9	5	5	14	7	7	17	9	9
40-44	6	3	3	7	3	4	9	5	4	14	7	7
45-49	5	2	3	6	3	3	7	3	4	9	4	4
50-54	4	2	2	4	2	2	6	3	3	7	3	3
55-59	3	1	1	3	1	2	4	2	2	5	3	3
60-64	2	1	1	2	1	1	3	1	2	4	2	2
65-69	3	1	1	2	1	1	2	1	1	3	1	2
70-74	2	1	1	2	1	1	2	1	1	2	1	1
75-79	1	1	1	1	1	1	2	1	1	1	0	1
80-84	1	0	0	1	0	0	1	0	0	1	0	1
85-89	0	0	0	0	0	0	0	0	0	0	0	0
90-94	0	0	0	0	0	0	0	0	0	0	0	0
95-99	0	0	0	0	0	0	0	0	0	0	0	0
100 +	0	0	0	0	0	0	0	0	0	0	0	0

Age group	2025 Both sexes	2025 Males	2025 Females	2030 Both sexes	2030 Males	2030 Females	2035 Both sexes	2035 Males	2035 Females	2040 Both sexes	2040 Males	2040 Females
All ages	238	119	119	259	129	130	281	140	141	303	151	152
0-4	27	14	13	28	14	14	30	15	15	31	16	15
5-9	27	14	13	27	14	13	28	14	14	29	15	14
10-14	26	13	13	27	14	13	27	14	13	28	14	14
15-19	25	13	12	26	13	13	27	13	13	27	13	13
20-24	22	11	11	25	12	12	26	13	13	26	13	13
25-29	19	10	9	21	11	10	24	12	12	25	13	13
30-34	17	9	8	19	9	9	21	10	10	24	12	12
35-39	16	8	8	17	8	8	18	9	9	20	10	10
40-44	17	9	9	16	8	8	16	8	8	18	9	9
45-49	13	7	7	17	8	8	16	8	8	16	8	8
50-54	8	4	4	13	6	7	16	8	8	15	8	8
55-59	6	3	3	8	4	4	12	6	6	16	8	8
60-64	5	2	3	6	3	3	8	4	4	12	6	6
65-69	3	1	2	5	2	3	6	3	3	7	3	4
70-74	2	1	2	3	1	2	4	2	2	5	2	3
75-79	1	1	1	2	1	1	2	1	1	3	1	2
80-84	1	0	0	1	0	1	1	0	1	1	1	1
85-89	0	0	0	0	0	0	0	0	0	0	0	0
90-94	0	0	0	0	0	0	0	0	0	0	0	0
95-99	0	0	0	0	0	0	0	0	0	0	0	0
100 +	0	0	0	0	0	0	0	0	0	0	0	0

Age group	2045 Both sexes	2045 Males	2045 Females	2050 Both sexes	2050 Males	2050 Females
All ages	325	162	163	346	172	173
0-4	31	16	15	31	16	15
5-9	30	15	15	31	16	15
10-14	29	15	14	30	15	15
15-19	27	14	14	29	15	14
20-24	26	13	13	27	14	13
25-29	26	13	13	26	13	13
30-34	25	13	12	25	13	13
35-39	23	12	12	25	12	12
40-44	20	10	10	23	12	11
45-49	18	9	9	20	10	10
50-54	16	8	8	17	9	9
55-59	15	7	8	15	8	8
60-64	15	7	8	14	7	7
65-69	11	5	6	14	7	7
70-74	6	3	3	10	4	5
75-79	4	2	2	5	2	3
80-84	2	1	1	2	1	1
85-89	1	0	0	1	0	1
90-94	0	0	0	0	0	0
95-99	0	0	0	0	0	0
100 +	0	0	0	0	0	0

United Nations Department of Economic and Social Affairs/Population Division
World Population Prospects: The 2004 Revision, Volume II: Sex and Age Distribution of the World Population

POPULATION BY AGE AND SEX (in thousands)

Age group	2005 Both sexes	2005 Males	2005 Females	2010 Both sexes	2010 Males	2010 Females	2015 Both sexes	2015 Males	2015 Females	2020 Both sexes	2020 Males	2020 Females
All ages	157	78	79	173	86	87	187	93	94	200	100	101
0-4	23	12	11	22	11	11	21	11	10	19	10	10
5-9	20	10	10	22	11	11	22	11	11	21	10	10
10-14	19	9	9	20	10	10	22	11	11	22	11	11
15-19	18	9	9	18	9	9	20	10	10	22	11	11
20-24	19	10	9	18	9	9	18	9	9	20	10	10
25-29	15	7	7	18	9	9	17	9	8	17	9	9
30-34	10	5	5	14	7	7	18	9	9	17	8	8
35-39	7	4	4	9	5	5	14	7	7	17	9	9
40-44	6	3	3	7	3	4	9	5	4	14	7	7
45-49	5	2	3	6	3	3	7	3	4	9	4	4
50-54	4	2	2	4	2	2	6	3	3	7	3	3
55-59	3	1	1	3	1	2	4	2	2	5	3	3
60-64	2	1	1	2	1	1	3	1	2	4	2	2
65-69	3	1	1	2	1	1	2	1	1	3	1	2
70-74	2	1	1	2	1	1	2	1	1	2	1	1
75-79	1	1	1	1	1	1	2	1	1	1	0	1
80-84	1	0	0	1	0	0	1	0	0	1	0	1
85-89	0	0	0	0	0	0	0	0	0	0	0	0
90-94	0	0	0	0	0	0	0	0	0	0	0	0
95-99	0	0	0	0	0	0	0	0	0	0	0	0
100 +	0	0	0	0	0	0	0	0	0	0	0	0

Age group	2025 Both sexes	2025 Males	2025 Females	2030 Both sexes	2030 Males	2030 Females	2035 Both sexes	2035 Males	2035 Females	2040 Both sexes	2040 Males	2040 Females
All ages	212	106	107	224	111	112	234	116	117	242	120	121
0-4	19	9	9	18	9	9	18	9	9	16	8	8
5-9	19	10	9	18	9	9	18	9	9	17	9	9
10-14	21	10	10	19	10	9	18	9	9	18	9	9
15-19	22	11	11	20	10	10	19	9	9	18	9	9
20-24	22	11	11	21	11	10	20	10	10	18	9	9
25-29	19	10	9	21	11	10	21	10	10	19	10	10
30-34	17	9	8	19	9	9	21	10	10	20	10	10
35-39	16	8	8	17	8	8	18	9	9	20	10	10
40-44	17	9	9	16	8	8	16	8	8	18	9	9
45-49	13	7	7	17	8	8	16	8	8	16	8	8
50-54	8	4	4	13	6	7	16	8	8	15	8	8
55-59	6	3	3	8	4	4	12	6	6	16	8	8
60-64	5	2	3	6	3	3	8	4	4	12	6	6
65-69	3	1	2	5	2	3	6	3	3	7	3	4
70-74	2	1	2	3	1	2	4	2	2	5	2	3
75-79	1	1	1	2	1	1	2	1	1	3	1	2
80-84	1	0	0	1	0	1	1	0	1	1	1	1
85-89	0	0	0	0	0	0	0	0	0	0	0	0
90-94	0	0	0	0	0	0	0	0	0	0	0	0
95-99	0	0	0	0	0	0	0	0	0	0	0	0
100 +	0	0	0	0	0	0	0	0	0	0	0	0

Age group	2045 Both sexes	2045 Males	2045 Females	2050 Both sexes	2050 Males	2050 Females
All ages	247	123	124	250	124	126
0-4	15	7	7	13	7	7
5-9	16	8	8	15	7	7
10-14	17	9	8	16	8	8
15-19	18	9	9	17	9	8
20-24	18	9	9	17	9	9
25-29	18	9	9	17	9	9
30-34	19	10	9	17	9	9
35-39	20	10	10	19	9	9
40-44	20	10	10	20	10	10
45-49	18	9	9	20	10	10
50-54	16	8	8	17	9	9
55-59	15	7	8	15	8	8
60-64	15	7	8	14	7	7
65-69	11	5	6	14	7	7
70-74	6	3	3	10	4	5
75-79	4	2	2	5	2	3
80-84	2	1	1	2	1	1
85-89	1	0	0	1	0	1
90-94	0	0	0	0	0	0
95-99	0	0	0	0	0	0
100 +	0	0	0	0	0	0

POPULATION BY AGE AND SEX (in thousands)

Age group	1950 Both sexes	1950 Males	1950 Females	1955 Both sexes	1955 Males	1955 Females	1960 Both sexes	1960 Males	1960 Females	1965 Both sexes	1965 Males	1965 Females
All ages	3 201	1 625	1 577	3 593	1 822	1 771	4 075	2 065	2 010	4 793	2 443	2 350
0-4	551	280	271	628	319	309	724	368	357	878	446	432
5-9	428	217	210	488	248	240	564	286	278	671	341	331
10-14	366	187	180	415	211	204	476	242	234	560	285	275
15-19	317	162	155	357	182	175	406	207	199	476	245	231
20-24	272	139	133	306	156	150	346	176	169	408	211	197
25-29	232	118	113	261	133	128	295	150	144	348	180	168
30-34	198	101	97	222	113	108	251	128	123	295	152	142
35-39	172	88	84	189	97	93	212	108	104	249	129	120
40-44	151	77	74	163	83	80	180	92	89	209	107	101
45-49	131	67	64	142	72	70	154	78	76	175	89	86
50-54	112	56	55	121	61	60	132	66	66	147	74	73
55-59	92	46	47	101	50	51	110	55	56	122	61	61
60-64	73	36	37	80	39	41	88	43	45	99	48	50
65-69	52	25	27	58	28	30	64	31	33	72	35	38
70-74	32	15	17	36	17	19	41	20	22	47	22	25
75-79	16	8	8	18	9	10	21	10	11	25	12	13
80 +	7	3	3	8	4	4	9	4	5	12	5	6

Age group	1970 Both sexes	1970 Males	1970 Females	1975 Both sexes	1975 Males	1975 Females	1980 Both sexes	1980 Males	1980 Females	1985 Both sexes	1985 Males	1985 Females
All ages	5 745	2 955	2 790	7 251	3 808	3 444	9 604	5 188	4 416	12 880	7 133	5 748
0-4	1 053	535	518	1 311	667	644	1 819	911	907	2 181	1 113	1 068
5-9	832	423	409	1 044	531	513	1 348	685	663	1 863	934	930
10-14	671	343	329	856	440	417	1 090	557	534	1 415	718	696
15-19	572	297	274	724	388	337	909	477	432	1 232	640	592
20-24	493	261	232	642	355	287	872	521	351	1 260	720	540
25-29	421	223	198	556	309	247	818	516	302	1 244	798	446
30-34	354	187	167	459	253	206	652	393	259	1 066	694	372
35-39	297	156	141	379	208	171	503	289	213	776	485	291
40-44	248	129	119	312	168	144	398	222	176	503	307	196
45-49	203	105	99	250	132	118	320	174	146	361	214	147
50-54	170	87	83	209	108	100	253	135	118	269	153	116
55-59	137	68	68	160	81	79	204	105	99	214	114	100
60-64	112	55	57	132	66	67	151	76	75	185	94	91
65-69	82	40	43	96	47	50	117	57	60	131	65	66
70-74	55	26	29	66	31	35	79	37	42	93	44	49
75-79	30	14	16	37	17	20	47	21	25	55	25	30
80 +	14	6	8	19	8	10	25	11	14	33	14	19

Age group	1990 Both sexes	1990 Males	1990 Females	1995 Both sexes	1995 Males	1995 Females	2000 Both sexes	2000 Males	2000 Females	2005 Both sexes	2005 Males	2005 Females
All ages	16 379	9 127	7 252	18 682	10 469	8 213	21 484	11 686	9 799	24 573	13 259	11 314
0-4	2 686	1 370	1 315	2 911	1 486	1 425	3 097	1 580	1 518	3 200	1 633	1 567
5-9	2 219	1 131	1 087	2 633	1 343	1 290	2 901	1 480	1 422	3 075	1 567	1 508
10-14	1 915	959	956	2 177	1 110	1 067	2 502	1 277	1 226	2 886	1 471	1 415
15-19	1 527	784	743	1 738	847	891	1 991	1 016	975	2 456	1 248	1 208
20-24	1 511	833	678	1 409	779	630	1 909	996	913	2 092	1 092	1 000
25-29	1 555	941	614	1 744	1 100	644	1 915	1 124	792	2 174	1 179	995
30-34	1 439	938	501	1 715	1 068	647	1 883	1 139	745	2 064	1 206	858
35-39	1 160	764	397	1 287	829	459	1 550	903	647	1 859	1 115	745
40-44	772	495	276	933	641	292	1 132	692	439	1 455	848	607
45-49	471	299	172	618	410	207	780	490	290	1 037	631	406
50-54	318	196	122	492	302	191	504	290	215	691	426	265
55-59	235	134	101	374	220	154	417	223	194	463	257	206
60-64	196	103	93	217	122	95	344	189	155	404	213	191
65-69	162	81	81	173	89	84	222	126	96	318	171	147
70-74	105	51	55	133	64	68	166	85	81	189	104	85
75-79	66	30	36	76	35	41	105	49	56	123	61	62
80 +	41	18	23	51	22	29	65	28	37	88	39	50

United Nations Department of Economic and Social Affairs/Population Division
World Population Prospects: The 2004 Revision, Volume II: Sex and Age Distribution of the World Population

750

POPULATION BY AGE AND SEX (in thousands)

Age group	2005 Both sexes	Males	Females	2010 Both sexes	Males	Females	2015 Both sexes	Males	Females	2020 Both sexes	Males	Females
All ages	24 573	13 259	11 314	27 664	14 810	12 854	30 828	16 391	14 437	34 024	17 981	16 043
0-4	3 200	1 633	1 567	3 346	1 708	1 638	3 477	1 776	1 701	3 583	1 832	1 751
5-9	3 075	1 567	1 508	3 180	1 622	1 558	3 328	1 698	1 631	3 460	1 767	1 693
10-14	2 886	1 471	1 415	3 061	1 559	1 501	3 166	1 614	1 552	3 315	1 691	1 624
15-19	2 456	1 248	1 208	2 837	1 439	1 398	3 013	1 528	1 485	3 119	1 584	1 535
20-24	2 092	1 092	1 000	2 543	1 317	1 226	2 924	1 509	1 415	3 100	1 598	1 502
25-29	2 174	1 179	995	2 335	1 260	1 075	2 786	1 486	1 300	3 167	1 678	1 490
30-34	2 064	1 206	858	2 293	1 239	1 054	2 455	1 322	1 134	2 906	1 547	1 359
35-39	1 859	1 115	745	2 017	1 166	851	2 247	1 200	1 047	2 409	1 283	1 127
40-44	1 455	848	607	1 759	1 054	705	1 918	1 106	811	2 148	1 142	1 006
45-49	1 037	631	406	1 358	785	573	1 660	990	670	1 820	1 043	776
50-54	691	426	265	943	565	379	1 261	717	543	1 560	919	641
55-59	463	257	206	643	388	255	889	522	367	1 199	671	528
60-64	404	213	191	449	245	204	621	369	252	856	496	360
65-69	318	171	147	375	193	181	418	223	194	576	336	240
70-74	189	104	85	272	142	130	324	162	162	363	188	175
75-79	123	61	62	141	76	66	208	104	103	251	120	131
80-84	63	28	35	76	36	40	89	45	44	135	63	72
85-89	20	8	12	28	12	16	35	15	20	43	20	24
90-94	4	2	3	6	2	3	9	3	6	11	4	7
95-99	1	0	0	1	0	0	1	0	1	2	0	1
100	0	0	0	0	0	0	0	0	0	0	0	0

Age group	2025 Both sexes	Males	Females	2030 Both sexes	Males	Females	2035 Both sexes	Males	Females	2040 Both sexes	Males	Females
All ages	37 160	19 530	17 629	40 132	20 985	19 147	42 865	22 305	20 560	45 309	23 465	21 844
0-4	3 618	1 851	1 767	3 570	1 828	1 743	3 470	1 777	1 693	3 345	1 713	1 632
5-9	3 568	1 823	1 744	3 603	1 843	1 760	3 556	1 820	1 736	3 456	1 770	1 687
10-14	3 447	1 760	1 687	3 555	1 817	1 738	3 591	1 836	1 754	3 544	1 814	1 730
15-19	3 268	1 660	1 608	3 400	1 730	1 671	3 509	1 787	1 722	3 545	1 807	1 738
20-24	3 207	1 654	1 553	3 357	1 731	1 626	3 490	1 801	1 689	3 598	1 858	1 740
25-29	3 344	1 767	1 577	3 452	1 824	1 628	3 602	1 901	1 700	3 735	1 972	1 764
30-34	3 287	1 739	1 548	3 465	1 830	1 635	3 574	1 887	1 687	3 724	1 964	1 760
35-39	2 860	1 508	1 351	3 241	1 701	1 541	3 420	1 792	1 628	3 528	1 849	1 680
40-44	2 311	1 225	1 086	2 761	1 450	1 310	3 142	1 643	1 499	3 320	1 733	1 587
45-49	2 050	1 079	970	2 214	1 163	1 050	2 662	1 388	1 274	3 041	1 579	1 462
50-54	1 719	973	746	1 949	1 010	938	2 113	1 095	1 018	2 557	1 317	1 240
55-59	1 492	868	624	1 651	922	729	1 879	960	919	2 043	1 044	998
60-64	1 155	638	517	1 437	826	611	1 594	880	714	1 819	920	899
65-69	795	452	343	1 076	583	493	1 341	757	584	1 495	811	684
70-74	502	284	218	697	384	312	949	499	451	1 190	654	536
75-79	285	141	144	397	215	182	559	294	264	773	388	385
80-84	167	74	93	193	88	105	271	136	135	392	192	201
85-89	68	28	40	88	33	55	104	41	64	150	66	84
90-94	15	5	9	25	8	17	34	10	24	42	13	29
95-99	2	1	2	3	1	2	6	1	5	9	2	7
100 +	0	0	0	0	0	0	0	0	0	1	0	1

Age group	2045 Both sexes	Males	Females	2050 Both sexes	Males	Females
All ages	47 466	24 471	22 995	49 464	25 394	24 070
0-4	3 243	1 660	1 582	3 284	1 681	1 602
5-9	3 332	1 706	1 626	3 230	1 654	1 576
10-14	3 444	1 764	1 681	3 320	1 700	1 620
15-19	3 499	1 785	1 714	3 399	1 734	1 665
20-24	3 635	1 879	1 756	3 589	1 857	1 733
25-29	3 844	2 029	1 815	3 881	2 050	1 832
30-34	3 857	2 035	1 823	3 966	2 092	1 874
35-39	3 679	1 926	1 753	3 812	1 996	1 816
40-44	3 429	1 791	1 639	3 580	1 868	1 712
45-49	3 220	1 670	1 550	3 329	1 728	1 602
50-54	2 934	1 507	1 428	3 113	1 597	1 516
55-59	2 480	1 262	1 218	2 853	1 449	1 403
60-64	1 981	1 003	979	2 408	1 214	1 194
65-69	1 715	852	862	1 873	933	940
70-74	1 338	707	631	1 548	749	799
75-79	978	516	463	1 113	565	548
80-84	556	259	297	714	352	362
85-89	226	97	129	331	136	196
90-94	63	22	41	99	34	65
95-99	12	2	9	18	4	14
100 +	1	0	1	2	0	2

United Nations Department of Economic and Social Affairs/Population Division
World Population Prospects: The 2004 Revision, Volume II: Sex and Age Distribution of the World Population

751

POPULATION BY AGE AND SEX (in thousands)

Age group	2005 Both sexes	Males	Females	2010 Both sexes	Males	Females	2015 Both sexes	Males	Females	2020 Both sexes	Males	Females
All ages	24 573	13 259	11 314	27 898	14 930	12 968	31 501	16 735	14 766	35 328	18 647	16 681
0-4	3 200	1 633	1 567	3 580	1 827	1 753	3 916	2 001	1 916	4 216	2 155	2 061
5-9	3 075	1 567	1 508	3 180	1 622	1 558	3 562	1 817	1 745	3 899	1 991	1 908
10-14	2 886	1 471	1 415	3 061	1 559	1 501	3 166	1 614	1 552	3 548	1 809	1 738
15-19	2 456	1 248	1 208	2 837	1 439	1 398	3 013	1 528	1 485	3 119	1 584	1 535
20-24	2 092	1 092	1 000	2 543	1 317	1 226	2 924	1 509	1 415	3 100	1 598	1 502
25-29	2 174	1 179	995	2 335	1 260	1 075	2 786	1 486	1 300	3 167	1 678	1 490
30-34	2 064	1 206	858	2 293	1 239	1 054	2 455	1 322	1 134	2 906	1 547	1 359
35-39	1 859	1 115	745	2 017	1 166	851	2 247	1 200	1 047	2 409	1 283	1 127
40-44	1 455	848	607	1 759	1 054	705	1 918	1 106	811	2 148	1 142	1 006
45-49	1 037	631	406	1 358	785	573	1 660	990	670	1 820	1 043	776
50-54	691	426	265	943	565	379	1 261	717	543	1 560	919	641
55-59	463	257	206	643	388	255	889	522	367	1 199	671	528
60-64	404	213	191	449	245	204	621	369	252	856	496	360
65-69	318	171	147	375	193	181	418	223	194	576	336	240
70-74	189	104	85	272	142	130	324	162	162	363	188	175
75-79	123	61	62	141	76	66	208	104	103	251	120	131
80-84	63	28	35	76	36	40	89	45	44	135	63	72
85-89	20	8	12	28	12	16	35	15	20	43	20	24
90-94	4	2	3	6	2	3	9	3	6	11	4	7
95-99	1	0	0	1	0	0	1	0	1	2	0	1
100 +	0	0	0	0	0	0	0	0	0	0	0	0

Age group	2025 Both sexes	Males	Females	2030 Both sexes	Males	Females	2035 Both sexes	Males	Females	2040 Both sexes	Males	Females
All ages	39 176	20 560	18 615	42 960	22 431	20 529	46 659	24 245	22 415	50 270	26 002	24 268
0-4	4 331	2 215	2 115	4 385	2 244	2 140	4 440	2 274	2 167	4 516	2 312	2 203
5-9	4 199	2 146	2 053	4 315	2 207	2 108	4 370	2 237	2 133	4 426	2 266	2 160
10-14	3 885	1 984	1 902	4 186	2 139	2 047	4 302	2 200	2 102	4 357	2 230	2 127
15-19	3 501	1 779	1 722	3 838	1 953	1 885	4 140	2 109	2 030	4 256	2 170	2 086
20-24	3 207	1 654	1 553	3 589	1 849	1 740	3 927	2 024	1 903	4 228	2 180	2 048
25-29	3 344	1 767	1 577	3 452	1 824	1 628	3 834	2 019	1 814	4 171	2 194	1 977
30-34	3 287	1 739	1 548	3 465	1 830	1 635	3 574	1 887	1 687	3 955	2 082	1 873
35-39	2 860	1 508	1 351	3 241	1 701	1 541	3 420	1 792	1 628	3 528	1 849	1 680
40-44	2 311	1 225	1 086	2 761	1 450	1 310	3 142	1 643	1 499	3 320	1 733	1 587
45-49	2 050	1 079	970	2 214	1 163	1 050	2 662	1 388	1 274	3 041	1 579	1 462
50-54	1 719	973	746	1 949	1 010	938	2 113	1 095	1 018	2 557	1 317	1 240
55-59	1 492	868	624	1 651	922	729	1 879	960	919	2 043	1 044	998
60-64	1 155	638	517	1 437	826	611	1 594	880	714	1 819	920	899
65-69	795	452	343	1 076	583	493	1 341	757	584	1 495	811	684
70-74	502	284	218	697	384	312	949	499	451	1 190	654	536
75-79	285	141	144	397	215	182	559	294	264	773	388	385
80-84	167	74	93	193	88	105	271	136	135	392	192	201
85-89	68	28	40	88	33	55	104	41	64	150	66	84
90-94	15	5	9	25	8	17	34	10	24	42	13	29
95-99	2	1	2	3	1	2	6	1	5	9	2	7
100 +	0	0	0	0	0	0	0	0	0	1	0	1

Age group	2045 Both sexes	Males	Females	2050 Both sexes	Males	Females
All ages	53 793	27 706	26 087	57 342	29 423	27 919
0-4	4 615	2 363	2 252	4 843	2 480	2 363
5-9	4 501	2 305	2 197	4 601	2 356	2 245
10-14	4 413	2 259	2 154	4 489	2 298	2 191
15-19	4 311	2 200	2 111	4 367	2 230	2 138
20-24	4 345	2 241	2 104	4 400	2 272	2 129
25-29	4 473	2 350	2 123	4 590	2 412	2 178
30-34	4 293	2 256	2 036	4 594	2 412	2 182
35-39	3 909	2 044	1 866	4 247	2 218	2 029
40-44	3 429	1 791	1 639	3 810	1 985	1 825
45-49	3 220	1 670	1 550	3 329	1 728	1 602
50-54	2 934	1 507	1 428	3 113	1 597	1 516
55-59	2 480	1 262	1 218	2 853	1 449	1 403
60-64	1 981	1 003	979	2 408	1 214	1 194
65-69	1 715	852	862	1 873	933	940
70-74	1 338	707	631	1 548	749	799
75-79	978	516	463	1 113	565	548
80-84	556	259	297	714	352	362
85-89	226	97	129	331	136	196
90-94	63	22	41	99	34	65
95-99	12	2	9	18	4	14
100 +	1	0	1	2	0	2

752

United Nations Department of Economic and Social Affairs/Population Division
World Population Prospects: The 2004 Revision, Volume II: Sex and Age Distribution of the World Population

POPULATION BY AGE AND SEX (in thousands)

Age group	2005 Both sexes	Males	Females	2010 Both sexes	Males	Females	2015 Both sexes	Males	Females	2020 Both sexes	Males	Females
All ages	24 573	13 259	11 314	27 430	14 691	12 739	30 155	16 048	14 107	32 719	17 314	15 405
0-4	3 200	1 633	1 567	3 112	1 588	1 524	3 037	1 551	1 486	2 950	1 508	1 442
5-9	3 075	1 567	1 508	3 180	1 622	1 558	3 095	1 579	1 516	3 021	1 543	1 478
10-14	2 886	1 471	1 415	3 061	1 559	1 501	3 166	1 614	1 552	3 082	1 572	1 510
15-19	2 456	1 248	1 208	2 837	1 439	1 398	3 013	1 528	1 485	3 119	1 584	1 535
20-24	2 092	1 092	1 000	2 543	1 317	1 226	2 924	1 509	1 415	3 100	1 598	1 502
25-29	2 174	1 179	995	2 335	1 260	1 075	2 786	1 486	1 300	3 167	1 678	1 490
30-34	2 064	1 206	858	2 293	1 239	1 054	2 455	1 322	1 134	2 906	1 547	1 359
35-39	1 859	1 115	745	2 017	1 166	851	2 247	1 200	1 047	2 409	1 283	1 127
40-44	1 455	848	607	1 759	1 054	705	1 918	1 106	811	2 148	1 142	1 006
45-49	1 037	631	406	1 358	785	573	1 660	990	670	1 820	1 043	776
50-54	691	426	265	943	565	379	1 261	717	543	1 560	919	641
55-59	463	257	206	643	388	255	889	522	367	1 199	671	528
60-64	404	213	191	449	245	204	621	369	252	856	496	360
65-69	318	171	147	375	193	181	418	223	194	576	336	240
70-74	189	104	85	272	142	130	324	162	162	363	188	175
75-79	123	61	62	141	76	66	208	104	103	251	120	131
80-84	63	28	35	76	36	40	89	45	44	135	63	72
85-89	20	8	12	28	12	16	35	15	20	43	20	24
90-94	4	2	3	6	2	3	9	3	6	11	4	7
95-99	1	0	0	1	0	0	1	0	1	2	0	1
100 +	0	0	0	0	0	0	0	0	0	0	0	0

Age group	2025 Both sexes	Males	Females	2030 Both sexes	Males	Females	2035 Both sexes	Males	Females	2040 Both sexes	Males	Females
All ages	35 146	18 502	16 645	37 325	19 550	17 774	39 151	20 406	18 745	40 562	21 037	19 524
0-4	2 907	1 487	1 420	2 774	1 420	1 354	2 561	1 311	1 250	2 306	1 181	1 125
5-9	2 936	1 500	1 435	2 893	1 480	1 413	2 761	1 413	1 348	2 548	1 305	1 244
10-14	3 008	1 536	1 472	2 923	1 494	1 429	2 881	1 474	1 408	2 749	1 407	1 342
15-19	3 035	1 541	1 494	2 963	1 506	1 456	2 878	1 465	1 413	2 836	1 445	1 392
20-24	3 207	1 654	1 553	3 124	1 613	1 512	3 053	1 578	1 475	2 969	1 537	1 432
25-29	3 344	1 767	1 577	3 452	1 824	1 628	3 370	1 783	1 587	3 299	1 749	1 550
30-34	3 287	1 739	1 548	3 465	1 830	1 635	3 574	1 887	1 687	3 492	1 846	1 646
35-39	2 860	1 508	1 351	3 241	1 701	1 541	3 420	1 792	1 628	3 528	1 849	1 680
40-44	2 311	1 225	1 086	2 761	1 450	1 310	3 142	1 643	1 499	3 320	1 733	1 587
45-49	2 050	1 079	970	2 214	1 163	1 050	2 662	1 388	1 274	3 041	1 579	1 462
50-54	1 719	973	746	1 949	1 010	938	2 113	1 095	1 018	2 557	1 317	1 240
55-59	1 492	868	624	1 651	922	729	1 879	960	919	2 043	1 044	998
60-64	1 155	638	517	1 437	826	611	1 594	880	714	1 819	920	899
65-69	795	452	343	1 076	583	493	1 341	757	584	1 495	811	684
70-74	502	284	218	697	384	312	949	499	451	1 190	654	536
75-79	285	141	144	397	215	182	559	294	264	773	388	385
80-84	167	74	93	193	88	105	271	136	135	392	192	201
85-89	68	28	40	88	33	55	104	41	64	150	66	84
90-94	15	5	9	25	8	17	34	10	24	42	13	29
95-99	2	1	2	3	1	2	6	1	5	9	2	7
100 +	0	0	0	0	0	0	0	0	0	1	0	1

Age group	2045 Both sexes	Males	Females	2050 Both sexes	Males	Females
All ages	41 564	21 453	20 112	42 298	21 729	20 569
0-4	2 083	1 067	1 016	2 012	1 030	982
5-9	2 294	1 175	1 119	2 071	1 061	1 011
10-14	2 537	1 299	1 238	2 283	1 169	1 114
15-19	2 704	1 378	1 326	2 493	1 270	1 222
20-24	2 927	1 517	1 410	2 796	1 451	1 345
25-29	3 216	1 708	1 507	3 175	1 689	1 486
30-34	3 422	1 813	1 609	3 339	1 772	1 567
35-39	3 448	1 809	1 639	3 378	1 775	1 603
40-44	3 429	1 791	1 639	3 350	1 751	1 599
45-49	3 220	1 670	1 550	3 329	1 728	1 602
50-54	2 934	1 507	1 428	3 113	1 597	1 516
55-59	2 480	1 262	1 218	2 853	1 449	1 403
60-64	1 981	1 003	979	2 408	1 214	1 194
65-69	1 715	852	862	1 873	933	940
70-74	1 338	707	631	1 548	749	799
75-79	978	516	463	1 113	565	548
80-84	556	259	297	714	352	362
85-89	226	97	129	331	136	196
90-94	63	22	41	99	34	65
95-99	12	2	9	18	4	14
100 +	1	0	1	2	0	2

United Nations Department of Economic and Social Affairs/Population Division
World Population Prospects: The 2004 Revision, Volume II: Sex and Age Distribution of the World Population

753

POPULATION BY AGE AND SEX (in thousands)

Age group	1950 Both sexes	Males	Females	1955 Both sexes	Males	Females	1960 Both sexes	Males	Females	1965 Both sexes	Males	Females
All ages	2 750	1 376	1 374	3 092	1 545	1 547	3 506	1 751	1 754	3 989	1 992	1 997
0-4	464	236	228	553	277	276	639	320	319	728	365	363
5-9	363	183	180	409	208	202	490	246	245	569	285	284
10-14	317	160	157	349	176	172	395	201	194	474	238	236
15-19	278	140	138	309	156	153	341	173	169	387	197	190
20-24	242	122	120	269	136	134	300	151	149	333	168	165
25-29	208	105	103	233	117	116	260	130	130	291	146	145
30-34	179	89	89	199	100	99	224	112	111	250	125	125
35-39	153	76	77	170	85	85	190	95	94	214	107	106
40-44	129	64	65	144	72	72	160	80	80	179	90	90
45-49	108	53	55	120	59	61	134	66	68	150	74	76
50-54	89	43	45	99	48	51	110	54	57	124	61	63
55-59	70	33	37	79	38	41	89	43	46	99	48	52
60-64	57	27	30	60	28	32	68	32	35	76	36	40
65-69	43	20	23	45	21	24	47	22	25	54	25	29
70-74	29	13	15	30	14	16	31	14	17	33	15	18
75-79	15	7	8	17	8	9	18	8	10	18	8	10
80 +	7	3	4	8	3	5	9	4	5	10	4	5

Age group	1970 Both sexes	Males	Females	1975 Both sexes	Males	Females	1980 Both sexes	Males	Females	1985 Both sexes	Males	Females
All ages	4 574	2 284	2 290	5 262	2 585	2 677	5 959	2 924	3 035	6 870	3 373	3 497
0-4	832	417	414	957	483	474	1 115	561	554	1 308	659	649
5-9	654	328	326	766	380	386	867	438	429	1 029	518	511
10-14	554	278	276	637	313	324	740	368	373	843	425	417
15-19	468	235	233	508	247	261	618	304	314	721	358	363
20-24	380	193	187	425	203	222	486	235	251	595	291	304
25-29	324	163	161	370	170	200	401	189	212	463	222	241
30-34	281	141	140	313	146	168	348	158	190	381	178	203
35-39	241	120	120	256	121	135	294	136	159	329	149	181
40-44	204	102	102	224	108	116	239	112	127	278	127	151
45-49	169	84	85	190	95	95	208	99	109	225	105	120
50-54	140	68	71	151	78	74	175	86	88	194	91	103
55-59	112	54	58	126	65	61	136	69	67	159	78	82
60-64	86	41	45	105	55	49	109	56	54	120	60	60
65-69	61	29	33	82	44	39	85	44	41	91	46	45
70-74	39	18	21	59	31	28	61	32	29	64	33	31
75-79	20	9	11	50	26	24	37	19	18	39	20	19
80 +	10	4	6	41	20	20	37	18	19	32	15	16

Age group	1990 Both sexes	Males	Females	1995 Both sexes	Males	Females	2000 Both sexes	Males	Females	2005 Both sexes	Males	Females
All ages	7 977	3 923	4 055	9 120	4 482	4 637	10 343	5 084	5 259	11 658	5 734	5 924
0-4	1 498	756	742	1 601	809	793	1 716	867	849	1 845	932	913
5-9	1 225	617	608	1 416	715	702	1 518	766	751	1 632	824	808
10-14	1 005	506	499	1 200	605	595	1 388	700	688	1 489	752	737
15-19	824	416	408	982	493	489	1 174	591	583	1 360	685	675
20-24	698	344	353	791	396	395	946	472	474	1 135	567	568
25-29	570	276	294	661	322	339	752	372	380	904	447	457
30-34	442	210	232	538	257	281	626	302	325	716	351	365
35-39	363	168	194	416	195	221	510	241	269	596	284	312
40-44	313	140	173	341	157	185	393	182	211	484	227	257
45-49	263	119	143	294	130	164	322	146	176	372	171	201
50-54	210	97	113	245	110	136	276	120	156	302	135	167
55-59	178	83	95	193	88	106	226	100	126	255	109	146
60-64	142	69	74	159	73	86	173	77	96	204	88	115
65-69	101	50	51	121	57	63	136	61	75	148	65	83
70-74	70	35	36	79	38	41	95	44	51	107	47	60
75-79	43	22	22	48	23	25	54	25	28	65	30	36
80 +	32	15	16	34	16	18	38	17	20	43	20	24

United Nations Department of Economic and Social Affairs/Population Division
World Population Prospects: The 2004 Revision, Volume II: Sex and Age Distribution of the World Population

754

POPULATION BY AGE AND SEX (in thousands)

Age group	2005 Both sexes	Males	Females	2010 Both sexes	Males	Females	2015 Both sexes	Males	Females	2020 Both sexes	Males	Females
All ages	11 658	5 734	5 924	13 082	6 443	6 638	14 538	7 169	7 369	15 970	7 882	8 088
0-4	1 845	932	913	1 956	988	968	2 019	1 020	999	2 028	1 024	1 004
5-9	1 632	824	808	1 764	891	874	1 880	949	931	1 949	983	965
10-14	1 489	752	737	1 604	810	795	1 738	877	861	1 854	935	919
15-19	1 360	685	675	1 463	738	725	1 579	796	783	1 712	863	849
20-24	1 135	567	568	1 323	663	660	1 426	716	710	1 542	774	768
25-29	904	447	457	1 095	544	551	1 281	638	643	1 384	690	694
30-34	716	351	365	869	427	443	1 058	522	536	1 242	615	627
35-39	596	284	312	687	335	353	838	409	429	1 024	503	521
40-44	484	227	257	571	271	300	661	320	341	809	393	416
45-49	372	171	201	462	215	247	547	258	289	635	305	329
50-54	302	135	167	352	160	192	438	202	236	521	243	277
55-59	255	109	146	281	124	157	329	148	181	411	188	224
60-64	204	88	115	231	98	133	256	112	144	301	133	167
65-69	148	65	83	176	75	101	201	84	117	224	96	128
70-74	107	47	60	118	51	67	141	59	82	163	66	96
75-79	65	30	36	75	32	43	84	35	48	101	41	60
80-84	30	14	16	37	16	21	43	18	25	49	20	29
85-89	11	5	6	12	5	7	16	7	9	19	7	11
90-94	2	1	1	3	1	2	3	1	2	4	2	3
95-99	0	0	0	0	0	0	0	0	0	1	0	0
100 +	0	0	0	0	0	0	0	0	0	0	0	0

Age group	2025 Both sexes	Males	Females	2030 Both sexes	Males	Females	2035 Both sexes	Males	Females	2040 Both sexes	Males	Females
All ages	17 348	8 565	8 783	18 678	9 222	9 455	19 956	9 851	10 105	21 146	10 431	10 714
0-4	2 010	1 015	996	1 990	1 004	986	1 961	990	972	1 906	962	944
5-9	1 964	990	974	1 957	986	971	1 948	981	967	1 929	971	957
10-14	1 925	970	954	1 943	979	964	1 940	976	963	1 934	973	961
15-19	1 829	921	908	1 901	957	944	1 923	967	956	1 922	965	956
20-24	1 675	840	835	1 793	899	894	1 867	936	931	1 891	947	944
25-29	1 499	748	751	1 633	814	818	1 752	874	878	1 828	911	917
30-34	1 344	667	677	1 460	724	735	1 595	791	803	1 716	851	864
35-39	1 205	594	611	1 308	646	663	1 426	704	722	1 562	771	790
40-44	991	484	507	1 171	574	596	1 275	627	648	1 394	685	708
45-49	779	376	403	958	466	493	1 137	555	582	1 242	608	634
50-54	606	289	316	747	358	389	922	445	477	1 098	533	565
55-59	490	227	263	572	271	301	709	337	372	880	422	458
60-64	378	170	207	452	207	246	532	249	283	663	312	351
65-69	264	115	149	334	148	186	404	182	222	478	220	258
70-74	183	77	106	218	93	124	279	121	157	340	150	190
75-79	118	47	71	134	55	79	162	68	95	211	89	121
80-84	60	24	36	71	27	44	83	33	50	102	41	61
85-89	22	8	13	27	10	17	33	12	21	39	15	24
90-94	5	2	3	6	2	4	8	3	5	11	4	7
95-99	1	0	1	1	0	1	1	0	1	2	0	1
100 +	0	0	0	0	0	0	0	0	0	0	0	0

Age group	2045 Both sexes	Males	Females	2050 Both sexes	Males	Females
All ages	22 207	10 945	11 263	23 108	11 375	11 734
0-4	1 826	922	905	1 728	872	856
5-9	1 882	948	935	1 809	911	898
10-14	1 918	965	953	1 874	942	931
15-19	1 918	963	955	1 904	956	948
20-24	1 892	947	946	1 891	946	946
25-29	1 855	924	931	1 859	925	934
30-34	1 794	890	904	1 823	904	920
35-39	1 684	832	852	1 765	871	893
40-44	1 531	753	778	1 654	814	841
45-49	1 361	666	695	1 498	734	764
50-54	1 203	585	618	1 322	644	678
55-59	1 051	506	545	1 156	558	598
60-64	826	392	435	991	473	519
65-69	600	278	322	752	351	401
70-74	406	184	222	514	233	280
75-79	260	112	148	314	139	176
80-84	135	55	79	169	71	98
85-89	49	19	30	66	26	40
90-94	13	4	8	16	6	10
95-99	2	1	1	2	1	2
100 +	0	0	0	0	0	0

POPULATION BY AGE AND SEX (in thousands)

Age group	2005 Both sexes	2005 Males	2005 Females	2010 Both sexes	2010 Males	2010 Females	2015 Both sexes	2015 Males	2015 Females	2020 Both sexes	2020 Males	2020 Females
All ages	11 658	5 734	5 924	13 192	6 499	6 693	14 851	7 327	7 524	16 571	8 185	8 386
0-4	1 845	932	913	2 066	1 044	1 022	2 226	1 125	1 102	2 324	1 173	1 151
5-9	1 632	824	808	1 764	891	874	1 986	1 002	983	2 149	1 084	1 065
10-14	1 489	752	737	1 604	810	795	1 738	877	861	1 959	988	971
15-19	1 360	685	675	1 463	738	725	1 579	796	783	1 712	863	849
20-24	1 135	567	568	1 323	663	660	1 426	716	710	1 542	774	768
25-29	904	447	457	1 095	544	551	1 281	638	643	1 384	690	694
30-34	716	351	365	869	427	443	1 058	522	536	1 242	615	627
35-39	596	284	312	687	335	353	838	409	429	1 024	503	521
40-44	484	227	257	571	271	300	661	320	341	809	393	416
45-49	372	171	201	462	215	247	547	258	289	635	305	329
50-54	302	135	167	352	160	192	438	202	236	521	243	277
55-59	255	109	146	281	124	157	329	148	181	411	188	224
60-64	204	88	115	231	98	133	256	112	144	301	133	167
65-69	148	65	83	176	75	101	201	84	117	224	96	128
70-74	107	47	60	118	51	67	141	59	82	163	66	96
75-79	65	30	36	75	32	43	84	35	48	101	41	60
80-84	30	14	16	37	16	21	43	18	25	49	20	29
85-89	11	5	6	12	5	7	16	7	9	19	7	11
90-94	2	1	1	3	1	2	3	1	2	4	2	3
95-99	0	0	0	0	0	0	0	0	0	1	0	0
100 +	0	0	0	0	0	0	0	0	0	0	0	0

Age group	2025 Both sexes	2025 Males	2025 Females	2030 Both sexes	2030 Males	2030 Females	2035 Both sexes	2035 Males	2035 Females	2040 Both sexes	2040 Males	2040 Females
All ages	18 274	9 032	9 242	19 994	9 886	10 109	21 764	10 761	11 003	23 555	11 644	11 912
0-4	2 348	1 185	1 163	2 395	1 209	1 187	2 470	1 246	1 223	2 527	1 275	1 252
5-9	2 252	1 135	1 117	2 286	1 151	1 134	2 345	1 181	1 164	2 429	1 223	1 206
10-14	2 123	1 070	1 052	2 228	1 122	1 106	2 266	1 140	1 125	2 329	1 172	1 157
15-19	1 932	973	959	2 097	1 056	1 041	2 205	1 109	1 096	2 245	1 128	1 117
20-24	1 675	840	835	1 894	950	944	2 061	1 033	1 028	2 170	1 087	1 083
25-29	1 499	748	751	1 633	814	818	1 852	924	928	2 020	1 007	1 012
30-34	1 344	667	677	1 460	724	735	1 595	791	803	1 815	901	914
35-39	1 205	594	611	1 308	646	663	1 426	704	722	1 562	771	790
40-44	991	484	507	1 171	574	596	1 275	627	648	1 394	685	708
45-49	779	376	403	958	466	493	1 137	555	582	1 242	608	634
50-54	606	289	316	747	358	389	922	445	477	1 098	533	565
55-59	490	227	263	572	271	301	709	337	372	880	422	458
60-64	378	170	207	452	207	246	532	249	283	663	312	351
65-69	264	115	149	334	148	186	404	182	222	478	220	258
70-74	183	77	106	218	93	124	279	121	157	340	150	190
75-79	118	47	71	134	55	79	162	68	95	211	89	121
80-84	60	24	36	71	27	44	83	33	50	102	41	61
85-89	22	8	13	27	10	17	33	12	21	39	15	24
90-94	5	2	3	6	2	4	8	3	5	11	4	7
95-99	1	0	1	1	0	1	1	0	1	2	0	1
100 +	0	0	0	0	0	0	0	0	0	0	0	0

Age group	2045 Both sexes	2045 Males	2045 Females	2050 Both sexes	2050 Males	2050 Females
All ages	25 312	12 505	12 807	26 981	13 320	13 661
0-4	2 543	1 283	1 260	2 521	1 272	1 249
5-9	2 496	1 257	1 239	2 519	1 268	1 251
10-14	2 416	1 215	1 201	2 485	1 250	1 235
15-19	2 311	1 160	1 150	2 399	1 205	1 195
20-24	2 213	1 107	1 106	2 281	1 141	1 140
25-29	2 131	1 062	1 069	2 177	1 084	1 093
30-34	1 983	984	999	2 097	1 040	1 057
35-39	1 782	880	901	1 951	964	987
40-44	1 531	753	778	1 750	861	889
45-49	1 361	666	695	1 498	734	764
50-54	1 203	585	618	1 322	644	678
55-59	1 051	506	545	1 156	558	598
60-64	826	392	435	991	473	519
65-69	600	278	322	752	351	401
70-74	406	184	222	514	233	280
75-79	260	112	148	314	139	176
80-84	135	55	79	169	71	98
85-89	49	19	30	66	26	40
90-94	13	4	8	16	6	10
95-99	2	1	1	2	1	2
100 +	0	0	0	0	0	0

United Nations Department of Economic and Social Affairs/Population Division
World Population Prospects: The 2004 Revision, Volume II: Sex and Age Distribution of the World Population

756

POPULATION BY AGE AND SEX (in thousands)

Age group	2005 Both sexes	2005 Males	2005 Females	2010 Both sexes	2010 Males	2010 Females	2015 Both sexes	2015 Males	2015 Females	2020 Both sexes	2020 Males	2020 Females
All ages	11 658	5 734	5 924	12 972	6 388	6 584	14 225	7 011	7 214	15 280	7 579	7 701
0-4	1 845	932	913	1 846	933	914	1 812	915	897	1 731	874	857
5-9	1 632	824	808	1 764	891	874	1 774	896	879	1 748	882	866
10-14	1 489	752	737	1 604	810	795	1 738	877	861	1 750	883	867
15-19	1 360	685	675	1 463	738	725	1 579	796	783	1 712	863	849
20-24	1 135	567	568	1 323	663	660	1 426	716	710	1 542	774	768
25-29	904	447	457	1 095	544	551	1 281	638	643	1 384	690	694
30-34	716	351	365	869	427	443	1 058	522	536	1 242	615	627
35-39	596	284	312	687	335	353	838	409	429	1 024	503	521
40-44	484	227	257	571	271	300	661	320	341	809	393	416
45-49	372	171	201	462	215	247	547	258	289	635	305	329
50-54	302	135	167	352	160	192	438	202	236	521	243	277
55-59	255	109	146	281	124	157	329	148	181	411	188	224
60-64	204	88	115	231	98	133	256	112	144	301	133	167
65-69	148	65	83	176	75	101	201	84	117	224	96	128
70-74	107	47	60	118	51	67	141	59	82	163	66	96
75-79	65	30	36	75	32	43	84	35	48	101	41	60
80-84	30	14	16	37	16	21	43	18	25	49	20	29
85-89	11	5	6	12	5	7	16	7	9	19	7	11
90-94	2	1	1	3	1	2	3	1	2	4	2	3
95-99	0	0	0	0	0	0	0	0	0	1	0	0
100 +	0	0	0	0	0	0	0	0	0	0	0	0

Age group	2025 Both sexes	2025 Males	2025 Females	2030 Both sexes	2030 Males	2030 Females	2035 Both sexes	2035 Males	2035 Females	2040 Both sexes	2040 Males	2040 Females
All ages	16 424	8 099	8 325	17 375	8 566	8 809	18 200	8 966	9 233	18 860	9 282	9 579
0-4	1 675	845	829	1 597	806	791	1 491	752	738	1 358	685	673
5-9	1 677	845	832	1 630	821	809	1 563	787	776	1 465	738	727
10-14	1 727	870	856	1 659	836	823	1 615	813	802	1 552	781	771
15-19	1 726	869	857	1 705	858	847	1 640	825	816	1 599	803	796
20-24	1 675	840	835	1 691	848	843	1 673	838	835	1 612	807	805
25-29	1 499	748	751	1 633	814	818	1 652	823	828	1 637	816	822
30-34	1 344	667	677	1 460	724	735	1 595	791	803	1 617	802	815
35-39	1 205	594	611	1 308	646	663	1 426	704	722	1 562	771	790
40-44	991	484	507	1 171	574	596	1 275	627	648	1 394	685	708
45-49	779	376	403	958	466	493	1 137	555	582	1 242	608	634
50-54	606	289	316	747	358	389	922	445	477	1 098	533	565
55-59	490	227	263	572	271	301	709	337	372	880	422	458
60-64	378	170	207	452	207	246	532	249	283	663	312	351
65-69	264	115	149	334	148	186	404	182	222	478	220	258
70-74	183	77	106	218	93	124	279	121	157	340	150	190
75-79	118	47	71	134	55	79	162	68	95	211	89	121
80-84	60	24	36	71	27	44	83	33	50	102	41	61
85-89	22	8	13	27	10	17	33	12	21	39	15	24
90-94	5	2	3	6	2	4	8	3	5	11	4	7
95-99	1	0	1	1	0	1	1	0	1	2	0	1
100 +	0	0	0	0	0	0	0	0	0	0	0	0

Age group	2045 Both sexes	2045 Males	2045 Females	2050 Both sexes	2050 Males	2050 Females
All ages	19 334	9 501	9 833	19 610	9 618	9 992
0-4	1 218	615	604	1 081	546	536
5-9	1 340	675	665	1 206	607	599
10-14	1 457	733	724	1 334	671	663
15-19	1 538	772	766	1 445	725	720
20-24	1 573	787	787	1 514	757	757
25-29	1 579	786	793	1 543	767	776
30-34	1 605	795	810	1 550	767	783
35-39	1 587	783	803	1 578	778	800
40-44	1 531	753	778	1 558	766	792
45-49	1 361	666	695	1 498	734	764
50-54	1 203	585	618	1 322	644	678
55-59	1 051	506	545	1 156	558	598
60-64	826	392	435	991	473	519
65-69	600	278	322	752	351	401
70-74	406	184	222	514	233	280
75-79	260	112	148	314	139	176
80-84	135	55	79	169	71	98
85-89	49	19	30	66	26	40
90-94	13	4	8	16	6	10
95-99	2	1	1	2	1	2
100 +	0	0	0	0	0	0

POPULATION BY AGE AND SEX (in thousands)

Age group	1950 Both sexes	Males	Females	1955 Both sexes	Males	Females	1960 Both sexes	Males	Females	1965 Both sexes	Males	Females
All ages	7 131	3 460	3 671	7 646	3 737	3 909	8 050	3 955	4 095	8 396	4 145	4 251
0-4	799	408	391	861	440	421	774	398	377	777	405	372
5-9	571	289	282	784	401	383	845	433	412	757	390	368
10-14	667	335	332	573	290	283	780	400	380	834	428	406
15-19	736	370	366	669	336	333	571	289	282	770	394	376
20-24	725	359	366	736	369	366	665	334	331	561	284	278
25-29	588	277	311	723	358	366	729	366	364	653	328	326
30-34	345	163	182	585	275	310	716	353	363	716	358	358
35-39	413	197	216	343	162	181	577	270	307	701	345	356
40-44	477	241	236	406	193	214	336	158	178	562	262	300
45-49	426	215	212	464	233	232	394	186	209	323	151	173
50-54	364	174	190	409	203	206	445	220	224	376	175	201
55-59	244	111	134	342	161	181	384	188	196	415	203	213
60-64	234	102	132	223	99	124	312	144	168	349	168	182
65-69	184	82	102	201	86	115	193	84	109	269	122	148
70-74	157	63	95	142	62	81	157	65	92	151	63	88
75-79	118	45	74	106	41	66	97	41	57	109	43	66
80 +	83	30	53	78	29	49	74	28	46	71	28	43

Age group	1970 Both sexes	Males	Females	1975 Both sexes	Males	Females	1980 Both sexes	Males	Females	1985 Both sexes	Males	Females
All ages	8 691	4 292	4 399	9 085	4 499	4 587	9 522	4 719	4 803	9 848	4 887	4 962
0-4	738	378	360	789	410	379	800	415	386	812	421	391
5-9	718	369	349	732	375	357	763	394	368	794	411	383
10-14	739	380	359	715	368	347	730	374	356	759	392	367
15-19	833	425	407	736	378	358	723	372	352	726	372	354
20-24	749	382	366	828	423	406	751	385	366	718	369	350
25-29	538	270	269	743	379	365	834	425	409	745	381	364
30-34	644	320	324	534	267	267	692	351	341	827	420	406
35-39	705	352	352	637	316	321	553	276	277	684	347	338
40-44	684	336	348	694	346	348	646	320	327	545	271	274
45-49	550	257	294	669	327	342	695	344	350	633	311	321
50-54	316	147	169	533	246	287	643	309	334	673	330	342
55-59	361	166	195	300	137	163	507	231	276	612	289	323
60-64	389	188	201	336	151	184	251	113	138	473	211	262
65-69	307	146	161	344	162	182	334	148	186	224	97	126
70-74	217	96	121	249	114	135	284	130	153	275	116	158
75-79	105	43	62	156	66	90	194	84	109	207	91	116
80 +	98	36	62	90	34	56	123	48	75	143	57	86

Age group	1990 Both sexes	Males	Females	1995 Both sexes	Males	Females	2000 Both sexes	Males	Females	2005 Both sexes	Males	Females
All ages	10 156	5 044	5 112	10 548	5 242	5 306	10 545	5 244	5 301	10 503	5 226	5 277
0-4	773	400	372	705	365	340	631	327	304	608	315	293
5-9	810	420	391	785	407	379	697	361	336	624	324	301
10-14	794	411	383	824	427	398	777	402	375	690	357	333
15-19	759	392	367	808	418	390	815	422	393	769	398	371
20-24	725	371	354	771	398	373	798	412	386	806	417	389
25-29	717	367	349	736	376	360	761	392	369	788	407	381
30-34	742	379	363	727	372	355	726	370	356	750	386	364
35-39	822	417	405	752	383	368	715	365	350	714	364	351
40-44	678	342	336	827	418	409	736	374	362	701	357	344
45-49	536	265	271	678	340	338	805	405	400	717	363	354
50-54	616	300	316	531	260	271	652	324	328	776	387	389
55-59	644	311	333	598	287	311	502	242	260	618	303	315
60-64	573	265	308	607	286	321	549	257	293	463	218	245
65-69	424	183	241	517	230	287	533	242	291	487	220	267
70-74	185	77	108	356	147	209	423	180	243	442	192	250
75-79	202	81	121	142	57	86	266	105	161	321	131	190
80 +	159	64	95	183	74	110	159	64	95	229	89	140

United Nations Department of Economic and Social Affairs/Population Division
World Population Prospects: The 2004 Revision, Volume II: Sex and Age Distribution of the World Population

758

SERBIA AND MONTENEGRO

POPULATION BY AGE AND SEX (in thousands)

Age group	2005 Both sexes	Males	Females	2010 Both sexes	Males	Females	2015 Both sexes	Males	Females	2020 Both sexes	Males	Females
All ages	10 503	5 226	5 277	10 479	5 217	5 262	10 416	5 190	5 227	10 005	5 152	5 183
0-4	608	315	293	584	303	281	571	296	275	564	293	271
5-9	624	324	301	605	314	291	582	302	280	569	295	273
10-14	690	357	333	622	322	300	603	312	290	580	301	279
15-19	769	398	371	687	355	332	619	321	299	600	311	289
20-24	806	417	389	765	395	369	684	353	330	616	319	297
25-29	788	407	381	801	414	387	761	393	368	680	351	329
30-34	750	386	364	783	403	379	796	411	385	756	390	366
35-39	714	364	351	744	382	362	777	400	377	790	408	383
40-44	701	357	344	706	359	348	736	378	359	769	396	374
45-49	717	363	354	689	350	340	695	352	343	725	371	354
50-54	776	387	389	697	350	347	672	338	333	678	341	337
55-59	618	303	315	744	366	378	670	332	338	646	322	324
60-64	463	218	245	577	276	301	697	335	361	629	306	324
65-69	487	220	267	415	189	227	520	241	279	632	295	337
70-74	442	192	250	410	177	233	353	153	199	445	198	247
75-79	321	131	190	341	142	199	320	132	189	278	115	163
80-84	169	65	105	210	82	128	227	89	138	217	84	133
85-89	41	16	25	82	30	51	105	39	66	117	43	74
90-94	17	7	9	13	5	8	27	10	17	36	13	24
95-99	2	1	1	3	1	2	3	1	1	6	2	4
100 +	0	0	0	0	0	0	0	0	0	0	0	0

Age group	2025 Both sexes	Males	Females	2030 Both sexes	Males	Females	2035 Both sexes	Males	Females	2040 Both sexes	Males	Females
All ages	10 234	5 104	5 130	10 114	5 043	5 071	9 973	4 969	5 004	9 806	4 883	4 923
0-4	547	284	263	532	276	256	522	271	251	506	263	243
5-9	562	292	270	545	283	262	530	275	255	520	270	250
10-14	567	294	273	560	291	269	543	282	261	528	274	254
15-19	577	299	278	564	293	272	558	290	268	541	281	260
20-24	598	310	288	575	298	277	562	291	270	555	288	267
25-29	613	317	296	595	308	287	572	296	276	559	290	269
30-34	676	349	327	610	315	294	592	306	285	569	295	274
35-39	751	387	364	672	347	325	606	313	293	588	304	284
40-44	783	403	380	745	384	361	668	344	323	601	311	291
45-49	758	389	369	773	397	376	736	379	357	659	339	320
50-54	709	361	349	743	379	364	758	388	370	722	370	352
55-59	654	326	329	685	345	340	719	364	356	735	373	363
60-64	609	298	312	619	302	317	650	321	329	684	340	344
65-69	573	270	303	557	264	293	569	270	299	600	289	311
70-74	545	244	301	497	225	272	487	222	265	500	228	272
75-79	355	150	205	438	186	252	403	173	230	399	172	227
80-84	191	74	117	247	97	150	310	121	189	291	115	176
85-89	114	40	74	104	36	68	138	48	90	178	62	117
90-94	42	14	28	43	13	30	41	12	29	57	17	41
95-99	8	3	5	10	3	7	11	3	8	11	3	8
100 +	1	0	0	1	0	1	1	0	1	2	0	1

Age group	2045 Both sexes	Males	Females	2050 Both sexes	Males	Females
All ages	9 621	4 789	4 832	9 426	4 691	4 735
0-4	493	256	237	482	250	232
5-9	504	262	242	491	255	236
10-14	518	269	249	502	261	241
15-19	526	273	253	516	268	248
20-24	539	280	259	524	272	252
25-29	553	287	266	536	278	258
30-34	556	288	268	550	285	265
35-39	566	293	273	553	286	267
40-44	584	302	282	561	290	271
45-49	595	307	288	577	298	279
50-54	647	331	316	584	300	284
55-59	702	356	345	630	320	310
60-64	701	350	351	671	335	335
65-69	634	307	327	652	318	335
70-74	531	246	285	564	264	301
75-79	414	179	235	443	195	248
80-84	292	117	176	308	123	184
85-89	172	60	112	177	62	115
90-94	78	22	55	78	23	55
95-99	16	4	12	23	5	18
100 +	2	0	1	3	0	2

United Nations Department of Economic and Social Affairs/Population Division
World Population Prospects: The 2004 Revision, Volume II: Sex and Age Distribution of the World Population

759

POPULATION BY AGE AND SEX (in thousands)

Age group	2005 Both sexes	Males	Females	2010 Both sexes	Males	Females	2015 Both sexes	Males	Females	2020 Both sexes	Males	Females
All ages	10 503	5 226	5 277	10 571	5 265	5 307	10 652	5 312	5 340	10 738	5 361	5 377
0-4	608	315	293	677	351	326	714	371	344	731	379	351
5-9	624	324	301	605	314	291	674	350	325	712	370	343
10-14	690	357	333	622	322	300	603	312	290	672	349	324
15-19	769	398	371	687	355	332	619	321	299	600	311	289
20-24	806	417	389	765	395	369	684	353	330	616	319	297
25-29	788	407	381	801	414	387	761	393	368	680	351	329
30-34	750	386	364	783	403	379	796	411	385	756	390	366
35-39	714	364	351	744	382	362	777	400	377	790	408	383
40-44	701	357	344	706	359	348	736	378	359	769	396	374
45-49	717	363	354	689	350	340	695	352	343	725	371	354
50-54	776	387	389	697	350	347	672	338	333	678	341	337
55-59	618	303	315	744	366	378	670	332	338	646	322	324
60-64	463	218	245	577	276	301	697	335	361	629	306	324
65-69	487	220	267	415	189	227	520	241	279	632	295	337
70-74	442	192	250	410	177	233	353	153	199	445	198	247
75-79	321	131	190	341	142	199	320	132	189	278	115	163
80-84	169	65	105	210	82	128	227	89	138	217	84	133
85-89	41	16	25	82	30	51	105	39	66	117	43	74
90-94	17	7	9	13	5	8	27	10	17	36	13	24
95-99	2	1	1	3	1	2	3	1	1	6	2	4
100 +	0	0	0	0	0	0	0	0	0	0	0	0

Age group	2025 Both sexes	Males	Females	2030 Both sexes	Males	Females	2035 Both sexes	Males	Females	2040 Both sexes	Males	Females
All ages	10 792	5 393	5 399	10 834	5 416	5 417	10 889	5 444	5 445	10 968	5 486	5 482
0-4	702	365	338	694	361	334	719	374	346	752	391	362
5-9	729	378	350	700	364	337	692	360	333	717	373	345
10-14	710	368	342	726	377	349	698	363	336	690	359	332
15-19	670	347	322	708	367	340	724	376	348	696	361	335
20-24	598	310	288	667	346	321	705	366	339	722	374	347
25-29	613	317	296	595	308	287	664	344	320	702	364	338
30-34	676	349	327	610	315	294	592	306	285	661	342	319
35-39	751	387	364	672	347	325	606	313	293	588	304	284
40-44	783	403	380	745	384	361	666	344	323	601	311	291
45-49	758	389	369	773	397	376	736	379	357	659	339	320
50-54	709	361	349	743	379	364	758	388	370	722	370	352
55-59	654	326	329	685	345	340	719	364	356	735	373	363
60-64	609	298	312	619	302	317	650	321	329	684	340	344
65-69	573	270	303	557	264	293	569	270	299	600	289	311
70-74	545	244	301	497	225	272	487	222	265	500	228	272
75-79	355	150	205	438	186	252	403	173	230	399	172	227
80-84	191	74	117	247	97	150	310	121	189	291	115	176
85-89	114	40	74	104	36	68	138	48	90	178	62	117
90-94	42	14	28	43	13	30	41	12	29	57	17	41
95-99	8	3	5	10	3	7	11	3	8	11	3	8
100 +	1	0	0	1	0	1	1	0	1	2	0	1

Age group	2045 Both sexes	Males	Females	2050 Both sexes	Males	Females
All ages	11 068	5 540	5 528	11 173	5 597	5 576
0-4	779	404	374	784	407	377
5-9	750	390	361	777	403	373
10-14	715	372	344	748	389	360
15-19	688	357	331	713	370	343
20-24	693	360	334	686	356	330
25-29	719	373	346	691	358	332
30-34	699	362	337	716	371	345
35-39	657	340	317	695	360	335
40-44	584	302	282	653	338	315
45-49	595	307	288	577	298	279
50-54	647	331	316	584	300	284
55-59	702	356	345	630	320	310
60-64	701	350	351	671	335	335
65-69	634	307	327	652	318	335
70-74	531	246	285	564	264	301
75-79	414	179	235	443	195	248
80-84	292	117	176	308	123	184
85-89	172	60	112	177	62	115
90-94	78	22	55	78	23	55
95-99	16	4	12	23	5	18
100 +	2	0	1	3	0	2

United Nations Department of Economic and Social Affairs/Population Division
World Population Prospects: The 2004 Revision, Volume II: Sex and Age Distribution of the World Population

760

POPULATION BY AGE AND SEX (in thousands)

Age group	2005			2010			2015			2020		
	Both sexes	Males	Females	Both sexes	Males	Females	Both sexes	Males	Females	Both sexes	Males	Females
All ages	10 503	5 226	5 277	10 386	5 168	5 217	10 179	5 066	5 113	9 929	4 942	4 987
0-4	608	315	293	491	255	236	427	221	205	395	205	190
5-9	624	324	301	605	314	291	489	254	235	424	220	204
10-14	690	357	333	622	322	300	603	312	290	487	253	234
15-19	769	398	371	687	355	332	619	321	299	600	311	289
20-24	806	417	389	765	395	369	684	353	330	616	319	297
25-29	788	407	381	801	414	387	761	393	368	680	351	329
30-34	750	386	364	783	403	379	796	411	385	756	390	366
35-39	714	364	351	744	382	362	777	400	377	790	408	383
40-44	701	357	344	706	359	348	736	378	359	769	396	374
45-49	717	363	354	689	350	340	695	352	343	725	371	354
50-54	776	387	389	697	350	347	672	338	333	678	341	337
55-59	618	303	315	744	366	378	670	332	338	646	322	324
60-64	463	218	245	577	276	301	697	335	361	629	306	324
65-69	487	220	267	415	189	227	520	241	279	632	295	337
70-74	442	192	250	410	177	233	353	153	199	445	198	247
75-79	321	131	190	341	142	199	320	132	189	278	115	163
80-84	169	65	105	210	82	128	227	89	138	217	84	133
85-89	41	16	25	82	30	51	105	39	66	117	43	74
90-94	17	7	9	13	5	8	27	10	17	36	13	24
95-99	2	1	1	3	1	2	3	1	1	6	2	4
100 +	0	0	0	0	0	0	0	0	0	0	0	0

Age group	2025			2030			2035			2040		
	Both sexes	Males	Females	Both sexes	Males	Females	Both sexes	Males	Females	Both sexes	Males	Females
All ages	9 671	4 812	4 860	9 399	4 672	4 727	9 094	4 512	4 581	8 740	4 330	4 410
0-4	390	203	188	379	197	182	357	186	172	318	165	153
5-9	393	204	189	388	202	187	377	196	181	355	185	171
10-14	423	219	203	391	203	188	386	201	186	375	195	180
15-19	485	251	233	420	218	202	389	202	187	385	200	185
20-24	598	310	288	482	250	232	418	217	201	387	201	186
25-29	613	317	296	595	308	287	480	249	231	416	216	200
30-34	676	349	327	610	315	294	592	306	285	477	247	230
35-39	751	387	364	672	347	325	605	313	290	588	304	284
40-44	783	403	380	745	384	361	666	344	323	601	311	291
45-49	758	389	369	773	397	376	736	379	357	659	339	320
50-54	709	361	348	743	379	364	758	388	370	722	370	352
55-59	654	326	329	685	345	340	719	364	356	735	373	363
60-64	609	298	312	619	302	317	650	321	329	684	340	344
65-69	573	270	303	557	264	293	569	270	299	600	289	311
70-74	545	244	301	497	225	272	487	222	265	500	228	272
75-79	355	150	205	438	186	252	403	173	230	399	172	227
80-84	191	74	117	247	97	150	310	121	189	291	115	176
85-89	114	40	74	104	36	68	138	48	90	178	62	117
90-94	42	14	28	43	13	30	41	12	29	57	17	41
95-99	8	3	5	10	3	7	11	3	8	11	3	8
100 +	1	0	0	1	0	1	1	0	1	2	0	1

Age group	2045			2050		
	Both sexes	Males	Females	Both sexes	Males	Females
All ages	8 345	4 127	4 218	7 926	3 912	4 014
0-4	281	146	135	256	133	123
5-9	317	164	152	279	145	134
10-14	354	184	170	315	164	151
15-19	373	194	179	352	183	169
20-24	382	198	184	371	193	178
25-29	385	199	185	380	197	183
30-34	413	214	199	382	198	184
35-39	474	245	229	410	213	198
40-44	584	302	282	470	243	227
45-49	595	307	288	577	298	279
50-54	647	331	316	584	300	284
55-59	702	356	345	630	320	310
60-64	701	350	351	671	335	335
65-69	634	307	327	652	318	335
70-74	531	246	285	564	264	301
75-79	414	179	235	443	195	248
80-84	292	117	176	308	123	184
85-89	172	60	112	177	62	115
90-94	78	22	55	78	23	55
95-99	16	4	12	23	5	18
100 +	2	0	1	3	0	2

POPULATION BY AGE AND SEX (in thousands)

Age group	1950 Both sexes	1950 Males	1950 Females	1955 Both sexes	1955 Males	1955 Females	1960 Both sexes	1960 Males	1960 Females	1965 Both sexes	1965 Males	1965 Females
All ages	1 944	952	992	2 085	1 021	1 064	2 256	1 105	1 151	2 458	1 205	1 254
0-4	311	155	156	328	163	166	364	180	183	404	201	203
5-9	242	120	122	258	128	130	275	136	140	308	152	156
10-14	213	106	107	232	115	117	249	124	125	266	131	134
15-19	192	95	97	206	102	103	225	112	113	241	120	121
20-24	172	85	87	182	91	92	196	97	99	214	107	108
25-29	152	75	77	162	80	82	172	85	87	185	92	94
30-34	133	66	68	143	70	73	152	75	77	163	80	82
35-39	116	57	59	125	61	64	134	66	68	144	71	73
40-44	100	49	51	108	53	55	117	57	60	126	61	64
45-49	85	41	44	92	44	48	100	48	52	108	52	56
50-54	70	33	37	77	36	40	84	40	44	91	43	48
55-59	57	26	30	62	29	33	68	32	36	74	35	40
60-64	43	19	24	47	21	26	52	23	28	57	26	31
65-69	30	13	17	32	14	18	35	16	20	39	18	22
70-74	18	8	10	19	8	11	21	9	12	23	10	13
75-79	8	3	5	8	4	5	9	4	5	10	4	6
80 +	3	1	2	3	1	2	3	1	2	4	1	2

Age group	1970 Both sexes	1970 Males	1970 Females	1975 Both sexes	1975 Males	1975 Females	1980 Both sexes	1980 Males	1980 Females	1985 Both sexes	1985 Males	1985 Females
All ages	2 697	1 322	1 375	2 945	1 444	1 500	3 236	1 588	1 647	3 580	1 759	1 821
0-4	450	224	226	471	234	236	523	261	262	593	296	297
5-9	346	171	175	389	193	196	410	204	207	457	227	230
10-14	298	147	150	335	166	169	377	187	190	399	198	201
15-19	258	127	130	289	143	146	326	161	164	368	182	185
20-24	231	115	116	247	122	125	278	137	141	314	155	158
25-29	203	101	103	219	109	111	236	116	120	266	131	135
30-34	176	87	89	193	96	98	209	104	106	225	111	115
35-39	154	76	78	167	82	84	184	91	93	199	99	101
40-44	135	66	69	145	71	74	157	77	80	174	86	89
45-49	117	57	61	126	61	65	136	66	70	148	72	76
50-54	100	47	52	108	51	56	116	56	61	126	61	66
55-59	82	38	43	89	42	47	97	46	52	105	49	56
60-64	63	29	34	69	32	38	76	35	41	84	38	45
65-69	44	20	24	49	22	27	54	24	30	60	27	33
70-74	26	11	15	30	13	17	33	15	19	37	16	21
75-79	12	5	7	14	6	8	16	7	9	18	8	10
80 +	4	2	3	5	2	3	6	2	4	7	3	4

Age group	1990 Both sexes	1990 Males	1990 Females	1995 Both sexes	1995 Males	1995 Females	2000 Both sexes	2000 Males	2000 Females	2005 Both sexes	2005 Males	2005 Females
All ages	4 078	2 006	2 072	4 137	2 036	2 100	4 509	2 221	2 288	5 525	2 725	2 801
0-4	707	353	354	706	353	354	777	389	388	958	479	479
5-9	530	264	266	567	282	284	609	303	306	758	378	380
10-14	453	225	228	469	234	236	539	269	270	650	324	326
15-19	396	197	199	402	200	202	447	223	224	576	287	289
20-24	361	179	182	347	172	175	378	188	190	473	236	238
25-29	306	151	155	314	155	159	321	159	162	395	196	199
30-34	259	128	132	266	131	135	290	143	147	331	164	167
35-39	219	107	112	225	110	114	245	120	125	296	146	150
40-44	192	95	98	189	92	97	207	101	106	250	122	128
45-49	167	81	86	165	81	84	173	84	89	211	102	109
50-54	140	67	73	141	68	73	149	72	77	175	84	92
55-59	116	55	61	115	55	61	125	59	66	148	70	78
60-64	93	43	50	91	42	49	98	45	52	119	55	64
65-69	68	31	37	67	30	37	72	33	39	87	39	47
70-74	42	19	24	42	19	24	46	20	26	56	25	31
75-79	20	9	12	21	9	12	23	10	13	29	12	16
80 +	8	3	5	9	3	5	10	4	6	13	5	8

United Nations Department of Economic and Social Affairs/Population Division
World Population Prospects: The 2004 Revision, Volume II: Sex and Age Distribution of the World Population

POPULATION BY AGE AND SEX (in thousands)

Age group	2005 Both sexes	Males	Females	2010 Both sexes	Males	Females	2015 Both sexes	Males	Females	2020 Both sexes	Males	Females
All ages	5 525	2 725	2 801	6 132	3 027	3 106	6 897	3 407	3 491	7 740	3 825	3 915
0-4	958	479	479	1 057	529	528	1 165	583	582	1 266	633	632
5-9	758	378	380	851	424	427	958	478	481	1 065	531	534
10-14	650	324	326	730	364	366	832	415	417	939	468	471
15-19	576	287	289	628	313	315	716	357	359	818	408	410
20-24	473	236	238	551	274	277	610	303	307	698	347	350
25-29	395	196	199	448	222	225	529	263	266	588	292	296
30-34	331	164	167	370	184	186	426	212	214	505	251	254
35-39	296	146	150	308	153	155	351	174	176	405	201	203
40-44	250	122	128	275	135	140	291	144	147	332	165	167
45-49	211	102	109	231	112	119	258	126	132	274	135	139
50-54	175	84	92	193	92	101	216	103	112	242	116	125
55-59	148	70	78	157	74	84	177	83	94	198	93	105
60-64	119	55	64	128	59	69	139	64	75	156	72	84
65-69	87	39	47	96	44	52	105	48	58	115	52	63
70-74	56	25	31	61	27	34	70	31	39	77	34	43
75-79	29	12	16	32	14	18	36	15	21	42	18	24
80-84	11	4	6	12	5	7	14	6	8	16	7	10
85-89	2	1	1	3	1	2	3	1	2	4	2	2
90-94	0	0	0	0	0	0	0	0	0	1	0	0
95-99	0	0	0	0	0	0	0	0	0	0	0	0
100 +	0	0	0	0	0	0	0	0	0	0	0	0

Age group	2025 Both sexes	Males	Females	2030 Both sexes	Males	Females	2035 Both sexes	Males	Females	2040 Both sexes	Males	Females
All ages	8 663	4 282	4 381	9 650	4 771	4 879	10 674	5 277	5 397	11 711	5 789	5 922
0-4	1 363	682	681	1 445	724	721	1 498	751	747	1 526	765	760
5-9	1 168	582	586	1 269	633	636	1 357	677	680	1 418	708	710
10-14	1 046	521	525	1 150	573	577	1 252	624	628	1 341	669	672
15-19	924	461	464	1 031	514	518	1 135	565	570	1 238	617	622
20-24	798	397	401	904	450	454	1 011	503	508	1 116	554	561
25-29	674	335	339	774	384	389	879	437	443	987	490	497
30-34	564	280	284	649	323	326	748	371	376	853	423	429
35-39	482	240	242	540	268	272	624	310	314	721	358	363
40-44	384	191	194	459	228	231	517	256	261	600	297	303
45-49	314	155	159	365	180	185	438	216	222	495	244	251
50-54	257	125	132	296	144	152	345	169	177	416	203	213
55-59	223	106	117	238	114	124	275	132	143	322	155	167
60-64	176	81	95	199	93	107	214	100	114	249	117	132
65-69	131	59	72	149	67	82	169	77	93	184	84	100
70-74	85	37	48	99	43	56	113	49	64	131	57	74
75-79	47	20	27	53	22	31	63	26	37	74	31	43
80-84	19	8	11	22	9	13	26	10	16	31	12	19
85-89	5	2	3	6	2	4	7	3	4	8	3	5
90-94	1	0	0	1	0	1	1	0	1	1	0	1
95-99	0	0	0	0	0	0	0	0	0	0	0	0
100 +	0	0	0	0	0	0	0	0	0	0	0	0

Age group	2045 Both sexes	Males	Females	2050 Both sexes	Males	Females
All ages	12 749	6 301	6 448	13 786	6 812	6 974
0-4	1 541	774	767	1 553	781	772
5-9	1 455	727	727	1 480	741	739
10-14	1 404	701	704	1 443	721	722
15-19	1 328	662	666	1 392	694	698
20-24	1 219	606	613	1 310	652	658
25-29	1 092	542	550	1 197	594	603
30-34	961	477	484	1 067	529	538
35-39	827	410	417	935	463	472
40-44	697	345	352	801	397	405
45-49	577	284	292	672	331	341
50-54	472	230	242	551	269	282
55-59	390	188	202	444	214	230
60-64	293	138	155	357	169	188
65-69	215	99	116	256	118	138
70-74	144	64	80	171	76	95
75-79	87	36	50	97	41	56
80-84	37	15	23	45	18	27
85-89	10	4	7	13	5	8
90-94	2	0	1	2	1	1
95-99	0	0	0	0	0	0
100 +	0	0	0	0	0	0

United Nations Department of Economic and Social Affairs/Population Division
World Population Prospects: The 2004 Revision, Volume II: Sex and Age Distribution of the World Population

763

POPULATION BY AGE AND SEX (in thousands)

Age group	2005 Both sexes	2005 Males	2005 Females	2010 Both sexes	2010 Males	2010 Females	2015 Both sexes	2015 Males	2015 Females	2020 Both sexes	2020 Males	2020 Females
All ages	5 525	2 725	2 801	6 137	3 029	3 108	6 967	3 441	3 525	7 914	3 912	4 002
0-4	958	479	479	1 062	531	531	1 230	615	614	1 376	688	688
5-9	758	378	380	851	424	427	963	480	483	1 124	560	564
10-14	650	324	326	730	364	366	832	415	417	944	470	473
15-19	576	287	289	628	313	315	716	357	359	818	408	410
20-24	473	236	238	551	274	277	610	303	307	698	347	350
25-29	395	196	199	448	222	225	529	263	266	588	292	296
30-34	331	164	167	370	184	186	426	212	214	505	251	254
35-39	296	146	150	308	153	155	351	174	176	405	201	203
40-44	250	122	128	275	135	140	291	144	147	332	165	167
45-49	211	102	109	231	112	119	258	126	132	274	135	139
50-54	175	84	92	193	92	101	216	103	112	242	116	125
55-59	148	70	78	157	74	84	177	83	94	198	93	105
60-64	119	55	64	128	59	69	139	64	75	156	72	84
65-69	87	39	47	96	44	52	105	48	58	115	52	63
70-74	56	25	31	61	27	34	70	31	39	77	34	43
75-79	29	12	16	32	14	18	36	15	21	42	18	24
80-84	11	4	6	12	5	7	14	6	8	16	7	10
85-89	2	1	1	3	1	2	3	1	2	4	2	2
90-94	0	0	0	0	0	0	0	0	0	1	0	0
95-99	0	0	0	0	0	0	0	0	0	0	0	0
100 +	0	0	0	0	0	0	0	0	0	0	0	0

Age group	2025 Both sexes	2025 Males	2025 Females	2030 Both sexes	2030 Males	2030 Females	2035 Both sexes	2035 Males	2035 Females	2040 Both sexes	2040 Males	2040 Females
All ages	8 957	4 429	4 528	10 093	4 992	5 101	11 317	5 598	5 719	12 620	6 243	6 377
0-4	1 493	747	746	1 606	804	802	1 712	858	854	1 810	908	902
5-9	1 270	633	637	1 390	693	697	1 508	752	756	1 620	809	811
10-14	1 105	550	554	1 250	623	628	1 372	684	688	1 491	743	747
15-19	928	463	466	1 089	542	547	1 234	615	620	1 356	675	681
20-24	798	397	401	908	452	456	1 067	531	537	1 213	603	610
25-29	674	335	339	774	384	389	883	439	445	1 042	517	525
30-34	564	280	284	649	323	326	748	371	376	857	425	431
35-39	482	240	242	540	268	272	624	310	314	721	358	363
40-44	384	191	194	459	228	231	517	256	261	600	297	303
45-49	314	155	159	365	180	185	438	216	222	495	244	251
50-54	257	125	132	296	144	152	345	169	177	416	203	213
55-59	223	106	117	238	114	124	275	132	143	322	155	167
60-64	176	81	95	199	93	107	214	100	114	249	117	132
65-69	131	59	72	149	67	82	169	77	93	184	84	100
70-74	85	37	48	99	43	56	113	49	64	131	57	74
75-79	47	20	27	53	22	31	63	26	37	74	31	43
80-84	19	8	11	22	9	13	26	10	16	31	12	19
85-89	5	2	3	6	2	4	7	3	4	8	3	5
90-94	1	0	0	1	0	1	1	0	1	1	0	1
95-99	0	0	0	0	0	0	0	0	0	0	0	0
100 +	0	0	0	0	0	0	0	0	0	0	0	0

Age group	2045 Both sexes	2045 Males	2045 Females	2050 Both sexes	2050 Males	2050 Females
All ages	13 991	6 922	7 069	15 423	7 630	7 793
0-4	1 896	952	944	1 974	992	982
5-9	1 725	863	863	1 820	911	909
10-14	1 604	801	804	1 711	855	856
15-19	1 476	735	740	1 590	793	797
20-24	1 335	664	672	1 456	724	732
25-29	1 187	589	598	1 311	651	660
30-34	1 014	503	511	1 160	575	585
35-39	830	412	418	987	489	498
40-44	697	345	352	805	398	407
45-49	577	284	292	672	331	341
50-54	472	230	242	551	269	282
55-59	390	188	202	444	214	230
60-64	293	138	155	357	169	188
65-69	215	99	116	256	118	138
70-74	144	64	80	171	76	95
75-79	87	36	50	97	41	56
80-84	37	15	23	45	18	27
85-89	10	4	7	13	5	8
90-94	2	0	1	2	1	1
95-99	0	0	0	0	0	0
100 +	0	0	0	0	0	0

United Nations Department of Economic and Social Affairs/Population Division
World Population Prospects: The 2004 Revision, Volume II: Sex and Age Distribution of the World Population

764

POPULATION BY AGE AND SEX (in thousands)

Age group	2005 Both sexes	Males	Females	2010 Both sexes	Males	Females	2015 Both sexes	Males	Females	2020 Both sexes	Males	Females
All ages	5 525	2 725	2 801	6 091	3 006	3 085	6 784	3 350	3 434	7 524	3 717	3 807
0-4	958	479	479	1 016	508	508	1 089	545	544	1 155	578	577
5-9	758	378	380	851	424	427	921	459	462	996	496	500
10-14	650	324	326	730	364	366	832	415	417	903	450	453
15-19	576	287	289	628	313	315	716	357	359	818	408	410
20-24	473	236	238	551	274	277	610	303	307	698	347	350
25-29	395	196	199	448	222	225	529	263	266	588	292	296
30-34	331	164	167	370	184	186	426	212	214	505	251	254
35-39	296	146	150	308	153	155	351	174	176	405	201	203
40-44	250	122	128	275	135	140	291	144	147	332	165	167
45-49	211	102	109	231	112	119	258	126	132	274	135	139
50-54	175	84	92	193	92	101	216	103	112	242	116	125
55-59	148	70	78	157	74	84	177	83	94	198	93	105
60-64	119	55	64	128	59	69	139	64	75	156	72	84
65-69	87	39	47	96	44	52	105	48	58	115	52	63
70-74	56	25	31	61	27	34	70	31	39	77	34	43
75-79	29	12	16	32	14	18	36	15	21	42	18	24
80-84	11	4	6	12	5	7	14	6	8	16	7	10
85-89	2	1	1	3	1	2	3	1	2	4	2	2
90-94	0	0	0	0	0	0	0	0	0	1	0	0
95-99	0	0	0	0	0	0	0	0	0	0	0	0
100 +	0	0	0	0	0	0	0	0	0	0	0	0

Age group	2025 Both sexes	Males	Females	2030 Both sexes	Males	Females	2035 Both sexes	Males	Females	2040 Both sexes	Males	Females
All ages	8 323	4 113	4 211	9 152	4 522	4 630	9 970	4 925	5 044	10 748	5 308	5 439
0-4	1 230	616	614	1 274	638	636	1 276	640	637	1 248	626	622
5-9	1 066	531	535	1 145	571	574	1 196	597	599	1 208	603	605
10-14	978	488	491	1 050	523	527	1 130	563	567	1 182	590	593
15-19	888	443	446	964	480	484	1 036	516	520	1 117	556	561
20-24	798	397	401	869	432	437	945	470	475	1 018	506	512
25-29	674	335	339	774	384	389	845	420	426	923	458	465
30-34	564	280	284	649	323	326	748	371	376	820	407	413
35-39	482	240	242	540	268	272	624	310	314	721	358	363
40-44	384	191	194	459	228	231	517	256	261	600	297	303
45-49	314	155	159	365	180	185	438	216	222	495	244	251
50-54	257	125	132	296	144	152	345	169	177	416	203	213
55-59	223	106	117	238	114	124	275	132	143	322	155	167
60-64	176	81	95	199	93	107	214	100	114	249	117	132
65-69	131	59	72	149	67	82	169	77	93	184	84	100
70-74	85	37	48	99	43	56	113	49	64	131	57	74
75-79	47	20	27	53	22	31	63	26	37	74	31	43
80-84	19	8	11	22	9	13	26	10	16	31	12	19
85-89	5	2	3	6	2	4	7	3	4	8	3	5
90-94	1	0	0	1	0	1	1	0	1	1	0	1
95-99	0	0	0	0	0	0	0	0	0	0	0	0
100 +	0	0	0	0	0	0	0	0	0	0	0	0

Age group	2045 Both sexes	Males	Females	2050 Both sexes	Males	Females
All ages	11 479	5 667	5 812	12 162	6 000	6 161
0-4	1 210	608	603	1 172	589	583
5-9	1 190	595	595	1 162	582	580
10-14	1 196	597	599	1 180	589	590
15-19	1 171	583	587	1 186	591	594
20-24	1 100	547	553	1 155	575	580
25-29	997	495	502	1 080	536	544
30-34	898	446	453	974	483	491
35-39	794	394	400	874	433	441
40-44	697	345	352	770	381	389
45-49	577	284	292	672	331	341
50-54	472	230	242	551	269	282
55-59	390	188	202	444	214	230
60-64	293	138	155	357	169	188
65-69	215	99	116	256	118	138
70-74	144	64	80	171	76	95
75-79	87	36	50	97	41	56
80-84	37	15	23	45	18	27
85-89	10	4	7	13	5	8
90-94	2	0	1	2	1	1
95-99	0	0	0	0	0	0
100 +	0	0	0	0	0	0

POPULATION BY AGE AND SEX (in thousands)

Age group	1950 Both sexes	Males	Females	1955 Both sexes	Males	Females	1960 Both sexes	Males	Females	1965 Both sexes	Males	Females
All ages	1 022	529	493	1 306	687	619	1 634	861	773	1 880	970	911
0-4	165	85	80	236	122	114	302	156	146	283	146	138
5-9	132	67	65	168	86	81	234	121	114	297	153	144
10-14	117	58	60	138	70	68	170	88	83	241	123	118
15-19	98	49	49	127	65	62	145	75	71	191	98	93
20-24	85	44	41	111	59	52	139	72	67	139	69	70
25-29	81	44	37	97	53	44	123	66	57	138	69	69
30-34	81	46	36	90	50	39	105	58	47	117	62	55
35-39	72	41	31	86	49	37	93	52	41	102	55	47
40-44	60	34	26	75	43	32	87	49	38	84	45	38
45-49	46	25	20	61	34	27	75	43	32	77	42	34
50-54	31	15	16	45	25	20	59	33	26	70	38	32
55-59	17	7	10	30	14	16	42	23	19	53	28	26
60-64	14	6	8	16	7	9	27	13	15	38	19	19
65-69	10	4	6	12	5	7	14	6	8	23	11	13
70-74	6	2	4	7	3	4	9	4	5	13	6	8
75-79	4	2	3	5	2	3	6	2	4	8	3	5
80 +	4	2	3	5	2	3	5	2	3	6	2	5

Age group	1970 Both sexes	Males	Females	1975 Both sexes	Males	Females	1980 Both sexes	Males	Females	1985 Both sexes	Males	Females
All ages	2 075	1 062	1 013	2 263	1 156	1 106	2 415	1 232	1 182	2 709	1 380	1 329
0-4	235	121	114	225	116	109	194	101	93	216	111	105
5-9	281	144	137	235	120	114	224	116	108	206	107	99
10-14	289	149	140	284	146	138	236	121	115	237	122	114
15-19	247	126	120	292	150	142	287	148	139	250	128	122
20-24	204	103	101	250	128	122	296	153	143	303	156	147
25-29	133	67	66	207	105	102	254	129	124	312	161	151
30-34	136	69	68	134	68	66	211	107	104	267	136	131
35-39	113	58	55	134	68	66	136	69	67	222	113	109
40-44	101	54	47	110	57	54	132	67	65	144	73	71
45-49	82	44	38	98	52	46	107	55	53	137	69	68
50-54	71	38	34	77	41	36	93	48	45	111	56	55
55-59	65	34	31	67	35	32	71	37	34	94	48	46
60-64	49	25	24	59	30	29	60	30	30	70	36	35
65-69	34	17	17	44	22	22	49	24	26	56	27	29
70-74	19	8	11	26	12	14	35	16	19	43	20	23
75-79	10	4	6	14	6	8	18	7	11	27	12	16
80 +	7	2	5	9	3	6	12	4	8	17	6	11

Age group	1990 Both sexes	Males	Females	1995 Both sexes	Males	Females	2000 Both sexes	Males	Females	2005 Both sexes	Males	Females
All ages	3 016	1 518	1 499	3 478	1 752	1 727	4 017	2 023	1 994	4 326	2 177	2 148
0-4	229	118	110	299	155	144	275	142	133	216	112	104
5-9	212	110	102	247	128	119	327	169	158	288	149	139
10-14	207	107	100	229	119	110	273	142	132	341	176	165
15-19	253	129	124	224	116	108	252	131	121	287	149	138
20-24	310	153	157	273	139	134	248	129	120	265	137	127
25-29	345	173	172	333	164	169	300	153	147	261	135	126
30-34	338	170	168	370	185	185	366	181	186	315	160	155
35-39	282	143	139	362	182	180	406	203	203	383	189	194
40-44	223	113	110	303	153	150	396	199	197	423	211	212
45-49	138	70	68	238	120	118	331	167	164	411	206	205
50-54	123	62	61	148	75	73	258	130	128	343	172	170
55-59	103	51	52	129	65	65	161	81	80	265	133	132
60-64	85	42	43	106	52	54	136	67	69	163	81	82
65-69	61	30	31	84	41	44	108	52	56	133	65	69
70-74	46	21	25	57	27	30	81	38	43	101	47	54
75-79	33	14	19	39	17	22	50	23	28	69	31	38
80 +	28	10	17	36	14	22	48	19	29	63	26	38

United Nations Department of Economic and Social Affairs/Population Division
World Population Prospects: The 2004 Revision, Volume II: Sex and Age Distribution of the World Population

766

POPULATION BY AGE AND SEX (in thousands)

Age group	2005 Both sexes	Males	Females	2010 Both sexes	Males	Females	2015 Both sexes	Males	Females	2020 Both sexes	Males	Females
All ages	4 326	2 177	2 148	4 590	2 309	2 282	4 815	2 419	2 396	4 986	2 502	2 484
0-4	216	112	104	192	99	92	200	104	97	223	116	108
5-9	288	149	139	226	117	109	199	103	96	205	106	99
10-14	341	176	165	301	156	145	235	122	113	204	106	99
15-19	287	149	138	356	184	172	312	161	150	241	125	116
20-24	265	137	127	300	155	145	367	190	178	319	165	154
25-29	261	135	126	276	143	133	311	161	150	376	194	182
30-34	315	160	155	273	141	132	286	148	138	319	165	154
35-39	383	189	194	328	167	161	283	146	137	293	152	142
40-44	423	211	212	398	196	202	339	172	167	289	149	140
45-49	411	206	205	439	219	220	410	202	208	346	175	171
50-54	343	172	170	425	212	212	450	224	226	416	204	212
55-59	265	133	132	351	176	176	432	215	217	453	224	229
60-64	163	81	82	266	132	134	352	174	178	429	212	217
65-69	133	65	69	160	78	82	261	127	133	342	167	175
70-74	101	47	54	125	59	66	151	72	79	243	116	127
75-79	69	31	38	87	39	48	109	50	59	132	61	71
80-84	38	16	22	53	23	31	68	29	39	85	37	48
85-89	18	7	11	24	10	14	35	14	21	45	18	27
90-94	6	2	4	9	3	6	12	5	8	18	7	11
95-99	1	0	1	2	1	1	3	1	2	4	2	3
100 +	0	0	0	0	0	0	0	0	0	1	0	0

Age group	2025 Both sexes	Males	Females	2030 Both sexes	Males	Females	2035 Both sexes	Males	Females	2040 Both sexes	Males	Females
All ages	5 144	2 578	2 566	5 265	2 635	2 630	5 321	2 659	2 662	5 313	2 651	2 662
0-4	246	127	119	248	129	120	228	118	110	209	108	101
5-9	229	118	110	252	130	121	254	131	122	233	121	113
10-14	211	109	102	234	121	113	258	133	124	260	134	125
15-19	209	108	101	216	112	104	240	124	116	263	136	127
20-24	247	128	119	215	111	104	221	114	106	245	127	118
25-29	326	169	158	253	131	122	220	114	106	226	117	109
30-34	384	198	186	334	172	161	259	134	125	225	116	109
35-39	326	168	158	391	202	189	341	170	165	265	137	128
40-44	300	155	146	333	172	161	399	206	193	348	179	168
45-49	295	152	143	305	158	148	340	175	165	406	209	197
50-54	351	178	174	300	154	146	310	160	150	345	178	167
55-59	420	205	214	355	179	176	303	155	148	313	161	152
60-64	451	222	229	419	203	215	354	177	177	303	155	149
65-69	418	204	214	440	214	226	410	197	213	348	172	175
70-74	321	154	167	394	189	205	417	199	218	390	185	205
75-79	214	100	115	286	133	152	353	165	188	377	176	201
80-84	106	47	59	173	78	96	234	105	129	293	132	161
85-89	58	24	34	74	31	43	123	52	71	170	72	98
90-94	24	9	15	32	12	20	42	17	26	73	29	44
95-99	7	2	4	10	3	6	13	5	9	18	6	12
100 +	1	0	1	2	1	1	2	1	2	4	1	2

Age group	2045 Both sexes	Males	Females	2050 Both sexes	Males	Females
All ages	5 268	2 627	2 641	5 213	2 601	2 612
0-4	209	108	101	225	116	108
5-9	214	111	103	214	111	103
10-14	239	124	115	219	113	106
15-19	266	138	128	245	127	118
20-24	269	139	130	272	141	131
25-29	251	130	121	276	143	133
30-34	231	119	112	256	133	124
35-39	230	119	111	236	122	114
40-44	271	140	131	235	121	114
45-49	354	183	172	276	143	134
50-54	412	212	200	360	185	175
55-59	349	179	170	416	213	203
60-64	314	160	153	350	179	171
65-69	299	151	148	310	157	153
70-74	333	163	170	287	143	144
75-79	355	164	191	305	146	159
80-84	316	142	174	302	135	167
85-89	217	92	124	238	102	137
90-94	103	41	62	134	53	81
95-99	32	11	21	47	17	30
100 +	5	2	4	9	3	6

United Nations Department of Economic and Social Affairs/Population Division
World Population Prospects: The 2004 Revision, Volume II: Sex and Age Distribution of the World Population

767

POPULATION BY AGE AND SEX (in thousands)

Age group	2005 Both sexes	Males	Females	2010 Both sexes	Males	Females	2015 Both sexes	Males	Females	2020 Both sexes	Males	Females
All ages	4 326	2 177	2 148	4 625	2 326	2 298	4 907	2 467	2 440	5 156	2 590	2 566
0-4	216	112	104	226	117	109	258	133	124	302	156	146
5-9	288	149	139	226	117	109	233	121	112	263	136	127
10-14	341	176	165	301	156	145	235	122	113	238	123	115
15-19	287	149	138	356	184	172	312	161	150	241	125	116
20-24	265	137	127	300	155	145	367	190	178	319	165	154
25-29	261	135	126	276	143	133	311	161	150	376	194	182
30-34	315	160	155	273	141	132	286	148	138	319	165	154
35-39	383	189	194	328	167	161	283	146	137	293	152	142
40-44	423	211	212	398	196	202	339	172	167	289	149	140
45-49	411	206	205	439	219	220	410	202	208	346	175	171
50-54	343	172	170	425	212	212	450	224	226	416	204	212
55-59	265	133	132	351	176	176	432	215	217	453	224	229
60-64	163	81	82	266	132	134	352	174	178	429	212	217
65-69	133	65	69	160	78	82	261	127	133	342	167	175
70-74	101	47	54	125	59	66	151	72	79	243	116	127
75-79	69	31	38	87	39	48	109	50	59	132	61	71
80-84	38	16	22	53	23	31	68	29	39	85	37	48
85-89	18	7	11	24	10	14	35	14	21	45	18	27
90-94	6	2	4	9	3	6	12	5	8	18	7	11
95-99	1	0	1	2	1	1	3	1	2	4	2	3
100 +	0	0	0	0	0	0	0	0	0	1	0	0

Age group	2025 Both sexes	Males	Females	2030 Both sexes	Males	Females	2035 Both sexes	Males	Females	2040 Both sexes	Males	Females
All ages	5 395	2 708	2 687	5 589	2 802	2 786	5 716	2 863	2 853	5 796	2 901	2 895
0-4	327	169	158	321	166	155	299	155	144	297	154	143
5-9	308	159	148	332	172	160	327	169	158	304	158	147
10-14	268	139	129	313	162	151	338	175	163	332	172	160
15-19	244	126	118	273	141	132	318	165	154	344	178	166
20-24	247	128	119	249	129	120	278	144	134	324	168	156
25-29	326	169	158	253	131	122	254	131	123	283	146	137
30-34	384	198	186	334	172	161	259	134	125	259	134	125
35-39	326	168	158	391	202	189	341	176	165	265	137	128
40-44	300	155	145	333	172	161	399	206	193	348	179	168
45-49	295	152	143	305	158	148	340	175	165	406	209	197
50-54	351	178	174	300	154	146	310	160	150	345	178	167
55-59	420	205	214	355	179	176	303	155	148	313	161	152
60-64	451	222	229	419	203	215	354	177	177	303	155	149
65-69	418	204	214	440	214	226	410	197	213	348	172	175
70-74	321	154	167	394	189	205	417	199	218	390	185	205
75-79	214	100	115	286	133	152	353	165	188	377	176	201
80-84	106	47	59	173	78	96	234	105	129	293	132	161
85-89	58	24	34	74	31	43	123	52	71	170	72	98
90-94	24	9	15	32	12	20	42	17	26	73	29	44
95-99	7	2	4	10	3	6	13	5	9	18	6	12
100 +	1	0	1	2	1	1	2	1	2	4	1	2

Age group	2045 Both sexes	Males	Females	2050 Both sexes	Males	Females
All ages	5 867	2 937	2 930	5 953	2 984	2 969
0-4	326	169	157	366	189	177
5-9	302	156	146	331	171	160
10-14	310	160	150	307	159	148
15-19	338	175	163	316	163	152
20-24	350	181	169	344	178	166
25-29	329	170	159	356	184	172
30-34	288	149	139	335	173	162
35-39	264	136	128	293	152	142
40-44	271	140	131	269	139	130
45-49	354	183	172	276	143	134
50-54	412	212	200	360	185	175
55-59	349	179	170	416	213	203
60-64	314	160	153	350	179	171
65-69	299	151	148	310	157	153
70-74	333	163	170	287	143	144
75-79	355	164	191	305	146	159
80-84	316	142	174	302	135	167
85-89	217	92	124	238	102	137
90-94	103	41	62	134	53	81
95-99	32	11	21	47	17	30
100 +	5	2	4	9	3	6

United Nations Department of Economic and Social Affairs/Population Division
World Population Prospects: The 2004 Revision, Volume II: Sex and Age Distribution of the World Population

768

POPULATION BY AGE AND SEX (in thousands)

Age group	2005 Both sexes	2005 Males	2005 Females	2010 Both sexes	2010 Males	2010 Females	2015 Both sexes	2015 Males	2015 Females	2020 Both sexes	2020 Males	2020 Females
All ages	4 326	2 177	2 148	4 556	2 291	2 265	4 724	2 372	2 352	4 816	2 414	2 402
0-4	216	112	104	157	81	76	143	74	69	146	75	70
5-9	288	149	139	226	117	109	164	85	79	148	77	72
10-14	341	176	165	301	156	145	235	122	113	170	88	82
15-19	287	149	138	356	184	172	312	161	150	241	125	116
20-24	265	137	127	300	155	145	367	190	178	319	165	154
25-29	261	135	126	276	143	133	311	161	150	376	194	182
30-34	315	160	155	273	141	132	286	148	138	319	165	154
35-39	383	189	194	328	167	161	283	146	137	293	152	142
40-44	423	211	212	398	196	202	339	172	167	289	149	140
45-49	411	206	205	439	219	220	410	202	208	346	175	171
50-54	343	172	170	425	212	212	450	224	226	416	204	212
55-59	265	133	132	351	176	176	432	215	217	453	224	229
60-64	163	81	82	266	132	134	352	174	178	429	212	217
65-69	133	65	69	160	78	82	261	127	133	342	167	175
70-74	101	47	54	125	59	66	151	72	79	243	116	127
75-79	69	31	38	87	39	48	109	50	59	132	61	71
80-84	38	16	22	53	23	31	68	29	39	85	37	48
85-89	18	7	11	24	10	14	35	14	21	45	18	27
90-94	6	2	4	9	3	6	12	5	8	18	7	11
95-99	1	0	1	2	1	1	3	1	2	4	2	3
100 +	0	0	0	0	0	0	0	0	0	1	0	0

Age group	2025 Both sexes	2025 Males	2025 Females	2030 Both sexes	2030 Males	2030 Females	2035 Both sexes	2035 Males	2035 Females	2040 Both sexes	2040 Males	2040 Females
All ages	4 894	2 449	2 445	4 940	2 467	2 473	4 929	2 456	2 473	4 852	2 412	2 439
0-4	165	85	80	173	90	84	161	83	78	139	72	67
5-9	151	78	73	171	88	82	179	93	86	166	86	80
10-14	154	79	74	157	81	76	177	91	85	185	96	89
15-19	175	91	84	159	82	77	162	84	78	182	94	88
20-24	247	128	119	180	93	87	164	85	79	168	87	81
25-29	326	169	158	253	131	122	185	96	89	169	87	82
30-34	384	198	186	334	172	161	259	134	125	190	98	92
35-39	326	168	158	391	202	189	341	176	165	265	137	128
40-44	300	155	145	333	172	161	399	206	193	348	179	168
45-49	295	152	143	305	158	148	340	175	165	406	209	197
50-54	351	178	174	300	154	146	310	160	150	345	178	167
55-59	420	205	214	355	179	176	303	155	148	313	161	152
60-64	451	222	229	419	203	215	354	177	177	303	155	149
65-69	418	204	214	440	214	226	410	197	213	348	172	175
70-74	321	154	167	394	189	205	417	199	218	390	185	205
75-79	214	100	115	280	100	152	353	165	188	377	176	201
80-84	106	47	59	173	78	96	234	105	129	293	132	161
85-89	58	24	34	74	31	43	123	52	71	170	72	98
90-94	24	9	15	32	12	20	42	17	26	73	29	44
95-99	7	2	4	10	3	6	13	5	9	18	6	12
100 +	1	0	1	2	1	1	2	1	2	4	1	2

Age group	2045 Both sexes	2045 Males	2045 Females	2050 Both sexes	2050 Males	2050 Females
All ages	4 722	2 344	2 377	4 564	2 266	2 299
0-4	124	64	60	122	63	59
5-9	144	75	70	129	67	62
10-14	172	89	83	149	77	72
15-19	191	99	92	178	92	86
20-24	189	98	91	197	102	95
25-29	173	90	84	195	101	94
30-34	174	90	84	179	93	87
35-39	196	101	95	180	93	87
40-44	271	140	131	201	104	97
45-49	354	183	172	276	143	134
50-54	412	212	200	360	185	175
55-59	349	179	170	416	213	203
60-64	314	160	153	350	179	171
65-69	299	151	148	310	157	153
70-74	333	163	170	287	143	144
75-79	355	164	191	305	146	159
80-84	316	142	174	302	135	167
85-89	217	92	124	238	102	137
90-94	103	41	62	134	53	81
95-99	32	11	21	47	17	30
100 +	5	2	4	9	3	6

POPULATION BY AGE AND SEX (in thousands)

Age group	1950 Both sexes	Males	Females	1955 Both sexes	Males	Females	1960 Both sexes	Males	Females	1965 Both sexes	Males	Females
All ages	3 463	1 681	1 782	3 798	1 849	1 950	4 145	2 023	2 122	4 362	2 135	2 226
0-4	381	194	187	486	251	235	476	245	231	428	220	207
5-9	321	163	158	381	194	187	489	252	236	470	242	228
10-14	301	152	149	322	163	159	384	196	189	483	250	233
15-19	305	152	153	294	152	142	320	164	156	376	193	183
20-24	285	133	152	305	151	154	296	153	143	315	162	154
25-29	302	145	156	285	133	153	306	152	155	291	150	141
30-34	168	82	86	300	144	156	286	133	153	301	149	152
35-39	261	128	132	167	81	86	300	143	156	280	130	151
40-44	250	124	127	256	125	131	166	80	86	292	139	153
45-49	225	110	115	242	118	125	251	121	130	160	76	83
50-54	187	89	98	214	102	112	234	111	122	239	113	125
55-59	135	61	74	173	80	94	202	94	108	218	101	117
60-64	113	49	64	122	53	69	158	70	88	182	82	101
65-69	90	39	51	97	40	57	106	44	63	137	58	80
70-74	67	29	38	72	29	43	79	30	49	86	33	53
75-79	44	19	24	48	19	29	53	20	33	58	21	37
80 +	30	13	17	35	14	20	41	16	25	46	17	30

Age group	1970 Both sexes	Males	Females	1975 Both sexes	Males	Females	1980 Both sexes	Males	Females	1985 Both sexes	Males	Females
All ages	4 528	2 235	2 294	4 735	2 336	2 400	4 976	2 446	2 531	5 140	2 525	2 616
0-4	380	195	186	450	230	221	481	246	236	456	232	223
5-9	410	210	200	380	194	185	440	224	215	479	244	235
10-14	440	225	215	410	209	200	379	194	185	438	223	215
15-19	457	233	224	439	225	215	407	208	199	377	193	185
20-24	378	192	186	456	232	224	432	222	210	404	206	198
25-29	296	147	149	376	191	185	439	223	216	428	219	209
30-34	272	134	138	294	145	149	363	183	180	436	221	215
35-39	282	139	143	270	132	138	288	142	147	359	180	179
40-44	290	143	148	278	137	142	264	128	136	284	138	146
45-49	297	144	153	284	138	146	272	132	140	258	124	134
50-54	169	82	87	286	137	149	274	131	143	262	125	137
55-59	223	108	115	159	76	83	271	127	144	257	120	137
60-64	215	103	112	202	95	107	147	69	79	246	111	135
65-69	171	78	93	182	84	98	185	84	101	125	56	70
70-74	126	54	72	131	58	73	156	67	89	142	62	81
75-79	70	28	42	82	35	47	101	40	61	103	43	60
80 +	50	18	32	59	20	39	76	27	50	87	28	59

Age group	1990 Both sexes	Males	Females	1995 Both sexes	Males	Females	2000 Both sexes	Males	Females	2005 Both sexes	Males	Females
All ages	5 256	2 570	2 686	5 364	2 612	2 751	5 400	2 625	2 775	5 401	2 620	2 781
0-4	409	209	200	358	183	175	289	148	141	255	131	125
5-9	445	227	218	406	207	199	358	183	175	289	148	141
10-14	474	242	232	446	228	218	407	208	199	359	183	175
15-19	429	219	210	475	242	233	446	228	218	406	207	199
20-24	371	189	182	429	218	211	475	242	233	445	227	218
25-29	394	201	193	369	187	182	428	217	211	474	241	233
30-34	420	214	206	393	199	194	367	186	182	426	216	210
35-39	426	215	210	417	211	206	390	197	193	366	184	181
40-44	344	171	173	420	210	210	413	207	205	387	194	193
45-49	275	132	143	337	165	172	412	204	208	406	202	204
50-54	246	116	130	267	126	141	327	158	169	401	196	205
55-59	247	114	133	234	107	127	254	117	138	313	148	165
60-64	236	105	130	229	101	127	218	96	122	238	105	132
65-69	217	92	124	209	88	122	204	86	119	196	82	114
70-74	104	43	61	180	71	109	176	68	108	173	67	106
75-79	114	45	69	79	30	49	137	49	88	136	47	88
80 +	107	36	71	115	38	77	99	33	66	133	42	90

United Nations Department of Economic and Social Affairs/Population Division
World Population Prospects: The 2004 Revision, Volume II: Sex and Age Distribution of the World Population

770

POPULATION BY AGE AND SEX (in thousands)

Age group	2005			2010			2015			2020		
	Both sexes	Males	Females	Both sexes	Males	Females	Both sexes	Males	Females	Both sexes	Males	Females
All ages	5 401	2 620	2 781	5 400	2 616	2 784	5 385	2 606	2 778	5 350	2 587	2 763
0-4	255	131	125	252	129	123	247	126	121	238	122	116
5-9	289	148	141	256	131	125	253	129	123	247	127	121
10-14	359	183	175	289	148	141	256	131	125	253	129	124
15-19	406	207	199	359	183	175	289	148	142	256	131	125
20-24	445	227	218	406	207	199	359	183	175	289	148	142
25-29	474	241	233	445	227	218	406	207	199	359	183	175
30-34	426	216	210	473	240	233	444	226	218	406	206	199
35-39	366	184	181	425	215	210	471	239	233	443	225	218
40-44	387	194	193	363	182	181	422	213	209	469	237	232
45-49	406	202	204	381	190	191	359	179	180	418	210	208
50-54	401	196	205	396	195	201	374	184	189	352	175	178
55-59	313	148	165	385	185	201	382	185	198	362	176	186
60-64	238	105	132	294	134	160	364	169	195	362	171	192
65-69	196	82	114	216	91	125	268	117	151	334	149	185
70-74	173	67	106	168	65	103	187	73	113	234	96	138
75-79	136	47	88	136	48	88	134	47	87	151	54	97
80-84	91	29	62	93	29	64	95	29	66	95	29	66
85-89	27	8	18	49	14	36	52	14	38	55	14	40
90-94	12	4	8	10	3	7	19	5	15	21	5	17
95-99	2	1	1	3	1	2	2	1	2	5	1	4
100 +	0	0	0	0	0	0	0	0	0	0	0	0

Age group	2025			2030			2035			2040		
	Both sexes	Males	Females	Both sexes	Males	Females	Both sexes	Males	Females	Both sexes	Males	Females
All ages	5 286	2 552	2 734	5 189	2 500	2 689	5 066	2 437	2 630	4 925	2 365	2 559
0-4	221	113	108	205	105	100	196	100	95	194	99	95
5-9	238	122	116	221	113	108	205	105	100	196	100	96
10-14	248	127	121	238	122	116	222	113	108	205	105	100
15-19	253	129	124	248	127	121	239	122	117	222	114	108
20-24	256	131	125	253	129	124	248	127	121	239	122	117
25-29	289	148	142	256	131	125	253	129	124	248	127	121
30-34	358	183	175	289	148	142	256	131	126	253	129	124
35-39	405	206	199	358	183	175	289	147	142	256	131	126
40-44	442	224	218	404	205	199	357	182	175	289	147	142
45-49	465	234	231	438	222	217	401	203	198	355	180	175
50-54	411	205	207	459	230	229	433	218	215	396	200	197
55-59	342	167	175	401	197	204	447	221	226	423	210	212
60-64	344	163	181	327	156	171	384	185	199	430	209	221
65-69	334	152	183	319	146	173	305	141	164	359	168	191
70-74	293	123	170	295	126	169	284	123	161	273	120	153
75-79	190	71	119	240	92	148	245	97	148	238	96	142
80-84	108	34	75	138	45	93	178	60	117	184	65	119
85-89	56	14	42	66	17	49	86	23	62	112	32	80
90-94	24	5	19	25	5	20	31	6	24	42	9	32
95-99	6	1	5	7	1	6	8	1	6	10	2	8
100 +	1	0	0	1	0	1	1	0	1	1	0	1

Age group	2045			2050		
	Both sexes	Males	Females	Both sexes	Males	Females
All ages	4 772	2 291	2 482	4 612	2 213	2 400
0-4	195	100	95	194	99	95
5-9	194	99	95	195	100	95
10-14	196	100	96	195	100	95
15-19	206	105	100	196	101	96
20-24	222	114	108	206	105	101
25-29	239	122	117	222	114	109
30-34	248	127	122	239	122	117
35-39	253	129	124	248	127	122
40-44	256	130	125	253	129	124
45-49	287	146	141	255	129	125
50-54	351	177	174	284	144	140
55-59	388	193	195	344	172	172
60-64	407	199	208	375	184	191
65-69	404	191	213	384	183	201
70-74	324	145	179	366	166	200
75-79	230	95	136	275	116	160
80-84	181	66	115	178	66	111
85-89	119	36	83	119	37	82
90-94	56	13	43	61	15	46
95-99	14	2	12	20	3	16
100 +	2	0	2	3	0	2

United Nations Department of Economic and Social Affairs/Population Division
World Population Prospects: The 2004 Revision, Volume II: Sex and Age Distribution of the World Population

771

POPULATION BY AGE AND SEX (in thousands)

Age group	2005 Both sexes	Males	Females	2010 Both sexes	Males	Females	2015 Both sexes	Males	Females	2020 Both sexes	Males	Females
All ages	5 401	2 620	2 781	5 453	2 643	2 810	5 517	2 674	2 843	5 571	2 700	2 871
0-4	255	131	125	305	156	149	327	167	160	326	167	159
5-9	289	148	141	256	131	125	306	156	149	327	167	160
10-14	359	183	175	289	148	141	256	131	125	306	156	149
15-19	406	207	199	359	183	175	289	148	142	256	131	125
20-24	445	227	218	406	207	199	359	183	175	289	148	142
25-29	474	241	233	445	227	218	406	207	199	359	183	175
30-34	426	216	210	473	240	233	444	226	218	406	206	199
35-39	366	184	181	425	215	210	471	239	233	443	225	218
40-44	387	194	193	363	182	181	422	213	209	469	237	232
45-49	406	202	204	381	190	191	359	179	180	418	210	208
50-54	401	196	205	396	195	201	374	184	189	352	175	178
55-59	313	148	165	385	185	201	382	185	198	362	176	186
60-64	238	105	132	294	134	160	364	169	195	362	171	192
65-69	196	82	114	216	91	125	268	117	151	334	149	185
70-74	173	67	106	168	65	103	187	73	113	234	96	138
75-79	136	47	88	136	48	88	134	47	87	151	54	97
80-84	91	29	62	93	29	64	95	29	66	95	29	66
85-89	27	8	18	49	14	36	52	14	38	55	14	40
90-94	12	4	8	10	3	7	19	5	15	21	5	17
95-99	2	1	1	3	1	2	2	1	2	5	1	4
100 +	0	0	0	0	0	0	0	0	0	0	0	0

Age group	2025 Both sexes	Males	Females	2030 Both sexes	Males	Females	2035 Both sexes	Males	Females	2040 Both sexes	Males	Females
All ages	5 585	2 705	2 879	5 563	2 692	2 871	5 531	2 674	2 856	5 505	2 662	2 842
0-4	298	153	146	281	144	137	287	147	140	310	158	151
5-9	326	167	159	298	153	146	281	144	137	287	147	140
10-14	327	167	160	327	167	160	299	153	146	281	144	137
15-19	306	157	150	328	168	160	327	167	160	299	153	146
20-24	256	131	125	306	156	150	328	167	160	327	167	160
25-29	289	148	142	256	131	125	306	156	150	328	167	160
30-34	358	183	175	289	148	142	256	131	126	306	156	150
35-39	405	206	199	358	183	175	289	147	142	256	131	126
40-44	442	224	218	404	205	199	357	182	175	289	147	142
45-49	465	234	231	438	222	217	401	203	198	355	180	175
50-54	411	205	207	459	230	229	433	218	215	396	200	197
55-59	342	167	175	401	197	204	447	221	226	423	210	212
60-64	344	163	181	327	156	171	384	185	199	430	209	221
65-69	334	152	183	319	146	173	305	141	164	359	168	191
70-74	293	123	170	295	126	169	284	123	161	273	120	153
75-79	190	71	119	240	92	148	245	97	148	238	96	142
80-84	108	34	75	138	45	93	178	60	117	184	65	119
85-89	56	14	42	66	17	49	86	23	62	112	32	80
90-94	24	5	19	25	5	20	31	6	24	42	9	32
95-99	6	1	5	7	1	6	8	1	6	10	2	8
100 +	1	0	0	1	0	1	1	0	1	1	0	1

Age group	2045 Both sexes	Males	Females	2050 Both sexes	Males	Females
All ages	5 486	2 656	2 830	5 465	2 649	2 816
0-4	329	169	161	334	171	163
5-9	310	159	151	330	169	161
10-14	287	147	140	310	159	151
15-19	281	144	137	287	147	140
20-24	299	153	146	282	144	138
25-29	327	167	160	299	153	146
30-34	328	167	160	327	167	160
35-39	306	156	150	327	167	160
40-44	256	130	125	305	156	150
45-49	287	146	141	255	129	125
50-54	351	177	174	284	144	140
55-59	388	193	195	344	172	172
60-64	407	199	208	375	184	191
65-69	404	191	213	384	183	201
70-74	324	145	179	366	166	200
75-79	230	95	136	275	116	160
80-84	181	66	115	178	66	111
85-89	119	36	83	119	37	82
90-94	56	13	43	61	15	46
95-99	14	2	12	20	3	16
100 +	2	0	2	3	0	2

POPULATION BY AGE AND SEX (in thousands)

Age group	2005 Both sexes	Males	Females	2010 Both sexes	Males	Females	2015 Both sexes	Males	Females	2020 Both sexes	Males	Females
All ages	5 401	2 620	2 781	5 346	2 589	2 758	5 251	2 538	2 713	5 126	2 473	2 653
0-4	255	131	125	199	102	97	167	85	81	147	75	72
5-9	289	148	141	256	131	125	199	102	97	167	86	82
10-14	359	183	175	289	148	141	256	131	125	200	102	98
15-19	406	207	199	359	183	175	289	148	142	256	131	125
20-24	445	227	218	406	207	199	359	183	175	289	148	142
25-29	474	241	233	445	227	218	406	207	199	359	183	175
30-34	426	216	210	473	240	233	444	226	218	406	206	199
35-39	366	184	181	425	215	210	471	239	233	443	225	218
40-44	387	194	193	363	182	181	422	213	209	469	237	232
45-49	406	202	204	381	190	191	359	179	180	418	210	208
50-54	401	196	205	396	195	201	374	184	189	352	175	178
55-59	313	148	165	385	185	201	382	185	198	362	176	186
60-64	238	105	132	294	134	160	364	169	195	362	171	192
65-69	196	82	114	216	91	125	268	117	151	334	149	185
70-74	173	67	106	168	65	103	187	73	113	234	96	138
75-79	136	47	88	136	48	88	134	47	87	151	54	97
80-84	91	29	62	93	29	64	95	29	66	95	29	66
85-89	27	8	18	49	14	36	52	14	38	55	14	40
90-94	12	4	8	10	3	7	19	5	15	21	5	17
95-99	2	1	1	3	1	2	2	1	2	5	1	4
100 +	0	0	0	0	0	0	0	0	0	0	0	0

Age group	2025 Both sexes	Males	Females	2030 Both sexes	Males	Females	2035 Both sexes	Males	Females	2040 Both sexes	Males	Females
All ages	4 983	2 397	2 586	4 814	2 309	2 506	4 617	2 207	2 410	4 392	2 093	2 299
0-4	142	73	69	133	68	65	121	62	59	110	56	54
5-9	147	75	72	142	73	69	133	68	65	122	62	59
10-14	168	86	82	148	76	72	142	73	70	133	68	65
15-19	200	102	98	168	86	82	148	76	72	143	73	70
20-24	256	131	125	200	102	98	168	86	82	149	76	73
25-29	289	148	142	256	131	125	200	102	98	168	86	82
30-34	358	183	175	289	148	142	256	131	126	201	102	98
35-39	405	206	199	358	183	175	289	147	142	256	131	126
40-44	442	224	218	404	205	199	357	182	175	289	147	142
45-49	465	234	231	438	222	217	401	203	198	355	180	175
50-54	411	205	207	459	230	229	433	218	215	396	200	197
55-59	342	167	176	401	197	204	447	221	226	423	210	212
60-64	344	163	181	327	156	171	384	185	199	430	209	221
65-69	334	152	183	319	146	173	305	141	164	359	168	191
70-74	293	123	170	295	126	169	284	123	161	273	120	153
75-79	190	71	119	240	92	148	245	97	148	238	96	142
80-84	108	34	75	138	48	90	178	60	117	184	65	119
85-89	56	14	42	66	17	49	86	23	62	112	32	80
90-94	24	5	19	25	5	20	31	6	24	42	9	32
95-99	6	1	5	7	1	6	8	1	6	10	2	8
100 +	1	0	0	1	0	1	1	0	1	1	0	1

Age group	2045 Both sexes	Males	Females	2050 Both sexes	Males	Females
All ages	4 145	1 970	2 175	3 884	1 840	2 043
0-4	99	51	48	92	47	45
5-9	110	56	54	99	51	49
10-14	122	62	60	111	57	54
15-19	134	68	65	122	63	60
20-24	143	73	70	134	69	65
25-29	149	76	73	143	73	70
30-34	169	86	82	149	76	73
35-39	201	102	98	169	86	83
40-44	256	130	125	200	102	98
45-49	287	146	141	255	129	125
50-54	351	177	174	284	144	140
55-59	388	193	195	344	172	172
60-64	407	199	208	375	184	191
65-69	404	191	213	384	183	201
70-74	324	145	179	366	166	200
75-79	230	95	136	275	116	160
80-84	181	66	115	178	66	111
85-89	119	36	83	119	37	82
90-94	56	13	43	61	15	46
95-99	14	2	12	20	3	16
100 +	2	0	2	3	0	2

POPULATION BY AGE AND SEX (in thousands)

Age group	1950 Both sexes	1950 Males	1950 Females	1955 Both sexes	1955 Males	1955 Females	1960 Both sexes	1960 Males	1960 Females	1965 Both sexes	1965 Males	1965 Females
All ages	1 473	704	769	1 533	732	800	1 580	755	825	1 630	781	850
0-4	149	75	74	153	78	75	138	70	68	139	72	68
5-9	127	65	62	146	74	72	150	76	74	137	70	67
10-14	129	66	63	124	63	61	144	73	71	148	76	73
15-19	136	69	67	127	65	62	122	62	60	142	72	70
20-24	134	66	68	132	67	65	124	63	61	120	61	59
25-29	114	49	65	131	64	67	129	65	64	122	62	60
30-34	72	32	40	111	48	63	128	62	65	127	64	63
35-39	99	46	53	69	30	39	108	46	62	125	61	64
40-44	109	52	57	95	44	51	67	29	37	105	45	61
45-49	101	48	53	103	49	54	91	42	49	64	28	36
50-54	86	40	47	94	44	50	97	45	52	86	39	47
55-59	63	28	35	79	36	44	87	40	47	91	41	49
60-64	52	23	29	56	24	32	71	31	40	79	35	44
65-69	41	19	22	44	19	26	49	20	29	62	26	36
70-74	28	13	15	32	14	19	36	14	22	39	15	24
75-79	20	9	11	19	8	11	23	9	14	26	9	17
80 +	15	6	9	16	6	9	16	6	10	18	7	12

Age group	1970 Both sexes	1970 Males	1970 Females	1975 Both sexes	1975 Males	1975 Females	1980 Both sexes	1980 Males	1980 Females	1985 Both sexes	1985 Males	1985 Females
All ages	1 670	808	862	1 742	843	899	1 832	885	947	1 884	912	973
0-4	134	69	66	141	72	68	146	76	70	133	68	65
5-9	136	70	67	135	69	66	142	73	69	147	76	71
10-14	132	68	65	137	70	67	137	70	67	142	73	69
15-19	148	76	72	133	68	65	141	71	69	138	70	67
20-24	142	74	68	149	76	72	147	73	74	144	72	72
25-29	116	60	56	143	74	68	157	81	76	150	74	75
30-34	121	63	58	116	60	56	138	71	67	158	81	76
35-39	124	63	61	121	62	59	110	56	54	137	70	67
40-44	121	58	63	123	62	61	119	59	59	109	55	54
45-49	102	43	59	119	57	62	119	58	61	117	58	59
50-54	62	27	35	99	41	58	115	54	62	116	55	60
55-59	82	36	46	59	25	34	96	39	57	110	50	60
60-64	84	37	46	76	33	44	57	23	34	90	35	55
65-69	68	29	39	75	32	43	70	29	41	51	20	31
70-74	50	19	31	57	22	34	63	25	38	59	23	36
75-79	27	9	17	37	13	24	42	15	27	48	18	30
80 +	20	7	13	23	7	15	33	10	23	37	12	26

Age group	1990 Both sexes	1990 Males	1990 Females	1995 Both sexes	1995 Males	1995 Females	2000 Both sexes	2000 Males	2000 Females	2005 Both sexes	2005 Males	2005 Females
All ages	1 926	935	992	1 964	957	1 007	1 967	959	1 008	1 967	960	1 007
0-4	119	61	58	98	50	48	89	46	43	86	44	42
5-9	135	69	66	121	62	59	98	50	48	89	46	44
10-14	148	77	72	137	70	67	121	62	59	98	50	48
15-19	144	74	70	150	78	73	137	70	67	122	62	59
20-24	141	72	69	146	75	71	150	78	73	138	70	68
25-29	149	75	74	143	73	70	146	75	71	152	78	73
30-34	152	76	77	152	77	75	144	73	70	147	75	71
35-39	157	81	76	155	78	77	152	77	75	144	74	71
40-44	135	69	66	159	82	77	155	78	77	152	77	75
45-49	107	54	53	136	69	66	157	81	76	154	77	77
50-54	113	55	58	105	52	53	133	67	66	154	79	75
55-59	110	52	59	110	53	57	102	50	52	128	64	64
60-64	103	45	57	105	48	57	104	48	55	96	46	50
65-69	81	30	51	94	40	55	96	42	54	95	43	52
70-74	43	16	28	71	25	46	82	32	50	84	34	50
75-79	45	16	29	34	11	23	57	18	39	66	24	42
80 +	44	14	30	47	15	33	45	12	33	61	15	45

POPULATION BY AGE AND SEX (in thousands)

Age group	2005 Both sexes	2005 Males	2005 Females	2010 Both sexes	2010 Males	2010 Females	2015 Both sexes	2015 Males	2015 Females	2020 Both sexes	2020 Males	2020 Females
All ages	1 967	960	1 007	1 959	957	1 001	1 942	950	992	1 917	939	978
0-4	86	44	42	84	43	41	81	42	39	77	40	38
5-9	89	46	44	86	44	42	84	43	41	81	42	40
10-14	98	50	48	90	46	44	87	44	42	84	43	41
15-19	122	62	59	99	51	48	90	46	44	87	45	42
20-24	138	70	68	123	63	60	100	52	49	92	47	44
25-29	152	78	73	140	71	68	125	64	60	102	53	49
30-34	147	75	71	153	79	74	141	72	69	126	65	61
35-39	144	74	71	147	76	71	153	80	74	142	73	69
40-44	152	77	75	144	74	70	147	76	71	153	80	74
45-49	154	77	77	151	76	75	143	73	70	146	75	71
50-54	154	79	75	151	75	76	149	74	74	141	72	70
55-59	128	64	64	150	76	74	147	73	75	145	72	73
60-64	96	46	50	122	60	62	143	71	72	141	68	73
65-69	95	43	52	89	41	48	113	54	60	133	64	69
70-74	84	34	50	84	36	48	79	35	44	101	46	56
75-79	66	24	42	68	26	43	69	27	42	66	27	39
80-84	40	11	29	47	15	32	50	16	33	51	18	33
85-89	13	3	10	24	5	18	28	7	21	30	8	22
90-94	6	1	5	6	1	5	11	1	9	13	2	11
95-99	1	0	1	2	0	1	2	0	2	3	0	3
100 +	0	0	0	0	0	0	0	0	0	0	0	0

Age group	2025 Both sexes	2025 Males	2025 Females	2030 Both sexes	2030 Males	2030 Females	2035 Both sexes	2035 Males	2035 Females	2040 Both sexes	2040 Males	2040 Females
All ages	1 883	923	960	1 842	903	939	1 794	879	916	1 742	852	890
0-4	72	37	35	69	35	33	68	35	33	68	35	33
5-9	77	40	38	72	37	35	69	35	34	68	35	33
10-14	81	42	40	78	40	38	73	37	35	69	35	34
15-19	85	44	41	82	42	40	78	40	38	73	38	36
20-24	89	46	43	86	45	42	83	43	40	80	41	38
25-29	93	48	45	90	47	44	88	46	42	85	44	41
30-34	103	54	50	95	49	45	92	48	44	90	47	43
35-39	127	66	61	104	54	50	96	50	46	93	48	44
40-44	142	73	69	127	66	61	105	55	50	96	50	46
45-49	153	79	73	141	73	69	127	66	61	105	54	50
50-54	145	74	71	151	78	73	140	72	68	126	65	61
55-59	138	70	69	142	72	70	148	76	72	137	70	67
60-64	130	60	71	130	63	67	137	69	68	144	73	71
65-69	132	62	70	131	63	69	126	61	65	130	64	66
70-74	120	56	65	120	54	66	120	55	65	115	54	61
75-79	85	36	49	102	44	57	102	44	59	103	45	58
80-84	49	18	31	64	24	40	78	31	47	80	31	49
85-89	32	9	23	32	9	22	42	13	29	52	17	35
90-94	15	3	12	16	3	13	16	3	13	22	5	17
95-99	4	0	4	5	1	5	6	1	5	6	1	5
100 +	1	0	1	1	0	1	1	0	1	1	0	1

Age group	2045 Both sexes	2045 Males	2045 Females	2050 Both sexes	2050 Males	2050 Females
All ages	1 687	826	861	1 630	799	832
0-4	69	35	34	69	35	33
5-9	69	35	33	69	35	34
10-14	68	35	33	69	35	33
15-19	70	36	34	69	35	33
20-24	75	39	36	71	37	34
25-29	81	42	39	77	40	37
30-34	87	45	42	83	43	40
35-39	91	47	43	88	46	42
40-44	93	49	44	91	48	43
45-49	96	50	46	93	49	44
50-54	104	54	50	95	50	46
55-59	123	63	60	102	53	49
60-64	133	67	66	120	61	59
65-69	136	68	68	127	63	64
70-74	119	57	63	126	61	65
75-79	100	44	55	104	47	57
80-84	81	32	49	79	32	47
85-89	54	18	36	56	19	37
90-94	28	7	21	30	8	22
95-99	8	1	7	11	2	9
100 +	1	0	1	2	0	2

POPULATION BY AGE AND SEX (in thousands)

Age group	2005 Both sexes	Males	Females	2010 Both sexes	Males	Females	2015 Both sexes	Males	Females	2020 Both sexes	Males	Females
All ages	1 967	960	1 007	1 976	966	1 010	1 984	972	1 012	1 987	975	1 012
0-4	86	44	42	101	52	49	106	55	52	105	54	51
5-9	89	46	44	86	44	42	101	52	49	107	55	52
10-14	98	50	48	90	46	44	87	44	42	101	52	49
15-19	122	62	59	99	51	48	90	46	44	87	45	42
20-24	138	70	68	123	63	60	100	52	49	92	47	44
25-29	152	78	73	140	71	68	125	64	60	102	53	49
30-34	147	75	71	153	79	74	141	72	69	126	65	61
35-39	144	74	71	147	76	71	153	80	74	142	73	69
40-44	152	77	75	144	74	70	147	76	71	153	80	74
45-49	154	77	77	151	76	75	143	73	70	146	75	71
50-54	154	79	75	151	75	76	149	74	74	141	72	70
55-59	128	64	64	150	76	74	147	73	75	145	72	73
60-64	96	46	50	122	60	62	143	71	72	141	68	73
65-69	95	43	52	89	41	48	113	54	60	133	64	69
70-74	84	34	50	84	36	48	79	35	44	101	46	56
75-79	66	24	42	68	26	43	69	27	42	66	27	39
80-84	40	11	29	47	15	32	50	16	33	51	18	33
85-89	13	3	10	24	5	18	28	7	21	30	8	22
90-94	6	1	5	6	1	5	11	1	9	13	2	11
95-99	1	0	1	2	0	1	2	0	2	3	0	3
100 +	0	0	0	0	0	0	0	0	0	0	0	0

Age group	2025 Both sexes	Males	Females	2030 Both sexes	Males	Females	2035 Both sexes	Males	Females	2040 Both sexes	Males	Females
All ages	1 978	972	1 006	1 960	964	997	1 940	954	987	1 923	945	978
0-4	97	50	47	92	47	45	95	49	46	104	53	50
5-9	105	54	51	97	50	47	93	48	45	96	49	47
10-14	107	55	52	106	54	51	97	50	47	93	48	45
15-19	102	52	50	107	55	52	106	55	52	98	50	47
20-24	89	46	43	103	53	50	109	56	53	108	55	52
25-29	93	48	45	90	47	44	105	54	51	111	57	53
30-34	103	54	50	95	49	45	92	48	44	107	55	51
35-39	127	66	61	104	54	50	96	50	46	93	48	44
40-44	142	73	69	127	66	61	105	55	50	96	50	46
45-49	153	79	73	141	73	69	127	66	61	105	54	50
50-54	145	74	71	151	78	73	140	72	68	126	65	61
55-59	138	70	69	142	72	70	148	76	72	137	70	67
60-64	139	68	71	133	66	67	137	69	68	144	73	71
65-69	132	62	70	131	63	69	126	61	65	130	64	66
70-74	120	56	65	120	54	66	120	55	65	115	54	61
75-79	85	36	49	102	44	57	102	44	59	103	45	58
80-84	49	18	31	64	24	40	78	31	47	80	31	49
85-89	32	9	23	32	9	22	42	13	29	52	17	35
90-94	15	3	12	16	3	13	16	3	13	22	5	17
95-99	4	0	4	5	1	5	6	1	5	6	1	5
100 +	1	0	1	1	0	1	1	0	1	1	0	1

Age group	2045 Both sexes	Males	Females	2050 Both sexes	Males	Females
All ages	1 911	940	970	1 900	937	963
0-4	112	57	54	115	59	56
5-9	104	53	51	112	57	54
10-14	96	49	47	104	53	51
15-19	93	48	45	96	50	47
20-24	99	51	48	95	49	46
25-29	109	57	53	101	52	49
30-34	112	58	54	111	58	53
35-39	108	56	52	113	59	54
40-44	93	49	44	108	56	52
45-49	96	50	46	93	49	44
50-54	104	54	50	95	50	46
55-59	123	63	60	102	53	49
60-64	133	67	66	120	61	59
65-69	136	68	68	127	63	64
70-74	119	57	63	126	61	65
75-79	100	44	55	104	47	57
80-84	81	32	49	79	32	47
85-89	54	18	36	56	19	37
90-94	28	7	21	30	8	22
95-99	8	1	7	11	2	9
100 +	1	0	1	2	0	2

United Nations Department of Economic and Social Affairs/Population Division
World Population Prospects: The 2004 Revision, Volume II: Sex and Age Distribution of the World Population

776

LOW VARIANT   SLOVENIA

POPULATION BY AGE AND SEX (in thousands)

Age group	2005 Both sexes	Males	Females	2010 Both sexes	Males	Females	2015 Both sexes	Males	Females	2020 Both sexes	Males	Females
All ages	1 967	960	1 007	1 942	949	993	1 899	928	971	1 845	902	943
0-4	86	44	42	67	34	32	55	28	27	48	25	24
5-9	89	46	44	86	44	42	67	34	33	56	29	27
10-14	98	50	48	90	46	44	87	44	42	67	34	33
15-19	122	62	59	99	51	48	90	46	44	87	45	42
20-24	138	70	68	123	63	60	100	52	49	92	47	44
25-29	152	78	73	140	71	68	125	64	60	102	53	49
30-34	147	75	71	153	79	74	141	72	69	126	65	61
35-39	144	74	71	147	76	71	153	80	74	142	73	69
40-44	152	77	75	144	74	70	147	76	71	153	80	74
45-49	154	77	77	151	76	75	143	73	70	146	75	71
50-54	154	79	75	151	75	76	149	74	74	141	72	70
55-59	128	64	64	150	76	74	147	73	75	145	72	73
60-64	96	46	50	122	60	62	143	71	72	141	68	73
65-69	95	43	52	89	41	48	113	54	60	133	64	69
70-74	84	34	50	84	36	48	79	35	44	101	46	56
75-79	66	24	42	68	26	43	69	27	42	66	27	39
80-84	40	11	29	47	15	32	50	16	33	51	18	33
85-89	13	3	10	24	5	18	28	7	21	30	8	22
90-94	6	1	5	6	1	5	11	1	9	13	2	11
95-99	1	0	1	2	0	1	2	0	2	3	0	3
100 +	0	0	0	0	0	0	0	0	0	0	0	0

Age group	2025 Both sexes	Males	Females	2030 Both sexes	Males	Females	2035 Both sexes	Males	Females	2040 Both sexes	Males	Females
All ages	1 786	873	913	1 722	841	881	1 650	805	846	1 572	765	807
0-4	47	24	23	45	23	22	44	23	21	42	21	20
5-9	49	25	24	47	24	23	46	23	22	44	23	22
10-14	56	29	27	49	25	24	47	24	23	46	24	22
15-19	68	35	33	56	29	27	50	25	24	48	25	23
20-24	89	46	43	69	36	33	58	30	28	51	26	25
25-29	93	48	45	90	47	44	71	37	34	60	31	29
30-34	103	54	50	95	49	45	92	48	44	72	38	35
35-39	127	66	61	104	54	50	96	50	46	93	48	44
40-44	142	73	69	127	66	61	106	55	50	96	50	46
45-49	153	79	73	141	73	69	127	66	61	105	54	50
50-54	145	74	71	151	78	73	140	72	68	126	65	61
55-59	138	70	69	142	72	70	148	76	72	137	70	67
60-64	139	68	71	133	66	67	137	69	68	144	73	71
65-69	132	62	70	131	63	69	126	61	65	130	64	66
70-74	120	56	65	120	54	66	120	55	65	115	54	61
75-79	85	36	49	102	44	57	102	44	59	103	45	58
80-84	49	18	31	64	24	40	78	31	47	80	31	49
85-89	32	9	23	32	9	22	42	13	29	52	17	35
90-94	15	3	12	16	3	13	16	3	13	22	5	17
95-99	4	0	4	5	1	5	6	1	5	6	1	5
100 +	1	0	1	1	0	1	1	0	1	1	0	1

Age group	2045 Both sexes	Males	Females	2050 Both sexes	Males	Females
All ages	1 486	722	763	1 396	678	717
0-4	38	19	18	35	18	17
5-9	42	21	20	38	20	19
10-14	44	23	22	42	22	20
15-19	46	24	23	45	23	22
20-24	50	26	24	48	25	23
25-29	53	28	25	51	27	24
30-34	61	32	29	54	29	26
35-39	73	39	35	62	33	29
40-44	93	49	44	74	39	35
45-49	96	50	46	93	49	44
50-54	104	54	50	95	50	46
55-59	123	63	60	102	53	49
60-64	133	67	66	120	61	59
65-69	136	68	68	127	63	64
70-74	119	57	63	126	61	65
75-79	100	44	55	104	47	57
80-84	81	32	49	79	32	47
85-89	54	18	36	56	19	37
90-94	28	7	21	30	8	22
95-99	8	1	7	11	2	9
100 +	1	0	1	2	0	2

POPULATION BY AGE AND SEX (in thousands)

Age group	1950 Both sexes	Males	Females	1955 Both sexes	Males	Females	1960 Both sexes	Males	Females	1965 Both sexes	Males	Females
All ages	90	49	40	102	55	47	118	64	55	137	73	65
0-4	14	7	7	18	9	8	22	11	10	25	13	12
5-9	13	7	7	13	7	7	16	9	8	20	11	10
10-14	11	6	5	13	7	7	13	6	6	16	8	8
15-19	10	5	5	10	5	5	13	6	6	12	6	6
20-24	8	4	4	10	5	5	10	5	5	12	6	6
25-29	7	4	3	7	4	4	9	5	5	10	5	5
30-34	5	3	2	7	4	3	7	4	3	9	5	4
35-39	5	3	2	5	3	2	7	3	3	7	4	3
40-44	4	2	2	4	3	2	5	3	2	6	3	3
45-49	3	2	1	4	2	2	4	2	2	5	3	2
50-54	4	3	1	3	2	1	3	2	1	4	2	2
55-59	3	2	1	4	3	1	3	2	1	3	2	1
60-64	1	1	0	2	2	1	3	2	1	2	2	1
65-69	1	1	0	1	1	0	2	1	1	3	2	1
70-74	1	0	0	1	0	0	1	1	0	1	1	0
75-79	0	0	0	0	0	0	0	0	0	0	0	0
80 +	0	0	0	0	0	0	0	0	0	0	0	0

Age group	1970 Both sexes	Males	Females	1975 Both sexes	Males	Females	1980 Both sexes	Males	Females	1985 Both sexes	Males	Females
All ages	161	85	76	193	101	92	229	119	110	272	141	131
0-4	27	14	13	40	21	19	44	23	21	49	25	24
5-9	24	12	12	30	16	14	36	19	17	42	22	20
10-14	21	11	10	23	12	11	29	15	14	38	20	18
15-19	16	9	8	19	10	9	23	12	11	28	14	14
20-24	12	6	6	14	7	7	18	9	9	23	11	12
25-29	12	6	6	13	7	7	16	8	8	18	9	9
30-34	10	5	5	11	6	5	13	7	6	15	8	7
35-39	9	5	4	9	5	5	11	6	5	12	6	6
40-44	7	4	3	7	4	4	9	5	4	11	6	5
45-49	6	3	3	7	4	3	8	4	4	9	5	4
50-54	4	3	2	5	3	2	6	3	3	7	4	3
55-59	4	2	2	5	3	2	5	3	3	6	3	3
60-64	3	2	1	3	2	1	4	2	1	5	3	2
65-69	2	1	1	3	2	1	3	2	1	4	2	1
70-74	2	2	1	2	1	1	2	1	1	3	2	1
75-79	1	1	0	1	1	0	1	1	0	2	1	1
80 +	0	0	0	1	0	0	1	1	0	1	1	0

Age group	1990 Both sexes	Males	Females	1995 Both sexes	Males	Females	2000 Both sexes	Males	Females	2005 Both sexes	Males	Females
All ages	317	164	153	364	188	176	419	216	203	478	247	231
0-4	55	29	26	58	30	28	67	35	32	72	37	34
5-9	48	25	23	54	28	26	57	30	27	66	34	32
10-14	42	22	20	48	25	23	54	28	26	56	29	27
15-19	37	19	18	42	22	20	47	25	23	53	28	26
20-24	28	14	14	37	19	18	41	21	20	47	24	23
25-29	22	11	11	27	14	14	36	19	17	40	21	19
30-34	18	9	9	22	11	11	27	14	13	36	19	17
35-39	15	7	7	18	9	9	21	11	11	26	13	13
40-44	12	6	6	14	7	7	17	9	9	21	10	11
45-49	10	6	5	12	6	6	14	7	7	17	8	8
50-54	8	4	4	10	5	5	11	6	5	13	7	6
55-59	7	4	3	8	4	4	9	5	4	10	5	5
60-64	6	3	3	6	3	3	7	3	3	8	4	4
65-69	4	2	2	5	2	2	5	3	2	6	3	3
70-74	3	2	1	3	1	1	3	2	2	3	2	2
75-79	1	1	1	1	1	1	1	1	1	2	1	1
80 +	1	1	0	1	0	0	1	0	0	1	0	0

United Nations Department of Economic and Social Affairs/Population Division
World Population Prospects: The 2004 Revision, Volume II: Sex and Age Distribution of the World Population

778

POPULATION BY AGE AND SEX (in thousands)

Age group	2005 Both sexes	Males	Females	2010 Both sexes	Males	Females	2015 Both sexes	Males	Females	2020 Both sexes	Males	Females
All ages	478	247	231	537	277	260	596	308	289	653	337	317
0-4	72	37	34	74	38	35	74	38	35	74	38	35
5-9	66	34	32	71	37	34	73	38	35	73	38	35
10-14	56	29	27	65	34	31	70	37	34	72	38	35
15-19	53	28	26	56	29	27	65	34	31	70	36	34
20-24	47	24	23	53	27	25	56	29	27	64	33	31
25-29	40	21	19	46	24	22	52	27	25	55	28	26
30-34	36	19	17	40	21	19	45	23	22	51	27	25
35-39	26	13	13	35	18	17	39	20	19	45	23	22
40-44	21	10	11	26	13	13	34	18	16	38	20	19
45-49	17	8	8	20	10	10	25	13	13	33	17	16
50-54	13	7	6	16	8	8	20	10	10	24	12	12
55-59	10	5	5	12	6	6	15	7	8	18	9	10
60-64	8	4	4	9	5	5	11	6	6	14	7	7
65-69	6	3	3	7	4	3	8	4	4	10	5	5
70-74	3	2	2	4	2	2	5	3	3	6	3	3
75-79	2	1	1	2	1	1	2	1	1	3	2	2
80-84	1	0	0	1	0	0	1	0	0	1	1	1
85-89	0	0	0	0	0	0	0	0	0	0	0	0
90-94	0	0	0	0	0	0	0	0	0	0	0	0
95-99	0	0	0	0	0	0	0	0	0	0	0	0
100	0	0	0	0	0	0	0	0	0	0	0	0

Age group	2025 Both sexes	Males	Females	2030 Both sexes	Males	Females	2035 Both sexes	Males	Females	2040 Both sexes	Males	Females
All ages	709	365	344	762	393	370	811	417	394	854	439	415
0-4	74	39	36	74	38	35	72	37	34	68	36	33
5-9	73	38	35	74	38	35	73	38	35	71	37	34
10-14	73	38	35	73	38	35	73	38	35	73	38	35
15-19	72	37	35	72	38	35	73	38	35	73	38	35
20-24	69	36	33	71	37	34	72	37	35	72	37	35
25-29	64	33	31	69	36	33	71	37	34	71	37	34
30-34	54	28	26	63	33	30	68	35	33	70	36	34
35-39	51	26	25	54	28	26	62	32	30	68	35	33
40-44	44	23	21	50	26	24	53	27	26	62	32	30
45-49	38	19	18	43	22	21	49	25	24	52	27	25
50-54	33	17	16	36	19	18	42	21	20	48	24	23
55-59	23	11	12	31	16	15	35	18	17	40	20	20
60-64	17	8	9	21	10	11	28	14	14	32	16	16
65-69	12	6	6	15	7	8	19	9	10	25	13	13
70-74	7	4	4	9	4	5	12	5	6	15	7	8
75-79	4	2	2	5	2	3	6	3	3	8	4	5
80-84	2	1	1	2	1	1	3	1	1	3	2	2
85-89	0	0	0	1	0	0	1	0	0	1	0	1
90-94	0	0	0	0	0	0	0	0	0	0	0	0
95-99	0	0	0	0	0	0	0	0	0	0	0	0
100 +	0	0	0	0	0	0	0	0	0	0	0	0

Age group	2045 Both sexes	Males	Females	2050 Both sexes	Males	Females
All ages	890	457	433	921	472	449
0-4	64	34	31	63	33	30
5-9	68	35	33	64	33	31
10-14	71	37	34	68	35	33
15-19	73	38	35	71	37	34
20-24	73	38	35	73	38	35
25-29	72	37	35	72	37	35
30-34	71	37	34	71	37	34
35-39	70	36	34	70	36	34
40-44	67	34	32	69	35	33
45-49	61	31	29	66	34	32
50-54	51	26	25	59	30	29
55-59	46	23	23	49	25	24
60-64	38	19	19	43	22	21
65-69	29	14	14	34	17	17
70-74	21	10	11	24	12	12
75-79	11	5	6	15	7	8
80-84	5	2	3	6	3	4
85-89	1	1	1	2	1	1
90-94	0	0	0	0	0	0
95-99	0	0	0	0	0	0
100 +	0	0	0	0	0	0

POPULATION BY AGE AND SEX (in thousands)

Age group	2005 Both sexes	Males	Females	2010 Both sexes	Males	Females	2015 Both sexes	Males	Females	2020 Both sexes	Males	Females
All ages	478	247	231	542	280	262	610	315	295	679	350	329
0-4	72	37	34	78	41	38	83	43	40	86	45	41
5-9	66	34	32	71	37	34	77	40	37	82	43	39
10-14	56	29	27	65	34	31	70	37	34	77	40	37
15-19	53	28	26	56	29	27	65	34	31	70	36	34
20-24	47	24	23	53	27	25	56	29	27	64	33	31
25-29	40	21	19	46	24	22	52	27	25	55	28	26
30-34	36	19	17	40	21	19	45	23	22	51	27	25
35-39	26	13	13	35	18	17	39	20	19	45	23	22
40-44	21	10	11	26	13	13	34	18	16	38	20	19
45-49	17	8	8	20	10	10	25	13	13	33	17	16
50-54	13	7	6	16	8	8	20	10	10	24	12	12
55-59	10	5	5	12	6	6	15	7	8	18	9	10
60-64	8	4	4	9	5	5	11	6	6	14	7	7
65-69	6	3	3	7	4	3	8	4	4	10	5	5
70-74	3	2	2	4	2	2	5	3	3	6	3	3
75-79	2	1	1	2	1	1	2	1	1	3	2	2
80-84	1	0	0	1	0	0	1	0	0	1	1	1
85-89	0	0	0	0	0	0	0	0	0	0	0	0
90-94	0	0	0	0	0	0	0	0	0	0	0	0
95-99	0	0	0	0	0	0	0	0	0	0	0	0
100 +	0	0	0	0	0	0	0	0	0	0	0	0

Age group	2025 Both sexes	Males	Females	2030 Both sexes	Males	Females	2035 Both sexes	Males	Females	2040 Both sexes	Males	Females
All ages	749	386	363	819	422	397	888	457	431	955	491	464
0-4	88	46	42	90	47	43	92	48	44	93	48	45
5-9	85	44	41	88	46	42	90	47	43	92	48	44
10-14	82	42	39	85	44	41	87	45	42	90	47	43
15-19	77	40	37	81	42	39	85	44	41	87	45	42
20-24	69	36	33	76	39	37	81	42	39	84	44	41
25-29	64	33	31	69	36	33	76	39	36	80	41	39
30-34	54	28	26	63	33	30	68	35	33	75	39	36
35-39	51	26	25	54	28	26	62	32	30	68	35	33
40-44	44	23	21	50	26	24	53	27	26	62	32	30
45-49	38	19	18	43	22	21	49	25	24	52	27	25
50-54	32	17	16	36	19	18	42	21	20	48	24	23
55-59	23	11	12	31	16	15	35	18	17	40	20	20
60-64	17	8	9	21	10	11	28	14	14	32	16	16
65-69	12	6	6	15	7	8	19	9	10	25	13	13
70-74	7	4	4	9	4	5	12	5	6	15	7	8
75-79	4	2	2	5	2	3	6	3	3	8	4	5
80-84	2	1	1	2	1	1	3	1	1	3	2	2
85-89	0	0	0	1	0	0	1	0	0	1	0	1
90-94	0	0	0	0	0	0	0	0	0	0	0	0
95-99	0	0	0	0	0	0	0	0	0	0	0	0
100 +	0	0	0	0	0	0	0	0	0	0	0	0

Age group	2045 Both sexes	Males	Females	2050 Both sexes	Males	Females
All ages	1 019	524	495	1 080	555	526
0-4	93	48	45	94	49	45
5-9	93	48	45	92	48	44
10-14	92	48	44	93	48	45
15-19	90	46	43	92	47	44
20-24	87	45	42	89	46	43
25-29	84	43	40	86	45	42
30-34	79	41	38	83	43	40
35-39	74	38	36	79	41	38
40-44	67	34	32	73	38	36
45-49	61	31	29	66	34	32
50-54	51	26	25	59	30	29
55-59	46	23	23	49	25	24
60-64	38	19	19	43	22	21
65-69	29	14	14	34	17	17
70-74	21	10	11	24	12	12
75-79	11	5	6	15	7	8
80-84	5	2	3	6	3	4
85-89	1	1	1	2	1	1
90-94	0	0	0	0	0	0
95-99	0	0	0	0	0	0
100 +	0	0	0	0	0	0

United Nations Department of Economic and Social Affairs/Population Division
World Population Prospects: The 2004 Revision, Volume II: Sex and Age Distribution of the World Population

780

POPULATION BY AGE AND SEX (in thousands)

Age group	2005			2010			2015			2020		
	Both sexes	Males	Females	Both sexes	Males	Females	Both sexes	Males	Females	Both sexes	Males	Females
All ages	478	247	231	533	275	258	593	300	282	627	323	304
0-4	72	37	34	69	36	33	65	34	31	61	32	29
5-9	66	34	32	71	37	34	68	35	33	64	33	31
10-14	56	29	27	65	34	31	70	37	34	68	35	32
15-19	53	28	26	56	29	27	65	34	31	70	36	34
20-24	47	24	23	53	27	25	56	29	27	64	33	31
25-29	40	21	19	46	24	22	52	27	25	55	28	26
30-34	36	19	17	40	21	19	45	23	22	51	27	25
35-39	26	13	13	35	18	17	39	20	19	45	23	22
40-44	21	10	11	26	13	13	34	18	16	38	20	19
45-49	17	8	8	20	10	10	25	13	13	33	17	16
50-54	13	7	6	16	8	8	20	10	10	24	12	12
55-59	10	5	5	12	6	6	15	7	8	18	9	10
60-64	8	4	4	9	5	5	11	6	6	14	7	7
65-69	6	3	3	7	4	3	8	4	4	10	5	5
70-74	3	2	2	4	2	2	5	3	3	6	3	3
75-79	2	1	1	2	1	1	2	1	1	3	2	2
80-84	1	0	0	1	0	0	1	0	0	1	1	1
85-89	0	0	0	0	0	0	0	0	0	0	0	0
90-94	0	0	0	0	0	0	0	0	0	0	0	0
95-99	0	0	0	0	0	0	0	0	0	0	0	0
100 +	0	0	0	0	0	0	0	0	0	0	0	0

Age group	2025			2030			2035			2040		
	Both sexes	Males	Females	Both sexes	Males	Females	Both sexes	Males	Females	Both sexes	Males	Females
All ages	669	345	325	707	364	343	737	379	358	759	389	369
0-4	60	31	29	58	30	28	53	28	25	47	24	22
5-9	61	32	29	60	31	29	57	30	28	53	27	25
10-14	64	33	31	61	31	29	60	31	29	57	30	28
15-19	67	35	32	64	33	31	60	31	29	59	31	29
20-24	69	36	33	67	35	32	63	33	31	60	31	29
25-29	64	33	31	69	36	33	66	34	32	63	33	30
30-34	54	28	26	63	33	30	68	35	33	66	34	32
35-39	51	26	25	54	28	26	62	32	30	68	35	33
40-44	44	23	21	50	26	24	53	27	26	62	32	30
45-49	38	19	18	43	22	21	49	25	24	52	27	25
50-54	32	17	16	36	19	18	42	21	20	48	24	23
55-59	23	11	12	31	16	15	35	18	17	40	20	20
60-64	17	8	9	21	10	11	28	14	14	32	16	16
65-69	12	6	6	15	7	8	19	9	10	25	13	13
70-74	7	4	4	9	4	5	12	5	6	15	7	8
75-79	4	2	2	5	2	3	6	3	3	8	4	5
80-84	2	1	1	2	1	1	3	1	1	3	2	2
85-89	0	0	0	1	0	0	1	0	0	1	0	1
90-94	0	0	0	0	0	0	0	0	0	0	0	0
95-99	0	0	0	0	0	0	0	0	0	0	0	0
100 +	0	0	0	0	0	0	0	0	0	0	0	0

Age group	2045			2050		
	Both sexes	Males	Females	Both sexes	Males	Females
All ages	771	395	376	777	398	380
0-4	41	21	20	38	20	18
5-9	47	24	22	41	21	20
10-14	53	27	25	47	24	22
15-19	57	30	27	52	27	25
20-24	59	31	29	57	29	27
25-29	60	31	29	59	30	28
30-34	62	32	30	59	31	29
35-39	65	34	32	62	32	30
40-44	67	34	32	64	33	31
45-49	61	31	29	66	34	32
50-54	51	26	25	59	30	29
55-59	46	23	23	49	25	24
60-64	38	19	19	43	22	21
65-69	29	14	14	34	17	17
70-74	21	10	11	24	12	12
75-79	11	5	6	15	7	8
80-84	5	2	3	6	3	4
85-89	1	1	1	2	1	1
90-94	0	0	0	0	0	0
95-99	0	0	0	0	0	0
100 +	0	0	0	0	0	0

POPULATION BY AGE AND SEX (in thousands)

Age group	1950 Both sexes	1950 Males	1950 Females	1955 Both sexes	1955 Males	1955 Females	1960 Both sexes	1960 Males	1960 Females	1965 Both sexes	1965 Males	1965 Females
All ages	2 264	1 124	1 140	2 522	1 249	1 273	2 820	1 395	1 425	3 173	1 568	1 604
0-4	389	195	194	472	235	237	526	262	264	591	294	296
5-9	287	142	144	330	165	165	406	201	205	459	228	231
10-14	258	128	130	271	135	137	314	157	157	388	192	196
15-19	218	111	107	248	123	125	261	130	131	303	152	151
20-24	195	99	96	208	105	103	237	117	120	251	124	127
25-29	173	87	86	184	93	91	197	99	98	226	111	115
30-34	153	77	76	163	82	81	174	88	86	187	94	93
35-39	133	67	67	142	71	71	152	76	76	164	82	81
40-44	114	56	57	123	61	62	132	66	66	142	71	71
45-49	96	47	49	104	51	53	113	56	57	122	60	62
50-54	79	38	41	86	42	44	94	45	48	102	50	52
55-59	63	30	33	69	33	36	76	36	40	83	39	43
60-64	46	21	25	52	24	28	58	27	31	64	30	34
65-69	31	14	18	35	16	20	40	18	22	45	21	25
70-74	17	7	10	21	9	12	24	10	14	28	12	16
75-79	8	3	5	9	4	6	11	5	7	14	6	8
80 +	3	1	2	3	1	2	4	2	3	6	2	4

Age group	1970 Both sexes	1970 Males	1970 Females	1975 Both sexes	1975 Males	1975 Females	1980 Both sexes	1980 Males	1980 Females	1985 Both sexes	1985 Males	1985 Females
All ages	3 601	1 779	1 822	4 134	2 043	2 091	6 487	3 206	3 280	6 470	3 199	3 272
0-4	678	339	340	797	399	399	1 268	634	634	1 151	576	575
5-9	521	259	262	605	301	304	971	484	487	1 010	504	506
10-14	440	218	222	501	249	252	793	395	398	824	411	413
15-19	376	186	190	427	212	215	662	329	333	677	337	340
20-24	292	146	146	363	179	184	560	277	283	563	279	284
25-29	240	118	121	279	139	141	470	231	239	473	233	240
30-34	215	105	110	228	112	116	365	180	184	396	194	202
35-39	176	88	88	204	100	104	296	146	151	304	150	154
40-44	153	77	77	166	83	83	259	127	133	246	120	125
45-49	132	65	67	143	71	72	211	105	107	214	104	110
50-54	111	54	57	121	59	62	179	88	91	171	84	87
55-59	91	44	47	100	48	52	148	71	76	142	69	73
60-64	71	33	38	79	37	41	117	56	62	113	54	59
65-69	51	23	27	57	26	31	86	40	46	84	39	45
70-74	32	14	18	36	16	20	56	25	31	55	25	30
75-79	16	7	9	19	8	11	30	13	17	30	13	17
80 +	7	3	5	9	4	6	15	6	9	16	6	10

Age group	1990 Both sexes	1990 Males	1990 Females	1995 Both sexes	1995 Males	1995 Females	2000 Both sexes	2000 Males	2000 Females	2005 Both sexes	2005 Males	2005 Females
All ages	6 674	3 301	3 373	6 312	3 118	3 193	7 012	3 472	3 540	8 228	4 081	4 147
0-4	1 205	604	601	1 084	541	543	1 291	649	642	1 482	746	736
5-9	940	470	471	905	452	453	948	473	475	1 207	607	600
10-14	885	441	443	760	380	381	848	424	424	941	470	472
15-19	724	361	363	730	364	366	716	358	358	846	423	423
20-24	592	294	298	590	293	297	685	341	344	711	354	357
25-29	489	241	248	478	236	242	549	272	277	676	335	341
30-34	409	201	208	393	193	200	444	219	225	540	267	273
35-39	342	167	175	328	161	167	363	178	185	434	214	221
40-44	260	128	132	272	133	140	300	147	153	353	173	180
45-49	208	101	107	203	100	104	248	120	128	290	141	149
50-54	180	86	93	160	77	83	182	88	94	236	113	123
55-59	140	68	72	136	64	72	141	67	74	170	82	89
60-64	112	54	58	101	48	53	115	53	62	127	59	67
65-69	84	39	45	75	35	40	80	38	42	97	45	53
70-74	56	26	30	50	23	27	54	25	29	61	28	33
75-79	32	14	18	28	12	16	30	13	17	35	16	19
80 +	17	7	10	16	6	10	18	7	11	22	9	13

United Nations Department of Economic and Social Affairs/Population Division
World Population Prospects: The 2004 Revision, Volume II: Sex and Age Distribution of the World Population

POPULATION BY AGE AND SEX (in thousands)

Age group	2005 Both sexes	2005 Males	2005 Females	2010 Both sexes	2010 Males	2010 Females	2015 Both sexes	2015 Males	2015 Females	2020 Both sexes	2020 Males	2020 Females
All ages	8 228	4 081	4 147	9 590	4 763	4 827	10 970	5 453	5 516	12 336	6 137	6 199
0-4	1 482	746	736	1 653	832	821	1 784	899	886	1 892	954	939
5-9	1 207	607	600	1 399	704	695	1 558	784	774	1 680	846	835
10-14	941	470	472	1 198	602	595	1 377	693	684	1 523	766	757
15-19	846	423	423	939	469	471	1 183	595	588	1 350	679	671
20-24	711	354	357	839	418	420	923	460	464	1 154	579	575
25-29	676	335	341	702	349	354	820	407	413	897	445	452
30-34	540	267	273	664	329	336	685	339	346	794	394	400
35-39	434	214	221	529	261	268	645	319	326	661	327	334
40-44	353	173	180	423	208	215	511	252	260	619	305	314
45-49	290	141	149	341	166	175	406	198	207	487	239	248
50-54	236	113	123	277	133	143	323	157	167	382	186	197
55-59	170	82	89	221	105	116	257	123	134	299	143	155
60-64	127	59	67	154	73	81	199	93	105	231	109	122
65-69	97	45	53	108	50	58	131	61	70	169	78	91
70-74	61	28	33	76	34	42	84	38	46	102	47	55
75-79	35	16	19	41	19	23	51	22	29	57	25	32
80-84	16	7	9	19	8	11	22	10	13	28	12	16
85-89	5	2	3	6	2	4	7	3	4	9	4	5
90-94	1	0	1	1	0	1	2	1	1	2	1	1
95-99	0	0	0	0	0	0	0	0	0	0	0	0
100 +	0	0	0	0	0	0	0	0	0	0	0	0

Age group	2025 Both sexes	2025 Males	2025 Females	2030 Both sexes	2030 Males	2030 Females	2035 Both sexes	2035 Males	2035 Females	2040 Both sexes	2040 Males	2040 Females
All ages	13 787	6 862	6 925	15 304	7 620	7 683	16 844	8 390	8 454	18 370	9 152	9 219
0-4	2 007	1 012	995	2 103	1 061	1 042	2 161	1 091	1 070	2 183	1 103	1 080
5-9	1 796	904	891	1 918	966	951	2 023	1 020	1 003	2 090	1 054	1 036
10-14	1 646	828	818	1 764	888	876	1 888	951	937	1 995	1 005	990
15-19	1 496	752	744	1 620	814	805	1 738	874	864	1 864	938	926
20-24	1 319	662	657	1 465	735	730	1 590	797	792	1 709	858	851
25-29	1 123	561	562	1 287	644	643	1 433	716	716	1 558	779	779
30-34	871	431	440	1 093	545	548	1 256	627	629	1 401	699	702
35-39	769	380	389	846	417	428	1 064	530	535	1 226	611	616
40-44	636	314	322	743	367	376	819	404	415	1 034	514	521
45-49	592	291	302	611	300	311	715	352	363	701	389	402
50-54	461	224	236	562	274	288	582	285	298	684	335	349
55-59	355	171	184	430	208	222	527	255	272	548	266	282
60-64	270	128	142	322	154	169	393	188	205	484	232	252
65-69	198	92	106	233	109	124	281	132	149	344	163	182
70-74	133	61	72	157	72	85	188	86	101	228	106	123
75-79	70	32	38	93	41	52	112	50	62	135	61	74
80-84	32	14	18	40	17	23	54	23	31	66	29	37
85-89	11	4	7	13	5	8	17	7	10	23	10	14
90-94	2	1	1	3	1	2	4	1	2	5	2	3
95-99	0	0	0	0	0	0	1	0	0	1	0	0
100 +	0	0	0	0	0	0	0	0	0	0	0	0

Age group	2045 Both sexes	2045 Males	2045 Females	2050 Both sexes	2050 Males	2050 Females
All ages	19 867	9 896	9 971	21 329	10 622	10 707
0-4	2 192	1 107	1 085	2 203	1 113	1 090
5-9	2 122	1 070	1 052	2 141	1 080	1 061
10-14	2 065	1 041	1 024	2 101	1 059	1 042
15-19	1 973	993	979	2 045	1 030	1 015
20-24	1 835	921	914	1 945	977	968
25-29	1 678	839	838	1 805	904	901
30-34	1 527	762	765	1 648	823	825
35-39	1 371	682	688	1 497	745	752
40-44	1 195	594	601	1 339	665	674
45-49	1 002	496	506	1 161	575	586
50-54	759	371	388	965	475	489
55-59	647	314	332	720	350	370
60-64	506	243	263	600	289	311
65-69	428	202	225	450	213	236
70-74	283	131	151	354	165	189
75-79	167	76	91	209	95	114
80-84	81	36	46	102	45	57
85-89	29	12	17	37	16	21
90-94	7	3	4	9	3	5
95-99	1	0	1	1	0	1
100 +	0	0	0	0	0	0

United Nations Department of Economic and Social Affairs/Population Division
World Population Prospects: The 2004 Revision, Volume II: Sex and Age Distribution of the World Population

783

POPULATION BY AGE AND SEX (in thousands)

Age group	2005 Both sexes	Males	Females	2010 Both sexes	Males	Females	2015 Both sexes	Males	Females	2020 Both sexes	Males	Females
All ages	8 228	4 081	4 147	9 657	4 797	4 861	11 160	5 549	5 611	12 702	6 321	6 381
0-4	1 482	746	736	1 720	866	854	1 911	963	948	2 077	1 047	1 030
5-9	1 207	607	600	1 399	704	695	1 622	816	806	1 800	906	894
10-14	941	470	472	1 198	602	595	1 377	693	684	1 585	797	788
15-19	846	423	423	939	469	471	1 183	595	588	1 350	679	671
20-24	711	354	357	839	418	420	923	460	464	1 154	579	575
25-29	676	335	341	702	349	354	820	407	413	897	445	452
30-34	540	267	273	664	329	336	685	339	346	794	394	400
35-39	434	214	221	529	261	268	645	319	326	661	327	334
40-44	353	173	180	423	208	215	511	252	260	619	305	314
45-49	290	141	149	341	166	175	406	198	207	487	239	248
50-54	236	113	123	277	133	143	323	157	167	382	186	197
55-59	170	82	89	221	105	116	257	123	134	299	143	155
60-64	127	59	67	154	73	81	199	93	105	231	109	122
65-69	97	45	53	108	50	58	131	61	70	169	78	91
70-74	61	28	33	76	34	42	84	38	46	102	47	55
75-79	35	16	19	41	19	23	51	22	29	57	25	32
80-84	16	7	9	19	8	11	22	10	13	28	12	16
85-89	5	2	3	6	2	4	7	3	4	9	4	5
90-94	1	0	1	1	0	1	2	1	1	2	1	1
95-99	0	0	0	0	0	0	0	0	0	0	0	0
100 +	0	0	0	0	0	0	0	0	0	0	0	0

Age group	2025 Both sexes	Males	Females	2030 Both sexes	Males	Females	2035 Both sexes	Males	Females	2040 Both sexes	Males	Females
All ages	14 362	7 152	7 210	16 142	8 043	8 099	18 027	8 986	9 041	19 997	9 971	10 026
0-4	2 228	1 124	1 104	2 382	1 202	1 180	2 525	1 275	1 250	2 649	1 338	1 311
5-9	1 971	992	979	2 129	1 073	1 056	2 291	1 155	1 136	2 442	1 232	1 210
10-14	1 764	887	876	1 936	975	962	2 096	1 056	1 040	2 261	1 139	1 121
15-19	1 557	783	774	1 736	873	863	1 909	960	949	2 070	1 042	1 028
20-24	1 319	662	657	1 525	765	760	1 703	854	849	1 877	942	935
25-29	1 123	561	562	1 287	644	643	1 491	746	746	1 669	835	834
30-34	871	431	440	1 093	545	548	1 256	627	629	1 459	728	731
35-39	769	380	388	845	417	428	1 064	530	535	1 226	611	616
40-44	636	314	322	743	367	376	819	404	415	1 034	514	521
45-49	592	291	302	611	300	311	715	352	363	791	389	402
50-54	461	224	236	562	274	288	582	285	298	684	335	349
55-59	355	171	184	430	208	222	527	255	272	548	266	282
60-64	270	128	142	322	154	169	393	188	205	484	232	252
65-69	198	92	106	233	109	124	281	132	149	344	163	182
70-74	133	61	72	157	72	85	188	86	101	228	106	123
75-79	70	32	39	93	41	52	112	50	62	135	61	74
80-84	32	14	18	40	17	23	54	23	31	66	29	37
85-89	11	4	7	13	5	8	17	7	10	23	10	14
90-94	2	1	1	3	1	2	4	1	2	5	2	3
95-99	0	0	0	0	0	0	1	0	0	1	0	0
100 +	0	0	0	0	0	0	0	0	0	0	0	0

Age group	2045 Both sexes	Males	Females	2050 Both sexes	Males	Females
All ages	22 036	10 988	11 048	24 133	12 033	12 100
0-4	2 763	1 396	1 367	2 870	1 450	1 420
5-9	2 576	1 300	1 276	2 698	1 361	1 337
10-14	2 414	1 217	1 197	2 551	1 286	1 265
15-19	2 235	1 125	1 110	2 390	1 204	1 186
20-24	2 038	1 023	1 015	2 205	1 107	1 097
25-29	1 842	922	921	2 005	1 004	1 001
30-34	1 636	817	820	1 810	904	906
35-39	1 427	711	717	1 604	799	806
40-44	1 195	594	601	1 394	692	702
45-49	1 002	496	506	1 161	575	586
50-54	759	371	388	965	475	489
55-59	647	314	332	720	350	370
60-64	506	243	263	600	289	311
65-69	428	202	225	450	213	236
70-74	283	131	151	354	165	189
75-79	167	76	91	209	95	114
80-84	81	36	46	102	45	57
85-89	29	12	17	37	16	21
90-94	7	3	4	9	3	5
95-99	1	0	1	1	0	1
100 +	0	0	0	0	0	0

United Nations Department of Economic and Social Affairs/Population Division
World Population Prospects: The 2004 Revision, Volume II: Sex and Age Distribution of the World Population

784

POPULATION BY AGE AND SEX (in thousands)

Age group	2005 Both sexes	2005 Males	2005 Females	2010 Both sexes	2010 Males	2010 Females	2015 Both sexes	2015 Males	2015 Females	2020 Both sexes	2020 Males	2020 Females
All ages	8 228	4 081	4 147	9 522	4 728	4 793	10 779	5 357	5 422	11 970	5 952	6 010
0-4	1 482	746	736	1 585	798	787	1 658	835	823	1 708	861	847
5-9	1 207	607	600	1 399	704	695	1 495	752	743	1 561	785	775
10-14	941	470	472	1 198	602	595	1 377	693	684	1 461	735	726
15-19	846	423	423	939	469	471	1 183	595	588	1 350	679	671
20-24	711	354	357	839	418	420	923	460	464	1 154	579	575
25-29	676	335	341	702	349	354	820	407	413	897	445	452
30-34	540	267	273	664	329	336	685	339	346	794	394	400
35-39	434	214	221	529	261	268	645	319	326	661	327	334
40-44	353	173	180	423	208	215	511	252	260	619	305	314
45-49	290	141	149	341	166	175	406	198	207	487	239	248
50-54	236	113	123	277	133	143	323	157	167	382	186	197
55-59	170	82	89	221	105	116	257	123	134	299	143	155
60-64	127	59	67	154	73	81	199	93	105	231	109	122
65-69	97	45	53	108	50	58	131	61	70	169	78	91
70-74	61	28	33	76	34	42	84	38	46	102	47	55
75-79	35	16	19	41	19	23	51	22	29	57	25	32
80-84	16	7	9	19	8	11	22	10	13	28	12	16
85-89	5	2	3	6	2	4	7	3	4	9	4	5
90-94	1	0	1	1	0	1	2	1	1	2	1	1
95-99	0	0	0	0	0	0	0	0	0	0	0	0
100 +	0	0	0	0	0	0	0	0	0	0	0	0

Age group	2025 Both sexes	2025 Males	2025 Females	2030 Both sexes	2030 Males	2030 Females	2035 Both sexes	2035 Males	2035 Females	2040 Both sexes	2040 Males	2040 Females
All ages	13 213	6 573	6 640	14 471	7 201	7 270	15 683	7 805	7 878	16 800	8 361	8 439
0-4	1 787	901	886	1 830	923	906	1 814	916	898	1 752	885	867
5-9	1 620	816	804	1 707	860	847	1 759	887	872	1 754	884	869
10-14	1 529	769	760	1 591	801	790	1 680	846	834	1 735	874	861
15-19	1 435	721	713	1 504	756	748	1 568	789	779	1 658	835	824
20-24	1 319	662	657	1 405	705	700	1 476	740	736	1 541	773	768
25-29	1 123	561	562	1 287	644	643	1 374	687	687	1 446	723	723
30-34	871	431	440	1 093	545	548	1 256	627	629	1 344	670	673
35-39	769	380	388	845	417	428	1 064	530	535	1 226	611	616
40-44	636	314	322	743	367	376	819	404	415	1 034	514	521
45-49	592	291	302	611	300	311	715	352	363	791	389	402
50-54	440	204	236	562	274	288	582	285	298	684	335	349
55-59	355	171	184	430	208	222	527	255	272	548	266	282
60-64	270	128	142	322	154	169	393	188	205	484	232	252
65-69	198	92	106	233	109	124	281	132	149	344	163	182
70-74	133	61	72	157	72	85	188	86	101	228	106	123
75-79	70	32	39	93	41	52	112	50	62	135	61	74
80-84	32	14	18	40	17	23	54	23	31	66	29	37
85-89	11	4	7	13	5	8	17	7	10	23	10	14
90-94	2	1	1	3	1	2	4	1	2	5	2	3
95-99	0	0	0	0	0	0	1	0	0	1	0	0
100 +	0	0	0	0	0	0	0	0	0	0	0	0

Age group	2045 Both sexes	2045 Males	2045 Females	2050 Both sexes	2050 Males	2050 Females
All ages	17 811	8 861	8 950	18 720	9 309	9 411
0-4	1 680	849	831	1 619	818	801
5-9	1 702	859	844	1 640	827	813
10-14	1 733	873	859	1 685	849	835
15-19	1 715	863	851	1 715	864	851
20-24	1 633	820	813	1 691	849	842
25-29	1 513	757	756	1 605	804	802
30-34	1 417	707	710	1 486	742	744
35-39	1 315	654	660	1 389	692	698
40-44	1 195	594	601	1 284	638	646
45-49	1 002	496	506	1 161	575	586
50-54	759	371	388	965	475	489
55-59	647	314	332	720	350	370
60-64	506	243	263	600	289	311
65-69	428	202	225	450	213	236
70-74	283	131	151	354	165	189
75-79	167	76	91	209	95	114
80-84	81	36	46	102	45	57
85-89	29	12	17	37	16	21
90-94	7	3	4	9	3	5
95-99	1	0	1	1	0	1
100 +	0	0	0	0	0	0

POPULATION BY AGE AND SEX (in thousands)

Age group	1950 Both sexes	Males	Females	1955 Both sexes	Males	Females	1960 Both sexes	Males	Females	1965 Both sexes	Males	Females
All ages	13 683	6 816	6 868	15 385	7 682	7 703	17 396	8 697	8 699	19 914	9 898	10 016
0-4	2 088	1 046	1 042	2 496	1 288	1 208	2 841	1 457	1 385	3 280	1 664	1 616
5-9	1 706	854	852	1 947	982	965	2 352	1 219	1 133	2 756	1 394	1 363
10-14	1 485	743	742	1 690	845	846	1 930	972	958	2 356	1 190	1 166
15-19	1 340	686	654	1 469	733	736	1 673	834	839	1 907	958	949
20-24	1 183	620	563	1 314	670	645	1 443	716	727	1 648	818	830
25-29	1 040	532	508	1 154	602	553	1 285	652	633	1 419	701	718
30-34	960	486	474	1 008	513	496	1 122	582	540	1 257	634	623
35-39	835	422	413	922	464	458	973	492	481	1 088	561	527
40-44	725	355	371	791	397	395	879	439	440	931	467	464
45-49	589	284	306	676	327	350	743	368	374	827	409	419
50-54	502	238	263	537	254	283	621	296	326	681	333	348
55-59	415	193	223	444	207	237	480	223	257	568	265	303
60-64	324	147	177	353	159	194	382	173	209	423	191	232
65-69	228	101	127	260	113	146	287	125	162	318	139	179
70-74	148	64	84	168	71	97	195	81	114	221	91	130
75-79	77	31	46	97	39	59	113	44	69	135	51	83
80 +	37	14	23	57	20	36	77	27	51	98	33	66

Age group	1970 Both sexes	Males	Females	1975 Both sexes	Males	Females	1980 Both sexes	Males	Females	1985 Both sexes	Males	Females
All ages	22 663	11 281	11 381	25 854	12 885	12 969	29 239	14 546	14 693	33 178	16 500	16 678
0-4	3 716	1 870	1 846	4 142	2 084	2 057	4 513	2 270	2 244	4 940	2 488	2 452
5-9	3 185	1 611	1 574	3 623	1 817	1 806	4 048	2 030	2 018	4 435	2 224	2 211
10-14	2 727	1 376	1 351	3 156	1 593	1 563	3 591	1 797	1 794	4 023	2 014	2 009
15-19	2 337	1 180	1 157	2 709	1 366	1 343	3 127	1 576	1 551	3 572	1 786	1 786
20-24	1 895	956	940	2 327	1 178	1 148	2 673	1 347	1 327	3 112	1 569	1 543
25-29	1 640	819	821	1 892	959	933	2 289	1 158	1 131	2 660	1 342	1 319
30-34	1 405	699	706	1 629	818	811	1 855	939	915	2 270	1 150	1 120
35-39	1 230	623	607	1 381	690	692	1 585	794	790	1 827	925	902
40-44	1 047	539	508	1 190	602	588	1 328	659	669	1 543	771	772
45-49	878	437	441	993	507	486	1 125	563	563	1 273	626	646
50-54	757	368	389	809	397	412	915	459	456	1 052	518	534
55-59	599	286	313	672	319	353	720	344	376	827	405	422
60-64	473	212	260	503	231	272	568	259	309	621	285	335
65-69	324	138	187	367	155	212	394	170	224	455	195	261
70-74	219	87	132	227	88	139	261	100	161	288	113	175
75-79	132	49	84	134	47	86	142	48	93	169	57	112
80 +	99	32	67	101	32	69	104	31	72	112	33	79

Age group	1990 Both sexes	Males	Females	1995 Both sexes	Males	Females	2000 Both sexes	Males	Females	2005 Both sexes	Males	Females
All ages	36 877	18 262	18 614	41 894	20 648	21 246	45 610	22 411	23 199	47 432	23 291	24 141
0-4	4 977	2 509	2 468	5 189	2 619	2 570	5 259	2 657	2 602	5 223	2 640	2 583
5-9	4 862	2 443	2 420	4 917	2 474	2 443	5 128	2 584	2 544	5 140	2 593	2 547
10-14	4 404	2 204	2 199	4 839	2 428	2 412	4 903	2 464	2 439	5 102	2 568	2 534
15-19	3 986	1 990	1 996	4 424	2 209	2 215	4 841	2 429	2 412	4 897	2 463	2 434
20-24	3 517	1 747	1 770	4 098	2 030	2 068	4 383	2 191	2 192	4 727	2 382	2 345
25-29	3 054	1 526	1 528	3 664	1 799	1 864	3 967	1 962	2 005	3 962	2 002	1 960
30-34	2 610	1 306	1 304	3 178	1 571	1 607	3 525	1 718	1 808	3 436	1 710	1 726
35-39	2 214	1 112	1 102	2 714	1 343	1 372	3 070	1 499	1 571	3 074	1 490	1 583
40-44	1 761	882	879	2 282	1 131	1 151	2 622	1 277	1 345	2 731	1 314	1 417
45-49	1 464	721	744	1 790	882	908	2 194	1 068	1 126	2 377	1 133	1 244
50-54	1 183	570	613	1 449	699	751	1 700	819	881	2 005	950	1 055
55-59	953	456	497	1 130	530	601	1 348	632	716	1 547	722	825
60-64	720	339	381	855	393	462	1 011	455	556	1 199	538	660
65-69	507	219	288	595	264	331	720	312	408	858	364	494
70-74	341	133	208	385	152	233	463	190	273	568	227	341
75-79	192	66	125	232	80	152	271	96	175	331	121	209
80 +	130	37	93	152	43	109	205	58	147	257	73	184

United Nations Department of Economic and Social Affairs/Population Division
World Population Prospects: The 2004 Revision, Volume II: Sex and Age Distribution of the World Population

786

POPULATION BY AGE AND SEX (in thousands)

Age group	2005			2010			2015			2020		
	Both sexes	Males	Females	Both sexes	Males	Females	Both sexes	Males	Females	Both sexes	Males	Females
All ages	47 432	23 291	24 141	47 819	23 618	24 201	47 902	23 843	24 059	48 100	24 108	23 992
0-4	5 223	2 640	2 583	4 960	2 509	2 451	4 758	2 409	2 350	4 660	2 360	2 300
5-9	5 140	2 593	2 547	5 046	2 548	2 498	4 812	2 432	2 380	4 661	2 358	2 303
10-14	5 102	2 568	2 534	5 052	2 546	2 505	4 901	2 473	2 428	4 691	2 369	2 321
15-19	4 897	2 463	2 434	5 094	2 566	2 528	5 033	2 539	2 494	4 877	2 463	2 414
20-24	4 727	2 382	2 345	4 811	2 430	2 381	5 017	2 538	2 478	4 964	2 514	2 449
25-29	3 962	2 002	1 960	4 291	2 203	2 088	4 447	2 284	2 163	4 666	2 397	2 269
30-34	3 436	1 710	1 726	3 247	1 700	1 547	3 619	1 930	1 689	3 824	2 032	1 792
35-39	3 074	1 490	1 583	2 752	1 408	1 345	2 587	1 415	1 172	2 972	1 649	1 323
40-44	2 731	1 314	1 417	2 533	1 238	1 296	2 219	1 164	1 054	2 125	1 194	931
45-49	2 377	1 133	1 244	2 341	1 116	1 225	2 126	1 043	1 083	1 879	994	886
50-54	2 005	950	1 055	2 097	979	1 119	2 038	959	1 079	1 861	905	956
55-59	1 547	722	825	1 791	824	967	1 862	847	1 015	1 819	837	982
60-64	1 199	538	660	1 366	612	754	1 582	700	882	1 655	727	929
65-69	858	364	494	1 019	431	588	1 167	494	673	1 363	571	791
70-74	568	227	341	684	267	417	820	321	499	950	373	577
75-79	331	121	209	413	148	265	505	177	328	613	216	397
80-84	168	52	116	208	67	141	265	83	182	331	101	229
85-89	68	17	51	84	22	62	106	29	77	138	37	102
90-94	18	4	14	25	5	20	32	7	25	41	9	32
95-99	3	0	3	4	1	4	6	1	5	8	1	7
100 +	0	0	0	0	0	0	1	0	1	1	0	1

Age group	2025			2030			2035			2040		
	Both sexes	Males	Females	Both sexes	Males	Females	Both sexes	Males	Females	Both sexes	Males	Females
All ages	48 297	24 347	23 950	48 405	24 505	23 900	48 430	24 586	23 844	48 445	24 640	23 805
0-4	4 541	2 301	2 240	4 363	2 212	2 151	4 161	2 110	2 051	3 981	2 020	1 962
5-9	4 594	2 326	2 269	4 497	2 278	2 219	4 334	2 197	2 138	4 143	2 100	2 042
10-14	4 584	2 318	2 267	4 545	2 300	2 245	4 466	2 261	2 205	4 316	2 186	2 129
15-19	4 675	2 364	2 311	4 577	2 317	2 260	4 543	2 302	2 241	4 468	2 266	2 202
20-24	4 816	2 442	2 374	4 623	2 347	2 276	4 532	2 303	2 229	4 504	2 291	2 213
25-29	4 638	2 380	2 259	4 522	2 316	2 206	4 367	2 235	2 132	4 305	2 204	2 101
30-34	4 054	2 145	1 909	4 068	2 136	1 931	4 011	2 091	1 920	3 920	2 035	1 885
35-39	3 190	1 756	1 434	3 426	1 865	1 562	3 484	1 869	1 615	3 487	1 847	1 640
40-44	2 487	1 413	1 074	2 707	1 517	1 190	2 944	1 622	1 322	3 035	1 640	1 395
45-49	1 825	1 002	793	2 163	1 235	928	2 379	1 335	1 044	2 618	1 439	1 178
50-54	1 659	871	789	1 625	913	713	1 943	1 100	843	2 157	1 198	959
55-59	1 673	797	876	1 501	774	727	1 478	816	662	1 780	991	789
60-64	1 628	725	903	1 507	696	811	1 358	681	678	1 344	724	621
65-69	1 439	600	839	1 426	605	821	1 328	586	742	1 202	578	624
70-74	1 121	437	683	1 195	465	730	1 194	474	720	1 120	465	655
75-79	720	255	464	860	304	556	928	328	600	930	339	597
80-84	408	126	282	486	152	335	590	183	407	644	201	444
85-89	176	46	130	223	58	165	272	71	201	336	88	249
90-94	55	12	44	73	15	58	95	19	76	118	24	94
95-99	11	2	9	15	2	13	21	3	18	28	4	24
100 +	1	0	1	2	0	2	3	0	2	4	0	3

Age group	2045			2050		
	Both sexes	Males	Females	Both sexes	Males	Females
All ages	48 507	24 704	23 803	48 660	24 798	23 862
0-4	3 833	1 945	1 888	3 712	1 884	1 828
5-9	3 969	2 013	1 956	3 825	1 941	1 884
10-14	4 132	2 095	2 038	3 964	2 010	1 954
15-19	4 321	2 192	2 128	4 139	2 102	2 038
20-24	4 435	2 258	2 177	4 294	2 189	2 105
25-29	4 303	2 204	2 099	4 262	2 184	2 077
30-34	3 909	2 027	1 883	3 955	2 048	1 907
35-39	3 459	1 818	1 640	3 502	1 836	1 667
40-44	3 082	1 640	1 441	3 101	1 636	1 465
45-49	2 730	1 470	1 260	2 805	1 487	1 318
50-54	2 395	1 303	1 092	2 522	1 344	1 178
55-59	1 991	1 088	903	2 227	1 193	1 034
60-64	1 628	885	743	1 833	979	854
65-69	1 195	620	575	1 456	765	691
70-74	1 019	464	555	1 017	503	515
75-79	884	337	548	808	340	468
80-84	657	211	446	626	212	414
85-89	374	98	277	387	104	283
90-94	150	30	120	171	34	137
95-99	36	5	31	47	7	41
100 +	5	0	5	7	1	6

United Nations Department of Economic and Social Affairs/Population Division
World Population Prospects: The 2004 Revision, Volume II: Sex and Age Distribution of the World Population

787

POPULATION BY AGE AND SEX (in thousands)

Age group	2005			2010			2015			2020		
	Both sexes	Males	Females	Both sexes	Males	Females	Both sexes	Males	Females	Both sexes	Males	Females
All ages	47 432	23 291	24 141	48 289	23 856	24 434	49 126	24 462	24 664	50 290	25 216	25 074
0-4	5 223	2 640	2 583	5 430	2 747	2 683	5 527	2 798	2 729	5 653	2 863	2 790
5-9	5 140	2 593	2 547	5 046	2 548	2 498	5 267	2 662	2 605	5 413	2 738	2 675
10-14	5 102	2 568	2 534	5 052	2 546	2 505	4 901	2 473	2 428	5 134	2 593	2 541
15-19	4 897	2 463	2 434	5 094	2 566	2 528	5 033	2 539	2 494	4 877	2 463	2 414
20-24	4 727	2 382	2 345	4 811	2 430	2 381	5 017	2 538	2 478	4 964	2 514	2 449
25-29	3 962	2 002	1 960	4 291	2 203	2 088	4 447	2 284	2 163	4 666	2 397	2 269
30-34	3 436	1 710	1 726	3 247	1 700	1 547	3 619	1 930	1 689	3 824	2 032	1 792
35-39	3 074	1 490	1 583	2 752	1 408	1 345	2 587	1 415	1 172	2 972	1 649	1 323
40-44	2 731	1 314	1 417	2 533	1 238	1 296	2 219	1 164	1 054	2 125	1 194	931
45-49	2 377	1 133	1 244	2 341	1 116	1 225	2 126	1 043	1 083	1 879	994	886
50-54	2 005	950	1 055	2 097	979	1 119	2 038	959	1 079	1 861	905	956
55-59	1 547	722	825	1 791	824	967	1 862	847	1 015	1 819	837	982
60-64	1 199	538	660	1 366	612	754	1 582	700	882	1 655	727	929
65-69	858	364	494	1 019	431	588	1 167	494	673	1 363	571	791
70-74	568	227	341	684	267	417	820	321	499	950	373	577
75-79	331	121	209	413	148	265	505	177	328	613	216	397
80-84	168	52	116	208	67	141	265	83	182	331	101	229
85-89	68	17	51	84	22	62	106	29	77	138	37	102
90-94	18	4	14	25	5	20	32	7	25	41	9	32
95-99	3	0	3	4	1	4	6	1	5	8	1	7
100 +	0	0	0	0	0	0	1	0	1	1	0	1

Age group	2025			2030			2035			2040		
	Both sexes	Males	Females	Both sexes	Males	Females	Both sexes	Males	Females	Both sexes	Males	Females
All ages	51 498	25 967	25 531	52 735	26 696	26 038	54 095	27 454	26 640	55 661	28 299	27 363
0-4	5 583	2 829	2 754	5 523	2 800	2 723	5 548	2 814	2 734	5 639	2 860	2 778
5-9	5 573	2 821	2 752	5 529	2 800	2 728	5 487	2 781	2 706	5 522	2 800	2 722
10-14	5 323	2 691	2 632	5 512	2 789	2 723	5 489	2 779	2 710	5 462	2 767	2 695
15-19	5 116	2 587	2 530	5 313	2 689	2 624	5 507	2 789	2 718	5 488	2 782	2 706
20-24	4 816	2 442	2 374	5 058	2 566	2 492	5 259	2 670	2 589	5 458	2 774	2 684
25-29	4 638	2 380	2 259	4 522	2 316	2 206	4 778	2 443	2 335	4 995	2 554	2 441
30-34	4 054	2 145	1 909	4 068	2 136	1 931	4 011	2 091	1 920	4 288	2 224	2 064
35-39	3 190	1 756	1 434	3 426	1 865	1 562	3 484	1 869	1 615	3 487	1 847	1 640
40-44	2 487	1 413	1 074	2 707	1 517	1 190	2 944	1 622	1 322	3 035	1 640	1 395
45-49	1 825	1 032	793	2 163	1 235	928	2 379	1 335	1 044	2 618	1 439	1 178
50-54	1 659	871	789	1 625	913	713	1 943	1 100	843	2 157	1 198	959
55-59	1 673	797	876	1 501	774	727	1 478	816	662	1 780	991	789
60-64	1 628	725	903	1 507	696	811	1 358	681	678	1 344	724	621
65-69	1 439	600	839	1 426	605	821	1 328	586	742	1 202	578	624
70-74	1 121	437	683	1 195	465	730	1 194	474	720	1 120	465	655
75-79	720	255	464	860	304	556	928	328	600	936	339	597
80-84	408	126	282	486	152	335	590	183	407	644	201	444
85-89	176	46	130	223	58	165	272	71	201	336	88	249
90-94	55	12	44	73	15	58	95	19	76	118	24	94
95-99	11	2	9	15	2	13	21	3	18	28	4	24
100 +	1	0	1	2	0	2	3	0	2	4	0	3

Age group	2045			2050		
	Both sexes	Males	Females	Both sexes	Males	Females
All ages	57 434	29 238	28 196	59 393	30 257	29 136
0-4	5 717	2 901	2 816	5 754	2 920	2 834
5-9	5 620	2 851	2 770	5 704	2 894	2 810
10-14	5 507	2 791	2 716	5 611	2 845	2 766
15-19	5 464	2 772	2 693	5 512	2 797	2 714
20-24	5 446	2 770	2 676	5 429	2 763	2 666
25-29	5 215	2 667	2 548	5 233	2 677	2 556
30-34	4 536	2 348	2 188	4 791	2 477	2 315
35-39	3 783	1 988	1 796	4 062	2 126	1 936
40-44	3 082	1 640	1 441	3 392	1 789	1 603
45-49	2 730	1 470	1 260	2 805	1 487	1 318
50-54	2 395	1 303	1 092	2 522	1 344	1 178
55-59	1 991	1 088	903	2 227	1 193	1 034
60-64	1 628	885	743	1 833	979	854
65-69	1 195	620	575	1 456	765	691
70-74	1 019	464	555	1 017	503	515
75-79	884	337	548	808	340	468
80-84	657	211	446	626	212	414
85-89	374	98	277	387	104	283
90-94	150	30	120	171	34	137
95-99	36	5	31	47	7	41
100 +	5	0	5	7	1	6

United Nations Department of Economic and Social Affairs/Population Division
World Population Prospects: The 2004 Revision, Volume II: Sex and Age Distribution of the World Population

788

POPULATION BY AGE AND SEX (in thousands)

Age group	2005 Both sexes	2005 Males	2005 Females	2010 Both sexes	2010 Males	2010 Females	2015 Both sexes	2015 Males	2015 Females	2020 Both sexes	2020 Males	2020 Females
All ages	47 432	23 291	24 141	47 349	23 380	23 969	46 679	23 224	23 454	45 911	23 000	22 911
0-4	5 223	2 640	2 583	4 490	2 271	2 219	3 990	2 020	1 970	3 666	1 857	1 809
5-9	5 140	2 593	2 547	5 046	2 548	2 498	4 356	2 202	2 154	3 909	1 977	1 932
10-14	5 102	2 568	2 534	5 052	2 546	2 505	4 901	2 473	2 428	4 247	2 145	2 102
15-19	4 897	2 463	2 434	5 094	2 566	2 528	5 033	2 539	2 494	4 877	2 463	2 414
20-24	4 727	2 382	2 345	4 811	2 430	2 381	5 017	2 538	2 478	4 964	2 514	2 449
25-29	3 962	2 002	1 960	4 291	2 203	2 088	4 447	2 284	2 163	4 666	2 397	2 269
30-34	3 436	1 710	1 726	3 247	1 700	1 547	3 619	1 930	1 689	3 824	2 032	1 792
35-39	3 074	1 490	1 583	2 752	1 408	1 345	2 587	1 415	1 172	2 972	1 649	1 323
40-44	2 731	1 314	1 417	2 533	1 238	1 296	2 219	1 164	1 054	2 125	1 194	931
45-49	2 377	1 133	1 244	2 341	1 116	1 225	2 126	1 043	1 083	1 879	994	886
50-54	2 005	950	1 055	2 097	979	1 119	2 038	959	1 079	1 861	905	956
55-59	1 547	722	825	1 791	824	967	1 862	847	1 015	1 819	837	982
60-64	1 199	538	660	1 366	612	754	1 582	700	882	1 655	727	929
65-69	858	364	494	1 019	431	588	1 167	494	673	1 363	571	791
70-74	568	227	341	684	267	417	820	321	499	950	373	577
75-79	331	121	209	413	148	265	505	177	328	613	216	397
80-84	168	52	116	208	67	141	265	83	182	331	101	229
85-89	68	17	51	84	22	62	106	29	77	138	37	102
90-94	18	4	14	25	5	20	32	7	25	41	9	32
95-99	3	0	3	4	1	4	6	1	5	8	1	7
100 +	0	0	0	0	0	0	1	0	1	1	0	1

Age group	2025 Both sexes	2025 Males	2025 Females	2030 Both sexes	2030 Males	2030 Females	2035 Both sexes	2035 Males	2035 Females	2040 Both sexes	2040 Males	2040 Females
All ages	45 105	22 732	22 373	44 136	22 345	21 791	42 973	21 823	21 150	41 697	21 218	20 479
0-4	3 508	1 778	1 730	3 255	1 650	1 605	2 920	1 481	1 439	2 587	1 312	1 274
5-9	3 615	1 830	1 785	3 475	1 760	1 715	3 234	1 639	1 595	2 908	1 475	1 434
10-14	3 846	1 944	1 901	3 577	1 810	1 767	3 452	1 748	1 704	3 222	1 632	1 589
15-19	4 234	2 142	2 093	3 842	1 945	1 896	3 579	1 814	1 765	3 457	1 754	1 703
20-24	4 016	2 442	2 374	4 188	2 127	2 061	3 805	1 936	1 869	3 550	1 809	1 741
25-29	4 638	2 380	2 259	4 522	2 316	2 206	3 956	2 026	1 929	3 614	1 854	1 760
30-34	4 054	2 145	1 909	4 068	2 136	1 931	4 011	2 091	1 920	3 551	1 845	1 706
35-39	3 190	1 756	1 434	3 426	1 865	1 562	3 484	1 869	1 615	3 487	1 847	1 640
40-44	2 487	1 413	1 074	2 707	1 517	1 190	2 944	1 622	1 322	3 035	1 640	1 395
45-49	1 825	1 032	793	2 163	1 235	928	2 379	1 335	1 044	2 618	1 439	1 178
50-54	1 659	871	789	1 625	913	713	1 943	1 100	843	2 157	1 198	959
55-59	1 673	797	876	1 501	774	727	1 478	816	662	1 780	991	789
60-64	1 628	725	903	1 507	696	811	1 358	681	678	1 344	724	621
65-69	1 439	600	839	1 426	605	821	1 328	586	742	1 202	578	624
70-74	1 121	437	683	1 195	465	730	1 194	474	720	1 120	465	655
75-79	720	255	464	860	304	556	928	328	600	936	339	597
80-84	408	126	282	486	152	335	590	183	407	644	201	444
85-89	176	46	130	223	58	165	272	71	201	336	88	249
90-94	55	12	44	73	15	58	95	19	76	118	24	94
95-99	11	2	9	15	2	13	21	3	18	28	4	24
100 +	1	0	1	2	0	2	3	0	2	4	0	3

Age group	2045 Both sexes	2045 Males	2045 Females	2050 Both sexes	2050 Males	2050 Females
All ages	40 415	20 594	19 821	39 211	19 990	19 221
0-4	2 316	1 175	1 141	2 122	1 077	1 045
5-9	2 580	1 308	1 271	2 312	1 173	1 139
10-14	2 902	1 471	1 431	2 578	1 307	1 271
15-19	3 229	1 639	1 589	2 911	1 480	1 432
20-24	3 433	1 751	1 681	3 211	1 641	1 571
25-29	3 391	1 742	1 649	3 298	1 696	1 603
30-34	3 283	1 705	1 578	3 118	1 619	1 499
35-39	3 134	1 649	1 485	2 943	1 545	1 398
40-44	3 082	1 640	1 441	2 810	1 484	1 327
45-49	2 730	1 470	1 260	2 805	1 487	1 318
50-54	2 395	1 303	1 092	2 522	1 344	1 178
55-59	1 991	1 088	903	2 227	1 193	1 034
60-64	1 628	885	743	1 833	979	854
65-69	1 195	620	575	1 456	765	691
70-74	1 019	464	555	1 017	503	515
75-79	884	337	548	808	340	468
80-84	657	211	446	626	212	414
85-89	374	98	277	387	104	283
90-94	150	30	120	171	34	137
95-99	36	5	31	47	7	41
100 +	5	0	5	7	1	6

POPULATION BY AGE AND SEX (in thousands)

Age group	1950 Both sexes	Males	Females	1955 Both sexes	Males	Females	1960 Both sexes	Males	Females	1965 Both sexes	Males	Females
All ages	28 009	13 526	14 483	29 199	14 153	15 046	30 455	14 777	15 678	32 056	15 547	16 509
0-4	2 742	1 399	1 343	2 779	1 434	1 345	3 016	1 539	1 477	3 074	1 571	1 503
5-9	2 530	1 274	1 255	2 667	1 351	1 316	2 701	1 401	1 300	2 978	1 518	1 461
10-14	2 316	1 177	1 139	2 492	1 250	1 242	2 636	1 335	1 302	2 712	1 409	1 303
15-19	2 624	1 306	1 319	2 288	1 163	1 126	2 421	1 194	1 227	2 631	1 330	1 301
20-24	2 517	1 255	1 261	2 533	1 253	1 280	2 225	1 125	1 100	2 385	1 162	1 222
25-29	2 378	1 170	1 208	2 424	1 211	1 213	2 440	1 190	1 250	2 178	1 084	1 094
30-34	1 936	928	1 008	2 307	1 128	1 180	2 355	1 174	1 181	2 390	1 146	1 244
35-39	1 882	903	980	1 874	889	985	2 231	1 075	1 156	2 323	1 144	1 179
40-44	1 794	860	934	1 814	860	954	1 809	847	962	2 202	1 054	1 148
45-49	1 613	778	835	1 727	821	906	1 747	820	927	1 785	831	954
50-54	1 444	678	766	1 545	742	803	1 658	781	877	1 709	794	915
55-59	1 170	536	634	1 379	634	745	1 460	690	770	1 591	736	855
60-64	1 019	463	556	1 079	482	597	1 255	572	683	1 354	625	729
65-69	744	324	420	892	395	497	947	411	536	1 098	484	614
70-74	627	245	382	668	274	394	737	311	426	764	322	442
75-79	381	138	243	414	160	254	463	187	276	482	195	287
80 +	292	92	200	316	107	209	353	126	227	401	143	258

Age group	1970 Both sexes	Males	Females	1975 Both sexes	Males	Females	1980 Both sexes	Males	Females	1985 Both sexes	Males	Females
All ages	33 779	16 489	17 290	35 596	17 362	18 234	37 542	18 429	19 112	38 474	18 879	19 595
0-4	3 209	1 655	1 554	3 317	1 700	1 616	3 362	1 738	1 624	2 487	1 288	1 199
5-9	3 228	1 644	1 585	3 289	1 685	1 604	3 311	1 695	1 615	3 103	1 596	1 507
10-14	3 001	1 534	1 467	3 223	1 647	1 575	3 303	1 692	1 611	3 291	1 692	1 599
15-19	2 655	1 333	1 322	2 947	1 492	1 456	3 182	1 623	1 559	3 306	1 693	1 613
20-24	2 523	1 281	1 243	2 653	1 317	1 336	2 879	1 457	1 422	3 214	1 631	1 583
25-29	2 190	1 087	1 103	2 498	1 253	1 244	2 572	1 299	1 272	2 867	1 441	1 425
30-34	2 034	998	1 036	2 130	1 054	1 076	2 453	1 224	1 229	2 518	1 266	1 252
35-39	2 375	1 178	1 197	2 121	1 040	1 082	2 090	1 046	1 045	2 443	1 221	1 222
40-44	2 305	1 134	1 171	2 410	1 187	1 223	2 304	1 140	1 164	2 184	1 090	1 094
45-49	2 122	1 044	1 077	2 241	1 096	1 145	2 413	1 188	1 224	2 062	1 016	1 046
50-54	1 703	799	904	2 026	979	1 047	2 202	1 076	1 126	2 319	1 135	1 184
55-59	1 632	752	879	1 622	741	881	1 891	900	991	2 164	1 045	1 119
60-64	1 497	684	813	1 550	697	853	1 570	709	862	1 897	894	1 003
65-69	1 285	573	713	1 326	586	739	1 439	628	811	1 475	647	828
70-74	915	380	535	1 010	423	587	1 157	489	669	1 269	529	740
75-79	576	229	347	634	252	382	784	306	477	964	379	585
80 +	528	185	343	601	214	387	630	218	412	912	314	597

Age group	1990 Both sexes	Males	Females	1995 Both sexes	Males	Females	2000 Both sexes	Males	Females	2005 Both sexes	Males	Females
All ages	39 303	19 247	20 056	39 921	19 568	20 353	40 717	19 970	20 747	43 064	21 148	21 916
0-4	2 032	1 043	989	1 925	993	932	1 915	984	931	2 217	1 146	1 072
5-9	2 464	1 264	1 200	2 055	1 053	1 002	1 915	980	935	1 999	1 026	973
10-14	3 120	1 598	1 522	2 508	1 285	1 223	2 107	1 081	1 026	1 961	1 003	958
15-19	3 377	1 727	1 649	3 190	1 633	1 557	2 615	1 343	1 273	2 237	1 145	1 092
20-24	3 273	1 670	1 604	3 458	1 767	1 691	3 348	1 713	1 635	2 919	1 494	1 425
25-29	3 139	1 588	1 550	3 324	1 693	1 631	3 606	1 843	1 763	3 722	1 902	1 821
30-34	2 894	1 453	1 441	3 177	1 604	1 573	3 333	1 696	1 637	3 917	2 001	1 916
35-39	2 535	1 270	1 265	2 930	1 467	1 464	3 224	1 621	1 603	3 549	1 806	1 743
40-44	2 432	1 213	1 219	2 544	1 270	1 274	2 990	1 491	1 499	3 358	1 689	1 669
45-49	2 217	1 102	1 115	2 418	1 201	1 217	2 510	1 250	1 260	3 063	1 526	1 537
50-54	1 995	976	1 019	2 194	1 083	1 111	2 380	1 177	1 203	2 539	1 261	1 279
55-59	2 264	1 098	1 166	1 936	937	999	2 166	1 058	1 108	2 370	1 163	1 207
60-64	2 131	1 013	1 118	2 184	1 041	1 142	1 812	865	947	2 120	1 021	1 099
65-69	1 854	854	1 001	2 021	934	1 087	2 119	987	1 131	1 731	807	925
70-74	1 350	568	783	1 669	736	933	1 898	845	1 053	1 946	872	1 075
75-79	1 064	416	649	1 122	440	682	1 368	565	803	1 633	681	952
80 +	1 161	396	765	1 267	431	836	1 413	472	941	1 782	608	1 174

United Nations Department of Economic and Social Affairs/Population Division
World Population Prospects: The 2004 Revision, Volume II: Sex and Age Distribution of the World Population

790

POPULATION BY AGE AND SEX (in thousands)

Age group	2005 Both sexes	2005 Males	2005 Females	2010 Both sexes	2010 Males	2010 Females	2015 Both sexes	2015 Males	2015 Females	2020 Both sexes	2020 Males	2020 Females
All ages	43 064	21 148	21 916	43 993	21 597	22 397	44 372	21 774	22 598	44 419	21 794	22 626
0-4	2 217	1 146	1 072	2 323	1 201	1 122	2 188	1 131	1 057	1 947	1 007	940
5-9	1 999	1 026	973	2 241	1 157	1 084	2 334	1 207	1 128	2 199	1 137	1 062
10-14	1 961	1 003	958	2 012	1 032	980	2 247	1 160	1 087	2 340	1 209	1 131
15-19	2 237	1 145	1 092	1 998	1 021	977	2 029	1 040	989	2 264	1 168	1 096
20-24	2 919	1 494	1 425	2 324	1 188	1 136	2 040	1 041	999	2 072	1 061	1 011
25-29	3 722	1 902	1 821	3 025	1 546	1 479	2 376	1 213	1 163	2 093	1 067	1 026
30-34	3 917	2 001	1 916	3 806	1 941	1 864	3 063	1 563	1 500	2 417	1 232	1 185
35-39	3 549	1 806	1 743	3 968	2 023	1 944	3 824	1 947	1 877	3 086	1 572	1 514
40-44	3 358	1 689	1 669	3 572	1 814	1 758	3 968	2 018	1 949	3 826	1 944	1 882
45-49	3 063	1 526	1 537	3 358	1 684	1 674	3 558	1 801	1 757	3 952	2 004	1 948
50-54	2 539	1 261	1 279	3 041	1 506	1 534	3 325	1 658	1 667	3 526	1 775	1 750
55-59	2 370	1 163	1 207	2 499	1 229	1 270	2 989	1 468	1 521	3 272	1 618	1 653
60-64	2 120	1 021	1 099	2 302	1 113	1 190	2 428	1 178	1 250	2 908	1 410	1 498
65-69	1 731	807	925	2 017	948	1 069	2 193	1 036	1 157	2 319	1 101	1 217
70-74	1 946	872	1 075	1 592	714	878	1 860	843	1 017	2 030	928	1 102
75-79	1 633	681	952	1 682	708	974	1 385	585	800	1 629	698	930
80-84	1 052	395	656	1 270	483	787	1 325	509	815	1 105	428	677
85-89	508	157	352	674	220	454	836	276	560	893	299	594
90-94	186	48	138	238	59	178	330	87	244	428	113	315
95-99	35	8	27	49	10	39	70	13	57	106	20	86
100 +	1	0	1	3	0	2	5	0	5	9	1	9

Age group	2025 Both sexes	2025 Males	2025 Females	2030 Both sexes	2030 Males	2030 Females	2035 Both sexes	2035 Males	2035 Females	2040 Both sexes	2040 Males	2040 Females
All ages	44 244	21 701	22 544	44 008	21 569	22 439	43 796	21 437	22 358	43 561	21 288	22 274
0-4	1 783	922	861	1 786	923	862	1 910	987	922	2 032	1 051	981
5-9	1 958	1 012	946	1 795	928	867	1 798	929	868	1 921	993	928
10-14	2 205	1 140	1 066	1 965	1 015	949	1 801	931	870	1 804	932	872
15-19	2 358	1 218	1 140	2 223	1 148	1 075	1 983	1 024	959	1 820	940	880
20-24	2 307	1 189	1 118	2 401	1 239	1 162	2 267	1 169	1 097	2 027	1 046	981
25-29	2 125	1 087	1 038	2 360	1 215	1 145	2 454	1 265	1 189	2 320	1 196	1 124
30-34	2 135	1 087	1 048	2 168	1 108	1 060	2 403	1 236	1 167	2 497	1 286	1 211
35-39	2 442	1 244	1 199	2 163	1 100	1 062	2 196	1 121	1 075	2 430	1 248	1 182
40-44	3 094	1 573	1 521	2 455	1 248	1 207	2 177	1 106	1 071	2 210	1 127	1 084
45-49	3 014	1 932	1 882	3 088	1 566	1 522	2 455	1 245	1 210	2 179	1 105	1 075
50-54	3 919	1 978	1 941	3 785	1 909	1 876	3 069	1 550	1 519	2 440	1 234	1 206
55-59	3 472	1 736	1 736	3 862	1 936	1 926	3 735	1 872	1 863	3 032	1 523	1 509
60-64	3 188	1 559	1 629	3 388	1 675	1 713	3 774	1 873	1 901	3 654	1 815	1 839
65-69	2 783	1 323	1 460	3 058	1 468	1 590	3 256	1 584	1 672	3 634	1 776	1 858
70-74	2 154	992	1 162	2 595	1 198	1 397	2 860	1 336	1 523	3 054	1 449	1 606
75-79	1 789	776	1 013	1 909	837	1 072	2 313	1 019	1 293	2 562	1 146	1 416
80-84	1 313	519	794	1 457	584	873	1 570	639	932	1 920	787	1 132
85-89	762	258	504	923	320	603	1 043	369	675	1 144	411	732
90-94	477	128	349	423	115	308	529	148	381	616	176	440
95-99	149	28	121	178	33	145	168	32	136	221	43	178
100 +	17	1	15	27	2	26	38	3	35	41	3	38

Age group	2045 Both sexes	2045 Males	2045 Females	2050 Both sexes	2050 Males	2050 Females
All ages	43 185	21 068	22 117	42 541	20 717	21 824
0-4	2 058	1 064	994	1 951	1 009	942
5-9	2 043	1 056	987	2 070	1 070	1 000
10-14	1 928	996	931	2 050	1 059	990
15-19	1 823	941	881	1 947	1 005	941
20-24	1 864	962	902	1 867	963	904
25-29	2 081	1 073	1 008	1 919	989	930
30-34	2 364	1 217	1 146	2 126	1 095	1 031
35-39	2 525	1 299	1 226	2 393	1 231	1 162
40-44	2 445	1 254	1 190	2 540	1 305	1 235
45-49	2 214	1 126	1 087	2 448	1 253	1 194
50-54	2 171	1 097	1 074	2 206	1 119	1 087
55-59	2 417	1 215	1 202	2 151	1 082	1 069
60-64	2 971	1 480	1 492	2 372	1 183	1 189
65-69	3 526	1 726	1 800	2 873	1 412	1 461
70-74	3 419	1 632	1 787	3 327	1 593	1 734
75-79	2 749	1 251	1 497	3 092	1 420	1 672
80-84	2 144	896	1 249	2 319	989	1 330
85-89	1 422	518	904	1 612	601	1 011
90-94	695	204	491	887	265	622
95-99	270	54	216	319	66	252
100 +	57	5	52	77	7	69

United Nations Department of Economic and Social Affairs/Population Division
World Population Prospects: The 2004 Revision, Volume II: Sex and Age Distribution of the World Population

791

POPULATION BY AGE AND SEX (in thousands)

Age group	2005 Both sexes	2005 Males	2005 Females	2010 Both sexes	2010 Males	2010 Females	2015 Both sexes	2015 Males	2015 Females	2020 Both sexes	2020 Males	2020 Females
All ages	43 064	21 148	21 916	44 412	21 813	22 599	45 366	22 288	23 078	46 006	22 614	23 392
0-4	2 217	1 146	1 072	2 742	1 418	1 324	2 764	1 429	1 335	2 541	1 314	1 227
5-9	1 999	1 026	973	2 241	1 157	1 084	2 752	1 423	1 330	2 775	1 434	1 340
10-14	1 961	1 003	958	2 012	1 032	980	2 247	1 160	1 087	2 758	1 425	1 333
15-19	2 237	1 145	1 092	1 998	1 021	977	2 029	1 040	989	2 264	1 168	1 096
20-24	2 919	1 494	1 425	2 324	1 188	1 136	2 040	1 041	999	2 072	1 061	1 011
25-29	3 722	1 902	1 821	3 025	1 546	1 479	2 376	1 213	1 163	2 093	1 067	1 026
30-34	3 917	2 001	1 916	3 806	1 941	1 864	3 063	1 563	1 500	2 417	1 232	1 185
35-39	3 549	1 806	1 743	3 968	2 023	1 944	3 824	1 947	1 877	3 086	1 572	1 514
40-44	3 358	1 689	1 669	3 572	1 814	1 758	3 968	2 018	1 949	3 826	1 944	1 882
45-49	3 063	1 526	1 537	3 358	1 684	1 674	3 558	1 801	1 757	3 952	2 004	1 948
50-54	2 539	1 261	1 279	3 041	1 506	1 534	3 325	1 658	1 667	3 526	1 775	1 750
55-59	2 370	1 163	1 207	2 499	1 229	1 270	2 989	1 468	1 521	3 272	1 618	1 653
60-64	2 120	1 021	1 099	2 302	1 113	1 190	2 428	1 178	1 250	2 908	1 410	1 498
65-69	1 731	807	925	2 017	948	1 069	2 193	1 036	1 157	2 319	1 101	1 217
70-74	1 946	872	1 075	1 592	714	878	1 860	843	1 017	2 030	928	1 102
75-79	1 633	681	952	1 682	708	974	1 385	585	800	1 629	698	930
80-84	1 052	395	656	1 270	483	787	1 325	509	815	1 105	428	677
85-89	508	157	352	674	220	454	836	276	560	893	299	594
90-94	186	48	138	238	59	178	330	87	244	428	113	315
95-99	35	8	27	49	10	39	70	13	57	106	20	86
100 +	1	0	1	3	0	2	5	0	5	9	1	9

Age group	2025 Both sexes	2025 Males	2025 Females	2030 Both sexes	2030 Males	2030 Females	2035 Both sexes	2035 Males	2035 Females	2040 Both sexes	2040 Males	2040 Females
All ages	46 362	22 796	23 567	46 697	22 959	23 738	47 207	23 201	24 007	47 901	23 530	24 371
0-4	2 315	1 197	1 118	2 359	1 220	1 139	2 634	1 362	1 272	2 963	1 532	1 431
5-9	2 552	1 319	1 233	2 327	1 203	1 124	2 370	1 225	1 145	2 646	1 368	1 278
10-14	2 781	1 437	1 343	2 558	1 322	1 236	2 333	1 206	1 127	2 376	1 228	1 148
15-19	2 776	1 434	1 342	2 798	1 446	1 353	2 576	1 331	1 245	2 351	1 214	1 137
20-24	2 307	1 189	1 118	2 818	1 454	1 364	2 841	1 466	1 375	2 619	1 352	1 267
25-29	2 125	1 087	1 038	2 360	1 215	1 145	2 870	1 479	1 391	2 894	1 492	1 402
30-34	2 135	1 087	1 048	2 168	1 108	1 060	2 403	1 236	1 167	2 912	1 500	1 413
35-39	2 442	1 244	1 199	2 163	1 100	1 062	2 196	1 121	1 075	2 430	1 248	1 182
40-44	3 094	1 573	1 521	2 455	1 248	1 207	2 177	1 106	1 071	2 210	1 127	1 084
45-49	3 814	1 932	1 882	3 088	1 566	1 522	2 455	1 245	1 210	2 179	1 105	1 075
50-54	3 919	1 978	1 941	3 785	1 909	1 876	3 069	1 550	1 519	2 443	1 234	1 208
55-59	3 472	1 736	1 736	3 862	1 936	1 926	3 735	1 872	1 863	3 032	1 523	1 509
60-64	3 188	1 559	1 629	3 388	1 675	1 713	3 774	1 873	1 901	3 654	1 815	1 839
65-69	2 783	1 323	1 460	3 058	1 468	1 590	3 256	1 584	1 672	3 634	1 776	1 858
70-74	2 154	992	1 162	2 595	1 198	1 397	2 860	1 336	1 523	3 054	1 449	1 606
75-79	1 789	776	1 013	1 909	837	1 072	2 313	1 019	1 293	2 562	1 146	1 416
80-84	1 313	519	794	1 457	584	873	1 570	639	932	1 920	787	1 132
85-89	762	258	504	923	320	603	1 043	369	675	1 144	411	732
90-94	477	128	349	423	115	308	529	148	381	616	176	440
95-99	149	28	121	178	33	145	168	32	136	221	43	178
100 +	17	1	15	27	2	25	38	3	35	41	3	38

Age group	2045 Both sexes	2045 Males	2045 Females	2050 Both sexes	2050 Males	2050 Females
All ages	48 597	23 864	24 733	49 055	24 082	24 973
0-4	3 135	1 621	1 514	3 058	1 581	1 477
5-9	2 974	1 538	1 437	3 146	1 627	1 520
10-14	2 652	1 371	1 281	2 980	1 541	1 440
15-19	2 395	1 237	1 158	2 670	1 380	1 291
20-24	2 395	1 236	1 159	2 439	1 259	1 180
25-29	2 672	1 378	1 294	2 449	1 263	1 186
30-34	2 936	1 513	1 424	2 716	1 399	1 317
35-39	2 939	1 512	1 427	2 964	1 525	1 438
40-44	2 445	1 254	1 190	2 952	1 517	1 436
45-49	2 214	1 126	1 087	2 448	1 253	1 194
50-54	2 171	1 097	1 074	2 206	1 119	1 087
55-59	2 417	1 215	1 202	2 151	1 082	1 069
60-64	2 971	1 480	1 492	2 372	1 183	1 189
65-69	3 526	1 726	1 800	2 873	1 412	1 461
70-74	3 419	1 632	1 787	3 327	1 593	1 734
75-79	2 749	1 251	1 497	3 092	1 420	1 672
80-84	2 144	896	1 249	2 319	989	1 330
85-89	1 422	518	904	1 612	601	1 011
90-94	695	204	491	887	265	622
95-99	270	54	216	319	66	252
100 +	57	5	52	77	7	69

United Nations Department of Economic and Social Affairs/Population Division
World Population Prospects: The 2004 Revision, Volume II: Sex and Age Distribution of the World Population

792

POPULATION BY AGE AND SEX (in thousands)

Age group	2005 Both sexes	2005 Males	2005 Females	2010 Both sexes	2010 Males	2010 Females	2015 Both sexes	2015 Males	2015 Females	2020 Both sexes	2020 Males	2020 Females
All ages	43 064	21 148	21 916	43 571	21 378	22 193	43 356	21 249	22 107	42 783	20 947	21 835
0-4	2 217	1 146	1 072	1 901	983	918	1 594	824	770	1 326	686	640
5-9	1 999	1 026	973	2 241	1 157	1 084	1 912	988	924	1 605	830	776
10-14	1 961	1 003	958	2 012	1 032	980	2 247	1 160	1 087	1 918	991	927
15-19	2 237	1 145	1 092	1 998	1 021	977	2 029	1 040	989	2 264	1 168	1 096
20-24	2 919	1 494	1 425	2 324	1 188	1 136	2 040	1 041	999	2 072	1 061	1 011
25-29	3 722	1 902	1 821	3 025	1 546	1 479	2 376	1 213	1 163	2 093	1 067	1 026
30-34	3 917	2 001	1 916	3 806	1 941	1 864	3 063	1 563	1 500	2 417	1 232	1 185
35-39	3 549	1 806	1 743	3 968	2 023	1 944	3 824	1 947	1 877	3 086	1 572	1 514
40-44	3 358	1 689	1 669	3 572	1 814	1 758	3 968	2 018	1 949	3 826	1 944	1 882
45-49	3 063	1 526	1 537	3 358	1 684	1 674	3 558	1 801	1 757	3 952	2 004	1 948
50-54	2 539	1 261	1 279	3 041	1 506	1 534	3 325	1 658	1 667	3 526	1 775	1 750
55-59	2 370	1 163	1 207	2 499	1 229	1 270	2 989	1 468	1 521	3 272	1 618	1 653
60-64	2 120	1 021	1 099	2 302	1 113	1 190	2 428	1 178	1 250	2 908	1 410	1 498
65-69	1 731	807	925	2 017	948	1 069	2 193	1 036	1 157	2 319	1 101	1 217
70-74	1 946	872	1 075	1 592	714	878	1 860	843	1 017	2 030	928	1 102
75-79	1 633	681	952	1 682	708	974	1 385	585	800	1 629	698	930
80-84	1 052	395	656	1 270	483	787	1 325	509	815	1 105	428	677
85-89	508	157	352	674	220	454	836	276	560	893	299	594
90-94	186	48	138	238	59	178	330	87	244	428	113	315
95-99	35	8	27	49	10	39	70	13	57	106	20	86
100 +	1	0	1	0	0	2	5	0	5	0	1	9

Age group	2025 Both sexes	2025 Males	2025 Females	2030 Both sexes	2030 Males	2030 Females	2035 Both sexes	2035 Males	2035 Females	2040 Both sexes	2040 Males	2040 Females
All ages	42 063	20 573	21 490	41 280	20 159	21 121	40 451	19 708	20 742	39 489	19 183	20 306
0-4	1 238	640	598	1 238	640	598	1 290	667	623	1 301	673	628
5-9	1 338	691	646	1 250	646	604	1 250	646	604	1 302	673	629
10-14	1 612	833	779	1 344	695	650	1 256	649	607	1 256	649	607
15-19	1 937	1 000	937	1 630	842	788	1 363	704	659	1 275	658	617
20-24	2 307	1 189	1 118	1 980	1 021	959	1 674	863	811	1 408	726	682
25-29	2 125	1 087	1 038	2 360	1 215	1 145	2 034	1 048	986	1 729	891	838
30-34	2 135	1 007	1 048	2 168	1 108	1 060	2 403	1 236	1 167	2 078	1 069	1 008
35-39	2 442	1 244	1 199	2 163	1 100	1 062	2 196	1 121	1 075	2 400	1 218	1 182
40-44	3 094	1 573	1 521	2 455	1 248	1 207	2 177	1 106	1 071	2 210	1 127	1 084
45-49	3 814	1 932	1 882	3 088	1 566	1 522	2 455	1 245	1 210	2 179	1 105	1 075
50-54	3 919	1 978	1 941	3 785	1 909	1 876	3 069	1 550	1 519	2 443	1 234	1 208
55-59	3 472	1 736	1 736	3 862	1 936	1 926	3 735	1 872	1 863	3 032	1 523	1 509
60-64	3 188	1 559	1 629	3 388	1 675	1 713	3 774	1 873	1 901	3 654	1 815	1 839
65-69	2 783	1 323	1 460	3 058	1 468	1 590	3 256	1 584	1 672	3 634	1 776	1 858
70-74	2 154	992	1 162	2 595	1 198	1 397	2 860	1 336	1 523	3 054	1 449	1 606
75-79	1 789	776	1 013	1 909	837	1 072	2 313	1 019	1 293	2 562	1 146	1 416
80-84	1 313	519	794	1 457	584	873	1 570	639	932	1 920	787	1 132
85-89	762	258	504	923	320	603	1 043	369	675	1 144	411	732
90-94	477	128	349	423	115	308	529	148	381	616	176	440
95-99	149	28	121	178	33	145	168	32	136	221	43	178
100 +	17	1	16	27	2	25	38	3	35	41	3	38

Age group	2045 Both sexes	2045 Males	2045 Females	2050 Both sexes	2050 Males	2050 Females
All ages	38 288	18 538	19 750	36 792	17 748	19 044
0-4	1 229	636	594	1 092	564	527
5-9	1 313	679	635	1 241	642	600
10-14	1 308	676	632	1 320	682	638
15-19	1 276	659	617	1 328	685	642
20-24	1 320	681	639	1 320	681	640
25-29	1 463	753	709	1 375	708	667
30-34	1 773	913	860	1 508	776	732
35-39	2 107	1 083	1 023	1 804	928	876
40-44	2 445	1 254	1 190	2 123	1 090	1 032
45-49	2 214	1 126	1 087	2 448	1 253	1 194
50-54	2 171	1 097	1 074	2 206	1 119	1 087
55-59	2 417	1 215	1 202	2 151	1 082	1 069
60-64	2 971	1 480	1 492	2 372	1 183	1 189
65-69	3 526	1 726	1 800	2 873	1 412	1 461
70-74	3 419	1 632	1 787	3 327	1 593	1 734
75-79	2 749	1 251	1 497	3 092	1 420	1 672
80-84	2 144	896	1 249	2 319	989	1 330
85-89	1 422	518	904	1 612	601	1 011
90-94	695	204	491	887	265	622
95-99	270	54	216	319	66	252
100 +	57	5	52	77	7	69

United Nations Department of Economic and Social Affairs/Population Division
World Population Prospects: The 2004 Revision, Volume II: Sex and Age Distribution of the World Population

793

POPULATION BY AGE AND SEX (in thousands)

Age group	1950 Both sexes	Males	Females	1955 Both sexes	Males	Females	1960 Both sexes	Males	Females	1965 Both sexes	Males	Females
All ages	7 782	4 094	3 688	8 805	4 620	4 185	10 066	5 265	4 800	11 348	5 915	5 433
0-4	1 258	669	589	1 462	752	710	1 687	866	821	1 737	887	850
5-9	1 008	501	507	1 207	646	561	1 411	729	681	1 636	842	794
10-14	859	433	427	995	496	499	1 193	639	554	1 396	722	674
15-19	737	368	368	847	427	419	982	490	492	1 177	631	545
20-24	715	348	367	721	361	360	831	420	411	959	480	479
25-29	594	340	254	696	340	356	705	354	351	806	409	397
30-34	497	258	239	577	331	246	679	332	346	682	344	339
35-39	439	250	188	481	251	230	561	322	238	656	322	334
40-44	347	202	145	422	241	181	464	242	222	540	311	229
45-49	308	168	140	330	192	138	404	230	173	444	231	212
50-54	258	160	98	289	157	132	311	180	131	382	217	165
55-59	190	107	82	236	146	90	266	144	122	289	166	123
60-64	144	83	61	167	94	73	209	128	81	238	127	111
65-69	134	57	77	119	68	51	140	77	62	176	107	70
70-74	131	67	64	102	42	59	91	51	40	108	59	49
75-79	92	47	45	85	43	42	67	27	40	61	33	27
80 +	71	35	36	70	34	36	67	33	35	60	26	34

Age group	1970 Both sexes	Males	Females	1975 Both sexes	Males	Females	1980 Both sexes	Males	Females	1985 Both sexes	Males	Females
All ages	12 734	6 603	6 131	14 042	7 248	6 794	15 235	7 854	7 382	16 437	8 464	7 973
0-4	1 829	931	899	1 805	917	888	1 932	980	952	2 002	1 015	988
5-9	1 696	867	829	1 795	913	882	1 766	896	870	1 896	961	935
10-14	1 623	835	787	1 684	861	823	1 776	903	873	1 748	887	861
15-19	1 380	715	666	1 605	826	779	1 649	845	804	1 739	887	852
20-24	1 155	620	534	1 352	701	651	1 533	795	738	1 570	811	759
25-29	936	469	467	1 123	605	518	1 267	664	602	1 437	754	683
30-34	785	399	386	909	456	453	1 050	573	477	1 185	629	556
35-39	663	335	329	762	388	374	853	432	422	988	545	443
40-44	636	312	324	642	324	318	719	368	352	808	410	397
45-49	521	299	221	613	300	313	607	307	300	682	349	333
50-54	424	220	204	496	284	212	588	286	302	585	294	291
55-59	357	201	155	396	204	193	476	269	206	569	274	295
60-64	261	148	113	323	180	143	368	186	182	445	248	197
65-69	204	107	97	224	125	99	284	155	129	329	162	166
70-74	138	82	56	161	82	79	181	99	83	234	124	110
75-79	73	39	35	95	55	40	115	57	58	131	69	62
80 +	54	26	28	58	28	30	71	37	34	89	43	45

Age group	1990 Both sexes	Males	Females	1995 Both sexes	Males	Females	2000 Both sexes	Males	Females	2005 Both sexes	Males	Females
All ages	17 786	9 114	8 672	18 872	9 642	9 230	19 848	10 111	9 736	20 743	10 541	10 202
0-4	1 830	927	902	1 757	890	867	1 648	836	812	1 628	826	802
5-9	1 990	1 007	983	1 812	917	895	1 743	882	861	1 634	828	806
10-14	1 890	957	933	1 981	1 002	979	1 804	913	891	1 735	878	857
15-19	1 740	882	858	1 871	948	923	1 964	994	970	1 788	905	883
20-24	1 725	879	846	1 701	865	837	1 837	932	904	1 930	979	952
25-29	1 554	802	751	1 677	857	820	1 660	846	814	1 795	914	881
30-34	1 422	746	676	1 512	783	729	1 640	840	800	1 624	830	794
35-39	1 171	621	550	1 388	730	658	1 482	769	713	1 611	826	785
40-44	974	537	437	1 143	607	536	1 362	716	646	1 457	756	701
45-49	791	401	390	948	522	426	1 118	593	526	1 336	701	635
50-54	663	338	325	770	388	382	925	507	418	1 094	577	517
55-59	560	279	281	640	322	318	745	372	374	896	487	410
60-64	530	251	279	527	258	269	605	299	305	706	346	360
65-69	396	216	180	478	220	257	478	228	250	552	266	285
70-74	272	130	142	330	175	156	406	180	226	409	188	222
75-79	171	87	84	203	93	110	249	126	123	313	131	182
80 +	106	52	54	135	65	70	181	78	103	234	103	131

United Nations Department of Economic and Social Affairs/Population Division
World Population Prospects: The 2004 Revision, Volume II: Sex and Age Distribution of the World Population

794

POPULATION BY AGE AND SEX (in thousands)

Age group	2005 Both sexes	Males	Females	2010 Both sexes	Males	Females	2015 Both sexes	Males	Females	2020 Both sexes	Males	Females
All ages	20 743	10 541	10 202	21 557	10 931	10 626	22 293	11 282	11 011	22 902	11 567	11 335
0-4	1 628	826	802	1 592	809	783	1 579	803	776	1 525	776	749
5-9	1 634	828	806	1 617	820	796	1 581	804	778	1 569	798	771
10-14	1 735	878	857	1 628	825	803	1 611	817	794	1 576	801	775
15-19	1 788	905	883	1 722	872	850	1 615	819	796	1 598	811	787
20-24	1 930	979	952	1 759	892	867	1 694	859	834	1 588	807	781
25-29	1 795	914	881	1 894	963	932	1 724	877	847	1 660	845	815
30-34	1 624	830	794	1 764	900	864	1 863	949	915	1 695	864	830
35-39	1 611	826	785	1 599	818	781	1 739	888	851	1 839	938	901
40-44	1 457	756	701	1 589	815	774	1 577	807	770	1 718	878	840
45-49	1 336	701	635	1 433	743	691	1 565	802	763	1 556	796	760
50-54	1 094	577	517	1 306	683	623	1 404	725	679	1 536	785	751
55-59	896	487	410	1 056	553	504	1 265	657	608	1 363	699	664
60-64	706	346	360	847	454	394	1 003	517	485	1 205	617	588
65-69	552	266	285	646	309	337	778	407	371	926	467	459
70-74	409	188	222	475	221	255	561	258	303	678	343	336
75-79	313	131	182	320	138	182	376	164	212	449	194	255
80-84	158	75	84	207	79	128	215	84	131	257	101	156
85-89	61	23	38	79	32	46	108	35	74	116	37	78
90-94	14	5	9	21	6	14	28	9	19	41	10	32
95-99	2	1	1	3	1	2	5	1	4	7	1	5
100 +	0	0	0	0	0	0	0	0	0	1	0	1

Age group	2025 Both sexes	Males	Females	2030 Both sexes	Males	Females	2035 Both sexes	Males	Females	2040 Both sexes	Males	Females
All ages	23 358	11 769	11 590	23 667	11 892	11 775	23 838	11 944	11 894	23 875	11 930	11 945
0-4	1 457	742	715	1 401	714	687	1 363	694	669	1 333	679	654
5-9	1 515	771	744	1 448	737	710	1 392	709	683	1 354	690	664
10-14	1 564	795	768	1 510	769	741	1 443	735	708	1 386	706	680
15-19	1 564	795	768	1 552	790	762	1 498	764	735	1 431	730	701
20-24	1 571	800	771	1 537	784	753	1 525	779	746	1 472	753	719
25-29	1 554	793	761	1 538	786	752	1 504	770	734	1 493	765	727
30-34	1 631	832	798	1 526	781	745	1 510	774	736	1 476	758	718
35-39	1 672	854	818	1 608	822	786	1 504	771	733	1 488	764	724
40-44	1 819	928	891	1 652	845	808	1 590	813	776	1 486	763	723
45-49	1 697	867	830	1 797	917	881	1 633	834	799	1 571	804	768
50-54	1 529	780	749	1 669	850	819	1 770	900	870	1 609	820	789
55-59	1 494	758	736	1 490	755	735	1 629	825	804	1 730	876	855
60-64	1 303	659	644	1 433	718	715	1 432	717	714	1 570	787	783
65-69	1 118	560	558	1 214	601	612	1 341	659	682	1 345	662	683
70-74	814	396	418	990	479	511	1 084	520	564	1 205	574	631
75-79	545	260	286	664	305	359	818	375	443	905	412	493
80-84	313	121	192	385	166	219	480	200	280	602	252	350
85-89	142	46	96	179	57	122	225	82	143	290	103	187
90-94	46	10	36	60	14	46	79	18	60	101	28	73
95-99	11	1	9	13	2	11	18	2	15	25	4	21
100 +	1	0	1	2	0	2	2	0	2	3	0	3

Age group	2045 Both sexes	Males	Females	2050 Both sexes	Males	Females
All ages	23 779	11 853	11 925	23 554	11 720	11 834
0-4	1 298	662	637	1 254	639	615
5-9	1 324	675	649	1 289	657	632
10-14	1 349	687	662	1 319	672	647
15-19	1 375	702	673	1 337	682	655
20-24	1 405	719	686	1 349	691	658
25-29	1 440	739	701	1 373	706	667
30-34	1 465	753	711	1 412	728	685
35-39	1 455	749	706	1 444	744	700
40-44	1 471	756	715	1 438	741	697
45-49	1 469	754	715	1 454	747	707
50-54	1 549	791	758	1 449	742	707
55-59	1 575	799	776	1 517	771	746
60-64	1 671	837	834	1 523	766	757
65-69	1 480	729	751	1 580	779	801
70-74	1 216	581	635	1 345	645	700
75-79	1 016	461	555	1 034	472	562
80-84	677	283	394	772	323	449
85-89	373	134	239	430	156	274
90-94	136	37	99	182	51	131
95-99	32	6	26	46	8	38
100 +	5	0	4	6	1	6

POPULATION BY AGE AND SEX (in thousands)

Age group	2005 Both sexes	Males	Females	2010 Both sexes	Males	Females	2015 Both sexes	Males	Females	2020 Both sexes	Males	Females
All ages	20 743	10 541	10 202	21 772	11 040	10 732	22 850	11 565	11 285	23 872	12 060	11 812
0-4	1 628	826	802	1 807	918	888	1 922	978	944	1 939	987	952
5-9	1 634	828	806	1 617	820	796	1 796	912	883	1 911	972	939
10-14	1 735	878	857	1 628	825	803	1 611	817	794	1 790	909	881
15-19	1 788	905	883	1 722	872	850	1 615	819	796	1 598	811	787
20-24	1 930	979	952	1 759	892	867	1 694	859	834	1 588	807	781
25-29	1 795	914	881	1 894	963	932	1 724	877	847	1 660	845	815
30-34	1 624	830	794	1 764	900	864	1 863	949	915	1 695	864	830
35-39	1 611	826	785	1 599	818	781	1 739	888	851	1 839	938	901
40-44	1 457	756	701	1 589	815	774	1 577	807	770	1 718	878	840
45-49	1 336	701	635	1 433	743	691	1 565	802	763	1 556	796	760
50-54	1 094	577	517	1 306	683	623	1 404	725	679	1 536	785	751
55-59	896	487	410	1 056	553	504	1 265	657	608	1 363	699	664
60-64	706	346	360	847	454	394	1 003	517	485	1 205	617	588
65-69	552	266	285	646	309	337	778	407	371	926	467	459
70-74	409	188	222	475	221	255	561	258	303	678	343	336
75-79	313	131	182	320	138	182	376	164	212	449	194	255
80-84	158	75	84	207	79	128	215	84	131	257	101	156
85-89	61	23	38	79	32	46	108	35	74	116	37	78
90-94	14	5	9	21	6	14	28	9	19	41	10	32
95-99	2	1	1	3	1	2	5	1	4	7	1	5
100 +	0	0	0	0	0	0	0	0	0	1	0	1

Age group	2025 Both sexes	Males	Females	2030 Both sexes	Males	Females	2035 Both sexes	Males	Females	2040 Both sexes	Males	Females
All ages	24 729	12 466	12 263	25 459	12 804	12 655	26 136	13 114	13 023	26 801	13 419	13 382
0-4	1 858	947	912	1 823	929	894	1 871	953	918	1 963	1 000	963
5-9	1 929	982	947	1 848	941	907	1 814	924	890	1 862	948	913
10-14	1 906	969	937	1 923	979	944	1 843	939	904	1 808	921	887
15-19	1 778	904	874	1 893	964	930	1 911	974	937	1 831	933	897
20-24	1 571	800	771	1 751	892	858	1 866	952	914	1 884	962	922
25-29	1 554	793	761	1 538	786	752	1 717	879	839	1 833	938	895
30-34	1 631	832	798	1 526	781	745	1 510	774	736	1 689	866	823
35-39	1 672	854	818	1 608	822	786	1 504	771	733	1 488	764	724
40-44	1 819	928	891	1 652	845	808	1 590	813	776	1 486	763	723
45-49	1 697	867	830	1 797	917	881	1 633	834	799	1 571	804	768
50-54	1 529	780	749	1 669	850	819	1 770	900	870	1 609	820	789
55-59	1 494	758	736	1 490	755	735	1 629	825	804	1 730	876	855
60-64	1 303	659	644	1 433	718	715	1 432	717	714	1 570	787	783
65-69	1 118	560	558	1 214	601	612	1 341	659	682	1 345	662	683
70-74	814	396	418	990	479	511	1 084	520	564	1 205	574	631
75-79	545	260	286	664	305	359	818	375	443	905	412	493
80-84	313	121	192	385	166	219	480	200	280	602	252	350
85-89	142	46	96	179	57	122	225	82	143	290	103	187
90-94	46	10	36	60	14	46	79	18	60	101	28	73
95-99	11	1	9	13	2	11	18	2	15	25	4	21
100 +	1	0	1	2	0	2	2	0	2	3	0	3

Age group	2045 Both sexes	Males	Females	2050 Both sexes	Males	Females
All ages	27 431	13 712	13 719	27 982	13 973	14 009
0-4	2 028	1 033	995	2 035	1 037	998
5-9	1 954	995	958	2 018	1 028	990
10-14	1 856	946	911	1 949	993	956
15-19	1 796	916	880	1 845	941	904
20-24	1 804	922	882	1 770	905	865
25-29	1 851	949	903	1 772	909	863
30-34	1 805	926	879	1 823	936	887
35-39	1 667	856	810	1 783	916	867
40-44	1 471	756	715	1 649	848	801
45-49	1 469	754	715	1 454	747	707
50-54	1 549	791	758	1 449	742	707
55-59	1 575	799	776	1 517	771	746
60-64	1 671	837	834	1 523	766	757
65-69	1 480	729	751	1 580	779	801
70-74	1 216	581	635	1 345	645	700
75-79	1 016	461	555	1 034	472	562
80-84	677	283	394	772	323	449
85-89	373	134	239	430	156	274
90-94	136	37	99	182	51	131
95-99	32	6	26	46	8	38
100 +	5	0	4	6	1	6

United Nations Department of Economic and Social Affairs/Population Division
World Population Prospects: The 2004 Revision, Volume II: Sex and Age Distribution of the World Population

796

POPULATION BY AGE AND SEX (in thousands)

Age group	2005 Both sexes	Males	Females	2010 Both sexes	Males	Females	2015 Both sexes	Males	Females	2020 Both sexes	Males	Females
All ages	20 743	10 541	10 202	21 343	10 822	10 521	21 735	10 999	10 737	21 932	11 073	10 850
0-4	1 628	826	802	1 377	700	677	1 237	629	608	1 112	566	546
5-9	1 634	828	806	1 617	820	796	1 367	695	672	1 227	624	603
10-14	1 735	878	857	1 628	825	803	1 611	817	794	1 361	692	670
15-19	1 788	905	883	1 722	872	850	1 615	819	796	1 598	811	787
20-24	1 930	979	952	1 759	892	867	1 694	859	834	1 588	807	781
25-29	1 795	914	881	1 894	963	932	1 724	877	847	1 660	845	815
30-34	1 624	830	794	1 764	900	864	1 863	949	915	1 695	864	830
35-39	1 611	826	785	1 599	818	781	1 739	888	851	1 839	938	901
40-44	1 457	756	701	1 589	815	774	1 577	807	770	1 718	878	840
45-49	1 336	701	635	1 433	743	691	1 565	802	763	1 556	796	760
50-54	1 094	577	517	1 306	683	623	1 404	725	679	1 536	785	751
55-59	896	487	410	1 056	553	504	1 265	657	608	1 363	699	664
60-64	706	346	360	847	454	394	1 003	517	485	1 205	617	588
65-69	552	266	285	646	309	337	778	407	371	926	467	459
70-74	409	188	222	475	221	255	561	258	303	678	343	336
75-79	313	131	182	320	138	182	376	164	212	449	194	255
80-84	158	75	84	207	79	128	215	84	131	257	101	156
85-89	61	23	38	79	32	46	108	35	74	116	37	78
90-94	14	5	9	21	6	14	28	9	19	41	10	32
95-99	2	1	1	3	1	2	5	1	4	7	1	5
100 +	0	0	0	0	0	0	0	0	0	1	0	1

Age group	2025 Both sexes	Males	Females	2030 Both sexes	Males	Females	2035 Both sexes	Males	Females	2040 Both sexes	Males	Females
All ages	21 990	11 073	10 918	21 896	10 991	10 905	21 620	10 815	10 804	21 143	10 540	10 603
0-4	1 059	539	519	996	508	489	914	466	448	817	416	401
5-9	1 102	561	541	1 050	535	515	987	503	484	905	461	444
10-14	1 222	621	600	1 097	559	539	1 045	532	512	983	501	482
15-19	1 349	687	663	1 210	616	594	1 086	554	532	1 033	527	506
20-24	1 571	800	771	1 323	676	648	1 184	606	578	1 060	543	517
25-29	1 554	793	761	1 538	786	752	1 291	662	629	1 152	592	560
30-34	1 631	832	798	1 526	781	745	1 510	774	736	1 263	650	613
35-39	1 672	854	818	1 608	822	786	1 504	771	733	1 488	764	724
40-44	1 819	928	891	1 652	845	808	1 590	813	776	1 486	763	723
45-49	1 697	867	830	1 797	917	881	1 633	834	799	1 571	804	768
50-54	1 529	780	749	1 669	850	819	1 770	900	870	1 609	820	789
55-59	1 494	758	736	1 490	755	735	1 629	825	804	1 730	876	855
60-64	1 303	659	644	1 433	718	715	1 432	717	714	1 570	787	783
65-69	1 118	560	558	1 214	601	612	1 341	659	682	1 345	662	683
70-74	814	396	418	990	479	511	1 084	520	564	1 205	574	631
75-79	545	260	286	664	305	359	818	375	443	905	412	493
80-84	313	121	192	385	166	219	480	200	280	602	252	350
85-89	142	46	96	179	57	122	225	82	143	290	103	187
90-94	46	10	36	60	14	46	79	18	60	101	28	73
95-99	11	1	9	13	2	11	18	2	15	25	4	21
100 +	1	0	1	2	0	2	2	0	2	3	0	3

Age group	2045 Both sexes	Males	Females	2050 Both sexes	Males	Females
All ages	20 481	10 175	10 306	19 669	9 743	9 926
0-4	730	372	358	663	338	325
5-9	808	412	396	721	367	354
10-14	900	459	441	804	410	394
15-19	971	496	475	889	454	435
20-24	1 008	517	491	946	486	460
25-29	1 028	530	498	976	504	472
30-34	1 125	581	544	1 001	519	483
35-39	1 242	641	601	1 104	572	532
40-44	1 471	756	715	1 226	633	592
45-49	1 469	754	715	1 454	747	707
50-54	1 549	791	758	1 449	742	707
55-59	1 575	799	776	1 517	771	746
60-64	1 671	837	834	1 523	766	757
65-69	1 480	729	751	1 580	779	801
70-74	1 216	581	635	1 345	645	700
75-79	1 016	461	555	1 034	472	562
80-84	677	283	394	772	323	449
85-89	373	134	239	430	156	274
90-94	136	37	99	182	51	131
95-99	32	6	26	46	8	38
100 +	5	0	4	6	1	6

POPULATION BY AGE AND SEX (in thousands)

Age group	1950 Both sexes	Males	Females	1955 Both sexes	Males	Females	1960 Both sexes	Males	Females	1965 Both sexes	Males	Females
All ages	9 190	4 582	4 608	10 250	5 111	5 139	11 513	5 743	5 770	12 963	6 471	6 492
0-4	1 654	833	821	1 802	912	891	2 051	1 038	1 013	2 337	1 184	1 153
5-9	1 285	645	640	1 457	732	725	1 596	806	791	1 821	920	901
10-14	1 086	545	541	1 231	618	613	1 398	703	696	1 529	772	757
15-19	930	467	464	1 050	527	523	1 192	599	593	1 351	679	672
20-24	795	398	397	895	447	447	1 012	506	505	1 145	574	572
25-29	676	336	340	759	378	381	855	426	430	965	481	484
30-34	569	283	286	642	318	324	722	358	363	812	403	409
35-39	480	239	241	537	266	270	608	301	307	682	338	343
40-44	400	199	202	449	223	226	503	249	254	569	281	288
45-49	327	161	166	371	183	188	417	206	212	467	230	238
50-54	268	132	136	298	145	153	340	165	174	382	186	196
55-59	229	110	119	238	116	122	266	128	138	303	146	158
60-64	186	91	95	195	92	102	204	97	106	228	108	120
65-69	138	67	72	147	71	77	155	72	83	163	77	86
70-74	92	43	49	97	46	51	104	49	55	111	51	60
75-79	50	23	27	54	24	29	57	26	31	63	28	34
80 +	25	12	13	28	12	15	31	13	18	34	14	19

Age group	1970 Both sexes	Males	Females	1975 Both sexes	Males	Females	1980 Both sexes	Males	Females	1985 Both sexes	Males	Females
All ages	14 699	7 345	7 353	17 056	8 535	8 521	19 970	10 008	9 962	23 382	11 734	11 648
0-4	2 680	1 359	1 321	3 124	1 586	1 538	3 594	1 827	1 766	4 080	2 078	2 002
5-9	2 094	1 059	1 035	2 468	1 250	1 218	2 934	1 488	1 446	3 419	1 737	1 682
10-14	1 749	883	865	2 051	1 037	1 014	2 442	1 237	1 205	2 918	1 480	1 438
15-19	1 479	747	732	1 724	871	853	2 041	1 032	1 009	2 440	1 235	1 205
20-24	1 300	652	648	1 450	730	720	1 706	860	847	2 028	1 023	1 005
25-29	1 095	546	549	1 267	632	634	1 428	716	712	1 687	847	840
30-34	919	457	462	1 063	529	534	1 243	619	624	1 408	705	703
35-39	769	381	388	888	441	447	1 038	516	523	1 220	607	613
40-44	640	317	324	738	365	373	862	427	435	1 014	502	511
45-49	530	260	270	610	300	310	711	350	361	835	412	423
50-54	429	209	220	498	242	256	580	283	297	681	332	349
55-59	343	165	178	395	190	205	465	223	241	545	263	282
60-64	262	124	138	304	144	160	356	169	187	423	201	222
65-69	185	86	99	218	102	117	259	121	138	306	143	163
70-74	118	55	64	139	63	75	168	77	91	202	93	110
75-79	68	30	38	76	34	42	92	41	51	114	50	63
80 +	38	16	22	44	18	25	51	21	30	62	26	36

Age group	1990 Both sexes	Males	Females	1995 Both sexes	Males	Females	2000 Both sexes	Males	Females	2005 Both sexes	Males	Females
All ages	26 066	13 094	12 972	29 352	14 755	14 597	32 902	16 550	16 353	36 233	18 235	17 998
0-4	4 258	2 169	2 088	4 628	2 359	2 269	5 001	2 550	2 450	5 216	2 660	2 556
5-9	3 761	1 913	1 848	4 009	2 040	1 969	4 394	2 237	2 157	4 738	2 412	2 326
10-14	3 280	1 666	1 614	3 667	1 865	1 803	3 916	1 992	1 924	4 264	2 170	2 095
15-19	2 809	1 424	1 385	3 206	1 627	1 578	3 589	1 824	1 765	3 806	1 934	1 872
20-24	2 336	1 179	1 156	2 731	1 381	1 350	3 118	1 579	1 539	3 466	1 757	1 709
25-29	1 932	971	961	2 258	1 136	1 122	2 637	1 330	1 308	2 979	1 505	1 474
30-34	1 603	803	800	1 862	933	929	2 172	1 090	1 082	2 503	1 261	1 242
35-39	1 333	666	667	1 540	769	771	1 787	893	894	2 057	1 031	1 026
40-44	1 149	570	579	1 274	635	640	1 472	733	739	1 689	842	847
45-49	948	468	480	1 091	539	552	1 212	601	611	1 388	688	700
50-54	772	378	394	891	436	454	1 028	504	524	1 133	558	575
55-59	618	299	319	712	345	367	825	401	425	948	460	487
60-64	479	229	251	554	265	289	642	308	334	742	356	386
65-69	352	165	187	407	192	216	475	224	251	551	260	290
70-74	232	107	126	274	126	148	322	149	173	376	174	202
75-79	133	59	74	157	70	87	190	85	105	225	102	123
80 +	75	31	43	90	38	53	122	51	71	154	65	89

United Nations Department of Economic and Social Affairs/Population Division
World Population Prospects: The 2004 Revision, Volume II: Sex and Age Distribution of the World Population

798

POPULATION BY AGE AND SEX (in thousands)

Age group	2005 Both sexes	Males	Females	2010 Both sexes	Males	Females	2015 Both sexes	Males	Females	2020 Both sexes	Males	Females
All ages	36 233	18 235	17 998	40 254	20 275	19 978	44 035	22 201	21 834	47 536	23 965	20 561
0-4	5 216	2 660	2 556	5 367	2 738	2 629	5 415	2 763	2 652	5 446	2 779	2 667
5-9	4 738	2 412	2 326	5 074	2 583	2 491	5 227	2 661	2 565	5 277	2 687	2 590
10-14	4 264	2 170	2 095	4 705	2 394	2 311	5 022	2 555	2 467	5 154	2 623	2 532
15-19	3 806	1 934	1 872	4 244	2 157	2 087	4 672	2 375	2 297	4 967	2 524	2 443
20-24	3 466	1 757	1 709	3 764	1 908	1 855	4 191	2 125	2 065	4 599	2 332	2 267
25-29	2 979	1 505	1 474	3 381	1 712	1 669	3 668	1 858	1 810	4 079	2 066	2 013
30-34	2 503	1 261	1 242	2 873	1 454	1 419	3 247	1 649	1 598	3 519	1 788	1 731
35-39	2 057	1 031	1 026	2 406	1 213	1 193	2 742	1 392	1 351	3 091	1 575	1 516
40-44	1 689	842	847	1 977	990	987	2 297	1 159	1 138	2 608	1 326	1 282
45-49	1 388	688	700	1 623	806	817	1 890	944	946	2 187	1 102	1 085
50-54	1 133	558	575	1 326	653	673	1 545	763	782	1 793	891	902
55-59	948	460	487	1 069	522	547	1 250	611	639	1 453	712	741
60-64	742	356	386	874	420	454	987	477	511	1 153	557	595
65-69	551	260	290	654	310	345	773	366	407	875	416	458
70-74	376	174	202	451	209	241	539	251	288	640	298	342
75-79	225	102	123	273	124	149	330	150	180	398	181	217
80-84	108	47	61	134	58	75	164	72	92	201	89	113
85-89	37	15	22	47	20	28	60	25	35	75	31	44
90-94	8	3	5	11	4	7	14	5	9	18	7	11
95-99	1	0	1	1	0	1	2	1	1	3	1	2
100 +	0	0	0	0	0	0	0	0	0	0	0	0

Age group	2025 Both sexes	Males	Females	2030 Both sexes	Males	Females	2035 Both sexes	Males	Females	2040 Both sexes	Males	Females
All ages	51 031	25 761	25 270	54 511	27 522	26 989	57 890	29 224	28 666	61 076	30 820	30 256
0-4	5 515	2 814	2 701	5 573	2 844	2 729	5 564	2 839	2 725	5 488	2 801	2 687
5-9	5 333	2 716	2 617	5 423	2 762	2 661	5 498	2 800	2 698	5 505	2 803	2 702
10-14	5 218	2 655	2 563	5 286	2 690	2 596	5 385	2 740	2 645	5 467	2 782	2 685
15-19	5 104	2 594	2 510	5 173	2 629	2 544	5 247	2 667	2 580	5 350	2 719	2 631
20-24	4 897	2 483	2 414	5 039	2 555	2 484	5 114	2 593	2 521	5 192	2 633	2 560
25-29	4 490	2 274	2 216	4 794	2 427	2 367	4 946	2 503	2 442	5 028	2 545	2 483
30-34	3 935	1 997	1 938	4 351	2 206	2 145	4 664	2 363	2 301	4 829	2 444	2 384
35-39	3 369	1 716	1 653	3 789	1 927	1 863	4 211	2 137	2 073	4 533	2 298	2 236
40-44	2 954	1 507	1 447	3 238	1 651	1 588	3 660	1 861	1 799	4 084	2 073	2 011
45-49	2 493	1 265	1 227	2 837	1 445	1 392	3 124	1 590	1 534	3 546	1 800	1 745
50-54	2 082	1 044	1 038	2 384	1 205	1 179	2 724	1 382	1 342	3 010	1 526	1 484
55-59	1 693	835	857	1 974	983	991	2 268	1 138	1 129	2 600	1 310	1 290
60-64	1 346	653	693	1 576	770	806	1 845	910	935	2 127	1 057	1 070
65-69	1 028	490	538	1 207	577	630	1 420	684	736	1 670	812	858
70-74	730	341	388	864	405	460	1 023	480	542	1 210	573	638
75-79	478	218	261	551	252	299	659	302	358	787	361	425
80-84	247	109	138	301	133	168	351	156	195	424	189	236
85-89	94	39	54	117	49	67	144	61	83	171	73	98
90-94	23	9	14	30	12	18	37	15	23	47	19	28
95-99	3	1	2	4	1	3	6	2	4	7	3	5
100 +	0	0	0	0	0	0	0	0	0	1	0	0

Age group	2045 Both sexes	Males	Females	2050 Both sexes	Males	Females
All ages	64 020	32 283	31 736	66 705	33 605	33 100
0-4	5 380	2 746	2 634	5 276	2 694	2 582
5-9	5 440	2 771	2 669	5 341	2 722	2 619
10-14	5 479	2 788	2 691	5 419	2 758	2 661
15-19	5 436	2 762	2 674	5 451	2 770	2 681
20-24	5 300	2 687	2 613	5 391	2 733	2 658
25-29	5 117	2 590	2 528	5 234	2 648	2 586
30-34	4 925	2 492	2 433	5 028	2 543	2 485
35-39	4 711	2 385	2 326	4 822	2 440	2 383
40-44	4 414	2 236	2 178	4 603	2 329	2 275
45-49	3 970	2 011	1 959	4 304	2 176	2 128
50-54	3 426	1 732	1 694	3 847	1 941	1 906
55-59	2 882	1 451	1 431	3 289	1 652	1 637
60-64	2 447	1 222	1 226	2 721	1 357	1 364
65-69	1 934	948	986	2 234	1 099	1 135
70-74	1 432	684	748	1 666	802	864
75-79	939	434	505	1 120	523	597
80-84	512	229	284	618	277	341
85-89	210	90	120	257	110	147
90-94	57	23	34	71	28	42
95-99	9	3	6	11	4	7
100 +	1	0	1	1	0	1

United Nations Department of Economic and Social Affairs/Population Division
World Population Prospects: The 2004 Revision, Volume II: Sex and Age Distribution of the World Population

799

POPULATION BY AGE AND SEX (in thousands)

Age group	2005 Both sexes	Males	Females	2010 Both sexes	Males	Females	2015 Both sexes	Males	Females	2020 Both sexes	Males	Females
All ages	36 233	18 235	17 998	40 592	20 448	20 144	44 979	22 682	22 297	49 322	24 895	24 426
0-4	5 216	2 660	2 556	5 706	2 910	2 795	6 030	3 077	2 954	6 307	3 218	3 089
5-9	4 738	2 412	2 326	5 074	2 583	2 491	5 555	2 828	2 727	5 877	2 993	2 884
10-14	4 264	2 170	2 095	4 705	2 394	2 311	5 022	2 555	2 467	5 479	2 788	2 691
15-19	3 806	1 934	1 872	4 244	2 157	2 087	4 672	2 375	2 297	4 967	2 524	2 443
20-24	3 466	1 757	1 709	3 764	1 908	1 855	4 191	2 125	2 065	4 599	2 332	2 267
25-29	2 979	1 505	1 474	3 381	1 712	1 669	3 668	1 858	1 810	4 079	2 066	2 013
30-34	2 503	1 261	1 242	2 873	1 454	1 419	3 247	1 649	1 598	3 519	1 788	1 731
35-39	2 057	1 031	1 026	2 406	1 213	1 193	2 742	1 392	1 351	3 091	1 575	1 516
40-44	1 689	842	847	1 977	990	987	2 297	1 159	1 138	2 608	1 326	1 282
45-49	1 388	688	700	1 623	806	817	1 890	944	946	2 187	1 102	1 085
50-54	1 133	558	575	1 326	653	673	1 545	763	782	1 793	891	902
55-59	948	460	487	1 069	522	547	1 250	611	639	1 453	712	741
60-64	742	356	386	874	420	454	987	477	511	1 153	557	595
65-69	551	260	290	654	310	345	773	366	407	875	416	458
70-74	376	174	202	451	209	241	539	251	288	640	298	342
75-79	225	102	123	273	124	149	330	150	180	398	181	217
80-84	108	47	61	134	58	75	164	72	92	201	89	113
85-89	37	15	22	47	20	28	60	25	35	75	31	44
90-94	8	3	5	11	4	7	14	5	9	18	7	11
95-99	1	0	1	1	0	1	2	1	1	3	1	2
100 +	0	0	0	0	0	0	0	0	0	0	0	0

Age group	2025 Both sexes	Males	Females	2030 Both sexes	Males	Females	2035 Both sexes	Males	Females	2040 Both sexes	Males	Females
All ages	53 760	27 151	26 609	58 341	29 472	28 869	63 063	31 856	31 207	67 896	34 289	33 608
0-4	6 484	3 308	3 175	6 704	3 421	3 283	6 945	3 544	3 401	7 184	3 666	3 518
5-9	6 178	3 146	3 032	6 376	3 247	3 129	6 615	3 369	3 246	6 872	3 499	3 373
10-14	5 812	2 957	2 854	6 124	3 116	3 007	6 332	3 222	3 110	6 578	3 347	3 231
15-19	5 426	2 758	2 668	5 763	2 929	2 834	6 079	3 090	2 990	6 292	3 198	3 094
20-24	4 897	2 483	2 414	5 357	2 716	2 641	5 697	2 889	2 808	6 017	3 051	2 966
25-29	4 490	2 274	2 216	4 794	2 427	2 367	5 258	2 661	2 596	5 602	2 836	2 767
30-34	3 935	1 997	1 938	4 351	2 206	2 145	4 664	2 363	2 301	5 133	2 599	2 535
35-39	3 369	1 716	1 653	3 789	1 927	1 863	4 211	2 137	2 073	4 533	2 298	2 236
40-44	2 954	1 507	1 447	3 238	1 651	1 588	3 660	1 861	1 799	4 084	2 073	2 011
45-49	2 493	1 265	1 227	2 837	1 445	1 392	3 124	1 590	1 534	3 545	1 800	1 745
50-54	2 082	1 044	1 038	2 384	1 205	1 179	2 724	1 382	1 342	3 010	1 526	1 484
55-59	1 693	835	857	1 974	983	991	2 268	1 138	1 129	2 600	1 310	1 290
60-64	1 346	653	693	1 576	770	806	1 845	910	935	2 127	1 057	1 070
65-69	1 028	490	538	1 207	577	630	1 420	684	736	1 670	812	858
70-74	730	341	388	864	405	460	1 023	480	542	1 210	573	638
75-79	478	218	261	551	252	299	659	302	358	787	361	425
80-84	247	109	138	301	133	168	351	156	195	424	189	236
85-89	94	39	54	117	49	67	144	61	83	171	73	98
90-94	23	9	14	30	12	18	37	15	23	47	19	28
95-99	3	1	2	4	1	3	6	2	4	7	3	5
100 +	0	0	0	0	0	0	0	0	0	1	0	0

Age group	2045 Both sexes	Males	Females	2050 Both sexes	Males	Females
All ages	72 782	36 739	36 043	77 653	39 171	38 482
0-4	7 384	3 769	3 615	7 536	3 848	3 688
5-9	7 123	3 628	3 495	7 332	3 736	3 596
10-14	6 841	3 481	3 360	7 096	3 611	3 485
15-19	6 542	3 324	3 218	6 808	3 459	3 349
20-24	6 234	3 161	3 074	6 489	3 290	3 200
25-29	5 931	3 001	2 929	6 157	3 115	3 042
30-34	5 488	2 777	2 710	5 828	2 947	2 880
35-39	5 009	2 536	2 473	5 374	2 719	2 655
40-44	4 414	2 236	2 178	4 894	2 476	2 419
45-49	3 970	2 011	1 959	4 304	2 176	2 128
50-54	3 426	1 732	1 694	3 847	1 941	1 906
55-59	2 882	1 451	1 431	3 289	1 652	1 637
60-64	2 447	1 222	1 226	2 721	1 357	1 364
65-69	1 934	948	986	2 234	1 099	1 135
70-74	1 432	684	748	1 666	802	864
75-79	939	434	505	1 120	523	597
80-84	512	229	284	618	277	341
85-89	210	90	120	257	110	147
90-94	57	23	34	71	28	42
95-99	9	3	6	11	4	7
100 +	1	0	1	1	0	1

United Nations Department of Economic and Social Affairs/Population Division
World Population Prospects: The 2004 Revision, Volume II: Sex and Age Distribution of the World Population

800

POPULATION BY AGE AND SEX (in thousands)

Age group	2005 Both sexes	Males	Females	2010 Both sexes	Males	Females	2015 Both sexes	Males	Females	2020 Both sexes	Males	Females
All ages	36 233	18 235	17 998	39 915	20 103	19 812	43 091	21 720	21 372	45 750	23 075	22 675
0-4	5 216	2 660	2 556	5 029	2 565	2 464	4 800	2 449	2 351	4 584	2 339	2 245
5-9	4 738	2 412	2 326	5 074	2 583	2 491	4 898	2 494	2 404	4 677	2 382	2 295
10-14	4 264	2 170	2 095	4 705	2 394	2 311	5 022	2 555	2 467	4 830	2 458	2 373
15-19	3 806	1 934	1 872	4 244	2 157	2 087	4 672	2 375	2 297	4 967	2 524	2 443
20-24	3 466	1 757	1 709	3 764	1 908	1 855	4 191	2 125	2 065	4 599	2 332	2 267
25-29	2 979	1 505	1 474	3 381	1 712	1 669	3 668	1 858	1 810	4 079	2 066	2 013
30-34	2 503	1 261	1 242	2 873	1 454	1 419	3 247	1 649	1 598	3 519	1 788	1 731
35-39	2 057	1 031	1 026	2 406	1 213	1 193	2 742	1 392	1 351	3 091	1 575	1 516
40-44	1 689	842	847	1 977	990	987	2 297	1 159	1 138	2 608	1 326	1 282
45-49	1 388	688	700	1 623	806	817	1 890	944	946	2 187	1 102	1 085
50-54	1 133	558	575	1 326	653	673	1 545	763	782	1 793	891	902
55-59	948	460	487	1 069	522	547	1 250	611	639	1 453	712	741
60-64	742	356	386	874	420	454	987	477	511	1 153	557	595
65-69	551	260	290	654	310	345	773	366	407	875	416	458
70-74	376	174	202	451	209	241	539	251	288	640	298	342
75-79	225	102	123	273	124	149	330	150	180	398	181	217
80-84	108	47	61	134	58	75	164	72	92	201	89	113
85-89	37	15	22	47	20	28	60	25	35	75	31	44
90-94	8	3	5	11	4	7	14	5	9	18	7	11
95-99	1	0	1	1	0	1	2	1	1	3	1	2
100 +	0	0	0	0	0	0	0	0	0	0	0	0

Age group	2025 Both sexes	Males	Females	2030 Both sexes	Males	Females	2035 Both sexes	Males	Females	2040 Both sexes	Males	Females
All ages	48 307	24 373	23 934	50 714	25 588	25 125	52 838	26 653	26 185	54 563	27 507	27 056
0-4	4 550	2 322	2 228	4 470	2 281	2 189	4 273	2 181	2 092	3 979	2 031	1 949
5-9	4 489	2 286	2 203	4 474	2 278	2 195	4 409	2 245	2 164	4 226	2 152	2 074
10-14	4 623	2 353	2 271	4 448	2 263	2 184	4 441	2 260	2 181	4 383	2 230	2 153
15-19	4 783	2 431	2 352	4 584	2 330	2 254	4 414	2 244	2 171	4 412	2 242	2 170
20-24	4 897	2 483	2 414	4 722	2 394	2 328	4 530	2 297	2 233	4 368	2 215	2 153
25-29	4 490	2 274	2 216	4 794	2 427	2 367	4 634	2 346	2 288	4 454	2 255	2 200
30-34	3 935	1 997	1 938	4 351	2 206	2 145	4 664	2 363	2 301	4 524	2 290	2 234
35-39	3 369	1 716	1 653	3 789	1 927	1 863	4 211	2 137	2 070	4 533	2 298	2 236
40-44	2 954	1 507	1 447	3 238	1 651	1 588	3 660	1 861	1 799	4 084	2 073	2 011
45-49	2 493	1 265	1 227	2 837	1 445	1 392	3 124	1 590	1 534	3 545	1 800	1 745
50-54	2 082	1 044	1 038	2 384	1 205	1 179	2 724	1 382	1 342	3 010	1 526	1 484
55-59	1 693	835	857	1 974	983	991	2 268	1 138	1 129	2 600	1 310	1 290
60-64	1 346	653	693	1 576	770	806	1 845	910	935	2 127	1 057	1 070
65-69	1 028	490	538	1 207	577	630	1 420	684	736	1 670	812	858
70-74	730	341	388	864	405	460	1 023	480	542	1 210	573	638
75-79	478	218	261	551	252	299	659	302	058	787	361	425
80-84	247	109	138	301	133	168	351	156	195	424	189	236
85-89	94	39	54	117	49	67	144	61	83	171	73	98
90-94	23	9	14	30	12	18	37	15	23	47	19	28
95-99	3	1	2	4	1	3	6	2	4	7	3	5
100 +	0	0	0	0	0	0	0	0	0	1	0	0

Age group	2045 Both sexes	Males	Females	2050 Both sexes	Males	Females
All ages	55 858	28 134	27 724	56 750	28 546	28 205
0-4	3 671	1 874	1 797	3 411	1 742	1 669
5-9	3 943	2 008	1 935	3 643	1 856	1 786
10-14	4 206	2 140	2 066	3 927	1 998	1 928
15-19	4 357	2 214	2 143	4 184	2 126	2 058
20-24	4 370	2 216	2 154	4 321	2 190	2 130
25-29	4 304	2 178	2 126	4 315	2 183	2 131
30-34	4 362	2 208	2 155	4 228	2 139	2 090
35-39	4 413	2 234	2 179	4 271	2 161	2 110
40-44	4 414	2 236	2 178	4 312	2 181	2 131
45-49	3 970	2 011	1 959	4 304	2 176	2 128
50-54	3 426	1 732	1 694	3 847	1 941	1 906
55-59	2 882	1 451	1 431	3 289	1 652	1 637
60-64	2 447	1 222	1 226	2 721	1 357	1 364
65-69	1 934	948	986	2 234	1 099	1 135
70-74	1 432	684	748	1 666	802	864
75-79	939	434	505	1 120	523	597
80-84	512	229	284	618	277	341
85-89	210	90	120	257	110	147
90-94	57	23	34	71	28	42
95-99	9	3	6	11	4	7
100 +	1	0	1	1	0	1

United Nations Department of Economic and Social Affairs/Population Division
World Population Prospects: The 2004 Revision, Volume II: Sex and Age Distribution of the World Population

801

POPULATION BY AGE AND SEX (in thousands)

Age group	1950 Both sexes	Males	Females	1955 Both sexes	Males	Females	1960 Both sexes	Males	Females	1965 Both sexes	Males	Females
All ages	215	107	108	250	126	124	290	145	145	332	165	167
0-4	37	19	18	47	24	23	59	30	29	64	33	32
5-9	26	13	13	35	18	17	45	23	22	54	27	27
10-14	23	11	12	26	13	13	34	17	17	42	21	21
15-19	21	10	11	22	11	11	24	12	12	31	15	15
20-24	18	9	9	20	10	10	21	10	11	23	11	12
25-29	16	8	8	18	9	9	20	10	10	21	10	11
30-34	12	6	6	16	8	8	17	8	9	19	9	10
35-39	12	6	6	12	6	6	14	7	7	17	8	8
40-44	10	5	5	11	6	5	11	5	6	14	7	7
45-49	8	4	4	10	5	5	11	6	5	10	5	5
50-54	8	4	4	8	4	4	8	4	4	10	5	5
55-59	6	3	3	7	4	3	8	4	4	8	4	4
60-64	5	3	2	6	3	3	6	3	3	7	3	3
65-69	4	2	2	4	2	2	4	2	2	5	3	3
70-74	4	2	2	3	1	2	4	2	2	4	2	2
75-79	3	1	2	3	1	2	2	1	1	2	1	1
80 +	2	1	1	2	1	1	2	1	1	2	1	1

Age group	1970 Both sexes	Males	Females	1975 Both sexes	Males	Females	1980 Both sexes	Males	Females	1985 Both sexes	Males	Females
All ages	372	186	186	364	183	182	356	177	179	383	191	192
0-4	64	32	31	56	29	28	47	24	23	53	28	26
5-9	63	32	31	62	31	31	49	25	25	45	23	22
10-14	54	27	27	55	28	27	50	25	25	46	23	23
15-19	40	21	20	42	21	21	47	24	23	46	23	23
20-24	27	13	14	27	13	13	33	16	17	44	22	22
25-29	20	9	11	20	10	11	23	11	12	31	15	16
30-34	19	9	10	18	9	9	18	9	9	22	11	11
35-39	18	9	9	18	9	9	16	7	8	17	8	9
40-44	16	8	8	15	7	7	15	7	8	15	7	8
45-49	13	7	7	13	6	6	14	7	7	15	7	8
50-54	10	5	5	9	5	5	12	6	6	14	7	7
55-59	9	5	4	8	4	4	9	5	5	11	5	6
60-64	7	3	4	7	4	4	6	3	3	8	4	4
65-69	6	3	3	5	3	3	5	3	3	5	3	3
70-74	4	2	2	4	2	2	4	2	2	4	2	2
75-79	3	1	1	3	1	1	3	1	2	3	1	2
80 +	2	1	1	1	1	1	4	2	2	3	1	2

Age group	1990 Both sexes	Males	Females	1995 Both sexes	Males	Females	2000 Both sexes	Males	Females	2005 Both sexes	Males	Females
All ages	402	201	201	415	207	207	434	217	217	449	224	225
0-4	49	25	24	45	23	22	49	25	24	45	23	22
5-9	51	26	25	48	25	23	44	23	21	47	24	23
10-14	42	22	20	49	25	24	47	24	23	42	22	20
15-19	42	21	21	39	20	19	47	24	24	44	23	22
20-24	42	21	21	39	19	19	36	18	18	44	22	22
25-29	40	20	20	38	19	19	35	18	18	33	17	17
30-34	28	14	14	37	19	18	34	17	17	32	16	16
35-39	21	10	11	26	13	13	33	17	16	32	16	16
40-44	16	8	9	20	10	10	24	12	12	32	16	16
45-49	14	7	8	16	7	8	19	9	10	23	11	12
50-54	14	7	7	14	6	7	15	7	8	19	9	10
55-59	13	6	7	13	6	7	13	6	7	14	7	7
60-64	10	5	5	12	6	6	12	6	6	12	5	6
65-69	7	3	4	9	4	4	10	5	5	11	5	6
70-74	4	2	2	6	3	3	7	3	4	8	4	5
75-79	3	1	2	3	1	2	4	2	2	5	2	3
80 +	3	2	2	3	2	2	4	2	2	4	2	2

United Nations Department of Economic and Social Affairs/Population Division
World Population Prospects: The 2004 Revision, Volume II: Sex and Age Distribution of the World Population

802

POPULATION BY AGE AND SEX (in thousands)

Age group	2005 Both sexes	Males	Females	2010 Both sexes	Males	Females	2015 Both sexes	Males	Females	2020 Both sexes	Males	Females
All ages	449	224	225	462	230	231	472	235	236	478	239	239
0-4	45	23	22	44	23	21	42	22	20	39	20	19
5-9	47	24	23	44	23	21	42	22	20	40	21	19
10-14	42	22	20	45	23	22	42	22	20	40	21	20
15-19	44	23	22	40	20	19	43	22	21	39	20	19
20-24	44	22	22	41	21	20	37	19	18	40	20	19
25-29	33	17	17	41	21	21	38	20	19	34	17	16
30-34	32	16	16	30	15	15	39	19	19	36	18	17
35-39	32	16	16	31	15	15	29	14	14	37	18	18
40-44	32	16	16	31	15	15	29	15	15	28	14	14
45-49	23	11	12	31	15	15	30	15	15	29	14	14
50-54	19	9	10	23	11	12	30	15	15	29	14	15
55-59	14	7	7	18	8	9	22	10	11	29	14	14
60-64	12	5	6	13	6	7	16	8	9	20	10	11
65-69	11	5	6	10	5	6	12	5	6	15	7	8
70-74	8	4	5	9	4	5	9	4	5	10	4	6
75-79	5	2	3	6	3	4	7	3	4	7	3	4
80-84	3	1	2	3	2	2	4	2	2	4	2	3
85-89	1	0	1	1	1	1	2	1	1	2	1	1
90-94	0	0	0	0	0	0	1	0	0	1	0	0
95-99	0	0	0	0	0	0	0	0	0	0	0	0
100 +	0	0	0	0	0	0	0	0	0	0	0	0

Age group	2025 Both sexes	Males	Females	2030 Both sexes	Males	Females	2035 Both sexes	Males	Females	2040 Both sexes	Males	Females
All ages	480	240	240	479	239	240	473	236	237	462	231	232
0-4	36	19	17	33	17	16	31	16	15	28	14	13
5-9	37	19	18	35	18	17	32	17	15	30	15	14
10-14	38	20	19	35	18	17	33	17	16	30	16	15
15-19	38	19	18	36	18	17	33	17	16	30	15	15
20-24	36	18	18	35	18	17	33	17	16	30	15	15
25-29	37	19	18	34	17	16	32	16	16	30	15	15
30-34	31	16	15	34	18	17	31	16	15	30	15	14
35-39	34	18	17	30	16	14	33	17	16	30	15	14
40-44	36	18	18	33	17	16	29	15	14	32	17	15
45-49	27	14	13	35	17	18	33	17	16	28	15	14
50-54	25	11	14	26	13	13	34	17	17	32	16	15
55-59	28	14	14	27	13	14	25	13	10	33	16	17
60-64	27	13	14	26	13	14	25	12	13	24	12	12
65-69	18	8	10	24	12	13	24	11	13	23	11	12
70-74	13	5	7	16	7	9	21	10	12	21	9	12
75-79	8	3	5	10	4	6	13	5	7	17	7	10
80-84	5	2	3	5	2	3	7	3	4	9	3	5
85-89	2	1	2	3	1	2	3	1	2	4	1	3
90-94	1	0	1	1	0	1	1	0	1	1	0	1
95-99	0	0	0	0	0	0	0	0	0	0	0	0
100 +	0	0	0	0	0	0	0	0	0	0	0	0

Age group	2045 Both sexes	Males	Females	2050 Both sexes	Males	Females
All ages	448	223	224	429	214	215
0-4	25	13	12	23	12	11
5-9	27	14	13	24	13	12
10-14	27	14	13	25	13	12
15-19	27	14	13	25	13	12
20-24	27	14	13	25	13	12
25-29	27	14	13	24	13	12
30-34	28	14	13	25	13	12
35-39	28	15	14	26	14	13
40-44	29	15	14	28	14	13
45-49	31	16	15	29	15	14
50-54	28	15	13	31	16	15
55-59	31	16	15	27	14	13
60-64	32	15	16	30	15	15
65-69	22	11	12	29	14	15
70-74	20	9	11	20	9	11
75-79	17	7	10	17	7	10
80-84	12	5	7	12	5	8
85-89	5	2	4	7	3	5
90-94	2	1	1	3	1	2
95-99	0	0	0	1	0	0
100 +	0	0	0	0	0	0

United Nations Department of Economic and Social Affairs/Population Division
World Population Prospects: The 2004 Revision, Volume II: Sex and Age Distribution of the World Population

803

POPULATION BY AGE AND SEX (in thousands)

Age group	2005 Both sexes	Males	Females	2010 Both sexes	Males	Females	2015 Both sexes	Males	Females	2020 Both sexes	Males	Females
All ages	449	224	225	466	233	234	483	241	242	498	249	249
0-4	45	23	22	48	25	23	49	25	24	48	25	23
5-9	47	24	23	44	23	21	47	24	23	48	25	23
10-14	42	22	20	45	23	22	42	22	20	45	23	22
15-19	44	23	22	40	20	19	43	22	21	39	20	19
20-24	44	22	22	41	21	20	37	19	18	40	20	19
25-29	33	17	17	41	21	21	38	20	19	34	17	16
30-34	32	16	16	30	15	15	39	19	19	36	18	17
35-39	32	16	16	31	15	15	29	14	14	37	18	18
40-44	32	16	16	31	15	15	29	15	15	28	14	14
45-49	23	11	12	31	15	15	30	15	15	29	14	14
50-54	19	9	10	23	11	12	30	15	15	29	14	15
55-59	14	7	7	18	8	9	22	10	11	29	14	14
60-64	12	5	6	13	6	7	16	8	9	20	10	11
65-69	11	5	6	10	5	6	12	5	6	15	7	8
70-74	8	4	5	9	4	5	9	4	5	10	4	6
75-79	5	2	3	6	3	4	7	3	4	7	3	4
80-84	3	1	2	3	2	2	4	2	2	4	2	3
85-89	1	0	1	1	1	1	2	1	1	2	1	1
90-94	0	0	0	0	0	0	1	0	0	1	0	0
95-99	0	0	0	0	0	0	0	0	0	0	0	0
100 +	0	0	0	0	0	0	0	0	0	0	0	0

Age group	2025 Both sexes	Males	Females	2030 Both sexes	Males	Females	2035 Both sexes	Males	Females	2040 Both sexes	Males	Females
All ages	509	255	254	517	259	258	522	262	261	525	263	262
0-4	45	23	22	43	22	21	42	22	20	41	21	20
5-9	46	24	22	43	23	21	41	22	20	40	21	19
10-14	45	23	22	44	23	21	41	21	20	39	20	19
15-19	42	21	21	43	22	21	41	21	20	39	20	19
20-24	36	18	18	39	20	19	40	20	19	39	20	19
25-29	37	19	18	34	17	16	36	19	18	37	19	18
30-34	31	16	15	34	18	17	31	16	15	34	18	17
35-39	34	18	17	30	16	14	33	17	16	30	15	14
40-44	36	18	18	33	17	16	29	15	14	32	17	15
45-49	27	14	13	35	17	18	33	17	16	28	15	14
50-54	28	14	14	26	13	13	34	17	17	32	16	15
55-59	28	14	14	27	13	14	25	13	13	33	16	17
60-64	27	13	14	26	13	14	25	12	13	24	12	12
65-69	18	8	10	24	12	13	24	11	13	23	11	12
70-74	13	5	7	16	7	9	21	10	12	21	9	12
75-79	8	3	5	10	4	6	13	5	7	17	7	10
80-84	5	2	3	5	2	3	7	3	4	9	3	5
85-89	2	1	2	3	1	2	3	1	2	4	1	3
90-94	1	0	1	1	0	1	1	0	1	1	0	1
95-99	0	0	0	0	0	0	0	0	0	0	0	0
100 +	0	0	0	0	0	0	0	0	0	0	0	0

Age group	2045 Both sexes	Males	Females	2050 Both sexes	Males	Females
All ages	525	263	262	522	262	260
0-4	40	21	19	39	20	19
5-9	40	21	19	39	20	19
10-14	38	20	19	38	20	18
15-19	37	19	18	36	18	17
20-24	36	18	17	34	17	17
25-29	36	18	17	33	17	16
30-34	35	18	17	34	17	16
35-39	33	17	16	33	17	16
40-44	29	15	14	32	17	15
45-49	31	16	15	29	15	14
50-54	28	15	13	31	16	15
55-59	31	16	15	27	14	13
60-64	32	15	16	30	15	15
65-69	22	11	12	29	14	15
70-74	20	9	11	20	9	11
75-79	17	7	10	17	7	10
80-84	12	5	7	12	5	8
85-89	5	2	4	7	3	5
90-94	2	1	1	3	1	2
95-99	0	0	0	1	0	0
100 +	0	0	0	0	0	0

United Nations Department of Economic and Social Affairs/Population Division
World Population Prospects: The 2004 Revision, Volume II: Sex and Age Distribution of the World Population

804

POPULATION BY AGE AND SEX (in thousands)

Age group	2005 Both sexes	2005 Males	2005 Females	2010 Both sexes	2010 Males	2010 Females	2015 Both sexes	2015 Males	2015 Females	2020 Both sexes	2020 Males	2020 Females
All ages	449	224	225	457	228	229	460	229	231	457	228	229
0-4	45	23	22	39	20	19	34	18	17	30	15	14
5-9	47	24	23	44	23	21	38	20	18	33	17	16
10-14	42	22	20	45	23	22	42	22	20	36	18	17
15-19	44	23	22	40	20	19	43	22	21	39	20	19
20-24	44	22	22	41	21	20	37	19	18	40	20	19
25-29	33	17	17	41	21	21	38	20	19	34	17	16
30-34	32	16	16	30	15	15	39	19	19	36	18	17
35-39	32	16	16	31	15	15	29	14	14	37	18	18
40-44	32	16	16	31	15	15	29	15	15	28	14	14
45-49	23	11	12	31	15	15	30	15	15	29	14	14
50-54	19	9	10	23	11	12	30	15	15	29	14	15
55-59	14	7	7	18	8	9	22	10	11	29	14	14
60-64	12	5	6	13	6	7	16	8	9	20	10	11
65-69	11	5	6	10	5	6	12	5	6	15	7	8
70-74	8	4	5	9	4	5	9	4	5	10	4	6
75-79	5	2	3	6	3	4	7	3	4	7	3	4
80-84	3	1	2	3	2	2	4	2	2	4	2	3
85-89	1	0	1	1	1	1	2	1	1	2	1	1
90-94	0	0	0	0	0	0	1	0	0	1	0	0
95-99	0	0	0	0	0	0	0	0	0	0	0	0
100 +	0	0	0	0	0	0	0	0	0	0	0	0

Age group	2025 Both sexes	2025 Males	2025 Females	2030 Both sexes	2030 Males	2030 Females	2035 Both sexes	2035 Males	2035 Females	2040 Both sexes	2040 Males	2040 Females
All ages	451	225	226	441	219	221	425	212	214	404	201	203
0-4	27	14	13	24	13	12	21	11	10	17	9	8
5-9	29	15	14	26	14	13	23	12	11	20	10	9
10-14	31	16	15	27	14	13	24	12	12	21	11	10
15-19	33	17	16	28	14	14	24	12	12	21	11	11
20-24	36	18	18	30	15	15	25	13	13	21	11	10
25-29	37	19	18	34	17	16	28	14	13	23	12	11
30-34	31	16	15	34	18	17	31	16	15	25	13	12
35-39	34	18	17	30	16	14	33	17	16	30	15	14
40-44	36	18	18	33	17	16	29	15	14	32	17	15
45-49	27	14	13	35	17	18	33	17	16	28	15	14
50-54	28	14	14	26	13	13	34	17	17	32	16	15
55-59	28	14	14	27	13	14	25	13	13	33	16	17
60-64	27	13	14	26	13	14	25	12	13	24	12	12
65-69	18	8	10	24	12	13	24	11	13	23	11	12
70-74	13	5	7	16	7	9	21	10	12	21	9	12
75-79	8	3	5	10	4	6	13	5	7	17	7	10
80-84	5	2	3	5	2	3	7	3	4	9	3	6
85-89	2	1	2	3	1	2	3	1	2	4	1	3
90-94	1	0	1	1	0	1	1	0	1	1	0	1
95-99	0	0	0	0	0	0	0	0	0	0	0	0
100 +	0	0	0	0	0	0	0	0	0	0	0	0

Age group	2045 Both sexes	2045 Males	2045 Females	2050 Both sexes	2050 Males	2050 Females
All ages	378	187	191	348	172	176
0-4	14	7	7	11	6	5
5-9	16	8	8	13	7	6
10-14	18	9	9	14	7	7
15-19	19	9	9	15	8	7
20-24	18	9	9	16	8	8
25-29	18	9	9	16	8	8
30-34	21	11	10	16	8	8
35-39	24	12	11	19	10	9
40-44	29	15	14	23	12	11
45-49	31	16	15	29	15	14
50-54	28	15	13	31	16	15
55-59	31	16	15	27	14	13
60-64	32	15	16	30	15	15
65-69	22	11	12	29	14	15
70-74	20	9	11	20	9	11
75-79	17	7	10	17	7	10
80-84	12	5	7	12	5	8
85-89	5	2	4	7	3	5
90-94	2	1	1	3	1	2
95-99	0	0	0	1	0	0
100 +	0	0	0	0	0	0

POPULATION BY AGE AND SEX (in thousands)

Age group	1950 Both sexes	1950 Males	1950 Females	1955 Both sexes	1955 Males	1955 Females	1960 Both sexes	1960 Males	1960 Females	1965 Both sexes	1965 Males	1965 Females
All ages	273	133	140	310	150	160	353	171	182	398	190	208
0-4	49	24	25	58	29	29	65	32	33	75	37	37
5-9	37	18	19	45	22	23	53	26	27	61	30	31
10-14	32	16	16	36	18	18	44	22	22	52	26	26
15-19	28	14	14	31	15	16	35	17	18	42	20	22
20-24	24	12	12	26	13	14	29	14	15	32	15	17
25-29	21	10	11	23	11	12	25	12	13	26	12	14
30-34	18	9	9	19	9	10	21	10	11	22	10	12
35-39	15	7	8	17	8	9	18	9	10	19	9	10
40-44	13	6	6	14	7	7	15	7	8	17	8	9
45-49	10	5	5	11	5	6	13	6	7	14	7	8
50-54	8	4	4	9	4	5	10	5	6	12	5	6
55-59	7	3	4	7	3	4	8	4	4	9	4	5
60-64	5	2	3	6	2	3	6	3	3	7	3	4
65-69	4	2	2	4	2	2	4	2	2	5	2	3
70-74	2	1	1	3	1	2	3	1	2	3	1	2
75-79	1	0	1	1	1	1	2	1	1	2	1	1
80 +	0	0	0	1	0	0	1	0	0	1	0	1

Age group	1970 Both sexes	1970 Males	1970 Females	1975 Both sexes	1975 Males	1975 Females	1980 Both sexes	1980 Males	1980 Females	1985 Both sexes	1985 Males	1985 Females
All ages	454	216	238	528	251	277	616	293	323	717	339	378
0-4	88	44	44	104	52	52	120	60	60	139	70	69
5-9	70	35	35	83	41	42	100	50	50	114	57	57
10-14	59	29	30	68	34	34	82	41	41	96	48	48
15-19	50	24	26	57	27	29	66	33	34	78	38	40
20-24	37	17	21	44	20	25	52	24	28	60	27	33
25-29	28	11	16	33	13	20	40	17	24	47	19	28
30-34	24	11	13	27	11	15	31	12	19	39	15	23
35-39	21	10	11	25	12	13	25	11	14	31	13	18
40-44	18	8	10	21	10	11	24	12	12	26	12	14
45-49	16	7	8	17	8	9	20	10	10	23	12	12
50-54	13	6	7	14	7	8	16	7	9	19	9	10
55-59	11	5	6	12	6	6	13	6	7	15	7	8
60-64	8	3	4	9	4	5	10	5	6	12	5	6
65-69	5	2	3	6	3	4	7	3	4	9	4	5
70-74	3	1	2	4	2	2	5	2	3	6	2	3
75-79	2	1	1	2	1	1	3	1	2	3	1	2
80 +	1	0	1	1	0	1	1	1	1	2	1	1

Age group	1990 Both sexes	1990 Males	1990 Females	1995 Both sexes	1995 Males	1995 Females	2000 Both sexes	2000 Males	2000 Females	2005 Both sexes	2005 Males	2005 Females
All ages	865	408	458	953	456	497	1 023	490	533	1 032	498	535
0-4	158	80	79	157	79	78	147	74	73	136	68	68
5-9	136	68	68	151	76	75	152	76	76	138	69	69
10-14	114	57	57	133	67	67	150	75	75	149	75	74
15-19	96	47	50	108	53	55	130	65	66	148	74	74
20-24	78	35	43	84	39	45	97	47	51	123	61	62
25-29	60	25	35	65	28	38	70	32	38	77	37	40
30-34	48	19	28	53	22	30	55	23	32	48	22	26
35-39	40	16	24	45	20	25	46	20	27	38	16	22
40-44	32	13	19	38	17	21	41	18	23	34	14	20
45-49	26	12	15	31	15	16	35	15	19	32	13	19
50-54	23	11	12	24	12	12	28	13	15	30	13	17
55-59	18	9	9	21	10	10	22	11	12	24	11	13
60-64	13	6	8	16	7	8	18	9	9	19	9	10
65-69	10	4	6	11	5	6	13	6	7	16	7	8
70-74	7	3	4	8	3	5	9	4	5	11	5	6
75-79	4	2	2	5	2	3	5	2	3	6	2	4
80 +	2	1	1	3	1	2	4	1	2	4	2	3

United Nations Department of Economic and Social Affairs/Population Division
World Population Prospects: The 2004 Revision, Volume II: Sex and Age Distribution of the World Population

POPULATION BY AGE AND SEX (in thousands)

Age group	2005 Both sexes	2005 Males	2005 Females	2010 Both sexes	2010 Males	2010 Females	2015 Both sexes	2015 Males	2015 Females	2020 Both sexes	2020 Males	2020 Females
All ages	1 032	498	535	1 010	495	516	992	494	499	983	496	406
0-4	136	68	68	130	65	64	131	66	65	128	65	64
5-9	138	69	69	125	63	62	122	61	60	126	63	63
10-14	149	75	74	131	66	65	117	59	58	115	58	57
15-19	148	74	74	147	74	74	129	64	64	114	57	57
20-24	123	61	62	141	70	71	141	71	71	124	62	62
25-29	77	37	40	100	50	49	119	61	58	122	62	60
30-34	48	22	26	49	25	24	69	38	31	87	48	39
35-39	38	16	22	28	14	14	29	17	12	45	27	18
40-44	34	14	20	24	10	13	17	9	8	18	11	7
45-49	32	13	19	24	10	14	16	7	9	11	6	5
50-54	30	13	17	25	10	15	18	7	11	12	5	6
55-59	24	11	13	25	10	14	21	8	12	15	6	9
60-64	19	9	10	21	9	12	21	8	12	17	7	11
65-69	16	7	8	16	7	9	17	7	10	18	7	11
70-74	11	5	6	12	6	7	13	6	7	14	6	8
75-79	6	2	4	7	3	4	9	4	5	9	4	6
80-84	3	1	2	4	1	2	4	2	3	5	2	3
85-89	1	0	1	1	0	1	1	1	1	2	1	1
90-94	0	0	0	0	0	0	0	0	0	0	0	0
95-99	0	0	0	0	0	0	0	0	0	0	0	0
100 +	0	0	0	0	0	0	0	0	0	0	0	0

Age group	2025 Both sexes	2025 Males	2025 Females	2030 Both sexes	2030 Males	2030 Females	2035 Both sexes	2035 Males	2035 Females	2040 Both sexes	2040 Males	2040 Females
All ages	975	498	477	973	501	472	976	504	471	985	510	475
0-4	121	61	60	112	57	56	108	55	54	108	55	54
5-9	126	63	63	119	60	59	111	56	55	108	54	53
10-14	122	61	61	124	62	62	118	59	59	111	56	55
15-19	113	57	56	121	61	60	123	62	61	117	59	58
20-24	111	55	56	110	55	55	118	58	59	120	60	60
25-29	110	55	55	99	49	50	99	49	50	107	53	54
30-34	94	51	43	88	46	42	81	41	39	82	42	40
35-39	59	36	23	68	40	20	66	37	30	63	33	29
40-44	29	19	10	42	27	15	52	31	20	52	29	22
45-49	12	8	4	22	15	7	33	22	11	41	25	16
50-54	8	5	3	10	7	3	18	12	5	27	18	9
55-59	9	4	5	7	4	3	8	6	3	15	11	5
60-64	12	5	8	8	4	5	6	3	3	7	5	2
65-69	15	6	9	11	4	7	7	3	4	5	3	2
70-74	14	5	9	12	4	8	9	3	6	6	3	3
75-79	10	4	6	11	4	7	9	3	6	7	2	4
80-84	6	2	3	6	2	4	6	2	4	6	2	4
85-89	2	1	1	2	1	2	3	1	2	3	1	2
90-94	0	0	0	1	0	0	1	0	0	1	0	1
95-99	0	0	0	0	0	0	0	0	0	0	0	0
100 +	0	0	0	0	0	0	0	0	0	0	0	0

Age group	2045 Both sexes	2045 Males	2045 Females	2050 Both sexes	2050 Males	2050 Females
All ages	1 003	519	484	1 026	530	496
0-4	108	54	53	105	53	52
5-9	108	54	53	107	54	53
10-14	107	54	53	107	54	53
15-19	110	55	55	107	54	53
20-24	115	57	58	108	54	54
25-29	111	55	56	107	53	54
30-34	91	46	45	97	48	48
35-39	65	34	31	75	39	37
40-44	50	27	23	54	28	25
45-49	42	24	18	42	23	19
50-54	35	22	14	37	21	16
55-59	24	16	8	32	19	12
60-64	14	9	4	22	14	8
65-69	6	4	2	12	8	4
70-74	4	2	2	5	3	2
75-79	4	2	3	3	2	2
80-84	4	1	3	3	1	2
85-89	3	1	2	2	1	1
90-94	1	0	1	1	0	1
95-99	0	0	0	0	0	0
100 +	0	0	0	0	0	0

POPULATION BY AGE AND SEX (in thousands)

Age group	2005 Both sexes	Males	Females	2010 Both sexes	Males	Females	2015 Both sexes	Males	Females	2020 Both sexes	Males	Females
All ages	1 032	498	535	1 020	499	520	1 018	507	511	1 029	520	510
0-4	136	68	68	139	70	69	147	74	73	151	76	75
5-9	138	69	69	125	63	62	130	65	65	142	71	71
10-14	149	75	74	131	66	65	117	59	58	123	62	61
15-19	148	74	74	147	74	74	129	64	64	114	57	57
20-24	123	61	62	141	70	71	141	71	71	124	62	62
25-29	77	37	40	100	50	49	119	61	58	122	62	60
30-34	48	22	26	49	25	24	69	38	31	87	48	39
35-39	38	16	22	28	14	14	29	17	12	45	27	18
40-44	34	14	20	24	10	13	17	9	8	18	11	7
45-49	32	13	19	24	10	14	16	7	9	11	6	5
50-54	30	13	17	25	10	15	18	7	11	12	5	6
55-59	24	11	13	25	10	14	21	8	12	15	6	9
60-64	19	9	10	21	9	12	21	8	12	17	7	11
65-69	16	7	8	16	7	9	17	7	10	18	7	11
70-74	11	5	6	12	6	7	13	6	7	14	6	8
75-79	6	2	4	7	3	4	9	4	5	9	4	6
80-84	3	1	2	4	1	2	4	2	3	5	2	3
85-89	1	0	1	1	0	1	1	1	1	2	1	1
90-94	0	0	0	0	0	0	0	0	0	0	0	0
95-99	0	0	0	0	0	0	0	0	0	0	0	0
100 +	0	0	0	0	0	0	0	0	0	0	0	0

Age group	2025 Both sexes	Males	Females	2030 Both sexes	Males	Females	2035 Both sexes	Males	Females	2040 Both sexes	Males	Females
All ages	1 044	533	511	1 066	548	518	1 098	566	532	1 143	589	554
0-4	144	72	71	137	69	68	139	70	69	147	74	73
5-9	148	74	74	142	71	70	136	68	68	138	70	68
10-14	138	69	69	146	73	72	141	71	70	135	68	67
15-19	121	61	61	136	68	68	144	72	72	140	70	70
20-24	111	55	56	118	59	59	133	66	67	141	70	71
25-29	110	55	55	99	49	50	106	53	53	121	60	61
30-34	94	51	43	88	46	42	81	41	39	88	45	43
35-39	59	36	23	68	40	29	66	37	30	63	33	29
40-44	29	19	10	42	27	15	52	31	20	52	29	22
45-49	12	8	4	22	15	7	33	22	11	41	25	16
50-54	8	5	3	10	7	3	18	12	5	27	18	9
55-59	9	4	5	7	4	3	8	6	3	15	11	5
60-64	12	5	8	8	4	5	6	3	3	7	5	2
65-69	15	6	9	11	4	7	7	3	4	5	3	2
70-74	14	5	9	12	4	8	9	3	6	6	3	3
75-79	10	4	6	11	4	7	9	3	6	7	2	4
80-84	6	2	3	6	2	4	6	2	4	6	2	4
85-89	2	1	1	2	1	2	3	1	2	3	1	2
90-94	0	0	0	1	0	0	1	0	0	1	0	1
95-99	0	0	0	0	0	0	0	0	0	0	0	0
100 +	0	0	0	0	0	0	0	0	0	0	0	0

Age group	2045 Both sexes	Males	Females	2050 Both sexes	Males	Females
All ages	1 200	619	582	1 267	651	615
0-4	153	77	76	154	78	76
5-9	146	74	72	153	77	76
10-14	138	69	68	146	73	72
15-19	135	68	67	137	69	68
20-24	137	68	69	132	66	66
25-29	131	65	66	128	64	65
30-34	103	52	51	114	57	57
35-39	70	37	34	85	44	41
40-44	50	27	23	58	31	27
45-49	42	24	18	42	23	19
50-54	35	22	14	37	21	16
55-59	24	16	8	32	19	12
60-64	14	9	4	22	14	8
65-69	6	4	2	12	8	4
70-74	4	2	2	5	3	2
75-79	4	2	3	3	2	2
80-84	4	1	3	3	1	2
85-89	3	1	2	2	1	1
90-94	1	0	1	1	0	1
95-99	0	0	0	0	0	0
100 +	0	0	0	0	0	0

POPULATION BY AGE AND SEX (in thousands)

Age group	2005 Both sexes	2005 Males	2005 Females	2010 Both sexes	2010 Males	2010 Females	2015 Both sexes	2015 Males	2015 Females	2020 Both sexes	2020 Males	2020 Females
All ages	1 032	498	535	1 001	490	511	967	481	480	936	473	463
0-4	136	68	68	120	61	60	114	57	57	106	53	53
5-9	138	69	69	125	63	62	113	57	56	110	55	55
10-14	149	75	74	131	66	65	117	59	58	107	53	53
15-19	148	74	74	147	74	74	129	64	64	114	57	57
20-24	123	61	62	141	70	71	141	71	71	124	62	62
25-29	77	37	40	100	50	49	119	61	58	122	62	60
30-34	48	22	26	49	25	24	69	38	31	87	48	39
35-39	38	16	22	28	14	14	29	17	12	45	27	18
40-44	34	14	20	24	10	13	17	9	8	18	11	7
45-49	32	13	19	24	10	14	16	7	9	11	6	5
50-54	30	13	17	25	10	15	18	7	11	12	5	6
55-59	24	11	13	25	10	14	21	8	12	15	6	9
60-64	19	9	10	21	9	12	21	8	12	17	7	11
65-69	16	7	8	16	7	9	17	7	10	18	7	11
70-74	11	5	6	12	6	7	13	6	7	14	6	8
75-79	6	2	4	7	3	4	9	4	5	9	4	6
80-84	3	1	2	4	1	2	4	2	3	5	2	3
85-89	1	0	1	1	0	1	1	1	1	2	1	1
90-94	0	0	0	0	0	0	0	0	0	0	0	0
95-99	0	0	0	0	0	0	0	0	0	0	0	0
100 +	0	0	0	0	0	0	0	0	0	0	0	0

Age group	2025 Both sexes	2025 Males	2025 Females	2030 Both sexes	2030 Males	2030 Females	2035 Both sexes	2035 Males	2035 Females	2040 Both sexes	2040 Males	2040 Females
All ages	906	464	442	881	455	426	857	445	412	837	435	402
0-4	98	49	48	88	44	44	80	41	40	75	38	37
5-9	104	52	52	96	49	48	87	44	43	80	40	40
10-14	106	53	53	102	51	51	96	48	48	87	44	43
15-19	105	52	52	105	53	53	101	51	51	95	48	47
20-24	111	55	56	102	51	51	102	51	52	99	49	50
25-29	110	55	55	99	49	50	92	46	46	93	46	47
30-34	94	51	43	88	46	42	81	41	39	76	38	37
35-39	59	36	23	68	40	29	66	37	30	63	33	29
40-44	29	19	10	42	27	15	52	31	20	62	29	22
45-49	12	8	4	22	15	7	33	22	11	41	25	16
50-54	8	5	3	10	7	3	18	12	5	27	18	9
55-59	9	4	5	7	4	3	8	6	3	15	11	5
60-64	12	5	8	8	4	5	6	3	3	7	5	2
65-69	15	6	9	11	4	7	7	3	4	5	3	2
70-74	14	5	9	12	4	8	9	3	6	6	3	3
75-79	10	4	6	11	4	7	9	3	6	7	2	4
80-84	6	2	3	6	2	4	6	2	4	6	2	4
85-89	2	1	1	2	1	2	3	1	2	3	1	2
90-94	0	0	0	1	0	0	1	0	0	1	0	1
95-99	0	0	0	0	0	0	0	0	0	0	0	0
100 +	0	0	0	0	0	0	0	0	0	0	0	0

Age group	2045 Both sexes	2045 Males	2045 Females	2050 Both sexes	2050 Males	2050 Females
All ages	821	427	394	811	421	390
0-4	70	35	35	65	33	32
5-9	74	38	37	70	35	35
10-14	79	40	39	74	37	37
15-19	86	43	43	79	40	39
20-24	93	46	47	84	42	42
25-29	91	45	46	86	43	44
30-34	79	39	39	79	39	40
35-39	60	31	29	65	33	32
40-44	50	27	23	50	26	24
45-49	42	24	18	42	23	19
50-54	35	22	14	37	21	16
55-59	24	16	8	32	19	12
60-64	14	9	4	22	14	8
65-69	6	4	2	12	8	4
70-74	4	2	2	5	3	2
75-79	4	2	3	3	2	2
80-84	4	1	3	3	1	2
85-89	3	1	2	2	1	1
90-94	1	0	1	1	0	1
95-99	0	0	0	0	0	0
100 +	0	0	0	0	0	0

United Nations Department of Economic and Social Affairs/Population Division
World Population Prospects: The 2004 Revision, Volume II: Sex and Age Distribution of the World Population

809

POPULATION BY AGE AND SEX (in thousands)

Age group	1950 Both sexes	1950 Males	1950 Females	1955 Both sexes	1955 Males	1955 Females	1960 Both sexes	1960 Males	1960 Females	1965 Both sexes	1965 Males	1965 Females
All ages	7 014	3 493	3 521	7 262	3 619	3 643	7 480	3 731	3 749	7 734	3 862	3 872
0-4	606	311	295	536	276	260	504	259	245	555	285	270
5-9	588	301	287	618	317	301	533	274	259	526	271	255
10-14	450	229	221	571	292	279	609	312	297	539	277	262
15-19	415	210	205	448	227	221	594	303	291	626	320	306
20-24	457	229	228	431	216	215	465	235	230	594	305	289
25-29	531	268	263	474	238	236	434	219	215	474	243	231
30-34	540	273	267	547	276	271	469	236	233	442	224	218
35-39	543	275	268	531	268	263	532	268	264	475	239	236
40-44	538	271	267	543	274	269	535	270	265	543	273	270
45-49	486	241	245	529	265	264	532	268	264	521	262	259
50-54	434	213	221	474	234	240	521	261	260	526	264	262
55-59	378	182	196	415	202	213	461	226	235	501	248	253
60-64	329	156	173	353	168	185	396	191	205	433	209	224
65-69	269	127	142	296	139	157	325	152	173	357	168	189
70-74	210	99	111	224	104	120	256	117	139	273	123	150
75-79	134	62	72	154	71	83	171	77	94	189	83	106
80 +	106	46	60	118	52	66	143	63	80	160	68	92

Age group	1970 Both sexes	1970 Males	1970 Females	1975 Both sexes	1975 Males	1975 Females	1980 Both sexes	1980 Males	1980 Females	1985 Both sexes	1985 Males	1985 Females
All ages	8 043	4 016	4 027	8 193	4 075	4 118	8 310	4 118	4 193	8 350	4 124	4 226
0-4	581	299	283	551	282	268	487	250	238	427	219	208
5-9	564	289	275	581	298	283	557	285	272	484	248	236
10-14	531	273	258	563	289	274	584	300	284	553	283	270
15-19	553	283	270	536	275	261	569	291	278	578	296	282
20-24	662	338	323	565	288	277	556	284	272	586	300	287
25-29	613	318	295	663	340	323	583	299	285	559	286	273
30-34	483	249	234	605	314	292	668	342	325	578	295	283
35-39	446	226	220	477	244	232	604	312	292	655	334	321
40-44	475	239	237	441	222	219	474	242	232	617	317	300
45-49	538	270	268	468	234	234	436	219	217	474	241	233
50-54	512	256	255	526	262	264	459	228	232	426	213	214
55-59	510	254	256	495	245	249	509	251	259	443	217	226
60-64	476	232	244	484	237	247	470	229	241	478	232	247
65-69	396	186	210	436	206	229	435	206	229	447	212	235
70-74	306	138	168	343	154	189	381	172	208	396	180	216
75-79	210	90	120	239	101	138	273	114	159	317	134	183
80 +	187	76	111	221	84	137	265	96	169	332	117	215

Age group	1990 Both sexes	1990 Males	1990 Females	1995 Both sexes	1995 Males	1995 Females	2000 Both sexes	2000 Males	2000 Females	2005 Both sexes	2005 Males	2005 Females
All ages	8 559	4 228	4 331	8 827	4 361	4 466	8 877	4 392	4 485	9 041	4 486	4 555
0-4	553	284	269	594	305	289	461	237	225	488	251	237
5-9	486	249	236	570	292	277	601	308	293	481	247	233
10-14	497	254	242	500	257	243	574	294	279	613	315	298
15-19	565	289	276	509	261	248	506	260	246	590	304	286
20-24	607	311	296	583	297	286	517	264	253	527	270	257
25-29	604	311	293	629	322	307	592	300	292	545	278	267
30-34	577	296	281	621	319	302	637	326	311	617	315	303
35-39	588	300	288	588	301	287	624	320	304	649	332	317
40-44	661	337	325	591	301	290	587	299	288	626	319	307
45-49	594	305	290	658	334	324	587	297	289	583	295	289
50-54	462	233	229	587	299	288	649	327	321	579	291	288
55-59	417	206	212	452	226	226	573	290	283	634	317	317
60-64	427	206	221	403	196	208	437	216	220	555	278	276
65-69	452	212	239	402	189	213	381	182	199	415	203	213
70-74	386	174	212	406	184	223	365	167	199	350	162	187
75-79	320	135	185	322	137	186	346	149	197	315	137	177
80 +	364	127	237	411	143	268	440	156	285	477	173	304

810

United Nations Department of Economic and Social Affairs/Population Division
World Population Prospects: The 2004 Revision, Volume II: Sex and Age Distribution of the World Population

POPULATION BY AGE AND SEX (in thousands)

Age group	2005 Both sexes	Males	Females	2010 Both sexes	Males	Females	2015 Both sexes	Males	Females	2020 Both sexes	Males	Females
All ages	9 041	4 486	4 555	9 168	4 560	4 607	9 315	4 643	4 672	9 488	4 735	4 753
0-4	488	251	237	494	255	240	516	265	250	546	281	265
5-9	481	247	233	500	258	242	507	261	245	528	272	256
10-14	613	315	298	488	252	236	507	262	245	514	266	248
15-19	590	304	286	623	321	302	498	258	240	518	269	249
20-24	527	270	257	602	310	292	636	327	308	512	265	247
25-29	545	278	267	544	279	265	620	319	301	653	336	317
30-34	617	315	303	560	287	274	560	288	272	636	328	308
35-39	649	332	317	624	318	306	568	291	277	568	292	276
40-44	626	319	307	649	330	318	625	317	308	569	290	279
45-49	583	295	289	622	315	307	645	327	318	622	314	308
50-54	579	291	288	577	290	287	616	311	305	639	322	317
55-59	634	317	317	567	283	284	566	282	283	605	303	302
60-64	555	278	276	615	305	310	551	273	278	551	273	278
65-69	415	203	213	528	261	267	587	288	300	528	258	270
70-74	350	162	187	382	182	200	488	236	252	545	261	284
75-79	315	137	177	303	135	168	333	153	181	428	200	229
80-84	261	104	157	242	99	144	236	99	138	263	114	150
85-89	145	50	95	164	58	105	156	57	99	156	59	98
90-94	57	16	42	65	19	46	77	23	54	78	24	54
95-99	12	2	10	16	3	12	19	4	15	25	6	19
100 +	1	0	1	2	0	2	3	0	2	4	1	3

Age group	2025 Both sexes	Males	Females	2030 Both sexes	Males	Females	2035 Both sexes	Males	Females	2040 Both sexes	Males	Females
All ages	9 650	4 818	4 832	9 769	4 877	4 892	9 845	4 914	4 931	9 906	4 946	4 960
0-4	551	284	267	532	274	258	513	264	249	514	265	249
5-9	559	288	271	563	290	273	544	281	263	526	271	255
10-14	535	277	259	566	293	273	570	295	276	551	285	266
15-19	524	272	252	546	283	262	576	299	277	581	301	280
20-24	531	275	256	538	279	259	559	290	269	590	306	284
25-29	530	274	256	549	285	264	556	288	268	577	299	278
30-34	669	346	324	546	283	263	565	294	271	572	298	275
35-39	644	302	311	677	350	327	554	288	266	573	298	275
40-44	569	292	277	645	332	313	678	349	329	555	287	268
45-49	567	287	279	567	289	278	643	329	313	676	347	329
50-54	616	310	300	562	284	278	563	285	277	638	326	312
55-59	629	315	313	607	304	303	554	278	276	555	280	275
60-64	590	294	296	614	306	308	594	295	299	542	270	272
65-69	529	259	270	568	280	288	592	292	300	574	282	291
70-74	492	236	256	495	238	257	532	257	275	557	270	287
75-79	482	223	259	438	203	235	442	206	236	479	225	254
80-84	343	151	192	390	171	219	358	157	201	365	161	204
85-89	178	70	108	237	95	142	275	110	165	257	103	154
90-94	81	26	55	96	32	64	132	45	87	158	54	104
95-99	27	6	20	30	7	22	37	10	28	54	14	39
100 +	5	1	4	6	1	5	7	1	6	9	2	8

Age group	2045 Both sexes	Males	Females	2050 Both sexes	Males	Females
All ages	9 973	4 984	4 989	10 054	5 030	5 024
0-4	529	272	256	544	280	264
5-9	527	272	255	541	279	262
10-14	533	276	257	534	276	258
15-19	562	291	270	544	282	261
20-24	594	308	286	575	298	277
25-29	608	315	293	613	318	295
30-34	594	309	285	625	325	300
35-39	580	302	278	602	313	289
40-44	575	298	277	582	302	280
45-49	554	285	269	574	296	278
50-54	672	343	329	551	282	268
55-59	630	320	310	664	337	326
60-64	544	273	271	618	312	306
65-69	525	260	266	528	263	265
70-74	542	262	279	497	242	255
75-79	504	237	266	492	232	260
80-84	399	178	221	423	190	233
85-89	267	108	159	297	122	175
90-94	153	53	100	163	58	106
95-99	68	18	49	68	19	49
100 +	14	3	11	19	4	16

United Nations Department of Economic and Social Affairs/Population Division
World Population Prospects: The 2004 Revision, Volume II: Sex and Age Distribution of the World Population

811

POPULATION BY AGE AND SEX (in thousands)

Age group	2005 Both sexes	Males	Females	2010 Both sexes	Males	Females	2015 Both sexes	Males	Females	2020 Both sexes	Males	Females
All ages	9 041	4 486	4 555	9 237	4 596	4 641	9 498	4 737	4 761	9 817	4 904	4 913
0-4	488	251	237	564	290	274	629	324	305	693	357	336
5-9	481	247	233	500	258	242	576	297	279	641	330	310
10-14	613	315	298	488	252	236	507	262	245	584	302	282
15-19	590	304	286	623	321	302	498	258	240	518	269	249
20-24	527	270	257	602	310	292	636	327	308	512	265	247
25-29	545	278	267	544	279	265	620	319	301	653	336	317
30-34	617	315	303	560	287	274	560	288	272	636	328	308
35-39	649	332	317	624	318	306	568	291	277	568	292	276
40-44	626	319	307	649	330	318	625	317	308	569	290	279
45-49	583	295	289	622	315	307	645	327	318	622	314	308
50-54	579	291	288	577	290	287	616	311	305	639	322	317
55-59	634	317	317	567	283	284	566	282	283	605	303	302
60-64	555	278	276	615	305	310	551	273	278	551	273	278
65-69	415	203	213	528	261	267	587	288	300	528	258	270
70-74	350	162	187	382	182	200	488	236	252	545	261	284
75-79	315	137	177	303	135	168	333	153	181	428	200	229
80-84	261	104	157	242	99	144	236	99	138	263	114	150
85-89	145	50	95	164	58	105	156	57	99	156	59	98
90-94	57	16	42	65	19	46	77	23	54	78	24	54
95-99	12	2	10	16	3	12	19	4	15	25	6	19
100 +	1	0	1	2	0	2	3	0	2	4	1	3

Age group	2025 Both sexes	Males	Females	2030 Both sexes	Males	Females	2035 Both sexes	Males	Females	2040 Both sexes	Males	Females
All ages	10 122	5 061	5 061	10 380	5 191	5 189	10 617	5 311	5 306	10 885	5 450	5 436
0-4	694	357	337	671	345	326	674	347	327	723	372	351
5-9	705	363	342	706	364	342	683	352	331	686	354	332
10-14	648	335	313	713	368	345	714	369	345	691	357	334
15-19	594	308	286	658	341	317	723	374	349	724	375	349
20-24	531	275	256	607	315	293	672	348	324	736	381	355
25-29	530	274	256	549	285	264	625	324	302	690	357	333
30-34	669	346	324	546	283	263	565	294	271	642	333	308
35-39	644	332	311	677	350	327	554	288	266	573	298	275
40-44	569	292	277	645	332	313	678	349	329	555	287	268
45-49	567	287	279	567	289	278	643	329	313	676	347	329
50-54	616	310	306	562	284	278	563	285	277	638	326	312
55-59	629	315	313	607	304	303	554	278	276	555	280	275
60-64	590	294	296	614	306	308	594	295	299	542	270	272
65-69	529	259	270	568	280	288	592	292	300	574	282	291
70-74	492	236	256	495	238	257	532	257	275	557	270	287
75-79	482	223	259	438	203	235	442	206	236	479	225	254
80-84	343	151	192	390	171	219	358	157	201	365	161	204
85-89	178	70	108	237	95	142	275	110	165	257	103	154
90-94	81	26	55	96	32	64	132	45	87	158	54	104
95-99	27	6	20	30	7	22	37	10	28	54	14	39
100 +	5	1	4	6	1	5	7	1	6	9	2	8

Age group	2045 Both sexes	Males	Females	2050 Both sexes	Males	Females
All ages	11 213	5 622	5 591	11 587	5 818	5 769
0-4	789	406	383	838	431	407
5-9	735	379	356	801	413	388
10-14	693	358	335	743	384	359
15-19	701	363	338	704	365	339
20-24	738	382	356	715	370	345
25-29	755	390	364	756	391	365
30-34	706	367	340	771	400	371
35-39	650	337	312	714	371	343
40-44	575	298	277	651	337	314
45-49	554	285	269	574	296	278
50-54	672	343	329	551	282	268
55-59	630	320	310	664	337	326
60-64	544	273	271	618	312	306
65-69	525	260	266	528	263	265
70-74	542	262	279	497	242	255
75-79	504	237	266	492	232	260
80-84	399	178	221	423	190	233
85-89	267	108	159	297	122	175
90-94	153	53	100	163	58	106
95-99	68	18	49	68	19	49
100 +	14	3	11	19	4	16

United Nations Department of Economic and Social Affairs/Population Division
World Population Prospects: The 2004 Revision, Volume II: Sex and Age Distribution of the World Population

812

POPULATION BY AGE AND SEX (in thousands)

Age group	2005 Both sexes	2005 Males	2005 Females	2010 Both sexes	2010 Males	2010 Females	2015 Both sexes	2015 Males	2015 Females	2020 Both sexes	2020 Males	2020 Females
All ages	9 041	4 486	4 555	9 098	4 524	4 573	9 133	4 549	4 584	9 159	4 566	4 593
0-4	488	251	237	425	219	206	403	207	195	400	206	194
5-9	481	247	233	500	258	242	437	225	211	415	214	201
10-14	613	315	298	488	252	236	507	262	245	444	230	214
15-19	590	304	286	623	321	302	498	258	240	518	269	249
20-24	527	270	257	602	310	292	636	327	308	512	265	247
25-29	545	278	267	544	279	265	620	319	301	653	336	317
30-34	617	315	303	560	287	274	560	288	272	636	328	308
35-39	649	332	317	624	318	306	568	291	277	568	292	276
40-44	626	319	307	649	330	318	625	317	308	569	290	279
45-49	583	295	289	622	315	307	645	327	318	622	314	308
50-54	579	291	288	577	290	287	616	311	305	639	322	317
55-59	634	317	317	567	283	284	566	282	283	605	303	302
60-64	555	278	276	615	305	310	551	273	278	551	273	278
65-69	415	203	213	528	261	267	587	288	300	528	258	270
70-74	350	162	187	382	182	200	488	236	252	545	261	284
75-79	315	137	177	303	135	168	333	153	181	428	200	229
80-84	261	104	157	242	99	144	236	99	138	263	114	150
85-89	145	50	95	164	58	105	156	57	99	156	59	98
90-94	57	16	42	65	19	46	77	23	54	78	24	54
95-99	12	2	10	16	3	12	19	4	15	25	6	19
100	1	0	1	2	0	2	3	0	2	4	1	3

Age group	2025 Both sexes	2025 Males	2025 Females	2030 Both sexes	2030 Males	2030 Females	2035 Both sexes	2035 Males	2035 Females	2040 Both sexes	2040 Males	2040 Females
All ages	9 176	4 574	4 602	9 156	4 561	4 595	9 090	4 525	4 564	8 983	4 471	4 512
0-4	406	209	197	393	202	190	370	191	179	347	179	168
5-9	413	213	200	418	216	202	405	209	196	383	198	185
10-14	422	219	204	420	217	202	425	220	205	413	214	199
15-19	455	236	218	433	225	208	430	224	207	436	227	209
20-24	531	275	256	468	243	225	446	232	214	444	231	213
25-29	530	274	256	549	285	264	486	252	234	465	241	223
30-34	669	346	324	546	283	263	565	294	271	503	262	241
35-39	644	332	311	677	350	327	554	288	266	573	298	275
40-44	569	292	277	645	332	313	678	349	329	555	287	268
45-49	567	287	279	567	289	278	643	329	313	676	347	329
50-54	618	310	308	562	284	278	563	285	277	638	326	312
55-59	629	315	313	607	304	303	554	278	276	555	280	275
60-64	590	294	296	614	306	308	594	295	299	542	270	272
65-69	529	259	270	568	280	288	592	292	300	574	282	291
70-74	492	236	256	495	238	257	532	257	275	557	270	287
75-79	482	223	259	438	203	236	442	206	236	479	225	254
80-84	343	151	192	390	171	219	358	157	201	365	161	204
85-89	178	70	108	237	95	142	275	110	165	257	103	154
90-94	81	26	55	96	32	64	132	45	87	158	54	104
95-99	27	6	20	30	7	22	37	10	28	54	14	39
100 +	5	1	4	6	1	5	7	1	6	9	2	8

Age group	2045 Both sexes	2045 Males	2045 Females	2050 Both sexes	2050 Males	2050 Females
All ages	8 852	4 408	4 445	8 710	4 339	4 371
0-4	330	170	160	320	165	155
5-9	360	186	174	342	177	165
10-14	390	202	188	367	190	177
15-19	423	220	203	401	209	192
20-24	449	234	216	437	227	210
25-29	462	240	222	468	243	225
30-34	481	251	230	479	250	229
35-39	511	266	245	489	255	234
40-44	575	298	277	513	266	247
45-49	554	285	269	574	296	278
50-54	672	343	329	551	282	268
55-59	630	320	310	664	337	326
60-64	544	273	271	618	312	306
65-69	525	260	266	528	263	265
70-74	542	262	279	497	242	255
75-79	504	237	266	492	232	260
80-84	399	178	221	423	190	233
85-89	267	108	159	297	122	175
90-94	153	53	100	163	58	106
95-99	68	18	49	68	19	49
100 +	14	3	11	19	4	16

POPULATION BY AGE AND SEX (in thousands)

Age group	1950 Both sexes	Males	Females	1955 Both sexes	Males	Females	1960 Both sexes	Males	Females	1965 Both sexes	Males	Females
All ages	4 694	2 262	2 432	4 980	2 407	2 573	5 362	2 630	2 732	5 857	2 853	3 004
0-4	410	210	200	405	207	198	438	224	214	515	263	252
5-9	390	199	191	418	214	204	407	208	199	455	232	223
10-14	305	155	150	385	196	189	422	216	206	443	225	218
15-19	326	163	163	322	163	159	420	214	206	486	245	241
20-24	348	167	181	350	171	179	404	207	197	479	243	236
25-29	356	172	184	364	171	193	402	207	195	424	214	210
30-34	318	157	161	368	178	190	381	191	190	405	203	202
35-39	344	168	176	321	159	162	373	185	188	382	187	195
40-44	358	173	185	356	175	181	316	156	160	374	182	192
45-49	334	159	175	358	174	184	345	168	177	314	154	160
50-54	297	138	159	329	157	172	346	167	179	341	165	176
55-59	249	114	135	283	131	152	309	145	164	332	156	176
60-64	208	94	114	230	103	127	260	117	143	291	132	159
65-69	176	79	97	184	81	103	202	88	114	235	101	134
70-74	138	59	79	144	62	82	152	64	88	172	71	101
75-79	82	34	48	97	40	57	105	43	62	114	45	69
80 +	55	21	34	66	25	41	80	30	50	95	35	60

Age group	1970 Both sexes	Males	Females	1975 Both sexes	Males	Females	1980 Both sexes	Males	Females	1985 Both sexes	Males	Females
All ages	6 187	3 022	3 164	6 339	3 090	3 249	6 319	3 074	3 245	6 536	3 185	3 351
0-4	502	256	246	424	218	206	356	182	174	371	190	181
5-9	506	258	248	493	252	241	407	209	198	366	187	179
10-14	462	236	227	505	258	247	484	248	237	406	208	197
15-19	451	229	222	466	235	231	505	258	247	488	250	238
20-24	502	250	252	462	226	236	465	232	233	524	265	259
25-29	499	254	246	516	259	257	463	229	234	500	251	249
30-34	437	223	214	493	252	241	503	254	249	487	244	243
35-39	412	208	204	425	216	210	473	241	233	512	259	253
40-44	386	190	197	405	203	202	408	205	203	483	246	238
45-49	374	182	191	379	185	194	390	194	196	407	204	203
50-54	310	151	159	364	176	188	365	176	189	385	190	194
55-59	330	157	172	299	144	155	346	165	182	354	169	185
60-64	313	143	169	310	144	166	279	132	148	328	152	176
65-69	263	115	148	283	125	158	269	122	148	262	119	143
70-74	199	81	118	227	93	133	247	103	144	248	105	143
75-79	131	50	81	155	59	97	185	71	114	204	79	125
80 +	109	39	71	132	45	87	174	56	118	211	67	144

Age group	1990 Both sexes	Males	Females	1995 Both sexes	Males	Females	2000 Both sexes	Males	Females	2005 Both sexes	Males	Females
All ages	6 834	3 371	3 463	7 003	3 426	3 577	7 167	3 481	3 687	7 252	3 512	3 740
0-4	400	205	195	423	217	207	396	203	193	353	181	172
5-9	381	195	186	410	210	199	433	222	211	401	206	195
10-14	373	191	182	399	203	196	427	218	209	442	226	215
15-19	421	217	204	388	197	192	414	209	205	435	221	214
20-24	535	276	258	444	222	222	411	202	209	425	211	214
25-29	602	313	289	560	282	279	471	228	242	424	205	219
30-34	561	292	269	612	316	296	571	285	286	475	229	246
35-39	512	263	249	571	295	276	622	318	303	575	286	289
40-44	514	262	252	507	257	250	566	288	278	618	314	304
45-49	474	241	233	502	251	251	496	246	250	558	282	277
50-54	391	195	196	460	229	231	488	239	249	487	239	248
55-59	363	177	185	377	183	194	446	217	229	477	231	246
60-64	326	152	174	336	157	179	352	165	187	426	203	223
65-69	296	132	164	295	134	161	306	141	166	328	151	177
70-74	231	99	131	261	111	150	263	115	147	278	124	154
75-79	203	80	124	191	77	114	221	89	132	226	94	132
80 +	251	80	171	267	85	181	284	94	190	324	110	215

United Nations Department of Economic and Social Affairs/Population Division
World Population Prospects: The 2004 Revision, Volume II: Sex and Age Distribution of the World Population

POPULATION BY AGE AND SEX (in thousands)

Age group	2005 Both sexes	Males	Females	2010 Both sexes	Males	Females	2015 Both sexes	Males	Females	2020 Both sexes	Males	Females
All ages	7 252	3 512	3 740	7 301	3 524	3 777	7 334	3 527	3 807	7 368	3 529	3 839
0-4	353	181	172	329	169	161	330	169	161	350	179	170
5-9	401	206	195	358	184	174	334	172	163	335	172	163
10-14	442	226	215	410	210	200	366	187	179	343	176	168
15-19	435	221	214	449	229	220	417	212	205	374	190	184
20-24	425	211	214	446	223	223	461	232	229	429	215	214
25-29	424	205	219	438	214	224	459	226	233	474	234	239
30-34	475	229	246	429	206	223	443	215	228	464	228	237
35-39	575	286	289	480	231	249	434	208	226	448	217	231
40-44	618	314	304	571	282	290	477	227	250	432	204	227
45-49	558	282	277	610	307	303	564	275	289	471	222	249
50-54	487	239	248	549	274	275	600	299	301	555	268	287
55-59	477	231	246	476	231	245	537	265	272	588	291	298
60-64	426	203	223	457	217	240	457	217	239	517	251	266
65-69	328	151	177	400	188	212	430	201	229	431	202	229
70-74	278	124	154	300	134	166	367	168	199	397	181	216
75-79	226	94	132	241	103	139	262	112	150	323	142	181
80-84	173	64	108	179	70	109	193	77	116	212	85	127
85-89	94	31	63	114	38	76	121	42	79	133	47	86
90-94	44	12	32	48	13	34	60	17	43	66	19	46
95-99	12	3	10	15	3	12	17	4	13	23	5	18
100 +	2	0	1	2	0	2	3	1	3	4	1	3

Age group	2025 Both sexes	Males	Females	2030 Both sexes	Males	Females	2035 Both sexes	Males	Females	2040 Both sexes	Males	Females
All ages	7 398	3 529	3 870	7 410	3 519	3 892	7 393	3 495	3 898	7 351	3 460	3 891
0-4	366	188	179	371	190	181	365	187	178	361	185	176
5-9	354	182	172	371	191	181	376	193	183	370	190	180
10-14	344	176	168	363	186	177	380	194	185	385	197	188
15-19	351	178	172	352	179	173	371	189	182	388	197	190
20-24	386	193	193	363	181	181	364	182	182	383	192	191
25-29	442	218	224	399	196	203	376	184	192	377	185	192
30-34	479	236	243	447	220	228	405	198	207	382	186	195
35-39	469	229	240	484	238	247	453	221	231	410	200	211
40-44	446	214	232	467	226	241	482	234	248	451	218	232
45-49	426	199	227	440	208	232	461	221	241	476	229	247
50-54	463	215	248	419	193	226	434	202	231	455	215	240
55-59	545	260	285	455	209	246	412	187	224	426	197	230
60-64	568	276	292	526	247	279	439	197	241	397	177	220
65-69	490	235	255	540	260	281	502	233	269	418	186	232
70-74	399	183	216	456	214	242	504	238	266	470	214	256
75-79	351	154	197	355	157	198	407	185	223	453	207	246
80-84	263	108	155	289	120	170	295	123	172	342	147	195
85-89	149	54	95	188	70	118	211	79	132	219	83	136
90-94	74	23	52	86	26	59	112	36	76	128	41	87
95-99	26	6	20	31	7	23	37	9	28	50	13	37
100 +	6	1	5	7	1	6	9	1	7	11	2	9

Age group	2045 Both sexes	Males	Females	2050 Both sexes	Males	Females
All ages	7 300	3 424	3 877	7 252	3 392	3 861
0-4	368	188	179	377	193	184
5-9	366	188	178	372	191	181
10-14	378	194	185	375	192	183
15-19	393	200	193	386	197	190
20-24	400	200	199	405	203	202
25-29	396	195	202	413	203	210
30-34	383	187	196	402	197	205
35-39	387	188	199	389	189	200
40-44	409	197	212	386	185	200
45-49	446	213	232	404	192	212
50-54	470	223	247	439	208	232
55-59	447	209	238	463	218	245
60-64	412	186	226	433	199	234
65-69	379	167	212	394	176	217
70-74	393	171	221	356	154	202
75-79	424	187	237	357	151	206
80-84	383	166	217	362	152	210
85-89	257	101	156	292	116	176
90-94	137	45	92	164	56	108
95-99	60	15	44	66	17	48
100 +	15	3	12	19	3	16

United Nations Department of Economic and Social Affairs/Population Division
World Population Prospects: The 2004 Revision, Volume II: Sex and Age Distribution of the World Population

815

POPULATION BY AGE AND SEX (in thousands)

Age group	2005 Both sexes	2005 Males	2005 Females	2010 Both sexes	2010 Males	2010 Females	2015 Both sexes	2015 Males	2015 Females	2020 Both sexes	2020 Males	2020 Females
All ages	7 252	3 512	3 740	7 357	3 553	3 804	7 480	3 602	3 878	7 629	3 663	3 966
0-4	353	181	172	386	197	188	420	215	205	464	238	227
5-9	401	206	195	358	184	174	390	200	190	425	218	207
10-14	442	226	215	410	210	200	366	187	179	399	204	195
15-19	435	221	214	449	229	220	417	212	205	374	190	184
20-24	425	211	214	446	223	223	461	232	229	429	215	214
25-29	424	205	219	438	214	224	459	226	233	474	234	239
30-34	475	229	246	429	206	223	443	215	228	464	228	237
35-39	575	286	289	480	231	249	434	208	226	448	217	231
40-44	618	314	304	571	282	290	477	227	250	432	204	227
45-49	558	282	277	610	307	303	564	275	289	471	222	249
50-54	487	239	248	549	274	275	600	299	301	555	268	287
55-59	477	231	246	476	231	245	537	265	272	588	291	298
60-64	426	203	223	457	217	240	457	217	239	517	251	266
65-69	328	151	177	400	188	212	430	201	229	431	202	229
70-74	278	124	154	300	134	166	367	168	199	397	181	216
75-79	226	94	132	241	103	139	262	112	150	323	142	181
80-84	173	64	108	179	70	109	193	77	116	212	85	127
85-89	94	31	63	114	38	76	121	42	79	133	47	86
90-94	44	12	32	48	13	34	60	17	43	66	19	46
95-99	12	3	10	15	3	12	17	4	13	23	5	18
100 +	2	0	1	2	0	2	3	1	3	4	1	3

Age group	2025 Both sexes	2025 Males	2025 Females	2030 Both sexes	2030 Males	2030 Females	2035 Both sexes	2035 Males	2035 Females	2040 Both sexes	2040 Males	2040 Females
All ages	7 772	3 720	4 052	7 894	3 767	4 127	7 995	3 803	4 192	8 104	3 846	4 258
0-4	479	246	234	481	246	234	484	248	236	512	262	250
5-9	469	241	228	484	248	236	485	249	236	489	251	238
10-14	434	222	212	478	245	233	493	252	241	494	253	241
15-19	407	207	200	442	225	217	486	248	238	501	255	246
20-24	386	193	193	419	210	209	454	228	226	498	250	247
25-29	442	218	224	399	196	203	432	213	219	467	231	236
30-34	479	236	243	447	220	228	405	198	207	437	215	223
35-39	469	229	240	484	238	247	453	221	231	410	200	211
40-44	446	214	232	467	226	241	482	234	248	451	218	232
45-49	426	199	227	440	208	232	461	221	241	476	229	247
50-54	463	215	248	419	193	226	434	202	231	455	215	240
55-59	545	260	285	455	209	246	412	187	224	426	197	230
60-64	568	276	292	526	247	279	439	197	241	397	177	220
65-69	490	235	255	540	260	281	502	233	269	418	186	232
70-74	399	183	216	456	214	242	504	238	266	470	214	256
75-79	351	154	197	355	157	198	407	185	223	453	207	246
80-84	263	108	155	289	120	170	295	123	172	342	147	195
85-89	149	54	95	188	70	118	211	79	132	219	83	136
90-94	74	23	52	86	26	59	112	36	76	128	41	87
95-99	26	6	20	31	7	23	37	9	28	50	13	37
100 +	6	1	5	7	1	6	9	1	7	11	2	9

Age group	2045 Both sexes	2045 Males	2045 Females	2050 Both sexes	2050 Males	2050 Females
All ages	8 244	3 907	4 337	8 413	3 986	4 427
0-4	558	286	272	595	305	290
5-9	517	265	251	563	289	274
10-14	498	255	243	525	269	256
15-19	502	256	246	506	258	248
20-24	513	258	254	514	259	255
25-29	511	253	257	526	261	265
30-34	473	233	240	517	255	261
35-39	443	217	226	478	235	244
40-44	409	197	212	441	214	228
45-49	446	213	232	404	192	212
50-54	470	223	247	439	208	232
55-59	447	209	238	463	218	245
60-64	412	186	226	433	199	234
65-69	379	167	212	394	176	217
70-74	393	171	221	356	154	202
75-79	424	187	237	357	151	206
80-84	383	166	217	362	152	210
85-89	257	101	156	292	116	176
90-94	137	45	92	164	56	108
95-99	60	15	44	66	17	48
100 +	15	3	12	19	3	16

United Nations Department of Economic and Social Affairs/Population Division
World Population Prospects: The 2004 Revision, Volume II: Sex and Age Distribution of the World Population

816

POPULATION BY AGE AND SEX (in thousands)

Age group	2005 Both sexes	Males	Females	2010 Both sexes	Males	Females	2015 Both sexes	Males	Females	2020 Both sexes	Males	Females
All ages	7 252	3 512	3 740	7 244	3 495	3 749	7 187	3 452	3 735	7 106	3 395	3 711
0-4	353	181	172	273	140	133	240	123	117	235	120	114
5-9	401	206	195	358	184	174	278	143	135	245	126	119
10-14	442	226	215	410	210	200	366	187	179	287	147	140
15-19	435	221	214	449	229	220	417	212	205	374	190	184
20-24	425	211	214	446	223	223	461	232	229	429	215	214
25-29	424	205	219	438	214	224	459	226	233	474	234	239
30-34	475	229	246	429	206	223	443	215	228	464	228	237
35-39	575	286	289	480	231	249	434	208	226	448	217	231
40-44	618	314	304	571	282	290	477	227	250	432	204	227
45-49	558	282	277	610	307	303	564	275	289	471	222	249
50-54	487	239	248	549	274	275	600	299	301	555	268	287
55-59	477	231	246	476	231	245	537	265	272	588	291	298
60-64	426	203	223	457	217	240	457	217	239	517	251	266
65-69	328	151	177	400	188	212	430	201	229	431	202	229
70-74	278	124	154	300	134	166	367	168	199	397	181	216
75-79	226	94	132	241	103	139	262	112	150	323	142	181
80-84	173	64	108	179	70	109	193	77	116	212	85	127
85-89	94	31	63	114	38	76	121	42	79	133	47	86
90-94	44	12	32	48	13	34	60	17	43	66	19	46
95-99	12	3	10	15	3	12	17	4	13	23	5	18
100 +	2	0	1	2	0	2	3	1	3	4	1	3

Age group	2025 Both sexes	Males	Females	2030 Both sexes	Males	Females	2035 Both sexes	Males	Females	2040 Both sexes	Males	Females
All ages	7 022	3 336	3 686	6 924	3 270	3 655	6 798	3 190	3 608	6 636	3 094	3 542
0-4	252	129	123	261	134	127	256	131	125	240	123	117
5-9	239	123	116	257	132	125	266	137	129	261	134	127
10-14	253	130	124	248	127	121	266	136	130	275	141	134
15-19	294	149	145	261	133	129	256	130	126	273	139	135
20-24	386	193	193	306	152	154	273	136	138	268	133	135
25-29	442	218	224	399	196	203	320	156	164	287	139	148
30-34	479	236	243	447	220	228	405	198	207	326	158	168
35-39	469	229	240	404	238	247	453	221	231	410	200	211
40-44	446	214	232	467	226	241	482	234	248	451	218	232
45-49	426	199	227	440	208	232	461	221	241	476	229	247
50-54	463	215	248	419	193	226	434	202	231	455	215	240
55-59	545	260	285	455	209	246	412	187	224	426	197	230
60-64	568	276	292	526	247	279	439	197	241	397	177	220
65-69	490	235	255	540	260	281	502	233	269	418	186	232
70-74	399	183	216	456	214	242	504	238	266	470	214	256
75-79	351	154	197	355	157	198	407	185	223	453	207	246
80-84	263	108	155	289	120	170	295	123	172	342	147	195
85-89	149	54	95	188	70	118	211	79	132	219	83	136
90-94	74	23	52	86	26	59	112	36	76	128	41	87
95-99	26	6	20	31	7	23	37	9	28	50	13	37
100 +	6	1	5	7	1	6	9	1	7	11	2	9

Age group	2045 Both sexes	Males	Females	2050 Both sexes	Males	Females
All ages	6 443	2 985	3 458	6 232	2 870	3 363
0-4	224	115	109	213	109	104
5-9	245	126	119	229	118	111
10-14	270	138	132	254	130	124
15-19	283	144	139	278	141	137
20-24	285	142	144	295	147	148
25-29	282	136	146	299	145	154
30-34	293	141	152	288	138	149
35-39	331	160	172	299	143	156
40-44	409	197	212	330	157	173
45-49	446	213	232	404	192	212
50-54	470	223	247	439	208	232
55-59	447	209	238	463	218	245
60-64	412	186	226	433	199	234
65-69	379	167	212	394	176	217
70-74	393	171	221	356	154	202
75-79	424	187	237	357	151	206
80-84	383	166	217	362	152	210
85-89	257	101	156	292	116	176
90-94	137	45	92	164	56	108
95-99	60	15	44	66	17	48
100 +	15	3	12	19	3	16

POPULATION BY AGE AND SEX (in thousands)

Age group	1950 Both sexes	1950 Males	1950 Females	1955 Both sexes	1955 Males	1955 Females	1960 Both sexes	1960 Males	1960 Females	1965 Both sexes	1965 Males	1965 Females
All ages	3 495	1 806	1 689	3 997	2 048	1 949	4 620	2 354	2 266	5 404	2 742	2 662
0-4	582	301	281	746	378	368	873	443	430	1 044	530	515
5-9	461	238	223	544	281	263	703	357	346	829	421	408
10-14	405	207	198	452	233	219	534	277	258	692	351	341
15-19	354	181	173	396	203	193	442	228	214	524	271	253
20-24	304	154	150	341	174	167	383	196	187	429	221	208
25-29	255	129	126	290	147	144	327	166	161	368	187	181
30-34	214	109	105	242	122	120	277	139	138	313	159	155
35-39	177	90	87	202	102	100	230	116	115	265	133	132
40-44	152	78	74	166	84	82	191	96	95	219	109	110
45-49	131	68	63	142	72	70	156	78	78	180	90	90
50-54	116	62	54	121	62	59	131	66	66	145	72	73
55-59	105	57	48	104	55	49	109	55	54	119	59	60
60-64	85	46	38	90	48	42	90	47	44	95	48	48
65-69	65	36	29	68	37	32	73	38	35	74	37	37
70-74	49	27	22	47	25	22	50	26	24	54	28	27
75-79	26	14	12	30	16	14	29	15	14	32	16	16
80 +	13	7	6	16	8	7	19	10	9	20	10	10

Age group	1970 Both sexes	1970 Males	1970 Females	1975 Both sexes	1975 Males	1975 Females	1980 Both sexes	1980 Males	1980 Females	1985 Both sexes	1985 Males	1985 Females
All ages	6 378	3 228	3 150	7 538	3 799	3 739	8 978	4 504	4 473	10 836	5 435	5 401
0-4	1 233	626	607	1 471	747	724	1 791	910	880	2 159	1 100	1 059
5-9	1 002	508	494	1 194	606	589	1 438	729	708	1 764	896	868
10-14	818	415	403	991	502	489	1 184	600	584	1 429	724	704
15-19	681	346	335	804	407	396	974	493	482	1 171	593	578
20-24	511	264	247	657	331	326	773	388	385	952	479	474
25-29	415	213	202	484	247	237	620	307	313	747	372	375
30-34	355	180	175	391	198	193	452	227	226	597	293	304
35-39	301	152	149	336	169	168	367	183	184	435	216	219
40-44	253	126	127	286	143	143	318	157	161	354	175	179
45-49	208	103	105	239	118	121	270	133	137	305	149	156
50-54	169	84	85	195	96	99	226	110	116	258	126	132
55-59	133	65	68	156	76	80	182	88	94	213	103	110
60-64	105	51	54	119	57	62	141	68	73	167	79	87
65-69	79	39	41	89	42	47	102	48	54	123	58	65
70-74	56	27	29	61	29	32	70	32	38	82	37	45
75-79	35	17	18	37	18	20	42	19	23	49	22	27
80 +	22	11	12	25	12	13	28	13	16	32	14	18

Age group	1990 Both sexes	1990 Males	1990 Females	1995 Both sexes	1995 Males	1995 Females	2000 Both sexes	2000 Males	2000 Females	2005 Both sexes	2005 Males	2005 Females
All ages	12 843	6 446	6 397	14 755	7 414	7 341	16 813	8 456	8 356	19 043	9 585	9 459
0-4	2 285	1 165	1 120	2 182	1 114	1 067	2 333	1 192	1 141	2 526	1 290	1 236
5-9	2 137	1 088	1 049	2 270	1 157	1 113	2 172	1 109	1 063	2 325	1 187	1 138
10-14	1 756	891	865	2 131	1 084	1 046	2 265	1 154	1 111	2 168	1 106	1 062
15-19	1 419	718	700	1 748	886	861	2 123	1 079	1 044	2 258	1 149	1 109
20-24	1 155	582	572	1 405	710	695	1 735	878	857	2 111	1 071	1 040
25-29	934	467	467	1 140	573	567	1 392	701	690	1 722	869	852
30-34	731	362	369	921	459	461	1 127	566	562	1 380	694	686
35-39	584	285	299	720	355	365	910	453	457	1 117	559	558
40-44	424	210	215	574	280	294	710	350	360	900	447	453
45-49	343	169	175	415	204	210	563	274	290	699	343	356
50-54	293	143	151	332	162	170	403	198	206	550	266	284
55-59	244	118	126	280	135	145	319	155	164	389	189	200
60-64	196	93	103	227	108	119	262	125	137	300	144	157
65-69	146	68	78	174	81	93	203	95	108	237	111	127
70-74	99	45	54	120	55	66	145	66	80	172	78	94
75-79	58	25	33	72	32	40	89	39	50	110	48	62
80 +	38	16	22	46	19	27	61	25	36	79	33	47

United Nations Department of Economic and Social Affairs/Population Division
World Population Prospects: The 2004 Revision, Volume II: Sex and Age Distribution of the World Population

818

POPULATION BY AGE AND SEX (in thousands)

Age group	2005			2010			2015			2020		
	Both sexes	Males	Females	Both sexes	Males	Females	Both sexes	Males	Females	Both sexes	Males	Females
All ages	19 043	9 585	9 459	21 432	10 798	10 634	23 802	12 000	11 802	26 029	13 127	12 902
0-4	2 526	1 290	1 236	2 680	1 370	1 310	2 715	1 389	1 327	2 624	1 343	1 281
5-9	2 325	1 187	1 138	2 521	1 287	1 234	2 674	1 367	1 308	2 711	1 386	1 325
10-14	2 168	1 106	1 062	2 323	1 186	1 137	2 518	1 285	1 233	2 672	1 365	1 307
15-19	2 258	1 149	1 109	2 165	1 104	1 061	2 319	1 183	1 136	2 514	1 283	1 231
20-24	2 111	1 071	1 040	2 253	1 146	1 107	2 158	1 099	1 058	2 312	1 179	1 134
25-29	1 722	869	852	2 105	1 068	1 037	2 244	1 140	1 104	2 150	1 095	1 055
30-34	1 380	694	686	1 716	866	850	2 096	1 062	1 034	2 236	1 135	1 101
35-39	1 117	559	558	1 374	691	683	1 708	862	846	2 087	1 057	1 030
40-44	900	447	453	1 110	555	554	1 364	685	679	1 698	856	842
45-49	699	343	356	890	441	448	1 098	548	549	1 351	678	673
50-54	550	266	284	685	335	350	874	432	442	1 080	538	542
55-59	389	189	200	532	256	277	665	323	342	849	417	432
60-64	300	144	157	368	177	191	506	240	266	634	304	330
65-69	237	111	127	274	128	146	338	159	179	467	216	250
70-74	172	78	94	203	92	111	236	107	129	294	134	160
75-79	110	48	62	132	57	75	158	68	90	187	81	106
80-84	55	23	32	70	29	41	87	35	52	106	42	64
85-89	19	8	12	26	10	16	34	13	22	44	16	29
90-94	4	1	3	6	2	4	9	3	6	12	3	9
95-99	0	0	0	1	0	0	1	0	1	2	0	1
100 +	0	0	0	0	0	0	0	0	0	0	0	0

Age group	2025			2030			2035			2040		
	Both sexes	Males	Females	Both sexes	Males	Females	Both sexes	Males	Females	Both sexes	Males	Females
All ages	28 081	14 164	13 918	29 983	15 121	14 862	31 724	15 993	15 732	33 297	16 774	16 523
0-4	2 512	1 287	1 226	2 444	1 252	1 192	2 386	1 222	1 164	2 342	1 200	1 143
5-9	2 621	1 341	1 280	2 509	1 285	1 224	2 441	1 250	1 191	2 383	1 220	1 163
10-14	2 709	1 385	1 324	2 619	1 340	1 279	2 508	1 284	1 224	2 440	1 249	1 191
15-19	2 668	1 363	1 306	2 706	1 383	1 323	2 616	1 338	1 278	2 505	1 282	1 223
20-24	2 508	1 278	1 229	2 662	1 359	1 303	2 700	1 379	1 321	2 611	1 335	1 276
25-29	2 305	1 174	1 131	2 500	1 274	1 226	2 655	1 354	1 301	2 693	1 375	1 318
30-34	2 143	1 090	1 052	2 297	1 170	1 128	2 493	1 270	1 223	2 648	1 350	1 298
35-39	2 227	1 130	1 097	2 135	1 086	1 049	2 290	1 166	1 124	2 485	1 265	1 220
40-44	2 076	1 051	1 025	2 216	1 125	1 092	2 125	1 081	1 044	2 280	1 160	1 120
45-49	1 683	848	835	2 059	1 042	1 017	2 200	1 115	1 085	2 110	1 072	1 038
50-54	1 331	666	665	1 659	834	825	2 032	1 026	1 006	2 173	1 099	1 074
55-59	1 052	521	531	1 299	646	652	1 622	811	811	1 989	999	990
60-64	812	394	418	1 008	494	514	1 248	615	633	1 563	774	789
65-69	587	276	311	756	360	396	942	453	489	1 171	568	604
70-74	409	184	226	519	236	283	673	311	362	845	395	449
75-79	235	101	134	332	141	191	426	185	241	559	247	312
80-84	128	50	78	165	65	100	238	93	145	311	124	186
85-89	56	19	37	71	24	47	94	32	62	140	48	93
90-94	16	4	12	22	6	16	29	8	22	41	11	30
95-99	3	1	2	4	1	3	6	1	5	8	1	7
100 +	0	0	0	0	0	0	1	0	1	1	0	1

Age group	2045			2050		
	Both sexes	Males	Females	Both sexes	Males	Females
All ages	34 723	17 476	17 247	35 935	18 065	17 870
0-4	2 344	1 200	1 144	2 295	1 175	1 120
5-9	2 340	1 198	1 142	2 342	1 199	1 143
10-14	2 382	1 220	1 162	2 339	1 198	1 141
15-19	2 437	1 248	1 190	2 380	1 218	1 162
20-24	2 500	1 279	1 221	2 433	1 245	1 188
25-29	2 604	1 331	1 274	2 494	1 275	1 219
30-34	2 686	1 371	1 315	2 597	1 326	1 271
35-39	2 640	1 345	1 294	2 678	1 366	1 312
40-44	2 475	1 259	1 215	2 629	1 340	1 290
45-49	2 264	1 151	1 113	2 459	1 250	1 209
50-54	2 086	1 057	1 028	2 240	1 136	1 104
55-59	2 129	1 072	1 057	2 046	1 033	1 013
60-64	1 921	956	964	2 060	1 029	1 031
65-69	1 472	718	754	1 815	891	924
70-74	1 056	499	558	1 334	635	699
75-79	708	317	391	893	405	488
80-84	414	170	244	532	222	310
85-89	188	66	122	257	93	164
90-94	64	17	46	89	25	63
95-99	12	2	10	20	4	16
100 +	1	0	1	2	0	2

United Nations Department of Economic and Social Affairs/Population Division
World Population Prospects: The 2004 Revision, Volume II: Sex and Age Distribution of the World Population

819

POPULATION BY AGE AND SEX (in thousands)

Age group	2005 Both sexes	2005 Males	2005 Females	2010 Both sexes	2010 Males	2010 Females	2015 Both sexes	2015 Males	2015 Females	2020 Both sexes	2020 Males	2020 Females
All ages	19 043	9 585	9 459	21 638	10 904	10 734	24 382	12 296	12 086	27 120	13 685	13 435
0-4	2 526	1 290	1 236	2 886	1 475	1 411	3 090	1 581	1 510	3 135	1 604	1 531
5-9	2 325	1 187	1 138	2 521	1 287	1 234	2 880	1 472	1 408	3 085	1 578	1 508
10-14	2 168	1 106	1 062	2 323	1 186	1 137	2 518	1 285	1 233	2 877	1 470	1 407
15-19	2 258	1 149	1 109	2 165	1 104	1 061	2 319	1 183	1 136	2 514	1 283	1 231
20-24	2 111	1 071	1 040	2 253	1 146	1 107	2 158	1 099	1 058	2 312	1 179	1 134
25-29	1 722	869	852	2 105	1 068	1 037	2 244	1 140	1 104	2 150	1 095	1 055
30-34	1 380	694	686	1 716	866	850	2 096	1 062	1 034	2 236	1 135	1 101
35-39	1 117	559	558	1 374	691	683	1 708	862	846	2 087	1 057	1 030
40-44	900	447	453	1 110	555	554	1 364	685	679	1 698	856	842
45-49	699	343	356	890	441	448	1 098	548	549	1 351	678	673
50-54	550	266	284	685	335	350	874	432	442	1 080	538	542
55-59	389	189	200	532	256	277	665	323	342	849	417	432
60-64	300	144	157	368	177	191	506	240	266	634	304	330
65-69	237	111	127	274	128	146	338	159	179	467	216	250
70-74	172	78	94	203	92	111	236	107	129	294	134	160
75-79	110	48	62	132	57	75	158	68	90	187	81	106
80-84	55	23	32	70	29	41	87	35	52	106	42	64
85-89	19	8	12	26	10	16	34	13	22	44	16	29
90-94	4	1	3	6	2	4	9	3	6	12	3	9
95-99	0	0	0	1	0	0	1	0	1	2	0	1
100 +	0	0	0	0	0	0	0	0	0	0	0	0

Age group	2025 Both sexes	2025 Males	2025 Females	2030 Both sexes	2030 Males	2030 Females	2035 Both sexes	2035 Males	2035 Females	2040 Both sexes	2040 Males	2040 Females
All ages	29 720	15 002	14 718	32 239	16 275	15 964	34 728	17 530	17 199	37 214	18 779	18 436
0-4	3 062	1 568	1 494	3 063	1 568	1 494	3 136	1 606	1 530	3 260	1 669	1 590
5-9	3 131	1 602	1 529	3 059	1 566	1 493	3 059	1 567	1 493	3 133	1 604	1 529
10-14	3 083	1 576	1 507	3 128	1 601	1 528	3 057	1 565	1 492	3 057	1 565	1 492
15-19	2 874	1 468	1 406	3 079	1 574	1 505	3 125	1 599	1 527	3 054	1 563	1 491
20-24	2 508	1 278	1 229	2 867	1 463	1 404	3 073	1 570	1 503	3 119	1 595	1 524
25-29	2 305	1 174	1 131	2 500	1 274	1 226	2 860	1 459	1 401	3 065	1 565	1 500
30-34	2 143	1 090	1 052	2 297	1 170	1 128	2 493	1 270	1 223	2 852	1 454	1 398
35-39	2 227	1 130	1 097	2 135	1 086	1 049	2 290	1 165	1 124	2 485	1 265	1 220
40-44	2 076	1 051	1 025	2 216	1 125	1 092	2 125	1 081	1 044	2 280	1 160	1 120
45-49	1 683	848	835	2 059	1 042	1 017	2 200	1 115	1 085	2 110	1 072	1 038
50-54	1 331	666	665	1 659	834	825	2 032	1 026	1 006	2 173	1 099	1 074
55-59	1 052	521	531	1 299	646	652	1 622	811	811	1 989	999	990
60-64	812	394	418	1 008	494	514	1 248	615	633	1 563	774	789
65-69	587	276	311	756	360	396	942	453	489	1 171	568	604
70-74	409	184	226	519	236	283	673	311	362	845	395	449
75-79	235	101	134	332	141	191	426	185	241	559	247	312
80-84	128	50	78	165	65	100	238	93	145	311	124	186
85-89	56	19	37	71	24	47	94	32	62	140	48	93
90-94	16	4	12	22	6	16	29	8	22	41	11	30
95-99	3	1	2	4	1	3	6	1	5	8	1	7
100 +	0	0	0	0	0	0	1	0	1	1	0	1

Age group	2045 Both sexes	2045 Males	2045 Females	2050 Both sexes	2050 Males	2050 Females
All ages	39 707	20 027	19 680	42 093	21 216	20 876
0-4	3 414	1 748	1 666	3 474	1 779	1 695
5-9	3 256	1 667	1 589	3 411	1 747	1 665
10-14	3 131	1 603	1 528	3 255	1 666	1 588
15-19	3 055	1 564	1 491	3 128	1 601	1 527
20-24	3 048	1 559	1 489	3 049	1 560	1 489
25-29	3 112	1 590	1 522	3 041	1 555	1 486
30-34	3 057	1 560	1 497	3 104	1 586	1 519
35-39	2 843	1 449	1 394	3 049	1 555	1 493
40-44	2 475	1 259	1 215	2 832	1 443	1 389
45-49	2 264	1 151	1 113	2 459	1 250	1 209
50-54	2 086	1 057	1 028	2 240	1 136	1 104
55-59	2 129	1 072	1 057	2 046	1 033	1 013
60-64	1 921	956	964	2 060	1 029	1 031
65-69	1 472	718	754	1 815	891	924
70-74	1 056	499	558	1 334	635	699
75-79	708	317	391	893	405	488
80-84	414	170	244	532	222	310
85-89	188	66	122	257	93	164
90-94	64	17	46	89	25	63
95-99	12	2	10	20	4	16
100 +	1	0	1	2	0	2

United Nations Department of Economic and Social Affairs/Population Division
World Population Prospects: The 2004 Revision, Volume II: Sex and Age Distribution of the World Population

820

POPULATION BY AGE AND SEX (in thousands)

Age group	2005 Both sexes	Males	Females	2010 Both sexes	Males	Females	2015 Both sexes	Males	Females	2020 Both sexes	Males	Females
All ages	19 043	9 585	9 459	21 224	10 692	10 532	23 215	11 699	11 515	24 927	12 563	12 363
0-4	2 526	1 290	1 236	2 472	1 264	1 208	2 336	1 195	1 141	2 108	1 079	1 029
5-9	2 325	1 187	1 138	2 521	1 287	1 234	2 467	1 261	1 206	2 332	1 193	1 140
10-14	2 168	1 106	1 062	2 323	1 186	1 137	2 518	1 285	1 233	2 465	1 259	1 205
15-19	2 258	1 149	1 109	2 165	1 104	1 061	2 319	1 183	1 136	2 514	1 283	1 231
20-24	2 111	1 071	1 040	2 253	1 146	1 107	2 158	1 099	1 058	2 312	1 179	1 134
25-29	1 722	869	852	2 105	1 068	1 037	2 244	1 140	1 104	2 150	1 095	1 055
30-34	1 380	694	686	1 716	866	850	2 096	1 062	1 034	2 236	1 135	1 101
35-39	1 117	559	558	1 374	691	683	1 708	862	846	2 087	1 057	1 030
40-44	900	447	453	1 110	555	554	1 364	685	679	1 698	856	842
45-49	699	343	356	890	441	448	1 098	548	549	1 351	678	673
50-54	550	266	284	685	335	350	874	432	442	1 080	538	542
55-59	389	189	200	532	256	277	665	323	342	849	417	432
60-64	300	144	157	368	177	191	506	240	266	634	304	330
65-69	237	111	127	274	128	146	338	159	179	467	216	250
70-74	172	78	94	203	92	111	236	107	129	294	134	160
75-79	110	48	62	132	57	75	158	68	90	187	81	106
80-84	55	23	32	70	29	41	87	35	52	106	42	64
85-89	19	8	12	26	10	16	34	13	22	44	16	29
90-94	4	1	3	6	2	4	9	3	6	12	3	9
95-99	0	0	0	1	0	0	1	0	1	2	0	1
100 +	0	0	0	0	0	0	0	0	0	0	0	0

Age group	2025 Both sexes	Males	Females	2030 Both sexes	Males	Females	2035 Both sexes	Males	Females	2040 Both sexes	Males	Females
All ages	26 429	13 318	13 111	27 726	13 966	13 760	28 772	14 482	14 290	29 545	14 854	14 691
0-4	1 962	1 005	957	1 838	941	897	1 688	864	823	1 541	789	752
5-9	2 105	1 077	1 028	1 959	1 003	956	1 836	940	896	1 686	863	823
10-14	2 330	1 191	1 139	2 103	1 076	1 027	1 958	1 002	955	1 834	939	895
15-19	2 461	1 257	1 204	2 327	1 190	1 138	2 101	1 074	1 026	1 956	1 001	955
20-24	2 508	1 278	1 229	2 456	1 253	1 202	2 322	1 186	1 136	2 096	1 072	1 025
25-29	2 305	1 174	1 131	2 500	1 274	1 226	2 449	1 249	1 200	2 316	1 182	1 134
30-34	2 143	1 090	1 052	2 297	1 170	1 128	2 493	1 270	1 223	2 442	1 245	1 197
35-39	2 227	1 130	1 097	2 135	1 086	1 049	2 290	1 165	1 124	2 485	1 265	1 220
40-44	2 076	1 051	1 025	2 216	1 125	1 092	2 125	1 081	1 044	2 280	1 160	1 120
45-49	1 683	848	835	2 059	1 042	1 017	2 200	1 115	1 085	2 110	1 072	1 038
50-54	1 331	666	665	1 659	834	825	2 032	1 026	1 006	2 173	1 099	1 074
55-59	1 052	521	531	1 299	646	652	1 622	811	811	1 989	999	990
60-64	812	394	418	1 008	494	514	1 248	615	633	1 563	774	789
65-69	587	276	311	756	360	396	942	453	489	1 171	568	604
70-74	409	184	226	519	236	283	673	311	362	845	395	449
75-79	235	101	134	332	141	191	426	185	241	559	247	312
80-84	128	50	78	165	65	100	238	93	145	311	124	186
85-89	56	19	37	71	24	47	94	32	62	140	48	93
90-94	16	4	12	22	6	16	29	8	22	41	11	30
95-99	3	1	2	4	1	3	6	1	5	8	1	7
100 +	0	0	0	0	0	0	1	0	1	1	0	1

Age group	2045 Both sexes	Males	Females	2050 Both sexes	Males	Females
All ages	30 085	15 103	14 982	30 359	15 212	15 147
0-4	1 454	744	709	1 351	692	659
5-9	1 539	788	751	1 452	744	709
10-14	1 685	863	822	1 538	788	751
15-19	1 832	938	894	1 683	861	822
20-24	1 952	998	953	1 829	936	893
25-29	2 090	1 068	1 022	1 946	995	951
30-34	2 309	1 178	1 131	2 085	1 064	1 020
35-39	2 434	1 241	1 194	2 303	1 174	1 128
40-44	2 475	1 259	1 215	2 425	1 235	1 190
45-49	2 264	1 151	1 113	2 459	1 250	1 209
50-54	2 086	1 057	1 028	2 240	1 136	1 104
55-59	2 129	1 072	1 057	2 046	1 033	1 013
60-64	1 921	956	964	2 060	1 029	1 031
65-69	1 472	718	754	1 815	891	924
70-74	1 056	499	558	1 334	635	699
75-79	708	317	391	893	405	488
80-84	414	170	244	532	222	310
85-89	188	66	122	257	93	164
90-94	64	17	46	89	25	63
95-99	12	2	10	20	4	16
100 +	1	0	1	2	0	2

POPULATION BY AGE AND SEX (in thousands)

Age group	1950 Both sexes	Males	Females	1955 Both sexes	Males	Females	1960 Both sexes	Males	Females	1965 Both sexes	Males	Females
All ages	1 532	741	790	1 782	863	920	2 082	1 016	1 066	2 512	1 233	1 279
0-4	172	81	91	280	140	140	394	203	191	498	255	243
5-9	149	77	72	168	78	89	266	132	134	382	196	186
10-14	197	100	97	152	79	73	165	77	88	267	132	134
15-19	172	85	87	201	102	99	150	78	72	166	77	89
20-24	163	83	80	175	87	88	198	100	97	150	78	72
25-29	105	46	58	164	84	80	171	85	86	197	100	97
30-34	75	32	44	105	47	59	160	82	78	170	84	86
35-39	92	38	53	76	32	44	102	45	57	158	81	78
40-44	89	40	49	91	38	53	73	30	42	100	44	56
45-49	88	41	46	87	39	48	87	36	51	71	29	41
50-54	69	34	35	85	40	45	82	36	46	83	34	49
55-59	48	26	22	65	32	33	78	36	42	77	33	44
60-64	47	24	23	44	23	21	57	27	30	71	32	39
65-69	31	16	15	41	20	21	37	19	18	50	23	27
70-74	19	10	9	25	12	13	33	16	17	30	15	16
75-79	10	5	5	14	7	7	18	8	10	24	11	13
80 +	6	3	3	9	4	5	12	5	7	16	7	9

Age group	1970 Both sexes	Males	Females	1975 Both sexes	Males	Females	1980 Both sexes	Males	Females	1985 Both sexes	Males	Females
All ages	2 942	1 448	1 493	3 442	1 699	1 743	3 953	1 955	1 998	4 567	2 268	2 299
0-4	501	254	247	585	296	289	632	319	313	769	390	379
5-9	486	248	238	506	256	250	564	285	279	615	311	304
10-14	384	197	187	472	241	231	500	253	247	558	282	276
15-19	268	133	135	367	187	180	468	236	232	488	245	243
20-24	167	78	89	275	135	140	366	179	187	461	232	229
25-29	150	78	72	177	87	90	271	133	137	364	180	184
30-34	196	99	96	150	80	71	182	91	91	264	131	134
35-39	169	83	85	194	98	96	137	73	63	176	88	88
40-44	156	79	77	161	79	82	189	96	93	131	71	61
45-49	98	43	55	149	75	74	157	77	79	180	91	89
50-54	68	28	40	105	42	64	146	73	73	150	73	77
55-59	79	32	47	68	26	42	98	40	58	139	68	70
60-64	71	30	41	71	30	42	65	24	40	88	36	53
65-69	62	27	35	59	24	35	61	25	36	56	21	36
70-74	42	18	23	48	21	27	48	20	28	50	20	30
75-79	23	11	12	27	12	15	37	16	21	35	14	21
80 +	22	9	13	27	11	16	33	14	19	42	17	24

Age group	1990 Both sexes	Males	Females	1995 Both sexes	Males	Females	2000 Both sexes	Males	Females	2005 Both sexes	Males	Females
All ages	5 303	2 634	2 669	5 770	2 886	2 884	6 159	3 086	3 072	6 507	3 230	3 277
0-4	934	474	461	914	466	449	871	444	427	834	425	409
5-9	746	378	368	889	450	439	873	444	429	839	427	413
10-14	609	307	301	720	364	356	862	436	426	863	438	425
15-19	543	275	269	580	292	287	686	347	340	837	421	415
20-24	471	231	240	509	257	253	540	270	270	630	314	316
25-29	447	219	227	438	215	223	472	235	237	470	229	241
30-34	360	179	181	417	206	211	409	200	209	411	199	213
35-39	256	126	129	333	167	166	391	195	196	364	173	191
40-44	169	84	84	230	114	116	301	150	151	357	175	182
45-49	126	68	58	148	74	74	200	98	102	276	135	141
50-54	171	85	85	110	59	51	127	63	64	181	86	95
55-59	141	68	73	148	73	75	93	51	43	113	54	59
60-64	128	62	66	113	54	59	121	60	62	81	42	38
65-69	77	30	47	99	48	51	79	37	42	104	49	55
70-74	47	17	30	56	22	34	68	33	35	64	28	35
75-79	37	14	23	29	10	19	36	14	22	49	22	27
80 +	42	16	25	36	14	22	28	10	18	35	12	23

United Nations Department of Economic and Social Affairs/Population Division
World Population Prospects: The 2004 Revision, Volume II: Sex and Age Distribution of the World Population

822

POPULATION BY AGE AND SEX (in thousands)

Age group	2005 Both sexes	Males	Females	2010 Both sexes	Males	Females	2015 Both sexes	Males	Females	2020 Both sexes	Males	Females
All ages	6 507	3 230	3 277	6 992	3 455	3 537	7 605	3 753	3 852	8 216	4 050	4 166
0-4	834	425	409	840	428	412	884	450	433	898	457	440
5-9	839	427	413	810	412	398	821	418	403	866	440	425
10-14	863	438	425	832	423	409	805	409	396	817	415	402
15-19	837	421	415	847	429	418	824	418	406	797	404	392
20-24	630	314	316	802	402	400	828	418	410	805	407	398
25-29	470	229	241	587	289	298	778	387	390	805	404	400
30-34	411	199	213	433	207	226	566	277	290	756	374	382
35-39	364	173	191	383	182	201	417	198	219	549	266	283
40-44	357	175	182	342	160	182	369	173	196	403	189	214
45-49	276	135	141	338	163	175	329	152	177	356	166	190
50-54	181	86	95	259	124	135	323	154	169	315	144	171
55-59	113	54	59	167	78	90	244	115	129	306	143	162
60-64	81	42	38	101	47	54	153	69	84	225	103	121
65-69	104	49	55	69	35	34	89	40	49	136	59	77
70-74	64	28	35	85	38	47	57	28	29	74	32	42
75-79	49	22	27	47	20	27	64	27	37	43	20	23
80-84	22	8	15	31	13	18	31	12	19	42	16	26
85-89	7	2	5	12	4	8	17	6	11	17	6	11
90-94	3	1	2	3	1	2	5	1	4	7	2	5
95-99	1	0	1	1	0	1	1	0	1	2	0	1
100 +	1	0	0	0	0	0	0	0	0	0	0	0

Age group	2025 Both sexes	Males	Females	2030 Both sexes	Males	Females	2035 Both sexes	Males	Females	2040 Both sexes	Males	Females
All ages	8 769	4 317	4 453	9 237	4 540	4 697	9 621	4 721	4 900	9 933	4 867	5 066
0-4	860	438	422	797	406	390	741	378	363	703	359	344
5-9	881	448	433	846	431	415	785	400	385	731	373	358
10-14	862	438	424	877	446	431	842	429	414	782	398	384
15-19	808	410	398	853	433	420	869	441	428	834	424	410
20-24	778	394	385	790	400	391	835	423	413	851	431	420
25-29	781	393	388	755	380	375	768	386	381	813	409	404
30-34	783	391	392	760	380	380	735	368	367	747	374	373
35-39	737	363	374	764	380	384	743	369	373	718	357	361
40-44	533	267	277	719	352	367	747	370	370	727	360	367
45-49	390	181	208	518	248	271	702	341	361	730	359	371
50-54	342	157	185	375	173	203	501	237	264	681	329	353
55-59	299	134	164	325	147	178	358	162	196	480	224	256
60-64	283	129	153	277	122	156	303	134	169	335	148	187
65-69	200	89	111	253	112	141	250	106	144	274	118	157
70-74	114	48	67	169	72	97	216	92	124	215	87	127
75-79	57	23	34	88	34	54	132	53	79	170	68	102
80-84	28	12	16	38	14	24	60	22	39	92	34	58
85-89	23	8	15	16	6	10	22	7	15	35	11	24
90-94	7	2	5	10	3	7	7	2	5	10	3	7
95-99	2	1	2	2	1	2	3	1	3	2	1	2
100 +	0	0	0	1	0	1	1	0	1	1	0	1

Age group	2045 Both sexes	Males	Females	2050 Both sexes	Males	Females
All ages	10 200	4 992	5 209	10 423	5 095	5 328
0-4	697	356	341	694	355	339
5-9	694	354	340	689	352	337
10-14	728	371	357	691	353	339
15-19	774	393	380	720	366	354
20-24	817	414	403	757	383	373
25-29	829	418	411	795	401	394
30-34	793	397	396	809	406	404
35-39	731	364	367	777	387	389
40-44	703	348	355	717	355	361
45-49	711	350	361	688	339	349
50-54	710	346	364	692	338	354
55-59	654	311	343	683	329	354
60-64	451	206	245	617	288	328
65-69	305	131	174	412	183	228
70-74	237	98	140	265	110	155
75-79	171	66	105	191	74	117
80-84	120	44	75	122	43	79
85-89	54	18	36	71	24	48
90-94	16	4	12	26	7	18
95-99	3	1	3	6	1	5
100 +	1	0	1	1	0	1

TAJIKISTAN

HIGH VARIANT

POPULATION BY AGE AND SEX (in thousands)

Age group	2005 Both sexes	Males	Females	2010 Both sexes	Males	Females	2015 Both sexes	Males	Females	2020 Both sexes	Males	Females
All ages	6 507	3 230	3 277	7 065	3 492	3 573	7 811	3 858	3 953	8 601	4 246	4 355
0-4	834	425	409	913	465	448	1 018	519	499	1 079	550	529
5-9	839	427	413	810	412	398	892	454	439	998	508	490
10-14	863	438	425	832	423	409	805	409	396	888	451	437
15-19	837	421	415	847	429	418	824	418	406	797	404	392
20-24	630	314	316	802	402	400	828	418	410	805	407	398
25-29	470	229	241	587	289	298	778	387	390	805	404	400
30-34	411	199	213	433	207	226	566	277	290	756	374	382
35-39	364	173	191	383	182	201	417	198	219	549	266	283
40-44	357	175	182	342	160	182	369	173	196	403	189	214
45-49	276	135	141	338	163	175	329	152	177	356	166	190
50-54	181	86	95	259	124	135	323	154	169	315	144	171
55-59	113	54	59	167	78	90	244	115	129	306	143	162
60-64	81	42	38	101	47	54	153	69	84	225	103	121
65-69	104	49	55	69	35	34	89	40	49	136	59	77
70-74	64	28	35	85	38	47	57	28	29	74	32	42
75-79	49	22	27	47	20	27	64	27	37	43	20	23
80-84	22	8	15	31	13	18	31	12	19	42	16	26
85-89	7	2	5	12	4	8	17	6	11	17	6	11
90-94	3	1	2	3	1	2	5	1	4	7	2	5
95-99	1	0	1	1	0	1	1	0	1	2	0	1
100 +	1	0	0	0	0	0	0	0	0	0	0	0

Age group	2025 Both sexes	Males	Females	2030 Both sexes	Males	Females	2035 Both sexes	Males	Females	2040 Both sexes	Males	Females
All ages	9 337	4 606	4 731	10 002	4 929	5 073	10 628	5 234	5 394	11 244	5 534	5 709
0-4	1 046	533	513	998	509	489	986	503	483	1 011	516	495
5-9	1 060	540	521	1 029	524	505	984	501	483	974	497	478
10-14	994	505	488	1 056	537	519	1 025	522	504	980	499	481
15-19	879	446	433	985	500	485	1 047	532	515	1 017	517	500
20-24	778	394	385	861	436	425	967	489	477	1 029	521	508
25-29	781	393	388	755	380	375	838	422	416	944	476	468
30-34	783	391	392	760	380	380	735	368	367	817	409	408
35-39	737	363	374	764	380	384	743	369	373	718	357	361
40-44	533	257	277	719	352	367	747	370	378	727	360	367
45-49	390	181	208	518	248	271	702	341	361	730	359	371
50-54	342	157	185	375	173	203	501	237	264	681	329	353
55-59	299	134	164	325	147	178	358	162	196	480	224	256
60-64	283	129	153	277	122	156	303	134	169	335	148	187
65-69	200	89	111	253	112	141	250	106	144	274	118	157
70-74	114	48	67	169	72	97	216	92	124	215	87	127
75-79	57	23	34	88	34	54	132	53	79	170	68	102
80-84	28	12	16	38	14	24	60	22	39	92	34	58
85-89	23	8	15	16	6	10	22	7	15	35	11	24
90-94	7	2	5	10	3	7	7	2	5	10	3	7
95-99	2	1	2	2	1	2	3	1	3	2	1	2
100 +	0	0	0	1	0	1	1	0	1	1	0	1

Age group	2045 Both sexes	Males	Females	2050 Both sexes	Males	Females
All ages	11 862	5 837	6 024	12 458	6 131	6 327
0-4	1 053	538	515	1 075	549	526
5-9	1 000	510	490	1 042	532	510
10-14	971	495	476	996	508	488
15-19	972	494	478	963	490	473
20-24	999	506	493	954	484	470
25-29	1 007	508	499	977	493	484
30-34	923	463	460	986	495	491
35-39	801	399	401	906	453	453
40-44	703	348	355	786	390	396
45-49	711	350	361	688	339	349
50-54	710	346	364	692	338	354
55-59	654	311	343	683	329	354
60-64	451	206	245	617	288	328
65-69	305	131	174	412	183	228
70-74	237	98	140	265	110	155
75-79	171	66	105	191	74	117
80-84	120	44	75	122	43	79
85-89	54	18	36	71	24	48
90-94	16	4	12	26	7	18
95-99	3	1	3	6	1	5
100 +	1	0	1	1	0	1

United Nations Department of Economic and Social Affairs/Population Division
World Population Prospects: The 2004 Revision, Volume II: Sex and Age Distribution of the World Population

824

POPULATION BY AGE AND SEX (in thousands)

Age group	2005 Both sexes	2005 Males	2005 Females	2010 Both sexes	2010 Males	2010 Females	2015 Both sexes	2015 Males	2015 Females	2020 Both sexes	2020 Males	2020 Females
All ages	6 507	3 230	3 277	6 921	3 419	3 503	7 406	3 652	3 754	7 844	3 860	3 983
0-4	834	425	409	769	392	377	754	384	370	722	368	354
5-9	839	427	413	810	412	398	752	382	369	738	376	363
10-14	863	438	425	832	423	409	805	409	396	747	380	367
15-19	837	421	415	847	429	418	824	418	406	797	404	392
20-24	630	314	316	802	402	400	828	418	410	805	407	398
25-29	470	229	241	587	289	298	778	387	390	805	404	400
30-34	411	199	213	433	207	226	566	277	290	756	374	382
35-39	364	173	191	383	182	201	417	198	219	549	266	283
40-44	357	175	182	342	160	182	369	173	196	403	189	214
45-49	276	135	141	338	163	175	329	152	177	356	166	190
50-54	181	86	95	259	124	135	323	154	169	315	144	171
55-59	113	54	59	167	78	90	244	115	129	306	143	162
60-64	81	42	38	101	47	54	153	69	84	225	103	121
65-69	104	49	55	69	35	34	89	40	49	136	59	77
70-74	64	28	35	85	38	47	57	28	29	74	32	42
75-79	49	22	27	47	20	27	64	27	37	43	20	23
80-84	22	8	15	31	13	18	31	12	19	42	16	26
85-89	7	2	5	12	4	8	17	6	11	17	6	11
90-94	3	1	2	3	1	2	5	1	4	7	2	5
95-99	1	0	1	1	0	1	1	0	1	2	0	1
100 +	1	0	0	0	0	0	0	0	0	0	0	0

Age group	2025 Both sexes	2025 Males	2025 Females	2030 Both sexes	2030 Males	2030 Females	2035 Both sexes	2035 Males	2035 Females	2040 Both sexes	2040 Males	2040 Females
All ages	8 220	4 037	4 183	8 502	4 166	4 336	8 681	4 243	4 438	8 755	4 268	4 487
0-4	680	346	333	609	311	298	532	271	260	462	236	226
5-9	708	360	348	668	340	328	599	305	294	523	267	257
10-14	734	373	361	705	358	346	664	338	326	596	304	293
15-19	739	375	364	726	369	358	697	354	343	657	334	323
20-24	778	394	385	721	365	357	709	358	350	680	344	336
25-29	781	393	388	755	380	375	699	351	347	687	345	341
30-34	783	391	392	760	380	380	735	368	367	679	339	340
35-39	737	363	374	704	000	384	743	369	373	718	357	361
40-44	533	257	277	719	352	367	747	370	378	727	360	367
45-49	390	181	208	518	248	271	702	341	361	730	359	371
50-54	342	157	185	375	173	203	501	237	264	681	329	353
55-59	299	134	164	325	147	178	358	162	196	480	224	256
60-64	283	129	153	277	122	156	303	134	169	335	148	187
65-69	200	89	111	253	112	141	250	106	144	274	118	157
70-74	114	48	67	169	72	97	216	92	124	215	87	127
75-79	57	23	34	00	34	54	132	53	79	170	68	102
80-84	28	12	16	38	14	24	60	22	39	92	34	58
85-89	23	8	15	16	6	10	22	7	15	35	11	24
90-94	7	2	5	10	3	7	7	2	5	10	3	7
95-99	2	1	2	2	1	2	3	1	3	2	1	2
100 +	0	0	0	1	0	1	1	0	1	1	0	1

Age group	2045 Both sexes	2045 Males	2045 Females	2050 Both sexes	2050 Males	2050 Females
All ages	8 755	4 256	4 499	8 695	4 215	4 479
0-4	426	217	208	405	207	198
5-9	455	232	223	419	214	205
10-14	521	265	255	452	231	222
15-19	589	299	290	513	261	252
20-24	640	324	316	572	290	283
25-29	658	331	327	619	311	308
30-34	667	334	334	639	319	320
35-39	663	330	333	652	324	328
40-44	703	348	355	649	321	328
45-49	711	350	361	688	339	349
50-54	710	346	364	692	338	354
55-59	654	311	343	683	329	354
60-64	451	206	245	617	288	328
65-69	305	131	174	412	183	228
70-74	237	98	140	265	110	155
75-79	171	66	105	191	74	117
80-84	120	44	75	122	43	79
85-89	54	18	36	71	24	48
90-94	16	4	12	26	7	18
95-99	3	1	3	6	1	5
100 +	1	0	1	1	0	1

POPULATION BY AGE AND SEX (in thousands)

Age group	1950 Both sexes	Males	Females	1955 Both sexes	Males	Females	1960 Both sexes	Males	Females	1965 Both sexes	Males	Females
All ages	19 626	9 845	9 781	22 759	11 397	11 362	26 603	13 308	13 295	31 209	15 605	15 604
0-4	3 226	1 639	1 588	4 081	2 050	2 031	4 834	2 432	2 401	5 634	2 840	2 794
5-9	2 583	1 321	1 262	3 082	1 561	1 521	3 928	1 967	1 961	4 687	2 353	2 335
10-14	2 460	1 234	1 225	2 547	1 302	1 245	3 045	1 542	1 503	3 889	1 947	1 942
15-19	2 132	1 059	1 072	2 421	1 214	1 207	2 512	1 284	1 229	3 010	1 523	1 487
20-24	1 818	918	900	2 084	1 034	1 050	2 373	1 189	1 184	2 470	1 260	1 210
25-29	1 439	730	710	1 768	891	877	2 034	1 008	1 026	2 325	1 162	1 162
30-34	1 198	604	594	1 395	706	689	1 721	866	855	1 988	983	1 005
35-39	1 046	533	513	1 156	582	575	1 352	683	670	1 676	841	834
40-44	910	455	455	1 002	508	494	1 113	558	556	1 309	658	650
45-49	757	381	376	864	428	436	957	482	475	1 068	532	536
50-54	617	307	310	707	352	355	812	399	414	905	451	453
55-59	449	223	226	563	276	287	650	319	331	752	364	388
60-64	354	161	193	394	192	202	499	239	259	580	279	301
65-69	281	126	155	293	130	163	329	156	173	421	197	224
70-74	165	74	91	212	92	120	224	96	128	254	116	137
75-79	110	48	63	107	46	61	139	58	82	150	61	89
80 +	81	32	49	81	32	49	81	32	49	93	36	57

Age group	1970 Both sexes	Males	Females	1975 Both sexes	Males	Females	1980 Both sexes	Males	Females	1985 Both sexes	Males	Females
All ages	36 257	18 118	18 138	41 292	20 617	20 675	46 334	23 111	23 223	50 612	25 215	25 396
0-4	6 143	3 098	3 045	6 190	3 122	3 068	6 175	3 115	3 060	5 869	2 966	2 903
5-9	5 491	2 761	2 730	6 016	3 025	2 991	6 105	3 071	3 035	6 099	3 070	3 029
10-14	4 647	2 331	2 316	5 452	2 739	2 713	5 995	3 012	2 983	6 053	3 041	3 013
15-19	3 850	1 926	1 924	4 608	2 309	2 299	5 426	2 723	2 703	5 886	2 950	2 936
20-24	2 965	1 498	1 467	3 801	1 898	1 903	4 568	2 285	2 284	5 266	2 630	2 635
25-29	2 426	1 235	1 190	2 919	1 472	1 448	3 758	1 872	1 886	4 448	2 215	2 233
30-34	2 279	1 137	1 141	2 384	1 212	1 172	2 882	1 450	1 432	3 702	1 841	1 860
35-39	1 942	958	983	2 233	1 112	1 120	2 347	1 191	1 157	2 839	1 426	1 413
40-44	1 627	814	813	1 893	931	962	2 188	1 086	1 102	2 302	1 165	1 137
45-49	1 260	630	630	1 573	783	791	1 841	901	940	2 130	1 053	1 077
50-54	1 015	501	514	1 202	596	606	1 511	746	765	1 770	860	910
55-59	841	414	427	948	462	486	1 132	555	578	1 426	696	730
60-64	675	321	355	760	367	393	865	414	452	1 037	499	538
65-69	493	231	262	579	268	312	659	310	349	755	352	403
70-74	328	148	180	389	176	213	463	207	256	530	241	289
75-79	172	75	97	225	97	128	272	118	154	320	137	183
80 +	104	40	64	118	47	71	147	59	88	179	72	107

Age group	1990 Both sexes	Males	Females	1995 Both sexes	Males	Females	2000 Both sexes	Males	Females	2005 Both sexes	Males	Females
All ages	54 639	27 188	27 451	58 336	28 932	29 404	61 438	30 301	31 137	64 233	31 543	32 690
0-4	5 534	2 797	2 737	5 299	2 683	2 616	5 041	2 554	2 486	5 012	2 542	2 470
5-9	5 819	2 935	2 884	5 502	2 776	2 726	5 274	2 667	2 607	5 020	2 541	2 479
10-14	6 068	3 051	3 017	5 736	2 890	2 845	5 423	2 734	2 689	5 263	2 660	2 603
15-19	5 989	3 003	2 986	5 868	2 952	2 916	5 541	2 794	2 747	5 404	2 721	2 682
20-24	5 780	2 887	2 892	5 569	2 791	2 778	5 458	2 746	2 711	5 491	2 762	2 729
25-29	5 179	2 578	2 601	5 356	2 649	2 707	5 124	2 536	2 588	5 378	2 694	2 684
30-34	4 399	2 186	2 213	5 045	2 469	2 576	5 173	2 502	2 672	5 013	2 459	2 553
35-39	3 658	1 816	1 842	4 413	2 172	2 241	5 009	2 414	2 595	5 048	2 414	2 634
40-44	2 794	1 400	1 394	3 772	1 881	1 891	4 489	2 205	2 284	4 888	2 330	2 558
45-49	2 250	1 133	1 116	2 939	1 477	1 462	3 884	1 932	1 952	4 374	2 125	2 248
50-54	2 058	1 010	1 047	2 319	1 155	1 164	2 987	1 482	1 505	3 764	1 852	1 912
55-59	1 680	807	873	2 077	998	1 079	2 331	1 136	1 196	2 861	1 400	1 461
60-64	1 315	630	685	1 662	779	883	2 041	957	1 084	2 187	1 045	1 142
65-69	912	427	485	1 243	581	662	1 566	716	850	1 845	842	1 003
70-74	614	276	338	797	364	433	1 083	492	591	1 324	583	741
75-79	374	163	211	466	203	263	614	271	344	819	354	465
80 +	217	87	130	274	112	162	400	163	237	543	219	325

United Nations Department of Economic and Social Affairs/Population Division
World Population Prospects: The 2004 Revision, Volume II: Sex and Age Distribution of the World Population

826

POPULATION BY AGE AND SEX (in thousands)

Age group	2005			2010			2015			2020		
	Both sexes	Males	Females	Both sexes	Males	Females	Both sexes	Males	Females	Both sexes	Males	Females
All ages	64 233	31 543	32 690	66 785	32 705	34 080	69 064	33 750	35 314	71 044	34 055	36 989
0-4	5 012	2 542	2 470	4 869	2 472	2 397	4 784	2 431	2 352	4 683	2 382	2 301
5-9	5 020	2 541	2 479	4 994	2 531	2 463	4 855	2 464	2 392	4 773	2 425	2 348
10-14	5 263	2 660	2 603	5 009	2 535	2 474	4 985	2 525	2 459	4 848	2 459	2 388
15-19	5 404	2 721	2 682	5 245	2 649	2 597	4 993	2 525	2 469	4 970	2 516	2 454
20-24	5 491	2 762	2 729	5 360	2 694	2 666	5 205	2 624	2 581	4 956	2 502	2 454
25-29	5 378	2 694	2 684	5 426	2 720	2 705	5 306	2 661	2 645	5 156	2 594	2 562
30-34	5 013	2 459	2 553	5 304	2 646	2 659	5 365	2 683	2 682	5 259	2 633	2 626
35-39	5 048	2 414	2 634	4 928	2 403	2 525	5 234	2 602	2 632	5 310	2 650	2 660
40-44	4 888	2 330	2 558	4 955	2 352	2 602	4 852	2 355	2 496	5 170	2 563	2 607
45-49	4 374	2 125	2 248	4 785	2 263	2 522	4 864	2 296	2 568	4 777	2 310	2 467
50-54	3 764	1 852	1 912	4 257	2 050	2 207	4 671	2 192	2 479	4 762	2 234	2 529
55-59	2 861	1 400	1 461	3 621	1 760	1 861	4 109	1 957	2 152	4 525	2 102	2 424
60-64	2 187	1 045	1 142	2 697	1 296	1 401	3 428	1 637	1 791	3 907	1 829	2 077
65-69	1 845	842	1 003	1 988	925	1 063	2 469	1 156	1 313	3 156	1 469	1 687
70-74	1 324	583	741	1 576	692	884	1 714	767	947	2 148	967	1 181
75-79	819	354	465	1 019	425	594	1 231	510	721	1 357	571	786
80-84	382	158	224	523	210	314	670	255	415	830	310	519
85-89	132	51	82	182	67	115	260	90	170	349	112	237
90-94	26	9	17	41	13	28	61	18	43	94	25	69
95-99	3	1	2	5	1	3	8	2	6	13	3	11
100 +	0	0	0	0	0	0	0	0	0	1	0	1

Age group	2025			2030			2035			2040		
	Both sexes	Males	Females	Both sexes	Males	Females	Both sexes	Males	Females	Both sexes	Males	Females
All ages	72 635	35 371	37 265	73 827	35 891	37 936	74 611	36 248	38 364	74 965	36 416	38 549
0-4	4 565	2 323	2 242	4 457	2 270	2 187	4 358	2 220	2 138	4 266	2 174	2 093
5-9	4 674	2 376	2 298	4 558	2 320	2 239	4 452	2 267	2 185	4 353	2 217	2 135
10-14	4 767	2 421	2 346	4 669	2 374	2 296	4 554	2 317	2 237	4 448	2 265	2 183
15-19	4 834	2 451	2 383	4 755	2 414	2 341	4 658	2 367	2 291	4 543	2 311	2 233
20-24	4 934	2 495	2 440	4 800	2 431	2 370	4 722	2 394	2 328	4 626	2 348	2 278
25-29	4 912	2 475	2 436	4 893	2 470	2 423	4 761	2 407	2 354	4 685	2 372	2 312
30-34	5 115	2 570	2 545	4 877	2 455	2 422	4 860	2 451	2 409	4 732	2 391	2 342
35-39	5 213	2 606	2 607	5 076	2 548	2 528	4 843	2 436	2 407	4 830	2 434	2 396
40-44	5 254	2 617	2 636	5 165	2 579	2 586	5 034	2 523	2 510	4 806	2 415	2 391
45-49	5 099	2 520	2 579	5 190	2 579	2 611	5 108	2 545	2 563	4 983	2 493	2 490
50-54	4 686	2 254	2 432	5 011	2 466	2 545	5 107	2 529	2 579	5 032	2 499	2 533
55-59	4 624	2 148	2 470	4 550	2 176	2 385	4 994	2 496	2 498	4 985	2 452	2 534
60-64	4 318	1 973	2 345	4 425	2 025	2 401	4 374	2 058	2 316	4 695	2 266	2 429
65-69	3 615	1 650	1 965	4 015	1 790	2 226	4 132	1 848	2 284	4 096	1 888	2 208
70-74	2 767	1 237	1 529	3 194	1 401	1 793	3 575	1 534	2 040	3 698	1 597	2 101
75-79	1 721	727	994	2 243	940	1 303	2 622	1 084	1 539	2 964	1 201	1 763
80-84	933	352	580	1 204	455	750	1 603	607	996	1 905	714	1 191
85-89	447	138	309	518	159	358	691	217	474	943	300	643
90-94	133	31	102	179	39	141	218	49	169	301	70	231
95-99	22	4	19	35	5	30	50	6	43	63	9	55
100 +	2	0	2	3	0	3	5	0	5	8	1	8

Age group	2045			2050		
	Both sexes	Males	Females	Both sexes	Males	Females
All ages	74 935	36 425	38 511	74 594	36 306	38 288
0-4	4 175	2 127	2 048	4 080	2 079	2 001
5-9	4 262	2 171	2 091	4 171	2 125	2 046
10-14	4 350	2 216	2 134	4 260	2 170	2 090
15-19	4 438	2 259	2 179	4 340	2 210	2 130
20-24	4 513	2 293	2 220	4 408	2 241	2 167
25-29	4 591	2 328	2 264	4 479	2 273	2 206
30-34	4 659	2 358	2 302	4 570	2 315	2 255
35-39	4 706	2 376	2 330	4 638	2 346	2 293
40-44	4 797	2 415	2 382	4 679	2 360	2 319
45-49	4 762	2 388	2 373	4 757	2 391	2 366
50-54	4 913	2 451	2 463	4 700	2 350	2 350
55-59	4 919	2 427	2 492	4 810	2 385	2 425
60-64	4 801	2 335	2 467	4 747	2 318	2 429
65-69	4 409	2 088	2 321	4 522	2 160	2 362
70-74	3 682	1 643	2 039	3 981	1 829	2 152
75-79	3 091	1 263	1 828	3 098	1 314	1 785
80-84	2 189	807	1 382	2 313	864	1 449
85-89	1 150	365	785	1 353	425	929
90-94	426	102	324	537	129	407
95-99	91	13	78	134	21	114
100 +	11	1	10	17	1	15

POPULATION BY AGE AND SEX (in thousands)

Age group	2005 Both sexes	2005 Males	2005 Females	2010 Both sexes	2010 Males	2010 Females	2015 Both sexes	2015 Males	2015 Females	2020 Both sexes	2020 Males	2020 Females
All ages	64 233	31 543	32 690	67 437	33 036	34 401	70 749	34 606	36 143	73 991	36 152	37 839
0-4	5 012	2 542	2 470	5 521	2 803	2 718	5 818	2 957	2 861	5 948	3 025	2 923
5-9	5 020	2 541	2 479	4 994	2 531	2 463	5 506	2 794	2 712	5 805	2 949	2 856
10-14	5 263	2 660	2 603	5 009	2 535	2 474	4 985	2 525	2 459	5 497	2 789	2 708
15-19	5 404	2 721	2 682	5 245	2 649	2 597	4 993	2 525	2 469	4 970	2 516	2 454
20-24	5 491	2 762	2 729	5 360	2 694	2 666	5 205	2 624	2 581	4 956	2 502	2 454
25-29	5 378	2 694	2 684	5 426	2 720	2 705	5 306	2 661	2 645	5 156	2 594	2 562
30-34	5 013	2 459	2 553	5 304	2 646	2 659	5 365	2 683	2 682	5 259	2 633	2 626
35-39	5 048	2 414	2 634	4 928	2 403	2 525	5 234	2 602	2 632	5 310	2 650	2 660
40-44	4 888	2 330	2 558	4 955	2 352	2 602	4 852	2 355	2 496	5 170	2 563	2 607
45-49	4 374	2 125	2 248	4 785	2 263	2 522	4 864	2 296	2 568	4 777	2 310	2 467
50-54	3 764	1 852	1 912	4 257	2 050	2 207	4 671	2 192	2 479	4 762	2 234	2 529
55-59	2 861	1 400	1 461	3 621	1 760	1 861	4 109	1 957	2 152	4 525	2 102	2 424
60-64	2 187	1 045	1 142	2 697	1 296	1 401	3 428	1 637	1 791	3 907	1 829	2 077
65-69	1 845	842	1 003	1 988	925	1 063	2 469	1 156	1 313	3 156	1 469	1 687
70-74	1 324	583	741	1 576	692	884	1 714	767	947	2 148	967	1 181
75-79	819	354	465	1 019	425	594	1 231	510	721	1 357	571	786
80-84	382	158	224	523	210	314	670	255	415	830	310	519
85-89	132	51	82	182	67	115	260	90	170	349	112	237
90-94	26	9	17	41	13	28	61	18	43	94	25	69
95-99	3	1	2	5	1	3	8	2	6	13	3	11
100 +	0	0	0	0	0	0	0	0	0	1	0	1

Age group	2025 Both sexes	2025 Males	2025 Females	2030 Both sexes	2030 Males	2030 Females	2035 Both sexes	2035 Males	2035 Females	2040 Both sexes	2040 Males	2040 Females
All ages	76 855	37 515	39 339	79 484	38 767	40 717	82 027	40 019	42 008	84 484	41 258	43 226
0-4	5 842	2 973	2 869	5 901	3 005	2 895	6 125	3 121	3 005	6 382	3 251	3 130
5-9	5 937	3 019	2 918	5 833	2 968	2 865	5 893	3 001	2 892	6 119	3 117	3 002
10-14	5 797	2 945	2 853	5 931	3 015	2 916	5 828	2 966	2 863	5 889	2 999	2 890
15-19	5 483	2 780	2 703	5 784	2 936	2 848	5 918	3 007	2 911	5 816	2 958	2 858
20-24	4 934	2 495	2 440	5 448	2 759	2 689	5 749	2 916	2 834	5 885	2 987	2 897
25-29	4 912	2 475	2 436	4 893	2 470	2 423	5 406	2 734	2 672	5 709	2 892	2 817
30-34	5 115	2 570	2 545	4 877	2 455	2 422	4 860	2 451	2 409	5 374	2 715	2 659
35-39	5 213	2 606	2 607	5 076	2 548	2 528	4 843	2 436	2 407	4 830	2 434	2 396
40-44	5 254	2 617	2 636	5 165	2 579	2 586	5 034	2 523	2 510	4 806	2 415	2 391
45-49	5 099	2 520	2 579	5 190	2 579	2 611	5 108	2 545	2 563	4 983	2 493	2 490
50-54	4 686	2 254	2 432	5 011	2 466	2 545	5 107	2 529	2 579	5 032	2 499	2 533
55-59	4 624	2 148	2 476	4 559	2 175	2 385	4 884	2 386	2 498	4 985	2 452	2 534
60-64	4 318	1 973	2 345	4 425	2 025	2 401	4 374	2 058	2 316	4 695	2 266	2 429
65-69	3 615	1 650	1 965	4 015	1 790	2 226	4 132	1 848	2 284	4 096	1 888	2 208
70-74	2 767	1 237	1 529	3 194	1 401	1 793	3 575	1 534	2 040	3 698	1 597	2 101
75-79	1 721	727	994	2 243	940	1 303	2 622	1 084	1 539	2 964	1 201	1 763
80-84	933	352	580	1 204	455	750	1 603	607	996	1 905	714	1 191
85-89	447	138	309	518	159	358	691	217	474	943	300	643
90-94	133	31	102	179	39	141	218	49	169	301	70	231
95-99	22	4	19	35	5	30	50	6	43	63	9	55
100 +	2	0	2	3	0	3	5	0	5	8	1	8

Age group	2045 Both sexes	2045 Males	2045 Females	2050 Both sexes	2050 Males	2050 Females
All ages	86 814	42 467	44 347	89 013	43 641	45 372
0-4	6 553	3 339	3 214	6 643	3 385	3 258
5-9	6 375	3 248	3 127	6 547	3 335	3 212
10-14	6 115	3 115	3 000	6 372	3 246	3 126
15-19	5 877	2 992	2 886	6 103	3 108	2 996
20-24	5 784	2 939	2 845	5 845	2 973	2 872
25-29	5 846	2 965	2 882	5 747	2 917	2 830
30-34	5 679	2 874	2 805	5 820	2 949	2 871
35-39	5 344	2 699	2 646	5 653	2 860	2 793
40-44	4 797	2 415	2 382	5 313	2 681	2 632
45-49	4 762	2 388	2 373	4 757	2 391	2 366
50-54	4 913	2 451	2 463	4 700	2 350	2 350
55-59	4 919	2 427	2 492	4 810	2 385	2 425
60-64	4 801	2 335	2 467	4 747	2 318	2 429
65-69	4 409	2 088	2 321	4 522	2 160	2 362
70-74	3 682	1 643	2 039	3 981	1 829	2 152
75-79	3 091	1 263	1 828	3 098	1 314	1 785
80-84	2 189	807	1 382	2 313	864	1 449
85-89	1 150	365	785	1 353	425	929
90-94	426	102	324	537	129	407
95-99	91	13	78	134	21	114
100 +	11	1	10	17	1	15

United Nations Department of Economic and Social Affairs/Population Division
World Population Prospects: The 2004 Revision, Volume II: Sex and Age Distribution of the World Population

POPULATION BY AGE AND SEX (in thousands)

Age group	2005 Both sexes	Males	Females	2010 Both sexes	Males	Females	2015 Both sexes	Males	Females	2020 Both sexes	Males	Females
All ages	64 233	31 543	32 690	66 122	32 374	33 750	67 380	32 804	34 485	68 097	33 157	34 940
0-4	5 012	2 542	2 470	4 217	2 141	2 076	3 749	1 906	1 844	3 417	1 738	1 679
5-9	5 020	2 541	2 479	4 994	2 531	2 463	4 205	2 134	2 071	3 741	1 901	1 840
10-14	5 263	2 660	2 603	5 009	2 535	2 474	4 985	2 525	2 459	4 198	2 130	2 068
15-19	5 404	2 721	2 682	5 245	2 649	2 597	4 993	2 525	2 469	4 970	2 516	2 454
20-24	5 491	2 762	2 729	5 360	2 694	2 666	5 205	2 624	2 581	4 956	2 502	2 454
25-29	5 378	2 694	2 684	5 426	2 720	2 705	5 306	2 661	2 645	5 156	2 594	2 562
30-34	5 013	2 459	2 553	5 304	2 646	2 659	5 365	2 683	2 682	5 259	2 633	2 626
35-39	5 048	2 414	2 634	4 928	2 403	2 525	5 234	2 602	2 632	5 310	2 650	2 660
40-44	4 888	2 330	2 558	4 955	2 352	2 602	4 852	2 355	2 496	5 170	2 563	2 607
45-49	4 374	2 125	2 248	4 785	2 263	2 522	4 864	2 296	2 568	4 777	2 310	2 467
50-54	3 764	1 852	1 912	4 257	2 050	2 207	4 671	2 192	2 479	4 762	2 234	2 529
55-59	2 861	1 400	1 461	3 621	1 760	1 861	4 109	1 957	2 152	4 525	2 102	2 424
60-64	2 187	1 045	1 142	2 697	1 296	1 401	3 428	1 637	1 791	3 907	1 829	2 077
65-69	1 845	842	1 003	1 988	925	1 063	2 469	1 156	1 313	3 156	1 469	1 687
70-74	1 324	583	741	1 576	692	884	1 714	767	947	2 148	967	1 181
75-79	819	354	465	1 019	425	594	1 231	510	721	1 357	571	786
80-84	382	158	224	523	210	314	670	255	415	830	310	519
85-89	132	51	82	182	67	115	260	90	170	349	112	237
90-94	26	9	17	41	13	28	61	18	43	94	25	69
95-99	3	1	2	5	1	3	8	2	6	13	3	11
100 +	0	0	0	0	0	0	0	0	0	1	0	1

Age group	2025 Both sexes	Males	Females	2030 Both sexes	Males	Females	2035 Both sexes	Males	Females	2040 Both sexes	Males	Females
All ages	68 434	33 235	35 199	68 290	33 076	35 214	67 566	32 665	34 901	66 227	31 973	34 255
0-4	3 306	1 683	1 623	3 115	1 587	1 529	2 841	1 447	1 394	2 561	1 305	1 256
5-9	3 411	1 734	1 677	3 301	1 680	1 621	3 112	1 585	1 527	2 838	1 446	1 392
10-14	3 736	1 898	1 838	3 408	1 732	1 675	3 299	1 678	1 620	3 109	1 583	1 526
15-19	4 186	2 122	2 064	3 725	1 891	1 834	3 397	1 726	1 671	3 289	1 673	1 616
20-24	4 934	2 495	2 440	4 153	2 103	2 050	3 694	1 873	1 821	3 368	1 709	1 659
25-29	4 912	2 475	2 436	4 893	2 470	2 423	4 116	2 081	2 035	3 660	1 853	1 807
30-34	5 115	2 570	2 545	4 877	2 455	2 422	4 860	2 451	2 409	4 090	2 066	2 025
35-39	5 213	2 606	2 607	5 076	2 548	2 528	4 843	2 436	2 407	4 830	2 434	2 396
40-44	5 254	2 617	2 636	5 165	2 579	2 586	5 034	2 523	2 510	4 806	2 415	2 391
45-49	5 099	2 520	2 579	5 190	2 579	2 611	5 108	2 545	2 563	4 983	2 493	2 490
50-54	4 686	2 254	2 432	5 011	2 466	2 545	5 107	2 529	2 579	5 032	2 499	2 533
55-59	4 624	2 148	2 476	4 559	2 175	2 385	4 884	2 386	2 498	4 985	2 452	2 534
60-64	4 318	1 973	2 345	4 425	2 025	2 401	4 374	2 058	2 316	4 695	2 266	2 429
65-69	3 615	1 650	1 965	4 015	1 790	2 226	4 132	1 848	2 284	4 096	1 888	2 208
70-74	2 767	1 237	1 529	3 194	1 401	1 793	3 575	1 534	2 040	3 698	1 597	2 101
75-79	1 721	727	994	2 243	940	1 303	2 622	1 084	1 539	2 964	1 201	1 763
80-84	933	352	580	1 204	455	750	1 600	607	990	1 905	714	1 191
85-89	447	138	309	518	159	358	691	217	474	943	300	643
90-94	133	31	102	179	39	141	218	49	169	301	70	231
95-99	22	4	19	35	5	30	50	6	43	63	9	55
100 +	2	0	2	3	0	3	5	0	5	8	1	8

Age group	2045 Both sexes	Males	Females	2050 Both sexes	Males	Females
All ages	64 375	31 054	33 321	62 143	29 974	32 169
0-4	2 335	1 190	1 145	2 167	1 104	1 063
5-9	2 559	1 304	1 255	2 333	1 188	1 144
10-14	2 836	1 445	1 392	2 558	1 303	1 255
15-19	3 100	1 578	1 522	2 828	1 440	1 388
20-24	3 260	1 656	1 604	3 072	1 562	1 510
25-29	3 336	1 690	1 646	3 230	1 638	1 592
30-34	3 640	1 841	1 799	3 319	1 680	1 639
35-39	4 069	2 053	2 015	3 623	1 831	1 792
40-44	4 797	2 415	2 382	4 045	2 040	2 005
45-49	4 762	2 388	2 373	4 757	2 391	2 366
50-54	4 913	2 451	2 463	4 700	2 350	2 350
55-59	4 919	2 427	2 492	4 810	2 385	2 425
60-64	4 801	2 335	2 467	4 747	2 318	2 429
65-69	4 409	2 088	2 321	4 522	2 160	2 362
70-74	3 682	1 643	2 039	3 981	1 829	2 152
75-79	3 091	1 263	1 828	3 098	1 314	1 785
80-84	2 189	807	1 382	2 313	864	1 449
85-89	1 150	365	785	1 353	425	929
90-94	426	102	324	537	129	407
95-99	91	13	78	134	21	114
100 +	11	1	10	17	1	15

POPULATION BY AGE AND SEX (in thousands)

Age group	1950 Both sexes	1950 Males	1950 Females	1955 Both sexes	1955 Males	1955 Females	1960 Both sexes	1960 Males	1960 Females	1965 Both sexes	1965 Males	1965 Females
All ages	1 230	616	613	1 354	681	672	1 392	703	689	1 481	750	731
0-4	175	90	86	193	99	94	186	96	90	189	98	91
5-9	132	67	65	169	86	82	175	90	85	176	91	85
10-14	129	65	64	131	67	65	157	81	76	169	87	82
15-19	128	64	64	128	65	64	122	62	60	151	78	74
20-24	111	55	56	127	63	64	119	60	59	117	59	58
25-29	92	45	47	110	54	56	118	59	59	114	57	57
30-34	62	31	31	92	45	47	102	50	52	113	56	57
35-39	70	36	33	62	31	31	85	41	43	97	48	50
40-44	64	34	30	68	36	33	56	28	28	80	39	41
45-49	55	29	26	63	33	30	62	32	30	52	26	27
50-54	42	21	22	52	28	25	56	30	27	58	30	28
55-59	31	15	16	40	19	20	46	24	22	51	27	25
60-64	33	15	18	28	14	15	34	16	18	41	21	20
65-69	28	14	14	28	13	15	23	11	12	29	14	15
70-74	36	17	19	22	10	11	21	9	11	17	8	9
75-79	24	11	13	24	12	13	14	7	7	14	6	8
80 +	17	7	9	17	8	9	17	8	9	13	7	7

Age group	1970 Both sexes	1970 Males	1970 Females	1975 Both sexes	1975 Males	1975 Females	1980 Both sexes	1980 Males	1980 Females	1985 Both sexes	1985 Males	1985 Females
All ages	1 568	795	773	1 676	849	826	1 795	909	886	1 828	920	909
0-4	173	89	84	179	92	87	176	91	85	169	87	82
5-9	170	87	83	169	87	82	167	86	81	169	87	82
10-14	169	87	82	167	86	81	171	88	83	160	82	78
15-19	165	84	80	166	85	81	168	86	82	161	82	79
20-24	145	74	70	162	83	79	168	86	82	158	81	77
25-29	111	56	55	142	73	69	162	83	79	156	80	76
30-34	110	55	55	109	55	54	135	69	66	151	77	74
35-39	109	55	54	108	54	54	110	55	54	125	63	62
40-44	94	46	48	106	53	53	108	54	54	105	52	53
45-49	78	38	40	91	45	46	105	52	52	103	51	52
50-54	51	25	26	75	36	39	87	42	45	100	49	51
55-59	56	28	27	48	23	24	72	35	37	82	40	43
60-64	49	25	23	51	26	26	42	20	22	68	32	36
65-69	37	19	18	43	22	21	50	25	25	38	18	20
70-74	25	12	13	29	15	15	34	17	17	38	18	20
75-79	13	6	7	18	8	10	24	12	13	25	12	13
80 +	16	8	9	14	6	7	15	7	8	20	9	11

Age group	1990 Both sexes	1990 Males	1990 Females	1995 Both sexes	1995 Males	1995 Females	2000 Both sexes	2000 Males	2000 Females	2005 Both sexes	2005 Males	2005 Females
All ages	1 909	958	951	1 963	983	981	2 010	1 004	1 005	2 034	1 015	1 019
0-4	164	84	79	154	79	75	130	67	63	117	61	56
5-9	168	86	82	161	83	78	153	79	74	129	67	62
10-14	167	86	81	168	86	82	160	82	78	152	79	74
15-19	158	81	77	165	84	81	167	86	82	159	82	77
20-24	158	80	78	155	79	76	164	84	80	166	85	81
25-29	155	79	76	152	77	75	154	79	76	163	83	80
30-34	154	78	75	149	75	74	151	76	74	153	78	75
35-39	148	75	73	147	75	72	148	75	73	149	76	74
40-44	122	61	61	141	71	70	145	74	71	146	74	72
45-49	102	50	52	115	56	58	138	69	69	142	72	70
50-54	100	49	51	101	49	51	112	55	57	134	67	67
55-59	95	46	49	96	46	49	96	47	50	107	52	55
60-64	77	36	41	90	43	47	89	43	47	90	43	47
65-69	61	28	33	70	32	38	80	37	43	80	37	43
70-74	31	14	17	53	24	29	58	26	32	67	30	37
75-79	28	13	15	24	11	13	39	16	23	44	18	26
80 +	22	10	12	24	11	13	24	10	14	34	12	22

(*) The former Yugoslav Republic of Macedonia.

830

United Nations Department of Economic and Social Affairs/Population Division
World Population Prospects: The 2004 Revision, Volume II: Sex and Age Distribution of the World Population

POPULATION BY AGE AND SEX (in thousands)

Age group	2005 Both sexes	Males	Females	2010 Both sexes	Males	Females	2015 Both sexes	Males	Females	2020 Both sexes	Males	Females
All ages	2 034	1 015	1 019	2 046	1 020	1 027	2 055	1 023	1 032	2 057	1 024	1 033
0-4	117	61	56	111	58	54	114	59	55	113	59	54
5-9	129	67	62	117	60	56	111	57	53	114	59	55
10-14	152	79	74	128	67	62	116	60	56	110	57	53
15-19	159	82	77	152	78	73	128	66	61	115	60	55
20-24	166	85	81	158	81	77	151	78	73	127	66	61
25-29	163	83	80	165	85	80	157	81	76	150	77	73
30-34	153	78	75	161	82	79	164	84	80	156	80	76
35-39	149	76	74	152	77	74	160	81	79	162	83	79
40-44	146	74	72	148	75	73	150	76	74	158	80	78
45-49	142	72	70	144	72	71	145	73	72	148	75	73
50-54	134	67	67	139	70	69	140	70	70	142	71	71
55-59	107	52	55	129	64	65	133	67	67	135	67	68
60-64	90	43	47	100	48	52	121	59	62	126	62	64
65-69	80	37	43	81	37	44	91	42	49	111	52	58
70-74	67	30	37	68	30	38	69	31	38	78	35	43
75-79	44	18	26	51	21	30	52	22	31	54	22	32
80-84	25	9	15	28	10	18	34	12	21	35	13	22
85-89	7	2	5	12	4	8	14	4	10	18	5	12
90-94	2	1	2	2	1	2	4	1	3	5	1	4
95-99	0	0	0	0	0	0	0	0	0	1	0	1
100 +	0	0	0	0	0	0	0	0	0	0	0	0

Age group	2025 Both sexes	Males	Females	2030 Both sexes	Males	Females	2035 Both sexes	Males	Females	2040 Both sexes	Males	Females
All ages	2 048	1 019	1 028	2 027	1 009	1 019	2 000	994	1 005	1 967	978	989
0-4	108	56	52	102	53	49	98	51	47	97	51	47
5-9	112	58	54	107	56	51	101	53	49	98	51	47
10-14	113	59	54	112	58	54	107	55	51	100	52	48
15-19	109	57	53	112	58	54	111	58	53	106	55	51
20-24	114	59	55	109	56	52	112	58	54	110	57	53
25-29	126	65	61	114	59	55	108	56	52	111	58	53
30-34	149	76	72	125	65	60	113	58	54	107	56	52
35-39	155	79	75	147	76	72	124	64	60	112	58	54
40-44	161	82	79	153	78	75	146	75	71	123	64	59
45-49	156	79	77	159	81	78	151	77	74	144	74	70
50-54	144	73	71	153	77	76	156	79	76	148	76	73
55-59	137	68	69	140	70	70	148	74	74	151	76	75
60-64	128	62	65	130	64	66	133	66	67	142	70	71
65-69	115	55	60	117	56	61	120	58	63	123	60	64
70-74	96	43	52	100	46	54	103	47	56	106	49	57
75-79	61	25	36	76	32	44	81	35	46	84	36	48
80-84	36	13	23	42	15	27	53	20	33	58	23	35
85-89	19	5	13	20	6	14	24	7	17	31	10	21
90-94	7	1	5	7	1	6	8	2	7	10	2	8
95-99	1	0	1	2	0	1	2	0	2	2	0	2
100 +	0	0	0	0	0	0	0	0	0	0	0	0

Age group	2045 Both sexes	Males	Females	2050 Both sexes	Males	Females
All ages	1 928	958	970	1 884	937	948
0-4	96	50	46	94	49	45
5-9	97	50	47	95	50	46
10-14	97	50	47	96	50	46
15-19	100	52	48	96	50	46
20-24	105	55	51	99	52	48
25-29	110	57	53	105	54	50
30-34	110	57	53	109	57	52
35-39	106	55	51	109	57	53
40-44	111	57	54	106	55	51
45-49	121	63	59	110	57	53
50-54	142	73	69	119	62	58
55-59	144	73	71	138	70	68
60-64	145	72	72	139	70	69
65-69	132	64	68	135	67	69
70-74	110	52	58	118	56	62
75-79	88	38	49	91	41	51
80-84	61	24	37	65	26	39
85-89	35	11	23	38	13	25
90-94	14	3	11	16	4	12
95-99	3	0	3	4	1	4
100 +	0	0	0	1	0	1

POPULATION BY AGE AND SEX (in thousands)

Age group	2005 Both sexes	Males	Females	2010 Both sexes	Males	Females	2015 Both sexes	Males	Females	2020 Both sexes	Males	Females
All ages	2 034	1 015	1 019	2 066	1 030	1 036	2 104	1 049	1 055	2 141	1 068	1 073
0-4	117	61	56	131	68	63	144	75	69	148	77	71
5-9	129	67	62	117	60	56	130	67	63	144	75	69
10-14	152	79	74	128	67	62	116	60	56	129	67	62
15-19	159	82	77	152	78	73	128	66	61	115	60	55
20-24	166	85	81	158	81	77	151	78	73	127	66	61
25-29	163	83	80	165	85	80	157	81	76	150	77	73
30-34	153	78	75	161	82	79	164	84	80	156	80	76
35-39	149	76	74	152	77	74	160	81	79	162	83	79
40-44	146	74	72	148	75	73	150	76	74	158	80	78
45-49	142	72	70	144	72	71	145	73	72	148	75	73
50-54	134	67	67	139	70	69	140	70	70	142	71	71
55-59	107	52	55	129	64	65	133	67	67	135	67	68
60-64	90	43	47	100	48	52	121	59	62	126	62	64
65-69	80	37	43	81	37	44	91	42	49	111	52	58
70-74	67	30	37	68	30	38	69	31	38	78	35	43
75-79	44	18	26	51	21	30	52	22	31	54	22	32
80-84	25	9	15	28	10	18	34	12	21	35	13	22
85-89	7	2	5	12	4	8	14	4	10	18	5	12
90-94	2	1	2	2	1	2	4	1	3	5	1	4
95-99	0	0	0	0	0	0	0	0	0	1	0	1
100 +	0	0	0	0	0	0	0	0	0	0	0	0

Age group	2025 Both sexes	Males	Females	2030 Both sexes	Males	Females	2035 Both sexes	Males	Females	2040 Both sexes	Males	Females
All ages	2 163	1 079	1 084	2 176	1 086	1 090	2 188	1 092	1 096	2 207	1 102	1 105
0-4	139	72	67	134	70	64	139	72	67	149	78	72
5-9	147	76	71	139	72	67	133	69	64	138	72	66
10-14	143	74	69	147	76	70	138	72	66	133	69	64
15-19	129	67	62	142	74	69	146	76	70	137	71	66
20-24	114	59	55	128	66	62	142	74	68	145	75	70
25-29	126	65	61	114	59	55	127	66	61	141	73	68
30-34	149	76	72	125	65	60	113	58	54	127	66	61
35-39	155	79	75	147	76	72	124	64	60	112	58	54
40-44	161	82	79	153	78	75	146	75	71	123	64	59
45-49	156	79	77	159	81	78	151	77	74	144	74	70
50-54	144	73	71	153	77	76	156	79	76	148	76	73
55-59	137	68	69	140	70	70	148	74	74	151	76	75
60-64	128	62	65	130	64	66	133	66	67	142	70	71
65-69	115	55	60	117	56	61	120	58	63	123	60	64
70-74	96	43	52	100	46	54	103	47	56	106	49	57
75-79	61	25	36	76	32	44	81	35	46	84	36	48
80-84	36	13	23	42	15	27	53	20	33	58	23	35
85-89	19	5	13	20	6	14	24	7	17	31	10	21
90-94	7	1	5	7	1	6	8	2	7	10	2	8
95-99	1	0	1	2	0	1	2	0	2	2	0	2
100 +	0	0	0	0	0	0	0	0	0	0	0	0

Age group	2045 Both sexes	Males	Females	2050 Both sexes	Males	Females
All ages	2 227	1 114	1 114	2 244	1 124	1 121
0-4	155	81	75	155	80	74
5-9	149	77	71	155	80	74
10-14	137	71	66	148	77	71
15-19	132	69	64	137	71	66
20-24	137	71	66	132	68	63
25-29	144	75	69	136	71	65
30-34	140	73	67	144	75	69
35-39	126	65	61	139	72	67
40-44	111	57	54	125	65	60
45-49	121	63	59	110	57	53
50-54	142	73	69	119	62	58
55-59	144	73	71	138	70	68
60-64	145	72	72	139	70	69
65-69	132	64	68	135	67	69
70-74	110	52	58	118	56	62
75-79	88	38	49	91	41	51
80-84	61	24	37	65	26	39
85-89	35	11	23	38	13	25
90-94	14	3	11	16	4	12
95-99	3	0	3	4	1	4
100 +	0	0	0	1	0	1

United Nations Department of Economic and Social Affairs/Population Division
World Population Prospects: The 2004 Revision, Volume II: Sex and Age Distribution of the World Population

832

POPULATION BY AGE AND SEX (in thousands)

Age group	2005 Both sexes	Males	Females	2010 Both sexes	Males	Females	2015 Both sexes	Males	Females	2020 Both sexes	Males	Females
All ages	2 034	1 015	1 019	2 027	1 010	1 017	2 005	998	1 008	1 972	980	992
0-4	117	61	56	92	48	44	84	44	41	78	40	37
5-9	129	67	62	117	60	56	91	47	44	84	43	40
10-14	152	79	74	128	67	62	116	60	56	91	47	44
15-19	159	82	77	152	78	73	128	66	61	115	60	55
20-24	166	85	81	158	81	77	151	78	73	127	66	61
25-29	163	83	80	165	85	80	157	81	76	150	77	73
30-34	153	78	75	161	82	79	164	84	80	156	80	76
35-39	149	76	74	152	77	74	160	81	79	162	83	79
40-44	146	74	72	148	75	73	150	76	74	158	80	78
45-49	142	72	70	144	72	71	145	73	72	148	75	73
50-54	134	67	67	139	70	69	140	70	70	142	71	71
55-59	107	52	55	129	64	65	133	67	67	135	67	68
60-64	90	43	47	100	48	52	121	59	62	126	62	64
65-69	80	37	43	81	37	44	91	42	49	111	52	58
70-74	67	30	37	68	30	38	69	31	38	78	35	43
75-79	44	18	26	51	21	30	52	22	31	54	22	32
80-84	25	9	15	28	10	18	34	12	21	35	13	22
85-89	7	2	5	12	4	8	14	4	10	18	5	12
90-94	2	1	2	2	1	2	4	1	3	5	1	4
95-99	0	0	0	0	0	0	0	0	0	1	0	1
100 +	0	0	0	0	0	0	0	0	0	0	0	0

Age group	2025 Both sexes	Males	Females	2030 Both sexes	Males	Females	2035 Both sexes	Males	Females	2040 Both sexes	Males	Females
All ages	1 931	959	972	1 880	932	948	1 820	901	919	1 749	864	884
0-4	76	39	36	71	37	34	65	34	31	59	31	28
5-9	77	40	37	75	39	36	71	37	34	65	34	31
10-14	83	43	40	76	40	37	75	39	36	70	36	34
15-19	90	47	43	82	43	40	76	39	36	74	38	36
20-24	114	59	55	89	46	43	82	42	39	75	39	36
25-29	126	65	61	114	59	55	89	46	43	81	42	39
30-34	149	76	72	125	65	60	113	58	54	88	46	42
35-39	155	79	75	147	76	72	124	64	60	112	58	54
40-44	161	82	79	153	78	75	146	75	71	123	64	59
45-49	156	79	77	159	81	78	151	77	74	144	74	70
50-54	144	73	71	153	77	76	156	79	76	148	76	73
55-59	137	68	69	140	70	70	148	74	74	151	76	75
60-64	128	62	65	130	64	66	133	66	67	142	70	71
65-69	115	55	60	117	56	61	120	58	63	123	60	64
70-74	96	43	52	100	46	54	103	47	56	106	49	57
75-79	61	25	36	76	32	44	81	35	46	84	36	48
80-84	36	13	23	42	15	27	53	20	33	58	23	35
85-89	19	5	13	20	6	14	24	7	17	31	10	21
90-94	7	1	5	7	1	6	8	2	7	10	2	8
95-99	1	0	1	2	0	1	2	0	2	2	0	2
100 +	0	0	0	0	0	0	0	0	0	0	0	0

Age group	2045 Both sexes	Males	Females	2050 Both sexes	Males	Females
All ages	1 667	823	844	1 578	778	800
0-4	52	27	25	48	25	23
5-9	59	30	28	52	27	25
10-14	64	33	31	58	30	28
15-19	70	36	33	64	33	31
20-24	73	38	35	69	36	33
25-29	75	39	36	73	38	35
30-34	80	42	39	74	38	36
35-39	87	45	42	80	41	38
40-44	111	57	54	86	45	42
45-49	121	63	59	110	57	53
50-54	142	73	69	119	62	58
55-59	144	73	71	138	70	68
60-64	145	72	72	139	70	69
65-69	132	64	68	135	67	69
70-74	110	52	58	118	56	62
75-79	88	38	49	91	41	51
80-84	61	24	37	65	26	39
85-89	35	11	23	38	13	25
90-94	14	3	11	16	4	12
95-99	3	0	3	4	1	4
100 +	0	0	0	1	0	1

United Nations Department of Economic and Social Affairs/Population Division
World Population Prospects: The 2004 Revision, Volume II: Sex and Age Distribution of the World Population

833

POPULATION BY AGE AND SEX (in thousands)

Age group	1950 Both sexes	Males	Females	1955 Both sexes	Males	Females	1960 Both sexes	Males	Females	1965 Both sexes	Males	Females
All ages	1 329	655	674	1 439	707	732	1 572	772	800	1 719	844	875
0-4	224	111	113	256	127	129	285	142	143	314	156	158
5-9	175	87	88	191	94	96	221	109	112	247	123	125
10-14	150	74	76	165	82	83	179	89	90	206	102	104
15-19	130	64	66	141	70	71	155	77	78	167	83	84
20-24	113	56	57	122	60	62	131	65	66	144	71	72
25-29	98	48	50	105	51	53	112	55	57	121	60	61
30-34	85	42	43	90	44	46	97	48	49	103	51	53
35-39	73	36	38	78	38	40	83	41	43	89	44	45
40-44	61	29	31	67	32	35	72	35	37	76	37	39
45-49	50	24	26	55	27	29	61	29	32	65	31	34
50-54	43	20	22	45	21	24	50	24	26	55	26	29
55-59	37	18	19	37	18	20	39	19	21	43	20	23
60-64	33	16	16	31	15	16	31	14	17	33	15	18
65-69	25	13	12	25	12	13	24	11	13	24	11	13
70-74	17	9	9	17	9	9	17	8	9	17	7	9
75-79	10	5	5	9	5	5	9	5	5	10	5	5
80 +	5	2	2	5	2	2	5	2	2	5	2	3

Age group	1970 Both sexes	Males	Females	1975 Both sexes	Males	Females	1980 Both sexes	Males	Females	1985 Both sexes	Males	Females
All ages	2 138	1 051	1 087	2 446	1 204	1 242	2 784	1 372	1 412	3 355	1 655	1 699
0-4	392	195	197	456	228	228	530	265	265	632	316	316
5-9	311	155	157	358	178	180	415	207	208	513	256	257
10-14	261	129	132	300	149	151	341	169	171	418	208	210
15-19	218	108	110	252	125	127	285	142	144	343	170	172
20-24	176	87	89	209	103	105	238	118	120	286	142	144
25-29	150	74	75	167	83	85	196	97	100	238	117	120
30-34	126	62	64	143	71	72	157	78	80	196	96	99
35-39	108	53	55	120	59	61	134	66	68	157	77	80
40-44	92	45	47	102	50	52	112	55	57	133	65	67
45-49	78	38	40	86	42	44	94	46	49	110	53	57
50-54	66	32	34	72	35	38	79	38	41	92	44	48
55-59	54	25	29	60	28	32	65	31	34	76	36	40
60-64	41	19	22	48	22	26	52	24	28	60	28	32
65-69	30	13	16	34	15	19	39	18	22	46	21	25
70-74	19	9	11	22	10	12	25	11	14	31	14	18
75-79	11	5	6	12	5	7	14	6	8	17	7	10
80 +	6	3	3	6	3	4	7	3	4	8	3	5

Age group	1990 Both sexes	Males	Females	1995 Both sexes	Males	Females	2000 Both sexes	Males	Females	2005 Both sexes	Males	Females
All ages	3 961	1 957	2 005	4 512	2 229	2 283	5 364	2 648	2 716	6 145	3 035	3 110
0-4	725	363	362	796	398	397	913	457	456	1 014	508	506
5-9	606	302	303	677	338	339	787	393	394	879	439	440
10-14	509	254	255	584	291	293	690	345	346	779	389	390
15-19	414	206	208	490	244	246	595	297	298	685	342	344
20-24	338	168	170	396	197	199	495	246	249	587	292	295
25-29	281	139	142	322	160	163	392	194	198	480	239	241
30-34	233	115	118	268	132	136	317	156	161	368	183	186
35-39	192	94	98	222	109	113	264	129	135	297	145	151
40-44	153	75	78	182	89	93	219	107	112	248	121	127
45-49	129	63	65	144	70	74	180	87	93	207	100	107
50-54	106	51	55	120	58	62	141	68	73	170	81	89
55-59	87	41	45	97	46	51	116	56	61	133	63	70
60-64	69	32	37	77	36	41	92	43	49	107	50	57
65-69	53	24	29	59	27	32	70	32	38	81	37	44
70-74	36	16	20	41	18	23	49	21	27	57	25	32
75-79	21	9	12	24	10	14	29	12	17	34	14	20
80 +	10	4	6	12	5	7	17	7	10	21	8	13

United Nations Department of Economic and Social Affairs/Population Division
World Population Prospects: The 2004 Revision, Volume II: Sex and Age Distribution of the World Population

834

POPULATION BY AGE AND SEX (in thousands)

Age group	2005 Both sexes	Males	Females	2010 Both sexes	Males	Females	2015 Both sexes	Males	Females	2020 Both sexes	Males	Females
All ages	6 145	3 035	3 110	6 977	3 448	3 529	7 847	3 882	3 966	8 731	4 322	4 409
0-4	1 014	508	506	1 085	543	542	1 133	567	566	1 160	581	579
5-9	879	439	440	980	489	491	1 055	527	528	1 108	554	555
10-14	779	389	390	869	434	435	970	484	486	1 046	522	524
15-19	685	342	344	773	386	388	863	430	433	965	481	484
20-24	587	292	295	676	337	340	765	381	384	856	426	430
25-29	480	239	241	571	284	287	661	329	331	750	374	377
30-34	368	183	186	459	229	230	548	274	274	637	319	318
35-39	297	145	151	347	172	174	437	219	218	523	263	261
40-44	248	121	127	280	137	143	330	164	166	417	209	208
45-49	207	100	107	235	113	121	266	130	137	315	156	159
50-54	170	81	89	196	94	103	223	107	117	254	123	131
55-59	133	63	70	160	75	84	185	87	98	211	100	112
60-64	107	50	57	122	57	65	148	68	80	172	79	93
65-69	81	37	44	94	43	51	109	49	60	133	60	73
70-74	57	25	32	66	29	37	78	34	43	91	40	51
75-79	34	14	20	40	17	23	47	20	27	57	24	33
80-84	15	6	9	18	7	11	22	9	13	27	10	16
85-89	5	2	3	6	2	4	7	2	4	8	3	5
90-94	1	0	0	1	0	1	1	0	1	1	0	1
95-99	0	0	0	0	0	0	0	0	0	0	0	0
100 +	0	0	0	0	0	0	0	0	0	0	0	0

Age group	2025 Both sexes	Males	Females	2030 Both sexes	Males	Females	2035 Both sexes	Males	Females	2040 Both sexes	Males	Females
All ages	9 613	4 763	4 851	10 486	5 198	5 289	11 334	5 620	5 714	12 135	6 018	6 117
0-4	1 177	589	587	1 185	594	591	1 180	592	589	1 157	580	577
5-9	1 140	570	570	1 160	580	580	1 172	586	585	1 169	585	584
10-14	1 102	550	552	1 135	567	568	1 157	578	579	1 169	584	584
15-19	1 041	519	522	1 098	548	550	1 132	565	567	1 154	576	578
20-24	957	477	481	1 035	515	519	1 092	544	548	1 126	562	565
25-29	841	419	422	942	470	473	1 020	508	512	1 079	538	541
30-34	726	363	363	816	408	408	918	459	459	998	498	499
35-39	610	306	304	699	351	349	789	396	393	891	447	445
40-44	500	252	249	586	295	292	675	339	336	765	384	381
45-49	399	199	199	481	241	240	566	284	282	654	328	326
50-54	301	148	153	383	190	193	463	231	232	547	273	274
55-59	241	115	126	287	139	148	366	180	186	444	219	225
60-64	198	91	106	226	106	120	270	129	141	346	167	179
65-69	156	70	86	180	81	99	207	95	112	249	116	133
70-74	112	49	63	133	58	75	155	67	87	180	79	100
75-79	67	28	39	84	35	49	101	42	59	120	50	70
80-84	33	13	20	40	15	24	51	20	31	62	24	38
85-89	10	4	7	13	5	9	17	6	11	22	8	14
90-94	2	1	1	2	1	2	3	1	2	4	1	3
95-99	0	0	0	0	0	0	0	0	0	0	0	0
100 +	0	0	0	0	0	0	0	0	0	0	0	0

Age group	2045 Both sexes	Males	Females	2050 Both sexes	Males	Females
All ages	12 877	6 385	6 492	13 544	6 711	6 833
0-4	1 120	562	558	1 072	538	534
5-9	1 148	575	573	1 112	557	555
10-14	1 167	584	583	1 146	574	573
15-19	1 166	583	584	1 165	582	582
20-24	1 149	573	576	1 162	580	582
25-29	1 115	556	559	1 140	569	571
30-34	1 059	529	530	1 098	549	550
35-39	973	487	486	1 037	519	518
40-44	867	435	432	951	476	474
45-49	744	372	371	847	424	423
50-54	634	316	318	724	361	363
55-59	526	260	267	612	302	310
60-64	422	205	217	502	244	258
65-69	320	151	169	392	186	206
70-74	218	98	119	282	129	153
75-79	141	59	81	172	74	98
80-84	75	29	46	89	35	54
85-89	27	9	18	33	12	22
90-94	5	2	4	7	2	5
95-99	1	0	0	1	0	1
100 +	0	0	0	0	0	0

United Nations Department of Economic and Social Affairs/Population Division
World Population Prospects: The 2004 Revision, Volume II: Sex and Age Distribution of the World Population

835

POPULATION BY AGE AND SEX (in thousands)

Age group	2005 Both sexes	Males	Females	2010 Both sexes	Males	Females	2015 Both sexes	Males	Females	2020 Both sexes	Males	Females
All ages	6 145	3 035	3 110	7 033	3 476	3 557	8 010	3 963	4 047	9 048	4 481	4 567
0-4	1 014	508	506	1 141	571	570	1 240	621	619	1 317	659	658
5-9	879	439	440	980	489	491	1 110	554	555	1 213	606	607
10-14	779	389	390	869	434	435	970	484	486	1 101	549	551
15-19	685	342	344	773	386	388	863	430	433	965	481	484
20-24	587	292	295	676	337	340	765	381	384	856	426	430
25-29	480	239	241	571	284	287	661	329	331	750	374	377
30-34	368	183	186	459	229	230	548	274	274	637	319	318
35-39	297	145	151	347	172	174	437	219	218	523	263	261
40-44	248	121	127	280	137	143	330	164	166	417	209	208
45-49	207	100	107	235	113	121	266	130	137	315	156	159
50-54	170	81	89	196	94	103	223	107	117	254	123	131
55-59	133	63	70	160	75	84	185	87	98	211	100	112
60-64	107	50	57	122	57	65	148	68	80	172	79	93
65-69	81	37	44	94	43	51	109	49	60	133	60	73
70-74	57	25	32	66	29	37	78	34	43	91	40	51
75-79	34	14	20	40	17	23	47	20	27	57	24	33
80-84	15	6	9	18	7	11	22	9	13	27	10	16
85-89	5	2	3	6	2	4	7	2	4	8	3	5
90-94	1	0	0	1	0	1	1	0	1	1	0	1
95-99	0	0	0	0	0	0	0	0	0	0	0	0
100 +	0	0	0	0	0	0	0	0	0	0	0	0

Age group	2025 Both sexes	Males	Females	2030 Both sexes	Males	Females	2035 Both sexes	Males	Females	2040 Both sexes	Males	Females
All ages	10 111	5 012	5 100	11 208	5 559	5 649	12 338	6 122	6 216	13 488	6 695	6 793
0-4	1 361	682	679	1 412	708	705	1 468	736	732	1 512	758	754
5-9	1 294	647	647	1 342	671	671	1 396	698	698	1 454	728	726
10-14	1 206	602	604	1 289	644	645	1 338	669	670	1 393	696	696
15-19	1 095	546	549	1 202	600	602	1 285	641	644	1 335	667	668
20-24	957	477	481	1 088	542	546	1 195	596	600	1 279	638	641
25-29	841	419	422	942	470	473	1 073	535	539	1 181	589	593
30-34	726	363	363	816	408	408	918	459	459	1 050	524	525
35-39	610	306	304	699	351	349	789	396	393	891	447	445
40-44	500	252	249	586	295	292	675	339	336	765	384	381
45-49	399	199	199	481	241	240	566	284	282	654	328	326
50-54	301	148	153	383	190	193	463	231	232	547	273	274
55-59	241	115	126	287	139	148	366	180	186	444	219	225
60-64	198	91	106	226	106	120	270	129	141	346	167	179
65-69	156	70	86	180	81	99	207	95	112	249	116	133
70-74	112	49	63	133	58	75	155	67	87	180	79	100
75-79	67	28	39	84	35	49	101	42	59	120	50	70
80-84	33	13	20	40	15	24	51	20	31	62	24	38
85-89	10	4	7	13	5	9	17	6	11	22	8	14
90-94	2	1	1	2	1	2	3	1	2	4	1	3
95-99	0	0	0	0	0	0	0	0	0	0	0	0
100 +	0	0	0	0	0	0	0	0	0	0	0	0

Age group	2045 Both sexes	Males	Females	2050 Both sexes	Males	Females
All ages	14 633	7 263	7 370	15 751	7 816	7 935
0-4	1 533	769	764	1 534	770	765
5-9	1 500	751	749	1 523	763	760
10-14	1 452	726	725	1 498	750	748
15-19	1 390	694	695	1 449	724	725
20-24	1 330	663	666	1 385	692	694
25-29	1 267	632	635	1 319	658	661
30-34	1 159	579	580	1 247	623	624
35-39	1 023	512	511	1 135	568	567
40-44	867	435	432	1 000	501	499
45-49	744	372	371	847	424	423
50-54	634	316	318	724	361	363
55-59	526	260	267	612	302	310
60-64	422	205	217	502	244	258
65-69	320	151	169	392	186	206
70-74	218	98	119	282	129	153
75-79	141	59	81	172	74	98
80-84	75	29	46	89	35	54
85-89	27	9	18	33	12	22
90-94	5	2	4	7	2	5
95-99	1	0	0	1	0	1
100 +	0	0	0	0	0	0

United Nations Department of Economic and Social Affairs/Population Division
World Population Prospects: The 2004 Revision, Volume II: Sex and Age Distribution of the World Population

POPULATION BY AGE AND SEX (in thousands)

Age group	2005 Both sexes	Males	Females	2010 Both sexes	Males	Females	2015 Both sexes	Males	Females	2020 Both sexes	Males	Females
All ages	6 145	3 035	3 110	6 920	3 420	3 501	7 685	3 800	3 885	8 414	4 164	4 250
0-4	1 014	508	506	1 028	515	514	1 025	513	512	1 002	502	501
5-9	879	439	440	980	489	491	1 000	499	500	1 003	501	502
10-14	779	389	390	869	434	435	970	484	486	992	495	497
15-19	685	342	344	773	386	388	863	430	433	965	481	484
20-24	587	292	295	676	337	340	765	381	384	856	426	430
25-29	480	239	241	571	284	287	661	329	331	750	374	377
30-34	368	183	186	459	229	230	548	274	274	637	319	318
35-39	297	145	151	347	172	174	437	219	218	523	263	261
40-44	248	121	127	280	137	143	330	164	166	417	209	208
45-49	207	100	107	235	113	121	266	130	137	315	156	159
50-54	170	81	89	196	94	103	223	107	117	254	123	131
55-59	133	63	70	160	75	84	185	87	98	211	100	112
60-64	107	50	57	122	57	65	148	68	80	172	79	93
65-69	81	37	44	94	43	51	109	49	60	133	60	73
70-74	57	25	32	66	29	37	78	34	43	91	40	51
75-79	34	14	20	40	17	23	47	20	27	57	24	33
80-84	15	6	9	18	7	11	22	9	13	27	10	16
85-89	5	2	3	6	2	4	7	2	4	8	3	5
90-94	1	0	0	1	0	1	1	0	1	1	0	1
95-99	0	0	0	0	0	0	0	0	0	0	0	0
100 +	0	0	0	0	0	0	0	0	0	0	0	0

Age group	2025 Both sexes	Males	Females	2030 Both sexes	Males	Females	2035 Both sexes	Males	Females	2040 Both sexes	Males	Females
All ages	9 116	4 514	4 602	9 773	4 841	4 932	10 357	5 132	5 225	10 850	5 375	5 474
0-4	993	497	496	965	483	481	912	457	455	842	422	420
5-9	985	492	493	979	490	490	954	477	477	904	452	451
10-14	997	498	499	981	490	491	976	488	488	951	476	476
15-19	987	492	495	994	496	498	978	488	490	974	486	487
20-24	957	477	481	981	488	492	988	492	496	974	486	488
25-29	841	419	422	942	470	473	967	482	485	977	487	490
30-34	726	363	363	816	408	408	918	459	459	946	472	473
35-39	610	306	304	699	351	349	789	396	393	891	447	445
40-44	500	252	249	586	295	292	675	339	336	766	384	381
45-49	399	199	199	481	241	240	566	284	282	654	328	326
50-54	301	148	153	383	190	193	463	231	232	547	273	274
55-59	241	115	126	287	139	148	366	180	186	444	219	225
60-64	198	91	106	226	106	120	270	129	141	346	167	179
65-69	156	70	86	180	81	99	207	95	112	249	116	133
70-74	112	49	63	133	58	75	155	67	87	180	79	100
75-79	67	28	39	84	35	49	101	42	59	120	50	70
80-84	33	13	20	40	15	24	51	20	31	62	24	38
85-89	10	4	7	13	5	9	17	6	11	22	8	14
90-94	2	1	1	2	1	2	3	1	2	4	1	3
95-99	0	0	0	0	0	0	0	0	0	0	0	0
100 +	0	0	0	0	0	0	0	0	0	0	0	0

Age group	2045 Both sexes	Males	Females	2050 Both sexes	Males	Females
All ages	11 246	5 569	5 677	11 541	5 709	5 832
0-4	766	384	382	690	346	344
5-9	835	418	417	760	381	379
10-14	902	451	451	834	417	416
15-19	949	474	475	900	450	450
20-24	970	484	486	946	472	474
25-29	964	481	483	962	480	482
30-34	958	479	480	949	474	475
35-39	922	462	460	938	470	469
40-44	867	435	432	901	451	450
45-49	744	372	371	847	424	423
50-54	634	316	318	724	361	363
55-59	526	260	267	612	302	310
60-64	422	205	217	502	244	258
65-69	320	151	169	392	186	206
70-74	218	98	119	282	129	153
75-79	141	59	81	172	74	98
80-84	75	29	46	89	35	54
85-89	27	9	18	33	12	22
90-94	5	2	4	7	2	5
95-99	1	0	0	1	0	1
100 +	0	0	0	0	0	0

United Nations Department of Economic and Social Affairs/Population Division
World Population Prospects: The 2004 Revision, Volume II: Sex and Age Distribution of the World Population

837

POPULATION BY AGE AND SEX (in thousands)

Age group	1950			1955			1960			1965		
	Both sexes	Males	Females	Both sexes	Males	Females	Both sexes	Males	Females	Both sexes	Males	Females
All ages	47	24	23	57	29	28	68	35	33	83	42	40
0-4	9	5	5	11	6	5	13	7	6	16	8	8
5-9	7	4	4	9	5	4	11	6	5	13	7	6
10-14	6	3	3	7	4	4	9	5	4	11	6	5
15-19	5	3	2	6	3	3	7	4	4	9	5	4
20-24	4	2	2	5	3	2	6	3	3	7	4	4
25-29	3	2	2	4	2	2	5	3	2	6	3	3
30-34	3	1	1	3	2	2	4	2	2	5	3	2
35-39	2	1	1	3	1	1	3	2	2	4	2	2
40-44	2	1	1	2	1	1	3	1	1	3	2	2
45-49	1	1	1	2	1	1	2	1	1	2	1	1
50-54	1	1	1	1	1	1	2	1	1	2	1	1
55-59	1	0	0	1	0	1	1	1	1	1	1	1
60-64	1	0	0	1	0	0	1	0	0	1	0	1
65-69	0	0	0	0	0	0	1	0	0	1	0	0
70-74	0	0	0	0	0	0	0	0	0	0	0	0
75-79	0	0	0	0	0	0	0	0	0	0	0	0
80 +	0	0	0	0	0	0	0	0	0	0	0	0

Age group	1970			1975			1980			1985		
	Both sexes	Males	Females	Both sexes	Males	Females	Both sexes	Males	Females	Both sexes	Males	Females
All ages	98	50	48	92	47	45	97	49	47	92	46	46
0-4	17	9	8	14	7	6	15	8	7	14	7	7
5-9	16	8	8	16	8	8	13	7	6	12	6	6
10-14	13	7	6	13	7	6	15	8	8	12	6	6
15-19	11	6	5	11	6	5	11	6	5	13	7	6
20-24	9	5	4	8	4	4	8	4	4	8	4	4
25-29	7	4	3	5	3	3	6	3	3	6	3	3
30-34	6	3	3	5	2	3	4	2	2	5	2	2
35-39	5	2	2	5	2	2	5	2	2	4	2	2
40-44	4	2	2	4	2	2	5	2	2	4	2	2
45-49	3	2	1	3	2	2	4	2	2	3	2	2
50-54	2	1	1	3	1	1	3	2	2	3	2	2
55-59	2	1	1	2	1	1	2	1	1	3	1	1
60-64	1	1	1	1	1	1	2	1	1	2	1	1
65-69	1	0	0	1	1	0	1	1	1	2	1	1
70-74	1	0	0	1	0	0	1	0	0	1	0	0
75-79	0	0	0	0	0	0	0	0	0	1	0	0
80 +	0	0	0	0	0	0	0	0	0	1	0	0

Age group	1990			1995			2000			2005		
	Both sexes	Males	Females	Both sexes	Males	Females	Both sexes	Males	Females	Both sexes	Males	Females
All ages	94	48	47	97	49	48	100	51	49	102	52	50
0-4	13	7	6	13	7	6	13	7	6	12	6	6
5-9	13	7	6	12	6	5	13	7	6	12	6	6
10-14	11	6	5	13	7	7	12	6	6	13	7	6
15-19	11	6	5	11	5	5	12	6	6	11	6	5
20-24	11	6	5	9	4	4	9	5	5	11	5	5
25-29	7	3	3	8	4	4	7	4	3	8	4	4
30-34	5	3	3	5	3	3	7	3	3	6	3	3
35-39	4	2	2	5	2	2	5	3	3	6	3	3
40-44	3	2	2	4	2	2	4	2	2	5	2	2
45-49	4	2	2	3	1	2	4	2	2	4	2	2
50-54	3	1	2	3	1	2	3	1	2	4	2	2
55-59	3	1	2	3	2	1	3	1	2	3	2	2
60-64	2	1	1	3	1	1	3	1	1	3	1	1
65-69	2	1	1	2	1	1	2	1	1	2	1	1
70-74	1	1	1	1	1	1	2	1	1	2	1	1
75-79	1	0	0	1	1	1	1	0	0	1	1	1
80 +	1	0	0	0	0	0	1	0	1	1	0	1

POPULATION BY AGE AND SEX (in thousands)

Age group	2005 Both sexes	Males	Females	2010 Both sexes	Males	Females	2015 Both sexes	Males	Females	2020 Both sexes	Males	Females
All ages	102	52	50	103	53	51	104	53	51	103	53	50
0-4	12	6	6	11	6	5	10	5	5	10	5	5
5-9	12	6	6	11	6	5	10	5	5	10	5	5
10-14	13	7	6	12	6	6	11	6	5	10	5	5
15-19	11	6	5	11	6	5	11	6	5	10	5	5
20-24	11	5	5	9	5	4	10	5	5	10	5	5
25-29	8	4	4	9	5	4	8	4	3	8	4	4
30-34	6	3	3	6	3	3	8	4	4	6	3	3
35-39	6	3	3	5	3	3	6	3	3	8	4	4
40-44	5	2	2	6	3	3	5	3	3	6	3	3
45-49	4	2	2	4	2	2	6	3	3	5	2	2
50-54	4	2	2	4	2	2	4	2	2	6	3	3
55-59	3	2	2	4	2	2	4	2	2	4	2	2
60-64	3	1	1	3	1	2	3	2	2	3	2	2
65-69	2	1	1	2	1	1	2	1	1	3	2	1
70-74	2	1	1	2	1	1	2	1	1	2	1	1
75-79	1	1	1	1	1	1	1	1	1	2	1	1
80-84	1	0	0	1	0	1	1	0	0	1	0	0
85-89	0	0	0	0	0	0	0	0	0	0	0	0
90-94	0	0	0	0	0	0	0	0	0	0	0	0
95-99	0	0	0	0	0	0	0	0	0	0	0	0
100 +	0	0	0	0	0	0	0	0	0	0	0	0

Age group	2025 Both sexes	Males	Females	2030 Both sexes	Males	Females	2035 Both sexes	Males	Females	2040 Both sexes	Males	Females
All ages	101	52	49	98	51	48	94	49	46	89	46	43
0-4	9	4	4	8	4	4	7	4	3	6	3	3
5-9	9	5	4	8	4	4	7	4	3	6	3	3
10-14	9	5	5	9	4	4	8	4	4	7	4	4
15-19	9	5	4	8	4	4	7	4	4	7	3	3
20-24	9	4	4	8	4	4	7	4	3	6	3	3
25-29	8	4	4	7	4	3	6	3	3	5	3	3
30-34	7	4	3	7	3	3	6	3	3	5	2	2
35-39	6	3	3	7	4	3	6	3	3	5	3	3
40-44	7	4	4	6	3	3	7	3	3	6	3	3
45-49	5	3	3	7	3	3	5	3	2	6	3	3
50-54	5	2	2	5	3	3	7	3	3	5	3	2
55-59	5	2	2	5	2	2	5	2	2	7	3	3
60-64	4	2	2	5	3	2	4	2	2	5	3	2
65-69	3	1	1	3	2	1	4	2	2	4	2	2
70-74	2	1	1	3	1	1	3	2	1	4	2	2
75-79	2	1	1	2	1	1	2	1	1	2	1	1
80-84	1	0	1	1	1	1	1	1	1	1	1	1
85-89	1	0	0	1	0	0	1	0	0	1	0	0
90-94	0	0	0	0	0	0	0	0	0	0	0	0
95-99	0	0	0	0	0	0	0	0	0	0	0	0
100 +	0	0	0	0	0	0	0	0	0	0	0	0

Age group	2045 Both sexes	Males	Females	2050 Both sexes	Males	Females
All ages	83	42	40	75	38	36
0-4	5	2	2	4	2	2
5-9	5	3	2	4	2	2
10-14	6	3	3	5	3	3
15-19	6	3	3	5	3	2
20-24	5	3	3	5	2	2
25-29	5	2	2	4	2	2
30-34	4	2	2	3	2	2
35-39	5	2	2	4	2	2
40-44	5	3	3	4	2	2
45-49	6	3	3	5	2	2
50-54	6	3	3	6	3	3
55-59	5	3	2	6	3	3
60-64	6	3	3	5	3	2
65-69	4	2	2	5	3	2
70-74	3	2	2	4	2	2
75-79	3	2	2	3	1	1
80-84	2	1	1	2	1	1
85-89	1	0	1	1	0	1
90-94	0	0	0	0	0	0
95-99	0	0	0	0	0	0
100 +	0	0	0	0	0	0

POPULATION BY AGE AND SEX (in thousands)

Age group	2005 Both sexes	Males	Females	2010 Both sexes	Males	Females	2015 Both sexes	Males	Females	2020 Both sexes	Males	Females
All ages	102	52	50	104	53	51	106	54	52	107	55	52
0-4	12	6	6	12	6	6	12	6	6	11	6	6
5-9	12	6	6	11	6	5	11	6	5	11	6	5
10-14	13	7	6	12	6	6	11	6	5	11	6	6
15-19	11	6	5	11	6	5	11	6	5	10	5	5
20-24	11	5	5	9	5	4	10	5	5	10	5	5
25-29	8	4	4	9	5	4	8	4	3	8	4	4
30-34	6	3	3	6	3	3	8	4	4	6	3	3
35-39	6	3	3	5	3	3	6	3	3	8	4	4
40-44	5	2	2	6	3	3	5	3	3	6	3	3
45-49	4	2	2	4	2	2	6	3	3	5	2	2
50-54	4	2	2	4	2	2	4	2	2	6	3	3
55-59	3	2	2	4	2	2	4	2	2	4	2	2
60-64	3	1	1	3	1	2	3	2	2	3	2	2
65-69	2	1	1	2	1	1	2	1	1	3	2	1
70-74	2	1	1	2	1	1	2	1	1	2	1	1
75-79	1	1	1	1	1	1	1	1	1	2	1	1
80-84	1	0	0	1	0	1	1	0	0	1	0	0
85-89	0	0	0	0	0	0	0	0	0	0	0	0
90-94	0	0	0	0	0	0	0	0	0	0	0	0
95-99	0	0	0	0	0	0	0	0	0	0	0	0
100 +	0	0	0	0	0	0	0	0	0	0	0	0

Age group	2025 Both sexes	Males	Females	2030 Both sexes	Males	Females	2035 Both sexes	Males	Females	2040 Both sexes	Males	Females
All ages	108	55	52	107	55	52	105	54	51	102	53	50
0-4	11	5	5	10	5	5	9	5	4	8	4	4
5-9	11	6	5	10	5	5	9	5	4	8	4	4
10-14	11	6	5	11	5	5	10	5	5	9	5	4
15-19	10	5	5	10	5	5	9	5	5	9	4	4
20-24	9	4	4	9	4	4	9	4	4	8	4	4
25-29	8	4	4	7	4	3	7	4	3	7	4	3
30-34	7	4	3	7	3	3	6	3	3	6	3	3
35-39	6	3	3	7	4	3	6	3	3	5	3	3
40-44	7	4	4	6	3	3	7	3	3	6	3	3
45-49	5	3	3	7	3	3	5	3	2	6	3	3
50-54	5	2	2	5	3	3	7	3	3	5	3	2
55-59	5	3	3	5	2	2	5	3	2	7	3	3
60-64	4	2	2	5	3	2	4	2	2	5	3	2
65-69	3	1	1	3	2	1	4	2	2	4	2	2
70-74	2	1	1	3	1	1	3	2	1	4	2	2
75-79	2	1	1	2	1	1	2	1	1	2	1	1
80-84	1	0	1	1	1	1	1	1	1	1	1	1
85-89	1	0	0	1	0	0	1	0	0	1	0	0
90-94	0	0	0	0	0	0	0	0	0	0	0	0
95-99	0	0	0	0	0	0	0	0	0	0	0	0
100 +	0	0	0	0	0	0	0	0	0	0	0	0

Age group	2045 Both sexes	Males	Females	2050 Both sexes	Males	Females
All ages	99	51	48	94	48	46
0-4	8	4	4	7	4	3
5-9	8	4	4	7	4	3
10-14	8	4	4	8	4	4
15-19	8	4	4	7	4	3
20-24	7	4	4	7	3	3
25-29	7	3	3	6	3	3
30-34	6	3	3	5	3	3
35-39	6	3	3	5	3	3
40-44	5	3	3	5	3	3
45-49	6	3	3	5	2	2
50-54	6	3	3	6	3	3
55-59	5	3	2	6	3	3
60-64	6	3	3	5	3	2
65-69	4	2	2	5	3	2
70-74	3	2	2	4	2	2
75-79	3	2	2	3	1	1
80-84	2	1	1	2	1	1
85-89	1	0	1	1	0	1
90-94	0	0	0	0	0	0
95-99	0	0	0	0	0	0
100 +	0	0	0	0	0	0

United Nations Department of Economic and Social Affairs/Population Division
World Population Prospects: The 2004 Revision, Volume II: Sex and Age Distribution of the World Population

840

POPULATION BY AGE AND SEX (in thousands)

Age group	2005 Both sexes	Males	Females	2010 Both sexes	Males	Females	2015 Both sexes	Males	Females	2020 Both sexes	Males	Females
All ages	102	52	50	102	52	50	101	52	49	98	50	48
0-4	12	6	6	10	5	5	9	4	4	8	4	4
5-9	12	6	6	11	6	5	9	5	5	8	4	4
10-14	13	7	6	12	6	6	11	6	5	9	5	5
15-19	11	6	5	11	6	5	11	6	5	10	5	5
20-24	11	5	5	9	5	4	10	5	5	10	5	5
25-29	8	4	4	9	5	4	8	4	3	8	4	4
30-34	6	3	3	6	3	3	8	4	4	6	3	3
35-39	6	3	3	5	3	3	6	3	3	8	4	4
40-44	5	2	2	6	3	3	5	3	3	6	3	3
45-49	4	2	2	4	2	2	6	3	3	5	2	2
50-54	4	2	2	4	2	2	4	2	2	6	3	3
55-59	3	2	2	4	2	2	4	2	2	4	2	2
60-64	3	1	1	3	1	2	3	2	2	3	2	2
65-69	2	1	1	2	1	1	2	1	1	3	2	1
70-74	2	1	1	2	1	1	2	1	1	2	1	1
75-79	1	1	1	1	1	1	1	1	1	2	1	1
80-84	1	0	0	1	0	1	1	0	0	1	0	0
85-89	0	0	0	0	0	0	0	0	0	0	0	0
90-94	0	0	0	0	0	0	0	0	0	0	0	0
95-99	0	0	0	0	0	0	0	0	0	0	0	0
100 +	0	0	0	0	0	0	0	0	0	0	0	0

Age group	2025 Both sexes	Males	Females	2030 Both sexes	Males	Females	2035 Both sexes	Males	Females	2040 Both sexes	Males	Females
All ages	95	49	46	90	46	44	85	43	41	77	40	38
0-4	7	4	3	6	3	3	5	3	3	4	2	2
5-9	7	4	3	6	3	3	5	3	3	4	2	2
10-14	8	4	4	7	3	3	6	3	3	5	3	3
15-19	8	4	4	7	3	3	6	3	3	5	2	2
20-24	9	4	4	7	3	3	5	3	3	4	2	2
25-29	8	4	4	7	4	3	5	3	3	4	2	2
30-34	7	4	3	7	3	3	6	3	3	4	2	2
35-39	6	3	3	7	4	3	6	3	3	5	3	3
40-44	7	4	4	6	3	3	7	3	3	6	3	3
45-49	5	3	3	7	3	3	5	3	2	6	3	3
50-54	5	2	2	5	3	3	7	3	3	5	3	2
55-59	5	3	3	5	2	2	5	3	2	7	3	3
60-64	4	2	2	5	3	2	4	2	2	5	3	2
65-69	3	1	1	3	2	1	4	2	2	4	2	2
70-74	2	1	1	3	1	1	3	2	1	4	2	2
75-79	2	1	1	2	1	1	2	1	1	2	1	1
80-84	1	0	1	1	1	1	1	1	1	1	1	1
85-89	1	0	0	1	0	0	1	0	0	1	0	0
90-94	0	0	0	0	0	0	0	0	0	0	0	0
95-99	0	0	0	0	0	0	0	0	0	0	0	0
100 +	0	0	0	0	0	0	0	0	0	0	0	0

Age group	2045 Both sexes	Males	Females	2050 Both sexes	Males	Females
All ages	69	35	33	59	30	29
0-4	3	1	1	2	1	1
5-9	3	2	2	2	1	1
10-14	4	2	2	3	2	2
15-19	4	2	2	3	2	2
20-24	4	2	2	3	1	1
25-29	3	1	1	2	1	1
30-34	2	1	1	1	1	1
35-39	4	2	2	2	1	1
40-44	5	3	3	3	2	2
45-49	6	3	3	5	2	2
50-54	6	3	3	6	3	3
55-59	5	3	2	6	3	3
60-64	6	3	3	5	3	2
65-69	4	2	2	5	3	2
70-74	3	2	2	4	2	2
75-79	3	2	2	3	1	1
80-84	2	1	1	2	1	1
85-89	1	0	1	1	0	1
90-94	0	0	0	0	0	0
95-99	0	0	0	0	0	0
100 +	0	0	0	0	0	0

POPULATION BY AGE AND SEX (in thousands)

Age group	1950 Both sexes	Males	Females	1955 Both sexes	Males	Females	1960 Both sexes	Males	Females	1965 Both sexes	Males	Females
All ages	636	317	319	721	360	361	843	419	424	896	447	450
0-4	106	53	53	119	60	59	140	71	69	146	74	72
5-9	86	43	43	102	51	51	120	60	60	127	65	63
10-14	65	33	32	84	42	42	103	52	52	109	55	55
15-19	54	27	27	64	32	32	81	40	42	93	47	47
20-24	50	24	26	52	26	26	66	33	34	75	37	39
25-29	48	23	25	49	24	25	53	25	27	60	30	31
30-34	45	23	22	47	23	24	50	24	25	52	25	27
35-39	41	21	20	43	22	21	48	23	24	44	22	22
40-44	35	18	17	39	20	19	43	22	20	44	22	22
45-49	29	15	14	33	17	16	38	19	18	38	19	18
50-54	22	11	11	25	13	12	29	15	14	33	17	16
55-59	16	8	8	20	10	10	23	12	11	24	13	12
60-64	14	7	7	16	8	8	16	8	8	20	10	10
65-69	10	5	5	11	5	6	13	6	7	13	6	7
70-74	7	3	4	9	4	5	10	4	6	10	4	6
75-79	5	2	3	5	2	3	6	2	3	6	2	3
80 +	3	1	2	3	1	2	5	2	3	4	1	3

Age group	1970 Both sexes	Males	Females	1975 Both sexes	Males	Females	1980 Both sexes	Males	Females	1985 Both sexes	Males	Females
All ages	971	479	492	1 012	503	509	1 082	541	541	1 178	587	591
0-4	126	63	63	124	63	61	128	65	63	151	77	75
5-9	151	76	75	121	61	60	121	61	60	128	65	63
10-14	132	66	65	140	70	70	121	61	61	117	59	58
15-19	109	53	56	120	60	60	134	67	67	122	61	61
20-24	85	41	43	97	48	49	113	57	56	125	63	62
25-29	61	29	31	77	38	39	89	45	44	109	54	54
30-34	51	24	26	58	29	29	72	37	36	87	44	44
35-39	45	22	24	49	24	25	57	29	29	69	34	34
40-44	42	20	22	42	20	22	48	24	24	56	28	28
45-49	40	20	20	39	19	20	40	20	21	46	23	23
50-54	36	18	17	36	18	18	37	18	19	39	19	20
55-59	29	15	14	31	16	15	32	16	16	34	17	17
60-64	22	11	11	27	13	14	27	14	13	29	14	14
65-69	19	9	11	19	9	10	25	12	13	24	12	13
70-74	11	5	6	15	7	8	16	8	9	19	9	10
75-79	6	3	4	9	4	5	10	4	6	13	5	7
80 +	7	2	4	7	3	4	8	3	5	10	4	6

Age group	1990 Both sexes	Males	Females	1995 Both sexes	Males	Females	2000 Both sexes	Males	Females	2005 Both sexes	Males	Females
All ages	1 215	608	607	1 259	627	632	1 285	637	648	1 305	644	662
0-4	132	67	65	106	54	52	87	44	43	90	46	44
5-9	147	74	73	131	66	65	105	53	52	86	44	43
10-14	128	65	63	146	74	72	130	66	64	105	53	52
15-19	115	58	56	126	64	62	145	73	72	129	65	64
20-24	104	52	52	110	56	54	122	62	61	141	71	70
25-29	111	56	55	99	49	50	105	53	52	116	58	58
30-34	96	48	48	106	53	53	94	46	48	99	49	49
35-39	80	40	40	92	46	47	102	50	52	88	43	46
40-44	66	34	33	77	38	39	89	44	46	97	47	50
45-49	53	26	26	64	32	32	74	36	38	86	41	44
50-54	43	22	22	50	25	25	61	30	31	71	35	36
55-59	34	17	18	41	20	21	47	23	24	58	28	29
60-64	30	15	15	32	15	16	38	18	20	44	21	23
65-69	28	13	14	27	13	14	28	13	15	34	16	18
70-74	20	10	10	23	11	12	23	10	12	24	11	13
75-79	14	7	8	15	7	8	18	8	10	18	8	10
80 +	14	5	8	15	6	9	17	7	10	20	8	12

United Nations Department of Economic and Social Affairs/Population Division
World Population Prospects: The 2004 Revision, Volume II: Sex and Age Distribution of the World Population

POPULATION BY AGE AND SEX (in thousands)

Age group	2005 Both sexes	2005 Males	2005 Females	2010 Both sexes	2010 Males	2010 Females	2015 Both sexes	2015 Males	2015 Females	2020 Both sexes	2020 Males	2020 Females
All ages	1 305	644	662	1 324	651	673	1 338	656	682	1 046	650	007
0-4	90	46	44	92	47	45	92	47	45	88	45	43
5-9	86	44	43	89	45	44	91	46	45	91	46	45
10-14	105	53	52	86	43	42	88	45	43	90	46	44
15-19	129	65	64	103	52	51	84	43	42	86	44	43
20-24	141	71	70	125	63	62	100	50	49	81	41	40
25-29	116	58	58	135	68	67	120	60	60	95	48	47
30-34	99	49	49	109	55	55	128	64	64	114	57	57
35-39	88	43	46	93	46	47	104	52	52	122	61	61
40-44	97	47	50	84	40	44	89	44	45	99	49	50
45-49	86	41	44	93	45	48	81	38	42	85	42	43
50-54	71	35	36	82	39	43	90	43	47	77	37	41
55-59	58	28	29	67	32	35	78	37	41	86	40	45
60-64	44	21	23	54	26	28	63	30	33	74	34	39
65-69	34	16	18	40	19	21	49	23	26	58	27	31
70-74	24	11	13	29	13	16	35	16	19	43	20	24
75-79	18	8	10	19	8	11	24	10	13	28	12	16
80-84	12	5	7	12	5	7	14	5	8	17	7	10
85-89	6	2	3	7	3	4	7	3	5	8	3	5
90-94	2	1	1	2	1	2	3	1	2	3	1	2
95-99	0	0	0	1	0	0	1	0	1	1	0	1
100 +	0	0	0	0	0	0	0	0	0	0	0	0

Age group	2025 Both sexes	2025 Males	2025 Females	2030 Both sexes	2030 Males	2030 Females	2035 Both sexes	2035 Males	2035 Females	2040 Both sexes	2040 Males	2040 Females
All ages	1 343	655	688	1 332	648	684	1 314	638	676	1 290	625	665
0-4	81	41	40	76	38	37	72	37	35	71	36	35
5-9	87	44	43	80	41	39	75	38	37	71	36	35
10-14	90	46	44	86	44	42	79	40	39	74	38	36
15-19	89	45	44	88	45	44	84	43	42	78	40	38
20-24	83	42	41	85	43	42	85	43	42	81	41	40
25-29	76	38	38	78	39	39	81	41	40	81	41	40
30-34	90	45	45	72	36	36	74	37	37	76	38	38
35-39	109	54	54	85	43	43	68	34	34	70	35	35
40-44	117	58	60	104	52	52	82	41	41	65	32	33
45-49	95	47	48	113	56	57	101	50	51	79	39	40
50-54	82	40	42	92	45	47	110	54	55	98	48	49
55-59	74	35	39	78	38	40	88	43	45	106	52	54
60-64	81	38	43	70	33	38	75	36	39	85	41	44
65-69	68	31	37	75	34	41	65	30	36	70	33	37
70-74	51	23	28	61	27	34	67	30	38	59	26	33
75-79	35	15	20	43	18	25	51	21	30	57	24	33
80-84	21	8	13	26	10	16	32	13	19	39	15	24
85-89	10	3	7	13	4	8	17	6	11	21	7	14
90-94	4	1	3	5	1	4	6	2	5	8	2	6
95-99	1	0	1	1	0	1	2	0	1	2	0	2
100 +	0	0	0	0	0	0	0	0	0	0	0	0

Age group	2045 Both sexes	2045 Males	2045 Females	2050 Both sexes	2050 Males	2050 Females
All ages	1 262	611	651	1 230	595	635
0-4	69	35	34	66	34	32
5-9	70	36	34	68	35	34
10-14	71	36	35	69	35	34
15-19	73	37	36	69	35	34
20-24	75	38	37	69	35	34
25-29	77	39	38	71	36	35
30-34	77	38	38	73	37	36
35-39	73	36	36	73	37	37
40-44	67	34	34	70	35	35
45-49	63	31	32	65	32	33
50-54	77	38	39	61	30	31
55-59	95	47	48	74	37	38
60-64	102	49	52	91	44	47
65-69	79	38	42	96	46	50
70-74	63	29	34	72	33	39
75-79	50	21	29	54	24	30
80-84	44	17	27	39	15	24
85-89	25	9	17	29	10	19
90-94	11	3	8	14	4	10
95-99	3	1	2	4	1	3
100 +	1	0	0	1	0	1

United Nations Department of Economic and Social Affairs/Population Division
World Population Prospects: The 2004 Revision, Volume II: Sex and Age Distribution of the World Population

843

POPULATION BY AGE AND SEX (in thousands)

Age group	2005 Both sexes	Males	Females	2010 Both sexes	Males	Females	2015 Both sexes	Males	Females	2020 Both sexes	Males	Females
All ages	1 305	644	662	1 338	658	680	1 375	675	700	1 408	690	718
0-4	90	46	44	107	54	52	114	58	56	113	58	56
5-9	86	44	43	89	45	44	105	54	52	113	57	55
10-14	105	53	52	86	43	42	88	45	43	104	53	51
15-19	129	65	64	103	52	51	84	43	42	86	44	43
20-24	141	71	70	125	63	62	100	50	49	81	41	40
25-29	116	58	58	135	68	67	120	60	60	95	48	47
30-34	99	49	49	109	55	55	128	64	64	114	57	57
35-39	88	43	46	93	46	47	104	52	52	122	61	61
40-44	97	47	50	84	40	44	89	44	45	99	49	50
45-49	86	41	44	93	45	48	81	38	42	85	42	43
50-54	71	35	36	82	39	43	90	43	47	77	37	41
55-59	58	28	29	67	32	35	78	37	41	86	40	45
60-64	44	21	23	54	26	28	63	30	33	74	34	39
65-69	34	16	18	40	19	21	49	23	26	58	27	31
70-74	24	11	13	29	13	16	35	16	19	43	20	24
75-79	18	8	10	19	8	11	24	10	13	28	12	16
80-84	12	5	7	12	5	7	14	5	8	17	7	10
85-89	6	2	3	7	3	4	7	3	5	8	3	5
90-94	2	1	1	2	1	2	3	1	2	3	1	2
95-99	0	0	0	1	0	0	1	0	1	1	0	1
100 +	0	0	0	0	0	0	0	0	0	0	0	0

Age group	2025 Both sexes	Males	Females	2030 Both sexes	Males	Females	2035 Both sexes	Males	Females	2040 Both sexes	Males	Females
All ages	1 429	699	730	1 442	704	738	1 452	708	744	1 463	713	750
0-4	104	53	51	100	51	49	101	51	50	106	54	52
5-9	112	57	55	103	53	51	99	50	48	100	51	49
10-14	112	57	55	111	57	55	103	52	50	98	50	48
15-19	103	52	51	111	56	54	110	56	54	101	51	50
20-24	83	42	41	100	50	49	107	54	53	107	54	53
25-29	76	38	38	78	39	39	95	48	47	103	52	51
30-34	90	45	45	72	36	36	74	37	37	90	45	45
35-39	109	54	54	85	43	43	68	34	34	70	35	35
40-44	117	58	59	104	52	52	82	41	41	65	32	33
45-49	95	47	48	113	56	57	101	50	51	79	39	40
50-54	82	40	42	92	45	47	110	54	55	98	48	49
55-59	74	35	39	78	38	40	88	43	45	106	52	54
60-64	81	38	43	70	33	38	75	36	39	85	41	44
65-69	68	31	37	75	34	41	65	30	36	70	33	37
70-74	51	23	28	61	27	34	67	30	38	59	26	33
75-79	35	15	20	43	18	25	51	21	30	57	24	33
80-84	21	8	13	26	10	16	32	13	19	39	15	24
85-89	10	3	7	13	4	8	17	6	11	21	7	14
90-94	4	1	3	5	1	4	6	2	5	8	2	6
95-99	1	0	1	1	0	1	2	0	1	2	0	2
100 +	0	0	0	0	0	0	0	0	0	0	0	0

Age group	2045 Both sexes	Males	Females	2050 Both sexes	Males	Females
All ages	1 475	719	756	1 485	724	760
0-4	110	56	54	110	56	54
5-9	105	54	52	109	56	54
10-14	99	51	49	105	53	51
15-19	96	49	47	98	50	48
20-24	98	50	48	93	47	46
25-29	102	52	51	94	47	46
30-34	98	49	49	98	49	49
35-39	86	43	43	95	48	47
40-44	67	34	34	84	42	42
45-49	63	31	32	65	32	33
50-54	77	38	39	61	30	31
55-59	95	47	48	74	37	38
60-64	102	49	52	91	44	47
65-69	79	38	42	96	46	50
70-74	63	29	34	72	33	39
75-79	50	21	29	54	24	30
80-84	44	17	27	39	15	24
85-89	25	9	17	29	10	19
90-94	11	3	8	14	4	10
95-99	3	1	2	4	1	3
100 +	1	0	0	1	0	1

United Nations Department of Economic and Social Affairs/Population Division
World Population Prospects: The 2004 Revision, Volume II: Sex and Age Distribution of the World Population

844

POPULATION BY AGE AND SEX (in thousands)

Age group	2005 Both sexes	Males	Females	2010 Both sexes	Males	Females	2015 Both sexes	Males	Females	2020 Both sexes	Males	Females
All ages	1 305	611	662	1 300	613	666	1 302	637	661	1 283	626	657
0-4	90	46	44	78	40	38	69	35	34	62	32	30
5-9	86	44	43	89	45	44	77	39	38	68	35	34
10-14	105	53	52	86	43	42	88	45	43	76	39	37
15-19	129	65	64	103	52	51	84	43	42	86	44	43
20-24	141	71	70	125	63	62	100	50	49	81	41	40
25-29	116	58	58	135	68	67	120	60	60	95	48	47
30-34	99	49	49	109	55	55	128	64	64	114	57	57
35-39	88	43	46	93	46	47	104	52	52	122	61	61
40-44	97	47	50	84	40	44	89	44	45	99	49	50
45-49	86	41	44	93	45	48	81	38	42	85	42	43
50-54	71	35	36	82	39	43	90	43	47	77	37	41
55-59	58	28	29	67	32	35	78	37	41	86	40	45
60-64	44	21	23	54	26	28	63	30	33	74	34	39
65-69	34	16	18	40	19	21	49	23	26	58	27	31
70-74	24	11	13	29	13	16	35	16	19	43	20	24
75-79	18	8	10	19	8	11	24	10	13	28	12	16
80-84	12	5	7	12	5	7	14	5	8	17	7	10
85-89	6	2	3	7	3	4	7	3	5	8	3	5
90-94	2	1	1	2	1	2	3	1	2	3	1	2
95-99	0	0	0	1	0	0	1	0	1	1	0	1
100 +	0	0	0	0	0	0	0	0	0	0	0	0

Age group	2025 Both sexes	Males	Females	2030 Both sexes	Males	Females	2035 Both sexes	Males	Females	2040 Both sexes	Males	Females
All ages	1 258	612	646	1 225	594	631	1 182	571	611	1 130	544	586
0-4	58	29	28	53	27	26	47	24	23	42	22	21
5-9	61	31	30	57	29	28	52	26	26	47	24	23
10-14	68	34	33	60	31	30	56	29	28	51	26	25
15-19	74	38	37	66	34	33	59	30	29	55	28	27
20-24	83	42	41	71	36	35	63	32	31	56	28	28
25-29	76	38	38	78	39	39	67	34	33	59	30	29
30-34	90	45	45	72	36	36	74	37	37	63	31	31
35-39	109	54	54	85	43	43	68	34	34	70	35	35
40-44	117	58	59	104	52	52	82	41	41	65	32	33
45-49	95	47	48	113	56	57	101	50	51	79	39	40
50-54	82	40	42	92	45	47	110	54	55	98	48	49
55-59	74	35	39	78	38	40	88	43	45	106	52	54
60-64	81	38	43	70	33	38	75	36	39	85	41	44
65-69	68	31	37	75	34	41	65	30	36	70	33	37
70-74	51	23	28	61	27	34	67	30	38	59	26	33
75-79	35	15	20	43	18	25	51	21	30	57	24	33
80-84	21	8	13	26	10	16	32	13	19	39	15	24
85-89	10	3	7	13	4	8	17	6	11	21	7	14
90-94	4	1	3	5	1	4	6	2	5	8	2	6
95-99	1	0	1	1	0	1	2	0	1	2	0	2
100 +	0	0	0	0	0	0	0	0	0	0	0	0

Age group	2045 Both sexes	Males	Females	2050 Both sexes	Males	Females
All ages	1 072	514	558	1 007	482	526
0-4	38	19	18	34	17	17
5-9	41	21	20	37	19	18
10-14	46	23	23	41	21	20
15-19	50	25	25	45	23	22
20-24	52	26	26	47	24	23
25-29	52	26	26	48	24	24
30-34	55	27	27	48	24	24
35-39	59	30	30	52	26	26
40-44	67	34	34	57	28	29
45-49	63	31	32	65	32	33
50-54	77	38	39	61	30	31
55-59	95	47	48	74	37	38
60-64	102	49	52	91	44	47
65-69	79	38	42	96	46	50
70-74	63	29	34	72	33	39
75-79	50	21	29	54	24	30
80-84	44	17	27	39	15	24
85-89	25	9	17	29	10	19
90-94	11	3	8	14	4	10
95-99	3	1	2	4	1	3
100 +	1	0	0	1	0	1

United Nations Department of Economic and Social Affairs/Population Division
World Population Prospects: The 2004 Revision, Volume II: Sex and Age Distribution of the World Population

845

POPULATION BY AGE AND SEX (in thousands)

Age group	1950 Both sexes	1950 Males	1950 Females	1955 Both sexes	1955 Males	1955 Females	1960 Both sexes	1960 Males	1960 Females	1965 Both sexes	1965 Males	1965 Females
All ages	3 530	1 759	1 771	3 860	1 916	1 944	4 221	2 131	2 090	4 630	2 364	2 266
0-4	576	290	286	637	321	315	765	392	372	858	437	421
5-9	427	215	212	525	264	261	609	313	296	704	365	339
10-14	369	188	181	415	209	206	457	230	227	583	306	277
15-19	336	170	166	355	178	177	357	177	180	389	196	193
20-24	305	155	150	317	158	159	328	161	167	300	145	154
25-29	269	138	131	285	142	143	306	151	155	303	145	158
30-34	231	118	113	251	126	126	276	138	138	295	144	151
35-39	202	102	100	217	109	108	228	115	113	266	134	133
40-44	171	86	85	190	94	95	198	101	97	205	104	102
45-49	143	71	72	161	80	81	174	89	84	179	94	85
50-54	120	59	61	134	66	68	146	76	70	158	84	74
55-59	98	45	52	110	53	57	114	58	56	132	73	60
60-64	82	39	43	86	39	47	88	45	43	94	50	44
65-69	69	31	38	67	31	36	64	30	33	67	37	30
70-74	49	22	27	50	22	29	46	23	24	42	22	20
75-79	53	20	32	29	13	17	40	19	20	25	14	11
80 +	32	12	20	32	12	20	26	12	14	31	16	15

Age group	1970 Both sexes	1970 Males	1970 Females	1975 Both sexes	1975 Males	1975 Females	1980 Both sexes	1980 Males	1980 Females	1985 Both sexes	1985 Males	1985 Females
All ages	5 127	2 537	2 590	5 668	2 873	2 794	6 454	3 270	3 184	7 332	3 710	3 622
0-4	874	446	428	907	463	444	999	515	484	1 081	556	525
5-9	811	412	400	830	424	406	885	452	433	980	503	477
10-14	686	348	338	745	383	362	823	421	402	874	443	431
15-19	543	269	274	639	327	313	737	378	359	811	411	400
20-24	361	177	184	490	242	248	625	318	307	719	366	353
25-29	260	123	137	323	151	172	475	233	242	600	301	299
30-34	260	118	143	264	125	139	311	144	167	463	227	236
35-39	264	125	139	299	145	155	255	120	135	315	151	164
40-44	238	116	122	274	136	138	293	141	151	258	123	135
45-49	194	96	98	233	118	115	269	133	136	289	138	151
50-54	169	85	84	183	95	88	227	114	113	264	131	133
55-59	152	76	76	149	80	69	175	91	84	219	111	108
60-64	124	61	63	131	75	57	137	74	63	165	86	78
65-69	89	42	47	88	48	39	113	64	49	122	67	56
70-74	57	26	31	59	34	25	68	37	31	94	54	40
75-79	33	14	19	26	14	12	39	22	17	50	28	22
80 +	15	6	9	26	13	12	22	11	11	28	16	12

Age group	1990 Both sexes	1990 Males	1990 Females	1995 Both sexes	1995 Males	1995 Females	2000 Both sexes	2000 Males	2000 Females	2005 Both sexes	2005 Males	2005 Females
All ages	8 219	4 155	4 064	8 977	4 535	4 441	9 563	4 824	4 740	10 102	5 090	5 013
0-4	1 102	567	536	984	506	478	838	432	406	806	416	390
5-9	1 050	538	512	1 075	550	524	980	504	476	835	431	404
10-14	969	496	472	1 039	532	507	1 072	549	523	978	503	476
15-19	863	437	426	959	491	468	1 036	530	506	1 069	547	522
20-24	791	400	391	842	424	418	952	487	465	1 029	526	503
25-29	697	352	345	759	376	383	834	420	414	944	483	462
30-34	582	289	293	674	334	340	752	372	380	827	416	411
35-39	456	224	232	583	293	290	667	330	337	746	368	377
40-44	323	160	164	471	239	232	577	290	287	661	326	334
45-49	266	130	136	332	167	165	463	234	229	569	285	284
50-54	286	137	149	264	129	135	324	162	162	453	228	225
55-59	254	125	129	274	131	142	254	123	131	312	154	158
60-64	209	105	104	245	123	122	257	121	136	240	114	126
65-69	151	78	72	199	99	100	221	108	113	234	107	127
70-74	105	56	50	133	66	67	167	81	86	188	89	99
75-79	71	40	31	81	42	40	99	47	51	126	58	67
80 +	44	23	21	63	33	30	71	35	35	85	40	46

United Nations Department of Economic and Social Affairs/Population Division
World Population Prospects: The 2004 Revision, Volume II: Sex and Age Distribution of the World Population

846

POPULATION BY AGE AND SEX (in thousands)

Age group	2005			2010			2015			2020		
	Both sexes	Males	Females	Both sexes	Males	Females	Both sexes	Males	Females	Both sexes	Males	Females
All ages	10 102	5 090	5 013	10 639	5 356	5 284	11 140	5 604	5 535	11 604	5 835	5 769
0-4	806	416	390	824	425	398	811	419	392	801	414	387
5-9	835	431	404	804	415	389	822	424	397	809	418	391
10-14	978	503	476	834	430	404	803	414	389	821	424	397
15-19	1 069	547	522	976	501	475	831	429	403	800	413	388
20-24	1 029	526	503	1 063	543	520	970	498	472	826	426	401
25-29	944	483	462	1 022	521	500	1 056	539	517	964	494	469
30-34	827	416	411	938	479	459	1 015	518	498	1 050	536	514
35-39	746	368	377	821	412	409	931	475	456	1 009	514	495
40-44	661	326	334	739	365	375	815	409	406	925	472	453
45-49	569	285	284	653	322	331	731	360	371	806	404	403
50-54	453	228	225	557	278	280	641	314	326	719	352	366
55-59	312	154	158	438	218	220	540	266	274	622	302	320
60-64	240	114	126	295	143	152	416	203	213	515	250	265
65-69	234	107	127	220	102	118	272	129	143	385	183	201
70-74	188	89	99	201	89	112	190	85	105	237	108	129
75-79	126	58	67	144	65	79	157	66	91	151	64	87
80-84	60	27	32	79	34	44	93	39	54	104	40	64
85-89	20	10	11	27	11	15	37	15	23	46	17	29
90-94	5	2	2	6	2	3	8	3	5	12	4	8
95-99	0	0	0	1	0	0	1	0	1	2	0	1
100 +	0	0	0	0	0	0	0	0	0	0	0	0

Age group	2025			2030			2035			2040		
	Both sexes	Males	Females	Both sexes	Males	Females	Both sexes	Males	Females	Both sexes	Males	Females
All ages	12 028	6 045	5 983	12 379	6 217	6 162	12 637	6 340	6 298	12 810	6 419	6 391
0-4	795	411	384	766	396	370	728	377	352	709	367	342
5-9	799	413	386	794	410	383	764	395	369	727	376	351
10-14	808	417	390	798	413	386	793	410	383	764	395	369
15-19	819	423	396	806	416	390	796	412	385	791	409	382
20-24	796	410	386	814	420	394	801	414	388	792	409	383
25-29	821	423	398	790	407	383	809	417	391	796	411	385
30-34	958	491	467	815	420	396	785	404	381	804	414	389
35-39	1 044	533	511	953	488	464	811	417	393	781	402	379
40-44	1 003	511	492	1 038	529	500	947	485	462	806	415	391
45-49	917	467	450	995	506	488	1 030	525	505	940	481	459
50-54	794	396	398	903	459	445	981	498	483	1 017	517	500
55-59	700	340	360	774	383	391	882	445	438	960	484	476
60-64	595	285	311	671	321	350	744	363	381	850	423	427
65-69	478	226	251	555	259	296	628	294	334	699	335	364
70-74	338	156	182	423	194	230	495	224	271	564	256	308
75-79	190	82	108	274	119	154	347	151	196	411	177	234
80-84	102	39	63	132	52	80	194	77	117	251	100	151
85-89	54	18	36	55	18	37	74	25	49	112	39	74
90-94	16	5	11	20	5	15	22	5	16	31	8	23
95-99	2	1	2	4	1	3	5	1	4	6	1	5
100 +	0	0	0	0	0	0	0	0	0	1	0	1

Age group	2045			2050		
	Both sexes	Males	Females	Both sexes	Males	Females
All ages	12 906	6 460	6 446	12 927	6 465	6 462
0-4	702	363	339	694	359	335
5-9	708	366	342	701	362	339
10-14	726	375	350	707	365	341
15-19	762	394	368	724	375	350
20-24	787	407	380	758	392	366
25-29	787	407	380	781	404	377
30-34	791	408	383	782	404	378
35-39	799	412	387	787	406	381
40-44	776	400	377	795	410	385
45-49	800	411	389	771	396	374
50-54	929	474	455	791	405	385
55-59	996	503	493	911	462	449
60-64	927	462	465	963	482	482
65-69	801	392	409	876	429	446
70-74	631	294	337	727	346	380
75-79	473	205	268	534	238	296
80-84	303	120	183	355	142	212
85-89	150	52	98	186	65	122
90-94	49	13	36	69	19	50
95-99	9	2	7	15	3	12
100 +	1	0	1	1	0	1

POPULATION BY AGE AND SEX (in thousands)

Age group	2005 Both sexes	2005 Males	2005 Females	2010 Both sexes	2010 Males	2010 Females	2015 Both sexes	2015 Males	2015 Females	2020 Both sexes	2020 Males	2020 Females
All ages	10 102	5 090	5 013	10 750	5 413	5 337	11 438	5 758	5 680	12 138	6 111	6 027
0-4	806	416	390	934	482	452	998	516	483	1 037	536	501
5-9	835	431	404	804	415	389	932	481	451	996	515	482
10-14	978	503	476	834	430	404	803	414	389	931	481	450
15-19	1 069	547	522	976	501	475	831	429	403	800	413	388
20-24	1 029	526	503	1 063	543	520	970	498	472	826	426	401
25-29	944	483	462	1 022	521	500	1 056	539	517	964	494	469
30-34	827	416	411	938	479	459	1 015	518	498	1 050	536	514
35-39	746	368	377	821	412	409	931	475	456	1 009	514	495
40-44	661	326	334	739	365	375	815	409	406	925	472	453
45-49	569	285	284	653	322	331	731	360	371	806	404	403
50-54	453	228	225	557	278	280	641	314	326	719	352	366
55-59	312	154	158	438	218	220	540	266	274	622	302	320
60-64	240	114	126	295	143	152	416	203	213	515	250	265
65-69	234	107	127	220	102	118	272	129	143	385	183	201
70-74	188	89	99	201	89	112	190	85	105	237	108	129
75-79	126	58	67	144	65	79	157	66	91	151	64	87
80-84	60	27	32	79	34	44	93	39	54	104	40	64
85-89	20	10	11	27	11	15	37	15	23	46	17	29
90-94	5	2	2	6	2	3	8	3	5	12	4	8
95-99	0	0	0	1	0	0	1	0	1	2	0	1
100 +	0	0	0	0	0	0	0	0	0	0	0	0

Age group	2025 Both sexes	2025 Males	2025 Females	2030 Both sexes	2030 Males	2030 Females	2035 Both sexes	2035 Males	2035 Females	2040 Both sexes	2040 Males	2040 Females
All ages	12 788	6 438	6 350	13 361	6 724	6 637	13 866	6 975	6 891	14 345	7 212	7 133
0-4	1 021	528	493	988	511	477	977	505	472	1 017	526	491
5-9	1 035	535	500	1 020	527	492	987	510	476	975	504	471
10-14	995	514	481	1 034	535	500	1 019	527	492	986	510	476
15-19	929	479	449	993	513	480	1 032	534	499	1 017	526	491
20-24	796	410	386	924	477	447	988	510	478	1 028	531	497
25-29	821	423	398	790	407	383	918	474	445	983	507	475
30-34	958	491	467	815	420	396	785	404	381	913	471	442
35-39	1 044	533	511	953	488	464	811	417	393	781	402	379
40-44	1 003	511	492	1 038	529	508	947	485	462	806	415	391
45-49	917	467	450	995	506	488	1 030	525	505	940	481	459
50-54	794	396	398	903	459	445	981	498	483	1 017	517	500
55-59	700	340	360	774	383	391	882	445	438	960	484	476
60-64	595	285	311	671	321	350	744	363	381	850	423	427
65-69	478	226	251	555	259	296	628	294	334	699	335	364
70-74	338	156	182	423	194	230	495	224	271	564	256	308
75-79	190	82	108	274	119	154	347	151	196	411	177	234
80-84	102	39	63	132	52	80	194	77	117	251	100	151
85-89	54	18	36	55	18	37	74	25	49	112	39	74
90-94	16	5	11	20	5	15	22	5	16	31	8	23
95-99	2	1	2	4	1	3	5	1	4	6	1	5
100 +	0	0	0	0	0	0	0	0	0	1	0	1

Age group	2045 Both sexes	2045 Males	2045 Females	2050 Both sexes	2050 Males	2050 Females
All ages	14 815	7 446	7 369	15 254	7 667	7 587
0-4	1 078	557	520	1 115	576	538
5-9	1 015	525	490	1 076	556	520
10-14	974	504	470	1 014	524	490
15-19	984	509	475	972	503	469
20-24	1 012	523	489	979	507	473
25-29	1 022	528	494	1 007	520	486
30-34	977	504	473	1 017	525	492
35-39	908	468	440	972	502	471
40-44	776	400	377	904	466	438
45-49	800	411	389	771	396	374
50-54	929	474	455	791	405	385
55-59	996	503	493	911	462	449
60-64	927	462	465	963	482	482
65-69	801	392	409	876	429	446
70-74	631	294	337	727	346	380
75-79	473	205	268	534	238	296
80-84	303	120	183	355	142	212
85-89	150	52	98	186	65	122
90-94	49	13	36	69	19	50
95-99	9	2	7	15	3	12
100 +	1	0	1	1	0	1

United Nations Department of Economic and Social Affairs/Population Division
World Population Prospects: The 2004 Revision, Volume II: Sex and Age Distribution of the World Population

848

POPULATION BY AGE AND SEX (in thousands)

Age group	2005 Both sexes	2005 Males	2005 Females	2010 Both sexes	2010 Males	2010 Females	2015 Both sexes	2015 Males	2015 Females	2020 Both sexes	2020 Males	2020 Females
All ages	10 102	5 090	5 013	10 529	5 299	5 230	10 842	5 450	5 391	11 070	5 560	5 510
0-4	806	416	390	713	368	345	623	322	301	565	292	273
5-9	835	431	404	804	415	389	711	367	344	621	321	300
10-14	978	503	476	834	430	404	803	414	389	710	367	344
15-19	1 069	547	522	976	501	475	831	429	403	800	413	388
20-24	1 029	526	503	1 063	543	520	970	498	472	826	426	401
25-29	944	483	462	1 022	521	500	1 056	539	517	964	494	469
30-34	827	416	411	938	479	459	1 015	518	498	1 050	536	514
35-39	746	368	377	821	412	409	931	475	456	1 009	514	495
40-44	661	326	334	739	365	375	815	409	406	925	472	453
45-49	569	285	284	653	322	331	731	360	371	806	404	403
50-54	453	228	225	557	278	280	641	314	326	719	352	366
55-59	312	154	158	438	218	220	540	266	274	622	302	320
60-64	240	114	126	295	143	152	416	203	213	515	250	265
65-69	234	107	127	220	102	118	272	129	143	385	183	201
70-74	188	89	99	201	89	112	190	85	105	237	108	129
75-79	126	58	67	144	65	79	157	66	91	151	64	87
80-84	60	27	32	79	34	44	93	39	54	104	40	64
85-89	20	10	11	27	11	15	37	15	23	46	17	29
90-94	5	2	2	6	2	3	8	3	5	12	4	8
95-99	0	0	0	1	0	0	1	0	1	2	0	1
100 +	0	0	0	0	0	0	0	0	0	0	0	0

Age group	2025 Both sexes	2025 Males	2025 Females	2030 Both sexes	2030 Males	2030 Females	2035 Both sexes	2035 Males	2035 Females	2040 Both sexes	2040 Males	2040 Females
All ages	11 269	5 653	5 616	11 404	5 713	5 691	11 436	5 719	5 717	11 352	5 665	5 687
0-4	569	294	275	549	284	265	502	259	242	450	233	218
5-9	563	291	272	568	294	274	548	283	264	500	259	242
10-14	620	321	300	562	291	272	567	293	274	547	283	264
15-19	708	366	343	619	320	299	561	290	271	565	292	273
20-24	796	410	386	704	363	341	614	317	297	557	288	269
25-29	821	423	398	790	407	383	699	361	338	609	315	295
30-34	958	491	467	815	420	396	785	404	381	694	358	336
35-39	1 044	533	511	953	488	464	811	417	393	781	402	379
40-44	1 003	511	492	1 038	529	508	947	485	462	806	415	391
45-49	917	467	450	995	506	488	1 030	525	505	940	481	459
50-54	794	396	398	903	459	445	981	498	483	1 017	517	500
55-59	700	340	360	774	383	391	882	445	438	960	484	476
60-64	595	285	311	671	321	350	744	363	381	850	423	427
65-69	478	226	251	555	259	296	628	294	334	699	335	364
70-74	338	156	182	423	194	230	495	224	271	564	256	308
75-79	190	82	108	274	119	154	347	151	196	411	177	234
80-84	102	39	63	132	52	80	194	77	117	251	100	151
85-89	54	18	36	55	18	37	74	25	49	112	39	74
90-94	16	5	11	20	5	15	22	5	16	31	8	23
95-99	2	1	2	4	1	3	5	1	4	6	1	5
100 +	0	0	0	0	0	0	0	0	0	1	0	1

Age group	2045 Both sexes	2045 Males	2045 Females	2050 Both sexes	2050 Males	2050 Females
All ages	11 153	5 554	5 599	10 855	5 395	5 461
0-4	406	210	196	373	193	180
5-9	449	232	217	405	209	195
10-14	500	258	241	449	232	217
15-19	546	282	263	498	258	240
20-24	562	290	271	542	280	262
25-29	552	285	267	557	288	269
30-34	605	312	293	547	283	265
35-39	690	356	334	601	310	291
40-44	776	400	377	686	353	332
45-49	800	411	389	771	396	374
50-54	929	474	455	791	405	385
55-59	996	503	493	911	462	449
60-64	927	462	465	963	482	482
65-69	801	392	409	876	429	446
70-74	631	294	337	727	346	380
75-79	473	205	268	534	238	296
80-84	303	120	183	355	142	212
85-89	150	52	98	186	65	122
90-94	49	13	36	69	19	50
95-99	9	2	7	15	3	12
100 +	1	0	1	1	0	1

POPULATION BY AGE AND SEX (in thousands)

Age group	1950 Both sexes	Males	Females	1955 Both sexes	Males	Females	1960 Both sexes	Males	Females	1965 Both sexes	Males	Females
All ages	21 484	10 722	10 762	24 610	12 351	12 259	28 233	14 328	13 905	31 997	16 328	15 669
0-4	3 425	1 750	1 675	4 150	2 125	2 025	4 735	2 425	2 310	5 080	2 600	2 480
5-9	2 675	1 375	1 300	3 325	1 700	1 625	4 050	2 075	1 975	4 695	2 415	2 280
10-14	2 500	1 300	1 200	2 575	1 325	1 250	3 175	1 675	1 500	3 945	2 055	1 890
15-19	2 425	1 275	1 150	2 350	1 225	1 125	2 400	1 250	1 150	3 000	1 600	1 400
20-24	1 952	984	968	2 301	1 199	1 102	2 286	1 168	1 118	2 370	1 235	1 135
25-29	1 470	722	748	1 964	951	1 013	2 315	1 148	1 167	2 260	1 150	1 110
30-34	1 108	521	587	1 468	743	725	1 996	1 019	977	2 272	1 147	1 125
35-39	1 281	684	597	1 036	515	521	1 431	743	688	1 930	990	940
40-44	1 140	548	592	1 278	662	616	1 046	502	544	1 390	710	680
45-49	940	496	444	1 035	520	515	1 165	605	560	944	474	470
50-54	856	387	469	982	502	480	1 064	544	520	1 121	561	560
55-59	472	213	259	704	324	380	856	421	435	991	491	500
60-64	553	196	357	625	241	384	741	366	375	745	365	380
65-69	267	114	153	296	125	171	377	165	212	648	298	350
70-74	241	94	147	295	115	180	338	132	206	350	142	208
75-79	123	45	78	153	56	97	175	64	111	177	68	109
80 +	56	18	38	73	23	50	83	26	57	79	27	52

Age group	1970 Both sexes	Males	Females	1975 Both sexes	Males	Females	1980 Both sexes	Males	Females	1985 Both sexes	Males	Females
All ages	36 207	18 398	17 809	41 211	21 048	20 163	46 316	23 434	22 881	52 150	26 400	25 751
0-4	5 672	2 904	2 768	6 355	3 249	3 106	6 922	3 555	3 367	7 057	3 587	3 471
5-9	4 987	2 538	2 449	5 607	2 888	2 719	6 298	3 229	3 069	6 762	3 468	3 294
10-14	4 384	2 260	2 124	5 097	2 614	2 483	5 499	2 826	2 673	6 249	3 199	3 050
15-19	3 802	1 916	1 886	4 399	2 288	2 111	4 966	2 549	2 417	5 471	2 809	2 663
20-24	2 930	1 535	1 395	3 587	1 864	1 722	4 151	2 125	2 026	4 979	2 558	2 421
25-29	2 310	1 166	1 144	2 892	1 522	1 370	3 460	1 762	1 698	4 192	2 152	2 039
30-34	2 135	1 042	1 092	2 281	1 129	1 151	2 762	1 407	1 355	3 489	1 783	1 707
35-39	2 195	1 125	1 070	2 141	1 033	1 108	2 253	1 105	1 148	2 772	1 421	1 351
40-44	1 832	935	897	2 105	1 099	1 006	2 109	1 013	1 095	2 223	1 088	1 135
45-49	1 388	703	686	1 840	942	898	2 058	1 069	989	2 062	987	1 075
50-54	964	481	483	1 260	651	609	1 764	875	889	1 987	1 026	961
55-59	1 152	597	554	903	438	465	1 162	595	567	1 672	822	850
60-64	907	461	446	937	478	459	801	377	424	1 070	540	530
65-69	762	374	388	831	398	433	863	410	453	707	326	381
70-74	449	220	229	532	259	273	592	262	330	701	323	378
75-79	219	95	123	303	140	163	348	160	188	425	180	245
80 +	120	46	74	142	55	87	308	115	192	331	132	199

Age group	1990 Both sexes	Males	Females	1995 Both sexes	Males	Females	2000 Both sexes	Males	Females	2005 Both sexes	Males	Females
All ages	57 300	28 985	28 315	62 620	31 640	30 980	68 234	34 437	33 798	73 193	36 878	36 314
0-4	6 772	3 443	3 328	6 982	3 555	3 427	7 288	3 713	3 574	7 212	3 676	3 536
5-9	6 958	3 532	3 426	6 712	3 410	3 303	6 940	3 531	3 409	7 233	3 683	3 550
10-14	6 732	3 451	3 281	6 936	3 519	3 417	6 696	3 400	3 296	6 916	3 517	3 399
15-19	6 224	3 184	3 040	6 707	3 435	3 272	6 919	3 507	3 412	6 656	3 376	3 280
20-24	5 446	2 791	2 655	6 190	3 161	3 030	6 688	3 419	3 269	6 840	3 460	3 381
25-29	4 953	2 540	2 413	5 412	2 768	2 644	6 170	3 145	3 025	6 594	3 363	3 231
30-34	4 166	2 137	2 029	4 917	2 518	2 399	5 389	2 752	2 636	6 085	3 095	2 990
35-39	3 456	1 764	1 693	4 126	2 113	2 013	4 883	2 497	2 386	5 311	2 707	2 604
40-44	2 732	1 398	1 335	3 409	1 736	1 673	4 081	2 086	1 995	4 803	2 450	2 353
45-49	2 173	1 059	1 114	2 676	1 363	1 313	3 348	1 699	1 649	3 992	2 032	1 960
50-54	1 989	944	1 045	2 102	1 017	1 085	2 597	1 314	1 283	3 240	1 632	1 608
55-59	1 874	955	919	1 888	883	1 004	2 004	956	1 048	2 469	1 233	1 237
60-64	1 528	736	792	1 724	862	863	1 750	802	948	1 857	867	990
65-69	927	457	471	1 341	629	712	1 523	742	781	1 552	691	861
70-74	561	251	310	746	356	390	1 092	495	597	1 244	586	659
75-79	478	212	266	392	168	224	529	242	286	780	339	441
80 +	330	132	198	360	148	212	339	138	201	407	173	234

United Nations Department of Economic and Social Affairs/Population Division
World Population Prospects: The 2004 Revision, Volume II: Sex and Age Distribution of the World Population

850

POPULATION BY AGE AND SEX (in thousands)

Age group	2005 Both sexes	2005 Males	2005 Females	2010 Both sexes	2010 Males	2010 Females	2015 Both sexes	2015 Males	2015 Females	2020 Both sexes	2020 Males	2020 Females
All ages	73 193	36 878	36 314	78 081	39 288	38 792	82 640	41 528	41 113	86 774	43 538	43 236
0-4	7 212	3 676	3 536	7 147	3 644	3 503	7 016	3 579	3 437	6 888	3 515	3 373
5-9	7 233	3 683	3 550	7 175	3 655	3 520	7 118	3 628	3 491	6 991	3 564	3 426
10-14	6 916	3 517	3 399	7 217	3 673	3 544	7 161	3 646	3 515	7 105	3 619	3 486
15-19	6 656	3 376	3 280	6 892	3 502	3 390	7 195	3 658	3 536	7 136	3 630	3 506
20-24	6 840	3 460	3 381	6 615	3 349	3 266	6 855	3 477	3 378	7 146	3 628	3 518
25-29	6 594	3 363	3 231	6 790	3 428	3 363	6 572	3 321	3 251	6 797	3 441	3 356
30-34	6 085	3 095	2 990	6 543	3 331	3 212	6 744	3 399	3 346	6 518	3 288	3 230
35-39	5 311	2 707	2 604	6 030	3 062	2 969	6 493	3 300	3 192	6 689	3 365	3 324
40-44	4 803	2 450	2 353	5 249	2 670	2 579	5 968	3 024	2 944	6 428	3 261	3 167
45-49	3 992	2 032	1 960	4 719	2 399	2 321	5 167	2 619	2 548	5 882	2 971	2 911
50-54	3 240	1 632	1 608	3 880	1 962	1 918	4 599	2 322	2 277	5 045	2 541	2 504
55-59	2 469	1 233	1 237	3 097	1 539	1 557	3 721	1 857	1 863	4 424	2 206	2 218
60-64	1 857	867	990	2 299	1 124	1 175	2 898	1 411	1 486	3 497	1 711	1 786
65-69	1 552	691	861	1 658	752	905	2 065	982	1 083	2 621	1 241	1 380
70-74	1 244	586	659	1 283	550	733	1 385	605	779	1 741	798	943
75-79	780	339	441	899	406	494	945	386	559	1 035	431	604
80-84	297	130	167	447	185	262	526	226	300	566	219	347
85-89	85	33	52	117	49	68	181	72	110	218	90	129
90-94	23	9	14	20	8	13	28	11	17	45	17	28
95-99	2	1	2	3	1	2	3	1	2	4	1	2
100 +	0	0	0	0	0	0	0	0	0	0	0	0

Age group	2025 Both sexes	2025 Males	2025 Females	2030 Both sexes	2030 Males	2030 Females	2035 Both sexes	2035 Males	2035 Females	2040 Both sexes	2040 Males	2040 Females
All ages	90 565	45 353	45 212	93 876	46 904	46 972	96 573	48 129	48 444	98 651	49 037	49 614
0-4	6 768	3 456	3 311	6 602	3 375	3 227	6 382	3 265	3 117	6 197	3 172	3 025
5-9	6 867	3 503	3 364	6 750	3 447	3 303	6 587	3 367	3 220	6 369	3 258	3 111
10-14	6 979	3 557	3 422	6 857	3 497	3 360	6 741	3 442	3 299	6 579	3 363	3 217
15-19	7 082	3 605	3 477	6 958	3 544	3 414	6 837	3 485	3 352	6 723	3 431	3 292
20-24	7 090	3 602	3 489	7 039	3 579	3 460	6 918	3 520	3 398	6 800	3 463	3 337
25-29	7 091	3 594	3 497	7 039	3 571	3 468	6 991	3 550	3 441	6 872	3 493	3 379
30-34	6 747	3 410	3 336	7 042	3 565	3 478	6 994	3 544	3 450	6 948	3 525	3 423
35-39	6 469	3 258	3 210	6 700	3 383	3 318	6 999	3 539	3 459	6 953	3 520	3 433
40-44	6 630	3 330	3 300	6 416	3 227	3 189	6 651	3 354	3 297	6 952	3 512	3 440
45-49	6 345	3 210	3 135	6 552	3 283	3 270	6 348	3 186	3 162	6 587	3 316	3 271
50-54	5 757	2 891	2 866	6 221	3 130	3 091	6 435	3 208	3 227	6 243	3 120	3 124
55-59	4 868	2 422	2 446	5 600	2 796	2 804	6 062	3 030	3 032	6 280	3 113	3 167
60-64	4 176	2 042	2 134	4 612	2 253	2 359	5 294	2 581	2 713	5 752	2 815	2 937
65-69	3 184	1 515	1 669	3 824	1 820	2 004	4 245	2 019	2 226	4 896	2 327	2 569
70-74	2 235	1 019	1 216	2 741	1 254	1 486	3 320	1 519	1 801	3 714	1 700	2 015
75-79	1 323	576	747	1 726	744	982	2 148	928	1 220	2 637	1 137	1 500
80-84	641	249	392	843	339	504	1 130	445	685	1 440	564	875
85-89	250	89	161	299	103	196	411	144	267	575	193	382
90-94	59	22	37	74	22	52	96	27	69	140	38	102
95-99	7	2	4	10	3	7	14	3	11	19	4	16
100 +	0	0	0	1	0	0	1	0	1	1	0	1

Age group	2045 Both sexes	2045 Males	2045 Females	2050 Both sexes	2050 Males	2050 Females
All ages	100 189	49 678	50 511	101 208	50 078	51 130
0-4	6 107	3 128	2 979	6 000	3 074	2 926
5-9	6 186	3 167	3 019	6 096	3 123	2 973
10-14	6 361	3 254	3 107	6 179	3 163	3 016
15-19	6 562	3 353	3 209	6 345	3 245	3 100
20-24	6 687	3 410	3 277	6 528	3 333	3 195
25-29	6 756	3 438	3 318	6 645	3 386	3 259
30-34	6 832	3 470	3 362	6 718	3 416	3 302
35-39	6 911	3 504	3 407	6 797	3 451	3 346
40-44	6 911	3 497	3 414	6 871	3 482	3 389
45-49	6 891	3 476	3 414	6 854	3 464	3 390
50-54	6 487	3 252	3 234	6 793	3 415	3 379
55-59	6 078	3 009	3 069	6 326	3 145	3 181
60-64	5 980	2 903	3 076	5 826	2 841	2 986
65-69	5 341	2 550	2 791	5 576	2 644	2 932
70-74	4 314	1 973	2 340	4 737	2 181	2 556
75-79	2 985	1 286	1 699	3 506	1 511	1 995
80-84	1 804	702	1 102	2 083	809	1 274
85-89	758	249	509	983	319	665
90-94	208	52	156	290	70	220
95-99	31	5	26	50	8	42
100 +	2	0	2	4	0	4

POPULATION BY AGE AND SEX (in thousands)

Age group	2005 Both sexes	Males	Females	2010 Both sexes	Males	Females	2015 Both sexes	Males	Females	2020 Both sexes	Males	Females
All ages	73 193	36 878	36 314	78 853	39 682	39 171	84 682	42 569	42 113	90 443	45 409	45 034
0-4	7 212	3 676	3 536	7 919	4 038	3 881	8 288	4 228	4 061	8 520	4 348	4 172
5-9	7 233	3 683	3 550	7 175	3 655	3 520	7 888	4 020	3 868	8 260	4 211	4 048
10-14	6 916	3 517	3 399	7 217	3 673	3 544	7 161	3 646	3 515	7 873	4 011	3 863
15-19	6 656	3 376	3 280	6 892	3 502	3 390	7 195	3 658	3 536	7 136	3 630	3 506
20-24	6 840	3 460	3 381	6 615	3 349	3 266	6 855	3 477	3 378	7 146	3 628	3 518
25-29	6 594	3 363	3 231	6 790	3 428	3 363	6 572	3 321	3 251	6 797	3 441	3 356
30-34	6 085	3 095	2 990	6 543	3 331	3 212	6 744	3 399	3 346	6 518	3 288	3 230
35-39	5 311	2 707	2 604	6 030	3 062	2 969	6 493	3 300	3 192	6 689	3 365	3 324
40-44	4 803	2 450	2 353	5 249	2 670	2 579	5 968	3 024	2 944	6 428	3 261	3 167
45-49	3 992	2 032	1 960	4 719	2 399	2 321	5 167	2 619	2 548	5 882	2 971	2 911
50-54	3 240	1 632	1 608	3 880	1 962	1 918	4 599	2 322	2 277	5 045	2 541	2 504
55-59	2 469	1 233	1 237	3 097	1 539	1 557	3 721	1 857	1 863	4 424	2 206	2 218
60-64	1 857	867	990	2 299	1 124	1 175	2 898	1 411	1 486	3 497	1 711	1 786
65-69	1 552	691	861	1 658	752	905	2 065	982	1 083	2 621	1 241	1 380
70-74	1 244	586	659	1 283	550	733	1 385	605	779	1 741	798	943
75-79	780	339	441	899	406	494	945	386	559	1 035	431	604
80-84	297	130	167	447	185	262	526	226	300	566	219	347
85-89	85	33	52	117	49	68	181	72	110	218	90	129
90-94	23	9	14	20	8	13	28	11	17	45	17	28
95-99	2	1	2	3	1	2	3	1	2	4	1	2
100 +	0	0	0	0	0	0	0	0	0	0	0	0

Age group	2025 Both sexes	Males	Females	2030 Both sexes	Males	Females	2035 Both sexes	Males	Females	2040 Both sexes	Males	Females
All ages	95 921	48 085	47 836	101 118	50 599	50 519	106 111	52 997	53 114	110 966	55 324	55 642
0-4	8 460	4 321	4 139	8 497	4 344	4 153	8 689	4 445	4 244	8 989	4 602	4 388
5-9	8 495	4 334	4 162	8 440	4 310	4 130	8 480	4 334	4 145	8 673	4 437	4 236
10-14	8 247	4 203	4 043	8 484	4 327	4 157	8 429	4 304	4 126	8 470	4 329	4 141
15-19	7 849	3 995	3 853	8 224	4 189	4 035	8 462	4 313	4 148	8 409	4 292	4 118
20-24	7 090	3 602	3 489	7 804	3 968	3 836	8 181	4 163	4 018	8 421	4 289	4 132
25-29	7 091	3 594	3 497	7 039	3 571	3 468	7 754	3 938	3 816	8 132	4 134	3 998
30-34	6 747	3 410	3 336	7 042	3 565	3 478	6 994	3 544	3 450	7 709	3 911	3 798
35-39	6 469	3 258	3 210	6 700	3 383	3 318	6 999	3 539	3 459	6 953	3 520	3 433
40-44	6 630	3 330	3 300	6 416	3 227	3 189	6 651	3 354	3 297	6 952	3 512	3 440
45-49	6 345	3 210	3 135	6 552	3 283	3 270	6 348	3 186	3 162	6 587	3 316	3 271
50-54	5 757	2 891	2 866	6 221	3 130	3 091	6 435	3 208	3 227	6 243	3 120	3 124
55-59	4 868	2 423	2 445	5 569	2 765	2 804	6 032	3 003	3 029	6 253	3 086	3 167
60-64	4 176	2 042	2 134	4 612	2 253	2 359	5 294	2 581	2 713	5 752	2 815	2 937
65-69	3 184	1 515	1 669	3 824	1 820	2 004	4 245	2 019	2 226	4 896	2 327	2 569
70-74	2 235	1 019	1 216	2 741	1 254	1 486	3 320	1 519	1 801	3 714	1 700	2 015
75-79	1 323	576	747	1 726	744	982	2 148	928	1 220	2 637	1 137	1 500
80-84	641	249	392	843	339	504	1 130	445	685	1 440	564	875
85-89	250	89	161	299	103	196	411	144	267	575	193	382
90-94	59	22	37	74	22	52	96	27	69	140	38	102
95-99	7	2	4	10	3	7	14	3	11	19	4	16
100 +	0	0	0	1	0	0	1	0	1	1	0	1

Age group	2045 Both sexes	Males	Females	2050 Both sexes	Males	Females
All ages	115 680	57 590	58 089	120 136	59 749	60 387
0-4	9 300	4 763	4 537	9 459	4 846	4 613
5-9	8 975	4 594	4 380	9 287	4 757	4 530
10-14	8 664	4 432	4 232	8 967	4 590	4 377
15-19	8 451	4 318	4 133	8 646	4 422	4 225
20-24	8 370	4 269	4 102	8 414	4 296	4 118
25-29	8 374	4 261	4 113	8 326	4 243	4 083
30-34	8 089	4 109	3 980	8 332	4 238	4 095
35-39	7 669	3 889	3 780	8 050	4 087	3 963
40-44	6 911	3 497	3 414	7 626	3 865	3 761
45-49	6 891	3 476	3 414	6 854	3 464	3 390
50-54	6 487	3 252	3 234	6 793	3 415	3 379
55-59	6 078	3 009	3 069	6 326	3 145	3 181
60-64	5 980	2 903	3 076	5 826	2 841	2 986
65-69	5 341	2 550	2 791	5 576	2 644	2 932
70-74	4 314	1 973	2 340	4 737	2 181	2 556
75-79	2 985	1 286	1 699	3 506	1 511	1 995
80-84	1 804	702	1 102	2 083	809	1 274
85-89	758	249	509	983	319	665
90-94	208	52	156	290	70	220
95-99	31	5	26	50	8	42
100 +	2	0	2	4	0	4

United Nations Department of Economic and Social Affairs/Population Division
World Population Prospects: The 2004 Revision, Volume II: Sex and Age Distribution of the World Population

852

POPULATION BY AGE AND SEX (in thousands)

Age group	2005 Both sexes	2005 Males	2005 Females	2010 Both sexes	2010 Males	2010 Females	2015 Both sexes	2015 Males	2015 Females	2020 Both sexes	2020 Males	2020 Females
All ages	73 193	36 878	36 314	77 308	38 894	38 414	80 598	40 486	40 112	83 105	41 667	41 438
0-4	7 212	3 676	3 536	6 375	3 251	3 124	5 743	2 930	2 814	5 256	2 682	2 574
5-9	7 233	3 683	3 550	7 175	3 655	3 520	6 349	3 235	3 113	5 722	2 917	2 804
10-14	6 916	3 517	3 399	7 217	3 673	3 544	7 161	3 646	3 515	6 337	3 228	3 109
15-19	6 656	3 376	3 280	6 892	3 502	3 390	7 195	3 658	3 536	7 136	3 630	3 506
20-24	6 840	3 460	3 381	6 615	3 349	3 266	6 855	3 477	3 378	7 146	3 628	3 518
25-29	6 594	3 363	3 231	6 790	3 428	3 363	6 572	3 321	3 251	6 797	3 441	3 356
30-34	6 085	3 095	2 990	6 543	3 331	3 212	6 744	3 399	3 346	6 518	3 288	3 230
35-39	5 311	2 707	2 604	6 030	3 062	2 969	6 493	3 300	3 192	6 689	3 365	3 324
40-44	4 803	2 450	2 353	5 249	2 670	2 579	5 968	3 024	2 944	6 428	3 261	3 167
45-49	3 992	2 032	1 960	4 719	2 399	2 321	5 167	2 619	2 548	5 882	2 971	2 911
50-54	3 240	1 632	1 608	3 880	1 962	1 918	4 599	2 322	2 277	5 045	2 541	2 504
55-59	2 469	1 233	1 237	3 097	1 539	1 557	3 721	1 857	1 863	4 424	2 206	2 218
60-64	1 857	867	990	2 299	1 124	1 175	2 898	1 411	1 486	3 497	1 711	1 786
65-69	1 552	691	861	1 658	752	905	2 065	982	1 083	2 621	1 241	1 380
70-74	1 244	586	659	1 283	550	733	1 385	605	779	1 741	798	943
75-79	780	339	441	899	406	494	945	386	559	1 035	431	604
80-84	297	130	167	447	185	262	526	226	300	566	219	347
85-89	85	33	52	117	49	68	181	72	110	218	90	129
90-94	23	9	14	20	8	13	28	11	17	45	17	28
95-99	2	1	2	3	1	2	3	1	2	4	1	2
100 +	0	0	0	0	0	0	0	0	0	0	0	0

Age group	2025 Both sexes	2025 Males	2025 Females	2030 Both sexes	2030 Males	2030 Females	2035 Both sexes	2035 Males	2035 Females	2040 Both sexes	2040 Males	2040 Females
All ages	85 219	42 626	42 593	86 727	43 257	43 470	87 386	43 441	43 945	87 161	43 172	43 989
0-4	5 084	2 597	2 488	4 791	2 449	2 342	4 333	2 217	2 116	3 880	1 986	1 894
5-9	5 239	2 673	2 566	5 070	2 589	2 481	4 778	2 442	2 336	4 322	2 211	2 111
10-14	5 712	2 911	2 800	5 230	2 668	2 563	5 062	2 585	2 478	4 772	2 439	2 333
15-19	6 315	3 215	3 100	5 693	2 900	2 793	5 213	2 657	2 556	5 046	2 575	2 471
20-24	7 090	3 602	3 489	6 274	3 190	3 084	5 655	2 878	2 778	5 178	2 637	2 541
25-29	7 091	3 594	3 497	7 039	3 571	3 468	6 228	3 163	3 066	5 613	2 853	2 760
30-34	6 747	3 410	3 336	7 042	3 565	3 478	6 994	3 544	3 450	6 188	3 139	3 049
35-39	6 469	3 258	3 210	6 700	3 383	3 318	6 999	3 539	3 459	6 953	3 520	3 433
40-44	6 630	3 330	3 300	6 416	3 227	3 189	6 651	3 354	3 297	6 952	3 512	3 440
45-49	6 345	3 210	3 135	6 552	3 283	3 270	6 348	3 186	3 162	6 587	3 316	3 271
50-54	5 757	2 891	2 866	6 221	3 130	3 091	6 435	3 208	3 227	6 243	3 120	3 124
55-59	4 900	2 420	2 445	5 600	2 755	2 845	6 033	3 003	3 030	6 263	3 096	3 167
60-64	4 176	2 042	2 134	4 612	2 253	2 359	5 294	2 581	2 713	5 752	2 815	2 937
65-69	3 184	1 515	1 669	3 824	1 820	2 004	4 245	2 019	2 226	4 896	2 327	2 569
70-74	2 235	1 019	1 216	2 741	1 254	1 486	3 320	1 519	1 801	3 714	1 700	2 015
75-79	1 323	576	747	1 726	744	982	2 148	928	1 220	2 637	1 137	1 500
80-84	641	249	392	843	339	504	1 130	445	685	1 440	564	875
85-89	250	89	161	299	103	196	411	144	267	575	193	382
90-94	59	22	37	74	22	52	96	27	69	140	38	102
95-99	7	2	4	10	3	7	14	3	11	19	4	16
100 +	0	0	0	1	0	0	1	0	1	1	0	1

Age group	2045 Both sexes	2045 Males	2045 Females	2050 Both sexes	2050 Males	2050 Females
All ages	86 181	42 525	43 656	84 559	41 574	42 986
0-4	3 572	1 829	1 742	3 337	1 710	1 627
5-9	3 871	1 982	1 889	3 563	1 825	1 738
10-14	4 316	2 208	2 108	3 865	1 979	1 887
15-19	4 756	2 430	2 326	4 302	2 200	2 102
20-24	5 013	2 556	2 457	4 725	2 412	2 312
25-29	5 139	2 614	2 524	4 974	2 534	2 440
30-34	5 576	2 832	2 744	5 104	2 595	2 509
35-39	6 152	3 119	3 033	5 544	2 814	2 730
40-44	6 911	3 497	3 414	6 116	3 099	3 017
45-49	6 891	3 476	3 414	6 854	3 464	3 390
50-54	6 487	3 252	3 234	6 793	3 415	3 379
55-59	6 078	3 009	3 069	6 326	3 145	3 181
60-64	5 980	2 903	3 076	5 826	2 841	2 986
65-69	5 341	2 550	2 791	5 576	2 644	2 932
70-74	4 314	1 973	2 340	4 737	2 181	2 556
75-79	2 985	1 286	1 699	3 506	1 511	1 995
80-84	1 804	702	1 102	2 083	809	1 274
85-89	758	249	509	983	319	665
90-94	208	52	156	290	70	220
95-99	31	5	26	50	8	42
100 +	2	0	2	4	0	4

POPULATION BY AGE AND SEX (in thousands)

Age group	1950 Both sexes	Males	Females	1955 Both sexes	Males	Females	1960 Both sexes	Males	Females	1965 Both sexes	Males	Females
All ages	1 211	594	617	1 356	664	691	1 594	782	812	1 890	929	961
0-4	142	73	69	207	107	100	286	146	140	351	179	173
5-9	110	57	53	137	70	67	204	105	99	281	144	138
10-14	146	75	70	110	57	53	139	71	68	206	106	100
15-19	122	63	59	145	75	70	112	58	54	141	72	69
20-24	121	61	60	121	62	59	146	75	71	113	58	54
25-29	80	35	45	120	60	60	122	63	59	146	75	71
30-34	62	27	36	79	34	45	120	60	60	122	62	60
35-39	80	33	46	61	26	35	79	34	45	119	59	60
40-44	73	33	40	78	32	46	60	25	35	78	33	44
45-49	68	32	36	70	32	39	76	31	45	59	24	35
50-54	51	25	26	63	29	34	67	29	38	72	29	44
55-59	41	22	19	46	22	24	58	26	32	62	26	35
60-64	44	23	22	35	18	17	40	19	22	52	23	29
65-69	31	16	16	36	18	18	29	14	15	34	15	19
70-74	20	10	11	23	11	12	27	13	15	22	10	12
75-79	12	5	6	14	6	8	16	7	9	19	8	11
80 +	7	3	4	9	4	5	11	4	6	13	5	8

Age group	1970 Both sexes	Males	Females	1975 Both sexes	Males	Females	1980 Both sexes	Males	Females	1985 Both sexes	Males	Females
All ages	2 189	1 077	1 111	2 520	1 241	1 279	2 861	1 406	1 455	3 230	1 587	1 642
0-4	354	179	175	399	201	197	437	220	217	497	252	245
5-9	346	176	171	356	180	176	391	197	195	425	214	211
10-14	284	145	139	341	173	168	354	179	175	386	194	192
15-19	208	106	101	282	143	139	333	168	165	343	174	169
20-24	141	72	69	216	108	108	288	146	143	333	166	168
25-29	113	58	55	144	73	71	214	105	108	284	141	143
30-34	146	75	71	111	57	54	148	74	74	206	101	106
35-39	121	62	60	143	73	70	100	51	49	139	69	71
40-44	117	58	59	115	58	57	137	69	68	95	48	47
45-49	76	32	44	112	54	58	108	54	54	129	64	65
50-54	57	23	34	76	31	45	107	51	56	102	50	52
55-59	67	26	41	55	21	34	71	28	43	99	47	53
60-64	55	23	33	58	23	35	50	18	31	63	25	39
65-69	44	18	26	45	18	27	47	18	29	42	15	27
70-74	27	11	16	32	13	19	34	13	21	38	13	24
75-79	16	7	9	18	7	11	23	9	14	24	8	15
80 +	16	6	9	18	7	11	19	7	12	22	8	14

Age group	1990 Both sexes	Males	Females	1995 Both sexes	Males	Females	2000 Both sexes	Males	Females	2005 Both sexes	Males	Females
All ages	3 668	1 809	1 859	4 193	2 069	2 124	4 502	2 220	2 282	4 833	2 380	2 453
0-4	579	294	285	592	300	292	485	246	239	488	247	241
5-9	484	244	240	576	292	284	575	291	284	476	241	235
10-14	421	212	209	489	246	242	568	288	280	572	289	283
15-19	375	189	186	425	214	211	481	242	239	564	285	279
20-24	339	172	166	377	190	188	417	210	208	476	240	237
25-29	325	158	167	339	172	167	369	185	184	412	206	206
30-34	276	136	140	325	157	167	331	167	164	363	181	182
35-39	200	98	102	275	134	141	315	152	164	324	162	162
40-44	134	66	68	198	96	102	265	128	137	307	146	161
45-49	91	46	46	131	64	67	190	90	99	256	122	134
50-54	122	59	62	88	43	45	123	59	65	180	84	96
55-59	94	45	49	115	55	60	81	39	42	115	53	62
60-64	89	40	48	87	41	46	104	48	56	74	34	39
65-69	54	20	34	78	34	44	75	33	41	90	40	50
70-74	34	11	22	45	16	30	63	26	37	60	25	35
75-79	27	9	18	25	8	18	33	10	23	45	17	29
80 +	24	8	16	26	8	18	26	7	19	30	8	22

United Nations Department of Economic and Social Affairs/Population Division
World Population Prospects: The 2004 Revision, Volume II: Sex and Age Distribution of the World Population

854

POPULATION BY AGE AND SEX (in thousands)

Age group	2005 Both sexes	Males	Females	2010 Both sexes	Males	Females	2015 Both sexes	Males	Females	2020 Both sexes	Males	Females
All ages	4 833	2 380	2 453	5 163	2 539	2 625	5 498	2 698	2 800	5 811	2 847	2 964
0-4	488	247	241	501	254	247	515	261	254	503	255	248
5-9	476	241	235	479	242	237	493	249	244	508	257	251
10-14	572	289	283	473	239	234	477	241	236	491	248	243
15-19	564	285	279	569	287	281	470	237	233	475	239	235
20-24	476	240	237	560	282	277	564	284	280	467	235	232
25-29	412	206	206	471	236	235	553	278	275	559	281	278
30-34	363	181	182	406	202	204	464	231	233	547	274	273
35-39	324	162	162	356	176	180	399	197	202	457	227	231
40-44	307	146	161	316	157	159	348	171	177	391	192	199
45-49	256	122	134	297	139	158	306	150	156	338	164	174
50-54	180	84	96	244	114	130	284	130	153	293	141	152
55-59	115	53	62	168	77	92	229	104	125	268	120	147
60-64	74	34	39	104	47	58	154	68	86	210	93	117
65-69	90	40	50	64	29	36	92	39	52	136	58	79
70-74	60	25	35	73	30	43	52	22	31	76	30	45
75-79	45	17	29	44	16	27	54	20	34	39	15	24
80-84	20	5	15	28	9	19	27	9	18	34	11	23
85-89	7	2	6	10	2	7	13	4	10	14	4	9
90-94	2	1	2	2	1	2	3	1	2	5	1	3
95-99	0	0	0	0	0	0	0	0	0	1	0	0
100 +	0	0	0	0	0	0	0	0	0	0	0	0

Age group	2025 Both sexes	Males	Females	2030 Both sexes	Males	Females	2035 Both sexes	Males	Females	2040 Both sexes	Males	Females
All ages	6 068	2 966	3 102	6 270	3 058	3 212	6 442	3 135	3 307	6 590	3 202	3 389
0-4	461	234	227	424	215	208	419	213	206	424	216	208
5-9	497	252	245	456	231	225	420	213	207	416	211	204
10-14	506	256	250	495	251	244	454	230	224	419	213	206
15-19	489	247	242	504	255	249	494	250	244	453	230	223
20-24	472	238	234	486	245	241	502	253	248	491	249	243
25-29	463	233	230	468	235	233	483	243	240	499	251	247
30-34	553	277	276	459	230	229	464	232	232	479	240	239
35-39	539	269	271	546	272	274	454	226	227	460	229	230
40-44	449	221	228	531	263	268	538	267	272	448	222	226
45-49	380	185	196	438	214	225	519	255	264	528	259	268
50-54	326	155	170	368	176	192	424	204	220	504	245	259
55-59	278	131	147	310	145	165	351	165	186	406	192	214
60-64	248	108	139	258	119	139	289	132	157	328	151	178
65-69	187	79	108	222	93	129	232	103	129	261	115	146
70-74	114	45	69	158	63	95	189	75	114	199	83	115
75-79	58	21	37	88	32	56	123	45	78	149	54	95
80-84	26	9	17	38	13	26	59	19	40	85	28	57
85-89	18	5	12	13	4	9	21	6	15	33	9	23
90-94	5	1	3	7	2	5	5	1	4	8	2	6
95-99	1	0	1	1	0	1	2	0	1	1	0	1
100 +	0	0	0	0	0	0	0	0	0	0	0	0

Age group	2045 Both sexes	Males	Females	2050 Both sexes	Males	Females
All ages	6 707	3 255	3 453	6 780	3 287	3 493
0-4	424	216	208	409	208	201
5-9	421	214	207	421	214	207
10-14	415	211	204	420	214	206
15-19	417	212	206	414	210	203
20-24	451	228	223	416	211	205
25-29	489	247	242	449	227	222
30-34	495	249	246	485	245	241
35-39	475	237	237	491	246	245
40-44	454	226	228	469	234	235
45-49	439	217	223	446	220	226
50-54	514	250	264	428	209	219
55-59	484	231	252	494	237	257
60-64	382	177	205	456	214	242
65-69	299	133	166	348	156	192
70-74	225	94	131	259	109	149
75-79	157	61	96	180	70	110
80-84	104	34	70	111	39	72
85-89	48	14	34	60	17	42
90-94	13	3	10	20	5	15
95-99	2	0	2	4	1	3
100 +	0	0	0	0	0	0

United Nations Department of Economic and Social Affairs/Population Division
World Population Prospects: The 2004 Revision, Volume II: Sex and Age Distribution of the World Population

855

POPULATION BY AGE AND SEX (in thousands)

Age group	2005 Both sexes	Males	Females	2010 Both sexes	Males	Females	2015 Both sexes	Males	Females	2020 Both sexes	Males	Females
All ages	4 833	2 380	2 453	5 218	2 566	2 652	5 647	2 774	2 873	6 080	2 983	3 097
0-4	488	247	241	555	281	274	611	310	301	625	317	308
5-9	476	241	235	479	242	237	546	276	270	602	305	297
10-14	572	289	283	473	239	234	477	241	236	544	275	269
15-19	564	285	279	569	287	281	470	237	233	475	239	235
20-24	476	240	237	560	282	277	564	284	280	467	235	232
25-29	412	206	206	471	236	235	553	278	275	559	281	278
30-34	363	181	182	406	202	204	464	231	233	547	274	273
35-39	324	162	162	356	176	180	399	197	202	457	227	231
40-44	307	146	161	316	157	159	348	171	177	391	192	199
45-49	256	122	134	297	139	158	306	150	156	338	164	174
50-54	180	84	96	244	114	130	284	130	153	293	141	152
55-59	115	53	62	168	77	92	229	104	125	268	120	147
60-64	74	34	39	104	47	58	154	68	86	210	93	117
65-69	90	40	50	64	29	36	92	39	52	136	58	79
70-74	60	25	35	73	30	43	52	22	31	76	30	45
75-79	45	17	29	44	16	27	54	20	34	39	15	24
80-84	20	5	15	28	9	19	27	9	18	34	11	23
85-89	7	2	6	10	2	7	13	4	10	14	4	9
90-94	2	1	2	2	1	2	3	1	2	5	1	3
95-99	0	0	0	0	0	0	0	0	0	1	0	0
100 +	0	0	0	0	0	0	0	0	0	0	0	0

Age group	2025 Both sexes	Males	Females	2030 Both sexes	Males	Females	2035 Both sexes	Males	Females	2040 Both sexes	Males	Females
All ages	6 453	3 161	3 292	6 777	3 315	3 462	7 102	3 470	3 633	7 445	3 635	3 810
0-4	578	294	284	548	278	269	574	292	282	621	316	305
5-9	618	313	305	572	290	282	543	276	267	570	290	280
10-14	600	304	296	616	312	304	571	289	281	542	275	267
15-19	542	274	268	598	302	296	614	311	303	569	288	280
20-24	472	238	234	539	272	267	595	301	295	611	309	302
25-29	463	233	230	468	235	233	535	269	266	592	298	293
30-34	553	277	276	459	230	229	464	232	232	531	267	265
35-39	539	269	271	546	272	274	454	226	227	460	229	230
40-44	449	221	228	531	263	268	538	267	272	448	222	226
45-49	380	185	196	438	214	225	519	255	264	528	259	268
50-54	326	155	170	368	176	192	424	204	220	504	245	259
55-59	278	131	147	310	145	165	351	165	186	406	192	214
60-64	248	108	139	258	119	139	289	132	157	328	151	178
65-69	187	79	108	222	93	129	232	103	129	261	115	146
70-74	114	45	69	158	63	95	189	75	114	199	83	115
75-79	58	21	37	88	32	56	123	45	78	149	54	95
80-84	26	9	17	38	13	26	59	19	40	85	28	57
85-89	18	5	12	13	4	9	21	6	15	33	9	23
90-94	5	1	3	7	2	5	5	1	4	8	2	6
95-99	1	0	1	1	0	1	2	0	1	1	0	1
100 +	0	0	0	0	0	0	0	0	0	0	0	0

Age group	2045 Both sexes	Males	Females	2050 Both sexes	Males	Females
All ages	7 782	3 800	3 982	8 084	3 949	4 136
0-4	648	330	318	643	327	315
5-9	617	314	303	644	328	316
10-14	568	289	279	615	313	302
15-19	540	274	266	567	288	279
20-24	567	287	280	538	273	265
25-29	608	307	301	564	285	279
30-34	588	295	292	604	304	300
35-39	527	263	263	583	292	291
40-44	454	226	228	521	259	261
45-49	439	217	223	446	220	226
50-54	514	250	264	428	209	219
55-59	484	231	252	494	237	257
60-64	382	177	205	456	214	242
65-69	299	133	166	348	156	192
70-74	225	94	131	259	109	149
75-79	157	61	96	180	70	110
80-84	104	34	70	111	39	72
85-89	48	14	34	60	17	42
90-94	13	3	10	20	5	15
95-99	2	0	2	4	1	3
100 +	0	0	0	0	0	0

United Nations Department of Economic and Social Affairs/Population Division
World Population Prospects: The 2004 Revision, Volume II: Sex and Age Distribution of the World Population

856

POPULATION BY AGE AND SEX (in thousands)

Age group	2005 Both sexes	Males	Females	2010 Both sexes	Males	Females	2015 Both sexes	Males	Females	2020 Both sexes	Males	Females
All ages	4 833	2 380	2 453	5 111	2 512	2 599	5 352	2 624	2 728	5 545	2 712	2 833
0-4	488	247	241	448	227	221	422	214	208	382	194	188
5-9	476	241	235	479	242	237	441	223	218	416	211	205
10-14	572	289	283	473	239	234	477	241	236	439	222	217
15-19	564	285	279	569	287	281	470	237	233	475	239	235
20-24	476	240	237	560	282	277	564	284	280	467	235	232
25-29	412	206	206	471	236	235	553	278	275	559	281	278
30-34	363	181	182	406	202	204	464	231	233	547	274	273
35-39	324	162	162	356	176	180	399	197	202	457	227	231
40-44	307	146	161	316	157	159	348	171	177	391	192	199
45-49	256	122	134	297	139	158	306	150	156	338	164	174
50-54	180	84	96	244	114	130	284	130	153	293	141	152
55-59	115	53	62	168	77	92	229	104	125	268	120	147
60-64	74	34	39	104	47	58	154	68	86	210	93	117
65-69	90	40	50	64	29	36	92	39	52	136	58	79
70-74	60	25	35	73	30	43	52	22	31	76	30	45
75-79	45	17	29	44	16	27	54	20	34	39	15	24
80-84	20	5	15	28	9	19	27	9	18	34	11	23
85-89	7	2	6	10	2	7	13	4	10	14	4	9
90-94	2	1	2	2	1	2	3	1	2	5	1	3
95-99	0	0	0	0	0	0	0	0	0	1	0	0
100 +	0	0	0	0	0	0	0	0	0	0	0	0

Age group	2025 Both sexes	Males	Females	2030 Both sexes	Males	Females	2035 Both sexes	Males	Females	2040 Both sexes	Males	Females
All ages	5 687	2 773	2 914	5 773	2 806	2 967	5 817	2 818	2 999	5 815	2 808	3 006
0-4	343	174	169	306	156	151	288	147	142	272	139	133
5-9	378	191	186	340	172	167	303	154	149	286	145	141
10-14	414	209	204	376	191	185	338	172	167	302	153	149
15-19	437	221	216	412	208	204	374	190	185	337	171	166
20-24	472	238	234	434	219	215	410	207	203	373	188	184
25-29	463	233	230	468	235	233	431	217	214	407	205	202
30-34	553	277	276	459	230	229	464	232	232	428	215	213
35-39	539	269	271	546	272	274	454	220	227	460	229	230
40-44	449	221	228	531	263	268	538	267	272	448	222	226
45-49	380	185	196	438	214	225	519	255	264	528	259	268
50-54	326	155	170	368	176	192	424	204	220	504	245	259
55-59	278	131	147	310	145	165	351	165	186	406	192	214
60-64	248	108	139	258	119	139	289	132	157	328	151	178
65-69	187	79	108	222	93	129	232	103	129	261	115	146
70-74	114	45	69	158	63	95	189	75	114	199	83	115
75-79	58	21	37	88	32	56	123	45	78	149	54	95
80-84	26	9	17	38	13	26	59	19	40	85	28	57
85-89	18	5	12	13	4	9	21	6	15	33	9	23
90-94	5	1	3	7	2	5	5	1	4	8	2	6
95-99	1	0	1	1	0	1	2	0	1	1	0	1
100 +	0	0	0	0	0	0	0	0	0	0	0	0

Age group	2045 Both sexes	Males	Females	2050 Both sexes	Males	Females
All ages	5 764	2 777	2 988	5 663	2 722	2 942
0-4	253	129	124	232	118	114
5-9	270	137	133	251	128	123
10-14	285	145	140	269	137	132
15-19	301	153	148	284	144	140
20-24	335	170	166	300	152	148
25-29	370	187	183	333	169	165
30-34	404	203	201	368	185	182
35-39	424	212	212	401	201	200
40-44	454	226	228	419	209	210
45-49	439	217	223	446	220	226
50-54	514	250	264	428	209	219
55-59	484	231	252	494	237	257
60-64	382	177	205	456	214	242
65-69	299	133	166	348	156	192
70-74	225	94	131	259	109	149
75-79	157	61	96	180	70	110
80-84	104	34	70	111	39	72
85-89	48	14	34	60	17	42
90-94	13	3	10	20	5	15
95-99	2	0	2	4	1	3
100 +	0	0	0	0	0	0

United Nations Department of Economic and Social Affairs/Population Division
World Population Prospects: The 2004 Revision, Volume II: Sex and Age Distribution of the World Population

857

POPULATION BY AGE AND SEX (in thousands)

Age group	1950 Both sexes	1950 Males	1950 Females	1955 Both sexes	1955 Males	1955 Females	1960 Both sexes	1960 Males	1960 Females	1965 Both sexes	1965 Males	1965 Females
All ages	5 054	2 527	2 527	5 759	2 872	2 888	6 620	3 297	3 324	7 821	3 892	3 929
0-4	957	481	476	1 090	544	545	1 256	629	627	1 498	751	747
5-9	731	367	364	849	426	424	980	489	492	1 165	582	583
10-14	554	278	276	702	353	350	819	410	409	966	482	485
15-19	530	266	263	537	270	267	683	343	340	813	407	406
20-24	452	227	225	511	256	255	519	260	259	674	337	336
25-29	381	190	191	432	216	216	490	245	246	510	254	256
30-34	314	158	156	362	180	182	413	206	208	479	239	240
35-39	255	129	127	297	149	148	345	171	173	402	200	202
40-44	210	106	104	240	120	119	281	141	140	333	165	168
45-49	173	86	87	195	97	98	224	112	112	269	134	135
50-54	143	70	73	159	78	81	180	89	91	212	105	107
55-59	111	54	57	128	62	66	143	69	74	167	81	85
60-64	90	43	47	95	46	50	111	53	58	128	61	67
65-69	68	32	36	72	34	38	77	36	41	93	44	49
70-74	46	21	25	48	22	26	52	24	28	59	27	32
75-79	26	12	14	27	12	15	30	13	16	34	15	19
80 +	13	6	7	15	6	8	17	7	10	19	8	11

Age group	1970 Both sexes	1970 Males	1970 Females	1975 Both sexes	1975 Males	1975 Females	1980 Both sexes	1980 Males	1980 Females	1985 Both sexes	1985 Males	1985 Females
All ages	9 278	4 617	4 661	10 766	5 360	5 406	12 577	6 264	6 313	14 772	7 357	7 414
0-4	1 844	926	918	2 157	1 085	1 072	2 491	1 253	1 238	2 931	1 474	1 457
5-9	1 393	697	696	1 686	845	840	1 989	999	990	2 304	1 158	1 147
10-14	1 140	569	571	1 328	664	664	1 624	814	810	1 925	967	958
15-19	951	474	477	1 092	545	547	1 284	642	642	1 579	791	787
20-24	796	397	398	906	450	456	1 050	523	527	1 241	618	622
25-29	656	327	329	754	375	379	867	429	438	1 009	500	509
30-34	495	246	249	620	308	311	720	357	362	831	410	421
35-39	463	230	233	465	231	234	589	293	297	687	340	347
40-44	386	191	195	433	215	219	439	218	222	560	277	283
45-49	317	156	161	359	177	182	407	201	206	414	204	210
50-54	253	125	128	292	143	149	333	163	170	379	186	194
55-59	196	96	100	228	111	117	265	128	137	304	147	157
60-64	149	72	77	171	82	88	201	97	104	235	112	122
65-69	108	51	57	123	58	64	142	68	75	168	80	88
70-74	71	33	38	81	37	44	93	43	50	108	50	58
75-79	39	17	21	46	21	26	53	24	29	61	27	34
80 +	22	9	13	26	11	15	30	13	18	35	15	21

Age group	1990 Both sexes	1990 Males	1990 Females	1995 Both sexes	1995 Males	1995 Females	2000 Both sexes	2000 Males	2000 Females	2005 Both sexes	2005 Males	2005 Females
All ages	17 758	8 833	8 925	20 892	10 390	10 502	24 309	12 128	12 181	28 816	14 416	14 400
0-4	3 571	1 798	1 773	4 246	2 141	2 105	4 973	2 508	2 465	5 970	3 011	2 959
5-9	2 800	1 406	1 394	3 378	1 698	1 680	3 981	2 004	1 977	4 713	2 374	2 340
10-14	2 290	1 150	1 140	2 764	1 387	1 377	3 272	1 644	1 627	3 857	1 941	1 916
15-19	1 919	963	955	2 269	1 139	1 130	2 713	1 361	1 352	3 213	1 614	1 599
20-24	1 547	772	775	1 872	937	934	2 208	1 106	1 102	2 652	1 327	1 325
25-29	1 193	589	604	1 413	704	708	1 755	882	874	2 119	1 061	1 058
30-34	967	474	493	1 052	517	535	1 217	617	600	1 624	823	801
35-39	797	390	408	858	416	442	883	439	444	1 077	555	522
40-44	660	324	336	719	346	373	733	355	378	776	389	387
45-49	536	263	273	605	292	313	631	301	330	654	317	337
50-54	394	192	202	495	239	256	540	257	283	570	269	301
55-59	355	172	183	362	174	189	444	211	234	489	229	259
60-64	277	132	144	319	152	167	321	151	170	396	185	211
65-69	202	95	107	238	112	126	271	127	144	274	127	147
70-74	132	62	71	160	74	86	187	86	101	214	98	116
75-79	74	33	41	91	41	50	110	50	61	130	58	72
80 +	43	18	25	52	22	30	70	30	40	88	38	51

United Nations Department of Economic and Social Affairs/Population Division
World Population Prospects: The 2004 Revision, Volume II: Sex and Age Distribution of the World Population

858

POPULATION BY AGE AND SEX (in thousands)

Age group	2005 Both sexes	Males	Females	2010 Both sexes	Males	Females	2015 Both sexes	Males	Females	2020 Both sexes	Males	Females
All ages	28 816	14 416	14 400	34 569	17 316	17 253	41 918	21 015	20 900	50 570	25 367	25 204
0-4	5 970	3 011	2 959	7 279	3 670	3 609	8 720	4 398	4 321	10 054	5 073	4 981
5-9	4 713	2 374	2 340	5 667	2 854	2 814	7 009	3 527	3 481	8 460	4 261	4 199
10-14	3 857	1 941	1 916	4 571	2 301	2 270	5 561	2 799	2 762	6 910	3 476	3 433
15-19	3 213	1 614	1 599	3 771	1 896	1 874	4 506	2 267	2 240	5 494	2 763	2 731
20-24	2 652	1 327	1 325	3 131	1 569	1 562	3 703	1 858	1 845	4 435	2 225	2 210
25-29	2 119	1 061	1 058	2 551	1 275	1 276	3 049	1 524	1 525	3 618	1 811	1 807
30-34	1 624	823	801	2 001	1 005	996	2 452	1 227	1 225	2 955	1 477	1 478
35-39	1 077	555	522	1 511	770	741	1 904	959	944	2 359	1 182	1 177
40-44	776	389	387	993	513	480	1 429	730	699	1 821	918	903
45-49	654	317	337	717	358	358	937	484	454	1 363	695	668
50-54	570	269	301	603	290	313	673	335	339	888	456	432
55-59	489	229	259	522	244	278	561	267	294	631	311	319
60-64	396	185	211	438	203	235	475	219	256	514	242	272
65-69	274	127	147	340	156	184	381	174	208	417	190	227
70-74	214	98	116	218	99	119	274	124	151	312	140	172
75-79	130	58	72	150	67	83	155	69	86	199	88	111
80-84	62	27	35	74	32	42	87	38	50	92	40	53
85-89	21	9	12	26	11	15	32	13	19	38	16	23
90-94	4	2	3	6	2	4	7	3	5	9	4	6
95-99	0	0	0	1	0	0	1	0	1	1	0	1
100 +	0	0	0	0	0	0	0	0	0	0	0	0

Age group	2025 Both sexes	Males	Females	2030 Both sexes	Males	Females	2035 Both sexes	Males	Females	2040 Both sexes	Males	Females
All ages	60 601	30 411	30 190	72 078	36 180	35 898	84 875	42 610	42 265	98 555	49 478	49 077
0-4	11 496	5 805	5 691	13 028	6 582	6 446	14 461	7 309	7 152	15 521	7 848	7 673
5-9	9 808	4 942	4 866	11 270	5 684	5 587	12 833	6 476	6 357	14 292	7 216	7 076
10-14	8 372	4 214	4 157	9 728	4 899	4 829	11 198	5 644	5 554	12 767	6 438	6 329
15-19	6 841	3 439	3 402	8 301	4 175	4 126	9 650	4 860	4 799	11 131	5 605	5 526
20-24	5 416	2 717	2 699	6 754	3 387	3 367	8 209	4 119	4 089	9 562	4 801	4 762
25-29	4 345	2 175	2 170	5 317	2 662	2 656	6 643	3 325	3 319	8 086	4 050	4 036
30-34	3 522	1 762	1 760	4 242	2 122	2 120	5 202	2 602	2 600	6 509	3 256	3 254
35-39	2 860	1 430	1 430	3 422	1 711	1 711	4 134	2 067	2 067	5 079	2 539	2 540
40-44	2 272	1 138	1 134	2 769	1 384	1 386	3 325	1 661	1 664	4 026	2 011	2 015
45-49	1 748	880	868	2 193	1 096	1 097	2 683	1 338	1 345	3 229	1 611	1 618
50-54	1 299	659	640	1 675	839	836	2 110	1 051	1 059	2 589	1 286	1 303
55-59	837	427	410	1 231	621	610	1 594	794	800	2 015	997	1 018
60-64	582	284	298	777	393	384	1 149	574	575	1 495	738	757
65-69	455	211	244	519	250	269	699	349	350	1 039	513	526
70-74	344	154	190	380	174	206	438	208	230	593	292	301
75-79	229	101	129	257	113	144	288	129	159	335	156	179
80-84	121	52	69	142	61	81	162	69	93	184	80	104
85-89	42	17	25	56	23	33	67	28	40	78	32	46
90-94	12	4	7	13	5	8	18	7	11	22	8	13
95-99	2	1	1	2	1	1	2	1	2	3	1	2
100 +	0	0	0	0	0	0	0	0	0	0	0	0

Age group	2045 Both sexes	Males	Females	2050 Both sexes	Males	Females
All ages	112 674	56 568	56 106	126 950	63 722	63 228
0-4	16 188	8 190	7 998	16 647	8 422	8 225
5-9	15 383	7 771	7 612	16 075	8 125	7 950
10-14	14 233	7 182	7 052	15 331	7 740	7 591
15-19	12 701	6 399	6 302	14 169	7 143	7 027
20-24	11 031	5 544	5 488	12 599	6 336	6 263
25-29	9 431	4 727	4 704	10 892	5 465	5 427
30-34	7 934	3 972	3 962	9 264	4 641	4 623
35-39	6 365	3 182	3 183	7 768	3 888	3 881
40-44	4 954	2 475	2 479	6 217	3 107	3 111
45-49	3 917	1 954	1 963	4 828	2 409	2 419
50-54	3 123	1 552	1 570	3 794	1 886	1 908
55-59	2 478	1 224	1 254	2 996	1 481	1 515
60-64	1 896	931	965	2 339	1 146	1 193
65-69	1 357	662	695	1 729	839	890
70-74	888	433	456	1 167	562	606
75-79	458	222	236	692	331	361
80-84	217	99	118	300	142	158
85-89	90	38	52	108	48	60
90-94	26	10	16	30	12	18
95-99	4	1	3	5	2	3
100 +	0	0	0	0	0	0

United Nations Department of Economic and Social Affairs/Population Division
World Population Prospects: The 2004 Revision, Volume II: Sex and Age Distribution of the World Population

859

POPULATION BY AGE AND SEX (in thousands)

Age group	2005			2010			2015			2020		
	Both sexes	Males	Females	Both sexes	Males	Females	Both sexes	Males	Females	Both sexes	Males	Females
All ages	28 816	14 416	14 400	34 569	17 316	17 253	42 162	21 138	21 024	51 582	25 877	25 705
0-4	5 970	3 011	2 959	7 279	3 670	3 609	8 963	4 521	4 442	10 828	5 464	5 364
5-9	4 713	2 374	2 340	5 667	2 854	2 814	7 009	3 527	3 481	8 697	4 380	4 317
10-14	3 857	1 941	1 916	4 571	2 301	2 270	5 561	2 799	2 762	6 910	3 476	3 433
15-19	3 213	1 614	1 599	3 771	1 896	1 874	4 506	2 267	2 240	5 494	2 763	2 731
20-24	2 652	1 327	1 325	3 131	1 569	1 562	3 703	1 858	1 845	4 435	2 225	2 210
25-29	2 119	1 061	1 058	2 551	1 275	1 276	3 049	1 524	1 525	3 618	1 811	1 807
30-34	1 624	823	801	2 001	1 005	996	2 452	1 227	1 225	2 955	1 477	1 478
35-39	1 077	555	522	1 511	770	741	1 904	959	944	2 359	1 182	1 177
40-44	776	389	387	993	513	480	1 429	730	699	1 821	918	903
45-49	654	317	337	717	358	358	937	484	454	1 363	695	668
50-54	570	269	301	603	290	313	673	335	339	888	456	432
55-59	489	229	259	522	244	278	561	267	294	631	311	319
60-64	396	185	211	438	203	235	475	219	256	514	242	272
65-69	274	127	147	340	156	184	381	174	208	417	190	227
70-74	214	98	116	218	99	119	274	124	151	312	140	172
75-79	130	58	72	150	67	83	155	69	86	199	88	111
80-84	62	27	35	74	32	42	87	38	50	92	40	53
85-89	21	9	12	26	11	15	32	13	19	38	16	23
90-94	4	2	3	6	2	4	7	3	5	9	4	6
95-99	0	0	0	1	0	0	1	0	1	1	0	1
100 +	0	0	0	0	0	0	0	0	0	0	0	0

Age group	2025			2030			2035			2040		
	Both sexes	Males	Females	Both sexes	Males	Females	Both sexes	Males	Females	Both sexes	Males	Females
All ages	62 541	31 389	31 152	75 205	37 758	37 448	89 642	45 014	44 627	105 659	53 061	52 598
0-4	12 447	6 285	6 162	14 242	7 195	7 047	16 132	8 154	7 978	17 899	9 050	8 849
5-9	10 563	5 322	5 240	12 203	6 154	6 049	14 029	7 079	6 950	15 944	8 050	7 894
10-14	8 606	4 332	4 274	10 476	5 276	5 200	12 125	6 111	6 014	13 957	7 038	6 918
15-19	6 841	3 439	3 402	8 533	4 292	4 242	10 403	5 234	5 169	12 052	6 068	5 984
20-24	5 416	2 717	2 699	6 754	3 387	3 367	8 438	4 234	4 204	10 299	5 170	5 128
25-29	4 345	2 175	2 170	5 317	2 662	2 656	6 643	3 325	3 319	8 312	4 163	4 149
30-34	3 522	1 762	1 760	4 242	2 122	2 120	5 202	2 602	2 600	6 509	3 256	3 254
35-39	2 860	1 430	1 430	3 422	1 711	1 711	4 134	2 067	2 067	5 079	2 539	2 540
40-44	2 272	1 138	1 134	2 769	1 384	1 386	3 325	1 661	1 664	4 026	2 011	2 015
45-49	1 748	880	868	2 193	1 096	1 097	2 683	1 338	1 345	3 229	1 611	1 618
50-54	1 299	659	640	1 675	839	836	2 110	1 051	1 059	2 589	1 286	1 303
55-59	837	427	410	1 231	621	610	1 594	794	800	2 015	997	1 018
60-64	582	284	298	777	393	384	1 149	574	575	1 495	738	757
65-69	455	211	244	519	250	269	699	349	350	1 039	513	526
70-74	344	154	190	380	174	206	438	208	230	593	292	301
75-79	229	101	129	257	113	144	288	129	159	335	156	179
80-84	121	52	69	142	61	81	162	69	93	184	80	104
85-89	42	17	25	56	23	33	67	28	40	78	32	46
90-94	12	4	7	13	5	8	18	7	11	22	8	13
95-99	2	1	1	2	1	1	2	1	2	3	1	2
100 +	0	0	0	0	0	0	0	0	0	0	0	0

Age group	2045			2050		
	Both sexes	Males	Females	Both sexes	Males	Females
All ages	122 913	61 733	61 179	141 060	70 841	70 219
0-4	19 378	9 804	9 574	20 595	10 419	10 176
5-9	17 740	8 961	8 778	19 243	9 726	9 517
10-14	15 879	8 012	7 867	17 680	8 926	8 754
15-19	13 885	6 996	6 889	15 808	7 968	7 839
20-24	11 944	6 002	5 942	13 773	6 926	6 847
25-29	10 157	5 091	5 066	11 794	5 917	5 876
30-34	8 156	4 083	4 073	9 978	4 999	4 979
35-39	6 365	3 182	3 183	7 985	3 996	3 989
40-44	4 954	2 475	2 479	6 217	3 107	3 111
45-49	3 917	1 954	1 963	4 828	2 409	2 419
50-54	3 123	1 552	1 570	3 794	1 886	1 908
55-59	2 478	1 224	1 254	2 996	1 481	1 515
60-64	1 896	931	965	2 339	1 146	1 193
65-69	1 357	662	695	1 729	839	890
70-74	888	433	456	1 167	562	606
75-79	458	222	236	692	331	361
80-84	217	99	118	300	142	158
85-89	90	38	52	108	48	60
90-94	26	10	16	30	12	18
95-99	4	1	3	5	2	3
100 +	0	0	0	0	0	0

United Nations Department of Economic and Social Affairs/Population Division
World Population Prospects: The 2004 Revision, Volume II: Sex and Age Distribution of the World Population

860

POPULATION BY AGE AND SEX (in thousands)

Age group	2005 Both sexes	Males	Females	2010 Both sexes	Males	Females	2015 Both sexes	Males	Females	2020 Both sexes	Males	Females
All ages	28 816	14 416	14 400	34 312	17 186	17 126	41 166	20 636	20 530	49 064	24 607	24 456
0-4	5 970	3 011	2 959	7 022	3 541	3 482	8 215	4 143	4 071	9 280	4 683	4 597
5-9	4 713	2 374	2 340	5 667	2 854	2 814	6 761	3 403	3 358	7 970	4 014	3 956
10-14	3 857	1 941	1 916	4 571	2 301	2 270	5 561	2 799	2 762	6 666	3 354	3 312
15-19	3 213	1 614	1 599	3 771	1 896	1 874	4 506	2 267	2 240	5 494	2 763	2 731
20-24	2 652	1 327	1 325	3 131	1 569	1 562	3 703	1 858	1 845	4 435	2 225	2 210
25-29	2 119	1 061	1 058	2 551	1 275	1 276	3 049	1 524	1 525	3 618	1 811	1 807
30-34	1 624	823	801	2 001	1 005	996	2 452	1 227	1 225	2 955	1 477	1 478
35-39	1 077	555	522	1 511	770	741	1 904	959	944	2 359	1 182	1 177
40-44	776	389	387	993	513	480	1 429	730	699	1 821	918	903
45-49	654	317	337	717	358	358	937	484	454	1 363	695	668
50-54	570	269	301	603	290	313	673	335	339	888	456	432
55-59	489	229	259	522	244	278	561	267	294	631	311	319
60-64	396	185	211	438	203	235	475	219	256	514	242	272
65-69	274	127	147	340	156	184	381	174	208	417	190	227
70-74	214	98	116	218	99	119	274	124	151	312	140	172
75-79	130	58	72	150	67	83	155	69	86	199	88	111
80-84	62	27	35	74	32	42	87	38	50	92	40	53
85-89	21	9	12	26	11	15	32	13	19	38	16	23
90-94	4	2	3	6	2	4	7	3	5	9	4	6
95-99	0	0	0	1	0	0	1	0	1	1	0	1
100 +	0	0	0	0	0	0	0	0	0	0	0	0

Age group	2025 Both sexes	Males	Females	2030 Both sexes	Males	Females	2035 Both sexes	Males	Females	2040 Both sexes	Males	Females
All ages	58 131	29 166	28 965	68 288	34 270	34 019	79 242	39 770	39 472	90 481	45 407	45 074
0-4	10 507	5 306	5 201	11 676	5 899	5 777	12 577	6 357	6 220	13 026	6 586	6 440
5-9	9 053	4 561	4 491	10 301	5 195	5 106	11 501	5 804	5 698	12 430	6 276	6 155
10-14	7 887	3 970	3 916	8 979	4 522	4 457	10 235	5 159	5 077	11 442	5 770	5 672
15-19	6 599	3 317	3 282	7 820	3 933	3 887	8 915	4 486	4 430	10 173	5 122	5 051
20-24	5 416	2 717	2 699	6 516	3 268	3 248	7 733	3 880	3 852	8 826	4 431	4 395
25-29	4 345	2 175	2 170	5 317	2 662	2 656	6 409	3 207	3 201	7 617	3 815	3 802
30-34	3 522	1 762	1 760	4 242	2 122	2 120	5 202	2 602	2 600	6 279	3 140	3 139
35-39	2 860	1 430	1 430	3 422	1 711	1 711	4 134	2 067	2 067	5 079	2 539	2 540
40-44	2 272	1 138	1 134	2 789	1 384	1 386	3 325	1 661	1 664	4 026	2 011	2 015
45-49	1 748	880	868	2 193	1 096	1 097	2 683	1 338	1 345	3 229	1 611	1 618
50-54	1 299	659	640	1 675	839	836	2 110	1 051	1 059	2 589	1 286	1 303
55-59	837	427	410	1 231	621	610	1 594	794	800	2 015	997	1 018
60-64	582	284	298	777	393	384	1 149	574	575	1 106	729	757
65-69	455	211	244	519	250	269	699	349	350	1 039	513	526
70-74	344	154	190	380	174	206	438	208	230	593	292	301
75-79	229	101	129	257	113	144	288	129	159	335	156	179
80-84	121	52	69	142	61	81	162	69	93	184	80	104
85-89	42	17	25	56	23	33	67	28	40	78	32	46
90-94	12	4	7	13	5	8	18	7	11	22	8	13
95-99	2	1	1	2	1	1	2	1	2	3	1	2
100 +	0	0	0	0	0	0	0	0	0	0	0	0

Age group	2045 Both sexes	Males	Females	2050 Both sexes	Males	Females
All ages	101 573	50 969	50 604	112 250	56 308	55 942
0-4	13 092	6 624	6 469	12 961	6 557	6 404
5-9	12 909	6 521	6 388	13 001	6 571	6 429
10-14	12 379	6 246	6 133	12 866	6 495	6 370
15-19	11 383	5 735	5 648	12 323	6 212	6 111
20-24	10 082	5 067	5 016	11 291	5 678	5 613
25-29	8 704	4 363	4 342	9 955	4 995	4 960
30-34	7 474	3 742	3 733	8 551	4 284	4 267
35-39	6 140	3 070	3 070	7 318	3 662	3 656
40-44	4 954	2 475	2 479	5 998	2 997	3 001
45-49	3 917	1 954	1 963	4 828	2 409	2 419
50-54	3 123	1 552	1 570	3 794	1 886	1 908
55-59	2 478	1 224	1 254	2 996	1 481	1 515
60-64	1 896	931	965	2 339	1 146	1 193
65-69	1 357	662	695	1 729	839	890
70-74	888	433	456	1 167	562	606
75-79	458	222	236	692	331	361
80-84	217	99	118	300	142	158
85-89	90	38	52	108	48	60
90-94	26	10	16	30	12	18
95-99	4	1	3	5	2	3
100 +	0	0	0	0	0	0

United Nations Department of Economic and Social Affairs/Population Division
World Population Prospects: The 2004 Revision, Volume II: Sex and Age Distribution of the World Population

861

POPULATION BY AGE AND SEX (in thousands)

Age group	1950 Both sexes	1950 Males	1950 Females	1955 Both sexes	1955 Males	1955 Females	1960 Both sexes	1960 Males	1960 Females	1965 Both sexes	1965 Males	1965 Females
All ages	37 298	16 009	21 289	40 099	17 522	22 577	42 783	18 965	23 818	45 341	20 343	24 998
0-4	2 988	1 476	1 512	3 803	1 947	1 856	4 178	2 134	2 043	4 087	2 091	1 996
5-9	2 870	1 394	1 476	3 045	1 508	1 538	3 818	1 953	1 865	4 192	2 142	2 050
10-14	4 302	2 102	2 200	2 935	1 428	1 507	3 068	1 518	1 551	3 835	1 962	1 873
15-19	3 056	1 504	1 551	4 372	2 139	2 232	2 959	1 438	1 521	3 081	1 524	1 557
20-24	3 927	1 808	2 119	3 111	1 530	1 581	4 364	2 129	2 234	2 965	1 439	1 527
25-29	2 856	1 140	1 716	3 968	1 821	2 147	3 123	1 529	1 595	4 358	2 120	2 238
30-34	2 014	794	1 220	2 888	1 149	1 739	3 950	1 803	2 147	3 120	1 521	1 599
35-39	3 056	1 164	1 892	2 036	798	1 238	2 876	1 137	1 739	3 927	1 782	2 145
40-44	2 685	1 079	1 606	3 052	1 153	1 899	2 027	786	1 241	2 850	1 117	1 733
45-49	2 293	884	1 409	2 656	1 052	1 604	2 984	1 111	1 874	1 994	764	1 231
50-54	1 710	688	1 022	2 234	843	1 391	2 566	995	1 571	2 895	1 056	1 839
55-59	1 459	594	864	1 634	638	996	2 120	777	1 343	2 449	923	1 525
60-64	1 244	470	774	1 351	529	822	1 508	566	942	1 973	695	1 278
65-69	1 023	362	661	1 104	396	708	1 193	444	749	1 349	481	868
70-74	798	260	538	844	281	563	911	307	603	1 000	350	650
75-79	571	168	403	579	176	402	617	192	425	685	215	470
80 +	445	119	326	488	133	355	520	145	375	580	162	418

Age group	1970 Both sexes	1970 Males	1970 Females	1975 Both sexes	1975 Males	1975 Females	1980 Both sexes	1980 Males	1980 Females	1985 Both sexes	1985 Males	1985 Females
All ages	47 317	21 403	25 913	49 016	22 257	26 759	50 044	22 865	27 179	50 941	23 415	27 526
0-4	3 467	1 769	1 697	3 697	1 883	1 814	3 628	1 848	1 781	3 789	1 932	1 856
5-9	4 120	2 108	2 012	3 489	1 773	1 716	3 625	1 843	1 782	3 619	1 840	1 779
10-14	4 231	2 161	2 069	4 087	2 099	1 988	3 459	1 757	1 702	3 624	1 845	1 779
15-19	3 868	1 977	1 890	4 126	2 108	2 018	3 942	2 016	1 926	3 432	1 745	1 688
20-24	3 102	1 531	1 571	3 821	1 907	1 914	4 059	2 050	2 009	3 830	1 937	1 894
25-29	2 983	1 442	1 541	3 129	1 530	1 600	3 785	1 874	1 911	4 014	2 004	2 010
30-34	4 363	2 113	2 250	2 987	1 432	1 555	3 288	1 607	1 681	3 772	1 858	1 914
35-39	3 124	1 514	1 610	4 328	2 077	2 251	2 759	1 315	1 445	3 246	1 575	1 671
40-44	3 903	1 757	2 146	3 071	1 472	1 599	4 278	2 029	2 249	2 716	1 282	1 434
45-49	2 814	1 089	1 725	3 825	1 706	2 119	2 950	1 401	1 549	4 162	1 951	2 211
50-54	1 950	731	1 219	2 815	1 052	1 763	3 724	1 650	2 074	2 845	1 321	1 524
55-59	2 776	983	1 793	1 905	690	1 214	2 795	1 027	1 769	3 547	1 520	2 027
60-64	2 290	828	1 462	2 611	900	1 711	1 775	615	1 160	2 582	908	1 673
65-69	1 777	592	1 185	2 047	699	1 348	2 277	738	1 539	1 574	512	1 061
70-74	1 140	381	760	1 452	461	991	1 735	551	1 184	1 892	566	1 326
75-79	757	245	512	858	259	598	1 101	318	784	1 284	368	916
80 +	652	182	470	770	210	560	862	226	636	1 014	251	763

Age group	1990 Both sexes	1990 Males	1990 Females	1995 Both sexes	1995 Males	1995 Females	2000 Both sexes	2000 Males	2000 Females	2005 Both sexes	2005 Males	2005 Females
All ages	51 891	24 002	27 890	51 531	23 932	27 599	49 116	22 699	26 417	46 481	21 310	25 171
0-4	3 683	1 882	1 801	2 953	1 514	1 439	2 114	1 087	1 027	1 924	989	935
5-9	3 794	1 930	1 864	3 779	1 926	1 853	2 924	1 498	1 426	2 088	1 073	1 015
10-14	3 644	1 851	1 792	3 812	1 937	1 874	3 748	1 909	1 838	2 895	1 482	1 412
15-19	3 693	1 881	1 812	3 658	1 850	1 807	3 758	1 905	1 853	3 694	1 877	1 817
20-24	3 341	1 681	1 660	3 654	1 867	1 788	3 537	1 772	1 766	3 636	1 826	1 811
25-29	3 793	1 889	1 904	3 323	1 664	1 658	3 463	1 737	1 725	3 334	1 635	1 699
30-34	3 987	1 968	2 019	3 878	1 916	1 962	3 154	1 550	1 604	3 270	1 606	1 664
35-39	3 742	1 828	1 914	3 921	1 914	2 007	3 711	1 799	1 912	2 986	1 433	1 552
40-44	3 200	1 536	1 664	3 686	1 774	1 912	3 744	1 788	1 956	3 524	1 666	1 858
45-49	2 682	1 254	1 428	2 936	1 382	1 554	3 513	1 649	1 863	3 560	1 654	1 905
50-54	4 028	1 858	2 171	2 731	1 242	1 488	2 756	1 256	1 501	3 298	1 497	1 802
55-59	2 708	1 222	1 485	3 732	1 666	2 066	2 506	1 092	1 414	2 534	1 105	1 429
60-64	3 302	1 358	1 944	2 477	1 060	1 418	3 327	1 401	1 926	2 233	915	1 318
65-69	2 314	771	1 543	2 855	1 085	1 770	2 123	845	1 277	2 868	1 121	1 747
70-74	1 323	400	923	1 816	551	1 264	2 301	800	1 501	1 713	624	1 089
75-79	1 426	389	1 038	964	263	701	1 332	361	971	1 687	526	1 162
80 +	1 231	303	928	1 358	321	1 037	1 107	250	857	1 236	280	956

United Nations Department of Economic and Social Affairs/Population Division
World Population Prospects: The 2004 Revision, Volume II: Sex and Age Distribution of the World Population

862

POPULATION BY AGE AND SEX (in thousands)

Age group	2005 Both sexes	Males	Females	2010 Both sexes	Males	Females	2015 Both sexes	Males	Females	2020 Both sexes	Males	Females
All ages	46 481	21 310	25 171	44 128	20 094	24 034	41 849	18 949	22 900	39 009	17 855	21 755
0-4	1 924	989	935	1 937	996	941	1 860	956	903	1 702	876	827
5-9	2 088	1 073	1 015	1 905	978	926	1 918	986	932	1 841	947	895
10-14	2 895	1 482	1 412	2 067	1 062	1 005	1 883	967	916	1 896	975	922
15-19	3 694	1 877	1 817	2 857	1 460	1 397	2 032	1 041	991	1 849	947	902
20-24	3 636	1 826	1 811	3 603	1 818	1 786	2 775	1 407	1 368	1 956	993	963
25-29	3 334	1 635	1 699	3 476	1 719	1 758	3 454	1 719	1 735	2 642	1 321	1 321
30-34	3 270	1 606	1 664	3 168	1 525	1 643	3 319	1 617	1 702	3 308	1 626	1 682
35-39	2 986	1 433	1 552	3 109	1 496	1 612	3 018	1 427	1 591	3 177	1 526	1 651
40-44	3 524	1 666	1 858	2 835	1 329	1 506	2 959	1 396	1 564	2 883	1 340	1 544
45-49	3 560	1 654	1 905	3 355	1 546	1 810	2 704	1 239	1 466	2 835	1 312	1 523
50-54	3 298	1 497	1 802	3 355	1 509	1 846	3 175	1 420	1 755	2 568	1 146	1 422
55-59	2 534	1 105	1 429	3 053	1 328	1 724	3 123	1 351	1 771	2 970	1 283	1 687
60-64	2 233	915	1 318	2 280	938	1 341	2 768	1 142	1 626	2 850	1 174	1 676
65-69	2 868	1 121	1 747	1 938	738	1 200	1 997	767	1 230	2 444	945	1 499
70-74	1 713	624	1 089	2 345	839	1 506	1 598	558	1 040	1 668	590	1 078
75-79	1 687	526	1 162	1 273	417	856	1 770	569	1 201	1 220	383	837
80-84	842	202	640	1 080	300	781	832	242	590	1 180	335	844
85-89	274	57	216	398	81	316	528	124	404	421	103	318
90-94	107	18	89	79	13	66	124	20	104	175	31	143
95-99	12	2	10	15	2	13	13	1	11	23	2	20
100 +	1	0	0	1	0	1	1	0	1	1	0	1

Age group	2025 Both sexes	Males	Females	2030 Both sexes	Males	Females	2035 Both sexes	Males	Females	2040 Both sexes	Males	Females
All ages	37 335	16 765	20 569	35 052	15 688	19 364	32 805	14 644	18 161	30 617	13 648	16 970
0-4	1 488	766	722	1 316	677	639	1 236	636	600	1 217	627	590
5-9	1 685	866	818	1 471	757	714	1 300	669	631	1 220	628	592
10-14	1 821	936	885	1 665	856	809	1 452	747	705	1 281	659	622
15-19	1 863	955	908	1 788	917	871	1 633	838	795	1 421	729	692
20-24	1 776	901	875	1 790	909	881	1 717	872	845	1 563	794	769
25-29	1 835	915	920	1 658	826	832	1 674	836	838	1 603	800	803
30-34	2 518	1 243	1 275	1 728	849	879	1 556	764	792	1 574	775	799
35-39	3 176	1 544	1 632	2 410	1 177	1 232	1 640	797	843	1 474	716	758
40-44	3 048	1 444	1 604	3 054	1 468	1 586	2 312	1 118	1 194	1 563	752	811
45-49	2 773	1 268	1 505	2 941	1 375	1 566	2 954	1 405	1 549	2 237	1 073	1 164
50-54	2 704	1 224	1 481	2 655	1 190	1 465	2 825	1 299	1 525	2 844	1 333	1 510
55-59	2 412	1 044	1 369	2 552	1 123	1 420	2 514	1 099	1 415	2 684	1 208	1 476
60-64	2 725	1 124	1 601	2 223	922	1 301	2 362	1 001	1 361	2 336	985	1 351
65-69	2 533	981	1 552	2 436	948	1 487	1 995	783	1 212	2 131	858	1 273
70-74	2 059	736	1 324	2 151	772	1 379	2 081	753	1 328	1 715	628	1 087
75-79	1 293	413	880	1 615	522	1 093	1 703	554	1 149	1 661	547	1 115
80-84	824	229	595	892	252	640	1 130	323	807	1 207	348	859
85-89	618	146	471	445	102	343	493	115	379	640	150	489
90-94	147	27	120	227	40	187	172	29	143	198	33	164
95-99	35	4	31	32	4	28	53	6	47	42	4	38
100 +	2	0	2	4	0	3	4	0	3	6	0	6

Age group	2045 Both sexes	Males	Females	2050 Both sexes	Males	Females
All ages	28 481	12 695	15 786	26 393	11 772	14 620
0-4	1 188	612	576	1 120	577	543
5-9	1 201	618	583	1 173	604	569
10-14	1 202	619	583	1 184	609	574
15-19	1 250	641	609	1 171	601	570
20-24	1 352	686	666	1 182	599	583
25-29	1 452	724	729	1 244	617	627
30-34	1 507	742	765	1 362	668	693
35-39	1 495	729	766	1 433	699	734
40-44	1 404	675	729	1 429	691	738
45-49	1 511	721	789	1 359	649	710
50-54	2 155	1 021	1 135	1 455	687	768
55-59	2 710	1 246	1 464	2 057	957	1 100
60-64	2 505	1 091	1 413	2 535	1 131	1 404
65-69	2 117	851	1 266	2 279	950	1 330
70-74	1 843	695	1 148	1 840	694	1 146
75-79	1 379	461	918	1 493	516	977
80-84	1 189	347	842	998	296	702
85-89	697	165	532	700	167	532
90-94	265	45	220	298	51	247
95-99	51	5	46	72	7	65
100 +	6	0	6	7	0	7

POPULATION BY AGE AND SEX (in thousands)

Age group	2005 Both sexes	Males	Females	2010 Both sexes	Males	Females	2015 Both sexes	Males	Females	2020 Both sexes	Males	Females
All ages	46 481	21 310	25 171	44 554	20 313	24 241	42 902	19 491	23 412	41 315	18 732	22 583
0-4	1 924	989	935	2 363	1 215	1 148	2 488	1 279	1 208	2 357	1 212	1 144
5-9	2 088	1 073	1 015	1 905	978	926	2 343	1 204	1 138	2 468	1 269	1 199
10-14	2 895	1 482	1 412	2 067	1 062	1 005	1 883	967	916	2 320	1 192	1 128
15-19	3 694	1 877	1 817	2 857	1 460	1 397	2 032	1 041	991	1 849	947	902
20-24	3 636	1 826	1 811	3 603	1 818	1 786	2 775	1 407	1 368	1 956	993	963
25-29	3 334	1 635	1 699	3 476	1 719	1 758	3 454	1 719	1 735	2 642	1 321	1 321
30-34	3 270	1 606	1 664	3 168	1 525	1 643	3 319	1 617	1 702	3 308	1 626	1 682
35-39	2 986	1 433	1 552	3 109	1 496	1 612	3 018	1 427	1 591	3 177	1 526	1 651
40-44	3 524	1 666	1 858	2 835	1 329	1 506	2 959	1 396	1 564	2 883	1 340	1 544
45-49	3 560	1 654	1 905	3 355	1 546	1 810	2 704	1 239	1 466	2 835	1 312	1 523
50-54	3 298	1 497	1 802	3 355	1 509	1 846	3 175	1 420	1 755	2 568	1 146	1 422
55-59	2 534	1 105	1 429	3 053	1 328	1 724	3 123	1 351	1 771	2 970	1 283	1 687
60-64	2 233	915	1 318	2 280	938	1 341	2 768	1 142	1 626	2 850	1 174	1 676
65-69	2 868	1 121	1 747	1 938	738	1 200	1 997	767	1 230	2 444	945	1 499
70-74	1 713	624	1 089	2 345	839	1 506	1 598	558	1 040	1 668	590	1 078
75-79	1 687	526	1 162	1 273	417	856	1 770	569	1 201	1 220	383	837
80-84	842	202	640	1 080	300	781	832	242	590	1 180	335	844
85-89	274	57	216	398	81	316	528	124	404	421	103	318
90-94	107	18	89	79	13	66	124	20	104	175	31	143
95-99	12	2	10	15	2	13	13	1	11	23	2	20
100 +	1	0	0	1	0	1	1	0	1	1	0	1

Age group	2025 Both sexes	Males	Females	2030 Both sexes	Males	Females	2035 Both sexes	Males	Females	2040 Both sexes	Males	Females
All ages	39 571	17 915	21 656	37 823	17 112	20 710	36 250	16 414	19 836	34 902	15 849	19 053
0-4	2 022	1 040	981	1 856	955	901	1 920	988	931	2 072	1 067	1 005
5-9	2 338	1 202	1 136	2 004	1 031	973	1 839	946	893	1 903	979	923
10-14	2 447	1 258	1 189	2 317	1 192	1 126	1 984	1 021	964	1 820	936	883
15-19	2 286	1 172	1 114	2 413	1 238	1 175	2 284	1 172	1 112	1 952	1 002	950
20-24	1 776	901	875	2 212	1 125	1 086	2 339	1 192	1 148	2 212	1 127	1 085
25-29	1 835	915	920	1 658	826	832	2 092	1 050	1 042	2 220	1 117	1 103
30-34	2 518	1 243	1 275	1 728	849	879	1 556	764	792	1 986	986	1 000
35-39	3 176	1 544	1 632	2 410	1 177	1 232	1 640	797	843	1 474	716	758
40-44	3 048	1 444	1 604	3 054	1 468	1 586	2 312	1 118	1 194	1 563	752	811
45-49	2 773	1 268	1 505	2 941	1 375	1 566	2 954	1 405	1 549	2 237	1 073	1 164
50-54	2 704	1 224	1 481	2 655	1 190	1 465	2 825	1 299	1 525	2 844	1 333	1 510
55-59	2 412	1 044	1 369	2 552	1 123	1 428	2 514	1 099	1 415	2 684	1 208	1 476
60-64	2 725	1 124	1 601	2 223	922	1 301	2 362	1 001	1 361	2 336	985	1 351
65-69	2 533	981	1 552	2 436	948	1 487	1 995	783	1 212	2 131	858	1 273
70-74	2 059	736	1 324	2 151	772	1 379	2 081	753	1 328	1 715	628	1 087
75-79	1 293	413	880	1 615	522	1 093	1 703	554	1 149	1 661	547	1 115
80-84	824	229	595	892	252	640	1 130	323	807	1 207	348	859
85-89	618	146	471	445	102	343	493	115	379	640	150	489
90-94	147	27	120	227	40	187	172	29	143	198	33	164
95-99	35	4	31	32	4	28	53	6	47	42	4	38
100 +	2	0	2	4	0	3	4	0	3	6	0	6

Age group	2045 Both sexes	Males	Females	2050 Both sexes	Males	Females
All ages	33 680	15 366	18 314	32 482	14 901	17 582
0-4	2 126	1 095	1 031	2 040	1 051	989
5-9	2 055	1 058	997	2 109	1 086	1 023
10-14	1 884	970	914	2 037	1 048	988
15-19	1 788	918	870	1 852	951	901
20-24	1 882	958	924	1 719	875	844
25-29	2 097	1 054	1 042	1 771	888	883
30-34	2 116	1 054	1 062	1 999	995	1 004
35-39	1 900	936	964	2 034	1 006	1 027
40-44	1 404	675	729	1 827	893	933
45-49	1 511	721	789	1 359	649	710
50-54	2 155	1 021	1 135	1 455	687	768
55-59	2 710	1 246	1 464	2 057	957	1 100
60-64	2 505	1 091	1 413	2 535	1 131	1 404
65-69	2 117	851	1 266	2 279	950	1 330
70-74	1 843	695	1 148	1 840	694	1 146
75-79	1 379	461	918	1 493	516	977
80-84	1 189	347	842	998	296	702
85-89	697	165	532	700	167	532
90-94	265	45	220	298	51	247
95-99	51	5	46	72	7	65
100 +	6	0	6	7	0	7

United Nations Department of Economic and Social Affairs/Population Division
World Population Prospects: The 2004 Revision, Volume II: Sex and Age Distribution of the World Population

864

POPULATION BY AGE AND SEX (in thousands)

Age group	2005			2010			2015			2020		
	Both sexes	Males	Females	Both sexes	Males	Females	Both sexes	Males	Females	Both sexes	Males	Females
All ages	46 481	21 310	25 171	43 703	19 875	23 827	40 794	18 406	22 387	37 883	16 967	20 916
0-4	1 924	989	935	1 511	777	734	1 228	632	597	1 030	530	500
5-9	2 088	1 073	1 015	1 905	978	926	1 493	768	726	1 211	623	589
10-14	2 895	1 482	1 412	2 067	1 062	1 005	1 883	967	916	1 473	757	716
15-19	3 694	1 877	1 817	2 857	1 460	1 397	2 032	1 041	991	1 849	947	902
20-24	3 636	1 826	1 811	3 603	1 818	1 786	2 775	1 407	1 368	1 956	993	963
25-29	3 334	1 635	1 699	3 476	1 719	1 758	3 454	1 719	1 735	2 642	1 321	1 321
30-34	3 270	1 606	1 664	3 168	1 525	1 643	3 319	1 617	1 702	3 308	1 626	1 682
35-39	2 986	1 433	1 552	3 109	1 496	1 612	3 018	1 427	1 591	3 177	1 526	1 651
40-44	3 524	1 666	1 858	2 835	1 329	1 506	2 959	1 396	1 564	2 883	1 340	1 544
45-49	3 560	1 654	1 905	3 355	1 546	1 810	2 704	1 239	1 466	2 835	1 312	1 523
50-54	3 298	1 497	1 802	3 355	1 509	1 846	3 175	1 420	1 755	2 568	1 146	1 422
55-59	2 534	1 105	1 429	3 053	1 328	1 724	3 123	1 351	1 771	2 970	1 283	1 687
60-64	2 233	915	1 318	2 280	938	1 341	2 768	1 142	1 626	2 850	1 174	1 676
65-69	2 868	1 121	1 747	1 938	738	1 200	1 997	767	1 230	2 444	945	1 499
70-74	1 713	624	1 089	2 345	839	1 506	1 598	558	1 040	1 668	590	1 078
75-79	1 687	526	1 162	1 273	417	856	1 770	569	1 201	1 220	383	837
80-84	842	202	640	1 080	300	781	832	242	590	1 180	335	844
85-89	274	57	216	398	81	316	528	124	404	421	103	318
90-94	107	18	89	79	13	66	124	20	104	175	31	143
95-99	12	2	10	15	2	13	13	1	11	23	2	20
100 +	1	0	0	1	0	1	1	0	1	1	0	1

Age group	2025			2030			2035			2040		
	Both sexes	Males	Females	Both sexes	Males	Females	Both sexes	Males	Females	Both sexes	Males	Females
All ages	35 062	15 597	19 465	32 292	14 270	18 023	29 535	12 963	16 571	26 770	11 671	15 099
0-4	938	482	455	824	424	400	717	369	348	624	321	303
5-9	1 013	521	492	922	474	448	809	416	393	702	361	341
10-14	1 192	613	579	995	512	483	904	465	439	791	407	384
15-19	1 440	738	702	1 161	595	566	964	494	470	873	447	426
20-24	1 776	901	875	1 369	694	676	1 091	551	540	896	451	445
25-29	1 835	915	920	1 658	826	832	1 257	622	635	983	482	500
30-34	2 518	1 243	1 275	1 728	849	879	1 556	764	792	1 164	565	598
35-39	3 176	1 544	1 632	2 410	1 177	1 232	1 640	797	843	1 474	716	758
40-44	3 048	1 444	1 604	3 054	1 468	1 586	2 312	1 118	1 104	1 663	752	811
45-49	2 773	1 268	1 505	2 941	1 375	1 566	2 954	1 405	1 549	2 237	1 073	1 104
50-54	2 704	1 224	1 481	2 655	1 190	1 465	2 825	1 299	1 525	2 844	1 333	1 510
55-59	2 412	1 044	1 369	2 552	1 123	1 428	2 514	1 099	1 415	2 684	1 208	1 476
60-64	2 725	1 124	1 601	2 223	922	1 301	2 362	1 001	1 361	2 336	985	1 351
65-69	2 533	981	1 552	2 436	948	1 487	1 995	783	1 212	2 131	858	1 273
70-74	2 059	736	1 324	2 151	772	1 379	2 081	753	1 328	1 715	628	1 087
75-79	1 293	413	880	1 615	522	1 093	1 703	554	1 149	1 661	547	1 115
80-84	824	229	595	892	252	640	1 130	323	807	1 207	348	859
85-89	618	146	471	445	102	343	493	115	379	640	150	489
90-94	147	27	120	227	40	187	172	29	143	198	33	164
95-99	35	4	31	32	4	28	53	6	47	42	4	38
100 +	2	0	2	4	0	3	4	0	3	6	0	6

Age group	2045			2050		
	Both sexes	Males	Females	Both sexes	Males	Females
All ages	24 003	10 395	13 608	21 290	9 152	12 138
0-4	534	275	259	467	240	226
5-9	609	314	296	520	268	252
10-14	685	352	332	592	305	287
15-19	760	389	371	654	335	319
20-24	805	405	400	694	348	346
25-29	790	384	406	701	339	362
30-34	895	429	466	706	332	374
35-39	1 091	523	568	829	390	439
40-44	1 404	675	729	1 032	488	543
45-49	1 511	721	789	1 359	649	710
50-54	2 155	1 021	1 135	1 455	687	768
55-59	2 710	1 246	1 464	2 057	957	1 100
60-64	2 505	1 091	1 413	2 535	1 131	1 404
65-69	2 117	851	1 266	2 279	950	1 330
70-74	1 843	695	1 148	1 840	694	1 146
75-79	1 379	461	918	1 493	516	977
80-84	1 189	347	842	998	296	702
85-89	697	165	532	700	167	532
90-94	265	45	220	298	51	247
95-99	51	5	46	72	7	65
100 +	6	0	6	7	0	7

United Nations Department of Economic and Social Affairs/Population Division
World Population Prospects: The 2004 Revision, Volume II: Sex and Age Distribution of the World Population

865

POPULATION BY AGE AND SEX (in thousands)

Age group	1950 Both sexes	Males	Females	1955 Both sexes	Males	Females	1960 Both sexes	Males	Females	1965 Both sexes	Males	Females
All ages	70	35	34	79	40	39	90	46	45	144	84	60
0-4	12	6	6	14	7	7	16	8	8	22	11	11
5-9	9	5	5	11	6	5	13	6	6	18	9	9
10-14	8	4	4	9	5	5	11	5	5	15	8	7
15-19	7	4	3	8	4	4	9	5	4	15	9	6
20-24	6	3	3	7	3	3	8	4	4	16	11	5
25-29	5	3	2	6	3	3	7	3	3	15	10	5
30-34	4	2	2	5	2	2	6	3	3	10	7	4
35-39	4	2	2	4	2	2	5	2	2	9	6	3
40-44	3	2	2	4	2	2	4	2	2	6	4	3
45-49	3	1	1	3	2	2	3	2	2	5	3	2
50-54	2	1	1	3	1	1	3	1	1	4	2	2
55-59	2	1	1	2	1	1	2	1	1	3	2	1
60-64	2	1	1	2	1	1	2	1	1	2	1	1
65-69	1	1	1	1	1	1	1	1	1	2	1	1
70-74	1	0	0	1	0	0	1	0	0	1	1	1
75-79	0	0	0	0	0	0	0	0	0	1	0	0
80 +	0	0	0	0	0	0	0	0	0	0	0	0

Age group	1970 Both sexes	Males	Females	1975 Both sexes	Males	Females	1980 Both sexes	Males	Females	1985 Both sexes	Males	Females
All ages	225	141	84	530	367	163	1 015	701	314	1 410	915	495
0-4	33	17	16	64	33	31	135	69	66	180	92	87
5-9	25	13	12	50	26	24	94	49	46	131	67	64
10-14	20	11	9	35	20	16	61	32	29	107	56	51
15-19	20	13	7	39	25	14	56	31	25	76	39	37
20-24	25	18	8	70	55	15	123	89	34	130	79	51
25-29	26	20	6	84	68	16	177	140	37	210	148	62
30-34	20	14	6	57	46	11	134	110	25	188	141	47
35-39	15	11	4	44	35	10	90	73	17	143	110	33
40-44	11	7	4	29	23	6	58	47	11	98	78	20
45-49	9	6	3	19	14	5	35	27	8	64	50	14
50-54	6	3	2	14	10	5	22	16	6	35	26	9
55-59	4	3	2	7	4	2	10	7	3	18	12	6
60-64	4	2	2	8	5	3	8	5	3	11	7	5
65-69	3	2	1	4	2	1	5	3	2	8	4	4
70-74	2	1	1	4	2	2	4	2	2	6	3	3
75-79	1	1	1	2	1	1	1	1	1	3	1	1
80 +	1	0	1	1	1	1	2	1	1	4	2	2

Age group	1990 Both sexes	Males	Females	1995 Both sexes	Males	Females	2000 Both sexes	Males	Females	2005 Both sexes	Males	Females
All ages	1 868	1 222	646	2 435	1 604	831	3 247	2 190	1 057	4 496	3 063	1 433
0-4	238	122	117	247	126	121	270	138	132	337	172	165
5-9	182	93	89	238	121	117	267	136	131	325	166	159
10-14	139	71	67	194	101	94	261	135	127	327	166	161
15-19	133	76	57	167	90	77	216	118	98	349	197	152
20-24	145	96	49	222	142	80	294	192	102	433	290	143
25-29	208	145	63	312	226	86	442	322	120	597	431	166
30-34	255	187	68	313	230	83	439	332	107	668	506	162
35-39	210	160	49	270	204	66	381	291	89	569	445	123
40-44	150	118	33	204	161	43	301	238	62	401	317	84
45-49	92	74	18	124	99	25	176	143	33	244	196	48
50-54	52	40	12	63	51	12	98	78	20	118	94	24
55-59	27	18	8	33	24	9	43	32	11	54	39	15
60-64	15	9	5	18	12	6	25	17	9	26	16	9
65-69	10	5	4	11	7	4	15	9	6	21	13	8
70-74	7	4	3	8	4	4	9	5	4	12	7	5
75-79	4	2	2	5	3	2	7	3	3	7	4	3
80 +	3	1	1	4	2	2	5	2	3	7	3	4

United Nations Department of Economic and Social Affairs/Population Division
World Population Prospects: The 2004 Revision, Volume II: Sex and Age Distribution of the World Population

866

POPULATION BY AGE AND SEX (in thousands)

Age group	2005			2010			2015			2020		
	Both sexes	Males	Females	Both sexes	Males	Females	Both sexes	Males	Females	Both sexes	Males	Females
All ages	4 496	3 063	1 433	5 035	3 380	1 654	5 588	3 703	1 885	6 144	4 025	2 119
0-4	337	172	165	369	189	180	389	199	190	401	205	196
5-9	325	166	159	341	174	167	373	191	182	393	201	192
10-14	327	166	161	328	167	161	344	176	168	376	192	183
15-19	349	197	152	372	204	168	373	205	168	389	214	175
20-24	433	290	143	452	284	168	474	291	183	470	287	183
25-29	597	431	166	548	387	161	566	381	185	579	378	201
30-34	668	506	162	704	522	182	655	479	176	665	464	201
35-39	569	445	123	705	534	171	741	550	191	688	502	185
40-44	401	317	84	525	402	123	661	490	170	698	508	190
45-49	244	196	48	341	262	79	464	347	117	602	437	165
50-54	118	94	24	184	141	43	279	206	73	411	300	111
55-59	54	39	15	74	56	19	139	102	37	244	177	67
60-64	26	16	9	35	25	11	55	41	14	120	88	32
65-69	21	13	8	20	12	8	29	20	9	48	35	12
70-74	12	7	5	19	11	8	18	11	7	26	18	8
75-79	7	4	3	10	6	5	16	9	7	15	9	6
80-84	5	2	2	5	3	3	8	4	4	12	7	6
85-89	2	1	1	3	1	2	3	2	2	5	2	3
90-94	1	0	0	1	0	1	1	0	1	2	1	1
95-99	0	0	0	0	0	0	0	0	0	0	0	0
100 +	0	0	0	0	0	0	0	0	0	0	0	0

Age group	2025			2030			2035			2040		
	Both sexes	Males	Females	Both sexes	Males	Females	Both sexes	Males	Females	Both sexes	Males	Females
All ages	6 693	4 340	2 353	7 225	4 640	2 585	7 734	4 921	2 813	8 213	5 177	3 036
0-4	408	209	199	411	210	200	415	212	202	421	216	206
5-9	406	208	198	412	211	201	415	212	203	419	214	204
10-14	396	203	193	408	209	199	415	212	202	418	214	204
15-19	421	231	191	441	241	200	454	247	206	460	250	210
20-24	486	295	191	518	312	206	538	322	216	551	328	222
25-29	574	374	201	591	383	208	623	399	223	643	409	233
30-34	677	461	216	673	457	216	689	466	224	721	482	239
35-39	698	488	210	710	485	225	706	481	225	723	490	233
40-44	645	461	185	655	446	200	668	443	225	664	440	225
45-49	639	455	184	587	408	179	597	394	204	610	391	219
50-54	548	390	159	586	407	178	534	361	173	545	347	197
55-59	374	269	105	509	357	152	546	375	171	496	330	166
60-64	222	160	62	349	250	99	481	336	145	519	354	165
65-69	110	80	30	207	148	58	328	234	95	456	316	140
70-74	44	32	12	101	72	28	190	135	55	304	214	90
75-79	22	15	7	37	27	11	87	61	26	166	116	51
80-84	12	7	5	17	11	6	29	20	9	69	47	22
85-89	8	4	4	8	4	4	12	7	5	20	13	7
90-94	3	1	2	4	2	2	4	2	2	6	3	3
95-99	1	0	0	1	0	1	2	1	1	2	1	1
100 +	0	0	0	0	0	0	0	0	0	0	0	0

Age group	2045			2050		
	Both sexes	Males	Females	Both sexes	Males	Females
All ages	8 657	5 403	3 255	9 056	5 593	3 463
0-4	435	223	212	447	229	218
5-9	425	218	208	440	225	215
10-14	422	216	206	428	219	209
15-19	463	252	211	467	254	213
20-24	557	332	225	560	333	227
25-29	655	416	239	662	419	242
30-34	741	493	249	754	499	255
35-39	755	506	248	775	517	258
40-44	680	448	232	712	465	248
45-49	606	387	219	623	396	227
50-54	558	345	213	554	341	213
55-59	507	317	191	521	315	206
60-64	471	311	160	482	298	184
65-69	493	334	159	448	294	154
70-74	424	291	133	461	309	152
75-79	268	185	83	377	254	123
80-84	134	90	44	218	146	72
85-89	48	31	17	95	61	35
90-94	11	7	5	28	16	11
95-99	3	1	1	5	2	2
100 +	0	0	0	1	0	0

United Nations Department of Economic and Social Affairs/Population Division
World Population Prospects: The 2004 Revision, Volume II: Sex and Age Distribution of the World Population

867

POPULATION BY AGE AND SEX (in thousands)

Age group	2005 Both sexes	Males	Females	2010 Both sexes	Males	Females	2015 Both sexes	Males	Females	2020 Both sexes	Males	Females
All ages	4 496	3 063	1 433	5 073	3 400	1 673	5 695	3 758	1 937	6 344	4 128	2 216
0-4	337	172	165	408	209	199	458	234	223	494	253	241
5-9	325	166	159	341	174	167	412	211	201	462	236	226
10-14	327	166	161	328	167	161	344	176	168	415	212	202
15-19	349	197	152	372	204	168	373	205	168	389	214	175
20-24	433	290	143	452	284	168	474	291	183	470	287	183
25-29	597	431	166	548	387	161	566	381	185	579	378	201
30-34	668	506	162	704	522	182	655	479	176	665	464	201
35-39	569	445	123	705	534	171	741	550	191	688	502	185
40-44	401	317	84	525	402	123	661	490	170	698	508	190
45-49	244	196	48	341	262	79	464	347	117	602	437	165
50-54	118	94	24	184	141	43	279	206	73	411	300	111
55-59	54	39	15	74	56	19	139	102	37	244	177	67
60-64	26	16	9	35	25	11	55	41	14	120	88	32
65-69	21	13	8	20	12	8	29	20	9	48	35	12
70-74	12	7	5	19	11	8	18	11	7	26	18	8
75-79	7	4	3	10	6	5	16	9	7	15	9	6
80-84	5	2	2	5	3	3	8	4	4	12	7	6
85-89	2	1	1	3	1	2	3	2	2	5	2	3
90-94	1	0	0	1	0	1	1	0	1	2	1	1
95-99	0	0	0	0	0	0	0	0	0	0	0	0
100 +	0	0	0	0	0	0	0	0	0	0	0	0

Age group	2025 Both sexes	Males	Females	2030 Both sexes	Males	Females	2035 Both sexes	Males	Females	2040 Both sexes	Males	Females
All ages	6 992	4 493	2 499	7 634	4 850	2 784	8 274	5 198	3 077	8 914	5 536	3 379
0-4	507	259	247	520	266	254	546	280	267	583	298	285
5-9	498	255	243	511	261	249	525	268	256	550	282	269
10-14	465	238	227	501	257	245	513	263	251	527	270	257
15-19	460	250	209	510	276	234	546	295	252	559	301	258
20-24	486	295	191	557	332	225	607	357	249	643	376	267
25-29	574	374	201	591	383	208	661	419	242	711	445	267
30-34	677	461	216	673	457	216	689	466	224	760	502	258
35-39	698	488	210	710	485	225	706	481	225	723	490	233
40-44	645	461	185	655	446	209	668	443	225	664	440	225
45-49	639	455	184	587	408	179	597	394	204	610	391	219
50-54	548	390	159	586	407	178	534	361	173	545	347	197
55-59	374	269	105	509	357	152	546	375	171	496	330	166
60-64	222	160	62	349	250	99	481	336	145	519	354	165
65-69	110	80	30	207	148	58	328	234	95	456	316	140
70-74	44	32	12	101	72	28	190	135	55	304	214	90
75-79	22	15	7	37	27	11	87	61	26	166	116	51
80-84	12	7	5	17	11	6	29	20	9	69	47	22
85-89	8	4	4	8	4	4	12	7	5	20	13	7
90-94	3	1	2	4	2	2	4	2	2	6	3	3
95-99	1	0	0	1	0	1	2	1	1	2	1	1
100 +	0	0	0	0	0	0	0	0	0	0	0	0

Age group	2045 Both sexes	Males	Females	2050 Both sexes	Males	Females
All ages	9 552	5 860	3 691	10 168	6 162	4 006
0-4	628	322	307	664	340	324
5-9	587	301	287	632	324	309
10-14	553	283	270	590	302	288
15-19	573	308	265	598	321	277
20-24	656	382	273	669	389	280
25-29	748	463	285	760	470	291
30-34	810	528	282	846	546	300
35-39	793	526	267	843	552	291
40-44	680	448	232	751	485	266
45-49	606	387	219	623	396	227
50-54	558	345	213	554	341	213
55-59	507	317	191	521	315	206
60-64	471	311	160	482	298	184
65-69	493	334	159	448	294	154
70-74	424	291	133	461	309	152
75-79	268	185	83	377	254	123
80-84	134	90	44	218	146	72
85-89	48	31	17	95	61	35
90-94	11	7	5	28	16	11
95-99	3	1	1	5	2	2
100 +	0	0	0	1	0	0

United Nations Department of Economic and Social Affairs/Population Division
World Population Prospects: The 2004 Revision, Volume II: Sex and Age Distribution of the World Population

POPULATION BY AGE AND SEX (in thousands)

Age group	2005			2010			2015			2020		
	Both sexes	Males	Females	Both sexes	Males	Females	Both sexes	Males	Females	Both sexes	Males	Females
All ages	4 496	3 063	1 433	4 996	3 360	1 636	5 480	3 648	1 832	5 044	3 023	2 021
0-4	337	172	165	330	169	161	320	164	156	309	158	151
5-9	325	166	159	341	174	167	334	171	163	324	166	158
10-14	327	166	161	328	167	161	344	176	168	337	173	164
15-19	349	197	152	372	204	168	373	205	168	389	214	175
20-24	433	290	143	452	284	168	474	291	183	470	287	183
25-29	597	431	166	548	387	161	566	381	185	579	378	201
30-34	668	506	162	704	522	182	655	479	176	665	464	201
35-39	569	445	123	705	534	171	741	550	191	688	502	185
40-44	401	317	84	525	402	123	661	490	170	698	508	190
45-49	244	196	48	341	262	79	464	347	117	602	437	165
50-54	118	94	24	184	141	43	279	206	73	411	300	111
55-59	54	39	15	74	56	19	139	102	37	244	177	67
60-64	26	16	9	35	25	11	55	41	14	120	88	32
65-69	21	13	8	20	12	8	29	20	9	48	35	12
70-74	12	7	5	19	11	8	18	11	7	26	18	8
75-79	7	4	3	10	6	5	16	9	7	15	9	6
80-84	5	2	2	5	3	3	8	4	4	12	7	6
85-89	2	1	1	3	1	2	3	2	2	5	2	3
90-94	1	0	0	1	0	1	1	0	1	2	1	1
95-99	0	0	0	0	0	0	0	0	0	0	0	0
100 +	0	0	0	0	0	0	0	0	0	0	0	0

Age group	2025			2030			2035			2040		
	Both sexes	Males	Females	Both sexes	Males	Females	Both sexes	Males	Females	Both sexes	Males	Females
All ages	6 394	4 187	2 207	6 819	4 433	2 387	7 207	4 652	2 555	7 545	4 835	2 710
0-4	309	158	151	303	155	148	293	150	143	280	143	137
5-9	313	160	153	313	160	153	308	157	150	297	152	145
10-14	327	168	160	316	162	154	316	162	154	311	159	151
15-19	383	211	172	373	206	167	361	200	161	361	200	161
20-24	486	295	191	479	292	187	469	287	182	458	281	177
25-29	574	374	201	591	383	208	584	379	205	574	374	200
30-34	677	461	216	673	457	216	689	466	224	683	463	220
35-39	698	488	210	710	485	225	706	481	225	723	490	233
40-44	645	461	185	655	446	209	668	443	225	664	440	225
45-49	639	455	184	587	408	179	597	394	204	610	391	219
50-54	548	390	159	586	407	178	534	361	173	545	347	197
55-59	374	269	105	500	357	162	546	375	171	496	330	166
60-64	222	160	62	349	250	99	481	336	145	519	354	165
65-69	110	80	30	207	148	58	328	234	95	456	316	140
70-74	44	32	12	101	72	28	190	135	55	304	214	90
75-79	22	15	7	37	27	11	87	61	26	166	116	51
80-84	12	7	5	17	11	6	29	20	9	69	47	22
85-89	8	4	4	8	4	4	12	7	5	20	13	7
90-94	3	1	2	4	2	2	4	2	2	6	3	3
95-99	1	0	0	1	0	1	2	1	1	2	1	1
100 +	0	0	0	0	0	0	0	0	0	0	0	0

Age group	2045			2050		
	Both sexes	Males	Females	Both sexes	Males	Females
All ages	7 829	4 979	2 850	8 053	5 080	2 974
0-4	275	141	134	271	139	132
5-9	285	146	139	279	143	136
10-14	300	154	146	287	147	140
15-19	356	197	159	346	192	154
20-24	458	281	177	453	279	174
25-29	563	369	194	563	369	194
30-34	673	458	215	662	452	210
35-39	716	487	229	706	482	225
40-44	680	448	232	674	445	229
45-49	606	387	219	623	396	227
50-54	558	345	213	554	341	213
55-59	507	317	191	521	315	206
60-64	471	311	160	482	298	184
65-69	493	334	159	448	294	154
70-74	424	291	133	461	309	152
75-79	268	185	83	377	254	123
80-84	134	90	44	218	146	72
85-89	48	31	17	96	61	35
90-94	11	7	5	28	16	11
95-99	3	1	1	5	2	2
100 +	0	0	0	1	0	0

POPULATION BY AGE AND SEX (in thousands)

Age group	1950 Both sexes	Males	Females	1955 Both sexes	Males	Females	1960 Both sexes	Males	Females	1965 Both sexes	Males	Females
All ages	49 816	24 187	25 629	50 399	24 340	26 059	51 572	24 885	26 687	53 550	25 980	27 570
0-4	4 278	2 190	2 088	3 794	1 944	1 850	4 079	2 087	1 992	4 671	2 391	2 280
5-9	3 554	1 814	1 740	4 221	2 159	2 062	3 734	1 906	1 828	4 040	2 066	1 974
10-14	3 295	1 675	1 620	3 514	1 795	1 720	4 182	2 132	2 051	3 727	1 901	1 826
15-19	3 264	1 649	1 615	3 260	1 643	1 617	3 517	1 784	1 734	4 210	2 147	2 064
20-24	3 511	1 773	1 738	3 243	1 628	1 614	3 341	1 687	1 654	3 615	1 829	1 786
25-29	3 818	1 922	1 896	3 407	1 703	1 704	3 240	1 635	1 606	3 371	1 712	1 659
30-34	3 443	1 727	1 715	3 753	1 865	1 888	3 365	1 678	1 687	3 277	1 676	1 601
35-39	3 830	1 905	1 924	3 332	1 641	1 691	3 702	1 830	1 871	3 366	1 696	1 670
40-44	3 796	1 879	1 917	3 725	1 831	1 894	3 287	1 610	1 676	3 697	1 840	1 857
45-49	3 509	1 705	1 804	3 679	1 811	1 867	3 646	1 782	1 865	3 241	1 592	1 649
50-54	3 092	1 437	1 655	3 413	1 649	1 764	3 551	1 726	1 825	3 542	1 712	1 830
55-59	2 698	1 216	1 481	2 903	1 320	1 583	3 230	1 533	1 697	3 378	1 617	1 761
60-64	2 387	1 061	1 326	2 475	1 078	1 397	2 672	1 177	1 494	2 984	1 380	1 605
65-69	2 024	880	1 145	2 076	874	1 202	2 172	894	1 278	2 339	974	1 366
70-74	1 567	667	900	1 641	665	976	1 694	661	1 033	1 778	680	1 098
75-79	1 016	421	594	1 117	434	683	1 175	434	741	1 229	431	797
80 +	736	266	470	847	299	547	985	330	655	1 085	337	748

Age group	1970 Both sexes	Males	Females	1975 Both sexes	Males	Females	1980 Both sexes	Males	Females	1985 Both sexes	Males	Females
All ages	54 832	26 675	28 157	55 426	27 013	28 413	55 530	27 046	28 484	56 008	27 277	28 731
0-4	4 454	2 284	2 170	3 911	2 013	1 898	3 339	1 715	1 624	3 572	1 830	1 741
5-9	4 644	2 381	2 263	4 449	2 284	2 165	3 862	1 986	1 876	3 362	1 727	1 635
10-14	4 198	2 157	2 042	4 575	2 347	2 228	4 402	2 259	2 144	3 846	1 976	1 870
15-19	3 837	1 968	1 869	4 100	2 105	1 995	4 531	2 315	2 216	4 491	2 303	2 188
20-24	4 223	2 140	2 083	3 836	1 960	1 875	4 067	2 076	1 991	4 696	2 386	2 310
25-29	3 660	1 856	1 804	4 150	2 104	2 047	3 772	1 916	1 855	4 059	2 051	2 008
30-34	3 216	1 635	1 581	3 438	1 746	1 692	4 121	2 065	2 056	3 729	1 879	1 850
35-39	3 120	1 576	1 544	3 218	1 635	1 583	3 413	1 722	1 691	4 100	2 053	2 047
40-44	3 266	1 631	1 636	3 125	1 575	1 550	3 196	1 621	1 575	3 387	1 704	1 683
45-49	3 459	1 710	1 749	3 256	1 619	1 637	3 084	1 553	1 531	3 137	1 572	1 565
50-54	3 230	1 573	1 656	3 497	1 716	1 780	3 180	1 572	1 608	3 008	1 498	1 510
55-59	3 295	1 584	1 711	2 996	1 438	1 558	3 376	1 638	1 739	3 046	1 490	1 556
60-64	3 135	1 466	1 669	3 143	1 472	1 672	2 817	1 326	1 492	3 112	1 478	1 634
65-69	2 650	1 168	1 481	2 800	1 248	1 552	2 789	1 253	1 536	2 513	1 137	1 375
70-74	1 961	755	1 206	2 188	889	1 299	2 372	992	1 379	2 374	1 005	1 370
75-79	1 263	435	828	1 430	491	940	1 679	620	1 059	1 806	684	1 122
80 +	1 221	357	864	1 314	371	943	1 531	419	1 112	1 772	505	1 267

Age group	1990 Both sexes	Males	Females	1995 Both sexes	Males	Females	2000 Both sexes	Males	Females	2005 Both sexes	Males	Females
All ages	56 761	27 318	29 443	57 670	27 900	29 771	58 670	28 513	30 156	59 668	29 153	30 515
0-4	3 830	1 974	1 856	3 743	1 915	1 828	3 545	1 816	1 729	3 367	1 725	1 642
5-9	3 535	1 773	1 762	3 794	1 956	1 838	3 757	1 924	1 833	3 554	1 820	1 734
10-14	3 447	1 732	1 715	3 555	1 778	1 777	3 884	1 992	1 892	3 778	1 935	1 842
15-19	3 710	1 861	1 849	3 481	1 762	1 719	3 612	1 837	1 775	4 023	2 069	1 954
20-24	4 262	2 061	2 201	3 740	1 865	1 876	3 524	1 753	1 770	3 804	1 938	1 866
25-29	4 415	2 129	2 286	4 350	2 083	2 267	3 903	1 913	1 990	3 683	1 853	1 830
30-34	4 043	1 963	2 080	4 556	2 208	2 348	4 572	2 229	2 342	3 962	1 952	2 010
35-39	3 796	1 846	1 950	4 130	2 027	2 104	4 623	2 275	2 348	4 585	2 238	2 347
40-44	4 117	2 066	2 051	3 797	1 865	1 933	4 072	2 016	2 055	4 613	2 270	2 344
45-49	3 489	1 756	1 733	4 047	2 043	2 003	3 690	1 826	1 864	4 033	1 997	2 036
50-54	3 131	1 571	1 560	3 476	1 738	1 738	4 099	2 039	2 060	3 638	1 794	1 844
55-59	2 984	1 481	1 503	2 990	1 484	1 506	3 247	1 607	1 640	3 998	1 975	2 023
60-64	2 953	1 422	1 531	2 811	1 373	1 438	2 836	1 389	1 447	3 105	1 519	1 586
65-69	2 824	1 323	1 501	2 702	1 269	1 433	2 592	1 238	1 353	2 642	1 274	1 368
70-74	2 275	994	1 281	2 442	1 097	1 345	2 351	1 061	1 290	2 298	1 064	1 234
75-79	1 859	731	1 128	1 813	732	1 080	1 973	820	1 153	1 936	829	1 107
80 +	2 092	636	1 456	2 242	703	1 538	2 390	777	1 613	2 649	901	1 748

United Nations Department of Economic and Social Affairs/Population Division
World Population Prospects: The 2004 Revision, Volume II: Sex and Age Distribution of the World Population

POPULATION BY AGE AND SEX (in thousands)

Age group	2005 Both sexes	2005 Males	2005 Females	2010 Both sexes	2010 Males	2010 Females	2015 Both sexes	2015 Males	2015 Females	2020 Both sexes	2020 Males	2020 Females
All ages	59 668	29 153	30 515	60 418	29 618	30 800	61 417	30 397	31 020	62 491	30 645	31 846
0-4	3 367	1 725	1 642	3 278	1 678	1 599	3 364	1 723	1 641	3 591	1 839	1 752
5-9	3 554	1 820	1 734	3 386	1 727	1 658	3 296	1 681	1 616	3 382	1 725	1 658
10-14	3 778	1 935	1 842	3 577	1 832	1 744	3 409	1 740	1 669	3 320	1 693	1 627
15-19	4 023	2 069	1 954	3 908	1 992	1 917	3 708	1 889	1 819	3 541	1 797	1 744
20-24	3 804	1 938	1 866	4 202	2 140	2 062	4 089	2 064	2 025	3 890	1 963	1 927
25-29	3 683	1 853	1 830	3 949	2 013	1 936	4 348	2 216	2 131	4 236	2 141	2 095
30-34	3 962	1 952	2 010	3 734	1 879	1 855	4 001	2 040	1 961	4 400	2 243	2 157
35-39	4 585	2 238	2 347	3 977	1 959	2 018	3 751	1 886	1 864	4 018	2 047	1 970
40-44	4 613	2 270	2 344	4 578	2 233	2 345	3 975	1 956	2 019	3 751	1 885	1 866
45-49	4 033	1 997	2 036	4 573	2 249	2 323	4 541	2 214	2 326	3 944	1 942	2 003
50-54	3 638	1 794	1 844	3 981	1 965	2 017	4 518	2 215	2 302	4 490	2 184	2 307
55-59	3 998	1 975	2 023	3 556	1 742	1 814	3 898	1 912	1 986	4 429	2 160	2 269
60-64	3 105	1 519	1 586	3 838	1 878	1 960	3 421	1 660	1 761	3 759	1 828	1 931
65-69	2 642	1 274	1 368	2 904	1 400	1 505	3 604	1 737	1 866	3 225	1 544	1 681
70-74	2 298	1 064	1 234	2 359	1 104	1 255	2 609	1 223	1 387	3 257	1 529	1 728
75-79	1 936	829	1 107	1 910	840	1 069	1 978	882	1 096	2 209	989	1 220
80-84	1 437	548	889	1 432	566	866	1 432	585	848	1 504	625	879
85-89	776	249	526	885	299	587	901	317	584	920	337	582
90-94	332	84	248	366	99	267	431	123	307	451	136	315
95-99	91	17	74	107	21	86	123	26	97	150	34	115
100 +	13	2	11	17	2	15	22	3	19	26	4	22

Age group	2025 Both sexes	2025 Males	2025 Females	2030 Both sexes	2030 Males	2030 Females	2035 Both sexes	2035 Males	2035 Females	2040 Both sexes	2040 Males	2040 Females
All ages	63 663	31 233	32 430	64 693	31 742	32 951	65 471	32 129	33 342	66 060	32 433	33 627
0-4	3 772	1 932	1 840	3 752	1 922	1 830	3 643	1 866	1 776	3 587	1 838	1 749
5-9	3 610	1 841	1 768	3 791	1 935	1 857	3 771	1 925	1 847	3 662	1 869	1 793
10-14	3 406	1 738	1 669	3 633	1 854	1 779	3 815	1 948	1 868	3 795	1 938	1 858
15-19	3 452	1 751	1 701	3 538	1 795	1 743	3 766	1 912	1 854	3 948	2 005	1 942
20-24	3 723	1 871	1 852	3 635	1 825	1 810	3 722	1 870	1 852	3 950	1 987	1 963
25-29	4 038	2 040	1 997	3 872	1 949	1 923	3 785	1 904	1 881	3 872	1 949	1 923
30-34	4 289	2 169	2 120	4 092	2 069	2 023	3 927	1 978	1 949	3 840	1 933	1 907
35-39	4 416	2 251	2 166	4 307	2 177	2 130	4 111	2 078	2 033	3 948	1 989	1 959
40-44	4 018	2 046	1 972	4 417	2 250	2 168	4 309	2 177	2 132	4 116	2 079	2 036
45-49	3 724	1 872	1 852	3 991	2 033	1 958	4 390	2 237	2 153	4 284	2 166	2 118
50-54	3 904	1 917	1 987	3 689	1 850	1 839	3 956	2 011	1 945	4 354	2 214	2 140
55-59	4 409	2 132	2 276	3 837	1 874	1 963	3 630	1 812	1 818	3 897	1 972	1 925
60-64	4 281	2 071	2 210	4 269	2 050	2 220	3 722	1 805	1 917	3 525	1 748	1 777
65-69	3 555	1 707	1 848	4 062	1 941	2 120	4 063	1 928	2 134	3 551	1 705	1 846
70-74	2 931	1 369	1 562	3 247	1 523	1 724	3 728	1 742	1 986	3 746	1 741	2 006
75-79	2 779	1 250	1 529	2 522	1 130	1 392	2 814	1 269	1 545	3 254	1 466	1 789
80-84	1 792	712	1 080	2 167	914	1 253	1 990	838	1 152	2 245	955	1 290
85-89	985	370	616	1 135	431	705	1 472	565	907	1 376	530	846
90-94	473	149	323	520	169	351	615	203	412	817	275	542
95-99	162	39	123	176	45	131	200	53	147	244	66	177
100 +	33	5	28	38	6	31	43	8	35	50	10	40

Age group	2045 Both sexes	2045 Males	2045 Females	2050 Both sexes	2050 Males	2050 Females
All ages	66 580	32 718	33 863	67 143	33 037	34 106
0-4	3 628	1 859	1 769	3 744	1 918	1 825
5-9	3 606	1 840	1 766	3 647	1 861	1 786
10-14	3 686	1 882	1 804	3 631	1 853	1 777
15-19	3 928	1 995	1 932	3 819	1 940	1 879
20-24	4 132	2 081	2 051	4 112	2 071	2 041
25-29	4 100	2 066	2 034	4 282	2 160	2 122
30-34	3 928	1 979	1 949	4 156	2 096	2 060
35-39	3 862	1 944	1 918	3 950	1 990	1 960
40-44	3 953	1 991	1 963	3 869	1 947	1 922
45-49	4 093	2 069	2 024	3 933	1 982	1 951
50-54	4 252	2 145	2 107	4 064	2 051	2 013
55-59	4 292	2 174	2 119	4 196	2 109	2 087
60-64	3 791	1 907	1 883	4 183	2 107	2 076
65-69	3 371	1 657	1 715	3 633	1 813	1 820
70-74	3 288	1 547	1 740	3 133	1 512	1 621
75-79	3 293	1 477	1 816	2 908	1 324	1 583
80-84	2 624	1 118	1 506	2 682	1 141	1 541
85-89	1 577	616	961	1 872	735	1 137
90-94	782	265	516	916	317	599
95-99	333	93	240	329	93	236
100 +	62	12	50	87	18	69

UNITED KINGDOM

HIGH VARIANT

POPULATION BY AGE AND SEX (in thousands)

Age group	2005 Both sexes	2005 Males	2005 Females	2010 Both sexes	2010 Males	2010 Females	2015 Both sexes	2015 Males	2015 Females	2020 Both sexes	2020 Males	2020 Females
All ages	59 668	29 153	30 515	60 999	29 865	31 134	62 690	30 746	31 944	64 782	31 819	32 963
0-4	3 367	1 725	1 642	3 760	1 925	1 834	4 155	2 128	2 027	4 610	2 361	2 248
5-9	3 554	1 820	1 734	3 386	1 727	1 658	3 778	1 927	1 851	4 173	2 130	2 043
10-14	3 778	1 935	1 842	3 577	1 832	1 744	3 409	1 740	1 669	3 801	1 940	1 862
15-19	4 023	2 069	1 954	3 908	1 992	1 917	3 708	1 889	1 819	3 541	1 797	1 744
20-24	3 804	1 938	1 866	4 202	2 140	2 062	4 089	2 064	2 025	3 890	1 963	1 927
25-29	3 683	1 853	1 830	3 949	2 013	1 936	4 348	2 216	2 131	4 236	2 141	2 095
30-34	3 962	1 952	2 010	3 734	1 879	1 855	4 001	2 040	1 961	4 400	2 243	2 157
35-39	4 585	2 238	2 347	3 977	1 959	2 018	3 751	1 886	1 864	4 018	2 047	1 970
40-44	4 613	2 270	2 344	4 578	2 233	2 345	3 975	1 956	2 019	3 751	1 885	1 866
45-49	4 033	1 997	2 036	4 573	2 249	2 323	4 541	2 214	2 326	3 944	1 942	2 003
50-54	3 638	1 794	1 844	3 981	1 965	2 017	4 518	2 215	2 302	4 490	2 184	2 307
55-59	3 998	1 975	2 023	3 556	1 742	1 814	3 898	1 912	1 986	4 429	2 160	2 269
60-64	3 105	1 519	1 586	3 838	1 878	1 960	3 421	1 660	1 761	3 759	1 828	1 931
65-69	2 642	1 274	1 368	2 904	1 400	1 505	3 604	1 737	1 866	3 225	1 544	1 681
70-74	2 298	1 064	1 234	2 359	1 104	1 255	2 609	1 223	1 387	3 257	1 529	1 728
75-79	1 936	829	1 107	1 910	840	1 069	1 978	882	1 096	2 209	989	1 220
80-84	1 437	548	889	1 432	566	866	1 432	585	848	1 504	625	879
85-89	776	249	526	885	299	587	901	317	584	920	337	582
90-94	332	84	248	366	99	267	431	123	307	451	136	315
95-99	91	17	74	107	21	86	123	26	97	150	34	115
100 +	13	2	11	17	2	15	22	3	19	26	4	22

Age group	2025 Both sexes	2025 Males	2025 Females	2030 Both sexes	2030 Males	2030 Females	2035 Both sexes	2035 Males	2035 Females	2040 Both sexes	2040 Males	2040 Females
All ages	66 966	32 925	34 041	69 003	33 950	35 052	70 922	34 922	36 000	72 958	35 967	36 991
0-4	4 786	2 452	2 334	4 760	2 439	2 321	4 786	2 452	2 334	5 039	2 582	2 457
5-9	4 628	2 363	2 265	4 804	2 454	2 351	4 778	2 441	2 338	4 805	2 455	2 350
10-14	4 197	2 143	2 054	4 651	2 376	2 276	4 828	2 466	2 361	4 802	2 454	2 349
15-19	3 933	1 997	1 936	4 328	2 200	2 129	4 783	2 433	2 350	4 960	2 524	2 436
20-24	3 723	1 871	1 852	4 116	2 071	2 045	4 511	2 274	2 237	4 966	2 508	2 458
25-29	4 038	2 040	1 997	3 872	1 949	1 923	4 265	2 150	2 115	4 660	2 353	2 308
30-34	4 289	2 169	2 120	4 092	2 069	2 023	3 927	1 978	1 949	4 320	2 179	2 141
35-39	4 416	2 251	2 166	4 307	2 177	2 130	4 111	2 078	2 033	3 948	1 989	1 959
40-44	4 018	2 046	1 972	4 417	2 250	2 168	4 309	2 177	2 132	4 116	2 079	2 036
45-49	3 724	1 872	1 852	3 991	2 033	1 958	4 390	2 237	2 153	4 284	2 166	2 118
50-54	3 904	1 917	1 987	3 689	1 850	1 839	3 956	2 011	1 945	4 354	2 214	2 140
55-59	4 409	2 132	2 276	3 837	1 874	1 963	3 630	1 812	1 818	3 897	1 972	1 925
60-64	4 281	2 071	2 210	4 269	2 050	2 220	3 722	1 805	1 917	3 525	1 748	1 777
65-69	3 555	1 707	1 848	4 062	1 941	2 120	4 063	1 928	2 134	3 551	1 705	1 846
70-74	2 931	1 369	1 562	3 247	1 523	1 724	3 728	1 742	1 986	3 746	1 741	2 006
75-79	2 779	1 250	1 529	2 522	1 130	1 392	2 814	1 269	1 545	3 254	1 466	1 789
80-84	1 702	712	989	2 167	914	1 253	1 990	838	1 152	2 245	955	1 290
85-89	985	370	616	1 135	431	705	1 472	565	907	1 376	530	846
90-94	473	149	323	520	169	351	615	203	412	817	275	542
95-99	162	39	123	176	45	131	200	53	147	244	66	177
100 +	33	5	28	38	6	31	43	8	35	50	10	40

Age group	2045 Both sexes	2045 Males	2045 Females	2050 Both sexes	2050 Males	2050 Females
All ages	75 284	37 178	38 107	77 910	38 554	39 356
0-4	5 438	2 787	2 651	5 812	2 979	2 834
5-9	5 058	2 584	2 473	5 457	2 789	2 668
10-14	4 829	2 467	2 361	5 081	2 597	2 484
15-19	4 934	2 511	2 423	4 961	2 525	2 436
20-24	5 143	2 599	2 544	5 118	2 586	2 532
25-29	5 115	2 586	2 529	5 293	2 678	2 615
30-34	4 715	2 382	2 334	5 170	2 615	2 555
35-39	4 340	2 189	2 151	4 736	2 392	2 344
40-44	3 953	1 991	1 963	4 346	2 191	2 155
45-49	4 093	2 069	2 024	3 933	1 982	1 951
50-54	4 252	2 145	2 107	4 064	2 051	2 013
55-59	4 292	2 174	2 119	4 196	2 109	2 087
60-64	3 791	1 907	1 883	4 183	2 107	2 076
65-69	3 371	1 657	1 715	3 633	1 813	1 820
70-74	3 288	1 547	1 740	3 133	1 512	1 621
75-79	3 293	1 477	1 816	2 908	1 324	1 583
80-84	2 624	1 118	1 506	2 682	1 141	1 541
85-89	1 577	616	961	1 872	735	1 137
90-94	782	265	516	916	317	599
95-99	333	93	240	329	93	236
100 +	62	12	50	87	18	69

872

United Nations Department of Economic and Social Affairs/Population Division
World Population Prospects: The 2004 Revision, Volume II: Sex and Age Distribution of the World Population

POPULATION BY AGE AND SEX (in thousands)

Age group	2005 Both sexes	Males	Females	2010 Both sexes	Males	Females	2015 Both sexes	Males	Females	2020 Both sexes	Males	Females
All ages	59 668	29 153	30 515	60 034	29 371	30 663	60 146	29 443	30 703	60 205	29 474	30 731
0-4	3 367	1 725	1 642	2 795	1 431	1 364	2 575	1 319	1 257	2 575	1 318	1 256
5-9	3 554	1 820	1 734	3 386	1 727	1 658	2 814	1 433	1 380	2 595	1 321	1 274
10-14	3 778	1 935	1 842	3 577	1 832	1 744	3 409	1 740	1 669	2 838	1 446	1 391
15-19	4 023	2 069	1 954	3 908	1 992	1 917	3 708	1 889	1 819	3 541	1 797	1 744
20-24	3 804	1 938	1 866	4 202	2 140	2 062	4 089	2 064	2 025	3 890	1 963	1 927
25-29	3 683	1 853	1 830	3 949	2 013	1 936	4 348	2 216	2 131	4 236	2 141	2 095
30-34	3 962	1 952	2 010	3 734	1 879	1 855	4 001	2 040	1 961	4 400	2 243	2 157
35-39	4 585	2 238	2 347	3 977	1 959	2 018	3 751	1 886	1 864	4 018	2 047	1 970
40-44	4 613	2 270	2 344	4 578	2 233	2 345	3 975	1 956	2 019	3 751	1 885	1 866
45-49	4 033	1 997	2 036	4 573	2 249	2 323	4 541	2 214	2 326	3 944	1 942	2 003
50-54	3 638	1 794	1 844	3 981	1 965	2 017	4 518	2 215	2 302	4 490	2 184	2 307
55-59	3 998	1 975	2 023	3 556	1 742	1 814	3 898	1 912	1 986	4 429	2 160	2 269
60-64	3 105	1 519	1 586	3 838	1 878	1 960	3 421	1 660	1 761	3 759	1 828	1 931
65-69	2 642	1 274	1 368	2 904	1 400	1 505	3 604	1 737	1 866	3 225	1 544	1 681
70-74	2 298	1 064	1 234	2 359	1 104	1 255	2 609	1 223	1 387	3 257	1 529	1 728
75-79	1 936	829	1 107	1 910	840	1 069	1 978	882	1 096	2 209	989	1 220
80-84	1 437	548	889	1 432	566	866	1 432	585	848	1 504	625	879
85-89	776	249	526	885	299	587	901	317	584	920	337	582
90-94	332	84	248	366	99	267	431	123	307	451	136	315
95-99	91	17	74	107	21	86	123	26	97	150	34	115
100 +	13	2	11	17	2	15	22	3	19	26	4	22

Age group	2025 Both sexes	Males	Females	2030 Both sexes	Males	Females	2035 Both sexes	Males	Females	2040 Both sexes	Males	Females
All ages	60 358	29 539	30 818	60 391	29 538	30 853	60 142	29 399	30 744	59 567	29 106	30 461
0-4	2 752	1 409	1 342	2 754	1 410	1 343	2 613	1 338	1 275	2 420	1 240	1 180
5-9	2 594	1 321	1 273	2 771	1 412	1 359	2 773	1 413	1 360	2 633	1 341	1 292
10-14	2 619	1 334	1 285	2 618	1 334	1 284	2 795	1 425	1 370	2 797	1 426	1 371
15-19	2 970	1 504	1 466	2 751	1 392	1 359	2 751	1 392	1 359	2 928	1 483	1 445
20-24	3 723	1 871	1 852	3 154	1 579	1 575	2 936	1 468	1 468	2 936	1 468	1 468
25-29	4 038	2 040	1 997	3 872	1 949	1 923	3 304	1 658	1 646	3 087	1 547	1 540
30-34	4 289	2 169	2 120	4 092	2 069	2 023	3 927	1 978	1 949	3 360	1 688	1 673
35-39	4 416	2 251	2 166	4 307	2 177	2 130	4 111	2 078	2 033	3 948	1 989	1 959
40-44	4 018	2 046	1 972	4 417	2 250	2 168	4 309	2 177	2 132	4 116	2 079	2 036
45-49	3 724	1 872	1 852	3 001	2 033	1 958	4 390	2 237	2 150	4 204	2 106	2 118
50-54	3 904	1 917	1 987	3 689	1 850	1 839	3 956	2 011	1 945	4 354	2 214	2 140
55-59	4 409	2 132	2 276	3 837	1 874	1 963	3 630	1 812	1 818	3 897	1 972	1 925
60-64	4 281	2 071	2 210	4 268	2 050	2 220	3 722	1 805	1 917	3 525	1 748	1 777
65-69	3 555	1 707	1 848	4 062	1 941	2 120	4 063	1 928	2 134	3 551	1 705	1 846
70-74	2 931	1 369	1 562	3 247	1 523	1 724	3 728	1 742	1 986	3 746	1 741	2 006
75-79	2 779	1 250	1 529	2 522	1 130	1 392	2 814	1 269	1 545	3 254	1 466	1 789
80-84	1 702	712	989	2 167	914	1 253	1 990	838	1 152	2 245	955	1 290
85-89	985	370	616	1 135	431	705	1 472	565	907	1 376	530	846
90-94	473	149	323	520	169	351	615	203	412	817	275	542
95-99	162	39	123	176	45	131	200	53	147	244	66	177
100 +	33	5	28	38	6	31	43	8	35	50	10	40

Age group	2045 Both sexes	Males	Females	2050 Both sexes	Males	Females
All ages	58 713	28 687	30 026	57 711	28 204	29 506
0-4	2 248	1 152	1 097	2 172	1 112	1 059
5-9	2 440	1 242	1 197	2 269	1 155	1 114
10-14	2 657	1 354	1 303	2 464	1 256	1 209
15-19	2 930	1 484	1 446	2 790	1 412	1 378
20-24	3 113	1 559	1 554	3 116	1 560	1 555
25-29	3 087	1 547	1 540	3 264	1 639	1 626
30-34	3 144	1 577	1 567	3 144	1 578	1 566
35-39	3 382	1 699	1 684	3 167	1 589	1 578
40-44	3 953	1 991	1 963	3 390	1 702	1 688
45-49	4 093	2 069	2 024	3 933	1 982	1 951
50-54	4 252	2 145	2 107	4 064	2 051	2 013
55-59	4 292	2 174	2 119	4 196	2 109	2 087
60-64	3 791	1 907	1 883	4 183	2 107	2 076
65-69	3 371	1 657	1 715	3 633	1 813	1 820
70-74	3 288	1 547	1 740	3 133	1 512	1 621
75-79	3 293	1 477	1 816	2 908	1 324	1 583
80-84	2 624	1 118	1 506	2 682	1 141	1 541
85-89	1 577	616	961	1 872	735	1 137
90-94	782	265	516	916	317	599
95-99	333	93	240	329	93	236
100 +	62	12	50	87	18	69

POPULATION BY AGE AND SEX (in thousands)

Age group	1950 Both sexes	Males	Females	1955 Both sexes	Males	Females	1960 Both sexes	Males	Females	1965 Both sexes	Males	Females
All ages	7 650	3 731	3 918	8 708	4 259	4 449	10 013	4 909	5 105	11 628	5 713	5 916
0-4	1 461	722	739	1 592	796	796	1 864	933	931	2 181	1 092	1 088
5-9	1 118	550	568	1 310	646	664	1 443	720	723	1 711	854	856
10-14	937	461	476	1 071	527	544	1 262	622	640	1 401	699	702
15-19	797	392	405	909	447	462	1 043	513	529	1 235	609	626
20-24	674	331	343	768	377	391	879	432	448	1 015	498	517
25-29	565	276	289	645	315	330	739	361	378	851	416	435
30-34	472	229	242	538	262	276	618	301	317	712	347	365
35-39	390	190	201	447	217	230	513	249	264	593	288	305
40-44	320	155	165	367	178	189	422	205	218	489	237	252
45-49	260	125	135	298	143	155	344	165	178	399	192	207
50-54	207	98	109	239	113	125	276	131	145	321	152	168
55-59	161	75	86	186	87	99	215	101	115	251	118	134
60-64	120	54	65	139	63	75	161	74	87	189	87	102
65-69	82	37	45	96	43	53	112	50	62	133	60	73
70-74	50	22	28	59	26	33	70	30	39	83	36	47
75-79	25	10	14	30	13	17	36	15	21	43	18	25
80 +	12	4	7	14	5	9	17	7	10	21	8	13

Age group	1970 Both sexes	Males	Females	1975 Both sexes	Males	Females	1980 Both sexes	Males	Females	1985 Both sexes	Males	Females
All ages	13 594	6 691	6 902	16 044	7 911	8 132	18 858	9 315	9 543	22 268	11 015	11 253
0-4	2 556	1 282	1 274	2 998	1 504	1 493	3 516	1 766	1 750	4 086	2 054	2 032
5-9	2 022	1 011	1 011	2 406	1 204	1 202	2 823	1 414	1 410	3 347	1 677	1 670
10-14	1 670	834	836	1 994	996	998	2 363	1 182	1 182	2 796	1 399	1 397
15-19	1 377	686	690	1 655	826	829	1 965	981	983	2 343	1 171	1 172
20-24	1 207	594	613	1 357	675	682	1 621	808	814	1 937	966	971
25-29	987	483	504	1 184	581	603	1 324	658	667	1 593	792	801
30-34	825	403	422	966	472	494	1 154	565	589	1 300	644	656
35-39	688	335	353	805	392	413	938	457	481	1 129	552	578
40-44	569	276	293	667	323	344	778	377	400	914	444	471
45-49	465	224	241	548	264	284	640	308	332	753	363	390
50-54	375	178	197	443	211	232	519	248	272	613	292	321
55-59	295	138	157	350	164	186	412	193	218	489	230	259
60-64	223	102	121	266	122	143	315	145	170	375	173	202
65-69	158	71	87	189	85	104	226	102	124	272	122	150
70-74	100	44	56	121	53	68	146	64	82	176	77	99
75-79	53	22	30	65	27	37	79	33	46	95	40	56
80 +	25	10	16	31	12	19	38	15	23	48	19	29

Age group	1990 Both sexes	Males	Females	1995 Both sexes	Males	Females	2000 Both sexes	Males	Females	2005 Both sexes	Males	Females
All ages	26 231	12 986	13 246	30 930	15 314	15 616	34 763	17 238	17 525	38 329	19 071	19 258
0-4	4 744	2 386	2 358	5 324	2 679	2 644	5 734	2 887	2 847	6 045	3 044	3 001
5-9	3 904	1 958	1 946	4 621	2 319	2 302	5 030	2 526	2 504	5 389	2 708	2 681
10-14	3 321	1 663	1 658	3 948	1 979	1 969	4 541	2 278	2 263	4 893	2 456	2 437
15-19	2 777	1 389	1 388	3 359	1 681	1 678	3 889	1 948	1 941	4 458	2 235	2 223
20-24	2 310	1 152	1 158	2 774	1 385	1 388	3 269	1 635	1 634	3 779	1 892	1 887
25-29	1 898	943	955	2 260	1 125	1 135	2 585	1 296	1 289	3 065	1 540	1 524
30-34	1 559	772	787	1 844	912	932	2 040	1 021	1 019	2 296	1 171	1 126
35-39	1 270	627	643	1 518	746	771	1 666	824	842	1 779	903	876
40-44	1 100	535	566	1 240	607	633	1 388	678	710	1 472	731	741
45-49	886	427	459	1 074	516	558	1 147	555	592	1 249	608	642
50-54	723	345	378	861	409	451	998	473	525	1 045	500	545
55-59	578	272	306	692	325	367	795	371	423	910	424	486
60-64	447	206	241	539	248	291	625	287	338	711	325	386
65-69	326	147	179	396	178	218	465	209	256	537	240	297
70-74	214	93	121	263	114	148	314	136	177	367	159	208
75-79	116	49	68	145	61	85	177	74	103	211	88	123
80 +	58	23	36	73	29	45	99	39	61	124	48	76

United Nations Department of Economic and Social Affairs/Population Division
World Population Prospects: The 2004 Revision, Volume II: Sex and Age Distribution of the World Population

874

POPULATION BY AGE AND SEX (in thousands)

Age group	2005 Both sexes	2005 Males	2005 Females	2010 Both sexes	2010 Males	2010 Females	2015 Both sexes	2015 Males	2015 Females	2020 Both sexes	2020 Males	2020 Females
All ages	38 020	10 071	19 950	41 838	20 881	20 957	45 598	22 820	22 777	49 265	24 722	24 543
0-4	6 045	3 044	3 001	6 156	3 101	3 056	6 262	3 156	3 106	6 275	3 164	3 111
5-9	5 389	2 708	2 681	5 697	2 863	2 834	5 875	2 953	2 922	6 029	3 032	2 997
10-14	4 893	2 456	2 437	5 237	2 630	2 607	5 585	2 805	2 780	5 776	2 902	2 875
15-19	4 458	2 235	2 223	4 806	2 411	2 395	5 184	2 602	2 582	5 535	2 778	2 757
20-24	3 779	1 892	1 887	4 340	2 174	2 166	4 723	2 367	2 356	5 105	2 560	2 545
25-29	3 065	1 540	1 524	3 563	1 791	1 772	4 135	2 081	2 055	4 526	2 278	2 248
30-34	2 296	1 171	1 126	2 772	1 413	1 359	3 264	1 663	1 601	3 814	1 945	1 870
35-39	1 779	903	876	2 025	1 049	976	2 492	1 289	1 204	2 951	1 526	1 425
40-44	1 472	731	741	1 577	807	770	1 827	954	873	2 260	1 179	1 081
45-49	1 249	608	642	1 325	657	668	1 441	737	704	1 677	876	801
50-54	1 045	500	545	1 138	549	590	1 223	601	622	1 334	677	657
55-59	910	424	486	952	448	504	1 049	498	551	1 131	548	583
60-64	711	325	386	815	372	444	863	398	465	956	445	511
65-69	537	240	297	612	272	340	710	315	395	757	340	417
70-74	367	159	208	424	183	241	491	211	279	575	247	328
75-79	211	88	123	248	103	145	292	121	171	343	141	201
80-84	92	37	56	110	44	67	132	52	80	159	62	97
85-89	27	10	17	33	12	21	41	15	26	50	18	32
90-94	4	1	3	6	2	4	7	2	5	9	3	6
95-99	0	0	0	1	0	0	1	0	1	1	0	1
100 +	0	0	0	0	0	0	0	0	0	0	0	0

Age group	2025 Both sexes	2025 Males	2025 Females	2030 Both sexes	2030 Males	2030 Females	2035 Both sexes	2035 Males	2035 Females	2040 Both sexes	2040 Males	2040 Females
All ages	52 807	26 561	26 245	56 178	28 312	27 866	59 314	29 938	29 376	62 170	31 410	30 759
0-4	6 217	3 136	3 081	6 097	3 076	3 021	5 916	2 985	2 931	5 690	2 871	2 819
5-9	6 090	3 066	3 024	6 069	3 057	3 012	5 980	3 013	2 967	5 824	2 935	2 889
10-14	5 954	2 993	2 961	6 033	3 035	2 998	6 026	3 034	2 992	5 948	2 995	2 953
15-19	5 733	2 878	2 855	5 917	2 972	2 945	6 003	3 018	2 985	6 001	3 019	2 982
20-24	5 461	2 739	2 722	5 666	2 842	2 824	5 857	2 940	2 917	5 949	2 989	2 960
25-29	4 913	2 473	2 440	5 274	2 655	2 619	5 492	2 764	2 728	5 694	2 867	2 827
30-34	4 208	2 143	2 065	4 597	2 340	2 258	4 965	2 525	2 440	5 199	2 642	2 557
35-39	3 479	1 798	1 681	3 871	1 996	1 875	4 261	2 194	2 066	4 634	2 383	2 251
40-44	2 895	1 405	1 290	3 205	1 669	1 536	3 594	1 867	1 727	3 982	2 065	1 918
45-49	2 086	1 088	997	2 505	1 307	1 198	2 999	1 563	1 437	3 383	1 750	1 625
50-54	1 559	809	750	1 951	1 012	939	2 357	1 222	1 134	2 836	1 470	1 366
55-59	1 239	621	619	1 456	746	710	1 831	938	893	2 223	1 140	1 083
60-64	1 036	492	544	1 141	561	580	1 348	679	669	1 704	859	846
65-69	844	383	462	922	428	494	1 023	491	532	1 217	599	618
70-74	620	270	350	700	308	393	773	347	426	866	403	463
75-79	408	168	240	448	186	261	514	216	298	575	247	328
00-04	191	74	117	233	90	143	261	102	159	306	121	185
85-89	61	22	39	76	27	49	96	34	62	110	40	70
90-94	12	4	8	15	5	10	19	6	13	24	8	17
95-99	1	0	1	1	0	1	2	1	1	3	1	2
100 +	0	0	0	0	0	0	0	0	0	0	0	0

Age group	2045 Both sexes	2045 Males	2045 Females	2050 Both sexes	2050 Males	2050 Females
All ages	64 695	32 699	31 996	66 845	33 776	33 069
0-4	5 416	2 733	2 682	5 106	2 578	2 529
5-9	5 617	2 831	2 786	5 359	2 702	2 657
10-14	5 800	2 921	2 879	5 599	2 821	2 778
15-19	5 927	2 982	2 945	5 783	2 911	2 872
20-24	5 955	2 994	2 961	5 888	2 961	2 927
25-29	5 802	2 924	2 879	5 826	2 937	2 890
30-34	5 421	2 754	2 667	5 556	2 822	2 734
35-39	4 886	2 508	2 378	5 130	2 630	2 500
40-44	4 360	2 256	2 104	4 628	2 389	2 239
45-49	3 771	1 956	1 815	4 152	2 149	2 003
50-54	3 216	1 662	1 553	3 601	1 858	1 742
55-59	2 687	1 378	1 310	3 060	1 565	1 495
60-64	2 080	1 049	1 031	2 526	1 274	1 252
65-69	1 549	763	786	1 902	939	964
70-74	1 041	497	543	1 336	639	697
75-79	653	291	362	796	364	432
80-84	350	141	209	404	169	235
85-89	132	48	84	154	57	97
90-94	29	9	20	35	11	24
95-99	3	1	2	4	1	3
100 +	0	0	0	0	0	0

United Nations Department of Economic and Social Affairs/Population Division
World Population Prospects: The 2004 Revision, Volume II: Sex and Age Distribution of the World Population

875

POPULATION BY AGE AND SEX (in thousands)

Age group	2005 Both sexes	Males	Females	2010 Both sexes	Males	Females	2015 Both sexes	Males	Females	2020 Both sexes	Males	Females
All ages	38 329	19 071	19 258	42 186	21 056	21 130	46 573	23 311	23 261	51 128	25 660	25 468
0-4	6 045	3 044	3 001	6 504	3 276	3 228	6 905	3 480	3 425	7 193	3 627	3 566
5-9	5 389	2 708	2 681	5 697	2 863	2 834	6 206	3 119	3 087	6 649	3 344	3 305
10-14	4 893	2 456	2 437	5 237	2 630	2 607	5 585	2 805	2 780	6 102	3 065	3 037
15-19	4 458	2 235	2 223	4 806	2 411	2 395	5 184	2 602	2 582	5 535	2 778	2 757
20-24	3 779	1 892	1 887	4 340	2 174	2 166	4 723	2 367	2 356	5 105	2 560	2 545
25-29	3 065	1 540	1 524	3 563	1 791	1 772	4 135	2 081	2 055	4 526	2 278	2 248
30-34	2 296	1 171	1 126	2 772	1 413	1 359	3 264	1 663	1 601	3 814	1 945	1 870
35-39	1 779	903	876	2 025	1 049	976	2 492	1 289	1 204	2 951	1 526	1 425
40-44	1 472	731	741	1 577	807	770	1 827	954	873	2 260	1 179	1 081
45-49	1 249	608	642	1 325	657	668	1 441	737	704	1 677	876	801
50-54	1 045	500	545	1 138	549	590	1 223	601	622	1 334	677	657
55-59	910	424	486	952	448	504	1 049	498	551	1 131	548	583
60-64	711	325	386	815	372	444	863	398	465	956	445	511
65-69	537	240	297	612	272	340	710	315	395	757	340	417
70-74	367	159	208	424	183	241	491	211	279	575	247	328
75-79	211	88	123	248	103	145	292	121	171	343	141	201
80-84	92	37	56	110	44	67	132	52	80	159	62	97
85-89	27	10	17	33	12	21	41	15	26	50	18	32
90-94	4	1	3	6	2	4	7	2	5	9	3	6
95-99	0	0	0	1	0	0	1	0	1	1	0	1
100 +	0	0	0	0	0	0	0	0	0	0	0	0

Age group	2025 Both sexes	Males	Females	2030 Both sexes	Males	Females	2035 Both sexes	Males	Females	2040 Both sexes	Males	Females
All ages	55 680	28 008	27 672	60 259	30 367	29 892	64 886	32 744	32 142	69 528	35 118	34 410
0-4	7 263	3 664	3 599	7 345	3 705	3 639	7 459	3 763	3 695	7 551	3 811	3 741
5-9	6 980	3 514	3 466	7 091	3 572	3 519	7 204	3 629	3 574	7 342	3 700	3 642
10-14	6 566	3 300	3 265	6 916	3 479	3 436	7 041	3 545	3 496	7 166	3 608	3 557
15-19	6 057	3 040	3 016	6 526	3 278	3 248	6 881	3 459	3 422	7 012	3 528	3 484
20-24	5 461	2 739	2 722	5 986	3 003	2 984	6 459	3 242	3 217	6 820	3 427	3 393
25-29	4 913	2 473	2 440	5 274	2 655	2 619	5 802	2 920	2 882	6 280	3 162	3 118
30-34	4 208	2 143	2 065	4 597	2 340	2 258	4 965	2 525	2 440	5 493	2 791	2 702
35-39	3 479	1 798	1 681	3 871	1 996	1 875	4 261	2 194	2 066	4 634	2 383	2 251
40-44	2 695	1 405	1 290	3 205	1 669	1 536	3 594	1 867	1 727	3 982	2 065	1 918
45-49	2 086	1 088	997	2 505	1 307	1 198	2 999	1 563	1 437	3 383	1 758	1 625
50-54	1 559	809	750	1 951	1 012	939	2 357	1 222	1 134	2 836	1 470	1 366
55-59	1 239	621	619	1 456	746	710	1 831	938	893	2 223	1 140	1 083
60-64	1 036	492	544	1 141	561	580	1 348	679	669	1 704	859	846
65-69	844	383	462	922	428	494	1 023	491	532	1 217	599	618
70-74	620	270	350	700	308	393	773	347	426	866	403	463
75-79	408	168	240	448	186	261	514	216	298	575	247	328
80-84	191	74	117	233	90	143	261	102	159	306	121	185
85-89	61	22	39	76	27	49	96	34	62	110	40	70
90-94	12	4	8	15	5	10	19	6	13	24	8	17
95-99	1	0	1	1	0	1	2	1	1	3	1	2
100 +	0	0	0	0	0	0	0	0	0	0	0	0

Age group	2045 Both sexes	Males	Females	2050 Both sexes	Males	Females
All ages	74 076	37 431	36 646	78 426	39 624	38 802
0-4	7 547	3 809	3 738	7 448	3 760	3 688
5-9	7 455	3 758	3 697	7 468	3 765	3 703
10-14	7 312	3 683	3 629	7 431	3 744	3 687
15-19	7 141	3 593	3 548	7 291	3 670	3 621
20-24	6 958	3 498	3 460	7 093	3 567	3 526
25-29	6 652	3 352	3 300	6 808	3 432	3 376
30-34	5 979	3 038	2 942	6 369	3 235	3 134
35-39	5 162	2 650	2 512	5 658	2 901	2 757
40-44	4 360	2 256	2 104	4 889	2 524	2 365
45-49	3 771	1 956	1 815	4 152	2 149	2 003
50-54	3 216	1 662	1 553	3 601	1 858	1 742
55-59	2 687	1 378	1 310	3 060	1 565	1 495
60-64	2 080	1 049	1 031	2 526	1 274	1 252
65-69	1 549	763	786	1 902	939	964
70-74	1 041	497	543	1 336	639	697
75-79	653	291	362	796	364	432
80-84	350	141	209	404	169	235
85-89	132	48	84	154	57	97
90-94	29	9	20	35	11	24
95-99	3	1	2	4	1	3
100 +	0	0	0	0	0	0

United Nations Department of Economic and Social Affairs/Population Division
World Population Prospects: The 2004 Revision, Volume II: Sex and Age Distribution of the World Population

876

LOW VARIANT   **UNITED REPUBLIC OF TANZANIA**

POPULATION BY AGE AND SEX (in thousands)

Age group	2005 Both sexes	Males	Females	2010 Both sexes	Males	Females	2015 Both sexes	Males	Females	2020 Both sexes	Males	Females
All ages	38 329	19 071	19 258	41 491	20 706	20 785	44 022	22 029	22 293	47 401	23 783	23 618
0-4	6 045	3 044	3 001	5 809	2 926	2 883	5 618	2 831	2 787	5 358	2 701	2 656
5-9	5 389	2 708	2 681	5 697	2 863	2 834	5 543	2 786	2 757	5 409	2 721	2 689
10-14	4 893	2 456	2 437	5 237	2 630	2 607	5 585	2 805	2 780	5 450	2 738	2 712
15-19	4 458	2 235	2 223	4 806	2 411	2 395	5 184	2 602	2 582	5 535	2 778	2 757
20-24	3 779	1 892	1 887	4 340	2 174	2 166	4 723	2 367	2 356	5 105	2 560	2 545
25-29	3 065	1 540	1 524	3 563	1 791	1 772	4 135	2 081	2 055	4 526	2 278	2 248
30-34	2 296	1 171	1 126	2 772	1 413	1 359	3 264	1 663	1 601	3 814	1 945	1 870
35-39	1 779	903	876	2 025	1 049	976	2 492	1 289	1 204	2 951	1 526	1 425
40-44	1 472	731	741	1 577	807	770	1 827	954	873	2 260	1 179	1 081
45-49	1 249	608	642	1 325	657	668	1 441	737	704	1 677	876	801
50-54	1 045	500	545	1 138	549	590	1 223	601	622	1 334	677	657
55-59	910	424	486	952	448	504	1 049	498	551	1 131	548	583
60-64	711	325	386	815	372	444	863	398	465	956	445	511
65-69	537	240	297	612	272	340	710	315	395	757	340	417
70-74	367	159	208	424	183	241	491	211	279	575	247	328
75-79	211	88	123	248	103	145	292	121	171	343	141	201
80-84	92	37	56	110	44	67	132	52	80	159	62	97
85-89	27	10	17	33	12	21	41	15	26	50	18	32
90-94	4	1	3	6	2	4	7	2	5	9	3	6
95-99	0	0	0	1	0	0	1	0	1	1	0	1
100 +	0	0	0	0	0	0	0	0	0	0	0	0

Age group	2025 Both sexes	Males	Females	2030 Both sexes	Males	Females	2035 Both sexes	Males	Females	2040 Both sexes	Males	Females
All ages	49 940	25 118	24 822	52 144	26 282	25 863	53 905	27 215	26 691	55 192	27 894	27 297
0-4	5 177	2 611	2 565	4 889	2 467	2 423	4 491	2 266	2 225	4 048	2 043	2 005
5-9	5 199	2 617	2 582	5 053	2 546	2 508	4 795	2 416	2 379	4 421	2 228	2 193
10-14	5 341	2 685	2 656	5 150	2 591	2 559	5 018	2 526	2 492	4 769	2 402	2 368
15-19	5 409	2 715	2 694	5 309	2 667	2 642	5 124	2 576	2 548	4 997	2 514	2 483
20-24	5 461	2 739	2 722	5 347	2 682	2 665	5 254	2 638	2 617	5 078	2 552	2 527
25-29	4 913	2 473	2 440	5 274	2 655	2 619	5 182	2 608	2 574	5 109	2 572	2 536
30-34	4 208	2 143	2 065	4 597	2 340	2 258	4 965	2 525	2 440	4 905	2 493	2 413
35-39	3 479	1 798	1 681	3 871	1 996	1 875	4 261	2 194	2 066	4 634	2 383	2 251
40-44	2 606	1 405	1 200	3 205	1 669	1 536	3 594	1 867	1 727	3 982	2 065	1 918
45-49	2 086	1 088	997	2 505	1 307	1 198	2 999	1 563	1 437	3 383	1 758	1 625
50-54	1 559	809	750	1 951	1 012	939	2 357	1 222	1 134	2 836	1 470	1 366
55-59	1 239	621	619	1 456	746	710	1 831	938	893	2 223	1 140	1 083
60-64	1 036	492	544	1 141	561	580	1 348	679	669	1 704	859	846
65-69	844	383	462	922	428	494	1 023	491	532	1 217	599	618
70-74	620	270	350	700	308	393	773	347	426	866	403	463
75-79	408	168	240	448	186	261	514	216	298	575	247	328
80-84	191	74	117	233	90	143	261	102	159	306	121	185
85-89	61	22	39	76	27	49	96	34	62	110	40	70
90-94	12	4	8	15	5	10	19	6	13	24	8	17
95-99	1	0	1	1	0	1	2	1	1	3	1	2
100 +	0	0	0	0	0	0	0	0	0	0	0	0

Age group	2045 Both sexes	Males	Females	2050 Both sexes	Males	Females
All ages	56 015	28 321	27 694	56 390	28 496	27 893
0-4	3 609	1 822	1 787	3 194	1 612	1 582
5-9	3 996	2 014	1 982	3 571	1 800	1 770
10-14	4 402	2 217	2 185	3 983	2 007	1 976
15-19	4 753	2 392	2 361	4 389	2 209	2 180
20-24	4 958	2 493	2 465	4 721	2 374	2 347
25-29	4 953	2 496	2 457	4 851	2 445	2 406
30-34	4 864	2 471	2 393	4 742	2 409	2 334
35-39	4 610	2 366	2 244	4 602	2 359	2 243
40-44	4 360	2 256	2 104	4 366	2 254	2 112
45-49	3 771	1 956	1 815	4 152	2 149	2 003
50-54	3 216	1 662	1 553	3 601	1 858	1 742
55-59	2 687	1 378	1 310	3 060	1 565	1 495
60-64	2 080	1 049	1 031	2 526	1 274	1 252
65-69	1 549	763	786	1 902	939	964
70-74	1 041	497	543	1 336	639	697
75-79	653	291	362	796	364	432
80-84	350	141	209	404	169	235
85-89	132	48	84	154	57	97
90-94	29	9	20	35	11	24
95-99	3	1	2	4	1	3
100 +	0	0	0	0	0	0

United Nations Department of Economic and Social Affairs/Population Division
World Population Prospects: The 2004 Revision, Volume II: Sex and Age Distribution of the World Population

877

POPULATION BY AGE AND SEX (in thousands)

Age group	1950 Both sexes	Males	Females	1955 Both sexes	Males	Females	1960 Both sexes	Males	Females	1965 Both sexes	Males	Females
All ages	157 813	78 830	78 983	171 074	84 911	86 163	186 158	92 132	94 026	199 796	98 543	101 252
0-4	17 237	8 812	8 425	19 263	9 842	9 420	20 849	10 646	10 203	20 444	10 442	10 002
5-9	13 785	7 044	6 741	17 207	8 796	8 412	19 263	9 835	9 428	20 958	10 690	10 268
10-14	11 574	5 890	5 684	14 003	7 146	6 856	17 286	8 828	8 458	19 398	9 900	9 498
15-19	11 217	5 668	5 549	11 399	5 713	5 686	13 791	6 974	6 817	17 336	8 797	8 539
20-24	12 250	6 105	6 145	10 923	5 333	5 590	11 509	5 714	5 795	13 978	6 939	7 040
25-29	12 872	6 407	6 465	12 267	6 118	6 149	11 365	5 687	5 678	11 736	5 858	5 878
30-34	12 143	6 045	6 099	12 907	6 414	6 493	12 398	6 181	6 217	11 490	5 765	5 725
35-39	11 563	5 751	5 812	12 126	6 034	6 092	12 895	6 403	6 492	12 376	6 160	6 216
40-44	10 682	5 328	5 354	11 416	5 675	5 742	11 990	5 947	6 043	12 788	6 325	6 463
45-49	8 491	4 325	4 166	9 929	4 970	4 959	11 260	5 560	5 700	11 777	5 803	5 974
50-54	8 636	4 287	4 349	9 120	4 510	4 610	10 162	4 991	5 171	10 857	5 325	5 533
55-59	7 635	3 782	3 853	8 082	3 933	4 149	8 717	4 204	4 513	9 816	4 708	5 108
60-64	6 685	3 304	3 381	7 358	3 537	3 822	7 573	3 564	4 009	7 897	3 712	4 185
65-69	5 485	2 613	2 872	6 005	2 838	3 167	6 466	2 989	3 476	6 693	3 021	3 672
70-74	3 541	1 673	1 868	4 190	1 930	2 260	4 791	2 158	2 633	5 402	2 341	3 061
75-79	2 216	1 023	1 193	2 655	1 195	1 460	3 201	1 394	1 807	3 695	1 550	2 145
80 +	1 801	774	1 026	2 223	927	1 296	2 643	1 057	1 586	3 154	1 207	1 947

Age group	1970 Both sexes	Males	Females	1975 Both sexes	Males	Females	1980 Both sexes	Males	Females	1985 Both sexes	Males	Females
All ages	210 111	103 108	107 003	220 165	108 140	112 025	230 917	113 165	117 752	243 056	119 176	123 880
0-4	17 814	9 103	8 710	16 583	8 490	8 094	16 777	8 587	8 190	18 318	9 370	8 948
5-9	20 574	10 500	10 074	18 015	9 195	8 820	16 852	8 624	8 228	16 977	8 685	8 292
10-14	21 171	10 800	10 371	20 826	10 631	10 195	18 276	9 330	8 946	17 309	8 855	8 453
15-19	19 504	9 894	9 610	21 360	10 862	10 498	21 143	10 772	10 370	18 916	9 656	9 259
20-24	17 025	8 349	8 676	19 743	9 975	9 768	21 836	11 048	10 788	21 711	11 025	10 686
25-29	14 163	7 092	7 071	17 764	8 966	8 798	20 282	10 231	10 050	22 378	11 257	11 120
30-34	11 964	5 980	5 984	14 518	7 284	7 234	18 067	9 058	9 009	20 682	10 376	10 307
35-39	11 495	5 720	5 775	11 935	5 941	5 995	14 445	7 209	7 236	18 182	9 062	9 121
40-44	12 369	6 138	6 231	11 514	5 757	5 757	12 075	6 010	6 065	14 410	7 143	7 268
45-49	12 630	6 223	6 407	12 176	6 019	6 157	11 386	5 631	5 755	11 957	5 909	6 048
50-54	11 450	5 598	5 852	12 228	5 963	6 265	11 901	5 828	6 074	11 179	5 479	5 700
55-59	10 371	4 976	5 395	10 902	5 231	5 671	11 777	5 652	6 126	11 505	5 556	5 949
60-64	8 916	4 165	4 751	9 566	4 477	5 090	10 230	4 800	5 430	11 109	5 223	5 886
65-69	7 124	3 186	3 938	8 135	3 614	4 521	8 753	3 907	4 846	9 335	4 244	5 090
70-74	5 581	2 348	3 233	5 832	2 451	3 382	6 832	2 869	3 963	7 624	3 250	4 374
75-79	4 124	1 651	2 473	4 378	1 688	2 690	4 825	1 854	2 971	5 548	2 179	3 369
80 +	3 837	1 386	2 451	4 690	1 598	3 092	5 460	1 757	3 704	5 916	1 907	4 009

Age group	1990 Both sexes	Males	Females	1995 Both sexes	Males	Females	2000 Both sexes	Males	Females	2005 Both sexes	Males	Females
All ages	255 539	125 396	130 143	269 603	132 388	137 215	284 154	139 643	144 511	298 213	146 680	151 533
0-4	19 710	10 090	9 620	20 465	10 481	9 984	19 830	10 159	9 671	20 408	10 457	9 951
5-9	18 493	9 457	9 036	19 966	10 220	9 746	20 777	10 640	10 137	20 126	10 311	9 815
10-14	17 383	8 891	8 491	19 062	9 748	9 314	20 646	10 569	10 077	21 413	10 967	10 446
15-19	17 877	9 146	8 731	18 192	9 312	8 880	20 035	10 256	9 779	21 557	11 045	10 512
20-24	19 420	9 881	9 539	18 633	9 505	9 128	19 119	9 761	9 358	20 901	10 676	10 225
25-29	22 160	11 185	10 975	20 125	10 170	9 954	19 535	9 901	9 635	19 967	10 136	9 831
30-34	22 681	11 344	11 338	22 636	11 349	11 287	20 800	10 455	10 345	20 188	10 185	10 003
35-39	20 728	10 334	10 393	22 790	11 321	11 469	22 857	11 399	11 458	21 045	10 534	10 511
40-44	18 083	8 953	9 130	20 643	10 221	10 422	22 749	11 239	11 510	22 833	11 336	11 497
45-49	14 252	7 017	7 235	17 904	8 807	9 097	20 472	10 084	10 388	22 570	11 103	11 467
50-54	11 747	5 759	5 988	14 037	6 859	7 177	17 651	8 630	9 021	20 188	9 891	10 297
55-59	10 833	5 245	5 588	11 436	5 542	5 894	13 688	6 625	7 063	17 216	8 344	8 873
60-64	10 889	5 166	5 723	10 312	4 910	5 402	10 917	5 214	5 703	13 091	6 249	6 842
65-69	10 188	4 661	5 527	10 052	4 649	5 403	9 553	4 446	5 107	10 150	4 742	5 409
70-74	8 188	3 577	4 611	9 007	3 970	5 037	8 916	3 988	4 928	8 517	3 835	4 682
75-79	6 249	2 511	3 738	6 779	2 803	3 976	7 470	3 135	4 336	7 438	3 168	4 270
80 +	6 658	2 179	4 479	7 565	2 522	5 042	9 138	3 144	5 995	10 605	3 703	6 902

878

United Nations Department of Economic and Social Affairs/Population Division
World Population Prospects: The 2004 Revision, Volume II: Sex and Age Distribution of the World Population

POPULATION BY AGE AND SEX (in thousands)

Age group	2005 Both sexes	2005 Males	2005 Females	2010 Both sexes	2010 Males	2010 Females	2015 Both sexes	2015 Males	2015 Females	2020 Both sexes	2020 Males	2020 Females
All ages	298 213	146 680	151 533	312 253	153 708	158 545	325 723	160 439	165 285	338 427	166 742	171 685
0-4	20 408	10 457	9 951	21 129	10 827	10 302	21 407	10 970	10 437	21 402	10 967	10 435
5-9	20 126	10 311	9 815	20 703	10 608	10 094	21 413	10 973	10 440	21 689	11 114	10 575
10-14	21 413	10 967	10 446	20 760	10 636	10 124	21 315	10 922	10 393	22 020	11 284	10 736
15-19	21 557	11 045	10 512	22 319	11 441	10 878	21 638	11 095	10 542	22 187	11 379	10 808
20-24	20 901	10 676	10 225	22 417	11 463	10 954	23 151	11 845	11 306	22 469	11 501	10 968
25-29	19 967	10 136	9 831	21 740	11 048	10 693	23 224	11 819	11 405	23 955	12 200	11 755
30-34	20 188	10 185	10 003	20 616	10 420	10 196	22 358	11 316	11 043	23 837	12 084	11 754
35-39	21 045	10 534	10 511	20 445	10 274	10 171	20 861	10 504	10 357	22 598	11 395	11 203
40-44	22 833	11 336	11 497	21 053	10 494	10 559	20 463	10 243	10 220	20 883	10 475	10 409
45-49	22 570	11 103	11 467	22 666	11 208	11 459	20 920	10 388	10 532	20 352	10 150	10 202
50-54	20 188	9 891	10 297	22 267	10 898	11 370	22 375	11 008	11 367	20 683	10 221	10 462
55-59	17 216	8 344	8 873	19 709	9 576	10 133	21 757	10 562	11 195	21 891	10 686	11 205
60-64	13 091	6 249	6 842	16 494	7 889	8 604	18 918	9 078	9 840	20 927	10 040	10 887
65-69	10 150	4 742	5 409	12 215	5 708	6 507	15 435	7 238	8 198	17 761	8 365	9 396
70-74	8 517	3 835	4 682	9 101	4 118	4 983	11 009	4 993	6 016	13 973	6 369	7 604
75-79	7 438	3 168	4 270	7 158	3 073	4 085	7 711	3 334	4 377	9 393	4 080	5 313
80-84	5 594	2 172	3 421	5 619	2 218	3 401	5 466	2 180	3 286	5 952	2 398	3 554
85-89	3 192	1 081	2 111	3 602	1 239	2 363	3 671	1 289	2 382	3 620	1 289	2 331
90-94	1 349	363	986	1 638	457	1 182	1 882	536	1 346	1 948	569	1 379
95-99	393	77	316	501	100	401	619	129	490	723	155	569
100 +	78	10	68	100	13	87	129	17	112	162	23	140

Age group	2025 Both sexes	2025 Males	2025 Females	2030 Both sexes	2030 Males	2030 Females	2035 Both sexes	2035 Males	2035 Females	2040 Both sexes	2040 Males	2040 Females
All ages	350 103	172 472	177 631	360 894	177 710	183 183	370 709	182 467	188 242	379 544	186 795	192 748
0-4	21 265	10 896	10 369	21 500	11 016	10 484	21 818	11 179	10 639	22 142	11 344	10 798
5-9	21 685	11 112	10 574	21 550	11 042	10 508	21 785	11 162	10 623	22 104	11 325	10 779
10-14	22 298	11 426	10 872	22 295	11 424	10 871	22 161	11 355	10 806	22 397	11 475	10 922
15-19	22 894	11 742	11 152	23 174	11 885	11 289	23 173	11 884	11 289	23 041	11 816	11 225
20-24	23 023	11 787	11 236	23 732	12 151	11 581	24 016	12 297	11 719	24 019	12 299	11 720
25-29	23 281	11 861	11 420	23 838	12 149	11 689	24 552	12 516	12 035	24 840	12 665	12 175
30-34	24 574	12 469	12 105	23 911	12 136	11 775	24 475	12 429	12 046	25 194	12 800	12 394
35-39	24 080	12 164	11 916	24 825	12 555	12 271	24 177	12 232	11 946	24 760	12 530	12 220
40-44	22 620	11 365	11 255	24 107	12 136	11 971	24 862	12 532	12 330	24 232	12 221	12 011
45-49	20 783	10 388	10 396	22 520	11 277	11 243	24 010	12 049	11 961	24 777	12 453	12 324
50-54	20 148	10 003	10 145	20 594	10 249	10 345	22 328	11 135	11 192	23 822	11 909	11 912
55-59	20 276	9 947	10 330	19 787	9 756	10 031	20 252	10 013	10 240	21 982	10 895	11 087
60-64	21 104	10 188	10 916	19 599	9 514	10 085	19 174	9 362	9 812	19 668	9 635	10 033
65-69	19 712	9 292	10 420	19 942	9 469	10 473	18 586	8 885	9 701	18 245	8 781	9 464
70-74	16 149	7 404	8 745	18 001	8 272	9 728	18 287	8 478	9 809	17 119	8 001	9 118
75-79	11 996	5 246	6 750	13 946	6 145	7 801	15 636	6 917	8 719	15 966	7 138	8 828
80-84	7 317	2 967	4 349	9 429	3 859	5 570	11 057	4 570	6 487	12 495	5 195	7 300
85-89	3 992	1 441	2 551	4 972	1 811	3 161	6 487	2 391	4 096	7 696	2 872	4 824
90-94	1 949	579	1 370	2 185	660	1 525	2 765	846	1 920	3 662	1 137	2 525
95-99	760	167	593	775	174	601	885	203	682	1 140	266	875
100 +	194	28	166	212	31	181	222	33	189	252	38	214

Age group	2045 Both sexes	2045 Males	2045 Females	2050 Both sexes	2050 Males	2050 Females
All ages	387 531	190 804	196 727	394 976	194 647	200 329
0-4	22 366	11 459	10 907	22 492	11 523	10 969
5-9	22 429	11 491	10 938	22 654	11 606	11 048
10-14	22 716	11 638	11 078	23 041	11 804	11 237
15-19	23 278	11 937	11 341	23 599	12 101	11 497
20-24	23 890	12 233	11 657	24 130	12 356	11 774
25-29	24 848	12 670	12 178	24 724	12 607	12 116
30-34	25 489	12 952	12 536	25 504	12 962	12 542
35-39	25 477	12 906	12 572	25 781	13 064	12 717
40-44	24 815	12 526	12 289	25 553	12 908	12 645
45-49	24 169	12 155	12 014	24 765	12 468	12 297
50-54	24 603	12 321	12 282	24 023	12 041	11 982
55-59	23 479	11 670	11 809	24 278	12 092	12 186
60-64	21 388	10 511	10 877	22 886	11 286	11 601
65-69	18 773	9 074	9 699	20 474	9 937	10 537
70-74	16 880	7 953	8 927	17 443	8 264	9 178
75-79	15 028	6 784	8 244	14 905	6 795	8 110
80-84	12 844	5 408	7 437	12 179	5 189	6 990
85-89	8 796	3 310	5 485	9 135	3 490	5 644
90-94	4 406	1 391	3 016	5 105	1 629	3 476
95-99	1 535	364	1 170	1 875	454	1 421
100 +	321	50	271	432	69	363

POPULATION BY AGE AND SEX (in thousands)

Age group	2005 Both sexes	2005 Males	2005 Females	2010 Both sexes	2010 Males	2010 Females	2015 Both sexes	2015 Males	2015 Females	2020 Both sexes	2020 Males	2020 Females
All ages	298 213	146 680	151 533	314 831	155 029	159 802	332 609	163 967	168 642	350 886	173 126	177 760
0-4	20 408	10 457	9 951	23 706	12 148	11 558	25 718	13 179	12 539	26 981	13 826	13 156
5-9	20 126	10 311	9 815	20 703	10 608	10 094	23 987	12 292	11 695	25 996	13 321	12 675
10-14	21 413	10 967	10 446	20 760	10 636	10 124	21 315	10 922	10 393	24 594	12 603	11 991
15-19	21 557	11 045	10 512	22 319	11 441	10 878	21 638	11 095	10 542	22 187	11 379	10 808
20-24	20 901	10 676	10 225	22 417	11 463	10 954	23 151	11 845	11 306	22 469	11 501	10 968
25-29	19 967	10 136	9 831	21 740	11 048	10 693	23 224	11 819	11 405	23 955	12 200	11 755
30-34	20 188	10 185	10 003	20 616	10 420	10 196	22 358	11 316	11 043	23 837	12 084	11 754
35-39	21 045	10 534	10 511	20 445	10 274	10 171	20 861	10 504	10 357	22 598	11 395	11 203
40-44	22 833	11 336	11 497	21 053	10 494	10 559	20 463	10 243	10 220	20 883	10 475	10 409
45-49	22 570	11 103	11 467	22 666	11 208	11 459	20 920	10 388	10 532	20 352	10 150	10 202
50-54	20 188	9 891	10 297	22 267	10 898	11 370	22 375	11 008	11 367	20 683	10 221	10 462
55-59	17 216	8 344	8 873	19 709	9 576	10 133	21 757	10 562	11 195	21 891	10 686	11 205
60-64	13 091	6 249	6 842	16 494	7 889	8 604	18 918	9 078	9 840	20 927	10 040	10 887
65-69	10 150	4 742	5 409	12 215	5 708	6 507	15 435	7 238	8 198	17 761	8 365	9 396
70-74	8 517	3 835	4 682	9 101	4 118	4 983	11 009	4 993	6 016	13 973	6 369	7 604
75-79	7 438	3 168	4 270	7 158	3 073	4 085	7 711	3 334	4 377	9 393	4 080	5 313
80-84	5 594	2 172	3 421	5 619	2 218	3 401	5 466	2 180	3 286	5 952	2 398	3 554
85-89	3 192	1 081	2 111	3 602	1 239	2 363	3 671	1 289	2 382	3 620	1 289	2 331
90-94	1 349	363	986	1 638	457	1 182	1 882	536	1 346	1 948	569	1 379
95-99	393	77	316	501	100	401	619	129	490	723	155	569
100 +	78	10	68	100	13	87	129	17	112	162	23	140

Age group	2025 Both sexes	2025 Males	2025 Females	2030 Both sexes	2030 Males	2030 Females	2035 Both sexes	2035 Males	2035 Females	2040 Both sexes	2040 Males	2040 Females
All ages	368 398	181 846	186 552	385 676	190 407	195 269	403 209	199 115	204 094	421 404	208 232	213 171
0-4	27 113	13 892	13 220	28 004	14 349	13 655	29 565	15 148	14 417	31 544	16 161	15 382
5-9	27 259	13 968	13 291	27 392	14 035	13 357	28 284	14 492	13 792	29 844	15 291	14 553
10-14	26 602	13 632	12 970	27 866	14 279	13 588	28 000	14 346	13 654	28 892	14 803	14 089
15-19	25 464	13 058	12 406	27 473	14 088	13 386	28 739	14 735	14 004	28 875	14 804	14 070
20-24	23 023	11 787	11 236	26 298	13 465	12 833	28 307	14 494	13 813	29 575	15 143	14 432
25-29	23 281	11 861	11 420	23 838	12 149	11 689	27 110	13 825	13 285	29 121	14 855	14 266
30-34	24 574	12 469	12 105	23 911	12 136	11 775	24 475	12 429	12 046	27 745	14 103	13 642
35-39	24 080	12 164	11 916	24 825	12 555	12 271	24 177	12 232	11 946	24 750	12 530	12 220
40-44	22 620	11 365	11 255	24 107	12 136	11 971	24 862	12 532	12 330	24 232	12 221	12 011
45-49	20 783	10 388	10 396	22 520	11 277	11 243	24 010	12 049	11 961	24 777	12 453	12 324
50-54	20 148	10 003	10 145	20 594	10 249	10 345	22 328	11 135	11 192	23 822	11 909	11 912
55-59	20 276	9 947	10 330	19 787	9 756	10 031	20 252	10 013	10 240	21 982	10 895	11 087
60-64	21 104	10 188	10 916	19 599	9 514	10 085	19 174	9 362	9 812	19 668	9 635	10 033
65-69	19 712	9 292	10 420	19 942	9 469	10 473	18 586	8 885	9 701	18 245	8 781	9 464
70-74	16 149	7 404	8 745	18 001	8 272	9 728	18 287	8 478	9 809	17 119	8 001	9 118
75-79	11 996	5 246	6 750	13 946	6 145	7 801	15 636	6 917	8 719	15 966	7 138	8 828
80-84	7 317	2 967	4 349	9 429	3 859	5 570	11 057	4 570	6 487	12 495	5 195	7 300
85-89	3 992	1 441	2 551	4 972	1 811	3 161	6 487	2 391	4 096	7 696	2 872	4 824
90-94	1 949	579	1 370	2 185	660	1 525	2 765	846	1 920	3 662	1 137	2 525
95-99	760	167	593	775	174	601	885	203	682	1 140	266	875
100 +	194	28	166	212	31	181	222	33	189	252	38	214

Age group	2045 Both sexes	2045 Males	2045 Females	2050 Both sexes	2050 Males	2050 Females
All ages	440 314	217 828	222 485	459 862	227 859	232 002
0-4	33 347	17 085	16 262	34 672	17 763	16 909
5-9	31 823	16 304	15 519	33 626	17 227	16 399
10-14	30 453	15 602	14 851	32 432	16 615	15 817
15-19	29 769	15 262	14 507	31 330	16 061	15 269
20-24	29 715	15 215	14 500	30 612	15 674	14 938
25-29	30 393	15 507	14 886	30 538	15 582	14 956
30-34	29 759	15 134	14 624	31 035	15 789	15 246
35-39	28 018	14 202	13 816	30 037	15 236	14 800
40-44	24 815	12 526	12 289	28 082	14 197	13 885
45-49	24 169	12 155	12 014	24 765	12 468	12 297
50-54	24 603	12 321	12 282	24 023	12 041	11 982
55-59	23 479	11 670	11 809	24 278	12 092	12 186
60-64	21 388	10 511	10 877	22 886	11 286	11 601
65-69	18 773	9 074	9 699	20 474	9 937	10 537
70-74	16 880	7 953	8 927	17 443	8 264	9 178
75-79	15 028	6 784	8 244	14 905	6 795	8 110
80-84	12 844	5 408	7 437	12 179	5 189	6 990
85-89	8 796	3 310	5 485	9 135	3 490	5 644
90-94	4 406	1 391	3 016	5 105	1 629	3 476
95-99	1 535	364	1 170	1 875	454	1 421
100 +	321	50	271	432	69	363

880

United Nations Department of Economic and Social Affairs/Population Division
World Population Prospects: The 2004 Revision, Volume II: Sex and Age Distribution of the World Population

POPULATION BY AGE AND SEX (in thousands)

Age group	2005 Both sexes	Males	Females	2010 Both sexes	Males	Females	2015 Both sexes	Males	Females	2020 Both sexes	Males	Females
All ages	298 213	146 680	151 522	309 676	152 387	157 290	312 835	150 910	161 925	325 968	160 358	165 611
0-4	20 408	10 457	9 951	18 551	9 506	9 045	17 096	8 761	8 336	15 822	8 107	7 715
5-9	20 126	10 311	9 815	20 703	10 608	10 094	18 838	9 653	9 184	17 383	8 908	8 475
10-14	21 413	10 967	10 446	20 760	10 636	10 124	21 315	10 922	10 393	19 447	9 966	9 482
15-19	21 557	11 045	10 512	22 319	11 441	10 878	21 638	11 095	10 542	22 187	11 379	10 808
20-24	20 901	10 676	10 225	22 417	11 463	10 954	23 151	11 845	11 306	22 469	11 501	10 968
25-29	19 967	10 136	9 831	21 740	11 048	10 693	23 224	11 819	11 405	23 955	12 200	11 755
30-34	20 188	10 185	10 003	20 616	10 420	10 196	22 358	11 316	11 043	23 837	12 084	11 754
35-39	21 045	10 534	10 511	20 445	10 274	10 171	20 861	10 504	10 357	22 598	11 395	11 203
40-44	22 833	11 336	11 497	21 053	10 494	10 559	20 463	10 243	10 220	20 883	10 475	10 409
45-49	22 570	11 103	11 467	22 666	11 208	11 459	20 920	10 388	10 532	20 352	10 150	10 202
50-54	20 188	9 891	10 297	22 267	10 898	11 370	22 375	11 008	11 367	20 683	10 221	10 462
55-59	17 216	8 344	8 873	19 709	9 576	10 133	21 757	10 562	11 195	21 891	10 686	11 205
60-64	13 091	6 249	6 842	16 494	7 889	8 604	18 918	9 078	9 840	20 927	10 040	10 887
65-69	10 150	4 742	5 409	12 215	5 708	6 507	15 435	7 238	8 198	17 761	8 365	9 396
70-74	8 517	3 835	4 682	9 101	4 118	4 983	11 009	4 993	6 016	13 973	6 369	7 604
75-79	7 438	3 168	4 270	7 158	3 073	4 085	7 711	3 334	4 377	9 393	4 080	5 313
80-84	5 594	2 172	3 421	5 619	2 218	3 401	5 466	2 180	3 286	5 952	2 398	3 554
85-89	3 192	1 081	2 111	3 602	1 239	2 363	3 671	1 289	2 382	3 620	1 289	2 331
90-94	1 349	363	986	1 638	457	1 182	1 882	536	1 346	1 948	569	1 379
95-99	393	77	316	501	100	401	619	129	490	723	155	569
100 +	78	10	68	100	13	87	129	17	112	162	23	140

Age group	2025 Both sexes	Males	Females	2030 Both sexes	Males	Females	2035 Both sexes	Males	Females	2040 Both sexes	Males	Females
All ages	331 870	163 129	168 741	336 483	165 204	171 279	339 379	166 420	172 959	340 321	166 710	173 612
0-4	15 481	7 932	7 549	15 303	7 841	7 462	14 871	7 619	7 252	14 209	7 280	6 929
5-9	16 112	8 256	7 856	15 771	8 081	7 690	15 595	7 990	7 604	15 164	7 769	7 395
10-14	17 994	9 221	8 773	16 724	8 570	8 155	16 385	8 395	7 990	16 208	8 305	7 904
15-19	20 324	10 425	9 899	18 874	9 682	9 192	17 607	9 033	8 574	17 269	8 860	8 410
20-24	23 023	11 787	11 236	21 167	10 838	10 329	19 724	10 100	9 624	18 462	9 454	9 008
25-29	23 281	11 861	11 420	23 838	12 149	11 689	21 993	11 208	10 785	20 558	10 475	10 083
30-34	24 574	12 469	12 105	23 911	12 136	11 775	24 475	12 429	12 046	22 643	11 496	11 147
35-39	24 080	12 164	11 916	24 825	12 555	12 271	24 177	12 232	11 946	24 750	12 530	12 220
40-44	22 620	11 365	11 255	24 107	12 136	11 971	24 862	12 532	12 330	24 232	12 221	12 011
45-49	20 783	10 388	10 396	22 520	11 277	11 243	24 010	12 049	11 961	24 777	12 453	12 324
50-54	20 148	10 003	10 145	20 594	10 249	10 345	22 328	11 135	11 192	23 822	11 909	11 912
55-59	20 276	9 947	10 330	19 787	9 756	10 031	20 252	10 013	10 240	21 992	10 905	11 097
60-64	21 104	10 188	10 916	19 599	9 514	10 085	19 174	9 362	9 812	19 668	9 635	10 033
65-69	19 712	9 292	10 420	19 942	9 469	10 473	18 586	8 885	9 701	18 245	8 781	9 464
70-74	16 149	7 404	8 745	18 001	8 272	9 728	18 287	8 478	9 809	17 119	8 001	9 118
75-79	11 996	5 246	6 750	13 946	6 145	7 801	15 636	6 917	8 719	15 966	7 138	8 828
80-84	7 317	2 977	4 340	9 429	3 859	5 570	11 057	4 570	6 487	12 495	5 195	7 300
85-89	3 992	1 441	2 551	4 972	1 811	3 161	6 487	2 391	4 096	7 696	2 872	4 824
90-94	1 949	579	1 370	2 185	660	1 525	2 765	846	1 920	3 662	1 137	2 525
95-99	760	167	593	775	174	601	885	203	682	1 140	266	875
100 +	194	28	166	212	31	181	222	33	189	252	38	214

Age group	2045 Both sexes	Males	Females	2050 Both sexes	Males	Females
All ages	339 511	166 220	173 291	337 519	165 240	172 279
0-4	13 513	6 923	6 590	12 979	6 649	6 330
5-9	14 502	7 430	7 072	13 807	7 073	6 734
10-14	15 778	8 084	7 694	15 118	7 745	7 373
15-19	17 095	8 770	8 325	16 666	8 550	8 116
20-24	18 127	9 283	8 845	17 955	9 195	8 761
25-29	19 303	9 833	9 469	18 972	9 665	9 307
30-34	21 219	10 771	10 449	19 973	10 135	9 838
35-39	22 936	11 609	11 327	21 526	10 893	10 634
40-44	24 815	12 526	12 289	23 024	11 620	11 404
45-49	24 169	12 155	12 014	24 765	12 468	12 297
50-54	24 603	12 321	12 282	24 023	12 041	11 982
55-59	23 479	11 670	11 809	24 278	12 092	12 186
60-64	21 388	10 511	10 877	22 886	11 286	11 601
65-69	18 773	9 074	9 699	20 474	9 937	10 537
70-74	16 880	7 953	8 927	17 443	8 264	9 178
75-79	15 028	6 784	8 244	14 905	6 795	8 110
80-84	12 844	5 408	7 437	12 179	5 189	6 990
85-89	8 796	3 310	5 485	9 135	3 490	5 644
90-94	4 406	1 391	3 016	5 105	1 629	3 476
95-99	1 535	364	1 170	1 875	454	1 421
100 +	321	50	271	432	69	363

United Nations Department of Economic and Social Affairs/Population Division
World Population Prospects: The 2004 Revision, Volume II: Sex and Age Distribution of the World Population

881

POPULATION BY AGE AND SEX (in thousands)

Age group	1950 Both sexes	Males	Females	1955 Both sexes	Males	Females	1960 Both sexes	Males	Females	1965 Both sexes	Males	Females
All ages	27	13	14	29	15	15	33	16	17	50	25	25
0-4	4	2	2	5	2	2	5	3	3	9	5	4
5-9	4	2	2	4	2	2	4	2	2	6	3	3
10-14	3	1	1	3	2	2	4	2	2	5	2	3
15-19	2	1	1	2	1	1	3	2	2	5	2	2
20-24	2	1	1	2	1	1	2	1	1	5	2	2
25-29	2	1	1	2	1	1	2	1	1	4	2	2
30-34	2	1	1	2	1	1	2	1	1	3	2	2
35-39	2	1	1	2	1	1	2	1	1	3	1	1
40-44	1	1	1	2	1	1	2	1	1	2	1	1
45-49	1	1	1	1	1	1	2	1	1	2	1	1
50-54	1	0	1	1	1	1	1	1	1	2	1	1
55-59	1	0	0	1	0	1	1	1	1	1	1	1
60-64	1	0	0	1	0	0	1	0	0	1	0	0
65-69	1	0	0	1	0	0	1	0	0	1	0	0
70-74	1	0	0	1	0	0	1	0	0	1	0	0
75-79	0	0	0	0	0	0	0	0	0	0	0	0
80 +	0	0	0	0	0	0	0	0	0	0	0	0

Age group	1970 Both sexes	Males	Females	1975 Both sexes	Males	Females	1980 Both sexes	Males	Females	1985 Both sexes	Males	Females
All ages	64	32	32	86	42	44	99	47	51	105	51	54
0-4	9	4	4	16	8	8	11	6	5	14	7	7
5-9	8	4	4	11	5	5	11	6	6	10	5	5
10-14	7	3	3	10	5	5	13	7	7	11	6	5
15-19	5	3	3	7	3	4	11	5	6	11	5	5
20-24	6	3	3	5	2	3	7	3	4	8	4	4
25-29	6	3	3	7	3	4	6	3	4	7	3	4
30-34	6	3	3	7	3	4	9	4	5	7	3	4
35-39	4	2	2	6	3	3	7	3	4	9	4	5
40-44	3	2	2	4	2	2	6	3	3	7	3	4
45-49	3	1	1	3	2	2	4	2	2	6	3	3
50-54	2	1	1	3	1	2	4	2	2	4	2	2
55-59	2	1	1	2	1	1	3	1	2	4	2	2
60-64	1	1	1	2	1	1	2	1	1	3	1	1
65-69	1	0	0	1	1	1	2	1	1	2	1	1
70-74	1	0	0	1	0	0	1	1	1	2	1	1
75-79	0	0	0	0	0	0	1	0	0	1	0	0
80 +	0	0	0	0	0	0	1	0	0	1	0	0

Age group	1990 Both sexes	Males	Females	1995 Both sexes	Males	Females	2000 Both sexes	Males	Females	2005 Both sexes	Males	Females
All ages	104	50	53	107	52	56	111	53	58	112	53	59
0-4	10	5	5	12	6	6	9	5	4	8	4	4
5-9	10	5	5	9	4	4	10	5	5	9	4	4
10-14	10	5	5	10	5	5	10	5	5	10	5	5
15-19	10	5	5	8	4	4	9	4	5	10	5	5
20-24	7	4	4	8	4	4	6	3	3	8	4	4
25-29	7	4	4	7	3	4	7	3	4	5	2	3
30-34	7	3	4	8	4	4	7	3	4	6	3	3
35-39	7	3	4	8	4	4	8	4	4	7	3	4
40-44	8	4	4	7	3	4	8	4	4	8	4	4
45-49	7	4	4	8	4	4	8	3	4	8	4	4
50-54	6	3	3	7	4	4	8	4	4	7	3	4
55-59	4	2	2	5	3	3	7	3	3	8	4	4
60-64	3	2	2	4	2	2	5	2	2	7	3	3
65-69	2	1	1	3	1	2	4	2	2	4	2	2
70-74	2	1	1	2	1	1	2	1	1	3	1	2
75-79	1	1	1	1	1	1	2	1	1	2	1	1
80 +	1	0	0	1	0	1	2	1	1	2	1	1

United Nations Department of Economic and Social Affairs/Population Division
World Population Prospects: The 2004 Revision, Volume II: Sex and Age Distribution of the World Population

MEDIUM VARIANT   **UNITED STATES VIRGIN ISLANDS**

POPULATION BY AGE AND SEX (in thousands)

Age group	2005 Both sexes	2005 Males	2005 Females	2010 Both sexes	2010 Males	2010 Females	2015 Both sexes	2015 Males	2015 Females	2020 Both sexes	2020 Males	2020 Females
All ages	112	53	59	112	62	50	111	52	58	109	51	58
0-4	8	4	4	7	4	4	7	4	3	7	4	3
5-9	9	4	4	8	4	4	7	4	3	7	4	3
10-14	10	5	5	9	4	4	8	4	4	7	4	3
15-19	10	5	5	10	5	5	8	4	4	7	4	4
20-24	8	4	4	9	4	5	9	5	5	8	4	4
25-29	5	2	3	8	4	4	8	4	4	9	4	4
30-34	6	3	3	4	2	2	7	3	4	7	4	4
35-39	7	3	4	5	2	3	4	2	2	6	3	3
40-44	8	4	4	6	3	3	5	2	3	4	2	2
45-49	8	4	4	7	3	4	6	3	3	5	2	3
50-54	7	3	4	7	3	4	7	3	4	6	3	3
55-59	8	4	4	7	3	4	7	3	4	7	3	4
60-64	7	3	3	7	3	4	7	3	4	7	3	4
65-69	4	2	2	6	3	3	7	3	4	6	3	4
70-74	3	1	2	4	2	2	5	2	3	6	3	4
75-79	2	1	1	3	1	2	3	1	2	5	2	3
80-84	1	0	1	1	1	1	2	1	1	3	1	2
85-89	1	0	0	1	0	1	1	0	1	1	0	1
90-94	0	0	0	0	0	0	0	0	0	1	0	0
95-99	0	0	0	0	0	0	0	0	0	0	0	0
100 +	0	0	0	0	0	0	0	0	0	0	0	0

Age group	2025 Both sexes	2025 Males	2025 Females	2030 Both sexes	2030 Males	2030 Females	2035 Both sexes	2035 Males	2035 Females	2040 Both sexes	2040 Males	2040 Females
All ages	107	50	57	104	49	55	99	46	53	94	44	50
0-4	7	4	3	6	3	3	5	3	3	5	2	2
5-9	7	4	3	7	3	3	6	3	3	5	3	2
10-14	7	4	3	7	4	3	7	3	3	6	3	3
15-19	7	3	3	7	3	3	7	3	3	6	3	3
20-24	7	4	3	6	3	3	6	3	3	6	3	3
25-29	7	4	3	6	3	3	5	3	3	5	3	2
30-34	8	4	4	6	3	3	5	3	3	5	2	2
35-39	7	3	4	8	4	4	6	3	3	5	3	2
40-44	6	3	0	7	3	3	7	4	4	6	3	3
45-49	3	2	2	6	3	3	6	3	3	7	4	3
50-54	5	2	3	3	1	2	6	3	3	6	3	3
55-59	6	3	3	5	2	3	3	1	2	5	2	2
60-64	7	3	4	6	2	3	4	2	3	3	1	2
65-69	6	3	4	6	3	4	5	2	3	4	2	3
70-74	6	2	3	6	3	3	6	2	3	5	2	3
75-79	5	2	3	5	2	3	5	2	3	5	2	3
80-84	4	1	2	4	2	3	4	1	3	4	2	3
85-89	2	1	1	3	1	2	3	1	2	3	1	2
90-94	1	0	1	1	0	1	1	0	1	2	0	1
95-99	0	0	0	0	0	0	0	0	0	1	0	1
100 +	0	0	0	0	0	0	0	0	0	0	0	0

Age group	2045 Both sexes	2045 Males	2045 Females	2050 Both sexes	2050 Males	2050 Females
All ages	88	42	46	82	39	43
0-4	4	2	2	4	2	2
5-9	4	2	2	4	2	2
10-14	5	3	2	4	2	2
15-19	5	3	3	5	2	2
20-24	6	3	3	5	3	2
25-29	5	3	2	5	3	2
30-34	5	2	2	5	2	2
35-39	4	2	2	4	2	2
40-44	5	2	2	4	2	2
45-49	5	3	3	4	2	2
50-54	7	3	3	5	3	2
55-59	6	3	3	7	3	3
60-64	5	3	3	6	3	3
65-69	3	1	2	5	2	3
70-74	4	1	2	3	1	2
75-79	4	2	3	3	1	2
80-84	4	2	3	4	1	2
85-89	3	1	2	3	1	2
90-94	2	0	1	2	0	1
95-99	1	0	1	1	0	1
100 +	0	0	0	0	0	0

POPULATION BY AGE AND SEX (in thousands)

Age group	2005 Both sexes	2005 Males	2005 Females	2010 Both sexes	2010 Males	2010 Females	2015 Both sexes	2015 Males	2015 Females	2020 Both sexes	2020 Males	2020 Females
All ages	112	53	59	112	53	59	113	54	60	114	54	60
0-4	8	4	4	8	4	4	9	4	4	9	5	4
5-9	9	4	4	8	4	4	8	4	4	9	4	4
10-14	10	5	5	9	4	4	8	4	4	8	4	4
15-19	10	5	5	10	5	5	8	4	4	7	4	4
20-24	8	4	4	9	4	5	9	5	5	8	4	4
25-29	5	2	3	8	4	4	8	4	4	9	4	4
30-34	6	3	3	4	2	2	7	3	4	7	4	4
35-39	7	3	4	5	2	3	4	2	2	6	3	3
40-44	8	4	4	6	3	3	5	2	3	4	2	2
45-49	8	4	4	7	3	4	6	3	3	5	2	3
50-54	7	3	4	7	3	4	7	3	4	6	3	3
55-59	8	4	4	7	3	4	7	3	4	7	3	4
60-64	7	3	3	7	3	4	7	3	4	7	3	4
65-69	4	2	2	6	3	3	7	3	4	6	3	4
70-74	3	1	2	4	2	2	5	2	3	6	3	4
75-79	2	1	1	3	1	2	3	1	2	5	2	3
80-84	1	0	1	1	1	1	2	1	1	3	1	2
85-89	1	0	0	1	0	1	1	0	1	1	0	1
90-94	0	0	0	0	0	0	0	0	0	1	0	0
95-99	0	0	0	0	0	0	0	0	0	0	0	0
100 +	0	0	0	0	0	0	0	0	0	0	0	0

Age group	2025 Both sexes	2025 Males	2025 Females	2030 Both sexes	2030 Males	2030 Females	2035 Both sexes	2035 Males	2035 Females	2040 Both sexes	2040 Males	2040 Females
All ages	114	54	60	112	53	59	109	51	57	106	50	56
0-4	9	4	4	8	4	4	7	4	3	7	3	3
5-9	9	5	4	9	4	4	8	4	4	7	3	3
10-14	8	4	4	9	5	4	8	4	4	7	4	4
15-19	8	4	4	8	4	4	9	4	4	8	4	4
20-24	7	4	3	7	4	3	8	4	4	8	4	4
25-29	7	4	3	6	3	3	6	3	3	7	4	3
30-34	8	4	4	6	3	3	5	3	3	6	3	3
35-39	7	3	4	8	4	4	6	3	3	5	3	2
40-44	6	3	3	7	3	3	7	4	4	6	3	3
45-49	3	2	2	6	3	3	6	3	3	7	4	3
50-54	5	2	3	3	1	2	6	3	3	6	3	3
55-59	6	3	3	5	2	3	3	1	2	5	3	3
60-64	7	3	4	6	2	3	4	2	3	3	1	2
65-69	6	3	4	6	3	4	5	2	3	4	2	3
70-74	6	2	3	6	3	3	6	2	3	5	2	3
75-79	5	2	3	5	2	3	5	2	3	5	2	3
80-84	4	1	2	4	2	3	4	1	3	4	2	3
85-89	2	1	1	3	1	2	3	1	2	3	1	2
90-94	1	0	1	1	0	1	1	0	1	2	0	1
95-99	0	0	0	0	0	0	0	0	0	1	0	1
100 +	0	0	0	0	0	0	0	0	0	0	0	0

Age group	2045 Both sexes	2045 Males	2045 Females	2050 Both sexes	2050 Males	2050 Females
All ages	103	49	54	100	48	52
0-4	7	4	3	7	4	3
5-9	7	3	3	7	4	3
10-14	7	3	3	6	3	3
15-19	7	4	3	6	3	3
20-24	8	4	4	7	3	3
25-29	7	4	3	7	4	3
30-34	6	3	3	7	3	3
35-39	5	3	2	6	3	3
40-44	5	2	2	5	3	2
45-49	5	3	3	4	2	2
50-54	7	3	3	5	3	2
55-59	6	3	3	7	3	3
60-64	5	3	3	6	3	3
65-69	3	1	2	5	2	3
70-74	4	1	2	3	1	2
75-79	4	2	3	3	1	2
80-84	4	2	3	4	1	2
85-89	3	1	2	3	1	2
90-94	2	0	1	2	0	1
95-99	1	0	1	1	0	1
100 +	0	0	0	0	0	0

United Nations Department of Economic and Social Affairs/Population Division
World Population Prospects: The 2004 Revision, Volume II: Sex and Age Distribution of the World Population

LOW VARIANT   **UNITED STATES VIRGIN ISLANDS**

POPULATION BY AGE AND SEX (in thousands)

Age group	2005 Both sexes	Males	Females	2010 Both sexes	Males	Females	2015 Both sexes	Males	Females	2020 Both sexes	Males	Females
All ages	112	53	59	111	52	59	108	51	57	105	49	56
0-4	8	4	4	6	3	3	6	3	3	5	3	3
5-9	9	4	4	8	4	4	6	3	3	5	3	3
10-14	10	5	5	9	4	4	8	4	4	6	3	3
15-19	10	5	5	10	5	5	8	4	4	7	4	4
20-24	8	4	4	9	4	5	9	5	5	8	4	4
25-29	5	2	3	8	4	4	8	4	4	9	4	4
30-34	6	3	3	4	2	2	7	3	4	7	4	4
35-39	7	3	4	5	2	3	4	2	2	6	3	3
40-44	8	4	4	6	3	3	5	2	3	4	2	2
45-49	8	4	4	7	3	4	6	3	3	5	2	3
50-54	7	3	4	7	3	4	7	3	4	6	3	3
55-59	8	4	4	7	3	4	7	3	4	7	3	4
60-64	7	3	3	7	3	4	7	3	4	7	3	4
65-69	4	2	2	6	3	3	7	3	4	6	3	4
70-74	3	1	2	4	2	2	5	2	3	6	3	4
75-79	2	1	1	3	1	2	3	1	2	5	2	3
80-84	1	0	1	1	1	1	2	1	1	3	1	2
85-89	1	0	0	1	0	1	1	0	1	1	0	1
90-94	0	0	0	0	0	0	0	0	0	1	0	0
95-99	0	0	0	0	0	0	0	0	0	0	0	0
100 +	0	0	0	0	0	0	0	0	0	0	0	0

Age group	2025 Both sexes	Males	Females	2030 Both sexes	Males	Females	2035 Both sexes	Males	Females	2040 Both sexes	Males	Females
All ages	101	47	54	96	45	51	90	42	48	83	38	44
0-4	5	3	2	4	2	2	4	2	2	3	1	1
5-9	5	3	2	5	2	2	4	2	2	3	2	2
10-14	5	3	3	5	3	2	5	2	2	4	2	2
15-19	6	3	3	5	3	2	5	2	2	4	2	2
20-24	7	4	3	5	3	3	4	2	2	4	2	2
25-29	7	4	3	6	3	3	4	2	2	4	2	2
30-34	8	4	4	6	3	3	5	3	3	4	2	2
35-39	7	3	4	8	4	4	6	3	3	5	3	2
40-44	6	3	3	7	3	3	7	4	4	6	3	3
45-49	3	2	2	6	3	3	6	3	3	7	4	3
50-54	5	2	3	3	1	2	6	3	3	6	3	3
55-59	6	3	3	5	2	3	3	1	2	5	3	3
60-64	7	3	4	6	2	3	4	2	3	3	1	2
65-69	6	3	4	6	3	4	5	2	3	4	2	3
70-74	6	2	3	6	3	3	6	2	3	5	2	3
75-79	5	2	3	5	2	3	5	2	3	5	2	3
80-84	4	1	2	4	2	3	4	1	3	4	2	3
85-89	2	1	1	3	1	2	3	1	2	3	1	2
90-94	1	0	1	1	0	1	1	0	1	2	0	1
95-99	0	0	0	0	0	0	0	0	0	1	0	1
100 +	0	0	0	0	0	0	0	0	0	0	0	0

Age group	2045 Both sexes	Males	Females	2050 Both sexes	Males	Females
All ages	75	35	40	67	31	36
0-4	2	1	1	2	1	1
5-9	3	1	1	2	1	1
10-14	3	2	2	3	1	1
15-19	4	2	2	3	2	1
20-24	4	2	2	3	2	2
25-29	3	2	2	3	2	1
30-34	3	2	1	3	1	1
35-39	3	2	2	3	1	1
40-44	5	2	2	3	2	1
45-49	5	3	3	4	2	2
50-54	7	3	3	5	3	2
55-59	6	3	3	7	3	3
60-64	5	3	3	6	3	3
65-69	3	1	2	5	2	3
70-74	4	1	2	3	1	2
75-79	4	2	3	3	1	2
80-84	4	2	3	4	1	2
85-89	3	1	2	3	1	2
90-94	2	0	1	2	0	1
95-99	1	0	1	1	0	1
100 +	0	0	0	0	0	0

POPULATION BY AGE AND SEX (in thousands)

Age group	1950 Both sexes	Males	Females	1955 Both sexes	Males	Females	1960 Both sexes	Males	Females	1965 Both sexes	Males	Females
All ages	2 239	1 132	1 106	2 372	1 193	1 179	2 538	1 270	1 268	2 693	1 343	1 350
0-4	220	111	109	231	118	113	256	130	125	272	139	133
5-9	204	103	101	219	110	109	232	118	114	254	129	124
10-14	200	101	100	204	103	101	220	111	110	231	117	113
15-19	200	101	99	200	101	100	204	103	102	219	110	109
20-24	195	98	97	200	100	99	201	101	100	202	102	101
25-29	177	90	87	195	98	97	202	101	101	198	99	99
30-34	154	79	75	177	89	87	196	98	98	200	100	100
35-39	158	81	78	154	79	75	177	89	88	194	97	97
40-44	138	72	66	156	79	77	153	78	75	174	87	87
45-49	126	66	60	135	70	65	153	77	76	149	75	74
50-54	109	56	52	121	63	58	130	67	63	148	74	74
55-59	94	48	46	102	52	50	115	59	56	123	62	61
60-64	80	40	40	85	42	43	94	46	47	105	52	53
65-69	66	33	33	69	33	36	75	36	39	83	39	43
70-74	51	25	26	53	25	28	56	26	31	62	28	34
75-79	35	16	19	37	17	20	39	17	22	42	18	24
80 +	32	13	19	34	14	20	36	14	22	39	15	24

Age group	1970 Both sexes	Males	Females	1975 Both sexes	Males	Females	1980 Both sexes	Males	Females	1985 Both sexes	Males	Females
All ages	2 808	1 396	1 412	2 829	1 401	1 427	2 914	1 430	1 484	3 009	1 468	1 541
0-4	266	136	130	276	140	135	277	141	136	263	134	129
5-9	267	136	131	250	127	122	267	137	131	280	143	138
10-14	251	128	123	258	132	127	241	123	118	264	135	129
15-19	227	115	111	237	120	117	246	124	122	235	118	116
20-24	212	106	106	204	103	101	222	110	112	232	115	117
25-29	196	98	98	190	95	96	199	99	100	218	107	111
30-34	193	96	97	180	89	90	186	91	95	196	97	99
35-39	194	97	97	179	90	89	175	86	89	183	89	94
40-44	189	94	95	184	91	92	171	84	87	172	84	88
45-49	169	84	84	179	89	91	178	88	90	165	80	86
50-54	143	72	71	159	79	80	173	84	88	171	84	88
55-59	139	68	71	134	66	68	151	73	78	164	78	85
60-64	113	56	57	127	61	67	123	59	64	139	66	74
65-69	93	44	48	99	47	52	113	52	62	110	50	60
70-74	68	31	37	76	35	42	83	37	46	96	41	54
75-79	46	19	27	51	21	30	58	24	34	63	26	37
80 +	42	16	26	46	17	29	51	18	32	58	21	37

Age group	1990 Both sexes	Males	Females	1995 Both sexes	Males	Females	2000 Both sexes	Males	Females	2005 Both sexes	Males	Females
All ages	3 106	1 507	1 598	3 218	1 561	1 658	3 342	1 620	1 722	3 463	1 680	1 783
0-4	271	139	133	281	143	137	283	145	139	282	144	138
5-9	260	133	127	268	137	131	278	142	136	281	144	138
10-14	278	141	136	257	131	126	266	136	130	277	141	135
15-19	260	132	128	275	140	135	255	130	125	264	135	130
20-24	229	114	115	257	130	126	272	138	134	253	129	124
25-29	225	111	115	225	112	113	253	128	125	269	136	133
30-34	214	104	110	222	109	113	222	110	112	250	127	124
35-39	192	94	98	211	102	108	219	107	112	219	109	111
40-44	179	87	92	188	92	96	207	100	107	217	106	111
45-49	167	81	86	175	84	91	185	90	95	204	98	106
50-54	159	76	83	162	78	84	170	81	89	180	87	93
55-59	163	78	85	152	71	81	155	73	82	163	77	86
60-64	152	70	81	151	70	81	142	65	78	146	67	79
65-69	125	56	69	137	61	76	137	61	76	130	57	73
70-74	93	40	53	107	45	62	118	50	69	120	51	69
75-79	74	29	45	73	29	45	86	33	52	97	38	59
80 +	66	23	43	79	27	52	93	31	62	111	36	75

United Nations Department of Economic and Social Affairs/Population Division
World Population Prospects: The 2004 Revision, Volume II: Sex and Age Distribution of the World Population

886

POPULATION BY AGE AND SEX (in thousands)

Age group	2005 Both sexes	2005 Males	2005 Females	2010 Both sexes	2010 Males	2010 Females	2015 Both sexes	2015 Males	2015 Females	2020 Both sexes	2020 Males	2020 Females
All ages	3 463	1 680	1 783	3 575	1 737	1 838	3 676	1 790	1 886	3 767	1 838	1 929
0-4	282	144	138	276	141	135	269	138	132	263	135	129
5-9	281	144	138	280	143	137	275	140	134	267	137	131
10-14	277	141	135	280	143	137	279	142	136	273	140	134
15-19	264	135	130	275	140	135	278	142	136	277	142	136
20-24	253	129	124	262	134	129	273	139	134	276	141	136
25-29	269	136	133	250	127	123	260	132	128	270	138	133
30-34	250	127	124	267	135	132	248	126	122	258	131	127
35-39	219	109	111	248	125	123	264	134	131	246	125	121
40-44	217	106	111	217	107	110	245	124	122	262	132	130
45-49	204	98	106	213	103	110	214	105	108	242	121	120
50-54	180	87	93	199	95	104	208	100	108	209	102	107
55-59	163	77	86	173	82	91	192	91	101	202	96	106
60-64	146	67	79	154	71	83	165	77	88	183	85	98
65-69	130	57	73	134	60	74	143	64	79	153	69	84
70-74	120	51	69	115	48	67	119	51	69	128	55	74
75-79	97	38	59	99	39	60	96	37	59	101	40	61
80-84	63	22	41	72	25	47	75	27	48	74	26	48
85-89	32	10	22	39	12	27	46	15	32	50	16	34
90-94	13	4	10	15	4	11	19	5	14	24	6	17
95-99	3	1	2	4	1	3	5	1	4	7	2	5
100 +	0	0	0	1	0	0	1	0	1	1	0	1

Age group	2025 Both sexes	2025 Males	2025 Females	2030 Both sexes	2030 Males	2030 Females	2035 Both sexes	2035 Males	2035 Females	2040 Both sexes	2040 Males	2040 Females
All ages	3 848	1 881	1 967	3 916	1 918	1 998	3 969	1 946	2 024	4 010	1 967	2 043
0-4	257	132	126	249	127	121	241	123	117	236	121	115
5-9	262	134	128	256	131	125	247	126	121	239	122	117
10-14	266	136	130	260	133	127	254	130	124	246	126	120
15-19	272	139	133	265	135	130	259	132	127	253	129	124
20-24	276	141	135	270	138	132	263	134	129	257	132	126
25-29	274	139	134	273	139	134	268	137	131	261	133	128
30-34	268	136	132	272	138	134	271	138	133	266	136	131
35-39	256	130	126	266	135	131	270	137	133	269	137	132
40-44	244	123	121	253	128	125	264	134	130	268	136	132
45-49	258	130	128	241	121	119	250	126	124	261	132	129
50-54	237	118	119	253	127	127	236	118	118	246	123	123
55-59	203	98	105	230	114	117	247	122	125	230	114	116
60-64	193	90	103	195	93	102	221	108	114	237	116	122
65-69	171	77	94	181	82	99	183	85	98	209	99	109
70-74	138	60	78	156	67	88	165	72	93	168	75	93
75-79	110	44	66	119	49	70	135	55	80	144	60	84
80-84	79	29	50	86	32	54	95	36	59	108	41	67
85-89	50	16	34	54	18	36	59	20	40	66	22	43
90-94	26	7	18	26	7	19	29	8	20	32	9	23
95-99	8	2	6	9	2	7	10	2	7	11	3	8
100 +	1	0	1	2	0	1	2	0	1	2	0	1

Age group	2045 Both sexes	2045 Males	2045 Females	2050 Both sexes	2050 Males	2050 Females
All ages	4 035	1 980	2 055	4 043	1 984	2 059
0-4	231	118	113	225	115	110
5-9	235	120	114	229	117	112
10-14	238	122	116	233	119	114
15-19	245	125	120	237	121	116
20-24	251	129	123	243	124	119
25-29	255	130	125	249	127	122
30-34	259	132	127	254	129	124
35-39	264	134	130	257	131	126
40-44	267	136	132	262	133	129
45-49	265	134	131	264	134	131
50-54	257	129	128	261	131	130
55-59	240	119	121	251	125	126
60-64	222	109	114	232	114	118
65-69	224	107	118	211	101	110
70-74	192	88	104	207	95	111
75-79	147	62	84	169	74	95
80-84	116	45	71	119	47	72
85-89	76	26	50	82	29	54
90-94	36	11	25	42	13	30
95-99	12	3	9	14	4	10
100 +	2	1	2	2	1	2

United Nations Department of Economic and Social Affairs/Population Division
World Population Prospects: The 2004 Revision, Volume II: Sex and Age Distribution of the World Population

887

POPULATION BY AGE AND SEX (in thousands)

Age group	2005 Both sexes	Males	Females	2010 Both sexes	Males	Females	2015 Both sexes	Males	Females	2020 Both sexes	Males	Females
All ages	3 463	1 680	1 783	3 605	1 753	1 853	3 756	1 831	1 925	3 910	1 911	1 999
0-4	282	144	138	307	157	150	319	163	156	326	167	159
5-9	281	144	138	280	143	137	305	156	149	317	162	155
10-14	277	141	135	280	143	137	279	142	136	304	155	148
15-19	264	135	130	275	140	135	278	142	136	277	142	136
20-24	253	129	124	262	134	129	273	139	134	276	141	136
25-29	269	136	133	250	127	123	260	132	128	270	138	133
30-34	250	127	124	267	135	132	248	126	122	258	131	127
35-39	219	109	111	248	125	123	264	134	131	246	125	121
40-44	217	106	111	217	107	110	245	124	122	262	132	130
45-49	204	98	106	213	103	110	214	105	108	242	121	120
50-54	180	87	93	199	95	104	208	100	108	209	102	107
55-59	163	77	86	173	82	91	192	91	101	202	96	106
60-64	146	67	79	154	71	83	165	77	88	183	85	98
65-69	130	57	73	134	60	74	143	64	79	153	69	84
70-74	120	51	69	115	48	67	119	51	69	128	55	74
75-79	97	38	59	99	39	60	96	37	59	101	40	61
80-84	63	22	41	72	25	47	75	27	48	74	26	48
85-89	32	10	22	39	12	27	46	15	32	50	16	34
90-94	13	4	10	15	4	11	19	5	14	24	6	17
95-99	3	1	2	4	1	3	5	1	4	7	2	5
100 +	0	0	0	1	0	0	1	0	1	1	0	1

Age group	2025 Both sexes	Males	Females	2030 Both sexes	Males	Females	2035 Both sexes	Males	Females	2040 Both sexes	Males	Females
All ages	4 057	1 988	2 069	4 201	2 063	2 138	4 346	2 138	2 208	4 494	2 214	2 280
0-4	324	166	158	325	166	159	332	170	162	344	176	168
5-9	324	166	159	322	165	157	324	166	158	331	169	161
10-14	316	161	154	323	165	158	321	164	157	322	165	157
15-19	302	154	148	314	161	154	322	164	157	319	163	156
20-24	276	141	135	300	153	147	312	160	153	320	163	157
25-29	274	139	134	273	139	134	298	152	146	310	158	152
30-34	268	136	132	272	138	134	271	138	133	296	151	145
35-39	256	130	126	266	135	131	270	137	133	269	137	132
40-44	244	123	121	253	128	125	264	134	130	268	136	132
45-49	258	130	128	241	121	119	250	126	124	261	132	129
50-54	237	118	119	253	127	127	236	118	118	246	123	123
55-59	203	98	105	230	114	117	247	122	125	230	114	116
60-64	193	90	103	195	93	102	221	108	114	237	116	122
65-69	171	77	94	181	82	99	183	85	98	209	99	109
70-74	138	60	78	156	67	88	165	72	93	168	75	93
75-79	110	44	66	119	49	70	135	55	80	144	60	84
80-84	79	29	50	86	32	54	95	36	59	108	41	67
85-89	50	16	34	54	18	36	59	20	40	66	22	43
90-94	26	7	18	26	7	19	29	8	20	32	9	23
95-99	8	2	6	9	2	7	10	2	7	11	3	8
100 +	1	0	1	2	0	1	2	0	1	2	0	1

Age group	2045 Both sexes	Males	Females	2050 Both sexes	Males	Females
All ages	4 641	2 289	2 352	4 784	2 362	2 421
0-4	354	181	173	360	184	175
5-9	343	175	167	352	180	172
10-14	329	169	161	342	175	167
15-19	321	164	157	328	168	160
20-24	318	162	155	319	163	156
25-29	318	162	155	315	161	154
30-34	308	157	151	316	161	155
35-39	294	150	144	306	156	150
40-44	267	136	132	292	148	144
45-49	265	134	131	264	134	131
50-54	257	129	128	261	131	130
55-59	240	119	121	251	125	126
60-64	222	109	114	232	114	118
65-69	224	107	118	211	101	110
70-74	192	88	104	207	95	111
75-79	147	62	84	169	74	95
80-84	116	45	71	119	47	72
85-89	76	26	50	82	29	54
90-94	36	11	25	42	13	30
95-99	12	3	9	14	4	10
100 +	2	1	2	2	1	2

United Nations Department of Economic and Social Affairs/Population Division
World Population Prospects: The 2004 Revision, Volume II: Sex and Age Distribution of the World Population

888

POPULATION BY AGE AND SEX (in thousands)

Age group	2005 Both sexes	Males	Females	2010 Both sexes	Males	Females	2015 Both sexes	Males	Females	2020 Both sexes	Males	Females
All ages	3 463	1 680	1 793	3 645	1 722	1 823	3 595	1 749	1 847	3 623	1 764	1 858
0-4	282	144	138	246	126	120	219	112	107	199	102	97
5-9	281	144	138	280	143	137	244	125	119	217	111	106
10-14	277	141	135	280	143	137	279	142	136	243	124	119
15-19	264	135	130	275	140	135	278	142	136	277	142	136
20-24	253	129	124	262	134	129	273	139	134	276	141	136
25-29	269	136	133	250	127	123	260	132	128	270	138	133
30-34	250	127	124	267	135	132	248	126	122	258	131	127
35-39	219	109	111	248	125	123	264	134	131	246	125	121
40-44	217	106	111	217	107	110	245	124	122	262	132	130
45-49	204	98	106	213	103	110	214	105	108	242	121	120
50-54	180	87	93	199	95	104	208	100	108	209	102	107
55-59	163	77	86	173	82	91	192	91	101	202	96	106
60-64	146	67	79	154	71	83	165	77	88	183	85	98
65-69	130	57	73	134	60	74	143	64	79	153	69	84
70-74	120	51	69	115	48	67	119	51	69	128	55	74
75-79	97	38	59	99	39	60	96	37	59	101	40	61
80-84	63	22	41	72	25	47	75	27	48	74	26	48
85-89	32	10	22	39	12	27	46	15	32	50	16	34
90-94	13	4	10	15	4	11	19	5	14	24	6	17
95-99	3	1	2	4	1	3	5	1	4	7	2	5
100 +	0	0	0	1	0	0	1	0	1	1	0	1

Age group	2025 Both sexes	Males	Females	2030 Both sexes	Males	Females	2035 Both sexes	Males	Females	2040 Both sexes	Males	Females
All ages	3 637	1 773	1 863	3 630	1 771	1 859	3 599	1 756	1 843	3 545	1 729	1 816
0-4	190	97	93	174	89	85	155	80	76	141	72	69
5-9	198	101	97	189	97	92	173	88	84	154	79	75
10-14	216	111	106	197	101	96	188	96	92	171	88	84
15-19	241	123	118	215	110	105	196	100	96	186	95	91
20-24	276	141	135	240	122	117	213	109	104	194	99	95
25-29	274	139	134	273	139	134	237	121	116	211	108	103
30-34	268	136	132	272	138	134	271	138	133	236	120	116
35-39	256	130	126	266	135	131	270	137	133	269	137	132
40-44	244	123	121	253	128	125	264	134	130	268	136	132
45-49	258	130	128	241	121	119	250	126	124	261	132	129
50-54	237	118	119	253	127	127	236	118	118	246	123	123
55-59	203	98	105	230	114	117	247	122	125	233	114	118
60-64	193	90	103	195	93	102	221	108	114	237	116	122
65-69	171	77	94	181	82	99	183	85	98	209	99	109
70-74	138	60	78	156	67	88	165	72	93	168	75	93
75-79	110	44	66	119	49	70	135	55	80	144	60	84
80-84	79	29	50	86	32	54	95	36	59	108	41	67
85-89	50	16	34	54	18	36	59	20	40	66	22	43
90-94	26	7	18	26	7	19	29	8	20	32	9	23
95-99	8	2	6	9	2	7	10	2	7	11	3	8
100 +	1	0	1	2	0	1	2	0	1	2	0	1

Age group	2045 Both sexes	Males	Females	2050 Both sexes	Males	Females
All ages	3 470	1 691	1 779	3 373	1 641	1 732
0-4	129	66	63	119	61	58
5-9	140	72	68	128	66	62
10-14	153	78	75	139	71	68
15-19	170	87	83	152	78	74
20-24	185	94	90	169	86	82
25-29	192	98	94	183	93	89
30-34	210	107	103	190	97	93
35-39	234	119	115	208	106	102
40-44	267	136	132	232	118	114
45-49	265	134	131	264	134	131
50-54	257	129	128	261	131	130
55-59	240	119	121	251	125	126
60-64	222	109	114	232	114	118
65-69	224	107	118	211	101	110
70-74	192	88	104	207	95	111
75-79	147	62	84	169	74	95
80-84	116	45	71	119	47	72
85-89	76	26	50	82	29	54
90-94	36	11	25	42	13	30
95-99	12	3	9	14	4	10
100 +	2	1	2	2	1	2

POPULATION BY AGE AND SEX (in thousands)

Age group	1950 Both sexes	1950 Males	1950 Females	1955 Both sexes	1955 Males	1955 Females	1960 Both sexes	1960 Males	1960 Females	1965 Both sexes	1965 Males	1965 Females
All ages	6 314	3 057	3 257	7 255	3 494	3 761	8 559	4 138	4 420	10 234	4 970	5 264
0-4	662	314	348	1 080	536	545	1 567	801	765	1 894	965	929
5-9	567	292	276	664	314	350	1 067	528	539	1 562	797	765
10-14	772	395	376	584	300	284	671	317	354	1 084	536	548
15-19	636	322	314	789	404	385	590	303	288	684	323	361
20-24	631	321	310	650	329	321	791	405	386	599	307	292
25-29	399	174	226	640	325	315	651	328	322	795	406	389
30-34	289	118	171	405	175	229	636	321	315	654	329	325
35-39	386	154	231	292	118	174	402	173	229	634	319	316
40-44	414	184	230	385	152	233	289	116	173	400	171	229
45-49	425	202	223	408	179	229	374	146	228	285	113	173
50-54	324	163	161	410	191	219	389	167	222	361	138	223
55-59	233	123	109	304	149	155	380	172	208	367	153	214
60-64	224	119	105	210	108	101	272	130	142	345	152	193
65-69	158	81	77	192	99	93	179	90	90	237	109	128
70-74	101	50	50	126	61	64	152	75	77	146	70	76
75-79	57	28	30	70	33	37	88	40	48	109	50	58
80 +	36	17	19	48	22	26	60	27	34	78	33	44

Age group	1970 Both sexes	1970 Males	1970 Females	1975 Both sexes	1975 Males	1975 Females	1980 Both sexes	1980 Males	1980 Females	1985 Both sexes	1985 Males	1985 Females
All ages	11 973	5 830	6 143	13 981	6 863	7 118	15 952	7 844	8 108	18 174	8 968	9 206
0-4	1 916	969	948	2 192	1 110	1 081	2 415	1 220	1 194	2 856	1 447	1 409
5-9	1 901	966	935	1 960	990	971	2 161	1 090	1 070	2 362	1 193	1 169
10-14	1 591	811	780	1 907	972	936	1 953	986	967	2 140	1 079	1 061
15-19	1 105	546	560	1 598	812	786	1 904	967	937	1 907	957	950
20-24	696	329	367	1 176	589	588	1 589	789	801	1 875	950	925
25-29	608	310	297	739	367	372	1 157	579	579	1 558	780	778
30-34	801	408	394	605	310	296	773	388	385	1 132	564	567
35-39	658	330	329	791	402	389	549	282	267	746	372	374
40-44	633	316	317	637	318	319	779	394	385	535	275	260
45-49	396	167	229	608	297	312	610	304	306	748	374	375
50-54	279	108	171	410	161	248	593	285	308	586	286	300
55-59	345	128	216	272	101	172	399	156	242	564	266	298
60-64	338	137	201	309	114	195	260	92	169	363	139	224
65-69	304	130	175	281	112	169	266	95	171	229	78	151
70-74	195	86	109	240	101	140	222	86	136	219	75	144
75-79	107	48	59	132	58	75	180	72	108	166	62	104
80 +	100	42	57	120	50	70	142	59	83	188	71	116

Age group	1990 Both sexes	1990 Males	1990 Females	1995 Both sexes	1995 Males	1995 Females	2000 Both sexes	2000 Males	2000 Females	2005 Both sexes	2005 Males	2005 Females
All ages	20 515	10 141	10 374	22 918	11 371	11 548	24 724	12 291	12 433	26 593	13 224	13 369
0-4	3 270	1 663	1 607	3 306	1 683	1 623	2 810	1 431	1 380	2 841	1 446	1 394
5-9	2 779	1 403	1 375	3 201	1 626	1 575	3 238	1 646	1 592	2 762	1 404	1 358
10-14	2 344	1 183	1 160	2 743	1 384	1 359	3 158	1 603	1 555	3 220	1 636	1 584
15-19	2 101	1 058	1 043	2 311	1 166	1 145	2 702	1 363	1 340	3 127	1 587	1 540
20-24	1 829	907	922	2 066	1 039	1 027	2 269	1 143	1 126	2 641	1 331	1 310
25-29	1 798	889	909	1 789	885	904	2 023	1 015	1 008	2 194	1 104	1 090
30-34	1 520	757	763	1 751	863	888	1 743	859	884	1 954	978	977
35-39	1 095	542	552	1 471	729	741	1 695	832	863	1 686	827	858
40-44	710	351	359	1 049	517	532	1 411	696	715	1 641	800	841
45-49	509	261	249	673	330	343	993	485	508	1 358	663	694
50-54	699	344	354	470	238	232	626	303	323	944	455	489
55-59	538	258	280	637	309	328	422	211	211	583	277	306
60-64	502	233	269	473	222	250	561	267	294	381	186	195
65-69	304	114	190	426	193	234	398	183	215	492	226	265
70-74	180	59	122	244	87	157	339	148	191	328	144	184
75-79	154	51	102	130	40	90	177	59	117	253	103	149
80 +	185	67	117	178	60	119	160	47	112	189	55	134

890

United Nations Department of Economic and Social Affairs/Population Division
World Population Prospects: The 2004 Revision, Volume II: Sex and Age Distribution of the World Population

POPULATION BY AGE AND SEX (in thousands)

Age group	2005 Both sexes	Males	Females	2010 Both sexes	Males	Females	2015 Both sexes	Males	Females	2020 Both sexes	Males	Females
All ages	26 590	13 224	13 369	28 578	14 209	14 368	30 651	15 234	15 417	32 515	16 148	16 367
0-4	2 841	1 446	1 394	2 929	1 491	1 437	2 985	1 521	1 464	2 838	1 447	1 391
5-9	2 762	1 404	1 358	2 798	1 423	1 375	2 894	1 472	1 422	2 954	1 504	1 450
10-14	3 220	1 636	1 584	2 748	1 397	1 352	2 788	1 417	1 371	2 884	1 466	1 418
15-19	3 127	1 587	1 540	3 195	1 623	1 573	2 733	1 388	1 345	2 774	1 409	1 365
20-24	2 641	1 331	1 310	3 080	1 562	1 518	3 165	1 606	1 559	2 706	1 374	1 333
25-29	2 194	1 104	1 090	2 583	1 300	1 283	3 040	1 540	1 500	3 127	1 585	1 543
30-34	1 954	978	977	2 141	1 074	1 067	2 545	1 278	1 267	3 001	1 517	1 485
35-39	1 686	827	858	1 908	951	957	2 106	1 053	1 053	2 509	1 256	1 253
40-44	1 641	800	841	1 641	801	840	1 870	927	943	2 068	1 030	1 039
45-49	1 358	663	694	1 589	768	821	1 597	773	824	1 824	898	926
50-54	944	455	489	1 299	627	673	1 529	730	799	1 542	738	804
55-59	583	277	306	887	419	467	1 228	582	646	1 452	681	770
60-64	381	186	195	532	247	286	815	377	439	1 136	526	610
65-69	492	226	265	335	159	176	473	212	260	729	327	402
70-74	328	144	184	408	180	228	280	127	153	400	172	228
75-79	253	103	149	247	101	145	311	128	182	216	92	124
80-84	116	36	80	166	63	103	164	62	102	210	80	130
85-89	43	11	32	64	18	46	93	32	61	93	32	61
90-94	21	6	15	19	4	15	28	7	21	41	13	28
95-99	7	2	5	7	2	5	6	1	5	9	2	7
100 +	2	1	1	2	1	1	2	1	1	2	0	1

Age group	2025 Both sexes	Males	Females	2030 Both sexes	Males	Females	2035 Both sexes	Males	Females	2040 Both sexes	Males	Females
All ages	34 042	16 887	17 154	35 329	17 501	17 828	36 490	18 050	18 440	37 482	18 515	18 967
0-4	2 580	1 316	1 264	2 446	1 249	1 197	2 460	1 256	1 204	2 458	1 255	1 203
5-9	2 812	1 432	1 379	2 559	1 305	1 254	2 428	1 239	1 189	2 443	1 247	1 196
10-14	2 945	1 498	1 447	2 804	1 428	1 376	2 552	1 301	1 251	2 422	1 235	1 186
15-19	2 870	1 459	1 412	2 932	1 491	1 441	2 792	1 422	1 371	2 542	1 295	1 246
20-24	2 748	1 395	1 353	2 846	1 446	1 400	2 909	1 479	1 430	2 769	1 410	1 360
25-29	2 674	1 355	1 318	2 717	1 378	1 339	2 815	1 429	1 387	2 879	1 462	1 417
30-34	3 091	1 563	1 528	2 642	1 337	1 305	2 686	1 360	1 326	2 786	1 411	1 374
35-39	2 964	1 493	1 470	3 055	1 541	1 514	2 612	1 319	1 293	2 658	1 343	1 315
40-44	2 469	1 231	1 238	2 922	1 467	1 455	3 015	1 516	1 499	2 579	1 298	1 281
45-49	2 023	1 000	1 022	2 420	1 199	1 221	2 868	1 432	1 436	2 964	1 483	1 481
50-54	1 766	860	905	1 963	962	1 001	2 354	1 156	1 197	2 795	1 385	1 410
55-59	1 469	692	777	1 699	810	870	1 882	905	972	2 262	1 097	1 165
60-64	1 350	620	730	1 372	633	739	1 582	745	837	1 769	839	930
65-69	1 022	460	562	1 221	545	676	1 246	559	687	1 442	662	781
70-74	621	267	354	877	379	498	1 054	453	602	1 083	468	615
75-79	312	126	186	490	198	292	698	284	414	847	343	504
80-84	148	58	89	217	81	136	346	129	216	498	188	310
85-89	121	42	79	86	31	55	129	44	85	208	70	138
90-94	42	13	29	56	17	38	40	13	27	61	18	43
95-99	14	4	10	14	4	10	19	5	14	14	4	10
100 +	2	1	2	3	1	2	4	1	3	5	1	4

Age group	2045 Both sexes	Males	Females	2050 Both sexes	Males	Females
All ages	38 222	18 859	19 363	38 665	19 058	19 607
0-4	2 386	1 219	1 168	2 270	1 159	1 111
5-9	2 443	1 247	1 196	2 373	1 211	1 162
10-14	2 437	1 244	1 194	2 438	1 244	1 194
15-19	2 411	1 230	1 182	2 427	1 238	1 189
20-24	2 520	1 284	1 236	2 391	1 219	1 172
25-29	2 741	1 394	1 347	2 493	1 270	1 224
30-34	2 850	1 446	1 404	2 714	1 379	1 335
35-39	2 758	1 395	1 363	2 823	1 430	1 393
40-44	2 626	1 323	1 303	2 727	1 376	1 351
45-49	2 537	1 271	1 265	2 586	1 298	1 288
50-54	2 893	1 437	1 456	2 479	1 234	1 245
55-59	2 692	1 318	1 374	2 792	1 372	1 420
60-64	2 133	1 017	1 116	2 545	1 226	1 319
65-69	1 619	750	870	1 959	912	1 047
70-74	1 259	557	702	1 420	635	785
75-79	876	358	518	1 025	430	595
80-84	610	229	381	637	242	395
85-89	304	104	200	377	128	249
90-94	100	30	70	148	45	104
95-99	21	6	16	36	9	26
100 +	4	1	3	5	1	4

United Nations Department of Economic and Social Affairs/Population Division
World Population Prospects: The 2004 Revision, Volume II: Sex and Age Distribution of the World Population

891

POPULATION BY AGE AND SEX (in thousands)

Age group	2005 Both sexes	Males	Females	2010 Both sexes	Males	Females	2015 Both sexes	Males	Females	2020 Both sexes	Males	Females
All ages	26 593	13 224	13 369	28 873	14 360	14 513	31 469	15 650	15 819	34 005	16 907	17 098
0-4	2 841	1 446	1 394	3 224	1 642	1 582	3 511	1 789	1 722	3 516	1 792	1 723
5-9	2 762	1 404	1 358	2 798	1 423	1 375	3 186	1 621	1 565	3 475	1 769	1 706
10-14	3 220	1 636	1 584	2 748	1 397	1 352	2 788	1 417	1 371	3 175	1 614	1 561
15-19	3 127	1 587	1 540	3 195	1 623	1 573	2 733	1 388	1 345	2 774	1 409	1 365
20-24	2 641	1 331	1 310	3 080	1 562	1 518	3 165	1 606	1 559	2 706	1 374	1 333
25-29	2 194	1 104	1 090	2 583	1 300	1 283	3 040	1 540	1 500	3 127	1 585	1 543
30-34	1 954	978	977	2 141	1 074	1 067	2 545	1 278	1 267	3 001	1 517	1 485
35-39	1 686	827	858	1 908	951	957	2 106	1 053	1 053	2 509	1 256	1 253
40-44	1 641	800	841	1 641	801	840	1 870	927	943	2 068	1 030	1 039
45-49	1 358	663	694	1 589	768	821	1 597	773	824	1 824	898	926
50-54	944	455	489	1 299	627	673	1 529	730	799	1 542	738	804
55-59	583	277	306	887	419	467	1 228	582	646	1 452	681	770
60-64	381	186	195	532	247	286	815	377	439	1 136	526	610
65-69	492	226	265	335	159	176	473	212	260	729	327	402
70-74	328	144	184	408	180	228	280	127	153	400	172	228
75-79	253	103	149	247	101	145	311	128	182	216	92	124
80-84	116	36	80	166	63	103	164	62	102	210	80	130
85-89	43	11	32	64	18	46	93	32	61	93	32	61
90-94	21	6	15	19	4	15	28	7	21	41	13	28
95-99	7	2	5	7	2	5	6	1	5	9	2	7
100 +	2	1	1	2	1	1	2	1	1	2	0	1

Age group	2025 Both sexes	Males	Females	2030 Both sexes	Males	Females	2035 Both sexes	Males	Females	2040 Both sexes	Males	Females
All ages	36 204	17 988	18 215	38 240	18 984	19 256	40 329	20 006	20 324	42 449	21 046	21 403
0-4	3 259	1 662	1 596	3 202	1 635	1 568	3 398	1 735	1 663	3 598	1 837	1 761
5-9	3 485	1 775	1 709	3 233	1 648	1 585	3 180	1 622	1 557	3 376	1 723	1 653
10-14	3 465	1 763	1 702	3 476	1 770	1 706	3 225	1 644	1 581	3 173	1 618	1 554
15-19	3 161	1 607	1 555	3 451	1 755	1 696	3 463	1 763	1 700	3 213	1 637	1 576
20-24	2 748	1 395	1 353	3 136	1 593	1 543	3 426	1 741	1 684	3 438	1 750	1 689
25-29	2 674	1 355	1 318	2 717	1 378	1 339	3 104	1 575	1 529	3 394	1 724	1 670
30-34	3 091	1 563	1 528	2 642	1 337	1 305	2 686	1 360	1 326	3 073	1 557	1 516
35-39	2 964	1 493	1 470	3 055	1 541	1 514	2 612	1 319	1 293	2 658	1 343	1 315
40-44	2 469	1 231	1 238	2 922	1 467	1 455	3 015	1 516	1 499	2 579	1 298	1 281
45-49	2 023	1 000	1 022	2 420	1 199	1 221	2 868	1 432	1 436	2 964	1 483	1 481
50-54	1 766	860	905	1 963	962	1 001	2 354	1 156	1 197	2 795	1 385	1 410
55-59	1 469	692	777	1 688	810	878	1 882	909	972	2 262	1 097	1 165
60-64	1 350	620	730	1 372	633	739	1 582	745	837	1 769	839	930
65-69	1 022	460	562	1 221	545	676	1 246	559	687	1 442	662	781
70-74	621	267	354	877	379	498	1 054	453	602	1 083	468	615
75-79	312	126	186	490	198	292	698	284	414	847	343	504
80-84	148	58	89	217	81	136	346	129	216	498	188	310
85-89	121	42	79	86	31	55	129	44	85	208	70	138
90-94	42	13	29	56	17	38	40	13	27	61	18	43
95-99	14	4	10	14	4	10	19	5	14	14	4	10
100 +	2	1	2	3	1	2	4	1	3	5	1	4

Age group	2045 Both sexes	Males	Females	2050 Both sexes	Males	Females
All ages	44 450	22 032	22 418	46 227	22 910	23 317
0-4	3 663	1 870	1 793	3 623	1 850	1 773
5-9	3 578	1 826	1 752	3 645	1 860	1 784
10-14	3 370	1 719	1 650	3 571	1 822	1 749
15-19	3 161	1 612	1 549	3 358	1 713	1 645
20-24	3 190	1 625	1 565	3 139	1 600	1 539
25-29	3 408	1 733	1 675	3 161	1 609	1 552
30-34	3 363	1 706	1 657	3 378	1 716	1 662
35-39	3 043	1 539	1 504	3 333	1 688	1 645
40-44	2 626	1 323	1 303	3 010	1 519	1 491
45-49	2 537	1 271	1 265	2 586	1 298	1 288
50-54	2 893	1 437	1 456	2 479	1 234	1 245
55-59	2 692	1 318	1 374	2 792	1 372	1 420
60-64	2 133	1 017	1 116	2 545	1 226	1 319
65-69	1 619	750	870	1 959	912	1 047
70-74	1 259	557	702	1 420	635	785
75-79	876	358	518	1 025	430	595
80-84	610	229	381	637	242	395
85-89	304	104	200	377	128	249
90-94	100	30	70	148	45	104
95-99	21	6	16	36	9	26
100 +	4	1	3	5	1	4

United Nations Department of Economic and Social Affairs/Population Division
World Population Prospects: The 2004 Revision, Volume II: Sex and Age Distribution of the World Population

POPULATION BY AGE AND SEX (in thousands)

Age group	2005 Both sexes	Males	Females	2010 Both sexes	Males	Females	2015 Both sexes	Males	Females	2020 Both sexes	Males	Females
All ages	26 593	13 224	13 369	28 283	14 059	14 224	29 834	14 818	15 016	31 024	15 389	15 635
0-4	2 841	1 446	1 394	2 634	1 341	1 293	2 459	1 253	1 206	2 159	1 101	1 058
5-9	2 762	1 404	1 358	2 798	1 423	1 375	2 601	1 323	1 278	2 433	1 238	1 195
10-14	3 220	1 636	1 584	2 748	1 397	1 352	2 788	1 417	1 371	2 592	1 318	1 274
15-19	3 127	1 587	1 540	3 195	1 623	1 573	2 733	1 388	1 345	2 774	1 409	1 365
20-24	2 641	1 331	1 310	3 080	1 562	1 518	3 165	1 606	1 559	2 706	1 374	1 333
25-29	2 194	1 104	1 090	2 583	1 300	1 283	3 040	1 540	1 500	3 127	1 585	1 543
30-34	1 954	978	977	2 141	1 074	1 067	2 545	1 278	1 267	3 001	1 517	1 485
35-39	1 686	827	858	1 908	951	957	2 106	1 053	1 053	2 509	1 256	1 253
40-44	1 641	800	841	1 641	801	840	1 870	927	943	2 068	1 030	1 039
45-49	1 358	663	694	1 589	768	821	1 597	773	824	1 824	898	926
50-54	944	455	489	1 299	627	673	1 529	730	799	1 542	738	804
55-59	583	277	306	887	419	467	1 228	582	646	1 452	681	770
60-64	381	186	195	532	247	286	815	377	439	1 136	526	610
65-69	492	226	265	335	159	176	473	212	260	729	327	402
70-74	328	144	184	408	180	228	280	127	153	400	172	228
75-79	253	103	149	247	101	145	311	128	182	216	92	124
80-84	116	36	80	166	63	103	164	62	102	210	80	130
85-89	43	11	32	64	18	46	93	32	61	93	32	61
90-94	21	6	15	19	4	15	28	7	21	41	13	28
95-99	7	2	5	7	2	5	6	1	5	9	2	7
100 +	2	1	1	2	1	1	2	1	1	2	0	1

Age group	2025 Both sexes	Males	Females	2030 Both sexes	Males	Females	2035 Both sexes	Males	Females	2040 Both sexes	Males	Females
All ages	31 885	15 789	16 096	32 464	16 042	16 422	32 812	16 176	16 636	32 877	16 170	16 708
0-4	1 907	973	934	1 730	883	847	1 637	836	801	1 521	776	744
5-9	2 138	1 089	1 049	1 890	964	926	1 716	875	840	1 625	829	796
10-14	2 425	1 234	1 191	2 132	1 086	1 046	1 884	960	924	1 711	873	838
15-19	2 580	1 311	1 269	2 414	1 228	1 186	2 121	1 080	1 041	1 875	955	919
20-24	2 748	1 395	1 353	2 556	1 299	1 258	2 391	1 216	1 176	2 101	1 069	1 031
25-29	2 674	1 355	1 318	2 717	1 378	1 339	2 527	1 282	1 245	2 364	1 201	1 163
30-34	3 091	1 563	1 528	2 642	1 337	1 305	2 686	1 360	1 326	2 499	1 266	1 232
35-39	2 964	1 493	1 470	3 055	1 541	1 514	2 612	1 319	1 293	2 658	1 343	1 315
40-44	2 469	1 231	1 238	2 922	1 467	1 455	3 015	1 516	1 499	2 579	1 298	1 281
45-49	2 023	1 000	1 022	2 420	1 199	1 221	2 868	1 432	1 436	2 964	1 483	1 481
50-54	1 766	860	905	1 963	962	1 001	2 354	1 156	1 197	2 795	1 385	1 410
55-59	1 460	692	777	1 688	810	878	1 882	909	972	2 262	1 097	1 165
60-64	1 350	620	730	1 372	633	739	1 582	745	837	1 769	839	930
65-69	1 022	460	562	1 221	545	676	1 246	559	687	1 442	662	781
70-74	621	267	354	877	379	498	1 054	453	602	1 083	468	615
75-79	312	126	186	490	198	292	698	284	414	847	343	504
80-84	148	58	89	217	81	136	346	129	216	498	188	310
85-89	121	42	79	86	31	55	129	44	85	208	70	138
90-94	42	13	29	56	17	38	40	13	27	61	18	43
95-99	14	4	10	14	4	10	19	5	14	14	4	10
100 +	2	1	2	3	1	2	4	1	3	5	1	4

Age group	2045 Both sexes	Males	Females	2050 Both sexes	Males	Females
All ages	32 625	16 008	16 616	32 057	15 693	16 364
0-4	1 380	705	675	1 241	634	607
5-9	1 510	771	739	1 370	699	671
10-14	1 620	827	794	1 506	768	737
15-19	1 702	868	834	1 612	822	789
20-24	1 855	945	910	1 683	858	824
25-29	2 074	1 055	1 019	1 830	932	898
30-34	2 337	1 186	1 151	2 050	1 042	1 008
35-39	2 472	1 251	1 222	2 313	1 172	1 141
40-44	2 626	1 323	1 303	2 444	1 233	1 210
45-49	2 537	1 271	1 265	2 586	1 298	1 288
50-54	2 893	1 437	1 456	2 479	1 234	1 245
55-59	2 692	1 318	1 374	2 792	1 372	1 420
60-64	2 133	1 017	1 116	2 545	1 226	1 319
65-69	1 619	750	870	1 959	912	1 047
70-74	1 259	557	702	1 420	635	785
75-79	876	358	518	1 025	430	595
80-84	610	229	381	637	242	395
85-89	304	104	200	377	128	249
90-94	100	30	70	148	45	104
95-99	21	6	16	36	9	26
100 +	4	1	3	5	1	4

POPULATION BY AGE AND SEX (in thousands)

Age group	1950 Both sexes	1950 Males	1950 Females	1955 Both sexes	1955 Males	1955 Females	1960 Both sexes	1960 Males	1960 Females	1965 Both sexes	1965 Males	1965 Females
All ages	48	25	23	55	29	26	64	33	31	75	38	36
0-4	9	5	4	10	5	5	12	6	6	14	7	7
5-9	7	4	3	8	4	4	10	5	5	11	6	6
10-14	6	3	3	7	4	3	8	4	4	10	5	5
15-19	5	3	2	6	3	3	7	4	3	8	4	4
20-24	4	2	2	5	3	2	6	3	3	7	3	3
25-29	3	2	2	4	2	2	5	2	2	5	3	3
30-34	3	2	1	3	2	2	4	2	2	4	2	2
35-39	2	1	1	3	1	1	3	2	2	4	2	2
40-44	2	1	1	2	1	1	3	1	1	3	2	1
45-49	2	1	1	2	1	1	2	1	1	2	1	1
50-54	1	1	1	1	1	1	2	1	1	2	1	1
55-59	1	1	0	1	1	1	1	1	1	1	1	1
60-64	1	0	0	1	0	0	1	0	0	1	1	1
65-69	1	0	0	1	0	0	1	0	0	1	0	0
70-74	0	0	0	0	0	0	0	0	0	0	0	0
75-79	0	0	0	0	0	0	0	0	0	0	0	0
80 +	0	0	0	0	0	0	0	0	0	0	0	0

Age group	1970 Both sexes	1970 Males	1970 Females	1975 Both sexes	1975 Males	1975 Females	1980 Both sexes	1980 Males	1980 Females	1985 Both sexes	1985 Males	1985 Females
All ages	86	46	40	101	54	47	117	62	55	132	69	63
0-4	15	8	7	17	9	8	20	11	10	22	12	11
5-9	13	7	6	15	8	7	18	9	8	20	11	9
10-14	11	6	5	13	7	6	15	8	7	17	9	8
15-19	9	5	4	11	6	5	13	7	6	13	7	7
20-24	7	4	4	9	5	4	11	5	5	12	6	6
25-29	7	4	3	8	4	4	9	4	4	10	5	5
30-34	5	3	2	6	3	3	7	3	3	8	4	4
35-39	5	3	2	5	3	3	6	3	3	7	4	3
40-44	3	2	1	4	2	2	5	2	2	5	3	3
45-49	3	2	1	4	2	1	4	2	2	5	3	2
50-54	2	1	1	2	1	1	3	1	1	3	2	1
55-59	2	1	1	2	1	1	2	1	1	3	2	1
60-64	1	1	1	2	1	1	2	1	1	2	1	1
65-69	1	1	0	1	1	1	1	1	1	2	1	1
70-74	1	0	0	1	0	0	1	1	0	1	1	0
75-79	0	0	0	1	0	0	1	1	0	1	1	0
80 +	0	0	0	0	0	0	0	0	0	1	0	0

Age group	1990 Both sexes	1990 Males	1990 Females	1995 Both sexes	1995 Males	1995 Females	2000 Both sexes	2000 Males	2000 Females	2005 Both sexes	2005 Males	2005 Females
All ages	149	77	72	172	88	84	191	98	94	211	108	104
0-4	25	13	12	28	14	13	29	15	14	30	15	15
5-9	22	12	11	25	13	12	27	14	13	28	15	14
10-14	18	10	9	22	11	10	25	13	12	26	13	13
15-19	14	7	7	17	8	8	20	10	10	23	12	11
20-24	13	6	7	15	7	8	16	8	8	19	10	10
25-29	12	6	6	14	7	7	15	7	8	16	8	8
30-34	10	5	5	11	6	6	13	7	7	15	7	8
35-39	8	4	4	10	5	5	11	5	5	13	6	6
40-44	6	3	3	7	4	4	9	5	4	10	5	5
45-49	6	3	2	6	3	3	7	3	3	8	4	4
50-54	4	2	2	5	2	2	6	3	3	6	3	3
55-59	3	2	1	4	2	2	4	2	2	5	3	3
60-64	3	1	1	3	2	1	3	2	2	4	2	2
65-69	2	1	1	2	1	1	2	1	1	3	2	1
70-74	1	1	1	1	1	1	2	1	1	2	1	1
75-79	1	1	1	1	1	1	1	1	0	1	1	1
80 +	1	0	0	1	1	0	1	1	0	1	0	0

894

United Nations Department of Economic and Social Affairs/Population Division
World Population Prospects: The 2004 Revision, Volume II: Sex and Age Distribution of the World Population

POPULATION BY AGE AND SEX (in thousands)

Age group	2005			2010			2015			2020		
	Both sexes	Males	Females	Both sexes	Males	Females	Both sexes	Males	Females	Both sexes	Males	Females
All ages	211	100	104	232	118	114	252	128	125	273	138	135
0-4	30	15	15	30	16	15	31	16	15	32	16	15
5-9	28	15	14	29	15	14	30	15	15	31	16	15
10-14	26	13	13	28	14	14	29	15	14	29	15	14
15-19	23	12	11	24	12	12	26	13	13	27	14	13
20-24	19	10	10	22	11	11	24	12	12	25	12	13
25-29	16	8	8	20	10	10	22	11	11	24	12	12
30-34	15	7	8	16	8	8	19	10	10	22	11	11
35-39	13	6	6	14	7	7	15	8	8	19	10	9
40-44	10	5	5	12	6	6	14	7	7	15	7	7
45-49	8	4	4	9	5	5	11	6	6	13	7	7
50-54	6	3	3	8	4	4	9	4	4	11	5	5
55-59	5	3	3	6	3	3	7	4	4	8	4	4
60-64	4	2	2	5	3	2	5	3	3	7	3	3
65-69	3	2	1	3	2	2	4	2	2	5	2	2
70-74	2	1	1	2	1	1	3	1	1	4	2	2
75-79	1	1	1	1	1	1	2	1	1	2	1	1
80-84	1	0	0	1	0	0	1	0	0	1	1	1
85-89	0	0	0	0	0	0	0	0	0	0	0	0
90-94	0	0	0	0	0	0	0	0	0	0	0	0
95-99	0	0	0	0	0	0	0	0	0	0	0	0
100 +	0	0	0	0	0	0	0	0	0	0	0	0

Age group	2025			2030			2035			2040		
	Both sexes	Males	Females	Both sexes	Males	Females	Both sexes	Males	Females	Both sexes	Males	Females
All ages	294	148	145	313	158	155	331	167	165	348	175	173
0-4	32	16	15	31	16	15	31	16	15	30	16	15
5-9	31	16	15	31	16	15	31	16	15	30	16	15
10-14	30	15	15	30	15	15	30	16	15	30	16	15
15-19	27	14	14	28	14	14	29	14	14	29	15	14
20-24	26	13	13	27	13	13	27	14	14	28	14	14
25-29	25	13	13	26	13	13	27	13	14	28	14	14
30-34	24	12	12	25	12	13	26	13	13	27	13	13
35-39	22	11	11	23	12	11	25	12	12	26	13	13
40-44	18	9	9	21	11	10	22	11	11	24	12	12
45-49	14	7	7	17	9	8	20	10	10	22	11	11
50-54	12	6	6	13	7	7	17	9	8	20	10	10
55-59	10	5	5	12	6	6	10	8	8	16	8	8
60-64	8	4	4	10	5	5	11	5	6	12	6	6
65-69	6	3	3	7	3	4	9	4	5	10	5	5
70-74	4	2	2	5	3	3	6	3	3	8	4	4
75-79	3	1	1	3	1	2	4	2	2	5	2	3
80-84	1	1	1	2	1	1	2	1	1	3	1	2
85-89	0	0	0	1	0	0	1	0	1	1	0	1
90-94	0	0	0	0	0	0	0	0	0	0	0	0
95-99	0	0	0	0	0	0	0	0	0	0	0	0
100 +	0	0	0	0	0	0	0	0	0	0	0	0

Age group	2045			2050		
	Both sexes	Males	Females	Both sexes	Males	Females
All ages	362	182	181	375	188	187
0-4	29	15	14	29	15	14
5-9	30	15	14	29	15	14
10-14	30	15	15	29	15	14
15-19	29	15	14	28	14	14
20-24	28	14	14	28	14	14
25-29	28	14	14	28	14	14
30-34	27	14	14	28	14	14
35-39	26	13	13	27	14	13
40-44	25	13	12	26	13	13
45-49	23	12	12	24	12	12
50-54	21	11	10	23	11	11
55-59	19	9	9	20	10	10
60-64	15	8	8	18	9	9
65-69	11	5	6	14	7	7
70-74	9	4	5	10	5	5
75-79	6	3	3	7	3	4
80-84	3	1	2	4	2	3
85-89	1	1	1	2	1	1
90-94	0	0	0	1	0	0
95-99	0	0	0	0	0	0
100 +	0	0	0	0	0	0

POPULATION BY AGE AND SEX (in thousands)

Age group	2005 Both sexes	Males	Females	2010 Both sexes	Males	Females	2015 Both sexes	Males	Females	2020 Both sexes	Males	Females
All ages	211	108	104	234	119	115	258	131	127	285	144	141
0-4	30	15	15	33	17	16	35	18	17	37	19	18
5-9	28	15	14	29	15	14	32	16	16	34	18	17
10-14	26	13	13	28	14	14	29	15	14	31	16	15
15-19	23	12	11	24	12	12	26	13	13	27	14	13
20-24	19	10	10	22	11	11	24	12	12	25	12	13
25-29	16	8	8	20	10	10	22	11	11	24	12	12
30-34	15	7	8	16	8	8	19	10	10	22	11	11
35-39	13	6	6	14	7	7	15	8	8	19	10	9
40-44	10	5	5	12	6	6	14	7	7	15	7	7
45-49	8	4	4	9	5	5	11	6	6	13	7	7
50-54	6	3	3	8	4	4	9	4	4	11	5	5
55-59	5	3	3	6	3	3	7	4	4	8	4	4
60-64	4	2	2	5	3	2	5	3	3	7	3	3
65-69	3	2	1	3	2	2	4	2	2	5	2	2
70-74	2	1	1	2	1	1	3	1	1	4	2	2
75-79	1	1	1	1	1	1	2	1	1	2	1	1
80-84	1	0	0	1	0	0	1	0	0	1	1	1
85-89	0	0	0	0	0	0	0	0	0	0	0	0
90-94	0	0	0	0	0	0	0	0	0	0	0	0
95-99	0	0	0	0	0	0	0	0	0	0	0	0
100 +	0	0	0	0	0	0	0	0	0	0	0	0

Age group	2025 Both sexes	Males	Females	2030 Both sexes	Males	Females	2035 Both sexes	Males	Females	2040 Both sexes	Males	Females
All ages	311	157	154	337	170	167	364	183	180	390	197	194
0-4	38	19	18	38	20	19	39	20	19	41	21	20
5-9	36	19	18	37	19	18	38	19	18	39	20	19
10-14	34	17	16	36	18	17	36	19	18	37	19	18
15-19	30	15	15	32	16	16	34	17	17	35	18	17
20-24	26	13	13	29	14	14	31	16	16	33	17	17
25-29	25	13	13	26	13	13	29	14	15	31	16	16
30-34	24	12	12	25	12	13	26	13	13	29	14	14
35-39	22	11	11	23	12	11	25	12	12	26	13	13
40-44	18	9	9	21	11	10	22	11	11	24	12	12
45-49	14	7	7	17	9	8	20	10	10	22	11	11
50-54	12	6	6	13	7	7	17	9	8	20	10	10
55-59	10	5	5	12	6	6	13	6	6	16	8	8
60-64	8	4	4	10	5	5	11	5	6	12	6	6
65-69	6	3	3	7	3	4	9	4	5	10	5	5
70-74	4	2	2	5	3	3	6	3	3	8	4	4
75-79	3	1	1	3	1	2	4	2	2	5	2	3
80-84	1	1	1	2	1	1	2	1	1	3	1	2
85-89	0	0	0	1	0	0	1	0	1	1	0	1
90-94	0	0	0	0	0	0	0	0	0	0	0	0
95-99	0	0	0	0	0	0	0	0	0	0	0	0
100 +	0	0	0	0	0	0	0	0	0	0	0	0

Age group	2045 Both sexes	Males	Females	2050 Both sexes	Males	Females
All ages	417	210	207	443	223	220
0-4	42	22	20	42	22	20
5-9	40	21	19	41	21	20
10-14	38	20	19	39	20	19
15-19	35	18	17	36	19	18
20-24	34	17	17	35	17	17
25-29	34	17	17	34	17	17
30-34	31	16	16	33	17	17
35-39	28	14	14	31	15	15
40-44	25	13	12	28	14	14
45-49	23	12	12	24	12	12
50-54	21	11	10	23	11	11
55-59	19	9	9	20	10	10
60-64	15	8	8	18	9	9
65-69	11	5	6	14	7	7
70-74	9	4	5	10	5	5
75-79	6	3	3	7	3	4
80-84	3	1	2	4	2	3
85-89	1	1	1	2	1	1
90-94	0	0	0	1	0	0
95-99	0	0	0	0	0	0
100 +	0	0	0	0	0	0

United Nations Department of Economic and Social Affairs/Population Division
World Population Prospects: The 2004 Revision, Volume II: Sex and Age Distribution of the World Population

896

POPULATION BY AGE AND SEX (in thousands)

Age group	2005 Both sexes	Males	Females	2010 Both sexes	Males	Females	2015 Both sexes	Males	Females	2020 Both sexes	Males	Females
All ages	211	108	104	230	117	113	247	125	122	262	132	130
0-4	30	15	15	28	15	14	27	14	13	26	13	13
5-9	28	15	14	29	15	14	28	14	14	27	14	13
10-14	26	13	13	28	14	14	29	15	14	27	14	13
15-19	23	12	11	24	12	12	26	13	13	27	14	13
20-24	19	10	10	22	11	11	24	12	12	25	12	13
25-29	16	8	8	20	10	10	22	11	11	24	12	12
30-34	15	7	8	16	8	8	19	10	10	22	11	11
35-39	13	6	6	14	7	7	15	8	8	19	10	9
40-44	10	5	5	12	6	6	14	7	7	15	7	7
45-49	8	4	4	9	5	5	11	6	6	13	7	7
50-54	6	3	3	8	4	4	9	4	4	11	5	5
55-59	5	3	3	6	3	3	7	4	4	8	4	4
60-64	4	2	2	5	3	2	5	3	3	7	3	3
65-69	3	2	1	3	2	2	4	2	2	5	2	2
70-74	2	1	1	2	1	1	3	1	1	4	2	2
75-79	1	1	1	1	1	1	2	1	1	2	1	1
80-84	1	0	0	1	0	0	1	0	0	1	1	1
85-89	0	0	0	0	0	0	0	0	0	0	0	0
90-94	0	0	0	0	0	0	0	0	0	0	0	0
95-99	0	0	0	0	0	0	0	0	0	0	0	0
100 +	0	0	0	0	0	0	0	0	0	0	0	0

Age group	2025 Both sexes	Males	Females	2030 Both sexes	Males	Females	2035 Both sexes	Males	Females	2040 Both sexes	Males	Females
All ages	277	139	137	289	146	144	300	150	150	307	154	154
0-4	26	13	12	25	13	12	23	12	11	21	11	10
5-9	26	13	12	25	13	12	24	13	12	23	12	11
10-14	26	13	13	25	13	12	25	13	12	24	12	12
15-19	25	13	13	24	12	12	23	12	12	23	12	11
20-24	26	13	13	25	12	12	24	12	12	23	11	11
25-29	25	13	13	26	13	13	25	12	13	24	12	12
30-34	24	12	12	25	12	13	26	13	13	25	12	12
35-39	22	11	11	23	12	11	25	12	12	26	13	13
40-44	18	9	9	21	11	10	22	11	11	24	12	12
45-49	14	7	7	17	9	8	20	10	10	22	11	11
50-54	12	6	6	13	7	7	17	9	8	20	10	10
55-59	10	5	5	12	6	6	13	6	6	16	8	8
60-64	8	4	4	10	5	5	11	5	6	12	6	6
65-69	6	3	3	7	3	4	9	4	5	10	5	5
70-74	4	2	2	5	3	3	6	3	3	8	4	4
75-79	3	1	1	3	1	2	4	2	2	5	2	3
80-84	1	1	1	2	1	1	2	1	1	3	1	2
85-89	0	0	0	1	0	0	1	0	1	1	0	1
90-94	0	0	0	0	0	0	0	0	0	0	0	0
95-99	0	0	0	0	0	0	0	0	0	0	0	0
100 +	0	0	0	0	0	0	0	0	0	0	0	0

Age group	2045 Both sexes	Males	Females	2050 Both sexes	Males	Females
All ages	312	156	156	313	156	158
0-4	19	10	9	18	9	8
5-9	21	11	10	19	10	9
10-14	22	11	11	20	10	10
15-19	22	11	11	20	10	10
20-24	22	11	11	21	11	11
25-29	23	11	12	23	11	11
30-34	24	12	12	23	11	11
35-39	24	12	12	23	12	12
40-44	25	13	12	24	12	12
45-49	23	12	12	24	12	12
50-54	21	11	10	23	11	11
55-59	19	9	9	20	10	10
60-64	15	8	8	18	9	9
65-69	11	5	6	14	7	7
70-74	9	4	5	10	5	5
75-79	6	3	3	7	3	4
80-84	3	1	2	4	2	3
85-89	1	1	1	2	1	1
90-94	0	0	0	1	0	0
95-99	0	0	0	0	0	0
100 +	0	0	0	0	0	0

United Nations Department of Economic and Social Affairs/Population Division
World Population Prospects: The 2004 Revision, Volume II: Sex and Age Distribution of the World Population

897

POPULATION BY AGE AND SEX (in thousands)

Age group	1950 Both sexes	1950 Males	1950 Females	1955 Both sexes	1955 Males	1955 Females	1960 Both sexes	1960 Males	1960 Females	1965 Both sexes	1965 Males	1965 Females
All ages	5 094	2 579	2 514	6 230	3 167	3 062	7 579	3 863	3 716	9 094	4 619	4 474
0-4	935	477	458	1 161	592	569	1 395	712	683	1 716	875	841
5-9	710	362	348	919	470	449	1 143	584	560	1 364	695	669
10-14	568	290	279	718	366	351	926	473	452	1 138	580	558
15-19	500	255	245	578	295	283	727	372	355	922	470	452
20-24	456	232	224	521	267	254	600	307	292	725	368	356
25-29	378	191	187	482	247	235	547	282	265	597	304	294
30-34	330	167	164	396	203	193	499	258	241	542	278	265
35-39	289	147	142	336	171	166	401	206	195	491	253	239
40-44	256	128	127	286	145	141	333	169	164	392	200	192
45-49	207	103	104	247	123	123	277	140	137	321	162	159
50-54	155	77	78	195	96	98	234	117	117	263	132	131
55-59	136	67	69	142	70	72	180	89	91	217	108	110
60-64	77	38	39	119	58	60	126	62	64	161	79	82
65-69	48	24	25	63	31	32	99	48	51	106	52	55
70-74	27	13	14	37	18	19	49	24	26	78	37	41
75-79	14	6	7	19	9	10	26	12	14	35	16	19
80 +	8	4	4	12	5	6	16	7	9	23	10	13

Age group	1970 Both sexes	1970 Males	1970 Females	1975 Both sexes	1975 Males	1975 Females	1980 Both sexes	1980 Males	1980 Females	1985 Both sexes	1985 Males	1985 Females
All ages	10 721	5 429	5 292	12 734	6 445	6 290	15 091	7 639	7 452	17 318	8 749	8 568
0-4	1 848	942	906	1 959	999	960	2 295	1 171	1 124	2 507	1 279	1 228
5-9	1 686	859	827	1 850	943	907	1 971	1 005	966	2 282	1 163	1 118
10-14	1 359	692	667	1 705	868	837	1 874	955	919	1 971	1 004	967
15-19	1 134	576	558	1 383	703	680	1 732	881	851	1 875	953	922
20-24	918	466	453	1 182	599	582	1 436	729	707	1 732	878	854
25-29	722	364	358	977	496	481	1 248	633	614	1 435	725	709
30-34	593	299	294	765	388	378	1 025	522	503	1 243	628	614
35-39	535	272	263	613	310	303	788	400	388	1 018	516	501
40-44	481	246	235	538	273	265	618	312	306	778	393	385
45-49	380	193	188	474	241	234	533	269	264	606	304	302
50-54	307	154	154	368	185	183	461	232	229	516	258	258
55-59	247	123	124	292	145	147	352	175	177	439	218	221
60-64	197	96	100	227	111	115	270	132	139	326	159	167
65-69	138	66	72	172	82	90	200	96	105	240	114	127
70-74	86	40	46	114	53	61	144	66	78	168	77	91
75-79	58	26	32	65	29	36	86	38	48	110	48	61
80 +	32	14	18	50	21	29	59	24	34	73	30	43

Age group	1990 Both sexes	1990 Males	1990 Females	1995 Both sexes	1995 Males	1995 Females	2000 Both sexes	2000 Males	2000 Females	2005 Both sexes	2005 Males	2005 Females
All ages	19 735	9 957	9 778	22 087	11 132	10 956	24 418	12 289	12 129	26 749	13 442	13 307
0-4	2 729	1 393	1 336	2 747	1 403	1 344	2 778	1 419	1 358	2 860	1 462	1 398
5-9	2 499	1 274	1 225	2 717	1 386	1 331	2 731	1 394	1 337	2 759	1 409	1 350
10-14	2 282	1 163	1 119	2 496	1 272	1 224	2 714	1 384	1 330	2 728	1 392	1 336
15-19	1 972	1 003	969	2 276	1 158	1 118	2 489	1 266	1 223	2 706	1 377	1 329
20-24	1 876	951	925	1 965	996	969	2 264	1 147	1 117	2 474	1 252	1 222
25-29	1 729	873	856	1 867	943	925	1 954	986	968	2 249	1 133	1 116
30-34	1 429	720	709	1 719	865	854	1 855	932	923	1 940	973	966
35-39	1 234	622	612	1 417	712	706	1 704	854	850	1 838	920	919
40-44	1 006	509	498	1 219	612	607	1 401	700	700	1 685	841	844
45-49	764	384	380	988	497	491	1 199	599	600	1 378	686	692
50-54	589	293	296	744	371	372	964	482	482	1 171	582	589
55-59	493	244	250	564	278	287	716	354	362	930	461	469
60-64	409	200	209	462	225	237	533	259	274	678	331	347
65-69	293	139	154	371	177	194	423	202	221	491	234	257
70-74	205	93	111	252	116	136	325	151	174	374	174	200
75-79	132	58	74	164	72	92	207	92	115	271	122	149
80 +	94	38	56	118	48	70	163	68	95	216	93	124

United Nations Department of Economic and Social Affairs/Population Division
World Population Prospects: The 2004 Revision, Volume II: Sex and Age Distribution of the World Population

898

MEDIUM VARIANT **VENEZUELA**

POPULATION BY AGE AND SEX (in thousands)

Age group	2005 Both sexes	Males	Females	2010 Both sexes	Males	Females	2015 Both sexes	Males	Females	2020 Both sexes	Males	Females
All ages	26 749	13 442	13 307	29 076	14 588	14 489	31 330	15 691	15 639	33 450	16 724	16 727
0-4	2 860	1 462	1 398	2 930	1 499	1 432	2 943	1 505	1 437	2 906	1 487	1 419
5-9	2 759	1 409	1 350	2 842	1 452	1 390	2 914	1 489	1 425	2 928	1 497	1 431
10-14	2 728	1 392	1 336	2 757	1 407	1 349	2 840	1 451	1 390	2 913	1 488	1 424
15-19	2 706	1 377	1 329	2 721	1 386	1 335	2 750	1 402	1 349	2 835	1 446	1 389
20-24	2 474	1 252	1 222	2 692	1 364	1 328	2 709	1 374	1 334	2 739	1 391	1 348
25-29	2 249	1 133	1 116	2 459	1 238	1 221	2 676	1 349	1 327	2 696	1 362	1 334
30-34	1 940	973	966	2 234	1 120	1 114	2 444	1 225	1 219	2 661	1 337	1 325
35-39	1 838	920	919	1 924	961	963	2 217	1 107	1 110	2 426	1 212	1 215
40-44	1 685	841	844	1 819	906	913	1 905	948	957	2 196	1 092	1 103
45-49	1 378	686	692	1 659	824	835	1 793	889	904	1 879	931	948
50-54	1 171	582	589	1 348	667	681	1 625	802	823	1 758	867	891
55-59	930	461	469	1 133	557	575	1 306	640	666	1 577	772	805
60-64	678	331	347	885	433	452	1 080	525	555	1 249	604	644
65-69	491	234	257	628	301	327	822	395	427	1 007	481	527
70-74	374	174	200	437	203	234	562	263	299	740	346	394
75-79	271	122	149	315	142	173	371	167	204	481	217	264
80-84	149	65	84	199	87	112	236	102	133	281	121	160
85-89	57	24	34	79	33	46	111	46	65	137	56	81
90-94	9	4	5	16	6	9	24	10	14	38	15	23
95-99	0	0	0	1	0	0	2	1	1	3	1	2
100 +	0	0	0	0	0	0	0	0	0	0	0	0

Age group	2025 Both sexes	Males	Females	2030 Both sexes	Males	Females	2035 Both sexes	Males	Females	2040 Both sexes	Males	Females
All ages	35 406	17 668	17 738	37 176	18 515	18 661	38 734	19 253	19 482	40 054	19 870	20 184
0-4	2 851	1 459	1 392	2 794	1 430	1 364	2 732	1 398	1 334	2 656	1 360	1 297
5-9	2 893	1 480	1 414	2 840	1 453	1 388	2 785	1 424	1 360	2 724	1 394	1 331
10-14	2 927	1 496	1 431	2 892	1 479	1 414	2 839	1 452	1 388	2 784	1 424	1 360
15-19	2 908	1 484	1 424	2 923	1 493	1 431	2 889	1 476	1 413	2 837	1 449	1 388
20-24	2 825	1 436	1 389	2 899	1 475	1 424	2 916	1 485	1 431	2 883	1 469	1 414
25-29	2 728	1 380	1 348	2 815	1 426	1 389	2 890	1 466	1 424	2 908	1 477	1 431
30-34	2 682	1 350	1 332	2 716	1 369	1 347	2 804	1 416	1 388	2 880	1 457	1 423
35-39	2 644	1 323	1 321	2 666	1 338	1 328	2 701	1 358	1 343	2 790	1 405	1 384
40-44	2 405	1 197	1 208	2 622	1 308	1 314	2 645	1 323	1 322	2 681	1 344	1 337
45-49	2 168	1 074	1 094	2 376	1 177	1 198	2 592	1 288	1 304	2 617	1 304	1 313
50-54	1 845	909	936	2 130	1 049	1 081	2 336	1 151	1 185	2 551	1 260	1 290
55-59	1 709	835	874	1 795	877	918	2 076	1 014	1 062	2 279	1 114	1 165
60-64	1 511	730	781	1 640	792	848	1 726	833	893	2 000	964	1 036
65-69	1 169	556	613	1 418	673	745	1 544	732	812	1 629	772	857
70-74	911	423	488	1 061	491	570	1 293	597	696	1 412	651	761
75-79	637	287	349	788	353	436	923	411	512	1 130	501	629
80-84	369	159	210	495	213	282	619	263	356	731	308	423
85-89	169	69	101	229	92	137	314	126	189	402	158	244
90-94	51	19	31	67	25	42	96	35	61	138	50	88
95-99	6	2	4	9	3	6	13	5	9	21	7	14
100 +	0	0	0	0	0	0	0	0	0	1	0	0

Age group	2045 Both sexes	Males	Females	2050 Both sexes	Males	Females
All ages	41 120	20 362	20 759	41 991	20 758	21 233
0-4	2 572	1 316	1 256	2 545	1 303	1 242
5-9	2 650	1 356	1 294	2 567	1 313	1 253
10-14	2 724	1 393	1 331	2 650	1 356	1 294
15-19	2 783	1 422	1 361	2 723	1 392	1 331
20-24	2 832	1 444	1 388	2 779	1 418	1 361
25-29	2 877	1 463	1 415	2 828	1 439	1 389
30-34	2 900	1 469	1 431	2 870	1 456	1 414
35-39	2 867	1 447	1 420	2 887	1 459	1 428
40-44	2 770	1 392	1 378	2 848	1 433	1 414
45-49	2 653	1 325	1 328	2 743	1 373	1 370
50-54	2 576	1 277	1 300	2 614	1 299	1 315
55-59	2 491	1 221	1 270	2 518	1 238	1 280
60-64	2 198	1 061	1 137	2 405	1 164	1 240
65-69	1 890	895	995	2 082	987	1 095
70-74	1 494	688	806	1 738	800	938
75-79	1 239	549	690	1 315	582	734
80-84	902	378	523	995	416	579
85-89	483	188	295	605	234	371
90-94	185	66	119	230	81	150
95-99	33	11	23	48	15	33
100 +	1	1	1	3	1	2

United Nations Department of Economic and Social Affairs/Population Division
World Population Prospects: The 2004 Revision, Volume II: Sex and Age Distribution of the World Population

899

POPULATION BY AGE AND SEX (in thousands)

Age group	2005 Both sexes	Males	Females	2010 Both sexes	Males	Females	2015 Both sexes	Males	Females	2020 Both sexes	Males	Females
All ages	26 749	13 442	13 307	29 349	14 727	14 622	32 074	16 072	16 002	34 817	17 423	17 395
0-4	2 860	1 462	1 398	3 202	1 638	1 565	3 417	1 748	1 669	3 532	1 807	1 725
5-9	2 759	1 409	1 350	2 842	1 452	1 390	3 185	1 628	1 557	3 399	1 738	1 661
10-14	2 728	1 392	1 336	2 757	1 407	1 349	2 840	1 451	1 390	3 183	1 626	1 556
15-19	2 706	1 377	1 329	2 721	1 386	1 335	2 750	1 402	1 349	2 835	1 446	1 389
20-24	2 474	1 252	1 222	2 692	1 364	1 328	2 709	1 374	1 334	2 739	1 391	1 348
25-29	2 249	1 133	1 116	2 459	1 238	1 221	2 676	1 349	1 327	2 696	1 362	1 334
30-34	1 940	973	966	2 234	1 120	1 114	2 444	1 225	1 219	2 661	1 337	1 325
35-39	1 838	920	919	1 924	961	963	2 217	1 107	1 110	2 426	1 212	1 215
40-44	1 685	841	844	1 819	906	913	1 905	948	957	2 196	1 092	1 103
45-49	1 378	686	692	1 659	824	835	1 793	889	904	1 879	931	948
50-54	1 171	582	589	1 348	667	681	1 625	802	823	1 758	867	891
55-59	930	461	469	1 133	557	575	1 306	640	666	1 577	772	805
60-64	678	331	347	885	433	452	1 080	525	555	1 249	604	644
65-69	491	234	257	628	301	327	822	395	427	1 007	481	527
70-74	374	174	200	437	203	234	562	263	299	740	346	394
75-79	271	122	149	315	142	173	371	167	204	481	217	264
80-84	149	65	84	199	87	112	236	102	133	281	121	160
85-89	57	24	34	79	33	46	111	46	65	137	56	81
90-94	9	4	5	16	6	9	24	10	14	38	15	23
95-99	0	0	0	1	0	0	2	1	1	3	1	2
100 +	0	0	0	0	0	0	0	0	0	0	0	0

Age group	2025 Both sexes	Males	Females	2030 Both sexes	Males	Females	2035 Both sexes	Males	Females	2040 Both sexes	Males	Females
All ages	37 451	18 714	18 737	40 014	19 965	20 048	42 532	21 193	21 340	44 983	22 386	22 597
0-4	3 534	1 808	1 725	3 593	1 839	1 754	3 702	1 895	1 807	3 800	1 945	1 855
5-9	3 516	1 798	1 718	3 520	1 800	1 719	3 580	1 831	1 749	3 690	1 888	1 803
10-14	3 398	1 737	1 661	3 514	1 797	1 717	3 518	1 799	1 719	3 579	1 831	1 749
15-19	3 177	1 621	1 556	3 392	1 732	1 660	3 509	1 792	1 717	3 514	1 795	1 719
20-24	2 825	1 436	1 389	3 167	1 611	1 556	3 383	1 723	1 660	3 501	1 784	1 717
25-29	2 728	1 380	1 348	2 815	1 426	1 389	3 156	1 601	1 556	3 373	1 713	1 660
30-34	2 682	1 350	1 332	2 716	1 369	1 347	2 804	1 416	1 388	3 145	1 591	1 554
35-39	2 644	1 323	1 321	2 666	1 338	1 328	2 701	1 358	1 343	2 790	1 405	1 384
40-44	2 405	1 197	1 208	2 622	1 308	1 314	2 645	1 323	1 322	2 681	1 344	1 337
45-49	2 168	1 074	1 094	2 376	1 177	1 198	2 592	1 288	1 304	2 617	1 304	1 313
50-54	1 845	909	936	2 130	1 049	1 081	2 336	1 151	1 185	2 551	1 260	1 290
55-59	1 709	835	874	1 795	877	918	2 076	1 014	1 062	2 279	1 114	1 165
60-64	1 511	730	781	1 640	792	848	1 726	833	893	1 999	964	1 035
65-69	1 169	556	613	1 418	673	745	1 544	732	812	1 629	772	857
70-74	911	423	488	1 061	491	570	1 293	597	696	1 412	651	761
75-79	637	287	349	788	353	436	923	411	512	1 130	501	629
80-84	369	159	210	495	213	282	619	263	356	731	308	423
85-89	169	69	101	229	92	137	314	126	189	402	158	244
90-94	51	19	31	67	25	42	96	35	61	138	50	88
95-99	6	2	4	9	3	6	13	5	9	21	7	14
100 +	0	0	0	0	0	0	0	0	0	1	0	0

Age group	2045 Both sexes	Males	Females	2050 Both sexes	Males	Females
All ages	47 327	23 528	23 799	49 614	24 645	24 969
0-4	3 866	1 979	1 887	3 982	2 038	1 944
5-9	3 790	1 939	1 851	3 857	1 973	1 883
10-14	3 690	1 887	1 802	3 789	1 938	1 851
15-19	3 576	1 827	1 748	3 686	1 884	1 802
20-24	3 507	1 788	1 719	3 570	1 821	1 749
25-29	3 492	1 775	1 717	3 499	1 780	1 720
30-34	3 361	1 703	1 659	3 481	1 765	1 716
35-39	3 130	1 579	1 550	3 346	1 691	1 655
40-44	2 770	1 392	1 378	3 109	1 564	1 544
45-49	2 653	1 325	1 328	2 743	1 373	1 370
50-54	2 576	1 277	1 300	2 614	1 299	1 315
55-59	2 491	1 221	1 270	2 518	1 238	1 280
60-64	2 198	1 061	1 137	2 405	1 164	1 240
65-69	1 890	895	995	2 082	987	1 095
70-74	1 494	688	806	1 738	800	938
75-79	1 239	549	690	1 315	582	734
80-84	902	378	523	995	416	579
85-89	483	188	295	605	234	371
90-94	185	66	119	230	81	150
95-99	33	11	23	48	15	33
100 +	1	1	1	3	1	2

900

United Nations Department of Economic and Social Affairs/Population Division
World Population Prospects: The 2004 Revision, Volume II: Sex and Age Distribution of the World Population

POPULATION BY AGE AND SEX (in thousands)

Age group	2005			2010			2015			2020		
	Both sexes	Males	Females	Both sexes	Males	Females	Both sexes	Males	Females	Both sexes	Males	Females
All ages	26 749	13 442	13 307	28 801	14 447	14 354	30 578	15 307	15 271	32 069	16 017	16 052
0-4	2 860	1 462	1 398	2 655	1 358	1 297	2 465	1 261	1 204	2 272	1 163	1 110
5-9	2 759	1 409	1 350	2 842	1 452	1 390	2 641	1 350	1 291	2 453	1 254	1 199
10-14	2 728	1 392	1 336	2 757	1 407	1 349	2 840	1 451	1 390	2 639	1 349	1 291
15-19	2 706	1 377	1 329	2 721	1 386	1 335	2 750	1 402	1 349	2 835	1 446	1 389
20-24	2 474	1 252	1 222	2 692	1 364	1 328	2 709	1 374	1 334	2 739	1 391	1 348
25-29	2 249	1 133	1 116	2 459	1 238	1 221	2 676	1 349	1 327	2 696	1 362	1 334
30-34	1 940	973	966	2 234	1 120	1 114	2 444	1 225	1 219	2 661	1 337	1 325
35-39	1 838	920	919	1 924	961	963	2 217	1 107	1 110	2 426	1 212	1 215
40-44	1 685	841	844	1 819	906	913	1 905	948	957	2 196	1 092	1 103
45-49	1 378	686	692	1 659	824	835	1 793	889	904	1 879	931	948
50-54	1 171	582	589	1 348	667	681	1 625	802	823	1 758	867	891
55-59	930	461	469	1 133	557	575	1 306	640	666	1 577	772	805
60-64	678	331	347	885	433	452	1 080	525	555	1 249	604	644
65-69	491	234	257	628	301	327	822	395	427	1 007	481	527
70-74	374	174	200	437	203	234	562	263	299	740	346	394
75-79	271	122	149	315	142	173	371	167	204	481	217	264
80-84	149	65	84	199	87	112	236	102	133	281	121	160
85-89	57	24	34	79	33	46	111	46	65	137	56	81
90-94	9	4	5	16	6	9	24	10	14	38	15	23
95-99	0	0	0	1	0	0	2	1	1	3	1	2
100 +	0	0	0	0	0	0	0	0	0	0	0	0

Age group	2025			2030			2035			2040		
	Both sexes	Males	Females	Both sexes	Males	Females	Both sexes	Males	Females	Both sexes	Males	Females
All ages	33 350	16 617	16 733	34 358	17 075	17 283	35 044	17 368	17 676	35 393	17 491	17 902
0-4	2 171	1 111	1 060	2 025	1 036	989	1 851	947	904	1 673	856	817
5-9	2 263	1 157	1 106	2 163	1 106	1 057	2 019	1 033	986	1 847	945	902
10-14	2 453	1 254	1 199	2 263	1 157	1 106	2 163	1 106	1 057	2 020	1 033	987
15-19	2 635	1 345	1 290	2 450	1 251	1 199	2 261	1 155	1 106	2 162	1 105	1 058
20-24	2 825	1 436	1 389	2 628	1 337	1 291	2 445	1 245	1 200	2 258	1 151	1 107
25-29	2 728	1 380	1 348	2 815	1 426	1 389	2 621	1 330	1 291	2 440	1 240	1 201
30-34	2 682	1 350	1 332	2 716	1 369	1 347	2 804	1 416	1 388	2 612	1 322	1 291
35-39	2 644	1 323	1 321	2 666	1 338	1 328	2 701	1 358	1 343	2 790	1 405	1 384
40-44	2 405	1 197	1 208	2 622	1 308	1 314	2 645	1 323	1 322	2 681	1 344	1 337
45-49	2 168	1 074	1 094	2 376	1 177	1 198	2 592	1 288	1 304	2 617	1 304	1 313
50-54	1 845	909	936	2 130	1 049	1 081	2 336	1 151	1 185	2 551	1 260	1 290
55-59	1 709	835	874	1 795	877	918	2 076	1 014	1 062	2 279	1 114	1 165
60-64	1 511	730	781	1 640	792	848	1 726	833	893	1 999	964	1 035
65-69	1 169	556	613	1 418	673	745	1 544	732	812	1 629	772	857
70-74	911	423	488	1 061	491	570	1 293	597	696	1 412	651	761
75-79	637	287	349	788	353	436	923	411	512	1 130	501	629
80-84	369	159	210	495	213	282	619	263	356	731	308	423
85-89	169	69	101	229	92	137	314	126	189	402	158	244
90-94	51	19	31	67	25	42	96	35	61	138	50	88
95-99	6	2	4	9	3	6	13	5	9	21	7	14
100 +	0	0	0	0	0	0	0	0	0	1	0	0

Age group	2045			2050		
	Both sexes	Males	Females	Both sexes	Males	Females
All ages	35 418	17 453	17 965	35 184	17 288	17 896
0-4	1 515	775	739	1 421	727	694
5-9	1 670	854	815	1 513	774	739
10-14	1 847	945	903	1 671	855	816
15-19	2 020	1 032	987	1 848	944	903
20-24	2 161	1 102	1 059	2 019	1 030	989
25-29	2 255	1 147	1 109	2 159	1 099	1 060
30-34	2 434	1 233	1 200	2 251	1 142	1 109
35-39	2 600	1 313	1 288	2 424	1 226	1 198
40-44	2 770	1 392	1 378	2 583	1 300	1 283
45-49	2 653	1 325	1 328	2 743	1 373	1 370
50-54	2 576	1 277	1 300	2 614	1 299	1 315
55-59	2 491	1 221	1 270	2 518	1 238	1 280
60-64	2 198	1 061	1 137	2 405	1 164	1 240
65-69	1 890	895	995	2 082	987	1 095
70-74	1 494	688	806	1 738	800	938
75-79	1 239	549	690	1 315	582	734
80-84	902	378	523	995	416	579
85-89	483	188	295	605	234	371
90-94	185	66	119	230	81	150
95-99	33	11	23	48	15	33
100 +	1	1	1	3	1	2

POPULATION BY AGE AND SEX (in thousands)

Age group	1950 Both sexes	Males	Females	1955 Both sexes	Males	Females	1960 Both sexes	Males	Females	1965 Both sexes	Males	Females
All ages	27 367	13 610	13 757	30 052	14 960	15 092	33 648	16 755	16 894	38 099	18 966	19 133
0-4	3 389	1 706	1 683	4 897	2 476	2 421	5 927	2 994	2 934	6 878	3 471	3 407
5-9	2 692	1 354	1 337	3 014	1 515	1 499	4 412	2 224	2 188	5 404	2 719	2 685
10-14	2 607	1 313	1 294	2 587	1 302	1 285	2 909	1 461	1 447	4 274	2 153	2 121
15-19	2 773	1 399	1 374	2 528	1 273	1 254	2 516	1 266	1 250	2 836	1 424	1 412
20-24	2 402	1 212	1 190	2 673	1 345	1 328	2 445	1 228	1 217	2 440	1 224	1 216
25-29	2 251	1 134	1 116	2 299	1 155	1 144	2 568	1 286	1 282	2 357	1 178	1 179
30-34	1 981	998	983	2 145	1 079	1 066	2 200	1 102	1 098	2 467	1 232	1 235
35-39	1 891	950	942	1 876	944	932	2 041	1 025	1 017	2 103	1 051	1 052
40-44	1 629	813	816	1 777	890	887	1 772	889	884	1 938	969	969
45-49	1 579	781	799	1 517	752	765	1 664	827	836	1 669	831	838
50-54	1 245	605	640	1 450	709	741	1 401	687	714	1 547	761	786
55-59	1 008	481	527	1 115	534	580	1 309	631	677	1 275	617	658
60-64	767	358	409	865	407	459	968	457	511	1 148	545	603
65-69	536	244	293	615	282	332	704	325	379	799	370	429
70-74	343	151	192	383	170	213	449	201	248	525	236	289
75-79	179	75	104	205	87	118	237	102	135	286	124	163
80 +	94	36	58	106	41	65	126	49	77	153	60	93

Age group	1970 Both sexes	Males	Females	1975 Both sexes	Males	Females	1980 Both sexes	Males	Females	1985 Both sexes	Males	Females
All ages	42 898	21 338	21 560	47 974	23 824	24 150	53 005	26 342	26 663	59 136	29 414	29 722
0-4	7 320	3 691	3 629	7 660	3 857	3 802	8 175	4 145	4 030	8 696	4 415	4 281
5-9	6 345	3 186	3 160	6 830	3 421	3 409	7 285	3 655	3 630	7 875	3 980	3 895
10-14	5 254	2 640	2 614	6 192	3 103	3 089	6 660	3 332	3 328	7 168	3 592	3 576
15-19	4 178	2 103	2 075	5 149	2 583	2 566	6 005	3 003	3 002	6 545	3 270	3 276
20-24	2 758	1 380	1 378	4 073	2 042	2 031	4 942	2 468	2 475	5 868	2 924	2 944
25-29	2 360	1 178	1 182	2 675	1 332	1 343	3 871	1 930	1 941	4 806	2 389	2 417
30-34	2 272	1 132	1 140	2 282	1 135	1 147	2 504	1 240	1 264	3 751	1 863	1 888
35-39	2 368	1 179	1 189	2 189	1 086	1 102	2 126	1 054	1 072	2 412	1 191	1 221
40-44	2 006	998	1 007	2 267	1 124	1 144	2 041	1 012	1 029	2 040	1 009	1 031
45-49	1 834	911	923	1 906	942	964	2 130	1 052	1 078	1 954	965	989
50-54	1 560	769	791	1 722	847	875	1 775	872	904	2 022	992	1 030
55-59	1 417	689	728	1 437	699	738	1 580	770	810	1 660	808	852
60-64	1 129	538	591	1 263	604	659	1 286	618	668	1 441	694	747
65-69	959	447	512	952	444	507	1 077	507	570	1 119	530	589
70-74	606	274	332	737	335	403	747	342	405	867	400	467
75-79	343	149	194	404	176	228	508	224	284	531	237	295
80 +	190	75	115	236	94	142	293	119	174	381	157	224

Age group	1990 Both sexes	Males	Females	1995 Both sexes	Males	Females	2000 Both sexes	Males	Females	2005 Both sexes	Males	Females
All ages	66 206	32 991	33 215	73 163	36 504	36 659	78 671	39 275	39 396	84 238	42 068	42 171
0-4	9 514	4 846	4 668	9 341	4 760	4 581	7 813	3 984	3 829	7 969	4 062	3 906
5-9	8 473	4 293	4 180	9 346	4 751	4 595	9 224	4 693	4 531	7 740	3 940	3 801
10-14	7 780	3 929	3 852	8 396	4 251	4 146	9 285	4 716	4 569	9 175	4 663	4 511
15-19	7 068	3 537	3 530	7 692	3 879	3 813	8 324	4 209	4 115	9 216	4 676	4 541
20-24	6 421	3 198	3 223	6 956	3 471	3 485	7 595	3 820	3 775	8 230	4 151	4 079
25-29	5 737	2 849	2 888	6 301	3 128	3 173	6 850	3 408	3 442	7 493	3 758	3 735
30-34	4 687	2 323	2 364	5 620	2 783	2 837	6 199	3 069	3 130	6 752	3 350	3 402
35-39	3 646	1 807	1 840	4 582	2 265	2 317	5 523	2 727	2 795	6 104	3 014	3 090
40-44	2 330	1 148	1 182	3 552	1 756	1 796	4 489	2 214	2 275	5 425	2 673	2 752
45-49	1 965	969	996	2 259	1 110	1 149	3 466	1 710	1 757	4 393	2 161	2 231
50-54	1 868	918	950	1 889	928	962	2 184	1 069	1 115	3 364	1 653	1 712
55-59	1 908	929	979	1 774	866	908	1 804	880	924	2 093	1 018	1 075
60-64	1 531	738	793	1 777	857	920	1 663	805	858	1 698	821	877
65-69	1 273	605	668	1 370	651	718	1 604	764	840	1 509	721	788
70-74	920	429	492	1 067	498	568	1 161	543	618	1 371	642	728
75-79	636	287	349	691	315	377	815	373	442	896	411	486
80 +	449	188	261	549	234	315	671	290	381	811	353	457

902

United Nations Department of Economic and Social Affairs/Population Division
World Population Prospects: The 2004 Revision, Volume II: Sex and Age Distribution of the World Population

POPULATION BY AGE AND SEX (in thousands)

Age group	2005 Both sexes	2005 Males	2005 Females	2010 Both sexes	2010 Males	2010 Females	2015 Both sexes	2015 Males	2015 Females	2020 Both sexes	2020 Males	2020 Females
All ages	84 238	42 068	42 171	89 718	44 814	44 905	95 029	47 470	47 559	99 928	49 909	50 019
0-4	7 969	4 062	3 906	7 982	4 072	3 910	7 933	4 049	3 885	7 672	3 918	3 754
5-9	7 740	3 940	3 801	7 913	4 029	3 884	7 938	4 045	3 893	7 896	4 026	3 870
10-14	9 175	4 663	4 511	7 704	3 918	3 786	7 880	4 009	3 871	7 908	4 028	3 881
15-19	9 216	4 676	4 541	9 114	4 627	4 487	7 654	3 888	3 766	7 834	3 982	3 852
20-24	8 230	4 151	4 079	9 127	4 619	4 508	9 035	4 576	4 459	7 589	3 847	3 742
25-29	7 493	3 758	3 735	8 134	4 092	4 043	9 035	4 561	4 474	8 952	4 524	4 428
30-34	6 752	3 350	3 402	7 399	3 702	3 697	8 046	4 038	4 008	8 948	4 508	4 440
35-39	6 104	3 014	3 090	6 662	3 298	3 364	7 313	3 650	3 663	7 961	3 987	3 974
40-44	5 425	2 673	2 752	6 009	2 961	3 049	6 570	3 246	3 325	7 222	3 598	3 624
45-49	4 393	2 161	2 231	5 322	2 616	2 706	5 908	2 904	3 004	6 470	3 189	3 281
50-54	3 364	1 653	1 712	4 276	2 095	2 181	5 194	2 543	2 651	5 778	2 829	2 949
55-59	2 093	1 018	1 075	3 237	1 580	1 657	4 129	2 011	2 117	5 029	2 448	2 581
60-64	1 698	821	877	1 979	954	1 025	3 074	1 488	1 587	3 935	1 901	2 035
65-69	1 509	721	788	1 550	740	810	1 817	865	953	2 840	1 357	1 483
70-74	1 371	642	728	1 300	611	689	1 347	632	715	1 593	745	848
75-79	896	411	486	1 071	491	580	1 029	473	556	1 080	495	585
80-84	526	235	292	589	263	327	717	320	397	705	313	391
85-89	216	92	123	264	113	150	302	130	172	382	162	220
90-94	59	23	36	73	29	43	92	37	54	111	44	67
95-99	8	3	6	12	4	8	15	5	9	20	7	13
100 +	1	0	1	1	0	1	1	0	1	2	0	1

Age group	2025 Both sexes	2025 Males	2025 Females	2030 Both sexes	2030 Males	2030 Females	2035 Both sexes	2035 Males	2035 Females	2040 Both sexes	2040 Males	2040 Females
All ages	104 343	52 096	52 247	108 128	53 954	54 174	111 304	55 492	55 811	113 827	56 695	57 132
0-4	7 413	3 788	3 625	7 120	3 640	3 480	6 979	3 569	3 410	6 900	3 529	3 371
5-9	7 642	3 900	3 742	7 387	3 773	3 615	7 099	3 627	3 471	6 960	3 558	3 402
10-14	7 869	4 011	3 859	7 617	3 886	3 731	7 365	3 760	3 605	7 077	3 615	3 462
15-19	7 865	4 002	3 863	7 829	3 986	3 843	7 579	3 863	3 716	7 329	3 739	3 590
20-24	7 773	3 943	3 830	7 807	3 965	3 843	7 774	3 951	3 823	7 529	3 831	3 698
25-29	7 521	3 804	3 717	7 708	3 902	3 806	7 746	3 927	3 819	7 717	3 916	3 801
30-34	8 873	4 476	4 397	7 455	3 764	3 691	7 645	3 864	3 781	7 687	3 891	3 796
35-39	8 864	4 457	4 407	8 795	4 429	4 366	7 390	3 726	3 664	7 583	3 827	3 756
40-44	7 873	3 936	3 937	8 775	4 406	4 369	8 712	4 381	4 332	7 322	3 687	3 635
45-49	7 122	3 542	3 581	7 773	3 879	3 894	8 673	4 347	4 326	8 618	4 326	4 291
50-54	6 340	3 114	3 226	6 989	3 464	3 525	7 638	3 800	3 838	8 532	4 264	4 269
55-59	5 608	2 731	2 877	6 166	3 013	3 153	6 809	3 358	3 451	7 453	3 690	3 763
60-64	4 809	2 323	2 487	5 378	2 599	2 779	5 926	2 874	3 052	6 557	3 210	3 347
65-69	3 653	1 742	1 911	4 483	2 138	2 345	5 031	2 401	2 629	5 561	2 664	2 897
70-74	2 509	1 178	1 331	3 249	1 522	1 726	4 010	1 878	2 132	4 522	2 119	2 403
75-79	1 293	590	703	2 058	942	1 116	2 689	1 227	1 463	3 346	1 524	1 822
80-84	755	333	421	919	402	517	1 485	649	836	1 970	857	1 114
85-89	387	162	225	426	175	251	531	215	317	880	354	526
90-94	146	56	90	154	57	97	176	63	113	229	80	149
95-99	26	9	17	36	11	25	40	12	28	49	14	35
100 +	2	1	2	3	1	3	5	1	4	6	1	5

Age group	2045 Both sexes	2045 Males	2045 Females	2050 Both sexes	2050 Males	2050 Females
All ages	115 625	57 532	58 093	116 654	57 986	58 669
0-4	6 793	3 475	3 319	6 622	3 388	3 234
5-9	6 882	3 519	3 364	6 778	3 466	3 312
10-14	6 940	3 547	3 393	6 863	3 508	3 355
15-19	7 044	3 596	3 448	6 908	3 528	3 379
20-24	7 283	3 710	3 573	7 001	3 570	3 431
25-29	7 476	3 799	3 677	7 234	3 680	3 553
30-34	7 661	3 882	3 779	7 424	3 768	3 656
35-39	7 628	3 856	3 772	7 606	3 850	3 756
40-44	7 518	3 790	3 728	7 566	3 821	3 746
45-49	7 245	3 642	3 603	7 444	3 747	3 697
50-54	8 486	4 248	4 238	7 140	3 579	3 560
55-59	8 337	4 146	4 190	8 301	4 137	4 165
60-64	7 189	3 534	3 655	8 056	3 979	4 077
65-69	6 171	2 985	3 186	6 783	3 295	3 489
70-74	5 022	2 362	2 660	5 595	2 657	2 938
75-79	3 802	1 731	2 071	4 252	1 941	2 311
80-84	2 485	1 077	1 408	2 859	1 237	1 622
85-89	1 195	477	718	1 540	611	929
90-94	393	136	257	552	189	363
95-99	66	18	48	120	32	87
100 +	8	2	6	11	2	9

United Nations Department of Economic and Social Affairs/Population Division
World Population Prospects: The 2004 Revision, Volume II: Sex and Age Distribution of the World Population

903

POPULATION BY AGE AND SEX (in thousands)

Age group	2005 Both sexes	Males	Females	2010 Both sexes	Males	Females	2015 Both sexes	Males	Females	2020 Both sexes	Males	Females
All ages	84 238	42 068	42 171	90 692	45 310	45 382	97 627	48 795	48 831	104 550	52 266	52 283
0-4	7 969	4 062	3 906	8 956	4 569	4 387	9 562	4 880	4 682	9 705	4 956	4 748
5-9	7 740	3 940	3 801	7 913	4 029	3 884	8 907	4 539	4 368	9 518	4 853	4 665
10-14	9 175	4 663	4 511	7 704	3 918	3 786	7 880	4 009	3 871	8 875	4 520	4 355
15-19	9 216	4 676	4 541	9 114	4 627	4 487	7 654	3 888	3 766	7 834	3 982	3 852
20-24	8 230	4 151	4 079	9 127	4 619	4 508	9 035	4 576	4 459	7 589	3 847	3 742
25-29	7 493	3 758	3 735	8 134	4 092	4 043	9 035	4 561	4 474	8 952	4 524	4 428
30-34	6 752	3 350	3 402	7 399	3 702	3 697	8 046	4 038	4 008	8 948	4 508	4 440
35-39	6 104	3 014	3 090	6 662	3 298	3 364	7 313	3 650	3 663	7 961	3 987	3 974
40-44	5 425	2 673	2 752	6 009	2 961	3 049	6 570	3 246	3 325	7 222	3 598	3 624
45-49	4 393	2 161	2 231	5 322	2 616	2 706	5 908	2 904	3 004	6 470	3 189	3 281
50-54	3 364	1 653	1 712	4 276	2 095	2 181	5 194	2 543	2 651	5 778	2 829	2 949
55-59	2 093	1 018	1 075	3 237	1 580	1 657	4 129	2 011	2 117	5 029	2 448	2 581
60-64	1 698	821	877	1 979	954	1 025	3 074	1 488	1 587	3 935	1 901	2 035
65-69	1 509	721	788	1 550	740	810	1 817	865	953	2 840	1 357	1 483
70-74	1 371	642	728	1 300	611	689	1 347	632	715	1 593	745	848
75-79	896	411	486	1 071	491	580	1 029	473	556	1 080	495	585
80-84	526	235	292	589	263	327	717	320	397	705	313	391
85-89	216	92	123	264	113	150	302	130	172	382	162	220
90-94	59	23	36	73	29	43	92	37	54	111	44	67
95-99	8	3	6	12	4	8	15	5	9	20	7	13
100 +	1	0	1	1	0	1	1	0	1	2	0	1

Age group	2025 Both sexes	Males	Females	2030 Both sexes	Males	Females	2035 Both sexes	Males	Females	2040 Both sexes	Males	Females
All ages	110 948	55 465	55 483	116 842	58 399	58 443	122 550	61 228	61 322	128 188	64 020	64 168
0-4	9 408	4 808	4 601	9 245	4 726	4 519	9 534	4 875	4 658	10 042	5 136	4 906
5-9	9 667	4 934	4 734	9 377	4 789	4 588	9 219	4 711	4 508	9 509	4 861	4 648
10-14	9 488	4 836	4 653	9 640	4 918	4 722	9 352	4 774	4 578	9 195	4 697	4 498
15-19	8 830	4 493	4 337	9 444	4 809	4 635	9 598	4 892	4 706	9 313	4 751	4 562
20-24	7 773	3 943	3 830	8 768	4 453	4 315	9 384	4 770	4 614	9 541	4 856	4 685
25-29	7 521	3 804	3 717	7 708	3 902	3 806	8 703	4 412	4 291	9 320	4 730	4 590
30-34	8 873	4 476	4 397	7 455	3 764	3 691	7 645	3 864	3 781	8 639	4 373	4 266
35-39	8 864	4 457	4 407	8 795	4 429	4 366	7 390	3 726	3 664	7 583	3 827	3 756
40-44	7 873	3 936	3 937	8 775	4 406	4 369	8 712	4 381	4 332	7 322	3 687	3 635
45-49	7 122	3 542	3 581	7 773	3 879	3 894	8 673	4 347	4 326	8 618	4 326	4 291
50-54	6 340	3 114	3 226	6 989	3 464	3 525	7 638	3 800	3 838	8 532	4 264	4 269
55-59	5 608	2 731	2 877	6 166	3 013	3 153	6 809	3 358	3 451	7 453	3 690	3 763
60-64	4 809	2 323	2 487	5 378	2 599	2 779	5 926	2 874	3 052	6 557	3 210	3 347
65-69	3 653	1 742	1 911	4 483	2 138	2 345	5 031	2 401	2 629	5 561	2 664	2 897
70-74	2 509	1 178	1 331	3 249	1 522	1 726	4 010	1 878	2 132	4 522	2 119	2 403
75-79	1 293	590	703	2 058	942	1 116	2 689	1 227	1 463	3 346	1 524	1 822
80-84	755	333	421	919	402	517	1 485	649	836	1 970	857	1 114
85-89	387	162	225	426	175	251	531	215	317	880	354	526
90-94	146	56	90	154	57	97	176	63	113	229	80	149
95-99	26	9	17	36	11	25	40	12	28	49	14	35
100 +	2	1	2	3	1	3	5	1	4	6	1	5

Age group	2045 Both sexes	Males	Females	2050 Both sexes	Males	Females
All ages	133 579	66 689	66 891	138 480	69 117	69 364
0-4	10 422	5 331	5 091	10 536	5 390	5 146
5-9	10 019	5 122	4 897	10 401	5 318	5 082
10-14	9 487	4 848	4 639	9 997	5 110	4 887
15-19	9 158	4 675	4 483	9 451	4 827	4 624
20-24	9 261	4 718	4 543	9 110	4 645	4 465
25-29	9 481	4 818	4 663	9 206	4 684	4 521
30-34	9 258	4 692	4 566	9 422	4 783	4 639
35-39	8 576	4 336	4 240	9 196	4 655	4 540
40-44	7 518	3 790	3 728	8 509	4 297	4 212
45-49	7 245	3 642	3 603	7 444	3 747	3 697
50-54	8 486	4 248	4 238	7 140	3 579	3 560
55-59	8 337	4 146	4 190	8 301	4 137	4 165
60-64	7 189	3 534	3 655	8 056	3 979	4 077
65-69	6 171	2 985	3 186	6 783	3 295	3 489
70-74	5 022	2 362	2 660	5 595	2 657	2 938
75-79	3 802	1 731	2 071	4 252	1 941	2 311
80-84	2 485	1 077	1 408	2 859	1 237	1 622
85-89	1 195	477	718	1 540	611	929
90-94	393	136	257	552	189	363
95-99	66	18	48	120	32	87
100 +	8	2	6	11	2	9

United Nations Department of Economic and Social Affairs/Population Division
World Population Prospects: The 2004 Revision, Volume II: Sex and Age Distribution of the World Population

904

POPULATION BY AGE AND SEX (in thousands)

Age group	2005 Both sexes	Males	Females	2010 Both sexes	Males	Females	2015 Both sexes	Males	Females	2020 Both sexes	Males	Females
All ages	84 238	42 068	42 171	88 779	44 335	44 445	92 487	46 174	46 313	95 331	47 564	47 767
0-4	7 969	4 062	3 906	7 043	3 593	3 450	6 325	3 228	3 097	5 608	2 864	2 744
5-9	7 740	3 940	3 801	7 913	4 029	3 884	7 004	3 569	3 435	6 295	3 210	3 085
10-14	9 175	4 663	4 511	7 704	3 918	3 786	7 880	4 009	3 871	6 976	3 553	3 423
15-19	9 216	4 676	4 541	9 114	4 627	4 487	7 654	3 888	3 766	7 834	3 982	3 852
20-24	8 230	4 151	4 079	9 127	4 619	4 508	9 035	4 576	4 459	7 589	3 847	3 742
25-29	7 493	3 758	3 735	8 134	4 092	4 043	9 035	4 561	4 474	8 952	4 524	4 428
30-34	6 752	3 350	3 402	7 399	3 702	3 697	8 046	4 038	4 008	8 948	4 508	4 440
35-39	6 104	3 014	3 090	6 662	3 298	3 364	7 313	3 650	3 663	7 961	3 987	3 974
40-44	5 425	2 673	2 752	6 009	2 961	3 049	6 570	3 246	3 325	7 222	3 598	3 624
45-49	4 393	2 161	2 231	5 322	2 616	2 706	5 908	2 904	3 004	6 470	3 189	3 281
50-54	3 364	1 653	1 712	4 276	2 095	2 181	5 194	2 543	2 651	5 778	2 829	2 949
55-59	2 093	1 018	1 075	3 237	1 580	1 657	4 129	2 011	2 117	5 029	2 448	2 581
60-64	1 698	821	877	1 979	954	1 025	3 074	1 488	1 587	3 935	1 901	2 035
65-69	1 509	721	788	1 550	740	810	1 817	865	953	2 840	1 357	1 483
70-74	1 371	642	728	1 300	611	689	1 347	632	715	1 593	745	848
75-79	896	411	486	1 071	491	580	1 029	473	556	1 080	495	585
80-84	526	235	292	589	263	327	717	320	397	705	313	391
85-89	216	92	123	264	113	150	302	130	172	382	162	220
90-94	59	23	36	73	29	43	92	37	54	111	44	67
95-99	8	3	6	12	4	8	15	5	9	20	7	13
100 +	1	0	1	1	0	1	1	0	1	2	0	1

Age group	2025 Both sexes	Males	Females	2030 Both sexes	Males	Females	2035 Both sexes	Males	Females	2040 Both sexes	Males	Females
All ages	97 742	48 728	49 013	99 519	49 563	49 956	100 480	49 972	50 508	100 456	49 877	50 579
0-4	5 397	2 758	2 639	5 096	2 605	2 491	4 743	2 426	2 317	4 325	2 212	2 113
5-9	5 585	2 850	2 735	5 377	2 746	2 631	5 079	2 595	2 484	4 728	2 417	2 311
10-14	6 271	3 196	3 075	5 563	2 838	2 725	5 357	2 735	2 622	5 060	2 585	2 475
15-19	6 935	3 529	3 407	6 234	3 174	3 060	5 529	2 818	2 711	5 325	2 716	2 608
20-24	7 773	3 943	3 830	6 881	3 494	3 387	6 185	3 144	3 042	5 486	2 791	2 694
25-29	7 521	3 804	3 717	7 708	3 902	3 806	6 824	3 459	3 365	6 134	3 113	3 022
30-34	8 873	4 476	4 397	7 455	3 764	3 691	7 645	3 864	3 781	6 769	3 426	3 343
35-39	8 864	4 457	4 407	8 795	4 429	4 366	7 390	3 726	3 664	7 583	3 827	3 756
40-44	7 873	3 936	3 937	8 775	4 406	4 369	8 712	4 381	4 332	7 322	3 687	3 635
45-49	7 122	3 542	3 581	7 773	3 870	3 904	8 673	4 347	4 326	8 618	4 326	4 291
50-54	6 340	3 114	3 226	6 989	3 464	3 525	7 638	3 800	3 838	8 532	4 264	4 269
55-59	5 608	2 731	2 877	6 166	3 013	3 153	6 809	3 358	3 451	7 453	3 690	3 763
60-64	4 809	2 323	2 487	5 378	2 599	2 779	5 926	2 874	3 052	6 557	3 210	3 347
65-69	3 653	1 742	1 911	4 483	2 138	2 345	5 031	2 401	2 629	5 561	2 664	2 897
70-74	2 509	1 178	1 331	3 249	1 522	1 726	4 010	1 878	2 132	4 522	2 119	2 403
75-79	1 293	590	703	2 058	942	1 116	2 689	1 227	1 463	3 346	1 524	1 822
80-84	755	333	421	919	402	517	1 485	649	836	1 970	857	1 114
85-89	387	162	225	426	175	251	531	215	317	880	354	526
90-94	146	56	90	154	57	97	176	63	113	229	80	149
95-99	26	9	17	36	11	25	40	12	28	49	14	35
100 +	2	1	2	3	1	3	5	1	4	6	1	5

Age group	2045 Both sexes	Males	Females	2050 Both sexes	Males	Females
All ages	99 422	49 271	50 152	97 481	48 211	49 270
0-4	3 929	2 010	1 919	3 612	1 848	1 764
5-9	4 313	2 205	2 108	3 917	2 003	1 914
10-14	4 711	2 407	2 303	4 296	2 196	2 100
15-19	5 030	2 568	2 462	4 681	2 391	2 290
20-24	5 284	2 692	2 592	4 992	2 545	2 447
25-29	5 440	2 764	2 676	5 241	2 666	2 575
30-34	6 085	3 083	3 002	5 395	2 738	2 657
35-39	6 715	3 394	3 320	6 036	3 055	2 981
40-44	7 518	3 790	3 728	6 658	3 362	3 296
45-49	7 245	3 642	3 603	7 444	3 747	3 697
50-54	8 486	4 248	4 238	7 140	3 579	3 560
55-59	8 337	4 146	4 190	8 301	4 137	4 165
60-64	7 189	3 534	3 655	8 056	3 979	4 077
65-69	6 171	2 985	3 186	6 783	3 295	3 489
70-74	5 022	2 362	2 660	5 595	2 657	2 938
75-79	3 802	1 731	2 071	4 252	1 941	2 311
80-84	2 485	1 077	1 408	2 859	1 237	1 622
85-89	1 195	477	718	1 540	611	929
90-94	393	136	257	552	189	363
95-99	66	18	48	120	32	87
100 +	8	2	6	11	2	9

POPULATION BY AGE AND SEX (in thousands)

Age group	1950 Both sexes	1950 Males	1950 Females	1955 Both sexes	1955 Males	1955 Females	1960 Both sexes	1960 Males	1960 Females	1965 Both sexes	1965 Males	1965 Females
All ages	14	7	7	21	11	10	33	17	15	50	27	23
0-4	2	1	1	3	2	2	5	3	3	8	4	4
5-9	2	1	1	2	1	1	3	2	2	6	3	3
10-14	2	1	1	2	1	1	3	2	2	5	2	2
15-19	1	1	1	2	1	1	4	2	2	5	3	2
20-24	1	1	1	2	1	1	4	2	2	6	3	3
25-29	1	1	1	2	1	1	3	2	2	6	3	2
30-34	1	0	0	1	1	1	2	1	1	4	2	2
35-39	1	0	0	1	1	0	2	1	1	3	2	1
40-44	1	0	0	1	1	0	1	1	1	2	1	1
45-49	1	0	0	1	0	0	1	1	0	2	1	1
50-54	0	0	0	1	0	0	1	0	0	1	1	1
55-59	0	0	0	0	0	0	1	0	0	1	1	0
60-64	0	0	0	0	0	0	1	0	0	1	0	0
65-69	0	0	0	0	0	0	0	0	0	1	0	0
70-74	0	0	0	0	0	0	0	0	0	0	0	0
75-79	0	0	0	0	0	0	0	0	0	0	0	0
80 +	0	0	0	0	0	0	0	0	0	0	0	0

Age group	1970 Both sexes	1970 Males	1970 Females	1975 Both sexes	1975 Males	1975 Females	1980 Both sexes	1980 Males	1980 Females	1985 Both sexes	1985 Males	1985 Females
All ages	76	42	34	75	41	34	151	81	69	183	97	86
0-4	13	6	6	13	7	7	23	11	11	32	16	16
5-9	9	5	5	11	6	6	15	8	8	22	11	11
10-14	8	4	4	9	5	4	14	7	7	15	8	8
15-19	8	4	4	8	4	4	15	8	7	15	7	7
20-24	8	4	4	8	4	3	17	9	8	16	8	8
25-29	8	4	3	6	4	3	16	9	7	18	9	8
30-34	6	4	3	4	2	2	13	7	5	17	9	8
35-39	5	3	2	3	2	2	9	5	4	13	7	6
40-44	4	2	1	3	2	1	8	4	3	10	5	4
45-49	3	2	1	3	2	1	6	3	2	8	4	3
50-54	2	1	1	2	1	1	4	3	2	6	3	2
55-59	1	1	1	2	1	1	3	2	1	4	3	2
60-64	1	1	0	1	1	0	3	2	1	3	2	1
65-69	1	0	0	1	0	0	2	1	1	2	1	1
70-74	1	0	0	1	0	0	1	1	1	2	1	1
75-79	0	0	0	0	0	0	1	0	0	1	0	0
80 +	0	0	0	0	0	0	1	0	0	1	0	0

Age group	1990 Both sexes	1990 Males	1990 Females	1995 Both sexes	1995 Males	1995 Females	2000 Both sexes	2000 Males	2000 Females	2005 Both sexes	2005 Males	2005 Females
All ages	218	115	104	259	136	124	300	156	144	341	176	165
0-4	35	18	17	37	19	18	39	20	19	42	21	21
5-9	31	16	16	35	18	17	36	18	18	39	20	19
10-14	22	11	11	31	16	16	35	18	17	36	18	18
15-19	16	8	8	22	11	11	32	16	16	35	18	17
20-24	16	8	8	17	9	9	24	12	12	33	17	16
25-29	17	9	8	18	9	9	19	10	9	25	13	12
30-34	19	10	9	19	10	9	19	10	9	20	10	10
35-39	17	10	8	20	10	9	19	10	9	20	10	10
40-44	13	7	6	18	10	8	20	11	9	20	10	9
45-49	10	5	4	13	7	6	18	10	8	20	11	9
50-54	7	4	3	10	5	4	13	7	6	17	9	8
55-59	5	3	2	7	4	3	9	5	4	12	7	6
60-64	4	2	2	5	3	2	7	4	3	8	5	4
65-69	3	2	1	3	2	1	4	2	2	6	3	3
70-74	2	1	1	2	1	1	3	2	1	3	2	1
75-79	1	1	1	1	1	1	1	1	1	2	1	1
80 +	1	0	0	1	0	0	1	1	0	1	1	1

United Nations Department of Economic and Social Affairs/Population Division
World Population Prospects: The 2004 Revision, Volume II: Sex and Age Distribution of the World Population

POPULATION BY AGE AND SEX (in thousands)

Age group	2005 Both sexes	2005 Males	2005 Females	2010 Both sexes	2010 Males	2010 Females	2015 Both sexes	2015 Males	2015 Females	2020 Both sexes	2020 Males	2020 Females
All ages	341	176	165	429	222	207	526	272	253	627	325	302
0-4	42	21	21	50	26	25	61	31	30	68	34	34
5-9	39	20	19	43	22	21	52	26	26	63	32	31
10-14	36	18	18	40	20	20	44	22	22	53	27	26
15-19	35	18	17	39	20	19	43	22	21	47	24	23
20-24	33	17	16	43	22	21	47	24	23	51	26	25
25-29	25	13	12	42	22	20	52	27	25	56	29	27
30-34	20	10	10	33	17	16	50	26	24	59	31	28
35-39	20	10	10	26	14	12	38	20	18	55	29	26
40-44	20	10	9	24	12	11	29	16	14	42	22	20
45-49	20	11	9	22	12	10	26	14	12	31	17	15
50-54	17	9	8	21	11	10	23	12	11	26	14	12
55-59	12	7	6	17	10	8	21	11	10	23	12	11
60-64	8	5	4	12	7	5	17	9	8	20	11	9
65-69	6	3	3	8	4	4	11	6	5	15	8	7
70-74	3	2	1	5	3	2	7	3	3	9	5	4
75-79	2	1	1	3	1	1	4	2	2	5	3	2
80-84	1	0	0	1	1	1	2	1	1	2	1	1
85-89	0	0	0	0	0	0	0	0	0	1	0	0
90-94	0	0	0	0	0	0	0	0	0	0	0	0
95-99	0	0	0	0	0	0	0	0	0	0	0	0
100 +	0	0	0	0	0	0	0	0	0	0	0	0

Age group	2025 Both sexes	2025 Males	2025 Females	2030 Both sexes	2030 Males	2030 Females	2035 Both sexes	2035 Males	2035 Females	2040 Both sexes	2040 Males	2040 Females
All ages	680	350	330	728	373	355	771	393	378	814	413	401
0-4	66	34	33	62	32	31	61	31	30	63	32	31
5-9	68	34	33	66	34	33	62	32	31	61	31	30
10-14	63	32	31	68	34	33	66	34	33	62	32	31
15-19	53	27	26	63	32	31	68	34	34	67	34	33
20-24	48	24	24	54	27	27	63	32	31	69	35	34
25-29	51	26	25	49	25	24	54	28	27	64	32	32
30-34	57	29	27	52	26	25	49	25	24	55	28	27
35-39	60	31	28	57	29	27	52	27	25	50	25	24
40-44	55	29	26	59	31	28	57	29	27	52	27	25
45-49	41	22	19	54	28	26	59	31	28	56	29	27
50-54	31	16	14	41	21	19	53	28	26	58	30	28
55-59	25	13	12	30	16	14	39	20	19	52	27	25
60-64	21	11	10	24	12	11	28	15	13	37	19	18
65-69	18	9	9	19	10	9	22	11	11	26	13	13
70-74	13	7	6	15	8	8	16	8	8	19	9	9
75-79	7	4	3	9	5	5	11	5	6	13	6	7
80-84	3	1	1	4	2	2	6	3	3	7	3	4
85-89	1	0	0	1	1	1	2	1	1	3	1	2
90-94	0	0	0	0	0	0	0	0	0	1	0	0
95-99	0	0	0	0	0	0	0	0	0	0	0	0
100 +	0	0	0	0	0	0	0	0	0	0	0	0

Age group	2045 Both sexes	2045 Males	2045 Females	2050 Both sexes	2050 Males	2050 Females
All ages	857	433	423	896	451	444
0-4	66	34	32	66	34	32
5-9	64	32	31	66	34	32
10-14	61	31	30	64	32	31
15-19	63	32	31	62	31	30
20-24	67	34	33	63	32	31
25-29	69	35	34	68	34	34
30-34	65	33	32	70	35	35
35-39	55	28	27	65	33	32
40-44	50	25	24	55	28	27
45-49	52	26	25	49	25	24
50-54	55	29	27	51	26	25
55-59	56	29	27	54	28	26
60-64	49	25	24	54	27	26
65-69	34	17	17	45	23	23
70-74	22	11	11	30	14	15
75-79	15	7	8	18	8	9
80-84	8	4	5	10	4	6
85-89	4	1	2	4	2	3
90-94	1	0	1	1	0	1
95-99	0	0	0	0	0	0
100 +	0	0	0	0	0	0

POPULATION BY AGE AND SEX (in thousands)

Age group	2005 Both sexes	2005 Males	2005 Females	2010 Both sexes	2010 Males	2010 Females	2015 Both sexes	2015 Males	2015 Females	2020 Both sexes	2020 Males	2020 Females
All ages	341	176	165	433	224	209	537	278	259	650	336	314
0-4	42	21	21	54	27	27	69	35	34	80	40	39
5-9	39	20	19	43	22	21	56	28	27	70	36	35
10-14	36	18	18	40	20	20	44	22	22	56	29	28
15-19	35	18	17	39	20	19	43	22	21	47	24	23
20-24	33	17	16	43	22	21	47	24	23	51	26	25
25-29	25	13	12	42	22	20	52	27	25	56	29	27
30-34	20	10	10	33	17	16	50	26	24	59	31	28
35-39	20	10	10	26	14	12	38	20	18	55	29	26
40-44	20	10	9	24	12	11	29	16	14	42	22	20
45-49	20	11	9	22	12	10	26	14	12	31	17	15
50-54	17	9	8	21	11	10	23	12	11	26	14	12
55-59	12	7	6	17	10	8	21	11	10	23	12	11
60-64	8	5	4	12	7	5	17	9	8	20	11	9
65-69	6	3	3	8	4	4	11	6	5	15	8	7
70-74	3	2	1	5	3	2	7	3	3	9	5	4
75-79	2	1	1	3	1	1	4	2	2	5	3	2
80-84	1	0	0	1	1	1	2	1	1	2	1	1
85-89	0	0	0	0	0	0	0	0	0	1	0	0
90-94	0	0	0	0	0	0	0	0	0	0	0	0
95-99	0	0	0	0	0	0	0	0	0	0	0	0
100 +	0	0	0	0	0	0	0	0	0	0	0	0

Age group	2025 Both sexes	2025 Males	2025 Females	2030 Both sexes	2030 Males	2030 Females	2035 Both sexes	2035 Males	2035 Females	2040 Both sexes	2040 Males	2040 Females
All ages	716	368	348	777	398	379	836	426	410	900	457	443
0-4	79	40	39	76	39	37	78	39	38	84	43	42
5-9	80	40	39	79	40	39	76	38	37	78	39	38
10-14	70	36	35	80	40	39	79	40	39	76	38	37
15-19	57	29	28	70	36	35	80	40	39	79	40	39
20-24	48	24	24	57	29	28	71	36	35	80	41	40
25-29	51	26	25	49	25	24	58	29	29	72	36	35
30-34	57	29	27	52	26	25	49	25	24	59	30	29
35-39	60	31	28	57	29	27	52	27	25	50	25	24
40-44	55	29	26	59	31	28	57	29	27	52	27	25
45-49	41	22	19	54	28	26	59	31	28	56	29	27
50-54	31	16	14	41	21	19	53	28	26	58	30	28
55-59	25	13	12	30	16	14	39	20	19	52	27	25
60-64	21	11	10	24	12	11	28	15	13	37	19	18
65-69	18	9	9	19	10	9	22	11	11	26	13	13
70-74	13	7	6	15	8	8	16	8	8	19	9	9
75-79	7	4	3	9	5	5	11	5	6	13	6	7
80-84	3	1	1	4	2	2	6	3	3	7	3	4
85-89	1	0	0	1	1	1	2	1	1	3	1	2
90-94	0	0	0	0	0	0	0	0	0	1	0	0
95-99	0	0	0	0	0	0	0	0	0	0	0	0
100 +	0	0	0	0	0	0	0	0	0	0	0	0

Age group	2045 Both sexes	2045 Males	2045 Females	2050 Both sexes	2050 Males	2050 Females
All ages	968	490	479	1 037	523	514
0-4	92	47	45	96	49	47
5-9	85	43	42	92	47	45
10-14	78	39	38	85	43	42
15-19	76	39	38	78	40	38
20-24	80	40	39	77	39	38
25-29	81	41	40	81	41	40
30-34	72	37	36	82	41	40
35-39	59	30	29	73	37	36
40-44	50	25	24	59	30	29
45-49	52	26	25	49	25	24
50-54	55	29	27	51	26	25
55-59	56	29	27	54	28	26
60-64	49	25	24	54	27	26
65-69	34	17	17	45	23	23
70-74	22	11	11	30	14	15
75-79	15	7	8	18	8	9
80-84	8	4	5	10	4	6
85-89	4	1	2	4	2	3
90-94	1	0	1	1	0	1
95-99	0	0	0	0	0	0
100 +	0	0	0	0	0	0

United Nations Department of Economic and Social Affairs/Population Division
World Population Prospects: The 2004 Revision, Volume II: Sex and Age Distribution of the World Population

POPULATION BY AGE AND SEX (in thousands)

Age group	2005 Both sexes	2005 Males	2005 Females	2010 Both sexes	2010 Males	2010 Females	2015 Both sexes	2015 Males	2015 Females	2020 Both sexes	2020 Males	2020 Females
All ages	341	176	165	426	221	205	515	267	248	604	313	291
0-4	42	21	21	47	24	23	53	27	26	56	29	28
5-9	39	20	19	43	22	21	48	25	24	55	28	27
10-14	36	18	18	40	20	20	44	22	22	49	25	24
15-19	35	18	17	39	20	19	43	22	21	47	24	23
20-24	33	17	16	43	22	21	47	24	23	51	26	25
25-29	25	13	12	42	22	20	52	27	25	56	29	27
30-34	20	10	10	33	17	16	50	26	24	59	31	28
35-39	20	10	10	26	14	12	38	20	18	55	29	26
40-44	20	10	9	24	12	11	29	16	14	42	22	20
45-49	20	11	9	22	12	10	26	14	12	31	17	15
50-54	17	9	8	21	11	10	23	12	11	26	14	12
55-59	12	7	6	17	10	8	21	11	10	23	12	11
60-64	8	5	4	12	7	5	17	9	8	20	11	9
65-69	6	3	3	8	4	4	11	6	5	15	8	7
70-74	3	2	1	5	3	2	7	3	3	9	5	4
75-79	2	1	1	3	1	1	4	2	2	5	3	2
80-84	1	0	0	1	1	1	2	1	1	2	1	1
85-89	0	0	0	0	0	0	0	0	0	1	0	0
90-94	0	0	0	0	0	0	0	0	0	0	0	0
95-99	0	0	0	0	0	0	0	0	0	0	0	0
100 +	0	0	0	0	0	0	0	0	0	0	0	0

Age group	2025 Both sexes	2025 Males	2025 Females	2030 Both sexes	2030 Males	2030 Females	2035 Both sexes	2035 Males	2035 Females	2040 Both sexes	2040 Males	2040 Females
All ages	645	332	313	679	348	331	707	361	346	732	372	360
0-4	54	27	27	49	25	24	46	23	23	45	23	22
5-9	56	28	28	54	27	27	49	25	24	46	23	23
10-14	55	28	27	56	28	28	54	27	27	49	25	24
15-19	50	25	25	55	28	27	56	29	28	54	27	27
20-24	48	24	24	50	25	25	56	28	28	57	29	28
25-29	51	26	25	49	25	24	51	26	25	57	29	28
30-34	57	29	27	52	26	25	49	25	24	52	26	25
35-39	60	31	28	57	29	27	52	27	25	50	25	24
40-44	55	29	26	59	31	28	57	29	27	52	27	25
45-49	41	22	19	54	28	26	59	31	28	56	29	27
50-54	31	16	14	41	21	19	53	28	26	58	30	28
55-59	25	13	12	30	16	14	39	20	19	52	27	25
60-64	21	11	10	24	12	11	28	15	13	37	19	18
65-69	18	9	9	19	10	9	22	11	11	26	13	13
70-74	13	7	6	15	8	8	16	8	8	19	9	9
75-79	7	4	3	9	5	5	11	5	6	13	6	7
80-84	3	1	1	4	2	2	6	3	3	7	3	4
85-89	1	0	0	1	1	1	2	1	1	3	1	2
90-94	0	0	0	0	0	0	0	0	0	1	0	0
95-99	0	0	0	0	0	0	0	0	0	0	0	0
100 +	0	0	0	0	0	0	0	0	0	0	0	0

Age group	2045 Both sexes	2045 Males	2045 Females	2050 Both sexes	2050 Males	2050 Females
All ages	753	381	372	768	387	381
0-4	44	22	22	42	21	21
5-9	45	23	22	44	22	22
10-14	46	24	23	45	23	22
15-19	50	25	24	47	24	23
20-24	55	28	27	50	25	25
25-29	58	29	29	56	28	27
30-34	57	29	28	58	30	29
35-39	52	26	26	58	29	28
40-44	50	25	24	52	26	26
45-49	52	26	25	49	25	24
50-54	55	29	27	51	26	25
55-59	56	29	27	54	28	26
60-64	49	25	24	54	27	26
65-69	34	17	17	45	23	23
70-74	22	11	11	30	14	15
75-79	15	7	8	18	8	9
80-84	8	4	5	10	4	6
85-89	4	1	2	4	2	3
90-94	1	0	1	1	0	1
95-99	0	0	0	0	0	0
100 +	0	0	0	0	0	0

POPULATION BY AGE AND SEX (in thousands)

Age group	1950 Both sexes	1950 Males	1950 Females	1955 Both sexes	1955 Males	1955 Females	1960 Both sexes	1960 Males	1960 Females	1965 Both sexes	1965 Males	1965 Females
All ages	4 316	2 179	2 137	4 733	2 391	2 342	5 223	2 637	2 586	5 800	2 926	2 874
0-4	755	383	372	884	450	434	988	503	485	1 110	565	544
5-9	575	292	283	663	338	325	782	400	382	878	449	429
10-14	495	252	243	554	283	272	640	327	313	756	387	368
15-19	430	219	211	474	242	232	530	271	259	612	313	299
20-24	369	188	181	401	204	197	440	224	216	491	250	241
25-29	315	160	154	338	171	167	365	184	180	397	200	197
30-34	268	136	131	286	145	141	304	153	151	326	163	163
35-39	228	116	112	241	122	119	256	129	127	272	135	137
40-44	194	99	95	204	103	101	216	108	108	228	113	115
45-49	165	83	82	172	87	86	181	90	91	191	94	97
50-54	140	70	71	143	71	72	150	74	76	158	77	81
55-59	114	55	59	118	58	61	121	59	63	128	61	66
60-64	97	46	51	91	43	48	95	45	50	98	46	51
65-69	76	36	40	71	33	38	67	31	36	70	33	38
70-74	52	25	28	49	22	26	47	21	25	44	20	24
75-79	28	13	16	28	13	15	26	12	15	25	11	14
80 +	14	6	8	14	6	8	14	6	8	14	6	8

Age group	1970 Both sexes	1970 Males	1970 Females	1975 Both sexes	1975 Males	1975 Females	1980 Both sexes	1980 Males	1980 Females	1985 Both sexes	1985 Males	1985 Females
All ages	6 327	3 171	3 156	6 968	3 469	3 499	8 197	4 101	4 097	9 951	5 005	4 946
0-4	1 233	628	604	1 406	717	688	1 702	869	832	2 188	1 120	1 068
5-9	991	507	484	1 114	570	544	1 303	668	636	1 607	824	783
10-14	848	435	413	959	492	467	1 089	558	530	1 281	657	624
15-19	714	366	348	802	410	391	932	478	453	1 066	547	518
20-24	544	275	269	634	320	314	765	391	374	900	462	438
25-29	414	205	209	453	221	232	595	299	296	731	373	359
30-34	331	161	170	337	159	178	421	204	217	566	284	283
35-39	274	132	141	271	126	145	312	146	166	399	192	206
40-44	231	111	120	228	106	123	250	115	135	293	136	157
45-49	195	94	102	195	90	105	210	95	114	234	106	127
50-54	163	77	85	165	76	89	177	80	96	193	87	106
55-59	132	62	69	136	62	73	146	66	80	159	71	88
60-64	102	47	54	105	48	57	115	52	63	126	56	70
65-69	72	33	39	76	34	42	83	37	46	93	41	52
70-74	46	21	26	48	21	27	54	24	31	62	27	35
75-79	24	10	14	26	11	15	29	12	17	34	14	20
80 +	14	6	8	14	5	8	16	6	10	19	7	11

Age group	1990 Both sexes	1990 Males	1990 Females	1995 Both sexes	1995 Males	1995 Females	2000 Both sexes	2000 Males	2000 Females	2005 Both sexes	2005 Males	2005 Females
All ages	12 086	6 102	5 983	15 219	7 731	7 487	17 937	9 104	8 832	20 975	10 635	10 340
0-4	2 578	1 318	1 260	2 957	1 510	1 447	3 287	1 676	1 612	3 668	1 871	1 797
5-9	2 093	1 074	1 019	2 524	1 292	1 232	2 869	1 465	1 404	3 209	1 636	1 574
10-14	1 585	814	771	2 099	1 080	1 019	2 499	1 279	1 220	2 845	1 452	1 392
15-19	1 258	646	612	1 587	821	766	2 072	1 066	1 006	2 469	1 263	1 206
20-24	1 035	531	504	1 209	622	587	1 553	802	751	2 028	1 041	987
25-29	867	444	423	987	492	495	1 176	603	572	1 508	776	732
30-34	702	357	345	880	432	449	957	476	481	1 138	582	556
35-39	541	271	271	744	372	372	852	416	435	924	458	466
40-44	379	182	197	587	294	293	717	357	360	821	400	422
45-49	276	127	149	435	217	218	562	280	282	687	340	347
50-54	217	98	120	345	175	170	410	203	207	531	262	269
55-59	176	78	98	266	135	131	318	160	159	380	186	194
60-64	140	61	78	205	104	101	237	118	119	286	141	145
65-69	105	45	59	159	78	81	173	85	87	202	98	103
70-74	70	30	40	116	55	61	123	59	64	135	65	70
75-79	40	17	23	70	32	38	78	36	42	83	38	45
80 +	23	9	14	47	21	27	54	23	31	60	26	35

United Nations Department of Economic and Social Affairs/Population Division
World Population Prospects: The 2004 Revision, Volume II: Sex and Age Distribution of the World Population

910

POPULATION BY AGE AND SEX (in thousands)

Age group	2005 Both sexes	Males	Females	2010 Both sexes	Males	Females	2015 Both sexes	Males	Females	2020 Both sexes	Males	Females
All ages	20 975	10 635	10 340	24 502	12 412	12 090	28 480	14 415	14 065	32 733	16 555	16 178
0-4	3 668	1 871	1 797	4 176	2 130	2 046	4 654	2 373	2 280	4 964	2 531	2 433
5-9	3 209	1 636	1 574	3 600	1 835	1 765	4 118	2 099	2 019	4 606	2 347	2 259
10-14	2 845	1 452	1 392	3 187	1 624	1 563	3 579	1 824	1 755	4 099	2 089	2 011
15-19	2 469	1 263	1 206	2 816	1 437	1 380	3 160	1 609	1 551	3 555	1 810	1 745
20-24	2 028	1 041	987	2 425	1 238	1 187	2 774	1 412	1 362	3 120	1 585	1 535
25-29	1 508	776	732	1 981	1 013	967	2 377	1 210	1 168	2 728	1 385	1 343
30-34	1 138	582	556	1 468	754	715	1 939	989	949	2 336	1 186	1 150
35-39	924	458	466	1 105	563	542	1 434	734	700	1 902	969	934
40-44	821	400	422	895	441	454	1 075	546	529	1 402	716	686
45-49	687	340	347	791	383	408	866	425	441	1 044	528	516
50-54	531	262	269	654	321	333	757	363	393	832	405	426
55-59	380	186	194	496	242	254	614	298	316	714	339	375
60-64	286	141	145	344	165	179	452	217	235	563	269	294
65-69	202	98	103	245	118	127	298	140	158	395	185	210
70-74	135	65	70	159	75	84	196	92	104	241	110	131
75-79	83	38	45	93	43	50	111	51	61	139	63	76
80-84	42	18	24	46	20	26	52	23	29	64	28	36
85-89	14	6	9	17	7	10	19	8	11	21	9	12
90-94	3	1	2	4	1	2	4	2	3	5	2	3
95-99	0	0	0	1	0	0	1	0	0	1	0	0
100 +	0	0	0	0	0	0	0	0	0	0	0	0

Age group	2025 Both sexes	Males	Females	2030 Both sexes	Males	Females	2035 Both sexes	Males	Females	2040 Both sexes	Males	Females
All ages	37 094	18 745	18 349	41 499	20 954	20 545	45 968	23 193	22 774	50 508	25 465	25 043
0-4	5 120	2 610	2 510	5 237	2 670	2 566	5 399	2 753	2 646	5 591	2 852	2 739
5-9	4 926	2 509	2 417	5 089	2 592	2 497	5 210	2 654	2 556	5 377	2 740	2 637
10-14	4 590	2 338	2 252	4 911	2 500	2 411	5 076	2 584	2 492	5 199	2 647	2 552
15-19	4 077	2 075	2 002	4 568	2 324	2 244	4 891	2 488	2 404	5 058	2 572	2 485
20-24	3 517	1 786	1 731	4 040	2 051	1 988	4 532	2 301	2 231	4 856	2 465	2 391
25-29	3 077	1 558	1 518	3 475	1 760	1 715	3 998	2 025	1 973	4 491	2 275	2 216
30-34	2 688	1 361	1 327	3 038	1 535	1 503	3 437	1 737	1 700	3 961	2 002	1 959
35-39	2 300	1 165	1 135	2 653	1 340	1 312	3 003	1 514	1 489	3 403	1 717	1 686
40-44	1 867	948	919	2 264	1 144	1 120	2 616	1 310	1 207	2 067	1 403	1 474
45-49	1 368	695	672	1 828	925	903	2 221	1 119	1 102	2 572	1 292	1 279
50-54	1 008	507	501	1 325	670	655	1 776	894	882	2 163	1 084	1 079
55-59	789	381	409	960	478	482	1 267	635	632	1 704	850	854
60-64	660	308	352	733	348	385	895	439	457	1 186	585	601
65-69	497	232	265	587	268	319	656	304	352	805	386	419
70-74	323	147	176	410	186	225	489	216	273	550	247	303
75-79	174	76	98	236	103	133	303	132	172	365	155	211
80-84	81	35	46	103	43	60	142	60	83	185	76	108
85-89	27	11	16	35	14	21	45	17	27	63	24	38
90-94	6	2	4	7	3	5	10	4	6	13	5	8
95-99	1	0	0	1	0	1	1	0	1	1	0	1
100 +	0	0	0	0	0	0	0	0	0	0	0	0

Age group	2045 Both sexes	Males	Females	2050 Both sexes	Males	Females
All ages	55 048	27 731	27 317	59 454	29 921	29 533
0-4	5 728	2 922	2 806	5 758	2 940	2 818
5-9	5 571	2 839	2 732	5 711	2 912	2 799
10-14	5 367	2 733	2 633	5 561	2 833	2 728
15-19	5 181	2 636	2 546	5 350	2 723	2 628
20-24	5 025	2 551	2 474	5 150	2 615	2 535
25-29	4 817	2 440	2 378	4 987	2 526	2 461
30-34	4 454	2 252	2 202	4 781	2 417	2 364
35-39	3 926	1 981	1 945	4 419	2 231	2 188
40-44	3 366	1 695	1 672	3 888	1 958	1 930
45-49	2 921	1 466	1 456	3 319	1 667	1 652
50-54	2 511	1 256	1 255	2 857	1 427	1 430
55-59	2 082	1 034	1 048	2 422	1 201	1 221
60-64	1 602	787	815	1 965	961	1 003
65-69	1 072	517	555	1 456	699	757
70-74	680	315	364	913	426	487
75-79	415	178	237	519	230	289
80-84	226	91	135	263	106	157
85-89	83	32	51	106	39	67
90-94	18	6	12	25	8	17
95-99	2	1	1	3	1	2
100 +	0	0	0	0	0	0

United Nations Department of Economic and Social Affairs/Population Division
World Population Prospects: The 2004 Revision, Volume II: Sex and Age Distribution of the World Population

911

POPULATION BY AGE AND SEX (in thousands)

Age group	2005 Both sexes	2005 Males	2005 Females	2010 Both sexes	2010 Males	2010 Females	2015 Both sexes	2015 Males	2015 Females	2020 Both sexes	2020 Males	2020 Females
All ages	20 975	10 635	10 340	24 687	12 506	12 181	29 028	14 695	14 333	33 828	17 113	16 715
0-4	3 668	1 871	1 797	4 361	2 224	2 137	5 019	2 560	2 460	5 516	2 812	2 703
5-9	3 209	1 636	1 574	3 600	1 835	1 765	4 300	2 192	2 108	4 968	2 532	2 436
10-14	2 845	1 452	1 392	3 187	1 624	1 563	3 579	1 824	1 755	4 281	2 181	2 100
15-19	2 469	1 263	1 206	2 816	1 437	1 380	3 160	1 609	1 551	3 555	1 810	1 745
20-24	2 028	1 041	987	2 425	1 238	1 187	2 774	1 412	1 362	3 120	1 585	1 535
25-29	1 508	776	732	1 981	1 013	967	2 377	1 210	1 168	2 728	1 385	1 343
30-34	1 138	582	556	1 468	754	715	1 939	989	949	2 336	1 186	1 150
35-39	924	458	466	1 105	563	542	1 434	734	700	1 902	969	934
40-44	821	400	422	895	441	454	1 075	546	529	1 402	716	686
45-49	687	340	347	791	383	408	866	425	441	1 044	528	516
50-54	531	262	269	654	321	333	757	363	393	832	405	426
55-59	380	186	194	496	242	254	614	298	316	714	339	375
60-64	286	141	145	344	165	179	452	217	235	563	269	294
65-69	202	98	103	245	118	127	298	140	158	395	185	210
70-74	135	65	70	159	75	84	196	92	104	241	110	131
75-79	83	38	45	93	43	50	111	51	61	139	63	76
80-84	42	18	24	46	20	26	52	23	29	64	28	36
85-89	14	6	9	17	7	10	19	8	11	21	9	12
90-94	3	1	2	4	1	2	4	2	3	5	2	3
95-99	0	0	0	1	0	0	1	0	0	1	0	0
100 +	0	0	0	0	0	0	0	0	0	0	0	0

Age group	2025 Both sexes	2025 Males	2025 Females	2030 Both sexes	2030 Males	2030 Females	2035 Both sexes	2035 Males	2035 Females	2040 Both sexes	2040 Males	2040 Females
All ages	38 847	19 638	19 209	44 068	22 263	21 805	49 590	25 038	24 553	55 490	28 001	27 488
0-4	5 784	2 949	2 835	6 060	3 090	2 970	6 463	3 296	3 167	6 961	3 550	3 410
5-9	5 474	2 788	2 686	5 749	2 928	2 821	6 030	3 072	2 958	6 436	3 280	3 157
10-14	4 951	2 521	2 429	5 458	2 779	2 679	5 734	2 919	2 815	6 017	3 064	2 953
15-19	4 257	2 167	2 091	4 928	2 507	2 421	5 436	2 765	2 671	5 714	2 906	2 808
20-24	3 517	1 786	1 731	4 220	2 143	2 077	4 890	2 483	2 407	5 399	2 741	2 659
25-29	3 077	1 558	1 518	3 475	1 760	1 715	4 177	2 116	2 061	4 847	2 456	2 392
30-34	2 688	1 361	1 327	3 038	1 535	1 503	3 437	1 737	1 700	4 139	2 092	2 046
35-39	2 300	1 165	1 135	2 653	1 340	1 312	3 003	1 514	1 489	3 403	1 717	1 686
40-44	1 867	948	919	2 264	1 144	1 120	2 616	1 319	1 297	2 967	1 493	1 474
45-49	1 368	695	672	1 828	925	903	2 221	1 119	1 102	2 572	1 292	1 279
50-54	1 008	507	501	1 325	670	655	1 776	894	882	2 163	1 084	1 079
55-59	789	381	409	960	478	482	1 267	635	632	1 704	850	854
60-64	660	308	352	733	348	385	895	439	457	1 186	585	601
65-69	497	232	265	587	268	319	656	304	352	805	386	419
70-74	323	147	176	410	186	225	489	216	273	550	247	303
75-79	174	76	98	236	103	133	303	132	172	365	155	211
80-84	81	35	46	103	43	60	142	59	83	185	76	108
85-89	27	11	16	35	14	21	45	17	27	63	24	38
90-94	6	2	4	7	3	5	10	4	6	13	5	8
95-99	1	0	0	1	0	1	1	0	1	1	0	1
100 +	0	0	0	0	0	0	0	0	0	0	0	0

Age group	2045 Both sexes	2045 Males	2045 Females	2050 Both sexes	2050 Males	2050 Females
All ages	61 701	31 118	30 583	68 054	34 299	33 755
0-4	7 415	3 783	3 632	7 723	3 943	3 780
5-9	6 937	3 536	3 401	7 393	3 770	3 624
10-14	6 424	3 272	3 152	6 926	3 528	3 397
15-19	5 998	3 051	2 947	6 406	3 260	3 146
20-24	5 679	2 883	2 796	5 964	3 029	2 935
25-29	5 358	2 714	2 644	5 639	2 857	2 782
30-34	4 809	2 432	2 377	5 319	2 690	2 629
35-39	4 103	2 070	2 032	4 772	2 409	2 362
40-44	3 366	1 695	1 672	4 064	2 047	2 016
45-49	2 921	1 466	1 456	3 319	1 667	1 652
50-54	2 511	1 256	1 255	2 857	1 427	1 430
55-59	2 082	1 034	1 048	2 422	1 201	1 221
60-64	1 602	787	815	1 965	961	1 003
65-69	1 072	517	555	1 456	699	757
70-74	680	315	364	913	426	487
75-79	415	178	237	519	230	289
80-84	226	91	135	263	106	157
85-89	83	32	51	106	39	67
90-94	18	6	12	25	8	17
95-99	2	1	1	3	1	2
100 +	0	0	0	0	0	0

United Nations Department of Economic and Social Affairs/Population Division
World Population Prospects: The 2004 Revision, Volume II: Sex and Age Distribution of the World Population

POPULATION BY AGE AND SEX (in thousands)

Age group	2005			2010			2015			2020		
	Both sexes	Males	Females	Both sexes	Males	Females	Both sexes	Males	Females	Both sexes	Males	Females
All ages	20 975	10 635	10 340	24 317	12 318	11 999	27 932	14 136	13 796	31 638	15 997	15 641
0-4	3 668	1 871	1 797	3 992	2 036	1 956	4 288	2 187	2 101	4 412	2 250	2 163
5-9	3 209	1 636	1 574	3 600	1 835	1 765	3 936	2 006	1 930	4 244	2 163	2 081
10-14	2 845	1 452	1 392	3 187	1 624	1 563	3 579	1 824	1 755	3 918	1 996	1 922
15-19	2 469	1 263	1 206	2 816	1 437	1 380	3 160	1 609	1 551	3 555	1 810	1 745
20-24	2 028	1 041	987	2 425	1 238	1 187	2 774	1 412	1 362	3 120	1 585	1 535
25-29	1 508	776	732	1 981	1 013	967	2 377	1 210	1 168	2 728	1 385	1 343
30-34	1 138	582	556	1 468	754	715	1 939	989	949	2 336	1 186	1 150
35-39	924	458	466	1 105	563	542	1 434	734	700	1 902	969	934
40-44	821	400	422	895	441	454	1 075	546	529	1 402	716	686
45-49	687	340	347	791	383	408	866	425	441	1 044	528	516
50-54	531	262	269	654	321	333	757	363	393	832	405	426
55-59	380	186	194	496	242	254	614	298	316	714	339	375
60-64	286	141	145	344	165	179	452	217	235	563	269	294
65-69	202	98	103	245	118	127	298	140	158	395	185	210
70-74	135	65	70	159	75	84	196	92	104	241	110	131
75-79	83	38	45	93	43	50	111	51	61	139	63	76
80-84	42	18	24	46	20	26	52	23	29	64	28	36
85-89	14	6	9	17	7	10	19	8	11	21	9	12
90-94	3	1	2	4	1	2	4	2	3	5	2	3
95-99	0	0	0	1	0	0	1	0	0	1	0	0
100 +	0	0	0	0	0	0	0	0	0	0	0	0

Age group	2025			2030			2035			2040		
	Both sexes	Males	Females	Both sexes	Males	Females	Both sexes	Males	Females	Both sexes	Males	Females
All ages	35 344	17 854	17 491	38 950	19 656	19 294	42 419	21 386	21 033	45 717	23 026	22 691
0-4	4 460	2 274	2 186	4 430	2 259	2 171	4 391	2 239	2 152	4 337	2 212	2 125
5-9	4 378	2 230	2 148	4 432	2 258	2 175	4 407	2 245	2 162	4 372	2 228	2 144
10-14	4 229	2 154	2 075	4 365	2 222	2 143	4 421	2 251	2 170	4 397	2 239	2 158
15-19	3 896	1 983	1 913	4 209	2 141	2 067	4 346	2 210	2 136	4 404	2 240	2 164
20-24	3 517	1 786	1 731	3 860	1 960	1 900	4 174	2 119	2 055	4 314	2 189	2 124
25-29	3 077	1 558	1 518	3 475	1 760	1 715	3 819	1 934	1 885	4 135	2 094	2 041
30-34	2 688	1 361	1 327	3 038	1 535	1 503	3 437	1 737	1 700	3 783	1 912	1 871
35-39	2 300	1 165	1 135	2 653	1 340	1 312	3 003	1 514	1 489	3 403	1 717	1 686
40-44	1 867	948	919	2 264	1 144	1 120	2 616	1 319	1 297	2 967	1 493	1 474
45-49	1 368	695	672	1 828	925	903	2 221	1 119	1 102	2 572	1 292	1 279
50-54	1 008	507	501	1 325	670	655	1 776	894	882	2 163	1 084	1 079
55-59	789	381	409	960	478	482	1 267	635	632	1 704	850	854
60-64	660	308	352	722	348	375	905	439	467	1 196	595	601
65-69	497	232	265	587	268	319	656	304	352	805	386	419
70-74	323	147	176	410	186	225	489	216	273	550	247	303
75-79	174	76	98	236	103	133	303	132	172	365	155	211
80-84	81	35	46	103	43	60	142	59	83	185	76	108
85-89	27	11	16	35	14	21	45	17	27	63	24	38
90-94	6	2	4	7	3	5	10	4	6	13	5	8
95-99	1	0	0	1	0	1	1	0	1	1	0	1
100 +	0	0	0	0	0	0	0	0	0	0	0	0

Age group	2045			2050		
	Both sexes	Males	Females	Both sexes	Males	Females
All ages	48 777	24 539	24 238	51 510	25 877	25 633
0-4	4 234	2 160	2 074	4 067	2 077	1 991
5-9	4 321	2 202	2 119	4 220	2 152	2 069
10-14	4 363	2 222	2 141	4 313	2 197	2 116
15-19	4 382	2 229	2 153	4 348	2 213	2 136
20-24	4 373	2 220	2 154	4 353	2 210	2 143
25-29	4 277	2 165	2 111	4 338	2 197	2 141
30-34	4 100	2 072	2 028	4 243	2 144	2 098
35-39	3 749	1 891	1 858	4 066	2 052	2 014
40-44	3 366	1 695	1 672	3 713	1 870	1 843
45-49	2 921	1 466	1 456	3 319	1 667	1 652
50-54	2 511	1 256	1 255	2 857	1 427	1 430
55-59	2 082	1 034	1 048	2 422	1 201	1 221
60-64	1 602	787	815	1 965	961	1 003
65-69	1 072	517	555	1 456	699	757
70-74	680	315	364	913	426	487
75-79	415	178	237	519	230	289
80-84	226	91	135	263	106	157
85-89	83	32	51	106	39	67
90-94	18	6	12	25	8	17
95-99	2	1	1	3	1	2
100 +	0	0	0	0	0	0

POPULATION BY AGE AND SEX (in thousands)

Age group	1950 Both sexes	Males	Females	1955 Both sexes	Males	Females	1960 Both sexes	Males	Females	1965 Both sexes	Males	Females
All ages	2 440	1 206	1 235	2 753	1 360	1 393	3 141	1 552	1 589	3 664	1 820	1 845
0-4	452	228	224	508	255	253	588	295	293	704	357	347
5-9	349	174	175	397	200	197	452	226	226	554	279	275
10-14	295	147	148	333	166	167	380	191	189	437	220	218
15-19	253	124	129	285	142	143	323	161	162	370	186	184
20-24	215	105	110	243	119	124	275	136	139	312	155	157
25-29	182	88	94	205	100	105	233	113	119	265	131	134
30-34	153	76	77	173	83	90	195	95	101	223	109	114
35-39	129	64	65	144	71	73	164	79	85	186	90	96
40-44	105	52	53	120	59	61	135	67	69	155	75	81
45-49	85	41	44	97	48	50	112	55	57	127	62	65
50-54	67	33	35	77	37	41	89	43	46	103	50	53
55-59	49	23	25	60	29	31	69	32	37	81	38	42
60-64	40	19	20	41	19	22	51	24	27	60	28	32
65-69	30	14	16	31	15	16	33	15	18	42	19	22
70-74	20	10	10	21	10	11	22	10	12	24	11	13
75-79	11	5	6	12	5	6	13	6	7	14	6	8
80 +	5	3	3	6	3	3	6	3	4	7	3	4

Age group	1970 Both sexes	Males	Females	1975 Both sexes	Males	Females	1980 Both sexes	Males	Females	1985 Both sexes	Males	Females
All ages	4 303	2 137	2 166	5 151	2 560	2 592	6 059	3 012	3 047	7 150	3 554	3 596
0-4	843	423	420	1 041	523	518	1 149	578	571	1 334	671	663
5-9	650	329	321	788	395	393	979	491	488	1 083	544	539
10-14	539	271	268	634	321	313	770	386	385	959	480	478
15-19	427	215	213	530	266	264	623	315	308	759	380	380
20-24	359	180	179	421	210	210	518	260	258	615	310	305
25-29	301	149	152	353	176	177	410	204	205	511	254	257
30-34	255	126	129	295	146	150	343	171	173	404	200	203
35-39	214	104	110	248	122	126	286	141	145	336	166	170
40-44	178	86	92	207	100	106	239	117	122	278	136	141
45-49	147	70	77	170	82	88	197	95	102	230	112	118
50-54	119	58	61	139	66	73	160	77	84	187	90	98
55-59	95	45	49	110	53	57	128	60	68	149	71	79
60-64	71	34	38	85	40	45	99	47	52	116	54	62
65-69	50	23	27	60	28	32	72	34	38	84	39	45
70-74	32	14	17	39	17	22	47	21	26	56	26	30
75-79	16	7	9	21	9	12	26	11	15	31	14	18
80 +	9	4	5	11	4	6	14	6	8	17	7	10

Age group	1990 Both sexes	Males	Females	1995 Both sexes	Males	Females	2000 Both sexes	Males	Females	2005 Both sexes	Males	Females
All ages	8 377	4 161	4 216	9 559	4 748	4 811	10 702	5 332	5 370	11 668	5 843	5 826
0-4	1 576	793	783	1 772	891	880	1 890	952	939	2 011	1 012	998
5-9	1 256	631	626	1 474	740	734	1 648	827	821	1 752	880	872
10-14	1 060	532	528	1 228	616	612	1 435	720	715	1 584	795	789
15-19	943	472	471	1 040	522	519	1 212	608	604	1 404	704	700
20-24	741	369	372	906	453	453	1 017	508	508	1 161	581	580
25-29	592	296	296	677	337	340	829	417	412	912	460	452
30-34	490	242	248	527	263	264	577	293	284	679	353	326
35-39	386	190	196	438	215	223	445	225	220	453	238	215
40-44	321	158	163	349	170	179	377	185	192	357	184	173
45-49	264	128	136	294	142	151	309	149	160	315	155	160
50-54	216	105	112	242	116	126	264	126	138	267	128	139
55-59	174	82	91	197	94	103	219	103	116	232	109	123
60-64	134	63	72	154	72	83	175	82	93	191	88	103
65-69	99	45	54	114	52	62	131	60	71	147	67	80
70-74	65	30	35	76	34	42	89	40	49	102	46	56
75-79	38	17	21	44	19	25	52	23	30	61	26	34
80 +	21	9	12	26	11	15	33	14	20	41	17	24

United Nations Department of Economic and Social Affairs/Population Division
World Population Prospects: The 2004 Revision, Volume II: Sex and Age Distribution of the World Population

914

POPULATION BY AGE AND SEX (in thousands)

Age group	2005 Both sexes	2005 Males	2005 Females	2010 Both sexes	2010 Males	2010 Females	2015 Both sexes	2015 Males	2015 Females	2020 Both sexes	2020 Males	2020 Females
All ages	11 668	5 843	5 826	12 673	6 369	6 304	13 841	6 979	6 862	15 128	7 652	7 476
0-4	2 011	1 012	998	2 122	1 068	1 053	2 245	1 130	1 114	2 325	1 172	1 153
5-9	1 752	880	872	1 871	940	931	1 998	1 003	995	2 147	1 079	1 068
10-14	1 584	795	789	1 680	843	837	1 800	903	897	1 938	972	965
15-19	1 404	704	700	1 546	775	771	1 645	825	820	1 770	887	882
20-24	1 161	581	580	1 342	672	670	1 494	748	747	1 605	803	802
25-29	912	460	452	1 042	525	516	1 231	620	610	1 396	702	694
30-34	679	353	326	759	393	366	890	460	430	1 079	556	523
35-39	453	238	215	543	291	252	627	334	293	751	399	351
40-44	357	184	173	365	196	169	451	247	204	529	288	241
45-49	315	155	160	298	154	144	311	168	143	390	215	175
50-54	267	128	139	272	133	139	261	134	127	275	148	127
55-59	232	109	123	235	111	124	242	117	125	234	119	115
60-64	191	88	103	203	94	109	207	96	111	215	102	113
65-69	147	67	80	161	73	88	173	78	95	178	81	97
70-74	102	46	56	115	51	64	127	56	71	139	61	77
75-79	61	26	34	70	30	40	81	35	46	91	39	52
80-84	29	12	17	34	14	20	40	17	23	47	20	27
85-89	10	4	6	12	5	7	14	6	9	17	7	10
90-94	2	1	1	3	1	2	3	1	2	4	1	3
95-99	0	0	0	0	0	0	0	0	0	1	0	0
100 +	0	0	0	0	0	0	0	0	0	0	0	0

Age group	2025 Both sexes	2025 Males	2025 Females	2030 Both sexes	2030 Males	2030 Females	2035 Both sexes	2035 Males	2035 Females	2040 Both sexes	2040 Males	2040 Females
All ages	16 419	8 321	8 097	17 706	8 978	8 728	18 989	9 619	9 369	20 271	10 251	10 020
0-4	2 352	1 185	1 167	2 358	1 189	1 169	2 375	1 198	1 178	2 397	1 209	1 188
5-9	2 247	1 130	1 117	2 289	1 151	1 138	2 308	1 161	1 147	2 333	1 174	1 159
10-14	2 103	1 056	1 047	2 214	1 113	1 102	2 265	1 138	1 127	2 289	1 151	1·138
15-19	1 910	958	952	2 079	1 043	1 036	2 193	1 101	1 092	2 247	1 127	1 119
20-24	1 729	865	864	1 870	935	935	2 040	1 020	1 019	2 155	1 079	1 077
25-29	1 509	757	752	1 632	816	815	1 774	886	888	1 944	971	973
30-34	1 240	634	606	1 353	686	667	1 475	743	732	1 618	812	807
35-39	921	486	435	1 077	559	517	1 188	608	580	1 309	663	646
40-44	639	346	292	797	426	371	944	493	450	1 052	540	512
45-49	459	252	207	561	306	256	709	379	330	847	442	405
50-54	345	190	155	410	224	186	506	274	232	645	342	303
55-59	247	131	115	312	170	142	373	202	171	463	248	215
60-64	208	105	104	221	117	105	282	152	130	339	181	158
65-69	186	87	99	181	90	92	194	101	94	248	132	117
70-74	144	64	80	152	70	82	150	73	77	161	82	79
75-79	100	43	57	105	46	60	112	50	62	112	53	59
80-84	54	22	31	60	25	35	65	27	38	70	30	40
85-89	21	8	12	24	10	15	28	11	17	30	12	18
90-94	5	2	3	6	2	4	7	3	5	9	3	6
95-99	1	0	0	1	0	1	1	0	1	1	0	1
100 +	0	0	0	0	0	0	0	0	0	0	0	0

Age group	2045 Both sexes	2045 Males	2045 Females	2050 Both sexes	2050 Males	2050 Females
All ages	21 542	10 869	10 673	22 781	11 466	11 315
0-4	2 402	1 211	1 190	2 381	1 201	1 180
5-9	2 362	1 189	1 174	2 374	1 195	1 179
10-14	2 318	1 165	1 153	2 350	1 181	1 169
15-19	2 273	1 141	1 132	2 304	1 157	1 147
20-24	2 212	1 107	1 105	2 241	1 122	1 119
25-29	2 065	1 032	1 033	2 129	1 063	1 065
30-34	1 790	897	893	1 918	961	957
35-39	1 453	732	721	1 627	818	809
40-44	1 173	594	578	1 318	663	654
45-49	954	487	467	1 074	542	532
50-54	776	401	375	882	446	435
55-59	594	311	282	720	368	352
60-64	424	224	200	547	283	264
65-69	301	158	143	379	197	182
70-74	208	108	100	254	131	123
75-79	122	61	61	159	81	78
80-84	71	32	38	78	38	40
85-89	33	14	20	34	15	19
90-94	10	4	6	11	4	7
95-99	2	1	1	2	1	1
100 +	0	0	0	0	0	0

POPULATION BY AGE AND SEX (in thousands)

Age group	2005 Both sexes	Males	Females	2010 Both sexes	Males	Females	2015 Both sexes	Males	Females	2020 Both sexes	Males	Females
All ages	11 668	5 843	5 826	12 759	6 412	6 346	14 084	7 101	6 982	15 602	7 890	7 712
0-4	2 011	1 012	998	2 207	1 111	1 096	2 407	1 212	1 195	2 566	1 293	1 273
5-9	1 752	880	872	1 871	940	931	2 078	1 044	1 035	2 302	1 157	1 145
10-14	1 584	795	789	1 680	843	837	1 800	903	897	2 016	1 012	1 004
15-19	1 404	704	700	1 546	775	771	1 645	825	820	1 770	887	882
20-24	1 161	581	580	1 342	672	670	1 494	748	747	1 605	803	802
25-29	912	460	452	1 042	525	516	1 231	620	610	1 396	702	694
30-34	679	353	326	759	393	366	890	460	430	1 079	556	523
35-39	453	238	215	543	291	252	627	334	293	751	399	351
40-44	357	184	173	365	196	169	451	247	204	529	288	241
45-49	315	155	160	298	154	144	311	168	143	390	215	175
50-54	267	128	139	272	133	139	261	134	127	275	148	127
55-59	232	109	123	235	111	124	242	117	125	234	119	115
60-64	191	88	103	203	94	109	207	96	111	215	102	113
65-69	147	67	80	161	73	88	173	78	95	178	81	97
70-74	102	46	56	115	51	64	127	56	71	139	61	77
75-79	61	26	34	70	30	40	81	35	46	91	39	52
80-84	29	12	17	34	14	20	40	17	23	47	20	27
85-89	10	4	6	12	5	7	14	6	9	17	7	10
90-94	2	1	1	3	1	2	3	1	2	4	1	3
95-99	0	0	0	0	0	0	0	0	0	1	0	0
100 +	0	0	0	0	0	0	0	0	0	0	0	0

Age group	2025 Both sexes	Males	Females	2030 Both sexes	Males	Females	2035 Both sexes	Males	Females	2040 Both sexes	Males	Females
All ages	17 172	8 700	8 472	18 812	9 534	9 278	20 545	10 402	10 143	22 386	11 314	11 072
0-4	2 644	1 332	1 311	2 725	1 374	1 351	2 846	1 435	1 411	2 985	1 506	1 480
5-9	2 480	1 247	1 233	2 573	1 294	1 279	2 667	1 342	1 325	2 796	1 407	1 389
10-14	2 255	1 133	1 122	2 444	1 228	1 216	2 546	1 279	1 267	2 645	1 330	1 316
15-19	1 987	996	991	2 229	1 118	1 111	2 421	1 215	1 206	2 525	1 267	1 258
20-24	1 729	865	864	1 946	973	973	2 187	1 094	1 093	2 379	1 191	1 188
25-29	1 509	757	752	1 632	816	815	1 845	922	924	2 085	1 041	1 043
30-34	1 240	634	606	1 353	686	667	1 475	743	732	1 683	844	839
35-39	921	486	435	1 077	559	517	1 188	608	580	1 309	663	646
40-44	639	346	292	797	426	371	944	493	450	1 052	540	512
45-49	459	252	207	561	306	256	709	379	330	847	442	405
50-54	345	190	155	410	224	186	506	274	232	645	342	303
55-59	247	131	115	312	170	142	373	202	171	463	248	215
60-64	208	105	104	221	117	105	282	152	130	339	181	158
65-69	186	87	99	181	90	92	194	101	94	248	132	117
70-74	144	64	80	152	70	82	150	73	77	161	82	79
75-79	100	43	57	105	46	60	112	50	62	112	53	59
80-84	54	22	31	60	25	35	65	27	38	70	30	40
85-89	21	8	12	24	10	15	28	11	17	30	12	18
90-94	5	2	3	6	2	4	7	3	5	9	3	6
95-99	1	0	0	1	0	1	1	0	1	1	0	1
100 +	0	0	0	0	0	0	0	0	0	0	0	0

Age group	2045 Both sexes	Males	Females	2050 Both sexes	Males	Females
All ages	24 316	12 263	12 053	26 307	13 238	13 069
0-4	3 106	1 566	1 539	3 194	1 611	1 583
5-9	2 943	1 481	1 462	3 070	1 545	1 525
10-14	2 778	1 396	1 382	2 927	1 472	1 456
15-19	2 626	1 318	1 308	2 761	1 386	1 375
20-24	2 486	1 244	1 242	2 590	1 297	1 294
25-29	2 279	1 139	1 140	2 393	1 195	1 197
30-34	1 919	962	958	2 118	1 061	1 057
35-39	1 512	761	750	1 744	877	867
40-44	1 173	594	578	1 371	690	681
45-49	954	487	467	1 074	542	532
50-54	776	401	375	882	446	435
55-59	594	311	282	720	368	352
60-64	424	224	200	547	283	264
65-69	301	158	143	379	197	182
70-74	208	108	100	254	131	123
75-79	122	61	61	159	81	78
80-84	71	32	38	78	38	40
85-89	33	14	20	34	15	19
90-94	10	4	6	11	4	7
95-99	2	1	1	2	1	1
100 +	0	0	0	0	0	0

United Nations Department of Economic and Social Affairs/Population Division
World Population Prospects: The 2004 Revision, Volume II: Sex and Age Distribution of the World Population

916

POPULATION BY AGE AND SEX (in thousands)

Age group	2005 Both sexes	Males	Females	2010 Both sexes	Males	Females	2015 Both sexes	Males	Females	2020 Both sexes	Males	Females
All ages	11 668	5 843	5 826	12 586	6 326	6 261	13 592	6 854	6 738	14 640	7 406	7 234
0-4	2 011	1 012	998	2 035	1 024	1 010	2 078	1 046	1 031	2 076	1 046	1 030
5-9	1 752	880	872	1 871	940	931	1 916	962	954	1 988	999	989
10-14	1 584	795	789	1 680	843	837	1 800	903	897	1 858	933	925
15-19	1 404	704	700	1 546	775	771	1 645	825	820	1 770	887	882
20-24	1 161	581	580	1 342	672	670	1 494	748	747	1 605	803	802
25-29	912	460	452	1 042	525	516	1 231	620	610	1 396	702	694
30-34	679	353	326	759	393	366	890	460	430	1 079	556	523
35-39	453	238	215	543	291	252	627	334	293	751	399	351
40-44	357	184	173	365	196	169	451	247	204	529	288	241
45-49	315	155	160	298	154	144	311	168	143	390	215	175
50-54	267	128	139	272	133	139	261	134	127	275	148	127
55-59	232	109	123	235	111	124	242	117	125	234	119	115
60-64	191	88	103	203	94	109	207	96	111	215	102	113
65-69	147	67	80	161	73	88	173	78	95	178	81	97
70-74	102	46	56	115	51	64	127	56	71	139	61	77
75-79	61	26	34	70	30	40	81	35	46	91	39	52
80-84	29	12	17	34	14	20	40	17	23	47	20	27
85-89	10	4	6	12	5	7	14	6	9	17	7	10
90-94	2	1	1	3	1	2	3	1	2	4	1	3
95-99	0	0	0	0	0	0	0	0	0	1	0	0
100 +	0	0	0	0	0	0	0	0	0	0	0	0

Age group	2025 Both sexes	Males	Females	2030 Both sexes	Males	Females	2035 Both sexes	Males	Females	2040 Both sexes	Males	Females
All ages	15 645	7 932	7 713	16 581	8 412	8 169	17 428	8 835	8 593	18 190	9 205	8 985
0-4	2 054	1 035	1 019	1 992	1 004	988	1 920	968	952	1 845	930	915
5-9	2 006	1 009	997	1 999	1 005	994	1 950	981	969	1 886	949	937
10-14	1 947	978	969	1 977	994	984	1 978	994	984	1 934	972	962
15-19	1 832	918	913	1 925	966	959	1 958	983	975	1 962	984	977
20-24	1 729	865	864	1 793	897	897	1 888	944	944	1 924	963	961
25-29	1 509	757	752	1 632	816	815	1 701	849	852	1 800	899	901
30-34	1 240	634	606	1 353	686	667	1 475	743	732	1 552	778	773
35-39	921	486	435	1 077	559	517	1 188	608	580	1 309	663	646
40-44	639	346	292	797	426	371	944	493	450	1 052	540	512
45-49	459	252	207	561	306	256	709	379	330	847	442	405
50-54	345	190	155	410	224	186	506	274	232	645	342	303
55-59	247	131	115	312	170	142	373	202	171	463	248	215
60-64	208	105	104	221	117	105	282	152	130	339	181	158
65-69	186	87	99	181	90	92	194	101	94	248	132	117
70-74	144	64	80	152	70	82	150	73	77	161	82	79
75-79	100	43	57	105	46	60	112	50	62	112	53	59
80-84	54	22	31	60	25	35	65	27	38	70	30	40
85-89	21	8	12	24	10	15	28	11	17	30	12	18
90-94	5	2	3	6	2	4	7	3	5	9	3	6
95-99	1	0	0	1	0	1	1	0	1	1	0	1
100 +	0	0	0	0	0	0	0	0	0	0	0	0

Age group	2045 Both sexes	Males	Females	2050 Both sexes	Males	Females
All ages	18 866	9 525	9 342	19 449	9 792	9 657
0-4	1 762	889	873	1 663	839	824
5-9	1 819	915	904	1 741	876	865
10-14	1 874	942	932	1 809	909	900
15-19	1 920	964	956	1 862	935	927
20-24	1 931	966	965	1 893	948	945
25-29	1 843	921	922	1 858	928	930
30-34	1 657	830	827	1 713	858	855
35-39	1 393	702	692	1 506	757	749
40-44	1 173	594	578	1 263	636	627
45-49	954	487	467	1 074	542	532
50-54	776	401	375	882	446	435
55-59	594	311	282	720	368	352
60-64	424	224	200	547	283	264
65-69	301	158	143	379	197	182
70-74	208	108	100	254	131	123
75-79	122	61	61	159	81	78
80-84	71	32	38	78	38	40
85-89	33	14	20	34	15	19
90-94	10	4	6	11	4	7
95-99	2	1	1	2	1	1
100 +	0	0	0	0	0	0

POPULATION BY AGE AND SEX (in thousands)

Age group	1950 Both sexes	Males	Females	1955 Both sexes	Males	Females	1960 Both sexes	Males	Females	1965 Both sexes	Males	Females
All ages	2 744	1 366	1 377	3 197	1 591	1 606	3 741	1 861	1 880	4 406	2 191	2 215
0-4	438	221	218	613	306	306	722	361	361	862	432	430
5-9	390	198	192	406	204	202	572	285	287	679	339	340
10-14	322	164	158	379	192	187	396	199	197	560	279	281
15-19	278	140	138	315	160	155	371	188	183	388	195	193
20-24	245	122	122	270	136	134	306	155	151	361	183	179
25-29	201	100	100	236	118	119	261	131	130	296	149	146
30-34	188	94	94	193	96	97	228	113	115	251	125	126
35-39	146	73	73	180	90	90	186	92	93	219	108	111
40-44	122	60	61	139	69	70	172	86	87	178	88	90
45-49	105	51	54	115	57	59	132	65	66	164	81	83
50-54	89	43	46	99	48	51	108	53	55	124	61	63
55-59	74	35	39	82	39	43	91	43	47	100	48	52
60-64	58	26	31	66	31	35	73	34	39	81	38	43
65-69	41	19	23	48	22	27	55	26	30	62	28	33
70-74	27	12	15	32	14	17	37	16	21	43	19	24
75-79	14	6	8	17	7	10	21	9	12	25	11	14
80 +	7	3	4	9	3	5	11	4	7	14	6	8

Age group	1970 Both sexes	Males	Females	1975 Both sexes	Males	Females	1980 Both sexes	Males	Females	1985 Both sexes	Males	Females
All ages	5 216	2 592	2 623	6 212	3 087	3 126	7 310	3 627	3 683	8 888	4 415	4 472
0-4	1 041	522	519	1 249	626	623	1 436	720	716	1 679	842	836
5-9	816	408	408	991	496	496	1 195	598	597	1 397	699	698
10-14	666	332	333	801	400	401	974	487	487	1 184	592	592
15-19	548	273	275	653	326	328	783	391	393	973	486	487
20-24	375	188	187	533	265	268	626	311	315	794	395	399
25-29	347	174	172	361	180	181	502	247	255	642	318	324
30-34	283	142	141	333	167	166	336	166	170	515	254	262
35-39	240	119	121	271	136	135	312	155	157	345	170	175
40-44	209	103	106	230	114	116	255	127	128	315	157	158
45-49	169	83	85	199	97	101	216	106	110	254	126	128
50-54	154	76	79	159	78	81	186	90	96	212	104	108
55-59	114	56	59	143	70	74	147	71	76	179	86	92
60-64	90	43	47	103	50	54	129	62	67	137	66	71
65-69	69	32	37	77	36	41	89	42	47	115	54	60
70-74	48	22	27	55	25	30	61	28	33	73	34	39
75-79	29	13	16	34	15	19	38	17	21	45	20	25
80 +	17	7	10	21	8	12	24	10	14	30	12	17

Age group	1990 Both sexes	Males	Females	1995 Both sexes	Males	Females	2000 Both sexes	Males	Females	2005 Both sexes	Males	Females
All ages	10 565	5 248	5 317	11 820	5 842	5 977	12 505	6 213	6 382	13 010	6 453	6 557
0-4	1 831	919	912	1 878	943	935	1 799	903	896	1 752	879	873
5-9	1 642	822	820	1 783	893	890	1 801	902	899	1 702	852	850
10-14	1 386	693	693	1 625	813	812	1 761	882	880	1 747	875	873
15-19	1 181	590	591	1 362	680	682	1 603	801	802	1 740	870	870
20-24	976	486	491	1 118	554	563	1 296	645	651	1 546	771	775
25-29	800	396	404	883	433	450	951	473	478	1 131	571	560
30-34	648	319	328	718	349	369	707	346	361	716	370	346
35-39	518	254	263	588	284	304	583	279	304	513	258	254
40-44	346	170	175	476	229	247	496	234	262	443	213	230
45-49	312	155	157	320	155	165	417	196	221	402	188	214
50-54	248	123	125	291	142	149	287	135	152	357	164	192
55-59	203	99	104	230	112	118	264	126	138	253	117	136
60-64	167	80	87	186	89	97	209	99	109	235	110	125
65-69	122	58	64	147	69	78	163	76	87	181	84	97
70-74	95	44	51	101	47	54	122	56	66	134	61	73
75-79	54	25	29	71	32	39	75	34	41	89	40	49
80 +	36	15	21	43	18	25	61	26	35	70	30	40

918

United Nations Department of Economic and Social Affairs/Population Division
World Population Prospects: The 2004 Revision, Volume II: Sex and Age Distribution of the World Population

POPULATION BY AGE AND SEX (in thousands)

Age group	2005 Both sexes	Males	Females	2010 Both sexes	Males	Females	2015 Both sexes	Males	Females	2020 Both sexes	Males	Females
All ages	13 010	6 453	6 557	13 402	6 696	6 705	13 804	6 948	6 856	14 144	7 171	6 973
0-4	1 752	879	873	1 762	884	878	1 777	891	885	1 729	867	861
5-9	1 702	852	850	1 659	830	829	1 681	841	840	1 717	859	857
10-14	1 747	875	873	1 634	818	816	1 594	797	797	1 625	812	813
15-19	1 740	870	870	1 722	861	861	1 610	805	805	1 573	786	787
20-24	1 546	771	775	1 685	841	843	1 674	836	838	1 569	783	786
25-29	1 131	571	560	1 379	697	681	1 513	767	746	1 521	770	751
30-34	716	370	346	897	473	425	1 114	587	527	1 242	656	586
35-39	513	258	254	524	285	238	686	379	306	864	479	385
40-44	443	213	230	382	199	183	403	227	176	537	308	229
45-49	402	188	214	351	171	181	308	162	146	329	189	141
50-54	357	164	192	338	157	182	299	144	155	264	139	125
55-59	253	117	136	312	141	171	298	136	162	265	126	138
60-64	235	110	125	224	101	123	278	123	155	267	120	147
65-69	181	84	97	204	93	111	196	86	109	244	106	138
70-74	134	61	73	148	67	81	168	75	93	163	70	93
75-79	89	40	49	98	44	55	111	49	62	127	55	72
80-84	45	20	26	55	24	31	61	26	35	70	30	40
85-89	20	8	11	21	9	12	25	10	15	29	12	17
90-94	4	2	3	6	2	4	6	2	4	8	3	5
95-99	1	0	0	1	0	0	1	0	1	1	0	1
100	0	0	0	0	0	0	0	0	0	0	0	0

Age group	2025 Both sexes	Males	Females	2030 Both sexes	Males	Females	2035 Both sexes	Males	Females	2040 Both sexes	Males	Females
All ages	14 430	7 357	7 073	14 700	7 516	7 184	14 972	7 658	7 313	15 251	7 794	7 458
0-4	1 647	826	820	1 581	793	787	1 544	775	769	1 514	761	754
5-9	1 687	844	842	1 618	810	808	1 561	782	779	1 529	766	763
10-14	1 676	838	838	1 659	830	830	1 600	800	800	1 548	775	774
15-19	1 607	802	804	1 661	829	832	1 647	823	825	1 590	794	796
20-24	1 536	766	771	1 572	783	789	1 628	810	817	1 617	805	812
25-29	1 438	724	714	1 415	709	706	1 456	727	729	1 518	757	761
30-34	1 273	666	607	1 219	630	590	1 213	619	594	1 263	639	624
35-39	905	544	441	1 031	558	473	1 002	530	472	1 011	525	486
40-44	689	395	294	803	455	349	854	470	385	841	449	392
45-49	445	259	186	581	337	244	687	391	296	739	406	333
50-54	284	163	121	389	227	163	513	296	217	612	345	267
55-59	235	123	113	255	145	110	351	202	149	466	266	200
60-64	238	112	126	213	109	103	232	130	102	321	182	138
65-69	236	104	133	212	98	114	190	96	94	207	114	93
70-74	205	87	118	200	86	114	180	81	99	162	80	82
75-79	124	52	72	158	65	93	155	64	90	140	62	79
80-84	81	34	47	80	33	48	103	41	62	102	41	61
85-89	34	14	20	39	16	24	40	15	24	52	20	32
90-94	9	4	6	11	4	7	13	5	8	14	5	9
95-99	2	1	1	2	1	1	2	1	1	3	1	2
100 +	0	0	0	0	0	0	0	0	0	0	0	0

Age group	2045 Both sexes	Males	Females	2050 Both sexes	Males	Females
All ages	15 530	7 922	7 609	15 805	8 041	7 764
0-4	1 469	738	731	1 407	707	700
5-9	1 503	754	749	1 460	733	727
10-14	1 520	761	759	1 497	750	747
15-19	1 541	770	771	1 514	757	757
20-24	1 564	779	785	1 518	757	762
25-29	1 518	757	762	1 480	737	742
30-34	1 334	673	661	1 354	681	673
35-39	1 070	549	521	1 150	586	564
40-44	861	450	412	927	477	450
45-49	737	392	345	764	397	367
50-54	664	362	303	669	352	316
55-59	560	312	248	613	329	283
60-64	428	241	187	517	284	233
65-69	289	161	127	387	214	173
70-74	178	96	82	249	137	113
75-79	127	61	66	141	75	67
80-84	94	40	54	86	40	46
85-89	52	20	32	49	20	30
90-94	18	6	12	19	7	12
95-99	3	1	2	4	1	3
100 +	0	0	0	0	0	0

POPULATION BY AGE AND SEX (in thousands)

Age group	2005 Both sexes	2005 Males	2005 Females	2010 Both sexes	2010 Males	2010 Females	2015 Both sexes	2015 Males	2015 Females	2020 Both sexes	2020 Males	2020 Females
All ages	13 010	6 453	6 557	13 518	6 755	6 763	14 121	7 106	7 014	14 726	7 462	7 263
0-4	1 752	879	873	1 879	942	936	1 982	994	988	2 004	1 005	999
5-9	1 702	852	850	1 659	830	829	1 793	897	896	1 915	958	956
10-14	1 747	875	873	1 634	818	816	1 594	797	797	1 733	866	866
15-19	1 740	870	870	1 722	861	861	1 610	805	805	1 573	786	787
20-24	1 546	771	775	1 685	841	843	1 674	836	838	1 569	783	786
25-29	1 131	571	560	1 379	697	681	1 513	767	746	1 521	770	751
30-34	716	370	346	897	473	425	1 114	587	527	1 242	656	586
35-39	513	258	254	524	285	238	686	379	306	864	479	385
40-44	443	213	230	382	199	183	403	227	176	537	308	229
45-49	402	188	214	351	171	181	308	162	146	329	189	141
50-54	357	164	192	338	157	182	299	144	155	264	139	125
55-59	253	117	136	312	141	171	298	136	162	265	126	138
60-64	235	110	125	224	101	123	278	123	155	267	120	147
65-69	181	84	97	204	93	111	196	86	109	244	106	138
70-74	134	61	73	148	67	81	168	75	93	163	70	93
75-79	89	40	49	98	44	55	111	49	62	127	55	72
80-84	45	20	26	55	24	31	61	26	35	70	30	40
85-89	20	8	11	21	9	12	25	10	15	29	12	17
90-94	4	2	3	6	2	4	6	2	4	8	3	5
95-99	1	0	0	1	0	0	1	0	1	1	0	1
100 +	0	0	0	0	0	0	0	0	0	0	0	0

Age group	2025 Both sexes	2025 Males	2025 Females	2030 Both sexes	2030 Males	2030 Females	2035 Both sexes	2035 Males	2035 Females	2040 Both sexes	2040 Males	2040 Females
All ages	15 300	7 792	7 507	15 906	8 120	7 787	16 585	8 466	8 119	17 339	8 839	8 500
0-4	1 947	977	970	1 931	969	962	1 971	990	982	2 027	1 018	1 009
5-9	1 955	979	977	1 913	958	955	1 907	955	952	1 953	979	974
10-14	1 870	935	935	1 924	962	962	1 892	946	946	1 892	947	945
15-19	1 713	855	858	1 853	925	928	1 910	954	956	1 881	939	942
20-24	1 536	766	771	1 676	835	842	1 816	904	912	1 876	934	942
25-29	1 438	724	714	1 415	709	706	1 553	776	778	1 693	844	849
30-34	1 273	666	607	1 219	630	590	1 213	619	594	1 347	682	666
35-39	985	544	441	1 031	558	473	1 002	530	472	1 011	525	486
40-44	689	395	294	803	455	349	854	470	385	841	449	392
45-49	445	259	186	581	337	244	687	391	296	739	406	333
50-54	284	163	121	389	227	163	513	296	217	612	345	267
55-59	235	123	113	255	145	110	351	202	149	466	266	200
60-64	238	112	126	213	109	103	232	130	102	321	182	138
65-69	236	104	133	212	98	114	190	96	94	207	114	93
70-74	205	87	118	200	86	114	180	81	99	162	80	82
75-79	124	52	72	158	65	93	155	64	90	140	62	79
80-84	81	34	47	80	33	48	103	41	62	102	41	61
85-89	34	14	20	39	16	24	40	15	24	52	20	32
90-94	9	4	6	11	4	7	13	5	8	14	5	9
95-99	2	1	1	2	1	1	2	1	1	3	1	2
100 +	0	0	0	0	0	0	0	0	0	0	0	0

Age group	2045 Both sexes	2045 Males	2045 Females	2050 Both sexes	2050 Males	2050 Females
All ages	18 143	9 231	8 912	18 981	9 634	9 347
0-4	2 054	1 032	1 022	2 054	1 033	1 022
5-9	2 012	1 009	1 003	2 042	1 025	1 018
10-14	1 942	972	969	2 003	1 004	999
15-19	1 882	941	942	1 933	967	967
20-24	1 851	922	929	1 855	925	931
25-29	1 761	878	883	1 751	872	878
30-34	1 488	751	738	1 570	790	780
35-39	1 141	585	556	1 284	654	629
40-44	861	450	412	989	509	480
45-49	737	392	345	764	397	367
50-54	664	362	303	669	352	316
55-59	560	312	248	613	329	283
60-64	428	241	187	517	284	233
65-69	289	161	127	387	214	173
70-74	178	96	82	249	137	113
75-79	127	61	66	141	75	67
80-84	94	40	54	86	40	46
85-89	52	20	32	49	20	30
90-94	18	6	12	19	7	12
95-99	3	1	2	4	1	3
100 +	0	0	0	0	0	0

United Nations Department of Economic and Social Affairs/Population Division
World Population Prospects: The 2004 Revision, Volume II: Sex and Age Distribution of the World Population

920

POPULATION BY AGE AND SEX (in thousands)

Age group	2005 Both sexes	2005 Males	2005 Females	2010 Both sexes	2010 Males	2010 Females	2015 Both sexes	2015 Males	2015 Females	2020 Both sexes	2020 Males	2020 Females
All ages	13 010	6 453	6 557	13 282	6 636	6 645	13 475	6 783	6 692	13 536	6 866	6 670
0-4	1 752	879	873	1 642	824	818	1 562	784	778	1 439	722	717
5-9	1 702	852	850	1 659	830	829	1 567	784	783	1 509	755	754
10-14	1 747	875	873	1 634	818	816	1 594	797	797	1 514	757	757
15-19	1 740	870	870	1 722	861	861	1 610	805	805	1 573	786	787
20-24	1 546	771	775	1 685	841	843	1 674	836	838	1 569	783	786
25-29	1 131	571	560	1 379	697	681	1 513	767	746	1 521	770	751
30-34	716	370	346	897	473	425	1 114	587	527	1 242	656	586
35-39	513	258	254	524	285	238	686	379	306	864	479	385
40-44	443	213	230	382	199	183	403	227	176	537	308	229
45-49	402	188	214	351	171	181	308	162	146	329	189	141
50-54	357	164	192	338	157	182	299	144	155	264	139	125
55-59	253	117	136	312	141	171	298	136	162	265	126	138
60-64	235	110	125	224	101	123	278	123	155	267	120	147
65-69	181	84	97	204	93	111	196	86	109	244	106	138
70-74	134	61	73	148	67	81	168	75	93	163	70	93
75-79	89	40	49	98	44	55	111	49	62	127	55	72
80-84	45	20	26	55	24	31	61	26	35	70	30	40
85-89	20	8	11	21	9	12	25	10	15	29	12	17
90-94	4	2	3	6	2	4	6	2	4	8	3	5
95-99	1	0	0	1	0	0	1	0	1	1	0	1
100 +	0	0	0	0	0	0	0	0	0	0	0	0

Age group	2025 Both sexes	2025 Males	2025 Females	2030 Both sexes	2030 Males	2030 Females	2035 Both sexes	2035 Males	2035 Females	2040 Both sexes	2040 Males	2040 Females
All ages	13 522	6 902	6 620	13 453	6 892	6 561	13 332	6 838	6 494	13 175	6 754	6 420
0-4	1 334	669	665	1 227	616	611	1 130	567	563	1 038	521	517
5-9	1 404	703	701	1 310	656	654	1 212	607	605	1 119	561	558
10-14	1 474	737	737	1 381	690	690	1 296	648	648	1 202	601	601
15-19	1 497	747	750	1 460	729	731	1 371	684	686	1 288	643	645
20-24	1 536	766	771	1 465	729	735	1 431	712	718	1 346	670	676
25-29	1 438	724	714	1 415	709	706	1 357	678	679	1 334	665	669
30-34	1 273	666	607	1 219	630	590	1 213	619	594	1 177	596	581
35-39	985	544	441	1 031	558	473	1 002	530	472	1 011	525	486
40-44	689	395	294	803	455	349	854	470	385	841	449	392
45-49	445	259	186	581	337	244	687	391	296	739	406	333
50-54	284	163	121	389	227	163	513	296	217	612	345	267
55-59	235	123	113	255	145	110	351	202	149	466	266	200
60-64	238	112	126	213	109	103	232	130	102	321	182	138
65-69	236	104	133	212	98	114	190	96	94	207	114	93
70-74	205	87	118	200	86	114	180	81	99	162	80	82
75-79	124	52	72	158	65	93	155	64	90	140	62	79
80-84	81	34	47	80	33	48	103	41	62	102	41	61
85-89	34	14	20	39	16	24	40	15	24	52	20	32
90-94	9	4	6	11	4	7	13	5	8	14	5	9
95-99	2	1	1	2	1	1	2	1	1	3	1	2
100 +	0	0	0	0	0	0	0	0	0	0	0	0

Age group	2045 Both sexes	2045 Males	2045 Females	2050 Both sexes	2050 Males	2050 Females
All ages	12 996	6 651	6 344	12 808	6 537	6 271
0-4	947	476	471	859	432	427
5-9	1 030	517	514	941	472	469
10-14	1 113	557	556	1 026	514	512
15-19	1 196	598	598	1 108	554	554
20-24	1 267	631	636	1 178	587	591
25-29	1 263	629	633	1 198	597	601
30-34	1 172	591	581	1 126	566	560
35-39	997	511	486	1 011	515	495
40-44	861	450	412	863	444	419
45-49	737	392	345	764	397	367
50-54	664	362	303	669	352	316
55-59	560	312	248	613	329	283
60-64	428	241	187	517	284	233
65-69	289	161	127	387	214	173
70-74	178	96	82	249	137	113
75-79	127	61	66	141	75	67
80-84	94	40	54	86	40	46
85-89	52	20	32	49	20	30
90-94	18	6	12	19	7	12
95-99	3	1	2	4	1	3
100 +	0	0	0	0	0	0

كيفيــة الحصــول على منشــورات الأمــم المتحـدة

يمكــن الحصول على منشــورات الأمم المتحـدة من المكتبـات ودور التوزيع في جميع أنحـاء العالم . استعلـم عنها من المكتبة
التي تتعامـل معها أو اكتـب إلى : الأمـم المتحـدة ، فسـم البيـع في نيويورك أو في جنيـف .

如何购取联合国出版物

联合国出版物在全世界各地的书店和经售处均有发售。请向书店询问或写信到纽约或日内瓦的
联合国销售组。

HOW TO OBTAIN UNITED NATIONS PUBLICATIONS

United Nations publications may be obtained from bookstores and distributors throughout the
world. Consult your bookstore or write to: United Nations, Sales Section, New York or Geneva.

COMMENT SE PROCURER LES PUBLICATIONS DES NATIONS UNIES

Les publications des Nations Unies sont en vente dans les librairies et les agences dépositaires
du monde entier. Informez-vous auprès de votre libraire ou adressez-vous à : Nations Unies,
Section des ventes, New York ou Genève.

КАК ПОЛУЧИТЬ ИЗДАНИЯ ОРГАНИЗАЦИИ ОБЪЕДИНЕННЫХ НАЦИЙ

Издания Организации Объединенных Наций можно купить в книжных магазинах
и агентствах во всех районах мира. Наводите справки об изданиях в вашем книжном
магазине или пишите по адресу: Организация Объединенных Наций, Секция по
продаже изданий, Нью-Йорк или Женева.

COMO CONSEGUIR PUBLICACIONES DE LAS NACIONES UNIDAS

Las publicaciones de las Naciones Unidas están en venta en librerías y casas distribuidoras en
todas partes del mundo. Consulte a su librero o diríjase a: Naciones Unidas, Sección de Ventas,
Nueva York o Ginebra.

Litho in United Nations, New York
36133—October 2005—4,485
ISBN 92-1-151408-8

United Nations publication
Sales No. E.05.XIII.6
ST/ESA/SER.A/245